LEONARDO DA VINCI
MASTER DRAFTSMAN

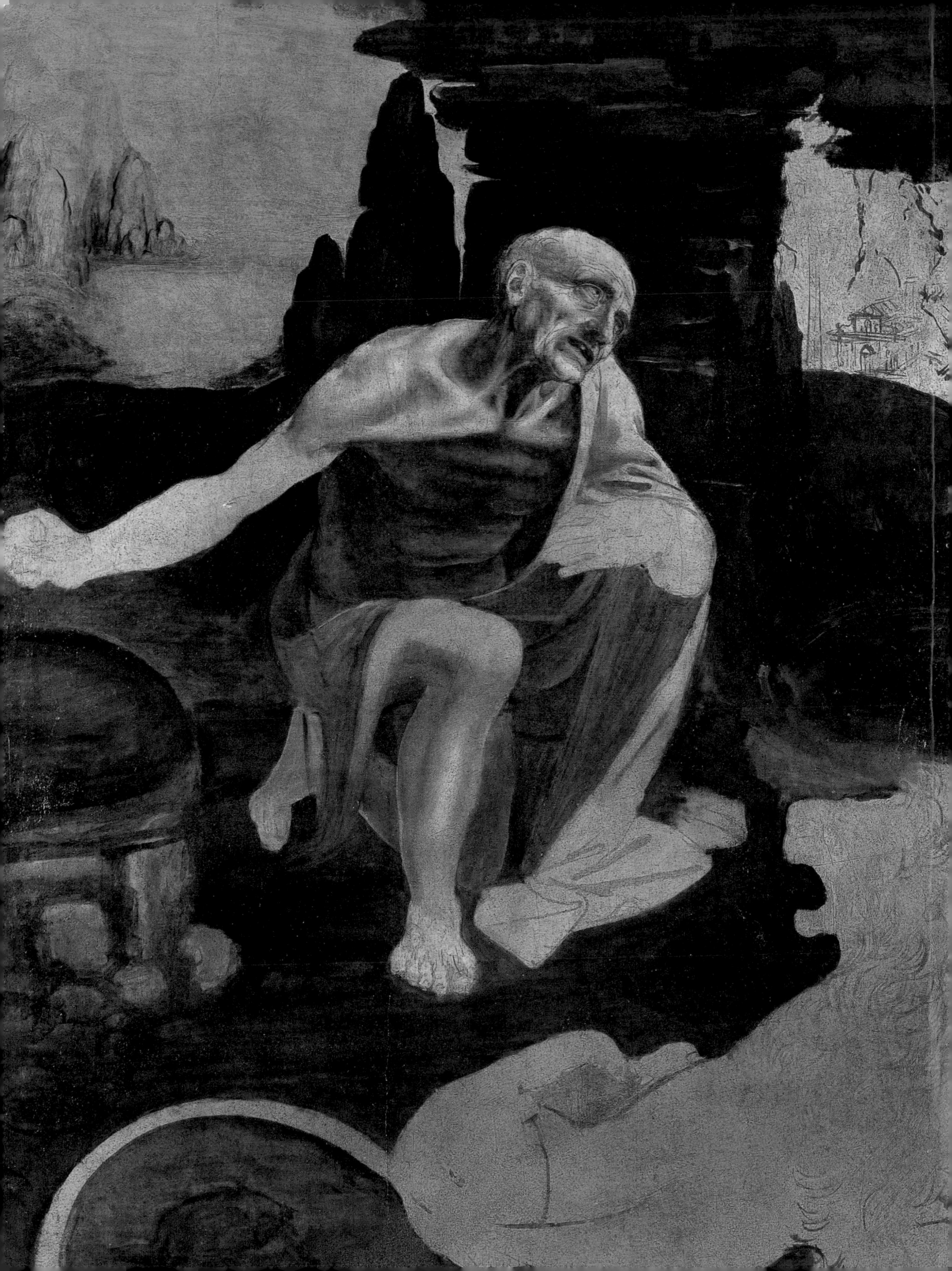

LEONARDO DA VINCI MASTER DRAFTSMAN

EDITED BY CARMEN C. BAMBACH

With contributions by Carmen C. Bambach, Alessandro Cecchi, Claire Farago, Varena Forcione, Martin Kemp, Anne-Marie Logan, Pietro C. Marani, Carlo Pedretti, Carlo Vecce, Françoise Viatte, and Linda Wolk-Simon

With the assistance of Rachel Stern and Alison Manges

THE METROPOLITAN MUSEUM OF ART, NEW YORK
YALE UNIVERSITY PRESS, NEW HAVEN AND LONDON

This volume has been published in conjunction with the exhibition "Leonardo da Vinci, Master Draftsman" organized by The Metropolitan Museum of Art, New York, and held there from January 22 to March 30, 2003.

Sponsored by Morgan Stanley

Additional support has been provided by the National Endowment for the Arts.

An indemnity has been granted by the Federal Council on the Arts and the Humanities.

The exhibition catalogue is made possible by The Drue E. Heinz Fund.

Published by The Metropolitan Museum of Art, New York

John P. O'Neill, Editor in Chief
Jane Bobko, Senior Editor, assisted by Margaret Aspinwall and Elizabeth Powers
Bruce Campbell, Designer
Peter Antony and Elisa Frohlich, Production
Robert Weisberg, Desktop Publishing
Penny Jones, Bibliographer

Typeset in Aldus and Michelangelo
Printed on New V Matte
Separations by Nissha Printing Co., Ltd.
Printed and bound by Nissha Printing Co., Ltd.

Translation from Italian by Lawrence Jenkens and Stephen Sartarelli; from French by Jane Marie Todd

Jacket/cover illustrations: cat. no. 94 (recto), *Studies of an Infant Holding a Lamb* (front); cat. no. 66, *Bearded Old Man in Half-Length, Three-Quarter View Facing to the Right (Saint Peter?)* (back)
Frontispiece: cat. no. 46, *Saint Jerome Praying in the Wilderness*

Cataloging-in-publication information is available from the Library of Congress.

ISBN: 1-58839-033-0 (hc), 1-58839-034-9 (pbk) (The Metropolitan Museum of Art)
ISBN: 0-300-09878-2 (Yale University Press)

CONTENTS

SPONSOR'S STATEMENT

Morgan Stanley is proud to collaborate with The Metropolitan Museum of Art in presenting "Leonardo da Vinci, Master Draftsman." For five hundred years Leonardo has embodied innovation in both art and science. As this exhibition makes clear, the common element of all Leonardo's achievements was his urge to expand the boundaries of human knowledge and to create a new vision. From anatomy to mathematics, from painting to engineering, Leonardo's many varied drawings demonstrate an insatiable drive to understand, explore, and experiment.

All of us can learn from Leonardo. By pursuing our own curiosity, we can always learn new things, create new possibilities, and increase our own expertise. At Morgan Stanley, this means constantly seeking to better understand our clients and finding new ways to help them achieve their financial aspirations. For us, today's intellectual curiosity is tomorrow's intellectual capital.

Leonardo inspires us with the possibilities of what one person can achieve and what the world may hold for each of us. Fueled by curiosity, we can embark on a journey to the heart of every mystery and accept and conquer every challenge. We hope everyone who sees this exhibition will discover the little bit of Leonardo that lies in each of us.

Philip J. Purcell
Chairman and Chief Executive Officer

Robert G. Scott
President and Chief Operating Officer

DIRECTOR'S FOREWORD

Few geniuses have come close to equaling the towering presence of Leonardo da Vinci; few have captured the imagination of so wide a public over so many centuries. The present exhibition includes one of the largest groups of original drawings by Leonardo ever assembled for a public display, as well as the invaluable loan of his unfinished painting *Saint Jerome Praying in the Wilderness*. Selected from public and private collections in Europe and the United States, this survey presents the great master's multifaceted career as artist, author, scientist, inventor, theorist, and teacher through his drawings, which, along with his myriad notebook pages, provide a most intimate insight into his monumental legacy. A substantial group of drawings by his teacher Andrea del Verrocchio, by some of his early Florentine colleagues, and by his Lombard pupils and most distinguished followers places Leonardo in a cultural and historical context.

The exhibition focuses on the hand of Leonardo, master draftsman, at work, highlighting the techniques and functions of his drawings (aspects not fully explored in the vast scholarly literature on the artist). To envision Leonardo quill pen in hand—sketching, brainstorming, reworking, discarding, recommencing, jumping from thought to analogous thought on the page—is to succumb entirely to the sorcery of a creative process of the highest order.

Forty years ago, for a month in the winter of 1963, The Metropolitan Museum of Art had the privilege of displaying in its Medieval Hall Leonardo's *Mona Lisa*, which was on loan from the Musée du Louvre. In 1981 and 1984 the Metropolitan Museum was also the fortunate venue for two beautiful thematic exhibitions offering selections of Leonardo's drawings of plants and anatomy from the magnificent holdings in the Royal Library at Windsor Castle. Happily, these two institutions have once again agreed to part with a significant number of their treasures for the Metropolitan's latest Leonardo undertaking. We are most grateful to Her Majesty Queen Elizabeth II, who graciously consented to lend a core of thirty-one drawings by Leonardo. We very much appreciate the early support and advice of Lady Jane Roberts, Chief Librarian and Keeper of the Print Room and the Royal Library, Windsor Castle. We are similarly indebted to Henri Loyrette, Director of the Musée du Louvre, for the unprecedented loan of twenty-nine drawings by Leonardo and his circle, and to Pierre Rosenberg, Président-Directeur de l'Académie Française du Musée du Louvre, for his immediate support of this initiative. We greatly benefited from

the learned counsel of Françoise Viatte, Conservateur Général Chargé du Département des Arts Graphiques of the Musée du Louvre, whose own exhibition, "Léonardo de Vinci, dessins et manuscrits," will open at the Musée du Louvre in May 2003. We wish to thank also our colleagues at the Réunion des Musées Nationaux for their assistance.

It is appropriate for me to express our immense gratitude to Professor Giuliano Urbani, the cultural minister of Italy, for his support in securing twenty masterpieces by Leonardo and his circle from Italian institutions. Here, I would also like to acknowledge the generosity of Francesco Buranelli, Director of the Musei Vaticani, for the exceptional loan of Leonardo's monumental *Saint Jerome*. Special thanks are also due to Giovanna Nepi Scirè, Soprintendente of the Patrimonio Storico Artistico Demoetnoantropologico di Venezia, for lending nearly the entire corpus of drawings by Leonardo from the Gallerie dell'Accademia, Venice, of which institution she is also director. Neil MacGregor, Director of The British Museum, generously lent nine critical drawings, and Antony Griffiths, Keeper of the Department of Drawings and Prints, The British Museum, provided encouragement from the outset of this endeavor.

Leonardo's drawings are among the most prized of Renaissance works, and this assemblage is the result of nearly five years of complex negotiations. I extend my deepest gratitude to the private collectors, as well as the directors and staffs of the following institutions for their superlative cooperation in lending what amount to be the most precious works of art entrusted to their care: Bill and Melinda Gates; the Duke of Devonshire, Chatsworth; the Woodner Family; the private collector who wished to remain anonymous; as well as the Staatliche Museen zu Berlin—Preussischer Kulturbesitz, Kupferstichkabinett, Berlin; Szépmüvészeti Múzeum, Budapest; The Syndics of the Fitzwilliam Museum, Cambridge; Wallraf-Richartz-Museum—Foundation Corboud, Graphische Sammlung, Cologne; National Gallery of Scotland, Edinburgh; Hamburger Kunsthalle, Hamburg; Victoria and Albert Museum, London; The J. Paul Getty Museum, Los Angeles; Biblioteca Pinacoteca Ambrosiana, Milan; The Pierpont Morgan Library, New York; Faculdade de Belas Artes, Universidade do Porto, Oporto; Visitors of the Ashmolean Museum, Oxford; Christ Church, Oxford; École Nationale Supérieure des Beaux-Arts, Paris; Istituto Nazionale per la Grafica, Rome; Museum Boijmans Van Beuningen, Rotterdam; Biblioteca Reale, Turin; Monumenti Musei e Gallerie Pontificie, Vatican City; Gallerie dell'Accademia, Venice; Graphische Sammlung Albertina, Vienna; National Gallery of Art, Washington, D.C.; and Sterling and Francine Clark Art Institute, Williamstown, Massachusetts.

The exhibition and accompanying catalogue were conceived by Carmen C. Bambach, Curator of Drawings and Prints; she served as the catalogue editor and wrote a number of its major texts. In offering new research and in summarizing the enormous, dauntingly complex Leonardo literature, the catalogue is directed toward both a general and a scholarly audience. We are most grateful to the distinguished experts on Leonardo's work who have contributed to this publication: Alessandro Cecchi, Claire Farago, Varena Forcione, Martin Kemp, Anne-Marie Logan, Pietro C. Marani, Carlo Pedretti, Carlo Vecce, Françoise Viatte, and Linda Wolk-Simon.

The Museum is most grateful to Morgan Stanley for its outstanding support of the exhibition. We are also indebted to the National Endowment for the Arts for its important contribution to the project. In addition, we would like to acknowledge the kind assistance provided by the Federal Council on the Arts and the Humanities. We would also like to recognize the generosity of The Drue E. Heinz Fund for its support of the exhibition catalogue.

Philippe de Montebello
Director
The Metropolitan Museum of Art

ACKNOWLEDGMENTS

An enormous debt of gratitude is owed to Philippe de Montebello, Director of the Metropolitan Museum, for bringing this exhibition to fruition with the kinds of resources and vision that can do justice to Leonardo's achievement. The lion's share of the credit for the project belongs to George R. Goldner, Drue Heinz Chairman of Drawings and Prints, who first invited me to entertain the possibility of an exhibition of Leonardo's drawings in 1995–96, granting me a leave of absence of six months for initial study and research in 1996–97, and then offering the staunch advocacy and sage guidance that took the project from dream to reality. The personal support and guidance of Mahrukh Tarapor, Associate Director for Exhibitions, have also been invaluable, for she prepared the way in the negotiations of many of the loans. The exhibition represents the collaboration of an enormous team of colleagues both inside and outside The Metropolitan Museum of Art. Words cannot properly acknowledge the steadfast advice, assistance, and encouragement of the numerous people who participated in this project with extraordinary effectiveness and great goodwill.

I am extremely grateful to my coauthors, not only for their extraordinary contributions to the catalogue but also for their intellectual generosity and their help in making inaccessible materials available: Alessandro Cecchi, Claire Farago, Varena Forcione, Martin Kemp, Anne-Marie Logan, Pietro C. Marani, Carlo Pedretti, Carlo Vecce, Françoise Viatte, and Linda Wolk-Simon.

It has been my great privilege to receive the counsel and warm collaboration of some of the most distinguished scholars in the field of old master drawings and Leonardo studies during the course of planning this exhibition, to whom I am deeply grateful: Lady Jane Roberts, Chief Librarian and Keeper of the Print Room and the Royal Library, Windsor Castle; Martin Clayton, Assistant Keeper of the Print Room and the Royal Library, Windsor Castle; Françoise Viatte, Conservateur Général Chargé du Département des Arts Graphiques of the Musée du Louvre; Varena Forcione, Conservateur du Département des Arts Graphiques of the Musée du Louvre; Antony Griffiths, Keeper of the Department of Drawings and Prints of The British Museum; Hugo Chapman, Assistant Keeper of the Department of Drawings and Prints of The British Museum; Professor Pietro C. Marani, Dipartimento di Storia e Conservazione dell'Architettura, Politecnico di Milano; Professor Carlo Pedretti, Department of the History of Art, University of California at Los Angeles; Professor Martin Kemp, Department of the History of Art, Oxford University, and Director, Wallace Kemp/Artakt; Giovanna Nepi Scirè, Soprintendente, Patrimonio Storico Artistico Demoetnoantropologico di Venezia; and Alessandro Cecchi, Direttore del Dipartimento della Pittura dal Medioevo al Primo Rinascimento, Galleria degli Uffizi.

At crucial points in the complex process of negotiations of loans from Italian institutions the following individuals intervened with great effectiveness: Professor Fabio Benzi; Ambassador Boris Biancheri, Chairman of ANSA; Adele Chatsfield-Taylor, President of the American Academy in Rome, who enlisted a number of her colleagues in the cause; Antonio Paolucci, Soprintendente per i Beni Artistici e Storici di Firenze e Pistoia; and Mr. and Mrs. Michael E. Pulitzer. The Metropolitan Museum of Art is greatly indebted to Daniel Berger for his generous and timely assistance with several important Italian loans.

I wish to thank Francesco Buranelli, Direttore Generale of the Monumenti Musei e Gallerie Pontificie, for making the impossible possible in granting the precious loan of Leonardo's unfinished painting of *Saint Jerome Praying in the Wilderness*. Heartfelt thanks are also owed to the private collectors, directors, and numerous colleagues at the following institutions for granting the loans of the magnificent drawings that presently enrich the walls of The Metropolitan Museum of Art. These colleagues also responded to innumerable requests for information, practical assistance, and photographs for which they are also gratefully thanked: Alexander Dückers and Hein-Thomas Schulze Altcappenberg of the Staatliche Museen zu Berlin—Preussischer Kulturbesitz, Kupferstichkabinett, Berlin; Miklós Mojzer, Loránd Zentai, Vilmos Tátrai, Andrea Czére, Ester Sabry, and Zsuzsa Gonda at the Szépművészeti Múzeum, Budapest; Duncan Robinson, David E. Scrase, Janie Munro, R. A. Crighton, Liz Woods, and Diane Hudson at the Fitzwilliam Museum, Cambridge, U.K.; His Grace the Duke of Devonshire and Peter Day, Keeper of the Devonshire Collection, Chatsworth; Rainer Budde, Uwe Westfehling, Barbara Schaefer, and Marina Fröhling at the Wallraf-Richartz-Museum— Foundation Corboud, Graphische Sammlung, Cologne; Michael Clarke, Aidan Weston-Lewis, and Anne Buddle at the National Gallery of Scotland, Edinburgh; Uwe M. Schneede, Andreas Stolzenburg, Peter Prange, and Meike Gerber at the Hamburger Kunsthalle, Hamburg; Neil MacGregor, Antony Griffiths, Hugo Chapman, Sheila O'Connell,

Giulia Bartrum, Mark McDonald, Janice Reading, and Joanna Laurie at The British Museum, London; Alan Borg, Michael Snowdin, Mark Evans, Jenny Ramkalawon, David Wright, and Annie Steinberg at the Victoria and Albert Museum, London; Deborah Gribbon, William H. Griswold, Lee Hendrix, Allegra Pesenti, Christine Giviskos, Sally Hibbard, Marc Harnly, and Jacklyn Burns at The J. Paul Getty Museum, Los Angeles; Monsignor Gianfranco Ravasi, Monsignor Pier Francesco Fumagalli, Angelo Colombo, Monsignor Marco Navoni, Agostino Fontana, and Valerio Brambilla at the Biblioteca Pinacoteca Ambrosiana, Milan; Diana Kunkel, curator, New York; Charles E. Pierce Jr., Rhoda Eitel-Porter, Cara D. Denison, Jennifer Tonkovich, and Lucy Eldridge at The Pierpont Morgan Library, New York; The Woodner Family and Jennifer Jones, Curator of The Woodner Collection, New York; Lúcia Almeida-Matos at the Faculdade de Belas Artes, Universidade do Porto, Oporto; Christopher Brown, Catherine Whistler, Geraldine Glynn, Caroline Campbell, and Katia Pisvin at the Ashmolean Museum, Oxford; Ian Watson, Richard B. Rutherford, Christopher Baker, and Dennis Harrington at Christ Church Picture Gallery, Oxford; Annie Jacques, Henry-Claude Cousseau, and Emmanuelle Brujerolles at the École Nationale Supérieure des Beaux-Arts, Paris; Henri Loyrette, Pierre Rosenberg, Françoise Viatte, Varena Forcione, Catherine Loisel, and Catherine Monbeig Goguel at the Musée du Louvre; Serenita Papaldo, Luigi Ficacci, and Rita Parma at the Istituto Nazionale per la Grafica, Rome; Chris P. E. Dercon, Hugo Bongers, Bram W. F. M. Meij, and Guido M. C. Jansen at the Museum Boijmans Van Beuningen, Rotterdam; Bill and Melinda Gates, Seattle, Washington, and their agent Frederick C. Schroeder of Resnicow Schroeder Associates, Inc., New York; Giovanna Giacobello Bernard and Clara Vitulo at the Biblioteca Reale, Turin; Arnold Nesselrath, Claudio Rossi de Gasperis, Guido Cornini, Filippo Petrignani, Karin Jansen Sagliocco, and Francesco Ricardi at the Monumenti Musei e Gallerie Pontificie, Vatican City; Giovanna Nepi Scirè, Roberto Fontanari, Annalisa Perissa Torrini, and Loretta Salvador at the Soprintendenza Patrimonio Storico Artistico Demoetno-antropologico di Venezia; Klaus Albrecht Schröder, Renata Antoniou, Heinz Widauer, and Margarete Heck at the Graphische Sammlung Albertina, Vienna; Earl Powell III, Alan Shestack, Andrew Robison, and Margaret Morgan Grasselli at the National Gallery of Art, Washington, D.C.; Michael Conforti, James Ganz, Mattie Kelley, and Kris Walton at the Sterling and Francine Clark Art Institute, Williamstown, Massachusetts; Lady Jane Roberts, Martin Clayton, Theresa-Mary Morton, Rhian Glover, and Sîan Cooksey at the Print Room and the Royal Library, Windsor Castle.

A fellowship at the Villa I Tatti, the Harvard University Center for Italian Renaissance Studies, in 1996–97 provided me with a significant period of research toward the planning of this exhibition, for which thanks are owed to I Tatti's staff and its director, Joseph Connors, and its former director Walter Kaiser. We are also deeply indebted to the following colleagues from nonlending institutions who offered advice and practical assistance (with apologies for inadvertent omissions): Francis Ames-Lewis, Noel Annesley, Anna Lou Ashby, Frank Bara, Geraldine Bass, Nicolò Orsi Battaglini, Nancy Bialler, Suzanne Boorsch, Giulio Bora, François Borne, Eve Borsook, David Alan Brown, David Bull, Andrew Butterfield, Lester Carissimi and Christian Lapeyre, Gianna Celli, Maria Luisa Cerrón Puga, Matthew Choberka, Anna Coliva, Roberto Contini, Elizabeth Cropper, Luis Alberto de Cuenca, Arnalda Dallaj, Angela Dillon, Francesco Paolo Di Teodoro, Nick Dorman, Colin Eisler, David Ekserdjian, Marisa Dalai Emiliani, Sylvia Ferino Pagden, Maria Teresa Fiorio, Howard Fox, Camila Gavazzi, Luisa Guarneri, Creighton E. Gilbert, Fiorella Superbi Gioffredo, Antonio Godoli, Egbert Haverkamp-Begeman, Marvin Hayes, Andrée Hayum, Jonathan Hynd, Robert Johnson, Gail Joice, Pamela Keech, Silvio Leydi, Lester K. Little, Annie Madec, Vittorio Menci, Lucia Monaci Moran, Giovanni Morello, Paolo Nannoni, Antonio Natali, Elena Ongania, Giovanni Pagliarulo, Roberta Panzanelli, Pina Pasquantonio, Mireille Pastoureau, Rossana Pedretti, Nicholas Penny, Ellen Perry, Claudia Roth Pierpont, Anna Maria Petrioli Tofani, Ivanoe Riboli, Cristiana Romalli, Ingrid Rowland, Rossana Sacchi, Fabiola Salcedo Garcés, Nicolas Schwed, Maurizio Seracini, Marina Sheriff, Michael Slade, Leo Steinberg, Claudio Strinati, Paolo Tosi, Caterina Bon Valsassina, Lisa Venturini, and Kathleen Weil-Garris Brandt. The following colleagues kindly provided access to important works of art in private collections: Joseph Baillio, Charles Hack, Michael Hall, and Eliot Rowlands. For assistance with translations and transcriptions of documents, thanks are owed to Virginia Budny, Gino Corti, Frank Dabell, and Katherine Welch.

The exhibition, accompanying catalogue, and various adjunct programs also involved numerous colleagues at The Metropolitan Museum of Art who have labored tirelessly on behalf of Leonardo. Heartfelt thanks are due to a number of colleagues in the Curatorial and Conservation Departments for making their unparalleled expertise available to the project: Maryan Ainsworth, Dita Amory, Katharine Baetjer, Andrea Bayer, George Bisacca, Barbara Drake Boehm, Thomas Campbell, Stefano Carboni, Keith Christiansen, James David Draper, Helen Evans, Everett Fahy, Laurence Kanter, Joan Mertens, Olga Raggio, Sabine Rewald, Hubert von Sonnenburg, Richard E. Stone, Ian Wardropper, and Linda Wolk-Simon.

Among my colleagues in the Department of Drawings and Prints, the following gave valuable help: Colta Ives, Michiel Plomp, Perrin Stein, Nadine Orenstein, Elizabeth Barker,

Wendy Thompson, Constance McPhee, Samantha Rippner, Jeff Guerrier, and Kit Basquin. Molly Carrott bravely and effectively resolved a myriad of administrative issues with great cheer. David del Gaizo and Ricky Luna are responsible for the handsome installation of the exhibition.

Marjorie Shelley, Sherman Fairchild Conservator in Charge for Works on Paper, generously shared her vast knowledge of Italian Renaissance drawing technique and undertook significant scientific analysis of the drawings by Leonardo and his circle in the Metropolitan's collections. In this endeavor she was expertly assisted by Rachel Mustalish, Silvia Centeno, and Kristi Dahm.

For their extremely important contributions to the exhibition, I should also like to single out the following members of the Metropolitan's staff: Emily Kernan Rafferty, Senior Vice President for External Affairs; Harold Holzer, Vice President for Communications and Marketing; and Doralynn Pines, Associate Director for Administration. Thanks are due as well to Nina Diefenbach, Christine Scornavacca, Kerstin Larsen, Christine Begley, Sarah Higby, Claire Gylphé, and Delphine Daniels in the Development Office; Andrew Ferren, Elyse Topalian, and Elizabeth Wilson in the Communications Department; Kent Lydecker, Stella Paul, Elizabeth Hammer-Munemura, Rebecca Arkenberg, and Barbara Woods in the Education Department; Barbara Bridgers, Mark Morosse, Joseph Coscia, Eileen Travell, Chad Beer, and Bruce Schwarz of the Photograph Studio; Carol Lekarew and Deanna Cross of the Photograph and Slide Library; and Sally Pearson and her dedicated staff in the Merchandising Activities Department. Special mention is due Martha Deese and Sian Wetherill in the office of the Associate Director for Exhibitions for tirelessly coming to the aid of the project on more occasions than they probably wish to remember, as well as to Rebecca Noonan in the office of the Vice President, Secretary and General Counsel. Kenneth Soehner and his staff at the Thomas J. Watson Library patiently accommodated our studies of a great body of research materials. Linda Seckelson and Katherine Yvinskas of the Watson Library are especially thanked for their exceptional efforts on behalf of Leonardo.

Linda Sylling, Manager of Special Exhibitions and Gallery Installation, has effectively overseen the installation of the show. Herbert M. Moskowitz, Chief Registrar, assisted by Elzbieta Myszczynski, admirably organized the participation of lending institutions, as well as addressing the challenges of indemnification and international insurance, transport, and customs. The display of Leonardo's precious drawings poses innumerable challenges, and these were thoughtfully addressed in the attractive exhibition design by Michael Batista, Sophia Geronimus, and Zack Zanolli, a collaboration under the guidance of Jeffrey L. Daly, Chief Designer.

Two years ago, at an advanced stage in the planning of the exhibition and in the writing of the catalogue, Rachel Stern and Alison Manges joined the Leonardo team as exhibition assistants, devoting their exceptional talents, as well as their great dedication and enthusiasm, to research still in progress and to the show's administration. During the last six months Maya Levy joined them, bringing untiring meticulousness to the project. Christine Begley, Silvia Borsotti, William Breazeale, Yvonne Elet, Anne Leader, Rachel McGarry, Donata Menci, Andreanne Saunier, and Jeanette Sisk substantially assisted with research at various points during the last five years. Xiomara Murray, Kelly Sidley, Risha Lee, and Sheila Hochberg have also kindly pitched in when needed. Additionally, the following talented graduate students devoted their efforts to Leonardo's drawings in the context of a seminar given at the Institute of Fine Arts, New York University, in autumn 1998, at the invitation of Marian Burleigh-Motley, director of its curatorial studies program: Susan Anderson, Holly Flora, John Garton, Lyle Humphrey, and Ashley Thomas.

I am immensely grateful to John P. O'Neill, Editor in Chief and General Manager of Publications, for the production of this book and for the inclusion of a generous number of illustrations that present the arguments of connoisseurship that the book pursues. My debt to Jane Bobko, the senior editor on this project, is enormous, for she worked with indefatigable dedication, patience, and precision. Heartfelt thanks are also owed to Margaret Chace, Managing Editor, and to the superb team of editors who worked under Jane Bobko's guidance: Margaret Aspinwall, Kathleen Howard, Elizabeth Powers, Jennifer C. Bernstein, Joan K. Holt, Ruth Lurie Kozodoy, Ellen Shultz, and Dale Tucker, as well as Penny Jones, bibliographic editor. It is a pleasure to acknowledge Peter Antony and Elisa Frohlich for their great attention to color and detail in this book's production. The complex tasks of desktop publishing were directed with great skill by Robert Weisberg. Bruce Campbell worked with exceptional grace to achieve the book's cogent and elegant design.

Last, I wish to thank my husband, Ronald Street, who lovingly, wisely, and steadfastly offered invaluable counsel and moral support in more ways than can be enumerated.

Carmen C. Bambach
Curator of Drawings and Prints
The Metropolitan Museum of Art

LENDERS TO THE EXHIBITION

CONTRIBUTORS TO THE CATALOGUE

CCB   Carmen C. Bambach, Curator, Department of
Drawings and Prints, The Metropolitan Museum of Art

Alessandro Cecchi, Direttore del Dipartimento della Pittura
dal Medioevo al Primo Rinascimento, Galleria degli Uffizi

CF   Professor Claire Farago, Department of Fine Arts,
University of Colorado at Boulder

VF   Varena Forcione, Conservateur du Département des
Arts Graphiques, Musée du Louvre

Professor Martin Kemp, Department of the History of Art,
Oxford University, and Director, Wallace Kemp/Artakt

A-ML   Anne-Marie Logan, Guest Research Curator,
Department of Drawings and Prints, The Metropolitan
Museum of Art

AM   Alison Manges, Exhibition Assistant, Department of
Drawings and Prints, The Metropolitan Museum of Art

PCM   Professor Pietro C. Marani, Dipartimento di Storia e
Conservazione dell'Architettura, Politecnico di Milano

Professor Carlo Pedretti, Department of the History of Art,
University of California at Los Angeles

Professor Carlo Vecce, Dipartimento di Ricerca Linguistica,
Letteraria e Filologica, Università di Macerata

FV   Françoise Viatte, Conservateur Général Chargé du
Département des Arts Graphiques, Musée du Louvre

LW-S   Linda Wolk-Simon, Associate Curator, Robert
Lehman Collection, The Metropolitan Museum of Art

NOTE TO THE READER

Drawings in the exhibition are reproduced as close as possible to actual size; lost or damaged areas appear in a tone lighter than that of the original sheet. In general the presentation of Leonardo's drawings follows the Chronology that appears in this volume.

Height precedes width in dimensions. "Metalpoint" signifies lead, silver, gold, tin, copper, or other metal alloys; the color of the paper is white unless otherwise indicated. Inscriptions by Leonardo have been retranscribed in this publication to achieve stylistic consistency; these transcriptions follow Leonardo's orthography as closely as possible, and his language has not been modernized. Abbreviations, as well as missing letters and words, are filled in within square brackets. Inscriptions by later hands on the drawings and mounts are transcribed when they have historical importance.

Translations of quoted text from primary sources are the authors' own unless otherwise noted. Leonardo's manuscripts are cited in abbreviated form in the essays, documented chronology, and catalogue entries; the bibliography gives a key to these forms. All of Leonardo's manuscripts are available in facsimile reproductions.

Citations are abbreviated throughout; full references are provided in the main bibliography, which also includes material not cited in the text. Each entry's bibliography, which is by no means complete, offers a large selection of publications, including exhibition catalogues.

Provenances are not a standard feature in catalogues of Leonardo's work. Here, however, they have been reconstructed within the limits of probability, and many are published for the first time. Leonardo's will of April 23, 1519, declared Francesco Melzi his artistic heir and presumably the majority owner of Leonardo's drawings. Provenances in this publication give Melzi as a past owner only when this fact is certain, as in the drawings from the Royal Library, Windsor Castle.

Attributions made by previous scholars are listed only if they differ from those offered by the present authors, and in these cases the name of the proposed artist is given within parentheses. A scholarly consensus is a rare event in the vast Leonardo literature, and like their predecessors, the present authors have not achieved complete agreement; on a small number of points the reader will notice a diversity of opinion.

LEONARDO DA VINCI
MASTER DRAFTSMAN

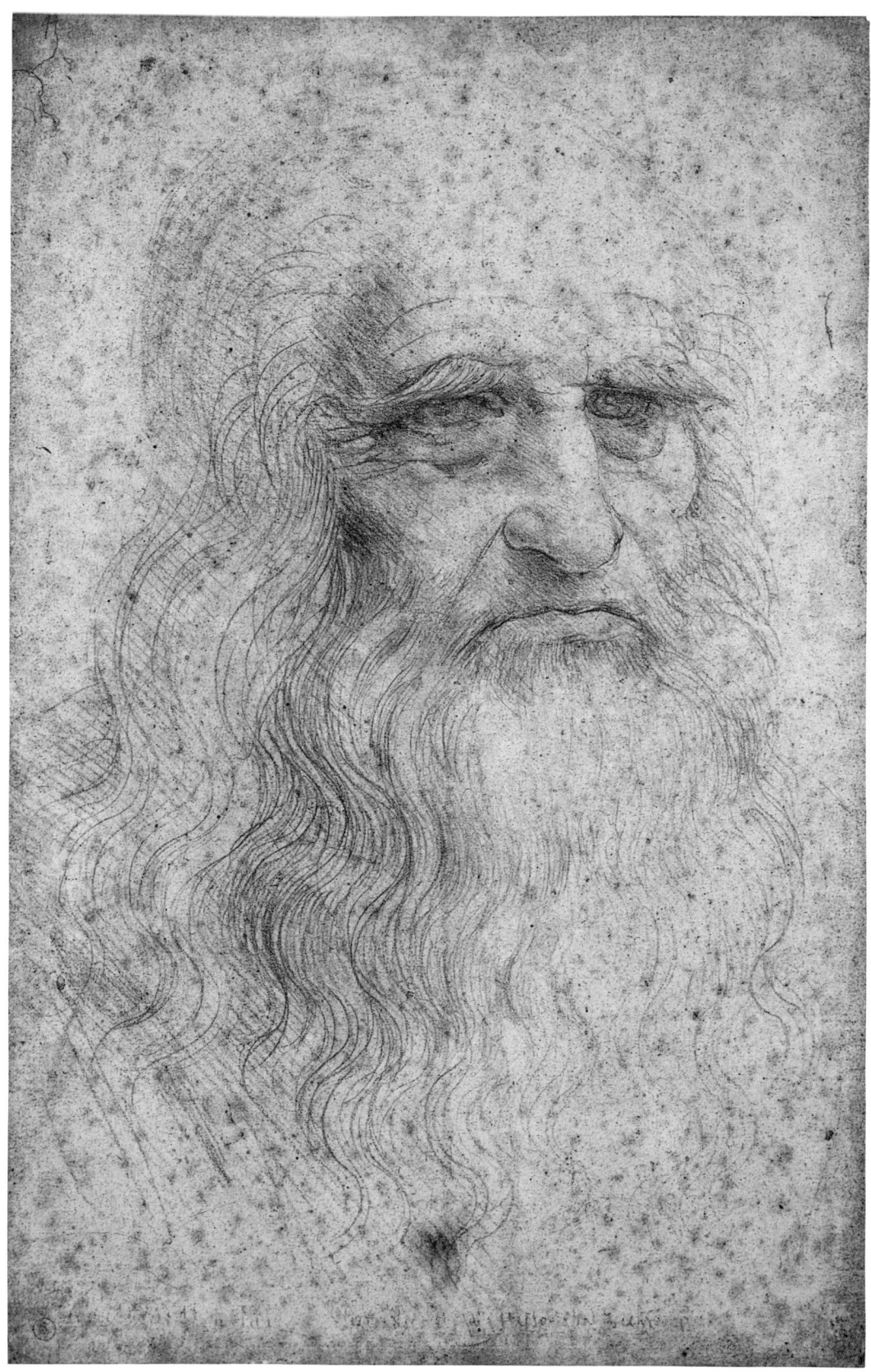

Fig. 1. Leonardo da Vinci, *Possible Self-Portrait*. Red chalk (selectively wetted), over some traces of stylus, on light brown paper, 333 × 213 mm. Biblioteca Reale, Turin 15571

INTRODUCTION TO LEONARDO AND HIS DRAWINGS

CARMEN C. BAMBACH

He who, without Fame, burns his life to waste
leaves no more vestige of himself on earth than
wind-blown smoke, or foam upon the water

Dante, *Inferno*, 24:49–51

EVEN IN AN ERA OF boundless scientific discovery and technological invention, and of sublime artistic and humanistic achievement, Leonardo da Vinci (1452–1519) stands as a supreme icon in Western consciousness—the very embodiment of the universal Renaissance genius (fig. 1). The essence of Dante's words on the theme of fame was not lost on Leonardo, for he even quoted the passage on a sheet of sketches for the casting of the colossal Sforza equestrian monument (see cat. no. 64 verso). He is possibly most famous as the artist who produced ineffably beautiful, mythical paintings. For example, when Leonardo's *Mona Lisa* (Musée du Louvre, Paris) was lent by the government of the French Republic to the president of the United States and the American people, it was seen by 1,077,521 visitors during its brief display at The Metropolitan Museum of Art, from February 7 to March 4, 1963 (figs. 2, 3). He is also celebrated as the polymath theorist, scientist, and inventor whose work has spoken across the centuries with an astonishingly modern voice. Yet Leonardo was hardly the prototypical artist of the Italian Renaissance, and his eventful life and somewhat itinerant career bear retelling (see Chronology). By temperament he never managed to fit within the traditions of production and socioeconomic structures of the Italian Renaissance, and he disappointed a good portion of the patrons who commissioned work from him. He was famously left-handed, and this had significant consequences for the way in which he drew and wrote (see my essay). Largely self-taught intellectually, he took on the task of writing a number of treatises but was barely able to master the rudiments of Latin, the language of most scientific texts and the lingua franca among the humanists who composed the intellectual elite of his day (see essay by Carlo Vecce). As an artist and scientist, Leonardo came to his revolutionary belief in empirical observation

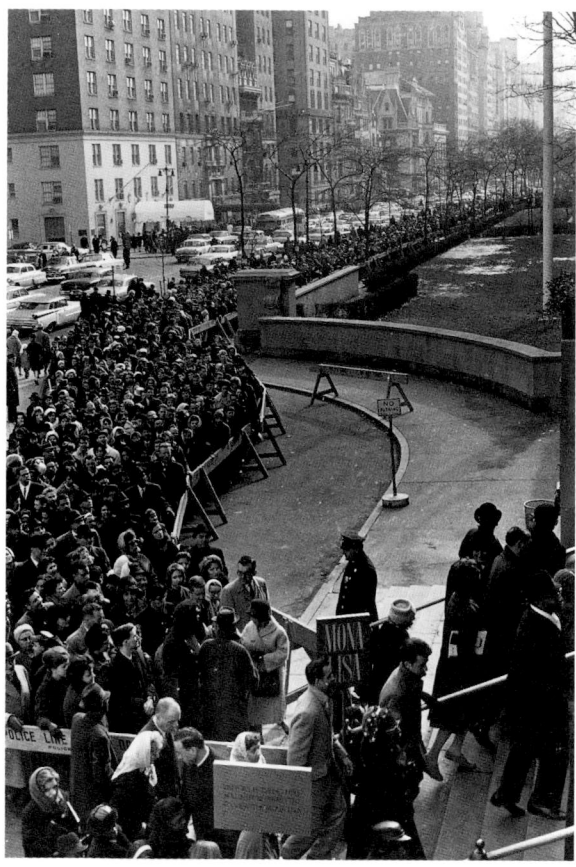

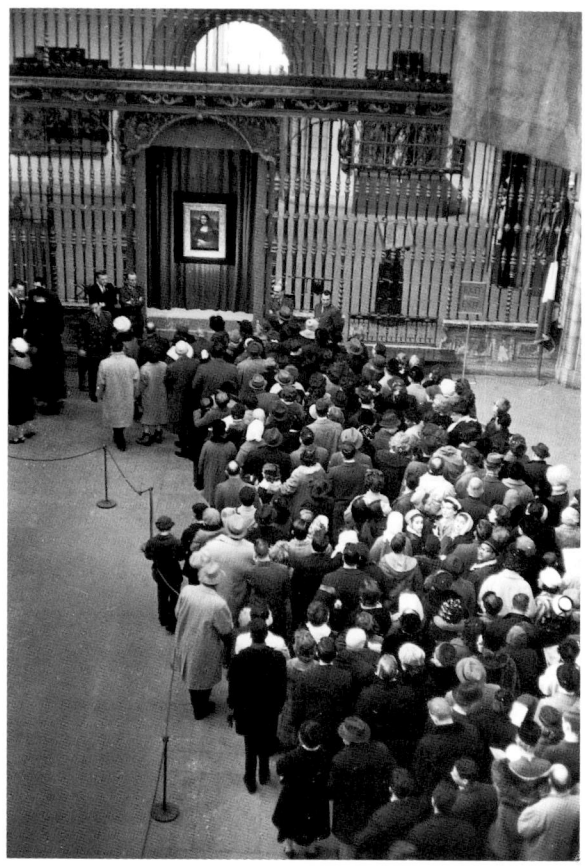

Fig. 2. Crowds lining up to see Leonardo's *Mona Lisa* (on loan from the Musée du Louvre, Paris) for its display at The Metropolitan Museum of Art in February 1963. The Metropolitan Museum of Art, New York

Fig. 3. Exhibition of Leonardo's *Mona Lisa* in the great Medieval Hall of The Metropolitan Museum of Art in February 1963. The Metropolitan Museum of Art, New York

as the foundation of all knowledge possibly out of necessity (so much book learning was out of his reach), leaving an unshakable intellectual legacy for centuries to come. This self-described "disciple of experience," this observer of the macrocosm and microcosm, transcended his time and was also very much defined by it. If the artist in him often got buried by the scientific investigator, the scientist's powers of observation also immeasurably amplified the artist's powers of evocation.

The key to Leonardo's legacy is without doubt to be found in his extant drawings and accompanying manuscript notes, for the number of his extant paintings is very small (at most fifteen, if one were to count generously finished and unfinished works, autograph and partly autograph works). None of his projects for sculptures seems to have reached a finished state (see cat. nos. 53, 63, 64, 101–4, 111, 118). At least two of his murals in Milan are in such damaged condition that they represent a pale semblance of his original intentions (the *Last Supper*, Refectory of Santa Maria delle Grazie [cat. no. 65], and the Sala delle Asse, Castello Sforzesco). Even during his lifetime, his inability to finish projects was legendary. Piero Soderini, the *gonfaloniere di giustizia* (the elected chief government official) of the Florentine

Republic, complained on October 9, 1506, to the representative of the French king in Milan about Leonardo's failed *Battle of Anghiari* mural: "he made a very small beginning of a very large thing."[1] When Pope Leo X, the brother of Giuliano de' Medici, Leonardo's patron in Rome from 1513 to 1516, learned that Leonardo was incessantly fussing over recipes for varnishes, instead of painting, he is said to have exclaimed, "Alas! This man will never do anything, for he begins by thinking about the end before the beginning of his work."[2] In this context it is nearly miraculous, especially if one considers the fragility of paper, that an enormous body of drawings by Leonardo survives—more than four thousand, if one counts every scrap of paper with sketches and diagrams, and all the pages bound in his notebooks. (Notebooks and albums offer a significant means of protecting works on paper.) The quantity of Leonardo's extant drawings is about four times the corpus of even the most prolific sixteenth-century draftsmen. Famous for their beauty and technical virtuosity, his drawings were avidly sought by collectors even during his lifetime.[3] Among the sixteenth-century collectors of his graphic work were Francesco Melzi (1491/93–ca. 1570), who was Leonardo's

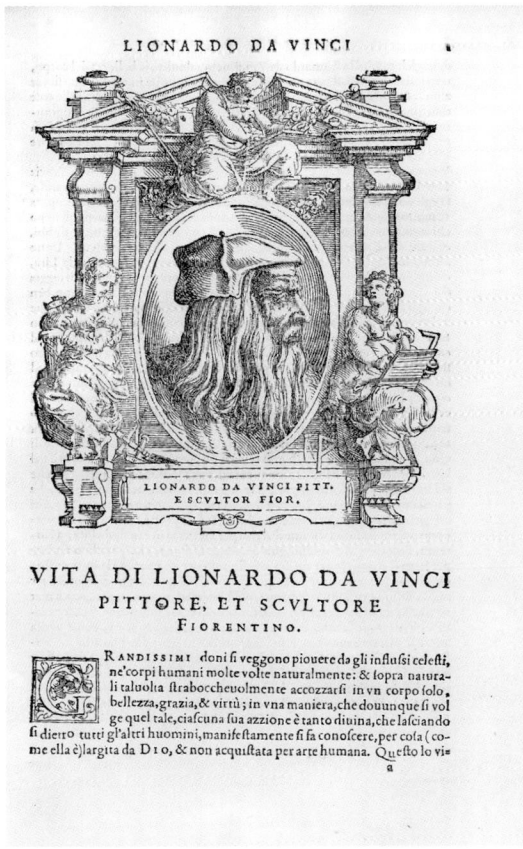

Fig. 4. Page in Giorgio Vasari, *Le vite de' più eccellenti pittori, scultori et architettori* (Florence: Giunti, 1568), showing the portrait and beginning of the biography of Leonardo. Woodcut, 245 × 166 mm. The Metropolitan Museum of Art, New York; Harris Brisbane Dick Fund, 1929 29.76 (2)

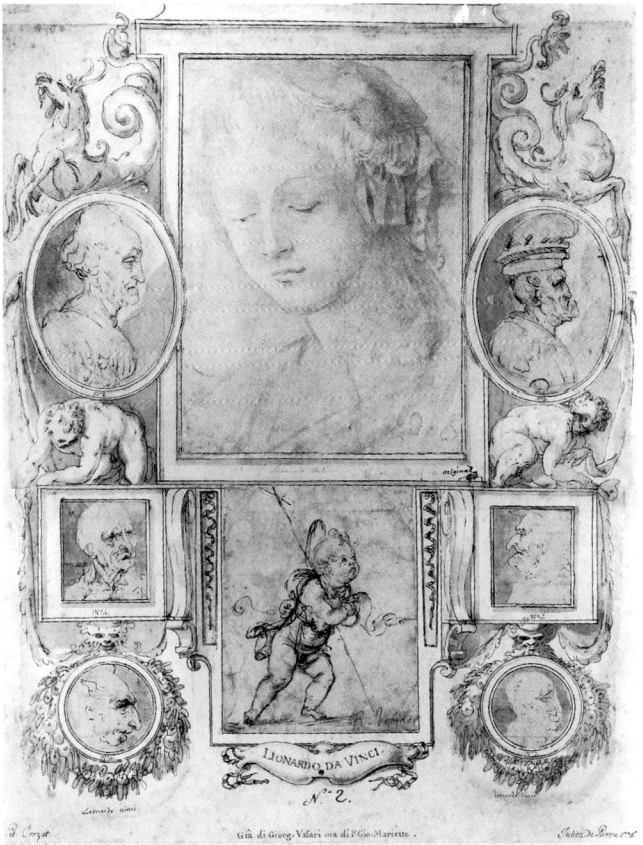

Fig. 5. Giorgio Vasari (with additions by Pierre-Jean Mariette), *Libro de' disegni* (dismembered), album page with pasted drawings thought to have been by Leonardo's hand. Pen and brown ink, brush and gray wash, traces of black chalk and leadpoint, 493 × 375 mm. Graphische Sammlung Albertina, Vienna 14179

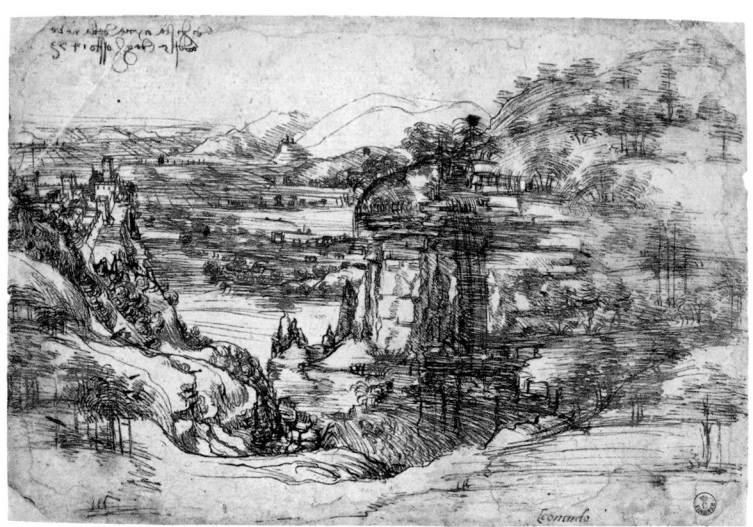

Fig. 6. Leonardo da Vinci, *Landscape of the Arno River and Valley* (recto). Pen and two colors of brown ink, 195 × 286 mm. Gabinetto Disegni e Stampe degli Uffizi, Florence 8 P

pupil and artistic heir and therefore the majority owner of the great master's drawings; Giorgio Vasari (1511–1574), who glued several examples onto the pages of his *libro de' disegni* (figs. 4, 5); and the sculptor Guglielmo della Porta (d. 1577), who owned the Codex Leicester (cat. no. 114).

The present exhibition aims to offer a unified portrait of Leonardo as a draftsman, integrating his diverse roles as an artist, author, scientist, inventor, theorist, and teacher within a chronological framework that can shed light on his development. Unlike most Italian Renaissance artists, Leonardo inscribed a number of his notebooks and drawings with dates and reminders of places and purposes. His earliest extant dated drawing is the double-sided sheet of landscape studies of the Arno River and valley (figs. 6, 7), which he inscribed on the upper left of the recto, "on the [feast] of Saint Mary of the Snow, on the day of August 5, 1473" (*dì di s[an]ta maria della neve / addj 5 daghossto 1473*). Leonardo's tendency toward record keeping may have stemmed from his family's traditional profession; his father, Ser Piero di Antonio da Vinci (1427–1504), was a notary, like many of the men in the artist's family going back to the late fourteenth century. A distinguished body of scholarship has settled numerous issues of connoisseurship in Leonardo's work, questions regarding content, context, dating, authenticity, and broad definitions of his corpus of drawings (see essay by Carlo Pedretti). However, the approach to Leonardo's drawings has often been thematic rather than chronologically integrated, which has led to fragmented discussions of his oeuvre. It is very clear from his writings that Leonardo considered his diverse endeavors complementary.

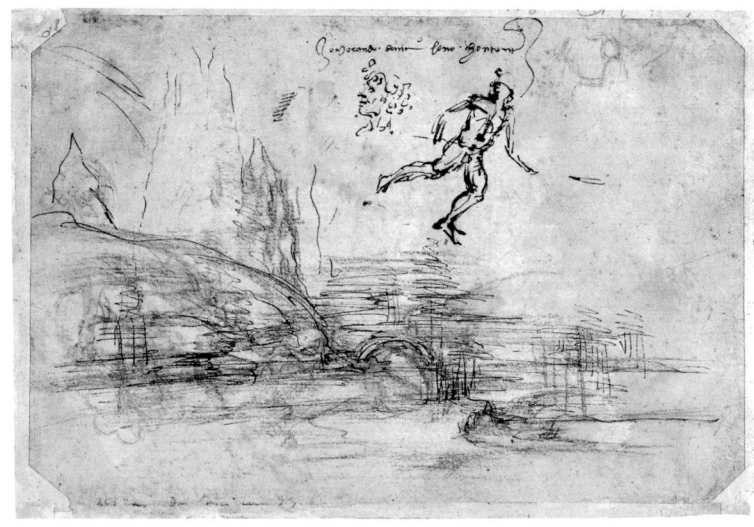

Fig. 7. Leonardo da Vinci, *Sketches of Landscape and Figures* (verso). Soft black chalk or charcoal, pen and brown ink, small traces of red chalk, 195 × 286 mm. Gabinetto Disegni e Stampe degli Uffizi, Florence 8 P

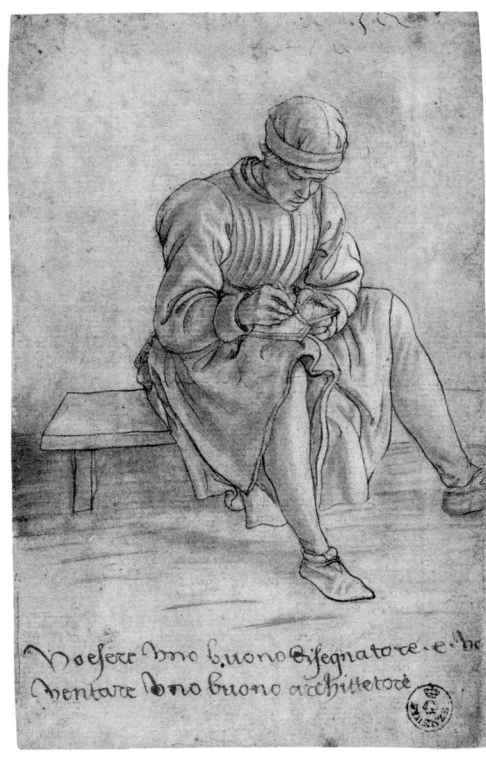

Fig. 8. Maso Finiguerra, *Apprentice Drawing.*
Pen and brown ink, brush and brown wash, over
traces of black chalk or leadpoint, on off white
paper partly tinted with red-pink wash, 194 ×
125 mm. Gabinetto Disegni e Stampe degli Uffizi,
Florence 115 F

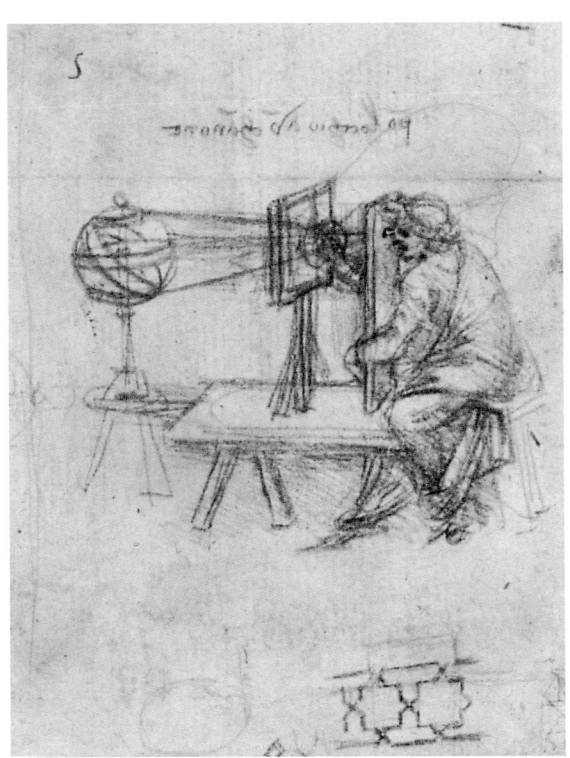

Fig. 9. Leonardo da Vinci, *Draftsman Drawing an Armillary
Sphere.* Silverpoint on pink-beige prepared paper, 297 ×
198 mm. Codex Atlanticus, vol. 1, fol. 5r (formerly fol.
Galibiati 1 bis r-a). Biblioteca Ambrosiana, Milan

This is the first comprehensive international-loan exhibition of Leonardo's work in
America, and it is among the largest ever attempted,[4] comprising 147 drawings and 1 painting, the unfinished *Saint Jerome Praying in the Wilderness* from the Vatican Museums (cat.
no. 46), which illustrates the artist's process of design in full scale. In the present selection,
118 works are by Leonardo, and 30 drawings are by artists relevant to his formation in
Florence and activity in Milan. An attempt is made to represent drawings for most of
Leonardo's major projects and through a diversity of types. Selected from public and private
collections in Europe and the United States, the display gives preference to drawings that are
less familiar, that have rarely been exhibited, and that have seldom been seen together.
Leonardo is possibly the most written-about artist of all time. Yet as a whole the enormous
literature on his drawings has neglected issues of their technique and function. In the last
twenty years scholarship has moved toward a clearer understanding of art production within
the socioeconomic structures of patronage in the Italian Renaissance. And during the last
decade especially, historians have also gradually clarified how art in this period was produced
within the material, businesslike world of the Renaissance artist's *bottega,* or workshop. It
is against this practical background that Leonardo the draftsman needs now to be reassessed.

An exhibition can offer an important first step toward such reassessments. Here, the primary objective is to offer the general public and art historians a context in which to look attentively at Leonardo's drawings as works of art full of telling clues about their making and their use, rather than as abstract illustrations of content. The skill of drawing was the backbone of artistic production and training in the Italian Renaissance. A study by Maso Finiguerra (1426–1464) from the early 1460s portrays a young apprentice, seated presumably in an artist's workshop, in the act of drawing in a small sketchbook (fig. 8). The sheet is inscribed along the bottom, "I would like to be a good draftsman and I would like to become a good architect."[5] Leonardo's sheet from the Codex Atlanticus, probably from the late 1470s to early 1480s, shows an artist drawing an armillary sphere onto a pane of glass by using a perspective frame (fig. 9). The great master had much advice to offer the young apprentices who were to be the readers of his intended painting treatise; the *Libro di pittura* (Codex Urbinas Latinus 1270, Biblioteca Apostolica Vaticana) was posthumously compiled from Leonardo's notes by Francesco Melzi (cat. nos. 120, 121). As Leonardo stated in the *Libro di pittura*, "A youth should first learn perspective, then the proportions of all things, then study with a good master.[6] . . . Study science, then follow the practice born of that science."[7] A note in the Codex Atlanticus, possibly dating from April 1490, further sums up Leonardo's teaching philosophy: "The painter who copies merely by practice and judgment of the eye, without reason, is like the mirror which imitates within itself all the things placed before it without cognition of their existence."[8] Sound theory was the foundation of practice.

Leonardo's early career in Florence (until his departure for Milan sometime between 1481 and 1483) merits particular attention, and here the reader of the present catalogue will find a number of proposed changes in the chronology of his drawings established by previous scholarship (cat. nos. 13–46). In an effort to clarify the young Leonardo's roots as a draftsman, the present exhibition gathers together a significant group of nine drawings by Andrea del Verrocchio (cat. nos. 1–6, 8 verso, 9, 10), the great sculptor and painter who was Leonardo's teacher. Only slightly more than a handful of sheets by Verrocchio are extant, and these reveal that innovations usually credited to Leonardo may have begun in Verrocchio's workshop. The innovations include the quick sketching of figures from different points of view (cat. no. 4), the sfumato technique of rendering shadows with charcoal or chalk (cat. nos. 1–3, 5, 6), and the measured survey drawings of the proportions of the horse (cat. nos. 9, 10). Leonardo probably entered Verrocchio's workshop in the 1460s (see Chronology), and it was there, one may argue, that he probably acquired a new approach to drawing, along with the more traditional skills and working habits that were largely expected in professions still governed by a medieval guild system. Speaking later from the vantage point of the teacher, Leonardo advised in a note from 1490–92, in Paris Ms. A, "the artist should first exercise his hand by copying drawings from the hand of a good master."[9] Among the highlights of Verrocchio's career as a draftsman are exquisite full-scale drawings, or cartoons, of the heads of young women (cat. nos. 1, 3), which according to Vasari the young Leonardo closely imitated in style and technique[10] but of which practically nothing survives in his oeuvre.[11] Unfortunately for modern connoisseurs, the practice of precise imitation favored in the workshops of Verrocchio and other artists of the period often makes it difficult to distinguish the hand of the master from that of his pupils. One such gifted pupil, Lorenzo di Credi, was Leonardo's younger colleague in Verrocchio's workshop and became the artistic heir of Verrocchio when he died in Venice in 1488. The exhibition includes two studies attributed to Credi (cat. nos. 7, 8 recto); one of these sheets may have come from a sketchbook by Verrocchio himself, to judge from the handwriting (cat. no. 8 verso). (All his life Leonardo would be a diligent keeper of sketchbooks and notebooks.) A page from another dismembered sketchbook (cat. no. 12), from 1487–88, is also by an artist connected with Verrocchio's workshop, who is probably to be identified as Francesco di Simone Ferrucci, and further illustrates the types of compendia that were current in Verrocchio's sphere of influence.

In 1472 the twenty-year-old Leonardo was inscribed in the account book (*Libro rosso: Debitori, creditori e ricordi*) of the painter's confraternity, the Compagnia di San Luca, in Florence, and the schedule of payment of his dues began in June of that year. This fact may be taken to mark the conclusion of Leonardo's apprenticeship and the beginning of his career as a professional painter, though he seems to have stayed with Verrocchio until at least 1476 (when he was accused twice of sodomy), probably as a collaborator. From Verrocchio, a highly successful master who was primarily a sculptor, Leonardo seems to have learned an approach to design and a visual culture that were fairly singular at a time when Renaissance painters looked to *disegno* (design and drawing) and *rilievo* (relief) as the shaping forces of their art. The young Leonardo's work from the 1470s onward reveals a refined plastic conception of form (cat. nos. 13–21). The exhibition gathers five early drapery studies attributed to him (cat. nos. 13–17), painted with the brush in ink, wash, and gouache on linen (see essay by Françoise Viatte). According to Vasari's biography of Leonardo, the precocious artist copied real draperies, which had been dipped in wet clay slip and then arranged on a clay mannequin.[12] Some of Verrocchio's other pupils also produced carefully executed drapery studies, and this has led to questions regarding the attribution to Leonardo of some of the early drapery studies painted on linen. The teaching practices in Verrocchio's workshop probably inspired Leonardo's later attempts (in his projected *Libro di pittura*) to describe the designs of draperies by means of a nearly academic classification of the disposition and movement of folds.[13]

For the young Leonardo, a potentially more significant legacy from his teacher Verrocchio may have been his method of inventing compositions in quick sketches. This process is recorded in Verrocchio's sheet in the Louvre (cat. no. 4), which explores a sequence of poses for an infant seen from a number of different points of view. It represents a sculptor's way of visualizing form. Leonardo's sketches for the so-called *Madonna of the Cat* (cat. no. 19) from about 1478–80 similarly portray the figural motifs from a variety of views. His initial sketches also integrate wash to obtain a remarkably sculptural chiaroscuro that functions as a dynamic, unifying element of the composition. Early examples of this technique are another sketch for the *Madonna of the Cat* (cat. no. 18) and the *Young Woman Bathing an Infant* (cat. no. 21) from Oporto.

The young Leonardo's refined control of tone with the traditional fifteenth-century technique of metalpoint drawing on prepared paper is already evident in sheets from the early to mid-1480s (cat. nos. 39–45, 53). These reveal an exquisitely unified use of parallel hatching, often with nearly pitch-straight lines for a soft relieflike effect of the forms on the paper (see my essay). Leonardo would continue to use the difficult, linear medium of metalpoint until the mid-1490s (cat. nos. 61–63, 66). Many of his drawings suggest that he first began sketching lightly and cautiously with the metal stylus (cat. nos. 41, 43, 53), then gradually reinforced strokes to define the final outlines and to build up a density of tone in the shadows; mistakes or unwanted lines in metalpoint cannot easily be erased. His materials essentially conform to those described in Cennino Cennini's *Libro dell'arte* (manuscript before 1437).[14] The paper is coated with a mixture of finely pulverized bone, color (from mineral sources), lead white, and glue; in his early drawings, this preparation is usually fairly thick and stiff and burnished to a slight shimmer. Leonardo appears to have favored the use of silverpoints (rather than styluses made with other alloyed metals), conforming again to the preference expressed in Cennino's *Libro;* two of Leonardo's fragmentary notes from 1490 and 1491 refer casually to silver styluses.[15] He often reworked his metalpoint drawings with pen and dark brown ink, to clarify the final outlines and to darken the shadows (cat. nos. 20, 25, 38, 40, 45, 66). He also frequently added white gouache highlights, according to Cennino's recipe of "a little lead white well worked up with gum arabic" dissolved in water. Three studies of animals in metalpoint on pink-beige prepared paper (cat. nos. 41–43) are here dated to 1480–85. The technique used in these drawings falls between that of the late studies for the *Adoration of the Magi* (cat. no. 40) and that of the study for the Sforza equestrian monument (cat. no. 53). The sheet of bear studies (cat. no. 43) also contains an underlying sketch of a pregnant woman who seems nearly identical in physical type to the Virgin in the British Museum double-sided sheet (cat. no. 20) that is associated with the *Benois Madonna* (State Hermitage Museum, Saint Petersburg) from 1478–80. The figural types in the British Museum sheet also reflect those of the early *Madonna of the Carnation* (Alte Pinakothek, Munich). Another reason for dating Leonardo's animal studies in metalpoint to the first half of the 1480s is that their style and technique more closely conform to the animal studies being done in this medium by contemporary Florentine artists.[16]

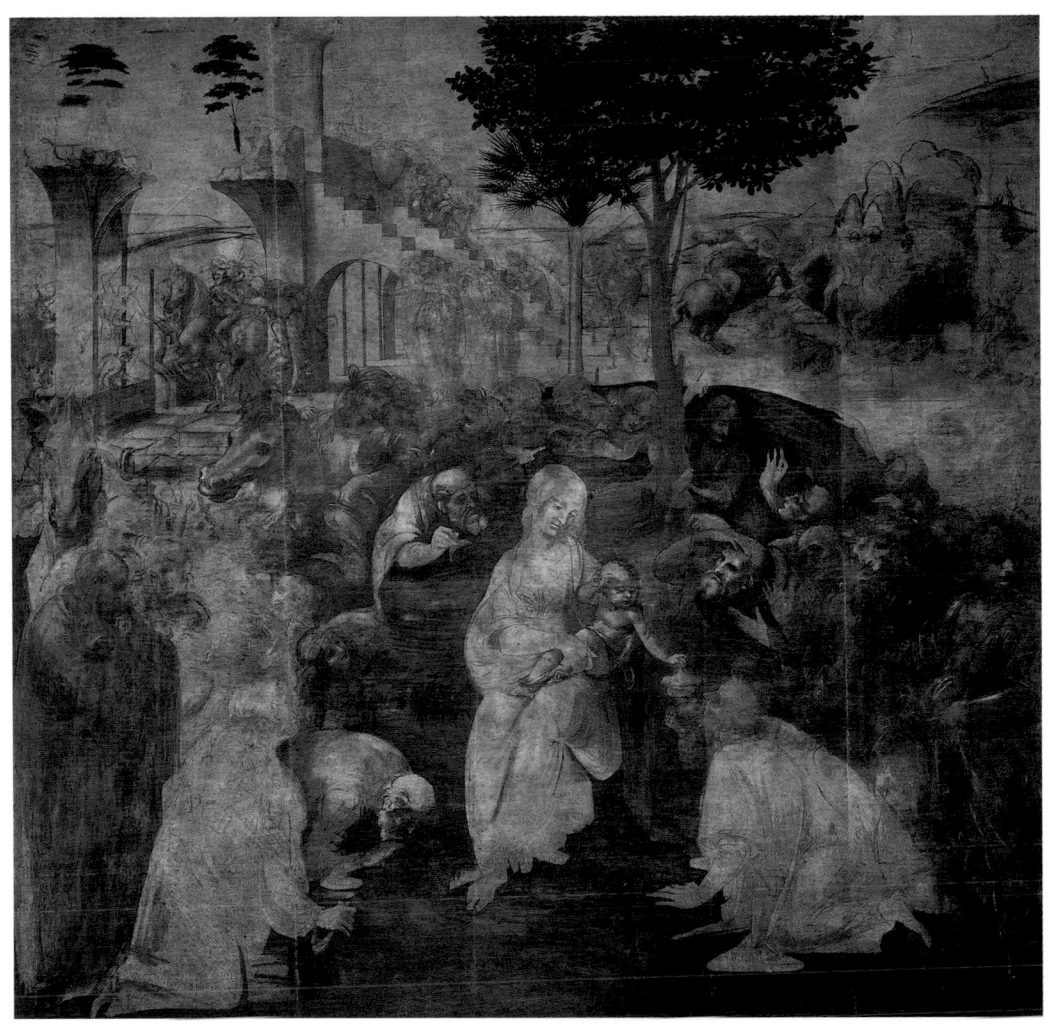

Fig. 10. Leonardo da Vinci, *The Adoration of the Magi*. Unfinished painting. Oil and some *tempera grassa* on wood, 243 × 246 cm. Galleria degli Uffizi, Florence 1594

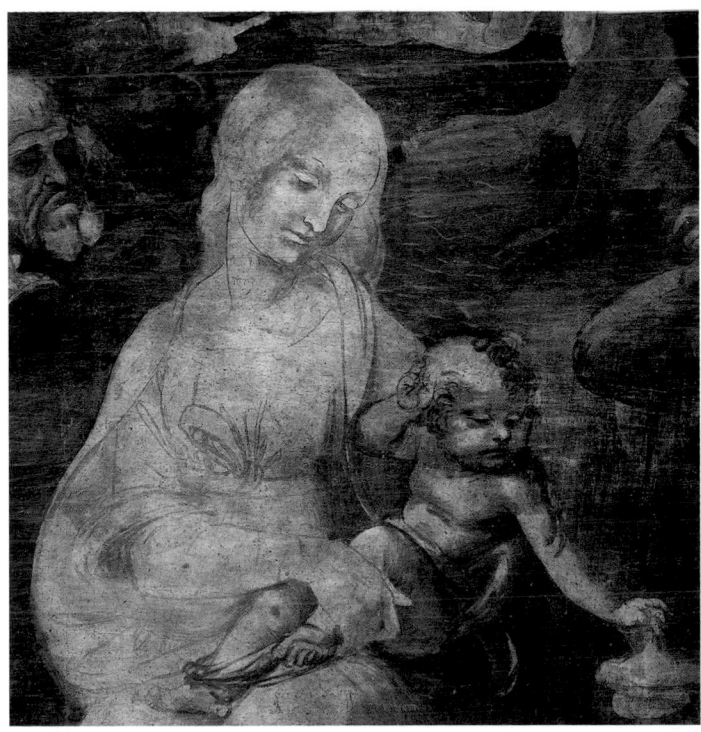

Fig. 11. Detail of fig. 10

Leonardo's work as an independent painter in Florence culminated in his altarpiece of the *Adoration of the Magi* (Uffizi, Florence), contracted by the monks, the Canonici Regolari, of San Donato a Scopeto in July 1481 and mediated by his father, Ser Piero da Vinci (figs. 10, 11). Alessandro Cecchi's essay offers new evidence of the role of Ser Piero in securing commissions for his son through his contacts as a practicing notary in Florence. The exhibition gathers almost half of the extant sketches and studies that seem related to the design of the *Adoration of the Magi* (cat. nos. 27–32, 36–40), which Leonardo left unfinished on his departure for Milan in 1481–83. The picture is a virtual brush drawing on the wood panel. Some of the animated quick sketches (cat. nos. 29–32, 38) call to mind Leonardo's advice to young painters to keep a small sketchbook for a nearly journalistic observation of the human figure in various poses or attitudes (*atti*):

> And with slight strokes take a note in a little book which you should always carry with you. It should be of tinted paper, that it may not be rubbed out, and when full exchange the old book for a new one; since these things should be preserved with great care. The forms and positions of objects are so infinite that the memory is incapable of retaining them. Keep these sketches as your guides and masters.[17]

If one considers the great expenditure of labor that would have been required to study each figure in drawings on paper and then to execute each one in paint (with Leonardo's nuanced techniques of oil glazes), one may be able to deduce some of the reasons why Leonardo abandoned the *Adoration of the Magi* altarpiece. The ambitious composition seems to contain at least sixty-six figures and eleven animals according to Jens Thiis's important early monograph, *The Florentine Years of Leonardo and Verrocchio* (London, 1914). Leonardo's patience was probably exhausted.

His panel of *Saint Jerome Praying in the Wilderness* (cat. no. 46), for which there are no extant directly preparatory studies, is in a state of unfinish similar to that of the *Adoration of the Magi* altarpiece. It therefore permits an extraordinary glimpse into Leonardo's creative process at a stage between the drawings on paper and the laying in of the full-scale design on the primed painting surface. The design of the saint's head was produced by means of a cartoon. Attentive examination of the paint surface reveals the presence of Leonardo's fingerprints on the upper left of the composition (see discussion in cat. no. 46). The Vatican *Saint Jerome* probably dates from not long after the Uffizi *Adoration,* considering that its composition is echoed in early designs for a *Nativity* (cat. no. 45; Windsor, RL 12560) and that it shares compositional elements with the Louvre *Virgin of the Rocks,* contracted in 1483. As scholars often note, the motif of the Virgin adoring the Christ Child in the center of catalogue number 45 may represent an initial idea from about 1483 to 1485 for the Louvre *Virgin of the Rocks,* the main panel of the altarpiece that is to be identified with Leonardo's earliest documented commission in 1483 on his arrival in Milan (fig. 12). (See Chronology for the complex, acrimonious development of this project.) Among Leonardo's great innovations as a draftsman was his emphasis on the freshness of the sketching process. In the sheet that seems to anticipate the conception of the *Virgin of the Rocks* (cat. no. 45), alternative designs for the composition and of other closely related motifs pour out in fluent sequences of sketches. One idea led to another idea, which he then completed with the outlines of the intended picture frames (see essay by Martin Kemp). A passage from Leonardo's notes, as it is recorded in the *Libro di pittura*, describes the creative flux of sketching:

> You, composer of pictures, however, do not draw the limbs on your figures with finished outlines or it will happen to you, as to many different painters who wish every little stroke of charcoal to be definitive. . . . Decide broadly on the position of the limbs of your figures and attend first to the movements appropriate to the mental attitudes of the creatures in the narrative, rather than to the beauty and quality of their limbs.[18]

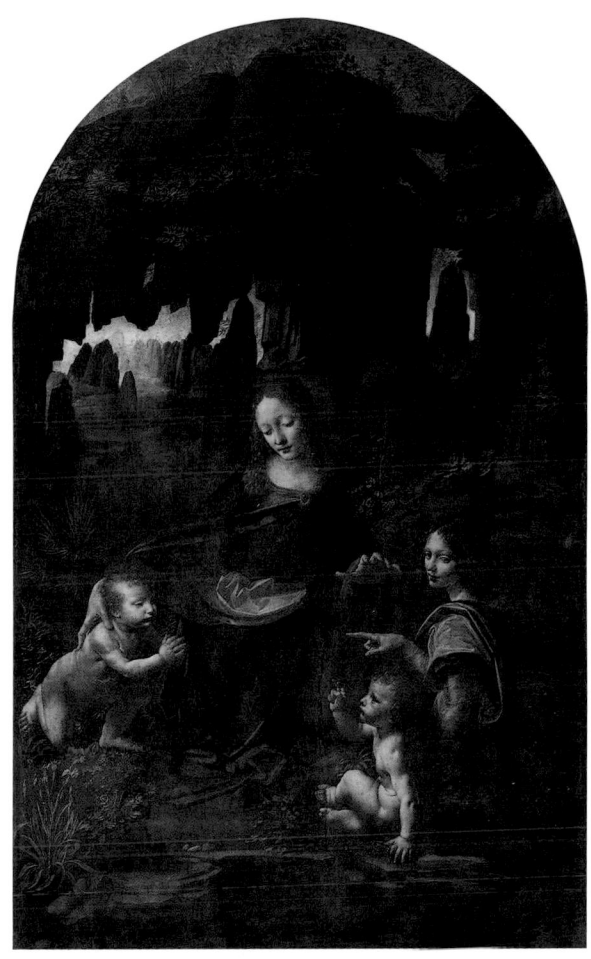

Fig. 12. Leonardo da Vinci, *The Virgin of the Rocks*. Oil on canvas transferred from wood, 199 × 122 cm. Musée du Louvre, Paris, 777

In his letter to Ludovico Sforza "Il Moro" from 1481–83 (known only from contemporary drafts), which he presumably wrote to seek employment at the ruler's court in Milan, Leonardo advertised himself as being a most ingenious military engineer.[19] His numerous drawings of lethal weapons and war machinery (cat. nos. 48–52, 55) seem unsurpassed in their narrative evocation of combat, giving some credence to the artist's claims. Yet even Leonardo might have agreed that his main endeavor for Ludovico Sforza in Milan was his design for a colossal bronze equestrian monument (cat. nos. 53, 63, 64) to commemorate the ruler's father, Francesco, who had died in 1466 (Leonardo's letter to Ludovico already casually alludes to the possibility of this undertaking). At some point in the complex history of the Sforza monument, which dates back to 1473, the project seems to have also involved the great Florentine sculptor and painter Antonio del Pollaiuolo.[20] The exhibition brings together, probably for the first time ever, Leonardo's exuberant early study for the Sforza monument (cat. no. 53), showing the horse in a rearing pose, and one of Pollaiuolo's strikingly similar working *modelli* for the same project (cat. no. 11). Leonardo's research in designing the statue

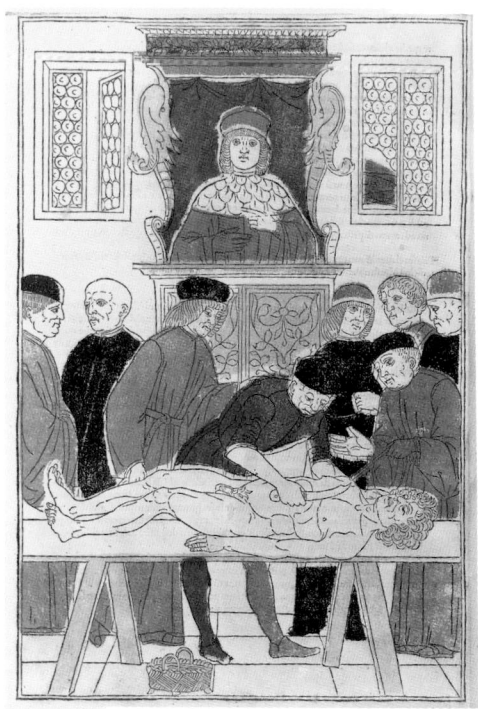

Fig. 13. Illustration of a human dissection in Johannes de Ketham, *Fascicolo di medicina* (Italian trans. by Sebastianus Manilius [Venice: Johannes and Gregorius de Gregoriis, February 5, 1493], unpaginated). Colored woodcut, 304 × 206 mm. The Metropolitan Museum of Art, New York; Harris Brisbane Dick Fund, 1938 38.52

entailed studies after nature of extraordinary nuance and cogitation, especially after he resolved to adopt a striding pose for the horse (cat. no. 63). Some of his ideas for the daunting task of casting the colossal statue in bronze are laid out in another sheet from Windsor (cat. no. 64).

As poetic exercises in the invention of subject matter, Leonardo's drawings of allegories (cat. nos. 54, 67, 68) appear to reflect the refined literary tastes of the Sforza court. In 1490 he staged the *Paradiso* by his friend the Florentine poet Bernardo Bellincioni (1452–1492), who arrived in Milan in 1485 and remained there until his death. Leonardo's apparent delight in actively participating in the pageantry of the Sforza court can also be inferred from extant records of other theatrical performances (particularly plentiful for the 1490s), as well as from his sketches of emblems, costumes, and stage sets (cat. no. 68). The nearly seventeen years that he spent at the Sforza court (from 1482–83 until 1499), which was a way station for some of the brilliant minds of the period, proved especially productive for his career, for he also emerged as a theorist, scientist, and author of treatises. Leonardo wrote a number of reminders and lists of the books in his possession (dating from the early 1490s to 1505), which suggest the diversity of his interests and reading (see essay by Carlo Vecce).[21] He also befriended Donato Bramante (1443/44?–1514), the great painter, architect, and geometrist from Urbino, who resided in Milan from at least 1481 onward, as well as Fra Luca Pacioli (ca. 1445–ca. 1514), the Franciscan mathematician and student of perspective, who arrived in 1496. During his brief journeys to Milan in 1490 and before, Francesco di Giorgio (1439–1501), the versatile Sienese artist, architect, and engineer, became Leonardo's friend and rival in the competition to design the domed crossing tower (*tiburio*) of Milan Cathedral (see discussion in cat. no. 55). Leonardo's exploration of proportion, perspective, geometry, and architectural design (cat. nos. 53 verso, 56) benefited from these exchanges in no small measure.

As Leonardo contemplated the writing of his treatises—on the human body; the elements of machines; the phenomena of light, shadow, and perspective; the movement of water; and the flight of birds—he sought a clarity of visual description that was equal to the logic of his empirical observation. He is often credited with devising the consistent method of depicting buildings and their parts in plan, section, and perspectival massing in architectural drawings from the late 1480s to 1490s. He would also gradually apply this more precise

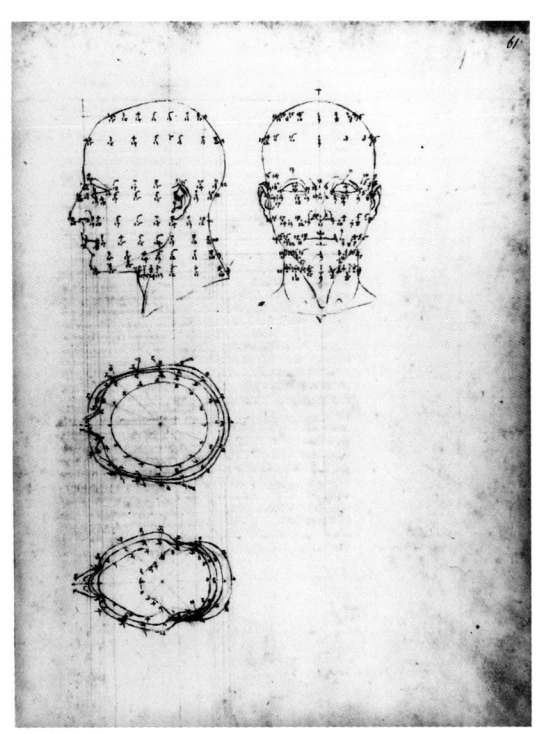

Fig. 14. Detail from Piero della Francesca, *De prospectiva pingendi,* showing a means of proportional measurement for the foreshortening of a head. Pen and brown ink, over black chalk or leadpoint, stylus, and compass construction, pin pricks for measurement, 290 × 219 mm. Biblioteca Palatina, Parma Ms. Parm. 1576, fol. 61r

system of describing three-dimensional form in a number of other endeavors. Leonardo's earliest anatomical drawings seem to date from 1488 to 1492. The illustration of the main organs related to the blood vessels (cat. no. 57), which he entitled the "Tree of the Veins" in an inscription between the man's legs, is partly based on animal dissection and partly derived from previous anatomical writings. Human dissections were extremely regulated and usually performed only on the corpses of criminals (fig. 13). Luca Landucci's *Diary* from 1450–1516 describes the dissection of the body of a young man who had been hanged on January 24, 1505; conducted for six days in rooms at Santa Croce in Florence, it was attended by many doctors and university scholars (including Landucci's son) after permission was granted by the republic's office, the Otto di Guardia e Balìa.[22] There is extant written evidence of

only one human full-body dissection by Leonardo, dating from much later, in 1510 (see cat. no. 113). Begun in 1489, his series of accurately observed studies of the human skull (cat. no. 58) reveal a neat, treatiselike disposition of image and text on the page (as well as the technique of exquisitely fine parallel hatching that is typical of engravings from this period). Leonardo's skull drawings offer the most original and lasting contribution of his early anatomical research. The rigorously systematic method of portrayal in sections and

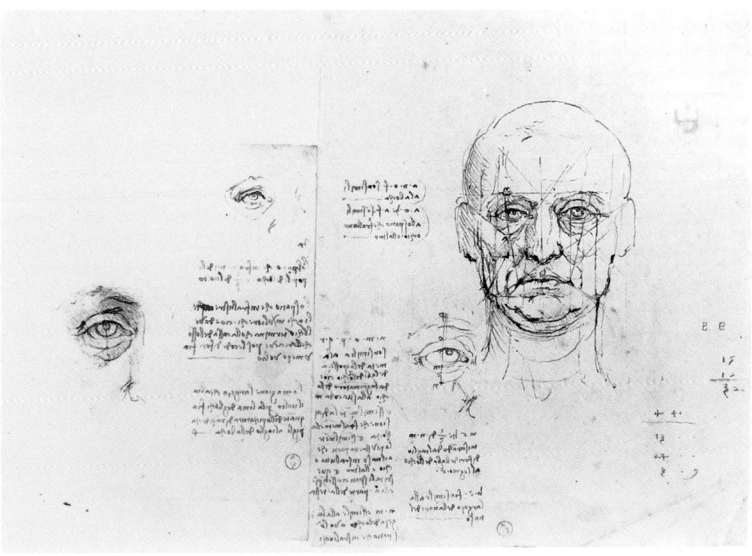

Fig. 15. Leonardo da Vinci, *Studies of Facial Proportion.* Pen and brown ink, over stylus and compass construction, pin pricks for measurement, on two joined sheets of paper, 145 × 117 mm (left), 197 × 160 mm (right). Biblioteca Reale, Turin 15574, 15576

in representative angles of view was unprecedented. His convention of illustrating anatomical details in sections, seen from the front, side, and top views, is indebted to the "plan and elevation" technique used in Piero della Francesca's *De prospectiva pingendi* (manuscript written before 1482),[23] a treatise that Leonardo knew from his experience as a perspectivist and as a friend of Fra Luca Pacioli (fig. 14). As the Renaissance understood it, "perspective" was the systematic application of "proportion" to form placed within space. For Leonardo, anatomy and proportion (fig. 15) were two sides of the same coin, and he planned to integrate the two aspects in his projected treatise on the human body (see cat. no. 86).

In his role as a theorist of painting, Leonardo repeatedly emphasized that the most formidable challenge facing a good painter was the portrayal of man and the intentions of the mind (*le passioni dell'anima*) through the body's physical capacity for gesture (cat. no. 66). His views are more fully recorded in the posthumously compiled *Libro di pittura*.[24] Leonardo appears to have finished writing a (lost) treatise on the *moti mentali*, or motions of the mind, before 1499, when he left Milan after the city fell to the French.[25] In his conception of the ages of man, the fleeting beauty of youth would often be pathetically juxtaposed with the decay and deformity of old age. From the late 1480s to the mid-1490s, his preoccupation with the human face (its proportions, expressions, and deterioration with age) would lead to some of his most penetrating studies of grotesque physiognomy (see cat. nos. 59, 60, 69–76). Yet not all his studies of grotesque physiognomy should be dated to this period, for such heads constitute a frequently recurring theme in Leonardo's drawings. Examples exist in his work ranging from the 1470s to the 1510s (see cat. nos. 24, 59, 60, 69–76, 92). Moreover, his pupil Francesco Melzi, who came to live in his household about 1508, closely imitated the series of small "caricatures" down to the left-handed strokes in Leonardo's originals (cat. no. 121). The drawings of grotesque heads also constitute the genre that made Leonardo famous in the seventeenth and eighteenth centuries, through the wide dissemination of countless copies and reproductive prints, when so much of his original work was inaccessible (see essay by Varena Forcione). A page from the *Libro di pittura* offers Leonardo's telling classification of nose types as a memory aid in drawing heads in profile; many of these are grotesquely deformed.[26] This type of classification was a teaching device primarily meant for pupils. The small selection of finished studies by Leonardo's Milanese pupils and followers that concludes the present exhibition reflects the fact that, at least in their drawings, the "Leonardeschi" were most often interested in renderings of the human head and its potential for expression. The theory of the *moti mentali* was yet another of Leonardo's major legacies as a teacher (see essay by Pietro C. Marani). The studies of heads by Giovanni Antonio Boltraffio, the Master of the Pala Sforzesca, Francesco Melzi, Andrea Solario, Bernardino Luini, and Giovanni Agostino da Lodi vividly attest that, at times, they could take Leonardo's styles and techniques to inspired heights (cat. nos. 120–33).

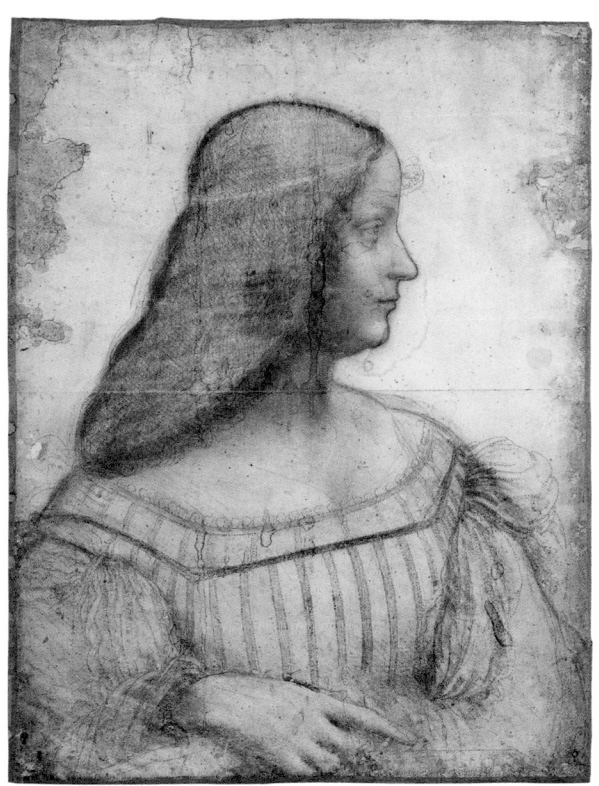

Fig. 16. Leonardo da Vinci, *Isabella d'Este*. Black, red, and white chalk, yellow pastel (?), over leadpoint, on paper prepared with a bone-color dry pigment, outlines pricked for transfer, 630 × 460 mm. Musée du Louvre, Paris MI 753

Leonardo's contribution to the design process of narrative compositions is arguably his greatest as a draftsman. Although one can identify a precedent in the second half of the fifteenth century for almost every drawing type used in the High Renaissance, it is clear that Leonardo expanded the nuances of narrative invention enormously. In the case of his mural of the *Last Supper* (Refectory of Santa Maria delle Grazie, Milan), painted in 1493–98, however, the evidence regarding his overall process of developing the composition is frustratingly sparse (this type of evidence seems more complete for his projects from after 1503). The spirited thumbnail sketches for the *Last Supper* on the upper part of the Windsor sheet (cat. no. 65) suggest that he began with a fairly conventional arrangement, with much less physical and psychological interaction among the figures, and with Judas seated on the opposite side of the table from Christ and the apostles. The early study in reworked metalpoint on blue prepared paper that is often thought to portray Saint Peter (cat. no. 66) seems closer in date to the Windsor composition sketch. The later studies in chalk for the heads and hands of the apostles are considerably more pictorial in effect (Windsor, RL 12543–12552).

In the mid- to late 1490s Leonardo turned increasingly to drawing media such as charcoal, black chalk, and red chalk that were easily smudged or blended to create exquisitely graded effects of light and shadow (cat. nos. 74–77).[27] He was among the earliest artists to use red chalk (cat. nos. 75–77). Giovanni Paolo Lomazzo's *Trattato dell'arte della pittura, scoltura et archittetura* (Milan, 1584) states that Leonardo also frequently used pastels (fabricated colored chalks) as a medium for drawing, citing the example of his studies for the heads of the apostles in the *Last Supper;* no such securely attributed drawings by Leonardo are extant.[28] The great master's own notes refer to pastels, and one describes a recipe for their making.[29] Attributed to Leonardo by a long tradition (but sometimes unjustly disputed), the fragile portrait cartoon of *Isabella d'Este* (Musée du Louvre, Paris) from 1500–1501 is regarded by most scholars as the first extant example in Italy to incorporate some pastel

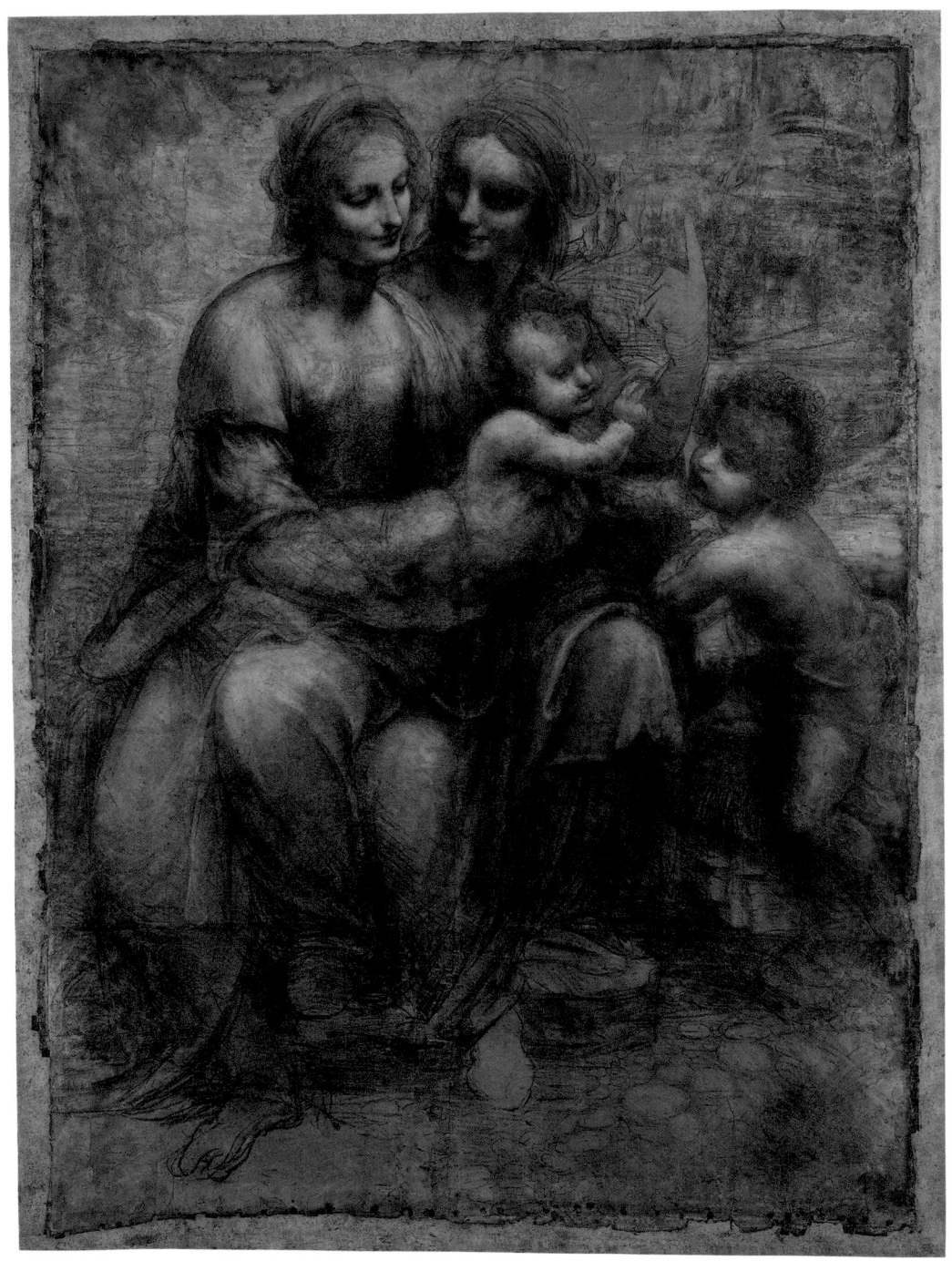

Fig. 17. Leonardo da Vinci, *Virgin and Child with Saints Anne and John the Baptist (The Burlington House Cartoon)*. Charcoal, soft black chalk, highlighted with white chalk, on light brown tinted paper, 1415 × 1060 mm. National Gallery, London 6337

pigments into its complex drawing technique (fig. 16). The present exhibition includes a selection of large-scale pastel drawings by Leonardo's earliest pupil, Giovanni Antonio Boltraffio (cat. nos. 127, 128), as well as by his more distant Lombard followers, Bernardino Luini (cat. no. 131) and Andrea Solario (cat. no. 129), to illustrate the impact of Leonardo's new pastel technique on North Italian artists.

Shortly after 1500–1501, when Leonardo returned to Florence after an absence of nearly seventeen years, he seems to have regained instant fame by publicly exhibiting a monumental cartoon portraying the *Virgin and Child with Saint Anne and a Lamb*. According to Vasari's biography of Leonardo, this cartoon enjoyed an enormously positive critical reception (which was more typically accorded to finished works of art), and for two days crowds of artists, women, and laymen came to admire Leonardo's cartoon in his private quarters at Santissima Annunziata.[30] This may or may not have been the same cartoon that Fra Pietro da Novellara carefully described in a letter from 1501 to Isabella d'Este.[31] The cartoon (or cartoons) of the *Virgin and Child with Saint Anne* from 1500–1501 has not survived, but one may judge Leonardo's exquisite drawing technique from the Burlington House cartoon (National Gallery, London), which depicts a similar subject and probably dates from 1507–8 (fig. 17). His scaled overall sketch for this later cartoon (cat. no. 96) demonstrates that movement and compositional unity were for him dominant artistic concerns. The greatly debated problem of Leonardo's versions on the theme of the *Virgin and Child with Saint Anne*, however, seems far from resolved. The studies relating to the composition of the *Virgin and Child with Saint Anne* that are exhibited here appear to conform better with Leonardo's ideas from 1506–8 and after (cat. nos. 95, 96, 105–9). In assessing Leonardo's drawings for the *Saint Annes*, as with those for the *Leda and the Swan* (cat. nos. 98–100), it may be necessary to distinguish between the dates of the original ideas or designs and the dates of execution of the studies.

According to Vasari and Benvenuto Cellini, Leonardo's cartoon for the *Battle of Anghiari* and Michelangelo's cartoon for the *Battle of Cascina* received spectacular critical acclaim, and the works served to teach the younger generation of artists — in Cellini's words, the cartoons were a "school for the world" (*scuola del mondo*).[32] Only partly completed and no longer extant, these much-admired cartoons by the greatest artistic rivals of the Renaissance were intended to serve as full-scale working drawings in painting murals on opposite walls in the Sala del Gran Consiglio (Great Council Hall) of the Palazzo della Signoria, Florence. The progress of the work on the projects can be charted from the detailed records of payment for materials and labor that are extant in the Archivio di Stato of Florence (see Chronology).[33] The *Battle of Anghiari* was commissioned from Leonardo about October 1503, and in the spring of 1505, although he had not completed the preliminary cartoon, he began executing a small part of the composition in a ruinous experimental technique of oil (apparently with some *tempera grassa*) on the dry wall (figs. 18, 19). Michelangelo's competing *Battle of Cascina* was commissioned almost a year later, in the late summer of 1504, and was meant to be painted in a traditional fresco technique, but may never have been begun on the wall (figs. 20, 21). The present exhibition gathers a group of ten drawings by Leonardo for the *Battle of Anghiari* cartoon (cat. nos. 81–88, 90, 91), as well as the famous monumental copy

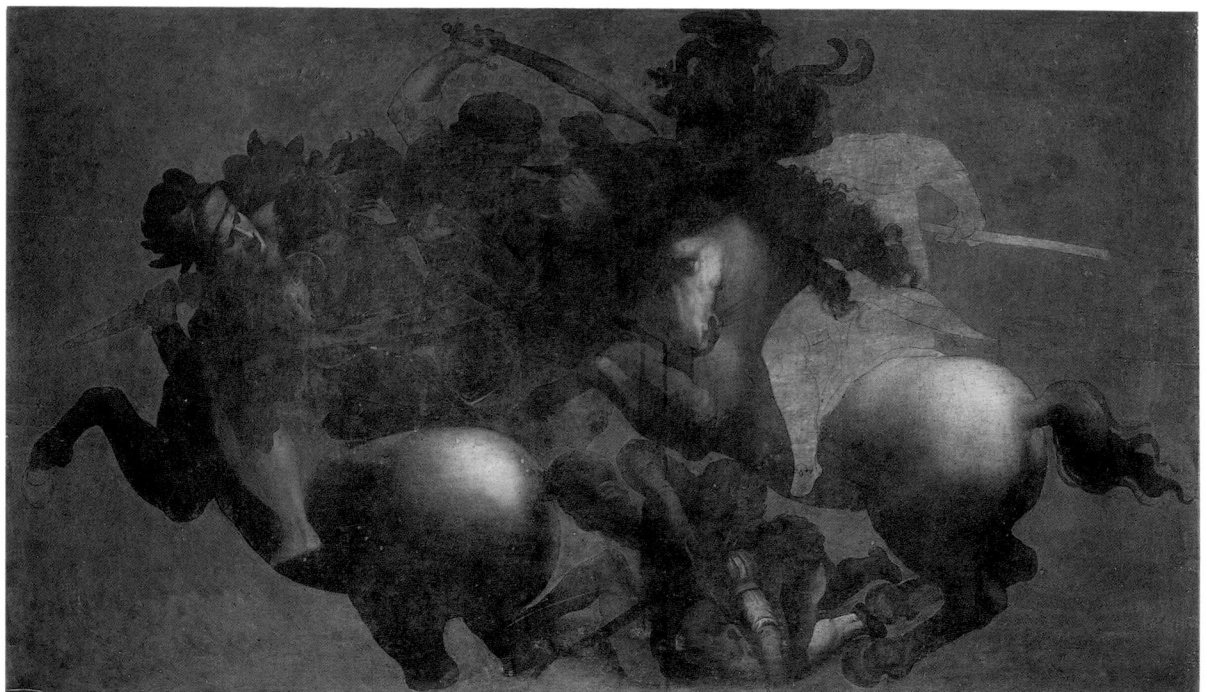

Fig. 18. Mid-sixteenth-century artist after Leonardo da Vinci, *Copy of the Fight for the Standard*, the central portion of the *Battle of Anghiari* that was executed in paint. Oil and some tempera on wood, 86 × 106 cm. Palazzo Vecchio (on deposit from the Gallerie Fiorentine), Florence 1890 no. 5376

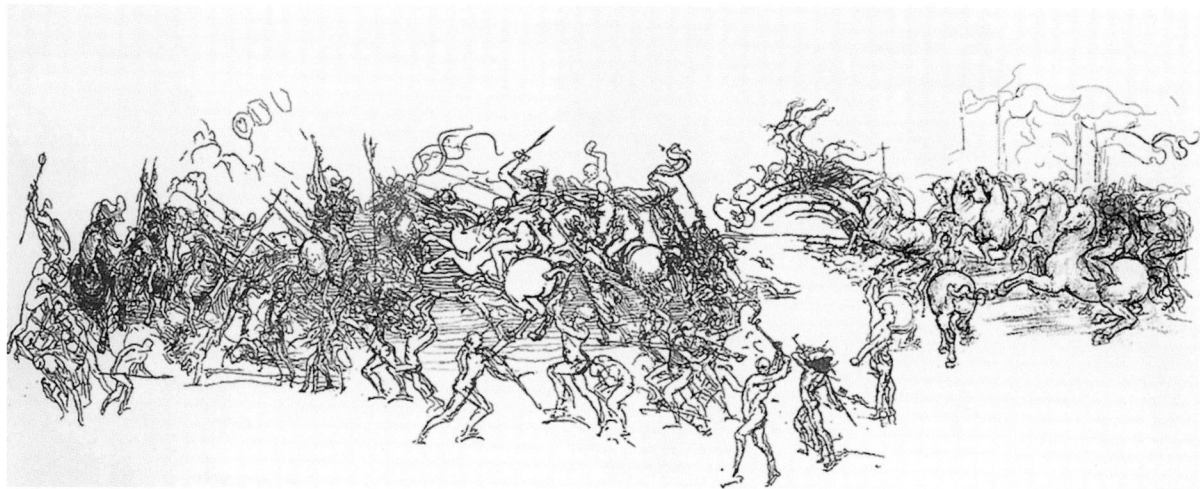

Fig. 19. Evocative reconstruction of Leonardo da Vinci's unfinished composition of the *Battle of Anghiari*, intended for the Sala del Gran Consiglio of the Palazzo della Signoria, Florence, based on Leonardo's sketches in cat. nos. 81–84 (digital image: Marvin Hayes)

after the main episode of the *Fight for the Standard* that was reworked by Peter Paul Rubens (cat. no. 135).

In the introduction to his *Vite de' più eccellenti pittori, scultori ed architettori* (Florence, 1550 and 1568),[34] Vasari described an orderly process of preliminary drawings based on the legacy of High Renaissance practice. According to Vasari, artists first drew *schizzi* (sketches). Sketches were supposed to resemble "the form of a stain" (*in forma di una macchia*) and

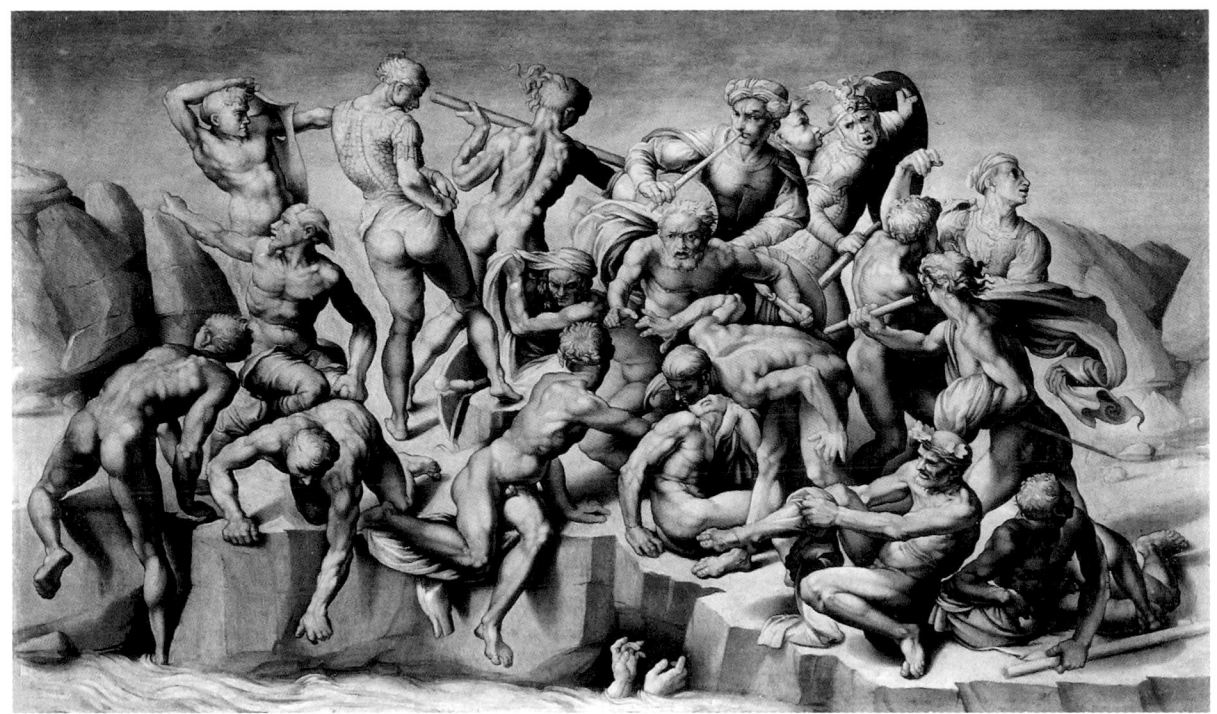

Fig. 20. Aristotile da Sangallo (after Michelangelo), *Copy of the Bathers*, the central portion of Michelangelo's lost cartoon for the *Battle of Cascina*. Oil on wood, 78.7 × 129 cm. Viscount Coke and the Trustees of the Holkham Estate, Norfolk

were meant only as a rough draft of the compositional idea, "to find the manner of the poses" (*per trovar il modo delle attitudine*). Leonardo's small pen-and-ink sketches for the *Battle of Anghiari* exemplify the extemporaneous and abstract quality of this drawing type (cat. nos. 81– 83). Here, the ideas pour onto the paper with little precision of pictorial notation. Leonardo spoke quite candidly about the stream-of-consciousness solutions arising from the intuitive process of exploration, and his approach was a great conceptual breakthrough for the history of art.[35] His justly famous passage in Paris Ms. A, from 1490–92, exhorts young apprenticing painters to look at the suggestive forms of stains and variegated patterns on stones in order to stir the creative juices and train the eye to a process of invention:

> I cannot refrain from mentioning among these precepts a new device for the imagination, which, although it may seem rather trivial and almost ludicrous, is nevertheless

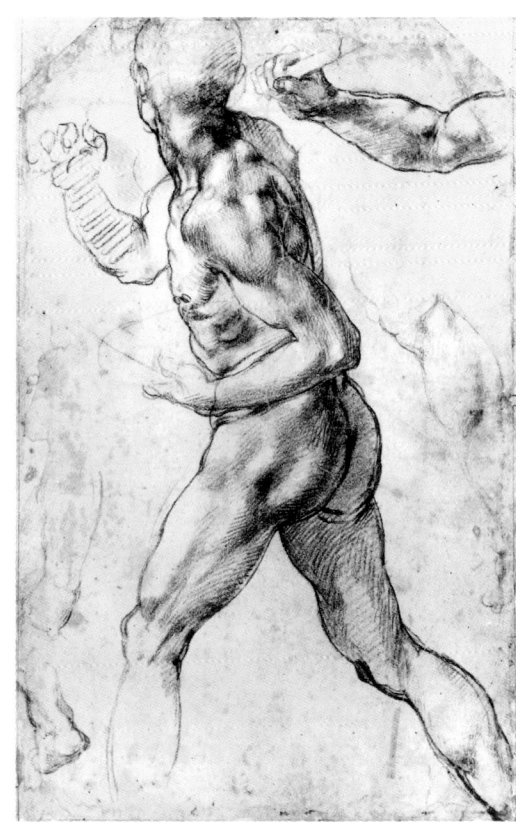

Fig. 21. Michelangelo Buonarroti, *Life Study for a Bathing Soldier in the Lost Cartoon for the Battle of Cascina*. Black chalk, 404 × 258 mm. Teyler Museum, Haarlem A 19

extremely useful in arousing the mind to various inventions. And, this is, when you look at any walls spotted with stains, or with stones of various patterns, if you have to invent some setting, you may be able to see therein a resemblance to various landscapes, graced with mountains, rivers, rocks, trees, plains, wide valleys, and hills in varied arrangement; or, again, you may see battles and figures in action; or strange faces and costumes, and an endless variety of things, which you can distill into well-drawn forms. And what happens with regard to such walls and variegated stones is just as with the sound of bells, in whose jangle you may find any name or word you choose to imagine.[36]

This inventive process seems most captivating in his "brainstorm" sketches for the composition of the kneeling *Leda and the Swan* (cat. no. 88). His repeated insistence on freshness in the sketching of initial ideas was quite new for the Renaissance: "Let your sketching of pictures be swift and the working out of the limbs not be too finished, but limited to their positioning."[37] Unfortunately, however, there are too many gaps in Leonardo's notes for one to be able to reconstruct his recommended step-by-step approach to drawing, and it is therefore very difficult to reconcile his notions of design sequence with Vasari's model. It may be that Leonardo's elaboration of more finished studies beyond composition sketches remained very flexible in approach.

Most probably drawn from life, the studies for the heads of the screaming soldiers in the *Fight for the Standard* (cat. nos. 90, 91), the central episode of the *Battle of Anghiari,* are the largest-scale drawings for the mural that are extant from Leonardo's own hand. After such detailed studies in chalk, and according to practices that were already typical by the mid-fifteenth century, artists enlarged the design of a composition to full scale by drawing a carefully rendered *cartone* (cartoon).[38] According to Leon Battista Alberti's theory, expressed in his treatise on painting (written in 1435–36), a drawing in large scale reveals errors in design more easily than a drawing in small scale; this advice was repeated by Leonardo in his notes and in his projected treatise on painting, the *Libro di pittura.*[39] In describing how to prepare wood panels for oil painting, Leonardo also recommended the use of pricked cartoons to transfer the design onto the working surface (see cat. no. 46).[40] This note from 1490–92 in Paris Ms. A is among the few fifteenth-century written allusions to cartoons. Leonardo's magnificent cartoon from 1503–5 portraying a monumental grotesque figure seen from the back (cat. no. 92) was probably very similar in drawing technique to the lost *Battle of Anghiari* cartoon. The bold, direct manner of rendering in black chalk and charcoal with aggressively hatched strokes, selective stumping in flesh areas, and vigorous reinforcement lines is typical of such large-scale drawings.

Leonardo's creative energies for the *Battle of Anghiari* seem to have been exhausted by 1506 (when he began to move back and forth between Florence and Milan); it is difficult to pinpoint when he stopped working on the mural project entirely. A magnificent sheet from 1506–8 (cat. no. 103) combines ideas related to the *Battle of Anghiari,* the standing *Leda and the Swan,* and possibly a statue of *Hercules.* His earliest thoughts for a composition of *Leda and the Swan* may have emerged in late 1504 or 1505, probably at the moment of his greatest involvement in the *Battle of Anghiari,* and thus stimulated by the problems of composing dynamic arrangements of intertwined figures. The simultaneity of conception in the two projects is evident in catalogue number 88. The sheet explores the kneeling pose of the sensuous Leda, tightly compressed within the picture field. The fairly finished Rotterdam and Chatsworth composition studies for Leda (cat. nos. 98, 99) are here displayed together, possibly for the first time. The extant copies after Leonardo's destroyed original painting show Leda standing (fig. 22; cat. no. 134), suggesting that, as would be true of his conception of the "Sforza Horse," when he resumed work on the *Leda* about 1508 he would opt for a final design that tamed agitated movement into classical

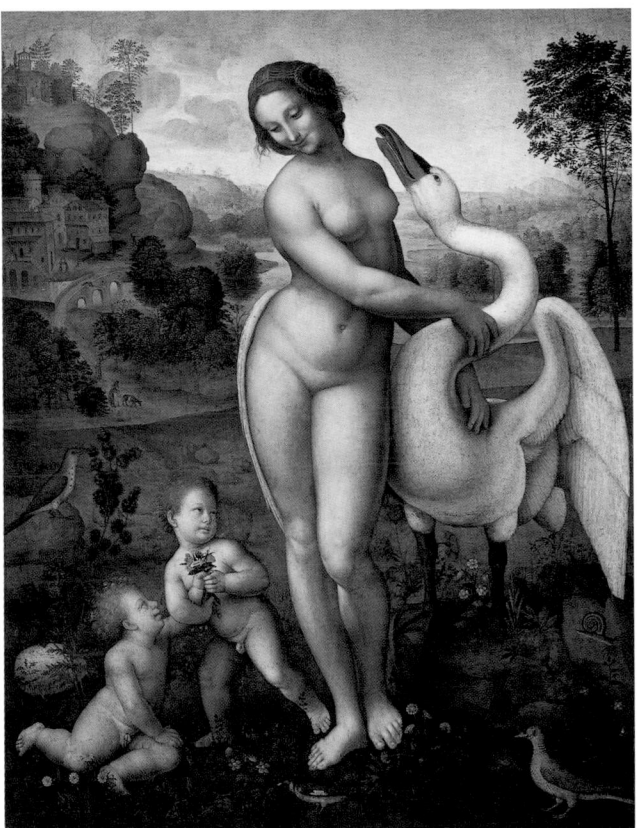

Fig. 22. Sixteenth-century artist after Leonardo da Vinci, *Leda and the Swan.* Oil and tempera on wood, 112 × 86 cm. Galleria Borghese, Rome 434

restraint of gesture. Some of Leonardo's most nuanced botanical studies correspond to the design of the foreground in the lost picture (cat. no. 100).

About 1506–8, Leonardo seems to have also contemplated the design for a statue of a standing vigilant *Hercules.* Until very recently this project had seemed hypothetical, only a scholar's house of cards. It can be reconstructed here for the first time with the relevant drawings (cat. nos. 101–4), thanks to the more concrete evidence offered by a small sheet of sketches discovered three years ago (cat. no. 101). This sheet includes sketches of water currents at the top similar to those in the Codex Leicester (cat. no. 114) and shows the figure of Hercules front and back, demonstrating that the design was intended for a statue (see discussion in cat. no. 101). Here, one may be unable to resist speculating on the possibility that Leonardo's statue was meant to compete with Michelangelo's giant marble *David,* placed in 1504 at the entrance of the Palazzo della Signoria in Florence. Toward the end of the *Anghiari* project, Leonardo also resumed anatomical research with great energy, as is suggested by a sheet from 1506–8 (cat. no. 104) that includes comparative studies of the legs of man and horse, along with views of the lower body of a Herculean figure. The larger-scale studies for the *Battle of Anghiari* (cat. nos. 90, 91), the *Leda and the Swan* (cat. nos. 98, 99), the *Hercules* (cat. no. 102), and the *Neptune Commanding His Quadriga of Seahorses* (cat. no. 93) illustrate the grandeur of expression of Leonardo's mature figural vocabulary.

His refined treatment of surface in some of his late drawings seems firmly grounded in his exacting scientific methods. About 1490 to 1492, as is especially apparent in Paris Ms. A and Paris Ms. C, Leonardo had begun to study empirically the physical properties of light and the gradations of shadows, describing their qualities, quantities, positioning, and shapes. His proposed treatise on light and shadow was to discuss "first the shadows and lights on opaque objects, and then on transparent bodies."[41] In his later notes in Paris Ms. E, dating from 1512 to 1515, he expanded on this research considerably. For example, he explored the effects from direct, diffused, restricted, and subdued light and recorded the motion of shadows with respect to moving or stationary light sources; he distinguished "simple derived shadows" from "compound derived shadows." He integrated this research with his theories on the perspective of color (*prospettiva de' colori*), aerial perspective (*prospettiva aerea*), and the perspective of disappearance (*prospettiva di perdimenti*). His descriptions of the minute optical effects produced by the atmosphere that interposes between the eye and visible objects are stunning for their precision of observation. Such findings seem to have stimulated his use of highly experimental pictorial drawing techniques, particularly for the studies of the painted *Virgin and Child with Saint Anne* (Musée du Louvre, Paris) from 1508–12 (fig. 23). The study for the head of the Virgin (cat. no. 108) makes use of an atmospheric technique of sfumato (as if a veil of mist stood between the viewer's eye and the forms); the black and red chalks are seamlessly blended in the "manner of smoke" (to rely on Leonardo's words for the technique). He used a similar technique of sfumato to render his studies for the landscape in the picture (cat. no. 109), which focus on the optical perception of the rock formations as they are affected by light and atmospheric perspective. In the drapery studies for the figure of the Virgin, he sought intensely luminous and seamlessly built-up effects of high relief (cat. nos. 106, 107), accentuating the intensity of highlights and shadows by blending white gouache, chalks, and brown ink washes. He had already used the nearly monochromatic red-on-red technique (red chalk on paper coated with a reddish ocher preparation) in some of his studies for the heads of the apostles in the *Last Supper* and in drawings from 1500–1504. Yet his application of this technique in the studies for the Louvre *Virgin and Child with Saint Anne* achieves a much more graded tonal scale and mimetic quality of surface (see especially cat. nos. 105, 106).

In his nonartistic endeavors, Leonardo's clarity of syntax for describing both the microcosmic complexity of three-dimensional form and its macrocosmic monumentality had attained an elegant coherence of visual language by 1507–10. The level of detail and accuracy of Leonardo's directly observed dissection of an old man's arms and veins (cat. no. 113 recto) sharply contrast with the fanciful anatomical abstraction of his "Tree of the Veins" (cat. no. 57) from 1488–92, which is largely based on the writings of Galen (A.D. ca. 130–

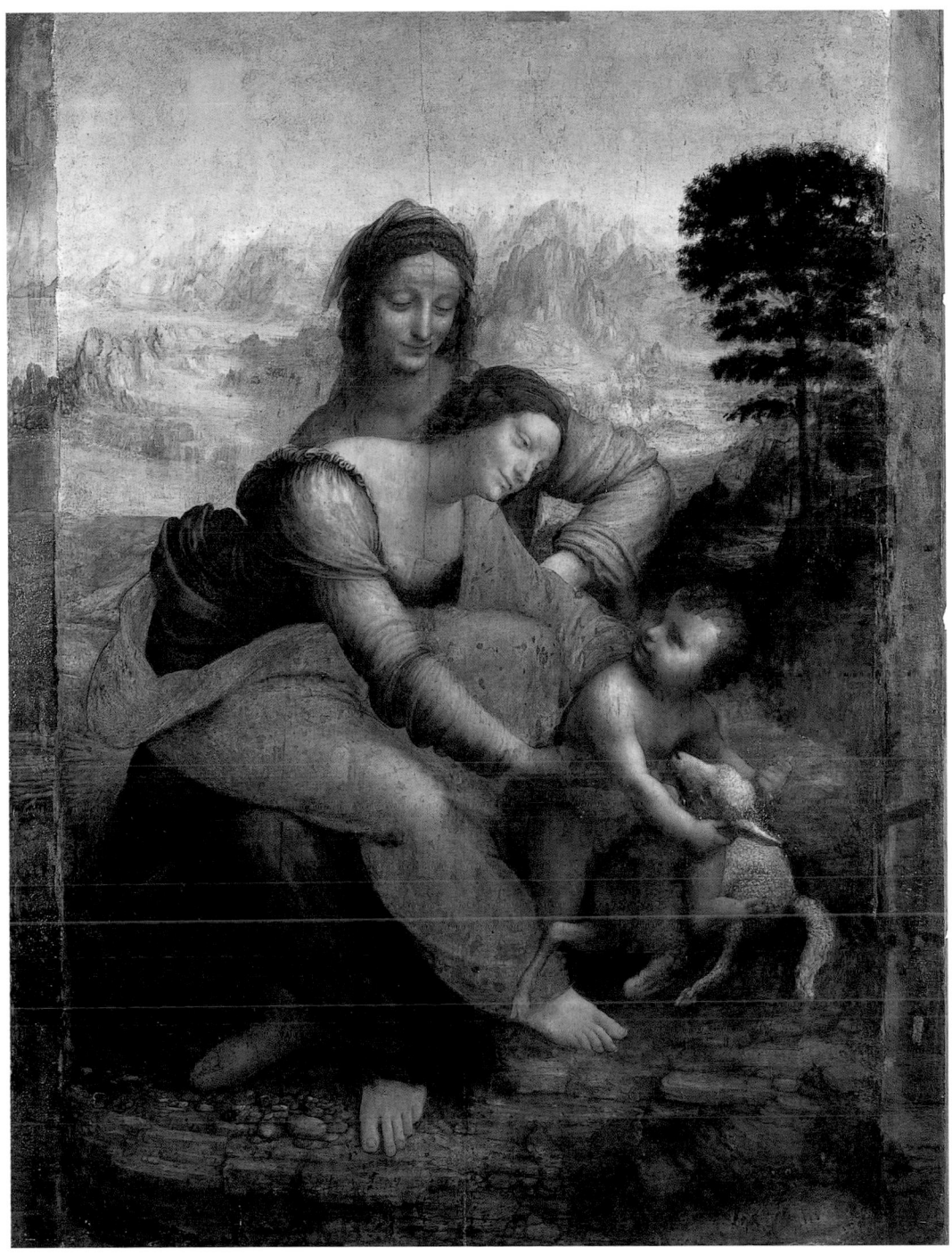

Fig. 23. Leonardo da Vinci, *Virgin and Child with Saint Anne and a Lamb in a Landscape*. Oil on wood, 168 × 130 cm. Musée du Louvre, Paris 776

200/210), the most celebrated of the ancient Greek medical writers, and Avicenna (980 – 1037), the great Arab philosopher and physician. The verso of catalogue number 113 further portrays the surface dissection of the muscles of the neck, shoulders, and arms in a sequence of rotated views of nearly cinematic effect. A similar consistency of visual description is found in the pages of Leonardo's Codex Leicester (cat. no. 114), which served as a draft for a treatise on the movement of water (see essay by Claire Farago).

The Codex Leicester is among the latest of Leonardo's extant notebooks. Eight double-sided pages of the Codex (dismembered in 1981; cat. no. 114), which offer a telling diversity of execution, are here exhibited with an array of Leonardo's other pen-and-ink drawings from 1508 to 1512. The Codex dates from the period broadly corresponding to his work on the famous though enigmatic funerary monument to Gian Giacomo Trivulzio (cat. no. 111), which included an equestrian statue that was never executed. The use of a tonal, somewhat scratchy curved hatching and straight parallel hatching is found in the Trivulzio design (cat. no. 111) and in some of the diagrams of the Codex (cat. no. 114, Sheet 3A, fol. 34v). In general, comparisons within the group of drawings from 1508–12 can clarify much about the artist's late pen-and-ink technique and modes of representing content. The devices in the portrayals of the minute, deeply rendered patterns of the water currents in the Codex—often seen in plans, sections, and perspectival three-quarter views—are as visually coherent as in the architectural rendering of a monumental mausoleum in an antique style (cat. no. 112). Some of the pages of the Codex vividly demonstrate that Leonardo continued to use parallel hatching in ways that can at first seem deceptively similar to his 1490s pen-and-ink drawings (cat. no. 114; Sheet 1A, fol. 1r; Sheet 2A, fol. 2r). Here, a rigorous precision of mark best served the expository functions of scientific illustration, but the hatching usually exhibits a subtly pictorial quality.[42] Leonardo rendered the intertwined patterns of some of the foamy water currents in curving, mimetic strands of parallel hatching of deeply tonal but atmospheric effect (cat. no. 114, Sheet 13B fols. 13v, 24r; Sheet 15B, fol. 22r).

Leonardo's closely observed, analytical studies of hydrodynamics in the Codex Leicester and other notes (Windsor, RL 12659–12665) are given a great expressive purpose in his *Deluge* drawings (cat. nos. 115, 116), which may date from 1515–17 (although there has been considerable debate on this point), just before he went to France at the invitation of King Francis I. With the poetic force of Dante's *Inferno* (quoted by Leonardo on catalogue number 64 verso), the *Deluge* drawings portray the destructive vortices of tidal waves furiously rebounding over the diminished forms of man and nature. They are powerful works of the imagination but conceived with an eminently rationalized knowledge of the dynamic principles governing the behavior of water.

As Martin Kemp has demonstrated, Leonardo understood imagination as *fantasia*, the ability to recombine images or parts of images into wholly new compounds or ideas, as in his sheet of animal sketches from 1513–17 (cat. no. 117).[43] Here, the artist portrayed more than twenty cats in fairly orderly rows and playfully inserted the form of a striding dragon in the lower center, thus transmogrifying the curving forms of real and imagined animals in a seamlessly veristic description. Since classical antiquity, poetry had been assessed in terms of "invention" of subject matter and composition, as put forth, for example, in Horace's *Ars poetica,* a work that was well known to Leonardo.[44] Inspired by an ancient literary topos, Leonardo forcefully argued in his *Paragone* (a comparison of the arts) of the early 1490s that the painter was superior to the poet, because sight was by far greater than all other mental capacities, and "the [poet's] imagination cannot see with such excellence as the eye."[45] In Leonardo's words, "he who loses his eyes leaves his soul in a dark prison without hope of ever again seeing the sun, light of all the world.[46] The eye, which is said to be the window of the soul, is the main organ whereby man's understanding can have the most complete and magnificent view of the infinite works of nature."[47] Drawing offered him a most essential tool in capturing this magnificence of sight.

1. Beltrami 1919a, p. 112, no. 180; Villata 1999, p. 203, no. 236; Marani 1999c, 2000b, p. 359, no. 73: "L[eonar]do da Vinci Il quale non si e portato come doueua con questa republica: perchè a preso buona somma de denaro et dato uno piccolo principio a una opera grande doueua fare."

2. Vasari–Milanesi 1906, vol. 4, p. 47: "Oimè! Costui non è per far nulla, da che comincia a pensare alla fine innanzi il principio dell'opera."

3. See esp. Roberts 1992.

4. Surveylike exhibitions with impressively large selections of works by Leonardo and related artists were held in 1939 at the Palazzo dell'Arte, Milan, as well as in 1952 at the Royal Academy of Arts, London, and at the Biblioteca Medicea Laurenziana, Florence, to celebrate the five-hundredth anniversary of Leonardo's birth in 1452. The catalogues accompanying these exhibitions offered essentially checklists of the works of art on display. Much smaller commemorative exhibitions were also held in 1952, notably that entitled *Hommage à Léonard de Vinci, 1452–1519* at the Musée du Louvre, Paris. In the United States, a loan exhibition organized in 1949 by Wilhelm Reinhold Valentiner (assisted by Wilhelm Suida) at the Los Angeles County Museum brought together seven original drawings by Leonardo with a body of facsimiles of his works, models of his machines, as well as drawings, paintings, and sculptures by related Florentine and Lombard artists (see Valentiner 1949). The last substantive monographic book on Leonardo as a draftsman was A. E. Popham's elegant essay-length treatment in 1945 (editions in 1946, 1947, 1949), reprinted most recently in 1994 with an introduction by Martin Kemp. Since Popham's groundbreaking book, significant drawings by Leonardo have come to light (notably the rediscovery in 1968 of his Codex Madrid in the Biblioteca Nacional, Madrid), opinions regarding attribution and chronology have been greatly revised, and methods of study have been considerably refined with the application of scientific technology to the investigation of Italian Renaissance drawing and painting techniques. A number of thematic exhibitions have explored specific aspects of Leonardo's draftsmanship, such as his studies of drapery, anatomy, horses, architecture, engineering, landscapes, and plants, as well as individual projects such as the mural of the *Last Supper,* the map of Imola, the *Madonna of the Yarnwinder,* the lost *Leda and the Swan,* and the Codex Leicester (formerly known as the Codex Hammer). These insightful displays have included relatively small selections of drawings by Leonardo, ranging from about 20 to 50 in number. Three ambitious exhibitions have attempted more surveylike treatments of Leonardo's drawings, and their accompanying catalogues have made significant scholarly contributions. The monumental exhibition in 1989 at the Hayward Gallery, London, organized by Martin Kemp and Jane Roberts, explored the universality of Leonardo's genius and offered 119 drawings with 15 three-dimensional reconstructions. *Leonardo e Venezia* at the Palazzo Grassi, Venice, in 1992 successfully integrated a selection of drawings by Leonardo with studies, paintings, and sculptures by artists related to him, in order to establish the great artist's relation to Venice, a city that he is known to have visited in 1500. The extraordinary exhibition at the Queen's Gallery (Buckingham Palace, London) in 1996, by Martin Clayton,

comprised 100 drawings by Leonardo, all selected from the rich holdings of the Royal Library at Windsor. See Kemp and Roberts 1989, Palazzo Grassi 1992, and Clayton 1996–97.

5. Uffizi, Florence, 115 F: "Vo esere uno buono disegnatore . e . do/ventare uno buono archittetore."

6. C. Urb., fol. 31r: "il giovane debbe prima imparare prospettiua puoi le misure dogni cosa poi di mano di bon maestro."

7. C. Urb, fol. 32r: "studia prima la scientia e poi seguita la praticha nata da essa scientia."

8. C. A., fol. 207 (formerly fol. 76r-a); Richter 1970, vol. 1, p. 119, no. 20: "Il pittore che ritrae per pratica e giuditio d'ochio, sanza ragione è come lo specchio, che in sé imita tutte le a sé co[n]traposte cose sanza cognitione d'esse."

9. Paris Ms. A, fol. 90r (Ms. B.N. 2038, fol. 10r); Richter 1970, vol. 1, p. 303, no. 485: "Il pictore debbe prima . suefare . la mano col ritrarre . disegni . di mano di bo[n] maestro."

10. Vasari–Milanesi 1906, vol. 3, pp. 333–34: "Sono alcuni disegni di sua mano nel nostro Libro, fatti con molta pacienza e grandissimo giudizio, infra i quali sono alcune teste di femina con bell'arie et acconciature di capelli, quali per la sua bellezza Lionardo da Vinci sempre imitò."

11. The only such extant drawing of a young woman's head with ornate coiffure that is in the present author's opinion convincingly attributed to the young Leonardo has also been given by scholars to Andrea del Verrocchio, or alternatively to Lorenzo di Credi. This is the study Florence, Uffizi 428 E (fig. 49). See Rosini 1843, vol. 4, pp. 10, 17 (n. 14); Ramirez di Montalvo 1849, no. 7; Turotti 1857, no. 7; Lagrange 1862, no. 207; Uzielli 1884, no. 11; Morelli 1890, p. 226 (Flemish copy after Verrocchio); Ferri 1890, pp. 162–63; Bayersdorfer 1893, pl. 3; Ferri 1895–1901, fol. 34v; Müller-Walde 1889, p. 40; Müller-Walde 1897, p. 6; Müntz 1898, vol. 1, p. 50, pl. 3; Morelli 1900, p. 177 (n. 8; Flemish copy after Verrocchio); Berenson 1903, vol. 2, p. 179, no. 2791 (school of Verrocchio); Jacobsen 1904, p. 417; Vasari–Milanesi 1906, vol. 4, p. 64, no. 7; Thiis 1913, p. 104 (copy of Verrocchio or Leonardo); Bode 1921, p. 20; Van Marle 1923–38, vol. 9, pp. 502–3; Venturi 1925, p. 110; Commissione Vinciana 1928– , vol. 1, pl. 16; Sirén 1928, vol. 1, p. 20, vol. 2, pl. 9B; Suida 1929, p. 20; MacCurdy 1930, p. 179; Berenson 1938, vol. 2, p. 111, no. 1015A; Degenhart 1932, p. 404; Berenson 1933–34, p. 206; Palazzo dell'Arte 1939, p. 148; Carusi 1940, p. 99; Valentiner 1950, p. 129; Castelfranco 1952b, pl. 3; Biblioteca Medicea Laurenziana 1952, p. 14, no. 11; Berenson 1961, vol. 2, p. 194, no. 1015A; Ottino della Chiesa 1967, pp. 90–91; Passavant 1969, p. 225; Pedretti 1973a, pp. 29, 32, 176; Annamaria Petroli Tofani in Forlani Tempesti and Petrioli Tofani 1974, no. 30; Ragghianti Collobi 1974, p. 92; Pedretti 1979c, no. 9; Petrioli Tofani 1980, no. 259; Pedretti 1982, p. 30; Vezzosi 1983–84b, pp. 134–35; Pedretti and Dalli Regoli 1985, pp. 53–54, no. 5; Petrioli Tofani 1986, p. 192, no. 428 E; Caterina Caneva in Petrioli Tofani 1992, pp. 114–15, no. 4.15; Brown 1998b, pp. 155–56, 211 (n. 42), fig. 149 (Lorenzo di Credi).

12. Vasari–Milanesi 1906, vol. 4, p. 20.

13. C. Urb., fols. 164v–174v.

14. Cennini 1991, pp. 26–33, 40; and Cennini 1933, pp. 5–12, 18 (English translation). Examination with X-ray fluorescence and infrared reflectography of metalpoint drawings by Leonardo and his circle at The Metropolitan Museum of Art, conducted by Kristi Dahm, confirms that the medium of the studies is silverpoint, but with varying metal inclusions (technical report, November 21, 2001); research conducted with X-ray fluorescence in 1996–97 suggested that the same was true in the case of the drawings by Filippino Lippi, the most prolific fifteenth-century user of the silverpoint medium. See more detailed discussion of fifteenth-century metalpoint technique in Bambach 1997.

15. Transcribed in Richter 1970, vol. 2, pp. 363–64, no. 1458; Beltrami 1919a, pp. 33–34, no. 52.

16. See sheets by Lorenzo di Credi (Windsor, RL 12365) and Piero di Cosimo (Windsor, RL 12796; Museum Boijmans Van Beuningen, Rotterdam).

17. Paris Ms. A, fol. 107v (B.N. 2038, fol. 27v); Richter 1970, vol. 1, p. 338, no. 571: "spesse volte nel tuo a[n]darti a spasso vedere e considerare i siti . e li atti delli omini in nel parlare, in nel co[n]te[n]dere o ridere o zuffare insieme, che atti fieno in loro . , che atti faccino i circu[m]stati . , i spartitori, i veditori d'esse cose . , e quelli

notare co[n] brevi segni in questa forma su un tuo piccolo libretto, il quale tu debi se[m]pre portar co[n] teco, e sia di crate ti[n]te, accio no[n] l'abbi a sca[n]cellare ma mutare di vechio in u[n] novo, chè . queste no[n] sono cose da essere sca[n]cellate ansi co[n] gra[n] dilige[n]za riserbate . , perchè gli sono ta[n]te le infinite forme e . atti delle cose che la memoria no[n] è capace a ritenerle, o[n]de queste riserberai come tua autori e maestri."

18. C. Urb., fols. 61v–62r: "Pero tu componitore delle istorie non membrifficare con terminati lineamenti le membrifficationi d'esse istorie che t'enteruera come a molti e' uari pittori interuenire suole liquali uogliono che ogni minimo segno di carbone sia ualido . . . componi grossamente le membra delle tue figure e' attendi prima alli mouimenti apropriati alli accidenti mentali de li animali componitori della storia." Leonardo's ideas on unfinish evoke the precepts given in Leon Battista Alberti's painting treatise (written in 1435–36); Alberti 1966, p. 97.

19. Transcriptions in Richter 1970, vol. 2, pp. 325–27, no. 1340; Beltrami 1919a, pp. 10–11, document no. 21; Pedretti 1977, vol. 2, p. 295; Villata 1999, pp. 16–17, no. 20.

20. See particularly the new documentary evidence published in Fusco and Corti 1992.

21. Pedretti 1977, vol. 2, pp. 353–75. See esp. C. A., fol. 559 (formerly fol. 210r-a); Richter 1970, vol. 2, pp. 366–68, no. 1469; Codex Madrid II, fols. 2v–3r; Ladislao Reti in Codex Madrid 1974, vol. 5, pp. 5–8.

22. Landucci 1927, p. 217.

23. Bambach [Cappel] 1994a; Bambach 1999a, pp. 224–28.

24. See C. Urb., fols. 122r–127v; selection translated in Kemp 1989c, pp. 144–46.

25. Kwakkelstein 1993b.

26. C. Urb., fol. 108v.

27. Bambach 1999a, pp. 249–64; Ames-Lewis 2001; Ames-Lewis 2002.

28. Lomazzo 1973–74, vol. 2, p. 170.

29. C. A., fol. 669 (formerly fol. 247r-a); Richter 1970, vol. 2, p. 349, no. 1379: "piglia da Gian di Paris il modo de colorire a secco"; Codex Forster II.2, fol. 159r; Richter 1970, vol. 1, p. 339, no. 612: "Per fare pu[n]te da colorire a secco; la te[m]pera co[n] vn po' di ciera e no[n] cascherà, la qual ciera disoluerai co[n] acqua, che, temperata la biacca, essa acqua stillata se ne vada in fumo a rima[n]ga la ciera sola, e farai bone pu[n]te; Ma sappi che bisogna macinare i colori colla pietra calda"; Fiorio 1997b; McGrath 1994; McGrath 1997.

30. Vasari–Milanesi 1906, vol. 4, p. 38; Bambach 1999a, pp. 249–59.

31. Beltrami 1919a, pp. 65–66, no. 107; Villata 1999, pp. 134–35, no. 150; Marani 1999c, 2000b, p. 349, no. 36.

32. Vasari–Milanesi 1906, vol. 4, pp. 41–42, vol. 7, pp. 159–61; Cellini 1971, p. 82: "Stetteno questi dua cartoni, uno innel palazzo de' Medici, ed uno alla sala del Papa. In mentre che gli stettono in piè, furno la scuola del mondo."

33. Transcribed in Frey 1909; Morozzi 1988–89; Bambach 1999b. Since Johannes Wilde's article in 1944, it has often been assumed that the *Battle* murals by Leonardo and Michelangelo were intended for the east wall of the Sala del Gran Consiglio of the Palazzo della Signoria (summary in Farago 1994). H. Travers Newton and John R. Spencer's complex and much debated proposal, however, argues instead for the murals' placement on the west wall (Travers Newton and Spencer 1982). That argument is strengthened by the reconstruction of the tribune ensemble proposed in Rubinstein 1995, pp. 104–15. Nicolai Rubinstein convincingly noted that the *gonfaloniere* and *signori* would have had more direct access to a tribune on the west wall, as their quarters were in the west wing of the palazzo. The general dimensions in Florentine braccia of the Sala del Gran Consiglio, before Vasari's drastic rebuilding are known from the vita of Simone Pollaiuolo "Il Cronaca"; Vasari 1966–, vol. 4 [testo], pp. 241–44. Francesco Albertini's *Memoriale* of 1510 more generally states the dimensions in braccia for the length and width of the Sala which agree—as much as can be expected—with Vasari's dimensions given in the vita of "Il Cronaca"; Horne 1909, p. 17. Based on the Florentine braccio at 58.36 cm, as well as on the quantities of paper that Leonardo and Michelangelo bought for their monumental preliminary cartoons, one can estimate the dimensions for the projected *Battle* murals in the Sala del Gran Consiglio to have been close to 8 meters in height and 20 meters in width. On this and other vexing questions regarding the reconstruction of Leonardo's *Battle of Anghiari* and Michelangelo's *Battle of Cascina*,

see Wilde 1944; Neufeld 1949; Wilde 1953; Gould 1954a; Isermeyer 1964; Pedretti 1968b, pp. 53–86; Kemp 1981, pp. 234–35, 245; Travers Newton and Spencer 1982; Rubinstein 1987; Morozzi 1988–89; Zöllner 1991; Rubinstein 1991; Farago 1994; Rubinstein 1995, pp. 43–46, 66–78, 97–101, 214–15; Farago 1996a; Cecchi 1996; Cecchi and Natali 1996–97, pp. 40–46, 102–29, nos. 15–24; Zöllner 1998; Bambach 1999a, pp. 33–80; Bambach 1999b.

34. Vasari–Milanesi 1906, vol. 1, pp. 174–77.

35. See esp. Gombrich 1954, 1976, pp. 58–63.

36. Paris Ms. A, fol. 102v (B.N. 2038, fol. 22v); Richter 1970, vol. 1, p. 311, no. 508: "Modo d'aume[n]tare e destare lo i[n]giegnio a varie i[n]ue[n]tioni./ Non resterò però di mettere i[n]tra questi precietti una nova i[n]ue[n]tione di speculatione, . la quale . be[n]chè paia . piccola . e quasi degnia di riso, no[n]dimeno è di grande vtilità . a destrare lo ingegno a varie inve[n]tioni, e questa . è . se tu riguarderai in alcuni mvri inbrattati di uarie machie o pietre di uari misti, se avrai a i[n]uentionare qualche sito . potrai . lì . uedere similitudine di diuersi paesi, ornati di mo[n]tagnie, fiumi, sassi, albori, pianvre, gra[n]di valli e colli in diuersi modi, . ancora vi potrai vedere diuerse battaglie e atti pro[n]ti di figure . , strane arie di uolti . e abiti . e infinite cose. , le quali potrai ridurre in i[n]tegra . e bona . forma . , e i[n]terviene i[n] simili mvri e misti come del suono di ca[m]pane . che ne' loro tochi vi troverai ogni nome e vocabolo che tu i[m]maginerai."

37. Paris Ms. A, fol. 88v (B.N. 2038, fol. 8v); Richter 1970, vol. 1, p. 340, no. 579: "Il bozzare delle storie sia pronto . e 'l me[m]brificare . no[n] sia troppo . finito , sia co[n]tenvto . solame[n]te a siti d'esse me[m]bra"; transcribed almost exactly by Francesco Melzi in the C. Urb., fol. 34r.

38. Vasari–Milanesi 1906, vol. 1, pp. 174–76.

39. Alberti 1966, p. 94. For Leonardo's elaboration, see Paris Ms. A, fol. 94v (B.N. 2038, fol. 14v); Richter 1970, vol. 1, p. 322, no. 533: "come . nelle . cose . piccole no[n] s'inte[n]de . li errori . come nelle gra[n]di." See C. Urb., fol. 46v.

40. Paris Ms. A, fol. 1r; Richter 1970, vol. 1, p. 362, no. 628.

41. Ar., fol. 171r; Richter 1970, vol. 1, p. 164, no. 110: "primo de o[n]bra e lumi de'corpi densi e poi de'corpi trasparenti."

42. Relevant comparisons are to anatomical drawings of 1508–9, the *Demonstration of the Bladder of Man* (Windsor, RL 19054r) and the *Cerebral Ventricles* (Windsor, RL 19127r).

43. Kemp 1977; Kemp 1981, pp. 152–212.

44. Paris Ms. G, fol. 8r; Richter 1970, vol. 2, p. 373, no. 1495: "vedi primo la poetica d'Oratio."

45. C. Urb. fol. 5v; Richter 1970, vol. 1, *Paragone*, p. 18, no. 18: "Non vede l'immaginatione cotal eccellentia qual vede l'occhio." See esp. Farago 1992.

46. C. Urb. fol. 13r; Richter 1970, vol. 1, *Paragone*, p. 40, no. 16: "ma chi li (occhi) perde, lascia essa anima in una oscura priggione, doue si perde ogni speranza di rivider il sole, luce di tutt' il mondo."

47. C. Urb. fol. 8r; Richter 1970, vol. 1, *Paragone*, p. 56, no. 23: "L'occhio, che si dice finestra dell'anima, è la principal uia, donde il comune senso pò più copiosa et magnificamente considerare l'infinite opere di natura."

LEONARDO, LEFT-HANDED DRAFTSMAN AND WRITER

CARMEN C. BAMBACH

I
N HIS DAY, Leonardo was known as a *mancino* ("lefty" and "southpaw" are modern-day
equivalents), with all the social, cultural, and psychological connotations—not all positive—that the word implied in the Renaissance and does even into our own time.[1] He
may be the most universally recognized left-handed artist of all time. In contrast, the natural left-handedness of other important masters in the history of Western art has not figured
as a prominent biographical fact about them or their work.[2] For example, the innate left-
handedness of Michelangelo, Leonardo's younger contemporary by twenty-three years, is
alluded to only in the autobiography of the Florentine sculptor and architect Raffaello da
Montelupo (ca. 1504/1505–1566), and then only by way of an anecdote when describing his
own left-handedness in drawing and writing.[3] Raffaello's eyewitness account is a footnote
in Michelangelo studies, for the famous biographies of Michelangelo written by Ascanio
Condivi (Rome, 1553) and Giorgio Vasari (Florence, 1550 and 1568), authors who were close
to the great artist, omit any such mention. However, many Renaissance authors writing
about Leonardo noted that he was left-handed. The difference in the level of documentation
regarding Leonardo's handedness, one may argue, can largely be explained by the fact that,
throughout his life, his manner of writing and drawing so conspicuously reflected his left-
handedness that it could not fail to be striking to his contemporaries.[4] Unlike many left-
handers from the Renaissance into our own time (such as Michelangelo), Leonardo may not
have retrained himself to use his right hand regularly for writing or drawing (more on this subject below). While Leonardo's left-handedness is well known to modern scholars of his work,[5]
it is treated much too summarily, considering the significant implications that it has both
for the connoisseurship of his drawings and for a reconstruction of his artistic personality.

The earliest record of Leonardo's left-handedness is that of the Franciscan mathematician and theorist Fra Luca Pacioli (ca. 1445–ca. 1514), the artist's intimate friend, frequent
collaborator, and near-contemporary. At the latest, Pacioli must have befriended Leonardo
during the years 1496 to 1499, when both were staying in Milan. They may have known
each other earlier, since Pacioli traveled extensively throughout Italy in the 1480s, before

residing in Venice in 1494 (publishing there his *Summa de arithmetica*, a copy of which Leonardo owned) and before arriving in Milan in 1496.[6] Pacioli and Leonardo became frequent traveling companions after both were forced to leave Milan in 1499, with the fall of the city and the flight of Ludovico Sforza "Il Moro," their patron. One of Pacioli's treatises on mathematics, the *De viribus quantitatis* (Ms. Università degli Studi di Bologna, 1496–1508), repeatedly states that Leonardo was a *mancino*. Pacioli stresses that he speaks from firsthand knowledge: he "wrote in reverse, [his script] is left-handed and could not be read except with a mirror or by holding the back of the sheet against the light. As I understand, and can say, this is the practice of our Leonardo da Vinci, lantern of Painting, who is left-handed" (fol. 239v).[7] The *De viribus* manuscript also alludes to Leonardo's collaboration with Pacioli in 1496, stating that Leonardo prepared and drew the studies of geometric solids "with his ineffable left hand" to illustrate the *De divina proportione*,[8] the famous treatise that Pacioli wrote in 1496–98 but that was not published until 1509 in Venice.[9] Pacioli is the only Renaissance source who makes overt reference to Leonardo's left-handedness as a draftsman.

The early accounts of Leonardo's left-handedness are most complete regarding his handwriting, which is not surprising, given the noteworthy character of this mirror script. Giorgio Vasari, one of the authors on the subject, corrected his posthumous vita of Leonardo after visiting Milan in 1566, where he met Francesco Melzi, the great master's faithful companion, pupil, and artistic heir (cat. nos. 120, 121). Vasari stated that a large portion of Leonardo's anatomical drawings and notes, which included the dissection studies guided by Marcantonio della Torre — the brilliant, young professor of philosophy and anatomy at the University of Pavia who died in 1511 — were owned by Melzi (for example, see cat. no. 113). In Vasari's words, Leonardo "made a notebook drawn in red chalk and hatched in pen," with illustrations of the frame of the bones, nerves, and muscles, and next to each drawing, "part by part, he wrote in letters of an ill-shaped character, which he made with the left hand, backward; and whoever is not practiced in reading them cannot understand them, since they are not to be read save with a mirror."[10] Vasari added that, besides the material in Melzi's possession that he saw in the city, some writings by Leonardo were also owned by a Milanese painter (probably Aurelio Luini), "with letters written with the left hand in reverse orientation."[11] Giovanni Paolo Lomazzo's *Trattato dell'arte della pittura, scoltura et archittetura* (Milan, 1584) records that Leonardo wrote his *Paragone* — a comparison of the arts — with the "tired hand" (*egli scrisse di mano stanca*), a common description of the left hand in the Renaissance.[12] A persistent mistake in the scholarly literature has it that Sabba da Castiglione's *Ricordi* (Bologna, 1546) mentions Leonardo's left-handedness in this context.[13] It is true that Sabba's *Ricordi* offer crucial testimony about Leonardo's work as an artist in Milan, especially about his mural of the *Last Supper* and the colossal model of the "Sforza Horse" that was destroyed by the Gascon bowmen in the French invasion of 1499.[14] But the treatise says nothing about Leonardo's left-handedness. Sabba da Castiglione (ca. 1480–1554), who was a minor writer, collector, and patron as well as a distant relation of the famous Baldassare, author of *The Courtier,* only noted his own left-handedness as a way of explaining his great difficulty in accomplishing the task of penning a treatise in his old age.[15]

Both early and modern authors have often attempted to explain the reason why Leonardo wrote in an unconventional right-to-left script, sometimes suggesting that it was a cryptographic writing concealing the secret contents of his work. The following note can be found on folio 2 verso of what was once part of the late-seventeenth- or early-eighteenth-century binding of the Codex Leicester (among the pages added by early collectors, preceding the pages of Leonardo's original manuscript; see cat. no. 114):[16] "Vinci used to write in a left-handed manner, according to the practice of the Jews, this being the manner in which those sixteen volumes are written that we have already mentioned, and the character [of the writing] being good, it could be read rather easily by means of a large mirror; it is probable that he did this so that not all could read his writings so easily."[17] This note as well as another, similarly alluding to Leonardo's left-handed script,[18] were written between 1690 and 1717–19, at the time that Leonardo's coveted manuscript had passed into the hands of the Roman painter Giuseppe Ghezzi (1634–1721), from whom Thomas William Coke, first earl of Leicester, directly purchased it in the first half of 1717.[19] Mario Baratta rightly pointed out in 1905 that in very specific circumstances Leonardo would invent code writing (for example, in the so-called Ligny memorandum of about 1499, recording the artist's secret journey to Rome with the count of Ligny). He also created playful rebuses and cryptic pictographs (Windsor, RL 12692). It is quite clear, however, that Leonardo's right-to-left script is not in itself sufficiently enigmatic to have functioned as a type of secret code.[20] With practice it can be read with little difficulty. The painter and brilliant early scholar Matteo Zaccolini of Cesena (1590–1630) is known to have become so absorbed by his studies of Leonardo's original writings that, according to the private notes of the erudite connoisseur Cassiano del Pozzo, "the said Matteo got used to that kind of [mirror] writing and began writing many of his own notes in that manner with great facility and in well-formed script, so that no one could at first understand them."[21] For Leonardo, his manner of writing was clearly one of practicality. Scientific research—old and new—seems to suggest that for "lefties" mirror writing may come more easily with practice than conventional left-to-right script,[22] as the hand moves with less effort and, staying ahead of the writing, does not smear the ink. Moreover, the fluent, expository manner of Leonardo's writings, their elegantly structured reasoning, their copious quantity, and the attractive calligraphic styles of some of his early notes in particular scarcely indicate a person suffering from dyslexia, as is often asserted concerning Leonardo in popular journalistic writings.[23]

A noteworthy point regarding Leonardo's handedness as a painter occurs in a well-known description by Antonio de' Beatis alluding to Leonardo's paralysis of the right hand, a reference that scholars have interpreted in a variety of ways. De' Beatis, who was secretary to Cardinal Luigi of Aragon, recorded in his diary on October 10, 1517, that he and his employer paid a visit to Leonardo in his living quarters at the castle of Cloux (near Amboise).[24] De' Beatis called the great artist an "old man of more than seventy years of age." Leonardo was actually sixty-five years old, but looked older, and nearly every sixteenth-century author seems to have misidentified his age at the time of his death in 1519. In this eyewitness account, de' Beatis also commented: "Quite true that, because he [Leonardo] was overcome by a certain paralysis of his right hand, one can no longer expect fine things from him . . . *messer* Leonardo can no longer paint with the sweetness of style that he used to have, and he can only make drawings and teach others."[25] It is not likely, as has often been claimed, that de' Beatis made a mistake regarding Leonardo's handedness; he was probably a good observer of social behavior in his service as secretary.[26] It is normal for an artist to engage much of the body in the physical act of painting, and the most likely implication to be drawn from this observation is that Leonardo probably engaged his right arm and hand for balance and support in painting with his left. Handedness can also be relative, as three later examples illustrate. First, the account of the naturally left-handed Adolph von Menzel (1815–1905): "When I paint in oils, [I do so] always with the right; drawing, watercolor, and gouache always with the left"; Menzel's paintings actually reveal right-handed and left-handed strokes, though his drawings seem predominantly left-handed.[27] A second case, in which left-handedness was forced upon a right-handed painter, is that of Jean Jouvenet (1644–1717). According to the biography by A. J. Dezallier d'Argenville (Paris, 1752), Jouvenet retrained himself to paint with his left hand at the age of sixty-nine, after suffering a stroke on the right side of his body, a fact that is also alluded to in the artist's own unpublished memoir. As if in curious confirmation of the written accounts, Jouvenet signed his altarpiece of the *Visitation of the Virgin (The Magnificat)* at Notre-Dame Cathedral in Paris, "J. Jouvenet, Dextra paralyticus Sinistra pinxit 1716" — that is, "paralyzed right hand, painted with the left hand in 1716."[28] Jouvenet was able to continue drawing with his right hand, with the aid of the left.[29] The third case concerns Henry Fuseli (1741–1825), who was ambidextrous until 1772, when, during a sojourn in Venice, a fever turned his hair white and gave him a permanent tremor of the right hand that forced him thereafter to draw only with his left.[30] For the sixty-five-year-old Leonardo, suffering from ill health, in contrast, the paralysis of the right hand did not impair his skill, since he was naturally left-handed, but taxed the physical strength of his arms in the demanding act of painting. Lomazzo's *Idea del tempio della pittura* (Milan, 1590) enigmatically notes, "so it seemed that Leonardo trembled each hour that he set out to paint."[31] Lomazzo's *Trattato* (Milan, 1584) also calls Leonardo "pittore di mano manca" (left-handed painter) along with numerous admiring citations of his genius,[32] and Giovanni Battista Armenini's *De' veri precetti della pittura* (Ravenna, 1586 and 1587) describes Leonardo's *Last Supper* (Refectory of Santa Maria delle Grazie, Milan), "which he painted with the *man manca* [left hand] in oil on the wall."[33] There is currently no body of archaeological data from the scientific investigation of Leonardo's paintings to shed conclusive light on his handedness (see discussion in cat. no. 46).[34]

The drawings are another matter. First published in 1903, exactly one hundred years ago, Bernard Berenson's *Drawings of the Florentine Painters* briefly singled out Leonardo's left-handedness as one of the fundamental criteria for establishing their authenticity. Although Berenson was not the first connoisseur to do so (that was Giovanni Morelli), he laid the groundwork for an extraordinary reevaluation of Leonardo's drawings.[35] While the archaeological evidence in Leonardo's drawings and handwriting can offer a solid basis for a discussion of his left-handedness, some distinctions need to be made. The evidence is clearest in the drawings in which the artist worked in a linear medium, either in metalpoint or, in his most common medium, pen and ink, but it is also distinguishable in many of his studies in chalk or charcoal. Broadly speaking, when Leonardo modeled areas of shadow with diagonal, parallel hatching, he very often drew lines that course from lower right to upper left (fig. 24) and, much less frequently, from upper left to lower right. Here, one may remember that, in writing, the comfortable direction for Leonardo's hand to travel was from right to left, hence,

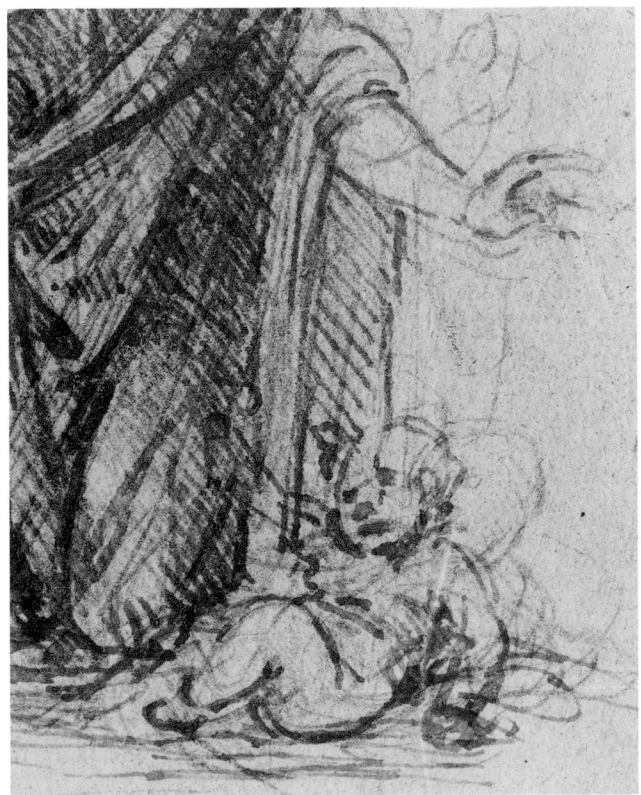

Fig. 24. Detail of cat. no. 45, Leonardo da Vinci, *Designs for the Adoration of the Christ Child; Perspectival Projection*. Metalpoint partly reworked with pen and dark brown ink on pink prepared paper, lines ruled with metalpoint, 194 × 163 mm. The Metropolitan Museum of Art, New York; Rogers Fund, 1917 17.142.1

Fig. 25. Detail of Michelangelo Buonarroti, *Studies for the Libyan Sibyl*. Red chalk, 289 × 214 mm. The Metropolitan Museum of Art, New York; Purchase, Joseph Pulitzer Bequest, 1924 24.197.2

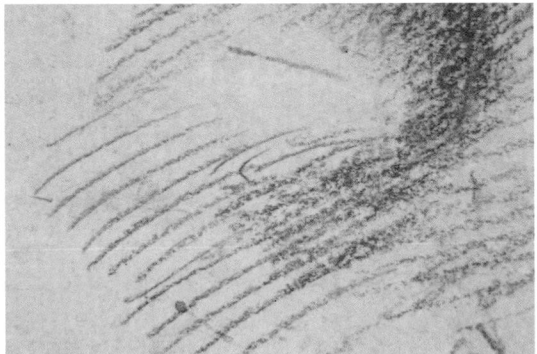

possibly the predominant direction in the hatching of his drawings. The overall effect of the parallel hatching lines is fluent and continuous, often suggesting that he moved the quill pen with great speed. Though the subject requires further research, one can generalize that artists of Leonardo's time who used the right hand to draw, in contrast, typically shaded forms with hatching in the opposite direction, with strokes coursing from upper right to lower left, or from lower left to upper right (fig. 25). For right-handed parallel hatching, see especially catalogue numbers 3 verso, 12 verso, and 122–27.

One can often determine where the artist began his hatching strokes by finding the tips of the lines of hatching that show a greater pressure of the hand wielding the pen or the chalk. Especially in drawings done with pen and ink or with a sharp red chalk stick, this tip at the beginning of a line sometimes appears to be marked by a slightly indented point from which the stroke departs, after which it curves slightly upward, at times also creating a very slight angular hook at the end (fig. 24). The initial pressure of the pen sometimes slightly indents the paper, because of the pressure of the hand, and the line, at the beginning, usually seems thicker because of the greater accumulation of ink. As the artist's hand continues to move rapidly across the paper, decreasing pressure causes the line to become thinner, tapering out at the end of a stroke, as the pen or chalk is lifted from the paper, or creating a very loopy, thin terminus. In Leonardo's case, therefore, it is not entirely correct to state that he consistently drew strokes in one direction, for, like artists working with their right hand, he did not always begin his strokes at the same place. There is also a great variety in the diagonal disposition of lines, with strokes sometimes traveling outward from the outlines of a form, thus departing from the outlines in divergent directions, say, from lower right to upper left or from upper left to lower right.

Whether Leonardo began the hatching from the lower right, and traveled upward, or (much less frequently) from the upper left, and moved downward, the patches of diagonal lines always appear oriented in the same direction. This characterization of left-handed strokes generally holds true, provided that the sheet of paper was always kept stationary. Artists, however, often shift the paper in the process of drawing. Left-handed parallel hatching is found in Leonardo's drawings from the very beginning of his artistic career in the early 1470s onward, though it would be greatly modified after 1500. To the connoisseur's great relief, Leonardo rarely used counterstrokes in hatching before 1500 (more on this below), unlike the young Michelangelo, who was innately left-handed, but who trained himself to draw right-handed. From the early 1480s to the early 1510s, Michelangelo used a dense pen-and-ink cross-hatching technique derived from a close study of Martin Schongauer's prints.[36] Leonardo's early drawings, from the 1470s and early 1480s, often exhibit shorter and more disorganized lines of parallel hatching than do his drawings from the 1490s, with the strokes characterized by an especially large loop at the end. The lines often

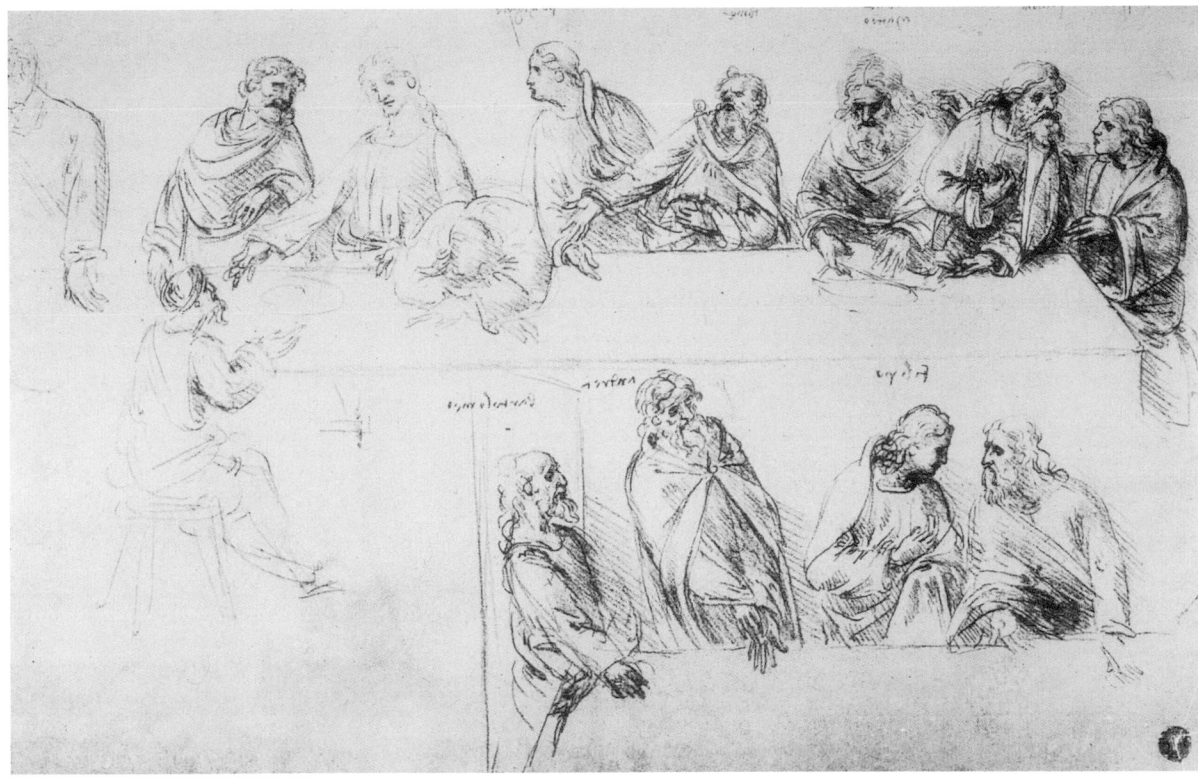

Fig. 26. Leonardo da Vinci (?), *Composition Sketches for the Last Supper*. Red chalk, 261 × 394 mm maximum. Gallerie dell'Accademia, Venice 254

start at the outline of the forms, or close to it, and the diagonal hatching is distributed in broad patches of shadow that are interrupted across the form, with little intermediate modeling (in the early drawings, Leonardo often reworked the intermediate shadows with brush and wash; cat. nos. 18, 21). Precisely because their rendering is painterly, rather than linear, however, the early drapery studies painted with brush on prepared linen (cat. nos. 13–17) present a challenging problem of attribution; the brushstrokes are totally blended in, and none are individually discernible. In drawings from the early 1470s to the early 1480s, the strokes in Leonardo's hatching are frequently not unified—they often visibly change in direction within the general "lower left to upper right" disposition—and expressively zigzag downward (cat. nos. 19, 21, 23, 31, 32). By the late 1480s and throughout the 1490s, however, his use of diagonal parallel hatching was often fluent, pitch-straight, and almost perfectly continuous (cat. nos. 58–73), much like Italian engravings of this period.

The question of the weight to give Leonardo's left-handedness in the connoisseurship of his drawings is both significant and complex. To a large extent (and here one may generalize broadly) Leonardo's drawings from his early years up to about 1500 do not present much difficulty in terms of attribution, because the diagonal parallel hatching courses across the surface of the forms (and into the background) with great fluidity and rapidity. In most of

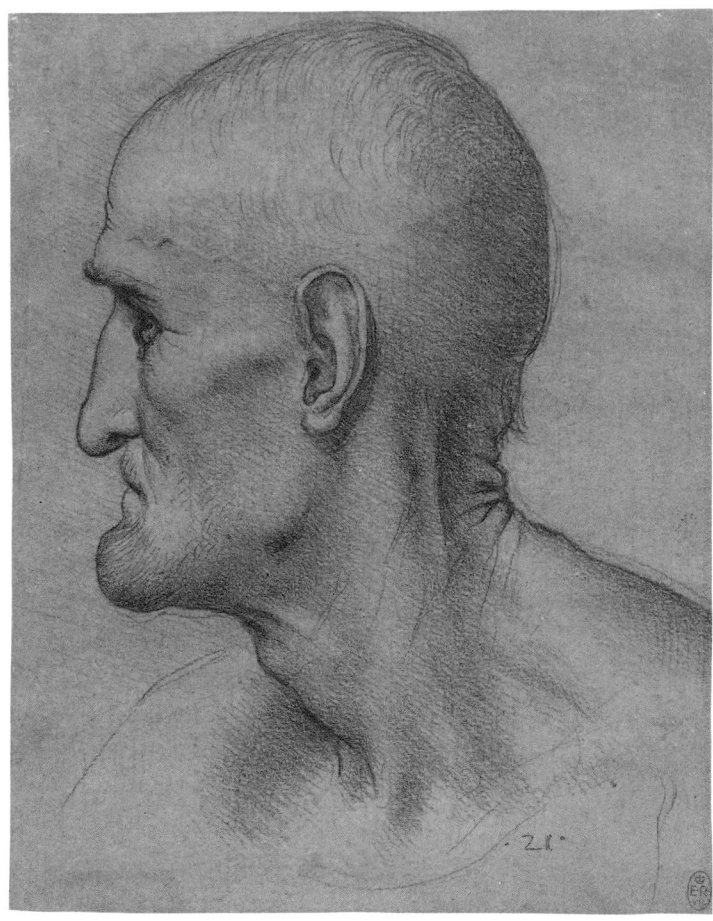

Fig. 27. Leonardo da Vinci (?), *Head of a Man in Profile Facing to the Left (Saint Simon?)*. Red chalk on red-ocher prepared paper, 192 × 151 mm. The Royal Collection, H.M. Queen Elizabeth II, Windsor Castle RL 12550

Leonardo's rendered drawings from the 1490s, the fine, nearly pitch-straight lines show an upper-left to lower-right orientation that is entirely clear. Yet even among drawings of the 1490s, the crudely executed, but definitely left-handed, *Last Supper* composition sketch in red chalk in Venice (inscribed in Leonardo's right-to-left script; fig. 26) has occasioned fierce debate regarding its authenticity.[37] While autograph drawings by Leonardo reveal left-handed parallel hatching (see the discussion below), it does not follow that all drawings with this type of parallel hatching are by Leonardo. Significant in any evaluation is the quality of execution. A number of surviving drawings that are executed in a Leonardesque style and that exhibit the hallmark of Leonardo's left-handedness — the lower right to upper left strokes — are demonstrably not by the master. These range from precise copies by enthusiastic pupils, to later imitations, to downright forgeries. It is known, for example, that Francesco Melzi reinforced drawings by Leonardo that were growing faint because of the physical properties of their medium, especially the studies in red chalk on reddish ocher prepared paper in which the contrasts between drawn form and colored ground are slight.[38] One such case is a much-discussed study of the head of an apostle (Simon?) in *profil perdu* that relates to Leonardo's *Last Supper* (fig. 27). The contours here seem harshly reinforced along the face, but the left-handed inner modeling of the features reveals a subtlety and beauty that are worthy of the great master himself.[39] A very detailed, left-handed copy in red chalk of this figure is also extant (fig. 28),[40] but the overall impression of the modeling of the forms is rather flat. Kenneth Clark first called attention to a number of similarly clean "replacement copies" drawn in red chalk (Royal Library, Windsor) in which the hatching with continuous, fairly fluent parallel diagonal lines seems fastidious and inert, and he convincingly attributed many of these to Melzi (see cat. nos. 120, 121).[41] In this connection, an original study by Leonardo of a horse's foreleg, probably dating about

1495–1500, can be compared with the partial copy derived from it by Melzi, both drawn in the same red chalk medium (figs. 29, 30).[42] The extent to which Leonardo's pupils and copyists imitated his left-handed manner of drawing is extraordinary, and in a number of cases both original prototypes and copies are extant.[43]

Of all Leonardo's drawings, his fascinating studies of grotesque physiognomy (including the so-called caricatures) were by far the most copied and can be instructive concerning the process by which copies begot further and even more distant copies (see also the essay by Varena Forcione). For example, in the present exhibition, one may trace the same motif of a small grotesque woman in bust length from Leonardo's original Chatsworth drawing (cat. no. 73b) to a copy attributed to Melzi (cat. no. 121), to another copy

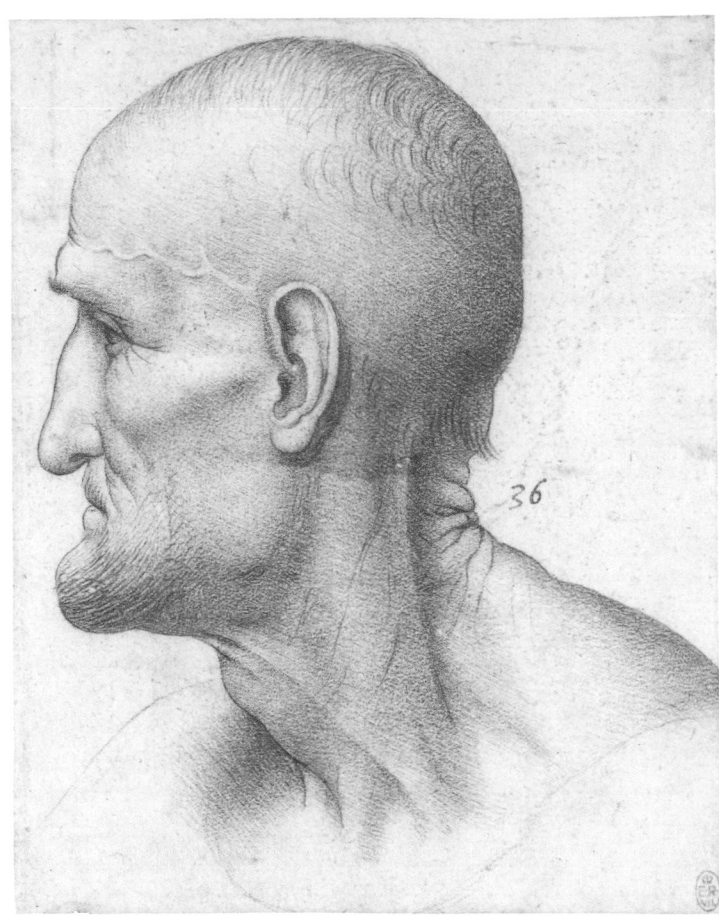

Fig. 28. Late-sixteenth-century copyist after Leonardo da Vinci, *Head of a Man in Profile Facing to the Left (Saint Simon?)*, copy of fig. 27. Red chalk, 188 × 152 mm. The Royal Collection, H.M. Queen Elizabeth II, Windsor Castle RL 12549

by a later sixteenth-century artist (cat. no. 136), and still further to a copy by a seventeenth-century artist found in the pages of the drawings album owned by the eighteenth-century French collector Pierre-Jean Mariette (cat. no. 137; RF 28749). These copies all simulate "left-handed" strokes, as in Leonardo's originals. This is also true of a more ambitious set of finished copies in soft leadpoint bound in a two-volume edition from 1669 of Rabelais's works (the Spencer Grotesques), which are probably by a late-sixteenth-century Lombard artist.[44] One of these copies may be compared to an original by Leonardo (figs. 31, 32). A sheet of caricatures in pen and ink (fig. 33) reveals just how Leonardo's left-handed parallel-hatching strokes were imitated. The pressure of the hand, the slight hook returns, and the greater ink deposits make clear that the strokes began at the lower right, tapering off toward the upper left, just as in many of Leonardo's originals. A further copy at The Metropolitan Museum of Art (fig. 34) after one of these heads is much less clever in its imitation of Leonardo's hatching, and most of the strokes end up looking like a salad of short lines running in very disparate directions. Thus, even in a case like this, when Leonardo's original is not extant for

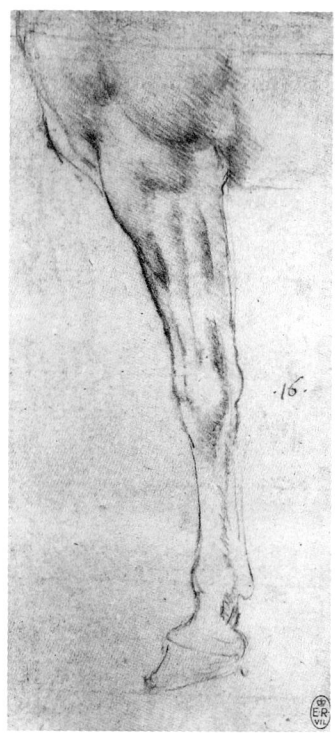

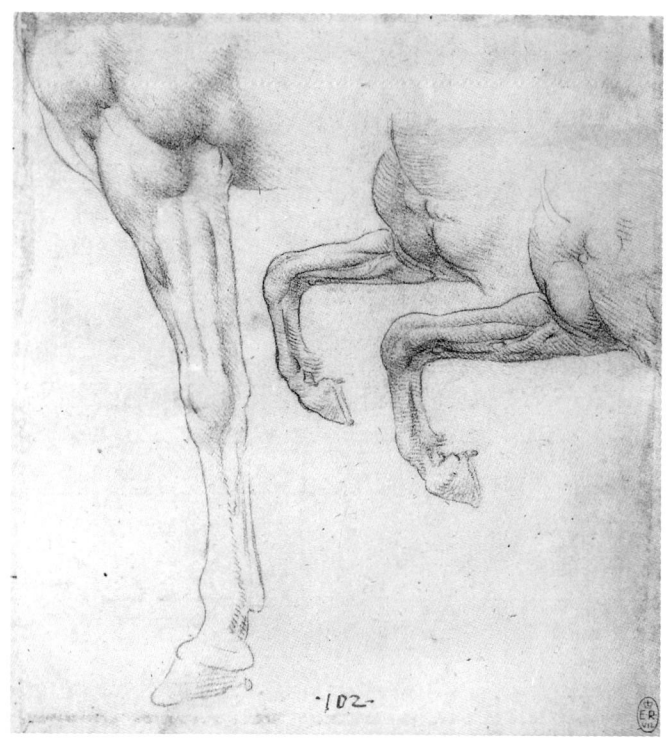

Fig. 29. Leonardo da Vinci, *Study of a Horse's Leg*. Red chalk, 180 × 82 mm. The Royal Collection, H.M. Queen Elizabeth II, Windsor Castle RL 12301

Fig. 30. Attributed to Francesco Melzi (after Leonardo da Vinci), *Studies of Horse's Legs*, partial copy of fig. 29. Red chalk, 174 × 157 mm. The Royal Collection, H.M. Queen Elizabeth II, Windsor Castle RL 12302

comparison, one can discern copies imitating left-handed hatching by the fact that the "left-handed" strokes appear forced and discontinuous. In comparing the originals and the resulting copies, it is crucial to be aware of the pen's or the chalk's natural and rapid movement across the paper in the autograph drawings. Leonardo let the pen glide quickly, and with beautiful, rhythmic tonal emphases. He knew exactly when a well-placed inkblot could produce a successful pictorial effect. He also knew how to create dynamic passages of finish and sketchy unfinish (*non finito*) in his drawings, and the strokes in the modeling always look unified, as they course over the forms and the background. By comparison, the penmanship in the copies often appears strained. It is as if the pen's tip scratched the surface of the paper, then encountered resistance, the result of the copyist drawing slowly and constantly pausing, timidly looking back and forth at the original, picking up the pen again, while checking continuously that he was following the original exactly. In order to get the angle of the lines to look left-handed, it is also not improbable that some copyists turned the paper around (rotating it ninety degrees) and drew sideways.[45] Copyists further removed from Leonardo's circle of pupils completely lost sight of the organic structure of the hatching in the master's drawings. These copyists also failed to leave any passages in a state of creative sketchiness, as is typical of Leonardo's originals.

Complicating matters further, from 1500 onward Leonardo modified his own evidently left-handed parallel-hatching technique in order to explore more diverse tonal rendering. He began to experiment with a pronounced curved hatching that follows form in a fairly exaggerated way (cat. nos. 94, 95, 97–99, 103) and to pursue sfumato effects of seamlessly blended tone (cat. nos. 91, 107–9). During these explorations, however, he also occasionally returned to the straight parallel-hatching technique, for instance, in 1508–12, as can be seen in some of the drawings in the Codex Leicester (cat. no. 114, Sheets 1, 2, and 3). Yet even in Leonardo's most densely pictorial drawings of his mature period some traces of his left-handed parallel hatching often remain underneath the layers of worked-up medium. The study for the head of the Virgin (cat. no. 108) has sometimes been doubted ex silentio as being by Leonardo (rather than stating their doubts about the drawing, scholars have omitted it in their publications of Leonardo's work), possibly because its magical beauty renders it suspicious, and possibly because it is also commonly agreed (not without reason) that Leonardo's pupils could be at times more Leonardesque in their pursuit of aesthetic effects than Leonardo himself. Most important, the head of the Virgin is drawn in a nearly seamless sfumato technique with a surprisingly homogeneous use of red and black chalks that reveals extensive, unified left-handed strokes in the rubbed-in intermediate

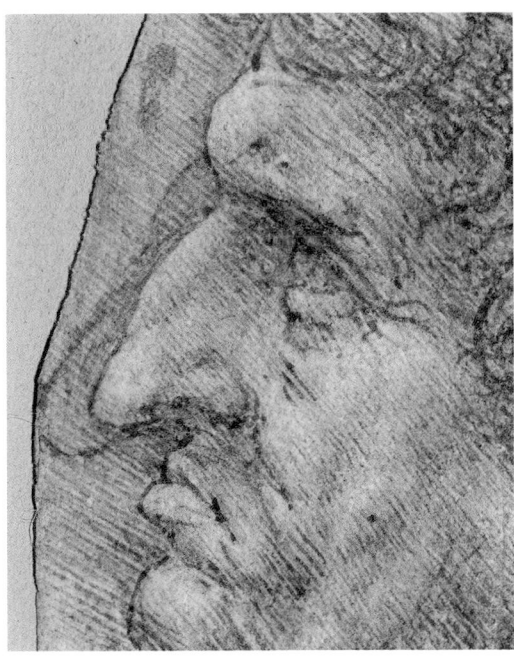

Fig. 31. Detail of cat. no. 60, Leonardo da Vinci, *Head of Grotesque Man in Profile Facing to the Left*. Pen and brown ink over charcoal or black chalk, 120 × 50 mm. The Metropolitan Museum of Art, New York; Rogers Fund, 1909 10.45.1

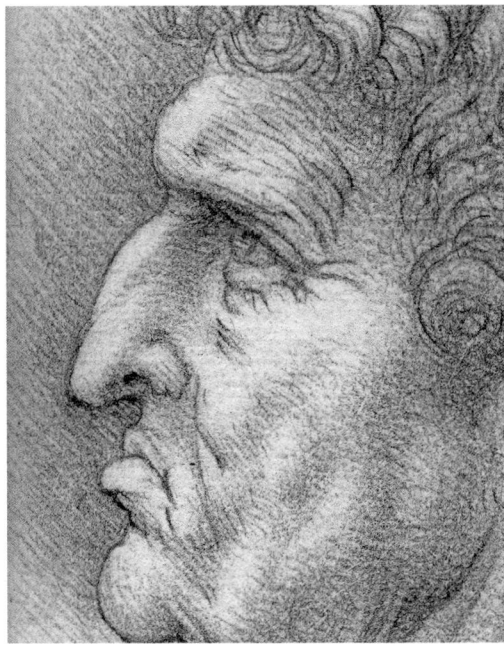

Fig. 32. Detail of late-sixteenth-century Lombard artist after Leonardo da Vinci, *Head of Grotesque Man* (from François Rabelais, *Les oeuvres de M. François Rabelais*, Rouen [?] 1659, 1669 [?]). Black chalk, 142 × 85 mm. The New York Public Library, Astor, Lenox and Tilden Foundations, New York; Spencer Collection. Spencer Grotesques, vol. 2, no. 36

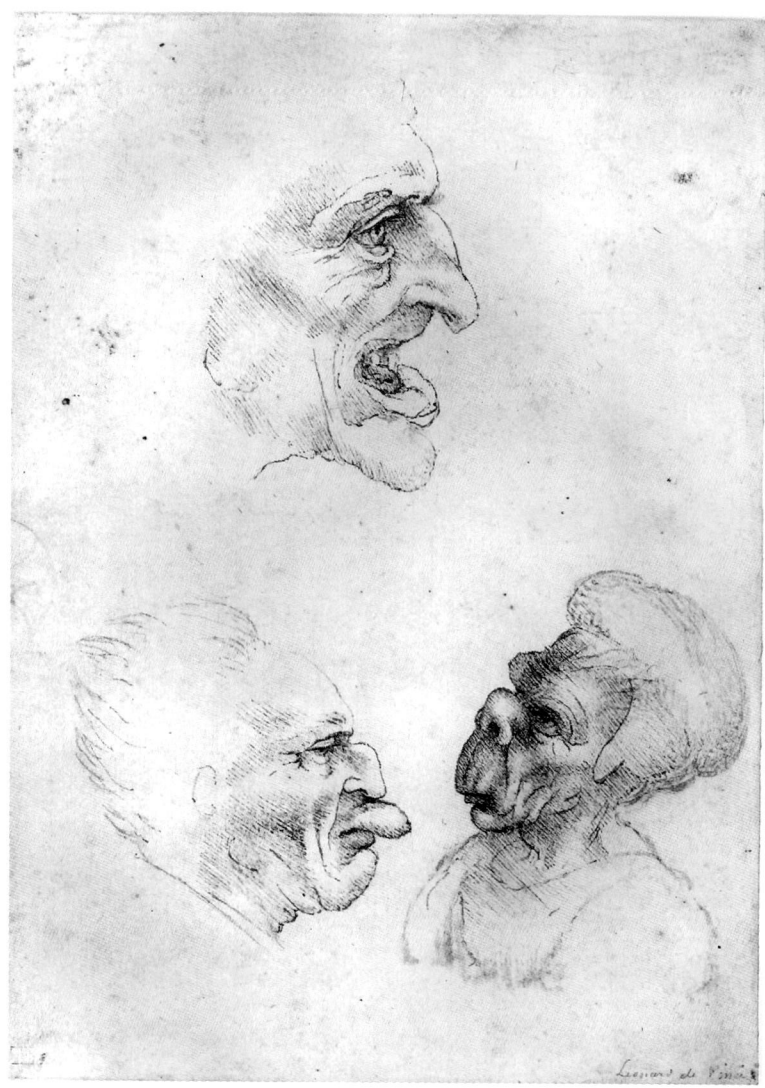

Fig. 33. Early sixteenth-century artist after Leonardo da Vinci, *Three Grotesque Heads*. Pen and brown ink, 185 × 134 mm. The British Museum, London 1946-7-13-223

shadows (fig. 35). The left-handed strokes have gone unnoticed, probably because the drawing is so often examined from photographs rather than from the original. The delicately curving strokes of silvery, soft black chalk, moving from lower right to upper left, are most evident to the unassisted eye in the area of the Virgin's forehead, while the short left-handed strokes in the red-chalk underdrawing, especially near the area of the Virgin's nose (fig. 35), can be seen only with microscopic enlargement.[46] Thus, there can be no doubt regarding Leonardo's authorship of this drawing.

Leonardo's highly rendered studies in pen and ink with a pronounced curved hatching have been among his most misunderstood drawing types (cat. nos. 95, 98, 99, 112). The parallel strokes change freely in direction, though in a unified way, as they follow the roundness of the forms. Thus, a survey of the early scholarly literature turns up doubts concerning the attribution of pen-and-ink composition studies with curved hatching for the *Leda and the Swan* from Rotterdam and Chatsworth (cat. nos. 98, 99), the *Virgin and Child with Saint Anne and a Lamb* from Venice (cat. no. 95), and the *Mausoleum* from the Louvre (cat. no. 112).[47] The early connoisseur Giovanni Morelli went so far as to attribute the *Leda* drawings to Giovanni Antonio Bazzi, "Il Sodoma" (1477–1549), the enigmatic painter from Varese who took Leonardo's sfumato technique to inspired heights. Today, most scholars rightly accept that these drawings with curved hatching—whether done with long or short strokes of the quill pen—represent examples of a genuine technique of rendering by Leonardo, which can be verified by comparing the sheets to his illustrations in the Codex Leicester (cat. no. 114) from 1508–10. There, one can see Leonardo's fine quill pen moving quickly back and forth from image to text written in his characteristic right-to-left script. Further confirmation of the authenticity of the *Ledas*, the Venice *Saint Anne*, or the Louvre *Mausoleum* comes from close study of the curved hatching technique in dark iron-gall ink in some of the drawings of Anatomical Manuscript C III (Windsor, RL 19101–19103, 19095), from 1508–12, which are also carefully inscribed with Leonardo's notes in his typical right-to-left script. Leonardo seems to have begun experimenting with this curved hatching technique in 1502–4 for his studies of fortifications and in 1503–5 for his sketches of the *Battle of Anghiari* (cat. nos. 81–83). He refined it into a wholly consistent and monumental graphic vocabulary in his drawings from 1508 to 1512.

As we have seen, some ambidexterity among artists is not unusual.[48] Given Leonardo's natural left-handedness, a crucial question

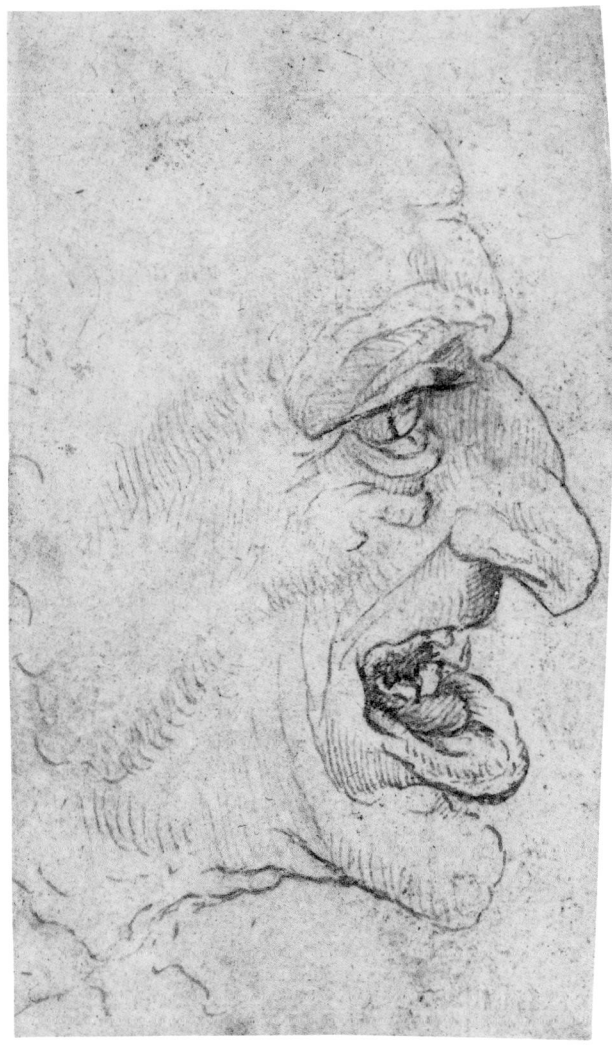

Fig. 34. Mid-sixteenth-century artist after Leonardo da Vinci, *Head of Grotesque Man in Profile Facing to the Right.* Pen and brown ink, 92 × 54 mm. The Metropolitan Museum of Art, New York; Rogers Fund, 1917 17.142.3

concerns whether the artist was ambidextrous as a draftsman, that is, a left-hander who learned to use his right hand. This was the subject of a heated dispute between two early connoisseurs of Leonardo's work, Giovanni Morelli and Luca Beltrami.[49] First, Morelli's contention: "In all these drawings by Leonardo, the shading . . . is from left to right—for Leonardo both wrote and drew with his left hand, and only occasionally made use of his right when representing spherical objects."[50] (Morelli, like other early connoisseurs, overlooked much archaeological evidence in assessing the creative process of Leonardo's drawings, and he therefore had difficulties with the great master's curved hatching technique.) Beltrami, pained by Morelli's indictment of the intuitive component in connoisseurship ("der geistige Gehalt," the inner or spiritual quality of works of art), fiercely advocated a less rigid view that took into account the possibility of a more ambidextrous Leonardo, both as a draftsman and as a writer. The view of Leonardo as an ambidextrous draftsman was endorsed by other early Italian connoisseurs (especially Gustavo Uzielli and Mario Baratta), while Anglo-American art historians have by and large agreed on an exclusively left-handed Leonardo as a drafts-man. One drawing in the present exhibition (cat. no. 92) reveals right-handed and left-handed strokes. This is the monumental Christ Church cartoon (full-scale drawing), dating from 1503–5, which portrays the head and shoulders of a grotesque man, vigorously executed in charcoal or soft black chalk. It exhibits much lower left to upper right parallel hatching in the face and hair, while the lower parts of the back are boldly drawn with lower right to upper left hatching. In such large-scale drawings as cartoons, which often demanded great physical effort to produce,[51] it seems almost possible to envision the artist drawing with both hands, though it cannot be discounted that the right-handed parts of the drawing were done by a pupil closely working with the master.

In the vast majority of Leonardo's notes, the script reads right to left in so-called mirror writing. This is true from the very beginnings of his artistic career, as is seen in the upper-left inscription on the recto of the famous *Landscape of the Arno River and Valley* (fig. 6), done in pen and ink and dated August 5, 1473, when the artist was twenty-one years old. His use of this script was continuous throughout his life, suggesting that it was a comfortable habit for him. Whether Leonardo sometimes wrote in conventional left-to-right script was also the subject of especially heated debate among early scholars, though the consensus now is that he did.[52] The verso of the *Arno River* drawing (fig. 7) is inscribed at the top in what appears to be an attractive calligraphic hand with a conventional, though somewhat strained, left-to-right script that may also possibly be by the young Leonardo. A more striking case is the drawing of an allegory on the verso of a sheet with studies relating to the *Adoration* (cat. no. 31), which establishes its date in 1481–83. The scene is labeled with four words in right-to-left script—"fortuna," "morte," "invidia," and "ingratitudine"—but two in conventional, though forced, left-to-right script—"ignoranza" (with a reversed letter "z") and "superbia." There can be no doubt that the latter words are also authentic, for the hand-writing of both types of lettering are in the identical metalpoint medium as the figural draw-ing on the sheet. The beautifully drawn maps in color (Royal Library, Windsor), from 1503 and later, one of which is exhibited here (cat. no. 80), are fluently labeled in conventional left-to-right script, for they were probably intended as presentation pieces for the patron. The boldly drawn preliminary sketches done to prepare these maps, however, bear Leonardo's usual right-to-left script (cat. nos. 78, 79). Functioning as official documents, the well-known letters from Leonardo to Ludovico Sforza (undated, ca. 1481–83) and to Cardinal Ippolito d'Este (September 18, 1507) are both written in conventional left-to-right script and are probably redactions of Leonardo's original text.[53] While scholars agree that these letters closely reflect Leonardo's intentions, the actual degree of his authorship has been hotly debated. Jean-Paul Richter and Luca Beltrami, for example, vehemently argued that the hand-writing in the letter to Ludovico was Leonardo's own. It is now commonly thought that they were written by scribes on Leonardo's behalf.[54] The well-educated and aristocratic Francesco Melzi (cat. nos. 120, 121) gradually took on the role of scribe for Leonardo, as well as of inter-preter of his notes, when he came to live in the master's household in Milan about 1508. Leonardo's numerals read often right to left and sometimes left to right, but not always with internal consistency (or with respect to the script; see cat. nos. 53 verso, 78, 79, 102), which suggests that he may have sometimes adapted them for the eyes of a reader other than him-self.[55] In his entire oeuvre, only the minuscule number of drawings and notes that were intended to be read by another—whether patron, collaborator, or friend—seem to be writ-ten in conventional left-to-right script.

The fragmentary autobiography by Raffaello da Montelupo, written in the 1560s when he was an old man, offers an unexpected glimpse of how left-handedness was perceived in the Renaissance, and what it meant to be a left-handed artist. The autobiography relates events in Raffaello's youth, in the early sixteenth century, before the brutal sack of Rome in 1527 by the army of Emperor Charles V, which is also vividly described:

> I will not omit to say that by nature I am left-handed, and, finding that hand more facile than the right one, I used to write with it, since my teacher did not mind, being satisfied that my handwriting was good. I have therefore always used the left hand, be it for writing, be it for drawing some designs from the *Morgante*,[56] which was used for reading at school. From the moment that I held the sheet [of paper] lengthwise, in order to write with the left hand, many were astonished, thinking that I wrote "all'ebraica" ["Hebrew-style," hence right to left] and that [my writing] could not be read later. Regarding this, I remember a curious case: when I found myself in Florence making a receipt for a notary for a certain amount of money, I laid the sheet lengthwise [to write], and the notary doubted that my writing could be read. When I had finished a sentence, he took the sheet and, realizing that it could be read extremely well, he called perhaps ten notaries to come watch me. Having finished the receipt, I then wrote some other words with the right hand because I could also use it well, even though I later stopped using it. As I have already said, I draw better with the left hand, and once when I found myself drawing the "Arco di Trasi al Colosseo" [the Arch of Constantine], Michelangelo and Sebastiano del Piombo passed by and stopped to watch me. It should be prefaced that both of them, though naturally left-handed, did everything with their right hand, except actions requiring force. So they stayed a long time to watch me with great won-der, because, as far as is known, the two of them never made anything with their left [hand].[57]

One of the important extant drawings by the left-handed Raffaello de Montelupo (fig. 36)[58] is shaded in pen and ink with hatching in a direction from lower right to upper left. This sheet also illustrates, in its inscriptions of "Vico mio caro" and other calligraphic exer-cises, the method of writing described by the artist in the above passage. Several striking points in Raffaello's account offer a more nuanced understanding of the left-handed Leonardo. First, Raffaello coped with his left-handedness in a clever, unusual way in order to

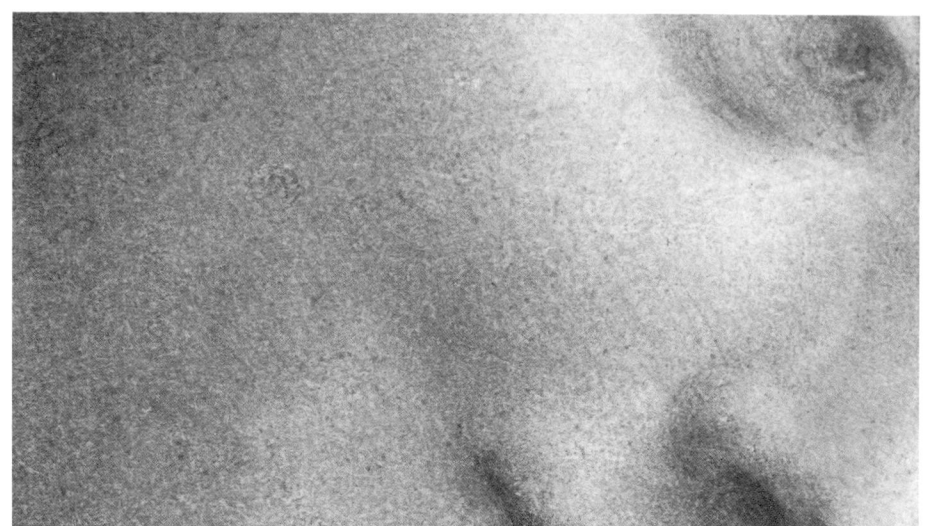

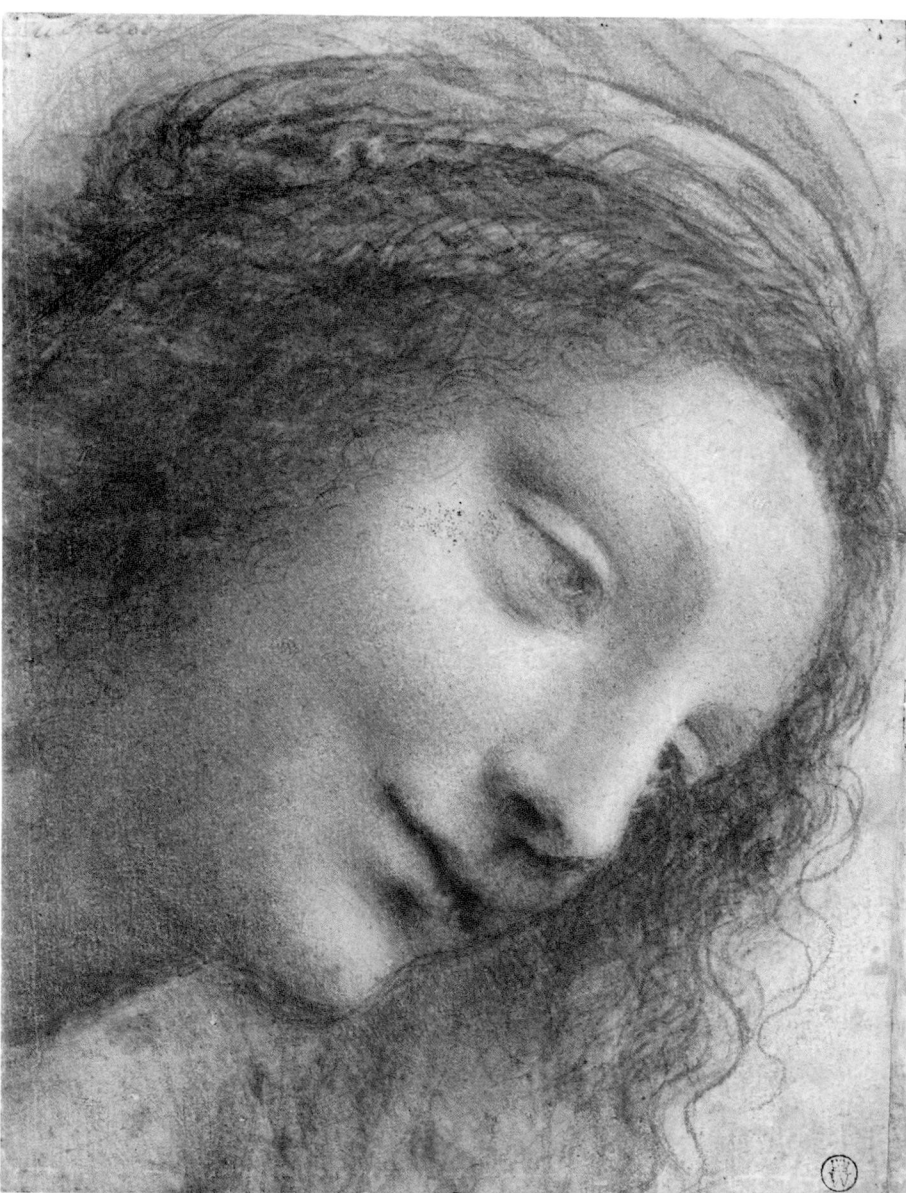

Fig. 35a, b, c, d. Digital image capturing Leonardo's left-handed strokes in cat. no. 108, *The Head of the Virgin.* Soft black and red chalks, 203 × 156 mm. The Metropolitan Museum of Art, New York; Harris Brisbane Dick Fund, 1951 51.90. Clockwise, starting at lower left: (*a*) overall view of the study showing the curved parallel, left-handed strokes in the upper layer of black chalk drawing on the Virgin's forehead, (*b* and *c*) two increasingly enlarged details of the Virgin's nose and cheek area, and (*d*) microphotograph of this area showing the short, parallel left-handed strokes in the red chalk underdrawing (digital photography: Barbara Bridgers and Rachel Mustalish)

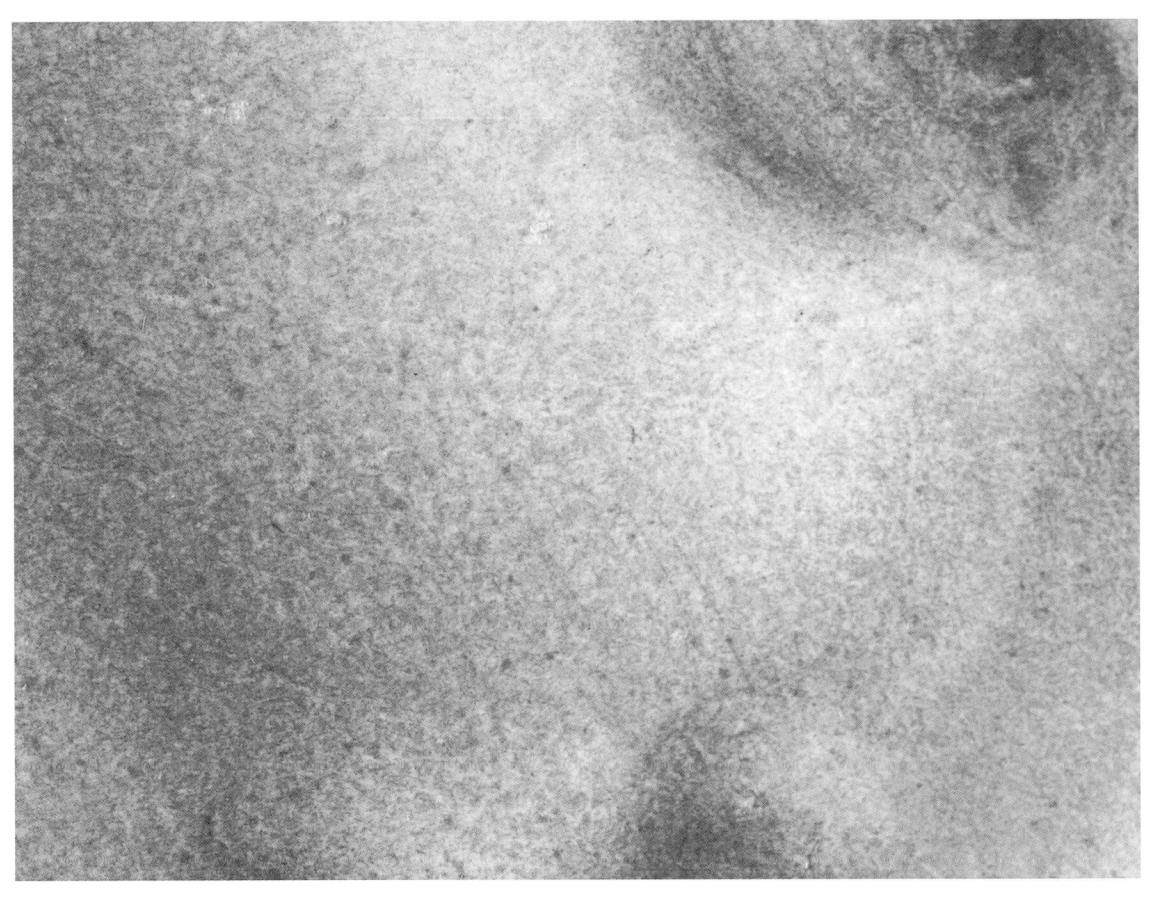

write and draw. His skill as a left-handed draftsman caught the attention of his contemporaries, including Michelangelo and Sebastiano del Piombo, who are certainly well known as artists but who are today virtually unknown as "lefties," for they seem to have retrained themselves into right-handedness. Raffaello's skill as a left-handed writer impressed the notaries, that is, the type of professionals who paid critical attention to the mechanics of script. Second, he could also write and draw with his right hand—a skill not atypical in left-handed people both then and now—but he eventually gave up right-handedness, because it was less comfortable. And third, Raffaello's teacher did not insist on retraining his young pupil out of his left-handedness.

One can learn a great deal about the emphasis on right-handedness in the Renaissance from printed calligraphy books of the period (they are often also illustrated with modest woodcuts),[59] though they are the type of resource that is rarely tapped by art historians. The detailed instructions of these popular manuals shed light on the mechanics of holding and moving the pen and ink across the paper, and the sum of the evidence argues (not unexpectedly) for a right-handed world.[60] Gerard Mercator's *Literarum latinarum . . .* (Antwerp, 1540), for example, illustrates the correct and incorrect ways of holding a quill pen in writing (fig. 37). Most manuals advise on how to maintain a steady posture of the body, as well as how to place the arm, right hand, and fingers, and warn that the pen be moved in only three strokes. In this regard, Leonardo's left-handedness would have posed a challenge to his writ-

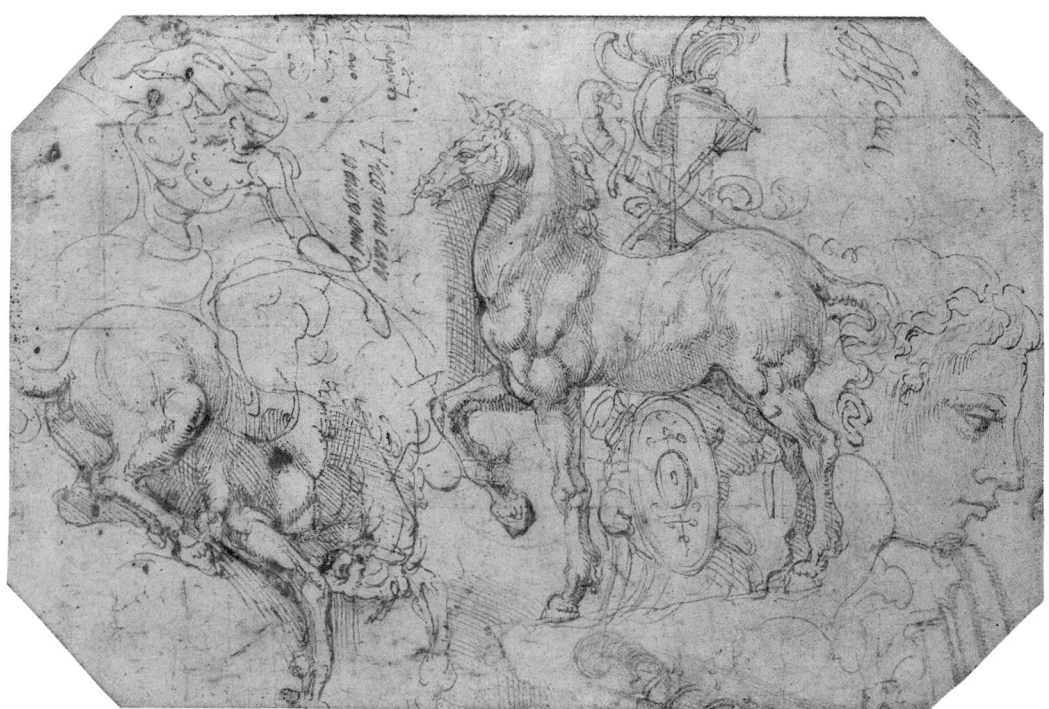

Fig. 36. Raffaello da Montelupo, *Phaeton, Horses, and Other Studies*. Pen and brown ink, red chalk, 190 × 281 mm. Ashmolean Museum, Oxford P II 405

ing teachers, especially because of the awkward placement of the left hand around the quill (for example, curling the hand and wrist above the line to be written or below it) in conventional left-to-right writing. The manuals give various recipes for inks, papers, and sizing, and describe how to make well-crafted quill pens for achieving the elegant, rapid movements necessary for cursive script (with attractive *legatura* and *incatenatura*). For instance, the best quill feathers were plucked from a domestic goose (*ocha domestica*), though a wild goose was also suitable, but from the bird's right wing so that the angle and curve would correspond to a right-handed writer (the tip then required cutting according to precise instructions; fig. 38). The calligraphy book by Marcello Scalino da Camerino, entitled *Regole nuove et avertimenti* (Venice, 1584; Brescia, 1591), also describes step-by-step how right-handed boys were taught handwriting.[61] Moreover, it is clear from Giovanni Francesco Cresci's *Perfetto scrittore* (Rome, 1570) that teachers gave up on the "defects" of some of their pupils (and one can imagine that left-handedness was at times one of them).[62] One may speculate that Leonardo, especially in his early years as an illegitimate child living outside the paternal household, may not have experienced ordinary patterns of schooling (see Chronology).[63] Giorgio Vasari's vita paints a portrait of the young Leonardo as a transgressive boy at the *abbaco,* the four-year secondary school that was attended by boys from the age of ten or eleven onward and where he was probably sent to learn the merchant's profession. The main subject was business arithmetic, though key books by such authors as Aesop and Dante were also read.[64] According to Vasari, "At the *abbaco* during the few months that he [Leonardo] attended it, he made such progress, that he often [deliberately] confounded his teacher by continually raising doubts and causing difficulties."[65] While the degree of veracity of the biographer's anecdote may be debated, it is probably not a complete fabrication. The boy's education must have also included learning good handwriting skills. Notaries were among the professionals in the Renaissance most required to possess a quick, self-confident, and clear cursive script, often not devoid of flourishes: their ideal was to write with a light hand (*scrivere con la mano leggiera*).[66] The artist's father, Ser Piero di Antonio da Vinci (1427–1504), was a notary, as were many men in the artist's family, excepting his grandfather, Antonio di Ser Piero da Vinci (ca. 1372–1465), going back to the fourteenth century.[67] Although in right-to-left direction, Leonardo's early handwriting, as in a sheet dated by him 1478 when he was twenty-six years old (fig. 39), is pleasingly ornate, and his initials sometimes reveal great calligraphic flourishes.[68] Moreover, the verso of a sheet from the late 1470s or early 1480s exhibited here (cat. no. 20) bears sketches that relate to the *Benois Madonna* and the *Madonna Litta* (State Hermitage Museum, Saint Petersburg), while the recto contains some small calligraphic exercises toward the top and bottom of the right border, written in right-to-left script. Also of concern to Leonardo, in his later career as author of a variety of treatises, the education of a Renaissance humanist was judged by the quality of his antique-style

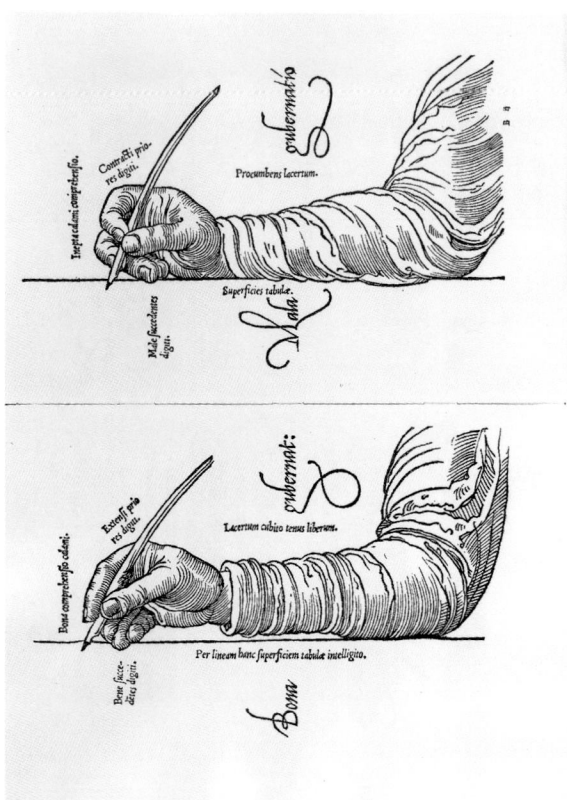

Fig. 37. Page in Gerard Mercator, *Literarum latinarum, quas italicas, cursoriasque vocant, scribendarum ratio* (Antwerp: Ioannes Richard, 1540), unpaginated, showing the incorrect and correct ways of holding a quill pen for writing, the *mala gubernatio* and the *bona gubernatio*. Woodcut, 282 × 201 mm. The Metropolitan Museum of Art, New York; Rogers Fund, 1931 231

lettering and script. Among his projects about 1498 may have been the preparation of drawings for the woodcuts of the alphabet of Roman epigraphic letters published in Fra Luca Pacioli's *De divina proportione* (Venice, 1509).[69] It also bears emphasizing that, in the 1480s and 1490s, Leonardo arduously taught himself a specialized vocabulary of expression by rote copying of words (*vocaboli*) from admired texts, compiling interminably long lists of individual words in alphabetical order for his lexicographic exercise (see cat. no. 21).[70] Calling himself a "man without a humanist's education" (*omo sanza lettere*), Leonardo was embarking on a career as an author of treatises.

Yet how odd was Leonardo's right-to-left handwriting considered to be? Beyond the case presented by Raffaello da Montelupo (fig. 36), it is difficult to offer concrete proof to substantiate the frequent claims that other Italian Renaissance artists and architects also wrote in left-handed script.[71] Nevertheless, the fact that Giovanni Battista Palatino's enormously popular calligraphy book *Libro nuovo d'imparare a scrivere* (Rome, 1540) illustrates a clever pattern for practicing "lettera mancina," mirror left-handed script, indicates that, however curious, left-handed script was not unheard of. According to the rhymed verse inscribed below Palatino's woodcut illustration, the writing can be read without straining the mind, with the aid of a mirror.[72] The variety of scripts that these books found acceptable seems to have been great: Giovanni Antonio Tagliente's *Excellente scrivere* pattern book (Venice, 1532) even illustrates a model for practicing a "lettera pendente," that is, a conventional left-to-right cursive that leans to the left in an otherwise deplorable and exaggerated way, as if it were left-handed (as opposed to the conventional rightward tilt).

If Leonardo's left-handedness was noteworthy in the Renaissance, it has fascinated posterity. Jean-Paul Richter, the author of the most important anthology of Leonardo's writings, speculated that the great artist became left-handed because "he was deprived of the normal use of his right hand by an accident, or in a fight."[73] Arthur Ewart Popham, the eminent connoisseur of Leonardo's drawings, suggested that a childhood accident had maimed the great artist's right hand, rendering him left-handed by necessity.[74] In a considerably more far-fetched attempt, Sigmund Freud wrote in a letter of October 9, 1898, to Wilhelm Fliess (his disciple in 1887–1902) that "perhaps the most famous left-handed individual was Leonardo, who is not known to have had any love affairs," thus linking the artist's left-handedness with sublimated sexuality.[75] Proceeding on the basis of a "childhood memory," Freud pressed this point (among others) quite far in his famous psychosexual interpretation of the artist's personality. (The study was published as *Eine Kindheitserinnerung des Leonardo da Vinci* in Leipzig and Vienna in 1909–10.)[76] Marie Bonaparte's 1927 interpretation misunderstood both the historical context of her subject and the study of Leonardo's drawings:

> From the psychoanalytic point of view, it is conceivable that this contiguity is not accidental and that there existed an unconscious connection between his [Leonardo's] undoubtedly extreme repression of infantile masturbation and his subsequent disgust of sexuality. This may even be true also of the fact that he was left-handed, or at least preferred the left hand for drawing, painting, and writing. For it is remarkable that the hands Leonardo drew on the page [Windsor, RL 19009 recto][77] on which he set down his thoughts about the disgust prompted in him by the sexual act are *all right hands.*[78]

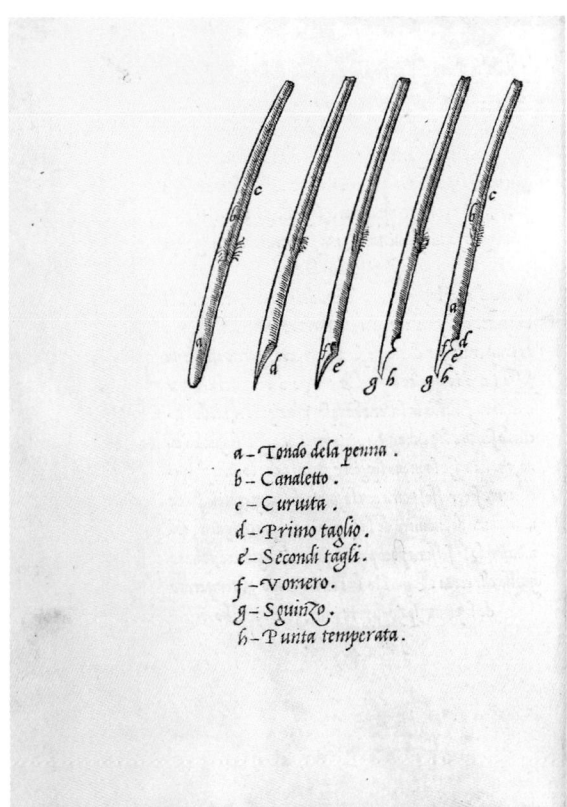

Fig. 38. Eustachio Celebrino, *The Making of a Good Quill Pen*, illustrated in Ludovico Arrighi "Il Vicentino," *Il modo de temperare le penne . . .* (Venice, 1523), fol. 78v. Woodcut, 204 × 142 mm. The Metropolitan Museum of Art, New York; Gift of Felix M. Warburg, 1928 28.106.3

Authors have puzzled about what causes left-handedness in human beings since at least the time of Plato's *Laws* (7:794).[79] Modern research in the fields of neurobiology, psychology, and sociology has continued to explore the origins, definitions, functions, patterns, and consequences of left-handedness among human beings as well as animals. If one considers the evidence as a whole, it is quite likely that Leonardo was a "natural" left-hander, like a substantial part of the population, then as now. He had an uncanny mental ability to reverse, as if in a mirror, both writing and images fluently; not all left-handed artists have this ability. Preliminary drawings show that he seems often to have tried out mirror images of a similar compositional idea, perhaps to stir up his creative juices in designing the figural arrangements of his pictures. This unusual, very prominent feature of his creative process has been little discussed by scholars. In at least three cases, preliminary sketches or studies survive for both early and late projects that portray the composition in a left and a right orientation: the *Madonna of the Cat,*[80] the *Adoration of the Magi,*[81] and the *Virgin and Child with Saint*

Anne.[82] The mirror also served Leonardo as a powerful metaphor for his work. During his late years in Rome, in 1513–16, when his patron was Giuliano de' Medici, Leonardo carried out highly innovative research on the optics of mirrors. He demonstrated "Alhazen's problem" (which concerns the spatial relation between an object and the projected image of the object produced by a curved mirror), and he pursued complex experiments with concave mirrors, both spherical and parabolic.[83] This was the culmination of a lifelong preoccupation with the science and mystery of mirrors. Representing his thoughts from almost twenty years earlier (in 1490–94), the posthumously compiled *Libro di pittura* records this advice to young painters: "When you wish to see whether your whole picture accords with what you have portrayed from nature, take a mirror and reflect the actual object in it. Compare what is reflected with your painting and carefully consider whether both likenesses of the subject correspond, particularly in regard to the mirror."[84] According to Leonardo: "The painter should be like a mirror which is transformed into as many colors as are placed before it, and in doing this, he will seem to be a second nature."[85]

1. A very slight sketch in red chalk from 1515–19 by one of Leonardo's pupils, too faint for reproduction, portrays a left hand holding a pen (Codex Atlanticus, vol. 9, fol. 770v [formerly, fol. 283v-b]; discussed in Möller 1926; Pedretti 1958b; and Pedretti 1978–79, vol. 2, p. 105, no. 770v. Historical research can be adduced to demonstrate that religions and cultures—across the ages—have at times stigmatized left-handedness. Negative connotations of character are evoked by the Latin and Italian words for "left" (*sinister* and *sinistra*), and in Italian the left hand is often figuratively called *la mano manca* (the lacking or injured hand). See lexicographic surveys in Battaglia 1975; Battaglia 1998.

2. Here, one would include, for example, Michelangelo, Hans Leonhard Schäufelein, Hans Holbein the Younger, Jan van Goyen, Francesco Borromini, Henry Fuseli (Johann Heinrich Füssli) late in his life, Adolph von Menzel, Edward Munch, Paul Klee, and Pablo Picasso. See Mongan 1987, p. 164; Jung 1977; Parker 1983, pp. 32–33; Beck 1987, pp. 12–13; Rowlands with Bartum 1993, vol. 1, p. 141; Reuterswärd 1993; and Gatteschi 1998, pp. 120–21.

3. Raffaello da Montelupo's autobiography (published in Vasari–Milanesi 1906, vol. 6, pp. 551–62; Gatteschi 1998, pp. 120–21). On Raffaello da Montelupo as a left-handed draftsman, see Berenson 1935, pp. 105–20; Berenson 1938, vol. 1, pp. 256–63; Berenson 1961, vol. 1, pp. 384–92.

4. Giovanni Paolo Lomazzo seems to refer to this in the *Idea del tempio della pittura* (Milan, 1590): "as one can see from many books written and drawn by him [Leonardo] with his left hand" ("come vedesi da molti libri da lui scritti e disegnati alla mancina"; quoted from Lomazzo 1973–74, vol. 1, p. 293).

5. The most substantive previous discussion of Leonardo's left-handed manner of writing is found in Baratta 1905a, pp. 3–55 ("perchè Leonardo da Vinci scriveva 'a rovescio'"), though imprecise in its details and outdated. For summary references to Leonardo's left-handedness, see Richter 1970, vol. 1, pp. 105–11; Beltrami 1909; Calvi 1916, pp. 437–45; Beltrami 1919b, pp. 144–54; Calvi 1925a; Berenson 1938, vol. 1, p. 168; Favaro 1930; Keller 1938; Venturi 1939; Pedretti 1953, pp. 176–86; Heydenreich 1954, vol. 1, pp. 53–54; Pedretti 1958b; Clark and Pedretti 1968–69, vol. 1, pp. xv–xix; Pedretti 1975b, pp. 1–38; Pedretti 1977, vol. 1, pp. 91–97; Jung 1977; Scaglia 1982; Mongan 1987; Reuterswärd 1993; and Holly 1996.

6. Pedretti 1953, pp. 176–93; Bambach [Cappel] 1994a, pp. 29–39.

7. Facsimile in Pedretti 1953, p. 183 (partial transcriptions in Baratta 1905a, pp. 30–31; Richter 1970, vol. 1, pp. 109–10, n. 1): "Cap. IX. Do scrivere ch[e] non se legi se no[n] con spechio / Scriuesi anchora alla rouescia

è mancina ch[e] non / si possono legere . se non con lo specchio . o, uero guarda/[n]do la carta dal suo rovescio contra la luce, come so / mentendi senzaltro, dica come fa il no[st]ro leonardo da / uinci, lume della pittura quale è. *mancino,* come piu / uolte è ditto."

8. Facsimile in Pedretti 1953, p. 179: "facte e formate per quella ineffabile senistra mano."

9. Two versions of the original manuscript of Pacioli's *De divina proportione* are extant, dating about 1496–98, in the Biblioteca Ambrosiana, Milan (of higher quality), and in the Bibliothèque Publique et Universitaire, Geneva.

10. Vasari 1966– , vol. 4, pp. 28–29: "Lionardo, che ne fece un libro disegnato di matita rossa e tratteggiato di penna) . . . et in quegli a parte per parte di brutti caratteri scrisse lettere che sono fatte con la mano mancina a rovescio, e chi non ha pratica a leggere con l'intende, perche non si leggono se non con lo spechio."

11. Vasari 1966– , vol. 4, p. 28: "Come anche sono nelle mani di [. . .], pittor milanese, alcuni scritti di Lionardo, pur di caratteri scritti con la mancina a rovescio, che trattano della pittura e de' modi del disegno e colorire. Costui non è molto che venne a Fiorenza a vedermi desiderando stampar questa opera, e la condusse a Roma per dargli esito, né so poi che di ciò sia seguito." Lomazzo's *Trattato* (Milan, 1584) identifies Aurelio Luini as one of the Milanese painter-collectors of Leonardo's drawings of grotesque heads (Lomazzo 1973–74, vol. 2, p. 315).

12. Lomazzo 1973–74, vol. 2, capitolo xiv, p. 138.

13. For example, see Solmi 1923, p. 227; Richter 1970, vol. 1, p. 110, n. 1 (with a misleading direct quotation).

14. Castiglione 1560, *Ricordo CIX*, "Circa gli ornamenti della casa," fols. 56v–57v.

15. Castiglione 1560, unpaginated preface: "& sopratutto co[n] la difficultà, e fatica gra[n]de del mio ritroso, & sconcio scriuere co[n] la sinistra mano a me naturale, il quale era si necessario, che no[n] si potea fare senza esso."

16. Pedretti 1980a, pp. 17–19; Pedretti 1994c, pp. 31–33.

17. Author's transcription: "Soleua il Vinci scriuere Alla Mancina, secondo luso degli / Ebrei, nella qual Maniera erano scritti quei sedici Volumi / de quali de già abiamo fatto Menzione, et esendo il cara/ttere buono, si legeua assai facilmente Mediante un spe/chio grande, è probabile ch'egli facessi questo, accio tu/tti non legessèro così facilmente i suoi scritti" (partially transcribed in Richter 1970, vol. 2, p. 413).

18. Author's transcription: "Libro Originale / Della Natura, peso, e moto delle Acque, / composto, scritto, e figurato di proprio carattere alla mancina dall insigne Pittore e Geometra / Leonardo da Vinci."

19. The earl of Leicester had the Codex handsomely rebound. The eighteenth-century brown leather slipcase (341 × 264 × 32 mm), which bears the arms of the earls of Leicester, is likewise inscribed: "DA VINCI/ DELLA NATURA &c./ DELLE ACQUE/ MS./ ORIGINALE/ DELL'AUTORE/ ALLA MANCINA./ 699." The Codex Leicester was disassembled in 1981, and the binding, slipcover, and added endpapers are now kept separately.

20. Baratta 1905a, pp. 34–40.

21. Bell 1991. Quotation of Cassiano del Pozzo's Montpellier Ms. H. 267, from Pedretti 1977, vol. 1, pp. 38–39: "nella quale ha spiegato molti[ssim]e cose che apartengono al Trattato di Lionardo da Vinci jnscritto opinione di Lionardo da Vinci, circa il modo di dipigner Prospettiue, ombre, lontananze, altezze, bassezze da presso e da discosto et altro. Del qual Trattato di Lionardo come haueua uisto molte cose da quello scritto con carattere alla rouescia, così il d[etto] Matteo s'assuefece à quella ragione di scriuere, e molte delle sue fatiche, acciò non fussero alla p[rim]a intense da ognuno le haueua con facilità grande e con caratteri assai aggiustato prese a scriuere in quella maniera."

22. Early scientific studies are cited in Baratta 1905a, pp. 41–46; Calvi 1916, pp. 438–39. Recent studies are cited in Schott 1979; Kirk and Kertesz 1989; Coren 1993, pp. 230–33; Kirk and Kertesz 1993; L'Anthony 1995; Zacharias and Kirk 1998; Schott 1999; Blank, Miller, and von Voss 2000 (my thanks to Alison Manges for some of this literature). See also "How to Teach Italic," Gunnlaugur SE Briem, January 1, 1999 (http://www.ismennt.is/not/briem/text/3/33/33.3/33.304.left.html).

23. Contra Røsstad 1995, pp. 112–25, "indications of visual dyslexia in Leonardo's texts." Davis 1997 and Sanders 2001 offer good working definitions of dyslexia (my thanks to Rachel Stern for this literature).

24. De' Beatis's diary entry is also discussed in Vecce 1990, pp. 51–59.

25. Marani 1999c, 2000b, pp. 364–65, document no. 94 (Vecce 1990, p. 56): "Ben vero che da lui per esserli venuta certa paralesi ne la dextra non se ne puo expectare piu cosa bona. Ha ben facto un creato milanese chi lavora assai bene et benche il prefato messer Lunardo non possa colorire con quella dulceza che solea pur serve ad fare disegni et insignare ad altri."

26. Contra Venturi 1939, p. 173.

27. Reuterswärd 1993, p. 10 (n. 10): "wenn ich Öl male immer mit der Rechten, Zeichnen, Aquarellieren, Gouache immer mit der Linken." See archival photograph of Adolph von Menzel drawing with his left hand, published in Keisch and Riemann-Reyher 1996–97, p. 43; and discussion in Jung 1977, p. 206.

28. Dezallier d'Argenville 1752, p. 352; and further Schnapper 1974, pp. 146, 222, no. 146 (my thanks to Nicolas Schwed and Perrin Stein).

29. Reuterswärd 1993, p. 10 (n. 6).

30. Powell 1951, pp. 12, 27; Reuterswärd 1993, p. 7.

31. Lomazzo's passage generally alludes to how artists approached their art. Lomazzo 1973–74, vol. 1, p. 333 (Beltrami 1919a, p. 188, document no. 263 [13a]), capitolo xxxi: "Così Leonardo parea che d'ogni ora tremasse, quando si ponea a dipingere; e però non diede mai fine ad alcuna cosa cominciata, considerando quanto fosse la grandezza dell'arte, talché egli scorgeva errori in quelle cose che egli altri pareano miracoli." Later painters used a "Malstick" to steady the hand, a device that in fact often renders the distinction between left-handed and right-handed brushstrokes difficult to discern.

32. Beltrami 1919a, p. 185, document no. 263 (8): "Leonardo Vinci Fiorentino, sommo e unico pittore e plastica-tore e acutissimo investigator de le sue arti, de le quali ne scrisse, e parimenti dell'acque e macchine molti libri, di mano manca, come già fece nel pingere l'antico Cavaliero Turpilio pittore Venetiano." Other evidence of Leonardo's genius is given in Lomazzo's writings (transcribed in ibid., pp. 182–206, no. 263).

33. Armenini 1587, 1977, p. 172: "Ma fra gli altri io vidi in Milano quello de' Frati di San Domenico in Santa Maria delle Gratie, nel quale à man manca vi è dipinto à oglio sul muro Un Cenacolo da Leonardo Vinci, che à benche fosse fino allhora mezo guasto." See also Pedretti 1953, p. 218.

34. David Alan Brown pointed out and illustrated the left-handed strokes in the hair of Tobias in the painting of *Tobias and the Angel* (National Gallery, London), part of which he attributed to the young Leonardo; Brown 1998b, pp. 55–56, 189 (n. 34), fig. 38. The curving brushstrokes in the highlights begin at the lower right, to judge from the greater thickness, and taper toward the upper left.

35. Berenson 1903, vol. 1, pp. 147–66; Berenson 1938, vol. 1, pp. 166–83; Berenson 1961, vol. 1, pp. 245–65.

36. The cross-hatching technique of the young Michelangelo is discussed in Hirst 1988, pp. 4–5, 59–68; Fischer 1994, pp. 245–53; Eike D. Schmidt and Letizia Treves in Weil-Garris Brandt 1999, pp. 326–31, nos. 44, 45.

37. A variety of discordant opinions on the attribution of this drawing are expressed in Richter 1883, vol. 1, pl. 46, p. 335; Müntz 1899, p. 189; Horne 1903, p. 25; Loeser 1903b, p. 183; MacCurdy 1904, p. 106; Gronau 1904; Seidlitz 1909, vol. 1, p. 197, pl. 34; Malaguzzi-Valeri 1913–23, vol. 2, p. 495, no. 536; Calvi 1916, p. 88; Poggi 1919, pl. 88; Venturi 1920, pp. 114–15, no. 76; Sirén 1928, p. 77, pl. 102; Bodmer 1931, pp. 252, 403–4; Berenson 1938, vol. 2, no. 1107; Popham 1994, p. 137, no. 162; Goldscheider 1952, no. 71; Pedretti 1968b, pp. 59–61 (n.); Cogliati Arano 1980, no. 22; Pedretti 1983, pp. 33, 62; Marani 1986b, p. 5 (n.); Clark and Pedretti 1988–89, pp. 150–51; Marani 1989, p. 70; Martin Clayton in Palazzo Grassi 1992, pp. 232–33, no. 19; Marani 2001a, pp. 152–53, no. 41; Steinberg 2001, pp. 288–87.

38. Clark and Pedretti 1968–69, vol. 1, pp. xvii–xix.

39. For a convincing proposal arguing Leonardo's partial authorship of this drawing, see Marani 2001a, pp. 144–45, no. 37, which also records the assenting opinion of Alessandro Ballarin. Clark and Pedretti 1968–69, vol. 1, p. 102, no. 12550, considered the drawing a copy.

40. Here, in agreement with Marani 2001a, pp. 146–47, no. 38; and Clark and Pedretti 1968–69, vol. 1, pp. 101, no. 12549.

41. Clark and Pedretti 1968–69, vol. 1, pp. xvii–xx.

42. A. E. Popham, in fact, published another such replacement copy in red chalk (Windsor, RL 12361), a sheet of studies of a dog, as autograph by Leonardo; Popham (1946) 1994, p. 116, no. 82.

43. For example, see the cleanly drawn copy in pen and ink (British Museum, P.p.1–33) of the small, delicately finished allegory at the Louvre (cat. no. 67). It includes some "left-handed" strokes that seem most evident in the figure of the seated man wearing a hat.

44. The Spencer Grotesques are discussed in Scott-Elliot 1958; Pedretti and Trutty-Coohill 1993. See also the essay by Varena Forcione in this volume.

45. Leonardo himself seems to have moved around the paper to draw his late pen-and-ink studies with pronounced curved hatching.

46. I am indebted to Marjorie Shelley, Paper Conservator at The Metropolitan Museum of Art, for conducting this insightful technical research (April 10, 2002).

47. Esp. Venturi 1939, p. 169, on the doubted Louvre *Mausoleum* drawing (cat. no. 112).

48. Reuterswärd 1993, pp. 7–10 (nn. 6–9).

49. Morelli 1900, pp. 177–79; Beltrami 1909; Beltrami 1919b, pp. 144–54.

50. Morelli 1900, pp. 177–78.

51. Bambach 1999a, pp. 33–80.

52. Richter 1970, vol. 1, pp. 105–11; Morelli 1900; Beltrami 1909; Beltrami 1919b, pp. 144–54.

53. Transcriptions with notes in Richter 1970, vol. 2, pp. 325–27, 332, nos. 1340, 1348; Beltrami 1919a, pp. 10–11, 123, document nos. 21, 193; Pedretti 1977, vol. 2, pp. 295, 298; Villata 1999, pp. 16–17, 219–20, nos. 20, 252.

54. See note above, with further opinions in Beltrami 1909; Calvi 1916, pp. 435–46; Calvi 1925a, pp. 65–70; Beltrami 1919b; Venturi 1939, pp. 167–73; Pedretti 1975, pp. 22–25; Vecce 1998a, pp. 77–79, 271; Marani 1999–2000, p. 362, no. 84.

55. Baratta 1905a, pp. 29–30, 52; Richter 1970, vol. 1, p. 107, under "24." Again, this was a matter of convention for him, and is probably not to be interpreted as an indication of dyslexia, as is often claimed in popular journalistic writing (see note 23).

56. *The Morgante* was a chivalric poem published by Luigi Pulci (1478), with a dedication to the mother of Lorenzo de' Medici. Leonardo copied 288 words from this book to teach himself an educated man's vocabulary of expression. For a discussion of Leonardo's list of 288 *vocaboli* in the Codex Trivulzianus (Biblioteca Trivulziana, Castello Sforzesco, Milan), see Marinoni 1980b, p. xv.

57. Raffaello da Montelupo in Gatteschi 1998, pp. 120–21: "Non mi asterrò dal dire come per natura io sia mancino, ed avendo quella mano più pronta della destra scrivevo con quella, dato che il maestro non ci faceva caso bastandogli che la mia scrittura sia buona. Dunque ho sempre usato la mano sinistra, sia per scrivere sia per fare qualche disegno che copiavo dal Morgante che veniva letto a scuola. Dal momento che per scrivere con la sinistra dovevo tenere il foglio per lungo, molti si meravigliavano, pensando che scrivessi "all ebraica" e che non si potesse leggere. A questo proposito ricordo un caso curioso: trovandomi a Firenze a fare una ricevuta ad un notaio per certi denari, misi il foglio per lungo e il notaio mi lasciò fare dubitando però che il mio scritto si potesse leggere. Quando ebbe terminato una frase, prese il foglio e, resosi conto che si leggeva benissimo, chiamò forse dieci notai perché venissero a guardarmi. Finita la ricevuta scrissi poi qualche altra parola con la mano destra perché riuscivo bene pure con quella, anche se poi l'ho abbandonata. Come ho già detto, disegno meglio con la mano sinistra e una volta che mi trovavo a disegnare l'Arco di Trasi al Colosseo, passarono da lì Michelangelo e fra Sebastiano del Piombo e si fermarono a guardarmi. C'e da premettere che tutt'e due sono mancini naturali pero facevano tutto con la mano destra, salvo le azioni di forza. Così rimasero a lungo ad osservarmi con grande meraviglia perché, che si sappia, loro due non hanno

fatto niente con la sinistra." The Arch of Constantine bore the name Arco di Trasi al Colosseo as far back as the twelfth century, a name that derives from the mistaken belief that the captive Dacians on the reliefs were Thracians (my thanks to Ellen Perry for this information).

58. This drawing was first presciently attributed to Raffaello da Montelupo by Bernard Berenson; Berenson 1935, pp. 105–6; Parker 1972, vol. 2, pp. 203–4, no. 405.

59. Casamassima 1966; Bambach [Cappel] 1991b, pp. 83–86; Bambach [Cappel] 1991a, pp. 99–101.

60. The research and conclusions that follow are based on the extensive collection of sixteenth-century calligraphy and alphabet books in The Metropolitan Museum of Art, Department of Drawings and Prints, and in particular on Pacioli 1509, Vicentino 1522, Vicentino 1523, Verini 1527, Tagliente 1532, Fanti 1535, Palatino 1540, Mercator 1540, Amphiareo 1554, Cresci 1570, Hercolani 1574, and Scalino 1591.

61. Scalino 1591, pp. 21–22, praises exercises of rote repetition and offers extremely rare evidence: "And finally that the pupil be [seated] to the left of the teacher, who will in turn place the fist of his left hand lightly touching on the right hand of the pupil in writing, to guide the pupil's hand with skill, helping the hand with the three fingers of the right hand, and so together [master and pupil] go on outlining many times over the letters one by one, in order that the boy feel the movement of the wrist in forming and linking the letters, and that he learn the ease of tracing the characters." Original text: "124. Modo che deve tener il maestro per inseg-/nar' à scriuere à fanciulli . . . & finalmente, che lo imparante stia nello scrivere che farà à man sinistra al Maestro, ilquale col pugno della / man sinistra, toccando leggiermente la mano dritta dello scolare, che scriue, la guidi con / destrezza, aiutandola con le tre dita della man destra, & cosi insieme vadano lineando, più, & / più volte quei caratteri ad vno ad vno, accioche il fanciullo senta il mouimento del polso, la for/matione, & l' andare de gli elementi, & che apprenda la facilità del lineare i caratteri."

62. Cresci 1570, unpaginated, folio 3 recto, explains: "The master ought to teach the student first how to hold the pen correctly, and remind him frequently of this, because he [will] frequently forget, because not everyone has the hand ready to hold the pen with grace, due to many defects, which in the case of some pupils are impossible to overcome; at least show them to hold the [quill] in a way that it can produce a good outline, and [let him] hold the pen as [he] wishes: telling him, however, that he hold something in his left hand [mano manca] that help him to hold the paper in place, so that it not turn around, as he writes, because this matters very much." Original text: "Delli modi che deve tener vn mastro / per insegna a scriuer bene a i suoi discepoli lettera corrente can-/cellaresca, & altri particolari./ Deve il mastro primieramente insegnar a tener ben la penna in mano allo scholaro, & ricordarli spesso tal modo, perche spesso se/ lo scorda: & perche ogn'uno non hà cosi la mano disposta à tener la penna con gratia, per diuersi difetti, a quali in alcuno sono / impossibili a rimediare, almeno gli mostri a tenerla in modo, che venghi a formar buona lineatura, & tenga poi la penna in che / modo si uoglia: auisandolo ancora che tenga alcuna cosa nella mano manca che l'aiuti a tener ferma la carta che non si dibatta quan/do scriue, perche questo importa molto."

63. Vecce 1998a, pp. 32–36.

64. Baxandall 1982, pp. 86–108, on the *abbaco*.

65. Vasari 1966– , vol. 4, p. 16: "Ecco, nell'abbaco, egli in pochi mesi ch'e'v'attese, fece tanto acquisto, che movendo di continuo dubbj e difficultà al maestro che gl'insegnava, bene speso lo confondeva." This allusion to the term *abbaco* has frequently been misinterpreted to mean generally "mathematics" or "arithmetic," despite the fact that it is quite clear from Vasari's wording that *abbaco* here means the school.

66. Fanti 1535, unpaginated, under "sesta ragione." A number of calligraphy books of the period offer patterns for the practice of a notary's script. It is called "littera per notari" in Vicentino 1523 and Fanti 1535, and "lettera notaresca" in Palatino 1540 and Palatino 1547.

67. Vecce 1998a, pp. 19–25.

68. Calvi 1925a, pp. 9–63; Pedretti 1975b pp. 10–11.

69. Bambach [Cappel] 1991b, p. 84 (nn. 79–81); Bambach [Cappel] 1991a, pp. 99–100 (n. 2).

70. Marinoni 1944–55; Marinoni 1980b, pp. vii–xxv.

71. Filippo Brunelleschi (1377–1446), the great Renaissance architect and engineer who was the son of a notary and who was a role model for the young Leonardo, is often said to have used mirror writing. This unreferenced claim, however, appears to be based on a rather contrived interpretation of an ambiguous passage about Brunelleschi's use of "graphs with numbers and symbols which Filippo alone understood," in Antonio di Tuccio Manetti's biography of Brunelleschi, written before 1489 (Manetti 1970, pp. 52–53). That passage deals with proportional measurements of antique ruins and is entirely unrelated. The most certain example of Brunelleschi's handwriting, his *portata del catasto* of 1427, is in conventional left-to-right script (illustrated in Milanesi 1876, vol. 1, no. 21). Moreover, Baratta 1905a, pp. 31–33, which is sometimes cited by later historians, also states that some architectural drawings attributed to Fra Giovanni Giocondo da Verona (1433–1515), the polymath antiquarian and theorist from a generation later who was Leonardo's close colleague, are inscribed with right-to-left words. A crude sketch in Florence (Uffizi 1530 A), now thought to be by an anonymous sixteenth-century draftsman, is inscribed with what appear to be a few garbled right-to-left words, while another sketch (Uffizi 1538 A), though most probably by Fra Giocondo himself, is not inscribed with mirror script. The vast majority of the extant documents and writings by Fra Giocondo are, in fact, written in a conventional left-to-right script (amply illustrated in Fontana 1988).

72. Transcribed in Baratta 1905a, pp. 31–33.

73. Richter 1970, vol. 1, p. 110.

74. Popham 1946, 1994, p. 9.

75. Letter quoted from Freud 1964, p. 7. See also Holly 1996.

76. Freud 1964, pp. 86–87; on Freud's Leonardo, Schapiro 1956, pp. 303–36; Schneider Adams 1993, pp. 14–140; Schapiro 1994; Benson 1994; Holly 1996; Oremland 1997, pp. xiii–xvi, 1–22, 109–21; Davis 1999, pp. 484–97 (my thanks to Rachel Stern for some of this literature).

77. See the thorough analysis of Leonardo's Windsor drawing of hands in Keele and Pedretti 1979–80, vol. 2, pp. 530–39, nos. 143 recto and verso.

78. Translation quoted from Eissler 1961, pp. 115–16 (with transcribed original French text).

79. Plato 2000, p. 152: "The practice which now prevails is almost universally misunderstood . . . that the right and left hand are supposed to be by nature differently suited for our various uses of them; whereas no difference is found in the use of the feet and lower limbs; but in the use of the hands we are, as it were, maimed by the folly of nurses and mothers; for although our several limbs are by nature balanced, we create a difference in them by bad habit."

80. See the double-sided sheet (figs. 71, 72) on which Leonardo drew the mirror designs of the composition by holding the paper to the light and tracing the design from one side of the sheet onto the other.

81. Compare the Uffizi drawing of a perspective projection for the stable appearing in the upper left of the *Adoration of the Magi* panel (fig. 139) and the very early, somewhat stiffly drawn sheet in the Louvre (cat. no. 27), which shows a number of design elements in reverse orientation.

82. Compare Leonardo's exploratory drawings on the theme of the *Virgin and Child with Saint Anne*: British Museum, London (cat. no. 96); Louvre, Paris, RF 460; Gallerie dell'Accademia, Venice (cat. no. 95).

83. See esp. Codex Arundel, Ms. 263, British Library, London.

84. Translation quoted from Kemp 1989c, p. 202. C. Urb., fol. 132r: "Come lo specchio e il maestro de pittori. / Quando tu uoi uedere se la tua pittura tutta insieme ha con / formita co'la cosa ritratta di naturale, habbi un specchio / et fai dentro specchiare la / cosa uiua, et parangona, la / cosa specchiata co' la tua pittura e' considera bene s'el tuo sub-/bietto del'una e l'altra similitudine ha conformita insie/me."

85. Translation quoted from Kemp 1989c, p. 202. C. Urb., fol. 33v: "facendo a'similitudine dello specchio / il quale si trasmutta in tanti colori quanti sono quelli delle co-/se, che se li pongano dinanzi, e' facendo cosi lui pa[r]à essere seconda / Natura."

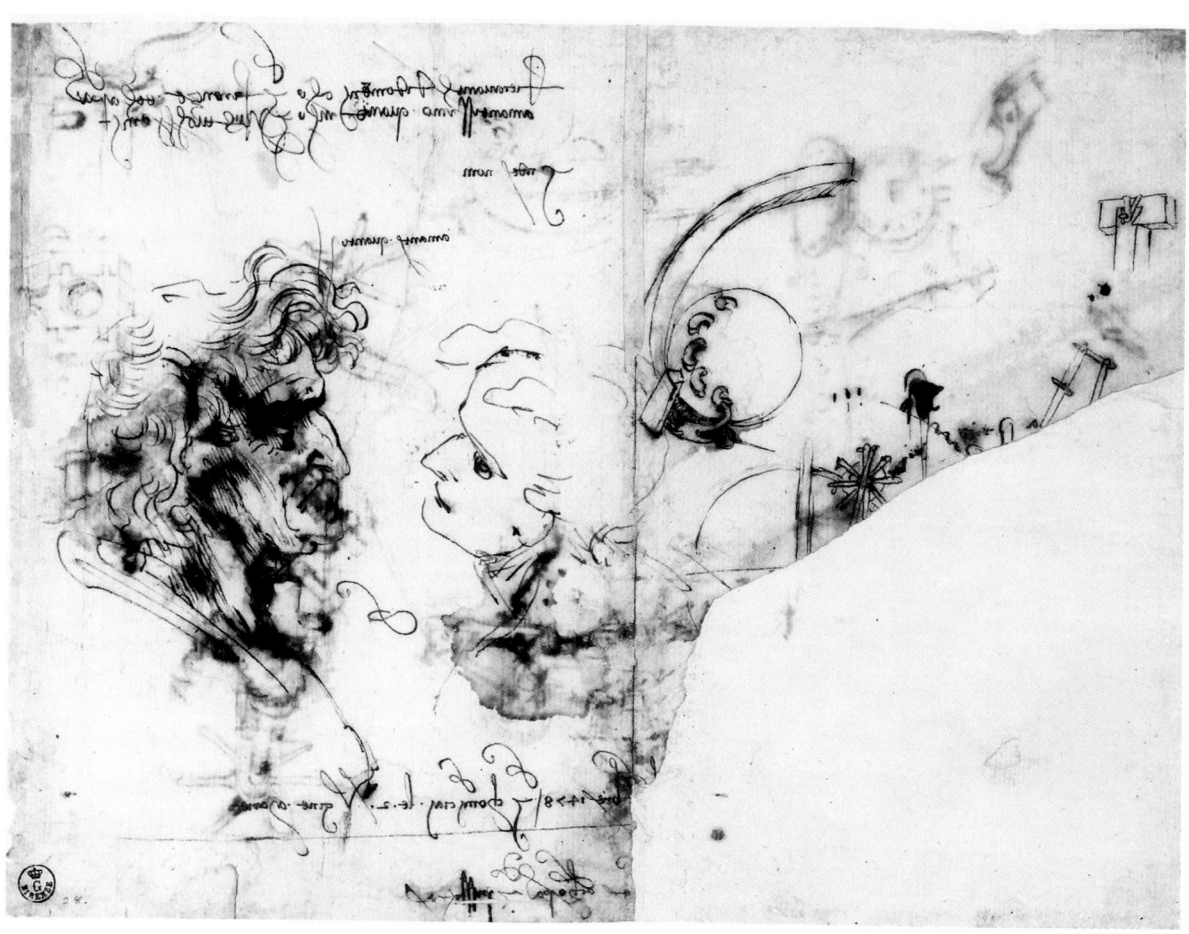

Fig. 39. Leonardo da Vinci, *Notes and Sketches of Heads and Machinery*. Pen and brown ink, 201 × 267 mm. Gabinetto Disegni e Stampe degli Uffizi, Florence 446 E

WORD AND IMAGE IN LEONARDO'S WRITINGS

CARLO VECCE

In terms of quantity alone, Leonardo the writer was far more productive than Leonardo the painter. Indeed, the physical act of writing probably occupied the largest part of his working day and was perhaps also the most satisfying part of it. The artist would have shut the door to his study, leaving behind his myriad daily tasks (the unavoidable but distracting requests of princes and patrons, visits from the curious, the squabbles and petty jealousies of his pupils, the haggling with workmen, carpenters, and suppliers). By the light of a candle or a lamp, he would don his "ceremonial robes" and take up the dialogue he had interrupted the evening before.

A dialogue with whom? In part it was with the classical *auctores* (authors) or, to use Leonardo's word, *altori*—just like Niccolò Machiavelli, who, in his famous letter to Francesco Vettori (1513), described his nightly communing with the ancients. To some, Leonardo was an uneducated man (an *omo sanza lettere*), because of his imperfect command of Latin and his lack of university training in disciplines like medicine, physics and mechanics, and natural philosophy. Leonardo himself, however, would have been dismissive of anyone who followed only the authority of ancient writers in his study of the natural sciences and ignored what was to be learned from Nature, the true teacher. Nonetheless, Leonardo had to ally himself with traditional schools of scientific and philosophical study even to take an independent position on them. To the self-taught man who stood as far from the university lecture room as the halls of the humanist academies, the ancient body of scientific learning, like that of ancient literature, was represented by an immense body of writing. For Leonardo it was a wall of words to be scaled only with some effort or a labyrinth that could be entered only with the help of humble but effective tools—elementary Latin grammars, abacus manuals, and lexicons, the most useful of which were vernacular dictionaries and lists of abbreviations. At the beginning of his career Leonardo juxtaposed images to this world of words and writing. He did this through painting, a form of expression he considered far superior because of the immediacy of its representation and its ability to communicate.

The extraordinary richness of the Italian vernacular, Leonardo's mother tongue, can be contrasted to the notable difficulties the artist had (until he was at least forty, and perhaps beyond) with Latin, his "paternal" tongue, that is to say, his second and learned language. Latin was the language of the scientific and humanist traditions, but it was also that used by notaries, the profession to which his own father, Ser Piero da Vinci, belonged (see essay by Alessandro Cecchi). A notary made his living by writing public documents, but these documents had a value different from writing in which learning was communicated and preserved. Notarial acts recorded, instead, the official events of social life in a performative and normative way, and notarial writing had its own characteristic decorative flourishes. These gave the script a great solemnity, and they included paraphs, which embellished the upper and lower strokes of certain letters, and graphic symbols in the documents themselves. The influence of this type of calligraphy can be seen in Leonardo's youthful writing, even in what must otherwise have been meaningless penmanship exercises. For example, in the notes accompanying two heads, one old and one young, on a sheet in the Uffizi (fig. 39) that is dated 1478 is a line that is transformed into purely expressive spiraling doodles. These flourishes seem almost to comment on or illustrate Leonardo's avowal of dear friendship for one Fieravanti: "Fieravanti di Domenico in Firenze e compa' amantissimo quanto mio"; "in dei nom"; "amant[issimo] quanto"; and "e compa' in Pistoia."[1]

In these instances the genesis of the writing is very close to that of the drawing: moving the tip of the pen across the white surface of the paper creates a line that can be transformed into a character, a word, or a drawing. Leonardo wrote: "the first picture was of a single line only, surrounding the shadow of a man cast by the sun onto the walls" (Paris Ms. A, fol. 97v = LDP no. 129, ca. 1492).[2] The reference here is to a story by Pliny the Elder (35:5: "umbra hominis lineis circumducta"), to which Leonardo adds the point, namely, that a line, an immaterial, purely imaginary entity, is nonetheless the origin of the science of painting: "The principle of the science of painting is the point; second is the line; third is the surface; fourth is the body which is enclosed by these surfaces. And this is just what it is to be represented, that is to say, the body which is represented, since in truth the scope of painting does not extend beyond the representation of the solid body or the shape of all the things that are visible"(LDP, no. 3, ca. 1510–15; and see LDP, no. 1).[3] Thus letters and drawings originate from the same operation—the movement of the pen over the blank surface of the paper—and in the act of separating them from oneself the idea is carried through the hand and is fixed in the material.

Leonardo was certainly aware that the spoken word, not writing, is the most natural way to transmit language. This was the world of the fables and stories that he had heard in the house of his mother, Caterina, or his grandfather, Antonio, or that were recited by singers in the town square in Vinci. Popular sacred plays were communicated orally, and so was the practical teaching in Florentine workshops like that of Andrea del Verrocchio. In the notes for his *Paragone*, a comparison of painting and poetry, which were begun in 1490 (now Paris Ms. A) and then expanded upon some ten years later in the texts collected in the first part of his planned *Libro di pittura*, Leonardo rooted his argument in the ways by which these art forms are transmitted (visually and orally) and received (by sight and hearing). His affirmation of the primacy of the eye, which he called the "window of the soul," has extraordinary anthropological value since it corresponds to the historical moment in which he lived, when the medieval world was passing into the modern period, a passage marked by the supremacy of visual perception over the senses of hearing and smelling in the representation of a human being's relationship to the natural world. The definition of poetry as "a painting one hears rather than sees" (LDP, no. 20) or a "blind painting" (LDP, no. 21) refers clearly to the oral quality of a text. In only one case does Leonardo acknowledge the presence of writing, which he considers a form of *disegno*, that is, design or drawing: "you writers are designing manually with the pen what is found in your mind" (Paris Ms. A, fol. 99v = LDP, no. 19).[4] It is painting, however, that "has found the signs used to express the different languages" (LDP, no. 23).

While advocating the primacy of seeing, Leonardo nonetheless remained deeply attached to the sense of hearing. Orality is dependent on memory, and, in an oral culture, even ideas and concepts tend to be articulated with formulae that allow them to be committed easily to memory, whether by such rhetorical strategies as repetition and antithesis, alliteration and assonance, epitaphs, verbal exercises, proverbs, and the like. The fundamental stylistic characteristics of oral literature are syntactical coordination (parataxis), aggregation, repetition, and redundancy, with a tendency to preserve structure while leaving the speaker (who might also intervene in the microstructure of the text) freedom and originality in his interpretation through, for instance, emphasis and participatory gestures. Orality is naturally collective, directed at a specific audience, reaching all members of an audience at the same time, and adapted to the actual circumstances of its reception. Hearing is a sense that unifies sounds into a sensory bundle that is then internalized by the listener. The phenomenology of sound gives value to the interior: it penetrates deeply; it tends to coalesce. Sacred writings that preserve the original, spoken quality of an utterance, even in its written form, seek to preserve this quality. The principal advantage of speaking comes in its interaction with other communicative activities (gesture, movement, proxemics) as well as other actions (and here one might recall the introduction to Benvenuto Cellini's *Autobiography*, in which the writer says of his assistant, "I set him to writing, and while I worked I dictated my autobiography to him"), allowing the listener to identify the speaker, and the speaker to verify that he is being heard in real time. The same rapidity of communication is also a disadvantage, however, because the sounds die on delivery; outside of memory, nothing remains, as the words dissolve into air, leaving that channel open for another message.[5]

Like Cellini, Leonardo sometimes dictated his texts, as can be seen in the nonautograph sheets of the Codex Arundel and the Codex Atlanticus. The earliest of these dictated texts, beginning with the artist's famous letter to Ludovico Sforza "Il Moro," were written in a variety of hands by his pupils and friends during his first sojourn in Milan. The later sheets show the more regular, almost humanist, script of Francesco Melzi, Leonardo's last pupil, whom he employed particularly to write letters. Dictation, like normal speaking, consists of much repetition, with the syntax developing directly from the flow of ideas. Linear development prevails, and completing the spoken text—or reaching the end of its recitation—requires time. While an image is immediately present in space, a spoken text, like music, occurs in time. Although an image does not allow for a polyphony of overlaid voices or for harmony, painting does permit the simultaneous reading of form and color: "The same occurs with the beauty of anything imagined by the poet, because such things are conceived [by him] separately at separate times, and the mind does not receive them in any harmony" (LDP, no. 21).[6] In this case, Leonardo wrote, "the painted imitation can provide a surrogate in large measure—a form of substitution not permitted the poet who, though wishing to rival the painter, cannot do so because the words with which he delineates the elements of beauty are separated from one another in time, which leaves voids between them and dismembers the proportions. He cannot delineate these elements without excessive wordiness and, not being able to depict them, he cannot construct the proportional harmonies that are produced by divine proportions. During the very time that it takes to embrace the contemplation of painted beauty, it is impossible to accomplish a beautiful description, and it is a sin against nature to send via the ear those things that should be sent via the eye" (LDP, no. 23).[7]

Beginning with his brief narratives, his fables and jokes, much of Leonardo's writing has the character of speech. This is true, more explicitly, of his "prophecies," which were intended to be recited at the festivals of the Sforza court. For instance, the stage directions for reciting the prediction "Della fossa" suggest that it be said "in a frenzied or berserk way, as of mental lunacy" (C.A., fol. 1033r, formerly fol. 370r-a).[8] In his scientific and technological texts this speech function is mostly connotative, with Leonardo often making use of an interlocutor (real or virtual or perhaps also just himself), in the role of teacher, to transmit a lesson or precept, to demonstrate a theorem, or to illustrate the course of an experiment.

For the young Leonardo in Verrocchio's workshop, a piece of paper was intended for drawing, for putting down sketches of compositional ideas, for copying the master's drawings, for tracing designs and projects for mechanical objects, and only occasionally for writing words or sentences. When these occur, they usually have no relationship to the drawings on the same sheet. A good example, on a page in the so-called Verrocchio Sketchbook that is attributed to Francesco di Simone Ferrucci, is the brief notes that Leonardo apparently made about his friends, his outstanding debts, and monies owed to him. Among Leonardo's jottings, written

Fig. 40. Workshop of Andrea del Verrocchio, *Figure Studies and Epigraphic Letters*, with words inscribed on the right by the young Leonardo. Pen and brown ink, 280 × 200 mm. Musée du Louvre, Paris RF 453

at the end of the 1470s, backward and next to a drawing by Francesco, we find the phrase "nicholo / di michele / debbe f. (?) ccc. s. (?) 50" (see also cat. no. 12). Another note, perhaps also by Leonardo, occurs a little farther down the sheet and to the left, but this time is written from left to right: "simone di miniato / b(er)nardo miniat [. . .]" (fig. 40). There are many similar texts on contemporary sheets, as, for example, a humorous recollection of his uncle: "Francesco d'Antonio in Firenze e compa' in Bacchereto deono dare fiorini MCCCCIIII" (C.A. fol. 878v, formerly fol. 320v-a); "Vante di Francesco da Castello Fiorentino e comp" (C.A. fol. 1112v, formerly fol. 400v-a); and "Io Lionardo," "in dei nomini amme[n]" (C.A. fol. 1054r, formerly fol. 379r-a). These brief notes are similar to a type of writing that must have been familiar to the young Leonardo, the *libri di ricordi*, literally "books of recollections," written by Florentine and Tuscan merchants and bourgeois citizens in the fifteenth century. These contained often brief notes on individual sheets that recorded the birth and death dates of children and other important events in a family's life and were not unlike that made by Leonardo's grandfather Antonio da Vinci to note the birth of his grandson in 1452.

Noting down events has nothing to do with orality; it is truly and properly writing—the recording of a memory that needs to be materially fixed in order to transmit its contents to another time or place. It is not accidental, then, that Leonardo wrote the names of friends on another sheet of paper next to the mysterious fragments of a letter, itself the type of text meant to be communicated across distances (C.A. fol. 18r–v, formerly fol. 4r-b–v-b). This sheet by the young Leonardo has drawings of machinery and gears. The writing on the recto (which Marinoni considered "idle scribbling," written from left to right in an "almost affected hand, idle, almost a game or trying the pen") is generally arranged in a column at the center of the left side, leaving the right side for drawings (tongs, an artillery piece, a three-wheeled cart, and a variety of gears). On the verso, however, the drawings are placed along the vertical axis of the sheet, ignoring its center line, and the text, also written from left to right, was added in the margins later.

Anyone familiar with Leonardo's manuscripts knows both how often they contain names of people and places and how valuable these are for determining a chronology of the individual sheets and the master's ideas. Similar observations can be made about dates, beginning with the earliest to be found on any sheet by Leonardo, "dì di s[an]ta Maria della neve / addj 5 daghossto 1473" (the [feast] of Saint Mary of the Snow, on the day of August 5, 1473; fig. 6). The date, too, is a distinct element of writing, as opposed to speaking, since it allows a text or drawing to be removed from the continuous and atemporal flow. Dates are temporal markers, and as such they verify the sheet.[9] It is interesting to note, though, that they are almost never put on individual drawings (and for this reason, too, the youthful drawing of a landscape in the Uffizi is exceptional). In his manuscripts, Leonardo used dates to fix important moments in his artistic career—beginnings or moments of starting anew. We find an example on the verso of figure 39: "[dice]mbre 1478 incominciai le 2 Vergine Marie" (December 1478 I began the two Virgins). The same is true of a note, "a dì 23 d'aprile 1490 cominciai questo libro e ricominciai il cavallo" (on April 23, 1490, I began this book and started again on the horse) (Paris Ms. C, fol. 15v), at the beginning of what was to be the first sheet of Paris Ms. C, in Claudio Scarpati's words "the first manuscript affirming Leonardo's decision in favor of the 'book.'"[10]

Drawing and writing have separate functions in Leonardo's earliest sheets. Usually the large drawings have no text, and the sheets on which text prevails have no drawings. The description of a sea monster and a cave in the Codex Atlanticus or the Codex Arundel demonstrates this point:

Oh, how many times were you seen through the waves of the swelling and great ocean, with your bristles and black back, like a mountain, with your heavy and imposing carriage! And often you were seen through the waves of the swelling and great ocean, with imposing and heavy movements turning in swirls in the waters of the sea, and with your bristles and black back, like a mountain that conquers and overwhelms. Oh, how many times were you seen through the waves of the swelling and great ocean, like a mountain that conquers and overwhelms, with your bristles and black back moving through the waters of the sea with your heavy and imposing carriage" (C.A., fol. 715r, formerly fol. 265r-a; see also Ar., fol. 155–56).[11]

These texts, dated to Leonardo's first Florentine period (1478–80), have a strongly visual character. From a rhetorical point of view, Leonardo uses description as the basic technique of his more creative writing. The object is presented as if it were in front of the painter, and it is analyzed in details that are "told" in linear succession. Such description allowed Leonardo to overcome, in writing, the problem of *inventio*—invention, which in contemporary schools was usually entrusted to the tiresome memorizing of *loci communes* and *flores sententiarum*—by using a strategy particular to painters. Nor is Leonardo's description static, merely decorative or juxtaposed to the narrative content (as it might be in the classical rhetorical technique of description—*ekphrasis*—or in Angelo Poliziano's contemporary *Stanze*); it becomes a dynamic representation of objects in movement, inserted in a temporal sequence that would be difficult to render with a symbol or in a painting. The things represented are most of all "seen," and then "described" according to a fairly common pattern—from the universal to the particular, from above to below according to angular and circular movements.[12] A "descriptive intentionality" predominates,[13] transforming, for example, the notes in Paris Ms. A into a coherent series of practical instructions destined for a book on painting based on the analogy between the modality of writing and the techniques of drawing. We also find here, however, that he has moved somewhat beyond orality. Latin constructions are adopted, vocabulary is enriched (these are the years of Leonardo's laborious study of Perotti's Latin grammar and memorization of the lists of learned vocabulary in the Codex Trivulzianus), and the rhetorical structure of the text is strengthened with the use of figures that depend for their effect on repetition, reversal of the order of words, and so on (chiasmus, anaphora, inversion, repetition, a crescendo of a lexical series and enumeration). The effect is to bring the prose to the rhythmical level of poetry.[14] We also find this quality in the structure of the fables and in autonomous passages that have nothing to do with the development of a narrative sequence. They describe movement and transformation with verbal imagery (the rhythmic cadence of the beating wings in the flight of the magpie, "ora qua ora in là") and anthropomorphic metaphor, such as the flame that sings "with sweet murmur . . . with its tail raised and its head lowered, it [the magpie] flies off the branch, putting its body's weight on the wings, which flapping above the displaced air, now here and now there, curiously using [uses] the tail for steering" (C.A., fol. 188r, formerly fol. 67r-b);[15] or "Now, the fire having rejoiced [exuberantly emerged] from the dry wood logs, begins to rise, catching the air in between the spaces of the logs, from which, with playful and mirthful passage [movement], it weaves itself into being. Having begun to exhale [emit] forth glittering [shining] and sparkling [flickering] little flames, [the fire] quickly dispels the gloomy darkness of the enclosed kitchen, and the flames that were already grown played [play] in the air around them and singing with sweet murmur they created [create] soft sound" (C.A., fol. 321r, formerly fol. 116v-b).[16]

We should also consider the reverse, the use of iconic signs or symbols as the equivalent of words or a verbal text. The icon, characterized by its resemblance to the object it replaces, had for Leonardo the qualities of universality and invariability, comprehensible even if its linguistic context changed. The image "speaks," but functions as a text. It was to explore the expressive potential of symbols that Leonardo embarked on what was perhaps the strangest intellectual experiment of his life — the compilation of his rebuses, or series of pictographs. Rebuses are pictures or symbols that suggest words or phrases and that can be combined into sentences with meanings that are very different from the original pictures.[17] The most interesting aspect of this exercise was the reduction in the size of the pictographs. They became small drawings consisting of only a few strokes of the pen, but representing the essential properties of the object, animal — even in motion — or acrobatic game.[18]

The pictographs are similar to the lists of learned vocabulary Leonardo compiled in the Codex Trivulzianus; they were his "libro di mia figure" (book of my figures), a repertory of images to be memorized, assembled on the basis of a figural mnemotechny that took advantage of the reproduction of images and their serial repetition (see Ar., fol. 250r; LDP, no. 173).[19] These drawings are not very different from ideograms and are thus not far removed from writing. It might be mentioned that Egyptian hieroglyphics were in vogue among Italian humanists — they appeared in the *Hypnerotomachia Poliphili* published by Aldo Manuzio in 1498 — at the time Leonardo was working on this project.

The association between images and words is also at the heart of the *imprese* and *emblemi*—devices and emblems—Leonardo made for members of the Sforza court (and they are one of the first examples of a fashion that would spread throughout Europe in the sixteenth century). The same is true for the artist's allegories, constructed with drawings and explanatory texts, in which instructions for painting, in anaphoric cadence, predominated: "a la fama si de' dipignere" (Paris Ms. B, fol. 2v); "la infamia sottosopra figurare si debbe" (Paris Ms. H, fol. 61r); "fannonsi," "figuransi," "questo si è," "qui si figura," "questa invidia si figura," "fassi–fassile" (see cat. no. 54 and Christ Church, Oxford, 0037).

In these, the correspondence between word and image was not always fixed as it had been in the pictographs. Leonardo's *imprese* and allegories were conceived in movement—as were many of his drawings and compositional sketches—and this process of transformation is

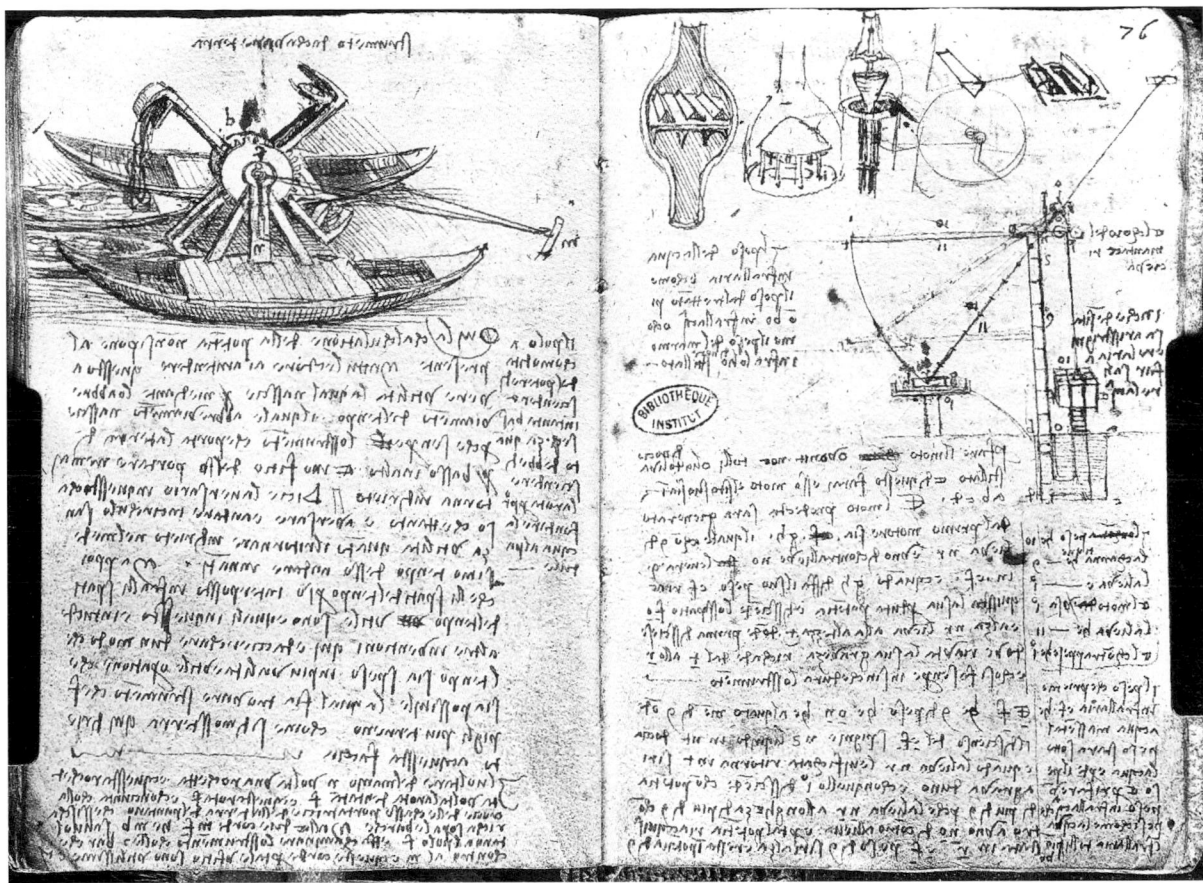

Fig. 41. Leonardo da Vinci, *Hydraulic Devices*. Manuscript E, fols. 75 verso and 76 recto. Pen and brown ink, 150 × 105 mm. Institut de France, Paris 2176

visible both in the iconic version and in the passages of text, such as those on a sheet at Windsor in the space left free by several geometric proofs (cat. no. 110 recto and verso). The recto has variations on the motto "non mi stanco nel giovare," which resemble different versions of an *Iris fiorentina*. It is worth noting that the various versions of text and image are independent of one another, which can be explained by Leonardo's quest to express himself better both verbally and graphically.

The variations in the allegories of truth and falsehood on the verso of the Windsor sheet are a laboratory for Leonardo's other and more complex allegories, and as such they are analogous to Botticelli's famous picture of the allegory of Calumny (Uffizi, Florence). The artist began at the center of the sheet (cat. no. 110) with an equivalence between image and abstract concept (Truth-sun, Falsehood-mask). He then added two further concepts without images (Innocence and Malignancy) but that can be identified in the two marginal figures. A brief text, however, ties fire to the action of unveiling Truth, and several drawings present variations on the theme of the mask (the "face," a symbol also used in the rebus) being destroyed by fire, while the rays of the sun illuminate the true face hidden beneath it. Other drawings

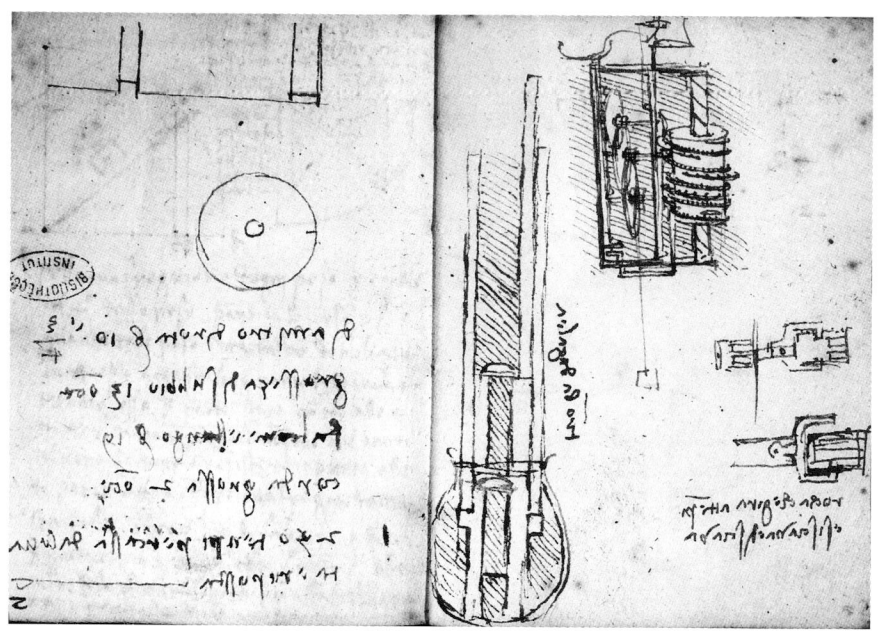

Fig. 42. Leonardo da Vinci, *Studies of Gears*. Ms. L, fols. 25v–26r. Institut de France, Paris 2182

return to the image of the sun, the heat of which seems to melt a mask evidently made of wax.[20]

The most common and even most natural arrangements of Leonardo's "writing spaces" are those that include text and drawing (fig. 41), and in these instances it is relatively easy to trace their genesis and find archetypes. The first of the surviving manuscripts, Paris Ms. B, which dates from about 1486–88, is in large part a collection of notes taken from the Italian edition of Roberto Valturio's *De re militari* produced by Paolo Ramusio (Verona, 1483). It reveals how close Leonardo's method of collecting texts was to that of contemporary humanists—for instance, Angelo Poliziano, Bartolomeo Fonzio, Aulo Giano Parrasio, Jacopo Sannazaro, and Pietro Bembo, who compiled so-called *zibaldoni,* or commonplace books.[21] These consisted of excerpts from classical texts and numerical references to the folios or pages of the books from which passages were copied—a procedure that arose in large part because the invention of printing now allowed for more than one copy or edition of the same book. This humanist technique allowed for new methods of organizing knowledge and, in a certain sense, created the foundations of the modern encyclopedia, namely, the compilation of knowledge tied to disciplinary hierarchies along with the principle of cited authorities. We find Leonardo using numerical cross-references for the first time in Paris Ms. B. Interestingly, these numbers correspond neither to the 1483 edition of Valturio's work nor to the original Latin text of 1472, but rather to an intermediate and now lost notebook of his own in which Leonardo had already transcribed these passages.[22]

We now know, thanks to the work of scholars like Nando De Toni, Girolamo Calvi, and Augusto Marinoni, that Valturio's was one of the books Leonardo referred to most often between 1486 and 1490 for his information about the military arts and war machines in Paris Ms. B (the result of the promises the artist-engineer had made to Ludovico "Il Moro") and for the list of vocabulary in the Codex Trivulzianus. Yet Valturio was not simply a textual source. The editions of his work were among the most beautiful illustrated books of the quattrocento, and Leonardo must also have appreciated them for this connection between text and image. An emphasis on the relationship between writing and illustration is a distinguishing characteristic of the architectural and engineering treatises of the Renaissance, for instance, those of Francesco di Giorgio Martini, Antonio Filarete, and Piero della Francesca, as well as of manuscripts by engineers and *omini pratici* (skilled or practical men) like Mariano di Taccola, Buonaccorso Ghiberti, and Lorenzo and Benvenuto della Golpaja.[23] These treatises represent, in addition to the *libri di ricordi* and *zibaldoni*, the third and most important model for Leonardo's writing.

These texts, even when they reach the conclusive form of a book or a treatise divided into books and chapters, all remained in manuscript form. (The only exception is the Latin edition of Leon Battista Alberti's *De re aedificatoria*, published by Poliziano in Florence in 1485, a text without illustrations that was of interest principally because of its humanistic and linguistic efforts to come to grips with Vitruvius's difficult text on architecture.) Because of the extreme difficulty of reproducing images in print, these books and treatises circulated in the form of sumptuous manuscripts that were carefully illuminated with illustrations made under the supervision of the authors themselves. Leonardo had, for example, seen the first edition of Francesco di Giorgio's treatise on military engineering—written at the court of Urbino and finished, after Duke Federico's death, in about 1484—by the time he was working on his Paris Ms. B. Leonardo became acquainted with Francesco di Giorgio himself in Milan and Pavia in 1490, and he then owned and annotated a lovely manuscript copy of the second edition of the treatise in about 1502–4 (Biblioteca Laurenziana, Florence, Ashburnham 361). Leonardo probably also knew about sketchbooks from Verrocchio's workshop (see cat. nos. 4, 8, 12); the first example we have is the Codex Forster III, circa 1487–90. These were small pocket-sized notebooks that engineers carried with them at work sites to note down technical problems and their solutions or to show pupils or workmen how to work a machine or mechanical device (fig. 42).

"Demonstration" is the key here. Drawings were used to make an object visible in a practical sense, immediately and without too much explanation (fig. 42). In rhetoric this technique of demonstration is called *evidentia*. It is based on a direct relationship between sender and receiver and is similar to what happens when one speaks to another. Here we find ourselves far from the utopian project (of substituting objects for words for the purpose of constructing a universal language and grammar) realized in the strange Academy in the continent of Lagado that Gulliver visited during his travels. It is also true, however, that we stand at the very beginning of modern science, when "things" (verifiable by experimentation) begin to take their revenge on "words," which had reigned supreme in ancient books and among Renaissance humanists. Leonardo had already substituted "things"—symbols—for words in his games of picture writing.

Scientific and technological illustration is not purely decorative, but it does go beyond a text by allowing a thing to be visualized more clearly than is possible in a verbal description

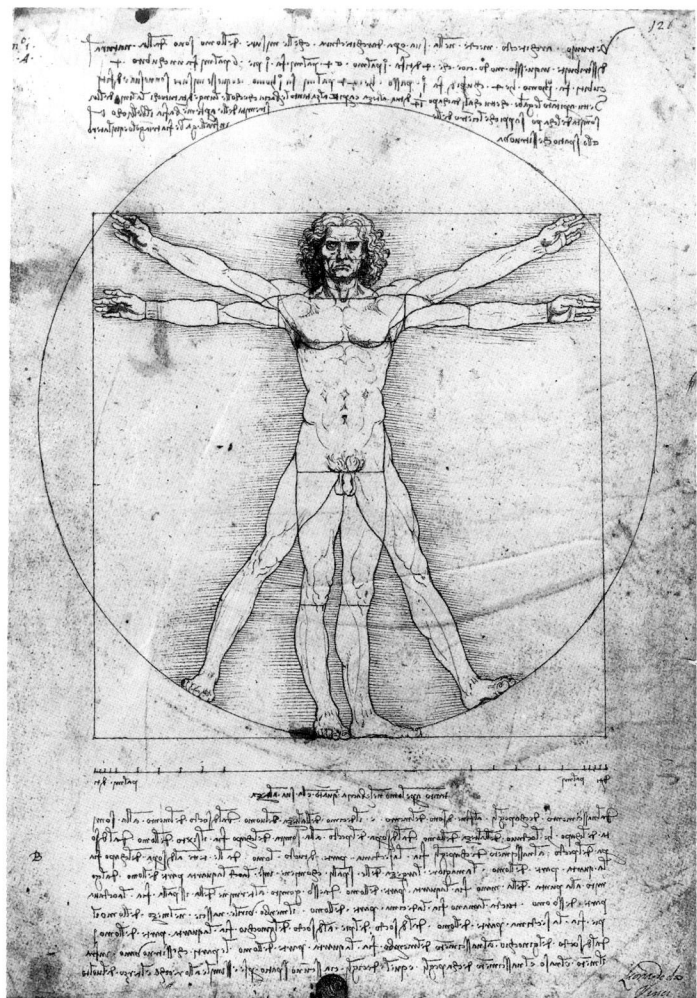

Fig. 43. Leonardo da Vinci, *The Proportions of the Human Body According to Vitruvius (The Vitruvian Man)*. Pen and brown ink, brush and some brown wash, over metalpoint, 344 × 245 mm. Gallerie dell'Accademia, Venice 228

alone. An example is the difficulty of reading and understanding Vitruvius's text, much corrupted through its long transmission from antiquity, without images. This challenge led Leon Battista Alberti to write his *De re aedificatoria* and Fra Giocondo da Verona (a humanist but also an engineer and architect who possessed the necessary technical skill) to produce the first illustrated edition of Vitruvius (Venice, 1511). And yet even the most exacting and detailed drawing cannot completely represent the reality of an object. The first difficulty comes in the transition from three dimensions to two, though this can be overcome by representing the object from several points of view (Leonardo's application of this technique, already in use in the fifteenth century, to his late anatomical drawings is nothing short of miraculous). Another apparently insurmountable difficulty is the representation of movement—a machine at work or an object being made—which a single, static drawing cannot convey. It was possible, however, to make a series of images that (like photographs) capture the different phases of movement, or one might also superimpose one image upon another. The latter technique has been noted in both the drawing of the so-called *Vitruvian Man* (fig. 43) and the extraordinary drawings—not by Leonardo but based on his work—in the Codex Huygens (Pierpont Morgan Library, New York).

Leonardo was certainly aware that images lacked something that only a text possessed. Thus he returned to writing, which for him was already and naturally strongly visual both in its *inventio* and *dispositio*. In general, writing that accompanied a drawing tended to be arranged rather formally around it, next to it, and sometimes within it, like the text in the circle traced by a hygrometer above the study of figures for an *Adoration* (cat. no. 29): "modo di pesare laria / eddi sap[er]e qua[n]do sa / arromp[er]e il te[m]po" (way of weighing the air and of knowing how time is interrupted); and, written outside the circle, "spugnja / ciera" (sponge/wax).

Headings were often placed at the top center of a sheet, and texts were then handled, in both appearance and execution, as if they were part of a single, intellectual unity (as indeed they were). Text and drawing gestated together, and, exercising mutual influence, were structured together in the formation of an idea. It is often difficult to discover which came first, especially when there are several subsequent variations of the same image and the same text on the same sheet. Leonardo worked intensely on variations, which was for him the most natural way to pursue the evolution of an idea. Thus textual variation, as part of the intellectual process, is like his continual variation of drawn images, an essential ingredient in Leonardo's permutatory technique.[24]

In Leonardo's drawings, an image outlined in red or black chalk was then reinforced with pen and ink. Similarly, texts were written first in red chalk (see cat. no. 64). Words would then be traced with pen and ink, character by character (and as in a palimpsest, one can distinguish the writing beneath and above), after which they would be transcribed in another notebook.

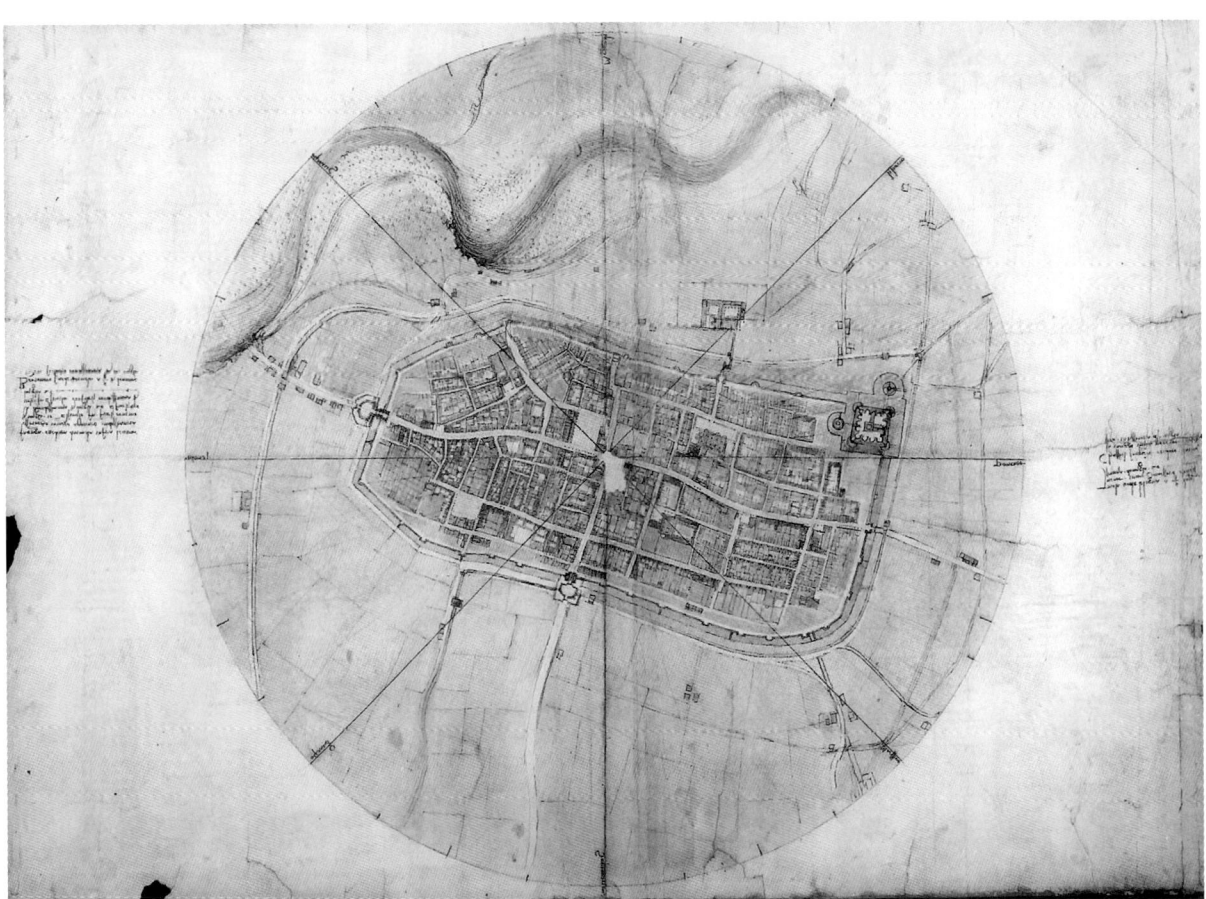

Fig. 44. Leonardo da Vinci, *Map of Imola*. Pen and brown ink, brush and watercolor, 440 × 602 mm. The Royal Collection, H.M. Queen Elizabeth II, Windsor Castle RL 12284

Rewriting and transcribing were never mechanical tasks. At each stage Leonardo introduced changes that create the sense of a text in perpetual movement. The page was freed to accommodate the different phases of this movement because writing had renounced the fixed quality it had throughout the history of civilization. Leonardo's scientific investigations were also liberated since they were no longer hindered by the need to assume the quality of permanence and thereby benefited from this mobility by formulating a new approach to the study of natural phenomena.

Locating, or "localization" (which for humanists had been restricted to the textual universe of their *zibaldoni*), worked in two directions—from the drawing to the text and from the text to the drawing—and was achieved by a system of alphabetical and numerical cross-references (which Leonardo had already made use of in his geometric drawings). By means of text on his maps Leonardo identified locations, cities, mountains, and rivers; often he did this himself, but in his later years he left the task to his pupil Francesco Melzi, who sometimes used regular capital letters. Renaissance cartography, surveying techniques (which Leonardo probably learned, for example, from Leon Battista Alberti and then used for his famous map of Imola [fig. 44]),[25] large manuscript maps, and published editions of Ptolemy all served Leonardo as models for the relationship between text and image. It had been known from antiquity that virtual representations of geographic or cosmological space were superior to what can be seen with the naked eye. The appearance of a valley or a mountain chain can be deceptive to a viewer (because of atmospheric or perspectival effects), while a faithful cartographic representation reveals in their totality elements that might otherwise be absent when seen from a particular point of view.

For this reason Leonardo loved to think of his representations of human anatomy as a form of mapping, comparing his anatomical charts to Ptolemy's maps of the cosmos (Windsor, RL 19061, ca. 1510). Certainly the analogies between the macrocosm and microcosm, between the larger and the smaller world, between bodies of land and human bodies, lay at the heart of this idea, but by the time Leonardo wrote the introduction to his anatomical books, he must have been no more certain of the correspondence between human functioning (especially the circulation of the blood) and the laws that governed grand geologic phenomena. (See essay by Claire Farago.) Ptolemy's map, the "cosmografia del minor mondo," was above all an analogy for charting the voyage undertaken in the miraculous universe inside the human body. The process of coming to know this body resembled a journey across oceans as yet unexplored (not unlike Christopher Columbus's of just a few years earlier), and the task of the returning sailor was to trace the territory he had just discovered on a map in order to make it visible to those who had not seen it. Every voyage takes place in time, and Leonardo's odyssey through anatomical dissection was an anguished struggle against time, against the rapid deterioration of muscle tissue and the vascular system before the eyes and under the hands of the anatomist. Drawings (from multiple points of view) thus succeeded in improving direct vision (just as does a map) because they preserved the details of the object even after it was lost to the corruption of the cadaver (Windsor, RL 19070v). In the extraordinary series of drawings of the muscles of an old man's arm, made on both sides of a sheet now at Windsor (cat. no. 113) and drawn from right to left, the descriptive texts concerning the functioning of the deltoid muscle "follow" the drawings in their physical rotation and are inserted into the empty spaces between them.

Words alone, as Leonardo writes in the text surrounding his sketch of the heart and a lung, are absolutely incapable of describing what the eye has seen (Windsor, RL 19071). The anatomical treatises then in circulation must have seemed inadequate to the artist, including Mondino de Luzzio's Italian edition of Johannes de Ketham's *Fasciculus de medicina*, published in Venice in 1493, which Leonardo owned and which was embellished with lovely woodcuts that had, however, only a decorative function (fig. 137). He found it necessary, instead, to "draw and describe" (Windsor, RL 19013v), and the value of the text was in naming the parts of the body and describing them. These descriptions accompanied the drawings and conveyed the impressions of the observer with greater accuracy. It is not accidental that we find Leonardo's most advanced reflections on verbal language, in which he sees potentiality and infinite variety, in his late anatomical writings (Windsor, RL 19045v). This kind of writing, far removed from orality, communicates across the distance of time and space. It also records an event, dissection, that Leonardo felt was truly revolutionary with respect to the ancient tradition of knowledge.

Even the peculiar characteristics of Leonardo's writing style have a metatextual dimension. This is especially true of the positioning of text on paper and of the delineation of the writing space itself, elements that can be interpreted only on a visual plane (figs. 41, 42). Everyone has noted that Leonardo wrote backward, from right to left, in what is often referred to as mirror writing because it can be easily read when reflected in a mirror. This manner of writing, which came naturally to a self-taught, left-handed person, was not entirely unusual among Renaissance artists (Raffaello da Montelupo is one example; see essay by Carmen C. Bambach). Originally Leonardo's calligraphic notes were placed next to drawings as isolated lines of text. As the mass of text increased and gained autonomy from the drawings (as, for example, in the sheets with descriptions of sea monsters and caves discussed above and, later, in Paris Mss. B, C, and A), the problem arose of where to put the text on a page that was conceived from right to left. As in Hebrew or Arabic manuscripts, the first page of the book for Leonardo was the last. (For this reason, Luca Pacioli recorded Leonardo's script as a form of secret writing.)[26] This reversal, both in the production and reception of the text, offered an alternative way of reading reality, following a reverse metonymic chain. A historian who traces the course of human history from the present backward does

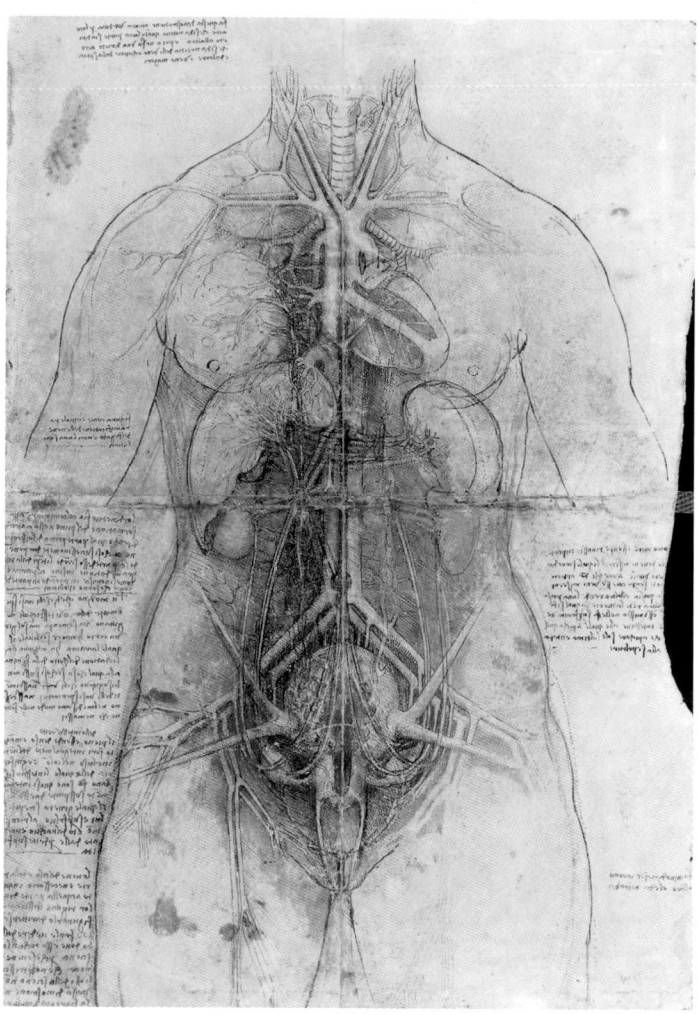

Fig. 45. Leonardo da Vinci, *Dissection of the Principal Organs and the Arterial System of a Female Figure* (recto). Pen and brown ink, brush and brown wash, over black chalk, outlines pricked for transfer, 470 × 328 mm. The Royal Collection, H.M. Queen Elizabeth II, Windsor Castle RL 12281

much the same thing, as does the physicist or natural philosopher who analyzes a succession of causes and effects in natural phenomena or anatomy.[27]

Leonardo's *mise en page* thus gives much more freedom to writing than in the normal production of books, whether mechanically or by hand, in the age of humanism. Mirror writing might suggest that some of Leonardo's more finished drawings (the Windsor anatomical sheets, for example) were to be published by means of the new technique of engraving on a metal plate (Ma. I, fol. 199r).[28] Yet Leonardo's position on printing, the most important and revolutionary invention of his time, was unique. He reproached it for creating infinite offspring—*infiniti figlioli* (LDP, no. 8)—thereby almost anticipating the later concerns of Martin Heidegger and Walter Benjamin. The reproducibility of prints diminishes the aura resulting from a unique artistic creation, while Leonardo wanted instead to preserve the distinctive character of his work, even of his writing and its textuality. Nonetheless, drawings like the *Vitruvian Man* and the female reproductive organs (figs. 43, 45) did become objects to be copied, though in these cases the method was the traditional one of pouncing. The latter was a true map of the human body, and it was destined to be reproduced like Leonardo's maps of the Arno or the Mugnone rivers (cat. nos. 78, 79).[29]

The book, reproduced by means of printing, also multiplies in its "infinite offspring" the idea of an end, a conclusion, or even death, which Leonardo's manuscripts constantly postpone. Their text is always in motion, the "books" (even when they are minutely outlined) remain open. Each text is an interchangeable form, able to combine in its parts with all the others, like the files in a hypertext.[30] Leonardo began, in the years of his second sojourn in Florence (from 1501–2 onward), to write on individual sheets of double-sized paper creased down the center that he left lying open on his desk, as if waiting to receive a continuous resystemizing of knowledge, which came through rereading and transcribing in new manuscripts (examples include a group of sheets in the Codex Arundel, fols. 1–14; and in the Codex Leicester, cat. no. 114) and which in turn triggered a continuous cycle of writing, reading, and more writing.[31] Even if the separate sheets were eventually put together in the form of a book, they always maintain their sense of openness, as one can see in Madrid Codex II, in which the planning of the book was guided by a constant need to locate and to recover texts and drawings from what must have seemed labyrinthine even to Leonardo.[32]

The Codex Leicester, the subject of new and important research, is also relevant to a discussion of the relationship between word and image. At the same time it is impossible not to notice that writing predominates in the pages of this disassembled notebook and that much of it consists of transcribing and reworking earlier manuscripts. Leafing through its pages, one has the sense that space for writing was very carefully planned. This space is filled with script that spread, as one might expect, over the entire page in a single line, leaving the right margin free for notes and drawings. The drawings themselves are small scientific illustrations that synthesize the essential elements of their subjects using a technique perfected in the two Madrid codices. They are extraordinarily effective sketches, especially in the representation of the movement of fluids through water (vortices, waves, currents; see cat. no. 114; Sheet 11A, fol. 26v; Sheet 9A, fol. 28v; Sheet 5B, fol. 32r).

Leonardo's writing should be regarded more as a "textual window" than as a sheet filled with script. Even when it is not perfectly set on the page, the text—if it does not need to fit around a preexisting drawing or adapt to the shape of the paper, as in the case of a page in the Codex Atlanticus (fol. 694v, formerly fol. 258v-a) that is round—is always placed within a square or rectangular frame and justified at its margins. When the text came to an end in the middle of the last line of the "window," Leonardo felt obliged (especially after 1500) to add a somewhat quivering terminal line that sometimes looks like the recording of small seismographic tremors or the beating of a heart. Sometimes this type of line grew out of the "et cetera" that closed a sequence in the text and referred it back to a mental discourse indissolubly linked, in a physical and biological continuum, to the act of writing.[33] A normal feature of notarial and chancery script, the et cetera was virtually nonexistent in Leonardo's writing before 1500 but became much more common in his work between 1503 and 1508 (a period, as we have noted, of intense rewriting). It then appears on almost every page of the late manuscripts (Paris Mss. E and G) and the last individual sheets.

The fundamental point to be made is that Leonardo did not like to finish things. "Scrittura infinita" (infinite writing) meant that there were no boundaries between forms of expression, languages, intellectual disciplines, and experience. It also meant, however, not recognizing the act of separation that constituted the closing of a text, the conclusion of the argument, the final word. The limits of writing are the word, the line, the paragraph, the page, and the book; those of the writer are the natural light of day or the artificial illumination of a lamp, his daily material needs (Leonardo's "la minesstra si fredda"), and his very life. This is so even when a single illusory victory of an "end" is achieved: "The night of Saint Andrew I found the solution to the squaring of the circle, and at the end of the light and of the night and of the paper on which I was writing it was finished, at the end of the hour" (Ma. II, fol. 112r).[34]

1. Arasse 1997, p. 136; Rosand 1988, p. 26.

2. "La prima pittura fu sol di una linea, la quale circondava l'ombra fatta dal sole ne' muri." English translation from Venerella 1999–, *Manuscript A*, p. 268. Herein LDP refers to the edition by Carlo Pedretti and Carlo Vecce of Leonardo's *Libro di pittura* (*Libro di pittura* 1995 in the Bibliography). Numbers refer to the passages in this edition.

3. "Il principio della scienza della pittura è il puonto, il secondo è la linea, il terzo è la superfizie, il quarto è il corpo che si veste de tal superfizie; e questo è in quanto a quello che si finge, cioè esso corpo che si finge, perché invero la pittura non s'astende più oltra che la superfizie, per la quale si finge il corpo figura di qualonque cosa evidente." English translation from Kemp 1989c, p. 15.

4. "Voi scrittori disegnando con la penna manualmente quello che nello ingegno vostro si trova." English translation from Venerella 1999–, *Manuscript A*, p. 277.

5. Vecce 2001, pp. 17–18.

6. "Il simile accade nelle bellezze di qualonque cosa finta dal poeta, le quali, per essere le sue parti dette separamente in separati tempi, la memoria non ne riceve alcuna armonia."

7. "Et in questo caso la pittura imitata da quella in gran parte supplisce, il che supplire non potrà la discrezione del poeta; il quale in questo caso si vole equiparare al pittore, ma non s'avede che'lle sue parole, nel far menzione delle membra di tal bellezze, il tempo le divide l'un dall'altro, e inframette la oblivione, e divide le proporzioni, le quali lui sanza gran prolissità non può nominare. E non potendole nominare, esso non può comporre l'armonica proporzionalità, la quale è composta de divine proporzioni. E per questo un medesimo tempo, nel quale s'include la speculazione d'una bellezza depinta, non può dare una bellezza descritta, e fa peccato contro natura quello che si dé mettere per l'occhio a volerlo mettere per l'orecchio." English translation adapted from Kemp 1989c, p. 24.

8. "Dilla in forma di frenesia o farnetico, d'insania di cervello." English translation from Kemp 1981, p. 163.

9. Rosand 1988, pp. 26–28; Zwijnenberg 1999, pp. 136–37.

10. Scarpati 2001, p. 16.

11. "O quante volte fusti tu veduto in fra l'onde del gonfiato e grande oceano, col setoluto e nero dosso, a guisa di montagna e con grave e superbo andamento! E spesse volte eri veduto in fra l'onde del gonfiato e grande oceano, e col superbo e grave moto gir volteggiando in fre le marine acque, e con setoluto e nero dosso, a guisa di montagna, quelle vincere e sopraffare. O quante volte fusti tu veduto in fra l'onde del gonfiato e grande oceano, a guisa di montagna quelle vincere e sopraffare, e col setoluto e nero dosso socare le marine acque, e con superbo e grave andamento."

12. Segre 1979.

13. Scarpati 2001, p. 12.

14. Scarpati 2001, p. 40.

15. "Con dolce mormorio," "alzato la coda e bassato le testa, e gittatasi del ramo, rendé il suo peso all'ali, e quelle battendo sopra la fuggitiva aria, ora qua, ora in là curiosamente col timon della coda dirizzandosi."

16. "Allora, rallegratosi il fo[co] delle sopra sé poste secche legne, comincia a elevarsi, [ca]cciando l'aria delli intervalli d'esse legne, infra quelle con ischerzevole e giocoso transito, se stessi tesseva. Cominciato a spirare fori di rilucenti e rutilanti fiammelle, subito discaccia le oscure tenebre della serrata cucina; e con galdio le

fiamme già cresciute scherzavano coll'aria d'esse circundatrice e con dolce mormorio cantando creava[n] suave sonito."

17. Marinoni 1954b; Vecce 1993a; Vecce 1995; Vecce 2000.

18. Carlo Pedretti, *Postilla* to Vecce 1993a, pp. 313–16.

19. Vecce 2000, pp. 31, 34.

20. Vecce 2000, pp. 33–34.

21. Vecce 1998c.

22. Calvi 1925b, pp. 101–6.

23. Maccagni 1971; Vecce 1993b; Galluzzi 1997.

24. Gombrich 1986b.

25. See Zwijnenberg 1999, pp. 106–8.

26. Pacioli 1997, p. 334.

27. Holly 1996, pp. 116, 146.

28. Zwijnenberg 1999, pp. 83–85; Farago 1999a, p. 437.

29. Bambach 1999a, pp. 304–9.

30. Vecce in Pedretti and Vecce 1998, p. 50.

31. Zwijnenberg 1999, pp. 91–92.

32. Farago 1993; Farago 1999a; Zwijnenberg 1999, pp. 181–87.

33. Pedretti 1975b; Vecce 1998b.

34. "La notte di Santo Andre' trovai il fine della quadratura del cerchio, e in fine del lume e della notte e della carta dove scrivevo fu concluso, al fine dell'ora."

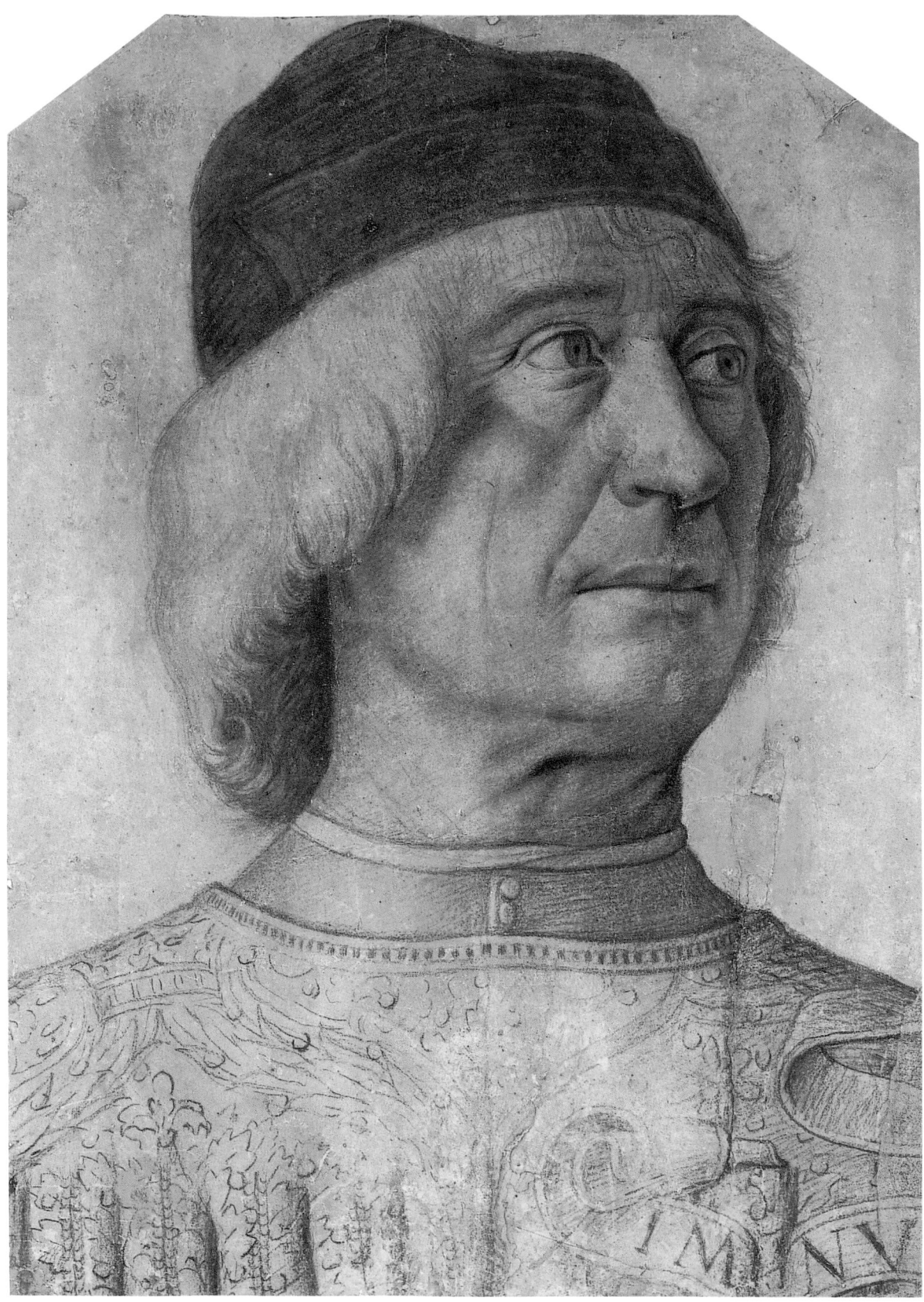

Fig. 46. Attributed to Giovanni Bellini, *Portrait of a Man*. Black chalk, brush, and some wash, 391 × 280 mm. Christ Church, Oxford JBS 702

THE CRITICAL FORTUNE OF LEONARDO'S DRAWINGS

CARLO PEDRETTI

A SPLENDID, LIFESIZE MALE PORTRAIT (fig. 46) in the Christ Church collection of old master drawings at Oxford—a front view, half-bust with a beautiful brocadelike robe, seen from slightly below, the head slightly lifted as if the man had turned his eyes to look up at something on his left—is now rightly attributed to Giovanni Bellini, though the style and character have also suggested in the recent past a comparison with portraits of members of the Gonzaga family by Andrea Mantegna at Mantua.[1]

Today, a glance informs us that both sitter and author of the drawing are Venetians. It would be pointless to argue over this. Since the publication of Sidney Colvin's scholarly catalogue of the whole Christ Church collection in 1902, this assessment of the drawing has been accepted.[2] Everything that was previously thought, said, or written about the drawing was forgotten, and no one today mentions that, shortly before the appearance of Colvin's publication, this Venetian portrait was taken to be a portrait of Ludovico Sforza "Il Moro," duke of Milan, made by no less an artist than Leonardo da Vinci. Doubts about such an identification did not concern the obviously Venetian character of the image or the undeniable incompatibility of the image with Ludovico Sforza's countenance, as well known then as now from all sorts of visual evidence—sculpture, painting, book illumination, and so on—but were based on a gradual understanding by the mid-nineteenth century, after much uncertainty and confusion in the seventeenth and eighteenth centuries, of Leonardo's style in painting and drawing. By 1877 one could read, regarding this drawing, "a fine portrait . . . but probably by a scholar of Leonardo's." This is in John William Brown's account of Leonardo's life and work appended to John Francis Rigaud's translation of Leonardo's *Libro di pittura*, entitled *A Treatise on Painting by Leonardo da Vinci*. At a time when so high a percentage of a pupil's work was freely given to the master, once the master's touch was no longer detected or was strongly doubted, the attribution to a pupil followed.[3] But the Christ Church portrait was such an extreme case that the emerging generation of scholars and trained connoisseurs, such as Giovanni Morelli (Ivan Lermolieff), Jean Paul Richter, Adolfo Venturi, and others, would not even bother discussing these misattributions.

Today, anyone writing about this drawing for a scholarly paper or an exhibition catalogue would hardly feel compelled to record the previous, striking, but wrong, attribution. It is therefore only because of the thoroughness of the information it offers that the pertinent entry (no. 702) in the updated catalogue of the Christ Church drawings collection, by James Byam Shaw in 1976, includes an opening statement concerning the earlier attribution. After the heading ("Attributed to Giovanni Bellini [ca. 1430–1516])," the subject description ("Bust of a man, wearing a cap and an embroidered coat; probably the portrait of Gentile Bellini, the artist's brother"), and the indication of the media and measurements ("Black chalk, washed over, on paper originally white, 391 × 280 mm"), we read the following: "There is no trace of any old ascription. Colvin [II. pl. 32, as Alvise Vivarini] says that the drawing was formerly called a portrait of Lodovico il Moro by Leonardo da Vinci; this information may have been cut away when the drawing was remounted about seventy years ago." This confirms that, with the operation of remounting the drawing about a century ago, the evidence of an earlier attribution to Leonardo was considered unworthy of being preserved. This decision was correct insofar as it recognized that the drawing was not by Leonardo, but it was unfortunate from a historical viewpoint, canceling as it did evidence of the unpredictable course of the critical fortune of Leonardo's drawings. This is a long-forgotten but instructive story that deserves to be told, for it involved some prominent scholars in a sort of a comedy of errors as late as the last years of the nineteenth century, when the whole corpus of Leonardo's manuscripts and drawings had already begun to be approached systematically, and drawings connoisseurship was about to undergo the revolutionary contribution of Bernard Berenson in 1903.[4]

The scenario opens with that masterpiece of scholarship, the second edition of the first series of Gustavo Uzielli's *Ricerche intorno a Leonardo da Vinci*, published in 1896.[5] In a long digression on Sforza portraiture, mostly attributed to Leonardo's pupils—notably the altarpiece once attributed to Leonardo and now known as the Sforza Altarpiece (Pala Sforzesca) of 1494–98—Uzielli attempts to evaluate Giorgio Vasari's attribution to Leonardo of the nearly faded effigies of members of the Sforza family, shown kneeling at the sides of Donato Montorfano's *Crucifixion*, which was painted in 1495 on the wall facing Leonardo's *Last Supper* (Refectory of Santa Maria delle Grazie, Milan). This digression serves as a preface for the question whether Leonardo could possibly have portrayed members of his patron's family, if not the patron himself. Hence, Uzielli mentions the Oxford drawing, which he knew from the references of other scholars: "Nel Christ Church College, a Oxford, è un ritratto, detto di Lodovico il Moro, in matita nera, in vera grandezza, attribuito a Leonardo" (At Christ Church College, Oxford, there is a portrait, said to be of Ludovico il Moro, in black chalk, in life size, attributed to Leonardo). Uzielli, in a footnote, gives the source of this information—"C. W. Heaton, *Leonardo da Vinci and his Work*, London, 1874, p. 290"—and then remarks: "Il Passavant lo dice assai bello; non lo crede però del Vinci, ma di uno dei suoi migliori allievi" (Passavant states that it is quite beautiful; however, he does not believe it to be by Leonardo, but by one of his best pupils). Passavant's opinion, as reported by Rigollot in his 1849 catalogue of Leonardo's works, goes back to 1833.[6]

These highlights of the attribution to Leonardo of an exquisitely Venetian drawing shed light on a curious misunderstanding of Leonardo's style. For next, Uzielli wonders whether Leonardo could also have portrayed Beatrice d'Este Sforza, the duke's wife, whose famous bust by Gian Cristoforo Romano in the Louvre had just come to be attributed to him by Louis Courajod.[7] Uzielli goes on to comment on a drawing in the Royal Library at Windsor Castle that Paul Müller-Walde, writing in 1889, thought could well be a portrait of Beatrice d'Este made by Leonardo and that the young German scholar included in his lavishly produced *Lebensskizze* of Leonardo:[8] Uzielli is referring to an authentic, truly unquestionable Leonardo, and now a famous one at that, *Woman Standing in a Landscape,* better known as the *Pointing Lady* (fig. 47).[9] Uzielli's ensuing remark deserves a place in the history of taste, and itself warrants a systematic study of the critical fortune of Leonardo's drawings: "Ma invero una certa durezza nei tratti e nell'espressione di quella figura," writes Uzielli, "e l'ondeggiare esagerato dei panneggiamenti, allontana dal mio pensiero qualsiasi ricordo della maniera semplice e vera del gran Pittore" (But a certain hardness of touch and expression in that figure, as well as the exaggerated fluttering of the drapery, truly removes from my mind any memory of the simple and spontaneous manner of the great Painter).[10] Thus, back in 1896, Uzielli dismissed Leonardo's authorship of one of the most beautiful and appealing figure studies in the Royal Library at Windsor Castle, a drawing that alone would make an exhibition! It could be, in fact, the centerpiece of a display of images and documents that Aby Warburg first investigated with his 1893 dissertation on Botticelli's *Primavera* and the *Birth of Venus.*[11] For Uzielli as for others at his time, the manner or style of Leonardo's drawings had to be *semplice e vera.*

If Müller-Walde's *Lebensskizze* of 1889 appears to be the first Leonardo monograph to include a reproduction of the *Pointing Lady* — and Warburg's first iconographic study of it is in fact based on that book, as well as on Richter's anthology of 1883 — it is also true that the drawing had been known since 1878, when it was first exhibited at the Grosvenor Gallery in London together with a vast selection of Leonardo drawings from the Queen's collection.[12] Although it was reproduced in the catalogue of that exhibition and made available in photographs, it seldom appeared in the more popular Leonardo publications.[13] It is therefore not surprising that an early copy of the Windsor *Pointing Lady* should have entered the collection of the Gabinetto Disegni e Stampe degli Uffizi with the Santarelli collection of old master drawings in 1870, which was not published until more than a century later. It is a most important and skillfully made copy (fig. 48), originally thought to be by Francesco Melzi, but possibly by Peter Paul Rubens, who must have seen the original in Milan in 1606 as a suitable

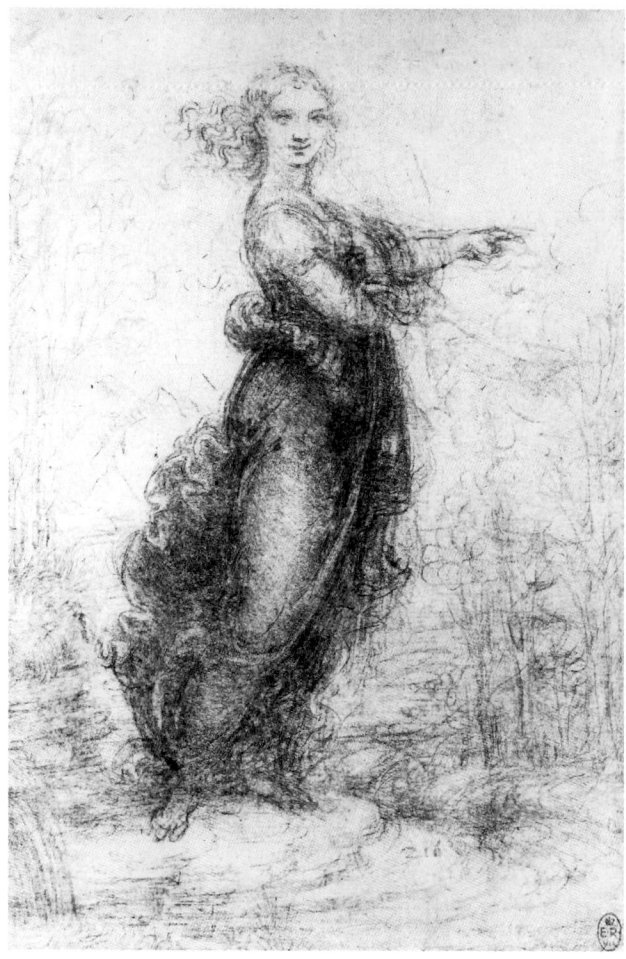

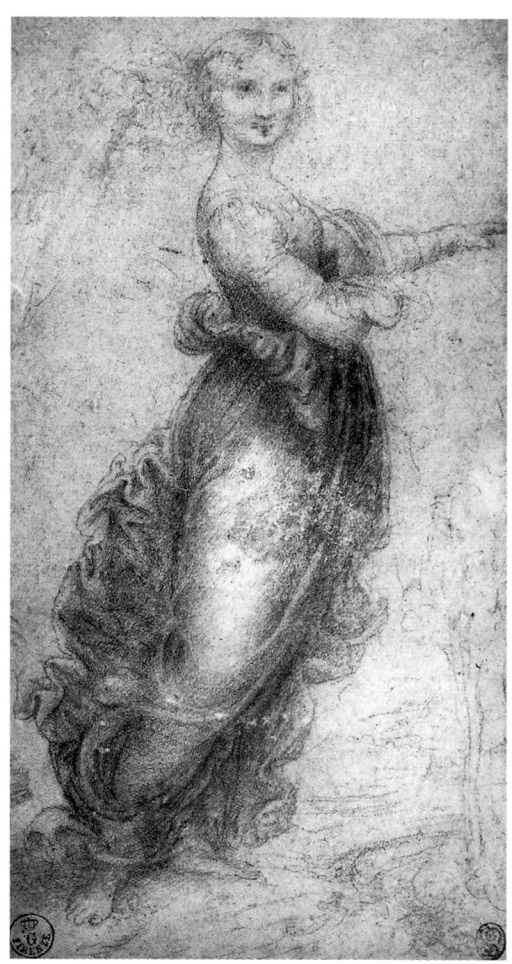

Fig. 47. Leonardo da Vinci, *Woman Standing in a Landscape (The Pointing Lady)*. Brown-hue black chalk, 210 × 135 mm. The Royal Collection, H.M. Queen Elizabeth II, Windsor Castle RL 12581

Fig. 48. Copy after Leonardo da Vinci, *The Pointing Lady*. Red chalk, 180 × 97 mm. Gabinetto Disegni e Stampe degli Uffizi, Florence 8953 S

model for his *Het Pelsken* of the 1630s (Kunsthistorisches Museum, Vienna).[14] A second series of Uzielli's *Ricerche* included a detailed catalogue of the drawings by Leonardo and his school in the Uffizi,[15] but the Santarelli version of the Windsor *Pointing Lady* was not included.

And so with Uzielli in 1896 one comes to a turning point in the critical fortune of Leonardo's drawings. The ultimate puzzle has taken place. A drawing that has nothing to do with Leonardo is given to the master without any hesitation, while doubts are cast on the authenticity of an unquestionable Leonardo. And there is more to make both the approach and the scholarship perplexing if not unreliable. The Windsor *Pointing Lady* is said to portray Beatrice d'Este, the wife of Ludovico "Il Moro," the man whose portrait by Leonardo is said to be the one in the all-too-obvious Venetian drawing in Christ Church. Uzielli refers to Müller-Walde for the proposed identification of the Windsor *Pointing Lady* with Beatrice, but the German scholar speaks of Dante's Beatrice, not of the duchess of Milan. In doing so he perceptively juxtaposes it to the small Venice sheet of studies of *Dancing Nymphs*,[16] concluding erroneously, however, that all such drawings of masqueraders were made at the time of a Medici *giostra* (joust) in Florence in 1475. In this way he explained their Botticellian character, an idea that Warburg was quick to elaborate upon as he turned Dante's Beatrice into the Simonetta Vespucci of Angelo Poliziano's *Giostra*.[17] It was a dangerous iconographic game that Müller-Walde himself was the first to give up. He had already perceived the impact of Leonardo's *Pointing Lady* on the mature work of Raphael, who alluded to it first in a figure in the *Disputa* and then in the Magdalene in the *Santa Cecilia* in Bologna. Twenty-five years later Müller-Walde had reached the best understanding of the development of Leonardo's style in drawings, so that the masqueraders as well as the *Pointing Lady*, the *Dancing Nymphs*, and the *Deluge* series would come to be dated at the very end of Leonardo's career.[18]

But the final act of the comedy of errors initiated by Uzielli in 1896 comes in an appendix to Eugène Müntz's imposing monograph of 1899, which contains the first attempt at a systematic catalogue of all the paintings, sculptures, and drawings by Leonardo or attributed to him in every part of Europe.[19] It includes a vast, painstaking account of all the drawings by Leonardo or by his pupils known to him, either published or unpublished, with a few real Leonardos published only in recent times, such as the fragment of a study for the *Madonna Litta* at the Staedel Museum in Frankfurt.[20] Errors are inevitable, but the shortcomings of this work are amply compensated for by the usefulness of the repertory, particularly from the viewpoint of the critical fortune of Leonardo's drawings. It is no surprise that, as eighth in the Müntz list, one again encounters the so-called portrait of Ludovico "Il Moro," the large Venetian drawing at Christ Church. According to the description, it is unquestionably the Bellini drawing: "Portrait of a beardless man, middle-aged; a bust, three-quarters to the right. The eyes cast slightly upward. Fifteenth century costume; a flowered doublet and a cap. Black chalk." No mention is made of Ludovico "Il Moro," but it is found to be "A good portrait, but not sufficiently free for Leonardo."[21] The real surprise, however, is in the preceding entry. The description leaves no doubt that it is the large caricature portrait that is sometimes identified with the so-called "Scaramuccia, capitano degli Zingari" recorded by Vasari (cat. no. 92).[22] Müntz reports Waagen's opinion that it should be ascribed "to one of Leonardo's best pupils."[23] Again a Leonardo drawing is given to a pupil. But to this Müntz adds a striking comment: "This portrait is certainly not that of Ludovico 'Il Moro,' to whom it does not bear the least resemblance." By the end of the nineteenth century a curious problem of style and iconography has resulted in a most amusing confusion.

A full-page reproduction in color of the Bellini drawing at Christ Church (fig. 46) is found in André Chastel's *The Flowering of the Italian Renaissance* (1965).[24] There is no mention of Leonardo in connection with the Bellini, but on the facing page is a full-page reproduction, also in color, of a Leonardo drawing of a girl's head nearly in profile with a most elaborate hairdo and a cascade of waving hair flowing over her shoulders (fig. 49).[25] The head is poised

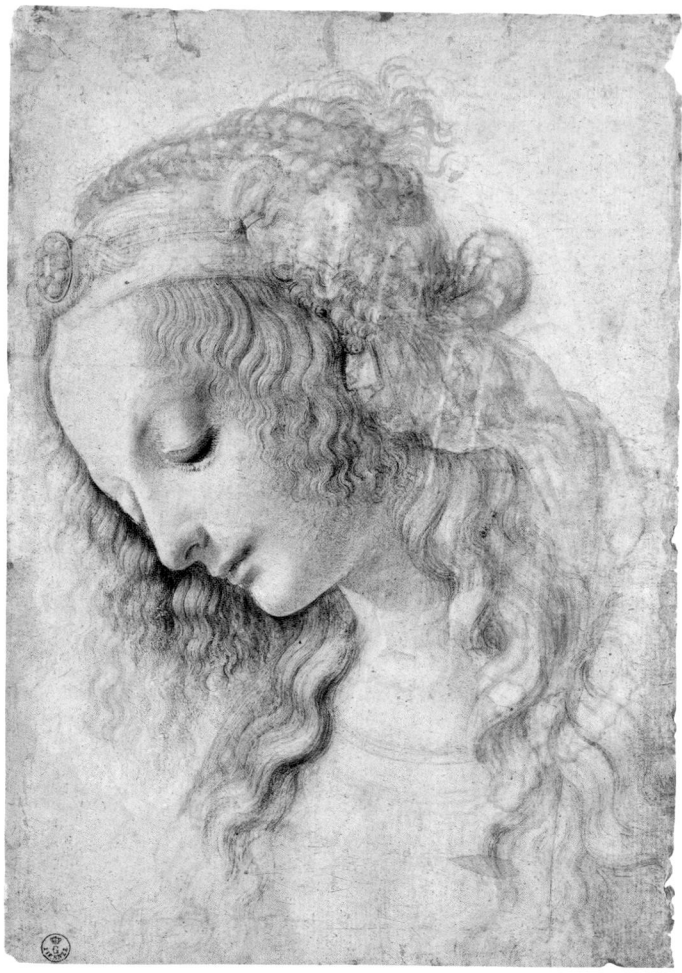

Fig. 49. Leonardo da Vinci, *Head of Young Woman*. Metalpoint, pen and brown ink, brush and brown wash, highlighted with white gouache, 281 × 199 mm. Gabinetto Disegni e Stampe degli Uffizi, Florence 428 E

like that of a Virgin at the Annunciation, and a large jewel adorns the top of her brow. It is a drawing carefully worked out to such a highly refined finish as to suggest the smoothness and translucency of a Donatello or a Duccio bas-relief. The eloquent juxtaposition in Chastel's book conveys at a glance a most effective characterization of the Italian Renaissance in Venice and in Florence—on one side a typical Venetian man, on the other a typical Florentine woman. But, in yet another aspect of the critical fortune of Leonardo's drawings, the Uffizi profile is not included in Popham's standard monograph on Leonardo's drawings of 1945, and, despite the favorable view of Berenson, Venturi, Castelfranco, and others, art criticism has long hesitated to return to the traditional attribution to Leonardo, while the Verrocchio and Lorenzo di Credi authorship still creeps in occasionally.[26]

It could be worse, of course. Morelli, for instance, dismissed the Uffizi drawing as the product of "a Flemish imitator of Verrocchio."[27] On the other hand, the Flemish influence on Verrocchio's talented pupil is a problem that art criticism has taken seriously only in recent years.[28] This kind of uncertainty prepares us to cope with a puzzling, fascinating dichotomy in Leonardo the draftsman—and not only in his years of apprenticeship: a minutely detailed and painstakingly finished drawing may appear alongside the roughest and scratchiest sketch, carelessly jotted down in a flash to record a fleeting impression, as in the case of a child clutching a cat. Perspective and human proportions may then be totally disregarded as in a sheet at Bayonne,[29] where the mother holding a cat-stroking child is so distorted along the upper margin of the sheet as to suggest the kind of exhilarating optical tricks that characterize *Alice's Adventures in Wonderland*.

In the process of drastically eliminating Leonardo's name from an all-too-long list of school drawings attributed to him almost everywhere in Europe, Morelli was particularly strict with the Uffizi collection. Out of some forty drawings, which form the whole collection of drawings by Leonardo and his circle as recently catalogued by Gigetta Dalli Regoli, Morelli accepted only five as genuine products of the master.[30] With reference to the reproductions in Popham's monograph of 1945, they are as follows: (1) The red-chalk epicene youth facing an old man (Popham, no. 141), which has on the verso an early attribution to Correggio;[31] (2) the perspective study for the *Adoration of the Magi* (Popham, no. 53; see cat. no. 32); (3) the 1478 sheet of technical studies, with two heads of shepherds facing each other (Popham, no. 127; fig. 39), and with other technical sketches on the verso; (4) the sketch of a condottiere-like profile (Popham, no. 130A), with a sketch of the profile of the angel in the Uffizi *Annunciation*, first recognized as such by David Alan Brown;[32] and (5) the famous 1473 Arno Valley landscape (Popham, no. 253; figs. 6, 7). Morelli left out six drawings now recognized as unquestionably by Leonardo, three of which (two drapery studies and the Verrocchiesque female profile) are not reproduced by Popham but are included in Giulia Brunetti's catalogue for the 1952 exhibition at the Biblioteca Medicea Laurenziana in Florence, commemorating the five hundredth anniversary of Leonardo's birth: (1) Monochrome drapery study on linen (Brunetti, no. 5); (2) study for the *Madonna of the Cat* (fig. 52); (3) the celebrated Verrocchiesque female profile (Brunetti, no. 11; fig. 49); (4) monochrome drapery study on linen (Brunetti, no. 8), occasionally related to the figure of Christ in Verrocchio's *Christ and Saint Thomas* for Orsanmichele (figs. 58, 59);[33] (5) a third drapery study (Popham, no. 7; Brunetti, no. 2); and (6) the red prepared sheet of *Adoration* and technical studies (Popham, no. 50; figs. 50, 51), with studies for a flying machine on the verso.[34]

A few short comments are in order. It is easy to understand why the drapery studies drawn with the brush on linen should have been eliminated, for the comparable ones in the Louvre were all attributed to Dürer in the nineteenth century (see cat. nos. 13–17).[35] The female profile (fig. 49), as we have seen, is a borderline case, where it is hard to indicate the precise contributions of teacher and pupil. The sheet of *Adoration* and technological studies even includes Leonardo's notes and must therefore have raised suspicions of forgery (figs. 50, 51). Heydenreich considered it one, even after the publication of the Popham monograph, where it was accepted as genuine.[36] A wealth of connections with other Leonardo drawings—notably one at Oxford (cat. no. 39) reproduced by Popham—as well as manuscript pages, particularly in the Codex Atlanticus, unearthed by recent scholarship, makes the recognition of authenticity of this sheet unassailable.[37] However paradoxically, the rejection of the study for the Uffizi *Madonna of the Cat* (fig. 52) can be considered Morelli's only justifiable mistake, the result of some sort of fixation that caused him to see Sodoma where Leonardo was, as in the studies for a *Kneeling Leda* in the now famous drawings at Chatsworth (cat. no. 99), Rotterdam (cat. no. 98), and Windsor (cat. no. 88). These are all late drawings, dating from after 1504 and showing the sculptural style that Leonardo had come to adopt about 1500, with a drawing technique characterized by long, parallel lines curved

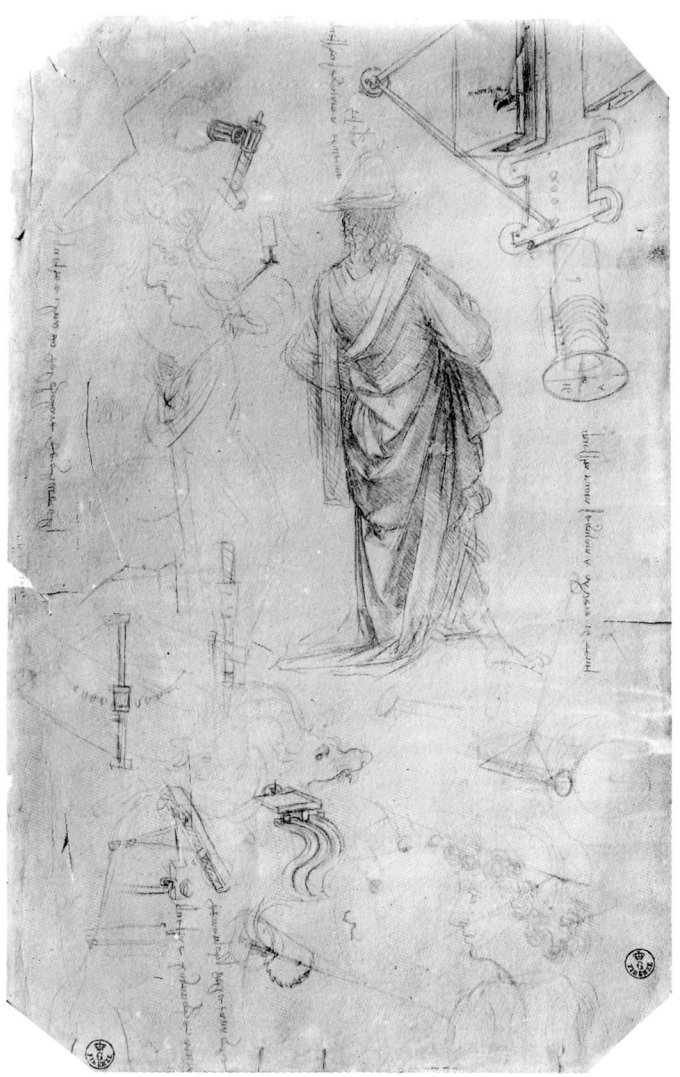

Fig. 50. Leonardo da Vinci, *Studies for the Adoration with Mechanical Studies and Notes* (recto). Metalpoint on red-ocher prepared paper, 303 × 194 mm. Gabinetto Disegni e Stampe degli Uffizi, Florence 447 E

Fig. 51. Leonardo da Vinci, *Technological Studies and Notes* (verso). Metalpoint, pen and brown ink, on red-ocher prepared paper, 194 × 303 mm. Gabinetto Disegni e Stampe degli Uffizi, Florence 447 E

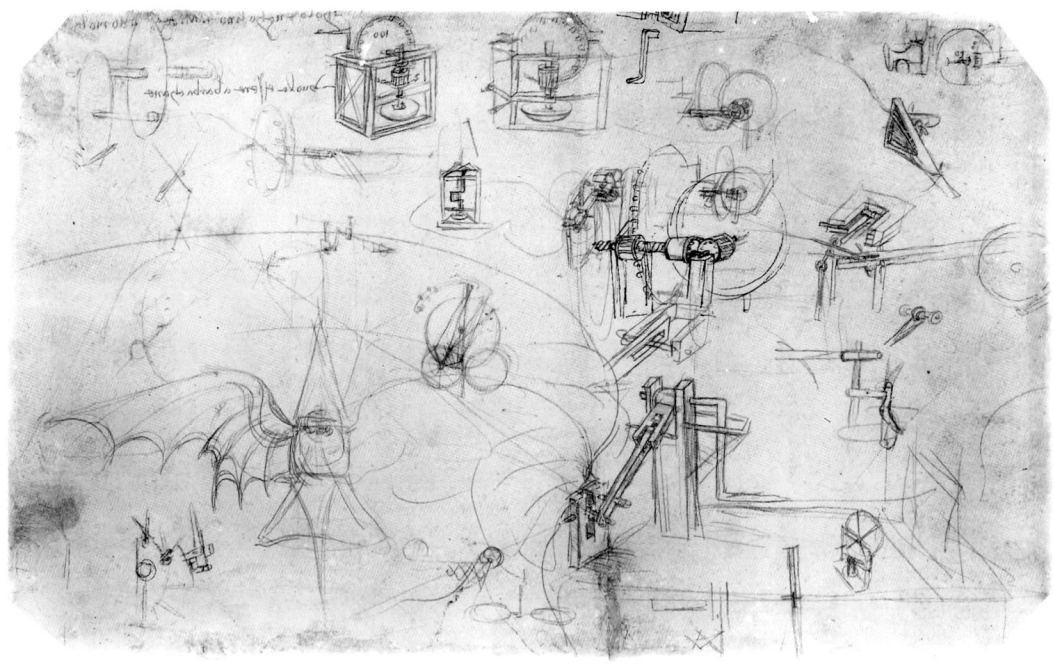

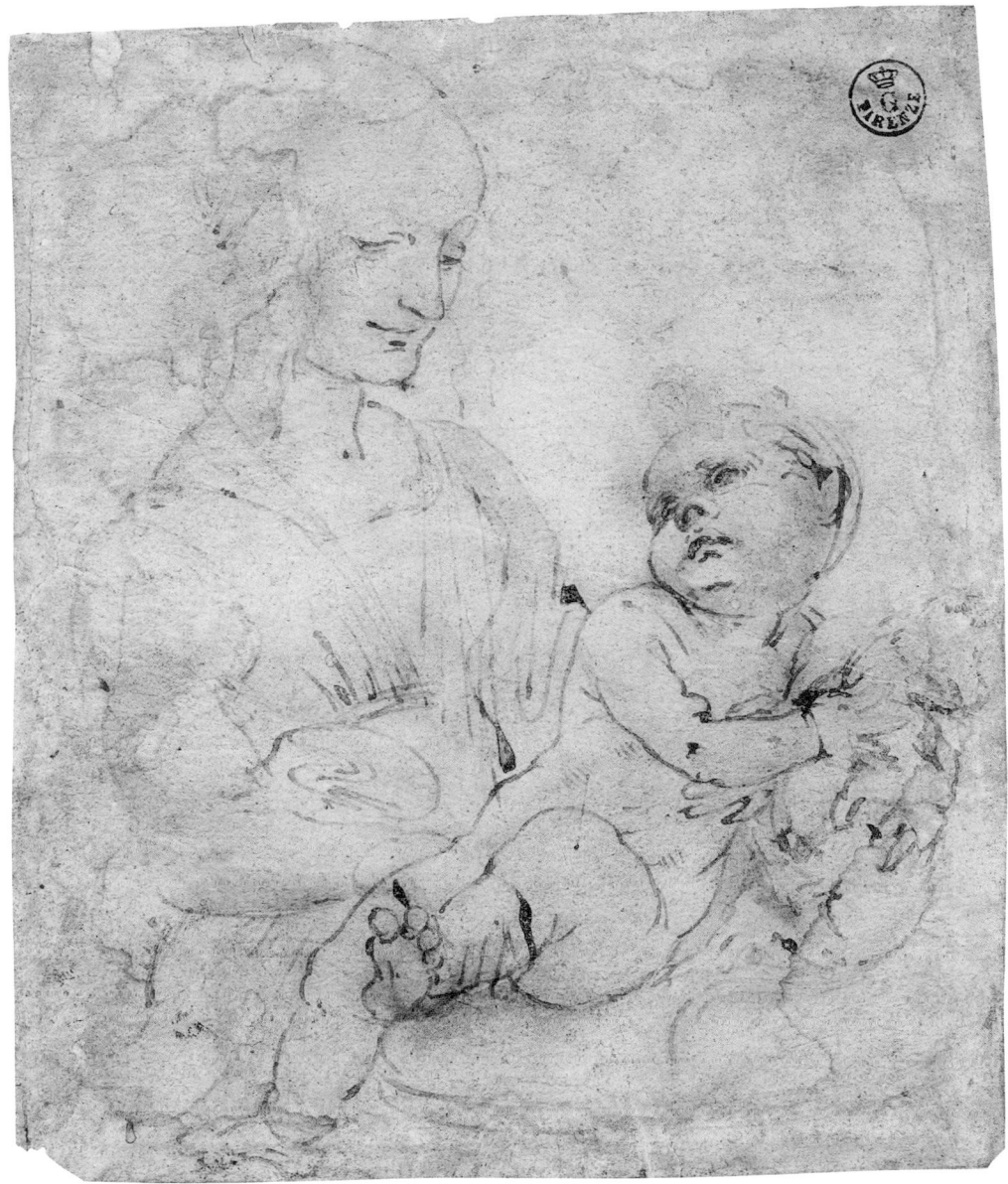

Fig. 52. Leonardo da Vinci, *Study for the Madonna of the Cat*. Pen and brown ink, brush and pale gray-brown wash, 125 × 110 mm. Gabinetto Disegni e Stampe degli Uffizi, Florence 421 E

to follow the form.[38] It is understandable that such a sensuous, deliberate type of drawing could make one think of Sodoma.

But the fresh, sketchy impression of the early Uffizi drawing shows the same whimsical mood and self-assurance of notation as the many figure studies for the *Adoration of the Magi* or that extraordinary, large drawing of the *Madonna and Child with a Bowl of Fruit* in the Louvre (cat. no. 22),[39] where the position of the child's legs is vigorously tested with pentimenti so as to convey the effect of an animated cartoon, a drawing that Passavant, in the mid-nineteenth century, had attributed to Raphael.[40] In the Uffizi drawing, it is not simply the unprecedented mastery of the pen but also the added accent of a flashy light wash that

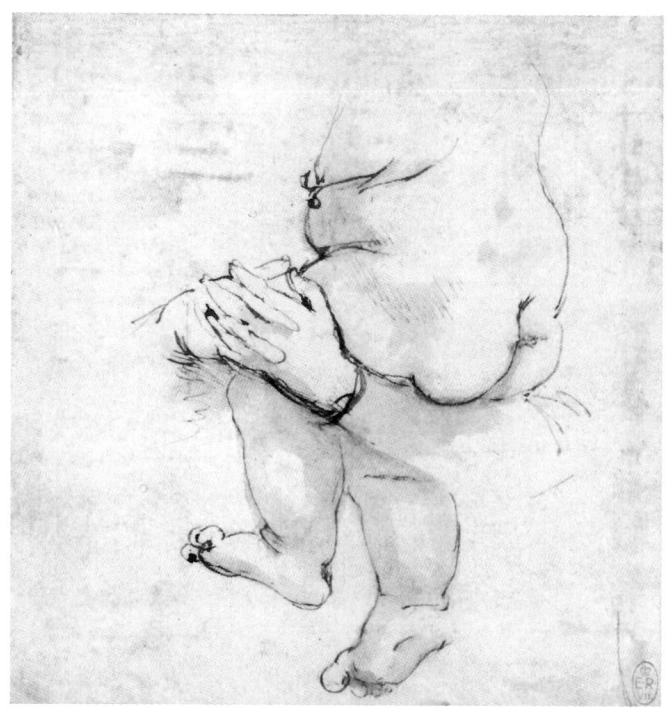

Fig. 53. Leonardo da Vinci, *Study of Woman's Arms Holding a Child.* Pen and brown ink, brush and brown wash, 133 × 130 mm. The Royal Collection, H.M. Queen Elizabeth II, Royal Windsor Castle RL 12561

suggests an urge to soften the harshness of the pen line. The result is a blurring effect, so that the form seems to emerge from its enveloping atmosphere, much as in a Tiepolo drawing of two centuries later. A similar effect can be seen in related drawings, for instance, in a Windsor fragment (fig. 53) showing a close-up of the bottom of a naked child. This drawing has come to be related, even physically, to a newly discovered drawing at Oporto in Portugal (cat. no. 21), long attributed to Raffaellino da Reggio, which shows the domestic, humorous scene of a young woman seated on the ground and holding a child with his feet in a basin of water for his bath.[41] At the time of the Oporto drawing, Sodoma was just such a child!

The Uffizi drawing needed a better advocate, and in 1903 Berenson wrote: "The finest by far of all the drawings for a *Madonna del Gatto* is the noble sketch in the Uffizi [fig. 52] . . . of the same early date, certainly, as is proved by the drawing of the bust and arms and hands, but with the added mystery, subtlety, and majesty of Leonardo's most magnificent haunting types of women."[42] Berenson has in mind here the kind of carefree, exuberant touch of Leonardo's pen, flowing like a brush or probing like the tool with which a sculptor gives a rough but proper shape to a clay figure.[43] And this is perhaps what Uzielli had in mind when he spoke of Leonardo's manner as "semplice e vera." Of course it would be simplicity in the sense of clarity and directness, and spontaneity as opposed to pretentiousness. Leonardo can be eloquent, even magniloquent, but never ostentatious.

And indeed the Uffizi *Adoration of the Magi* (figs. 10, 11), a painting commissioned in 1481 and left unfinished when Leonardo moved to Milan the following year, is eloquent, if not magniloquent. It can be called a large-scale drawing, and as such Popham includes it in his 1945 monograph.[44] The composition is built up directly on the panel, bypassing the cartoon stage. The architectural setting, so carefully planned in one of the Uffizi drawings (see cat. no. 32),[45] is done with a sharp black chalk or metalpoint and a straightedge, while the individual figures are sketched in with the point of a brush, its pressure varying from a delicate touch to an emphatic stroke or blotching, progressing all the way up to the first phase of an elaborate modeling with which to give shape to a sculptural form ready to be colored.

This large composition is the occasion for Leonardo to try out a number of subsidiary episodes that can be singled out and developed into independent subjects. Such is the case with the confronting horsemen high up in the right background, a motif that prefigures the central group of the *Battle of Anghiari* of some twenty-five years later. The evidence of preliminary studies suggests that Leonardo may originally have been considering the emblematic motif of a Dragon Fight, following a quattrocento print tradition that seems to have been inspired by Paolo Uccello, and testing as well the emblematic and still unexplained motif of a dragon attacking a lion.[46] A small metalpoint drawing at Oxford includes the structural element of the hut of the Nativity, corresponding approximately to that area of the painting where the confrontation between the horsemen occurs.[47] In the Oxford drawing the dragon bears clear connotations of a heraldically poised griffin. Early in the 1950s the British Museum acquired a much larger drawing of the same subject (cat. no. 33). The formally outlined griffin is replaced by the impetuous vortex of a fierce dragon, blood gushing from its chest after the first blow of the attacking horseman, whose shield the beast has desperately seized with its teeth and front paws.[48] The medium, too, has changed. It is no longer the sharp, cold metalpoint, but pen and ink and wash, with an overall colorist effect that causes form to vibrate as under a flashing light. Pen and brush alternate in producing an explosive quality of warm and dense strokes, such as the one with which the brush makes a quick and perfect spiral out of the dragon's tail.

Once more, as with the Uffizi sketch for the *Madonna of the Cat* (fig. 52), drawings from the time of the *Adoration of the Magi* show the experimental nature of a technique that allows the pen to move as a brush and the brush to move as a pen (cat. nos. 30–34). Hence the combined used of the two, as in another drawing in the British Museum (cat. no. 34), a drawing even more enigmatic—and indescribable—from an iconographic viewpoint.[49] It has been called an allegory of Victory or Fortune, or both. Prominently displayed in the foreground below is a heraldic shield appended to a tree stump, as in a later allegory by Lorenzo Lotto on which is a rampant lion.[50]

As for the critical fortune of this drawing (cat. no. 34), there is nothing worth recording before it entered the British Museum with the Malcom collection in 1895. Its subject more than its style has attracted the attention of scholars and critics, but no satisfactory explanation of its meaning has so far been offered. As early as 1939 no less an iconographer than Edgar Wind ventured into the problem of style by claiming that much of the lower part of the drawing was an eighteenth-century fabrication possibly involving no less a figure than the artist Sir Joshua Reynolds.[51] For Wind the brushwork on the lower figure and on the trophy, and some of the wash on the upper figure, could not possibly be by Leonardo, the exaggerated fluttering of ribbons and drapes bespeaking a touch of typical eighteenth-century mimicry.

In their 1950 catalogue of the British Museum collection of old master drawings, A. E. Popham and Philip Pouncey mention Wind's thesis only to dismiss it as "quite absurd."[52] On the other hand, it is instructive, if not revealing, that the character and style of this early allegory should be regarded as so striking a departure from Leonardo's other drawings of the same time as to suggest that it was reworked two centuries later. Of course, as we have just seen, the same brushwork and the same touch of the pen appear time and again in the studies for the *Adoration of the Magi,* and in particular in the large *Rider on a Rearing Horse Fighting a Dragon* (cat. no. 33), which is now part of the same drawing collection at the British Museum.[53] It is time then, and above all appropriate, to return to previous positions, say, the refreshing judgment of Berenson, writing in 1903: "In such a drawing as the bold, dashing bistre-sketch in the Malcom Collection . . . we are scarcely any longer in the realm of symbolism. It is a plain representation of Victory. But what loveliness of the nude, and what action! And this reminds me that nowhere as in these subjects is there so close a parallelism between Leonardo and his not unworthy contemporary, Sandro Botticelli. We cannot help recalling Botticelli's *Calumny* and certain pages of his illustrations to the last cantos of the *Purgatorio.*"[54] Berenson's conclusion is then fully predictable: "And there is also the beautiful woman pointing—so like Sandro's Beatrice." The reference is of course to the Windsor *Pointing Lady,* which, as we have seen, is one of Leonardo's latest drawings, possibly made in France more than thirty years after the Victory allegory. "The quality of its inspiration," writes Popham in 1945, "and its ethereal charm seems to place it beyond the confines of any objective reality. The flavour of the *quattrocento* which it retains is the reminiscence of an ageing man; it represents the sum of that romantic feeling which underlies Leonardo's work as a painter and a draughtsman, but which the scientist so ruthlessly suppresses."[55]

In the past, when a drawing by a pupil was attributed to Leonardo, a bona fide collector would write on the back or on the mount, but seldom on the drawing itself.[56] In the case of one such early attribution, the Venice sheet of red-chalk studies for the *Last Supper,* there is a good chance that the drawing, if not by Leonardo, is not by a faker either. Broadly speaking, forgeries were not a widespread phenomenon until the eighteenth century. In that century Leonardo originals became increasingly scarce on the market and rapidly increased in value so that they could be acquired only with *la gran forza dell'oro*—the great power of gold.[57] It was then that forgeries started to appear, but so far nothing has been settled in this regard. The claim that Leonardo's famous self-portrait at Turin is a fake made by Giuseppe Bossi (1777–1814) at the beginning of the nineteenth century has failed to offer a reasonable ground for discussion and has quickly been dropped (fig. 1).[58] The same should apply to claims regarding the Venice sheet of studies for the *Last Supper* (fig. 26), which still has more than one advocate. It, too, has been attributed to Bossi, though his private notes specify how he acquired it in 1811, the year after the publication of his book on the *Cenacolo.*[59] It is a slow, almost clumsy drawing, and even Leonardo's writing has been said to be a forgery, which can be shown to be an impossibility. It is indeed a special case that is best approached with the sort of humorous wisdom that Berenson was to contribute to a comparable debate over the authenticity of another drawing in Venice, the sheet of studies for the Christ Child in the Louvre *Saint Anne* (cat. no. 105).[60] The 1938 revised edition of his *Florentine Drawings* appeared with this additional remark: "I used to see the hand of a kindred imitator in a rather puzzling sheet in the Venice Academy.... I am old enough now ... to question whether an artist is always his highest self. The sheet is perhaps by the great artist in a moment when, like nodding Homer, he faltered."[61] More recently the attribution has again been questioned and the forgery thesis resumed.[62]

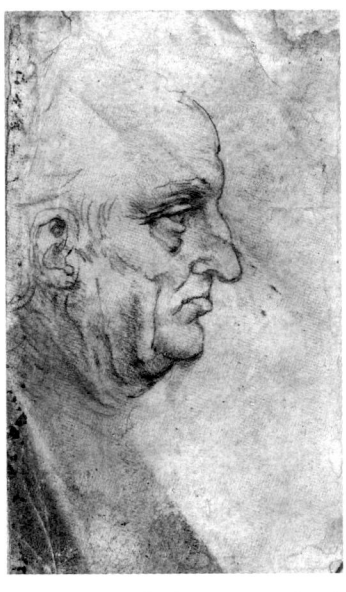

Fig. 54. Leonardo da Vinci, *Study of Grotesque Head (The 300 Dollar Leonardo)*. Red chalk, 129 × 78 mm. Pinacoteca di Brera, Milan 7415

Here the case involves a drawing of questionable quality. In other words, this is a problem that deserves to be addressed rather than dismissed, in that there are "bad drawings" even among those unquestionably by Leonardo. A case in point is that of a man's head on a sheet of anatomical studies at Windsor (RL 12624r), which Kenneth Clark was not shy to designate "the worst piece of drawing that must reasonably be attributed to Leonardo."[63] Of course, one's eye is better trained today to see the positive side of a bad drawing and thus able to recognize Leonardo's hand even when it is not up to expectations. Good judgment should be prepared to favor the rough sketch or careless scrawl endowed with energy and verve to a suspiciously diligent but tame, if not lifeless, figure or head study. When the Hammer drawing now at the National Gallery of Art in Washington (cat. no. 24) was still in a private collection in San Francisco, just before its London auction in 1972, it was seen by Kenneth Clark, who stated in a private letter of that year that he was inclined to accept it as authentic and see it as very late, adding that it was so bad that "for Leonardo's reputation it would have been better had it not turned up."[64]

Goodness and beauty are often a matter of opinion, and the Hammer sheet was eventually recognized as an important document for a better assessment of Leonardo's late style, even in connection with his celebrated water studies.[65] The same can be said of the small Hercules sheet recently acquired by the Metropolitan Museum (cat. no. 101), which settles for good the long-debated attribution to Leonardo of the large and magnificent Hercules drawing at Turin (cat. no. 102).[66] It has taken time to overcome the negative opinion expressed by the eminent scholar and critic Aldo Bertini, who in 1958 relegated the Turin drawing to the much later circle of Bartolomeo Ammannati (1511–1592), because of its "qualità che non è degna di Leonardo" —its quality being unworthy of Leonardo.[67]

An unquestionable Leonardo drawing (fig. 54) was auctioned in Milan in 1982, but the official assessment of the item was: "Head of a man by Boltraffio with a Leonardo note on the back." Because of the high expectations concerning the quality of a Leonardo drawing, it fetched the staggeringly low figure of 260,000 Italian lire, then the equivalent of about $300! It is now in the Pinacoteca di Brera, Milan, with the rest of the works of art bequeathed by Lamberto Vitali, the scholar and collector who had purchased it in disregard of the opinion of all those who had advised the auctioneer.[68] It is a red-chalk profile of a man showing the style of Leonardo's late drawings and has a brief autograph technological notation on the back that links the small sheet to the contents of Leonardo's Paris Ms. G of about 1510–15. Leonardo's touch is unmistakable, however, and this is certainly not a bad drawing. Because of the pensive expression so brilliantly conveyed, it may look tame and hesitant, but it is not. After my publication of it in 1979, Kenneth Clark remarked: "It is so typical of Leonardo's drawings."[69]

This brings us to a problem of attribution that has ceased to be a problem. This concerns the Cologne sheet of *Adoration* studies (cat. no. 28), apparently for the Uffizi *Adoration of the Magi*, though all the figures rather suggest the subject of an *Adoration of the Shepherds*, which seems to have occupied Leonardo about 1478.[70] So unusually slow and tentative is the line with which the different attitudes of the young men are defined that Müller-Walde harshly denied Leonardo's authorship, rejecting as well that of the drawings of crabs on the verso.[71] It was a dangerous thought for Müller-Walde to entertain. In 1907, outraged by the insistence with which the beautiful drawing of aquilegia studies by Francesco Melzi at Windsor was always reproduced as a genuine Leonardo, he simply destroyed it in a fit of madness.[72] But the crabs are certainly not bad drawings—"almost nearer to Dürer than to Leonardo," says Berenson[73]—and, though Müller-Walde wrongly argued that Leonardo could not have seen crabs in Tuscany, they are far better than the figures on the recto, particularly those at bottom left, which lack the Leonardo touch that one is used to. Yet all must be taken as his.[74] A badly reworked sheet of a comparable weak drawing is in the Isabella Stewart Gardner Museum in Boston.[75] It was acquired in 1902 at the London sale of the renowned Robinson collection, apparently on Berenson's advice, though it is not mentioned in his 1903 publication. But Berenson does include the Cologne drawing, remarking that, as a study for the Uffizi *Adoration of the Magi*, it is "a trifle weaker than the other studies for the same." Some of the underdrawing of the Uffizi *Adoration*, made visible through spectography, is just as bad as the Hamburg and even the Robinson drawings.[76]

In looking at the first page of Leonardo's Codex Trivulzianus, a manuscript of about 1487–90 (Biblioteca Trivulziana, Castello Sforzesco, Milan), one cannot fail to be perplexed at the cluster of grotesque heads in the middle of the sheet.[77] They are crude and weak, without any sense of form.[78] And yet, the few sentences in Leonardo's hand that precede and follow them show that the pen and ink with which they are written are the same as in

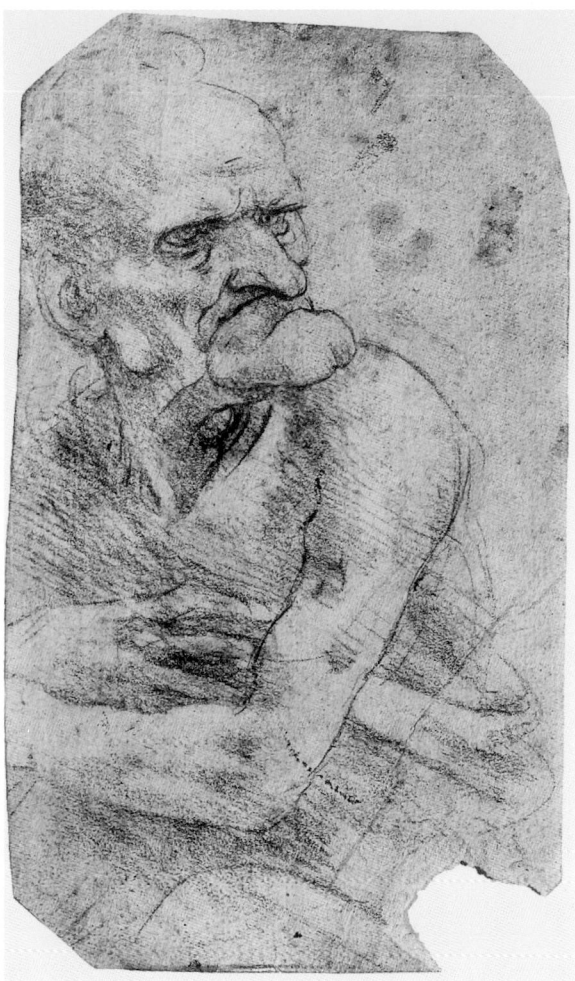 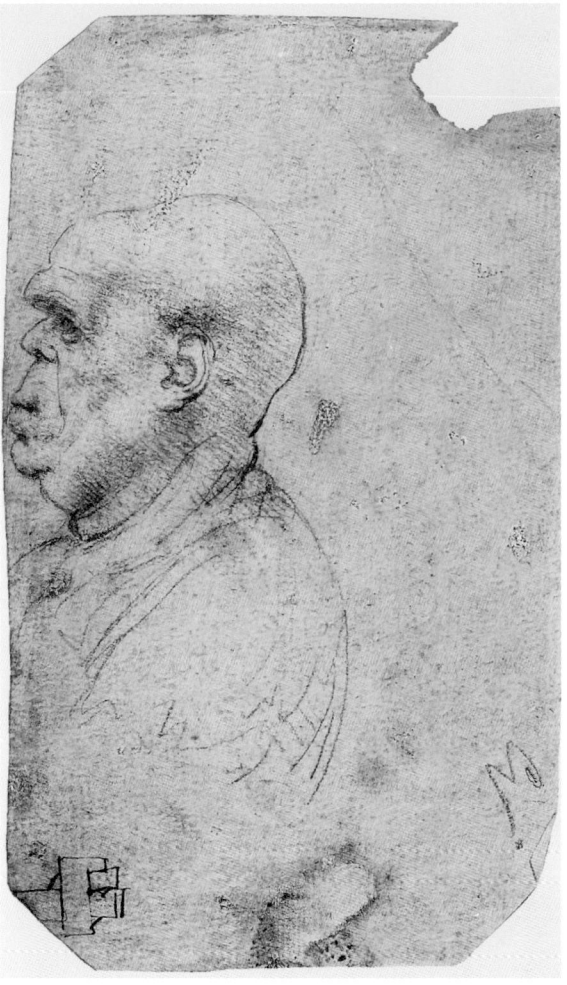

Fig. 55. Leonardo da Vinci, *Study of Grotesque Man in Three-Quarter View Facing to the Right* (recto). Red chalk, 182 × 105 mm. Istituto per la Grafica, Rome F.N. 4

Fig. 56. Leonardo da Vinci, *Study of Grotesque Man in Profile Facing Left* (verso). Red chalk, 182 × 105 mm. Istituto per la Grafica, Rome F.N. 4

the sketches. These are what E. H. Gombrich calls "Leonardo's doodles."[79] Comparable ones are found throughout the sheets of the Codex Atlanticus, mostly from the same time, and in particular on a sheet of geometrical and anatomical studies at Windsor (RL 12669r) that, though much later, are surprisingly unchanged in character. Gombrich notes the "strangely hesitant stroke" of some of these scribbles, including those in the Codex Trivulzianus, and adds: "If we would meet them in isolation we might well doubt whether they could be authentic."[80]

Here again it is a matter of bad drawings, which might seem appropriate for the portrayal of ugliness. And yet some of Leonardo's so-called caricatures (cat. nos. 59, 60, 69–73, 75, 76) are masterpieces of draftsmanship.[81] They were among the first of Leonardo's drawings to appeal to collectors, beginning as early as the sixteenth century when Leonardo's pupils and followers not only collected originals but also set themselves the tedious task of gathering them in a corpus of copies, at times so accurate as to appear by the master himself, and occasionally even producing a finished drawing out of a simple scrawl (cat. nos. 121, 136, 137).[82] It was perhaps this passion by collectors of Leonardo's "caricatures" and other studies that triggered the necessity, still in the sixteenth century, of systematically extracting all possible profiles, heads, and figure studies that could be found in manuscript pages, such as those that came to be collected in the Codex Atlanticus, namely, "Leonardo's doodles."[83] Six fragments of comparable origin and all very early—though not yet properly studied—were mounted in the sixteenth century on a large, elaborate page of the famous *libro de' disegni* (album of drawings) assembled by Giorgio Vasari that later passed through the prestigious Pierre-Jean Mariette and Pierre Crozat collections before entering the Graphische Sammlung Albertina in Vienna (fig. 5).[84] Nearly seventy such fragments are now at Windsor, a few found their way into other collections, and many are lost.[85] A good number of them, however small, are surprisingly highly finished. Such are the grotesques at Chatsworth (cat. nos. 69–73), which Kenneth Clark reluctantly accepts as authentic. Having noticed that they are drawn as carefully as the studies of skulls in the anatomical manuscript of 1489, he concludes: "It is partly the scientific precision of the style that makes them so distasteful."[86]

No doubt can possibly be cast on the authenticity of one such grotesque, the *Head of Old Man or Woman in Profile Facing to the Left* at Hamburg (cat. no. 75), which bears comparison with Giorgione's *La vecchia*.[87] As such it cannot be called a bad drawing or a distasteful one, and the same can be said of the larger double-sided sheet of grotesques (figs. 55, 56).[88] But there are grotesques of comparable quality and size that are never included in the publications on the collections that preserve them, an omission suggesting implicitly that they are considered unworthy of Leonardo. I am referring to a pair in the Ambrosiana.[89] Another one, reproduced in facsimile by the Commisione Vinciana,[90] is now considered to be by an "Imitatore di Leonardo da Vinci."[91]

Leonardo's projected treatise on painting, the *Libro di pittura*, which was posthumously compiled by Francesco Melzi, includes a text based on a lost original note by Leonardo, which can be taken to record the sort of drawing experience that Leonardo seems to have acquired early in Florence, in a cultural climate dominated by intellectuals, notably poets and writers.[92] The text concerns the use of drawing in planning a composition, and the implication is that drawing, like poetry, was not only a tool but also above all a medium for communicating feelings, impressions, and ideas. Drawing's function as a visual commentary on a technical or scientific text, hence as a diagram or a text figure, was, in this cultural climate, rapidly becoming a necessity. The tool, drawing, was becoming a language, and as such could adopt a variety of expository or rhetorical devices, with the aim of reproducing objective reality with the utmost accuracy—hence the use of a perspectograph, the draftsman's tool that Leonardo knew well but avoided[93]—the resulting image would lack only color. Leonardo detected a dangerous side of this appealing process and advised the painter to follow the example of the poets:

> And to you, composer of narrative paintings, I have to say: refrain from finishing with sharp outlines the limbs of the figures in your compositions, or it will happen to you what happens to many painters who want every minutest touch of the charcoal to stand. These may well acquire riches but not praise for their art, because many are the times when the body of the living creature so represented does not move in a way representative of its thoughts and emotions. But having made a finished, beautiful, and agreeable arrangement of the limbs, it would seem to the painter an outrageous thing to alter those limbs, placing them higher or lower, or farther back or forward. He who so behaves deserves no praise for the knowledge he shows. Now, haven't you ever considered how poets compose their verses? It does not matter to them, after having written them in beautiful letters,[94] to cross some of them out, so as to write them anew in a better form. Therefore, painter, compose the parts of your figures only roughly, and before being concerned with their beauty and goodness, see to it that their movement be properly represented, so as to have it in keeping with the mental attitudes of those which form your narrative painting.[95]

Leonardo's foremost preoccupation as a draftsman is to give priority to the study of gestures, attitudes, and figural actions that may best convey the thought and emotions that provoke them. This can be done in quick, abbreviated form, as shorthand is to writing.[96] But the rough sketch cannot replace the final product; hence the most elaborate drawing that is just one step from a *modello* or a cartoon. There is even historical evidence that Leonardo had indeed produced such elaborate drawings, which Armenini, writing in 1586, recorded: "I saw already some minute drawings from his hand, which were shown to me by certain old painters when I was staying in Milan, and this in addition to his marvelous paintings, drawings which were finished in such a way, and truly extraordinary for their handling of light and shade, that the more I was pondering over them the more I was convincing myself of the impossibility of imitating them or having them made by others."[97] Armenini's comments indicate, however indirectly, how such finished drawings became models for pupils and followers to imitate. And one can see how a good drawing by a pupil may occasionally be taken to be by the master. Such is the case, for instance, with the famous sheet of flowers at Venice, which is even included in Popham's monograph among studies for the Louvre *Virgin of the Rocks* of 1483 (fig. 12). It is, however, demonstrably the work of Francesco Melzi, whose comparable examples of "replacement drawings" —as Clark was to designate this type of most successful copies—were produced certainly not before 1510.[98]

The question is often asked whether the *Adoration of the Magi* (figs. 10, 11), had Leonardo finished it, would have looked like his first Milanese commission, the *Virgin of the Rocks* of a few years later. The answer could well be yes, but the means of achieving the same result might have been quite different. Unfortunately, nothing is known of Leonardo's preparatory work. The picture was transferred from panel to canvas in the mid-nineteenth century, and laboratory examination has not been able to ascertain whether it was sketched directly on the panel or done from a cartoon.[99] Again, documentary evidence, however indirect, may offer assistance. Ludovico Sforza's court poet, Bernardo Bellincioni, who died in 1492, must have watched Leonardo at work on this commission and seen the preparatory drawings that made that masterpiece possible. In his *Rime* (published posthumously in 1493) he praised Leonardo for his drawings first and then for his colors: "Del Vinci a suoi disegni e suoi colori / e moderni e gli antichi hanno paura" (Both the modern and the ancient fear Leonardo's drawings and colors).[100] The only drawing left of the many that Leonardo must have produced in preparation for the first version of the *Virgin of the Rocks* is the Turin study for the head of the kneeling angel (fig. 80).[101] This is where modern criticism is at its best in its evaluation of Leonardo's draftsmanship as even subservient to psychology. Suffice it to quote the Scandinavian critic Osvald Sirén writing in 1911 (and again, in French, in 1928): "There is something elusive in this image, the big, half-mischievous eyes open upon us with that expression which is so peculiar to Leonardo's figures, and which does not fail to become somewhat disquieting as the intellectual is made to blend with the sentimental."[102] But this drawing is also an exceptional document for showing how best to approach the problem of defining the borderline between Leonardo's drawings and those of his pupils. We know now that Leonardo portrayed the same model from a different angle in a sketch at Windsor (RL 12512) and let a pupil, possibly Boltraffio, work it out to a comparable finish. Like the paintings—for instance, the *Madonna Litta* (State Hermitage Museum, Saint Petersburg), which is now attributed to Boltraffio alone in spite of Leonardo's preparatory studies for it —drawings, too, could have been finished or reworked by a pupil under Leonardo's eyes.[103] This is undeniable, yet the implications of this process are still to be fully assessed as part of the ongoing research on the critical fortune of Leonardo's drawings.

Another drawing, in the Louvre, first reproduced by Richter in 1883 as a study for the head of the kneeling infant Saint John (cat. no. 61), is a fragment of heavy paper cut nearly to the contour of the head and mounted on paper tinted dark green.[104] At one time in the Vallardi collection in Milan, it was described by its former owner in 1855 as a fragment of the cartoon for the *Madonna and Child* (Sant'Onofrio, Rome), a fresco by Cesare da Sesto then believed to be by Leonardo.[105] It is in metalpoint, reworked with pen and ink on prepared paper, and it is pricked for transfer. A horizontal fold in the paper going through the child's cheek shows the original position of the fragment. This drawing was omitted by Popham and never included in more recent books on Leonardo, but I have no doubt that it is genuine, and from about the time of the *Adoration of the Magi*. The hair shows precisely the touch of the pen resembling brushstrokes as in, for instance, the *Dragon Fight*, the *Victory*, and other early drawings. Its outline corresponds exactly to that of the head of the young Saint John in the Louvre painting, though unfortunately it is not possible to ascertain the presence of traces of charcoal dust or *spolvero* corresponding to the pricked outlines. An alternative suggested by a number of minor details is that this drawing could be all that is left of the cartoon for the lost *Madonna of the Cat.*[106]

Sketchy or impressionistic as the child's hair is, the rest of the head is highly finished. This cameo quality is often regarded with suspicion. The unwritten rule is that when a Leonardo drawing is too slick it should be given to a pupil, as is exemplified by the Venice sheet of studies for the child in the Louvre *Saint Anne* (cat. no. 105) and related drawings in the same collection and elsewhere.[107] Now that they are

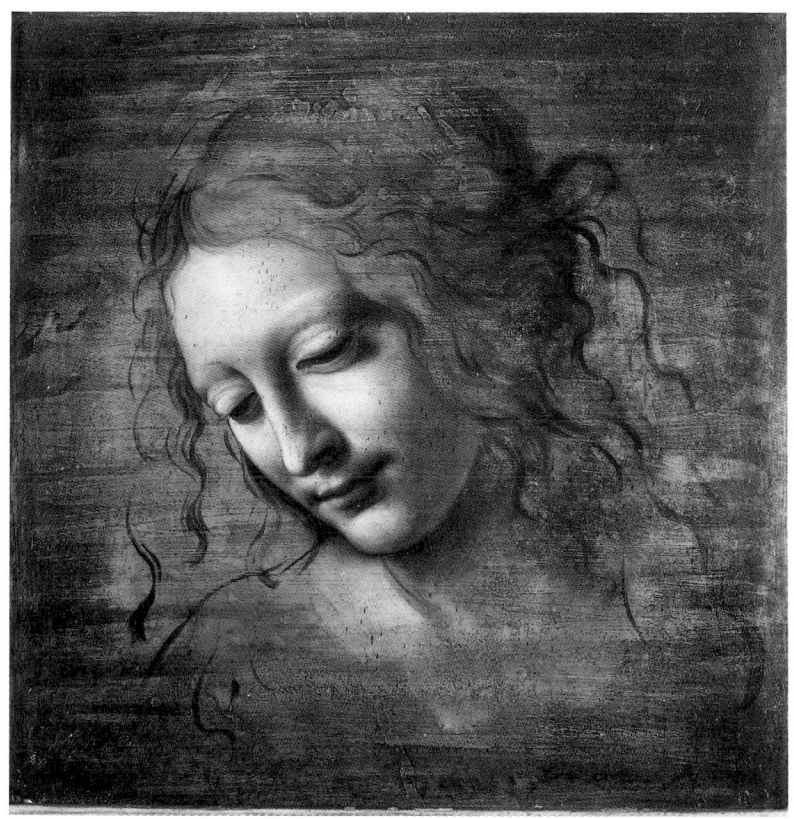

Fig. 57. Attributed to Leonardo da Vinci, *Head of Young Woman (La Scapiliata).* Unfinished painting. Oil on wood, 24.7 × 21 cm. Pinacoteca Nazionale, Parma 362

once again attributed to Leonardo, nobody cares to record why and when they were taken away from him. And everybody becomes nervous when confronted with a Leonardo drawing that is too sweet and sentimental, in the manner of Bernardino Luini, as shown by the beautiful female head at the Fogg Art Museum in Cambridge.[108] The painted sketch of the head of a young woman, the *Scapiliata* (fig. 57), long waited in limbo before being recognized as one of Leonardo's most appealing creations.[109] And the catalogue of Leonardo's drawings rarely includes the red-chalk study for the head of *Leda* (Castello Sforzesca, Milan), which has been given to Giampietrino, or the Metropolitan Museum study for the head of the Virgin in the Louvre *Saint Anne* (cat. no. 108).[110] A third drawing of this kind, a red-chalk, cameolike study for the head of the Virgin in the *Saint Anne* cartoon in London, disappeared from the Pembroke collection at Wilton House after it was reproduced in facsimile in 1902. It was, however, accepted by Berenson as a genuine Leonardo, if retouched, and then forgotten until it was recently shown to have been taken by Giampietrino as a model for his *Madonna di Castel Vitoni.*[111] Such drawings should be viewed next to the most repulsive examples of human deformity as depicted in Leonardo's grotesques. Such a comparison would verify Leonardo's own conclusion about beauty and ugliness being reciprocally enhanced by their juxtaposition: "Le bellezze con le bruttezze paiono più potenti l'una per l'altra."[112]

So unacceptable was the idea of Leonardo working a drawing to a refined finish that some drawings were said to have been gone over and beautified in the nineteenth century. This is what one reads in the catalogues by Müntz and Demonts about, for instance, the large drapery study for the Virgin in the Louvre *Saint Anne* (cat. no. 107), a very late drawing in the typical style of Leonardo's French period, black chalk on paper lightly tinted black as in comparable studies at Windsor.[113] Still, in 1921 Demonts writes: "entièrement retravaillé par la main d'un artiste plus moderne."[114] No such information appears in a 1990 catalogue of a Louvre exhibition. Figure studies have not been the only target of such demolition, a process still going on. A Louvre drawing showing the architectural project of a monumental mausoleum (cat. no. 112), first published by Richter in 1883 and left out by Popham, was soon ascribed to Francesco di Giorgio and has returned to Leonardo only recently.[115]

The study of the critical fortune of Leonardo's drawings is far from over. During the last thirty years or so I have dedicated much effort to the task of sorting out so heterogeneous an amount of material involving Leonardo, his pupils and followers, as well as imitators and later fakers. Drawings that used to be set aside with contempt are gradually being recognized as invaluable documents concerning the many aspects of Leonardo's draftsmanship. This study should be not simply an exercise in connoisseurship but a relentless philological process that leaves no stone unturned.

1. Christ Church, Oxford, no. 263; Byam Shaw 1976a, vol. 1, no. 702, pp. 188–90, with an account of the attributions, ranging from Giovanni Bellini to Mantegna and from Alvise Vivarini to Bonsignori and Gentile Bellini, and even to Grünewald. More recently, David Ekserdjian has again attributed the drawing to Mantegna (Metropolitan Museum of Art and Royal Academy of Arts 1992, no. 104, pp. 341–43). While the issue of attribution seems now more or less settled—though it may still be debated whether in favor of Giovanni Bellini or, as less convincingly suggested, of his older brother-in-law Andrea Mantegna—it is unquestionable that the author of the drawing is an artist from northeastern Italy.

2. Colvin 1907, vol. 2, pl. 32 (as Alvise Vivarini); Bell 1914, no. H. 9, p. 93 and pl. 125 (as Alvise Vivarini).

3. Rigaud and Brown 1877, p. 235: "At Christ Church College, Oxford. . . . Ludovico Sforza, a fine portrait. In black chalk, life size, but probably by a scholar of Leonardo's."

4. Berenson 1903; Berenson 1938 (hereafter the edition cited); and Berenson 1961.

5. Uzielli 1896, pp. 262–63.

6. Rigollot 1849, p. 75: "M. Passavant parle, dans son voyage en Angleterre, page 247, d'un très-beau portrait de Louis-le-Maure, dessiné au crayon noir, de grandeur naturelle, attribué à Léonard, mais qu'il croit plutôt être d'un de ses meilleurs élèves; il est conservé à Oxford." (See Passavant 1833, p. 247.)

7. Courajod and Ravaisson Mollien 1877, pp. 330–54.

8. Müller-Walde 1889, p. 75 and pl. 29.

9. Pedretti 1969. See Pedretti 1982a, no. 55r, pp. 122–23, as well as pp. 4, 10, 43, 115, 116, 118, 119, 139.

10. Uzielli 1896, pp. 262–63. Another instance of Uzielli's perplexing way of viewing the style and character of a Leonardo drawing occurs in the second series of his *Ricerche* (Uzielli 1884), pp. 394–95. As shown by anecdotes related by Adolfo Venturi (Venturi 1927, pp. 79–80), Uzielli's meticulous scholarship was dominated by a persistent positivism, which might account for his lack of understanding of problems of style (discussed in Pedretti 1972a, pp. 134–35).

11. On this problem, see Warburg 1893. The concluding chapter of Warburg's early work on Botticelli concerns the relation of Botticelli to Leonardo, with a discussion (English ed., pp. 139–41; Italian ed., pp. 54–57) of Leonardo's masquerader costumes at Windsor that Müller-Walde (1889, pp. 74–75, pls. 36–38) had just referred to Poliziano's *Giostra* of 1475. The *Pointing Lady* that Müller-Walde (1889, pp. 75–76, pl. 39) thought represented Beatrice, as in Botticelli's illustrations to Dante's *Divine Comedy*, is then suggested by Warburg to represent Simonetta Vespucci, the heroine of that *Giostra*. In his 1883 anthology of Leonardo's writings, Richter had regarded the *Pointing Lady* as an illustration of Leonardo's description of a nymph that appears in a text on painting in the early Paris Ms. A, fol. 18r, ca. 1490–92 (Richter, §391). Hence its facsimile reproduction as pl. 26 as the obvious source of Warburg's thesis about its connection to Poliziano's *Nymph*. A later interpretation by Peter Meller, which takes the drawing for what it is, that is, a very late one, proposes a more convincing identification, namely, a representation of the mysterious Matelda who, suddenly appearing to Dante at the end of *Purgatorio*, canto 28, becomes his guide until his encounter with Beatrice (Meller 1955, in particular pp. 135ff., fig. 1). Compelling as any such interpretation can possibly be, the drawing seems to rely for its hidden meaning precisely on the turbulent effect of the fluttering drapery, which was so perplexing to Uzielli and which has come to be recognized as an unquestionable earmark of Leonardo's latest drawings.

12. Grosvenor Gallery 1877, vol. 2, p. 14; see Clark and Pedretti 1968–69, vol. 1, p. 114 (RL 12581). See also Suida 1929, p. 50, fig. 127; and Pedretti 1969.

13. A small reproduction of it is in Müntz 1899, p. 123, as "Étude de jeune femme" (Müntz 1898, vol. 1, p. 121), without any reference in the text, except for the catalogue entry (Müntz 1898, p. 533; Müntz 1899, vol. 2, p. 268) in the category "C" of the "Figures isolés" at Windsor: "Jeune Femme debout, étendant la main gauche. Au fond, un paysage." Although it appears as a full-page facsimile reproduction in Richter 1883, pl. 26, no. 391 n., it is not included, for instance, in such a popular book as Rosenberg 1898 (in English, Rosenberg 1903).

14. Gotti 1870, p. 605: "Imitazione da Leonardo, *Figura muliebre in piedi panneggiata*." The drawing now has the number 8953 S, is in red chalk on white paper, and measures 180 by 97 mm. It was first published in Pedretti 1969, p. 345. See also my edition of the corpus of Leonardo's landscape drawings at Windsor (Pedretti 1982, pp. 122–23, fig. 117, as by Melzi), and Pedretti and Dalli Regoli 1985, p. 23 and fig. 26.

15. Uzielli 1896, pp. 262–69. A comparable list had been published in Turotti 1857, pp. 8–11; Vasari–Milanesi 1906, vol. 4, pp. 63–66.

16. Gallerie dell'Accademia, Venice, 233, originally joined to no. 258; Pedretti 1982, pp. 8 (n. 2), 117, 139, fig. 138; Pedretti 1987a, pp. 126, 128, fig. 163. See Müller-Walde 1889, p. 76, fig. 40, and exhibition catalogue Biblioteca Medicea Laurenziana 1952, nos. 64, 65.

17. See note 11 above.

18. Müller-Walde 1897, 1898, 1899. For a contextual evaluation of Müller-Walde's contributions, see Gould 1954, in particular pp. 190–91.

19. The catalogue of drawings given in the appendix by Müntz 1898, vol. 2, pp. 248–77, is preceded by a note useful for the historiography of the subject and also for some observations on matters of style and conservation.

20. See Pedretti 1989a.

21. Müntz 1898, vol. 2, p. 264, no. 8 (with reference to the Grosvenor Gallery exhibition catalogue, no. 3).

22. The tentative identification of the Oxford drawing or cartoon (black chalk, 382 × 275 mm, pricked for transfer) with "Scaramuccia, chief of the gypsies," mentioned by Vasari (Vasari–Milanesi 1906, vol. 4, pp. 26–27) goes back to Berenson 1938, vol. 1, p. 178, and vol. 2, no. 1050.

23. Waagen as quoted by Müntz 1898b, no. 7 (with reference to the Grosvenor Gallery exhibition catalogue, no. 2), is most probably Waagen 1854, vol. 2, p. 48.

24. Chastel 1965, p. 222, fig. 209.

25. Gabinetto Disegni e Stampe degli Uffizi, Florence, 428 E (Pedretti and Dalli Regoli 1985, no. 5).

26. Published for the first time as Leonardo's with an aquatint by Stefano Mulinari in 1774 (illustrated in Pedretti and Dalli Regoli 1985, fig. 22). Passavant 1969, p. 177 and pl. 92, claims that this is a study for the figure of Christ in Verrocchio's group of *Christ and Saint Thomas*. Even if this were taken as proof of Verrocchio's authorship, it should not be overlooked that the model is a female, with clearly pronounced breasts (as pointed out by Berenson 1938, 1015 B). And yet the Louvre exhibition catalogue (Louvre 1989, no. 15 on pp. 72–73) is inclined to accept the alleged Verrocchio connection. It may be appropriate to mention that Brunetti in the exhibition catalogue of 1952 (see note 16 above) simply suggests the reference to a comparable drawing in the Rennes Museum, namely, one of two included in the Louvre exhibition of 1989, nos. 13 and 14, that carry the early collector's Roman numerals III and V (possibly Melzi's), just as do several of the drapery studies now recognized as Leonardo's.

27. Morelli 1890, p. 226.

28. See Hills 1980, which considers Leonardo's first Florentine period. Leonardo's ties with Flemish art are also evident in drawings of a much later period, e.g., the two drapery studies at Windsor for a *Salvator Mundi*, first studied as such in Heydenreich 1964.

29. Popham 1945, pl. 14; Bean 1960, no. 41.

30. A simple table of concordance confined to the eleven drawings recognized as Leonardo's in Pedretti and Dalli Regoli 1985 might help to evaluate at a glance Morelli's elimination process:

Uffizi inv. no.	Dalli Regoli no.	Popham pl.	Subject	Morelli
420 E	3	—	Drapery study	no
421 E	10	10	*Madonna of the Cat*	no
423 E	11	141	Epicene youth facing an old man	yes (1)
428 E	5	—	Female profile	no
433 E	4	—	Drapery study	no
436 E	8	53	Perspective study for the *Adoration of the Magi*	yes (2)
437 E	2	7	Drapery study	no
446 E	7	127	1478 sheet	yes (3)
447 E	9	50	*Adoration* and technological studies	no
449 E	6	130 A	Profile of a man	yes (4)
8 P	1	253	1473 landscape	yes (5)

31. The note in pen and ink reads as follows: "del Corezo." See facsimile in Pedretti and Dalli Regoli 1985, pl. 11. The red-chalk medium might have contributed to this early attribution.

32. Brown 1971.

33. For a recent attribution of this drawing to Verrocchio, see note 26 above; see Pedretti 1969, esp. p. 17 n. 18, and figs. 11, 12.

34. The verso of this drawing was first reproduced (from a Brogi photograph), but not discussed, in *Leonardo da Vinci: Conferenze fiorentine* 1910, on a plate facing p. 265. It was then published in Pedretti 1954b, pp. 468–71, and again in Pedretti 1957b, pp. 211–16. After the facsimile reproduction in Pedretti and Dalli Regoli 1985 (no. 9), it was the subject of a paper by Domenico Laurenza (1998). See also Pedretti 1999, p. 78, fig. 4. See also note 37 below.

35. See Demonts 1921, notes to pls. 1–4 ("Autrefois attribué à Albert Dürer"), the first three corresponding to Popham 1945, nos. 2, 3, 4. For the last one, which carries the early collector's Roman numeral IX, see Louvre 1989, no. 12, pp. 66–67.

36. Popham 1945, no. 50. Rejected by Morelli in 1890 as a fake, it is dismissed by the organizers of the 1952 Florence exhibition (i.e., Giulia Brunetti in Biblioteca Medicea Laurenzia 1952) in that it is excluded from their selection. See Pedretti and Dalli Regoli 1985, no. 9 on pp. 58–59, as well as my introduction to it, p. 15, particularly for Heydenreich's personal communication ("sixteenth-century forgery").

37. In addition to the evidence offered by the publications mentioned in note 34 above, a strong argument in favor

of Leonardo's authorship of this sheet of *Adoration* and technical studies is provided by the light sketch of a dragon that also appears in a drawing after Leonardo in the Uffizi collection, 435 E, *Dragon Attacking a Lion,* reproduced in facsimile in Pedretti and Dalli Regoli 1985 (no. 32 on pp. 81–83). This is fully discussed in my introduction to that catalogue, p. 15, figs. 3–6. See also my edition of Leonardo's horse studies (Pedretti 1987a, pp. 37–38, figs. 15, 16). This may be important for iconography as well, since the confrontation of horsemen in the right background of Leonardo's *Adoration of the Magi* may have developed out of the Dragon Fight theme at the same time as he was considering the emblematic motif of the *Dragon Attacking a Lion.* See notes 46 and 93 below.

38. On this particular aspect of Müller-Walde's contribution, see Gould 1954, in particular pp. 190–91. See also Clark and Pedretti 1968–69, vol. 1, p. xv. A good insight into what a Sodoma drawing should look like, and thus into Morelli's rationale, is offered in Strong 1902, p. 14, pl. 35: On the *Kneeling Leda,* then ascribed to Sodoma, Strong writes: "Sodoma has for critics the attraction of a nature complicated and responsive, with that dash of the morbid which is apt to simulate every form but its own. In the present drawing he shows himself markedly under the influence of Leonardo, though his rendering of the master's wave-like flow of line is only approximate. The drawing has evidently been retouched here and there by a hand that has coarsened the outline and marred the effect of relief." The drawing is still in pristine condition, without any retouching. For an unfortunate restoration of the Rotterdam version of the same subject (see cat. no. 98), see Pedretti 1997, pp. 258–59, figs. 1–10.

39. Louvre RF 486, from His de la Salle collection (1878); Popham, no. 25.

40. See Demonts 1921, p. 10, pl 5: "Autrefois attribué à Raphaël (Passavant, no 363)." See Both Tauzia 1881, pp. 60ff., where doubts on the traditional attribution to Raphael are first voiced on the basis of a comparison with Leonardo drawings of the same style at the British Museum. In 1903 Berenson finally gave the drawing back to Leonardo (Berenson 1903, no. 1069, fig. 475), specifying that in 1900 it was still ascribed to Raphael "despite the fact that M. de Tauzia and M. Ephrussi had long since recognized its authorship." A systematic account of the critical fortune of each drawing by Leonardo, and of those formerly or still attributed to him, is yet to be done, but, as the necessary sources of information are particularly difficult to locate, it would be best to have such project entrusted to a well-organized research institution.

41. Faculdade de Belas Artes, Universidade do Porto, Oporto (cat. no. 21).

42. Berenson 1938, vol. 1, p. 169.

43. It may not be coincidental that the sketch portrays a young mother who has placed her child on the kind of high modeling stand that sculptors use, suggesting a studio activity, for instance, a live model simulating the act of holding a child. The artist's quick notation through sketches must be akin to the facility with which a sculptor rapidly works the clay into a rough but accurate impression of a portrayed figure. One is reminded of what Vasari says in the Introduction to the *Lives* (I. 169): "E perché alcuni scultori talvolta non hanno molta pratica nelle linee e ne' dintorni, onde non possono disegnare in carta: eglino, in quel cambio, con bella proporzione e misura facendo con terra o cera uomini, animali ed altre cose di rilievo, fanno il medesimo che fa colui, il quale perfettamente disegna in carta o in su altri piani" (And seeing that there are certain sculptors who have not much practice in strokes and outlines, and consequently cannot draw on paper, these work instead in clay or wax, fashioning men, animals, and other things in relief, with beautiful proportion and balance. Thus they effect the same thing as does he who draws well on paper or other flat surface). The presence of the sculptor's stand in Leonardo's sketch was first noted by Thiis 1913, p. 168. Thiis, after having rejected Morelli's attribution of the drawing to Sodoma, here recalls how, in 1901, together with Berenson, he discovered the figure of the child alone sketched on the verso.

44. Popham 1945, nos. 30–38. "It is not inherently different from a cartoon or a large drawing," explains Popham on p. 43, "and, if a precedent were needed to justify its appearance among the drawings proper, this is afforded by the Olschki publication of the Uffizi drawings, where it also finds a place." The publication mentioned by Popham is not recorded in Verga 1931. It is a large portfolio (55 × 40.4 cm) containing fifteen plates of the

Adoration of the Magi with details, plus five plates of Leonardo drawings (8 P, 446 E, 436 E, 421 E, and 423 E). The plates are preceded by a sheet numbered as two pages with catalogue entries signed by Giuseppe Poggi. On the cover is the title *I disegni della R. Galleria degli Uffizi in Firenze. Serie Quinta—Fascicolo Terzo: Disegni di Leonardo da Vinci*, Firenze, Leo S. Olschki Editore, 1920. The convoluted Italian of the opening paragraph of the first entry explains: "Here for the first time are reproduced details of the famous painting from photographs taken after the 1914 restoration, when the cleaning of darkened areas came to be newly glazed so as to enhance every minutest part of the drawing. This work, in fact, ought to be considered as one of Leonardo's most precious drawings, in that it was left unfinished with very light traces of color."

45. Gabinetto Disegni e Stampe degli Uffizi, Florence, 436 E (Pedretti and Dalli Regoli 1985, no. 8, with full bibliography). Popham 1945, no. 53. Errors in the perspective construction were detected in Sanpaolesi 1954, in particular p. 40, pl. L*b*. See also the analysis by Giovanni Degli Innocenti in Pedretti 1978a, p. 282.

46. The Paolo Uccello antecedent is known through Vasari's description (vol. 2, p. 208) of "alcune storie di animali" painted for the house of Medici, which included "una storia dove un serpente combattendo con un leone mostrava con movimento gagliardo la sua fierezza e il veleno che gli schizzava per bocca e per gli occhi" (De Vere trans., vol. 2, p. 135: [a story] wherein a serpent, combating with a lion, was showing its ferocity with violent movements, with the venom spurting from its mouth and eyes). These lost subjects are reflected in Florentine prints of about 1460. See Degenhart and Schmitt 1968, pt. 1, vol. 2, pp. 399–402, figs. 531–33. See also Walcher Casotti 1960, vol. 1, pp. 43–44 and n. 52.

47. Ashmolean Museum, Oxford; Popham 1945, pl. 60B.

48. British Museum, London, 1952-10-11-2 (cat. no. 33).

49. British Museum, London, 1895-9-15-482 (cat. no. 34). Popham 1945, no. 103, describes it as "An Angel Placing a Shield on a Trophy and Separate Studies of the Angel." The upper-left figure, which Berenson calls "a plain representation of Victory" (see note 54 below), may be called an angel, but the lower one on the right is clearly a young woman with bare breasts and no wings, her hair blown forward by the wind as in the traditional representation of Fortuna, just as in the upper-right detail. Compare the allegorical sketches on the verso of a sheet of studies for the *Adoration of the Magi*, also at the British Museum (Popham 1945, no. 104). A rotating figure of Fortuna is shown atop the spire on the temple of Fortuna in the *Hypnerotomachia Poliphili* of 1499. See Calvesi 1980, esp. pp. 66–135, fig. 3 (with full bibliography). Because of the way Leonardo's winged figure is balanced on one foot, it seems that he had something comparable in mind. See also the following note.

50. National Gallery of Art, Washington, 267. This is a panel (56 × 43 cm) that served as a cover to Lotto's *Portrait of Bishop Bernardo de' Rossi* in the National Gallery at Naples, as evidenced by the painter's inscription on the back, dated 1505. See Berenson 1955, pp. 2–3, pls. 7, 8. Emblematic imagery, such as the *Maiden with the Unicorn*, considered by Leonardo at the time of his early Madonnas, ca. 1478 (Popham 1945, nos. 27, 28 B), could have been intended for a comparable destination, and so the Victory or Fortuna motif as well.

51. Wind 1938–39. Even before the electronic age, Wind could easily have reproduced the Leonardo drawing, with the alleged eighteenth-century additions removed, and would have been the first to see the absurdity of his claim. If anything, it was Leonardo's zestful flourish that Reynolds might have found so appropriate to imitate in his own drawings, only to turn it into mimicry. On the other hand, whatever artists in the past have said about Leonardo drawings that they saw or even acquired may be of interest. Jonathan Richardson, for instance, wrote of a Leonardo drawing of a horse's skull that he owned, saying that the identical skull could be seen in the Uffizi *Adoration of the Magi*. No skull is to be seen there, not even with the aid of spectograms. Richardson must have meant that in the painting Leonardo started out to build up with flesh the same skull as in the drawing, the prominent one halfway up in the immediate background on the left. Confirmation of this comes from an account of Richardson's son, concerning the horsemen in that painting: "These my father has the studies of in several drawings (small ones) and one large one of a horse's skull which is here just as in the drawing, only in oil as this picture is painted. Probably this was a whim of Lionardo

which is intended to cloth with flesh and skin, but a bare skull could have no meaning in this place." See Richardson 1722, p. 63. The only *Adoration* studies known to have belonged to Richardson are the horsemen studies now at Cambridge (Popham 1945, pl. 65) and the sheet from the Rothschild collection in the Louvre (7810r–v), which also includes a sketch of the *Dragon Fight* first published by Richter in 1883 (pl. 30 A). Both recto and verso of the sheet, along with Dürer's copy of the verso, are reproduced in my edition of the horse studies at Windsor (as in note 16 above), figs. 10–12. A horse's head (not a skull, but resembling one) appears often in Leonardo's drawings, beginning with a fragment in the Ambrosiana, F 263 Inf. 10v, which is precisely a study for the horse in the mid-background of the *Adoration* on the left. See Pedretti 1988c, fig. 2. Compare also the early engraving among the Leonardo drawings at Windsor (RL 12287). The motif also appears in the context of Leonardo's studies for the *Battle of Anghiari* (e.g., RL 12327r) and in a related lost original that was copied in two drawings made in Pesaro in 1527 (now in Fossombrone), and another copy by Ambrogio Figino (now in Venice). See my edition of the horse studies at Windsor (Pedretti 1987a, p. 78, figs. 102–4).

52. Popham and Pouncey 1950, no. 104. Wind's thesis had already been discussed and rejected in Popham 1945 (p. 130).

53. In his comment on the newly discovered *Dragon Fight* sheet (Popham 1954, p. 225), Popham states: "Technically the sheet which most nearly resembles it is the 'Allegory of Fortune', also in the British Museum."

54. Berenson 1938, p. 182.

55. Popham 1945, pp. 60–61.

56. The Boltraffio drawing *Head of a Woman* (Sterling and Francine Clark Art Institute, Williamstown, Massachusetts; cat. no. 124) is inscribed by an early collector at bottom left: "Leonardo da Vinci." A comparable inscription is found on Leonardo's *Kneeling Leda* in Rotterdam (cat. no. 98).

57. These words occur in the concluding line of the calligraphic title page, written by Giuseppe Ghezzi on the Leonardo codex that he sold in 1717 to Thomas Coke, later Lord Leicester. See *The Codex Hammer of Leonardo da Vinci*, trans. and annotated by Carlo Pedretti (Florence, 1987), p. liii, fig. 32.

58. See Ost 1980, reviewed in Ferino-Pagden 1982, with additional discussion in the same periodical, pp. 163–72.

59. In support of her claim that the drawing should be regarded as a modern forgery, Anna Maria Brizio (1960a, pp. 45–52) speaks of a "dubbia provenienza del disegno," contradicting the evidence of Bossi's purchase in 1811 and all the other historical information that I had made available to her.

60. Gallerie dell'Accademia, Venice, 257 (cat. no. 105).

61. Berenson 1938, p. 168.

62. In 1980 the drawing was given to either Cesare da Sesto or Ambrogio de' Predis. See Cogliati Arano 1980, no. 30 on pp. 67–69. Because of this attribution, it was possible to obtain the loan of the drawing for an exhibition in Vinci two years later, where it was presented as a Leonardo. See *Leonardo dopo Milano* 1982, no. 17, and p. 23 of the introduction. With a catalogue entry by Martin Clayton for the Venetian exhibition of 1992 (Palazzo Grassi 1992, pp. 250–51), the drawing went back to Leonardo.

63. Clark in Clark and Pedretti 1968–69, vol. 1, p. 129, where the drawing is described as follows: "A man's head with the top of his head sawn off flat and four flaps like a cock's hanging down; above, the words: 'de corpo vmano' / 'de corpo e figura vmana.'"

64. To Kate T. Steinitz. A copy of the letter is in my files. See Pedretti and Trutty-Coohill 1993, no. 15 on pp. 50–52, giving the provenance as follows: "Albert M. Shapiro, Berkeley, California (1972). New York, private collection (1972). Colnaghi's, London, sold to Dr. Armand Hammer (1972)."

65. This is fully discussed in my edition of the Codex Hammer (as in note 57 above), pp. 167–72, with a facsimile reproduction of the drawing.

66. For both the New York and Turin Hercules sheets (cat. nos. 101, 102), see Bambach 2001, pp. 16–23 (with updated bibliography). A facsimile reproduction of the Turin sheet is in Pedretti 1990a, no. 8 on pp. 93–94 (see also pp. 23–24 of the introduction).

67. Bertini 1958, no. 479 on p. 61.

68. Pedretti 1979a.

69. This in a letter to me of that year.

70. Wallraf-Richartz-Museum, Cologne (cat. no. 28). Reproduced by Popham 1945, pl. 47 (recto only). Included in Biblioteca Medicea Laurenziana 1952, no. 19, with reproduction of the verso as well.

71. The letter from Müller-Walde to Emil Möller of February 7, 1917, is in my possession.

72. The story is hinted at by Kenneth Clark in Clark and Pedretti 1968–69, vol. 1, p. xv. The Melzi drawing, catalogued as "unnumbered" in the same volume, pp. 188–89, is reproduced in the second volume.

73. Berenson 1938, vol. 2, no. 1014 on p. 110.

74. See Pedretti 1990a, p. 30 and n. 39.

75. Isabella Stewart Gardner Museum, Boston (I.I.r/13). See Trutty-Coohill 1989, esp. pp. 164–65 and figs. 4, 5. See also Pedretti and Trutty-Coohill 1993, no. 16 on pp. 52–54, with facsimile reproduction.

76. Much of what has surfaced through spectrography was already published ten years ago in Baldini 1992. An examination of a new spectrographic study carried out by Dr. Maurizio Seracini in late 2001, taken in conjunction with a prolonged, close-up examination of the original, enables me to come to such a conclusion. There is even the indisputable evidence of a later hand that extensively reworked Leonardo's initial drawings and added the date 1630. This information had not come out in the recent discussions concerning the proposed restoration of the Uffizi painting.

77. Reproduced in Biblioteca Medicea Laurenziana 1952, no. 71.

78. The drawing is just as weak as a comparable one in the Ambrosiana, F 263 Inf. 24 (engraved by Gerli in 1784, but not included in Cogliati Arano's catalogue), and might therefore be by Leonardo. It is no surprise, then, that in Gombrich 1954, 1976, p. 68 and fig. 165, it should have been considered a possible Leonardo drawing.

79. Gombrich 1954, pp. 197–219, reprinted in expanded version as Gombrich 1954, 1976.

80. Gombrich 1954, p. 207, figs. 3, 4, or Gombrich 1954, 1976, p. 66, figs. 115, 138.

81. It is enough to mention the large sheet of the *Five Grotesque Heads* at Windsor (RL 12495), which is central to Gombrich's discussion. See Gombrich 1954, 1976, pp. 71–72, fig. 183.

82. One such case is discussed in Gombrich 1954, 1976, p. 66, figs. 135, 136, with reference to my note, Pedretti 1962b, where I present a finished drawing in the Rijksmuseum in Amsterdam, possibly by Melzi, showing a fantastic, humanlike animal. See also Pedretti 1987a, pp. 121, figs. 148, 149. The pupil's drawing gives full shape to a faint image just hinted at by Leonardo with a red-chalk sketch on a sheet of the Codex Atlanticus, fol. 193r-a (524r), ca. 1493–95.

83. On the subject of these cut-out "doodles," see Pedretti 1957a, as well as the chapter "I 'disegni fantasma' del Codice Atlantico" in Pedretti 1957b, pp. 188–200.

84. Albertina, Vienna, 14179, included with reproductions in the catalogue of the 1952 exhibition in Florence (as in note 16 above), no. 45. On Mariette and Crozat as collectors of Leonardo drawings, see Steinitz 1974.

85. For two fragments not at Windsor identified as extracted from sheets of the Codex Atlanticus, see Pedretti 1957b, pp. 242–43, figs. 95, 96, and pls. 18a and b.

86. Clark and Pedretti 1968–69, vol. 1, p. xliv. Only after Gombrich's seminal paper of 1954 did the psychological dimension of the Chatsworth grotesques come to be considered as evidence in Leonardo's art. I am referring in particular to the contributions of Flavio Caroli, Michael W. Kwakkelstein, Domenico Laurenza, and others published during the last ten years. But it would be wrong to suggest that these "doodles," with their immediate appeal to collectors, had been previously regarded only as curiosities, as a caricature might be understood as a witty form of divertissement. Strong 1902, pp. 6–7, pl. 28, showing a Darwinian cast of mind, took the first step in the right direction: "The object of Leonardo in these studies has never been thoroughly explained. That he ever did anything without purpose is out of the question. On the whole, it seems most probable that he was experimenting with the lines that express character and govern or reveal the changes of emotion in the human countenance. His method was akin to that of the geometry of projection. Just as the shadow of a circle is an ellipse, so by projecting the lines of a human face of a certain marked type

he was enabled to detect and exhibit, as in a shadow, the secret but most real kinship between the *bête humaine* and the dog, the ape or the swine, as the case might be. In a sheet of drawings at Windsor [RL 12326r] we see the same process applied to the head of a lion until it quickens into a lower canine form."

All the Leonardo drawings at Chatsworth are now catalogued and reproduced in Jaffé 1994. In my note, Pedretti 1988i, I reproduce two Chatsworth drawings "which have so far escaped publication possibly because believed not to be by Leonardo." The first one, the head of an old man with sparse, fluffy hair on the sides and in the back (yellowish coarse paper, 65 × 53 mm), is particularly important because it is demonstrably one of Leonardo's latest drawings, ca. 1517–18. The other drawing is the original of the so-called caricature of Dante known in copies at Windsor and elsewhere. It is even recorded by Clark in the Windsor catalogue (RL 12493) but as a copy, when it is unquestionably the original, of about 1490.

87. Hamburger Kunsthalle, 21482 (Popham 1945, pl. 134 A). See Caroli 1995, p. 168, figs. 1, 2.

88. Istituto per la Grafica, Rome, F.C. 31645. Gift of the Fogg Museum of Art (1927), formerly in the Bocciarelli collection, Turin. The American "gift" was an alternative to confiscation, since the drawing was sold by an Italian private collector without an exportation permit. As by right it should belong to America, I wanted it included in Pedretti and Trutty-Coohill 1993, no. 8 on p. 42, with reproduction in facsimile. It is sometimes related, at least in character and style, to the studies for the *Last Supper,* and I have read somewhere that it could have been intended as a study for Judas. Elsewhere, I have read that the greedy old man is supposedly captured in a spirited attitude conceptually related to that of the *Lady with the Ermine!*

89. Ambrosiana, Milan, F 274 Inf. 31 and F 274 Inf. 21, as discussed and reproduced in Fabrizio-Costa 1997, p. 91 and figs. 4, 5.

90. Ambrosiana, Milan, F 263 Inf. 90, reproduced in facsimile by the Commissione Vinciana (V. 215 iii).

91. Marinoni and Cogliati Arano 1982, no. 30, p. 122. Along with the prevailing tendency to ascribe authentic Leonardo drawings to pupils, the reverse may still occur today, namely, upgrading a pupil's or even a follower's drawing to the status of the master, a move that is understandable if not excusable on the part of a private collector, but not so on the part of a reputable museum. Shortly before Gombrich's essay of 1954, the Detroit Institute of Arts labeled as a Leonardo one of the Pembroke series of Melzi's "replacement drawings." See Valentiner 1949, no. 80. It would be tedious to record all such anomalies that, sooner or later, are gradually being rectified. But it is indeed surprising that a comparable upgrading has blatantly taken place in the Uffizi collection, of all places: a sheet of sketches of fighting horsemen (150 F), which is a sixteenth-century drawing resembling Leonardo's studies for the *Battle of Anghiari* at Venice, but not necessarily after Leonardo (see Pedretti and Dalli Regoli 1985, no. 45), is ascribed in an official publication to Leonardo and, as such, has just been selected for an exhibition in Japan. See Petrioli Tofani 1991, no. 150 F. Of course, I cannot deny that I have not at times been tempted to see Leonardo where he is not, but when I do, as in the case of a drawing in the Metropolitan Museum, *Head of an Old Man in Profile to the Right,* the attribution is always, as it should be, the result of a working hypothesis, not of a guessing game. See Pedretti and Trutty-Coohill 1993, no. 19 on pp. 55–57. In the case of another drawing at the Uffizi, 424 E (Pedretti and Dalli Regoli 1985, no. 24), *Head of an Old Man in Profile to the Left* (metalpoint on ivory prepared paper, 223 × 160 mm), I am still convinced that it was an original Leonardo reworked by a pupil. This drawing should be the occasion for a systematic study of the collection from which it came, that of Fra Sebastiano Resta, a late-seventeenth-century amateur who assembled an enormous number of old master drawings, including several of Leonardo's. He was in the habit of writing long explanations on the mount of each drawing and occasionally on the drawing itself, front and back. However unreliable his comments might be, they may still throw light on the early history of Leonardo drawings. In 1707 he published an account of the content of two of his many large books of old master drawings, the *Arena dell'anfiteatro pittorico* and the *Parnaso de pittori.* The Leonardo drawings he mentions in his possession include "two half-anatomies" (possibly meaning the figures of two half-dissected bodies), the portrait of the prior of Santa Maria delle Grazie in Milan, and a "bambino mirabilissimo." But greater importance is attached to a large drawing after Verrocchio's *Baptism of Christ,*

allegedly made by Leonardo as a boy, along with a finished study for the head of the angel that Vasari records as having been added by Leonardo to that painting. Resta also mentions these drawings in one of his marginal notes to a copy of the 1550 edition of Vasari's *Lives*, which belonged to Giuseppe Bossi and which is now in the Vatican Library. No drawing after Verrocchio's *Baptism of Christ* is known today, but the head of the angel could well be the one now at Turin (BR 232), possibly a real Leonardo.

92. Lu 189 (McM 261). This is the traditional way of quoting the chapters in Leonardo's *Treatise on Painting*, with reference to the old and still valuable critical edition by Heinrich Ludwig of 1882 and to the only available English edition, McMahon 1956. There is now my own critical edition, which restores the original title of *Libro di pittura*—just as Ludwig had correctly adopted the title *Malerbuch*—and which follows every detail of the original apograph, the Codex Urbinas Latinus 1270, Vatican Library. A full-color facsimile is also given. The transcription has been entrusted to the philologist and Leonardo scholar Carlo Vecce, and I have done the rest—concordances, dates, and, I hope, all that a researcher may reasonably expect from such an edition: *Libro di pittura* 1995. In the original the chapters are not numbered. The numbering adopted between square brackets is that of the Ludwig edition.

93. Leonardo's warning against the use of the perspectograph as detrimental to the painter's creativity is found in his *Libro di pittura*, Lu 42 (McM 48), to which see note in *Libro di pittura* 1995. For a full discussion of the perspectograph in context, from Alberti to Dürer, see Camerota 2001, to which I have contributed the section on Leonardo (pp. 167–88). The only known example of a profile portrait executed by Leonardo with a perspectograph is a drawing at Windsor (RL 12808), in black chalk or charcoal, pricked for transfer, touched in with pen and ink on finely squared paper. It is impossible to recognize this outline drawing as Leonardo's, except for its provenance in the same Leoni volume that contained all the other Leonardo drawings. It is catalogued but not reproduced by Kenneth Clark, who says: "A Florentine drawing of the type usually connected with the [Pollaiuoli brothers] but evidently common in all contemporary workshops. It is hard to explain how Melzi came to include this drawing in his Leonardo collection, unless indeed it were a very early drawing by Leonardo himself. But such a suggestion has nothing but provenance to support it." I dare say that the type is Lombard, not Florentine. This could well be an experiment from the time of Leonardo's descriptions of two types of perspectograph (both illustrated by Dürer in 1525) in Paris Ms. A (fol. 104r [Ash. I, fol. 24r]) in the early 1490s (Richter, §523; Lu 90 and 97; McM 118 and 119). His lively depiction of the instrument with its operator in Codex Atlanticus (fol. 1 bis r-a [5r]) dates from his first Florentine period, at the time of the *Adoration of the Magi*, ca. 1480–82. In the first publication of this drawing, which escaped the facsimile edition of the entire codex (1894–1904), Calvi 1923–25, p. 169, fig. 2, states that the seated figure of the operator shows the same character as those in the *Adoration of the Magi*, in particular that of the young man standing at the far right and looking out of the picture as if to perform the role of "commentator" (as Leon Battista Alberti recommended in his treatise on painting) so appropriate to a self-portrait of the painter. One could add that the same style, character, and even attitude of the Codex Atlanticus figure are found in the figure shown seated with a mirror in the small allegory in the Louvre, 2247 (Popham, no. 110 A). The latter might have been a later outcome, ca. 1489–90, of the series of allegories with fighting animals apparently intended at first for the background of the *Adoration of the Magi*. See notes 37 and 46 above. See Pedretti 1987a, pp. 115–16, fig. 132.

94. The original has "non dà noia il fare bella lettera," meaning, indeed, "it does not matter to write in beautiful letters," that is, in calligraphy. McMahon has it right, though his translation of the whole text is not satisfactory. A more satisfactory one, that by Martin Kemp and Margaret Walker, gets the "bella lettera" curiously wrong: "Have you never reflected on the poets who in composing their verses are unrelenting in their pursuit of fine literature and think nothing of erasing some of these verses in order to improve upon them?" See Kemp and Walker 1989, p. 222.

95. "Però tu, compositore delle istorie, non membrificare con terminati lineamenti le membrificazioni d'esse istorie, ché te 'nteverrà come a molti e vari pittori intervenire suole, li quali vogliano che ogni minimo segno

di carbone sia valido. E questi tali ponno bene acquistare ricchezze, ma non laude della sua arte, perché molte sono le volte che lo animale figurato non ha li moti delle membra apropriate al moto mentale, et avendo lui fatta bella e grata membrificazione ben finita, li parrà cosa ingiuriosa a trasmutare esse membra più alte, o basse, o più indietro che inanzi. E questi tali non sono meritevoli d'alcuna laude nella sua scienzia. Or non hai tu mai considerato li poeti compositori de' lor versi, alli quali non dà noia il fare bella lettera, né si cura di canzellare alcuni d'essi versi, rifacendoli migliori? Adonque, pittore, componi grossamente le membra delle tue figure, e attendi prima alli movimenti apropriati alli accidenti mentali de li animali compositori della storia che alla bellezza e bontà delle loro membra. Perché tu hai a intendere che, se tal componimento inculto ti reuscirà apropriato alla sua invenzione, tanto maggiormente satisfarà, essendo poi ornato della perfezzione apropriata a tutte le sue parte." For a possible date after 1500, see my comment in *Libro di pittura* 1995.

96. This aspect of Leonardo drawings is fully discussed in Pedretti 1975b.

97. "Io viddi già alcuni dissegni minuti di sua mano, che mi furono mostrati da certi pittori vecchi, mentre io stetti in Milano, oltre alle sue meravigliose pitture, i quali erano finiti con un modo, et per lumi et per l'ombre tanto straordinari, che quanto più io vi considerava, tanto più mi pareva impossibile ad imitarsi, non che a farsi per le mani d'altrui." Armenini (1586) 1989, p. 132. The first edition is normally cited with the date 1587, but there are copies with the 1586 date, e.g., Biblioteca Universitaria, Bologna, IV, Q. X, 71. See Pedretti 1953, p. 218.

98. Gallerie dell'Accademia, Venice, 237 (Popham 1945, no. 256), catalogued with exemplary objectivity (and with a question mark as to the attribution to Leonardo) by Giovanna Nepi Scirè in Palazzo Grassi 1992, no. 46 on pp. 300–301. This drawing has always been regarded as by Leonardo and very early, ca. 1480. It is not by him, however, and is very late, after 1510. Not only is the touch of the pen as cold and lifeless as it could be, typical of Melzi's "replacement drawings," as shown by the two sheets of caricatures also in the Venice collection (227, 229; Cogliati Arano [as in note 6 above], nos. 23, 24), but there is even a piece of documentary evidence that proves the late origin of these sheets. This is a double sheet in the Codex Arundel (fols. 243r and 248v). When this sheet is spread open as it was originally, it shows Leonardo's notes and diagrams pertaining to a particular problem of light and shade that occupied him about 1508–10 and after, particularly in 1513. Close to the upper margin and to the middle vertical fold is the pen-and-ink drawing of the same flower bud seen at the top left of the Venice drawing. As Leonardo's note moves around it, it is clear that the drawing was already there. It is identical to the Venice one in style as well, except that the lines of shading show the use of the right hand. Hence this may safely be taken as evidence of Melzi's testing the pen at the time he would make the copies on the Venice sheet. The new facsimile edition of the Codex Arundel shows the sheet open flat. See Leonardo da Vinci, *Il Codice Arundel 263 nella British Library. Edizione in facsimile nel riordinamento cronologico dei suoi fascicoli a cura di* Carlo Pedretti. *Trascrizioni e note critiche a cura di Carlo Vecce* (Florence, 1997), fol. P 143r. See also Pedretti 1982a, p. 21 n. 1, figs. 4, 5. For Melzi's "replacement drawings," see Clark 1967. In Clark and Pedretti 1968–69, the Venice drawing is mentioned in a note to no. 12363.

99. The painting was transferred from the original wood panel in 1841 and has since been undergoing periodic cleaning. See *Musée du Louvre. Hommage a Léonard de Vinci. Exposition en l'honneur du cinquième centenaire de la naissance*, exh. cat. by Michel Florisoone and Sylvie Beguin (Paris, 1952), pp. 7–14, esp. p. 8. For the results of a laboratory examination carried out in 1952, see Hours 1954, pp. 18–19, pls. 15–17.

100. *Rime del argvto et faceto poeta Bernardo Belizone fiorentino . . .* (Milan, 1493), fol. e ii r, reproduced in Pedretti 1993 (see ill. on p. 135).

101. Biblioteca Reale, Turin, 15572 (Popham 1945, pl. 157). See the catalogue entry in Pedretti 1990a, pp. 18–21 and no. 2 on pp. 84–86. See also the catalogue of the Camaiore exhibition, Pedretti 1998b, no. 1 on pp. 45–47.

102. Sirén 1911. A revised and expanded edition in English was published in London in 1916 (Sirén 1916), and a definitive one, in French, in 1928 (Sirén 1928). See vol. 1, p. 54: "En quelques traits, quelques frottis d'ombre, le maître transfigure un modèle quelconque pour en faire un être plein de grâce et de vie. La pose de la tête a quelque chose de fugitif, les grands yeux à demi malicieux s'ouvrent un instant sur nous avec

cette exsspression particulière aux personnages de Léonard, et qui ne laisse pas que d'être un peu inquiétante par son mélange d'intellectualité et de sentiment."

103. For the Leonardo drawing gone over by a pupil, see my introduction to Pedretti and Dalli Regoli 1985, p. 12, figs. 1, 2. For the latest attribution of the *Madonna Litta* to Boltraffio, see Fiorio 2000. See also Pedretti 1989a.

104. Département des Arts Graphiques du Musée du Louvre, Paris, 2347 (cat. no. 61). First reproduced by Richter 1970, vol. 1, p. 342 (first ed., 1883), in facsimile, pl. 51 A (second ed., 1939), and then in 1934 by *Comm. Vinc.* fasc. 3, pl. 87. (As a curiosity, an earlier, actual-size woodcut reproduction might be mentioned, in Clément 1861, p. 278.) In Berenson 1903, no. 1067, he says "retouched," adding, in 1938, "but still very fine." A reference to the Paris version of the *Virgin of the Rocks* was unanimously agreed upon until the publication of Beltrami 1919c, where it is proposed (pp. 165–67, figs. 35, 36) that the fragment refers to the *Saint Anne* cartoon in London. The early style of the drawing makes this impossible. And yet even Gerolamo Calvi changed his mind, as shown by his review of MacCurdy's 1932 *The Mind of Leonardo da Vinci* (Calvi 1930–34, p. 305), contradicting his paper Calvi 1916. There he still favored the reference to the *Virgin of the Rocks* (pp. 501–3), adding the curious observation (p. 502, n. 1) that the green coat in the paper of support seems to conceal lines of handwriting. The original shows that this is not the case.

105. Leonardo's authorship of the Sant'Onofrio fresco began to be questioned by Müntz in 1899 (Müntz 1899, vol. 2, pp. 200–203). For recent scholarship on the subject, see Vezzozi 1983 with my introductory essays, no. 454, and pp. 218–25.

106. In my essay on the date of the *Madonna of the Cat* appended to Pedretti and Dalli Regoli 1985, pp. 99–101, I compare (figs. 49–50) the child's hair to that of the condottiere-like profile in the Uffizi drawing 449 E. I also suggest (figs. 44, 49) the juxtaposition with a British Museum sketch for the *Madonna of the Cat*.

107. Gallerie dell'Accademia, Venice, 257 (cat. no. 105).

108. See Trutty-Coohill 1993, no. 41 on p. 78.

109. See Pedretti 1977, and Eugenio Riccòmini, "Il Leonardo di Parma," in Palazzo del Podestà 1985, pp. 141–42.

110. For the drawing of *Leda*'s head, see Pedretti 1988d, fig. 1. For that of the *Saint Anne* head, see Pedretti and Trutty-Coohill 1993, no. 18 on p. 55.

111. See Geddo 1994, in particular the "Appendicei. Per i disegni del Giampietrino," on p. 67, with a facsimile reproduction of the drawing formerly at Wilton House.

112. Lu 139 (McM 277), from the lost *Libro A*, carta 27. See Pedretti 1964, p. 51.

113. Département des Arts Graphiques du Musée du Louvre, Paris, 2257 (cat. no. 107). Black chalk and bistre with wash, heightened with white, on paper lightly tinted black, 230 × 245 mm. See Biblioteca Medicea Laurenziana 1952, no. 52. For comparable late drapery studies at Windsor, see Pedretti 1970, esp. pp. 300–303.

114. Demonts 1921, note to pl. 19.

115. Département des Arts Graphiques du Musée du Louvre, Paris, 2386 (cat. no. 112). Demonts 1921, p. 5, mentions it only with reference to Seidlitz 1909, vol. 1, p. 126. After it was first reproduced in facsimile by Richter in 1883, pl. 98, pp. 58–59 (2nd ed., 1939, vol. 2, pp. 44–45), in the section on architecture entrusted to Henry de Geymüller, it was seldom considered, except for a proposal in 1911 to take it as a model for a monument to Dante. Cf. Laureti 1911. Some forty years later it appears again in Sartoris 1952, p. 120. Meanwhile Adolfo Venturi had published the last volume of his *Storia dell'arte italiana*, XI. *Architettura del cinquecento*, Parte I, Milan, 1938 (Venturi 1901–39), where a five-line footnote on p. 49 dismisses the possibility that the drawing is by Leonardo and assigns it to Francesco di Giorgio on the basis of comparable drawings in the codex of that architect (Biblioteca Nazionale, Florence). This was further stressed in Venturi 1939, so that a few years later the drawing was officially no longer by Leonardo, as shown by Allen Stuart Weller, in Chicago 1943, p. 276, n. 115. And this with serious consequences, in that even Chastel agreed. See Chastel (1959) 1982, p. 69, pl. 13. "Le dessin est assez froid," writes Chastel, "il n'est pas tracé de la main gauche et l'attribution à Léonard est a bon droit contestée; on pense plutôt à Francesco di Giorgio, mais on ne peut guere hésiter sur

sa source d'inspiration." At least he was right on "sa source d'inspiration," i.e., Etruscan funerary chambers. Martelli 1977 was to show how the Leonardo drawing could be explained by its correspondence with just one such type of tomb discovered in Castellina in Chianti in 1507—exactly the date that I had proposed for the Leonardo drawing, on the basis of style alone, in my 1977 commentary to the Richter anthology (as in note 11 above), vol. 2, pp. 80–81. See also Pedretti 1986, pp. 122–23, figs. 180–84.

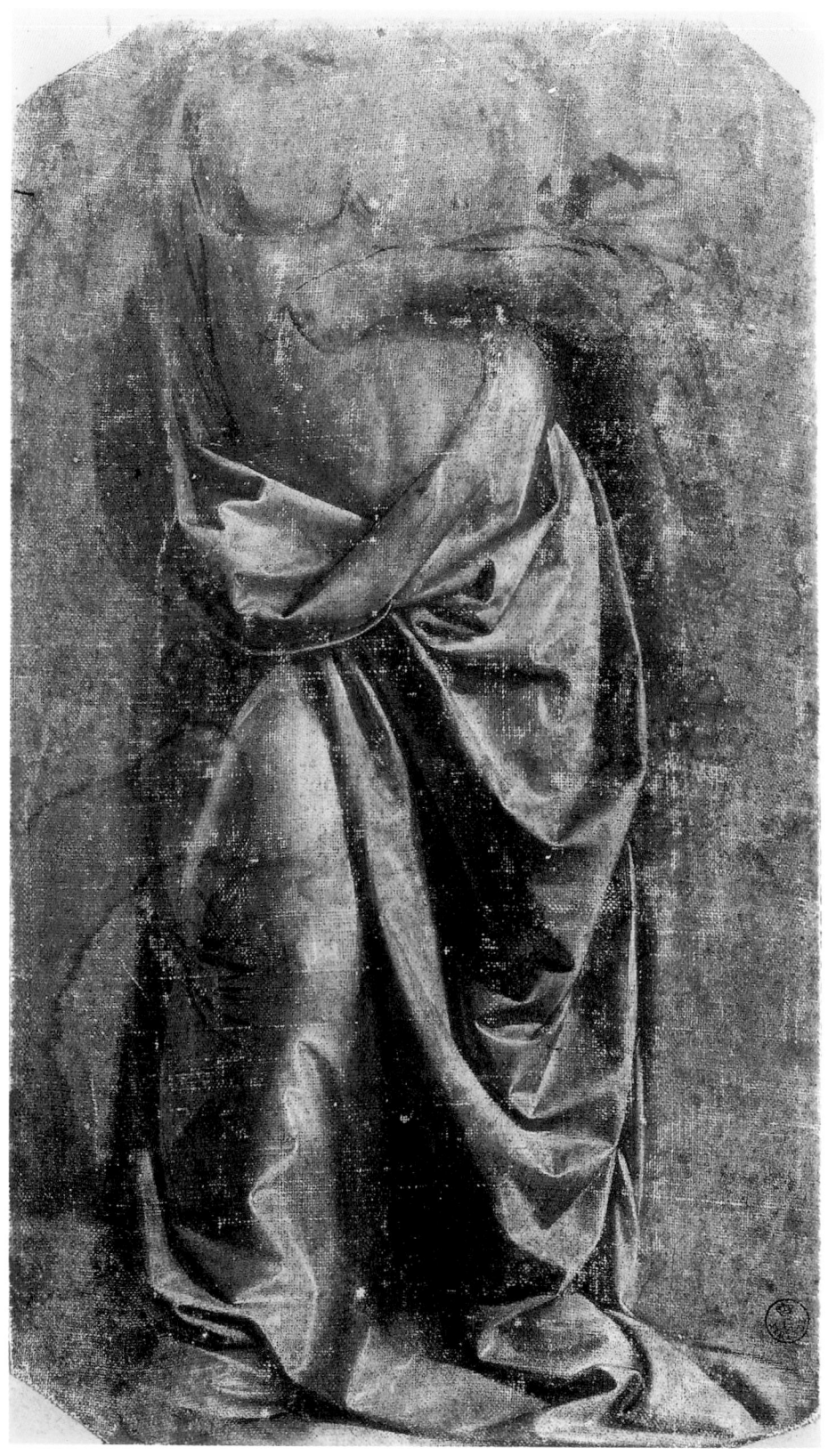

Fig. 58. Leonardo da Vinci, *Study of Drapery for a Figure Standing in Frontal View.* Brush with brown ink, gray and white gouache, on gray-brown prepared linen, 282 × 158 mm, maximum. Gabinetto Disegni e Stampe degli Uffizi, Florence 433 E

THE EARLY DRAPERY STUDIES

FRANÇOISE VIATTE

His vocation was painting; he often studied from life and some-
times manufactured clay models, on which he placed moist fabric
coated with clay, which he patiently undertook to paint on very
fine canvas or prepared linen. He thus obtained, in black and
white, marvelous effects with the tip of his brush; we have
authentic evidence of this in our album of drawings.

—Giorgio Vasari,
Le vite de' più eccellenti pittori, scultori ed architettori

I N 1989, WHEN THE Musée du Louvre acquired two drapery studies, complementing the
four already located there, an exhibition was mounted that displayed sixteen of these little sketches on cloth (cat. nos. 13–17). Their reunion was based on Vasari's commentary,
which, through the clarity of its terms, justified the compilation of a sort of dossier, inasmuch as a great deal of the analysis already advanced by historians had been repeatedly challenged. The juxtaposition of the drawings gave way to an intense reconsideration regarding
the nature, date, and even attribution of the studies, addressing the genesis of Leonardo's
early works and the works created collectively in Andrea del Verrocchio's studio. The exhibition at the Louvre marked the first time these sketches have been reunited since their dispersion, which probably occurred in the late sixteenth century. Inquiry about them has been
conducted for nearly a century and is still pertinent today. It has even returned to the point
where it began with Heinrich Wöllflin and Franz Wickhoff, then Bernard Berenson and
Bernhard Degenhart; however, new factors now make possible an attempt to synthesize the
arguments that have been suggested since the Louvre exhibition. Insisting on the impersonal character of the technique—monochrome drawing with brush on cloth—I argued at
the time that it should be acknowledged as "the armature of perfection," that is, paraphras-
ing Paul Valéry's text,[1] as the recognition of the genesis of a work to come, its "inhuman"
character, "a set of knowledge to which no name is attached." Perfection is anonymous. It is

also mute: all we do is grant it its place without claiming to retrace its generation ("one does not often remember that they have not always been," wrote Valéry of human works). To what extent do these monochromes "on very fine canvas or prepared linen" allow us better to understand Leonardo's activity during his apprenticeship in Verrocchio's studio between 1469 and 1476? Or does the raison d'être for this series elude any wrongheaded desire for classification? Did this group of sketches even constitute a series during the painter's lifetime? His writings tell us nothing about them.

The expertise, which was characteristic of several quattrocento studios, is precisely the element that arouses speculation: is this a collective work or the remnants of independent studies conducted simultaneously by several hands? The article Gigetta Dalli Regoli devoted to the *piegar de' panni*[2] (folding of the cloth) in 1976 mentions studies from models done by painters and sculptors who arranged *tele sottilissime* (extremely thin cloth) on clay or wax figures or wood mannequins and then drew them on cloth. *Piegare* means not only "to fold" but also "to curve," "to bend," "to twist." The reflexive form of the verb means "to surrender." André Chastel uses the old word *ammaccature* (bruises) to describe the breaks in the pleats in reference to the sculptor's dressing of the model.[3] When understood as a summation of the lessons Leonardo received in Verrocchio's studio, these are not studies of draped figures but studies dissociated from the human model. Their technique can be compared to that recommended by Cennino Cennini for preparing canvas, and the adjustment of the folds is consistent with Filarete's recommendations: "Drapery as well has to do with the study of nature," he says, but it is a composed nature like a three-dimensional sketch that—once it has been modeled according to the painter's wish—can be put to use more than once if necessary. Cennini recommends observing the surface of the drapery in preference to that of the anatomy it covers. The drapery is *constructed* fold by fold; the wash serves to shade the outlines. Studying the draped model is different from studying the nude. It concerns solid forms, even though, for Alberti, drawing the nude body under the clothing that covers it is an indispensable preliminary to drawing a clothed figure.[4] Vasari recommends this method in the chapter devoted to sculpture in the introduction to his *Lives of the Most Eminent Painters, Sculptors, and Architects:* models ought to be molded in clay, wax, or stucco, which can be used even for a large model, the same size as the final marble statue. "Once completed, if you wish to put fine clothes on it [the figure], use fine cloth; if you want coarse ones, use coarse cloth." The cloth, moist and covered with clay, is placed "around the figure by arranging the folds and modeling it according to [the artist's] intention; once dry, it will harden and hold the drape."[5]

In addition to the comments formulated after the Louvre exhibition, let me address the various hypotheses made in the monographs published since that time, which have to do with the date and formal analysis of the paintings, primarily the *Baptism of Christ* and the

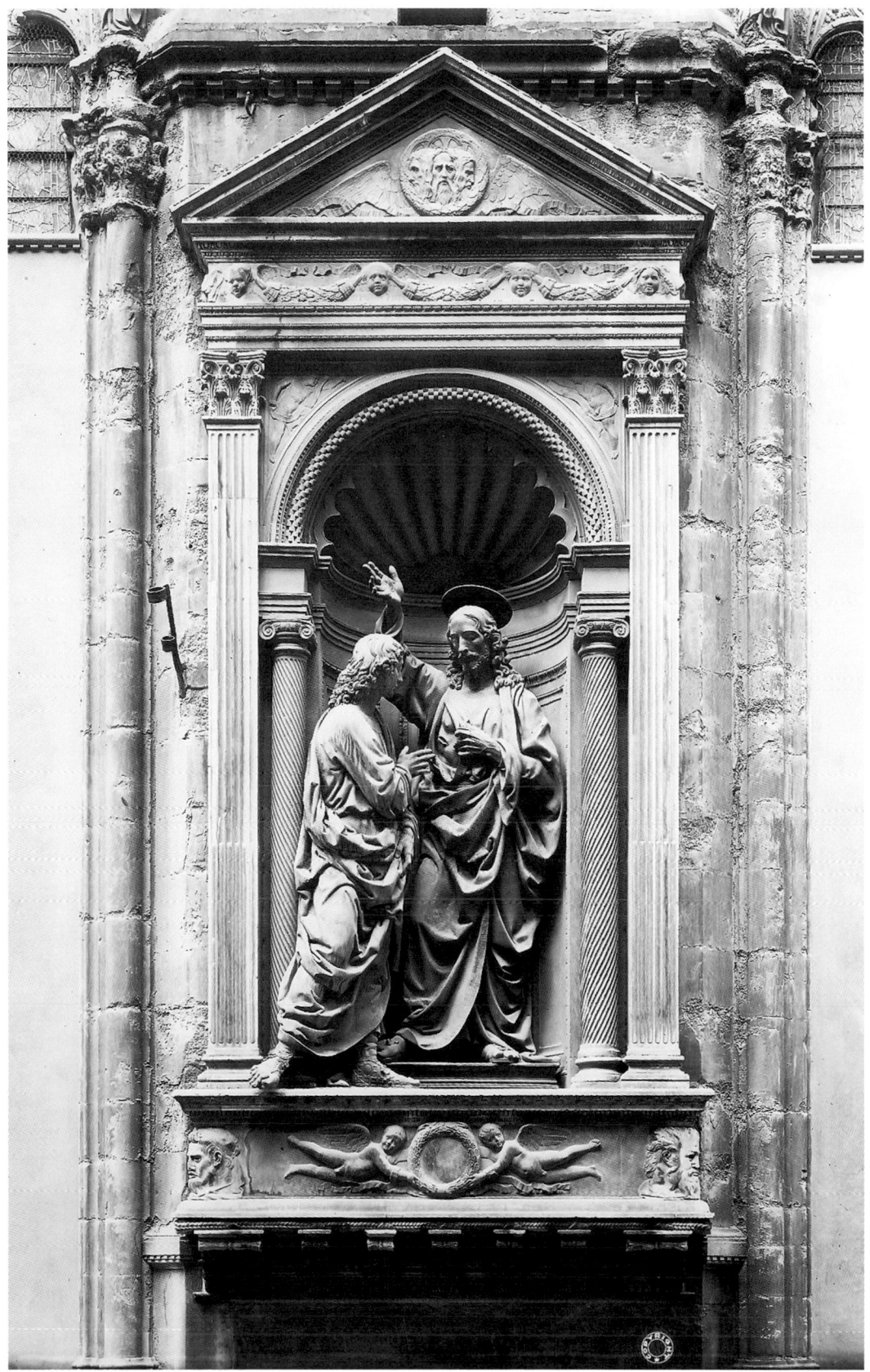

Fig. 59. Andrea del Verrocchio, *Christ and Saint Thomas*. Bronze, figure of Christ 230 cm high. Niche on east façade of Orsanmichele, Florence

Annunciation, related to the drapery group. The studies devoted to Verrocchio and to Florentine art in the 1470s are also pertinent to any discussion of the attribution of the series because the works are attributed either to a single person, Leonardo da Vinci in Verrocchio's studio in about 1470, or to a group effort directed by Verrocchio but realized by several hands. Keith Christiansen (1990), echoing an argument already made by Jean K. Cadogan (1983a), maintains that the studies of drapery as they appeared in the Paris exhibition were produced by a group of artists active in Verrocchio's studio in the late 1460s and early 1470s. The practice of studying the figure, in a suitable light, from sculpted models covered with fabric arranged in a certain manner, then covered with glue or clay, and dried to retain the shape, was so common, says Christiansen, that it can be discerned in Masaccio, Gentile da Fabriano, and Donatello. Unfortunately, there are no surviving drawings by these artists or by Piero della Francesca, who, Vasari said, habitually made models in clay covered with soft drapery in order to copy them and put them to use. For Christiansen, the formal nature of the study dictated that it be painted on canvas or linen and dictated as well the choice technique: a wet brush applying only white, black, and shades of gray. The differences, according to him, did not stem from the mode of transcribing the model but from the intellectual level of the project and each artist's power of observation. In attempting to understand the genesis and function of these studies, we should accept the idea that labor was organized collectively in Verrocchio's studio and that several artists would have used a single mannequin but each according to his own explorations.

Three "coherent" groups have been distinguished by Christiansen, who rejects the idea of a single inquiry conducted by one master and evolving during the gradual adjustment of his intentions. Rather, Christiansen sees the groups as three distinct approaches to a formal problem. The first is centered around the study in the Kupferstichkabinett in Berlin, done in preparation for the *Saint Matthew* painted by Domenico Ghirlandaio on the vault of the chapel of Santa Fina at the collegiate church of San Gimignano.[6] A second set of six or perhaps seven studies is, according to Christiansen, connected by a common reference to the risen Christ in Verrocchio's bronze sculpture *Christ and Saint Thomas* (figs. 58, 59). These studies would have been by Verrocchio himself and would be closely linked to his work as a sculptor, but "the analytical mind to which they testify is scarcely inferior to that of the young Leonardo."[7] Some, almost indistinguishable from one another, compromise the distinction between the master and the student. According to Christiansen, Leonardo was responsible for two studies of kneeling figures, one in the Louvre (cat. no. 14) and the other in the Gabinetto Disegni e Stampe degli Uffizi, and for the most famous of them all, the study of a seated figure (cat. no. 17).[8]

David Alan Brown took up the discussion of the drapery studies in the monograph that he devoted to Leonardo da Vinci in 1998. He considers all sixteen to be consistent with the procedure described by Vasari. According to Brown, they are a clearly identifiable and homogeneous group, all treating the same object: the way light falls on folded cloth. Although he feels that the studies resulted from an individual initiative—that of Verrocchio at the head of his studio—the differences in style point to several hands: Verrocchio's own but also those of his students. While identifying connections between some of the studies and the Orsanmichele group and insisting on the chiaroscuro effects and on the utilitarian function of the exercise, Brown nonetheless states that the whole idea of assigning them to particular artists remains difficult. In his opinion, the drawings of drapery are the expression of a style tending toward the impersonal. They were not created for their own sake or for a specific project but rather as an exercise that could be used if needed. Hence, Brown supports the theory of a collective effort, subject to the discipline of a studio. The failure of attempts to attribute the sketches to particular artists can be imputed to historians' desire to analyze the style of the drapery sketches rather than consider them individually. Of the drapery studies recently acquired by the Louvre (with the exception of the one related to the bronze Christ in *Christ and Saint Thomas*), Brown believes that seven are closely linked to the *Annunciation,* although none of these corresponds exactly to the painting.[9]

The attribution of the group to several different artists and the relation between the drapery studies and Verrocchio's sculpted works continue to be debated: Pietro C. Marani (1999) pursues the comparison between the standing figure in the Galleria degli Uffizi and the bronze Christ in *Christ and Saint Thomas,* the first of the two figures in the group, commissioned in late 1466 or early 1467 and executed between 1470 and 1476. According to Marani, the Uffizi drawing cannot have been done after 1470, even though Leonardo was no more than fifteen at that date: he entered Verrocchio's studio in 1469. Like Christiansen and Brown, Marani posits three main groups of studies, which he distributes among Leonardo himself,[10] Verrocchio,[11] and Lorenzo di Credi.[12] Marani formulates the same hypothesis of collective research—a sort of "testing ground"—made by the artists frequenting Verrocchio's studio. Marani also notes the impossibility of distinguishing Leonardo's sheets within the group even while acknowledging that they were a "reflection" of the convictions the young painter had formed during his years of apprenticeship.

To return to the origin of that discussion, let us refer to Berenson's argument in the first edition of *The Drawings of Florentine Painters* (1903), repeated with modifications in the two following editions and in his article of 1933–34. Berenson writes, "Some give them to Verrocchio and others, as I used to do, to a nameless pupil of that artist." For him, the first and oldest study is the one in the British Museum,[13] despite strong similarities, in the draping and the indication of the face, to Verrocchio's painted works. Like all the historians who have studied the group, Berenson tries to identify a precise figure based on its attitude, in this case, the Virgin for an Annunciation. He therefore hypothesizes that characteristics of the drawing—the "internal structure" of the folds, their arrangement, the rhythm of the line, and the quality of the chiaroscuro—transcend Verrocchio's personality and, even more certainly, that of his followers. In 1938 Berenson wrote that he was tempted "to ascribe it to Leonardo. . . . The date need be no earlier than 1470 and may even be slightly later." He added, "Leonardo was then eighteen years old and quite able not only to equal his master but to surpass him." As a result, the whole group of drapery studies, Berenson said, needed to be examined with reference to the British Museum drawing and attributed to the same artist. Even the pieces that might display the most similarities with Verrocchio's works, like the one in the Uffizi or the one in the Musée des Beaux-Arts in Rennes, do not stand up to a comparison with the master's paintings or sculptures.[14]

The group's provenance remains mysterious, as the Louvre exhibition catalogue indicates,[15] and it cannot be established whether any of the studies were part of the Vasari collection. All the same, recent research has made it possible to identify their former owners since the late seventeenth century, that is, prior to the mention, still considered the first, of fourteen drapery studies in Pierre Crozat's sales catalogue of 1741. We are indebted to Bernadette Py for this important discovery, which demonstrates that the fourteen pieces, now dispersed among different collections, were united in Everard Jabach's collection.[16] Py's examination of the *Inventaire après décès 1695* (Posthumous inventory of 1695), conducted in an attempt to reconstitute the second Jabach collection, which was assembled after the sale of his first collection to Louis XIV in 1671, unearthed the following mention on the list of drawings contained in portfolio E: "14 studies of dalberdur [Albrecht Dürer] drapery on fabric pasted on paper and highlighted in white tempera." Crozat acquired these fourteen studies, and Pierre-Jean Mariette attributed them to Leonardo da Vinci in the 1741 Crozat sales catalogue. As Py was able to establish, thanks to a handwritten annotation by Mariette in the sales catalogue, the batch was sold to Nourri for sixteen francs, and two of the studies can be found in the Nourri sales catalogue in 1785, where, described under number 736, they are once again attributed to Dürer.[17] It was therefore beginning with the 1741 Crozat sale that the set, which had remained together, was dispersed: Py gives new provenances for the drawings, now divided among the Musée du Louvre, the Fondation Custodia, the Musée des Beaux-Arts in Rennes, the Staatliche Museen in Berlin, the British Museum, and the collection of Barbara Piasecka Johnson in Philadelphia.[18] The two studies belonging to Nourri came to the Louvre from the Saint-Morys collection (cat. nos. 14, 17) when property was seized from the emigrants fleeing the Revolution in 1793; two others were bequeathed by Édouard Gatteaux in 1881 (cat. nos. 15, 16). The last two came to the Louvre in 1989, one donated, one acquired (cat. no. 13), from the collection of Marquis Jean-Louis de Ganay and his brothers. The four drapery studies that entered the collection in 1793 and 1881 are listed under Dürer's name in the museum's handwritten inventories, even though Frédéric Reiset reestablished the proper attribution of the first two studies in his inventory completed in the 1860s. It is difficult to know how many drawings Vasari selected for his book, but it is unlikely that he used all fourteen studies collected by Jabach, inasmuch as Vasari himself describes them as only "a few": "alcuni che ne ho di sua mano in sul nostro libro de' disegni" (a few that I have from his hand for our album of drawings). There is no support for the generally held view[19] that his drawings are those in the Uffizi, part of a volume received by Francesco I de' Medici from Vasari's nephew Pietro.

It must therefore be taken into account that, beginning in the seventeenth century, the entire series of drapery studies or at least fourteen of them belonged to a single collector. Therein may lie an argument in favor of their unity: their common origin in the collection from which they were acquired by Jabach but which we still cannot identify. The hypothesis that they were consolidated at that time is incompatible with the notion that they were produced by several artists in a single studio and that works dealing with just one theme, drapery, were brought together. There is, in addition, a similarity in the surfaces and pigments used, as I noted in 1989–90, with the help of the laboratory analysis conducted at the Uffizi and in Paris.[20] Another element, related to their technical execution, complements these questions of provenance. Let us recall, first, that microscopic examinations done at the laboratory for the museums of France revealed that eight of the works exhibited were painted on cloth of similar texture—a plain weave with twenty threads warp and twenty-two threads woof per square centimeter. An almost identical texture was observed in one of the Uffizi drawings; and a preliminary drawing for the series, in black chalk or charcoal, was identified.[21] Furthermore, the paper lining seems to be identical in five of the pieces in the Musée du Louvre; the sixth, like the drapery for a seated figure in the Uffizi, is not lined.[22] Nine studies are numbered in Roman numerals in the upper part of the canvas, but this old numbering is discontinuous. There are no numbers on the pieces in the Uffizi. All these factors support the idea that the studies were once together.

The physical differences as they appear today may lie in the variations in tonality, both in the draperies themselves and in the ground. Some are rather gray or gray-green (cat. nos. 15, 16); others are lighter, pinkish beige (cat. no. 13); still others are almost brown (RF 41905). They also vary in how finished they are, both in terms of the accents of light and in the degree of modeling. Finally, they are not always inscribed the same way within the dimensions of the cloth. I shall only point out, with the greatest caution, the particularities identified on the works in Paris; but the examination ought to extend to the seventeen studies on *tela di lino* (linen cloth), based on observations collected in May 2001 by Pietro C. Marani (cat. no. 17).

The first particularity has to do with the most famous of these studies, the drapery for a seated figure, sometimes attributed to Ghirlandaio (cat. no. 17): its placement on a wide white strip of ground, thick and heavily reworked in the lower right-hand corner, is difficult to understand. It contradicts the illusion of suspended forms that Leonardo was seeking in his studies. In addition, one zone, at the right edge, seems to be on a different plane from the figures. The nature of the pigment used for these whites (perhaps white lead) seems to be the same as that most heavily applied to the folds of fabric. The very dense, very thick whites contrast to the shadows, and the whites are much lighter and more subtly applied in the upper part of the figure. Let me suggest that these white highlights, found on the folds, in the central part, and around the figure, were added or perhaps simply reworked by a hand other than Leonardo's. A similar observation can be made regarding the other drapery studies. Let us remember that certain massive dark areas, applied uniformly, weigh down the shape and give it a rigid unwieldiness. In other cases, thickness is added to the figure by mat applications with the brush, which take the place of the original volume—a coil creased with folds—and create the false appearance of a standing draped figure and no longer a crumpled drapery studied for its own sake. Similarly, indications of the body, the torso, and the arm (in cat. no. 14, for example) might serve the same purpose, that of making the abstract forms that the painter studied—how they fall, how they bend, how light catches them—into "habited" representations intended to take their place within a larger whole. The culmination of the "retouching" exercise, if we adopt both the idea and the term, is found in the large seated figure, which could have been retouched—in the folds of the lower part and in the way they fall, in the inclination of the ground, and on the right edge (cat. no. 17).

To conclude with the question of this group's attribution, I now believe there is no need to modify the statement I made in 1989–90, even though my views have wavered over the last ten years. Contrary to what was advanced at the time, it appears that these draperies on *tela di lino* are to be regarded as having been modeled for their own sake with no specific aim and not as figures defined by the clothing that covers them[23] nor as illustrations that anticipate works to come, like the drapery for the Virgin of the *Saint Anne* (cat. no. 107), for example. The unity of the series as a whole, both from a technical point of view and in its conception, is forcefully apparent as soon as one attentively examines the technique of these sketches. They could be understood as exercises with no other purpose than to develop a skill commonly practiced in several studios in the fifteenth and early sixteenth centuries. Fra Bartolommeo and Giovanni Sogliani would use it in their turn for draping and also for portraits. Leonardo da Vinci was the only one, even at this young age, to achieve such mastery as is demonstrated by the similarity between these studies and his early painted works. Neither Lorenzo di Credi nor Verrocchio nor Ghirlandaio displayed in their drawings true perfection of the kind found here. Furthermore, there is no work of this type among these artists' drawings. Leonardo undertook an unconventional exploration of draping, the details of which correspond to abstract schemata, abandoned later in his writings from the last decade of the century.[24] In conclusion, I suggest that the difficulties of attribution apparent in the diverse statements made by historians (who tend to divide these studies into groups related to several painted or sculpted works) can be understood as a consequence of the retouching done after the fact. Although it is not possible to ascertain the date of these additions, we have reason to believe that they came after the dispersal of the studies and may have been done in the seventeenth century, after Everard Jabach had acquired them as works by Albrecht Dürer. This retouching had less to do with actual additions than with an intensification, a reworking of the dark parts or the white highlights to give them the appearance of completeness that was considered appropriate in the seventeenth century.

1. Valéry 1894, 1975, vol. 1, pp. 1157–58.
2. Dalli Regoli 1976.
3. Chastel in Louvre 1989–90, pp. 11–12.
4. Alberti 1992, p. 163; Louvre 1989–90, pp. 38–39.
5. Vasari–Milanesi 1878–85, vol. 1, p. 154; Louvre 1989–90, p. 39.
6. Staatliche Museen, Kupferstichkabinett, Berlin, 5039; Louvre 1989–90, no. 9. The other pieces in the group are the drapery study in the Piasecka Johnson collection (Louvre 1989–90, no. 8) and the one in the Musée des Beaux-Arts of Rennes (794-1-2507; Louvre 1989–90, no. 14).
7. Christiansen 1990, p. 573. The group, composed solely of standing figures, combines studies from the Musée du Louvre (RF 41905, RF 41904, RF 1081, RF 1082), a second study in the Piasecka Johnson collection, and one in the Galleria degli Uffizi (433 E; Louvre 1989–90, nos. 3, 4, 10, 11, 12, 13, and 15).
8. Musée du Louvre, Paris, 2255 and 2256; Galleria degli Uffizi, Florence, 420 E; Louvre 1989–90, nos. 1, 2, and 16.
9. Musée du Louvre, Paris, RF 41905; Brown 1998b, pp. 78–80.
10. For the Rome drawings, FC. 125770; in the Louvre, 2255, 2256, RF 41905, and RF 1081; at the Fondation Custodia, Paris, 6632 (but reproduced as by Domenico Ghirlandaio, Marani 1999b, p. 17).
11. Musée des Beaux-Arts, Rennes, 794-1-2507; and Kupferstichkabinett, Berlin, 5039.
12. Fondation Custodia, Paris, 2491; Louvre 1989–90, no. 21.
13. British Museum, London, 1895-9-15-489; Berenson 1903, no. 1037A.
14. Galleria degli Uffizi, Florence, 433 E; Berenson 1903, no. 1015B; Musée des Beaux-Arts, Rennes, 794-1-2507; Berenson 1903, no. 1082B.
15. Louvre 1989–90, pp. 23–24.
16. Py 2001, pp. 270–74.
17. Py 2001, p. 270.
18. Py 2001, pp. 270–74.
19. Ragghianti and Dalli Regoli 1975, pp. 6, 31 n. 10.
20. Louvre 1989–90, pp. 40–41.
21. Galleria degli Uffizi, Florence, 420 E; Louvre 1989–90, no. 2.
22. Musée du Louvre, RF 41905; Galleria degli Uffizi, Florence, 437 E; Louvre 1989–90, no. 5.
23. Louvre 1989–90, pp. 21–22.
24. Pedretti and Dalli Regoli 1985, pp. 50–51.

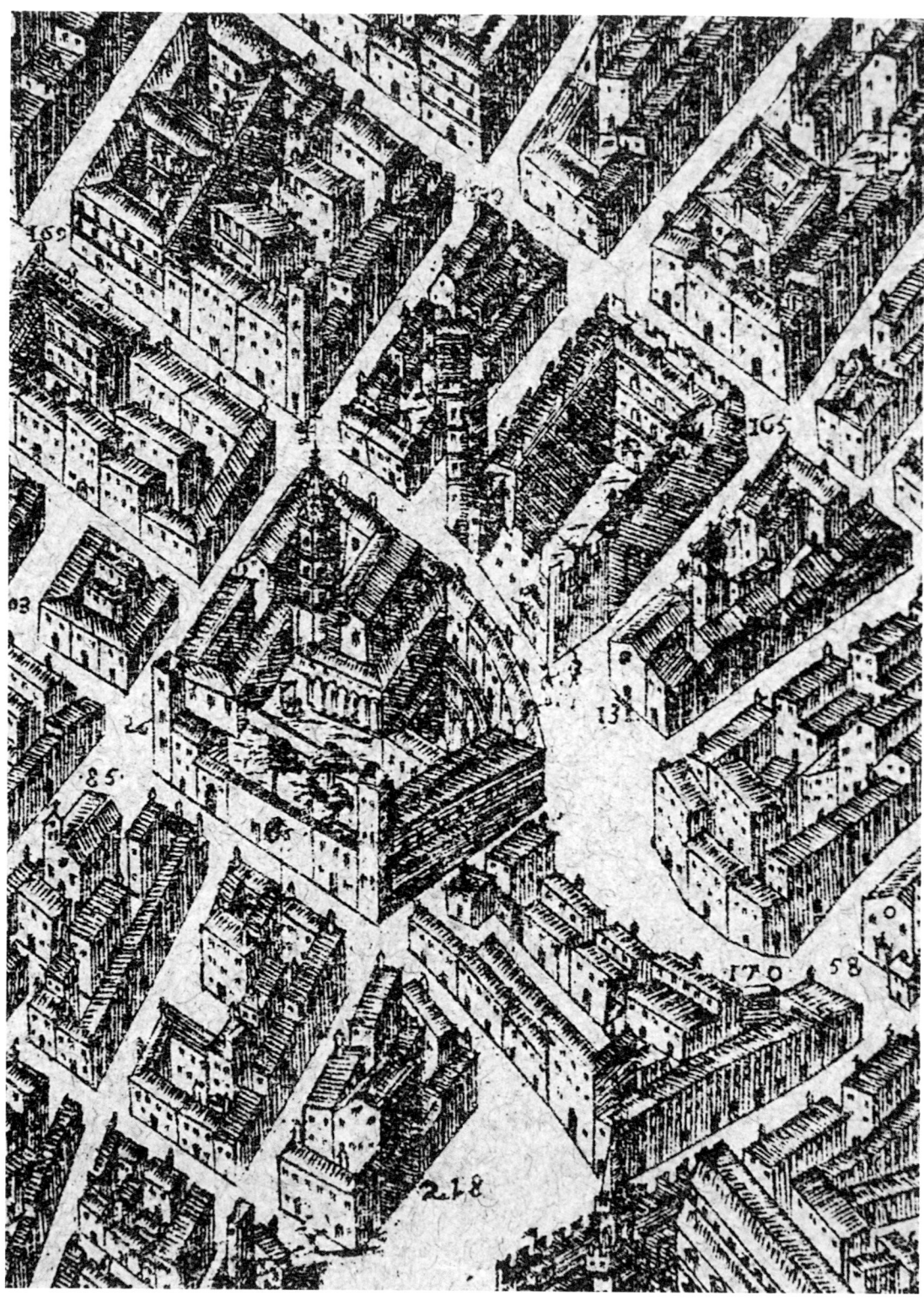

Fig. 60. Detail of Fra Stefano Buonsignori, *View of Florence,* showing the area around Piazza di Sant'Apollinare and the Badia Fiorentina (Ser Piero da Vinci's neighborhood) in 1584. Etching printed on six sheets of glued paper, 1250 × 1380 mm. Gabinetto Disegni e Stampe degli Uffizi, Florence 2614 (st.sc.)

NEW LIGHT ON LEONARDO'S FLORENTINE PATRONS

ALESSANDRO CECCHI

A S LEONARDO'S HORIZONS broadened, this increasingly passionate student of antique art, master of human anatomy, and curious investigator of nature came to command the most varied of artistic techniques employed in Florentine drawing of the second half of the quattrocento—a feat unimaginable in the first half of the century. The ground for this innovation was prepared by the workshops of Antonio and Piero del Pollaiuolo and of Andrea del Verrocchio, which, with exceptional versatility, strove to meet the demands of increasingly exacting, cultured, and refined patrons. Besides paintings, sculpture, and work in precious metals, these workshops provided drawings for embroidery and for banners and decorations for banquets, festivals, and jousts.[1] Leonardo entered Verrocchio's workshop in the 1460s and was deeply influenced by the Pollaiuolo brothers throughout his first Florentine period (see cat. nos. 1–6, 9–11).

Leonardo's career as a painter seems to be studded with unfulfilled commissions: works not even begun, others left at the planning stage or barely outlined, and still others marred by technical failure. This makes the surviving preparatory drawings in the artist's vast graphic production all the more precious. They are singular documents of what might be defined as genius made ineffectual owing to interests too vast.

Some of Leonardo's drawings, perhaps only those most refined, those finished for presentation, were, apparently, left with his patrons, public or private. These works are astonishing in their intelligence and inventiveness, and they make one regret the artist's failure to realize the intended paintings, including the *Adoration of the Magi* for the Augustinian Canonici Regolari of San Donato a Scopeto (Uffizi, Florence), which was for some time in the possession of the Benci family (figs. 10, 11; see cat. nos. 27–32, 36–40 for related drawings), and the *Saint Jerome* (cat. no. 46) of unknown patronage.[2] One likewise laments the incompletion of, for example, the *Battle of Anghiari*, which was left as a small, ruined painted fragment on one of the walls of the Sala del Maggior Consiglio in the Palazzo Vecchio, a monument to genius and unfinishedness (for related drawings, see cat. nos. 81–88, 90, 91).

In many cases, Leonardo did not get beyond the stage of a cartoon (full-scale drawing) for his paintings, as with the *Virgin and Child with Saints Anne and John the Baptist* in the National Gallery, London (fig. 17), one of three versions of the subject mentioned in contemporary letters. And when he did manage to bring such celebrated works as *Leda and the Swan* to completion, these were destroyed, as if fate wished to vent its rage on the little he had produced in the field of painting and to render the copies made of Leonardo's paintings, and the master's preparatory drawings, that much more valuable. (On the preparatory phase of the *Saint Anne,* see cat. nos. 94–97, 105–9; for *Leda and the Swan,* see cat. nos. 98–100, 134.)

We know about certain projects of his only indirectly, thanks to studies such as the one made for a *Hercules Holding a Club* (cat. no. 101), recently acquired by The Metropolitan Museum of Art, or the *Hercules and the Nemean Lion* (cat. no. 102)—perhaps intended for a sculptural group to counter Michelangelo's *David.*[3] In other cases Leonardo did not disdain to execute occasional drawings such as the lost *Neptune,* a gift to his friend Antonio Segni and mentioned by Vasari, of which the sheet from the Royal Library, Windsor (cat. no. 93), is an early formulation.

Any discussion of Leonardo's drawings entails tracing the commissioning from him of his few ultimately executed or surviving works. And the art historian's task, beyond the stylistic analysis and iconographic interpretation of the works, therefore also involves looking backward, to the past, to the world of contacts and acquaintances which—in a city like Florence, where everyone knew each other—favored Leonardo's rise from a promising assistant in Verrocchio's workshop to an established, independent artist. Much remains to be investigated before we have even a remote picture of the cultural and artistic environment of Florence between the quattrocento and the cinquecento. My work is a start in this direction.

One figure until now unjustly neglected by scholars is the artist's father, the famous notary Ser Piero di Antonio di Guido da Vinci, who early on set up his professional headquarters "within the Palazzo del Podestà of the city of Florence," the present-day Bargello, as attested by one of his first documents, notarized on June 5, 1451, that is, a little less than a year before Leonardo's birth (figs. 60, 61).[4] This was not, however, the only context in which he practiced his profession, as is suggested by the evidence of the documents. At least twenty rows of documents notarized by him are extant in the Archivio di Stato of Florence (ASF), spanning a rather long period of time, from March 20, 1449, to June 26, 1504.[5] The list of documents ends just a few days before Ser Piero met his death at the ripe old age of eighty, according to a note made by his son Leonardo (see Chronology).[6]

Although long officially a resident of Vinci, in the home of his father, Antonio, in the parish of Santa Croce,[7] Ser Piero was quick to move to Florence, where he is known to have been living in 1469 with his brother Francesco in a rented house in Via delle Prestanze, the present-day Via dei Gondi.[8] The documents suggest that in Florence Ser Piero continued to expand his dense web of connections—begun in the 1450s after an early period of activity in the province of Pisa[9]—with laymen and religious orders, and that the Tuscan capital soon became the principal center of his business. He established significant professional ties with the Jewish community, who had chosen him from among various Florentine notaries,[10] as well as with the major Florentine monasteries, whose official notary he thereafter became.

Among the first to avail themselves of his services were the institutions dependent on the Vallombrosian Order, such as, in an

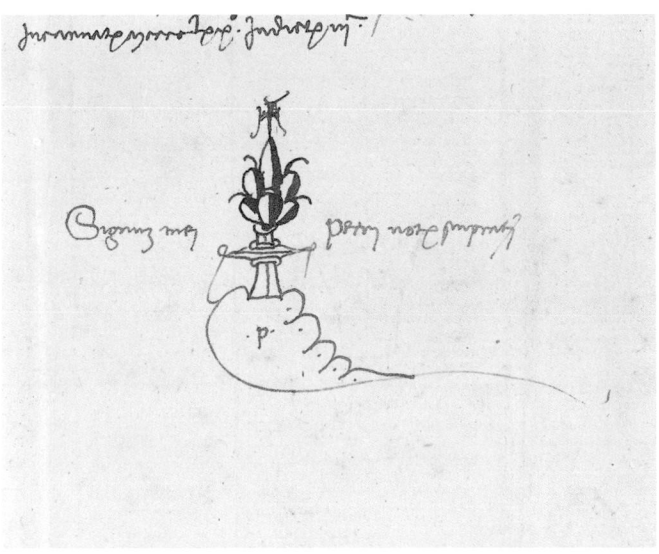

Fig. 61. Ser Piero da Vinci's emblem as a notary. Notarile Antecosimiano 16826, carta 1 recto. Archivio di Stato, Florence

exceptional case, the Badia at Passignano,[11] or the convent of San Giovanni Evangelista outside Porta a Faenza—destroyed in 1529 at the time of the siege of Florence—whose official deeds and interests he had always handled.[12] In addition, there were the monasteries of great opulence and prestige, such as the Badia Fiorentina of the "black" Benedictines, whose first deed notarized by Ser Piero dates from September 22, 1453, to be followed by many others till the end of the notary's life in 1504.[13] In fact, Ser Piero was apparently so closely associated with the Badia that he chose it, in 1472, as the site of his and his family's tomb, as attested by the inscriptions bearing this date on the sepulchral lid, which was described by such early authors as Rosselli, Puccinelli, and Dei and has since been lost (fig. 62).[14]

Worthy of mention among the other monasteries recorded in the surviving documents as employers of Ser Piero are San Lorenzo di Monteaguto, also known as the Charterhouse of Florence,[15] and Sant'Apollonia, which made Ser Piero its trusted notary. Others that used his services more intermittently include San Miniato al Monte, the monastery of San Giusto degli Ingesuati outside Porta a Pinti, and San Salvatore of Camaldoli.[16]

From March 22, 1464,[17] Ser Piero began drafting the minutes of the chapters and looking after the interests of the Augustinian Canonici Regolari of the outlying monastery of San Donato a Scopeto. The friars were the future patrons of the unfinished *Adoration of the Magi* (Uffizi, Florence; figs. 10, 11), which in all probability was commissioned from Leonardo thanks to his father's intercession.[18]

On June 24, 1466, the convent of Santa Brigida del Paradiso also appears to have become Ser Piero's steady client,[19] followed, on August 20 of the same year,[20] by the monastery of Santa Maria dei Servi, better known as the Santissima Annunziata, which likewise chose him as the sole overseer of its legal deeds.[21] The *frati* of Santissima Annunziata later provided

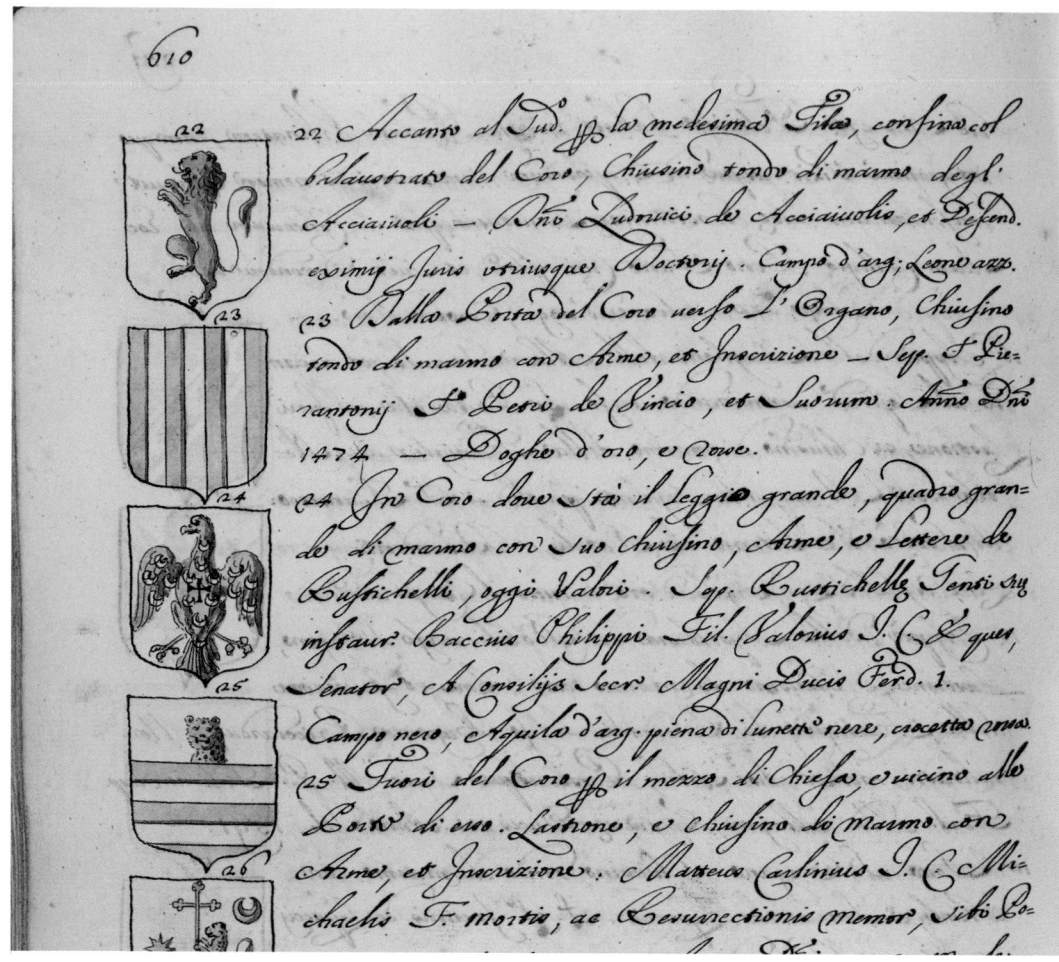

Fig. 62. Coat of arms and inscription on the lid of the funerary monument of Ser Piero da Vinci formerly in the Badia Fiorentina, as recorded in the *Sepoltuario Rosselli*, 1657, vol. 1, Ms. 624, carta 610 recto. Archivio di Stato, Florence

lodging to Leonardo, along with his retinue of pupils and servants, starting on April 3, 1501, if not earlier.[22] In the latter case Ser Piero, who was nearly seventy-two years old and still notary of the Annunziata, certainly did recommend Leonardo, as Giorgio Vasari says, to succeed Filippino Lippi in painting the altarpiece of the main altar.[23]

An examination of the deeds notarized by Ser Piero over the course of his long and busy life reveals quite a few other surprises as well, including confirmation of Vasari's assertion that the sculptor Andrea del Verrocchio was a "good friend" of Ser Piero.[24] Whether Verrocchio was in fact a friend of the notary cannot be known for certain, but Ser Piero did enjoy Verrocchio's trust, since the sculptor, on at least four occasions from 1465 to 1471, turned to him to have documents notarized.

The sculptor and the notary had known each other from at least December 13, 1465, the date of a deed relating to a quarrel arising between "Andrea [son] of the deceased Michele [son of] Francesco, master of sculpture of the parish of Sant'Ambrogio in Florence, on one side, and Maso, carnal brother of the said Andrea and son of the said deceased Michele [son of] Francesco, weaver of cloth,"[25] over their paternal inheritance[26] (their father, Michele, had died on March 10, 1454[27]). Five years later, when it became a question of renting the house inherited from his father, Verrocchio again turned to the father of his assistant Leonardo. On August 15, 1470, Ser Piero, at his house in the parish of Sant'Apollinare in Via delle Prestanze, notarized the rental contract of a house with workshop in the parish of Sant'Ambrogio, "at the corner of Via dell'Agnolo, which is bounded on the first and second sides by a street, on the third, the landlord, on the fourth, Francesco, weaver of cloth," owned by "Andrea son of the deceased Michele son of Francesco, called Andrea del Verrocchio," rented out by him to "Giovanni son of Agnolo son of Giovanni, called Giovanni di Strochardo, of the parish of San Giuliano, pieve of Settimo, county of Florence."[28]

The house "at the corner of Via dell'Agnolo" was, however, to change tenant shortly thereafter, since on August 4 of the following year, Ser Piero at his house in the parish of Sant'Apollinare notarized another rental contract for five years, starting from the first of May next, for 10 florins annually, between "Andrea son of the deceased Michele son of Francesco, called Andrea del Verrocchio, of the parish of San Michele" and "Domenico son of Giovanni son of Ottaviano, weaver of cloth of the parish of San Pietro Maggiore in Florence, and Francesco and Matteo his sons"(fig. 63).[29]

Domenico, however, did not stay long in the house in the parish of Sant'Ambrogio, since, on December 15 of that year, Verrocchio, described in the document as a "scultor," rented it again, this time to a certain "Niccolò son of Tommaso di Mellino, washer of cloths of the parish of Sant'Ambrogio in Florence," with a contract notarized by the same Ser Piero in the parish of Santo Stefano of Sant'Apollinare, and therefore probably again in his own home, which was in that parish.[30]

The contract of August 4, 1471, contains information of great value to us, as it indicates, in passing, that Verrocchio's residence was in the parish of San Michele Visdomini, not that of Sant'Ambrogio, thus implying that he had moved across town—an event that must have occurred after his declaration in the *catasto* (income-tax assessment declaration) of 1469. His new residence was a little house with workshop near the Opera del Duomo which belonged to the Bischeri family (fig. 64). The premises had been previously rented to Donatello and Michelozzo, and Verrocchio was living and working there at the time of his entry in the 1480 *catasto*.[31]

Undoubtedly, the growing number of commissions, especially for sculptural works,[32] which required larger spaces than those needed for the practice of painting, must have quickly compelled Verrocchio to abandon his ancestral home for a new and more appropriate arrangement. Verrocchio's choice of this site had a definite meaning, moreover, emphasizing the continuity between himself and his predecessor Donatello, who was considered the greatest

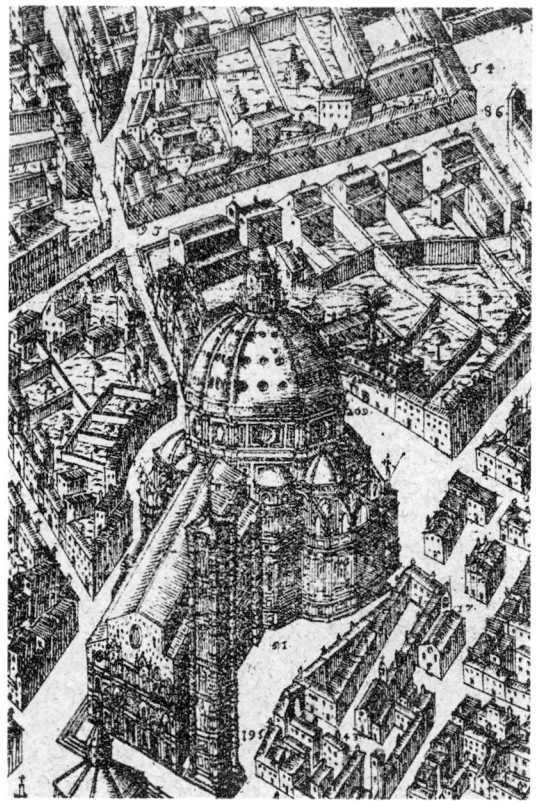

Fig. 63. Detail of Fra Stefano Buonsignori, *View of Florence*, showing the area behind the the cathedral and near the Opera del Duomo in 1584. Etching printed on six sheets of glued paper, 1250 × 1380 mm. Gabinetto Disegni e Stampe degli Uffizi, Florence 2614 (st.sc.)

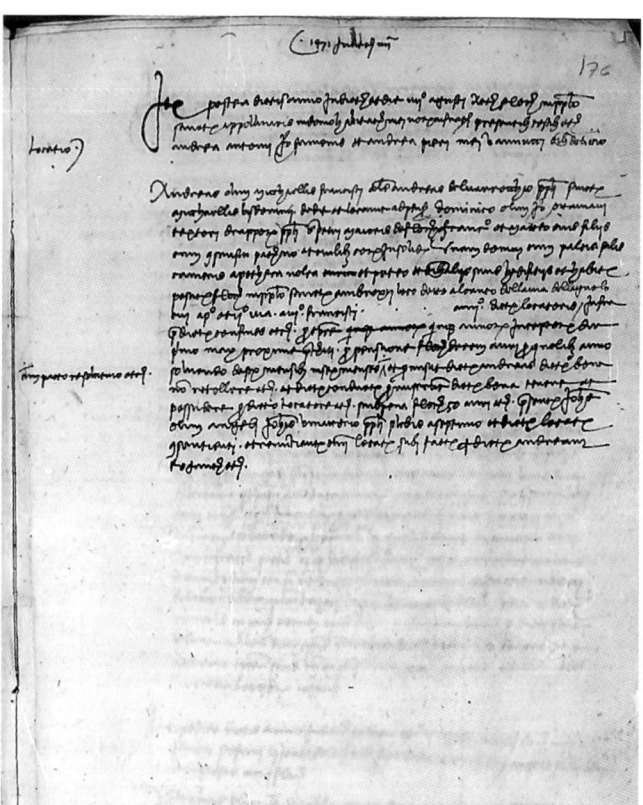

Fig. 64. Contract for the rental of Andrea del Verrocchio's house on August 4, 1471. Notarile Antecosimiano 16828, carta 176 recto. Archivio di Stato, Florence

sculptor of the fifteenth century; this significance was underscored by the favor shown Verrocchio by the Medici.[33] In this light, the knowledge that Leonardo took his first steps as an artist in the famous workshop that had once been Donatello's, in the shadow of Brunelleschi's dome, takes on great importance, as it did for his contemporaries, for it demonstrates the continuation of a glorious artistic tradition.

The friendly relations between Verrocchio and Ser Piero apparently also influenced the notary's already established ties to the Vallombrosian Order, of which Verrocchio's brother Don Simone was an important member and several times abbot of San Salvi and other monasteries observing the rule of San Giovanni Gualberto, as Antonio Natali has shown.[34] Although the order's official notary, to judge by the quantity of deeds notarized, appears to have been Ser Griso di Giovanni Griselli,[35] on October 17, 1468, it fell to Ser Piero to confer legal status upon the gathering of the chapter of monks of San Salvi, all of whom are listed, starting with "Don Simone of Florence, their abbot."[36] He performed the same function again on May 24, 1476, and on October 17, 1478, also during the period of Don Simone's service as abbot.[37] While Verrocchio must have acted as an intermediary between Ser Piero and Don Simone in arranging these occasional assignments for the notary, it is likely that it was the abbot himself, as Antonio Natali has concluded, who commissioned the *Baptism of Christ* (Uffizi, Florence) from Verrocchio, who was assisted on this project by the young Leonardo and others from his workshop (fig. 65).

Verrocchio's is not, however, the only artist's name to appear in the archives alongside Ser Piero's. As the documents vividly confirm, Ser Piero seems to have assisted other artists and craftsmen; these references can be easily overlooked, however, because they are usually unrelated to the professional activity of the artists. Among the recipients of Ser Piero's services the documents give the names of the famous wax-worker "Benintendi, maker of images";[38] a not well known "Bartolomeo son of the deceased Donato di Filippo, painter";[39] an "Andrea di Marco di Simone, sculptor,"

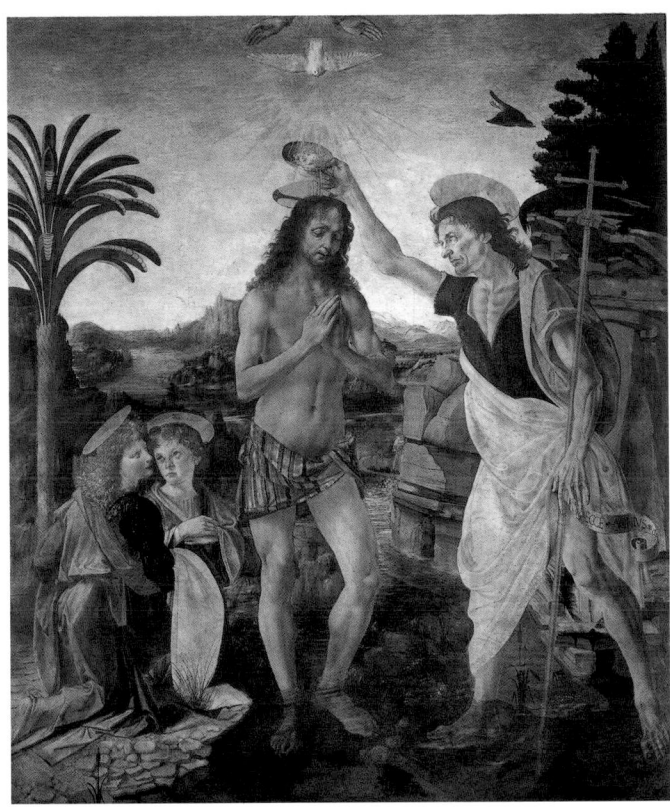

Fig. 65. Andrea del Verrocchio and Leonardo da Vinci (with workshop), *Baptism of Christ* (after cleaning). Oil and tempera on wood, 17.7 × 15.1 cm. Uffizi, Florence 1890 no. 8358

identifiable as Andrea della Robbia;[40] Antonio di Jacopo del Pollaiuolo, goldsmith, and Neri di Bicci di Lorenzo, painter, both engaged in an arbitration on behalf of their colleague the painter Stefano di Antonio di Vanni;[41] Giuliano di Leonardo da Maiano and Giovanni da Gaiole, who on January 18, 1477, appraised a house in the parish of Santa Lucia d'Ognissanti;[42] "Francesco son of Domenico, called Monciatto, woodworker," and "Niccolò son of Francesco delle Tarsie," referees on June 30, 1486, in a legal arbitration;[43] and, finally, "Alessio son of the deceased Baldovinetto, called Baldovinetto, painter," who on November 24, 1479, hired Leonardo's father to oversee the documents of his marriage to "Daria daughter of the said deceased Matteo the son of Migliore de' Guadagni."[44]

Ser Piero also managed to serve the monks of San Bartolomeo di Monteoliveto, though only once, on July 6, 1470 — and therefore a number of years before his son Leonardo was commissioned by the same order to paint an *Annunciation* (Uffizi, Florence; fig. 66).[45] The notary's assignment is attested to by a deed bearing that date and involving Fra Lorenzo di Antonio Salvetti, representative and attorney of that monastery.[46]

Of no significance, in terms of obtaining public commissions for Leonardo, was Ser Piero's employment as notary of the Signoria, which occurred only once, in the months of March and April 1485.[47] The inconsequentiality of this engagement was due either to its brief dura-

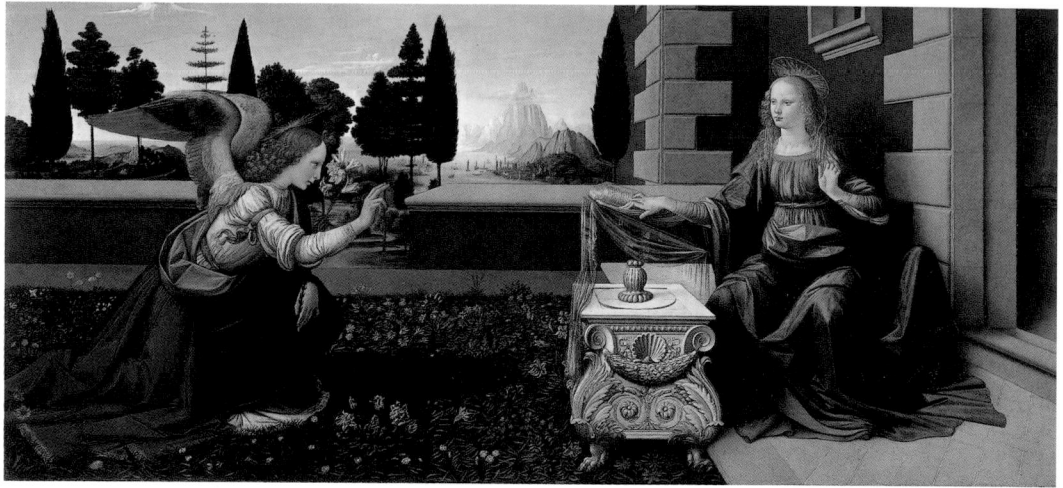

Fig. 66. Leonardo da Vinci, *Annunciation* (after cleaning). Oil on wood, 98 × 217 cm. Uffizi, Florence 1890 no. 1618

tion or to the significant fact that Leonardo at the time was in Milan, in the service of Duke Ludovico Sforza "Il Moro." The artist, indeed, may already have squandered any chance to obtain a commission from the Signoria, after having failed to meet the commitment he had made on January 10, 1478, to replace Piero del Pollaiuolo in painting the altarpiece for the Chapel of San Bernardo in the Palazzo dei Priori, for which on March 16 he had received, as advance payment, 25 florins, which he was of course required to give back.[48]

On that occasion he must have been summoned by one of the new *operai di palazzo* (palace work supervisors) — whose number had increased from three to five for a term of one year by a law of November 1477[49] — rather than by the *priori* or by the *gonfaloniere di giustizia* of the first Signoria, who served for only two months and were not among those whom Leonardo or his father could claim as acquaintances.[50] Lorenzo de' Medici "Il Magnifico" was one of the five new *operai*.[51] Thus we must trace back to him the project to have an altarpiece painted for the San Bernardo Chapel, as well as the decision to commission first Piero del Pollaiuolo, on December 24, 1477, and, later, Leonardo for this work.[52]

During Leonardo's years in Florence, from his entry into Verrocchio's workshop about 1469–70 — an event facilitated, as we have seen, by Verrocchio's close relationship with Ser Piero — up to his departure in 1482–83 for Milan, where the artist went to serve Ludovico Sforza "Il Moro," only one public religious commission, as far as we know, was independently fulfilled by Leonardo: the *Annunciation* formerly in San Bartolomeo di Monteoliveto and now in the Uffizi (fig. 66). The one other undertaking was the monumental *Adoration of the Magi* for San Donato a Scopeto — the most significant project of Leonardo's early career; it was destined to remain unfinished (figs. 10, 11). Leonardo obtained the commission, in all probability, thanks to the good offices of his father, notary of the Canonici and a dependable, scrupulous, and precise person, to judge even from the appearance of the deeds and the clear handwriting on them.

After having been granted the commission for the *Adoration* in March of 1481, and having received various sums—including for the painting of the monastery's clock (*uriolo*)—Leonardo apparently did not hesitate to abandon the altarpiece at an early stage of work; as we can still see today, only the underdrawing and underpainting with washes were executed on the wood panel. It put his father, who must have vouched for his son, in a terribly embarrassing predicament.[53] According to Vasari, the work remained "in the house of Amerigo Benci opposite the loggia of the Peruzzi," most likely in late 1482 or early 1483, when Leonardo left Florence for Milan. It was later moved to an unknown location as documented in 1568, at the moment of the Giunti publication of Giorgio Vasari's *Vite de' più eccellenti pittori, scultori ed architettori* (Lives of the most eminent painters, sculptors, and architects).[54]

The choice of this Florentine family as caretakers of the great panel he perhaps intended to complete later is an indication of the familiarity and friendship that existed between Leonardo and the Benci del Sanna family, who were among the most important citizens of the Santa Croce quarter. For some time, between 1458 and 1465, they were also clients of Leonardo's father, who was trustee of legal documents for Bartolomeo, Niccolò, Donato, Amerigo, and Francesco—sons of Giovanni di Amerigo Benci (1394–mid-July 1455). On May 13, 1460, at the home of Amerigo di Giovanni Benci, Ser Piero drafted the last will and testament of Maddalena Bandini Baroncelli, widow of Giovanni di Amerigo Benci. He later drafted and notarized, on April 9 and 27, 1465, respectively, at the Benci home in the parish of San Jacopo fra' Fossi, a letter of attorney for Amerigo di Giovanni Benci and a deed on behalf of Francesco di Giovanni di Amerigo, his brother.[55]

After having directed, respectively, the affiliates of the Medici Bank in Geneva and Avignon,[56] Amerigo di Giovanni (1432–1468) and his brother Francesco left their posts, most likely because of disagreements with the Medici. They settled in Florence in the parish of San Jacopo fra' Fossi, in the Gonfalone Lion Nero of the Santa Croce quarter, in the "two houses located in the Via degli Alberti that are bounded first by a street, second, Pagola della Casa, third Bartolomeo Gianfigl[i]azzi, fourth Francesco Dini, which houses were taken in payment from Francesco son of Altobianco degli Alberti for 5,300 florins at the Palazzo del Podestà on June 13, 1462, in the declaration or first *catasto* [of 1427] in . . . of which we have made a house for our residence." The houses were recorded in the 1469 *catasto* declaration of the family, registered among the taxpayers of the Vaio Gonfalon of the San Giovanni quarter.[57] The structures were probably later transformed into the building identifiable at number 16 of the actual via de' Benci.[58]

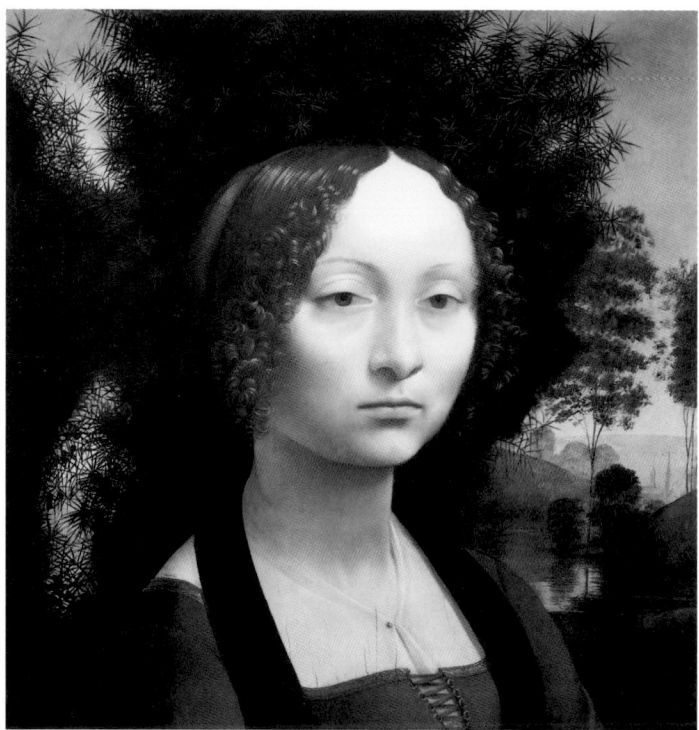

Fig. 67. Leonardo da Vinci, *Portrait of Ginevra de' Benci* (after cleaning). Oil on wood, obverse 38.8 × 36.7 cm (reverse 38.2 × 36.7 cm). National Gallery of Art, Washington D.C.; Ailsa Mellon Bruce Fund 2326

It was not with Amerigo—who was long dead by 1481 and buried in the family tomb in the little church of Santissima Annunziata delle Murate, run by Benedictine nuns[59]—that Leonardo had dealings, but with his firstborn, Giovanni (1456–1523). In 1469 and 1480 Giovanni was living in the two aforementioned houses with the various members of his entourage, that is, his mother, Mona Antonia di Lorenzo Cresci (ca. 1438–1484); his brother Carlo (b. 1458); his sisters Ginevra (1457–by 1521), Margherita, Marietta (married to Antonio di Tommaso di Jacopo Nori), Nannina, and Lucrezia (married to Francesco Scali); his uncles Francesco, Bartolomeo (ca. 1440–1518), Niccolò, and Donato di Giovanni Benci; Mona Ginevra di Niccolò di Piero Capponi (married to Francesco in 1456); Mona Maddalena (widow of Giovanni Benci) and her grandmother (b. 1415); Mona Maria, sister of Giovanni Benci; Ghostanza and Piero di Francesco Benci; Luigi di Nicholo Benci, Benci di Miniato Benci (b. 1414); Marco di Marco Strozzi, and entire vast progeny.[60]

It must have been Giovanni's uncle Bartolomeo—the oldest of Giovanni di Amerigo's sons—who, as head of the family and proprietor of the most important entry in the 1480 *catasto*[61] (in which the descendants of his brother Amerigo di Giovanni were also registered, among others), oversaw the negotiations for the marriage of Giovanni's sister Ginevra to Luigi di Bernardo di Lapo Niccolini (1442–1505), which were concluded on January 15, 1474, with the nuptial contract notarized by Ser Simone Grazzini da Staggia.[62] On the other hand, in all likelihood it was through Giovanni's mediation that Leonardo, at a date not long before the marriage,[63] received, most probably from Bernardo Bembo (1433–1519), humanist and Venetian ambassador to the Florentine Republic, the commission to portray Ginevra in a painting Vasari called "a most beautiful thing."[64] The work is now in the National Gallery, Washington, D.C. (fig. 67).[65] For a drawing that may be related to this painting, see catalogue number 23.

The exquisite plant allegory adorning the back of the portrait of Ginevra de' Benci, with wreaths of laurel and palm intertwined around a juniper and linked by a scroll displaying the motto "Virtutem forma decorat" (Virtue adorned by form), bears eloquent witness to the refined cultural climate surrounding the scarcely seventeen-year-old bride. She was celebrated for her virtues by Bembo, remembered in an anecdote by Angelo Poliziano, and made the dedicatory object of two sonnets by Lorenzo de' Medici "Il Magnifico."[66] This cultural climate, one might add, was experienced firsthand by the members of this branch of the Benci family. Indeed, as early as 1462, Amerigo, author of a number of spiritual lauds and sonnets,[67] made a gift of a codex "in cloth fiber" of several Platonic dialogues to Marsilio Ficino, having attended, with his nephews Tommaso and Giovanni di Lorenzo Benci, the lessons of the Accademia Platonica.[68] And his son Giovanni must not have been any less remarkable, having well-demonstrated, vast literary[69] and scientific interests that ranged as far as veterinary medicine, as witnessed by his possession of the ancient *Liber de medicina veterinaria* by the Calabrian author Giordano Rufo, a veterinary physician of the court of Frederick II.[70] Benci's interest in this discipline, it must be said, had a personal aspect, for Giovanni was a superb horseman and used to ride about Florence, richly decked out, on purebred steeds dearly purchased. These included the Barbary horse for which he paid the enormous sum of six hundred florins, creating a general scandal in a businesslike, parsimonious city.[71]

Between Leonardo and Giovanni, who was four years his junior and the wealthy scion of a cultured family, there must have been a special relationship of friendship and confidence for the artist first to have entrusted him with the large unfinished *Adoration*—one wonders, given the panel's considerable size, whether the artist hadn't perhaps taken advantage of his friend's hospitality to work on it in a room in the latter's palazzo, which was, in any case, quite populous, as we have seen—and later to have exchanged books and scientific tools with him, including a map of the world. One may deduce as much from the numerous times in which Benci's name appears in the Codex Atlanticus, in hurried notes that nevertheless eloquently express their relations: "a book of Giovanni Benci"; "my world map which is with Giovanni Be[n]ci"; "Benci's map of the world"; "Giovanni Benci, my book, jaspers, brass for eyeglasses."[72]

We do not know what instructions Leonardo gave regarding the San Donato altarpiece (figs. 10, 11) and any other objects belonging to him that he may have left with Giovanni at the time of his departure for France in 1517. Presumably he would have left everything to his friend, as tokens of remembrance. Upon Benci's death six years later, on September 9, 1523,[73] the painting, along with whatever else there was, most likely passed to Amerigo (1498–after 1560),[74] his firstborn son, who was perhaps the same Amerigo in whose house the *Adoration* remained until 1568.

In the same quarter of Santa Croce and the same Gonfalone Lion Nero lived another friend of Leonardo's, the until now mysterious Antonio Segni, remembered by history for the magnificent gifts he received from Leonardo and Botticelli, as recorded by Vasari.

According to Vasari's *Vite*, Leonardo gave Segni, his "very good friend," a drawing he had made of a "Neptune, drafted so well and with such diligence that he looked utterly alive. One could see the stormy sea and his chariot pulled by sea horses, with Phantoms, Monsters and Winds, and a few very beautiful heads of sea Gods" (see cat. no. 93).[75] Along with this sheet Segni received the famous painting of *Calumny* (Uffizi, Florence), executed by Botticelli presumably in the 1490s.[76] Leonardo's sheet was lost after Segni's son Fabio gave it in turn to Giovanni Gaddi.

This Segni has been identified incorrectly until now as Antonio di Carlo Segni, a Florentine pontifical minter in Rome from the late quattrocento.[77] He is instead Antonio di Neri di Antonio di Segna Guidi, the descendant of a family of armorers, who later practiced the profession of retail dealer or broker in silk (*setaiuolo a minuto*)[78] and lived in the San Remigio parish of the Gonfalone Lion Nero of the Santa Croce quarter. His father, Neri, had been a prominent person in the Florence of his day, having been a member of the Signori and Collegi on more than one occasion.[79] There is therefore no explanation for the absolute absence of official posts for Antonio, who was born on May 8, 1457, and is included in the lists of those eligible for posts.[80] Based on his entry in the 1480 *catasto*, he was living at the time with his mother, Nanna di Piero Angelini, widow of Neri; his sister Marietta possessed of a dowry of 800 florins in assets; and a serving girl in the father's house with cottage, carrying out occasional professional activity, as he himself affirms: "I do not stay at a shop, I habitually go to the vault at the bank of the Bartolini."[81]

The little confirmed information we have on him to date stops with that provided in his tax declaration (the Decima Repubblicana) of 1498, which shows that he is not particularly affluent, that he conducts no professional activity, and resides, with his sister Lisabetta, in half of the house registered in the 1470 and 1480 *catasti*, the other half having been rented out to his brother-in-law the physician Francesco di Jacopo Rampini d'Asti, who also bought the remaining plot of family land.[82] Segni's marriage the following year to Francesca di Bartolo Corsi, who belonged to one of the prominent families in the district, must have won him greater prestige. Their union was blessed, three years later, on November 1, 1502, by the birth of their firstborn son, Fabio, the future man of letters and friend of Vasari.[83]

As we have seen, the information we have on Antonio is not nearly enough to corroborate Vasari's assertion that he was a friend of Botticelli and Leonardo. We may plausibly hypothesize that Segni fell out of favor in Florence—and was therefore excluded from official positions of the sort his father had held—because he was a victim of one of the many purges of real or presumed enemies conducted after the advent in 1494 of the republic led by Girolamo Savonarola. Segni already might have chosen the path of sea trade, far from his native city, if he is indeed to be identified with the same Antonio Segni, citizen of Florence, who, together with two associates, was granted on November 12, 1493, a safe-conduct by the doge of the Republic of Genoa, Agostino Adorno.[84] If we assume this familiarity with the sea on his part, then it was probably to him that Niccolò Machiavelli turned, in 1502, at the time of his first Roman legation, when seeking to take on in the employ of the Florentine Republic the Genoese captain Mottino, whose ships were later used to break up the flow of supplies to a Pisa under siege.[85] Segni may have met a tragic end, tortured and ultimately put to death by the Medici some time before September 13, 1512.[86]

Such information as the above may serve to explain Leonardo's gift of the Neptune drawing to a landlocked Florentine, for whom it would have seemed out of context, as the god, since antiquity, had been the tutelary deity of navigators and protector of sea trade—of the sort in which Segni perhaps was engaged. However, the gift of a painting such as Botticelli's *Calumny* can be explained only, in my opinion, as an act motivated by a personal association.

Aside from Giovanni Benci and Antonio Segni, Leonardo also had ties with Piero di Braccio di Domenico Martelli (1468–1525), the patron, according to Vasari,[87] of the painter-sculptor Giovan Francesco Rustici, when he was involved in the creation of the bronze group of Saint John the Baptist preaching to a Levite and a Pharisee for Florence's Baptistery (1506–11). Leonardo was staying with Martelli when, on March 22, 1508, he began the notebook of mathematical and physics notations in the Codex Arundel.[88] His host, a member of a perpetually pro-Medici family, seems to have been one of the family's most prominent cultural figures in the early cinquecento and, after a period of study under Francesco da Diacceto, continued to frequent the master even in his mature years, taking part in the literary, historical, political, and philosophical discussions that were held from 1513 to 1522 in the Orti Oricellari, presided over by Bernardo Rucellai and animated by the most eminent men of culture of the age.[89]

When in 1517 Leonardo, at the age of sixty-five, left Italy for good to serve the king of France, he probably had no regrets, being the citizen of the world that he was. But he would miss, forever after, that world of acquaintances that had surrounded him since his youth and in which he had been educated, as well as the constant, invaluable support of his father—dead thirteen years earlier—and the people his father frequented, who had become Leonardo's friends and patrons.

1. See Brown 1998b, pp. 5–21.
2. It has been hypothesized that this commission was connected with the Florentine Badia since the commission for the San Donato *Adoration*, like that for the Uffizi *Saint Jerome,* was later fulfilled by Filippino Lippi. The Uffizi *Saint Jerome* is known to come from the Badia (Cecchi 1988, p. 70 n. 10).
3. Bambach 2001.
4. "[I]nfra pallatio potestatis civitatis florentie."ASF, Notarile Antecosimiano 16823, c. 53r.
5. From 1455 to 1457, Ser Piero frequently notarized "in popolo Sancti Stefani Abbatie florentine in apotheca residentia mei notari infrascripti" (in the Saint Stephen's Abbey parish of Florence in the office-residence of undersigned notary), which leads one to think that, like many other notaries, he rented a shop from the

Badia. Sometimes, though more rarely, he notarized documents in the Palazzo dei Priori; he did so more frequently in the Palazzo del Podestà, and in his own home or in that of his client, whether lay or religious (ASF, Notarile Antecosimiano 16840, cc. n.n.).

6. "[O]n Wednesday, July 9, 1504, at 7 o'clock, Ser Piero da Vinci, notary at the Palazzo del Podestà, and my father, died. He was 80 years old, left behind ten male children and two females." Autograph note by Leonardo in the British Museum, London, Codex Arundel 263 Plut CLXV; see Uzielli 1872, p. 73 n., and Richter 1970, vol. 2, p. 344 nn. 1372–73.

7. This is borne out by the father Antonio's entries in the *catasto* for August 15, 1451 and 1457 (see Uzielli 1872, docs. I and II, pp. 139–44).

8. *Catasto* of 1469; see Uzielli 1872, pp. 145–47. The house was near the Palazzo del Podestà, where he notarized many of his documents; the seat of the Arte dei Giudici or Proconsul in the present-day Via del Proconsolo; and the Badia Fiorentina, which he chose as the site of the family tombs.

9. Uzielli 1872, pp. 43, 46–47.

10. Luzzati 1987, p. 433 n. 30. This article was kindly brought to my attention by Andrea Bruscino, to whom I express my thanks. In the same note one finds the mention—which has eluded prior Leonardo scholars—of the loan of one lira and fourteen *soldi* which the artist obtained from the Jewish bank of Empoli on November 22, 1478.

11. We know of only one deed notarized for this monastery, on August 11, 1457 (ASF, Notarile Antecosimiano 16823, c. n.n.).

12. The first document we know of dates from February 26, 1451, 1452, s.c. (see ASF, Notarile Antecosimiano 16823, c. 87r) and the last from 1498 (ASF, Notarile Antecosimiano 16837, c. 931).

13. ASF, Notarile Antecosimiano 16823, c. 142v.

14. ASF, Ms. 624, *Sepoltuario fiorentino ovvero Descrizione delle chiese cappelle e sepolture loro armi et inscrizioni della città di Firenze e suoi contorni fatta da Stefano Rosselli, MDCLVII*, vol. 1, c. 610: "23. By the Choir Door near the Organ the round marble sepulchral lid with arms and the inscription—Sep. Ser Pierantonij Ser Petri de Vincio et Suorum. Anno Domini 1474—Golden and red pales." In 1664 the tomb marker was located in the Capitolo Nuovo of the Badia Fiorentina (see Puccinelli 1664, vol. 5, p. 23 n. 129); in the eighteenth century it was moved into the cloister: "in the Badia, on the western wall of the cloister, round marble sepulchral lids with arms of red marble and bronze, with around it the writing: 'SS. Petr Antonii S.Petri de Vincio et suorum A.D. 1472'" (Uzielli 1872, pp. 64, 109–11; Beltrami 1919a, doc. 6, p. 3). The notary was buried there on July 10, 1504: "Ser Piero da Vinci on day 10 laid to rest in Badia" (ASF, Arte dei Medici e Speziali 247, c. 186r).

15. The church and monastery, dedicated to Saint Lawrence, are located on a picturesque hill, called Monte Acuto, near the village of Galluzzo (see Repetti 1833–46, vol. 1, p. 672). The first deed for San Lorenzo di Monteaguto dates from July 28, 1457 (ASF, Notarile Antecosimiano 16823, c. n.n.). Its mayor (*sindaco*) and procurator, from December 17, 1490, was apparently "Domino Leonardus Johannis Bonafe de Florentia monacus" (ASF, Notarile Antecosimiano 16835, cc. 246v, 257r, 272v, 284r, 287v, 297v–298r and v), the future hospital director of Santa Maria Nuova, the guarantor for Leonardo da Vinci on May 30, 1506, the eve of his departure for Milan (Beltrami 1919a, p. 110 n. 176).

16. ASF, Notarile Antecosimiano 16823, cc. 330r and v, 350r, 380r.

17. ASF, Notarile Antecosimiano 16824, cc. 186r–195v.

18. Cecchi 1988, p. 70 n. 8.

19. ASF, Notarile Antecosimiano 16834, cc. 205r–209v.

20. Ibid., cc. 210r and v.

21. Of particular importance among these are the papers concerning the granting, on September 7, 1470, of the Tribune's patronage to Giovanfrancesco Gonzaga, marquis of Mantua, in the presence of Francesco di Simone di Giovanni, stonecutter from the parish of San Michele; Giovanni di Leonardo di Antonio, carpenter from

the parish of San Lorenzo; and Tommaso Ridolfi (ASF, Notarile Antecosimiano 16828, cc. 53v–57r, 58r; other pertinent papers in ASF, Notarile Antecosimiano 16829, cc. 24, 31, and ff.) These documents are not mentioned in Brown 1981.

22. In May of 1470, Ser Piero was paid by the brothers of the Santissima Annunziata for service as "prochurator della casa," performed the previous year (Uzielli 1872, doc. IV, p. 148; Beltrami 1919a, doc. 4, p. 3).

23. Nelson 1997, pp. 86–87.

24. Vasari 1966– , vol. 4, pp. 16–17.

25. "Andrea olim Michaellis Francisci magister sculture populi Sancti Ambroxii de Florentia per una et Masius frater carnalis dicti Andreae et filius dicti olim michellis francisci textor drapporum." Tommaso must have been born in 1439, taking the name of a brother who died at a tender age sometime after 1433 (ASF, Catasto 41, Quartiere di Santa Croce, Gonfalone Ruote, c. 150; Covi 1987, p. 160 nn. 5, 6).

26. ASF, Notarile Antecosimiano 16826, c. 87v. To settle the controversy, it became necessary to appoint an arbitrator, the painter Pier Francesco di Bartolomeo from the parish of San Jacopo fra' Fossi, who would draft an award by the following December 15 (ibid., cc. 87v–89v).

27. Carl 1982, pp. 140–41, 154 n. 118.

28. "[S]uper angulo via dellagnolo cui aprimo et secondo via, IIIo locatoris, a IIII francisci textoris drapporum . . . Andreas olim Michaellis Francisci alias Andrea del Verrocchio . . . Johanni olim Angeli Johannis vocato ser G[i]ovanni di Strochardo [?] populi Santi Juliani plebis septimi comitatis florentie" (ASF, Notarile Antecosimiano 16828, cc. 43v–44r). It could not have been a question of another house, bought by Michele from the Compagnia del Tempio and registered among the alienated possessions in the *catasto* entry for 1470 as having been granted in dowry by the father to Verrocchio's sister Apollonia (Cruttwell 1904, doc. II, pp. 236–38; Passavant 1959, doc. IV, pp. 217–18). From the description, it seems plausible that Verrocchio had rented out half the house, reserving the other half with workshop for himself and his assistants. One gathers as much from the cited entry from 1470, in which the tenant was, however, one "Nicholo di . . . sta choglioficiali del monte." The artist had already been called "del Verrocchio" in a payment document for *Christ and Saint Thomas* dating from January 15, 1466, 1467 s.c. (Covi 1987, pp. 158, 160 n. 23).

29. "[I]n loco detto alcanto dellavia dellagnolo . . . Andreas olim Micchaellis Francisci alias andrea delverrocchio populi sancti michaellis bisdomini . . . Dominico olim Io[hannis] Ottaviani textori drapporum populi sancti petri maioris de Florentia et Francisco et Mattio eius filiis."ASF, Notarile Antecosimiano 16828, c. 176r.

30. Ibid., c. 205r.

31. "Nicholao Thomasii di Mellino purgatori populi Sancti Ambroxii de Florentina." The house of Verrocchio "posta nel popolo di Santo Ambruogio di Firenze in sul chanto della via dellagniolo da primo via 1/2 rede di Pagholo di Domenico Lanino terzo rede di Piergianni 1/4 messer Dietaiuti chalonico" was at this date rented for twelve *fiorini di suggello* to one "Giovanni di Bartolommeo, grocer"; Verrochio rented, from "Ghuglielmo Bischeri, deacon," the house with workshop formerly rented by Donatello (Del Badia 1886; Passavant 1959, doc. V, pp. 218–19; Procacci 1968, pp. 13–14; Caglioti 2000, app. IV, doc. 33, p. 428). Evidence of the rental can also be found in the 1480 *catasto* entry for Battista di Giovanni di Nofri Bischeri: "It is currently held in rent by Andrea di Michele, chiseler known as Andrea del Verrocchio, for 16 florins" (ASF, Catasto 1024, cc. 387r and v).

32. In 1461, he was competing to furnish the sculptural decoration for a chapel in Orvieto cathedral, and by the end of 1466, he had won from the Tribunale della Mercatanzia the commission for the bronze group *Christ and Saint Thomas* at Orsanmichele; later still, by October of 1467, he was sculpting the tombstone of Cosimo de' Medici "Il Vecchio" in San Lorenzo and providing Luca della Robbia and Michelozzo with part of the bronze used for the door of the cathedral's Sagrestia delle Messe or Sacristy of Masses; in 1468, he won the commission for the great gilt-bronze ball for the lantern of Brunelleschi's dome, executed before May of 1471, probably at the Opera del Duomo's worksite, if not earlier, in the workshop of Bischeri, which was adjacent thereto. To this activity as sculptor, which reached its apex with the tomb of Piero and Giovanni de'

Medici in the Old Sacristy of San Lorenzo (1470–72), Verrocchio—defined, in the deed of his enrollment in the Compagnia di San Luca, in the dual role of "painter and carver"—added that of painter. He executed the standard of Lorenzo de' Medici "Il Magnifico" for the joust in honor of Lucrezia Donati, tried the following year to obtain the commission for some of the *Virtues* begun by Piero Pollaiuolo for the audience hall of the Tribunale della Mercatanzia, and oversaw, at the Medicis' behest, the pomp and display for the solemn entry into Florence of Galeazzo Maria Sforza, duke of Milan, as well as making the standard of Giuliano de' Medici for the 1475 joust in honor of Simonetta Vespucci (Passavant 1969, pp. 5–7).

33. In his *De Sculptura*, published in Florence in 1504, Pomponio Gaurico had already defined the late Verrocchio as an "aeumulus" of Donatello (Passavant 1969, p. 7).

34. Don Simone, then a Vallombrosian at San Salvi, is remembered in the will of Michele di Francesco Cioni, father of Verrocchio, dated March 4, 1453, 1454 s.c. He was apparently abbot of that monastery several times, in 1464 and for a few months in 1465, again on December 1, 1468, then from 1471 to 1473, and again from 1475 to 1478, only to assume the same office in 1479 at San Pancrazio in Florence. He again became abbot of San Salvi in 1481; see Natali 1998, p. 94 n. 62; Natali 1998a, pp. 269–70, 272 nn. 44–59. On September 5, 1487, with his brother absent, having gone to work on the equestrian monument of Bartolomeo Colleoni in Venice, Don Simone represented him as proxy (Carl 1982, no. 1, p. 154 n. 120; Covi 1987, pp. 157, 160).

35. ASF, Notarile Antecosimiano, 10045–10048, and ASF, Corporazioni Religiose soppresse dal Governo Francese 89, filza 49, Ricordanze relative ai beni di San Salvi dal 1469 al 1478, cited by Natali 1998, p. 94 n. 62, and Natali 1998a, p. 272.

36. ASF, Notarile Antecosimiano 16827, cc. 90r–91v, 137r.

37. ASF, Notarile Antecosimiano 16831, cc. 66r–66v, 68r and v; ASF, Notarile Antecosimiano 16829, file dated 1470–81, actually miscellaneous, with documents relating to the entire range of Ser Piero's work as a notary, especially for San Salvi, from 1478 to 1494, cc. 80r–84v, 627v–631r, 838, 846–47, 849, 851; ASF, Notarile Antecosimiano 16833, cc. 245, 247, 447, 451, 452, 536, 551.

38. "Benintendi fale[i]magini." A "Niccholaus olim Benintendi falemagini" (Niccolò son of Benintendi, image maker) rented a shop on October 16, 1454, with a contract notarized by Ser Piero (ASF, Notarile Antecosimiano 16823, cc. 170r–171r); Piero was again the guarantor of the agreement between "Zanobi Benintendi fa leimagine" (Zanobio Benintendi, maker of images) and the Servites of the Santissima Annunziata, for whom Zanobio made ex-voto images in wax, on November 5, 1484 (ASF, Notarile Antecosimiano 16829, cc. 374v–376v).

39. "Bartolomeus olim donati filippi pittor." The document is dated July 31, 1460 (ASF, Notarile Antecosimiano 16825, cc. 146r and v).

40. "Andreas Marci Simonis scultor populi santi laurentii." The deed was drafted on October 19, 1461 (ASF, Notarile Antecosimiano 16825, c. 199r).

41. The two were summoned on November 30, 1465, to pronounce their opinions on an altarpiece painted by Stefano d'Antonio for the chapel of Felice di Simone Salvucci in San Pietro di Cascia, on which they made a detailed report (ASF, Notarile Antecosimiano 16826, cc. 83r–84v, 86r).

42. ASF, Notarile Antecosimiano 16831, cc. 186r–187r.

43. "Franciscus Dominici vocato monc[i]atto legnaiuolus populi Sancti Michaellis Vice Dominorum de Florentie et Niccholaus Francisci delletarsie populi Sancte Trinitatis de Florentie." ASF, Notarile Antecosimiano 16834, cc. 263r–264r.

44. "Alexius olim Baldovinetti, alias ilbaldovinettis pictor . . . Daria filia dicti olim Mathei Migloris de Guadagnis" (ASF, Notarile Antecosimiano 16832, cc. 361r and v, 375r–377r). The marriage contract was not known to Kennedy (1938, pp. 185, 231 n. 383). Baldovinetti apparently again used Ser Piero's services for a document drafted between 1493 and 1495 (ASF, Notarile Antecosimiano 16836, c. 274).

45. For doubts about the original location of the painting in San Bartolomeo di Monteoliveto, see Natali 2000, pp. 37–40, 55 n. 2, 56 n. 36.

46. ASF, Notarile Antecosimiano, 16828, c. 36r.

47. He was chosen by lot as the notary for the Santo Spirito quarter (Marzi 1910, vol. 2, app. I, p. 505).

48. ASF, Signori e Collegi. Deliberazioni in forza di ordinaria aurtorità 94, cc. 5v, 27r, published in Beltrami 1919a, docs. 10, 11, pp. 5–6.

49. On the Operai di Palazzo, see Rubinstein 1995, app. X, pp. 118–21.

50. That Signoria was made up of Lorenzo di Antonio Ridolfi and Francesco di Antonio Antinori for the Santo Spirito quarter; Alessandro di Francesco, "fornaciaio" (kiln owner), and Salvi di Bartolo, "galigaio" (chicken merchant), for the Santa Croce quarter; Jacopo di Dino Gucci and Mariotto di Marco alla Palla, "speziale" (spice seller) for the Santa Maria Novella quarter; Conte di Bartolomeo Pecori and Apollonio di Giovanni Baldovini for the San Giovanni quarter; and Berlinghieri di Francesco Berlinghieri Gonfaloniere di Giustizia for the Santa Croce quarter (ASF, Priorista di Palazzo, c. 214r).

51. The others were Tommaso Ridolfi, Francesco Dini, Antonio de' Nobili, and Francesco Romoli (see Rubinstein 1995, p. 120). Ser Piero had notarized a number of documents concerning Lorenzo di Piero de' Medici (ASF, Notarile Antecosimiano 16829, cc. 265, 268–69, 273).

52. Rubinstein 1995, p. 59 n. 122.

53. On April 8, 1496, Ser Piero probably drafted the act for the convocation of the Canonici Regolari of San Donato a Scopeto, in which the Canonici arc all listed after the prior, Frate Giovanbattista di Lorenzo di Bologna. From this meeting emerged the commitment, pursuant to a donation, to have an altarpiece for the church of San Donato painted, as one gathers from a document notarized by "ser Simonis olim pogginis Jacobi depogginis civis et notarius publicus florentinus" (the contract, dated August 25, 1479, between Fra Simone di Antonio di Piero, "bastaio" [packsaddle maker], and the brothers, is published in Poggi 1910, pp. 96–98). Also recorded is the granting of the commission to Filippino Lippi (of whom there is some autograph writing on the back of the panel, with the date March 29, 1496) and the agreed compensation of three hundred *fiorini di suggello*; the document was notarized by Ser Piero da Vinci (ASF, Notarile Antecosimiano 16837, cc. 180r–184r; the document is published in part in Poggi 1910, pp. 98–101). For the publication of the payments for the altarpiece in 1497 and 1498, see Cecchi 1998, pp. 60–63, 70–71 nn. 24–43. On June 7, 1497, in a deed notarized by Ser Piero, Filippino Lippi named as his attorneys Ser Mariano di Rinieri di Giovanni di Mariano and Ser Jacopo di Francesco, Florentine citizens and notaries (ASF, Notarile Antecosimiano 16837, c. 320v).

54. Vasari 1966– , vol. 4, p. 24. The work is not cited in the 1550 Torrentini edition.

55. ASF, Notarile Antecosimiano 16825, c. 322v; ASF, Notarile Antecosimiano 16842, cc. 1r–v; ASF, Notarile Antecosimiano 16826, cc. 8r–v, 16r and v.

56. De Roover 1970, p. 106.

57. "Duo chase poste nellavia deglialberti che da primo via secondo pagholo della chasa 1/3 Bartolomeo Gianfigliazzi, 1/4 Francesco Dini prese in pagamento da francescho d'altobiancho deglialberti [for 5300 florins at the] Palazzo del Podestà sino a di 13 di giugno 1462 in scritta nel primo catasto in . . . delle quali abiamo fatto una chasa attegnalla per nostro abitare." ASF, Catasto 929, c. 280r.

58. Möller 1937–38, p. 196.

59. Giovanni had financed the church's expansion projects between 1439 and 1443 (Paatz 1940–54, vol. 4, p. 344). Amerigo was buried at le Murate on July 5, 1468 (Möller 1937–38, p. 196; De Roover 1970, p. 412).

60. ASF, Catasto 929, cc. 280r–286v; ASF, Catasto 1024, cc. 371r–375v. On the family, see BNCF, Poligrafo Gargani 251.

61. In his entry are registered the greatest number of the land properties enumerated in the earlier 1469 entry (ASF, Catasto 1024, cc. 371r–375v). Born about 1440 and dead in 1518, Bartolomeo in 1469 married Bartolomea di Angelo di Lorenzo della Stufa (d. May 25, 1471). He held important public offices, such as that of *priore* for the San Giovanni quarter, on September 1, 1474, and July 1, 1499 (BNCF, Poliografo Gargani 251). On February 14, 1464, Palazzo Benci was the starting point of the Carnival of Bartolomeo, in honor of

Marietta di Lorenzo di Palla Strozzi (Möller 1937–38, p. 196). Also known are the 1480 *catasto* entries of Niccolò di Giovanni Benci (ASF, Cataso 1024, cc. 376r and v) and Donato di Giovanni Benci (ibid., cc. 380r and v), also residents of the houses in Via degli Alberti, today called Via de' Benci.

62. Alessandrini 1966, p. 193.

63. Brown 1998b, p. 105.

64. Vasari 1966– , vol. 4, p. 30.

65. See David A. Brown in Brown 2001–2, pp. 142–45, n. 16 (with bibliography).

66. Alessandrini 1966; Brown 1998b, p. 104.

67. Bandini 1791–93, vol. 5, 1792, col. 372 n. XVII, col. 373 n. XXVIII, col. 375 n. LII; Mazzucchelli 1753–63, vol. 2, pt. 2, pp. 787–88; Flammini 1891, pp. 543 n.4 and 563.

68. Della Torre 1902, pp. 29, 547, 550, 555.

69. Giovanni is the author of orations (BNCF, Strozziane VIII, misc. sec. XVI; see Kristeller 1963, vol. 1, p. 125) and a "Protesto fatto per giovanni damerigho benci dinanzi e nostri magnifici signori elloro venerabili chollegi e capitudini" (BNCF, Magliab VIII, 1385 [II, 1, 71], c. 38v, see Della Torre 1902, p. 555 nn. 1, 2; Magl. VIII n.345, misc. sec. XVI, see Kristeller 1963, vol. 1, p. 121).

70. Based on the note of possession, the work turns out to have belonged to Benci from 1485 on (Bandini 1792, vol. 2, cols. 590–91).

71. So much so that it gave rise, in Florence, to the saying: "Ecco Seicento, solito dirsi nel vedere persona che sfoggia soverchia pompa nelle vesti" (Here comes Six Hundred, one customarily says upon seeing somebody who displays excessive ostentation in his dress; Ademollo and Passerini 1845, vol. 2, pp. 421–22).

72. Richter 1883, vol. 2, pt. 2, no. 1416 p. 428, no. 1444 p. 433, no. 1454 p. 437; Renouard and Ragni 1966, p. 182.

73. Möller 1937–38, pp. 196–97.

74. Amerigo was born on January 30, 1498 (ASF, Cittadinario fiorentino, Quartiere di Santa Croce, I, c. 47to). He held many important offices over the course of the first half of the sixteenth century, after the return of the Medici to power in 1530 (see the list in ASF, Raccolta Sebregondi 547).

75. Vasari 1966– , vol. 4, p. 23.

76. On Botticelli's friend Segni, see Cecchi-Natali 2000, pp. 31, 264–65 nn. 24–34.

77. On this Segni, who was enrolled at the Compagnia di San Luca from 1503 to 1505 (ASF, Accademia del Disegno 2, Debitori, creditori e ricordi, ad annum), see Solmi 1911, pp. 399–404; Martinori 1918, pp. 42, 46–49, 58, 403, doc. on pp. 70–73, 75–76, 78, 82; Polverini Fossi 1991, pp. 133, 140–141 n. 44, 156–57 n. 85, 161.

78. Bearing witness to this is the entry of his workshop in Calimala, which figured among the alienated properties of Neri di Antonio in the 1470 *catasto* entry.

79. Born on March 8, 1411 (see ASF, Tratte 777 Libri d'Età [1347–1468]), and dead sometime between 1477 and 1480, he was a fairly prominent figure, since he was enrolled at the Collegio in 1433 with his brothers Segna and Tuccio (ASF, Ms. 361, Carte Dell'Ancisa NN, c. 353r), among the members of the Arte dei Corazzai on July 5, 1440 (ASF, Arte dei Corazzai e Spadai, ad annum), of the Otto (the Eight) in 1448 (BNCF, Poligrafo Gargani 1850, Cod. 140 Cl. 26, Magl. 118), of the XVI Gonfalonieri on January 8, 1451; he was *pennoniere* (standard bearer) the same year, *priore* for his quarter and *gonfalone* in September and October of 1460, a member of the XII Buonomini on December 15, 1461, again *priore* in May and June of 1469, scrutinized with his brother Tuccio for the major guilds in 1473 (ASF, Ms. 361 cit.), again with the XVI Gonfalonieri on September 8, 1474, and Podestà of Castelfranco Inferiore for six months starting June 1, 1477 (ASF, Raccolta Sebregondi 4845, famiglia Segni Guidi).

80. ASF, Tratte 80, Libro delle Età (1379–1521). He was baptized on May 9 (AOSMF, Registro dei Battessati maschi e femmine 1450–1460, alla data).

81. ASF, Catasto 1005, cc. 17r and v; see Horne 1908, p.352, doc. XXXIX, p. 486.

82. ASF, Decima Repubblicana 16, c. 30r.

83. AOSMF, *Registro dei Battezzati maschi 1501–1511*, alla data.

84. ASF, MAP, file XCIII, n. 579, cited by Cast 1981, pp. 49–50 n. 24.

85. Machiavelli 1971, pp. 559 n. 72, 564, 566.

86. One Antonio Segni, perhaps our own and the one in contact with Machiavelli, who was in Rome on October 31, 1505, among the domestic staff of Cardinal Francesco Soderini, apparently died while serving this same Soderini, when acting as messenger between Cardinal Francesco and his brother Piero, the former *gonfaloniere perpetuo* of Florence deposed by the Medici (Lowe 1993, pp. 55 n. 8, pp. 119, 241).

87. "E [il Rustici] perché abitò un tempo nella via de' Martegli, fu amicissimo di tutti ql'uomini di quella famiglia, che ha sempre avuto uomini virtuosissimi e di valore, e particolarmente di Piero, al quale fece (come a suo più intrinseco) alcune figurette di tondo rilievo, e fra l'altre una Nostra Donna col Figlio in collo, a sedere sopra certe nuvole piene di Cherubini; simile alla quale ne dipinse poi col tempo un'altra in un gran quadro a olio, con una ghirlanda di Cherubini che intorno alla testa le fa diadema" (Vasari 1966– , vol. 4, p. 476).

88. See Richter 1883, vol. 1, p. 112; Civai 1990, pp. 41, 47 n. 45.

89. Civai 1990, pp. 40–41, 47 nn. 39, 40, 120–21. Much remains to be investigated before we have even a remote picture of the cultural and artistic environment of Florence during the quattrocento and cinquecento. I nourish the hope that this research of mine will help to pave the way for those who come after me and wish to further explore these subjects.

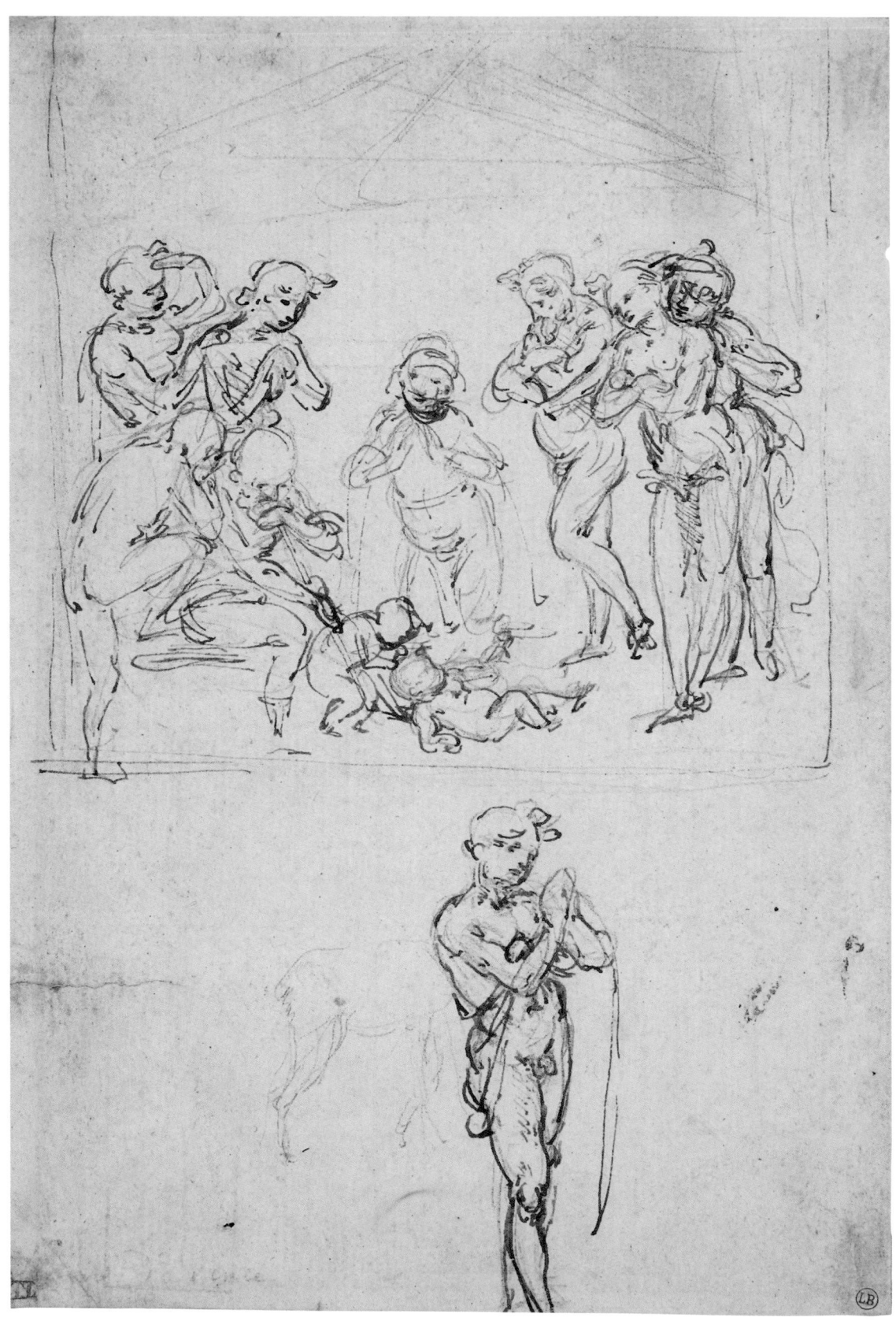

Fig. 68. Leonardo da Vinci, *Adoration*. Metalpoint, reworked with pen and brown ink, on pale pink prepared paper, 222 × 152 mm. Musée Bonnat, Bayonne 658

DRAWING
THE BOUNDARIES

MARTIN KEMP

HEN FRA PIETRO DA NOVELLARA wrote from Florence to Isabella d'Este in Mantua in 1501, reporting to the marchesa about Leonardo's apparently intermittent engagement with painting and describing a cartoon of the *Virgin and Child with Saint Anne and a Lamb* that the artist was making, he was particularly impressed by the way in which substantial figures could be compressed into a composition of modest dimensions: "These figures are all as large as life, but they exist within a small cartoon, because they are either seated or in curved poses."[1] The subject of the cartoon, sometimes in a variant form with the infant Saint John, was one to which Leonardo returned repeatedly over the course of almost two decades (see cat. nos. 95–97, 105–9). One reason for his recurrent interest, even in the apparent absence of any direct commission, is that the subject permitted a dramatic enlargement of the scale of the figures within the constraints of the frame.

Comparable effects of compression could be achieved if the main figure or figures were to be depicted kneeling, and he became fascinated by protagonists who sustained improbably active poses even while on their knees. He utterly transformed the decorous piety normally associated with a kneeling figure in religious subjects into something altogether more emotionally dynamic and spatially assertive. This is true particularly with a series of schemes for the Virgin with either one or two children, best represented in the drawing in the Metropolitan Museum (cat. no. 45), but it also extends to secular subjects, as is evident in the project for a kneeling *Leda* (cat. nos. 88, 98–100), which drew at least part of its inspiration from ancient Roman statues of a kneeling Venus.[2]

To achieve the compression of interlocked and spatially integrated figures Leonardo utilized his famous "brainstorm" drawing technique to the full. In swirls of crashing lines, sometimes augmented by mid-tone wash and white heightening, he would virtually sculpt forms into the surface of the paper. Unsurprisingly, this innovatory feature of his design process has attracted much comment, not least for its revolutionary effect on younger draftsmen, especially Raphael. What has been largely overlooked is the special role of drawn frames or boundaries in Leonardo's composition drawings (cat. nos. 23, 45, 65, 68, 88, 95, 96, 110) when

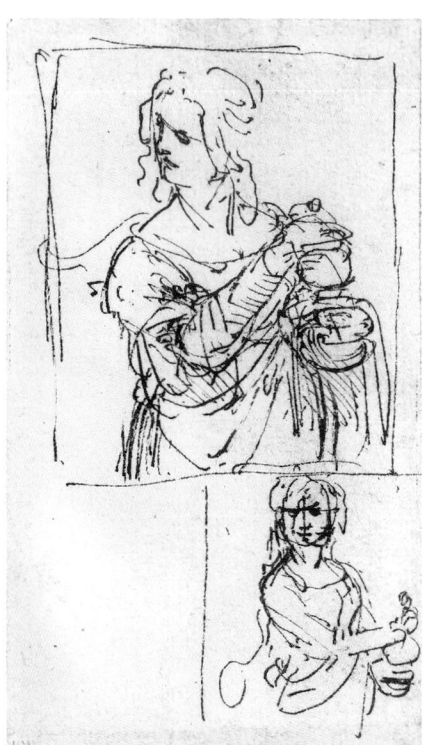

Fig. 69. Leonardo da Vinci, *Studies for Saint Mary Magdalen.* Pen and brown ink, 135 × 80 mm. Courtauld Institute Gallery, Somerset House, London; Seilern Collection

plotting the necessary containment of the graphic mêlée in relation to the planned shape and proportions of the picture.

A frame around a compositional drawing is not unexpected or exceptional in the Renaissance. It was natural for a painter faced with a commission for a painting of a certain shape and proportions to think from the first about the containing boundaries of the composition. The arched top of an altarpiece, for example, would need to be accommodated when plotting the figures and their settings, both on the surface and within the pictorial space. Perugino, and following him, Raphael, was particularly adept at the construction of such pictorial architecture within the framing of the composition. Leonardo, for his part, naturally laid in the outlines of the pictorial field for the almost square altarpiece he was planning for San Donato a Scopeto in 1481, which resulted in the unfinished *Adoration of the Magi* (figs. 10, 11). The sketch of naked figures for an *Adoration* (fig. 68) — apparently involving shepherds rather than kings at this stage — includes a roughly outlined frame. At the right, the first boundary (Leonardo was a left-hander and tended to begin on the right side) is drawn in with some confidence, while the base line gets into difficulties at the far left as it collides at ankle level with the stooping worshiper next to Joseph. Two rapid horizontals below the left corner impatiently acknowledge the problem, while alternatives for the left boundary are casually dashed in.

In a similar manner, indications of the framing boundaries of the field are included in the drawing at Windsor representing some of his earliest thoughts on the *Last Supper* (cat. no. 65). Concerned here with defining the behavior of Judas (as yet still traditionally isolated on the near side of the table), rather than with the whole span of the composition, Leonardo sketches in the lower and right boundaries of the planned mural. Along the top, he adds a series of lunettes, which does not correspond to the architecture of the end wall of the Refectory of Santa Maria delle Grazie but appears to represent an intended articulation of the wall of the painted room behind the table and figures.

On the smaller scale of devotional images intended primarily for domestic settings, it was also natural to sketch in the frame to judge the setting of the figure or figures within the confines of the panel. The two quick sketches of *Mary Magdalen* with her jar of ointment are unremarkably set within rectangular boundaries (fig. 69). Comparably, for secular compositions of emblems and allegories, either as freestanding images or as part of decorative ensembles, Leonardo found it natural to lay down the boundaries of the field. A series of emblematic and allegorical subjects is placed within the kind of round frames (cat. nos. 68, 110) that infer the destination of these subjects within an ornamental scheme, such as an embroidery or festival decoration. By contrast, studies in the British Museum and Ashmolean Museum (see cat. no. 23) for the smug virgin who has captured the elusive unicorn are assigned to conventionally rectangular fields. And a long, horizontal frame surrounds the elaborate and incomprehensible allegorical composition at Windsor that appears to involve a supplicant menaced by a monstrous animal that has intruded itself into a grand building. The identity of the person appealing for protection from the female figure, who is accompanied by an angelic host, is unclear, as are all the other elements in this bizarre subject (fig. 70).

All these drawn frames are relatively unremarkable, at least in terms of design procedures. The framing lines become more actively participatory in those studies where alternative ideas for dynamic forms—either in overlaid or successive compositions—are compressed within confined boundaries. Six such drawings, ranging approximately from 1480 to 1507, show how the frame was involved as an integral component in the "brainstorming" process, serving to contain and discipline the potentially wayward inventions—just as a poetic form, such as a sonnet or a madrigal, provides the container against which the poet's imagination can creatively press. The design process within the frame may be seen as tensely stretching the boundaries of what is possible within the confines of what is preordained by convention or necessity. This kind of tension has provided a source of inspiration for artists in all visual and auditory media through the ages.

The earliest case study is provided by the double-sided sheet depicting the *Madonna of the Cat*, dating from about 1480, when Leonardo was beginning to work on the *Adoration*

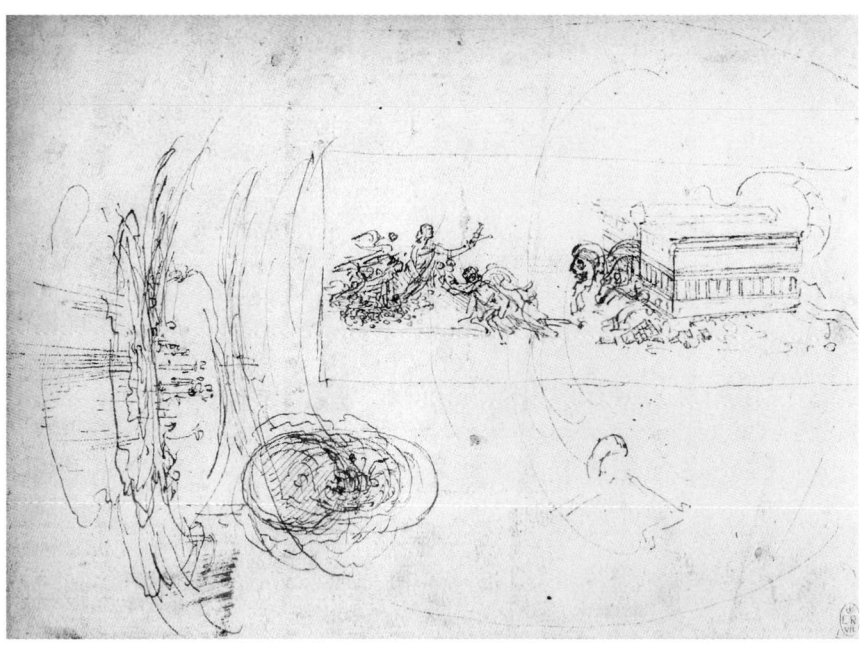

Fig. 70. Leonardo da Vinci, *Sheet of Sketches for an Allegory*. Pen and brown ink, 157 × 215 mm. The Royal Collection, H.M. Queen Elizabeth II, Windsor Castle RL 12497

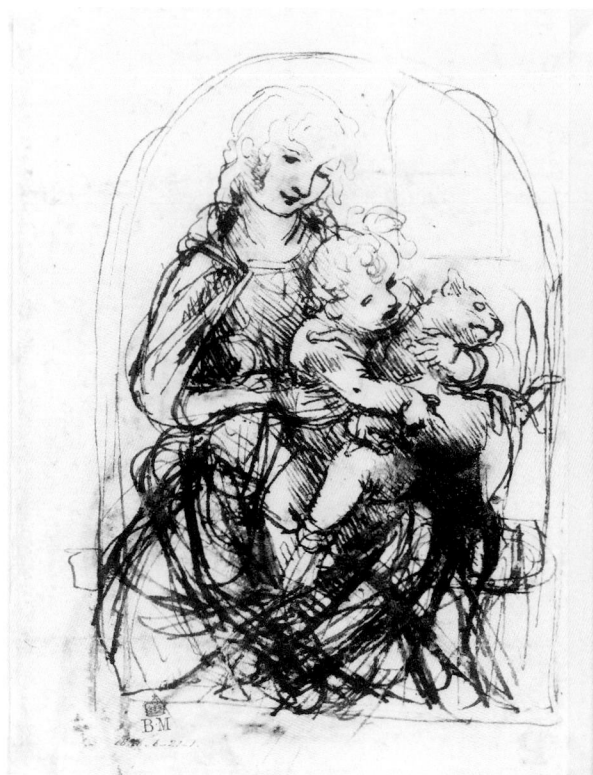

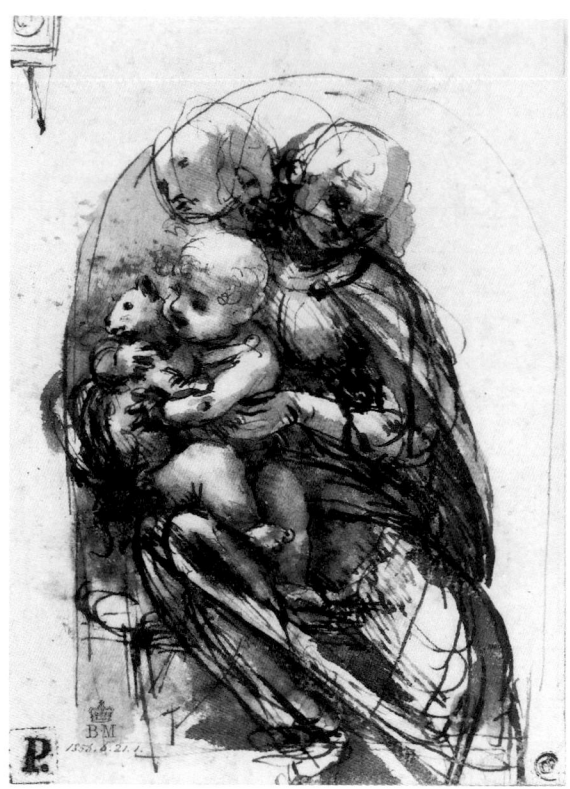

Fig. 71. Leonardo da Vinci, *Sketch for the Madonna of the Cat* (verso). Pen and brown ink, stylus incised, 132 × 96 mm. The British Museum, London 1856-6-21-1

Fig. 72. Leonardo da Vinci, *Sketch for the Madonna of the Cat* (recto). Pen and brown ink, brush and brown wash, stylus incised, 132 × 96 mm. The British Museum, London 1856-6-21-1

(figs. 71, 72). The cat's presence is explained less by domestic anecdote than by the legend that a cat gave birth at exactly the moment when Christ entered the world. A rich series of drawings survives for the project (cat. nos. 18, 19), into which Leonardo poured substantial creative thought, but which was not apparently to result in an autograph painting. In other studies of the subject, the poses of the three participants are orchestrated, sometimes separately and sometimes together, with apparently boundless fertility. Leonardo particularly enjoyed speculating graphically on the range of potential relationships between the child and the cat, as the animal is alternately stroked, cuddled, and bear-hugged to its obvious pleasure or discomfort (cat. nos. 18, 19). In one of the double-sided sheets (fig. 71), Leonardo appears at first to be reasonably settled on the descending curve of the three heads, while the participants' legs and the cat's thrashing tail are scribbled in a maelstrom of alternative positions. Turning over the densely worked sheet (fig. 72) to view the composition in reverse—as he specifically recommended—Leonardo both attempts to clarify his preferred arrangement for the legs and to adjust the formal-cum-emotional balance in the light of its reversal. The Virgin's head is laid down in three positions, one corresponding to his first idea and two positions radically different in compositional and psychological effect.

When was the frame added on either side of the British Museum sheet (figs. 71, 72)? There are clear signs on the recto that the basic form of the arched frame with its lower boundary was added quite early, since the rapidly drawn lines tend to stay within its confines. Even the outlines of the double-arched window behind the figures may have been sketched in after the framing lines, though they overlap at the upper right. On the left, however, the Virgin's actively thrusting knees demanded a leftward extrusion of the edge of the composition, which is achieved with a looping line to the left of the original edge. On the verso, the frame again appears to have been laid in at an early stage, certainly predating the definition of the ledge and schematic cushion and the addition of the wash. Again, characteristically of Leonardo as a left-hander, he has run into difficulties as he proceeds from right to left, ending up with an uncomfortable mash of forms against the left-hand boundary, which he again considers extending. It is clear that the rhythm of the arched top, with the restriction of the free space around the Virgin's head, is crucial to his design method. More radically, the compressed crowding of figures that are on a large scale relative to the pictorial field is a vital element in the effect that Leonardo was intending. The sketched frames thus play a potent role in the process of graphic invention.

The Metropolitan sheet (cat. no. 45), by contrast, essays alternative solutions in separate compositions and serves to emphasize how diverse were the design resources on which Leonardo could draw. The sketched "pictures" are best regarded as spin-off variations from the *Virgin of the Rocks* (the painting he devised in response to the commission for the decoration of the large wooden altarpiece for the Confraternity of the Immaculate Conception in Milan in 1483; fig. 12). The idea for a kneeling Madonna, making general allusion to Saint Bridget's vision of the Virgin on her knees at the moment of Christ's birth, appears to have occupied the painter at various stages of his career. It is likely that the present drawing dates from after the designing of the *Virgin of the Rocks*. The optical diagram on the sheet (to be discussed below) would tend to suggest that the drawing is from about 1490, if the sets of studies were made around the same time, though it might have originated from later in the 1490s, when he was in all probability making his second attempt to provide a finished picture for the troubled project of the Milanese altarpiece (see Chronology).

It is reasonable to assume that the central study, for the Virgin with both the infant Saint John and the Christ Child, was the first on the sheet (cat. no. 45), as Leonardo considered how to organize the children under the overarching spread of the Virgin's arms, a gesture that is generally reminiscent of a Madonna della Misericordia. Moving away from the *Virgin of the Rocks* motif with the two infants, he then appears to have simplified the composition by eliminating the infant John, perhaps in response to the smaller projected scale of the picture. The arched frame appears as he begins to think in terms of a specific format. In the developed composition at the lower left, the frame must have been added very early, since almost all the lines respect its boundaries. It is clear that the balletic sway and turn of the Virgin, the arch of the stable, and the diagonals of its roof are very much organized to tie the dynamism of the composition into the shape of the field as a whole.

It may even be that the apparently unrelated optical diagram on the lower part of the sheet was triggered by the nature of the picture he was planning. The diagram is part of Leonardo's investigation of the "fallacies" of orthodox perspective.[3] The basic setup involves a horizontal ground plane, a vertical picture plane standing on this ground plane, and an eyepoint from which the artist/spectator looks at the section of the ground plane on the other side of the picture plane. The picture plane may be considered to be like a glass window on which the things behind it are traced. In the Metropolitan drawing (cat. no. 45), Leonardo is showing the setup from the side, so that the picture plane is a simple vertical line while the ground plane is a horizontal line divided into equal intervals. He uses this setup to demonstrate how a viewpoint very close to the picture plane results in the equal intervals immediately behind the plane appearing to be of wildly different sizes on the surface of the picture. He does this by connecting the rays that run from the eyepoint at the right of the vertical picture plane to the two intervals on the ground immediately to the left of the vertical. As an alternative, he considers what happens if the plane that intersects the rays is formed by a circle centered on the eyepoint. In this case the diminution of apparent size of the horizontal intervals, as registered by the intersections on the curved plane, is less extreme and more akin to what we perceive when looking at equal intervals on an actual ground plane. The diagram is part of a complex debate in his notebooks about the problems of orthodox perspective.

It may be that it was just this kind of small-scale devotional painting, to be seen from close range and in which the figures are by implication very near the spectator, which occasioned Leonardo's analyses of the problems of close viewing positions. There is indeed something slightly uncomfortable about the looming Virgin in the most developed of the sketches, even though in this instance perspectival geometry is not overtly apparent in the foreground.

When, about ten years later, Leonardo took up the theme again, he retained the method of the framed sketch. At the top of a sheet at Windsor (fig. 73), he first established the basic disposition of forms in black chalk, surrounded by a quickly delineated frame. Only the rock behind Christ on the right significantly extrudes

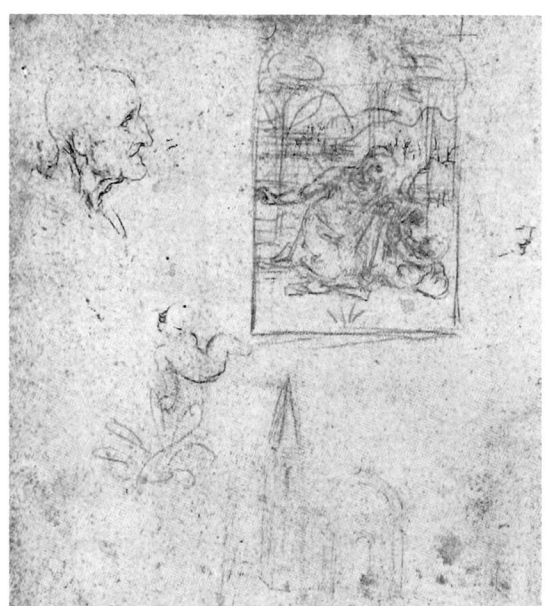

Fig. 73. Detail of Leonardo da Vinci, *Sheet of Sketches with a Nativity.* Metalpoint, reworked with pen and brown ink, on pale blue prepared paper, 183 × 137 mm. The Royal Collection, H.M. Queen Elizabeth II, Windsor Castle RL 12560

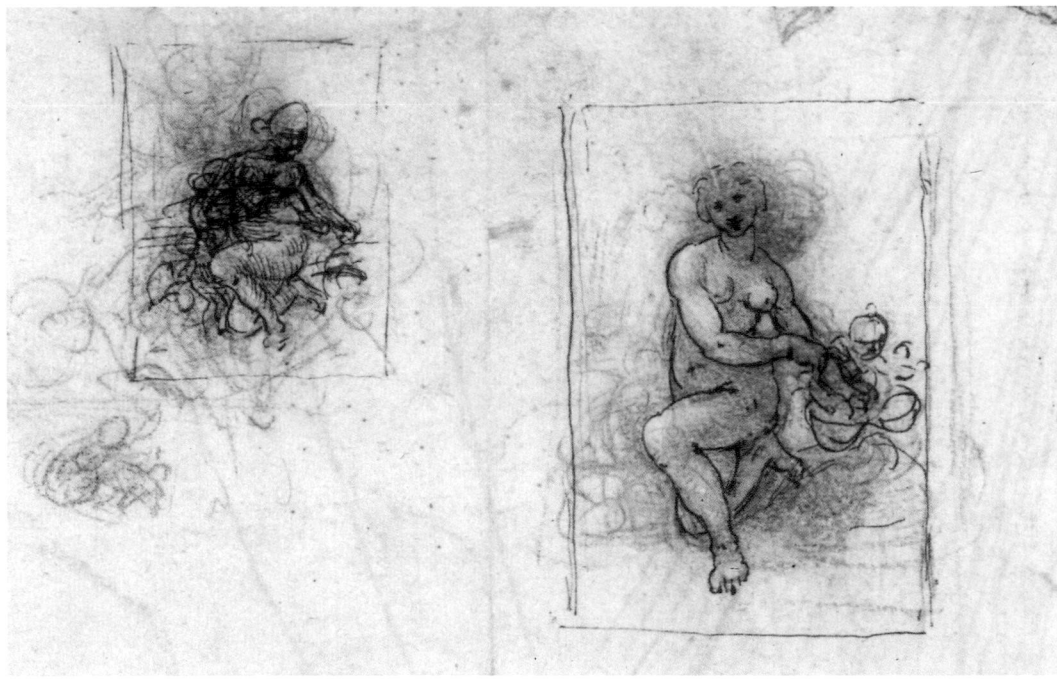

Fig. 74. Detail of cat. no. 88, Leonardo da Vinci, *Studies for Leda and the Swan* (recto). Charcoal or soft black chalk partly reworked with pen and brown ink, 292 × 412 mm. The Royal Collection, H.M. Queen Elizabeth II, Windsor Castle RL 12337

beyond its confines. Then, in keeping with a technique he exploited extensively in his later career, he excavated the preferred contours with firm strokes of the pen, while characteristically extending the left border to accommodate the Virgin's outstretched arm and lowering the base to set the group slightly further back into space. The extra area of foreground is signaled schematically by the insertion of a typically spiky plant. The upper boundary appears to be flat rather than arched, its position at first marked by a small horizontal line at the top right and subsequently lowered in response to the lower base of the composition as a whole. The spaces between the Virgin's head and the upper corners (which had been effectively eliminated in the arched-top format) are now busily occupied by mountains, trees, and buildings on the right and by a plunging perspective vista on the left behind a slender tree.

Like his plans for the *Madonna of the Cat*, the project for a kneeling Virgin with one or two infants does not seem to have resulted in an autograph painting (see cat. no. 45). However, a number of versions of variable quality and condition show that the composition (finally involving both the Christ Child and Saint John) did reach a definitive point as a model for the kind of small-scale studio pictures in which Leonardo's workshop seems to have specialized after 1500.

The dense plasticity resulting from the combination of black chalk with dark ink features conspicuously in three other examples, all apparently from the unsettled period when Leonardo was struggling with the mural of the *Battle of Anghiari* and being tugged back and forth between Florence and Milan by the conflicting demands of the Florentine and French regimes in either city. The first is the project for a kneeling *Leda* accompanied by the children sired by Zeus in his disguise as a swan. The theme first appears on a sheet that contains a spirited study for a rearing horse with a sketchy rider, made in connection with the battle mural he was supposed to be painting in the Great Council Hall of the Florentine Republic (cat. no. 88 recto; fig. 74). In both the framed sketches for the *Leda,* the problem posed by the naked figure and her energetic progeny (whose number is unclear) has elicited a frantic bout of brainstorming, more akin to the studies for the *Madonna of the Cat* than to the relatively cut-and-dried alternatives for the kneeling Madonna. Leda's convoluted pose, which set welcome challenges for Leonardo as an ambitious draftsman and makes uncomfortable demands on the tolerance and confidence of the spectator, is knotted intricately into each of the framed spaces. Here, the frame is less involved with strict containment than in defining a rectangular field or plane against which the tangled plasticity of the group can be thrown into relief. As if alert to the way that the torsions of the pose were becoming too extreme, even by his own adventurous standards, Leonardo seems to allow Leda to rise to a half-standing position in the unframed sketch below the horse. It was as a fully standing figure that Leda was eventually to feature in a finished painting (now accompanied by her amorous swan), which was recorded by Cassiano del Pozzo in 1625 and seems to have perished in the French royal collection in the eighteenth century.

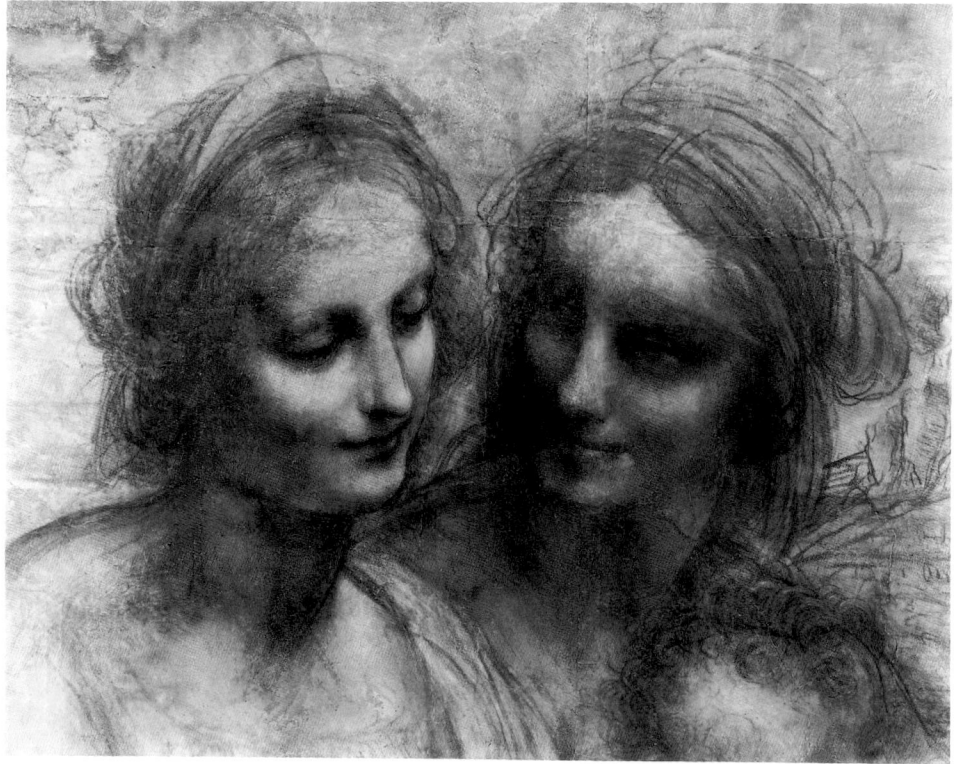

Fig. 75. Detail of fig. 76

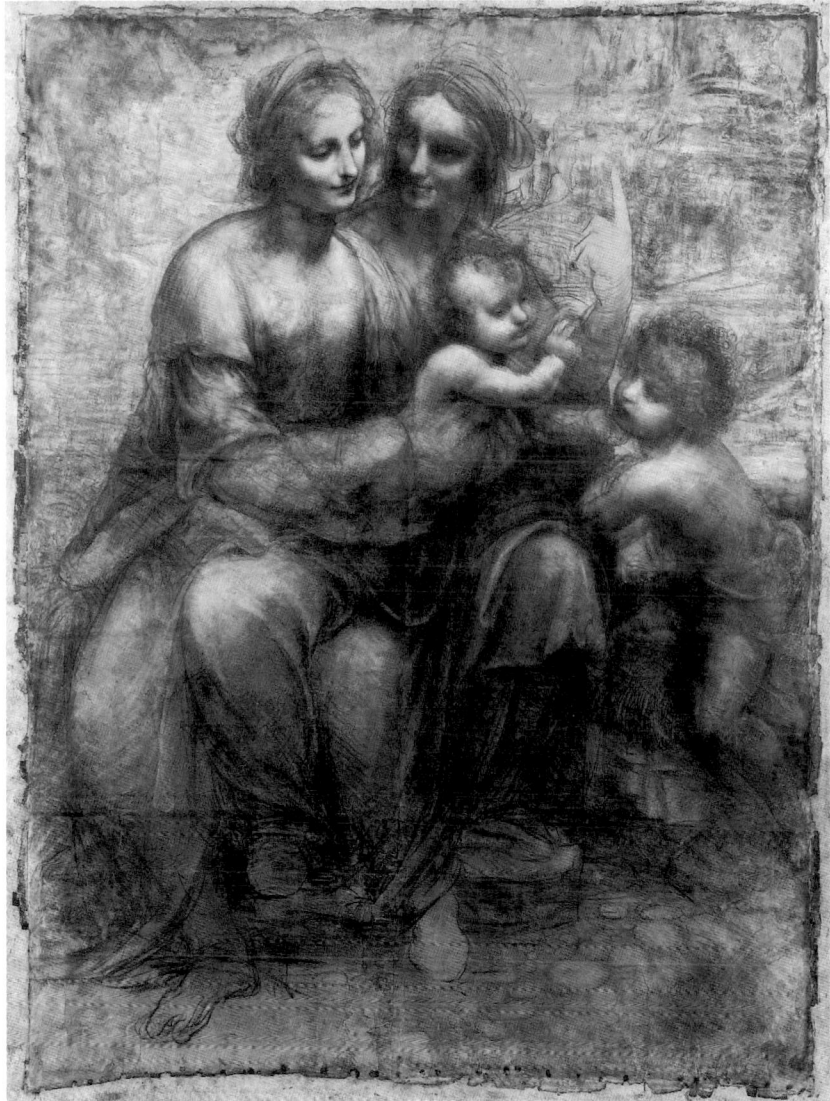

The final two examples are both connected with his return to the Virgin and Child with Saint Anne (or Elizabeth) project, perhaps in connection with a picture planned for presentation to the French king, Louis XII (see cat. nos. 95, 96). The king's wife was Anne of Brittany, and a subject including her namesake was therefore highly appropriate.

The first, a small sheet in Venice (cat. no. 95), has generally been connected to the composition described by Fra Pietro in 1501, but, as Carmen Bambach is arguing, the hooked ink lines over a black chalk substrate are more characteristic of Leonardo's design methods about 1507 and thus closer in date to the cartoon in the National Gallery, London (figs. 75, 76). Any interpretation of the framing lines, drawn in black chalk and ink, is not helped by the obvious trimming of the edges of the sheet, but it is possible to reconstruct some of the framing maneuvers that we will encounter in more elaborate form in our final example. Generally speaking, it is safe to assume that the vaguer black chalk preceded the pen work in two different inks, but

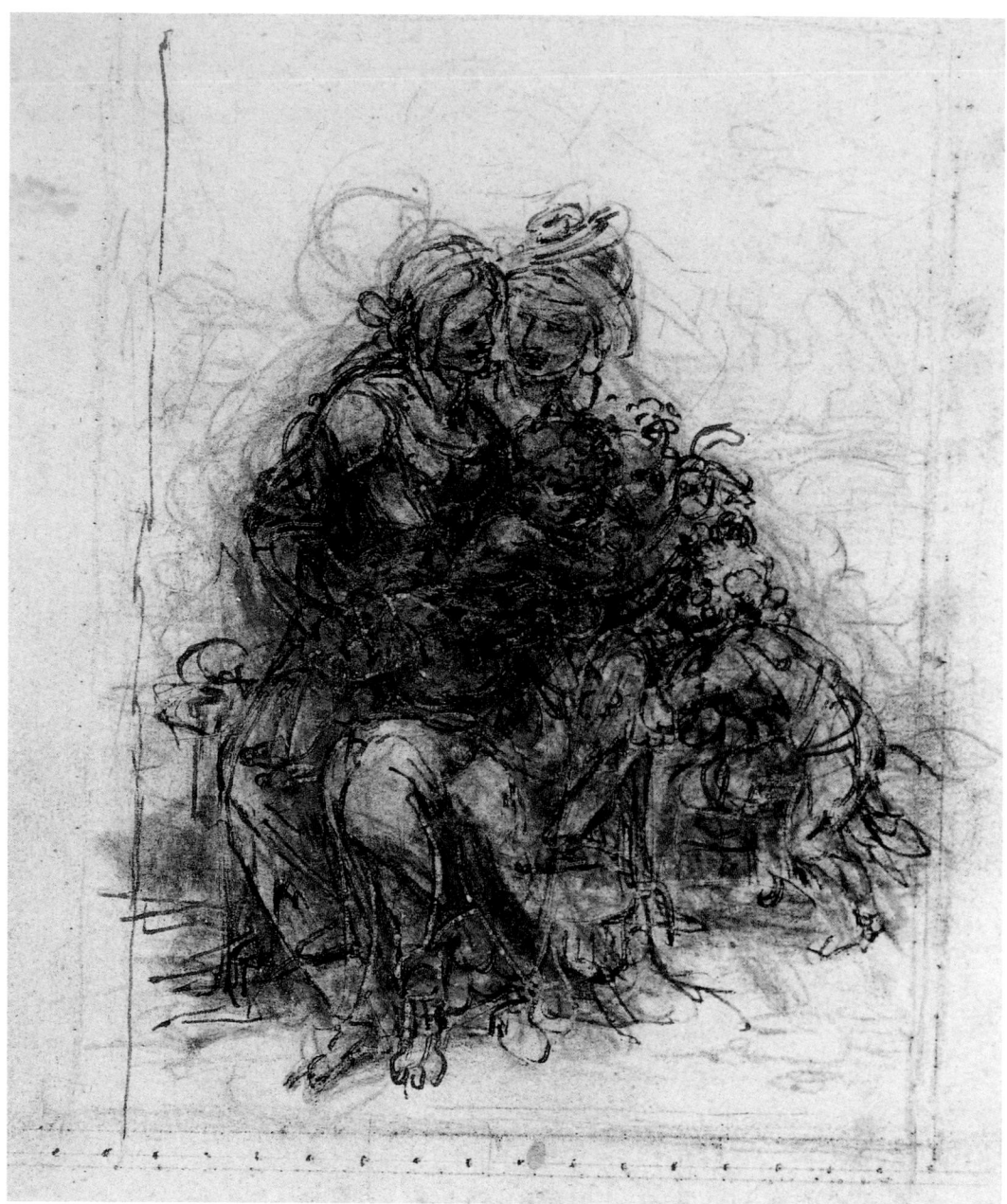

Fig. 77. Detail of cat. no. 96, Leonardo da Vinci, *Sketches for the Virgin and Child with Saint Anne.* Pen and brown ink, brush and brown wash, over black chalk, 266 × 200 mm. The British Museum, London 1875-6-12-17

in this case the alternative positions for the head of Saint Anne appear in both chalk and ink. Since the lighter, sepia ink, used especially in the landscape and outer frame, appears to have been added after the blacker ink, it looks as if the left-hand alternative was the later option. This suggests either that Leonardo decided at different stages to ink in both the head positions he had previously considered in black chalk, or that he took up his black chalk again, after adding the lines in dark ink, and then used the sepia ink to go over the new form that was emerging. So densely has the second head been worked in the two inks that the highly corrosive iron gall ink has caused the paper to disintegrate in the region of Saint Anne's eyes.

In any event, the first framing motif was almost certainly that in black chalk, since the landscape in sepia ink on the right passes beyond it and up to the inked frame, which is now at the very edge of the trimmed sheet. At top left, two faint chalk verticals appear to originate from two marked points well inside the boundary subsequently drawn in pen. Then, before the landscape was added, new frames were roughly inked in, as if Leonardo now has a reasonably clear idea of how much space the figure group needs—though at the bottom right he made one false shot before settling on the lower border. There is a clear sense that he has moved from a process of compression, within a tight frame, toward a more expansive sense of the figures "breathing" in the context of a more expansive landscape vista.

Our final example of the internally framed sketch, the drawing in the British Museum that appears to represent the vital preparatory step in the design of the so-called Burlington House cartoon (National Gallery, London), is in all senses the most remarkable (cat. no. 96; fig. 77). It again involves four participants, all "either seated or in curved poses" as Fra Pietro da Novellara had said in 1501 of its forerunner. The challenge of four figures triggered a process of extraordinary elaboration, above all with respect to the frames and measured lines that surround the main sketch. It is upon this study that I will now concentrate.

The drawing began in black chalk, like the *Leda* studies (fig. 74), with a tangle of ghostly protagonists, whose poses were progressively established with more strongly drawn contours. Leonardo then intervened, almost aggressively, with curving pen strokes, the impetus of which energized the interlocked bodies and draperies. Touches of white heightening and darker wash were next added to cast some prominent forms into the "relief" (*relievo*) upon which he set such store. Finally, he pressed the surface of the sheet with a blank tool (cat. no. 96 recto; fig. 77), transferring to the other side of the sheet the basic outline of the design that was emerging (cat. no. 96 verso). This transfer was accomplished by placing a sheet rubbed with charcoal or black chalk face up against the reverse of the page containing the drawing. The result is to clarify the most extreme of all his "brainstorm" studies, in which it is otherwise difficult for us in retrospect to sort out what is emerging.

Amid such freewheeling and serendipitous scribbling, it is extraordinary to discover how elaborately calculated are the framing elements around the tornado of lines. In connection with the Leonardo exhibition in 1989 at the Hayward Gallery in London, I made some inroads into the analysis of the frames and measurements.[4] More recently, one of my doctoral students, Edward Ford, has undertaken a minutely detailed and productive scrutiny of the sheet, including the use of raking light to pick up incised marks.[5] The following draws on his observations and adapts his conclusions (fig. 78). The detailed examination of the framing motifs allows us to reconstruct the design process, even if it is not possible to establish with absolute certainty a tidy sequence of events (if such ever existed). It is also possible to reconstruct the tool kit with which Leonardo worked on the surface of the paper: a stick of

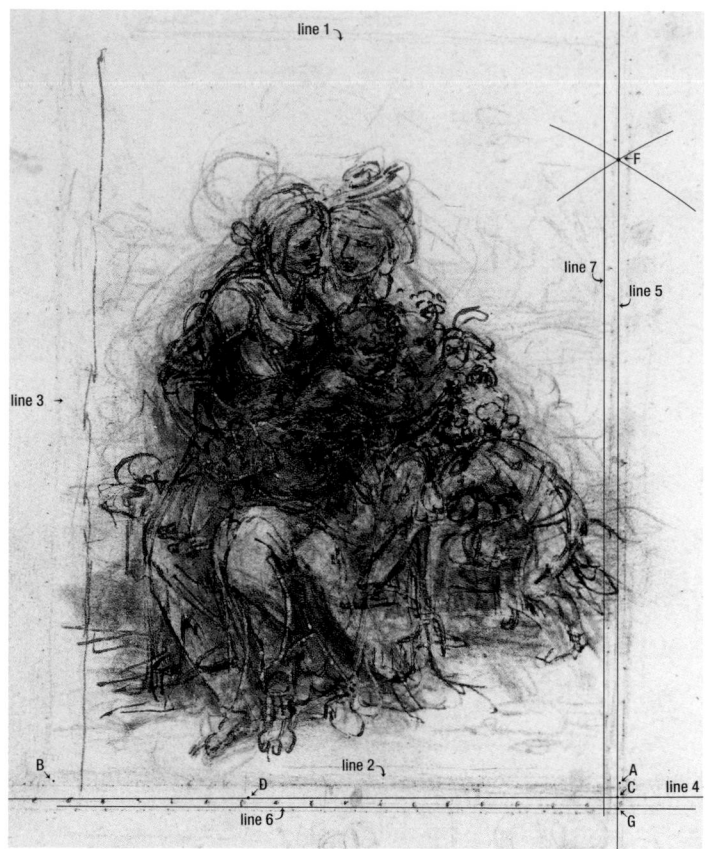

Fig. 78. Diagram showing the archaeological evidence on cat. no. 96,
Leonardo da Vinci, *Sketches for the Virgin and Child with Saint Anne*
(after Edward Ford)

black chalk with a not especially sharp point, a pen loaded with dark brown ink, a brush dipped into a dilute gray-brown wash and another used for white gouache, a blank stylus (quite blunt), and a pair of dividers. The dividers possessed a sharp and a blunt point, which made significantly different marks, the former tending to puncture the paper. It is possible that the sharper point was at the tip of a removable arm which was subject to less regular wear than the fixed arm. Along the left-hand border of the main sketch on the recto, it can be seen that he occasionally dragged the free point in an arc across the paper as he stepped out the equal measures. Did he also press the dividers into service as the blank stylus when he roughly pressed the design through the sheet?

The first, lightly sketched frame in chalk establishes the general proportions of the frame in relation to the knot of figures. Only the upper border (line 1 in fig. 78) was not to be redrawn during the whole design process. The lower border, by contrast, was subject to repeated reworking. What appears to be the earliest attempt to define the lower boundary is incised amid the main run of chalk alternatives (line 2). From two endpoints (A and B), the dividers were used for determining the midpoint in a hit-or-miss method: one point was placed at A and the necessary extension of the dividers was estimated. From this inaccurate midpoint, Leonardo swung the first foot of the dividers toward B, only to find that he had overestimated. A cluster of indentations bears witness to a series of increasingly accurate shots, until the true center was found, after which he worked toward the quarter points along the line, which he unexpectedly used to estimate the placing of seventeen equal divisions between points A and B. From point B, he stepped out twenty-five of these units up a free-hand vertical line in chalk, taking it to approximately three units above the designated upper boundary. A similar use of such construction appears in the large Hercules drawing from Turin exhibited here (cat. no. 102), which dates from about 1506–8.

This effort did not prove definitive, and he incised a lower base line (4 on the diagram; fig. 78) across the page, which was used to establish the right border as a precise perpendicular. From points D and E, equidistant from the intended bottom right corner at C, he incised intersecting arcs to determine point F, vertically above C. The intersecting arcs are just visible in a good photograph. From C he then stepped out a second set of seventeen units, slightly larger than the first, effectively extending the left border very slightly. It was probably his anticipation of the need for space to construct this vertical that explains why he set the study off-center on the sheet. Each of the intervals is reinforced with an inked dot. He measured another set of twenty-five units up the vertical line of the right border.

Even this is not the final solution. A further lower border (line 6; fig. 78) is drawn in a slightly lower position (passing through point G) and divided into eighteen marginally smaller units that do not quite reach to the earlier boundary on the left. Then five units are measured vertically from point G. Next he remeasured, with a very slightly diminished interval, eighteen units from the left corner as established by line 3, which means that he arrived at a point to the left of line 5, the right boundary. From this new corner, a fresh vertical is drawn and divided to a height of twenty-four units, coinciding with the first and only position for the upper boundary. Apparently as the last of these maneuvers, he scrawled in a new left border in ink, the broken pen line moving in an upward direction from the bottom corner, downward from the top corner, and erratically in between. The new border leaves seventeen units across the base line once more.

However we might reconstruct Leonardo's thought process during these repeated adjustments and remeasurements, he was clearly trying to accomplish something very precise around the maelstrom of central sketching. The seventeen-unit division is so odd and unnatural that we may guess that it related to the predetermined dimensions of the panel on which the painting was to be made. It may well be that the joinery of the panel had already been accomplished, with the kind of integral frame that was common in Renaissance painting. There is, of course, no finished painting that allows us to determine its dimensions, but we are fortunate to possess the cartoon (figs. 75, 76). The problem with using the cartoon to predict the size of the painting is that its present borders are irregular and unreliable. However, using the British Museum drawing as a guide (fig. 77; cat. no. 96), we can infer that the width of the cartoon (now 104–105.5 cm) would originally have extended to about 114 to 124 centimeters. Can we make sense of the seventeen units in the light of these likely dimensions?

Taking the famous drawing of the *Vitruvian Man* in Venice (fig. 43) as a guide, we know that one of the units of measurement used by Leonardo was a palmo of one-eighth of a braccio (that is, a little under 7.3 cm).[6] Seventeen palmo units would thus give a width of between 123 and 124 centimeters. The twenty-four– to twenty-five–unit height would be equivalent to about 175 to 182 centimeters, which is also within the predictable bounds for the London cartoon, which is currently 140 to 142 centimeters high and has almost certainly been reduced at the top. None of the present edges of the cartoon (fig. 76), composed from eight sheets of paper glued in two vertical rows of four each, can be taken as original. Precision in such estimates is impossible, given the nature of the evidence, but we can reasonably surmise that Leonardo was working toward a composition seventeen palmi wide and twenty-four or twenty-five palmi high. As a point of comparison, the Louvre painting of the *Virgin and Child with Saint Anne and a Lamb* (fig. 23) presently measures 169 by 112 centimeters, that is to say, about 7 to 13 centimeters shorter and 11 centimeters narrower.

Although we have been dealing with little more than a dozen drawings with drawn frames, we may, given the severe attrition of Leonardo's drawn oeuvre, assume that it would have been a regular habit to introduce defined boundaries into the design process for the majority of his planned paintings and decorative designs. Much of this would have been unexceptional in Renaissance practice. Where Leonardo did have recourse to exceptional measures was in response to the unprecedented dynamism of his methods of preliminary sketching, in which the apparent anarchy of invention needed to be constrained by the practical bounds of the configuration and the dimensions of a planned picture. In the case of the smaller devotional subjects, he often but not invariably used small framed studies to explore successive alternatives for the composition. For larger paintings, like the *Leda* and the *Virgin and Child with Saint Anne* series, the writhing plasticity of the main motif is set within boundaries that are maneuvered to give the group just enough space to breathe while emphasizing the ingenious compression that Fra Pietro da Novellara so admired in 1501. The creative tension between set form and unbridled freedom reaches its peak in the British Museum drawing, in which, as in some of his maps, the highest degree of improvisation is paradoxically combined with the most meticulous efforts at measured scaling. Leonardo is a draftsman who perpetually surprises even the most experienced of his observers.

1. Villata 1999, no. 150, revising Beltrami 1919a, no. 106.
2. Bober and Rubinstein 1986, pp. 62–63, no. 18. For the *Leda*, see more generally Dalli Regoli, Nanni, and Natali 2001.
3. For his problems with orthodox perspective in the 1490s, see Kemp 1990b, p. 49.
4. Kemp and Roberts 1989, no. 77, p. 150.
5. Ford 2002.
6. Kemp and Roberts 1989. The results suggested in that catalogue have now been adjusted in the light of the further work by Ford and myself.

LEONARDO'S DRAWINGS IN MILAN AND THEIR INFLUENCE ON THE GRAPHIC WORK OF MILANESE ARTISTS

PIETRO C. MARANI

T HE PAINTER OUGHT FIRST to accustom his hand by portraying drawings from the hands of able masters; and having developed this habit with the judgment of his preceptor, he ought then to accustom himself to portraying things in good relief, using those rules that will be told below."[1] Leonardo wrote this precept for the young painter, his *putto pittore,* in Milan in about 1490–92 in what is now known as his Paris Ms. A. He meant it to introduce a method to teach a student to draw from life and in particular to render three-dimensional objects. It was repeated later in the *Trattato della pittura* compiled by Francesco Melzi (Codex Urbinas Latinus 1270, fol. 34r). Although the rules for "portraying in relief" follow the above-quoted passage immediately in Leonardo's Paris Ms. A, Melzi inexplicably put them seven folios later in transcribing Leonardo's notes for the Codex Urbinas Latinus (fol. 41r). The result in the posthumously compiled *Trattato* is the loss of the relationship between learning to draw and studying from life that Leonardo had emphasized in his original manuscript by giving his rules for the two activities one after the other. In that passage about portraying things in relief Leonardo wrote: "One who portrays in relief ought to position himself so that the eye of the figure being portrayed is equal with the eye of the one portraying. And this is to be done for a head that you have to portray from life, because, universally, the figures, or rather, the persons whom you encounter on the street, all have their eyes at the height of yours, and if you made them higher or lower, you would cause your portrait to appear dissimilar."[2] There is a clear relationship between the practice—the *praticha*—of drawing and the rendering of heads, which Leonardo himself then refers to as portraits—*ritratti*—immediately afterward.

Reading these two passages in sequence, possible only in the original Paris Ms. A manuscript by Leonardo or in modern editions of it, may explain why Leonardo's followers in Milan focused almost exclusively on heads, faces, and facial expressions in the enormous number of drawings they left behind.³ Such studies might also be called a type of portrait even though they are not exactly that; they do not seem to be mere generalized drawings of limbs, anatomical details, compositional studies, or the blocking out of an entire narrative. The prevalence of the study of heads and faces in the drawings of Leonardo's followers, which has already been noted in the literature,⁴ is especially evident when one examines the work of his first and closest pupils, material largely concentrated in the decade from 1490 to 1500 and immediately afterward. These years must have seen the earliest diffusion of Leonardo's theories, as expressed in Paris Ms. A, about drawing as well as his ideas of how to teach in the workshop; or perhaps better, the thoughts and theories in Ms. A may be notes based on Leonardo's desire to find a method by which to transmit his teaching. I have recently observed elsewhere that Leonardo's system for training his pupils, his hypothetical *putti pittori*, seems to reproduce the instructional method he himself learned in Verrocchio's shop.⁵ Verrocchio's drawings of "heads of women, beautiful in expression and in the adornment of the hair," as Vasari put it, and his monochromatic drapery studies on linen such as that (fig. 58) for the bronze *Christ and Saint Thomas* at Orsanmichele (Florence),⁶ and similar drawings by Leonardo of heads of laughing women and drapery studies on linen such as those in the Louvre (cat. nos. 13–17) and the Uffizi, which Vasari noted and perhaps also owned, confirm that Leonardo, like Domenico Ghirlandaio, Lorenzo di Credi, and other young artists who worked in or around Verrocchio's shop, was trained by studying and copying the master's drawings.⁷ This group of drawings does not include those by Verrocchio that Leonardo may also have had a hand in, as has recently been suggested for the black-chalk drawing *Head of a Woman* in the British Museum (1875-9-15-785).⁸ The reading of multiple layers on this sheet (an underlying black-chalk drawing by Verrocchio reworked in metalpoint and pen and ink by Leonardo) is the same as that already used to explain the so-called *Study for a Standard* (fig. 79) now in the Uffizi.⁹

Leonardo must have learned a variety of drawing techniques in Verrocchio's shop, including brush drawings on linen, silverpoint on prepared paper, pen and ink, and black chalk, though he only later grasped the importance and flexibility of the last technique, especially during his first stay in Milan (ca. 1481–99)—the period of interest to us here. These were the practical tools he used for the various preparatory phases of the work he executed in the 1470s and 1480s. They soon proved insufficient, however, when early in the 1490s he began his broad exploration of the natural world and the things in it. At the same time the traditional drawing and painting media he had already experimented with became inadequate to represent the "motions of the mind" (*moti mentali*) and to portray from life.

Leonardo's recommendations as recorded in about 1490–92 in Paris Ms. A fit perfectly with the artist's situation as well as with his own evolving needs at a time when he had been in Milan for almost a decade and was surrounded by his first pupils, including Giovanni

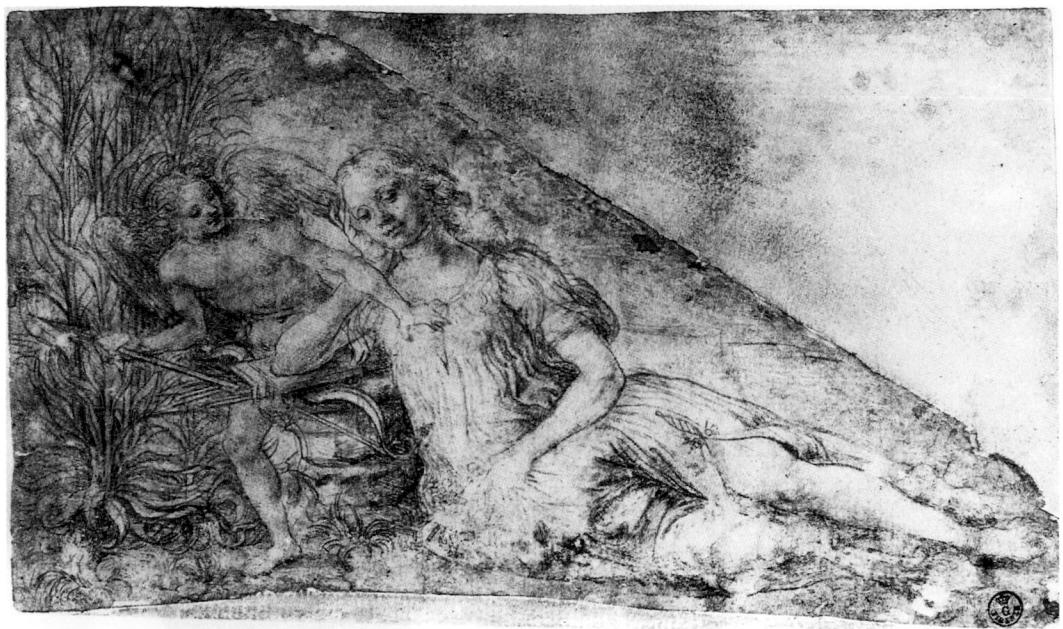

Fig. 79. Andrea del Verrocchio and Leonardo da Vinci, *Study for a Standard* (or *Cupid and a Nymph*).
Metalpoint, some black chalk, on ivory prepared paper, 147 × 258 mm. Gabinetto Disegni e Stampe degli Uffizi,
Florence 212 E

Antonio Boltraffio and Marco d'Oggiono. At that moment he was becoming increasingly interested in theory; at the same time he was changing the way he drew and would soon also change his medium from silverpoint and pen-and-ink drawings to studies in black and red chalk. This fundamental shift was first pointed out in Anny E. Popp's groundbreaking book of 1928,[10] on which much of Kenneth Clark's 1935 reconstruction of Leonardo's development as a draftsman was based,[11] and with which A. E. Popham was largely in agreement.[12] In the second edition of 1968–69 of his catalogue of Leonardo's drawings at Windsor Castle, Clark also implicitly underscored the fundamental importance of the artist's move from Florence to Milan. Although his drawing style was more influenced, after 1480, by Antonio del Pollaiuolo than Verrocchio—evident in his typical use, for example, of brown washes— the style of Leonardo's silverpoint and pen-and-ink drawings seems to have remained more or less the same from 1482 to about 1493, that is, during the first decade of his stay in Milan. A comparison of a drawing of a horse (Windsor, RL 12290) of about 1481–82 and a similar study of a horse, also at Windsor (RL 12321), for the second phase of the Sforza monument about 1490–93 makes this clear. Clark noted, however, that the "comparison shows how much Leonardo has learned in ten years," given that, in the first drawing, "the patches of shadow do not define the form, as they do in the later, and the modelling is less learned and continuous," while in the second study Leonardo "has adopted a finer and more fused line."[13]

The first ten years in Milan were in fact fundamental for Leonardo and not just because of the development of his graphic style. In this decade he began to write down his ideas, and his earliest-known manuscripts date from the period: Ms. B (Institut de France, Paris), to which the date 1483 seems to have been added but which should be dated instead to about 1487–90 (or just a few years earlier, as Clark suggested), has Leonardo's first tentative notes about architecture and the military arts; the Codex Trivulzianus (Biblioteca Trivulziano, Castello Sforzesco, Milan) of about 1490 contains his efforts to appropriate the humanist lexicon and the language of scholars; and finally, Paris Ms. A, certainly begun about 1490, with the first formulations of his artistic precepts and contemporary with or slightly later than Paris Ms. C, also dated 1490, which reports the results of the initial experiments with optics and the studies "of light and shade." And if, as both Clark and Popham have noted, Leonardo's drawing style, in silverpoint or pen and ink, appears to vary little in this decade, it seems significant that at the beginning of the 1490s the changes in his style and technique are also evident in the drawings of his pupils. This was true first of all of the artists who worked with him or in his shop; they immediately reflect his experiments with new techniques and media as well as the drawing practices he brought with him from Florence and the evolution of his style. A brief examination and comparison of the graphic production of Leonardo and of his closest followers, traditionally called the "Leonardeschi," ought to provide some useful clues about the importance of the master's teaching, the diffusion of his *praticha*, and the changes in drawing techniques he introduced in Milan, as well as about the effects his style had in Lombardy well into the sixteenth century.

Leonardo's first decade in Milan began with the commission for the altarpiece for the chapel of the Confraternity of the Immaculate Conception in San Francesco Grande, awarded to him and the brothers Giovanni Ambrogio and Evangelista de' Predis on April 25, 1483. The drawings Leonardo made for the central panel of the polyptych, a representation of "Our Lady" today known as the *Virgin of the Rocks* (Louvre, Paris), would offer extremely useful visual evidence of his graphic style when he arrived in Milan. Unfortunately, however, very little if anything survives of the preparatory drawings for this first version of the painting, certainly finished between 1486 and 1489 (and perhaps never delivered to the members of the confraternity; they later received a second version of the altarpiece, now at the National Gallery in London, begun in 1490–93 and still not finished in 1506).[14]

A drawing of a child's head in the Louvre (cat. no. 61), possibly a study for the head of the Christ Child in the *Virgin of the Rocks*, serves to indicate the variety of techniques Leonardo employed. It is a silverpoint drawing reworked with pen and ink, brush and brown wash, highlighted with white gouache, on light gray-blue prepared paper. The complexity of the technique is indicative of the expressive potential of Leonardo's graphic vocabulary at the beginning of the 1480s. It is also worth noting that this drawing has been pricked and pounced, though we do not know if it was transferred onto the painting surface of a panel (its measurements seem to correspond with those of the picture now in the Louvre) or if it was

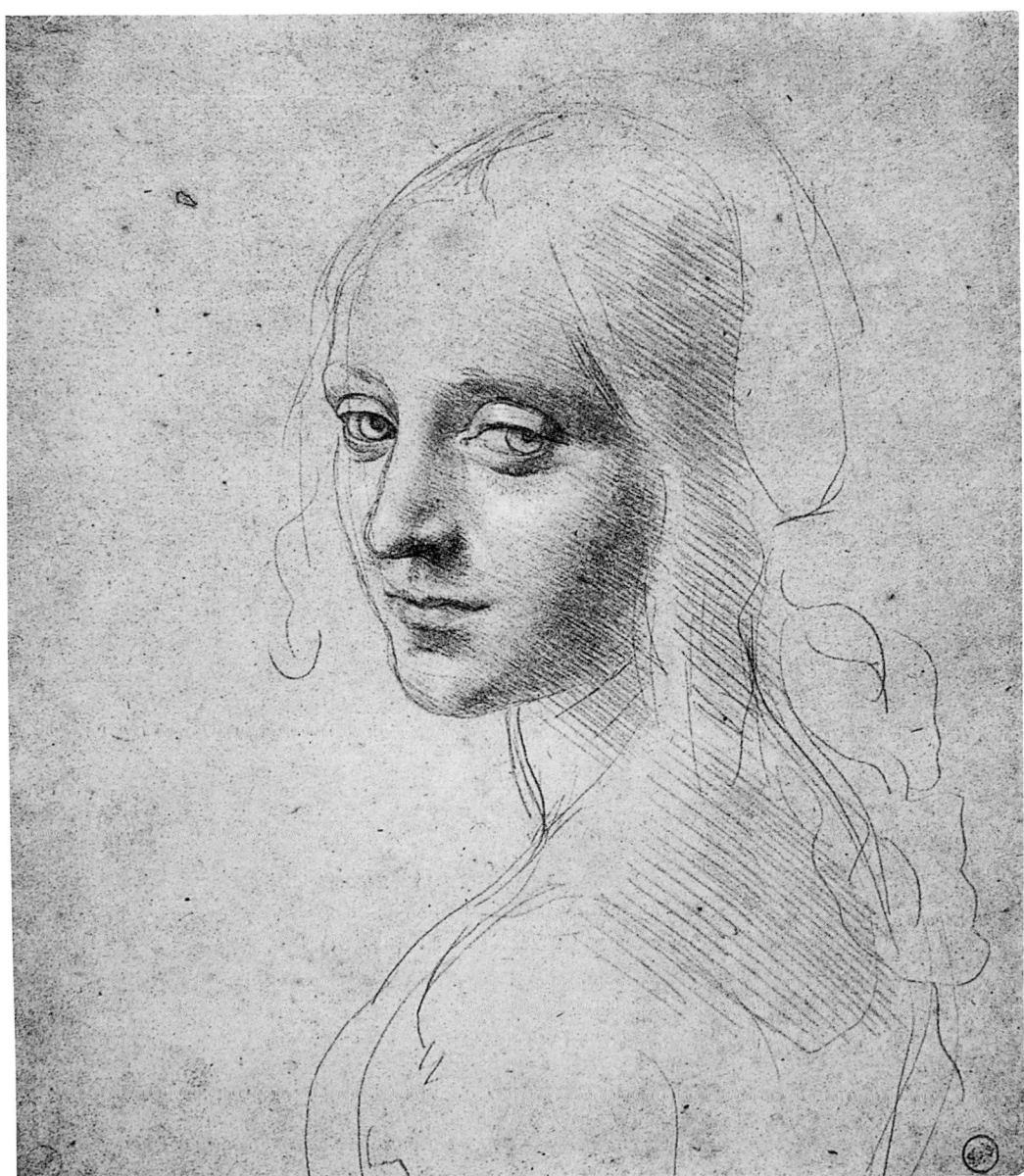

Fig. 80. Leonardo da Vinci, *Study of a Young Woman's Face*. Silverpoint, with traces of leadpoint, and white gouache highlights, on very pale ocher prepared paper, 181 × 159 mm. Biblioteca Reale, Turin 15572

to be copied by pupils. Indeed, there is an exact copy of this head on a sheet in the Devonshire Collection at Chatsworth (893), attributed to Boltraffio, one of Leonardo's earliest followers. Some of its characteristics (the outline of the left cheek, for example) are identical to the Louvre drawing (though the hatching in the Chatsworth drawing is more fastidious and stiffer, and it lacks the ringlets on the forehead and above the right ear), and they do give reasons to pause concerning the Louvre sheet. Recent observations of the latter suggest, furthermore, that some of the right-handed hatching (on the nape of the child's neck, his chin, and his ear, which is completely reworked) as well as some of the white gouache highlights are the result of later retouchings.[15]

A drapery study at Windsor (RL 12521) has until now been identified with the kneeling figure of the angel in the Louvre version of the *Virgin of the Rocks*; it seems, however, to be later and is probably related to the second version of the composition (National Gallery, London), but it seems difficult to explain why Leonardo would have undertaken a new drapery study from life at such a late date.[16] For this reason, therefore, the Windsor study should be dated to the 1490s. The famous drawing traditionally thought to be a study for the face of the angel in the first version of the *Virgin of the Rocks* (Louvre)[17] does not seem on closer examination to coincide with the typology or the position of the youthful angel in the Louvre painting (see figs. 12, 80). (The angel's head is inclined slightly backward in the painting while in the drawing it is more upright.) The hairstyle and age of the woman in the Turin drawing indicate that it is a study made from life, probably in the late 1480s but without any specific relationship to the Virgin in the Louvre painting. Indeed, it was most likely a portrait made in a style very close to the silverpoint drawings dating from the end of the 1480s. The variations in and sensitivity of the hatching, which, as Marco Rosci has pointed out, show every gradation of sfumato,[18] create "the fullest plastic statement," according to Clark, who called this drawing "one of the most beautiful . . . in the world").[19] This suggests, and in my opinion without much room for doubt, a date very close to the anatomical drawings of 1489 and especially the famous studies of skulls now at Windsor (cat. no. 58). The pen-and-ink hatching in the latter is a marvelous translation of the silverpoint technique used in the Turin drawing of the woman's head. One further sheet of studies (cat. no. 45), now in The Metropolitan Museum of Art, has also sometimes been associated with the *Virgin of the Rocks*. It, too, was executed in metalpoint on pink prepared paper and then reworked with pen and ink (perhaps at two separate moments, with the reworking in pen and ink done in the 1490s). It is linked to a sheet at Windsor (fig. 73), also done in metalpoint and then reworked with pen and ink on blue prepared paper. These studies may have been executed later, well into the 1490s; thus the only drawing for the first version of the *Virgin of the Rocks* of about 1483–89 that survives is the Louvre *Head of a Child* (cat. no. 61).

This drawing, then, takes on additional importance as an example of Leonardo's drawing style and technique in Milan in the 1480s, the style, too, that his pupils absorbed and closely imitated. The Louvre drawing (cat. no. 61), formerly in the collection of Giuseppe Vallardi, should thus be examined very carefully as a rare testament of the artist's silverpoint technique (highlighted with white gouache on a light gray-blue prepared paper) in the early 1480s. One must, however, read out the incidental (and irrelevant) white highlights that seem to have been added in the background and beneath the chin (and perhaps also retouched on the child's face) and which seem to present an instance similar to the later retouchings that have been detected on drawings from the collection of Everard Jabach; the retouchings of the Jabach drawings were made when they entered the Louvre.[20] The pen-and-ink rendering of the locks of hair on the Louvre head of the Christ Child, quivering like tufts of vegetation or lance-shaped leaves stirred by the wind such as those in the foreground of the *Virgin of the Rocks* in the Louvre, and the left-handed silverpoint hatching, visible on the child's temple and above his ear, are surely the work of Leonardo's own hand.

Leonardo's drawings of military machines give a more precise idea of his stylistic preferences at the beginning of the 1480s (cat. nos. 48–52); indeed, these drawings seem to illustrate the contents of the letter the artist sent Ludovico Sforza "Il Moro" in about 1483, which is preserved in a nonautograph copy in the Codex Atlanticus (fol. 1082r, formerly fol. 391). A drawing portraying chariots with revolving scythes (Biblioteca Reale, Turin, 15583), executed in pen and ink with brown wash and dated to 1483–85 on the basis of its dependence on Roberto Valturio's *De re militari,* published in the vernacular by Paolo Ramusio in 1483 (a text that Leonardo knew well),[21] confirms the persistence of Antonio del Pollaiuolo's influence on Leonardo. Indeed, the older artist's nervous definition of form with broken outlines and strokes of wash is not far from the style of this drawing. Another sheet that may date from about 1483–85, now in the Accademia in Venice (cat. no. 49), is a silverpoint drawing reworked with pen and brown ink: on the recto are studies of arms, horses, and mounted men and foot soldiers engaged in battle; shown on the verso is a type of catapult with another sketch of how to dig a trench in front of a tower. This sheet is related to the series of rough pen-and-ink drawings that seem to have been jotted down rapidly as immediate, almost crude records of ideas. In a similar sheet in the Louvre (cat. no. 48), however, the studies of weapons drawn in pen and ink over metalpoint were executed on blue prepared paper.[22] The stylistic references to Pollaiuolo and the very Florentine style of these drawings recall Leonardo's studies for the *Adoration of the Magi* (figs. 10, 11), the altarpiece for the monks of San Donato a Scopeto that he left unfinished in Florence in 1482, as an indication of the drawing technique he took with him to Milan and then passed on to his first pupils and followers.

Among the many metalpoint drawings on prepared paper, two sheets at Windsor (RL 12306, 12325) are particularly useful in understanding this style. They both have studies of horses; the silverpoint drawing on red-orange prepared paper has been greatly reworked with pen and ink. There are two exceptional drawings by Lombard followers of Leonardo that exhibit preparations of the paper of this unusual red-orange color (red, pink, or blue preparations of the paper are far more typical in Lombard drawings of the fifteenth century; however, red-orange prepared paper was used in northern Italy much earlier, by Gothic artists) contrasted with lead-white highlighting: one is a sheet in the Ambrosiana with two studies of female heads recently associated with Francesco Napoletano but in my opinion more likely to be by the Master of the Pala Sforzesca,[23] and the other a sheet recently found at the Brera in Milan with a study of three feet, attributed to Cesare da Sesto (fig. 81).[24] It is

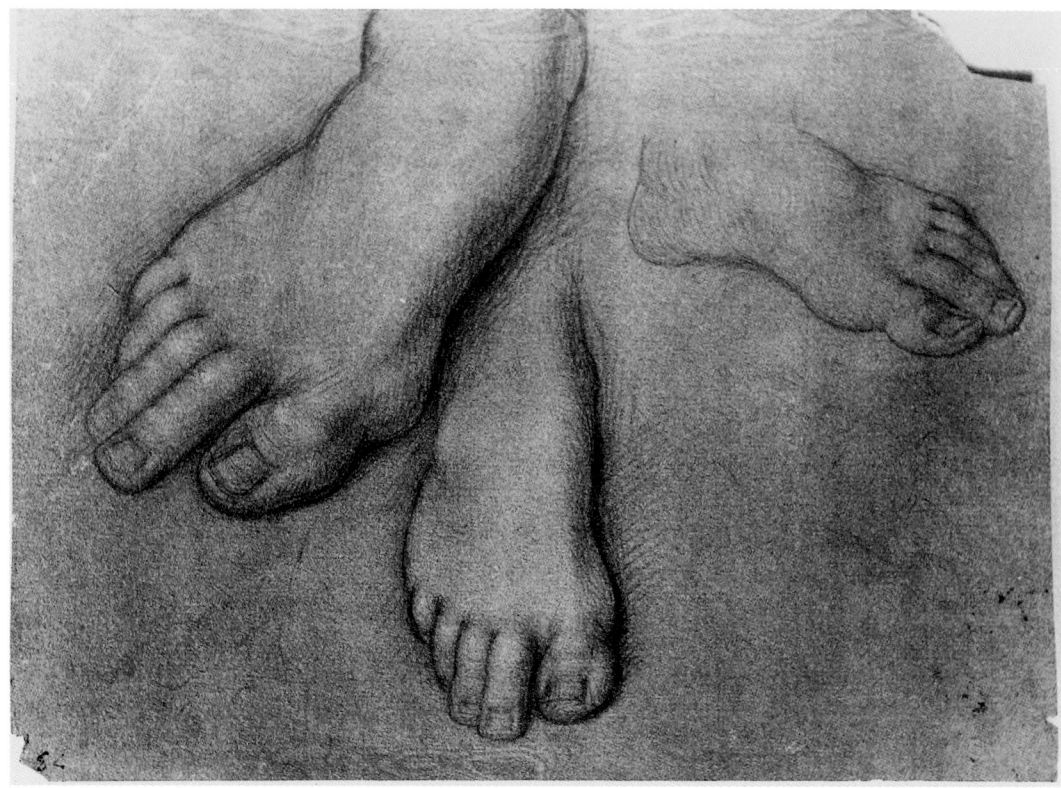

Fig. 81. Cesare da Sesto, *Study of Feet*. Red chalk, highlighted with white gouache, on red-ocher prepared paper, 216 × 255 mm. Accademia di Belle Arti di Brera, Milan s.n.i.

reasonable to assume that Leonardo took his studies for the *Adoration of the Magi* with him to Milan, and Milanese artists would thus certainly have seen them (as well as his drawings for the *Dragon Fight* executed in pen and ink and brown wash such as cat. no. 33 and the sheet now at the Musée du Louvre, Collection Edmond de Rothschild).[25] One cannot exclude, however, the possibility that these drawings by Lombard masters on red-orange prepared paper may have been influenced by the later "red-on-red" studies Leonardo made in the mid-1490s, that is, during the final phase of his preparations for the *Last Supper*. We will return to these drawings in due course.

The equestrian monument of Francesco Sforza was another of Leonardo's important Milanese commissions, generating a great many studies. Given that this monument was perhaps one of the reasons Leonardo had been summoned to Milan, he is likely to have begun work on the project in the very first years of his stay in the city (see cat. no. 53).[26] Drawings from the first phase of the project can be dated to before 1489–90. Representing a rider on a rearing horse above a fallen foot soldier, they were done with pen and ink over silverpoint on prepared, generally blue paper. The second phase began in 1490 and is today better documented thanks to the drawings now bound into Codex Madrid II (8936). These sheets date from 1491 to 1493 and represent a pacing horse overturning a water jar with its right rear hoof. They indicate that the artist was moving steadily away from the pen-and-ink technique, though he still used it occasionally, in favor of red chalk.

Catalogue number 53 is probably one of the earliest studies for the first phase of the Sforza project. With its rapid, darting line in silverpoint on prepared blue paper, it dates to about 1488.[27] Drawings that belong to the second phase include the very fine pen-and-ink drawing of about 1490 in the Ambrosiana (Cod. F 263 inf. 91),[28] those in Codex Madrid II, especially the studies on fols. 151v, 153v, and 157r (there are, of course, other drawings of horses in pen and ink as well as one, on fol. 147r, in black chalk), and the drawing in the Codex Atlanticus (fol. 577v, formerly 216v-a), which cannot be later than 1493.[29] The silverpoint drawings on blue prepared paper, heightened with white, for the Sforza monument are concentrated in the period from 1489 to 1490. Their manner and especially the decisive and accentuated handling of the line and the use of white gouache highlights are important to the argument being made here, and the drawing in Turin (cat. no. 63) is a good example.[30] These studies help to explain the experimental drawings by artists such as Giovanni Ambrogio de' Predis, the Master of the Pala Sforzesca, and especially Giovanni Antonio Boltraffio and Marco d'Oggiono, all of which can be dated to about 1490 or slightly later (see cat. nos. 122–26). The artists in question were certainly also influenced by the series of anatomical drawings and studies of the proportions of the human body that Leonardo made between 1489 and 1490. Many of the sheets, Windsor RL 12601 and 12637, for example, were also done with metalpoint on blue prepared paper and highlighted with white gouache.[31] The combination of silverpoint and very subtle white highlights in these extraordinary anatomical drawings allowed Leonardo to communicate the sense of form as it is struck by light. There are several problematic studies by artists who were almost certainly Milanese but are as yet unidentified that clearly derive stylistically from Leonardo's example but that are less vibrant. These drawings are also similar in technique to Leonardo's; they include the *Study of Legs* in the Uffizi (202 Fr) and the sheet in the Kupferstichkabinett, Berlin (50-1881), with two studies of legs.[32] Further examples can be found in drawings of women's faces such as those at Windsor (RL 12511, 12512), which I have tentatively attributed to Boltraffio and which were inspired by similar but more sophisticated, idealized models by Leonardo.[33]

It seems to me that the chronology of the drawings discussed above, as well as the style of Leonardo's silverpoint studies and the change in his technique that occurred between 1490 and 1493, allows us to date two problematic but autograph drawings to about 1490. The first, in Vienna (cat. no. 66), is a study of a male figure associated with Leonardo's first ideas for the *Last Supper*, done in silverpoint reinforced with pen and ink on blue prepared paper. The second, *Christ Carrying the Cross* in the Accademia in Venice (cat. no. 62), is a silverpoint drawing on gray prepared paper. Clark dated both well into the 1490s and suggested that they were late and unusual examples of a technique Leonardo had almost completely abandoned after 1490. He based his opinion on the fact that the Vienna drawing must be related to the studies for the *Last Supper*, traditionally dated to about 1495. The recent redating of the entire group of studies for the *Last Supper*, however, allows us to move up the date of the Vienna drawing to about 1490, which puts it in perfect harmony with Leonardo's silverpoint drawings on prepared blue paper for the Sforza monument.[34] The fine silverpoint hatching here moves away for a moment from the more nervous, quivering touches in pen and ink and is thus close to Windsor RL 12321, a sheet with studies of horses in silverpoint on blue prepared paper that is related to the second version of the Sforza monument of about 1490.[35] One might also ask if the *Study of Hands* (Windsor, RL 12558), in metalpoint over charcoal and highlighted with gouache on pink prepared paper, which is traditionally dated to 1474, though more likely to have been done in 1478–80 if it were inspired by Andrea del Verrocchio's famous marble sculpture of a woman with a bouquet of flowers (Museo Nazionale del Bargello, Florence), should not instead be assigned to the 1480s. It can perhaps also be associated with the *Lady with the Ermine* (Muzeum Czartoryskich, Kraków), securely dated to about 1488–89, in which the position of the arms is identical except that they are seen from a different viewpoint.[36]

The studies for the second version of the Sforza monument document the important transition from a silverpoint technique on prepared paper to red chalk. This apparently happened before Leonardo's red-chalk studies for the *Last Supper*, which were, as we shall see, contemporary with the last phases of the Sforza monument. This shift in drawing medium is subsequently confirmed by the use of red chalk in the notebooks dated between 1493 and 1494—Paris Ms. H is a good example—and it can thus be used in dating the drawings in silverpoint on prepared (usually blue) paper by many of Leonardo's Milanese pupils. These include Giovanni Antonio Boltraffio, Marco d'Oggiono, the Master of the Pala Sforzesca, and others who remain anonymous. It is fair to assume that these artists, Leonardo's first followers in Milan and working in close contact with him, would imitate his technique carefully. This would mean their abandoning the use of metalpoint when Leonardo switched definitively, in about 1493–94, to red chalk for his studies "from life" (*di naturale*). It is very interesting, then, that Leonardo's pupils were making silverpoint drawings in about 1490. Leonardo himself recorded in 1490 (in Paris Ms. C, fol. 15v) the theft by Salaì (Gian Giacomo Caprotti) of a silverpoint stylus from Marco d'Oggiono and another from Giovanni Antonio Boltraffio, who had left it "on a drawing of his" which was clearly being done in that technique.[37] Scholars have rightly noted that this passage in Paris Ms. C confirms that Salaì as well as Boltraffio and Marco d'Oggiono, all of them members of Leonardo's workshop, were making silverpoint drawings, whether copies or originals, under the master's direction in 1490. Given that silverpoint is not, as Clark has pointed out, "a high Renaissance medium.

It is sharp, brittle and precise like the *maniera secca* which men of the high Renaissance disliked,"[38] its use must not have continued for long even among the students. A silverpoint profile to the right of a young man on blue prepared paper, recently on the art market and now in a private collection in Geneva, suggests the slightly mechanical quality of the metalpoint drawings that Giovanni Ambrogio de' Predis made in the early 1490s following Leonardo's example.[39] The other drawings that we can almost certainly attribute to this artist are done in red chalk and are thus slightly later in date (for example, the *Head of a Lady in Profile to the Left* at the Ambrosiana in Milan [Cod. F 273 inf. 36]),[40] or in pen and black ink and wash, such as the sheet in the Accademia in Venice (260) with studies of a putto for the *Madonna Litta* in the State Hermitage Museum, Saint Petersburg, and for two portraits, one of Maximilian I and the other of Bianca Maria Sforza; because of its connection with the *Portrait of Maximilian I* in the Kunsthistorisches Museum in Vienna, this can be dated to about 1502.[41] Another drawing, in the Hamburger Kunsthalle (21478), that was first attributed to Ambrogio de' Predis by Woldemar Von Seidlitz in 1906, shows three studies of a youth done in silverpoint and heightened with lead white on blue prepared paper.[42] It suggests the possibility that this technique, combined with influences from German graphic artists evident in the very dry and precise quality of the drawing, continued to be used over time.

The controversial *Madonna Litta* (fig. 82), formerly attributed to Leonardo but now more convincingly ascribed to Boltraffio and dated to the 1490s, also offers some evidence that the technique was still current at that date.[43] In addition to Leonardo's famous silverpoint drawing for the *Madonna Litta* (cat. no. 44), there are at least two other drawings by his pupils that can be associated with the painting. These were executed in silverpoint on blue prepared paper. One (fig. 83) is a study of the Virgin's torso that must be, given its quality, by Boltraffio.[44] The other is a study of the head of a woman in The Metropolitan Museum of Art (fig. 84). This shows the Virgin's head in pure profile rather than at its slightly three-quarters angle in the painting, and it has thus been associated by Carlo Pedretti, Mauro Natale, and David Alan Brown with the rather free copy of the *Madonna Litta* now in the Museo Poldi Pezzoli in Milan (1655/39), traditionally attributed to Bernardino de' Conti and dated about 1500–1510.[45] The New York drawing is, however, certainly earlier and should also be dated about 1490. Its quality is sufficiently good to suggest that it, too, might be by Boltraffio.[46]

Boltraffio's drawings dated after 1490 include the drapery study at Christ Church, Oxford (23), for the *Virgin and Child* in the Museo Poldi Pezzoli (1609/1642). Maria Teresa Fiorio begins her catalogue of the artist's work with this study, but I think it should be dated later perhaps to the 1490s. Alessandro Ballarin first correctly identified the subject of the drawing, which is done in a traditional metalpoint technique on blue prepared paper but with the addition of brown wash and a sense of chiaroscuro that demonstrates a greater freedom

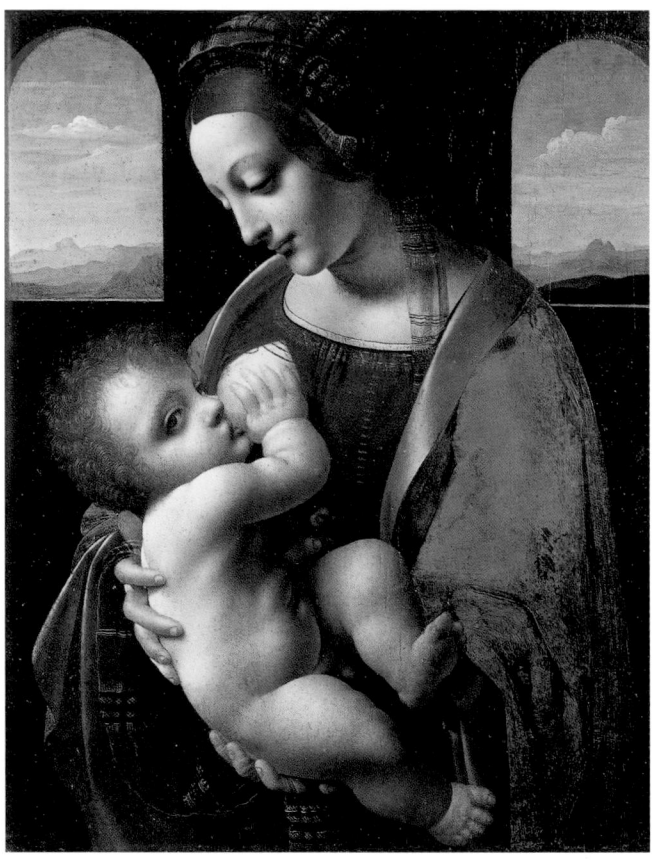

Fig. 82. Here attributed to Giovanni Antonio Boltraffio, *Madonna Nursing the Christ Child (Madonna Litta).* Oil with some tempera on canvas, transferred from wood, 42 × 33 cm. State Hermitage Museum, Saint Petersburg 249

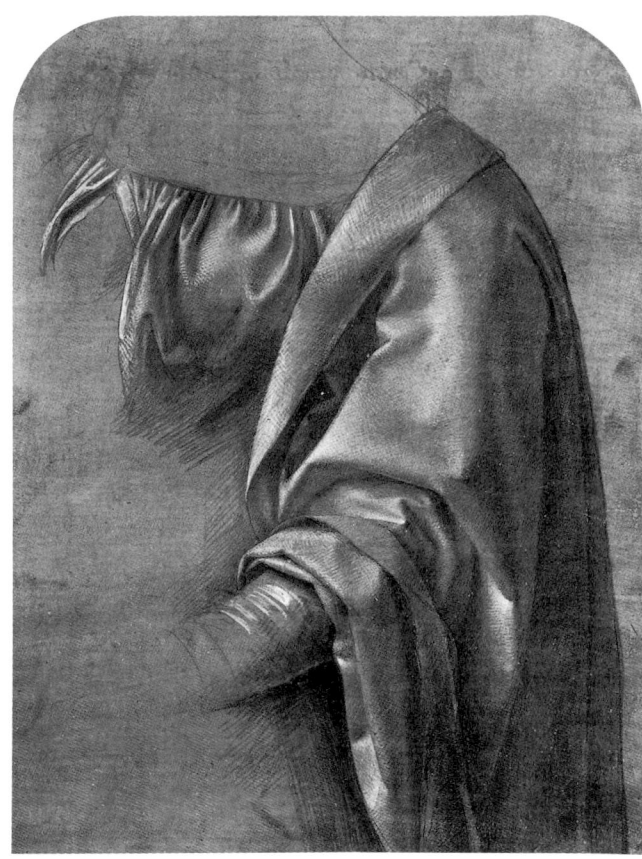

Fig. 83. Giovanni Antonio Boltraffio, *Study for the Torso of the Madonna Litta.* Metalpoint, highlighted with white gouache, on blue prepared paper, 285 × 213 mm. Kupferstichkabinett, Staatliche Museen zu Berlin – Preussischer Kulturbesitz 4144.12

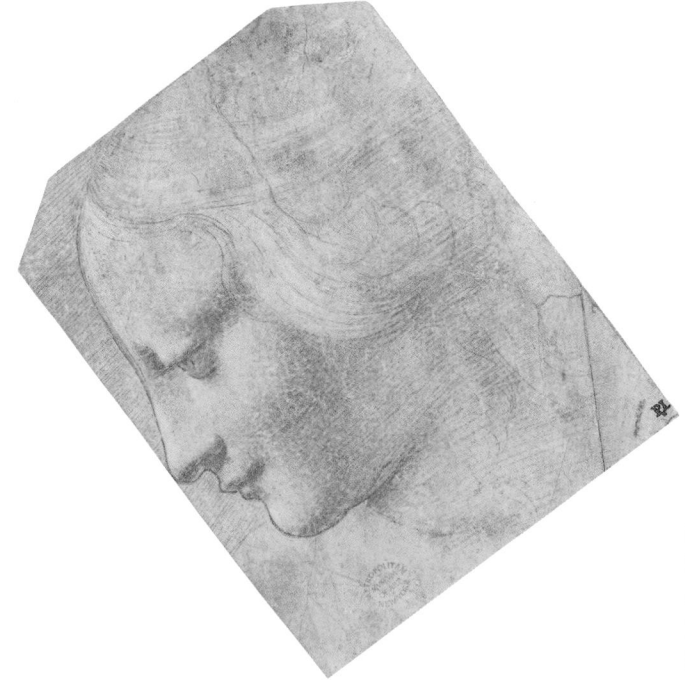

Fig. 84. Here attributed to Giovanni Antonio Boltraffio, *Head of a Woman in Profile Facing to the Left.* Metalpoint, highlighted with white gouache, on pale blue-green prepared paper, 154 × 127 mm. The Metropolitan Museum of Art, New York; Frederick C. Hewitt Fund, 1917 19.76.3

in interpreting Leonardo's models and techniques.[47] Although it is very close to Boltraffio's Berlin drawing, discussed above, it must be dated later.

A sheet in the British Museum (fig. 85) is similar in style and technique to the two discussed above. It is a preparatory study for Christ's drapery in the *Resurrection of Christ with Saints Leonard and Lucy* (Gemäldegalerie, Staatliche Museen, Berlin), a picture that Wilhelm von Bode believed to be by Leonardo but that is now attributed to Boltraffio and d'Oggiono on the basis of abundant documentary evidence.[48] Boltraffio was responsible for the two kneeling saints, Leonard and Lucy, while d'Oggiono painted the figure of Christ, his drapery, and the rock formation and landscape behind him. The latter are executed with a more flowing style and fewer of the subtle passages of chiaroscuro that mark Boltraffio's pictorial technique. It makes sense, then, to attribute the drapery study in the British Museum to

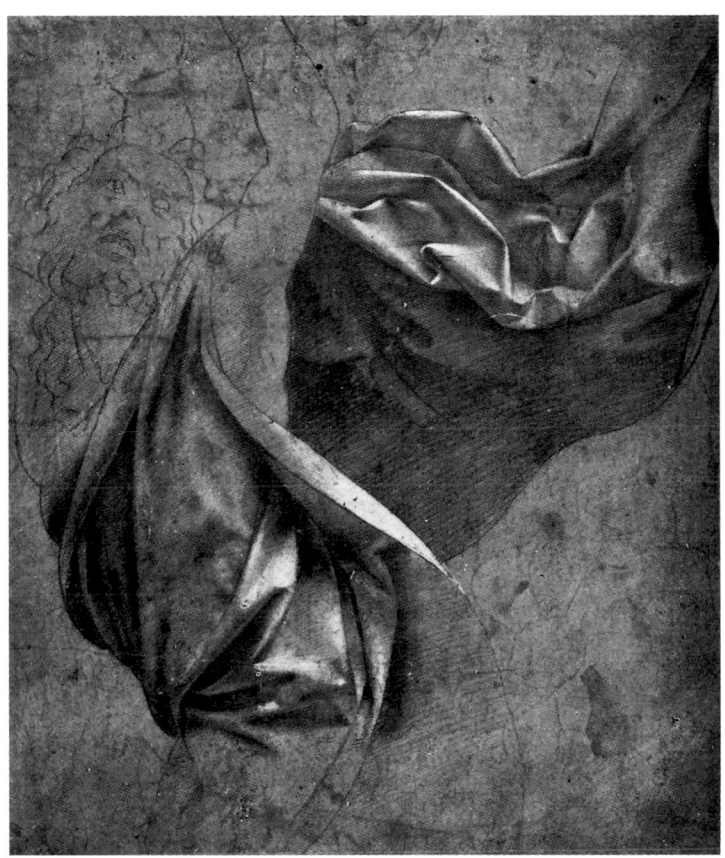

Fig. 85. Marco d'Oggiono (and Giovanni Antonio Boltraffio?), *Study for the Draperies of Christ in the Resurrection Altarpiece* (Staatliche Museen zu Berlin – Preussischer Kulturbesitz). Metalpoint, highlighted with white gouache, on blue prepared paper, 180 × 156 mm. The British Museum, London 1895 9 15 485

Marco d'Oggiono, though it has been suggested that Boltraffio was responsible for it.[49] This drawing shows a sharper and more angular handling of line, especially in the drapery,[50] than one finds in Boltraffio's preparatory study for the *Madonna Litta* in Berlin (fig. 83). There are, however, many similarities of technique between the two, and one cannot completely exclude the possibility that Marco based his part of the painting on a study prepared by his collaborator.[51] The summary definition of Christ's torso and especially the simplified line used to draw his face seem to me to suggest the style and hand of Marco d'Oggiono. Regardless of the artist responsible, the drawing can certainly be dated to about 1491, the year when the first contract for the altarpiece was drawn up, and not to about 1494 when a final agreement gave the two men three months in which to finish the work. Because it can be dated so precisely to 1491, the British Museum drawing (fig. 85) is an important piece of evidence in reconstructing the diffusion of that technique in Marco d'Oggiono's and Boltraffio's circle. This is especially true of the drawings closely related to Leonardo's work in silverpoint, a technique he was shortly to abandon, as these followers did later (see below for Marco d'Oggiono's and Boltraffio's later drawings).

Another important silverpoint drawing is that now in the Ambrosiana (cat. no. 122). Executed on gray-blue prepared paper, it shows Cesare Sforza in profile just as he is represented in the Pala Sforzesca (Brera, Milan), a work that Ludovico "Il Moro" is known to have commissioned in 1494 and that was painted, at the very latest, by the end of the following year. The drawing offers a secure reference for the graphic style of the still-anonymous Master of the Pala Sforzesca. His authorship of a small group of drawings in the Uffizi and the Ambrosiana has recently been confirmed.[52]

The drawings of the artists discussed above are fairly well documented as dating to the 1490s. The case of Bartolomeo Suardi, called "Il Bramantino," on the other hand, is different. Recent studies have revealed his strict dependence on and continuing dialogue with Leonardo's work.[53] What we know of Bramantino's drawing style, though, comes from his work in the first years of the sixteenth century—the lost cartoons for the Trivulzio tapestries (Castello Sforzesco, Milan) of about 1503–9 and his paintings of this period. There are only a few examples of drawings by him from an earlier period, and perhaps the famous sheet in the Uffizi with a pen-and-ink *Martyrdom of Saint Sebastian* can be dated to the last years of the quattrocento. We might, then, look carefully at a group of studies in the Biblioteca Ambrosiana in Milan that has been tentatively associated with Bramantino.[54] They are drawings of male figures, executed in metalpoint and heightened with lead white on blue prepared paper. The metalpoint drawing on blue prepared paper of the head of a man (Ambrosiana, Cod. F 274 inf. 44), rendered in three-quarter profile and in *di sotto in sù* perspective, seems especially to reflect the training he received as a goldsmith in Antonio de Caxeriis's shop from 1486 to 1490. It also reveals Bramantino's proximity to the painter Bernardino Butinone, though he was influenced too by a knowledge of Leonardesque drawings of the late 1480s.[55] An early date of 1490 for this drawing is sustained by its stylistic similarity to the *Adoration of the Magi* in the Pinacoteca Ambrosiana, a painting full of references to Butinone and the Ferrarese culture in which Bramantino was immersed before the exploit of the *Argus* frescoed on a wall of the Sala del Tesoro (Castello Sforzesco, Milan) about 1491–93. (One should note that the head of the shepherd on the right in the *Adoration* recalls in particular the head in the drawing.) The Ambrosiana drawing also demonstrates that Bramantino, too, quickly became aware of the style and technique of Leonardo's metalpoint drawings in which hatching was used to create the effect of light on form.

Marco d'Oggiono's graphic production remains badly documented. Despite the many drawings attributed to him in the past (by Wilhelm Suida and Luisa Cogliati Arano), his style as a draftsman is not clear. This is especially true in the last decade of the fifteenth century, when, as we have seen, his drawings seem to have been confused with other first-generation

Leonardeschi whose "group style" makes their work indistinguishable from that of Boltraffio and the Master of the Pala Sforzesca. Giulio Bora has recently attributed two drawings, both in the Ambrosiana, to Marco d'Oggiono. The first (Cod. F 263 inf. 37) is a silverpoint study on blue prepared paper of a torso related to the figure of Saint Sebastian in the polyptych in the church of Sant'Eufemia in Oggiono.[56] The other (Cod. F 268 inf. 144) is a red-chalk drawing of a crouching male figure related to the fresco of Adam and Eve originally in the Bagarotti Chapel in Santa Maria della Pace in Milan and now at the Pinacoteca di Brera.[57] Although it does not perfectly correspond to the painting, the first drawing may document d'Oggiono's style in the 1490s (the polyptych in Oggiono, however, is certainly later, and the artist may have reused an earlier study for it). The red-chalk drawing, on the other hand, definitely reflects both Leonardo's later drawing style in the same medium and an exposure to Raphael (as well as a trip to Rome) in the first decade of the cinquecento.

The silverpoint drawing in the Ambrosiana seems to be related to the sheets in the Uffizi and in Berlin, discussed above, with anatomical studies of legs. It is different, however, from another drawing in the Kupferstichkabinett in Berlin (KdZ 5103), which has also been attributed to Marco d'Oggiono and identified by Bora as a preparatory study for the artist's *Visitation* now in the Museé des Beaux Arts, Strasbourg. The latter is a late painting, executed in the 1510s.[58] Rather than reflecting Leonardo's evolving graphic style, d'Oggiono seems to have remained tied to a technique of brush drawings, heightened with lead white on prepared paper (a technique used in Berlin KdZ 5103), which he assimilated from Leonardo at the very beginning of his apprenticeship with the Tuscan artist in the 1490s, if not earlier, and on which he grafted his own later stylistic development.

The *Study of the Head of a Bearded Man* (fig. 86), now preserved among the drawings attributed to Francesco Granacci, may be a good example of Marco d'Oggiono's technique in the middle of the 1490s. This very delicate drawing, which has been cut into a tondo, was executed in metalpoint and black chalk highlighted with white gouache on a faintly pink-orange paper.[59] Attributed to Granacci by Bernard Berenson in 1903, it has, however, nothing to do either with Granacci's autograph drawings from his youth or, as Christian Von Holst suggested in 1974, with those that date after 1500.[60] The physiognomy of the man in the Uffizi is unmistakably characteristic of Marco's work—fleshy eyelids, small mouth, and knitted brows—and the artist used the type frequently in his compositions over the course of time until the results become almost idealized masks. This physiognomic formula can be found, for example, in his late *Assumption of the Virgin* now in the Brera and in the frescoes for Santa Maria della Pace in Milan, discussed above, which can be dated to the 1520s.

The Uffizi study (fig. 86), however, should, like the drawings discussed above, be dated to the mid-1490s on the basis of both style and technique. In the second edition of his catalogue of the drawings of Florentine painters, Berenson suggested that in this case Granacci

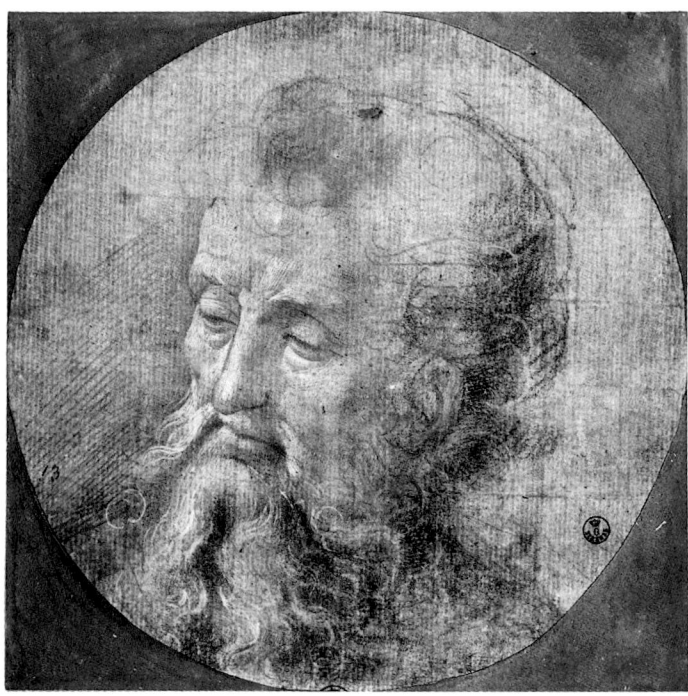

Fig. 86. Marco d'Oggiono, *Study of the Head of a Bearded Man*. Metal-point, black chalk, highlighted with white gouache, on pale red-ocher prepared paper, diam. 220 mm. Gabinetto Disegni e Stampe degli Uffizi, Florence 127 F

(to whom he still attributed Uffizi 127 F) might have been influenced by Perugino and especially by the drawing of a head in the British Museum in London (Pp. 28), and he emphasized that Granacci's drawing was much more three-dimensional than its models.[61] Perugino's drawing of the head of an old man in three-quarter profile to the right — in London and perhaps the one to which Berenson was referring — was done in metalpoint, highlighted with white chalk. It is in fact a study for the saint on the left side of his altarpiece *Virgin and Child with Two Saints* in the church of Sant'Agostino in Cremona, dated 1494 on its base.[62] Marco d'Oggiono reproduced the head of Perugino's saint but in reverse in figure 86, and it is clear that he must have had the opportunity to study the Cremona altarpiece not long after it was delivered in 1494 and then used it as a model for the head of the bearded man in the Uffizi drawing.

Even the most up-to-date artists in Lombardy, that is, those who worked in Leonardo's circle and perhaps including the master himself, must have looked carefully at the stylistic novelties Perugino introduced into the region. They would have been, furthermore, well disposed to assimilate the Umbrian's "sweetness and gentleness of manner" (which Giovanni Santi had already noted in Leonardo's figures) into their own work. Thus we find that Marco d'Oggiono's Uffizi drawing is done both in metalpoint with very subtle white highlights in gouache, consistent with his graphic style in the first years of the 1490s, and in black chalk. The latter was clearly used at the suggestion of Leonardo (who, as we shall see shortly, adopted black chalk for his more mature studies for the *Last Supper* in about 1494) in order to give the drawing a sense of atmosphere and sfumato not possible with silverpoint alone. The Uffizi drawing offers a sort of double check. It signals Marco d'Oggiono's immediate reception of Leonardo's shift in drawing technique a little before the middle of the 1490s, as we see in the black-chalk studies for the heads of the apostles in the *Last Supper*, and it also reveals his interest in Perugino's new, sweet, and easier style.

Leonardo used black chalk for the first time methodically and with a full sense of its expressive potential in his study for the *Head of Saint Philip* (fig. 87).[63] This sheet is correctly dated to about 1493–94 on the basis of its reflection in the head of Saint Lucy in the Berlin *Resurrection of Christ with Saints Leonard and Lucy* painted, as we have noted, by Boltraffio and d'Oggiono between 1491 and 1494 or immediately afterward.[64] Even if Boltraffio's Saint Lucy is not a literal citation of Leonardo's drawing, there can be little doubt that the sense of sweetness created by the passages of sfumato and chiaroscuro, as well as by the "science of emotions" (*scienza degli affetti*) manifest in it, must be derived from Leonardo's new technique of drawing with black chalk that matured in his preparatory studies for the *Last Supper*.[65]

The apostles' emotions and their more subtle expressiveness were created by gestures, expressions, and postures that would have been difficult to work out successfully in metal-point or pen-and-ink drawings. Only a much softer medium like chalk, which was easy to manipulate with the tip of a finger, would allow the artist to achieve the resonating effects of light and emotion he sought. Leonardo continued to use pen and ink to capture his ideal subjects in something like a photographic instant, and the series of caricatures or grotesque heads he made in the last decade of the fifteenth century, works that parallel his draw-

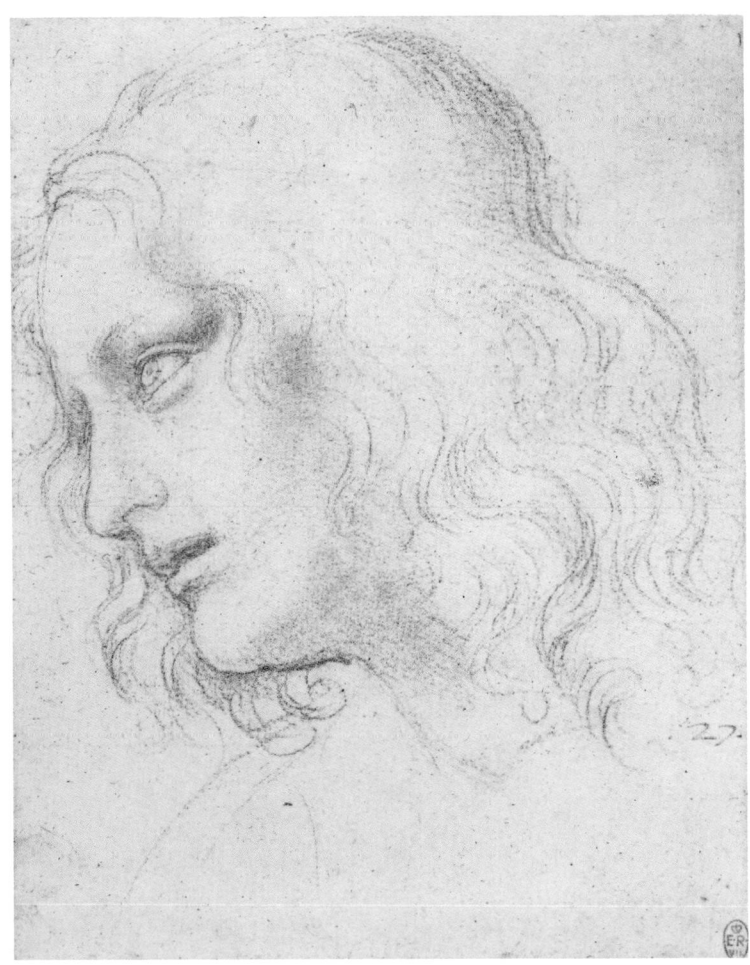

ings from nature and his studies of idealized heads, bear witness to the fact that he still practiced that rapidly executed technique.[66] Yet he began to explore the possibilities of chalk—gray, black, and red—when he started to experiment with reproducing the effects of light and atmosphere he wanted in his paintings, whether they be in oil or tempera (and the choice of a secco technique for the *Last Supper* was a consequence of this desire, given that fresco would never have allowed him to achieve such results).[67]

It is telling that Leonardo also used black chalk in his studies of details for the *Last Supper*. We have already seen that he used it to draw the head of Saint Philip, and he employed the same technique for the hands of Saint John in a drawing (Windsor, RL 12543) that, though it might be "flat and

Fig. 87. Leonardo da Vinci, *Head of Saint Philip*. Black chalk, 252 × 172 mm. The Royal Collection, H.M. Queen Elizabeth II, Windsor Castle RL 12551

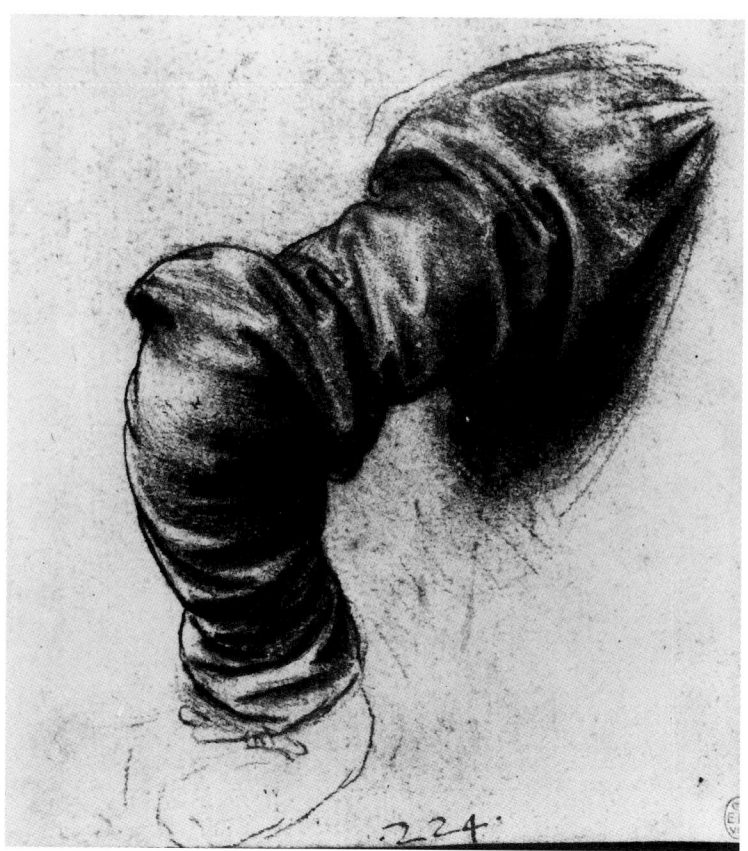

Fig. 88. Leonardo da Vinci, *Study of Arm with Sleeve*. Black chalk, pen and brown ink, highlighted with white gouache, 166 × 154 mm. The Royal Collection, H.M. Queen Elizabeth II, Windsor Castle RL 12546

tame" as Clark deemed it, is certainly an autograph work (and should perhaps be dated to the period of the artist's earliest experimentation with the medium). Black chalk is used with more skill in the drawing of Saint Peter's right arm (fig. 88), which is one of Leonardo's most extraordinary drawings of this period. Traditionally dated to about 1495–96, it has recently been moved up to about 1493–94 on the basis of the fact, noted first by Pedretti and more recently by Edoardo Villata, that this detail of Peter's arm seems to have influenced the anonymous artist who engraved the figure in the frontispiece of Bernardo Bellincioni's *Rime*, published in Milan in July 1493.[68] The drawing is outlined in black chalk, highlighted with white gouache, reworked with pen and brown ink, and then probably smudged with a finger to create a sfumato effect. It has in the past been associated with the *Saint Anne* in the Louvre, especially because it anticipates later studies at Windsor for that painting.[69]

These studies date to the first years of the sixteenth century and anticipate Leonardo's drawings in black chalk and stumping (the seamless blending of tone by rubbing the chalks) for the *Virgin and Child with Saints Anne and John the Baptist* cartoon in the National Gallery in London (fig. 17); they were also quickly absorbed by his Milanese followers,[70] whose work reflects the new stimuli provided by Leonardo in the direction of a more "modern" style. Boltraffio's drawing in the Uffizi (17184 F) of 1498–99 is in this sense a masterpiece. Executed in black chalk, charcoal, and white chalk, it is a study of a bust-length female figure for the Virgin in his Casio Altarpiece, painted in 1500 (on which he defines himself as a "discepolo di Leonardo") for the church of Santa Maria della Misericordia in Bologna (Louvre, Paris).[71] The strong chiaroscuro and "modern" technique Boltraffio adopted clarifies the development of the artist's drawing style, his instinctive appropriation of Leonardo's inventions, and his definitive abandonment of silverpoint. This also opened the way for his later experiments with color charcoals, to which we shall return shortly.

The influence of Leonardo's black-chalk drawings can be seen in another sheet in the Uffizi (1724 F), a *Bust of a Child in Profile to the Left*. Giovanni Agosti has argued that it should be attributed to Giovanni Ambrogio de' Predis.[72] The drawing is especially interesting because it reveals influences of artists from the Veneto and Germany, and it might document de' Predis's tendency at the end of the quattrocento toward a softer and more "modern" handling of line.

Giovanni Agostino da Lodi seems also to have been moving in the same direction; his drawings in the last years of the fifteenth century balance the influence of Leonardo's innovations with elements absorbed from artists of the Veneto. Giovanni Agostino da Lodi's *Study of the Head of a Man* (Gabinetto dei Disegni, Castello Sforzesco, Milan, Sc. B. 36), executed in black chalk on white paper, must come at the beginning of the period when he was thinking about both Leonardo's new style and his use of the medium of black chalk.[73]

There are several examples of black-chalk drawings by the first and second generation of Leonardeschi made after 1500 — today they are found in the collections at the Uffizi, Windsor, Venice, and Milan — and what remains differs from the examples discussed above. They include: Andrea Solario's early black-chalk drawing, with brown wash, for the *Expulsion of Adam and Eve* (Gallerie dell'Accademia, Venice, 269), a drawing often attributed to Bernardino Luini that is, instead, a precocious example of Solario's graphic style;[74] the same artist's later cartoons such as those at the Brera in Milan (*Virgin and Child* and *Saint John the Baptist*, Reg. Cron. 969 and 1228); works by anonymous artists such as the *Head of a Youth* at Windsor (RL 12809, in black chalk with traces of red chalk), perhaps one of Giampietrino's earliest works; the *Head of a Man* (Gallerie dell'Accademia, Venice, 232); and finally Bernardino Luini's drawings, such as the black-chalk and charcoal study on red prepared paper of a woman reading in the Ambrosiana, Milan (Cod. F 290 inf. 9).[75] A discussion of these drawings could take us well into the sixteenth century. Solario's black-chalk and wash drawing at Windsor, the *Lamentation over the Body of Christ* (RL 12819), and his *Head of Christ* in the same medium at the Louvre (2574), for example, can both be dated about 1505. They also earn for the artist the distinction of being one of the best interpreters of this style of black-chalk drawing in which the medium, first used to define folds and contours with a calligraphic line, is then employed more flexibly to achieve soft atmospheric effects like those in the Louvre drawing.[76] It is of greater interest, however, to look again at the last five years of the fifteenth century and to trace the development of another new technique: the use of red chalk and the combination of multicolored chalks that Leonardo seems to have adopted in the final years of his preparation for the *Last Supper*.

It is indeed extraordinary to find that there are two red-chalk copies of now-lost studies by Leonardo for the hands of an apostle in the *Last Supper* (Windsor, RL 12544, 12545) — the originals of which may have been similar to the *Hands of Saint John* discussed above.

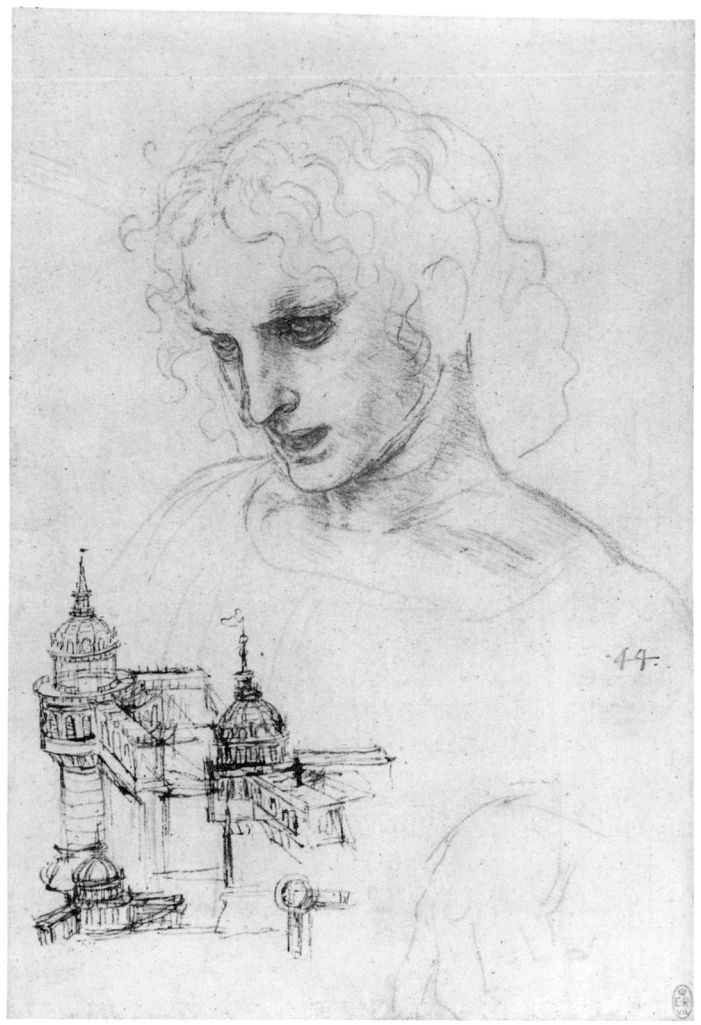

Fig. 89. Leonardo da Vinci, *Head of a Youth Looking Down*. Red chalk, pen and brown ink, 252 × 172 mm. The Royal Collection, H.M. Queen Elizabeth II, Windsor Castle RL 12552

These two drawings by pupils of the master seem to have been done at the same time as those in black chalk. They are drawn, furthermore, on red prepared paper, a combination of material and medium that appears for the first time in the late studies for the *Last Supper*, though Carlo Pedretti has dated them considerably later.[77]

Leonardo first systematically used red chalk in his notes on the casting of the "Sforza Horse" of 1491–93 (Codex Madrid II, 8936) and his nature studies of 1493–94. (Clark has noted that Leonardo's sporadic use of red chalk earlier does not reduce the impact of his full embrace of the medium in these years.) The artist's use of red chalk developed, furthermore, at the same time as his experiments with black chalk, and its influence was immediate and profound. More than black chalk, red chalk could be used with a great degree of naturalism to describe the vibrations of light and atmosphere as well as the vital forces that course beneath a figure's skin.[78]

That red chalk first appears, however, in Leonardo's pocket-sized notebooks (Paris Ms. H, for example, or Codex Forster II and III [Victoria and Albert Museum, London], dated 1493–96) may suggest that the artist used it while traveling or drawing out-of-doors because it was less cumbersome than the more complicated pen-and-ink technique. In these early manuscripts, the red chalk is still used, as Clark has noted, as an incisive and well-sharpened tool, comparable to the pen-and-ink technique. I am also not convinced by Francis Ames-Lewis's argument that Leonardo used black chalk specifically to depict physiognomic awkwardnesses or ingrained features such as wrinkles and expression lines, and, more generally, the heads of the aged while reserving red chalk for the young.[79] This may have happened later, in the artist's second Florentine period, but in the last decade of the fifteenth century black chalk was also used to create effects of sfumato and atmosphere, as the drawings discussed above demonstrate.

A sheet at Windsor with a red-chalk study from life of the head and torso of a youth playing an instrument, later used as a model for the head of Saint James Major in the *Last Supper* (fig. 89), also has pen-and-ink drawings, apparently later, that Pedretti has suggested are related to the work Leonardo did for Cecilia Gallerani at the Palazzo Carmagnola in 1493. It seems clear that the head is a study done from life in about 1493 and then only later adapted for the figure of Saint James in the *Last Supper*. This proves that the red-chalk study is almost contemporary with the black-chalk drawing for the *Head of Saint Philip* (fig. 87) discussed above. The red-chalk drawings on red prepared paper at Windsor of the heads of Bartholomew and Judas (figs. 90, 91) are slightly later, that is, about 1496–97, when Leonardo was already at work painting the mural. Drawings for details like the red-chalk *Study of a Foot* (Windsor, RL 12635) and a group of original studies for the *Last Supper* (which are lost, but known through copies) must then date sometime during 1496–97, based on the chronology of drawings discussed above.[80]

These studies of heads and perhaps also drawings contemporary with them but not associated with the *Last Supper*—the juxtaposed *Profiles of an Old and a Young Man* in the Uffizi (423 E), dated about 1495, is a good example—exerted the largest influence on the drawing styles and techniques of Lombard artists. It seems likely that some of the studies of heads by Giovanni Agostino da Lodi, which must have been already in Venice in the last five years of the century, should be dated to the very end of the fifteenth century or the first years of the next (fig. 92). These include the *Head of a Man* (Kupferstichkabinett, Dresden, C 1923-14), the drawing in Venice (Accademia 262),[81] and the study for a *David with the Head of Goliath* (Kupferstichkabinett, Berlin, KdZ 1543), which Hein-Thomas Schulze Altcappenberg dated to about 1500.[82] The latter already seems to incorporate ideas gleaned from Boccaccio Boccaccino and Giorgione.

Andrea Solario was also among the first Lombard artists to sense the unusual potential of red chalk to achieve natural effects very close to life. Brown considers his drawing *Christ Crucified* (Fitzwilliam Museum, Cambridge, 2116), a preparatory study for the Louvre *Crucifixion* of 1503, to be, for its realism, "a true rarity in Lombard art of the time: a drawing from life."[83] He dates the Cambridge drawing early, to 1502–3. It is interesting to note that artists who were quick to adopt red chalk—and Solario and Giovanni Agostino da Lodi are good examples from Leonardo's circle—had spent a long time in Venice and had had early contact with Venetian artists who were certainly more interested in interpreting the phenomena of light and color and in a manner completely different from that of Lombard artists. But the possibility that a drawing by Solario in red chalk was done from nature also confirms the medium's potential that Leonardo foresaw. The greatest diffusion of the technique of drawing in red chalk on red prepared paper in Lombardy, however, came after Leonardo's second visit there in 1508. This time he used red chalk with a new flexibility. Red-chalk drawings,

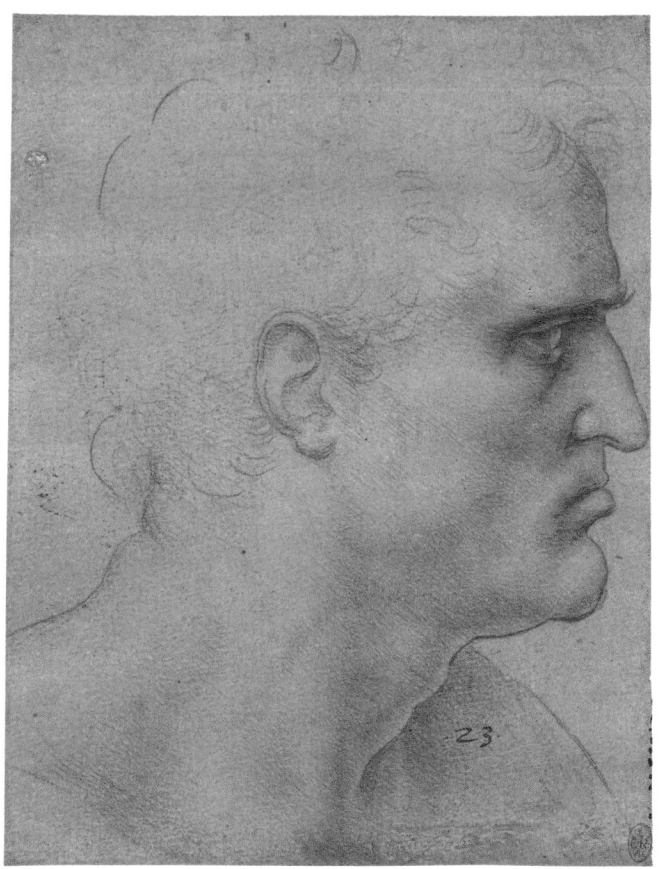

Fig. 90. Leonardo da Vinci, *Bust of Man in Profile Facing to the Right.* Red chalk on red-ocher prepared paper, 190 × 146 mm. The Royal Collection, H.M. Queen Elizabeth II, Windsor Castle RL 12548

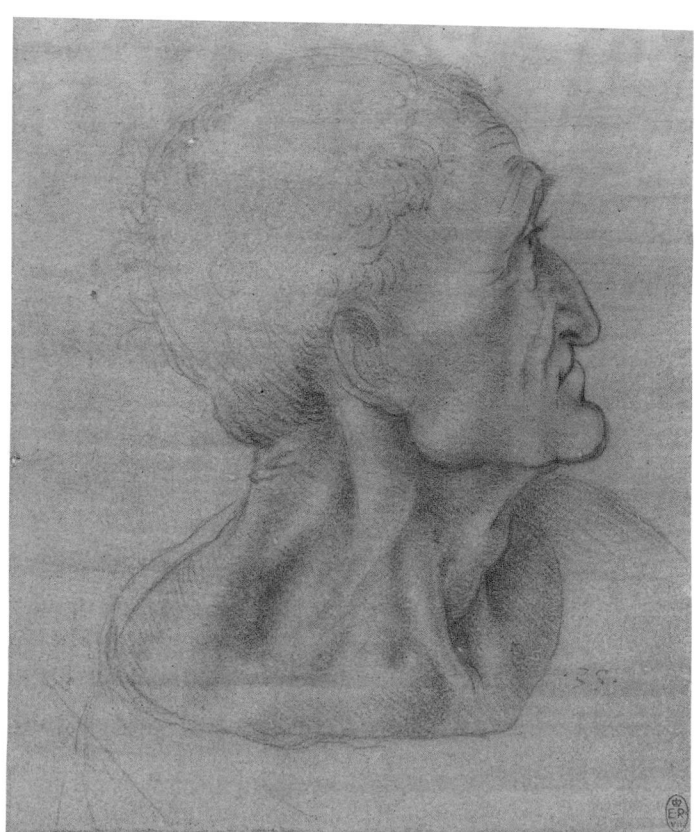

Fig. 91. Leonardo da Vinci, *Bust of Man in Three-Quarter View Facing to the Right.* Red chalk on red-ocher prepared paper, 180 × 150 mm. The Royal Collection, H.M. Queen Elizabeth II, Windsor Castle RL 12547

often combined or reinforced with pen and ink, by artists such as Cesare da Sesto, Francesco Melzi, Giampietrino, and Cesare Magni can now be dated to the last years of the first decade of the century and the early years of the next. The drawings of the first three of these artists are, furthermore, fairly easy to distinguish and characterize stylistically since they have recently been the subjects of exhaustive specialist studies.[84]

Scholars have pointed out the quality of Cesare da Sesto's red-chalk drawings and noted the degree to which he assimilated both Leonardo's style and spirit, though these works also reveal the influence of Raphael and Andrea del Sarto. The group of red-chalk drawings on red prepared paper at the Accademia in Venice, dated to 1511–17, are fundamental to understanding his use of this medium (figs. 93–97).[85] It is interesting to note, too, that Cesare da Sesto had not abandoned the use of pen and ink, as we see in the classicizing drawings dating from the same period to be found in his sketchbook in the Pierpont Morgan Library, New York.[86]

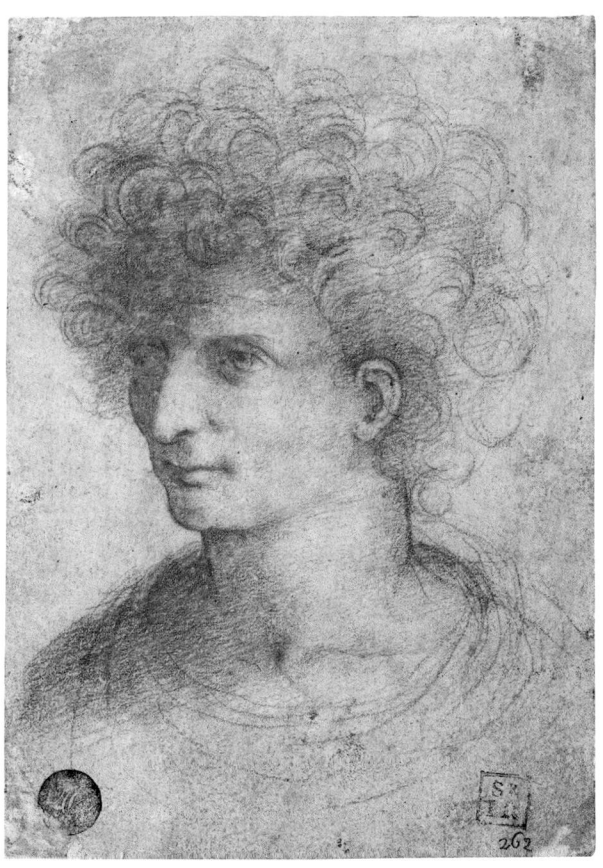

Fig. 92. Giovanni Agostino da Lodi, *Bust of a Young Man*. Red chalk, 145 × 103 mm. Gallerie dell'Accademia, Venice 262

Francesco Melzi's most important red-chalk drawing is the profile of a man (probably based on a statue) on a sheet signed and twice dated 1510 (cat. no. 120). Here the artist's use of red chalk is sharper and his line more insistently incisive. A page in the Codex Resta (fol. 35bis), in the Ambrosiana, contains a study on pink prepared paper of the right foot of Pomona for the Berlin *Pomona and Vertumnus,* dated to 1515–20.[87] Here, however, the use of red chalk reveals the development of a more academic and frozen manner in Melzi's drawing that also betrays the imitation of Cesare da Sesto's style.

Giampietrino's use of red chalk was certainly more original, and one sees this especially in his anatomical studies such as the study of an arm (fig. 98) for his *Mary Magdalen,* now in the Museo d'Arte Antica del Castello Sforzesco, Milan. Here the soft but sometimes quite vigorous line (which creates a strong chiaroscuro effect) is also crosshatched more than in his other compositional studies of later date (the *Holy Family* drawing in the Pierpont Morgan Library, for example, or that for his San Marino Altarpiece, Pavia, now in the Louvre and dated 1520–21).[88] His drawings are characterized by a soft, evanescent use of the chalk, which anticipates the mannerists of the late sixteenth century.

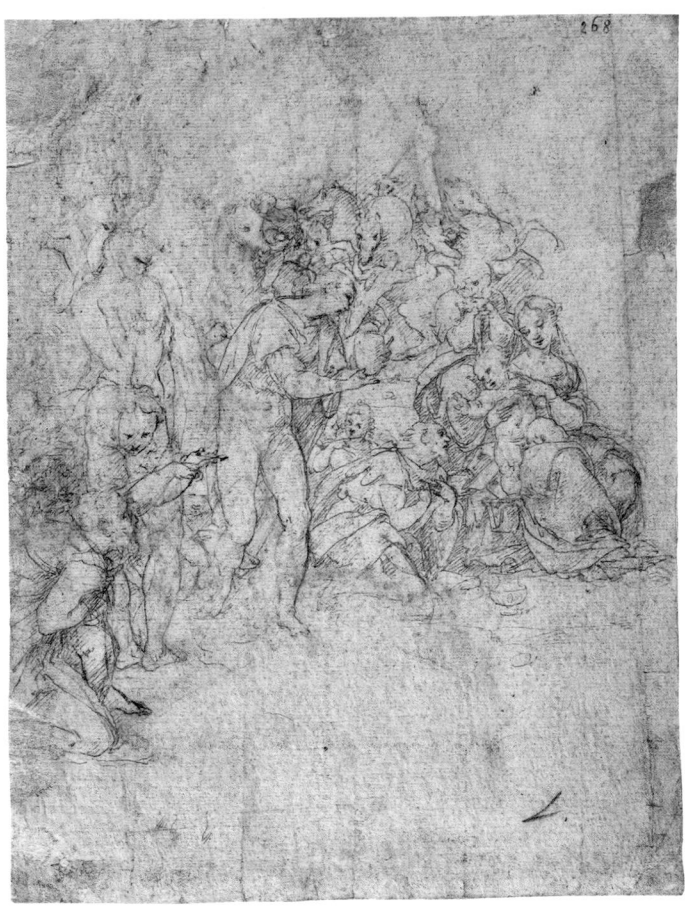

Fig. 93. Cesare da Sesto, *Study for an Adoration of the Magi*. Red chalk, pen and brown ink, traces of black chalk, on pale brown paper, 210 × 161 mm. Gallerie dell'Accademia, Venice 268

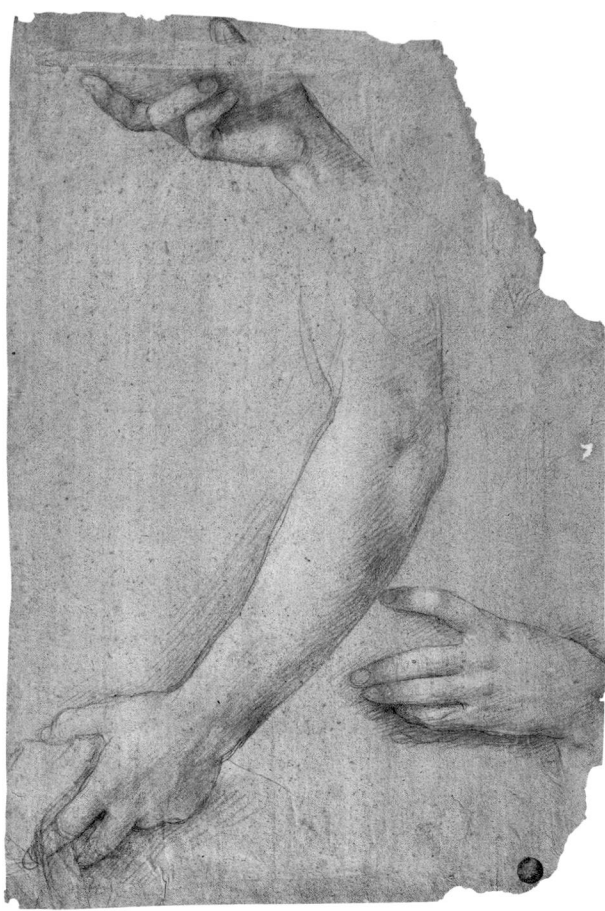

Fig. 94. Cesare da Sesto, *Study of Hands and an Arm*. Red chalk, highlighted with white gouache, on red tinted paper, 390 × 260 mm. Gallerie dell'Accademia, Venice 137

Fig. 95. Cesare da Sesto, *Studies of Arms and Hands*. Red chalk on red tinted paper, 302 × 261 mm. Gallerie dell'Accademia, Venice 143

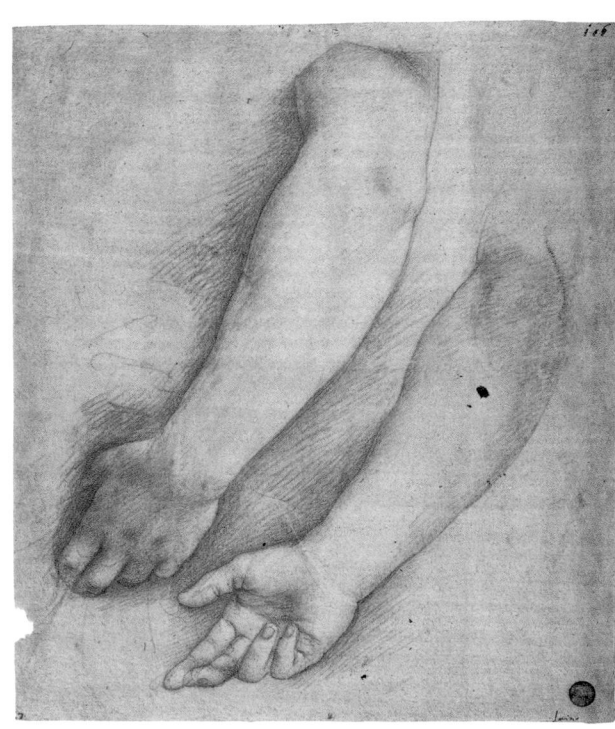

Fig. 96. Cesare da Sesto, *Study of an Arm and a Shoulder, with Caricature*. Red chalk, highlighted with white gouache, on red tinted paper, 395 × 238 mm. Gallerie dell'Accademia, Venice 139

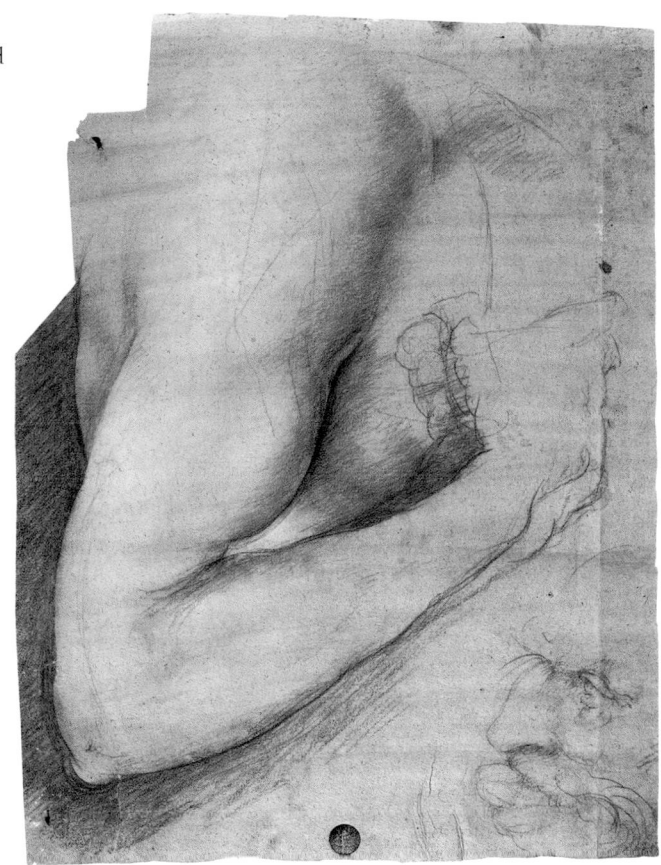

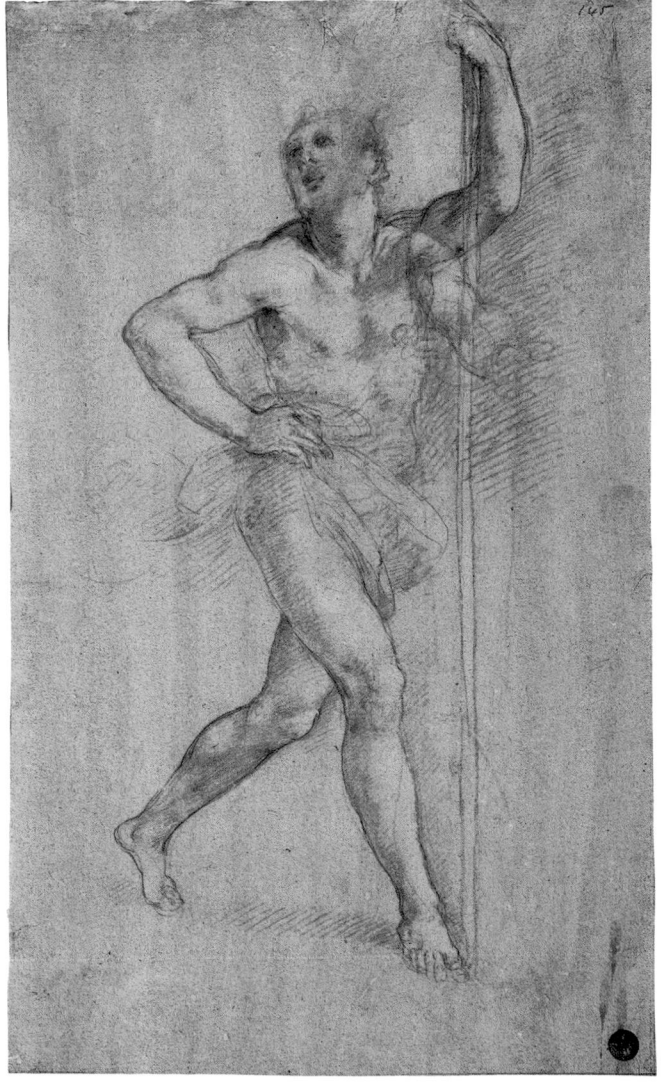

Fig. 97. Cesare da Sesto, *Study for Saint Christopher*. Red chalk on red tinted paper, 310 × 235 mm. Gallerie dell'Accademia, Venice 145

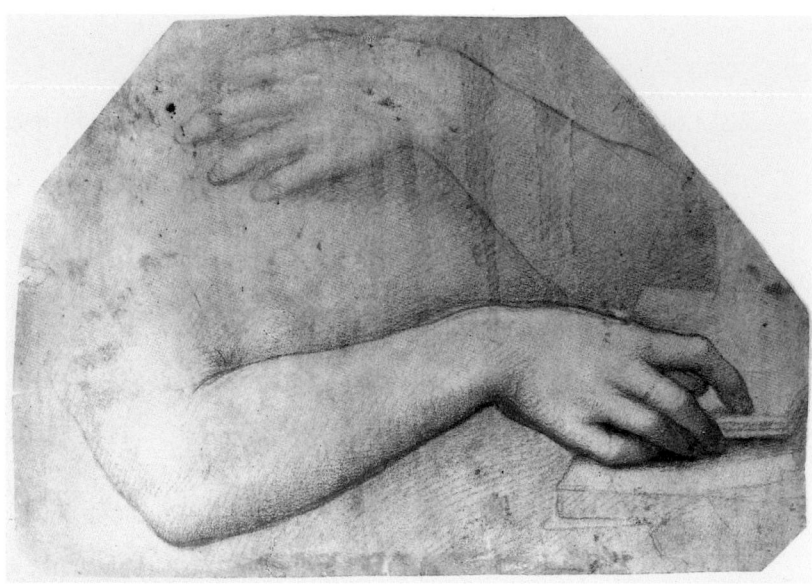

Fig. 98. Giovan Pietro Rizzoli, called "Il Giampietrino," *Study of an Arm for Saint Mary Magdalen*. Red chalk, on lightly prepared paper, 234 × 338 mm. Gabinetto dei Disegni, Castello Sforzesco, Milan C 425

Cesare Magni's identity as a draftsman has yet to be reconstructed. It is worth noting, though, the rediscovery of a sheet at the Louvre that can be attributed to him (fig. 99). The unpublished drawing in red chalk on white paper is a copy of the version of Leonardo's *Virgin of the Rocks* in the National Gallery, London, which was on view in the church of San Francesco Grande, Milan, from at least 1508.[89] We know that Magni made a drawing of the altarpiece on "papiro" (vellum?) or parchment, which he gave to the church of Santa Maria delle Grazie in 1524 in exchange for the saying of masses in perpetuity. The drawing's characteristics are very close both to the style and typology of Magni's pictures and in particular to his free copy of the *Virgin of the Rocks* now in a private collection in Germany and recently published (fig. 100).[90] The style of the Louvre drawing also confirms his authorship of a perhaps earlier drawing in the Ambrosiana (Cod. F 274 inf. 5) of the heads of Judas and Peter from Leonardo's *Last Supper*, in which the handling of the red chalk is the same.[91] The Louvre drawing might likewise be compared to a drawing at the Accademia in Venice (27), also in red chalk on white paper, which was inspired by Bernardo Zenale's altarpiece for the church of San Francesco Grande (Denver Art Museum). The style of the drawing and the handling of line (including its weaknesses) are identical in the two drawings.[92] These three drawings give us some notion of Cesare Magni's graphic style as well as a sense of the last echoes in Milan of the technical and expressive innovations that Leonardo's red-chalk drawings introduced there in the middle of the 1490s.

A discussion of the innovations Leonardo brought to the style and practice of drawing in Lombardy at about the turn of the sixteenth century cannot be concluded without some mention of his experimentation with multicolored chalk at the end of the 1490s. Giovanni Paolo Lomazzo noted this technique in his *Trattato della pittura* (Milan, 1584) when he discussed Leonardo's drawings for the *Last Supper*: "I cannot fail to mention another way of coloring known as with *pastello* [colored chalk]. This is done with sticks composed of colored powder of which [colors] all can be made. It is used on paper and was much employed by Leonardo da Vinci, who drew the exquisite and miraculous heads of Christ and the apostles in this way on paper. But how difficult is it to color in this new manner and how easy is it for it to be ruined!"[93] Lomazzo seems to be referring to these same drawings in his *Idea del tempio della pittura* (Milan, 1590), when, after lamenting the loss of the *Battle of Anghiari* and the *Last Supper*, he consoles himself with the fact that of these masterpieces "only the drawings remain, but neither time, nor death, nor other accidents can vanquish them. With great praise and glory for the artist they will live forever."[94] I have noted elsewhere that these statements seem to suggest that Lomazzo had seen and perhaps owned Leonardo's drawings for the *Last Supper*, even though it must also be said that none of the surviving autograph sheets for the painting can really be said to have been done with multicolored chalks.

Critics have, on the other hand, connected Lomazzo's recollections with a note Leonardo himself made in the Codex Atlanticus (fol. 699r), in which he says, "Obtain from Gian di Paris the method of coloring with dry pigment." "Gian di Paris" has long been identified with Jean Perréal, an artist who went to Italy with the two French military expeditions to the peninsula in 1494–95 and 1499. It was he who first developed a type of drawing "au crayon" that was then very popular in France, in the work of François Clouet, for instance, and throughout Europe, as in the drawings of Hans Holbein. Even Raphael seems to have tried this technique on occasion; for example, in the drawing of a papal procession (Isabella Stewart Gardner Museum, Boston),

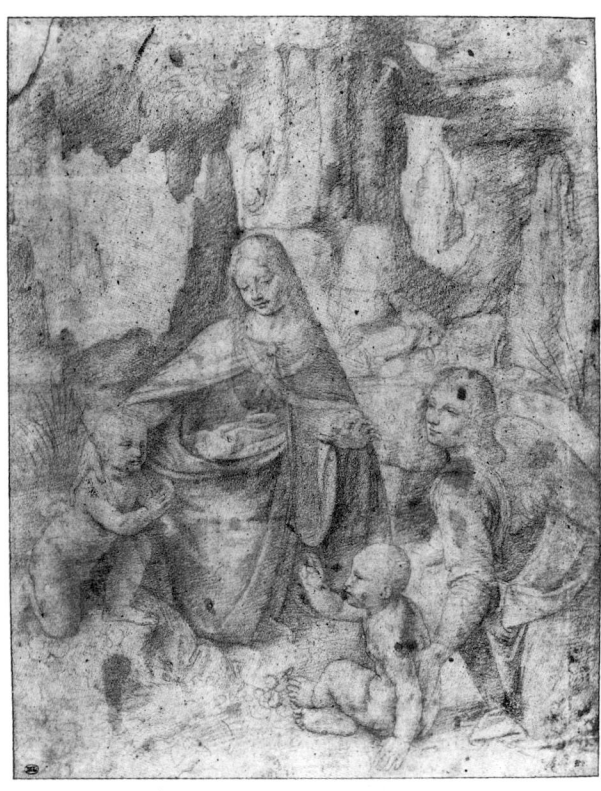

Fig. 99. Cesare Magni, *Copy of Leonardo da Vinci's Virgin of the Rocks*. Red chalk, 265 × 205 mm. Département des Arts Graphiques, Musée du Louvre, Paris 2556

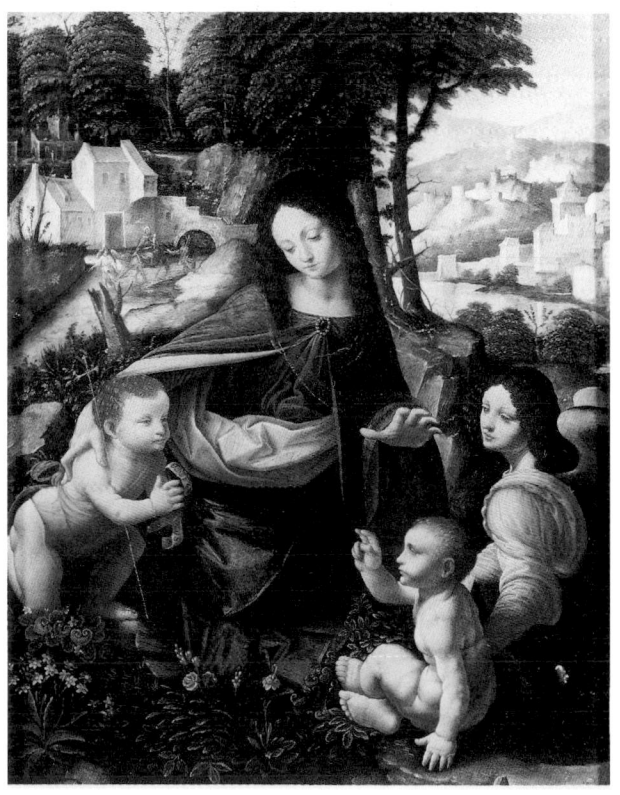

Fig. 100. Cesare Magni, *Copy of Leonardo da Vinci's Virgin of the Rocks*. Oil on wood, 37.4 × 28.5 cm. Private collection, Germany

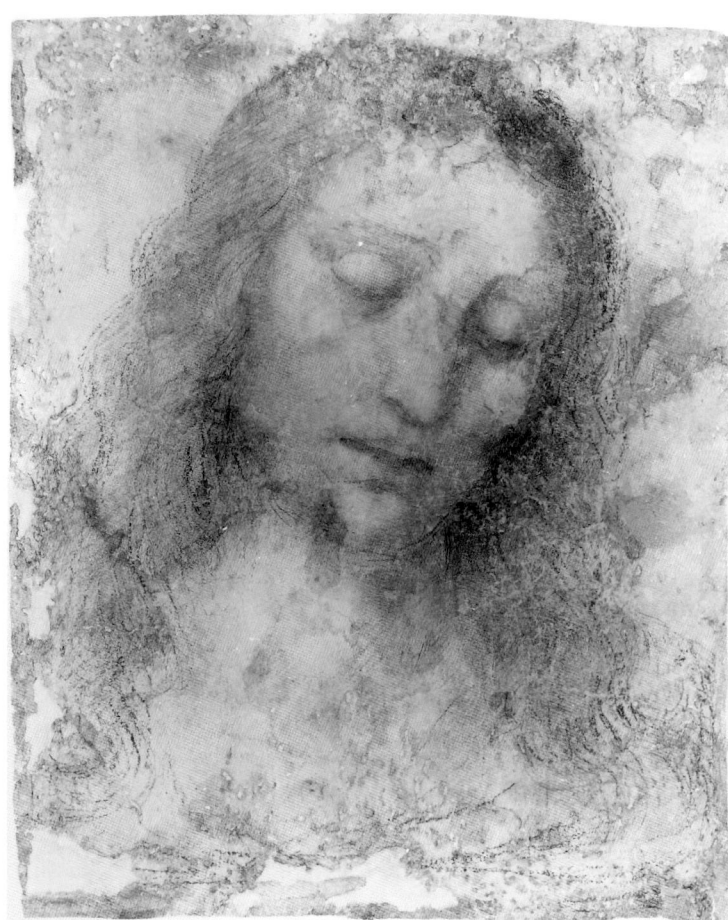

Fig. 101. Leonardo da Vinci (reworked by later hand), *Head of Christ for the Last Supper*. Black and red chalk, pastel, reworked with charcoal, brush and tempera and brown ink wash, 400 × 320 mm. Pinacoteca di Brera, Milan Reg. Cron. 862

which is dated about 1519 and was executed in red, yellow, and black chalk.[95] The attribution of Raphael's drawing has been debated, though Konrad Oberhuber has recently restored it to Raphael's oeuvre. The technique was, however, unusual for an Italian artist outside French-influenced Lombardy at such an early date.

The Brera *Head of Christ* (fig. 101), which was executed in black, red, and colored chalk on pale green paper, and the two series of cartoons for the apostles—that is, six cartoons in the Musée des Beaux-Arts, Strasbourg, attributed alternatively to Boltraffio and Giampietrino, and a second series, of contested date and attribution, formerly in Weimar and now scattered among private collections in Australia, the United States, and England, are the only surviving visual evidence to sustain Lomazzo's claim that Leonardo made colored-chalk studies for the apostles.[96] It seems unlikely that Leonardo had to learn about colored chalks from Jean Perréal, given that he had already made drawings in red and black chalk for the heads of the apostles for the *Last Supper,* if not by 1494 then certainly by 1499, and it is also possible that Lomazzo's statement itself is not accurate (he may in fact have seen the series of cartoons now in Strasbourg and thought them to be by Leonardo). Yet in addition to the Brera drawing (only partially from Leonardo's hand and ruined by repeated retouching), Leonardo's portrait of *Isabella d'Este* at the Louvre, made in the winter of 1499–1500 (specifically between December 1499 and February 1500) while the master was in Mantua, is certainly executed in multicolored chalks (fig. 16). We can see the use of yellow as well as red and black chalk, and the drawing was also carefully and precisely pricked for transfer to a panel or to another cartoon in order to make a copy of it.[97]

Boltraffio was, again, among the first Milanese artists to find inspiration in this combination of media and to make an original use of its potential. He must have learned the technique both by studying Leonardo's lost drawings for the heads of the apostles and from his direct knowledge of the Louvre cartoon portrait of *Isabella d'Este* (Leonardo went from Mantua to Venice; Boltraffio was in Bologna). Two of his large drawings in multicolored chalk are now in the Ambrosiana (cat. nos. 127, 128): *Bust of a Woman* and *Bust of a Man with a Hat*. The first is certainly a study for the *Saint Barbara* now in the Staatliche Museen in Berlin and dated 1502, and thus the drawing must have been made in 1501–2.[98]

Boltraffio's immediate reception both of specific works by Leonardo and of the latter's experiments with technique and medium offers an important tool for dating his other drawings, as well as those made by other followers of Leonardo in Milan. In view, for example, of the connection between techniques in Leonardo's drawings and paintings, the controversial *Bust of a Youth with a Crown of Leaves* can only be dated to several years after 1501–2. This drawing (Uffizi, Florence, 566 E) previously attributed to Sodoma or an unknown Milanese artist but ascribed to Boltraffio by Fiorio,[99] is less confident and so full of Leonardesque references taken from the *Mona Lisa* that it seems more likely to date after 1504, though it also reveals a knowledge of the *Portrait of Charles d'Amboise* (Louvre), a copy of the original by Andrea Solario dated to about 1507–9.[100] The work cannot be by Boltraffio because it is weaker than the two drawings in the Ambrosiana, which also date to about 1502.

There is a multicolored-chalk drawing in the Uffizi (427 Er) that can be associated with the portrait of *Isabella d'Este* at the Louvre. It shows a profile of a man to the left, and on the verso there is a small, red-chalk drawing of the bust of a woman, which Françoise Viatte has associated with the *Isabella d'Este* cartoon. She has thus assigned it a date of about 1500.[101] Giovanni Morelli attributed it to de' Predis, and the undulating, calligraphic quality of the hair seems to reflect a knowledge of Leonardo's drawings of the 1490s, such as the so-called *Self-Portrait* in the Biblioteca Reale in Turin (fig. 1). This famous image does not represent Leonardo himself, but he might have done it about 1495 as a study of a head (perhaps as a sort of elderly counterpart to the head of an ideal youth) related to the heads of the apostles for the *Last Supper*. Indeed, it was even copied in the background of a recently recovered painting by Sodoma, which can be dated, at the very latest, to the first years of the cinquecento.[102] Andrea Solario's 1505–7 *Portrait of a Man in Three-Quarter Profile to the Left with a Hat* in the Uffizi (1917 F), done in red and black chalk with traces of white-chalk highlights, is perhaps one of the earliest examples of the use of multicolored chalk.[103] Solario's drawing takes advantage of the warm color of the paper, as heavy as parchment, as a base for his flesh tones, an expedient that closely recalls Leonardo's efforts to achieve a strong naturalistic illusion (using his fingertip to manipulate the painted surface). Multicolored chalk was employed shortly afterward by Luini in his *Portrait of a Woman* in the Albertina (cat. no. 131), perhaps a portrait done from life of Ippolita Bentivoglio and then used later, about 1521, by the same artist in the church of San Maurizio al Monasterio Maggiore in Milan.[104]

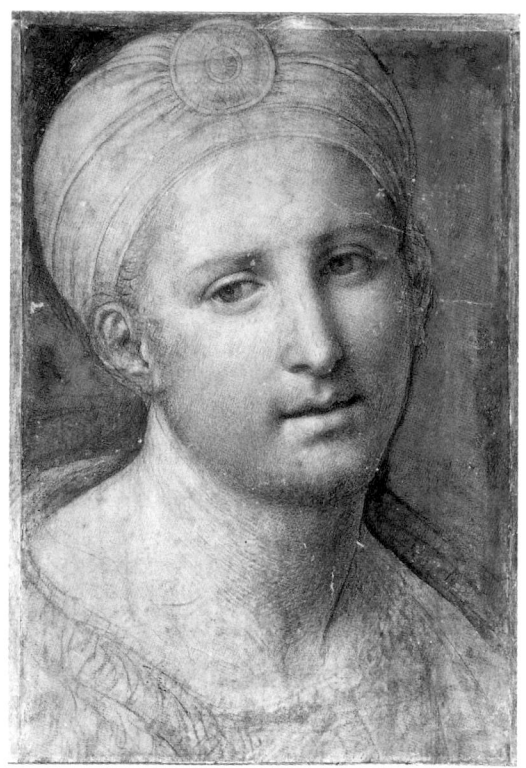

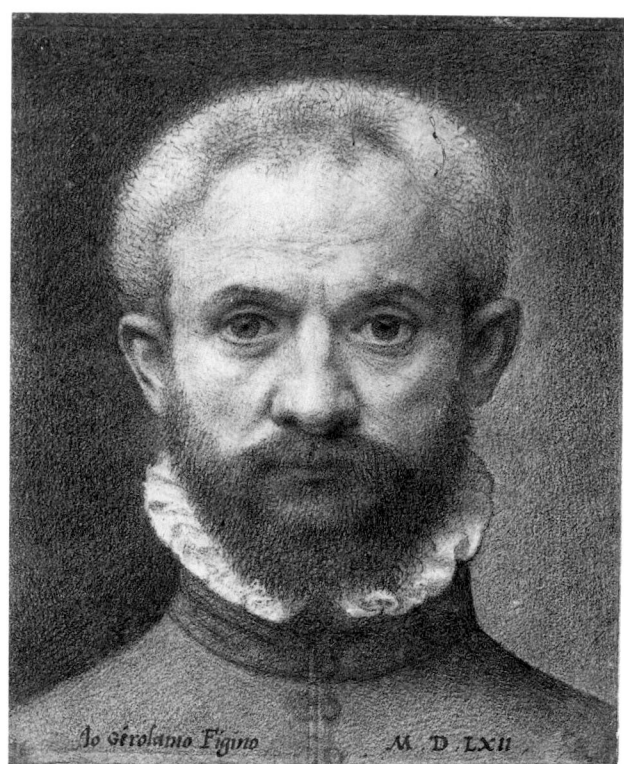

Fig. 102. Andrea Solario, *Young Man with Turban*. Black chalk, pen and brown ink, brush and brown wash, traces of white gouache highlights, 374 × 246 mm. Graphische Sammlung Albertina, Vienna 243

Fig. 103. Gerolamo Figino, *Self-Portrait*. Black and red chalk, 194 × 158 mm. Pinacoteca di Brera, Milan Dis. 250

This brief review of drawings by Leonardo's followers in Lombardy, necessarily based on only a few examples, comes to a close with another extraordinary example of a large drawing by Solario, a *Young Man with Turban*, in the Albertina (fig. 102), which almost certainly dates from the artist's stay in France. Here Solario offers an example of a mixed-media technique that must have taken its cue from Leonardo's own graphic experiments; he reinforced a charcoal and wash drawing with pen and ink and then heightened it with lead white.[105]

Later developments in drawing techniques in Lombardy and Emilia, that is, from the middle of the sixteenth century onward, demonstrate the vitality of Leonardo's teaching. The impressive optical realism of Gerolamo Figino's *Self-Portrait* of 1562 (fig. 103), which was drawn with black and red chalk on white paper,[106] seems to recall the precise precepts that Leonardo set down on how to draw from nature and that we took as a starting point for this essay.

1. Venerella 1999– , *Manuscript A*, p. 246. This is a better translation than that of Richter 1883, vol. 1, p. 244. For Melzi's transcription, see *Libro di pittura* 1995, vol. 1, p. 175, par. 63: "Il pittore debbe prima suefare la mano col ritrarre disegni di mano di boni maestri, e fatto detta suefazione col giudizio del suo precettore, debbe di poi suefarsi col ritrarre cose di rilevo bone, con quelle regole che del ritrar de rilevo si dirà."

2. Venerella 1999– , *Manuscript A*, p. 246. "[Quello] che ritrae de rilevo, si debbe aconciare in modo tale, che l'occhio della figura ritratta sia al pari de l'occhio di quello che ritrae; e questo si farà ['n] una testa, la quale avessi a ritrarre di naturale, perché universalmente le figure over [le] persone che scontri per le strade tutti hanno i loro occhi a l'altezza dei tuoi, e se tu li facessi o più alti o più bassi, verresti a dissimigliare il tuo ritratto"; *Libro di pittura* 1995, p. 187, par. 89. Richter 1883, vol. 1, p. 270, par. 541, also separated these two passages, by more than twenty-five pages, even though they follow each other on the same page in Paris Ms. A.

3. For a modern edition of Leonardo's manuscript, see Marinoni 1990.

4. See, for example, Bora 1987b.

5. Marani 1998e.

6. I believe that Uffizi 433 E is most likely by Verrocchio rather than Leonardo. It is significant that A. E. Popham, in his *Drawings of Leonardo da Vinci* (Popham 1945), does not include it among the series of drapery studies he attributes to Leonardo, beginning with the famous drawings in the Fondo Corsini (125770) in the Istituto Per la Grafica, Rome, and the Cabinet des Dessins at the Louvre (2255). See Marani 1999c, pp. 12–18; 2000b, pp. 12–17. For Vasari's comment on Verrocchio's drawings of women's heads, see Vasari 1912–15, vol. 3, p. 270. For the women's heads, see Viatte 1994.

7. For the monochromatic drapery studies, see Louvre 1989–90, and Christiansen 1990. See also Cadogan 1983b and Cadogan 1983a. Françoise Viatte and I have new findings on the Louvre studies, which she reports in this catalogue.

8. Leonardo's additions to this cartoon include the delicate left-handed hatching in gray wash over Verrocchio's black chalk; see Bambach 1999a, pp. 260–61. This hypothesis has been accepted in Ames-Lewis 2001.

9. I first noted Leonardo's reworking of this drawing in Marani 1989, pp. 13–14. See also Brown 1994b. G. Dillon, on the other hand, reaffirms the traditional attribution of the drawing to Verrocchio alone (see Petrioli Tofani 1992, pp. 150–51) and is followed in this by C. Morandi in Scalini 2001–2, p. 134.

10. Popp 1928.

11. Clark 1935.

12. See Popham 1945, and the revised edition of his study with an introduction by Martin Kemp (Popham 1994).

13. Clark and Pedretti 1968–69, vol. 1, pp. xxv–xxvi.

14. For the history of the commission for the *Virgin of the Rocks* and the two extant versions of the altarpiece, see Marani 1999c, 2000b, pp. 123–55, including bibliography. See also the recent work, Shell and Sironi 2000.

15. For the Louvre drawing (2347), which came from the Vallardi collection, see Françoise Viatte's entry for catalogue number 61. See also Bambach 1999a, pp. 83–85 and 403–4. The head of the Christ Child in the painting in the Louvre is, however, smaller than it is in the London version, though it is not possible to get exact measurements. Bambach has reported that the height of the Child's head in the Louvre drawing is 121 mm; when I measured it on the original on February 16, 2002, I found that it was 125 mm in total, from the chin to the top of the head. For the Chatsworth drawing, attributed to Boltraffio, see Fiorio 2000a, pp. 170–71, no. C9, with a discussion of the earlier bibliography. The drawing, which Fiorio rejects as by Boltraffio, is inverted in the reproduction. As Varena Forcione of the Cabinet des Dessins at the Louvre kindly pointed out to me, the two white marks below the Child's chin hide the collection marks of Sir Peter Lely and J. Richardson. See also note 20 below.

16. Clark (Clark and Pedretti 1968–69, vol. 1, p. 93) dates the Windsor drawing (RL 12521) to about 1496. The idea that Leonardo meant radically to transform the first version of the *Virgin of the Rocks* and began new studies for the figures and draperies should be abandoned. Nor does the Windsor drawing correspond with the drapery of the angel in the second version of the picture in the National Gallery in London. Stylistically, it is a problematic drawing (though I believe it is autograph; see Marani 2000b, p. 133). Edoardo Villata has suggested (in an oral communciation, 2002) that it might be a drawing made afterward by Bramantino—an interesting suggestion, yet to be sustained. Windsor RL 12520, which has been related to the angel's right

hand, is also problematic (again I believe it to be an autograph drawing; see Marani 2000b, p. 133) and should perhaps be considered a derivative work, though of very high quality, by a pupil.

17. For which, see Pietro C. Marani in Palazzo Reale 2001, p. 120, no. 25, with a discussion of the earlier bibliography. Carlo Pedretti in Sciolla 1990, pp. 42–43, no. 11, rightly dates this drawing "più verso la fine che all'inizio degli anni ottanta." He notes technical and stylistic similarities with the studies of horses at Windsor Castle for the Sforza monument.

18. Rosci 1979, pp. 90–91.

19. Clark 1988, p. 94.

20. See above, note 15, for these retouchings and the marks they hide. Even if these white retouchings are from the nineteenth century, we cannot exclude the possibility that the ex-Vallardi drawing had also been partially reworked by one of Leonardo's pupils. Another drawing in the Louvre (RF 5635) has similar, though not identical, characteristics. It represents the body of a child without a head and is executed in metalpoint on a deep blue prepared paper, which, the retouchings and restorations notwithstanding, may well be by Boltraffio or perhaps more precisely, an early sixteenth-century drawing of about 1515–20 (when Boltraffio's style had changed completely), attributable to Melzi or a copyist (the child drawn on Louvre RF 5635 is similar to a Holy Family in Prague at the Národní Galerie that I believe to be a copy after Melzi; see Marani 1988a, p. 381, fig. 265). For the retouching of many of the Louvre drawings that came from the Jabach Collection in 1671, see Monbeig Goguel 1988.

21. For the derivation of this drawing from Ramusio's translation of Valturio, see Marani 1984, pp. 31–33.

22. For the drawings in Turin, Venice, and Paris, see also Pietro C. Marani in Palazzo Grassi 1992, pp. 206–13, where I have suggested a date of about 1485 for all of them.

23. The two drawings that I believe to be by the Master of the Pala Sforzesca are Uffizi, Florence, 425 E, 426 E. See, however, Bora 1998c, pp. 99–101, fig. 4.8. Francesco Napoletano's personality as a draftsman is still not clear (his last name, Galli, we now know thanks to research by J. Shell and G. Sironi). Bora's suggestions were not accepted by G. Agosti (Agosti 2001, pp. 183–88), who attributes Uffizi 426 E (assigned to Francesco Napoletano by Bora; see Palazzo Grassi 1992, p. 370) to the Master of the Pala Sforzesca, an attribution that I had also made and with which I agree. I think that Uffizi 425 E (attributed to Boltraffio by A. Ballarin and G. Agosti in Agosti 2001, pp. 188–94) should also be attributed to the Master of the Pala Sforzesca; it is very closely related to Uffizi 426 E and to a study of a woman's head in the British Museum (1895.9.15.475) correctly attributed to the Master of the Pala Sforzesca by Bora in 1987 (in Palazzo Reale 1987–88, p. 162). The Ambrosiana drawing, first laid down with a brown wash and then highlighted with white gouache, can be associated in terms of both style and the characteristics of the woman's face with drawings by the Master of the Pala Sforzesca such as Uffizi 426 E and British Museum 1895-9-15-475, both reproduced by Fiorio 2000a, pp. 198–99, nos. D37, D38.

24. This drawing was first published by Pietro C. Marani in Brambilla Barcilon and Marani 1999c, pp. 35–36. See also A. Rovetta in Palazzo Reale 2001, p. 199, whose proposed date of 1515–18 might perhaps be moved to the first decade of the sixteenth century.

25. For the drawings for the *Dragon Fight*, see Popham 1954. See also Marani 1999c, 2000b, pp. 101–6.

26. For the Sforza monument, see Brugnoli 1974, and Fusco and Corti 1992.

27. For this drawing, see Martin Kemp in Kemp and Roberts 1989, p. 56, no. 8.

28. See A. Rovetta in Ambrosiana 1998–99, pp. 72–73.

29. For the transition from silverpoint to red chalk, see Clark and Pedretti 1968–69, vol. 1, p. xxvi and n. 3. (Clark observes that occasionally a drawing of about 1480, such as Windsor RL 12568, might have been done in red chalk without implying habitual use of this medium at this time.) For the drawings for the Sforza monument cited here, see Marani in Ambrosiana 1998–99, pp. 40–43.

30. For this drawing, see L. Tongiorgi Tomasi in Petrioli Tofani 1992, p. 194, no. 9, with earlier bibliography.

31. Clayton 1996–97, pp. 41–43, nos. 18, 19, which dates the first drawing to 1488–89 and the second to about 1490.

32. For Uffizi 202 Fr, which I pointed out to Carlo Pedretti in 1982 (see Pedretti and Dalli Regoli 1985, pp. 72–73, who suggest a possible attribution to Boltraffio), see Fiorio 2000a, p. 198, no. D36 (who rejects the attribution to Boltraffio). For the Berlin drawing, see Schulze Altcappenberg 1995, p. 216, no. 65 (where it is attributed to the school of Leonardo da Vinci).

33. The two Windsor drawings, RL 12511 and 12512, are silverpoint on blue prepared paper. Clark attributed the first to Marco d'Oggiono and the second to Boltraffio (Clark and Pedretti 1968–69, vol. 1, p. 90). See also Marani 1999c, 2000b, p. 181, for the attribution of both to Boltraffio, keeping in mind that the second may have been heavily reworked. M. T. Fiorio (Fiorio 2000a, pp. 203, 209) has rejected Boltraffio's authorship of either drawing, though without any valid reason.

34. See Palazzo Reale 2001, pp. 103–53; and for the Vienna drawing, see esp. the entry on p. 122. For the *Christ Carrying the Cross* in Venice, see the entry for cat. no. 62, and most recently, G. Nepi Scirè in Nepi Scirè and Torrini 1999, p. 68, no. 19.

35. For this sheet, see Kemp 1989b, p. 99, no. 40.

36. This proposal has already been put forward in Marani 2000b, p. 31, where the drawing is associated with a Milanese portrait. The drawing (see Kemp 1989b, p. 51, no. 4, where it is dated about 1474; Clayton 1996–97, pp. 14–15, no. 1; and P. L. Rubin in Rubin and Wright 1999–2000, p. 189, no. 30) was dated by Clark to about 1478–80, though he also noted its similarities to the metalpoint drawings executed about 1490. See also Brown 1998b, pp. 106–9, which offers again the debatable suggestion that the arms and hands in this drawing (though in a different position) can be associated with the *Ginevra de' Benci* (National Gallery of Art, Washington, D.C.). See also Brown 2001–2, pp. 142–45. This study may have been done in preparation for the portrait of Cecilia Gallerani, in which the arm holding the ermine and the raised right arm repeat exactly—though from the right rather than the left—the position of the arms in the Windsor drawing. For the *Lady with an Ermine*, see Fabjan and Marani 1998–99.

37. For this incident, see Marani 1998e, pp. 9–10.

38. Clark and Pedretti 1968–69, vol. 1, p. xxvi.

39. Trinity Fine Art Ltd., Salon du Dessin, Paris, 2001, correctly attributed to de' Predis (11.3 × 14.9 mm) and thought to be a portrait of Massimiliano Sforza on the basis of a comparison with the miniature on the inside cover of Codex 2167 (Biblioteca Trivulziana, Milan). See Testori 2001, pp. 18–19, no. 2. Massimiliano was born in 1493, but the drawing is not identical to the miniature and might also represent Cesare, son of Ludovico "Il Moro" by Cecilia Gallerani, who was born in 1490. My thanks to Françoise Viatte for bringing this drawing to my attention.

40. See M. T. Fiorio in Palazzo Reale 1987–88, no. 19, attributed with a question mark to de' Predis.

41. See Cogliati Arano 1980, pp. 106–7, no. 54, and Kwakkelstein 1999, esp. pp. 186–88, fig. 10.

42. See Bora 1998c, pp. 97 fig. 4.7, 100, with earlier bibliography.

43. For the *Madonna Litta*, see Brown 1990b. Fiorio has now confirmed the attribution of this painting to Boltraffio (Fiorio 2000a, pp. 81–83, no. A3).

44. See Schulze Altcappenberg 1995, pp. 110–12.

45. For this painting, see Natale 1982, pp. 90–91, with earlier bibliography.

46. The drawing was first catalogued in Bean 1982, pp. 121–22, no. 112. Fiorio includes it among the works with an uncertain attribution to Boltraffio (Fiorio 2000a, p. 175, no. C15).

47. See Ballarin 1992, p. 2, fig. 23. For the relationship of the drawing to the painting, see Fiorio 2000a, pp. 76–77, 138.

48. See Shell and Sironi 1989b, with a discussion of the critical and historical literature and the texts of the contracts for the work dated 1491 and 1494.

49. This hypothesis has been put forward by Alessandro Ballarin (Cittadella, forthcoming).

50. See Popham and Pouncey 1950, vol. 2, fig. CXIV (recto). See, too, the verso of this sheet (fig. XCV) and comments by Schulze Altcappenberg 1995, p. 112.

51. Fiorio 2000a, p. 138, explores this possibility.

52. See Agosti 2001, pp. 180–88. On drawings by the Master of the Pala Sforzesca, see the literature cited in note 23 above.

53. See Tomio 2002, with a discussion of the recent bibliography. For a first attempt at a catalogue of Bramantino's drawings, see Suida 1953, pp. 71ff. The chronology proposed in Bora 1980, pp. 3–5, has been superseded by recent studies.

54. See Palazzo Reale 1987–88, pp. 64–67, nos. 13–15.

55. On the *Head of a Man*, see Rossi in Ambrosiana 1998–99, pp. 122–23, no. 52, who dates it 1497–1503. The drawing, however, is without a doubt earlier than that.

56. See Palazzo Reale 1987–88, pp. 88–89. For the related painting, see Sedini 1989, p. 188, no. 94, who rejects an attribution to Marco d'Oggiono of both the drawing and the painting. It seems unlikely that another drawing in red chalk on white paper in the Ambrosiana (Cod. F 271 inf. 8), attributed to Marco by Bora (Palazzo Reale 1987–88, pp. 90–91), is indeed autograph. Sedini 1989, p. 32, accepts the attribution to Marco of this unattractive drawing and relates it to the *Saint Sebastian* in the Museo Poldi Pezzoli in Milan (Sedini 1989, p. 31, no. 3b). It clearly has nothing to do with this painting, from which it differs in the position of the torso, the arms, and the head. For Marco d'Oggiono's graphic oeuvre as a whole, see Bora 1998c, pp. 99ff.

57. See, for this drawing, Bora in Palazzo Reale 1987–88, pp. 114–15; and for the fresco and the drawing, Sedini 1989, pp. 143–45, nos. 53, 54.

58. For the drawing, see Bora in Palazzo Reale 1987–88, pp. 17–18, and Schulze Altcappenberg 1995, pp. 113–14 (who dates it to about 1520). For the Strasbourg picture and the related drawing, see Sedini 1989, pp. 168–69, nos. 64, 65.

59. Berenson 1903, vol. 2, no. 914. In making this attribution, Berenson was perhaps thinking of the head of God the Father in Granacci's tondo now in the Staatliche Museen in Berlin (229), for which see Bock 1996, pp. 57, 450. Berenson's attribution was repeated without comment in Petrioli Tofani 1991, pp. 58–59.

60. Von Holst 1974, for example, nos. 13–15, 18, 21, 29. Uffizi 189 F, a pen-and-ink drawing on blue prepared paper, for example, was identified by von Holst (no. 13) as a preparatory study for the head of Saint Francis in the Covoni Altarpiece at the Accademia in Florence, and Uffizi 435 F (no. 15), on blue prepared paper, as securely attributed to Granacci. Neither has any technical or stylistic similarity with Uffizi 127 F, which I first identified on the mat in 1992 as by Marco d'Oggiono. This attribution escaped Agosti 2001.

61. Berenson 1938, vol. 1, p. 103, no. 970A.

62. For Perugino's drawing in the British Museum, see Popham and Pouncey 1950, no. 188. It is also reproduced in Scarpellini 1984, p. 183, fig. 92, with reference to the entry for the Cremona Altarpiece, pp. 88–89, no. 61. For Perugino's prestige and influence in Milan and Lombardy in these years, see Fabjan 1986, with preceding bibliography. The Perugino drawing in the British Museum (Pp. 28) was first in Giorgio Vasari's collection and then in that of Pierre-Jean Mariette. See Bacou 1967, p. 84, no. 101.

63. For the use of black chalk, see Ames-Lewis 2001, with bibliography.

64. Marani in Palazzo Reale 2001, p. 132.

65. As observed in Bertelli 2001, p. 43. He noted that the female saint in the Berlin painting gazes upward while in Leonardo's drawing the apostle looks down. Bertelli believes that Leonardo's Milanese followers would have absorbed older models from the Master's Florentine period into their compositions. Apart from the fact that the chiaroscuro which allows Boltraffio's Saint Lucy to display her feelings would have been impossible without the example of the *Head of Saint Philip* (Windsor, RL 12551), it should be noted that in current scholarly opinion the cartoon, or project for the composition, of the Berlin altarpiece (among the other Leonardesque features are the unified composition, the dramatic reactions of the saints to Christ's appearance, the monumentality of the drapery, and so on) must reflect Leonardo's style in about 1490.

66. For Leonardo's grotesque heads, see Gombrich 1954, 1976. For the various sources relative to the caricatures,

see L. Cogliati Arano in Ambrosiana 1982; A. Rovetta in Ambrosiana 1998–99, pp. 80–98; Pietro C. Marani in Grasselli 1995–96, pp. 80–83, with bibliography.

67. For the mural technique of the *Last Supper,* see Brambilla Barcilon and Marani 2000b.

68. For this drawing and the relevant bibliography, see Pedretti and Trutty-Coohill 1993, pp. 131–35, and Villata 2000. For the earlier dating of the drawing, see Marani 2001, pp. 134–35.

69. Clark and Pedretti 1968–69, vol. 1, p. 101.

70. For an earlier date for the London cartoon, just after 1501, see Marani 1999c, 2000b, pp. 262–75. See also Marani 1999a.

71. For Uffizi 17184 F, see Agosti 2001, pp. 194–97, no. 34, with bibliography.

72. Agosti 2001, pp. 178–80, no. 30. This is, I think, a drawing of the last years of the fifteenth century.

73. The drawing was first published by G. Bora in Palazzo Grassi 1992, pp. 122, 125–27, 135 n. 53.

74. See Brown 1987, p. 139, no. 11, where it is dated to the earliest years of the sixteenth century, just after the *Christ Carrying the Cross* in the Pinacoteca Tosio Martinengo in Brescia (Brown 1987, no. 10). It seems to me, rather, to be from the last years of the quattrocento and related to the *Christ Carrying the Cross with Carthusian Monks* by Bergognone (Pinacoteca Malaspina, Pavia), dated to about 1497.

75. For these drawings, see the relevant entries in the previously cited catalogues: Clark and Pedretti 1968–69 (for Windsor, RL 12809); Cogliati Arano 1980 (for the two drawings in Venice); and Ambrosiana 1998–99 (for Ambrosiana F 290 inf. 9).

76. Brown 1987, pp. 148–49, nos. 29–30.

77. Pedretti 1983, pp. 106–10.

78. For Leonardo's red-chalk drawings, see Tordella 1996b, pp. 187ff.; Spagnolo 2000; and Ames-Lewis 2001, pp. 14–32.

79. Ames-Lewis 2001, pp. 26–34.

80. For the reconstruction of the sequence of red-chalk drawings for the *Last Supper,* the confirmation of their authenticity, and for copies after them, see Marani in Palazzo Reale 2001, pp. 103–15 and the entries for the drawings at Windsor, RL 12552 (Saint James), 12635 (Christ's foot), 12548 (Saint Bartholomew), 12550 (Saint Simon), and 12549 (copy of Saint Simon's head), pp. 130–31, 136–37, 142–47.

81. Bora, in Palazzo Grassi 1992, pp. 372–73, no. 79 (and related to the *Christ Washing the Feet of His Disciples* in the Accademia in Venice, about 1500), who also refers to the sixteenth-century course of Giovanni Agostino da Lodi's drawings, of which attention should at least be called to the Louvre drawing (Cabinet des Dessins, 2252) and that at the Accademia in Venice (262), both executed in red chalk.

82. Schulze Altcappenberg 1995, pp. 118–20.

83. Brown 1987, p. 141.

84. For the graphic work of these artists, see the studies cited in the above notes by Giulio Bora, Luisa Cogliati Arano, and Carlo Pedretti. In particular, see Bora 1998c.

85. See Perissa Torrini in Palazzo Grassi 1992, pp. 400–419.

86. See, for example, Carminati 1994, pp. 242–86, with bibliography.

87. For these two drawings by Melzi, see Rossi and Rovetta in Ambrosiana 1998–99, pp. 78–79, 114–15, with bibliography. Many sheets at Windsor were attributed to Melzi in the second edition of Clark's catalogue (Clark and Pedretti 1968–69). See also Pietro C. Marani, in Palazzo Reale 1987–88, pp. 92–95, nos. 36–38.

88. The drawing in the Castello Sforzesco was published for the first time in Marani 1987a, p. 204, no. 37. For the drawings in New York and at the Louvre, see Bora 1987–88, p. 15, fig. 7. I have also tried to attribute to Giampietrino a drawing of Saint Barbara that was recently on the art market in New York; see Samsum 2001, no. 1, red chalk on buff paper, 198 × 146 mm.

89. I intend to publish this drawing in *La revue de l'art.*

90. See Fiorio 2000b, fig. 2.

91. For this drawing, which I first attributed to Cesare Magni but which Bora later ascribed to Marco d'Oggiono,

see A. Rovetta in Palazzo Reale 2001, p. 202, for a discussion of the proposed attributions and a confirmation of Magni's authorship.

92. For this drawing and the altarpiece, which has also been attributed to Cesare Magni, see M. Natale in Milan 1982, pp. 182–84; Ruggeri 1982, p. 27, no. 16.

93. "Non tacerò anco d'un altro certo modo di colorare che si dice a pastello, il quale si fa con punte composte particolarmente in polvere di colori che tutti si possano comporre. Il che si fa in carta, e molto fu usato da Leonardo da Vinci, il qual fece le teste di Cristo e de gl'Apostoli a questo modo, eccellenti e miracolose, in carta. Ma quanto è difficile il colorire in questo nuovo modo, tanto è egli facile a guastarsi." For this passage and the vast literature on the subject, see Marani 2001, pp. 103–15.

94. There remain "solamente i disegni, i quali certo né il tempo, né la morte, né altro accidente sarà mai per vincere, ma con grandissima lode e gloria di lui vivranno in eterno."

95. See Hadley 1968, pp. 16–19, no. 8. See also Oberhuber 1999, pp. 230–31, no. 159.

96. For the Brera *Head of Christ* and the two series of cartoons, see Marani and Rovetta in Palazzo Reale 2001, pp. 150–51, 192–98, nos. 40, 54–59, 60–64.

97. For the Louvre cartoon, see Bambach 1999a, pp. 111–14.

98. Rovetta in Ambrosiana 1998–99, pp. 100–103, dates both drawings between 1494 and 1502. He sees in them a reflection of Leonardo's studies for the *Last Supper* and notes that the position of the woman's face reveals that of Christ in the mural. For these two extraordinary drawings, see also Agosti 2001, p. 197, with additional bibliography. For the two drawings in the Ambrosiana and two others dated to this period, see Fiorio 2000a, pp. 153–57, 159–60, nos. B13–B15, B17.

99. Fiorio 2000a, pp. 158–59, no. B16, dates it to about 1502 and relates it to the Casio portraits. Agosti 2001, did not include it, and I, too, in 1989 and 1990 have viewed it as by a "Milanese artist."

100. For this painting, see Brown 1987, pp. 278–79, no. 55, fig. on p. 218.

101. Viatte 1999, p. 46, fig. 30. Agosti 2001, pp. 202–6, dates the portrait on Uffizi 427 Er to the second decade of the sixteenth century.

102. For the Turin drawing, see Pedretti in Sciolla 1990, pp. 40–41, no. 10. For an earlier dating of the drawing and the painting by Sodoma, see Marani in Palazzo Reale 2001, pp. 109ff., 180–81, no. 47.

103. Brown 1987, p. 209, no. 44, dates it to about 1505 and calls the support parchment. Agosti 2001, pp. 197–201, no. 35, says that it is done on yellowed paper, places a question mark after the attribution, and dates it to after Solario's trip to France, begun in 1507. The drawing is in fact on heavy paper, as Lucia Monaci Moran confirmed to me following our close examination of the sheet in February 2002.

104. For this drawing and the frescoes at San Maurizio, see Marani 2000a.

105. Brown 1987, p. 209, no. 45.

106. See P. C. Marani (Florence 1986), pp. 56–57, no. 11.

THE CODEX LEICESTER

CLAIRE FARAGO

THE CODEX LEICESTER is the product of Leonardo da Vinci's mature activities as a writer who worked by combining the visual and verbal registers into a single, syntactic model of exposition. The present exhibition displays eight double-sided pages from the disassembled Codex Leicester (cat. no. 114). As a text, the codex offers a significant example of what Italo Calvino once described as Leonardo's "battle with language to capture something that evaded his powers of expression."[1] It is a preliminary draft for a treatise—in the most advanced state of any surviving treatise in Leonardo's corpus—on the dynamics of water, compiled when he was in his mid-fifties. The manuscript deals with the forces of nature on a cosmological scale. It documents Leonardo's observations and attendant theoretical considerations about the movement of water in rivers and canals and, conversely, about the non-movement of water in the standing waves of the sea. The text records numerous controlled experiments, including some that are classics in a textual heritage established since antiquity, and describes many additional imagined thought experiments of Leonardo's own devising. Without duplicating his procedures in an actual laboratory setting, scholars may find it difficult to distinguish between drawings that are thought experiments and ones that document actual trials, although some distinctions have been made in recent years through experiments.[2] The discussion of specific cases in the codex shows Leonardo's testing of inherited theories using models, thought experiments, and direct observation of natural phenomena. The manuscript also offers numerous practical solutions to real-life engineering problems that arose during his employment as a consultant engineer. It is clear throughout that Leonardo's intention is not just observation and explanation of phenomena but also a quest for an understanding of nature's basic principles in order to apply that knowledge to the needs of the world.

Leonardo's dual occupation as an artist and engineer may seem strange today, but the combination was not uncommon among his contemporaries. During most of his adult life, Leonardo worked successfully as a consulting water engineer for a "superhighway" canal system in an emerging capitalist economy. The graphic techniques essential to his artistic training enhanced his scientific expertise. Judging from the systematic compilation of nearly a lifetime's worth of notes on the movements of water in the Codex Leicester, Leonardo planned to publish an illustrated book for an emerging market geared to practitioners. If this is the case, the large format of the codex suggests that he envisioned a publication on an extravagantly large scale, comparable to Giorgio Valla's folio-size encyclopedia, *De fugiendis et expetendis rebus* (Venice, 1501). Leonardo framed his studies on the movement of rivers and seas in a lofty theoretical framework sanctioned not only by his expertise as an engineer but also by a philosophical tradition institutionalized in medieval universities and the scientific literature associated with them. At the same time, the printing revolution, especially the new technology that made it increasingly possible to combine text with sophisticated illustrations on a single page, opened the possibility for a new class of treatise writers (such as Leonardo) to work outside the context of the university.

Carlo Pedretti has suggested that Leonardo was preparing the material gathered in the codex as a treatise for publication with copperplate engravings, a luxurious and technically sophisticated method of printing that may help explain the consistent format of a body of text combined with marginal illustrations, seen frequently in printed texts of the time.[3] Leonardo also developed a simple but effective technique to aid the busy reader: each new "case" begins with a highly visible capital letter in the text, another device he borrowed from manuscripts and printed texts. In the Codex Leicester, Leonardo transmitted practical information on the best method of harnessing the power of water in rivers and canals, together with an analysis of the causes of observed effects. Inclusion of theoretical information encouraged readers to develop their own applications. Had it been published at the time it was written, such a text would have far exceeded the scope of any existing technical manual directed to a professional class of artisans and applied engineers. In addition to serving this specialist audience, the treatise, with its wide theoretical compass, might have appealed to a highly educated leisure class, as did perspective treatises and handbooks of geometry of the time.[4]

The practical purpose that Leonardo may have intended the text to serve is a significant factor to bear in mind in studying the interplay of the visual and the verbal register. This purpose is visually documented in the traces of Leonardo's thought process on the page. The Codex Leicester contains approximately 360 small sketches and visual diagrams, most of which serve as components of the arguments and investigations recorded in words. Typically, Leonardo employed a range of graphic strategies to express a sequence of thoughts. For example, on Sheet 3 (fol. 34v), Leonardo begins in the top right margin with a geometric diagram representing the crust of the earth in cross section. Below this are two geometric sketches showing in elevation and plan the transformation in shape of a drop of water as it incorporates bits of solid matter, which he observes in order to model the action of water on the scale of the body of the earth. Elsewhere on this page is a series of beakers sketched in pen and ink that show a variety of configurations of siphons. These drawings accompany his further considerations of a received theory concerning the circulation of water throughout the earth's "body" (see cat. no. 114, Sheet 3A, fol. 3r, for further discussion). In other instances, however, Leonardo drew one idea directly on top of another, nearly to the point of

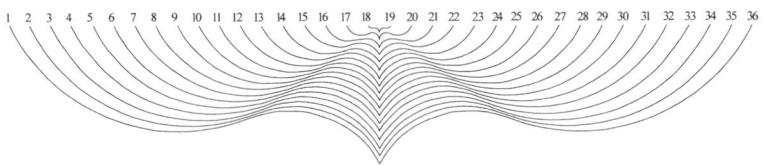

Fig. 104. Diagram showing the nestling of the double pages of the Codex Leicester, cat. no. 114 (after Gerolamo Calvi)

illegibility. For example on Sheet 9, in a sketch at the bottom of folio 28 verso, in a consideration of the complex action of waves rebounding against the banks of a river, he simulates this action via an experiment conducted in a glass tank.

Although text predominates over image to a greater degree than in any other notebook surviving from Leonardo's own hand, the range of notational means employed in the Codex Leicester offers the remarkable testimony of more than four decades of experimentation in a variety of graphic media. The sheer diversity of representational strategies provides an invaluable resource for understanding his graphic techniques at the time the codex was compiled, about 1508 to 1510. For example, Leonardo's use of parallel hatching is conventionally associated with his early work, but his utilization of this device in many pen-and-ink sketches in the codex demonstrates that the technique continued to serve him in certain contexts. In the case of the codex illustrations, parallel hatching provides an economical means for rendering volume that can be readily transposed to the medium of line engraving.

The codex consists of eighteen large sheets of paper, folded in half to form a quire, written on all four sides, and bound in a single signature whose pages are numbered 1 to 36 by an unknown sixteenth-century hand. Figure 104 offers a reconstruction of the nestling of the original folios of the codex, based on a diagram published by Gerolamo Calvi. In addition, Leonardo numbered "cases," "propositions," "conclusions," and "concetti" (ideas) at the top of many of the folios. At the point when Leonardo counted these examples, the bifolded sheets were already written and perhaps stacked in a certain order. This is corroborated by archaeological evidence. A series of paleographical indications permit the solid conclusion that the individual sheets were folded, and in one case stacked, while the ink and other writing materials, such as red chalk, were not fully dry.[5] When the notebook was first rediscovered, it was stacked and numbered in the way just described and sewn into cardboard covers of a kind used by Leonardo that are reinforced at the center seam with tape. The binding is exactly in the manner of Paris Ms. C, from about 1490.[6] The individuality of the binding technique is, however, difficult to gauge.

There is insufficient evidence to determine the exact provenance of the manuscript before 1625, when it was in Rome in the possession of heirs of the Milanese sculptor Guglielmo della

Porta (d. 1577).[7] Pedretti hypothesizes that della Porta may have acquired the manuscript from Leonardo's artistic heir and pupil Francesco Melzi, but it is just as likely that it was passed from one generation of Milanese artists to another, beginning with one directly associated with Leonardo. Evidence for this consists of a notice of 1689 in the Milanese archives placing the notebook in the possession of Giuseppe Ghezzi (1634–1721), who found it, perhaps already bound in brown leather, or perhaps not, in a trunk containing the books, manuscripts, and drawings of della Porta. Guglielmo della Porta was trained by his uncle Giacomo della Porta, who was trained by the sculptor and architect Cristoforo Solari, an associate of Leonardo's documented in Milan around 1510, when Leonardo may have still been working on the treatise. (See further discussion in the entry to Sheet 13.)

The manuscript left the Italian peninsula in 1717, when Ghezzi sold it to the erudite English collector Thomas Coke, later the first earl of Leicester, who commissioned three copies and had the brown leather-bound manuscript bound additionally in red Moroccan leather stamped in gold with the earl's impresa of an ostrich grasping the proverbial worm with its beak. Coke's descendants still owned the manuscript when it was first exhibited in 1952, at the Royal Academy of Arts in London, to celebrate the five hundredth anniversary of Leonardo's birth. In 1980, the Leicester manuscript was sold at auction to Dr. Armand Hammer, who lent it to the Elmer Belt Library of Vinciana, University of California at Los Angeles. The following year, when the manuscript was renamed in Hammer's honor, Carlo Pedretti recommended unbinding the notebook, which emphasized the autonomy of the individual folios at the expense of the coherence of the manuscript as a whole. This act also enables the pages of the codex to be exhibited. In 1994, the manuscript in its disassembled state was sold at auction to its present owner, Bill Gates, who restored the work's former name.

The Codex Leicester is neither a finished treatise with a beginning, middle, and end nor a catchall journal, like some of the small pocket notebooks such as Paris Mss. K or H in which Leonardo recorded daily memoranda. The Codex Leicester is a work in progress. The manner in which Leonardo compiled his draft for a treatise on water, as well as the range of his ideas about the origins of rivers and occasional concrete references to rivers, bridges, places, and the like, securely dates the manuscript to about 1508–10. The dating is corroborated by the circumstances of Leonardo's life. A note written in Florence about 1508 to one of his French patrons in Milan describes instruments and experiments Leonardo planned to perform on the Naviglio Grande, the great canal linked to Milan that was donated to him for this purpose by the French king Louis XII.[8] This opportunity to experiment provides an important context for the theoretical and empirical work on the the main subject of the manuscript, namely, the most effective construction of canals and navigable rivers for transporting goods. Maintenance of canals for the transportation of goods was the primary application for Leonardo's studies of hydraulics, alongside irrigation and fortification projects.

The eighteen sheets composing the codex also preserve the process by which Leonardo reassessed the analogy between the macrocosm of the world and the microcosm of the human body that had been fundamental to his thinking since the early 1490s. Leonardo regularly questioned inherited theories about the circulation of water in the earth, which were based on a long-standing analogy between the circulation of water through the planet earth and the circulation of blood in the human body. Ultimately, Leonardo came to understand that there exists no adequate explanation for the manner in which the planet behaves like a living body. The Codex Leicester documents his significant, gradually emerging, realization that no known type of siphonic action—the leading theory and the one Leonardo considered the most promising—accounts for the internal circulation of water from the seas to the tops of mountains. The unfolding story in the codex tells of his diminishing confidence in traditional analogies between the body of the earth and the human body and his formulation of a more complex, more modern, and more original view of the world.

Aside from the treatise on painting (the *Libro di pittura* that was compiled posthumously from his surviving notes), published in abridged form in 1651, Leonardo's study of water is the only subject among his extensive writings that was systematically studied by his immediate successors and printed before the end of the nineteenth century, when facsimiles of his notebooks and anthologies culled from his manuscripts began to appear. But long before technological advances in printing enabled this modern revival of interest in Leonardo, there were attempts to acknowledge the scientific importance of his writings on water to the history of hydraulics. In 1717, the same year that the notebook went to England, Tommaso Buonaventuri, the scholar of Galileo, contemplated publishing a selection, but he did not have access to a manuscript. Notes on water derived from original manuscripts of Leonardo then in the Biblioteca Ambrosiana, Milan, similar to those contained in the Codex Leicester, were the first of his writings on the subject ever set in print. *Del moto e misura dell'acqua* (On the motion and measure of water) consists of 566 passages edited as nine chapters by F. Luigi Maria Arconati (published in Bologna by Francesco Cardinali in 1826), based on a copy of other autograph writings made for Cardinal Francesco Barberini in Rome in the early seventeenth century.[9]

The first scholarly study of the codex was published by Mario Baratta in 1903, who studied one of the copies commissioned by Lord Leicester.[10] Some Leonardo manuscript experts find no rhyme or reason to the bewildering diversity of entries typical in Leonardo's notes. Yet knowledge of Leonardo's compilation habits has been growing over several generations of scholarship, yielding evidence of various kinds of order in Leonardo's literary remains. Credit for a change of attitude belongs, above all, to Gerolamo Calvi, who established his scholarly reputation with a facsimile edition of the Codex Leicester that was published in 1909. Calvi recognized that Leonardo developed a system of canceling notes when he transferred them from one manuscript to another. From Leonardo's system of striking through passages and from other discoveries about his compilation habits, we know that he transferred ideas to the Codex Leicester that had been recorded as early as Paris Ms. C., about 1490, and that he copied specific passages from at least five surviving manuscripts: Paris Ms. H, 1493–94; Codex Madrid I, 1497–1500; Codex Madrid II, about 1504; Codex Arundel, dated March 1508 in Florence; and Paris Ms. F, dated September 1508 in Milan. Early testimony, references by Leonardo himself, and dismembered sheets surviving from lost notebooks tell us that other writings were integrated in the Codex Leicester compilation. Leonardo completed at least one other treatise devoted to the subject of water, the lost Libro M.

From the surviving evidence, it is difficult to say whether Leonardo "was more interested in the process of inquiry than in the completion of a text for publication," as Calvino and most scholars today maintain.[11] Like his other projects for treatises on specific subjects, the Codex Leicester demonstrates that Leonardo was experimenting with organizational techniques. In this case, Leonardo's major challenge was to integrate notes recorded over many years on a variety of interrelated subjects. Scholars hold a variety of opinions about the order in which Leonardo compiled the Codex Leicester and how he intended it to be read. Calvi hypothesized that Leonardo filled each folio of the codex as if it were an autonomous document. He concluded that the folios that record Leonardo's rejection of the analogy between the circulation of water and blood were the last to be written because the arguments are the most advanced. Therefore, Leonardo must have begun with the folios at the centerfold in its bound form and ended with the pages at the beginning and end of the codex that reject this analogy. Pedretti follows Calvi's argument that the folios are autonomous units but, because the discussions at the centerfold include nothing to signify a beginning, disagrees with Calvi's hypothesis about the order of compilation. Pedretti hypothesizes that the exterior folios are the earliest, and the centerfold is the latest stage of the compilation.

Yet there are other alternatives. Scholars have long labored over questions of sequence and order without reaching definitive conclusions. The linear format of a bound book does not provide the best representation of Leonardo's working habits. Nor is the order in which Leonardo compiled the manuscript necessarily the order he meant his intended readers to follow. The advantage of loose-leaf folios in an era when paper was sold by stationers as unbound quires is precisely that Leonardo did not have to determine the order of his ideas or the amount of space for any subsection in advance. The Codex Leicester, like the somewhat earlier Codex Madrid II, of about 1504, brings together an enormous range of notes in a way that allowed the maximum amount of flexibility for adding new notes while keeping track of existing ones.[12] In the case of the Codex Leicester, the compilation defines a subject that Leonardo largely invented in its current form. The practice of making each folio autonomous turned Leonardo's long-standing, nonlinear habits of compilation into an advantage. The author, anticipating his own habitual thought processes, gave himself as much flexibility as possible in this manner.

It is reasonable to infer on the basis of the physical evidence that the sheets were all loose during the compilation process. Leonardo was thus able to organize the subject matter on the folded sheets as he was recopying information from other sources. Many sheets of the manuscript attest to this procedure: they are devoted to the same or related subjects, though not necessarily in a single unified argument. Moreover, some pages derive from more than one source in Leonardo's autograph notes (for example, fol. 13r on Sheet 13A, discussed below). The famous statement on folio 2 recto of the codex makes sense if one considers that he was drafting a treatise from earlier notes: "My concern now is to find subjects and inventions, gathering them as they occur to me; then I will get them in order." Other sheets do not appear planned out completely in advance and contain original observations not found in any of the surviving notes used to compile the codex. Sheet 3 is an excellent example of the improvisatory aspect of Leonardo's compilation process that records his ongoing thoughts on specific problems. Anatomical Ms. A (Windsor, RL 19000–19017), which postdates the Codex Leicester by a few years and is widely considered a project that Leonardo intended for publication, indicates that its method of compilation is a refinement of the same procedure. Leonardo again adopted the four-sided, folded-folio format, and recopied earlier notes carefully and neatly. The subject of each folio is autonomous to an even greater degree.

In addition to procedural aspects of the compilation process, Leonardo left clues about his conceptual framework internal to the manuscript. His knowledge of hydraulics was extensive, informed by such classical texts as Pliny the Elder's *Natural History* and Heron of Alexander's treatise on water, and by Scholastic literature, including commentaries on Aristotle by Albertus Magnus, Albert of Saxony, and others. Yet Leonardo, whose knowledge of Latin was rudimentary at best, relied on a limited range of direct sources, notably on the compendium of theories about the composition of the earth written in Italian by Ristoro d'Arezzo in 1282 (entitled *Composizione del mondo*).[13] In 1277, Church authorities in Paris condemned the view that the cosmos is a living creature, along with many other unorthodox ideas. Perhaps contrary to the effect intended by theologians, this clash between science and religion encouraged the scientific study of the heavens.

The Codex Leicester contains crucial evidence of Leonardo's changing views of the world. These changes were precipitated by his intensive study of the body of the earth, but before the establishment of the geological sciences as such. According to notes preserved in Paris Ms. A, folios 55 to 58, about 1490–92, Leonardo initially planned to organize his writings on the science of water around the analogy between the macrocosm of the world and the microcosm of the human body. By the time of the Codex Leicester, he had moved away from this literal analogy, questioning ancient authority on the basis of his ongoing study of geological formations (see, further, cat. no. 114, Sheet 3). His most articulate statements postdate the codex, but the reasons for his disenchantment with the older view are already clear there: Leonardo came to believe that the rivers of the earth originated as vaporized water, that is, as clouds. The renewal of rivers is not, in other words, due to the continuous circulation of subterranean rivers, as is the case with the human body, with its analogous veins and internal "lake of blood." In notes of slightly later date, such as RL 19003 recto (Windsor, Anatomical Ms. A, fol. 4r), cited by Pedretti and dated by him after 1510, Leonardo maintained that "the origin of the sea is contrary to the origin of the blood because the sea receives unto itself all the rivers, which are caused solely by the aqueous vapors raised up to the air. But the sea of blood is caused by all the veins." Similar statements to the effect that clouds are the origin of rivers (Paris Ms. G, fol. 48v, about 1510–15, for example) are preserved among Leonardo's writings to the end of his life.

Besides the macrocosm/microcosm analogy, Leonardo considered three other modes of organization for his newly invented science of water. The codex contains notes on water and the moon copied from the first thirty pages of the heterogeneous compilation known as the Codex Arundel (British Library, London), begun in Florence on March 22, 1508. On pages of the Codex Arundel studied by Anna Maria Brizio, who dated them after the Codex Leicester, Leonardo drafted definitions from which to begin the science of the movement of water on deductive principles, along the lines of Euclid's *Elements of Geometry*.[14] On Sheet 15B (fol. 15v) of the Codex Leicester, in keeping with this deductive approach, Leonardo recorded an extensive list of chapters he called "books" for his projected treatise. He proposed beginning with chapters on the general nature of water itself, on the sea, on veins (i.e., subterranean rivers and springs), on rivers, on the bottoms of rivers, and so on, culminating with details such as "things worn away by water," the title of his last projected chapter. Yet he was evidently not entirely committed to this approach, for he also drafted introductions in the form of literary descriptions praising the beauty of the earth, preserved in both the Codex Arundel and the Codex Leicester (Sheet 3, for example). In the contemporary Paris Ms. F and in the same section of the Codex Arundel (fols. 1–30), Leonardo also contemplated an alternative, empirical mode of organization that simply lists the numerous effects of water. This approach is also recorded on several pages of the Codex Leicester, including folio 15 verso (see further discussion in cat. no. 114, Sheet 15).

In the Codex Leicester, all four conceptual frameworks described above are present, but Leonardo went beyond simply combining their individual characteristics and instead appealed to the Aristotelian science of cosmology. Sheets 1, 2, and 3, containing some of his most sophisticated thinking about the circulation of water through siphonic action and the composition of the body of the earth, are also the most significant folios with respect to Leonardo's ongoing thoughts on both organizational and conceptual matters. These three outermost sheets, forming the front and back of the notebook in its nested and bound form, are unique in that the halves of the sheets located at the front of the bound codex *differ* in subject from those portions of the same sheets located at the end. In the front, on Sheets 1 and 2 (fols. 1r–2v), Leonardo treats a classic problem in the science of lunar cosmology, the composition of the moon, which is discussed in terms of the moon's appearance when the moon is viewed from the earth. On the halves of the same Sheets 1 and 2 (fols. 35r–36v) located at the end of the codex in its nested, bound format, Leonardo instead discusses the composition of the body of the earth, the subject of the back half of Sheet 3 (located on fol. 34r and v), that is, on the adjacent page when the folios were nested and stacked as a single signature.

No other folios in the Codex Leicester exhibit such a clear division of subject matter, with the left-hand side of the sheet (i.e., the recto and verso at the beginning of the signature) devoted to one set of ideas, while the right-hand side (the recto and verso at the end of the signature) is devoted to a different subject. In most other cases, the same subject ranges over the entire sheet. Significant inferences about Leonardo's planned treatise can be drawn from this physical evidence. Traditionally, treatises on cosmology follow the order established by Aristotle in *De caelo et mundo* (On the heavens and the earth). By beginning with a discussion of the lunary sphere and proceeding to a discussion of the sublunary sphere of the earth, to which the rest of the codex is devoted, Leonardo followed Aristotle's order of exposition, thus situating his newly invented science of the movement of water among the theoretical sciences, as part of (subalternate to) the science of cosmology. With this strategy, Leonardo seems to have been well on his way to resolving the long-standing question of how to present his investigations of the dynamics of water. The solution glimpsed on the opening three sheets of the Codex Leicester combines a deductive method of investigation, which proceeds from first principles or known causes, with a method of investigation that proceeds in the opposite direction, from observation of effects in nature to their causes.

Leonardo conceived the science of pictorial perspective in the same way, that is, as a *scientia media*, a mixture of theory and experience. In his study of perspective and of water, he bestowed new theoretical status on what had been merely one of the mechanical arts in Hugh of St. Victor's classification of knowledge, which was widely diffused in Scholastic writings. In this respect, Leonardo participated in current trends for reclassifying the practical sciences. At the end of the fifteenth century, new classifications of the productive sciences were proposed by humanists such as Giorgio Valla, whose encyclopedia (mentioned above) Leonardo owned by 1504. In Valla's scheme, theoretical sciences ordered to practical use replaced the seven mechanical arts that were traditional throughout the later Middle Ages and made them equal to the practical liberal arts. In constructing the science of water along these lines, Leonardo participated in current trends for reclassifying the practical sciences while still understanding the term "scientia" in its medieval sense, as a field of intellectual endeavor in which true causal explanations could be discovered.[15]

It is probable that Leonardo developed this organizational scheme and innovative conceptualization of the science of the movement of water during the process of gathering his research for the Codex Leicester. Closely related notes from 1508 preserved in the Codex Arundel and Paris Ms. F suggest that he also developed his ideas about the moon in the context of thinking about the composition of the earth. In his writings both moon and earth are concerned with the behavior of water, but beyond his study of water the subjects are related in the Aristotelian cosmology, which treats the elements and the spheres of the planets, stars, and other heavenly bodies. In this connection, Leonardo offered an original answer to the ancient question concerning the composition of the moon, a topic that arose in the context of explaining why some parts of the moon's surface were brighter than others. By the end of the fifteenth century, there was broad consensus that the moon did not have a light of its own. His energies in the Codex Leicester are largely directed to explaining the particular luminosity of the moon. Arguing against contemporary explanations—primarily in order to contest the position that the moon has a smooth reflective surface that behaves according to the same principle as a mirror—Leonardo postulated, on the basis of his extensive knowledge of optics, that the uneven brightness of the moon's surface is due to the corrugated surface of the watery sphere that envelops the moon's core.

The historical importance of the Codex Leicester is currently incompletely understood. As the codex especially demonstrates, Leonardo maintained that the moon, like the earth, has standing waves and its own center of gravity. The solution that he proposed in this connection to explain the source of the moon's light was similar to the definitive answer given by Galileo a century later. In her 1997 study of Galileo, Eileen Reeves investigated continuities between art and science and the compatibility of religious and scientific knowledge during the opening decades of the seventeenth century.[16] She described Galileo's contact with Paolo Sarpi, the Servite friar and historian of the Council of Trent who had suggested twenty years before the publication of Galileo's *Sidereus nuncius* (the book placed on the Index in 1616 that partly brought about the great astronomer's arrest and trial by the Inquisition) that the ashen or bluish surface barely visible between the horns of the moon in its crescent phase might be due to sunlight reflected from the earth's atmosphere. Since the understanding of the moon's composition was inherited from ancient sources, the similarities among authors are most likely due to shared sources. Nonetheless, Reeves emphasized that resonances between Galileo's and Sarpi's discussions of lunar substance suggest that they had direct knowledge of Leonardo's empirical observations about reflected light and color and shadow. According to Reeves, the sequence of argumentation and missteps in Sarpi's thinking, as well as his correct conjectures, suggests such a direct transmission of ideas. In the Codex Leicester, which contains Leonardo's most extensive and mature notes on the subject of the moon's light (though Reeves does not discuss this manuscript), the artist hypothesized correctly that the light of the sun reflecting from the uneven surface of the moon accounts for the moon's unusual, soft luminescence. The artist also correctly hypothesized that the pale ashen light visible between the horns of the moon in its crescent phase is due to sunlight reflecting onto the moon from the earth's own uneven surface, one covered by seas and land masses. While the exact location of the Codex Leicester at the time that Galileo and Sarpi developed their own similar theories is unknown, the manuscript could easily have been among Leonardo's writings that then circulated in artistic, humanist, and scientific circles. If so, the Codex Leicester is one of the rare instances in which Leonardo's writings had an effect on the future of scientific discovery. Unlike Galileo, neither Leonardo nor Sarpi considered the moon's ashen light as possible evidence of the Copernican world system, but the transmission and attendant transformation of ideas leading to this historic, paradigm-shifting theory deserve further investigation and comment.

1. Calvino 1992, p. 77. The text includes the following synoptic understanding of Leonardo's writing process: "The various phases in the treatment of an idea . . . are, for Leonardo as writer, the proof of the effort he invested in writing as an instrument of knowledge; and also of the fact that, in the case of all the books he thought of writing, he was more interested in the process of inquiry than in the completion of a text for publication."

2. Kemp 1986 has re-created some of Leonardo's experiments, thus distinguishing between laboratory trials and thought experiments. An abbreviated version of this article is published as Kemp 1996a. Kemp 1996c includes videotaped reconstructions of Leonardo's water tank experiments, described throughout the Codex Leicester and in related notes, which were produced in the hydraulics laboratory at the University of Washington, Seattle. The essential, classic study of Leonardo's artistic and scientific interest in the movement of water is Gombrich 1969, 1976.

3. Pedretti 1987a, pp. xxxv–xxxvi; see, further, Reti 1971.

4. On practical handbooks of geometry, called *abbacchi*, see Van Egmond 1980; Piochi 1984; Goldthwaite 1972.

5. Pedretti 1987a, pp. 182–83.

6. Pedretti 1987a, p. 165.

7. Pedretti 1987a, pp. liii, 166, noting that the codex was in possession of Guglielmo's heirs in Rome in 1625, precisely when twelve of Leonardo's manuscripts were acquired by Count Galeazzo Arconati in Milan from the collection of Pompeo Leoni.

8. C.A., fol. 317r-b; Richter 1970, vol. 2, p. 333, no. 1349.

9. Carusi and Favaro 1923.

10. Baratta 1903.

11. Calvino 1992.

12. See, further, Farago 1993.

13. Narducci 1859.

14. Brizio 1951.

15. On *scientia media*, see Weisheipl 1965; Gagné 1986; Farago 1992, pp. 63–65.

16. Reeves 1997.

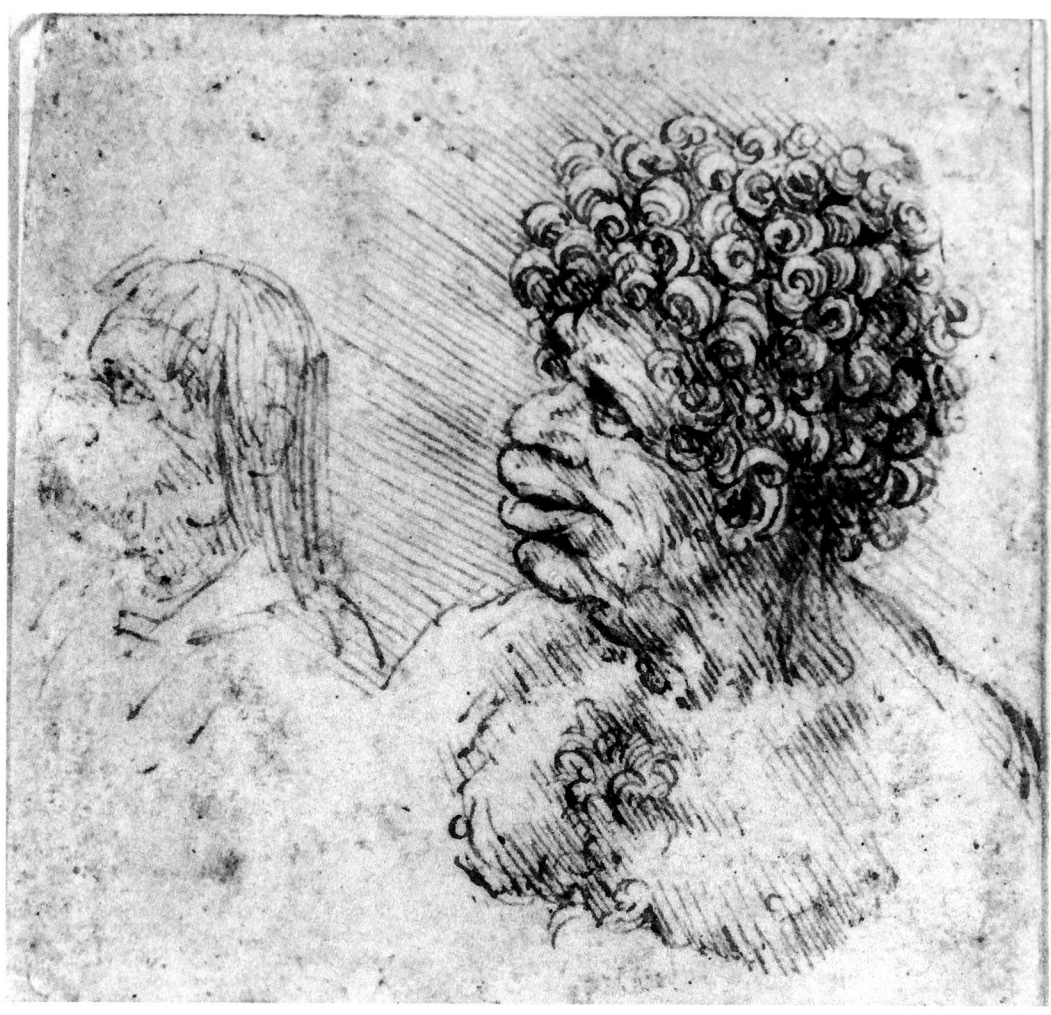

Fig. 105. Leonardo da Vinci, *Two Grotesque Heads in Profile.* Pen and brown ink, 57 × 62 mm. Graphische Sammlung Albertina, Vienna 66

LEONARDO'S GROTESQUES: ORIGINALS AND COPIES

VARENA FORCIONE

Cosa bella mortal passa e non dura.
> —Leonardo da Vinci, *Codex Forster*

The mind throws up fragments of weeds and dirt which float
about on its surface and betray us into tuneless humming or
stupid reiterated words: and such, it seems to me, was the origin
of most of Leonardo's caricatures.   —Kenneth Clark,
> *A Catalogue of the Drawings of Leonardo da Vinci*
> *in the Collection of His Majesty the King at Windsor Castle*

T HE COMPLEX HISTORY of the dispersion of Leonardo's drawings after his death in 1519 is a fascinating subject unto itself and has received much scholarly attention.[1] A neglected aspect of this history is the way in which Leonardo's drawings of grotesque physiognomies ("caricatures") came to be admired, copied, engraved, and disseminated.[2] This essay will focus on Leonardo's original drawings in the Devonshire Collection at Chatsworth (and those sold at auction in 1984; cat. nos. 69–73) vis-à-vis the copies in the Louvre album that belonged to the eighteenth-century French collector Pierre-Jean Mariette (cat. no. 137), the starting point for this study. This history begins with the English collector Lord Arundel in London and proceeds to the Sir Peter Lely collection, then to the Van Bergesteyn collection in The Hague, then to Nicolaes Flinck in Rotterdam, and finally to the collection of the second duke of Devonshire at Chatsworth. It should be noted that only the Flinck provenance is certain, since that collector's mark appears on some of the originals (see cat. no. 72). The transfer from Arundel to Flinck was reconstituted on the basis of annotations made in 1775 by Antoni Rutgers, an art lover and art dealer in Amsterdam, that appear only on the copy of the album of prints of the count of Caylus (Kunsthistorisch Instituut, Leiden).[3]

Leonardo's caricatures circulated widely immediately after they were executed.[4] For example, beginning in 1506, they were copied in frescoes decorating an oratory in Santa Maria di

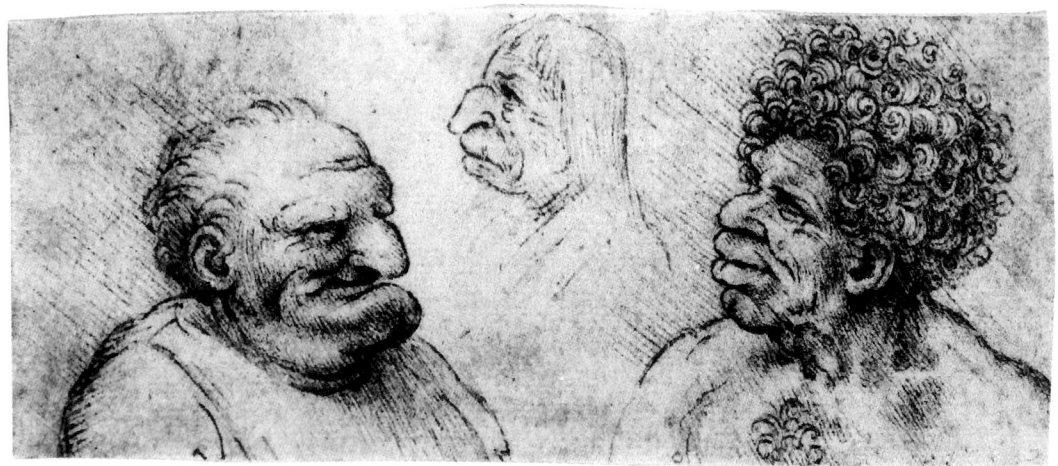

Fig. 106. Attributed to Francesco Melzi (after Leonardo da Vinci), *Three Grotesque Heads.* Pen and brown ink, 44 × 103 mm. The Pierpont Morgan Library, New York; Gift of Mrs. Edward J. Fowles 1968.11

Rivolta d'Adda, near Milan, and, north of the Alps, in paintings by Antwerp masters. After Leonardo's death in France in 1519, his pupil Francesco Melzi was named his principal heir[5] and returned to Italy with much of his master's collection of works, which he kept in his villa in Vaprio d'Adda, near Milan. Melzi, who had come to Leonardo's studio about 1506, looked after his master's drawings and writings, which he venerated like "relics,"[6] for fifty-one years following Leonardo's death, trying to give them a certain order. According to recent research on the collection at the Royal Library, Windsor,[7] Melzi arranged Leonardo's drawings by subject and numbered them within these divisions. Although some drawings may have been taken from Leonardo's studio during his lifetime (or been lost or left behind in the master's frequent moves), and Melzi may have given away some of his master's works,[8] it was not until Melzi's death in 1570 that the breakup of the drawings collection truly began.

The man principally responsible for this dispersion was Pompeo Leoni, who, like his father, Leone, was a sculptor at the royal court of Spain in Madrid. Between 1582 and 1590, Leoni managed to take possession of most of the drawings thought to be by Leonardo.[9] Once he had them, and without taking into account Melzi's numbering system, Leoni assembled them into bound volumes, which later became part of the collections of the Royal Library at Windsor and the Biblioteca Ambrosiana in Milan. Carlo Pedretti has demonstrated that Leoni even cut out small heads or figures from the pages of the Codex Atlanticus, which Pedretti has identified in the collections at Windsor[10] and the Ambrosiana.[11] According to Roger de Piles, Rubens may have consulted Leonardo's drawings at Leoni's home in the early seventeenth century.[12]

In his *Trattato dell'arte della pittura* (1584), Giovanni Paolo Lomazzo spoke of a "libricciuolo" of "misshapen" figures by Leonardo still in Milan at the time he was writing.[13] He also reported that Leonardo planned meals at which he provoked the laughter of his servants in order to reproduce the expressions on their faces.[14] The small grotesque heads exhibited here (cat. nos. 69–73), which are now glued onto an eighteenth-century mount, may have been part, not of the *libricciuolo*, but of that exercise at capturing expressions. In my opinion (which takes into account previous scholarly research) these drawings of grotesques originally portrayed two figures facing each other—generally as couples, a man and a woman—in experiments that sought both diversity and contrast.[15] This original layout of the grotesques, as envisioned by Leonardo, still exists in the copies in the Pembroke collection (cat. no. 121), which serve as a reference in seeking to understand the original arrangement of the series as a whole (see discussion below), but, to my knowledge, no original couple remains intact. A fragment comprising two heads can be found in the Albertina in Vienna,[16] but it was initially composed of three figures as can be seen from the extant copies (figs. 105–7; cat. no. 137, RF 28741, RF 28742, RF 28746).[17] Given the current absence of a drawing depicting a couple in its initial configuration, one would like to identify the person responsible for dividing the couples in the original sheets into several fragments.

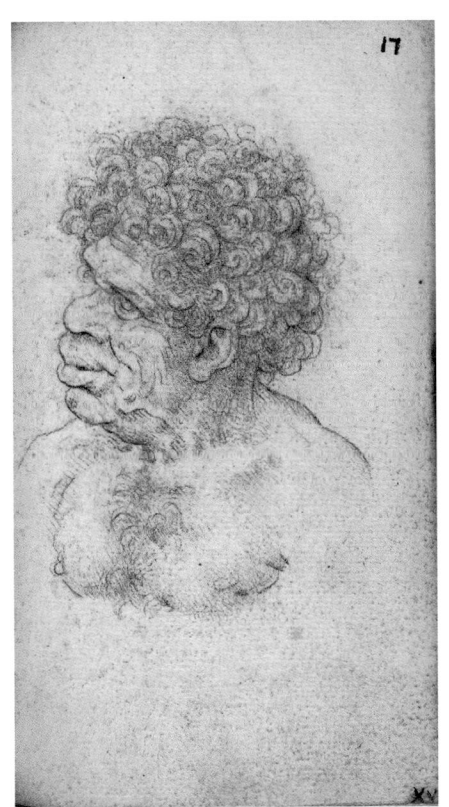

Fig. 107. Late-sixteenth-century Lombard artist after Leonardo da Vinci, *Head of Grotesque Black Man* (from François Rabelais, *Les oeuvres de M. François Rabelais*, Rouen [?] 1659, 1669 [?]). Black chalk, 142 × 85 mm. The New York Public Library, Astor, Lenox and Tilden Foundations, New York; Spencer Collection. Spencer Grotesques, vol. 1, no. 17

One candidate may be Francesco Melzi, since he was engaged in the process of reorganizing Leonardo's drawings and notes. Another candidate is Pompeo Leoni, who rearranged Leonardo's drawings between 1590, when he acquired the collection, and his death in Spain in 1608. What these series looked like also remains to be established: were they arranged on a large sheet with the drawings side by side, or were they bound into a small sketchbook, a *libricciuolo*?

The grotesques arrived in England thanks to Thomas Howard, earl of Arundel (1585–1646),[18] a diplomat and major collector who purchased a large number of Leonardo's drawings while in Italy and brought them back to his London residences. In the late eighteenth century, Horace Walpole called him "the Father of Vertue in England."[19] According to Cust,[20] Lord Arundel was a "pioneer" among art collectors in England. In 1613 he traveled Italy from north to south, from Milan and Venice to Naples, with Lady Arundel and the architect Inigo Jones.[21] White writes that Arundel was the first English aristocrat to visit that country with the declared intention of studying its art and architecture.[22] The Arundels' collection was constituted with the help of several agents who went in search of artworks on their behalf in different Italian cities.[23] The presence in England of at least part of the Arundel drawings is attested by a copy of a Leonardo drawing, dated "Sept. 21, 162[6?]," that is hypothetically attributed to Inigo Jones (Devonshire Collection, Chatsworth).[24] The Arundel collection as a whole, which included sculptures, paintings, drawings, tapestries, and furniture, was in England between 1615–20 and 1642. It was fully accessible to other art lovers: in fact, in 1617, when Arundel composed his first will, he wrote: "My desire is that all gentlemen of Vertue or Artistes wch are honest men may allways be used, wth curtesy & humanity when they shall come to see them before sonne of the House & doe not hurt them wth theyre handling."[25] In 1637, there was a room in Arundel House called the "Academy," where guests could see "three large portfolios with drawings by Michelangelo, Raphael, and Leonardo, as well as more than two hundred similar books filled with excellent drawings by various masters."[26]

The civil war that erupted in 1642 forced Lord and Lady Arundel to leave their homeland for the continent and to settle there permanently. The part of their art collection that could be transported was transferred to Holland in 1643, but another part remained in England, in their residences of Arundel House and Tart Hall.[27] Lady Arundel established her residence in Amsterdam, while Lord Arundel chose Padua, where he died in 1646. The collection remained with Lady Arundel in Holland until her death in 1654, but it was very quickly broken apart. We know that in 1653 Lady Arundel sold a thousand drawings for ten thousand guldens to the collector Everard Jabach.[28] After Lady Arundel's death,[29] the long dispute among her heirs led to the dispersion, as late as 1720, of the entire Arundel collection in Holland and England.[30]

The transfer of a portion of the works to Holland, the disagreement between the spouses that led them to adopt separate residences, and, finally, lawsuits among the heirs lasting several decades are some of the reasons it is difficult to retrace with any certainty the dispersion of works from that prestigious collection.

A large portion of the collections of drawings assembled by the Arundels now belongs to the royal collection at Windsor Castle and comes from the "Leoni-Windsor" volume, that is, the volume of drawings assembled by Pompeo Leoni from Leonardo's legacy to Francesco Melzi. Oddly, there is no exact record of when the volume, which was taken apart in the nineteenth century[31] and hence no longer exists as such, became part of the royal collection. The first precise mention dates from January 22, 1690,[32] when the drawings were admired at Kensington Palace by Constantijn Huygens Jr. (1628–1697), secretary to the stadtholder William of Orange, who had been proclaimed King William III of England, Scotland, and Ireland the previous year. It is believed they were probably acquired by King Charles II on the European continent about 1660–70.[33] The Leoni-Windsor volume contained several of Leonardo's grotesques, some of the most famous, but none is found copied in the Louvre album (discussed below) known as the Mariette album.

The second player in the history of the complex journey of the Arundel drawings was Sir Peter Lely (1618–1680).[34] A Dutch painter who settled in England, he acquired from the Arundel collection[35] the grotesques that are now at Chatsworth. It is these drawings that are copied in the Louvre album.

The first sale of drawings that had belonged to Sir Peter Lely took place in London on April 16, 1688, eight years after his death. Roger North, the architect and lawyer, was the executor of the estate and, in his autobiography, he describes with humor the milieu of English collectors of the time, who pounced on the drawings as if on bread during a famine.[36] The details of the sale of these drawings can be found in the account book of the Lely house.[37] There is no mention of individual drawings, only the total value of the sale: "drawings in the portfolios £1848.9.6"; "Prints in books and portfolios, cartoons of prints, Books of prints bound £597.18.6"; "Totall proceed of the whole sale £2446.8."[38] It is interesting to note that the major purchasers at the Lely sale were the same people who had organized it: Frederick Sonnius, Lely's close friend, who also made purchases on behalf of a certain Van Bergesteyn,[39] spent "£814.8"; Prosper Henry Lankrinck, a painter and former aide to Lely, spent "£243.3"; and William Gibson, a miniaturist painter, spent "£328.10."[40] The sale went on for eight days;[41] the decision was then made to suspend it and await a "fitter opportunity." During that time, the rest of the drawing collection was left "in the custody of Mr. Sonnius." The sale was conducted with great care. There were two books. One was kept by Sonnius, with the list of all the drawings for sale; next to each drawing, Sonnius indicated the buyer and the price. The other book was kept by Thomas Mills, who was also in charge of the cashbox, and he noted the purchaser and the amount paid. North writes that there were ten thousand drawings at the sale and that the crowd rushed to see them. He reports that he placed the mark PL on every drawing prior to the sale and arranged them all into portfolios. Each portfolio was recorded on a list and bore a letter of the alphabet, which also appeared on the drawing itself, so that anything could be found at any time. Unfortunately, these valuable books mentioned by North have not been recovered, which deprives us of the detailed list of drawings and a written record of the buyers' names. Nevertheless, traces of Roger North's numbering system may remain on drawings that were in the Lely sale. In the reproductions in Arthur Strong's 1900 book on the Pembroke collection, several drawings bear an annotation in pen and brown ink, on the lower right of the sheet, indicating the artist, the volume, and the number of the drawing in the volume.[42] Everything remaining from the 1688 sale was sold in London in November 1694.[43]

The most beautiful sheets at the Lely sale in 1688 seem to have been purchased by Sonnius, acting as an agent for a collector and dealer from The Hague. Little is known about this individual, Jonckheer Jan van der Does, lord of Bergesteyn or Berghestein, also called Van der Dous or Van der Douse (1621–1704).[44] In the correspondence between Christiaan Huygens and his brother Constantijn, the latter, in a letter sent from The Hague and dated October 31, 1663, wants to know what profession Van der Does is practicing in England and if it is true "what one says here, that he had a private shop in Whitehall where people went to play raffle."[45] On December 20, 1663, he persisted, asking "if he runs a shop for curious gentlemen." Christiaan replied from Paris that "Mr. van der Does has the privilege in the court of England of being able personally to supply merchandise that people bid on there. He orders it from here, and sometimes comes to do the shopping himself. People say he makes money that way, but in return, it seems to me, his honor suffers a great deal. He has never spoken to me of that traffic but quite a great deal about others." And Constantijn comments: "Van der Does's profession is not very noble, but in France and England I hear that even great men, if they do not themselves have several sorts of monopolies, at least have a share, an interest, in them."[46] Van Bergesteyn appears throughout the correspondence between the two brothers, becoming their friend and rival in the purchase of drawings. He is mentioned by the seventeenth-century diarist John Evelyn, who reports that in 1683 he paid a visit to the duke of Norfolk, grandson of Arundel, on behalf of a certain Van der Douse, for the purpose of buying cartoons or drawings by Raphael, but that he was told that Lely had already taken the most beautiful sheets.[47] Van Bergesteyn and Sonnius were with Constantijn Huygens at Kensington Palace in September 1690 when they saw the Leoni-Windsor volume[48] containing Leonardo da Vinci's drawings.

The Van Bergesteyn sale took place in The Hague on April 14, 1705.[49] According to Van Heel,[50] on December 20, 1704, an announcement was made that the sale was to take place in early 1705 at the "Confrery-Kamer" in The Hague, with one catalogue in Dutch and another in French, but neither has yet been found. As in the case of the Lely sale, we do not have a list of the drawings or a written record of the names of the buyers.

The man who purchased Leonardo's grotesques from the Van Bergesteyn sale was Nicolaes Anthonis Flinck of Rotterdam (1646–1723),[51] son of the painter Govaert Flinck, one of Rembrandt's pupils. Nicolaes did not follow in his father's footsteps but became a director of the Dutch India Company in Rotterdam. Besides inheriting his father's collection of paintings, he purchased many works at sales, since he shared his father's taste for art: Lugt says that the Flinck collection was famous. Arnold Houbraken[52] wrote that it included the most beautiful drawings from the famous collection of Van Bergesteyn and of the lord of Zuylichem (Constantijn Huygens Jr.). It is believed that the Leonardo originals now at Chatsworth and elsewhere (cat. nos. 69–73) were already separated and that each head stood alone in the Flinck collection, since his stamp F, which he was accustomed to placing in the lower margin of the sheet, is sometimes missing or partly cut off on certain drawings. At other times, the stamp is placed directly beneath a head, which would have been unlikely if there had been two heads facing each other on a larger sheet.[53] The Flinck sale took place in Rotterdam in 1724.

At this point in their travels, the drawings again became part of an English collection. William, second duke of Devonshire (1665–1729),[54] purchased 225 drawings at the Flinck sale.[55] Michael Jaffé[56] observed that he was almost certain that all of Leonardo's grotesque heads at Chatsworth[57] once belonged to Nicolaes Flinck. According to Jaffé, these drawings were cut up and remounted[58] by the duke,[59] which might explain the absence on them of the mark PL, indicating the Peter Lely provenance, as well as the absence on several of them of the mark F, indicating the Flinck provenance. It is therefore in the Devonshire Collection at Chatsworth that, since 1724, the originals of Leonardo's grotesques have been located, including seventeen copied in the Louvre album.

In the Département des Arts Graphiques at the Musée du Louvre are two albums that belonged to Pierre-Jean Mariette (1694–1774).[60] One contains drawings in pen and brown ink of small grotesque heads,[61] the other etchings done from these drawings.[62] The first is known as the Mariette album (cat. no. 137), the second as the Caylus album (cat. no. 138).

The album of drawings (cat. no. 137) was first purchased by Pierre-Jean Mariette's father, Jean Mariette, from Salomon Gautier, who had bought it in Amsterdam in 1719. The younger Mariette attached great importance to the drawings because he believed they were originals by Leonardo da Vinci. In 1730, after his father "had just" bought the volume of grotesques, he had etchings made of them by his friend the count of Caylus and reassembled them in a volume to "share with his friends" (cat. no. 138).[63] The reproductive prints were preceded by a twenty-two-page introduction composed by Mariette himself and titled "La lettre sur Léonard de Vinci" (The letter on Leonardo da Vinci), where the album of drawings is discussed in detail.

This text was translated into Italian and published by Giovanni Bottari[64] in 1757, in volume 2 of his *Raccolta di lettere sulla pittura, scultura e architettura*.[65] In a note,[66] Bottari discussed Mariette's introduction and disputed the attribution of the drawings to Leonardo, writing that "the true originals were purchased in Holland by Monsignor Cardinal Silvio Valenti."[67] In volume 4 of the *Raccolta*, Bottari published a letter Luigi Crespi had sent him in 1752, in which the cardinal's purchase, in Holland, of a "book of caricatures done in pen by the hand of Leonardo da Vinci himself" was again at issue.[68] To reaffirm the authenticity of the volume in his possession, Mariette wrote as follows in the 1767 edition of the volume of etchings:

> It is much more for love of the truth than in my capacity as owner of this beautiful collection of drawings that I feel obliged to take up their defense and to maintain against anyone wishing to advance a contrary view that the drawings composing them are indisputably originals and are absolutely without parallel whatsoever in that respect. I make this observation because, in the second volume of *Lettere su la pittura*, published in Rome in 1757, which, while doing me the honor of inserting that letter, translated into Italian, expounds in a note on page 170 on the fact that the late Cardinal Silvio Valenti had a collection of drawings purchased in Holland and that the present drawings are apparently only copies of the latter, since his own are judged to be the only *true originals*. If I were not afraid of raising

suspicions about myself, I would say that I had them examined by good connoisseurs when the book was for sale, and that, on the basis of the report I received about them, I was not tempted to acquire them.[69]

Hence, thirty-seven years after the first edition of the album of etchings, Mariette was still convinced that he owned the original drawings.

That dispute about whether it was the Mariette album or Cardinal Valenti Gonzaga's album, now lost, that contained the "true originals" demonstrates not only the popularity of Leonardo's drawings, which became known and were reproduced immediately after the artist's death and throughout the following centuries, but also the difficulty in distinguishing the originals from the copies. On this matter, Roger North's autobiography, after describing the mob in London that rushed to the Lely sale of 1688 to make purchases, spoke of the diffusion of copies that "deprecated" the drawings and expressed the author's astonishment at how sure some people were that they could distinguish between the originals and the copies.[70] In her 1996 article on Cardinal Valenti Gonzaga's collection of drawings, Simonetta Prosperi Valenti Rodinò also noted that the copies were spread throughout the largest graphic collections of the eighteenth century and wondered whether refined connoisseurs of that century were able to make the subtle distinction between originals and copies.[71]

Mariette believed his drawings came from the Arundel collection[72] because several had been engraved by Wenceslaus (Wenceslas, Venceslas, or Wenzel) Hollar, a Prague artist who had been in the service of Lord Arundel. In fact, the originals were those that had been with Arundel, whereas Mariette's drawings were later copies. Mariette also wrote that his album could be the one Lomazzo spoke of in his *Trattato* of 1584 as being in the hands of Aurelio Luini, and which remains unidentified. The drawings in that album, however, were done in red chalk (as Lomazzo stated), whereas the Mariette album drawings were in pen and brown ink. Finally, of the heads copied in the latter album, only the first thirty-eight are after Leonardo; the twenty-two that follow were copied from other artists. Mariette himself noticed the difference in hand and said that "the drawings that follow the first thirty-eight, though of the same character, were added by a few curiosos."[73]

There are no pairs in the Mariette album, only individual heads. As for the first thirty-eight, copies after Leonardo—the object of my research within the framework of this essay— I would like to suggest that they were executed when the original sheets were still in Holland, between the time of Lady Arundel's death in 1654 and 1719, when Gautier purchased them as an album. The hand seems to be Dutch, and it is the same hand for the entire group. The frontispiece was executed after Agostino Carracci and is different from all the caricatures that follow. The first thirty-eight heads, which are derived from originals by Leonardo, must be considered separately from the other twenty-two, which were added after the fact to that first series and do not belong to it. Seventeen of the Leonardo originals from which the thirty-eight heads in the Mariette album were copied are now in Chatsworth;[74] two, of Dutch provenance (Ploos van Amstel), are in the British Museum;[75] and two are at the Albertina (with Crozat-Mariette provenance).[76] These originals were part of the group that remained in Holland after the Leoni-Windsor volume left that country in about 1660, the probable date of purchase by King Charles II for the English royal collection.

We may well wonder who the copyist was. In an attempt to identify the artist who drew the grotesques in the Louvre album, I will trace, in chronological order, the owners of the originals, in order to see when the copyist might have executed his work and hence to explore all the possibilities.

The first possibility is that the copies were done at Arundel's home in London. The earl had in his service artists whose task it was to copy the artworks in his collection: a father and son bearing the same name, Lucas Vorsterman; Hendrick van der Borcht Jr.; and Wenceslaus Hollar,[77] any of whom might therefore have copied the originals of the small heads. Nevertheless, the Mariette album contains copies of only some of the grotesques that belonged to Arundel, namely, those that went to Holland; the Mariette album does not contain any copies of the Windsor grotesques.

Hollar worked at Arundel's home in England, etching the collection between 1636 and 1642; then he lived in Antwerp between 1644 and 1652.[78] A first volume of Hollar's etchings, including grotesques after Leonardo, appeared in Antwerp in 1645. There were further editions in 1648 and 1666. Hollar has often been cited as the artist responsible for the Louvre

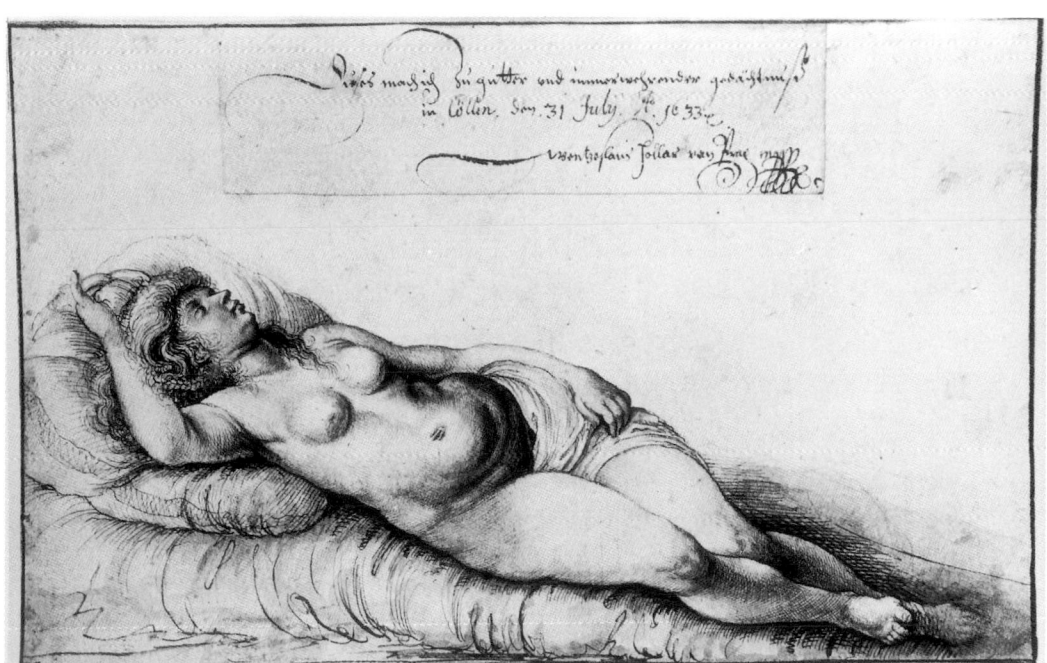

Fig. 108. Wenceslaus Hollar, *Sleeping Female Nude.* Pen and brown ink with watercolor, 171 × 104 mm. Národní Galerie, Prague K 31216

heads, which seems logical, given that he was employed by Lord Arundel. All the same, Hollar's prints do not closely follow Leonardo's originals, to the point that Pierre-Jean Mariette remarked of them: "One might wish for a bit more taste, and that the artist's manner was a little less disguised."[79] Hollar's etchings include twenty-one of the heads that appear in the Caylus album; but the difference between the Mariette album, Hollar's known drawings, and his prints is too great for it to be possible to attribute the Louvre drawings to him (fig. 108). The same difference in hand can be seen in the drawings by Lucas Vorsterman[80] and by Van der Borcht Jr. As for Van der Borcht, it should be noted that he was still residing at the home of Lady Arundel when she died in 1654.[81]

Other individuals in the Arundel entourage may have copied the caricatures, for example, Nicholas Lanier,[82] a composer who became Master of Musick to King Charles I of England. He was not well known as a draftsman, but he was an extremely important dealer, purchasing works in Italy on behalf of the king and Arundel. Jeremy Wood's study on Lanier, which can help us understand Lanier's manner of copying the works of Italian artists, allows us to rule him out as a possible copyist of the Mariette grotesques.[83] Another artist to consider is the miniature painter Peter Oliver, also well known to the English court.[84] Wood's studies can again persuade us that it would be very difficult, because of a significant difference in the strokes, to connect Oliver's hand to the one that executed the copies in the Mariette album.

Might Peter Lely, who owned the originals subsequent to Arundel, have copied them or had them copied before his death in 1680? Lely was known to use drawings in his possession as a source of inspiration for his works.[85] He wanted to acquire the originals, and Constantijn Huygens even accused him of stealing drawings from the royal collection and substituting copies for them.[86] The style of the copies in the Louvre, however, which is very different from his own, rules Lely out as a possible copyist.

The most plausible hypothesis is that the copies were executed in Holland, where Van Bergesteyn had taken the originals after purchasing them at the Lely sale in 1688.[87] Is it possible that the "little book with forty-five pretty little heads . . . by Leonardo da Vinci, done in pen,"[88] which had belonged to the wealthy Dutch collector and patron Jan Six and which was sold in Amsterdam in 1702, contained the thirty-eight heads copied from Leonardo, which were then later bound with the other twenty-two now found in the Mariette album? Peter Schatborn has kindly suggested to me the names of two individuals who might have been responsible for the copies in the album: Constantijn Huygens Jr. and the draftsman and etcher Jan de Bisschop.

We know that these two individuals wanted to collaborate on a "noble book," but we do not know just what it would have been.[89] For his book *Paradigmata graphices variorum artificum* (1671), a collection of engravings after drawings by old masters, Bisschop copied drawings located in the Netherlands at the time,[90] including some from Jan Six's and Nicolaes

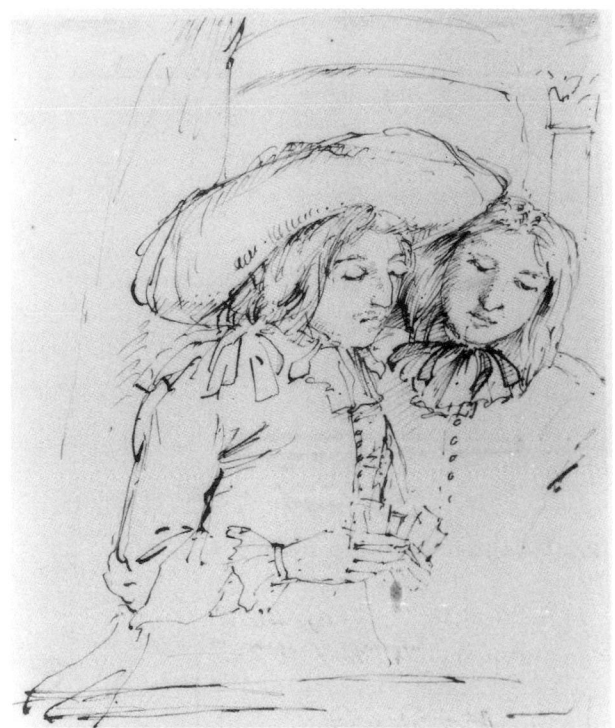

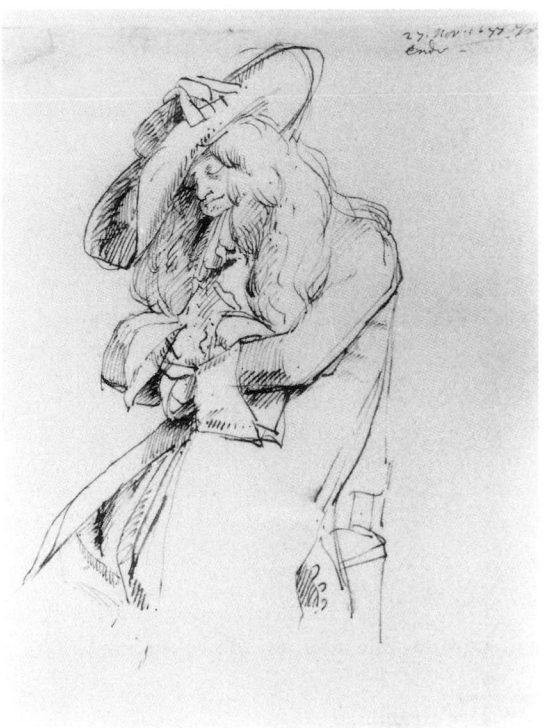

Fig. 109. Here attributed to Constantijn Huygens Jr., *Portrait of Two Young Men*. Pen and brown ink, 172 × 143 mm. Prentenkabinet, Universiteit Leiden AW 1035

Fig. 110. Here attributed to Constantijn Huygens Jr., *Portrait of a Gentleman with a Large Hat*. Pen and brown ink, 170 × 130 mm. Prentenkabinet, Universiteit Leiden AW 1036

Flinck's collections. I do not see any similarity between Bisschop's manner of drawing and the Mariette album, even though it is very tempting to attribute the Louvre copies to him. Conversely, Huygens might be responsible for these copies, since he was not only a collector but also an amateur artist excited about drawing, copperplate engraving, and pastels, who, moreover, practiced drawing by copying the masters.[91] In addition, Christiaan Huygens boasted of having a brother who drew "like Raphael."[92]

A drawing in Leiden[93] depicting two young men (fig. 109) and another of a man in a large hat (fig. 110)[94] reveal a meticulous and flexible stroke that may be linked to the first thirty-eight heads in the Mariette album. I note as well a certain similarity in the lines of the hatching and in the application of the shadows. Another drawing by Constantijn Huygens—a copy of a figure from Dürer's woodcut *Death of the Virgin* (Hollstein, 7, no. 205)—displays the same hand.[95] If we accept Constantijn Huygens as the artist who made the Mariette copies, it follows that they were done before 1697, the year of his death. Nor can we rule out the possibility that Constantijn even owned Leonardo's originals, since we know he purchased drawings at the second Lely sale in 1694,[96] and Houbraken cited him as the owner of some drawings from the Flinck collection. But in that case one would have expected Huygens to mention them in his writings, just as he proudly indicated his acquisition of what is now

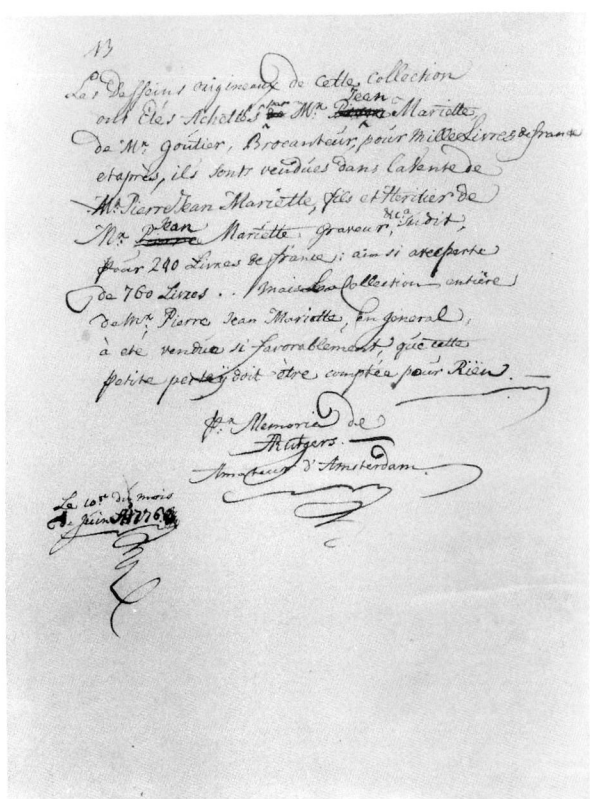

Fig. 111. Annotations by Antoni Rutgers in the Caylus album in Leiden. Pen and brown ink, 286 × 212 mm. Kunsthistorisch Instituut, Universiteit Leiden RB I B 14

called the Huygens Codex, which he believed was written by Leonardo.[97]

Thanks to Antoni Rutgers's handwritten annotations on the album of Caylus prints in Leiden (figs. 111, 112), we know that the collector Siewert van der Schelling of Amsterdam bound the Mariette album,[98] placing the drawings in the order in which they are now found. The binding has been linked to bindings done in Amsterdam between 1700 and 1719 (see cat. no. 137).[99]

Mariette, believing his album contained originals, attributed its origin to Arundel: "The collection of drawings of heads I just spoke of may have belonged to that illustrious curioso. I base my conjecture on the fact that several of these heads were previously engraved by Venceslas Hollar."[100] Antoni Rutgers, annotating the copy of the volume of engravings, also endorsed that view, giving the volume's provenance and adding the names of Lely, Van Berghesteyn, and Van der Schelling. His first annotation is dated immediately after the death of Mariette in 1775 and the second the following year, with details on the price paid. Rutgers makes no distinction, however, between originals and copies, whereas we know that the originals remained in Holland, at the home of Nicolaes Anthonis Flinck, until his death in 1723, and that Van der Schelling thus could only have had copies.

Siewert van der Schelling had in his possession the thirty-eight copies after Leonardo that he bound with another twenty-two drawings he owned. He must have known that the "Leonardos" were copies because the originals were still in Holland and the world of collectors was also a circle of friends. Conversely, when Jean Mariette purchased the album from Gautier, who had bought it in 1719,[101] he must not have known that the originals were still in Holland, since he would not have concealed that fact from his son. In 1767 Pierre-Jean Mariette was still insisting on the authenticity of his album.

We may now turn to two series of copies of Leonardo's grotesques (see cat. nos. 69–75, 121; figs. 32, 107) that contain several heads that appear in the Mariette album: the Pembroke series, which in my view was the first to be executed; and the Spencer series. The former series, which no longer exists as a set, was a group of twelve sheets previously mounted on one large page.[102] It was in the Pembroke collection at Wilton House, near Salisbury, before

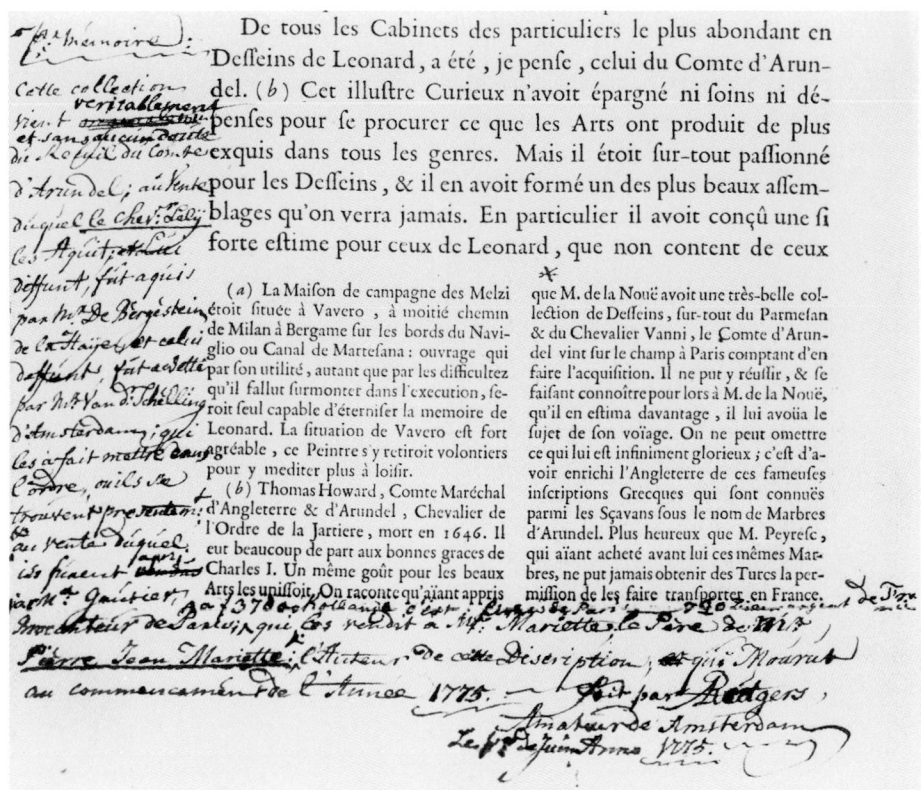

Fig. 112. Annotations by Antoni Rutgers on page 4 of the Caylus album in Leiden. Pen and brown ink. Kunsthistorisch Instituut, Universiteit Leiden RB I B 14

1772; the collection was dispersed in 1917.[103] The dimensions of the sheets are very similar to those of the originals in Chatsworth. The layout of the heads in the Pembroke series, in profile facing each other, the diversity of expressions, the intelligence of the composition, and the dialogue suggested by the strong presence of the figures all indicate that this was how Leonardo wanted the pages put together. That is how we ought to imagine the isolated grotesques today at Chatsworth. Every detail both complements and stands in opposition to every other. Ascending lines correspond to other, falling lines. A mouth with protruding teeth is juxtaposed with a toothless mouth. A hairstyle rising like a tower confronts a beard projecting horizontally. Every "vignette" gives a glimpse of the aging process, the deterioration of the faces, the wear and tear on relationships between human beings who know each other well. In contrast, when the couples are separated, split up, and paired off indifferently (cat. no. 136; figs. 113, 114),[104] the force of the psychological study is lost, and the combinations no longer have any significance. When the figures are presented individually, as in the case of the Mariette album, the individual heads end up isolated from their context and become mute.

Patricia Trutty-Coohill suggested that the two folios mounted in the upper part of the Chatsworth sheet exhibited here (cat. no. 73), given their dimensions, composition, and execution, may have been part of the Pembroke series.[105] The present exhibition will make

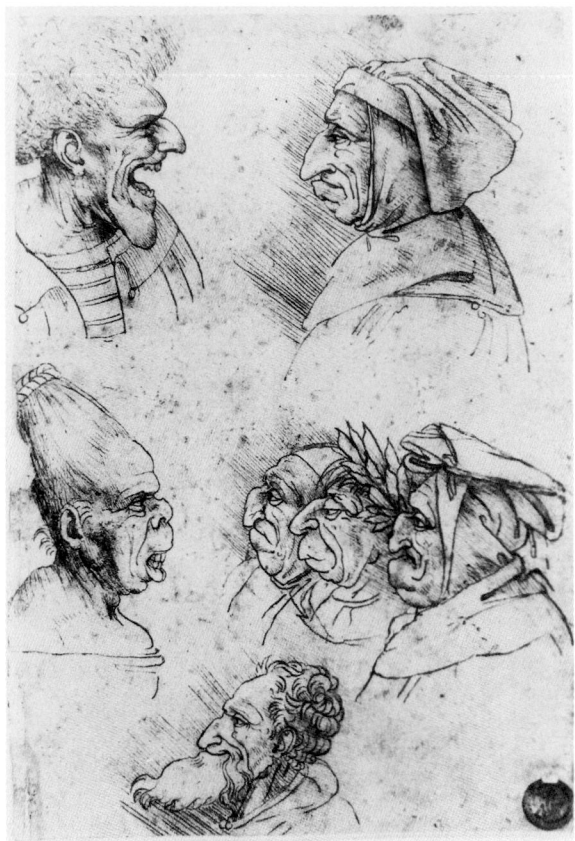

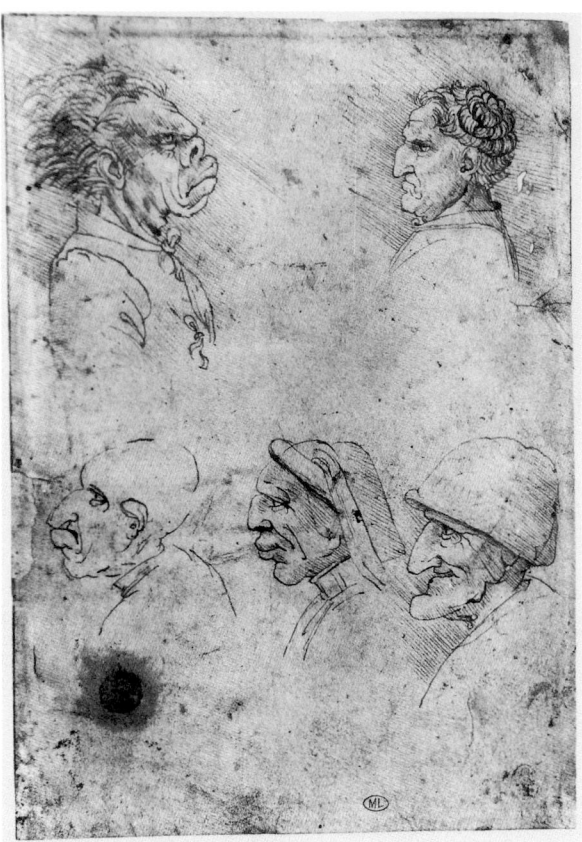

Fig. 113. Copy after Leonardo, *Seven Grotesque Heads*. Pen and brown ink, 180 × 120 mm. Gallerie dell'Accademia, Venice 229

Fig. 114. Copy after Leonardo, *Five Grotesque Heads*. Pen and brown ink, 192 × 127 mm. Musée du Louvre, Paris 2297

it possible to compare them with the Pembroke sheet now in The Metropolitan Museum of Art (cat. no. 121), in order to find support for that supposition.

Carlo Pedretti attributed the drawings in the Pembroke series to Francesco Melzi,[106] an attribution scholars have accepted. Let us note, however, that Melzi's hand is not well known, especially for pen drawings. Also, the Pembroke copies are not similar to copies attributed to Melzi in the collection of the Royal Library in Windsor,[107] which display a subtlety of line, hatching, and shading missing from the Pembroke sheets. All the same, it would be possible to argue that Leonardo's originals in Chatsworth were sketchily drawn, which would explain the lack of subtlety in the copies. All but five of the figures on the Pembroke sheets[108] were copied individually in the Mariette album in the Louvre, as were three of the four figures on the two Chatsworth sheets previously mentioned.[109]

The Spencer copies occur at the end of the first two volumes of *Les oeuvres de M. François Rabelais. Augmentées de la vie de l'auteur de quelques remarques sur sa vie et sur l'histoire* (The works of M. François Rabelais. With the life of the author and a few remarks on his life and on history), in the Spencer Collection at the New York Public Library.[110] There are 42 heads in volume 1 and 62 in volume 2; of a total of 104 heads, 35 are found in the Mariette album. The grotesques, though unrelated to the text, were bound into it in about 1800. Aydua H. Scott-Elliot, in a 1958 article, analyzed this series in depth. She wrote that the paper used is the same for all the sheets containing grotesques, sometimes with a watermark (Briquet 536–38), which can be dated approximately to the last quarter of the sixteenth century in northern Italy. These are individual heads derived, for the most part, from Leonardo's originals, which were in Milan after Melzi's death in 1570 and were subsequently dispersed. Each folio measures about 5⅜ by 3¼ inches (13.5 × 8.3 cm). The Spencer images of the group we are studying here are about twice the size of the originals at Chatsworth, and the copies were made with a desire to reproduce folds, facial wrinkles, and head coverings; most have no hatching to indicate placement in space.

The originals from which this series was copied are now scattered throughout the world. The Spencer copies are after two originals at Windsor Castle; three at the Biblioteca Ambrosiana, Milan; twenty-four at Chatsworth; one at the Albertina, Vienna (fig. 105); two at the British Museum, London; one at The Metropolitan Museum of Art (cat. no. 60; figs. 31, 32); one at the Pierpont Morgan Library, New York (fig. 106); one at the Hamburger Kunsthalle (cat. no. 75); the recto and verso of a sheet at the Istituto per la Grafica, Rome (figs. 55, 56); and one at the École Nationale Supérieure des Beaux-Arts, Paris (cat. no. 47). The last sheet was discovered by art historians only in 1992, at the time of the exhibition "Leonardo e Venezia." In addition, let us note that the Spencer series also includes drawings executed by artists belonging to the Accademia de la Val di Blenio, founded in 1560,[111] and others that seem very different from those of Leonardo.[112]

Since the Spencer grotesques are on watermarked paper from the late sixteenth century and contain drawings by members of the Accademia de la Val di Blenio,[113] I would like to suggest that they were executed in Milan between about 1570 and the first decade of the 1600s. Scholars have suggested the names of Francesco Melzi and Bernardino Lanino as the artists responsible for the Spencer grotesques. Unfortunately, the drawings were retouched with solid, uniform, and regular strokes that are disturbing for their heaviness. This strengthening masks and distorts the original stroke, making attribution difficult[114]—even distinguishing among several hands is risky. Indisputably, certain sheets are of very fine quality, such as the copy of the "old duchess" of Windsor or the man with the long chin.[115] On the back of some sheets[116] one finds an offset from a drawing on the front, which cannot be explained since the medium is black chalk. At other times, the verso bears the trace of the image on the front of the following sheet, even though there is now a sheet of transparent paper placed between the two.[117]

Leonardo's physiognomic types in his series of caricatures became widely disseminated and celebrated thanks to the drawings' reproduction in the count of Caylus's etchings (cat. no. 138). The etchings Mariette ordered done from his album of drawings in order to share them with his friends, preceded by his introductory text, "La lettre sur Léonard de Vinci,"[118] were a source of knowledge about Leonardo's grotesques that spread rapidly among art lovers. Copies of these etchings are found in many collections and, even today, Caylus's prints are used to discuss Leonardo's grotesques. Mariette's text on Leonardo, written at Caylus's insistence, became known very quickly. Kate Steinitz, who studied the different editions of the volume,[119] noted that there was a German translation in about 1750, which was followed by Bottari's Italian translation in 1757. The importance of that text lies in Mariette's extensive knowledge of art and painters. His erudition, his method of analysis, and his connoisseur's eye have secured him an important place at the origins of modern art history.

The long friendship between Pierre-Jean Mariette and Anne-Claude-Philippe de Thubières, count of Caylus,[120] began in about 1719 and continued until Caylus's death in 1765, "despite the difference in their character and training."[121] They belonged to the same circle of scholars and art lovers, who met in the home of the collector and patron Pierre Crozat with artists such as Watteau and Rosalba Carriera. For the count, the friendship with Antoine Coypel, premier painter to the king and director of paintings and drawings in the king's collection, opened the doors to the French royal collection. Within that milieu, he developed his taste for prints and in 1729 published some of the plates that appeared in the first volume of the *Recueil Crozat*,[122] a famous art-publishing project that Francis Haskell called "the first art book in history."[123] Etchings from the Mariette album were published at the same time. When he etched the plates for Mariette, Caylus did not try to interpret the drawings but rather followed the draftsman's lines to make the works known through his reproductive prints. "He is a true master . . . of the rapid transcription of the gesture, the accent, the life, in a word, the style. . . . It is impossible to be more other while remaining oneself, to push resemblance farther toward illusion."[124] These etchings exude Leonardo's spirit even though they were done from copies of his drawings.

1. See the introduction by Dame Jane Roberts in Palazzo Grassi 1992, pp. 155–78, for a detailed overview of the provenance of Leonardo's drawings; Clark and Pedretti 1968–69, vol. 1, introduction, for the provenance of the Windsor drawings; Mazenta 1919, and Ravasi in Ambrosiana 1998–99, pp. 9–13, for the history of their dispersion, in particular, the origin of the Biblioteca Ambrosiana collection, as well as the importance of the role played by Pompeo Leoni; and Bora 1991, on the collecting and dispersion of drawings by Leonardo's followers.

2. The definitive work on Leonardo's grotesques is Gombrich 1954, 1976. See also appendix B in the first edition of Clark's catalogue of Leonardo's drawings (Clark 1935) and the later 1968 edition (Clark and Pedretti 1968–69); and Popham 1947, pp. 42–47. The subject is discussed in Caroli 1991 and examined in detail by Kwakkelstein 1991, 1993a, 1993c, and 1994 and by Laurenza 1996, 1997, and 2001.

3. See note 98 below for the full transcription of the annotations, and figs. 111 and 112, where they are reproduced.

4. Recent research has established that the works painted on the vault of Santa Maria di Rivolta d'Adda were done in 1506 (Bora, oral communication, January 2002). Giulio Bora (1991, p. 206) pointed out that, as of 1540, there were frescoes at the Villa Medici in Frascarola, near Varese, with grotesque heads very faithful to Leonardo's models. For Leonardo's influence on the Antwerp painters, see Friedländer 1947. B. Meijer (1971) has analyzed the close relation between Leonardo's drawings and Quentin Metsys's paintings. In 1998

the same author returned to the question of the reciprocal influence between northern Europe and Italy (Meijer 1998). J. Białostocki (1959) established a connection between Leonardo's grotesques and a work by Dürer and advanced the hypothesis that there was a concrete connection between Leonardo and Antwerp. Cécile Scailliérez (1991, pp. 57–61) uses the expression "Antwerpian Leonardism." Popham (1945) points out that one of Leonardo's caricatures, no. 138B (fig. 56), was engraved by Hans Liefrinck in 1573; see Muylle 1994, p. 253, fig. 2, and Muylle 2001, p. 189, fig. 11.

5. Beltrami 1919a, document no. 244, pp. 152–54.

6. Vasari–Milanesi 1878–85, vol. 4, p. 35: "che le ha care et tiene come per reliquie tal carte."

7. Clayton, oral communication, December 2001, and Clayton 2002–3.

8. Rosci 1984 (p. 58 n. 14) writes that, in 1542, Cellini reported that he had purchased a book on perspective in France, copied from a manuscript by Leonardo; and that, in 1566, one of Leonardo's manuscripts was listed in the library left by Alfonso Piccolomini II upon his death.

9. Clark and Pedretti 1968–69, vol. 1, p. x.

10. For example, Windsor 12438, 12439, 12460, and 12464; see Pedretti 1957a, pp. 11ff.; and Marinoni 1991, p. 164. According to Clayton, in an oral communication of December 2001, it was Melzi, not Leoni, who cut them out.

11. Cod. F. 263 inf. 28, Biblioteca Ambrosiana, Milan.

12. Clark and Pedretti 1968–69, vol. 1, p. x; Roberts 1992, p. 166 and n. 69; Kwakkelstein 1994, p. 144.

13. Lomazzo 1584, pp. 359–60; Lomazzo 1973–74, vol. 2, p. 315: "Leonardo: il quale perciò molto si dilettò di disegnare vecchi e villani e villane diformi che ridessero, i quali si veggono ancora in diversi luoghi, tra quali forsi da cinquanta, designati di sua mano, ne tiene Aurelio Lovino uno libricciuolo"; and Lomazzo 1590, pp. 54–55; Lomazzo 1973–74, vol. 1, p. 290: "quelle disegnate co'l lapis rosso, che tiene Aurelio Lovino, pittore milanese; ove ne sono alcune che ridono tanto alla gagliarda per forza d'un arte grandissima che appena lo può far l'istessa natura."

14. Lomazzo 1973–74, pp. 96–97.

15. Gombrich 1954, 1976, p. 68; Kwakkelstein 1991, p. 134 n. 47, "the originals are at Chatsworth and were probably also conceived as pairs."

16. Inv. no. 66.

17. The original sheet with three figures is copied on one of the sheets that were part of the Pembroke collection, now in the Pierpont Morgan Library, New York (fig. 106). The whereabouts of a third figure, on the left on the original sheet, are unknown, but it, with others, is copied on a sheet in the Gallerie dell'Accademia, Venice (inv. 227), and in the Spencer series (vol. 2, no. 30). The original Vienna fragment (fig. 105) comprising two heads is copied on a sheet in the Biblioteca Ambrosiana, Milan (F. 274 inf. 54). Finally, the three heads are copied separately in the Louvre album (RF 28741, RF 28742, RF 28746; see cat. no. 137).

18. The definitive work on Lord Arundel is Hervey 1921; on the history of the formation of his collection and its dispersion, see Cust 1911–12, Watson 1944, Sutton 1947, Newman 1980, and the August 1996 issue of *Apollo*, which is entirely devoted to the Arundel collection, with articles by various authors. See also Ashmolean Museum 1985–86, and White 1995. I take this opportunity to thank Dame Jane Roberts for her kindness in meeting with me and for generously sharing her research on Lord Arundel.

19. Walpole 1849, vol. 1, p. 293 n. 1.

20. Cust 1911–12, p. 278.

21. On Lady Aletheia Arundel, a personality as interesting as her husband and just as much a collector, see Howarth 1998.

22. White 1995, p. 16.

23. For example, Hervey (1921, p. 398) has published excerpts of letters from George Conn, the pope's agent in England, to Cardinal Francesco Barberini in Rome: "January 22, 1637: . . . The Earl told me he had bought, at the recommendation of your Eminence, the drawings of Gaddi."

24. Roberts forthcoming, fig. 2, where the partial copies of Windsor RL 12582 and RL 12515 are shown. Wood (1998, p. 131) attributes this drawing to Peter Oliver. It is interesting to note that the Chatsworth drawing also reproduces, along the left edge, a profile of a young man (RL 12276) and, at the top of the sheet, three profiles of the old men depicted on an anonymous sheet in the Edmond de Rothschild collection at the Musée du Louvre, Paris, d.R. 782.

25. Newman 1980, p. 695.

26. Francis Junius, *Painting of the Ancients* (1638), quoted in Van Gelder and Jost 1985, p. 198 n. 16; Howarth 1980, p. 691.

27. See "A Memorial of All the Rooms at Tart Hall: and an Inventory of All the Household Stuffs and Goods There Belonging to the Rt. Hon. The Countess of Arundel. 8th September, 1641," in Cust 1911–12, pt. 2, pp. 98–100, 233–36.

28. Howarth 1998, p. 135 and n. 45, in which he gives the reference to the Public Record Office in London, Court of Delegates Processes, vol. 7, no. 14, p. 882.

29. The posthumous inventory of all Arundel works in England and Holland was done in 1655, one year after Lady Arundel's death. It was published in Cust 1911–12, pp. 278–86.

30. Watson 1944, p. 224.

31. Scott-Elliot 1956, p. 11.

32. Roberts 1992, p. 167.

33. Watson 1944, p. 226; Roberts 1992, p. 167.

34. Lugt 2092 (Lugt 1921, 1956, here and in references below); Dethloff 1996.

35. Richardson 1728, p. 160: "That collection was composed above all of the debris from those of Mylord Arundel and the Laniers."

36. Jessop 1887, pp. 199–200: "It was wonderful to see with what earnestness people attended this sale. One would have thought bread was exposed in a famine."

37. "Executors' Account Book of Sir Peter Lely" (1679–91), British Library, London, Add. Ms. 16174, published and studied in detail in Dethloff 1996.

38. "Executors' Account Book" 1679–91, fol. 85v.

39. See Lugt, under 959; Huygens 1888–1905, vol. 9, no. 2569.

40. "Executors' Account Book" 1679–91, fol. 86r; Dethloff 1996, pp. 18–19.

41. "Executors' Account Book" 1679–91, fol. 85v.

42. Strong 1900: for example, no. 2 with the mark PL and the notation: "Cor. From vol. 2nd N. 6" (*La notte*, today at the Fitzwilliam Museum, Cambridge, PD. 119-1961), and no. 28 with the mark PL and the notation: "L. da V. from vol. 2nd N. 3" (*Head of a Young Woman in Profile Facing to the Left*, now attributed to Boltraffio, in The Metropolitan Museum of Art, New York, 19.76.3; fig. 84).

43. Lugt 2092.

44. Van Bergesteyn (Van Bergestein) is mentioned under Lugt 718–19, 959, 2092, and 2668; Jaffé (1995–96, p. 16 and no. 22) repeats the story told by Roger North in his autobiography (see Jessop 1887, p. 1999), regarding a drawing from the Lely collection purchased by Sonnius for Van Bergesteyn—a drawing that was considered a Raphael at the time and is today attributed to Giovan Francesco Penni—which was the occasion for a rather lively battle among purchasers. This drawing became part of the Flinck collection, where Jonathan Richardson Sr. saw it when he visited the collection (see Dethloff 1996, p. 49 n. 84). Constantijn Huygens mentions it to his brother in a letter of March 3, 1690, and reports that Van Bergesteyn was furious that he had been forced to pay such a high price (Huygens 1901, no. 2569). The drawing is now at Chatsworth, 175.

45. Huygens 1888–1905, vol. 4, no. 1159.

46. Huygens 1888–1905, vol. 4, no. 1188, quoted in Van Gelder 1972, pp. 56–57.

47. Sutton 1947, p. 75.

48. Roberts 1992, p. 167.

49. Unlocated catalogue, cited by Lugt under 959. Bernadette Py, to whom I express my gratitude, told me about a drawing by Taddeo Zuccaro in Turin, 15800 D.C., *A Roman Army Crossing a River*, which bears an annotation in Dutch on the back of the old mount, in red chalk: "No. 607 uyt bergestein Auctie N.° 47."

50. Van Heel 1975, p. 164, no. 83. My thanks to Michiel Plomp for his kindness in sharing with me his research on eighteenth-century Dutch collectors.

51. Lugt 959.

52. Houbraken 1753, vol. 2, p. 27; Jaffé 1995–96, p. 14.

53. See Pedretti 1988, p. 156, fig. 2, where the Flinck mark on Chatsworth 818A is placed on the mounting sheet, not on the original sheet itself. Drawing 820B, which originally formed a pair with 822C, bears a Flinck mark lower right (partly cut off), thus in the center of the confronted couple.

54. Lugt 718 and 719.

55. Richardson 1728, ed. 1972, p. 162: "The perfectly beautiful and well-chosen collection of the great connoisseur Mr. Flinck of Rotterdam, which after his death was added in its entirety to that of the duke of Devonshire."

56. Jaffé 1995–96, p. 14.

57. Leonardo's caricatures formerly or still at Chatsworth: see cat. nos. 69–73.

58. See Flinck mark, partly cut off, on the former Chatsworth 820 B (National Gallery of Art, Washington, D.C.; cat. no. 72), the former Chatsworth 820 C (J. Paul Getty Museum, Los Angeles; cat. no. 69), and Chatsworth 818 A, 824 B, and 826 D.

59. Jaffé 1994, p. 171.

60. Lugt 1852. On Pierre-Jean Mariette, see the catalogue of the exhibition devoted to him at the Musée du Louvre, Paris, in 1967 (Bacou 1967). Let me simply cite here the titles he had acquired by the time he died, which were published in the funeral announcement: "Messire Pierre-Jean Mariette Ecuyer, Conseiller du Roi en ses Conseils, Secrétaire de Sa Majesté, Maison-Couronne de France et de ses Finances, Contrôleur-Général de la Grande Chancellerie de France, Amateur-Honoraire de l'Académie Royale de Peinture et Sculpture, et de l'Académie de France, ancien Marguillier de la Paroisse" (Pierre-Jean Mariette, squire, councillor to the king in his councils, secretary to His Majesty, House of the Crown of France and of Its Finances, controller general of the Great Chancellery of France, honorary art lover of the Académie Royale de Peinture et Sculpture, former churchwarden of the parish). Viatte in Bacou 1967, no. 337.

61. RF 28725 to RF 28785, composed of a frontispiece and sixty individual heads: thirty-eight copied from Leonardo, followed by twenty-two others.

62. RF 28786, composed of a frontispiece, fifty-five heads copied from the album of drawings, and eleven heads with a different provenance.

63. See Chennevières and Montaiglon 1851–60, vol. 3, n. on p. 145. In the 1730 edition (p. 18), the younger Mariette says that the album "has just become part of my father's collection." Given that the introductory text on the Caylus prints was first published in 1726 (see, below, n. 118), we may assume that the album had just been purchased.

64. On Giovanni Bottari, see Cormio 1986 and Prosperi Valenti Rodinò 1996; on the correspondence between Bottari and Mariette, see Prosperi Valenti Rodinò 1978.

65. *Raccolta di lettere sulla pittura, scultura e architettura* (1757–68) was a collection of letters culled from Roman archives, libraries, and private collections containing much useful information for art historians and artists' biographies. See Bottari 1822–25 in the Bibliography, where the different editions of the work and the publication dates for the volumes are indicated.

66. Bottari 1822–25, vol. 2, no. 84, p. 209 n. 1, "Queste teste sono caricature toccate in penna meravigliosamente. Gli originali veri furono comprati in Olanda dal signor card. Silvio Valenti; e le stampe di cui si parla, sono nella famosissima Raccolta della Libreria Corsini." It should be noted that Bottari had been a librarian for Neri Corsini.

67. On Cardinal Silvio Valenti (1690–1756)—also known as Valenti Gonzaga—his ecclesiastical career, and his collection, see Cormio 1986 and Prosperi Valenti Rodinò 1996.

68. Bottari 1822–25, vol. 4, letter no. 170, February 9, 1752, p. 402 n. 1, "Il detto Sig. Card. Valenti Gonzaga comprò in Olanda all'incanto un libro di Caricature fatte in penna di pugno proprio di Lionardo da Vinci." Could this be the "Teste Capriciose di Lionardo da Vinci" sold at the sale of the count of Wassenaer d'Obdam's collection in The Hague on August 19, 1750? The sales catalogue mentions Book A, composed of forty drawings, each containing two heads drawn in pen. My thanks to Peter Schatborn for sending me a photocopy of the pages in the sales catalogue. The volume that belonged to the cardinal can no longer be located, according to Simonetta Prosperi Valenti Rodinò (written communication, December 1999).

69. Chennevières and Montaiglon 1851–60, vol. 3, p. 145 n. 1. After Mariette's note, Chennevières and Montaiglon add, regarding the authenticity of the drawings in Mariette's possession: "It is obvious that the vast majority of the drawings in this collection were originals."

70. Lugt 1921, under no. 2092, p. 388; Jessop 1887, p. 200: "This aptness to be copied deprecates drawings much; but the masters will seem to be very much assured of copies and originals, and will turn up the nose at some, and say that others as originals stare you in the face."

71. Prosperi Valenti Rodinò 1996, p. 145: "Viene spontaneo di domandarsi fino a che punto i raffinati collezionisti del Settecento fossero consapevoli del sottile distinguo che differenzia un originale da una copia."

72. Mariette 1730, p. 5; Chennevières and Montaiglon 1851–60, vol. 3, p. 143.

73. Chennevières and Montaiglon 1851–60, vol. 3, p. 158 n. 1.

74. See note 57 above.

75. Inv. nos. Pp I-37 and 38; Popham and Pouncey (1950, p. 71) waver between the idea that these are originals and the belief that they are excellent copies.

76. Inv. no. 66 (fig. 105).

77. See Faber Kolb 1996 on the engravers used by Arundel; and Griffiths 1998.

78. On Wenceslas Hollar, his life, career, and works, see Pennington 1982.

79. Chennevières and Montaiglon 1851–60, vol. 3, p. 144.

80. See Popham 1971, pl. 424 O.C. 14, British Museum; pl. 444 O.C. 13, British Museum; pl. 416 O.C. 12, British Museum.

81. Howarth 1998, p. 136.

82. Lugt 2885 and 2886.

83. Wood 2002, figs. 24, 26, 29.

84. On Peter Oliver, see Wood 1998.

85. Dethloff 1996, p. 22.

86. Kurz 1936, p. 135.

87. Even in 1966, Frits Lugt expressed the opinion (cited by Rezniceck 1981, n. 8) that the drawings were executed in Holland in the seventeenth century.

88. Jan Six sale, Amsterdam, April 6, 1702, "Een Omslagje, daar in 45 aardige Tronitjes, en 11 Paarde Hoofdjes, konstig, door Leonard da Vinci, met de pen getekent." My thanks to Michiel Plomp for his kindness in sharing his research with me.

89. Huygens 1888–1905, vol. 6, no. 1784, letter of November 14, 1669, from Christiaan to Constantijn. "I'd like to know what you're plotting with Bisschop, where you're going to put the content of that noble book"; quoted in Van Gelder 1972, p. 59 and n. 39.

90. Van Gelder 1972, p. 25. On Bisschop, see Van Gelder and Jost 1985.

91. See Van Gelder 1972, p. 55; Huygens 1888–1905, vol. 1, no. 834: letter from Christiaan to Constantijn, Paris, February 4, 1661: "the original belonging to the marquis del Guasto and his wife, whose copy you copied."

92. Huygens 1888–1905, vol. 6, no. 1691, Christiaan to Constantijn, January 5, 1669: "I often boast about having a brother who draws like Raphael."

93. Prentenkabinet, Universiteit Leiden, AW 1035. Peter Schatborn examined the album in the Louvre with me; I thank him for kindly pointing out this drawing, which supports the attribution to Constantijn Huygens.

94. Prentenkabinet, Universiteit Leiden, AW 1036.

95. See fig. p. 30 in Amsterdam 1982–83.

96. Huygens 1905, vol. 5, no. 2888, letter from Christiaan in The Hague to Constantijn in London, January 7, 1695: "Berckestein also let me know that you purchased a few more drawings at the last sale of Lely's things"; Constantijn replied on February 23, 1695 (no. 2890): "In addition to the drawings and prints I got a little while ago from the Lilly collection, I have found five or six very pretty ones and I got them at a good price because of the owner's ignorance. All that will contribute to Monsr. De Berkestein's phthisis."

97. Huygens 1888–1905, vol. 9, no. 2569. The Pierpont Morgan Library, New York, Codex M.A. 1139; the volume is now attributed to the painter and draftsman Carlo Urbino (d. after 1585). See Panofsky 1940 and Cremante 1998–99.

98. Lugt indicated it under no. 1852. Annotation in pen and brown ink by Antoni Rutgers on the copy at the Prentenkabinet, Universiteit Leiden, transcribed by Jef Schaeps, assistant curator, whom I sincerely thank for his help:

[Facing frontispiece] Note: The original drawings in this collection were purchased by Mr. Jean [written over a crossed-out "Pierre"] Mariette, from Mr. Goutier, a bric-a-brac dealer, for one thousand French livres and afterward were sold at the sale of Mr. Pierre-Jean Mariette, son and heir to Mr. Jean [written over a crossed-out "Pierre"] Mariette, engraver etc.; the aforementioned, for 240 French livres: hence at a loss of 760 livres. But the entire collection of Mr. Pierre Jean Mariette was, in general, sold to such advantage that this little loss ought to be counted for nothing.
Recorded by ARutgers, art lover of Amsterdam
The tenth day of June A.D. 1776.

[Next to the paragraph describing Lord Arundel's collection, in the margin of p. 4]: Note: This collection truly [written over a crossed-out "originally"] and without a doubt comes from the album belonging to the count of Arundel; at whose sale *the chevalier Lelij* acquired them; and, after his death, it was acquired by Mr. De Bergestein of The Hague; after his death, it was purchased by Mr. Van d. Schelling of Amsterdam, who had them placed in the order in which they are presently found; at whose sale they were acquired [written over a crossed-out "sold"] by Mr. Gautier, bric-a-brac salesman from Paris [inserted above the line] for 370 Dutch guldens, that is, 740 silver livres in French currency; who sold them to Mr. Mariette, father of Mr. *Pierre Jean Mariette*, the author of this description, who died at the beginning of the year 1775.
Attested by ARutgers, art lover of Amsterdam.
The [?] of June Anno 1775.

99. Reznicek 1981, pp. 248–49 n. 9.

100. Mariette 1730, p. 5; Chennevières and Montaiglon, 1851–60, vol. 3, p. 143.

101. From the van der Schelling sale; see Van Heel 1977, p. 114, no. 191.

102. For the original mount of the sheet, see Pedretti and Trutty-Coohill 1993, p. 16, fig. 1. According to Bora 1991, p. 280, this is a rather common pagination system, also found in other seventeenth-century collections.

103. See Pembroke sale 1917, p. 23. The catalogue indicates that the drawings were in four large volumes, bound in "old morocco or calf and numbered respectively XU, 1, XU, 2, XU, 3, XU, 4. Each volume was lettered in gold 'Wilton House Library Drawings.'" The drawings of couples after Leonardo were in volume XU, 3, dated November 25, 1772. They were sold in lot 466: "Leonardo da Vinci? Drawings of some twenty-six grotesque heads in the style so characteristic of the artist, on twelve sheets of paper laid down on one sheet, which measures 12 in. by 8½ in. Pen and sepia." See Pedretti and Trutty-Coohill 1993, fig. 1, p. 16, and pp. 66–71, no. 30a-l, for a discussion of each couple and its current location. On William Herbert (1580–1630), third earl of Pembroke, lord chamberlain, and brother-in-law to Lord Arundel, see Lugt 2636b. For the formation of the Pembroke collection, see Pembroke 1968.

104. In a drawing at the Accademia, Venice (fig. 113), the laughing man with copious hair and his partner (Pedretti and Trutty-Coohill 1993, no. 30c) are paired with the man with the pointed beard (Pedretti and Trutty-Coohill 1993, no. 30g), but the woman who formed a couple with that man now faces the three poets (Pedretti and

Trutty-Coohill 1993, 30h). Conversely, the Louvre sheet 2296 (cat. no. 136) reunites three couples, respecting the original assemblage, whereas the other Louvre sheet, 2297, is a set of individual heads (fig. 114).

105. Inv. nos. 827A and 827B; Trutty-Coohill 1993, p. 53 n. 16.

106. Pedretti 1973b, no. 2.

107. For the pen drawing, RL 12491; for the red chalk drawings, RL 12492, 12493, and 12494.

108. Missing caricatures: the woman on the sheet in a private collection (Pedretti and Trutty-Coohill 1993, no. 30a), the original of which is Chatsworth 824D; the laughing man in the Elmer Belt Library, Los Angeles (Pedretti and Trutty-Coohill 1993, no. 30c), the original of which is at the J. Paul Getty Museum, Los Angeles, 84. GA. 647 (cat. no. 69); and three for which the whereabouts of the originals are unknown: the man with the pointed beard in the Elmer Belt Library (Pedretti and Trutty-Coohill 1993, no. 30g); the woman with the crushed nose on the sheet in the Pierpont Morgan Library, New York (Pedretti and Trutty-Coohill 1993, no. 30j); and the man on the sheet now in the Fogg Art Museum, Cambridge, Mass. (Pedretti and Trutty-Coohill 1993, no. 30l).

109. Chatsworth 827A, 827B; the man in 827B is missing.

110. Rabelais 1669. The Spencer drawings are studied in detail in Scott-Elliot 1958, Pedretti and Trutty-Coohill 1993, and Trutty-Coohill 1993.

111. On that academy, established in Milan in 1560, with Lomazzo as a founding member, see the exhibition devoted to it in Lugano 1998. Paliaga 1995 underscores the relation between the Spencer drawings and the members of the Accademia de la Val di Blenio; Berra 1998 analyzes the Milanese milieu at the end of the cinquecento. Let me add that Aurelio Luini ("Lovino"), whom Lomazzo mentions as the owner of Leonardo's *libricciuolo,* was one of the principal members of the Accademia.

112. Spencer Grotesques, vol. 1, no. 1; vol. 2, no. 43.

113. For example, *La Cipolla;* see Bora 1998d, p. 47, fig. 14, copied in Spencer Grotesques, vol. 1, no. 34. Already identified in Scott-Elliot 1958, p. 284.

114. Scott-Elliot (1958) writes that Fairfax Murray, the owner of the volumes in the early part of the century, attributed the drawings to Hollar; Bacall (1968), following Pedretti, attributed them to Melzi; Pedretti (1990d) reaffirms that attribution. Pedretti (1990d) attributes a Louvre drawing, 2567, to the "Master of the Spencer Grotesques," but it seems to be of later date and is not similar to any of the Spencer drawings. Kwakkelstein (1993a) attributes it to Bernardino Lanino. Another Louvre drawing, RF 28781, part of the Mariette album, was also attributed to the "Master of the Spencer Grotesques"; see Barryte 1990, p. 137. I discuss it in the entry on that sheet in this volume (cat. no. 137).

115. Spencer Grotesques, vol. 2, no. 22, copy of RL 12492; vol. 2, no. 17, copy of figs. 55, 56 (Rome).

116. For example, Spencer Grotesques, vol. 1, nos. 5, 7, 10; vol. 2, no. 4; and so on.

117. For example, Spencer Grotesques, vol. 1, nos. 8, 39; vol. 2, no. 2; and so on.

118. The text was published without the plates in 1726, according to Dumesnil (1858, p. 39) and Viatte (in Bacou 1967, p. 26). Chennevières and Montaiglon (1851–60, vol. 3, p. 139 n. 1) give the date of publication for the text by itself as 1730, noting that the publication bore neither Caylus's full name ("M. le C. de C."; see title page) nor that of Mariette ("Votre très humble et très obéissant serviteur M." [Your very humble and very obedient servant M.]; see Mariette 1730, p. 22). Chennevières and Montaiglon thus had not seen the 1730 edition with the text and the plates. See, in the Bibliography, Mariette 1730, where the different editions of the work are indicated.

119. Steinitz 1974, p. 14.

120. On Caylus (1692–1765), see Rocheblave 1889; Viatte in Bacou 1967, no. 304; and Borea 2001.

121. Viatte in Bacou 1967, p. 176, under no. 304.

122. Bacou 1967, no. 300.

123. Cited in Borea 2001, p. 105.

124. Rocheblave 1889, pp. 159–60.

CATALOGUE

Chronology

Entries

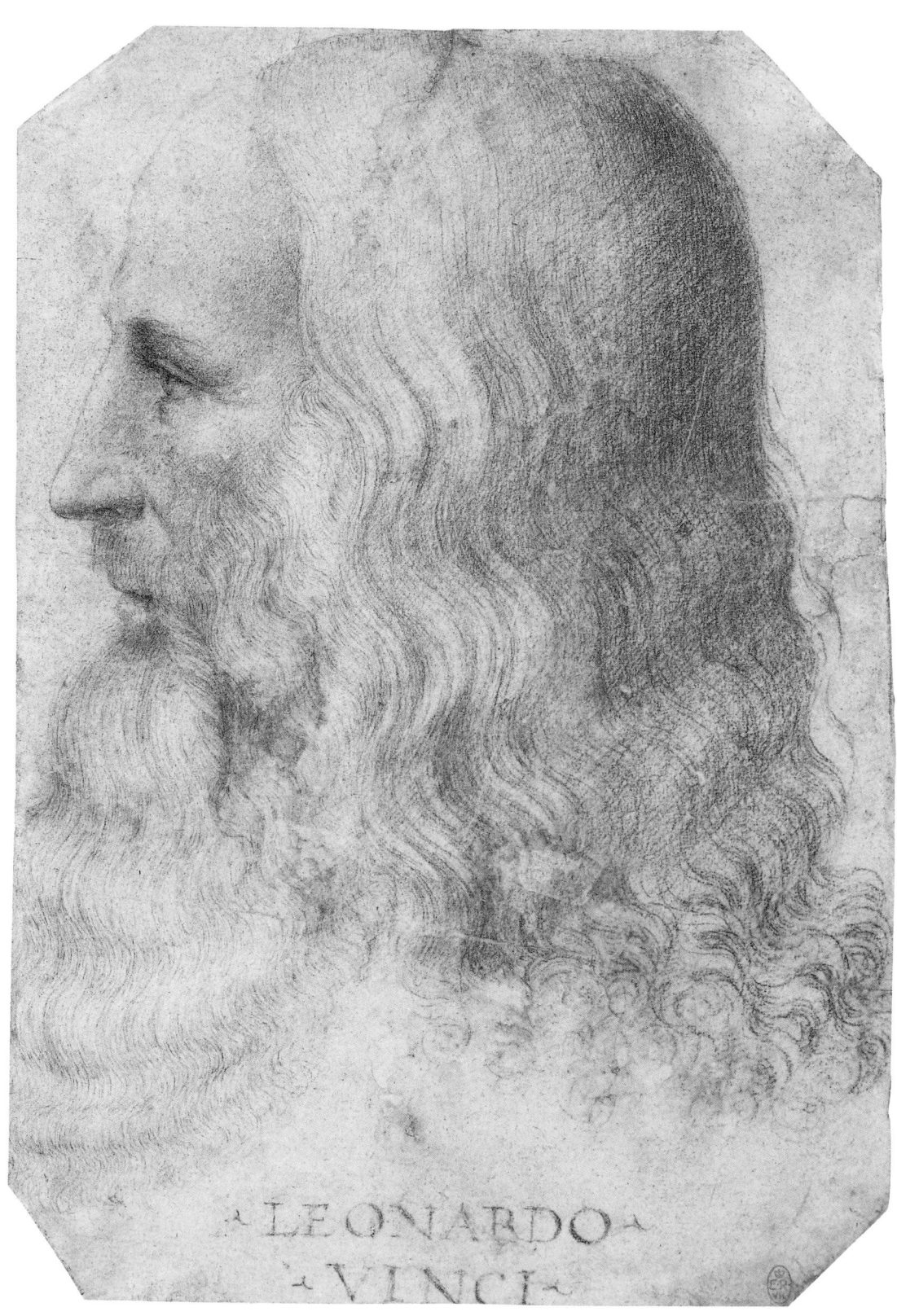

Fig. 115. Pupil of Leonardo da Vinci (Francesco Melzi?), *Portrait of Leonardo da Vinci*. Red chalk, 274 × 190 mm. The Royal Collection, H. M. Queen Elizabeth II, Windsor Castle RL 12726

DOCUMENTED CHRONOLOGY OF LEONARDO'S LIFE AND WORK

CARMEN C. BAMBACH

All dates are given in modern style.

1452

April 15, on Saturday, about 10:30 P.M. Leonardo is born out of wedlock. The event, with the time of night, is recorded by the artist's paternal grandfather, Antonio di Ser Piero da Vinci (ca. 1372–1465), in a family notebook (*zibaldone*) begun in the fourteenth century (Vecce 1998, p. 20; M 1–2; V 1). Leonardo's father is the notary (*notaio*) Ser Piero di Antonio di Ser Piero di Ser Guido da Vinci (1427– 1504), and his mother is a young farmer's daughter, Caterina, who in 1453 would marry Accattabriga di Piero del Vacca. Although a nineteenth-century tradition identifies Leonardo's birthplace as the hill of Anchiano, near Vinci (some twenty miles west of Florence), scholars now agree that Vinci was more probably his birthplace. A few months after Leonardo's birth, Ser Piero marries Albiera di Giovanni Amadori, who remains childless and who will adopt the young Leonardo. The history of the da Vinci family can be traced from 1339 to the late nineteenth century through Leonardo's half brother Domenico [1]

1457

February 28 The four-year-old Leonardo is listed as a dependent (*bocca*) in the extant tax assessment declaration (*portata del catasto*) of his paternal grandfather, Antonio di Ser Piero da Vinci, who is living in the *popolo* (neighborhood) of Santa Croce in Vinci (B 2; M 2; V 2, 2b). The young boy is called the illegitimate son of Ser Piero and Caterina.

1461

April Leonardo's future teacher, the Florentine sculptor Andrea del Verrocchio (1434/37–1488), is recorded as an independent artist.

1464

Ser Piero's wife, Albiera di Giovanni Amadori, dies in childbirth in Florence, and Leonardo's paternal grandfather, Antonio di Ser Piero, dies in Vinci.

FIRST FLORENTINE PERIOD
CA. 1464/69 – 1481/83

1464–69

At the death of his grandfather in 1464, the twelve-year-old Leonardo probably moves to his father's household in Florence. He may have then begun his apprenticeship in Verrocchio's workshop and house at via dell'Agnolo (parish of Sant'Ambrogio).

1465

Leonardo's father, Ser Piero di Antonio da Vinci, marries his second wife, Francesca di Ser Giuliano Lanfredini.

1467

January 15 Verrocchio is first recorded as being at work on the bronze sculpture *Christ and Saint Thomas*, which was commissioned by the Università della Mercanzia (Merchant's Tribunal) for its niche on Orsanmichele in Florence (fig. 59). *October 22* Verrocchio apparently completes the floor marker and tomb of Cosimo de' Medici "Il Vecchio" in the church of San Lorenzo in Florence. *October* He also probably executes his first major bronze statue, *David* (Museo Nazionale del Bargello, Florence), for the Medici family. Leonardo is fifteen years old.

1469

The tax assessment declaration (*portata del catasto*) of Leonardo's father, Ser Piero, and of his uncle Francesco, the sons of Antonio da Vinci, suggests that Ser Piero is already working as notary (*notaio*) at the *palagio del podestà* (today Palazzo del Bargello) in Florence: "Ser Piero da Vinci sta al palagio del podesta" (B 3; M 3; V 3).

1470

May The convent of Santo Martire in Florence records that an annual salary is to be paid to Ser Piero da Vinci for his service from *1469 to April 1470* as *procurator della casa* (the convent's legal agent and public administrator; B 4). Ser Piero moves with his family to a house on via delle Prestanze (via dei Gondi; fig. 61), opposite the Palazzo della Signoria, on the site where the Palazzo Gondi would be built in 1490 by Leonardo's friend and influential colleague Giuliano da Sangallo (ca. 1445–1516). Verrocchio's model of the Christ in the Orsanmichele *Christ and Saint Thomas* bronze group is finished and is cast between 1470 and 1476.

1471

May 27 By this time Verrocchio builds and mounts the famous copper orb (*palla*) on the lantern of the dome of Florence Cathedral, which had been commissioned in *September 1468*. Leonardo recalls this groundbreaking engineering project in a note about 1515, when he is in Rome (Paris Ms. G, fol. 84v).

1472

The twenty-year-old Leonardo is inscribed in the account book (*Libro rosso: Debitori, creditori e ricordi*) of the painter's confraternity, the Compagnia di San Luca, in Florence, and is thus presumably a professionally established painter in his own right. The schedule of fees he was required to pay begins in the month of June; also mentioned are the offering to be made on the feast day of Saint Luke, *October 18*, and the payment of sixteen soldi for "the subvention and subsidy" of the guild each year (B 5; M 4; V 5). In this year Verrocchio is also inscribed as "painter and sculptor" (*dipintore e intagliatore*) in the same account book of the Compagnia di San Luca. Verrocchio probably executes the tomb of Piero de' Medici and his brother Giovanni between the Old Sacristy and the Chapel of Saints Cosmas and Damian in the church of San Lorenzo (it is inscribed with this year but is documented as still incomplete in *March 1473*).

1473

August 5 Leonardo inscribes a landscape drawing portraying the Arno River with a view of Montalbano toward Valdarno and Valdinievole: "[feast] of Saint Mary of the Snow / day of August 5, 1473 (figs. 6, 7; Gabinetto Disegni e Stampe degli Uffizi, Florence, 8 P; B 7; V 6).[2]

1473–76

At this time he presumably paints the *Annunciation* (fig. 66; Galleria degli Uffizi, Florence) and the *Madonna of the Carnation* (fig. 132; Alte Pinakothek, Munich). In these years Verrocchio collaborates with the young Leonardo in painting the *Baptism of Christ* (fig. 65; Galleria degli Uffizi, Florence), an altarpiece commissioned by the monks of San Salvi for their monastery outside the city walls of Florence.

1475–78

Leonardo apparently paints the *Portrait of Ginevra de' Benci* (fig. 67; National Gallery of Art, Washington, D.C.).

1475–82

The young artist seems to study and work in the garden of Lorenzo de' Medici "Il Magnifico" at San Marco under his patronage, as recorded in the Codice Magliabechiano.[3] A reference to this Medici garden (*lorto de medicj*) appears in one of Leonardo's own notes of 1508 (P 1447, p. 345).

1476

April 9 and June 7 While still in Verrocchio's employ but as a collaborator rather than an assistant, the twenty-four-year-old Leonardo is among those charged with having committed sodomy with Jacopo Saltarelli, a seventeen-year-old apprentice in a goldsmith's workshop. The first accusation lists "Lionardo di ser piero da vinci, sta con andrea del verrochio" and the second "Leonardo pieri de vincio manet cum andrea del verrochio" (Leonardo son of Piero da Vinci works with Andrea del Verrocchio) (B 8; M 5–6; V 7, 8). *May 15* Lorenzo and Giuliano de' Medici sell Verrocchio's famous bronze *David* (Museo Nazionale del Bargello, Florence) to the Palazzo della Signoria. *May 15* Verrocchio wins the commission for the marble cenotaph of Cardinal Niccolò Forteguerri in Pistoia Cathedral (San Zeno), which he leaves unfinished at his death in 1488.

1478

January 10 The first commission of Leonardo's professional career is recorded, an altarpiece for the Chapel of San Bernardo in the Palazzo della Signoria of Florence, whose decoration had shortly before been entrusted to Piero del Pollaiuolo; Leonardo never finishes the altarpiece (B 10, with the incorrect date January 1; M 7; V 9). *January 13* The Arte della Calimala awards Verrocchio the commission to adorn the silver altar of the Florence Baptistery with the *Beheading of Saint John the Baptist*, a relief that he finishes by 1480 but which is not installed until 1483. *March 16* A payment of twenty-five florins to Leonardo is authorized for his work on the Chapel of San Bernardo altarpiece (B 11; M 8). The altarpiece was probably intended to depict the Virgin and Child with Saints. *December 28* or in the following days, Leonardo draws an eyewitness sketch of the hanged corpse of Bernardo di Bandino Baroncelli and inscribes the sheet with color notes for the criminal's clothing (Musée Bonnat, Bayonne, 659; B 14). Baroncelli had been one of the chief instigators of the Pazzi Conspiracy (*April 26, 1478*) and had murdered Giuliano de' Medici. According to the diary of the sixteenth-century Florentine author Luca Landucci, Baroncelli had been arrested in Constantinople on *December 23* and hanged from a window in the Palazzo del Capitano on the via dei Gondi in Florence five days later. In this year Leonardo seems to undertake the first drawings and notes contained in the Codex Atlanticus (Biblioteca Ambrosiana, Milan) and in the Codex Arundel (British Library, London), 1478–1518. He also presumably paints the *Benois Madonna* (fig. 133; State Hermitage Museum, Saint Petersburg), 1478–82. Possibly in reference to the latter, Leonardo cites two paintings of the Madonna in a fragmentary sheet of sketches (Gabinetto Disegni e Stampe degli Uffizi, Florence, 446 E) that is enigmatically inscribed: ". . . 1478, I began the two Virgin Marys" (R 663; P 663, p. 380; B 13; V 11).[4] By this year Verrocchio receives a commission from Bishop Donato de' Medici for the *Madonna di Piazza* altarpiece (fig. 122; Pistoia Cathedral); he executes some preparatory drawings but entrusts the painting of it to his assistant Lorenzo di Credi (finished in *November 1485*).

1479

Verrocchio's model of the Thomas in the Orsanmichele *Christ and Saint Thomas* bronze group is finished, although the final sculpture is not installed at its intended site until *June 21, 1483*.

1480

The twenty-eight-year-old Leonardo is no longer mentioned in the extant tax assessment declaration (*portata del catasto*) of his fifty-three-year-old father, Ser Piero da Vinci, who at this time lives on via Ghibellina in Florence (B 15).

1481

Leonardo undertakes the *Adoration of the Magi* altarpiece (unfinished; figs. 10, 11, 140; Galleria degli Uffizi, Florence). *July* The extant dated contractual document for the *Adoration* altarpiece, which the Augustinian Canonici Regolari commission for the main altar of their convent church of San Donato a Scopeto, states that Leonardo is to complete it within twenty-four months (or at the most thirty months; B 16; M 9; V 14). The artist had actually begun the painting in *March 1481*, and he seems to have obtained the commission through the

influence of his father. *June to September* The payment records appear to indicate that Leonardo worked on the *Adoration of the Magi* altarpiece continuously (B 17–19; M 10–13; V 15–18). *September 28* The last payment record for Leonardo's *Adoration* altarpiece (the artist was paid in wine rather than money) is also the last dated document that confirms his presence in Florence (B 19; M 13).

FIRST MILANESE PERIOD
1481/83 – 1499

1481–83

Between September 1481 and April 1483 Leonardo leaves Florence for Milan. The Codice Magliabechiano (Anonimo Gaddiano) of about 1540 states that the artist was thirty years old when he departed and that he and the musician Atalante Migliorotti were entrusted by Lorenzo de' Medici "Il Magnifico" to deliver a lyre to the duke of Milan, Ludovico Sforza "Il Moro" (B 20; Frey 1892; Vecce 1998, pp. 360–63). In his famous letter (known only from extant contemporary drafts) to Ludovico, Leonardo offers his services as military engineer, architect, sculptor, and painter and mentions that he could work on the gigantic equestrian monument which had long been planned to commemorate Francesco Sforza, Ludovico's father and the first Sforza duke of Milan (the "Sforza Horse"; C.A., fol. 1082r [formerly fol. 391r-a; B 21; R 1340; P 1340–45, p. 295; V 20). *Sometime between July 1481 and May 1483* Leonardo's master Verrocchio secures the commission from the Venetian Republic for the enormous bronze equestrian monument of Bartolomeo Colleoni (figs. 125, 162; Campo Santi Giovanni e Paolo, Venice), following a competition among three unnamed sculptors, one of whom may be Verrocchio.[5] *Sometime between 1481 and 1485,* Leonardo paints the Vatican *Saint Jerome Praying in the Wilderness* (unfinished; cat. no. 46).

1483

Leonardo undertakes the first version of the *Virgin of the Rocks* (most likely that in the Musée du Louvre, Paris; fig. 12), 1483–1503, in Milan. *April 25* Leonardo, along with the brothers Evangelista and Giovan Ambrogio de' Predis (who were notable Milanese painters), sign a long and detailed contract for a sumptuous altarpiece that was to include the *Virgin of the Rocks* as its main panel (B 23–24; M 14; V 23). The patrons are the members of the Confraternity of the

Immaculate Conception (Confraternita della Concezione), and the altarpiece is intended for their chapel in the church of San Francesco Grande in Milan. Giacomo del Maino had been contracted to carve an elaborate wood frame for the altarpiece on *April 8, 1480,* and had received his final payment on *August 7, 1482.*

1485

March 16 Leonardo witnesses a total eclipse of the sun. *April 23* Ludovico Sforza sends a letter to Maffeo da Treviglio, ambassador to the court of Matthias Corvinus, king of Hungary, in which he states that he has commissioned a Madonna from Leonardo on the king's behalf: "a figure of Our Lady as beautiful, as superb, and as devout as he knows how to make without sparing any effort" (B 22; M 15; V 24).[6] By this year Leonardo probably begins the drawings and notes of Ms. B (Institut de France, Paris), 1485–88.

1487

The thirty-five-year-old Leonardo prepares design drawings for a domed crossing tower (*tiburio*) for Milan Cathedral and hires the carpenter's assistant Bernardino de' Madis to build a wood model of the proposed *tiburio*. Payments to Leonardo for the model are recorded on *July 30, August 8, August 18, August 27, September 28, and September 30* (B 25–31; V 25–31). In this project he competes against the architects Donato Bramante, Francesco di Giorgio, Giovanni Battagio, Luca Fancelli, Giovanni Antonio Amadeo, and Giacomo Dolcebuono. He produces the drawings and notes in the Codex Trivulzianus (Castello Sforzesco, Milan), as well as the second part of the Codex Forster I (Victoria and Albert Museum, London), 1487–90.

1488

January Leonardo collects additional payment for the project of the *tiburio* of Milan Cathedral (B 32–33; V 33). *End of June* His master, the sculptor Verrocchio, dies in Venice. Also in this year, Leonardo is known to be working on the "Sforza Horse." His friend the architect and painter Donato Bramante (1443/44?–1514) undertakes his most ambitious project in Lombardy, the rebuilding of Pavia Cathedral (which he continues until 1497, when Giovanni Antonio Amadeo and Giovanni Giacomo Dolcebuono take over). Leonardo and Bramante probably become close collaborators on Bramante's arrival in Milan in the late 1470s. Leonardo probably begins the *Lady with the Ermine* (*Portrait of Cecilia Gallerani*; Muzeum Czartoryskich, Kraków), 1488–90.

1489

April 2 Leonardo begins a sequence of skull studies (cat. no. 58) and other anatomical drawings including a sheet that he dates and inscribes (*a dj 2 daprile 1489*), adding also "book entitled 'On the Human Figure'" (Windsor, RL 19059r; R 1370; B 35; V 37). *July 22* Piero Alamanni, the Florentine ambassador to the Sforza court in Milan, writes to Lorenzo de' Medici in Florence stating that Ludovico Sforza intends to commemorate his father "with an enormous horse in bronze, on which rides Duke Francesco in armor." The letter states that Ludovico has already entrusted the model of the "Sforza Horse" to Leonardo and that he wishes for "a master or two capable of doing such work" ("maestro o dua apti a tale opera") from Florence (B 36; M 16; V 44). Ludovico appears to doubt that Leonardo himself would be able to cast the "Sforza Horse" in bronze.

1490

January 13 Leonardo produces the stage set for the *Feast of Paradise* (*La festa del paradiso*) by Bernardo Bellincioni, performed in the Castello Sforzesco, Milan, to celebrate the wedding of Gian Galeazzo Sforza and Isabella of Aragon, as recounted in his friend Bellincioni's *Sonetti, canzoni, capitoli,* published in Milan in 1493 (B 40–41; V 49). *April 23* Leonardo begins Ms. C (Institut de France, Paris), 1490–91, and resumes work on the "Sforza Horse," as he states in a note (Ms. C, fol. 15v; R 720; B 44; V 53).[7] *May 10, 17* He continues to collect payments for the model of the Milan Cathedral *tiburio* (B 46–47; V 55–57). *June 8* The Sienese artist, architect, and engineer Francesco di Giorgio (1439–1501) is expected to arrive in Milan, invited by Ludovico Sforza, to advise Amadeo on building the lantern for the *tiburio* of Milan Cathedral (B 48). *June 21* Leonardo accompanies Francesco di Giorgio to Pavia in connection with the project to rebuild the cathedral; they are both paid for their expertise (B 50). *June 27* Leonardo loses the design competition for the *tiburio,* which is awarded to Giovanni Antonio Amadeo (ca. 1447–1522) and Giovanni Giacomo Dolcebuono (doc. 1465–1504), the local Lombard architect-sculptors who worked in professional partnership; the *tiburio* of Milan Cathedral is completed in 1500. It is clear that Leonardo and the other foreign architects in this competition could not circumvent the guild system that controlled Milan's building trades. *July 22* Salaì (Gian Giacomo Caprotti di Oreno), who is ten years old, arrives in Leonardo's workshop as an apprentice and quickly earns a reputation as a glutton and thief (V 53). *September 7* Salaì steals a silverpoint from one of Leonardo's assistants named Marco, who is probably to be identified as the painter Marco d'Oggiono (R 1458; B 52; V 53). In this year Leonardo may have begun writing the *Paragone* (Comparison of the arts).

1491

January 26 Leonardo is "in the house of Galeazzo da Sanseverino" to prepare a festival and tournament (*la festa della sua giostra*) honoring the wedding of Ludovico Sforza and Beatrice d'Este (R 1458; B 52; V 53). Leonardo's note on a sheet relating to the "Sforza Horse" indicates his ideas for the casting of the monument (Ma. II, fol. 157v; V 64). *April 2* Salaì steals a silverpoint from yet another of Leonardo's workshop assistants named Giovan Antonio, who is most likely to be identified as the painter Giovanni Antonio Boltraffio (R 1458; B 52; V 53).

1491–95

In an undated letter that was probably written about this time, Leonardo and Giovan Ambrogio de' Predis—Evangelista de' Predis had died in 1491—complain to Ludovico Sforza "Il Moro" (B 120; M 19). The artists state that the Confraternity of the Immaculate Conception (Confraternita della Concezione) at San Francesco Grande in Milan had grossly underpaid them for the panel *Virgin of the Rocks* and the two flanking paintings of angels and that none of the members understood the art of painting "because a blind man cannot judge color."[8] The artists ask that the paintings be reappraised.

1492

March 29 Bramante begins the project for the new eastern end (*tribuna*) of Santa Maria delle Grazie, commissioned by Ludovico Sforza. In this same year, and with the collaboration of the forty-year-old Leonardo, Bramante lays out the new square in Vigevano (southwest of Milan), work that continues until 1496. *April 8* Lorenzo de' Medici "Il Magnifico" dies in Florence. *August 11* Rodrigo Borgia becomes Pope Alexander VI and reigns until *August 18, 1503*. *October* This is the probable date when Giuliano da Sangallo discusses problems of bronze casting with Leonardo in Milan, as is mentioned in Giorgio Vasari's life of Leonardo (Vasari 1906, vol. 4; B 55). In this year Leonardo travels to the Lake Como region in Lombardy, visiting Valtellina, Valsassina, Bellagio, and Ivrea (C.A., fol. 573b-r [formerly fol. 214r-e]; R 1030), possibly motivated by the civil engineering projects in the Valtellina that occupied his rival, Giovanni Antonio Amadeo, from the late 1480s to the early 1490s. By this year Leonardo probably

begins his drawings and notes in the Ms. A (Institut de France, Paris).

1493

Leonardo dates his notes in the Codex Madrid I and II (Biblioteca Nacional, Madrid), "*January 1*" (Ma. I, fol. 1v, a volume containing material from 1493–95) and "*December 21*" (Ma. II, fol. 151v, a volume that he continues in 1503–4). The forty-one-year-old artist begins Ms. H (Institut de France, Paris), 1493–94 (V 80), as well as the Codex Forster III (Victoria and Albert Museum, London), 1493–97 (V 77). *July 16* A woman named Caterina joins Leonardo's household (B 56). *November* An equestrian effigy of Francesco Sforza (which may have been Leonardo's actual model of the "Sforza Horse" or more likely a version based on his design) is displayed under a triumphal arch inside Milan Cathedral during the festivities for the marriage of Ludovico's niece Bianca Maria Sforza to the Hapsburg emperor Maximilian I (as recorded in a letter of *December 29* from Beatrice d'Este to her sister Isabella d'Este in Mantua; V 73). A poem written by Baldassare Taccone to celebrate the event states that Leonardo is "still working on the clay model" in his studio at the Corte Vecchia (V 73).[9] *December 20* Leonardo decides to cast the "Sforza Horse" sideways without the tail (Ma. II, fol. 151v; V 81), implying that the clay model of the "Sforza Horse" is finished. Bernardo Bellincioni's *Rime. . .*, published in Florence in 1493 praises Leonardo's *Portrait of Cecilia Gallerani* (M, p. 201 n. 37; V 72a-e).

1494

January The artist begins his short stay in Vigevano, dating a note about the stairs in the nearby villa La Sforzesca *February 2*, and another about the vineyard at Vigevano *March 20* (B 62; V 86). *November 17* Ludovico Sforza sends the bronze that had been set aside for the casting of the "Sforza Horse" to his father-in-law, Ercole d'Este, duke of Ferrara, who was to make a cannon from it. In this year Ludovico becomes duke of Milan at the death of his young nephew Gian Galeazzo Sforza (1476–1494), whom he may have poisoned, and his political ally Charles VIII, king of France (1470–1498), begins his invasion of Italy.[10] *November 9* The Florentine magistrates rebel against Piero de' Medici after he yields Tuscan territory to the invading French, and he and his family are forced to flee Florence for safety. *December 9* The Medici are officially exiled from Florence, and a republic is established. *December 15* The war between Florence and Pisa resumes, lasting until *May 25, 1509*.

At a date that is not precisely known, Ludovico Sforza or possibly the Dominican monks of Santa Maria delle Grazie commission Leonardo to paint the *Last Supper,* a mural on the north wall of the Refectory of Santa Maria delle Grazie in Milan, as well as three surmounting lunettes with foliage and the Sforza ducal arms (figs. 168, 169).

1495

November 14 A record suggests that Leonardo may be at work on the decoration of rooms in the Castello Sforzesco in Milan (B 67; M 21; V 101). He then briefly goes to Florence, where he acts as a consultant in the building of the Sala del Gran Consiglio (1495–97) on the main floor of the Palazzo della Signoria. Here, he presumably works with the architect of the Sala, Simone Pollaiuolo "Il Cronaca" (1457–1508). Giovanni da Montorfano signs and dates the *Crucifixion* fresco on the south wall (opposite Leonardo's *Last Supper*) of the Refectory of Santa Maria delle Grazie in Milan. In this fresco the portraits of Ludovico Sforza and Beatrice d'Este with their two small sons—painted in oils rather than in *buon fresco*—are inserted in the foreground, presumably by Leonardo. In this year Leonardo apparently begins Codex Forster II (Victoria and Albert Museum, London), 1495–97, as well as Ms. M (Institut de France, Paris), 1495–99.

1496

Leonardo drafts a detailed letter about the manufacture of bronze doors to the administrators (*fabbricieri*) of Piacenza Cathedral (R 1346; B 92; V 121). Letters of *June 8, 13* note that the painter (Leonardo?) decorating rooms in the Castello Sforzesco has abandoned the project in a huff, and another artist is suggested for the job, namely Pietro Perugino (B 70–71; M 22 b; V 108, 109). The Franciscan monk, theorist, mathematician, and writer Fra Luca Pacioli (ca. 1445–ca. 1514) arrives in Milan, where he stays until 1499 and collaborates with Leonardo on studies of proportion, geometry, and mathematics.

1497

June 29 Ludovico Sforza sends a letter with a memorandum to his secretary, Marchesino Stanga [Stange], expressing his hope that Leonardo will soon finish the *Last Supper* so that he may begin work on another wall in the Refectory of Santa Maria delle Grazie (B 76; M 24; V 116). A payment of 37 lire and 16.5 soldi "for work in the refectory where Leonardo is painting the Apostles, with one window" is recorded without the month (B 77; M 25; V 117). Also in this year, Matteo Bandello writes his famous novella *La prigionia di Filippo Lippi . . .* (*The Imprisonment of Filippo Lippi;* published in Florence, 1554), which describes Leonardo on the scaffolding in the Refectory of Santa Maria delle Grazie, at work on the *Last Supper,* and on the monumental clay model of the "Sforza Horse" at the Corte Vecchia, the foundry to which it had been transferred (B 79). Leonardo designs the suburban villa of Mariolo de' Guiscardi near the Porta Vercellina in Milan. *September 28* Leonardo dates the cover of Codex Madrid I (Biblioteca Nacional, Madrid) and begins Ms. I and Ms. L (Institut de France, Paris), 1497–1502.

1498

February 9 Fra Luca Pacioli dedicates the treatise *De divina proportione* to Ludovico "Il Moro" (published in Venice, 1509; B 82; V 124). It greatly praises Leonardo, suggesting that the *Last Supper* is finished and that his model of the "Sforza Horse" measures 12 braccia ("the said height from the nape to the flat ground") and is of a bronze mass of 200,000 libbre.[11] The 12-braccia height of the lost "Sforza Horse" from nape to ground is equivalent to 23 feet 11 inches, and therefore it might have stood as tall as 31 feet 6 inches from head to ground (without the rider). The 200,000 libbre of bronze amounts to about 150,000 pounds. *March 17* Leonardo travels to Genoa and makes notes on the ruined quay in the harbor (C.A., fol. 10r [formerly fol. 2r-a]; R 1370c). *March 22* A letter to Ludovico Sforza states that the work in the Refectory of Santa Maria delle Grazie is progressing with no time wasted ("non si perde tempo alcuno"; B 84; M 26; V 125). *April 20, 21, and 23* Leonardo is recorded at work on the murals in the Saletta Negra and the Sala delle Asse in the northwest tower of the Castello Sforzesco of Milan, which he may have finished later in the year (B 85–87; M 27–29; V 126–28). *April 26, 29* Isabella d'Este, the marchioness of Mantua and famous collector of works of art, asks Cecilia Bergamini Gallerani, who was Ludovico Sforza's mistress in her youth and a literary figure of some accomplishment, for the portrait that Leonardo painted of her that is in her possession, but she is gracefully turned down (B 88–89; V 129–31). Also in this year Leonardo continues to compile drawings and notes in Ms. L and Ms. M (Institut de France, Paris). *May 23* Girolamo Savonarola, the Dominican monk who had helped forge a new republican government in Florence, is executed in Florence. *December 6* Charles VIII dies, and Louis XII (1462–1515) is crowned king of France. Louis is no longer an ally of Ludovico Sforza in Milan. Also in this year the political theorist and statesman Niccolò Machiavelli (1469–1527), who was a patron of Leonardo, becomes chancellor of the Florentine Republic.

1499

April 26 It is officially recorded that Ludovico Sforza has given to Leonardo the present of a vineyard near Porta Vercellina, between the monasteries of San Vittore and Santa Maria delle Grazie in Milan, although the artist may have actually received the gift a year or two earlier (B 95; M 32a, 32b; V 136–36b). Leonardo explores designs to decorate a bathroom for Isabella d'Este and prepares notes on a bridge by Bramante. *August 1* He begins his notes on "moto e peso" (motion and weight) (C.A., fol. 289r [formerly fol. 104r-b]; R 1371; B 96; V 138). *August* Ludovico "Il Moro" is forced out of Milan. *September 9 and 10* The French troops of Louis XII storm the city, led by the mercenary general Gian Giacomo Trivulzio, who was to be Leonardo's future patron.[12] As Trivulzio and the French soldiers enter Milan through the Porta Vercellina, they probably see Leonardo's monumental clay model of the "Sforza Horse" in a corner of his vineyard. In his *Ricordi* (Bologna, 1546), Sabba da Castiglione, the prelate who as a boy may have met Leonardo in Milan, condemns the destruction of the "Sforza Horse," on which Leonardo had labored "for sixteen continuous years.... But the ignorance and negligence of some who by failing to acknowledge virtue show that they do not value it, allowed it to be shamefully ruined, for I remember—and I cannot speak of it without grief and indignation—so noble and masterly a work made a target for the Gascon bowmen (*balestrieri Guasconi*)." *October* Louis XII enters Milan and, according to Giorgio Vasari's life of Leonardo, grieves that Leonardo's *Last Supper* cannot be taken to France (B 260). *December 14* Milan falls to the French, and Leonardo is forced to leave the city. He sends his money to his bank account at the hospital of Santa Maria Nuova in Florence in anticipation of his return to that city (B 98, 101; V 143). Fra Luca Pacioli records in the *De divina proportione* that he and Leonardo left Milan together for Florence.

Second Florentine Period
1500 – 1506/8

1500

Ludovico Sforza "Il Moro" returns briefly to Milan in *February*, but following his final defeat and capture in *April* of this year, he is sent to prison in France, where he dies in 1508.

Early in the year Leonardo appears to have accompanied Count Louis de Ligny (a courtier to Charles VIII and later to Louis XII) on a mysterious trip to Rome, and possibly Naples, as is suggested by a manuscript list of things and people—the so-called Ligny memorandum—that Leonardo writes in code (R 1379; P 1379, p. 326). *February* On his way to Florence Leonardo stops in Mantua as the guest of the Gonzaga family. *March 13* The lute player Lorenzo Gusnasco da Pavia sends a letter to Isabella d'Este stating that while in Venice Leonardo showed him a portrait of her (B 103; V 144). This portrait may or may not be the same as the famous monumental portrait cartoon of Isabella d'Este (fig. 16; Musée du Louvre, Paris). In Venice Leonardo possibly meets Giorgione (ca. 1478–ca. 1510) while working for the Venetian Republic on a proposal for a defense system against the threat of a Turkish invasion in the Friuli region. With Giovanni Antonio Boltraffio, Leonardo is possibly the guest of the poet Gerolamo Casio in Bologna; Boltraffio, as well as Leonardo's *Virgin and Child with Saint Anne,* is mentioned in the poet's books published in 1525 (V 335, 336). *April 24* Leonardo arrives in Florence and seems to stay in the church complex of Santissima Annunziata (hosted by the Servite brothers), where he draws the famous cartoon *Virgin and Child with Saint Anne* (lost) so praised by Giorgio Vasari. He offers advice on the damages to the foundation of the church of San Salvatore dell'Osservanza (San Francesco al Monte) above Florence and on the construction of a campanile for the church of San Miniato, based on a drawing by Baccio d'Agnolo (B 99; V 142). *August 11* Leonardo sends Francesco Gonzaga a proposed design for the villa of Angelo del Tovaglia near Florence (V 146).

1501

March 20 Leonardo is probably briefly in Rome (V 147). *March 29* From Mantua, Isabella d'Este inquires of Fra Pietro da Novellara (head of the Carmelites order in Florence), "if Leonardo the Florentine painter is to be found there in Florence . . . inform yourself what is his life like, that is, if he has begun any work." She asks whether Leonardo can sketch another portrait of her, because her husband has given away the one the artist made earlier (B 106, as March 27; M 35; V 149). *April 3* Fra Pietro da Novellara replies to Isabella d'Este that Leonardo is at work on a lifesize cartoon (*figure grande al naturale*) for a *Virgin and Child with Saint Anne and a Lamb* (B 107; M 36; V 150). *April 14* Fra Pietro sends another letter to Isabella, noting that Leonardo is painting a "little picture" (*quadrettino*) of the *Madonna of the Yarn Winder* (*Madonna dei fusi*), a lost painting known only from copies (B 108, as

April 4; M 37; V 151). The patron is Florimond Robertet (1459–1527), who had become secretary of Louis XII in 1499. *Spring* Piero Soderini, who would commission Leonardo's *Battle of Anghiari*, comes to power as *gonfaloniere di giustizia* (chief government official) of the Florentine Republic. *August 16* Michelangelo is awarded the commission for the immense marble *David*, which Soderini seems to have considered giving to Leonardo (Vasari 1906, vol. 4; B 114). *September 19 and 24* Letters by Giovanni Valla, ambassador to Ercole I d'Este, duke of Ferrara, ask the French authorities in Milan if the duke may use the molds of the "Sforza Horse," which were "exposed to daily decay as the result of neglect," to cast his own equestrian monument in Ferrara (B 111–12; V 155–56). Although Valla responds that the king of France is to be informed of the duke's request, nothing seems to have come of this project.

1502

May 12 As stated in a letter, the fifty-year-old Leonardo evaluates drawings of antique vases from Lorenzo de' Medici's collection being offered to Isabella d'Este (B 116; V 159). *Between May and August 18* Cesare Borgia "Il Valentino" (1475–1507), captain general of the papal armies, names Leonardo "family architect and general engineer" in the Marches and Romagna (B 117; V 160).[13] *July to September* Leonardo travels to Urbino, Cesena, Porto Cesenatico, Pesaro, and Rimini in Cesare's service (B 116; V 163–68). He studies military architecture, field defense, and cartography. He drafts the presentation map of Imola, as well as maps of Tuscany, Umbria, Val di Chiana, Castiglion Fiorentino, and he undertakes hydraulic studies in Tuscany, Umbria, and the Marches (Ms. L, Institut de France, Paris). *September* or thereabouts, Piero Soderini becomes *gonfaloniere* for life of the Florentine Republic.

1503

February Leonardo possibly ends his service for Cesare Borgia and returns to Florence. He writes to the sultan Baiazeth offering his services, promising a project for a bridge on the Bosporus (V 177). *March 9 and June 23* The notary for the Confraternity of the Immaculate Conception (Confraternita della Concezione) makes a summary of events regarding the *Virgin of the Rocks* commission, noting the appeal made by Giovan Ambrogio de' Predis and Leonardo's problematic absence from Milan (B 121–22; M 43; V 175). De' Predis's plea to Louis XII of France seems to indicate that the *Virgin of the Rocks* is unfinished. *June and July* During the siege of Pisa, Leonardo stays in that city's Camposanto and makes topographical sketches and designs for military machines and

fortifications for the Signoria of Florence. *July 24* A letter by Francesco Guiducci states that Leonardo and others have come to show him and the governor a drawing regarding the diversion and canalization of the Arno (B 126; V 180). *July 26* Leonardo is officially being paid by the Signoria of Florence to straighten (*livellare*) the Arno at Pisa (B 127; V 181),[14] and he himself notes the projects (Ma. II, fol. 1v). Leonardo appears reinscribed in the account book (*Libro rosso: Debitori, creditori e ricordi*) of the painter's confraternity (Compagnia di San Luca) in Florence starting on the feast day of Saint Luke, *October 18* (partly and imprecisely in B 128; not in M; V 182). *October 24* Leonardo receives keys to the Sala del Papa and adjacent rooms in the great cloister of Santa Maria Novella, Florence, which will serve as his workshop and living quarters during his preparation of his cartoon for the *Battle of Anghiari* (B 130; M 44; V 183). *November 1* Julius II becomes pope and reigns until *February 21, 1513*. *November 11* In a letter to Niccolò Machiavelli, the captain Luca Ugolino praises a portrait of "Mona Marietta": "Leonardo da Vinci would not have portrayed her better" (M 45; V 184). Leonardo makes an inventory of the books in the convent of Santa Maria Novella. *December 16* The roofing in his newly allocated working space in the Sala del Papa is being repaired (F 153; B 132). Leonardo probably produces the lost original of the *Neptune* presentation drawing for Fabio Segni (see cat. no. 93), 1503–4, and the lost painting *Salvator Mundi*, 1503–4, known from copies. He begins planning the lost *Leda and the Swan* composition (cat. nos. 88, 98–100), as well as the *Mona Lisa* (*La Gioconda*; Musée du Louvre, Paris), pictures that he probably continues to refine until 1516–17. Also in this year Leonardo undertakes the notes and drawings in Ms. K (Institut de France, Paris), 1503–8.

1504

January 8 Further repairs are done to Leonardo's working space in the Sala del Papa (F 158; B 134; M 46; V 187). *January 25* Along with twenty-nine other artists and artisans, Leonardo participates in a meeting to discuss the final placement of Michelangelo's giant marble *David*. After Giuliano da Sangallo's impassioned plea for the Loggia dei Lanzi as a site, Leonardo concurs, "I confirm that it be in the loggia" (B 135; M 47; V 186).[15] In the end, this opinion is disregarded, and the *David* is placed at the entrance of the Palazzo della Signoria. *February to October* Leonardo is paid a steady salary for his work on the *Battle of Anghiari* cartoon. *February 28* Payments are recorded for the ingenious movable scaffolding that Leonardo invents to work on the *Anghiari* cartoon, as well as for a very large quantity of cartoon paper (F 159–73; B 137; M 48; V 188). *May 4* The *signori* of the Florentine Republic, led by the chancellor Niccolò Machiavelli, sign a contractual document that summarizes the state of Leonardo's work on the *Battle of Anghiari* cartoon (F 175; B 140; M 49; V 189). It reiterates his monthly salary of fifteen fiorini for the project and also stipulates the order of execution in designing and painting the mural in the Sala del Gran Consiglio of the Palazzo della Signoria; his deadline for finishing the cartoon is given as *February 1505. May 14 and 27 and October 31* Letters record Isabella d'Este's intention to commission from Leonardo a devotional painting of "a youthful Christ of about twelve years old" (B 141–43, B 152; M 50–52, 55).[16] *June 30* Further payments to various artisans are recorded for work on the *Battle of Anghiari* cartoon, including reimbursement to the baker who furnished eighty-eight libbre (pounds) of sifted white flour to make gluing paste for the cartoon (F 176–80; B 145; M 53; V 194). *July 9, in the evening,* Leonardo's father, Ser Piero di Antonio da Vinci, who had until then been a notary at the Palazzo del Podestà (now Palazzo del Bargello), dies in Florence. The artist records this fact twice in his notes, but giving the wrong weekday, Wednesday rather than Tuesday (Ar., fol. 272r; C.A., fol. 196v [formerly fol. 71v-b]; R 1372, 1373; B 148; V 185, 197). Ser Piero was father to ten sons and two daughters, and the settlement of his estate caused acrimonious disputes for almost six years, between Leonardo and his seven living, legitimate half brothers (B 172, 190, 193). *August 30* The *funaiuoli* are paid for iron wheels and parts for Leonardo's scaffolding for the *Battle of Anghiari* cartoon (F 181; B 146, 151; M 54). *August* Leonardo's uncle Francesco bequeaths property to him. *August to September* Michelangelo receives the commission to paint the mural *Battle of Cascina* as a pendant to Leonardo's *Battle of Anghiari* in the Sala del Gran Consiglio of the Palazzo della Signoria. *October 31 to December 31* Payments are recorded for the purchase of paper and for the manual labor of assembling Michelangelo's cartoon for the *Battle of Cascina*, which the artist draws in a room at the Ospedale dei Tintori in Sant'Onofrio in Florence (F 188–205). *By November 1* Leonardo goes to Piombino to work on the city walls, citadel, main gate, and other military engineering projects at the request of Jacopo IV Appiani, lord of Piombino, an ally of Florence during the Pisan war (Ma. II, fol. 24v; V 202–3). *November 30* Leonardo records that he has solved the problem of squaring the circle (V 204). He adds notes and other marginalia on a codex by his friend Francesco di Giorgio (Biblioteca Laurenziana, Florence). *December 31* Payment records suggest that Leonardo incurs further expenses for supplies (F 198–205).

1505

February 28 and March 14 Expenses for Leonardo's scaffolding for the *Battle of Anghiari* in the Palazzo della Signoria are reimbursed (F 206–10; B 159; M 59–60; V 211–12). *March 14* or thereabouts, to judge from a related note, Leonardo undertakes the Codice del Volo degli Uccelli (Biblioteca Reale, Turin), composed of notes and sketches on the flight of birds (CUV, fol. 18v; R 1374 A; V 216). *April 14* The seventeen-year-old Lorenzo (called "Il Fangoia") arrives in the artist's household (B 164). *April 30* Additional expenses for Leonardo's *Battle of Anghiari* are recorded: various scaffolding materials, construction laborers, another large amount of cartoon paper, and assistants to paint the mural (which suggest a pyramid of delegated labor). The painting assistants are Raffaello d'Antonio di Biagio (called a *dipintore*), Ferrando Spagnolo (also called a *dipintore*), and Thomaso di Giovanni, who "grinds colors" for Ferrando (F 211–27; B 165; M 61; V 218).[17] This *April 30* account also mentions a reimbursement to Leonardo for the customs tax he paid when a bundle of clothes he had left behind in Rome was sent to Florence. Finally ready to paint, on *June 6* Leonardo writes, "(On Friday in June at the 13th hour) On the 6th day of June, 1505, Friday, at the stroke of the 13th hour I began to paint in the palace. At that moment when [I] applied the brush the weather became bad, and the bell tolled calling the men to assemble. The cartoon ripped. The water spilled and the vessel containing it broke. And suddenly the weather became bad, and it rained so much that the waters were great. And the weather was dark as night" (Ma. II, fol. 2r; P 669, p. 382; V 219).[18] *July 12* Leonardo records that he begins the first part of the Codex Forster I (Victoria and Albert Museum, London; Fo.I, fol. 3v; R 1374; V 220). *August 31* Further payments are recorded directly to Leonardo's assistant Ferrando Spagnolo and Ferrando's assistant the "color grinder" Tomaso di Giovanni (F 230–38; B 165; M 62). *August 31 and October 31* Expenses for painting supplies for the *Anghiari* mural and the cloth covers for the scaffolding are reimbursed (F 235–38; B 165–66; M 62–63; V 222).

SECOND MILANESE PERIOD
1506/8 – 1513

1506

For much of the year the fifty-three-year-old Leonardo is in Florence. *February 13* He and the heir of Evangelista de' Predis (who died in 1491) designate Giovan Ambrogio de' Predis to represent them in the ongoing dispute with the Confraternity of the Immaculate Conception (*scolari della Concezione*) over the *Virgin of the Rocks* altarpiece (B 168; not in M). *April 4* Arbitrators are appointed to resolve the dispute over the price of the *Virgin of the Rocks* altarpiece, and Leonardo is mentioned as being absent from Milan (B 169; M 64, 65; V 224–25). *April 27* Giovan Ambrogio de' Predis, on behalf of Leonardo who is in Florence, comes to an agreement with the Confraternity of the Immaculate Conception (*scole conceptionis beate Virginis Marie*) regarding the *Virgin of the Rocks* altarpiece, which the tense of the verb in the document[19] seems to indicate is still unfinished. The artists are to finish the incomplete work in two years, by their own hand, for a fee of two hundred lire imperiali (B 170; M 66; V 226). *May 3 and 12* Letters between Isabella d'Este and Alessandro Amadori (brother of the first wife of Ser Piero da Vinci) mention "those figures, which we have beseeched from Leonardo" (B 173–74; M 67–68; V 227–28).[20] *May 30* A contract between Leonardo and the Signoria of Florence requires that before Leonardo can depart for Milan, he is to guarantee his return to Florence within three months to finish the *Battle of Anghiari* or else incur a stiff penalty (B 176; M 69; V 229). *August 18* Charles II d'Amboise (1473–1511), the governor of Milan who had become a marshal of France in 1504, writes to the Signoria in Florence requesting Leonardo's services in Milan (B 177; M 70; V 233). *August 19 and 28* Letters between the French court in Milan and the Signoria of Florence vividly record the negotiations to allow Leonardo to go to Milan without penalty (B 178–79; M 71–72; V 234–35). *Early September* Leonardo sets out for Milan with his apprentice Salaì and Lorenzo "Il Fanfoia." Their host is Charles d'Amboise, who commissions Leonardo to design a suburban villa and garden. He also undertakes studies of the Adda River and of the environs of Charles's villa near San Babila. *October 9* In a well-known letter Piero Soderini, the frustrated *gonfaloniere* of the Florentine Republic, accuses Leonardo of impropriety, "Because he has taken a good portion of the money and has made a small beginning of a large work he was supposed to do" (B 180; M 73; V 236).[21] *December 16* In a letter to the Signoria of Florence, Charles d'Amboise expresses his satisfaction with and admiration for Leonardo's work (B 181; V 237). In this year Leonardo apparently begins the third part of Ms. K (Institut de France, Paris), 1506–8.

1507

Leonardo is still in Milan. *January 12, 14, and 22* In an exchange of letters among Francesco Pandolfini, the Signoria of Florence, and the French court at Blois it is agreed that Leonardo should stay in Milan to serve the French (B 183–86;

M 75–79; V 240–43). *April 27* A decree finally restores to Leonardo his vineyard at San Vittore near the Porta Vercellina, which had been expropriated during the fall of Milan in December 1499 (B 187; V 244). *July 23* Leonardo designates representatives in an unidentified legal case (possibly the dispute over the *Virgin of the Rocks*) and seems to be living within the parish of San Babila in Milan (S doc IV; not in B or M). *July 26* Florimond Robertet intervenes in Leonardo's dispute with the Signoria of Florence over the unfinished *Battle of Anghiari* project, and he requests the presence in Milan of "our dear and well-loved Leonardo da Vinci painter and engineer of our trust" (B 189; M 78; V 247).[22] *August 3* A member of the Dominican order is appointed arbitrator in a dispute between Leonardo and Giovan Ambrogio de' Predis (S doc V; M 80; V 248). Leonardo executes an aerial view and schematic plan of Milan. He also produces studies for *Orfeo*, a play by Angelo Poliziano, of a stage set for a "mountain which opens" (Ar., fols. 139–40, 231). *August 15* Charles d'Amboise demands that the Signoria of Florence ensure that Leonardo can return to Milan again "because he is obliged to make a [painted] panel" for Louis XII (B 191; M 81).[23] *August 20* Leonardo finds someone to represent him in Milan (*procura spetialis domini Leonardi de venzijs*; S doc VI; M 82; V 250). *August 26* The tedious arbitration decisions regarding the *Virgin of the Rocks* commission are summarized in a long report (B 192; M 83). *September 18* Leonardo writes a letter from Florence to Cardinal Ippolito d'Este in Ferrara, stating that "it is a few days since I arrived from Milan, to find that one of my older brothers does not want to honor the will made three years ago at the death of our father," and requests a letter of recommendation from the cardinal to serve in the legal case (B 193; M 84; V 252).[24] In 1507–8 Leonardo probably begins the *Virgin and Child with Saint Anne* cartoon (figs. 17, 75, 76; National Gallery, London), and in Milan, he meets Francesco Melzi (1491/93–ca. 1570), the nobleman from Vaprio d'Adda who was to be his devoted pupil, companion, and major heir to his artistic production. Leonardo's uncle Francesco dies and leaves Leonardo as sole heir.

1508

The fifty-six-year-old Leonardo returns to Florence. *In the winter* Leonardo dissects a male corpse, supposedly one hundred years old (called the "centenarian" in the artist's notes), at the hospital of Santa Maria Nuova in Florence (see cat. no. 113). *March 22* Leonardo is staying at the house of Piero di Braccio Martelli, where he begins the Codex Arundel, which he describes as "a collection [of notes] without order, composed of many pages which I have copied, hoping then to put them in their appropriate place, according to the topics that they treat" (Ar. fol. 1r; B 194; V 254).[25] *April 23* By this date Leonardo seems to have returned to Milan to serve Louis XII of France. In Milan he continues to live in the parish church of San Babila (S VII–VIII). *May 27* Leonardo's most important patron, Ludovico Sforza, dies in France after being imprisoned for ten years in the château of Loches in Touraine. *July 1508 to April 1509* Leonardo records the fees that he is being paid by the French king (C.A., fol. 522r [formerly fol. 192r-a]; R 1529). *August 18* Giovan Ambrogio de' Predis and Leonardo receive permission to remove the *Virgin of the Rocks* altarpiece, newly installed in San Francesco Grande in Milan, so that Giovan Ambrogio can copy it (*retrahere*), under Leonardo's supervision, presumably to sell one version; it is also stipulated that the proceeds of this sale shall be divided "equally in good faith and without fraud" (S doc VII; M 85; V 258).[26] This copy may be identified with the second extant version of the *Virgin of the Rocks* (National Gallery, London), 1506–8. *September 12* Leonardo notes that he began Ms. F (Institut de France, Paris) in Milan, 1508–13 (R 1375; B 195; V 259). *October 12* He authorizes a release of a quittance regarding the *Virgin of the Rocks* (S VIII; M 86); another unrelated note in his hand records that he is in Milan (B 198). *October 23* Giovan Ambrogio de' Predis receives a final payment of one hundred lire imperiali regarding the *Virgin of the Rocks* copy, and Leonardo confirms the settlement of the confraternity's debt for the *Virgin of the Rocks* altarpiece (B 199; M 87). During his stay in Milan Leonardo compiles his notes in the lost Libro A on painting, later copied selectively by Francesco Melzi to create the *Libro di pittura*, a treatise on painting (Codex Urbinas Latinus 1270, Biblioteca Vaticana). Leonardo probably begins work on the funerary equestrian monument to Gian Giacomo Trivulzio, intended for the church of San Nazaro, and compiles the notes and drawings of Ms. D (Institut de France, Paris). He also undertakes the Codex Leicester (cat. 114; Collection of Bill and Melinda Gates, Seattle, Washington), 1508–12, as well as the *Virgin and Child with Saint Anne* (fig. 23; Musée du Louvre, Paris), in progress until 1513–14.

1509

Leonardo appears to have begun Ms. K (Institut de France, Paris). He notes his trip to Savoy. He executes hydraulic and geological studies of valleys in Lombardy and of Lake Iseo. *April 28* Leonardo notes that he has solved the geometric prob-

lem of squaring two curved outlines (*falcate*, or scythelike surfaces; Windsor, RL 19145; B 201). *May 3* Leonardo records the making of the canal (*naviglio*) of San Cristoforo in Milan (C.A., fol. 1097r [formerly fol. 395r-a]; R 1009; B 202; V 268). *May 14* The French defeat the Venetians at Agnadello. Leonardo prepares the triumphal celebration of Louis XII of France.

1510

Leonardo is still in Milan and is paid a salary of 104 livres for the year by the French state under Louis XII (B 206–7; M 89). *March 6* He is allowed to build a wall separating his vineyard from the garden of the monks of San Vittore (B 204; V 270). *August 14* The only securely autograph drawing by his beloved assistant Francesco Melzi is thus dated; the youth states that he is seventeen years old (cat. no. 120). *October 21* Leonardo is asked to advise on the design of the choir stalls of Milan Cathedral (B 205; M 88; V 272). *Winter* He works with Marcantonio della Torre, the brilliant professor of anatomy at the University of Pavia, to refine his technique of anatomical investigation and produces the so-called Windsor Anatomical Ms. A (R 1376; B 205; V 273),[27] the most exquisite and precise anatomical drawings of his career. In this year Leonardo also undertakes the drawings and notes in Ms. G (Institut de France, Paris), 1510–15. Published in this year, Francesco Albertini's guidebook admiringly mentions "Leonardo's drawings" (presumably for the *Battle of Anghiari*) in the "second cloister" of Santa Maria Novella, as well as "the horses of Leonardo da Vinci and the drawings of Michelangelo" in the Sala del Gran Consiglio of the Palazzo della Signoria (B 203; V 277, 277c). The "horses" presumably refer to the portion of the *Battle of Anghiari* mural that Leonardo actually painted on the wall, and the "drawings of Michelangelo" possibly refer to the fragments of the *Battle of Cascina* cartoon. Albertini also lists the *Baptism of Christ* at San Salvi among the "most beautiful panels . . . and with an angel by Leonardo da Vinci."[28]

1511

January 5 Leonardo writes that a quarry "above Saluzzo" has marble of the hardness of porphyry "if not greater" and that his friend *maestro* Benedetto has promised to give him a piece to use as a palette for mixing colors (Ms. G, fol. 1v; B 212; V 282). In this year the painter Bramantino is commissioned to carry out the architecture of Leonardo's funerary equestrian monument to Gian Giacomo Trivulzio. *December 16 and 18* He records that the invading Swiss soldiers have set fires in Milan (B 215; V 283), marking an end to French domination of the city. *December 18* This date appears inscribed in one of

Leonardo's landscape drawings in red chalk on ocher prepared paper (Windsor, RL 12416). The fifty-nine-year-old Leonardo and his household are forced to abandon the fallen city, going east to settle for some time at the Melzi family villa in Vaprio d'Adda.

1512

In this year Leonardo executes additional landscape and river and canal studies in the region of Lombardy. Also in this year the Florentine Republic falls and the Medici family returns to power.

ROMAN PERIOD
1513–16

1513

January 9 Leonardo produces the so-called Windsor Anatomical Ms. C II. *March 11* Giovanni de' Medici is elected Pope Leo X, reigning until *December 1, 1521*. *March 25* Leonardo appears to have returned to Milan for he is listed in one of the register books of the Milan Cathedral masons' works (*Fabbrica del Duomo*; B 215). *April 30* Certain that Leonardo had abandoned the *Battle of Anghiari* mural, the administrators of the Palazzo della Signoria in Florence have a carpenter erect a wood structure to protect the small portion of the mural that he had painted in the Sala del Gran Consiglio (F 244; partly in B 216 and M 90). Leonardo writes, "I departed from Milan to go to Rome on *September 24* with Giovan Francesco [Melzi], Salaì, Lorenzo, and Il Fanfoia" (Ms. E, fol. 1r; R 1465; B 217; V 287). This record also marks the beginning of Leonardo's notes and sketches in Ms. E (Institut de France, Paris), 1513–14. *October* He and his four companions probably pass through Florence (C.A., fol. 1113r [formerly fol. 400r-b]; B 217). *December 1* By this date Leonardo is in Rome as part of the household of Giuliano de' Medici (brother of Leo X), who sets up the artist in a workshop in the Belvedere wing of the Vatican Palace. An account book records the expenses for the labor and materials required to refurbish Leonardo's Belvedere living quarters (B 218; M 91; V 288).

1514

April 11 Bramante dies in Rome. Regarding the proof of a geometric problem, Leonardo writes, "finished on *July 7* at the 23rd hour at the Belvedere, in the studio made for me by Il Magnifico [Giuliano de' Medici]" (C.A., fol. 244v [formerly fol. 90v-a]; R 1376 B; B 219; V 290). He writes that he is "in

Parma on *September 25*" and "on the banks of the Po, *September 27*" (Paris Ms. E, fol. 80r; B 220–21; V 291–92). He also visits Civitavecchia to undertake studies of the harbor and archaeological ruins. For Leo X he produces the delicately colored map showing a project for draining the Pontine marshes. *October 8* Leonardo appears inscribed in the confraternity of San Giovanni dei Fiorentini in Rome (not in B; M 92; V 293). In this year Leonardo works on his notes for the *Libro di pittura*, a treatise on painting. In this year and the next he writes drafts of letters to Giuliano de' Medici that mostly describe his quarrels with Giovanni degli Specchi, a German mirror maker (C.A., fols. 500v, 671r, 768r [formerly fols. 182v-c, 247v-b, 283r-a]; R 1351–53; B 225–28).

1515

January 1 Louis XII dies, and Francis I (1494–1547) becomes king of France. *January 9* Leonardo notes that his master, Giuliano de' Medici, departed at dawn from Rome for his marriage in Savoy and also notes incorrectly that Louis XII had died that day (Paris Ms. G, verso of cover; R 1377; B 230; V 298). He probably writes about the *Diluvii* (the descriptions of the Deluge). *July 12* At a banquet honoring the entry of Francis I into Lyons on his return from Italy, a mechanical lion invented by Leonardo is presented as a gift of Lorenzo di Piero de' Medici, the duke of Urbino, the governor of Florence, and a nephew of Leo X. *November 30* The pope makes a triumphal entry into Florence, and Leonardo and his employer Giuliano de' Medici (Leo's brother) go to the city as part of the papal entourage. In Florence Leonardo plans a new palace for Lorenzo di Piero de' Medici, across from Michelozzo's majestic Palazzo Medici. *December 7 to December 17* He leaves Florence, passing through Firenzuola, on his way to Bologna, where the pope is to meet the French king. For his trip to Bologna, Leonardo receives forty ducati from Giuliano de' Medici (B 224; M 93; V 299). The artist and his employer soon return to Rome.

1516

March 3 Leonardo records the solution to a mathematical problem (C.A., fol. 627r [formerly fol. 230v-a]; V 308). *March 17* Giuliano de' Medici dies, and Leonardo writes "The Medici made me and destroyed me" (C.A., fol. 429r [formerly fol. 159r-c]; R 1368A).[29] *August* He takes measurements of the large early Christian basilica of San Paolo fuori le Mura in Rome (C.A., fol. 471r [formerly fol. 172v-a]; R 757A; B 235; V 309). *October 20* Leonardo's old friend and influential colleague Giuliano da Sangallo dies in Rome.

French Period
1516 – 19

1516

In this year (the precise date is not known), the sixty-four-year-old Leonardo goes to France. He is invited as "paintre du Roy" by Francis I, who grants him a house at the château of Cloux, not far from the royal court at Amboise (B 241; V 315). Leonardo is accompanied by the loyal Francesco Melzi and his roguish servant Salaì.

1517

May Leonardo is the guest of Francis I at Cloux. *May 21 (Ascension Day)* The artist writes that he is in Amboise and Cloux (C.A., fol. 284r [formerly fol. 103r-b]; R 1377B; B 236; V 310). *October 1* A letter from Rinaldo Ariosto to Federico Gonzaga in Mantua describes a celebration for Francis I in Argentan, mentioning Leonardo's mechanical "lion which opened, and in the inside it was all blue, which signified love according to the customs here" (B 237; V 311).[30] *October 10* Leonardo receives a visit from Cardinal Lugi d'Aragona and his secretary Antonio De Beatis, who records the event at some length in his diary (B 238; M 94; V 314).[31] De Beatis calls the artist an "old man of more than seventy years of age" (Leonardo was actually sixty-five years old) and states that he showed the cardinal three paintings, "all most perfect": a mysterious portrait of "a certain Florentine woman done from life at the request of the said magnificent Giuliano de' Medici," which may or may not be identified with the famous *Mona Lisa* (Musée du Louvre, Paris); a young Saint John the Baptist; and a Virgin and Child seated on the lap of Saint Anne. According to De Beatis, Leonardo had trained a Milanese pupil — Francesco Melzi — who "works very well." And because Leonardo suffered from paralysis of his right side, possibly caused by a stroke, "he can no longer paint with the sweetness of style that he used to have, and he can only make drawings and teach others." De Beatis also marvels at Leonardo's anatomical investigations, noting that the artist "says that he has dissected more than thirty bodies of men and women of all ages." Along with the anatomical drawings, the visitors peruse volumes of notes on the nature of water and on hydraulics, machines, and "other things." Apparently during this year Leonardo reorganizes his manuscripts and drawings in an attempt to issue them as treatises. *October 11* An entry in De Beatis's diary amends the facts slightly regarding the visit to the royal castle of Blois the previous day: "there was also a picture in which a certain lady from Lombardy is painted in oil, from life, quite beautiful, but in my opinion not as much as the lady Gualanda, the lady Isabella Gualanda" (not in B; M 94; V 314).[32] It is far from clear whether the so-called portrait of Isabella Gualanda is to be identified with the female portrait seen by De Beatis the day before, "a certain Florentine woman done from life at the request of the said magnificent Giuliano de' Medici," since the historical Isabella Gualanda was a young widow from the circle of Vittoria Colonna in Rome. *December 29* Yet another entry in De Beatis's diary records his visit to Leonardo's *Last Supper* at the Refectory of Santa Maria delle Grazie in Milan (figs. 168, 169): "although most excellent, it is beginning to deteriorate, I do not know whether it is because of the humidity that the wall produces or because of another inadvertent problem" (B 240; M 94; V 314).[33] *At the end of the year* Leonardo is recorded at work in Romorantin in connection with a proposed palace for Francis I (Royal Library, Windsor; C.A., Biblioteca Ambrosiana, Milan; Ar., British Library, London). For the year 1517–18, the royal pension for the "master Leonardo da Vinci, Italian painter" amounts to two thousand ecus soleil for two years. "Francesco Melzi, Italian nobleman" receives eight hundred ecus for two years, and "Salaì, servant of master Leonardo da Vinci," one hundred ecus (B 241; M 96; V 316).[34]

1518

Until January 16 The sixty-six-year-old artist remains in Romorantin, where he continues to work on the plans for the king's palace and for the canals to irrigate the lands between the Loire and the Saône Rivers (V 317). He also executes topographical studies of the Loire Valley and designs a royal fountain in Amboise. *May 3–6* The wedding of Lorenzo de' Medici and Maddalena de la Tour d'Auvergne, the niece of Francis I, is celebrated in Amboise (B 240; V 318). Leonardo designs a ring with the emblems of the Medici family, probably at the request of Piero de' Medici during a visit to the French court. *June 19* Also in celebration of this wedding, the musical play *Feast of Paradise* (*La festa del paradiso*), originally staged by Leonardo for the Castello Sforzesco in Milan in 1490, is performed in Cloux with mechanical scenery (B 240). *June 24* Leonardo writes that he has left Romorantin to go to Amboise, to the castle of Cloux (C.A., fols. 673r, 918r [formerly fols. 249rb-a, 336r]; R 1378; B 243). In this year the artist also prepares studies for an arena, volumetric analyses of churches, among them Bramante's Saint Peter's Basilica (C.A., Biblioteca Ambrosiana, Milan), and studies of perspective and architecture (Geigy-Hagenbach Collection, University Library, Basel).

Leonardo, sixty-seven years old and ailing, appears at the royal court at Amboise to acknowledge his will, dated *April 23* (extant only in a notarial copy by Venanzio de Pagave; R 1566; B 244; M 97; V 323). Francesco Melzi is the executor of Leonardo's estate and is bequeathed all the drawings, manuscripts, tools, and "works of the painter" (*instrumenti et portracti*), which Melzi brings back to Italy in 1520 and jealously guards in his family villa at Vaprio d'Adda. Among the other heirs are the servants Salaì and Battista de Vilanis, as well as the artist's half brothers and half sisters. Salaì inherits Leonardo's vineyard in Milan, where he builds himself a house, and obtains some of the master's major paintings: the *Leda and the Swan, Virgin and Child with Saint Anne, Mona Lisa, Saint John the Baptist,* and *Saint Jerome.*[35] *May 2* Leonardo dies in the château of Cloux. Following his wish, he is buried in the cloister of the church of Saint-Florentin in Amboise (destroyed). *June 1* His beloved companion and artistic heir, Francesco Melzi, writes to Leonardo's half brother Ser Giuliano da Vinci to inform the family of the master's death (B 245; V 324).

SOURCES

Adorno 1991; Bambach 1999a; Bambach 1999b; B=Beltrami 1919a; Bernacchioni 1992; Brown 1998b; Butterfield 1997; Calvi 1916; Calvi 1925a; Davies and Hemsoll 1996; Elam 1996a; Elam 1996b; Fiorio 1996a; Fiorio 1996b; Frey 1892; F=Frey 1909; Fusco and Corti 1992; Guicciardini 1984; Kemp 1989; Kemp 1995; Kirwin 1995; *Legacy of Leonardo,* 1998; Letze and Buchsteiner 1997; Marani 1989; Marani 1996; M=Marani 2000b; Morozzi 1988–89; Passavant 1969; Pedretti 1953; Pedretti 1973a; P=Pedretti 1977; Pedretti 1995a; Pedretti and Roberts 1984–96; R=Richter 1970; Schofield and Shell 1996; Shell and Sironi 1991; S=Sironi 1981; Smiraglia Scognamiglio 1900; Uzielli 1896; Vasari–Milanesi 1906; Vecce 1998a; V=Villata 1999; Wilde 1944.

1. See further Uzielli 1896, pp. 3–618; family tree in Vasari–Milanesi 1906, vol. 4, pp. 54–55.
2. "[D]ì di s[an]ta maria della neve / addj 5 daghosto 1473." The feast day of Our Lady of the Snow commemorated a miraculous snowfall in August at the site on which the basilica of Santa Maria Maggiore was later built in Rome.
3. Transcribed in Frey 1892, p. 110; B 9; Vecce 1998a, p. 358.
4. "[B]re 1478 incominciai le due vergini marie." The *bre* ending in the month's name can refer to various autumn months, September to December. Gerolamo Calvi and Carlo Pedretti interpreted the month as probably December (Calvi 1925a, p. 12; Pedretti 1977, vol. 1, p. 381, no. 663).
5. Butterfield 1997, pp. 6, 159–83, 232–36, no. 26. See cat. nos. 9, 10. The precise date that Andrea del Verrocchio received the commission for the Colleoni equestrian monument is not clear. By April 1486 Verrocchio appears to have been in Venice working on the models for the sculpture. At the time of his death in June 1488 he had brought the models to an advanced state of completion. The casting of the sculpture in bronze was entrusted to Alessandro Leopardi in 1490 and was finished in the spring of 1496.
6. (M 15): "una figura de Nostra Dona quanto bella excellente et diuota la sapia piu fare senza sparagno de spesa alcuna."

7. (B 44; V 53): "di. 23 d'aprile. 1.4.9.0 chominciaj. questo. libro e richominciaj. il cauallo."
8. (M 19): "et che dicti Scolari non sono in talibus experti et quod cechus non iudicat de colore."
9. "[Q]ual di presente tanto ben l'impronta."
10. Ludovico Sforza "Il Moro" had assumed the title of duke of Milan in 1494 after prolonged plotting. In 1476, following the murder of Ludovico's brother Galeazzo Maria (duke of Milan, 1466–76), his wife, Duchess Bona of Savoy, became regent for their son and heir, Gian Galeazzo, who was only seven years old. In 1479, on the death of Ludovico's other brother, Sforza Maria, the tyrant finally inherited the title of duke of Bari. In 1480, when Bona was exiled from Milan, "Il Moro" became the de facto ruler of the city. He continued his campaign to usurp the title of duke of Milan and take control of the duchy throughout the decade. In 1493 Ludovico even secretly paid Emperor Maximilian I to appropriate the position of Gian Galeazzo in order to be granted the ducal title. In the same year Ludovico had arranged the marriage of the emperor to his niece Bianca Maria Sforza.
11. On Leonardo, see Pacioli 1509, Pars prima, fols. 1r, 8r, 22r, 28v, 30v; and on his "Sforza Horse": "Com[m]o ladmira[n]da e stupenda eq[ue]stre statua. La cui alteçça dala cervice a piana terra sonno bracia.12.cioe 37 4/5 ta[n]ti dela quale p[un]te li[n]ea.a.b e tutta la sua ennea massa alire circa 200,000." As Pacioli's *De divina proportione* also suggests, Leonardo seems to have executed the drawings of the five geometric solids (*cinque corpi regolari*) for Pacioli's treatise in 1499 (B 97). Written about 1498, the manuscript of the treatise exists in two versions, one at the Biblioteca Ambrosiana, Milan, and the other at the Biblioteca Civica, Geneva.
12. Gian Giacomo Trivulzio had become condottiere under Ferdinand I, king of Naples, and then transferred his services first to Charles VIII of France, and later to Louis XII.
13. (B 117; V 160): "Familiare Architecto et Ingengero Generale." Cesare Borgia was the illegitimate son of Pope Alexander VI, who reigned from August 11, 1492, to August 18, 1503. He became duke of Valentino and married Carlotta d'Albret on May 10, 1499, an alliance that gave him an indirect claim to the French throne.
14. (B 127; V 181): "livellare arno in quello di pisa e levallo del letto suo."
15. That is, the Loggia della Signoria, today also called the Loggia dei Lanzi.
16. (M 51): "uno Christo giouenetto de anni circa duodeci che seria de quella eta quando lhaueua quando disputo nel tempio."
17. *Dipintore* (literally, painter) implies that they were professional painters, while the other was an assistant who ground colors, "che macina i colori."
18. (P 669, p. 382): "(In venerdj dj gugno/ aore 13)// Addj 6 dj gugno^1505^invenerdj altocho/ delle 13 ore comj[n]caj acolorire in/ palazo . nel qual p-u[n]to del posare il/penelo si guasto il te[m]po essono aba[n]cho richiedendo li omjnj aragone il/cartone sistracco lacqua siuerso eru/pesi il uaso dellacqua chessi portaua/ esubito si guasto il tenpo eppiove/ insino assere acqua gra[n]djssima/ estette il tenpo come notte."
19. The verb is in the future tense (M 66): "deberent dare anchonam capelle suprascripte."
20. (M 68): "quelle figure che gli hauimo rechieste."
21. (M 73): "L.do da vinci Il quale non si e portato come doueua con questa republica: perchè a preso buona somma de denaro e dato uno piccolo principio a una opera grande doueua fare."
22. (M 79): "nostre chier et bien amé Léonardo de vincy nostre paintre et ingenieur ordinaire."
23. (M 81): "Vene li m.ro Leonardo vinci pittore del X.mo Re: al quale cum grandissima dificulta hauemo dato Licentia per essere obligato fare una tauola ad essa m.ta X.ma."
24. (M 84): "Pochi giorni sono chio venni da Milano et trouando che uno mio fratello maggiore non mi vuol seruare uno [te]stamento: facto da 3 anni in qua che e morto nostro padre: ancor che la ragione sia per me: non di

meno per non mancare a me medesmo in una cosa che io stimo assai non ho voluto ommettere di richiedere la R.ma S. V. di una littera commendatizia et di fauore qui a el S.or Raphaello Iheronymo che e al presente uno de n.ri excelsi Sig.ri ne quali questa mia causa si agita."

25. (B 194; V 254): "Chom[inc]jcato add in firenze incasa di bacco martellj addi 22 di marzo 1508: ecquesto sia un raccolto sanza ordine, tratto di molte carte lequali io ho qui copiate sperando poi di metterle alli lochi loro, se condo le materie di che esse tratteranno."

26. (M 85): "parte altera bona fide et sine fraude."

27. (B 205; V 273): "Questa vernata del 510 credo spedire tutta tal notomia."

28. Francesco Albertini and Baccio da Montelupo, *Memoriale di molte statue e pitture della Città di Firenze* (Florence: Antonio Turbini), 1510 (B 203; V 277): "Quartieri di S. M. Novella: . . . nel secundo (claustro) il quale è lungo br. 120 è una cappella bellissima presso alla Sala pontificale dove sono I disegni di Leonardo Vinci. . . . In Palazzo majore: nella Sala Grande nuova del consiglio majore, lunga br. 104 larga br. 40, è una tavola di fra Philippo, li cavalli di Leonardo Vinci, et li disegni di Michelangelo . . . Nelli Ingesuati et altri lochi: . . . Lascio in Sancto Salvi tavole bellissime, et un Angelo di Leonardo Vinci."

29. (R 1368A): "Li Medici mi creorono e destrussono."

30. (B 237): "et epso Leone se aperse et dentro era tutto d'azuro, che significava amore secondo il modo di qua."

31. See Vecce 1990, pp. 51–59. (M 94): "In uno deli borghi il signore con noi altri ando ad videre messer Lunardo Vinci firentino, vecchio de piu di LXX anj pictore en la eta mostra excellentissimo, quale mostro ad usa s. Ill.ma tre quattri, uno di certa donnafirentina facto di naturale ad instantia del quondam Mag.co Juliano de Medici: laltrodi san Johanne Baptista giovane et uno de la Madonna e del figliolo che stan posti in gremmo de s.ta Anna : tucti perfectissimi. Ben vero che da lui per esserli venuta certa paralesi ne la dextra non se ne puo expectare piu cosa bona. Ha ben facto un creato

milanese chi lavora assai bene et benche il prefato messer Lunardo non possa colorire con quella dulceza che solea pur serve ad fare disegni et insignare ad altri. Questo gentilhuomo ha composto de notomia tanto particolarmente cun la demostrazione de la pictura si de membri come de muscoli, nervi, vene, giunture dintestini et di quanto si puo ragionare tanto di corpi di huomini come di donne, de modo non e stato mai anchora facto da altra persona. Il che habbiamo visto oculatamente et gia lui disse haver facta notomia de piu de xxx corpi tra mascoli et femine de ogni eta. Ha anche composto de la natura de l'acque, de diverse machine et d'altre cose, secondo ha riferito lui, infinita de volumi, et tucti in lingua volgare, quali se vengono in luce, saranno profigue et molto delectevoli. Esso ultra le spese et stantie da re di Franza ha 1000 scuti l'anno di pensione et lo creato trecento."

32. (M 94): "Vi era ancho [nel castello reale di Blois] un quatro dove e pintata ad oglio una certa signura di Lombardia di naturale assai bella, ma al mio iuditio non tanto come la signora Gualanda [added along the border:] s.ra Isabella Gualanda."

33. (M 94): "In lo monastero di Santa Maria de le Gratie, quale fo facto dal signor Ludovico Sforza, assai bello e bene acteso, fo visto nel refectorio de frati chi sonno del ordine di san Dominico de observantia, una cena picta al muro da messer Lunardo Vinci, qual trovaimo in Amboys, che e excellentissima, benche incomincia ad guastarse non so si per la humidita che rende il muro o per altra [in]advertentia. Li personaggi di quella son de naturale retracti de piu persone de la corte et de Milanesi di quel tempo, di vera statura."

34. Of note, the Florentine sculptor Benvenuto Cellini writes in his famous autobiography that he received the same pension from the king of France as Leonardo, seven hundred scudi a year, which is incorrect (B 234).

35. See inventory of Salai's property dated April 21, 1525, transcribed in Shell and Sironi 1991.

ANDREA DEL VERROCCHIO (ANDREA DI MICHELE CIONE)

(Florence, 1434/37 – Venice, 1488)

1. *Young Woman in Bust Length in Three-Quarter View Facing to the Left*

Soft black chalk or charcoal, partly reworked in pen and golden brown ink, brush with brown ink and gray wash; outlines pricked for transfer, 411 × 327 mm (16 3/16 × 12 7/8 in.)
Christ Church, Oxford 0005

PROVENANCE: Giorgio Vasari (?), Arezzo, Florence, and Rome (1511–1574); General John Guise, Winterbourne and London (1682/83–1765; under Lugt 2754); his bequest, 1765.

LITERATURE: Berenson 1903, vol. 2, p. 180, no. 2800 (school of Verrocchio); Colvin 1907, vol. 3, p. 1; Bell 1914, A.5, p. 92; Van Marle 1923–38, vol. 11, p. 534; Royal Academy of Arts 1930, no. 452; Popham 1930–31, no. 51; Petit Palais 1935, no. 735; Berenson 1938, vol. 1, pp. 48 n. 2, 59, vol. 2, p. 359, vol. 3, fig. 127, no. 2782 (Verrocchio); Mathey 1951, no. 7; Matthiesen Gallery 1960, no. 79; Berenson 1961, vol. 1, p. 99, vol. 2, p. 608, vol. 3, fig. 121, no. 2782A; Gratchenkov 1963, pl. 29; Walker Art Gallery 1964, no. 50; Passavant 1969, p. 193, no. D8; Byam Shaw 1972–73a, no. 84; Ragghianti Collobi 1974, p. 83; Byam Shaw 1976a, vol. 1, p. 36, no. 15; Ames-Lewis and Wright 1983, pp. 310–13, no. 72; Cadogan 1983c, pp. 373, 375, 378, fig. 10; Adorno 1991, p. 269; Caterina Caneva in Petrioli Tofani 1992, pp. 110–11, no. 4.13; Wiemers 1996, pp. 144–47; Butterfield 1997, pp. 184–85, fig. 244; Bambach 1999a, pp. 82, 242, 259–62, 414 n. 176; Rubin and Wright 1999–2000, pp. 194–97, no. 31; Ames-Lewis 2001, p. 9, n. 9; Baker 2002, pp. 22–23, no. 2.

"That your shadows and highlights fuse without hatching or strokes, as smoke does [*a uso di fumo*]." With these words, Leonardo described a new technique of drawing in 1490–92 that would make him famous in the history of art.[1] Yet as can be surmised from sadly fragmentary evidence, the lion's share of the credit for exploring this new manner of drawing should probably go to Leonardo's teacher, Andrea del Verrocchio. Along with Piero del Pollaiuolo, Verrocchio was one of the first Tuscan artists to experiment successfully with the sfumato technique of rendering shadows, especially in cartoons, or full-scale drawings. (See also cat. nos. 2, 3, 5, 6.) In 1903, the great connoisseur Bernard Berenson catalogued the large-scale Christ Church drawing (and the stylistically related cartoon of a boy's head in Berlin, cat. no. 2) as by the school of Andrea del Verrocchio. By 1938, Berenson had come around to appreciate the magnificence of the drawing, reattributing it to Verrocchio and calling it "one of the boldest and most inspiring achievements of the Quattrocento."[2] Berenson's enthusiastic opinion has been unanimously endorsed by later scholars.

Probably dating from the late 1460s to the early 1470s, the Christ Church drawing offers proof of Verrocchio's extraordinary

Fig. 116. Andrea del Verrocchio, *Madonna and Child*. Oil and tempera on wood, 73.8 × 54.7 cm (original painting surface). Gemäldegalerie, Staatliche Museen zu Berlin—Preussischer Kulturbesitz 104A

Fig. 117. Andrea del Verrocchio, *Head of an Angel*. Soft black chalk or charcoal, reworked with pen and brown ink, outlines pricked for transfer, 210 × 181 mm. Gabinetto Disegni e Stampe degli Uffizi, Florence 130 E

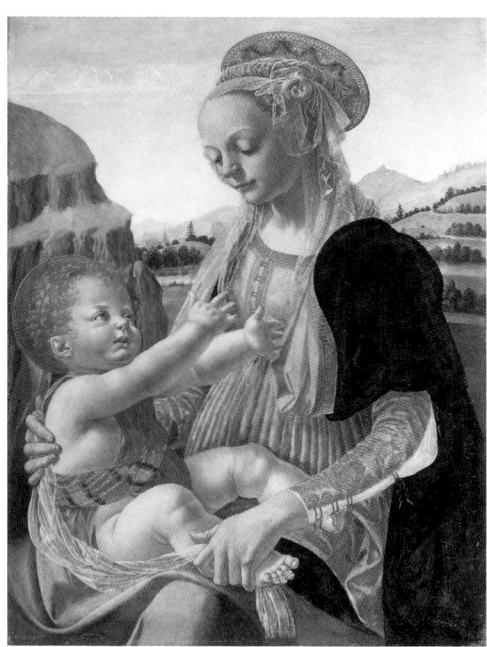

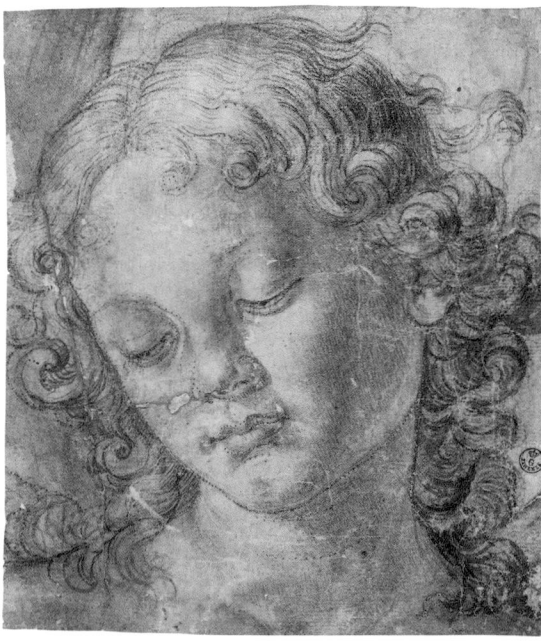

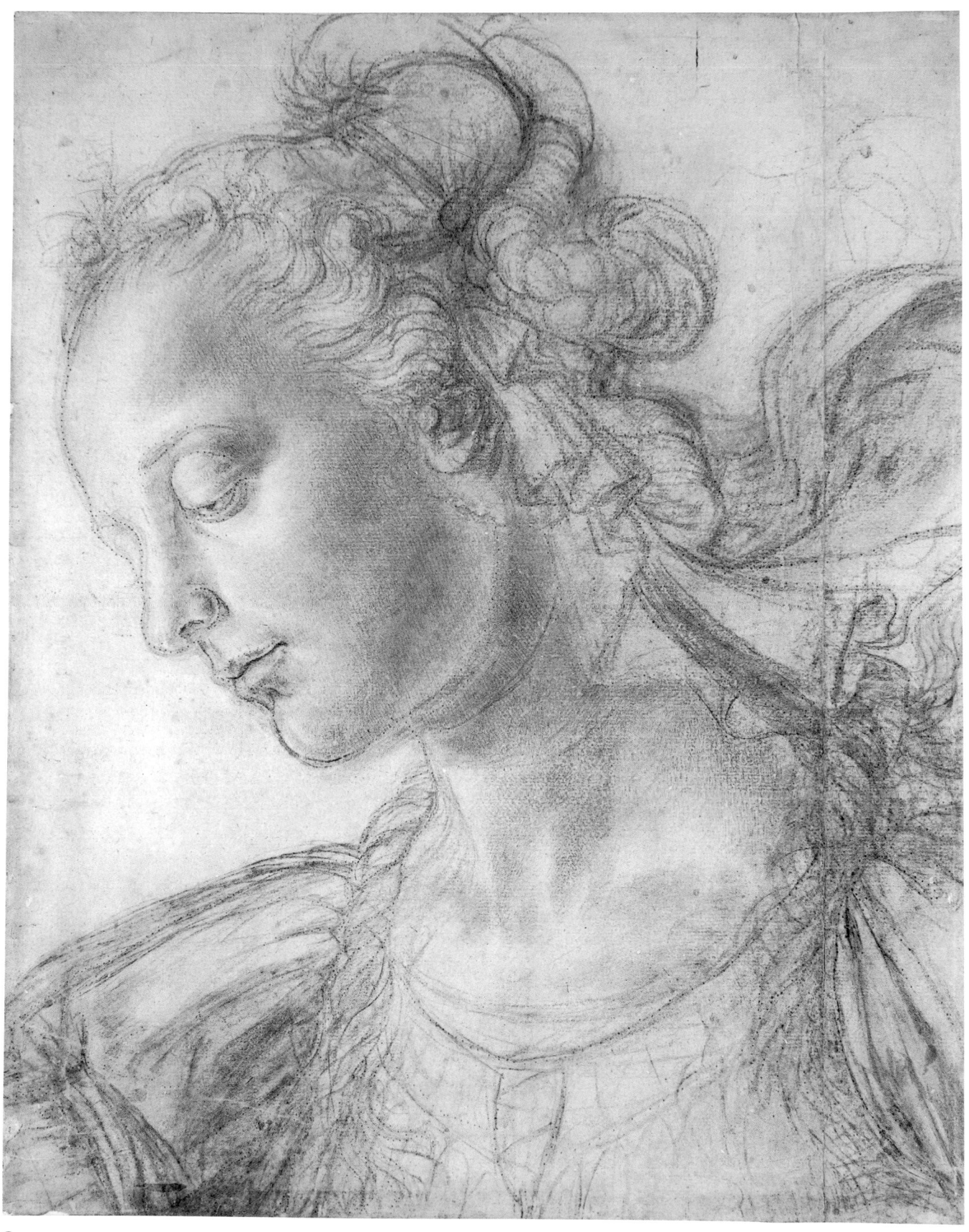

Cat. 1

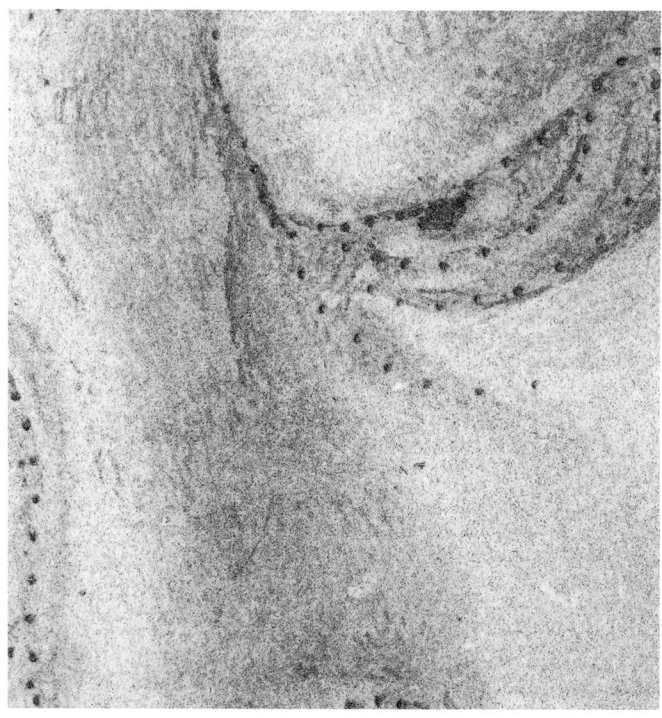

Cat. 1 *(detail)*

innovation as a draftsman. The drawing soars on the paper
with light and movement, even poetry, partly as a result of the
artist's dynamic use of contrasts. Verrocchio played off passages
of great finish against ones left intentionally unfinished. He
selected the flesh areas for a luminous refinement of surface
resembling the luster of polished marble. He smudged the silvery black chalk or charcoal to its darkest, seamlessly blended
tone just short of the edges of the planes of the face, neck,
and cleavage, creating an effect of flickering reflected light. By
contrast, he treated the dress, braided hair, and crinkled gauze
veil with an airy impressionistic touch, everywhere leaving bold,
reinforced strokes that are virtually unblended. The drawing
was originally executed on a single large sheet of paper; the
paper later separated along a crease and was rejoined by an
early restorer. It served as a cartoon to transfer the design
onto a working surface. This cartoon was actually used, for the
outlines of the design are pricked, and the perforated holes
still bear evidence of rubbed charcoal pouncing dust, from the
transfer process.

The woman in the cartoon, an idealized beauty with an
ornate headdress, is a type that frequently occurs in Verrocchio's oeuvre of the 1470s (the years when Leonardo was
present in his workshop), though no precise correspondence of
design between the drawing and any finished work is known.

Her general type is that of the Virgin in a painted panel
(fig. 116) and a stucco after a lost Verrocchio prototype (Allen
Memorial Art Museum, Oberlin) — such images of the
Madonna and Child were the bread and butter of the Verrocchio
workshop. Her type is also generally recognizable in the allegorical figure of a Christian virtue in the unexecuted project
for the Vendramin tomb (cat. no. 5) and in the marble funerary monument of Cardinal Niccolò Forteguerri (Pistoia
Cathedral), begun by the great sculptor in 1477–83, with
the assistance of his workshop.

The Christ Church cartoon was useful beyond its application in the production of finished works, however. Verrocchio
was famous as a teacher, as one can gather from the praise by
Ugolino Verino in 1502/1503[3] and by Giorgio Vasari in
1550–68. The artist probably offered the cartoon as a model
for his pupils to copy in learning to draw. It may have been
this type of drawing of idealized female beauty that Vasari
had in mind when he extolled Verrocchio: "there are some
drawings by his hand in our album [Vasari's famous *libro de'
disegni*] made with much patience and very great mastery,
and among these are some heads of women, with graceful
manner and hair arrangements that because of their great
beauty Leonardo always imitated."[4]

The cartoon is delicately reworked with short, left-handed
parallel hatching in brush and gray wash that unifies the tonal
structure of the shadows on the woman's temple and cheek.[5]
Two other drawings by Verrocchio also exhibit some reworking with apparently left-handed parallel hatching (Uffizi,
Florence, 130 E and 212 E; figs. 117, 79). In the Christ Church
cartoon, the intermediate grade of shadows in the flesh areas
are also further reworked with delicate parallel hatching on
top, done with a fine-tipped pen and a wash of light brown
ink. This type of hatching is especially visible on the woman's
forehead, temple, cheek, and neck. Both the wash and ink
reworkings have been regarded as later retouchings. Their
beauty and logic of placement, however, argue that they were
functional surface refinements. This reworking of drawings in
leadpoint, charcoal, or black chalk on top with a layer in pen
and ink or wash was a typical technique in Verrocchio's workshop (cat. nos. 4–8) and one that Leonardo also practiced, even
late in his career. Without pressing the point too far, it seems
worth pondering whether the left-handed parts in the Christ
Church cartoon are not in fact the work of the young Leonardo.
Telling evidence for the young Leonardo's style of drawing

with the tip of the brush in the 1470s is found in the small drapery study (Istituto Nazionale per la Grafica, Rome, 125770), which is done in metalpoint with his characteristic lower right to upper left strokes, on cinnabar red prepared paper. In the Rome sheet, the original passages of white gouache highlights, however, are applied with the very fine tip of the brush and consist mostly of short, tiny parallel and crosshatched strokes, which change in directions (as if the artist turned around the sheet in drawing the minute strokes), and therefore seem somewhat disunified.[6]

Artists of Verrocchio's generation and later calibrated the drawing in large cartoons to be seen from a distance. Thus, when Verrocchio's Christ Church drawing is held far from the eye, even at arm's length, the delicate, ink-hatched modeling is perceived no longer as a pattern but as a golden hue, suggesting the warmth of living flesh that the smudged silvery black chalk or charcoal alone cannot evoke. The artist (whether this was Verrocchio or someone else) seems also to have corrected the outlines of the woman's nostril, mouth, and chin with fine, gently swelling brushstrokes in brown ink wash, to inflect their slightly foreshortened turns in space. The effect of these reworked outlines when studied from a distance is also successful. The technique recalls Leonardo's later advice on drawing: "regarding the outlines, note which way they go; and in the lines, how much is curved to one side or the other, and where they are more or less evident, and if they are broad or fine."[7] Despite the calibrations of chiaroscuro and outline, the overall manner of drawing in Verrocchio's cartoon seems still too delicate for such a large-scale design, and the beautiful woman's figure consequently appears as if carved in low relief, rather than in the round.   CCB

1. Paris Ms. A, fol. 107v (B.N. 2038, fol. 27v); Richter 1970, vol. 1, p. 306, no. 492: "che le tue o[m]bre e lumi sieno uniti sa[n]za tratti o segni, a uso di fumo"; Bambach 1999a, pp. 249–64.
2. Berenson 1938, vol. 1, pp. 59–60.
3. Butterfield 1997, p. 195.
4. Vasari–Milanesi 1906, vol. 3, pp. 363–64: "Sono alcuni disegni di sua mano nel nostro Libro, fatti con molta pacienza e grandissimo giudizio; infra i quali sono alcune teste di femina con bell'arie ed acconciature di capelli, quali, per la sua bellezza, Lionardo da Vinci sempre imitò."
5. For a discussion of left-handed drawings, see my essay in the present catalogue.
6. Many drawings in pen and ink or metalpoint by the young Leonardo also exhibit a somewhat disunified left-handed parallel hatching.
7. This passage directly precedes the famous note on sfumato drawing in the Paris Ms. A, fol. 107v (B.N. 2038, fol. 27v); Richter 1970, vol. 1, p. 306, no. 492: "i lineame[n]ti . a che parte si dirizzino, e nelle linie qua[n]te parte d'esse torcie per vno o altro verso, e dove più o meno evide[n]ti e se sia larga o sottile."

ANDREA DEL VERROCCHIO

2. *Head of a Young Boy* (recto)
Fragment of a Head of a Young Boy (verso)

Soft black chalk or charcoal, highlighted with white chalk, outlines pricked for transfer; traces of framing outlines in pen and brown ink, 185 × 160 mm (7 5/16 × 6 5/16 in.)
Inscribed in pen and brown ink on recto at lower right corner: *da Vinci*
Staatliche Museen zu Berlin — Preussischer Kulturbesitz, Kupferstichkabinett, Berlin KdZ 5095

PROVENANCE: Sir John Charles Robinson (1824–1913; Lugt 1433); Adolf von Beckerath (1834–1915; Lugt 1612 and 2504); 1902, acquired by the Berliner Museen; museum stamp (Lugt 1612).

LITERATURE: Mackowsky 1901, p. 89, no. 72; Berenson 1903, vol. 1, pp. 36, 37, vol. 2, p. 179, no. 2784 (school of Verrocchio); Loeser 1903a, p. 54; Beckerath 1904, pp. 239–40, nos. 5 and 6; von Beckerath 1905, pp. 125–26; Kupferstichkabinett Berlin 1910, nos. 14a, 14b; Van Marle 1923–38, pp. 534 n. 2, 580; Dussler 1926, p. 295; Bertini 1935, p. 471 (Verrocchio?); Berenson 1938, vol. 1, pp. 48 n. 2, 59, vol. 2, p. 359, vol. 3, fig. 126, no. 2780E (formerly 2784); Arnolds 1949, p. 10; Berenson 1961, vol. 2, p. 606, no. 2780E (formerly 2784); Pouncey and Gere 1962, vol. 1, pp. 5–6, no. 5, vol. 2, p. 6; Passavant 1969, p. 59, 192–93, no. 7; Ragghianti and Dalli Regoli 1975, p. 28 n. 2, p. 42 n. 36, no. 11 (Botticelli; incorrectly listed as KdZ 5093); Dreyer 1979, no. 6; Ames-Lewis and Wright 1983, under no. 72; Cadogan 1983b, p. 277; Cadogan 1983c, pp. 373–80 n. 32, figs. 11, 12; Bambach [Cappel] 1988, pp. 463–64, no. 336; Adorno 1991, pp. 262–63 (workshop of Verrocchio, under his direct supervision); Kupferstichkabinett Berlin 1994, v.4; Schulze Altcappenberg 1995, pp. 141–43; Wiemers 1996, pp. 148–50, figs. 135–36; Butterfield 1997, p. 185 n. 11, fig. 250; Bambach 1999a, pp. 33–80, 259–62, 465 n. 80; Rubin and Wright 1999–2000, pp. 198–99, no. 32.

To judge from the cropping of the boy's head on the verso, it is clear that the double-sided Berlin sheet was originally much larger and that the unfinished drawing on the verso was considered to be of lesser importance. The boy's head on the recto, sharply foreshortened in a difficult *sotto in sù pose* (as if seen from below) that is rare in drawings of this scale and function from the second half of the fifteenth century, represents a virtuosic exercise in figural draftsmanship—a *scorto*, or foreshortening—that was much admired during this period.[1] For this reason, it may have been saved by the artist as a useful *exemplum* in teaching drawing skills to his pupils. This exquisitely rendered head also exemplifies the innovative sfumato drawing technique of Andrea del Verrrocchio that would greatly influence the younger generation of artists apprenticing in the great sculptor's workshop: Leonardo, Lorenzo di Credi (cat. nos. 7, 8), and Domenico Ghirlandaio. Like the Christ Church *Young Woman* (cat. no. 1), this double-sided cartoon, or full-scale drawing, probably dates from the early 1470s, when Leonardo is known to have been part of Verrocchio's *bottega*, though increasingly in the role of a collaborator after his matriculation in 1472 in the painters' confraternity, the Compagnia di San Luca.[2] An early collector erroneously attributed the Berlin cartoon to Leonardo himself, writing his name on the lower right of the recto.

The Berlin sheet is rightly recognized as one of the very few, little-disputed extant drawings by Verrocchio, for it closely conforms to the sculptor's drawing technique, style, and figural types. In 1903 Bernard Berenson first considered the Berlin cartoon to be merely a workshop piece (as he did in the case of the Christ Church cartoon), but by 1938 he had entirely changed his mind, following in the footsteps of Hans Mackowsky, Charles Loeser, and Adolf von Beckerath, the early champions of the Berlin sheet. More recently, only Carlo Ragghianti, Gigetta Dalli Regoli, and Pietro Adorno have expressed reservations about the attribution to Verrocchio, the last-named scholar noting—quite puzzlingly—the absence of the great sculptor's characteristic plasticism.[3]

The drawing technique of the recto is nearly identical to

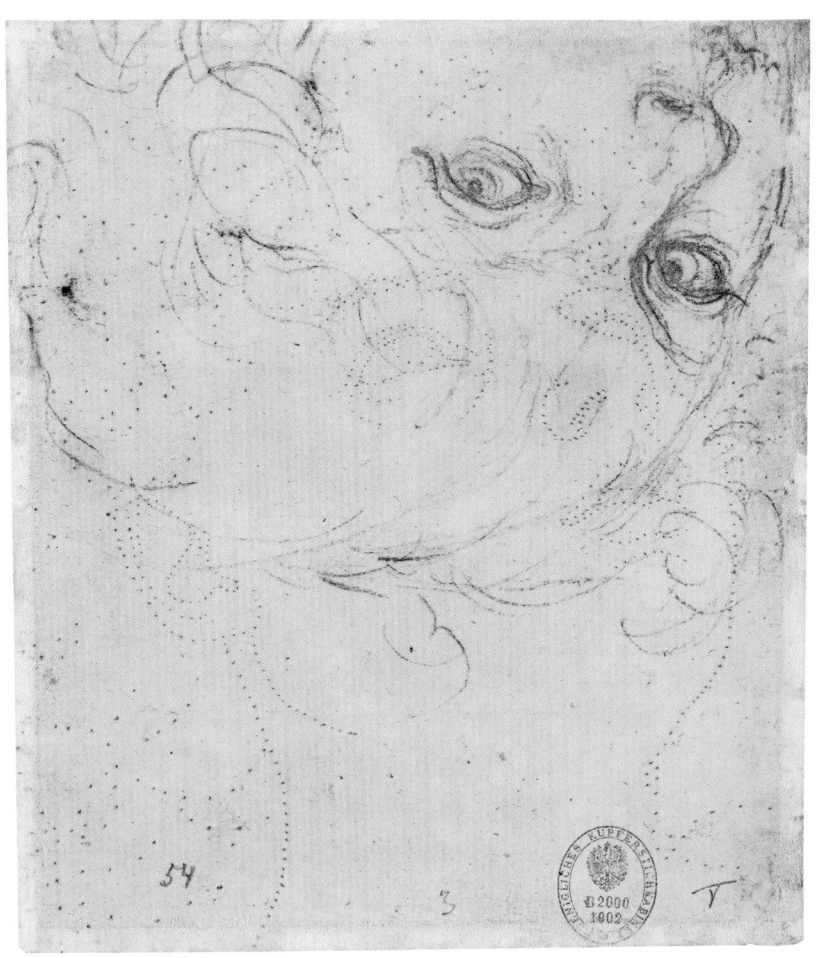

Cat. 2v

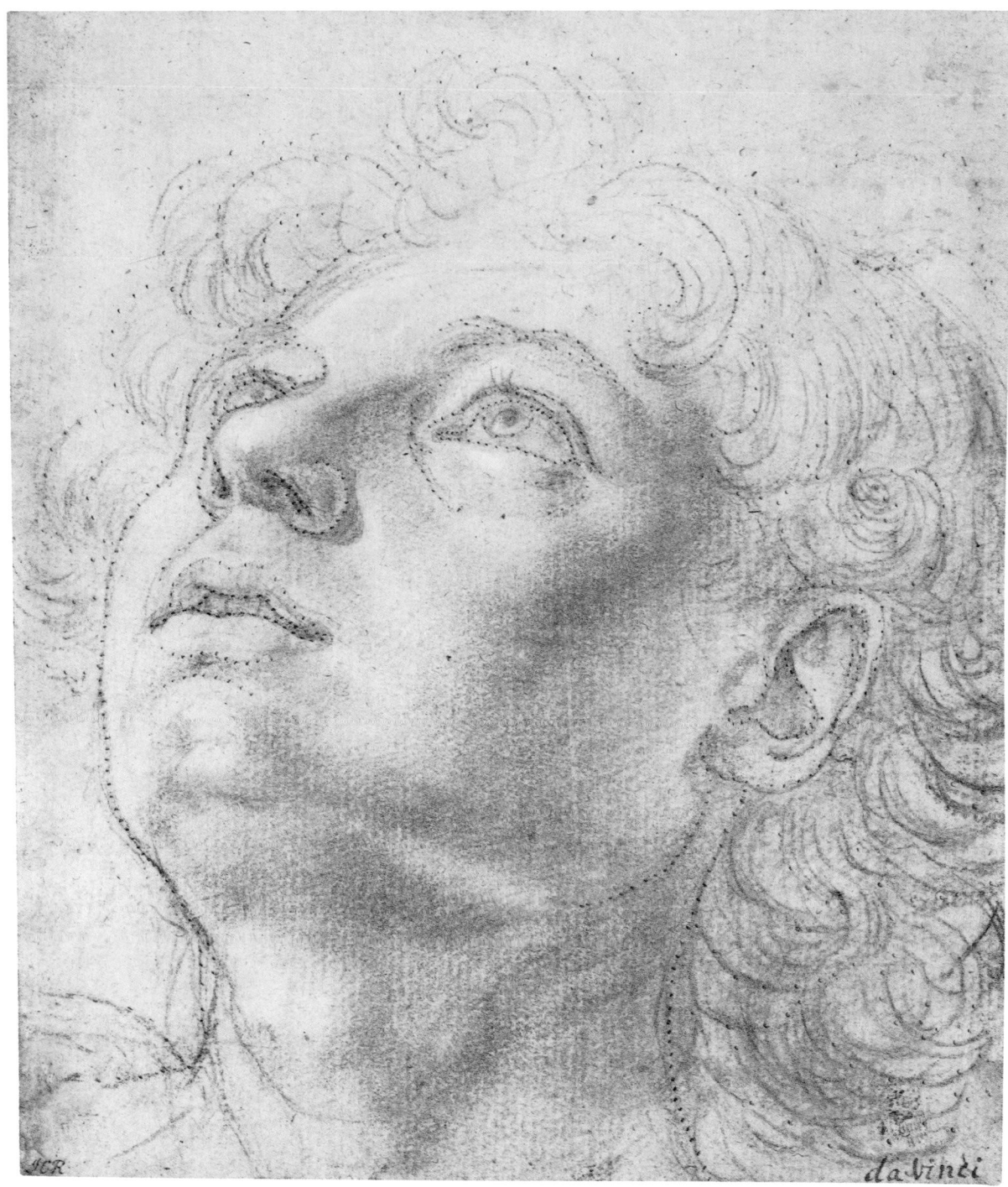

Cat. 2R *(actual size)*

that of the Christ Church cartoon, but without the reworking with ink and wash partly done by a left-handed artist. As Berenson rightly observed in 1961, the two cartoons must date from nearly the same moment in Verrocchio's career,[4] about the time of his painted panel of the *Madonna and Child* in Berlin (fig. 116), which critics have variously dated between 1465 and 1475, on the basis of style, but which is most likely from the early 1470s. The drawing on the Berlin recto is highly finished, and the outlines of the design are pricked for transfer onto another working surface. The unfinished, unpricked sketch on the verso, which is also in the scale of a cartoon, reveals vigorous, fairly sculptural outlines. The artist would have softened these considerably, had he carried out the sketch to the advanced stage of rendering that is seen on the

247

recto. An analogous situation, of a highly finished full-scale study on one side of the sheet and a bold, unfinished sketch on the reverse, is found in the later British Museum double-sided cartoon by Verrocchio (cat. no. 3). This sheet, however, does not exhibit pricked outlines. The boy's head on the Berlin recto probably served as a preparatory study for the figure of an angel (or, much less likely, of a Christ Child or an infant Saint John the Baptist), but a precise correspondence of the design to a painting or sculpture by Verrocchio, or to an artist closely related to his workshop, has not been identified. The boy's facial type is generally reminiscent of that of an angel on the left portion of a much-discussed painted panel of the *Madonna and Child* (National Gallery, London, 296), which has also been dated about 1466–75, though the angel there faces in the opposite direction and appears older. Similarly, the boy's facial type on the Berlin verso is generally comparable to that of the angel on the right portion of the same National Gallery panel.[5] It is evocative, as well, of the slightly younger-looking infants in catalogue number 4 and in several relief sculptures by Verrocchio and his workshop. Günther Passavant, who inexplicably thought that the figures on the two sides of the Berlin sheet could be a girl or a boy, unconvincingly connected the recto to the design of Verrocchio's cenotaph for Cardinal Niccolò Forteguerri. He suggested that it was "certainly a study for the head of Faith," but that it was more closely comparable to the terracotta model (*bozzetto*) for the project (Victoria and Albert Museum, London; fig. 121) than to the final marble monument in Pistoia Cathedral.[6] As stated above, the Christ Church cartoon (cat. no. 1) may be more closely related in design to this allegorical figure in the Forteguerri cenotaph.

For the boy's head on the Berlin recto, as in catalogue number 1, Verrocchio greatly varied his handling of the soft, silvery, friable medium (whether it is black chalk or charcoal is not entirely clear) to capture the diversity in the effects of reflected and absorbed light as the textures change from flesh to hair. The artist positioned the light source to fall from the upper left on the boy's head, thereby accentuating the sculptural definition of the forms; this use of an upper left light source for the figure is also evident in Verrocchio's other cartoons of heads (cat. nos. 1, 3). A later note by Leonardo, from 1490–92, recommends much the same practice to young, apprenticing painters, namely, placing the light source in the upper left when drawing after the model.[7] Here, Leonardo was most probably repeating the tradi-

tional advice that masters passed on orally to pupils in Italian Renaissance workshops and that he probably heard from Verrocchio himself. In Verrocchio's Berlin cartoon, sketchy, undisguised curving strokes articulate the curls of the boy's hair and the small portion of his clothing that is seen on the lower left corner of the sheet. The opaque tone of the hair and clothing offers a subtle foil for the high luster of the marblelike flesh areas, drawn with seamlessly blended shadows, in which the artist stumped, or rubbed in, the individual strokes, probably with his fingers, a piece of soft cloth,[8] or a stumping tool. The boy's foreshortened facial features are defined in a tonal way (in terms of architectural planes of smoky shadows) rather than in a linear way (in terms of outlines, parallel hatching, or cross-hatching), as was more typical in cartoons of the second half of the fifteenth century.[9] Observed close-up, Verrocchio's technique appears to capture at once the smoothness of plump young skin and the structure of the underlying bones. The artist gradually built up the intensity of the evenly blended shadows just short of the edges of planes and allowed the smudged charcoal gradually to give way to shining highlight. The white chalk highlights may or may not be a later retouching; on the boy's forehead the white attempts to hide pentimenti. Even in this very polished study, numerous reinforcement outlines in the underdrawing also attest to the artist's creative process of exploring the design. In such a tonal drawing, only the general outlines could be pricked in order to use the design as a cartoon. The pricking is done neatly, with the Verrocchio workshop's characteristically large, closely spaced holes, more or less carefully aligned with the drawing. As is typical of Verrocchio's cartoons, the boy's face was pricked more densely and carefully than his sketchily drawn hair.   CCB

1. Bambach 1999a, pp. 186–248.
2. See Chronology.
3. Adorno 1991, p. 263.
4. Berenson 1961, vol. 2, p. 607, no. 2708E.
5. Cadogan 1983c, p. 374, called the Berlin verso a preparatory study for the angel on the right in the National Gallery painting, but the connection between drawing and painting seems much less direct, for they exhibit the same general figural type but not the same design.
6. Passavant 1969, p. 59.
7. Paris Ms. A, fol. 112r (B.N. 2038, fol. 33r); Richter 1970, vol. 1, p. 315, no. 515: "Come de'e essere alto il lume da ritrare di naturale"; Pedretti 1977, vol. 1, p. 331. See also Leonardo's posthumously compiled painting treatise, the *Libro di pittura* 1995 (C. Urb., fol. 40r); McMahon 1956, vol. 1, no. 129; translated in Kemp 1981, p. 214.
8. Such techniques of rubbing in the strokes for shadows (stumping) are described in Armenini 1587, 1977, p. 107.
9. Bambach 1999a, pp. 257–62.

ANDREA DEL VERROCCHIO

3. *Head of a Young Woman in Three-Quarter View Facing to the Left* (recto)
Head of a Young Woman in Three-Quarter View (verso)

Charcoal reworked with black chalk, highlighted with white chalk, on paper with a layer of cream color preparation (recto); charcoal on paper with a layer of cream color preparation (verso), 324 × 273 mm (12¾ × 10¾ in.)
The British Museum, London 1895-9-15-785

PROVENANCE: Jean Pietersz Zoomer, Amsterdam (1641–1724; Lugt 1511); Count Antoine François Andréossy, London, Vienna, and Constantinople (1761–1828; Lugt under 119, 2445) (according to Robinson: perhaps sold, Paris [Pérignon], March 11, 1816, lot 70: *Louini* [sic], *Rome, XVe siècle. Une tête de jeune fille, élégamment coiffée en cheveux, beau dessin à la pierre noir*); John Malcolm, Poltalloch and London (1805–1893; Lugt 1780).

LITERATURE: Robinson 1876, no. 333; Morelli 1893, pp. 270–71; British Museum 1895, no. 18; Mackowsky 1901, pp. 89ff., fig. 73; Berenson 1903, vol. 1, p. 34, vol. 2, p. 179, no. 2782; Cruttwell 1904, pp. 112–14, pls. 26, 27; Thiis 1913, p. 119; Van Marle 1923–38, vol. 11, pp. 529–31, fig. 328f; Popp 1927a, pl. 38; Popp 1928, p. 36, no. 15; Valentiner 1930, pp. 50, 52–54, fig. 4; Bertini 1935, pp. 470f.; Berenson 1938, vol. 1, pp. 47, 48, 55, 75, vol. 2, p. 359, vol. 3, fig. 125, no. 2782; Popham and Pouncey 1950, pp. 160–61, no. 258; Berenson 1961, vol. 1, pp. 85, 92, 99, 117, vol. 2, p. 608, vol. 3, fig. 120, no. 2782; Valentiner 1966, pp. 66–67, fig. 14; Pliny the Elder 1968, book 35, pp. 318–19, chap. 36, l. 79; Passavant 1969, pp. 58, 192, no. D5; Richter 1970, vol. 1, p. 341, no. 583; Seymour 1971, pp. 78, 172, no. 5; Pedretti 1982a, pp. 29–30, figs. 17, 18; Cadogan 1983c, pp. 373–75, figs. 6, 7; British Museum 1996, pp. 30–31, no. 7; Wiemers 1996, pp. 140–41, fig. 125; Butterfield 1997, pp. 185–86, figs. 246–47; Brown 1998b, pp. 126–27, fig. 118; Bambach 1999a, p. 259; Rubin and Wright 1999, pp. 184–87, no. 29; Marani 2000b, pp. 12, 15; Ames-Lewis 2001, p. 10, n. 13; Ames-Lewis 2002, p. 8, nos. 7, 8; Clayton 2002–3, pp. 143–44, fig. 47.

By the late 1470s and early 1480s, Andrea del Verrocchio's style attained an extraordinary monumentality and sculptural presence of form. Here, these qualities are exquisitely integrated with his pioneering sfumato technique of drawing. Verrocchio's authorship of the large-scale drawings on each side of this sheet has not been questioned since Giovanni Morelli first made the attribution in 1893, regarding them as the very foundation in the connoisseurship of the master's corpus. The design of the young woman's head, especially on the more boldly sketched verso of the sheet, is similar to that of the reclining goddess in a much discussed drawing, *Venus Wounded by Love* (Uffizi, Florence, 212 E; fig. 79), which is thought to be by Verrocchio, with the possible collaboration of the young Leonardo.[1] The Uffizi drawing is often linked to a recorded but lost painted banner that Verrocchio designed to celebrate Giuliano de' Medici's victory on January 29, 1475, in a tournament held in the Piazza Santa Croce in Florence and which became known as "La giostra di Giuliano." More convincingly, the British Museum sheet has also been compared to the Pistoia Cathedral altarpiece (the *Madonna di Piazza*; fig. 122), where the enthroned Virgin appears in a very similar pose, though more simply coiffed. The famous altarpiece was commissioned from Verrocchio by the executors of Bishop Donato de' Medici's will, probably about 1478–79; it was intended for the Chiesino della Madonna di Piazza, an oratory originally adjacent to the cathedral that was still unfinished in November 1485 (see cat. nos. 7, 8). Stylistic analysis of the altarpiece suggests the extensive participation of Lorenzo di Credi (cat. nos. 7, 8), to whom Giorgio Vasari attributed the painting. According to the present scholarly consensus, Verrocchio probably executed at least some of the preparatory drawings for the altarpiece, since the documents attest to his being awarded the commission on the basis of a contractual drawing. To judge from its monumental scale, the British Museum *Head of a Young Woman* must be an unused cartoon. Considering the extraordinary labor and cost of producing carefully drawn cartoons, it seems hardly worth an artist's effort to have made one for a painted banner, however prestigious the commission of the *giostra* of Giuliano de' Medici may have been. It appears more likely that the British Museum drawings were produced for an important painting in which some of the labor of execution was to be delegated to assistants, and their relation to an early planning stage for the *Madonna di Piazza* seems worthy of exploration.

Verrocchio used the black chalk in extremely subtle pictorial ways to intensify the tonal depth of the drawing against the warm cream color of the paper, combining the techniques of smudging, wetting of the laid-in chalk with the brush, and accenting with cool white highlights. This sheet with its deli-

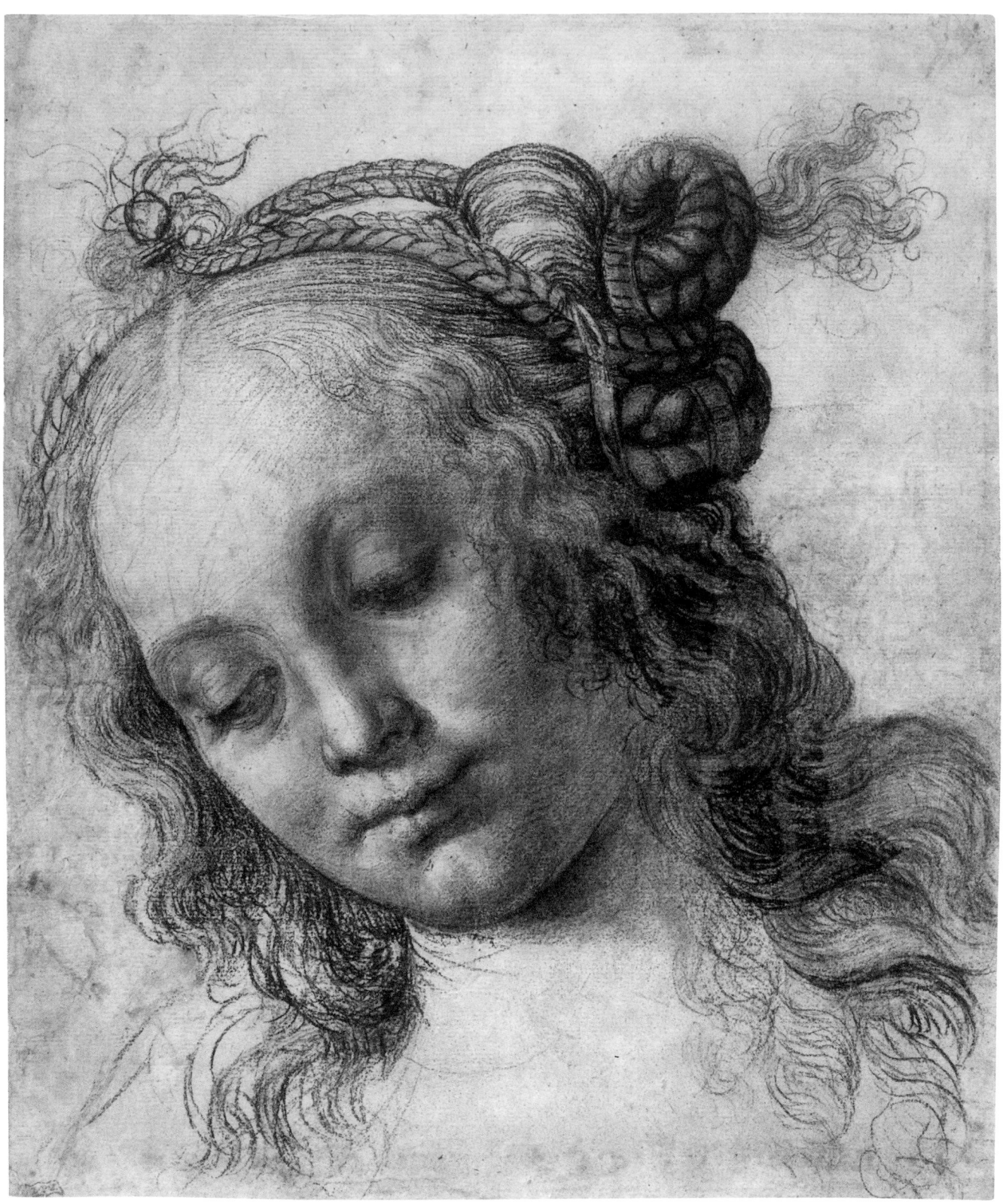

Cat. 3r

cately calibrated axes of the woman's facial features, and the more boldly sketched verso, can only hint at the scope of the artist's innovation.   CCB

1. Opinions on the authorship of the famous Uffizi drawing (fig. 79) vary greatly. See Berenson 1903, no. 2788 (Lorenzo di Credi); Passavant 1969, pp. 58, 192, no. d6 (Verrocchio); Petrioli Tofani 1986, pp. 93–94, no. 212 E (Verrocchio); Marani 1989, pp. 13–14, fig. 9 (Leonardo);

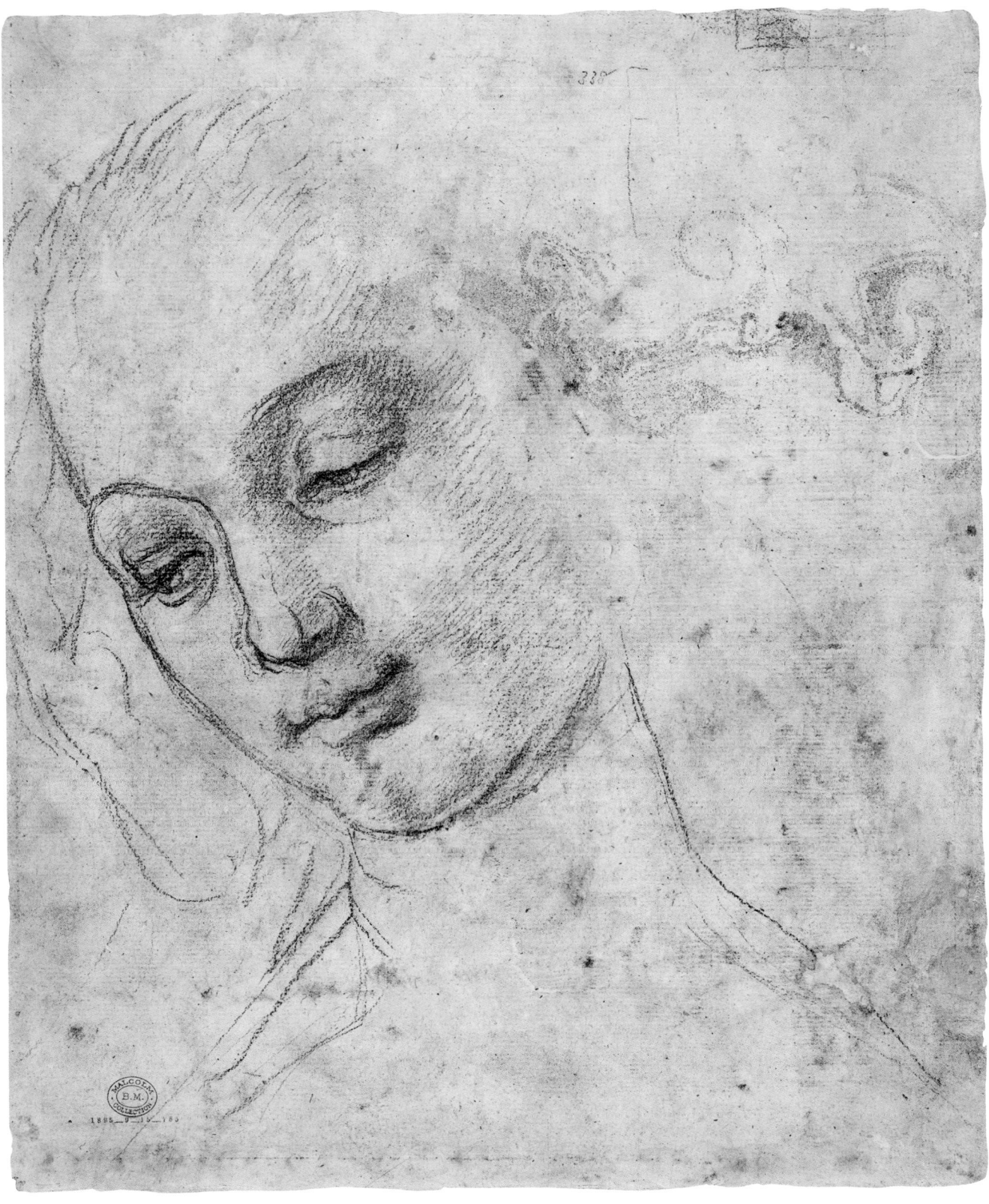

Cat. 3v

Gianvittorio Dillon in Petrioli Tofani 1992, pp. 150–51, no. 7.5 (Verrocchio); Brown 1994b (Verrocchio and Leonardo); Butterfield 1997, pp. 185, 188, 253, fig. 249 (Verrocchio and Leonardo); Brown 1998b, pp. 123–26, 207, nn. 17–19 (Verrocchio and Leonardo); Marani 2000b, pp. 31–34 (Verrocchio and Leonardo); and Pietro C. Marani's essay in the present catalogue.

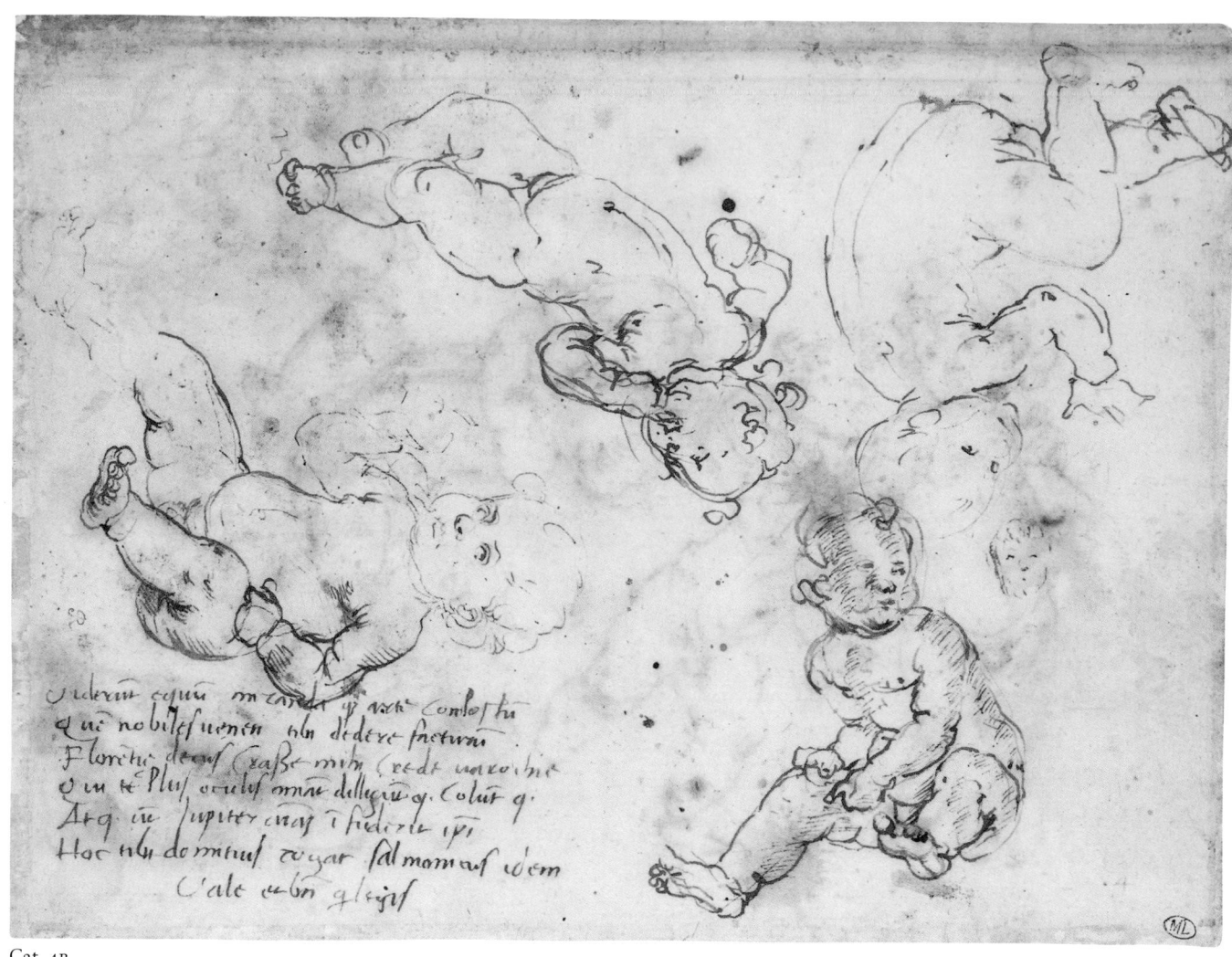

Cat. 4R

ANDREA DEL VERROCCHIO

4. *Sketches of Infants* (recto and verso)

Pen and dark brown ink, over traces of leadpoint or soft black chalk, 158 × 210 mm (6¼ × 8¼ in.)

Inscribed in pen and brown ink on recto by late-fifteenth- or early-sixteenth-century hand with a poem: *Videru[n]t equu[m] miranda q[u]e arte confectu[m] / Que[m] nobiles ueneti tibi dedere facturu[m] / Flore[n]tiae decus Crasse mihi crede varochie / Qui te Plus oculis ama[n]t dilligu[n]tq[ue] colu[n]tq[ue] / Atq[ue] cu[m] Jupiter animas[?] i[n]fuderit ip[s]i / Hoc tibi dominus rogat Salmonicus idem / Vale et bene [?] q[ui] legis.*

Watermark: Six-pointed star (not in Briquet)

Département des Arts Graphiques du Musée du Louvre, Paris RF 2

PROVENANCE: Jonathan Richardson, Senior, London (1665–1745; Lugt 2183, 2184, Suppl. 2183, 2983, 2984, 2993–2996); Comte Nils Barck, Paris and Madrid (1820–1896; Lugt 1959); Comte Thibaudeau-Wertheimer; his sale, December 1871; acquired then by the Louvre, museum stamp (Lugt 1886a).

LITERATURE: Morelli 1893, p. 271; Mackowsky 1901, pp. 90–91; Berenson 1903, vol. 1, p. 33, vol. 2, p. 179, no. 2783; Cruttwell 1904, pp. 70–71; Thiis 1913, p. 161; Van Marle 1923–38, vol. 11, pp. 532–33; Berenson 1938, vol. 1, pp. 46–47, vol. 2, p. 359; Berenson 1961, vol. 1, pp. 85, 98, vol. 2, p. 608; Heil 1969, p. 274, fig. 8; Passavant 1969, pp. 60, 193–94, no. D10; Seymour 1971, p. 173, n. 7; Ames-Lewis 1981, p. 108; Vertova 1981, p. 48; Cadogan 1983c, pp. 371–73, figs. 4, 5; Adorno 1991, pp. 154, 269–70, figs. 94, 95; Antonio Natali in Petrioli Tofani 1992, pp. 132–33, no. 6.5; Butterfield 1997, pp. 12–15, 189, 202, figs. 13, 251; Brown 1998b, pp. 37–38, fig. 28; Bambach 1999a, pp. 83, 403, n. 20; Rubin and Wright 1999, pp. 206–7, no. 36.

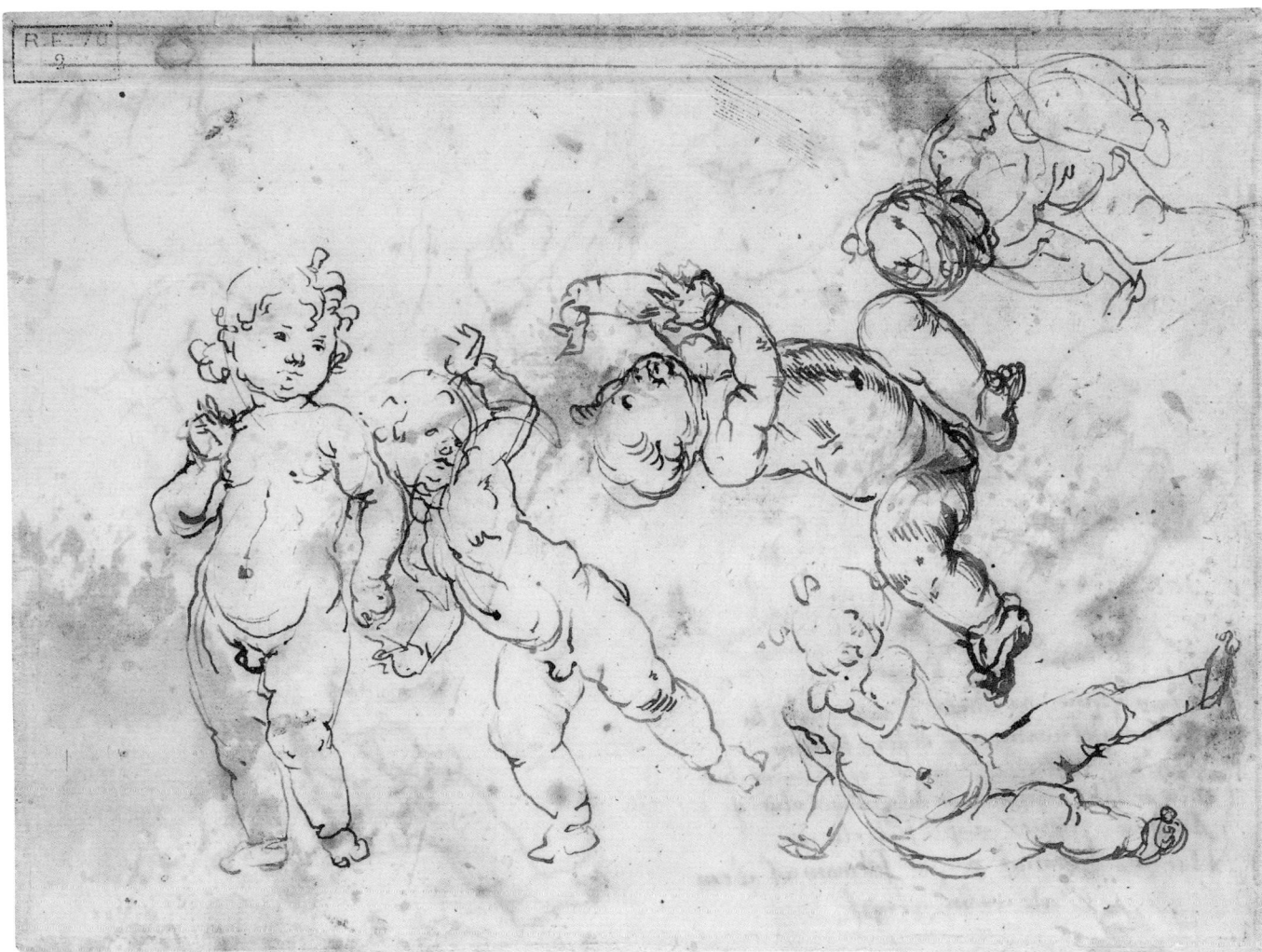

Cat. 4v

An unknown contemporary author wrote a Roman-style encomium in Latin on the lower left of the recto of this sheet of animated life sketches, praising Andrea del Verrocchio's bronze equestrian statue of Bartolomeo Colleoni (Campo Santi Giovanni e Paolo, Venice; figs. 125, 162):

> They see the horse, constructed by that marvelous art
> Which, about to be made, the Venetian nobles give to you.
> Crasius, the glory of Florence, believe me Varochie [Verrocchio]
> Those who love you and esteem you and cultivate you with
>   more than their eyes
> And when Jupiter will pour souls into the thing itself,
> Lord Salmonicus asks you this same thing.
> Goodbye and good health to you who read.[1]

In 1481–82 Verrocchio had secured the commission from the Venetian Republic for the enormous Colleoni monument, and by April 1486 he was in Venice working on the models for the sculpture.[2] By the time Verrocchio died, in June 1488, he had brought the models to an advanced state of completion; the casting of the statue in bronze was entrusted to Alessandro Leopardi in 1490 and was finished in the spring of 1496. The allusions in the poem inscribed on the Louvre sheet (which is posthumous) provided a basis for the Marquis de Chennevière's attribution of the studies to Verrocchio in 1879, in his review of an exhibition of old master drawings at the École des Beaux-Arts, Paris. Reaffirmed by the great connoisseur Giovanni Morelli in 1893, the attribution of the Louvre draw-

253

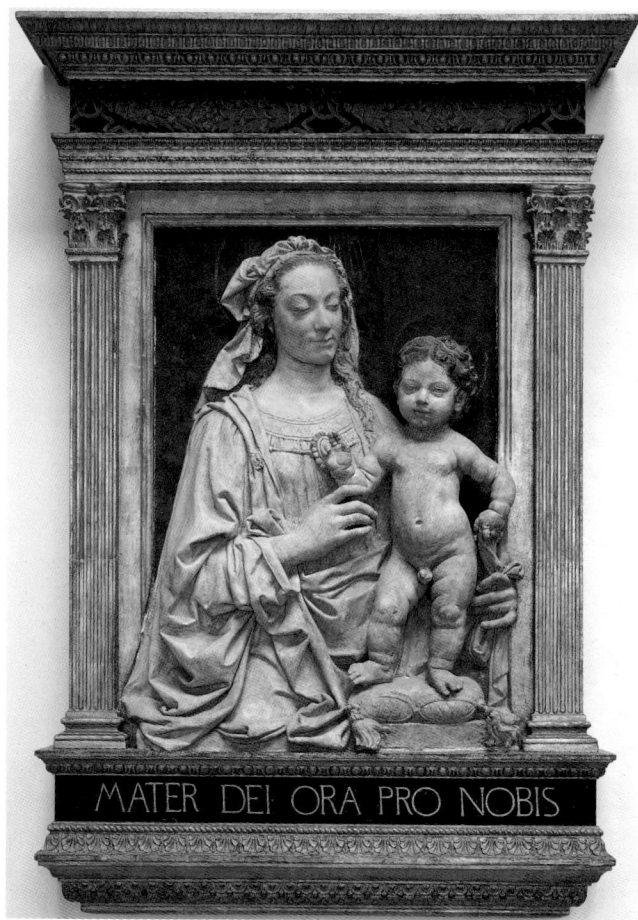

Fig. 118. Andrea del Verrocchio, *Madonna and Child*. Polychromed terracotta relief (from the Ospedale di Santa Maria Nuova), 86 × 66 cm. Museo Nazionale del Bargello, Florence 415

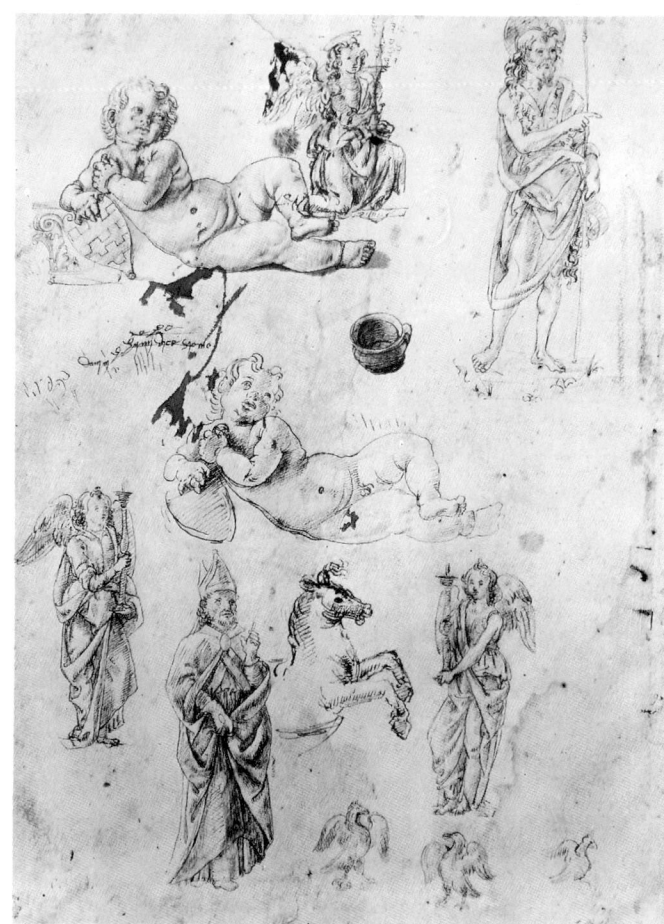

Fig. 120. Attributed to Francesco di Simone Ferrucci, *Sheet of Studies* (recto). Pen and brown ink, brush and brown wash, over traces of black chalk or leadpoint, some red chalk, on paper partly washed rose, 276 × 195 mm. Musée Condé, Chantilly 20 (14)

ing to Verrocchio has been accepted by scholars ever since, on the strength of stylistic comparisons with the great master's sculptures, particularly with the *Madonna and Child* reliefs (fig. 118).

The Louvre sheet probably dates from the 1470s at the latest, based on the similarity of the facial and the body type of the putti to those of the infant Christ in the *Madonna and Child* terracotta (Museo Nazionale del Bargello, Florence; fig. 118).[3] On the recto, the pose of the reclining putto toward the center of the left border of the sheet closely evokes that of the *Sleeping Youth* terracotta (Staatliche Museen zu Berlin), from the 1470s as well. The design of this recumbent putto goes back to a lost prototype, for it also turns up in fairly precise form among Verrocchio's workshop pieces: a lost terracotta (formerly Kaiser-Friedrich Museum, Berlin),[4] a bronze (Metropolitan Museum of Art, New York, 09.155.1), and a marble that has sometimes been attributed to the great sculptor himself (M. H. de Young Memorial Museum, San

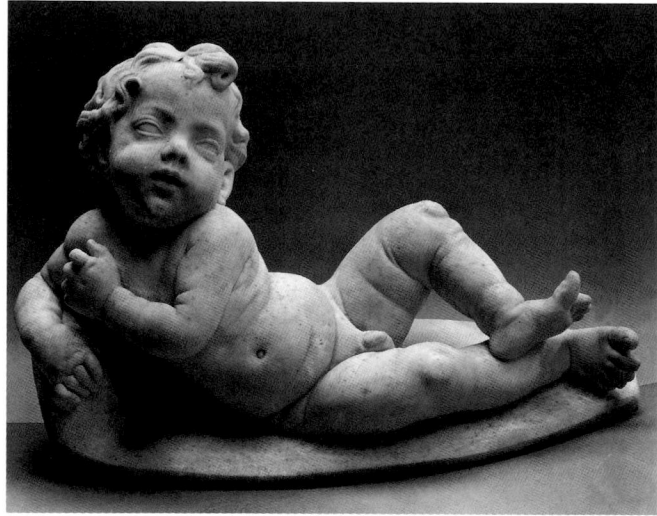

Fig. 119. Andrea del Verrocchio (?), *Reclining Putto*. Marble, 28.6 × 52.1 cm. M. H. de Young Memorial Museum, San Francisco

Francisco; fig. 119). One of the pages from the sketchbook that is traditionally attributed to Francesco di Simone Ferrucci (Musée Condé, Chantilly, 20[14]; fig. 120) also records such a reclining infant statue, which shows the unidentified coat of arms of a family.[5] Moreover, Andrew Butterfield rightly pointed out the stylistic connection between the poses of the putti on the verso of the Louvre sheet and the frieze of dancing putti adorning the monumental bronze bell of San Marco, *La Piagnona*, a commission by Cosimo de' Medici that Verrocchio probably finished about 1468.

The artist's bravura with the pen in the Louvre sheet is innovative in the history of figural sketching. Verrocchio captured the kinetic vitality of the children's movement, seen from different points of view in space, with only a few well-placed strokes of the pen. The spontaneity of his drawing and his command of volume are simply breathtaking, and in the lower two sketches, especially, the artist conveyed the pleasing roundness of the forms almost entirely through the rapidly turning contours, with almost no internal modeling at all. This rapid, sculptural manner of summarizing the figure was formative for the young Leonardo. It characterizes his sketches for the *Madonna of the Cat* and the *Madonna and Child with a Bowl of Fruit* from the late 1470s (cat. nos. 18, 19, 22), and even his mature drawings of nearly thirty years later (cat. nos. 94, 97).

CCB

1. Translated by Katherine Welch, June 18, 2002.
2. Summary of documents and history of the Colleoni project in Butterfield 1997, pp. 159–83, 232–36, no. 26.
3. On the dating of the terracottas, see Butterfield 1997, pp. 215–16, nos. 12, 13.
4. Illustrated in Heil 1969, p. 275, figs. 5, 6.
5. Discussed in Musée Condé 1995, pp. 51–54, no. 6.

ANDREA DEL VERROCCHIO

5. *Study for a Funerary Monument to Doge Andrea Vendramin*

Leadpoint, partly reworked with pen and brown ink, brush and brown wash, and some ruling in leadpoint; glued to secondary paper support, 272 × 174 mm (10¾ × 6⅞ in.)
Victoria and Albert Museum, London 2314

PROVENANCE: Vincenzo (Maria) Borghini (?), Florence (1515–1580; Lugt under 929); Sir Thomas Lawrence, Bristol and London (1769–1830; Lugt 2445); Samuel Woodburn, London (1786–1853; Lugt 2584, 2591; Suppl. 2378a); Woodburn sale, Christie's, London, June 8, 1860, lot 1053, bought for the museum.

LITERATURE: Van Marle 1923–38, vol. 9, p. 582 n., vol. 13, p. 269; Dussler 1926, p. 295; Clark 1929; Degenhart 1932a; Degenhart 1932b, p. 105, n. 65; Berenson 1933–34, pp. 262–63, fig. 27; Middeldorf 1934; Möller 1935; Berenson 1938, vol. 1, pp. 68, 75, n. 1, vol. 2, p. 73, vol. 3, fig. 130, no. 699 B (Lorenzo di Credi); Valentiner 1950, p. 119 n.; Berenson 1961, vol. 1, p. 117, vol. 2, p. 132, no. 699 B (Lorenzo di Credi); Dalli Regoli 1965; Dalli Regoli 1966, pp. 133–34, no. 66 (Lorenzo di Credi), pl. 53; Passavant 1969, p. 194, no. D11 (reworked by another hand); Seymour 1971, pp. 28–29, pl. 24; Grossman 1972, p. 18, fig. 5; Stedman Sheard 1978; Ward-Jackson 1979, pp. 24–26, no. 18 (partly reworked by another hand, Lorenzo di Credi?); Cadogan 1983c, pp. 378, 380, 383, fig. 16; Pedretti 1989f, p. 33, fig. 39; Stedman Sheard 1992, pp. 78–85; Antonio Natali in Petrioli Tofani 1992, p. 244, under no. 12.4; Butterfield 1997, pp. 185, 191, fig. 256; Rubin and Wright 1999–2000, pp. 146–47, no. 11; Marani 2000b, pp. 251, 296, n. 51.

With his sfumato technique Verrocchio achieved in this magnificent working sketch an ineffable delicacy of touch. The dynamic, highly graded tonal balance of the drawing layers—that in leadpoint and those of the reworkings in pen and ink with wash—shows the technique at its most original and effective. The ink reworkings of the allegorical figures and putti delineate details with greater precision and deepen the shadows, while the wash reworkings softly unify the modeling, for a sculptural effect. Although the pen-and-ink reworking of the bowl part of the monument seems slightly harsh in its linearity, it may be original, as it advances the level of detail in the design. These reworkings of the leadpoint drawing, therefore, seem to be highly integrated and highly functional and are not likely to be retouchings by another artist or by a later restorer.

The artist proposed a large, unusually elaborate console wall tomb under an arched canopy that is decorated with an antique-style coffered vault and flanking pairs of garland-bearing putti on the side brackets. He conceived the funerary urn below, intended to hold the ashes of the deceased, in the shape of a corbel, a typical fifteenth-century Venetian tomb type. In the best late-fifteenth-century Florentine tradition, however, the monument soars like a goldsmith's fantasy of precious filigree and small solidly carved figures against the dramatic backdrop of a curtain. The artist omitted an effigy of the deceased, focusing instead on symbolic representations of his virtue. At the top, the urn is surmounted by three standing female allegorical figures: the one standing higher and in the center is Justice, holding in her left hand her attribute of the scales. The attributes of the two fluttering female figures on either side are less clear in the exquisite gray smoke of the leadpoint drawing. That on the right probably holds the laurel wreath of Fame, and that on the left the cornucopia of Plenty and the olive branch of Peace. The soaring figures recall those in the marble funerary monument of Cardinal Niccolò Forteguerri (Pistoia Cathedral), begun by Verrocchio and his workshop in 1477–83 and exquisitely prepared in a terracotta *bozzetto*, or sketch model (Victoria and Albert Museum, London; fig. 121). On the shoulder of the urn in the present drawing, two flanking seated putti hold heraldic shields containing what appears to be the faintly drawn arms of the Vendramin family, while the ovals at the belly of the urn are decorated with three additional heraldic devices. Within the lateral ovals are crossed cornucopias, and within the central oval is the lion of Saint Mark, the emblem of the Venetian Republic and of its highest magistrate, the doge. Three delightful putti below, standing on a base at the bottom tip of the corbel, act as the Atlas-like weight bearers of the large cinerary urn.

This unfinished working drawing may be identified with a reference in Giorgio Vasari's vita of Verrocchio (1550 and 1568) to "a design for a tomb, made by him in Venice for a doge" that was among the drawings by Verrocchio that Vasari had admired in the collector's album (*libro de' disegni*) of his friend the Florentine humanist Vincenzo Borghini.[1] Since Verrocchio's drawing includes the lion of Saint Mark and, apparently, the arms of the Vendramin family, it seems safe to assume that the patron of the tomb was Andrea Vendramin, who was elected doge in 1476 and who died in 1478. Moreover,

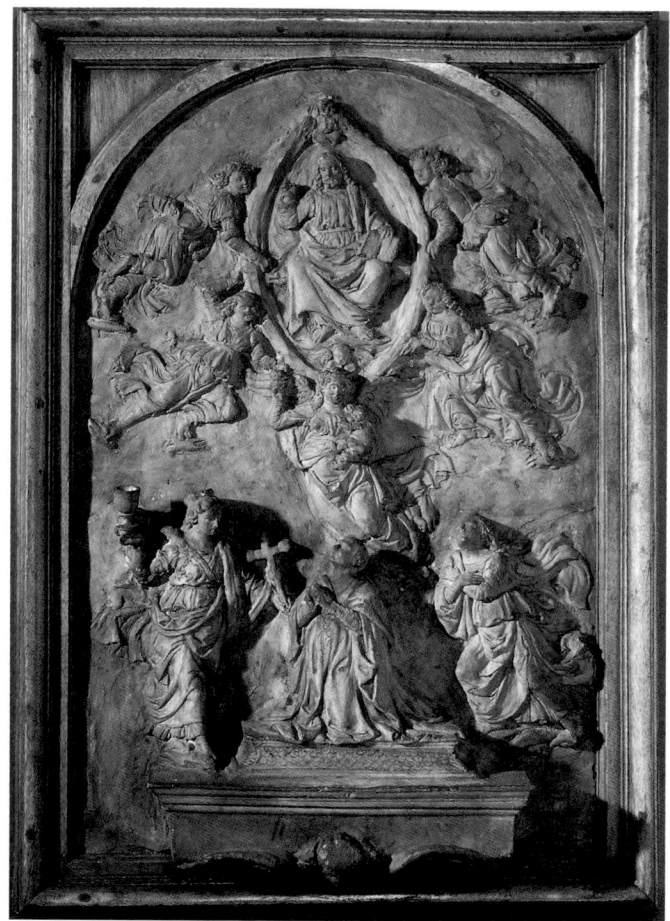

Fig. 121. Andrea del Verrocchio, *Christ in Glory*. Sketch model for the Monument of Cardinal Niccolò Forteguerri. Terracotta relief, 39.4 × 26.7 cm. Victoria and Albert Museum, London 7599-1861

Vendramin's heraldic motto prominently alluded to the virtue of Justice, a feature that conforms with the iconography seen in Verrocchio's drawing.[2] A few years earlier, when the wealthy Vendramin was procurator of Saint Mark's, he had made a will, on March 24, 1472, in which he stipulated that his heirs erect him a lavish tomb. Verrocchio's tomb design must date from sometime between 1478 and 1488; the patron died in 1478, and the artist died in Venice in 1488. Whether or not it was death that impeded the artist from executing the project, the tomb was completely redesigned and finished in 1493–94 by the sculptor Tullio Lombardo. It was finally erected in the church of Santa Maria dei Servi and was moved to its present location, in the church of Santi Giovanni e Paolo, in the nineteenth century.

Verrocchio's tomb design must have achieved some fame, since it was emulated by artists of his workshop and also

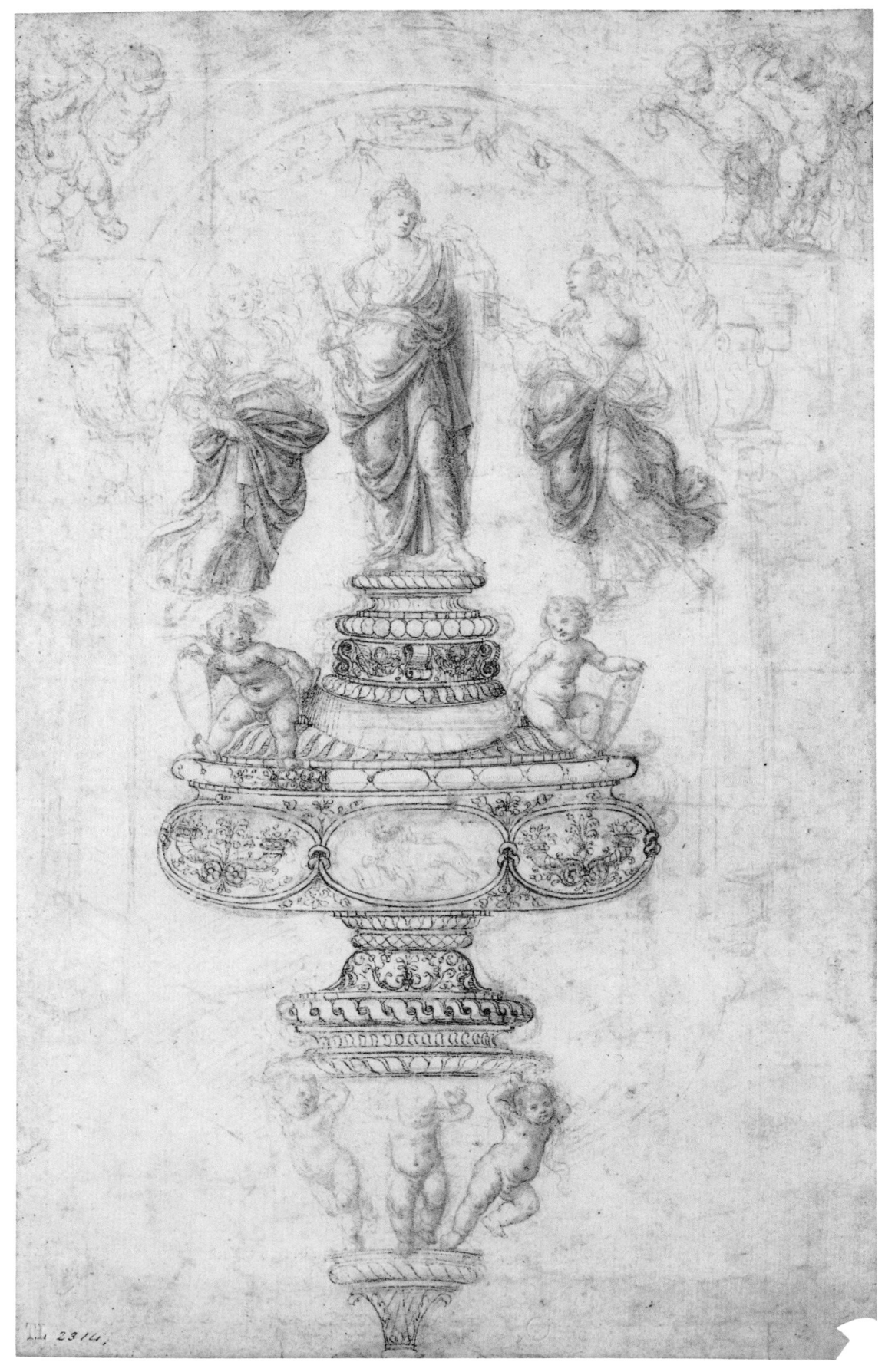

elicited a positive mention by Vasari. A drawing in pen and ink with wash, of much less inspired execution, reprises Verrocchio's tomb design with only variations of iconographic detail (Musée du Louvre, Paris, 1788). The Louvre tomb design was in Vasari's own *libro de' disegni,* and his probably correct attribution of the drawing to Lorenzo di Credi is inscribed on the mount. Seen in this context, Vasari's succinct reference to Verrocchio's tomb design in the drawings album of Vincenzo Borghini seems quite informed and should carry some weight as evidence for the attribution of the Victoria and Albert Museum sheet to Verrocchio himself. Lorenzo di Credi has sometimes been proposed as the author of the Victoria and Albert sheet. According to Vasari, Lorenzo was trained by a goldsmith before his arrival in Verrocchio's workshop,[3] and he apparently became Verrocchio's right hand, especially as a painter, when Leonardo left the workshop. Verrocchio's will of June 25, 1488, declared Lorenzo his heir and executor and also entrusted him to see to completion the Colleoni equestrian monument in Venice, a project in which Lorenzo was apparently uninterested, for soon afterward he sold the rights to the sculpture to the Florentine sculptor Giovanni d'Andrea di Domenico.[4] Since Lorenzo is not known to have been a sculptor of note, the attribution to him of an innovative sculptural project, and of the sketchy drawing in progress that details this project, does not seem convincing.   CCB

1. Vasari–Milanesi 1906, vol. 3, p. 364: "e fra gli altri, un disegno di sepoltura, da lui fatto a Vinegia per un doge."
2. Möller 1935: "Domi justitia adeo colui ut proprio nec pepercerit filio."
3. Vasari–Milanesi 1906, vol. 4, p. 563.
4. Butterfield 1997, pp. 234–35, no. 26.

ATTRIBUTED TO ANDREA DEL VERROCCHIO

6. *Child in Bust Length in Three-Quarter View Facing to the Right*

Metalpoint reworked with brush and brown wash, highlighted with white gouache on beige prepared paper; arch motif in pen and brown ink, brush and brown wash with reddish wash accents, 229 × 158 mm (9 × 6 3/16 in.)
The Syndics of the Fitzwilliam Museum, Cambridge, England. Purchased with grants from the National Lottery through the Heritage Lottery Fund, the National Art Collections Fund and the Pilgrim Trust 2930

PROVENANCE: Giorgio Vasari (?), Arezzo, Florence, and Rome (1511–1574); Augustus Arthur VanSittart, Cambridge (1824–1882; Lugt Suppl. 2479ter) (1862; as Baccio Bandinelli).

LITERATURE: Vasari Society 1905–15, part 2, p. 5, no. 1 (school of Verrocchio); Royal Academy of Arts 1930, p. 17, no. 56 (Verrocchio School); Popham 1930–31, p. 17, no. 56, pl. 47A (school of Verrocchio); Degenhart 1932a, p. 444; Berenson 1933–34, p. 262 (Lorenzo di Credi, Verrocchio School); Trombetti 1936, pp. 378–79; Berenson 1938, vol. 1, p. 67, vol. 2, p. 70, no. 670C (Lorenzo di Credi); Hasselt 1960, pp. 17–19 (Verrocchio); Berenson 1961, vol. 1, p. 114, vol. 2, p. 127, no. 670 C (Lorenzo di Credi); Dalli Regoli 1966, p. 108, no. 19 (Lorenzo di Credi); Grossman 1968, p. 67 (Verrocchio); Passavant 1969, p. 194, no. D2, p. 101; Grossman 1974, pp. 7–8 (Verrocchio); Brown 1987, pp. 51, 64–65, n. 88 (Verrocchio); Brown 1998b, pp. 126, 208 n. 30, fig. 117 (Verrocchio).

Acquired in 1862 with an illogical attribution to the Florentine sculptor Baccio Bandinelli (1493–1560), this delicately rendered life study was then attributed to Andrea del Verrocchio by tradition until 1933–34, when Bernard Berenson gave it to Lorenzo di Credi, Leonardo's younger colleague in Verrocchio's workshop, at the moment of Credi's greatest emulation of Leonardo.[1] Berenson thought the Fitzwilliam sheet to be an early work and also attributed to the artist much of the actual painting of the Pistoia altarpiece, the *Madonna di Piazza* (see cat. nos. 7, 8; fig. 122). Berenson's penetrating reasoning regarding the Fitzwilliam sheet is worth quoting: "[I]t is so Leonardesque, however, that Leonardo could scarcely have disclaimed it. If it is [Credi's] it offers a good instance of what a mediocre artist can achieve with the example of a great but kindred genius before him, if he has the luck to encounter it when this technical training is complete but custom and customers have not yet shaped him into a mould for producing the same article to the end of his days."[2] Berenson's statement leaves the door open for an attribution to a more accomplished artist, and it seems probable to the present author that the early traditional attribution to

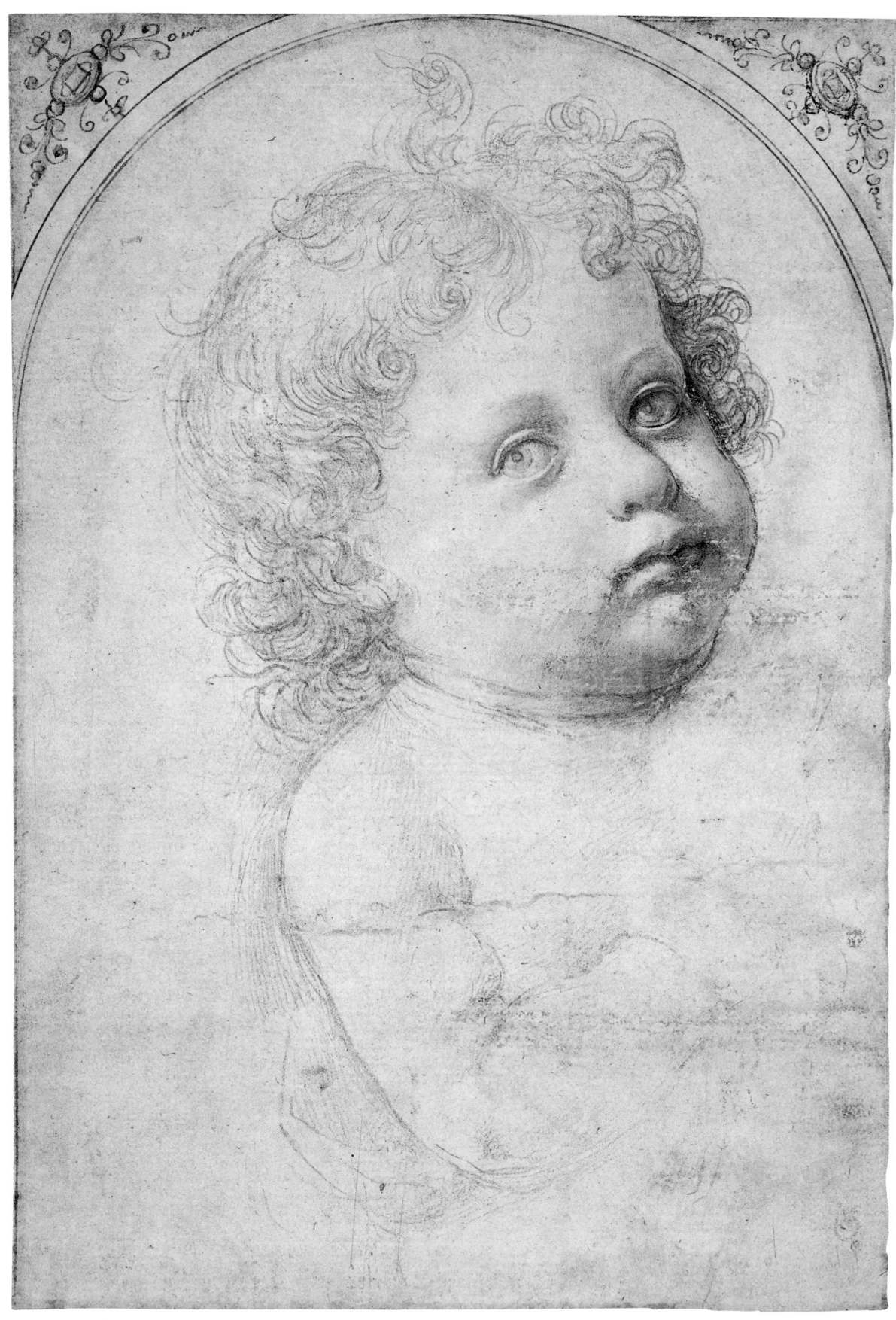

Cat. 6 *(actual size)*

259

Andrea del Verrocchio himself is correct, particularly if one considers the high quality of execution and stylistic vocabulary of the Fitzwilliam sheet. The attribution to Verrocchio has been advocated repeatedly by Sheldon Grossman and David Alan Brown, as well as by Nicholas Turner in an oral communication in 1987.[3] The figural type of the child is similar to that of the seated infant seen toward the lower right in the Louvre sheet that is securely attributed to Verrocchio (cat. no. 4).

The infant's head is refined with a complex sfumato technique of drawing that, though in a different medium, seems identical in its extraordinary tonal subtleties to that of the beautiful, larger *Head of a Young Woman* by Verrocchio at the British Museum (cat. no. 3). Moreover, the Fitzwilliam drawing exhibits a similar sculptural monumentality of form, a crucial element that all too often escaped the accomplished

Lorenzo di Credi in the 1470s and 1480s. The delightful infant on the Fitzwilliam sheet is a physical type that does not seem to occur in any of Lorenzo's extant drawings or numerous paintings but evokes instead the standing Christ in Verrocchio's exquisite *Madonna and Child* terracotta (Museo Nazionale del Bargello, Florence; fig. 118), from the 1470s.[4] The Fitzwilliam study probably served as an exploration of the figure of Christ or Saint John the Baptist for a relief or a painting, and probably dates from the 1470s, rather than a full decade later, as Grossman and Brown have proposed.   CCB

1. Berenson 1933–34, pp. 193–214, 241–64.
2. Berenson 1938, vol. 2, p. 70.
3. Oral communication to David Scrase, as conveyed to the author, August 2002.
4. Butterfield 1997, pp. 215–16, no. 13.

LORENZO DI CREDI (LORENZO DI ANDREA DI ODERIGO)

(Florence, ca. 1457–Florence, 1536)

7. *Standing Saint John the Baptist (Study for the Pistoia Altarpiece)*

Metalpoint, reworked with pen and brown ink, brush with brown and gray wash, highlighted with white gouache, on light red-orange prepared paper; glued to secondary paper support, 262 × 101 mm (10⁵⁄₁₆ × 3¹⁵⁄₁₆ in.); enlarged with similar paper, 276 × 128 mm (10⁷⁄₈ × 5 in.)
Département des Arts Graphiques du Musée du Louvre, Paris RF 455

PROVENANCE: Pierre-Jean Mariette, Paris (1694–1774; Lugt 1852); his sale, Paris, 1775, part of lot 186 (Bellini); Comte Moriz von Fries, Vienna (1777–1826; Lugt 2903); Comte Nils Barck, Paris and Madrid (1820–1896; Lugt 1959); Aimé-Charles-Horace His de la Salle, Paris (1795–1878; Lugt 1333); by bequest to the Musée du Louvre in 1878; museum stamp (Lugt 1886).

LITERATURE: Louvre 1881, p. 34; Ephrussi 1882, p. 242; Bode 1899, pp. 393–94; Mackowsky 1901, p. 96; Berenson 1903, vol. 1, pp. 44–45, vol. 2, p. 37, no. 725; Frizzoni 1904, p. 98; Liphart 1912, p. 202; Gronau 1913; Chiappelli 1925–26, p. 60 (Verrocchio); Trombetti 1929, p. 210; Valentiner 1930, pp. 57–58, fig. 11; Van Marle 1923–38, vol. 13, p. 321; Degenhart 1932a, p. 412, fig. 29 (Verrocchio and Credi); Berenson 1938, vol. 1, pp. 66, 74 n. 2, vol. 2, p. 75, vol. 3, fig. 138, no. 725 (Lorenzo di Credi); Chastel 1950, p. 16 (Verrocchio); Valentiner 1950, p. 142; Passavant 1959, pp. 53, 238 (Verrocchio and Credi); Berenson 1961, vol. 1, p. 114, vol. 2, p. 135, vol. 3, fig. 134, no. 725; Dalli Regoli 1965, pp. 113–14, 37–38, fig. 31, p. 43 n. 12; Dalli

Regoli 1966, pp. 15–16, 105–6, 113–14, no. 13, fig. 30; Andrews 1968, p. 43, under no. D642; Passavant 1969, pp. 191–92, no. D4, fig. 91 (Verrocchio and Credi); Bacou 1981, p. 251; Louvre 1989–90, pp. 88–89, no. 22; Roberta Bartoli in Petrioli Tofani 1992, pp. 74–75, no. 2.30; Wiemers 1996, pp. 153–54, fig. 40; Brown 1998b, pp. 153–54, fig. 146; Kemp 1998, p. 33 n. 6 (Verrocchio); Rubin and Wright 1999–2000, pp. 166–67, no. 20.

This preliminary study, characterized by sculptural presence and delicate luminosity, was for the figure of Saint John the Baptist standing on the left of the enthroned Virgin and Child in the famous Pistoia altarpiece (the *Madonna di Piazza*; fig. 122; cat. nos. 3, 8). The altarpiece was originally conceived for the oratory that was adjacent to the Pistoia Cathedral, the Chiesino della Madonna di Piazza (now the Chapel of the Sacrament in the Cathedral). The Louvre study was drawn from a posed live model (presumably a workshop assistant, or *garzone*), to judge from the man's less idealized features. As is clear from the pentimenti outlines, it took the artist a few attempts to find the correct balance of the body for the pose, especially the placement of the legs and feet on the ground. Unlike the final painted saint, the figure in the Louvre

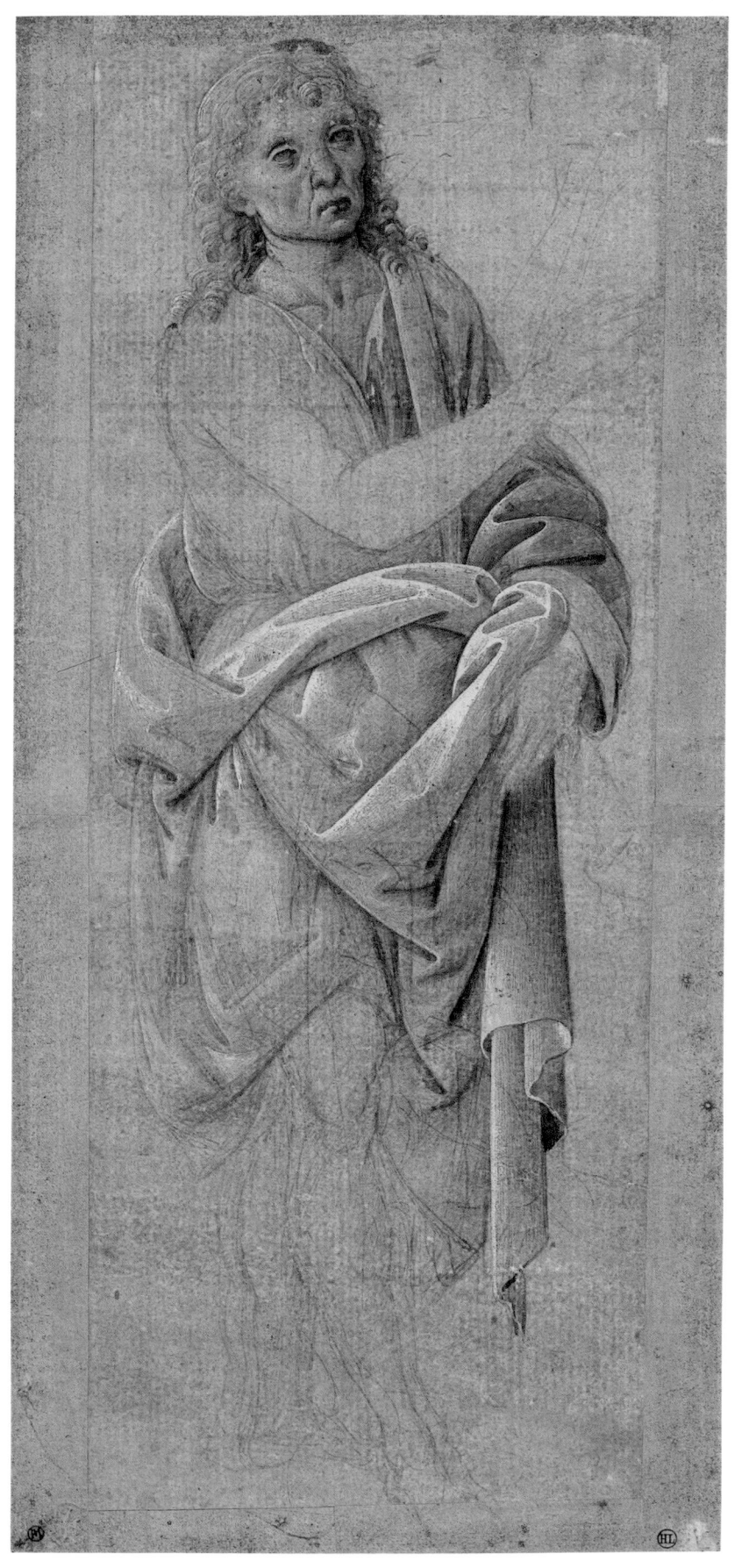

Cat. 7

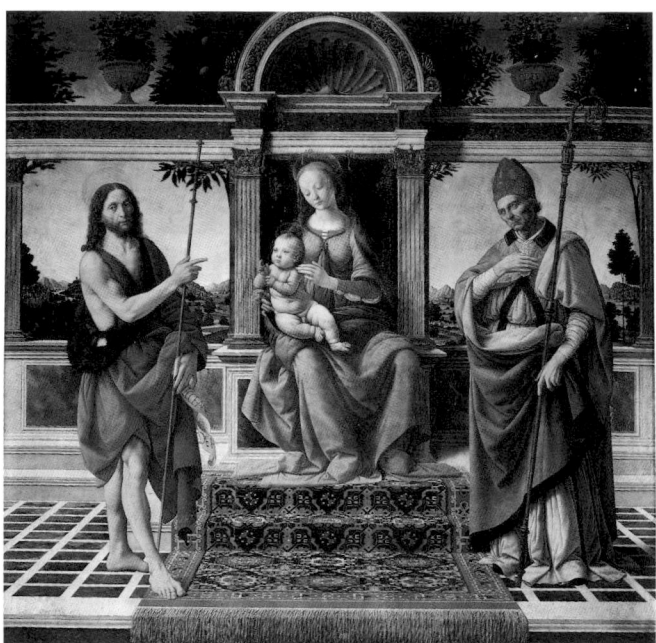

Fig. 122. Attributed to Lorenzo di Credi, *Enthroned Madonna and Child with Saints John the Baptist and Donatus.* Oil on wood, 189 × 191 cm. Chapel of the Sacrament, Duomo, Pistoia

study is beardless; delicate locks of hair fall on his forehead; his face is squarer and craggier; his draperies are not individualized to show the animal's pelt on his torso; and the configuration of the folds seems more animated.

The attribution of the drawings connected to the Pistoia altarpiece (see cat. no. 8) in part depends on who the author of the final painting is thought to be, a vexing question and one on which scholars have disagreed intensely.[1] The documents from November 21, 22, and 25, 1485, suggest that the altarpiece that was commissioned from Verrocchio by the executors of the will of Donato de' Medici, bishop of Pistoia, was "finished or was almost finished" ("facta o mancarvi poco"). Although the documents do not state the date of the commission precisely, it is implied that if Verrocchio had been paid in full he would have delivered the painting "more than six years ago," which suggests that the project originated about 1478 or

1479. According to Giorgio Vasari's vita of Lorenzo di Credi (1568), however, the latter was the author of the painting: "from Lorenzo's hand is a painting of Our Lady on a panel, very well executed, and which is at the corner of the great church of San Jacopo."[2] Since the 1485 documents mention Verrocchio by name, and since he was given the commission based on a contractual drawing, he must have executed at least some preliminary studies. Yet stylistic analysis of the finished Pistoia altarpiece suggests that Vasari was right, as Gigetta Dalli Regoli and David Alan Brown have noted. Verrocchio clearly delegated the execution of the altarpiece to Lorenzo di Credi—if not all of it, at least a great part of it.

Despite the apparently Verrocchiesque conception of the figure of the Baptist, the artist of the Louvre study is probably also Lorenzo di Credi. Unlike many life drawings from this period, the Louvre study seems somewhat inert because it is so carefully worked to a fairly high finish, with ink, washes, and white gouache over the metalpoint underdrawing. This slightly belabored technique of drawing is characteristic of Lorenzo. And the same is true of his paintings. As Vasari noted of Lorenzo's paintings, "he showed such a perfection of finish in his works, that any other painting, in comparison with his, will always seem merely sketched and dirty."[3] Recent research by Bernadette Py on the provenance of the Louvre drawing suggests that it was most probably not in the collections of Vasari, Everard Jabach, and Pierre Crozat, as has previously been published.[4]   CCB

1. Summaries of the evidence and scholarly opinions in Dalli Regoli 1966, pp. 111–12, no. 30; Brown 1998b, pp. 151–55, 210–11 nn. 16–38.
2. Vasari–Milanesi 1906, vol. 4, p. 566: "È di mano di Lorenzo una Nostra Donna in una tavola, molto ben condotta, la quale è a canto alla chiesa grande di San Iacopo di Pistoia."
3. Vasari–Milanesi 1906, p. 569: "Fu costui tanto finito e pulito ne'suoi lavori, che ogni altra pittura, a comparazione delle sue, parrà sempre abbozzata e mal netta."
4. Varena Forcione, communication on February 26, 2002. See Giorgio Vasari, Arezzo, Florence, and Rome (1511–1574); Everard Jabach, Cologne and Paris (1618–1695); Pierre Crozat, Toulouse and Paris (1665?–1740).

LORENZO DI CREDI (AND ANDREA DEL VERROCCHIO?)

8. *Standing Bishop Saint Donatus (Study for the Pistoia Altarpiece) and Other Figures* (recto)
A Male Head in Three-Quarter View Facing to the Left and Other Figural Sketches (verso)

Metalpoint, pen and brown ink, brush and brown wash, highlighted with white gouache, on pink prepared paper (recto); pen and brown ink on off-white unprepared paper (verso), 285 × 201 mm (11 ¼ × 7 ⅞ in.)

Inscribed in pen and dark brown ink on verso along right border (toward upper right): *Al mondo . non fuma[i] . piu . bella . chosa / Al mondo . no[n] fumaj piu . bel chosa / n[..];* along right border (toward lower right): *Et [or El] di che noj A . . . ino . . . chosa / [? simone ma ? Mona chaterina] di mariano / simone di domenicho [? di g[i]ovan[n]i e chonpagni] / Simone [?] d [?] dono / deno / da[?] re;* along left border (toward upper left): *chome g[io]van[n]j . dantonio . di michele e chonpagnj . / di napolj . de[v]ono . dare f[iorini] . 5 l[ire] 8;* along left border (toward lower left), the mostly cropped text possibly reads: *Simone di iacho / po/ dolm . . . / no/d . . . che.*

National Gallery of Scotland, Edinburgh 642

PROVENANCE: David Laing, Edinburgh (1793–1878; Lugt Suppl. 1656d); bequest of David Laing to the Royal Scottish Academy (1879; Lugt 2188 and Suppl. 1656d), transferred to National Galleries of Scotland, Edinburgh, in 1910.

LITERATURE: Vasari Society 1905–15, vol. 7, n. 3; Van Marle 1923–38, vol. 13, p. 269; Degenhardt 1932a, p. 416; Douglas 1933, pp. 1–36; Dalli Regoli 1966, pp. 106, 113–14, no. 14 (retouched and difficult to judge, probably a copy); Andrews 1968, vol. 1, pp. 43–44, D 642, figs. 315, 316 (Saint Donatus by Credi, gone over in a later hand); Ames-Lewis and Wright 1983, pp. 66–69, no. 6 (Verrocchio workshop); Cadogan 1983b, pp. 280, 288–89, fig. 12; Cadogan 1983c, pp. 385–89, fig. 21 (Verrocchio); Macandrew 1990, p. 26, no. 3 (Verrocchio, reworked in pen and ink by a later hand); Roberta Bartoli in Petrioli Tofani 1992, pp. 74–75, under no. 2.30; Anna Padoa Rizzo in Falletti 1996, p. 71 (workshop of Agnolo di Donnino del Mazziere); Wiemers 1996, p. 155, fig. 141; Kemp 1998, pp. 25, 34 n. 6 (metalpoint underdrawing possibly by Verrocchio); Rubin and Wright 1999, p. 165, no. 19 (Verrocchio and Credi).

This double-sided sheet is among the most fascinating of the late quattrocento for the diversity of drawings types that it exhibits and the problems of attribution that it raises. To judge from the array of different studies, rapid sketches, doodles, and passages of writing on the verso, this appears to have been a page torn from a sketchbook. (See cat. no. 12 for a sketchbook page by another artist associated with Andrea del Verrocchio's circle.) The main study on the recto of the Edinburgh sheet relates to the figure of the bishop Saint Donatus of Arezzo (not Saint Zenobius, as some early scholars state), who stands to the right of the enthroned Virgin and Child in the *Madonna di Piazza* (Pistoia Cathedral; fig. 122; cat. nos. 3, 7), which was commissioned from Verrocchio by the executors of Donato de' Medici's will about 1478 or 1479. As is known from the documents, the painting was still unfinished in November 1485. Saint Donatus of Arezzo was the namesake of Donato de' Medici, bishop of Pistoia, who had died in 1466. The figure of Saint Donatus in the Edinburgh drawing is heavily reworked in pen and ink with wash, much more so than catalogue number 7, and there is little agreement in the literature as to how original these layers are. The delicate, more rapidly drawn studies of youths and a bearded old man do seem to be by the same hand as the underlayers of metalpoint drawing in the figure of Saint Donatus. As is true of catalogue number 7, the attribution of the Edinburgh double-sided sheet has gone back and forth between Andrea del Verrocchio and his brilliant pupil Lorenzo di Credi. (See the discussion under cat. no. 7.) The Edinburgh sheet entered the museum's collection with an attribution to Lorenzo di Credi; most early scholars have generally designated it as by the "school of Verrocchio." According to recent scholarly opinion (with which the present author concurs), however, the hand of Verrocchio appears to be evident in the pen-and-ink drawings on the verso of the sheet. It is even possible that Verrocchio also drew the metalpoint studies on the recto, including the figure of the bishop-saint, before the figure was reworked with pen and ink with wash. These issues of authorship are far from being resolved.

The sketches on the verso are confidently drawn in pen and ink and display an interesting range of subjects; the abrasions of the drawing surface make the strokes in pen and ink seem less fluid than they actually are. The general appearance of the sheet is reminiscent of the so-called Verrocchio Sketchbook, attributed, with some debate, to Francesco di Simone Ferrucci (cat. no. 12; figs. 40, 120), but the draftsmanship of the Edinburgh verso is without doubt far superior. As has been pointed out, the hand responsible for the various passages of writing on the verso is almost certainly that of Verrocchio. The slightly disorderly, rounded manner of the script by

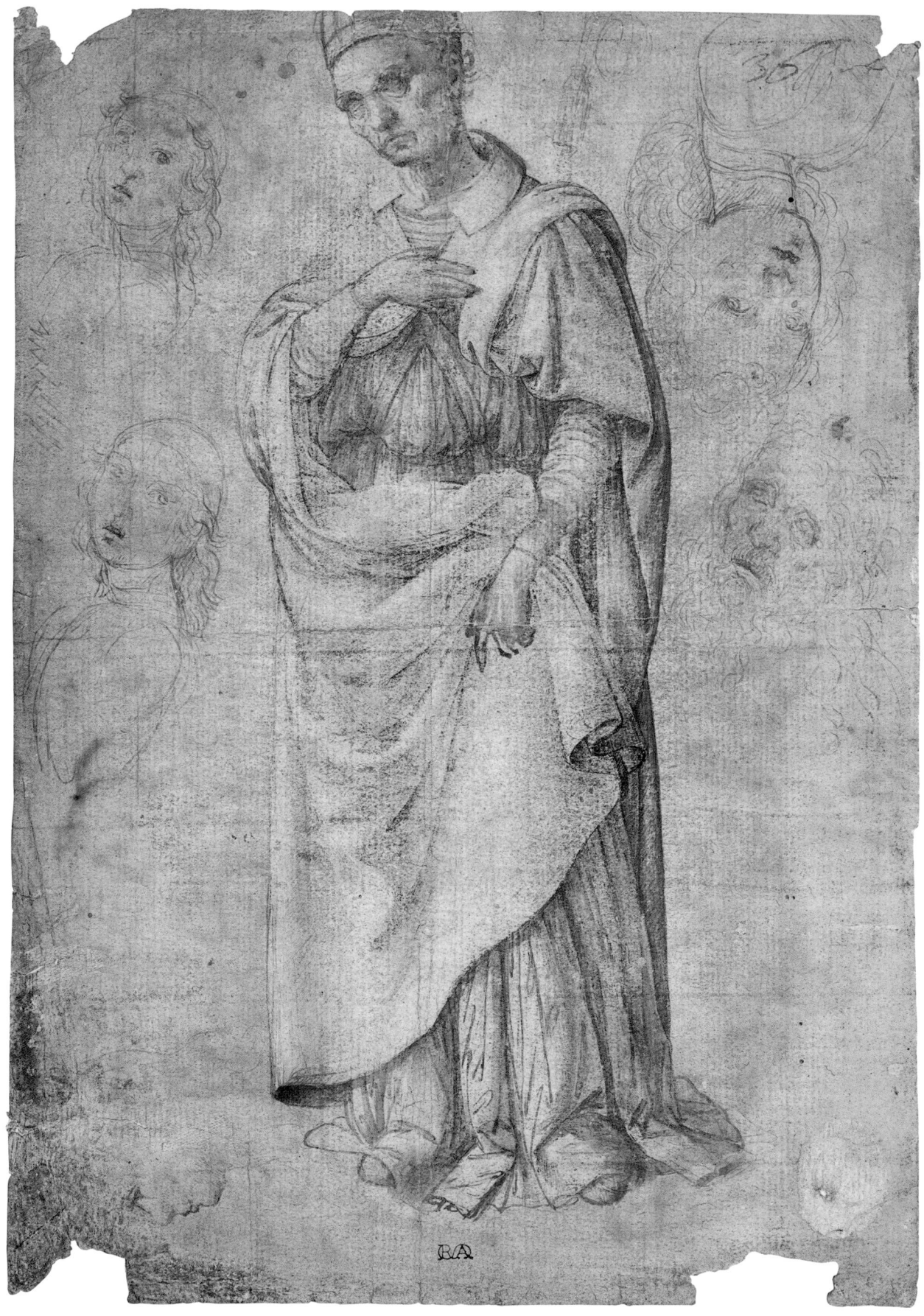

Cat. 8R

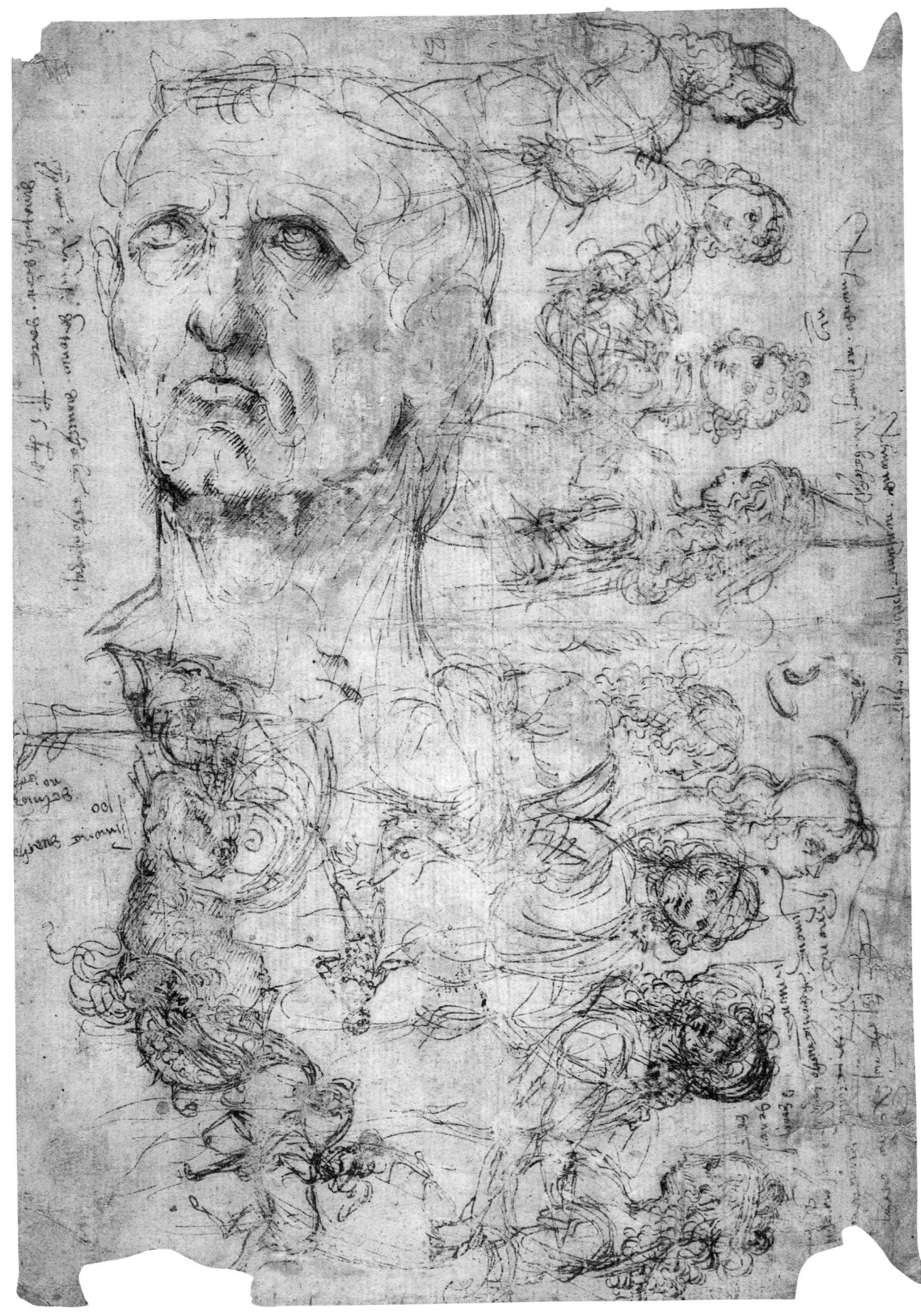

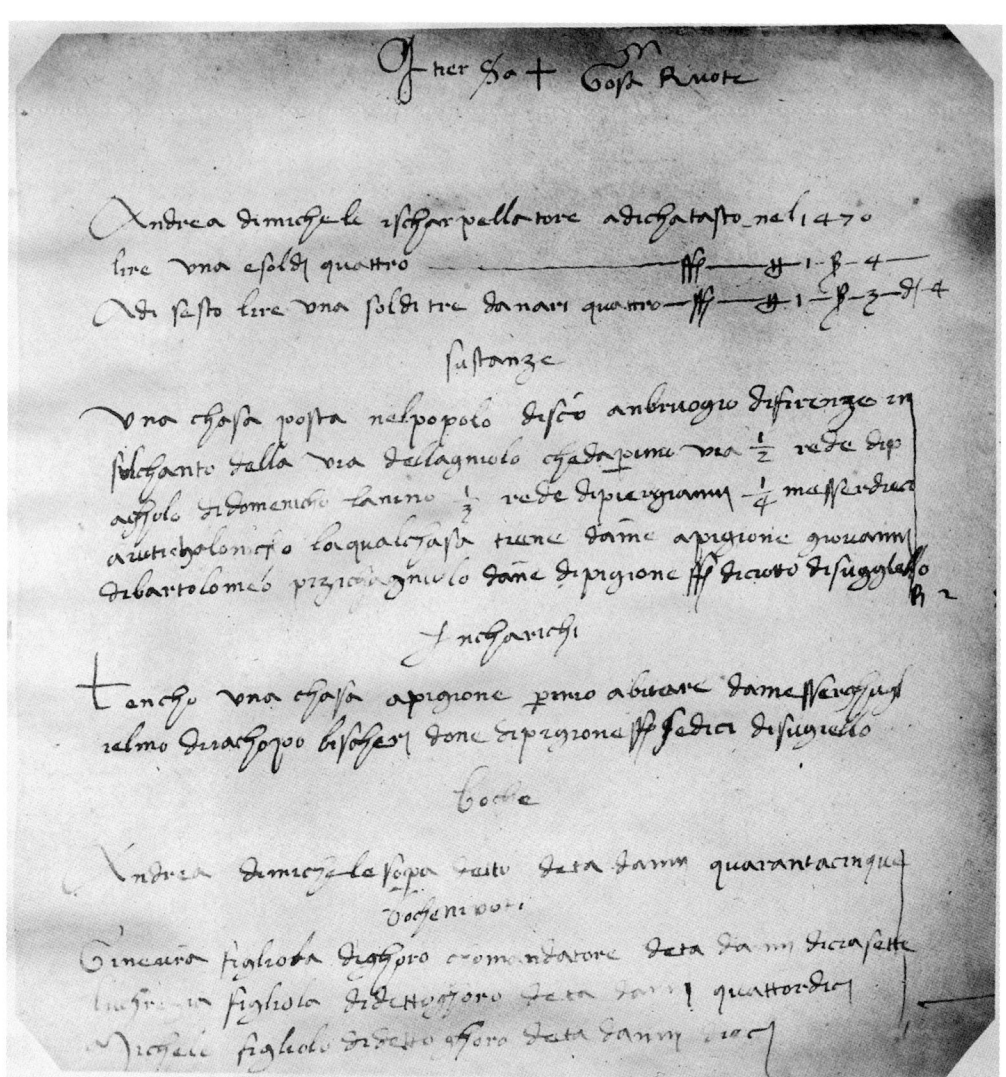

Fig. 123. Andrea del Verrocchio, *Catasto* (tax assessment declaration) of 1481. Quartiere Santa Croce, Gonfalone Ruote, Archivio di Stato, Florence

Verrocchio in his *catasto* declaration (tax assessment of wealth of a Florentine citizen) of 1481 seems extremely close, if not identical (fig. 123).[1] The script also compares favorably to Verrocchio's studies of a horse's proportions, which is inscribed with measurements (see cat. nos. 9, 10). In the Edinburgh verso, which evidently is drawn by a right-handed artist and with spidery, scratchy reinforced contours, the scattered motifs in diverse scale nevertheless recall the large sheets of sketches by the young Leonardo from the early 1470s. The bust-length young beautiful women and men, as well as the small standing male nude, seem especially reminiscent of the motifs included in a large sheet by Leonardo with rapid studies of a woman nursing a child (Windsor, RL 12276 recto and verso; fig. 136). A similar sketch of a standing nude man also appears on the verso of Leonardo's famous drawing of the Arno landscape (fig. 7), dated by him August 5, 1473, on the recto of the sheet. The more detailed sketch of the warrior in antique-style armor on the Edinburgh verso is reminiscent of Leonardo's famous metalpoint study on beige prepared paper (British Museum, London, 1895-9-15-474), from the early to mid-1470s. The boldness of the pen-and-ink sketching style seen in the Edinburgh verso seems to have little to do with the typically diligent and more tonally refined style of Lorenzo di Credi. Of imposing sculptural presence and *terribilità* of expression, the large-scale head is reminiscent of antique Roman busts and may be based on a cast or terracotta *bozzetto* kept in Verrocchio's workshop. This large head study appears to have served as the model for the more idealized face of the bishop-saint on the recto of the sheet. The general facial expression and distinctive gaze are very similar.

CCB

1. See Milanesi 1876.

ANDREA DEL VERROCCHIO

9. *Measured Drawing of a Horse in Profile Facing to the Left*

Pen and dark brown ink, over traces of black chalk, 249 × 298 mm (9 ¹³⁄₁₆ × 11 ¾ in.)

Inscribed in pen and the same brown ink as the drawing with measurements, starting at upper left, from ear to chest: *u[na] T 5/16 1/2 / dal osso del orechio insino al petto una testa e cinque sedecimi e mezo;* from ear to withers: *u[na] T 3 1/6 1/2 / dal orechio al guidalescho un testa e tre sedecimi 1/2;* from chest to withers: *una T e 1/2 sedecimo / dal petto al guidalescho una testa e mezo sedecimo;* from chest to front side of upper leg: *sei 1 /6 1/2 / dal petto alacchomincio dela ghanba se sedecimi;* from chest to back side of upper leg: *10 sedecimi e nezo [sic: mezzo]/ dal petto al chomincio de la ghanba dieci sedecimi;* from beginning of front leg to withers: *una T e dua 1 /6 / dal chomincio dela chanba insino al guidalescho una testa e dua sedecimi;* at front left hoof: *tre sedecimi 1/2 / 3 1/6 1/2;* from front fetlock to knee: *nove sedecimi / da questo nodello al ginochio 9 16;* from front left knee to belly: *undici 16 1/2 / dal ginochio al chomincamento / undici parti e mezo;* from withers to top of the rump: *una T e 11 1/6 / dal gudalesch a p[r]incipia dela groppa una testa e undici sede-cimi;* from chest to rump: *dua T e 10 1/6 / dal petto alla groppa dua teste e dieci sedecimi;* from top of front leg bone to top of back leg bone: *una T e 4 1/6 / dal ginocho al chomincio dela choscia una testa e quaettro 1 6;* across front thickness of belly: *una T 5 1/6 1/2 / grosso una testa [canceled: e mez] e cinque 1/6;* from top of back leg to the rump: *undici 1/6 / da qu al osso dela gropa undici 1 /6;* from rump (or crupper) to tail: *nove 16 / dal gropa alla choda nove 16;* from lower rump to top of tail: *14 16 1/2 / du qui alla choda di sop[r]a 14 1/6 e 1/2;* from top of haunch bone to knee. *u[na] T e 10 1/6 / da questo o dela groppa insino al gnochio una testa e dieci sedecimi;* from top of back leg to knee of back leg: *da questo o insino al ginochio 13 1/6 1/2;* from rear knee to lower rump: *otto sedecimi / dal ginochio a questo 8;* from rear fetlock to above the knee: *dodici 16 / da questa guntura al disop[r]a del ginochio dodici 1/6;*[1] in pen and a darker brown ink on lower left by an early hand: *And: Verrocchio.*

The Metropolitan Museum of Art, New York; Frederick C. Hewitt Fund, 1917 19.76.5

PROVENANCE: Giorgio Vasari, Arezzo, Florence, and Rome (1511–1574); Jonathan Richardson, Senior (?), London (1665–1745; Lugt 2183, 2184, Suppl. 2183, 2983, 2984, 2993–2996); Earls of Pembroke (Lugt under 2183, under 2585, under 2957); Pembroke sale, Sotheby's, London, July 5–6, 9–10, 1917, lot 358 (Verrocchio); purchased by The Metropolitan Museum of Art in 1917.

LITERATURE: Strong 1900, pt. 6, no. 58; Berenson 1903, vol. 2, p. 136, no. 1951 A (School of Antonio Pollaiuolo); Burroughs 1919, p. 137 (Antonio del Pollaiuolo); Sirén 1928, vol. 2, pl. 81B (Leonardo da Vinci); Suida 1929, pp. 64–65; Valentiner 1933, p. 232; Kurz 1937, p. 14; Berenson 1938, vol. 2, p. 271, no. 1947 B (School of Antonio Pollaiuolo); Degenhart 1939, pp. 140–41, fig. 57 (Antonio Federighi); Metropolitan Museum of Art 1942, no. 4; Berenson 1961, vol. 2, p. 453, no. 1947 B (School of Antonio Pollaiuolo); Ragghianti Collobi 1974, vol. 1, p. 82, vol. 2, fig. 230; Beltrame Quattrocchi 1979, pp. 25–26, under no. 7, fig. 1obis; Metropolitan Museum of Art 1980, no. 82 (follower of Verrocchio); Palazzo Reale 1981, no. 47 (follower of Verrocchio); Bean 1982, pp. 264–66, no. 270 (Verrocchio?); Scaglia 1982, figs. 7, 8; Pedretti and Roberts 1984–86, pp. 38–39, under no. 8; Pedretti 1987b, p. 44, fig. 31; Kemp and Roberts 1989, pp. 168–69, under no. 92; Butterfield 1997, pp. 185, 191, fig. 255; Clayton 2002–3 p. 34, under no. 6, fig. 7.

The attribution of line drawings, such as the present example, is notoriously difficult. As Gustina Scaglia rightly noted in 1982, however, there is no reason to doubt the traditional attribution to Andrea del Verrocchio of this and the following drawing (cat. no. 10), as the rapid cursive script seen here is identical to that in Verrocchio's declaration for the *catasto* (tax assessment of wealth of a Florentine citizen) of 1481, which is extant in the Archivio di Stato in Florence (fig. 123).[2] Attributed to Lorenzo di Credi and Verrocchio, the sketchbook page from Edinburgh also offers an example of Verrocchio's script (cat. no. 8). Recent scholars have unanimously agreed with the attribution of the Metropolitan Museum drawing to Verrocchio. This and catalogue number 10 probably correspond to the type of drawings that Giorgio Vasari mentioned as being in his famous *libro de' disegni:* "in our book, also, are two horses, with the due measures and protractors for reproducing them on a larger scale from a smaller, so that there may not be any errors in their proportions."[3]

The Metropolitan Museum study of the horse is of great draftsmanly quality and conceptual elegance. This innovative drawing relates to the basic techniques of proportional division that Leonardo adopted in his earliest horse studies (see fig. 124; and Windsor, RL 12319). After producing the outlines of the horse, Verrocchio identified each joint of movement in the horse's body. He marked these articulations with a small circle and then proceeded to inscribe the measurements. The artist probably worked originally from a live horse, presumably taking notes on a sheet of paper or in a bound notebook

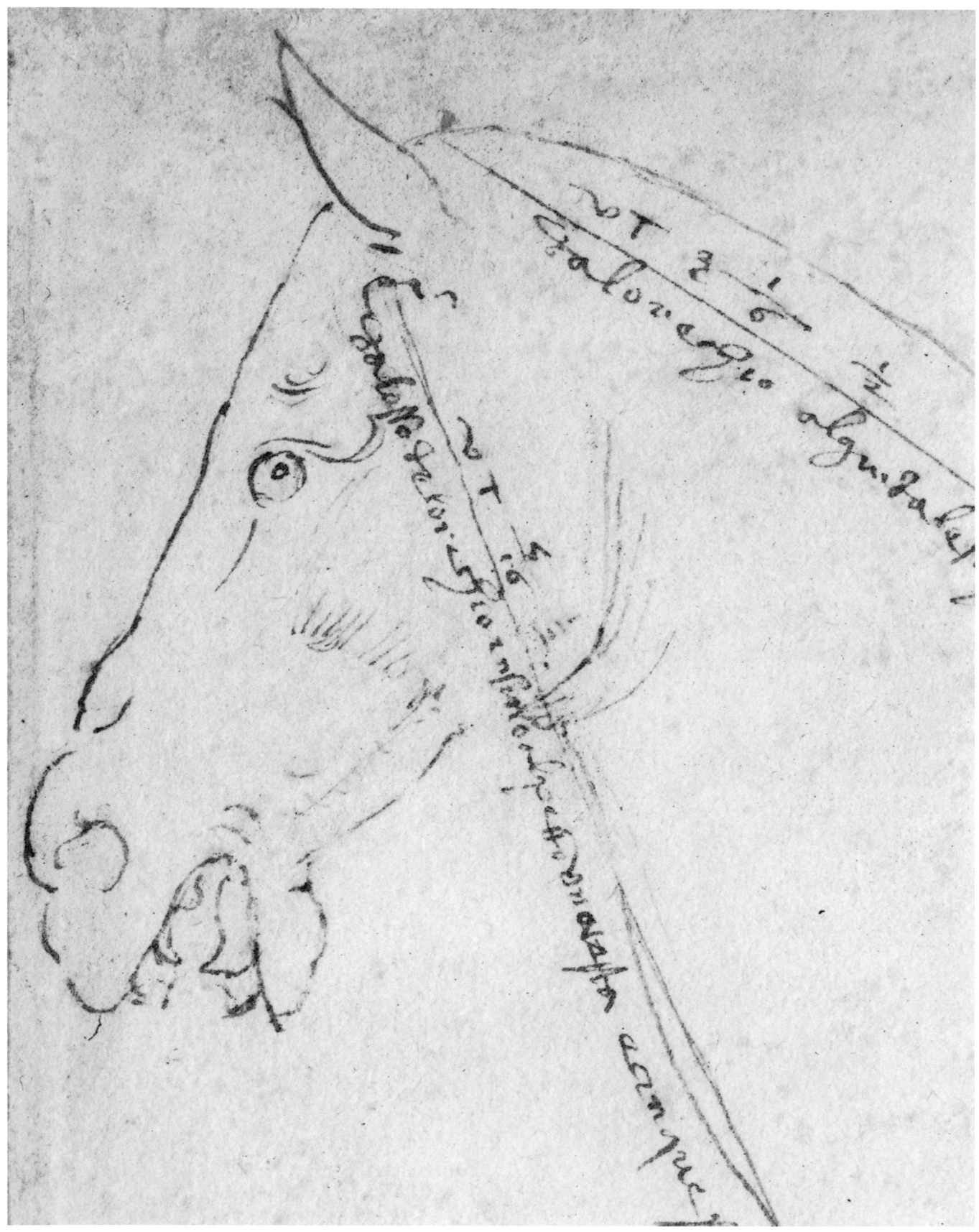

Cat. 9 *(detail)*

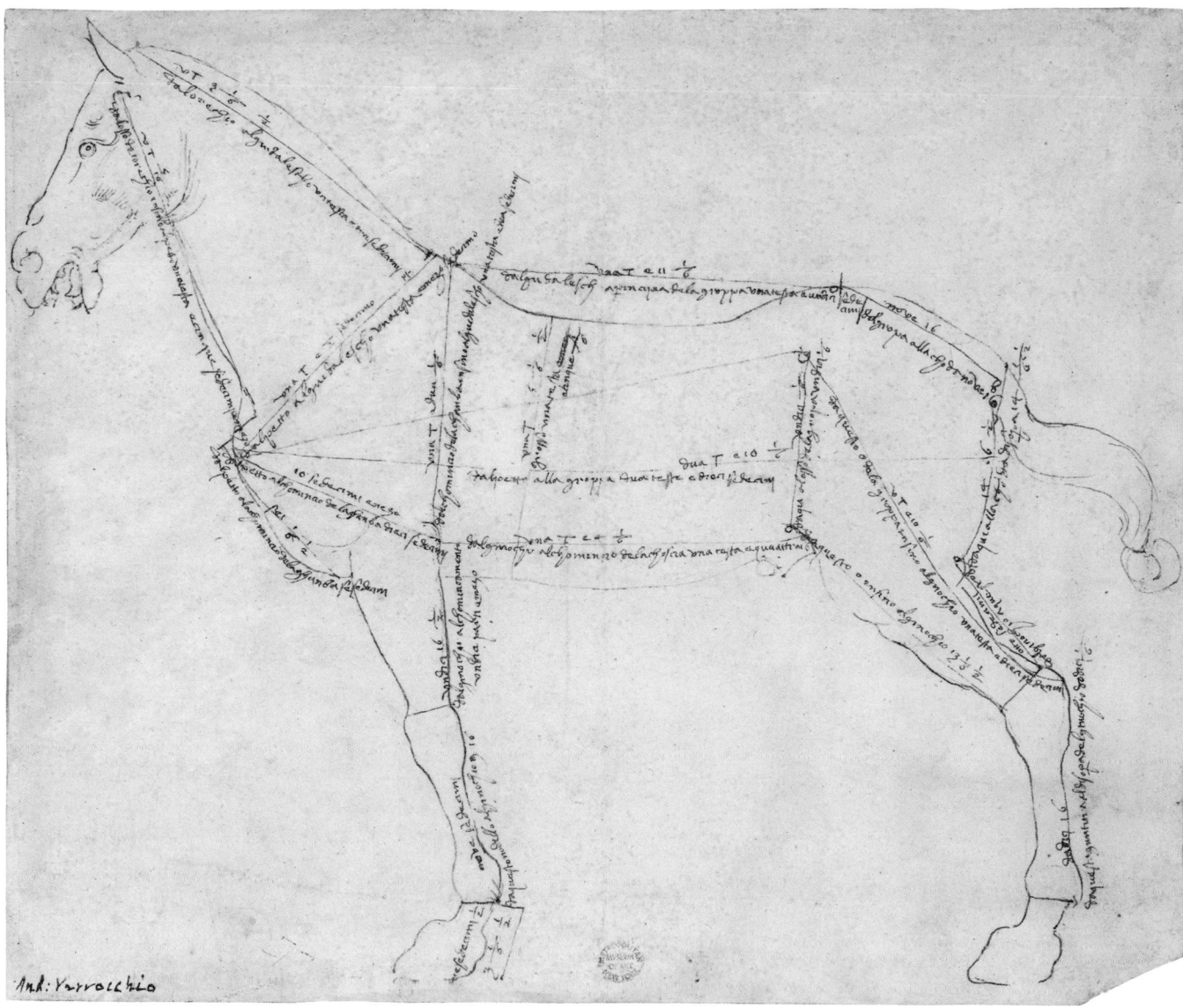

Cat. 9

and later transferring them to the present sheet. The inscriptions detailing the measurements of the horse are a great deal simpler than they may at first appear to the viewer. Verrocchio seems to have taken the head of the horse as the unit of measurement, and then divided the head itself into sixteen parts to obtain more precise subunits. Each line of measurement gives the dimensions both in numerals and spelled out in words. But with both these systems in operation, a number of inconsistencies crept in. For example, Verrocchio all too often writes "1/6" when "1/16" is correct and is what he writes in longhand. The measurement of the horse's body in terms of head lengths is a Vitruvian concept: the human body was also measured according to the height of the head. The eight heads to the human body may have determined the sixteen subunits of Verrocchio's horse.

Verrocchio probably undertook these detailed studies of the horse's proportions (cat. nos. 9, 10) when he faced the challenge of designing the enormous bronze equestrian monument of Bartolomeo Colleoni (Campo Santi Giovanni e Paolo, Venice; figs. 125, 162) in the 1480s. Based on the circumstances of the commission of the Colleoni project, one may be able to pinpoint the date of Verrocchio's drawings more precisely to 1483–88. Leonardo undertook his proportion studies of the horse, probably almost concurrently—certainly from the late

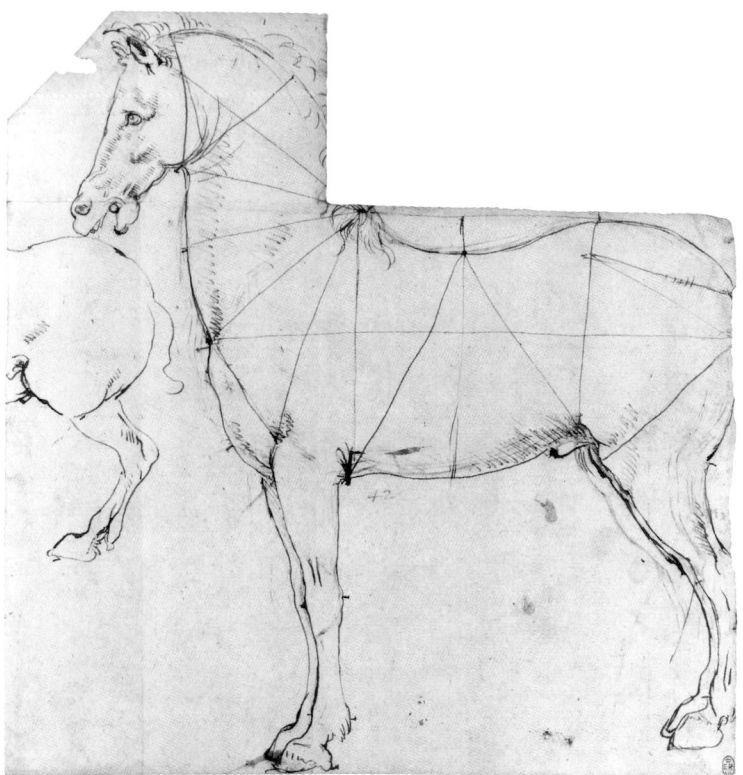

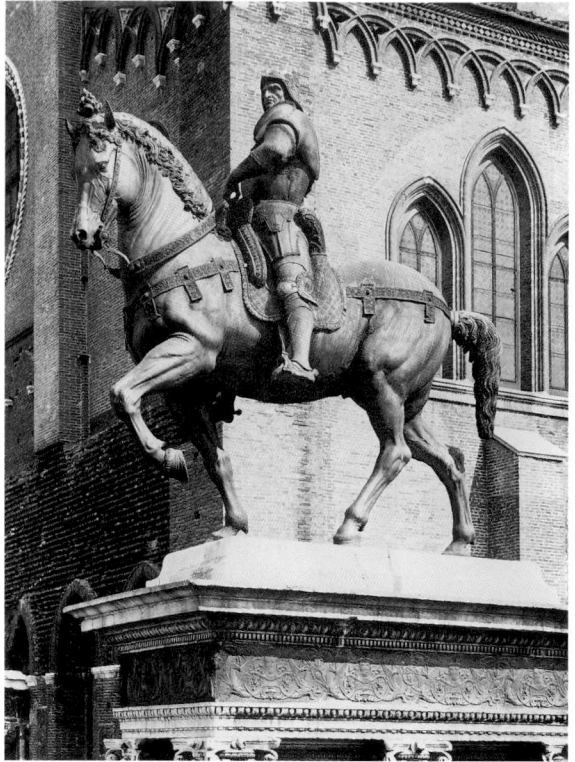

Fig. 124. Leonardo da Vinci, *Study of a Horse*. Pen and brown ink over black chalk, 298 × 290 mm. The Royal Collection, H.M. Queen Elizabeth II, Windsor Castle RL 12318

Fig. 125. Andrea del Verrocchio, *Equestrian Monument to Bartolommeo Colleoni*. Bronze on a marble and Istrian stone pedestal with a bronze frieze, H. of horse and rider (without marble plinth) 395 cm. Campo Santi Giovanni e Paolo, Venice

1480s to early 1490s — in designing his colossal equestrian monument to Francesco Sforza, the "Sforza Horse" (cat. nos. 53, 63, 64). Sometime between July 1481 and May 1483, Verrocchio secured the prestigious commission from the Venetian Republic for the Colleoni, following a competition among three sculptors of unknown name; it has been speculated that Verrocchio's two other rivals for the Colleoni commission may have been Antonio del Pollaiuolo (see cat. no. 11) and Leonardo.[4] The precise date when Verrocchio received the commission for the Colleoni equestrian monument, however, is not clear. A competition model for the commission of the Colleoni statue, by an unnamed sculptor, is mentioned in a letter of July 12, 1481, addressed to Duke Ercole d'Este by his ambassador. Models by three unnamed sculptors competing for the project are also mentioned in the diary of the German Dominican monk Felix Fabri, in an entry written in Venice on May 3, 1483. Fabri described a wax model of a horse — the

winner of the competition — and this may well be the one produced by Verrocchio. By April 1486 Verrocchio appears to have been in Venice working on the models for the sculpture. By the time of his death, in June 1488, he had brought the models to an advanced state of completion. The casting of the sculpture in bronze was entrusted to Alessandro Leopardi in 1490, and it was finished in the spring of 1496. The production of the Colleoni monument almost precisely overlapped in time Leonardo's planning of the design for his "Sforza Horse" (cat. nos. 53, 63, 64).   CCB

1. Transcribed with the assistance of Silvia Borsotti, August 24, 2001.
2. See Milanesi 1876; Scaglia 1982.
3. Translation quoted from Vasari–Milanesi 1996, vol. 1, p. 552; Vasari 1906, vol. 3, p. 364: "Sonvi [nel nostro libro] ancora due cavalli, con il modo delle misure e centine da farli di piccoli grandi, che venghino proporzionati e senza errori."
4. Discussion below based on Butterfield 1997, pp. 6, 159–83, 232–36, no. 26.

ANDREA DEL VERROCCHIO

10. *Horse in Profile Facing to the Right; Unrelated Small Figural Sketch at Bottom Center* (recto) *Measured Drawings of a Horse in Rear View, a Horse in Frontal View, and Detail of Its Foreleg in Profile* (verso)

Pen and dark brown ink, over traces of black chalk (recto and verso), 293 × 275 mm (11 ½ × 10 ¹³⁄₁₆ in.), irregular borders

Inscribed on verso in pen and the same dark brown ink as the drawings, with measurements, starting at left, across the flank of the left horse: *parte tredici / dalluno osso allaltro 15 1/6 / dallunosso alaltro tredici 1/6;* across the neck of the horse at center: *13 1/6 / da questa forcella insotto la ghola 13 1/6;* across the chest of the horse at center: *undici 1/6 1/2 / larcheza del petto undici sedecimi e mezo;* across the height of the leg in the detail at right: *dalginochio atter[r]a un[a] testa e sei sedecimi T un[a] 6 1/6 / T una sei 1/6;* in pen and brown ink by an early-sixteenth-century hand along lower border: *Di lionardo da vinci* and with numbers by later hands

Watermark: Scales within a circle (not in Briquet)

Istituto Nazionale per la Grafica, Rome F. C. 127615

PROVENANCE: Corsini Collection, Rome; Reale Accademia dei Lincei (Lugt 2187); unidentified stamp at lower right of recto (star? not in Lugt); Gabinetto [Reale] Nazionale delle Stampe (Lugt 1183).

LITERATURE: Giovanni Morelli in Flores 1896, p. 144, no. 8; Beltrame Quattrocchi 1979, pp. 24–26, 84–85, no. 7; Pedretti and Roberts 1984–86, pp. 38–39, under no. 8; Pedretti 1987b, p. 44, figs. 31–33.

This double-sided sheet of drawings, as innovative for its time as catalogue number 9, has often fallen through the cracks of the scholarly literature; it is little published and rarely exhibited. The profile pose of the horse on the recto of the sheet recalls that in Verrocchio's equestrian monument of Bartolomeo Colleoni (fig. 125), as well as Leonardo's early proportion studies (fig. 124). The pose here is more active than it may at first appear—close to a spirited amble—for the horse's bent far foreleg is outlined only faintly in pen and ink (there may have been a greater articulation of the form in the underdrawing in chalk, but this has completely disappeared).

Verrocchio captured the agitated animation of the heaving standing horse with deftly reinforced outlines that manage to evoke fully the volume of the forms, without relying on internal modeling. The self-confident immediacy of the outline sketch suggests that he worked from a live horse. The artist observed quickly, but closely, the structural articulation of the muscles on the neck, chest, and tense near foreleg, using abbreviated internal strokes—small dots and dashes—rather than long contours.

The verso of the Rome sheet is drawn quickly and with considerably more synthetic, deliberately simplified outlines. For example, the head of the horse is blocked out as a large rectangle, and then the forms of the neck are refined with pen-and-ink outlines. This suggests that Verrocchio copied the forms from preliminary studies that he had previously done from life (like the type of life study that is seen on the recto of the sheet). Here, the artist's purpose was to record rather than to explore. In style, technique, and function, the verso can be considered the companion to catalogue number 9, as it offers the measurements (though less detailed) of the horse in foreshortened views from the front and the rear. The head of the horse is still the unit of measurement; in the inscriptions the letter T stands for *testa* (head), and the subunits are given in fractions of the head's measurement. As the great paleographer Armando Petrucci long ago pointed out, the *mercatesca* script here (and in cat. no. 9) is closely comparable to that in Verrocchio's *catasto* of 1481 (fig. 123).[1] Catalogue number 8 probably offers yet another example of Verrocchio's handwriting.

CCB

1. Quoted in Beltrame Quattrochi 1979, p. 26; see Milanesi 1876.

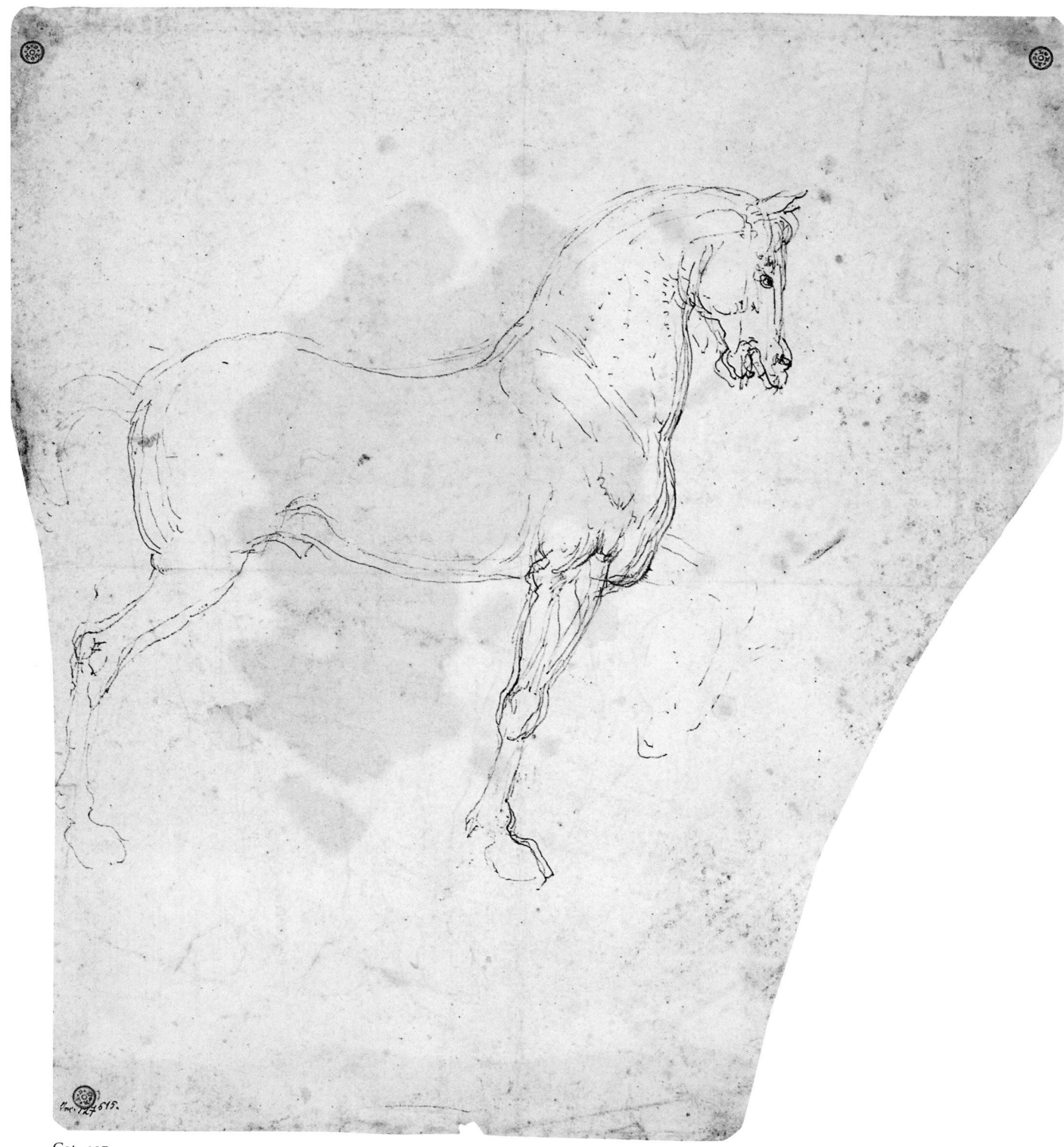

Cat. 10R

272

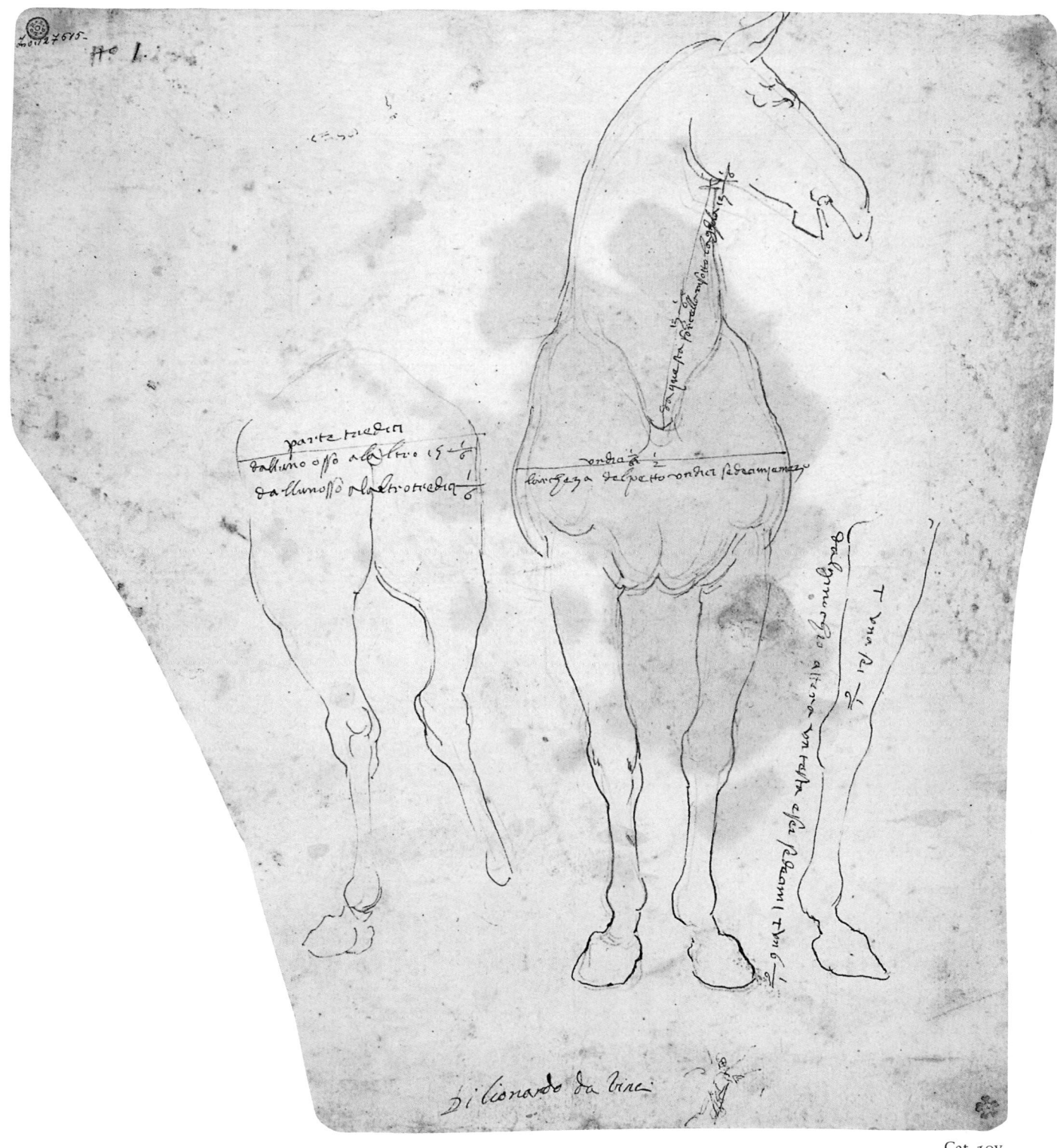

parte media

dalluno osso ala[...]ro 15 ½ /6

da llunosso ola[...]trovedia 1/6

ondia ½

longeza delpetto ondia sedeamjam[...]

[vertical text right side] dalgineghio altura vntesta esſa ſe[...]ami tvn 6 1/2

[vertical text] t vna [...] ½

di lionardo da vinci

ANTONIO DEL POLLAIUOLO (ANTONIO BENCI)

(Florence, 1431/32 – Rome, 1498)

11. *Study for an Equestrian Monument*

Pen and brown ink, brush with light and dark brown wash, over faint black chalk underdrawing; outlines of the horse and rider are selectively pricked for transfer; the background was reworked with dark brown ink, possibly by Giorgio Vasari, 288 × 255 mm (11⅜ × 10¹⁄₁₆ in.), irregular borders
The Metropolitan Museum of Art, New York; Robert Lehman Collection, 1975 1975.1.410

PROVENANCE: Giorgio Vasari, Arezzo, Florence, and Rome (1511–1574); Simon Meller (?), Budapest and Paris; Philip Hofer, Cambridge, Massachusetts (1898–1984; Lugt Suppl. 2087a); Robert Lehman, New York (1892–1969).

LITERATURE: Vasari–Milanesi 1906, vol. 3, p. 297; Van Marle 1923–38, vol. 11, p. 370; Meller 1934, pp. 204–5, fig. 124; López-Rey 1935, pp. 41–42, 49, fig. 35; Kurz 1937, p. 13; Berenson 1938, vol. 1, p. 27 n. 4, vol. 2, p. 266, vol. 3, fig. 78, no. 1908A (Antonio Pollaiuolo); Colacicchi 1943, pl. 77; De Tolnay 1943, p. 111, pl. 42; Sabatini 1944, p. 88; Tietze 1947, no. 13; Ortolani 1948, pp. 169, 220–21, pl. 134; Philadelphia Museum of Art 1950, no. 12; Ettlinger 1953, p. 243; Halm, Degenhart, and Wegner 1958, p. 26, pl. 2; Pope-Hennessy 1985, pp. 55–56, fig. 87; Goldscheider 1959, pp. 177–78, under no. 106; Berenson 1961, vol. 1, p. 59, vol. 2, p. 446, vol. 3, fig. 75, no. 1908 A (Antonio Pollaiuolo); Degenhart and Schmitt 1964, pp. 57–59, fig. 12; Bean and Stampfle 1965, p. 21, no. 6, pl. 6; Degenhart and Schmitt 1967, p. 71, under no. 60; Degenhart and Schmitt 1968, vols. 1–2, pp. 632–33, fig. 971; Busignani 1970, pls. 178, 179; Spencer 1972, pp. 741–42; Spencer 1973, p. 35, fig. 10; Tietze 1973, no. 13; Ragghianti Collobi 1974, p. 78, fig. 209; Szabo 1975, p. 103, no. 173; Los Angeles County Museum of Art 1976, p. 18; Bush 1978, pp. 47–49; Ettlinger 1978, no. 34, pl. 106; Szabo 1978, no. 19; Hibbard 1980, pp. 233, 236, fig. 409; Metropolitan Museum of Art 1980, no. 83; Szabo 1981, fig. 3; Vertova 1981, pp. 43–48; Szabo 1983, no. 12; Cocke 1984, pp. 174, 177; Pedretti and Roberts 1984–86, p. 46, under no. 18; Pope-Hennessy 1985, pp. 55–56, fig. 87; Metropolitan Museum of Art 1987, p. 72, fig. 50; Pedretti 1987a, p. 54, fig. 69; Forlani Tempesti 1991, pp. 197–202, no. 69; Fusco and Corti 1992, pp. 11, 14, 18–20, fig. 12; Butterfield 1997, p. 167, fig. 221; Arasse 1998, pp. 242–43, fig. 174; Fiorio 1998e, pp. 40–41, fig. 2.1; Bambach 1999a, pp. 57–58, 328–29, 394 n. 149, 395 n. 170; Pope-Hennessy 2000, pp. 210–13, pl. 193; Clayton 2002b, p. 20.

Besides Verrocchio, Antonio del Pollaiuolo was the artist who most influenced the young Leonardo during the 1470s in Florence. Their paths again intersected — though it is not known precisely how this came about — regarding the project in Milan to sculpt a bronze equestrian monument commemorating Francesco Sforza (1401–1466), the famous condottiere (mercenary general) of the Visconti family in Milan who became duke of the city and its dominions. The patron was Francesco's son, Ludovico Sforza "Il Moro," who himself had pretentions to the Duchy of Milan. Expelled from Milan, Ludovico Sforza was in exile in Pisa from 1477 to 1479; when he visited Lorenzo de' Medici "Il Magnifico" in Florence, he probably also became acquainted with some of the artists and humanists in Lorenzo's circle. On his return to Milan in 1479 (after almost a decade of political infighting to solidify his power), Ludovico was ready to recommence his plans for the commission of the statue honoring his father. The carefully finished drawing by Pollaiuolo exhibited here offers an extremely accurate portrait of Francesco Sforza (fig. 126). As numerous scholars have pointed out, Pollaiuolo's drawing uncannily resembles Leonardo's own design for the Sforza equestrian monument (cat. no. 53). As seen here, Pollaiuolo's firmly traced pen-and-ink outlines and sculptural wash technique are typical of his drawings from the 1470s (note especially his *Adam* and *Eve* studies; Uffizi, Florence, 95 F, 97 F). The style and metalpoint technique of Leonardo's study (cat. no. 53) are characteristic of his work from the 1480s. Although previous scholars have often dated Leonardo's sheet around 1488–89, a date closer to the mid-1480s is preferred by the present author (see discussion in cat. no. 53). Leonardo's letter to "Il Moro" (known only from contemporary drafts) probably dates from 1481–83 and mentions that he could execute the horse in bronze; Leonardo presumably wrote the letter to seek employment at the ruler's court in Milan.[1] In noting the destruction of Leonardo's model (*forma*) for the "Sforza Horse" in 1499, Sabba da Castiglione's *Ricordi* (Bologna, 1546) points out that Leonardo had labored on the model for sixteen continuous years, which puts the starting date at about 1483; Castiglione personally remembered Leonardo's model.[2] The evidence is frustratingly sparse, but it can be inferred that by 1489 Ludovico Sforza "Il Moro" doubted Leonardo's ability to cast the "Sforza Horse" in bronze. An exchange of letters in July 1489 and August 1489 between "Il Moro" and "Il Magnifico" suggests the possibility

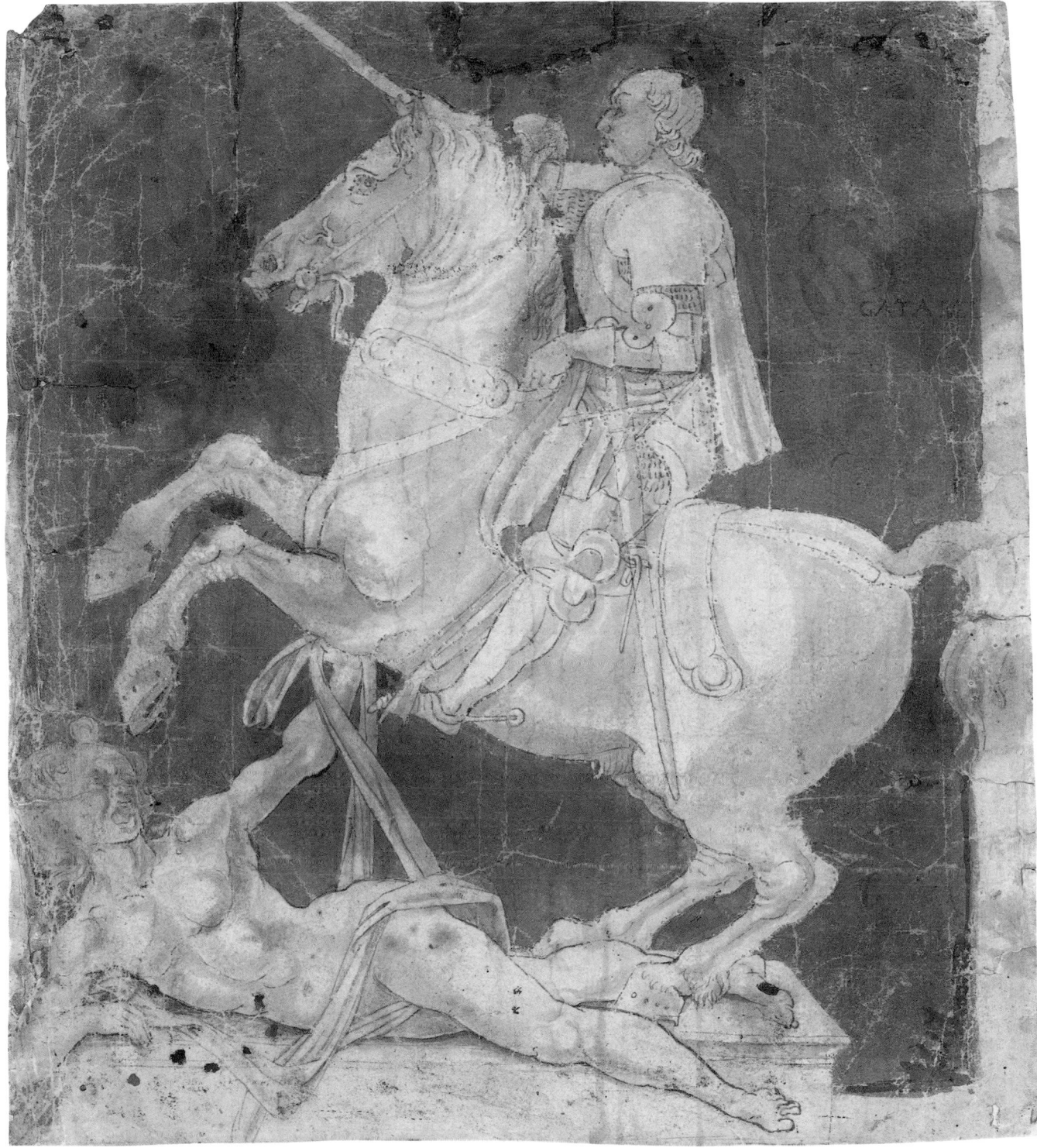

Cat. 11

that Antonio del Pollaiuolo was being considered as one of the two masters "apt in such work" to replace Leonardo in the project.[3] Although it seems difficult to resolve the question regarding who influenced whom based on a chronology (there are no firmly documented dates for the drawings or the proj-

ect at this early phase), it seems worth considering the possibility that Pollaiuolo's and Leonardo's drawings are roughly contemporaneous. Both sheets may date sometime during the crucial years from 1481 to 1485, when "Il Moro" was beginning to revisit his plans for the monument to his father. It seems

275

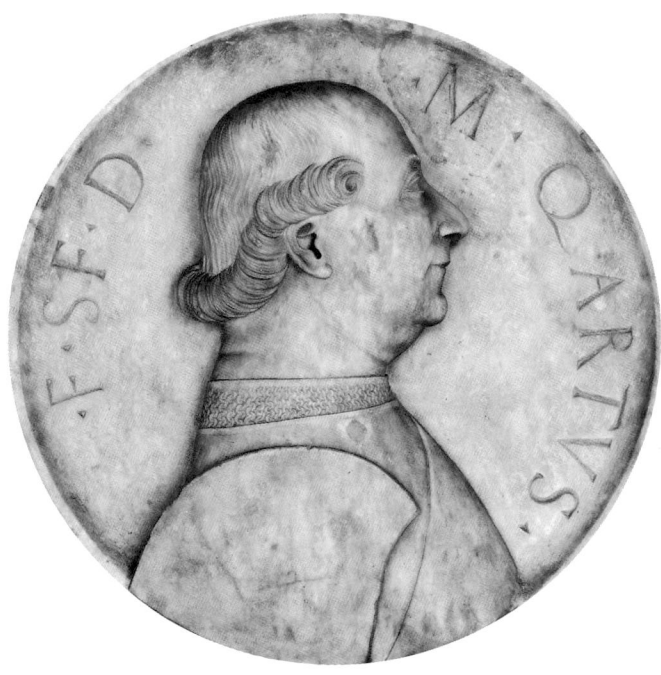

Fig. 126. Artist unknown, *Portrait of Francesco Sforza*. Marble relief, diam. 54.3 cm. The Metropolitan Museum of Art, New York; Rogers Fund, 1911 11.182.1

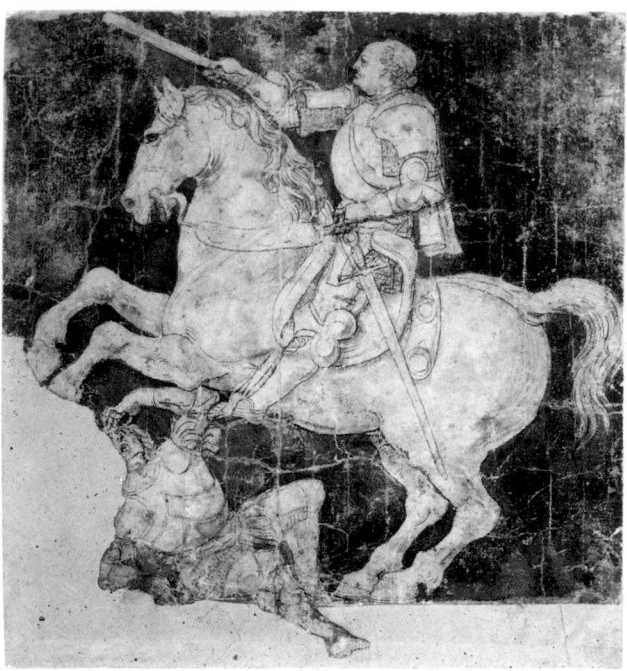

Fig. 127. Antonio del Pollaiuolo, *Design for an Equestrian Monument to Francesco Sforza*. Pen and brown ink, brush and brown wash, 208 × 217 mm. Staatliche Graphische Sammlung, Munich 1908.168

also worth speculating that the drawings by the two artists may represent preliminary drafts (of course, at different stages in the design process, since Leonardo's sheet is much sketchier; cat. no. 53) in preparing competing presentation drawings for submission to the patron. The 1568 edition of Vasari's vita of Antonio del Pollaiuolo notes that two *disegni* (drawings) by Pollaiuolo, for the monument of Francesco Sforza, were in the biographer's *libro de' disegni*: "discovered after his death were the drawing and model he made for Ludovico Sforza for a statue of Francesco Sforza, duke of Milan, on a horse; and that design is in our album in two versions: in one he [Francesco] has Verona beneath him, in the other he is in full armor and, above a base full of battle scenes, he makes his horse rear up over an armed man. But the reason why he did not execute these designs I have not been able to find out."[4] The sheet at the Metropolitan Museum as well as a similarly executed variant drawing in Munich (fig. 127), without pricked outlines, have traditionally been identified with Vasari's passage. It is often assumed that Vasari added the dark brown wash to the background of both the New York and Munich sheets to harmonize the formats of the composition with respect to each other. Both carefully rendered drawings by Pollaiuolo exhibit the characteristic appearance of a *modello* (demonstration drawing for a patron) that is already at an advanced stage in the design process.

In the Metropolitan Museum drawing, Pollaiuolo used a pricking technique as a shortcut to draw the horse-and-rider motif, which suggests that he was intent on replicating generally consistent variations of the motifs in other drafts. The shortcut that Pollaiuolo used was primarily helpful in elaborating preliminary drawings from draft to draft, rather than in transferring the design to a final working surface.[5] He seems to have stacked a number of sheets of paper and pricked through the outlines of the horse-and-rider motif to obtain a general design on each sheet. He then drew on the pricked-through sheet by connecting the holes one by one with pen and ink, refining the design greatly according to his intentions and exploring alternative ideas on subsequent drafts. This explains why the pricking in the Metropolitan sheet is only partial and done coarsely with large holes placed far apart, and why in most passages the holes are greatly misaligned with respect to the drawing. The pricked outlines on Pollaiuolo's sheet served only as a general guideline in drawing. The shortcut procedure accounts for the entirely unpricked portions of Pollaiuolo's drawing: the horse's right rear leg and genitals, the female allegorical figure representing the city of Verona, and the pedestal on which she reclines. These details were clearly added by the artist after he had finished pricking the outlines of the design; significantly, the details that are

276

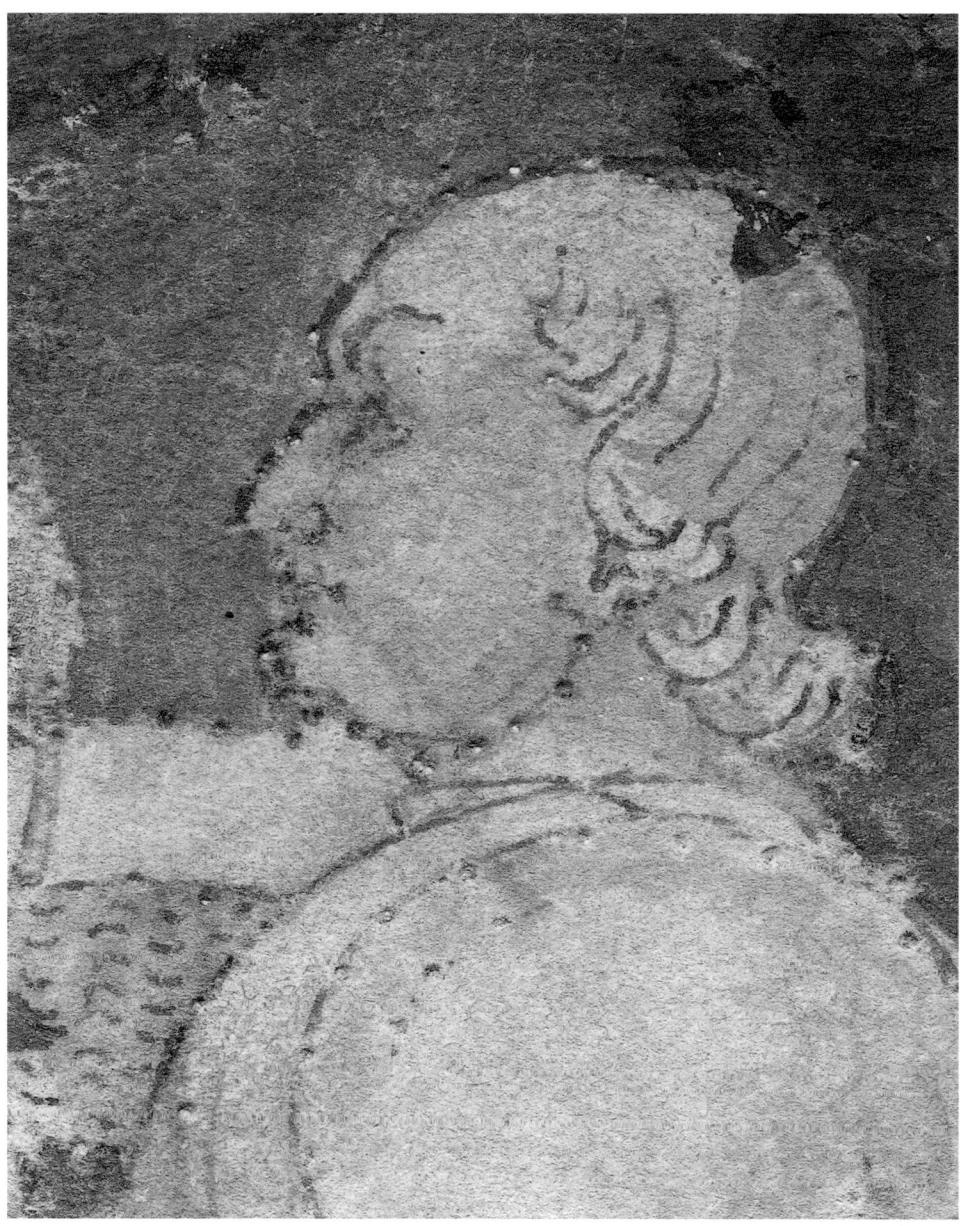

Cat. 11 *(detail)*

unpricked in the Metropolitan Museum drawing are precisely among the details that were modified in the Munich variant. The sizes of the two drawings are close but not identical, and thus the relationship between the Metropolitan and Munich drawings must be indirect.   CCB

1. C.A., fol. 1082r (formerly fol. 391r-a); Richter 1970, vol. 2, pp. 325–27, no. 1340: "Ancora si potrà dare opera al cauallo di bronzo." See Beltrami 1919a, pp. 10–11, doc. no. 21; Pedretti 1977, vol. 2, p. 295; Villata 1999, pp. 16–17, no. 20.

2. Castiglione 1560, fol. 57r: "si occupò nella forma del cauallo di Milano, oue sedici anni co[n]tinui consumò."

3. "[U]no maestro o dua, apti a tale opera." Another letter from Lorenzo de' Medici to Giovanni Lanfredini in Rome on November 12, 1489, mentioning Pollaiuolo helps complete this interpretation; transcribed and discussed in Fusco and Corti 1992, pp. 16–18.

4. Vasari 1966– , vol. 3 (text), p. 507: "E si trovò dopo la morte sua il disegno e modello che a Lodovico Sforza egli aveva fatto per la statua a cavallo di Francesco Sforza duca di Milano; il quale disegno è nel nostro libro in due modi: in uno egli ha sotto Verona, nell'altro egli, tutto armato e sopra un basamento pieno di battaglie, fa saltare il cavallo addosso a uno armato. Ma la cagione perché non mettesse questi disegni in opera non ho già potuto sapere."

5. An artist in the circle of Antonio del Pollaiuolo may have similarly drawn two battle scenes (Uffizi, Florence, 14531 F and 14532 F) by connecting with pen and ink the holes one by one in the preliminary coarsely pricked outlines.

FRANCESCO DI SIMONE FERRUCCI

(Fiesole, 1437–Florence, 1493)

12. *Sketches of Figures of the Virgin Kneeling, Saint Peter Standing, Seated Allegorical Figures of Faith and Charity, and Child Standing on a Corbel (?)* (recto)
Sketches of Figures of Saint Sebastian Standing and the Virgin and Child with Angels (verso)

Pen and brown ink, over leadpoint or black chalk, on rose-washed paper, 274 mm × 198 mm (10 13/16 × 7 13/16 in.)
Inscribed in pen and dark brown ink on verso at lower left: *m. 53*
The Metropolitan Museum of Art, New York; Bequest of Walter C. Baker, 1971 1972.118.252

PROVENANCE: Earl of Brownlow; sale, Sotheby's, London, July 14, 1926, lot 17; Philip Hofer, Cambridge, Massachusetts (1898–1984; Lugt Suppl. 2087a); Walter C. Baker, New York.

LITERATURE: Berenson 1938, vol. 1, p. 48 n. 3, vol. 3, fig. 129; Popham and Pouncy 1950, pp. 39–40; Kurz 1955, pp. 40, 44, pl. 18c; Berenson 1961, vol. 1, p. 108; Virch 1962, no. 3; Bean and Stampfle 1965, no. 9; Grossman 1972, p. 15, fig. 1; Ames-Lewis 1981, pp. 84–85, 161, 183, n. 16; Bean 1982, pp. 92–94, no. 82; Ames-Lewis and Wright 1983, pp. 140–43, no. 25 (with general mention of the sketchbook only); Schulze-Altcappenberg 1995, pp. 144–45; Musée Condé 1995, pp. 48–50, 71, under no. 12; Elen 1995, pp. 253–55; Rubin and Wright 1999–2000, p. 220, under no. 42 (with general mention of the sketchbook only).

This boldly drawn double-sided sheet is part of a well-known dismembered Florentine sketchbook (now dispersed in a variety of collections; fig. 120) that apparently records sculptural models, most of which can be associated with the style of Andrea del Verrocchio's workshop. It also includes, however, motifs inspired by the work of such other Florentine sculptors as Antonio del Pollaiuolo, Benedetto da Maiano, Desiderio da Settignano, Luca della Robbia, and Bernardo Rossellino. This and nineteen other pages of the sketchbook are currently known, all of a similar size and drawing technique on rose-washed paper, and at least nine of these bear the same watermark (a Gothic M). The codicological evidence has been examined with particular attention by Albert J. Elen. Like catalogue number 8, most of the sheets are also drawn on both sides and bear inscriptions of many types, from dates to debit accounts to the names of individuals. The following collections own pages of this sketchbook: the Musée Condé, Chantilly (eight); Musée du Louvre, Paris (three); École des Beaux-Arts, Paris (two); British Museum, London (two); Kupferstichkabinett, Berlin (one); Musée des Beaux-

Arts, Dijon (one); Hamburger Kunsthalle (one). An additional sheet was last recorded in a private collection in 1983.[1] Two of the Chantilly sheets (21[15]; 22[16]) bear the date 1487, while one of the sheets in the École des Beaux-Arts, Paris (374 v), bears the date 1488. To judge from the very eclectic choices of sculptural motifs and styles, the sketchbook may have served as a visual record or sourcebook for the use of a modestly talented sculptor, or even a sculptor's apprentice. (Similar motifs are sometimes naively repeated in page after page of the sketchbook.) About 1850, when the sketchbook seems to have gotten noticed by scholars, it was ascribed to Andrea del Verrocchio himself, since his name is inscribed on one of the sheets used for the purpose of settling an account, and thus it became nicknamed the Verrocchio Sketchbook. In 1893, Giovanni Morelli (Ivan Lermolieff) attributed the sketchbook to the sculptor Francesco di Simone Ferrucci da Fiesole (Francesco di Simone Fiorentino), who was said by Giorgio Vasari to have been Verrocchio's pupil but who was in actuality Verrocchio's near contemporary.[2] From the little that is known about Francesco di Simone (he is not documented until 1463), he was likely a collaborator in the Verrocchio workshop. Scholars have usually accepted Morelli's attribution, though often with reservations (Georg Gronau expressing the most doubt in 1896), for the inscriptions on the pages seem to be by another hand than that of the artist of the sketches, and the names "Lorenzo" and "Gabrielo" also turn up.[3]

That the draftsman of the sketchbook is probably not the author of the actual motifs can be surmised from the fact that the main motif of the kneeling Virgin seen here in the center of the recto seems to be copied repeatedly on the other sheets, recording the incomplete state of the original work that served as a model. One such kneeling Virgin appears in a sheet at Chantilly (Musée Condé, 23[17] verso), while at least two further variants in drawings that were not part of the so-called Verrocchio Sketchbook are at the Palazzo Abatellis, Palermo, and the British Museum, London (1963-11-9-23). On the one hand, the drawings are close in style to a design in the Nationalmuseum, Stockholm, that may well be Francesco di

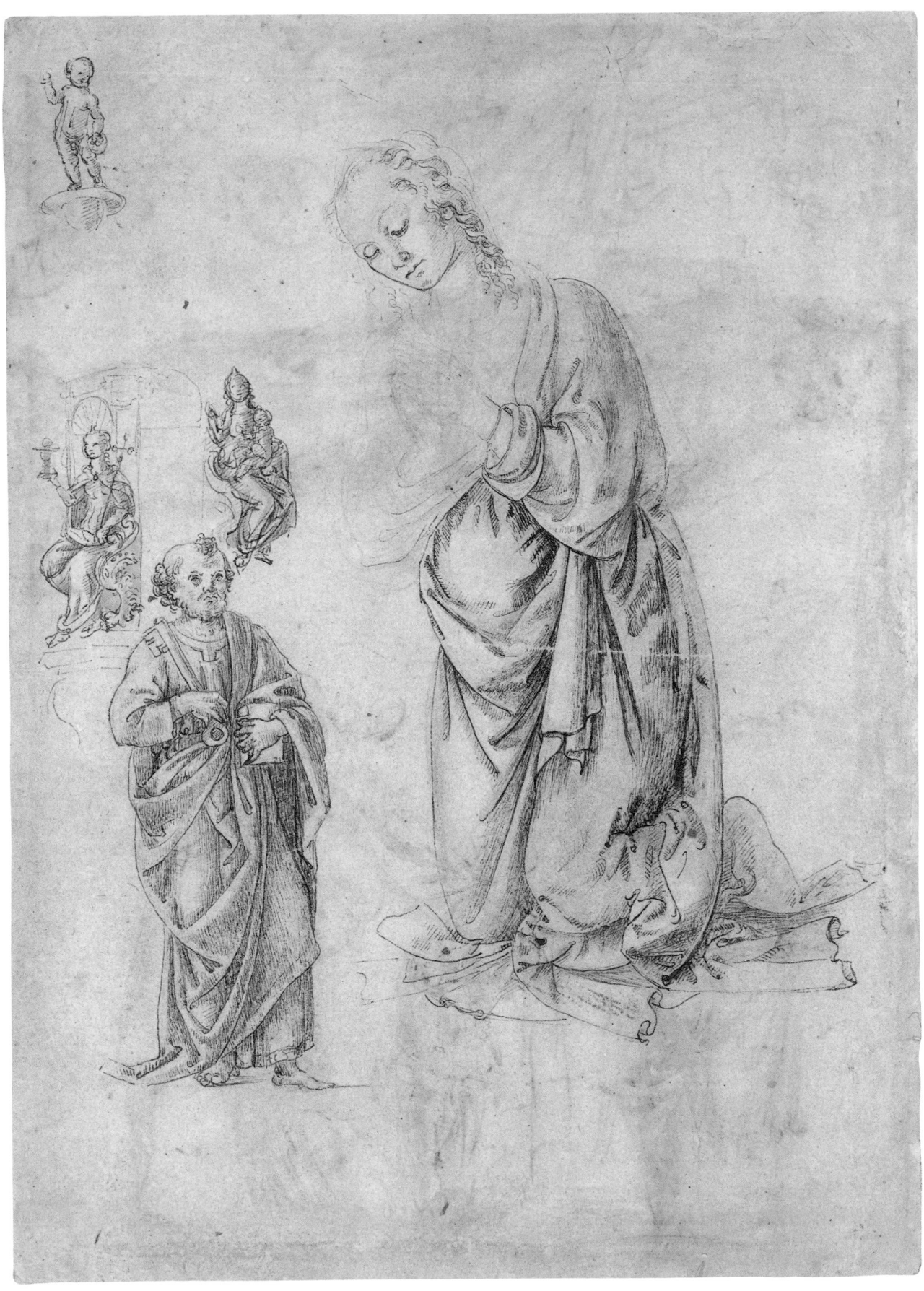

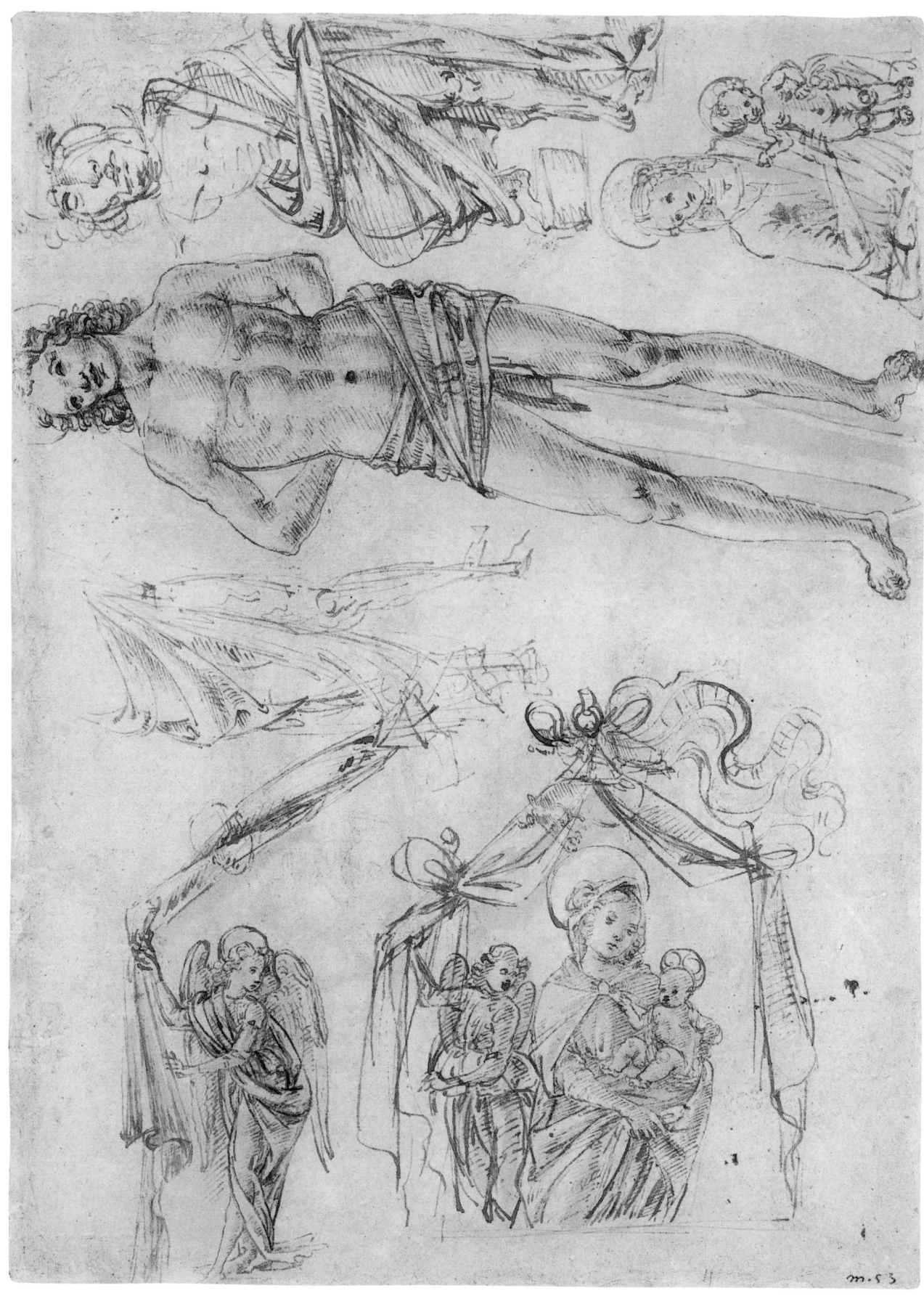

Cat. 12v

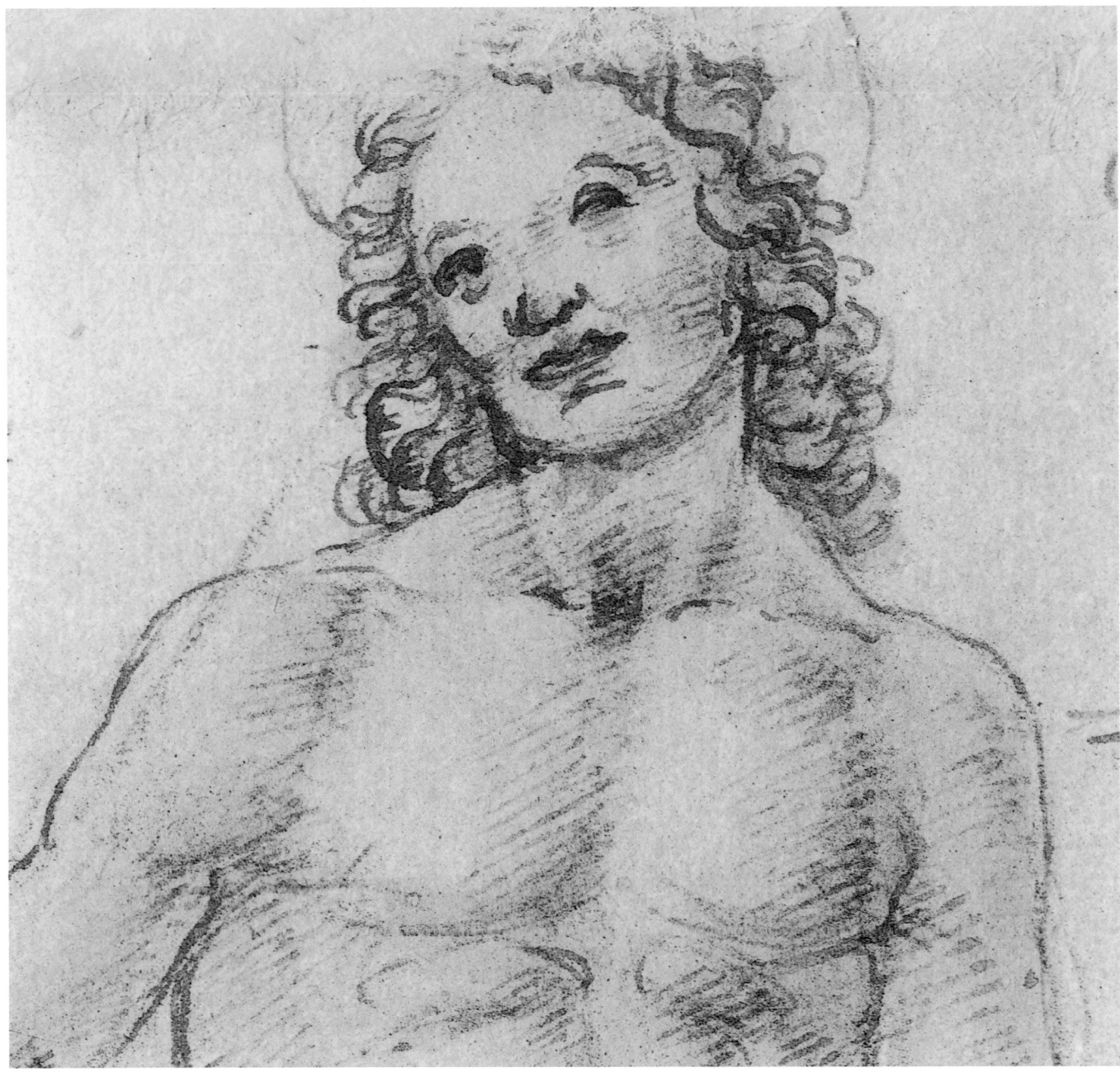

Cat. 12v *(detail)*

Simone's original study for the tomb of the jurist Alessandro Tartagni (San Domenico, Bologna), from about 1477 to 1480 and mentioned by Vasari. On the other hand, some of the annotations on the sheets conflict with the thesis of Francesco's authorship.   CCB

1. Elen 1995, p. 253.
2. Vasari–Milanesi 1906, vol. 3, pp. 371–72.
3. "Lorenzo" might refer to Lorenzo di Credi; "Gabriele" was the name of one of Francesco di Simone Ferrucci's sons.

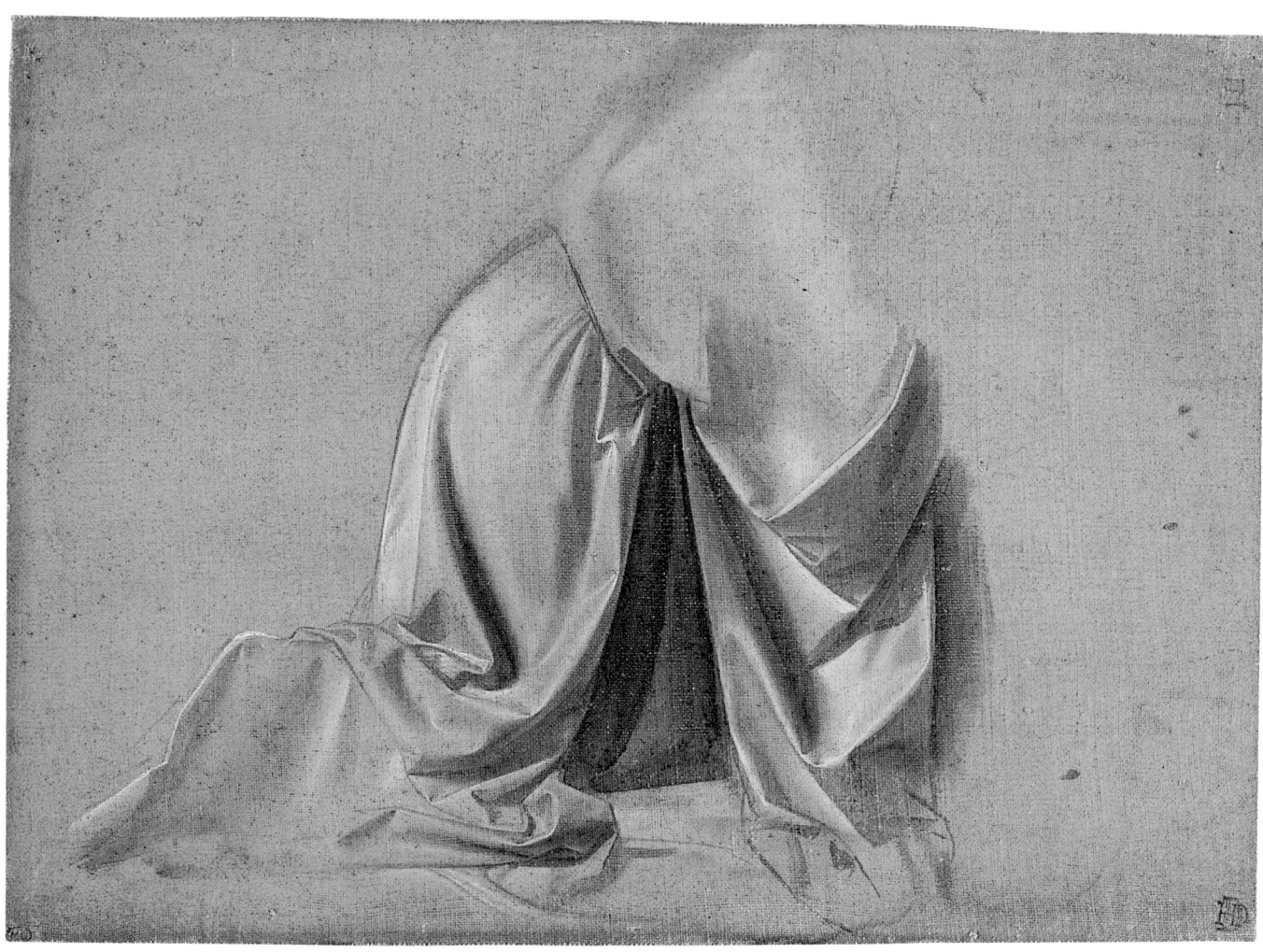

Cat. 13

LEONARDO DA VINCI

13. *Drapery for a Kneeling Figure*

Brush and gray-brown tempera, highlighted with white, on gray prepared linen; glued to secondary support, 206 × 281 mm (8 ⅛ × 11 ⅟₁₆ in.); perforations in upper right and left corners; yellowing around edges

Inscribed in brown ink in upper right of recto, partially erased: *IIII*; on verso: modern paraph in black chalk

Département des Arts Graphiques du Musée du Louvre, Paris RF 41904

PROVENANCE: Everard Jabach; *Inventaire après décès 1695–1696*, portfolio E: "14. Estudes de draperie dalberdur sur toile collee sur papier et rehaussé de blanc en detrempe"; P. Defer; H. Dumesnil (Lugt 739); 1900, sale, Paris, no. 251; Comtesse M. M.-P. de Béhague; Marquis H. de Ganay; Marquis J.-L. de Ganay; 1989, acquired by the Musée du Louvre; museum mark (Lugt 1886a).

LITERATURE: École des Beaux-Arts 1879, no. 61 (Florentine School, late fifteenth century); Louvre 1919, no. 34; Degenhart 1934, p. 224 n. 6 (Fra Bartolommeo); Berenson 1938, vol. 1, p. 62, vol. 2, no. 1071B, vol. 3, fig. 522; Popham 1947, p. 20; Biblioteca Medicea Laurenziana 1952, no. 7; Florisoone and Bacou 1952, no. 3; Berenson 1961, no. 1071B, vol. 3, fig. 440; Ragghianti and Dalli Regoli 1975, pp. 9, 31; Dalli Regoli 1976, p. 47 n. 16; Vezzosi 1980, fig. 3; Byam Shaw 1983, p. 11 n. 7, under no. 6; Cadogan 1983a, pp. 57–58, fig. 24; Pedretti and Dalli Regoli 1985, p. 51, under no. 3; Louvre 1989–90, no. 3; Pedretti 1989d, p. 178, fig. 2; Christiansen 1990, p. 573 (Verrocchio?); Arasse 1997, pp. 48, 52, fig. 22; Rubin and Wright 1999–2000, under no. 39, fig. 105 (with incorrect inv. no.); Baldinotti 2000, p. 87, fig. 17 (with incorrect inv. no.); Py 2001, p. 272.

Most authors connect this study to one with a similar motif in the Uffizi, Florence (420 E). For Bernard Berenson, it was a repetition of the latter and of another drapery study in the Musée du Louvre (cat. no. 14). Jean K. Cadogan denied this relationship, however, because the viewing angle in this drawing is different from that in catalogue number 14. In addition, part of Cadogan's argument hinges on the fact that none of the drapery studies can be linked to Leonardo's early works and that, therefore, comparisons and analogies within the group must remain purely stylistic. In opposition to the view later advanced by Keith Christiansen—that the sketch exhibited here may be related to the group that he attributes to Andrea del Verrocchio (see Musée du Louvre,

RF 41095)—she proposes that the drawings be divided between Verrocchio and Leonardo, based in great part on the differences in their approach to the treatment of light. By that reasoning, this drapery study would be by Leonardo's own hand: it displays a skill that far surpasses Verrocchio's in the rendering of light and anticipates—or accompanies, without being a preliminary study—the execution of the early paintings, in particular the angel in the *Baptism of Christ* (fig. 65). Let us keep in mind that the studies on *tela di lino* are primarily experimental and that forcing a relationship between them and sculptures or paintings undermines more than it enhances the quality of our assessment. FV

LEONARDO DA VINCI

14. *Drapery for a Kneeling Figure*

Brush and gray tempera, highlighted with white, on gray prepared linen; torso and right arm sketched with tip of the brush, 181 × 234 mm (7⅛ × 9¼ in.); trace of framing outline in pen and brown ink; glued to secondary support
Inscribed in brown ink in upper left corner of recto: *I*
Département des Arts Graphiques du Musée du Louvre, Paris 2256

PROVENANCE: Everard Jabach; *Inventaire après décès 1695–1696*, portfolio E: "14. Estudes de draperie dalberdur sur toile collee sur papier et rehaussé de blanc en detrempe"; Pierre Crozat, Paris sale, 1741, under no. 5 (Leonardo da Vinci); Nourri, Paris sale, 1785, no. 736 (Dürer); Ch.-P. J.-B. de Bourgevin Vialart de Saint-Morys; 1793, seized from emigrants fleeing the Revolution; 1796–97, placed in the collection of the Museum; mark of the Conservatoire (Lugt 2207); inv. MS Morel d'Arleux, vol. 6, 7752 (Albrecht Dürer); museum mark (Lugt 1886).

LITERATURE: Louvre 1879, no. 1641; Rosenberg 1898, p. 27, fig. 10; Müntz 1899, p. 520, no. 43; Berenson 1903, vol. 2, no. 2801 (school of Verrocchio); Louvre 1919, no. 31; Demonts 1921, no. 2; Demonts 1922, no. 2; Sirén 1928, pl. 19B (Verrocchio); Suida 1929, p. 30, pl. 7; Berenson 1933–34, p. 246, fig. 4; Degenhart 1934, pp. 224–26 nn. 4, 9, fig. 6 (Fra Bartolommeo); Berenson 1938, vol. 1, p. 61, vol. 2, no. 1067A, vol. 3, fig. 521; Popham 1945, p. 12, no. 3; Amboise 1952; Biblioteca Medicea Laurenziana 1952, no. 6; Florisoone and Bacou 1952, no. 2; Berenson 1961, vol. 1, p. 101, vol. 2, no. 1067A, and

under no. 1071B; Sérullaz 1965, no. 3; Clark and Pedretti 1968–69, under no. 12521; Ragghianti and Dalli Regoli 1975, p. 32, fig. 15; Palais de Tokyo 1980; Béguin 1983, p. 83; Cadogan 1983a, pp. 54–56, fig. 21; Pedretti and Dalli Regoli 1985, p. 51, under no. 3; Arquié-Bruley, Labbé, and Bicart-Sée 1987, vol. 1, no. 55, vol. 2, p. 68; Kemp and Roberts 1989, no. 3; Louvre 1989–90, no. 1; Christiansen 1990, p. 573; Bull 1992, pp. 70–73, fig. 5; Arasse 1997, pp. 48, 52, fig. 23; Rubin and Wright 1999–2000, under no. 39; Py 2001, p. 271, fig. p. 272.

Art historians have often linked this study to the drapery study for a seated figure (cat. no. 17), perhaps because the two works were formerly placed on a single mount. Unlike the other sheet, however, the attribution of this drawing has not been placed in doubt except by Bernhard Degenhart (1934). Nevertheless, when looking at it, we must take into account the retouching that has modified its nature. The indication of a torso and the sketch of one arm have transformed what was merely a study of falling folds of fabric arranged on a piece of furniture into a figure bending forward, arm extended. Like another drawing, at the Uffizi, Florence (420 E), it is often understood as a study for the angel's robe in the *Annunciation*

283

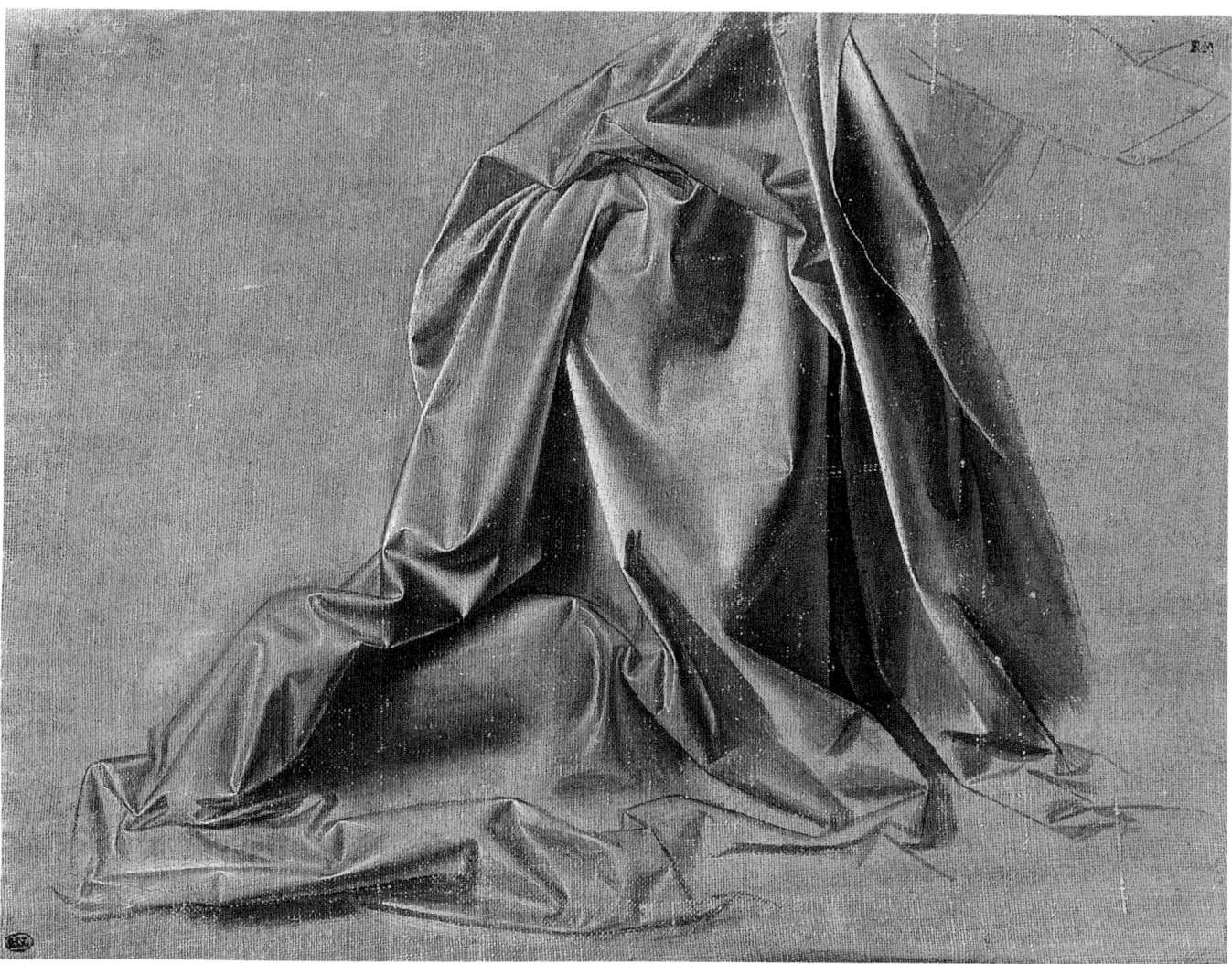

Cat. 14

(Cadogan 1983a) or, more justifiably, for that of the angel on the left in the *Baptism of Christ* (figs. 65, 66). The Louvre drawing exhibited here and the Uffizi study are not directly related to the elaboration of these two paintings, done several years apart; the drawings should be considered works in themselves. Nonetheless, they are to be interpreted within the same context as that surrounding the paintings: the inscription of forms in space, of which the angel in the *Baptism* is one of the first and most masterful demonstrations, especially because of the oblique perspective in the turning motion of the figure. There is no precise correspondence between these drawings and the two paintings: the poses and the choices made in the studies are different. In the elaboration of these draperies, modeled "with a sure and decisive gesture, at once compact and resplendent," there is an evident desire to complicate

rather than simplify, a desire the painter would later renounce.[1] Leonardo's art as it existed at the time can best be perceived in the unretouched parts of the drawing, that is, the entire central part of the figure but not the lower part, where brushstrokes have been added. The placement of the *lumi*, tapering along the crest of the folds and arranged in fine layers of hatching in the brighter areas, is again found in the angel of the *Annunciation* and the one in the *Baptism*. The motifs studied on *tela di lino* are not "habited forms" but are indicative of Leonardo's research at that date, which he would conduct ever after, aimed at creating living forms captured in the movement proper to them.   FV

1. Pedretti and Dalli Regoli 1985, p. 51.

LEONARDO DA VINCI

15. *Standing Draped Figure*

Brush and gray tempera, highlighted with white, on dark gray prepared linen; traces of black chalk in bust and head; glued to secondary support, 315 × 168 mm (12 7/16 × 6 5/8 in.)
Inscribed in brown ink in upper left corner of recto: *III*; on verso: modern paraph in black chalk
Département des Arts Graphiques du Musée du Louvre, Paris RF 1081

PROVENANCE: Everard Jabach; *Inventaire après décès 1695–1696*, portfolio E: "14. Estudes de draperie sur toile collee sur papier et rehaussé de blanc en detrempe"; Édouard Gatteaux (Lugt 852); 1881, bequeathed to the Musée du Louvre; museum mark (Lugt 1886a).

LITERATURE: Louvre 1919, no. 32; Demonts 1921, no. 3; Demonts 1922, no. 3; Berenson 1933–34, pp. 245–48, fig. 6; Degenhart 1934, pp. 224–25 nn. 4, 9 (Fra Bartolommeo); Berenson 1938, vol. 1, p. 62, vol. 2, no. 1070A, vol. 3, fig. 526; Popham 1945, p. 12, no. 4; Amboise 1952; Biblioteca Medicea Laurenziana 1952, no. 9; Florisoone and Bacou 1952, no. 7; Bouchot-Saupique 1953–54, fig. 2; Laclotte 1956, p. 101, under no. 139; Berenson 1961, vol. 1, pp. 102–3, vol. 2, no. 1070A, and under no. 1071D; Sérullaz 1965, no. 4; Dalli Regoli 1976, pp. 47–48 n. 16; Palais de Tokyo 1980; Cadogan 1983a, pp. 57–59, fig. 25; Louvre 1989; Louvre 1989–90, no. 10; Christiansen 1990, p. 573 (Verrocchio); Py 2001, p. 272.

Bernard Berenson, Jean K. Cadogan, and Keith Christiansen connect this drawing and catalogue number 16 to another study for a standing figure in profile, in the collection of Barbara Piasecka Johnson in Philadelphia.[1] All three were understood to be studies for an Adoration of the Magi. Although Christiansen attributes the present drawing to Verrocchio, Cadogan cites it and the other two as works by Leonardo, slightly predating the *Annunciation* or part of the first phase in the development of that painting (fig. 66). The highlights give the cloth a palpable texture, simulating a three-dimensional effect.

It seems that the shaded part on the left, running along the entire upper half of the figure, was original to the drawing, as were the lines rapidly tracing the face and bust with the tip of the brush. The hesitations and reworking of that part seem to have been intended to transform the "abstract" drapery into a living form, corresponding to a typology Leonardo would later develop.   FV

1. Louvre 1989–1990, no. 11; sale, Sotheby's, Monaco, December 1, 1989, no. 74.

LEONARDO DA VINCI

16. *Drapery for a Standing Figure*

Brush and gray tempera, highlighted with white, on gray prepared linen; glued to secondary support, 196 × 153 mm (7 3/4 × 6 1/8 in.); cloth probably cut along all four borders
Inscribed in brown ink in upper right corner of recto: *IX*; on verso: modern paraph in black chalk
Département des Arts Graphiques du Musée du Louvre, Paris RF 1082

PROVENANCE: Everard Jabach; *Inventaire après décès 1695–1696*, portfolio E: "14. Estudes de draperie dalbedur sur toile collee sur papier et rehaussé de blanc en detrempe"; Édouard Gatteaux (Lugt 852); 1881, bequeathed to the Musée du Louvre; museum mark (Lugt 1886a).

LITERATURE: Louvre 1919, no. 33; Demonts 1921, no. 4, pl. 4; Demonts 1922, no. 4; Degenhart 1934, pp. 224–25 nn. 4, 9, fig. 7 (Fra Bartolommeo); Berenson 1938, vol. 1, p. 62, vol. 2, 1070B; Florisoone and Bacou 1952, no. 78; Tours 1956, no. 27; Berenson 1961, vol. 1, p. 102, vol. 2, no. 1070B, and under no. 1071D; Sérullaz 1965, no. 5; Dalli Regoli 1976, pp. 47–48 n. 16; Cadogan 1983a, pp. 57–59, fig. 6; Louvre 1989–90, no. 12; Christiansen 1990, p. 573 (Verrocchio); Arasse 1997, p. 48, fig. 37; Py 2001, p. 272.

The pattern of folds at the waist is among the motifs found in Leonardo's painted works both at this time and later: gathers that pleat by pleat accentuate the volumes and render the weight of the fabric. This can be seen in the drapery of the angel in the *Annunciation* (fig. 66), the yellow and blue drapery in the *Madonna of the Carnation* (fig. 132), the drapery in the *Benois Madonna* (fig. 133), and even in the fold under the shoulder of the angel's robe in the *Baptism of Christ* (fig. 65). Jean K. Cadogan thinks the upper part of the drawing has been cut off.

See also the discussion under catalogue number 15.

                                                        FV

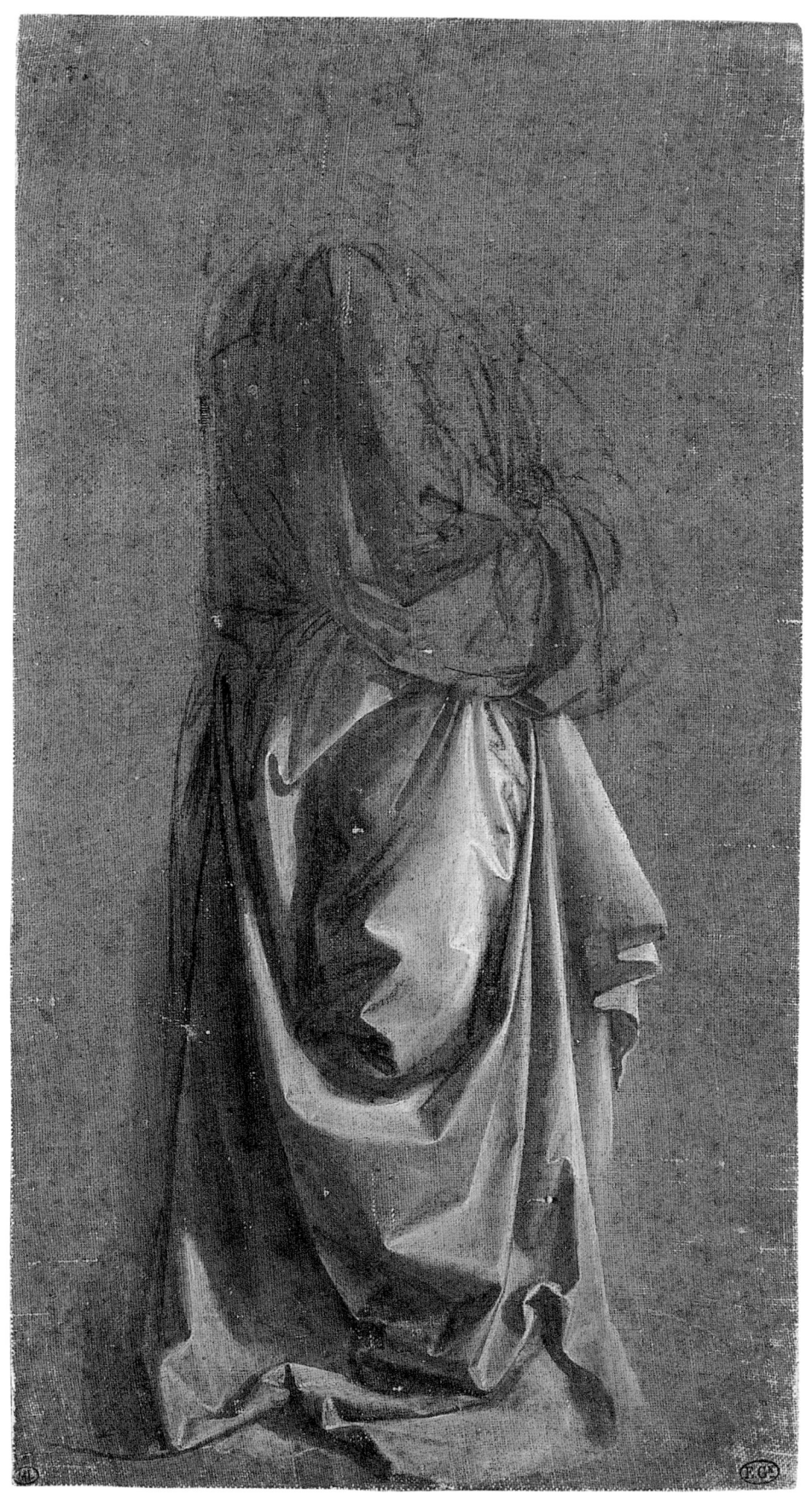

Cat. 15

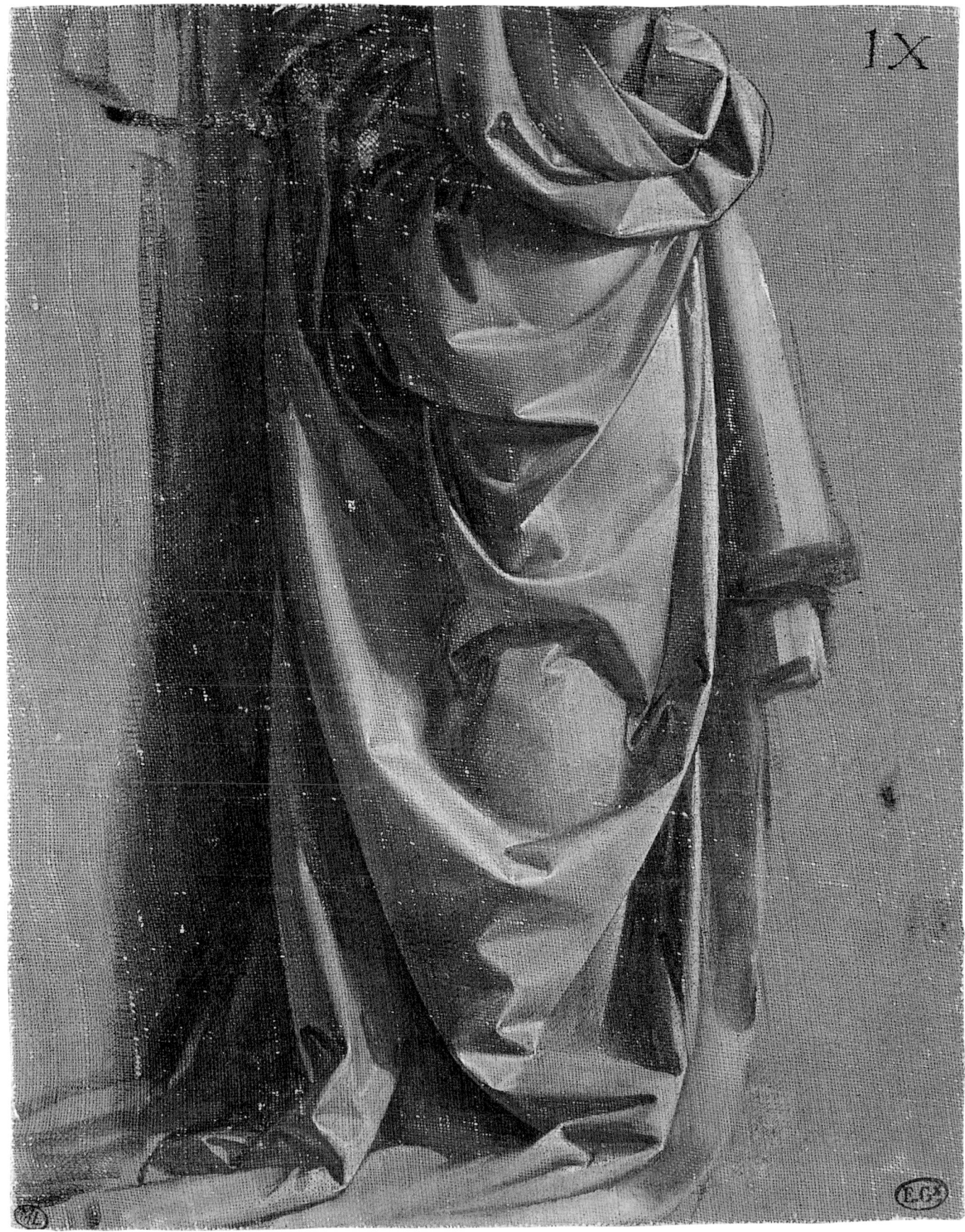

IX

Cat. 16

LEONARDO DA VINCI

17. Drapery for a Seated Figure

Brush and gray tempera, highlighted with white, on gray prepared linen; 266 × 233 mm (10½ × 9¼ in.); traces of framing outline in pen and black ink; worn spots in preparation; upper and lower left corners reconstituted and gray-tinted; glued to secondary support

Département des Arts Graphiques du Musée du Louvre, Paris 2255

PROVENANCE: Everard Jabach; *Inventaire après décès 1695–1696*, portfolio E: "14. Estudes de draperie dalberdur sur toile collee sur papier et rehaussé de blanc en detrempe"; Pierre Crozat, Paris sale, 1741, under no. 5 (Leonardo da Vinci); Nourri, Paris sale, 1785, no. 736 (Dürer); Ch.-P. J -B. de Bourgevin Vialart de Saint-Morys; 1793, seized from emigrants fleeing the Revolution; 1796–97, placed in the collection of the Museum; mark of the Conservatoire (Lugt 2207); inv. MS Morel d'Arleux, vol. 6, 7752 (Albrecht Dürer).

LITERATURE: Louvre 1866, no. 389; Gruyer 1887, p. 472, fig. p. 469; Müller-Walde 1889, p. 53, pl. 18; Gruyer 1891, p. 33 n. 1; Rosenberg 1898, p. 28, fig. 12; Müntz 1899, p. 521, pl. 11, no. 44; Wickhoff 1899, pp. 212–13 nn. 1, 2 (Domenico Ghirlandaio); Wölfflin 1899, p. 247 n. 1; Berenson 1903, vol. 1, p. 158, pl. 112, vol. 2, no. 1061, vol. 3, pl. 112; Seidlitz 1909, vol. 1, pp. 36, 384 n. 19 (Credi?); Thiis 1913, pp. 72–74, repr. p. 73; Gronau 1914, pp. 55–56, fig. p. 55; Küppers 1915, pp. 293–94 (Domenico Ghirlandaio); Louvre 1919, no. 29; Meder 1919, p. 448, fig. 194; Poggi 1919, p. lix, pl. 115; Demonts 1921, no. 1; Demonts 1922, no. 1; Commissione Vinciana 1928– , vol. 1, p. 15; Suida 1929, pp. 29–30 (Verrocchio?); Valentiner 1930, pp. 60–61, pl. 1-E; Degenhart 1932a, p. 299 (Domenico Ghirlandaio); Berenson 1933–34, pp. 247, 248, 252, fig. 8; Degenhart 1934, pp. 224–25 nn. 4, 9, 226, 230–31 (after Ghirlandaio?); Petit Palais 1935, no. 568; Berenson 1938, vol. 1, p. 62, vol. 2, no. 1061, vol. 3, fig. 530; Palazzo dell'Arte 1939, p. 159; Popham 1945, p. 11, no. 2; Bovi 1952, p. 72, fig. p. 75; Florisoone and Bacou 1952, no. 1; Berenson 1961, vol. 1, pp. 103, 104, 105 n.; Louvre 1962, no. 7; Sérullaz 1965, no. 2; Bacou 1968, no. 11; Fahy 1969, p. 151 n. 56, fig. 34 (Domenico Ghirlandaio); Dalli Regoli 1976, pp. 47–48 n. 16; Arasse 1978, p. 51; Grossman 1979, pp. 108, 123 n. 29; Ames-Lewis and Wright 1983, p. 147, fig. 3 B; Byam Shaw 1983, p. 11, under no. 6, p. 16, under no. 10; Cadogan 1983a, pp. 33–36, fig. 2; Cadogan 1983b, p. 283, fig. 17 (Domenico Ghirlandaio); Kustodieva 1984, p. 15, fig. 13; Pedretti and Dalli Regoli 1985, p. 68, under no. 17; Marchini 1985a, p. 26, fig. 10; Arquié-Bruley, Labbé, and Bicart Sée 1987, vol. 2, p. 68; Louvre 1989–90, no. 16; Christiansen 1990, pp. 572–73; Scrase 1990, p. 151; Pedretti 1990a, p. 166, fig. 4; Sérullaz 1996, p. 565, fig. 4; Arasse 1997, pp. 48, 53, fig. 20; Brown 1998b, pp. 79–80, 82, fig. 67; Bambach 1999a, p. 464 n. 65; Marani 1999b, pp. 17, 60–61, fig. p. 16; Rubin and Wright 1999–2000, p. 105, fig. 79; Baldinotti 2000, p. 87, fig. 18; Cadogan 2000, no. 104, pl. 106 (Ghirlandaio); Fornasari 2001, p. 44, fig. 25; Py 2001, p. 270, fig. p. 271.

The study exhibited here is the most famous of all the sketches on *tela di lino*, which total sixteen, or more than twenty if one adds the studies of heads and figures in the same medium and today divided among various museums.[1] This sketch is often believed to be related to the elaboration of the figure of the Virgin in the Uffizi *Annunciation* (fig. 66), like the drawing from the former Ganay collection exhibited here (cat. no. 13) and another study of a seated figure at the Uffizi, Florence (437 E). Unlike the two others, the Louvre figure displays a contrapposto pose; the figure is initiating a turn, perceptible in the way the legs are drawn and accentuated by the orientation of the torso, which is implied more than actually presented, thanks to the angle of the fold in the upper left section. That motif tends toward a roundness by means of which Leonardo defines the form he wishes to represent. This bend of the fold, which suggests the curving drape without showing it altogether, can be seen, for example, in the *Benois Madonna* of about 1478 (fig. 133) and, later, in the *Virgin and Saint Anne* (see cat. no. 107). That turning movement, which shifts the figure toward the right and is accompanied by a raised arm — the gesture of the Virgin in the Uffizi painting (fig. 66) — is already indicated here. Similarly, in the drapery drawing and in the *Annunciation* (fig. 66), Leonardo studied what could be called the fall of the folds, the way the heavy fabric cascades in waves and is held in place all around the form as if the original momentum remained in force even far from its origin. The sculptures done between 1408 and 1415 by a group of artists that included Donatello, for the lower niches in the main portal of the Cathedral in Florence, display that same monumentality. We are indebted to Bernard Berenson for an appreciation of the studies' modernity. In 1938 he clearly saw the unity of the group done during the master's youth: "Leonardo was perhaps the first modern artist who treated drapery neither as mere calligraphy nor as ornament [but as] . . . real tissues, made up as real clothing."[2] Contrary to the present author's opinion in 1989–90, these studies are not, strictly speaking, preliminaries to other works as some critics continue to maintain; but they are also not "uninhabited," that is, without visible forms.

Leonardo's research had a formal, objective exactitude. The arrangement of folds, studied from inert forms — clay models

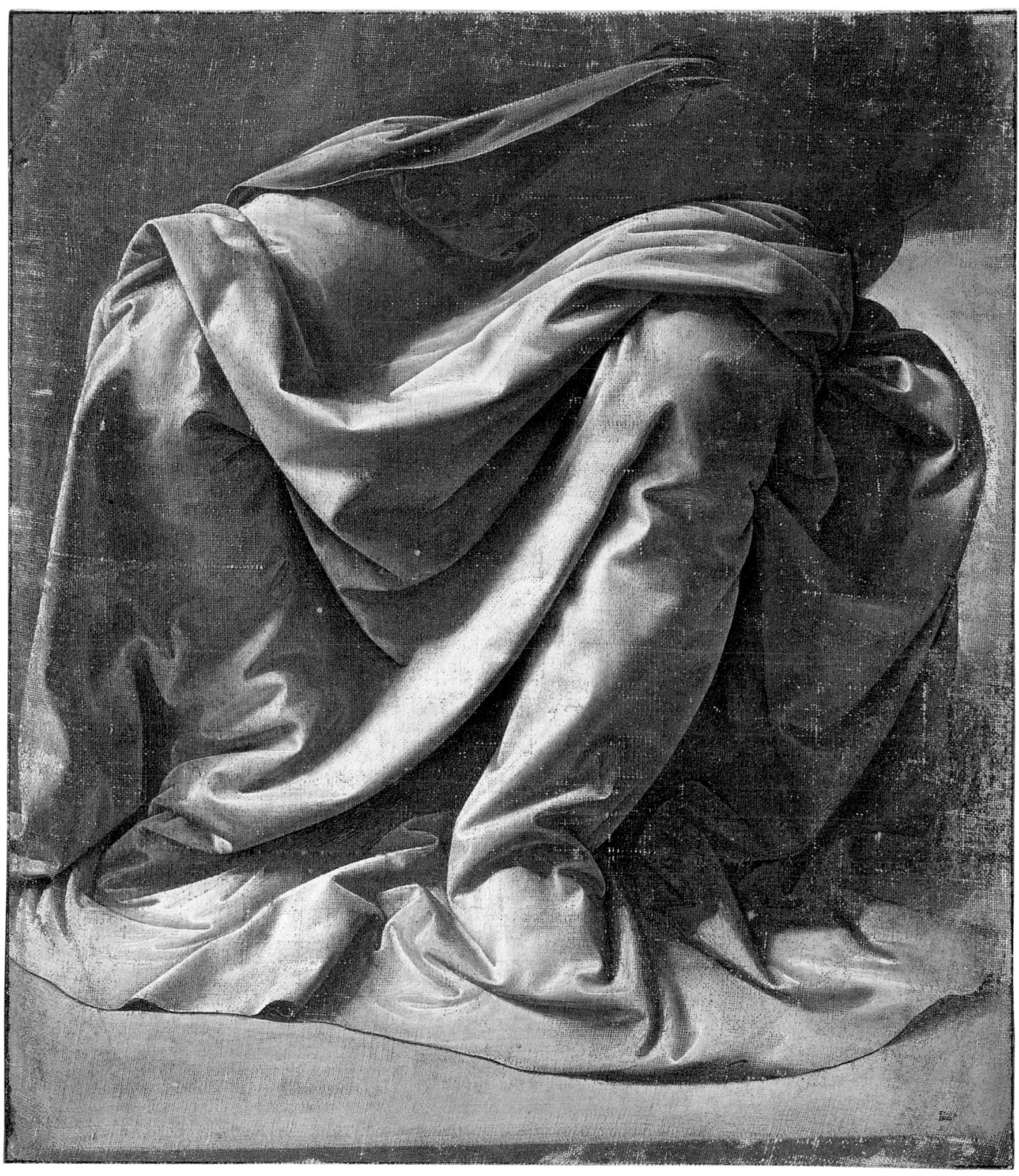

Cat. 17

covered with draperies — was determined by the nature of the cloth chosen. It has long been established that the description of Leonardo's method for modeling the clay figures, as it was given by Vasari, is identical to that which Vasari himself recommends in the introduction to his *Lives*.

Paradoxically, the attribution of the Louvre drapery study displayed here is the least in dispute because of its very high quality; yet it is the only one that (in 1899) was linked to a painting by another artist. Heinrich Wölfflin was the first to draw attention to the close analogy between that drapery and the one covering the Virgin in Domenico Ghirlandaio's *Virgin and Child with Saints,* known as the San Giusto altarpiece, now in the Uffizi (881). Did Ghirlandaio really copy Leonardo? Wölfflin chose to concur with the traditional attribution. Franz Wickhoff, while also noting the similarity, rejected the idea of a copy and argued that the Louvre study was a Ghirlandaio original like several studies in that same group in the Uffizi.[3] This hypothesis was embraced until very recently by some authors, including Jean K. Cadogan, who believed it was a preparatory study for the drapery in the San Giusto altarpiece, which dates from about 1479–80. This writer links it to the Berlin drawing for the fresco *Saint Matthew and the Angel* on the vault of the chapel of Santa Fina in San Gimignano (5039),[4] while at the same time recognizing differences in style between the two and in relation to others of the group (437 E, for example). The entire discussion, undertaken following Wickhoff's proposal and hinging, in succession, on the names Verrocchio, Ghirlandaio, and Fra Bartolommeo as possible authors of the drawing in question, did not take into account the essential fact, pointed out by Gigetta Dalli Regoli,[5] that these are not so much works to be compared to paintings or sculptures as studies devoted to the use of supple surfaces and fluid materials; above all, they are a meditation on light.

Keith Christiansen, discussing the views advanced by Cadogan, remarks that the complexity of the Louvre study—the delicacy with which shadow and light are indicated—makes it impossible to credit any relation to the geometric clarity of Ghirlandaio's work, In this context, he suggests that the same model may have been used collectively, that is, may have served several artists in the same studio.

I would like to reconsider the entire question of drapery studies, at least those in the Musée du Louvre, based on an observation of their technique. These draperies were reworked by a later hand at an indeterminate date. Pietro C. Marani came to this opinion in May 2001, after he studied the technical execution of these sketches in conjunction with the curators of the Département des Arts Graphiques. The reworking is most visible in the study under discussion, and this fact has certainly played a role in the diversity of attributions that have been proposed. The retouching is visible on the lower edge in the part located under the drapery. Other additions can be seen on the right side, in the outline of the drapery, and in the background. In addition, there is substantial highlighting of the folds of the figure itself, reinforcing the sculptural effect of that form, which thereby achieves a timeless perfection. It is in the upper part of the underside of the draping, at waist level, that the light touch of the *lumi* on the hem of the fabric, left intact, allows one to discern the work as it probably appeared originally.

This drawing and catalogue number 14 entered the Musée du Louvre in 1793 under Albrecht Dürer's name and, listed thus in the first inventory, appeared on the same mount until they were identified by Frédéric Reiset. They were placed one above the other and since 1866 have been exhibited in the galleries of the museum.

FV

1. See Pedretti and Dalli Regoli 1985, p. 66, under no. 15.
2. Berenson 1938, p. 176.
3. See Pedretti and Dalli Regoli 1985, pp. 49–50.
4. Cadogan 2000, no. 75, pl. 105.
5. Pedretti and Dalli Regoli 1985, p. 50.

LEONARDO DA VINCI

18. *Virgin and Child Holding a Cat*

Pen and brown ink, brush and brown wash, over stylus and traces of leadpoint, 84 × 71 mm (3 $\frac{5}{16}$ × 2 $\frac{13}{16}$ in.) maximum
Private collection, New York

PROVENANCE: Comte Moritz von Fries, Vienna (1777–1826; Lugt 2903); Arthur Hungersford Pollen, London; Mrs. A. H. Pollen; Bodmer Foundation, Geneva.

LITERATURE: Venturi 1922, p. 2; Commissione Vinciana 1928– , vol. 1, p. 23, pl. 27; Bodmer 1931, pp. 125 (left), 381; Berenson 1938, vol. 2, p. 116, no. 1045 A; Palazzo dell'Arte 1939, p. 158; Popham and Pouncey 1950, pp. 59–60, under no. 99; Biblioteca Medicea Laurenziana 1952, p. 21, under no. 23; Berenson 1968, vol. 2, p. 202, no. 1045 A; Nicodemi 1980a, p. 39; Vezzosi 1982, fig. 74; Marani 1989, p. 128, under no. 5A; Popham 1994, no. 8B; Wiemers 1996, pp. 275–76, fig. 261.

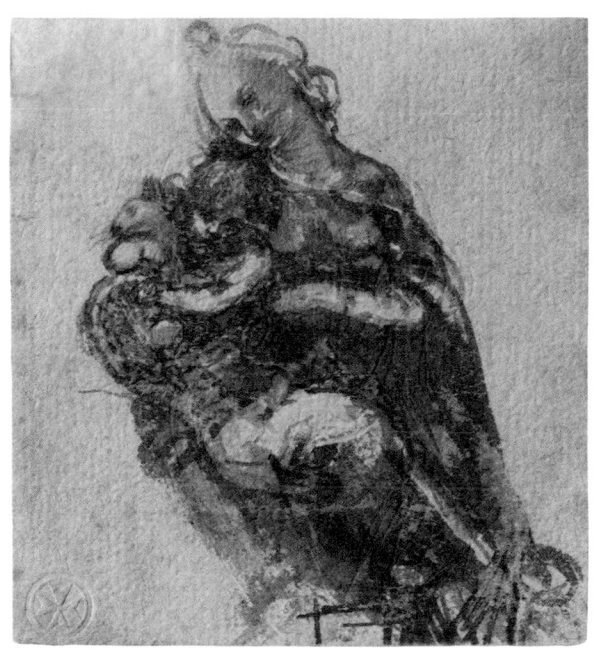

Cat. 18 *(actual size)*

This rarely exhibited drawing is of great sculptural presence. It offers one of Leonardo's earliest exercises on the theme of the Madonna of the Cat and probably dates from the mid- to late 1470s, to judge from the Virgin's delicate facial type, three-quarter-view pose, and apparently elaborate headdress, all elements that are still strongly reminiscent of his teacher Andrea del Verrocchio. Here, the child holds the cat to the left. In a double-sided sheet of studies Leonardo experimented with reversing the orientation of the design (figs. 71, 72), which he drew by holding the paper against the light and tracing the composition through from one side of the sheet onto the other.[1] In the drawing on the recto (fig. 72) the child holds the cat to the left, as in the present sketch, and in the drawing on the verso (fig. 71) he holds the cat to the right. The figural group in the lower part of a sheet in Bayonne (fig. 128) offers another closely related idea for the composition in the present sketch, though the Virgin and Child face to the right, toward the cat.[2] A number of other sketches of the general subject exist (cat. no. 19), but these do not seem to fall into an order that can readily be reconstructed, and the reversals of the design left to right, or right to left, in such drawings should probably not be interpreted as forming a linear sequence. A painted panel by one of Leonardo's pupils (fig. 129) closely reprises the figural group seen in the present drawing but shows the motif cropped to a three-quarter length.[3] The Brera

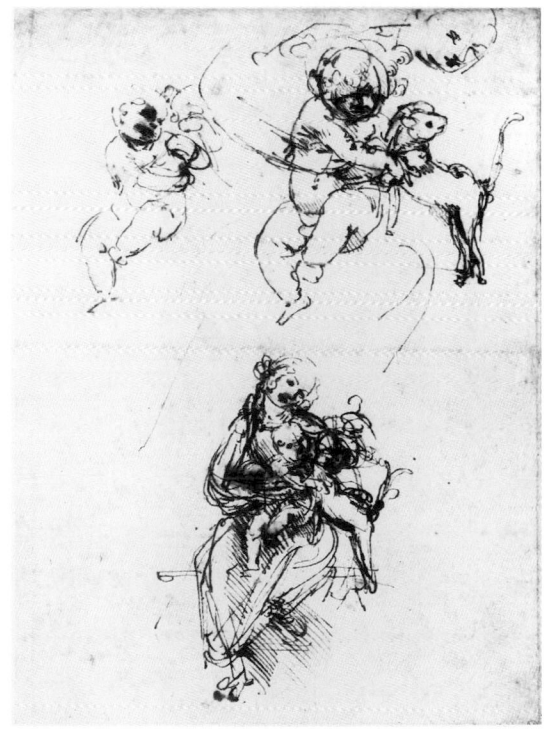

Fig. 128. Leonardo da Vinci, *Studies for the Madonna of the Cat.* Pen and brown ink, 232 × 175 mm. Musée Bonnat, Bayonne 152

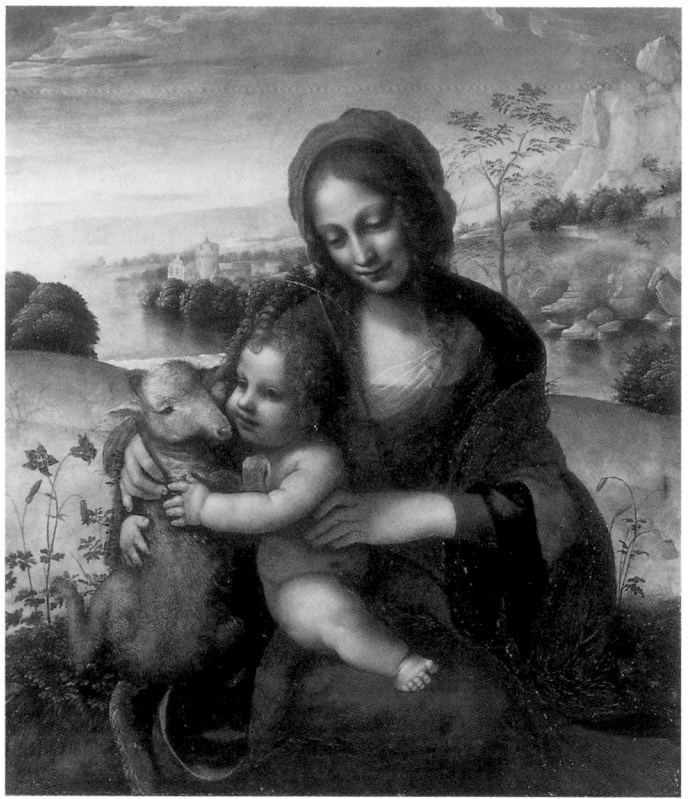

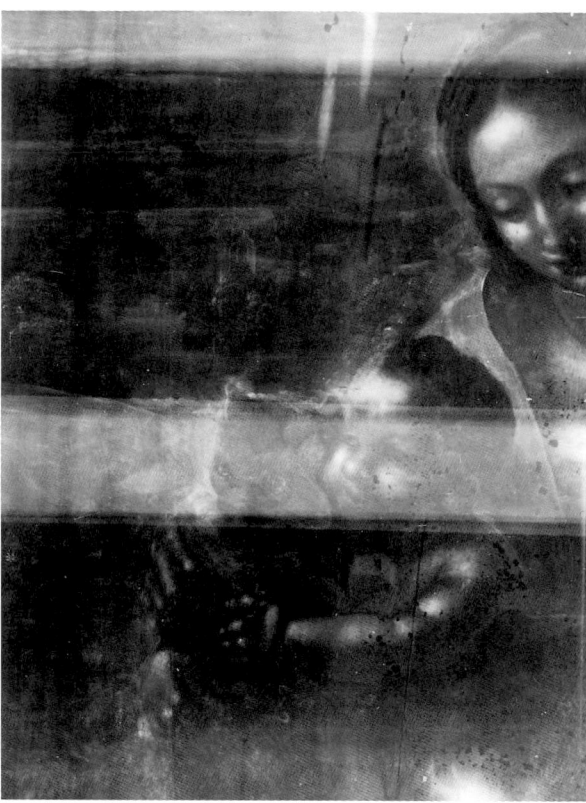

Fig. 129. Circle of Leonardo da Vinci (Cesare da Sesto?), *Virgin and Child with Lamb.* Oil on wood, 52 × 60 cm. Pinacoteca di Brera, Milan 286

Fig. 130. Radiograph of fig. 129

panel (fig. 129) also substitutes a lamb, in allusion to the Agnus Dei, for the cat in Leonardo's drawings, but X-radiographs of the painting confirm that the artist originally attempted to depict a cat much like the animal seen in the present drawing by Leonardo, before he finally overpainted it with the lamb (fig. 130).[4] As is often explained, the ostensible reason for the cat in Leonardo's drawings comes from the legend that a cat was born at the same time that the Christ Child was born. One may well wonder, however, whether in all of Leonardo's compositional drawings the cat

may not have been meant to be a stand-in for a lamb in the final painting. In many of the quick sketches that scholars have often associated with the *Madonna of the Cat*, the cat does not always look like a cat and at times oddly resembles a dog or a lamb.   CCB

1. Popham and Pouncey 1950, pp. 58–60, no. 97.
2. Bean 1960, no. 41.
3. Suida (1929, p. 24, fig. 35) attributed the Brera painting to Giovanni Antonio Bazzi "Il Sodoma," whereas Pietro C. Marani has more recently given it to Cesare da Sesto (?); Marani 1987a, pp. 115–23.
4. Discussed in Marani 1987a, pp. 118–20.

LEONARDO DA VINCI

19. *Sketches of a Child Holding and Playing with a Cat; a Cat* (recto)
Sketches of the Virgin and Child with a Cat; a Child with a Cat; a Cat (verso)

Pen and dark brown ink over traces of leadpoint (recto); pen and
dark brown ink over a sketch with a stylus (verso), 213 × 149 mm
(8 ³⁄₈ × 5 ⁷⁄₈ in.)
Watermark: Flower (close to Briquet 6645)
The British Museum, London 1857-1-10-1

PROVENANCE: Comte Moritz von Fries, Vienna (1777–1826; Lugt
2903); Rev. Dr. Henry Wellesley, Oxford (1791–1866; Lugt 1384),
museum stamp (Lugt Suppl. 302).

LITERATURE: British Museum 1858, no. 48; Berenson 1903, vol. 2,
p. 58, no. 1025; Seidlitz 1909, vol. 1, p. 76; Thiis 1913, pp. 168–70;
Poggi 1919, pls. 52, 53; Venturi 1920, pp. 79–80, figs. 18, 19; De
Rinaldis 1926, p. 45, fig. 11; Commissione Vinciana 1928– , vol. 1,
p. 23, pls. 19, 20; Sirén 1928, pls. 25A, 25B; Bodmer 1931, pp. 123–24,
381; Berenson 1938, vol. 2, p. 113, no. 1025; Bottari 1942, pls. 25, 26;
Giglioli 1944, p. 95, pls. 52, 53; Popham and Pouncey 1950, pp. 59–
60, no. 99; Berenson 1961, vol. 2, p. 197, vol. 3, fig. 454, no. 1025;
Richter 1970, vol. 1, pp. 303, 308, nos. 483, 498; Gould 1975,
pp. 40–41, fig. 14; Nicodemi 1980a, p. 38; Kemp 1981, p. 54;
Vezzosi 1982, figs. 80, 81; Pedretti and Dalli Regoli 1985, p. 60,
under no. 10, fig. 39; Turner 1986, p. 27, no. 4; Pedretti 1990b, p. 32,
fig. 5; Moro 1991, p. 120; Popham 1994, nos. 12, 13; Wiemers 1996,
pp. 270–71, figs. 254, 254a; Rubin and Wright 1999–2000,
pp. 210–11, no. 37.

The rapid pen-and-ink sketches on this sheet seem dazzling in their economy of stroke and immediacy and also
appear to have been inspired by the challenge of composing
the design for the *Madonna of the Cat*. Although more passive, the pose of the child holding the lovely, rebelling animal
in catalogue number 18 resembles that portrayed in the lower
left of the recto and lower right of the verso of the present
sheet. Here, these motifs also seem to relate to the solutions
that are depicted in mirror images on the British Museum
double-sided sheet of studies (figs. 71, 72), arranged in a composition with an arched top. Leonardo drew that sheet by
holding the paper against the light and tracing the composition through from the verso onto the recto in order to reverse
the designs. That practice is yet one more example of Leonardo's
supreme ability to consider reversals of form by turning in
space, which in the present sheet seems everywhere demonstrated in the subtle considerations of each motif. As a whole,

however, the various poses of the child playing with the cat
most directly resemble those seen in yet another sheet of
sketches of identical technique and style at the British Museum
(1860-6-16-98), which also frequently integrates the figure of
the Virgin into the groupings. That sheet may have preceded
the present sketches in Leonardo's sequence of design. The
present sheet of sketches omits the Virgin almost entirely (she
is very lightly indicated only on the verso), in order to focus
on the interaction of the Christ Child with the cat.

The sketches here clearly take on a life of their own, as the
artist—pen and paper in hand, ready to record every movement, and apparently with no preconceived final picture guid-
ing his hand as he draws—follows the child playing with the
cat. (The experience seems not unlike that of a cinematogra-
pher letting the camera track his subject, open to the suggestions of the moment.) This is a profoundly modern way of
drawing. It is clear that the rich variety of poses emerging on
the page would not all make it into the final picture; the composition would be born, rather, from the brainstorm. At the
top of the recto of the drawing, the seated child struggles to
hold the half-reluctant cat, which can almost be heard purring
into his ear. Below, toward the center, the squatting child pets
the escaping cat as it prances away with elegant indifference.
In the lower left, the cat twists away from the tight embrace
of the seated child, in a struggle that makes for one of the
most dynamic effects of contrapposto before Mannerism. If
more compact in mass, it rivals Andrea del Verrocchio's bronze
Putto with a Dolphin (fig. 131), probably produced contempo-
raneously, at the latest in the last years of the 1470s or in the
early 1480s.[1] Of no less interest, in one of the verso sketches
toward the center, the cat scurries from the child's embrace, and
the boldly reinforced outlines on its body suggest each progressive step in the sequential motion (an almost cinematic effect).

Precisely because of Leonardo's manner of composing
designs with the "brainstorm technique," however, it seems
clear that one set of ideas often led to another, related picture.
Thus, to complicate matters, the lower left motif on the recto
of the present sheet is not only close to the final conception of
the *Madonna of the Cat*, as it is portrayed in the double-sided

293

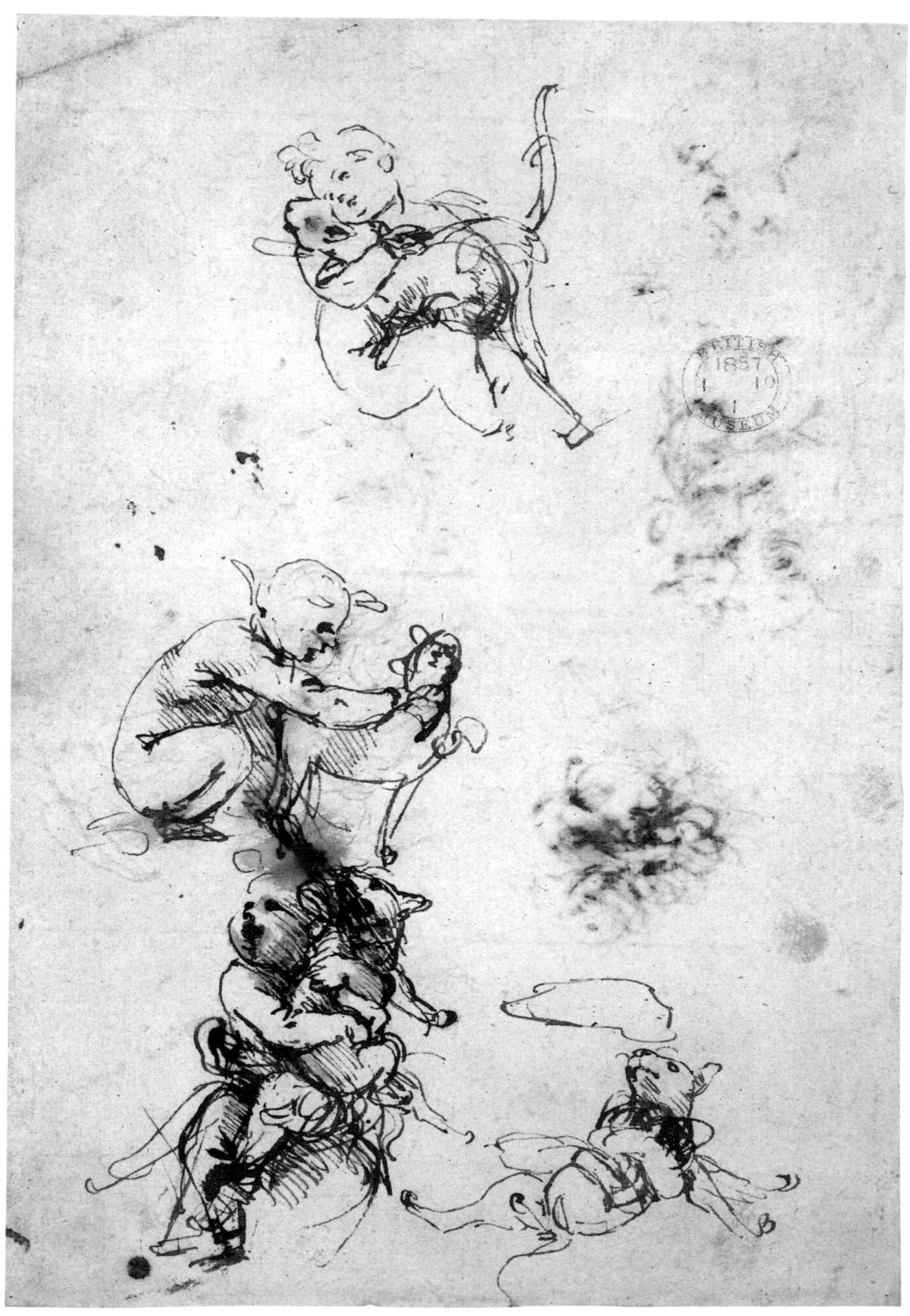

Cat. 19R *(actual size)*

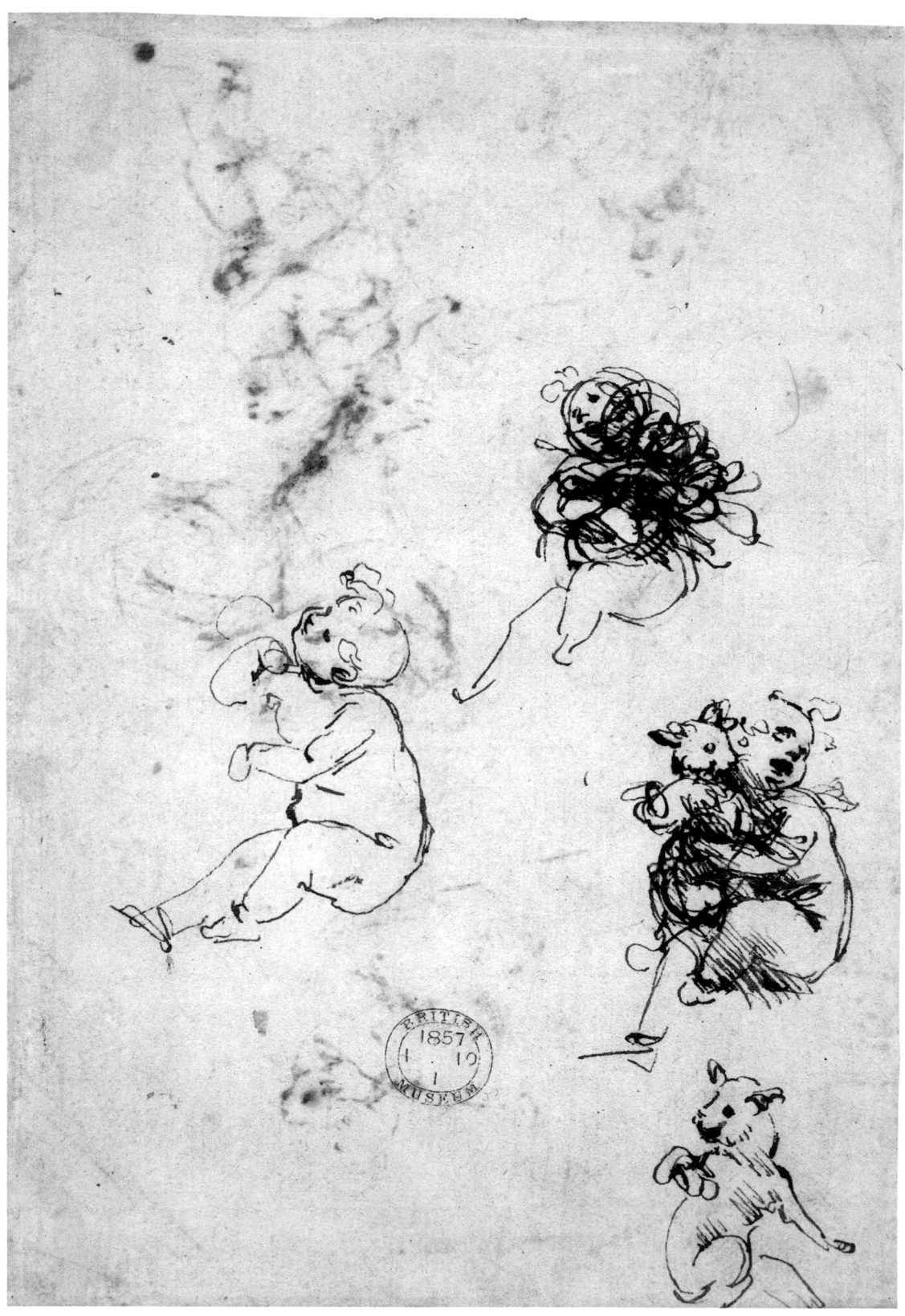

Cat. 19v *(actual size)*

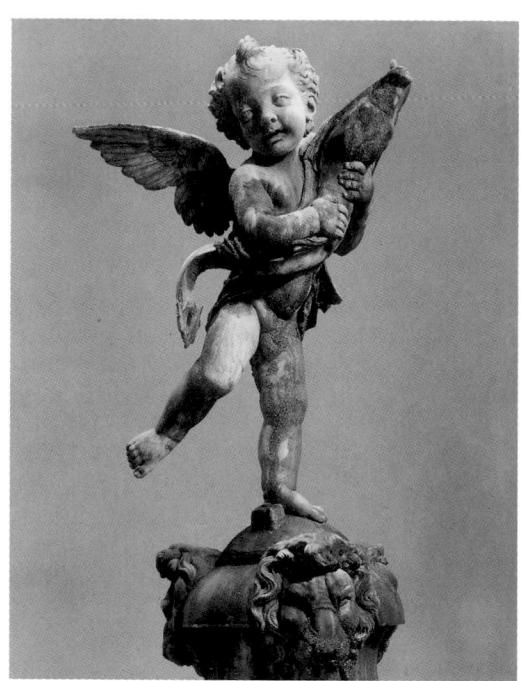

Fig. 131. Andrea del Verrocchio, *Putto with a Dolphin*. Bronze, H. 67 cm. Palazzo Vecchio, Florence

sheet at the British Museum (figs. 71, 72); it is also curiously like a motif seen on the upper right in a copy after a lost original drawing by Leonardo (Windsor, RL 12564). The motif in the dry Windsor copy is part of an entirely different pictorial conception, and since it seems very finished in its details, it may record a final idea for a painting. There, the figure who is presumably the Virgin sits, apparently on the ground, head seen in profile facing to the left, and legs sprawled open to support the child nursing at her breast; another child plays by her side with a cat. The iconography of the recombined image in the Windsor copy adds yet another layer of mystery to the *Madonna of the Cat* project.   CCB

1. On Verrocchio's sculpture, see Butterfield 1997, pp. 132, 222–23, no. 20.

LEONARDO DA VINCI

20. *The Virgin and Child; Profiles; Technical Sketches* (recto)
The Virgin and Child (verso)

Silverpoint and leadpoint, reworked with pen and brown ink on pale salmon-pink prepared paper (recto); pen and medium brown ink over leadpoint on unprepared cream paper, small sketch in leadpoint only (verso), 202 × 157 mm (7 ^{15}/16 × 6 ^{3}/16 in.)
Inscribed in metalpoint on recto at bottom right in right-to-left script: *in principio era;* at upper right: *iesus e V[ergine]*
The British Museum, London 1860-6-16-100

PROVENANCE: Sir Thomas Lawrence, Bristol and London (1769–1830; Lugt 2445); Samuel Woodburn, London (1786–1853; Lugt 2584, 2591; Suppl. 2378a); Woodburn sale, Christie's, London, June 8, 1860, lot 1056; museum stamp (Lugt Suppl. 302).

LITERATURE: Berenson 1903, vol. 2, p. 58, no. 1027; Colvin 1912, pls. A, B; Gronau 1912, pp. 253–59, fig. 1; Thiis 1913, pp. 165–67; Poggi 1919, pls. 56, 57; Venturi 1920, pp. 74–76, figs. 14, 15; De Rinaldis 1926, p. 45, fig. 7; Commissione Vinciana 1928– , vol. 1, p. 23, pls. 28, 29; Sirén 1928, pls. 26A, 26B; Bodmer 1931, pp. 117,

118, 379–80; Clark 1933b, p. 139; Clark 1935, under no. 12569; Berenson 1938, vol. 2, p. 113, no. 1027; Bottari 1942, pl. 22; Giglioli 1944, pp. 95–96, pls. 56, 57; Popham and Pouncey 1950, p. 60, no. 100; Heydenreich 1954, vol. 1, pp. 30, 183, vol. 2, p. 18, pls. 23, 25; Castelfranco 1956, pp. 35, 55–56, pls. 8b, 11; Berenson 1961, vol. 2, p. 197, no. 1027; Castelfranco 1966, p. 71, fig. 7; Gould 1975, pp. 40–41, fig. 15; Nicodemi 1980a, p. 40; Kustodieva 1985, pp. 49–50, fig. 19; Pedretti 1987b, p. 34; Parronchi 1989, p. 49, fig. 9; Popham 1994, nos. 15, 16; Arasse 1998, pp. 340–41, fig. 232; Marani 2000b, pp. 90–92; Butterfield 2001.

The soft metalpoint drawing technique, reworked with pen and ink on pink prepared paper, of these dainty studies for a Madonna and Child helps date the work to the very late 1470s. The figural types are much like those in the *Madonna of the Carnation* (fig. 132). The British Museum *Madonna*

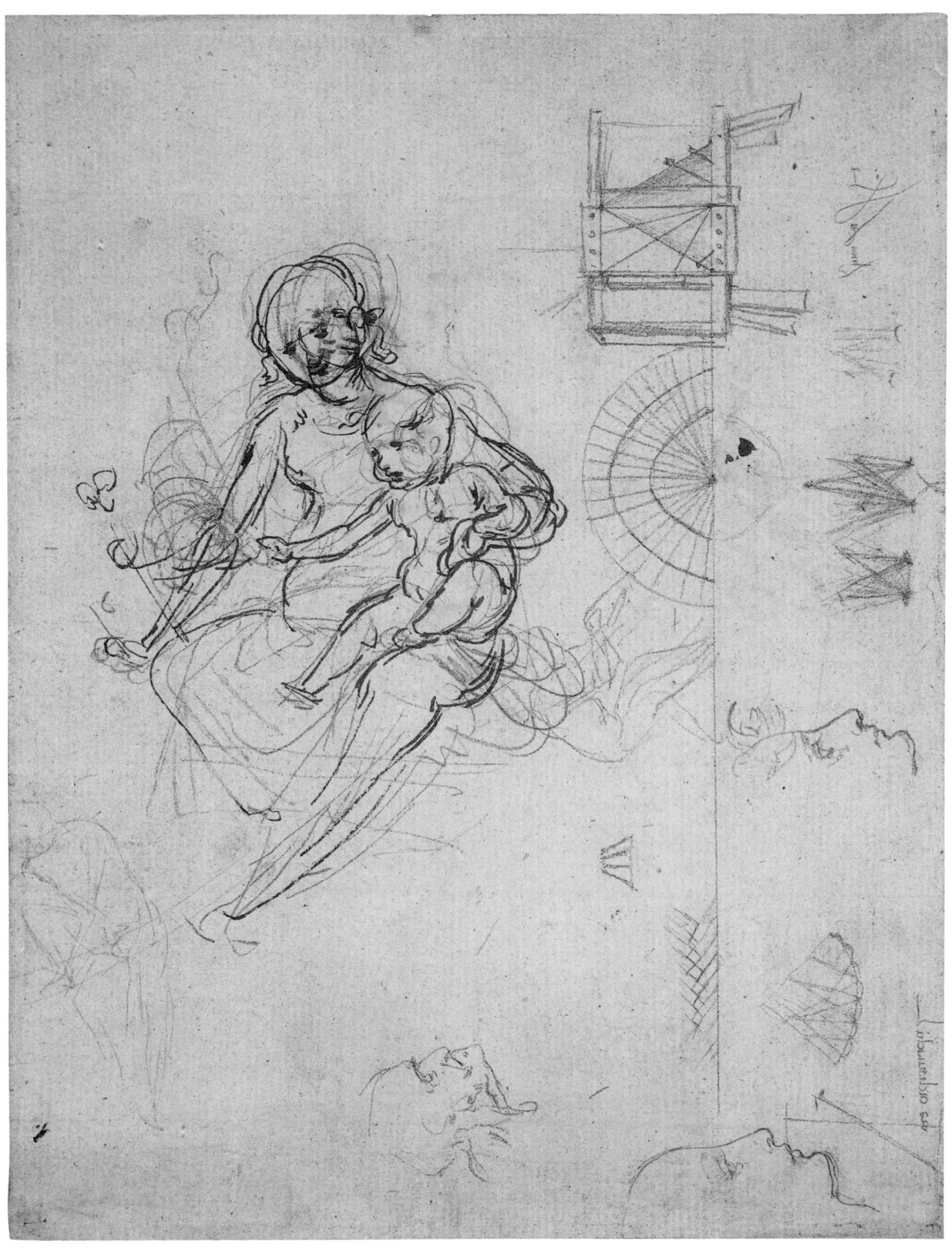

Cat. 20R *(actual size)*

studies can probably be identified with an enigmatic reference to two paintings mentioned in a note by Leonardo that is inscribed on a fragmentary sheet with pen-and-ink sketches (fig. 39): "1478, I began the two Virgin Marys."[1] On the recto of the British Museum sheet, toward the center of the lower border and seen sideways, is a small sketch of an old man with grotesque profile (nearly a "nutcracker" type) that is of almost exactly the same design as the old man on the left in the Uffizi sheet with Leonardo's inscription about the *Madonnas* of 1478 (fig. 39). Moreover, both sheets of figural sketches bear unrelated technological studies, as well as an identical neat, deliberate style of script with sumptuous flourishes, though Leonardo's inscriptions in the British Museum sheet are brief. The Uffizi and British Museum sheets must consequently be of the same date.

On the verso of the British Museum sheet, the sketch of the Virgin and Child on the right includes the arched top of the

intended painting. Since the arrangement of the figures, with the Virgin seated in a three-quarter view facing to the right, exactly matches the composition of the *Benois Madonna* (fig. 133), the British Museum sketches must represent Leonardo's early ideas for the picture. The artist probably drew the studies of the Virgin and Child on the recto first, and these, too, seem to relate to the conception of the *Benois Madonna*, for the infant sits on the legs of his mother in a similar three-quarter view, facing to the left, and the Virgin holds a four-petaled flower. This initial idea for the composition, on the recto, also seems connected in its overall rhombic shape to the earliest of the sketches for the *Madonna of the Cat* (cat. no. 18). Kenneth Clark plausibly proposed that the faint leadpoint composition sketch on the lower part of the verso, showing a woman in profile facing to the left, was a preliminary idea for the *Madonna Litta* (fig. 82). Clark then linked the composition to a list, written by Leonardo about 1481–83, either before he

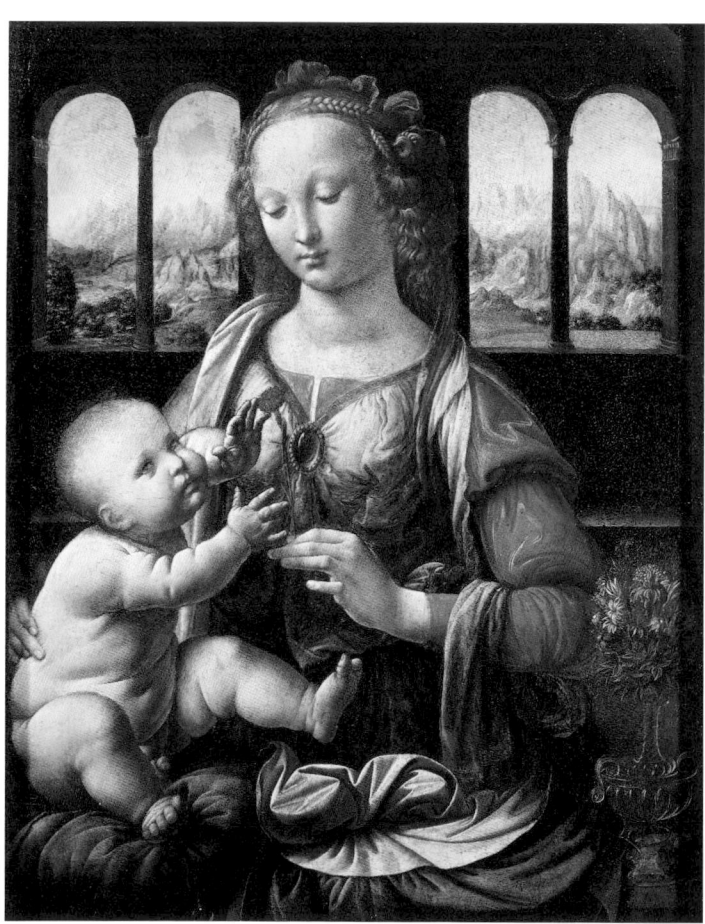

Fig. 132. Leonardo da Vinci, *Madonna of the Carnation*. Oil on wood, 62.2 × 47.6 cm. Alte Pinakothek, Munich 7776

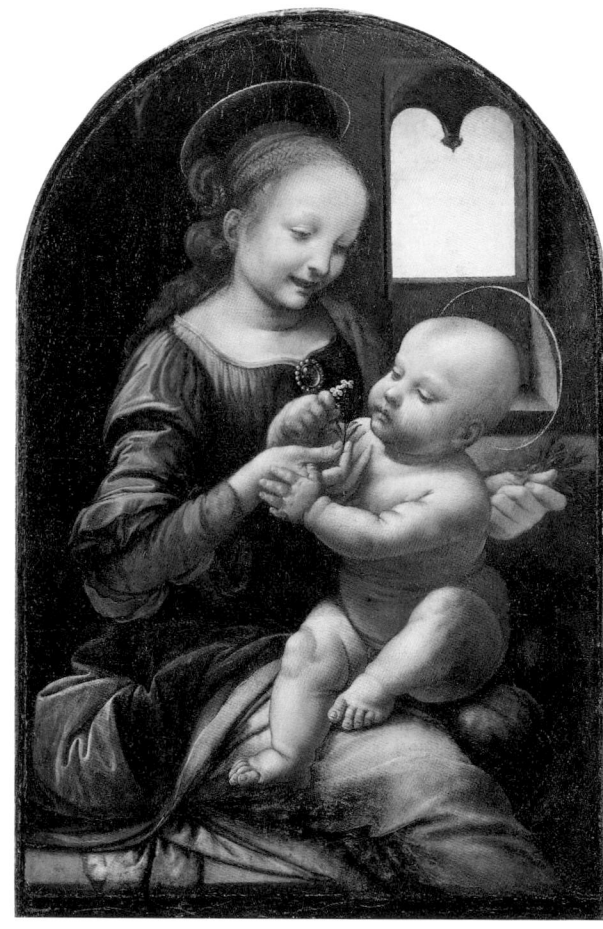

Fig. 133. Leonardo da Vinci, *Madonna and Child (Benois Madonna)*. Oil on canvas transferred from wood, 49.5 × 31.5 cm. State Hermitage Museum, Saint Petersburg 2773

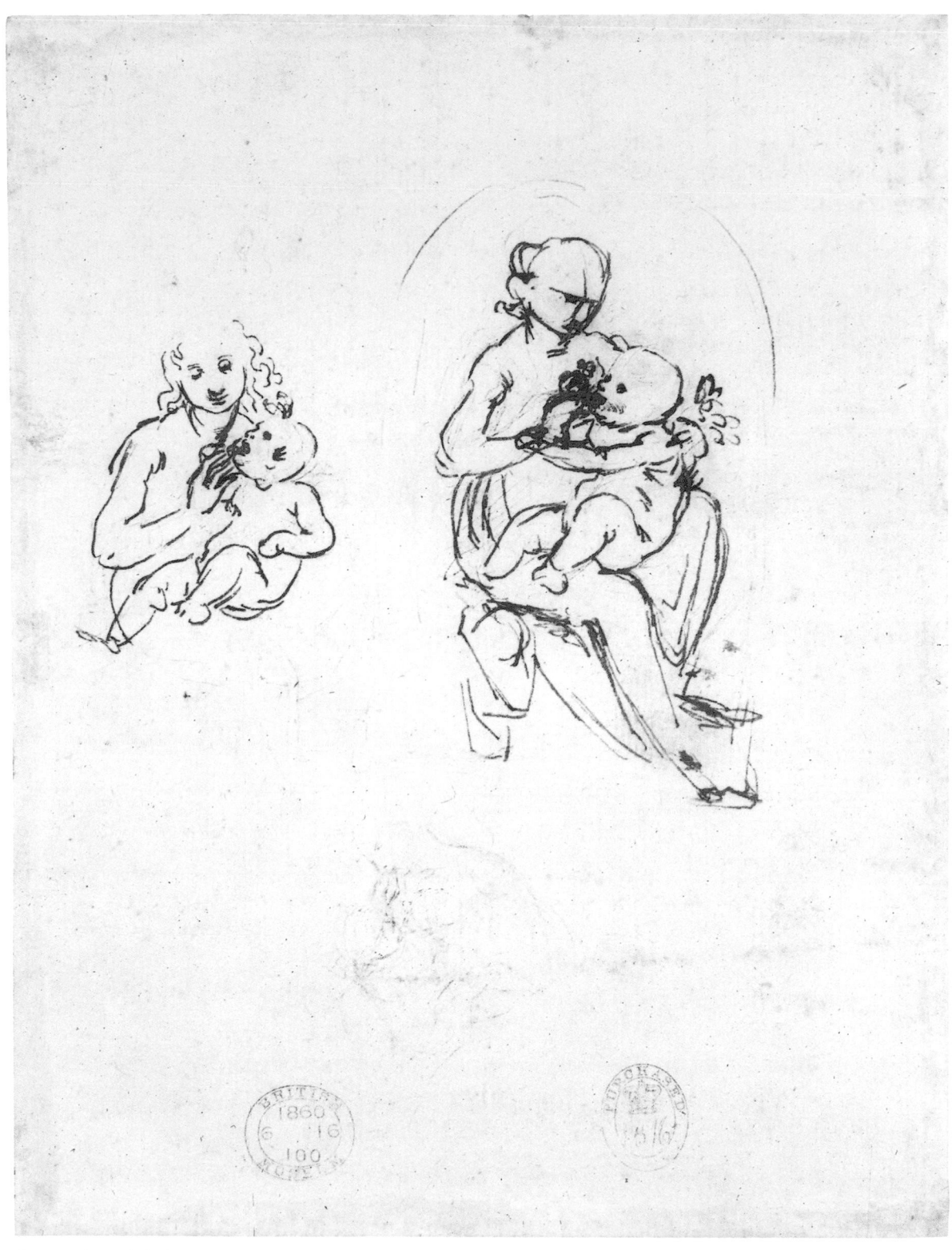

Cat. 20v *(actual size)*

left Florence or soon after he arrived in Milan, of works of art that he was to take with him; they included "another [Madonna] almost [finished], which is in profile."[2] This assertion is not entirely convincing and is basically unprovable.   CCB

1. Uffizi, Florence, 446 E, inscribed on upper left: *Fieravante di Domenicho in Firenze e chompar / amantissimo . quanto mio . . .;* below it, on upper left: *in dei nom . . . / amant . quanto;* lower left: . . . *bre 1478 jnchominciaj . le . 2 . V[er]gine marie / . . . e chompa in Pisstoja.* Partly transcribed in Richter 1970, vol. 1, p. 379, no. 663; see Chronology.
2. C.A., fol. 888r (formerly, fol. 324r); Richter 1970, vol. 1, p. 388, no. 680: "vn' altra [nostra donna] quasi [finita], che' [in] proffilo."

LEONARDO DA VINCI

21. *Young Woman Bathing an Infant* (Il Bagnetto); *the Buttocks of an Infant*

Pen and brown ink, brush and brown wash, over black chalk; glued to secondary paper support, 185 × 114 mm (7¼ × 4½ in.)
Inscribed in pen and brown ink on verso in right-to-left script legible from recto, although sheet is glued to a collector's mount; upper right column of recto (upper left column of verso): *affabile / assu[n]to / adussto / armonja / anicchillare / antepossto / attonito;* upper left column of recto (upper right column of verso): traces of a column of four words of which the second seems to be *tremebo[n]do*

and the fourth *taciturno;* two or more lines barely visible at lower left, of which only the word *forte* or *forse* can be read
Faculdade de Belas Artes, Universidade do Porto, Oporto 99.1.1174

PROVENANCE: Commendatore Vittorio Genevosio, Turin (called also Cavaliere Gelozzi or Gelosi; Lugt 545; probably his mount); Marchese Giovanni Antonio Turinetti di Priero (probably the sheet cited in Turinetti's inventory of April 2, 1801, as by Raffaellino da Reggio); unidentified Portuguese collector; Academia de Marinha e Comercio, Oporto; 1835 Academia de Belas Artes, Oporto (light purple stamp of the academy's collection; not in Lugt).[1]

LITERATURE: Vasconcelos 1962–63, no. 2 (Rafaelino da Regio [*sic*]); Vasconcelos 1963 (Rafaelino da Regio [*sic*]); Pouncey 1978, p. 405; Pedretti 1979c, p. 15; Vezzosi 1982, p. 74, fig. 83; Pedretti and Dalli Regoli 1985, pp. 18–19, figs. 17, 37; Scrase and Stock 1985, no. 28; Pereira Viana 1987, no. 26; Pouncey in Di Giampaolo 1994, pp. 233–35, fig. 3; Weston-Lewis 1994, pp. 130–31, 143 n. 21; Letze and Buchsteiner 1997 (hors catalogue); Pedretti 1997a; Almeida-Matos 1998; Moreira 1998, pp. 27, 29–31; Pedretti 1998a; Pedretti 1998b, pp. 22–25; Pouncey 1998; Pedretti 1998–99, pp. 48–53, no. 2; Turner 2000–1, pp. 20–21, no. 2; Turner 2002, pp. 22–23, no. 2.

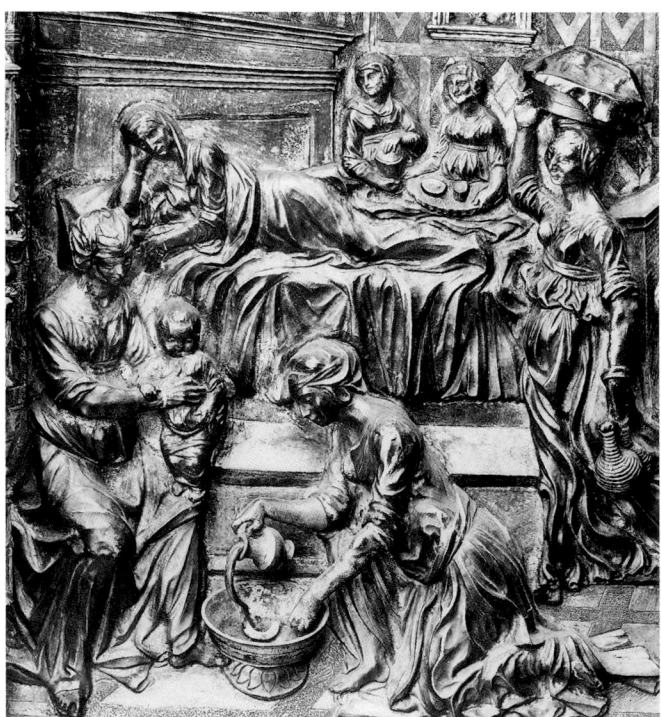

Fig. 134. Detail of Antonio del Pollaiuolo, *The Birth of Saint John the Baptist.* Silver relief on the altar from the Florence Baptistery, 31.5 × 42 cm. Museo dell'Opera del Duomo, Florence 2569B

The great connoisseur Philip Pouncey first attributed the Oporto drawing correctly to Leonardo in 1965 on the basis of a photograph and later reaffirmed this authorship when he studied the original in 1977. The sheet had previously been ascribed to the much less inspired, though proficient, Mannerist painter Raffaello Motta da Reggio, nicknamed Raffaellino da Reggio (1550–1578), who was a young follower of Taddeo Zuccaro. This attribution seems somewhat mysterious, and Eduardo Batarda (cited in Turner 2000) recently proposed that the ascription to Raffaello may have come about by

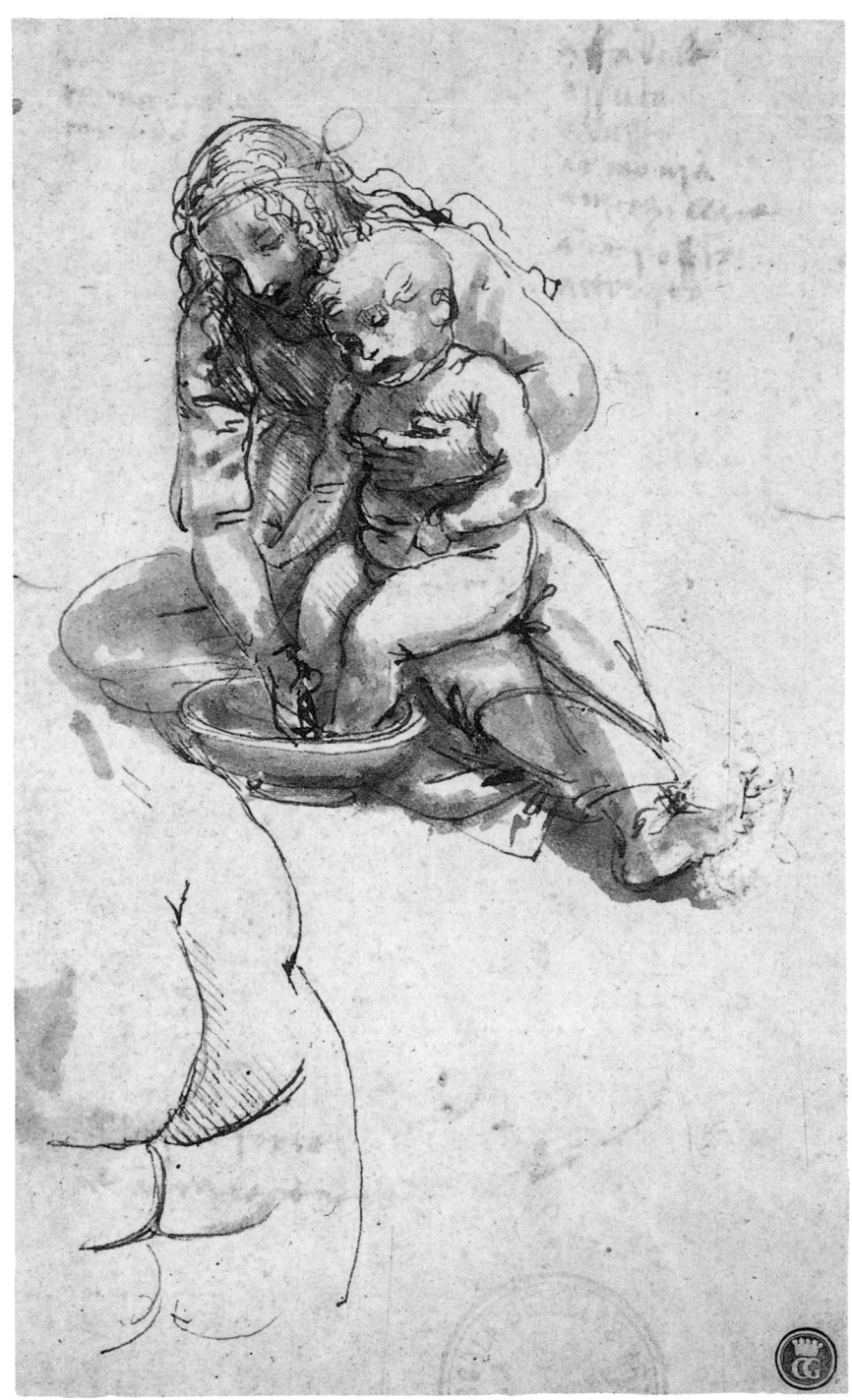

Cat. 21 *(actual size)*

mistake, for the name passed on by hearsay (before it was annotated on the mount) actually may have alluded to Raffaello da
Montelupo (1504–1566), the left-handed Tuscan sculptor and
draftsman. It was probably always evident to previous owners
of the Oporto drawing that it had been done by a left-handed
artist. Pouncey published the Oporto drawing only in 1978, and
the sheet is therefore a latecomer to the Leonardo literature.

Here, the drawings on the recto of the sheet are dated to the
late 1470s (certainly before Leonardo left Florence for Milan
sometime between 1481 and 1483) — more or less in agreement with Pouncey's tentative proposal of 1480 — on the basis
of style and technique. The relevant stylistic comparisons are
to catalogue number 18, as well as to the magnificent double-
sided sheet for the *Madonna of the Cat* in the British Museum

301

(figs. 71, 72). The woman's facial type anticipates that of the Virgin in the Uffizi *Adoration of the Magi* (fig. 11). As in his other early *Madonna* studies, Leonardo relied here mostly on the brown wash to do the work of modeling the figures, using little parallel hatching over the wash, and this only to indicate areas in very deep shadow. The figural types of the woman and infant in the Oporto drawing are the same as those in another early sheet in the British Museum (1913–6–17–2). Moreover, the right hand of the woman in the Oporto sheet is abbreviated in the form of a "mitten," a typical shorthand notation in Leonardo's earliest drawings of the human figure. The young artist's dazzling pen-and-ink-with-wash technique in the Oporto sheet has been likened to that of the great later virtuosi of the medium, Giovanni Francesco Barbieri (Il Guercino; 1591–1666) and Giovanni Battista Tiepolo (1696–1770).

This tender depiction of a woman bathing a child is one of the few extant representations of unguarded, intimate domesticity by Leonardo. The awkwardly drawn child's buttocks on the lower left are also autograph and clearly the work of a young artist, who may have been looking at a sculpture (to judge from the broad reductive modeling with hatching and wash). The Oporto study can be connected to an early fragmentary sketch of an infant's lower body being held in a woman's arms (fig. 53), a sheet whose verso likewise bears inscribed words from a lexicographic exercise (on which see below). The general stylistic moment of the Oporto drawing seems also to be that of two sheets of studies of infants, some of which are seen nursing (Windsor, RL 12568, 12569), drawings that were independently dated by Kenneth Clark and Carlo Pedretti to about 1478–80.[2] The motif of the woman and child, as well as that of the buttocks below, can also be stylistically related to a series of lost drawings by Leonardo (identified by Pedretti), as recorded in three early-sixteenth-century copies done by an anonymous Tuscan artist in pen and ink with wash (Uffizi, Florence, 17050 F, 17051 F, and 17052 F).

Seen in isolation on the page, the woman bathing the child in the Oporto drawing would seem an unusual subject for the Renaissance. It can easily be explained, however, as part of a larger context: it would be a fitting foreground motif, portraying the apocryphal holy infant's first bath, in a scene of the birth of the Christ Child, of the Virgin, or of Saint John the Baptist. Of the same probable date as Leonardo's Oporto drawing, Antonio del Pollaiuolo's exquisite silver relief of *The Birth of Saint John the Baptist* (Museo dell'Opera del Duomo, Florence), originally produced for the altar in the Baptistery in 1478–80, includes in the left foreground the traditional apocryphal motif of the holy child's first bath (fig. 134).[3] Commissioned by the Arte della Calimala in 1477–78, Pollaiuolo and Andrea del Verrocchio both submitted models, drawings, and, finally, executed silver reliefs (of different subjects) for the Baptistery altar, and there was probably an element of competition between them in the overall project. The young Leonardo often turned to Pollaiuolo's work as a source, and it would not be surprising if the famous project for the Baptistery silver altar stimulated his creative juices. Be that as it may, the Oporto drawing of the woman bathing the child is remarkably sculptural in conception. Yet another sheet of the late 1470s by Leonardo shows a striding Pollaiuolesque young woman carrying a child that may fit the motif of the beautiful nursemaid bringing the holy child to the bath (British Museum, London, 1913-6-17-2). In Leonardo's own work, the motif of the young nursemaids (or the Virgin) bathing the holy child would be fitting in an Adoration of the Shepherds or large Nativity scene. A similar inclusion of the apocryphal motif of the Infant Christ being bathed is found, for example, in Parmigianino's drawings from 1524–26 of the *Adoration of the Shepherds*.[4] The young Leonardo was contemplating the Adoration and Nativity subjects in 1478–82/83 (cat. nos. 27, 36, 37, 38, 45), as he reworked the composition of the *Adoration of the Magi* altarpiece for the monks of San Donato a Scopeto (figs. 10, 11).

The most recent tendency in the Leonardo literature has been to date the Oporto drawing based on the evidence of the inscriptions on the verso. The verso of the Oporto sheet is inscribed with a partial list of words in alphabetical order (*vocaboli*) that was part of a lexicographic exercise. Carlo Pedretti rightly connected these inscriptions to the rigorous, interminable lists of words in the Codex Trivulzianus (Castello Sforzesco, Milan, Biblioteca Trivulziana 2162) with which Leonardo taught himself a Latin-Italian vocabulary of expression (in order to become a writer of treatises) and which encompass entire signatures of that notebook. According to Edmondo Solmi (1908), Augusto Marinoni (1980), and others, however, Leonardo derived many of his lexicographic lists in the Codex Trivulzianus from the Milanese edition of the *Novellino* by Masuccio Salernitano, published in 1483, as well as from the Italian translation of Roberto Valturio's *De re militari* (Ms., 1446–55) by Paolo Ramusio, which was printed in Verona in 1483.[5] Leonardo most likely listed a copy of

Valturio's treatise in his record of books in the Codex Atlanticus (fol. 559r [formerly fol. 210r-a]) and of those "that I left locked in the chest" in the Codex Madrid II (fols. 2v–3r).[6] Valturio's treatise offered Leonardo important sources of inspiration in his designs of military technology; see catalogue numbers 51, 52, 55. Moreover, Leonardo also recorded in the Codex Trivulzianus a solar eclipse that took place in Milan in March 1485 (which he presumably witnessed), and the Codex includes, as well, his studies for the design of the domed crossing tower (*tiburio*) of Milan Cathedral; the earliest payment records for the latter project date to July and August 1487. (See Chronology.) These facts establish that the Codex Trivulzianus must be closer in date to 1487–90; some scholars have dated it into 1493. The date of the *vocaboli* on the verso of the Oporto sheet, however, does not necessarily determine the date of the drawing on the recto, for it is well known that Leonardo often later reused the backs of sheets of paper with drawings for note taking.   CCB

1. Provenance based on Weston-Lewis 1994, Turner 2000–1, and Turner 2002. An alternative, less convincing provenance for Leonardo's Oporto drawing was hypothesized in Moreira 1998, pp. 30–31, based on the mount of the drawing and the inscription in old Portuguese, which may suggest that the drawing was possibly part of an album owned by Luís da Costa (1595–ca. 1650) that was passed on to his son Félix da Costa (1639–1712), and which at some point was also owned by Bento Coelho da Silveira (1620–1708), by André Gonçalves (1685–1762), and by Jerónimo de Barros Ferreira (1750–1803), and then was dismembered and sold to the Portuguese state in 1801.
2. See Clark and Pedretti 1968–69, vol. 1, p. 109, nos. 12568, 12569.
3. The cruder embroidery of the *Birth of Saint John the Baptist* (Museo dell'Opera del Duomo, Florence), from 1469–80, after Pollaiuolo's cartoon also contains the first bath motif.
4. British Museum, London, 1853-10-8-3; Metropolitan Museum of Art, New York, 46.80.3; see Carmen C. Bambach in British Museum and Metropolitan Museum of Art 2000–1, pp. 126–27, nos. 80–81.
5. Marinoni 1980b, pp. vii–xxvi.
6. Richter 1970, vol. 2, pp. 366–69, no. 1469; Pedretti 1977, p. 353, nos. 1469–1508; Ladislao Reti in Codex Madrid 1974, vol. 3, pp. 56–58, vol. 5, pp. 5–6.

LEONARDO DA VINCI

22. *Madonna and Child with a Bowl of Fruit* (recto)
Architectural Study for a Vault (verso)

Pen and brown ink with brown wash over stylus and metalpoint (leadpoint?) (recto), leadpoint, traces of stylus (verso), 355 × 253 mm (14 × 10 in.); horizontal fold in the center; oxidation; worn along all four edges (recto), added piece of paper (verso)
Département des Arts Graphiques du Musée du Louvre, Paris RF 486

PROVENANCE: A.-C.-H. His de la Salle (Lugt 1333); his sale, *État des dessins . . . His de la Salle*, no. 69 (Raphael); 1878, bequeathed to the Musée du Louvre; museum mark (Lugt 1886a).

LITERATURE: Passavant 1860, no. 363; Louvre 1881, no. 101; Ephrussi 1882, p. 242, fig. p. 233; Morelli 1890, p. 197 n. 1; Müntz 1899, p. 519, no. 2; Berenson 1903, vol. 1, p. 151, pl. c, vol. 2, no. 1069; Seidlitz 1909, vol. 1, p. 75, pl. 3; Liphart 1912, p. 207, fig. 6; Thiis 1913, p. 163, fig. p. 164; Gronau 1914, fig. p. 54; Calvi 1919, pp. 2, 21, fig. p. 18; Louvre 1919, no. 11; Poggi 1919, p. xliv, pl. 58; Suida 1919–20, p. 279; Venturi 1920, pp. 76–78, fig. 16; Demonts 1921, no. 5; Demonts 1922, no. 5; Venturi 1925, p. 88, fig. 28; Commissione Vinciana 1928–, vol. 1, p. 31; Popp 1928, p. 4, no. 16; Sirén 1928, p. 28, pl. 31; Suida 1929, pp. 33, 271; Bodmer 1931, p. 380, fig. 119; Orangerie 1931, no. 11; Petit Palais 1935, no. 572; Palazzo dell'Arte 1939, p. 160; Goldscheider 1945, no. 59; Popham 1945, pp. 6, 17, no. 25; Amboise 1952; Biblioteca Medicea Laurenziana 1952, no. 24; Florisoone and Bacou 1952, no. 9; Bouchot-Saupique 1953–54, p. 58, fig. 4; Heydenreich 1954, vol. 1, p. 202; Tours 1956, no. 46; Bouchot-Saupique 1957, no. 67; Goldscheider 1959, p. 164, no. 56; Louvre 1962, no. 8; Sérullaz 1965, no. 6; Richter 1970, vol. 1, p. 343 n.; Pedretti 1973a, p. 53, fig. 44; Pedretti 1977, vol. 1, no. 663; Arasse 1978, p. 73; Rosci 1978, p. 180, no. 7; Pedretti 1984, fig. 24; Dalli Regoli 1982, p. 25, fig. 69; Béguin 1983, p. 83; Alpatov 1984, p. 7; Alpatov 1985, p. 45, fig. 17; Clark 1988, p. 64, fig. 16; Louvre 1989; Marani 1989, p. 53; Viatte 1991, no. 1; Meyer zu Capellen 1996, p. 165, fig. 102; Perrig 1997, p. 13, fig. 10; Vecce 1998a, p. 64; Marani 1999b, pp. 84, 87, fig p. 86.

The preliminary work in metalpoint remains visible through the pen-and-ink drawing on the Virgin's face, the Child's profile, and the gesture of his right arm but is at variance with the final lines in these places. This indicates the attention Leonardo gave to the essential part of his research in this series of Virgins with Child: the relationship between the

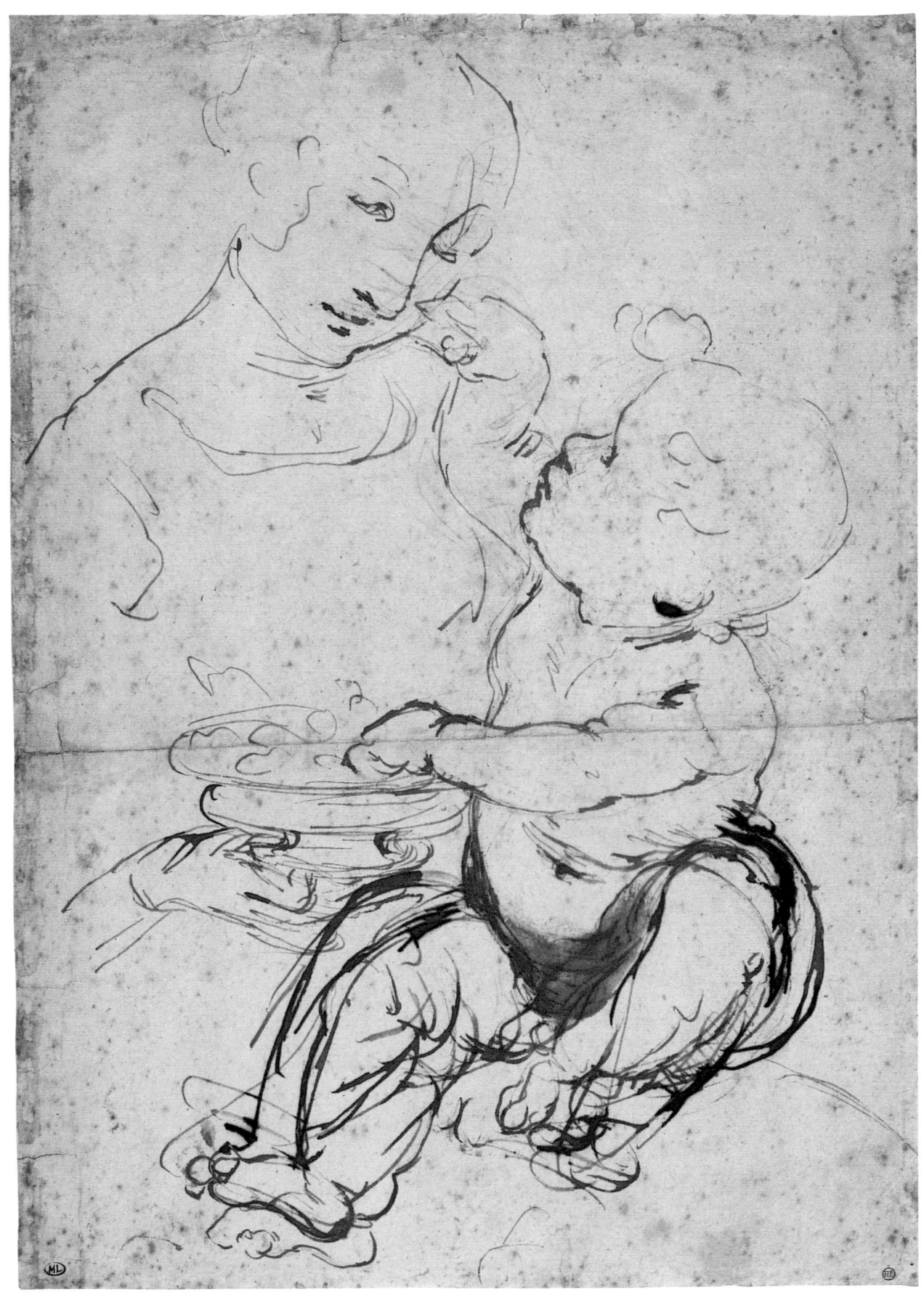

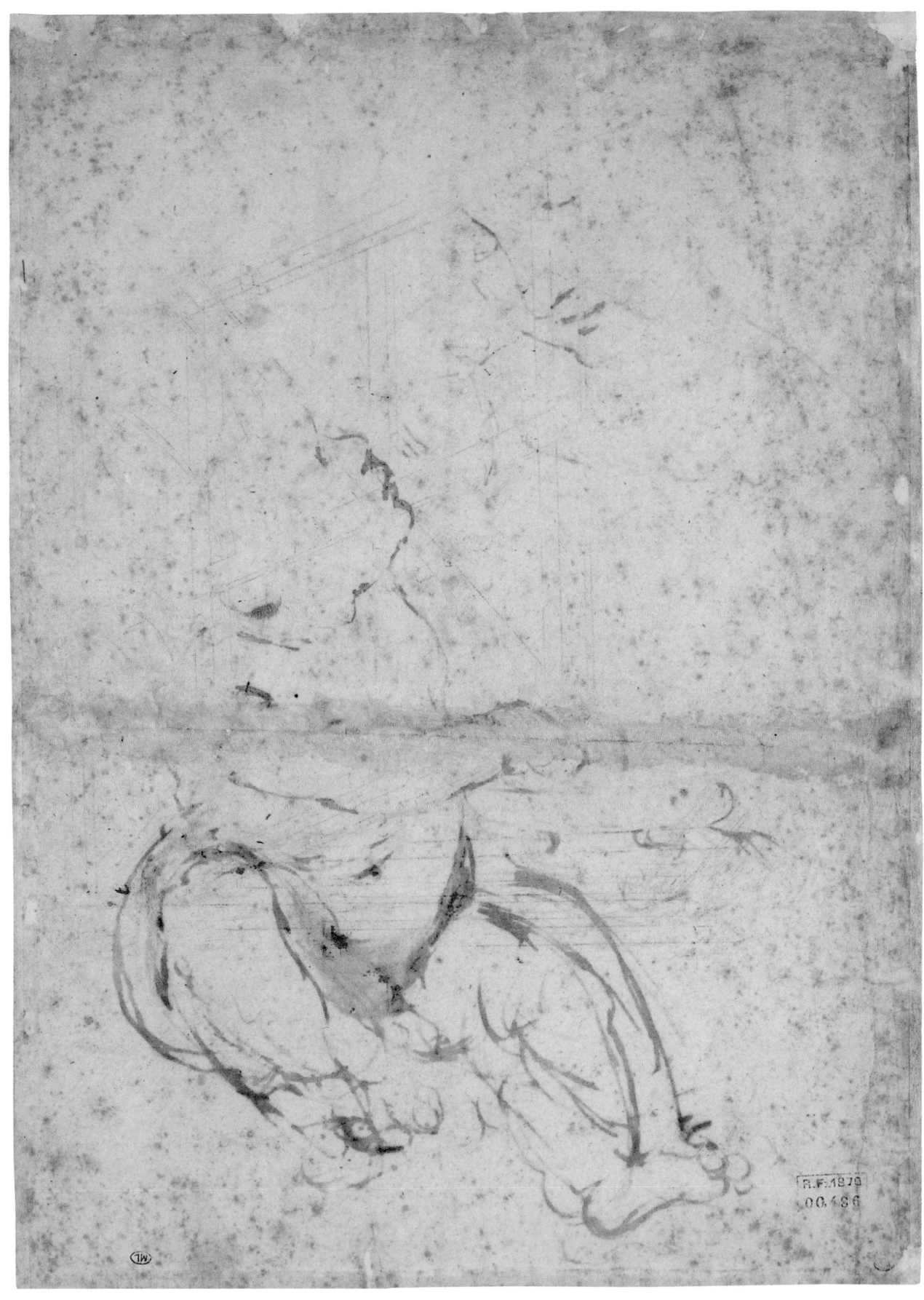

Cat. 22v

two figures and their direction of movement, sometimes perceptible in only a single detail. It is the full dynamic of action and reaction, flight and return, that animates the principal group and the living forms that surround it—flower, fruit, plant, or animal—here and in the *Benois Madonna* (fig. 133), providing them with both their familiarity and their mystery. This expressiveness of a form identified by its movement has been linked to the influence in these drawings of sculpture, particularly the flat planes of Donatello's bas-reliefs, such as those in the *Dudley Madonna* (Victoria and Albert Museum, London), which was sometimes attributed to Leonardo himself.[1]

When the present study was in the His de la Salle collection, it was attributed to Raphael, and it was included under that name in Passavant. The attribution was corrected by Giovanni Morelli, following an argument advanced by Both de Tauzia and Charles Ephrussi. Tauzia had pointed out the similarity in the treatment of the Child's hair to the British Museum studies for the *Madonna of the Cat* (cat. no. 19; figs. 71, 72). Heinrich Bodmer dated the drawing to the end of the 1470s based on a comparison with the principal group in the *Adoration of the Magi* (cat. no. 27). Bernard Berenson linked it to the profile of the Child on the recto of a sheet of studies in the British Museum (1860–6–16–98 recto), of which it might appear to be a version developed to focus on the intensity of the Virgin and Child's face-to-face relationship. He also compared it to the face of the Virgin in a drawing that depicts the Virgin and Child with Saint John the Baptist and other figures (Windsor, RL 12276), in which the principal motif—the Virgin on her knees—displays the same vivacity as the rough pen treatment of the Child in the present drawing. Kenneth Clark and Carlo Pedretti dated the Windsor drawing to about 1478–80.[2]

All the commentators on the sheet shown here have insisted on the close connection between it and studies for the *Madonna of the Cat*, though they considered it almost certain that these drawings were studies for the *Benois Madonna* (fig. 133). That painting was probably conceived and begun in 1478, according to a note attached to the drawing in the Uffizi (fig. 39)—that is, if the "two Virgin Marys" referred to in the note are paintings and not bas-reliefs.[3] In the present drawing the Child takes a piece of fruit from a dish and offers it to his mother. It is the largest of the variations on this theme, and it is also the most masterful, with its stages of work perfectly legible. Leonardo erased nothing; all his lines are visible because he did not hesitate, he thought with his hand in motion.

As Berenson said, "It is perhaps as near an approach to the actual transfer to paper of a visual thought as man has ever achieved."[4] According to Clark's excellent analysis, it is these drawings that best inform us of the painter's true intentions in his early Virgins. By the time the paintings were finally undertaken, the weight of the preliminary work and the accompanying preoccupations were such that the works would remain unfinished or, as in the case of the *Benois Madonna* (fig. 133), would lose the vitality of their original concept.[5]

On the verso of the present sheet is a faint architectural drawing (executed in part with metalpoint, in part with stylus) of a structure consisting of several columns on two levels and topped with a pitched roof. At the left, two or three marks indicating a vault seem to complete the structure. On the lower part of the sheet, there are suggestions of a threshold consisting of several steps with many pentimenti and, at right, some hatching.

I am inclined to link this drawing to the background of the *Adoration of the Magi*, because of its similarity to the recto of catalogue number 27 and also to the perspective study for the composition's background in the Uffizi (436 E). The structure on the verso of the present sheet could be the one that, in the Uffizi drawing, joins the top of the stairs to the ruins.[6] This hypothesis is strengthened by the existence of two column elements on the back of catalogue number 27 which complement the Uffizi study. In addition, if such a connection exists, the chronological relationship between the Louvre drawing for the *Madonna and Child with a Bowl of Fruit* and the *Adoration of the Magi* would be supported.

Keeping in mind the probable link between the early Virgins and the *Adoration*, between the verso of catalogue number 22 and the background of the *Adoration*, note the sketch of a plan for an unidentified architectural vault on the recto of the British Museum drawing for the *Virgin and Child* (cat. no. 20).

FV

1. Parronchi 1989, pp. 49–50. Some historians still attribute the two marble bas-reliefs at the Victoria and Albert Museum to Desiderio da Settignano.
2. Clark and Pedretti 1968–69.
3. See Parronchi 1989.
4. Berenson 1938, vol. 1, p. 170.
5. Clark 1988, p. 65.
6. Pedretti 1988e, fig. 405. See the series of arcades associated with the Adoration on fol. 28r-b in the Codex Atlanticus, dating from 1479; Marinoni 2000, fol. 80.

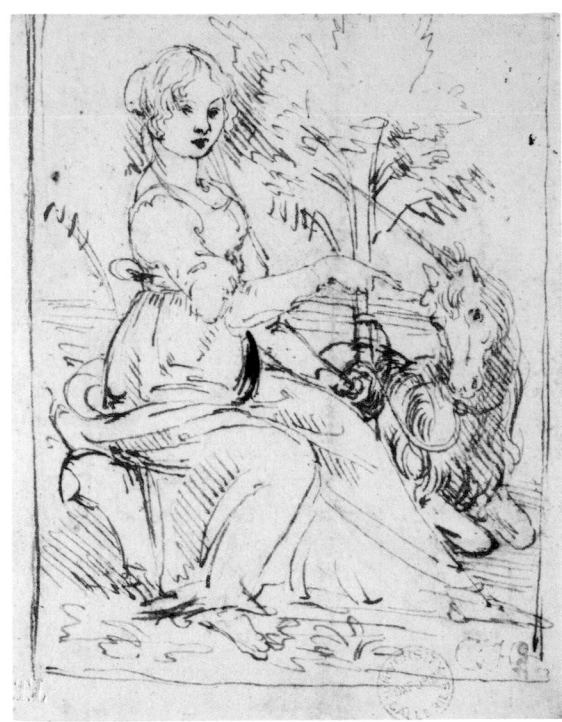

Cat. 23 *(actual size)*

LEONARDO DA VINCI

23. *Young Woman Seated in a Landscape with a Unicorn*

Pen and dark brown ink, 94 × 74 mm (3¹¹/₁₆ × 2¹⁵/₁₆ in.)
Visitors of the Ashmolean Museum, Oxford Chambers Hall Gift,
Oxford, 1855 KPII 15

PROVENANCE: Sir Thomas Lawrence, Bristol and London (1769–
1830; Lugt 2445); Samuel Woodburn, London (1786–1853; Lugt
2584, 2591; Suppl. 2378a); Chambers Hall (1786–1855; Lugt 551).

LITERATURE: Berenson 1903, vol. 2, p. 54, no. 1057; Colvin 1907,
vol. 1, pl. 15A; Seidlitz 1909, p. 76; Poggi 1919, pl. 48; Venturi 1920,
pl. 5; Commissione Vinciana 1928– , vol. 1, p. 22, pl. 5; Popham
1930–31, no. 64; Bodmer 1931, pp. 126 right, 381; Berenson 1938,
vol. 2, p. 117, no. 1057; Giglioli 1944, pl. 48; Royal Academy of Arts
1952, no. 11; Heydenreich 1954, vol. 1, p. 59, vol. 2, p. 62, pl. 77;
Berenson 1961, vol. 2, p. 206, no. 1057; Sutton 1970, no. 5; Parker
1972, no. 15; Nicodemi 1980a, p. 20; Pedretti 1982a, p. 29; Pedretti
1987b, p. 115, fig. 130; Kemp and Roberts 1989, p. 154, nos. 80, 81;
Agghàzy 1989, p. 69, fig. 80; White, Whistler, and Harrison 1992,
p. 24, no. 3; Popham 1994, no. 28 B; Brown 1998b pp. 116,
205 n. 70, fig. 107; Brown 2001–2, pp. 150–53, no. 18.

This delightful drawing of a young woman pointing at the
placid unicorn that she holds by a leash at her left side
may date from the mid- to late 1470s, to judge from its style
and figural type. When the viewer takes a second look at the
drawing, once having been appropriately seduced by the brilliant lightness of touch of the young Leonardo's pen, it
becomes more apparent that the technique of diagonal parallel
hatching is still somewhat disunified, especially with respect
to the outlines. The outlines themselves appear less boldly
economical than they are just a few years later in the composition sketch for the *Adoration* at the Musée du Louvre (cat.
no. 27). Leonardo often drew, as he did here, framing outlines
around small composition sketches that he intended for paintings. The Ashmolean composition resembles that in a much
larger, fragile sheet (fig. 135), which is similarly outlined but
which may be slightly later in date, about 1478–80 (rapid
studies for the *Madonna of the Cat* appear on the recto). The
British Museum sheet seems more self-confident in its bold,
lively sketch, showing the maiden pointing at (or caressing)

307

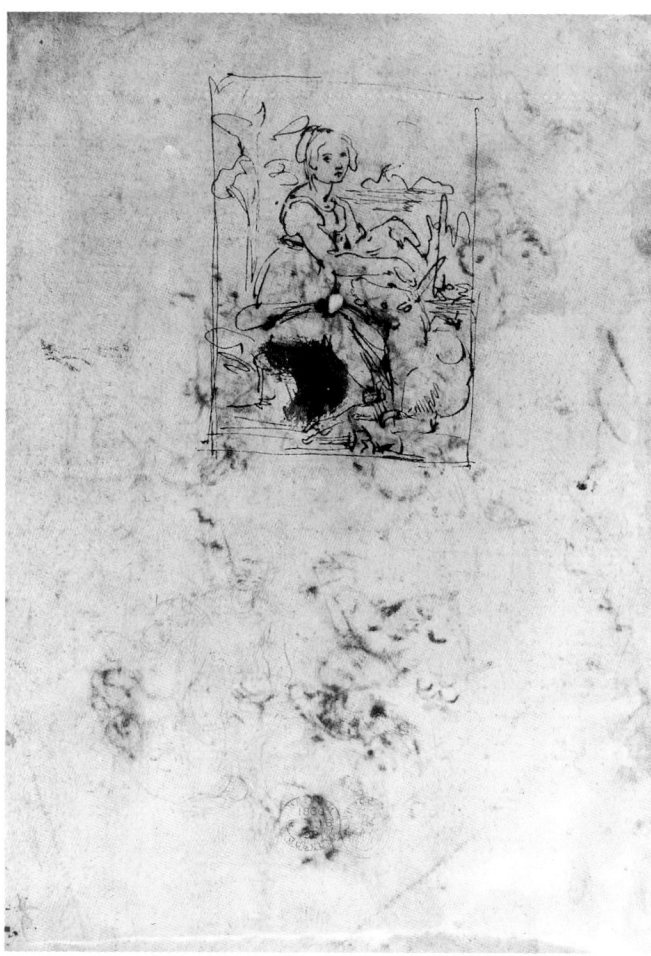

Fig. 135. Leonardo da Vinci, *Studies of a Maiden with a Unicorn* (verso). Pen and brown ink over leadpoint; leadpoint only on lower studies, 281 × 199 mm. The British Museum, London 1860-6-16-98

Ginevra de' Benci (fig. 67), before the artist decided to paint the present wreath of laurel, palm, and juniper with a scroll that was the emblem of Bernardo Bembo, the Venetian humanist and ambassador to Florence.[2] Born into a prosperous family of bankers in Florence, the young Ginevra de' Benci married Luigi Niccolini on January 15, 1474, and seems to have become Bembo's object of platonic love, during one of his diplomatic missions to Florence in 1475–76 and in 1478–80, occasioning the repainting of the reverse of the portrait.[3] As portraits of young women were usually commissioned at the time of their marriage, Ginevra's portrait is most frequently dated by scholars in the mid-1470s. In support of the tantalizing yet basically unprovable theory, some painted and medal portraits of this period do include reverses with depictions of unicorns and the Ashmolean drawing can be independently dated to the mid-1470s on the basis of style.

The unicorn, however, was an oddly ambiguous symbol of sacred and profane chastity in medieval bestiaries. Leonardo, curiously, singled it out as an emblem of incontinence (*intemperanza*) in the fantastic tales and fables of animals that he recorded in his notes: "The unicorn . . . because of its intemperance, not knowing how to control itself before the delight it feels toward fair maidens, forgets its ferocity and wildness, and casting aside all fear it will go up to the seated maiden and sleep in her lap, and thus the hunters take it."[4] In the Ashmolean drawing, the maiden and the unicorn leashed at her side thus offer a nuanced range of meanings, from chastity, virtue, and docility to lust.

CCB

1. Parker 1972, p. 11.
2. Brown 2001–2, pp. 142–53, nos. 16–18. See also essay by Alessandro Cecchi.
3. Leonardo's portrait and Bembo's love for Ginevra are discussed in Fletcher 1989.
4. Paris Ms. H[1], fol. 11r; Richter 1970, vol. 2, p. 265, no. 1232: "Inte[n]peranza/ Il liocorno overo vnicorno . per la sua inte[n]pera[n]za e no[n] sapersi ui[n]cere per lo diletto che à delle donzelle . dime[n]tica la sua ferocità e saluatichezza pone[n]do da ca[n]to ogni sospetto va alla sedente donzella e se le adorme[n]ta in gre[n]bo , e i cacciatori in tal modo lo pigliano."

the unicorn with both hands in a pose that also seems less iconic than that of the maiden in the Ashmolean sheet. The small Ashmolean sketch of a unicorn dipping its horn into a pool of water (cat. no. 26) is probably also from this slightly later moment, about 1480–82, and is unlike the animal here in that it is of the *similis haedo* type, with divided hooves.[1]

It was recently suggested that the composition sketches of the young woman with the unicorn represent Leonardo's early idea for a painting on the reverse of the portrait of

LEONARDO DA VINCI

24. *Figural Sketches* (recto)
Figural Studies (for a Madonna?) (verso)

Pen and brown ink over traces of stylus, and leadpoint or black chalk (recto); soft black chalk or charcoal (verso), 164 × 139 mm (6½ × 5½ in.)
Watermark: Tulip (close to Briquet 6645–6659).
National Gallery of Art, Washington, D.C.; The Armand Hammer Collection 1991 1991.217.2.a

PROVENANCE: Albert M. Shapiro, Berkeley, California (1972); private collection, New York (1972); P. and D. Colnaghi and Co., Ltd., London; sold to Armand Hammer, New York (1898–1990) and Los Angeles in 1972.

LITERATURE: Los Angeles County Museum of Art 1971, no. 104; National Gallery of Art 1974, no. 65; Los Angeles County Museum of Art 1976, no. 12; National Gallery of Art 1978, p. 32; Keele and Pedretti 1979–80, vol. 2, pp. 841, 859 (under no. 26), 890–91 (under no. 199 verso), figs. 148, 149 (verso not by Leonardo); Pedretti 1979b, pp. 43, 46; Los Angeles County Museum of Art 1981, p. 20 (as "Hammer 20"); Pedretti and Roberts 1981–82, pp. 10, 47, 122, no. 20 (as "Hammer 20"); Pedretti 1982a, p. 107, under nos. 47 and 48, fig. 82; Walker 1984, p. 622, no. 1045 (color reproduction of recto); Palazzo del Podestà 1985, p. 63, no. 20; Konrad Oberhuber in Natinal Gallery of Art 1987, pp. 15, 76–77, no. 1; Pedretti 1987a, pp. 167–72, figs. 35–39; Trutty-Coohill 1988, pp. 28–29, figs. 8, 9; Caroli 1991, p. 207, no. 20r (detail of recto is identified as part of the Codex Leicester [cat. no. 114; formerly known as the Codex Hammer]); Pedretti and Trutty-Coohill 1993, pp. 9, 15, 50–52, 105, 111, no. 15; Kwakkelstein 1994, pl. 19; Caroli 1995, p. 169, fig. 21; Howze and Mittler 2001, p. 213, fig. 11.11.

The relatively orderly *mise en page*—disposition of motifs on the sheet—suggests that these lively sketches of an old man's head and of a dainty young woman in half length were primarily an exercise in draftsmanship, and in all likelihood they were part of a page from a sketchbook. This *mise en page* seems still reminiscent of mid- to late-fifteenth-century Florentine sketchbooks (see, for example, cat. no. 12). On the basis of style, the Washington sketches may be dated somewhere between the mid- to late 1470s and Leonardo's departure from Florence in 1481–83. A date about 1478 was first proposed by Konrad Oberhuber, on the evidence of style, a date with which the present author generally concurs. In several publications, however, Carlo Pedretti has dated the Washington sheet (when it was still in the collection of Armand Hammer), quite late in Leonardo's career, about 1508, or after 1506–10, noting that it corresponds stylistically and technically with the Codex Leicester (cat. no. 114; formerly Codex Hammer), with which it also shares a similar watermark and structure of the paper.[1] The evidence of watermarks (which often had a long life span in Italian paper manufacturing mills) and the disposition of chain lines and laid lines in the structure of at least average linen-rag, off-white papers can at times be much too ambiguous in order to serve for definitive conclusions in dating drawings.[2]

If a date in the 1470s is accepted, then the Washington sheet may be considered to represent an early example of Leonardo's preoccupation with the varieties of human physiognomy. Increasingly in his work, the idealized beauty of youth was mockingly paired with the deformity of old age.

Even in the young Leonardo's earliest drawings it is apparent that he brought a sculptor's eye to the process of inventing, sketching, and studying figural types. The top portion of the Washington sheet shows the head of a bearded old man of chiseled features and intent gaze seen in profile, and next to it are enlarged detail studies, of his eye in a three-quarter view and of the upper right portion of the face seen frontally. The deliberate, overly descriptive drawing of the forms—with parallel hatching of short, slightly curving strokes coursing from lower right to upper left—suggests that the young artist may have done these exercise sketches from a sculptural model. Although bearded, the old man's face—with a fine, overhanging nose—is a type reminiscent of Andrea del Verrocchio's figural vocabulary, as in the famous lost relief of *Darius* that was copied by the Della Robbia workshop (formerly Kaiser-Friedrich Museum, Berlin).[3] On the lower part of the sheet, by contrast, the artist let his pen loose, quickly summing up two poses for the half-length figure of a young woman (perhaps even based on the same model), seen in an elegant three-quarter view from the back. In the left sketch, she turns her head to gaze directly at the viewer in an exquisite contrapposto pose; in the larger sketch on the right, she turns her body more fully, and her head upward and slightly away from the viewer, in a sinuous *profil perdu*.

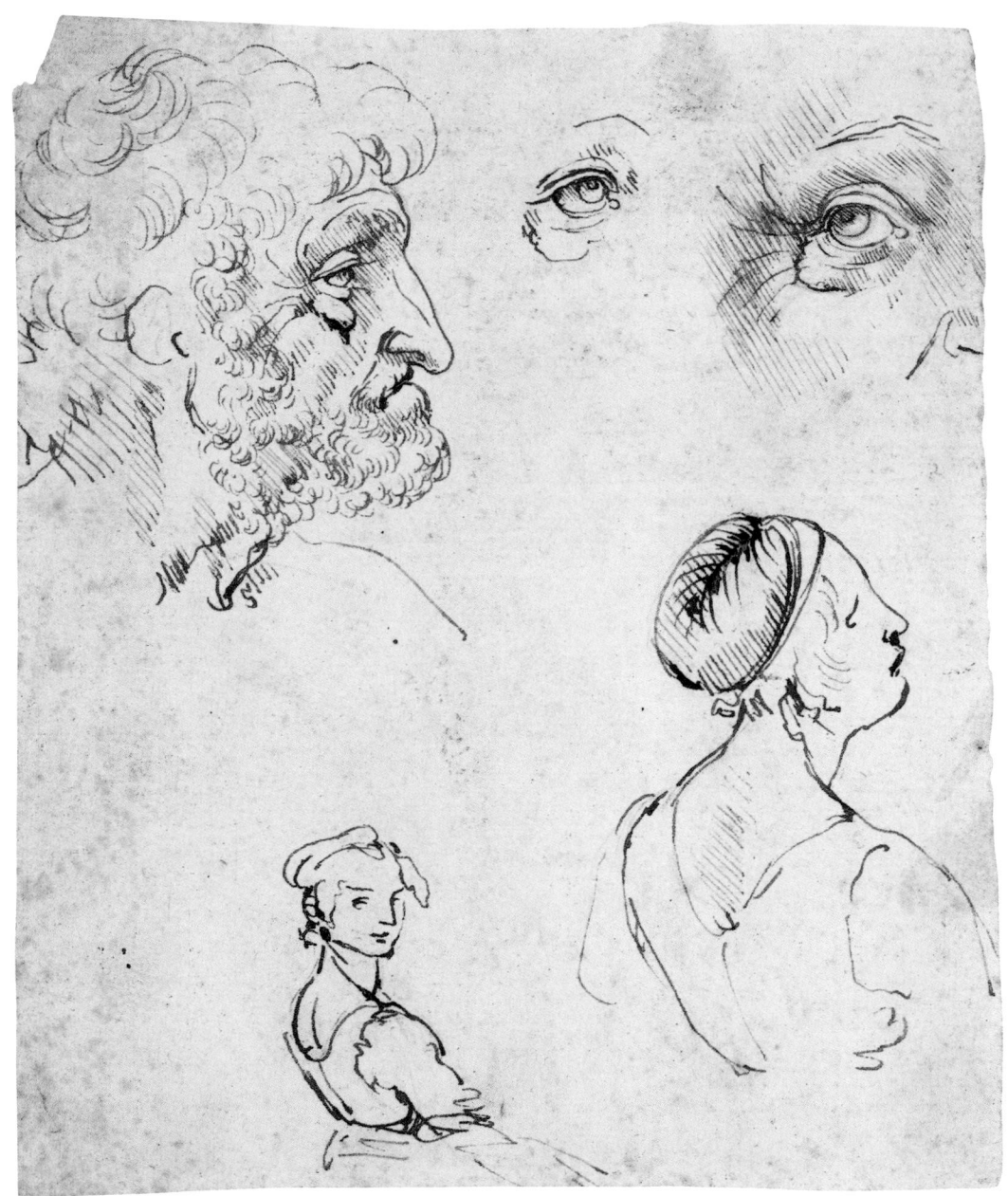

Cat. 24R *(actual size)*

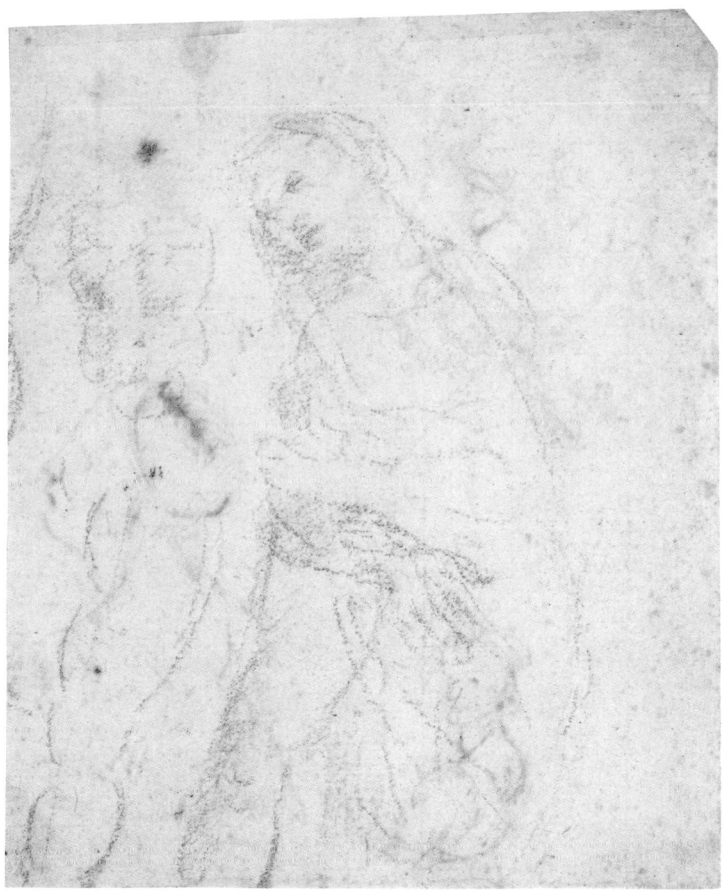

Cat. 24v

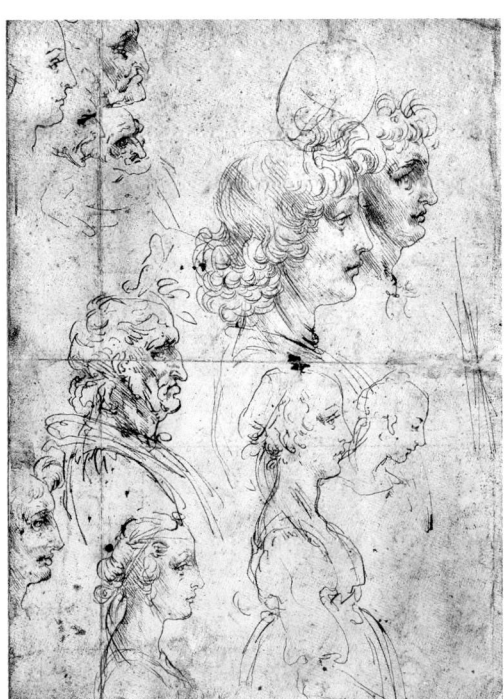

Fig. 136. Leonardo da Vinci, *Figure Studies* (verso). Pen
and brown ink, 405 × 290 mm. The Royal Collection,
H.M. Queen Elizabeth II, Windsor Castle RL 12276

A sheet that is drawn delicately in metalpoint on pink prepared paper, from 1475–80 (Windsor, RL 12513), shows a
sequence of more detailed studies after a woman's upper body
from different angles, which allows us to understand better
the process of exploration. As the artist's eye considered the
human form from different points of view, this opened the
possibilities for fluent variations of the pose. The small sketch
of the woman on the lower left in the Washington sheet,
which is drawn over extensive stylus underdrawing, may well
have been prepared for an independent composition. Her
figure is surrounded by a rectangular framing outline that is
drawn only with the stylus (especially evident in raking
light),[4] and, as we know, Leonardo frequently drew framing
outlines around compositions that he intended for pictures
(cat. nos. 23, 45, 65, 68, 88, 95, 96, 110). The style of this
delightful sketch is similar to that of the maiden with a unicorn seated in a landscape (cat. no. 23; see also fig. 135), both
drawings from Leonardo's first Florentine period. The male
and female figural types in the Washington sheet turn up in a
variety of poses on the verso of a monumental sheet of even

311

looser sketches (fig. 136); the recto of the sheet includes a large Madonna and Child nursing (Windsor, RL 12276), drawn in a style that seems typical of Leonardo's work in the 1470s. The transformations of one physiognomic type into another by association may have been yet another element of invention that Leonardo learned in Andrea del Verrocchio's workshop.

On the verso of the Washington sheet are slight, difficult-to-read sketches, probably portraying a woman standing in three-quarter view, a male torso in frontal view, and other anatomical details. These awkward sketches in soft black chalk or charcoal contain areas of right-handed diagonal parallel hatching, and possibly were intended for a Madonna. They most likely are not by Leonardo and are illustrated here, although not exhibited.

CCB

1. Pedretti 1987a, pp. 167–72.
2. The manufacture and structure of Renaissance drawing papers are discussed in Bambach 1999a, pp. 34–50, 283–95; and Bambach 1999b.
3. Illustrated in Butterfield 1997, p. 157, fig. 207.
4. These stylus lines around the figure have alternatively been interpreted as a doorway framing the woman at an angle (Pedretti 1987b, p. 167, Hammer 20). If examined in raking light, however, the stylus lines appear to conform to the rectilinear disposition of a frame, rather than a doorway seen in perspective.

LEONARDO DA VINCI

25. *Phyllis (or Campaspe) Riding Aristotle* (recto)

Pen and dark brown ink over metalpoint on pale blue-gray paper; traces of framing outlines in pen and dark brown ink (recto); unprepared paper (verso), 96 × 135 mm (3¾ × 5 5⁄16 in.)
Inscribed in graphite on recto along lower right: [illegible]; in pen and brown ink on verso in right-to-left script: *co[m]pagnje / volupta . dispiacere / amore . gielosia / felicita . I[n]vidia . / fortuna . penjte[n]za / sospetto*
Hamburger Kunsthalle 21487

PROVENANCE: Alexandre Pierre François Robert Dumesnil, Paris (1778–1864; Lugt 2199); Georg Ernst Harzen, Hamburg (1790–1863); ca. 1842–56 manuscript inventory by G. E. Harzen (NH.Ad:01:04), fol. 116 (stating the Robert provenance); ca. 1860 manuscript inventory by G. E. Harzen (NH.Ad:02:01), p. 222; 1863, Harzen bequest.

LITERATURE: Koopmann 1891, p. 40; Müntz 1899, p. 525, no. 1; Berenson 1903, vol. 1, p. 153, vol. 2, p. 57, no. 1020; Seidlitz 1909, p. 156, pl. 22; Pauli 1927, pl. 8; Commissione Vinciana 1928– , vol. 7, p. 17, pl. 296.2; Valentiner 1930, pp. 76–77, 81, fig. 28; Bodmer 1931, pp. 110, 378; Berenson 1938, vol. 2, p. 112, no. 1020C; Valentiner 1949, pp. 26, 109, fig. 75; Biblioteca Medicea Laurenziana 1952, pp. 20–21, no. 22; Hamburger Kunsthalle 1957, no. 13; Berenson 1961, vol. 2, p. 196, no. 1020C; Pedretti 1977, vol. 1, p. 384; Agghazy 1989, p. 69, fig. 81; Kiang 1994, figs. 1, 2; Popham 1994, no. 110B; Butterfield 1997, p. 214; Hamburger Kunsthalle 1997, p. 92, no. 25; Brown 1998b, pp. 96–97, fig. 84.

This humorous drawing can be dated to the mid- to late 1470s (in general agreement with Wilhelm Reinhold Valentiner and Heinrich Bodmer). The figural types seem still strongly influenced by Antonio del Pollaiuolo and Andrea del Verrocchio. The woman's body is awkwardly proportioned, and she exhibits lumpy, mittenlike hands; the face of Aristotle recalls the physiognomy of some of the male figures in the Cologne *Adoration* sheet (cat. no. 28). Leonardo began the drawing (which has suffered from abrasions and water stains) with a fine metal point and then rapidly reworked the outlines and the modeling with a quill pen; the thickly corrected final outlines on the architecture are done with a fairly blunt quill pen. The composition portrays an allegory of woman's power

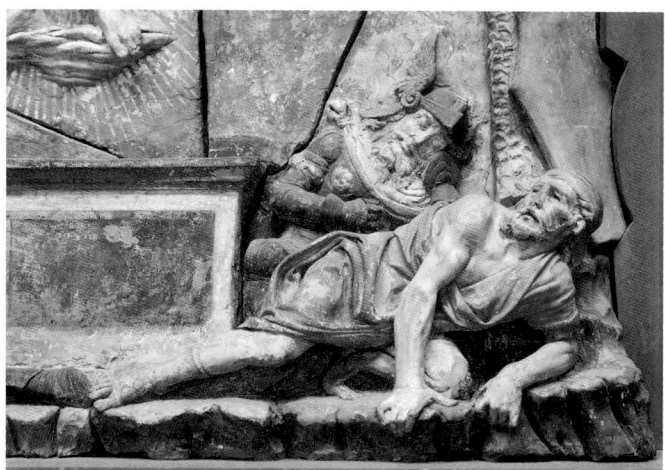

Fig. 137. Detail showing sleeping Roman soldiers at the tomb, Andrea del Verrocchio, *The Resurrection*. Polychromed terracotta relief, painted and gilded, 135 × 150 cm. Museo Nazionale del Bargello, Florence 472

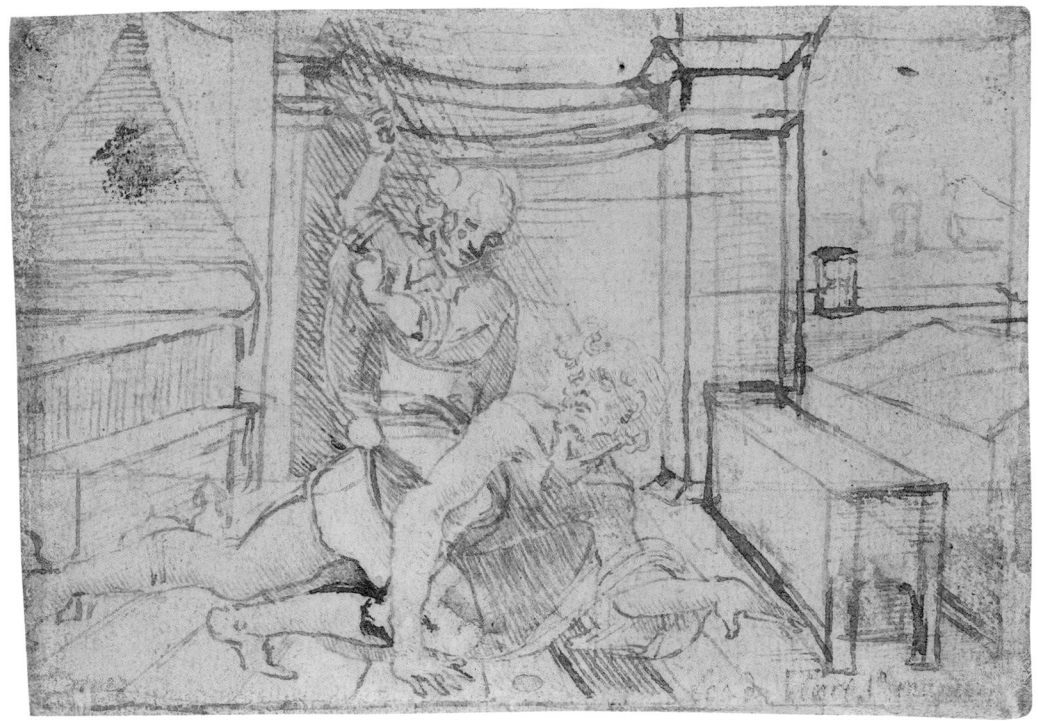

Cat. 25R *(actual size)*

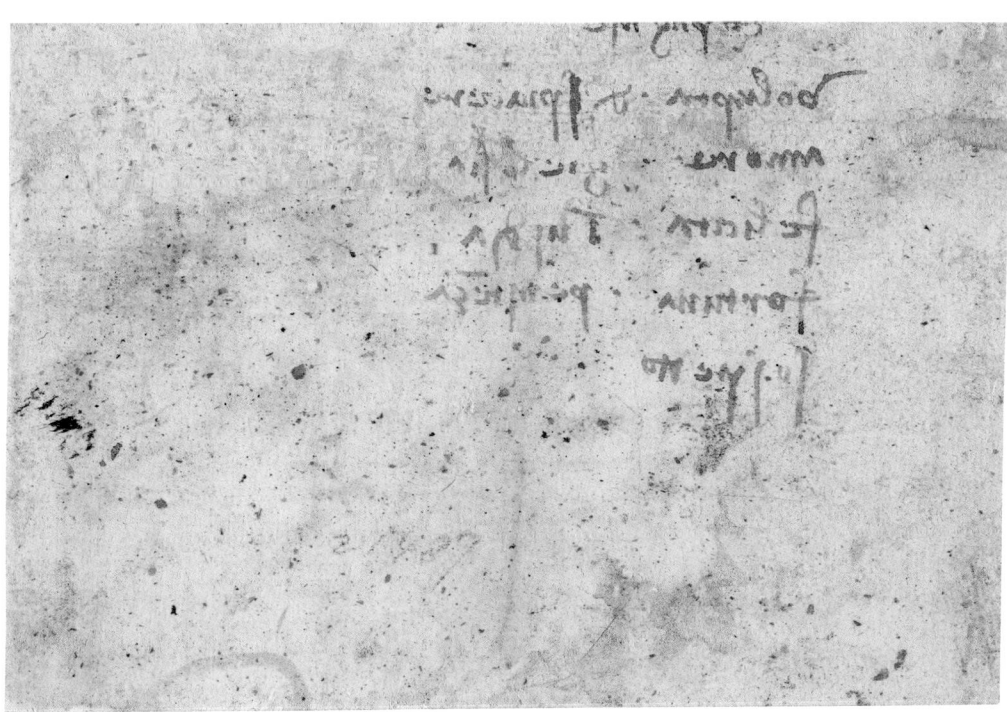

Cat. 25V *(actual size)*

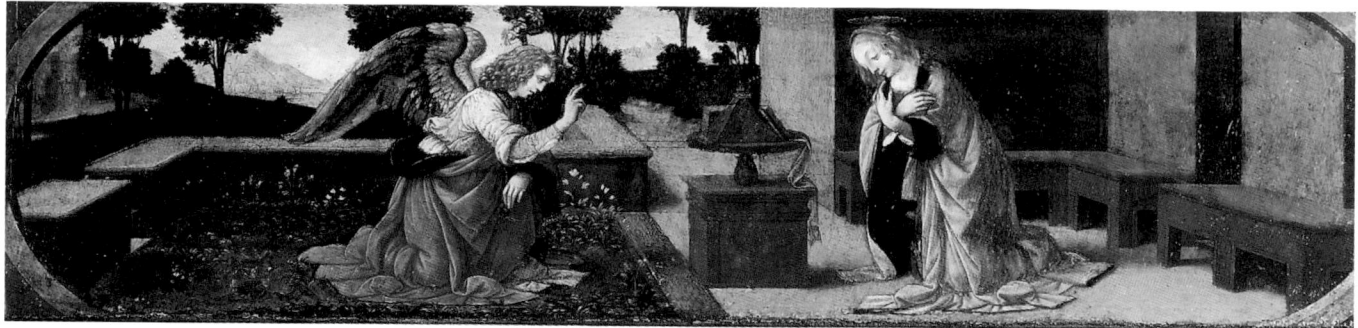

Fig. 138. Attributed to Leonardo da Vinci, *The Annunciation*. Oil on wood, 16 × 60 cm. Musée du Louvre, Paris M.I. 598

over man, a subject that seems to have been especially popular in quattrocento Florence. Here, the old philosopher Aristotle crawls pathetically as if he were a beaten horse, but the identity of the merciless woman riding him has caused some debate in the Leonardo literature. It is not clear whether she is Phyllis or, less likely, Campaspe. According to one legend, Aristotle (384 – 322 B.C.) let his young beautiful mistress Phyllis ride on his back in exchange for her favors. According to a conflation with another myth, Aristotle, who was the tutor of Alexander the Great, tried to dissuade the young emperor from his love for his mistress Campaspe but himself fell under her spell and let her ride on his back. The theme of a woman riding Aristotle occurs in early Florentine engravings of the "fine manner" from the 1460s and 1470s (Hind A.I.20; Hind A.I.79; Hind A.IV.20). This motif is the centerpiece in a tondo with the blind Cupid shooting arrows at a youth and his beloved who holds a ribbon inscribed "Fede" (Faith), and it is a secondary detail in the lower right corner of the *Triumph of Love* illustrating Petrarch's *Trionfi* (though the story is not part of Petrarch's text). Leonardo's re-creation of the allegory, by contrast, shows it as an independent scene teeming with anecdotal detail. Some of the prints were probably known to Leonardo, and they may have served to reinforce the moralizing message of his imagery. He inscribed the verso of the Hamburg sheet with a list of moralizing words (the staccato style of his lettering is typical of his early handwriting) that seems evocative in the context of the *Aristotle* scene on the recto, "companionship, lust, displeasure, love, jealousy, happiness, envy, fortune, penance, suspicion."

In Leonardo's vivid retelling of the allegory, as the woman raises her right hand to whip Aristotle, he turns his head back to look at her in pain and humiliation. For the figure of Aristotle, Leonardo seems to have borrowed the stance and doleful expression of a crawling soldier seen on the extreme right in Verrocchio's polychromed terracotta of the *Resurrection* (fig. 137), originally from the Medici villa in Careggi and which most likely dates from the 1470s, if not earlier.[1] The similarity of the male figural types in the Hamburg sheet and the Careggi terracotta relief of the *Resurrection* led Valentiner to propose rather unconvincingly that the latter sculpture was a collaboration between the young Leonardo and his teacher. In the Hamburg drawing, Leonardo set the scene of his allegory in the interior of a bedroom (this is among the rare depictions of a domestic setting by the artist), which is clearly meant to be identified with the philosopher's private quarters. The bed on a raised platform on the left symbolizes his lust, and the scriptorium with a tall bench by a window with an hourglass on the right symbolizes his intellect. Both the architectural style of the simple furnishings and the gently upward-tilting perspectival projection recall those of the background in the small Louvre painting of the *Annunciation* that is often attributed to the young Leonardo (fig. 138). That painting has long been thought to form part of the predella panel of the Pistoia altarpiece, the so-called *Madonna di Piazza* (see cat. nos. 3, 7, 8).   CCB

1. Valentiner 1930, p. 81; Butterfield 1997, pp. 82 – 86, 214; Brown 1998b, pp. 96 – 97.

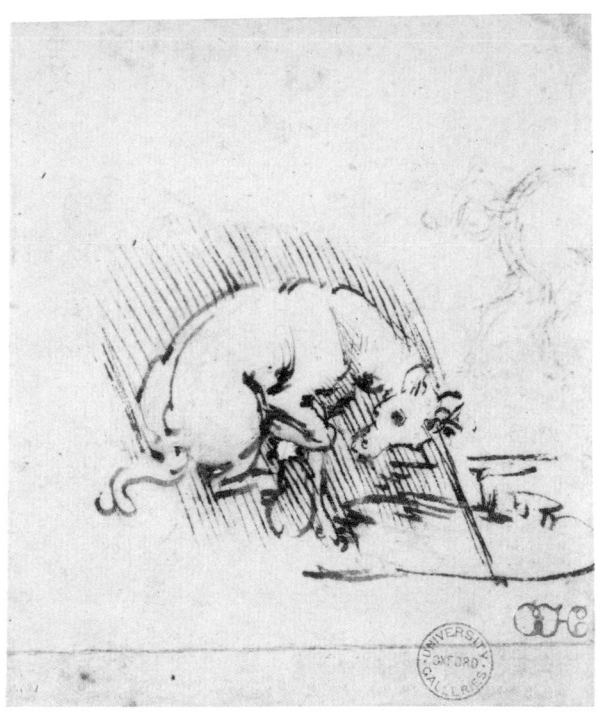

Cat. 26 *(actual size)*

LEONARDO DA VINCI

26. *A Unicorn Dipping its Horn into a Pool of Water; Unrelated Fragment of a Study of the Hindquarters of a Horse or Unicorn*

Pen and dark brown ink (unicorn); leadpoint (hindquarters of horse or unicorn), 92 × 80 mm (3⅝ × 3³⁄₁₆ in.)

Visitors of the Ashmolean Museum, Oxford Chambers Hall Gift, 1855, Oxford KPII 16

PROVENANCE: Sir Thomas Lawrence, Bristol and London (1769–1830; Lugt 2445); Samuel Woodburn, London (1786–1853; Lugt 2584, 2591; Suppl. 2378a); Chambers Hall (1786–1855; Lugt 551).

LITERATURE: Colvin 1907, vol. 1, pl. 15B; Commissione Vinciana 1928– , vol. 2, p. 28, pl. 70; Bodmer 1931, pp. 182 (right), 392; Berenson 1938, vol. 2, p. 118, no. 1059A; Royal Academy of Arts 1952, no. 12; Berenson 1961, vol. 2, p. 207, no. 1059A; Sutton 1970, no. 6; Parker 1972, no. 16; Pedretti 1987b, p. 115, fig. 131; Kemp and Roberts 1989, p. 154, no. 81; White, Whistler, and Harrison 1992, p. 26, no. 4; Popham 1994, no. 60A; Brown 2001–2, p. 153 n. 6.

In a charming flight of the imagination, Leonardo alluded here to a legend told in the Greek *Physiologus* (2nd century A.D. and later), a fanciful natural history based on the Bible, Aristotle, Pliny the Elder, and other antique writings that had wide circulation in the Middle Ages and Renaissance. According to this text and the medieval bestiaries that followed, a unicorn could miraculously purify a pool of water that was poisoned by serpents by dipping its horn into the water and making the sign of the cross with its horn (*Physiologus*, 22).[1] Because of the medieval iconographic tradition in which the unicorn was also a symbolic attribute of the Virgin Mary's virginity, the unicorn dipping its horn into the water also alluded to the mystic purification of the Virgin. Leonardo's drawing is clearly a fragment and offers little evidence of its intended context. The dates that scholars have proposed for the sketch have varied widely, from 1478–81 to 1485–89. A date around 1480–83 is probable given the stylistic similarities to catalogue number 27. CCB

1. Parker 1972, p. 11.

LEONARDO DA VINCI

27. *Adoration of the Magi* (recto)
Sketch of a Seated Nude Man, His Left Leg Bent; Two Sketches of Paired Columns (verso)

Pen and brown ink over leadpoint tracing (recto); leadpoint (verso), 284 × 213 mm (11 ⅛ × 8 ⅜ in.); oxidation and stains, reconstituted in upper right corner (recto)

Inscribed in pencil in upper part of verso: *N° 8*

Département des Arts Graphiques du Musée du Louvre, Paris RF 1978

PROVENANCE: Émile Galichon, Paris sale, 1875, no. 162; Louis Galichon (Lugt 1060 on verso); 1894, bequeathed to the Musée du Louvre; museum marks (Lugt 1886a recto and verso).

LITERATURE: Galichon 1867, p. 535, fig. p. 534; Chennevières 1879, p. 518; École des Beaux-Arts 1879, no. 37; Müller-Walde 1889, p. 128, fig. 69; Rosenberg 1898, pp. 33–34, fig. 20; Müntz 1899, p. 63 n. 1, fig. p. 65, pp. 70–71, p. 519, no. 12; Berenson 1903, vol. 1, p. 152, pl. 101, vol. 2, no. 1068; Seidlitz 1909, vol. 1, p. 63, pl. 11; Thiis 1913, pp. 195–200, 211–13, fig. p. 194; Gronau 1914, fig. p. 14; Calvi 1919, pp. 9 n. 2, 11–14, 20, fig. p. 12; Louvre 1919, no. 8; Poggi 1919, p. xlv, pl. 62; Suida 1919–20, p. 280; Bode 1921, pp. 69, 70, fig. 33; Demonts 1921, no. 8; Demonts 1922, no. 8; Venturi 1925, pp. 130, 132, 136, fig. 69; Commissione Vinciana 1928– , vol. 2, p. 46; Popp 1928, pp. 34–35, pl. 10; Sirén 1928, pp. 34, 35, pl. 38; Suida 1929, pp. 32, 33, 269; Bodmer 1931, pp. 382–83, fig. 132; Orangerie 1931, no. 12; Petit Palais 1935, no. 567; Palazzo dell'Arte 1939, p. 159; Goldscheider 1945, no. 71; Popham 1945, pp. 22, 24, 32, no. 42; Popham and Pouncey 1950, under no. 106; Florisoone and Bacou 1952, no. 11; Bouchot-Saupique 1953–54, p. 61, fig. 5; Heydenreich 1954, p. 31, fig. 9; Rosenberg 1957, p. 21, fig. 38; De Tolnay 1962, no. 2 (verso), fig. 6; Louvre 1962, no. 9; Sérullaz 1965, no. 7; Bacou 1968, no. 12; Clark and Pedretti 1968–69, under no. 12362; Pedretti 1973a, p. 32, fig. 40; Wasserman 1975, fig. 25; Vertova 1976, p. 80, no. 32; Arasse 1978, p. 89; Carpiceci 1978, figs. 22, 29; Rosci 1978, fig. p. 37, p. 181, no. 14e; Hills 1980, p. 613, fig. 15; Ames-Lewis 1981, pp. 161–67, fig. 167; Lisner 1981, pp. 203, 204, 206, 208, 213, 214, 223, 232, fig. 2; Kemp 1981, p. 68, fig. 24; Chastel 1982, pp. 430–31; Béguin 1983, pp. 83–84; Budny 1983, p. 43 n. 45; Pedretti and Clark 1983, p. 58, fig. 47; Becherucci 1985, pp. 41–42; Pedretti and Dalli Regoli 1985, p. 57, under no. 8; Marchini 1985b, pp. 180–81, fig. 2; Veltman and Keele 1986, pp. 338, 352, figs. 4.1, 48.1, 49.1 (detail); Westfehling 1986, under no. 8a; Clark 1988, pp. 73–74, fig. 21; Louvre 1989; Marani 1989, p. 48; Parronchi 1989, p. 59; Trutty-Coohill 1989a, p. 165; Palazzo Grassi 1992, no. 1; Petrioli Tofani 1992, p. 156, under no. 7.10; Natali 1994, pp. 150, 156, fig. 4; Wiemers 1996, pp. 294, 296, 297 fig., 298, 299, fig. 289 (verso); Arasse 1997, p. 297, fig. 207; Marani 1999b, fig. p. 107, pp. 108, 109; Weil-Garris Brandt 1999, p. 28, fig. 44; Butterfield 2001, p. 49, fig. 3; Marani 2001b, pp. 110, 112, under no. 24; Natali 2001, pp. 48, 53, fig. p. 49.

This drawing, which came to the Louvre through a bequest from Louis Galichon, was acquired by his brother Émile in Turin, along with a sheet of studies now at the École Nationale Supérieure des Beaux-Arts, Paris (cat. no. 30), according to Philippe de Chennevières. Émile Galichon had discussed the drawing and illustrated it with a line engraving in the *Gazette des beaux-arts*, of which he was publisher. In 1875, in the Galichon sale catalogue, the drawing was described by the appraiser Clément, who wrote that on the verso was "une étude d'homme assis, á la mine d'argent" (a study of a seated man, in silverpoint). This important detail was overlooked in all the studies devoted to the drawing, even when it was published in 1962 by Tolnay, who believed he had discovered an unpublished drawing.

A careful examination of the sheet reveals a preparatory sketch in stylus for the Virgin and Child under two worshipers in the left foreground. Further preliminary drawing in leadpoint is clearly distinguishable under the pen drawing of the figure of the Virgin. She is identified through the procedure, common in Leonardo's work, of achieving gradually an idea by moving a figure around an axis, experimenting with three —perhaps four—different positions for the head and the legs. The distance between the main group and the circle of visitors is already under consideration: here it is smaller than it would be in the painting. The drawing is also more intimate than the painting in the leaning of the Child toward the kneeling king bearing a vase, from whom he is separated by a horizontal plane, perhaps a piece of stiff fabric; in the painting the Child's gesture would become a more distant and formal one of bene-diction. Preparation in leadpoint can be seen also in the group of spectators on the right and in several elements in the back-ground—in the forward flight of stairs, the central structure at roof level, and the tree trunk supporting the roof.

The composition is conceived in two distinct parts. They are not yet connected but reflect Leonardo's work in its appar-ently initial phase, that is, before he opened up the space to strongly set off the Virgin and Child from the worshipers. Here, they are confined within a triangle, itself set within a sort of ellipsis that is echoed in the ruins and processions in

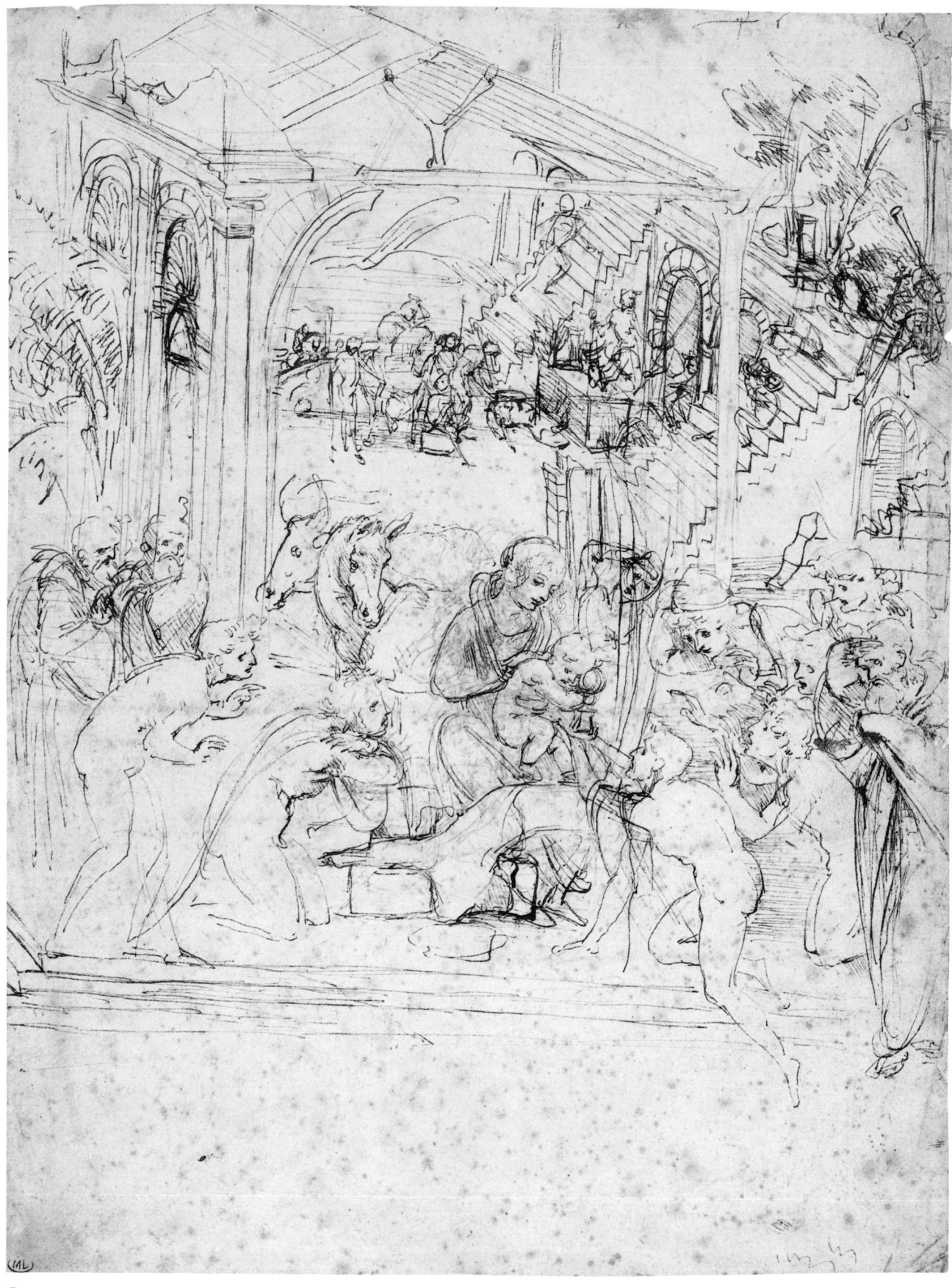

Cat. 27R

Cat. 27v

the background. Investigating Leonardo's possible sources for this composition, Luisa Becherucci cited Lorenzo Ghiberti's *Gates of Paradise* for the Baptistery in Florence (1425–52).[1] In the episodes depicted on those doors, the figures are situated at the edge of the architecture on separate planes, without penetrating it. However, Leonardo seems to have eliminated any reference point, seeking in the haphazard grouping of men and ruins in undefined planes the basis for solutions that would derive from rhythm, movement, and above all, human emotions.[2] All the components of the painting are already in place in the drawings, though differently arranged. The axes are indicated, but the plane containing the figures around the Virgin would acquire more openness and more depth. In the drawing the roof allows representation of both inside and outside spaces; it would be replaced in the painting by the verticality of two trees. These circular spaces recall the solution adopted in the two *Adoration of the Magi* tondi by Filippo Lippi and Botticelli (about 1455, National Gallery of Art, Washington; and about 1476, National Gallery, London).[3] As drawn here, the Virgin and Child are very reminiscent of the *Madonna and Child with a Bowl of Fruit* (cat. no. 22), which with its architectural study on the verso can be seen as a first independent study for the *Adoration*, anticipating in monumental form the composition to come—if one accepts the dating of the so-called early Virgins series as the period between 1478 and 1480, or slightly later.

The dramatic character of the scene would take final shape only in the last stages of its execution, but the painter's key intentions are already present in the attitudes and gestures of the figures, whose variety enhances the quality of the narrative. That "diversity," wrote André Chastel, "forms a clear chain: the gestures correspond to one another like a succession of breaking waves, the features, the faces . . . point to one another ad infinitum."[4] In this drawing and in the other sheets exhibited here treating the same subject, the figures are nude so the shepherds and magi are undifferentiated from each other. There are obvious pentimenti, as in the kneeling figure at lower right that would become King Balthazar offering myrrh. The figures' gestures would develop toward an attitude of extreme fervor, depicted according to the Eastern ritual of *proskynesis* or *prostratio*, a Byzantine manifestation of the Adoration.[5]

The scene is arranged around a structure, which is off center. That pushes the entire foreground to the right and, combined with the composition's high viewpoint, creates a diagonal perspective. The figures occupying the foreground are positioned on a sort of three-step podium that closes off the composition along the front but is interrupted on the left by a corner. The structure itself consists of antique architectural ruins, over which two roof panels resting on a forked branch and supported at right by a tree trunk are added to form a makeshift shelter. On the left are a square pillar and an arcature supported by columns with decorated tympana. Part of an arch at right angles to the square pillar at the forward corner can also be made out. In the opening thus created and in the right background is another diagonally placed antique structure, which terminates in a wall at right angles. Two flights of stairs bracket double arches, which are extended to the back of the scene by a few additional strokes. The stairs lead up to a horizontal plane on which there are elements of vegetation and three musicians playing trumpets. The background is like a piercing of the central structure, populated by a throng of small silhouettes: on horseback, standing, sitting, conversing, drinking, running up and down the stairs.

Although the Louvre drawing reflects a fairly early stage in the arrangement of the composition, as a whole it could be understood as anticipating the drawing for the background at the Uffizi (fig. 139).[6] That drawing, much more precise in its indication of perspective and meticulously delineated with a dense web of lines and vanishing points, is often considered the last of the studies for the corresponding part of the painting. Motifs seen in the Louvre drawing are found again in the Uffizi drawing, but reversed, particularly the double flight of stairs, the battling horsemen, and the people occupying the steps and the terrace. It is possible that Leonardo very quickly formulated his ideas at the beginning of his work on the Adoration theme and also in drawings that are thought to be for an Adoration of the Shepherds. The grouping of the figures in a drawing in the Musée Bonnat in Bayonne (fig. 68),[7] the typology of figural postures, and even the way the scene is centered show the overall composition of the final work that would soon follow. The presence of the ass and ox in the Louvre drawing leads me to the theory that Leonardo was exploring both Adoration themes on these sheets.

The place in Leonardo's researches of the present drawing has been variously interpreted, however. According to Jens Thiis, it is not a summing up of the preliminary studies or a "first idea," as Wilhelm Suida and Carlo Pedretti would later claim. Thiis saw the drawing rather as the basis for a series of new drawings in which isolated figures are reworked. The 1481 date for the sheet was doubted by Bernard Berenson, who argued that the Adoration theme had been treated in drawings datable to 1478, before Leonardo had received the commission for the *Adoration of the Magi*. This idea can be accepted if one considers that Leonardo treated various themes simultaneously: for instance, note the sketch on the verso depicting a seated nude man leaning on his right hand. Tolnay connected it with another Louvre study for the Adoration (cat. no. 29) and with the British Museum sheet exhibited here. He concluded that there existed a plan for the apostle figures visualized at the same time as the studies for the Adoration and intended to be part of that same composition (see cat. no. 29).   FV

1. Becherucci 1985, p. 42.
2. See Chastel 1982, p. 430.
3. See Kemp 1981, p. 68.
4. "[Cette] diversité doit manifester un enchaînement: les gestes se répondent comme les moments successifs d'une onde, les traits, les visages . . . se faisant voir les uns les autres à l'infini"; Chastel 1982, p. 430.
5. Réau 1957, p. 247.
6. Pedretti and Dalli Regoli 1985, no. 8r; see De Marchi in Petrioli Tofani 1992, nos. 7–10.
7. Popham 1945, no. 39.

LEONARDO DA VINCI

28. *Figure Studies for the Adoration of the Magi* (recto)
Two Studies of a Crab (verso)

Pen and brown ink over traces of leadpoint or black chalk (recto); pen and brown ink (verso), 274 × 180 mm (10¾ × 7 1/16 in.)
Wallraf-Richartz-Museum — Foundation Corboud, Graphische Sammlung, Cologne   Z 2003

PROVENANCE: Probably from the Collection of Ferdinand Franz Wallraf, Cologne (1748–1824); museum stamp (Lugt Suppl. 2547a).

LITERATURE: Müntz 1892, pp. 31–35; Müller-Walde 1898, p. 251; Müntz 1898, vol. 1, p. 77 (detail); Müntz 1899, p. 67; Venturi 1901–39, vol. 9, pt. 1, p. 126, fig. 60; Berenson 1903, vol. 2, p. 57, no. 1014; Seidlitz 1909, vol. 1, p. 390 n. 7; Thiis 1913, pp. 137, 187–89, 200–201, 204–5; Calvi 1919, p. 23 n. 2; Poggi 1919, p. 46, pl. 66; Venturi 1920, p. 92, fig. 43; De Toni 1922, fig. 35; De Rinaldis 1926, p. 52, fig. 25; Hildebrandt 1927, pp. 229, 334, figs. 171, 278; Commissione Vinciana 1928– , vol. 2, pp. 27–28, pls. 62, 63; Sirén 1928, vol. 1, p. 34; Suida 1929, pp. 46, 269; Bodmer 1931, pp. 133, 383; Berenson 1938, vol. 2, p. 110, no. 1014; Giglioli 1944, p. 99, pl. 66; Valentiner 1949, p. 110, no. 77; Biblioteca Medicea Laurenziana 1952, p. 19, no. 19; Goldscheider 1952, p. 36, fig. 132; Möller 1952b (as copy); Royal Academy of Arts 1952, no. 13; Wallraf-Richartz-Museum 1953, no. 48; Heydenreich 1954, vol. 1, p. 31, vol. 2, p. 13, fig. 16; Goldscheider 1959, p. 176 (under no. 101); Rosenberg 1959, p. 20, fig. 37; Huyghe 1960, figs. 116–17; Berenson 1961, vol. 2, p. 193, no. 1014; Hale 1965, pp. 132–33; Martindale 1966, p. 47, fig. 33; Venturi 1980, p. 90; Marinoni 1980a, p. 215; Westfehling 1986, pp. 54–57, no. 8a, b; Kemp and Roberts 1989, p. 55, no. 7; Popham 1994, no. 47; Marani 2000b, pp. 108–13; Natali 2001, p. 55, fig. 41.

L eonardo's posthumously compiled *Libro di pittura* admonished young painters, "do not repeat the same movements in the same figure, be it in their limbs, hands or fingers. Nor should the same pose be repeated in one narrative composition [*storia*]."[1] In the workshops of late-fifteenth-century Florentine artists, this was traditional advice for young painters, and already found in Leon Battista Alberti's painting treatise of 1435–36. To the same end, young artists of the late 1470s and 1480s (the young Filippino Lippi is an example) explored variations of pose in drawing after drawing of the live model. As can be surmised, however, from the present sheet of figure studies, which probably dates to the years 1478 to 1481–82 (hence, at the cusp of the new practice), Leonardo's great contribution was the completely fluid, tireless variation after variation of each pose, and viewed from different angles. He developed this design approach into nuanced theory in the *Libro di pittura*, in which he wrote, "the same pose [*attitudine*] will display infinite variety, because it can be seen from infinite places."[2]

   Although none of the nude and nearly nude male figures on the Cologne sheet bear noticeable attributes that might help establish either their identity or the context for which they were intended, the somewhat ill-proportioned young man at the upper left seems to wear boots and a short frock tied at the waist, possibly those of a modest shepherd. The Cologne sheet is usually thought to be preparatory for the unfinished *Adoration of the Magi* altarpiece (figs. 10, 11) that the monks, the Augustinian Canonici Regolari, of San Donato a Scopeto commissioned from Leonardo in 1481, because the

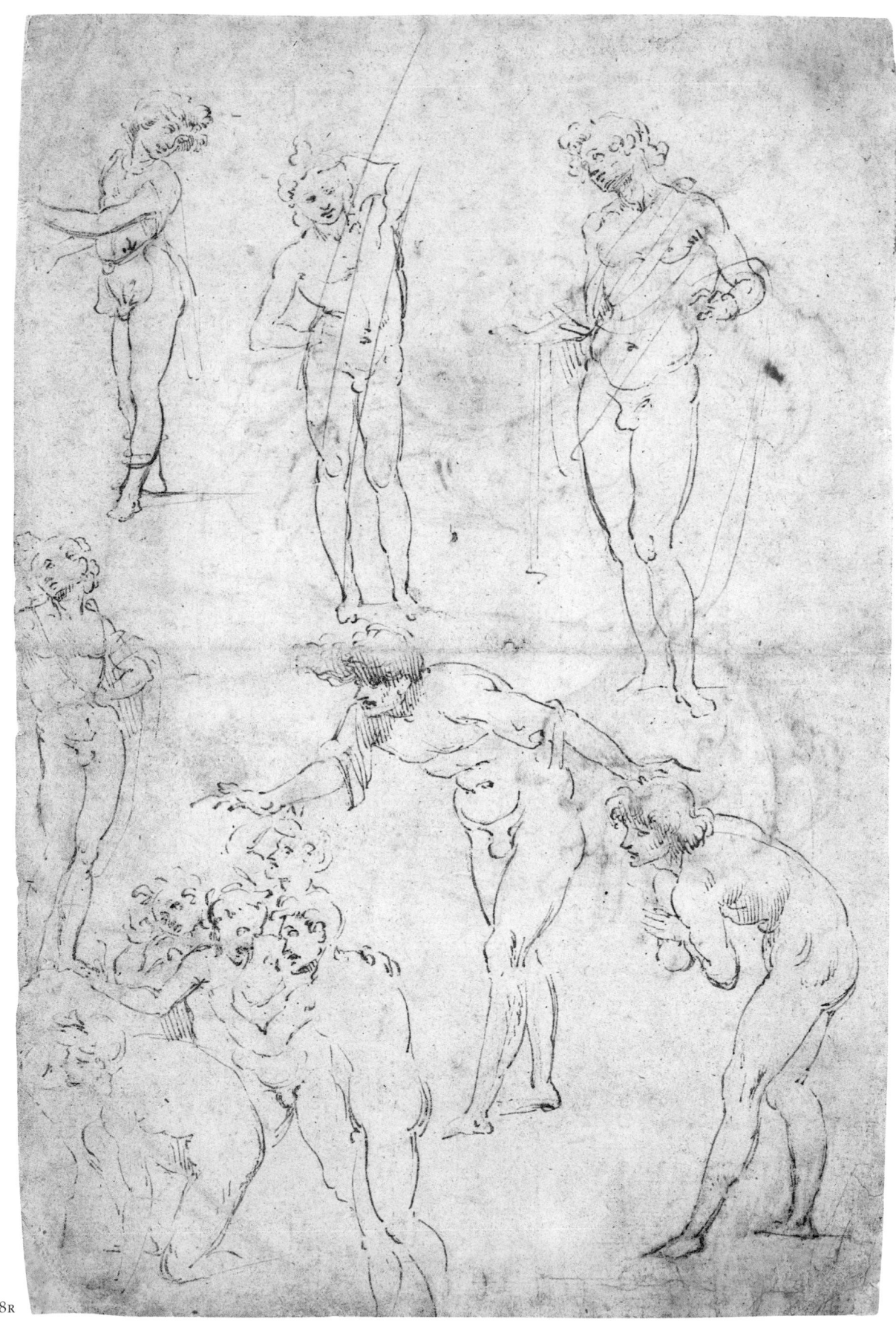

Cat. 28R

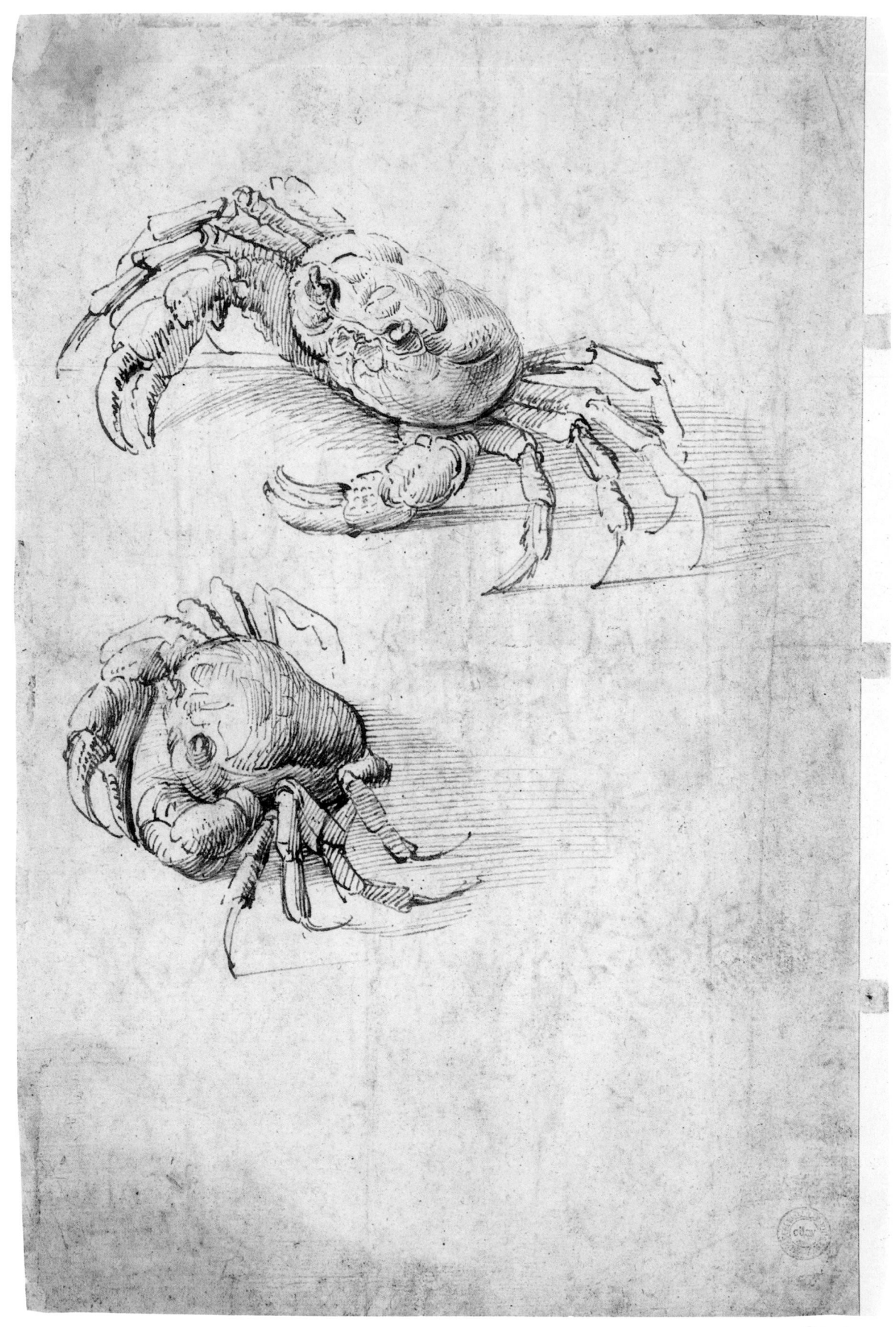

Cat. 28v

drawings on the lower portion portray the nude and nearly nude men in poses that generally recall those of the onlookers in the left foreground of the panel. The men's poses are also quite similar to those of the figures on the left in the magnificent Louvre composition drawing (cat. no. 27), which was evidently an early idea for the Uffizi altarpiece. The poses and figural types on the Cologne sheet, however, might be equally suited for an Adoration of the Shepherds, a subject that may or may not be connected with Leonardo's mysterious commission for an altarpiece for the Chapel of San Bernardo (Palazzo della Signoria, Florence), which is documented in January and March of 1478, and a subject that may or may not constitute an early idea for the San Donato a Scopeto altarpiece. (See cat. nos. 36–38; Chronology.) In any case, the slightly awkward bodily proportions of some of the figures may suggest a date for the sheet closer to 1478.

The rapid, summary figure sketches on the Cologne sheet consist primarily of outlines, with little or no internal modeling. Their somewhat dry character (they are much less fluent than the Venice sketches, cat. nos. 36, 37) suggests that the young artist was probably synthesizing the poses of the various figures, based on antecedent drafts, rather than exploring them anew. In contrast, others of Leonardo's more exploratory figure sketches teem with reinforcement lines (cat. nos. 30–32,

36–38). As he proceeded to articulate the poses of the figures into final form, he tamed the agitated movement of the contours to gain clarity, even if this resulted in a loss in the overall vivacity of the drawing. At this point, Leonardo still abbreviated the eyes of the figures as empty sockets.

The less well known, detailed studies of crabs on the verso of the Cologne sheet (illustrated here, although not exhibited) have elicited doubts among scholars and are frequently omitted from the Leonardo drawings literature; they were accepted as autograph by Ludwig Goldscheider. If this is correct, the studies do not seem easily datable, for, to quote Bernard Berenson in 1961, "in quality they seem almost closer to Dürer than to Leonardo."[3] It is not readily apparent that the parallel hatching is left-handed.   CCB

1. C. Urb., fol. 106v: "D'attitvdine e' mouimenti e' loro membra. / Non sia replicato li mededesimi [sic] mouimenti in una medesima figura, che'le sua membra, o' mani, o' dita, ne ancora si replichi le medesime attitvdini in una storia."
2. C. Urb., fol. 110v: "Dvn medesimo atto ueduto da uarij siti. / Una medesima attitudine si dimostrera uariata in infinito perche d'infiniti lochi po essere ueduta li quali lochi hanno quantita continua, e' la quantita continua e'diuisibile i[n] infinito, adunque infinitamente uarij siti mostra ogni action' humana in se medesima."
3. Berenson 1961, vol. 2, p. 193, no. 1014: "Per qualità sembrano quasi più vicini al Dürer che a Leonardo."

LEONARDO DA VINCI

29. *Studies of Male Nude Figures; a Virgin and Child; a Hygrometer* (recto) *Six Studies of Nude or Draped Men* (verso)

Pen and brown ink over leadpoint, leadpoint for the Virgin and Child (recto); pen and brown ink over leadpoint; leadpoint for sketch at lower left (verso), 277 × 209 mm (11 × 8¼ in.); oxidation and a few lacunae

Inscribed in pen and ink, in right-to-left script, on recto in center of circle: *modo di pesare laria / eddi sap[e]re qua[n]do sa / arromp[er]e il te[m]po;* outside circle: *spugnja; ciera;* in metalpoint at top: *una benta [?] di 16 annj;*[1] on verso in black chalk at top: *Dessin double* Département des Arts Graphiques du Musée du Louvre, Paris 2258

PROVENANCE: Probably Sir Thomas Lawrence; William II of the Netherlands; 1850, his sale, The Hague, no. 232 (not 233); acquired at that sale by the Musée du Louvre; museum mark (Lugt 1886).

LITERATURE: *Le Moniteur* 1850; Montaiglon 1852, pp. 211–12; Chennevières 1879, p. 518; Richter 1880, fig. p. 30 (recto, detail); Richter 1883, no. 594 n., fig. p. 297 (recto), no. 999 n.; Louvre 1888, no. 2022 (recto and verso); Rosenberg 1898, p. 36, fig. 23; Müller-Walde 1889, p. 17, figs. 71 (verso), 73 (recto); Müntz 1899, p. 189, figs. pp. 61, 72, 179 (details, recto), pp. 66, 69–71, fig. p. 80 (verso), p. 519, no. 13; Berenson 1903, vol. 1, p. 155, vol. 2, no. 1065; Seidlitz 1909, vol. 1, p. 63, pl. 10 (verso), pl. 33 (recto); Thiis 1913, pp. 200–202, 204–6, 216, fig. p. 197 (verso), fig. p. 203 (recto); Malaguzzi Valeri 1913–23, vol. 2, p. 489, fig. 534 (recto, detail); Calvi 1919, p. 23 n. 2, p. 44 (verso); Louvre 1919, no. 9 (verso?); Poggi 1919, pl. 64, p. xlv (verso), pl. 68, p. xlvi (recto); Demonts 1921, no. 7 (recto); Demonts 1922, no. 7 (recto); Venturi 1925, p. 126, fig. 59 (verso); Commissione Vinciana 1928–, vol. 2, pp. 56, 57; Sirén 1928, p. 34, pl. 39 (verso), p. 76, pl. 99 (recto); Suida 1929, p. 73 (recto); Bodmer 1931, p. 383, fig. pp. 134, 135; Clark 1933b, p. 139; Petit Palais 1935 (recto); Goldscheider 1945, no. 77 (recto), no. 80 (verso); Popham 1945, p. 24, no. 43 (verso), pp. 15, 24, 46, no. 44 (recto); Popham and Pouncey 1950, under no. 106 (recto); Amboise 1952; Biblioteca Medicea Laurenziana 1952, no. 18 (recto); Bovi 1952, p. 96, fig. p. 98 (verso), fig. p. 167 (recto); Florisoone and Bacou 1952, no. 12 (recto); Bouchot-Saupique 1953–54, p. 58; Heydenreich 1954, p. 31, fig. 15 (recto); Louvre 1955, no. 1 (verso); Parker 1956, under no. 18; De Tolnay 1962, under no. 2, figs. 5, 7 (recto); Sérullaz 1965, no. 8 (text, verso; fig., recto); Bacou 1968, no. 13 (verso); Clark and Pedretti 1968, vol. 1, under no. 12702 (verso); Heydenreich 1974a, p. 44, fig. 33 (recto); Louvre 1977; Pedretti 1977, vol. 1, p. 95, no. 38, p. 351 under no. 594, pl. 33B (recto), no. 999 n.; Salvini 1977, p. 388, fig. 1; Pedretti 1978b, p. 153, fig. 3 (verso); Rosci 1978, p. 183, no. 25b (recto); Pedretti 1979b, p. 11, fig. 4 (verso); Ames-Lewis 1981, pp. 163–64, 169, 178, fig. 169 (recto), pp. 110, 163, 178, fig. 89 (verso); Kemp 1981, p. 68, fig. 25 (recto); Lisner 1981, p. 201; Chastel 1982, p. 431 n. 3; Pedretti

and Clark 1983, pp. 27, 58, fig. 11 (recto); Louvre 1986, no. 73 (recto); Veltman and Keele 1986, pp. 338, 352, figs. 4.1, 48.1, 49.1 (detail); Westfehling 1986, under no. 8a (verso); Bassi 1989, p. 114, fig. p. 115; Parronchi 1989, p. 57, fig. 52 (recto); Wasserman 1989, figs. 1, 2 (recto); Palazzo Grassi 1992, no. 2 (verso); Roberts 1992, p. 171 n. 111; Arasse 1997, p. 367, figs. 254, 255 (recto), p. 352, fig. 244 (verso); Marani 1999b, p. 108 (verso), p. 109 (recto); Bertelli 2001, p. 39; Marani 2001, p. 112; Natali 2001, p. 55, fig. 40 (verso).

This drawing was probably in the collection of Sir Thomas Lawrence, as the manuscript inventory of the Louvre drawings indicates. However, it does not appear in the catalogue of the fifth exhibition of Lawrence's collection, held posthumously in London in February 1836, and the *Adoration of the Shepherds* that appeared there corresponds in its dimensions to a drawing in the Musée Bonnat, Bayonne (fig. 68).[2] In an anonymous article published in *Le Moniteur* in 1850, at the time the Louvre acquired two paintings and sixteen drawings, including the present sheet, at the sale of King William II of the Netherlands, this drawing was called a "dessin double" (double drawing), which repeats the inscription on the verso. The drawing was part of the same collection as a sheet of studies in the Wallraf-Richartz-Museum (cat. no. 28), which has the same "double drawing" inscription and is of similar dimensions. Their common provenance prior to the collection of William II for this drawing and of Wallraf Richartz for the other has yet to be determined. This very well known sheet of studies was exhibited at the Louvre in the late nineteenth century: it was displayed in 1888 and could still be found "in the revolving case placed at the entrance to the Thiers rooms" in 1899, when Eugène Müntz saw it there.[3]

The recto and verso of the sheet are related to the *Adoration of the Magi* in the Uffizi (figs. 10, 11). In the figures on both sides, Leonardo set out to define, individually and in groups, some of the major participants in that scene. These are, wrote André Chastel, "intermediaries set up to draw one's eyes gradually to the scene." The figures come into sharper focus as their roles are progressively clarified: "meditating figure," "dazzled spectator," "group in discussion."[4] As in other preparatory drawings (see cat. no. 27), the postures here are

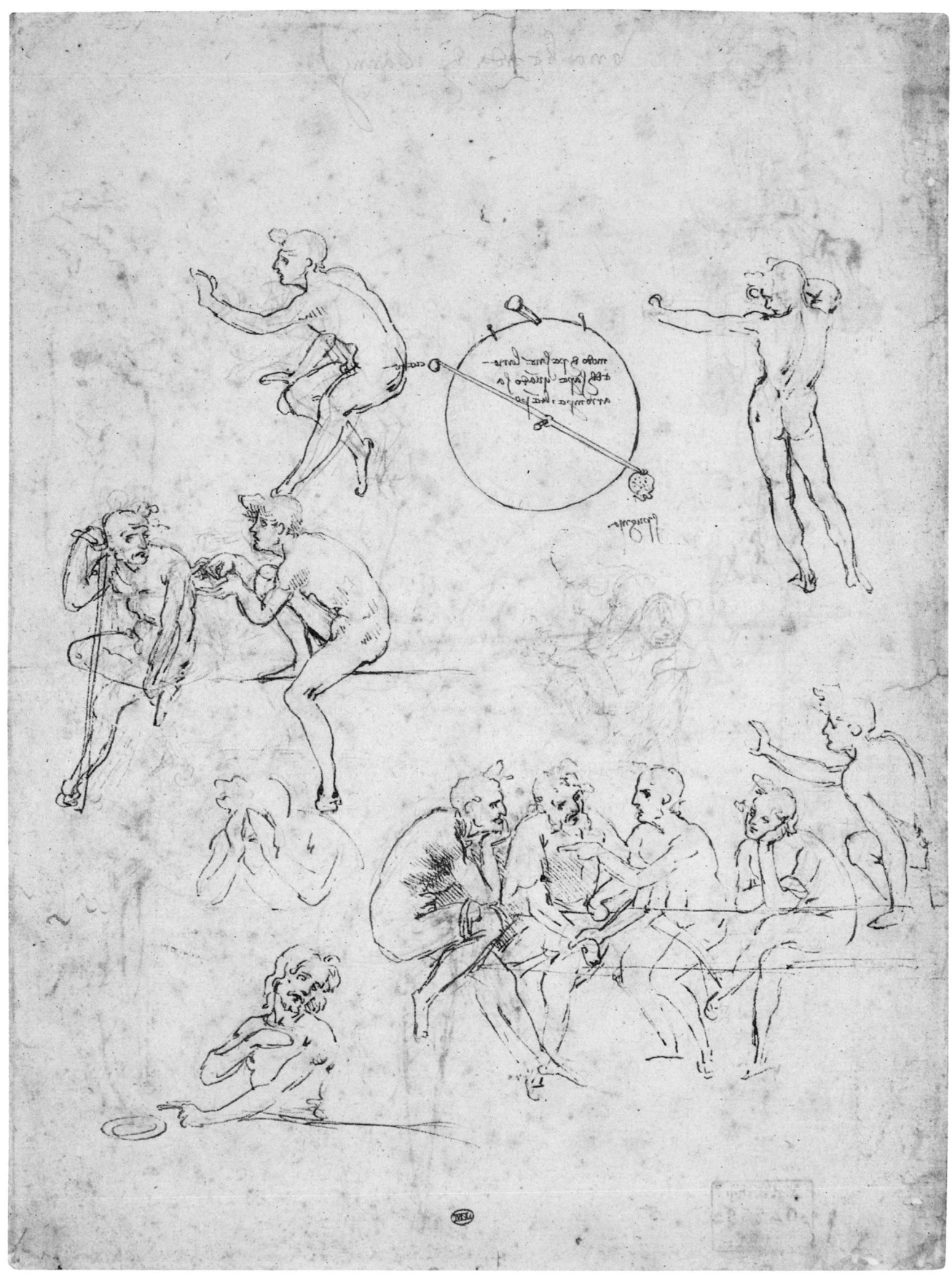

Cat. 29R

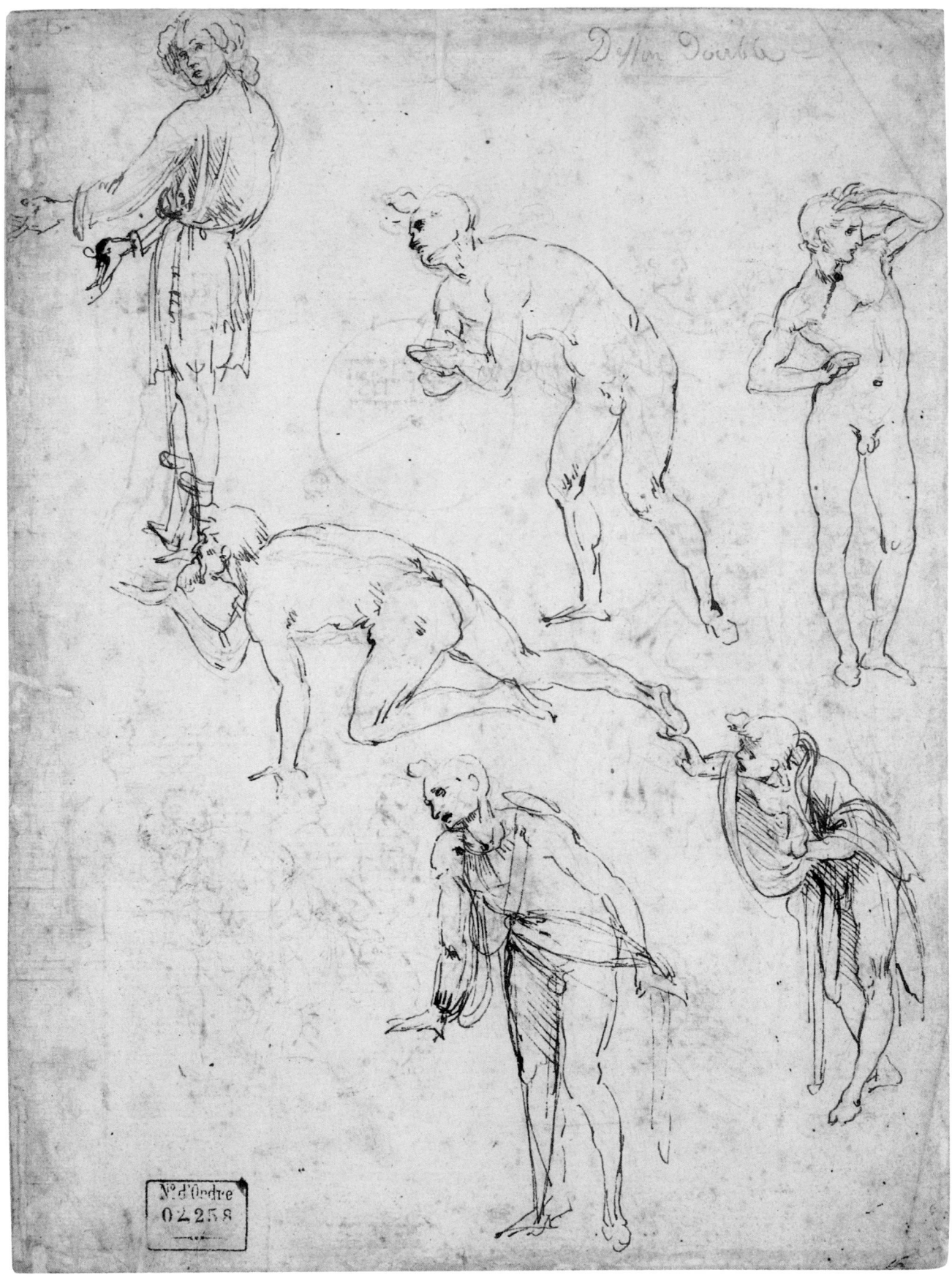

Cat. 29v

326

not identical to those in the painting. They differ sufficiently that they look like variations of motifs of which many were not used. An exception, however, is the bearded, kneeling man in the center of the verso, who forms a line, more extreme than it would be in the painting, which establishes the diagonal of the composition and, along with the Virgin and Child, the dramatic effect of the foreground.[5] The other figures are utterly expressive, set down with a single stroke of a pen that never retraces its steps, that makes few hatch marks and occasional superimposed designs, as if it were intently following its own train of thought. That is how we can understand the pentimento on the face of the man in the upper left corner of the verso who turns his back to the viewer, or the suggestion of clothing that partly covers the body of the left-hand man advancing along the bottom. That and the other half-draped figure are perhaps found again, reversed, in the left part of the overall drawing (cat. no. 27). They may also be interpreted as variants of the nude figure with hands joined in the upper part of the present sheet, and they are reworked in the lower right part of the Wallraf-Richartz drawing (cat. no. 28). These, in turn, may relate to the bent figures with hands raised found in the painting to the right of the Virgin. The figure shading his eyes, at the upper right of the sheet, can be connected with the "dazzled spectator"; that figure is also studied on the Ashmolean Museum sheet (cat. no. 39). One of the principal actors in the group at the right of the painting, this figure expresses the "effort of contemplative attention" that, according to Chastel, translates into "the spontaneous act of covering one's eyes when struck by a blinding light."[6] The gestures and postures recorded on both sides of the sheet give form to an illumination, not simply a narration, of a particular event. They can be understood as an anticipatory illustration of the groundwork of Leonardo's painting, studies and observations of the *moti corporali* (motions of the body) that reveal the *atti e moti mentali* (attitudes and motions of the mind).[7] All the emotions that overwhelm human beings are *accidenti mentali* and, wrote Leonardo, "and these mental attitudes should accompany the hands with the face, and thus also with the person."[8]

The recto of the sheet is more complicated because it involves another composition that was also being developed during 1480–81. Art historians have seen in some of the sketches prefigurations of work for the *Last Supper*, later painted in Milan. In addition, the tondo-type composition at the center of the sheet is a sketch of the Virgin and Child that is close to the early Virgins group in this exhibition, attesting to the fact that Leonardo treated these various themes simultaneously (cat. nos. 18, 20–22). This motif is treated as a circular composition, showing the child lying flat on the Virgin's knees, their heads facing in opposite directions. The drawing is done in leadpoint, with the Virgin's profile reworked in pen and ink; circular strokes close the circle in the lower part.

In the upper part of the recto is a study of a hygrometer, annotated by Leonardo, writing from right to left, inside and outside the circle. The hygrometer, used to measure moisture in the atmosphere, had a sponge attached to the end of the arm of a scale and a piece of wax (*ciera*?) to the other. A depiction of a hygrometer in the Codex Atlanticus is inscribed: "A cognoscere le qualità e grossezze dell'aria, e quando ha a piovere."[9] Carlo Vecce notes the importance accorded by Leonardo to the arrangement of the words in a drawing (see his essay). Jean Paul Richter linked the inscription on the present drawing that begins "modo di pesare laria" with a passage in the Paris Ms. H: "Per cognosciere meglio i vēti"; however, that connection is not valid.[10] Richter was also the first to recognize the seated figures in the lower part as an anticipation of the *Last Supper*. Through an analysis of Leonardo's handwriting, Richter dated the inscription on the hygrometer on the present sheet to the 1490s, which would imply—but not verify—that the drawing was reworked then, a hypothesis supported by the fact that the word *ciera* is written over the figure of the man seated at upper left.

Interpretation of the sheet's theme as a double one was adopted by most historians, following studies by Bernard Berenson (1903) and Jens Thiis (1913). The motif of conversation and debate is inserted into and developed among studies for the Adoration, not independently from them. As in other studies, Leonardo moved from one theme to the other by allowing images associated with each theme to work upon those of the other. In studying on paper the animation of figures for the background, Leonardo arrived at ideas he would later rework, including that of the charged interpersonal discussion. On the present sheet, the rightmost among the five half-seated and half-standing figures appears with variations in the scene at center left and also perhaps in the single figure just above. Differing in arm gestures and position of the legs, these figures might represent three variations of a single attitude. Richter linked this group to a text in the Paris Ms. A titled "Del figurare uno che parli in fra più persone."[11]

This text perfectly describes the relationship between the two figures on the left of the sheet and even, to a degree, the animated group at the right. In the Paris Ms. A, which was written after the Louvre drawing was done, Leonardo set out to determine the modes of spoken expression and the gestures and attitudes attached to them, which depended, he said, on the nature of the discourse: "Cioè se l'è materia persuasiva, che li atti sieno al proposito, se l'è materia dichiarativa per diverse ragioni." Hence, as we see in the left part of the drawing, the speaker should reinforce his outward expression with a two-handed gesture—"pigli colle pri[me] 2 dita della mano destra un dito de la sinistra, avendone serrate le 2 minori"—and accompany it with an echoing facial expression.[12] These studies may initially have been conceived for the background of an Adoration, then abandoned. It is not certain whether in the five-figure group the horizontal plane indicated by two strokes is a table or just a delimiter of the space of that conversation. A well-defined axis—like that in the *Last Supper*—would give coherence to the gestures and the rhythm of the figures' placement. A drawing in metalpoint on prepared paper at Windsor (RL 12702),[13] which shows a group of three seated figures on a low wall or parapet, has similarly been linked to the *Adoration of the Magi* and considered from the perspective of studies for the *Last Supper*. To these two sheets can be connected a third study (cat. no. 32). It shows an exchange between two people, with, above it, a sketch of a man blowing a trumpet in the ear of his interlocutor, his din contrasting with the calm of the intelligent discourse.

Within the context of studies for the *Adoration*, Leonardo reflected on an incipient idea for a Last Supper twelve years prior to that Milan project.[14] It is not possible to determine whether these studies for the *Adoration* predate the composition sketch in the Louvre or instead to see them as the development of individual figures once the composition had been established. Jack Wasserman, reiterating that the presumed subject of the five-figure group on the recto of the present sheet is the Last Supper, considered that the study in the lower left corner depicting a nude figure seated at a table and pointing his right hand in front of him to his left represents Christ pointing to Judas, seated across from him.[15] Richter had already connected this figure to the central motif of the composition sketch for the *Last Supper* at Windsor (cat. no. 65).[16] According to him, Leonardo was not, in 1480–81, yet following one specific gospel text or another, as he would later do, but was already envisioning the theme he would treat. The present two-sided Louvre sheet is one of the most complex of the studies for that composition, but it is also the most pertinent for assessing the importance, the innovativeness, and the complexity of research that constituted the germ of what was to come in Leonardo's first years in Milan.

FV

1. This previously unpublished inscription in Leonardo's hand was deciphered by Pietro C. Marani.
2. Popham 1945, no. 39; Bean 1960, no. 42.
3. Müntz 1899.
4. "Intermédiaires disposés pour attirer peu à peu le regard vers la scène"; "personnage qui médite"; "spectateur ébloui"; "groupe en discussion"; Chastel 1982, p. 430.
5. Clayton in Palazzo Grassi 1992, no. 2.
6. "L'effort d'attention contemplative"; "par l'acte spontané de se couvrir les yeux en face d'une lumière aveuglante"; Chastel 1982, p. 432.
7. *Libro di pittura* 1995, fols. 285b, 286a.
8. *Libro di pittura* 1995, vol. 2, p. 260: "questi tali accidenti debbono accompagnare le mani col volto, e così la persona."
9. C.A., fol. 675r; ed. Marinoni 1990, p. 1324.
10. Pedretti 1977, no. 999, Ms. H3, fol. 100r.
11. Pedretti 1977, no. 594; ed. Marinoni 1990, fol. 101, p. 200.
12. See Chomentovskaya 1938.
13. Pedretti and Clark 1983, no. 1.
14. Ames-Lewis 1981.
15. Wasserman 1989.
16. Richter 1883.

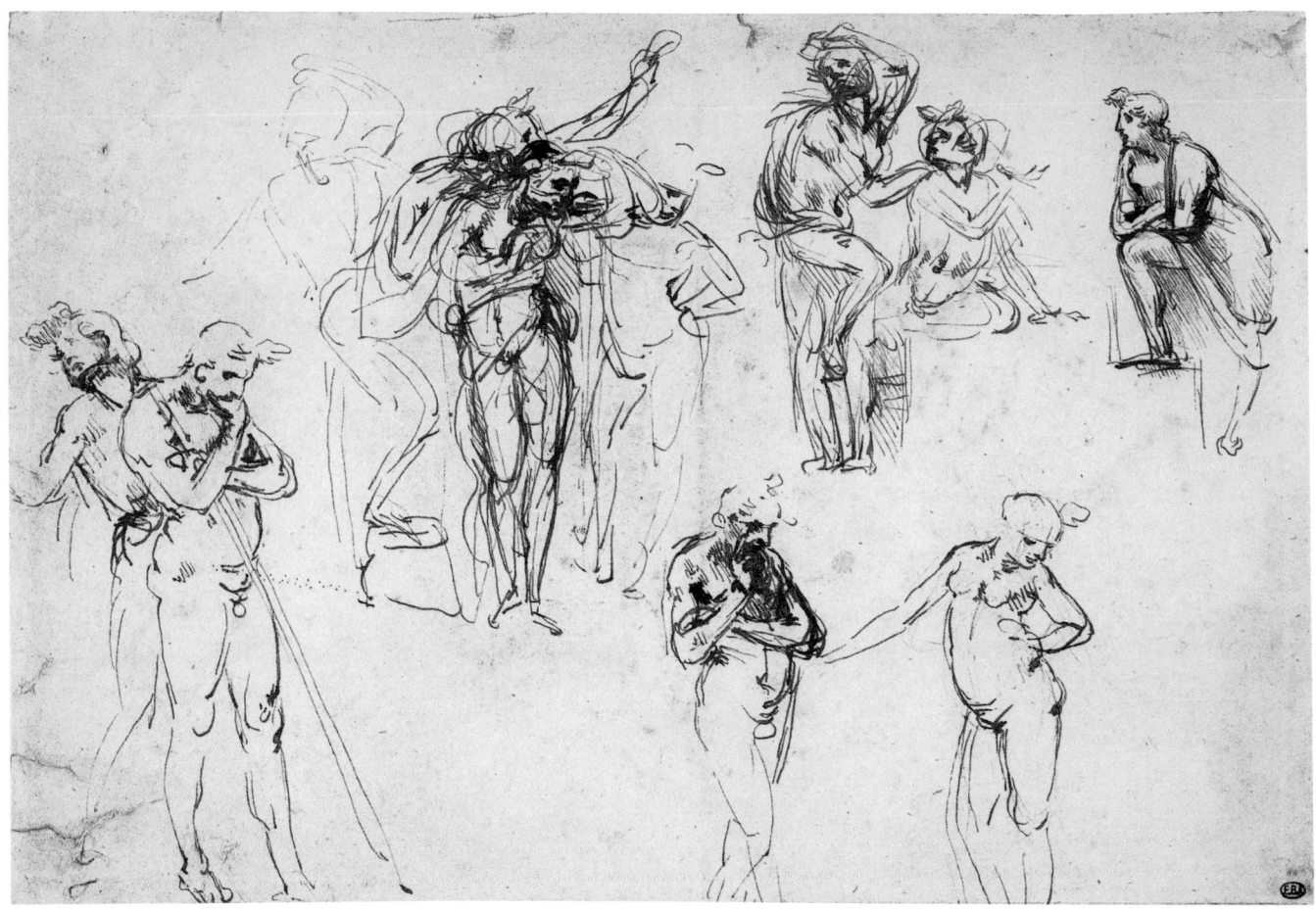

LEONARDO DA VINCI

30. *Studies for the Adoration of the Magi* (recto and verso)

Pen and brown ink over stylus (recto); leadpoint for the child, pen and brown ink for the woman's head (in another hand?), center of sheet rubbed with charcoal (verso), 179 × 263 mm (7⅛ × 10⅜ in.) Bibliothèque de l'École Nationale Supérieure des Beaux-Arts, Paris 424

PROVENANCE: Émile Galichon, mark (Lugt 1058) on verso; 1875, sale, Paris, no. 165; Alfred Armand and Prosper Valton; 1907, bequeathed to the École Nationale Supérieure des Beaux-Arts with mark (Lugt 829).

LITERATURE: Chennevières 1879, p. 518; École des Beaux-Arts 1879, no. 34; Müller-Walde 1889, p. 137, fig. 76; Rosenberg 1898, p. 36, fig. 25; Müntz 1899, p. 523 ; Berenson 1903, vol. 2, no. 1081; Seidlitz 1909, vol. 1, pl. 13; Thiis 1913, p. 190, fig. p. 206; Gronau 1914, fig. p. 46; Calvi 1919, p. 30 n. 1; Poggi 1919, p. xlvi, pl. 65; Bode 1921, pp. 45, 46, fig. 24 (detail; with incorrect location); Venturi 1925, p. 126, fig. 58; Commissione Vinciana 1928–, vol. 2, p. 61; Sirén 1928, p. 37, pl. 41; Bodmer 1931, p. 384, fig. 137; École des Beaux-Arts 1935, no. 157; Goldscheider 1945, no. 79; Popham 1945, pp. 23, 25, no. 48; Biblioteca Medicea Laurenziana 1952, no. 20; Bovi 1952, p. 102, fig. p. 95; Florisoone and Bacou 1952, no. 13; Bouchot-Saupique 1953–54, pp. 61–67, fig. 8; École des Beaux-Arts 1958, no. 60; De Tolnay 1962, no. 1 (verso), figs. 1, 2; Petit Palais 1965–66, no. 183; Pedretti 1973a, fig. 110; Lisner 1981, p. 201; École des Beaux-Arts 1981–82, no. 49; Chastel 1982, pp. 430–31; École des Beaux-Arts 1984, no. 117; Veltman and Keele 1986, p. 352, fig. 49.2–3; Trutty-Coohill 1989a, p. 165; Palazzo Grassi 1992, no. 3; Wiemers 1996, p. 272, fig. 257; Marani 1999b, fig. 112.

This drawing belonged to Émile Galichon, as did the overall composition sketch for the *Adoration of the Magi* at the Louvre (cat. no. 27). Philippe de Chennevières indicated that both were acquired in Turin, but the date of that purchase, like the provenance of the drawings, remains unknown.

There is a significant amount of preliminary work with a

stylus, as in the Louvre preparatory sketch; it was used for almost all the figures, particularly the group of three at the left, as well as the man leaning on a staff in the lower left corner and the man turning away in the lower right corner. In the last case, there are also traces of leadpoint. In some instances, this first work with the stylus reflects ideas that are very different from those made finally with the pen, especially in the position of the heads. It is less a preliminary laying out than a sort of on-the-spot reading, with the stylus playing as important a role as the pen. In several places the pen strokes themselves appear almost as a first indication, but where they are more precise, heavily worked and reworked, with an agitation characteristic of these years in Florence, they make this drawing one of the most striking of the group of studies for the *Adoration*. The hatching may correspond to intended shaded areas in the painting, and the indication of planes on which the figures are placed implies that planning is well advanced, even though almost none of the figures appears in identical form in the painting. This composition process can also be observed on the two-sided sheet in the Louvre (cat. no. 29). Note also the line of fine perforations between the two groups on the left, which the artist may have employed to calculate distance or indicate perspective.

Only one of the figures here, seen at lower left and again at lower center, is found in the *Adoration of the Magi* in the Uffizi: he is the pensive figure leaning on a staff in the left foreground and is known as the "philosopher" (figs. 10, 11). He appears in reverse in the composition sketch (cat. no. 27), and also figures twice on the sheet in the British Museum (cat. no. 31). That sheet has dimensions very similar to catalogue number 30 and displays the same unusual overlapping of forms. Another figure on the present sheet, the one that is turning away in the lower left group, may have been a study in connection with the man in armor in the lower right of the painting (fig. 10). His youth contrasts with the maturity of the "philosopher," the two extremes bracketing the principal scene.

The complexity of the lines in the three-figure group on this same side of the sheet makes it difficult to interpret. The figures might be a variant of the two figures below and to the right, but they lack an indication of the horizontal plane that would position them in space. One of the figures, arm raised and turning away, is itself delineated over a standing silhouette, a technique used on the British Museum sheet. André Chastel has argued that this "grappe humaine" (cluster of humans) can be viewed as a version of the "group in discussion" on the recto of catalogue number 29. These figures, arms extended, heads lifted, are studied with particular regard to their placement and their distance from each other in a space that is barely defined, but in which the perspective effects of the background and the jumble of worshipers in the middle ground around the Virgin can already be discerned (figs. 10, 11). I suggest that there is a connection between this group and the spectators at the foot of the stairs in the left background of the painting who are pointing to the eager throng of horsemen arriving through the ruined arcade. Martin Clayton has observed that these animated horsemen and spectators are looking toward the sky, where their attention is drawn to a comet, an event often linked to the Adoration of the Magi.[1]

The verso of the present sheet was first studied by Charles de Tolnay in 1962.[2] He remarked that the black chalk (or charcoal) rubbing is not original. Indeed, it is unlikely that the substance was applied by Leonardo himself so that he could, by tracing or pouncing, transfer the designs on the front onto another surface. By contrast, as Tolnay noted, the very light leadpoint drawing of a child holding a cat is analogous specifically to a drawing in the Musée Bonnat in Bayonne[3] and to the two-sided sheet in the British Museum (1860-6-16-98 recto). The present sheet, like the Louvre drawing (cat. no. 29), confirms that Leonardo's studies for the early Virgins were simultaneous with those he undertook for the *Adoration of the Magi*.

FV

1. Martin Clayton in Palazzo Grassi 1992, no. 3.
2. De Tolnay 1962, no. 1.
3. Popham 1945, p. 14.

LEONARDO DA VINCI

31. *Six Figures and the Profile of an Old Man Facing to the Right* (recto)
Allegory with Fortune (verso)

Pen and dark brown ink on unprepared paper (recto); metalpoint partly reworked with pen and brown ink and brush and brown wash on warm pink prepared paper (verso), 166 × 265 mm (6½ × 10⁷⁄₁₆ in.) Inscribed on verso with identifications of many of the figures in metalpoint, in conventional left-to-right script: *ignoranzia; sup[er]bia;* in right-to-left script: *ingratitudine; morte; invidia; fortuna*
The British Museum, London 1886-6-9-42

PROVENANCE: Marquis of Breadalbane, Scotland (d. 1862); sale, Christie's, London, June 4, 1886, lot 42; (Alphonse Wyatt Thibaudeau); purchased by the museum.

LITERATURE: British Museum 1888–94, vol. 1, pp. 4–5, pls. 7, 8; Müller-Walde 1889, pp. 139–40, 154–55, figs. 77, 82; British Museum 1891, no. 22; Müller-Walde 1898, p. 256; Berenson 1903, vol. 1, p. 152, vol. 2, p. 58, no. 1023; Seidlitz 1909, vol. 1, pp. 155, 293; Thiis 1913, pp. 184–88, 191, 200 (incorrectly listed as Valton Collection), 201; Venturi 1920, p. 91, figs. 38, 39; Commissione Vinciana 1928– , vol. 2, p. 27, pl. 60, 1934, vol. 3, p. 23, pl. 98; Popp 1928, p. 41, no. 31; Sirén 1928, pl. 42; Suida 1929, p. 46; Bodmer 1931, pp. 138, 144, 384–85; Berenson 1938, vol. 1, p. 170, vol. 2, p. 112, vol. 3, fig. 478, no. 1023; Nicodemi 1939, pl. 58; Popham and Pouncey 1950, pp. 62–64, no. 105; Castelfranco 1952b, no. 11; Castelfranco 1956, pp. 26, 57, pl. 27b; Berenson 1961, vol. 1, p. 249, vol. 2, p. 196, no. 1023; Wasserman 1984, p. 39, fig. 34; Pedretti 1987b, pp. 56, 91; Caroli 1991, p. 175. Popham 1994, nos. 49, 104; Wiemers 1996, pp. 301–2, fig. 292.

On the recto of the sheet, two of the standing male figures—the one in the center and the one second from the left leaning on a staff—are drawn in a larger scale, and these can be connected definitively with figures of onlookers in the extreme left portion of the unfinished *Adoration of the Magi* altarpiece (fig. 10), which Leonardo began painting in March 1481 for the monks of San Donato a Scopeto. These two larger-scale male figures seem also recognizable in the extreme left of the early Louvre composition sketch for the picture (cat. no. 27), where they are drawn in a closely similar pen technique. The correspondences of design between the British Museum sketches and the final painting are fewer, however, for the angles of view are somewhat changed, especially that of the pensive bearded man in the center, who is usually nicknamed the "philosopher." As a monumental anchoring figure, the "philosopher" type is turned in a nearly profile view in the

painting, enveloped in deep shadow, and clothed in draperies of extraordinary sculptural presence. He was the subject of two additional studies rapidly drawn in pen and ink (cat. no. 30).

As a whole, the drawing technique of the British Museum sheet, with jagged reinforced contours, short, slightly zigzagging diagonal hatching, and small pools of ink along some of the reinforced outlines (as if the artist had inked the pen too much), is the same as that of the École des Beaux-Arts sheet (cat. no. 30). Leonardo therefore must have drawn the two sheets in quick succession of each other. On the lower left of the British Museum sheet, the head of the old man in profile may be a detail study also intended for the magnificent "philosopher" type. Since Leonardo habitually added unrelated head motifs in preparatory sketches, however, the possibility also exists that the head is no more than an inspired doodle (cat. nos. 20 recto, 24). More mysterious are the neighboring four small-scale figures portrayed in full length, which may or may not relate to the *Adoration*. A sketch of a standing seminude man facing to the left, who may be leaning on a staff with outstretched arms, can be discerned below the waist of the large-scale study of the man leaning on a staff; the motif may easily be overlooked. (Leonardo most likely drew the larger figures first on the sheet.) On the extreme right, the general pose of the man standing with open arms and gazing upward is much like that of some of the gesticulating figures that stand by the arch with stairs in the background ruin of the *Adoration of the Magi* (fig. 10), without being precisely identical in design. Similarly, the seated female figure at the upper left of the British Museum sheet (whom some scholars have called a sibyl) puts her hand to her forehead as if gazing into the distance. Although her gesture is not a perfect match, she seems to resemble the seated figures on the stairs in the background ruin of the altarpiece (the stairs slope in the opposite direction).

The allegorical composition on the verso is here redated to 1478–81, with the proposal that the subject alludes to the Pazzi conspiracy, possibly even specifically to Lorenzo de' Medici's narrow escape from the assassins' blows in 1478. The scene depicts the works of Fortune in a political context, and the artist curiously inscribed it—using the same metalpoint

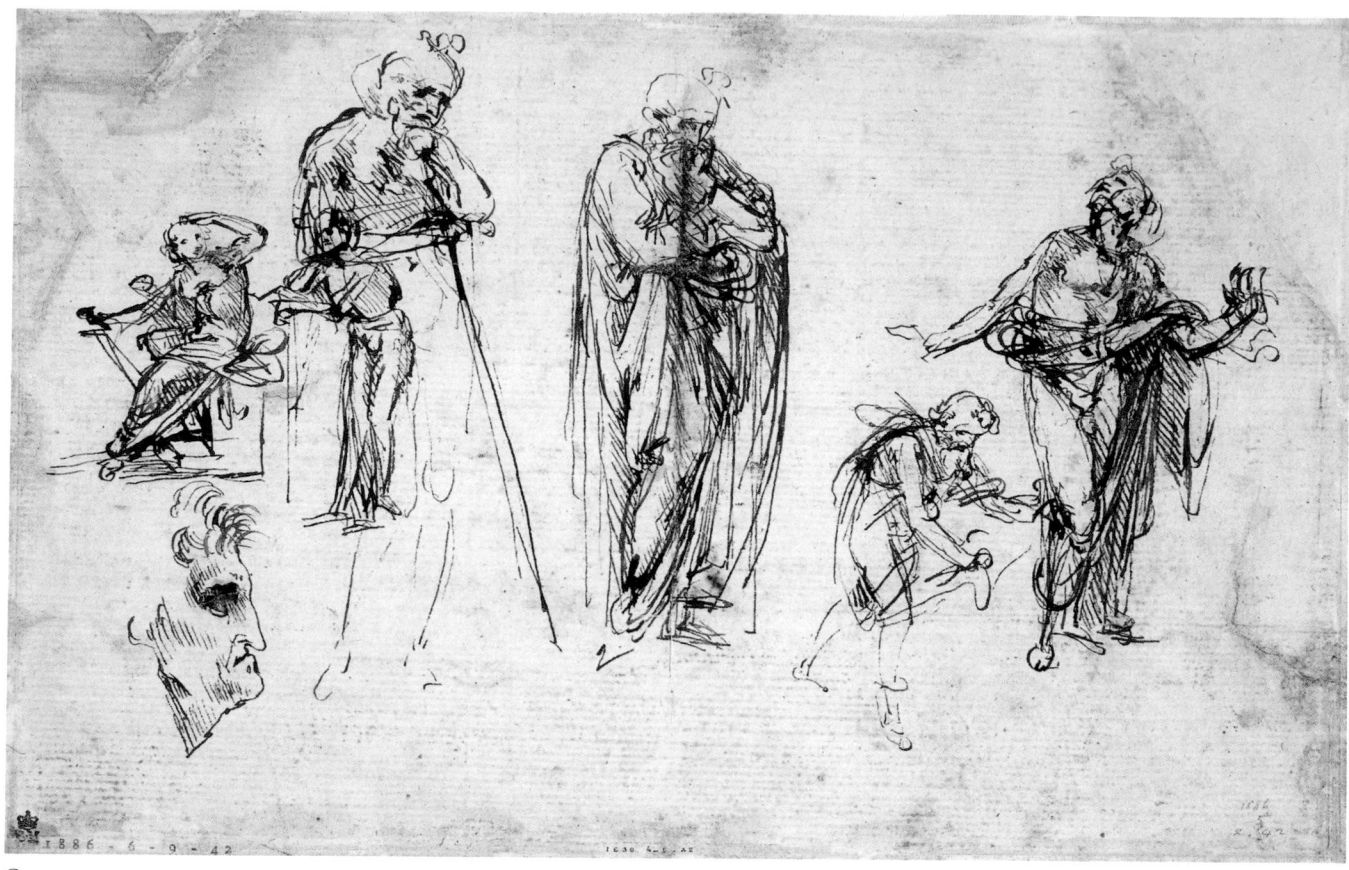

Cat. 31R

as in the drawing—with allegorical names sometimes reading right to left, and other times left to right. Leonardo reworked the delicate metalpoint drawing extensively with pen, brown ink, brush and wash to deepen its tonal range against the warm pink prepared paper. The allegorical scene unfolds around a tree (which may be a laurel, Lorenzo's emblem), set on a rocky promontory.[1] At the upper right, the flying, long-haired female figure of Fortuna holds by the waist a putto who energetically blows wind through a trumpet to halt the doings of Morte (Death). The agitated, hunched-over figure of Death (whether it is a man or a woman is not clear) aggressively pushes forward a flaming torch above the tree and straddles Invidia (Envy), the bent woman on the right, and Ingratitudine (Ingratitude), the mournful woman on the left. The menacing group of Ingratitudine, Invidia, and Morte stands below, at the

crag of the rocky promontory with the tree. On the far left, Leonardo sketched the motif of Ignoranza hovering above the seated Superbia (Pride) only roughly in metalpoint, without reworking it in pen and ink, and quite uncharacteristically wrote the names of the figures from left to right.

A. E. Popham wavered in his opinion on the date of this sheet in 1946 and 1950, settling in the end, like many scholars, for a date in Leonardo's first Milanese period,[2] based on the iconographic argument that the allegory, like two related sheets in Christ Church (see 0037 [JBS 18] and cat. no. 54), probably refers to a failed plot to murder Ludovico Sforza "Il Moro" (for example, that of his sister-in-law Duchess Bona, at Christmas 1485). He also noted that Ludovico's favorite device was a mulberry tree;[3] the genus of the tree in the present drawing is not precisely distinguishable. Leaving the difficult

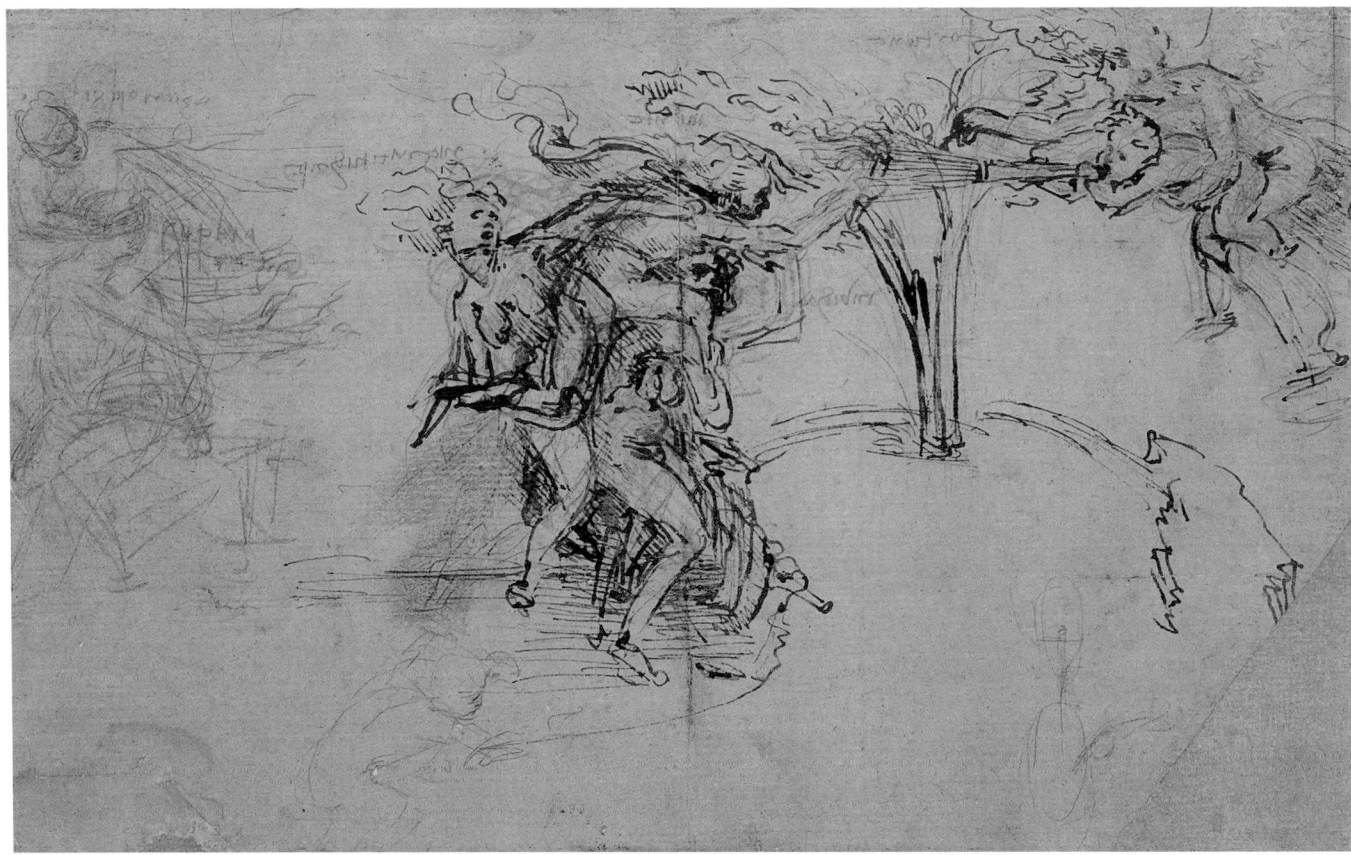

Cat. 31v

question of subject matter aside, one can demonstrate that the drawing technique and the articulation of the figural types in the British Museum allegory are both typical of Leonardo's work from the late 1470s to 1482/83. First (and as Popham and others have usually agreed), the recto of the British Museum sheet has studies of six figures, some of whom are, in physical type and pose, just like the early small figure drawings for the *Adoration of the Magi*. Like them, the British Museum figures on the recto are executed in pen and brown ink on the unprepared buff color of the paper. Second, the style of drawing on the recto and verso of the British Museum sheet is entirely consistent and thus from the same moment. Both the recto and verso exhibit the scratchy, angular, reinforced outlines, jagged parallel hatching, and the hands and feet of the figures abbreviated as "mittens" that are character-

istic of Leonardo's sketches throughout the 1470s. Third, the type of warm pink preparation on the paper of the verso is much like that on the early sheet of sketches of conversing figures intended for either an *Adoration* or a *Last Supper* (Windsor, RL 12702). The same is true of the figural notation. In the British Museum allegory, the putto in particular is identical in figural type to the infants portrayed in the various sketches and studies for the *Madonna of the Cat* (cat. nos. 18, 19), datable in the late 1470s to 1480/81.

CCB

1. Compare examples of laurel-tree motifs in illuminated manuscripts commissioned by Lorenzo de' Medici "Il Magnifico" in the 1470s; Lenzuni 1992, p. 151 for Plut. 54.23, c. 1, Florence; p. 154 for Bibl. Nat. Ital. 548, Paris.
2. For Popham's opinion in 1946, see Popham 1994, pp. 119–20, no. 104; and in 1950, see Popham and Pouncey 1950, vol. 1, pp. 62–64, no. 105 verso.
3. Popham and Pouncey 1950, vol. 1, p. 64.

32. *Man Blowing a Trumpet into the Ear of Another Man; Two Seated Men Disputing*

Pen and dark brown ink over leadpoint, 258 × 192 mm (10⅛ × 7⁹⁄₁₆ in.)
The British Museum, London 1895-9-15-478

PROVENANCE: Abbé Luigi Celotti [Cellotti], Venice (1765–1846; Lugt under no. 188) (according to the Lawrence Gallery Catalogue); Sir Thomas Lawrence, Bristol and London (1769–1830; Lugt 2445); Miss C. Goodrich; John Malcolm, Poltalloch and London (1805–1893; Lugt 1489, 1780, 1781, Suppl. 1489).

LITERATURE: Lawrence Gallery 1835–36, Fifth Exhibition, no. 66; Robinson 1869, p. 16; Robinson 1876, no. 42; Müller-Walde 1889, p. 132, fig. 72; British Museum 1895, no. 37; Müntz 1898, vol. 1, pp. 72 (detail), 225 (detail); Berenson 1903, vol. 2, p. 58, no. 1036; Seidlitz 1909, vol. 1, p. 197; Thiis 1913, pp. 202, 204–5, 241; Poggi 1919, pl. 67; Venturi 1920, pp. 91–92, fig. 40; Commissione Vinciana 1928–, vol. 2, p. 27, pl. 59; Popp 1928, no. 15; Sirén 1928, pl. 40; Bodmer 1931, pp. 136, 383–84; Clark 1935, under no. 12702; Berenson 1938, vol. 1, p. 172, vol. 2, p. 114, vol. 3, fig. 491, no. 1036; Nicodemi 1939, pl. 60; Bottari 1942, pl. 48; Giglioli 1944, p. 100, pl. 67; Popham and Pouncey 1950, p. 64, no. 106; Berenson 1961, vol. 1, p. 251, vol. 2, p. 199, vol. 3, fig. 462, no. 1036; Gould 1975, pp. 47–48, fig. 20; Nicodemi 1980a, p. 29; Pedretti and Clark 1983, p. 58, fig. 48, under no. 1; Popham 1994, no. 46; Wiemers 1996, pp. 298–99, fig. 288.

The style and technique of these animated though enigmatic figural sketches are those of the drawings more securely connected with the *Adoration of the Magi* altarpiece (figs. 10, 11) for the monks of San Donato a Scopeto (cat. nos. 27–32). Although they are not clearly present in the final unfinished Uffizi altarpiece, groups of men blowing long trumpets do appear on the upper right of the early Louvre composition sketch for the picture (cat. no. 27), a sheet that seems also closely comparable in pen technique to the present drawing. In the Louvre composition sketch, however, the trumpeters face left, rather than right as in the present drawing (which is of only minor importance, since the orientation of the architectural background of the Louvre composition sketch is also the reverse of that in the final Uffizi altarpiece), and no trumpeter blows into another man's ear. The motifs of seated conversing figures—sometimes even disputing heatedly—also occur repeatedly among the figures populating the architectural background of the Louvre composition sketch (cat. no. 27), the well-known Uffizi perspective study (fig. 139), and the unfinished Uffizi altarpiece (fig. 10). Groups of conversing or disputing figures are the subject of separate studies, and these were most probably also intended for the San Donato a Scopeto altarpiece (cat. nos. 28–31, 38). Some of the conversing figure studies, however, are mysteriously arranged into a composition type that evokes the *Last Supper* (cat. nos. 29, 39, with one man crouching on the table!). If such studies date as early as 1481, as in fact they must, to judge from their drawing technique, it would mean that Leonardo was contemplating the Last Supper as a subject nearly fifteen years earlier than in his famous mural at the refectory of Santa Maria delle Grazie, Milan.

CCB

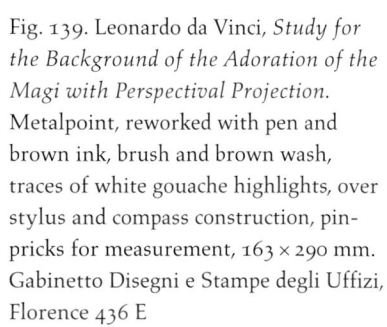
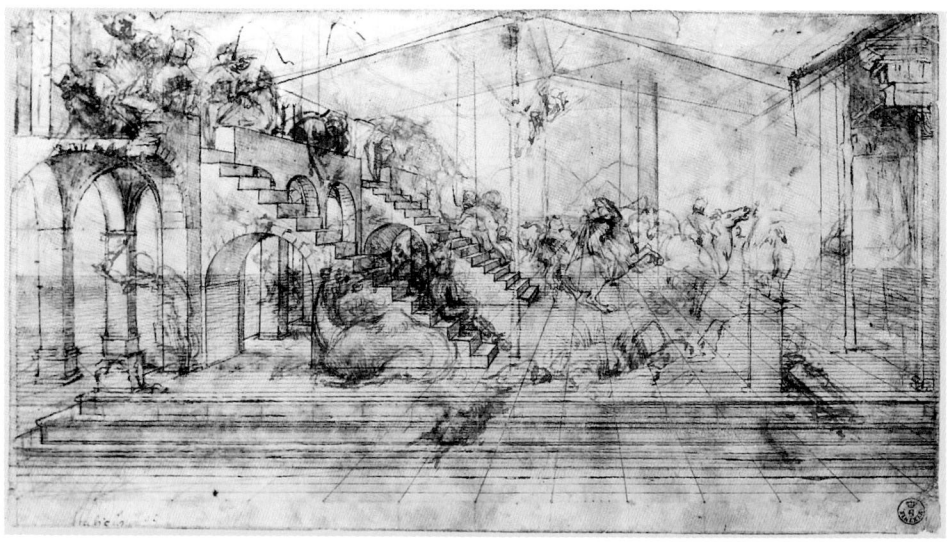

Fig. 139. Leonardo da Vinci, *Study for the Background of the Adoration of the Magi with Perspectival Projection.* Metalpoint, reworked with pen and brown ink, brush and brown wash, traces of white gouache highlights, over stylus and compass construction, pinpricks for measurement, 163 × 290 mm. Gabinetto Disegni e Stampe degli Uffizi, Florence 436 E

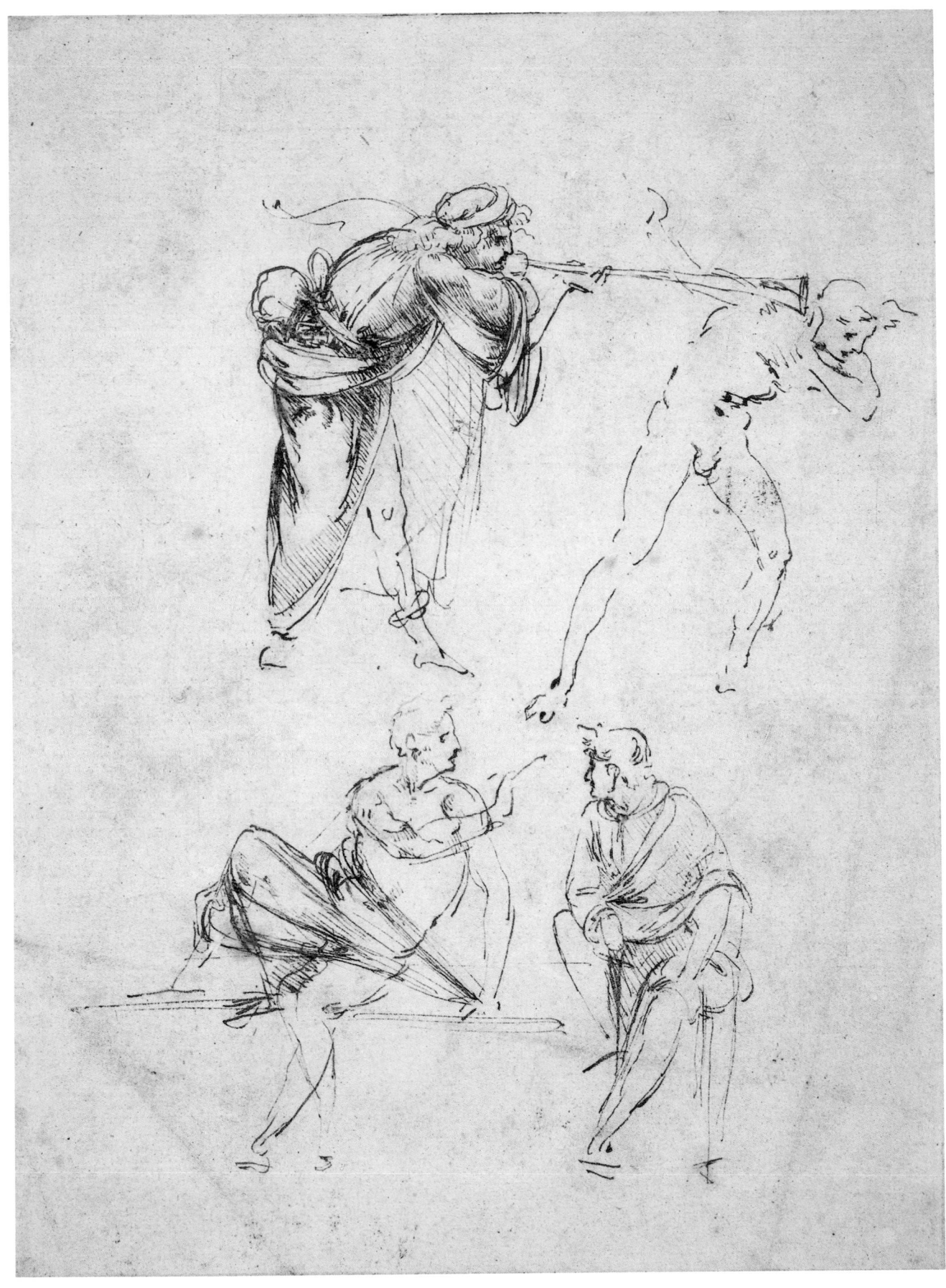

Cat. 32

LEONARDO DA VINCI

33. *Rider on a Rearing Horse Fighting a Dragon*

Pen and dark gray-brown ink, brush and gray-brown wash, over traces of preliminary stylus underdrawing, on light brown paper, 136 × 189 mm (5 3/8 × 7 7/16 in.)
Inscribed in pen and dark black-brown ink on verso by a later hand: *Leonardo Vinci [?]*
The British Museum, London 1952-10-11-2

PROVENANCE: George Henry Haydon (d. 1891; Goldscheider 1959); his granddaughter Mrs. Winifred E. Reavell; 1952, purchased from Mrs. Winifred Reavell.

LITERATURE: Unsigned article in *The Illustrated London News*, October 25, 1952, p. 687; Popham 1954, pp. 223–27, pl. 113, fig. 1; Castelfranco 1956, p. 58, pl. 40b; Goldscheider 1959, p. 177, pl. 104; Berenson 1961, vol. 2, p. 201, vol. 3, fig. 467, no. 1038A; Pouncey 1964, p. 286; Parker 1972, p. 12, under no. 17; Pedretti 1982a, p. 33; Pedretti and Roberts 1984–86, p. 33; Pedretti 1987b, pp. 31–32, 37, 76, 125, fig. 9; Wiemers 1996, pp. 311–13, fig. 301; Marani 2000b, pp. 101–6.

The poses of this shouting rider and vigorously rearing horse, with head swung to the left, are identical to a motif in the background of Leonardo's unfinished Uffizi altarpiece of the *Adoration of the Magi* (fig. 140); the drawing therefore probably also dates about 1482–83, or, at the latest, 1485. The figural types of the London rider and horse are comparable to those in extant studies for the unfinished altarpiece (cat. nos. 27, 40), and the pen and ink with gray-brown wash technique is the same as that of the horses and figures in the background of the Uffizi perspectival study for the *Adoration* (fig. 139). No less important, however, the drawing with wash technique of the London rider and horse is the same as that of the mounted soldiers in Leonardo's drawings of fantastic military machines in London, Windsor, and Turin, which date to 1482–85, soon after the artist arrived in Milan

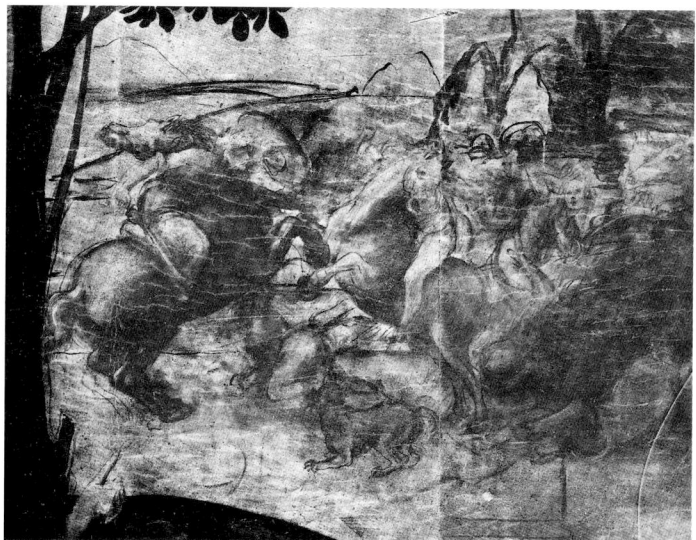

Fig. 140. Detail of Leonardo da Vinci, *The Adoration of the Magi*. Unfinished painting. Oil and some *tempera grassa* on wood, 243 × 246 cm. Galleria degli Uffizi, Florence 1594

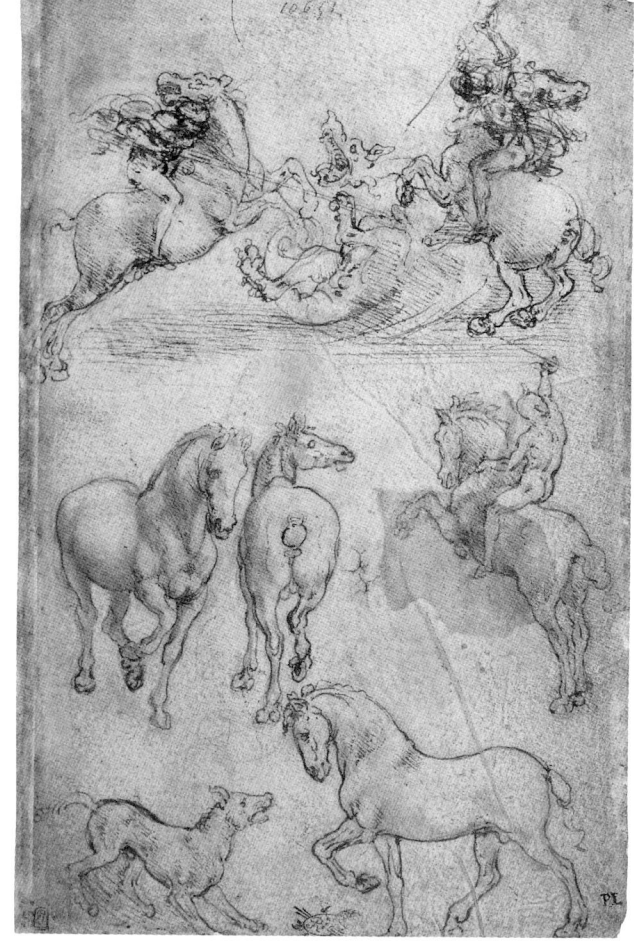

Fig. 141. Leonardo da Vinci, *Studies of Horsemen, Dragons, Horses, and a Dog* (recto). Pen and brown ink, 192 × 123 cm. Musée du Louvre, Paris, Collection Edmond de Rothschild 781 DR

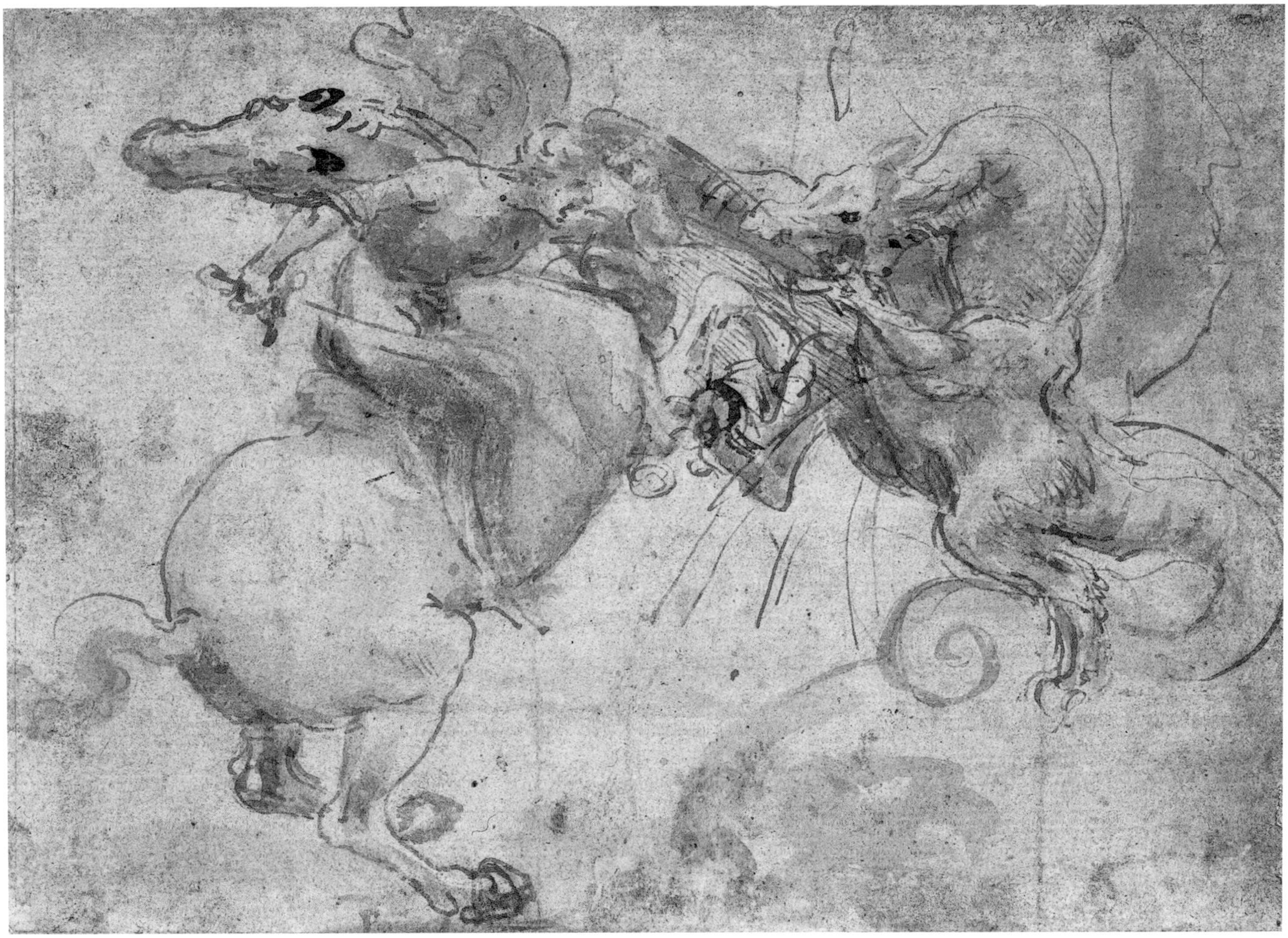

Cat. 33R

Cat. 33V

and sought employment from Ludovico Sforza "Il Moro" as military engineer.[1] In the unfinished Uffizi *Adoration* altarpiece, the rider on the rearing horse (fig. 140) is attacked from the right by another equally spirited horseman. In the London drawing, however, Leonardo substituted a rearing dragon for the opponent rider on the right thus transforming the composition into a scene much like a Saint George fighting the dragon, though of ferocious intensity. This inventive act of transformation is typical of the young Leonardo's process of design (cat. nos. 19, 28–32). Although no painting of the subject by Leonardo is known to have survived, three sheets of sketches seem to allude to the general theme. The most closely related is a fragile, abraded drawing in the Ashmolean Museum, Oxford, showing the rider on a rearing horse much like the motif in the London sheet, but,in yet another act of transmogrification, fighting a griffin. The griffin in the Ashmolean sheet is lightly sketched over a preliminary underdrawing

portraying a dragon.[2] A double-sided sheet of studies with two horsemen attacking a dragon with spears (fig. 141)[3] and another with studies of a seething dragon in motion (though not rearing) may also be connected to this otherwise unknown project and date from the same moment.[4]

The London drawing became known to Leonardo scholars belatedly, and it has apparently not been exhibited before. The connoisseurs A. E. Popham and Karl T. Parker considered it superior to the closely related Ashmolean Museum drawing.

CCB

1. British Museum, London, 1860-6-16-99 (Popham and Pouncey 1950, pp. 64–65, no. 107); Windsor, RL 12653 (Clayton 1996–97, pp. 30–33, no. 10); Biblioteca Reale, Turin, 15583 (Carlo Pedretti in Scuderie Papali al Quirinale 2001–2, pp. 162–63, no. 3.3).
2. Illustrated in Popham 60B; discussed in Parker 1972, pp. 12–13, no. 17.
3. Collection Edmond de Rothschild 781 DR (recto and verso), Musée du Louvre, Paris; Berenson 1961, vol. 2, p. 212, no. 1080.
4. Windsor, RL 12370 recto; Kemp and Roberts 1989, p. 158, no. 84.

LEONARDO DA VINCI

34. *Flying Winged Figures; Allegorical Figure of Fortune; Tree Stump with a Shield Bearing a Lion Rampant Hanging from a Branch, Other Emblems Beside*

Pen and dark brown ink, brush and brown wash, over leadpoint and stylus; the upper right figure largely sketched with the stylus only, 249 × 202 mm (9 13/16 × 7 15/16 in.)
Inscribed in pen and black-gray ink on recto at lower right: *Léonard de Vinci*; in pen and the same ink on verso along center: *Ecriture de Léonard de Vinci*, indicating the partially cropped text of a letter that is to the side and below in pen and brown ink: *[da poj?] la partita / [l]asso pensare in che dispiacer[e] / [t]empo de scriver[e] dua . . . / ripesa de li miei affan[n]i e tribulatione e voliative / avertire se riplianino de po fare damno, e max[ime] de le v[ost]re scriture / p[er]che qui Milano à tolto copia certi v[ost]ri depi[n]tori di grado che li d . . . / scodere*[1]
The British Museum, London 1895-9-15-482

PROVENANCE: E. Despéret (1804–65; Lugt 721); Émile Galichon, Paris (1829–75; Lugt 856); sale, Clément, Paris, May 10–14, 1875, lot 167; John Malcolm, Poltalloch and London (1805–93; Lugt 1489, 1780, 1781, suppl. 1489).

LITERATURE: Robinson 1876, no. 44; Müller-Walde 1889, p. 77, fig. 41; British Museum 1895, no. 38; Berenson 1903, vol. 1, p. 164, vol. 2, p. 58, no. 1037, pl. 121; Seidlitz 1909, vol. 1, pp. 155, 293, pl. 25; Thiis 1913, p. 175; Poggi 1919, pl. 178; Venturi 1920, pp. 100–101, fig. 52; Commissione Vinciana 1928– , vol. 3, p. 24, pl. 104; Sirén 1928, pl. 96; Valentiner 1930, pp. 64–67, 73, 82, fig. 16; Bodmer 1931, pp. 160, 388–89; Berenson 1938, vol. 1, p. 182, vol. 2, p. 114, vol. 3, fig. 559, no. 1037; Nicodemi 1939, pl. 80; Wind 1939, pp. 49–50, pl. 49; Bottari 1942, pl. 31; Giglioli 1944, pp. 157–58, pl. 185; Popham and Pouncey 1950, pp. 62–64, no. 104, and under no. 105; Heydenreich 1954, vol. 1, p. 59, vol. 2, p. 60, pl. 74; Goldscheider 1959, p. 162, pl. 47; Berenson 1961, vol. 1, p. 263, vol. 2, p. 200, vol. 3, fig. 456, no. 1037; Valentiner 1966, pp. 78–79, 84–85, 90, pl. 26; Gould 1975, pp. 48–49, fig. 21; Pedretti 1989f, pp. 19 n. 27, 37 n. 71, fig. 51 (incorrect inv. no.); Popham 1994, no. 103.

The brushwork in this sheet stands out as one of the great exercises of technical virtuosity in the history of Renaissance drawing. In its painterliness and economy of stroke, the handling of the brush seems exactly comparable to that of the quickly sketched groups of figures, horses, and landscape features in the background of Leonardo's unfinished *Adoration of the Magi* altarpiece for San Donato a Scopeto

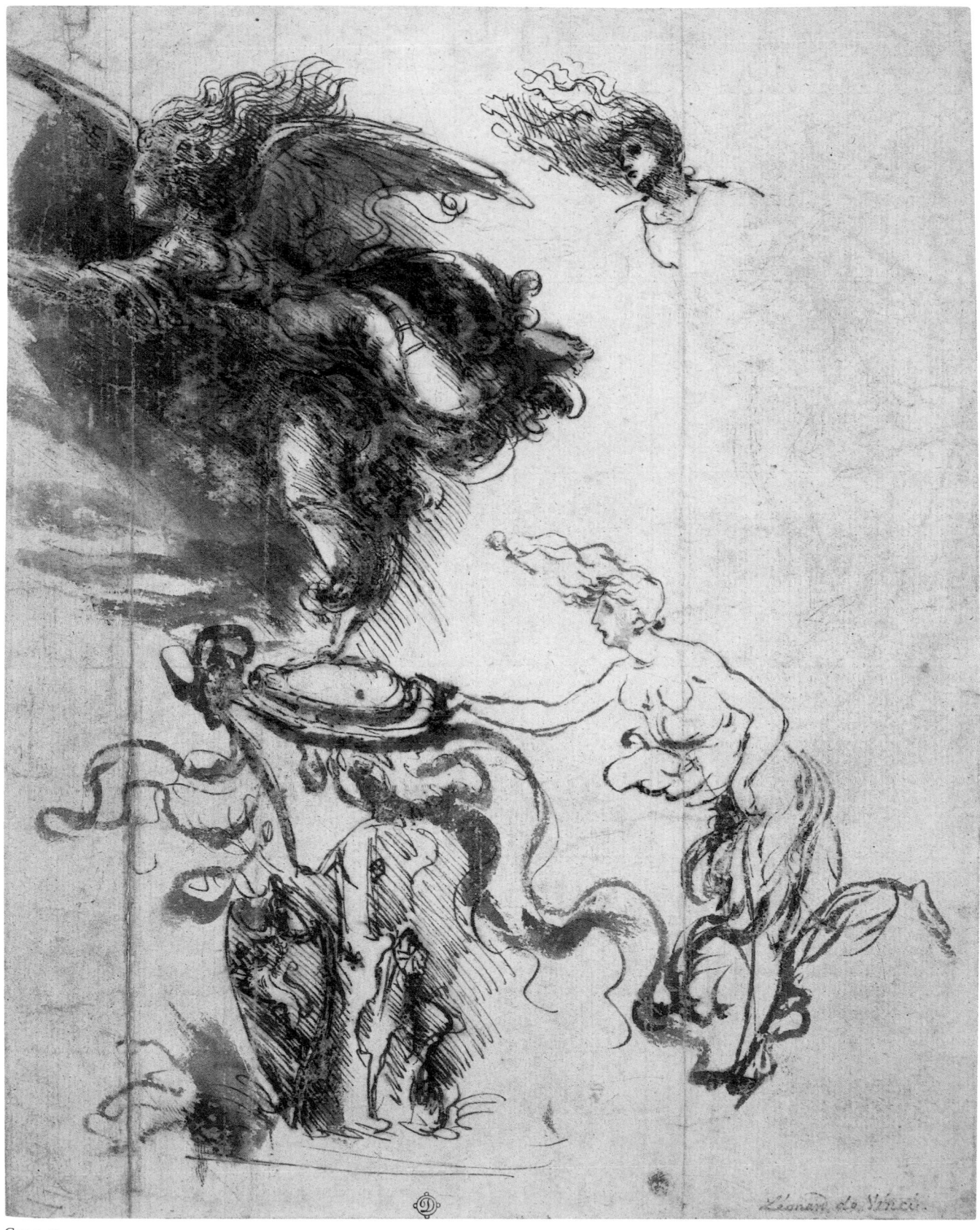

Cat. 34R

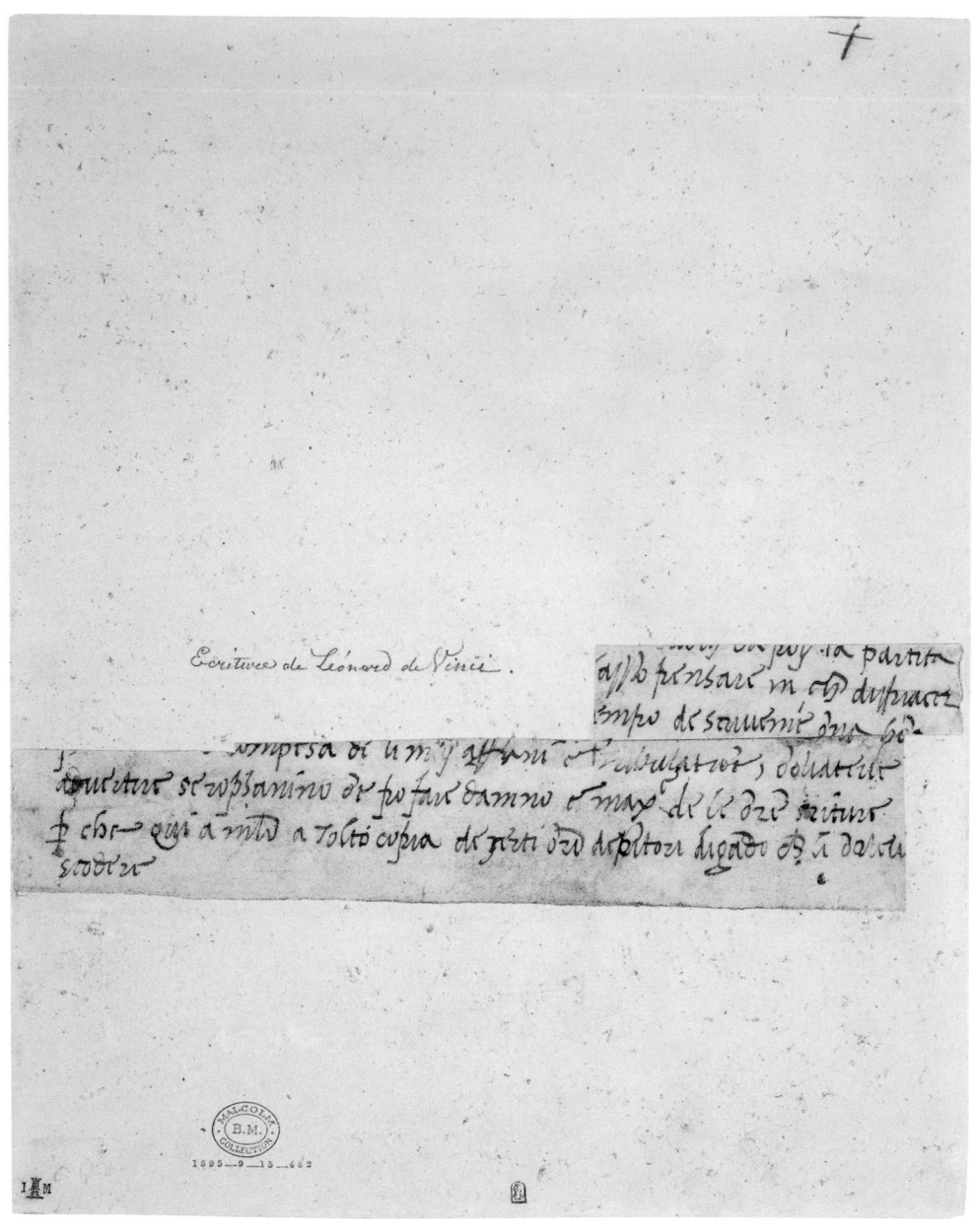

Cat. 34v

(figs. 10, 140). The figural types of the androgynous youths seen in the altarpiece (and the preparatory studies for it) are comparable, as well, to the three figures in the present sheet. It is, therefore, most likely that the sheet dates about 1482–85, that is, sometime between Leonardo's departure from Florence and arrival in Milan. The brushwork could not possibly be eighteenth-century retouching, as has sometimes been claimed.

In the upper portion of the sketch, the flying winged figure on the left and the apparently wingless woman (who is largely outlined with the stylus only) on the right may or may not be related to the allegorical composition below. The winged figure probably represents Fame, for in Leonardo's words, "Fame flies and raises herself to heaven, because virtuous things find favor with God."[2] The figural type is reminiscent of Verrocchio's small Louvre terracotta reliefs of angels (fig. 142) of the late 1470s to early 1480s. According to Ludwig Goldscheider, however, Leonardo's winged figure forms part of the motif below; he therefore regards the upper and lower registers of the

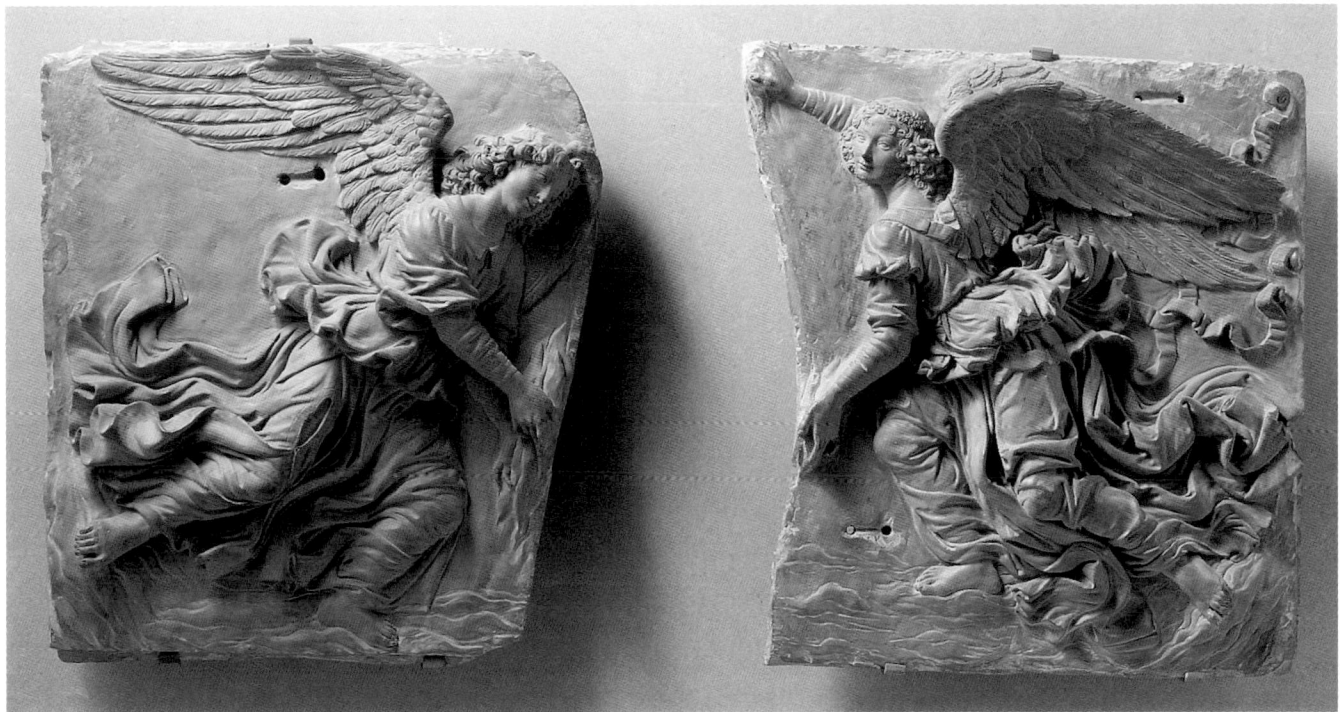

Fig. 142. Andrea del Verrocchio, *Flying Angels*. Unpainted terracotta relief, left angel 365 × 328 mm, right angel 370 × 340 mm. Musée du Louvre, Paris 98DE8672

British Museum sheet as one composition. On the lower right, the female figure can be identified as Fortune (because of her luscious mane of hair blowing in the wind, forward of her head); the partial sketch of the woman on the upper right may represent Fortune as well, but seen in a frontal three-quarter view. Because of the quick and abstract character of the brilliant brush sketch on the lower part of the sheet, however, neither the precise gesture nor the attributes of Fortune seem clear. Suspended in the air, she elegantly strides toward a group of trophies by a tree stump, where a shield containing a lion rampant hangs from a branch on the left. The family heraldic device of Ludovico Sforza "Il Moro" was the *biscione* (dragon), rather than a lion rampant, as has been claimed, and so the allegory may not allude to him. A slight sketch of an emblem labeled by Leonardo "Prudence" and "Strength" in Paris Ms. H depicts a shield containing a dragon and a facing lion rampant.[3] In the British Museum drawing, Fortune appears to hold a convex disk (another shield? a mirror?) in her right hand, seeming to lower it over the flames and billowing clouds of smoke that emanate, perhaps, from the triangular form (another shield?) above the tree stump.

The meanings of the allegories, and whether the drawings are part of one scene or two, seem inaccessible without an explanatory text by Leonardo (see cat. no. 54), for his imagery was uniquely personal and rich in layers of fantastic allusion. The lower composition (which may be cropped along the left side) possibly alludes to the providential intervention of Fortune. In catalogue number 31 verso, it is the flying, long-haired Fortune who holds a putto by the waist as he blows wind through a trumpet to halt the doings of Death. The script in the partially cropped text of the letter that is glued onto the verso of the drawing resembles that of Francesco Melzi (Leonardo's loyal companion and artistic heir), as it is exemplified in the posthumously compiled *Libro di pittura* (Codex Urbinas Latinus 1270, Biblioteca Apostolica Vaticana), but it is not identical. See catalogue numbers 120 and 121 for early drawings by Melzi.   CCB

1. Transcribed with the assistance of Gino Corti, Virginia Budny, and Frank Dabell.
2. Paris Ms. H², fol. 61r; Richter 1970, vol. 1, p. 390, no. 693: "La fama vola e si leva al cielo, perche le cose virtuose sono amiche di dio."
3. Paris Ms. H², fol. 49v; Richter 1970, vol. 1, p. 390, no. 692.

35. *Saint Sebastian Standing in Three-Quarter View Tied to a Tree* (recto)
Diagrams of Perspective (verso)

Pen and dark brown ink over leadpoint, 174 × 63 mm (6 $^{13}/_{16}$ × 2 $^3/_8$ in.)
maximum; irregular borders
Inscribed faintly in graphite on recto toward lower left by a modern
hand: *Leo . . . ;* in pen and dark brown ink, in right-to-left script, on
verso at bottom by Leonardo: *Quella parte dell[ocho all a quale]*
Hamburger Kunsthalle 21489

PROVENANCE: Alexandre Pierre François Robert Dumesnil, Paris
(1778–1864; Lugt 2199); Georg Ernst Harzen, Hamburg (1790–
1863); ca. 1842–56 manuscript inventory by G. E. Harzen
(NH.Ad:01:04), fol. 117 (stating the Robert provenance); ca. 1860
manuscript inventory by G. E. Harzen (NH.Ad:02:01), p. 222; 1863,
Harzen bequest; museum stamp (Lugt 1328).

LITERATURE: Koopmann 1891, p. 40; Müller-Walde 1898, pp. 250–62
(p. 250, pl.); Müntz 1899, p. 535 (under no. 5); Berenson 1903, vol. 1,
p. 163, vol. 2, p. 58, no. 1022 (incorrect inv. no.); Commissione Vinciana
1928– , vol. 2, p. 28, pl. 69; Suida 1929, pp. 83, 160, 274, fig. 87;
Bodmer 1931, pp. 178 (right), 392; Berenson 1938, vol. 1, p. 180, vol. 2,
p. 112, no. 1022; Heydenreich 1943, p. 194; Valentiner 1949, p. 111,
no. 79; Biblioteca Medicea Laurenziana 1952, p. 23, no. 25; Brugnoli
1954, p. 366, pl. 149, no. 5 (incorrect inv. no.); Heydenreich 1954, vol. 2,
p. 130, pl. 181; Hamburger Kunsthalle 1957, no. 12; Bean 1960, under
no. 44; Berenson 1961, vol. 1, p. 262, vol. 2, p. 196, no. 1022; Clark
and Pedretti 1968–69, vol. 1, p. 115, under no. 12583A; Ragghianti
and Dalli Regoli 1975, p. 38; Nicodemi 1980a, p. 62; Popham 1994,
no. 213B; Hamburger Kunsthalle 1997, p. 93, no. 26; Dalli Regoli
1998, p. 61, fig. 5; Dalli Regoli, Nanni, and Natali 2001, p. 18, fig. 12
(incorrect inv. no.).

In a long, cryptic list of works in his possession, Leonardo
alluded to "eight Saint Sebastians," and from the wording
it can be deduced that several of these items were probably
drawings and that at least some of these works related to his
early activity in Florence, before 1481–83; Leonardo usually
drafted such lists when he was about to leave a place and take
objects with him.[1] Although the precise project for which the
small Hamburg sketch was preparatory has not been identified,
the subject might have been suitable for an ex-voto (the
extremely popular cult of Saint Sebastian as protector against
the plague began in the 4th century A.D.), or a small-scale
work to be used in private devotion.

Here, Leonardo repeatedly reworked the contorted figure
of the saint, as is clear from the agitated underdrawing in

leadpoint. He seems to have first faintly drawn Sebastian's
head foreshortened in an almost frontal view, nearly centered
above his body. He then reworked the saint's head in a sharply
foreshortened view facing to the right, considering it a fairly
definitive solution, for he also drew it in pen and ink. Only
later he seems to have changed his mind again—for a third
time—redrawing the head in a slightly raised, lost-profile
view facing to the left. A much weaker drawing in Bayonne of
Saint Sebastian, executed in soft black chalk (with left-handed
hatching, so the attribution to Leonardo may well be correct),
shows the saint's foreshortened head raised to the right in a

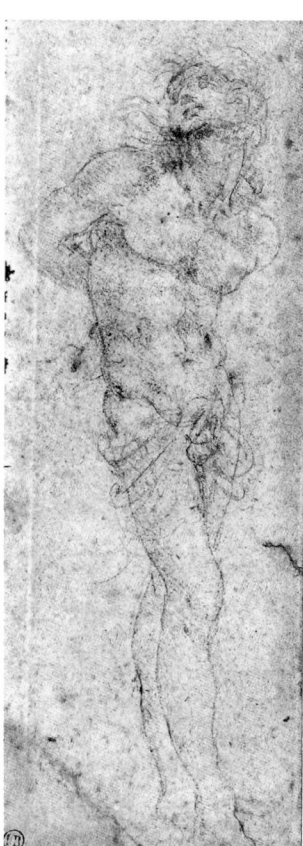

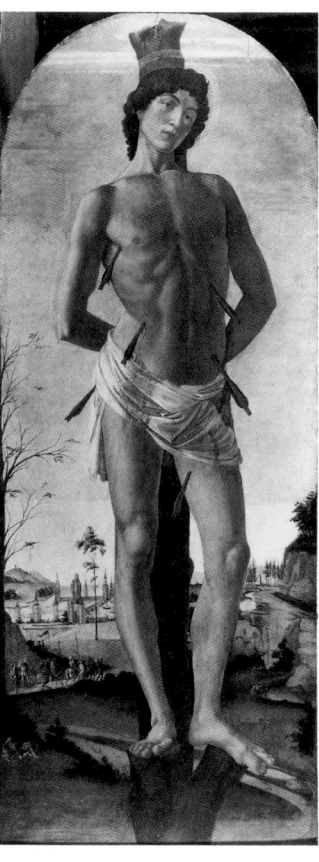

Fig. 143. Leonardo da Vinci,
Saint Sebastian. Black chalk,
148 × 54 mm. Musée Bonnat,
Bayonne 1211

Fig. 144. Sandro Botticelli, *Saint
Sebastian.* Originally from Santa
Maria Maggiore, Florence. Oil
and tempera on wood, 195 × 75 cm
(arched top). Gemäldegalerie,
Staatliche Museen zu Berlin –
Preussischer Kulturbesitz 1128

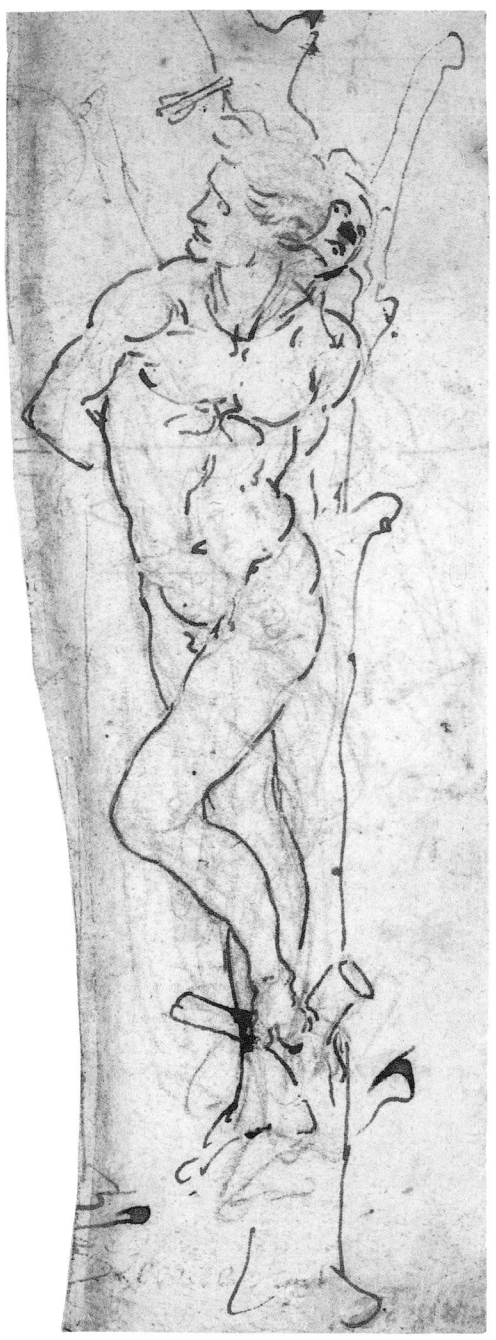

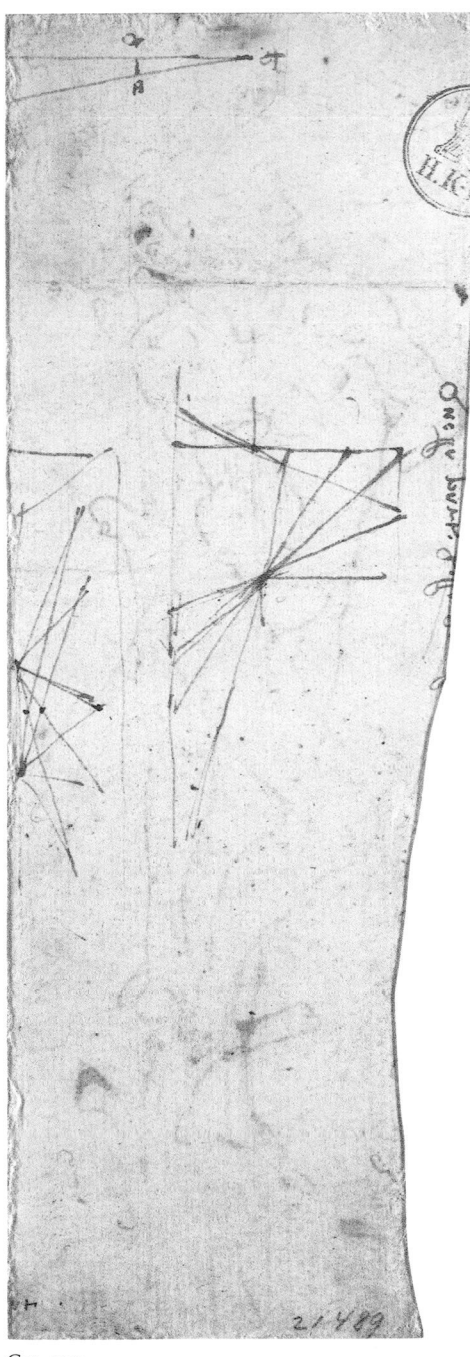

Cat. 35R   Cat. 35V

pose that evokes the saint's upturned head in the inked pentimento of the Hamburg sketch, but his lower body twists to
the right, and his feet are planted on the ground (fig. 143).[2]

Most likely, the Hamburg drawing dates from about 1478–
83, to judge from the quickly traced facial type and the summary bodily outlines reminiscent of the early sheets for the
Adoration (cat. nos. 28, 29). This was a period in the young
Leonardo's career for which few documented references to

projects survive, but a period when the young artist must have
produced numerous designs for proposed pictures in an effort
to cultivate patrons.

Although more active and in a pronounced three-quarter
view, the pose of the figure in Leonardo's Hamburg sketch
nevertheless recalls that in Sandro Botticelli's tall, narrow
early panel of *Saint Sebastian* (Gemäldegalerie, Berlin), which
was probably intended as an ex-voto, and which was placed on

343

a pier in the church of Santa Maria Maggiore, Florence, that was dedicated in January 1474, as is recorded in the sixteenth-century Codice Magliabechiano (fig. 144).[3] Both figures are conceived in a slight *sotto in sù* perspective (as if seen from below). Leonardo's design of *Saint Sebastian* may have in turn inspired a much later painted rendition of the subject by his pupil Marco d'Oggiono (Gemäldegalerie, Berlin). The line diagrams on the verso of the Hamburg sheet seem to represent Leonardo's attempts at resolving the problem of a spectator's viewpoint with respect to a form placed on a pictorial plane. The truncated inscription on the verso ("that part of the eye to which . . .") appears to allude to the anatomy of the eye. It is possible, although not necessarily so, that the text and diagrams on the sheet were added at a later point in Leonardo's career. His more sustained anatomical studies of the eye, the optic nerve, and the mechanics of vision seem to date from 1489–93.

CCB

1. C.A., fol. 888r (formerly fol. 324r); Richter 1970, vol. 1, p. 387, no. 680; Pedretti 1977, vol. 1, p. 388, no. 680: "8 sa[n]n Bastiani."
2. Musée Bonnat, Bayonne, 1211; Bean 1960, no. 44.
3. Transcribed in Frey 1892, p. 105; on Botticelli's *Saint Sebastian*, see Lightbown 1978, vol. 2, pp. 27–28, no. B14.

LEONARDO DA VINCI

36. *The Virgin and Child with Saint Joseph (?), Shepherds, and Angels (Studies for an Adoration of the Christ Child)* (recto)
Cropped Outlines of a Youth's Head in Profile (verso)

Pen and two brown inks, over black chalk or leadpoint (recto); pen and brown ink, black chalk or leadpoint (verso), 119 × 135 mm (4 $\frac{11}{16}$ × 5 $\frac{5}{16}$ in.); irregular borders in the shape of an upside-down L
Inscribed in pen and brown ink on recto at lower center: *42*
Gallerie dell'Accademia, Venice 256

PROVENANCE: Cardinal Cesare Monti, Milan (1635–1650); Contessa Anna Luisa Monti, Milan; 1770, Venanzio de Pagave, Milan; his son Gaudenzio de Pagave; ca. 1808 or before, Giuseppe Bossi, Milan and Venice (1777–1815; album marked K); auction, Milan, February 1818, vol. 2; February 24, 1818, purchase by Abbate Luigi Celotti [Cellotti], Venice (1765–1846); in deposit (under custody of Carlo Porta and Nicola Cassoni) Accademia di Belle Arti, Milan; 1820–22, proposal of purchase of Bossi's collection from Celotti submitted to Austrian government on behalf of Accademia delle Belle Arti, Venice; 1822, purchase by Franz I (Habsburg), emperor of Austria, Florence and Vienna (1768–1835), for Accademia delle Belle Arti, Venice; ca. 1832 manuscript inventory; December 31, 1870, manuscript inventory; museum stamp (Lugt 188).

LITERATURE: Selvatico 1854, cornice V, no. 7; Uzielli 1884, p. 279, no. 23; Berenson 1903, vol. 2, p. 62, no. 1109; Seidlitz 1909, vol. 1, no. 33; Fogolari 1913, p. 14, no. 10; Thiis 1913, pp. 183, 257; Beltrami 1919b, pp. 158, 160, 209, fig. 4B; Poggi 1919, pl. 60; Venturi 1920, p. 85, no. 29; Commissione Vinciana 1928–, vol. 2, p. 26, pl. 43.a; Popp 1928, pp. 6, 36, no. 17; Suida 1929, p. 46, no. 23; Popham 1930–31, no. 68; Bodmer 1931, pp. 128, 382; Berenson 1938, vol. 1, p. 171, vol. 2, p. 123, vol. 3, fig. 479, no. 1109; Palazzo dell'Arte 1939, p. 153; Giglioli 1944, pl. 60; Heydenreich 1949, pls. 1, 2; Biblioteca Medicea Laurenziana 1952, pp. 16–17, no. 15; Berenson 1961, vol. 1, p. 251, vol. 2, p. 217, vol. 3, fig. 472, no. 1109; Cogliati Arano 1966–67, p. 18, no. 3, fig. 3; Valentiner 1966, pp. 78–79, 84–85, fig. 24; Pedretti 1973a, pp. 26–27; Cogliati Arano 1980, p. 22, no. 3; Pedretti 1982a, p. 56; Pedretti and Roberts 1984–86, p. 33; Pedretti 1987b, p. 31; Clark 1988, pp. 71–72; Martin Clayton in Palazzo Grassi 1992, pp. 196–97, no. 4; Popham 1994, no. 40A; Ambrosiana 1998–99, p. 26; Annalisa Perissa Torrini in Nepi Scirè and Torrini 1999, pp. 44–45, no. 12; Marani 2000b, pp. 78–83.

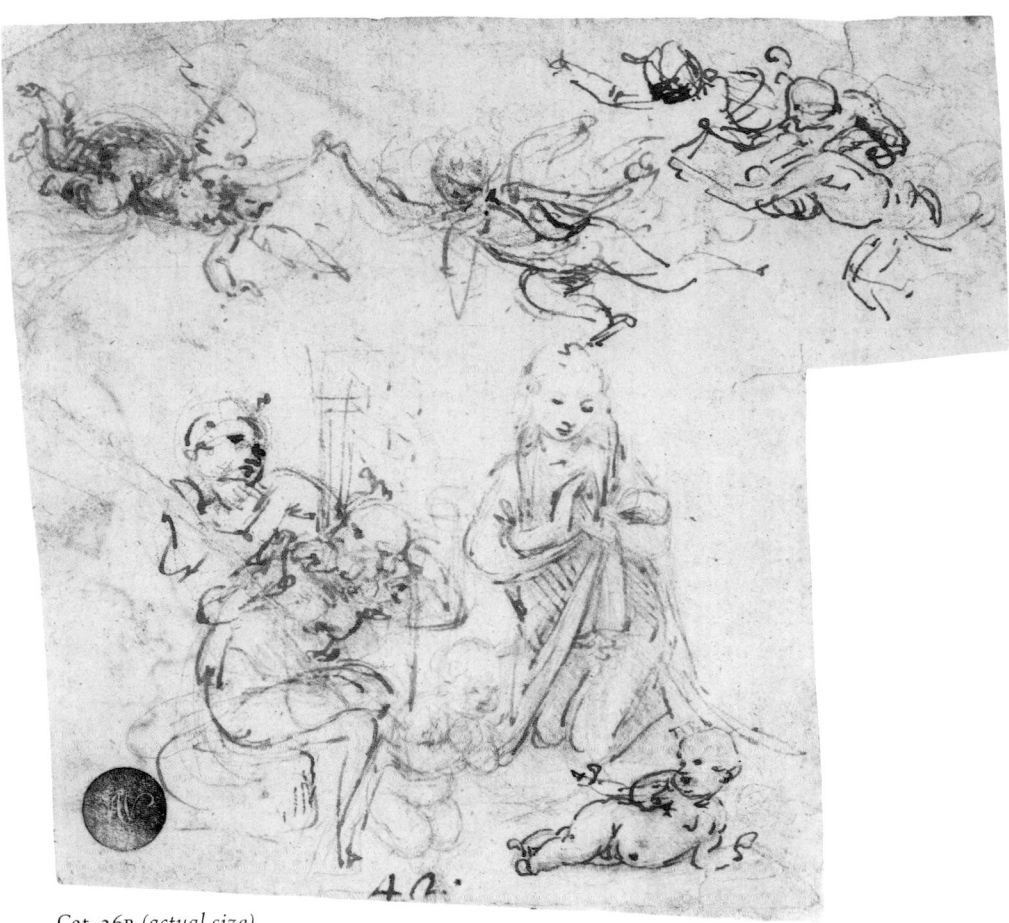

Cat. 36R *(actual size)*

37. Kneeling Figure, Infants, and Angels
(Studies for an Adoration of the Christ Child) (recto)
Cropped Outlines of a Lira or Viola "da Braccio" (verso)

Pen and brown ink, brush and brown wash, over black chalk or
lead point (recto); pen and brown ink (verso), 110 × 122 mm
(4⅛ × 4¹³⁄₁₆ in.); irregular borders in the shape of an L
Gallerie dell'Accademia, Venice 259

PROVENANCE: Cardinal Cesare Monti, Milan (1635–1650); Contessa
Anna Luisa Monti, Milan; 1770, Venanzio de Pagave, Milan; his son
Gaudenzio de Pagave; ca. 1808 or before, Giuseppe Bossi, Milan and
Venice (1777–1815; album marked K); auction, Milan, February
1818, vol. 2; February 24, 1818, purchase by Abbate Luigi Celotti
[Cellotti], Venice (1765–1846); in deposit (under custody of Carlo
Porta and Nicola Cassoni) Accademia di Belle Arti, Milan; 1820–22,
proposal of purchase of Bossi's collection from Celotti submitted to
Austrian government on behalf of Accademia delle Belle Arti,
Venice; 1822, purchase by Franz I (Habsburg), emperor of Austria,
Florence and Vienna (1768–1835), for Accademia delle Belle Arti,
Venice; ca. 1832 manuscript inventory; December 31, 1870 manu-
script inventory; museum stamp (Lugt 188).

LITERATURE: Uzielli 1884, p. 282, no. 37; Berenson 1903, vol. 2, p. 62,
no. 1110; Fogolari 1913, p. 14, no. 11; Poggi 1919, pl. 61; Commissione
Vinciana 1928– , vol. 2, p. 26, pl. 43.b; Popp 1928, pp. 6, 36, no. 18;
Sirén 1928, vol. 1, p. 41, pl. 55B; Popham 1930–31, no. 69; Bodmer
1931, pp. 129, 382; Berenson 1938, vol. 1, p. 171, vol. 2, p. 123, vol. 3,
fig. 481, no. 1110; Giglioli 1944, pl. 61; Heydenreich 1949, pl. 3;
Biblioteca Medicea Laurenziana 1952, p. 17, no. 16; Berenson 1961,
vol. 1, p. 251, vol. 2, p. 218, vol. 3, fig. 471, no. 1110; Cogliati Arano
1966–67, p. 17, no. 2, fig. 2; Valentiner 1966, pp. 78–79, 84–85,
pl. 25; Wasserman 1971, pp. 316–17, fig. 9; Pedretti 1973a, p. 26;
Cogliati Arano 1980, p. 20, no. 2; De Vecchi 1982, pp. 46–47, 49;
fig. 23; Pedretti 1982a, p. 56; Vezzosi 1982, fig. 90; Pedretti and
Roberts 1984–86, p. 33; Pedretti 1987b, p. 31; Clark 1988, pp. 71–72;
Martin Clayton in Palazzo Grassi 1992, pp. 198–99, no. 5; Popham
1994, no. 40B; Wiemers 1996, pp. 280–81, fig. 264; Annalisa Perissa
Torrini in Nepi Scirè and Torrini 1999, pp. 46–47, no. 13; Marani
2000b, pp. 78–83.

These two fragmentary sketches must date from early in
Leonardo's graphic oeuvre, from the late 1470s to the
early 1480s, to judge from both the rapid drawing technique,
with shadows modeled in wash and scant, bold parallel hatching in pen and ink, and the style of figural types, with hands
gracefully abbreviated as fingerless mittens and feet as tiny
hooked stumps. The Venice fragments were most likely originally part of one sheet of sketches for a Nativity or an
Adoration of the Christ Child, in which the Virgin, Saint
Joseph, shepherds, and angels behold the holy infant. (The
Venice fragments, however, were already separated when
glued into the album assembled by Giuseppe Bossi in 1808–
15, and they remained so in the Bossi album at the Gallerie
dell'Accademia for a long time.) There is no scholarly consensus regarding the final work for which the Accademia drawings were intended. This is hardly surprising, because the
sheer inventiveness, dazzling fluency of notation, and simultaneity of contrasting ideas in Leonardo's composition drawings can make it at times frustratingly difficult for the viewer
to identify when the artist has stopped pursuing one subject
and moved on to the next one. Most frequently, and probably
quite rightly, the Accademia fragments are grouped with studies relating to an Adoration of the Shepherds, a subject that is
thought to have been an initial or at least an early compositional idea for the unfinished Adoration of the Magi altarpiece
(fig. 10), which was commissioned from Leonardo in 1481 by
the monks of San Donato a Scopeto for the main altar of their
convent church in Florence. (See Chronology.) The extant contractual document for the Adoration of the Magi altarpiece,
dated July 1481, does not state the subject of the commissioned painting, though it does stipulate that Leonardo was
to complete it within twenty-four or at most thirty months,
and it is clear that the artist had in fact begun the painting in
March 1481; he may have secured the commission on the
basis of drawings done even earlier than that date. It is therefore very plausible that Leonardo and his patrons may have
considered the theme of the Adoration of the Shepherds for
the altarpiece.

In both style and technique, the two Venice fragments
closely resemble the composition sketches for a populous
Adoration that seems to include the shepherds (fig. 68), and
they also seem generally comparable to the magnificent composition sketch in the Musée du Louvre (cat. no. 27), in which
Leonardo had already begun to reshape the subject into an
Adoration of the Magi. But the motif of the kneeling Virgin in

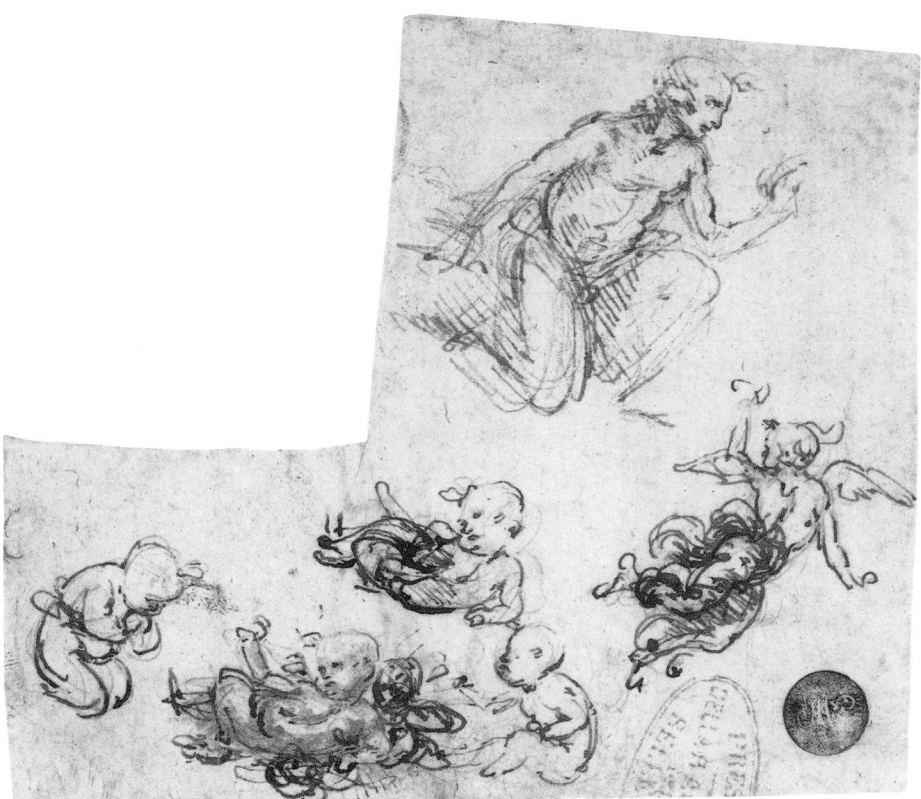

Cat. 37R *(actual size)*

catalogue number 36 also recurs in other drawings showing a simpler Nativity composition of a tall rectangular shape, sometimes with an arched top (cat. no. 45; figs. 73, 150), in which the Virgin appears adoring the Christ Child either alone or with the infant Saint John the Baptist and angels. Thus it has also been posited that the Venice drawings may relate to a very elusive inscription on a fragmentary drawing by Leonardo in which he cited two paintings of the Madonna (fig. 39), "1478, I began the two Virgin Marys";[1] or to the altarpiece that Leonardo was to paint for the Chapel of San Bernardo in the Palazzo della Signoria of Florence, which is recorded in documents in January and March of 1478 but which he seems to have abandoned (the Chapel of San Bernardo altarpiece probably would have depicted a Madonna and Child with Saints, much like Filippino Lippi's *Pala degli Otto* [Uffizi, Florence]). Although the drawing technique and style of the Venice fragments make these possibilities generally plausible within the chronology of Leonardo's career, they seem much less likely on iconographic grounds, given the inclusion in the Venice fragments of hovering angels in a Gloria in Excelsis Deo disposition and of shepherdlike onlookers. The present author therefore favors a broad connection to the San Donato

altarpiece. The schematic outline drawing of a musical instrument on the verso of catalogue number 37 may be related to the music-making angels of the *Adoration*, although it is difficult to conclude whether the drawing is by Leonardo.

The last payment record for Leonardo's San Donato a Scopeto altarpiece (the unfinished *Adoration of the Magi*), on September 28, 1481, is also the last documented date of the artist's presence in Florence; the first documented date of his presence in Milan is April 25, 1483, when he was cosigning the contract for the altarpiece whose central panel included the *Virgin of the Rocks*.[2] It is true that as a more general motif, the kneeling Virgin in catalogue number 36 turns up also in Nativity scenes of a slightly later date, to judge from the drawing technique in metalpoint reworked with pen and ink (cat. no. 45; fig. 73). The compositional idea in the main sketch in the center of catalogue number 45, in fact, anticipates the arrangement seen in the *Virgin of the Rocks,* though not the iconography in its full complexity. On these Nativity compositions (cat. no. 45), however, Leonardo also drew a framing outline to indicate the final effect of the intended picture. The compositions are more compressed and sparse in figures, thus quite different from the Venice drawings.

347

In the end, because of the great gaps in evidence and the paucity of documents, the question of how these various compositions relate to each other must remain open, for they seem to have been executed within a span of about five years, to judge solely by drawing style and technique, and Leonardo almost habitually considered ideas for related pictures in very quick succession. The metalpoint technique with pen and ink in the sketches of infants and onlookers for an Adoration of the Shepherds or Magi in Hamburg (cat. no. 38) seems similar to that in catalogue numbers 36 and 37, and the Christ Child on the lower right in the Hamburg sheet appears in a pose very similar to that seen in the center motif of catalogue number 45, which seems to anticipate the *Virgin of the Rocks*. Yet that same pose of the Christ Child in the Hamburg sheet also appears in two of the infants in the Venice sheet.

CCB

1. "[B]re 1478 incominciai le due vergini marie." The "bre" ending in the month's name can refer to various autumn months, September to December. Gerolamo Calvi and Carlo Pedretti interpreted the month as probably "December" (Calvi 1925a, p. 12; Pedretti 1977, vol. 1, p. 381, no. 663). See Beltrami 1919a, p. 6, no. 13; Richter 1970, vol. 1, p. 379, no. 663.
2. See Chronology.

LEONARDO DA VINCI

38. *Studies for an Adoration of the Christ Child*

Fine pen with dark brown ink, thick pen and lighter brown ink, over metalpoint on pale purple prepared paper (recto); unprepared paper (verso), 173×111 mm ($6\,{}^{13}\!/_{16} \times 4\,{}^{3}\!/_{8}$ in.)
Watermark: fleur de lys (close to Piccard 422; not in Briquet)
Hamburger Kunsthalle 21488

PROVENANCE: Alexandre Pierre François Robert Dumesnil, Paris (1778–1864; Lugt 2199); Georg Ernst Harzen, Hamburg (1790–1863); ca. 1842–56 manuscript inventory by G. E. Harzen (NH.Ad:01:04), fol. 117 (stating the Robert provenance); ca. 1860 manuscript inventory by G. E. Harzen (NH.Ad:02:01), p. 222; 1863, Harzen bequest; museum stamp (Lugt 1328).

LITERATURE: Müntz 1899, p. 525; Berenson 1903, vol. 2, p. 58, no. 1021; Seidlitz 1909, vol. 1, pp. 62–63, 390, no. 9; Thiis 1913, p. 183; Suida 1919–20, p. 281; Venturi 1920, p. 87, fig. 31; Pauli 1927, no. 7; Commissione Vinciana 1928– , vol. 2, p. 26, pl. 44; Bodmer 1931, pp. 130, 382; Berenson 1938, vol. 1, p. 171, vol. 2, p. 112, vol. 3, fig. 483, no. 1021; Heydenreich 1943, pp. 36–42; Valentiner 1949, p. 110, no. 76; Belt 1952, p. 206; Biblioteca Medicea Laurenziana 1952, pp. 17–18 (under no. 15), no. 17; Royal Academy of Arts 1952, no. 27; Hamburger Kunsthalle 1957, no. 11; Bean 1960, under no. 42; Berenson 1961, vol. 1, p. 251, vol. 2, p. 196, vol. 3, fig. 474, no. 1021; Stubbe 1967, p. 22, no. 8; Clark and Pedretti 1968–69, vol. 1, pp. xxxv–xxxvi; Pedretti 1973a, p. 26; De Vecchi 1982, p. 49; Pedretti 1982a, p. 56; Clark 1988, pp. 70–83, fig. 19; Martin Clayton in Palazzo Grassi 1992, pp. 200–201, no. 6; Popham 1994, no. 41; Wiemers 1996, pp. 279–80, fig. 263; Hamburger Kunsthalle 1997, pp. 93–94, no. 27; Rubin and Wright 1999–2000, pp. 307–9, no. 76; Marani 2000b, pp. 79–83; Hamburger Kunsthalle 2001, pp. 14–15, no. 2.

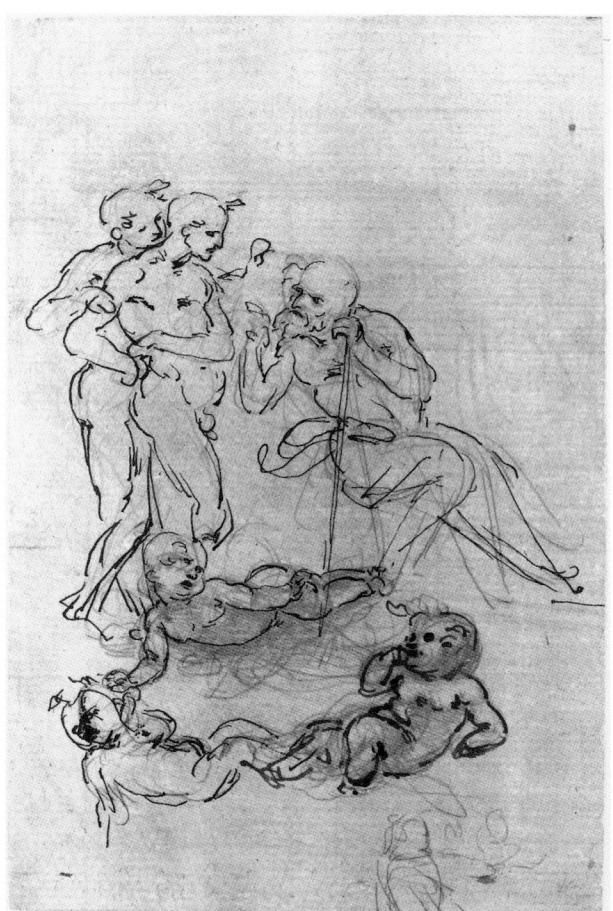

Fig. 145. Infrared photograph of cat. no. 38

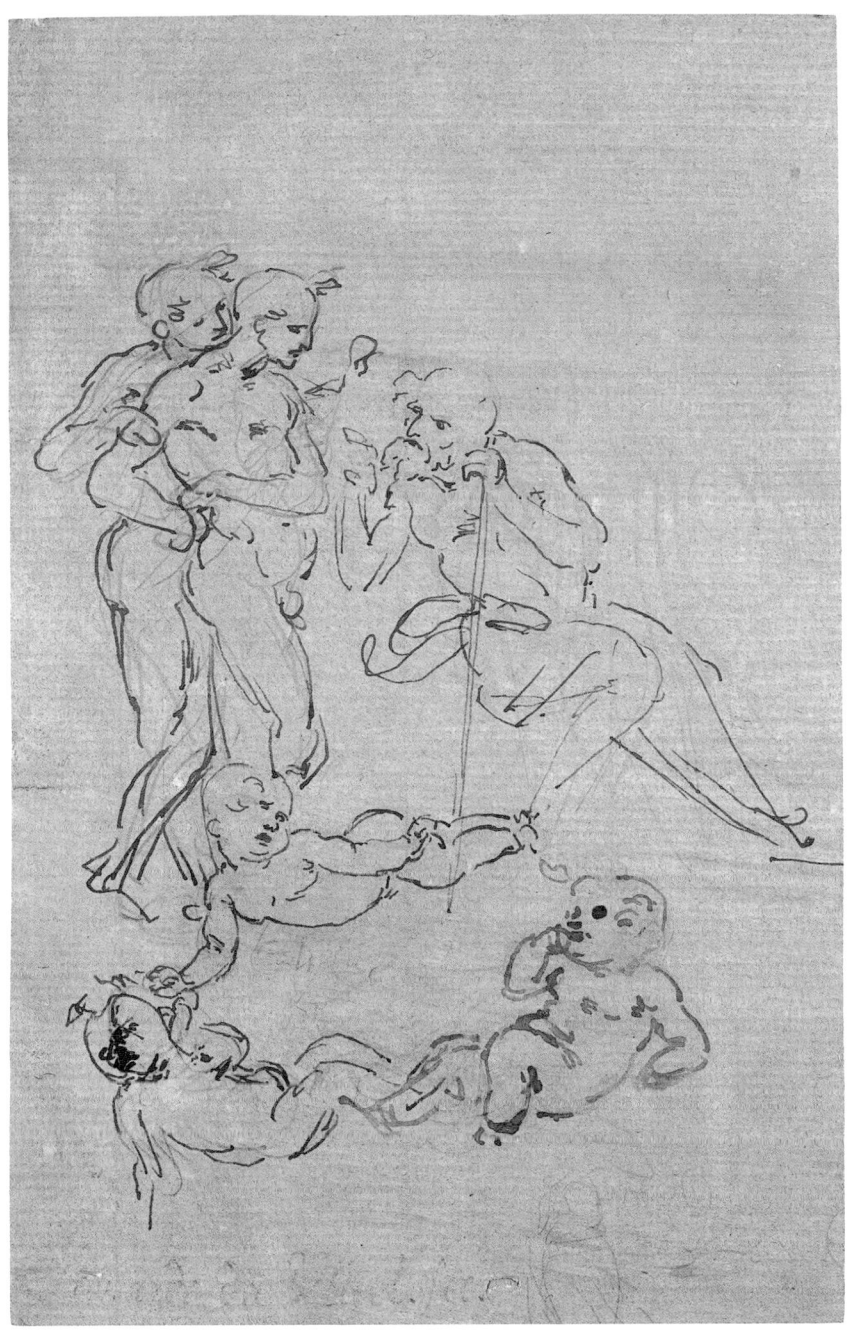

Cat. 38 *(actual size)*

This bold, expressive sketch, drawn with rapid, summary strokes of the quill pen over an extensive, much reinforced underdrawing in metalpoint, is a masterpiece of shorthand figural notation. Leonardo outlined most of the figures with a very fine pen in nearly black brown ink, and probably later added the infant's sketch on the lower right with a fairly blunted quill pen and much lighter ink. This was probably a page from a sketchbook (*libretto*), possibly even one that the artist carried with him, sketching and taking notes on site

with the metalpoint, then strengthening the outlines of the drawings with ink, perhaps in his studio. The underdrawing in metalpoint differs considerably with respect to the ink reworking on top, and it seems better visible in photographs with ultraviolet light (fig. 145). Leonardo used here a relatively thick paper (the presence of a large watermark somewhat obscures the drawing on the right side), much as in the Fitzwilliam study of a horseman (cat. no. 40). He seems to have applied the watery pale purple preparation thinly and quite quickly with the brush in horizontal strokes, following the direction of the laid lines on the paper. The cropped form of a torso (drawn faintly in metalpoint) on the lower right suggests that the original size of the page was cut down.

In composing the *Adoration of the Shepherds* (cat. nos. 36, 37; fig. 68), Leonardo sought to animate the main group of the Virgin worshiping the Christ Child by exploring a great variety of poses for the conversing secondary figures, and this he achieved in draft after draft of rapid figural sketching. When he recast the composition in the form of the *Adoration of the Magi* that is depicted in the unfinished San Donato a Scopeto altarpiece (figs, 10, 11), he continued the same approach for the secondary figures. As one of Leonardo's later notes stated, "where natural vivacity is lacking it must be supplied by art."[1] To this end, the artist also advised young painters,

> you must go about, and often when you are walking, observe and consider the positions and actions of men in talking, debating, or laughing, or fighting together, what actions there might be among them, what actions there might be among the bystanders, among the participants, and among those who look on. And take note of them with slight strokes thus, in a little sketchbook, which you should always carry with you. And it should be of paper that is prepared with color, so that it may not be rubbed out, but change the old [book when full] for a new one; since these things should not be rubbed out but preserved with great care; for the forms and positions of objects are so infinite that the memory is incapable of retaining them, wherefore keep these [sketches] as your guides and masters.[2]

As seems particularly evident here, Leonardo considered the poses of the figures in a composition as counterpoints. He experimented with reversing the designs left and right, and thereby attempted to echo the pose of one figure in the reactive pose of another. The Hamburg sheet portrays a seated bearded man in the center, who is presumably Saint Joseph, with one hand leaning on a staff, straddled legs positioned to the right, and torso turned to the left in a pronounced but seemingly effortless contrapposto, as he intently points with his right hand to address the beautiful nude youths standing on the left, who are presumably shepherds. The motif of Saint Joseph announcing to the shepherds the news of the Christ Child's birth is unusual. The closely intertwined standing poses of the youths on the left are rhythmic echoes of each other and counterbalance the thrusting impact of the bearded seated figure of Saint Joseph. Below, the artist tried out three poses for the Christ Child reclining on the ground, moving him left and right, belly down and belly up, and the rather crudely drawn anatomical details of the infant's figure suggest that the artist was barely satisfied with each of the solutions before he moved on to articulate the next one. The belly-down pose of the Christ Child in the upper center motif is nearly the same as in catalogue number 36, but in reverse. Yet the belly-up pose of the Christ Child in the right motif of the Hamburg sheet is essentially the same as in catalogue number 37, and in the same orientation. Leonardo later repeated this pose in his composition sketches for a Nativity (cat. no. 45) that seems connected with the design of the *Virgin of the Rocks*, which was to be the central panel of the altarpiece that he contracted on April 25, 1483, along with the brothers Evangelista and Giovan Ambrogio de' Predis, in Milan.

CCB

1. C.A., fol. 399r (formerly fol. 147r-b); Richter 1970, vol. 2, p. 359, no. 1445: "Doue . manca . la uiuacità naturale, bisogna farne una accidentale."
2. Paris Ms. A., fol. 107v (B.N. 2038, fol. 27v); Richter 1970, vol. 1, p. 338, no. 571: "spesse volte nel tuo andati a spasso vedere e considerare i siti . e li atti delli omini in nel parlare, in nel contendere o ridere o zuffare insieme, che atti fieno in loro . , che atti faccino i circumsta[n]ti . , i spartitori, i veditori d'esse cose . , e quelli notare con brevi segni in questa forma su un tuo piccolo libretto, il quale tu debi sempre portar con teco, e sia di carte tinte, accio non l'abbi a scancellare ma mutare di vechio in un novo, che . queste non sono cose da essere scancellate ansi con gran diligenza riserbate . , perchè gli sono tante le infinite forme e . atti delle cose che la memoria non è capace a ritenerle, onde queste riserberai come tua autori e maestri."

LEONARDO DA VINCI

39. *Three Figures; Gears, Wheels, and Other Mechanical Devices*

Metalpoint on pale pink prepared paper, 204 × 180 mm (8 1/16 × 7 1/8 in.) Visitors of the Ashmolean Museum, Oxford; Chambers Hall Gift, 1855 KPII 18

PROVENANCE: Sir Thomas Lawrence, Bristol and London (1769–1830; Lugt 2445); Samuel Woodburn, London (1786–1853; Lugt 2584, 2591; Suppl. 2378a); Chambers Hall (1786–1855; Lugt 551).

LITERATURE: Berenson 1903, vol. 2, p. 59, no. 1058; Colvin 1907, vol. 3, pl. 2B; Seidlitz 1909, p. 83; Thiis 1913, pp. 205–9; Poggi 1919, pl. 69; Venturi 1920, p. 100, fig. 51; Bodmer 1931, pp. 140, 384; Berenson 1938, vol. 2, p. 117, no. 1058; Royal Academy of Arts 1952, no. 33;

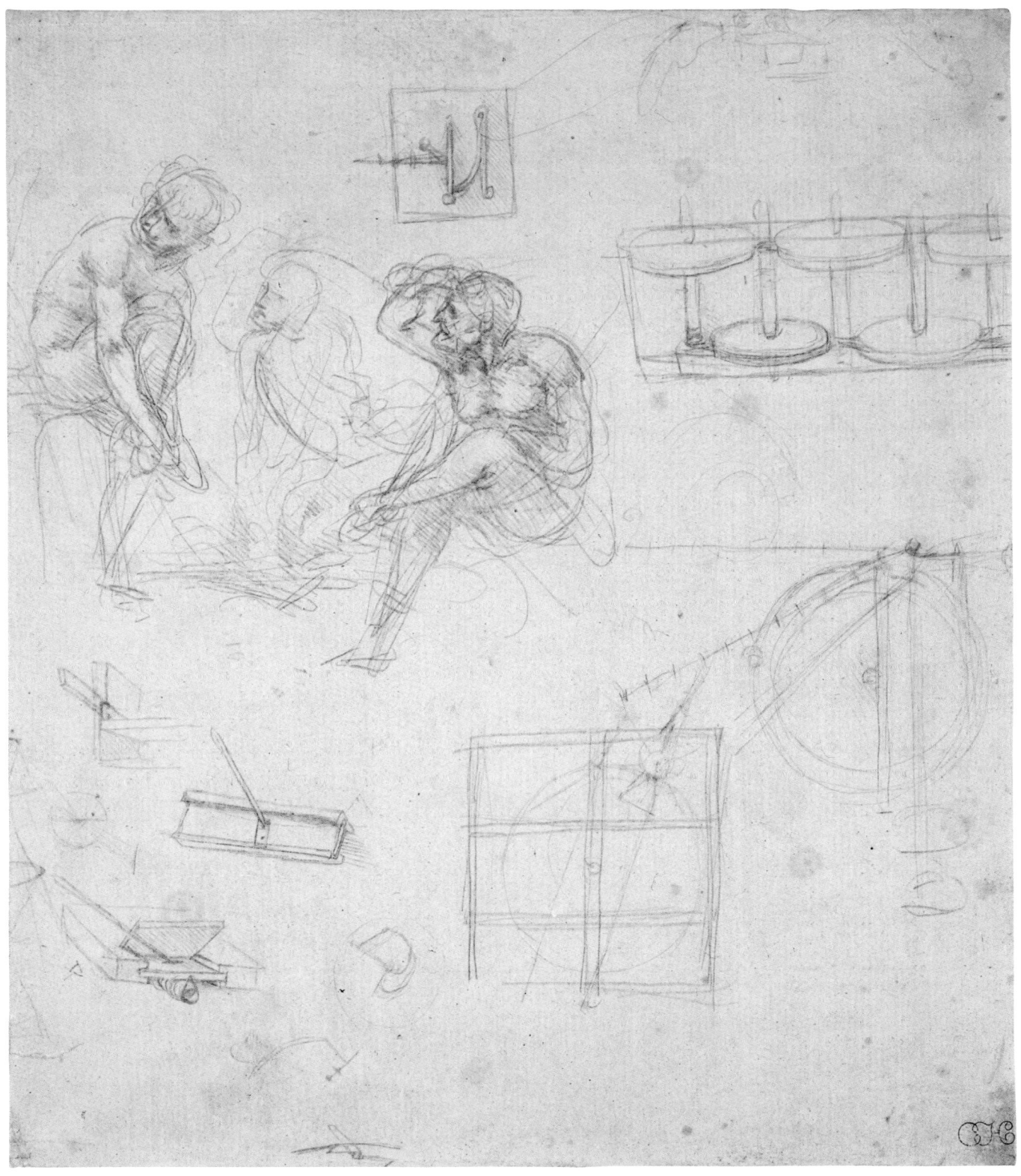

Cat. 39 *(actual size)*

Berenson 1961, vol. 2, p. 207, no. 1058; Clark and Pedretti 1968–69, vol. 1, p. 180, under no. 12702; Parker 1972, no. 18; Keele and Pedretti 1979 80, vol. 2, p. 804; Pedretti and Clark 1983, p. 59, fig. 49, under no. 1, fig. 49; Pedretti 1987b, p. 61; Popham 1994, no. 51.

The arrangement of the figures—sitting or crouching as if engaged in lively conversation—links the delicately drawn sketches on the upper left both with sheets that contain motifs loosely related to the *Adoration of the Shepherds* and with the later reworking of the composition as the unfinished *Adoration of the Magi* altarpiece, commissioned in 1481 by the monks of San Donato a Scopeto (cat. nos. 27–32). Both the fragmentary state and the vibrant sketchiness of the Ashmolean Museum drawing, however, make the subject seem fairly ambiguous, and the scene has even been described as Christ Washing the Feet of the Disciples, a proposal that does not seem entirely convincing. The physical types of the figures themselves (all portrayed nude and apparently beardless, and one exhibiting a Dantesque profile) do not appear to be those of Christ or of his apostles. More probably, the figures relate in a general sense to the groups of conversing onlookers—sitting or crouching on steps or stone slabs—that populate the architectural background of the Louvre composition sketch (cat. no. 27), of the Uffizi perspective study (fig. 139), and of the unfinished *Adoration* altarpiece (fig. 10). In the Ashmolean sheet, the gesture of the more monumental seated figure with the Dantesque profile (to the right in the group)—holding up his right hand to his brow to enhance or shield his vision—is the same as that of the seated woman on the left of catalogue number 31, a drawing more evidently connected with the *Adoration*, and the general gesture recurs in a variety of permutations throughout the composition of the unfinished altarpiece, among standing, sitting, or kneeling figures, as well as among riders on horses (figs. 10, 11, 140).

The motif of the three conversing figures in the Ashmolean drawing also relates to a small sketchy sheet portraying a multitude of conversing figures, who are apparently seated on a type of bench, as if grouped around a table (Windsor, RL 12702). The small Windsor sheet is drawn in a similar metalpoint technique as the present sheet,[1] and it has reasonably been identified as a preliminary study for a Last Supper, although the gestures of some of the figures seem overly animated for such a holy scene. A group of conversing figures around a table appears also on the lower right of catalogue number 29 recto, and there the mischievous figure at the extreme right is about to get up on the table. Seen together, the three drawings suggest that Leonardo was experimenting with a type of compositional arrangement that resembled a Last Supper but may have served a more playfully whimsical purpose.

The schematic studies of gears and cogwheels scattered on the Ashmolean sheet give little sense of the elegant quality of mechanical detail and graphic synthesis of structure that characterized Leonardo's technological studies of the 1480s and 1490s (cat. nos. 55, 64 recto, 65 verso). The designs evoke those in the highly detailed drawings of Bonaccorso Ghiberti's *Zibaldone* (Biblioteca Nazionale Centrale, Florence, BR 228), compiled in 1472–83 and the 1490s, that record earlier devices utilized by Filippo Brunelleschi for the dome of Florence Cathedral and other projects. Bonaccorso Ghiberti (1451–1516), an architect, engineer, and bronze caster, was Leonardo's nearly exact contemporary. Bonaccorso was privy to the vast engineering expertise that had made the construction of Brunelleschi's dome possible, for he was the grandson of the great sculptor, architect, and theorist Lorenzo Ghiberti (whose writings on optics Leonardo read attentively). Leonardo might have come in contact with Bonaccorso when Andrea del Verrocchio built and mounted the famous copper orb, or *palla*, on top of the lantern to the dome of Florence Cathedral (the orb, commissioned in September 1468, was installed on May 27, 1471). It is clear that Leonardo was greatly indebted to Bonaccorso during his first and second Florentine periods. The other source that is evoked by Leonardo's technological studies in the Ashmolean sheet is Giuliano da Sangallo's sketchbook (Biblioteca Apostolica Vaticana, Codex Barberinus Lat. 4424), begun in 1463 and continued until at least 1483. The polymath Giuliano was a long-standing friend and influence on Leonardo. (See Chronology.)   CCB

1. Clark and Pedretti 1968–69, vol. 1, pp. 179–80, no. 12702; Pedretti and Clark 1983, pp. 56–59, no. 1.

LEONARDO DA VINCI

40. *A Rider on a Rearing Horse in a Profile View*

Metalpoint, reworked with pen and dark brown ink, on pink-beige prepared paper, 144 × 122 mm (5 $^{11}/_{16}$ × 4 $^{13}/_{16}$ in.)
The Syndics of the Fitzwilliam Museum, Cambridge, England. Purchased with grants from the National Lottery through the Heritage Lottery Fund, the National Art Collections Fund and the Pilgrim Trust PD. 44–1999

PROVENANCE: Sir Peter Lely (1618–1680; Lugt 2092); the earls of Pembroke (Lugt under 2183, under 2585, under 2957); Pembroke sale, Sotheby's, London, July 10, 1917, lot 467; Henry Oppenheimer, London (1859–1932; Lugt 1351, Suppl. 1351); Oppenheimer sale, Christie's, London, July 10–14, 1936, lot 106; bought Colnaghi for Captain Norman Colville; acquired from the Trustees of Colonel Norman R. Colville, deceased, by private treaty sale, from the Gow,

Cunliffe, Leverton Harris, Perrins, and Reitlinger Funds with a contribution from the National Art Collections Fund, The National Lottery through the Heritage Lottery Fund and a grant from the Pilgrim Trust, with contributions from Mrs. Monica Beck and two anonymous donors, 1999.

LITERATURE: Strong 1900, no. 1; Berenson 1903, vol. 2, p. 62, no. 1116; Malaguzzi Valeri 1915, vol. 2, pp. 454, 439, fig. 493; Vasari Society 1920–35, pt. 1, no. 2; Commissione Vinciana 1928– , vol. 2, p. 28, pl. 66.b; Popp 1928, pp. 7, 35–36, no. 14; Royal Academy of Arts 1930, pp. 272 73, no. 546; Valentiner 1930, p. 69, fig. 19; Bodmer 1931, pp. 147, 386; De Hevesy 1931, p. 107, fig. 4; Berenson 1938, vol. 2, p. 115, no. 1044A; Palazzo dell'Arte 1939, p. 158; Goldscheider 1945, no. 128; Royal Academy of Arts 1952, no. 36; Popham 1957, p. 131; Bovi 1959, pl. 3; Berenson 1961, vol. 2, p. 202, vol. 3, fig. 483, no. 1044A;

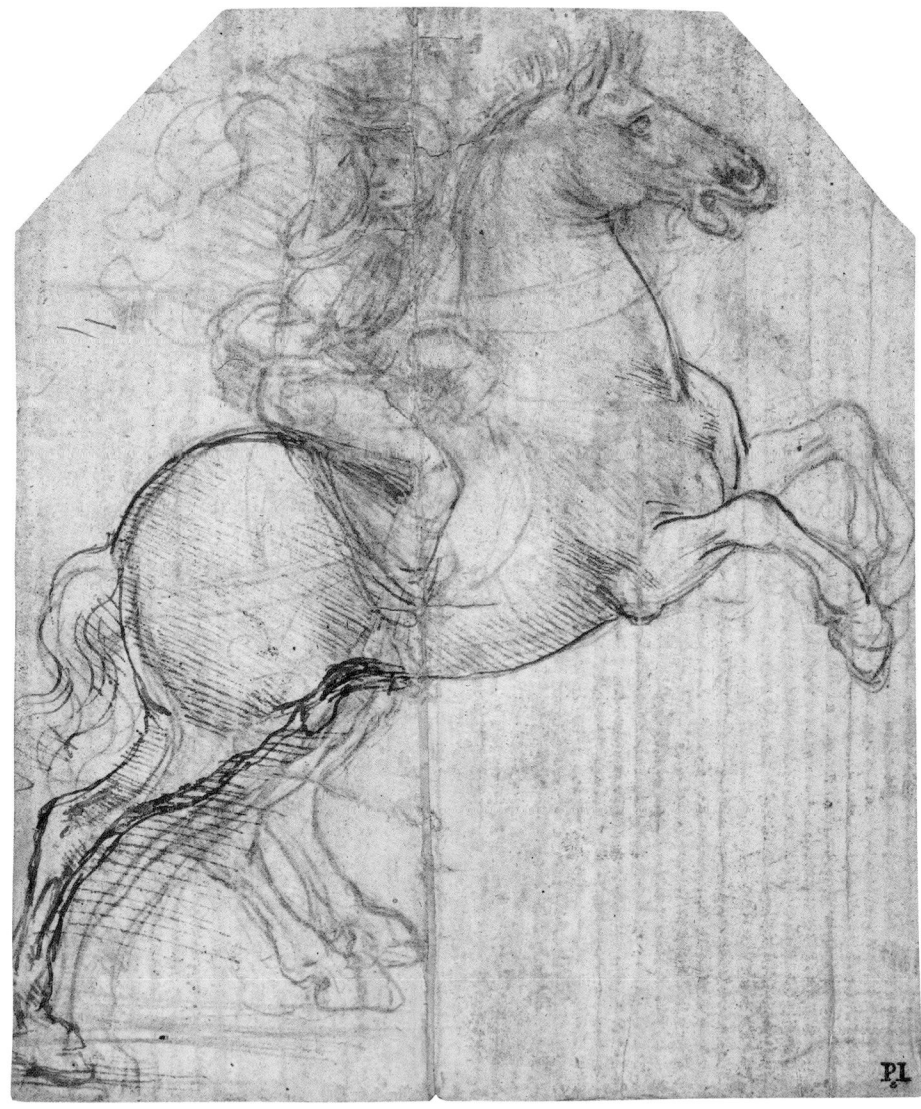

Cat. 40 *(actual size)*

Valentiner 1966, pl. 29; Pedretti 1987b, pp. 36, 39, 45, 108, fig. 18;
Luijten and Meij 1990–91, p. 164; Popham 1994, no. 64; Borne 2001;
Scrase 2002, no. 1.

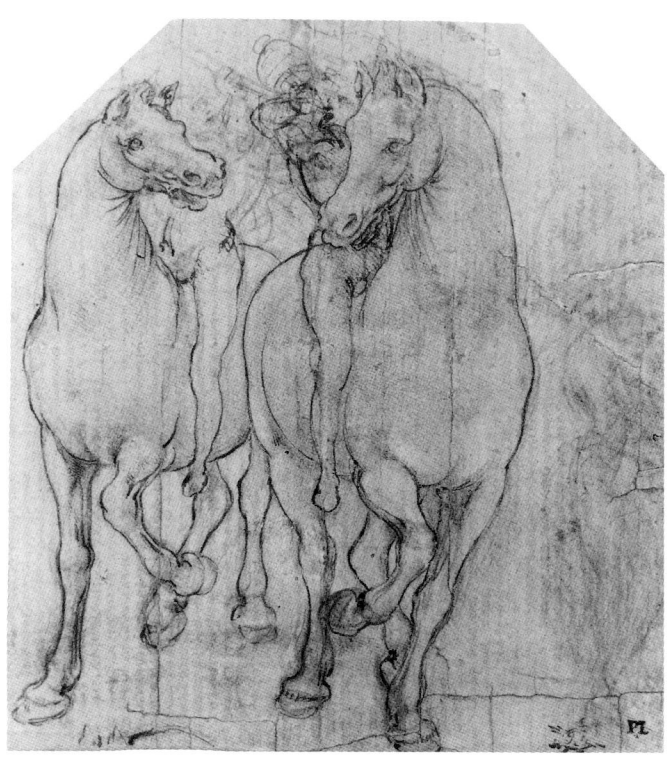

Fig. 146. Leonardo da Vinci, *Two Horsemen*. Metalpoint, reinforced
with pen and brown ink, 143 × 128 mm. Fitzwilliam Museum,
University of Cambridge PD.121-1961

Although Leonardo did not in the end use the precise
design of this exuberant horseman in the background
of the composition of the *Adoration of the Magi* altarpiece for
San Donato a Scopeto, there can be no doubt that he originally
conceived the dazzling Fitzwilliam study with the painting in
mind (fig. 10). A similar design of a rearing horse and rider
shading his eyes with his right hand seems recognizable in the
Adoration altarpiece, though enveloped in murky shadow and
much more broadly sketched with the brush. The motif forms
part of the agitated cavalry group toward the extreme right of
the composition (fig. 140).

The present study and a companion sheet also at the
Fitzwilliam Museum (fig. 146), portraying frontal views of
riders mounted on ambling horses, are drawn in an identical
metalpoint with-pen-and-ink technique on pink prepared
paper (with thick laid lines) and therefore must have been
part of the same sketchbook page. Especially in the present
study, Leonardo used the difficult medium of metalpoint with

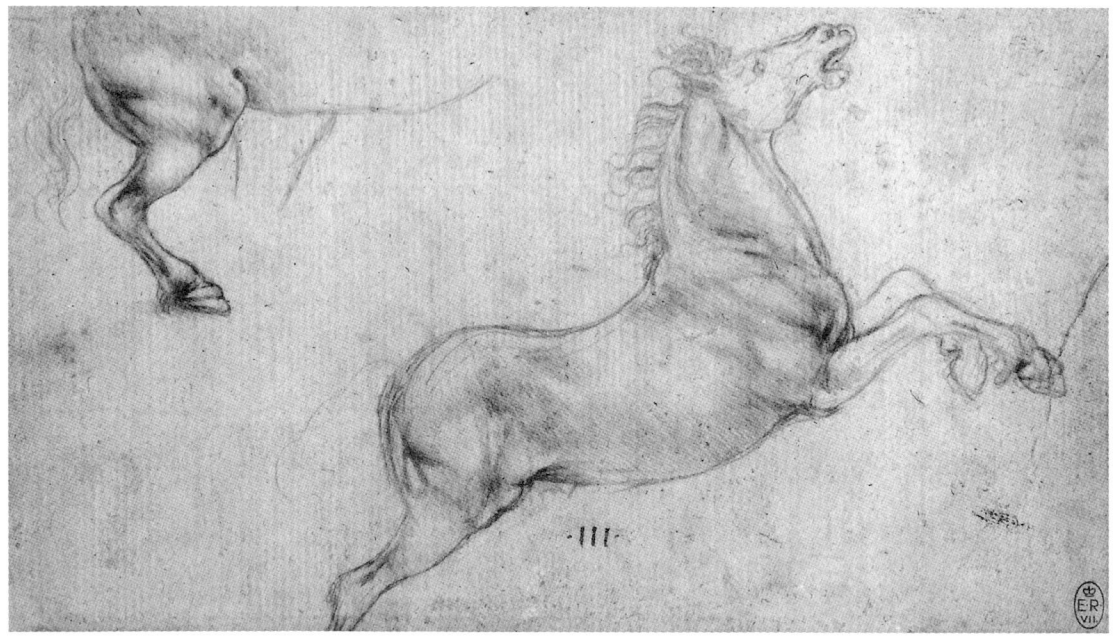

Fig. 147. Leonardo da Vinci, *Study of a Rearing Horse*. Metalpoint, 112 × 196 mm. The Royal Collection, H.M.
Queen Elizabeth II, Windsor Castle RL 12315

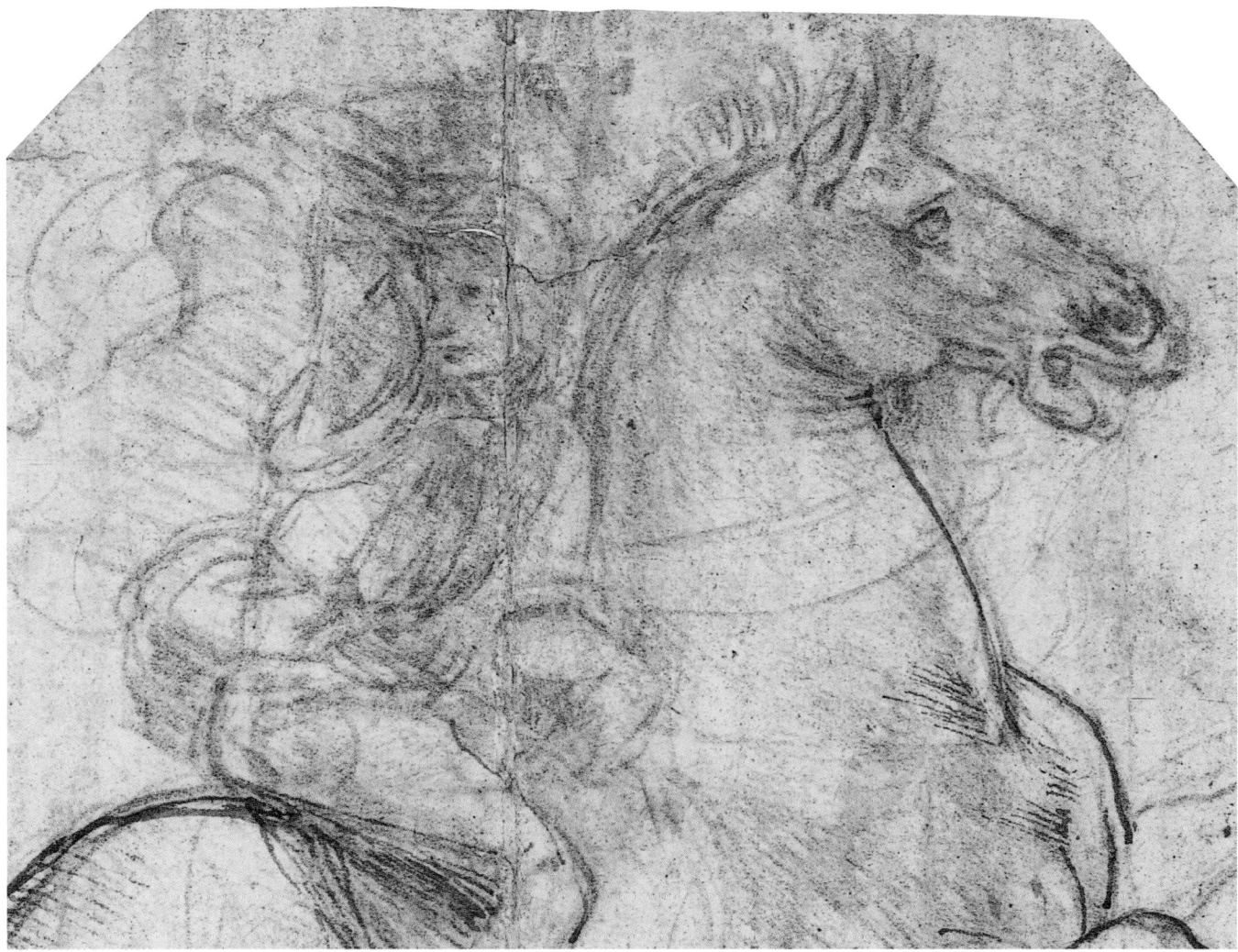

Cat. 40 *(detail)*

breathtaking freshness to capture the figures in arrested movement, then reworked the final outlines of the design in pen and ink, giving it in the process an imposing sculptural presence. Both Fitzwilliam studies were probably among the last drawings that Leonardo undertook for the *Adoration of the Magi* altarpiece before his departure for Milan in 1481–83 (leaving the work unfinished), since the confident metalpoint technique with animated reinforcement lines, as well as the figural type of the horse, already anticipate the study for the equestrian monument to Francesco Sforza (cat. no. 53), drawn in metalpoint on blue prepared paper.

The level of detail in the present drawing seems far greater than that of the underpainting in the unfinished San Donato a Scopeto altarpiece. The overall design evokes the monumental grandeur of the famous, much-copied Roman marble sculpture of the *Dioscuri* (the "Horse Tamers of Montecavallo"), now in the Piazza del Quirinale, Rome, and one of the few antique colossal statues visible throughout the Middle Ages and Renaissance. The source may seem unexpected, considering the relatively small size of Leonardo's drawing. Another study of a rearing horse for the *Adoration*, drawn in a similar technique, echoes more closely still the pose of the horses of the *Dioscuri* (fig. 147). Together, the two drawings therefore attest to the young Leonardo's gradual achievement of a monumental vocabulary of form, also through his nuanced exploration of antique sculpture and a possible trip to Rome.　CCB

355

LEONARDO DA VINCI

41. *Two Studies for a Cat, Study of a Dog*

Metalpoint on pale gray prepared paper, 137 × 103 mm (5 ⅜ × 4 ¹⁄₁₆ in.)
The British Museum, London 1895-9-15-477

PROVENANCE: Sir Thomas Lawrence, Bristol and London (1769–
1830; Lugt 2445); Miss C. Goodrich; John Malcolm, Poltalloch and
London (1805–1893; Lugt 1489, 1780, 1781, Suppl. 1489).

LITERATURE: Robinson 1869, no. 39; Robinson 1876, no. 41;
Berenson 1903, vol. 1, p. 160, vol. 2, p. 58, no. 1035; Sirén 1928,
pl. 160A; Bodmer 1931, pp. 181, 392; Berenson 1938, vol. 2, p. 115,
no. 1035A; Popham and Pouncey 1950, p. 61, no. 101; Berenson 1961,
vol. 2, p. 199, no. 1035A; Leinati 1980, p. 397; Marinoni 1980a,
p. 216; Pedretti 1987b, p. 43, fig. 30; Popham 1994, no. 63A.

The style and fine, sharply indented metalpoint technique
on pink prepared paper can help one broadly date this
delightful sheet of studies of a cat and a dog to sometime
between the late 1470s and 1485. A date closer to 1478–82
seems probable to the present author, during the period of
Leonardo's work on the *Madonna of the Cat* (cat. nos. 18, 19;
figs. 71, 72). The general challenge of composing the *Madonna
of the Cat* must have led Leonardo to produce a variety of
studies of cats from life, especially to capture their movements. Such life studies would have in turn served him in
reinventing the cat as a linking element between the figures in
the composition of the painting. It is clear from the various
extant sketches that the overall arrangement of the figures in

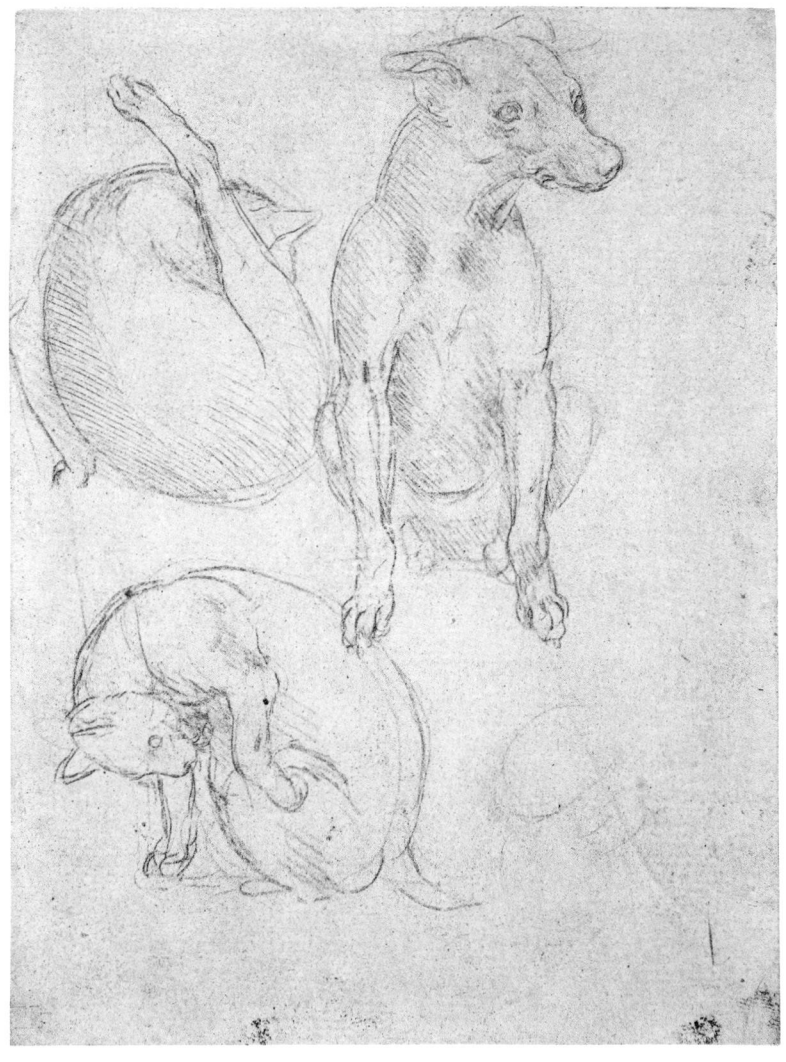

Cat. 41 *(actual size)*

the intended painting greatly depended on a structural under-standing of the cat's agility and the movement of its spine. In the sketches of the child playing alone with the cat (cat. no. 19), Leonardo suggested the animal's agitated movements with only a few well-placed outlines of the pen, and this rapidity and evocative freshness of mark were undoubtedly grounded in his sustained empirical observations. For the present stud-ies, the artist turned to a delicate metalpoint technique on pale pink prepared paper (the drawing surface is slightly abraded), rather than pen and ink, to achieve a cleaner draft, with more

precise detail and greater tonal subtlety. The spontaneity of the animals' poses in the drawing is striking. In the 1470s and early 1480s Leonardo must have drawn considerably more such life studies after domestic animals than has survived in his work. The studies of what are presumably a dog's paws from Edinburgh (cat. no. 42) are closely related in style and technique to the present sheet. Although more generally artic-ulated, the anatomy of the dog's paws in the British Museum sheet is similar to that of the hairy paws in the detail studies in the Edinburgh sheet. CCB

LEONARDO DA VINCI

42. *Studies of a Dog's Paw* (recto and verso)

Metalpoint on pale pink prepared paper (recto and verso), 141 × 107 mm (5 9/16 × 4 3/16 in.)
Inscribed on recto along lower left: illegible and partly cropped; along lower right: *Leonard de V [...]*.
National Gallery of Scotland, Edinburgh D5189

PROVENANCE: Sir Thomas Lawrence, Bristol and London (1769–1830; Lugt 2445); Samuel Woodburn, London (1786–1853; Lugt 2584, 2591; Suppl. 2378a); Woodburn sale, Christie's, London, June 4, 1860, lot 1039B; by 1937, Colonel Norman R. Colville; purchased by private treaty with the aid of the National Art Collections Fund, 1991.

LITERATURE: Popham 1937, pp. 86–87, pl. B; Berenson 1938, vol. 2, p. 115, no. 1044B; Palazzo dell'Arte 1939, p. 158 (no. 45?), Royal Academy of Arts 1952, nos. 32, 33; Berenson 1961, vol. 2, p. 202, no. 1044B; Pedretti 1987b, p. 57; Kemp and Roberts 1989, no. 37; National Gallery of Scotland 1991, no. 69; Kemp 1992c, pp. 64–65, no. 14; Pedretti 1992f, p. 188, figs. 12, 13; National Gallery of Scotland and Hazlitt Gooden and Fox 1994, no. 31; Popham 1994, nos. 79A, B; Aidan Weston-Lewis in National Gallery of Scotland 1999, pp. 14–15, 172, no. 1.

This sheet of detailed paw studies can also broadly be dated to the end of Leonardo's first Florentine period, or the beginning of his first Milanese period—that is, about 1478–85—based on the metalpoint technique and color of the paper preparation (see cat. nos. 20, 39–41). In support of generally dating Leonardo's animal studies on pink prepared paper in the artist's first Florentine period is the relationship of these sheets to the tradition of highly descriptive drawings in metalpoint on delicately colored paper preparations from

the 1470s to the 1490s produced by Florentine draftsmen (for example, by Domenico Ghirlandaio, Sandro Botticelli, and the young Filippino Lippi). Leonardo's other famous sheets in metalpoint on pink or beige prepared paper are also unani-mously dated in his first Florentine period.[1] In contrast, no such tradition of metalpoint drawings on pink prepared paper seems to have emerged among Lombard artists following Leonardo's arrival in Milan in 1481–83, although they were quick to adopt his technique of blue prepared grounds (see cat. nos. 53, 61, 66, 122–26). Detailed studies of animals in metal-point on prepared paper by Florentine artists also exist.[2] Leonardo's paw studies are clearly drawn from an actual ani-mal, with an attentive description of the animal's hirsute hair and of the overall forms as they are seen from different angles of view, although it is difficult to know whether the animal was dead or alive. Aidan Weston-Lewis has convincingly pro-posed that the paws in the present sheet of studies are those of a dog (see cat. no. 41) rather than of a wolf or of a bear, as has sometimes been suggested. Comparisons to the studies of a bear also exhibited here (cat. no. 43) can demonstrate that the proportions of the paws seen in the present sheet seem much more compact. The paws are closer in shape to those of the sketchily drawn dog on the right in catalogue number 41.

CCB

1. See Windsor, RL 12513, 12558; British Museum, London, 1895-9-15-474.
2. See sheets by Lorenzo di Credi (Windsor, RL 12365; Uffizi, Florence, 789 Orn.) and Piero di Cosimo (Windsor, RL 12796; Boijmans Van Beuningen Museum, Rotterdam).

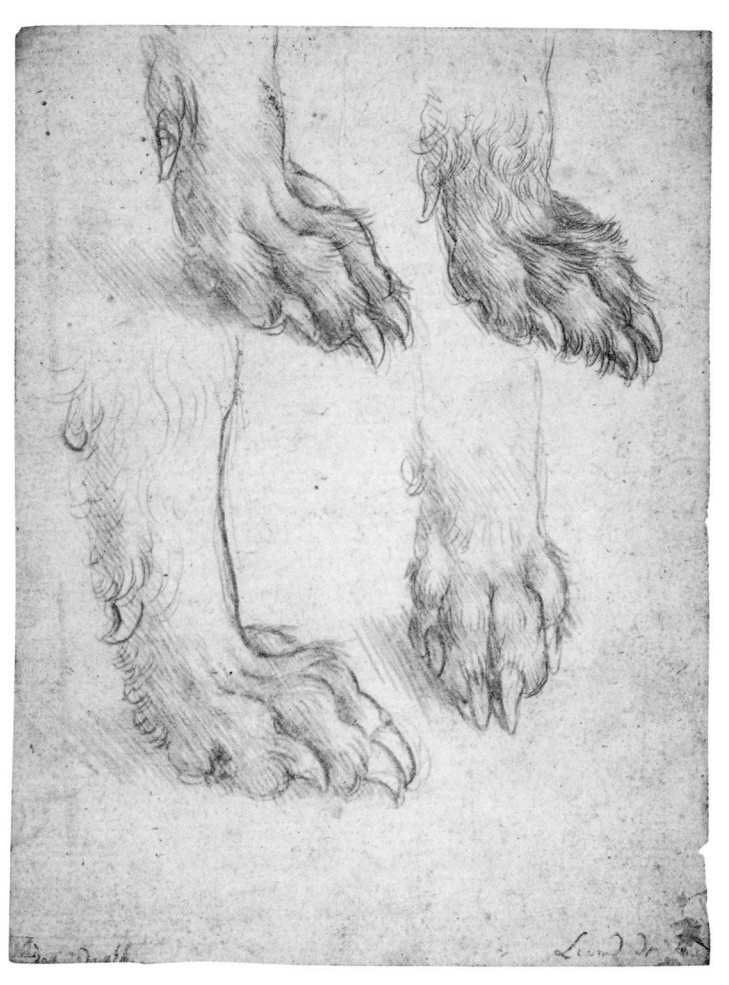

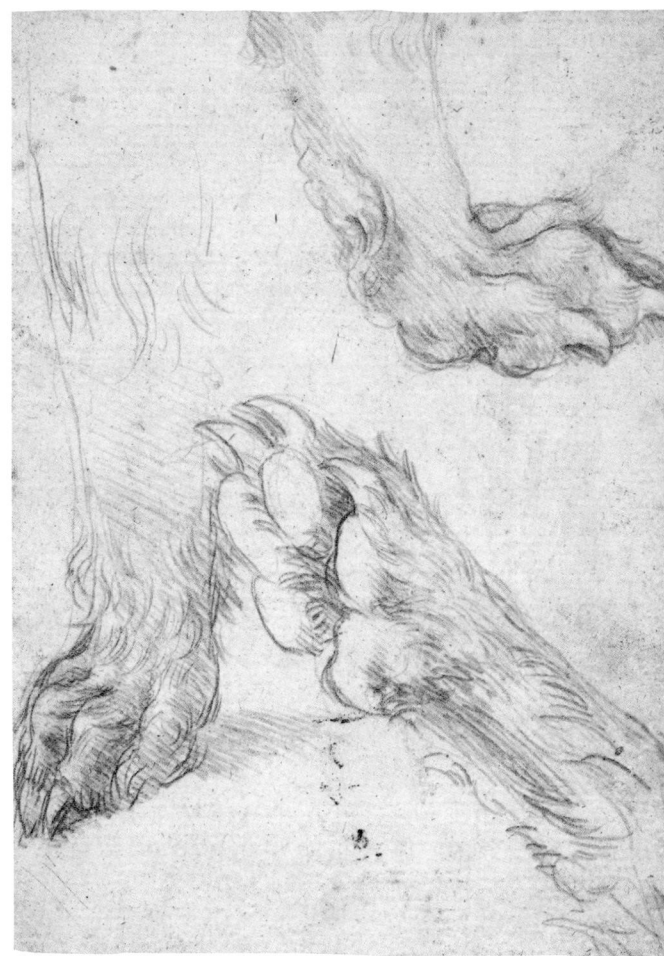

Cat. 42R

Cat. 42V

LEONARDO DA VINCI

43. *Studies for a Bear Walking; Faint Underdrawing of an Unrelated Design of a Pregnant Woman's Body*

Metalpoint on pink-light brown prepared paper, 103 × 134 mm (4 1/16 × 5 5/16 in.)
The Metropolitan Museum of Art, New York; Robert Lehman Collection, 1975 1975.1.369

PROVENANCE: Sir Thomas Lawrence, Bristol and London (1769–1830; Lugt 2445); Samuel Woodburn, London (1786–1853; Lugt 2584, 2591; Suppl. 2378a); Lawrence-Woodburn sale, London, June 8, 1860, lot 1038; private collection, England; [P. and D. Colnaghi and Co., London]; Ludwig Rosenthal, Bern (later L. V. Randall, Montreal); [Schaeffer Galleries, New York]; acquired by Robert Lehman (1892–1969) from Schaeffer Galleries in February 1945.

LITERATURE: Clark 1937; Popham 1937, p. 87; Berenson 1938, vol. 2, p. 110, no. 1010J; Cetto 1950, p. 15; Philadelphia Museum of Art 1950, no. 22; Royal Academy of Arts 1952, no. 41; Sterling 1957, no. 106; Goldscheider 1959, p. 101, pl. 101; Van Groschwitz 1959, no. 206; Berenson 1961, vol. 2, p. 205, no. 1049E; Schaeffer 1961, p. 27; Pouncey 1964, p. 286; Bean and Stampfle 1965, pp. 27–28, no. 18; Bacall 1968, no. 1; Clark and Pedretti 1968–69, vol. 1, p. 52, under no. 12372; Szabo 1975, p. 103, pl. 174; Szabo 1978, no. 27; Keele and

Pedretti 1979–80, vol. 1, p. 22, fig. 13, vol. 2, p. 810; Pedretti 1980b, p. 238; Szabo 1983, no. 17; Pedretti 1987b, p. 57, fig. 71; Trutty-Coohill 1989b, pp. 161–62; Forlani Tempesti 1991, pp. 237–40, no. 80 (accession no. incorrectly listed as 1976.1.369); Kemp 1992c, p. 65, under no. 14; Pedretti and Trutty-Coohill 1993, pp. 37–39, no. 5; Popham 1994, no. 5; Fairbrother and Ishikawa 1997–98, pp. 23–24, no. 23, fig. 3; National Gallery of Scotland 1999, p. 14.

Leonardo produced exquisitely refined, small-scale studies of bears on pink-beige prepared paper, such as this one and a related fragment (fig. 148). He also undertook detailed dissections of their paws, as is recorded in an extant group of four larger-scale anatomical drawings probably done in 1485–90, to judge from their technique in metalpoint on blue or gray-blue prepared paper that he then reworked in pen and brown ink.[1] In great contrast to the bold handling of the anatomical dissections of the bear's paws, the artist rendered here the figure of the bear and the detail of its paw on the left

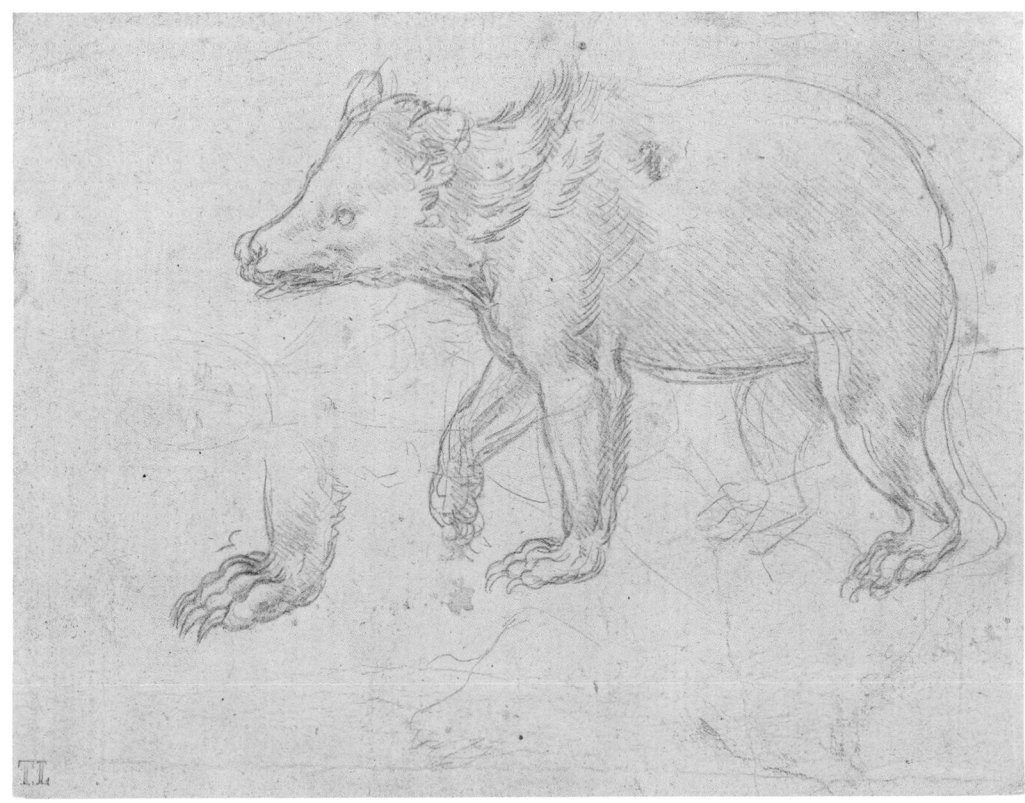

Cat. 43

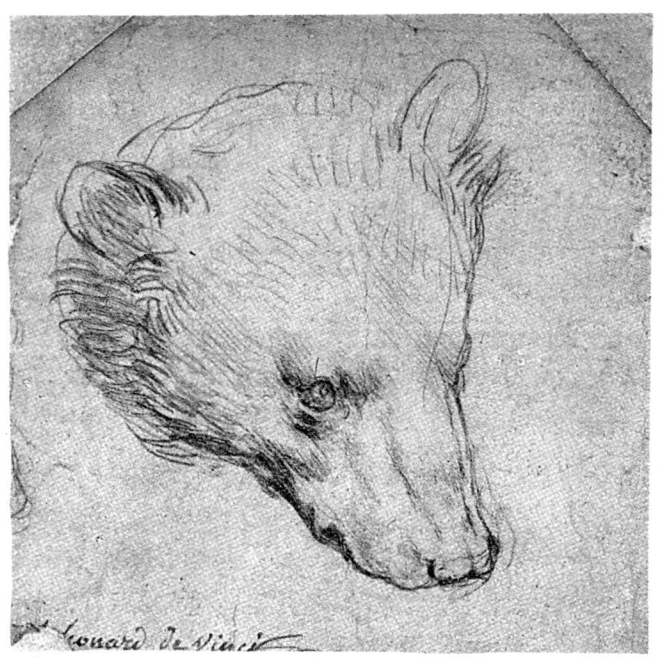

Fig. 148. Leonardo da Vinci, *Head of a Bear*. Metalpoint on prepared pink paper, 70 × 70 mm. Private collection, Great Britain

the stylized illustrations of the *Gravida* figure (pregnant woman) in anatomical treatises, as is found in some early-fifteenth-century Persian manuscripts and Johannes de Ketham's *Fasciculus medicinae* (Venice, 1491 and 1493–94).[2] Leonardo's figure, however, exhibits a narrative quality that would seem to be counterintuitive in an anatomical illustration.

Leonardo was fascinated by bears. The docile specimen seen walking in the Metropolitan sheet may have been drawn after a live animal in captivity, although there is a possibility that the drawing is an "animated" study after a dead beast. In Leonardo's time, wild bears abounded in the mountains of Tuscany and Lombardy. In contrast to the lively drawing technique, the fairly strict profile view of the bear seems somewhat static and suggests a pose descended from the traditions of medieval bestiaries and Renaissance model books. In such

in extremely delicate relief, using a fine, dense, and superbly uniform parallel hatching within the spirited, relatively emphatic outlines. The economy of Leonardo's drawing style is extraordinary. He was able to suggest the bear's fur with just a few well-placed short parallel ticks of the metalpoint on the head, torso, and legs. The soft, but animated, metalpoint drawing technique and the pale color of the paper preparation suggest a date in the early to mid-1480s (Leonardo left Florence for Milan in 1481–83) for both the present sheet and figure 148, hence much earlier than is usually proposed by scholars. In style and technique they seem related to those of the studies of two cats and a dog from the British Museum (cat. no. 41) and the larger-scale dog's paws from Edinburgh (cat. no. 42). The present sheet exhibits underneath the main study of the bear the sketch of a seated woman apparently with a pregnant belly, seen in a frontal view with legs apart, and with her dress partially lifted. This design, which Leonardo abandoned, is here reconstructed on the basis of infrared light (fig. 149). Reminiscent of Antonio del Pollaiuolo's relief sculptures, the female figure seems generally related in bodily type and pose to the Virgin in the British Museum sheet on pink prepared paper that appears to offer an early idea for the *Benois Madonna* (cat. no. 20 recto) from around 1478. The frontal design of the woman in the present sheet is also generally similar to

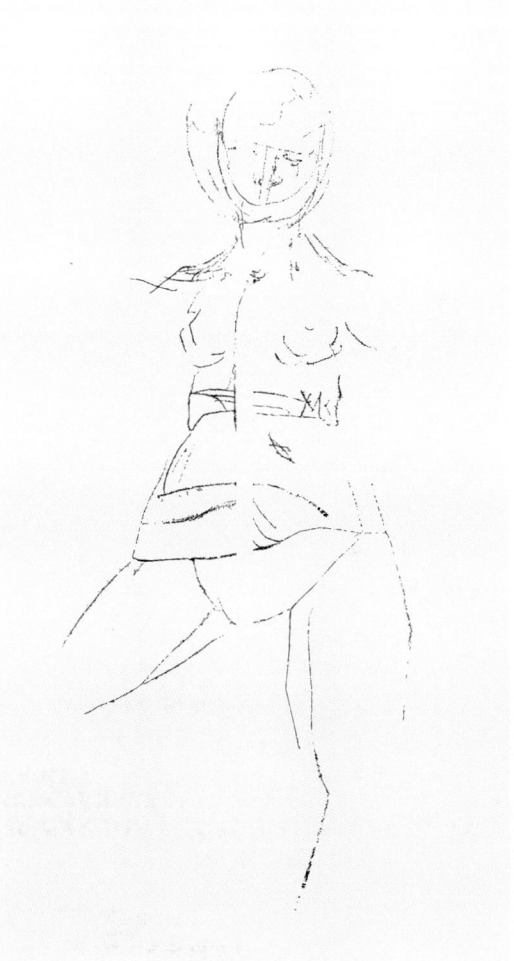

Fig. 149. Manual extraction using Adobe Photoshop (Leica S1 Pro) of the background area of cat. no. 43, showing a human figure (Barbara Bridgers)

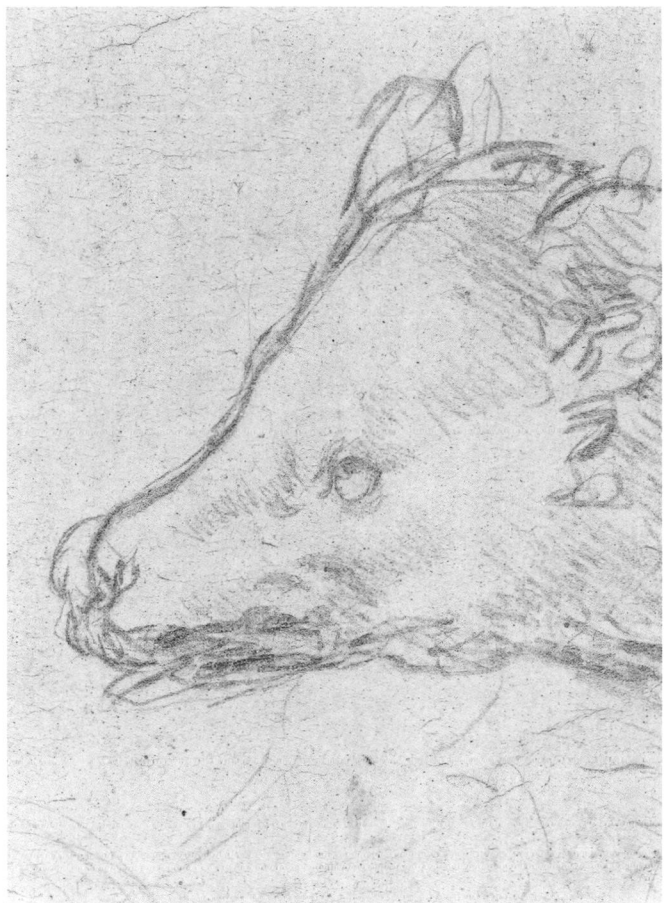

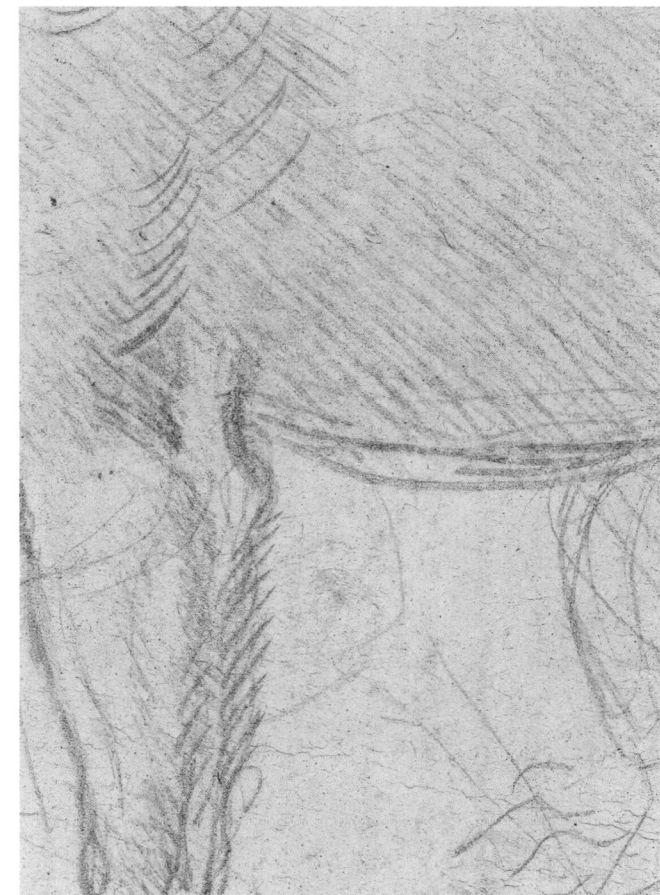

Cat. 43 *(detail)*

Cat. 43 *(detail)*

anthologies of animal illustrations, artists usually portrayed the specimens in orderly, highly descriptive profile or three-quarter views on the page. In a later passage copied from one of the popular bestiaries of his day, the *Fiore di virtù* (Venice, 1488), Leonardo recorded a short moralizing fable about the bear as a symbol of ire, a story that is based on Pliny the Elder's *Historia naturalis.*[3] He also planned to include a discussion of the bear's paw, "which has the ligatures of the sinews of the toes joined above the instep," in his great projected treatise on comparative anatomy.[4] Leonardo seems to have repeatedly traveled to the mountainous Valtellina region near Lake Como, in northern Lombardy, and described in a note from 1490–92 how the ingenious hunters of the Valchiavenna cast bears down the steep mountain cliffs.[5] The style and technique of

the Metropolitan Museum bear anticipate those of the spirited study for the Sforza equestrian monument (cat. no. 53), carefully drawn in metalpoint on blue prepared paper.　　CCB

1. Windsor, RL 12372–12375.
2. Ketham's illustration of the *"Gravida"* figure in the Venice 1493–94 edition is entitled "Figura dela matrice dal natural.du[n]a Dona." For earlier illustrations, see Keele and Pedretti 1979–80, vol. 1, pp. xxii–xxv.
3. Paris Ms. H[1], fol. 6r; Richter 1970, vol. 2, p. 261, no. 1222. See De Toni 1922, p. 58.
4. Windsor, RL 19061 r; Richter 1970, vol. 2, p. 95, no. 822: "Farai poi un discorso delle mani di ciascun animale per mostrare in che si uariano, come nell'orso che agiugne la legatura delle corde de' diti del piè sopra il collo d'esso piè."
5. C.A., fol. 570ar (formerly fol. 214r-a); transcribed in Richter 1970, vol. 2, p. 189, no. 1, no. 1030.

LEONARDO DA VINCI

44. *Woman's Head Almost in Profile* (recto and verso)

Metalpoint highlighted with white on pale blue prepared paper; at lower left, black-chalk sketch of a half-length nude man by a different, right hand, 179 × 168 mm (7 1/16 × 6 5/8 in.); several stains; reworking of outline of the face, eye, and neck (recto); reworking of facial features on recto in another hand in pen and brown ink and red chalk (verso)

Département des Arts Graphiques du Musée du Louvre, Paris 2376

PROVENANCE: Giuseppe Vallardi (Lugt 1223, in green on verso); 1856, acquired by the Musée du Louvre; museum mark (Lugt 1886a).

LITERATURE: Vallardi 1855, pp. 35–36, fol. 170; Müller-Walde 1890, p. 95, fig. 51; Rosenberg 1898, p. 106, fig. 99; Müntz 1899, pp. 177, 424, pl. 11, p. 520, no. 61; Seidlitz 1909, vol. 1, p. 291, p. xlii; Thiis 1913, p. 104, fig. p. 103; Malaguzzi Valeri 1913–23, vol. 2, p. 568, fig. 633; Louvre 1919, no. 20; Poggi 1919, pl. 123, p. lxi; Suida 1919–20, vol. 13, pp. 43, 285–86; Demonts 1921, no. 14; Demonts 1922, no. 14; Venturi 1925, pp. 150–51, fig. 81; Commissione Vinciana 1928–, vol. 3, p. 95; Sirén 1928, p. 57; Suida 1929, pp. 57, 60, fig. 56; Bodmer 1931, p. 399, fig. 230; Clark 1933b, p. 139; Petit Palais 1935, no. 570; Berenson 1938, vol. 1, pp. 55, 60, vol. 2, no. 1067c, vol. 3, fig. 562; Palazzo dell'Arte 1939, p. 161 (Leonardo?); Goldscheider 1945, no. 69; Popham 1945, pp. 15, 16, no. 19; Bovi 1952, p. 126; Florisoone and Bacou 1952, no. 14; Heydenreich 1954, vol. 2, p. v, fig. 32; Sérullaz 1965, no. 9; Clark and Pedretti 1968–69, under no. 12572; Petit Palais 1968–69, no. 361; Gould 1975, pp. 63–65, fig. 30; Rosci 1978, fig. p. 66, p. 182, no. 20a; Grossman 1979, p. 120, fig. 27; Kemp 1981, pp. 53–54, fig. 12; Béguin 1983, p. 84; Alpatov 1984, p. 8, fig. 3; Kustodieva 1985, p. 53, fig. 20; Clark 1988, p. 90, fig. 32; Pedretti 1989b, p. 166; Brown 1990b, pp. 5, 6, 10, 13, 15–19, fig. 2; Pedretti 1990a, p. 85, under no. 2; Brown 1991, pp. 25, 27, fig. 23; Brown 1998b, p. 212 n. 49; Marani 1998e, p. 34 n. 66; Kwakkelstein 1999, p. 196 n. 35; Fiorio 2000a, pp. 28, 82, fig. p. 29; Zöllner 2000, p. 35, fig.

The relation between this drawing and the Virgin and Child known as the *Madonna Litta* at the State Hermitage Museum, Saint Petersburg, was established when Giuseppe Vallardi published the drawing in 1855 (fig. 82).[1] The paper is described as "ash colored," but the medium is incorrectly indicated as "black lead and pen." The three-quarter profile of the left side of the face is specifically pointed out, as is the inward-looking expression; both aspects would continue to be mentioned in characterizations of the drawing. "This drawing was used by Leonardo as a study for painting the head of the Virgin and Child in the precious panel once belonging to the Visconti family and today in the Litta-Visconti-Arese collection," wrote Vallardi. The engraving of the *Madonna Litta* cited by Vallardi was executed by Iacopo Bernardi about 1830,[2] but in the sixteenth century, a burin engraving of the panel was executed by a master identified as Zoan Andrea.[3]

The authenticity of the drawing has never been questioned, although William Suida rejected its relationship specifically to the Hermitage painting in preference to other compositions on the theme of the Holy Family. When Eugène Müntz described it in 1899, it was on view at the Louvre in the same case as the sheet of studies of weapons (cat. no. 48). Nonetheless, the complexity of the painting's genesis and the unresolved question of its attribution make evaluating this drawing a more delicate matter than it at first appears.

Lionello Venturi was the first to emphasize the drawing's quality, venturing a poetic description that evokes both the light touch of the line and the "crepuscular" melancholy of the gaze "lending its dying glimmer to that delicate shade flower, with the face seemingly immersed in a liquid atmosphere." In the 1930s, Bernard Berenson and Kenneth Clark proposed a very early date for the drawing—even earlier, according to Berenson, than the *Annunciation* (fig. 66) and a drawing of a face in profile at the Uffizi (fig. 49) that has been linked to the small *Annunciation* at the Louvre (fig. 138).[4] Similarly, in 1933 Clark, followed in 1945 by A. E. Popham, set out a genealogy for the *Madonna Litta* that made the present drawing—in my opinion, the only one directly related to the painting that is in Leonardo's hand—the mooring onto which a group of preliminary studies for the composition was fastened. First came a sketch in leadpoint on the verso of a sheet in the British Museum that also includes two studies in pen of the Virgin and Child (cat. no. 20). It is a very light sketch showing the Virgin, her face in left profile, with the Child pressed to her breast. Another leadpoint drawing appears on a sheet of studies for the *Adoration of the Magi* at the Louvre (cat. no. 29). However, instead of showing the Virgin suckling the Child, as the study has often been described, it depicts the Virgin holding the Child on her knees.

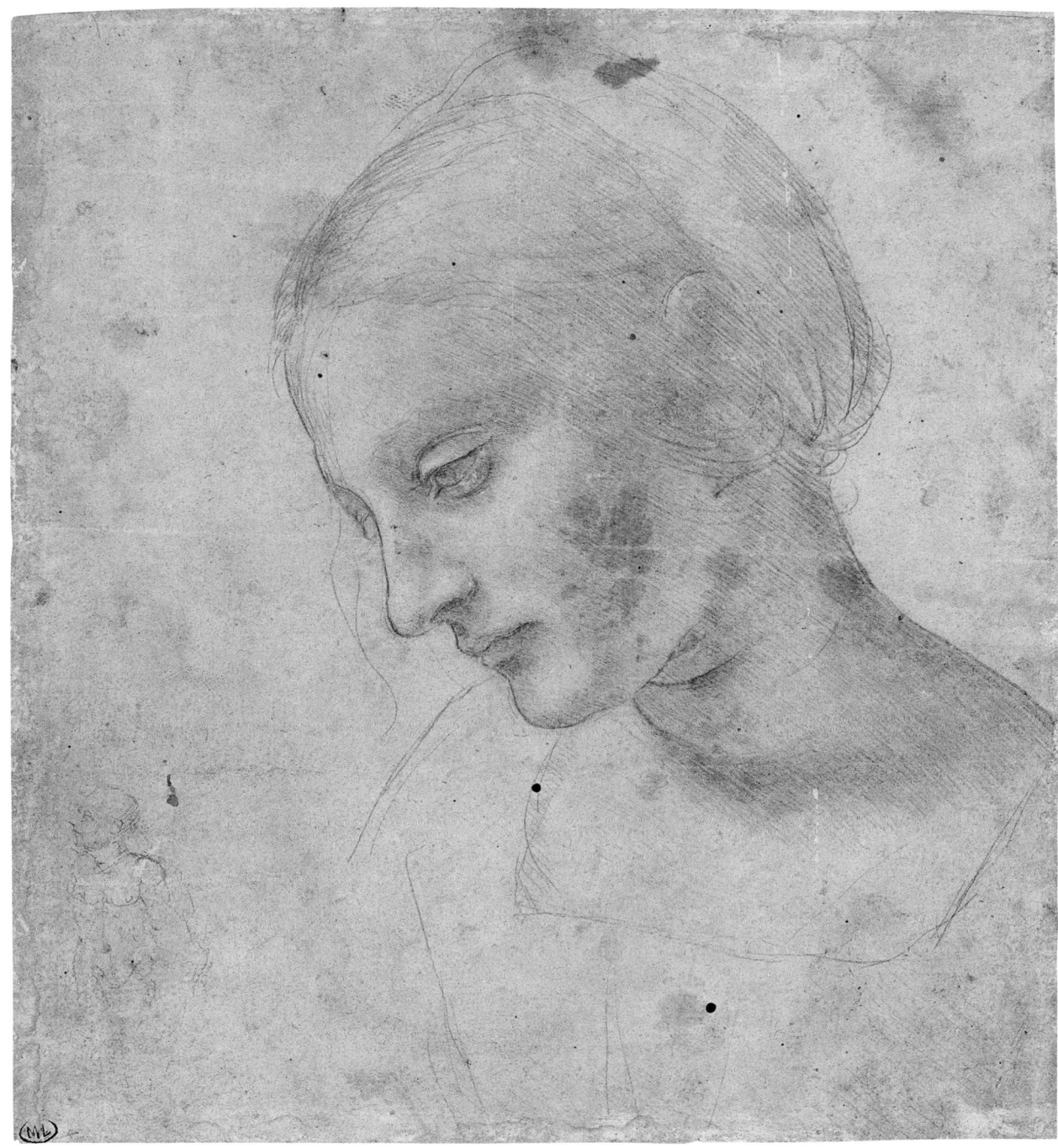

Cat. 44R *(actual size)*

Clark and then Popham suggested relating the study of the head exhibited here, the sketch in the British Museum and the sketch in the Louvre, and a sheet at Windsor (RL 12568) that shows several studies of children to a list of works compiled by Leonardo about 1482, found on folio 888r of the Codex Atlanticus, where he mentioned two Virgins: "Una nostra donna finita. Un'alta qu[a]si, ch'è 'n proffilo." Hinging on this are various interpretations of the chronology of the *Madonna Litta* and thus of its attribution. According to Clark, this Virgin is "quasi finita di profilo" (almost finished, in profile)[5] — although according to Carlo Pedretti, the Virgin is "quasi di profilo" (almost in profile).[6] In the first hypothesis, the *Madonna Litta* may have been begun in Florence about 1480 and completed in Milan, by a student, after a long hiatus.

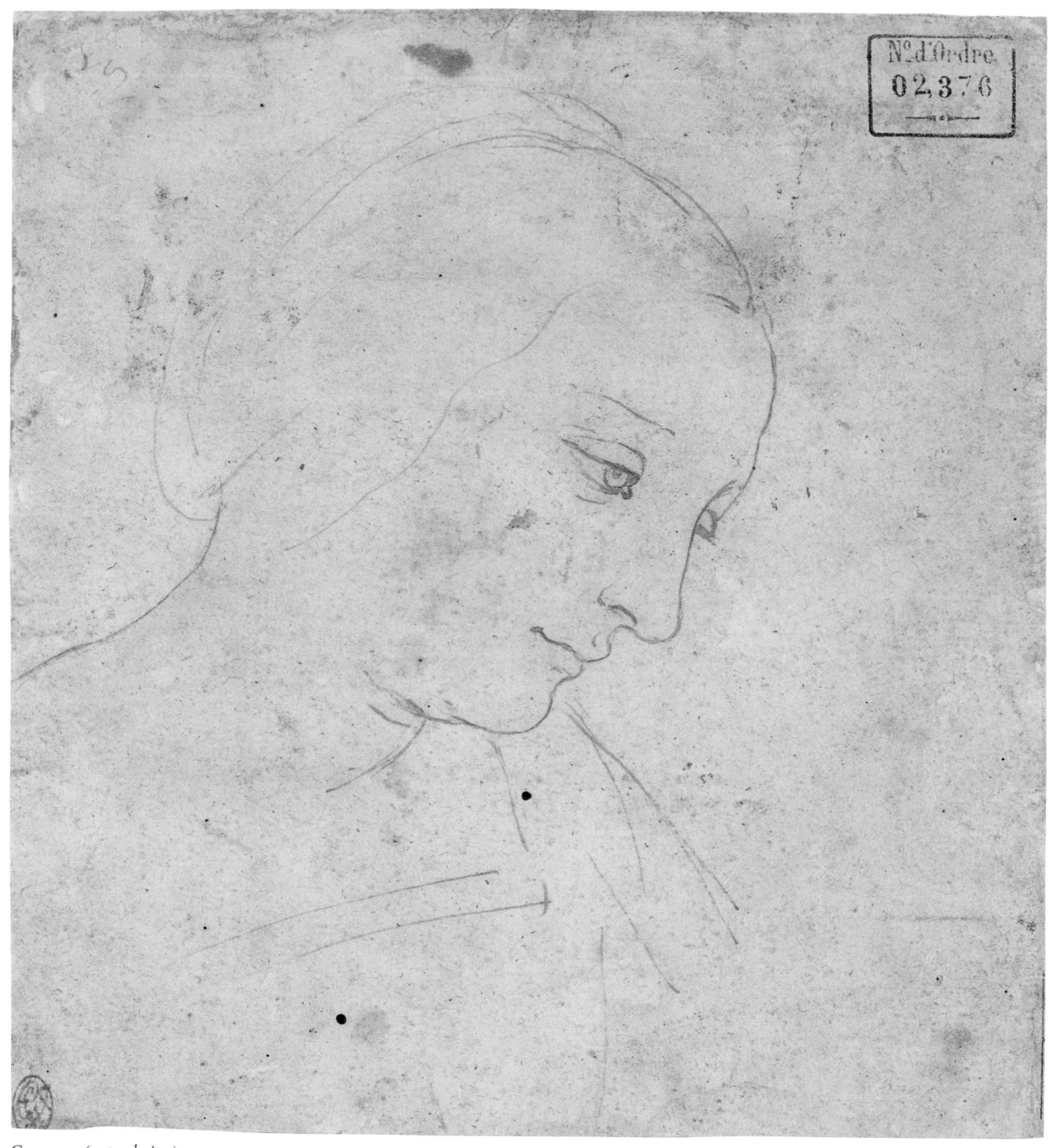

Cat. 44v *(actual size)*

According to Clark and then Popham, the three studies involving variations in the Child's position that they linked to the Hermitage painting would all have to be dated before 1482. But it should be noted that the British Museum sketch is on the same sheet as the *Virgin and Child,* which is identified as one of the Virgins begun in the autumn of 1478 (cat. no. 20). The Louvre sketch of the Virgin appears on a sheet of studies for the *Adoration* that dates to 1480–81 (cat. no. 29). In the opinion of Berenson, Clark, and Popham, the present study of a face predates Leonardo's departure for Milan—predates even the study of hands at Windsor done at a time, about 1478–80, close to that of the portrait of Ginevra de' Benci (ca. 1474–78; fig. 67); however, in 1968 Clark and Pedretti proposed a later date, about 1490, for the sheet.[7] In that hypothetical reconstruction of the genesis of drawings for the *Madonna Litta*, the sketch in the British Museum (cat. no. 20 verso), the one in the Louvre (cat. no. 29), and the two studies at Windsor in red chalk and leadpoint (RL 12568, RL 12569) would be contemporary, all executed about 1480 and related to the Madonna "quasi finita," identified as being either the *Madonna Litta* or the *Virgin with a Flower*.[8] The principal variation between the Louvre drawing studied here and the Hermitage painting (fig. 82) would thus be in the head of the Virgin and that of the Child, Leonardo's Milanese student having intervened more freely in this part.

David Alan Brown and, more recently, Maria Teresa Fiorio rejected the argument made by Clark, who was the first to study the theme of the Virgin in profile based on the notation in the Codex Atlanticus. In two successive analyses (1990, 1991) Brown proposed a very different development of the *Madonna Litta* (fig. 82): the painting, which shows no evidence of successive stages of work, thus eliminating the possibility that it was completed at a later date, cannot be the Virgin "in profile" that Leonardo painted before leaving Florence. It is rather a work realized in Milan in the late 1480s. Once the hypothesis that this work was begun by Leonardo and completed by somebody else at a different time and place has been abandoned, Leonardo's exact role in its elaboration still remains to be determined. Even if the present drawing is the only remnant of the master's intervention in the painting's genesis, the very conception of the painting was completely his own: the motif of the Child at the Virgin's breast turning his gaze as if interrupted by an invisible spectator and the motif of the captive lark, a symbol of the Passion, in his left hand are elements that argue for precedents in the Lombard tradition, which Brown has meticulously detailed.[9] If we accept Brown's idea that a student may have transcribed one of the master's ideas, we need to clarify what may have been the model. A now-lost sketch may have set the overall composition before the detail studies, the conception thereby passing intact from master to student. The preparatory studies, with the exception of the one discussed here, are not by Leonardo and suggest the possibility of a project conceived in the studio based on the master's ideas. The first of these is a study of the garments draping the Virgin's torso and left arm, now in the Berlin Kupferstichkabinett (fig. 83). A second study, in the Frits Lugt Collection, treats the head of the Child; it is also attributed to Boltraffio.[10] According to Brown, this study, as

well as others that have not survived, must have predated the overall cartoon for the painting. This would also be true of a study of a female head in left profile, in metalpoint on blue prepared paper, which, though done at a different angle, may be a drawing for the face of the Virgin.[11] It was modified in the *Madonna Litta* but is identical in appearance to an anonymous copy of that painting in the Museo Poldi Pezzoli, Milan.

According to Brown's hypothesis concerning an attribution of the *Madonna Litta*, the present drawing corresponds to the motif conceived by Leonardo himself of the angle of the Virgin's torso and head, the "almost in profile" motif around which the entire composition is articulated. The contrapposto of the Child echoes the turning movement suggested in the face of his Mother, the concept of a twofold shift in space, which interested Leonardo from his first sketches of Virgins with Child. Brown concluded with the proposal that the present drawing, done in preparation for the face and shoulders of the *Madonna Litta*, be regarded as a relatively late stage in the elaboration of the painting, coming after the study at the Metropolitan Museum (fig. 84) and the cartoon for the Museo Poldi Pezzoli painting.

Leonardo's drawing is an investigation of structure. The movement tends to give the clearest possible definition to this face, "not only to increase the sharpness of the notation but also to confer on the figure the emotion befitting it."[12] It is a timeless moment of perfection achieved without perceptible effort. Leonardo's study of the face is on the same scale as the painting so that the student could use it as a model to better master the perspective of the half profile. If we accept this "suspended" conception of the *Madonna Litta*, its genesis can be seen as an example of how Leonardo's studio operated: it was at once a place where models were developed and handed over to students to use for their own work and a place where there was active participation in a specific project carried out under Leonardo's direction. However, even though the foreshortening of the face in the painting corresponds to that in the Louvre drawing and was therefore executed in a manner consistent with the master's plan, the head has not preserved its grace and is closer to the Metropolitan Museum drawing (fig. 84), which cannot be considered as by Leonardo, and to the version of the painting at the Museo Poldi Pezzoli. There is in the Hermitage painting nothing of Leonardo's interiority of expression or his extraordinary economy of line. During 1485–90 his work was marked by an absolute mastery of stroke, which can be found again in the Turin study related to the Louvre's *Virgin of the Rocks* (fig. 80)[13] and in the *Profile of a Woman* at Windsor (RL 12505). Clark dated the latter to Leonardo's stay in Milan, "between 1482, the period of the last silver-point drawings for the Adoration, and 1495, when he seems to have abandoned this medium altogether."[14]

In the conclusion to his 1991 study, Brown proposed that the *Litta Madonna* was painted not by Boltraffio but by Marco d'Oggiono who joined Leonardo's studio on September 7, 1490, revisiting a hypothesis advanced decades previously by Suida. Vasari, Brown reminded us, mentions both Boltraffio and Marco d'Oggiono as students of Leonardo.[15] Leonardo also mentioned them in a note he wrote in 1490–91 regarding the theft of metalpoint pencils by Salaì.[16] In 1491 Boltraffio and d'Oggiono together painted the *Resurrection of Christ with Saint Leonard and Saint Lucy* (see fig. 85).

Suida attributed the Hermitage painting to Boltraffio[17] and in 1920 wrote that the Louvre drawing is unrelated to that painting. He later changed his mind, publishing the painting as a work by Marco d'Oggiono that had been retouched by Leonardo, and ultimately as a work by Leonardo himself.[18] Finally, Brown, in comparing the motif of the Child turning away from his mother's breast in the *Madonna Litta* to Marco d'Oggiono's *Virgin and Child* at the Louvre,[19] rallied behind the proposition that d'Oggiono was the artist of that work.

FV

1. Vallardi 1855, pp. 35–36, fol. 170 (Leonardo da Vinci): "su carta alquanto tinta in cenerognolo eseguito a matita nera ed a penna: busto della Vergine veduto di profilo dal lato sinistro, un quarto il vero, in atto di contemplazione, col capo coperto da velo, e colla veste appena segnata intorno al petto.—Da un lato semplice indicazione della metà superiore d'una macchietta nuda. Al rovescio, trovasi ripetuto a penna il semplice contorno dello stesso busto. Questo disegno servì a Leonardo di studio per dipingere la testa della Vergine col Bimbo nella preziosa tavola già appartenente alla famiglia Visconti ed ora a quella di Litta-Visconti-Arese. Bernardi ne eseguì l'intaglio. Una piccola tavola ma non meno interessante trovasi nella raccolta Vallardi, di eguale composizione, descritta per opera di Bernardino Zenale da Treviglio al N. 9 a pag. 5 del Catalogo a stampa della suddetta raccolta. La Vergine in atto di soave amore contempla il divin fanciullo tenendolo colle braccie stretto al seno: questi poppa, mentre colla sinistra mano stringe un uccelletto, volgendo altrove la ricciuta testa. Le chiome della regale donna sono chiuse da un ricco panno i cui lmebi cadono sotto il manto. E' mezza figura, stante in piedi, con sfondo di camera, ove si aprono due finestrelle sopra la campagna. / Alto poll. 7. 1. largo poll. 4. 5."
2. Alberici and De Biasi 1984, no. 231.
3. Lambert 1999, no. 514.
4. Berenson 1938, no. 1015A, fig. 561; Petrioli Tofani 1992, no. 4.15.
5. Clark and Pedretti 1968–69, under no. RL 12568; Clark 1988 (1939), p. 89.
6. Fiorio 2000a, p. 82.
7. Clark and Pedretti 1968–69, under no. RL 12558.
8. Clark and Pedretti 1968–69, under no. RL 12569; cat. no. 20.
9. Brown 1990b, pp. 10–11.
10. Fondation Custodia, Paris, 2886; Byam Shaw 1983, no. 387, pl. 440.
11. Brown 1990b, p. 15 and fig. 13.
12. Brown 1990b, pp. 16–18.
13. Berenson 1938, no. 1084; Popham 1945, no. 157.
14. Clark and Pedretti 1968–69, no. RL 12505.
15. Vasari–Milanesi 1878–85, vol. 4, pp. 51–52; Brown 1991, p. 25.
16. Richter 1883, vol. 2, p. 363, no. 1458.
17. Suida 1929, pp. 57, 271, 287.
18. Brown 1991, p. 25 and nn. 12, 13.
19. Brown 1991, fig. 9.

LEONARDO DA VINCI

45. *Designs for a Nativity or Adoration of the Christ Child; Perspectival Projection* (recto) *Slight Doodles* (not by the artist; verso)

Metalpoint partly reworked with pen and dark brown ink on pink prepared paper; lines ruled with metalpoint (recto); pen and brown ink (verso), 194 × 163 mm (7⅝ × 6⅜ in.)
The Metropolitan Museum of Art, New York; Rogers Fund, 1917 17.142.1

PROVENANCE: Jacques-Guillaume Legrand, Paris (1743–1807); Joseph Allen Smith, London and Charleston (S.C.); possibly Thomas Sully, London and Philadelphia (1783–1872); possibly Sully passed it on to his grandson Francis T. S. Darley; Darley bequeathed it to

Thomas Nash, New York (1861–1926); purchased by The Metropolitan Museum of Art, New York, in 1917.

LITERATURE: Burroughs 1918; Möller 1918, pp. 219–20; Lieb 1919, pp. 259–60; Venturi 1920, p. 89; Berenson 1923, pp. 21, 29; Venturi 1925, p. 120; De Rinaldis 1926, p. 51; Commissione Vinciana 1928–, vol. 2, p. 25, pl. 40; Popp 1928, pp. 6, 37, no. 19; Sirén 1928, p. 41, pl. 54; Möller 1928–29, pp. 219–20; Suida 1929, pp. 51, 270, pl. 49; Borenius 1930; Bodmer 1931, pp. 149, 386; Seidlitz 1935, pl. 54; Berenson 1938, vol. 1, pp. 171, 172 n. 1, vol. 2, p. 116, vol. 3, fig. 484,

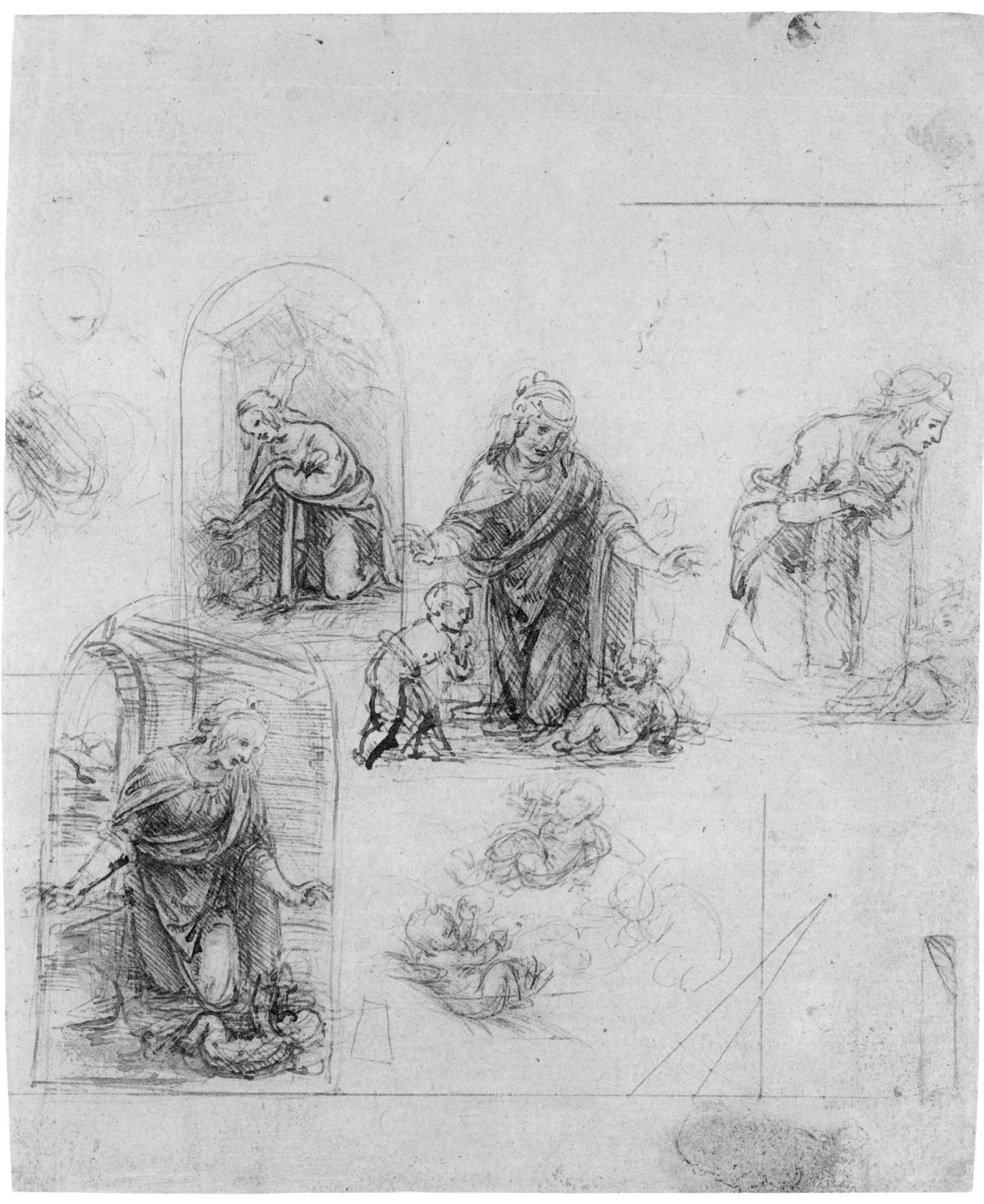

Cat. 45R *(actual size)*

no. 1049C; Tryon Art Gallery 1941, fig. 35; Metropolitan Museum of Art 1942, no. 8; Goldscheider 1943, no. 81; Douglas 1944, pp. 77–78; Metropolitan Museum of Art 1944, no. N.S.2; Heydenreich 1946, p. 182; Tietze 1947, pp. 42–43, pl. 159, no. 21; Philadelphia Museum of Art 1950, no. 21; Biblioteca Medicea Laurenziana 1952, p. 17, under no. 15; Heydenreich 1954, vol. 1, p. 60, vol. 2, p. 25, pl. 34; Castelfranco 1956, pp. 32, 58, pl. 43; Goldscheider 1959, p. 168, pl. 70; Rosenberg 1959, p. 22; Berenson 1961, vol. 1, pp. 251–52, vol. 2, p. 205, vol. 3, fig. 475, no. 1049C; Ames 1962, no. 153; De Tolnay 1962, pp. 110–11, fig. 13; Ames 1963, no. 153; Bean 1964, no. 3; Bean and Stampfle 1965, p. 26, no. 15; Castelfranco 1966, pp. 203, 212, figs. 23, 24; Bacall 1968, no. 3; Clark and Pedretti 1968–69, vol. 1, pp. 105–6,

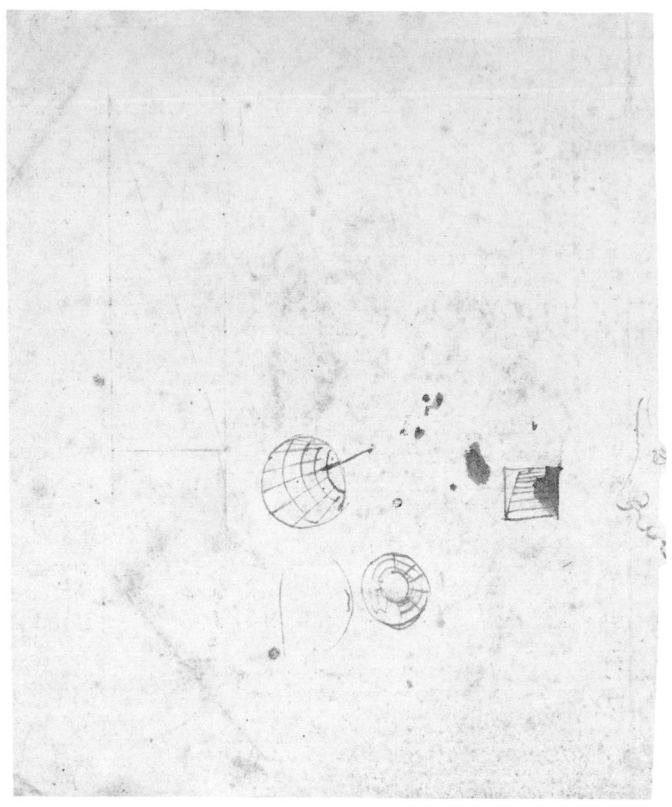

Cat. 45v

These sketches show a breathtaking sequence of invention on the theme of the Virgin kneeling in humility before the Christ Child, who lies on the ground. Leonardo adapted the general motif for the *Virgin of the Rocks* (versions in the Musée du Louvre, Paris [fig. 12], and National Gallery, London), in which the Virgin kneels facing the spectator, her right hand raised in blessing over the seated Infant Jesus. The composition seen here in the center is closest to the *Virgin of the Rocks*. These sketches seem more closely related, however, to an undocumented painting by Leonardo of a Nativity that includes the infant Saint John the Baptist, from about 1480–85, which must have been brought at least to the stage of a complete cartoon (full-scale drawing). Several contemporary copies of this composition survive; it is possible either that the painting was not executed or that it disappeared (fig. 150).[1]

under no. 12560; Metropolitan Museum of Art 1970, p. 222, fig. 218; Wasserman 1970, p. 198; Pedretti 1973a, pp. 59–60; Pedretti 1973b, pp. 13–17, 31–34, fig. 4; Gould 1975, pp. 75–76, fig. 35; Pedretti 1977, vol. 1, note to no. 86 and p. 378; Bean 1982, pp. 114–15, no. 107; De Vecchi 1982, p. 50, figs. 19, 20; Gigetta Dalli Regoli in Vezzosi 1982, pp. 27, 31 n. 24, fig. 84; Marani 1984, p. 13; Ottino della Chiesa 1985, p. 111; Carlo Pedretti in Galluzzi 1987, pp. 17–18; Clark 1988, pp. 90–93, fig. 34; Marani 1989, p. 114, under no. 23; Martin Clayton in Palazzo Grassi 1992, pp. 202–3, no. 7; Metropolitan Museum of Art 1993, p. 108; Pedretti and Trutty-Coohill 1993, pp. 40–42, no. 7; Marani 1994, p. 13; Pedretti 1994a, p. 96, fig. 8; Popham 1994, no. 159; Wiemers 1996, pp. 282–84, fig. 270; Arasse 1997, pp. 320, 322, fig. 219; Letze and Buchsteiner 1997, p. 72; Arasse 1998, pp. 319, 322, fig. 219; Echinger-Maurach 1998, pp. 278–82, fig. 7; Pietro C. Marani in Rossi and Rovetta 1998, pp. 26–27, under no. 1; Carmen C. Bambach and Lance Humphries in Gibbes Museum of Art 1999, pp. 183–87, under nos. 48–49, fig. 81; Villata 1999, p. 92, no. 107; Marani 2000b, pp. 79–83; Dalli Regoli, Nanni, and Natali 2001, pp. 19–20, fig. 13; Marani 2001a, pp. 118–19, no. 24.

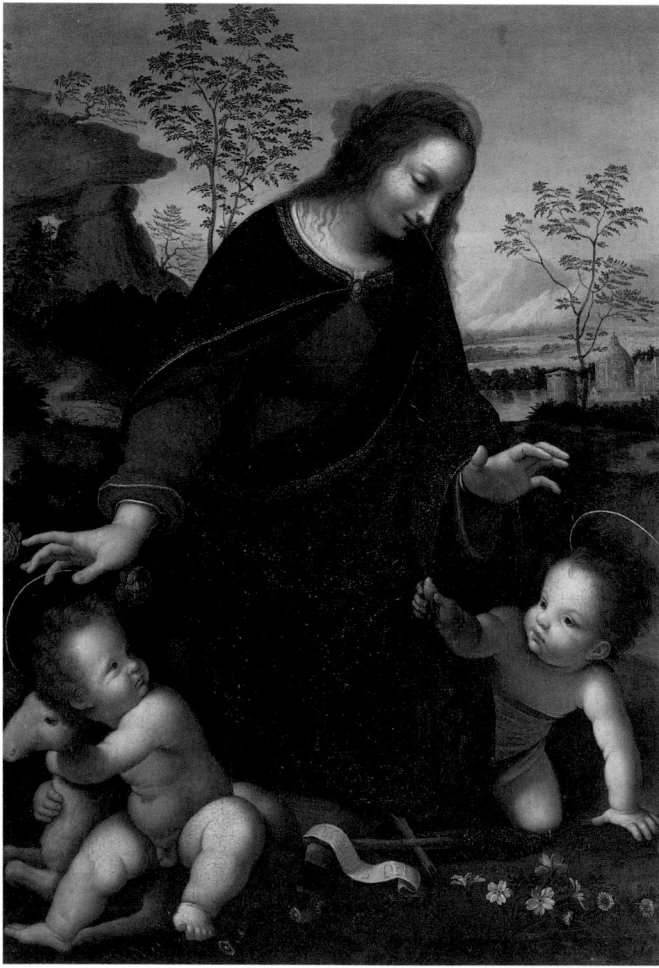

Fig. 150. Copy after Leonardo da Vinci, *Nativity*. Oil on wood, 73 × 50 cm. Galleria Palatina, Palazzo Pitti (on deposit from the Gallerie Fiorentine), Florence 1890 no. 1335

The Getty sketches of the Christ Child playing with the lamb of the Agnus Dei in catalogue number 94 may also have been intended for that lost project, though those drawings seem stylistically later. The exquisite motifs at the center and at the lower left corner of the Metropolitan Museum sheet, where the Virgin raises both hands in devotional wonder, are especially close to a small composition study on a sheet at Windsor (fig. 73). The Windsor sheet includes several architectural studies that seem to be connected to Leonardo's first work for the Milan Cathedral, about 1485.[2]

In the Metropolitan Museum sheet, Leonardo reworked the delicate effect of the metalpoint drawing with pen and dark ink to deepen the shadows. The artist was seeking a graphic equivalent for the rich effects of chiaroscuro that he was investigating in his paintings, of which the Louvre *Virgin of the Rocks* is a superb example. (One cannot produce much dark tone with the medium of metalpoint alone.) His sketches are dazzling for their fluency, energy, and variety of compositional motif. The geometric constructions at the lower right of the sheet apparently represent Leonardo's attempts to work out the perspective for the figures within the composition, with respect to the spectator's vantage point.

The controversy over the chronology of the Paris and London versions of the *Virgin of the Rocks* (particularly after the discovery of new documents in 1981) complicates the dating of the Metropolitan drawing; see Chronology. If, as has generally been assumed, the Paris *Virgin of the Rocks* was the picture commissioned in 1483 by the confraternity of the Immaculate Conception for the church of San Francesco in Milan (fig. 12), then the Metropolitan Museum drawing may be dated around that time. However, if the London version, which reveals all the hallmarks of Leonardo's late style about 1506, is the altarpiece commissioned in 1483, and the Paris picture was painted in Florence before the artist's departure for Milan, as Martin Davies and Kenneth Clark long ago contended, then the Metropolitan Museum drawing would have to date considerably earlier and from Leonardo's first Florentine period (before 1482/83). In contrast, Carlo Pedretti has proposed a dating on stylistic grounds to the late 1490s.

Presented as gifts by Jacques-Guillaume Legrand to Joseph Allen Smith before he resettled in Charleston, South Carolina, this vibrant sheet of compositional sketches and catalogue number 68 seem to have been among the earliest works by Leonardo to have entered a collection in the United States. When the pres-

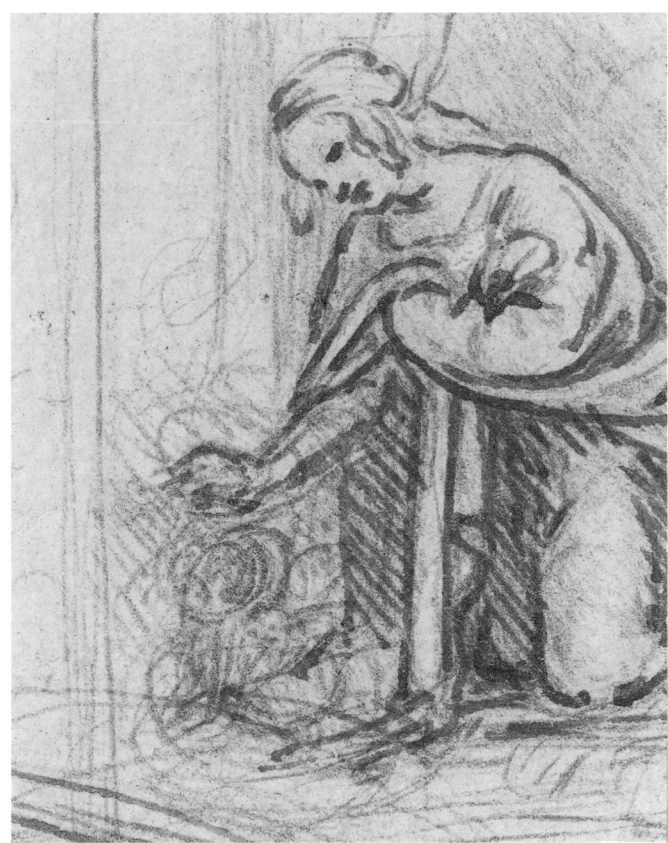

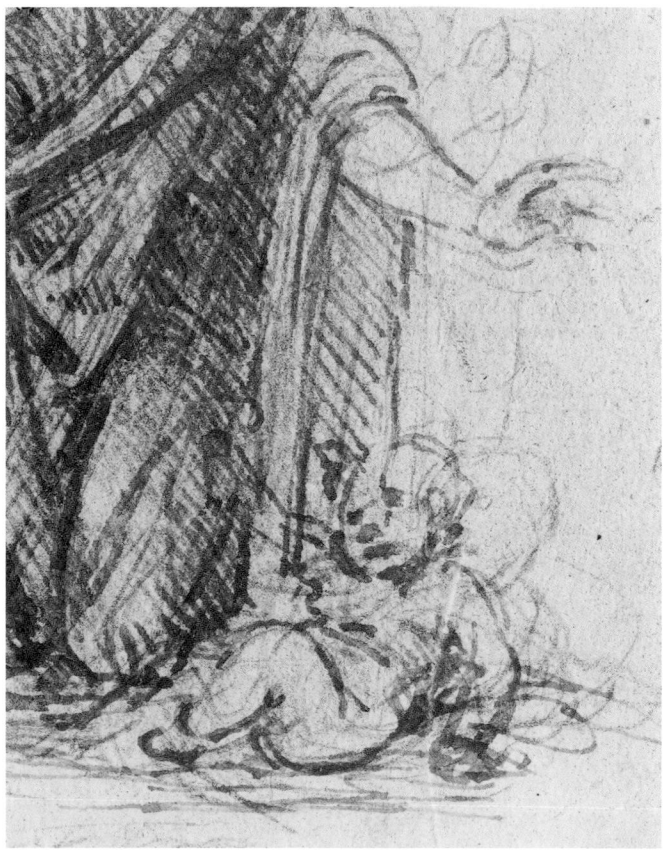

Cat. 45R *(details)*

369

ent sheet and catalogue number 68 were purchased by The Metropolitan Museum of Art from Thomas Nash in October 1917, they were still pasted onto pages of blue paper from the *album amicorum* that Legrand gave to Smith (Department of Drawings and Prints, The Metropolitan Museum of Art). A photograph from the 1950s records the drawing on Legrand's original blue paper mount (The Metropolitan Museum of Art, negative no. 37134). The mount bears only Legrand's succinct

inscription along the top, "De la main de Leonardo da Vinci" (from the hand of Leonardo da Vinci). As is suggested by the annotation on the mount of catalogue number 68, Joseph Allen Smith seems to have acquired the two sheets as early as 1801.

CCB

1. Other versions of the painting are discussed in Casa Buonarroti 1998, pp. 204–7, no. 3; Dalli Regoli, Nanni, and Natali 2001, pp. 122–25, no. 2.8.
2. Clark and Pedretti 1968–69, vol. 1, p. 105, under no. 12560.

LEONARDO DA VINCI

46. *Saint Jerome Praying in the Wilderness*

Unfinished painting in a mixed technique of oil and tempera on walnut wood, 102.8 × 73.5 cm (40½ × 28¹⁵⁄₁₆ in.)
Monumenti, Musei e Gallerie Pontificie, Vatican City 40337

PROVENANCE: After 1787–88 and before 1802–3, Angelica Kauffmann (1741–1807), Rome; probably after 1813, Cardinal Joseph Fesch (1763–1839), Rome; about 1845, Alessandro Aducci (a dealer), Rome; in dowry to his daughter on her marriage to Cesare Lanciani; until 1856 in deposit, Galleria del Monte di Pietà (Rome's official pawnshop); September 5, 1856, under Pope Pius IX, acquired by the Italian state for the Musei Vaticani as a result of a commission led by the painters Tommaso Minardi and Luigi Agricola for the Ministero del Commercio, Belle Arti e Lavori Pubblici.

LITERATURE: Amoretti 1804, p. 161; Fesch Sale 1841, p. 38, no. 750; Fesch Sale 1845, vol. 2, pp. 174–76, no. 838–750; Moroni 1858, p. 244; Wey 1878, pp. 31–32; Langl 1889, p. 298; Müller-Walde 1891, p. 126; Strzygowski 1895, pp. 166–68, 171, 173; Müntz 1898, vol. 1, pp. 79–81; Brockhaus 1902, p. 73; D'Achiardi 1913, pp. 69–70, no. 151, fig. 10; Thiis 1913, pp. 140–41, 147, 185, 229; D'Achiardi 1914, p. 25, pl. 18; Urbini 1919; Suida 1929, pp. 80–82; Bodmer 1931, pp. 18–19, 357; Meinhof 1931, fig. 1; Nogara 1931, pp. 243–45, figs. 1–4; Verga 1931, pp. 158, 245, 394, 667, 690, nos. 411, 763, 1402, 2503, 2594; Pinacoteca Vaticana 1934, p. 143, no. 337 (151), pl. 11; Clark 1939, pp. 33, 42, pl. 18; Goldscheider 1943, p. 37, nos. 97, 98; Giglioli 1944, p. 62, pls. 12, 13; Heydenreich 1954, vol. 1, pp. 11, 27–28, 33 n. 1, 180, vol. 2, pp. 15, iv, pl. 19; Suida 1954, pp. 318–19; Castelfranco 1956, pp. 26, 29–30, 32, 58, pl. 42; Pedretti 1957b, pp. 155–56; Heydenreich 1958b, cols. 562, 566, pl. 171; Réau 1958, pp. 743–44;

Goldscheider 1959, p. 173, nos. 76, 77; Francia 1960, pp. 61–62, pl. 227; Castelfranco 1966, pp. 76, 202, fig. 22; Ottino della Chiesa 1967, p. 92, no. 13, pls. 25, 26; Pedretti 1973a, pp. 53, 66, 68, pl. 10; Reti 1974, p. 14; Gould 1975, pp. 43–45, fig. 16; Ost 1975a, pls. 1–3, 17; Meller 1977; Royal Academy of Arts 1977, pp. 14–15; Pedretti 1979c, pp. 28, 30, 36, nos. 16, 17; Keele and Pedretti 1979–80, vol. 1, p. 28, fig. 14; Favaro 1980, p. 362; Nicodemi 1980a, pp. 30, 31, 48; Mancinelli and Nahmad 1981, pp. 38–39, no. 26; Pedretti 1981b, pp. 116–18, 280–82, no. 3, figs. 417–19; Bora 1982, p. 138; Fabrizio Mancinelli in Metropolitan Museum of Art 1983, pp. 156–57, no. 80; Cecchi 1984, pp. 59, 70 n. 10; Wasserman 1984, pp. 74–75, pl. 14; Brizio 1985; Redig De Campos 1985, pls. 18, 19; Pietrangeli 1987; Vannini 1987, p. 305; Fabrizio Mancinelli in Baldini 1988, nos. 20, 20a; Clark 1988, pp. 86–89, pl. 30; Kemp and Roberts 1989, p. 24, fig. 17; Marani 1989, pp. 50–52, no. 8; Pedretti 1989e; Frangi 1991, pp. 71–74, fig. 3; Martin Clayton in Palazzo Grassi 1992, p. 204; Parronchi 1992, pp. 33–36, figs. 1, 6; Pinacoteca Vaticana 1992, pp. 23, 60–61, 257, figs. pp. 47–49, 258–59; Colalucci 1993; Mancinelli 1993, pp. 106–8, no. 92; Marani 1994, pp. 11, 18, 23, 52–57, 147; Pedretti 1995c, p. 239; Pedretti 1995d; Clayton 1996–97, pp. 7, 28; Geraldine Bass in Pedretti 1996e; Pedretti 1996c, p. 128 n. 36; Pietrangeli 1996, pp. 150–51, no. 140; Campbell 1997, pp. 80, 82, 179 nn. 54–56, pl. 65; Letze and Buchsteiner 1997, pp. 38–39; Fairbrother and Ishikawa 1997–98, p. 26, fig. 7; Arasse 1998, pp. 344–50, 361, 427, figs. 238, 239; Brown 1998b, pp. 147, 150, fig. 140; Nesselrath 1999; Marani 2000b, pp. 95–101; Carlo Pedretti in Palazzo Reale 2000, p. 133, no. 3.31; Laurenza 2001, p. 41, fig. 30; Campbell 2002, pp. 125–27.

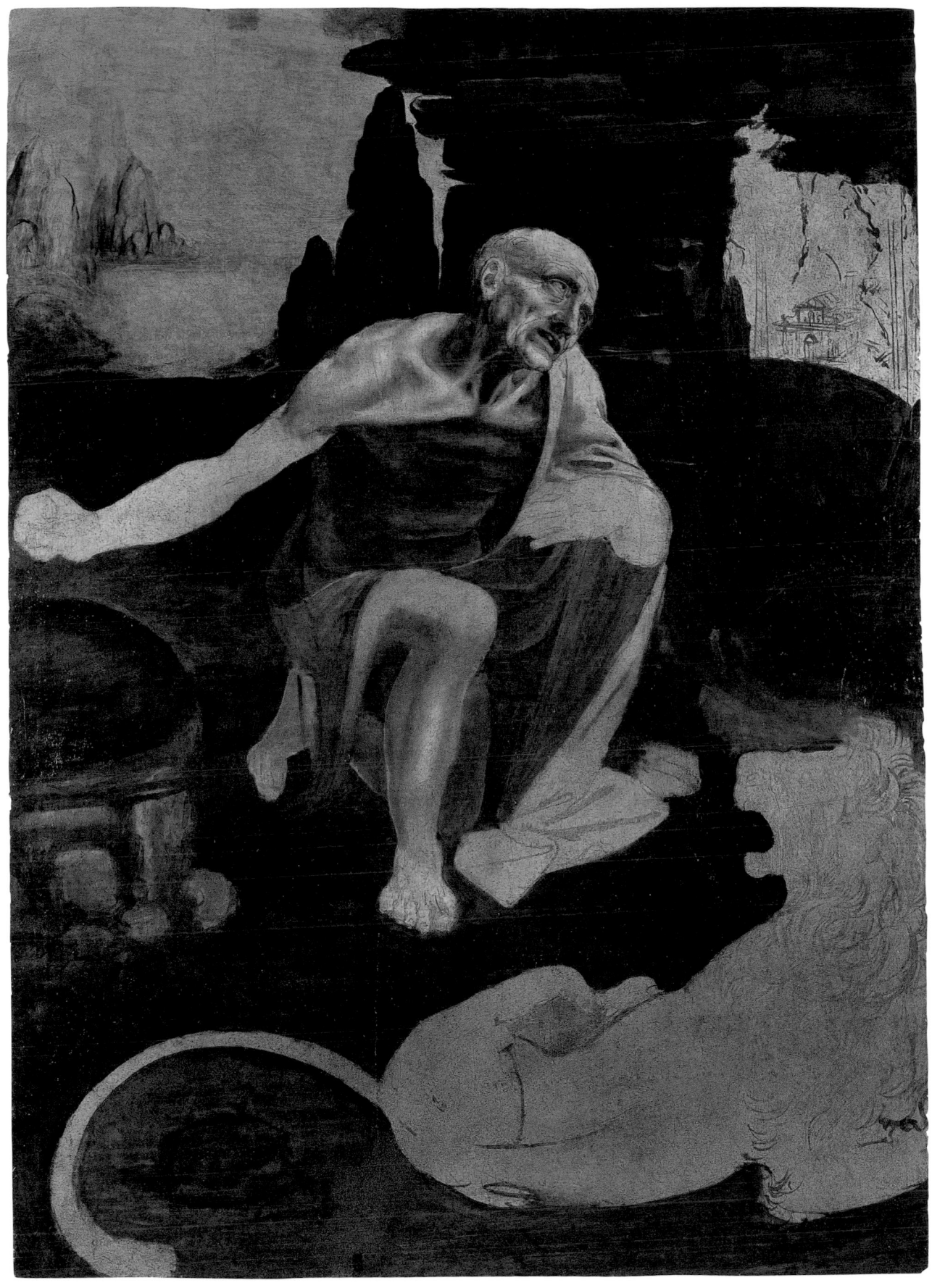

Cat. 46

For reasons that are still entirely unknown, Leonardo abandoned this monumental, exquisitely rendered portrayal of *Saint Jerome Praying in the Wilderness* at the very initial stages of painting. In its unfinished state, it is a virtual drawing on the wood panel, revealing a breathtaking glimpse of Leonardo's creative process at the stage between the final designs on paper and the painting surface. (Cartoons, or full-scale drawings, by Andrea del Verrocchio and Leonardo, also exhibited here, likewise illustrate this process; cat. nos. 1–3, 92.) The Vatican *Saint Jerome* and the earlier, larger *Adoration of the Magi* altarpiece (Galleria degli Uffizi, Florence), begun in March 1481 for the monks of San Donato a Scopeto in Florence, are the only securely attributed unfinished paintings by Leonardo.

The panel represents Saint Jerome (A.D. 347–420), the Latin Church Father and one of the original four Doctors of the Church, in a scene that was probably inspired by the fanciful story of the hermit's later life, as narrated in Jacobus de Voragine's *Golden Legend*.[1] According to this thirteenth-century work, Jerome had already lived in the desert and in the town of Bethlehem, "dwelling at the Lord's Crib like a domestic animal" in ascetic contemplation, when Pope Damasus committed him to the task of "putting the offices of the Church in order" in the Holy Land, for he was "skilled in the Latin, Greek, and Hebrew languages." "Thereafter, Jerome built his tomb at the mouth of a cave where Our Lord had lain, and was buried there, at the age of ninety-eight years and six months."[2] In Leonardo's Vatican panel, the penitent Jerome—old, gaunt, and nearly toothless— kneels in a rocky landscape. Although it is not entirely clear from the design or the tonal modeling in its present state, it is probable that much of the setting that is portrayed in Leonardo's panel is meant to represent the interior of a cave.[3] A similar setting is depicted in Leonardo's *Virgin of the Rocks* (Musée du Louvre, Paris; fig. 12), which constituted the central panel of an altarpiece that was contracted on April 25, 1483, and which was in progress until at least 1490.[4] In the Vatican panel, a stalactite formation on the upper right (which may or may not constitute an opening of a cave) frames a distant view of a church, which perhaps alludes to Jerome's work of standardizing the ritual of the mass in the Holy Land. The church itself is hastily sketched on the lead-white priming and is set deeply into the background, seen in sharp foreshortening. It exhibits a three-bay, pedimented façade that resembles the general style of Leon Battista Alberti's façade for Santa Maria Novella in Florence,

but that more closely reflects the style of Leonardo's Milanese drawings of churches (Paris Ms. B, fol. 11v; Gallerie dell'Accademia 238). On the upper left, a freely sketched mountain range in blue-greens recedes into the magical haze of the atmosphere, partly enclosing a plane of an evanescent blue-green form that may be a body of water or a valley. Here the increased transparency of the thin paint layer (due to the natural aging process of materials) reveals the design of a palm set against the sky, an early idea that Leonardo seems to have discarded. This upper left portion of the landscape with the monumental rocks seen against a distant plane and mountains recalls the effect of the grotto in the Louvre *Virgin of the Rocks*. A reconstruction of the complex perspective that forms the pictorial space of this *Saint Jerome* was proposed by Carlo Pedretti.[5]

The blocklike, compact form of the kneeling Jerome occupies the center of the Vatican composition and commands the space around him with his sweeping gesture. The saint stretches his right arm to the side, holding in his fist the rock with which (according to the *Golden Legend*) he beat his breast, and places his pointing left hand near his uncovered chest. Jerome's gesture enacts the motions of the soul (*i moti dell'anima*) with a grandeur of expression anticipating that of the apostles in Leonardo's mural of the *Last Supper* (Refectory of Santa Maria delle Grazie, Milan), begun in 1493–94. This figural type seems reminiscent of the *Anatomical Male Figure Showing the Heart, Lungs, and Main Arteries* (cat. no. 57), from 1488–90. The saint's poignant face offers the pictorial dimension of Leonardo's anatomical quest for the seat of the soul and the "meeting place of all the senses" (the *senso comune* of Aristotelian thought), in his studies of the human skull at Windsor (cat. no. 58), begun in April 1489. According to Leonardo's note on the Windsor study (cat. no. 58 recto), the mathematically proportioned chambers of the skull house the intellectual, psychological, and imaginative faculties of man, as well as his memory. The saint directs his gaze to the upper right at a crucifix, possibly marking the place where, according to the *Golden Legend*, he "built his tomb at the mouth of a cave where Our Lord had lain." The crucifix is sketchily outlined in a profile view, close to the right border of the panel. Reclining before Saint Jerome is the tame lion, his companion in the desert and one of the saint's main attributes according to a popular fable (the lion's miraculous deeds are also narrated in the *Golden Legend*).[6] The animal's elegant serpentine form, hardly more than a silhouette, defines much of the fore-

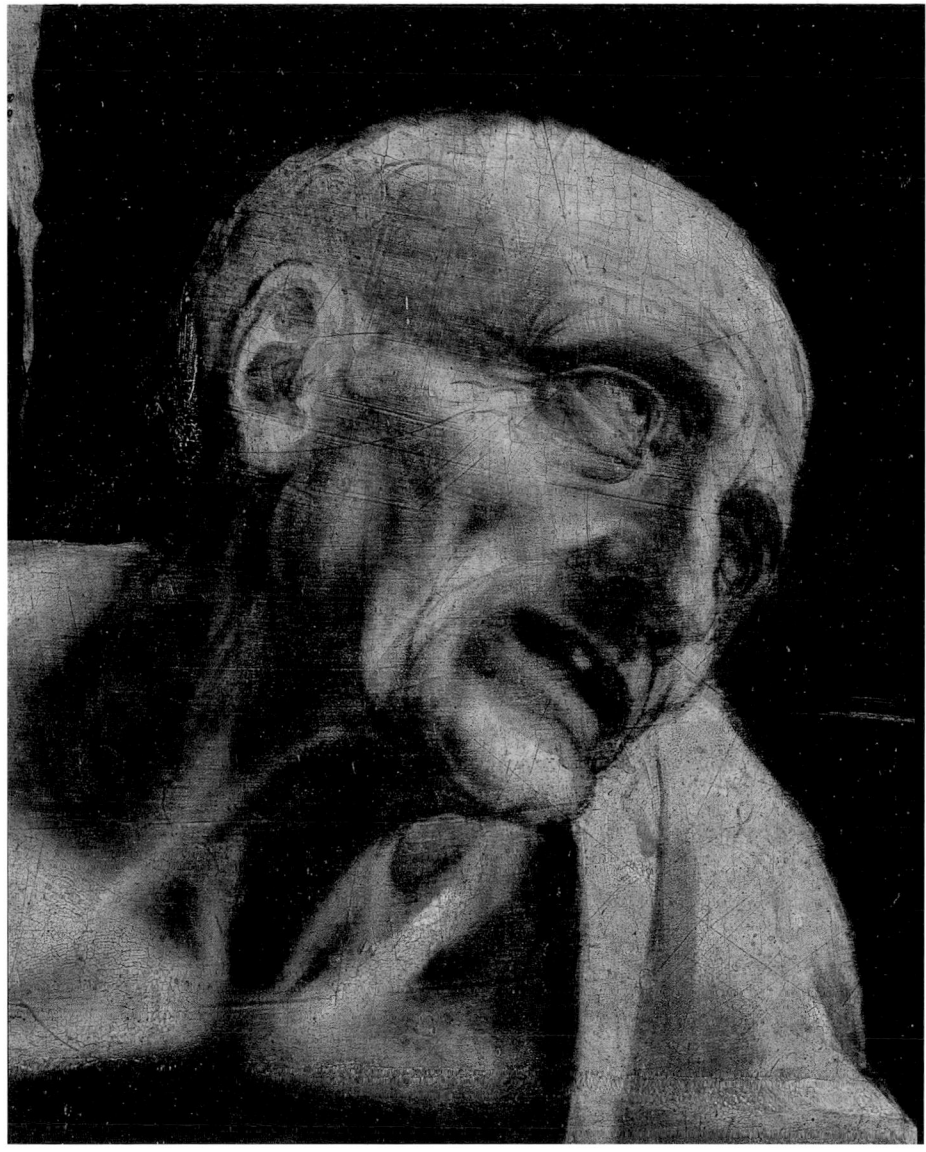

Cat. 46 *(detail)*

ground of the painting and mediates between the spectator and the figure of the venerable saint.

The most recent campaign of conservation and cleaning of the Vatican *Saint Jerome,* conducted by Gianluigi Colalucci (finished on January 20, 1993), brought important technical data to light.[7] Now in stable condition, the painting surface still bears traces of the layers of old discolored varnishes (which affect the chromatic scale of the original palette) and some repainting by early restorers. The support of the painting is a rectangular panel of walnut wood that was originally composed of two boards glued vertically; there are three butterfly inserts reinforcing the pieces (visible in X ray). There is no extant physical evidence to substantiate the hypothesis by Alessandro Parronchi that Leonardo originally conceived the composition of the Vatican *Saint Jerome* in the shape of a tondo that was subsequently cropped.[8] The wood on the back of the panel was thinned by early restorers to a 1.5 – 1.6 cm depth, and a rigid cradle was applied to the reverse in 1929. Leonardo used a priming of traditional gesso with the addition of lead white, which he applied in four layers, the first of these being quite liquid and containing a greater quantity of size. In many parts of the panel the underdrawing that he finely outlined with the tip of the brush appears directly applied to the lead-white priming. Only the head and shoulders of the saint, his bent muscular right leg (though not his foot), and the rocks in the atmospheric haze of the distance on the upper left seem to be worked up to an advanced stage of modeling, exhibiting also more finished passages in paint. In highlights, Leonardo seems to have used a blue (azurite) pigment mixed with iron oxide to produce pale tones tending to gray-blue. In shadows, he used a brown color (mostly iron oxide), and in many of these passages he also mixed the browns with green (copper carbonate).

From what can be discerned, Leonardo seems to have begun the Vatican *Saint Jerome* in a mixed technique that may not be very different from the practice seen in other late-fifteenth-century Italian panel paintings, particularly those that are associated with the more progressive workshops of Andrea del Verrocchio and the Pollaiuolo brothers, Antonio and Piero. The medium consists primarily of egg tempera with a high percentage of oil (*tempera grassa*), with many of the brown and green pigments, and the brown and delicate red lake glazes, diluted only with oil, which has soaked into the priming.[9] On the upper left, the sky and the mountains in the distance were painted with azurite blue. Although it has previously been stated that Leonardo spread many of the pigments on the upper left background with his fingers and the palm of his hand,[10] reexamination of one of the laboratory photographs (fig. 151) suggests another, more plausible scenario. It is clear that the artist's fingerprints press down on the paint and therefore sit on top of the long, mostly horizontal strokes, many of which seem to run from right to left.[11] Contrary to what is sometimes stated, the presence of artists' fingerprints is not uncommon in paintings of this period,[12] and they are found, for example, in the London (National Gallery) version of the *Virgin of the Rocks* by Leonardo and his workshop, especially in the flesh areas of the figures.[13] Fingerprints and handprints of various kinds have also been identified in Leonardo's *Portrait of Ginevra de' Benci* (fig. 67), from 1474–75, and in his *Portrait of Cecilia Gallerani* (*The Lady with the Ermine*, Muzeum Czartoryskich, Kraków), from 1488–90.[14] In the latter two instances, as David Bull has cogently observed, Leonardo seems to have dabbed his fingers after he had blended the colors with the brush in order to obtain a "soft focus" effect of modeling. Similarly in the case of the Vatican *Saint Jerome*, Leonardo may have painted primarily with the brush and then attempted a soft focus effect (though the work is unfinished); not coincidentally, the finger-

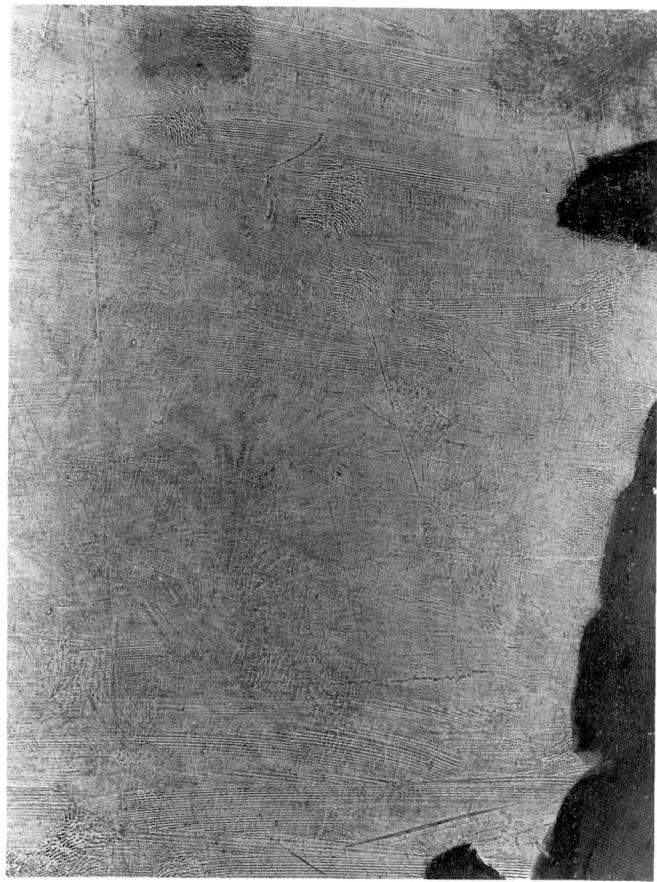

Fig. 151. Detail showing brushstrokes and fingerprints in cat. no. 46

prints appear in the area of the panel where the paint is most worked up.

In order to design the intricately detailed head of the saint—seen in a *sotto in sù* perspective (as if viewed from below) with a turn to the right—Leonardo appears to have first developed a cartoon (full-scale drawing) on paper. He would have pricked the outlines of the cartoon with a point (a needle or a stylus) and placed it on top of the primed surface of the panel, tapping a small bag filled with charcoal dust over the perforations. This technique, called pouncing (*spolvero*), created a dotted charcoal underdrawing on the primed panel underneath, and the dots served as a guide in outlining the forms freehand with the tip of the brush. The telltale *spolvero* dots from this process are visible only in some infrared fluorescence photographs of the saint's face, taken with a blue filter (fig. 152).[15] The same evidence of *spolvero* dots from a cartoon occurs in the *Portrait of Ginevra de' Benci* and in the *Portrait of Cecilia Gallerani* (*The Lady with the Ermine*),

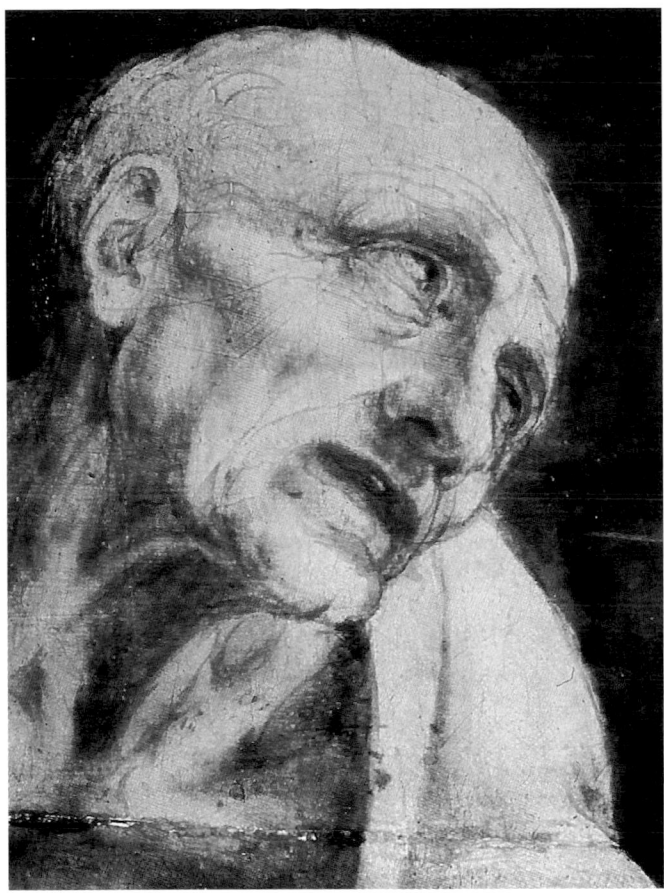

Fig. 152. Detail infrared photograph showing *spolvero* dots in cat. no. 46

especially in the women's faces.[16] Leonardo mentioned the use of pricked cartoons transferred by means of pouncing in a fragmentary note from 1490–92 in the Paris Ms. Λ (rarely cited by art historians) that also describes a technique of preparing a wood panel for oil painting. His note is not written according to an entirely consistent sequence of steps: it glosses over some details and conflates two separate steps (the preparation of the ground and the priming). His recipe for the priming of the painting surface is elaborate, and somewhat enigmatic:

> The panel should be cypress or pear or service tree or walnut. You must seal it over with mastic and twice-distilled turpentine and lead white or, if you like, lime,[17] and put it in a frame so that it may expand and shrink according to its moisture and dryness. Then give it [a coat] of aqua vitae[18] in which you have dissolved arsenic or [corrosive] sublimate, two or three times. Then apply boiled linseed oil in such a way that it may penetrate every part, and, before it is cold, rub it well with a cloth to dry it. Over this apply spirit varnish and lead white with a stick [brush?], then wash it with urine when it is dry.

Then pounce and outline your drawing finely and over it lay a priming of thirty parts of copper resinate and one more of copper resinate with two of yellow.[19]

Leonardo's authorship of the Vatican *Saint Jerome Praying in the Wilderness* has never been doubted,[20] and the panel is one of possibly five never-disputed paintings by the great master, the others being the *Adoration of the Magi*, the Louvre version of the *Virgin of the Rocks*, the *Last Supper*, and the *Mona Lisa*. The date and the circumstances of the Vatican panel's production, however, are entirely unknown. The picture is not clearly mentioned by any of the early biographers of the artist, nor is it specifically recorded in any other written source, until its dramatic reappearance in Rome in Angelica Kauffmann's collection (see below). The dating of the Vatican *Saint Jerome* is therefore extremely difficult, and proposals by scholars have ranged between 1473 and 1495, based on stylistic analysis. In the present author's opinion, a date about 1482–85 seems likely.

Most frequently, the picture has been assigned to Leonardo's first Florentine period, from 1478 to 1483, roughly contemporary with his similarly unfinished altarpiece for the monks of San Donato a Scopeto, the Uffizi *Adoration of the Magi*, which he began in March 1481 and left unfinished in 1482–83, when he departed Florence for Milan (figs. 10, 11, 140). Both works are in a state of mostly monochromatic underpainting, but their apparent similarity of technique and style may require some reassessment.[21] The foreshortened head of a bald, old man of similar anatomical type, but in much smaller scale and turned to the left (rather than to the right), appears among the onlookers on the right in the *Adoration of the Magi*. In contrast to the *Adoration*, however, the *Saint Jerome* exhibits a monumentality of figure and space that seems unprecedented in Florentine art. Moreover, the extraordinary individualization of anatomical detail in the portrayal of the head and body of the saint and the atmospheric handling of the pigments that can be discerned in the landscape and the figure are absent in the *Adoration*.

Nevertheless, a good deal of circumstantial evidence can be marshaled for a Florentine dating of the Vatican *Saint Jerome*. The general motif of the seminude, kneeling Saint Jerome in a landscape is anticipated in Florentine works from the 1460s to 1470s. Examples are the marble reliefs by Benedetto da Maiano (fig. 153), which is a recent discovery,[22] and by Desiderio da Settignano (National Gallery of Art, Washington, D.C.), as

375

well as a drawing (Uffizi, Florence, 101 F) and an engraving (Hind A.I.58) associated with Antonio del Pollaiuolo and his workshop. The ascetic, doleful, anatomical type of the saint is also generally evocative of works attributed to Andrea del Verrocchio and his *bottega*. Among the painted examples are a *Head of Saint Jerome* (Palazzo Pitti, Florence), a *Crucifixion* (formerly in Santa Maria e Angelo, Argiano), and a fresco fragment (Museo di San Domenico, Pistoia). Among sculpted examples are two expressive terracotta busts (Victoria and Albert Museum, London). Giorgio Vasari's biography of Verrocchio notes his terracotta "head of Saint Jerome, which is thought to be marvelous."[23] Leonardo himself alludes to "certain Saint Jeromes" in a long, cryptic list of works of art in his possession. It is not clear, however, whether these works, some of which apparently relate to his early activity in Florence, before 1482–83,[24] were drawings, paintings, or sculptures, and whether these were made by him or by other artists. Leonardo usually drafted such inventories when he was about to depart from a place and take objects with him. Geraldine Ruth Bass has proposed the possibility that the panel was commissioned by a confraternity of Saint Jerome in Florence.[25] Alessandro

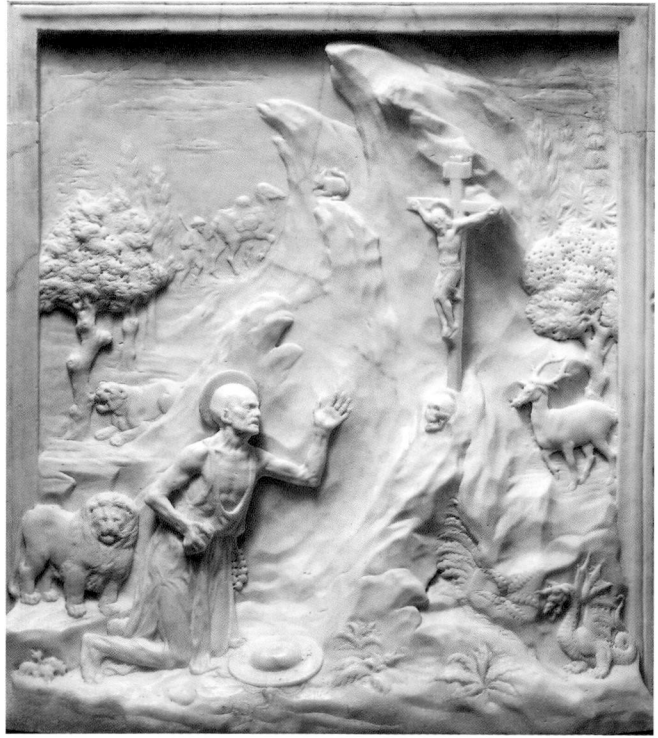

Fig. 153. Benedetto da Maiano, *Saint Jerome Praying in the Wilderness*. Marble relief, 42.5 × 38 cm. The Metropolitan Museum of Art, New York; Purchase, Rogers Fund and Lila Acheson Wallace Gift, 2001 2001.593

Cecchi has hypothesized that the patrons commissioning the *Saint Jerome* panel from Leonardo may have been the Benedictine monks of the Badia Fiorentina, based on the fact that Filippino Lippi (1457/58–1504), who appears to have been Leonardo's friend and who was his somewhat younger Florentine colleague, eventually painted a Saint Jerome for the Badia, the place where Leonardo's family also had its tomb.[26] There are indeed some echoes of Leonardo's Vatican composition in Filippino's kneeling *Saint Jerome* for the Badia (Uffizi, Florence, 8652), a taller, rectangular oil painting that may be dated about 1485–90.[27] The Filippinesque (rather than Leonardesque) conception reverberates further in a tondo from around 1490, attributed to Francesco Granacci (Collection of the Marquess of Bath, Longleat House, Warminster).[28] Filippino Lippi frequently seems to have picked up commissions to produce paintings for projects on which Leonardo had defaulted.[29] This appears to be true of the altarpiece that was planned for the Chapel of San Bernardo in the Palazzo della Signoria; Filippino's large painting is now in the Uffizi, signed and dated 1486.[30] It is also true of the *Adoration of the Magi* for the monks of San Donato a Scopeto; Filippino's panel, square like Leonardo's *Adoration*, is now in the Uffizi, signed and dated 1496.[31] The most precise Florentine evocation of Leonardo's composition, however, is found in a much later painted tondo, the *Penitent Saint Jerome* from the 1520s by Pontormo (Niedersächsisches Landesmuseum, Hannover), who, according to Vasari, was Leonardo's pupil before landing in Andrea del Sarto's workshop in 1512.[32] Pontormo's picture is in reverse design.

There is also plausible evidence for dating the Vatican panel in Leonardo's first Milanese period (from 1482–83 onward), beginning with the marked resemblance of the setting in the Vatican *Saint Jerome* to the Louvre *Virgin of the Rocks*.[33] Leonardo's panel may have responded to an iconographic tradition in North Italian art. For example, a similar compositional arrangement showing the seminude penitent saint kneeling before a rocky landscape is found in the small predella panel for the signed altarpiece of the Collegio di Spagna in Bologna by Marco Zoppo (1433–1478) that was painted in the 1450s.[34] Another very similar compositional arrangement of the figure in a landscape appears in Leonardo's own small sketch of a *Nativity* (fig. 73), which can be independently dated about 1485.[35] The Windsor sheet includes several engineering and architectural studies (better visible in ultraviolet

light, for they are extremely faint), which can be securely connected to Leonardo's first work for the Milan Cathedral in
1485–87.[36] Even scholars who have favored a Florentine date,
before 1482–83, for the *Saint Jerome* have noted its great stylistic similarities to works from the artist's Milanese years and
have also cited the various echoes of the figural type and the
composition in designs by artists working in Lombardy.[37]
Examples are Cesare da Sesto's painting (Nationalmuseum,
Stockholm) and preparatory pen-and-ink sketches (Windsor,
RL 064), as well as a metalpoint study by a Milanese artist
from the 1490s (Windsor, RL 12571 recto), in all of which the
figure appears in a pose similar to Leonardo's saint, though
seen from the back. A drawn copy of the latter Windsor sheet
also exists (Biblioteca Ambrosiana Cod. F 263 inf. 96, Milan).
The physical type of the figure is also used in a painted panel
of the *Penitent Saint Jerome* (Pinacoteca Ambrosiana, Milan, 83)
by one of Leonardo's followers, who in this case is sometimes
identified as Andrea Solario. The composition of Leonardo's
Saint Jerome is re-created fairly precisely in a recently discovered panel painting by an anonymous Lombard follower close
to Bramantino (Datrino Collection, Torre Canavese).[38] The
impact of Leonardo's composition in the Vatican panel is
strongest, however, on the anonymous author of the woodcut
frontispiece of the *Antiquarie prospetiche romane . . .* (fig. 154),
a poem that was written in 1496–98 with a gushing laudatory
dedication to Leonardo.[39] The woodcut on the frontispiece of
this *opusculum* offers the most exact reprise — that is extant —
of the pose in Leonardo's Vatican *Saint Jerome.* The meaning
of the nude figure is transformed: instead of the ascetic saint,
he embodies the ideal artist, kneeling before the classical ruins
of Rome with a compass and armillary sphere in his hands.
The author of the *Antiquarie prospetiche,* who called himself
only a "prospectivo Melanese depictore" (a Milanese painter
who was a master of perspective), has been variously
identified as Bramante or Bramantino.

According to an undocumented tradition, Leonardo's *Saint
Jerome* belonged to the Vatican collections early on, but this is
difficult to substantiate.[40] Early scholars also mistakenly
identified this work with a picture attributed to him in an inventory from 1680 of the Farnese collection in the Palazzo del
Giardino in Parma,[41] but the painting matching exactly the
description of that inventory has been recently identified.[42] The
first known modern owner of the Vatican painting was Angelica
Kauffmann (the discerning Swiss painter and art collector),

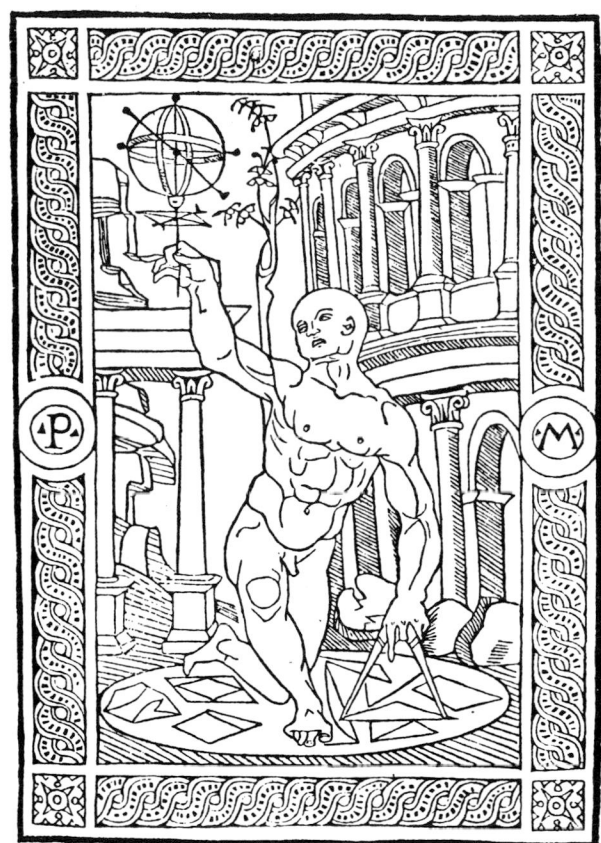

Fig. 154. Anonymous Italian artist ca. 1498, *Le antiquarie
prospetiche romane.* Woodcut. Biblioteca Casanatense, Rome

who probably acquired it after 1787–88, since it is not mentioned by her intimate friend Johann Wolfgang von Goethe in
his *Italienische Reise* (Goethe stopped in Rome in 1787–88,
during his journey to Italy in 1786–88). She probably acquired
the painting before 1802–3, since the Vatican *Saint Jerome*
may be identified with an unspecific reference to a "painting
thought to be by [*creduto di*] Leonardo da Vinci"; this wording
appears in an official declaration made by her cousin Johann
Kauffmann in 1802 to the Italian state (this was mandated by
law, and Angelica was absent from Rome).[43] A year later, on
June 17, 1803, the picture appears fully described in the Swiss
painter's last will and testament, drafted by the Roman notary
public Bartolo.[44] Kauffmann's wish — at least in 1803 — was for
the majority of her paintings to be sold. The erudite Leonardo
scholar Carlo Amoretti seems to have been the first modern
author to publish a reference to the picture in Kauffmann's collection in his groundbreaking *Memorie storiche* (Milan, 1804),
though he may not have seen the work firsthand.[45]

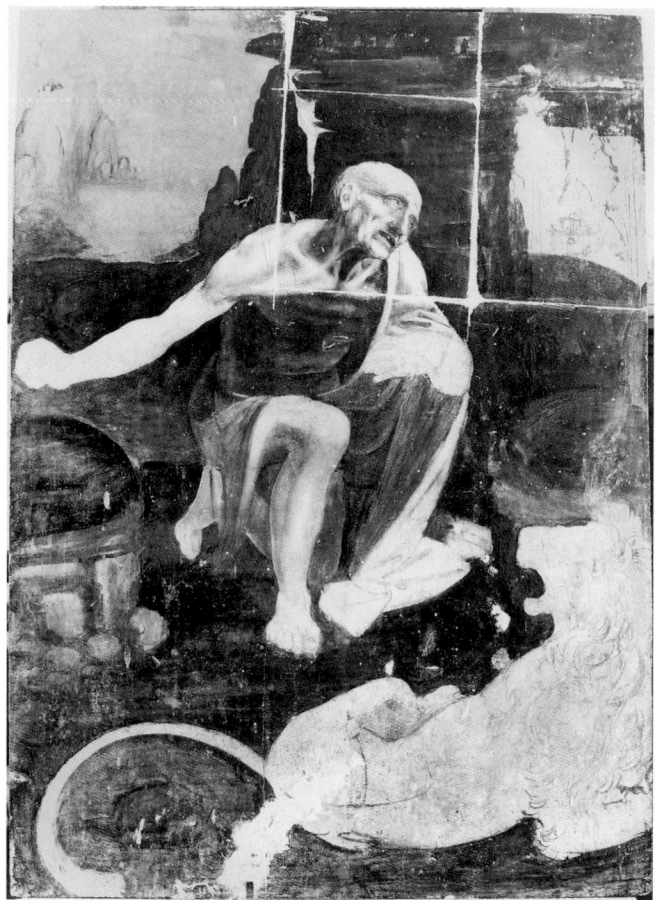

Fig. 155. *Saint Jerome*. Cat. no. 46 before inpainting of pigment losses (during restoration) in 1993

ture, the story of the recovery of the two portions is not related in the cardinal's posthumous biography by the Abbé J. B. Lyonnet in 1841, while some of the incidental details regarding precisely what the separated panels depicted are not entirely comprehensible.[47] The physical evidence corroborates that the wood panel was finely sawn into pieces at an unknown date (perhaps in the early nineteenth century; fig. 155). This operation was apparently done in order to extract the head of the saint, the most compelling detail of the composition, and possibly the most commercially valuable. To judge from the disposition of the seams on the upper right of the panel, it is likely that the removal of the saint's head in a square portion led to a further division of at least two rectangular pieces, one containing the rocks above the saint's head, and another including the landscape on the right side. This operation seems to have been performed rather neatly, for the rejoined panel exhibits relatively few losses of original paint considering the ordeal.[48] The reverse of the Saint Jerome panel is said to bear the marks from cuts by a shoemaker's knife.[49] After the death of Cardinal Fesch in 1839, it eluded sale at the auction of his estate in 1841 (the prelate's collection was to be sold in block). At the Fesch auction in 1845, the picture seems to have been bought privately and shortly thereafter fell into the hands of the art dealer Alessandro Aducci.[50] Leonardo's *Saint Jerome* was finally acquired by the Italian state for the Vatican Museums on September 5, 1856,[51] in large part due to the long-standing efforts of a commission that included the painters Tommaso Minardi and Luigi Agricola.

CCB

After Angelica Kauffmann's death in 1807, the history of Leonardo's painting takes on the overtones of legend. Cardinal Joseph Fesch, the influential uncle of Napoleon and stepbrother of his mother, Maria Letizia Ramolino, is said to have acquired the divided pieces of Leonardo's painting on two separate occasions. Fesch was in Rome as early as 1803 (when he was made cardinal), and then repeatedly thereafter during his prominent political career. During the twilight years and after the abdication of Napoleon he took up more permanent residence in the city, first at the Palazzo Falconieri on Via Giulia on May 12, 1813, and later at the nearby Palazzo Ricci. Anecdote has it that he found the greater part of the panel first in the shop of a *rigattiere* (junk or antiques dealer), who used the fragment as the door for a cupboard (or chest). A few years later, another part seems to have turned up in the shop of the cardinal's shoemaker, who was using the board as the seat for his stool.[46] Contrary to some accounts in the scholarly litera-

1. Voragine 1969, pp. 587–92.
2. Voragine 1969, pp. 589–91.
3. Mancinelli 1993, p. 107.
4. See Chronology.
5. Pedretti 1981b, p. 281.
6. Voragine 1969, pp. 589–90.
7. The following summary is based on my conversations with George Bisacca, Conservator of Paintings, The Metropolitan Museum of Art, and on the unpublished, detailed conservation report by Gianluigi Colalucci, "Nota sulla tecnica, lo stato di conservazione e intervento (Protocolo 1339/93)," made available to me by Francesco Buranelli. It is supplemented by the abbreviated publication of those findings in Colalucci 1993 (with an account of the conservation treatment).
8. Parronchi 1992, pp. 33–36.
9. Colalucci 1993, p. 109.
10. Colalucci 1993, p. 109; Marani 2000b, pp. 95–101.
11. Confirmed by Claudio Rossi de Gasperis, Restorer of Paintings, Vatican Museums (May 24, 2002).
12. George Bisacca points to, among others, the example of Giovanni Bellini's *Madonna and Child* (Metropolitan Museum of Art, 08.183.1).

13. Davies 1986, pp. 262, 271 n. 4.

14. Gibson 1991; Bull 1992, pp. 70, 80–82.

15. Hitherto unnoticed, and confirmed by Claudio Rossi de Gasperis (May 24, 2002). The *spolvero* dots in the underdrawing are less visible in infrared fluorescence with a yellow filter.

16. Gibson 1991, pp. 164; David Bull in Fabjan and Marani 1998–99, pp. 83–90.

17. Leonardo used the word *calcina,* which may be a colloquialism for calcium sulfate or calcium carbonate. The term is here translated as "lime" (in Italian, *calce*).

18. Leonardo's word *acquavite* (a distilled vine residue) may refer to a common household alcohol liquid, such as, for example, *grappa* for drinking.

19. Translated with the assistance of George Bisacca. Paris Ms. A, fol. 1r; Richter 1970, vol. 1, p. 362, no. 628: "Il legnio sarà d'arcipresso o pero o sorbo o noce, il quale salderai co[n] mastico e treme[n]tina seco[n]da destillata . e biacca o vuoi calcina, e metti i[n] telaio i[n] modo possa cresciere e discresciere seco[n]do l'umido o secco; dipoi li dà con acquavite . , che vi sia dentro disoluto arsenico o solimato 2 o 3 volte, di poi da olio di lino bolito in modo penitri per tutto, e inanzi si freddi fregalo bene con v[n] panno in modo parrà ascivtto . , e dalli di sopra vernice liquida e biacca colla stecca, poi laua con orina, qua[n]do è ascivtta . ; e poi spoluerezza e proffila il tuo disegno sottilme[n]te e dà di sopra l'imprimitura di 30 parti di uerde rame e vna di uerderame e 2 di giallo."

20. Except in the unintelligent article in 1919 by Giulio Urbini, who doubted the *Saint Jerome* along with other canonical paintings by the great artist.

21. As pointed out in Suida 1929, pp. 80–82; but Suida 1954, p. 318, drastically reversed his opinion on the dating of the Vatican *Saint Jerome.* Recent evidence uncovered by Maurizio Seracini (Editech, Florence) in diagnostic tests of the Uffizi *Adoration of the Magi* indicates that Leonardo's brush drawing on this panel was extensively reinforced by a later hand. Thus, a degree of caution seems necessary in statements regarding the picture's style and technique.

22. See Draper 2002, p. 14.

23. Vasari–Milanesi 1906, vol. 3, p. 375: "ed alcune cose di terra . . . una testa di San Girolamo, che è tenuta maravigliosa."

24. C.A., fol. 888r (formerly fol. 324r); Richter 1970, vol. 1, p. 387, no. 680; Pedretti 1977, vol. 1, p. 388, no. 680: "cierti sa[n] Girolami."

25. Cited in Pedretti 1995c, p. 239, and Pedretti 1996e.

26. Cecchi 1984, pp. 59, 70 n. 10.

27. On Filippino's Badia *Saint Jerome,* see Uffizi 1979, p. 332, no. P866; Berti and Baldini 1991, pp. 172–73, 188. Although the width of the two panels is similar (within a 1.5 cm difference), Leonardo's *Saint Jerome* is shorter by about 33 cm.

28. Everett Fahy in Barocchi 1992, pp. 49–52, no. 11.

29. Cecchi 1984, pp. 59–84.

30. On the succession from Leonardo to Filippino Lippi in the Chapel of San Bernardo commission, see the account of about 1540 in the anonymous Codice Magliabechiano (Anonimo Gaddiano; transcribed in Frey 1892, p. 116; Vecce 1998, p. 362) and Marani 1989, pp. 125–27.

31. According to the somewhat garbled account in Vasari–Milanesi 1906, vol. 4, p. 38 (which has led to heated discussion by art historians), Filippino Lippi reentered Leonardo's career at the time that the great master displayed his cartoon of the *Virgin and Child with Saint Anne and a Lamb* in his quarters at Santissima Annunziata in Florence, soon after he returned to the city in 1500–1501.

32. Vasari–Milanesi 1906, vol. 4, p. 246.

33. Strzygowski 1895, pp. 166–67; Goldscheider 1959, pp. 173–74, nos. 76–77.

34. Campbell 1997, pp. 80–82, 179 nn. 54–56; Campbell 2002, pp. 125–27.

35. Müller-Walde 1891, p. 126; Strzygowski 1895, pp. 167–68; Martin Clayton in Palazzo Grassi 1992, p. 204, no. 8.

36. Clark and Pedretti 1968–69, vol. 1, p. 105, under no. 12560.

37. Marani 1989, pp. 50–52, no. 8.

38. This picture was first published by Carlo Pedretti, though without the stylistic connection to Bramantino here proposed (see Palazzo Reale 2000, p. 133, no. 3.31).

39. The *Antiquarie prospetiche* must have been written between 1496 and 1498, for the "Genoese cardinal" to whom the author refers is Cardinal Campofregoso of Genoa, who occupied the house of Cardinal Giuliano della Rovere (later Pope Julius II) from 1496 until his death in 1498. See Pedretti 1981b; Brown 1986; Agosti 1990, pp. 103–33; Robertson 1990; Pedretti 1991a.

40. D'Achiardi 1913; D'Achiardi 1914; Suida 1929, p. 80.

41. Palazzo del Giardino, "Terza camera detta della Madonna della Gatta," fol. 12v, no. 110; transcribed in Bertini 1987, p. 95, no. 31.

42. See Pierluigi Leone de Castris in Spinosa 1995, p. 46. The canvas, attributed to Giovan Girolamo Savoldo, portrays the figure of Saint Jerome in half length with a book (Museo Nazionale di Capodimonte, Naples).

43. Redig De Campos 1985; Pietrangeli 1987, p. 104.

44. Angelica Kauffmann's testament is transcribed in Langl 1889 (p. 298): "Ein anderes schönes auf eine Tafel gemaltes Gemälde, welches den hl. Hieronimus in der Wildniß vorstellet, eine ganz halb natürliche Figur vor dem Kreuze knieend, es wurde dießes Gemälde von mir für einen Leonard da Vinzi erhalten, ein dieses Autors würdiges sehr gut bewahrtes Stük."

45. Hitherto unnoticed, Amoretti 1804, p. 161: "e la sig. Kauffmann ha un San Gerolamo, del quale un disegno è quello che ha pubblicato Gerli (Tav. 31)." The reproductive engraving by Carlo Giuseppe Gerli that Amoretti mentioned is after another composition, the drawn copy in the Biblioteca Ambrosiana Cod. F 263 inf. 96, which is after the original drawing by a Milanese artist of the 1490s (Windsor, RL 12571 recto). Both drawings and Gerli's print show the figure in a pose similar to that of Leonardo's Saint Jerome, but seen from the back. This fact does not cast doubts on Kauffmann's ownership of Leonardo's Vatican *Saint Jerome,* but suggests that the Milanese Amoretti probably wrote from hearsay, rather than from firsthand knowledge.

46. D'Achiardi 1914, p. 25; Redig De Campos 1985; Pietrangeli 1987, pp. 106–7; Mancinelli 1993, p. 106.

47. A detailed direct description of the cardinal's discovery is quoted in Vannini 1987, pp. 305, 308 n. 19; and Mancinelli 1993, p. 106, but contrary to their citation it does not appear in Lyonnet 1841, vol. 1, pp. 72–73, vol. 2, pp. 703–9. Lyonnet mentions two paintings by Leonardo incidentally, neither of which is the *Saint Jerome.*

48. Mancinelli 1993, pp. 106–8; Colalucci 1993; Nesselrath 1999, p. 552, no. 326.

49. Redig De Campos 1985.

50. More detailed (though somewhat contradictory) accounts are given in Redig De Campos 1985; Pietrangeli 1987; Mancinelli 1993, p. 106.

51. Document of acquisition discovered by Francesco Buranelli (Pietrangeli 1987, pp. 108–10).

379

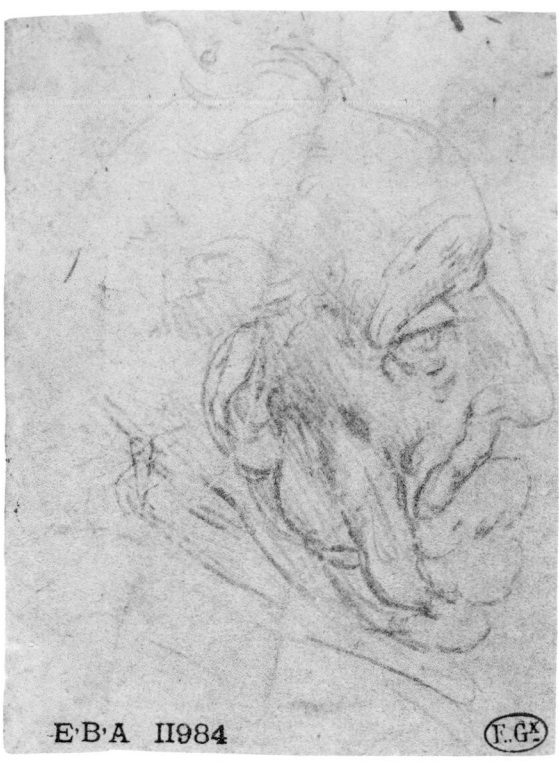

Cat. 47R *(actual size)*

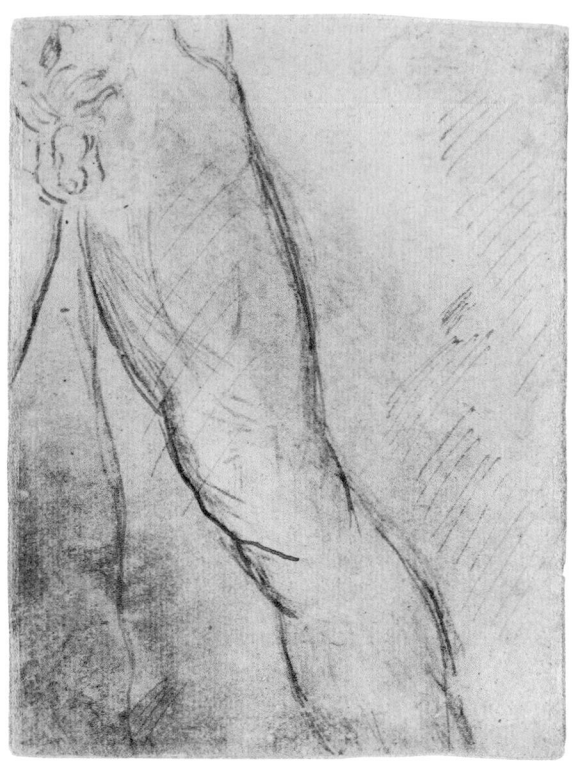

Cat. 47V *(actual size)*

LEONARDO DA VINCI

47. *Old Man in Profile Turning to the Right* (recto) *Fragment of a Nude Man* (verso)

Metalpoint on lightly prepared pink-ocher paper (recto), pen and brown ink over metalpoint (verso), 98 × 75 mm (3 ⅞ × 3 in.); diagonal vertical fold; pink-ocher color of paper more intense on verso than on recto
Inscribed on two joined mount fragments: *Léonard de Vinci / Collection Gatteaux; pourrait être de Léonard d'après M. le Dr. Moeller; Dessin original de Léonard Emil Möller*
École Nationale Supérieure des Beaux-Arts, Paris EBA 426

PROVENANCE: Édouard Gatteaux (Lugt 852); 1883, bequest to the École Nationale Supérieure des Beaux-Arts (mark EBA 11984; not in Lugt).

LITERATURE: Palazzo Grassi 1992, no. 50; Pedretti 1992a, fig. 1 (recto), fig. 3 (verso); Laurenza 1997, p. 283, fig. 9, p. 285; Musée d'Art et d'Histoire, Geneva 1998, no. 183 (verso).

Until the 1992 exhibition at the Palazzo Grassi in Venice, when this drawing was shown as a work by Leonardo for the first time since its acquisition by the École des Beaux-Arts in 1883, its authenticity had always been doubted. There

is a copy of it in the Spencer Collection at the New York Public Library (2.18).[1] In the Venice exhibition, Luisa Cogliati Arano grouped it with "caricatures" rather than "classical profiles" and linked it to a series of portraits of middle-aged men in the Biblioteca Ambrosiana, Milan.[2] These small drawings, almost all executed in pen and brown ink, were dated by Cogliati Arano to 1485–90 and by Carlo Pedretti to a slightly earlier date, about 1480. The present drawing is the only one among these male portraits to be executed in metalpoint on prepared paper, which would tend to support Pedretti's dating. In addition, Pedretti argued that the study of a leg on the verso, apparently original, should be linked to several sheets in the Royal Library at Windsor and the Biblioteca Reale in Turin that were executed about 1487–90.[3] Within the group of middle-aged male portraits, the closest analogy to the present sheet is a study of a profile in which the nose, mouth, and chin, though less prominent than in this work, are treated the same way, displaying, through increasingly loose strokes,

380

attention to the passage of time and to the gradual deterioration of a face or a gaze marked by fatigue, then old age.[4] "Onde tal membrificazione tra pel continuo peso della pelle e pel gran umore, si vengono alungare e discostare la pelle da' muscoli e da l'ossa, e comporre diversi sacchi pieni di rappe e grinze," wrote Leonardo.[5]

Cogliati Arano related these Leonardesque sheets from the Ambrosiana to the painter's writings on time, endurance, and the power of the mind as the pledge for survival, as they are recorded in the Codex Trivulzianus, compiled during 1487–88.[6] Leonardo was thirty-five. This is the very first manuscript—the one, says André Chastel, "that begins the written works . . . and marks his entirely modern preoccupation with noting down, pell-mell, ideas, quotations, sketches, and studies."[7] Cogliati Arano went so far as to propose that we consider the above-mentioned Ambrosiana drawing an illustration of a phrase erected into a maxim on the verso of a sheet in the Codex Atlanticus: "Si come il ferro s'arrugginisce sanza esercizio e l'acqua si putrefa o nel freddo s'addiaccia, cosi lo'ngegno sanza esercizio si guasta."[8] "The mind deteriorates without exercise" applies to the face in the École des Beaux-Arts drawing, for the intensity of the eye's gaze mutely contradicts the facial deformations.

Domenico Laurenza, in his *Sur les traces de patognomica chez Léonard* (1997)—pathognomy is the expression of emotions in the body and face—focused on portions of the painter's notes and sketches that deal with old age. Leonardo approached the concept the same way the classical Greek philosophers did, as "part of the set of somatic modifications that, across the different ages of life, constitute a natural event."[9] According to Laurenza, Leonardo, following the medical theories of his time, contrasted youth, maturity, and old age in terms of different temperaments: "sanguine," "choleric," and, for old age, "melancholic" and "phlegmatic." In the group of drawings in the Ambrosiana and, by association, in the drawing in the École des Beaux-Arts, the expression of psychic and physical weakness is transcribed as a sort of excess, which, in the harshness of the artist's line, manages to preserve in this pensive face something of the energy that marks the so-called classic or ideal portraits—further manifestation of the precariousness of classification of the different moods considered by Leonardo.   FV

1. Pedretti 1992a and fig. 2; Forcione essay in this volume.
2. Cogliati Arano in Palazzo Grassi 1992, p. 310.
3. Pedretti 1992a, p. 112 n. 1, figs. 5, 8–10.
4. Cod. F. 263 inf. 94; Cogliati Arano 1982, no. 7.
5. *Libro di pittura* 1995, p. 339; quoted in Laurenza 1997, p. 285.
6. Cogliati Arano 1991, p. 6.
7. "[Q]ui engage l'oeuvre écrite . . . et marque sa préoccupation, toute moderne, de noter pêle-mêle, idées, citations, esquisses, études"; Chastel 1980, quoted in Cogliati Arano 1991, p. 6 n. 3.
8. Marinoni 2000, fol. 785b verso; Cogliati Arano 1991, p. 7.
9. "[P]artie de l'ensemble des modifications somatiques qui, à travers les différents âges de la vie, constituent un événement naturel"; Laurenza 1997, p. 282.

LEONARDO DA VINCI

48. *Studies of Weapons*

Metalpoint and pen and brown ink on blue prepared paper, partly reworked in pen and brown ink, 209 × 308 mm (8¼ × 12⅛ in.); vertical center fold with perforations; sketch in lower right corner in another hand; trace of fold from papermaking process on lower edge of sheet

Inscribed in pen and brown ink, in right-to-left script, on right folio, top to bottom: *Prima tona* [?] / *fronda* / *mazza di ferro* / *e scoppietto* / *d'osso* / *d'acciaio* / *di legno* / *per passare un fiume a ca* / *vallo e con uno in groppa* / *da nor* [?] *la spada*; on left folio, top to bottom: *somma scoppietto 100* / *Questo si dimanda cacciafrusto e fassi bracci 3.* / *Gitta grosse pietre a lontano 2/3 della distanzia*

Département des Arts Graphiques du Musée du Louvre, Paris 2260

PROVENANCE: Giuseppe Vallardi (L. 1223, in green on verso); 1856, acquired by the Musée du Louvre; museum mark (Lugt 1886a).

LITERATURE: Vallardi 1855, p. 2, fol. 2; Müntz 1899, p. 521, under no. 61; Seidlitz 1909, vol. 1, p. 292; Louvre 1919, no. 27; Commissione Vinciana 1928– , vol. 3, pp. 17, 21, pl. 71; Bodmer 1931, p. 394, fig. 197; Berenson 1938, vol. 2, no. 1065a; Popham 1945, pp. 83, 85, no. 307; Amboise 1952; Biblioteca Medicea Laurenziana 1952, no. 29; Florisoone and Bacou 1952, no. 16; Palais de la Découverte 1952–53, p. 34; Tours 1956, no. 25; Sérullaz 1965, no. 221; Vertova 1976, under no. 35; Pedretti 1977, p. 95, no. 39; Pedretti and Roberts 1981–82, p. 125; Béguin 1983, p. 84; Louvre 1986, no. 72; Kemp and Roberts 1989, no. 67; Palazzo Grassi 1992, no. 10; Arasse 1997, p. 235, fig. 165.

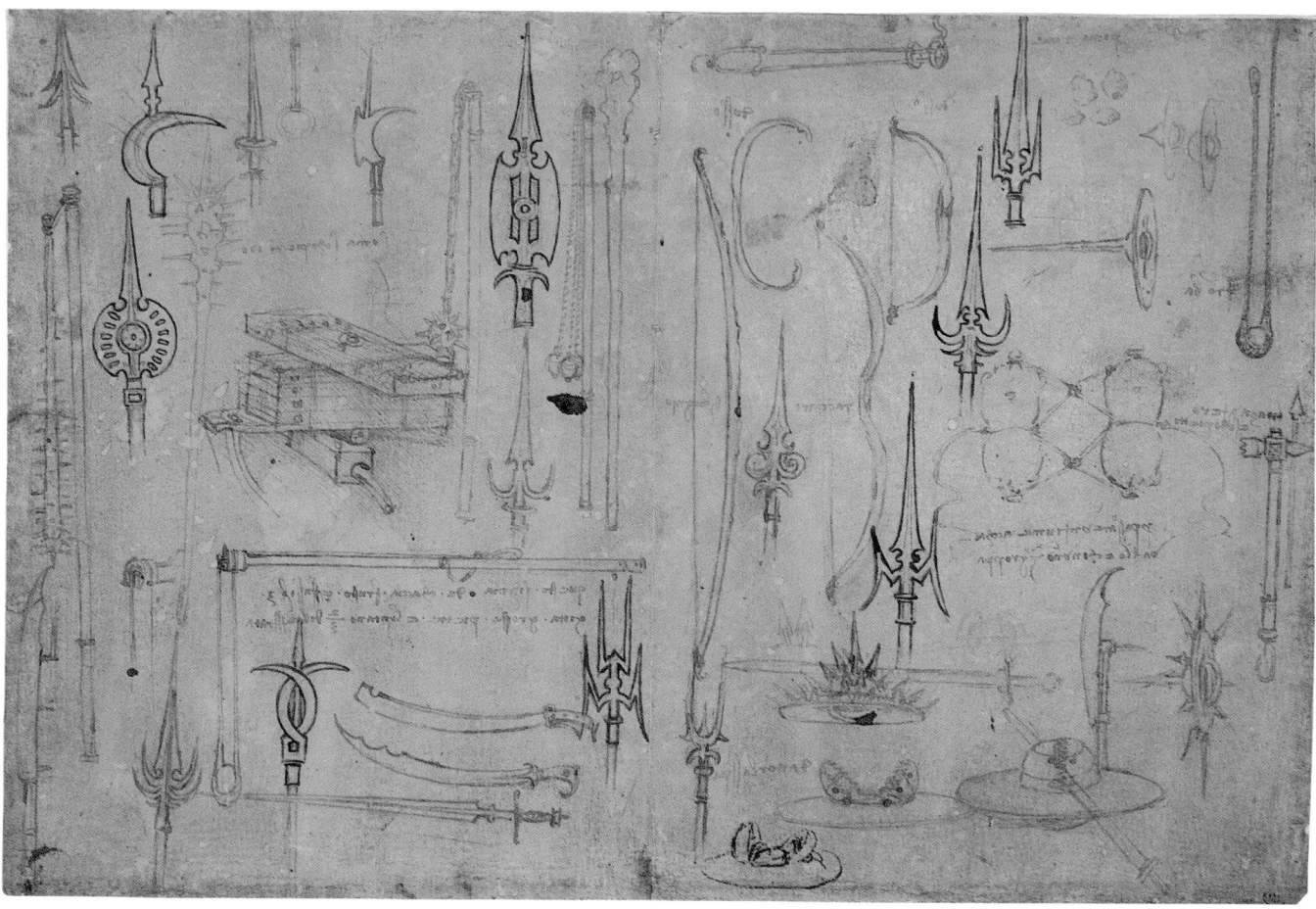

Cat. 48

This drawing must have been part of a bound collection, since it is composed of two adjoining leaves, and three stitching holes are visible along the fold. Giuseppe Vallardi enumerated the weapons, which are identified by the notations in Leonardo's hand: "Drawing on blue paper, which originally constituted two sheets in one of those little pocket-size books Leonardo used to carry with him: it depicts spearheads, various extravagantly shaped halberds, iron sledgehammers, daggers, catapults, arrows, crossbows, defensive shields, etc.; as well as the drawing for a machine of unknown function, perhaps an oil press."[1]

On the right folio is a draft of four goatskins that Leonardo described as designed "for crossing a river on horseback and with one [riding] pillion." Pietro C. Marani pointed out that this system of floats used to ford a river was already recorded in a manuscript by Francesco di Giorgio Martini, studied by Luisa Vertova.[2] By contrast, Leonardo seems to have invented

the snare in the lower left corner of the right folio, drawn three times, which was meant to catch the sword of an inattentive warrior by closing around it. In the center of the left folio, the device consisting of three boxes or crates one on top of each other, drawn in metalpoint, has not yet been identified. The suggestion of wheels and a handle suggest that this machine, undoubtedly filled with explosives, was intended to be mobile.

This Louvre drawing belongs to more or less the same period, about 1487–88, as the sheet of studies in the Accademia in Venice (cat. no. 49), according to Marani.[3] The dimensions and the technique are different, and the two sheets must have been gathered into separate collections. The writing is nevertheless comparable, and the use of metalpoint on prepared paper suggests a date before 1490 for the Louvre sheet. However, there is reason to wonder whether the reworking in pen is original; its somewhat painstaking character contradicts the light touch of the delineation and hatching in the parts drawn only in metalpoint.

In addition, there are precise similarities in style and motif between the Louvre drawing and folios B.1 and B.2 in Ashburnham Manuscript 2184 (Institut de France, Paris). The paper on those two folios is prepared in blue, but the dimensions are larger than those of the Louvre drawing. The similarity of the designs for spearheads, halberds, and scythes indicates that these sheets were part of a single coherent group that was scattered among several collections.　　　　FV

1. Vallardi 1855, p. 2, fol. 2 (Leonardo da Vinci): "Disegno in carta cerulea, che già costituiva due fogli di altro dei libricciuoli da tasca che Leonardo soleva portar seco: rappresenta estremità di aste con lance, alabarde diverse a stravaganti forme, mazze ferrate, daghe, fionde, dardi, balestre, scudi per difesa, ecc.; non che lo schizzo di una macchina d'ignoto uso, forse strettojo da olio, con varie indicazioni scritte di mano dello stesso *Leonardo*. / Alto poll. 1.2 largo poll. 8.2. E' disegno con armi dei più complicati che abbia veduto fra le Collezioni."
2. Marani 1992, p. 210; Vertova 1976, pl. 25.
3. See Marani in cat. no. 49.

LEONARDO DA VINCI

49. *Two Horsemen Attacking a Position Defended by Two Foot Soldiers; Drawings of Weapons* (recto) *Drawing of a War Machine and Other Studies* (verso)

Metalpoint, pen and ink on white paper, 293 × 208 mm (11 ½ × 8 ⅛ in.) Inscribed on recto: *Quessto istrumento è molto al proposito della fanteria chontro a li omjnj d'arme / Anchora quando que' de le lance lunghe avessino soffionj sulle punte delle lance / darebbon grande spavento a chavalli, onde li omjnj d'arme facilmente si rompereno / e cquesto si è il più [u]til modo ch'e fant[i] a pié posino usare a risitere alla furia de' chavagli / e degli omjnj d'arme*; further down, beneath drawing: *chol da trarre*; on upper left: *N.2 B*; on the right: *235*; on the verso: *questo strumento vuol essere (v) ne . . .* ; next to small drawing of crossbow: *dardj*; on the upper right: *131*; at bottom: *Leonardo da Vinci*
Gallerie dell'Accademia, Venice 235

PROVENANCE: Cardinal Cesare Monti, Milan (1635–1650); Contessa Anna Luisa Monti, Milan; 1770, Venanzio de Pagave, Milan; his son Gaudenzio de Pagave; ca. 1808 or before, Guiseppe Bossi, Milan and Venice (1777–1815; album marked K); auction, Milan, February 1818, vol. 2; February 24, 1818, purchase by Abbate Luigi Celotti [Cellotti], Venice (1765–1846); in deposit (under custody of Carlo Porta and Nicola Cassoni) Accademia de Belle Arti, Milan; 1820–22, proposal of purchase of Bossi's collection from Celotti submitted to Austrian government on behalf of Accademia delle Belle Arti, Venice; 1822, purchase by Franz I (Habsburg), emperor of Austria, Florence and Vienna (1768–1835), for Accademia delle Belle Arti, Venice; ca. 1832 manuscript inventory; December 31, 1870 manuscript inventory; museum stamp (Lugt 188).

LITERATURE: Gerli 1784, pls. 14, 15; Selvatico 1854, vol. 5, p. 5; Uzielli 1884, p. 279, no. 21; Commissione Vinciana 1928– , vol. 3, p. 21, nos. 72 (recto), 82 (verso); Popp 1928, pp. 37–38, no. 22; Suida 1929, fig. 155; Berenson 1938, vol. 2, p. 123, no. 1104; Popham 1946, no. 304; Heydenreich 1949, pls. 21 (recto), 22 (verso); Brunetti 1952, p. 24, fig. 28b; Berenson 1961, vol. 2, p. 217, no. 1104; Cogliati Arano 1966–67, p. 19; Cogliati Arano 1980, pp. 26–27; Marani 1984, p. 95, fig. 2a (verso), p. 96, fig. 2b (recto); Marani 1985a, p. 9, fig. 4 (verso); Marani in Palazzo Grassi 1992, pp. 208–9, nos. 9, 9a; Popham 1994, pp. 162–63, no. 304.

This sheet must once have been part of an album or notebook, since the center of the right edge of the recto has tears that seem to be evidence of stitching holes. The number "131" on the verso, old and written in the normal direction, suggests successive numbering after the sheet was already loose. Anny E. Popp (1928) and especially Ludwig Heinrich Heydenreich (1949) associated this sheet and the notebook from which it came with Giovanni Paolo Lomazzo's description of drawings of horsemen and foot soldiers that Leonardo made for the Milanese nobleman Gentile de' Borri. Lomazzo took particular note of Leonardo's drawings of mounted soldiers and of the way "one might defend himself from the other, with one on foot, and how those on foot might both defend themselves and attack using a variety of arms."[1] This is precisely what is illustrated on the recto of the sheet in Venice. Pietro C. Marani (1992) has, furthermore, associated the drawing of a weapon with two points near the lower right corner of the page with that wielded by the *Man with a Halberd*

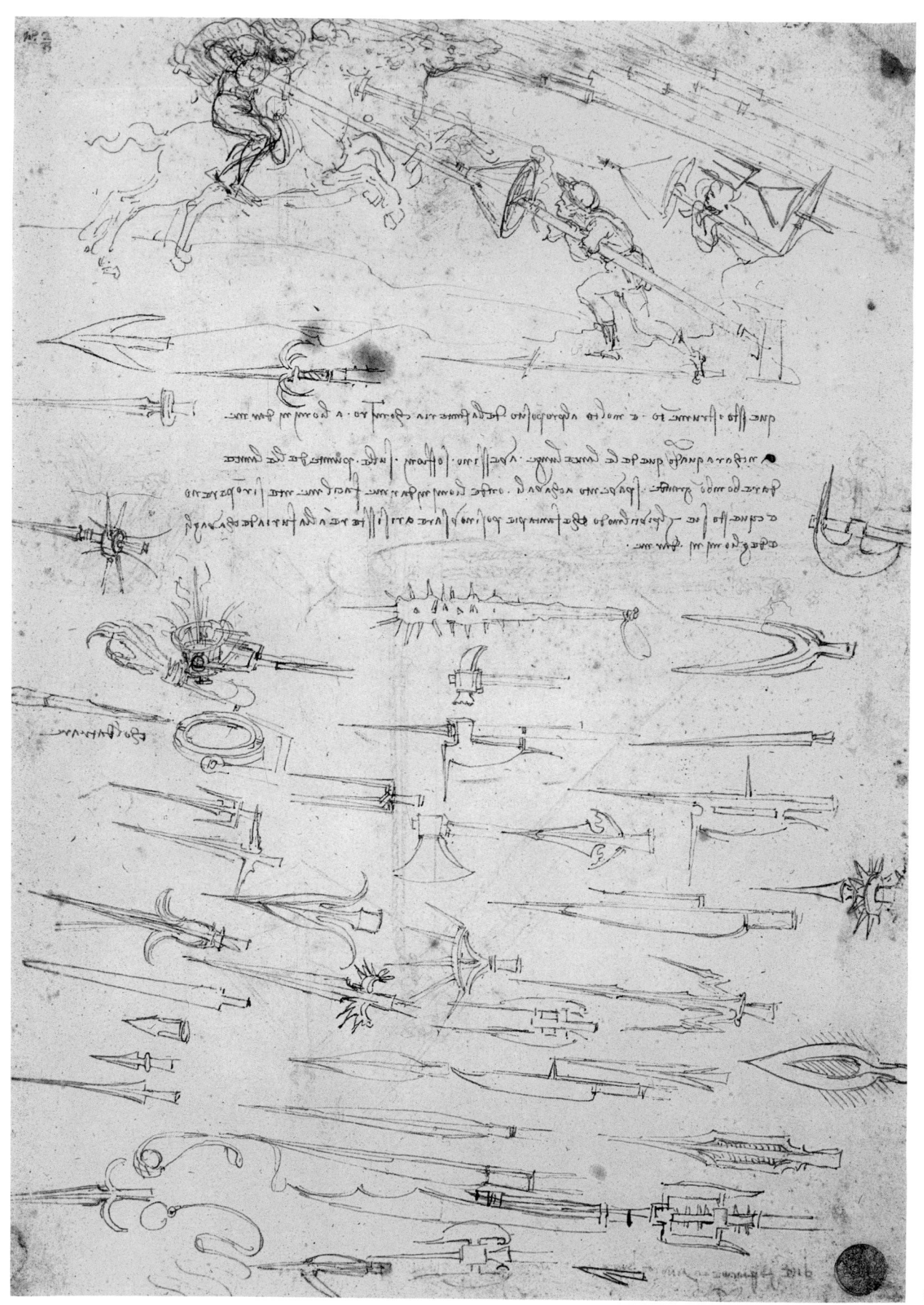

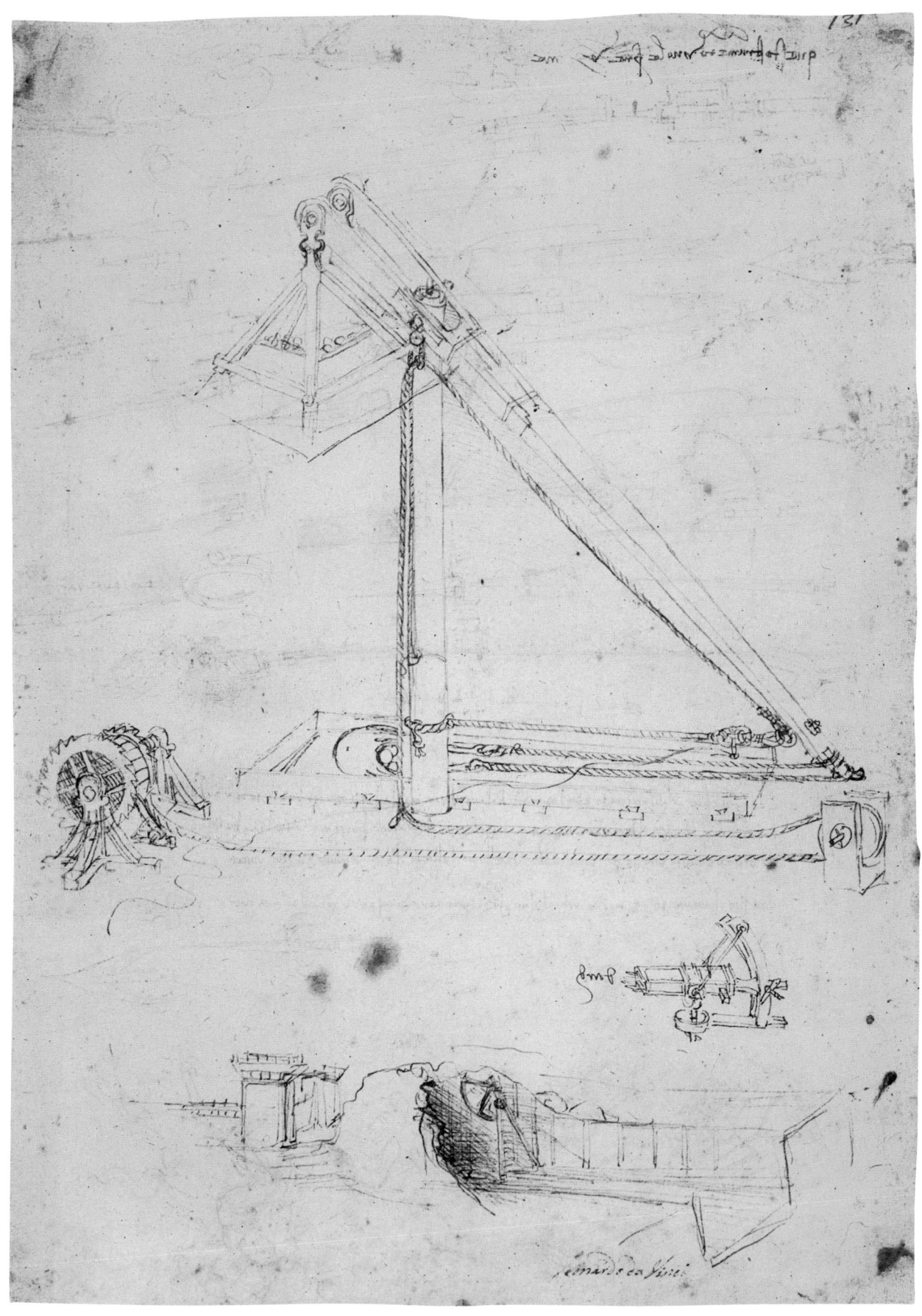

Cat. 49v

painted by Bramante in Gaspare Ambrogio Visconti's house in Milan about 1487 (now in the Brera, reg. cron. 1240); and more generally with the series of Men at Arms (to which the painting belongs), in which, according to Lomazzo, Bramante portrayed prominent members of the Sforza court—in particular, Pietro Suola, Ludovico Sforza "Il Moro's" master-at-arms, as well as Beltramo de Stuchis, another *magister armorum*. In this connection, the small drawing of a kind of crossbow on the verso of the sheet, inscribed "dardj" (arrows), may point to Leonardo's later relationship with Pietro Monti, master-at-arms at the Sforza court in the 1480s. Leonardo mentions him in a note of about 1497 in Ms. I at the Institut de France, folio 120v: "Parla con Pietro Monti di questi tali modi di trarre i dardi" (Spoke with Pietro Monti about the kinds of ways of drawing the arrows). An expert crossbowman and swordsman, Monti also wrote various treatises on the military arts (one of which, on fencing, was published in 1509), and the influence of his ideas about combat can be traced in Leonardo's work.[2] Drawings similar to those on the recto of this sheet, although more analytically rendered (with hatching, shading, and greater detail), can be found on four of the folios now bound into Ashburnham 2184 at the Bibliothèque de l'Institut de France in Paris, the last part of what is now known as Ms. B. Several halberd blades on folios A.1 and A.2 are identical to those in the Venice drawing; it is as if the latter were initial, rapid sketches that were then developed on the two folios in the Ashburnham manuscript. Similar blades can be found on folios B.1 and B.2 but in pen and ink on blue prepared paper. On folio 10r of the Ashburnham manuscript, written in four columns, is a list of mysterious weapons. It includes the terms *fulminea, tridente,* and *fistula* and was later enlarged (Ms. B, fol. 40r) with *acinace, daga, gladjo, spata,* and many other names—all of which suggest the infinite number of weapons for striking and cutting.[3] These weapons are further illustrated on folios 40v–46v of Ms. B. The horseman in the upper left corner of the recto of the present sheet (the position of his right leg was corrected—to bend more sharply at the knee—at a later time and with different ink) is elaborated in a rapid sketch in Ms. B, folio 46v. On the same page are drawings of two kinds of crossbows (the one above is called "scorpione" and the one at the center of the page has the explanatory title "Natura di balestro"), as well as an outline of mounted crossbowmen. Apparently in the drawings on the Venice sheet and in Ms. B, Leonardo was preparing to try the infinite variety of

points and blades that he later drew more carefully on four folios of Ashburnham 2184. He undoubtedly learned about them by reading military treatises and through his relationships with masters-at-arms such as Pietro Monti and the others mentioned above.

The date of the Venice sheet should be earlier than that generally assigned to Ms. B and to the drawings now bound into the Ashburnham manuscript, usually dated 1487–90. Bernard Berenson (1938) cautiously dated the Venice sheet to Leonardo's Milanese period, 1482–99; Heydenreich (1949) dated it to about 1482–85; A. E. Popham (1946) to 1485–88; Carlo Pedretti (in a written communication to Luisa Cogliati Arano, 1980) suggested 1483–85; my own preference (Marani 1992) is for a date of about 1485. A drawing in the Cabinet des Dessins at the Louvre (cat. no. 48), executed in metalpoint and pen and ink on blue prepared paper (a technique that Leonardo abandoned after 1490), with similar drawings of lance and halberd blades as well as studies of slings, shields, bows, and swords is contemporary,[4] as is the famous drawing of *carri falcati,* war carts mounted with scythes in the Biblioteca Reale in Turin (15583). The latter derives from Roberto Valturio's *De re militari,* first published in Latin in 1472 and then by Ramusio in 1483 in both Latin and the vernacular.[5] A date of about 1485 for the Venice sheet also takes into account Leonardo's interest in other authors who wrote on the military arts after the publication of Valturio's work. It reflects, too, Leonardo's vision of architecture and the military arts as it was characterized by his attempt to assimilate the views of ancient authors—an approach that was more literary than practical and which the artist abandoned in the mid-1490s.

An examination of the drawings on the verso of catalogue number 49 confirms this dating at the beginning of Leonardo's interest in military affairs. The drawing of a *trabucco,* or catapult, can be connected to passages in the famous letter Leonardo wrote to Ludovico "Il Moro" (Codex Atlanticus, fol. 1082r) and especially to the eighth paragraph in which he says he can make "briccole, mangani, trabucchi et altri instrumenti di mirabile efficacia et fora de l'usato . . . et infinite cose da offender e di[fender]"—a series of catapults and launching devices that he claims will be most effective both as defensive and offensive weapons. This passage links the Venice drawing to the things Leonardo was offering to make for the lord of Milan about 1483. Finally, the drawing at the foot of the page, and especially its allusion to a fortress with tall, crenellated towers, can be connected to a drawing in the Royal Library at Windsor (cat. no. 52 verso) that demonstrates a way to mine the towers of a fortress (on the recto of this sheet are drawings of weapons that can be linked to the drawings in Ms. B), which has been dated 1485–87. It can also be associated with another page in Ms. B, folio 63v, which illustrates the explosion of a cylindrical tower still medieval in plan.[7] Thus both sides of the Venice sheet can be connected with Ms. B, and the date when the latter was begun should be moved forward to about 1482.[8]

The technique (pen and ink) and style of Leonardo's drawings on the Venice sheet confirm its early dating at a time in his life when the artist was not completely comfortable with penmanship. Indeed, some of the flourishes of the pen and the minute handwriting suggest a date in the first half of the 1480s. The drawings of horsemen, horses, and foot soldiers are close to the Florentine studies for the *Adoration of the Magi*, the painting that Leonardo left unfinished in Florence in 1482 (now at the Uffizi). The drawing of the rearing horse, especially, should be compared with a sheet in the Ashmolean Museum, Oxford, a study for a horse and rider fighting a dragon, the subject that marks the beginning of the studies for the background of the *Adoration*.[9] It might also be compared with the silverpoint drawing, reinforced with pen and ink (cat. no. 40), which has a horse in the identical pose as that on the Venice

sheet and which must date to about 1480.[10] In both these drawings as well as in the Venice sheet, however, Leonardo seems to have moved beyond the influence of Verrocchio's drawing style (although there is still a trace of it in the facial profile of the foot soldier in the foreground). He has also here transformed Antonio Pollaiuolo's sinuous, nervous line into a new sense of dynamism, as seen in his representation of the horse's hind legs with repeated simple and summary lines which seem almost to disappear, suggesting both the animal's movement and the instability of its stance.   PCM

1. "[P]otevano l'uno dall'altro difendersi con uno a piedi, e ancora quelli ch'erano a piedi come si potevano l'uno e l'altro difendere e offendere per cagioni delle diverse armi"; Lomazzo 1584, p. 384. See also Beltrami 1919a, docs. 263–69.
2. See Anglo 1989.
3. For these names and their possible derivation from treatises on the military arts such as Valturio's, see Marinoni 1990.
4. See Marani in Palazzo Grassi 1992, pp. 210–11, no. 10.
5. For a comparison of the woodcuts of *carri falcati* in the 1483 edition of Valturio's treatise and Leonardo's drawings, see Marani 1984, figs. 12–14.
6. See Clark and Pedretti 1968–69, p. 143; Kemp in Kemp and Roberts 1989, p. 137, no. 67.
7. For Ms. B, fol. 63v, as well as Windsor RL 12652v, see Marani 1984, pp. 94–96, nos. 1, 2.
8. Pedretti 1964 notes the existence of the date "1482" on a lost page from this manuscript, although it was not written in Leonardo's hand.
9. See Popham 1946, no. 60B; and Marani 2000a, pp. 101–6.
10. Popham 1946, no. 46.

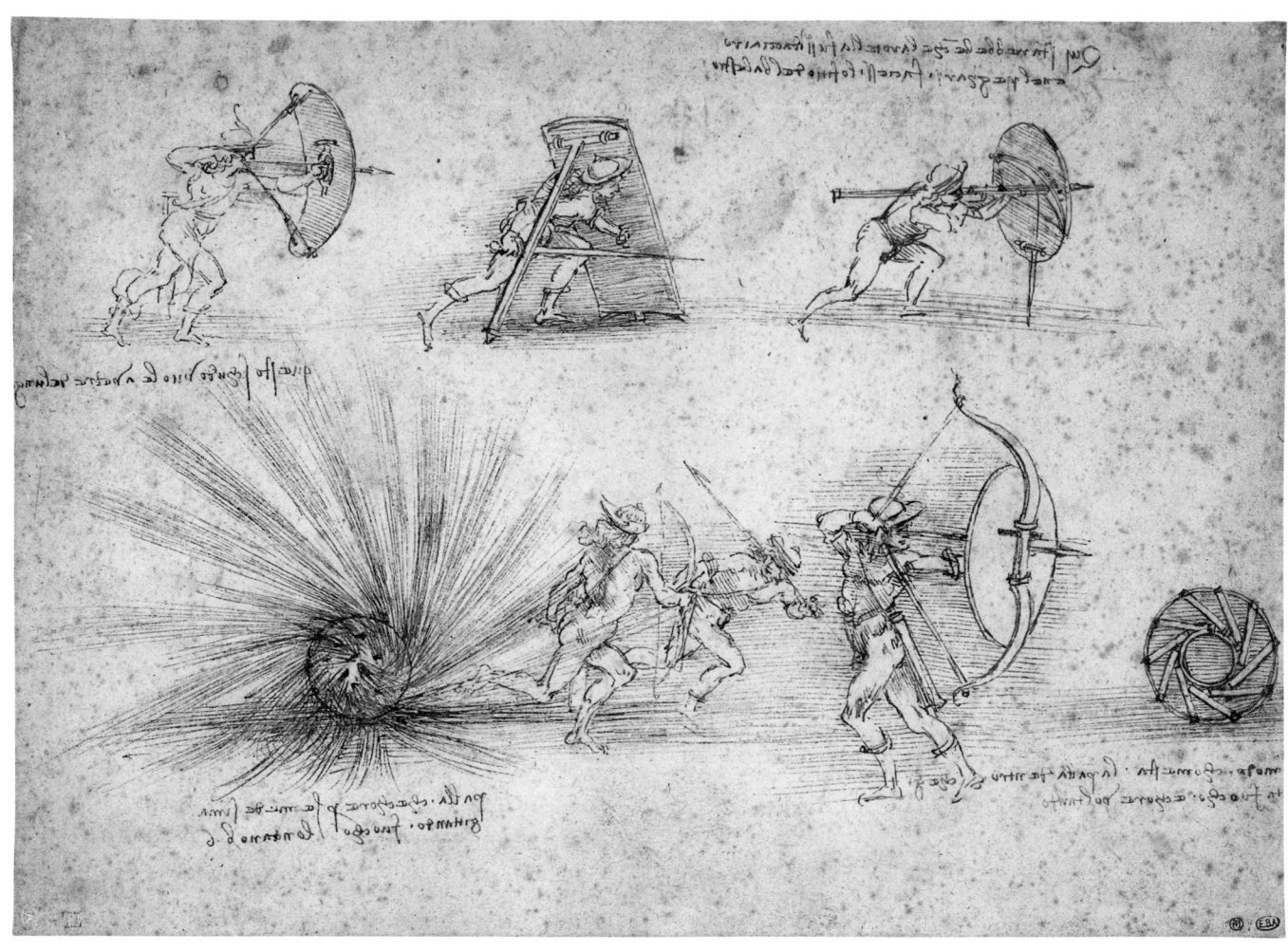

LEONARDO DA VINCI

50. *Studies of Ballistics*

Pen and brown ink, 200 × 280 mm (7 7/8 × 11 1/16 in.); framing outline in pen and brown ink; oxidation; glued to secondary support
Inscribed in pen and brown ink, in right-to-left script, in the upper register from left to right: *questo schudo vuole avere . . . de lungo / qui starebbe ben che la rotella fussi d'acciaro / e nel pegarsi faciessi l'ofitio del balestro*; in the lower register: *palla che chore per se medesima / gittando fuocho lontano br. 6. / modo chome sta la palla dentro che gitta fuoco e chore voltando.*
École Nationale Supérieure des Beaux-Arts, Paris EBA 423

PROVENANCE: 1775, Pierre-Jean Mariette (Lugt 2097) sale, Paris, possibly part of no. 788; Moritz von Fries (Lugt 2903); Sir Thomas Lawrence (Lugt 2445); Raffaello Tosoni; 1907, Armand-Valton bequest to the École Nationale Supérieure des Beaux-Arts (Lugt 829).

LITERATURE: Chennevières and Montaiglon 1851–60, vol. 3, pp. 174–75; Turotti 1857, p. 11; Vasari–Milanesi 1878–85, vol. 4, p. 66; Chennevières 1879, p. 516; École des Beaux-Arts 1879, no. 35; Müller-Walde 1890, pp. 185, 186, fig. 100; Rosenberg 1898, p. 41, fig. 28; Müntz 1899, p. 523; Berenson 1903, vol. 2, no. 1082; Marcheix 1909, p. 257, pl. 1, p. 259; Seidlitz 1909, vol. 1, p. 115; Poggi 1919, p. lxxvi, pl. 200; Popp 1928, p. 38, under no. 22; Sirén 1928, p. 48, pl. 60; Bodmer 1931, p. 394, no. 194; Commissione Vinciana 1928– , vol. 3, pp. 17, 22, pl. 77; École des Beaux-Arts 1935, no. 158; Popham 1945, pp. 83, 84, no. 301; Biblioteca Medicea Laurenziana 1952, no. 30; Florisoone and Bacou 1952, no. 17; Lebel 1952, p. 60, pl. 6; École des Beaux-Arts 1958, no. 61; Petit Palais 1965–66, no. 185; Bacou 1967, no. 74; Clark and Pedretti 1968–69, under no. 12653; Pedretti 1977, p. 95, no. 40; École des Beaux-Arts 1981–82, no. 50; École des Beaux-Arts 1984, no. 118; Pedretti 1988b.

In the upper register, the sheet shows three warriors in right profile, from left to right, a man shooting an arrow through an opening in the shield affixed to his bow; a man with a sword behind a tall supported shield; a man shooting an arrow through a shield affixed to a bow and supports. From left to right in the lower register we see a shell or grenade catching fire as it rolls; two fleeing warriors armed with crossbows; a warrior shooting an arrow through a shield attached to a crossbow; a shell or grenade, seen in cross section with the channels for propellant indicated.

In 1857 Felice Turotti was the first to publish the provenance of this drawing. At that time it belonged to Professor Raffaello Tosoni of Cetona, living in Florence, whose collection was dispersed in 1877. Tosoni owned another drawing by Leonardo, a lifesize portrait of a woman that had belonged to King Charles I of England; that has not been identified. The *Studies of Ballistics* had earlier belonged to Pierre-Jean Mariette, who described it in two different accounts, one of which was included in the *Abecedario*: "a fire balloon and . . . a few war machines consisting of shields designed to approach the enemy without being discovered and without danger."[1]

Like the sheets of weapons and ballistics discussed by Pietro C. Marani in his study of Ms. B, the present drawing was linked by Giovanni Paolo Lomazzo to works executed for Gentile de' Barri,[2] either upon Leonardo's arrival in Milan in 1483–85[3] or, according to Marani, between 1487 and 1489 or later. The date of the sheet exhibited here may be close to that of folio 4 in Ms. B, on which two plans for incendiary bombs corresponding to those depicted here can be found, with an explanation of how they were set off: "Questa palla nel gettare va spinta e, giunta in terra, la canne fasciate in testa di panno-lino acceso, si ficca in dentro e dà fuoco alla polvere."[4] The relationship between the style of the present drawing and the figure of the archer on a sheet at Windsor (RL 12653) would imply a fairly early date for the Paris drawing, according to Kenneth Clark, who underscored its kinship with the *Dragon Fight* from the Rothschild collection (fig. 141).[5] This again supports the theory of a project dating to the first years in Milan, still stylistically close to studies for the *Adoration of the Magi*.   FV

1. "[U]n ballon d'artifice et . . . quelques machines de guerre consistant en des boucliers faits pour approcher de son ennemi sans être découvert et sans danger"; Mariette in Chennevières and Montaiglon 1851–60, vol. 3, pp. 174–75; see Monbeig Goguel in Bacou 1967, no. 74.
2. These works were listed by Giovanni Paolo Lomazzo in his 1584 *Trattato dell'arte de la pittura* (Lomazzo 1584, p. 335).
3. Clark and Pedretti 1968–69, under no. RL 12653.
4. Marinoni 1990, fol. 4r.
5. Clark and Pedretti 1968–69, no. RL 12653.

LEONARDO DA VINCI

51. *A Cannon Factory*

Pen and dark brown ink over traces of black chalk or leadpoint (?), 247 × 183 mm (9¾ × 7³⁄₁₆ in.)
Lent by Her Majesty Queen Elizabeth II, Royal Library, Windsor Castle 12647

PROVENANCE: Windsor Leoni volume: 1519, Francesco Melzi, Milan and Rome (1491/93–ca. 1570); ca. 1570, Orazio Melzi; by 1590, Pompeo Leoni, Madrid and Milan (ca. 1533–1608; Lugt under 2885); ca. 1613, Thomas Howard, second earl of Arundel (1586–1646); before 1690, British Royal Collection (inventory of King George III's collection, ca. 1810).

LITERATURE: Chamberlaine 1812, pl. 5; Grosvenor 1878, vol. 2, p. 36; Müller-Walde 1889, p. 214, pl. 113; Müntz 1898, vol. 1, p. 101; Müntz 1899, p. 361; Berenson 1903, vol. 1, p. 165, vol. 2, p. 67, no. 1261; Seidlitz 1909, pl. 19; Seidlitz 1911, p. 274, no. 101; Malaguzzi Valeri 1913–23, vol. 2, fig. 678; Poggi 1919, pl. 189; Commissione Vinciana 1928– , vol. 3, p. 22, pl. 83; MacCurdy 1928, pl. 7; Popp 1928, p. 38, no. 24; Sirén 1928, p. 48, pl. 59; Popham 1930–31, p. 22, no. 74, pl. 62; Bodmer 1931, pp. 199, 394; Berenson 1938, vol. 1, p. 182, vol. 2, p. 138, vol. 3, fig. 560, no. 1261; MacCurdy 1938, vol. 2, pl. 6; Palazzo dell'Arte 1939, p. 156; Giglioli 1944, pl. 196; Castelfranco 1952b, pl. 14; Royal Academy of Arts 1952, p. 47, no. 172; Clark 1954, pl. 14; Heydenreich 1954, vol. 2, p. 99, pl. 134; Arthur Ewart Popham in Royal Academy of Arts 1960, p. 197, no. 479; Berenson 1961, vol. 1, p. 264, vol. 2, p. 244, no. 1261; Clark and Pedretti 1968–69, vol. 1, p. 140, no. 12647; Clark 1969–70, p. 5, no. 23, pl. 16; Heydenreich 1974b, pp. 168–69, fig. 169/1; Calvi 1980, p. 306; Kemp 1981, pp. 177–78, pl. 47; Bora 1982, pp. 136–37, fig. 93; Wasserman 1984, p. 46, fig. 47; Galluzzi 1987, p. 344; Roberts 1988, pp. 22–23, no. 5; Kemp and Roberts 1989, pp. 198–99, no. 113; Kemp 1992b, p. 284, no. 185; Popham 1994, no. 305; Kirwin 1995, pp. 90–96; Arasse 1998, pp. 202–3, fig. 139 (incorrect inv. no.).

As Leonardo understood only too well, warfare was possibly the art most prized by the princely patrons of his day, and so he advertised in a letter to his prospective employer Ludovico Sforza "Il Moro," "in case of need I will make cannon, mortars, and light ordnances of most beautiful and functional design that are quite out of the ordinary."[1] Although the extant draft of this famous letter is most probably not autograph, it nevertheless records Leonardo's intentions to "Il Moro," indicating also the scope of his talents as military engineer. The Windsor drawing dates from 1482–85, Leonardo's first years in Milan, to judge from its technique and figural style (see cat. nos. 48–50, 52). It portrays a panoramic view of foundrymen and other laborers at work in a cannon yard, and it has an immediacy possibly inspired by the artist's visits to the Sforza arsenals. Yet the source for the main motif of the composition lies buried in an illustration from the treatise by Roberto Valturio, the *De re militari* (manuscript 1446–55), that was printed in Verona in an *editio princeps* in 1472 and in Latin and Italian editions in 1483 (fig. 156). Valturio intended the device for raising and lowering cannons ("Instrumento da alzar et arbasar bombarde").[2] The illustration in the different manuscripts and editions of Valturio varies in the details and quality of execution, but it is clear that Leonardo transformed the inert military diagram into a powerful scene of human toil in the service of warfare. Leonardo repeatedly quoted the military vocabulary of Valturio (see cat. nos. 21, 52), and he likely listed a copy of Valturio's treatise in his record of books in the Codex Atlanticus (fol. 559r [formerly fol. 210r-a]) and of those "that I left locked in the chest" in the Codex Madrid II (fols. 2v–3r).[3] The Italian translation of Valturio by Paolo Ramusio published in 1483 seems almost exactly contemporary with Leonardo's Windsor drawing.

The scene by Leonardo depicted here is among a small number of extant, relatively finished composition drawings by him, and it may be the only surviving example of this type from his early period. Because the Windsor drawing presents the military-technological subject in a unified narrative context (in contrast to other military designs by him; cat. nos. 48–52), and with clear expository detail, it was possibly intended to serve as a preliminary study for a frontispiece or illustration to an accompanying text (perhaps even his own military treatise). Seen as a whole, Leonardo's drawings and notes from the 1470s until his death in 1519 offer one of the most complete accounts of the weapons industry during the Renaissance, and

especially of the evolving technology of the cannon.[4] Leonardo drew many of his studies on site or after closely observed sketches done at the cannon foundries. The rigor of his investigations anticipated by several decades that of the treatise on metallurgy and bronze casting of the period, Vannoccio Biringuccio's *Pirotechnia*, published in Venice in 1540.

Although there has been disagreement about what precisely is represented in Leonardo's Windsor drawing, much can be clarified by comparing it to the illustration from Valturio's treatise (fig. 156) and to Leonardo's own detailed studies of breech-loading cannons in the Codex Atlanticus (fol. 37r [formerly fol. 10v-a]). The cradle on the lower right in the foreground of the Windsor drawing evidently served as a means of transport, as it is on rollers. It is similar to the sled or cradle shown at the center of the page of the Codex Atlanticus (fol. 37r), fourth from the top, that accommodates the barrel of a breech-loading cannon cast in bronze. The prominent diagonal placement of this transportation cradle within the pictorial space of the Windsor drawing leads the eye directly to the heart of the scene in the middle ground, where a vast number of muscular, nude laborers toil and struggle as they hoist an enormous, apparently overwhelmingly heavy cylindrical form onto a cart with wheels on an axle. A wheeled cart would support each end of the cylinder as it was transported to an area of assembly or storage. As the illustration from Valturio proves (fig. 156), the cylinder being hoisted is the barrel of a breech-loading cannon cast in metal,

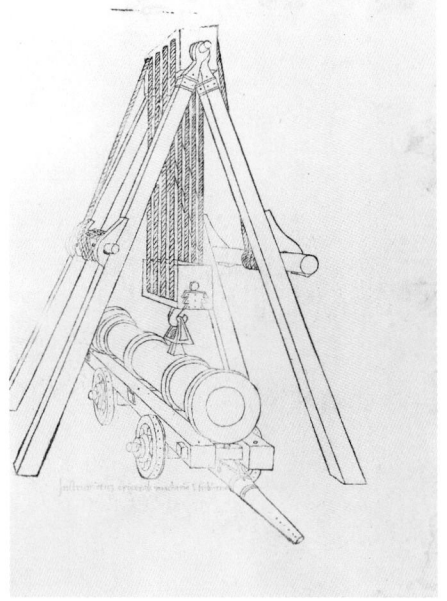

Fig. 156. Roberto Valturio, *De re militari* (Verona: Johannes ex Verona, 1472). *Instrumentus erigendi di machina sublime*, fol. 187r. Woodcut, 326 × 227 mm. The Metropolitan Museum of Art, New York; Harris Brisbane Dick Fund, 1926 26.71.4

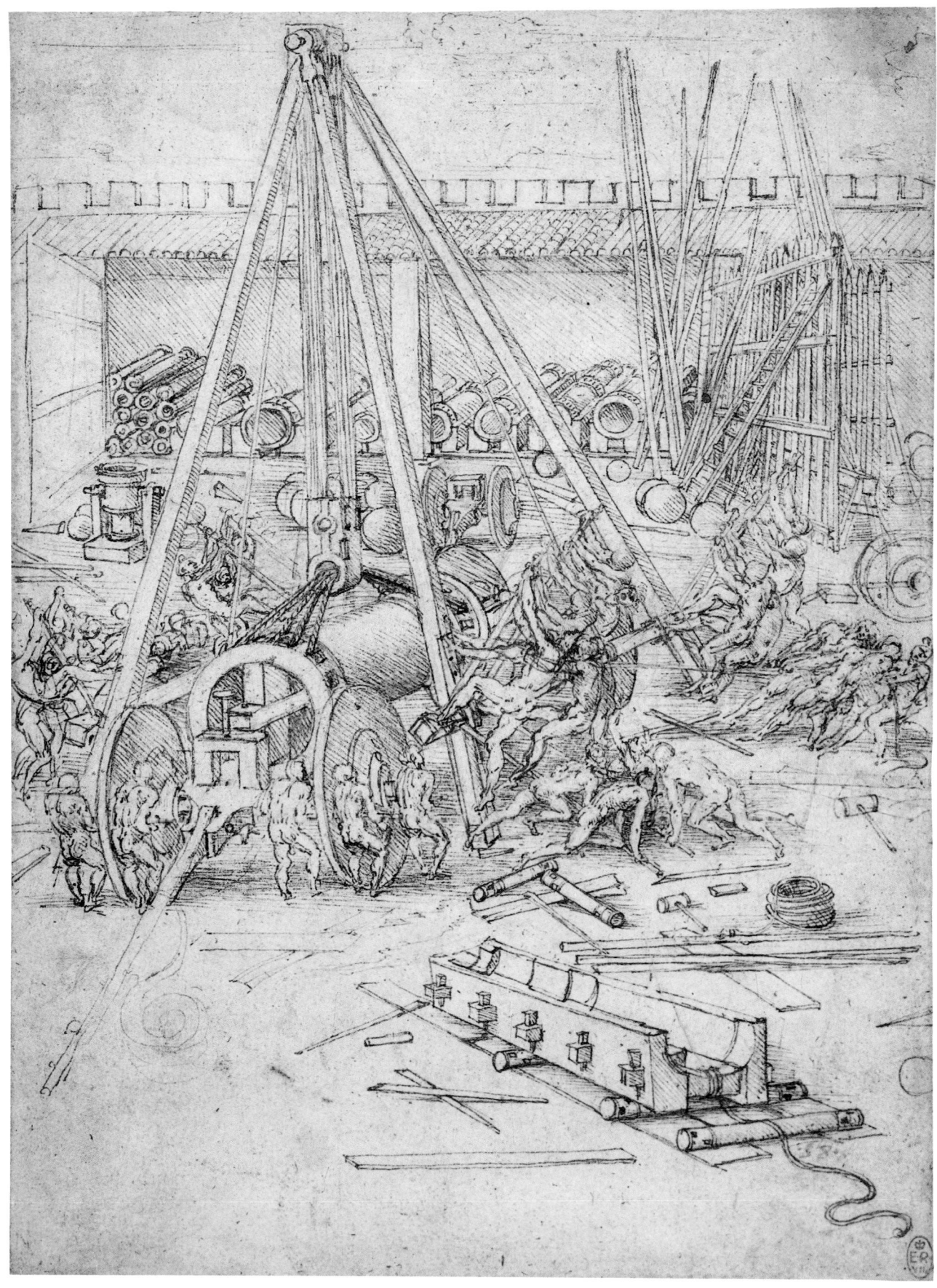

Cat. 51

which explains the enormous manual and technological labor involved in lifting its weight. This is the very subject of Leonardo's drawing. The cylinder, therefore, cannot represent the outer reinforced female mold (*cappa*) made of clay from which the barrel of a breech-loading bombard would be cast (Kirwin 1995); also, no comprehensive external fastenings for a *cappa* mold seem visible in the drawing. There is no doubt, either, that the sixth motif from the top in catalogue number 52 — a short, thick cylindrical form emitting smoke and fire (labeled "a" by Leonardo) — is a unit of a metal cannon barrel, probably a breechloader, and that it looks much like the cylindrical form in the center of the present Windsor drawing. The page with details of breechloaders from the Codex Atlanticus also portrays such thick cylinders in blown-up scale, with joins and ends from which protrude bands of rectangular perforations; the Windsor drawing shows ropes strung through these perforations at either end of the barrel.

The tall pyramidal wood armature with pulleys, winches, and ropes being used to hoist the cannon functions as a compositional device of formidable presence. It articulates the depth of the pictorial space in the scene and offers a context for the dramatic action that unfolds around it, as the foundrymen go about their work. The men's sweaty, infernal labor appears to go into turning the long levers for the winches, into pulling the long ropes along the left and right of the wood armature, or into pushing the axled wheels into place at the front and back ends of the heavy barrel. In the background,

cannonballs are strewn about in groups; to the right, a mortar in a cradle stands upright. In the background, a storage shed with a tile roof along the battlement is stacked with various types of cannon barrels, resting on the same types of cradles as the example seen in the foreground to the lower right.

This scene vividly describes the colossal toils of foundry work and its place within the bronze-casting process that was the backbone of the warfare industry. As Vannoccio Biringuccio's treatise of 1540 aptly notes, "concerning the art of casting . . . having considered this work many times, with its extraordinary obstacles and the bodily labors as heavy as a stevedore's . . . it is such that a man of noble birth, even though he be gifted or be drawn to it by pleasure, should not practice it and could not unless he is accustomed to the sweat and many discomforts it brings . . . In addition to this, he who wishes to practice this art must not be of a weak nature . . . Nor do I doubt that whoever considers this art well will fail to recognize a certain brutishness in it."[5]   CCB

1. C. A., fol. 1082r (formerly fol. 391r-a); Richter 1970, vol. 2, p. 326, no. 1340; Pedretti 1977, vol. 2, p. 295, nos. 1340–45: "Item occorrendo di bisogno, farò bo[m]barde, mortari et passauolanti di bellissime e utili forme furi del comune uso."
2. Other versions of this device are illustrated in Bassignana 1988, p. 120, pl. 34, fig. 4.
3. Richter 1970, vol. 2, pp. 366–69, no. 1469; Pedretti 1977, vol. 2, p. 353, nos. 1469–1508; Ladislao Reti in Codex Madrid 1974, vol. 3, pp. 56–58, vol. 5, pp. 5–8 ("Ricordo de' libri ch'io lasscio serati nel cassone . . . / De re militari.").
4. Kirwin 1995.
5. Translation quoted from Biringuccio 1942, pp. 213–14.

LEONARDO DA VINCI

52. *Mortars, Guns, and Other Military Devices Intended for a Boat* (recto)
The Tower of a Military Fortress Being Blown Up; A Hill Town Being Blown Up (verso)

Pen and dark brown ink with some brown wash over leadpoint on unprepared paper (recto); pen and dark brown ink on blue prepared paper (verso), 285 × 207 mm (11 ¼ × 8 3⁄16 in.)
Inscribed in pen and brown ink, in right-to-left script, on recto at top: *se maj . gliomjnj dj mjlano feciono . chosa . che fussi fuora dj propo[s]itto semmaj*; below base of gun cradle: *qua; questo e strume[n]to da galea e debesi fare / dj piastra sottil dj rame salda chon arie[n]to*; at mouth of barrel of gun: *fuocho*; below barrel: *b[r] 2 e largho 1/3*; to right of larger-barreled device: *questo e[n]tra J[n] quel dj sopra*; to left of device for tinders and above waves: *questa gita chal/cina avenenata / e debesi trare su la*; continuing at bottom left, below waves: *[. . .]ra a il ch[ochone] / [. . .] / fa dj bronzo e st [. . .] e*

ser[. . .] / cho[n] chorda; on small device for tinders for six-barreled gun: *per dar / foco*; on boxes of mortar at lower left, on larger box: *calcina*; on smaller box: *poluere*; at bottom of sheet: *questa . macchina vuole avere un ase dopo Jl chochone che sia v[. . .] cho grosa e sugieli e sia be[n] / [crossed out: j] chalafatata chonjstopa e peghola elchoperchio serato cho[n] chorda*"; devices are inscribed with letters
Lent by Her Majesty Queen Elizabeth II, Royal Library, Windsor Castle 12652

PROVENANCE: Windsor Leoni volume: 1519, Francesco Melzi, Milan and Rome (1491/93 – ca. 1570); ca. 1570, Orazio Melzi; by 1590, Pompeo Leoni, Madrid and Milan (ca. 1533 – 1608; Lugt under 2885);

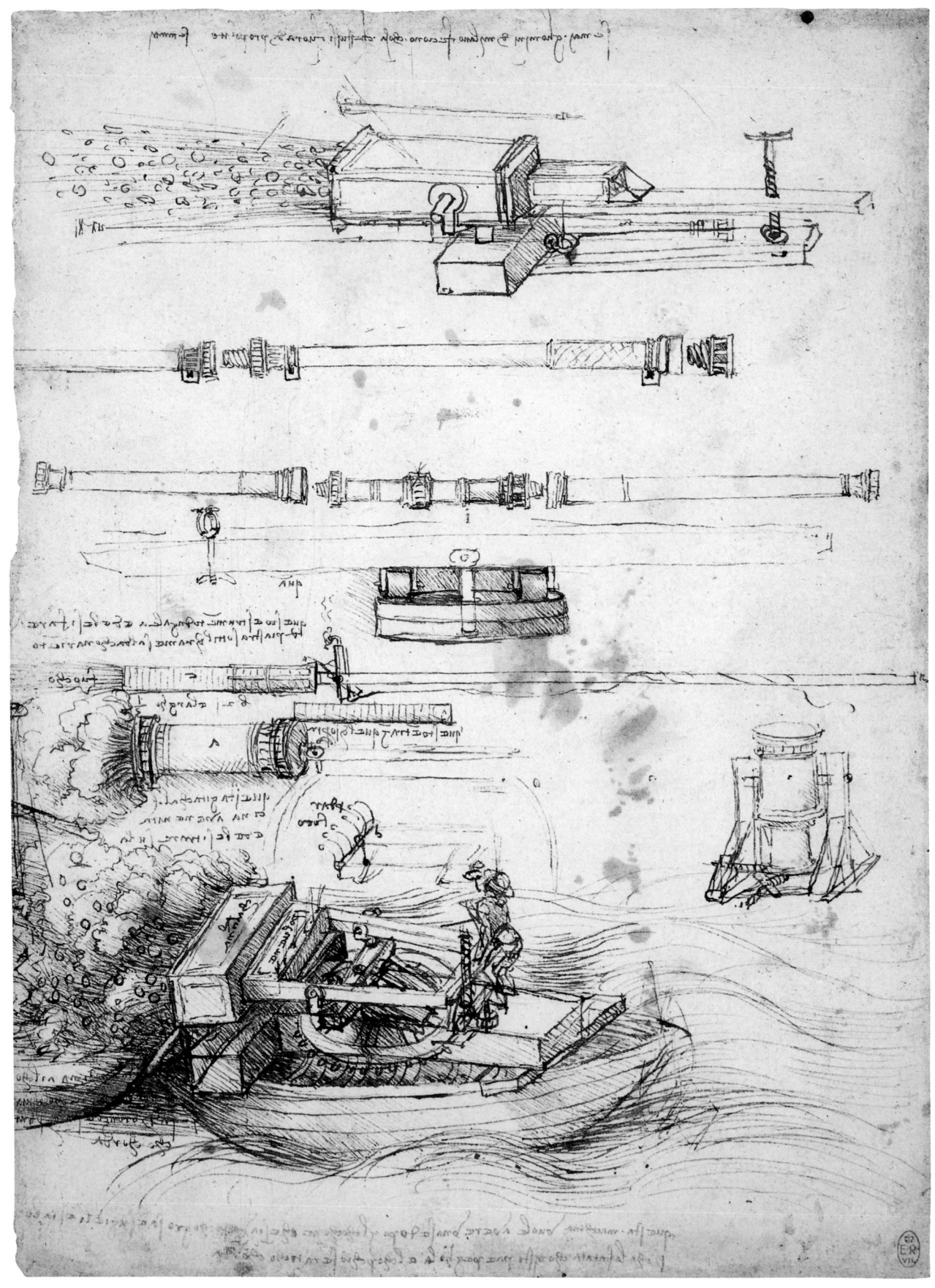

Cat. 52R

ca. 1613, Thomas Howard, second earl of Arundel (1586–1646); before 1690, British Royal Collection (inventory of King George III's collection, ca. 1810).

LITERATURE: Müller-Walde 1899, p. 67; Seidlitz 1911, p. 274, nos. 103–4; Commissione Vinciana 1928–, vol. 3, p. 22, pl. 81; Bodmer 1931, pp. 196, 394; Berenson 1938, vol. 2, p. 133, no. 1191C; Royal Academy of Arts 1952, no. 174 (hors catalogue); Berenson 1961, vol. 2, p. 234, no. 1191C; Eissler 1961, pl. 61; Clark and Pedretti 1968–69, vol. 1, pp. 142–44, no. 12652; Clark 1969–70, p. 6, no. 26, pl. 1; Heydenreich 1974b, p. 187, fig. 187/1; Calvi 1980, p. 276; Pedretti 1982a, pp. 121–22, fig. 114; Gombrich 1984, pp. 12–13, pl. 3; Marani 1984, pp. 94–95, no. 1; Clark 1988, p. 85, fig. 28; Kemp and Roberts 1989, p. 139, no. 69; Schofield 1991, pp. 115–16, figs. 1, 2; Kemp 1992c, pp. 62–63, no. 13; Popham 1994, no. 306; Clayton 1996–97, pp. 30–33, no. 11.

The drawings of military technology and inventions by Leonardo—in great contrast to the fifteenth-century imagery by Mariano Jacopo "Il Taccola," Matteo de' Pasti (who worked for Roberto Valturio), Guido da Vigevano, Antonio Averlino "Il Filarete," Bonaccorso Ghiberti, Francesco di Giorgio Martini, or Giuliano da Sangallo—attain an extraordinary power of persuasion, because the artist deployed an unparalleled mastery of pictorial techniques to illustrate his ideas. He drew the fascinating studies of naval weapons on the recto of this sheet with an elegantly rationalized clarity of structure and a flair for narrative theatricality. Whether the ingenious contraptions were actually functional seems beside the point, next to the graphic presence of the drawings. Leonardo wrote on the upper border of the sheet a caustic comment on the grudging practicality of the Milanese, who may have been unmoved by his genius as a military draftsman: "[Tell me] if ever the men of Milan did anything beyond that which was required . . . if ever." The inscription helps date this and other drawings of extravagant weaponry of related technique and figural style to Leonardo's early Milanese years (cat. nos. 49–51), in 1482–84, when he probably first sought work as a military engineer to Ludovico Sforza "Il Moro."

The Codex Atlanticus contains related notes and designs of naval weapons (fols. 1062r, 1044r [formerly fols. 384r-a, 394r-b]), and the Paris Ms. B has studies of similar long-barreled guns (fol. 31r). The present sheet and one of the sheets from the Codex Atlanticus (fol. 1044r [formerly 394r-b]) may originally have formed part of the same page in Leonardo's notebook, to judge from their similar styles and their blue prepared versos. The extant draft (which is probably not in Leonardo's own hand) of the famous undated letter of "job application" to Ludovico Sforza reveals that, in times of war, Leonardo promoted his ingenuity as a military engineer, minimizing entirely his artistic prowess as architect, sculptor, and painter.[1] The letter probably dates from 1482–83 and is written in conventional left-to-right script, rather than in the artist's habitual right to left, signaling its official purpose.[2]

The detail study at the top of the recto of the present sheet depicts a mortar in the shape of an oblong box that fires a deadly whiff of small stones. The types of attachment mechanisms suggest that the weapon was intended to ride on a boat, as in the motif at the bottom left. The middle section of the sheet includes a variety of designs for long gun barrels. Here, the two slender, somewhat decorative gun barrels permitted a more or less simultaneous front-end and back-end loading, and the component barrels are all drawn apart to show the screw joins. The study immediately below portrays the corresponding gun cradle with a revolving mechanism at its base, labeled with the word *qua* (here), and inscribed with a note that "this instrument is for a galley and must be made of thin sheets of copper soldered with silver." The gun mounted on a cradle with the revolving mechanism seems to be a takeoff on the two *torre tormentaria* devices illustrated in Roberto Valturio's *De re militari* (manuscript 1446–55) that was printed in Verona in an *editio princeps* in 1472 and in Latin and Italian editions in 1483 (figs. 156, 157). Leonardo seems to have owned a copy of the treatise; it may appear in the Codex Atlanticus and Codex Madrid II book lists.[3] The fierce *torre tormentaria* devices were among the most

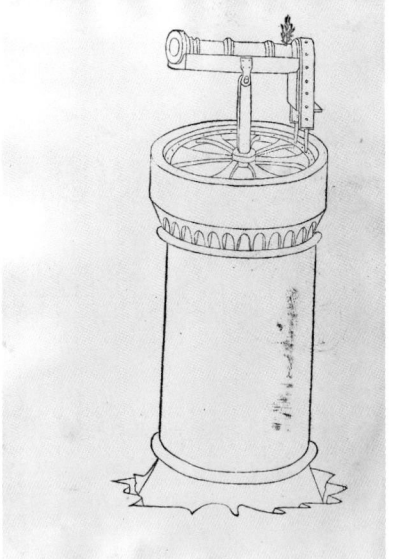

Fig. 157. Roberto Valturio, *De re militari* (Verona: Johannes ex Verona, 1472). *Instrumentus erigendi di machina sublime*, fol. 189v. Woodcut, 327 × 225 mm. The Metropolitan Museum of Art, New York; Harris Brisbane Dick Fund, 1926 26.71.4

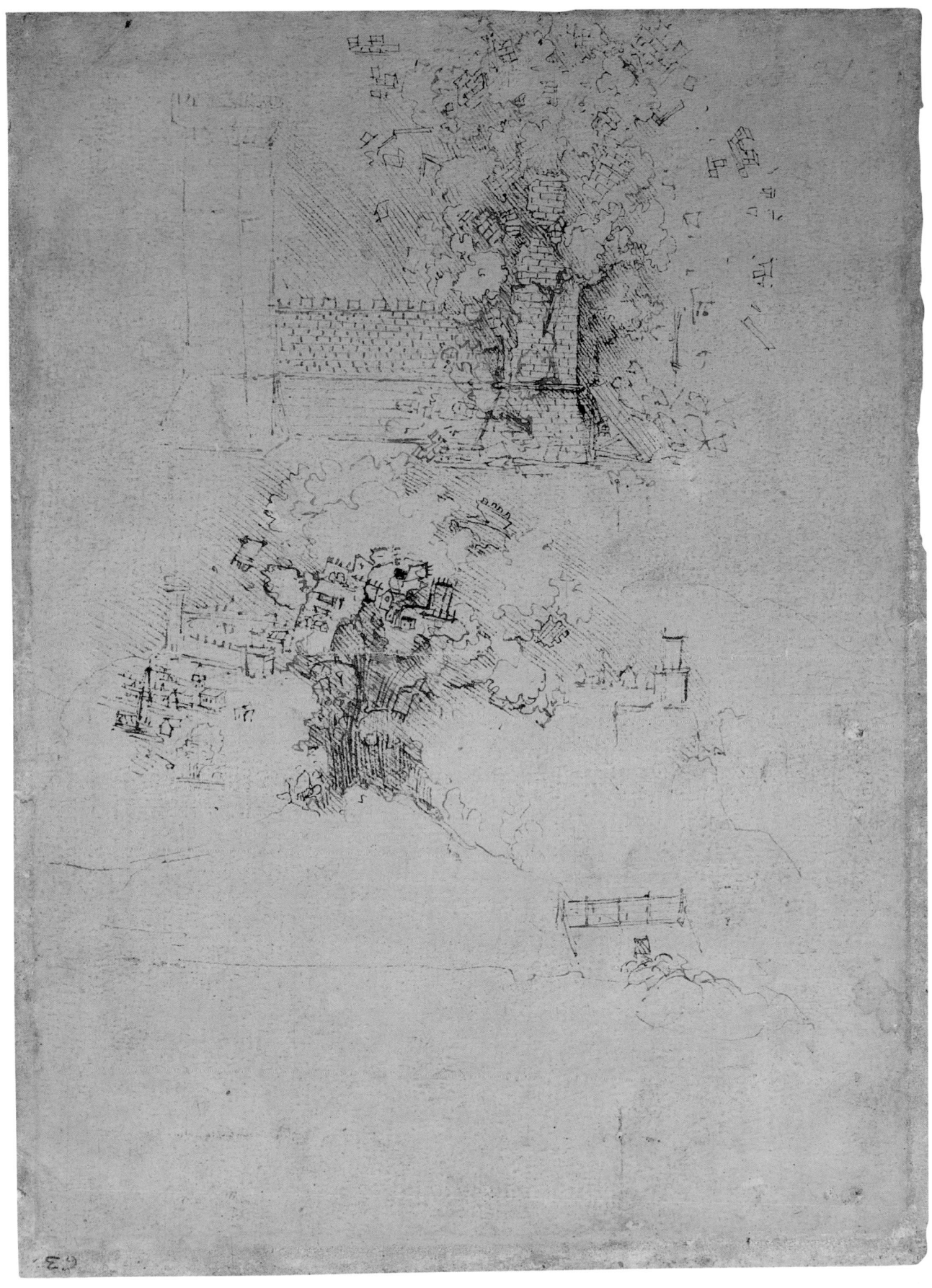

Cat. 52v

famous images of Valturio's treatise, and in adapting them Leonardo gave them a superb sense of immediacy.

One of the gun barrels below is attached to a long pole and was to be fired by pulling the long string through the lever. In drawing the loading mechanism for the thicker gun barrel further below, Leonardo omitted the handle and labeled the threaded cylinder device to put in the gunpowder "this enters into the one above." More difficult to interpret is the blown-up sketch of a six-barrel ignition device (indicated with six dots and labeled "to fire"). It probably offers a version of the design for the part seen in the oblong mortar on the boat below. Toward the lower right of the sheet, Leonardo also boldly sketched a round upright mortar in a wood cradle, which may have been intended for a boat as well. The prominent drawing on the lower left offers an overall view of Leonardo's elaborate invention in all its lethal grandeur, put to use in a naval battle. Here, the helmeted soldier steers the coracle-like war boat in frantic movement, as the oblong mortar (buttressed somewhat precariously on the shell) fires off a storm of deadly missiles at a vaguely sketched vessel with soldiers on the extreme left, which is being swallowed up by the smoke, fire, and waters. The contents of the oblong mortar are labeled "lime" (*chalcina*) and "powder" (*polvere*). It is not clear whether the boat would propel forward or backward in the process of firing. The waves of the sea partly efface Leonardo's inscriptions above and below the magnificent study: "this one throws poisonous lime." In a narrative way, this drawing vividly brings together some of the motifs and component parts that are the subject of the individual studies on the rest of the sheet. As Leonardo wrote to Ludovico Sforza, "I have also certain types of cannon that are most convenient and easy to carry: and these can fling small stones almost like a storm, and with the smoke of this [storm] cause great terror to the enemy, bringing about great damage and confusion. . . . And if the combat should take place at sea, I have many kinds of machines that are most efficient for offense and defense; and sea vessels that will resist the attack of the largest mortars, and powder and fumes."[4] As is usual with Leonardo, the expressive power of his images far surpasses that of his words.

The artist prepared the verso of the sheet with a blue ground on which to draw the blowing up of a fortification wall and a hill town in metalpoint, which he then reworked in pen and brown ink to gain tonal definition of form. The evocative close-up detail at the top of the sheet portrays the shattered masonry on the towers of the fortification going up in puffs of smoke and gunpowder. Pietro C. Marani has noted the similarity of design of these towers to the Torre di Bona di Savoia (Castello Sforzesco, Milan), begun in 1477. The bird's-eye view below shows the craggy landscape, the fortified town, and its buildings being blown up, with a church steeple recognizable toward the lower left. These drawings seem close in date to those on the recto, about 1482–84, and they likewise evoke one of Leonardo's statements in the letter of application to Ludovico Sforza "Il Moro": "If by reason of the height of the embankment, or the strength of the place and its position, it is impossible, when besieging a place, to use the plan of bombardment: I have methods for destroying any stronghold or fortress, even if it were founded on a rock."[5] The style and technique of the verso have also been compared to those of the apocalyptic sketches on a very late sheet that depicts the powers of destruction unleashed on a town, with water, flames, and smoke raining from heaven (Windsor, RL 12388). As the subject matter of that sheet seems loosely connected to the *Deluge* drawings (cat. no. 115), it has been dated anywhere between 1511–12 and 1517.[6] The themes of the verso of the present drawing and RL 12388, however, do not seem directly related, for Leonardo's concern here is with the *pazzia bestialissima* (his words for the madness of war), with military destruction, rather than with the cataclysmic forces of nature and the Second Coming.

CCB

1. C.A., fol. 1082r (formerly fol. 391r-a); Beltrami 1919a, pp. 10–11, no. 21; Richter 1970, vol. 2, pp. 325–26, no. 1340; Pedretti 1977, p. 295, nos. 1340–45; Villata 1999, pp. 16–17, no. 20.
2. For opinions on the degree of Leonardo's authorship of this letter, see also Beltrami 1909; Calvi 1916, pp. 433–39; Beltrami 1919b; Calvi 1925a, pp. 65–70; Venturi 1939; Pedretti 1975a, pp. 22–25; Vecce 1998a, pp. 77–79.
3. On Leonardo's book lists, Richter 1970, vol. 2, pp. 366–69, no. 1469; Pedretti 1977, vol. 2, p. 353, nos. 1469–1508; Ladislao Reti in Codex Madrid 1974, vol. 3, pp. 56–58, vol. 5, pp. 5–8 ("Ricordo de' libri ch'io lasscio serati nel cassone . . . / De re militari"). The *torre tormentaria* devices in the Latin manuscript of Valturio's *De re militari* (fols. 93r and v; Amma) are illustrated in Bassignana 1988, pls. 39, 40.
4. Richter 1970, vol. 2, p. 326, no. 1340: "4. Ho ancora modi di bombarde co[m]modissime e facili a portare: Et con quelle buttare minuti sassi a similitudine quasi di tempesta .; E con il fumo di quella dando gra[n]de spaue[n]to al' inimico con graue suo danno e confusione."
5. Richter 1970, vol. 2, p. 326, no. 1340: "3. Ite[m] se per altezza di argine o per . fortezza di loco e di sito no[n] si potesse i[n] la ossidione di vna terra usare l'officio delle bombarde: ho modi di ruinare omni rocca o altra fortezza, se già no[n] fusse fondata i[n] su el sasso ecc."
6. Clark and Pedretti 1968–69, vol. 1, p. 56, no. 12388; Kemp and Roberts 1989, p. 159, no. 85.

LEONARDO DA VINCI

53. *A Rider on a Rearing Horse Trampling on a Fallen Foe (Study for the Sforza Monument)* (recto)
Sketches of Walls; Triangles; Wave; Crossbow; Water (verso)

Metalpoint on blue prepared paper (recto); pen and dark brown ink on unprepared paper (verso), 151 × 188 mm (5 15/16 × 7 7/16 in.)
Inscribed in pen and brown ink, in right-to-left script, on verso in left column: *la / il ue[n]to che chapita / duna . valle . invno orga[no] / dell acq[u]ª che ve[rsa] . . . / sapere sela osse[r]/va do[n]de z a sopr/a la[n]golo della s[ua] / chaduta / acqua / qua[n]to . chadera . piv . presto / lacq[u]ª per la . linja . a . b. che / p[er] la . linja . b . c. / acqua / lacqua in questo locho fa jº retroso;* in right column: *il cho[n]tatto de djrettj murj . sara piv . forte / dove . il suo . a[n]golo fia . piv achuto c . d . / apocho cho[n]tatto e p[er]o fia . pocho forte a . b . / perche la . magiore p[er]ro . fia . me[n] debole c . f / fia . piv . forte . che . nessuno / [crossed out: semo] sele . base dj moltj*

tria[n]golj / equj . laterj . fieno . situate . sulantera . basa / del magiore tria[n]golo . equilatero . i tria[n]golj / mjnori . circhu[n]derano . [crossed out: qua[n]to] . tuttj . insieme / qua[n]to . il magiore . tria[n]golo———- / londa . che chade [crossed out: p] dj piv alto . sito / e[n]tra . sotto acquella che chade dj piv . basso / il balesstro largo 2 o[n]ce / e altura trara ta[n]to / qua[n] / to . quelo . che ffia alto 2 o[n]cie / e llargo . jª . p[er]che . quello . cheffia / piv grosso ara meno dj portata / insino alla noce maffia piv gagliardo / laltra ara magiore tratto . insino . alla noce . [crossed out: maffia . piv . debole]

Lent by Her Majesty Queen Elizabeth II, Royal Library, Windsor Castle 12358

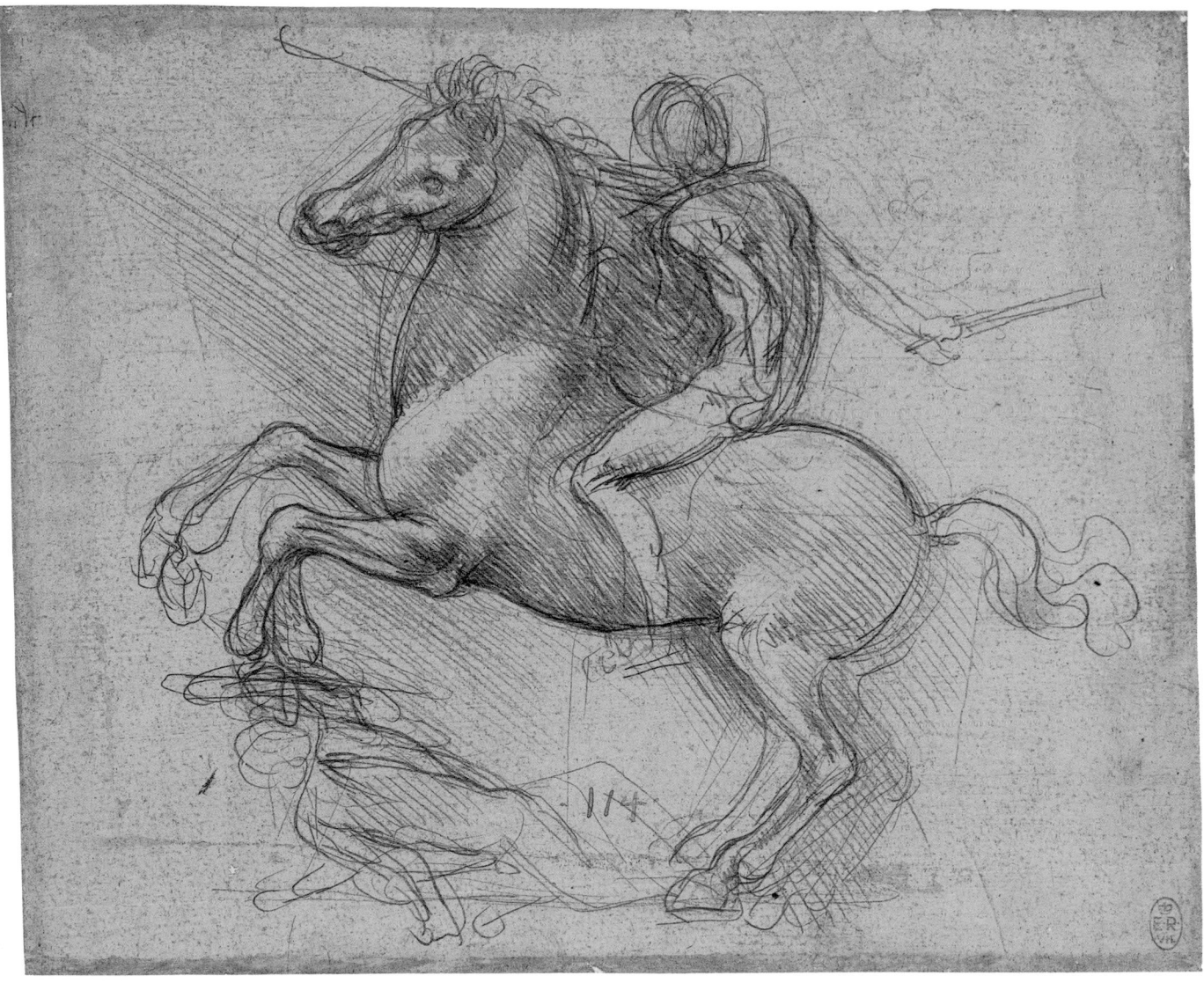

Cat. 53R

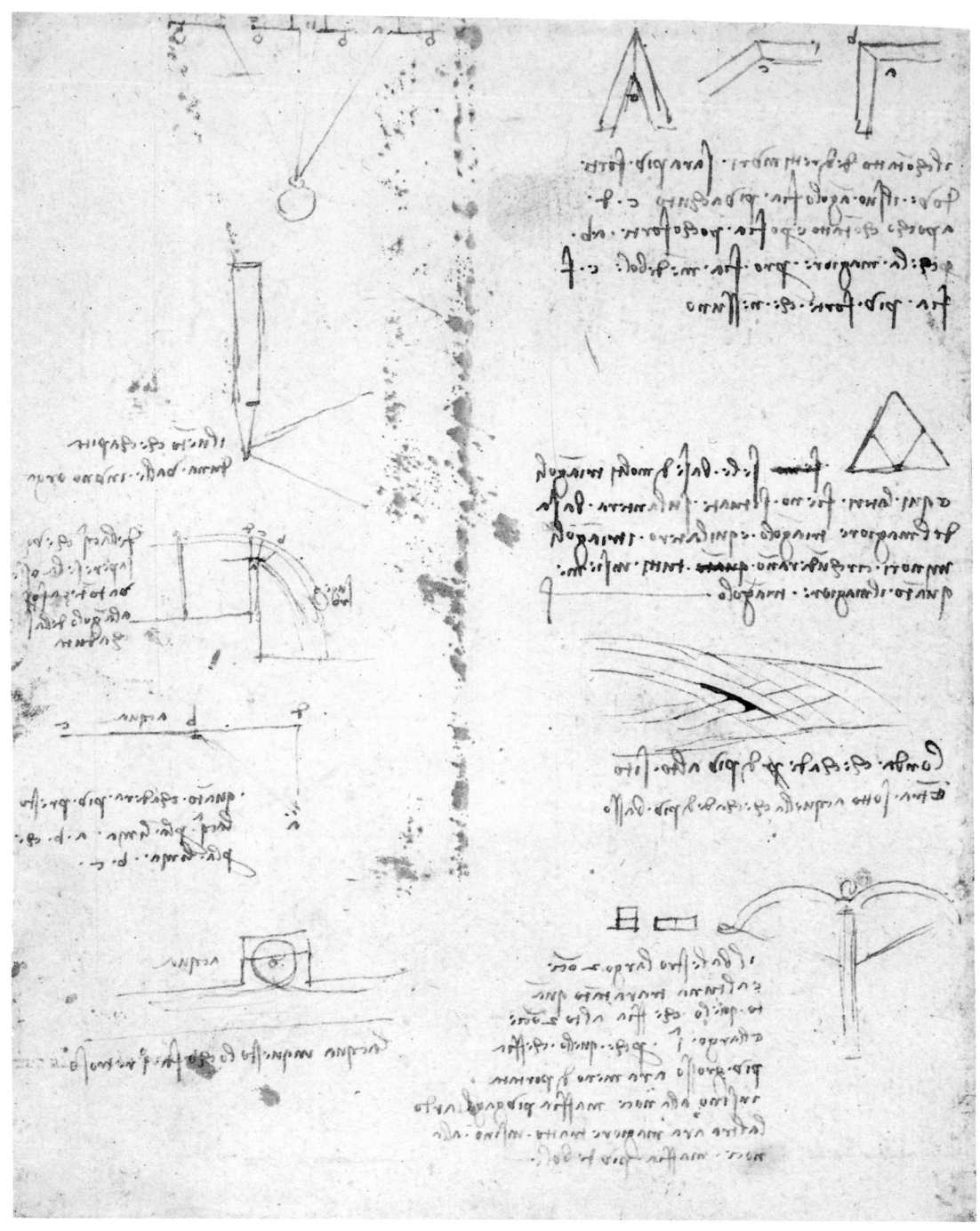

Cat. 53v

PROVENANCE: Windsor Leoni volume: 1519, Francesco Melzi, Milan and Rome (1491/93–ca. 1570); ca. 1570, Orazio Melzi; by 1590, Pompeo Leoni, Madrid and Milan (ca. 1533–1608; Lugt under 2885); ca. 1613, Thomas Howard, second earl of Arundel (1586–1646); before 1690, British Royal Collection (inventory of King George III's collection, ca. 1810).

LITERATURE: Grosvenor 1878, vol. 2, p. 33 (bottom); Richter 1883, vol. 2, pp. 2–3, 5, pl. 67; Müller-Walde 1897, p. 95; Müntz 1898, vol. 1, pp. 44, 145–46, 213–14; Müntz 1899, p. 215; Berenson 1903, vol. 1, p. 155, vol. 2, p. 66, no. 1214, pl. 104; Seidlitz 1909, vol. 1, p. 178, pl. 30; Seidlitz 1911, p. 283, nos. 619–20; Malaguzzi Valeri 1913–23, vol. 2, fig. 492; Meller 1916, p. 224, fig. 4; Poggi 1919, pl. 81; Malaguzzi Valeri 1922, p. 98, fig. 70 (printed in reverse); Popp 1926–27; Commissione Vinciana 1928– , vol. 6, p. 24, pl. 276.1; Popp 1928, pp. 7–8, 24–25, 40, no. 30; Sirén 1928, p. 60, pl. 79; Bodmer 1931, pp. 185, 392–93; Hevesy 1931, p. 106; Berenson 1938, vol. 1, p. 173, vol. 2, p. 135, vol. 3, fig. 496, no. 1214; Royal Academy of Arts

1952, p. 10, no. 76; Brugnoli 1954, pp. 367, 373, 375, pl. 146, fig. 1; Clark 1954, pl. 11; Heydenreich 1954, vol. 1, pp. 66–69; Bovi 1959, pl. 14; Goldscheider 1959, pp. 177–78, pl. 106; Royal Academy of Arts 1960, no. 494; Berenson 1961, vol. 1, p. 253, vol. 2, p. 238, vol. 3, fig. 484, no. 1214; Salvini 1964; Castelfranco 1966, p. 226, fig. 38; Clark and Pedretti 1968–69, vol. 1, pp. 46–47, no. 12358; Clark 1969–70, p. 8, no. 34b; Richter 1970, vol. 2, pl. 67; Queen's Gallery 1972–73, pp. 24–25, no. 19b; Brugnoli 1974, p. 91, fig. 91/1; Gould 1975, pp. 58, pl. 2; Bush 1978; Visconti 1980, p. 116; Kemp 1981, pp. 203–4, pl. 57; Brugnoli 1982, pp. 94, 97, fig. 60; Pedretti and Roberts 1984–86, pp. 46–47, no. 19, colorpl. 6; Pedretti 1987b, pp. 61–63, no. 106; Clark 1988, pp. 139–41, fig. 51; Kemp and Roberts 1989, pp. 56–57, no. 8; Fusco and Corti 1992, pp. 11, 16, 18–20, fig. 1; Cunnally 1993, pp. 74–75, fig. 16; Popham 1994, no. 68; Clayton 1996–97, pp. 49–55, no. 23; Butterfield 1997, pp. 166–68; Arasse 1998, pp. 243, 245, fig. 176; Fiorio 1998e, pp. 41–42, fig. 2.2; Butterfield 2001; Clayton 2002b, pp. 18, 20, fig. 10, under no. 1.

Leonardo's drawing of a nude rider mounted on a rearing horse indicates different solutions for the rider's arms. Although here Leonardo seems first to have lightly sketched the rider holding the reins of the horse with his left hand closer to the animal's neck, the artist more emphatically redrew the left arm to hold the reins tightly behind the rider's back, near the buttocks. Similarly, he drew the rider holding the baton of command both forward with his right hand and also stretched backward behind the body. Leonardo's vigorous reworking of the outlines left the marks of the metalpoint heavily incised on the paper. This spirited study probably dates at the latest from the mid-1480s, to judge from the figural types, as well as the soft metalpoint technique and pictorial rather than sculptural conception of the horse. The sheet seems unexpectedly close in technique and style to the Fitzwilliam horse study for the unfinished *Adoration of the Magi* (cat. no. 40). Compare, for example, the horse's forelock, large head, and flaring nostrils. The abstracted figural types of the rider and the fallen foe, with little internal description, seem very similar to those of the nude men toiling at a cannon foundry (cat. no. 51). The present drawing is dated here, therefore, a few years earlier than is usually proposed by Leonardo scholars. Kenneth Clark and Carlo Pedretti dated the scattered notes and diagrams on the verso of the sheet to 1489–90, based on comparisons to the Codex Atlanticus, for the spherical weight suspended from a rope, and to the Paris Ms. C, for the diagrams of water. The recto and verso of the sheet do not have to have been produced at the same time, and the paper on the verso is unprepared.

The exuberant study on the recto of the sheet was correctly identified long ago by scholars as being a preparatory design for the equestrian monument to Francesco Sforza (1401–1466). The "Sforza Horse" would occupy Leonardo on and off until he was forced to flee Milan in 1499, and his colossal model for the statue was destroyed (see cat. nos. 63, 64). The history of the "Sforza Horse" appears to have also involved the great Florentine sculptor Antonio del Pollaiuolo, if the account in Giorgio Vasari's vita of that artist is correct in its details (see cat. no. 11). The two drawings by Pollaiuolo that are extant in New York and Munich seem to represent his idea for the equestrian monument. The evidence of technique in Pollaiuolo's New York sheet seems to suggest that it was probably a relatively finished working draft for a demonstration drawing (*modello*). The resemblances of design in the projects by Pollaiuolo and Leonardo—at least to the extent that they can be assessed in the two drawings that are here exhibited—seem undeniable, and the matter therefore bears some reconsideration. It is clear that Galeazzo Maria Sforza had already intended to commission a sculptor to produce an equestrian monument to his father, Francesco Sforza, about ten years before Leonardo expressed his interest in the project to Ludovico Sforza "Il Moro." A letter dated November 26, 1473, by Galeazzo Maria instructed the commissar of the ducal works, Bartolomeo da Cremona, to search for a sculptor—in Rome, Florence, or any other city—capable of executing a bronze monument of the defunct duke in a lifesize scale ("sia grande quanto era la persona de soa Signoria").[1] The last of the letters relating to Galeazzo Maria's inquiry dates from December 1473, and since no further record of the Sforza equestrian project exists from the 1470s, it is presumed that nothing came of it. Galeazzo Maria was murdered in 1476, and his brother Ludovico Sforza "Il Moro" was exiled from Milan from 1477 to 1479.

It is quite possible that on returning to power in Milan, Ludovico may have considered a competition, as was traditional in such cases, or at the very least may have had drawings sent to him by artists whose work interested him. One such drawing may have been by Pollaiuolo, and another may have been by Leonardo; until 1481–83, both artists were in Florence. An analogous competition was unfolding in Venice. Sometime between July 1481 and May 1483, Leonardo's master Andrea del Verrocchio had secured the commission from the Venetian Republic for the great bronze equestrian monument of Bartolomeo Colleoni (Campo Santi Giovanni e Paolo, Venice), following a competition among three sculptors of unknown name; Andew Butterfield has reasonably speculated that Verrocchio's two unnamed rivals for the Colleoni may, in fact, have been Leonardo and Pollaiuolo.[2] Scholars agree that the undated extant draft of the famous letter addressed to "Il Moro" (which is not actually in Leonardo's own hand, but which was certainly written on his behalf) has all the character of an employment solicitation, and can be broadly dated in 1481–83.[3] There, Leonardo advertised his services as a military engineer in times of war and as an architect, sculptor, and painter in times of peace. He concluded the letter by noting his wish to work on the equestrian statue of Francesco Sforza: "the work on the bronze horse could still be undertaken, which shall be to the immortal glory and eternal honor, in happy memory, of the lord, your father, and of the illustrious house of Sforza."[4]

Leonardo's drawings from 1490 to 1494 for the Sforza equestrian monument (cat. nos. 63, 64) suggest that he, or his patron, gave up on the earlier, more dynamic idea of a rearing horse, which seemed virtually impracticable given the bronze-casting technologies available at the time. The casting of monumental bronze equestrian statues showing a rearing horse would become feasible only much later.[5] Leonardo finally adopted a solution showing the horse in a more traditional striding pose that also rendered the rider more triumphant. The new design of the horse in Leonardo's monument appears to have resembled Andrea del Verrocchio's much smaller equestrian bronze of *Bartolomeo Colleoni,* the casting of which was being carried out at precisely this time, having been entrusted in 1490 to Alessandro Leopardi, who finished it in the spring of 1496 (see cat. nos. 9, 10; figs. 125, 162). Verrocchio had left the *Colleoni* incomplete at his death in 1488, probably at the stage of the full-size model. Leonardo appears to have changed his mind regarding the final pose of the "Sforza Horse," stimulated by his study of the *Regisole* (the most famous Roman equestrian monument besides the *Marcus Aurelius* in Rome), during a visit to Pavia, probably in June 1490.[6]   CCB

1. Transcribed in Fusco and Corti 1992, pp. 12–13 nn. 2–4.
2. See Chronology.
3. C.A., fols. 1082r (formerly fol. 391r-a); Richter 1970, vol. 2, pp. 325–27, no. 1340; Beltrami 1919a, pp. 10–11, document no. 21; Pedretti 1977, vol. 2, p. 295; Villata 1999, pp. 16–17, no. 20.
4. C.A., fol. 1082r (formerly fol. 391r-a); Richter 1970, vol. 2, pp. 325–27: "Ancora si potrà dare opera al cauallo di bronzo, che sarà gloria i[m]mortale e eterno onore della felice memoria del signore vostro padre e dela i[n]cljta casa Sforzesca."
5. Examples are Pietro Tacca's statue of King Philip IV of Spain (Plaza del Oriente, Madrid), produced in 1634–40, and Étienne-Maurice Falconet's monument to Emperor Peter the Great of Russia (Ploshchad Dekabristov, Saint Petersburg), unveiled in 1782.
6. The letter by Ludovico Sforza "Il Moro" on June 8, 1490, establishes the date of Leonardo's visit, for it notes that Leonardo is expected to go to Pavia, with Giovanni Antonio Amadeo, to join Francesco di Giorgio, in working out a project for a new cathedral in the town (transcribed in Beltrami 1919a, pp. 30–31, no. 48; Richter 1970, vol. 2, pp. 41 nn. 1, 2, 359, no. 1445).

LEONARDO DA VINCI

54. *Two Allegories of Envy* (recto)
Two Allegories (verso)

Pen and brown ink, traces of red chalk (recto and verso), 210 × 289 mm (8¼ × 11⅜ in.)
Inscribed in pen and brown ink, in right-to-left script on recto in left column: *Questa j[n] vid[ia] si figura chole fiche v[er]so 'l cielo / p[er]che se potessi vs[er]e[b]be le sue forze cho[n]tro a dio / fasi cola maschera j[n] volto dj be[l]la dimostratio / ne fassi chela ferita nella vissta da palma / e olivo fassi ferito lorechio di lavro e / mirto a ssignificare che vettoria e vertu loffendono fassi le vsscire molti folgori / a ssignificare il suo mal djre fassi magra / e ssecha p[er]che*

sempre j[n] continuo strvgime[n]to / fasse le jl core roso da vn serpe[n]te e[n]fian / te fassi le vn turchasso che le frecie / lingue p[er]che speso cho[n] quela offe[n]de / fasse le vna pe[l]le dj liopardo p[er]che chuel[lo] / p[er] invidja ama[z]za i[l] lione chon i[n]ga[n]no / fasse le vn uaso j[n] mano pie[n] dj fiori essi / acque li pie[n] dj scorpioni e rosspi e altri / veneni fasse le chavalchare la morte / p[er]che la invidia no[n] more[n]do mai languisce a signoreg[g]iare fassele la briglia [chari] / cha e charicha dj djv[er]si armj p[er]che / tuti strume[n]ti de la morte; toward center of upper

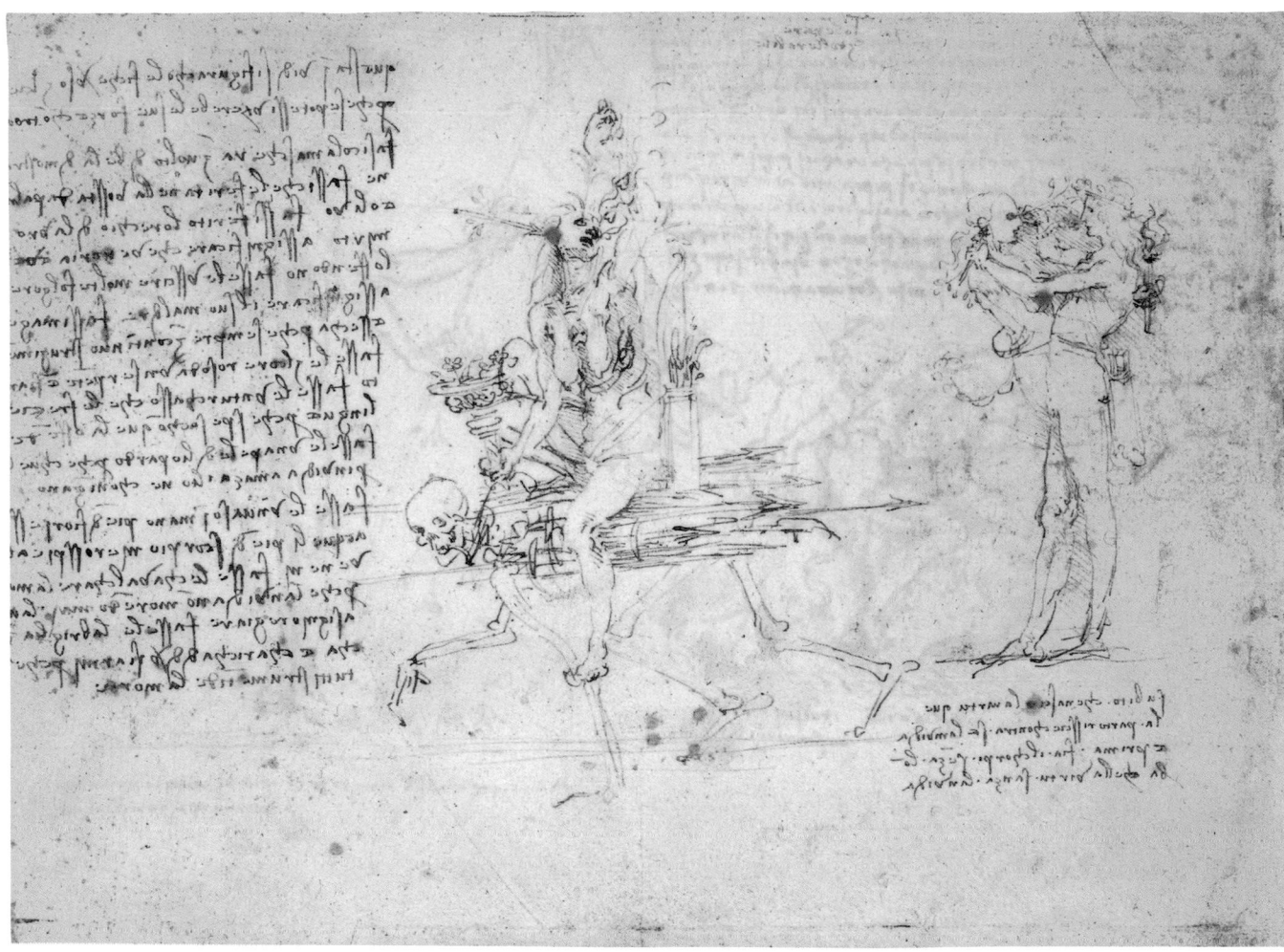

Cat. 54R

border: *Tolerare. / J[n]tolerabile*; on right below figures: *subito che nascie la uirtu quel / la partorisscie chontra se la invidja / e prima . sia . il chorpo . se[n]za . lo[m]b[r]a chella virtù . sanza . la invidja*; on verso, in right-to-left script, on upper left: *questo si e . il piacere · i[n]sieme chol dispiacere . e figuransi binati p[er]che mai luno e spiccato dal altro / fan[n]osi cholle schiene voltate . p[er]che son chontrari l'uno a l'altro fan[n]osi fondati sopra vn me / desimo corpo p[er]che an[n]o vn medesimo fondame[n]to j[n]p[er]oche l fondame[n]to del piaciere / si e la faticha chol dispiacere il fon- dame[n]to del dispiacere si sono j vani e lascivi piacieri E pero qui si figura chola channa nella ma[n] destra ch e vana e se[n]za forza / e le pvnture fatte cho quela so[n] uenenose metto[n]si j[n] Toscana al sostegnio / de letti a significare che quivi si fan[n]o j vani sogni e quivi si chonsuma / gra[n] parte della vita quiui si gitta di molto vtile tempo c[i]oe quel della mattina / che la me[n]te e sobria e riposata e chosi il corpo atto a ripigliare nove fatiche / anchora li si pigliano molti vani piaceri e chola me[n]te jmagina[n]do cho/se j[n]possibili a se e chol chorpo piglia[n]do que' piacieri che spesso*

son cha/gione di ma[n]chame[n]to di uita siche per questo si tiene la cha[n]na per tali fo[n]damenti; below figures on left: *Il mal pe[n]siero e[n] i[n]vidia / over j[n]gratitudjne*; on upper right: *Piacere e dispiacere / fannosi binati p[er]che maj luno e sanza . lal- tro cho/me se fussin appiccati volta[n]si / le schiene p[er]che so[n] co[n]trari*; labeled near the groundline for the figures: *fango, oro*; below figures on the right: *se piglieraj il piacere sap[p]i che lui a djrieto asse chi ti porgiera / tribolatione e pe[n]time[n]to* Christ Church, Oxford 0034

PROVENANCE: General John Guise, Winterbourne and London (1682/83–1765; Lugt under 2754); his bequest, 1765.

LITERATURE: Passavant 1836, vol. 2, p. 136l; Richter 1883, vol. 1, pp. 352–53, nos. 676, 677, pls. 59–61; Müntz 1898, vol. 1, p. 136; Müntz 1899, p. 138; Berenson 1903, vol. 2, p. 59, no. 1051; Colvin 1907, vol. 1, nos. 18, 19; Seidlitz 1909, p. 154; Thiis 1913, pp. 138, 193; Bell 1914, p. 60, A. 29; Poggi 1919, pls. 173, 174; Commissione Vinciana 1928–‚ vol. 1, pp. 99, 100, vol. 3, p. 23, pls. 99, 100; Suida

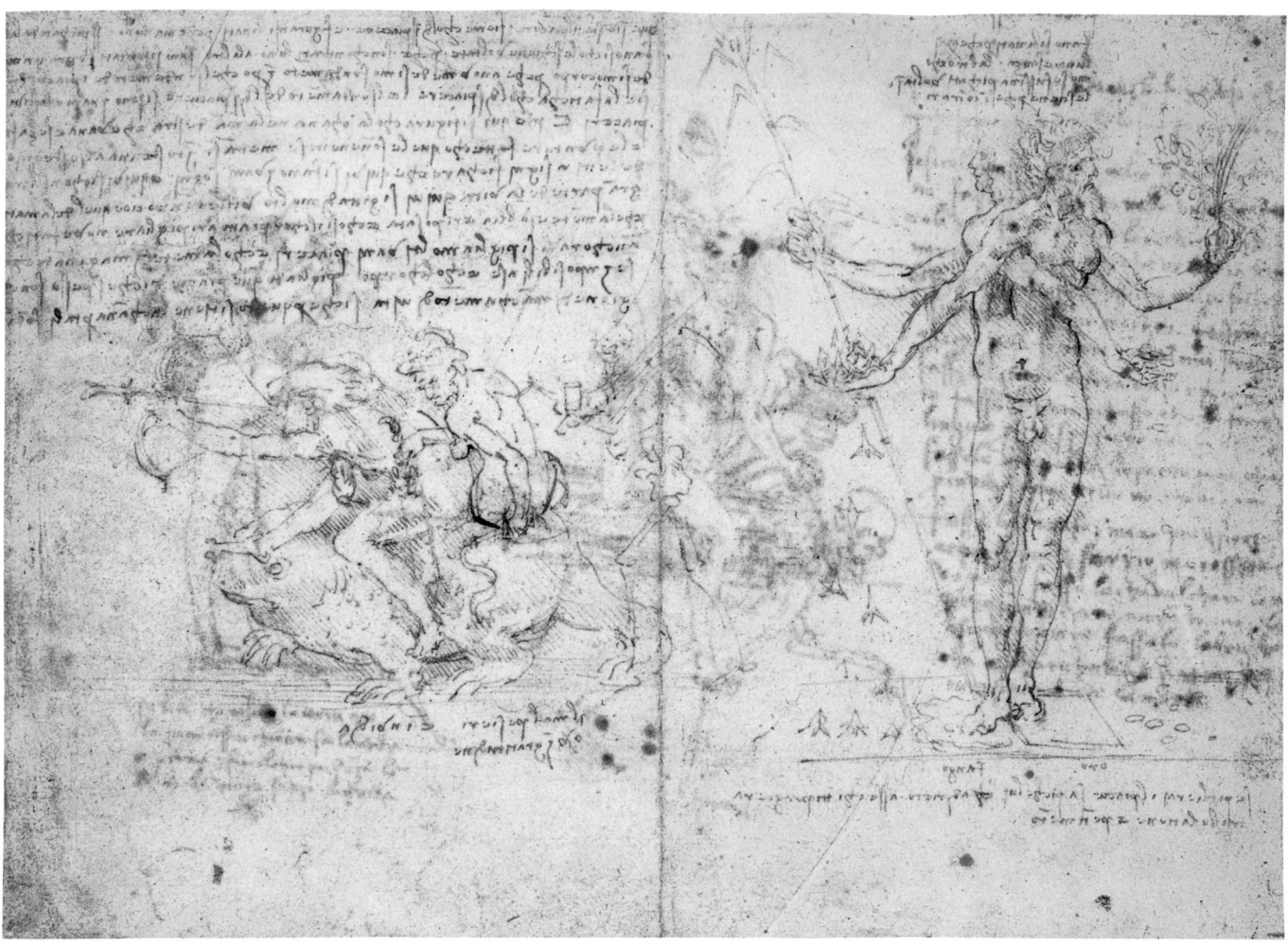

Cat. 54v

1929, p. 102, fig. 120; Bodmer 1931, pp. 158–59, 388; Berenson 1938, vol. 1, p. 181, vol. 2, p. 117, vol. 3, figs. 553, 554, no. 1051; MacCurdy 1938, vol. 2, pp. 492–93; Giglioli 1944, pl. 131; Royal Academy of Arts 1952, no. 55; Pedretti 1954; Pedretti 1957b, pp. 54–61; Matthiesen Gallery 1960, no. 38; Berenson 1961, vol. 1, p. 263, vol. 2, p. 205, no. 1051; Walker Art Gallery 1964, no. 34; Richter 1970, vol. 1, p. 386, no. 677 n., pl. 61; Byam Shaw 1972–73, no. 34; Lomazzo 1973–74, vol. 2, pp. 390–91 n. 1; Byam Shaw 1976a, vol. 1, pp. 36–37, no. 17; Pedretti 1977, vol. 1, pp. 384–86, nos. 676, 677; Gentile 1980, pp. 166–67; Kemp 1989c, pp. 239–40; Popham 1994, nos. 107, 108.

Envy as the born enemy of radiant virtue is a recurrent theme in Leonardo's drawings (cat. nos. 31 verso, 110) and writings. A number of such images in his sketches are inscribed with just the word *invidia* (envy), or with such aphorisms as "envy wounds with false accusations, that is with detraction, a thing which frightens virtue."[1] In contrast, the sketches in the well-preserved Christ Church sheet seem to have been conceived by Leonardo as ambitious exercises in the invention of allegorical subject matter, much as a painter would in a competition with a poet (a subject described in Leonardo's *Paragone*, a comparison of the arts). Although by itself the meaning of the fantastic imagery of the Christ Church drawings might seem impenetrable, the texts accompanying each of the motifs interpret the mute poetry—in some cases, step by step—in the clear, didactic style of "how to" instructions for a young artist. The author's voice in the long note along the left border of the recto of the Christ Church sheet is similar to that of Leonardo's intended painting treatise, the *Libro di pittura*.

The recto of the sheet offers two complex and quite different facets of the theme of envy. Toward the center, Envy is the

402

nude old woman with pendulous breasts who wears a mask that makes her youthfully attractive; she is attacked in the eyes and ear as she rides a skeleton that represents Death. Death is saddled with a quiver of arrows. The text to the left explains the negative character of Envy:

This [figure of] Envy should be represented making an obscene gesture toward heaven, because if she could, she would use her strength against God. Make her with a mask on her face of beautiful appearance. Make her appear wounded in the eye by palm and olive. Make her wounded in the ear by laurel and myrtle, to signify that victory and virtue offend her. Make her spew out many thunderbolts to denote her evil speaking. Make her thin and gaunt, because she is in constant contortion. Make her heart gnawed by a swelling serpent, and make her with a quiver with tongues serving as arrows, because she often offends with it. Give her the pelt of a leopard because that animal kills the lion out of envy and deceit. Put a vase in her hand full of flowers, scorpions, and toads, and other poisons. Make her ride Death, because envy never dies and never stops to rule. Show her bridled and loaded with various weapons, all of them instruments of death.

Toward the right, Leonardo attempted to illustrate the twin origins of Virtue and Envy, seen as two struggling figures growing out of the same pair of legs, like branches growing from one tree trunk. The sinuous, beautiful, long-haired figure on the right is Virtue, and the masked hag on the left is Envy, being attacked in the eye and ear. Envy is about to torch the hair of Virtue. The motif is inscribed below, "as soon as Virtue is born, Envy comes to the world in opposition to it, and sooner will the body be without a shadow, than Virtue without Envy." Another sheet of allegorical sketches at Christ Church is similarly inscribed at the top, "a body may sooner be without its shadow, than Virtue be without Envy."[2]

The verso of the present Christ Church sheet portrays two more allegories. The most inaccessible of the images on the Christ Church page, the group on the left, Leonardo did not explain, but merely labeled: "Evil-thinking (Il mal pensiero) is either Envy or Ingratitude." Here, as Carlo Pedretti has shown, one may rely on Giovanni Paolo Lomazzo's *Trattato dell'arte della pittura, scoltura et archittetura* (Milan, 1584), which further describes the images on the Christ Church sheet. It is apparently based on notes by Leonardo that are no longer extant; the Christ Church sheet may originally have

been double its present size, and the lost portion may have contained the text paraphrased in Lomazzo's treatise.[3] According to Lomazzo, "One can also make, for [the purpose of] teaching and educating about human life, other figures of this kind, such as Evil Thinking with Envy or Ingratitude, who is to be represented precariously placed on a frog, symbol of imperfection, and Evil-Thinking, that is the purpose of Envy, should be in front of her lean, dry, thin, pale, and choleric. . . . But Envy, who follows her wicked thought, is portrayed as an old, ugly, and pale woman, in the way that Apelles had already portrayed her."[4] The two nude figures riding the swollen frog are therefore Evil-Thinking and Envy, and they are followed by Death striding with the scythe and hourglass.

On the right of the Christ Church sheet, Leonardo represented Pleasure and Pain as two standing intertwined male figures, one young and the other old and bearded. The artist exhorted in his note above the group: "represent Pleasure and Pain as twins, since there is never one without the other, and as if they were joined back to back, since they are opposite to each other." The much longer paragraph on the upper left repeats the analogy of the twin figures of Pleasure and Pain with much the same wording, then expands on the attribute of Pleasure (the young man): "vain and wanton pleasures are the origins of pain, and therefore he is here represented with a reed in his right hand which is useless and without strength, and the wounds it inflicts are poisoned. In Tuscany they [reeds] are used to support beds, to mean that it is here that vain dreams come, and that it is here that a great part of life is consumed. It is here that much precious time is wasted."

CCB

1. Paris Ms. H², fol. 60v; Richter 1970, vol. 2, p. 248, no. 1197: "La invidia offe[n]de colla fitta infamia cioè col detrarre, la qual cosa spave[n]ta."
2. Christ Church, Oxford, 0037 verso; Richter 1970, vol. 2, p. 246, no. 1183A: "Prima sia il corpo sanza l'ombra che la virtù sanza Invidia."
3. Transcribed and translated in Pedretti 1977, vol. 1, pp. 384–86.
4. Lomazzo 1973–74, vol. 2, p. 391: "Formansi ancora, per ammaestramento et instruttione della vita umana, altre figuree in questo genere, come il mal pensiero con l'invidia, overo ingratitudine, la quale si rappresenta sconcertata e mal accommodata sopra una rana che è l'imperfezioni, e dinanzi il mal pensiero, cioè l'intento dell'invidia, tutto magro, asciuto, secco, pallido e collerico, con faccia malvagia e gesto iniquo, che scocca a mira una saetta, essendo tutto ignudo . . . Ma l'invidia la quale è di dietro, sequendo il suo malvagio pensiero, si dipinge vecchia, brutta e pallida, come già la fece Apelle."

LEONARDO DA VINCI

55. *Designs for a Maritime Assault Mechanism and a Device for Bending Beams*

Pen and brown ink over traces of black chalk, 283 × 201 mm
(11 ⅛ × 7 ¹⁵⁄₁₆ in.)
Inscribed in pen and brown ink, in right-to-left script, on recto above
upper drawing: *pie[n] di fieno bagnjato*; to the left and lower:
*strume[n]to di vrno / p[er] damare p[er] ichalare / vnatore di sopra
esse lle / fusino due torrj va p[er] / tale linia chelluna . fa / cj scudo.
allaltra ma / fa chel mare . sia cho[n]tu / tj . isegnj di tranqujlita*;
above lower drawing: *questibuchi . vo liano. essere dipari alteça . a 2
. a 2.*; at center of lower drawing: *sotterra*; beneath lower drawing:
modo di torciere vna trave p[e]r fare ichavalettj; at lower border in
graphite in a modern hand: *Ecriture de Leonard de Vinci — Le facsimile de cet fragment a été publié à Londres*; on verso in pen and
black ink in a nineteenth-century hand, presumably that of M.
Lefebvre: *Vendu par moi pour la somme de cent francs a Monsieur
Picchioni ce dessin autogra/phe de Leonard de Vinci, provenant de la
Collection de Mr Garnier President du tribunal / de la Rochelle, et
qui m'a été saisi par ordre de Mr hallon juge d'instruction il y a /
environ un mois et rendu au bout de quelques jours Paris ce 11 Juin
1849 / Lefebvre / Libraire 9 rue rameau*; in another hand (probably
that of Stefan Zweig): *gut*; unrelated fragment of an account
inscribed in a different pen and brown ink in a late-fifteenth-century
hand (in another direction) at right border
The Pierpont Morgan Library, New York; Gift of Otto Manley,
1986 1986.50

PROVENANCE: Presumably Francesco Melzi, Milan and Rome
(1491/93–ca. 1570) (heir to Leonardo's drawings); Garnier (accord-
ing to Lefebvre's inscription; Jean Garnier [?] [1754–1820]);
Lefebvre, Paris; probably Luigi Picchioni (active first half of the
nineteenth century); possibly Count Guglielmo Libri; his sale,
Sotheby's, London, June 1, 1864, part of lot 142; Alfred Morrison,
London (see Richter 1883, vol. 1, p. 7, no. 50); his sale, Sotheby's,
London, April 17, 1918, lot 174; Enrico Fatio, Geneva; Stefan Zweig,
Geneva (1881–1942); private collection, Germany; Edmund
Schilling, London; private collection, Switzerland; acquired by the
museum in 1986.

LITERATURE: Richter 1883, vol. 1, p. 7, no. 50; Morrison 1892, vol. 6,
p. 325, pl. 161; Carusi 1926, n.p. [following x]; Richter 1939, vol. 2,
p. 109, no. 45; Steinitz 1948, p. 41; De Toni 1975, pp. 6–7; Pedretti
1977, vol. 1, p. 95, no. 46; Denison 1984–86, pp. 304–7; Pedretti
1988f, pp. 142–43; Kemp and Roberts 1989, pp. 200–201, no. 114;
Paolo Galluzzi in Petrioli Tofani 1992, p. 200, no. 9.20; Pedretti and
Trutty-Coohill 1993, pp. 39–40, no. 6; Scaglia 1995; Letze and
Buchsteiner 1997, p. 146.

The drawing on the upper part of the sheet portrays a
monumental device intended to be attached to the bow of
a large boat attacking an enemy fortification on the coast.
Leonardo's note on the left of the image explains, "device to be
used during daytime from the sea to climb a tower above, and
if these are two towers put them in line so that one shields the
other, but make sure that the sea shows all signs of being
calm." The artist illustrated similar military offensive devices
in the Codex Atlanticus (fols. 49r and v, 50r, 977r and v, 1084r,
1088r, 1095a, 1095b; formerly fols. 15r-a, 15v-a, 15r-b, 353r-a,
353v-a, 391v-a, 392v-b, 394v-b) and in the Codex Trivulzianus
(fols. 2r, 28v) and described the defense of towers in the Paris
Ms. B (fols. 21r, 48r). The Morgan drawing is greatly more
detailed and shows the attacking device not in use, rather than
in action, reaching for a military fortification. Despite the
increased detail in the Morgan drawing, it is far from clear
just how the mechanism worked. The device generally operated according to a fulcrum principle: the long arm at right
would swing upright with a counterweight—that is, when the
curved receptacle on the left was filled with heavy wet hay.
The long arm on the right seems to represent the ladders that
would have swung upright, allowing soldiers to climb the
fortified walls or towers. It was clear to Leonardo himself
that the ingenuity and persuasive power of his drawing were
well ahead of the practicality of the device, for as he cautioned
in his note, the waters had to be perfectly calm. The boat
might otherwise have sunk in the operation of the tall,
swinging mechanism.

The drawing on the lower part of the sheet is in a much
larger proportional scale than that of the device above. It
shows a wedge-and-lever contraption, on upright posts buried
in the ground for stability, used to apply pressure to make a
wood beam curve. As Leonardo's note below the image says,
this was the "manner of bending a beam to make frameworks." Curved wood beams would have served a variety of
structural purposes in small-scale and large-scale construction. Scholars usually date the Morgan sheet, like the Paris
Ms. B, to 1487–90, based on the clear expository drawing
technique and style of script. The fifteenth-century inscription
on the verso of the Morgan sheet apparently represents a

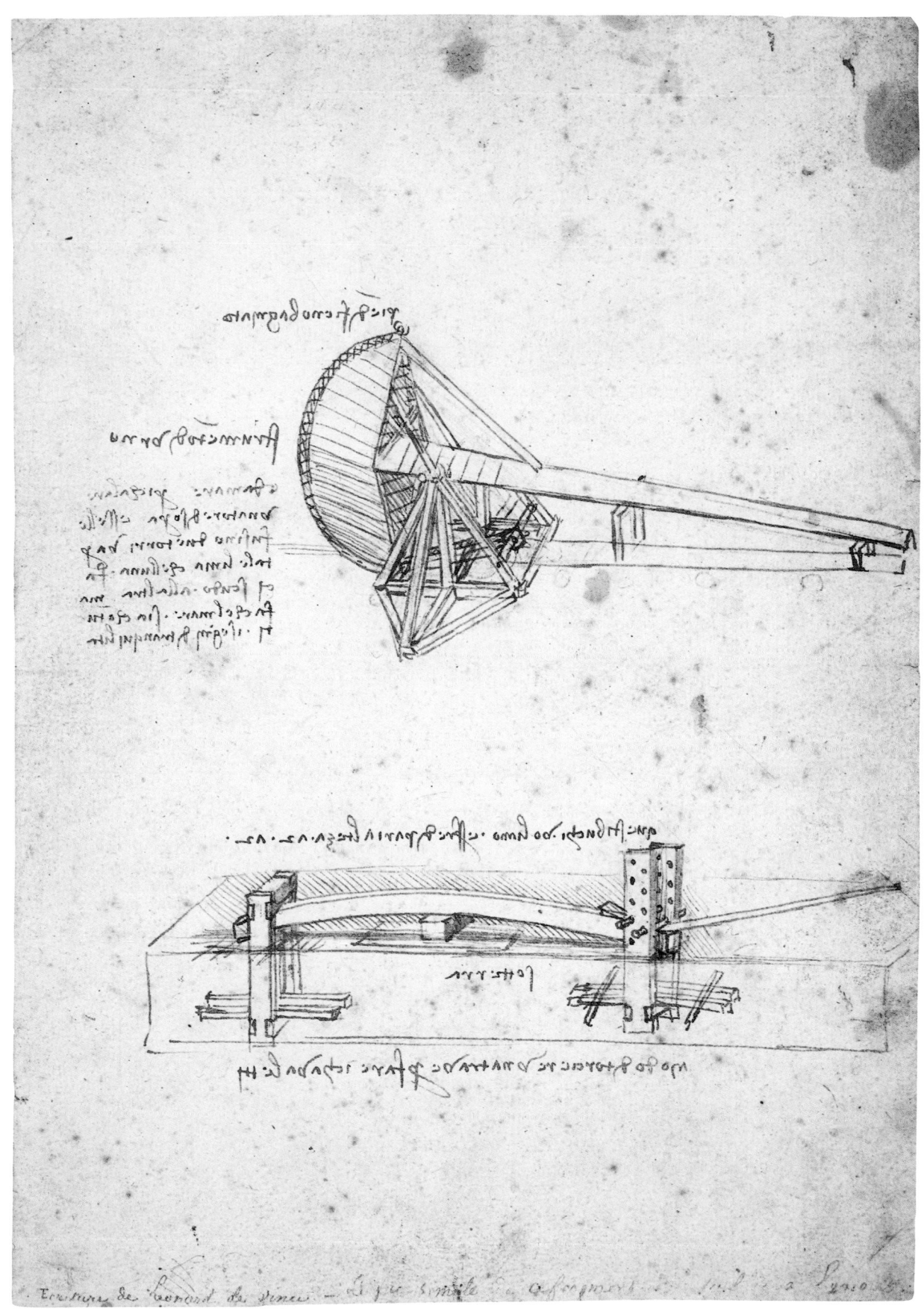

Cat. 55

405

fragment of an account of credits and debits related to the Milan Cathedral masons' works (Fabbrica del Duomo). From 1487 to 1490, Leonardo prepared designs for the domed crossing tower (*tiburio*) of Milan Cathedral; he hired the carpenter's assistant Bernardino de' Madis to build a wood model of the proposed *tiburio* based on his drawings. (See Chronology.) It may well be that the device to bend wood in the Morgan drawing served also in preparing the architectural model. The word *cavaletti*, which Leonardo used in his inscription beneath the drawing, was sometimes used in its specific meaning of wood roof support, as in the *Trattato I* by Francesco di Giorgio, the polymath Sienese architect, engineer, and artist who was Leonardo's friend and close associate in 1490.[1] At the time Leonardo was at work on the drawings for the design of the *tiburio* of Milan Cathedral, he seems to have reused a number of sheets with accounts from the Fabbrica del Duomo.[2] According to Carlo Pedretti, the Morgan sheet may have formed part of the Codex Atlanticus assembled by Pompeo Leoni in the 1560s, though Gustina Scaglia has questioned this hypothesis.

CCB

1. Scaglia 1995, p. 28.
2. Paolo Galluzzi in Petrioli Tofani 1992; inscriptions illustrated in Scaglia 1995, pp. 28–32 (figs. 2, 7).

LEONARDO DA VINCI

56. *Architectural Studies* (recto and verso)

Pen and brown ink, 145 × 219 mm (5¾ × 8⅝ in.); traces of former mount (recto); traces of former blue mount; piece glued to lower edge on left (verso)

Inscribed in pen and brown ink on recto, partly effaced: *193*

Département des Arts Graphiques du Musée du Louvre, Paris 2282

PROVENANCE: Giuseppe Vallardi (Lugt 1223, in green on verso);[1] 1856, acquired by the Musée du Louvre; museum mark (Lugt 1886a).

LITERATURE: Richter 1883, vol. 2, pp. 24, 32, pl. 80; Müntz 1899, p. 521, no. 49; Seidlitz 1909, vol. 1, p. 239; Malaguzzi Valeri 1913, vol. 1, fig. p. 311; Louvre 1919, no. 28; Demonts 1921, no. 15; Demonts 1922, no. 15; Commissione Vinciana 1928– , vol. 5, p. 21 and pl. 177; Bodmer 1931, p. 394, no. 200; Orangerie 1931, no. 15; Palazzo dell'Arte 1939, p. 159; Florisoone and Bacou 1952, no. 18; Palais de la Découverte 1952–53, p. 34; Tours 1956, no. 26; Sérullaz 1965, no. 222; Carpiceci 1978, p. 119, fig. 14 (verso), fig. 15 (verso), fig. 26 (recto), fig. 45 (verso), fig. 92 (verso); Pedretti and Roberts 1981–82, p. 125; Béguin 1983, p. 84; Marani 1984, pp. 130–31, no. 35, fig. and p. 130, under no. 34; Galluzzi 1987; Guillaume 1987, p. 208, fig. 200 (recto), p. 232 (verso); Schofield 1991, p. 134, fig. 13; Pedretti 1995a, p. 35; Ambrosiana 1998–99, under no. 4.

On the recto are a square enclosure with base; several towers, including one in the center with several stories; a sketch for a covered gallery with arcades on the right; a study of fortifications in the foreground; and in the upper part, a plan on the left and a design for a staircase on the right. Two studies of a building with a central plan appear on the verso.

This drawing was studied for the first time by Jean Paul Richter, who did not adopt Giuseppe Vallardi's identification of it as a plan for the Castello Sforzesco, but did recognize the defensive function of the central watchtower. Richter linked it to the fortress plan with three towers found on the verso of folio 23 of Paris Ms. B.[2]

The most complete study of this drawing was done by Pietro C. Marani (1984), who describes it this way: "a quadrangular fortress with circular keeps in the corners and a colossal watchtower overhanging the approaches. The approaches are, in turn, protected by a ravelin equipped with small cylindrical towers." The same motif of the ravelin—a sort of small spur that reinforced the outer walls—is explored at the upper left of the drawing; an interior courtyard and the indication of a round tower can be seen there. Marani considers this sketch to be the development of plans for a ravelin that are studied on folios 5r and 57v of Ms B.[3] One ought to read the entire sheet of drawings as a series of projects independent of one another: ravelin, watchtower, and fortress. The principal design, drawn from a bird's-eye view, is reworked at the upper left, where a fortress is laid out in a triangular plan with a square interior courtyard, bordered by a gallery on two sides. The ravelin sketched in the foreground is a smaller version of the principal motif. The detail of a tower in the left center is a variant of the section of the large tower that is

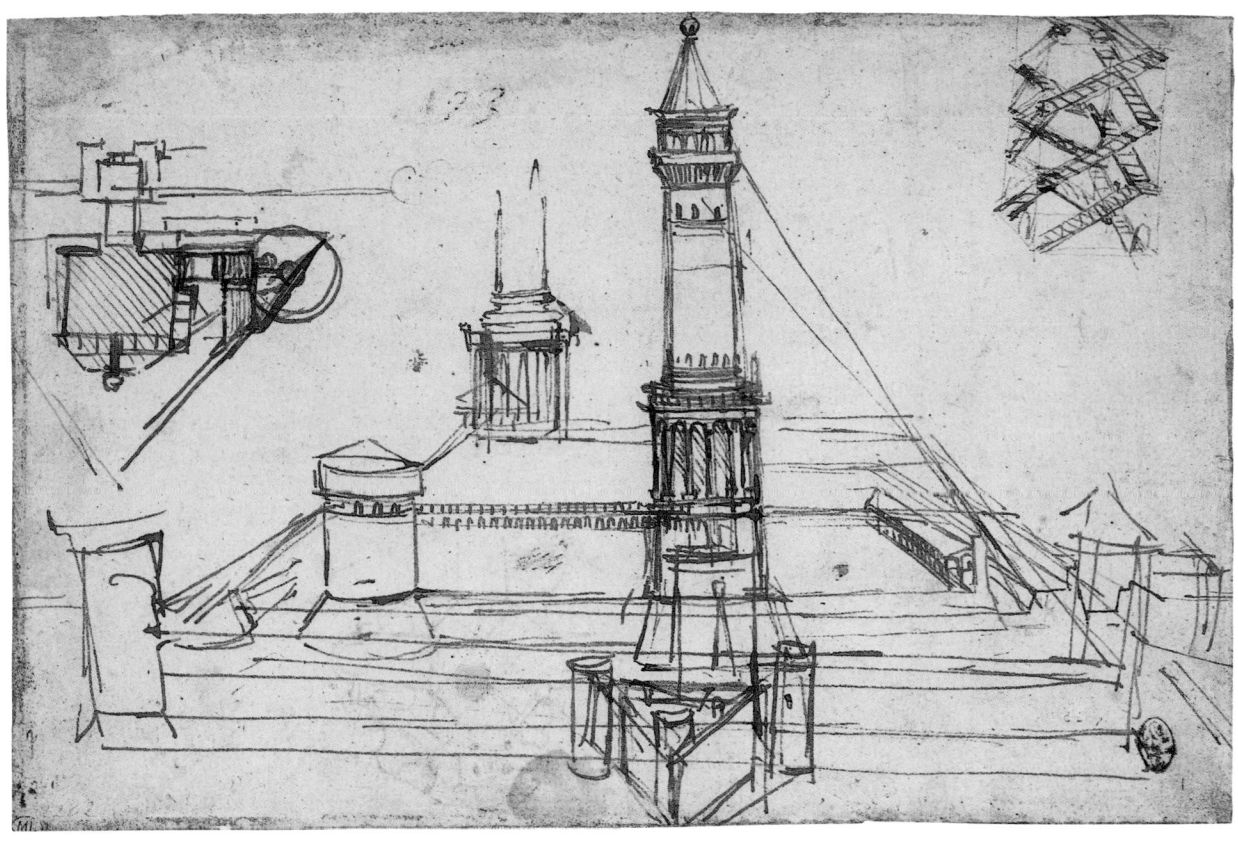

Cat. 56ʀ

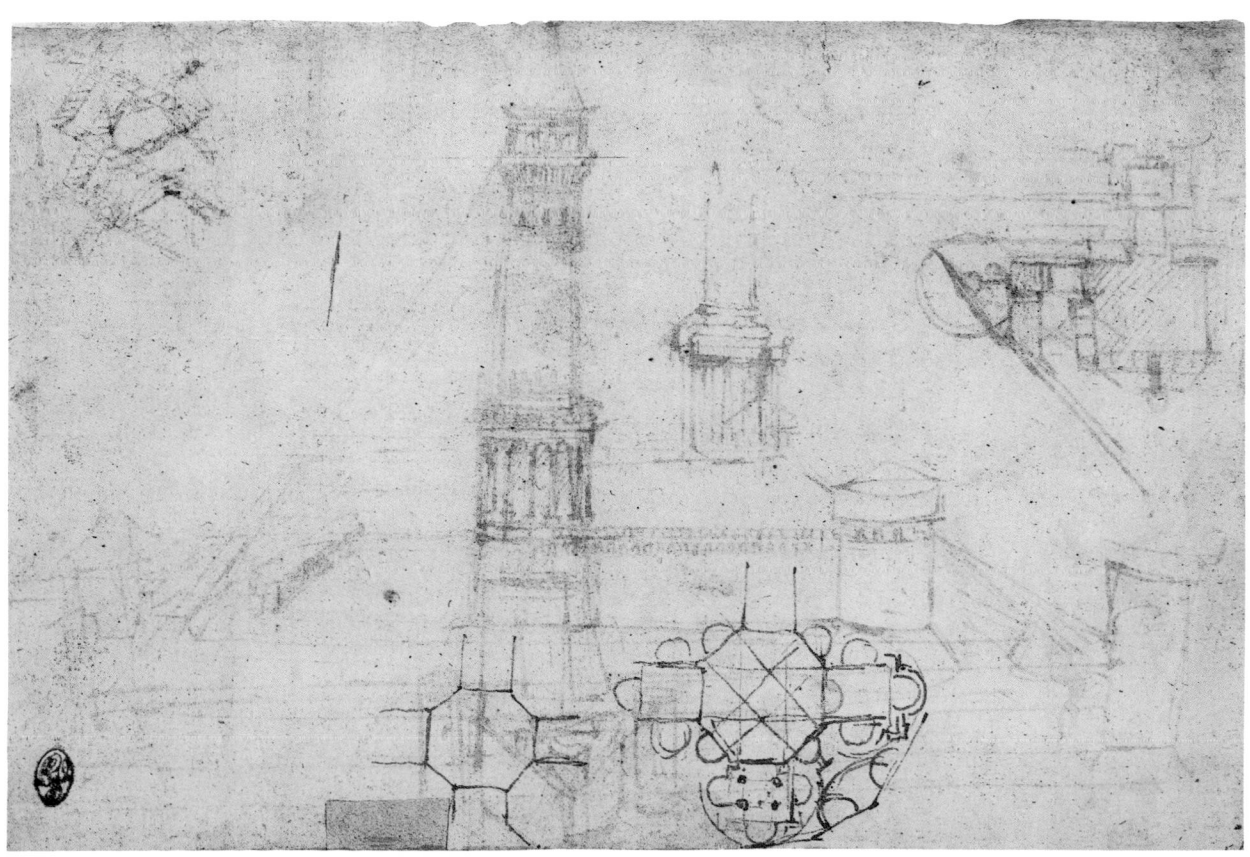

Cat. 56v

adorned with columns. Similarly, different types of roofing for the towers are indicated on the bastions.

In the upper right corner, Leonardo has drawn what seems to be the design (Vallardi writes, "rope ladder") for a staircase containing three completely separate stairways, a scheme that is developed several times on folios 68v and 47r in the same manuscript.[4] Multiple means of access to a building allowed uninterrupted movement without danger, as Leonardo explains in the note on fol. 47r: "qui è 5 scale con 5 entrate e l'una non vede l'altra, e chi fussi nell'una, non puo entrare nell'altra."[5]

Marani concludes that this drawing is not a bit of ideal, abstract architecture or a project connected to the construction of the Castello Sforzesco, but consists instead of studies directly related to projects undertaken at the request of Ludovico Sforza (as is the case with folio 23v of Ms. B).

The two studies on the verso, of a building with a central plan, which Vallardi already noted, are similarly related to the plan and elevation of the church in Ms. B (fols. 19r and 18v). They confirm the close chronological connection between these two works.[6]

FV

1. Vallardi 1855, p. 7, fol. 39 (Leonardo da Vinci): "Disegno su carta bianca a penna: schizzo di un progetto per l'abbellimento della torre del Castello di Milano a porta Giovia. — Da un lato, altro schizzo di una macchina. — Dall'altro lato, primo pensiero di una scala a corda. Al rovescio, vedesi indicato a penna la pianta di un edifizio ottagono. / Alto poll. 5.7. largo poll. 8.5. Il Castello venne fatto costruire da Francesco Sforza, IV Duca di Milano, con torri di pietra a punta di diamante. E' qui che tenevano gli Sforzeschi la loro Corte, o Rocca come pur si chiamava. Bramante e Leonardo concorsero ad abbellirlo e quest'ultimo vi fece il modello del gran cavallo di Francesco Sforza, che doveva essere fuso in bronzo, e che dai Francesi fu distrutto nell'anno 1500."
2. Marinoni 1990; Marani 1984, pp. 128–31.
3. Marani 1984, nos. 29, 33.
4. Marani 1984, nos. 36, 37.
5. See Marinoni 1990, fol. 47r.
6. Marani 1984, nos. 26, 27.

LEONARDO DA VINCI

57. *Anatomical Male Figure Showing Heart, Lungs, and Main Arteries*

Pen and dark brown ink with brush and green watercolor and wash that ranges from yellow to green to blue, over charcoal, 278 × 197 mm (10 15/16 × 7 3/4 in.)
Inscribed in pen and brown ink, in right-to-left script, on recto at upper left: *parte spiritualj / taglia p[er] mezzo core fegato e polmone e i [rog] / njonj accio tu possi interamen[n]te* ^*ve*^ *figurare / [crossed out: il] lalbero delle vene*; toward bottom, between legs of figure: *alb[ero] di vene.* The words inside the *vena cava* (labeling it "vena cilis") may not be by Leonardo.
Lent by Her Majesty Queen Elizabeth II, Royal Library, Windsor Castle 12597

PROVENANCE: Windsor Leoni volume: 1519, Francesco Melzi, Milan and Rome (1491/93–ca. 1570); ca. 1570, Orazio Melzi; by 1590, Pompeo Leoni, Madrid and Milan (ca. 1533–1608; Lugt under 2885); ca. 1613, Thomas Howard, second earl of Arundel (1586–1646); before 1690, British Royal Collection (inventory of King George III's collection, ca. 1810).

LITERATURE: *Quaderni d'anatomia* 1911–16, vol. 5, fol. 1 recto; Commissione Vinciana 1928– , vol. 6, p. 24, pl. 289.1; O'Malley and Saunders 1952, no. 116; Royal Academy of Arts 1952, no. 299 (hors catalogue); Esche 1954, pp. 153–54, fig. 21; Clark and Pedretti 1968–69, vol. 1, pp. 120–21, no. 12597; Royal Academy of Arts 1977, p. 22, no. 1; Keele and Pedretti 1979–80, vol. 1, pp. 82–83, no. 36; Favaro 1980, p. 371; Keele and Roberts 1983, pp. 28–29, no. 1; Baur 1984, pp. 56, 207, 279, fig. 43; Wasserman 1984, p. 18, fig. 11; Kemp and Roberts 1989, p. 112, no. 50; Caroli 1991, pp. 90–91; Clayton and Philo 1992–93, pp. 42–44, no. 4; Popham 1994, no. 232.

Leonardo inscribed this comprehensive anatomical drawing the "tree of the veins" at the bottom between the figure's legs, and "spiritual parts" on the upper left at the shoulder. The drawing may have been intended to illustrate a treatise on anatomy, to judge from its neat expository style of image and text. It may also have served in the construction of a three-dimensional anatomical model, because of its relationship to another sheet with studies of the viscera of a horse (Windsor, RL 19097r) that is inscribed, "when you have finished enlarging the man, you will make the statue with all its superficial measurements."[1] As is true of much of his anatomical illustration, Leonardo's chief concern in the pres-

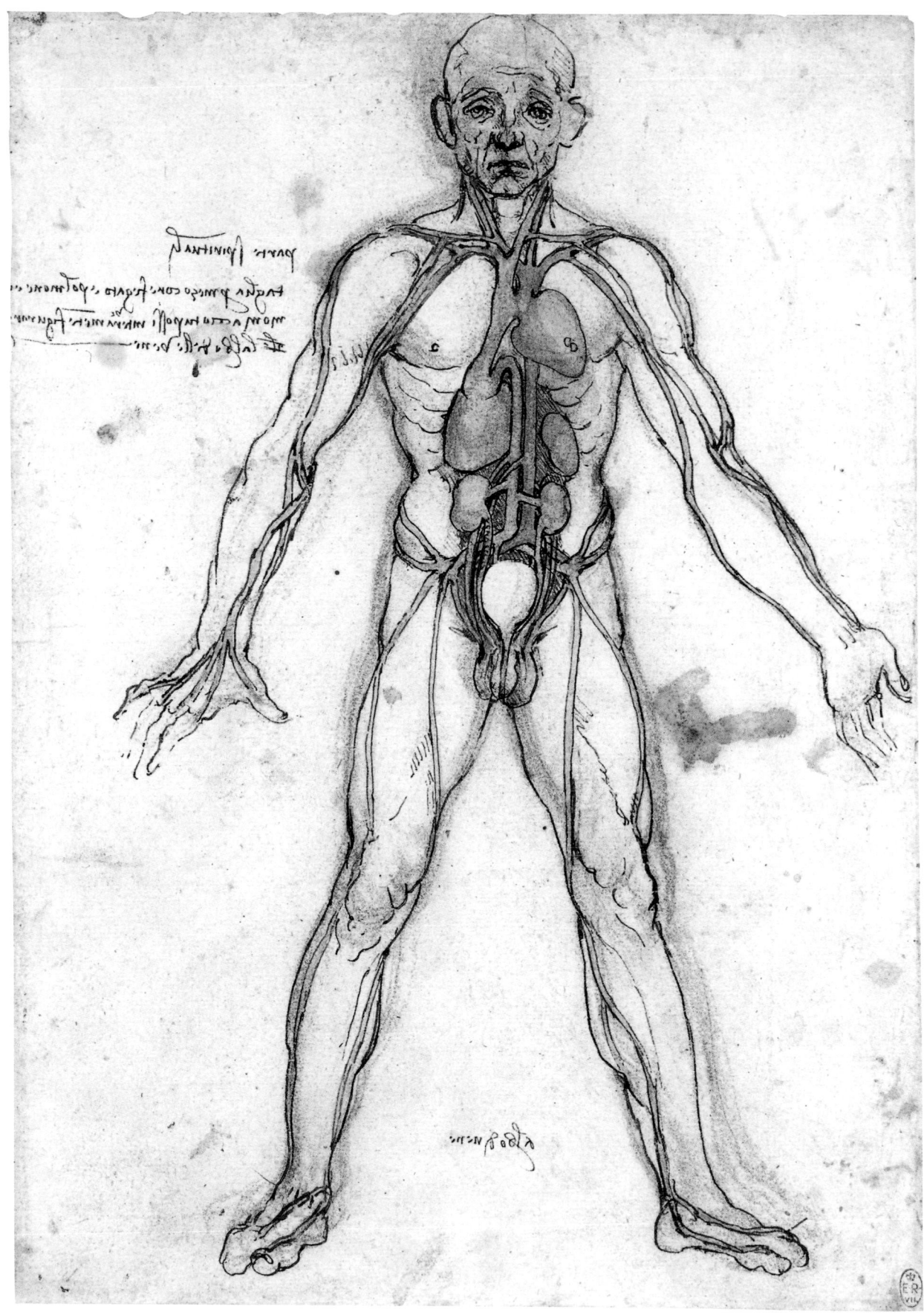

Cat. 57

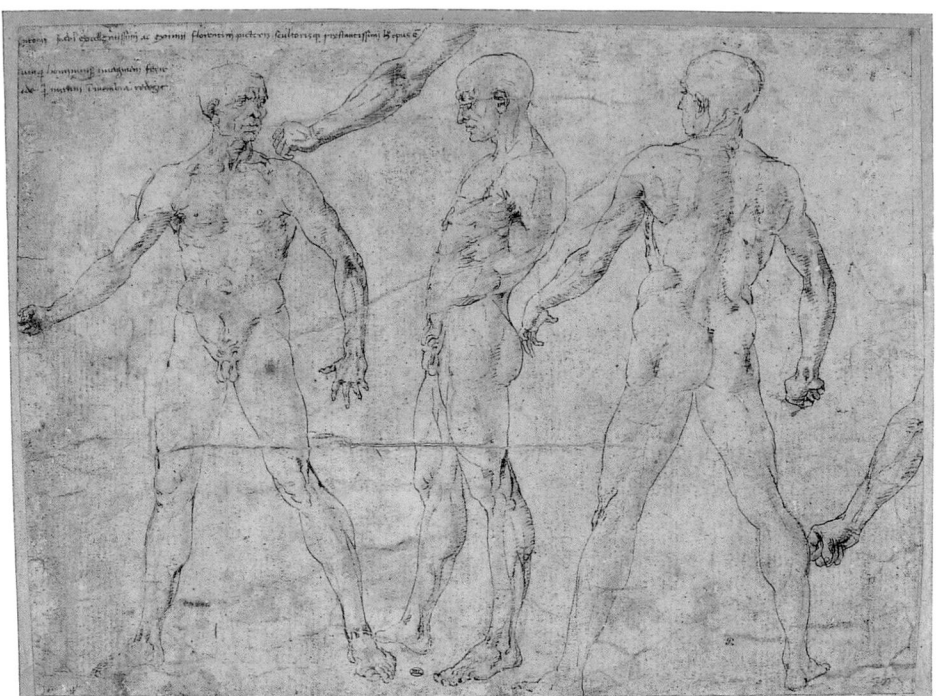

Fig. 158. Antonio del Pollaiuolo, *Nude Man seen from Three Angles*. Pen and brown ink, brush and brown wash, on darkened paper, outlines stylus incised, maximum 265 × 360 mm. Musée du Louvre, Paris 1486

ent drawing was to demonstrate the relationship of the anatomical organs to the surface of the body. He therefore experimented with a sculptural technique of illustration, bringing forward the vascular system and the main organs (the heart, liver, small right lung, kidneys, and bladder) from the plane of the man's external outlines, rather than drawing them as if the body were transparent or in cross-section. His general technique of using color as a means of distinguishing anatomical features is still found in anatomical illustration today (albeit in very modified form). In the note on the left, he explained that he intended "to cut through the middle of the heart, liver, lung, and kidneys so that you can represent the tree of the veins in its entirety." He would have drawn his findings from such a cross section onto a detailed study on another sheet.

According to the physiology of the great Greek anatomist Galen (A.D. ca. 130–200/210), and of subsequent medieval tracts that Leonardo read (especially Mondino di Luzzio's *Anathomia* of 1316, first published without illustrations in Venice in 1478), it was the blood vessels that transmitted the spirits or "humors" throughout the human body. In the Galenic system, the "natural spirits" emanated from the liver and were carried by the venous side, and the "vital spirits" originated from the heart and were carried by the arterial side. In the drawing, Leonardo also depicted the *vena cava* (which

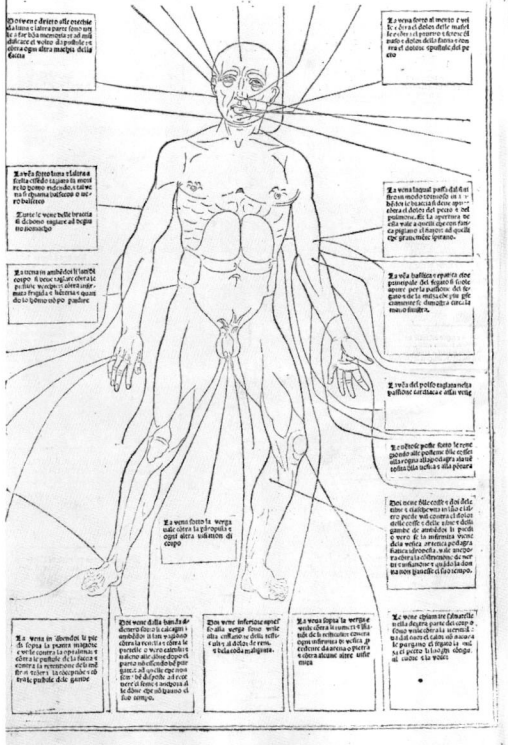

Fig. 159. Illustration of blood-letting (the "Vessel Man" or Phebotomy), in Johannes de Ketham, *Fascicolo di medicina* (Italian trans. by Sebastianus Manilius [Venice: Johannes and Gregorius de Gregoriis], February 5, 1493, unpaginated). Woodcut, 304 × 206 mm. The Metropolitan Museum of Art, New York; Harris Brisbane Dick Fund, 1938 38.52

he called the "vena chilis," but was here thus labeled by another hand) as the conduit of nourishment to the upper body, branching into the kidneys and testicles. His portrayal of the main organs related to the blood vessels was partly based on animal dissection and partly derived from previous anatomical writings. Although regarded as a relatively crude illustration by most modern scientists, this is the earliest extant attempt at an accurate representation of the vascular and urinary-genital systems in a complete human figure.

The "Tree of the Veins" drawing is here dated to 1488–90, in agreement with Martin Kemp, for, as he pointed out, the style, anatomical content, and ornamental script suggest such an early date. Other opinions on the date have differed widely, with A. E. Popham suggesting about 1504–6 (and later settling on the 1490s), Kenneth Clark and Carlo Pedretti about 1490–1500, and Martin Clayton about the mid-1490s. In support of the early date, in 1488–90, it should be noted that the figural type of the man in Leonardo's drawing recalls the male nudes in Antonio del Pollaiuolo's exercises in anatomical drawing, as in the much-copied, stylus-incised *Man Seen from Three Angles* (of which the best version is Musée du Louvre, Paris, 1486), which probably dates from the 1470s at the latest.[2] The figural type most closely comparable to Leonardo is on the left of Pollaiuolo's sheet (fig. 158). Next to Andrea del Verrocchio, Pollaiuolo was the artist who most influenced the young Leonardo in the 1470s in Florence. Also crucial is the relationship of Leonardo's present drawing to the Venice editions of 1491 and 1493–94 of the *Fasciculus medicinae*, the illustrated collection of short anatomical treatises to which the name of Johannes de Ketham is usually attached as author. It is often rightly pointed out that the man's pose in Leonardo's "Tree of the Veins" drawing (note the disposition of his hands and the doleful expression of his face) resembles a woodcut illustration of bloodletting (the "Vessel Man" or Phlebotomy) in the 1493–94 Italian edition of Ketham's *Fasciculo di medicina* (fig. 159). It is usually surmised that Leonardo borrowed the figure from the woodcut, as a point of departure for his diagram.

However, it bears emphasizing the well-known fact that Leonardo came to object violently to the medium of woodcut for the illustration of anatomy, as his notes attest. Moreover, based on stylistic comparisons to the illustrations in the Venetian editions of Ketham, it is possible to advance that Leonardo's "Tree of the Veins" drawing was innovative, rather

than derivative. The Latin edition of 1491, published in Venice, includes woodcut illustrations in the traditional medieval style of the "Urine Chart," as well as of the situs figures — the "Bloodletting Man" (the "Vessel Man" or Phlebotomy), the "Zodiac Man" (the phlebotomy chart with the signs of the zodiac), the *"Gravida"* (Pregnant Woman), the "Wound Man" (Surgery), and the "Disease Man" (Anatomy).[3] However, of the corresponding illustrations in the Italian translation published in Venice in 1493–94, only two are recomposed in a Renaissance figural vocabulary, the "Bloodletting Man" and the *"Gravida"*; the others are either the same or reworked only in small details. The "Bloodletting Man" stands out among the five illustration types. The addition of the illustrations of scenes (the dissection and the teaching of anatomy, for example) in the new Renaissance figural vocabulary no doubt helped modernize the book. Yet it is also clear that these illustrations are only partly new, and that the style of illustration of the book as a whole is internally inconsistent. The anonymous Venetian artist of the 1493–94 book illustrations was obviously looking at a variety of sources, unafraid to mix the old with the more up-to-date figural vocabularies of Giovanni Bellini, Antonio del Pollaiuolo, Andrea Mantegna (for the *"Gravida"* figure), and, we would argue, Leonardo. Leonardo's relationship to the traditions of printmaking and book illustration in late-fifteenth-century Milan and Venice is a largely uncharted topic, yet the little we know suggests that his drawings and designs offered a source to other artists.[4] It is worth pondering that the re-imaging of the woodcut illustrations in the 1493–94 Italian edition of Ketham's treatise was a response (whether direct or indirect) to the new figural vocabulary of anatomical illustration being pioneered by Leonardo. For example, the "Tree of the Veins" drawing here exhibited offers external anatomical detail and pictorial description far beyond those offered by the Venetian woodcut artist illustrating Ketham in the new Renaissance style. Given the conceptual difference between the woodcut illustrations of Ketham's treatise from 1491 and those of 1493–94, it would seem more difficult to demonstrate the contrary: that Ketham's 1493–94 Italian edition stimulated Leonardo's drawing, and that Leonardo's Windsor sheet must therefore date to the mid-1490s. Lastly, Leonardo seems to have owned not the Italian 1493–94 edition but Ketham's Latin 1491 edition; a *Fassciculu medicine latino* appears in his record of books "that I left locked in the chest," in the Codex Madrid II (fols. 2v–3r).[5]

Already in the late 1480s, in the anatomical metalpoint sketches that are partly reworked with pen on prepared blue paper, Leonardo had drawn situs figures with the organs pushed forth, as well as in transparencies and cross sections.[6] There, the awkward visual effects of his technique suggest that it was still a work in progress. It is clear that he was also pioneering similar techniques of perspective rendering, transparency, and cross section in his architectural drawings, and, in fact, one of the anatomical sheets on blue paper also contains minute architectural plans and elevations.   CCB

1. "Qua[n]do tu . aj finito dj / cressciere lomo . ettu / faraj . lasstatua . cho[n]tu / tte . sue misure—superfitialj." Clark and Pedretti 1968–69, vol. 1, p. 120, vol. 3, p. 37, nos. 12597, 19097.
2. Département des Arts Graphiques du Musée du Louvre, Paris, 1486; pen and dark brown ink, brush and pale brown wash, over stylus, on darkened paper; 265 × 360 mm (10⅜ × 14⅛ in.) (max.). Discussed with bibliography in Rubin and Wright 1999–2000, pp. 244–47, no. 50.
3. Cazort and Kornell 1996, pp. 105–6.
4. Alberici and De Biasi 1984; Bambach [Cappel] 1991b; Landau and Parshall 1994, pp. 33–38, 381 nn. 7–25; Ambrosiana 1998–99, pp. 140–41, no. 59.
5. Ladislao Reti in Codex Madrid 1974, vol. 3, pp. 56–58, vol. 5, pp. 5–6.
6. Windsor, RL 12626–12627.

LEONARDO DA VINCI

58. *Studies of the Human Skull* (recto and verso)

Pen and dark brown ink over traces of leadpoint (recto); pen and brown ink over black chalk or leadpoint (verso), 189 × 139 mm (7⁷⁄₁₆ × 5½ in.)

Inscribed in pen and brown ink, in right-to-left script, on recto from top to bottom: *Jlchoncorso dj tuttj . isensi assotto . se . p[er] linja . p[er]pe[n]dichulare luuola . dove sigusta . ilcibo a djsia[n]tia [sic: distantia] di 2 . djta / essidjriza . sop[r]a . lachan[n]a . delpolmone . e ssop[r]a . ilbuso . delchore . p[er]isspatjo . duno . pie E a . sop[r]a . se la / givntura . dellosso delcraneo jᵃ . [una] meza . tessta E a djna[n]zi . asse p[er] linja . [crossed out: emjspericha] orizo[n]tiale / ilagrimatoio . delliochi . a jᵃ [una] terza . testa E djrieto . asse . alla . nvcha a 2/3 duna . testa E a da / ilati . i . 2 polsi . delle . tenpie p[er] equale djsta[n]tja . e alteza . leuene chessifigurano . de[n]tro al crane / i nelloro . ramjfichare . siuano . in pronta[n]do . lameta . della . loro . grosseza . inellosso del craneo / ellaltra . meta . sinasschonde ne panjcholj . che uesstano ilcieruello . E doue . losso . e charestioso . dj de[n]tro / djuene . ellj . erisstorato . djforj . p[er]la . uena . a . m . la quale usscita delcraneo . passa . nellochio e poi nella* [here Leonardo left the text unfinished]; skull inscribed with letters; at lower right corner in a sixteenth-century hand: *F*; on verso in pen and brown ink, in right-to-left script, in a column at left border, above teeth: *djsop[r]a 4 2 4 6; / below teeth: 6 . massciellari dj / sop[r]a . an[n]o 3 radjce / p[er] ciasschuno iqualj / te[n]gano 2 . radjce / dj forj della massciel[a] / e jᵃ [una] . dj de[n]tro che i / 2 vltjmj mettano / in . 24 a[n]nj o circha / dj poj se 4 de[n]ti mascj/ellarj . dj 2 . radjcj p[er] / ciasschuno jᵃ [una] dj de[n]tro / ellaltra dj forj poj / seguita . le 2 . maestre / cho jᵃ [una] sola radjce E / djna[n]zi sonoj 4 de[n]ti / che tagliano e ano / jᵃ [una] sola radjce—— lamassciela . djsotta / aanchora. lej . 16 . de[n]tj . chome djsop[r]a / ma i sua massciellarj / nonanno . se no[n] . 2 . ra/djce . lialtri de[n]ti sta[n]no / chome quelj djsop[r]a / il de[n]te . 2 . ferma* [crossed out: 4] / *ineglianjma . lj. la preda / 4 . taglia . 6 . macina*; in center immediately below drawing of skull: *Jluachuo . della . chassa . dellochio . eluachuo dellosso sosstenjtore . della / ghuancja . e quello . del naso . e della bocha . sono . dequale . frofondjta [sic: profondjta] / e ttermjnano . sotto . il senso . chomune . p[er]linj . p[er]pe[n]dichulare [. . .] / eccjasschuna . desse . vachujta . atanto . dj profondjta qua[n]te / la . terza . parte . deluolto . dellomo . cioe dalme[n]to achapeglj*

Lent by Her Majesty Queen Elizabeth II, Royal Library, Windsor Castle 19058

PROVENANCE: Windsor Leoni volume: 1519, Francesco Melzi, Milan and Rome (1491/93–ca. 1570); ca. 1570, Orazio Melzi; by 1590, Pompeo Leoni, Madrid and Milan (ca. 1533–1608; Lugt under 2885); ca. 1613, Thomas Howard, second earl of Arundel (1586–1646); before 1690, British Royal Collection (inventory of King George III's collection, ca. 1810).

LITERATURE: Berenson 1903, vol. 2, p. 66, no. 1206; Poggi 1919, pls. 169, 170; Bodmer 1931, pp. 176, 391; Berenson 1938, vol. 2, p. 134, nos. 1206, 1209; O'Malley and Saunders 1952, nos. 3, 6; Royal Academy of Arts 1952, nos. 284, 286 (hors catalogue); Esche 1954, p. 124, figs. 13, 14; Heydenreich 1954, vol. 1, p. 126, vol. 2, p. 132, pl. 183; Berenson 1961, vol. 2, p. 237, nos. 1206, 1209; Clark and Pedretti 1968–69, vol. 3, p. 24, no. 19058; Woodburne 1978, pp. 262–73; Keele and Pedretti 1979–80, vol. 2, pp. 102–5, no. 42; Baur 1984, pp. 19–20, 180, 272, fig. 16; Philo 1985, nos. 23, 26; Kemp and Roberts 1989, pp. 58–59, no. 9; Caroli 1991, pp. 119–20; Clayton and Philo 1992–93, pp. 33–37, nos. 2A, 2B; Kornell 1992, p. 126; Popham 1994, nos. 218, 219; Galluzzi 1996, p. 235, no. 3.3.q; Clayton 1996–97, pp. 44–45, 47, no. 21; Arasse 1998, p. 72, fig. 38 (as Windsor RL 19059), pp. 275, 278, fig. 194; Zwijnenberg 1999, pp. 156–59; Kemp and Wallace 2000, pp. 72, 224, no. 189; Laurenza 2001, pp. xxviii, 18–23, 28–29, 37, 44, 176, figs. 17, 19; Clayton 2002b, pp. 10, 11, fig. 5.

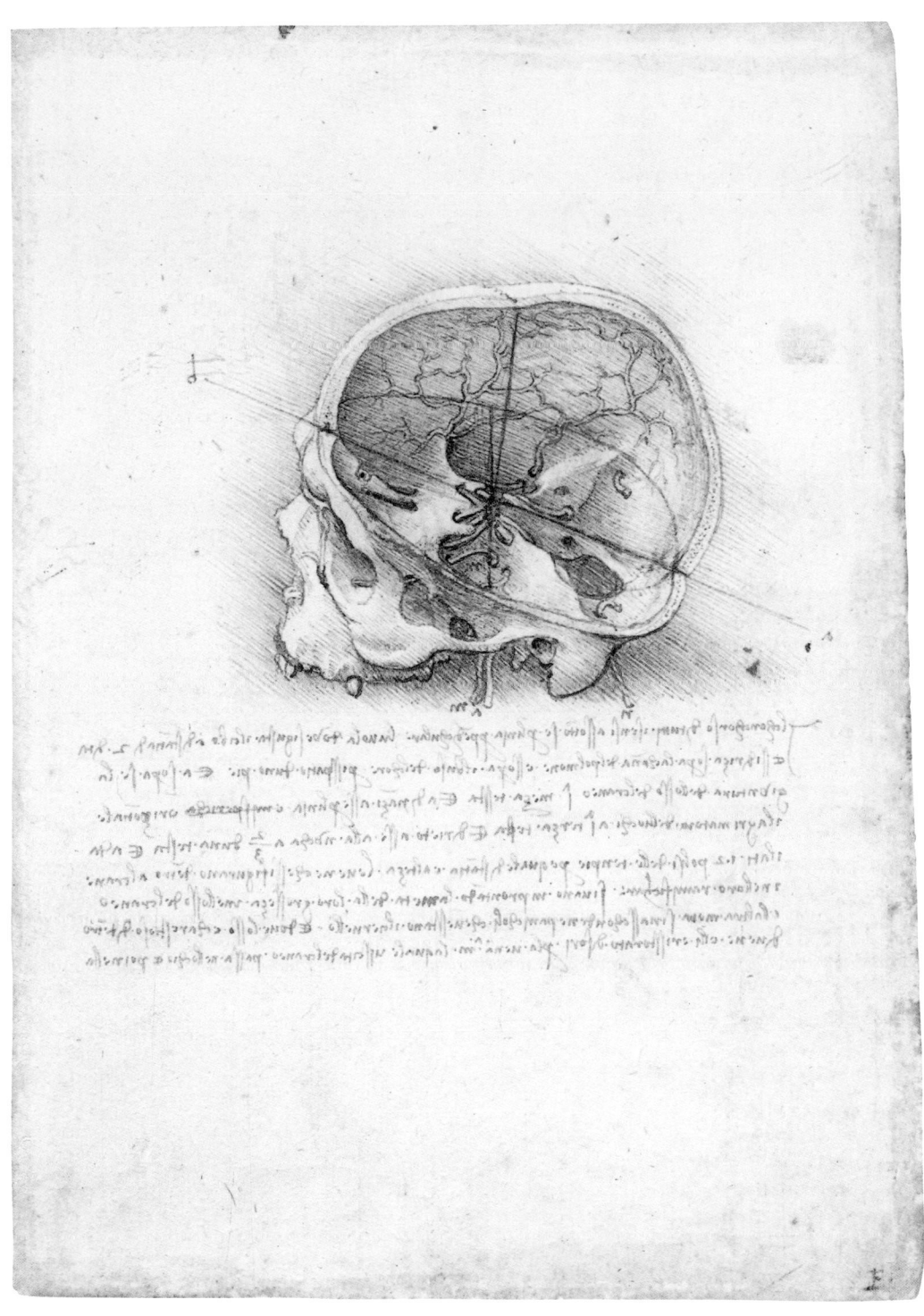

Cat. 58R *(actual size)*

The object of much scholarly study, this double-sided sheet is justly famous, for it is drawn with a breathtaking virtuosity of the pen. The style of parallel hatching is extraordinary for its fineness of line, nuance of tone, and overall sculptural impact. The recto of the sheet offers a meticulously observed side view of the sagittal section, to demonstrate the location of what Leonardo called the *sensus communis*, or confluence of the mental and imaginative faculties of man and the seat of the soul. The verso represents a large-scale frontal view of the human skull cut in section along the sagittal suture, which divides the cranium into left and right halves. Leonardo adopted this illustration technique (which is still used in anatomical studies today) to show the correspondence of the parts of the exterior of the skull seen on the right half to the interior parts and cavities seen on the left half. The section on the left also reveals the positioning of the teeth. Farther to the left, he drew and numbered four types of teeth "4, 2, 4, 6" to correspond to the formula indicating the presence in each skull of four incisors, two canines, four premolars, and six molars.

Based on direct observation, the series of studies of the human skull (Windsor, RL 19057–19059) represent the most innovative aspect of Leonardo's early anatomical research. The artist probably began the skull drawings on April 2, 1489, to judge from his inscription on the upper border of the recto of one of the sheets (Windsor, RL 19059). That sheet appears to be the first in the skull series, for the handling of the pen seems still timid, and the forms somewhat flat and disunified, by comparison to the present sheet. The skull drawings offer Leonardo's most lasting contribution in scientific terms, because of the superb accuracy of his observation. As is seen here and in the third of the Windsor skull drawings (RL 19057 recto and verso; fig. 160), the rigorously systematic method of illustration in sections and in highly descriptive angles of view constituted a groundbreaking innovation for the history of anatomical illustration.

Leonardo's skull studies were at least partly stimulated by his nearly quixotic search for the precise location of the *sensus communis*. Leonardo noted, "The soul seems to reside in the part of judgment, and the part of judgment appears to reside in that place where all the senses meet; and this is called *senso comune*; and [the soul] is not all-pervading throughout the body, as many have thought, rather it is entirely in one part. Because if it [the soul] were all-pervading and the same in every part, there would have been no need to make the instru-

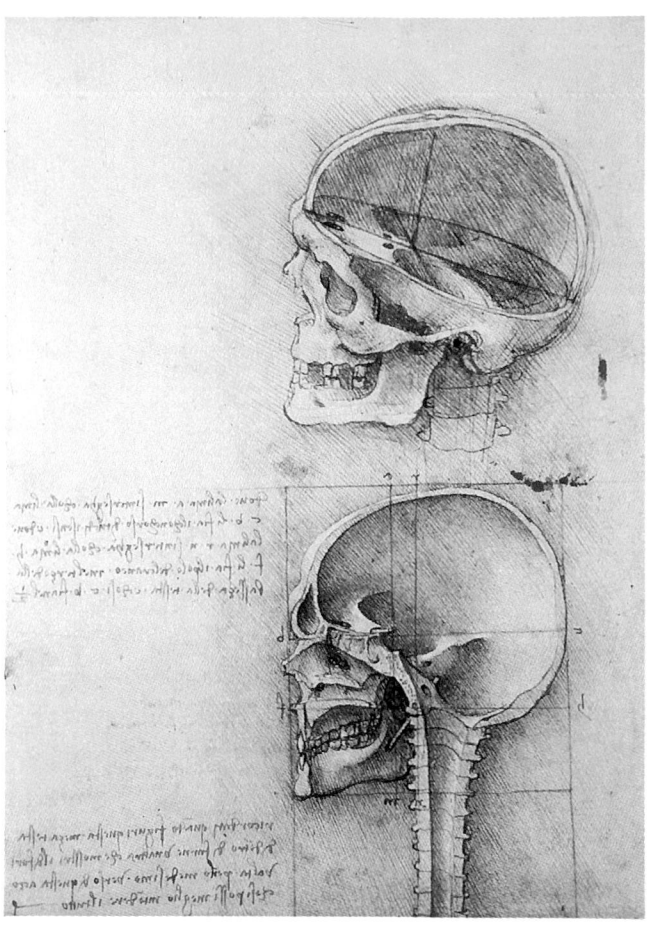

Fig. 160. Leonardo da Vinci, *Two Views of the Skull*. Pen and brown ink, 190 × 133 mm. The Royal Collection, H.M. Queen Elizabeth II, Windsor Castle RL 19057

ments of the senses follow the same path to meet in one single spot."[1] Leonardo identified the *sensus communis* at the intersection of upright and diagonal lines seen within the tilted plane inside the skull on the recto of the present sheet. Leonardo's words are poignant in their attempt to grapple with the similitude: "Avicenna will have it that soul gives birth to soul, as body to body, and each member to itself."[2]   CCB

1. Windsor, RL 19019r; Richter 1970, vol. 2, p. 101, no. 838: "L'anima . pare . risedere . nella parte juditiale, . e la . parte juditiale pare essere nel loco . doue . concorrono . tutti i se[n]si . , il quale è detto . senso comvne, e non è tutta per tutto . il corpo. , come molti . àn[n] . creduto . , anzi . tutta in nella . parte . , imperochè se ella (sc. anima) fusse . tutta per tutto . e tutta . in ogni . parte . , non era . necessario . li strume[n]ti . de' sensi fare infra loro . uno . medesimo co[n]corso a uno . solo loco."
2. Richter 1970, vol. 2, p. 371, no. 1482: "Avicenna vole che l'anima partorisca l'anima, e 'l corpo il corpo, e ogni me[m]bro per rata."

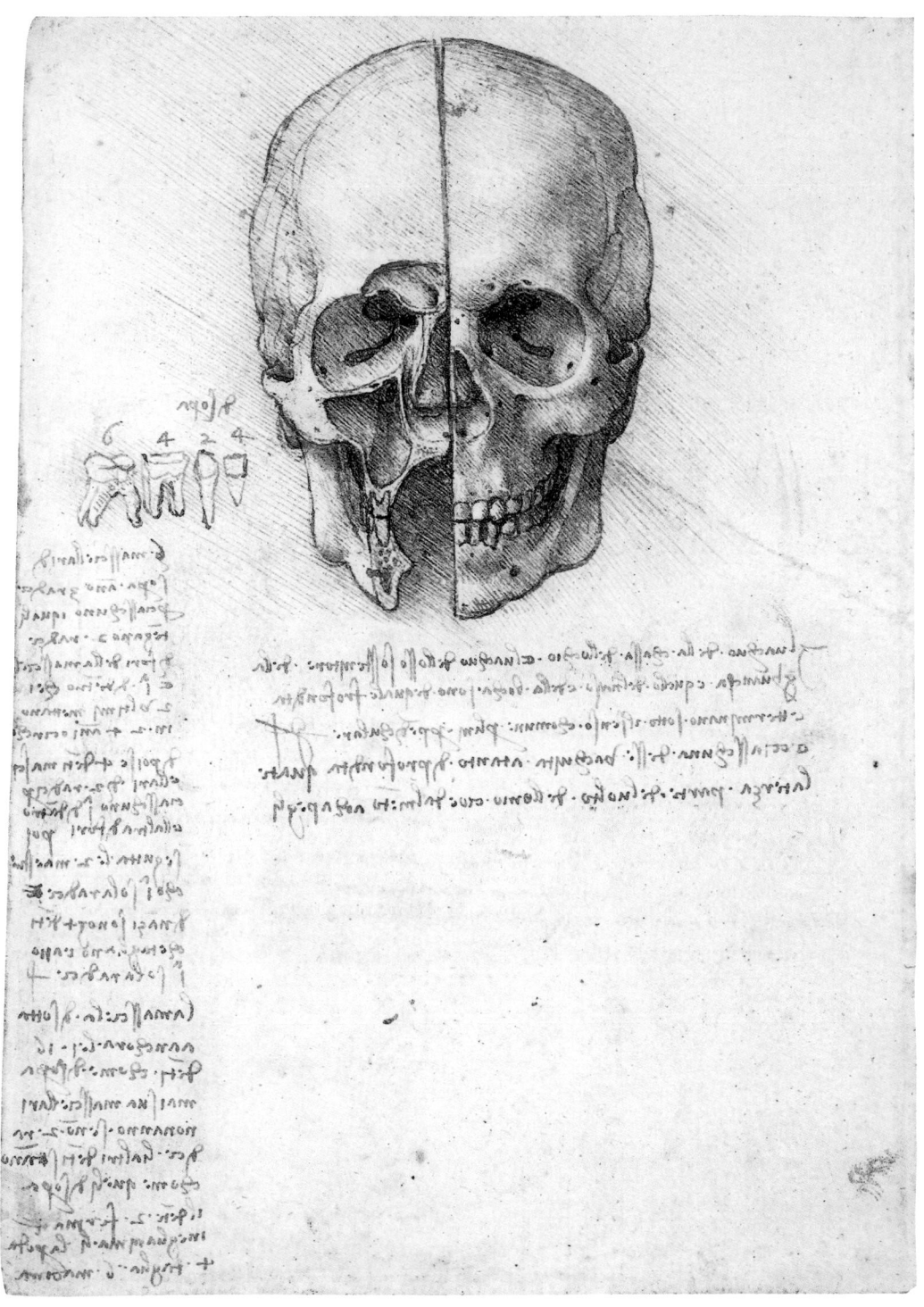

Cat. 58v *(actual size)*

415

LEONARDO DA VINCI

59. *Head of an Old Man in Profile Facing to the Right*

Pen and brown ink, 126 × 104 mm (4 15/16 × 4 1/16 in.); irregular borders; glued onto secondary paper support
Biblioteca Pinacoteca Ambrosiana, Milan Cod. F. 263 inf. 78

PROVENANCE: Part of the Accademia Ambrosiana (as suggested by the stamp of interlacing letters ACAMSN), possibly since the time of its opening in 1620–21 by Cardinal Federico Borromeo, Milan (1564–1631).

LITERATURE: Gerli 1784, pl. 23 (inscribed no. 14); Beltrami and Fumagalli 1904, p. 14, no. 18; Malaguzzi Valeri 1915, vol. 2, p. 621, fig. 683, p. 623; Commissione Vinciana 1928– , vol. 5, pp. 24–25, pl. 216.1; Bodmer 1931, pp. 166, 390; Berenson 1938, vol. 2, p. 116, no. 1048A; Venturi 1942, p. 48; Kunstmuseum Lucerne 1946, no. 134; Berenson 1961, vol. 2, p. 203, no. 1048A; Gombrich 1976, p. 93, fig. 161; Cogliati Arano 1980, p. 124, pl. 23; Marinoni 1980a, p. 222; Marinoni and Cogliati Arano 1982, p. 97, no. 3; Marani 1990, pp. 47–48; Caroli 1991, p. 149; Cogliati Arano 1992b, pp. 9–10; Luisa Cogliati Arano in Palazzo Grassi 1992, p. 314, no. 53; Kwakkelstein 1994, p. 106, fig. 46; Popham 1994, no. 137A; Marco Rossi in Ambrosiana 1998–99, pp. 66–69, 84, no. 23, p. 88, under no. 37; Marani 2001b, pp. 140–41, no. 35.

The serene dignity of the old man's gaze offsets the deformity of his profile—a "nutcracker" type with an enormous clenched jaw and a nose abruptly broken at the bridge and arching down, its tip nearly touching the curved lower lip. Both the drawing technique and the physiognomic type of the old man are closely related to a monumental sheet at Windsor with five grotesque figures in bust and half-length arranged in the mode of a conversation piece (fig. 161). Although scholars have dated the Ambrosiana drawing anywhere between 1485 and 1495, the precise connection to the Windsor sheet establishes in this author's opinion a date closer to 1490. In the small Ambrosiana drawing, the arresting psychological presence of the bust-length profile commands a space much beyond the actual size of the sheet of paper. The drawing is a fragment cut from a larger page, to judge from the cropped summary sketch of a head at upper right and the slight outlines in the same pen and ink on the lower right, which may suggest a facing figure in at least bust length. It may be that the composition of Leonardo's original Ambrosiana page included a group of grotesque figures engaged in "conversa-

tion," as in figure 161 and as in other extant sheets of this type, technique, and date.[1] In type, technique, and date the *Head of an Old Man* does not seem similar to the other single grotesque figure drawings in the Biblioteca Ambrosiana, as has been adduced, for the latter are considerably less animated in their draftsmanship.[2]

The reproduction of the Ambrosiana *Head of an Old Man* published in Carlo Giuseppe Gerli's *Disegni di Leonardo da Vinci* (Milan, 1784) is engraved in the same direction as Leonardo's original design and is in the identical size. Gerli's reproductive engraving suggests that Leonardo's Ambrosiana sheet was already in a fragmentary state in 1784, for the cropped sketch of a head on the upper right was but an unintel-

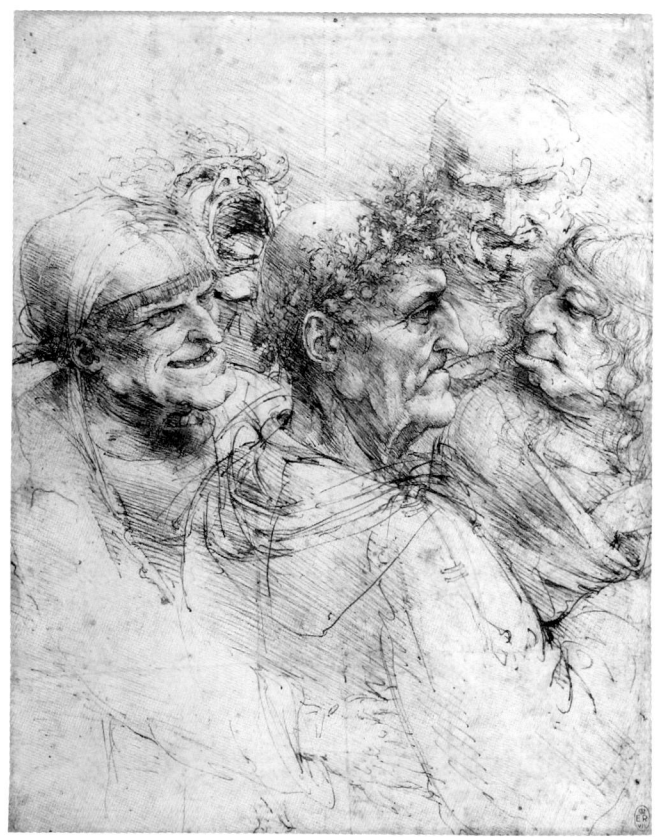

Fig. 161. Leonardo da Vinci, *A Group of Five Grotesque Figures*. Pen and brown ink, 260 × 205 mm. The Royal Collection, H.M. Queen Elizabeth II, Windsor Castle RL 12495

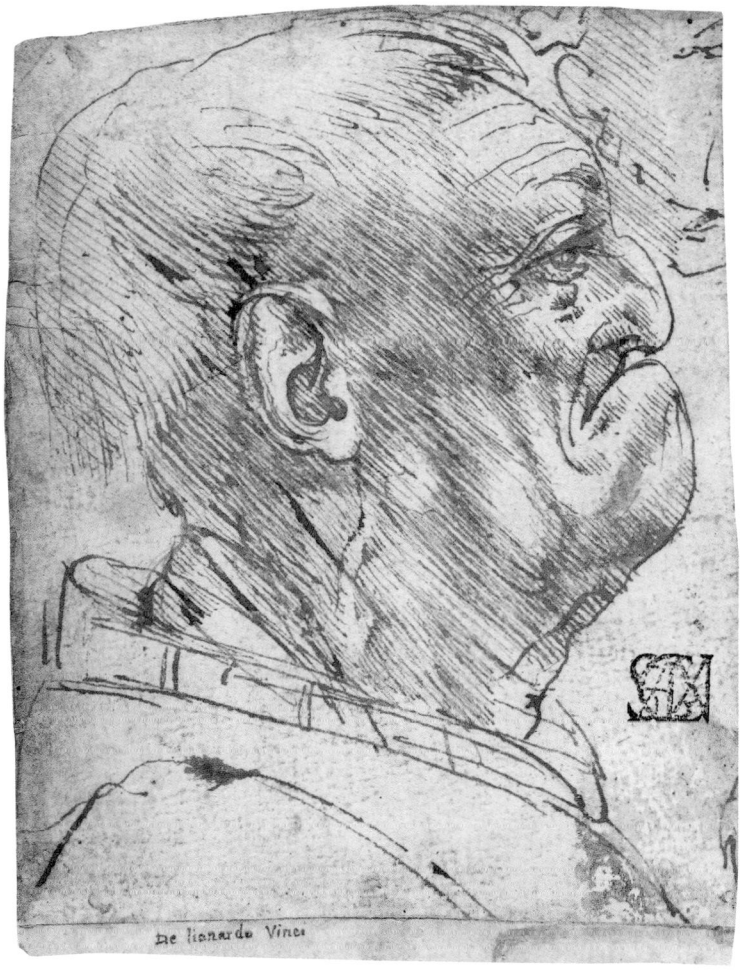

Cat. 59 *(actual size)*

ligible scrawl to the copyist. As Gerli himself noted, in order to produce his engraved copies, he traced the original drawings with translucent paper, exercising great diligence.[3] Although Gerli's reproductive engraving of the Ambrosiana *Head of an Old Man* is fairly true to Leonardo's manner of drawing, as it re-creates much of the original left-handed hatching, the engraving introduces cross-hatching into the shadows.   CCB

1. Windsor, RL 12449, 12490, 12453, 12463.
2. See Cod. F 263 inf. 93, 94; Ambrosiana 1998–99, pp. 82–84, nos. 21–23.
3. Gerli 1784, p. 3: "diligenza somma nel lucidare."

LEONARDO DA VINCI

60. *Head of Man in Profile Facing to the Left*

Pen and brown ink over charcoal or black chalk, 120 × 50 mm
(4¾ × 2 in.)
The Metropolitan Museum of Art, New York; Rogers Fund,
1909 10.45.1

PROVENANCE: Sir Peter Lely, London (1618–1680; Lugt 2092);
[Roger Fry]; purchased in London by The Metropolitan Museum of
Art in 1909.

LITERATURE: Vasari Society 1905–15, vol. 7, no. 2; Malaguzzi
Valeri 1913–23, vol. 2, p. 510; Seidlitz 1935, pl. 88; Berenson 1938,
vol. 2, p. 117, no. 1049D; Metropolitan Museum of Art 1942, no. 10;
Scott-Elliot 1958, pp. 282, 287, 298, pl. 3B; Berenson 1961, vol. 2,
p. 205, no. 1049D; De Tolnay 1962; Bean 1964, no. 4; Bean and
Stampfle 1965, p. 27, no. 16; "Drawings from the Roger Fry
Purchase," *Apollo* 82 (1965), p. 247, fig. 3; Bacall 1968, no. 4; Clark
and Pedretti 1968–69, under no. 12475A; Pedretti 1973b, p. 16,
no. 2; Bean 1982, p. 118, no. 109; Pedretti 1982a, pp. 25–26; Caroli
1991, p. 213; Trutty-Coohill and Pedretti 1993, pp. 44–45, no. 10;
Kwakkelstein 1994, pp. 102–3, fig. 19; Popham 1994, no. 140C; Letze
and Buchsteiner 1997, p. 78; Trutty-Coohill 1997, p. 194, fig. 5
(incorrect inv. no.); Trutty-Coohill 1998b, p. 193.

In his studies from the late 1480s onward, Leonardo would
increasingly link his exploration of human physiognomy to
that of the "ages of man." While he often portrayed youth as
possessing perfectly proportioned features, he would depict
old age as marred by caricaturesque deformity. In this fragmentary study from about 1490–94, Leonardo began to draw
the grotesque aquiline profile of an old man in charcoal or soft
black chalk, as is seen in the underdrawing, but then transformed it by carefully reworking the drawing in pen and ink
to portray a younger man. The most dramatic change occurs
in the nose, which in the pen-and-ink drawing appears shorter
and straighter. The noble mature profile in the finished form
evokes the portraits of Roman emperors seen in antique
medals, cameos, and coins, but it bears an uncanny resemblance
to the profile of Bartolommeo Colleoni (which may not be an
actual portrait of the condottiere) in Andrea del Verrocchio's
monumental bronze equestrian monument (Campo Santi
Giovanni e Paolo, Venice; fig. 162). Leonardo's master had
secured the commission in 1481–83 from the Venetian
Republic but had finished only the models at his death in June
1488. The casting of the Colleoni monument in bronze was

entrusted to Alessandro Leopardi in 1490 and was finished in
the spring of 1496 (all of which falls more or less within the
dates of Leonardo's Metropolitan Museum drawing).

The manner of pen-and-ink drawing, with dense, fine, perfectly straight parallel hatching that goes over form into background in unified strokes and achieves great depth of tone, is
typical of Leonardo's style from about 1490–95. As is evident
here, it may have come to fruition as the result of his involvement with the art of engraving, directly or indirectly through
his collaboration with the Milanese printmakers who were
beginning to engrave after his designs in the 1490s. The
Metropolitan Museum drawing may have been cut from a
larger page of Leonardo's notebooks. Irregularly cropped fragments of a similar kind from the Codex Atlanticus exist at the
Royal Library in Windsor.[1]

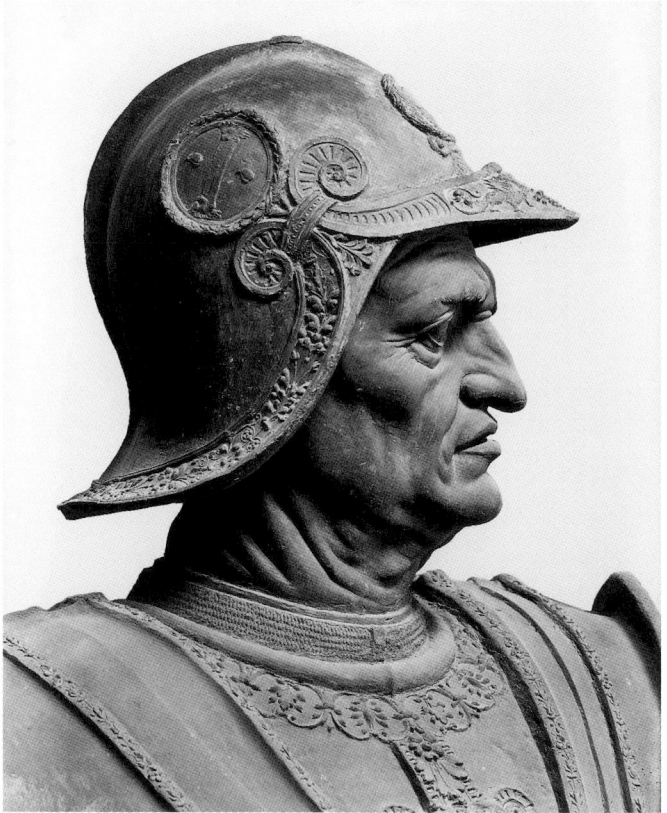

Fig. 162. Detail of Andrea del Verrocchio, *Equestrian Monument to
Bartolommeo Colleoni.* Bronze on a marble and Istrian stone pedestal
with a bronze frieze, H. of horse and rider (without marble plinth)
395 cm. Campo Santi Giovanni e Paolo, Venice

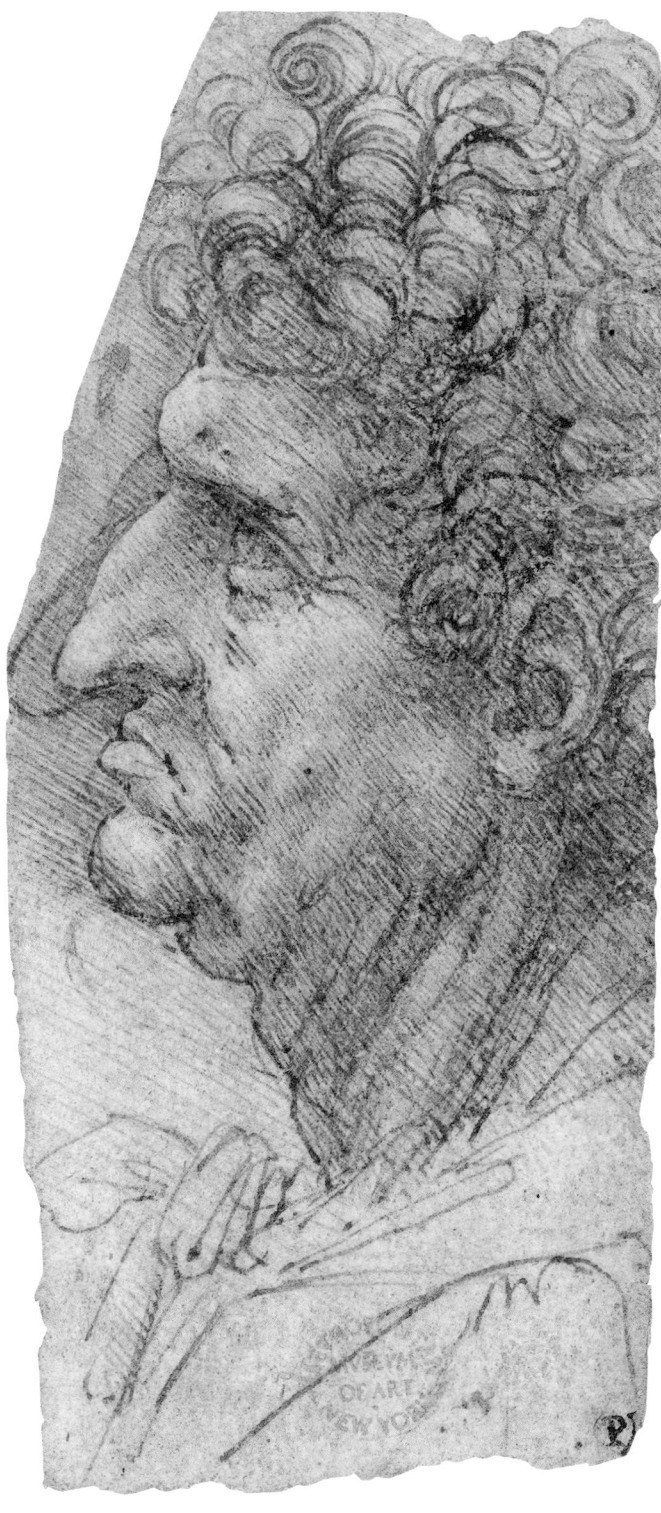

Cat. 60

Some scholars have dated the Metropolitan Museum sheet much earlier than is here proposed and have considered it a conscious recollection of the idealized *Darius* by Verrocchio. Verrocchio's relief, sent by Lorenzo de' Medici "Il Magnifico" to Matthias Corvinus, king of Hungary, is lost, but the profile is recorded in a terracotta relief by the Della Robbia workshop (Bodemuseum, Berlin).[2] There also is a generic resemblance of physical types between the Metropolitan Museum drawing and the early, highly finished metalpoint study of a warrior (British Museum, London, 1895-9-15-474), which seems to have been directly inspired by Verrocchio's original relief. A. E. Popham dated the British Museum warrior to about 1480, though more recent scholars concur that Leonardo executed it in 1472–76. However, Leonardo returned to certain figural and compositional types throughout his career, and thus the physiognomic resemblance in the two drawings is not at all a factor in considering their dates. Underscoring this point, the grotesque conception of the old man's profile in the underdrawing of the Metropolitan sheet resembles the boldly drawn charcoal study of a deformed old man's head in profile (Windsor, RL 12500), a work that is universally recognized to be from Leonardo's late years.

An early, direct copy of the Metropolitan Museum drawing is found among the "Spencer Grotesques" bound in a two-volume edition from 1669 of Rabelais's works (Spencer Collection II.36, New York Public Library; for a detail, see fig. 32). The "Spencer Grotesques" are possibly by a Lombard artist working about 1590–1600; the watermarks suggest that the paper was manufactured in Italy in the late sixteenth century.[3] The copy among the "Spencer Grotesques" already reflects the cropped state of Leonardo's original, as the rendering ends fairly abruptly on the right border. The Spencer copyist also emphasized the man's droopy nose, because he was undoubtedly swayed by the design of the deformed nose in the underdrawing of the original. CCB

1. See Pedretti 1957a.
2. Reproduced in Passavant 1969, fig. 50.
3. The "Spencer Grotesques" were attributed to a Venetian artist from the second half of the sixteenth century by Aydua H. Scott-Elliot in 1958. Illustrated and also discussed in Pedretti and Trutty-Coohill 1993, p. 98, no. 55 (2.36).

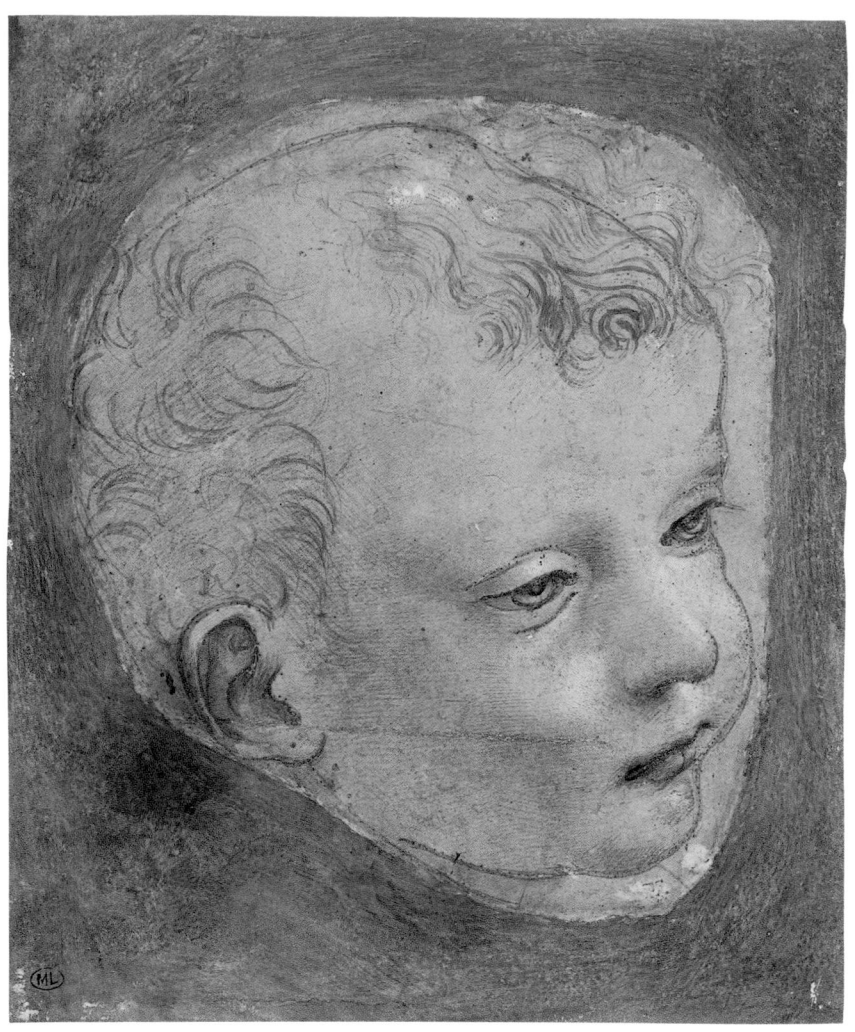

Cat. 61R *(actual size)*

LEONARDO DA VINCI

61. *Head of a Child in Three-Quarter View*

Metalpoint, highlighted with white gouache, on prepared gray-beige paper, irregularly cut, max. 134 × 119 mm (5 ⁵⁄₁₆ × 4 ¹¹⁄₁₆ in.), glued to prepared gray-brown paper, 169 × 140 mm (6 ¹¹⁄₁₆ × 5 ½ in.); largely reworked in pen, brush, and brown wash; pricked for transfer; hatching on the lower part of the chin and cheek done by a right-handed person; spots of white gouache on the upper part; creased on the cheek and ear; annotated curving lines on verso of mount
Département des Arts Graphiques du Musée du Louvre, Paris 2347

PROVENANCE: Peter Lely (Lugt 2092, mark scratched out and covered over); Jonathan Richardson Senior (Lugt 2184, mark scratched out and covered over); Giuseppe Vallardi (Lugt 1223, in green on verso); 1856, acquired by the Musée du Louvre; museum mark (Lugt 1886a).

LITERATURE: *Magasin pittoresque* 1858, p. 14, fig. p. 13; Richter 1883, vol. 1, p. 345 n. 4, pl. p. 342; Louvre 1888, no. 2024; Müller-Walde 1889, p. 111, fig. 63; Gruyer 1891, p. 29 n. 4 (with erroneous reference to Louvre 1866, no. 383); Müntz 1899, pp. 168–69, 213, fig. p. 178, p. 519, no. 7; Berenson 1903, vol. 1, p. 154 n., vol. 2, no. 1067 (with incorrect inv. no.); Seidlitz 1906, p. 31, fig. 13 (de' Predis); Seidlitz 1909, vol. 1, p. 170 (de' Predis); Malaguzzi Valeri 1913–23, vol. 2, pp. 414–15, fig. 454; Beltrami 1919b, p. 212, fig. 35; Louvre 1919, no. 17; Suida 1919–20, p. 283; Demonts 1921, no. 13; Demonts 1922, no. 13; Commissione Vinciana 1928– , vol. 3, p. 18, no. 87; Suida 1929, p. 130, fig. 129; Orangerie 1931, no. 13; Calvi 1934–39, p. 106, fig. 22; Davies 1951, p. 210; Amboise 1952; Biblioteca Medicea Laurenziana 1952, no. 33; Florisoone and Bacou 1952, no. 19 and

420

p. 13; Popham 1952, p. 128 n. 2 (student of Leonardo, or copy); Tours 1956, no. 47; Sérullaz 1965, no. 10; Petit Palais 1968, no. 251; Pedretti 1977, vol. 1, p. 377; Rosci 1978, p. 185, no. 29f; Pedretti 1984, p. 24; Ballarin 1985, pp. 16–18; Pedretti and Dalli Regoli 1985, pp. 22 n. 21, 99, fig. 49; Bora 1987–88, p. 46, under no. 2; Nathan 1990, p. 21; Pedretti 1990a, p. 34 n. 48; Kemp 1991, pp. 36–37; Kemp 1992a, no. 19; Carminati 1994, p. 156; Jaffé 1994, p. 167, under no. 881; Ballarin 1998–99, pp. 52, 85; Bambach 1999a, p. 83, fig. 71, p. 404 n. 29; Marani 1999b, p. 125; Fiorio 2000, p. 170, under no. c9; Ballarin 2002; Zöllner 2002.

This drawing was published in the *Magasin pittoresque* soon after its acquisition by the Louvre and was connected with the head of the Infant Saint John the Baptist in the *Virgin of the Rocks* at the Louvre. In 1883 Jean Paul Richter pointed out the importance of the white highlights and the restorations, "visible in the outlines, particularly the head and ear." These alterations led most art historians to doubt the drawing's authenticity. Nonetheless, with the exception of Wilhelm Suida who in 1929 saw it as a study for the head of the Infant Christ in the cartoon of the *Virgin and Child with Saint Anne,* most scholars have confirmed its link with the Louvre painting. More recently, in 1985, Carlo Pedretti and Alessandro Ballarin have proposed other interpretations. The drawing's provenance was established during preparation of the present exhibition: Varena Forcione noted that two marks pertaining to English collectors—Peter Lely and Jonathan Richardson Senior—had been scratched out and covered with the same thick white that was used for the retouching. This English provenance, previously unknown, might provide additional information about the Giuseppe Vallardi collection,[1] although the time elapsed between the dispersal of the Richardson collection in 1747 and Vallardi's purchases does not permit inference.

The sheet is irregularly cut and glued on a fragment of paper that is itself unevenly shaped. In the outlines of the head, the eyes, the nose, the mouth, the ear, and the hair, it was largely reworked and sometimes even incised. The outlines pricked for transfer, separate from the reworked lines, have hardened its appearance. It is impossible to prove that the pricking was done by Leonardo himself, as Johannes Nathan wrote in 1990. Finally, the white highlights, thickened by another than the author of the original drawing, make this little cartoon—perhaps part of a larger work, now lost—the harder to appreciate. "The Louvre head for Saint John has preserved little of da Vinci's own work," wrote Bernard Berenson

in 1903, admitting that it was nevertheless "very beautiful." With close study almost in profile, the quality of the drawing becomes apparent, for under the reworking in pen, brush, and brown wash, the original metalpoint delineations of the hair and the facial features are perfectly distinguishable. The shaded part of the right cheek and temple is treated in Leonardo's characteristic and inimitable style, which consists of an imperceptible play of strokes and cross strokes that lets reflected light show. Here the light is coming from the right, indicated by a thin application of white that dims the hatching on the forehead and the left part of the face. The angle of the head, which suggests rather than actually indicates a turning motion toward the right, recalls the female head study almost in profile (cat. no. 44) for the *Madonna Litta,* at the end of the Florentine studies for the early Virgins and Child. The child's face is captured in all its fullness, and the beauty of its gaze— the clear pupils undamaged by the reworking—give the face a somewhat pensive interiority, which conveys the essence of the mystery expressed in the encounter between the Infant Saint John the Baptist and the Infant Christ depicted in the *Virgin of the Rocks.*

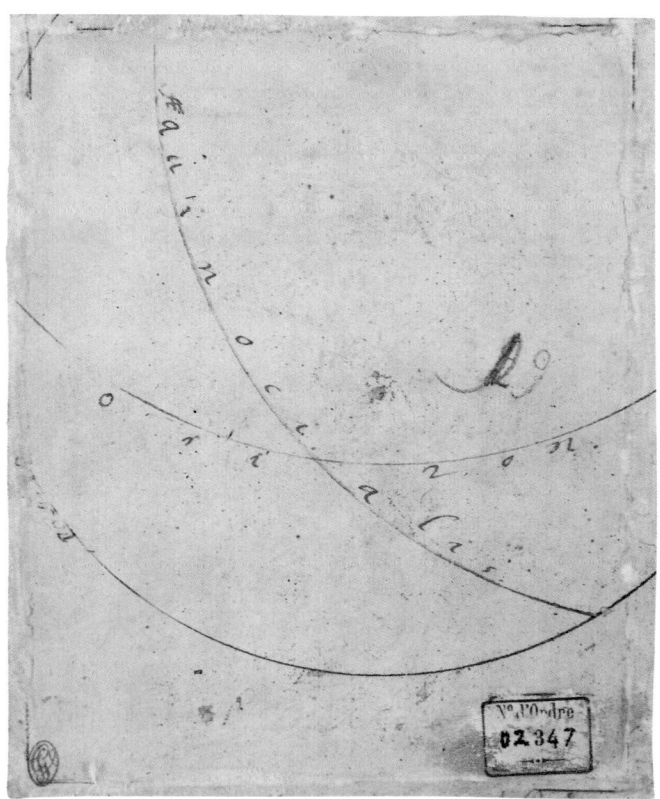

Cat. 61v

421

In December 2001, a comparative study of the Louvre and National Gallery, London, versions of the *Virgin of the Rocks* was conducted by the Conservation du Département des Peintures at the Louvre, the Laboratoire des Musées de France, and the National Gallery. This examination enabled the already established relationship between the present drawing and the Louvre painting to be clarified. A tracing was made of the drawing and placed over the head of Saint John in the painting, which showed that the two heads correspond in both their dimensions and the angle of the heads. The drawing of the eyelids is different, as is the direction of the light. Coming from the right in the drawing, in the painting the source of light is high in the left background, far behind the rocks of the background. In addition, when the tracing of the present drawing was reversed, it seemed to correspond to the head of the Infant Christ as it appears in underdrawing on the London version of *Virgin of the Rocks*. The examination showed that there the child's head was initially larger and in a different position.

Pedretti has linked the strong definition of the metalpoint drawing and the meticulous *tratteggio* of the left part with the technique in a drawing at the Uffizi (424 E), perhaps a study for one of the apostles at the Last Supper, also clumsily reworked by a pupil.[2] According to Pedretti, the technique, especially of the hair, is still close to the Florentine period and might suggest that the present drawing is a fragment of a cartoon for a *Madonna of the Cat,* as it is sketched in a drawing at the British Museum (fig. 71).[3]

Pedretti further noted that in the present drawing the beginning of the child's left shoulder is indicated by a line beneath the middle of the chin, whereas in the Louvre painting the shoulder begins higher up. Vallardi called this cartoon a "brano" (scrap)—which might suggest that he knew of other pieces—and linked it to the lunette fresco *Virgin and Child with Donor,* painted by Cesare da Sesto in the monastery of Sant'Onofrio al Gianicolo in Rome.[4]

Lionello Venturi (*Commissione Vinciana* 1934) ascribed the very obvious reworking of the present drawing to Ambrogio de' Predis, an argument already put forth by Malaguzzi Valeri for this sheet as well as for other children's heads that are attributed here to Giovanni Antonio Boltraffio (cat. no. 125).[5] A relationship noted between this study and two other sheets from Leonardo's studio highlights the complexity of the working methods in the studio in his first years in Milan. Giulio Bora (1987–88) and then Maria Teresa Fiorio (2000)

linked this drawing to the child's head on a sheet in the Devonshire Collection, Chatsworth (893): it has the same dimensions as the Louvre drawing and is also in metalpoint on prepared paper.[6] On the upper part of the Chatsworth sheet is a female head that may be the completed version of a drawing in the Biblioteca Ambrosiana.[7] The child, by contrast, could be Boltraffio's initial idea for the motif that Leonardo developed in the Louvre drawing. Conversely, Martin Kemp advanced the more plausible hypothesis that the Chatsworth design was a transfer drawing that Boltraffio obtained from the Louvre sheet.[8]

In 1985 and again in 2002, Ballarin revisited that issue by considering the Chatsworth drawing in relation to the *Madonna and Child,* called the *Esterházy Madonna,* in the Szépművészeti Múzeum, Budapest (52), painted by Boltraffio in the last decade of the fifteenth century and contemporary with the second version of the *Virgin of the Rocks.* According to Ballarin, the Chatsworth drawing represents an earlier stage of the Louvre drawing for the head of the Infant Saint John. The similarity of technique—in the outlines and indications of shadows—would be evidence that the same artist, Boltraffio, used the Chatsworth drawing as the model for the small Louvre cartoon. Both would thus be related to the Budapest painting, as would the female head above the child's on the Chatsworth sheet. In addition, Ballarin suggested that the Louvre cartoon is the missing part of a study of a headless putto (Louvre RF 5635), and his montage of the two drawings would support this hypothesis. This author does not subscribe to that theory, however.

Taking into account the fact that the Louvre drawing was used as a cartoon—though the pricking was not done by Leonardo—and the precise correspondence between it and the two versions of the *Virgin of the Rocks*, we propose the following interpretation: The drawing was done by Leonardo and is, to my knowledge, the only study that can be associated with the Louvre painting. The drawing in the Biblioteca Reale, Turin (fig. 80), long held to be a study for the angel Uriel, is now considered one of the most beautiful portraits drawn by Leonardo in the late 1480s but has no direct relation to the *Virgin of the Rocks.*[9] The drapery study for a kneeling figure in the Royal Library at Windsor (RL 12521) should be considered related to the figure of the angel in the National Gallery painting. Finally, on a sheet inserted in the Arundel Codex in 1952, a sketch in metalpoint on blue prepared paper becomes visible through photography under ultraviolet light.[10] A. E. Popham believed it was a study for the Infant Christ in the

Louvre version of *Virgin of the Rocks*; instead, it should be linked to the nursing Child in the *Madonna Litta* and to two sheets of studies at Windsor (RL 12568, RL 12569).

The inclusion in this exhibition of a drawing by Boltraffio (cat. no. 125) makes it possible to assess the significant difference in style between the present cartoon and the faces in full profile that Boltraffio drew around the same time—about 1490—and in a perspective close to that of his master (see essay by Pietro C. Marani). Here, in the acuity of the expression and in the rendering of the volume solely through the treatment of light, this face is the achievement of Leonardo and of no one else.   FV

1. The present drawing is listed in Vallardi 1855, p. 38, fol. 132 (Leonardo da Vinci): "Disegno su carta tinta in ceruleo, riportato su carta consimile più grande, eseguito a matita nera ed a penna, lumeggiato di bianco: testa di un bambino. Brano del cartone che servì per l'affresco che vedesi nel Convento di sant'Onofrio a Roma, siccome riscontrasi infatti il contorno minutamente punteggiato. / Alto poll. 6.5. largo poll. 5.5."
2. Pedretti and Dalli Regoli 1985, no. 24.
3. Popham 1945, no. 9A.
4. Vallardi 1855, p. 38, fol. 132. Carminati (1994, pp. 154–56) calls the drawing located.
5. Commissione Vinciana 1928– , vol. 3, no. 87; Malaguzzi Valeri 1915, vol. 2, p. 414.
6. See the essay by Pietro C. Marani in this volume.
7. Cod. F 263 inf. 99; Fiorio 2000, no. C13.
8. Kemp 1992a, p. 77, no. 20.
9. Marani in Palazzo Reale 2001, no. 25.
10. Arundel Codex, fols. 253v and 256r; Pedretti and Vecce 1998, p. 17 n. 19, fig. 17.

LEONARDO DA VINCI

62. *The Head and Shoulders of Christ Being Held by His Hair by a Hand (Study for a Christ Carrying the Cross)*

Metalpoint on pale gray-blue prepared paper, 116 × 91 (4⅝ × 3⅝ in.)
Inscribed at lower right corner: *231*; at lower left corner: *Leonardo da Vinci*
Gallerie dell'Accademia, Venice 231

PROVENANCE: Cardinal Cesare Monti, Milan (1635–1650); Contessa Anna Luisa Monti, Milan; 1770, Venanzio De Pagave, Milan; his son Gaudenzio De Pagave, ca. 1808 or before, Giuseppe Bossi, Milan and Venice (1777–1815; album marked K); auction, Milan, February 1818, vol. 2; February 24, 1818, purchase by Abbate Luigi Celotti [Cellotti], Venice (1765–1846); in deposit (under custody of Carlo Porta and Nicola Casonni) Accademia di Belle Arti, Milan; 1820–22, proposal of purchase of Bossi's collection from Celotti submitted to Austrian government on behalf of Accademia delle Belle Arti, Venice; 1822, purchase by Franz I (Habsburg), emperor of Austria, Florence and Vienna (1768–1835), for Accademia delle Belle Arti, Venice; ca. 1832 manuscript inventory; December 31, 1870, manuscript inventory; museum stamp (Lugt 188).

LITERATURE: Bossi 1810, pl. facing p. 102, p. 263; Selvatico 1854, vol. 4, no. 8; Uzielli 1884, no. 8; Berenson 1903, vol. 2, p. 62, no. 1103; Loeser 1903b, p. 183; Malaguzzi Valeri 1913–23, vol. 2, p. 504; Poggi 1919, p. lx, pl. 120; Commissione Vinciana 1928– , vol. 5, p. 23, pl. 198.1; Suida 1929, fig. 97; Bodmer 1931, p. 261; Berenson 1938, vol. 2, p. 123, no. 1103; Suida in Giglioli 1944, pl. 124; Popham 1946, pp. 120, 131, no. 171B; Heydenreich 1949, pp. 5, 10, pl. 7; Biblioteca Medicea Laurenziana 1952, p. 32, no. 43; Goldscheider 1952, p. 34, pl. 98; Möller 1952a, p. 124; Castelfranco 1954b, p. 455; Heydenreich 1954, vol. 1, p. 202; Berenson 1961, vol. 2, p. 217, no. 1103; Cogliati Arano 1966–67, p. 28; Clark and Pedretti 1968–69, vol. 1, p. xxvi, n. 2; Pedretti 1978a; Pedretti 1979a; Cogliati Arano 1980, pp. 36–37, no. 10; Pedretti 1981a, p. 498; Pedretti and Clark 1983, pp. 39–40, fig. 26; Brown 1987, p. 88; Marani 1987a, pp. 37–38, fig. 19; Lucco 1989, p. 22; Pedretti 1990a, p. 19, fig. 5; Renouard de Bussierre 1991, pp. 120–25, no. 13; Marani in Palazzo Grassi 1992, pp. 344–47, no. 69; Popham 1994, p. 138, no. 171B; Marani in Brambilla Barcilon and Marani 1999, p. 25; Giovanna Nepi Scirè in Nepi Scirè and Torrini 1999, pp. 68–69, no. 19; Marani 2001a, pp. 107–9, 122, 107, fig.

The drawing of Christ's face, seen in three-quarter view, looking back over his left shoulder as he is held by his hair by a disembodied hand, was done in metalpoint on pale gray-blue prepared paper. The artist perhaps used a gold-point stylus (a suggestion first made by Carlo Pedretti in an oral communication cited in Cogliati Arano 1980, which has been put forward again by Nepi Scirè 1999); this would explain the "unusual sparkle of the image." Although it is an appealing hypothesis, there is no documentation to support it. Furthermore, we know that the only metalpoint technique employed in Leonardo's workshop about 1490 was silverpoint.[1]

This drawing was engraved for the first time by Giuseppe Longhi in 1810 and published as an *hors-texte* illustration in Giuseppe Bossi's book on Leonardo's *Last Supper*, where he described it as "done after an original drawing by Leonardo."[2] Since all the other drawings illustrated with engravings in Bossi's volume belonged to him and were all then acquired by the Accademia in Venice in 1822, there is no reason to assume that this one had a different provenance, despite Giulia Brunetti's suggestion that it came from "the collection of the painter Andrea Appiani."[3] Appiani was simply trying to secure the deposit of Bossi's collection of drawings at the Brera in Milan.

Scholars have been unanimous in attributing this drawing to Leonardo; the only one to reject the attribution, calling it "truly defamatory," was Charles Loeser (1903). Luisa Cogliati Arano (1966) expressed some doubt about it, before becoming "completely" convinced of its authenticity (1980). Kenneth Clark (1968) associated its technique with that of a similar sheet in the Albertina, Vienna, that has a study of a draped male figure, probably for Saint Peter in the *Last Supper* (cat. no. 66). He considered both drawings "unusual . . . in other respects," given that they were executed with metalpoint on prepared paper (the Venice sheet is pale gray-blue and the one in Vienna an intense blue) and that Leonardo seems to have abandoned that technique after 1490.[4] Yet their style and strong, almost dramatic expressiveness suggested to Clark that they were executed in or after the middle of the last decade of the quattrocento. A. E. Popham (1946) dated the Venice drawing to 1495–97 but with a question mark, and Ludwig Heinrich Heydenreich (1949) and Cogliati Arano proposed a date of 1495–99, which is the period traditionally associated with the execution of the *Last Supper*. Indeed, the dramatic quality of the drawing and its sense of tension seem to reflect similar concerns in the painting. Pedretti (1979), on the other hand, assigned the Venice drawing to about 1490, although he pointed out that in its almost incised quality it could be compared to the mechanical studies in Codex Madrid I that date to the second half of the 1490s. When he returned to this drawing in the course of analyzing Leonardo's studies for the *Last Supper*, Pedretti (1983) noted its similarity to catalogue number 66 (which he dated to about 1495), and in 1990 he suggested that the Venice sheet, too, dates to 1495. The sharp, incised quality of the drawing also recalls the influence

of German prints on Leonardo (Pedretti 1979), especially works by Martin Schongauer (Brown 1987) and Albrecht Dürer; Dürer's later woodcut *Men Bathing*, of 1498, includes a figure seen from over his shoulder (Marani 1992). Other analogies, useful in defining the context of this drawing in Leonardo's work, are found in the work of Ambrogio Bergognone (Marani 1992), for example, his *Christ Carrying the Cross with Carthusian Monks* in the Certosa of Pavia (now at the Pinacoteca Malaspina, Pavia), probably executed about 1490.[5] Leonardo is likely to have seen the Certosa in 1490, when he was visiting Pavia with Francesco di Giorgio Martini, and this would also explain the unusual pietistic and devotional quality of the Christ represented in the Venice drawing. For these reasons, the drawing was recently dated to the years 1490–95 (Marani 1992). A reconstruction of the chronological sequence of Leonardo's studies for the *Last Supper*, our belief that catalogue number 66 represents the beginning of the artist's preparatory work for it, and, finally, an understanding of the evolution of Leonardo's drawing techniques and medium over the long creative process for the *Last Supper*, which began as early as 1488–90 and came to a close about 1497, have contributed to the latest hypothesis that the *Study for a Christ Carrying the Cross* in Venice must date to about 1490 (Marani 2001). A stylistic and technical comparison of the Venice sheet to a whole series of studies (which begins with drawings for the Sforza monument—for example, Windsor, RL 12358, about 1488–89—and includes the studies of the human skull, also at Windsor, such as RL 19058 and 19059, dated 1489, as well as cat. no. 58) reveals similar incisive hatching and allows us, without hesitation, to date the *Christ Carrying the Cross* study to about 1490, if not, as Carmen Bambach suggests, even to a few years earlier (about 1488).[6]

The motif of Christ held by the hair by one of his executioners, represented here only by a hand, who drags his head around so that Christ fixes his eyes on the viewer though presented as a *ritratto di spalla*, may have served Leonardo as an opportunity to experiment with the complicated three-by-three groupings of figures that he envisioned for the apostles in the *Last Supper*. Leonardo may also have intended to develop the idea of a *Christ Carrying the Cross* in terms of a group of three figures: a tormentor in front and to the left of Christ who drags him forward, while another behind him pulls him by the hair in the opposite direction. Such a group can be found reflected in varying degrees of development in

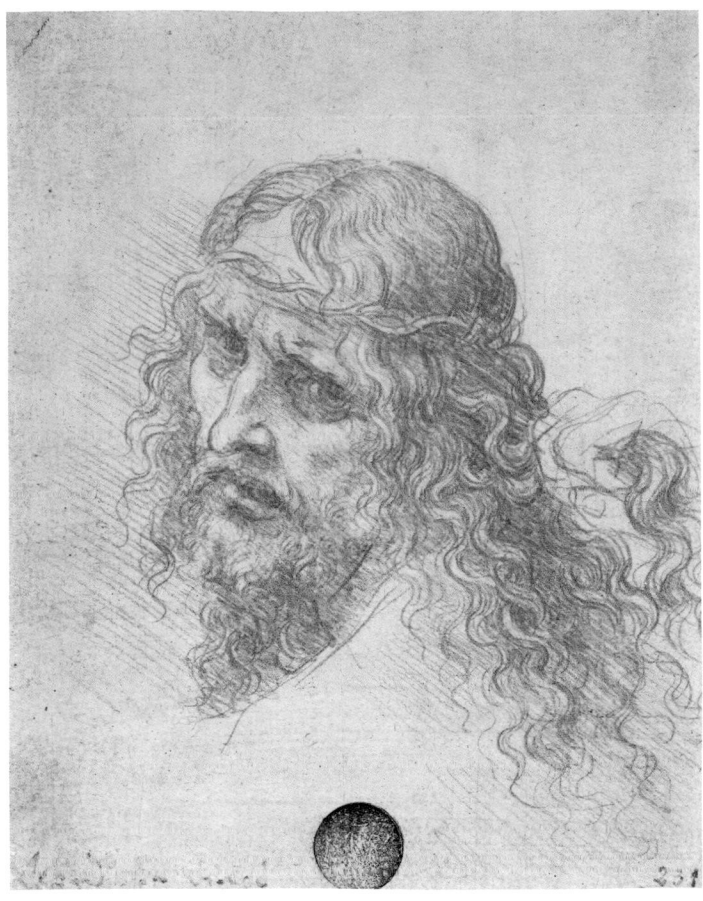

Cat. 62 *(actual size)*

works by members of Leonardo's school. Examples include a drawing in the Albertina and a painting in the Galleria Borghese, Rome, both by Andrea Solario,[7] and two paintings from Giampietrino's workshop now in Pavia and in the Castello Sforzesco in Milan.[8] These works are faithful enough to the detail of the hand holding Christ's hair in the Venice drawing to suggest that they derive from a Leonardesque model but one more finished than the drawing. The possibility that the drawing may be a first idea for a more articulated composition later elaborated by Leonardo in a cartoon that he intended to make into a painting cannot be excluded,[9] even though there is no indication in the documents that Leonardo ever received such a commission. Indeed, the *Last Supper* aside, the artist seems not to have painted scenes of the Passion of Christ. According to Pedretti (1979), the small black-chalk drawing now in the Biblioteca Ambrosiana (Milan, Cod. F 263, inf. no. 27) can be identified as a study for the tormentor in front of Christ, since it is close to the figure in

Giorgione's later *Christ Carrying the Cross* at the Scuola Grande di San Rocco in Venice (even if in the latter the man's head is looking down and seen in a slightly three-quarter view, while in the Ambrosiana drawing it is erect and strictly in profile). Giorgione's painting can be dated to 1508–9, and it is an incontestable reflection (along with the so-called *Three Ages of Man* in the Galleria Palatina of the Palazzo Pitti, Florence) of the influence Leonardo exercised on the younger artist from Castelfranco, even though Giorgione painted four figures rather than three (he inserted another head in *profil perdu* at the extreme left that is also Lombard and perhaps Bramantesque in its origins). Knowledge of the Venice drawing, and of the possible lost cartoon that might have been the source for these works, can be traced as far, perhaps, as Sodoma, who, passing through Milan at the end of the fifteenth century or at the beginning of the sixteenth, painted an *Ecce Homo between Two Executioners* (now in the Brera, Milan). The strong pathos of this image comes from a combination of

425

Leonardesque models contemporary with the *Last Supper*. It also includes a reference to Leonardo's so-called *Self-Portrait* in the Biblioteca Reale, Turin (fig. 1),[10] which is the model for the head of the tormentor on the right. The *Self-Portrait* is in reality a study from the 1490s in which Leonardo used red chalk to repeat the incised and calligraphic effects that characterize the Venice drawing. In the latter, the fluid rhythm of the hair, the passages of chiaroscuro which define the masses, the strong areas of shadow in the eye sockets and half-closed mouth, and the delicate hatching on the right are the most fascinating elements of a drawing that should certainly be included among Leonardo's most vibrant and successful graphic works of the last decade of the fifteenth century.

PCM

1. See my essay in this volume.
2. Bossi 1810, p. 263.
3. Biblioteca Medicea Laurenziana 1952, p. 32.
4. For the evolution of Leonardo's drawing style in the crucial decade of the 1490s, see my essay in this volume.
5. See L. Baini in Sciolla 1998, p. 230.
6. See my essay in this volume.
7. See Bora and Brown in Palazzo Grassi 1992, pp. 354–57.
8. See Marani 1987a, p. 31, figs. 20, 21. A third, unpublished picture might be added to these, better in quality than the other two though not by Giampietrino himself, which is now in the Rolla Collection in Novara.
9. Such a cartoon might thus be assigned to about 1495, the date of the *Last Supper*; see Marani 1992a.
10. See Marani 2001b, pp. 180–81.

LEONARDO DA VINCI

63. *Four Studies of Horses' Legs*

Metalpoint, highlighted with brush and white gouache, on dark blue prepared paper; glued onto secondary paper support, 155 × 204 mm (6⅛ × 8 1/16 in.)
Biblioteca Reale, Turin 15580

PROVENANCE: According to tradition, Ambrogio Mazenta, Milan; Alessandro and Guido Mazenta, Milan; Duke Charles Emmanuel I of Savoy (r. 1580–1630); or alternatively Giovanni Volpato ([1797–1871], private sale in 1839); documented after the reconstitution of the Biblioteca Reale of Turin by King Charles Albert of Sardinia-Piedmont (r. 1831–49); museum stamp (Lugt 2724).

LITERATURE: Uzielli 1884, p. 271, no. 10; Loeser 1899, p. 19; Müntz 1899, p. 517 n. 8; Berenson 1903, vol. 2, p. 61, no. 1092; Carotti 1921, p. 35, pl. 21; Popp 1926–27, p. 55–56; Commissione Vinciana 1928– , vol. 4, p. 18, pl. 141; Bodmer 1931, pp. 240, 401; Berenson 1938, vol. 2, p. 122, no. 1092; Biblioteca Medicea Laurenziana 1952, p. 30, no. 39; Bertini 1958, p. 36, no. 223; Goldscheider 1959, p. 178, no. 107; Berenson 1961, vol. 2, p. 215, no. 1092; Clark and Pedretti 1968–69, vol. 1, p. xxxvii n. 2; Pedretti 1975a, p. 27, no. 11; Keele and Pedretti 1979–80, vol. 2, p. 804; Leinati 1980, p. 394; Sciolla 1985, p. 40; Pedretti 1987b, pp. 48, 50, 59, fig. 40; Pedretti 1990a, no. 11; Carlo Pedretti in Sciolla 1990, pp. 50–51, no. 15; Fusco and Corti 1992, p. 21 n. 37, fig. 9; Lucia Tongiorgi Tomasi in Petrioli Tofani 1992, p. 194, no. 9.16; Popham 1994, no. 73; Letze and Buchsteiner 1997, p. 70; Giacobello Bernard 1998, pp. 96–97, no. 2.11.

Drawn in connection with the design of the "Sforza Horse" about 1490–92, the present sheet was probably originally part of a dismembered sketchbook (*libro* or *libretto*) that may have been filled with similar life studies of horses. A number of Leonardo's other studies for the "Sforza Horse" datable to this time are drawn in a similar (though not uniform) metalpoint technique on blue prepared paper.[1] We also know of one such sketchbook in which a little more than a decade later Leonardo compiled studies of horses for the unfinished cartoon and mural of the *Battle of Anghiari*.[2] The Turin sheet with animated studies of the horse's forelegs has not received the attention it deserves, despite serving to document the later, striding pose of the "Sforza Horse," which is also recorded in an impressive array of preparatory sketches, studies, and measured diagrams (figs. 163–65). Leonardo's Windsor sheet of studies of the horse's proportions and anatomical details already takes into account this later redesign of the pose for the Sforza equestrian monument (fig. 164). Like the Turin sheet, it is executed in metalpoint on blue prepared paper, though the overall tonal calibration of the Windsor sheet is much more delicate and omits the white gouache highlights. Leonardo's examination of the antique *Regisole*

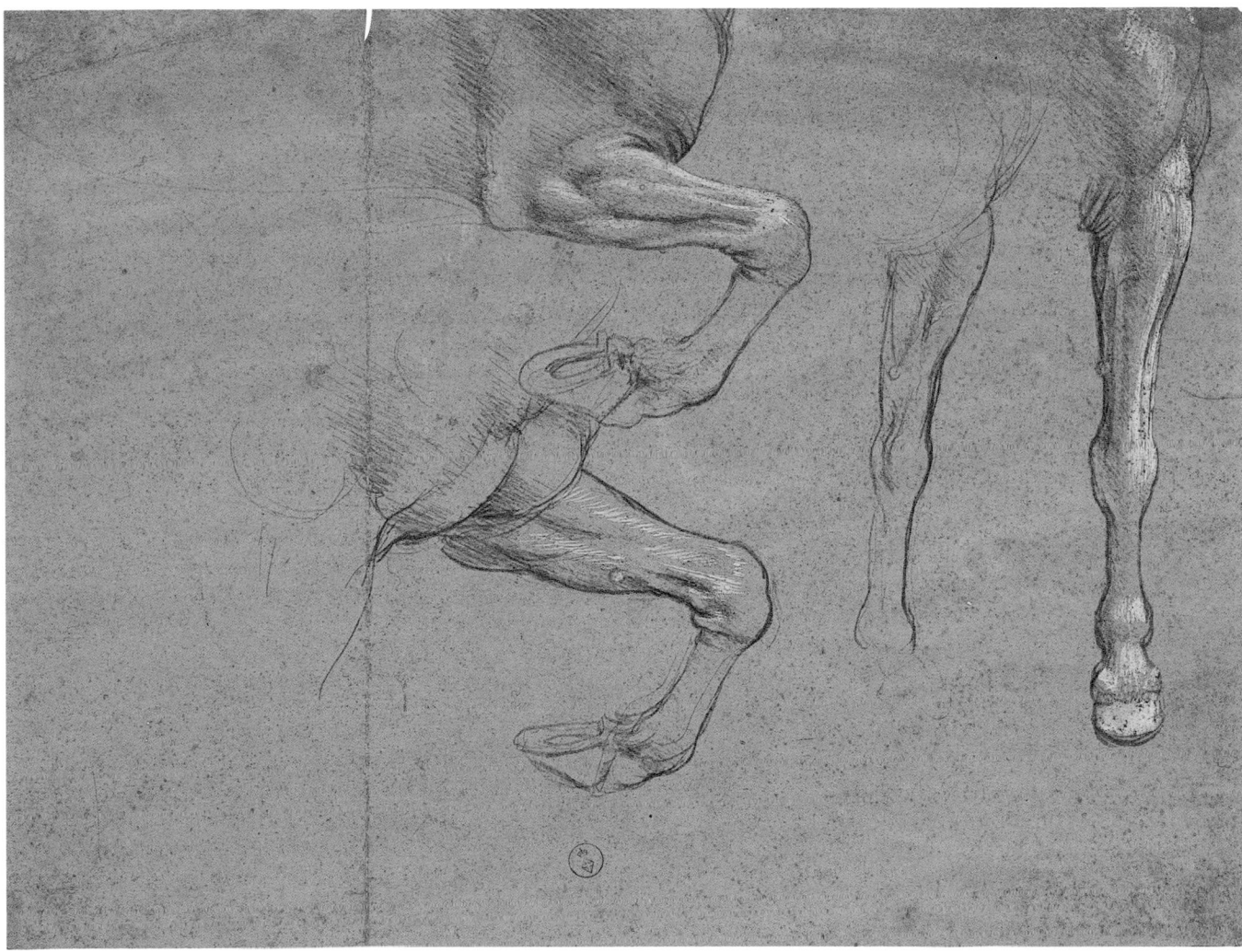

Cat. 63

(the most famous Roman equestrian monument besides the *Marcus Aurelius* in Rome), probably during a visit to Pavia with his friend Francesco di Giorgio in June 1490, may have pointed the way for the pose of the "Sforza Horse."[3] As Leonardo himself commented on the *Regisole*: "In that [monument] of Pavia the movement more than anything else is the most praiseworthy. The imitation of antique works is more praiseworthy than that of modern ones."[4] His renewed experience of classical antiquity must have also reinvigorated his interest in recording the proportional measurements of the horse, a subject that had been previously undertaken by his teacher, Andrea del Verrocchio (cat. nos. 9, 10; fig. 124). Leonardo himself had produced some measured proportion studies of the horse for the design in the background of the *Adoration of the Magi* altarpiece.

The challenge of animating this artistic legacy was formidable. Based on the precision of detail in the Turin sheet of studies, one can almost imagine the artist working in the famous stables of Ludovico Sforza "Il Moro" and the Milanese gentry, where he moved about the fine figures of stallions and mares for hours at a time, observing, deliberating, drawing, measuring, and taking notes. Here, the motifs appear neatly arranged on the page (as if the artist were intentionally posing the forelegs of the horse), and the studies seem already the result of some process of synthesis that was probably based on a previous step of more spontaneous, purely investigative sketches. This initial stage—a kind of on-site unedited reportage—may be illustrated in a fairly large, relatively little known sheet that is drawn faintly in metalpoint on gray-cream prepared paper, also in the Biblioteca Reale in Turin (fig. 163).

427

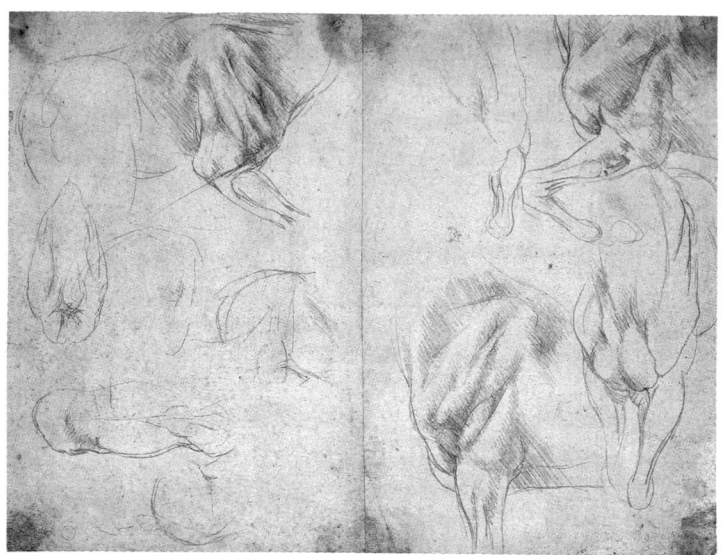

Fig. 163. Leonardo da Vinci, *Studies of a Horse*. Metalpoint, highlighted with white gouache, on gray-cream prepared paper, 217 × 287 mm. Biblioteca Reale, Turin 15579

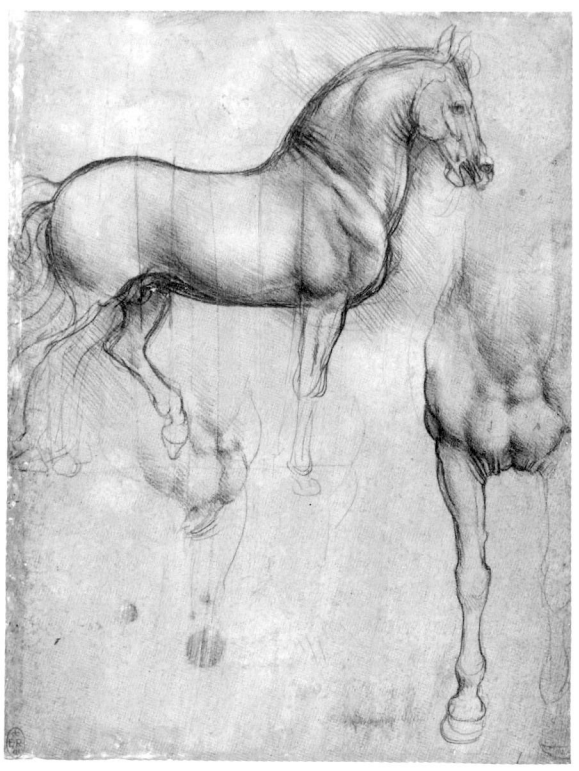

Fig. 164. Leonardo da Vinci, *Proportion Studies of a Horse*. Silverpoint on blue prepared paper, 214 × 160 mm. The Royal Collection, H.M. Queen Elizabeth II, Windsor Castle RL 12321

Fig. 165. Leonardo da Vinci, *Studies of a Horse*. Black chalk, 215 × 145 mm. Szépmüvészeti Múzeum, Budapest 1776

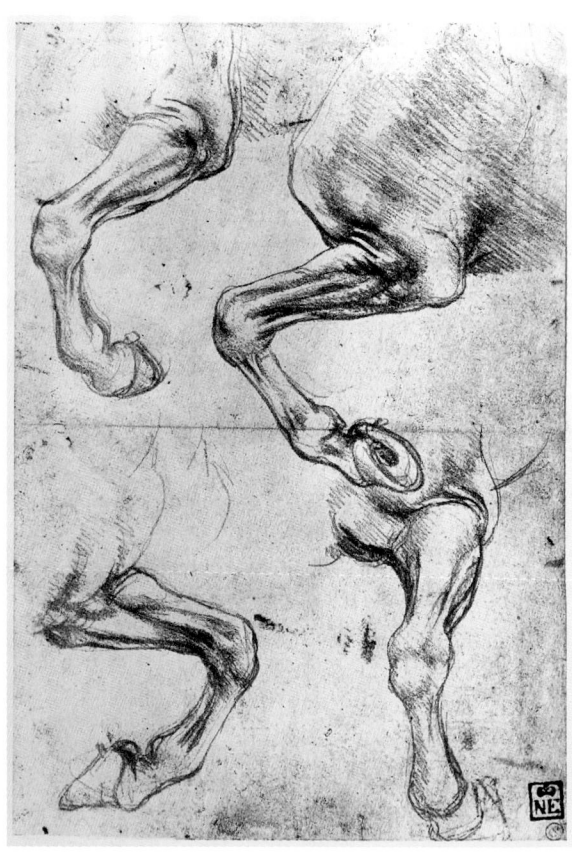

There, with greater immediacy—and awkwardness (for he drew quickly to capture the poses of the moving animals)—than is seen here, Leonardo drew the disorderly, though delicate, sketches of the side, three-quarter, and top views of the horse on the left portion of the sheet and of the front parts of the horse with bent and straight forelegs on the right.[5]

In the present sheet, Leonardo focused on a much more sculptural technique of drawing. One can almost see him translating form, from live animal to equine statue. He chose a fairly dark ground for greater tonal contrasts and applied a relatively thin layer of the blue preparation onto the paper, though not very uniformly, with right-to-left brushstrokes. He seems to have begun drawing the horse's forelegs in a standing position at the right of the sheet. On the extreme right, he first depicted the frontal view of the horse's standing left foreleg in great detail (even the chestnut, the horny inner knob above the horse's knee, is visible), and then next to it, on the left, he sketched the same horse's standing left foreleg, but in a more summary side view. Examination with raking light more clearly reveals the fainter parts of this particular drawing, including the overlapping outlines of the horse's chest and belly at the top of the leg and the outline of the hoof in strict profile at the bottom. The two drawings of the erect forelegs in the Turin sheet are similar in style to the Windsor sheet of proportions and details (fig. 164). After this study of the left foreleg in an erect position, Leonardo went on to the side views of the bent foreleg on the larger left portion of the paper. Here, he tried out the bent foreleg pose on both legs of the horse—right and left—which makes the Turin sheet an unusual document of Leonardo's gestating ideas for the "Sforza Horse." He developed these studies to a similarly high finish. The top drawing, which is the first of the side views of the horse that Leonardo drew on the sheet, shows the animal's bent right foreleg, that is, the natural counterpart to the erect left forelegs in the studies on the right of the sheet. When he concluded with the bottom drawing, however, he exchanged the pose of the legs, showing the animal now with a bent left foreleg (the chestnut can be seen there, on the inner side above the knee).

Leonardo pressed fairly hard on the metalpoint, which deeply incised the paper. He first lightly outlined the forms, then reinforced the contours repeatedly with increasing force, as he also gradually built up the interior modeling to a high relief. He applied the white gouache highlights first quite broadly in a very diluted base layer, after which he parallel-hatched on top with drier pigment and with the very fine tip of the brush. There is great movement in the strokes of white gouache, many of them being entirely upright, and others coursing from lower left to upper right. The white gouache highlights seem for the most part intact, but the areas along the contours in the study on the extreme right, from the top of the horse's leg down to at least the knee, were gone over with a gouache of a slightly cream color, probably by a restorer. The gouache highlights in the cool white hue are certainly original.

A number of Leonardo's extant studies for the "Sforza Horse" (and copies after his lost original drawings) suggest a bent right foreleg pose for the equestrian monument, as is illustrated on the upper left in the Turin sheet. Yet it is the bent left foreleg pose seen on the lower left of the Turin sheet—the last of the four studies that Leonardo drew on the page (and almost as if it had been an afterthought)—that apparently reflects the final solution adopted in the colossal full-scale model for the statue. The half-mold for the statue on the lower right of the Windsor sheet, with preliminary sketches and notes for the casting of the "Sforza Horse" (cat. no. 64), is for the bent left foreleg pose. One of his last extant drawings for the "Sforza Horse," a sketch in red chalk showing the transport of the gigantic full-scale model enveloped in scaffolding (Codex Atlanticus), also shows this pose. Leonardo seems to have pondered this particular detail of the design a great deal. It was the subject of a close-up drawing with remarkably precise measurements (Windsor, RL 12294). The artist also took up the motif in a sheet in Budapest (fig. 165), vigorously rendered in black chalk, which portrays four studies of the bent left foreleg each from a different angle of view, in a more continuous sequence than the metalpoint studies in Turin and in a larger scale. Most scholars concur that Leonardo did not produce preliminary drawings for the "Sforza Horse" after 1494–95, though he probably continued to work sporadically on the colossal model.[6] On November 17, 1494, the bronze that had been set aside for the casting of the statue was sent by Ludovico Sforza to his father-in-law, Ercole d'Este, to cast artillery. In 1499, probably between September and December, the colossal model was destroyed by the Gascon bowmen (*bulestrieri Guasconi*) of the invading French king, according to the account in Sabba da Castiglione's *Ricordi*, first published in Bologna in 1546.[7]

CCB

1. Windsor, RL 12289, 12290, 12319, 12320, 12321.
2. Leonardo's Codex Madrid II (fols. 2v–3r) gives a list of books that the artist had left "locked in the chest" about 1503–5, which includes a reference to "a book of horse sketches for the cartoon" (*libro di cavalli schizzati pel cartone*) under no. 104.
3. The *Regisole* was installed on a high column or pilaster in the square of the Duomo of Pavia, until its destruction in the eighteenth century.
4. C.A., fol. 399r (formerly fol. 147r-b); Richter 1970, vol. 2, p. 359, no. 1445: "Di quel di Pavia si lauda . piv . il movime[n]to che nessun altra cosa; / L'imitatione . delle cose . antiche . è piv laudabile . che quella delle . moderne." Leonardo's small sketch of the *Regisole*, extracted from the Codex Atlanticus as a fragment by a late-sixteenth-century collector, is still extant (Windsor, RL 12345).
5. Other sketches of this more spontaneous type for the "Sforza Horse" are Windsor, RL 12310, 12317.
6. Clark and Pedretti 1968–69, vol. 1, p. xxxvii.
7. Castiglione 1560, p. 57.

LEONARDO DA VINCI

64. *Designs of Furnaces in Ground Plan and Perspectival Section for the Casting of the "Sforza Horse"; Cogwheel and Pulley Mechanisms; Armatures for the Core of the "Sforza Horse"; and a Man in Bust-Length Profile Facing to the Right* (recto)
Further Designs of Furnaces in Ground Plan and Section for the Casting of the "Sforza Horse" (verso)

Pen and golden brown ink (recto and verso); notes in red chalk on recto, 278 × 191 mm ($10\,^{15}/_{16}$ × $7\,^{1}/_{2}$ in.)

Inscribed in pen and brown ink, in right-to-left script, at upper left, above and below ground plan of furnaces: *sop[r]a*; within the plan: *sotto* four times; at upper right: *lacq^a . benche ssia libera no[n] si partira / dj loco allocho . sela . no[n] trova aria piv / bassa dj se. / p[er]che la sspera de lacqua e cholochata sotto quella / dellaria . chonequidjsta[n]te superfitie dal cie[n]tro della / tera qua[n]do ella fia i[n] sua liberta senpre chacie/ra laria che del suo sito chessi tro-vera / piv . bassa . dj lej* [crossed out: *Jl movime[n]to . no[n] po essere durabile / in chosa . mvorta] nessuna chosa . sanza .vita . ara durabi/lita . dj moto accide[n]tale / Siccome ma[n]giare . sanza voglia si co[n]uerte / i[n] fastidioso . notrimento . cosi lo stud[i]o sa[n]/za* [crossed out: . . .] *desiderio . guasta la / memoria,* [crossed out: . . .] *col no[n] ritenere cosa ch'ella pigli*; near center: *24*; at lower right border, near two drawings of sections of molds for casting a horse: *queste legature va[n]o dj dentro; ferro*; in red chalk: *doma[n] sella superfitie del/lacqua posta piv alta che la / sua . spera osseruera quella parte / del circhulo simjle a quello della sua spera*; on verso in conventional left-to-right script: *Johannes . Antonius . di Johannes Ambrosius de Bolate / Chi perde il Tempo e virtu non aquista* [crossed out: *q,qu] quanto piu* [crossed out: . . .] *pensa l'animo piu s'attrista / Virtu non ha in potere le [lo] auere chi lassa [lasscia]a honore p[er] acquistare hauere / Non vale fortuna achi non s'affatica // perfecto don no[n] sa sanza gran pena / Coluy [colui] si fa felice ch[e] Xtum [Christum] vestiga / Passano nostri triumfi nostre pompe / La gola . e 'l sonno e l'otiose piume Anno dal mondo ogni virtu sbandita / tal che dal corso suo quasi e[?]ssmarita Nostra natura e vinta dal costume / Ormai convien cosi che tu ti spoltri Disse il maestro che sseggiendo [segiendo] in piuma / infama non si viene ne sotto choltri Sanza la qual chi sua vita consuma / tal uestigia interra di se lascia . Qual fumo in aria o nell'acqua la schiu-ma*; in right-to-left script on plans of furnaces at bottom: *sopra, sotto, dj sop[r]a, sop[r]a, sotto, sop[r]a, esse[n]do sotto, dj sopra*

Watermark: Serpent (close to Briquet 13665–13668)

Lent by Her Majesty Queen Elizabeth II, Royal Library, Windsor Castle 12349

PROVENANCE: Windsor Leoni volume: 1519, Francesco Melzi, Milan and Rome (1491/93–ca. 1570); ca. 1570, Orazio Melzi; by 1590, Pompeo Leoni, Madrid and Milan (ca. 1533–1608; Lugt under 2885); ca. 1613, Thomas Howard, second earl of Arundel (1586–1646); before 1690, British Royal Collection (inventory of King George III's collection, ca. 1810).

LITERATURE: Richter 1883, vol. 2, pp. 13–14, 294, 463, nos. 713, 715, 1175, 1547; Uzielli 1892, vol. 1, pp. 374–75; Solmi 1908, pp. 120, 321; Seidlitz 1909, vol. 1, p. 188; Seidlitz 1911, p. 283, nos. 613, 639; Malaguzzi Valeri 1922, figs. 53–54; Commissione Vinciana 1928–, vol. 7, pp. 17, 42, pls. 311, 312; Berenson 1938, vol. 2, p. 135, no. 1220A; Royal Academy of Arts 1952, no. 170 (hors catalogue); Brugnoli 1954, p. 367, pl. 155, fig. 14; Heydenreich 1954, vol. 1, pp. 64–66, 134, vol. 2, p. 73, pl. 95; Bovi 1959, pls. 23, 30; Goldscheider 1959, p. 184, pl. 8C; Berenson 1961, vol. 2, p. 239, no. 1220 A; Clark and Pedretti 1968–69, vol. 1, pp. 39–40, no. 12349; Clark 1969–70, p. 9, no. 38; Richter 1970, vol. 2, pp. 7–8, 244, 384, nos. 713, 715, 1175, 1547; Brugnoli 1974, p. 91, fig. 91/2; Visconti 1980, p. 118; Pedretti and Roberts 1984–86, pp. 44, 47–49, nos. 21A, B; Pedretti 1987b, pp. 71–73, no. 112 recto and verso; Aggházy 1989, p. 21, fig. 11; Caroli 1991, p. 53; Kemp 1995, p. 77; Clayton 1996–97, pp. 49–55, no. 27.

Leonardo's work on the colossal, ultimately unrealized "Sforza Horse" (cat. no. 53) seems to have reached a virtual standstill after the summer of 1489, when Ludovico Sforza "Il Moro" lost confidence in Leonardo's abilities. On July 22, 1489, the Florentine emissary Piero Alamanni wrote from Pavia to Lorenzo de' Medici "Il Magnifico" in Florence, stating that Ludovico had entrusted Leonardo with designing an enormous and magnificent equestrian statue for his father Francesco's tomb. Alamanni, however, expressed Ludovico's doubts that Leonardo could finish the project.[1] According to the dedication text in Fra Luca Pacioli's *De divina proportione* (written in 1498 and published in 1509), Leonardo's lost model for the "Sforza Horse" measured 12 braccia high from nape to ground, which is equivalent to 23 feet 11 inches.[2] If one were to estimate from this the height of the finished project, the "Sforza Horse" might have stood as tall as 31 feet 6 inches from head to ground without the rider.[3] The technical feat required to cast such an enormous monument in bronze must have seemed impossible, giving Ludovico good reason for pause and for requesting Lorenzo de' Medici's assistance,

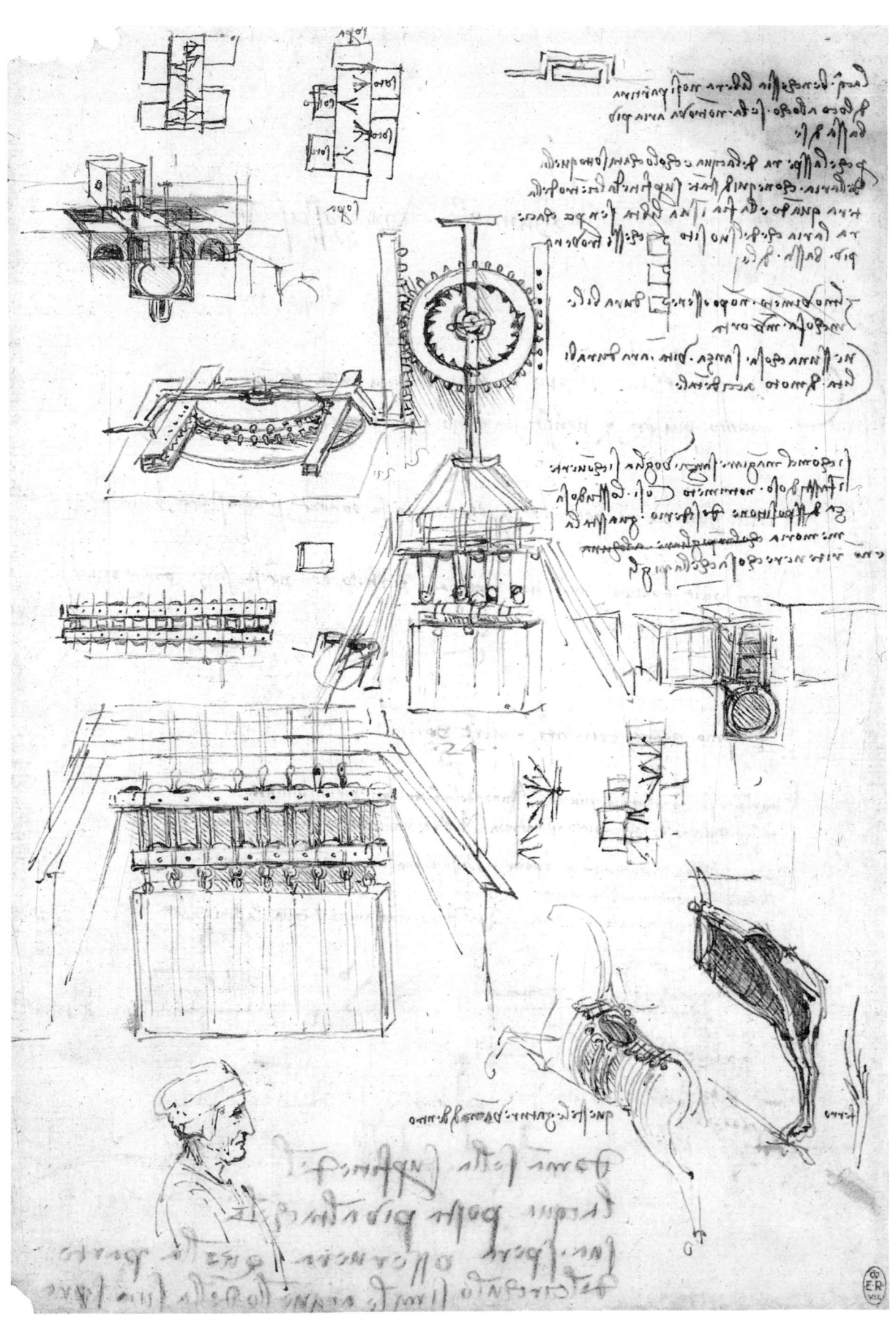

Cat. 64r

Johannes antonius di Johannes Ambrossius de bolate

Chi perde il Tempo e virtu non aquista
quanto piu se g pense l'animo piu satrista

Virtu non ha m poterebe avere chi lassa honore p aquistare havere

Non vale fortuna achi non sa faticha / perfecto don no sa senza gran pena
Colui si fa felice ch l'otru m destipa

Passano nostri triunfi nostre pompi

l'agola e l'onno e l'orose piume, Anno del mondo ogni virtu banxia
tal g tal gorso suo quasi ismarrita. Nostra natura e vinta dal costume

Ormai convien cosi restuti spolra. Disse il maestro che sfuggiendo in piuma
infama non sinen nel lotto e l'otri. Sanza laqual chi sua vita consuma
tal vestigia in terra di se lassia. Qual fumo in aria o nnellacqua la schiuma

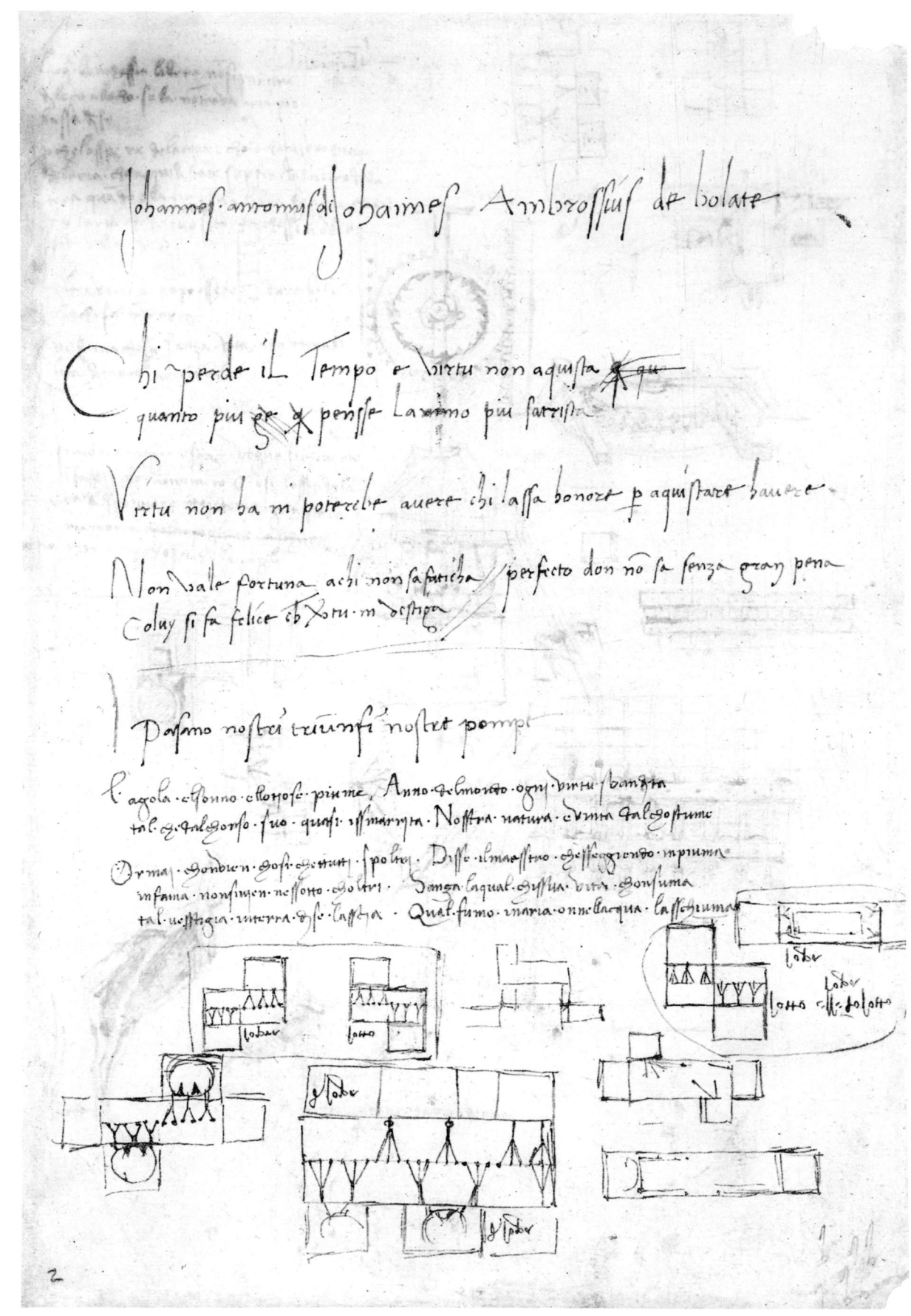

2

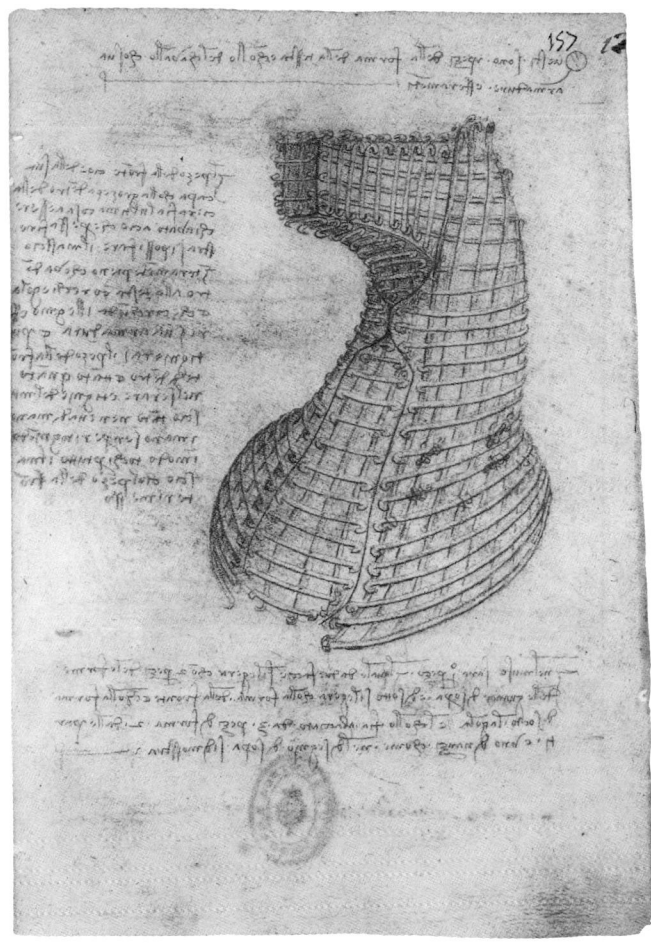

Fig. 166. Leonardo da Vinci, *Model for the Casting of the "Sforza Horse."* Red chalk, 210 × 148 mm. Codex Madrid II, fol. 157r. Biblioteca Nacional, Madrid 8936

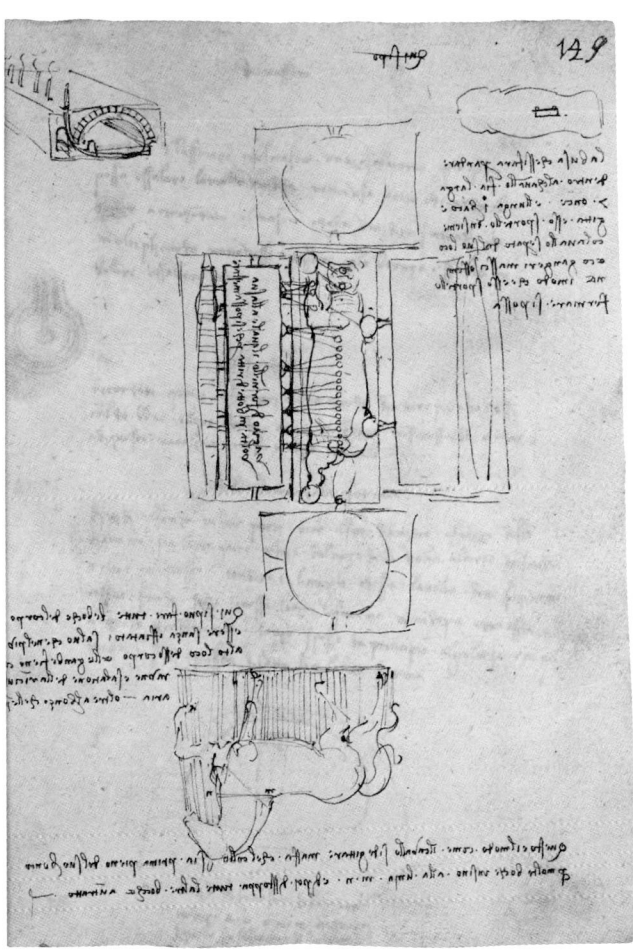

Fig. 167. Leonardo da Vinci, *Studies for the Casting of the "Sforza Horse."* Pen and brown ink, 212 × 147 mm. Codex Madrid II, fol. 149r. Biblioteca Nacional, Madrid 8936

"if you could kindly send . . . a master or two capable of doing such work" (*maestro o dua apti a tale opera*) from Florence (see cat. nos. 11, 53). Leonardo seems to have returned to the project with renewed energy about April 23, 1490, when he wrote in the Paris Ms. C, "I commenced this book, and recommenced the horse." During this second phase of work, he devoted most of his ingenuity and effort to the enormously complex technological problems of casting the statue in bronze.[4] It is clear that during 1493–94 he was at the cusp of viable solutions. But on November 17, 1494, or thereabouts, he experienced another blow, one from which, perhaps, he did not entirely recuperate. His patron Ludovico Sforza sent the bronze that had been saved for the "Sforza Horse" to his father-in-law, Ercole d'Este, duke of Ferrara, to cast from it a cannon, since he was in need of artillery. According to the dedication text in Pacioli's *De divina proportione*, the weight in

bronze of the statue was to have been 200,000 libbre (the equivalent of almost 150,000 pounds).

The present sheet of drawings and notes belongs to the second phase of work on the "Sforza Horse" and can be dated with some confidence to 1492–93. The Paris Ms. A (fol. 114v; B.N. 2038, fol. 34v) is dated July 10, 1492, and the recto of that page repeats, almost word for word, the unrelated five-line note toward the center of the right border in the recto of the Windsor sheet, which admonishes those who do not study with interest. Moreover, Leonardo's old friend Giuliano da Sangallo (ca. 1445–1516), the polymath architect, engineer, and sculptor who had a good claim to be considered among the Florentine masters "capable of doing such work," passed through Milan in October 1492. According to Giorgio Vasari, he offered Leonardo advice on casting the "Sforza Horse."[5] Most important, however, seventeen pages bound at the end

433

of the Codex Madrid II (figs. 166, 167) deal with the project of casting the "Sforza Horse," and two of these pages are dated. The first is inscribed May 17, 1491 (fol. 157v), and states, "here a record shall be kept of everything related to the bronze horse presently in production."[6] The second of the relevant pages is dated December 20, 1493 (fol. 151v), and notes, "I have decided to cast the horse without its tail and lying on the side. And because the horse measures twelve braccia, if I cast it upside down, the water [water table] would be as close as one braccio. And as I cannot raise up the ground, the humidity could cause harm, since the mold [forma], staying underground for many hours and the head, as close to the water as one braccio, would become filled with humidity and the cast would not turn out well."[7] Leonardo reached this decision after he had exhaustively considered the problem of casting the horse in an upside-down position, but even after his resolution in December 1493, he seems to have gone back and forth on the possibilities of the upside-down casting position.

The present sheet shows the model of the "Sforza Horse" upside down in the foundry pit; this is clearest in the recto, in the perspectival section of the aboveground and belowground furnaces toward the upper left corner, in which the trunk of the horse in section appears abbreviated as a circle, and two of its legs as thin upright sticks (see also fig. 167).[8] Next to the horse appear the sections of two arched underground furnaces. Two of the somewhat enigmatic notes on the recto of the sheet allude to the problematic interaction of air and the water table. It may be recalled that Leonardo's major reason for abandoning the idea of putting the gigantic model of the "Sforza Horse" upside down into the ground was that the humidity from the proximity to the water table at that depth would cause severe damage. On the lower right, the two representations seen in three-quarter oblique view probably depict the iron armature for the hollow core (the maschio) that would be coated with clay. The outer reinforced female mold (the cappa) would then be built from this hollow, clay-modeled core. Leonardo rightly thought of lightening the weight of the core by making it hollow (a solid core of the size that was required would have been unmovable because of its weight). He noted next to the lower sketch, "these armatures go inside" (queste legature vanno di dentro). This lower sketch shows that the halves of the hollow core's armature were fastened by metal stays hooked at the top like a corset, and this was also true of the outer cappa (illustrated in the Codex Madrid II, fols. 156v–

157r; fig. 166). The upper sketch offers a view of the core in hemisection with a reinforcement rod as armature in place inside, next to the overall sketch a detail diagram of this rod is labeled ferro for iron. Both representations omit the horse's tail.

Leonardo devoted a good portion of the present sheet of sketches and notes to exploring designs for a complex system of multiple aboveground and belowground furnaces (which apparently would prove unworkable) that would be necessary to melt the enormous mass of bronze. He also carefully drew several alternatives for the network of runners that would feed the molten bronze into the gates leading to the buried molds of the horse. His ideas are most clearly articulated in the sketches on the upper left of the recto and in those toward the lower border of the verso. At this point, Leonardo seems to have abandoned the traditional lost-wax method of bronze casting, which he may have earlier considered, in favor of a bronze-casting technology that was more typically used in foundries to produce cannons and bells. In that method, the molten bronze was poured directly into the space between the cappa (outer mold) and the maschio, the sculpted inner core.[9] The three sketches on the upper left of the sheet show the designs of the furnaces in plan and perspectival section; the two levels of furnaces, above and below ground, are carefully distinguished, for they could not be stacked one on top of the other. In the plans, the furnaces are represented as squares, marked with the words sopra (for above ground) and sotto (for below ground); the arteries leading from the squares represent the runners feeding the molten bronze from the furnaces to the gates into the earth. The sketches on the verso adopt similar conventions.

Toward the center of the recto, the technological studies show variations of designs for a device for lifting extremely heavy weights. The device is operated at the top by cogwheels and at the level of the suspended weight by neatly aligned rows of numerous interconnected pulleys. Ever fascinated by the nature of movement, Leonardo dedicated detail studies to the mechanisms of motion in the device—the cogwheel and pulleys. In the context of the sheet, these technological drawings suggest that the problems of lowering and raising the massive molds of the "Sforza Horse" into and out of the pit may have weighed no less on Leonardo's mind than the problems of its casting.

On the verso of the sheet, Leonardo seems to have continued the sketches and notes of furnaces from the recto holding what is now the lower border of the sheet upright, then apparently turned it around to add (in a larger, conventional left-to-right script) the quotations from Dante, Petrarch, and Cecco d'Ascoli's *L'Acerba*. Leonardo's extensive quote from Dante's *Inferno* (24:46–51) on the theme of fame concludes the notes on the verso: "'Now, it would be good for you to shake sloth thus,' / said the teacher, 'for by sitting on down / one does not attain Fame, nor by resting underneath the covers; / he who, without Fame, burns his life to waste / leaves no more vestige of himself on earth than / wind-blown smoke, or foam upon the water.'" As has been pointed out, there is little reason to doubt the authenticity of the larger left-to-right script; the smaller left-to-right script closely resembles the left-to-right script of Leonardo's presentation maps (cat. no. 80). The small portrait of the man in bust length at the bottom of the recto may be an idealized portrait of Dante. CCB

1. Transcribed in Fusco and Corti 1992, pp. 16–17.
2. Pacioli 1509, Pars prima, fol. 1r.
3. See Kirwin 1995.
4. Paris Ms. C, fol. 15v; Beltrami 1919a, p. 29, no. 44; Richter 1970, vol. 2, p. 8, no. 720: "a dì . 23 d'aprile . 1.4.90. chomi[n]ciaj . questo libro e richomi[n]ciaj. il cavallo."
5. Vasari–Milanesi 1906, vol. 4, p. 276.
6. Ladislao Reti in Codex Madrid 1974, vol. 5, p. 327: "A sere 17 di maggio 1491. / Qui si farà ricordo di tucte quelle cose le quale fieno / al proposito del cavallo de bronzo del quale al presente / sono inn opera."
7. Ladislao Reti in Codex Madrid 1974, vol. 5, p. 321: "A dì 20 di diciembre 1493 conchiudo gittare il cavallo sanza coda / e a diacere, perchè essendo esso cavallo braccia 12, a gittarllo pe' piede andere/be vicino all'acqua uno braccio, e levare il terren non posso, e ll'umido mi potrebe no/cere, perchè la forma starà assai ore sotto terra, e lla testa vicino all'acqua / uno braccio s' inpregnierebbe di umidità. E l'gietto non verrebbe—"
8. A clearer view of the model of the "Sforza Horse" set upside down into the pit is found in Codex Madrid II, fol. 149r (fig. 167).
9. Kirwin 1995.

LEONARDO DA VINCI

65. *Sketches for the Last Supper; Architectural and Geometric Sketches* (recto) *Calculations with Architectural, Engineering, and Geometric Sketches* (verso)

Pen and golden brown ink (recto); pen and brown ink, soft black chalk or charcoal (verso), 266 × 214 mm (10½ × 8⁷⁄₁₆ in.)
Inscribed in pen and brown ink, in right-to-left script, on recto toward lower border, and canceled: *Jo voglio sop[r]a . vna linja data . fare la figura dj 8 lati equali . effaro inquesto modo / sia la linja data . a . b . io tor[r]o il suo mez[z]o . in . n . e faro la p[er]pe[n]djcu-lare . m . n . dj poi po[n]/go il pie del sessto nel mez[z]o della . linja . data . a.b . effo il circulo . a . c . b . dj poj apro il se/sto dalo stremo della linja data . in . b insino dove il p[r] circulo sinp[er]tersega sop[r]a la p[er]pe[n]/djculare della linja . data . cioe . in . c . ap[er]to chio ho il stesto intale largeza e io lo pongo / cosi ap[er]to sop[ra] la p[er]pe[n]djculare che ava[n]za sop[r]a la intersegatione . cio he fo tanto la linja . m / c . quanta la linja . c . b . he in . m fo il cientro dj tale circhulo ilquale tocha[n]do li stremi / della data . linja . cho[n]tiene dentro asse 8 desse linje date chosi fo hesso ottango.lo;* on verso in pen and brown ink, with numerous calculations: *Tal pro-portione quale . ha / il moto . della forza . primaria / col moto della forza djriuatiua / Tale . ara la pote[n]tia . della forza / djrivatiua . co[n] quella della / primitjva—*
Lent by Her Majesty Queen Elizabeth II, Royal Library, Windsor Castle 12542

PROVENANCE: Windsor Leoni volume: 1519, Francesco Melzi, Milan and Rome (1491/93–ca. 1570); ca. 1570, Orazio Melzi; by 1590, Pompeo Leoni, Madrid and Milan (ca. 1533–1608; Lugt under 2885); ca. 1613, Thomas Howard, second earl of Arundel (1586–1646); before 1690, British Royal Collection (inventory of King George III's collection, ca. 1810).

LITERATURE: Grosvenor 1878, vol. 2, p. 25; Richter 1883, vol. 1, p. 335, pl. 45; Müller-Walde 1889, p. 148, pl. 80; Müntz 1898, vol. 1, pp. 177–78, 189–90, vol. 2, p. 53; Müntz 1899, pp. 179, 191; Berenson 1903, vol. 1, p. 156, vol. 2, p. 65, no. 1188; Seidlitz 1909, vol. 1, pp. 110, 197; Seidlitz 1911, pp. 40–41; Malaguzzi Valeri 1913–23, vol. 2, p. 493, fig. 535; Thiis 1913, pp. 244, 246; Poggi 1919, pl. 87; Venturi 1920, pp. 133–34, fig. 75; De Rinaldis 1926, p. 104, fig. 34; Commissione Vinciana 1928– , vol. 5, p. 23, pl. 198.2; Popp 1928, pp. 41–42, no. 35; Sirén 1928, p. 77, pl. 101; Bodmer 1931, pp. 251, 403; Berenson 1938, vol. 1, p. 174, vol. 2, p. 135, vol. 3, fig. 500, no. 1188; Giglioli 1944, pl. 77; Heydenreich 1946, p. 182; Möller 1952a, vol. 1, fig. 15; Royal Academy of Arts 1952, no. 59 (hors catalogue); Clark 1954, pl. 21; Castelfranco 1957, p. 516; Heydenreich 1958a, fig. 11; Goldscheider 1959, p. 172, pl. 4a; Berenson 1961, vol. 1, p. 254, vol. 2, p. 233, vol. 3, fig. 485, no. 1188; Chastel 1961, p. 69; Eissler 1961, pl. 33; Castelfranco 1966, p. 230; Clark and Pedretti 1968–69, vol. 1, pp. 99–100, no. 12542; Clark 1969–70, p. 10, no. 41; Richter 1970, vol. 1, p. 373, pl. 45; Brachert 1971, p. 464; Pedretti 1973a, p. 69, fig. 62; Steinberg 1973; Brizio 1974b, pp. 32–33, fig. 32/3; Heydenreich 1974a, pp. 40–41,

116, fig. 28; Gould 1975, pp. 92–94, fig. 44; Pedretti 1978–79, pp. 18, 105, figs. 16, 151; Kemp 1981, pp. 191–92, pl. 53; Pedretti 1981b, p. 99; Heydenreich 1982, p. 44; Kemp 1982b, p. 176, pl. 45; Mazzini 1982, pp. 62–63, 69, figs. 36, 42; Pedretti and Clark 1983, pp. 33, 64–71, no. 3; Brizio 1985, pp. 76, 82, 89, fig. 27; Marani 1986a, pp. 5–9; Clark 1988, pp. 144–55, fig. 57; Kemp 1989a, no. 10; Kemp and Roberts 1989, pp. 60–61, no. 10; Marani 1989, pp. 18–19, 70, fig. 17; Martin Clayton in Palazzo Grassi 1992, pp. 230–31, no. 18; Popham 1994, no. 161; Arasse 1997, p. 364, fig. 1; Dragstra 1997, pp. 84, 96–97, fig. 2a; Arasse 1998, p. 364, fig. 251; Eichholz 1998, pp. 487–93, pls. 26, 110; Pietro Marani in Brambilla Barcilon and Marani 1999, pp. 1–20; Marani 2000b, pp. 222–26; Marani 2001a, pp. 124–26, no. 27; Steinberg 2001, pp. 273–87.

The upper portion of this dazzling sheet of rapid sketches from 1493–95 is of extraordinary historical importance, as it offers the earliest extant compositional ideas by Leonardo for his famous mural of the *Last Supper* (Refectory of Santa Maria delle Grazie, Milan), one of the masterpieces of Western art. These figural sketches, however, seem to have been almost an afterthought on the page. To judge from the overall disposition of motifs on the paper, Leonardo probably first drew the large diagram about the construction of an octagon on the lower portion of the sheet, then wrote the explanatory notes below. (Similar studies of geometry occur among Leonardo's notes of 1487–92 in Paris Ms. A and Ms. B.) He may have next added the four architectural designs on the left, which depict a partial view of an interior elevation with an arch, two sketches for octagonal architectural forms (an inlay pavement of interlacing ornament and a ribbed dome?), and three bays of an arcade (sketched upside down). The column of numbers close to the left border of the sheet may have been a list of daily household expenses.[1] The studies of geometry deal with the contruction of a polygon from a particular line; the verso describes mechnical devices for hoisting weights.

The sketches for the *Last Supper* on the recto have received the lion's share of the scholarly attention in the Leonardo literature. Yet surprisingly little is known about the circumstances of the commission and initial stages of planning of the *Last Supper* (fig. 168), beyond a few of Leonardo's own scattered iconographic notes and a handful of extant contemporary documents.[2] On March 29, 1492, Leonardo's friend the painter and architect Donato Bramante (1443/44?–1514) had begun building the new eastern end (*tribuna*) of Santa Maria delle Grazie, commissioned by Ludovico Sforza "Il Moro," as part of a plan to turn the church into a grandiose quasi mausoleum for the Sforza family. In 1493–95 (the date is uncertain), Leonardo seems to have obtained the commission for the *Last Supper*. It is not clear whether the direct patron was indeed Ludovico (whose arms appear in the lunettes and whom early written sources name), or whether it was the Dominican monks of Santa Maria delle Grazie; in any case, Ludovico's good friend Vincenzo Bandello was appointed prior of Santa Maria delle Grazie in 1495.[3] The significant documents are less precise than one would wish. A letter with memorandum, dated June 29, 1497, from Ludovico to his secretary, Marchesino Stanga, expresses his hope that Leonardo will soon "finish the work that was begun in the refectory delle Gratie so that he may attend to the other wall of the said refectory."[4] It is presumed that "Il Moro" was impatiently referring to the *Last Supper* still being unfinished. There is

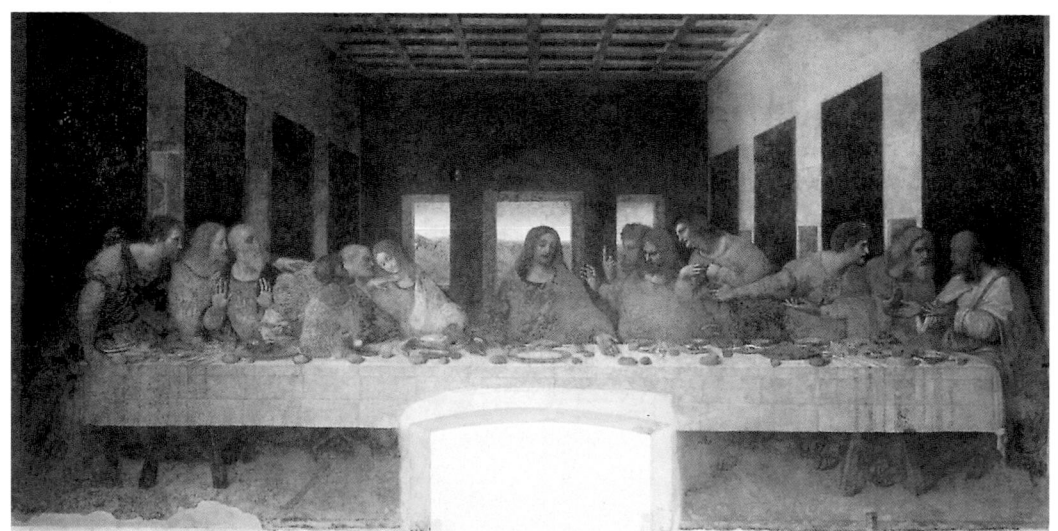

Fig. 168. Leonardo da Vinci, *Last Supper* (after restoration). Oil with some *tempera grassa*, 460 × 880 cm. Refectory of Santa Maria delle Grazie, Milan

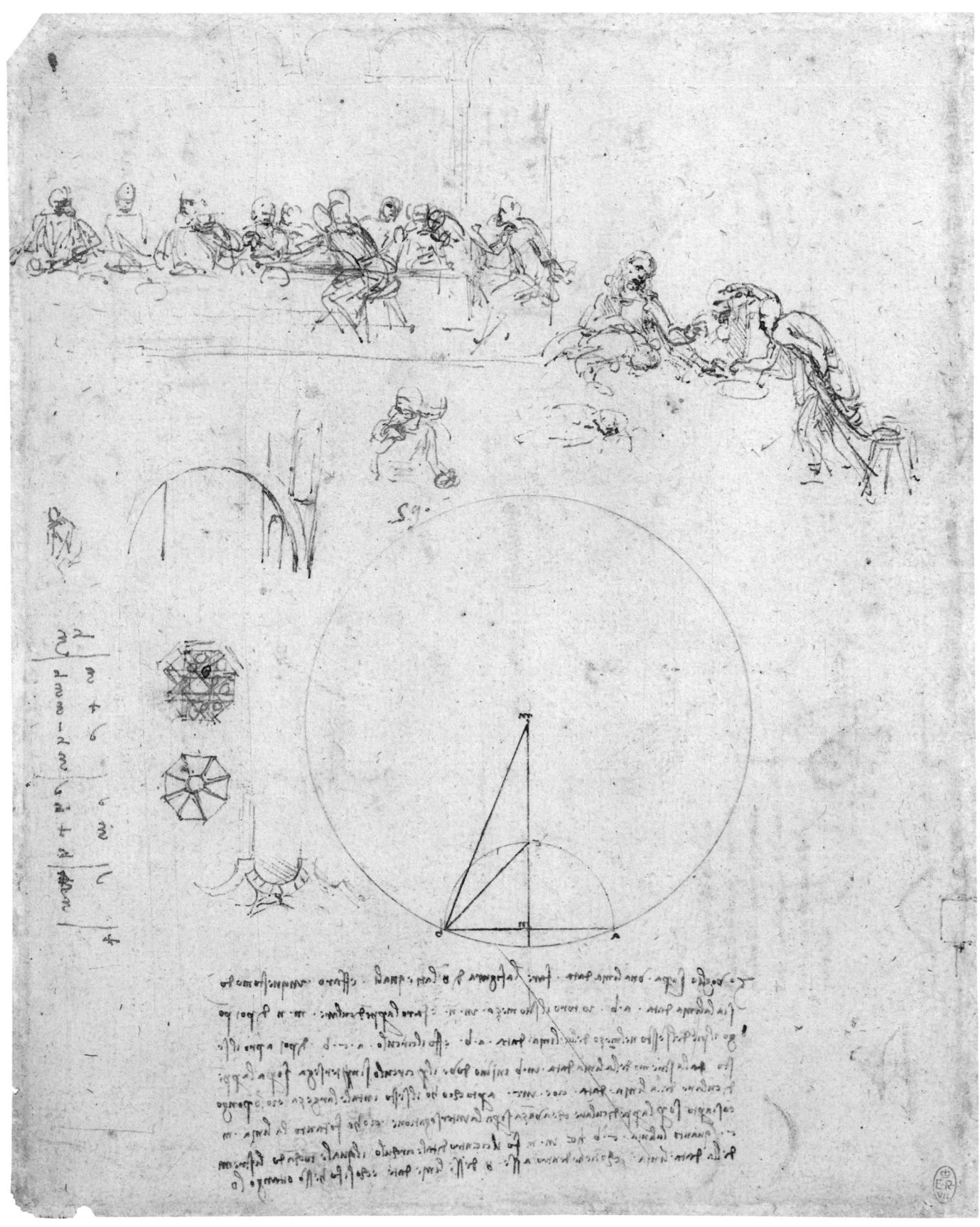

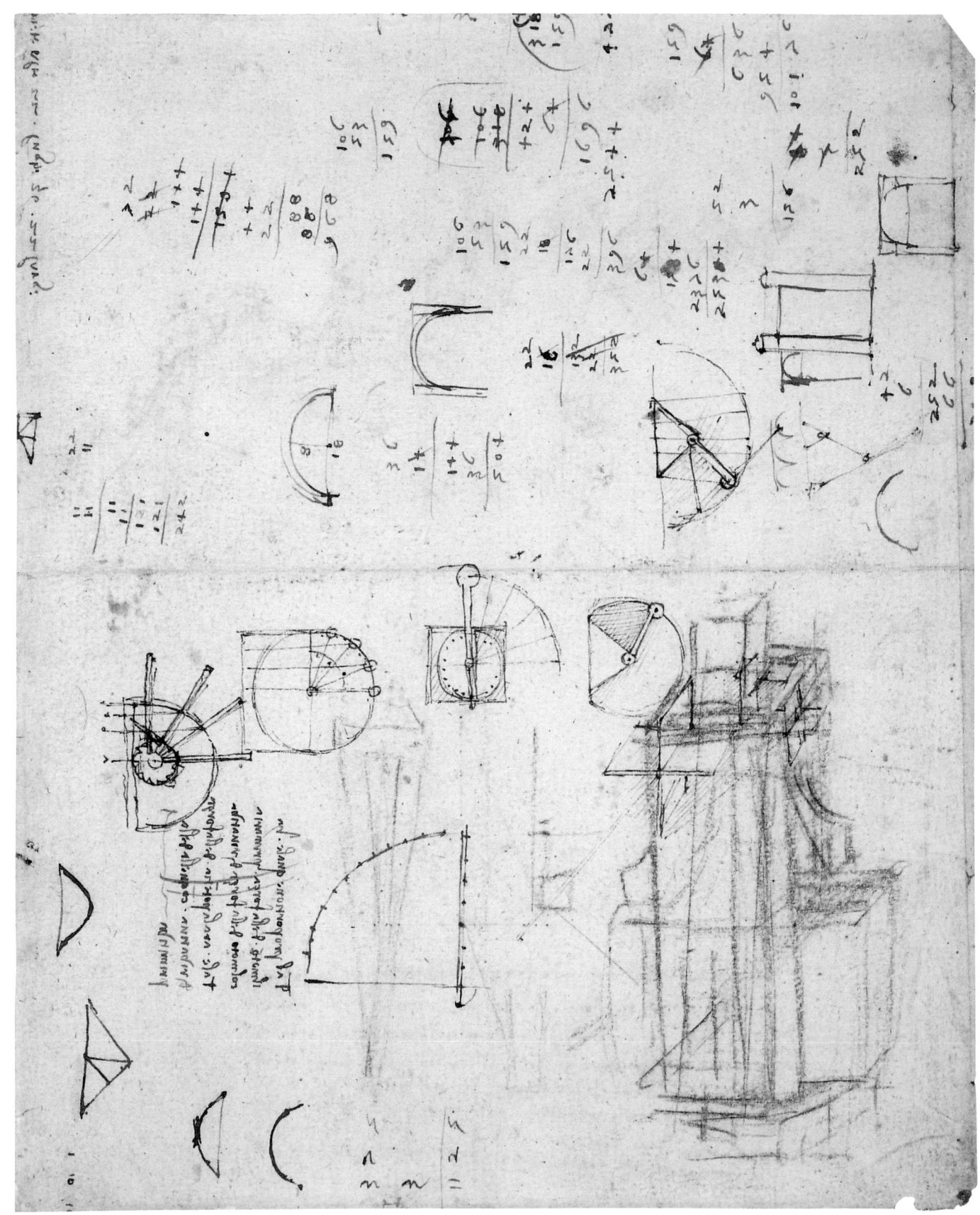

also a payment record of 1497 for "work made in the refectory, where Leonardo is painting the Apostles [the *Last Supper*], with a window."[5] Matteo Bandello's fifty-eighth *novella* in part one of his anthology (published in Florence in 1554) offers an eyewitness account of Leonardo's ponderous method of work on the *Last Supper* at the Refectory of Santa Maria delle Grazie and on the monumental clay model of the "Sforza Horse" at the Corte Vecchia.[6] Scholars usually place Bandello's description about 1497. Fra Luca Pacioli's *De divina proportione* (published in Venice in 1509) bears a dedication to Ludovico Sforza, dated February 8, 1498, which greatly praises Leonardo and mentions that the *Last Supper* is finished.

Leonardo painted the *Last Supper* composition in tempera and oil over two layers of preparation on the north wall of the long, austere refectory of Santa Maria delle Grazie; above it he painted three lunettes with foliage and the arms of Ludovico Sforza and his family.[7] The upper left composition in the Windsor sheet is the most significant document of Leonardo's initial design process, though it is frustratingly unclear in its details. It shows that from the very beginning the artist thought of integrating the pictorial architecture that forms the setting of the composition with the real architecture of the room, but it surprisingly portrays the scene within an architectural space that is considerably different from that of the final mural. In the sketch, the multiple lunettes at the top (at least four are drawn, though a greater number are suggested, possibly eight or ten) imply that the real architecture had a groin vault with multiple corbels and lunettes. In the north wall of the refectory where the final mural is placed, there are only three lunettes (separated by two corbels); Leonardo's fictive architecture within the *Last Supper* responds to the real architecture of these three lunettes, without actually making them part of the scene. In the sketch, there is little anticipation of the immensely complex perspectival framework of the final composition, and a full pilaster supports the corbel in the bay on the extreme right. Therefore, it is difficult to discern in the sketch which is the intended fictive architecture of the painting and which is the intended actual architecture of the room.

The identification of the figure of Christ in the upper left of the Windsor sketch has led to considerable scholarly disagreement (wittily summed up in Steinberg 2001), and given the fragmentary nature of the sketch, it would seem futile to attempt clarification. But Christ is the protagonist of the story. By turns, therefore, he has been identified as the second figure from the left (a mere sketch of an oval above a box sugestive of a slight and angular body), the third figure from the left (hairy, bearded, and somewhat massive), and the fourth from the left (balding and bearded, with a gaze seemingly directed at Judas). Judas is seen on the opposite side of the table, according to the traditional iconography of the *Last Supper*. The proposal that Christ is the slight and angular figure second from the left seems convincing,[8] because it is by far the sketchiest figure in technique and the least individualized in physical appearance, as if Leonardo had postponed to the last thinking about the Savior's characterization. The top sketch is probably cropped along the left, for Christ presumably would have been seated at the center with an equal number of apostles on either side.

Slightly below and to the right is a more fragmentary sketch that reworks the main figural group around Christ. Here, John throws himself dramatically over the table close to the Savior's bosom, and two solutions are offered for Christ's left hand. In the first, he reaches for the same dish as Judas; in the second, he holds up his hand as if in a gesture of blessing, admonishment, or speech. Judas may or may not be the figure at the end of the table, getting up to reach for the sop on the table near Christ. The apostle seated on Christ's left, who holds his left hand to his brow to shield or enhance his vision, may be Peter, but his identity is not certain. Farther to the left, a schematic sketch appears to portray two embracing figures, possibly two apostles, or Christ with an apostle. The main function of this slight but evocative sketch is to explore solutions for the intertwined poses of figures, which in general recall those on the left portion of the final mural (Andrew and James the Less; John and Peter). CCB

1. Pedretti and Clark 1983, pp. 67–68, under no. 3.
2. See esp. Brambilla Barcilon and Marani 1999, pp. 1–5, 86, 328–426.
3. Brambilla Barcilon and Marani 1999, pp. 1–5.
4. Transcribed in Beltrami 1919a, pp. 43–44, no. 76; Marani 2000b, pp. 346–47, no. 24: "Item de solicitare Leonardo fior.no perché finischa lopera del Refittorio delle Gratie principiata per attendere poi ad altra Fazada desso Refittorio."
5. Brambilla Barcilon and Marani 1999; document transcribed in Beltrami 1919a, p. 45, no. 77; Marani 2000b, p. 347, no. 25: "Item per lavori facti in lo refettorio, dove dipinge Leonardo li Apostoli, con una finestra."
6. Bandello's *novella* is entitled *Fra Filippo Lippi . . . fiorentino pittore e presso da Mori e fatto schiavo, et per l'arte della Pittura è fatto libero et honorato*; partly transcribed in Beltrami 1919a, pp. 45–46, no. 79.
7. Brambilla Barcilon and Marani 1999, pp. 1–5.
8. Eichholz 1998, pp. 489–90.

LEONARDO DA VINCI

66. *Bearded Old Man in Half-Length, Three-Quarter View Facing to the Right (Saint Peter?)*

Metalpoint, reworked with pen and brown ink, on blue prepared paper, 145 × 113 mm (5¾ × 4⁷⁄₁₆ in.)

Graphische Sammlung Albertina, Vienna 17614 (S.R. 64)

PROVENANCE: Prince Charles de Ligne; Duke Albert of Sachsen-Teschen (1738–1822; Lugt 174); museum stamp.

LITERATURE: Recueil de Ligne, no. 25; Bartsch 1794, p. 34, no. 5; Schönbrunner and Meder 1896, no. 590; Berenson 1903, vol. 1, p. 156, vol. 2, p. 62, no. 1113; Seidlitz 1909, vol. 1, p. 199; Malaguzzi Valeri 1913–23, vol. 2, pp. 507–8, fig. 552; Meder 1923, pl. 23; Popp 1928, p. 41, no. 33; Suida 1929, p. 74; Bodmer 1931, pp. 257, 404; Stix and Fröhlich-Bum 1932, vol. 3, p. 5, no. 18, pl. 6; Berenson 1938, vol. 1, p. 174, vol. 2, p. 124, vol. 3, fig. 502, no. 1113; Heydenreich 1946, p. 182; Popham 1948, no. 13; Biblioteca Medicea Laurenziana 1952, p. 31, no. 42; Möller 1952a, vol. 1, pp. 24, 28, fig. 21; Goldscheider 1959, p. 154, no. 14; Berenson 1961, vol. 1, p. 254, vol. 2, p. 218, vol. 3, p. 488, no. 1113; Benesch 1964, p. 320, pl. 1; Clark and Pedretti 1968–69, vol. 1, p. xxvi n. 2; Koschatzky and Krasa 1969, no. 247; Albertina 1971, no. 12; Louvre 1975, pp. 28–29, no. 6; Ames-Lewis 1981, p. 164, pl. 173; Heydenreich 1982, pp. 41, 44, fig. p. 73; Pedretti 1982a, p. 27; Pedretti and Clark 1983, pp. 38–40, fig. 25, p. 30; Zöllner 1989b, p. 146, fig. 11; Birke 1991, pp. 42, 44, no. 41; Caroli 1991, p. 191; Sciolla 1991b, p. 214, fig. 238; Kemp in Palazzo Grassi 1992, p. 46; Birke and Kertész 1992–97, vol. 4, p. 2167, inv. 17614; Brown 1994a, fig. 4, p. 77; Popham 1994, no. 164; Arasse 1998, p. 332, fig. 227; Eichholz 1998, pp. 490, 498, pl. 112; Brambilla Barcilon and Marani 1999, pp. 24, 27; Dossi 1999, p. 185, no. 12; Marani 2000b, p. 242; Ames-Lewis 2001, p. 20, fig. 4; Laurenza 2001, pp. 41–42 n. 87, 45, 169–70, fig. 35; Marani 2001b, pp. 122–23, no. 26.

Following Bernard Berenson's tentative suggestion in 1903, and firmer statements in 1938 and 1961, the luminous Albertina study has been traditionally connected to the mural of the *Last Supper* (Refectory of Santa Maria delle Grazie, Milan), which Leonardo seems to have begun in 1493–95 — the precise date is not documented — and finished in 1498, to judge from Fra Luca Pacioli's mention of it as being complete in the preface to his *De divina proportione* (see Chronology). It bears emphasizing, however, that the figure in the powerful Albertina drawing seems quite far from both the design and the classical grandeur of expression of the apostles in the *Last Supper*, as the mural was finally painted on the end wall of the Refectory of Santa Maria delle Grazie (fig. 169). Moreover, the

figure of the old man in the Albertina study is lit from the upper right, whereas the pictorial light in the mural emanates from the upper left, coinciding with the light source from the actual windows of the refectory.[1] There is also little indication that the figure in the Albertina study was meant to be part of a larger narrative whole, even if one takes into account that the sheet has been cropped considerably along the borders. For example, the man's body appears to continue below the waist; the planes of his lap seem to be indicated along the lower left with a few deft outlines and parallel-hatched shadows. There do not appear to be signs of a horizontal plane suggestive of a table, as might be expected in a composition of the *Last Supper* (it is possible, however, that the original sheet of the Albertina drawing was cropped above this detail in the composition). In its present state, the Albertina study appears to portray the old man's figure as if it were an independent composition, more or less complete in and of itself; in this respect, it seems comparable to many extant Renaissance devotional images in which the single figures of saints are portrayed in half-length or three-quarter length. In Leonardo's final mural in the Refectory of Santa Maria delle Grazie (fig. 168), by contrast, the apostles appear dramatically intertwined in groups of three figures as they react to the

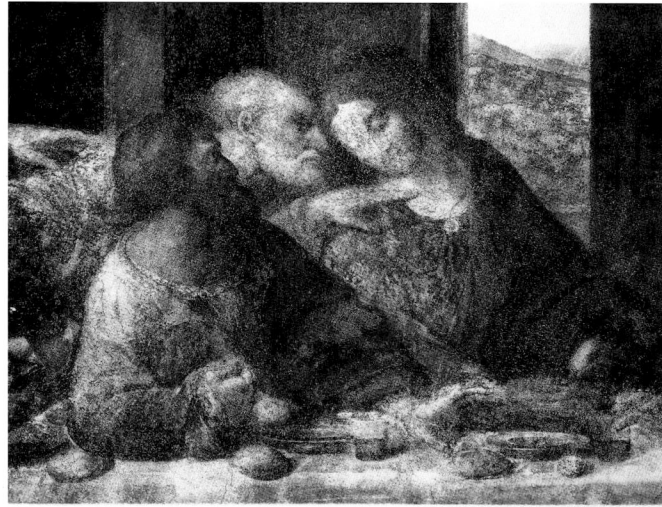

Fig. 169. Detail of Leonardo da Vinci, *Last Supper* (fig. 168), showing Saints Peter and John with Judas

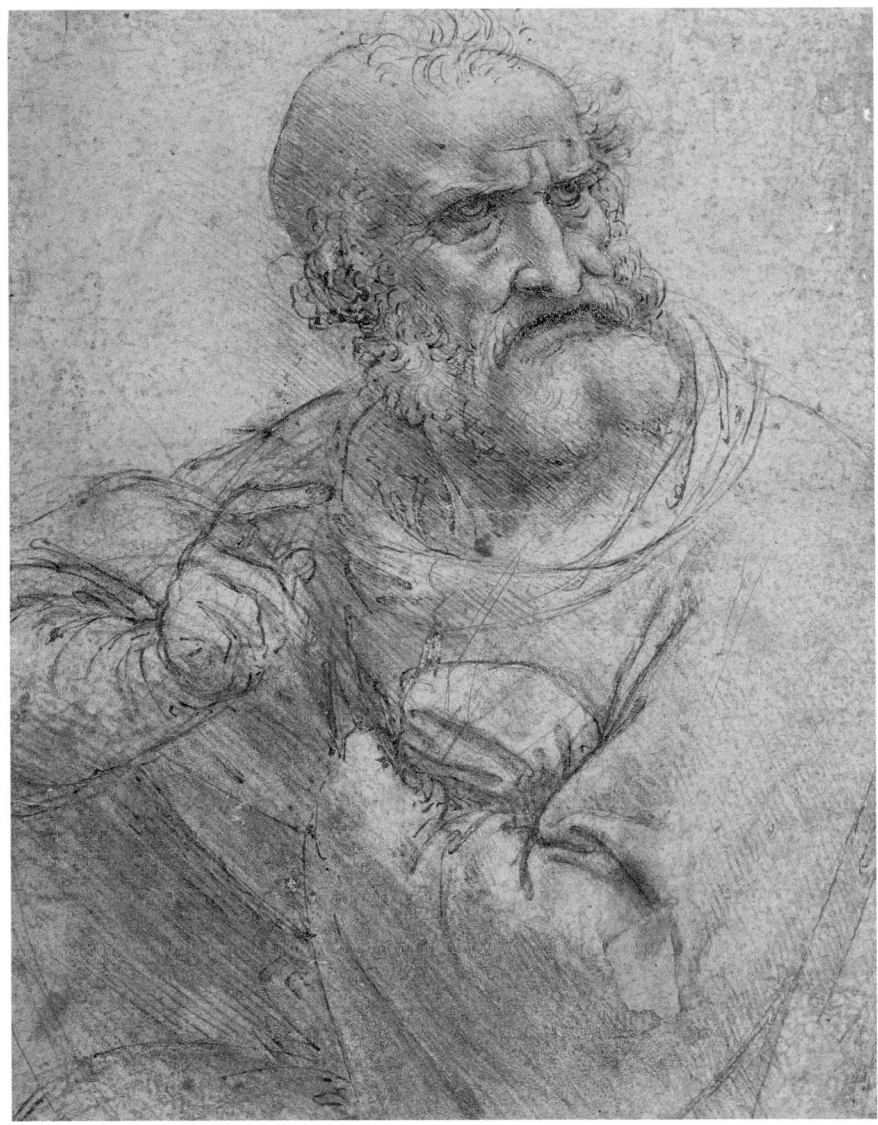

Cat. 66 *(actual size)*

mystery of Christ's words instituting the sacrament of the Eucharist and foretelling his betrayal by Judas.[2]

Despite such objections, it does not seem possible to rule out the connection of the Albertina study to the mural of the *Last Supper,* as it probably corresponds to a very early stage of planning in the project. In the author's opinion (in agreement with a number of previous scholars), the study is to be dated to the same moment, in 1493–95, as the dazzling com-

positional sketches from the Royal Library, Windsor (cat. no. 65), and is here exhibited next to those sketches in order to focus attention on Leonardo's early design of the mural's composition. The Windsor sheet shows the figures of Christ and the apostles sitting around the table in relative isolation from one another and offers no suggestion of the lighting source for the scene. Although it is drawn with a great degree of finish, the iconic blessing figure in the Albertina study would seem to fit well visually within the arrangement that Leonardo envisioned in the Windsor sketch. The figure on the extreme upper left in the Windsor sheet especially resembles the apostle in the Albertina study.

The subject of the Albertina study has traditionally—and probably correctly—been identified as Saint Peter, prince of the apostles. The possibility that the study portrays another of Christ's disciples is not to be ruled out entirely (perhaps he is Peter's brother Andrew, who is placed to Peter's left in the final mural, or Simeon, who is seated second from the right border of the composition, as Ludwig Goldscheider maintained). The saint's pose is iconic, with the right hand extended in blessing and the left clutching the ends of a voluminous mantle and holding what appears to be a conventional apostolic attribute; whether it is Peter's gold and silver keys (or just one of the keys) is not clear, as the outlines are only slightly indicated in the metalpoint underdrawing on the chest and seem too tentative in their repeatedly reinforced contours for a definitive conclusion. Characteristic of Leonardo's graphic work from the late 1480s to the early 1490s are both the sculptural style of drawing, with effects of exquisitely calibrated light, and the metalpoint technique. In the latter fairly long, pitch-straight parallel lines of hatching, which course over the form of the apostle's figure into the background in a unified, continuous manner, are then reworked in pen and ink to deepen the contrasts of tone. The hatching technique is much like that of his pen-and-ink studies of grotesque physiognomy (cat. nos. 60, 61). Following Ludwig Goldscheider's hesitant observations in 1959, Bernard Berenson would more strongly state in 1961 that the pen-and-ink reworking of the Albertina study was by another hand (no such doubts had troubled Berenson's mind in 1903 or 1938); this opinion is sometimes upheld in the later Leonardo literature.[3] Attentive examination of the drawing layers, however, can demonstrate that most of these passages in pen and ink are original. They deepen the shadows (it is not possible to achieve extremely dark tone with the metalpoint) and are a thoroughly integrated extension of the tonal scale of the metalpoint outlines and rendering. Moreover, the pen-and-ink reworkings of some of the shadows are fluently executed with left-handed parallel hatching. Leonardo often reworked metalpoint drawings with pen and ink in his early years (see cat. nos. 20, 25, 31 verso, 38, 40, 45). His use of the metalpoint medium in drawing the Albertina study, as well as the small related sheet of *Christ*

Carrying the Cross, the so-called *Cristo Portacroce* from Venice (cat. no. 62), has also caused debate in the literature. The use of the metalpoint medium in Italian drawings from the early 1490s, however, is not as rare as some scholars maintain, and it does not—in itself—adduce definitive evidence for a dating of Leonardo's studies. As in his other endeavors, Leonardo can surprise us in matters of drawing technique with both his experimental approaches and his reliance on traditional methods. The rare evidence of the medium offered by the Albertina and Venice studies has led to the somewhat dogmatic assertion that "silver-point is not a high Renaissance medium,"[4] which can be countered with the significant example of Raphael's silverpoint studies on pink-beige prepared paper for the *Madonna del Granduca* of 1507, the Vatican *stanze* of 1508–10, or the *Madonna of the Veil* of 1510–12. Numerous other cases exist of less famous artists using this medium between 1490 and 1510, such as Filippino Lippi, Piero di Cosimo, Lorenzo di Credi, and Pietro Perugino (as well as various Umbrian artists in his circle). Documented references also exist regarding the use of metalpoint as a drawing medium in Leonardo's workshop from 1490 and 1491, when the scoundrel "Salaì" (Gian Giacomo Caprotti di Oreno), who was ten years old and newly arrived in Leonardo's workshop as an apprentice, absconded with silverpoints of two assistants.[5] The metalpoint drawings on blue-gray prepared paper by one of these assistants—Giovanni Antonio Boltraffio—are directly inspired by the master's own technique (in addition to the present drawing, see cat. no. 61). Three such studies by Boltraffio from the 1490s are exhibited here (cat. nos. 124–26). In the late 1470s, and throughout the 1480s, Leonardo had used the metalpoint medium in drawing in order to obtain a delicate relieflike inflection of form against the color of the prepared paper. His nuanced explorations of the metalpoint medium culminate, for example, in his studies for the "Sforza Horse" (cat. no. 53), the *Saint John the Baptist* (cat. no. 61), the angel in the *Virgin of the Rocks* (Biblioteca Reale, Turin, 15572; fig. 80), and the *Madonna Litta* (cat. no. 44). In the case of the Albertina study from the early 1490s, it seems that Leonardo had pushed the tonal possibilities of the subtle linear medium of metalpoint to its limits, hence his more pictorial reworking of the study with pen and ink.

The conception of the apostle's figure in the Albertina study borders on caricature. The old, bearded man, with a bald, prominent cranium touched by small tufts of forelocks, exhibits the bony, broken, long nose and clenched, protruding jaw seen in many of Leonardo's "nutcracker" grotesques — the *visi mostruosi*, to use Leonardo's own words for facial deformity — of the late 1480s and early 1490s (see cat. no. 59). A fragile study in red chalk on the recto of a sheet at the Istituto per la Grafica di Roma, which may date from the early 1490s, portrays such a nutcracker, a nude old man in a pose closely similar to that in the Albertina sheet, but with a physiognomy and body otherwise pathetically malformed (fig. 55). By comparison, the psychological presence and monumentality of the apostle's figure in the Albertina study are arresting. It would also be precisely at this time, in the early 1490s, when Leonardo would most compellingly write about the power of gesture to amplify the "motions of the mind" (*i moti mentali*). Here, the saint turns his head and directs his intent gaze to the right, apparently seized by divine furor. His raised light eyes partially pierce through the bushy, tightly knit eyebrows, as is typical in many of Leonardo's physiognomic studies of old men from the 1490s and 1500s. To create mass and animated movement in counterpoint to the saint's extraordinary head, Leonardo showed the holy man turning his body sharply to the left and agitatedly gathering his mantle in an inflated, zigzagging knot across his chest, while pointing his blessing right hand to the upper right.

Carlo Pedretti, Georg Eichholz, and Pietro C. Marani have more recently favored an earlier date for the Albertina study,

about 1490, linking it especially to the style and use of the metalpoint technique in the Venice study for *Christ Carrying the Cross* (cat. no. 62).[6] Marani has also disassociated the Albertina study from the *Last Supper* and considers it instead a premonition of the powerful studies in physiognomy for the mural that was to come. Catalogue numbers 29 and 39, which may be dated on the basis of style about 1478 – 83 (they are loosely connected with the *Adoration of the Shepherds* and the Uffizi altarpiece of the *Adoration of the Magi*), suggest that Leonardo had considered the challenges of designing a figural composition in the style of a *Last Supper* composition in his earlier years in Florence.   CCB

1. Marani 2001b, pp. 122 – 23, no. 26.
2. Steinberg 2001.
3. Goldscheider 1959, p. 154, no. 14 ("some of the ink lines are perhaps by a later hand"); Berenson 1961, vol. 2, p. 218, no. 1113 ("ripassato a penna da altra mano").
4. Clark and Pedretti 1968 – 69, vol. 1, p. xxvi n. 2.
5. Leonardo himself recorded in a note dated September 7, 1490, that "Salaì" stole a silverpoint from one of his workshop assistants called Marco, who is sometimes identified as the painter Marco d'Oggiono (transcribed in Richter 1970, vol. 2, pp. 363 – 64, no. 1458; Beltrami 1919a, pp. 33 – 34, no. 52). The artist also noted on April 2, 1491, that "Salaì" had stolen the silverpoint of yet another workshop assistant, called Giovan Antonio, who may be identified as the painter Giovanni Antonio Boltraffio (transcribed in Richter 1970, vol. 2, pp. 363 – 64, no. 1458; Beltrami 1919a, pp. 33 – 34, no. 52).
6. Pedretti and Clark 1983, p. 39, fig. 25, p. 30; Eichholz 1998, p. 498; Marani 2001b, pp. 122 – 23, no. 26.

LEONARDO DA VINCI

67. *Allegory with Solar Mirror*

Pen and brown ink, framing lines in pen and brown ink, 104 × 124 mm (4⅛ × 4⅞ in.); traces of mounting outlines in pen and brown ink; paper yellowed, worn in spots, glued to secondary support
Inscribed in pen and brown ink, lower center: *Lionardo da Vinci*
Département des Arts Graphiques, Musée du Louvre, Paris 2247

PROVENANCE: Everard Jabach (inv. MS school of Florence, no. 12 [Leonardo davincij]); 1671, acquired for the Cabinet du Roi initials of J.-C. Garnier d'Isle (Lugt 2961); inv. MS Morel d'Arleux, vol. 1, no. 42 (Leonardo da Vinci).

LITERATURE: *Recueil Caylus*, fol. 58, no. 146; Mariette 1730, after p. 22; Louvre 1802, no. 166; Louvre 1811, no. 196; Louvre 1814, no. 155; Louvre 1817, no. 182; Louvre 1820, no. 208; Louvre 1838,

no. 361; Chennevières and Montaiglon 1851 – 60, vol. 3, p. 168 n. 1; Passavant 1864, p. 256 (with incorrect location); Galichon 1865, p. 547; Louvre 1879, no. 1640; Müller-Walde 1889, p. 61, fig. 23 (with incorrect location); Müntz 1899, pp. 476, 519, no. 18; Solmi 1900, p. 504 n. 1, no. 18 (with incorrect location); Berenson 1903, vol. 1, p. 164, pl. 120, vol. 2, no. 1064; Seidlitz 1909, p. 155, fig. p. 231 (with incorrect location); Solmi 1912, p. 504 n. 1; Kristeller 1913, pp. 21 – 22; Fumagalli 1915, pp. 360 – 61 (with incorrect location); Louvre 1919, no. 12; Poggi 1919, pl. 176b, p. lxxii; Demonts 1921, no. 9; Demonts 1922, no. 9; Commissione Vinciana 1928 – , vol. 6, p. 265; Popp 1928, no. 21, pl. 21; Suida 1929, p. 104, fig. 118; Bodmer 1931, p. 389, fig. 164; Angoulvent 1933, no. 193; Roux 1940, no. 459; Goldscheider 1945, no. 54; Popham 1945, p. 36, no. 110A; Hind 1948, vol. 5, p. 98, under no. 2; Popham and Pouncey 1950, under no. 116; Amboise 1952; Biblioteca Medicea Laurenziana 1952, no. 41; Florisoone and Bacou 1952, no. 41; Chastel 1959, 1982, p. 274; Clark and Pedretti 1968–69, under no. 12395; Levenson, Oberhuber, Sheehan 1973, under no. 159; Orangerie 1977–78, no. 6; Eisler 1979, p. 322, fig. 47; Béguin 1983, p. 84; Pedretti 1985–86, p. 70; Pedretti 1990a, p. 29, fig. 47; Lambert 1999, pp. 272–73, under no. 526.

We are indebted to Paul Müller-Walde for the initial attempt to describe this scene, whose meaning is still not completely understood. Müller-Walde's and most early-twentieth-century studies, except that by Bernard Berenson, perpetuate a confusion between the original drawing in the Louvre and the copy in the British Museum (I-33) either by misstating its location or by listing it as the copy. A. E. Popham, writing about the copies of Parmigianino's drawings that came to the British Museum in the bequest of Payne Knight, suggested that the author of those copies, Lucas Vorsterman, might also have drawn the version of the *Allegory* in the Louvre.[1]

In 1730 Pierre-Jean Mariette, who knew the drawing and the engraving of it by the count of Caylus, noted its hermetism and interpreted the scene as symbolic. An inked framing line confines the composition and gives it its compressed aspect. A seated man, his head turned in three-quarter profile, holds a convex mirror that is reflecting a blazing sun. With the mirror, the man directs the sun's rays toward animals fighting in front of him, as if to illuminate them or to keep them at a distance. Reflecting the brilliant, petrifying image of the sun (as if it were that of Medusa) on the clashing group, the fiery mirror becomes a sort of shield. The animals were first identified in 1915 by Giuseppina Fumagalli. A lion has fallen under the claws of a winged dragon, which is biting its ear, even as the dragon itself is being attacked in the neck by a wolf. On the left a unicorn seems ready to attack the lion; in the foreground, another lion, seen from the back, menaces the dragon. In the left background, a wild boar emerges from a rocky mountain pass.

Edmondo Solmi, whose hypotheses have been fiercely disputed, limited himself to the motif of the animal fight, arguing that we should recognize it as a specific allusion to contemporary events in the duchy of Milan. Solmi saw in the Louvre drawing a representation of Calumny in the form of a nocturnal procession of animals, led by a dragon personifying the house of Aragon, rulers of Naples, and a unicorn symbolizing the role of Gian Giacomo Trivulzio in antagonistic relation to Ludovico Sforza, duke of Milan. The procession goes up toward a narrow passage between rocky crags symbolizing Lombardy, but Truth, diffusing the sunlight, breaks up the struggle. The allusion here would be to the conflict between Ludovico and the house of Aragon.

Nevertheless, Solmi recognized that the true meaning of the battle between the lion and the dragon was still not apparent. Fumagalli, by contrast, refuting Solmi's political reading and interpretation of the drawing, understood it as a moral allegory closely linked to Leonardo's writings. In this context, she evoked the notations on the recto of a drawing at Windsor (RL 12700 recto; cat. no. 110). These inscriptions on the lower part of the sheet, *verità / il sole; bugia / maschera*,[2] link Truth to the sun and Falsehood to the mask, referring particularly to the mask melting under the sun's rays.

In the Louvre drawing, then, the sun would symbolize Truth and the figure with the mirror would be Virtue or Science; the rays of Truth illuminate the struggle between the victorious dragon and the defeated lion. Müller-Walde had already connected the latter motif to a drawing at the Uffizi, Florence (435 E), which Carlo Pedretti and Gigetta Dalli Regoli (1985) consider a copy from about 1550 of a lost original by Leonardo. And, as Solmi had established in 1915, both authors remind us of a passage in book 2, chapter 20, of Lomazzo's *Trattato dell'arte della pittura*.[3] Lomazzo mentions a Leonardo drawing he had owned depicting a dragon attacking a lion: "Come già fece Leonardo da Vinci, il quale dipinse un drago in zuffa con un leone con tanta arte, che mette in dubbio chiunque lo riguarda chi di loro debba restare vittorioso, tanto espresse egli in ciascuno i moti difensivi et offensivi; della qual pittura io ne ebbi già un disegno, che molto m'era caro." In book 6, chapter 20, of the *Trattato*, Lomazzo points out that, according to Francesco Melzi, Leonardo had painted a dragon doing battle with a lion, "cosa molto mirabile a vedere."[4] Finally, in the first quarter of the sixteenth century, two engravings diffused the theme of the battle between a lion and a dragon: Lucantonio degli Uberti's *Lion, Lioness, and Dragon Doing Battle*[5] and a plate attributed to Zoan Andrea.[6] The dragon motif is found again in several texts of Paris Ms. H, a collection of most of Leonardo's writings about fables, dated 1494, the same as that proposed by A. E. Popham for the *Allegory* in the Louvre. Jean Paul Richter indicated that among the sources of inspiration in Ms. H are the *Historia naturalis* of Pliny and the *Physiologus*.[7] That treatise is an encyclopedia from A.D. 140–200, which sets up a system of

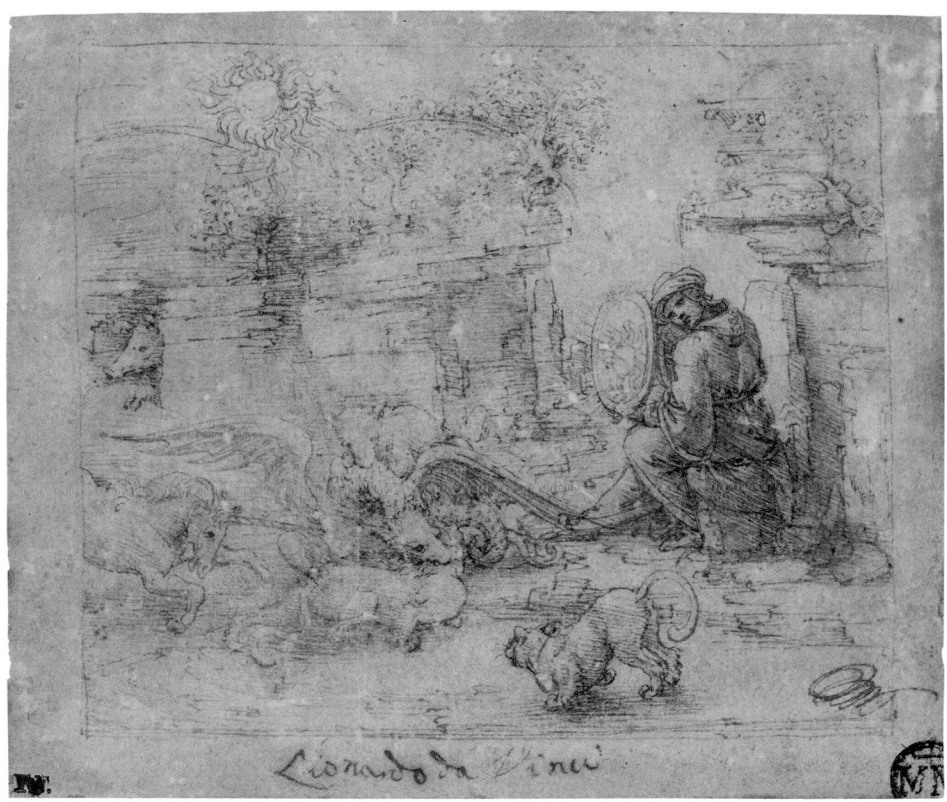

Cat. 67 *(actual size)*

analogies between animals and the vices. The bear is described as the symbol of Anger, for example, and the unicorn as that of Intemperance.[8] In addition, Leonardo took some of his Paris Ms. H texts from books that he listed on folio 210a of the Codex Atlanticus.[9] The motif of the fight between the lion and the dragon can be linked to Leonardo's description of the attack on an elephant by a dragon on folio 19r–20v of Ms. H, and which Fumagalli compares to the drawing described by Lomazzo: "Il drago se li gitta sotto il corpo, colla coda l'annoda le gambe e coll'ali e colle branche li cigne le coste e co' denti lo scanna."[10]

The Louvre *Allegory* can be interpreted simply as a moral allegory, perhaps referring to Ludovico Sforza, according to Anny E. Popp, through the motifs of the blazing sun, one of Ludovico's emblems, and the mulberry trees (*gelsomoro*) at the upper right, which allude to the name Ludovico "Il Moro." The animals might represent the passions, at war with one another, which the mirror, reflecting the purifying light of the sun, holds at bay; man is protected from evil by the shield-mirror. In a passage from Paris Ms. H on the tiger (fol. 23v),[11] Leonardo describes the capture of young cats by a hunter who, as a ruse, substitutes mirrors for them to fool the panther,

which believes it has found them when it sees its own image in the mirrors. Here again, the theme is artifice, falsehood, deceit, the two-faced image.

In 1959 André Chastel opened an entirely new interpretive perspective on the Louvre *Allegory*, proposing a link to the Platonic theme of Orpheus. In this view, the animal fight around the blazing mirror—which functions like a dazzling shield—would be a variation on the theme of Orpheus "pulled to the magic of light."

Finally, Pedretti (1990) established an interesting connection between the Louvre *Allegory* and the verso of a sheet in the Biblioteca Reale in Turin (15578), which shows a very rough sketch of a figure seated on swampy ground, leaning forward toward a fire, above which many moths are flying. According to Pedretti, that may have indicated a later development of the typology in the Louvre *Allegory*. Moreover, Pedretti remarked that the figure with sloped shoulders seen in profile in the Louvre *Allegory* is found again in the lower right corner of folio 43 of the Codex Atlanticus, where a man is observing an armillary sphere.[12]

Allegory with Solar Mirror can thus be understood as a struggle between the world of evil, of darkness, symbolized by the procession of animals fighting among themselves, and the world of Truth, symbolized by the blazing sun, whose rays are reflected on the shield-mirror.

Like Leonardo's other allegories,[13] the Louvre drawing is framed as if for a panel or a tondo, unlike the larger sheets belonging to the British Museum and to Christ Church, Oxford (cat. nos. 31, 54). The dimensions of these scenes located in well-defined spaces are similar for the sheets in the Louvre and in the museums in Bayonne and Hamburg. This suggests that they were cut and were originally as large as the *Allegory* in the Metropolitan Museum (cat. no. 68). The scene here displays in the treatment of the landscape a sharpness that evokes the precision of drawings from Leonardo's first Florentine period. The figure on the right, a *ritratto di spalla*, is also related to that time. Pedretti linked the rocks with sprouting roots to the landscape in the *Virgin of the Rocks,* even though the *Allegory* is generally dated about 1494. That is also the date advanced by Clark for a drawing at Windsor (RL 12395) depicting a rocky landscape and a riverbed, whose harsh, mineral appearance is comparable to that in the Louvre drawing. A passage in Leonardo's *Trattato della pittura* on vegetation and rocky passages in landscape settings could be describing the Louvre image, which depicts a savage natural environment that echoes the battle in the foreground, "et le minute piante, stentate et invecchiate in minima grandezza, con corte e spesse ramificattioni e con poche foglie, scoprendo in gran' parte le rugin ti et aride radici tessute co' le falde e rotture delli ruginosi scogli, nate dalli storpiati cieppi dalli huomini e da venti."[14] About four years later, in decorating the Sala delle Asse in the Castello Sforzesco, Milan, Leonardo would choose similar motifs of rocky strata entangled with roots. That commission was not completed, and in the upper part of the northeast wall we can see in the monochromatic state of the work this beautiful naturalistic motif integrated into a design based on curves and interlacings.[15]

During the nineteenth century, the Louvre drawing was exhibited regularly, mounted with a copy (2516) after Leonardo's *Grotesque Heads* now at Windsor (RL 12495). In 1879 the Louvre sheet was recognized to be a copy and the *Allegory* was exhibited separately. Its fame can probably be attributed to Mariette's commentary of 1730 on the Caylus engravings.

In an engraving—anonymous, but long attributed to Jean Duvet—the composition was enlarged, reversed, and modified. The group of animals fighting underwent few changes except for the body of the dragon, which was given a human male torso, and the background landscape, where a city was inserted. In addition, the blazing mirror is depicted in the engraving as a shield. Passavant, recognizing that the source of the print was the Louvre drawing, suggested it was done by an Italian follower of Leonardo in Gaillon, perhaps Andrea Solario.[16] Mariette called the printmaker anonymous and argued that the work "retained so little of da Vinci's manner" that no one would recognize him as its author if it were not for the drawing in the royal collection. Émile Galichon,[17] followed by Paul Oskar Kristeller,[18] listed the print, which they titled *Poison and Counterpoison,* as a work of the Master of the Beheading of Saint John the Baptist,[19] an engraver of four plates active in the first quarter of the sixteenth century, probably in Milan. That is the hypothesis most frequently accepted today.[20] Popham suggested that the engraving may derive from another, more finished—but now lost—drawing by Leonardo on the same subject.

FV

1. Popham 1971, vol. 1, p. 234.
2. Pedretti 1977, no. 684.
3. Lomazzo 1973–74, p. 156 and n. 2.
4. Lomazzo 1973–74, p. 291 and n. 2.
5. Hind 1948, vol. 1, D.3.4, vol. 3, pl. 309.
6. Hind 1948, vol. 5, p. 65, no. 7, vol. 6, pl. 579.
7. Richter 1970, nos. 1220–63.
8. Paris Ms. H, fols. 6r and 11r, respectively; Richter 1970, nos. 1222, 1232.
9. Richter 1970, no. 1469.
10. Fumagalli 1970, p. 255, n. 6.
11. Richter 1970, no. 1254.
12. C.A., fol. 54; Pedretti 1990, fig. 48.
13. Popham 1945, nos. 109A–111.
14. Fumagalli 1970, pp. 152–53 and pl. 10; Urb. 72.
15. Kemp 1981, p. 182, pl. 51; Marani 1999b, pp. 248–49.
16. Passavant 1864, p. 255.
17. Galichon 1856, p. 552.
18. Kristeller 1913, pp. 21–22.
19. Hind 1948, no. E.3.18.
20. Lambert 1999, pp. 272–73, under no. 526.

LEONARDO DA VINCI

68. *Allegory on the Fidelity of the Lizard* (recto)
Design for a Stage Setting (verso)

Pen and brown ink (recto and verso), 202 × 133 mm (7¹⁵⁄₁₆ × 5¼ in.)
Inscribed in pen and medium brown ink, in right-to-left script, on
recto toward center of upper border: *ilramarro . fedele allomo
vede[n]do quello adorme[n] / tato . co[n] batte . cholla bisscia esse
vede no[n]lla potere / vincere core sopra ilvolto dello mo . ello dessta
accioche / essa . bisscia nonoffenda loadorme[n]tato . homo
[paraph]*; on verso in pen and medium brown ink, in right-to-left
script, but with numbered fractions reading conventionally left to
right, on upper left quadrant: *6 3/4 _____ . 2 . 4 3/4 acrissio
gia[n]cristofano / 13 1/4 _____ acriso _____ 1 . 1 1/4 . 3 . 2 . 3/4*
[reworked and fraction separated with a long line from numbers
below] *. 1 . 2 siro tacho[n] / 15 _____ 2 1/3 . 1 . 8 . 3 1/4 danae
franc° romano / 14 _____ 1 . 1 . 4 . 3 . 2 . 1 . 2 merchurio . gian-
batista da osimo [or, daossmo] / 8 _____ 2 . 1 . 2 . 2 giove
gia[n]franc° tantio / 1/3 servo* [canceled: *piac*] *. / anu[n]tiatore
[annuntiatore] dellafesta / +* [or possibly, a faded 4] *i quali si mia-
ravigliano / della nova stella essinginochiano / e quella adorano
essingino / chiano e co[n] musicha finisscha / no la fessta _____ /
annv[tia]tore*
The Metropolitan Museum of Art, New York; Rogers Fund,
1917 17.142.2

PROVENANCE: Jacques-Guillaume Legrand, Paris (1743–1807);
Legrand gave it in 1801 to Joseph Allen Smith, London and
Charleston, South Carolina (according to an inscription on the old
mount that reads: "Souvenir d'amitie a J. allen Smith par J.G.
Legrand en floréal an 9"); possibly Thomas Sully (1783–1872); possibly Sully passed it on to his grandson Francis T. S. Darley; Darley
bequeathed it to Thomas Nash, New York; purchased in New York
by The Metropolitan Museum of Art in 1917.

LITERATURE: Burroughs 1918; Lieb 1919, pp. 259–62; Herzfeld 1922,
p. 226; Commissione Vinciana 1928– , vol. 3, p. 24, pl. 106, 1939, vol. 5,
p. 21, pl. 183; Popp 1928, pp. 12, 39, no. 27; Bodmer 1931, pp. 233,
399–400; Berenson 1938, vol. 2, p. 116, no. 1049B; Richter 1939, vol. 1,
p. 45, no. 705A, vol. 2, no. 1264A; Metropolitan Museum of Art 1942,
no. 9; Goldscheider 1943, fig. 33, pl. 53; Mayor in Jebb 1946, p. 100;
Heydenreich 1954, vol. 1, p. 60, vol. 2, p. 64, pl. 81; Goldscheider 1959,
p. 187; Berenson 1961, vol. 2, p. 204, no. 1049B; Bean 1964, no. 5;
Steinitz 1964, pp. 35–40, pl. 1, fig. 1; Bean and Stampfle 1965, p. 27,
no. 17; Bacall 1968, no. 6; Clark and Pedretti 1968–69, vol. 1, p. 58,
no. 12395; Richter 1970, pp. 392–93, no. 705, vol. 2, pp. 276, 418,
no. 1264A; Steinitz 1970, pp. 257–61; Pedretti 1973b, p. 16 n. 4;
Fitzwilliam Museum 1976–77, p. 15, no. 21; Pedretti 1977, vol. 1, p. 402,
vol. 2, p. 265; Angiolillo 1979, pp. 57–58, 77–79, fig. 37; Gentile
1980, p. 169; Pedretti 1980b, p. 238; Visconti 1980, p. 114; Bean 1982,
pp. 117–18, no. 108; Pedretti 1982a, p. 117; Winternitz 1982, pp. 77–
78, fig. 6.1; Mazzocchi Doglio 1983, pp. 49–55, fig. 41; Mazzocchi
Doglio and Tintori 1983, pp. 58–62; Carpiceci 1984, nos. 3, 4, fig. 216;
Pedretti 1987b, p. 116, fig. 135; Clark 1988, pp. 118–20, fig. 46; Kemp
1989c, p. 247; Maria Teresa Fiorio 1991, pp. 95–99, fig. 14; Parronchi
1992, p. 35 n. 11, fig. 12; Pedretti and Trutty-Coohill 1993, pp. 42–44,
no. 9; Popham 1994, no. 111 (recto); Venturelli 1994, p. 117, fig. 2;
Arasse 1998, pp. 236–37, fig. 167; Vecce 1998a, pp. 159–61; Carmen
C. Bambach and Lance Humphries in Gibbes Museum of Art 1999,
pp. 183–87, under nos. 48–49; Villata 1999, pp. 92–93, no. 107.

The small circular sketch on the recto was possibly
intended for a medal and is rendered with the quick, reinforced outlines, full of movement, and the delicate horizontal
parallel hatching that are typical of Leonardo's drawings from
the first half of the 1490s. As he noted in his inscription, the
sketch portrays a man sleeping by a tree while, to his right, a
green lizard (*ramarro*) loyally attempts to overcome a grass
snake (*biscia*) that threatens him: "The lizard faithful to man,
seeing him asleep, fights with the snake, and as he [the lizard]
sees that [he] cannot conquer her [the snake], he [the lizard]
runs over the face of the man to wake him so that the snake
may not harm the sleeping man." This fable of the lizard and
the sleeping man may be interpreted as an allegory on the
virtues of fidelity, alertness, and protectiveness. It derives from
the tradition of medieval bestiaries and Leonardo's close reading of Pliny the Elder's *Historia naturalis* (first century A.D.).

On the verso Leonardo produced sketches and notes to
stage a musical comedy in rhyme, *La Danae*, on January 31,
1496. As related in Ovid's *Metamorphoses* (4:611), Danae, the
daughter of Acrisius, king of Argos, was seduced by the god
Jupiter in the form of a shower of gold. The comedy in five
acts was written by Baldassare Taccone, who was the chancellor to Ludovico Sforza "Il Moro," duke of Milan, and was performed in Milan at the house of Gian Francesco Sanseverino,
count of Carazzo, who was captain of the Sforza army.
Taccone's dated text helps establish the date for Leonardo's
drawings on the sheet.

The meaning of Leonardo's numbers and fractions remains
unclear, but the list of names on the upper left quadrant of the

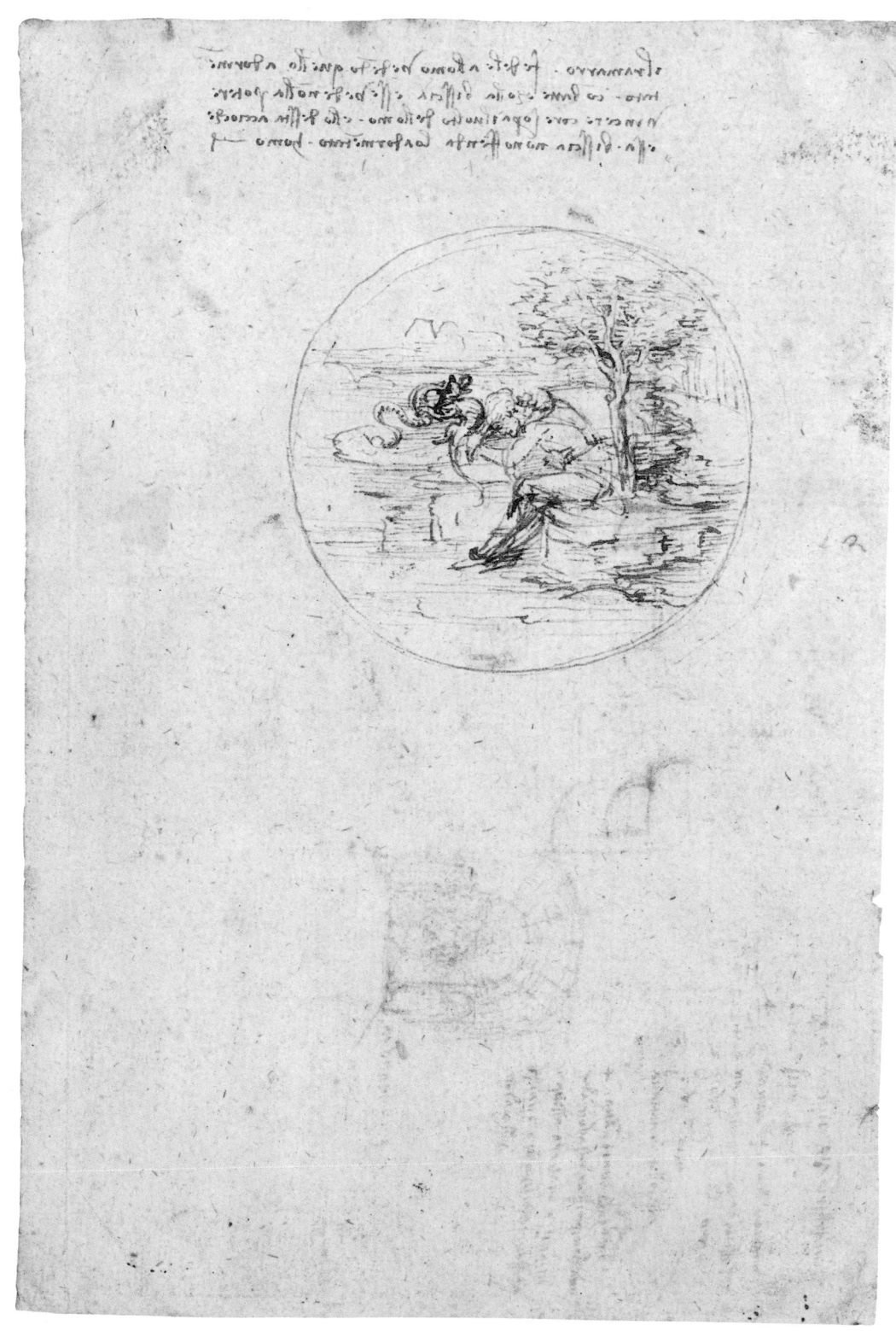

Cat. 68R *(actual size)*

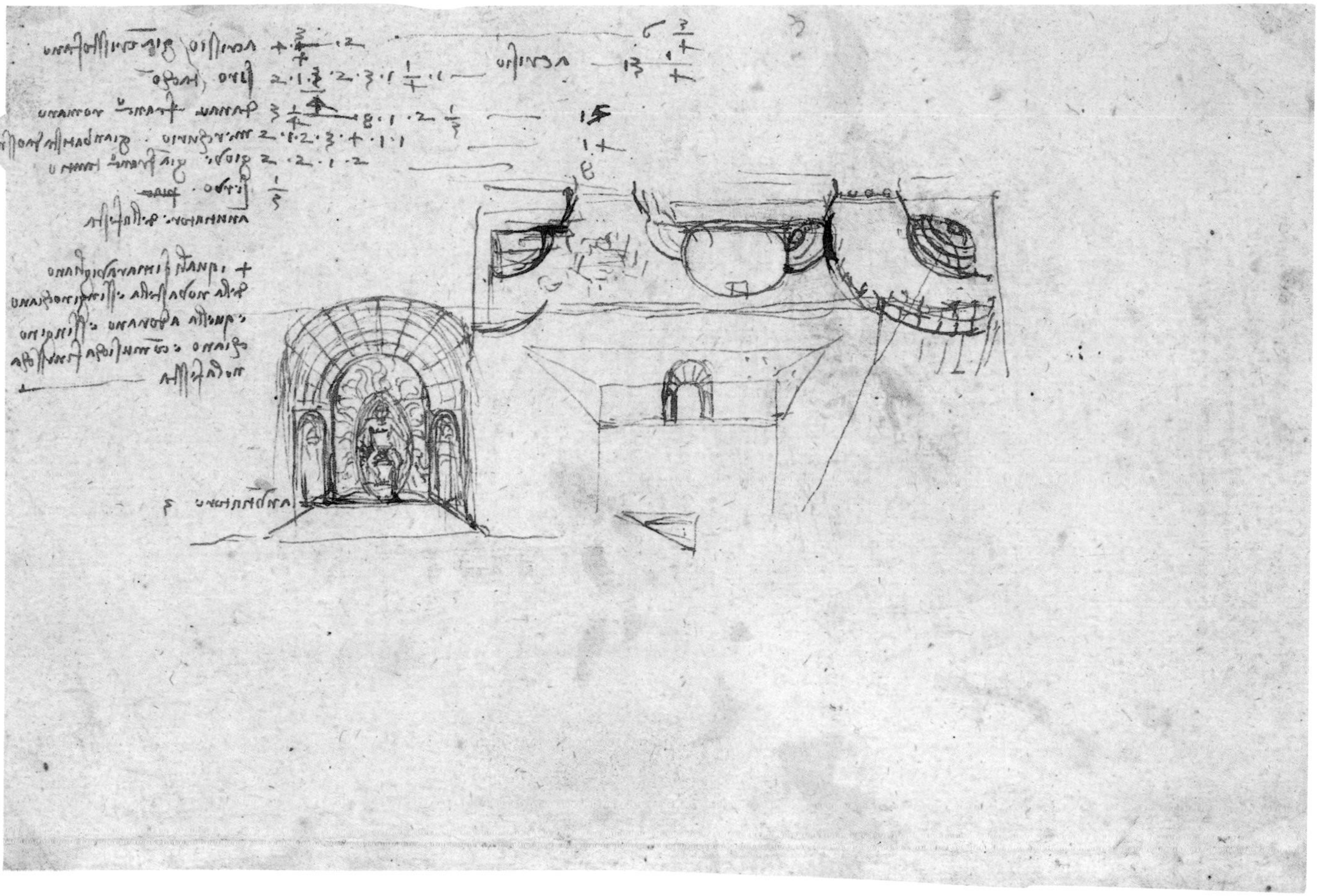

Cat. 68v

sheet identifies the actors for the roles in the performance, in columns right to left. Acrisius, king of Argos and the father of Danae, was to be played by Gian Cristofano (presumably the sculptor Gian Cristoforo Romano), the gardener Sirus by Taccone (the playwright), while Danae, the headstrong princess and main character, was to be acted by a man (not unusual for the time), a certain Francesco Romano. The god Mercury, who was to descend from Olympus hoisted from a rope and pulley, was to be played by Gian Battista da Osimo. The lecherous god Jupiter, who transformed himself into a rain of gold to impregnate Danae, was to be portrayed by Gian Francesco Tanzio, a well-known literary figure and the editor of Bernardo Bellincioni's *Rime*, published in 1493. The piece also included roles for a servant and for at least one "heavenly messenger" (*annunziatore*). Leonardo produced a floor plan of the stage setting with two perspectival elevation sketches (at center). In the sketch on the left, the figure seated on a throne

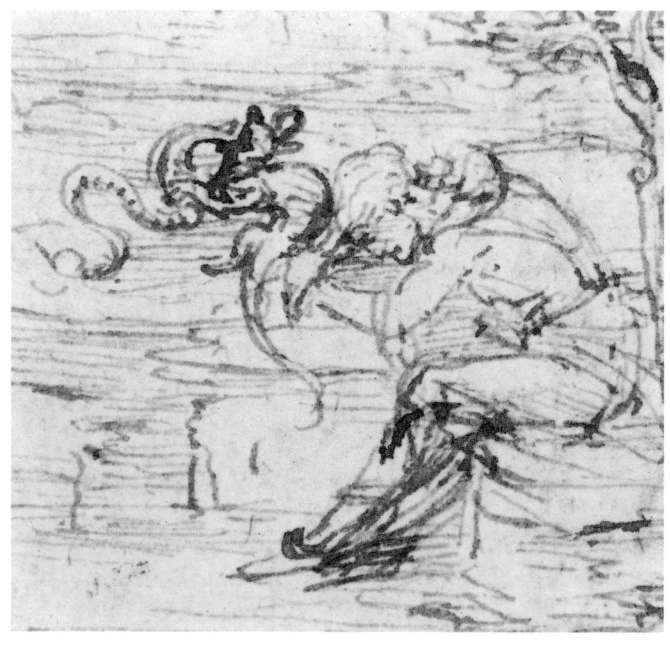

Cat. 68R *(detail)*

449

surrounded by an aureole of flames can be identified as Jupiter; the flanking figures represent other gods, for according to the play, "beautiful sky became visible, with Jupiter and the other gods, lit by an infinite number of lamps like stars." The barrel vault of the theatrical space was transformed to accommodate lighting machinery. Other drawings may be connected to the staging of the *Danae* (Ar., fol. 250r; Windsor, RL 12582, 12461, 12720).

Like catalogue number 45, this drawing was presented as a gift by Jacques-Guillaume Legrand to Joseph Allen Smith before he resettled in Charleston, South Carolina, and is also among the earliest works by Leonardo to have entered a collection in the United States. For Legrand, the small sketch and fable on the recto may have had personal meaning, summing up the spirit of a great friendship. The present double-sided sheet was originally glued on a thin blue paper mount that was a page from a now dispersed *album amicorum*. As stated in a letter by Bryson Burroughs to Thomas Nash, Esquire (a later owner), on October 19, 1917, just four days after the acquisition of catalogue numbers 45 and 68 (Archive of The Metropolitan Museum of Art), another sketch, a grotesque head of a man in profile, was discovered glued underneath (fig. 34).[1] This is the drawing referred to in Jacques-Guillaume Legrand's inscription on the verso of the mount, at the bottom center, as being by Francesco Parmigianino (Italian, 1503–1540); the drawing was still thought to be by Parmigianino when Burroughs wrote of it in his letter to Nash, cited above. It is now rightly considered to be a copy after Leonardo.

Archival photographs taken before the removal of both sheets of drawings from the blue paper mount document that Legrand had attached Leonardo's large double-sided sheet in vertical orientation, showing the recto, that is, the side that portrays the circular allegorical scene; the small sketch of the grotesque man was centered in the upper half of the mount (see Metropolitan Museum of Art, Department of Drawings and Prints, negative nos. 37135, 37139). Some of this evidence is still clear today from the glue residue and the disposition of Legrand's inscriptions on the blue paper mount's verso. On the upper left, Legrand's explanation of Leonardo's mirror handwriting (which we now know to have been an adaptation to his left-handedness) would have been exactly aligned with the artist's own lines of text above the circular allegorical design. The verso of Leonardo's sheet, containing his notations and sketches for staging elements of the *Danae*, may or may not have been glued down along all four borders. It is therefore possible that it was not always viewable.   CCB

1. Bean 1982, pp. 120–21, no. 111.

LEONARDO DA VINCI

69. *Laughing Man with Bushy Hair in Bust-Length Profile*

Pen and medium brown ink; glued onto secondary paper support,
66 × 55 mm (2⅝ × 2⅛ in.)
The J. Paul Getty Museum, Los Angeles 84.GA.647

PROVENANCE: Thomas Howard, second earl of Arundel (1586–1646);
presumably Nicholaes Anthoni Flinck, Rotterdam (1646–1723;
cropped stamp Lugt 959 at lower left, which also appears whole on
Chatsworth 824B, hence most of the small "caricatures" with a
Chatsworth provenance are from this same collection); possibly
from Flinck sale in 1723, William Cavendish, second duke of
Devonshire, Chatsworth (1672–1739; Lugt 718, 719, Suppl. 719; his
mount; Chatsworth 820C; by descent to the eleventh duke; sale,
Christie's, London, July 3, 1984, lot 24; Ars Libri, Boston.

LITERATURE: Habich 1892, p. 544; Strong 1905, p. 114; Commissione
Vinciana 1928– , vol. 5, p. 24, pl. 212.6; Scott-Elliot 1958, pp. 282,
294, no. 31; Clark and Pedretti 1968–69, vol. 1, p. xliv; Pedretti
1973b, p. 40, under no. 12; Cogliati Arano 1981, p. 16, under no. 29i;
Marinoni and Cogliati Arano 1982, p. 120, under no. 29i; Goldner
1985, p. 191, no. 96; Stock 1985, p. 119; Goldner 1988, pp. 58–59,
under no. 19; Caroli 1991, pp. 154, 159, no. 15; Pedretti and Trutty-
Coohill 1993, pp. 46–47, no. 12; Jaffé 1994, p. 169, no. 883, 820C;
Kwakkelstein 1994, pp. 107–9, pl. 49i; Letze and Buchsteiner 1997,
p. 78; Trutty-Coohill 1998b, p. 193.

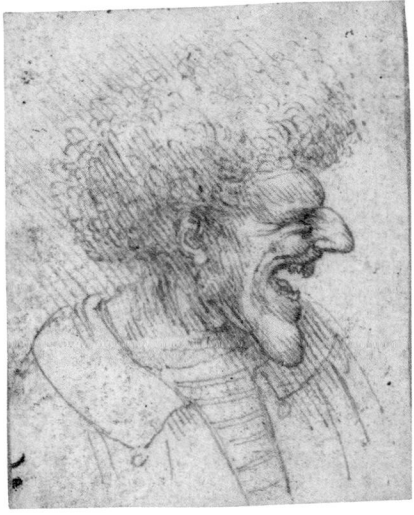

Cat. 69 *(actual size)*

The following four drawings (cat. nos. 69–72) formed part
of a fascinating group of small sheets portraying the
grotesque heads of men and women (the so-called caricatures)
that had been together in the collection of the dukes of
Devonshire at Chatsworth, probably since 1723, until their
sale at auction in 1984 (cat. no. 73). Now dispersed in United
States collections, the four sheets are reunited here with some
of their companions still at Chatsworth (cat. no. 73). The
Getty laughing man and the two related drawings in a private
collection (cat. nos. 70, 71) are exhibited here apparently for the
first time since their sale. Leonardo scholars have not always
been complimentary about the small Chatsworth "caricature"
drawings. It bears emphasizing, however, that the small sheets
from the Chatsworth group were all glued onto mounts by
early collectors. This has tended to flatten the pen-and-ink
drawing, which also affects the original tonal calibration of
the outlines and shadows. Approximately twenty-five of the
Chatsworth sheets have a reasonable probability of being
originals by Leonardo (although the question continues to be

much discussed), and many of the drawings seem to have provided models for scores of later copies (cat. nos. 121, 136–38).
The problems raised by the originals and the copies have been
attentively studied by Aydua H. Scott-Elliot, Ernst Gombrich,
Kenneth Clark, Michael Kwakkelstein, Domenico Laurenza,
and in the present volume, by Varena Forcione.

Leonardo's term for these types of grotesquely deformed
faces was *visi mostruosi* (the relatively modern term "caricature" is therefore not entirely apt). There is enough extant
evidence to suggest that he conceived of the small Chatsworth
drawings as didactic exercises in the portrayal of physiognomy (cat. nos. 69–73) and, to judge from some of the extant
copies (cat. no. 121), that the figures were arranged originally
as facing couples or groups of three. A long passage in the
manuscript of his projected painting treatise, the *libro di pittura* (Codex Urbinas Latinus, 1270) that was posthumously
compiled by Francesco Melzi after Leonardo's notes, helps
clarify the intended effect of the small drawings:

> It is true that the signs of faces display in part the nature of
> men, their vices and temperaments. If in the face the signs
> which separate the cheeks from the lips of the mouth and the
> nostrils of the nose and sockets of the eyes are pronounced,
> the men are cheerful and often laughing, and those with slight
> signs are men who engage in thought. And those who have
> facial features of great relief and depth are bestial and wrathful

men of little reason, and those who have strongly pronounced lines between their eyebrows are evidently wrathful, and those who have strongly delineated lines crossing the forehead are men who are full of hidden or overt regrets. And it is possible to discuss many features in this way.[1]

Here, the great master was attempting to read human temperament according to a classification of facial features. In his vita of Leonardo, Giorgio Vasari, who seems to have collected many of Leonardo's pen-and-ink drawings of freakish heads of men and women for his celebrated *libro de' disegni* (album of drawings), pointed out that the artist "was so delighted when he saw certain bizarre heads [*teste bizzarre*] of men, with the beard or hair growing wildly, that he would follow one that pleased him a whole day, and he memorized it to such an extent [*e se lo metteva talmente nella idea*], that afterward, on arriving home, he drew him as if he had had him in his presence."[2] In fact, a number of Leonardo's notes allude to memorable faces: "Cristofano da Castiglione, who lives at the Pietà, has a fine face."[3] Another such aide-mémoire by Leonardo states: "Giovannina has a fantastic face; she is at Santa Caterina, at the hospital."[4] These tantalizing tidbits give us glimpses of just how much evidence about Leonardo's working process has been forever lost to us, and especially about the various types of drawings that he must have prepared. For example, it is no longer possible to reconstruct any of the small drawing books (*piccoli libretti*) that he thought indispensable for his note-taking in the study of bodily and facial gesture.[5] In this regard, Leonardo's description of types of facial features in a passage that probably dates about 1508–10 (and which was transcribed into the *Libro di pittura*) is worth quoting in full, to convey the rigorous process that he advocated in attempting to memorize a human face:

If you want to acquire facility for bearing in mind the expression of a face, first make yourself familiar with a variety of [forms of] several heads, eyes, noses, mouths, chins, and throats, and necks and shoulders. And to give an example, noses are of ten types: straight, bulbous, concave, prominent above or below the center [of the length], aquiline, regular, flat, round, or pointed. These hold good as to profile. In full face they are of eleven types; these are equal, thick in the middle, thin in the middle, with the tip thick and the root narrow, or narrow at the tip and wide at the root; with the nostrils wide or narrow, high or low, and the openings wide or hidden by the point; and you will find an equal variety in the other details; which things you must draw from nature and fix them

in your mind. Or else, when you have to draw a face by heart, carry with you a little book in which you have noted such features; and when you have cast a glance at the face of the person you wish to draw, you can observe in private, which nose or mouth is most like, and there make a little mark to recognize it at home. Of grotesque faces [*visi mostruosi*] I need say nothing, because they are kept in mind without difficulty.[6]

As this passage makes clear, Leonardo thought one could enhance one's visual memory by classifying the facial features by type, and by consulting the models of faces that were recorded in a *piccolo libretto*. This is the voice of Leonardo the teacher. The dryly pedagogic *Libro di pittura*, which somewhat crudely explains Leonardo's exercises in physiognomic drawing, illustrates on folio 108, verso, a telling classification of nose types as a guide in sketching profiles. Leonardo's original drawing of this does not survive.

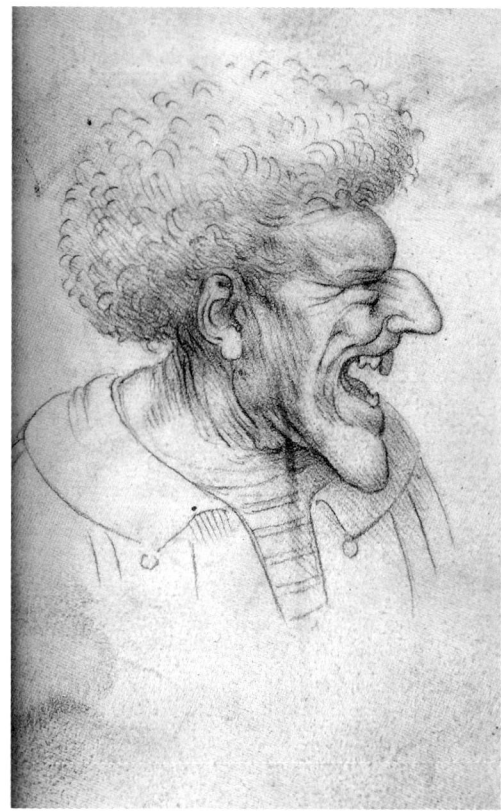

Fig. 170. Late sixteenth-century Lombard artist after Leonardo da Vinci, *Head of Grotesque Man* (from François Rabelais, *Les oeuvres de M. François Rabelais*, Rouen [?] 1659, 1669 [?]). Black chalk, 142 × 85 mm. The New York Public Library, Astor, Lenox and Tilden Foundations, New York; Spencer Collection. Spencer Grotesques, vol. 1, no. 31

It can be tentatively suggested (too much evidence is lost for definitive conclusions) that Leonardo's small grotesque heads, or *visi mostruosi*, were so frequently copied by his pupils precisely because they served his didactic purposes. The scholars who have accepted the small Chatsworth grotesques have usually dated them in the late 1480s or early 1490s, though tentatively so, and have tended to group them en masse with Leonardo's other, much larger studies of grotesque physiognomy (cat. nos. 59, 60). It is a truism, however, that in his later years Leonardo frequently revisited favorite early themes and figural types. He repeatedly returned to the study of grotesque physiognomy (cat. nos. 74–76, 91, 92) and the exaggerated movements of the human face when expressing strong emotions. The studies for the screaming soldiers in the unfinished *Battle of Anghiari* (cat. no. 91), dating about 1503–6, are a case in point. In the present author's opinion, many of the small-scale Chatsworth *visi mostruosi* (cat. nos. 69–73) exhibit the type of parallel hatching with short strokes that seems much more atmospheric and tonal in effect than in Leonardo's drawings of the 1490s, suggesting a later date. Even a date as late as 1506–8, close to the time that such designs were being copied in the frescoes of the oratory in Santa Maria di Rivolta d'Adda (near Milan), is not implausible. An extraordinary atmospheric treatment of form is evident in the short, curving strokes articulating the bushy hair of the Getty laughing man. Here, the sfumato effect of the drawn curls of hair is striking; in some respects, the meticulous drawing technique is not unlike that of the small illustrations of water and silt in the Codex Leicester (cat. no. 114), which can be dated in 1508–10 on the basis of their contents. The diverse Codex Leicester illustrations also demonstrate that at this much later date Leonardo still sometimes employed parallel hatching with fine, short strokes (in addition to curving strokes of greater freedom) and that his pen-and-ink technique had a considerable range of graphic mark, at times achieving highly tonal and atmospheric effects. For the sake of caution, however, one may wish to retain a broad range of dates, between 1495 and 1506–8, for the small Chatsworth "caricatures."

The first and most dedicated copyist of Leonardo's original models was his pupil and artistic heir, Francesco Melzi (cat. no. 121), who arrived in the master's household about 1508 and who even imitated, as best as he could, Leonardo's left-handed style of parallel hatching. The close connections of design between Leonardo's small original drawings and the copies produced by Melzi, and his role as the compiler of Leonardo's notes (including those on physiognomy), might offer yet another basis for a later dating of the Chatsworth "caricatures." A finely drawn copy of the Getty laughing man, convincingly attributed to Melzi by Carlo Pedretti in 1973 (and endorsed by Patricia Trutty-Coohill and Michael Kwakkelstein), is now at the Elmer Belt Library of Vinciana (University of California at Los Angeles).[7] Melzi's sketch formed part of the so-called Pembroke Grotesques, a series of twelve precisely drawn sheets copying Chatsworth "caricatures" that were mounted together on a page when they were in the collection of the earls of Pembroke at Wilton House (see cat. no. 121). The Pembroke Grotesques were sold at auction in 1917, were acquired by Edward J. Fowles, and then became dispersed in various collections. Like Melzi, many of the later right-handed artists who imitated Leonardo's female and male "caricature" types in copy after copy also attempted to imitate the master's left-handed style of parallel hatching. The effect of these copies, though neat, seems always dry and forced, and the lines in the hatching often appear fine and scratchy.

In two anonymous sixteenth-century copies in pen and ink, the Getty laughing man with bushy hair appears paired with the same grotesque man, who wears academic headdress of the fourteenth or early fifteenth centuries and who exhibits a long nose and receding chin, along with a rather dour expression (see fig. 113).[8] The Getty laughing man type also turns up in the ambitious Spencer Grotesques volumes carefully drawn in left-handed imitation in soft leadpoint, possibly by a Lombard artist of about 1590–1600; the watermarks on the paper of the Spencer drawings point to late-sixteenth-century northern Italy (fig. 170).[9] Like many of the Chatsworth group of "caricatures," the Getty figural type was also etched by Wenceslaus Hollar (1607–1677), the great artist from Prague who settled in England; the etching appears to be the same size as the original but in a reversed design, and it is signed and dated 1645.[10] When Hollar made his etching, the Getty head was paired with that of an old woman with a hooked nose and swollen lips, wearing a close-fitting cap and a transparent veil. Yet another version of the Getty laughing-man type appears engraved in Carlo Giuseppe Gerli's anthology of Leonardo's drawings of 1784, but this image is most likely based on the Ambrosiana or Venice copies.[11] The Getty figural type was not included, however, among the copy drawings in the album of the great French collector Pierre-Jean Mariette,

453

and it therefore does not appear in the book of etchings by the count of Caylus, *Recueil de testes de caractère & de charges dessinées par Leonardo da Vinci* (Paris, 1730; see cat. nos. 137, 138). According to the evidence of such copies, the Chatsworth small "caricatures" seem to have been by far the most copied type of drawing that Leonardo ever produced.   CCB

1. Translation quoted from Kemp 1989a, p. 147. See C. Urb., fol. 109v: "li segni de uolti mostrano in parte la natura degli huomini di lor uitij e' complessioni, ma nel uolto li segni che separano le guancie da labri della bocca elle' nari del naso e' casce d'e gli occhi sono euidenti sono huomini allegri e'spesso ridenti, e' quelli chi poco li segnano sono huomini, operatori della cogitatione, et quelli ch'anno le parti del uiso di gran rilievo e' profondita sono huomini bestiali et iracondi con pocha raggione et quelli ch'anno le linee interposte infra le ciglia forteeuidenti sono iracondi e'quelli che hanno le linee trauersali dela fronte forte lineate sono huomini copiosi di lamentationi occulte o palesi."

2. Vasari–Milanesi 1906, vol. 4, p. 26: "Piacevagli tanto quando egli vedeva certe teste bizzarre, o con barbe o con capegli degli uomini naturali, che arebbe seguitato uno che gli fussi piaciuto, un giorno intero; e se lo metteva talmente nella idea, che poi arrivato a casa lo disegnava come se l'avesse avuto presente."

3. Codex Forster[III], fol. 1v; Richter 1970, vol. 2, p. 351, no. 1387: "Cristofano da Castiglione sta alla Pietà, a bona testa."

4. Codex Forster[II], fol. 1.3r; Richter 1970, vol. 2, p. 352, no. 1404: "Giovannina, viso fantastico, sta a Sta Caterina, all'ospedale."

5. Two such references to *piccoli libretti* for drawing in Leonardo's notes are transcribed in Richter 1970, vol. 1, pp. 338–39, nos. 571, 572.

6. C. Urb., fols. 108v–109r. See also Paris Ms. A, fol. 106v (B.N. 2038, fol. 26v); Richter 1970, vol. 1, pp. 338–39, no. 572: "*Del modo del tenere in me[n]te la forma d' u[n] volto.* Se uolli avere facilità in tenere a me[n]te una . aria d'uno volto . i[m]para a me[n]te una . aria d'uno volto . , i(m)para . prima a me[n]te di molte teste, occhi, nasi, boche, me[n]ti . e gole . . e colli e spalle: e poniamo caso: j[n] nasi sono di 10 ragioni . , dritto . , gobbo, cavo, col rilievo più sù o piv che 'l mezzo , aquilino, pari . , simo . e to[n]do e acuto; questi sono boni in qua[n]to al proffilo; In faccia i nasi sono di 11 ragioni: equale, grosso in mezzo, sottil' in mezzo, la pv[n]ta grossa e sottile nell'appicatura . , sottile nella . pu[n]ta e grosso nell' appicatura ., di larghe narici . , di strette, d'alte e basse, di busi scoperti e di busi occupati dalla pu[n]ta, e così troverai diversità nelle altre particole, delle quali . cose tu de' ritrare di naturale e metterle a me[n]te, overo qua[n]do ài a fare uno volto a me[n]te . porta con teco uno piccolo libretto, doue sieno notate simili fationi . , e qua[n]do ài dato una ochiata al uolto della persona che uoi ritrare, guarderai poi i[n] parte quale naso o bocca se le somiglia e fa ui uno piccolo segnio, per riconoscerle poi a casa. De' visi mostruosi no[n] parlo perchè sa[n]za fatica si te[n]gono a me[n]te."

7. Pedretti 1973, p. 40.

8. Biblioteca Ambrosiana, Milan, Cod. F. 274 inf. 54; Gallerie dell'Accademia, Venice, 229.

9. Illustrated and discussed in Pedretti and Trutty-Coohill 1993, p. 94, no. 55 (I.31).

10. Pennington 1982, no. 1591, p. 275.

11. Gerli 1784, pl. 24 (inscribed 39), on the extreme right of the second row from the top.

LEONARDO DA VINCI

70. *Old Woman with Beetling Brow, Wearing a Tall Pointy Hat, in Bust-Length Profile*

Pen and brown ink; glued onto secondary paper support, 69 × 56 mm (2¾ × 2¼ in.)
Private collection, New York

PROVENANCE: Thomas Howard, second earl of Arundel (1586–1646); presumably Nicholaes Anthoni Flinck, Rotterdam (1646–1723; Lugt 959 stamp appears whole on Chatsworth 824B, hence most of the small "caricatures" with a Chatsworth provenance are from this same collection); possibly from Flinck sale in 1723, William Cavendish, second duke of Devonshire, Chatsworth (1672–1739; Lugt 718, 719, Suppl. 719; his mount?); Chatsworth 820D; by descent to the eleventh duke; sale, Christie's, London, July 3, 1984, lot 25.

LITERATURE: Strong 1905, p. 114; Commissione Vinciana 1928–, vol. 5, p. 24, pl. 212.5; Scott-Elliot 1958, p. 282; Stock 1985, p. 119; Caroli 1991, pp. 154, 159, no, 14; Jaffé 1994, p. 169, no. 883, 820D; Kwakkelstein 1994, pp. 107–9, pl. 49e.

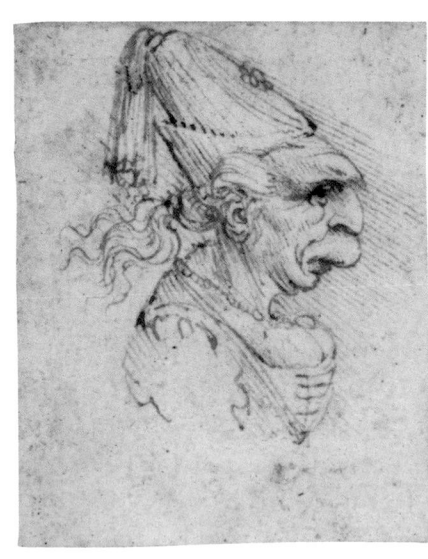

Cat. 70 *(actual size)*

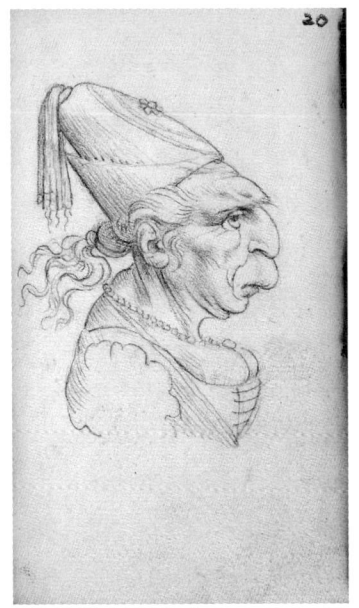

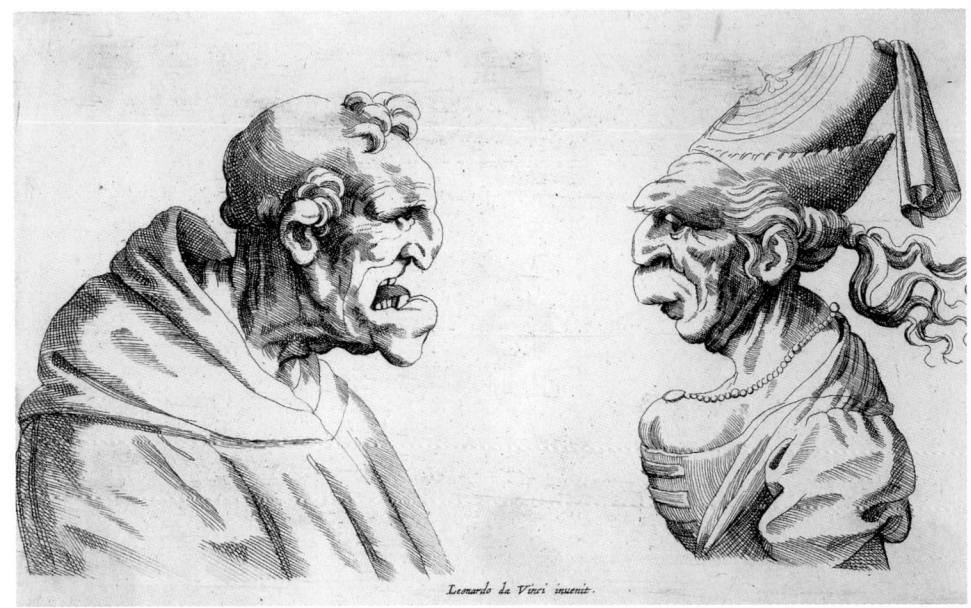

Fig. 171. Late-sixteenth-century Lombard artist after Leonardo da Vinci, *Head of Grotesque Man* (from François Rabelais, *Les oeuvres de M. François Rabelais*, Rouen [?] 1659, 1669 [?]). Black chalk, 142 × 85 mm. The New York Public Library, Astor, Lenox and Tilden Foundations, New York; Spencer Collection. Spencer Grotesques, vol. 1, no. 20

Fig. 172. Wenceslaus Hollar (after Leonardo da Vinci), *Grotesque Couple*. Etching, 106 × 167 mm. The Metropolitan Museum of Art, New York; Purchase, Joseph Pulitzer Bequest, 1917 17.50.18-164

Like catalogue number 69, the present drawing may be dated broadly between 1495 and 1506–8. The woman with beetling brow, wearing a string of beads, seems noteworthy for her tall, medieval-style hat with veil. She and two greatly deformed old men are the subject of a sixteenth-century copy, carefully drawn with "left-handed" parallel hatching in pen and ink, that seems related in style to the so-called Pembroke Grotesques attributed to Francesco Melzi.[1] Her type also turns up in the Spencer Grotesques volumes of copies carefully drawn in left-handed imitation in soft leadpoint, possibly by a Lombard artist of about 1590–1600 (fig. 171).[2] Wenceslaus Hollar's exquisite etching copying the figure pairs her with the man in catalogue number 73d, and both are depicted in a much larger scale and in reverse design (fig. 172).[3] Hollar's print, probably produced in the 1640s (it is undated), interprets the woman's pointy hat in fascinating detail—much beyond what seems apparent in Leonardo's drawing. According to Hollar, the hat

contains a series of concentric circles from which erupts, not unlike a volcano, a tiny face blowing air or wind from the mouth; Leonardo's drawing depicts here a flower. Hollar's print appears to interpret Leonardo's original drawing as an embodiment of the "choleric" temperament. The figure was not included, however, among the copy drawings in the album of the great French collector Pierre-Jean Mariette, and it therefore does not appear in the book of etchings by the count of Caylus, *Recueil de testes de caractère & de charges dessinées par Leonardo da Vinci* (Paris, 1730; see cat. nos. 137, 138.)

CCB

1. Illustrated and discussed in Pedretti and Trutty-Coohill 1993, p. 65, no. 29.
2. The Spencer Grotesques were attributed to a Venetian artist from the second half of the sixteenth century by Aydua H. Scott-Elliot. Illustrated and also discussed in Pedretti and Trutty-Coohill 1993, p. 92, no. 55 (I.20).
3. Pennington 1982, p. 275, no. 1601A.

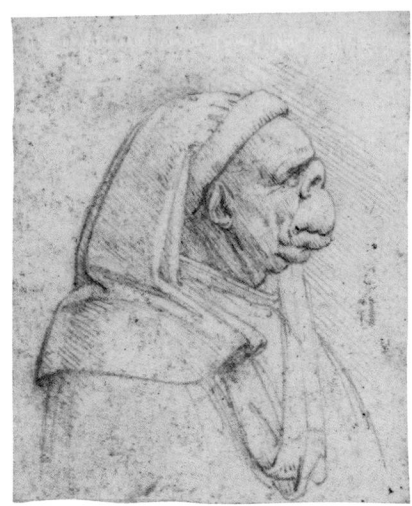

Cat. 71 *(actual size)*

LEONARDO DA VINCI

71. *Snub-Nosed Old Man with a Cowled Hat in Bust-Length Profile*

Pen and brown ink; glued to secondary paper support, 65 × 53 mm
(2 ½ × 2 ⅛ in.)
Private collection, New York

PROVENANCE: Thomas Howard, second earl of Arundel (1586–
1646); presumably Nicholaes Anthoni Flinck, Rotterdam (1646–
1723; Lugt 959 stamp appears whole on Chatsworth 824B, hence
most of the small "caricatures" with a Chatsworth provenance are
from this same collection); possibly from Flinck sale in 1723,
William Cavendish, second duke of Devonshire, Chatsworth (1672–
1739; Lugt 718, 719, Suppl. 719); Chatsworth 820A; by descent to
the eleventh duke; sale, Christie's, London, July 3, 1984, lot 22.

LITERATURE: Strong 1905, p. 114; Commissione Vinciana 1928–,
vol. 5, p. 24, pl. 212.4; Scott-Elliot 1958, p. 282; Clark and Pedretti 1968–
69, vol. 1, p. 44; Pedretti 1973a, p. 40, under no. 13; Stock 1985, p. 119;
Goldner 1988, p. 58, no. 19; Caroli 1991, pp. 154, 158, no. 13; Jaffé 1994,
p. 168, no. 883, 820A; Kwakkelstein 1994, pp. 107–9, pl. 49g.

This drawing of a snub-nosed man with long upper lip
may also be dated broadly between 1495 and 1506–8.

His costume may be that of a merchant.[1] A copy of the man
in the present sheet, coupled with a tired, rather masculine
hag, appears among the Pembroke Grotesques attributed to
Francesco Melzi.[2] This man's type also turns up in the Spencer
Grotesques volumes of copies carefully drawn in left-handed
imitation in soft leadpoint, possibly by a Lombard artist of
about 1590–1600 (fig. 173).[3] Yet another related late-sixteenth-
century or early-seventeenth-century copy, but in pen and ink
with cross-hatching and close to the style of the Bolognese
artist Bartolomeo Passarotti (1529–1592), is in the Crocker
Art Museum at Sacramento.[4] The type of the New York man
wearing a cowled hat was included among the copy drawings
in the album of the great French collector Pierre-Jean Mariette
(RF 28757); it therefore was reproduced in the book of etchings made by the count of Caylus, *Recueil de testes de caractère
& de charges dessinées par Leonardo da Vinci*, no. 32 (Paris,
1730; see cat. nos. 137, 138). There, the design is in reverse
orientation with respect to Leonardo's original. (See also cat.
no. 71.) The type of this man with cowled hat was also

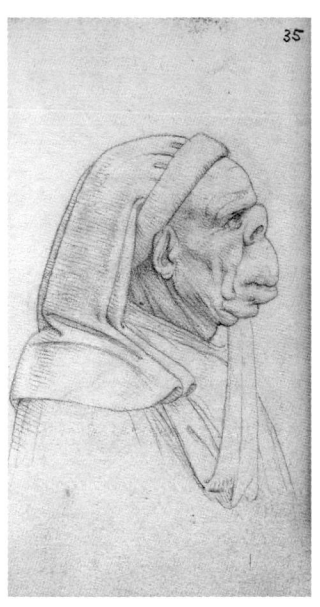

Fig. 173. Late-sixteenth-century Lombard artist after Leonardo da Vinci, *Head of Grotesque Man* (from François Rabelais, *Les oeuvres de M. François Rabelais,* Rouen [?] 1659, 1669 [?]). Black chalk, 142 × 85 mm. The New York Public Library, Astor, Lenox and Tilden Foundations, New York; Spencer Collection. Spencer Grotesques, vol. 1, no. 35

engraved by Carlo Giuseppe Gerli in his anthology of Leonardo's drawings of 1784, though his source seems to have been traced from a copy after the present drawing.[5]

CCB

1. The man in an engraving from about 1465 by the Master of the Tarocchi, which is inscribed *Merchadante* (Merchant), wears exactly the same costume as the snub-nosed man in Leonardo's small drawing (Hind 1938–48, vol. 1, p. 234, no. E.1.42).
2. Illustrated and discussed in Pedretti and Trutty-Coohill 1993, pp. 66–68, no. 30a. Art market, Christie's, London, July 7, 1998, lot 59.
3. The Spencer Grotesques were attributed by Aydua H. Scott-Elliot to a Venetian artist from the second half of the sixteenth century. Illustrated and also discussed in Pedretti and Trutty-Coohill 1993, p. 94, no. 55 (I.35).
4. Illustrated and discussed in Pedretti and Trutty-Coohill 1993, p. 87, no. 54a.
5. Gerli 1784, pl. 27 (inscribed 40), in the center of the bottom row.

LEONARDO DA VINCI

72. *Old Woman with Horned Head Dress, Wearing a Carnation, in Bust-Length Profile*

Pen and dark brown ink; glued to secondary paper support, 64 × 52 mm (2 ½ × 2 1/16 in.)
The Woodner Collections, on deposit at the National Gallery of Art, Washington, D.C. 74585

PROVENANCE: Thomas Howard, second earl of Arundel (1586–1646); presumably Nicholaes Anthoni Flinck, Rotterdam (1646–1723; Lugt 959, stamp at lower right partly cropped; Lugt 959 stamp appears whole on Chatsworth 824B, hence most of the small "caricatures"with a Chatsworth provenance are from this same collection); possibly from Flinck sale in 1723, William Cavendish, second duke of Devonshire, Chatsworth (1672–1739; Lugt 718, 719, Suppl. 719; his mount?); Chatsworth 820B; by descent to the eleventh duke; sale, Christie's, London, July 3, 1984, lot 23; Ian Woodner, New York; 1990, by inheritance to his daughters, Andrea and Dian Woodner, New York.

LITERATURE: Strong 1905, p. 114; Stix and Spitzmüller 1926–41, no. 19; Commissione Vinciana 1928– , vol. 5, p. 24, pl. 212.7; Venturi 1939, vol. 5, p. 24, pl. 212; Popham and Pouncey 1950, p. 73; Gombrich 1954, pp. 208–10, fig. 6; Scott-Elliot 1958, p. 293, no. 24; Gombrich 1976, p. 67, fig. 152 (Leonardo?); Stock 1985, p. 119; Piel 1986, pp. 12–14, no. 6; Rocha 1986–87, pp. 31–33, no. 7; Royal Academy of Arts 1987, pp. 30–31, no. 6; Metropolitan Museum of Art 1990, no. 8;

Caroli 1991, pp. 154, 159, no. 16; Pedretti and Trutty-Coohill 1993, pp. 9, 15, 45–46, 69, 103, no. 11; Jaffé 1994, p. 168, no. 883, 820B; Annesley 1995, p. 54; Pietro C. Marani in Grasselli 1995–96, pp. 80–83, no. 11; Fairbrother and Ishikawa 1997, pp. 32–33, 68, no. 22, fig. 14; Letze and Buchsteiner 1997, p. 78; Trutty-Coohill 1998b.

The position of the partly cropped stamp of the Dutch collector Nicholaes Anthoni Flinck (the son of one of Rembrandt's pupils) on this sheet indicates that this and the other Chatsworth "caricatures" (cat. nos. 69–71, 73), which Leonardo probably originally conceived as couples or groups of three, may have been separated after Flinck's time. The present drawing may likewise be dated broadly between 1495 and 1506–8. As is poignantly clear here, Leonardo was obsessed with the deterioration of beauty due to age. In the artist's own words, "what is fair in mortal beings passes and does not last."[1] He was fascinated by the facial deformities caused by toothlessness in the elderly, and the uncompromising portrayals seen among the small Chatsworth "caricatures" are often repulsive in effect.

457

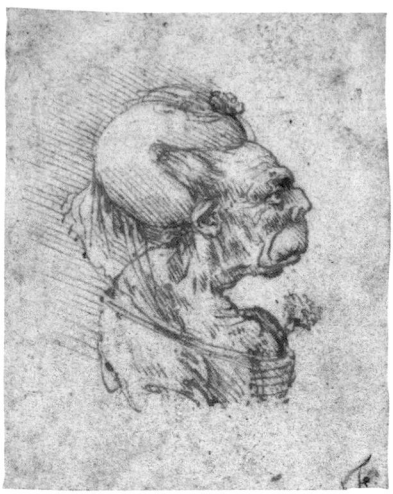

Cat. 72 *(actual size)*

There, the design is in reverse orientation with respect to Leonardo's original.

CCB

1. Codex Forster[III], fol. 72r; Richter 1970, vol. 1, p. 367, no. 651: "Cosa bella mortal passa e no[n] dura."
2. National Gallery of Art, Washington, 1980. 63.1 (Gift of Mrs. Edward Fowles).
3. The Spencer Grotesques were attributed by Aydua H. Scott-Elliot to a Venetian artist from the second half of the sixteenth century. Illustrated and also discussed in Pedretti and Trutty-Coohill 1993, p. 93, no. 55 (I.24).

The old woman in the Woodner study is drawn with extraordinary vivacity. The artist moved the pen quickly and self-assuredly, with a well-placed tick here or there, suggesting rather than fully describing. The thickish strokes of his parallel hatching course from lower left to upper right. He also allowed the ink to settle in minute, suggestive pools of liquid along selected passages of the outlines to achieve inflections of varying darkness. In contrast to Leonardo's pen heavy with ink, Francesco Melzi's pen in the copy from the Pembroke Grotesques—which is in the same museum and thus allows for a side-by-side comparison of drawing technique—seems quite fine, scratchy, and timid.[2] The Woodner old woman wears an outdated, early-fifteenth-century style of coiffure and dress, which contributes to the irony of her portraitlike representation. Her profile pose and the detail of a carnation flirtatiously tucked into the low neckline of her tight bodice are typical of late-fifteenth-century painted portraits of young women (which were often intended to celebrate the occasion of their betrothal or marriage).

The Woodner old woman turns up in the Spencer Grotesques volumes of copies carefully drawn in left-handed imitation in soft leadpoint, possibly by a Lombard artist of about 1590–1600 (fig. 174).[3] She was also included among the copy drawings in the album of the great French collector Pierre-Jean Mariette (RF 28731) and therefore was reproduced in the book of etchings by the count of Caylus, *Recueil de testes de caractère & de charges dessinées par Leonardo da Vinci*, no. 6 (Paris, 1730; see cat. nos. 137, 138).

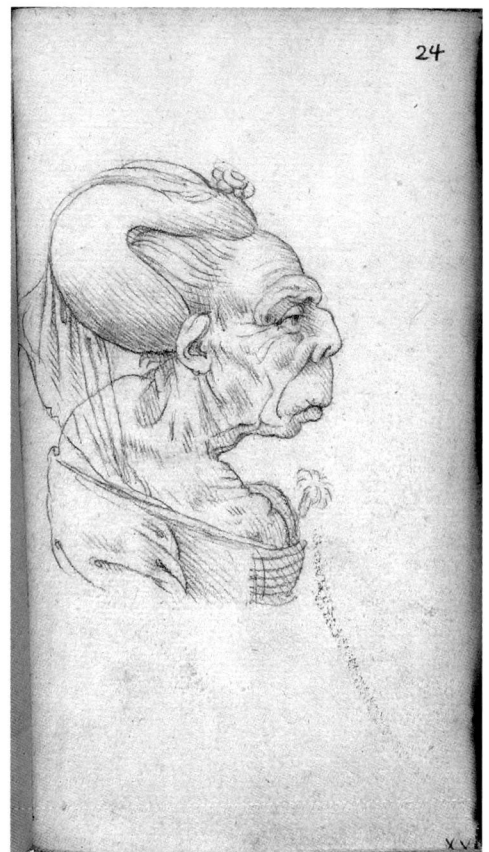

Fig. 174. Late-sixteenth-century Lombard artist after Leonardo da Vinci, *Head of Grotesque Man* (from François Rabelais, *Les oeuvres de M. François Rabelais*, Rouen [?] 1659, 1669 [?]). Black chalk, 142 × 85 mm. The New York Public Library, Astor, Lenox and Tilden Foundations, New York; Spencer Collection. Spencer Grotesques, vol. 1, no. 24

458

LEONARDO DA VINCI

73. *Four Fragments with Grotesque Heads*

Pen and brown ink, glued onto secondary paper support, a: 51 × 37 mm
(2 × 1 7/16 in.), b: 52 × 37 mm (2 1/16 × 1 7/16 in.), c: 50 × 42 mm
(2 × 1 5/8 in.), d: 52 × 45 mm (2 1/16 × 1 3/4 in.)
The Duke of Devonshire and the Chatsworth Settlement Trustees,
Chatsworth 823A, B, C, D

PROVENANCE: Thomas Howard, second earl of Arundel (1586–1646);
Nicholaes Anthoni Flinck, Rotterdam (1646–1723; stamp Lugt 959
appears whole on Chatsworth 824B, hence most of the small "caricatures" with a Chatsworth provenance are from this same collection);
possibly from Flinck sale in 1723, William Cavendish, second duke
of Devonshire, Chatsworth (1672–1739; Lugt 718, 719, Suppl. 719),
his mount.

LITERATURE: Strong 1905, p. 114; Commissione Vinciana 1928–,
vol. 5, p. 212, no. 16; Clark and Pedretti 1968–69, vol. 1 p. 59
(under no. 12398); Bean 1982, p. 136, under no. 129; Caroli 1991,
pp. 154, 156, nos. 5, 6, 7, p. 157, no. 9; Pedretti and Trutty-Coohill
1993, pp. 70–71; Jaffé 1994, p. 171, no. 886; Kwakkelstein 1994,
pp. 107–12, pls. 49b, 49f.

The arbitrary mounting of the small, individually cut
sheets seen here most probably dates from the 1720s to
1730s, when the drawings were in the possession of the second
duke of Devonshire, and when the appreciation for Leonardo's
studies of grotesque physiognomy was at its height. To judge
from the frequent pairings of such motifs in many of the later
copies (and especially in the dispersed early sheets known as
the Pembroke Grotesques; cat. no. 121), Leonardo's small
studies were conceived for the most part as orderly couples, or
trios, of men and women facing each other, and displaying a
variety of sometimes extreme, though complementary, emotive states. These deformed heads (which, as we have seen,
Leonardo called *visi mostruosi*, and Giovanni Paolo Lomazzo,
faccie mostruose) can hardly be considered mere "doodles," as
they have sometimes been termed, if one takes into account
their arresting psychological presence. Yet their meaning as a
whole has proved extremely elusive. Beyond Leonardo's own
fragmentary notes,[1] early sources offer general evidence of his

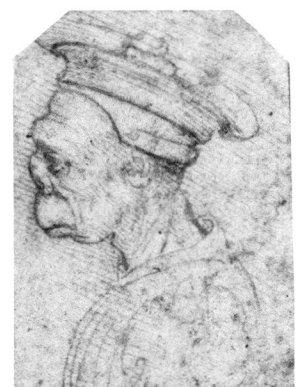

Cat. 73a *(actual size)*

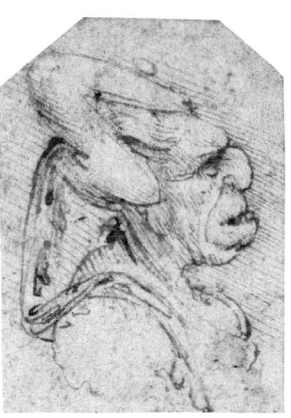

Cat. 73b *(actual size)*

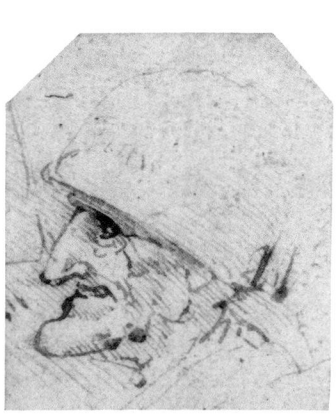

Cat. 73c *(actual size)*

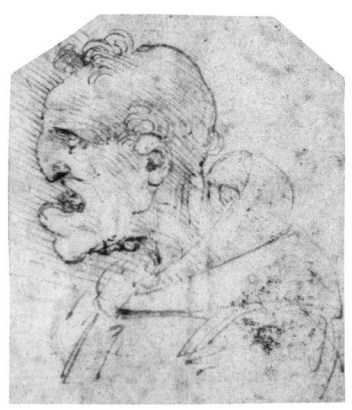

Cat. 73d *(actual size)*

interest in the capacities of physical gesture, particularly among the acutely physically deformed, to reflect inner dispositions of character and emotive state. Such texts include Giovanni Battista Giraldi Cinthio's *Discorsi . . . intorno al comporre de i romanzi* (Venice, 1554), Giorgio Vasari's *Vite de' più eccellenti pittori, scultori ed architettori* (Florence, 1568), Giovanni Paolo Lomazzo's *Trattato dell'arte della pittura, scoltura et archittetura* (Milan, 1584), and Giovanni Battista Armenini's *De' veri precetti della pittura* (Ravenna, 1586 and 1587).[2]

Like catalogue numbers 69–72, which were also recognized by the Commissione Vinciana in 1939 as originals by Leonardo, these four small sheets (mounted together with a complete misunderstanding of their original context) exhibit a range of mark from spirited sketchy outlines to subtly modulated parallel hatching. This fact sheds some light on Leonardo's creative process, and the relative disparities of finish help establish that these are most probably originals by him, for, by contrast, the lines in the contours and hatching in the outright copies seem scratchy and uniform in their tonal weight (see cat. nos. 121, 136). Such copies, for example, lack the increased and decreased tonal emphases that are normally the result of Leonardo's rapidly gliding pen. Especially in catalogue numbers 73b and 73c, one finds dynamic passages of sketchiness with small, suggestively placed blots of ink. As is true of catalogue numbers 69–72, the dating of these "grotesques" is difficult; they were probably produced sometime between 1495 and 1506–8 (at which date such motifs were being copied in the frescoes of the oratory of Santa Maria di Rivolta d'Adda). Catalogue number 73c is the sketchiest of the small grotesque drawings and seems to have been rarely (if ever) copied by later imitators of Leonardo. It can be said to resemble the "caricatures" on folio 2 verso of the Codex Trivulzianus, dating from 1487–90, although only superficially, for the codex sketches are little more than exaggerated outline drawings, lacking the modeling with diagonal parallel hatching that is the hallmark of most of the Chatsworth *visi mostruosi*. Although the type of parallel hatching in many of the Chatsworth small sheets has been likened to that found on the larger-scale studies of the human skull from about 1489 (cat. no. 58; Windsor, RL 19057, 19059), this is a technique that, as we have seen, recurs also in some of Leonardo's very late drawings, as in some of the sheets of the Codex Leicester (cat. no. 114). The best known of the larger-scale Windsor drawings of

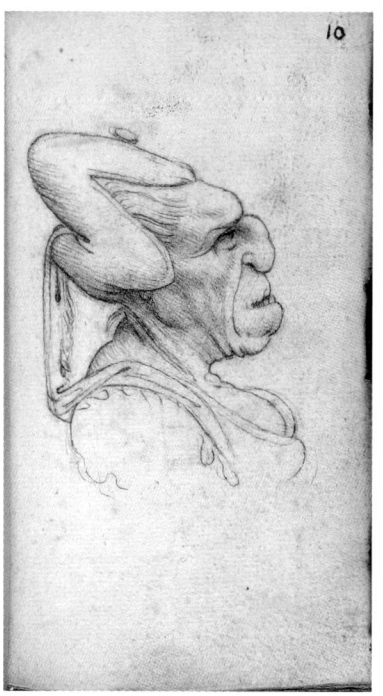

Fig. 175. Late sixteenth-century Lombard artist after Leonardo da Vinci, *Head of Grotesque Woman* (from François Rabelais, *Les oeuvres de M. François Rabelais*, Rouen [?] 1659, 1669 [?]). Black chalk, 142 × 85 mm. The New York Public Library, Astor, Lenox and Tilden Foundations, New York; Spencer Collection. Spencer Grotesques, vol. 1, no. 10

grotesque physiognomy in pen and ink can be confidently dated to somewhere between 1485 and 1495 (Windsor, RL 12449, 12489, 12490, 12495). However, a number of much smaller fragmentary sketches of such heads (Windsor, RL 12452, 12455, 12456, 12459)—some with straight parallel hatching—that were extracted from the Codex Atlanticus were convincingly dated by Kenneth Clark and Carlo Pedretti to about 1503–5 on the basis of the content of the parent sheets.[3]

The woman with the horned headdress (cat. no. 73b), which seems to reflect fashions of the 1440s rather than of Leonardo's time, is especially carefully detailed and seems comparable to catalogue numbers 69–72, like them revealing an atmospheric use of the pen. This figure was copied exactly in one of the sheets of the Pembroke Grotesques attributed to Francesco Melzi (cat. no. 121; another sheet of the Pembroke Grotesques includes a copy after cat. no. 73a), down to the left-handed strokes. On the upper left of catalogue number 136, the woman with horned headdress was more freely copied, also with imitation left-handed strokes, and with a slightly less compact facial anatomy by an anonymous later sixteenth-century draftsman. The deformed woman's type, as well as types seen in catalogue numbers 73a and 73d, are included among the copy drawings in the album of the great French collector Pierre-Jean Mariette (RF 28732, 28734, 28749) and were thus reproduced in etchings by the count of Caylus as nos. 7, 9, and 24 of his *Recueil de testes de caractère & de charges dessinées par Leonardo da Vinci* (Paris, 1730; see cat. nos. 137, 138). The prototype for the snub-nosed dejected man portrayed in catalogue number 73a appears to have been another, much larger pen-and-ink drawing by Leonardo (Biblioteca Ambrosiana, Milan, F. 274 inf. 53) that scholars have rightly dated to 1485–90, based on comparison with the pitch-straight parallel hatching technique of Paris Ms. B. This fact does not at all preclude, however, that Leonardo (and his

pupils) would return to such types in later years. Attractively executed copies of catalogue numbers 73a, 73b, and 73d are also found among the Spencer Grotesques (fig. 175 and Spencer Collection, New York Public Library, I.21; I.23).

CCB

1. Transcribed in Caroli 1991, pp. 30–43; Kwakkelstein 1994, pp. 147–48.
2. Transcribed in Kwakkelstein 1994, pp. 139–43.
3. Clark and Pedretti 1968–69, vol. 1, pp. 74–75.

LEONARDO DA VINCI

74. *Old Man Standing in Profile Facing to the Right*

Leadpoint or soft pale black chalk with some red chalk offsetting, 211 × 156 mm (8⁵/₁₆ × 6⅛ in.)
Lent by Her Majesty Queen Elizabeth II, Royal Library, Windsor Castle 12582

PROVENANCE: Windsor Leoni volume: 1519, Francesco Melzi, Milan and Rome (1491/93–ca. 1570); ca. 1570, Orazio Melzi; by 1590, Pompeo Leoni, Madrid and Milan (ca. 1533–1608; Lugt under 2885); ca. 1613, Thomas Howard, second earl of Arundel (1586–1646); before 1690, British Royal Collection (inventory of King George III's collection, ca. 1810).

LITERATURE: Chamberlaine 1812, pl. 8; Grosvenor 1878, vol. 2, p. 34; Müntz 1898, vol. 1, p. 245; Müntz 1899, p. 249; Berenson 1903, vol. 2, p. 63, no. 1137; Seidlitz 1911, p. 271, no. 36; Commissione Vinciana 1928–, vol. 5, p. 22, pl. 190; Bodmer 1931, pp. 208, 396; Berenson 1938, vol. 2, p. 126, no. 1137; Royal Academy of Arts 1952, p. 55, no. 79; Berenson 1961, vol. 2, p. 223, no. 1137; Chastel 1961, p. 145; Clark and Pedretti 1968–69, vol. 1, p. 114, no. 12582; Clark 1969–70, p. 4, no. 16; Pedretti and Clark 1983, pp. 114–15, 128–29, figs. 81, 88, under nos. 14, 18; Caroli 1991, p. 86; Kwakkelstein 1994, p. 110, fig. 52; Popham 1994, no. 145.

The elderly man portrayed here in a full-length standing pose and clutching a scroll with his right hand wears classical dress (a tunic with wide sleeves, cowl, and long stole) that

seems to identify him as a philosopher, scholar, chancellor, or chamberlain. Although the characterization of the figure appears to be intentionally sardonic, the touch of melancholy on his face arouses the viewer's empathy. The strict profile view of the old man's head calls attention to his grotesquely deformed broken nose, apparently toothless mouth, receding chin, puckered throat, and goiterous cheek. It is not clear whether his thick hair—stiffly undulating backward—is a wig showing a seam at the hairline or his natural hair tied with a band or ribbon at the highest point of the forehead. Leonardo may well have intended the man as a mocking portrayal of pedantry. Both the general subject matter and the regular manner of the parallel hatching (though in chalk, rather than in pen and ink) connect the present study to the group of grotesque figures, often portrayed in bust-length, that were produced by Leonardo in the late 1480s to 1490s (cat. nos. 59, 60). The whimsical conception of the old man's head in the present drawing, with his highly particularized details of costume, also evokes the style of the small so-called Chatsworth "caricatures" (cat. nos. 69–73). The monumental presence of the draperies on the figure and the subtlety of the tonal modeling indicate a date for the present study closer to

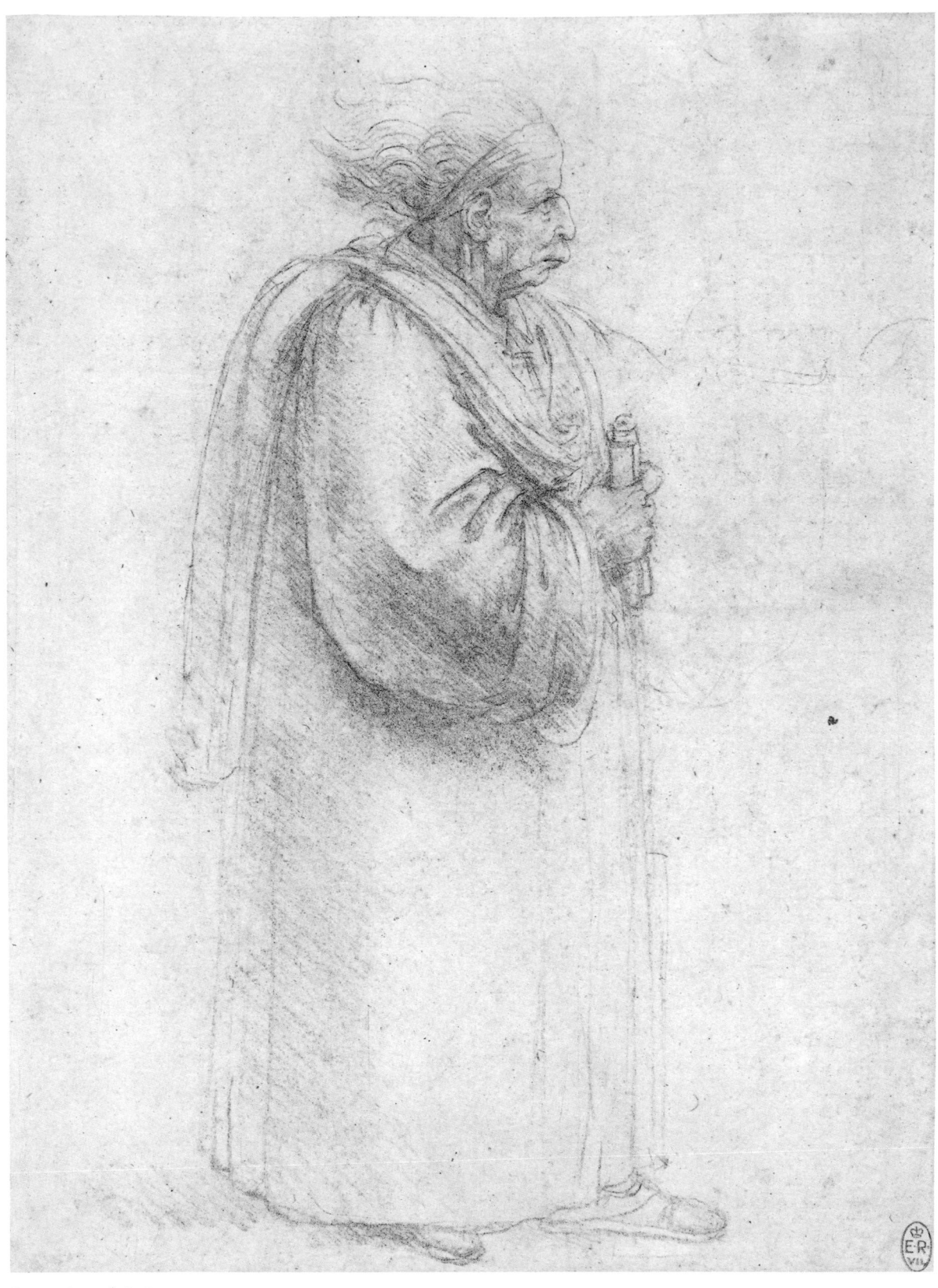

Cat. 74 *(actual size)*

1495–99, a few years later than is often suggested. Bernard Berenson less convincingly dated the drawing as late as Leonardo's second Milanese period, in 1506–13.

Wenceslaus Hollar (1607–1677), the great artist from Prague who settled in England, copied Leonardo's drawing in an exquisitely rendered etching that is signed and dated 1648.[1]

Hollar's print shows the Windsor old man cropped to a half-length, in a reversed design orientation, and interprets the old man's expression as more dour. The print also clearly suggests that the man's long, backward-streaming hair is a wig.

CCB

1. Pennington 1982, p. 273, no. 1576.

LEONARDO DA VINCI

75. *Head of Old Man or Woman in Profile Facing to the Left*

Red chalk; outlines along the profile of the front part of the cranium, face, and neck pricked for transfer, 100 × 80 mm (3 $\frac{15}{16}$ × 3 $\frac{3}{16}$ in.) Inscribed in pen and brown ink, in right-to-left script, on verso: *[anatom]ja dellochio / [fa la natomi]a dellochio chomellj sta de[n]tro cholle sue tonjche / [e per questo] che si facci vna uesta simile acquella dellouo / [e se la terra] i fresscha talieraj detta cholla* [crossed out: *l*] *dellochio co[n] / [? cre]ssciere de[n]tro a essi vasi la . . . a . a dell ochio / [che e dentr]o i[n] modo . ue[n]ghi il proposito . tuo . appu[n]to.*[1]

Hamburger Kunsthalle 21482

PROVENANCE: Johann Goll van Franckenstein (1722–1785), Amsterdam; his son (1756–1821); Georg Ernst Harzen, Hamburg (1790–1863); ca. 1842–56 manuscript inventory by G. E. Harzen (NH.Ad:01:04), fol. 116 (stating the Goll van Franckenstein provenance); ca. 1860 manuscript inventory by G. E. Harzen (NH.Ad:02:01), p. 222; 1863, Harzen bequest; museum stamp (Lugt 1328).

LITERATURE: Gerli 1/84, pl. 19, Müntz 1899, p. 525, no. 5; Pauli 1927, no. 10; Berenson 1938, vol. 2, p. 112, no. 1020B; Gombrich 1954, p. 208; Pedretti 1957b, pp. 230–31; Scott-Elliot 1958, pp. 282, 287; Berenson 1961, vol. 2, p. 195, no. 1020B; Clark and Pedretti 1968–69, vol. 1, pp. 83–84, under no. 12493; Gombrich 1976, pp. 66–67, fig. 146; Keele and Pedretti 1979–80, vol. 2, pp. 808, 816–17, 861, figs. 64, 65; Marani 1985b, p. 864; Gombrich 1986b, p. 92, no. 151; Giulio Bora in Palazzo Reale 1987–88, pp. 122–23, under no. 58; Caroli 1991, p. 212; Luisa Cogliati Arano in Palazzo Grassi 1992, pp. 324–25, no. 61; Pedretti and Trutty-Coohill 1993, p. 96, under no. 7; Kwakkelstein 1994, pp. 116–17, fig. 83; Popham 1994, no. 134A; Caroli 1995, p. 168, fig. 1; Hamburger Kunsthalle 1997, p. 94, no. 28; Clayton 2002–3, p. 89, under no. 38.

Catalogue number 76 and this poignant bust in red chalk of a grotesque man or woman (the gender is not clear) may have been pages from the same small notebook, to judge from their similar scale and drawing technique with a very fine pointy red chalk stick. The psychological intensity of the small Hamburg portraitlike head study is arresting. Like many studies of grotesque physiognomy by Leonardo, the figure was probably conceived as part of a pair; in numerous extant early copies of such drawings by Leonardo, the various head types face each other as couples. A number of copies exist of the head seen on the Hamburg sheet. A sheet in Windsor (fig. 177) includes it with three other heads, in pairs. Other single copies of the head are in the Biblioteca Ambrosiana (Milan, Cod. F 263 inf. 19), ex-Rudolf Collection (Courtauld Institute of Art, negative no. 293/22.39), and in the Spencer Grotesques volumes (fig. 176). This particular head design became widely appreciated as the result of reproductive prints, in particular the etching by Wenceslaus Hollar (1607–1677), the great artist from Prague who settled in England,[2] and the engraving by Carlo Giuseppe Gerli published in his anthology of Leonardo's drawings (Milan, 1784). Hollar's etching seems to be based on the Windsor copy of the Hamburg head type and clearly portrays the figure as a man (in contrast to the androgynous figure in Leonardo's original). Gerli's engraving may be based on the Biblioteca Ambrosiana copy, though it includes the Hamburg head type as part of a couple. Executed in red chalk, like the Hamburg original, the Windsor drawn copy (fig. 177) is possibly the earliest. It shows the Hamburg head type coupled with a buxom grotesque woman—with a swollen upper lip that nearly swallows her nose and wearing a veiled headdress—facing to the right. It may be that the Hamburg design was pricked so a pupil of Leonardo (Francesco Melzi?) could transfer the motif to another sheet for replication, by the *spolvero* technique.

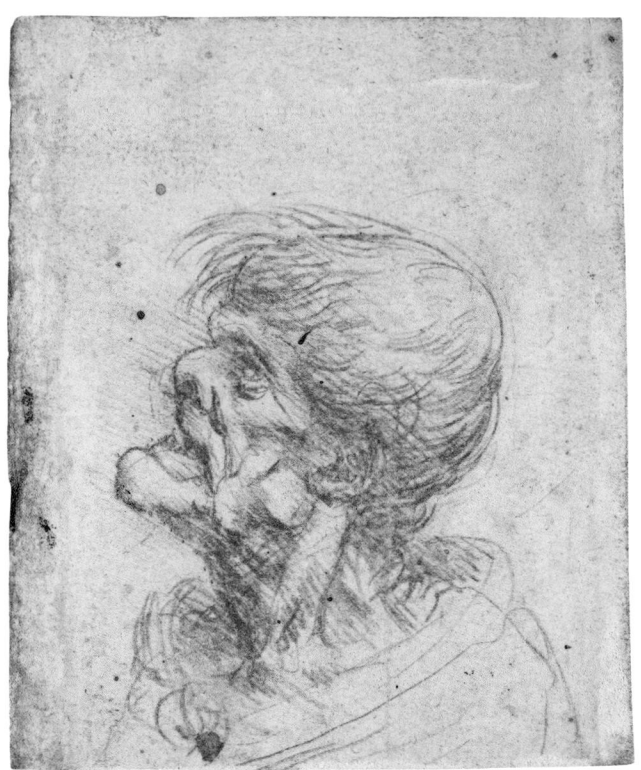

Cat. 75R *(actual size)*

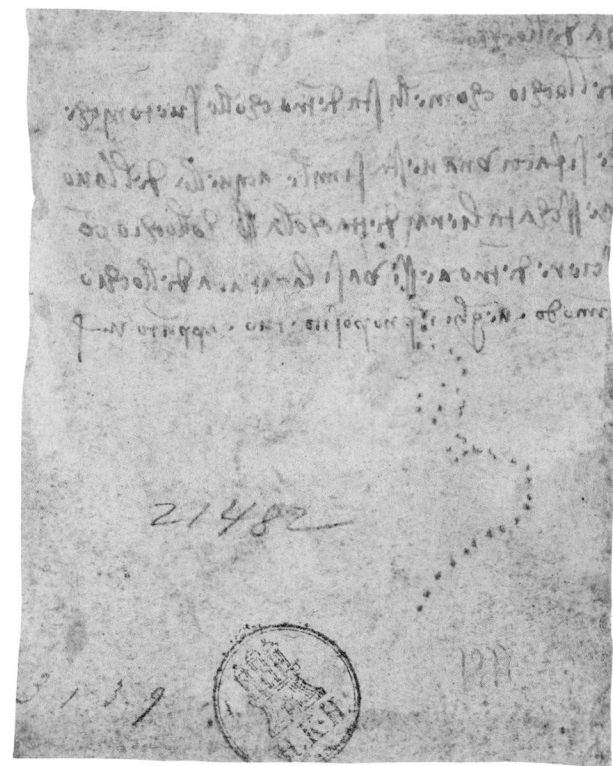

Cat. 75V *(actual size)*

The gender of the model for the Hamburg study has caused considerable debate in the Leonardo literature (it may be a man, because in the copies it is coupled with a woman), as has the dating of the drawing. The careful technique of drawing with a fine, pointy red chalk, using regular parallel hatching that is often subtly blended for a unified depth of tone, suggests to this author a date about 1495–1505 (rather than 1490–93, as has sometimes been proposed); the inscribed text on the verso of the sheet reinforces a dating after 1500. Also typical of this period (around 1500) in Leonardo's draftsmanship are darkest shadows, emphasized by wetting the tip of the red chalk stick, or by pressing it down hard on the paper, and the refined modeling of intermediate shadows.

The artist inscribed the verso of the Hamburg sheet with a somewhat repetitive note on the anatomy of the eye that is fairly elusive in meaning, which scholars have transcribed and translated in a variety of ways. One of these translations reads, "The eye is structured in such a way that it fits into its tunic; and it is for this reason that it forms a membrane similar to that of the egg; and if you keep it fresh, you can dissect this glue-like substance, with the eye that is inside, so that

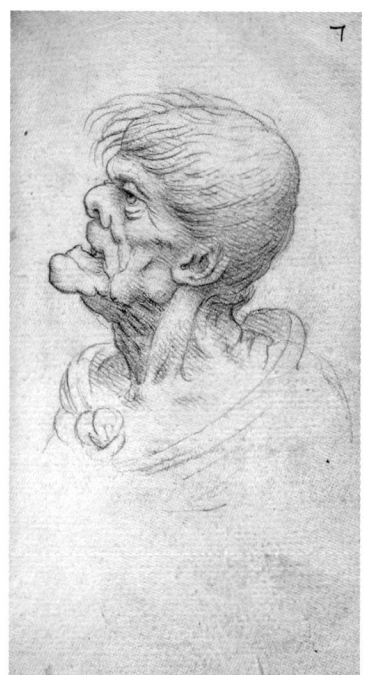

Fig. 176. Late-sixteenth-century Lombard artist after Leonardo da Vinci, *Head of Grotesque Man or Woman* (from François Rabelais, *Les oeuvres de M. François Rabelais*, Rouen [?] 1659, 1669 [?]). Black chalk, 142 × 85 mm. The New York Public Library, Astor, Lenox and Tilden Foundations, New York; Spencer Collection. Spencer Grotesques, vol. 2, no. 7

464

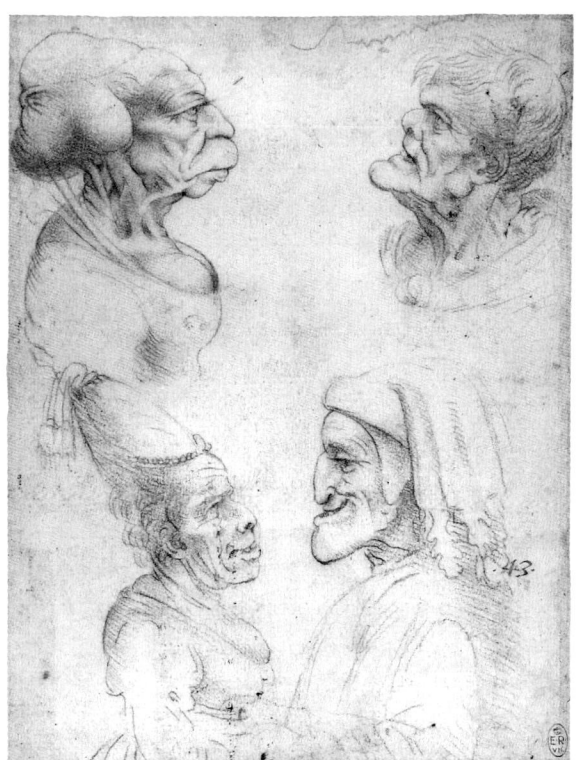

Fig. 177. Copy after Leonardo da Vinci, *Four Grotesque Heads*. Red chalk, 195 × 146 mm. The Royal Collection, H.M. Queen Elizabeth II, Windsor Castle RL 12493

produce the desired result."[4] It seems extremely difficult to arrive at a refined translation of Leonardo's wording, beyond an evocation of the general content of his description, given the significant lacunae in the text. Leonardo described a similar method of studying the dissection of the eye in Paris Ms. K[III], fol. 119r, which Kenneth Keele and Carlo Pedretti rightly dated to about 1507.[5] Although the artist's first sustained anatomical studies of the eye, the optic nerve, and the mechanics of vision seem to date from 1489–93, his practical reasoning about the structure of the eye in both the Hamburg sheet and his Paris Ms. K should be dated much later, probably between 1500 and 1507–8. Leonardo's discourse grew out of his profound interest in the phenomenon of optical perception, and he gathered more such research in his Paris Ms. D. This scientific investigation seems to have had its equivalent in the nuanced tonal exploration of the red chalk medium, as is clear also in the sheet of studies of trees (cat. no. 77).

CCB

you will be able to do exactly what you intended."[3] Another states, "Dissect the eye as it is within its coats, and to do so, have it enveloped in glue as if it were an egg, and when the glue is still fresh cut it together with the eye inside it, so as to

1. Here retranscribed (reconstructions of lacunae based on Carlo Pedretti in Keele and Pedretti 1979–80, vol. 2, p. 816). An alternative reconstruction of this text is given by Luisa Cogliati Arano in Palazzo Grassi 1992, p. 324 (Marani 1985b, p. 864): "Anatomia dell'occhio . / Fa' l'anatomia dell'occhio / come li sta dentro colle sue / tuniche; e per questo che si / facci una vesta simile a / quella dell'ovo; e se la / terrai fresca, táliérai [meaning, taglierai] / detta colla / coll'occhio che è dentro, / in modo [ch]e venghi / il proposito tuo a punto."
2. Pennington 1982, p. 273, no. 1575.
3. Translation by Luisa Cogliati Arano in Palazzo Grassi 1992, p. 324, no. 61.
4. Translation by Carlo Pedretti in Keele and Pedretti 1979–80, vol. 2, p. 816.
5. Discussed and transcribed in Keele and Pedretti 1979–80, vol. 2, p. 816.

LEONARDO DA VINCI

76. *Head of an Old Man*

Red chalk, traces of stylus, 94 × 61 mm (3 ¾ × 2 ⅜ in.); traces of framing outlines in pen and brown ink, gold particles; slight oxidation stain; glued to secondary support
Département des Arts Graphiques du Musée du Louvre, Paris 2249

PROVENANCE: Charles Le Brun; 1690, entered the Cabinet du Roi (Lugt 2953: Prioult paraph); Commission du Museum (Lugt 1899); Commission du Conservatoire (Lugt 2207); Morel d'Arleux, inv. MS vol. 1, no. 44 (Leonardo da Vinci); *Inventaire Napoléon*, no. 44.

LITERATURE: *Recueil Caylus*, no. 118, fol. 49; Mariette 1730, pp. 19–20; Louvre 1802, no. 167bis; Louvre 1811, no. 195; Louvre 1814, no. 154; Louvre 1817, no. 180; Louvre 1820, no. 207; Louvre 1838, no. 363, Chennevières and Montaiglon 1851–60, vol. 3, pp. 161–62; Louvre 1866, no. 385; Müntz 1899, p. 411 n., fig. p. 241, p. 520, no. 27; Berenson 1903, vol. 2, no. 1060; Seidlitz 1909, vol. 1, fig. p. 190; Malaguzzi Valeri 1913–23, vol. 2, pp. 510, 513, fig. 560; Louvre 1919, no. 24; Demonts 1921, no. 16; Demonts 1922, no. 16; Commissione Vinciana 1928– , vol. 5, no. 224; Popp 1928, p. 55, no. 81;

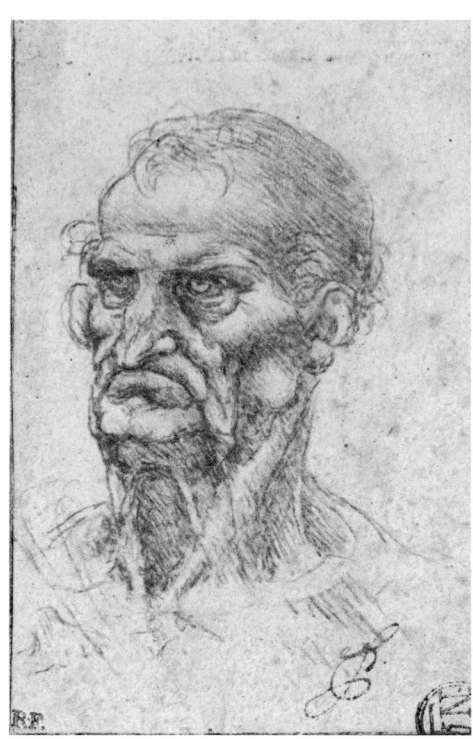

Cat. 76 *(actual size)*

Bodmer 1931, p. 397, fig. 221; Angoulvent 1933, no. 195 (attributed to Leonardo); Roux 1940, no. 456; Popham 1945, p. 41, no. 139B; Amboise 1952; Bibilioteca Medicea Laurenziana 1952, no. 48; Florisoone and Bacou 1952, no. 23; Tours 1956, no. 48; Cogliati Arano 1966–67, under no. 26; Cogliati Arano 1980, under no. 26; Béguin 1983, p. 86; Caroli 1991, p. 204; Cogliati Arano 1992, p. 318 n. 50; Palazzo Grassi 1992, no. 57; Kwakkelstein 1993c, pp. 47, 52, 60 n. 22, and 25, fig. 8; Kwakkelstein 1994, p. 105, fig. 32; Paliaga 1995a, p. 223; Giannattasio 1999, p. 38, fig. 23; Pinault Sørensen 2001, p. 227, fig. 8; Propeck 2002, forthcoming.

Thanks to the *Inventaire Napoléon,* we know that this drawing was mounted with the *Head of a Young Man Seen in Profile* (school of Leonardo; 2248) and that they were exhibited this way at least from 1802 to 1866. The celebrity of this study undoubtedly lies in that fact, but also in Pierre-Jean Mariette's description of it in his 1730 letter to the count of Caylus, who engraved it[1] to include in his *Recueil:* "You have again dipped into the royal collection of drawings, and have pulled from it this beautiful head of an old man seen full face, with such a proud character. It is drawn in a manner that was very familiar to Leonardo, I mean in red chalk crayon, which

he handled in the same spirit as his pen. That is how he drew the figures for his anatomy course."[2] In just a few words, Mariette accounted for the essential qualities of this portrait: the search for expressiveness through the chiseled treatment of the face and the anatomical rendering of the muscle structure in the neck. Before becoming part of the royal collection, the drawing belonged to Charles Le Brun, whose studio was seized upon his death for Louis XIV, with no distinction made between Le Brun's own work and his collection. This last point, which we owe to recent research by Lina Propeck, is of particular significance in light of Le Brun's interest in the expressive heads.[3]

The exhibited drawing is often understood as a study of a model whom Leonardo had previously drawn. The most striking analogy is found in a red-chalk drawing of a male profile, executed about 1490, that has nearly the same dimensions (Popham 1945, no. 140B) . He can similarly be recognized as the model in a drawing in the Accademia, Venice (236), done during the same years and depicting a younger face (cat. no. 86). The date that various scholars have proposed for the Louvre drawing varies a great deal: according to Bernard Berenson, between 1482 and 1499; according to Heinrich Bodmer, during the time of the *Last Supper*; and much later, according to A. E. Popham (1506–8), Luisa Cogliato Arano (about 1505), and Pietro C. Marani.[4] The assignment of a later date, which would link it to the time of the *Battle of Anghiari*, is based on the model's physical resemblance to other portraits of "warriors," such as those at Windsor (RL 12502, RL 12556) and in the Biblioteca Reale, Turin (15575).[5] A last connection has been made, to a full-face male portrait in Turin (15585), which Carlo Pedretti has attributed to Cesare da Sesto.[6] Correspondences can be established with several sheets from the school of Leonardo,[7] especially a *Bust of an Old Man*, catalogued at the Louvre as school of Leonardo da Vinci (2624), published by Eugène Müntz as by Leonardo,[8] and attributed successively to Giovanni Agostino da Lodi by Jean-Christophe Baudequin[9] and, hypothetically, to Pedro Fernàndez by Paolo Giannattasio.[10]

Even if the drawing is to be dated within Leonardo's second Florentine period, which has not been demonstrated, it is a finely structured study, very intense in its small format. It is as explicit as the pen-and-ink studies of more distorted faces of elderly men at the Biblioteca Ambrosiana that date from 1485–90 (see cat. no. 59).[11]

Kenneth Clark revealed this shift from warrior-condottiere faces to ones with sharp prominent features like those in the *Adoration of the Magi*[12] during Leonardo's early years in Florence. A profile with winged helmet, beside which Leonardo included a lion's-head breastplate,[13] shows the influence he derived from Florentine sculpture, particularly that by Andrea del Verrocchio, which itself traces its origins to Roman, especially medallic, portraits.[14] The basis of Leonardo's experimentation, which took place about 1478–80, involved gradually transforming the features by shifting the viewpoint. It is perceptible on a sheet at Windsor (RL 12276), a masterful early variation on the theme of youth versus old age in facing profiles. The profile motif is gone over and over in successive layers, somewhat like the pentimenti in the heads of the early Virgins (see cat. no. 22). A profile in a Windsor drawing (RL 12599), which Popham dates about 1503 and compares to the one at the Louvre,[15] incorporates in its right section a reworking in red chalk of a youthful mouth and chin, which are like an idealized variation.

Michael W. Kwakkelstein compared the entire group of head studies, emphasizing these contradistinctions and the correspondences of human and animal facial features—

man/lion, man/dragon—to Giovanni Paolo Lomazzo's text on Leonardo's sculpture in the *Libro dei sogni*: "Piacevami sopra ogni cosa il far vecchi, di modo che solamente in dissegno ne feci, e tutti mirabili, tra di lapisso e di inchiostro."[16] Leonardo's interest in sculpture is attested by his entry in his inventory of completed work, compiled when he left Florence for Milan in 1482, that he had modeled "molte teste di vecchi."[17] The connection between the "many heads of old men," as well as the "female heads" and the "putti heads," and the drawings serves as the foundation in the attempt to interpret these studies, whose specific purpose continues to elude us but which likely relates to the very narrow distinction in Leonardo's work between expression and anatomy. Domenico Laurenza approaches these questions in penetrating studies on what he calls Leonardo's *fisionomia naturale*.[18] He bases his observations on those already formulated by Clark[19] and Ernst Gombrich[20] and goes on to point out that the relationship between physiognomics and medical treatises is often mentioned but never evaluated in terms of the exact place it occupies in Leonardo's work. Treatises on physiogomy from classical antiquity were known during the Renaissance and influenced the theory of the facial expression. Leonardo's ideas belong to the tradition that grew up during the Middle Ages of so-called natural physiognomics—"natural" because founded on scientific observation. The drawing at Windsor (RL 12276) is the first indication of the attention Leonardo would grant to the antithesis between two profiles, and through this examination of the morphology of the face, he would approach studies of anatomy and proportions of the body. FV

1. Musée du Louvre, RF 28786, fol. 42r, no. Caylus 55.
2. Mariette 1730, pp. 19–20: "Vous avez encore puisé dans la collection de Desseins du Roi, & vous en avez tiré cette belle tête de vieillard vûë de face, dont le caractère est si fier. Elle est dessinée dans une manière qui était très familière à Léonard, je veux dire au craïon de sanguine qu'il manioit dans le même esprit que sa plume. C'est de cette façon qu'il dessina les figures de son cours d'Anatomie."
3. Propeck 2002, forthcoming.
4. Marani, oral communication, 2002.
5. Kwakkelstein 1993c, p. 47 and n. 24.
6. Pedretti 1975a, no. 6; see Kwakkelstein 1993, pp. 47, 61, n. 26.
7. Kwakkelstein 1993c, p. 60, n. 25.
8. Müntz 1899, p. 521, no. 58.
9. Note on back of mount.
10. Giannattasio 1999, p. 46, fig. 24, n. 49.
11. Biblioteca Ambrosiana, Milan, Cod. F. 263 inf. 93, inf. 94, inf. 78; Venice 1992, nos. 51–53.
12. Popham 1945, pls. 30–32.

13. See Laurenza 1993, p. 17, regarding the sheet of studies at Windsor, RL 12276.
14. For example, British Museum, 1895-9-15-474; Popham-Pouncy 1950, no. 96.
15. Popham 1945, no. 139A.
16. Lomazzo 1973–74, vol. 1, p. 153.

17. Codex Atlanticus, Marinoni 2000, fol. 888r (324r); see Kwakkelstein 1993, p. 58, n. 8.
18. Laurenza 2001.
19. Clark 1935, pp. xlvii–xlix; Clark and Pedretti 1968, pp. xlii–xliv.
20. Gombrich 1976, pp. 6off.

LEONARDO DA VINCI

77. *A Copse of Trees Seen in Sunlight* (recto)
Tree (verso)

Red chalk, 194 × 153 mm (7⅝ × 6 1/16 in.)

Inscribed in red chalk, in right-to-left script, on verso toward lower right: *Quella parte dellalb[er]o checanpegia / djuerso lonb[r]a etutta du[n]cholore e do/ve lialb[er]i* [crossed out: *si*] *ov[er]o rami so[n] piv spe/si ivi epiv scuro p[er]che lì ma[n]cho / si sta[n]pissce laria . Ma dove lira/mj ca[n]pegiano sop[ra]a altri ra/mj qujvi le parte lumjnose / sidjmostra[n] piv chiarj ele foglie / lustra[n] p[er] lo sole chellalumjna*—

Lent by Her Majesty Queen Elizabeth II, Royal Library, Windsor Castle 12431

PROVENANCE: Windsor Leoni volume: 1519, Francesco Melzi, Milan and Rome (1491/93–ca. 1570); ca. 1570, Orazio Melzi; by 1590, Pompeo Leoni, Madrid and Milan (ca. 1533–1608; Lugt under 2885); ca. 1613, Thomas Howard, second earl of Arundel (1586–1646); before 1690, British Royal Collection (inventory of King George III's collection, ca. 1810).

LITERATURE: Grosvenor 1878, vol. 1, p. 40; Richter 1883, vol. 1, p. 229, no. 456; New Gallery 1893–94, p. 166, no. 1518; 1925, fig. 84; Berenson 1903, vol. 2, p. 67, no. 1238; Seidlitz 1909, vol. 1, p. 294, vol. 2, p. 11; Seidlitz 1911, p. 287, nos. 753–54; De Toni 1922, p. 16, fig. 2; Baldacci 1922–23, p. 80; Venturi 1925, pp. 109–10, fig. 69; Commissione Vinciana 1928– , vol. 3, p. 23, pls. 92, 93; Bodmer 1931, pp. 346–47, 419; Berenson 1938, vol. 1, p. 182, vol. 2, p. 137, no. 1238; Castelfranco 1952a, pl. 28; Goldscheider 1952, pls. 21, 22; Royal Academy of Arts 1952, no. 196 (hors catalogue); Heydenreich 1954, vol. 1, p. 104, vol. 2, p. 118, pl. 160; McMahon 1956, pl. 9; Berenson 1961, vol. 1, p. 264, vol. 2, p. 243, no. 1238; Chastel 1961, p. 117; Clark and Pedretti 1968–69, vol. 1, p. 69, no. 12431; Clark 1969–70, p. 27, no. 110; Richter 1970, vol. 1, p. 292, no. 456; Baldacci 1980, pp. 450, 452; Pedretti and Clark 1980–81, p. 32, nos. 7A–7B; Kemp 1981, pp. 334–35, pl. 87; Pedretti 1982a, pp. 44–46, no. 8 recto and verso; Gombrich 1984, pp. 14–15, pl. 7; Roberts 1986, p. 36, no. 17; Emboden 1987, pp. 143–44; Kemp 1989, pp. 186–87; Kemp and Roberts 1989, p. 63, no. 12; Popham 1994, no. 262A, B; Clayton 1996–97, pp. 64–65, no. 33; Letze and Buchsteiner 1997, p. 82; Pedretti 1997c, pp. 83–84, figs. 15, 16; Arasse 1998, pp. 315–16, fig. 215.

Scholars have attempted to identify the species of the trees depicted on the recto of this delicately drawn sheet of studies (as *Betula, Robinia,* and *Ulmus*). Definitive conclusions, at least based on the present drawing, are difficult to reach, however. Although Leonardo individualized the sturdy forest trees, giving attention to their ramification, as well as their type and density of foliage, the note on the verso of the sheet demonstrates that he was more concerned with the

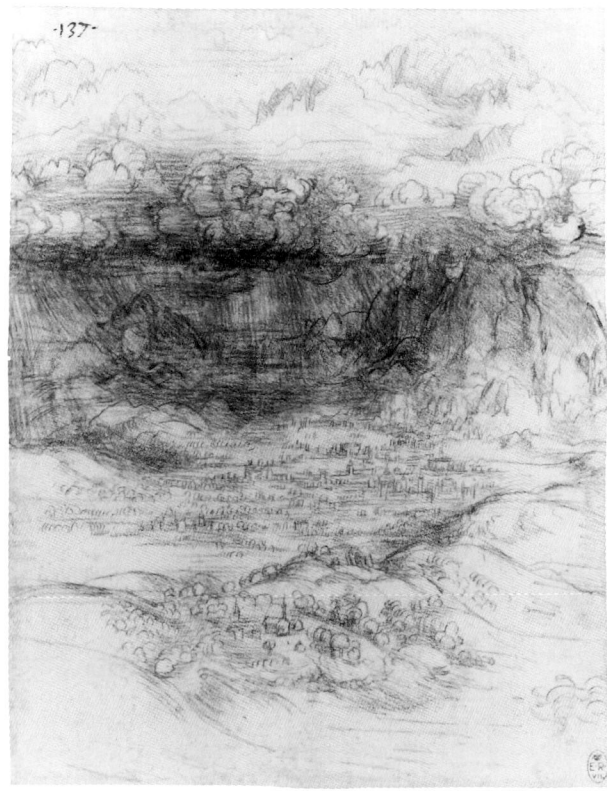

Fig. 178. Leonardo da Vinci, *Storm Breaking over a Valley.* Red chalk, 200 × 150 mm. The Royal Collection, H.M. Queen Elizabeth II, Windsor Castle RL 12409

Cat. 77R *(actual size)*

469

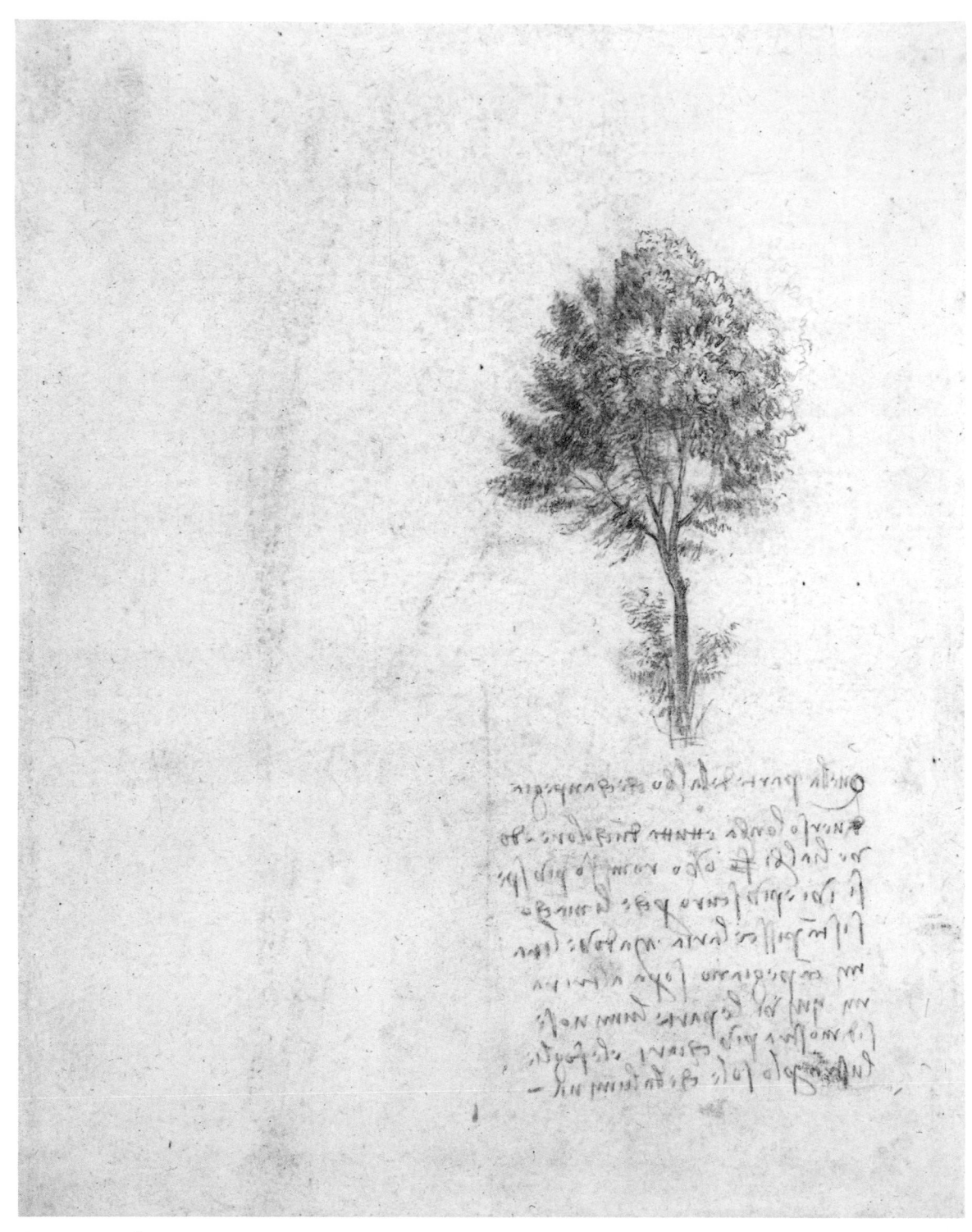

Cat. 77v *(actual size)*

general phenomenon of visual perception than with the individual trees in a scientific, botanical sense. More detailed than the copse on the recto, the birch tree on the verso can probably be recognized as the *Robinia* or *Ulmus* genus.

Between 1500 and 1510, Leonardo's study of landscape would increasingly focus on the optical perception of form as it was affected by light and atmospheric perspective. He investigated the structure of plants and trees—and the effects of light and shadow that modified their forms—mainly to distill detailed principles of portraying landscapes. He probably intended to include these notes in his projected treatise on painting, and such passages—in woefully truncated form—do appear in the posthumously compiled manuscript of his *Libro di pittura* (Codex Urbinas Latinus, 1270). Much of this research is contained in his Paris Ms. G. His note on the verso of this sheet describes the foliage of trees and the atmospheric effects of sunlight. It also offers a clue to the subtlety of the pictorial handling of the red chalk that is manifest in the drawings: "That part of the tree's foliage that is seen against the shadow of a background is all of one tone, and wherever the trees or branches are thickest they will be darkest, because

there are no openings for the light to penetrate. But, where the branches are against other branches, the bright parts seem lighter, and the leaves lustrous from the sunlight falling on them." After the artist rendered the base tone of the forms, he gradually went over some contours and shadows with the fine tip of a sharp chalk to apply minute accents. He seems to have touched broad areas with a damp brush to unify shadows (the chalk seems pinker in hue). In the author's opinion, the exquisitely pictorial handling of the red chalk suggests a date about 1500–1502, that is, slightly later than the storm over a valley in the foothills of the Alps (fig. 178) of analogous technique. The copse of trees on the recto also resembles folio 81v in the Paris Ms. L, dated about 1498–1502. The proposed date is generally in agreement with Martin Kemp and Jane Roberts (1989), as well as with Martin Clayton (1996). Other proposed dates have ranged from 1495, based on a perceived similarity to the red-chalk study of Saint James for the *Last Supper* (Windsor, RL 12552), to about 1510, based on a comparison to Leonardo's handwriting in a sheet of horse studies for the monument to Gian Giacomo Trivulzio (Windsor, RL 12303).

CCB

LEONARDO DA VINCI

78. *Topographic View of the Countryside around the Plain of Arezzo and the Val di Chiana*

Charcoal or soft black chalk, reworked with pen and dark brown ink, brush and brown wash, 208 × 283 mm (8 3/16 × 11 1/8 in.)
Inscribed in pen and brown ink, in right-to-left script, on recto at upper left: *arezzo*; near center of left border: *quarata*; in center above lake: *el brolio colle*; the four towns on near side of lake are labeled: *cesa, foiano, marciano,* and *lucignano*; in black chalk upside down on near side of lake, to the right: *torite, sena*; at right border: *po[n]te auaglano*; on left, below map: *da laualle [la valle] infral brolio e castiglone e 2 magla [migla] / da castiglone a montechio mjgla 1° —— / da castiglone a mamj mjgla 1° / da castiglone alla montanjna miglia 4 / da castiglone a cortona miglia 5 / da castiglone a ujtiano mjgla 2 / da castiglone a robuttino mjgla 3 / da castiglone appuliccano mjgla 5 / da castiglone a pigli mjgla —— 6 / da castiglone allolmo c[i]oe il taglio del colle chessina arezo mjgla 8*; on right, below map: *da foiano a cortona mjgla 8 / da foiano a lucignano —— 2 [3 corrected to 2] / da foiano a marcano 3*; on recto in pen and brown ink by a later hand (Francesco Melzi?) at lower left: *156*

Lent by Her Majesty Queen Elizabeth II, Royal Library, Windsor Castle 12682

PROVENANCE: Windsor Leoni volume: 1519, Francesco Melzi, Milan and Rome (1491/93–ca. 1570); ca. 1570, Orazio Melzi; by 1590, Pompeo Leoni, Madrid and Milan (ca. 1533–1608; Lugt under 2885); ca. 1613, Thomas Howard, second earl of Arundel (1586–1646); before 1690, British Royal Collection (inventory of King George III's collection, ca. 1810).

LITERATURE: Seidlitz 1911, p. 289, no. 833; Solmi 1911, pp. 133–37; Solmi 1912, p. 123; Commissione Vinciana 1928– , 1940–70, p. 42, pl. 13; Gantner 1958, p. 157; Castelfranco 1966, fig. 69; Clark and Pedretti 1968–69, vol. 1, p. 170, no. 12682; Heydenreich 1974b, p. 149, fig. 149/1; Wasserman 1975, fig. 85; Sacco 1980, p. 458; Kemp 1981, p. 232; Pedretti 1982a, pp. 50, 162, fig. 34; Marani 1984, p. 183, no. 104; Clayton 1996–97, pp. 97–98, under no. 52; Starnazzi 1996b, p. 696; Starnazzi 1998, pp. 151–53; Clayton 2002b, p. 24, fig. 12, under no. 3.

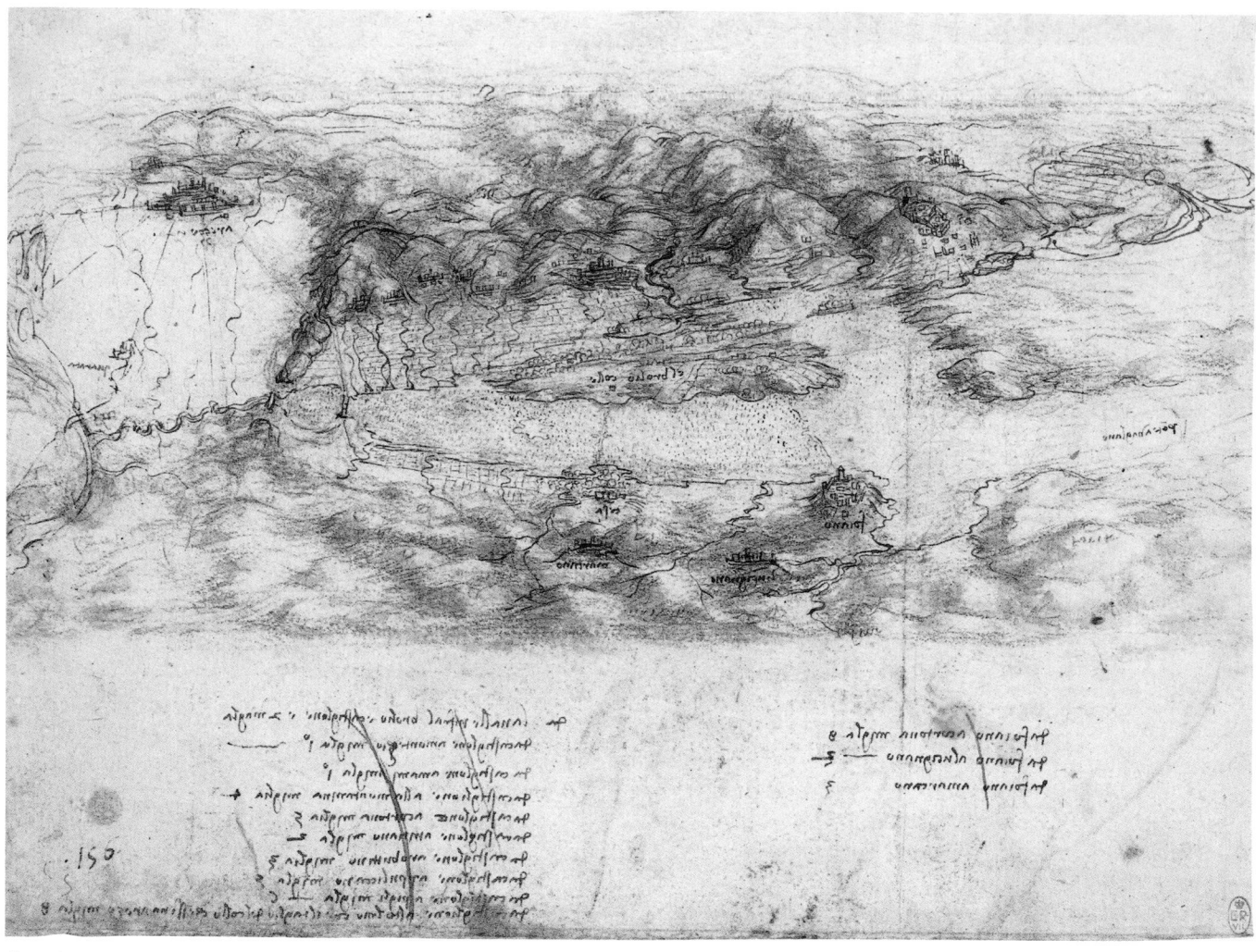

Cat. 78

This expressive preliminary study was probably intended to prepare a presentation map. The portion of territory that it portrays broadly corresponds to that seen in the upper left quadrant of a monumental map, carefully drawn in pen and brown ink with watercolor over black chalk, showing the towns of Arezzo, Borgo Sansepolcro, Perugia, Chiusi, and Siena, among others, all labeled in Leonardo's formal left-to-right script (Windsor, RL 12278). The present drawing depicts a bird's-eye view of the towns, citadels, and countryside that were part of the much-disputed dominions of the Republic of Florence, the Republic of Siena, and the states of the Church (the modern-day regions of Tuscany and the Marches). Scholars have often agreed with Edmondo Solmi's hypothesis that Leonardo produced this topographical drawing for a military purpose, following the revolts of Arezzo and the Val di Chiana against Florentine domination, which began on June 4, 1502

(at the instigation of the vengeful Vitelozzo Vitelli, captain of Cesare Borgia's army). Leonardo became military engineer to Cesare Borgia "Il Valentino" (1475–1507), duke of Valentinois and captain general of the papal armies, perhaps as early as May 1502, but he certainly served him in this capacity by August 18, 1502, and worked closely with Vitelli. The artist labeled many of the sites. The view is from Arezzo (inscribed at upper left) and Quarata (near the center of the left border), looking across the large lake of Chiana toward the center, and as far southwest as Lucignano and Foiano (near the center of the lower border). Nearby, the towns of Cesa and Marciano are also designated, and toward the extreme right is Ponte a Vagliare (*ponte auaglano*). These were strategic sites in Cesare Borgia's military campaigns from 1501 to 1503. Alternatively the drawing has been identified with Leonardo's ambitious plan to transform the huge, marshy valley of Chiana into an artificial lake that was to

472

serve as a retention basin. The drawing technique of pen and ink with wash over charcoal or soft black chalk is generally consistent with a date about 1502 to 1504.

Here Leonardo reworked the spirited underdrawing—full of repeated outlines, especially in the rivers—with pen and ink to finalize the form, adding the towns and citadels in sketchy strokes of pen and ink. Below the topographical view, the notes in two columns of text give the distance in miles (*miglie*) from Foiano and Castiglion Fiorentino (two critical stations for Cesare Borgia's armies) to other towns and citadels; these notes are canceled with slashes, presumably because they represent content that the artist had already addressed (he may have transcribed them to the final presentation map, or he may have discussed them with his patron). He hardly rendered the plain of Arezzo stretching along the left border of the sheet, or the lake of Chiana toward the right, focusing the tonal calibration instead on the magnificent ranges of hills and mountains surrounding the lake at the center of the sheet. The drawing noticeably compresses and foreshortens the geography of the sites. Some proportional imprecision is to be expected in a rough preliminary study (which was probably measured by pacing the distances), and also in a drawing that was done long before the development of refined instrumentation and cartographic projection methods in the seventeenth century. A similar list of measured distances dealing with the same area is found in the Paris Ms. L (fol. 94v), a manuscript that Leonardo is known to have used during his service for Cesare Borgia. Another related representation of the Val di Chiana occurs in the Codex Atlanticus (fol. 918r [formerly fol. 336r]).   CCB

LEONARDO DA VINCI

79. *Map of the River Arno*

Charcoal or soft black chalk, reworked with pen and dark brown ink, brush with brown wash and some gray wash, 334 × 482 mm (13 3/16 × 19 in.)

Inscribed in pen and brown ink, in right-to-left script, on recto with names of towns and geographic sites, and with columns of text; at upper left: *no[n] sanno p[er]che arno / no[n] stara [?] mai in cana / nale [canale] — —p[er]che i fiumi che vi mettano / nella loro entrata po[n] / ga[no] terreno e dallu [op]po / sita parte leuano e / pieganvi il fiume*; bottom left. *6 / miglia si fa p[cr] ar / no [Arno] dalla caprona a lli / vorno [Livorno] e 12 si fa p[er] li stagni che s ava[n]zano 32 miglia e 16 dallacaprona [Caprona] in su che fa[n] 48 p[er] arno da fire[n]ze / avanzasi 16 miglia / a vico miglia 16 / e l canale a 5*; to right of upper left corner: *Il minor fiume che mette nel magore / isscarica nella p[er]chussione dj quella il suo ca / richo e cosi spigne la sua argine inuer / rso il mezo del fiume magore ella* [crossed out: *o(n)dadjtio/ne*] *p[er]chussione desso fiume mjnore fa piegare / lacque del magore alloposita riua e cosi la / piega e consuma——*; at center of upper border: *cor[so dac]qua torbida e / adu[n]que [l]acqua . darno no[n] uale*; at center of bottom border: *da firenze a fucecchio miglia 40 per acq[u]ᵃ darno* [a calculation to the right]; toward center of right border: *miglia 56 . p[er]arno [Arno] da fire[n]ze a vicho—/ e pel canale di pisstoia e miglia 44 . adu[n] / que e piv chorta 12 miglia p[er] canale che p[er] arno*; in pen and brown ink toward lower center by later hand: *190*

Lent by Her Majesty Queen Elizabeth II, Royal Library, Windsor Castle 12279

LITERATURE: Richter 1883, vol. 2, p. 229, no. 1006 n.; Baratta 1905b, pl. 2; Seidlitz 1909, vol. 2, p. 96; Seidlitz 1911, p. 288, no. 819; Commissione Vinciana 1928– , 1940–70, pp. 38–39, pl. 5; Royal Academy of Arts 1952, p. 232; Castelfranco 1955b, pp. 56–58; Castelfranco 1966, p. 158, fig. 75; Clark and Pedretti 1968–69, vol. 1, pp. 5–6, no. 12279; Clark 1969–70, p. 19, no. 77; Heydenreich 1974b, p. 145, fig. 145/2; Zammattio 1980, p. 471; Galluzzi 1987, p. 344; Kemp and Roberts 1989, p. 111, no. 49; Clayton 1996–97, pp. 101–2, no. 55; Galuzzi 1996, pp. 71, 76, fig. 74; Arasse 1998, pp. 210, 213, fig. 151; Bambach 1999a, p. 308.

During the siege of Pisa in 1503–4, the Florentines sought to deprive their enemy of direct access to the sea by diverting the Arno River, bypassing Pisa via canalization. The ambitious, costly idea was favored above all by the statesman Niccolò Machiavelli (who would be the chief magistrate signing Leonardo's revised contract for the *Battle of Anghiari* cartoon in May 1504, as will be discussed). Francesco

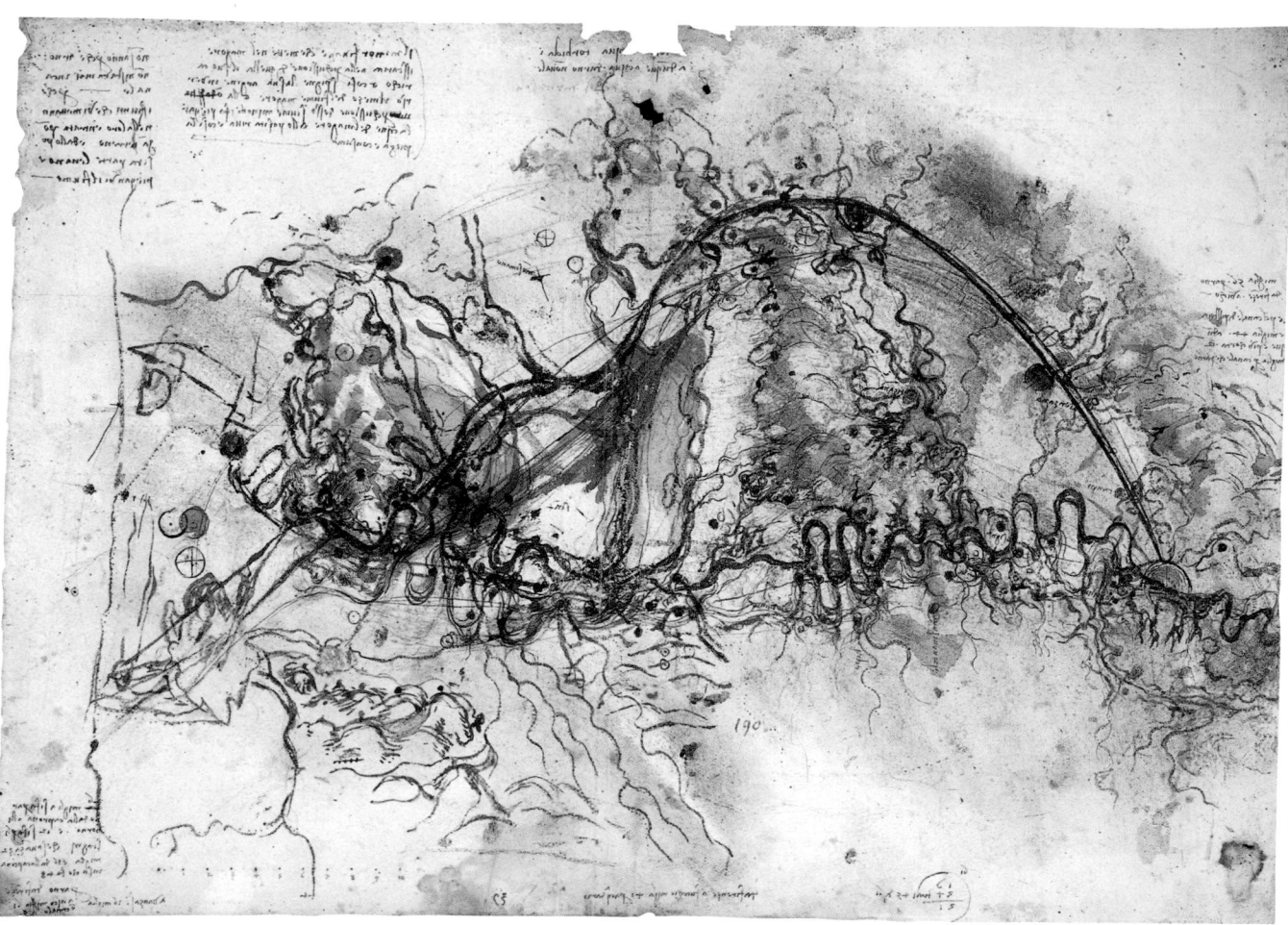

Cat. 79

Guicciardini, Machiavelli's rival in the arena of Florentine politics, later described the reasons for diverting the Arno, as well as the idea's shortcomings in his *History of Italy* (written in 1537–40). With the exquisitely pragmatic irony that the Florentines—then and now—are famous for, he wrote, "But this enterprise which was begun with the greatest hope and carried on with even greater expenses, proved to be in vain: because as often happens, although such-like projects may be almost palpably demonstrated in the measured plans, yet experience will find them failing (which is the most certain proof of how great a distance there is between planning things and putting them in operation)."[1] Guicciardini might well have been describing Leonardo's inspired but impractical designs, though he never mentioned the artist by name.

Leonardo's spirited map of the Arno in pen and ink and washes is full of pentimenti in the charcoal or soft black chalk underdrawing and was probably prepared largely on-site. It can generally be dated on the basis of style and technique in 1502–4, like catalogue number 78; in June 1503, Leonardo stayed at the Camposanto in Pisa to work out the problem of diverting the Arno. The present drawing is quite messy in appearance, as is typical of a working draft. The outlines of the intricately meandering path of the river and its arteries are pricked rather freely with a needle or stylus and are rubbed with carbon pouncing dust for transfer to another sheet of paper, which presumably served for drawing a final presentation draft of the map for the patron. The simple arched path of the proposed canal is seen toward the top of the sheet.   CCB

1. Translation quoted from Guicciardini 1984, pp. 185–86.

474

LEONARDO DA VINCI

80. *Map of the Arno and Mugnone Rivers to the West of Florence*

Pen and brown ink, brush with blue and green watercolor, 442 × 241 mm (17$\frac{7}{16}$ × 9½ in.)

Inscribed in pen and brown ink, in conventional left-to-right script, on recto (from top to bottom, left to right): *1000 / sardj / gna / porta al prato / f. mvgnone; Isola lu[n]gha / b[raccia] 1600 . ellargha / b[raccia] 700 ellacq^a che / la spicha dj legna / ia e lu[n]gha b[raccia] 2300; po[n]te alle mosse / f. rifredj / N; casa dj ser ama[n]zo; [crossed out: 13] 1300 / b[raccia] e quj largho / il renaio cholle 2 / largeze de ramj / darno — — / M; Lisola . M . he staiora / 825 che a 10 f[iorini] lo stu [io] / vale f[iorini] 8250 el simj / le djcho dellisola . N .; backward S; da . S . alla pesscaia / dognj santj son . b[raccia]. 5000 / c[i]oe vn mjglo e 2/3 — —; peretola / se sara fattj 3 fossj picho / lj i quali sastendjno da . S . / alla uolta dj sotto darno e[l] / fiume corera si forte che abandone/[ra]*; in pen and brown ink by another hand, toward center right: *167*

Watermark: Eagle inscribed within a circle (not in Briquet)

Lent by Her Majesty Queen Elizabeth II, Royal Library, Windsor Castle 126781

PROVENANCE: Windsor Leoni volume: 1519, Francesco Melzi, Milan and Rome (1491/93 ca. 1570); ca. 1570, Orazio Melzi; by 1590, Pompeo Leoni, Madrid and Milan (ca. 1533–1608; Lugt under 2885); ca. 1613, Thomas Howard, second earl of Arundel (1586–1646); before 1690, British Royal Collection (inventory of King George III's collection, ca. 1810).

LITERATURE: Rouvèyre 1901, *Can.* 1; Baratta 1905b, *Arno*, fig. 1; Seidlitz 1911, p. 288, no. 814; Commissione Vinciana 1928– , 1941 70, p. 39, pl. 7; Gantner 1958, p. 157; Clark and Pedretti 1968–69, vol. 1, p. 168, no. 12678; Sacco 1980, p. 466; Vezzosi 1982, pp. 94–95, fig. 136; Kemp and Roberts 1989, p. 110, no. 48; Clayton 1996–97, pp. 103–5, no. 57; Bambach 1999a, p. 308.

This vigorously drawn map in color, which Leonardo inscribed with names and distances in a conventional left-to-right script, shows the stretch of the Arno River immediately to the west of Florence and between that city and the town of Peretola. This was the key area in Leonardo's and the Florentine Republic's efforts to make the Arno a navigable waterway connecting Florence to the sea. The inscribed text orients the design upright rather than sideways (Leonardo thought of the Arno as being "above and below" Florence), and the city of Florence (not depicted) lies, therefore, toward the upper border of the sheet, from the center to the left. The large inscribed letters "N" and "S" are not directionals but

identification points for a discussion of the price and the measurements of distance in the text. The city's thirteenth-century western gate—the Porta al Prato—is labeled toward the upper left, with the Mugnone River (a tributary of the Arno) also clearly labeled nearby. The Rifredi River (another tributary) and the Ponte alle Mosse appear halfway down toward the left border, and the town of Peretola toward the lower left. Leonardo portrayed the wide riverbed of the Arno by leaving the white of the paper blank (which at first glance can be deceptive); he colored the complex curves of the river's actual stream in blue and the surrounding countryside in green.

Although more expressive, the drawing style and technique of the map are closely similar to those of the large plan in watercolor of the city of Imola (Windsor, RL 12284) done by Leonardo in 1502 for Cesare Borgia. The present map is usually associated with hydraulic projects on the Arno River that Leonardo undertook in 1504, probably at the commission of the Florentine Republic; these are to be distinguished from the grandiose schemes of diverting the river during the siege of Pisa in 1503–4 (cat. no. 80). In his efforts to "straighten out" (*dirizare*) the curving Arno, Leonardo seems to have surveyed the riverbed between May and September 1504. He recorded his findings in the Codex Arundel (fols. 148v–149r, 271v–275r, 278r), where his dated notes are all written in conventional left-to-right script. In a schematic plan of the Arno's flow through Florence, he showed how to straighten the river into an "up and down" course (Windsor, RL 12681). He considered the hydraulic project financially rewarding, explaining in a note, "to straighten out the Arno below and above, a treasure will be put forward, at such and such a rate per acre, to whomever may wish for it."[1] The present map offers prices in fiorini in the paragraph of text on the lower right border, possibly an allusion to such financial gain. In the present map, the area of tiny dots within the two parting blue streams of the Arno, just by the Mugnone River (toward the upper center), represents the silt or sediment deposits at the mouth of the tributary, a problem Leonardo studied and alluded to specifically in the notes on a companion map (Windsor, RL 12679). At this time, he seems to have observed closely the problems with the existing embankment and

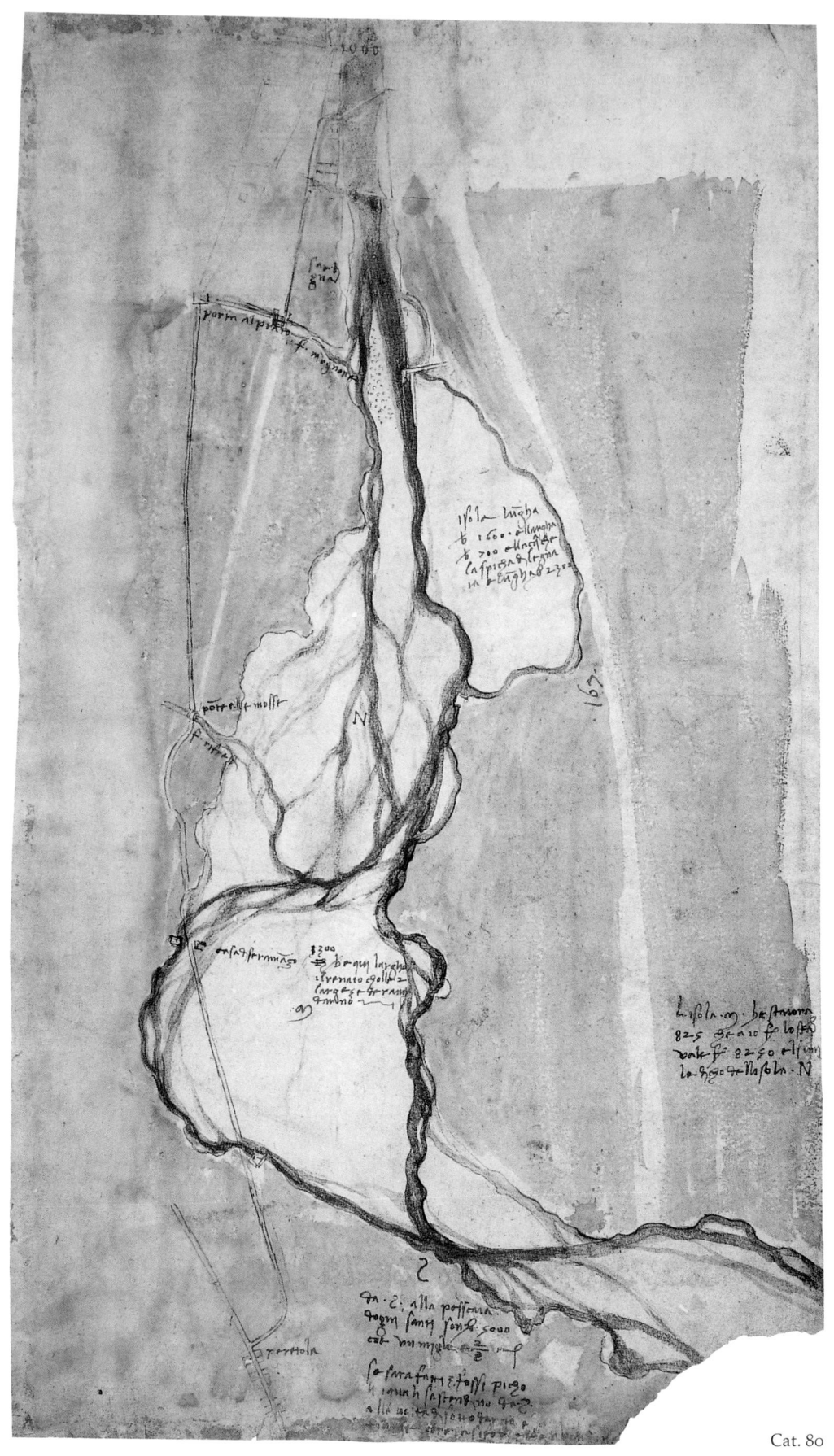

Cat. 80

system of weirs used to narrow the Arno's flow as it entered Florence (the river's flooding has posed an age-old threat to the city), recording the damage to the walls in detailed drawings (Windsor, RL 12680, 12679).

As may be true of those maps, Leonardo probably intended the present map not so much as a proposal for a project but as a record of the existing topography of the river, to be of use to his employers in the practical management of the waterway (hence his conventional left-to-right script). He must have considered it the clean, presentation draft of the design, for it synthesized the information that he had gathered in preliminary sketches and notes, including those in red chalk and pen

and ink in the Codex Arundel (fols. 149r, 272–75, 278r). A boldly drawn, precisely constructed working draft for the present map (Windsor, RL 12677) details the same geographic area in the same scale; it is possible that Leonardo traced the sketch map to obtain the clean presentation map here. Full of functional notation, the working draft is drawn in pen and ink over an underdrawing in charcoal, a preliminary stylus-ruled construction, and a framework of pinpricked measurements.

CCB

1. C.A. fol. 785br (formerly fol. 289r-e); transcribed in Clark and Pedretti 1968–69, vol. 1, p. 168: "Dirizare Arno di sotto e di sopra s'avanzera un tesoro, a tanto per istaioro a chi lo vole."

LEONARDO DA VINCI

81. *Two Skirmishes between Horsemen and Foot Soldiers*

Pen and brown ink, brush and brown wash, over traces of stylus (?), 147×154 mm ($5\frac{3}{4} \times 6\frac{1}{16}$ in.)

Inscribed in pen and brown ink, in right-to-left script, on verso: *rio . . . que[s]te fie[n] piu propi[n]qui al mezo dessa corda——/ Gienerasi la potentia . del moto dentro ai motori . de corpi gravi . p[er] 3 djverse cause / delle quali . la prima* [crossed out: *dell'altre 2*] *e chausatrice laltre 2 da cquesta son causate // la / causale e quella che ssi trova ne corpi animatj;* below, near figure of five balls on curving stick: *Segna queste pallotte colnumero o alfabeto e ffa che / nel lor[o] fugire terminjno il lor[o] moto sop[r]a del fango o nneve / ma ffalle illoco alto a cio che lla p[er]cussione sia fatta dal discienso / p[er]pe[n]diculare delle ballotte / ogni potentia di gravita motiva da charestia e dovitia con equal tenpo* ^nate he ^*opositame[n]te /* [crossed out: *se gie son gienerate*] *situate e gienerata e con equal te[m]po e co[n]sumata / con equal tenpo opositame[n]te nate e gienerate;* below, near figure of balls falling: *generasi la potentia . del moto . dentro ai motori de corpi gravi p[er] 3 djverse cause / delle quale la prima e ssensibile . la 2ª insensibile determinata la terza e insensibile / indeterminata / sono i motori de corpi gravi di 3 varie nature delle quali la prima e de corpi animati / e ssensibili la 2ª e de corpi insensibili determinati la 3ª e de corpi insensibili / de indeterminata figura . le 3 dette pote[n]tie movano i corpi po[n]derosi p[er] 2 djverse / cause delle quali luna he detta attratione [attrazione] laltra [crossed out: remo ?] discacciatrice quella che / attrae asse i pesi [crossed out: sol per care] sol da carestia e neciessitata . quella che djscaccia da sse tali / corpi da sop[r] [a]bondanzia e cosstretta* Gallerie dell'Accademia, Venice 215 A

PROVENANCE: Cardinal Cesare Monti, Milan (1635–1650); Contessa Anna Luisa Monti, Milan; 1770, Venanzio de Pagave, Milan; his son Gaudenzio de Pagave; ca. 1808 or before, Giuseppe Bossi, Milan and Venice (1777–1815; album marked K); auction, Milan, February 1818, II; February 24, 1818, purchase by Abbate Luigi Celotti [Cellotti], Venice (1765–1846); in deposit (under custody of Carlo Porta and Nicola Cassoni) Accademia di Belle Arti, Milan; 1820–22, proposal of purchase of Bossi's collection from Celotti submitted to Austrian government on behalf of Accademia delle Belle Arti, Venice; 1822, purchase by Franz I (Habsburg), emperor of Austria, Florence and Vienna (1768–1835), for Accademia delle Belle Arti, Venice; ca. 1832 manuscript inventory; December 31, 1870, manuscript inventory; museum stamp (Lugt 188).

LITERATURE: Selvatico 1854, frame 5, no. 4; Richter 1883, vol. 1, pp. 337, 339–40, pl. 55; Uzielli 1884, p. 278, no. 20; Müntz 1898, vol. 2, p. 141 (detail); Berenson 1903, vol. 2, p. 61, no. 1098; Seidlitz 1909, vol. 2, p. 80; Fogolari 1913, p. 14; Meller 1916, p. 238; Poggi 1919, pl. 96; Venturi 1920, p. 134, fig. 116; De Rinaldis 1926, p. 210, fig. 53; Popp 1928, p. 47, no. 52; Sirén 1928, p. 139, pl. 174B; Suida 1929, fig. 153; Bodmer 1931, pp. 294, 410; Berenson 1938, vol. 2, p. 122, no. 1098; Palazzo dell'Arte 1939, p. 151; Venturi 1942, fig. 63; Giglioli 1944, pl. 96; Commissione Vinciana 1928– , vol. 6, p. 24, pl. 256.2; Heydenreich 1949, pl. 9; Neufeld 1949, pp. 176–82, fig. 2; Biblioteca Medicea Laurenziana 1952, no. 56; Goldscheider 1952, fig. 138; Pedretti 1953, pp. 282–83; Castelfranco 1954b, p. 457, pl. 168, fig. 10 (incorrect inv. no.); Gould 1954b, p. 124, fig. 16; Heydenreich 1954, vol. 1, p. 45, vol. 2, p. 47, fig. 58; Castelfranco 1956, p. 60, pl. 74; Goldscheider 1959, p. 179, pl. 109; Barocchi, Forlani, and Fossi Todorow 1961, no. 28; Berenson 1961, vol. 2, p. 216, no. 1098; Cogliati Arano 1966–67, pp. 27–28, no. 16, fig. 20; Pedretti 1968b, fig. 50; Richter 1970, vol. 1, p. 376, pl. 55; Gould 1975, pp. 136, 138, fig. 74; De Toni 1979, pp. 16–21; Keele and Pedretti 1979–80, vol. 2, p. 839; Cogliati Arano 1980, pp. 42–43, no. 13 (with transcriptions by

Augusto Marinoni); Lavagnino 1980, p. 129; Kemp 1981, pp. 240–41, 245, pl. 66; Hochstetler 1984, pp. 367 n. 4, 368, fig. 2; Meller 1985, pp. 134–35, fig. 65; Pedretti 1987a, pp. 19, 86, 89, fig. 96; Clark 1988, pp. 192–96; Joannides 1988, p. 85; Marani 1989, pp. 132–35, under no. 8A, fig. 32; Wasserman 1990, fig. 58; Giovanna Nepi Scirè in Palazzo Grassi 1992, pp. 258–61, nos. 28–28a; Farago 1994, pp. 301–10; Popham 1994, no. 192B; Cecchi and Natali 1996, pp. 106–7, under no. 17; Arasse 1998, pp. 438, 440–41, fig. 298; Giovanna Nepi Scirè in Nepi Scirè and Torrini 1999, pp. 70–75, no. 20.

LEONARDO DA VINCI

82. *Skirmish between Horsemen and Foot Soldiers; Foot Soldiers Wielding Long Weapons*

Pen and brown ink, over black chalk and traces of stylus (?), 164 × 152 mm (6 $\frac{7}{16}$ × 6 $\frac{1}{16}$ in.)

Inscribed in pen and brown ink, in right-to-left script, on verso: *Sono e motori de corpi gravi di tre varie nature delle quali . la prima / he de corpi anjmatj . e ssensibilj . la 2ᵃ e de corpi . insensibilj . di termi-nata / figura 3ᵃ he de corpi insensibili* [crossed out: *de diterminati*] *de figura indeterminata / Le 3 varie* [crossed out: *potentie*] *nature de corpi nelle quali sinclude la pote[n]tia motrice de corpi / gravi sol p[er] 2 diverse cause in se gienerano la pote[n]tia* [crossed out: *del moto*] *motiva delle quali luna / e detta . carestia laltra sop[r]a bon-dante e nominata queste 2 cause* [crossed out: *di moto / locale*] *dj pote[n]tia motiva gieneratricj .* [crossed out: *p*] *sol p[er] 2* [crossed out: *vie*] *co[n]trarie vie adop[er]ano loro / pote[n]tie, co[i]e luna e attrattiva . laltra scacciatrice e nomjnata lattrattiva / e creata dalla pote[n]tia . della carestia . la scaciatrice dalla sop[r]a bonantia e gienerata* [crossed out: *le 2 dette*] *ciasscuna delle 2 pote[n]tie . p[er] 3 diverse linie puo* [crossed out: *ade*] *movere i sua / mobili . delle quali la prima e retta . la 2ᵃ e obbliqua . la 3ᵃ e curva dj queste / 3 linje di moti . puo nasscire 3 varie* ˡⁱⁿⁱᵉ [crossed out: *moti cioe nella retta perpendiculare nasscie/ra senplice moto*] *puo nasscire 4 vari moti delli quali luno e se[m]plice naturale / il 2° e semplice violente il 3°* [crossed out: *e misto co*] *e naturale viole[n]te* [crossed out: *cioe misto*] *il se[m]plice / naturale . cade p[er] la linja retta p[er]pe[n]diculare el senplice violente sinalza p[er] la / medesima linja p[er]pe[n]diculare el 3° natural v[i]olente discie[n]de p[er] la / retta obliqua e p[er] la / curva el quarto e violente composto* [crossed out: *che si va*] *si leva per la linia obliqua e per la / curva j motori de pesi sol p[er] due vie scacciano ottirano a sse e corpi gravi / luna . el mo bile e congiunto col motore insino al fine del moto . lal-tra* [crossed out: *subito si*] */ disgiun*[crossed out: *gie*]ᵗᵒ *cacia[n] o ttira[n] a sse il mo bile come la calamjta o bo[m]barta inoposito \\ / puossi gienerare il moto pel mobile* [reconstructed: *per 3 diverse*] Gallerie dell'Accademia, Venice 215

PROVENANCE: Cardinal Cesare Monti, Milan (1635–1650); Contessa Anna Luisa Monti, Milan; 1770, Venanzio de Pagave, Milan; his son Gaudenzio de Pagave; ca. 1808 or before, Giuseppe Bossi, Milan and Venice (1777–1815; album marked K); auction, Milan, February 1818, II; February 24, 1818, purchase by Abbate Luigi Celotti [Cellotti], Venice (1765–1846); in deposit (under custody of Carlo Porta and Nicola Cassoni) Accademia di Belle Arti, Milan; 1820–22, proposal of purchase of Bossi's collection from Celotti submitted to Austrian government on behalf of Accademia delle Belle Arti, Venice; 1822, purchase by Franz I (Habsburg), emperor of Austria, Florence and Vienna (1768–1835), for Accademia delle Belle Arti, Venice; ca. 1832 manuscript inventory; December 31, 1870, manuscript inventory; museum stamp (Lugt 188).

LITERATURE: Selvatico 1854, frame 5, no. 9; Richter 1883, vol. 1, p. 336, pl. 54; Uzielli 1884, p. 280, no. 25; Müntz 1899, p. 409; Berenson 1903, vol. 2, p. 61, no. 1097; Loeser 1903, p. 183; Seidlitz 1909, vol. 2, p. 80, fig. 86; Fogolari 1913, no. 12; Meller 1916, p. 236; Poggi 1919, pl. 95; Popp 1928, pp. 24, 47, no. 53; Bodmer 1931, pp. 296, 410–11; Berenson 1938, vol. 2, p. 122, no. 1097; Venturi 1942, fig. 62; Giglioli 1944, pl. 97; Commissione Vinciana 1928– , vol. 6, p. 24, pl. 256.1; Heydenreich 1949, pl. 10; Neufeld 1949, pp. 175, 181, fig. 3; Biblioteca Medicea Laurenziana 1952, p. 40, no. 57; Castelfranco 1952b, pl. 24; Goldscheider 1952, fig. 138; Castelfranco 1954, p. 457, pl. 169, fig. 12; Gould 1954a, p. 123, fig. 9; Heydenreich 1954, vol. 1, p. 45, vol. 2, p. 47, pl. 59; Goldscheider 1959, p. 179, pl. 110; Berenson 1961, vol. 2, pp. 215, 216, no. 1097; Castelfranco 1966, p. 114, 195, fig. 76; Cogliati Arano 1966–67, pp. 26–27, no. 15, fig. 17; Pedretti 1968a, fig. 49; Richter 1970, vol. 1, p. 375, pl. 54; Gould 1975, pp. 138, 141, fig. 75; Cogliati Arano 1980, pp. 38–39, no. 11 (with transcriptions by Augusto Marinoni); Lavagnino 1980, p. 129; Kemp 1981, pp. 240–41, 245, pl. 66; Hochstetler 1984, pp. 367 n. 4, 368, fig. 1; Meller 1985, pp. 134–35, fig. 64; Pedretti 1987a, pp. 75, 79, 84, fig. 94; Clark 1988, pp. 192–96, fig. 80; Joannides 1988, p. 85, fig. 18; Rosand 1988, pp. 29–30, fig. 36; Kemp 1989a, pp. 228–33; Marani 1989, pp. 132–35, under no. 8A, fig. 33; Zöllner 1991, p. 189 n. 78, fig. 16; Giovanna Nepi Scirè in Palazzo Grassi 1992, pp. 262–63, nos. 29–29a; Paolo Spezzani in Palazzo Grassi 1992, p. 184; Farago 1994, pp. 301–10; Popham 1994, no. 194; Cecchi and Natali 1996, pp. 106–7, under no. 17; Farago 1997, pp. 13–14, fig. 1; Zöllner 1997, pp. 11, 31, no. 1, pl. 1; Arasse 1998, pp. 319–20, fig. 217; Giovanna Nepi Scirè in Nepi Scirè and Torrini 1999, pp. 70–71, 76–79, no. 21.

LEONARDO DA VINCI

83. *Fight for the Standard at the Bridge and Two Foot Soldiers*

Pen and brown ink, 99 × 141 mm (3 $^{15}/_{16}$ × 5 $^9/_{16}$ in.)
Gallerie dell'Accademia, Venice 216

PROVENANCE: Cardinal Cesare Monti, Milan (1635–1650); Contessa
Anna Luisa Monti, Milan; 1770, Venanzio de Pagave, Milan; his son
Gaudenzio de Pagave; ca. 1808 or before, Giuseppe Bossi, Milan and
Venice (1777–1815; album marked K); auction, Milan, February
1818, II; February 24, 1818, purchase by Abbate Luigi Celotti
[Cellotti], Venice (1765–1846); in deposit (under custody of Carlo
Porta and Nicola Cassoni) Accademia di Belle Arti, Milan; 1820–22,
proposal of purchase of Bossi's collection from Celotti submitted to
Austrian government on behalf of Accademia delle Belle Arti,
Venice; 1822, purchase by Franz I (Habsburg), emperor of Austria,
Florence and Vienna (1768–1835), for Accademia delle Belle Arti,
Venice; ca. 1832 manuscript inventory; December 31, 1870, manu-
script inventory; museum stamp (Lugt 188).

LITERATURE: Richter 1883, vol. 1, p. 336, pl. 53; Uzielli 1884, p. 282,
no. 34; Müller-Walde 1899, pp. 95, 109, 113–14; Berenson 1903,
vol. 2, p. 61, no. 1096; Loeser 1903, p. 183; Seidlitz 1909, vol. 2, pp. 66,
80; Commissione Vinciana 1928– , vol. 6, p. 24, pl. 256.4; Popp 1928,
p. 47, no. 54; Suida 1929, p. 143, fig. 154; Popham 1930–31, no. 83;
Bodmer 1931, pp. 295, 410; Clark 1935, p. 29; Berenson 1938, vol. 2,
p. 122, no. 1096; Giglioli 1944, pl. 95; Heydenreich 1949, pl. 11;
Neufeld 1949, pp. 171–83, fig. 4; Biblioteca Medicea Laurenziana
1952, p. 40, no. 58; Goldscheider 1952, fig. 140; Gould 1954a, p. 22,
fig. 5; Berenson 1961, vol. 2, p. 215, no. 1096; Cogliati Arano 1966–67,
p. 26, no. 14, fig. 21; Pedretti 1968a, fig. 60; Richter 1970, vol. 1, p. 375,
pl. 53; Gould 1975, pp. 136–37, fig. 71; Cogliati Arano 1980, p. 45,
no. 14; Lavagnino 1980, p. 132; Kemp 1981, p. 245; Rosci 1982, pp. 129,
144; Hochstetler 1984, pp. 367 n. 4, 368, fig. 3; Meller 1985, p. 133,
fig. 63; Pedretti 1987a, pp. 87–88, fig. 97; Clark 1988, pp. 192–96;
Joannides 1988, pp. 80, 85, fig. 17; Agghàzy 1989, p. 51, fig. 53;
Marani 1989, pp. 132–35, under no. 8A; Zöllner 1991, p. 189, fig. 17;
Giovanna Nepi Scirè in Palazzo Grassi 1992, pp. 264–65, no. 30;
Farago 1994, pp. 301–10; Popham 1994, no. 193B; Cecchi and Natali
1996, pp. 106–7, under no. 17; Clayton 1996, p. 72, under no. 37;
Zöllner 1997, pp. 11, 31, no. 2, pl. 2; Arasse 1998, pp. 319–21, 438,
fig. 218; Giovanna Nepi Scirè in Nepi Scirè and Torrini 1999, pp. 70–
71, 80–81, no. 22.

These three small sheets of rapid, abstract sketches (cat.
nos. 81–83) offer *primi pensieri* (first ideas) for the
complex composition of the cartoon (full-scale drawing) of
Leonardo's lost *Battle of Anghiari*. Although fragmentary,
they provide the most important visual record of Leonardo's

intended composition, together with catalogue number 84; no
complete copy of the Anghiari composition is extant. The
Venice sketches probably formed part of the same notebook,
for two of the sheets (cat. nos. 81, 82) are inscribed with long
notes that are closely linked narratively and deal with the
mechanics of weights, a subject related to the artist's undertaking in the *Battle of Anghiari* composition, where many of
the soldiers dressed in armor would have wielded heavy
weapons in ferocious poses of combat.

About October 1503 (the exact date is not known),
Leonardo was commissioned to paint the mural of the *Battle
of Anghiari* for the Sala del Gran Consiglio, the recently
rebuilt and refurnished Great Council Hall of the Palazzo della
Signoria (today, Palazzo Vecchio) in Florence, during the city's
first years of republican government. If Giorgio Vasari's *vite*
are correct, Leonardo may even have advised the architect of
the refurbished hall, Simone Pollaiuolo "Il Cronaca," in 1494.
(See Chronology.) As most scholars agree (a rare occurrence
in the Leonardo literature), the small Venice sketches probably
date from 1503–4, soon after the artist received the *Anghiari*
commission from the *signori* of the republic. On October 24,
1503, Leonardo was given the keys to his apartment in the
Sala del Papa at the Chiostro Grande of Santa Maria Novella,
where he would live and where he would also produce the
Battle of Anghiari cartoon, but roofing and other major repairs
were being made in his work space there into January 1504.
Less than a year after Leonardo received the Anghiari commission (certainly by the late summer of 1504), Michelangelo
received the commission for his competing fresco of the *Battle
of Cascina*. The murals by the rival artists were designed to
commemorate famous Florentine military victories; although
their intended locations have been much disputed, the evidence as it presently stands suggests that they were to occupy
the politically significant west wall of the hall flanking the
seats of the *gonfaloniere di giustizia* and the *priori*,
Leonardo's to the left and Michelangelo's to the right.[1]

Scholars have made numerous attempts at reconstructing
the intended composition of the lost *Battle of Anghiari*,
beginning with Giorgio Vasari in his *vita* of Leonardo
(Florence, 1550 and 1568). The task of reconstruction seems

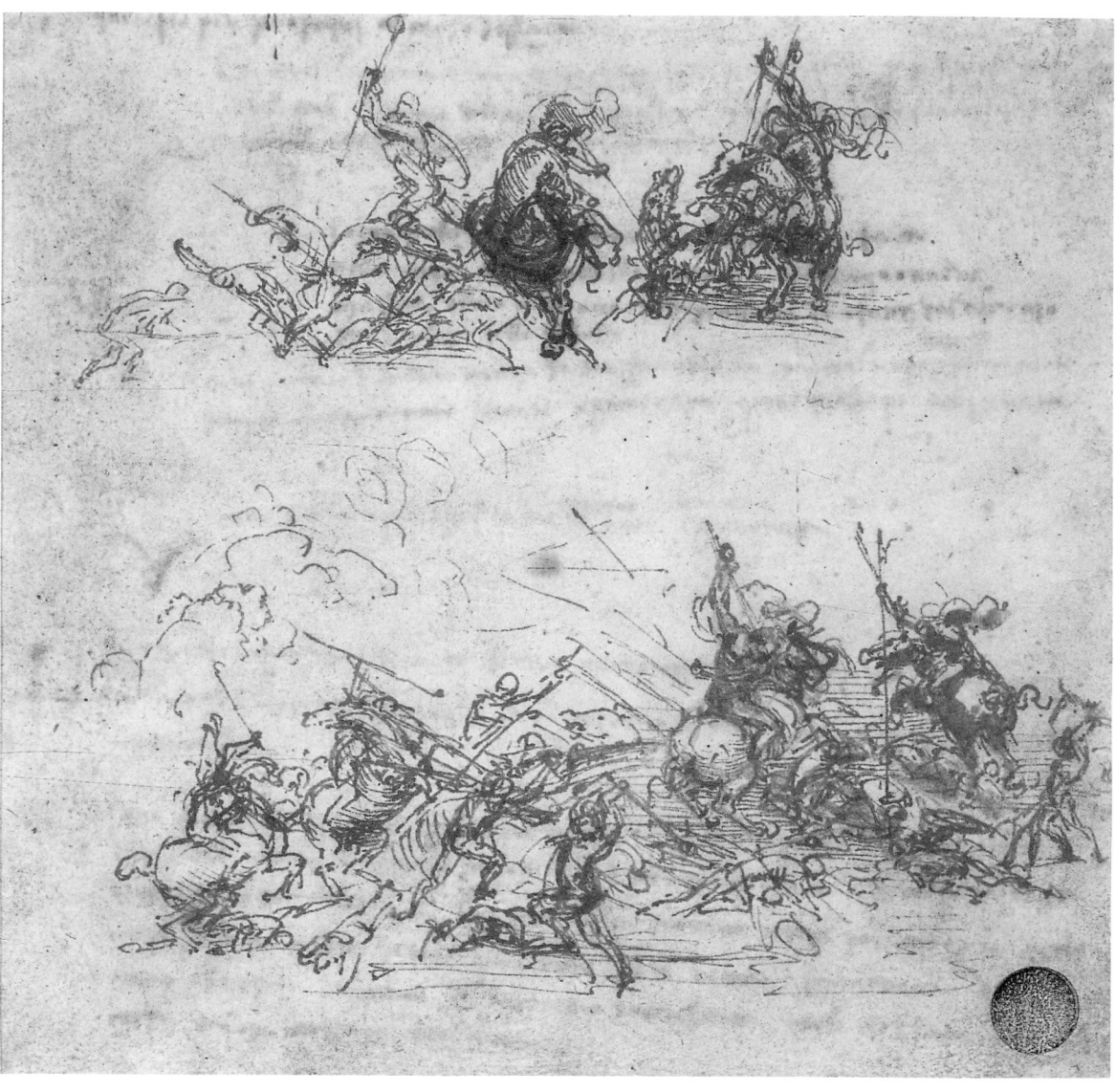

Cat. 81R *(actual size)*

quixotic, considering that Leonardo may not even have finished the composition of the cartoon before he began to paint the central section with the *Fight for the Standard.* (His revised contract of May 1504 permitted him to work in this unconventional way.) Moreover, nothing remains of the original *Anghiari* cartoon—little if anything may have been extant even in Vasari's time[2]—or of the damaged painted central section of the *Fight for the Standard* (done in an unsuccessful experimental oil technique), which Vasari covered over about 1563, when he remodeled the room and painted his own monumental fresco cycle of battle scenes from Florentine history. All that survives of Leonardo's and Michelangelo's projects are autograph partial preliminary

drawings (cat. nos. 81–91) and partial copies (cat. no. 135). With this caveat, the Venice sheets and the closely related Windsor sheet (cat. no. 84) are here arranged in a proposed reconstruction of the episodes of the composition from left to right; the present reconstruction does not drastically differ in substance from that of other scholars (fig. 19).[3]

The Venice and Windsor sketches begin to suggest the enormous scale and complexity of the *Battle of Anghiari* as a composition, as well as its dramatic impact as a story. In his evocation of the historical event, however, Leonardo seems to have ignored much that was narrated in the textual sources, other than the episode for the *Fight for the Standard.* He was apparently given a detailed account of the actual Battle of

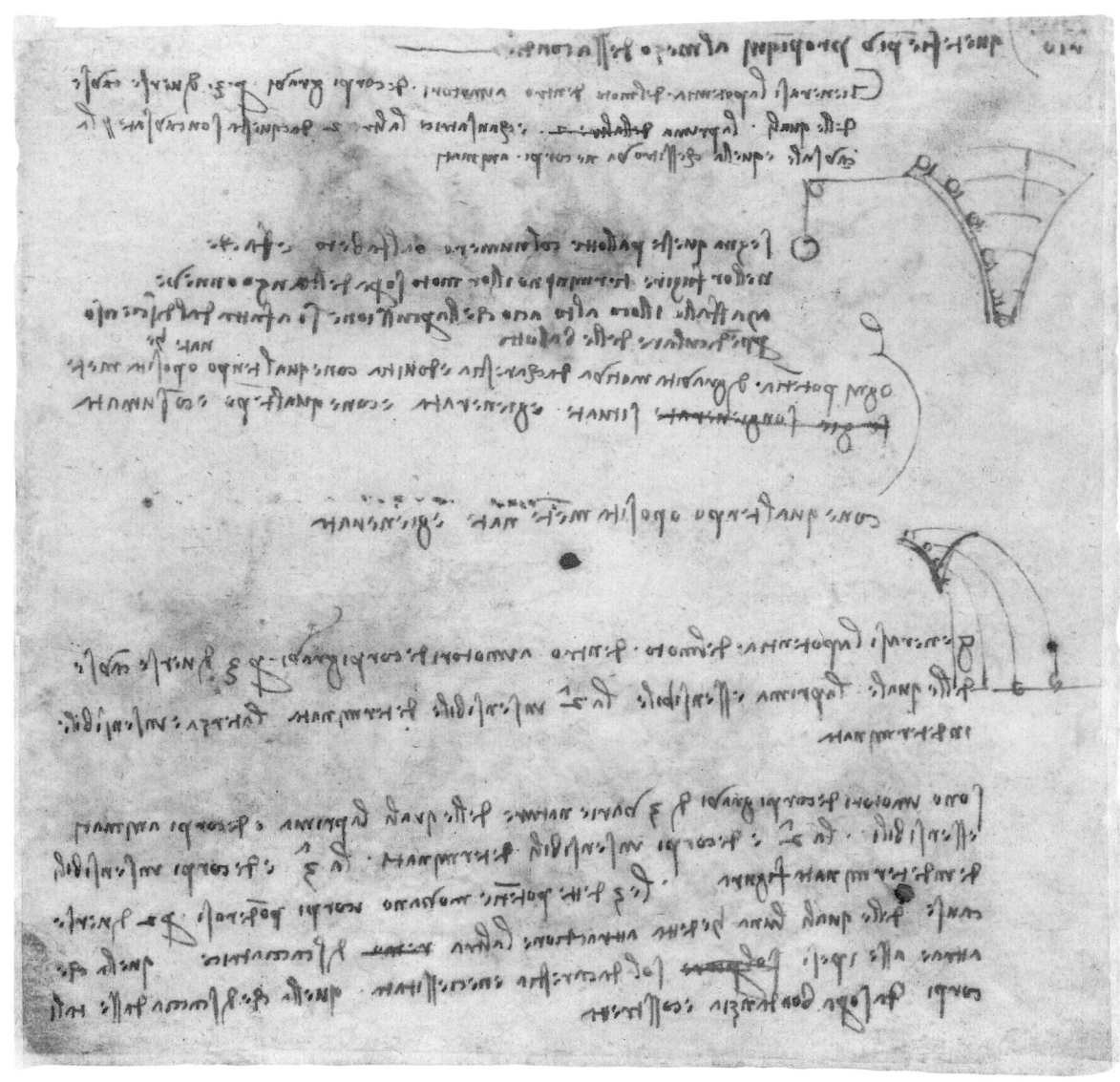

Cat. 81v *(actual size)*

Anghiari, with a list of its participants, as a guide for the iconography he was to depict, and this is preserved in a note that is not written in his hand.[4] The author of the note seems to have been a clerk of the Florentine Republic, presumably Agostino Vespucci, the secretary of Niccolò Machiavelli, who was then chancellor and was a cosigner of the revised contract of May 1504 for Leonardo's *Battle of Anghiari*. The clerk's note translated passages from Pietro Dati's *Trophaeum angelicarum*. The Florentine statesman Marcello Virgilio Adriani may also have had a hand in directing some of the political iconography in Leonardo's *Battle of Anghiari*.[5]

Early accounts of the Battle of Anghiari include Flavio Biondo's *Decades*, Neri di Gino Capponi's *Commentarii*, and

Machiavelli's own *Istorie fiorentine*.[6] As can be gathered from these sources, the historic battle was fought on June 29, 1440, in the plain of Anghiari in Tuscany, near the road that leads from Borgo Sansepolcro (a few miles east of Arezzo) to the castle of Anghiari. The victorious Florentines were commanded by Pier Giampaolo Orsini, who aided the militia of Pope Eugenius IV under the leadership of Ludovico degli Scarampi. The Milanese army was led by Niccolò Piccinino, the condottiere hired by Filippo Maria Visconti, duke of Milan. The strategic turning point in the battle occurred when the Florentines finally seized the bridge over the Tiber River (Ponte della Giustizia)—which had passed repeatedly between Florentine and Milanese hands in previous skirmishes—and

481

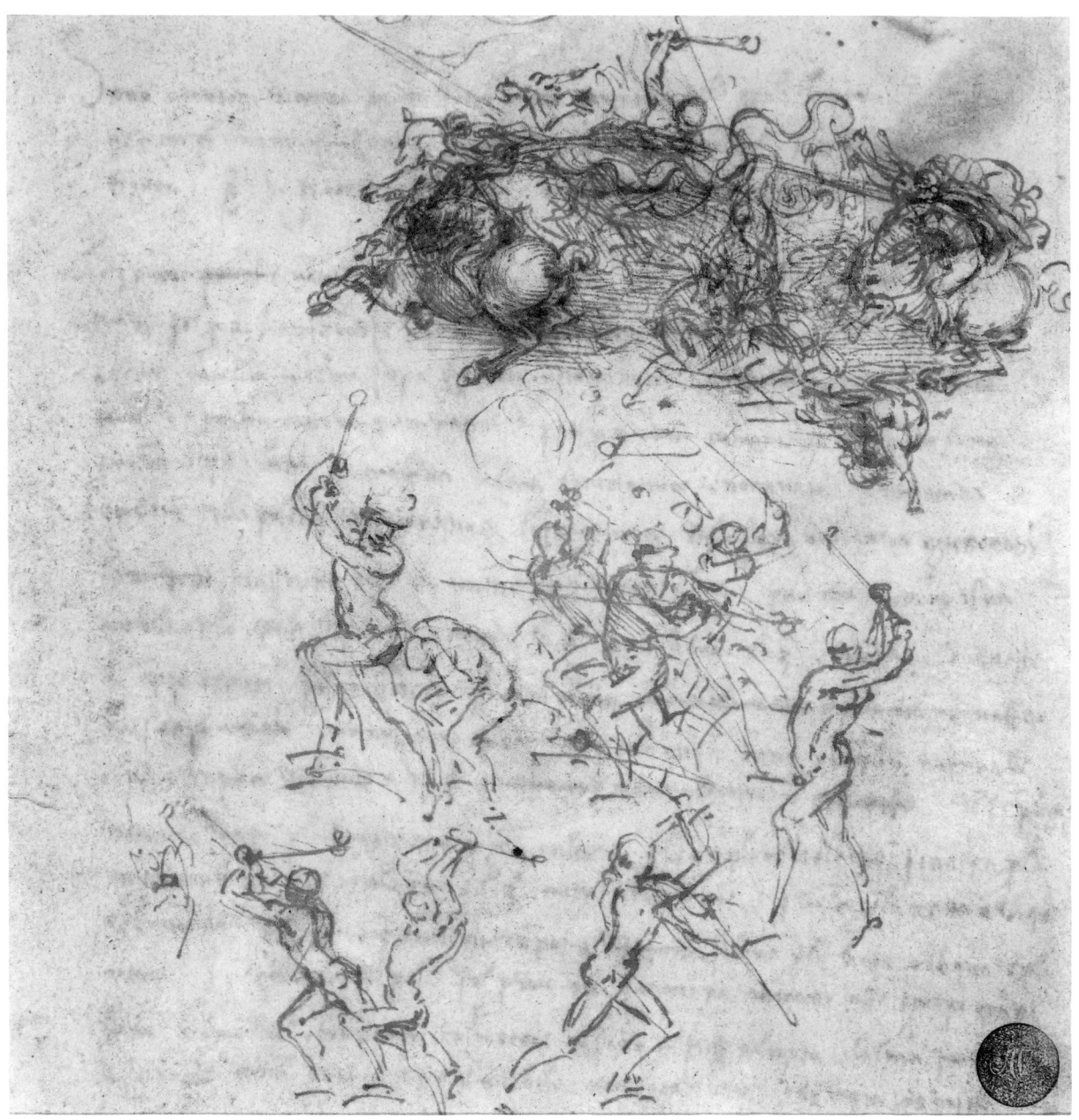

Cat. 82R *(actual size)*

forced the enormous Milanese army to retreat east toward Borgo Sansepolcro. The somewhat dry account from Dati's *Trophaeum* that is compiled with Leonardo's notes emphasizes the Florentines' valor, the imposing size of the Milanese cavalry (at least forty squadrons), the large number of Milanese foot soldiers, and the fury of the slaughter—with ferocious face-to-face combat—that ended the daylong battle. It sets the stage, though not the mood, for the artist's portrayal. For his projected painting treatise, the *Libro di pittura*, Leonardo

created his own text on "how to depict a battle" (*modo di figurare una battaglia*), describing all manner of atmospheric effects, such as the clouds of rising artillery smoke mixed with the dust-laden air, the distant puffs of ground dust from galloping horses, and the reddened faces of the musketeers in the forefront of the military action.[7]

The effects of smoke, dust, and clouds are indicated with a few deft lines on the lower left of catalogue number 81, which suggests that Leonardo considered such pictorial details of

Cat. 82v *(actual size)*

mood and setting to be an integral part of a painting, to be dealt with from the very start of the design process. The left portion of Leonardo's composition is the most problematic to reconstruct. It seems to have included a long display of charging cavalry in which a lunging horseman, as he is portrayed at the center in catalogue number 85, was a prominent and constant figure, for he also turns up in sheets of summary pen-and-ink sketches now in Turin (cat. no.103), Windsor (RL 12328), and London (British Museum, 1854-5-13-17). However, it is arguable that an abstract pen-and-ink sketch by Michelangelo (British Museum, 1895-9-15-496 recto; fig.179), which depicts charging horsemen and foot soldiers, also re-creates this passage from Leonardo's *Anghiari* composition, for it seems probable that Michelangelo intended his sketch for his own composition, the *Battle of Cascina*. The lunging horseman does not seem to appear in any of the Venice sketches, but he is seen in reverse design and faintly drawn on the upper left of the Windsor sheet (cat. no. 84). Toward the right and at the

483

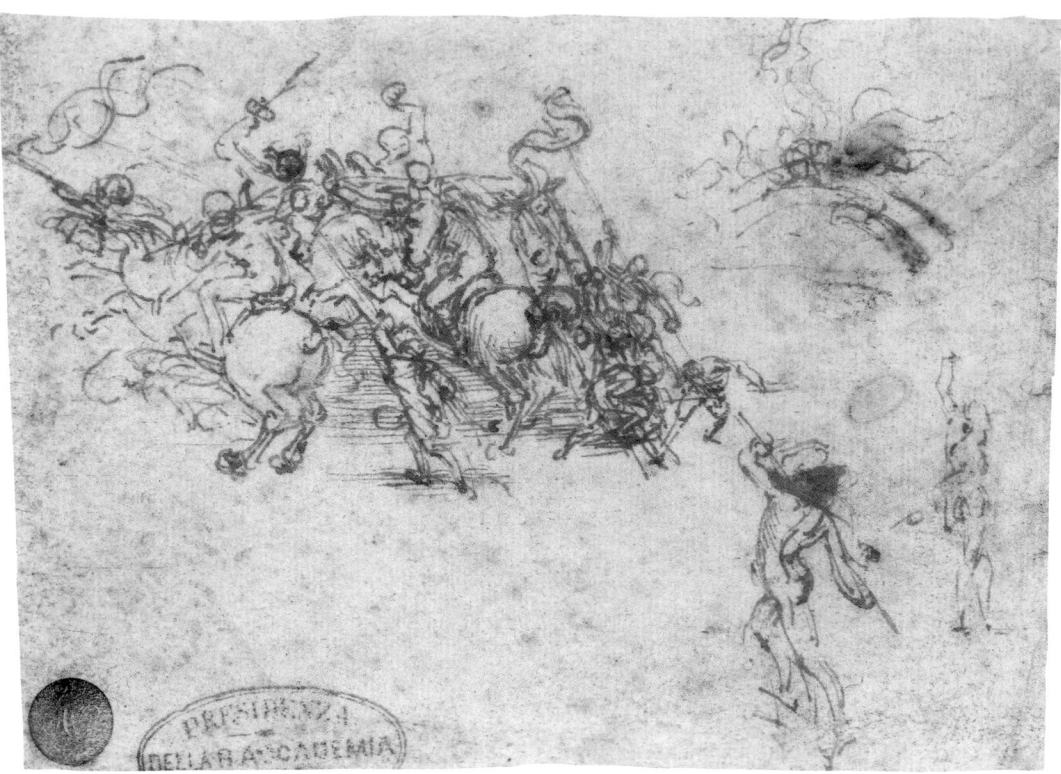

Cat. 83 *(actual size)*

center of the composition was the *Fight for the Standard* (see cat. nos. 83, 90, 91, 135; fig. 18), and farthest to the right was the taking of the bridge over the Tiber River with another flanking cavalry (cat. no. 84). The two episodes portrayed at the top and bottom of catalogue number 81 are probably meant to be seen side by side as a continuation, right to left (the direction in which the left-handed Leonardo usually drew and wrote).[8] These probably render the little-known charging cavalry in the long area to the left of the *Fight for the Standard.* The design on the top portion of catalogue number 82 seems to represent an early idea for the dazzling group of horsemen and foot soldiers in the *Fight for the Standard,* but with an expansive arrangement of the figures in their pictorial space. Leonardo then clarified this design on the top right of catalogue number 83, compressing the forms in the composition. The resulting sketch essentially represents the final design Leonardo apparently produced in the cartoon and in the section he began painting in the Sala del Gran Consiglio at the Palazzo della Signoria (fig. 18). Dating from 1505 or so, Raphael's sketchy copy after Leonardo's *Fight for the Standard* (Ashmolean Museum, Oxford) conveys the same immediacy of mark as Leonardo's Venice sketch (cat. no. 83);

that Raphael probably had access not only to Leonardo's finished designs for the *Fight* but also to the master's dazzling rapid sketches is worth pondering. On the lower right of catalogue number 83, the sketch of the foot soldier wielding a long weapon in a sinuous contrapposto pose seen from the back is an enlarged, clearer reprise of the design of the soldier seen above, striding at the lower center of the group of horses and soldiers. Catalogue number 83 also shows the slight sketch of a bridge (a crucial linking element) on the upper right, which further establishes that the group of horses and soldiers to the left of the bridge is to be identified with the *Fight for the Standard.* The choice of the *Fight for the Standard* as the focus of the composition was politically significant, because the standards of the defeated Niccolò Piccinino and the duke of Milan—which the Florentine soldiers captured in the Battle of Anghiari, as the Milanese forces retreated from the bridge over the Tiber River—were kept as trophies in the room of the *gonfaloniere di giustizia,* the chief magistrate of the Florentine Republic.[9]

However fragmentary, catalogue numbers 82 and 83 are the only autograph compositional drawings by Leonardo for the *Fight for the Standard* that are extant. The groups of foot

484

soldiers wielding long weapons at each other—seen in the lower portion of catalogue number 82—may have populated the foreground to either side of the *Fight for the Standard.* The slight sketch of the bridge on the upper right of catalogue number 83 links it to the following episode, the cavalcade on the extreme right that is the subject of catalogue number 84 (Windsor, RL 12339).

CCB

1. On the vexing question of the location of the murals in the Sala del Gran Consiglio, compare Pedretti 1968a; Kemp 1981; Travers Newton and Spencer 1983; Farago 1994; Rubinstein 1995; Cecchi 1997; Zöllner 1997; Bambach 1999b.
2. See Vasari–Milanesi 1906, vol. 4, pp. 41–43. In referring to the cartoon, Vasari described only the part of the *Battle of Anghiari* composition that Leonardo painted, *The Fight for the Standard,* rather than the actual full-scale drawing; he mentions the "old soldier in a red cap" ("soldato vecchio, con un berretton rosso"). This was the part that Vasari was familiar with, since he covered it over in remodeling the room.
3. Compare Neufeld 1949; Gould 1954a; Pedretti 1968a, fig. 61; Giovanna Nepi Scirè in Palazzo Grassi 1992, pp. 256–79; Farago 1994, pp. 301–30; and, regarding the size of the intended cartoon and mural, Wilde 1944; Isermeyer 1964 (with an incorrect reading of the documents); Bambach 1999a, pp. 39–54, 283–95; Bambach 1999b (with new archival research).
4. C.A., fols. 202ar–202bv (formerly fols. 74r-b–74r-c); Beltrami 1919a, pp. 85–87, no. 138; Richter 1970, vol. 1, pp. 381–82, no. 669; Marinoni 1975; Pedretti 1977, vol. 1, p. 381, no. 669.
5. Cecchi 1997.
6. Rubinstein 1991, pp. 275–85; Rubinstein 1995, pp. 74–75; Cecchi 1997.
7. Paris Ms. A, fols. 110v, 111r (B.N. 2038, fols. 30v, 31r); Richter 1970, vol. 1, pp. 348–50, nos. 601, 602.
8. A similar way of laying out sketches for a long composition is seen in the sketch for the *Last Supper* (Gallerie dell'Accademia, Venice, 254), in which the right half of the composition is shown at the top of the sheet and the continuing left part at the bottom.
9. Rubinstein 1995, pp. 74–75; Cecchi 1997; Zöllner 1997.

LEONARDO DA VINCI

84. *Cavalcade* (recto)
Insignificant Sketches Possibly Representing Horsemen (verso)

Charcoal and black chalk (?), possibly slightly reworked with brush and brown wash in some shadows (recto); charcoal or black chalk (verso), 159 × 197 mm (6¼ × 7¾ in.)
Lent by Her Majesty Queen Elizabeth II, Royal Library, Windsor Castle 12339

PROVENANCE: Windsor Leoni volume: 1519, Francesco Melzi, Milan and Rome (1491/93–ca. 1570); ca. 1570, Orazio Melzi; by 1590, Pompeo Leoni, Madrid and Milan (ca. 1533–1608; Lugt under 2885); ca. 1613, Thomas Howard, second earl of Arundel (1586–1646); before 1690, British Royal Collection (inventory of King George III's collection, ca. 1810).

LITERATURE: Richter 1883, vol. 1, p. 337, pl. 57; Geymüller 1886, p. 160; Müntz 1898, vol. 2, p. 145; Müntz 1899, p. 407; Seidlitz 1911, p. 273, no.75; Commissione Vinciana 1928– , vol. 6, p. 24, pl. 250.2; Popp 1928, pp. 10, 47–49, no. 55; Sirén 1928, pl. 175; Neufeld 1949, pp. 171, 179–82, figs. 5, 9; Royal Academy of Arts 1952, p. 17, no. 121; Gould 1954a, fig. 13; Goldscheider 1959, p. 179, under no. 108; Pedretti 1968a, p. 73, fig. 51; Clark and Pedretti 1968–69, vol. 1, p. 34, no. 12339; Clark 1969–70, p. 11, no. 48; Richter 1970, vol. 1, p. 376, pl. 57; Gould 1975, pp. 135–36, 139, fig. 70; Pedretti 1977, vol. 1, p. 376, no. 26; Lavagnino 1980, p. 131; Kemp 1981, p. 246, pl. 68; Rosci 1982, p. 122; Hochstetler Meyer 1984, pp. 367–69, fig. 5; Pedretti and Roberts 1984–86, pp. 56–57, no. 31; Meller 1985, p. 135, fig. 66; Pedretti 1987a, pp. 88–89, no. 123 recto; Clark 1988, pp. 192–96, fig. 81; Agghàzy 1989, p. 51, fig. 54; Zambrano 1990, p. 60, no. 53a; Giovanna Nepi Scirè in Palazzo Grassi 1992, pp. 270–71, no. 33; Farago 1994, pp. 301–10; Popham 1994, no. 201; Clayton 1996, pp. 68–75, no. 35; Simon 1997, pp. 20–21, figs. 1, 4; Zöllner 1997, pl. 6; Arasse 1998, pp. 438, 441, fig. 300; Bambach 1999a, pp. 50, 391 n. 98; Marani 2000b, pp. 264–68.

This sheet portrays a mounted cavalry of furiously rearing horses on a terrain of gentle hills much like the actual plain of Anghiari, where the historical battle was fought. The soldiers at the extreme right hold numerous banners (*gonfaloni*), probably alluding to the distinctive symbols for the Florentine Republic: the standards of the defeated Milanese army that after the battle were kept by the chief magistrate, the *gonfaloniere di giustizia.* On the extreme left of the sheet,

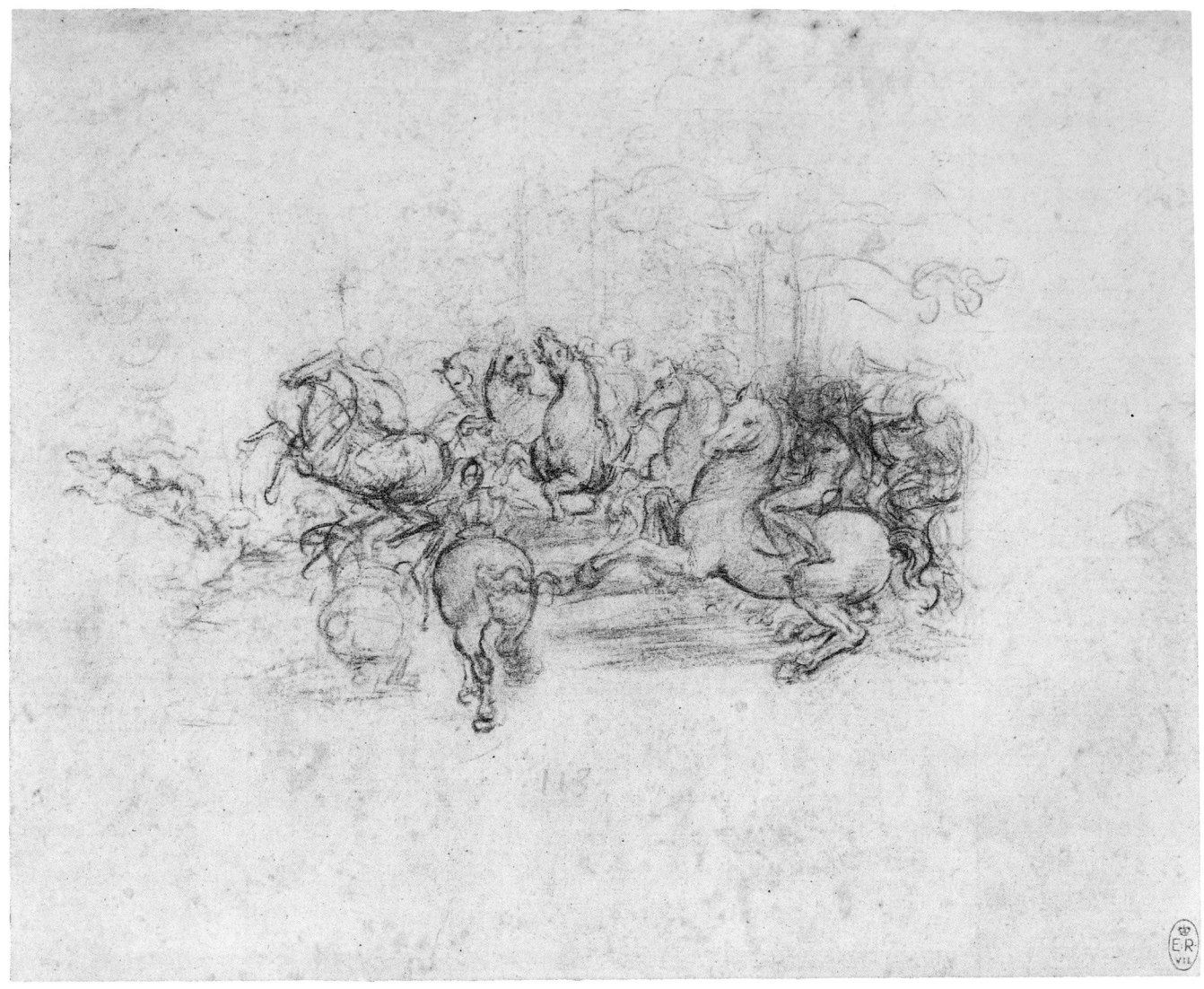

Cat. 84R

and quickly sketched, a horse leaps toward the left, which sug-
gests that it faces the Tiber River in the bridge episode of the
Battle of Anghiari. The main episode of the *Fight for the
Standard* (see cat. no. 135) would have been farther to the left.

Some scholars have perceived a lack of quality of execution
in the present drawing, without taking note of the way in
which it was produced. It seems clear that this expressive
study exhibits left-handed hatching. Short diagonal strokes
(from lower right to upper left) are especially visible in the
interior modeling of the buttocks of the rearing horses in the
foreground. Relatively long, right-to-left strokes are evident
in the horizontal parallel hatching on the ground; the thickness from the pressure of the hand is on the right in each line.

Moreover, the doughy, stylized character of many of the
horses and soldiers suggests that Leonardo (there can be no
doubt as to his authorship) probably did not draw them from
life, but from small three-dimensional models of either wax or
clay. Confirmation of such a procedure may be found in a
sheet by Leonardo that contains some minute pen-and-ink
sketches of rearing and charging horses for the *Battle of
Anghiari* at Windsor (RL 12328r). It is inscribed, "make one of
wax the length of a finger" (*fanne uno piccolo di cera lungo
un ditto*). Moreover, Giorgio Vasari's introduction to the *Vite
de' più eccellenti pittori, scultori ed architettori* (Florence,
1550 and 1568) describes the practice of artists drawing after
such models of clay or wax to compose figures in difficult

486

poses of foreshortening (*scorti*) for paintings; he notes that Michelangelo was among the famous artists who did so.[1] In his *Rime* (manuscript, 1560s), Benvenuto Cellini also referred to the use of small three-dimensional models to compose pictures, a method that he said Masaccio had introduced and that Leonardo had adopted in "some beautiful things in Milan and Florence."[2] One can envision Leonardo moving the little soldiers and horses around the table like a general preparing his strategy for the battlefield.[3]

In a note written in 1490–92, Leonardo emphasized the importance of studying the height and placement of the figures in a composition according to their final execution on the wall, and that preparatory studies be drawn consistently from the same viewpoint.[4] This Windsor study for the extreme right portion of the *Battle of Anghiari* cartoon can therefore serve as

a visual document regarding the viewing angle that Leonardo intended for the composition: *di sotto in sù* (as if seen from below) and in an oblique perspective from right to left.

CCB

1. Vasari–Milanesi 1906, vol. 1, pp. 177–78: "Degli scorti delle figure al di sotto in sù, e di quegli in piano."
2. Cellini 1971, p. 921: "Avvenga che la sua lucerna viene ad essere la scultura, e da quella tutti, gli eccellentissimi pittori, ogni cosa che loro hanno voluto fare di pittura, in prima l'hanno fatte in piccola scultura, e da quelle ritratte. E con quella mirabile lucerna, come dice il nostro maravigliosissimo Michelagnolo, si sono fatti lume, sì come si vede in nel Carmine, in Firenze, per Masaccio pittore; e in Milano e in Firenze alcune belle cose per Lionardo da Vinci pittore; e in Roma per mano del nostro gran Michelagnolo, scultore, pittore e architettore."
3. Carlo Pedretti in Galluzzi 1987, p. 13.
4. Paris Ms. A, fol. 90r (B.N. 2038, fol. 10r); Richter 1970, vol. 1, p. 324, no. 537; Pedretti 1977, vol. 1, p. 335, no. 537: "Del modo di ritrare figure per istorie."

LEONARDO DA VINCI

85. *Studies of Charging Soldiers and Horses*

Brick-red chalk on cream paper, 167 × 240 mm (6⁹⁄₁₆ × 9⁷⁄₁₆ in.), irregular
Lent by Her Majesty Queen Elizabeth II, Royal Library, Windsor Castle 12340

PROVENANCE: Windsor Leoni volume: 1519, Francesco Melzi, Milan and Rome (1491/93–ca. 1570); ca. 1570, Orazio Melzi; by 1590, Pompeo Leoni, Madrid and Milan (ca. 1533–1608, Lugt under 2885); ca. 1613, Thomas Howard, second earl of Arundel (1586–1646); before 1690, British Royal Collection (inventory of King George III's collection, ca. 1810).

LITERATURE: Müntz 1898, vol. 2, p. 17; Berenson 1903, vol. 1, p. 155, vol. 2, p. 67, no. 1224; Seidlitz 1909, vol. 2, pp. 68, 80; Seidlitz 1911, p. 273, no. 80; Venturi 1919, p. 170, fig. 4; Venturi 1920, p. 133, fig. 108; Venturi 1925, fig. 118; De Rinaldis 1926, p. 210, fig. 48; Sirén 1928, pl. 171; Bodmer 1931, pp. 290, 410; Berenson 1938, vol. 1, p. 173, vol. 2, p. 135, vol. 3, fig. 495; MacCurdy 1938, vol. 1, pl. 32; Commissione Vinciana 1928– , vol. 6, p. 24, pl. 252.1; Castelfranco 1952b, pl. 25; Royal Academy of Arts 1952, p. 36, no. 130; Gould 1954a, fig. 8; Berenson 1961, vol. 1, p. 253, vol. 2, p. 239, vol. 3, fig. 509, no. 1224; Pedretti 1968a, fig. 58; Clark and Pedretti 1968–69, vol. 1, pp. 34–35, no. 12340; Clark 1969–70, p. 12, no. 52; Lavagnino 1980, p. 132; Pedretti and Roberts 1984, pp. 55–56, no. 28; Meller 1985, p. 132, fig. 61; Pedretti 1987a, pp. 86–87, no. 121 recto; Palazzo Grassi 1992, pp. 276–77, no. 36; Popham 1994, no. 200; Clayton 1996–97, pp. 68–75, no. 36; Farago 1996, pp. 81, 84, fig. 8; Simon 1997, pp. 20–21, fig. 7; Arasse 1998, pp. 438, 442, fig. 302.

Dating to about 1503–4, these action studies of soldiers and horses are breathtakingly bold and abstract in character, even for Leonardo. In their exuberance and immediacy, they anticipate Edgar Degas's from the 1860s of sketches of jockeys and racehorses. Both the figural style, with a nearly cinematic sequence of repeating outlines, and the grainy drawing technique, achieved with a blunt stick of red chalk and little internal modeling, seem similar to the sheet in Venice (cat. no. 86), which elaborates on the figures of the charging riders in a larger scale and raises complexities in its dating. The motif of the galloping horse and rider appears also in two other sheets (Windsor, RL 12348; British Museum, London, 1854-5-13-17) as well as in a more schematic form in the center of the bottom row in the sheet from the Biblioteca Reale, Turin (cat. no. 103), exhibited here. These drawings seem to have been preparatory for the left part of the *Battle of Anghiari* composition, a passage that scholars believed Michelangelo may have re-created in an abstract sketch now

487

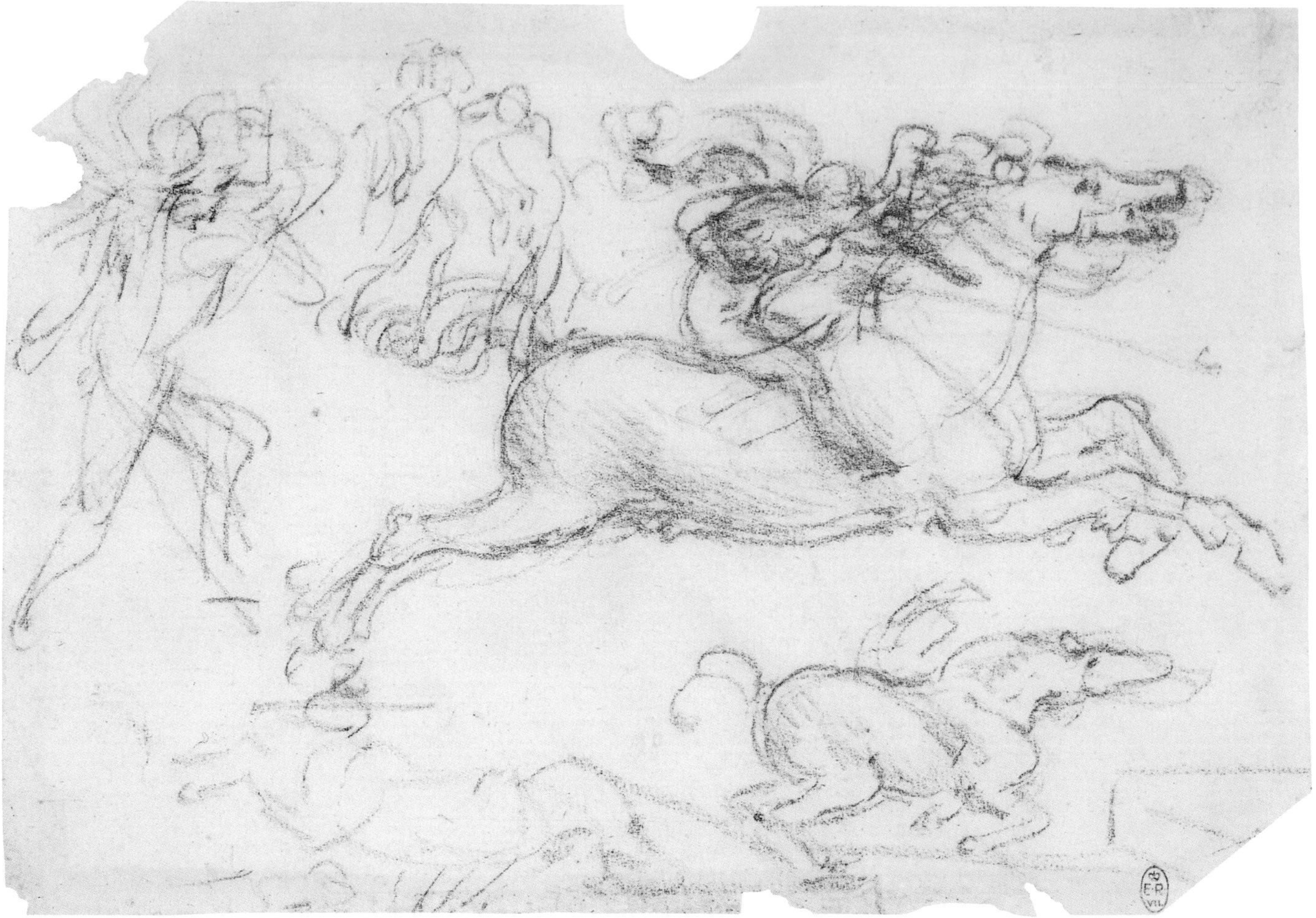

Cat. 85

in the British Museum (fig. 179). However, this seems to stack hypothesis on hypothesis, for simply too much evidence is lost about Leonardo's and Michelangelo's working procedures in designing their rival *Battle* scenes, and the extent of their unfinished work. Michelangelo's British Museum sketch of the charging horsemen and foot soldiers may have been intended for the artist's own fresco of the *Battle of Cascina*. Because the left portion of Leonardo's *Anghiari* composition seems to be the least documented—there is very little surviving evidence, even if we count autograph preliminary studies and copies—it may also have been the portion that the artist had developed the least. It is probable that a large section of the *Anghiari* cartoon was not finished when Leonardo abandoned the project sometime between 1506 and 1508 (see Chronology), as a clause in the revised contract of May 1504 allowed him to begin painting the mural in the Sala del Gran Consiglio at the Palazzo della Signoria before finishing the cartoon.

CCB

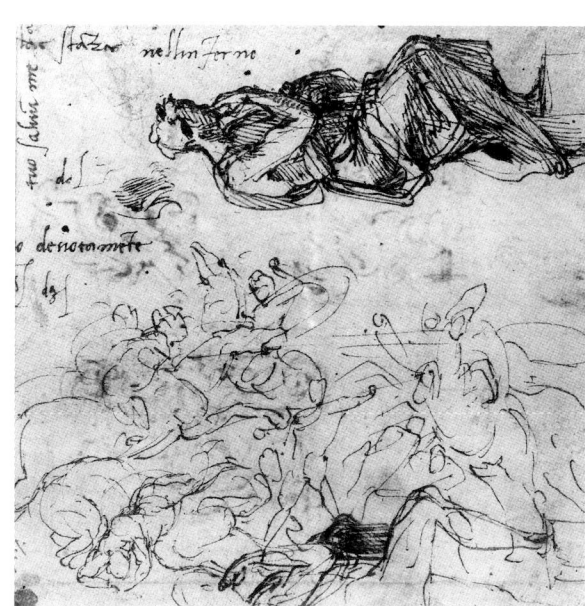

Fig. 179. Michelangelo Buonarroti, *Sketch of a Battle and Other Figure Studies*. Pen and brown ink, 186 × 183 mm. The British Museum, London 1895-9-15-496

LEONARDO DA VINCI

86. *The Facial Proportions of a Man in Profile; Study of Soldiers and Horses* (recto) *Studies of the Proportions of a Man in Bust Length in Profile Inscribed within a Rectangle* (verso)

Pen and two colors of brown ink over traces of stylus, black chalk, or charcoal, selectively pinpricked holes for the construction of the grid over the figure in profile, red chalk (recto); pen and two colors of brown ink over black chalk or charcoal, densely pinpricked holes close to the figure's profile (verso), 280 × 224 mm (11 × 8 ¹³⁄₁₆ in.) Inscribed in pen and brown ink on recto, in right-to-left script, at upper left: *Dal ciglio alla co[n]giuntione / dellabro chol me[n]to . ella . punta / della massciella . el fine disop[r]a dello / orecchio . cholla tenpia . fia un qua/drato perfetto . E cciasscuna faccja p[er] se . e meza tessta . — / El chavo dellosso della guancja / si truova . in mezo fralla punta del / naso . el confine della massciella cho/lla . punta . di sotto dello . orecchjo / in . nella figurata . isstella — / Dal chan-tone dellosso dellocchio allo / orecchio . e ttanto . spatio quanto . e lla / lungheza . dello . orecchio . ovuol . il / terzo . della tessta —*; on verso in pen and brown ink, in right-to-left script, on grid and along figure in profile with letters *a* to *t* in a successive order, and the measurements of the anatomical features are referenced with respect to these letters; to the left of the bust: h i *1/6 del* [crossed out: *capo*] *volto / g i 1/5 del capo / g i 1/4 del volto / f i 1/3 del volto / c f 1/3 del volto/ b c 1/3 del volto / k l 1/2 del volto / h f e 1/6 del volto*; below the bust: *Ta chel capo . cioe dalla som[m]ita dell omo . al disotto del me[n]to . sia* [crossed out: *divi*] *lottava . parte di tucto lomo / il quale chapo . divjderaj in 5 . parti e una desse parti fa che ssia dal nasscime[n]to de chapelli insino / al pari della soma alteza del capo un altra . parte metti dal taglio . della boccha al fine di sotto del me[n]to e llultre di mezo ressteranno infra [i]l taglio dessa boccha . al fine del v[i]so coi chapegli —*.

Annotated on recto with crossed-out *o* above the head and text on left; annotated on verso above column of proportions with repeating symbol of the crossed-out *o*, which generally indicates a transcription by one of the sixteenth-century compilers of anthologies based on Leonardo's notes, who most likely may be identified with Giovanni Francesco Melzi; also annotated with several numbers, *Lionardo da Vinci* at bottom right, and *Leonardo* at upper left Watermark: Eight-petaled flower (Briquet 6597) Gallerie dell'Accademia, Venice 236

PROVENANCE: Cardinal Cesare Monti, Milan (1635–1650); Contessa Anna Luisa Monti, Milan; 1770, Venanzio De Pagave, Milan; his son Gaudenzio De Pagave; ca. 1808 or before, Giuseppe Bossi, Milan and Venice (1777–1815; album marked K); auction, Milan, February 1818, II; February 24, 1818, purchase by Abbate Luigi Celotti [Cellotti], Venice (1765–1846); on deposit (under custody of Carlo Porta and Nicola Cassoni), Accademia di Belle Arti, Milan; 1820–22, proposal of purchase of Bossi's collection from Celotti submitted to Austrian government on behalf of Accademia

delle Belle Arti, Venice; 1822, purchase by Franz I (Habsburg), emperor of Austria, Florence and Vienna (1768–1835), for Accademia delle Belle Arti, Venice; ca. 1832 manuscript inventory; December 31, 1870, manuscript inventory; museum stamp (Lugt 188).

LITERATURE: Gerli 1784, pls. 2 (inscribed 2; verso only), 3 (inscribed 13; male proportion study on recto only), 13 (inscribed 11; horsemen on recto only); Bossi 1810, p. 204; Selvatico 1854, frame 4, no. 16; Richter 1883, vol. 1, p. 172, no. 315 n., pl. 9; Uzielli 1884, pp. 276–78, no. 16; Berenson 1903, vol. 2, p. 62, no. 1106; Seidlitz 1909, vol. 2, p. 81; Fogolari 1913, no. 16; Malaguzzi Valeri 1913–23, vol. 2, p. 467, fig. 520; Favaro 1917, pp. 167–227.; Beltrami 1919b, p. 161; Poggi 1919, pls. 152, 154; Venturi 1920, p. 133, fig. 107; De Rinaldis 1926, p. 210, fig. 50; Commissione Vinciana 1928– , vol. 6, p. 24, pls. 257, 286; Popp 1928, p. 39, no. 26; Bodmer 1931, pp. 298, 409–10; Clark 1935, pp. 30, 38, 103; Berenson 1938, vol. 2, p. 123, no. 1106; Palazzo dell'Arte 1939, p. 150; Panofsky 1940, p. 44, figs. 28, 75; Richter 1941, pp. 335–38; Giglioli 1944, pls. 157, 159; Meller 1948, p. 14; Heydenreich 1949, pp. 13–14, nos. 55–56, pls. 15, 16; Biblioteca Medicea Laurenziana 1952, pp. 38–39, no. 55; Goldscheider 1952, fig. 47; Lambertini 1953, pl. 9, fig. 4; Heydenreich 1954, vol. 1, p. 101, vol. 2, p. 111, vol. 3, pl. 152; Berenson 1961, vol. 2, p. 217, vol. 3, fig. 510, no. 1106; Monti 1966, fig. 76; Cogliati Arano 1966–67, pp. 21–22, no. 8, figs. 9–10; Richter 1970, vol. 1, p. 247, no. 315 n., pl. 9; Pedretti 1975a, p. 13; Pedretti 1977, vol. 1, pp. 234–35; Keele and Pedretti 1979–80, vol. 2, p. 812, fig. 54; Cogliati Arano 1980, pp. 29–31, no. 7; Lavagnino 1980, p. 134; Nicodemi 1980b, pp. 13–14; Marinoni and Meneguzzo 1981a, pp. 126–27; Bora 1982, p. 140, fig. 96; Pedretti and Clark 1983, p. 76, fig. 59, under no. 4; Pedretti 1987a, p. 87, fig. 114; Caroli 1991, pp. 165–66; Giovanna Nepi Scirè in Palazzo Grassi 1992, pp. 224–25; Loretta Salvador in Palazzo Grassi 1992, pp. 424–25, nos. 15–15a; Kwakkelstein 1994, pp. 102–3, pl. 15; Popham 1994, no. 191; Letze and Buchsteiner 1997, p. 108; Arasse 1998, p. 329, fig. 226; Giovanna Nepi Scirè in Nepi Scirè and Torrini 1999, pp. 58–59, 64–67, no. 18; Laurenza 2001, p. 20, fig. 23; Giovanna Nepi Scirè in National Museum of Western Art 2001–2, pp. 158–59, no. 3.004; Giovanna Nepi Scirè in Scuderie Papali al Quirinale 2001–2, pp. 163–64, no. 3.4; Clayton 2002–3, p. 31, fig. 6, under no. 4.

This magnificent double-sided sheet appears to combine work from two different moments in Leonardo's career. The artist undertook the studies of the proportions of the bald man's head about 1490–95, probably not long after he had embarked on his detailed investigation of the proportions and

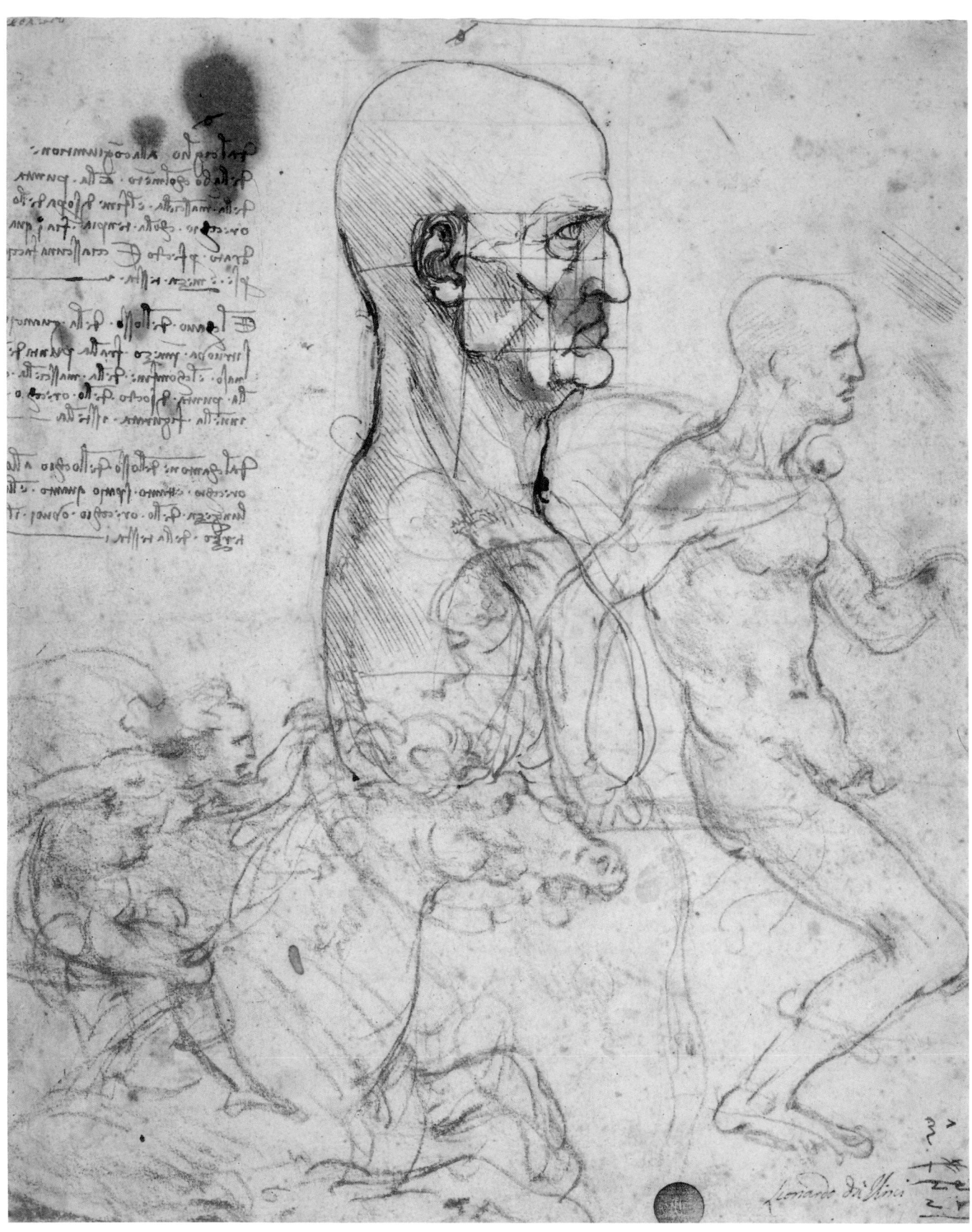

Cat. 86r

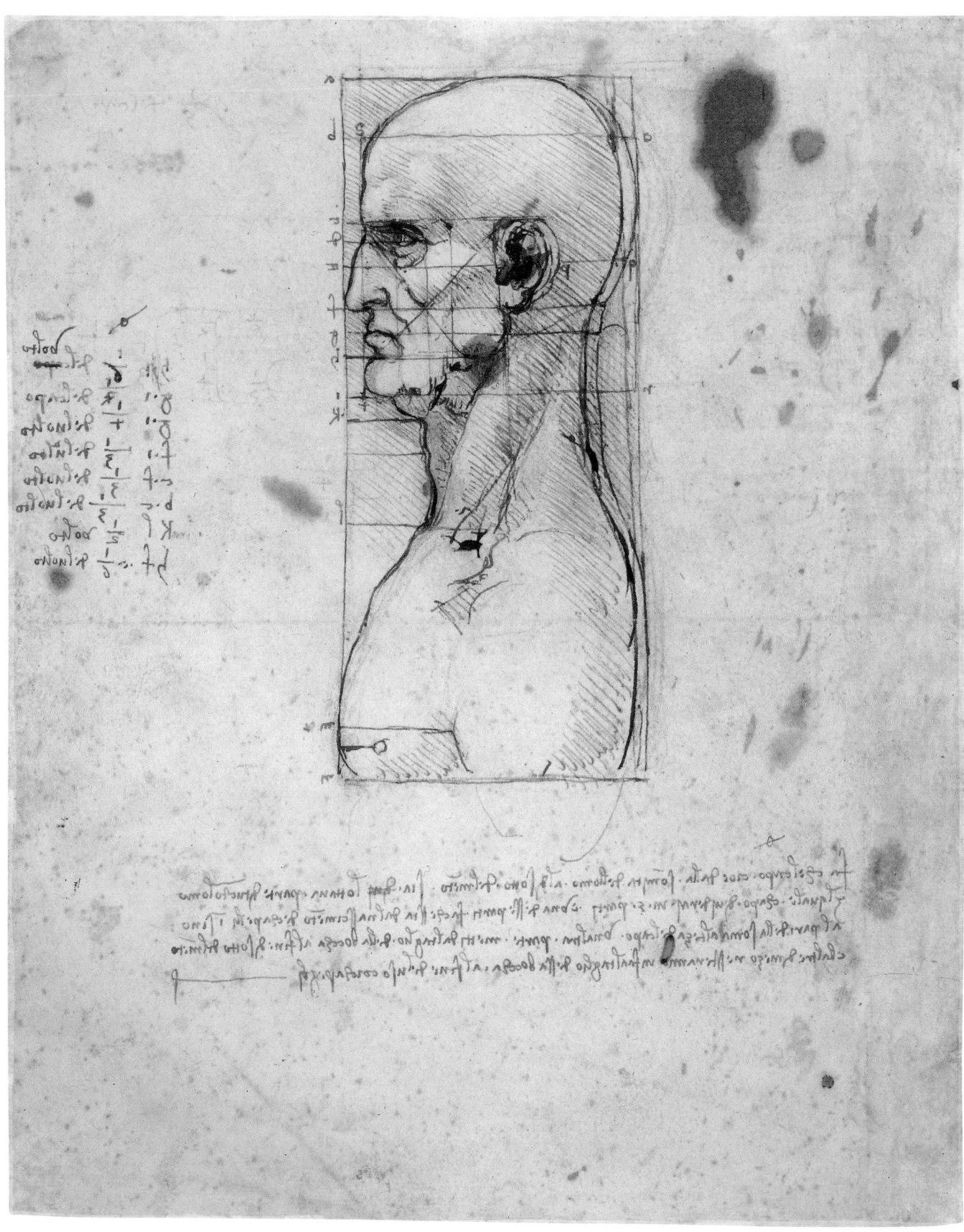

Cat. 86v

movements of the human figure, which he seems to have begun in 1488–90. These proportion studies of the head were the external counterpart to his anatomical studies of the skull begun in 1489 (cat. no. 58), in which he detailed the relationship of the measurements of the parts to the whole. For Leonardo, human proportions and human anatomy were two facets of the same enterprise: a microcosmic study of man. In his words, "man is said to be a 'little world' by the ancients."[1] The lower portion of the recto of the Venice sheet, by contrast, contains dazzling composition sketches in red chalk of two charging soldiers mounted on horses that appear to relate to the cavalry in the little-known left part of Leonardo's unfinished cartoon and mural of the *Battle of Anghiari* (cat. nos. 81, 85, 103). These red-chalk sketches seem analogous in conception and technique to catalogue number 85 and probably may be dated to about 1503–4, an early stage in the project. The proportion studies of the man's head first were more delicately drawn in pen and a light-to-medium brown ink with fine, almost pitch-straight parallel hatching, typical of Leonardo's pen technique in the 1490s. The text and individual letters accompanying the proportion drawings were also inscribed at this point, for the color of the ink is the same. The outlines of the man's head and face, however, were boldly reworked in an almost-black brown ink, especially heavily on the verso of the sheet, giving the final design of the heads on both sides greater sculptural effect and an impressive monumentality of form. It may be that Leonardo reworked these studies at the time that he reused the sheet to draw the *Battle of Anghiari* red-chalk sketches on the recto. The same fierce physiognomic type of the bald man in the Venice proportion studies is recognizable in the soldier identified as the Milanese condottiere Niccolò Piccinino in the *Fight for the Standard* episode of the *Battle of Anghiari* (cat. no. 91). This is not surprising, since Leonardo regarded an understanding of the proportions of the human head as the foundation for the study of expression, gesture, and "the motions of the mind" (*i moti mentali*).

Leonardo's quest for an ideal of human proportions was stimulated by Plato's *Timaeus* and by book 3 of Vitruvius's treatise *De architectura*, which pointed out analogies between the symmetry and proportionate parts of a well-constructed temple and those of the human body, and proposed a module of measurement for the *homo bene figuratus* (the well-proportioned man).[2] In the late 1480s and the 1490s, two of

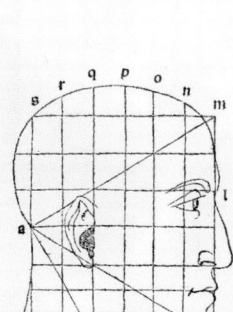

Fig. 180. Fra Luca Pacioli, *De divina proportione*. Venice: Paganinus de Paganinis, June 1, 1509, p. 17 verso. Woodcut, 289 × 198 mm. The Metropolitan Museum of Art, New York; Rogers Fund, 1919 19.50

Leonardo's friends sojourning in Milan, Francesco di Giorgio (the Sienese polymath, architect, and engineer) and Fra Luca Pacioli (the Franciscan mathematician and theorist from Borgo Sansepolcro), also studied Vitruvius's treatise dealing with the proportions of the human body and the head (fig. 180). While many fifteenth-century artists and theorists investigated proportion, Leonardo approached his research with an unparalleled level of detail and coherence of vision. Only Piero della Francesca's *De prospectiva pingendi* (manuscript, written before 1482) offers a comparably nuanced discussion in his passage on the proportional foreshortening of the head (*la testa proportionalmente degradata*; fig. 14).[3] Leonardo probably knew of Piero's principles through Fra Luca Pacioli (who was accused by Giorgio Vasari of plagiarizing Piero), for the heads in Leonardo's Venice proportion drawings manifest divisions that are remarkably similar to those articulated in the *De prospec-*

tiva. As can be gathered from the fragmentary evidence of his extant drawings and notes, Leonardo refined modules for the human body at rest and in motion, detailing the proportions of the various parts of the body and individualizing the proportions of men, women, and children. He may have accomplished a large part of this investigation by 1498, to judge from a contemporaneous reference in the manuscript of Fra Luca Pacioli's *De divina proportione* (published later, in Venice, in 1509). Leonardo's "proportional" box is carefully constructed on both sides of the Venice sheet, and, in fact, Pacioli's *De divina proportione* illustrates a male head in profile with a similar proportional grid (fig. 180). Leonardo may have written a treatise on human proportion separate from that on anatomy, for allusions to it occur in the posthumously compiled manuscript of his *Libro di pittura* (Codex Urbinas Latinus, 1270) and in Giovanni Paolo Lomazzo's *Idea del tempio della pittura* (Milan, 1590).

As Leonardo gradually considered the proportions of each of the parts constituting the human figure, he increased the level of detail. His studies of the proportional measurements of the facial features with respect to the head are the culmination of this systematic approach. In the Venice sheet, Leonardo's choice of a distinctive model—a mature, bald man with sharp facial features and a strong, square jaw—partly reflects the system of facial proportions based on the unit and subunits of the rectangle and square that he employed. For a frontal study of facial proportions (Biblioteca Reale, Turin, 15574, 15576; fig. 15), Leonardo used a similar model with a strong, square jaw and well-defined cranium who likewise seems suited to the squaring up and triangulation of the features that the artist had in mind. The same male model seen in the Venice sheet turns up in a few other proportion studies and sketches (Windsor, RL 12601, 12607).

Comparisons of the proportional relationships stated in Leonardo's inscriptions and the corresponding details in the drawings on the Venice sheet reveal that the drawings represent a draft done by eyeing the dimensions, rather than a precisely constructed illustration. For example, we may compare the slightly unequal squares in the face sketched on the recto with Leonardo's inscription, "the join of the lower lip with the chin and tip of the jaw and the upper tip of the ear with the temple forms a perfect square: and each face is half a head." The mature, sagging facial and body type of the male model in the Venice sheet offers a sharp contrast to the idealized male beauty that Leonardo portrayed in his proportion studies of the entire body (see fig. 43 and Windsor, RL 19132). When studying the overall proportions of the body in a Vitruvian canon, his choice of model seemed closer to that of a man of "the utmost grace," and of "a body that is naturally of praiseworthy proportions."[4] As the present sheet of studies vividly documents, Leonardo intended to take the systems that he explored for the entire body as the points of departure for his investigation of the proportions of individualized heads and faces, according to gender, age, and physiognomic type. Inspired by the Vitruvian model, though not precisely adhering to it, Leonardo divided the total height from the crown of the bald man's head to the top of his chest into five parts of unequal measurements,[5] and these general divisions he articulated more clearly in the drawing of the profile on the verso: from the crown to the forehead, point a to b; from the forehead to the eyebrow, point b to c; from the eyebrow to the tip of the nose, point c to f; from the tip of the nose to the chin, point f to j; from the tip of the chin to the top of the chest, point i to l. He then subdivided the measurements according to the horizontal and vertical lines tangential to the main features.

Both the recto and verso of the Venice sheet are marked throughout with the sign of a crossed-out *o*, which signifies that the passages were transcribed by an early hand.[6] The scheme of proportions on the recto and the corresponding notes were copied onto folio 54 recto of the Codex Huygens (Pierpont Morgan Library, New York).[7] These facts suggest that Francesco Melzi probably owned the Venice sheet of drawings, and that sometime before his death in about 1570 he offered the compiler of the Codex Huygens access to it to transcribe the diagram and notes. Carlo Giuseppe Gerli's *Disegni di Leonardo da Vinci* (Milan, 1784) reproduces Leonardo's complex double-sided Venice sheet, based on tracings done in the exact size of Leonardo's originals. Gerli was aware of the great difference in style between the male proportion study and the horsemen on the recto of the Venice sheet, for he reproduced them in separate engravings. These engravings are also in the correct orientation with regard to the original designs, and render some of Leonardo's inscriptions on the verso of the Venice sheet in readable mirror script, suggesting that Leonardo's hand could be imitated by others in quite competent fashion.[8]

CCB

493

1. "L'uomo e detto da li antichi mondo minore."
2. Zöllner 1987.
3. Bambach [Cappel] 1994, pp. 17–43; Bambach 1999a, pp. 222–28.
4. "Di miglior grazia"; "corpo naturale il quale comunemente sia di proporzione laudabile."
5. The *Vitruvian Man* (Accademia, Venice, 228; fig. 43) also has this five-part division from the crown of the head to the top of the chest

drawn in with short horizontal dashes of the pen.
6. Pedretti 1977, vol. 1, pp. 235–36.
7. Giovanna Nepi Scirè in Palazzo Grassi 1992, and in Scuderie Papali al Quirinale 2001–2.
8. For another example of Gerli's relatively proficient imitation of Leonardo's right-to-left script in a technological drawing, see Gerli 1784, pl. 39 (inscribed 31).

LEONARDO DA VINCI

87. *Rearing Horse*

Red chalk, with traces of pen and brown ink reworking, 153 × 142 mm (6 1/16 × 5 5/8 in.)
Lent by Her Majesty Queen Elizabeth II, Royal Library, Windsor Castle 12336

PROVENANCE: Windsor Leoni volume: 1519, Francesco Melzi, Milan and Rome (1491/93–ca. 1570); ca. 1570, Orazio Melzi; by 1590, Pompeo Leoni, Madrid and Milan (ca. 1533–1608; Lugt under 2885); ca. 1613, Thomas Howard, second earl of Arundel (1586–1646); before 1690, British Royal Collection (inventory of King George III's collection, ca. 1810).

LITERATURE: Seidlitz 1909, vol. 1, no. 94; Seidlitz 1911, p. 273, no. 86; Malaguzzi Valeri 1922, p. 92, fig. 47; Commissione Vinciana 1928– , vol. 2, p. 27, pl. 55.b; Popp 1928, p. 49, no. 56; Sirén 1928, pl. 165a; Bodmer 1931, pp. 317, 414; Berenson 1938, vol. 2, p. 136, no. 1228A; Royal Academy of Arts 1952, p. 124; Clark 1954, pl. 27; Berenson 1961, vol. 2, p. 241, no. 1228A; Valentiner 1966, p. 82, pl. 31a; Clark and Pedretti 1968–69, pp. 31–32, no. 12336; Clark 1969–70, p. 12, no. 51; Pedretti and Roberts 1984–86, p. 51, no. 22; Pedretti 1987a, pp. 75–76, no. 113 recto; Roberts 1988, pp. 30–31, no. 9; Rosand 1988, pp. 28, 30, fig. 34; Kemp and Roberts 1989, p. 146, no. 73; Kemp 1992a, p. 157, fig. 7; Popham 1994, no. 84B; Clayton 1996–97, pp. 72–74, under nos. 37–39; Pedretti 1999, p. 133, fig. 1.

The bravura of the main red-chalk study—of superbly refined tonal structure—seems unparalleled among the more detailed of Leonardo's horse studies for the *Battle of Anghiari*. Evidently drawn from life, the rearing horse is depicted here as if recoiling in fear. The figure of a tense rider, leaning tightly against the horse's neck, is summarily indicated. In continuously pivoting movements, the magnificent animal shifts its hind legs on the ground, kicking its forelegs in the air and violently throwing its head forward, upward, sideways, and backward. The agitated outlines quiver with life. Leonardo may have decided finally to portray the horse's head violently twisted back, as this is the solution that seems most emphatically drawn on the present sheet. In contrast to the boldness of mark seen in catalogue number 85, Leonardo seems to have begun to draw quite lightly with a fine-pointed, brownish red stick of chalk, to judge from the slight underdrawing. He gradually built up the rendering with dense, curved parallel hatching, as in the belly and hindquarters, varying the pressure on the chalk as he drew to increase the tonal depth, and wetting the tip of the chalk for the darkest accents. He further reworked the drawing with pen and light brown ink to select the final contours among the reinforced outlines drawn in red chalk; the pen and ink does not appear to be from a later retouching, as it seems structurally integral to the drawing.

A number of other Windsor drawings for the *Battle of Anghiari* portray the motif of the rearing horse, as represented in the present study (to be cautious, it may be recalled that the position of the animal's head is somewhat undetermined). The motif appears, for example, on the right in catalogue number 88; in dotted charcoal underdrawings (*spolvero* marks) in the upper right in a damaged sheet of designs of charging horsemen (RL 12338); in pen and ink on the right in a powerful sheet of sketches of heads and full figures (RL 12326); and in pen and ink in the lower left of a sheet with sketches of an angel, horsemen, and cogwheel mechanisms (RL 12328). Two other highly modeled charcoal studies may also relate to the motif. One shows the rearing horse's head fiercely turned back (RL 12334), much as in the most emphatic solution seen in the present sheet, and the other is a detail of the hindquarters of the same rearing horse (RL 12335). The recurrence of the motif suggests its significance as a compositional element. To judge from the pose of the rider and rearing horse, the motif was either intended for the episode immediately to the right of the main *Fight for the Standard*—seen in the upper right of catalogue number 82 (Accademia, Venice, 215), although none of the later copies apparently records it—or for the

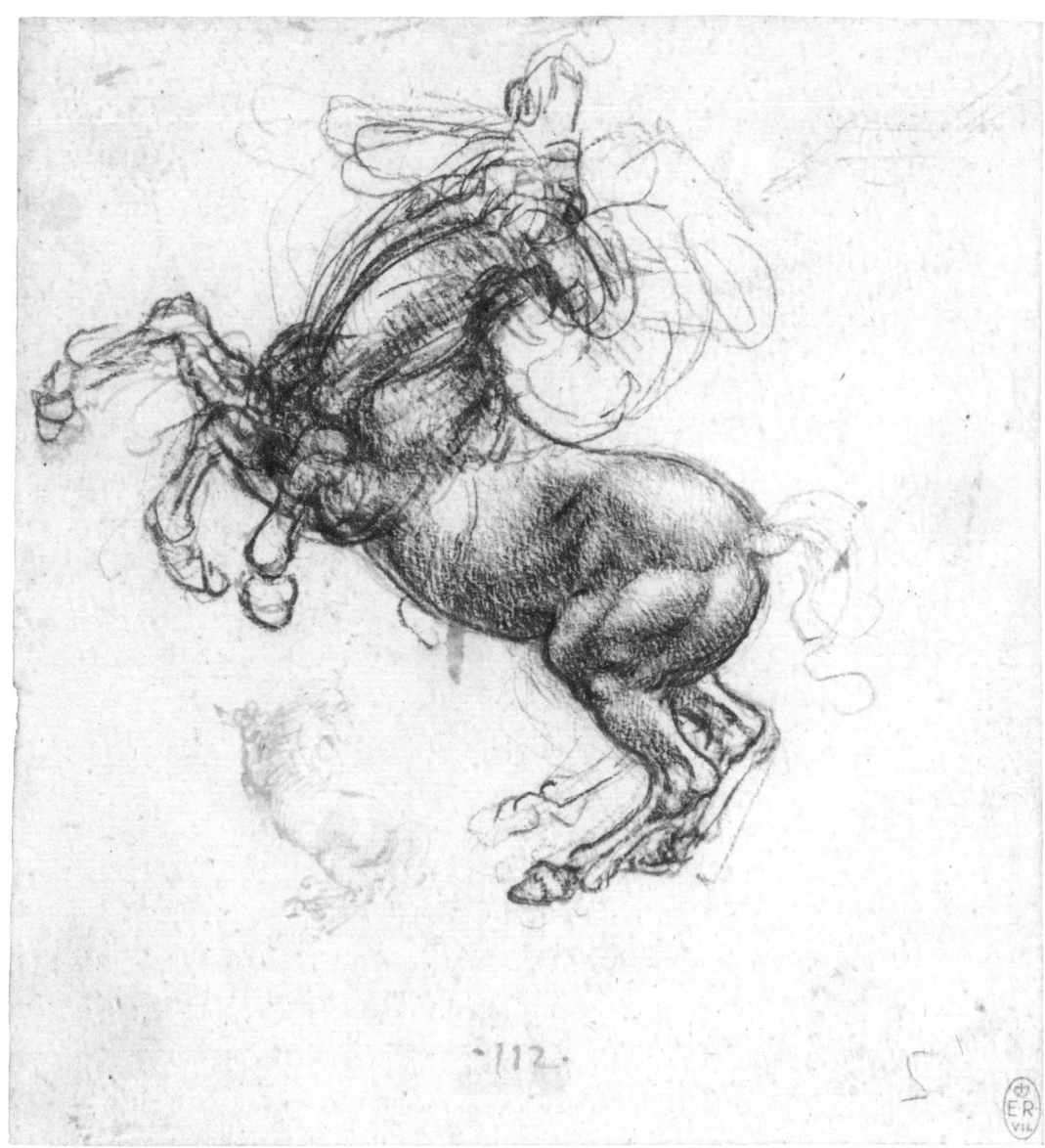

Cat. 87 *(actual size)*

cavalcade on the extreme right of the composition, documented in catalogue number 84 (RL 12339). In the present sheet, below the main drawing in red chalk and to the left, the slight sketch in pen and faded brown ink portrays a similar rider and rearing horse, although the animal is more upright. The style and technique of this sketch do not seem far from those of the Venice *primi pensieri,* the famous "early idea" sketches for the *Battle of Anghiari* (cat. nos. 81–83).

About 1502–4, when Leonardo was preparing to leave Florence (for Piombino?), he included "a book of horses sketched for the cartoon"[1] in a list of books stored "in a crate at the monastery" (Codex Madrid II, fols. 2v–3r). The Windsor horse sketches and studies probably formed part of such a *libro.* The reference to an entire preparatory sketchbook for the production of the *Battle of Anghiari* cartoon suggests the extent of the tragic dismemberment and losses in Leonardo's corpus of drawings, for not a single sketchbook by him of preparatory drawings for a pictorial project survives intact.

CCB

1. "Un libro di cavalli schizzati pel cartone" (fol. 3r). See Ladislao Reti in Codex Madrid 1974, vol. 3, pp. 56–58, vol. 5, pp. 7–8.

LEONARDO DA VINCI

88. *Studies of a Rearing Horse and Rider; Leda and the Swan* (recto)
Mortars Firing Stones or Cannonballs across the Walls of a Fort or Town (verso, upside down)

Charcoal or soft black chalk partly reworked with pen and brown ink, 292 × 412 mm (11½ × 16¼ in.)

Inscribed in pen and brown ink on verso, in right-to-left script, left column: *prima sia ruinate tutte / le djfese delle mura ettorri / le mura sono alte 16 [braccie] io voglio pigliare vna / largheza dj br[accie] 200 e gittare gu 10 br[accie] dessa alteza / dj muro e largheza dj 200 [crossed out: e no] effatto questo / sia colli rottamj etterrato e ramj dalb[e]ri con / posto quatt[r]o posste dj 25 br[accie] lina e djsta[n]te lu / na dallaltra altre 25 br[accie]*; middle column: *son molte caue cop[er]te / le quali rispondano / a bonbardiere sotterane / le quali battano [crossed out: le basseze] / [crossed out: de fossi] in basso le lun / geze de fossi assciutti e ac / questi riparereno col dare / lacqva——; right column: esse no[n] uolete i mortaj / sia dato lacqua alla fosse / e poi che trabocheranno / enpieranno le altre fos / se che no[n] sono vnjte colle / prime e cosi are cacci / ato le djuese [difese] delle fosse / per testa e p[er] fiancho fatte / da difensori che in quelle / sasscondeano——/ lacqua data anegera / li fochi [crossed out: sotterranj] i quali / possano essere ordjnati in / caue sotterane co[n] molti / tudjne dj legniamj i qua / fochi siscop[r]ano arequjsitio / ne del nemjco——*

Lent by Her Majesty Queen Elizabeth II, Royal Library, Windsor Castle 12337

PROVENANCE: Windsor Leoni volume: 1519, Francesco Melzi, Milan and Rome (1491/93–ca. 1570); ca. 1570, Orazio Melzi; by 1590, Pompeo Leoni, Madrid and Milan (ca. 1533–1608; Lugt under 2885); ca. 1613, Thomas Howard, second earl of Arundel (1586–1646); before 1690, British Royal Collection (inventory of King George III's collection, ca. 1810).

LITERATURE: Berenson 1903, vol. 1, p. 163, vol. 2, p. 62, no. 1123; Seidlitz 1909, vol. 2, p. 130; Seidlitz 1911, p. 273, nos. 89–90; Poggi 1919, pl. 110; Venturi 1920, p. 136, fig. 123; Venturi 1925, fig. 140; De Rinaldis 1926, p. 221; Commissione Vinciana 1928– , vol. 5, p. 24, pls. 208, 209; Sirén 1928, pl. 194; Bodmer 1931, pp. 328, 416–17; Berenson 1938, vol. 1, p. 180, vol. 2, p. 125, vol. 3, fig. 547, no. 1123; Royal Academy of Arts 1952, no. 129; Goldscheider 1959, pp. 158–59, under pl. 36; Berenson 1961, vol. 1, p. 262, vol. 2, p. 220, vol. 3, fig. 512, no. 1123; Clark and Pedretti 1968–69, vol. 1, pp. 32–33, no. 12337; Wasserman 1969, p. 130, figs. 30, 32; Clark 1969–70, p. 13, no. 55; Wasserman 1970, pp. 200, 203, fig. 14; Konrad Oberhuber in Levenson, Oberhuber, and Sheehan 1973, pp. 450–51, under no. 162; Weil-Garris Posner 1974, pp. 33–34, fig. 33; Allison 1974, pp. 375–76, figs. 1, 10, 11, 12; Smart and Kemp 1980, pp. 160–71; Kemp 1981, p. 270; Pedretti and Roberts 1984–86, p. 55, no. 27A, B; Calvesi 1985, p. 137, fig. 69; Marani 1987a, p. 48, fig. 30;

Pedretti 1987a, pp. 81–83, no. 118 recto and verso; Clark 1988, pp. 183–86, fig. 76; Ames-Lewis 1989, pp. 73–76, fig. 104; Kemp and Roberts 1989, p. 147, no. 74; Popham 1994, no. 212; Cecchi and Natali 1996, pp. 106–7, under no. 17; Arasse 1997, pp. 420, 424, figs. 279, 280; Arasse 1998, pp. 420–21, 424, figs. 279, 280; Bambach 2001, fig. 10; Dalli Regoli, Nanni, and Natali 2001, pp. 65–67, figs. 52–54.

This large, complex, double-sided sheet vividly attests to the spontaneity and dynamic plasticity of Leonardo's drawing technique about 1504–5, when his powers of invention seemed inexhaustible. The exquisitely rendered study of a rearing horse at the upper right with a barely indicated rider is likely connected with the cavalcade at the extreme right in the intended *Battle of Anghiari* composition, for it evokes the less violently rearing poses of the horses seen at the extreme left and right in catalogue number 84 (Windsor, RL 12339). In the present study, however, the faintly drawn rider bends down as though holding a long weapon, and thus the head of man and horse overlap. Nearly the same motif recurs in the upper right in one of the Venice sketches with early ideas for the *Fight for the Standard* (cat. no. 82). The rear legs of the horse in the present study are also drawn in different positions on the ground. It therefore is probable that Leonardo undertook his studies of riders on rearing horses, such as the one seen here, with great flexibility of purpose in mind, adapting and moving the figures around the composition as he refined the design. To this end, he seems to have also relied on tiny movable wax models of horses (see cat. no. 84).

As most scholars agree, the two small compositional sketches within framing outlines toward the center and the left on the sheet portray the nude Leda kneeling on her right knee (cat. nos. 98, 99) in a tightly compressed pose. The small sketch on the left seems to show Leda holding a child to her right breast while turning to the left. The larger sketch at the center portrays her sustaining an impossibly complex contrapposto pose, with her head seen in two positions, and her right arm and hand stretched across her body reaching to a child on her left. The "right arm across the body" solution would reemerge in the standing version of Leda and the Swan

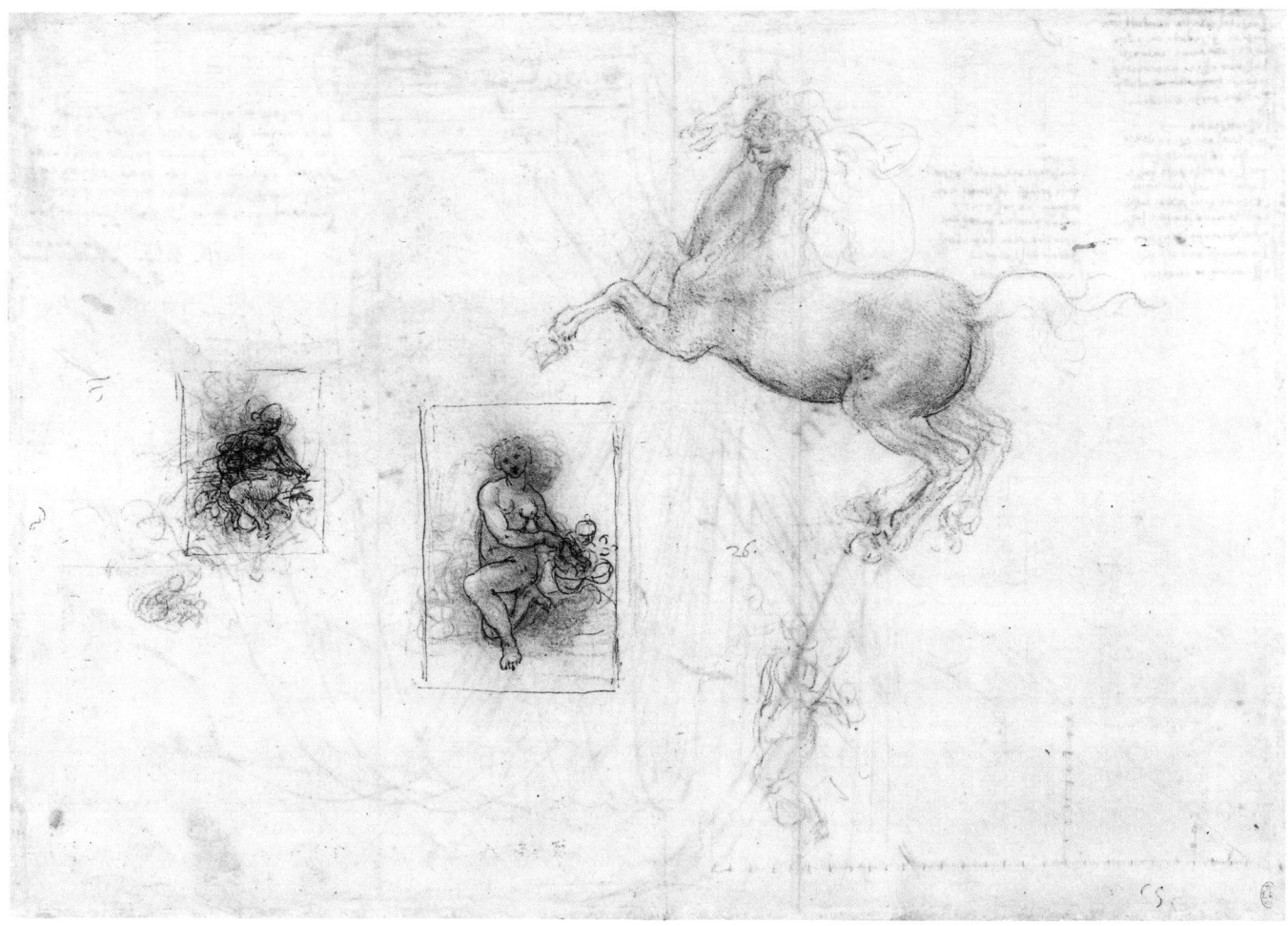

Cat. 88R

(cat. nos. 98, 99, 134). The present *Leda* sketches, perhaps more than any others by Leonardo for paintings, capture the intimate process of the artist's creation in the very act of unfolding, with a breathtaking sense of immediacy for the viewer. The two framed compositional sketches are fairly abstract in their details, and their contents have led to a variety of interpretations. What is clear is that the alternatives for the elegantly agitated twists of the figure's head and body are developed over very small areas of the paper in a nearly cinematic sequence, and with a sense of effortless simultaneity of invention. Leonardo firmly reworked the blurs of gestating

forms in the charcoal underdrawing with pen and brown ink, picking out the outlines of one part of the design from the alternatives. In a quick, highly abstract sketch toward the right of the framed compositional sketches, the figure of the kneeling Leda is decompressed and appears almost to be standing, although apparently still without the swan. The somewhat crude sketch toward the lower left of the sheet seems to represent a child seated on the ground.

On the verso of the sheet, the large, broadly drawn military design depicts rows of mortars firing a great shower of stones or cannonballs into the fortified walls of a town. The

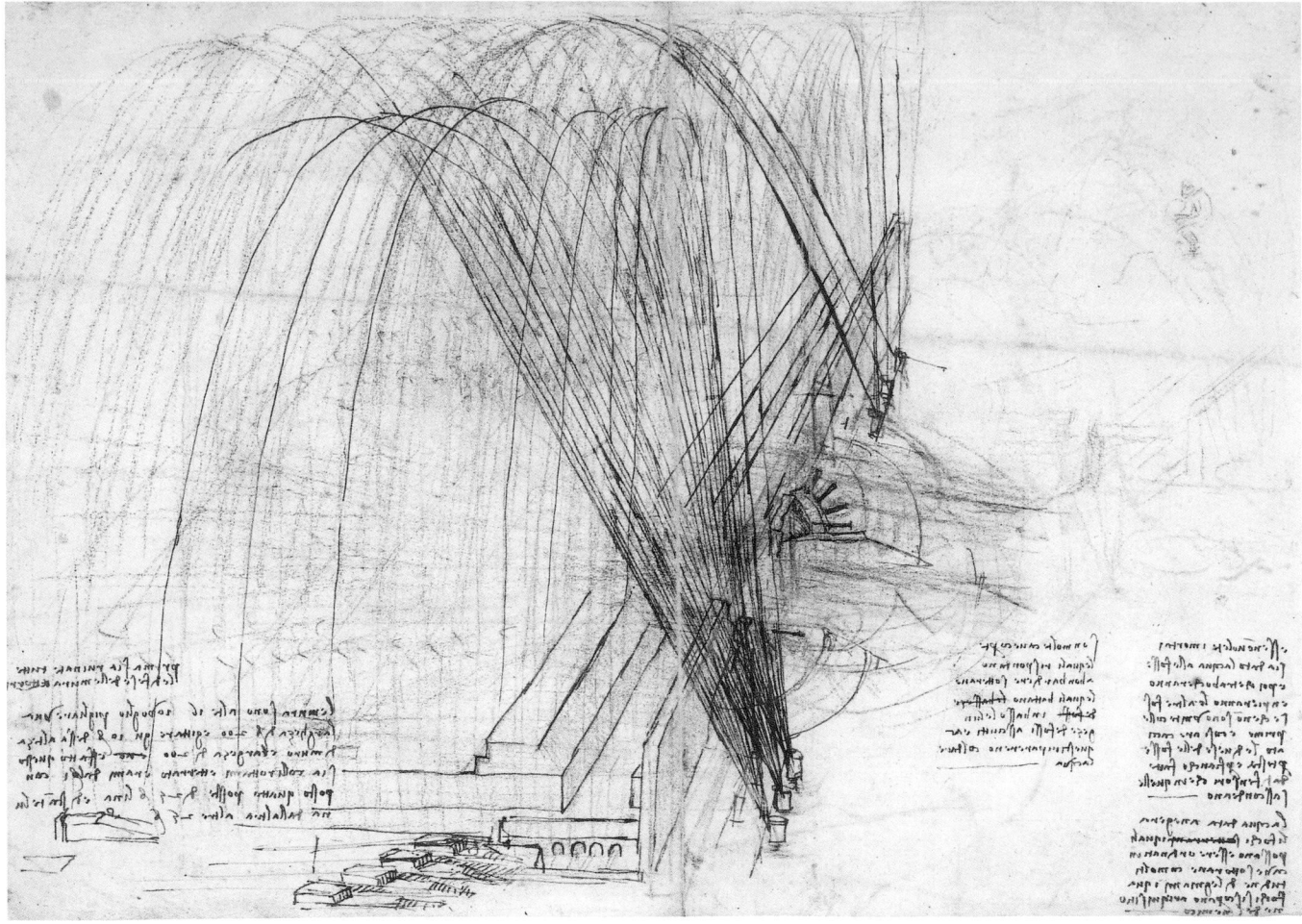

Cat. 88v

impressive trajectories of the fired stones or balls are clearly reinforced in pen and ink. To the lower left and right, Leonardo's notes describe tactics for demolishing the defenses of walls and towers, and for disposing of mines and guns buried in the ground by inundating the ditches before them.[1] This boldly sketched composition probably served as a preliminary draft in preparing a larger, pristinely executed presentation drawing of the subject (cat. no. 89). A similar drawing of mortars firing stones occurs also in the Codex Atlanticus (fol. 72r [formerly fol. 24r-a), and Kenneth Clark and Carlo Pedretti offered the tantalizing suggestion that the Codex Atlanticus sheet and the present one were once part of the same large page, a page similar in size to the *Map of Imola* (Windsor, RL 12284), from 1502. Reconstructed, this original page would be of a *foglio reale* format, a common size in this period. The drawing on the verso, which is in the opposite direction from the study and sketches on the recto, may have preceded the recto in date, for it probably relates to Leonardo's earlier military endeavors for Cesare Borgia and the Florentine Republic, of 1502–3 (see Chronology). CCB

1. Transcribed and translated in Clark and Pedretti 1968–69, vol. 1, p. 32.

LEONARDO DA VINCI

89. *A Row of Four Mortars Firing into the Courtyard of a Fortification*

Pen and brown ink, brush with gray-brown and yellow-brown
(originally green?) wash, over traces of charcoal or soft black chalk,
326 × 476 mm (12⅞ × 18¾ in.)
Lent by Her Majesty Queen Elizabeth II, Royal Library, Windsor
Castle 12275

PROVENANCE: Windsor Leoni volume: 1519, Francesco Melzi, Milan
and Rome (1491/93–ca. 1570); ca. 1570, Orazio Melzi; by 1590,
Pompeo Leoni, Madrid and Milan (ca. 1533–1608; Lugt under 2885);
ca. 1613, Thomas Howard, second earl of Arundel (1586–1646);
before 1690, British Royal Collection (inventory of King George III's
collection, ca. 1810).

LITERATURE: Commissione Vinciana 1928– , vol. 6, p. 24, pl. 273;
MacCurdy 1938, vol. 2, pl. 5; Royal Academy of Arts 1952, p. 171;
Clark and Pedretti 1968–69, vol. 1, p. 3, no. 12275; Clark 1969–70,
p. 11, no. 47; Calvi 1980, p. 285; Marani 1984, pp. 212–13, no. 126;

Rosand 1988, pp. 42–43, fig. 52; Kemp and Roberts 1989, p. 140,
no. 70; Kemp 1992a, p. 157, fig. 6; Kemp 1992b, p. 285, no. 187; Arasse
1998, pp. 208–10, fig. 147; Clayton 2002b, pp. 28–30, no. 4.

Here, four mortars buried in a row of ditches before the
crenellated walls of a fortress fire a lethal rain of stones
into the *piazzaforte*, the courtyard of the enemy stronghold,
the ammunition achieving a gigantic height and a dizzying
density. Leonardo exploited the tunneling perspective created
by the trajectories of the missiles with a surrealistic sense of
immediacy. To quote Kenneth Clark, "the violence of gunfire is
rendered as a graceful play of water."[1] Like catalogue number 80,
this design for a military defense, from 1503–4, probably was
intended as a presentation piece for a patron, to judge from

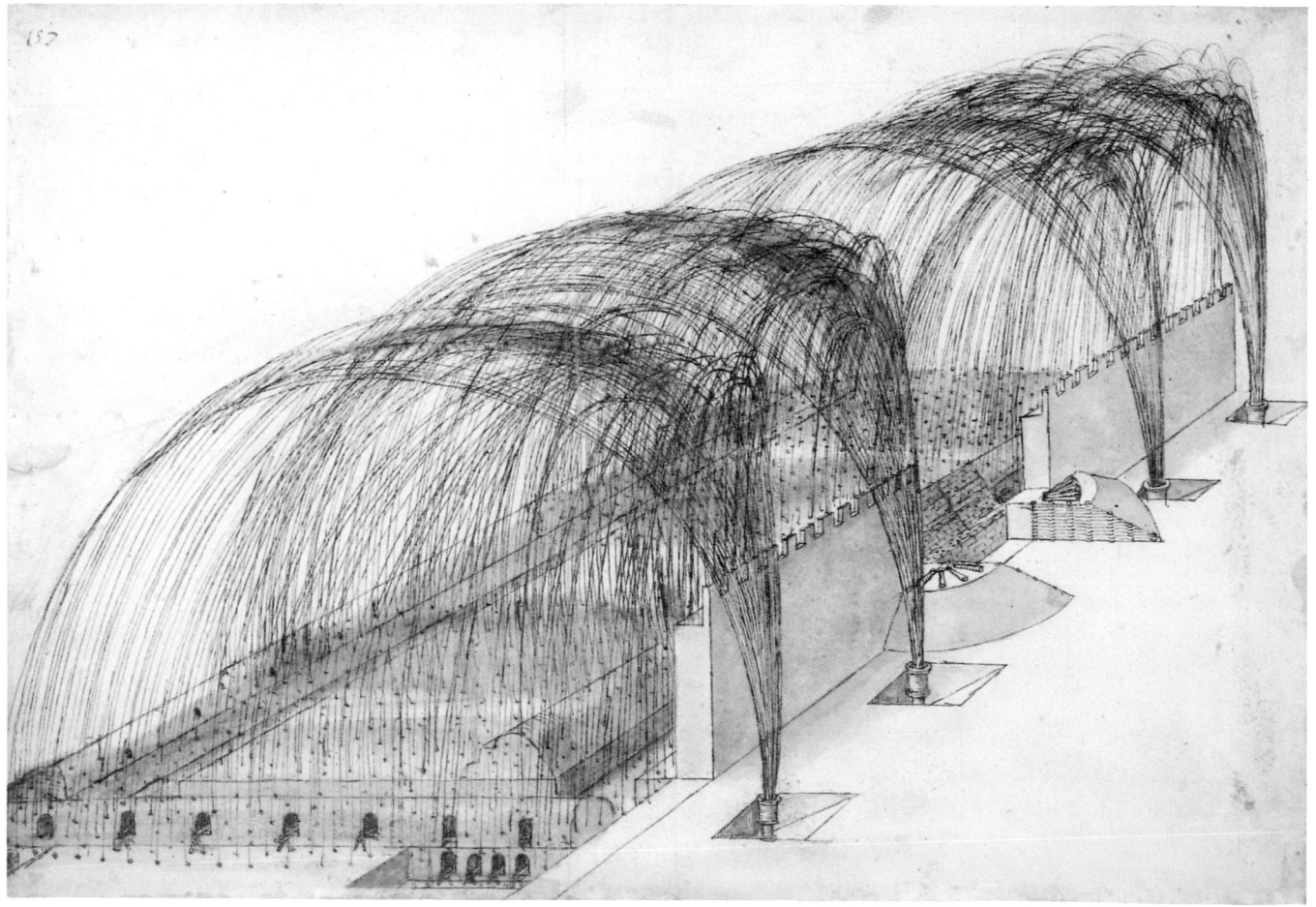

Cat. 89

the large size of the sheet and the clear, expository manner of drawing. It constitutes the cleaned-up draft of the expressive sketch seen on the verso of catalogue number 88, which bears early studies for both the *Battle of Anghiari* and the *Leda and the Swan* on the recto, and thus helps establish the date. The notes accompanying the rough sketch on the verso of catalogue number 88 clarify Leonardo's intentions in the present drawing: "Let the defenses of walls and towers be ruined first. . . . The walls are 16 braccia high. . . . There are many covered mines to house guns, which are placed below ground level and which fire along the dry ditches. We shall dispose of them by means of inundation. And if you do not want the mortars, let us fill the ditches with water, and as they overflow, the water will fill up the other ditches . . . and so we shall have eliminated the defenses of the ditches."[2]

The maps of 1502–4 prepared by Leonardo during his service to Cesare Borgia "Il Valentino" (1475–1507) and the Florentine Republic offer a touchstone for the neat drawing technique in color seen in the present sheet.[3] Niccolò Machiavelli, the author of *Il Principe* (The Prince), which he modeled after Cesare Borgia, was sent by the Florentine Republic on a diplomatic mission to Cesare's court in June 1502. That very summer— between May and August 18—Cesare would name Leonardo the Borgias' "family architect and general engineer" in the Marche and Romagna regions (see Chronology). The type of military defense seen in the present drawing—with an internal ditch instead of the usual external ditch—seems to correspond with a description in book 7 of Machiavelli's military treatise,

the *Arte della guerra*.[4] Another significant comparison for the technique and use of color in the present drawing is Leonardo's nine sketches of plans for a city gate and fortification at Piombino (C.A., fol. 125v [formerly 45v-b]), connected with his service there under Cesare Borgia's orders, rather than his later stint in the town. The mood and grandeur of the present drawing are paralleled also in an enigmatic project for a *piazzaforte* of polygonal plan that is neatly drafted in a panoramic perspective and in color (C.A., fol. 116r [formerly 41v-a]) .

The delicate use of color and the eerily subdued panoramic style of illustration seen in the present drawing, as well as in the presentation maps, contrast greatly with the narrative theatricality of Leonardo's drawings of military subjects from the 1480s (cat. nos. 49–52). Returning to military engineering, Leonardo explored the more dispassionate, clear, expository style of traditional fifteenth-century illustrated treatises on military architecture, without sacrificing his unparalleled powers of description. He apparently still had his copy of Roberto Valturio's *De re militari* (the most famous military treatise of its day), published in 1472 and 1483, recording it among the books that he "left locked in the chest" in 1502–4 (Codex Madrid II, fols. 2v–3r). CCB

1. Quoted in Clark and Pedretti 1968–69, vol. 1, p. 32; full transcription in cat. no. 88.
2. Clark and Pedretti 1968–69, vol. 1, p. 3; Marani 1984, p. 212.
3. Windsor, RL 12284, 12277, 12278, 12279, 12682, 12683, 12679, and cat. no. 80.
4. Marani 1984, pp. 175–76, no. 95.

LEONARDO DA VINCI

90. *Study for the Head of a Soldier in the "Battle of Anghiari"* (recto)   *Study for the Same Soldier on a Horse* (verso)

Red chalk on very pale ocher-pink prepared paper; outlines along facial profile slightly incised (recto); red chalk on unprepared paper (verso), 227 × 186 mm (8 15/16 × 7 5/16 in.)
Inscribed faintly by modern hand on verso in graphite: *B 1.5*
Szépmüvészeti Múzeum, Budapest 1774

PROVENANCE: Antonio Cesare Poggi (1744–1836), London and Paris (Lugt 617); Prince Miklós (Nikolaus) Esterházy, Vienna (1765–1833; Lugt 1965); by inheritance, Prince Paul Esterházy (1785–1866); acquired from the family in 1870 by the Hungarian government;

Országos Képtár (Hungarian National Picture Gallery; Lugt 2000); museum stamp (Lugt 2328).

LITERATURE: Richter 1883, vol. 1, pp. 339–40; Schönbrunner and Meder 1896, vol. 5, p. 490; Müntz 1899, p. 410; Berenson 1903, vol. 1, p. 162, vol. 2, p. 57, no. 1012, pl. 116; Seidlitz 1909, vol. 2, p. 81, pl. 56; Poggi 1919, pl. 99; Venturi 1920, p. 133, fig. 111; De Rinaldis 1926, p. 209, fig. 42; Commissione Vinciana 1928– , vol. 6, p. 24, pl. 258.2; Sirén 1928, vol. 1, p. 142, vol. 3, pl. 177B; Suida 1929, p. 142 (copy after Leonardo); Popham 1930–31, no. 82; Bodmer 1931,

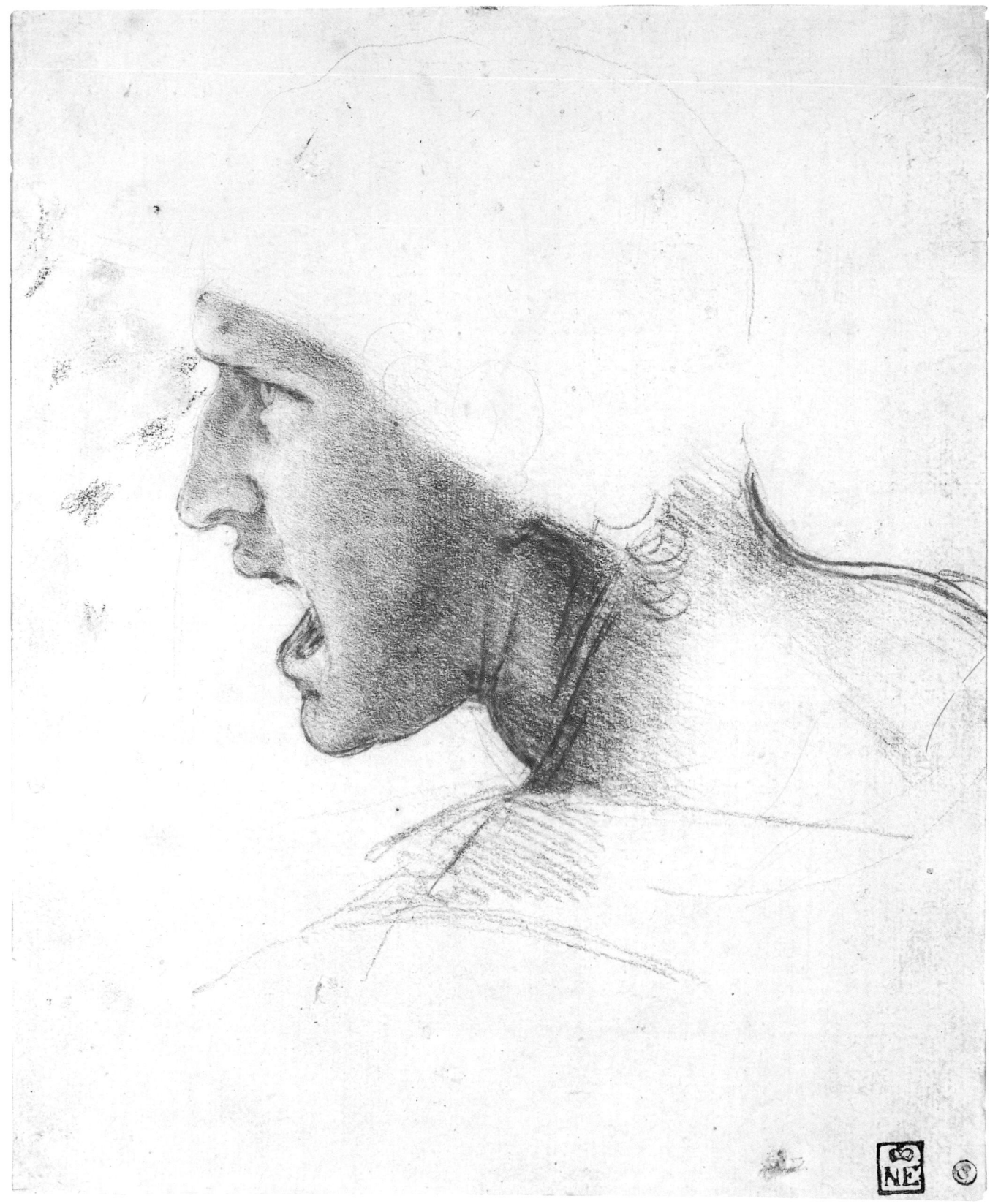

Cat. 90R

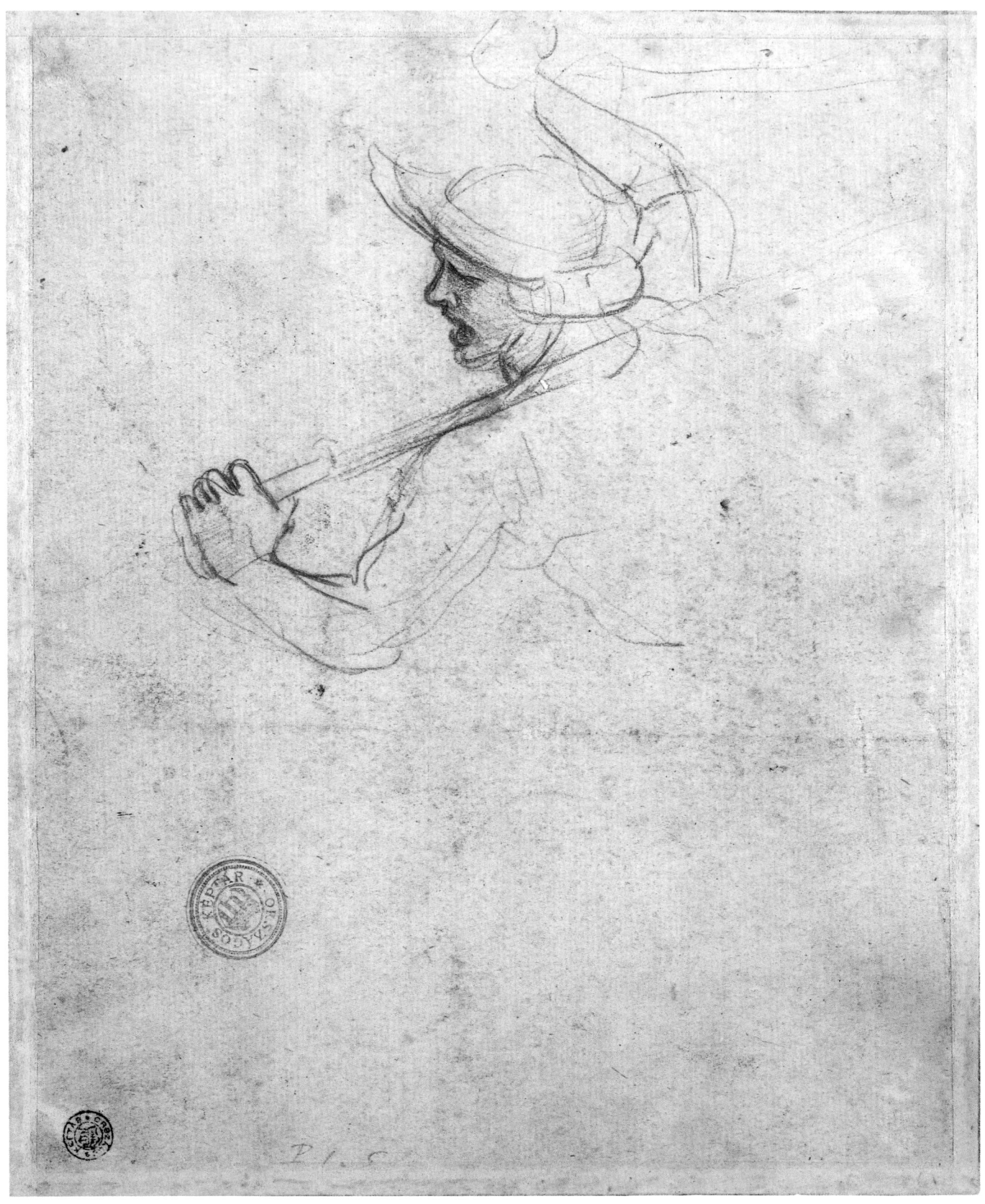

Cat. 90v

502

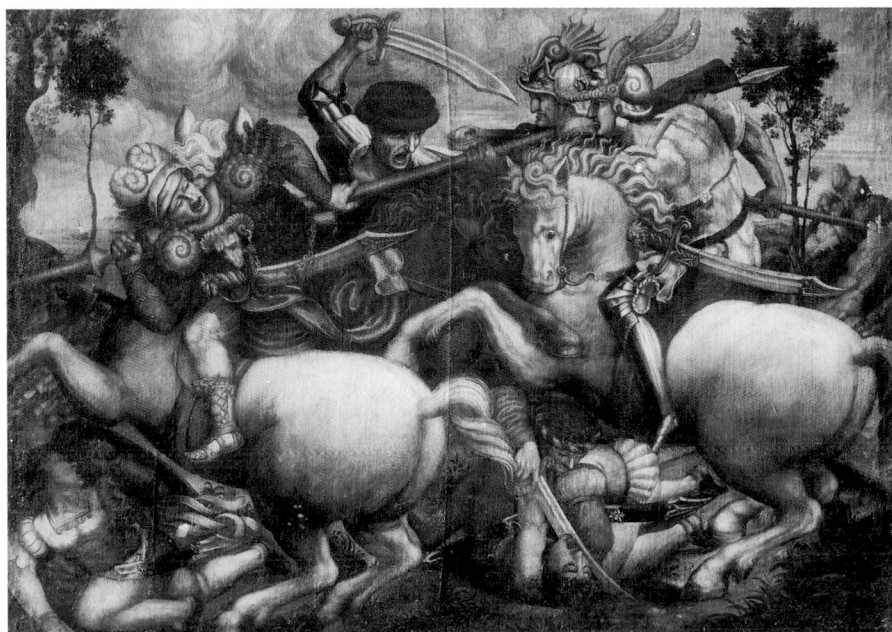

pp. 307, 412; Berenson 1938, vol. 1, p. 179, vol. 2, p. 110, vol. 3, fig. 541, no. 1012; Giglioli 1944, pl. 99; Castelfranco 1952a, pl. 27; Heydenreich 1954, vol. 1, pp. 45–46, vol. 2, p. 49, pl. 61 (incorrect inv. no.); Castelfranco 1956, p. 60, pl. 73 (incorrect inv. no.); Vayer 1957, nos. 18–19; Goldscheider 1959, p. 154, pl. 12; Berenson 1961, vol. 1, p. 260, vol. 2, p. 192, no. 1012; Castelfranco 1966, fig. 79; Pedretti 1968a, fig. 43; Richter 1970, vol. 1, p. 376, pl. 50c; Brizio 1974b, p. 47, fig. 47/2; Gould 1975, pp. 135–36, pl. 7; Pedretti 1977, vol. 1, p. 376, fig. 29; Keele and Pedretti 1979–80, vol. 2, pp. 840, 852; Rosci 1980, p. 508; Rosci 1982, p. 127; Meller 1985, p. 136, fig. 68; Yakush 1985, pp. 26–27, no. 5; Joannides 1988, pp. 78–79, fig. 13; Marani 1989, pp. 132–38, under no. 8a; Caroli 1991, pp. 196–97; Giovanna Nepi Scirè in Palazzo Grassi 1992, pp. 274–75, nos. 35–35a; Marani 1994, p. 14; Kwakkelstein 1994, pp. 115–16, pl. 80; Popham 1994, no. 199; Cecchi and Natali 1996, pp. 106–7, no. 17; Kemp 1996b, p. 192; Zöllner 1997, pp. 10–15, 32, pl. 5; Arasse 1998, pp. 437, 439, fig. 297; Zentai 1998, pp. 18–22, no. 4; Loránd Zentai in Gerszi 1999, pp. 26–27, no. 5; Mras and Galavics 1999, pp. 189–91; Marani 2000b, pp. 264–68; Ames-Lewis 2001, pp. 4–7, fig. 1; Laurenza 2001, p. 127, 150–51, 158, fig. 77; Ames-Lewis 2002, pp. 9–10, no. 13; Clayton 2002a, pp. 120–23, fig. 39.

Jean Paul Richter was one of the first scholars to recognize in 1883 that Leonardo produced this magnificent sheet of life studies as well as catalogue number 91, also from the Szépmüvészeti Múzeum, Budapest, to prepare the over-lifesize designs for the main figures of the angry soldiers in the *Fight for the Standard*, which was to be the central episode of the ill-fated *Battle of Anghiari*. The *Fight for the Standard* became

justly famous as a composition, for, to quote Vasari's vita of Leonardo, "in it rage, fury, and revenge are perceived as much in the men as in the horses."[1] The monumental sixteenth-century copy that was reworked by Peter Paul Rubens (cat. no. 135) is among the few reprises of Leonardo's lost masterpiece to capture the feral spirit of the original composition. The two imposing Budapest studies of the screaming soldiers (cat. nos. 90, 91) are all that remains of what must have been Leonardo's numerous penetrating studies of physiognomy for the *Battle of Anghiari*. The soldiers' faces rage with the *pazzia bestialissima*—the human madness of war that Leonardo repeatedly described in his notes. As is well known, the *Fight for the Standard* was the only portion of the *Battle of Anghiari* that Leonardo actually began painting on the wall of the Sala del Gran Consiglio of the Palazzo della Signoria. According to the Codice Magliabechiano (Anonimo Gaddiano) of about 1540, he used an experimental *secco* painting technique that caused the colors to run with the heat of the fire that he lit to dry them,[2] and whatever remained as a sadly ruined fragment was covered up in Giorgio Vasari's remodeling of the room in 1563. The lost composition of the *Fight for the Standard* is known from numerous copies (drawings, prints, and paintings cat. no. 135; figs. 18, 181), and these help clarify the context of the Budapest head studies (cat. nos. 90, 91). The design of the carefully drawn heads in both sheets is in identical scale: the heads are, broadly speaking, half lifesize. In all likelihood, therefore, the Budapest sheets were among the last preliminary drawings that Leonardo undertook for the heads of these particular figures in the *Fight for the Standard* before he enlarged their design to the full scale of the cartoon.

Drawn from the live model, the figure on the recto and verso of the present sheet corresponds to the soldier on the extreme right in the *Fight for the Standard*. He can possibly be identified as Pier Giampaolo Orsini, the young Florentine condottiere sent by Ludovico degli Scarampi to recapture the standard of the Florentine Republic from Milanese hands. The overall effect of the rendering in the present study is deeply tonal, and the modeling of the forms displays an exquisite range of gradations from the darkest shadows to the most intense highlights. Leonardo first outlined the head broadly and modeled the shadows with parallel strokes in his characteristic lower right to upper left direction. He rubbed in the strokes for a seamless effect, and to strengthen the final contours he pressed rather hard with the chalk on the paper. The present sheet probably dates after the revised contract of May 1504, which gave a status report on Leonardo's progress on the *Battle of Anghiari* project, suggesting that he was still at work on the cartoon in the Sala del Papa of the Chiostro Grande at Santa Maria Novella, and closer to the time that he began to paint in the Sala of the Palazzo della Signoria during the spring of 1505 (see Chronology). Leonardo drew the young soldier's head largely in reserve, omitting the elaborate plumed helmet that he was supposed to wear in the final composition, to focus attention on his screaming countenance. Some indications of a close-fitting helmet with a concentric coil around the ear appear lightly sketched in outline. The verso of the sheet offers a more synthetic overall view of the same soldier on horseback.

A number of the copies after Leonardo's central episode of the *Fight for the Standard* curiously omit the screaming figure that is portrayed in the present sheet as a young man of idealized beauty, or conflate him with that of another screaming but older soldier of grotesque physiognomy. Two of the mid-sixteenth-century painted copies representing the most archaeologically precise record of the portion of the *Fight for the Standard* that Leonardo began to execute on the wall of the Sala del Gran Consiglio demonstrate that he left this figure largely unpainted on the plaster except for the head (private collection [ex collections Doria d'Angri, Naples; Hoffmann, Munich]; fig. 18). There, the soldier of the present

Budapest study appears as a bold silhouette in reserve, mounted on a rearing horse that is painted with great finish. A relatively accomplished copy in the British Museum (fig. 182), drawn in pen and ink with wash on pink prepared paper, shows the screaming figure in full length on horseback, with a fairly idealized young face, similar to that in the Budapest study. The design of the frontal parts of his body is relatively complete, which suggests that the British Museum copy was presumably drawn after the original cartoon or another smaller-scale study by Leonardo (of the type that is seen here on both sides of the sheet), rather than after the mural. In great contrast, all the copies, whether direct or indirect, show the main figure of the soldier seen in catalogue number 91 consistently with more or less the same facial features, suggesting that Leonardo must have actually carried out this part of the design in paint, in its entirety.

As inconceivable as it may seem, the arresting drawing on the recto of the present Budapest sheet has had some detractors among Leonardo scholars (in such cases, the drawing is simply omitted by the skeptics, rather than explicitly rejected). In 1998, Loránd Zentai rightly discussed some of the problems of condition caused by early restorations that mar the drawing surface of this exquisite sheet. We know of one of these restorers' early attempts at cleaning from Paul Müller-Walde, who published the present sheet in 1899 (along with cat. no. 91) in a groundbreaking article in which he also proudly announced that the Budapest drawings had been cleaned before being photographed for his publication.[3] The main results of such interventions by restorers appear to be here a blank area in the background around the soldier's cap and facial profile, as well as a slight flattening of the drawing's surface in the area of the soldier's upper back. The outline in the upper part of the face is also somewhat abraded. One can see that the pale, ocher-pink prepared paper has been lightened around the head, probably in an effort to clean stains (some of the gray spots on the left appear to be oxidized lead white). This has probably diminished the subtle tones of the red chalk on the paper, which originally were probably similar to those of the nearly contemporary, strikingly beautiful plant studies often associated with the *Leda and the Swan* (Windsor, RL 12419–12422). The superb tonal control of the chalk, however, closely comparable to that of catalogue number 91, can leave no doubt that this is among the great masterpieces of Leonardo's mature draftsmanship.

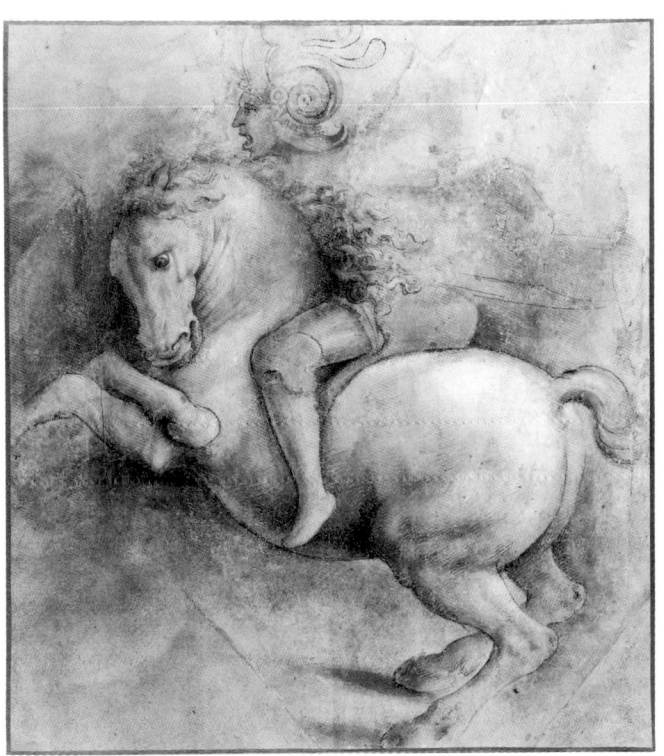

Fig. 182. Copy after Leonardo da Vinci, *Horseman from the "Fight for the Standard" ("Battle of Anghiari")*. Pen and brown ink, brush and gray wash, highlighted with white gouache, on pink-washed paper, 267 × 237 mm. The British Museum, London 1895-9-15-479

Doubts have been expressed more often regarding Leonardo's authorship of the accomplished figure sketch on the verso of the Budapest sheet (it was rejected by A. E. Popham in 1946).

However, such skepticism can be laid to rest if one considers the animated movement of the reinforced contours, the subtle modulation of the chiaroscuro rendering, and the obviously fluent left-handed manner of curved parallel hatching in the lightly modeled face of the soldier. There are also very slight, somewhat curving strokes of lower left to upper right curved parallel hatching on the hand and helmet of the figure; these are also most probably original, for they follow the form closely (as in a number of pen-and-ink drawings from this period; cat. nos. 95, 97–99). The verso has been accepted as autograph by Bernard Berenson, Carlo Pedretti, Loránd Zentai, and, with some hesitation, by Paul Joannides. It bears emphasizing that the sketchy red-chalk drawing technique on the verso of the Budapest sheet is quite similar to that of the so-called portrait of Cesare Borgia (Biblioteca Reale, Turin, 15573 D.C.), a drawing datable stylistically to about 1502–5.[4]

CCB

1. Vasari–Milanesi 1906, vol. 4, p. 41: "perciocchè in essa non si conosce meno la rabbia, lo sdegno e la vendetta negli uomini, che ne' cavalli."
2. Transcribed in Frey 1892, p. 114; Vecce 1998, p. 362.
3. Paul Müller-Walde noted that before the sheet was photographed, "he freed the drawing of later accretions"; see Zentai 1998, p. 18, nos. 3, 4.
4. If the Turin drawing in red chalk is, indeed, a portrait of Cesare Borgia (in this author's opinion, the resemblance of the head to portrait medals of Cesare supports that proposal by Wilhelm Reinhold Valentiner in 1930), then the drawing would have to be dated closer in time to Leonardo's service to Cesare Borgia in 1502–3 (see Chronology; see also Carlo Pedretti in Biblioteca Reale 1990, pp. 46–47, no. 13).

LEONARDO DA VINCI

91. *Studies for the Heads of Two Soldiers in the "Battle of Anghiari"*

Charcoal, or soft black chalk; some traces of red chalk on left, 192 × 188 mm (7⁹⁄₁₆ × 7⁷⁄₁₆ in.)
Inscribed in graphite on verso by modern hand: *1.5a*
Szépmüvészeti Múzeum, Budapest 1775

LITERATURE: Richter 1883, vol. 1, pp. 338–40; Schönbrunner and Meder 1896, vol. 3, p. 267; Müntz 1899, p. 410; Berenson 1903, vol. 1, p. 162, vol. 2, p. 57, no. 1011, pl. 115; Seidlitz 1909, vol. 2, p. 81, pl. 55; Poggi 1919, pl. 100; Venturi 1920, p. 133, fig. 110; De Rinaldis 1926, p. 209, fig. 43; Commissione Vinciana 1928– , vol. 6, p. 24, pl. 258.1; Popp 1928, pp. 9, 49, no. 58; Sirén 1928, vol. 1, p. 142, vol. 3, pl. 177A; Suida 1929, p. 142 (copy after Leonardo?); Valentiner 1930, pp. 79, fig. 33; Popham 1930–31, no. 81; Bodmer 1931, pp. 306, 412; Suter 1937, pl. 10; Berenson 1938, vol. 1, p. 179, vol. 2, p. 110, vol. 3, fig. 538; Giglioli 1944, pl. 100; Neufeld 1949, pp. 179–83; Castelfranco 1954, pl. 169, fig. 11; Heydenreich 1954, vol. 1, pp. 45–46, vol. 2, p. 48, pl. 60 (incorrect inv. no.); Castelfranco 1956, p. 60, pl. 75 (incorrect inv. no.); Vayer 1957, no. 20; Goldscheider 1959, p. 154, pl. 13; Berenson 1961, vol. 1, p. 260, vol. 2, p. 192, no. 1011; Freedberg

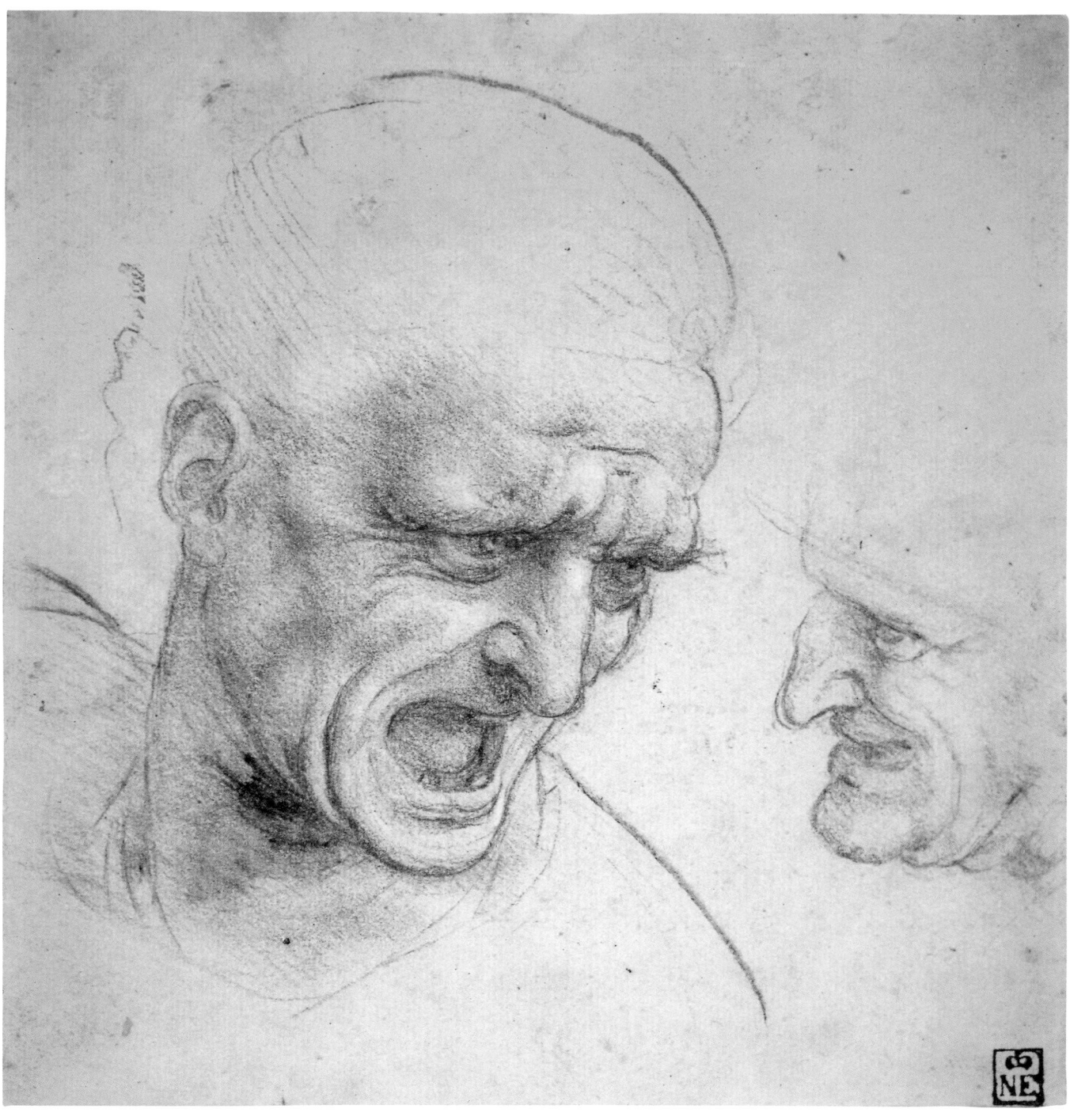

Cat. 91

1961, fig. 32; Moskovits 1962, no. 164; Castelfranco 1966, fig. 78; Fenyö 1967, pp. 16–17, no. 4; Pedretti 1968a, fig. 42; Richter 1970, vol. 1, p. 376, pl. 50B; Gould 1975, pp. 134–36, fig. 69; Cogliati Arano 1980, p. 54, under no. 20; Lavagnino 1980, p. 133; Kemp 1981, pp. 240, 242, pl. 67; Rosci 1982, p. 126; Meller 1985, p. 136, fig. 67; Yakush 1985, pp. 24–25, no. 4; Clark 1988, pp. 198–200, fig. 83; Kemp

1989c, pp. 228–32; Marani 1989, pp. 132–38, no. 8A, fig. 35; Caroli 1991, pp. 194–95; Zöllner 1991, p. 189, fig. 21; Giovanna Nepi Scirè in Palazzo Grassi 1992, pp. 272–73, no. 34; Kwakkelstein 1994, pp. 115–16; pl. 79; Popham 1994, no. 198; Caroli 1995, p. 169, fig. 13; Zöllner 1997, pp. 10–15, 32, pl. 4; Arasse 1998, pp. 414, 437, fig. 278; Zentai 1998, pp. 18–22, no. 3; Bambach 1999b; Loránd Zentai in

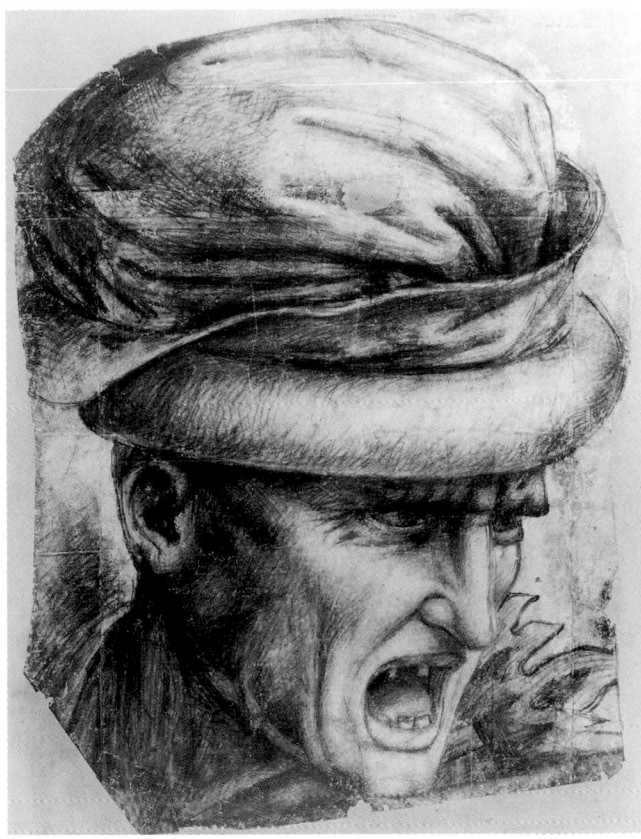

Fig. 183. Copy after Leonardo da Vinci, *Head of a Warrior (Niccolò Piccinino) from the "Fight for the Standard" ("Battle of Anghiari")*. Black chalk on gray-blue paper, 505 × 375 mm (irregular). Ashmolean Museum, Oxford 20

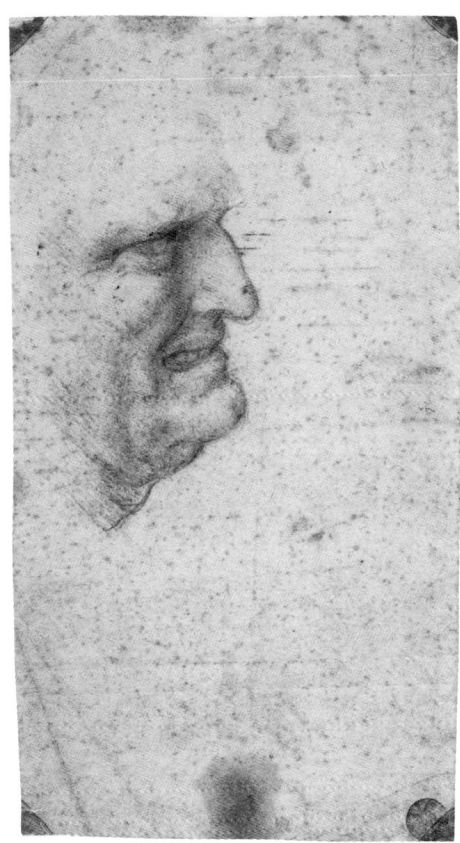

Fig. 184. Leonardo da Vinci, *Head of a Warrior in Profile*. Black chalk, 220 × 116 mm. Gallerie dell'Accademia, Venice 232

Gerszi 1999, pp. 24–25, no. 4; Marani 2000b, pp. 264–68; Ames-Lewis 2001, pp. 4–7, n. 5, fig. 2; Ames-Lewis 2002, pp. 9–10, no. 14; Laurenza 2001, p. 127, 150–51, 158, figs. 76, 84; Clayton 2002–3, pp. 120–23, fig. 38.

This justly famous study portrays the head of the protagonist in the episode of the *Fight for the Standard* (appearing near the top toward the center), from whose hands the Milanese standard is wrested by the victorious Florentine soldiers, and the profile of the soldier immediately on his right. The well-known sixteenth-century copy that was reworked by Peter Paul Rubens can help clarify the positioning of these figures in Leonardo's lost composition (cat. no. 135). The main figure—the screaming soldier whose head is seen in three-quarter view, facing right, in the Budapest study—is usually identified as Niccolò Piccinino, the condottiere in command of the Milanese troops of Duke Filippo Maria Visconti that were defeated by the Florentines. The upper parts of the soldiers' heads are barely rendered, since in the final design they were to be portrayed wearing sumptuously ornamented military costumes. As is suggested by the painted copies after the small portion of the mural that Leonardo began to execute on the wall of the Sala del Gran Consiglio of the Palazzo della Signoria, the figure of Niccolò Piccinino wore a large red cap ("un soldato vecchio, con un berrettone rosso," as Vasari's vita of the great master notes), and the adjoining soldier a fanciful antique-style helmet (see fig. 18).[1] The neckline of the armor of the main figure in the Budapest study is also indicated with faint outlines.

Like catalogue number 90, this sheet was cleaned by early restorers (as is documented in Paul Müller-Walde's article of 1899), though apparently with less severe results. There is a slight reinforcement of the dark shadows on the wrinkles of the main soldier's back and jaw line with brush and dark gray wash that probably is not original. Loránd Zentai has observed that technical analysis reveals that Leonardo seems to have begun the present study with an underdrawing in red chalk on the left part of the figure, which he abandoned; this red underdrawing is what gives the charcoal or soft black chalk outlines a slightly brown color.[2] It is possible, however, that the slight touches of red chalk may lie on top of the charcoal or soft black chalk. Leonardo used a much more extensive version of this technique of red-chalk underdrawing and overdrawing, combined with charcoal or soft black chalk, in the later study of the *Head of the Virgin* (cat. no. 108). Here, the artist turned to the medium of a rather grainy, charcoal or soft black chalk in order to create a seamlessly blended sfumato effect in the rendering of shadows with greater ease. It is more labor intensive to rub in the individual strokes of hatching with a stick of red chalk, as in catalogue number 90, for red chalk is harder and denser. It is clear, particularly on the left portion of the main soldier's cranium, that Leonardo began by applying the charcoal or soft black chalk with pronounced curved parallel hatching (in a technique that is comparable to that in the Venice composition sketch for the *Virgin and Child with Saint Anne*; cat. no. 95), before he smudged the individual strokes to obtain uniform shadows. Nevertheless, the tonal articulation of the figure's eye sockets, pupils, and eyelids is nearly identical to that in catalogue number 90. Here, the tonal modulation of the outlines along the right profile of the face is superb. The sketchy outlines on the man's cranium indicate that he originally wore a tightly fitted cloth turban, knotted on the front of the head, not unlike like that of the formidable standing warrior seen from the back in the Turin sheet (cat. no. 103).

A large, anonymous sixteenth-century fragment in the Ashmolean Museum, Oxford, copies the main figure seen in the Budapest study in probably the same scale as Leonardo's original cartoon (fig. 183). A puzzling drawing in Venice reproduces the head seen in profile on the right in the Budapest sheet in the exact medium, technique, and size, but in reverse orientation (fig. 184). Although less vigorous in technique, the Venice drawing is nevertheless rendered with left-handed parallel hatching. Deemed autograph by the connoisseurs of Leonardo's drawings, Bernard Berenson and A. E. Popham (as well as others), the Venice sheet is considered to be a copy in more recent scholarly literature.[3]   CCB

1. Zentai 1998, p. 22, nos. 3–4.
2. Vasari–Milanesi 1906, vol. 4, p. 41.
3. Cogliati Arano 1980, p. 54, no. 20, with early bibliography. See Giovanna Nepi Scirè in Palazzo Grassi 1992, pp. 272–73; Caroli 1991, p. 232.

LEONARDO DA VINCI

92. *Bust of Grotesque Man in Profile Facing to the Right*

Charcoal or black chalk, with some right-handed reworking, with contours pricked for transfer, 382 × 275 mm (15 1/16 × 10 13/16 in.) Inscribed on recto in pen and brown ink, at left, in epigraphic letters by a sixteenth-century hand resembling that of Giorgio Vasari (according to Byam Shaw 1976) or, much less likely, that of Francisco de Holanda (according to Franklin 2000): *LIONARDO DA VINCI*; in pen and brown ink on the backing in an eighteenth-century hand: *Leonardo da Vinci* and *G.30*
Christ Church, Oxford 0033

PROVENANCE: Giorgio Vasari (?), Arezzo, Florence, and Rome (1511–1574) or, much less likely, Francisco de Holanda (?), Rome and Lisbon (1517–1584); General John Guise, Winterbourne and London (1682/83–1765; under Lugt 2754); his bequest, 1765.

LITERATURE: Berenson 1903, vol. 1, p. 160, vol. 2, p. 59, no, 1050; Colvin 1907, vol. 1, no. 21; Thiis 1913, p. 40; Bell 1914, p. 60, A.28; Poggi 1919, p. 160; Bodmer 1931, pp. 305, 412; Berenson 1938, vol. 1, p. 178, vol. 2, p. 117, vol. 3, fig. 536, no. 1050; Giglioli 1944, pl. 167; Royal Academy of Arts 1952, no. 88; Gombrich 1954, pp. 197–220; Heydenreich 1954, vol. 2, p. 40, pl. 50; Matthiesen Gallery 1960, no. 40; Berenson 1961, vol. 1, p. 259, vol. 2, p. 205, no. 1050; Walker Art Gallery 1964, no. 22; National Gallery of Art 1972, no. 35; Ragghianti Collobi 1974, vol. 1, p. 92, vol. 2, p. 128, fig. 249; Byam Shaw 1976, vol. 1, p. 38, no. 19; Gombrich 1976, pp. 57–75; Bora 1982, p. 152, fig. 108; Kemp and Roberts 1989, p. 91, no. 34; Caroli 1991, pp. 208–9, no. A.28; Pedretti 1991d, pp. 44–47; Palazzo Grassi 1992, p. 158; Gianvittorio Dillon in Petrioli Tofani 1992, p. 126, no. 5.5; Kwakkelstein 1994, pp. 105–7, fig. 47; Popham 1994, no. 146; Marani 1997, pp. 165–66, fig. 8; Arasse 1998, pp. 124–25, fig. 69; Marco Rossi in Ambrosiana 1998–99, pp. 80–98; Bambach 1999a, pp. 51, 111, 262, 414 n. 176; Marani 2000b, pp. 195–98, 207 n. 96; Franklin 2000, fig. 7; Ames-Lewis 2002, p. 9, no. 10; Baker 2002, pp. 30–31, no. 6.

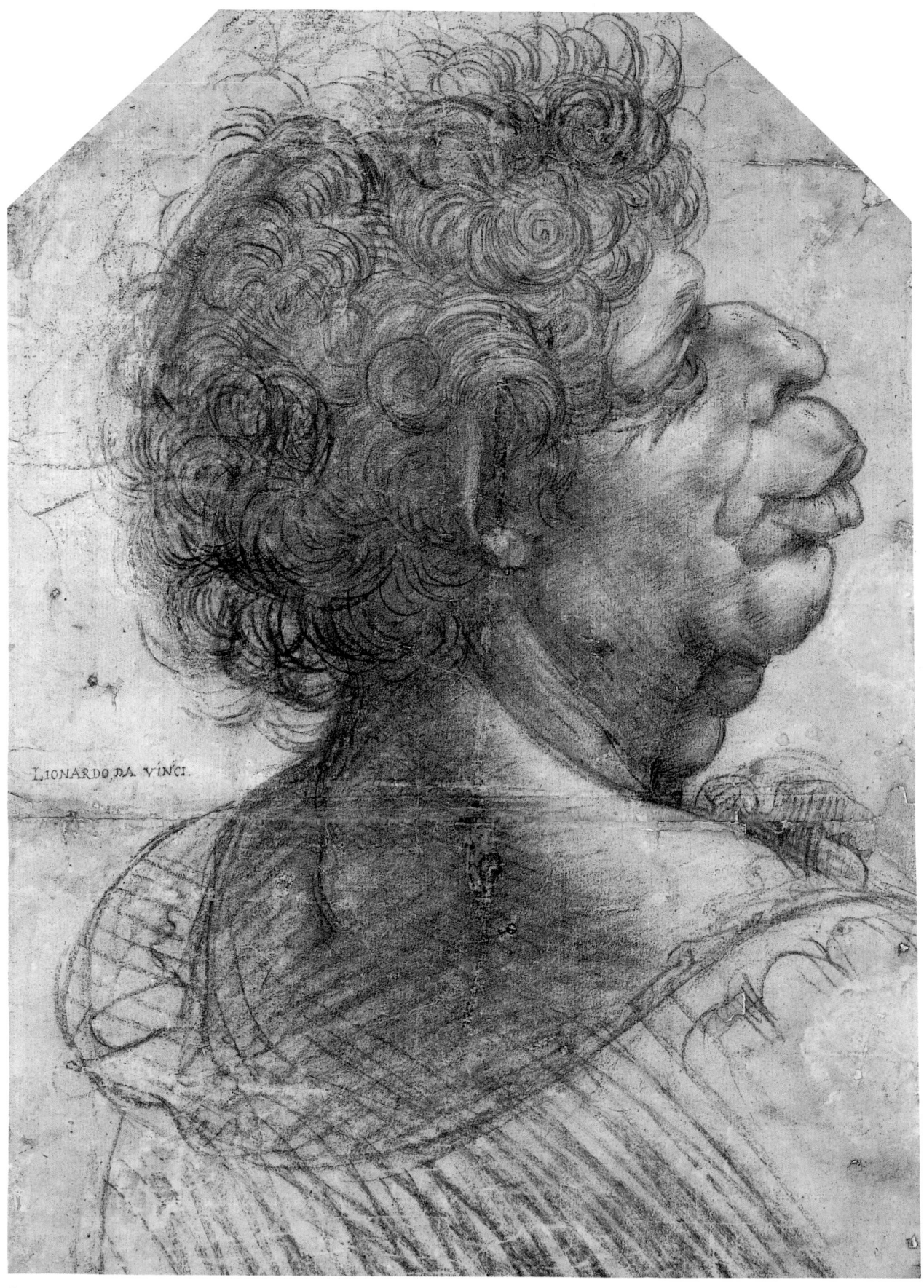

LIONARDO DA VINCI.

Cat. 92

509

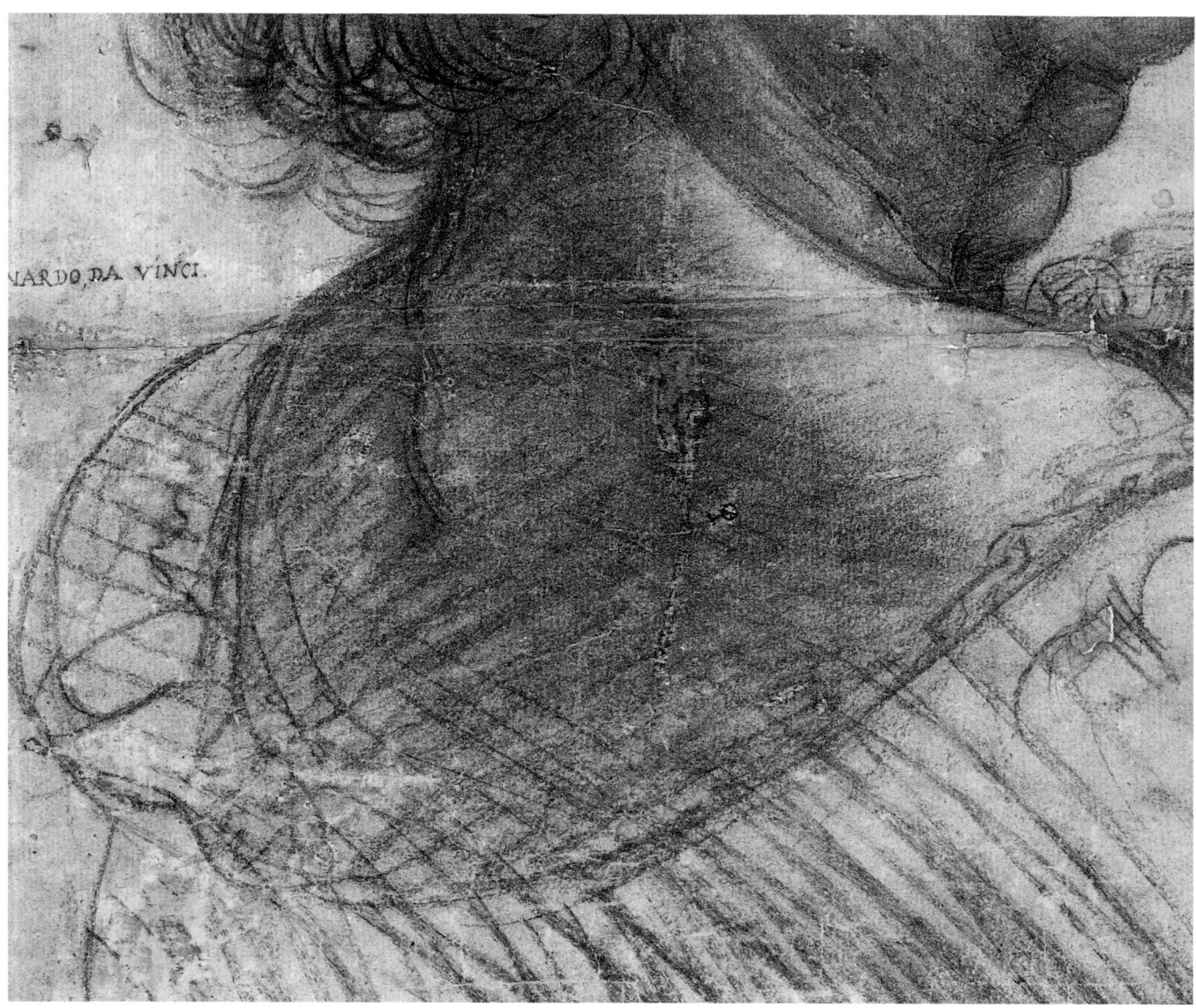

Cat. 92 *(detail)*

Among Leonardo's extant studies, this imposing, nearly lifesize cartoon (full-scale drawing) represents the culmination of his exploration of the physiognomy of the ugly. It is doubtful that the Christ Church cartoon is based on the likeness of an actual person. Giorgio Vasari aptly called Leonardo's magnificent physiognomic inventions and re-creations *teste bizzarre* (bizarre heads; see cat. nos. 69–73). The Christ Church cartoon can be dated about 1503–5, during Leonardo's most energetic work on the *Battle of Anghiari* project. The dynamic contrapposto of the man, with the torso seen boldly from the back and the head turned sharply to the upper right in a nearly strict profile view, lends him a powerful sculptural

presence, and leads the spectator's gaze directly to the deformity of his features. This monumental figure, more so than any others in Leonardo's smaller-scale drawings, evokes the artist's description of physiognomic types in the posthumously compiled manuscript of his *Libro di pittura* (Codex Urbinas Latinus, 1270): "and those who have facial features of great relief and depth are bestial and wrathful men, men of little reason."[1] Leonardo's classification of physiognomy offers yet another reason why it is unlikely that his drawings of deformed human faces are taken directly from life.

Bernard Berenson's tentative identification of the male figure portrayed in the Christ Church cartoon as "Scaramuccia" derives from an ambiguous passage in Giorgio Vasari's vita of the artist concerning Leonardo's *teste bizzarre*. The passage begins by describing a famous (lost) portrait drawing in charcoal of the head of Amerigo Vespucci, and then incidentally alludes to a head of "Scaramuccia, Captain of the Gypsies, which was later owned by Messer Donato Valdambrini of Arezzo, Canon of San Lorenzo, left to him by Giambullari."[2] Berenson's identification, however, may not be correct, for Vasari's admittedly elusive passage seems to allude to a specific likeness, in the sense of a portrait. It is also not entirely clear that the head of "Scaramuccia" was a charcoal drawing (like that of Amerigo Vespucci). Although in reverse orientation, the same figure type seen in the Christ Church cartoon is also represented in a small autograph caricature (Graphische Sammlung Albertina, Vienna; fig. 105), which is related to the Chatsworth caricature series (cat. nos. 69–73), and which, like them, was frequently copied by contemporary and later draftsmen. Therefore, it seems quite probable that the monumental portraitlike drawing at Christ Church exemplifies a more general physiognomic exercise in Leonardo's work.

The bold manner of handling the charcoal (or black chalk) with aggressively hatched strokes, selective stumping in the flesh areas, and vigorous reinforcement lines is typical of Leonardo's larger-scale drawings, and it may be very similar in technique to that of the lost *Battle of Anghiari* cartoon. In order to draw in such a large scale, the artist must have relied at least partly on the whole span of his arm. As Renaissance and Baroque treatises attest, cartoons required a very physical manner of drawing, and the involvement of much of the body in the process. In Leonardo's Christ Church cartoon, the parallel hatching in the rendering of shadows exhibits strokes that course in both directions: from upper left to lower right, as is most evident on the back of the figure, and from upper right to lower left, as in the more delicate modeling of flesh areas. Scholars often have noted that the Christ Church cartoon is retouched (in Berenson's words, "sadly retouched"), because of the passages of right-handed shading that are especially noticeable in the face but are also present elsewhere. As James Byam Shaw observed, the contours of the profile have been reworked as well, apparently with the brush. Retouchings of cartoons by restorers are inevitable, considering the great size

of the drawings and also the damage to the surface caused by their highly functional application in the working process. Many of the strokes in both directions, however—left to right and right to left—are in the same charcoal or black chalk medium (there is, indeed, also some reinforcement of the modeling from old restorations). The original charcoal or black chalk strokes could therefore be interpreted as left-handed and right-handed. It is possible, in view of the monumental scale of the Christ Church drawing in particular and the great physical effort of producing cartoons in general (whose large size often required the artist to engage his entire body in the action of drawing), that here Leonardo drew with both hands. In other words, the usually left-handed artist also relied on his right hand to draw. He may have worked with both hands to cover the large areas of shadow more rapidly with the chalk or charcoal. The rendering of broad areas of shadow in large-scale cartoons was considered sufficiently labor intensive that Giovanni Battista Armenini's *De' veri precetti della pittura* (Ravenna, 1586–87) advocated a shortcut that consisted of dusting—literally, *spolverare*—passages of shadow with a pouncing bag, thus reducing the effort of achieving a gray base tone.[3] It is also possible that Leonardo enlisted his pupils to help him model the vast shadows in the Christ Church cartoon, in order to achieve results quickly and with less effort on his part. It was not necessary to obtain as fine and precisely calibrated a line as when drawing on a small scale.

The outlines in the Christ Church cartoon are pricked to transfer the design: the artist or his assistants rubbed charcoal dust through the perforations, which created a dotted underdrawing on the working surface. Although the pricked outlines of the face and features are quite carefully done, they are much more selective in areas of the body and hair.

CCB

1. C. Urb., fol. 109v: "et quelli ch' anno le parti del uiso di gran' rileuo e' profondita sono huomini bestiali et iracondi con pocha raggione." See also Kemp 1989c, p. 147.
2. Vasari–Milanesi 1906, vol. 4, pp. 25–26: "come fu quella di Amerigo Vespucci, ch' è una testa di vecchio bellissima, disegnata di carbone, e parimenti quella di Scaramucci capitano de' Zingani, che poi ebbe messer Donato Valdambrini d'Arezzo, canonico di San Lorenzo, lassatagli dal Giambullari."
3. Armenini 1587, pp. 102–3; Bambach 1999a, pp. 51, 392 n. 109.

LEONARDO DA VINCI

93. *The Sea God Neptune Commanding His Quadriga of Sea Horses*

Charcoal or soft black chalk, 252 × 389 mm (9 15/16 × 15 5/16 in.)
Inscribed on recto in charcoal, in right-to-left script, on upper
border toward left: *abassa icha valli [abassa i cavalli]*
Lent by Her Majesty Queen Elizabeth II, Royal Library, Windsor
Castle 12570

PROVENANCE: According to Giorgio Vasari: Antonio Segni, his son
Fabio Segni, and Giovanni Gaddi; Windsor Leoni volume: 1519,
Francesco Melzi, Milan and Rome (1491/93–ca. 1570); ca. 1570,
Orazio Melzi; by 1590, Pompeo Leoni, Madrid and Milan (ca. 1533–
1608; Lugt under 2885); ca. 1613, Thomas Howard, second earl of
Arundel (1586–1646); before 1690, British Royal Collection (inven-
tory of King George III's collection, ca. 1810).

LITERATURE: Grosvenor 1878, vol. 1, p. 42; Müntz 1898, vol. 1,
p. 140; Müller-Walde 1899, p. 88, pl. 48; Müntz 1899, pp. 426–34;
Berenson 1903, vol. 1, p. 162, vol. 2, p. 165, pl. 118, no. 1117; Horne
1903, p. 17; Seidlitz 1909, vol. 2, p. 66, pl. 58; Seidlitz 1911, p. 272,
no. 65; Thiis 1913, pp. 37, 40; Poggi 1919, p. 10, pl. 114; Venturi
1920, p. 134, fig. 118; De Toni 1922, p. 122, fig. 40; Malaguzzi Valeri
1922, p. 29, fig. 28; Venturi 1925, fig. 52; De Rinaldis 1926, p. 215,
fig. 57; Commissione Vinciana 1928– , vol. 6, p. 24, pl. 279; Popp
1928, p. 45, no. 48; Sirén 1928, p. 150, pl. 182; Suida 1929, no. 151;
Stites 1930, pp. 265–66, fig. 21; Bodmer 1931, pp. 315, 413–14;
Berenson 1938, vol. 1, p. 180, vol. 2, p. 124, vol. 3, fig. 542, no. 1117;
Palazzo dell'Arte 1939, p. 155; Giglioli 1944, no. 118; Clark 1952,
p. 128, pl. 43; Gould 1952, pp. 289ff., fig. 18; Royal Academy of Arts
1952, no. 119 (hors catalogue); Brugnoli 1954, p. 373; Clark 1954, pl. 29;
Heydenreich 1954, vol. 1, p. 62, vol. 2, p. 61, pl. 76; Goldscheider
1959, pp. 161–62, pl. 46; Berenson 1961, vol. 1, p. 261, vol. 2, p. 219,
no. 1117; Chastel 1961, p. 188; Castelfranco 1966, p. 113; Clark and
Pedretti 1968–69, vol. 1, pp. 109–10, no. 12570; Clark 1969–70,
p. 18, no. 73; Gould 1975, pp. 115, 117, fig. 56; Nees 1978, pp. 24–26;
Leonardo da Vinci 1980, p. 4; Pedretti and Roberts 1984–96, pp. 58,
59–60, no. 32, colorpl. 9; Wasserman 1984, p. 33, fig. 25; Bober and
Rubinstein 1986, p. 131, pl. 99a; Pedretti 1987a, pp. 89, 108, fig. 117;
Clark 1988, pp. 188–90, fig. 78; Roberts 1988, pp. 28–29, no. 8;
Rosand 1988, pp. 29–30, fig. 37; Kemp 1989, p. 237; Kemp and
Roberts 1989, p. 144, no. 71; Marani 1989, pp. 139–40, no. 9A;
Zöllner 1991, p. 189, fig. 18; Popham 1994, no. 205; Dolev 1995,
p. 134, fig. 6; Marani 1995, p. 220, fig. 49; Marani 1997, pp. 175–76,
fig. 10; Arasse 1998, pp. 251, 254, 285, 319, fig. 184; Marani 2000b,
pp. 268, 278; Bambach 2001, pp. 20–23; Ames-Lewis 2001, p. 23,
n. 33, fig. 7; Clayton 2002b, pp. 31–33, no. 5.

The grandeur and tempestuous action of Leonardo's *Neptune and Sea Horses* evoke those of the central episode portraying the *Fight for the Standard* in the unfinished *Battle of Anghiari*. Scholars usually have identified the impos- ing Windsor sheet as a preparatory sketch for the presentation drawing that is described in Giorgio Vasari's vita of Leonardo (1550 and 1568 editions): "For Antonio Segni, his dear friend, he made a drawing of Neptune executed with such draftsman- ship and diligence that it seemed absolutely alive. It showed the turbulent sea and Neptune's chariot drawn by sea horses, with fantastic creatures, sea monsters, and figures of the winds, and some most beautiful heads of marine gods."[1] Since the function of the magnificent Windsor sketch was to explore the main figures of the composition, it is not unusual that it omits the fantastic creatures, sea monsters, figures of winds, and heads of marine gods that Vasari mentioned. Antonio Segni, who was Sandro Botticelli's frequent patron, left for Rome in 1504, which would offer a terminus ante quem for Leonardo's *Neptune* drawing. Vasari's vita of Leonardo also states that Fabio Segni (Antonio's son) gave the *Neptune* drawing to Giovanni Gaddi, with a rhymed epigram in Latin.[2]

The *Neptune* and the *Leda* compositions (cat. nos. 88, 98, 99) constitute Leonardo's most ambitious re-creations of classical subject matter. Certainly by 1502–5 Leonardo owned a copy of Ovid's *Metamorphoses*; he recorded "Ovidio metamorfoseos" among the books that he "left locked in the chest" in the Codex Madrid II (fols. 2v–3r).[3] It is not known, however, whether he owned a copy of Virgil's *Aeneid*, with its famous storm scene in book 1 (125–43) in which Neptune utters his threat to punish the winds, "Quos Ego" (Whom I). The Latin epigram written by either Antonio or Fabio Segni to celebrate Leonardo's *Neptune* drawing mentions Virgil (quoted in Vasari's vita). In any case, the sea god also figures prominently in Ovid's *Metamorphoses*. The verses of book 1, telling of Jupiter's wrath and his command to Neptune to unleash all his powers of cata- clysmic destruction, seem especially evocative of the Windsor sketch: "Put forth all your strength, for there is need. Open wide your doors, away with all restraining dykes, and give full rein to all your river steeds."[4]

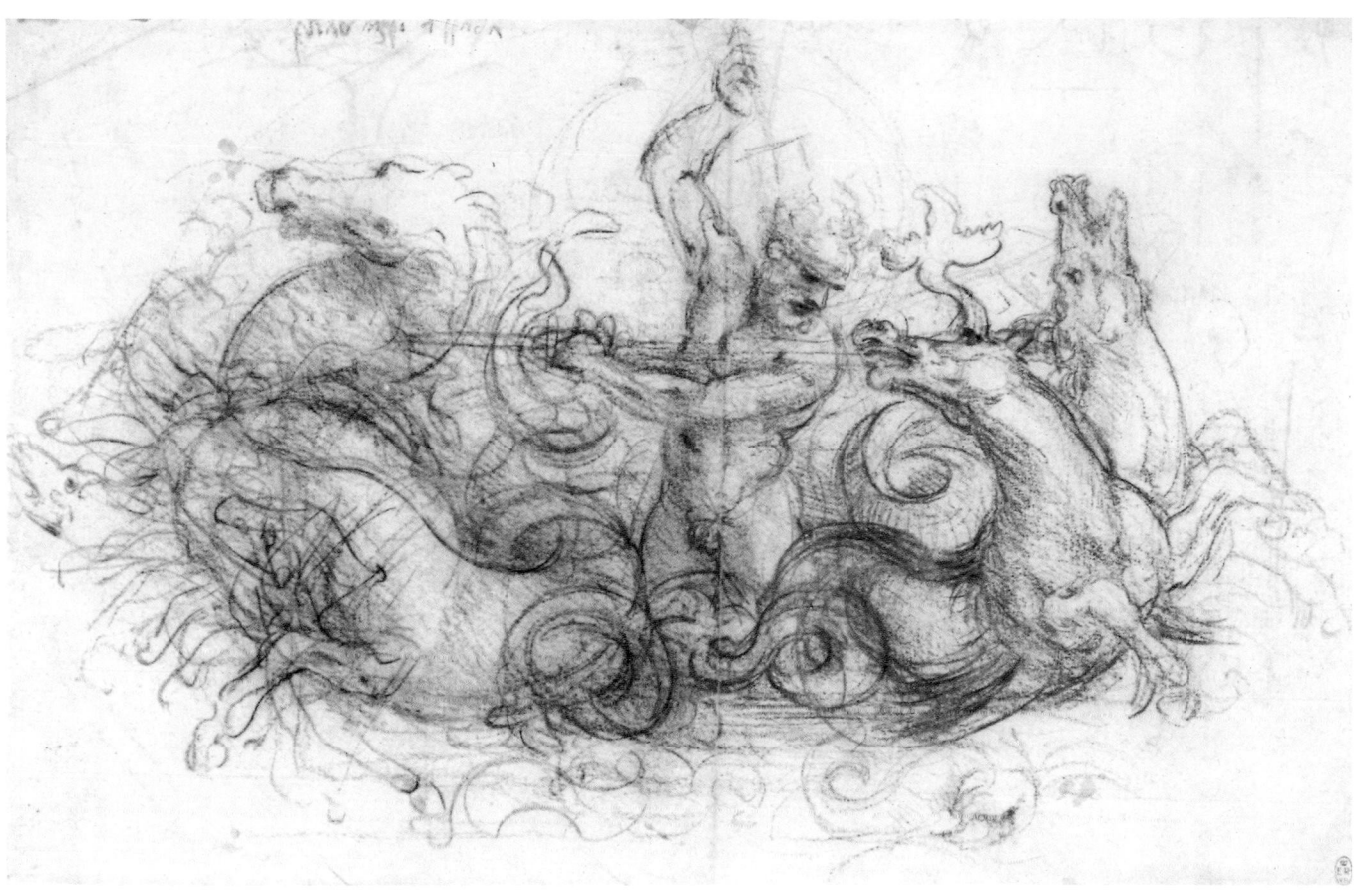

Cat. 93

The composition of Leonardo's Windsor sketch appears to be an adaptation of the central portion of a Roman sarcophagus from the early third century A.D. (Giardino della Pigna, Musei Vaticani), which likely depicts the marriage of Neptune and Amphitrite attended by Nereids and Tritons. The sarcophagus was set out on the steps of the church of Santa Maria in Aracoeli in Rome by the end of the fifteenth century, if not earlier. Leonardo was briefly in Rome during the winter of 1499–1500, apparently in the company of Count Louis of Ligny (see Chronology). Andrea Mantegna's imposing engraving *Battle of the Sea Gods* (possibly 1470s, but before 1494), itself a poetic evocation of antique relief sculpture, probably inspired Leonardo's Neptune composition as well.[5] Both relieflike

scenes display sharply foreshortened figures in frenzied movement. A resident of Mantua until his death in 1506, Mantegna may have met Leonardo (if the younger artist actually visited Mantua in 1500), and they shared a common patron, Isabella d'Este, who is documented as a presence in Leonardo's career from at least 1498 until 1506 (see Chronology). Leonardo's expertise on antiquities was such that, as is recorded in a letter of May 12, 1502, he evaluated drawings of antique vases from Lorenzo de' Medici's collection being offered to Isabella d'Este. Leonardo's *Neptune and Sea Horses*, in turn, was among the visual sources that inspired Raphael's preparatory drawings for two projects, the *Triumph of Galatea* fresco (Villa Farnesina, Rome) in 1511–12, and

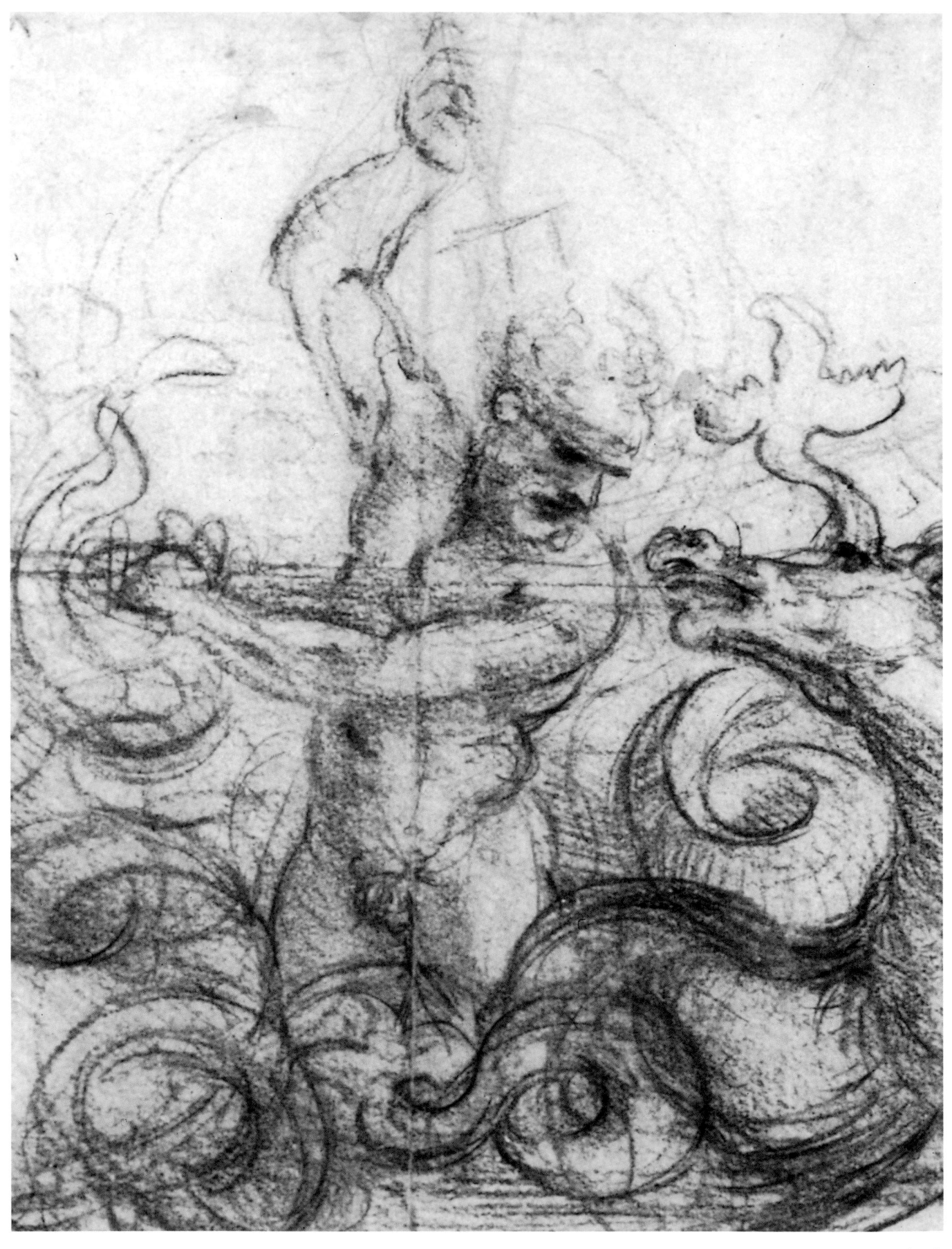

Cat. 93 *(detail)*

the *Quos Ego* of 1515–16, which would be engraved by Marcantonio Raimondi (Bartsch XIV.264, 352).

Raphael's and Leonardo's paths seem to have intersected only between 1503 and 1508 in Florence (see cat. nos. 98, 99 on Raphael's copy after Leonardo's *Leda and the Swan*) and between 1513 and 1516 in Rome. Leonardo's *Neptune* composition therefore must have been known to Raphael (whether directly or indirectly through preparatory drawings) during his Florentine period—that is, before 1506–8; the patron, Antonio Segni, would have taken Leonardo's final original drawing with him to Rome in 1504. A large copy, carefully drawn in red chalk by a mid-sixteenth-century central Italian artist, shows the sea horses around Neptune in a lower position, with respect to the extant Windsor drawing, and is carefully finished with cross-hatching (Accademia Carrara, Bergamo). There is little agreement, however, whether the Bergamo copy reflects the drawing that Leonardo finally presented to Antonio Segni, or one of Raphael's lost drawings for the *Quos Ego* that Marcantonio Raimondi engraved.[6]

Leonardo captured the sea god Neptune in a charged pose, struggling with his quadriga of sea horses. The sheet contains the artist's working note to himself, along the upper border toward the left, "abassa icha valli" (bring down the horses), in the same charcoal as the drawing. The lowering of the group of sea horses in the final composition would have led to a more iconic portrayal of the myth, presenting Neptune in the majesty of repose, unobstructed. This solution also seems closer to the conception of Neptune on the Roman sarcophagus from Santa Maria in Aracoeli. An additional sheet of small sketches and notes by Leonardo in Windsor shows another such reworked conception of Neptune.[7] There, his pose echoes that of Michelangelo's marble *David*, although the sheet is probably related to a fountain project, rather than to the presentation drawing for Antonio Segni. CCB

1. Vasari–Milanesi 1906, vol. 4, p. 25: "Ad Antonio Segni, suo amicissimo, fece in su un foglio un Nettuno, condotto così di disegno con tanta diligenzia che e' pareva del tutto vivo. Vedevasi il mare turbato ed il carro suo tirato da' cavalli marini con le fantasime, l'orche e i noti, ed alcune teste di Dei marini bellissime."
2. Vasari–Milanesi 1906, vol. 4, p. 25: "Pinxit Virgilius Neptunum, pinxit Homerus; / Dum maris undisoni per vada flectit equos. / Mente quidem vates illum conspexit uterque, / Vincius ast oculis; jureque vincit eos."
3. Transcribed in Ladislao Reti in Codex Madrid 1974, vol. 3, pp. 56–58, vol. 5, pp. 5–6.
4. Ovid 1977 (Book 1:274–85), p. 23.
5. The date 1494 is inscribed on Albrecht Dürer's copy of the right half of Andrea Mantegna's engraving; David Landau in Metropolitan Museum of Art and Royal Academy of Arts 1992, pp. 285–86, no. 79.
6. Gould 1952; Nees 1978, pp. 24–26, fig. 9; Marani 1989, p. 140, fig. 38.
7. Windsor, RL 12591. See Clark and Pedretti 1968–69, pp. 117–18, *sub numero*; and Clayton 1996–97, pp. 108–9, no. 58.

LEONARDO DA VINCI

94. *Studies of an Infant Holding a Lamb* (recto)
Technological Studies; Head of a Grotesque Old Man (verso)

Soft black chalk, partly reworked in pen and brown ink (recto); soft black chalk, pen and brown ink (verso), 210 × 142 mm (8¼ × 5⁹⁄₁₆ in.) Inscribed in pen and brown ink on recto, in right-to-left script, along upper border: *ji[n]cipit liber.endabor[um] . assauasorda . judeo inʰebraico . conposit[us] et a platone . / tiburtinj inlatin[o] sermone[s] translat[us] . anno . arabu[m?] . dx. m[en]se saphar \\ / capi / tulum primu[s? or m?] ingeometrie arithmetice p[er] vnyversalia p[ro]posita /;* in chalk below left: *franco.o dif.;* in pen and brown ink on verso, in right-to-left script, along upper border: *vedj la testa dello altovitj sella tenvto . il fermo / essapi dalcaiano . . . / il zendato . inv[er]njcia[to e] stacciatovi . suso la cimatura co[n] uarj colori / a vso . dj gianbellotto . e altre op[er]e . regie [regge] . allacq[u]a;* below, on the diagram: *a;* in a paragraph to the left: *a . sia un ferro da ri /mettere . quando . fussi / chonsummato . dal polo /*

essimilmente . si debbi . f[a] /re da potere . rimectere / ilpolo . quando . fussi ch[on] /summato———; below, on the drawing of the axle: *polo . [crossed out: s] rimessibile*
The J. Paul Getty Museum, Los Angeles 86.GG.725

PROVENANCE: Abbate Luigi Celotti [Cellotti] (?), Venice (1765–1846; Lugt under 188); Sir Thomas Lawrence, Bristol and London (1769–1830; Lugt 2445); perhaps sold with the Lawrence collection at Christie's, June 17–19, 1830, or February 1836; King William II of Holland (1792–1849); sale, Het Paleis, The Hague, August 12–20, 1850, part of lot 136; Grand Duke Charles Alexander of Saxe-Weimar-Eisenbach (Granducal Collection), Schlossmuseum Weimar (Lugt under 2445); S. Schwartz, New York; John Ryan Gaines, Lexington, Kentucky; Gaines sale, Sotheby's, New York, November 17, 1986, lot 3.

LITERATURE: Lawrence Gallery 1835–36, no. 70; Solmi 1908, pp. 263–64; Seidlitz 1909, vol. 1, pp. 76, 80; Suida 1920, p. 284; Venturi 1922, pp. 3–6; Verga 1926–29, pp. 219–23; Commissione Vinciana 1928– , vol. 6, p. 23, pl. 243.2; Möller 1928–29, pp. 221, 226; Borenius 1930, p. 142; Möller 1930–34, p. 66; De Toni 1930–34, p. 58; Verga 1931, vol. 1, p. 172, no. 475; Seidlitz 1935, p. 66; Marcolongo 1937, pp. 37–39 n. 19; Richter 1939, vol. 2, pp. 368–69; Pedretti 1957b, pp. 225–29; Steinitz 1961–63, pp. 343–44; Pedretti 1968a, p. 26; Clark and Pedretti 1968–69, pp. 98–99, under no. 12540; Wasserman 1970, pp. 198, 200, 201 (with n. 26), 203, fig. 13; Pedretti 1973a, p. 60; Pedretti 1973b, p. 33; Kemp 1982a, p. 788; Pedretti 1982a, pp. 30, 82–85; Carlo Pedretti in Vezzosi 1982, pp. 82–85, figs. 110, 111; Vezzosi 1982, p. 30 (nos. 22, 82–85, 87–89); Fogg Art Museum 1983a; Vezzosi 1983–84, pp. 72–73; Pedretti 1986a, p. 3; letter by Jack Wasserman quoted in sale catalogue, Sotheby's, New York, November 17, 1986, lot 3; Galluzzi 1987, pp. 86–89; Marani in Galluzi 1987, p. 121; Goldner 1987, pp. 202–3, no. 84; Marani 1987, pp. 120–21, figs. 94, 95; Pedretti in Galluzzi 1987, pp. 16–21; Pedretti 1987b; Vente record 1987, p. 26; Walker 1987; Pedretti 1988b, figs. 1, 2; Goldner and Hendrix 1992, pp. 64–67, no. 22, pl. 2; Kwakkelstein 1993c, p. 52, fig. 12; Pedretti and Trutty-Coohill 1993, pp. 48–50, no. 14; Pedretti 1994a, fig. 1; Popham 1994, no. 123; Clayton 1996–97, pp. 66–67, under no. 34; Letze and Buchsteiner 1997, pp. 80–81; Turner and Hendrix 1997, p. 9, no. 2; Arasse 1998, p. 427; Bambach 1999a, pp. 83, 403 n. 21; Marani 2000b, p. 275.

The present sheet may represent a page with notes and technical studies in pen and ink that Leonardo reused to develop the captivating figure studies for the composition of a painting or a cartoon (full-scale) drawing that is no longer extant. The three sketches reworked in pen and brown ink on the recto of the Getty sheet show the seated Christ Child tightly holding a lamb. In a fourth and a fifth sketch, toward the upper center of the sheet and the lower right, respectively, a similar group is lightly indicated in soft black chalk, and yet another such motif is also faintly discernible at the lower center. A similar sketch of the Christ Child holding a lamb appears on the verso, and although the boldly reinforced lines suggest that it was merely another sketch for the composition, it is considerably larger in scale and is worked up in soft, silvery black chalk, creating an exquisite sfumato effect. The delightful sketches of the recumbent holy infant on this double-sided sheet often have been connected with Leonardo's famous lost cartoon for the *Virgin and Child with Saint Anne and a Lamb*, which was described in a letter of April 3, 1501, from Fra Pietro da Novellara in Florence to Isabella d'Este in Mantua (see cat. no. 95 and Chronology). Supporting this hypothesis is the

position of Christ playing with the Lamb, which is similar, although by no means identical, to that in the presumed painted copy by Andrea Brescianino after Leonardo's lost cartoon (destroyed in World War II; formerly Kaiser-Friedrich Museum, Berlin)—this, despite the fact that there the infant is standing with his knees bent rather than sitting, as in the Getty sheet. The drawing technique, achieved with soft, silvery black chalk and densely reworked with fine, curved hatching in pen and dark brown ink, is seen in the most refined of the studies on the Getty sheet (for example, on the recto, near the left border), and it is virtually the same as that of the Venice compositional sketch for the *Virgin and Child with Saint Anne and a Lamb* (cat. no. 95). The motif of the Child playing with the lamb is also analogous in mood. The Getty sheet, therefore, probably dates as well to Leonardo's second Florentine period, about 1503–6. Curiously, the motif of the Christ and the lamb in the Getty sheet seems closely connected in design to an entirely different composition by

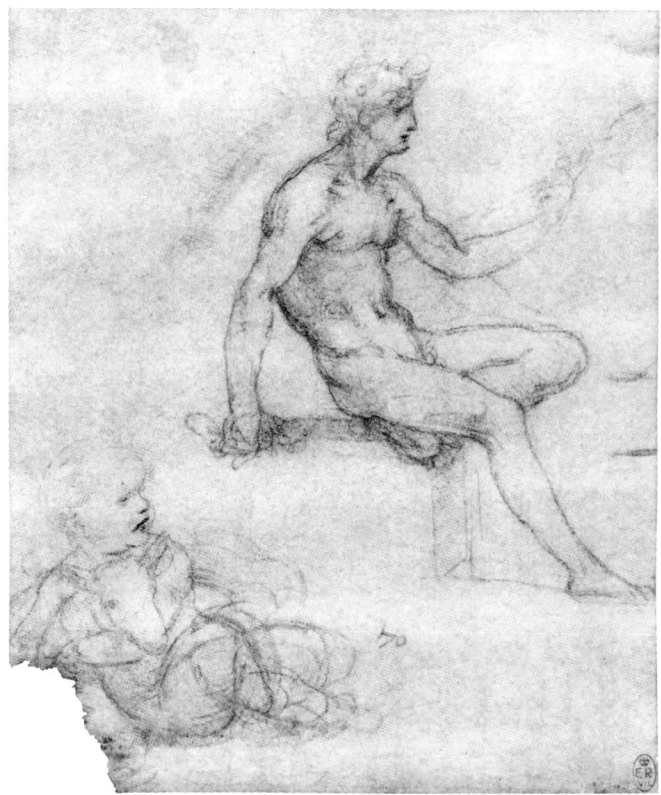

Fig. 185. Leonardo da Vinci, *Seated Nude Young Man and Seated Child with the Lamb*. Black chalk, 173 × 140 mm. The Royal Collection, H.M. Queen Elizabeth II, Windsor Castle RL 12540

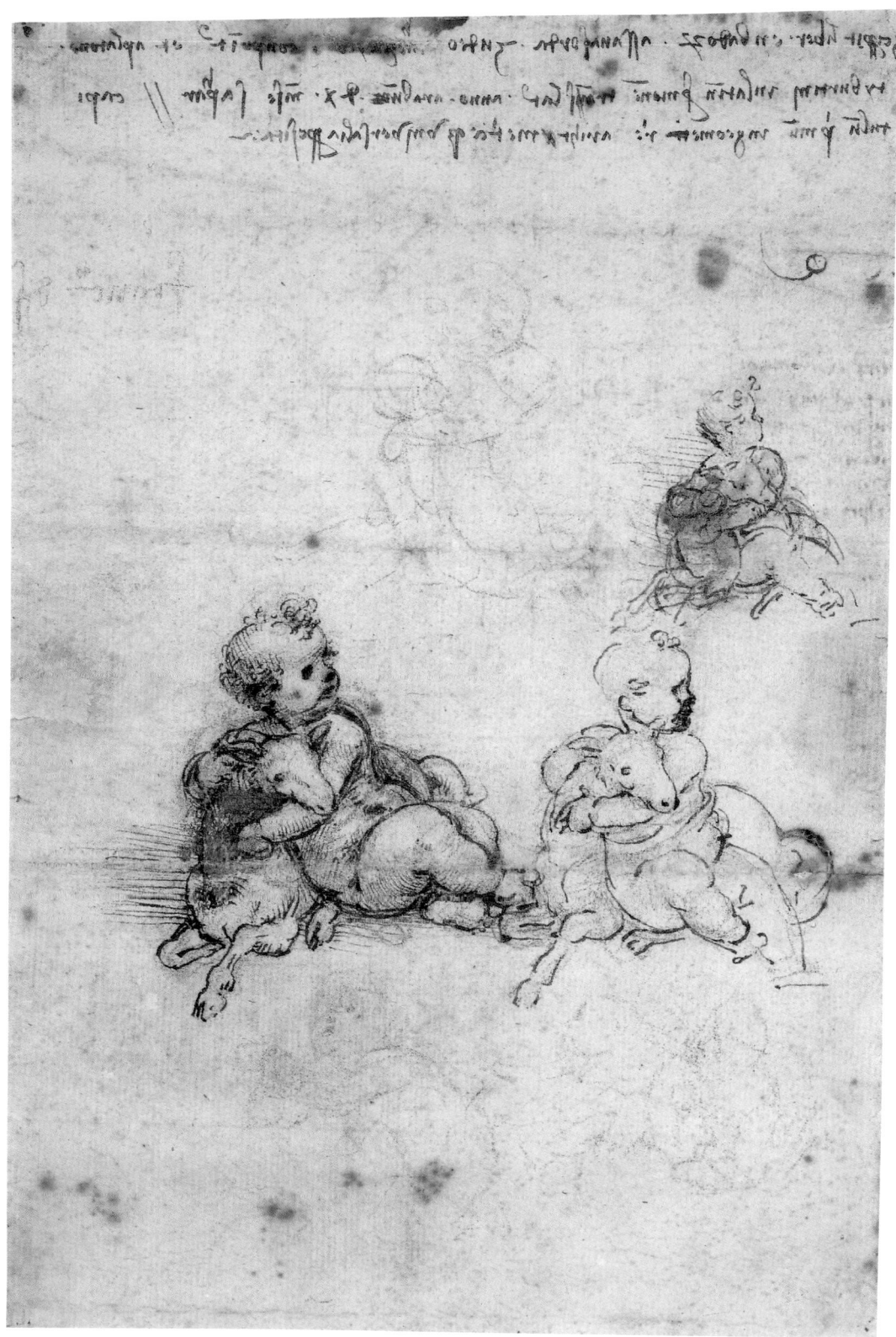

Cat. 94R *(actual size)*

517

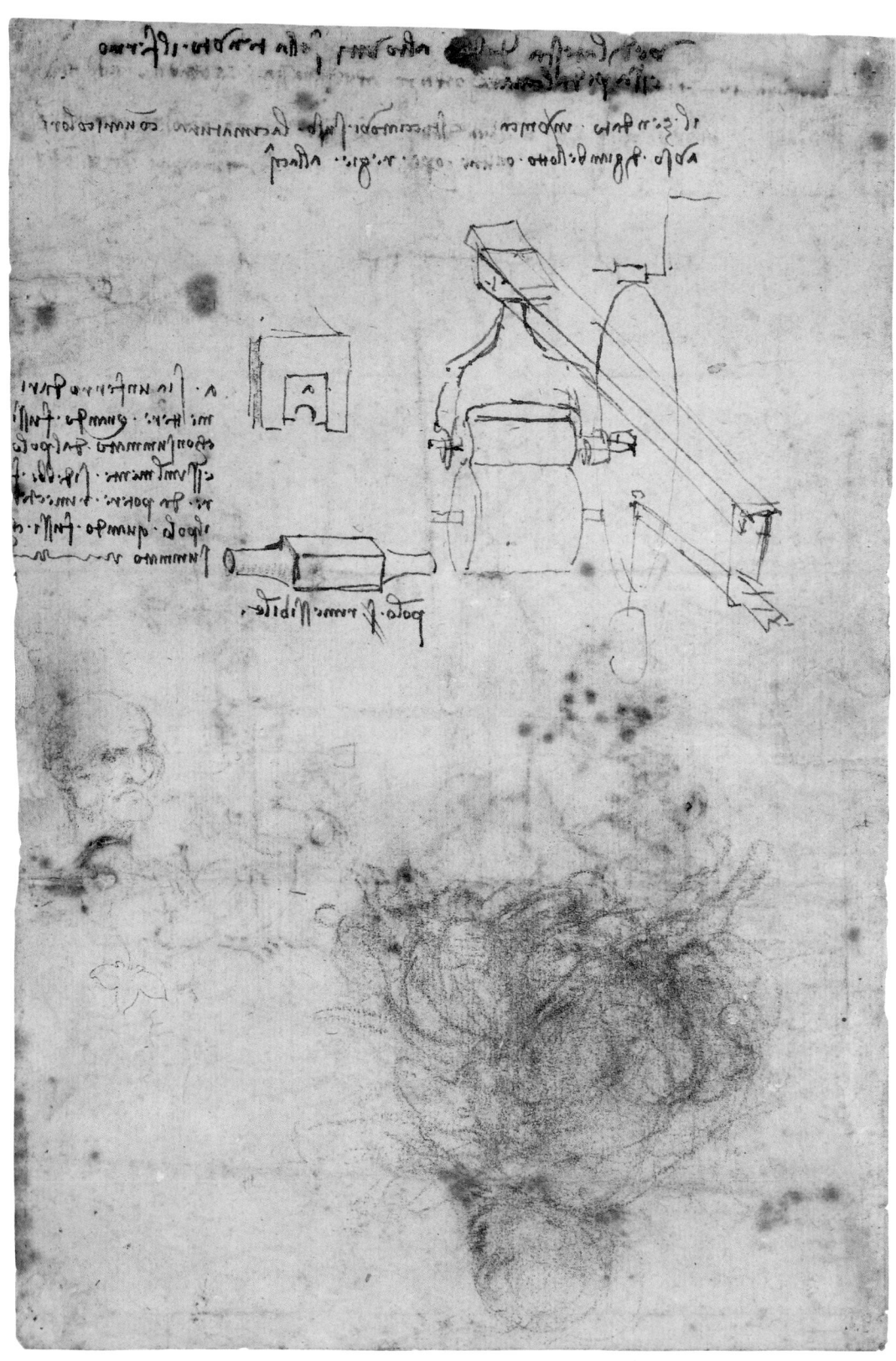

Cat. 94v *(actual size)*

Leonardo—an undocumented painting of a *Nativity* (fig. 150), which the artist may have developed as far as the cartoon or final painting stage, although neither is extant. A metalpoint drawing reworked in pen and ink (cat. no. 45) represents Leonardo's original preparatory sketches for this lost composition (fig. 150), and its technique and style help establish a date for that project between about 1480 and 1485,[1] or about twenty years earlier than that of the Getty sheet. While several painted copies of Leonardo's original design exist, it is not possible to determine whether the original painting ever was executed or if it simply disappeared.[2] To complicate matters, because it is not always clear when Leonardo's followers produced faithful copies and when they merely created pastiches, the dating and reconstruction of Leonardo's lost original designs become extremely difficult.

A date for the Getty sheet of about 1503–6—possibly even 1503–4—can be demonstrated by a comparison with the design for the Christ Child and the lamb in a sketch in soft black chalk at the lower left of another drawing in Windsor (fig. 185). This Windsor sheet includes a study after an antique chalcedony intaglio that was in Lorenzo de' Medici's collection but was lost when his family was expelled from Florence in 1494; the design of the gem was re-created by Donatello's workshop (Palazzo Medici, Florence) in a marble roundel relief portraying Diomedes. These circumstances tie Leonardo's conception of the Christ Child with the lamb to his work in Florence, rather than Milan. The soft black-chalk technique and the style of the sketch of Diomedes in Windsor— typical of Leonardo's second Florentine period—are comparable to the *Neptune Commanding His Quadriga of Sea Horses*, intended for the presentation drawing offered to Antonio Segni (who left Florence in 1504; see cat. no. 93), as well as to the sheet combining early ideas for the *Leda and the Swan* and the *Battle of Anghiari* (cat. no. 88), all of which can be dated more precisely to about 1503–4. The sfumato technique of the Windsor studies is the same as that of the soft black-chalk drawing on the verso of the Getty sheet, which includes a faint sketch near the center of the left border, also in black-chalk, of the head of a grotesque old man in three-quarter view and facing to the right. In technique, style, and physiognomic type, the old man evokes the Budapest study of the bald screaming soldier (cat. no. 91) for the *Fight for the Standard* in the *Battle of Anghiari*, as well as a red-chalk study in the Louvre (cat. no. 76).

Leonardo inscribed the verso of the Getty sheet "head of Altoviti," a mysterious note apparently referring to the likeness of a member of the noble Altoviti family of Florence.[3] The artist often wrote such notes to remind himself of the identities of the highly unusual people he encountered (see cat. no. 69). Also on the Getty verso are hesitant technological studies in pen and ink over black chalk of blown-up details of the parts of a laminating device (containing a square core and a corresponding removable axle), their timidity perhaps indicating that they precede the pictorial composition sketches, and date to about 1497–1500, during the last years of Leonardo's stay in Milan.[4] The note immediately below them describes a translucent varnish that could render taffeta (Leonardo writes *zendato*, for *zendado*) waterproof, giving the cloth an attractive texture and color. As Carlo Pedretti related at greater length, Leonardo's invention of this type of taffeta may have been in the context of his costume designs for the Sforza court. In the enlarged details and accompanying text at the left, the artist expressed his concern with the wear and tear caused by the continuous friction of operating such a device, and he provided a solution: the replaceable axle, or *polo rimessibile*.

Leonardo's note on the Getty recto, an allusion to the "*incipit* [beginning] of the *Liber embadorum* by Savasorda the Jew, written in Hebrew and translated into Latin by Plato," refers to the treatise of about 1145 on trigonometry, measurement, and calculation by the great Spanish Jewish mathematician, philosopher, and astronomer Abraham Bar Hiyya Hanasi (ca. 1065–ca. 1136), known as Savasorda, which became an important textbook in the period. The Latin translation of Savasorda's treatise, by the Spanish scholar Plato of Tivoli (fl. 1135–45), was entitled the *Liber embadorum*. It is possible that Leonardo's source was a manuscript (rather than a printed edition) of Savasorda's treatise, two of which are known to have been in the Biblioteca di San Marco, the Dominican library in Florence;[5] one is now in the Biblioteca Medicea Laurenziana, Florence. Perhaps it was the mathematician and theorist Fra Luca Pacioli, Leonardo's intimate friend with whom he traveled to Florence in 1499–1501, who brought Savasorda's magisterial work to the artist's attention.

Crucial evidence regarding the artistic and mathematical contexts alluded to on the Getty sheet is found in Fra Pietro da Novellara's letter from Florence of April 3, 1501, to Isabella d'Este in Mantua. Fra Pietro (head of the Carmelite order in Florence) reported that Leonardo was leading a haphazard life in the city, producing little else but the cartoon of the *Virgin and Child with Saint Anne and a Lamb,* and with great alarm he noted that the artist was obsessed with problems of geometry, which distracted him from his art (see Chronology).

CCB

1. Another version of this early composition is found in Windsor (RL 12650).
2. Other versions of the painting are discussed in Casa Buonarroti 1998, pp. 204–7, no. 3; Dalli Regoli, Nanni, and Natali 2001, pp. 122–25, no. 2.8.
3. Bindo Altoviti (1491–1557), for example, famously handsome as a youth, became the friend of Michelangelo and Raphael.
4. Pedretti 1986a, p. 3.
5. Pedretti 1986a, p. 3.

LEONARDO DA VINCI

95. *Virgin and Child with Saint Anne and a Lamb in a Landscape*

Pen and two colors of brown ink, over black chalk and some stylus; traces of framing outlines in pen and brown ink, 121 × 100 mm (4¾ × 3¹⁵⁄₁₆ in.)
Gallerie dell'Accademia, Venice 230

PROVENANCE: Cardinal Cesare Monti, Milan (1635–1650); Contessa Anna Luisa Monti, Milan; 1770, Venanzio De Pagave, Milan; his son Gaudenzio De Pagave; ca. 1808 or before, Giuseppe Bossi, Milan and Venice (1777–1815; album marked K); auction, Milan, February 1818, II; February 24, 1818, purchase by Abbate Luigi Celotti [Cellotti], Venice (1765–1846); in deposit (under custody of Carlo Porta and Nicola Cassoni), Accademia di Belle Arti, Milan; 1820–22, proposal of purchase of Bossi's collection from Celotti submitted to Austrian government on behalf of Accademia delle Belle Arti, Venice; 1822, purchase by Franz I (Habsburg), emperor of Austria, Florence and Vienna (1768–1835), for Accademia delle Belle Arti, Venice; ca. 1832 manuscript inventory; December 31, 1870, manuscript inventory; museum stamp (Lugt 188).

LITERATURE: Müntz 1898, vol. 2, p. 121; Müntz 1899, pp. 383, 389; Berenson 1903, vol. 1, p. 158, vol. 2, p. 62, no. 1102; Seidlitz 1909, vol. 2, p. 26; Fogolari 1913, p. 15; Poggi 1919, pl. 106; Venturi 1920, pp. 120–21, fig. 87; Shapley 1925, p. 96; De Rinaldis 1926, p. 230, fig. 68; Commissione Vinciana 1928– , vol. 6, p. 23, pl. 238.2; Popp 1928, pp. 9, 44–45; Sirén 1928, p. 111, pl. 128b; no. 45; Popham 1930–31, no. 80; Bodmer 1931, pp. 277, 407; Berenson 1938, vol. 1, p. 176, vol. 2, p. 123, vol. 3, fig. 515, no. 1102; Palazzo dell'Arte 1939, p. 151; Giglioli 1944, pl. 108; Heydenreich 1949, pl. 17; Biblioteca Medicea Laurenziana 1952, pp. 35–36, no. 50; Goldscheider 1952, no. 95; Castelfranco 1954b, pl. 170, fig. 13; Castelfranco 1956, p. 61, pl. 84; Berenson 1961, vol. 1, p. 256, vol. 2, p. 216, vol. 3, fig. 504, no. 1102; Castelfranco 1966, p. 117; Cogliati Arano 1966–67, pp. 22–23, no. 10, fig. 7; Wasserman 1970, pp. 196–98, fig. 7 (anonymous, attributed to Leonardo); Pedretti 1973a, pp. 104–7, fig. 120; Brizio 1974b, p. 42,

fig. 42/3; Gould 1975, pp. 104–9, fig. 54; Pedretti 1979c, p. 29; Cogliati Arano 1980, pp. 34–35, no. 9; Nicodemi 1980a, p. 76; Dalli Regoli 1982, p. 27, fig. 31; Pedretti 1982a, p. 40; Pedretti 1982c, p. 18, fig. 31; Budny 1983, pp. 34–50; Marani 1989, pp. 22–25, fig. 21; Martin Clayton in Palazzo Grassi 1992, pp. 244–45, no. 22; Maidani Gerard and Krause-Zimmer 1993, p. 80, fig. 4; Popham 1994, no. 174A; Posèq 1994, p. 95, fig. 16; Arasse 1998, pp. 450–55, fig. 311; Annalisa Perissa Torrini in Nepi Scirè and Torrini 1999, pp. 84–85, no. 24; Marani 2000b, pp. 262–64.

Early written sources and Leonardo's various extant small-scale studies, one full-scale cartoon (the so-called Burlington House cartoon; figs. 17, 75, 76), and one surviving painting (fig. 23) suggest that the artist pondered the subject of the Virgin and Child with Saint Anne during the last two decades of his life, from about 1500–1501 to 1515–17. The compositions represent the main figures with and without (as in the Venice sheet) the infant Saint John the Baptist, and with and without the lamb. Since critical visual evidence is lost, it is extremely difficult to separate the individual projects and related drawings on this theme. As a working hypothesis, the drawings, here, are grouped stylistically around two general nuclei: those that seem related to the National Gallery cartoon (cat. nos. 95, 96) and those that appear to be connected to the Louvre painting (cat. nos. 105–9). Some scholars have posited that Leonardo produced as many as four final compositions of the *Virgin and Child with Saint Anne* (three cartoons and a painting), based on perceived internal discrepancies of design between Leonardo's originals and the copies after his lost

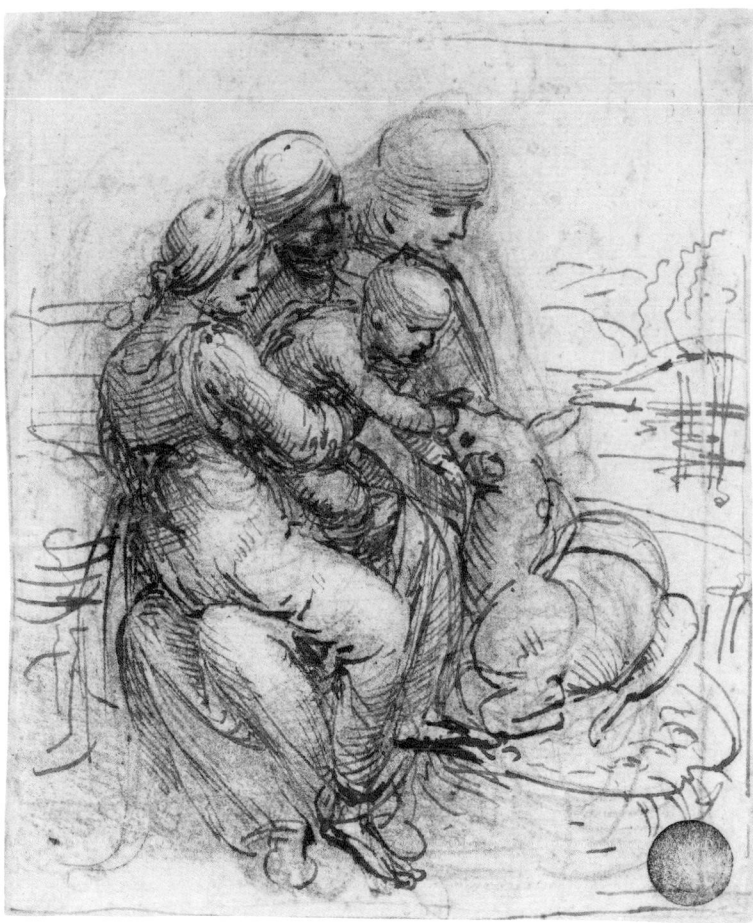

Cat. 95 *(actual size)*

works, and between the visual and the complex textual evidence. While the problems are far from resolved, the present drawing is considered to be one of the key developments in the early history of the Saint Anne compositions.

The main written sources that mention compositions by Leonardo on the theme of the Virgin and Child with Saint Anne will be quoted directly, rather than paraphrased, to clarify their reliability. These sources are two letters of 1501 from Fra Pietro da Novellara in Florence to Isabella d'Este in Mantua (Fra Pietro was Isabella's agent); the second, more complete edition of Giorgio Vasari's *Le vite de' più eccellenti pittori, scultori ed architettori* of 1568 (the 1550 edition is shorter, but does not differ substantially on the present subject); and a considerably later, undated letter from Padre Sebastiano Resta (1635–1714) to Giovanni Pietro Bellori (1615–1696). Resta, the noted drawings collector, was writing to Bellori in his role as a well-known author of artists' biographies, and the reliability of his letter should not be discounted

too quickly, for, in its favor, it offers an explanation for the existence of multiple versions of the Virgin and Child with Saint Anne, even if one assumes that the historical details are not all correct. Ambiguities in wording in the sources are at the root of the scholarly debate about the Saint Anne projects, and the problem also has been compounded (and sometimes unnecessarily complicated) by fragmentary paraphrases of the original texts.

Fra Pietro da Novellara's letter of April 3, 1501, to Isabella d'Este states:

> Since he came to Florence he has done the drawing of a cartoon ["a sketch on a cartoon"]. He is portraying a Christ Child of about a year old who is almost slipping out of his Mother's arms to take hold of a lamb, which he then appears to embrace. His Mother, half-rising from the lap of Saint Anne, takes hold of the Child to separate him from the lamb (a sacrificial animal), signifying the Passion. Saint Anne, rising slightly from her sitting position, appears to want to restrain her daughter from separating the Child from the lamb. She is perhaps

intended to represent the Church, which would not want the Passion of Christ impeded. And these figures are life-size but can fit into a small cartoon because all are either seated or bending over and each one is positioned a little in front of the other and facing to the left-hand side. And this drawing ["sketch"] is as yet unfinished. He has done nothing else save for the fact that two of his apprentices are making copies on which he puts his hand from time to time. He is hard at work on geometry and has no time for the brush.[1]

It can be deduced from this letter that the composition of the cartoon of the *Virgin and Child with Saint Anne* in 1501 included the lamb (but no infant Saint John) and that the figures faced left. The letter also is among the earliest testimony that Leonardo's pupils produced copies that the master then retouched. The wording of Fra Pietro's letter implies that Leonardo's cartoon was only at the very preliminary stage of a sketch ("vno schizo in vno Cartone"). The composition of this lost cartoon—with the Virgin, the Child, Saint Anne, and a lamb facing left—is probably reflected in a painted copy (formerly Kaiser-Friedrich-Museum, Berlin) by Andrea Brescianino that was destroyed in World War II, and in a problematic drawing that sometimes has been attributed to Leonardo or a follower (private collection, Switzerland).

On April 14, 1501, Fra Pietro again wrote to Isabella d'Este. Although this letter does not mention the composition of the *Virgin and Child with Saint Anne,* some scholars have interpreted the oblique reference to Leonardo's obligation to the French king as pertaining to one of the versions of this project. All that is patently clear from the letter, however, is the information that Leonardo is working on the (lost) *Madonna of the Yarn Winder* for Florimond Robertet (1459–1527), who had become secretary to King Louis XII of France in 1499. In Fra Pietro's words:

During this Holy Week I have learned [of] the intention of Leonardo the painter through Salai, his pupil, and from some other ones dear to him, who, in order that I might obtain more information, brought him to me on Holy Wednesday. In short, his mathematical experiments have so greatly distracted him from painting that he cannot bear the brush. However, I tactfully made sure he understood Your Excellency's wishes . . . seeing that he was most eagerly inclined to please Your Excellency by reason of the kindness you showed to him at Mantua, I spoke to him freely about everything. The conclusion was that if he could discharge himself without dishonor from his obligations to His Majesty the King of France as he hoped to do within a month at the most, then he would rather

serve Your Excellency than anyone else in the world. But that in any event, once he has finished a little picture that he is doing for one Robertet, a favorite of the King of France, he will immediately do the portrait and send it to Your Excellency. I leave him well entreated. The little picture that he is doing is of a Madonna seated as if she were about to spin yarn. The Child has placed his foot on the basket of yarns and has grasped the yarn-winder and gazes attentively at the four spokes that are in the form of a cross.[2]

Next in reliability as evidence is the 1568 edition of Vasari's vita of Leonardo, which attempts to describe the events of 1500–1501:

He returned to Florence, where he found that the Servite Friars had entrusted to Filippino [Lippi] the painting of the panel for the high altar of the Nunziata; whereupon Leonardo said that he would willingly have done such a work. Filippino, having understood this, like the amiable person that he was, withdrew from the undertaking; and the friars, to the end that Leonardo might paint it, took him into their house, meeting the expenses both of himself and of all his household. And thus he kept them in expectation for a long time, but never began anything. In the end, he made a cartoon containing a Madonna and a Saint Anne, with a Christ, which not only caused all the craftsmen to marvel, but, when it was finished, men and women, young and old, continued for two days to flock for a sight of it to the room where it was, as if to a solemn festival, in order to gaze at the marvels of Leonardo, which caused all those people to be amazed. For in the face of that Madonna was seen whatever of the simple and the beautiful can by simplicity and beauty confer grace on a picture of the Mother of Christ, since he wished to show that modesty and that humility which are looked for in an image of the Virgin, supremely content with happiness at seeing the beauty of her Son, whom she was holding with tenderness in her lap, while with most chastened gaze she was looking down at Saint John, as a little boy, who was playing with a lamb; not without a smile from Saint Anne, who, overflowing with joy, was beholding her earthly progeny become divine—ideas truly worthy of the brain and genius of Leonardo. This cartoon, as will be told below, afterward went to France.[3]

From Vasari's passage it seems clear that the altarpiece for the high altar of Santissima Annunziata in Florence that Filippino Lippi was painting for the Servite friars was a commission that he supposedly was ready to graciously cede to Leonardo, but this work was not necessarily the one for which Leonardo's cartoon of the *Virgin and Child with Saint Anne and the Infant Saint John the Baptist* was preparatory. In fact, as a number of scholars rightly have pointed out, the two projects most likely are quite unrelated. Moreover, if this cartoon were executed about 1500–1501, it cannot be the one seen by Fra Pietro da Novellara, for it includes the lamb as well as the infant Saint John the Baptist. Further on in the text of the 1568 edition of Vasari's vita of the artist, he concludes: "Leonardo, understanding this, departed and went to France, where the king, having had works by his hand, bore him great affection; and he wished that he should color the cartoon of Saint Anne, but Leonardo, according to his custom, put him off for a long time with words."[4] Vasari does not seem to have been aware of the Louvre painting on the subject.

Advocates of the theory that a cartoon of the *Virgin and Child with Saint Anne* was commissioned from Leonardo by King Louis XII of France before 1500 have given special weight to a letter from Sebastiano Resta to Giovanni Pietro Bellori, which states:

Here, *Signore* Giampietro, [is] the news that you desire about my cartoon. Lodovico [Louis] XII, king of France, before 1500 commissioned a cartoon of Saint Anne from Leonardo, who was residing in Milan in the service of Ludovico il Moro. Leonardo made a first drawing ["sketch"] that is with the *signori conti* Arconati in Milan. After that first one, he made this second more finished [drawing], and the present one is [well] preserved as one can see, even though it is 200 years old more or less. Residing then in Florence, after the death of Louis XII, to whom he had never sent [the drawing], he made a third work, re-creating it from this second [drawing], and sent it to King Francis I, successor of Lodovico [Louis], which therefore was in 1515. It pleased the king, and he invited [Leonardo] to France to produce it in paint. Leonardo went [to France] but he never painted it, even though he lived in France until 1542 [*sic*; the artist died in 1519], when the *Last Judgment* of Michelangelo was unveiled in Rome.[5]

According to many Leonardo scholars, the vibrant Venice sheet may be the earliest of Leonardo's extant small composition drawings on the theme of the Virgin and Child with Saint Anne. Leonardo's use of the corrosive medium of iron gall ink has caused a conspicuous dark area but only a minimal loss in the paper on the face of Saint Anne (in the pentimento in the center); otherwise, the Venice sketch seems in good condition. The arrangement in this drawing includes a rather large, recumbent lamb on the right, the object of the Christ Child's affectionate caresses and his attribute, symbolizing the Passion. Both the Venice sketch and the late, Louvre painting accord

with the description in Fra Pietro da Novellara's 1501 letter to Isabella d'Este, except that the figures face right rather than left. Leonardo began the Venice composition sketch with a nebulous blur of charcoal or soft black chalk, then reworked the design for greater definition with pen and two types of brown ink. The main purpose of the Venice sketch seems to have been to explore the massing of the forms. At the time that Leonardo began inking the design, he still thought of portraying Saint Anne leaning closer toward her holy grandchild and apparently caressing the lamb herself. Yet, once the artist began the hatching in pen of the form of Saint Anne, he decided to distance her from the lamb (probably to reduce her prominence in the composition) and move her head and body closer to the figure of her daughter, the Virgin, on the left. Leonardo also adjusted the proportions of Saint Anne's head with respect to the heads of the Virgin and the Christ Child. However, as a result of this adjustment of limbs in recomposing the figure of Saint Anne within the group, the final conception of her body in the Venice sheet seems weak (especially noticeable is the disproportionate relationship between her short lower legs and towering upper body), and the depiction of her anatomy requires further refinement. The figural group is rather tightly compressed within the pictorial field, and, in addition, Leonardo sketchily drew framing outlines around the composition in pen and brown ink.

The sparsely drawn landscape includes two trees on the extreme right, a feature present as well in Leonardo's only extant painting on the subject, the Louvre's *Virgin and Child with Saint Anne and the Lamb* (fig. 23). The painting paradoxically is his latest version of the theme, dating between 1508 and 1515–17; the trees are not in any of Leonardo's other drawings or in extant direct copies after his lost originals. The contrapposto stance of Saint Anne in the Venice composition sketch also more closely resembles that in the late, Louvre painting, for Saint Anne's torso is turned halfway to the left, her head and shoulders above those of the Virgin, and her left arm apparently bent. Saint Anne's legs are turned to the left, too, and the Virgin sits sidesaddle on her lap with her legs facing right. Of the various drawings, only the Venice sketch includes the lamb at the right—an element also included in the Louvre painting.

Catalogue number 96 is much closer in design to the cartoon of the *Virgin and Child with Saint Anne and the Infant Saint John the Baptist* (figs. 17, 75, 76) in the National

Gallery, London, which can be dated about 1506–8. The Venice sketch, however, shares an important overall stylistic feature with the National Gallery cartoon: emphatically rounded, articulated volumes, most evident in the curved hatching of the heads (figs. 17, 75, 76). Much of this curved hatching in the London cartoon was later blurred when the charcoal was blended for a sfumato effect, but it nevertheless is present in the underlayers of the drawing.

The actual date of the Venice sketch is uncertain, although scholars often have placed it between 1500 and 1503, based on the complex external evidence supplied by the elusive chronology of the various *Virgin and Child with Saint Anne* projects. On the internal evidence of drawing technique and style alone, the fragile Venice sheet could be dated quite late, about 1508, in the present author's opinion. For example, the curved hatching and the baby's figural type do not seem much different from their counterparts in the anatomical sheet of *Five Views of the Fetus in the Womb* (Windsor, RL 19101), of 1510–12. In design, the Venice sheet resembles one of the composition sketches for the National Gallery cartoon, seen at the lower right of the British Museum sheet (cat. no. 96), even more than the cartoon itself.[6]

Ultimately, the discrepancies of design that the texts suggest may add up to a simpler scenario—namely, fewer final versions of the Saint Anne theme, which would then be the lost cartoon described by Fra Pietro and by Giorgio Vasari, the National Gallery cartoon, and the Louvre painting. A great deal probably can be explained by Leonardo's working methods, the production of endless variations in the preliminary sketch and study stages in the design of a single project, as well as by his habitual practice of reversing compositions—and parts of compositions—left and right.

CCB

1. Translation based on Kemp 1989c, p. 273. Original text (Marani 1999c, p. 349, no. 36): "A facto solo dopoi che e ad firenci vno schizo in vno Cartone: finge vno christo bambino de eta cerca vno anno che vscindo quasi de bracci ad la mamma piglia vno agnello et pare che lo stringa. La mamma quasi leuandose de grembo ad s.ta Anna piglia el bambino per spicarlo dalo agnellino (animale immolatile) che significa la passione. S.ta Anna alquanto leuandose da sedere pare che uoglia retenere la figliola che non spica el bambino da lo agnellino. Che forsi uole figurare la chiesa che non uorebbe fussi impedita la passione di christo. Et sono queste figure grande al naturale ma stano in picolo cartone perche Tutte o sedeno o stano curue et una stae alquanto dinanti ad laltra uerso la man sinistra. Et questo schizo ancora non e finito. Altro non ha facto senon che dui suoi garzoni fano retrati et lui ale uolte in alcuno mette mano. Da opra forte ad la geometria Impacientissimo al pennello."

2. Translation based on Kemp 1989c, p. 273. Original text (Marani 1999c, pp. 349–50, no. 37): "Questa septimana s.ta ho inteso la intentione de Leonardo pictore per mezo de Salai suo discipulo et de alcuni altri suoi affectionati li quali per farmila piu nota melo menorno el merchordi s.to. Insumma li suoi experimenti Mathematici lhano distracto tanto dal dipingere, che non puo patire el pennello. Pur me asegurai di farli intendere cum destreza el parere di V. ex. Prima como da me poi vedendolo molto disposto al uolere gratificare v. ex. per la humanita gli monstroe a Mantua, (*e se resolti*) gli disse el tutto liberamente. Rimase in questa Conclusione se si potea spiccare da la maesta del Re de Franza senza sua disgratia Como speraua ala piu longa fra meso vno: che seruirebbe piu presto v. ex. che persona del mondo. Mah che ad ogni modo fornito chegli hauesse vn quadretino che fa a uno Roberteto fauorito del Re de Franza, farebbe subito el retrato elo mandarebbe a v. ex. Gli lasso dui boni sollicitadori. El quadretino che fa e vna Madona che sede como se uolesse inaspare fusi, el Bambino posto el piede nel Canestino dei fusi e ha preso laspo e mira atentamente que quattro raggi che sono in forma di Croce."

3. Translation based on Vasari 1996, vol. 1, p. 635. Original text (Vasari 1966– , vol. 4, pp. 29–30): "Ritornò a Fiorenza, dove trovò che i frati de' Servi avevano allogato a Filippino l'opere della tavola dell'altar maggiore della Nunziata; per il che fu detto da Lionardo che volentieri avrebbe fatta una simil cosa. Onde Filippino inteso ciò, come gentil persona ch'egli era, se ne tolse giù; et i frati, perché Lionardo la dipignesse, se lo tolsero in casa, facendo le spese a lui et a tutta la sua famiglia: e così li tenne in practica lungo tempo, né mai cominciò nulla. Finalmente fece un cartone, dentrovi una Nostra Donna et una S. Anna con un Cristo, la quale non pure fece maravigliare tutti gl'artefici, ma finita ch'ella fu. nella stanza durarono due giorni d'andare a vederla gl'uomini e le donne, i giovani et i vecchi, come si va a le feste solenni, per veder le maraviglie di Lionardo, che fecero stupire tutto quel popolo; perché si vedeva nel viso di quella Nostra Donna tutto quello che di semplice e di bello può con semplicità e bellezza dare grazia a una madre di Cristo, volendo mostrare quella modestia e quella umiltà ch'è in una Vergine, contentissima d'allegrezza del vedere la bellezza del suo figliuolo che con tenerezza sosteneva in grembo, e mentre che ella, con onestissima guardatura, abasso scorgeva un S. Giovanni piccol fanciullo che si andava trastullando con un pecorino, non senza un ghigno d'una S. Anna che, colma di letizia, vedeva la sua progenie terrena esser divenuta celeste: considerazioni veramente dallo intelletto et ingegno di Lionardo. Questo cartone, come di sotto si dirà, andò poi in Francia."

4. Translation based on Vasari 1996, vol. 1, p. 639. Original text (Vasari 1966– , vol. 4, pp. 35–36): "Lionardo intendendo ciò, partì et andò in Francia, dove il re, avendo avuto opere sue, gli era molto affezionato e desiderava ch'e' colorisse il cartone della S. Anna; ma egli, secondo il suo costume, lo tenne gran tempo in parole."

5. Author's translation. Original text (Bottari and Ticozzi 1822, vol. 3, p. 481): "Eccole, sig. Giampietro, le notizie ch'ella desidera circa il mio cartone. Lodovico XII, re di Francia, prima del 1500 ordinò un cartone di s. Anna a lionardo da Vinci, dimorante in Milano al servizio di Lodovico il Moro. Ne fece Leonardo un primo schizzo, che sta presso a'signori conti Arconati in Milano. Dopo il primo, ne fece questo secondo più condotto, ed il presente conservato come si vede, benche abbia 200 anni o poco meno. In Firenze poi dimorando Leonardo dopo la morte di Lodovico XII, al quale non lo aveva mai mandato, ne fece un terzo compito, ricavandolo da questo secondo, e lo mandò al re Francesco primo successore di Lodovico, e ciò fu del 1515. Piacque al Re, e lo invitò in Francia ad eseguirlo in pittura. V'andò Leonardo, ma non perciò lo dipinse mai, benchè sopravvivesse in Francia sino al 1542, quando si scoperse il Giudizio di Michelagnolo in Roma."

6. Wasserman 1970, pp. 197–98 (although with some doubt about Leonardo's authorship of the Venice drawing).

LEONARDO DA VINCI

96. *Sketches for the Virgin and Child with Saint Anne; Wheels; a Weir, Dam, or Bridge* (recto) *Profile of an Old Man Facing to the Right; Traced-through Composition of the Virgin and Child with Saint Anne* (verso)

Pen and brown ink and wash over black chalk (recto); black chalk (verso), 266 × 200 mm (10⁷/₁₆ × 7⁷/₈ in.)
Inscribed in pen and brown ink on recto, in right-to-left script, close to right border, on bottom quadrant: *pagol data vechia p[er] / vedere le machie de/lle pietre tedessce*; cropped along lower left: *fa co[n]che dove lac[qu]a*
The British Museum, London 1875-6-12-17

PROVENANCE: Émile Galichon, Paris (1829–1875; Lugt 856); sale, Clément, Paris, May 10–14, 1975, lot 163; (Colnaghi); museum stamp (Lugt 296-305, Suppl. 302).

LITERATURE: Marks 1882, p. 41; Berenson 1903, vol. 1, p. 157, vol. 2, p. 58, no. 1028; Seidlitz 1909, vol. 2, p. 33, pl. 50; Poggi 1919, pls. 105, 157; Pettorelli 1920, p. 197; Venturi 1920, p. 119, figs. 84, 85; De Rinaldis 1926, pp. 228–29, figs. 27, 66; Commissione Vinciana 1928–, vol. 6, p. 23 pls. 235.2, 239.2; Popp 1928, p. 44, no. 44; Sirén 1928, p. 111, pl. 127; Suida 1929, p. 129; Bodmer 1931, pp. 279, 312, 407 8, 413; Heydenreich 1933, pp. 205–9, 211; Berenson 1938, vol. 1, p. 175, vol. 2, p. 113, vol. 3, fig. 511, no. 1028; Richter 1939, vol. 2, no. 1457; Bottari 1942, pl. 100; Giglioli 1944, pp. 122, 145, pls. 105, 164; Popham and Pouncey 1950, pp. 65–69, no. 108; Heydenreich 1954, vol. 2, p. 42, pl. 53; Castelfranco 1956, p. 61, pl. 82; Berenson 1961, vol. 1, p. 256, vol. 2, p. 198, no. 1028; Wasserman 1970, pp. 197–98, 201–4, figs. 9, 10; Wasserman 1971, pp. 316–17, fig. 7; Gould 1975, pp. 154–56, figs. 86, 88; Pedretti 1979c, p. 33; Keele and Pedretti 1979–80, vol. 2, p. 865; Nicodemi 1980a, p. 76; Kemp 1981, pp. 223, 225, pl. 63; Pedretti 1982a, pp. 54, 104, figs. 78–79; Pedretti 1982c, pp. 18, 21, fig. 33; Budny 1983, pp. 34, 36, figs. 1–4; Clark 1985, p. 112, figs. 55–56; Pedretti 1987b, pp. 82, 105; Clark 1988, pp. 162–66, fig. 63; Pedretti 1988k, p. 123, fig. 1; Kemp 1989a; Kemp and Roberts 1989, pp. 150–51, no. 77; Caroli 1991, p. 174; Martin Clayton in Palazzo Grassi 1992, pp. 246–47, nos. 23–23a; Maidani Gerard and Krause-Zimmer 1993, p. 80, fig. 7; Popham 1994, nos. 144, 175; Farago 1996b, p. 81, fig. 5; Arasse 1998, pp. 284–85, fig. 201; Zwijnenberg 1999, pp. 67–71; Marani 2000b, p. 292.

This imposing sheet of sketches offers a fascinating juxtaposition of highly pictorial solutions for the composition of the Virgin and Child with Saint Anne (cat. no. 95), here including the infant Saint John the Baptist at the right, with various technological designs. Leonardo apparently first drew the large, nearly black mass of the framed compositional sketch on the page, building up the rough drawing so heavily in charcoal with ink and wash that the forms became indistinguishable. For clarity, it was necessary to indent the final forms with a stylus (carbon-traced outlines are visible on the verso) and also to elaborate on the various possibilities for the poses of the figures in the small jottings in the lower portion of the sheet. He seems to have added the technological studies last, near the right and bottom borders. Represented here are a wheel with an axle shaft, a mill wheel with running water, a pair of wheels on an axle (part of a cart?), and what appear to be two details of the same hydraulic project (a weir, dam, or bridge). The sheet clearly has been cropped along the borders, especially at the bottom.

Much scholarly debate surrounds the date of the British Museum sheet and its place in the sequence of composition drawings on the Saint Anne theme. A. E. Popham first dated the Saint Anne sketches on the British Museum sheet to 1498–99 in his monograph of Leonardo's drawings, espousing the theory of French patronage, by King Louis XII, of the Burlington House cartoon. Popham later revised his opinion in the British Museum catalogue of 1950 (coauthored with Philip Pouncey), dating the drawings about 1507, based on stylistic evidence. The hydraulic projects in the lower left provide an especially significant clue, for the British Museum sheet and another fragment from 1506–8 with water studies (Windsor, RL 12666) originally formed part of the same page, as pointed out by Carlo Pedretti. While this is not definitive proof of a 1506–8 date for the Saint Anne sketches on the recto of the British Museum sheet, it seems more than likely, as can be confirmed by the independent evidence of the drawing style and technique.

The main sketch on the British Museum sheet portrays the Virgin on the left, seated sidesaddle on the lap of Saint Anne, her legs facing left; the ink and the stylus outlines show the Virgin's left leg in two different positions. The carbon-traced outlines on the verso help in deciphering the final composition. Although the figural groups in the Venice (cat. no. 95) and British Museum sheets are more or less emphatically oriented

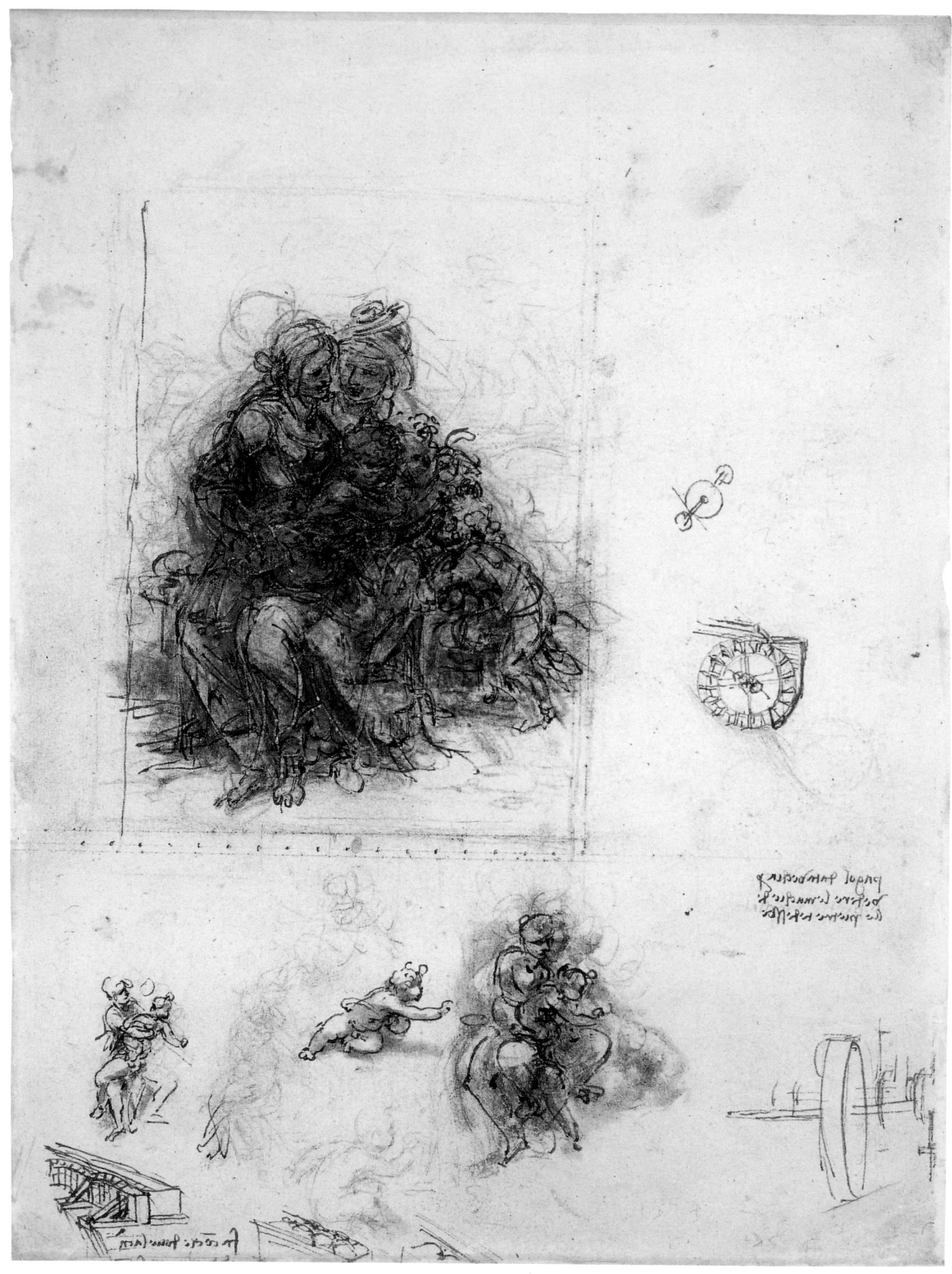

Cat. 96R

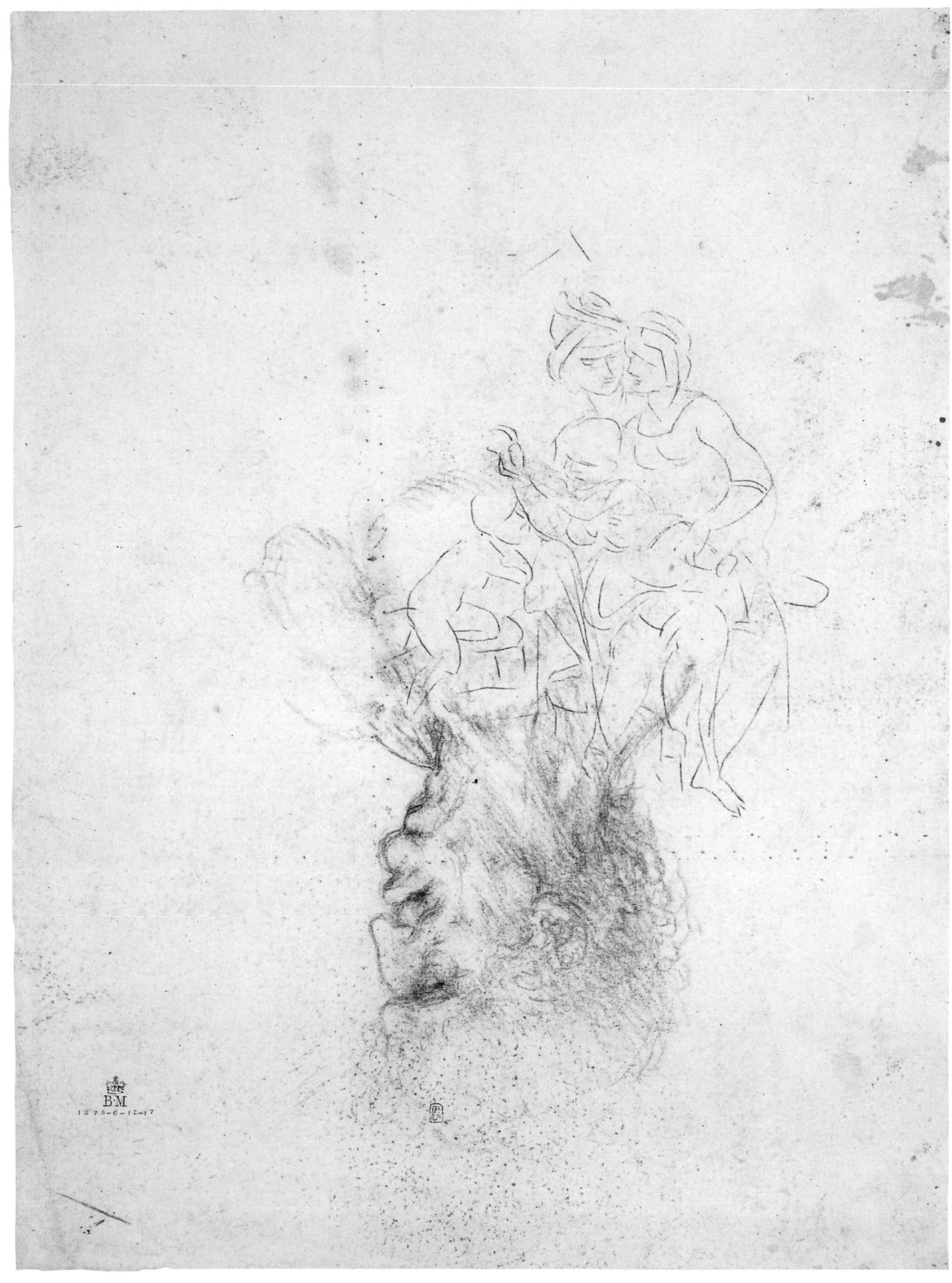

Cat. 96v

527

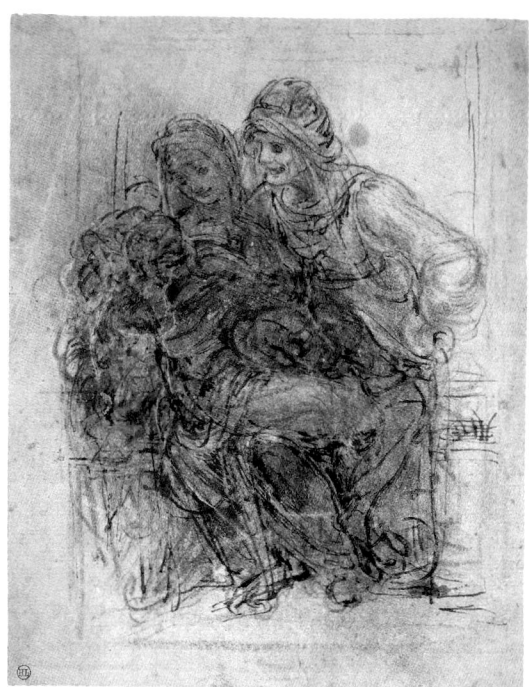

Fig. 186. Leonardo da Vinci, *Sketch for the Virgin and Child with Saint Anne*. Black chalk, reworked with pen and brown ink, 100 × 120 mm. Musée du Louvre, Paris RF 460

seated Saint Anne, who turns her face to her daughter, while the recumbent blessing Christ Child bridges the laps of the two women in a shallow diagonal line. He reaches out to the infant Saint John the Baptist, who half kneels and half stands nearly in profile on the right. This general arrangement conforms fairly closely to the composition of the extant monumental cartoon of the *Virgin and Child with Saint Anne and the Infant Saint John the Baptist* (the Burlington House cartoon; National Gallery, London). Even such details as the design of the headdresses of the women are quite similar.

Here, as he did so often, Leonardo drew a rough framing outline around the composition (cat. nos. 45, 88, 95), and the pinpricked scale at the lower border of the frame may give an indication of the proportional enlargement of the design on the final surface. Since Leonardo may have used the same unit of the palmo (one-eighth of a braccio, equaling 7.25 cm) as in his *Proportions of the Human Body According to Vitruvius* (Accademia, Venice, 228; fig. 43), the completed work may have measured between 108 and 116 centimeters at the base, which is not too far from the dimensions of the National Gallery cartoon.[1] A lamb does not appear to be part of the main sketch, but the largest of the motifs in the lower part of the sheet may include the animal to the right of the figures. The small sketches in the lower part of the sheet explore alternative solutions for the figures in the main composition. The artist was concerned with the placement of the Virgin sidesaddle on the lap of Saint Anne, as well as the crossing of the women's legs, one's facing left and the other's right.

CCB

to the right, Leonardo also experimented with more subtle turns of the figures, varying their dispositions left and right, as in figure 186 and in the monumental cartoon or full-scale drawing in the National Gallery, London (figs. 17, 75, 76). In the fragile compositional drawing in the Musée du Louvre, Paris (RF 460; fig. 186), the figures are turned resolutely to the left. The reversed image on the verso of the British Museum sheet is close to that of the Louvre composition sketch. In the recto of the sheet, to the Virgin's right is the

1. Convincingly pointed out in Kemp and Roberts 1989, p. 150, no. 77. See Martin Kemp's essay in this volume.

LEONARDO DA VINCI

97. *Studies and Sketches of a Young Child*

Black chalk or charcoal with some red chalk offsetting, partly reworked with pen and medium brown ink, 204 × 152 mm (8 1/16 × 6 in.)
Lent by Her Majesty Queen Elizabeth II, Royal Library, Windsor Castle 12562

PROVENANCE: Windsor Leoni volume: 1519, Francesco Melzi, Milan and Rome (1491/93–ca. 1570); ca. 1570, Orazio Melzi; by 1590, Pompeo Leoni, Madrid and Milan (ca. 1533–1608; Lugt under 2885);

ca. 1613, Thomas Howard, second earl of Arundel (1586–1646); before 1690, British Royal Collection (inventory of King George III's collection, ca. 1810).

LITERATURE: Möller 1926, p. 18, fig. 26; Berenson 1938, vol. 2, p. 125, no. 1129B; Royal Academy of Arts 1952, p. 9, no. 106; Clark 1954, pl. 35; Berenson 1961, vol. 2, pp. 221–22, no. 1129B; Clark and Pedretti 1968–69, vol. 1, pp. 106–7, no. 12562; Wasserman 1969, p. 130; Clark

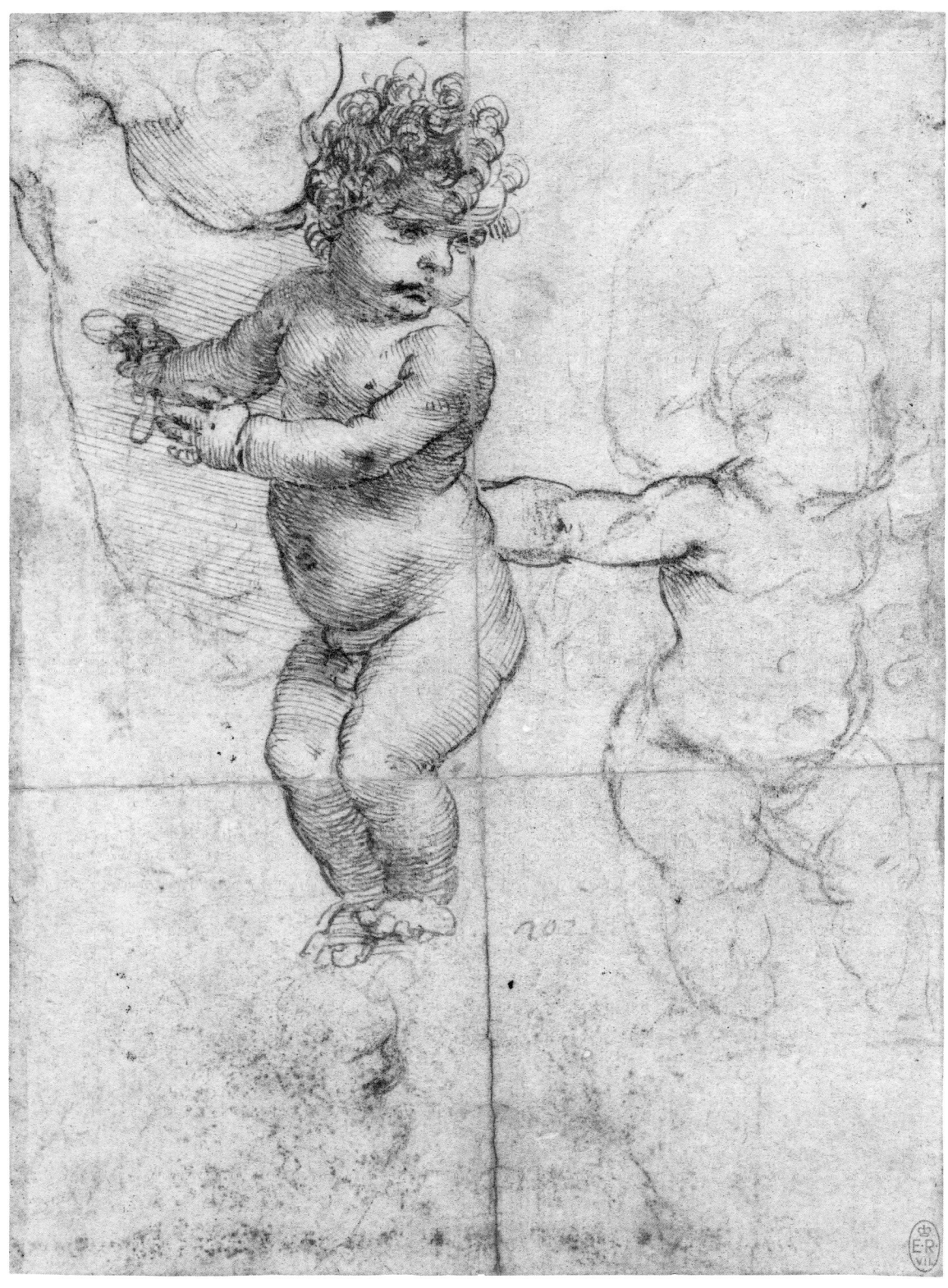

Cat. 97 *(actual size)*

1969–70, p. 20, no. 83; Gould 1975, p. 161, fig. 91; Nicodemi 1980a, p. 23; Pedretti 1982c, p. 21, fig. 46; Kemp and Roberts 1989, p. 86, no. 29; Kemp 1992a, pp. 62–63, no. 13; Pedretti 1992d, p. 172, fig. 4; Popham 1994, no. 181; Bambach 1999a, pp. 83, 403 n. 20; Laurenza 2001, p. 85 n. 115, fig. 65.

L eonardo most probably drew these studies of an infant from a live model, to judge especially from the freshness and economy of the contours in the charcoal underdrawings. As an exercise in life drawing, the sheet evokes an example by his teacher, Andrea del Verrocchio, executed nearly three decades earlier (cat. no. 4). Bernard Berenson noted that these studies are among the drawings by Leonardo that are most reminiscent of Michelangelo, and probably date to about 1506–8. The broad, partial sketch that is cropped by the edges of the paper on the upper left of the present sheet shows the naked child with his head in a nearly lost-profile view, facing right, and his distended body turned almost frontally, as if he were held by an unseen adult. The most highly worked-up study, toward the center of the sheet, portrays the child at rest in a full-length contrapposto, his head and gaze directed to the right and his body and limbs turned to the left, clearly suggesting his function as a major linking element in a figural composition. The small, slight study of a child's head toward the lower left of the sheet, although autograph, seems quite unrelated to the other drawings in scale, style, and technique. Perhaps the most spontaneous and lifelike is the sketch in the right foreground, which evocatively captures the movement of the child's body in the unsteady effort of standing up. His pose, in three-quarter view facing right, with outstretched arms, suggests that he, too, is a major linking element in a figural composition. Behind him is an extremely fragmentary sketch of the shoulders and arms of a figure that may be an infant (or an adult woman).

The Windsor sheet of studies often has been connected with the compositions of the *Virgin and Child with Saint Anne* (with or without the young Saint John the Baptist and the lamb), and especially with the monumental National Gallery cartoon (figs. 17, 75, 76), but a comparison of the present studies with either of the infant figure types in the London cartoon definitively confirms that they are quite unrelated. Simply too few other studies of infants by Leonardo for the *Saint Anne* compositions survive, and those that do also seem totally unrelated to the present large-scale studies of infants. The pose of the infant that is most highly worked up, toward the center of the Windsor sheet, evokes that of the Christ Child playing with a lamb in Andrea Brescianino's lost painting (formerly Kaiser-Friedrich-Museum, Berlin), which often has been presumed to represent a fairly accurate rendition of Leonardo's (lost) early cartoon of the *Virgin and Child with Saint Anne and a Lamb* that was described by Giorgio Vasari as having been publicly exhibited at Santissima Annunziata in Florence, to great acclaim. As has rightly been remarked, the style and drawing technique of the present sheet, with deep modeling and dense and pronounced curved hatching, seem remarkably close to the studies for the *Leda and the Swan* (cat. nos. 98, 99). The small, incidental sketch toward the lower left of the sheet, which is quite unlike the large sketches in style and technique, resembles one of the studies at Windsor (RL 12536) for the National Gallery cartoon.

CCB

LEONARDO DA VINCI

98. *Kneeling Leda and the Swan*

Pen and brown ink (with losses of pigment), over extensive charcoal or soft black chalk; traces of a framing outline in pen and brown ink, 126 × 109 mm (4 15/16 × 4 5/16 in.)
Inscribed on recto in pen and brown ink, toward lower right border, in a seventeenth- or early-eighteenth-century hand: *Lionardo da Vinci* Museum Boijmans Van Beuningen, Rotterdam I 466

PROVENANCE: Sir Thomas Lawrence, Bristol and London (1769–1830; Lugt 2445); King William II of Holland, The Hague (1792–1849); his sale, Amsterdam, August 12, 1850 (withdrawn); his daughter Sophie, grand duchess of Saxe-Weimar, Weimar; Karl Alexander, grand duke of Saxe-Weimar, Weimar; Wilhelm Ernst, grand duke of Saxe-Weimar, Weimar; ca. 1923, J. W. Boehler, Lucerne; 1929, Franz Koenigs, Haarlem; 1940, D. G. van Beuningen, Rotterdam; 1941, his gift to the Museum Boijmans Foundation.

LITERATURE: Ottley 1823, p. 20, no. 18; von Ritgen 1865, no. 32; Morelli 1890, p. 196 (Giovanni Antonio Bazzi "Il Sodoma"); Morelli 1900, pp. 154–57 (Sodoma); MacCurdy 1904, pp. 65–66; Frizzoni 1905, p. 66; Seidlitz 1909, vol. 2, p. 131 (copy); Poggi 1919, p. 58, pl. 112; Venturi 1920, p. 136 (copy), fig. 125; De Toni 1922, p. 115, fig. 31; Popp 1928, p. 50, no. 61; Sirén 1928, vol. 1, p. 157, vol. 3, pl. 195A; Bodmer 1931, pp. 329, 417; Stedelijk Museum 1934, p. 148, no. 571; Berenson 1938, vol. 1, p. 180 n. 5, vol. 2, p. 112, vol. 3, fig. 546, no. 1020A; Giglioli 1944, pp. 125–26 (rejected), pl. 114; Valentiner 1949, pp. 111–12, no. 81; Biblioteca Medicea Laurenziana 1952, pp. 37–38, no. 54; Castelfranco 1954b, pl. 170, fig. 14; Heydenreich 1954, vol. 1, pp. 54, 184, vol. 2, p. 54, pl. 66; Goldscheider 1959, pp. 158–59, under pl. 36; Haverkamp Begemann 1957, pp. 37–39, no. 40; Berenson 1961, vol. 1, p. 262, vol. 2, p. 213, vol. 3, fig. 513, no. 1082C-1; Museum Boymans-Van Beuningen 1962, vol. 1, pp. 42–43, no. 49, vol. 2, pl. 38, no. 49; Clark and Pedretti 1968–69, vol. 1, p. 33, under no. 12337; Pedretti 1973a, p. 98; Konrad Oberhuber in Levenson, Oberhuber, and Sheehan 1973, pp. 450–41 n. 5, under no. 162; Allison 1974, fig. 2; Weil-Garris Posner 1974, pp. 33–34, fig. 32; Gould 1975, pp. 117–18, fig. 59; Pedretti 1979c, no. 39; Keele and Pedretti 1979–80, vol. 2, p. 835; Kemp and Smart 1980, pp. 160–71; Pedretti 1982a, pp. 53–57, fig. 36; Carlo Pedretti in Vezzosi 1982, p. 21, fig. 96; Calvesi 1985, p. 139, fig. 70; Emboden 1987, pp. 108–9; Pedretti 1987a, p. 82, fig. 106; Rosand 1988, p. 30, fig. 38; Ames-Lewis 1989, fig. 5; Kemp and Roberts 1989, p. 65, no. 14; Dalli Regoli 1991, pp. 12–13; Zeri 1991, p. 179; Pedretti 1993b, p. 188; Popham 1994, no. 208; Marani 1995, p. 220 n. 74, fig. 47; Clayton 1996–97, p. 76; Pedretti 1996a, p. 63, fig. 6; Ames-Lewis 1997, pp. 119, 121, fig. 4; Pedretti 1997b, figs. 1–3, 5; Arasse 1998, pp. 422, 425, fig. 281; Marani 2000b, pp. 269–75; Meijer and van der Sman 2000, pp. 9–10, no. 1; Dalli Regoli, Nanni, and Natali 2001, pp. 36–37, fig. 18, pp. 112–13, no. 2.4; Laurenza 2001, pp. 88–89, fig. 67; Clayton 2002–3, p. 150.

LEONARDO DA VINCI

99. *Kneeling Leda and the Swan*

Pen and brown ink, brush and brown wash, over charcoal or soft black chalk, 160 × 139 mm (6 5/16 × 5 1/2 in.)

Inscribed on recto in pen and brown ink, in lower right, in a seventeenth- or early eighteenth-century hand: *Leonardo da Vinci*

The Duke of Devonshire and the Chatsworth Settlement Trustees, Chatsworth 717

PROVENANCE: Possibly William Cavendish, second duke of Devonshire, Chatsworth (1672–1739); by descent to the eleventh duke of Devonshire.

LITERATURE: Morelli 1890, p. 196 (Giovanni Antonio Bazzi "Il Sodoma"); Morelli 1900, pp. 154–57 (Sodoma); Strong 1902, no. 35; MacCurdy 1904, pp. 65–66; Frizzoni 1905, p. 66; Seidlitz 1909, vol. 2, p. 131 (copy); Sirén 1928, vol. 1, p. 157, vol. 3, pl. 195B; Berenson 1938, vol. 1, p. 180 n. 5, vol. 2, p. 110, no. 1013A; Palazzo dell'Arte 1939, p. 157, no. 78; Giglioli 1944, pp. 125–26 (rejected), pl. 113; Popham 1949, no. 7; Biblioteca Medicea Laurenziana 1952, p. 38, under no. 54; Royal Academy of Arts 1952, no. 135; Clark 1959, pp. 116–17; Goldscheider 1959, pp. 158–59, pl. 36; Haverkamp Begemann 1957, pp. 37–39, under no. 40 (possibly by Leonardo); Berenson 1961, vol. 1, p. 262, vol. 2, p. 193, no. 1013B; Popham 1962, no. 32; Clark and Pedretti 1968–69, vol. 1, p. 33, under no. 12337; Wasserman 1969, p. 130, fig. 31; Konrad Oberhuber in Levenson, Oberhuber, and Sheehan 1973, pp. 450–51 n. 5, under no. 162 ("probably only a copy"); Pedretti 1973a, p. 98; Allison 1974, fig. 3; Museum of Fine Arts, Blunt 1979–80, no. 54; Nicodemi 1980a, p. 66; Kemp and Smart 1980, pp. 160–71; Kemp 1981, pp. 270–72, pl. 73; Pedretti 1982a, pp. 48, 53–57, fig. 37; Vezzosi 1982, fig. 97; Ames-Lewis and Wright 1983, no. 45, pl. 16; British Museum 1983–84, no. 79; Wasserman 1984, pp. 23–24, fig. 15; Calvesi 1985, p. 139, fig. 71; Emboden 1987, pp. 108–9; Pedretti 1987a, p. 82, fig. 107; Ward 1988, no. 1; Pedretti 1988i, fig. 3; Ames-Lewis 1989, fig. 6; Kemp and Roberts 1989, no. 75; Dalli Regoli 1991, pp. 12–13; Jaffé 1993, pp. 73–75, no. 79; Geddo 1994, pp. 58–59, fig. 5; Jaffé 1994, p. 165, no. 880; Popham 1994, under no. 208; Marani 1995, p. 220, fig. 48; Clayton 1996–97, pp. 76–77, under nos. 40–42; Arasse 1998, pp. 422, 425, fig. 282; Marani 2000b, pp. 269–75; Bambach 2001, pp. 20–21; Dalli Regoli, Nanni, and Natali 2001, pp. 114–15, no. 2.5; Clayton 2002–3, p. 150.

The Rotterdam and Chatsworth drawings, together with the large Windsor sheet that includes sketches of the *Leda* along with studies for the *Battle of Anghiari* (cat. no. 88), depict with some differences the Greek myth of Leda: she was seduced by the god Zeus, who came to her illicitly at the river in the guise of a swan. Leonardo's recasting of the classical myth speaks of the timeless notions of fecundity, birth, and the regenerative power of nature; in fact, he undertook some of the most nuanced of his botanical studies in connection with his portrayal of the flowered meadow in the foreground of the compositions (cat. no. 100).

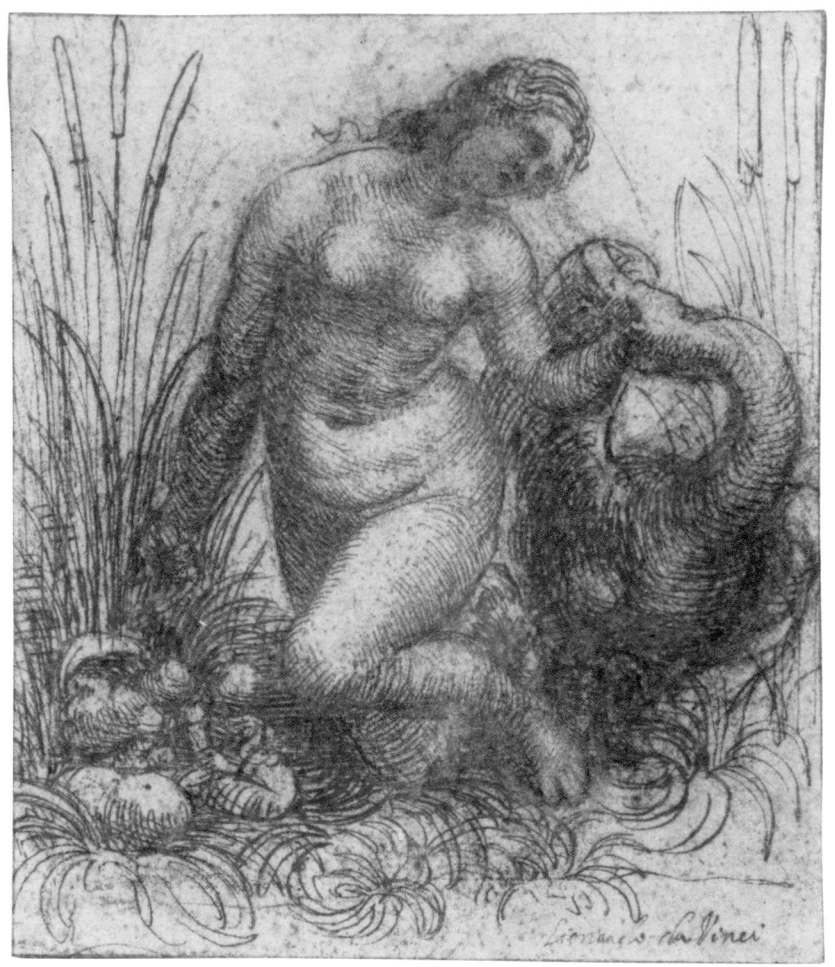

Cat. 98 *(actual size)*

Leda's kneeling pose was inspired by Roman copies of Hellenistic sculptures of the crouching or kneeling Venus of the "Doidalsas type." The example closest in design to Leonardo's kneeling *Leda*s seems to be a rare variant of the "Doidalsas type," a marble *Venus Kneeling on a Tortoise* (Museo del Prado, Madrid) that was repeatedly copied by sixteenth-century North Italian artists, and which can be documented as having been in Rome from at least the seventeenth century onward, in the collection of Cardinal Azzolini, if not earlier; it may very well have already been in the eternal city in the 1490s.[1] Similar motifs of the kneeling *Venus* also exist on *Nereid* sarcophagi (for example, Musée du Louvre, Paris; Villa Borghese, Rome), all of which suggests that Leonardo and his contemporaries would have had access to such antique designs through a variety of variants. Leda was the daughter of King Thestius of Aetolia and the wife of King Tyndareus of Sparta, but the classical accounts of the myth vary in several details. Hygenus has Leda giving birth to two eggs (as in Leonardo's Rotterdam and Chatsworth drawings), from which hatched four infants, often identified as Helen of Troy,

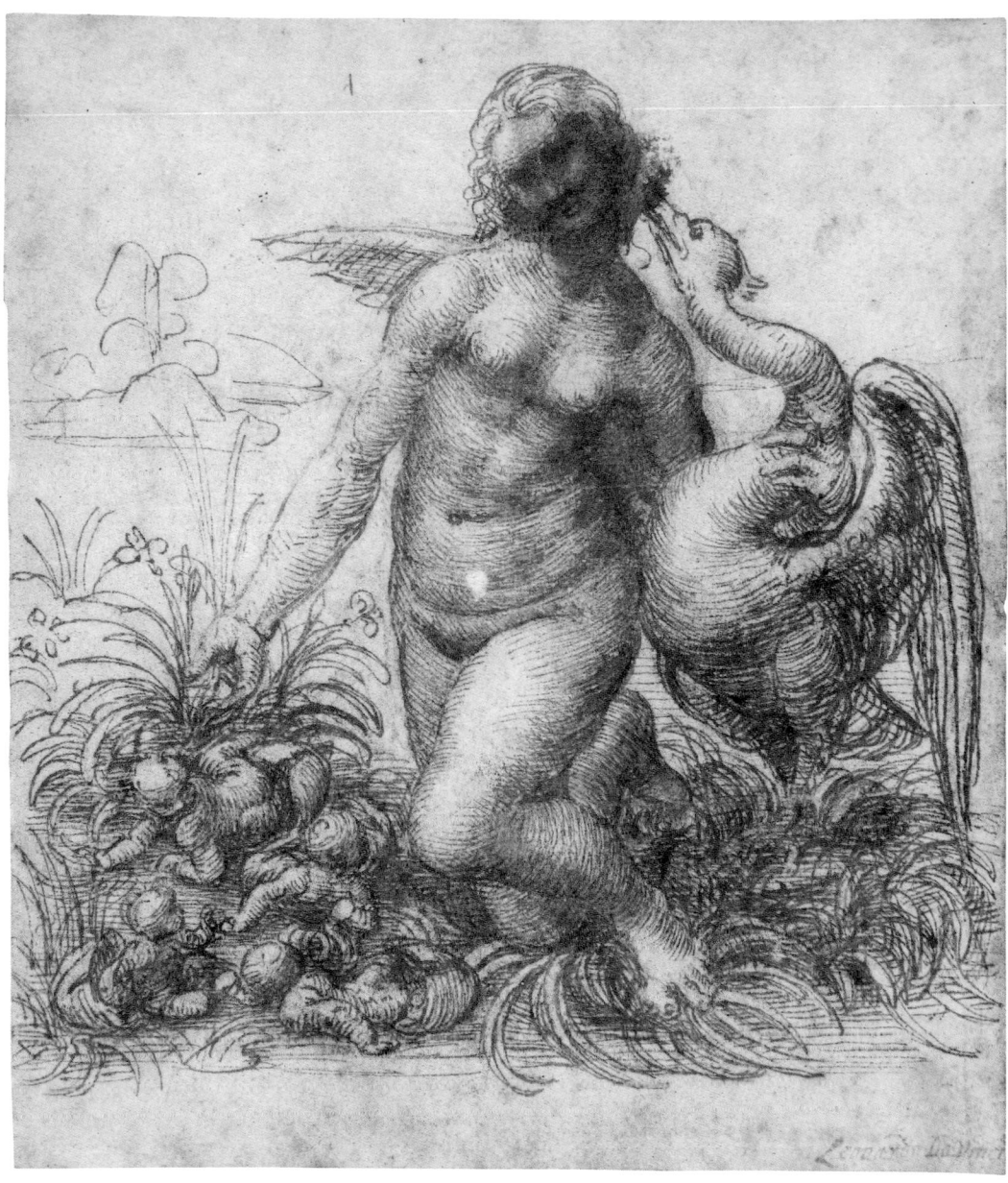

Cat. 99 *(actual size)*

Clytemnestra, and the heavenly twins Castor and Pollux. In both drawings, Leda is shown with her right knee on the ground, and the vortices of the star-of-Bethlehem plant (studied separately in cat. no. 100) in the foreground echo her agitated contrapposto. Her four infants, in different poses and groupings, are seen in the lower left. In the Rotterdam sheet, Leda turns her face to the swan, chastely caressing it with her left hand, but the tall, upright reeds (*Typha latifolia*) on the extreme left of the composition heighten the erotic content of the scene. Leonardo heavily reworked the swan's neck and

head several times, in charcoal or soft black chalk, before the final drawing in pen and ink. He then reworked again the design of the swan's neck and head with charcoal or black chalk over the ink. In the passages in charcoal or black chalk, the beak of the swan reaches quite closely to Leda's head. In the more agitated Chatsworth composition (probably a later conception), the swan embraces Leda with its right wing as it sinks its beak into her elaborately dressed hair, while the Aetolian princess coyly looks away.

It seems extremely difficult to propose a chronology for

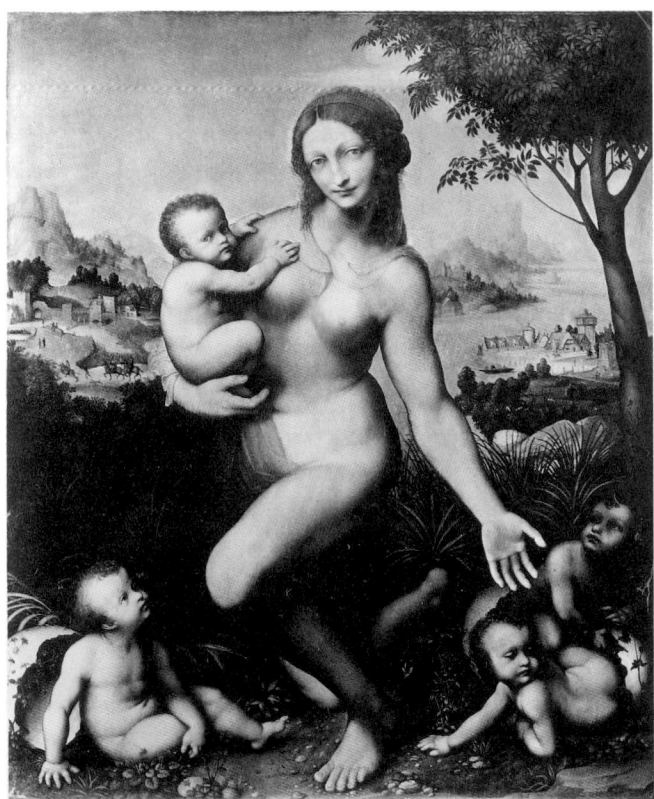

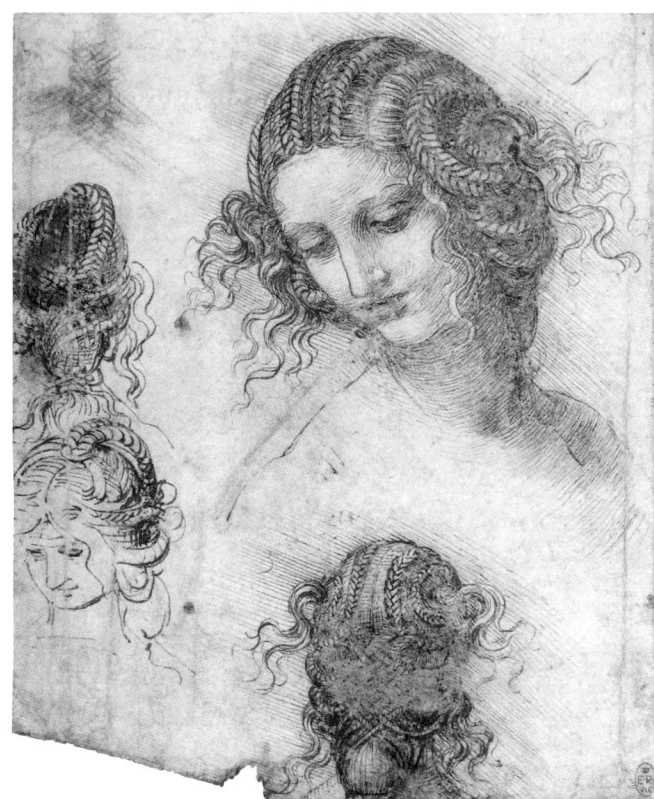

Fig. 187. Attributed to Giovanni Pietro Rizzoli, called "Il Giampietrino" (after Leonardo da Vinci), *Leda*. Oil on wood, 128 × 105.5 cm. Gemäldegalerie Alte Meister, Schloss Wilhelmshöhe, Staatliche Museen Kassel GK 966; inv. 1749 no. 850

Fig. 188. Leonardo da Vinci, *Studies for the Head of Leda*. Pen and brown ink over black chalk, 200 × 162 mm. The Royal Collection, H.M. Queen Elizabeth II, Windsor Castle RL 12516

Leonardo's *Leda and the Swan* drawings, given that the date and intended destination of the *Leda* project are totally uncertain. No original paintings survive, and the early biographies of Leonardo (most surprisingly, that by Giorgio Vasari) are silent about such a work. The only secure early document is a mention of a *Leda and the Swan* in an inventory of the property owned by Leonardo's hapless pupil Salai that is dated April 21, 1525, shortly after he was murdered. The inventory lists an extremely high value for this painting, which therefore suggests that it was by Leonardo's hand (if this is the case, Salai would have inherited the *Leda* at Leonardo's death in 1519, along with other major paintings by the master).[2] The Codice Magliabechiano (Anonimo Gaddiano) of about 1540 notes that Leonardo painted a Leda ("Et anchora [una Leda]").[3] Additional sources that refer to a *Leda and the Swan* painting by Leonardo are rather late: Giovanni Paolo Lomazzo's *Trattato dell'arte della pittura, scoltura et archittetura* (1584), his sonnet *Grotteschi* (1587), and his *Idea del tempio della pittura* (1590), all published in Milan. The erudite connoisseur Cassiano del Pozzo wrote about works that he had seen at

the Château de Fontainebleau in 1625, describing a rather damaged painting by Leonardo of a "standing nearly nude Leda, with the swan and two eggs from whose shells one sees that four children have issued (Castor and Pollux, Helen and Clytemnestra)."[4] It is assumed that this is the picture that was destroyed sometime between 1692–94 and 1775, as is suggested by the gaps in the extant written evidence.

Of great historical importance, therefore, the Rotterdam and Chatsworth drawings probably can be dated to about 1506–8, based on the style and the densely tonal technique of curved parallel hatching (hence, a few years later than is often suggested). The drawings seem generally comparable in style and technique to the Turin sheet of sketches connected with a variety of projects (cat. no. 103), including the later phase of work on the *Battle of Anghiari*. There is no doubt that Leonardo already was considering a composition of a kneeling Leda and the Swan about 1504–5, during his most energetic work on the *Battle of Anghiari* cartoon. The magnificent sheet at Windsor (cat. no. 88) includes three sketches for such a *Leda* painting (two of which have the drawn framing outlines around the composition, signifying an intended picture), together with a study of a rearing horse and rider for the cavalry portion planned for the right of the *Anghiari* cartoon. The larger composition sketch toward the center of the Windsor sheet (cat. no. 88) shows Leda's head both frontally (the version that is inked) and with her face turned to the right, thus combining in one design several of the solutions seen in the Chatsworth and the Rotterdam sheets respectively. That some years elapsed between the Windsor sheet (cat. no. 88) and the present drawings, however, seems clear from the very different techniques, for the latter are highly modeled in dark brown iron gall ink with the dense, pronounced curved hatching that anticipates the embryo-anatomical studies of 1508–10.[5] It is most probable that Leonardo continued to revise the *Leda* composition until his years in Rome (1513–17), and the sheet of botanical studies (cat. no. 100) may thus relate to a rather late phase of work on the project, about 1508–10.

A painting that is often attributed to Leonardo's pupil Giampietrino (fig. 187; Staatliche Museen Kassel, ex-Schloss Neuwied) vividly evokes the master's ideas for a kneeling Leda that he explored in the Windsor, Rotterdam, and Chatsworth sheets. The pose of Leda in this painted copy seems closest to that in the Chatsworth sheet, though the extended arms are reversed; as for the motif of the child at the breast, the painting seems most like the left composition sketch on the Windsor sheet. Leda's pose, with her right arm across her body, as depicted in the larger composition sketch toward the center of the Windsor sheet (cat. no. 88), would become an important feature of the standing Leda.

It is not known exactly when Leonardo produced the figure of Leda in a standing pose (see the copy exhibited here as cat. no. 134), though he must have been designing such a figure by about 1508, while still in Florence—either in small drawings or in the form of a full-scale cartoon—since Raphael, who probably left Florence for Rome late in 1508, made a sketch of it (Windsor, RL 12759), using Leonardo's technique of bold curved hatching in pen and ink. To judge from the many painted and drawn copies by Leonardo's Milanese followers (Galleria Borghese, Rome, fig. 22; cat. no. 134), the master must have presumably produced an original painting of a standing Leda, when he returned to Milan in 1508 (see Chronology). It seems no less worthy of note, however, that an engraving from about 1510 by Giovanni Battista Palumba (the "Master I. B. with the Bird") takes on the subject of a crouching *Leda and the Swan* in a Leonardesque vocabulary and in a design that is very reminiscent of Giampietrino's painting in Kassel, which itself probably dates from 1510–15.[6] It seems therefore worth pondering that the kneeling and standing *Leda*s may have constituted separate projects, in and of themselves, that Leonardo possibly developed concurrently, and during a long period of time.

Four sheets at Windsor portray the elaborately coiffed head of Leda, which Leonardo based on a wig (fig. 188).[7] These detailed, deeply modeled coiffure studies would seem equally suited for a kneeling or a standing Leda, though their design is closest to the copies of the standing Leda. They are drawn in the same technique, pen and dark brown iron gall ink, as the Rotterdam and Chatsworth studies, with a very dense, pronounced curved hatching. The most dryly executed of the Windsor coiffure sketches is also the one that bears a note in Leonardo's hand explaining, "this [wig] can be removed and put on without damaging it."[8] These well-known Windsor coiffure studies were all accepted by the brilliant scholar of Leonardo's drawings A. E. Popham, who dated them about 1505–6.

By comparison to these Windsor sheets, the Rotterdam and Chatsworth compositional studies were apparently much less accessible in their early history, especially during the critical years from the mid-nineteenth to the mid-twentieth century, when drawings connoisseurs were attempting rigorously to define Leonardo's oeuvre. In contrast to many other drawings by Leonardo, even today the Rotterdam and Chatsworth sheets (although well known from reproductions) do not seem to be as frequently studied in the original by scholars. To the best of the present author's knowledge, the two sheets have never been exhibited side by side.[9] The damaged state of the Rotterdam and Chatsworth sheets has sometimes unjustly detracted attention from the obvious skill of their execution. The drawing surface on the Rotterdam sheet appears somewhat flat, which is probably the result of having been drymounted by an early collector (Sir Thomas Lawrence?); the sheet was detached from its backing in 1996. Moreover, at some point after 1962 and before 1970, the Rotterdam sheet was washed with a watery solution to clean it. The restoration technique of washing can especially adversely affect drawings in iron gall ink (this is the medium of all the extant pen *Leda* studies by Leonardo), and in the case of the Rotterdam sheet, this removed a great amount of ink from the darkest outlines and shadows, which now seem lighter than areas that were originally intended to be of a lighter, intermediate tone.[10] The passages showing the greatest depletion of pigment are in the outlines of Leda's facial features (the nose, mouth, and cheeks), her right knee, the lower contours on the beak and neck of the swan, and the portion around the eggs and the children. In contrast to the Rotterdam sheet, the untreated Chatsworth drawing is still mounted down and exhibits stains, as well as a loss on the paper on Leda's belly.[11] The corrosive iron gall ink that Leonardo used has slightly disfigured some of the darkest shadows in the composition.

Obviously very closely related in the details of their designs, the two sheets present challenging issues of connoisseurship, not least because of Leonardo's use of the dense, somewhat heavy-handed curved-hatching technique that follows the roundness of forms in an almost exaggerated way. This modeling technique sometimes makes it quite difficult to identify whether the strokes are left-handed, since Leonardo often turned the paper around as he worked. It is therefore not surprising that the noted and highly influential connoisseur Giovanni Morelli (who was quite attuned to Leonardo's left-handedness, at least in the master's early drawings) attributed both the Rotterdam and Chatsworth sheets to Giovanni Antonio Bazzi "Il Sodoma," following apparently the (verbal) skeptical opinion of Jean Paul Richter. It was Oskar Fischel (one of the foremost Raphael scholars) who in 1928 insisted that the Chatsworth sheet was by Leonardo, and who can largely be credited with leading the reinstitution of the drawing into Leonardo's oeuvre. Popham illustrated the Rotterdam sheet and dated it about 1504, adding, laconically, that "a version is at Chatsworth." It can be assumed that Popham accepted the Chatsworth sheet as autograph (though grudgingly), for he usually noted if drawings were copies, and the drawings that he did not accept—which included the versos of well-known sheets—he omitted entirely from his book. The opinion expressed by Kenneth Clark and Carlo Pedretti (1968–69) conveys a similar emphasis: "The drawing at

Rotterdam is certainly by Leonardo." While the authenticity of the Chatsworth sheet has received fewer positive assessments from scholars, both drawings nevertheless have figured prominently in the Leonardo literature. Any lingering doubts regarding Leonardo's authorship of both the Rotterdam and Chatsworth sheet easily can be assuaged. One need only compare the handling of the pen and brown iron gall ink to that in the imposing Windsor sheet of studies of young children (cat. no. 97), which must date from exactly the same period as the present *Leda* drawings. It is entirely probable that the Chatsworth *Leda* represents Leonardo's synthesis of composition drawings previously studied on other sheets, and that its function as a summary draft would explain its slightly inert quality of execution.

CCB

1. The complex antique iconography is summarized in Allison 1974; and Maria Chiara Monaco in Dalli Regoli, Nanni, and Natali 2001, pp. 106–7, no. 2.1.
2. This inventory is discussed and transcribed in Shell and Sironi 1991.
3. Transcribed in Vecce 1998, p. 362; not in Frey 1892.
4. Transcribed in Marani 1989, p. 142: "Una Leda in piedi, quasi tutta ignuda, col cigno e due uova a piè della figura dalle guscia delle quali si vede esser usciti quattro bambini (Castore e Polluce, Elena e Clitemnestra). Questo pezzo è finitissimo, ma alquanto secco, in specie il petto della donna, del resto il paese e la verdura è condotta con grandissima diligenza; ed è molto per la mala via, perchè come che è fatto di tre tavole per lo lungo, quelle scostate vi han fatto staccare assai del colorito."
5. See Windsor, RL 19101, 19102, 19095.
6. Palumba's engraving is discussed by Konrad Oberhuber in Levenson, Oberhuber, and Sheehan 1973, pp. 450–51, no. 162.
7. See Windsor, RL 12515, 12517, 12516, 12518.
8. See Windsor, RL 12515: "questo si po / levare e ppo/re sanza gu/astarrsi."
9. Although both the Rotterdam and Chatsworth sheets were included in the magnificent Leonardo exhibition at the Hayward Gallery in London in 1989 (Kemp and Roberts 1989, nos. 14, 75), they were not hung together, as the purpose of that show was to study the thematic relationships between Leonardo's artistic and scientific vision.
10. Bram Meij in discussion with the author (September 5, 2002). The photograph published in the Museum Boymans-Van Beuningen 1962 catalogue was taken before restoration, while the official Gernsheim Corpus photograph of the late 1960s was taken after restoration.
11. The loss on Leda's belly dates between 1939 and 1946; Peter Day in a letter to the author (summer 2002).

LEONARDO DA VINCI

100. *Botanical Studies with Star-of-Bethlehem, Grasses, Crowfoot, Wood Anemone, and Another Genus*

Red chalk, reworked with pen and dark brown ink, 196 × 158 mm
($7^{11}/_{16}$ × $6^{3}/_{16}$ in.)
Watermark: Part of an anvil? (not in Briquet); cropped at upper right
Lent by Her Majesty Queen Elizabeth II, Royal Library, Windsor
Castle 12424

PROVENANCE: Windsor Leoni volume: 1519, Francesco Melzi,
Milan and Rome (1491/93–ca. 1570); ca. 1570, Orazio Melzi; by
1590, Pompeo Leoni, Madrid and Milan (ca. 1533–1608; Lugt
under 2885); ca. 1613, Thomas Howard, second earl of Arundel
(1586–1646); before 1690, British Royal Collection (inventory of
King George III's collection, ca. 1810).

LITERATURE: Grosvenor Gallery 1878, vol. 1, p. 27; Müntz 1898,
vol. 1, p. 256 (detail); Müntz 1899, p. 260; Berenson 1903, vol. 2, p. 67,
no. 1236; Seidlitz 1909, vol. 1, p. 294, vol. 2, p. 7; Seidlitz 1911, p. 738;
Malaguzzi Valeri 1913–23, vol. 2, fig. 440; Poggi 1919, pl. 131; Venturi
1920, p. 105, fig. 61; De Toni 1922, p. 18, fig. 7; Baldacci 1922–23,
p. 81; Venturi 1925, fig. 143; Commissione Vinciana 1928–,
vol. 5, p. 25, pl. 231; Popp 1928, pp. 16, 53, no. 74; Bodmer 1931,
pp. 335, 418; Popham 1931, p. 26, no. 90, pl. 85B; Berenson 1938,
vol. 1, p. 182, vol. 2, p. 137, no. 1236; MacCurdy 1938, vol. 1, pl. 14;
Palazzo dell'Arte 1939, p. 155; Goldscheider 1952, pl. 38; Royal
Academy of Arts 1952, p. 38, no. 148; Clark 1954, pl. 31; Heydenreich
1954, vol. 1, p. 139, vol. 2, p. 155, pl. 212 (incorrect inv. no.; as
12427); Heydenreich 1958b, col. 583; Goldscheider 1959, pp. 171–
72, pl. 91; Berenson 1961, vol. 1, p. 264, vol. 2, p. 242, vol. 3, fig. 516,
no. 1236; Chastel 1961, p. 154; Clark and Pedretti 1968–69, vol. 1,
p. 67, no. 12424; Clark 1969–70, p. 14, no. 61b; Queen's Gallery
1972–73, p. 26, no. 24; Brizio 1974b, p. 36, fig. 36/5; Morley 1979,
pp. 556, 559, 562, fig. 21; Baldacci 1980, p. 448; Pedretti and Clark
1980–81, p. 36, no. 13, pl. 4; Kemp 1981, pp. 273–74, pl. 74; De
Vecchi 1982, p. 58, fig. 33; Pedretti 1982a, p. 56, no. 16 recto; Baur
1984, pp. 179, 271, fig. 15; Wasserman 1984, p. 45, fig. 46; Calvesi
1985, p. 140. fig. 72; Emboden 1987, pp. 23, 144–45; Clark 1988,
pp. 179–80, fig. 72; Rosand 1988, pp. 32, 36, fig. 44; Kemp and
Roberts 1989, p. 123, no. 57; Kemp 1992b, p. 283, no. 184; Popham
1994, no. 273; Clayton 1996–97, pp. 76–77, 79, no. 41; Ames-Lewis
1997, pp. 119, 122, fig. 3; Letze and Buchsteiner 1997, p. 106; Arasse
1998, pp. 101–2, fig. 50; Dalli Regoli, Nanni, and Natali 2001, p. 69,
fig. 59.

Represented here are several varieties of plants, although the protagonist is clearly the elegantly stylized star-of-Bethlehem (*Ornithogalum umbellatum*), with its pointy-petaled flowers and long, spiraling leaves, which eloquently articulates Leonardo's concern with the vortex as a compositional element. Scholars have differed greatly regarding the identification of the species of the other flowers, sketched more lightly on the page. The species to the immediate left of the magnificent star has been called a crowfoot (*Anemone bulbosa*), a *Ranunculus bulbosus*, and a *Pulsatilla vernalis*. The daintier variety on the right has been identified as both a wood anemone (*Anemone ranunculoides*) and an *Anemone nemerosa*. Below, the delicate spray and seed vessels of the Euphorbia flower (it is not clear whether the genus is *Helioscopi* or *Amygdaloides*) are drawn in a considerably finer manner in pen and brown ink, without a red-chalk underdrawing, and with extremely precise parallel hatching. The two different drawing techniques seen in the sheet—red chalk reworked with dark brown ink and fine, plain pen and dark brown ink with exact parallel hatching— in this author's opinion establish a date between about 1508 and 1513 for the studies; hence, they appear to be a number of years later than is usually favored in the literature.[1]

In notes from 1508–12, Leonardo expressed the wish to order his representations of plants and verdure according to individualized topics, which suggests that he intended to compile a botanical treatise, in the modern sense, with neatly laid-out scientific illustrations and an expository text.[2] It would have been the first such treatise of its kind, and rather different in conception from traditional medieval and Renaissance herbals, which served a largely medical function. As is vividly clear from his drawings and notes, Leonardo's knowledge of botanical science about 1508–10 seems to have far surpassed that of the leading professors of the subject then teaching at the renowned universities of Padua and Pisa.[3]

Leonardo seems originally to have produced the present drawing, as well as possibly ten other sheets of botanical studies, at Windsor,[4] in connection with his designs for the lush vegetation in the foreground of the lost composition of *Leda and the Swan*, which he began about 1504 and largely reworked in 1514–15, keeping it in his possession until his death in 1519 in France. From the very beginning, even when

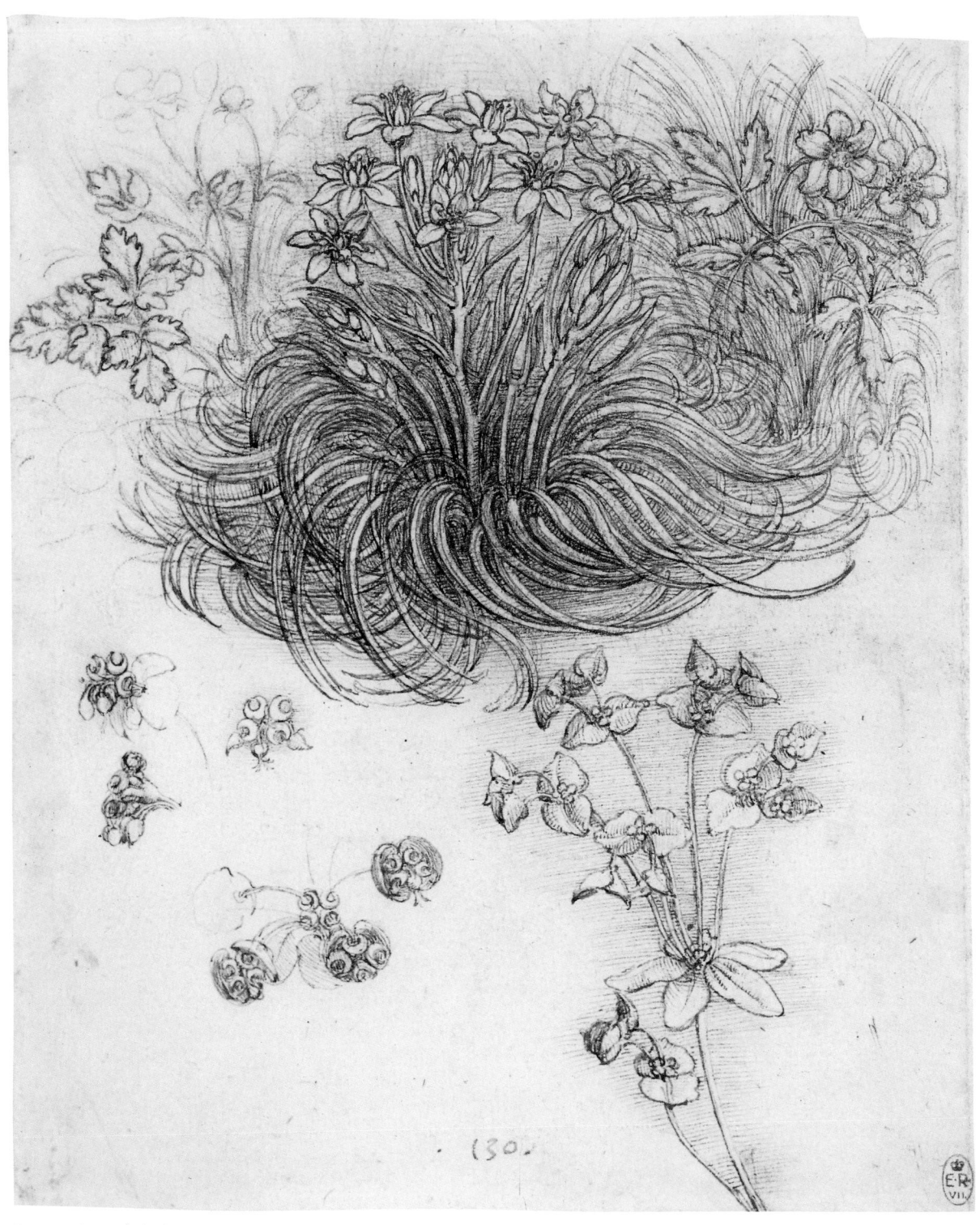

Cat. 100 *(actual size)*

the artist was considering a composition for a kneeling Leda, a form of the star-of-Bethlehem seems to have been vaguely present amid the tall grass (see cat. nos. 98, 99). Many copies attest to the details of the composition (see fig. 22 and cat. no. 134) of an original final painting of a standing *Leda and the Swan* by Leonardo, which also was seen and described by the erudite Cassiano del Pozzo. In this painting, which was destroyed sometime between 1694 and 1775, the star-of-Bethlehem occupied an essential place on the ground between the two main figures, for it served to camouflage the rocky promontory on which the monstrous swan had to stand in order to embrace the now upright graceful nymph. This composition by Leonardo of a standing *Leda* already must have been in progress about 1508, whether in drawings or as a full-scale cartoon, when Raphael copied it in a sketch.[5] It could be argued that it was at the stage of reworking the composition into a standing *Leda* that the star-of-Bethlehem assumed its crucial role and that the present sheet of studies was undertaken. Although the copies after Leonardo's final painting include variations and, at best, only selections of the total number of flower and plant species that must have been depicted in the original (to judge from the great diversity of Leonardo's extant botanical studies), the star-of-Bethlehem is among the constants of the composition.

CCB

1. In discussions of the dating of this sheet of studies, the drawing technique has not been duly taken into account. For instance, it should be noted that Leonardo used red chalk reworked with brown ink for anatomical drawings that usually are independently dated about 1510–12 on the basis of their scientific content (Windsor, RL 19102, 19101), for his studies of flowing water that can be dated to about 1509 because of their subject and allusion to a Lombard town (Windsor, RL 12660, 12661), as well as for the famous design of the monument to Gian Giacomo Trivulzio, usually dated 1508–10 on the basis of its intended patron (Windsor, RL 12356; fig. 197). The artist employed the fine, plain pen-and-ink technique for the osteological and myological drawings found in Anatomical Ms. A (Windsor, RL 19000–19017), one of which is dated "this winter of 1510." Lastly, he used both techniques on the same sheet for studies of architecture and a bird's wing (Windsor, RL 19107 verso); this relates to yet another study for the Villa Melzi project that Leonardo himself dated January 13, 1513.

2. See Windsor, RL 19120, 19121; Paris Ms. G; C.A., fols. 207r, 207v (formerly fols. 76r-a, 76v-a); as well as the discussion in Clark and Pedretti 1968–69, vol. 3, p. 48; and Emboden 1987, pp. 141–61.

3. Emboden 1987, p. 141.

4. See Windsor, RL 12419, 12420, 12421, 12422, 12423, 12424, 12425, 12427, 12429, and 12430.

5. See Windsor, RL 12759.

LEONARDO DA VINCI

101. *Sketches for the Flow of Water; Standing Hercules, Holding a Club, Seen from the Front; and a Man Sheathing or Unsheathing a Sword* (recto) *Standing Hercules, Holding a Club, Seen from the Rear* (verso)

Pen and brown ink, with charcoal or soft black chalk (recto); charcoal or soft black chalk (verso), 137 × 140 mm (5 ⅜ × 5 ½ in.)
Inscribed on recto in graphite, lower left, by a later hand: *Leon. da Vinci*; on verso in pen and brown ink on lower border by a later hand: *Leonard da Vinci*; along top: *205…*
Watermark: Cropped fleur-de-lis (?)
The Metropolitan Museum of Art, New York; Purchase, Florence B. Selden Bequest and Rogers Fund, and Promised Gift of Leon D. and Debra R. Black, 2000 2000.328

PROVENANCE: E. Desperet, Paris (1804–1865; Lugt 721); sale, Hôtel Drouot, Paris, June 7–13, 1865, lot 152; C. Paravey; sale, Hôtel Drouot, Paris, April 13, 1878, lot 135; Émile Colando (father), Paris (Lugt 837, Suppl. 837); Emile Colando (son), Paris and Grasse (d. 1953; Lugt Suppl. 426b).

LITERATURE: Sotheby's London catalogue, July 5, 2000, lot 7; Bambach 2001, figs. 1–2.

This drawing and the three that follow (cat. nos. 102–4) are exhibited together for the first time in an attempt to reconstruct Leonardo's ideas for a sculpture of Hercules that is otherwise unrecorded in the extant early biographies of the master and was little known to scholars until recently. This project from Leonardo's mature years still remains mysterious in many of its details, and the present double-sided sheet of sketches only came to light at an auction in 2000, providing an important key to the puzzle of the Hercules sculpture. Carlo Pedretti first hypothesized in 1958 that Leonardo had considered a statue of this subject, based on the existence of a large study of Hercules and the Nemean Lion, seen from the back, now in the Biblioteca Reale, Turin (cat. no. 102).[1] The Hercules project seems to have evolved during the late phase of Leonardo's work on the cartoon and mural of the *Battle of*

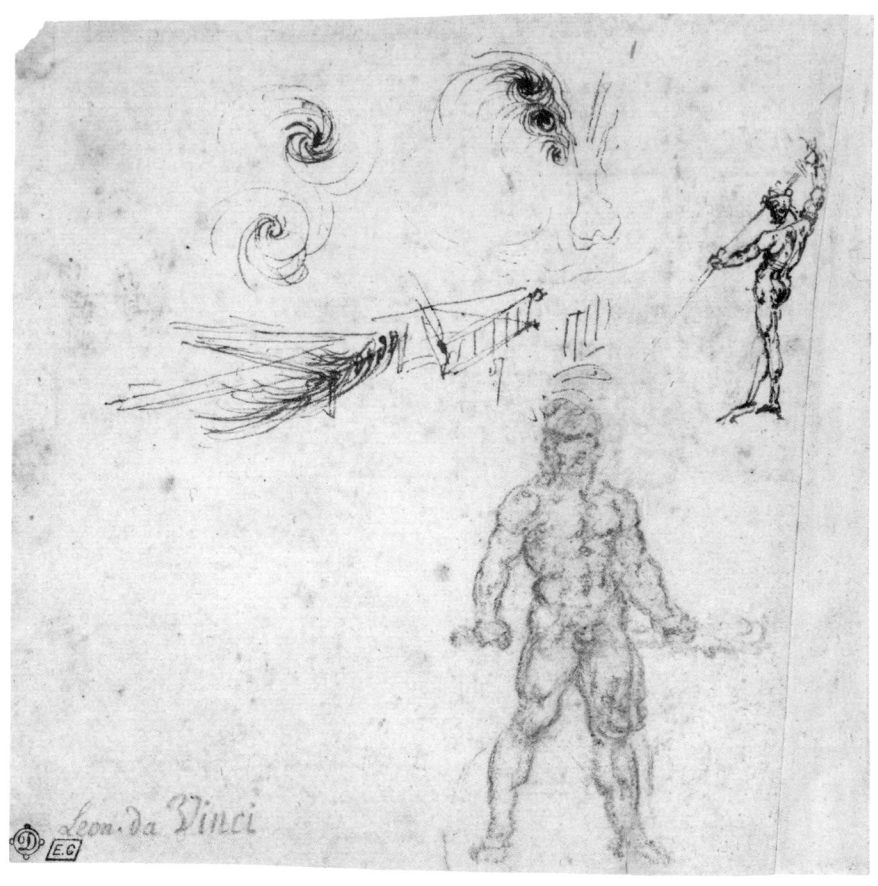

Anghiari, planned for the Sala del Gran Consiglio in the Palazzo della Signoria in Florence in 1506–8. Another sheet in Turin (cat. no. 103) includes two large, neatly drawn studies of a nearly identical Herculean figure seen from the back—which probably was envisioned as a warrior for the left portion of the *Battle of Anghiari*—as well as a number of thumbnail sketches of soldiers and horsemen. On the upper left of the Turin sheet (cat. no. 103), a more elusive design echoes the final composition of the standing *Leda,* elaborated by Leonardo about 1508 (see cat. no. 134). Attentive analysis suggests that a few of Leonardo's anatomical and proportion studies from 1506–8 also may have been inspired by the challenge of the Hercules project. One such study, of the comparative anatomy of the legs of a man and a horse (cat. no. 104), is included in the present selection of Hercules drawings. Although from 1506 to 1508 Leonardo moved back and forth between Florence and Milan while in the service of both the Florentine Republic and the French rulers occupying the city of Milan,[2] it is most likely that the Hercules sculpture was intended for a Florentine patron. The present sheet, which probably represents the first

idea for the Hercules statue, combines a variety of other sketches that together vividly illustrate the parallel paths of Leonardo's artistic and scientific genius. The figural style, drawing technique, and scientific content of the Metropolitan Museum sheet also confirm independently a general date of 1506–10.

Three sketches on the upper portion of the recto show the centrifugal swirling currents of water around obstacles, all seen from above, as if they were plans for some project. The style of these sketches is closely related to those documenting Leonardo's experiments on the flow of water, in the Codex Leicester (see cat. no. 114); to his larger, more detailed study of water passing through obstacles and falling into a pool (Windsor, RL 12660 verso); and to some of the folios in the Paris Ms. F (Institut de France, Paris), a notebook that he inscribed, "begun in Milan on September 12, 1508."[3] We know, however, that about six months earlier Leonardo had been living in Florence, for he inscribed the first page of the disorderly notebook known as the Codex Arundel (British Library, London), "begun in Florence in the house of Piero di Braccio Martelli on March 22, 1508."[4] The pen-and-ink drawing

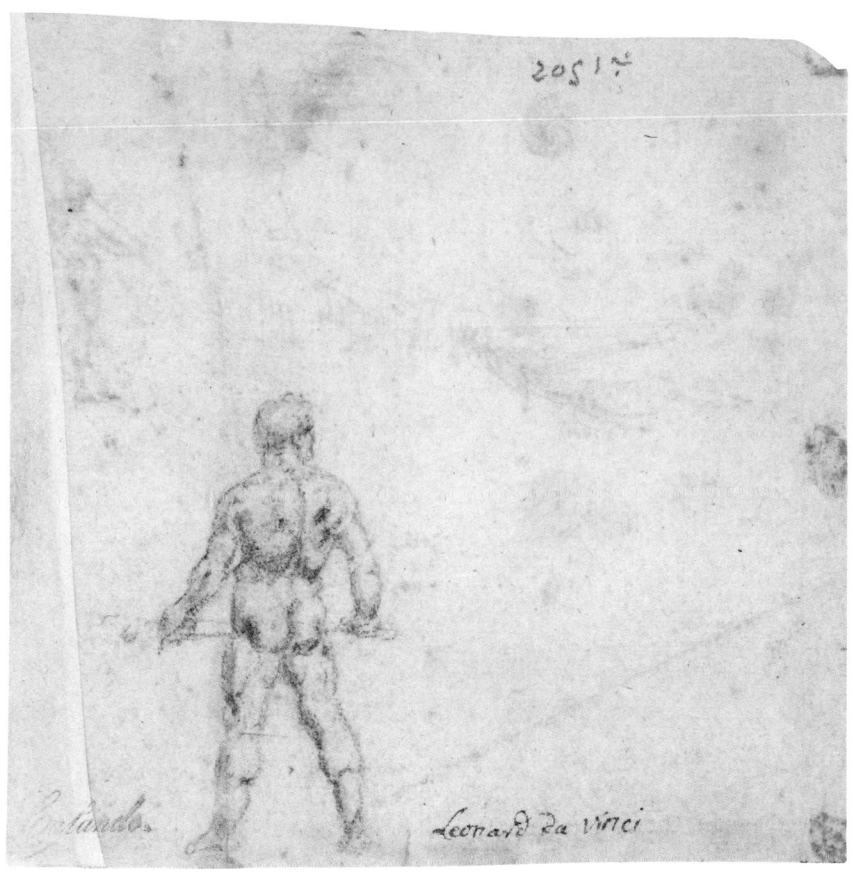

Cat. 101v

technique of the water sketches on the Metropolitan Museum sheet as well as on Sheets 9, 13, 14, and 15 of the Codex Leicester (cat. no. 114) is nearly identical, exhibiting a free, deeply tonal, curved hatching. Immediately below, on the Metropolitan sheet, is a three-quarter view of water currents flowing by a bridge. Sheet 9A of the Codex Leicester (cat. no. 114) illustrates what appears to be a similarly constructed type of wooden bridge over a stream, seen in three-quarter view. The other diagrams on this sheet illustrate the rise in the water level as it approaches an obstacle (for example, the wooden pier of a bridge), and the water current flowing through a narrow pass. The lengthy text alongside the drawings provides a history of how the geography of the Arno River valley (Val d'Arno) was formed, and describes the area around Florence and the rock at Gonfolina (in Leonardo's words, the "gola della Golfolina") that kept the river contained, mentioning Girone, Arezzo, and the Prato Magno.[5] The immediacy and specificity of Leonardo's references to Tuscan sites on Sheet 9 suggest that he worked out these ideas for the codex while he was still living in Florence.

The sketch at the right on the Metropolitan Museum sheet portrays a slender, nude man sheathing or unsheathing a sword. Both the quick pen-and-ink drawing technique and the figure type seem reminiscent of the soldiers and horsemen in the thumbnail sketches for the unfinished *Battle of Anghiari* (cat. nos. 81–83, 103). The Venice *Anghiari* sketches (cat. nos. 81–83) may be dated close to 1503, when Leonardo received the commission for the mural from the *signori* of the Florentine Republic, whereas the Turin sketches (cat. no. 103) more likely date from 1506–8, toward the end of Leonardo's involvement with the project. At this late date, the artist was probably still making sketches, since parts of the composition of the cartoon, beyond the main episode of the *Fight for the Standard*, still had to be worked out, and a vast portion of the mural had not yet been painted.

Toward the bottom right of the Metropolitan's sheet is the magnificent sketch of the nude, muscular Hercules seen from the front and holding a club horizontally, while, on the verso, the same figure of Hercules is depicted from the rear; both of these sketches are drawn with a grainy, soft black chalk or

541

charcoal. One of Leonardo's impassioned statements about a sculptor's work—which he voiced in his *Paragone* (a comparison of the arts), recorded in the posthumously compiled *Libro di pittura* (Codex Urbinas Latinus 1270)—can be adduced as new evidence that the sketches were intended for a sculpture. Leonardo argued that "the sculptor says that he cannot make a figure without at the same time making an infinite number of drawings, due to the infinite number of outlines that are . . . continuous. One answers that this infinite number can be reduced to two half figures: that is, one half composed of the back view and the other of the front [view]. If these two halves are well proportioned, they will together make up the figure in the round, and if all their parts are in the proper relief, they will of themselves and without further work correspond to the infinite number of outlines that the sculptor says he must draw."[6] Such a representation of Hercules—front and back, in "two half figures"—is seen in the Metropolitan Museum sheet. No less significantly, and again true to the spirit of Leonardo's argument, if the Metropolitan's sheet is held up to the light, it is evident that the artist traced through the profile of the front view onto the other side to create the outlines of the figure in the corresponding back view. Other examples exist of Leonardo's practice of tracing a design from one side of a sheet onto the other (figs. 71, 72; Windsor, RL 12356). The process of envisioning the pose of Hercules, front and back, is related to the exercises in anatomical drawing practiced by Antonio Pollaiuolo in his famous, much-copied *Man Seen from Three Views* (the best version is in the Musée du Louvre, Paris, 1486; fig. 158), which Leonardo's Hercules sketches resemble in design.[7]

What is strikingly new about Leonardo's conception of Hercules is the figure's tense and alert stance. This vigilant Hercules is quite anticlassical in mood, for, unless Hercules is actually performing one of his twelve mythical labors, the depictions from antiquity always show the figure in repose. Examples of this passive type are the colossal bronze *Hercules Standing* discovered during the reign of Pope Sixtus IV in the Forum Boarium, in the Temple of Hercules Victor in Rome, and the *Hercules Resting*, after Lysippus, a replica of which was in the palace of Cardinal Francesco Piccolomini (Pope Pius III) near the church of Sant'Andrea della Valle in Rome before 1503. (The Farnese *Hercules* unearthed in 1546 is the most famous version of this latter type.)[8] Still other Roman marble copies of the *Hercules Resting* already had been dis-

covered by the end of the fifteenth century. In all these examples, the hero usually leans on his club, which is placed more or less upright on the ground, unlike the Metropolitan Museum or Turin drawings (cat. nos. 101, 102), in which Leonardo shows him holding the weapon in his hands. The iconography of Hercules was well established in Florence[9] by the last quarter of the fifteenth century, when the sculptor Bertoldo di Giovanni produced a number of such statuettes.[10] The most celebrated monumental public statue of Hercules predating Leonardo's design seems to have been Michelangelo's lost marble of 1493–94, which stood about 2.33 meters high (in a resting pose, to judge from the surviving visual evidence) and wound up in the collection of King Francis I of France (Leonardo's patron, from 1517 to 1519), installed in the gardens at Fontainebleau.[11]

The polychrome terracotta *Hercules* atop the fireplace of the Sala Grande in the Palazzo Gondi in Florence (fig. 189), executed between 1497 and 1503 for the Florentine banker Giuliano Gondi, represents the most important precursor of Leonardo's vigilant Hercules type.[12] This sculpture can be firmly attributed to Giuliano da Sangallo, the architect of the Palazzo Gondi and the designer of the fireplace.[13] Giuliano and Leonardo had been friends since the late 1470s, when they were both in Florence, but especially from 1492 on, during their overlapping stays in Milan.[14] Giuliano da Sangallo first traveled to Milan on October 13, 1492, to present Ludovico Sforza "Il Moro" with the *modello* for a palazzo.[15] When Leonardo resettled in Florence in 1500–1501, both he and Giuliano served as consulting architects for the foundations of the church of San Salvatore, work that lasted on and off into 1506.[16] In his vita of Giuliano da Sangallo, Vasari recounts that during Giuliano's stay in Milan Leonardo sought advice from him on the casting of the Sforza equestrian monument.[17] Leonardo's studies for the casting of the "Sforza Horse" unfolded in two phases, in December 1491 and in December 1493 (cat. no. 64), which helps confirm Vasari's statement.[18]

Much about Leonardo's Hercules statue remains unknown, including the circumstances of its patronage, its intended final setting, and its scale. One may speculate that it was meant to be a monumental sculpture possibly for a public setting, considering the colossal size of much of the sculpture and many of the painting programs commissioned from the 1480s to the 1510s in Italy; artists and patrons were thinking large, not small. Leonardo's reinvention of the hero as an image of pre-

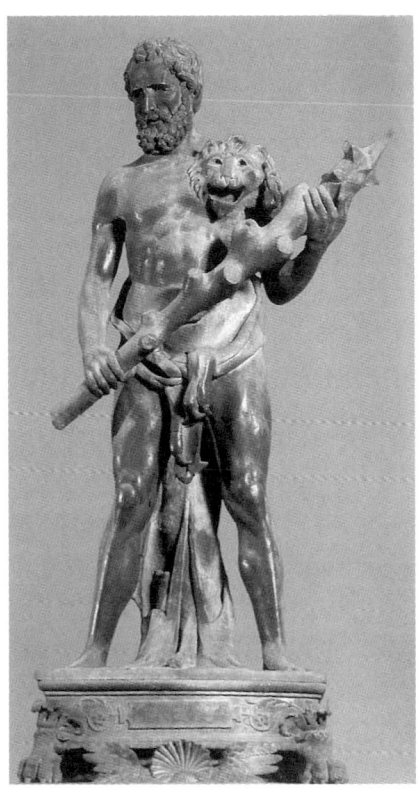

Fig. 189. Giuliano da Sangallo, *Hercules*. Polychromed terracotta, H. without base 131 cm. Sala Grande, Palazzo Gondi, Florence

paredness, tensely holding the club in his hand—an allusion to civic vigilance—similarly is evoked by Michelangelo's gigantic marble *David* (Galleria dell'Accademia, Florence), a figure that, in its embodiment of physical and moral strength, represents liberty and a Christianized Hercules. According to Vasari, the *gonfaloniere di giustizia* Piero Soderini originally had thought of giving Leonardo the marble block that became the *David*, but that story was often discredited by scholars because Vasari's account did not fit into the chronology of historical events. Recent research shows, however, that Soderini had been a key political player in the Florentine Republic since 1500, and occupied his post in the spring of 1501; the *David* was commissioned from Michelangelo on August 16, 1501.[19] Leonardo's small sketch of *Neptune with Sea Horses* (Windsor, RL 12591) is an inspired reworking of Michelangelo's *David* in terms of the Herculean physical type that the older master had come to prefer by 1507–8.

Leonardo (as well as Giuliano da Sangallo, also a trusted colleague of Michelangelo) was among the artists and artisans who participated in the decision, by vote on January 25, 1504, to install the colossal *David* at the entrance to the Palazzo della Signoria, facing the Piazza of the same name.[20] Leonardo had been Michelangelo's notorious rival for the decoration of

the Sala del Gran Consiglio of the Palazzo della Signoria from 1503 to 1508. Although neither project was finished, Leonardo's *Battle of Anghiari* mural (cat. nos. 81–91) was meant to compete with Michelangelo's *Battle of Cascina* fresco on the flanking wall of the Sala (figs. 18–21). Considering the charged professional interaction between the two great artists during these years, it is worth speculating whether Leonardo conceived of his *Hercules* sculpture with a civic function in mind, and in competition with Michelangelo. Recently analyzed documents suggest that Michelangelo was working on his own ideas for a colossal *Hercules* statue about 1506 (even going as far as roughing out a sketch for the marble block) as a pendant to the newly installed *David*,[21] but nothing seems to have come of this project. At a much later date, between 1525 and 1534, Baccio Bandinelli planned and went on to produce a *Hercules* group for the site; it was reviled by some of his contemporaries for its weaknesses in design in comparison to Michelangelo's heroic *David*.[22] Vasari's vita of Bandinelli (1488–1560) offers two insights regarding his connection to Leonardo that suggest that he became aware of Leonardo's ideas for a statue of Hercules about 1508.[23] According to Vasari, Bandinelli was trained by the sculptor Giovanni Francesco Rustici (1474–1554), Leonardo's close associate and friend, and when still a young apprentice to Rustici Bandinelli's drawings were assessed favorably by Leonardo himself. (This probably occurred about 1504–8.) Also, according to Vasari (but stated in a somewhat contradictory account), Bandinelli was accused by some of his contemporaries of causing the destruction of Michelangelo's famous *Battle of Cascina* cartoon, out of his affection for Leonardo.

The Hercules figure in the Metropolitan's sketch is presented in a more defined context in the large Turin working drawing (cat. no. 102) with the addition of the Nemean lion at the hero's feet.   CCB

1. Pedretti 1958a, pp. 163–70 (see cat. no. 000).

2. See Chronology.

3. Paris Ms. F, fol. 1r; Richter 1970, vol. 2, p. 345: "Comi[n]ciato a Milano a dì 12 di sette[m]bre 1508."

4. Ar., fol. 1r; Richter 1970, vol. 2, p. 112: "Comi[n]ciato in Firenze in casa Piero di Braccio Martelli addì 22 di marzo 1508: e questo fia vn racolto sanza ordine."

5. Pedretti 1987a; Pedretti 1994c; Pedretti and Roberts 1981–83 (with transcriptions).

6. C. Urb. fol. 26v: "dice lo scultore che no[n] po fare / una figura che non ne faccia infinite per gli infiniti / termini c'hano le quantita continue, rispondesi che'gli in/finiti termini di tal figura si riduccono in due mezze fi/gure cioe' una mezza dal mezzo indietro et l'altra mezza / dal mezzo in anzi le

quali sendo ben proportionate com/pongono una figura tonda e'queste tali mezze [figure] hauen/do li loro debiti rileui intutte le loro parti rispondera[n]no / per se sanz'altro magistero tutte l'infinite figure che tale scultore dice hauer fatte chel medesimo sipo dire a uno / che faccia un uaso al torno perche anchora si po mostra/re il suo uaso per infiniti aspetti."

7. See Rubin and Wright 1999–2000, pp. 244–47, no. 50.

8. Haskell and Penny 1981, pp. 227–32, nos. 45–46; Bober and Rubinstein 1986, pp. 164–65, nos. 129–130.

9. Ettlinger 1972.

10. Draper 1992, pp. 146–59, nos. 12–14.

11. On Michelangelo's early *Hercules* statue see De Tolnay 1969, vol. 1, pp. 197–98, no. 14; Harprath 1994; Cox-Rearick 1996, pp. 302–13, no. 9-5.

12. Bambach 2001. On Giuliano da Sangallo's Palazzo Gondi fireplace, see Giancarlo Gentilini in Barocchi 1992, pp. 45–46, nos. 7–8.

13. Vasari–Milanesi 1906 vol. 4, p. 275–76.

14. Bambach 2001, pp. 18–19, 23.

15. Vasari–Milanesi 1906, vol. 4, p. 276.

16. Pedretti 1981b, pp. 52–55, 137; Pedretti 1977, vol. 2, p. 32; Pedretti 1981b, pp. 188–90.

17. Vasari–Milanesi 1906, vol. 4, p. 276.

18. Pedretti 1995a, p. 32.

19. Pedretti 1975a, p. 23, no. 8. A more refined chronology for Michelangelo's *David* is given in Hirst 2000.

20. Levine 1974; Parks 1975.

21. Donato 1991; Hirst 2000, pp. 490–92.

22. Bush 1980, pp. 163–89.

23. Vasari–Milanesi 1906, vol. 4, pp. 136–37, 138.

LEONARDO DA VINCI

102. *Standing Hercules Holding a Club, with a Recumbent Lion, Seen from the Rear (Hercules and the Nemean Lion)*

Soft black chalk or charcoal, incised with the stylus for transfer; two sections of a circle incised with a compass; ruled lines; pinpricks to determine intervals and to transcribe measurement; verso rubbed with black chalk or charcoal dust for transfer, 279 × 192 mm (11 × 7 9/16 in.)

Inscribed on recto, close to upper border, probably by the artist, in pen and dark brown ink: numbers, in left-to-right script, for accounting

Watermark: Close to Briquet 7388–7389 (Pedretti 1958b, p. 164)

Biblioteca Reale, Turin 15630

PROVENANCE: According to tradition, Ambrogio Mazenta, Milan; Alessandro and Guido Mazenta, Milan; Duke Charles Emmanuel I of Savoy (r. 1580–1630); or alternatively Giovanni Volpato (1797–1871; private sale in 1839); documented after the reconstitution of the Biblioteca Reale of Turin by King Charles Albert of Sardinia-Piedmont (r. 1831–49); museum stamp (Lugt 2724).

LITERATURE: Frizzoni 1910; Beltrami 1919c, p. 264; Lesca 1919, p. 31; Berenson 1938, vol. 2, p. 139, no. 1262A (imitation of Leonardo); Bertini 1950b, p. 21, no. 58 (by a Michelangelesque sculptor); Bertini 1958, p. 61, no. 479 (Florentine school, first half of the sixteenth century); Middeldorf 1958, p. 175, pl. 10, fig. 1 (anonymous early-sixteenth-century artist); Pedretti 1958a, pp. 163–70; Brizio 1960, p. 261 (not by Leonardo); Berenson 1961, vol. 2, p. 245, no. 1262A (imitation of Leonardo); Pedretti 1968b, p. 25 n. 39, pl. 20; Clark and Pedretti 1968–69, vol. 1, pp. 116, 117, vol. 3, p. 19; Clark 1969, p. 21, fig. 23; Pedretti 1973a, p. 80, fig. 69; Pedretti 1975a, pp. 21–23, no. 8; Pedretti 1979b, p. 19, fig. 9; Keele and Pedretti 1979–80, vol. 2, pp. 820, 827–28, 838–40, fig. 76; Agghàzy 1989, p. 60, fig. 70; Marani 1997, pp. 176–77, fig. 11; Giacobello Bernard 1998, pp. 88–89, no. 2.8; Bambach 2001, fig. 3.

This bold and imposing study would have followed the small sketches of Hercules on The Metropolitan Museum of Art sheet (cat. no. 101), according to the artist's design process. The present study, likewise drawn with a grainy, soft black chalk or charcoal, is a rare surviving example of a highly utilitarian working drawing in Leonardo's oeuvre, and consequently it represents a much less familiar aspect of Leonardo's draftsmanship. Although the drawing is primarily a study of the outlines defining the massive forms of the figure (rather than an articulation of the interior modeling), there is nevertheless extensive shading with fluent, left-handed parallel hatching on the lion as well as on the torso and legs of the figure of Hercules. Until the Metropolitan's small sheet of sketches came to light at auction in 2000, the present study from the Biblioteca Reale of Turin provided the only concrete visual clue that Leonardo had contemplated a statue of Hercules.

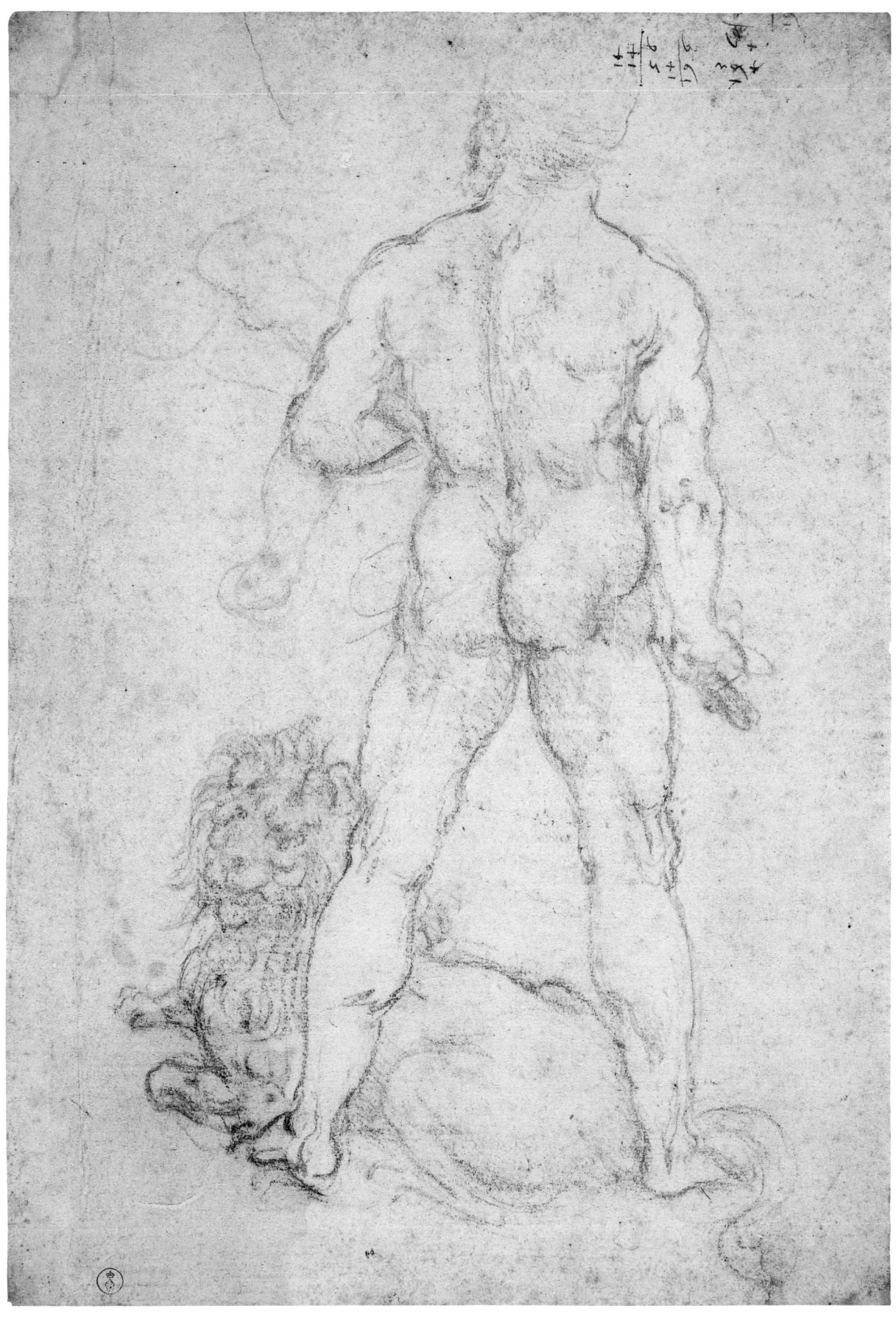

Cat. 102

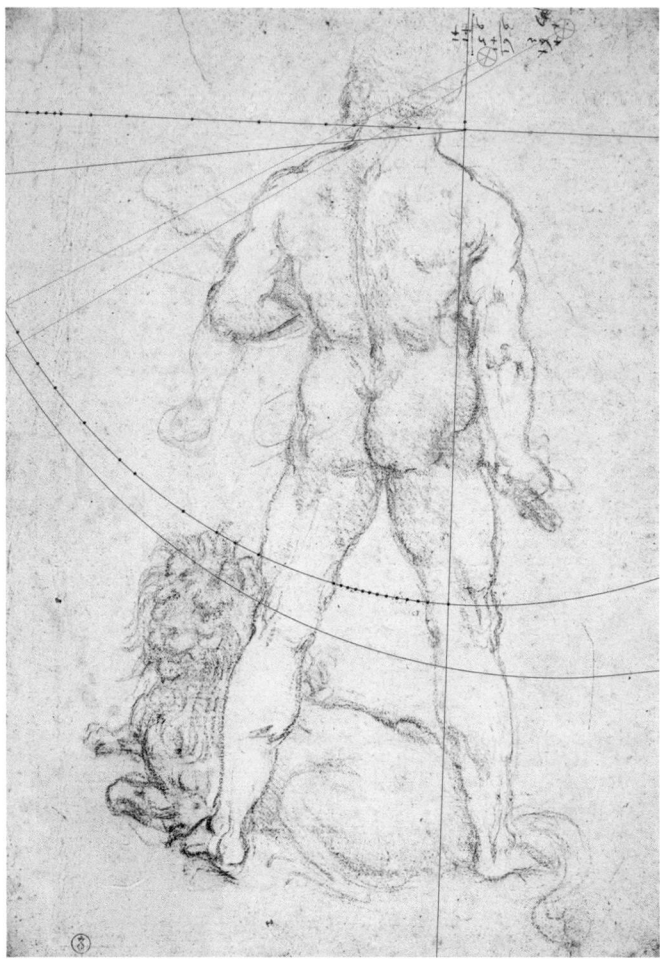

Fig. 190. Diagram showing the prick marks and compass and stylus construction on cat. no. 102 (digital image: Marvin Hayes).

In 1910 Gustavo Frizzoni was among the first scholars to attribute the Turin *Hercules* to Leonardo, but the drawing did not fare well in the Leonardo literature for some time afterward, counting among its detractors Bernard Berenson, Aldo Bertini, Anna Maria Brizio, and Ulrich Middeldorf. Berenson published the Turin sheet in 1938 and 1961 as a copy after catalogue number 103, "but done in a Michelangelesque way."[1] Bertini, who also repeatedly insisted that the Turin drawing was not up to the quality of Leonardo's hand, preferred to see it as the work of a sculptor from Bartolommeo Ammanati's generation, strongly influenced by the mature Michelangelo.[2] Leonardo's authorship of the Turin sheet rightly has been accepted by a number of scholars, among them, for example, Kenneth Clark, Carlo Pedretti (who has written repeatedly about this work),[3] and Heinrich Bodmer, the astute early connoisseur of Leonardo's drawings, who, sometime before the

late 1930s, wrote on the old mount of the Turin drawing, "without doubt Leonardo in 1503."[4] The distinctive use of soft black chalk or charcoal and the smoky effect of the repeatedly reinforced outlines are typical of Leonardo's mature draftsmanship. The drawing technique is much like that of the Hercules sketches on the Metropolitan Museum sheet (cat. no. 101); the Windsor *Neptune Commanding His Quadriga of Sea Horses* (cat. no. 93), which was preparatory for the presentation drawing given by Leonardo to Antonio Segni in 1503–4; the Windsor sheet, combining sketches for the *Battle of Anghiari* and *Leda and the Swan* (cat. no. 88), from about 1506; and the verso of the Getty *Child Playing with a Lamb* (cat. no. 94), from 1506–8. The numbers at the upper right on the Turin sheet read in a conventional left-to-right direction and, according to Pedretti, are also by Leonardo, for they correspond to examples in the Codex Atlanticus (fols. 374r, 514v, 541v, 544r [formerly fols. 136r-b, 188v-a, 202v-a, 203r-b]), dating to about 1506–8. The master seems to have written out numbers conventionally from left to right when counting, but from right to left when he was crossing them out.[5]

The delicate hue of the Turin drawing does not reproduce well in photographs, and a brown stain (possibly oil) on the lower left of the sheet has distorted the color of the soft black chalk or charcoal, making it seem intensely black. Moreover, sharp incisions with the stylus, used by the artist to transfer the outlines of the design onto another work surface, have spliced the chalk or charcoal pigmentation along the contours. These are problems of condition rather than signs of the artist's weak draftsmanship. The sheet bears archaeological evidence characteristic of a carefully thought-out working drawing. The preliminary incisions with the stylus and the pricked holes, best seen in raking light, are reconstructed here (fig. 190). Leonardo seems to have made two attempts each at preliminary incisions for the horizontal line and for the compass-drawn circle, and for this reason the lines appear slightly syncopated with respect to each other. Such "trial-and-error" misalignments provide vivid proof that the Turin sheet is a draft in progress.

As he often described in his notes,[6] Leonardo first ruled an exact plumb line, or axis, with the stylus (but without ink) to fix the pose of the figure, who is seen here from the back, with feet firmly planted on the ground and the body turned slightly asymmetrically in space. The figure stands at an angle to the picture plane, with the plumb line tangentially touching its head, waist, and right calf. Leonardo thought precisely about the distribution of the body weight along its axis as he established the opening between the legs. He drew two large arcs with the compass from two closely spaced points to the right of the figure's head to help him determine the movement of the lower body and the space between the figure's legs. An analogous conception of the movement and the opening between the legs is seen in Leonardo's much earlier *Vitruvian Man* (Accademia, Venice; fig. 43), measured similarly with pinpricked intervals on stylus-ruled lines and in relation to a compass-constructed circle; however, there, the frontal view of the figure is flat, and parallel to the picture plane. The proportion drawings of the figure in motion in the Codex Huygens (Pierpont Morgan Library, New York), by a later Lombard artist after Leonardo's ideas, also take up this problem. In the Turin Hercules study, the final arc of the compass exhibits the precisely pinpricked measurements of the intervals on the arc marking the opening between the legs. This is the only portion of the compass-thrown circle that has dense pinpricking. The careful calculation of this opening between the legs of the figure would have been crucial in the engineering of a large sculpture to be carried out in bronze or in marble.

After these calculations, with black chalk or charcoal in hand Leonardo began to draw the figure. He turned the head and gaze of Hercules in the opposite direction, with respect to the Metropolitan Museum sketches (cat. no. 101). The faint underdrawing also shows that he first envisioned the figure of Hercules with his left arm and hand tensely lowered, as in the Metropolitan sketches, before finally deciding to show the club left side up. Leonardo also raised the outlines of the right arm and hand much higher than in the preliminary underdrawing. As a last step, once the artist had finished the study, he blackened the verso of the Turin sheet with charcoal, and then incised the outlines of the large, complex drawing with a stylus or some such pointed instrument to transfer the design with precision, and in the exact dimensions, onto another work surface, probably another sheet of paper. The Turin sheet

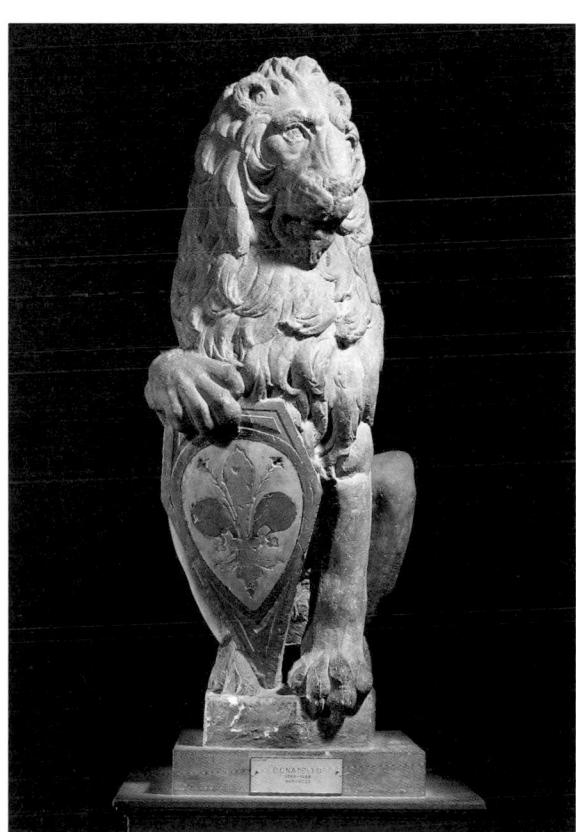

Fig. 191. Donatello, *Marzocco (Florentine Lion)*. Sandstone, 135.5 × 38 × 60 cm. Museo Nazionale del Bargello, Florence

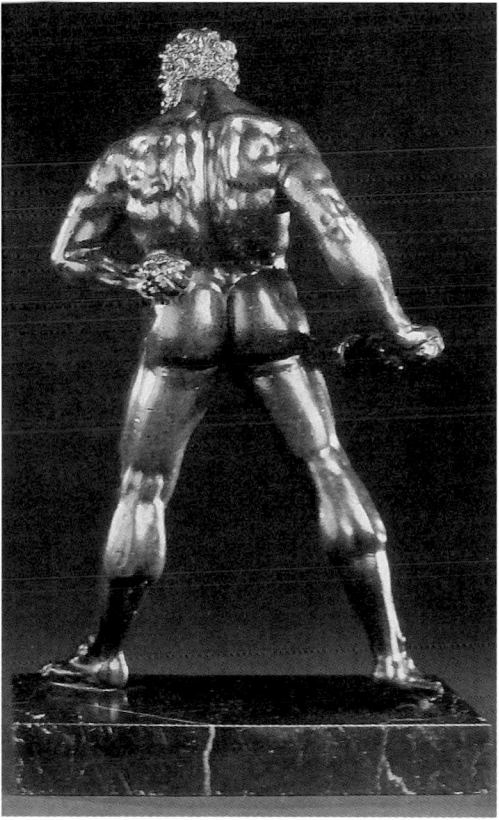

Fig. 192. Willem Danielsz. van Tetrode, back view of *Hercules Pomarius*. Bronze, H. 39.4 cm. Private collection, New York

does not look like a cartoon for the design of a painting. In order to produce an intermediate draft of the design, Leonardo probably traced the Turin drawing with a stylus, as a shortcut, perhaps to determine the complex front view in the design of the Hercules statue from the precise outlines of the rear view (he then would have had to reverse the design that he had traced with the stylus). From the passage in the posthumously compiled *Libro di pittura* (Codex Urbinas Latinus 1270) discussed in catalogue number 101, we know that Leonardo thought that a sculpture should represent primarily the front and back views, and therefore that he sketched the front and rear views of the Hercules on the Metropolitan sheet in an analogous technique to that of the Turin sheet: he held the Metropolitan sheet against a light source, tracing the outlines of the figure from one side onto the other, to produce both front and rear views.

In the Turin drawing, Leonardo added the distinctive attribute of the Nemean lion reclining at the feet of Hercules—an allusion to the first of the hero's twelve mythical labors. Leonardo's project for a Hercules statue thus may be connected with a cryptic mention in one of his notes from 1508 in the Codex Atlanticus: "The labors of Hercules for Pier Francesco Ginori; the Medici garden."[7] The recto of the sheet on which this reference is inscribed includes sketches of the courtyard of a villa or a palazzo.[8] In Pedretti's reconstruction of the fragments extracted from the Codex Atlanticus, now in the Royal Library at Windsor Castle, the overall image on folio 575br (formerly fol. 215r-a) included a large, stocky, nude standing male figure with his legs spread apart in a Hercules-like stance that is crudely outlined in charcoal, as well as other, much smaller figural and architectural sketches in pen and brown ink. The Windsor sheet is inscribed in Leonardo's right-to-left script, "a g[i]an martelli" (for Gian Martelli), at the upper right, and "orto" (garden), in the lower right on one of the architectural sketches.[9] This evidence helps to further establish Leonardo's whereabouts during the period that is relevant to the dating of the Hercules statue, for he settled in Florence between September 18, 1507,[10] and March 22, 1508,[11] residing in the house of Piero di Braccio Martelli. At this time, he also began work on the Codex Arundel (see cat. no. 101) and renewed his ties with the sculptor Giovanni Francesco Rustici, whom he had met while both were members of Andrea del Verrocchio's workshop. Martelli's house was not far from that of Pier Francesco Ginori, who was host to Leonardo in 1508.

The reference to the "Medici garden" in Leonardo's note must refer to the famous Giardino di San Marco (which Lorenzo de' Medici "Il Magnifico" had established by 1475), a garden that Leonardo apparently knew well in his youth and probably began to frequent again during his second Florentine sojourn.[12]

For Leonardo, Hercules embodied the ideal physical type of the mature male, and he used the ancient hero as the point of departure for a number of studies of male proportion and anatomy (cat. no. 104). A study in Windsor (RL 19043) that may represent an underdrawing by Leonardo and that was weakly reworked by a pupil (Francesco Melzi?) renders the same back view of the Turin *Hercules,* but the figure holds a pole rather than a club and is without the lion.[13] The somewhat stocky male type is also generally recognizable among the abbreviated figure drawings in the *Libro di pittura* (Codex Urbinas Latinus 1270, fols. 120r, 128r), the posthumously compiled manuscript, as well as in Leonardo's drawing of the god Neptune for Antonio Segni (cat. no. 93) and in the soldiers in the *Battle of Anghiari* (cat. no. 103). In addition, Leonardo likened the physiognomy of the ideal Herculean warrior to the features of a lion, as seen in a bust-length study (Windsor, RL 12502), from about 1508, which anticipates the theories of facial expression by Giovanni Battista della Porta.[14]

In the Turin drawing, the head of the recumbent lion at the feet of Hercules seems especially archaic in characterization. One may argue that this stylization was deliberate, since the lion's physiognomy is reminiscent of the Gothic-style face of Donatello's *Marzocco* (fig. 191), carved in 1419–20. The knitted brow, stylized curls, chiseled planes of the face, and long, curving snout are all remarkably similar. It would not have been out of place for Leonardo to quote Donatello's *Marzocco,* as it was the most famous representation of the heraldic animal, the symbol of the city of Florence and of the proud spirit of its citizens, and was itself a re-creation of medieval emblematic images. Carved in *pietra di macigno,* Donatello's sculpture originally adorned the staircase of the Sala del Papa in the Chiostro Grande of Santa Maria Novella, where it stood until the staircase was demolished in 1515.[15] It was in the Sala del Papa that, from 1503 on, Leonardo was at work on the *Battle of Anghiari.* The charged emblematic character of the lion of Hercules further suggests the possibility that the sculpture was intended for a prominent public setting, such as the Piazza della Signoria.

Leonardo's Hercules project was influential for later sixteenth-century artists working in Florence, such as Baccio Bandinelli, as is clear from the latter's early preparatory studies for the marble group of *Hercules and Cacus* (see cat. no. 101), completed in 1534, which was to flank Michelangelo's marble *David* at the entrance to the Palazzo della Signoria. One of Bandinelli's pen-and-ink drawings of Hercules (Christ Church, Oxford, 0085), from about 1525, is a mirror image of Leonardo's design; the tense, vigilant hero, holding his club horizontally, is quite different in mood from the passive figure in the monument that Bandinelli finally carved.[16] A sketch of Hercules in pen-and-ink with wash by Domenico Beccafumi, from about 1525 (Musée du Louvre, Paris, 255), is remarkably similar in physical type and pose to Leonardo's and shows the alert muscular hero from the rear, holding his club upright on the ground.[17] The plastic conception of Beccafumi's figure indicates that it probably was modeled after a statue. It is also clear that Leonardo's design of a vigilant Hercules became a paradigm for artists of the next generation. A reprise is seen in the bronze *Hercules Pomarius* (in which the hero holds the apple of his eleventh labor in his left hand), attributed to Willem Danielsz. van Tetrode and known in several versions (fig. 192).[18] Van Tetrode's sculpture has often been dated to the artist's Delft period (1568–73), soon after his return from an extensive stay in Italy. More recently, an earlier dating of about 1545–65, coinciding with the sculptor's Italian period, has been advanced.[19] Called "Guglielmo Fiammingo" and "Guglielmo Tedesco," Van Tetrode is documented in Florence as an assistant to Benvenuto Cellini in 1549, and he also worked with Bartolommeo Ammanati on the base of the *Neptune* fountain in the Piazza della Signoria in the early 1560s.

CCB

1. Berenson 1938, vol. 2, p. 139, no. 1262A; Berenson 1961, vol. 2, p. 245, no. 1262A.
2. Bertini 1958, p. 61, no. 479.
3. Pedretti 1975a, p. 21, no. 8, records additional opinions in favor of Leonardo's authorship by A. E. Popham and Cecil Gould (in written communications to the author).
4. The old mount is annotated, "Scuola Fiorentina" (crossed out), "Leonardo da Vinci," and "senza dubbio Leonardo in 1503" (Bodmer).
5. Pedretti 1973a, p. 80; Pedretti 1975a, pp. 21–23, no. 8.
6. Leonardo's notes regarding life drawing and the axis or plumb line of the body are transcribed in Richter 1970, vol. 1, pp. 317–18, 345–46, nos. 521, 523, 594–95.
7. C.A., fol. 783v (formerly fol. 288v-b); Pedretti 1958a, p. 165; Pedretti 1977, vol. 2, p. 345: "fatiche derchole a pier f / ginori—/ lorto de medjcj."
8. See Pedretti 1972a, fig. 59.
9. See Pedretti 1957a, p. 38, nos. 12482, 12723 (from C.A., fols. 575br, 575bv [formerly fols. 215r-a, 215v-b]), pl. 12.
10. The date of Leonardo's letter to Cardinal Ippolito d'Este, written from Florence.
11. Pedretti 1980a, pp. 7–8.
12. The evidence for Leonardo's association with the Giardino di San Marco as a youth is provided by the reference in the account in the Codice Magliabechiano (Anonimo Gaddiano) of about 1540 (transcribed in Frey 1892, p. 110; Vecce 1998, p. 360); Elam 1992, pp. 159–74.
13. Pedretti 1958a, pp. 169–70; Clark and Pedretti 1968–69, vol. 3, p. 19, no. 19043. Clark and Pedretti considered the sixteenth-century letter K identical to that on RL 19080r, and thus probably by Francesco Melzi, who was also possibly the author of the delicate reworking in ink.
14. Pedretti 1958a, p. 164 n. 7.
15. Pope-Hennessy 1993, p. 62; Wirtz 1998, p. 25.
16. Byam-Shaw 1976a, vol. 1, pp. 58–59, no. 89; Ward 1988, pp. 49–51, no. 26.
17. Ragghianti Collobi 1974, vol. 1, pp. 132–33, vol. 2, p. 231, pl. 408; Bacou 1981, pp. 20–33; Paolo Giannattasio in Torriti 1998, pp. 282–84, no. d 78. A close copy exists of Beccafumi's Louvre *Hercules* study (École des Beaux-Arts, Paris, EBA 45).
18. Bambach 2001; James Draper in Metropolitan Museum of Art 2001, pp. 522–24, no. 141. Beccafumi's Louvre *Hercules* drawing on the Vasari mount has been thought to be the model for Van Tetrode's sculpture.
19. James Draper in Metropolitan Museum of Art 2001, pp. 522–24, no. 141.

LEONARDO DA VINCI

103. *Figural Sketches* (recto)
Faintly Traced Through Figure of a Soldier Holding a Sword; probably not by Leonardo (verso)

Pen and dark brown ink, with traces of soft black chalk or lead-point (recto); soft black chalk or leadpoint (verso), 253 × 197 mm (10 × 7¾ in.)
Watermark: Flower (similar to Briquet 6599)
Biblioteca Reale, Turin 15577

PROVENANCE: According to tradition, Ambrogio Mazenta, Milan; Alessandro and Guido Mazenta, Milan; Duke Charles Emmanuel I of Savoy (r. 1580–1630); or alternatively Giovanni Volpato (1797–1871; private sale in 1839); documented after the reconstitution of the Biblioteca Reale of Turin by King Charles Albert of Sardinia-Piedmont (r. 1831–49); museum stamp (Lugt 2724).

LITERATURE: Uzielli 1884, p. 271, no. 7; Müller-Walde 1897, pp. 140–42; Müntz 1898, vol. 2, p. 153 (detail); Loeser 1899, p. 19; Müntz 1899, p. 411, 415, 517, n. 4; Berenson 1903, vol. 2, p. 61, no. 1089; Poggi 1919, p. 66, pl. 148; Sirén 1928, vol. 1, p. 138, vol. 3, pl. 169; Bodmer 1931, pp. 301, 411; Herzfeld 1932, p. 8; Berenson 1938, vol. 2, p. 122, no. 1089; Goldscheider 1943, p. 28, pl. 46; Giglioli 1944, pp. 140–41, pl. 153; Neufeld 1949, p. 177, n. 21, fig. 7; Bertini 1950b, no. 28, pl. 18; Biblioteca Medicea Laurenziana 1952, pp. 41–42, no. 62; Esche 1954, p. 46, fig. 81; Gould 1954a, pp. 126–27, fig. 6; Gould 1954b, p. 190; Heydenreich 1954, vol. 1, p. 103, vol. 2, fig. 158; Bertini 1958, p. 36, no. 227; Middeldorf 1958, p. 175, pl. 10, fig. 2; Pedretti 1958a, p. 168; Rosenberg 1959, p. 27, pl. 53a; Berenson 1961, vol. 2, p. 215, no. 1089; Pedretti 1968b, pp. 23 n. 36, 24, 73–74, pl. 17; Clark and Pedretti 1968–69, vol. 1, pp. 27, 34, 129, 137, 146, vol. 3, pp. 15, 19; Pedretti 1973a, p. 80, fig. 68; Gould 1975, pp. 139, 143, fig. 77; Pedretti 1975a, pp. 17–20, no. 7; Griseri 1978, n. 11; Pedretti 1979c, p. 37; Keele and Pedretti 1979–80, vol. 2, pp. 811, 826–27, fig. 75; Favaro 1980, p. 372; Mobilleau 1980, p. 156; Pedretti 1982a, p. 54; Sciolla 1985, p. 40; Pedretti 1987a, pp. 84, 87, fig. 110; Carlo Pedretti in Sciolla 1990, pp. 48–49, no. 14; Pedretti 1990a, no. 7; Giovanna Nepi Scirè in Palazzo Grassi 1992, pp. 278–79, no. 37; Popham 1994, no. 197; Letze and Buchsteiner 1997, p. 80; Villata 1997, pp. 191–93, fig. 2; Giacobello Bernard 1998, pp. 86–87, no. 2.7; Bambach 2001, fig. 5.

This dazzling sheet of small sketches and more finished studies, representing ideas for a variety of compositions, is probably to be dated to 1506–8. The design for the heroic nude man seen from behind that Leonardo explored elsewhere (cat. nos. 101, 102) and that is apparently related to the enigmatic statue of Hercules from 1506–8 can also be identified here

in the two figures at the top center and upper right. The intricately detailed muscles of the lower body of the second of these male nudes are, in fact, identical in the Turin *Hercules* (cat. no. 102) and in the study of comparative anatomy (cat. no. 104). The abrupt cropping of the larger of these two suggests that the original sheet has been greatly cut down.

Seen as a whole, the sheet displays a unique breadth of pictorial inventions and suggests the extent to which Leonardo's ideas for compositions may have emerged from a spontaneous discovery of formal analogies between one subject and another. The artist probably "brainstormed" the diverse motifs in rapid succession, beginning on the upper right (as he was left-handed) with the two motifs of the standing Herculean nude man seen from the back, which he executed cleanly and with an astonishing bravura of outline and curved cross-hatching. He may have relied on a three-dimensional model of a figure in either clay or wax to draw the difficult pose, according to the practice that was later described in Giorgio Vasari's introduction to *Le vite de' più eccellenti pittori, scultori ed architettori* (Florence, 1550 and 1568) and Benvenuto Cellini's *Rime* (manuscript, 1560s).[1] The larger of these nude studies is rendered with the precision of an écorché, and the descriptive, curved cross-hatching courses over the protrusions of the musculature with great consistency and complexity. It is a tour de force of draftsmanship that is rarely seen in the graphic arts before the Dutch engraver Hendrik Goltzius (1558–1617). The fine, dense strokes of Leonardo's curved cross-hatching are like those of the myologies illustrated in the Anatomical Ms. A (Royal Library, Windsor),[2] from 1508–10, and anticipate the more expressive use of this hatching technique in the Windsor studies of the female reproductive organs and the fetus, from 1510–12.[3] In drawing the Turin studies, the artist must have turned the sheet around repeatedly in order to achieve the intricate, superbly unified technique of curved cross-hatching.

In the study of the male nude at top center, the man's left arm is sharply turned to the right, accentuating the contrapposto movement—the action in repose—of the standing figure. The man wields a sword with his right hand and wears

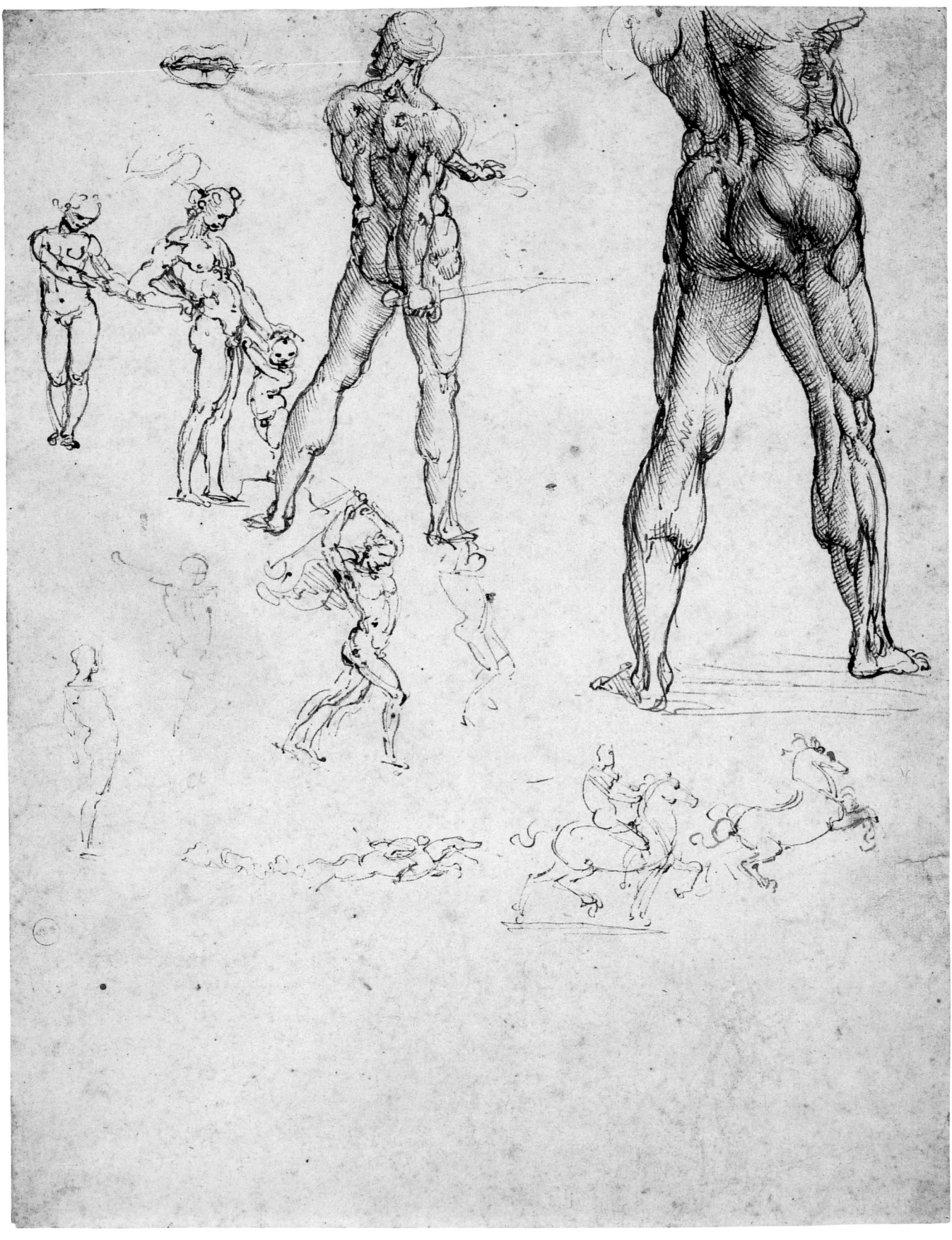

Cat. 103R

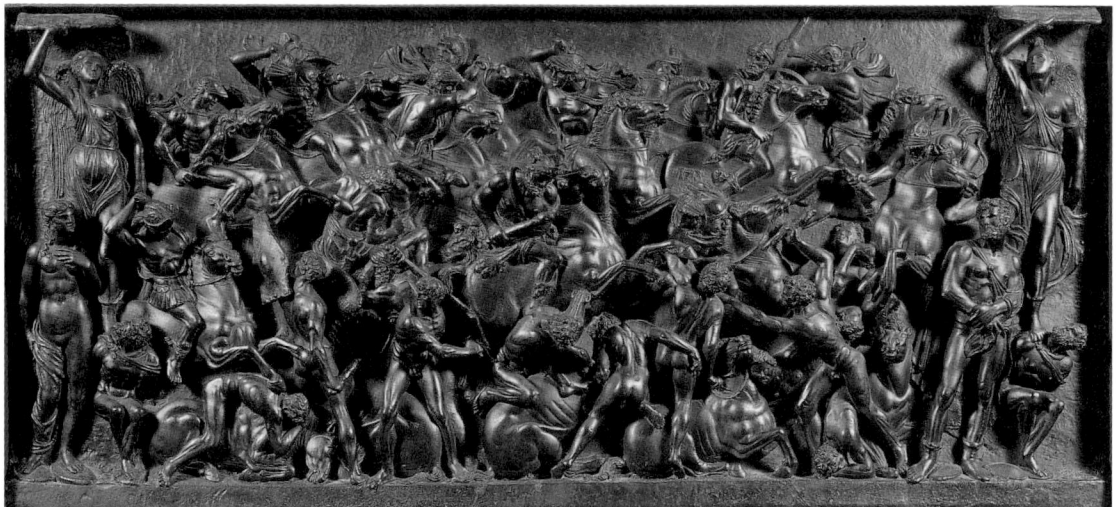

what appears to be either a tight turban or a skullcap, which sets off his distinctive aquiline profile. The design of this figure was weakly traced through from the recto onto the verso, by holding the sheet against the light (see also cat. nos. 44, 101). The faint, awkward outlines in soft black chalk or leadpoint on the verso, a crude tracing that is probably not original, depict the figure with an outstretched left arm. In the larger study of the Herculean man on the upper right, Leonardo left the stump of his left arm fairly undetermined, though the summary pen-and-ink outlines possibly suggest the beginnings of a raised arm. The right arm of the figure in this larger study appears like the neatly leveled truncation of a limb in a classical statue. This truncation is also a detail seen in some of Leonardo's anatomical drawings of this period illustrating a Herculean type.[4]

It is noteworthy that the two designs of a male nude with deeply chiseled musculature so specifically recall a variety of undertakings about 1506–8. They relate to the warriors in the unfinished *Battle of Anghiari*, the enigmatic Hercules statue (cat. nos. 101, 102; Windsor, RL 19043 verso), the models in many anatomical drawings (cat. no. 104),[5] and studies of standing male nudes.[6] The smaller study of the two shows the male figure in the act of wielding a sword, much like the *Anghiari* soldiers. He is copied exactly in the figure of an executioner on the right side of Raphael's *Judgment of Solomon* ceiling fresco (Stanza della Segnatura, Vatican Palace), from 1508–10, thus probably not long after the date of the Turin sheet. Of all of Leonardo's drawings, the Turin sheet records the Herculean nude man in the greatest detail. It is still not clear, however, whether the design corresponds to that of a

struggling foot soldier that, according to some scholars, occupied the extreme left portion of the *Battle of Anghiari*.[7] The reconstruction of the left portion of this unfinished painting is extremely problematic (cat. nos. 81, 85) and was probably the most unresolved portion for the artist when he abandoned the project. Scholars have thought that this portion is partly re-created in a very rough sketch by Michelangelo (fig. 179), but this raises the question as to why Michelangelo might have "copied" Leonardo. Two of Michelangelo's own drawings for the *Battle of Cascina* appear to have included a similarly Herculean standing warrior (British Museum, London, 1859-6-25-564; Uffizi, Florence, 233 F recto). Leonardo may have drawn inspiration for his heroic male figure from a similar motif seen toward the left in Bertoldo's bronze relief of a *Battle Scene* (fig. 193), which is recorded in the inventory of Lorenzo de' Medici's possessions at his death in 1492 (it was "nella saletta rimpetto alla sala grande" of the Medici palace). If the Codice Magliabechiano (Anonimo Gaddiano) of about 1540 is a reliable source, Leonardo may have even met Bertoldo (who was Michelangelo's teacher in the early 1490s) before 1482/83 at the famous Medici sculpture garden at San Marco, where the sculptor taught and also curated Lorenzo's collections.[8]

To the left is a much smaller unrelated sketch of a male nude with odd clumps of hair, who stands in a nearly profile contrapposto pose, caressing the head of an infant boy at his side. He has been variously identified as the god Hermes with the young Cupid, Dionysos with the young Hermes, and as a transgendered version of the goddess Venus with the young Cupid. To the left of that pair is the still smaller sketch of an androgynous figure, standing in a frontal contrapposto pose, with arms outstretched to the right. It recalls the standing *Leda and the Swan*, which Leonardo had been reworking in 1505–8 (see cat. nos. 88, 98, 99) and which Raphael also closely copied about 1508 (Windsor, RL 12759). The sketch of a mouth with defined parted lips and teeth, seen above these two small figural sketches, relates to Leonardo's scientific studies of the motor muscles of the mouth (Windsor, RL 19055 verso), which he undertook about 1508. The lips have also been compared to those of David in Michelangelo's statue (Galleria dell'Accademia, Florence). Leonardo's reinvention of Michelangelo's *David* for a figure of Neptune is found in another drawing from 1506–9 (Windsor, RL 12591).

In the lower register of the Turin sheet, the slight sketches of the male nudes in a nearly profile view, wielding weapons over their heads, and of the horsemen in the bottom row also seem to have their origins in Leonardo's ideas for the *Battle of Anghiari*. The rider on the charging horse on the left galloping at a high speed, the horse and rider in the center trotting somewhat majestically, and the agitated rearing horse on the right were conceived as isolated motifs, rather than as an integrated group. Although the thumbnail style of these sketches of warriors, riders, and horses is generally comparable to that of the earliest Venice sketches for the *Battle of Anghiari* (cat. nos. 81–83, especially cat. no. 83), the Turin drawings seem quite a bit later in date. The nude men delivering blows are like the tiny figural sketches on a sheet that illustrates principles of human movement (Windsor, RL 12641 verso) and that also includes small drawings of siphons of exactly the same type that is represented in the Codex Leicester (cat. no. 114). Hence, this related Windsor sheet is more or less precisely datable to 1508–10.[9] Moreover, other sketches in Windsor (RL 12328) and the British Museum (1895-5-13-17), which also display riders and horses in galloping or charging poses similar to those of the Turin sheet, have been rightly dated about 1505, or later.[10] The small, schematic forms of the three horsemen in the bottom row of the Turin sheet possibly indicate that they were drawn from small three-dimensional models. One of the related Windsor sheets with such tiny riders and horses is curiously inscribed by Leonardo with a note reminding himself of such models: "Make a small [horse] of wax the length of a finger."[11] The Turin, Windsor, and London small sketches of horsemen may not all have been necessarily

used in the actual design of the *Battle of Anghiari* and could equally well represent playful scribbles done at the time of the project and shortly thereafter, pouring forth onto the pages of Leonardo's sketchbook when his mind still teemed with ideas of such forms.[12] Among these horsemen, the one charging from the left in the group is similar to the larger, bold study in red chalk at Windsor (cat. no. 85) that is associated with the problematic left portion of the *Anghiari* composition. Several scholars, however, have also interpreted the rider and prancing horse in the center of the group, standing on a groundline that is drawn with two horizontal dashes, as a slight sketch, or *primo pensiero*, for the equestrian monument of Gian Giacomo Trivulzio (cat. no. 111). The dashes are thought to indicate the base for the statue.

The attribution of the Turin sheet has never been doubted since Paul Müller-Walde discovered it among the neglected drawings of the Biblioteca Reale of Turin and published it as a work by Leonardo. The dating proposed here is in agreement with the more recent studies by Carlo Pedretti (1989 and 1990a) and Giovanna Nepi Scirè (1992). The Turin sheet has also often been dated a few years earlier, to about 1503–6, in closer proximity to the *Anghiari* sketches in Venice (cat. nos. 81–83), for example, by its discoverer Paul Müller-Walde as well as by Heinrich Bodmer, Bernard Berenson, Sigrid Esche, and Cecil Gould. CCB

1. Vasari–Milanesi 1906, vol. 1, pp. 177–78: "Degli scorti delle figure al di sotto in sù, e di quegli in piano"; Cellini 1971, p. 921: "in prima l' hanno fatte in piccola scultura, e da quelle ritratte."
2. Especially Windsor, RL 19006, 19012, 19013, 19014, and 19015.
3. Windsor, RL 19101, 19102.
4. Other, more strictly anatomical drawings of the male nude exhibit this peculiar cropping of the arms: Windsor, RL 12636, 12540, 12601, and 19032 verso.
5. Windsor, RL 12592, 12629, 12630, 12631, 12636, 19014, and 19044.
6. Windsor, RL 12593–12596.
7. Neufeld 1949, p. 177; Gould 1954a, 1954b; and Giovanna Nepi Scirè in Palazzo Grassi 1992.
8. Leonardo's presence in the Giardino di San Marco as a youth is mentioned in the Codice Magliabechiano (Anonimo Gaddiano; transcribed in Frey 1892, p. 110; Vecce 1998, p. 360); Caroline Elam in Barocchi 1992. On Bertoldo and Michelangelo at the Giardino di San Marco, see Vasari–Milanesi 1906, vol. 7, pp. 141–42.
9. In agreement with Clark and Pedretti 1968–69, vol. 1, p. 137, no. 12641.
10. Clark and Pedretti 1968–69, vol. 1, pp. 27–28, 129.
11. Clark and Pedretti 1968–69, vol. 1, p. 27, Windsor, no. 12328: "fanne un picho/lo dj cera lu[n]gho / un djto—."
12. A similar point is made in Clark and Pedretti 1968–69, vol. 1, p. 27, no. 12328.

104. *Comparative Studies of Human and Horse Legs*

Pen and brown ink, brush and brown wash over traces of red chalk on ocher or brick-red prepared paper (recto); unprepared off-white paper (verso), 284 × 204 mm (11 3/16 × 8 1/16 in.)

Inscribed in pen and brown ink on recto, in right-to-left script (from top to bottom, and left to right), cropped at top: *[. . .]g[. . .] sta alla stadera / del corduso*—; at left border, to left of thigh of profile of a man: *descriuj qualj mus/scolj si perdano nello i[n]/grassare e nel djmagra/re qualj musscolj si sco/prano —— / e nota che quelochi del/lla superfitie del grasso . / chessara piu co[n]cuata / qua[n]do si djssgrassa fia / piu eleuata ——.*; in middle, to right of profile study of a man: *della vicinjta / che anno le co[n]/formjta delle / ossa e mussco/li dellj anjma/li colle ossa e / musscoli delo/mo ——.*; near right border, near hip of rightmost study: *conguntjone de mvs/scoli carnoso colle os/sa sanza alcun ner/vo o cartilagine —— / elsimile farai dj / piu anjmale e / ucellj ——.*; at bottom left corner: *doue li musscolj / siseparano lu[n] dal/laltro farai p/roffjlj e doue s/apichano insiem^e / ettu solame[n]te pe/negeraj——.*; near center of lower border, to right of lower leg of man in profile: *fa prima los/sa seperate co / le sassule doue si / co[n]gungano e poi / li co[n]gugnj insieme / e massima mente la/sscia over gu[n]tura / della cosscia ——.*; to left of central skeletal study of leg and hip: *figura il ginochio / dellomo piegato co/me quel del cauallo*; below: *p[er] equjparare los/satura delcauallo ac/quella dellomo faraj / lomo in pu[n]ta dj piedj / nella figuratione delle / ganbe ——.*; at lower right corner: *fa lomo in pu[n]ta / di piedj acco che ttu / assimjgli meglio / lomo allj altri anj/malj ——.*

Lent by Her Majesty Queen Elizabeth II, Royal Library, Windsor Castle 12625

PROVENANCE: Windsor Leoni volume: 1519, Francesco Melzi, Milan and Rome (1491/93–ca. 1570); ca. 1570, Orazio Melzi; by 1590, Pompeo Leoni, Madrid and Milan (ca. 1533–1608; Lugt under 2885); ca. 1613, Thomas Howard, second earl of Arundel (1586–1646); before 1690, British Royal Collection (inventory of King George III's collection, ca. 1810).

LITERATURE: Richter 1883, vol. 2, p. 115, no. 810; Seidlitz 1909, pl. 46; Seidlitz 1911, p. 281, no. 559; *Quaderni d'anatomia* 1911–16, vol. 5, fol. 22; Popham 1930–31, p. 25, no. 87, pl. 72; O'Malley and Saunders 1952, p. 58; Royal Academy of Arts 1952, p. 51, nos. 162, 263 (hors catalogue); Clark 1954, pl. 36; Esche 1954, p. 160, fig. 83; Heydenreich 1954, vol. 1, pp. 127, 134, vol. 2, p. 138, pl. 192; Chastel 1961, p. 55; Hale 1965, pp. 132–33; Clark and Pedretti 1968–69, vol. 1, pp. 129–30, no. 12625; Clark 1969–70, p. 43, no. 159; Richter 1970, vol. 2, p. 91, no. 810; Keele 1976, p. 26, no. 7; Royal Academy of Arts 1977, pp. 133–34, no. 42; Keele and Pedretti 1979–80, vol. 1, pp. 298–99, no. 95; Biaggi 1980, p. 439; Leinati 1980, p. 398; Keele and Roberts 1983, pp. 139, 141, no. 42; Baur 1984, pp. 62, 193, 274, fig. 29; Philo 1985, pp. 273, 276; Pietro C. Marani in Palazzo Reale 1987–88, p. 78, under no. 25a; Pedretti 1988g, p. 91, fig. 1; Kemp and Roberts 1989, pp. 66–67, no. 15; Clayton and Philo 1992–93, pp. 106–7, no. 17; Kornell 1992, p. 203 n. 131; Popham 1994, no. 230; Letze and Buchsteiner 1997, p. 92; Arasse 1998, pp. 74–76, fig. 40; Laurenza 2001, p. 181, fig. 92.

The design of the heroic nude man seen from the back, as in the drawings associated with the mysterious statue of Hercules of 1506–8 (cat. nos. 101, 102) and in the Turin sheet of sketches discussed in the previous entry, is also recognizable here in the three studies of the male lower body. In fact, the complex musculature of the figure on the upper right in this breathtaking sheet of studies is in the exact configuration of that of the nude on the upper right in that sheet (cat. no. 103) and very close in design to the Turin Hercules (cat. no. 102). Here, the pronounced musculature of the standing Herculean warrior is transformed into an object of scientific demonstration, leading to a detailed exploration of the surface muscles as seen through the skin. The male figural type portrayed in these studies of the lower body is also reminiscent of the soldiers in the unfinished *Battle of Anghiari* project. Thus, on the evidence of style the present sheet of drawings can be dated more or less precisely. The subject matter of the studies on the lower part of the sheet—the anatomical comparison of man to horse—also evokes the great battle scene. During the years 1506–8, when his incomplete work on the *Battle of Anghiari* had become a sore point with his patrons, Piero Soderini (the *gonfaloniere di giustizia*) and the *signori* of the Florentine Republic, Leonardo left Florence for extended stays in Milan, where he tried to reconnect with the French, who were in power.[1] It is reasonably certain that Leonardo produced the present sheet of anatomical studies when he was in Milan, for he wrote on the upper border of the recto, "is at the steelyard of Cordusio," referring to the district with the market in the old center of Milan, immediately northwest of the cathedral. Although the subtle drawing technique of red on red (red chalk on red-ocher prepared paper) was first explored

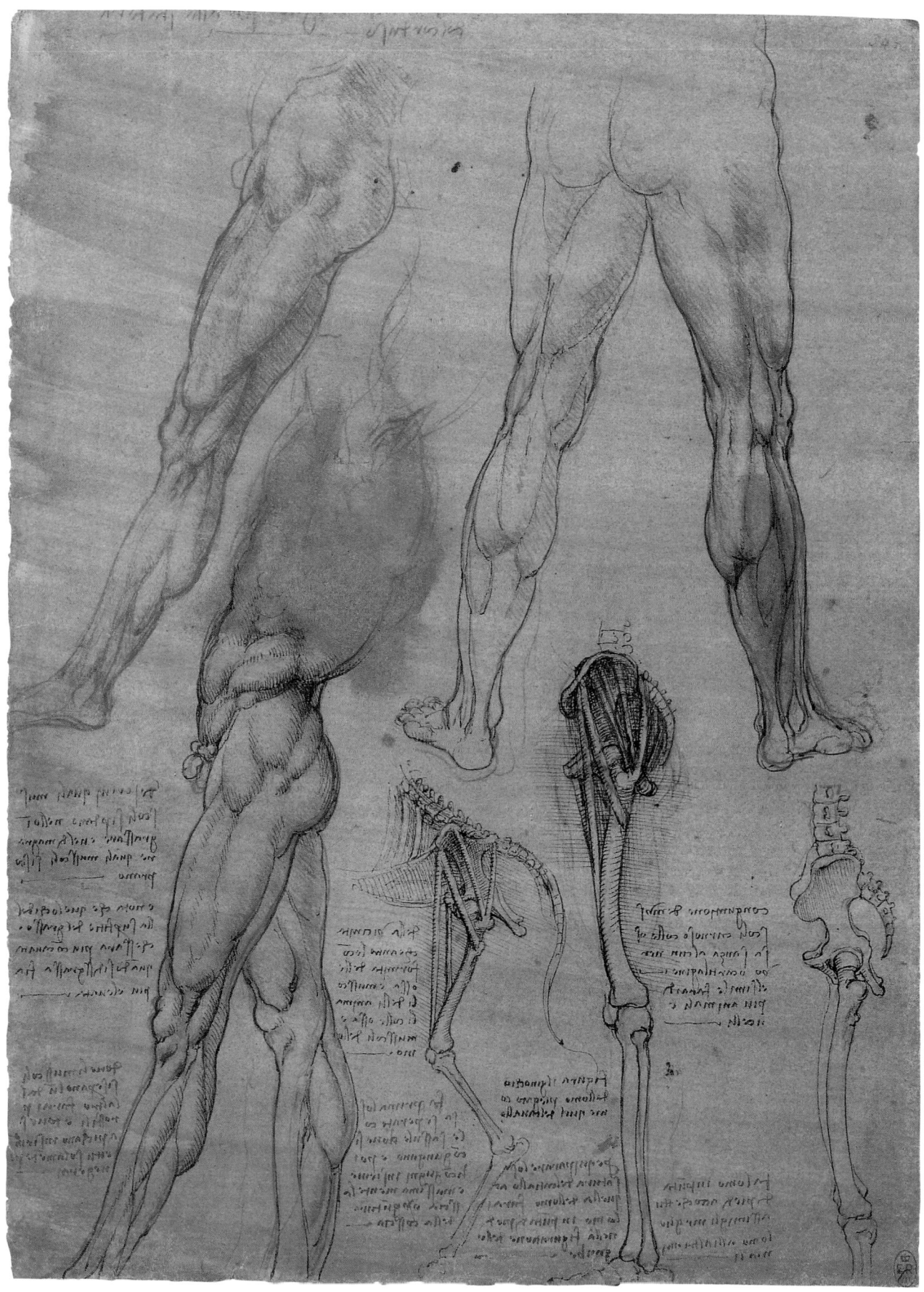

Cat. 104

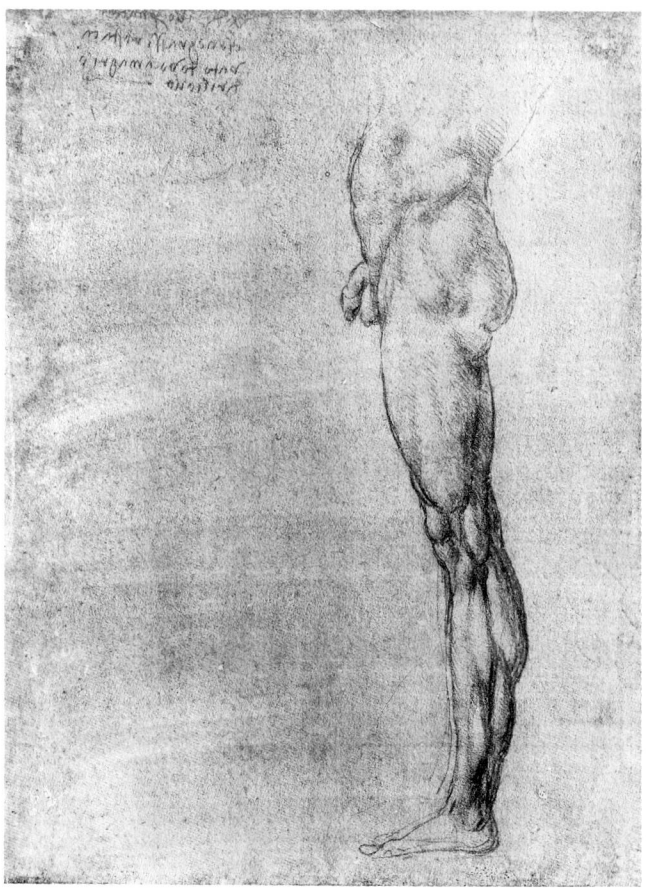

Fig. 194. Leonardo da Vinci, *Abdomen and Left Leg of a Nude Man Standing in Profile.* Red chalk on ocher prepared paper, 252 × 198 mm. The British Museum, London 1886-6-9-41

by Leonardo in studies for the apostles' heads in the *Last Supper,* it is also typical of his work during the first decade of the century. It is here reworked with pen and ink for more precise descriptive detail. Leonardo used the identical technique in a number of anatomical drawings datable to 1506–8, for example, in another closely related study showing the surface muscles of the legs of a man seen from the rear in a straddling position (Windsor, RL 12623). Another related study of the male lower body (fig. 194), in a similar red-on-red drawing technique, shows the figure in profile, as in the studies on the left in the present sheet. These may have all been pages of a sketchbook devoted to such anatomical drawings. At this time, Leonardo also produced a number of his botanical studies for *Leda and the Swan* in red chalk on very pale, ocher-red prepared paper (Windsor, RL 12419–12422). Preparatory

sketches for the present exquisitely finished anatomical studies are to be found in pages of the Paris Ms. K (fols. 102r and 109v), also executed in this technique, in a section of the small notebook that Leonardo used in Milan.

The studies on the lower right illustrate the internal anatomy of a horse's leg compared to that of a man's. In order to show more clearly the exact position where the muscles are attached to the bones, Leonardo used a shorthand notation, abbreviating the muscles as cords. This is among the earliest applications of the "cord" shorthand notation in his anatomical drawings. Toward the center at the bottom, the artist offered a partial view of the skeleton and muscular structure of the rear legs and tail of a horse, comparing them, to the right of this, to the bones and muscular structure of the legs of a man. At the extreme lower right, he drew a partial view of just the skeleton of the lower body of the man. A note on the side by the artist— "to compare the structure of the bones of the horse to that of man you shall represent the man on tiptoe in figuring the legs" —indicates that the tiptoe portion has been lost in the cropping of the drawing along the lower border of the sheet. Leonardo, who had already undertaken a number of dissections of animals in the 1490s, often sought to understand and illustrate the anatomy of the human figure by comparing it to that of various animals. (To some extent he supposed erroneously, like Galen, that much evidence on human anatomy could be derived from animal dissection; human corpses were not often readily available for dissection.) For instance, he inscribed another sheet of studies of the muscles of a man (Windsor, RL 12631 recto), "You will represent for the sake of comparison the legs of a frog, which have a great resemblance to the legs of man, both as to the bones and their muscles; then you should follow with the hind limbs of a hare, which are very muscular and which have active muscles because they are not encumbered with fat."[2]   CCB

1. See Chronology.
2. Keele and Pedretti 1979–80, vol. 1, p. 286, no. 89r: "figureraj a cquessto p/aragone le ganbe dera/nochi le quali anno gran / simjlitudjne colle ganbe / dellomo si nellossa com[e] / nesua musscoli dj poj / seguirai le gambe djrieto / della lepre le quali son / molte [crossed out: p] muscolose e dj / muvsscoli spedjti perche non / sono inpedjte dagrasse [crossed out: ss]/zza—."

LEONARDO DA VINCI

105. *Studies for the Christ Child* (recto)
Slight Diagramatic Sketches (verso)

Red chalk, brush and red wash (head at center), small traces of white gouache highlights over traces of stylus, on ocher-red prepared paper (recto); pen and brown ink (verso), 285 × 198 mm (11 ¼ × 7 ¹³/₁₆ in.)

Inscribed in red chalk on recto, in right-to-left script, toward center of upper border: *anbroso*; in pen and black ink toward lower right, by a later hand: *di Leonardo*; on verso in pen and brown ink, by the artist in right-to-left script, toward bottom of sheet: *Se io so co[n] certezza lospatio che e dal [punto] e f all o[g]chio . g . che qui lometto 1500 miglia / la qua[n]tita c d che meincognita p[er] magnitudine e p[er] distantia m[iglia] 10 la misuro tal / quale elle e poi la re movo quella medesima unaltro spatio incognito e l / c[i]oe in a b, e lla trovo diminuta e 4/5 della prima qua[n]to giudichero io ch ella / sia piu remota dallochio che essa p[rima] in questa regola io cerco colla prima / notitia acquisstare la notitia della distantia e gra[n]dezza dun corpo c[i]oe del sole / Adu[n]que mjsura prima lospatio dunora qua[nt]e elle piu propi[n]quo e poi mjsura lultima / ora qua[n]t elle e piu remoto e tal quale e il ma[n]came[n]to tal sara lecesso della remotio/[ne]*

Gallerie dell'Accademia, Venice 257

PROVENANCE: Cardinal Cesare Monti, Milan (1635–50); Contessa Anna Luisa Monti, Milan; 1770, Venanzio De Pagave, Milan; his son Gaudenzio De Pagave; ca. 1808 or before, Giuseppe Bossi, Milan and Venice (1777–1815; album marked K); auction, Milan, February 1818, II; February 24, 1818, purchase by Abbate Luigi Celotti [Cellotti], Venice (1765–1846); in deposit (under custody of Carlo Porta and Nicola Cassoni) Accademia di Belle Arti, Milan; 1820–22, proposal of purchase of Bossi's collection from Celotti submitted to Austrian government on behalf of Accademia delle Belle Arti, Venice; 1822, purchase by Franz I (Habsburg), emperor of Austria, Florence and Vienna (1768–1835), for Accademia delle Belle Arti, Venice; ca. 1832, manuscript inventory; December 31, 1870, manuscript inventory; museum stamp (Lugt 188).

LITERATURE: Gerli 1784, pl. 8 (inscribed as no. 9; inverts the top and bottom halves of the sheet in the reproduction); Selvatico 1854, frame 6, no. 2; Uzielli 1884, p. 280, no. 27; Venturi 1896, p. 44; Berenson 1903, vol. 2, p. 62, no. 1264 (as imitation of Leonardo); Loeser 1903b, p. 183; Fogolari 1913, no. 20; Berenson 1938, vol. 1, p. 168, vol. 2, p. 123, vol. 3, p. 563, no. 1109A; Heydenreich 1949, pl. 28; Biblioteca Medicea Laurenziana 1952, p. 36, no. 51; Berenson 1961, vol. 1, pp. 247–48, vol. 2, p. 217, no. 1109A; Cogliati Arano 1966–67, pp. 37–38, no. 37, figs. 43–44 (Cesare da Sesto); Cogliati Arano 1980, pp. 67–69, no. 30 (as Cesare da Sesto [?], Ambrogio de' Predis [?]); Pedretti 1982c, p. 23, figs. 17, 23, 24; Pedretti 1982a, p. 78;

Pedretti and Clark 1983, p. 46, fig. 35, p. 51; Marani 1987a, p. 240, fig. 163; Kemp 1991, p. 37; Martin Clayton in Palazzo Grassi 1992, pp. 250–51, nos. 25–25a; Popham 1994, no. 185; Caroline Lanfranc de Panthou in Musée Condé 1995, pp. 94–95, no. 23; Tordella 1995, p. 415; Arasse 1998, pp. 452–55, fig. 313; Annalisa Perissa Torrini in Nepi Scirè and Torrini 1999, pp. 92–95, no. 28.

This delicately rendered sheet in red chalk on ocher-red prepared paper offers several studies of gradually increased scale for the figure of the infant Jesus as he is represented in the extant Louvre painting of the *Virgin and Child with Saint Anne and a Lamb* (fig. 23). The red-on-red drawing technique helps date the Venice drawing to about 1508–10. The note and diagrammatic sketches on the verso help confirm this date, for they pertain to the proportional measurement of distances (as, for example, the distance between the eye and the sun), which suggests an analogy of purpose to the early pages of the Codex Leicester illustrated here (cat. no. 114). On the recto of the Venice sheet, the red-on-red drawing technique reduces the contrast between form and ground tone, and seems therefore especially apt for the Christ Child's figure, which appears in a penumbra of intermediate shadow in the final painting, except for the concentrated highlights on the forehead, cheek, right shoulder, and arm. Leonardo seems to have first drawn the smaller study of the child on the upper right of the sheet. The virtually nude child model is here posed holding a curved stick—a frequent prop in life drawings of the period—substituting for the lamb in the painting, but the details of his face and hands are still relatively undefined. The right side of the child's head in this study exhibits the use of a purpler red chalk (next to the lighter, more orange chalk), as do some of the shadows in the body, suggesting the extent of Leonardo's experiments with tonal refinement. (The parallel hatching is left-handed in the passages of "orange" and "purple" red chalk.) In the larger study on the upper left Leonardo maintained the general design of the pose but began to soften and idealize the leaning angle of the infant's body in a manner that seems closer to the final painting. The study of the torso toward the center of the right

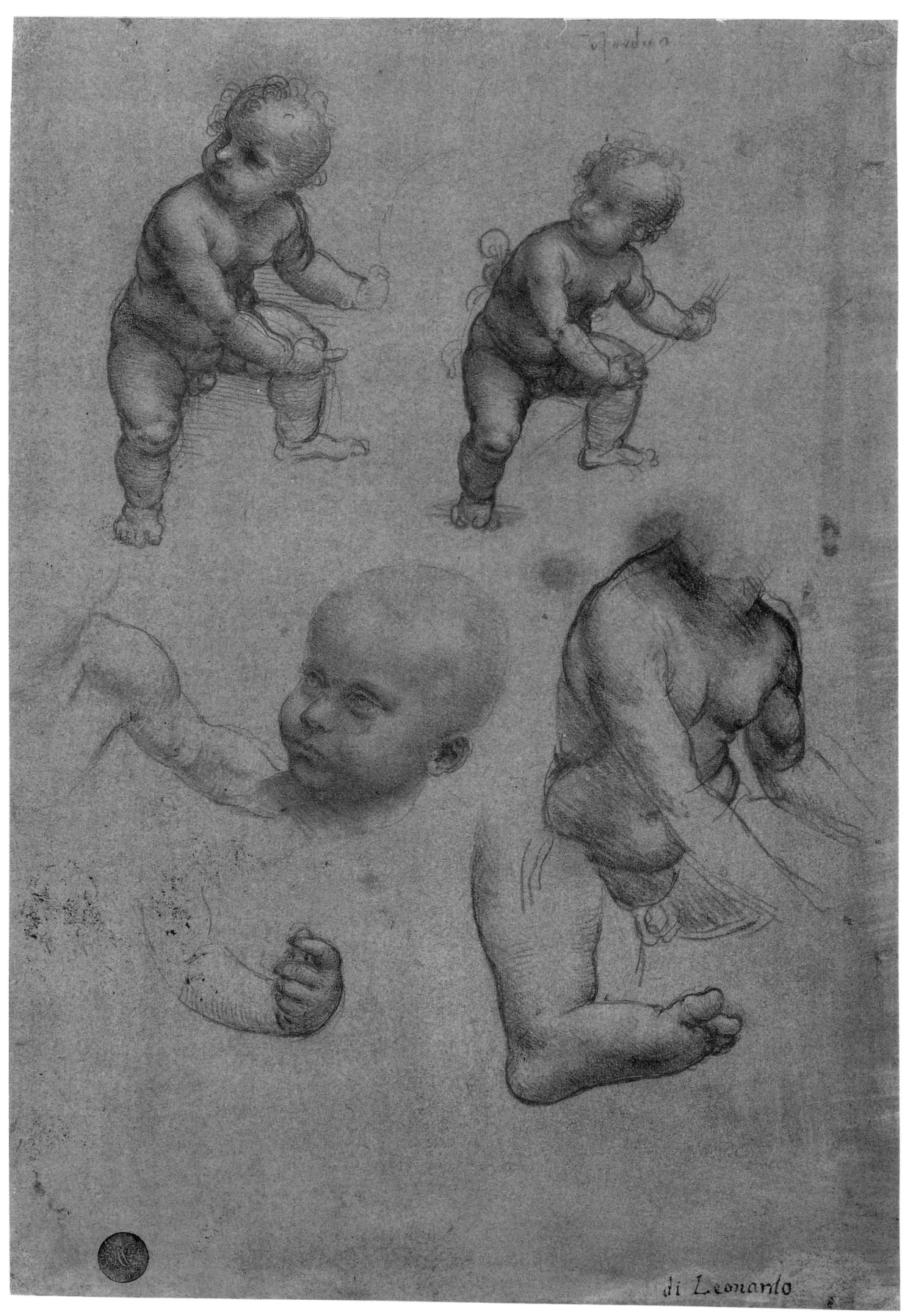

di Leonardo

Cat. 105v

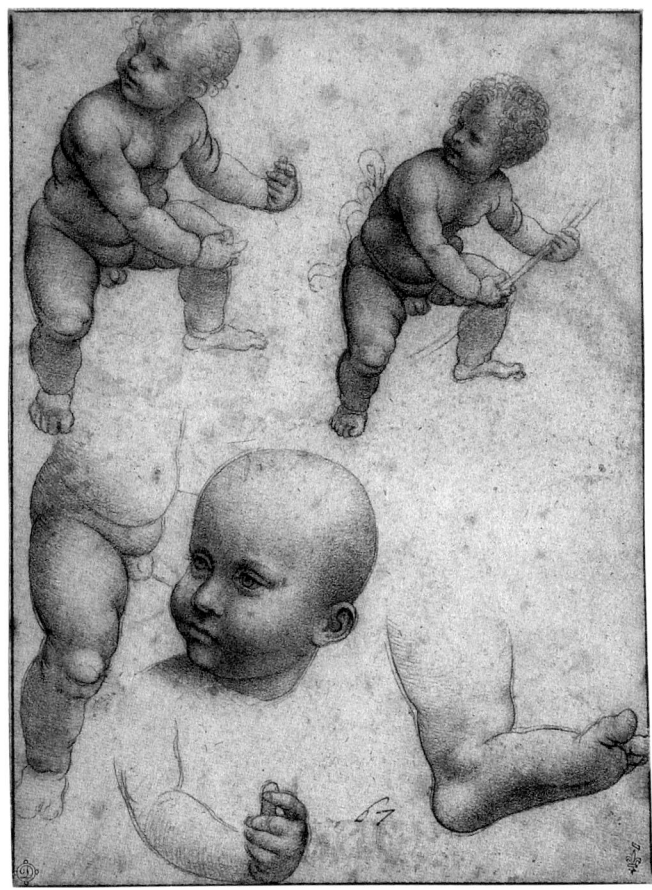

Fig. 195. Copy after Leonardo da Vinci, *Copy of Studies of an Infant.*
Red chalk, 202 × 149 mm. Musée Condé, Chantilly 33 (27 bis).

ows more seamlessly. Last, he seems to have lightly high-lighted a small area of the child's brow, nose, and cheekbones with traces of white gouache, blending the tones exquisitely. Indeed, the tonal perfection is so good in photographic repro-ductions that the drawing has been doubted to be by Leonardo. Without pressing the point too far, it is precisely because of the animated and highly innovative experimental technique that this study of the child's head is most probably also by Leonardo.

The attribution of the Venice sheet to Leonardo has been disputed (as a whole and in its parts), in the present author's opinion unreasonably so, given the exquisitely nuanced tonal modeling achieved with left-handed hatching in most of the sheet. A copy in Chantilly (fig. 195) exhibits the rather stiff, dull outlines suggestive of a reworked *spolvero* underdrawing or some other such semimechanical means of design transfer. The dry manner of shading also attempts to imitate the left-handed hatching of Leonardo. The proposed author of the Chantilly copy is Francesco Melzi, who was extremely adept at imitating Leonardo's "left-handed" manner of drawing (see my essay and cat. no. 121) and who produced a number of clean-looking "left-handed" replacement copies that are extant at the Royal Library, Windsor.[1] Drawn in red chalk on uncolored paper, the Chantilly copy differs from the Venice original in the disposition of the motifs on the lower part of the sheet. Interestingly, it is clear that these motifs do not constitute merely reshufflings from the original to the copy. For instance, on the left of the Chantilly copy is a study of a torso and right leg instead of the left shoulder and arm. The copy also omits the study of the upper body seen at the right border of the Venice sheet. Curiously, this study of the torso and right leg is apparently based on an original study on another sheet also in Venice (Gallerie dell'Accademia, 217). By comparison with the Chantilly copy, the present drawing exhibits dynamic passages of unfinish as well as vigorous reinforcement outlines and pentimenti that seem particularly evident in the extremities. Last, and not to be overlooked, the notes on the verso of the present sheet, which discuss the position of the sun in language that is reminiscent of the early notes in the Codex Leicester (cat. no. 114), are written in Leonardo's typical right-to-left script.   CCB

border details the tonal articulation of the forms, specifically, the ineffable highlights that describe the infant's soft adipose skin on the right shoulder and arm and chest area. Unfortunately, the contours along the shoulders and the infant's left arm seem to have been somewhat crudely reinforced by another hand. This motif of the torso and right shoulder was the sub-ject of a separate, still more tonally refined study in the same red-on-red technique (Windsor, RL 12538). The study of a left foot near the bottom of the Venice sheet is intended to explore the soft effect of the intermediate shadows; it is this foot of the child that is visible in the painting. Toward the center of the sheet, the child's head in three-quarter view is in an unusually polished technique. First, Leonardo drew the child's head with light strokes of red chalk. A passage of left-handed parallel hatching is especially evident, with magnification, on the lower part of the child's cranium. The artist then stumped the red chalk to blend in the strokes and seems to have applied on top a layer of red wash or wet red chalk to unify the shad-

1. See Windsor, RL 12492, 12493, 12549, 12559, and 12584.

560

LEONARDO DA VINCI

106. *Arm, Hand, and Sleeve of Drapery*

Charcoal and orange red chalk, brush with brown ink and brown wash, highlighted with white gouache, 167 × 84 mm (6⁹⁄₁₆ × 3⁵⁄₁₆ in.) Lent by Her Majesty Queen Elizabeth II, Royal Library, Windsor Castle 12532

PROVENANCE: Windsor Leoni volume: 1519, Francesco Melzi, Milan and Rome (1491/93–ca. 1570); ca. 1570, Orazio Melzi; by 1590, Pompeo Leoni, Madrid and Milan (ca. 1533–1608; Lugt under 2885); ca. 1613, Thomas Howard, second earl of Arundel (1586–1646); before 1690, British Royal Collection (inventory of King George III's collection, ca. 1810).

LITERATURE: Grosvenor Gallery 1878, vol. 2, p. 17; Müller-Walde 1899, p. 56; Berenson 1903, vol. 2, p. 65, no. 1182; Seidlitz 1909, vol. 1, p. 167; Seidlitz 1911, p. 282, no. 597; Poggi 1919, pl. 109; Venturi 1919, p. 170, fig. 6; Venturi 1920, p. 123, fig. 90; Venturi 1925, fig. 135; De Rinaldis 1926, p. 235, fig. 74; Commissione Vinciana 1928– , vol. 6, p. 23, pl. 241.3; Berenson 1938, vol. 2, p. 132, no. 1182; Royal Academy of Arts 1952, no. 113 (hors catalogue); Goldscheider 1959, p. 160, pl. 40; Berenson 1961, vol. 2, p. 233, no. 1182; Eissler 1961, pl. 64; Clark and Pedretti 1968–69, vol. 1, p. 96, no. 12532; Clark 1969–70, p. 21, no. 89b, pl. 4a; Pedretti and Clark 1983, pp. 114–15, fig. 79, under no. 14; Clark 1985, p. 109, fig. 49; Kemp and Roberts 1989, p. 122, no. 56; Popham 1994, no. 184B; Franck 1997, p. 169, fig. 6; Marani 2000b, p. 290.

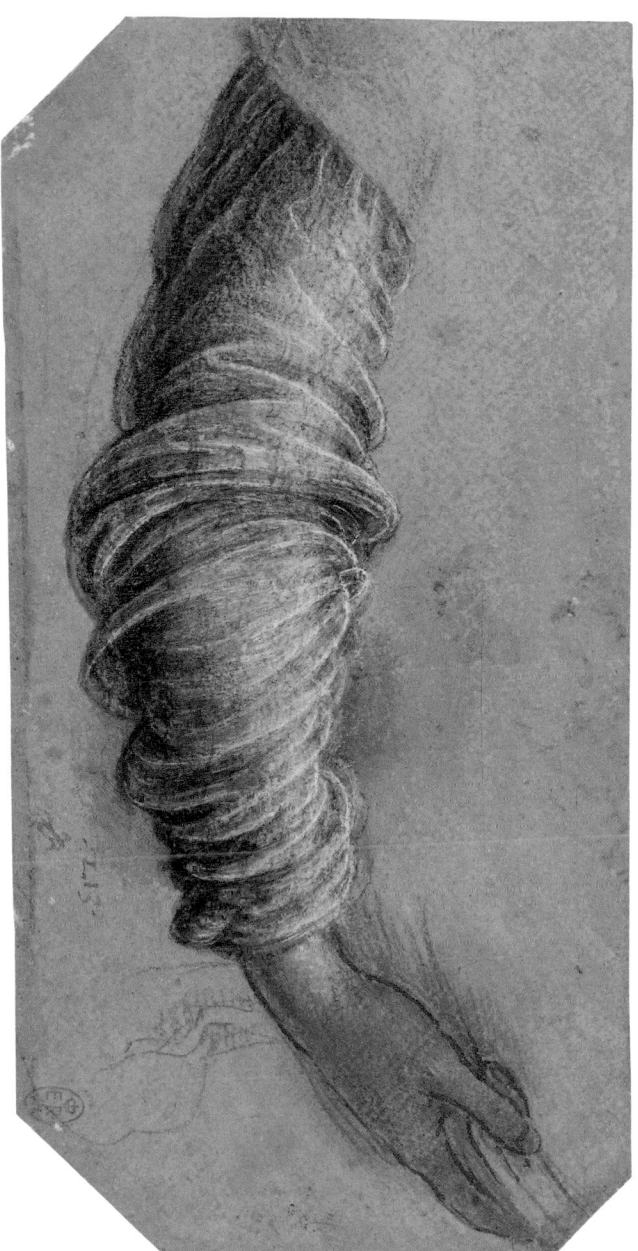

Cat. 106 *(actual size)*

The extant studies for the Louvre *Virgin and Child with Saint Anne* (fig. 23), of 1508–12, richly illustrate Leonardo's increasingly complex pictorial techniques in connection with his scientific studies of color, form, light and shadow. In the drapery studies connected with the Louvre composition (see cat. no. 107), the artist experimented with highly unusual, not always successful, combinations of drawing media—quite diverse in color and composition—to attain effects of modeling that seem luminous, chromatically saturated, and seamlessly built up.

This delicate study on ocher prepared paper for the Virgin's right arm in the Louvre painting makes use of an extremely dense combination of media. Leonardo seems to have begun modeling the forms broadly with charcoal or a soft black chalk, rubbing the strokes together for a soft sfumato effect in the intermediate shadows. He then reworked areas of deeper shadows with brush and brown wash (the aqueous layer gave the forms a greater definition over the smoky chalk layer), also accenting outlines with pen and dark brown inks (it is difficult to dismiss the pen and ink outlines as a later retouching). He added selective white gouache highlights to describe a play of gauzy, but tubelike, drapery folds, while the hand is drawn fleshlike in red chalk reinforced with pen and brown ink.

The complex red-on-red drawing technique suggests a date about 1508–10. The similar use of this technique reworked with pen and dark brown ink for the study of the comparative anatomy of human and horse legs (cat. no. 104) can offer a terminus post quem for the present sheet. The extremely subtle pictorial effects achieved here correspond to Leonardo's later studies of optics.

CCB

LEONARDO DA VINCI

107. *Drapery Enveloping the Legs of a Seated Figure*

Initial drawing in black chalk and black-chalk wash, white and black pigments applied with a tempera technique, 230 × 245 mm (9 1/16 × 9 5/8 in.); damaged corners
Watermark: Eight-petaled flower (close to Briquet 6601, Lombard paper in use from 1480 to 1487). This type of watermark appears on the sheets of the *Nodi* at the Bibliothèque Nationale de France[1] and on several studies by Leonardo and Giovanni Antonio Boltraffio[2]
Département des Arts Graphiques du Musée du Louvre, Paris 2257

PROVENANCE: J. B. J. Wicar ("Chevalier Vicar," according to the catalogue of the Lawrence Gallery, London, 1836, purchased by Woodburn for Thomas Lawrence in Rome in 1823); Sir Thomas Lawrence (Lugt 2445); William II of the Netherlands, sale, The Hague, 1850, no. 182; S. Woodburn; October 1851, acquired from the latter by the Musée du Louvre; museum mark (Lugt 1886).

LITERATURE: Lawrence Gallery 1835–36, vol. 2, no. 51; *Athenaeum* 1836; Montaiglon 1852, pp. 211–12; Louvre 1866, no. 391; Geymüller 1886, p. 149; Müntz 1899, p. 372, pl. 17, p. 519, no. 4; Berenson 1903, vol. 1, p. 158, pl. 111, vol. 2, no. 1063; Louvre 1919, no. 30; Poggi 1919, pl. 107, p. lvii; Demonts 1921, no. 19; Demonts 1922, no. 19; Sirén 1928, p. 112, pl. 132; Suida 1929, pp. 133–34; Valentiner 1932, pp. 60–61; Berenson 1938, vol. 1, p. 177; Popham 1945, pp. 8, 51, no. 188; Pedretti 1951, p. 23; Amboise 1952; Biblioteca Medicea Laurenziana 1952, no. 52; Florisoone and Bacou 1952, no. 22; Valentiner 1957, p. 136, fig. 10; Sérullaz 1965, no. 12; Forlani Tempesti 1970, p. 81, pl. 3; Pedretti 1973a, p. 130, fig. 134; Arasse 1978, p. 48; Rosci 1978, fig. p. 16; Béguin 1983, p. 86; Dalli Regoli 1983–84, p. 71, fig. 71; Pedretti 1988b, p. 145; Hinterding and Horsch 1989, p. 53 n. 215; Marani 1989, p. 114; Louvre 1989–90, no. 18; Pedretti 1990a, p. 168, fig. 5; Roberts 1992, p. 177 n. 111; Clayton 1996–97, under no. 80; Arasse 1997, pp. 455, 456, 459, fig. 316; Marani 1999b, fig. p. 290; Scailliérez 2000, p. 49, fig. 7.

If it is true, as now believed, that the conception of the *Virgin and Child with Saint Anne* developed over a long period of time, the changes in motifs that accompanied it were not divorced from its complex scheme. The theme of the trinitarian Saint Anne, that is, her place in three generations— Anne the mother, her daughter the Virgin Mary, and Jesus— can be understood as an extension of studies conducted for the simpler group of the Virgin with Child beginning in Leonardo's first Florentine period (cat. nos. 18–22). The presence of Saint Anne in the later painting, however, by conferring her solemnity on the group, transforms the movements of offering and withdrawal that organize scenes of mother-child play into a symbolic representation of the mystery of the Incarnation and the Passion of Christ. To understand the genesis of the painting, we need to consider anew the early Virgins drawings, that is, the "reproduction, on the basis of a motionless motif, of the dynamic energy and movement of the human figures."[3]

To appreciate the proper place of the Louvre drapery sketch in relation to the depiction of the Virgin's left hip and leg in the painting, we must examine the hypotheses previously advanced about Leonardo's work. The one generally adopted today is that the Louvre painting was a commission received in Milan in 1499 from the French king Louis XII. The work was begun in 1500 and defined in an overall cartoon in 1501 but was still unfinished in 1517, two years before Leonardo's death.[4] The elaboration of the *Virgin and Child with Saint Anne* is believed to have resulted in two works in a large format, only one of which has survived: the cartoon in the National Gallery, London (figs. 17, 75, 76). Two letters, dated April 3 and April 14, 1501, written by Fra Pietro da Novellara, tell us that Leonardo was in Florence at that time working on the sketch for a composition of the Christ Child with Saint Anne and also under obligation to fulfill commitments that he had made in Milan at the time of the French rule. In the still-

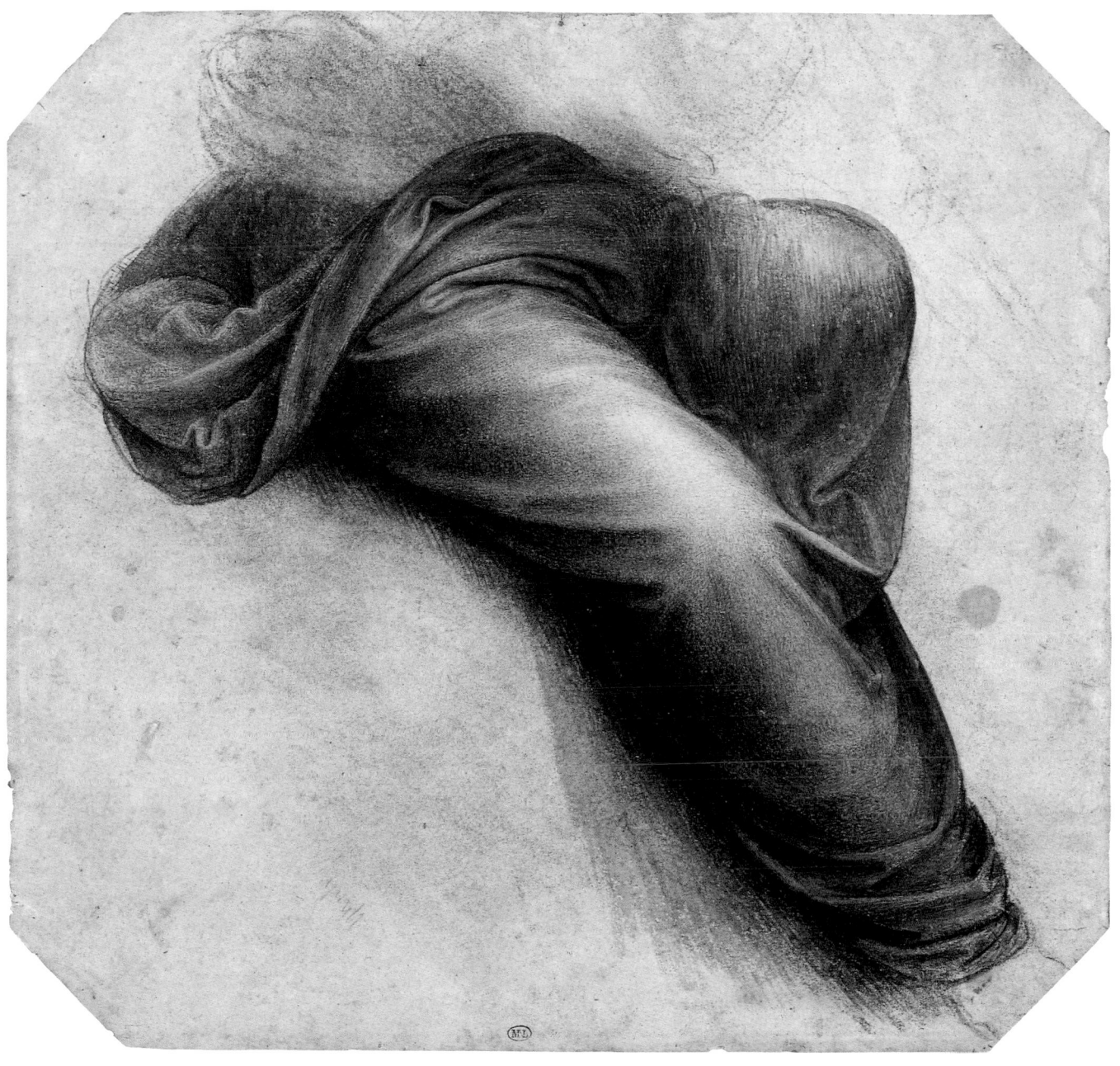

Cat. 107

unfinished cartoon, the figures were lifesize but, writes Novellara, "of small dimensions because all are seated or leaning over, one behind the other, positioned toward the left."[5] That cartoon disappeared, and only two works retained a trace of it: one heavily retouched drawing in a private collection in Geneva[6] and a painting attributed to Andrea Brescianino, formerly in the Kaiser-Friedrich-Museum in Berlin.[7]

The date of the so-called Burlington House cartoon, now in the National Gallery, London (figs. 17, 75, 76), is itself open to discussion. Some historians agree that it is the "sketch" mentioned in an undated letter from Padre Sebastiano Resta to Giovanni Pietro Bellori, prior to 1696.[8] In that case, it would date from the same period as Leonardo's commission from the king of France. Others tend to see it as a later work—after 1505 and perhaps even later, from 1508–10—based on a comparison with the studies for *Leda* (see fig. 186).[9] A second version, possibly identifiable as the one described by Fra Pietro da Novellara, displays an important change in iconography: the motif of the two children (Jesus and John the Baptist) is replaced by that of Jesus escaping from the arms of his mother to embrace a lamb. Therefore, shortly after the execution of the London cartoon—preparatory studies for which are in the British Museum (1875-6-12-17; cat. no. 96) and the Louvre (fig. 186)—Leonardo may have conceived another project that served as the model for the painting in the Louvre. Most of the drawings for the painting—all studies of isolated motifs—would stem from that lost composition. On the other hand, the London cartoon was "adjusted," masterfully in its general effect, on the basis of the two preparatory studies just mentioned.[10] All the studies relating to the Louvre painting seem contemporary with one another, as if, once the overall composition was set down, the painter focused on each of the chosen forms. Once again, the question of the chronology of these works arises, in particular for the Virgin's drapery exhibited here. For a time, it was considered an early work, connected to the *Benois Madonna* (fig. 133) and, simply by virtue of similarities, to sketches for that painting, such as the one in the British Museum (1860-6-16-100; cat. no. 20). According to Valentiner (1932), it differs from the definitive version in the arrangement of the folds and in the substance of the fabric. Valentiner considers it a much earlier drawing, dating from about 1478 and used later for *Virgin and Child with Saint Anne*.[11] That hypothesis is no longer tenable, however, because the drapery sketches on *tela di lino* have revealed

the character of Leonardo's work at that early date. Nonetheless, the style of the drawing and the nature of its support lead us to wonder about its place in the elaboration of the painting, done between 1510 and 1513 but still unfinished—particularly the Virgin's face and drapery—when Antonio de' Beatis saw and described it in Cloux in 1517.

The drapery unfolding around Mary's legs and hips—the extreme point of tension between the two principal figures, Saint Anne and the Virgin—was a matter of study by Leonardo from the beginning of his work in the *Virgin and Child with Saint Anne* and was retained in the London cartoon. It could on its own testify to the ambition of the painter, who may have been inspired by classical sculpture.[12] It also conveys the grandeur of the scene, a scene "of an extreme serenity, in which one perceives no tension about to break it."[13] Cécile Scaillierez has aptly pointed out that the shift from the cartoon to the painting is marked by a clarification of the forms, "an equilibrium in a stable but asymmetrical group, which aligns along one side four heads and four gazes."[14] The entire movement of the Virgin, simultaneously leaning forward and about to straighten up again—a "totally ambiguous" movement[15]—is contained in this drawing, which clearly indicates the oblique angle of the right leg. The withdrawn left leg establishes the perpendicular and suggests, through a few strokes of black chalk on the upper part, the inclination of the torso and the gesture of the arm. The right arm, which will be placed almost in the center, does not appear here but is studied separately in a drawing at Windsor (cat. no. 106). All the same, the angle of vision chosen for the drawing is different from that of the painting. In the drawing, the seated figure is turning away, pivoting. The pronounced oblique, which gives the lower part all its weight, is not yet shown. Finally (compared to the painting, no doubt, because it is unfinished) the drawing is infinitely polished, pushed to an extreme. Its technique is almost pictorial in its definition: in the refining of the drawing with a wash, in the meticulous application of the pigments, in the very diversity of technical inventions, which look as if a number of different ideas were pursued at various times on a single sheet—preliminary and masterful at the same time in the treatment of the creases and the gathers at the waist.[16]

The detail studies for the *Virgin and Child with Saint Anne* can be dated, it seems, to the years 1510–13; four of the studies appear in this exhibition (cat. nos. 106–9). The drapery sketches (cat. no. 106; Windsor RL 12527, 12530) belong to the group that Martin Clayton calls "technical innovations."[17] Pointing out that two of them are on paper with French watermarks (RL 12527 and RL 12526), he suggests a date of execution in the last years of Leonardo's life.[18]

The question raised by the Louvre drapery study has to do with the sheet's very recognizable watermark, which is found again, notably, on the study for Saint James the Greater at Windsor (fig. 89). If, as is generally believed today, the London cartoon was preliminary to the first version of the *Virgin and Child with Saint Anne*, it must have been executed immediately after the *Last Supper*, for which the study of Saint James the Greater was made. The recently exhibited study for the arm of Saint Peter (fig. 88),[19] done in a technique close to that of the Louvre drapery sketch, leads us in the same direction, toward pushing back the date of the Louvre drawing or even establishing a relationship between it and the figure of an apostle at the Last Supper, which may have been reused later for the Virgin in the Louvre painting.[20] Marani has connected the drawing for Saint Peter's arm with a text from Leonardo's projected *Libro di pittura*, dating about 1490–92, which describes the representation of the folds of cloth surrounding the limbs ("questa discrezzione nelle pieghe che circondano le braccia, gambe od altro").[21] There is a great similarity in style, and the position of the bent arm on the hip is close to Saint Anne's in the painting and in the small Louvre study (fig. 186). Without abandoning the connection between the study for the Virgin's drapery and the form that would finally be chosen but which the painter did not pursue to its conclusion, we may wonder about the date of the study. It is very different in technique from the other studies, particularly the so-called French-watermark drapery sketches at Windsor; might it not represent an intermediate stage between the cartoon and the painting, still close to the Milanese works—provided we accept the date (about 1501) now assigned to the London cartoon?

In view of historians' current eagerness to establish the chronological order of Leonardo's studies for the *Virgin and Child with Saint Anne*, studies that occupied the artist's attention for more than a decade, it should be remembered that neither the drawings nor the texts reconstruct the painting's genesis completely. Whatever the distance separating the cartoon from the painting, it is clear that one stems directly from the other, that the pyramidal composition in which the forms overlap was chosen very early by Leonardo, and that the bending motion was already in place for one or the other of the "plural mothers."   FV

1. Lambert 1999, nos. 522, 524a.
2. See A. de la Chapelle in the Paris catalogue of this exhibition.
3. Clark 1985, p. 106.
4. Scailliérez 2000, p. 35.
5. Scailliérez 2000, p. 34; Villata 1999, p. 135.
6. Clayton 1996–97, p. 451, fig. 310.
7. Bodmer 1931, p. 61.
8. Popham and Pouncey 1950, p. 67, under no. 108.
9. Pedretti 1968a, p. 26; Dalli Regoli 1982, p. 28.
10. Scailliérez 2000, pp. 47–48.
11. Bode 1921; Suida 1929; Valentiner 1932.
12. Marani 1999b, p. 262.
13. Clark 1985, p. 108.
14. Scailliérez 2000, p. 47.
15. Scailliérez 2000.
16. See Arasse 1997, p. 456.
17. Clayton 1996–97, pp. 133–34, nos. 75–80.
18. Scailliérez 2000, p. 49.
19. Palazzo Reale 2001, no. 32.
20. Pietro C. Marani, oral communication, May 2001.
21. *Libro di pittura* 1995, vol. 2, no. 540, p. 358.

LEONARDO DA VINCI

108. *Head of the Virgin in Three-Quarter View Facing to the Right*

Soft black and red chalks; traces of framing outline in pen and brown ink at upper right (not by Leonardo), 203 × 156 mm (8 × 6⅛ in.)

Inscribed on recto at upper left with script in faded pen and brown ink (not legible); on verso at upper center in pen and brown ink possibly by a sixteenth- or early-seventeenth-century hand: *i20. R.Vr*

The Metropolitan Museum of Art, New York; Harris Brisbane Dick Fund, 1951 51.90

PROVENANCE: Sir Charles Greville (1763–1832; Lugt 549); George Guy, fourth earl of Warwick (1818–1893; Lugt 2600); Warwick sale, Christie's, London, May 20–21, 1896, lot 213; Dr. Ludwig Mond, London (1839–1909); Right Honorable Gwen Lady Melchett of Landford; Melchett sale, Sotheby's, London, May 23–24, 1951, lot 7; purchased by The Metropolitan Museum of Art in 1951.

LITERATURE: Grosvenor Gallery 1877, no. 675; Christie's, Manson and Woods 1896, p. 26, no. 213; Berenson 1903, vol. 1, p. 158, vol. 2, p. 59, no. 1045; Richter 1910, pp. 323–35, pl. 19; Frizzoni 1911, p. 43, fig. 6; Sirén 1916, p. 137; Poggi 1919, pp. 20–21; Venturi 1925, p. 208, fig. 138; De Rinaldis 1926, p. 235, pl. 69; Sirén 1928, vol. 1, p. 112; Berenson 1938, vol. 1, p. 176, vol. 2, p. 116, vol. 3, fig. 514, no. 1045; Metropolitan Museum of Art 1951, cover; Bernardi 1952, p. 105; Metropolitan Museum of Art 1952, p. 68, no. 60; Pedretti 1953, p. 76; Berenson 1961, vol. 1, p. 256, vol. 2, p. 205, vol. 3, fig. 499, no. 1049D-1; Bean and Stampfle 1965, pp. 28–29, no. 19; Vitzthum 1966, p. 109; Vitzthum 1967, p. 109; Bacall 1968, no. 7; Bean 1982, pp. 119–20, no. 110; Ottino della Chiesa 1985, p. 109; Agnews 1968; Vezzosi 1987b, p. 17; Pedretti and Trutty-Coohill 1993, pp. 53–55, no. 18; Marani 2000b, p. 288; Ames-Lewis 2001b, p. 13, no. 23; Clayton 2002–3, p. 149, fig. 50.

This hauntingly beautiful drawing closely relates to the Louvre *Virgin and Child with Saint Anne* (fig. 23), from about 1508–12, and was probably a preparatory study for it. Although the delicately finished drawing surface has suffered somewhat from a slight abrasion throughout, it is still possible to appreciate the atmospheric dissolution of the Virgin's relieflike features as a work of superb technical virtuosity. The sheet vividly illustrates the depth of Leonardo's explorations of optical phenomena late in his career. The artist would increasingly rely on complex pictorial techniques of drawing to articulate the results of his scientific research on color perspective, the disappearance of form, and the gradations of light and shadow. Here, using the sfumato technique, Leonardo reworked the soft black-chalk drawing with red chalk, especially evident in the face (but also extending less noticeably to the locks of hair in the underdrawing), softly smudging all the drawing strokes to achieve a seamlessly blended tone "in the manner of smoke" (*fumo*), as he called it in a note from 1490–92.[1] The technique conforms to the observable phenomenon of disappearing edges in the secondary planes of a perspectival space, a subject that the artist amply discussed in his scientific writings. Further preparatory studies for the *Virgin and Child with Saint Anne* composition,

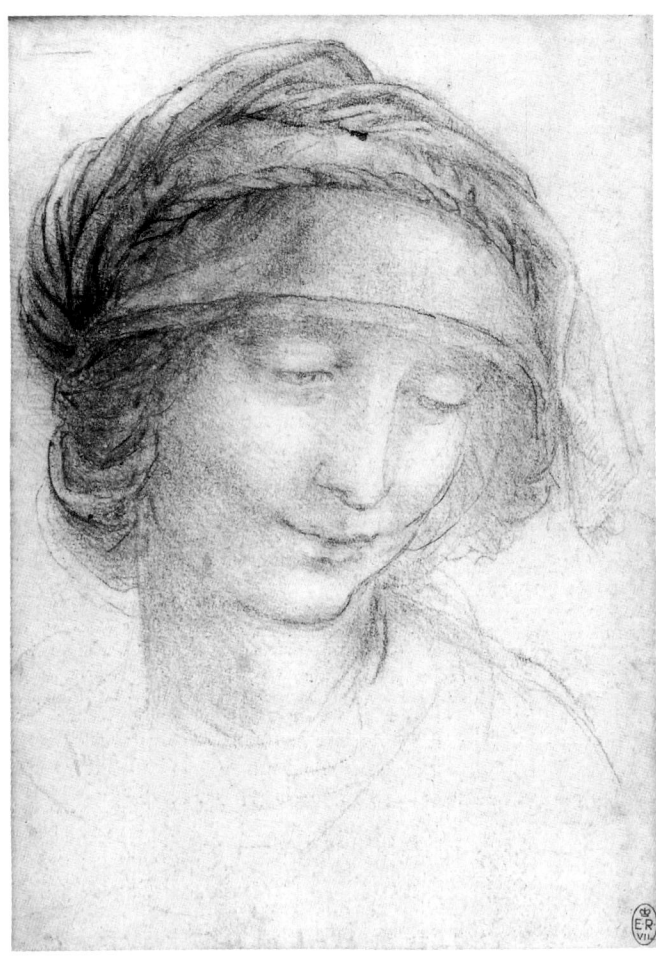

Fig. 196. Leonardo da Vinci, *Study of Saint Anne's Head.* Black chalk, 188 × 130 mm. The Royal Collection, H.M. Queen Elizabeth II, Windsor Castle RL 12533

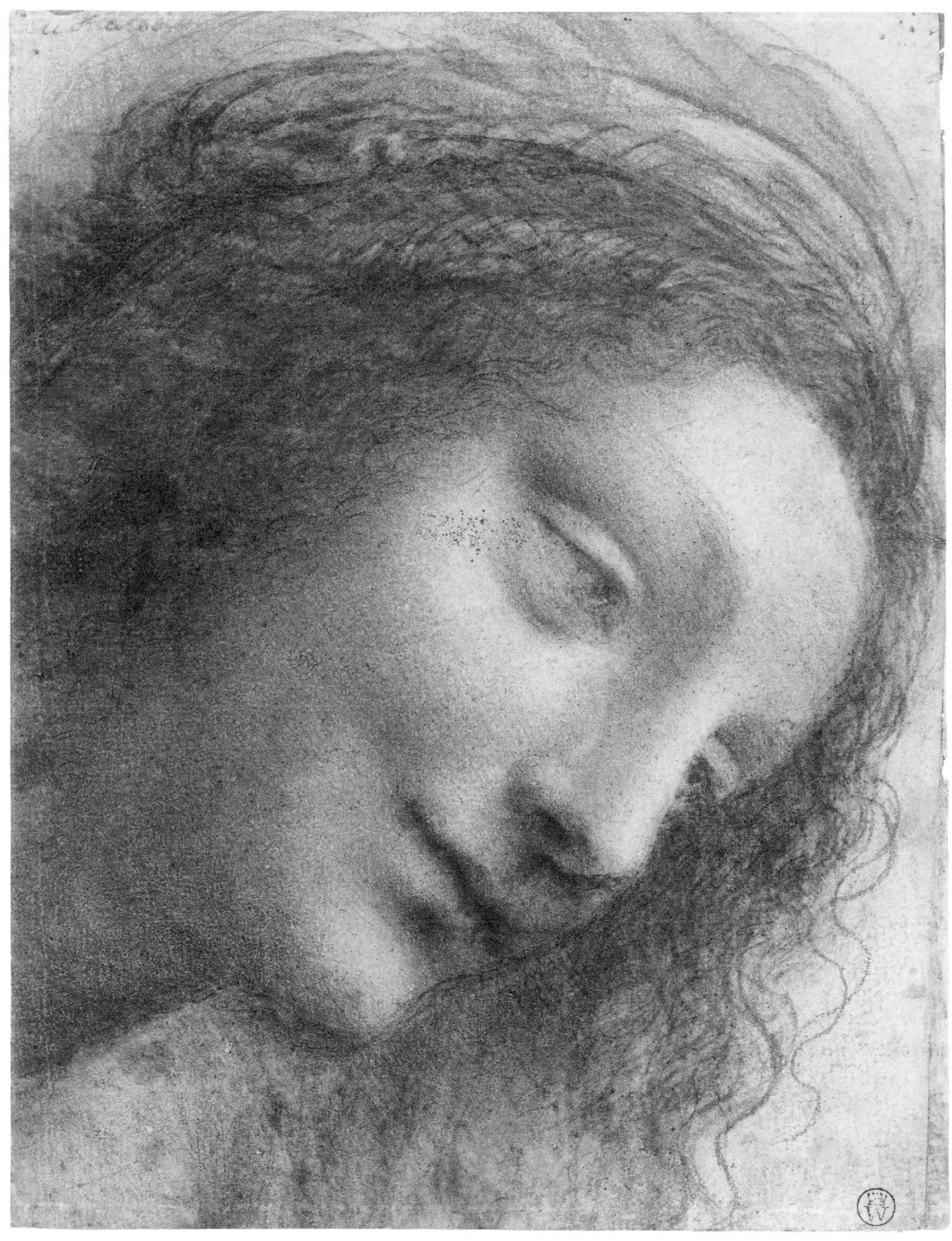

Cat. 108 *(actual size)*

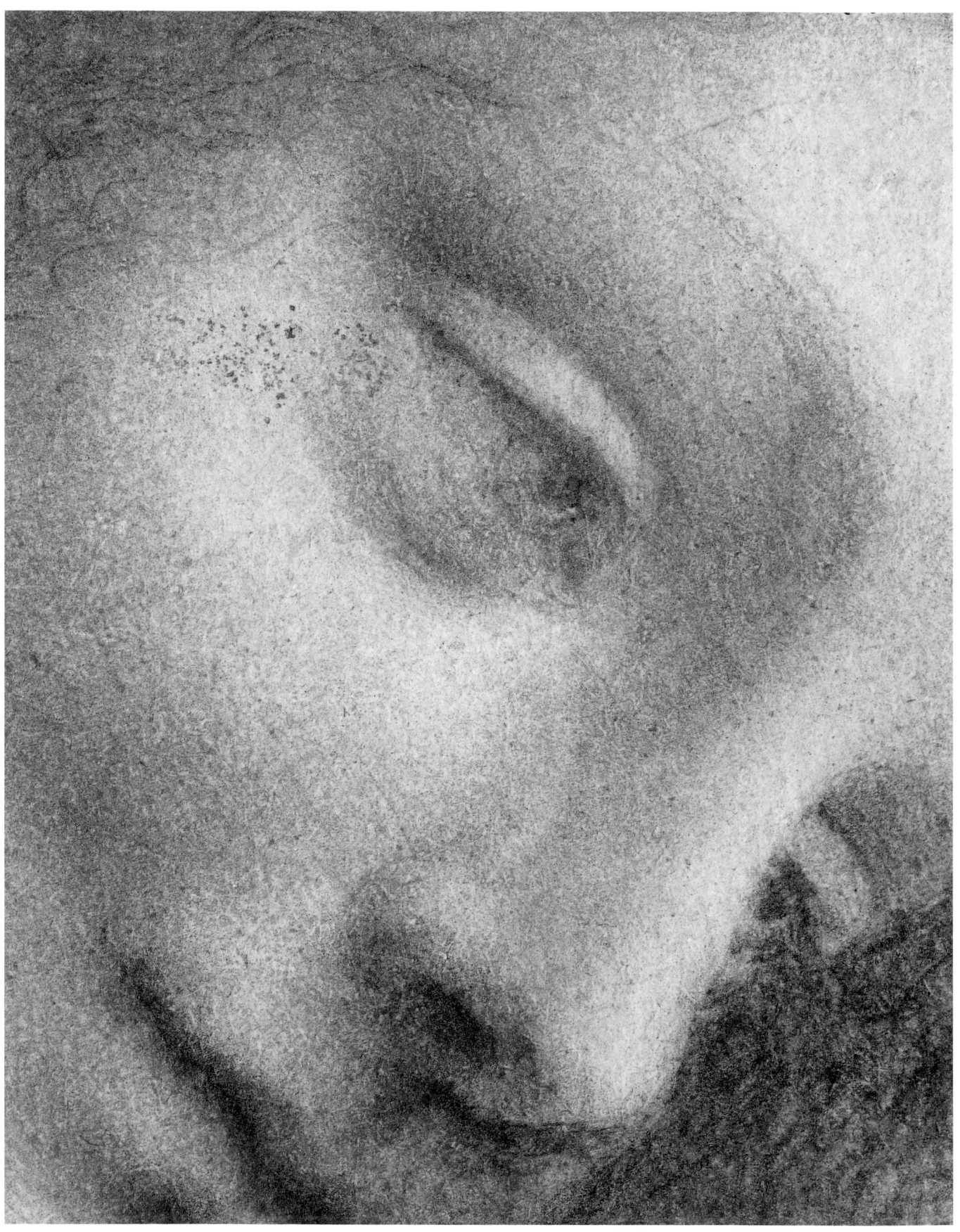

Cat. 108 *(detail)*

at Windsor (fig. 196), transform scientific principles into a pictorial language of magical force and nuance. The present drawing, as well as a study for the head of a screaming soldier from Budapest (cat. no. 91), which was similarly begun with a red-chalk underdrawing, are among the early examples in Italy of the "twin chalk technique," in which red and black chalks are blended for a subtly complementary pictorial effect. This technique would be more typically used, and to great effect, by Late Mannerist artists of two generations later.

As Jacob Bean rightly emphasized, most authors writing on Leonardo before 1982—and Bernard Berenson first and foremost—accepted the present drawing as an original work by Leonardo and as a study for the Louvre picture. It was hesitantly discussed in 1993 by Patricia Trutty-Coohill and Carlo Pedretti, and it has also more recently been accepted as autograph by Martin Clayton.[2] Although no serious doubts as to Leonardo's authorship have been published, its omission from the scholarship on the artist's drawings may reflect skepticism ex silentio. The exquisite degree of finish of the drawing complicates the issue of authorship, for the seamless sfumato drawing technique of soft black chalk with red chalk greatly obscures the artist's individual strokes. Attentive study of the sheet with the unassisted eye shows that there are nevertheless extensive curved left-handed strokes in the soft black-chalk layer on the intermediate shadows of the Virgin's face, especially visible on her forehead (see my essay). These left-handed strokes begin on the lower right and gently curve upward. They have gone unnoticed, probably because the Metropolitan Museum drawing is all too often examined from photographs rather than from the original. No less important, there are also short, delicately curving left-handed strokes in the underdrawing of red chalk that are evident with microscopic enlargement, and these are especially clear near the area of the Virgin's nose (see fig. 35).[3] This evidence in the layer of the underdrawing provides proof of Leonardo's authorship that may be difficult to refute.

It is true that the Milanese followers of Leonardo were quick to adopt the master's innovative colored chalk techniques, achieving at times extraordinarily beautiful results (cat. nos. 127–29, 131–33). Yet none of the head studies by such artists, however directly inspired by Leonardo they may be, approaches the poetry and beauty of the drawing technique seen in the present head study. Slight restorations by a later hand may account for minute dark passages in the right cheek, nostril, and lips. An old, inertly drawn copy is in the Graphische Sammlung Albertina, Vienna. CCB

1. For Leonardo's note on sfumato, see Paris Ms. A, fol. 107v (B.N. 2038, fol. 27v); Richter 1970, vol. 1, p. 306, no. 492: "che le tue o[m]bre e lumi sieno uniti sa[n]za tratti o segni, a uso di fumo."
2. Clayton 1996–97, p. 133; Clayton 2002–3, p. 149.
3. Examination by Marjorie Shelley, Paper Conservator, The Metropolitan Museum of Art (April 10, 2002).

LEONARDO DA VINCI

109. *Rock Formations*

Charcoal or very soft black chalk, probably reworked with pale brown wash to unify some of the deeper shadows, 160 × 198 mm (6 5/16 × 7 13/16 in.), maximum, irregular shape
Lent by Her Majesty Queen Elizabeth II, Royal Library, Windsor Castle 12397

Provenance: Windsor Leoni volume: 1519, Francesco Melzi, Milan and Rome (1491/93–ca. 1570); ca. 1570, Orazio Melzi; by 1590, Pompeo Leoni, Madrid and Milan (ca. 1533–1608; Lugt under 2885); ca. 1613, Thomas Howard, second earl of Arundel (1586–1646); before 1690, British Royal Collection (inventory of King George III's collection, ca. 1810).

Literature: Berenson 1903, vol. 2, p. 67, no. 1260; Seidlitz 1911, p. 287, no. 778; Venturi 1919, p. 173, fig. 11 (printed in reverse); Venturi 1920, p. 110, fig. 72; Commissione Vinciana 1928– , vol. 6, p. 24, pl. 268.1; Popp 1928, pp. 14, 50, pl. 64; Sirén 1928, pl. 153; Berenson 1938, vol. 1, p. 182, vol. 2, p. 138, no. 1260; MacCurdy 1938, vol. 1, pl. 18; Castelfranco 1952a, pl. 30; Goldscheider 1952, pl. 55; Royal Academy of Arts 1952, no. 206 (hors catalogue); Heydenreich 1954, vol. 1, p. 143, vol. 2, p. 157, pl. 216; Gantner 1958, pp. 184, 186–88, fig. 37; Pedretti 1959, pl. 9; Berenson 1961, vol. 2, p. 244, no. 1260; Castelfranco 1966, p. 71, 118, 150; Clark and Pedretti 1968–69, vol. 1, p. 58, no. 12397; Clark 1969–70, p. 30, no. 122b; Pedretti and Clark 1980–81, p. 34, no. 8; Pedretti 1982a, pp. 46–50, no. 9 recto; Marani 1989, pp. 24–26, fig. 22; Popham 1994, no. 284B; Clayton 1996, pp. 132–36, no. 77; Letze and Buchsteiner 1997, p. 82; Marani 2000b, pp. 304–5.

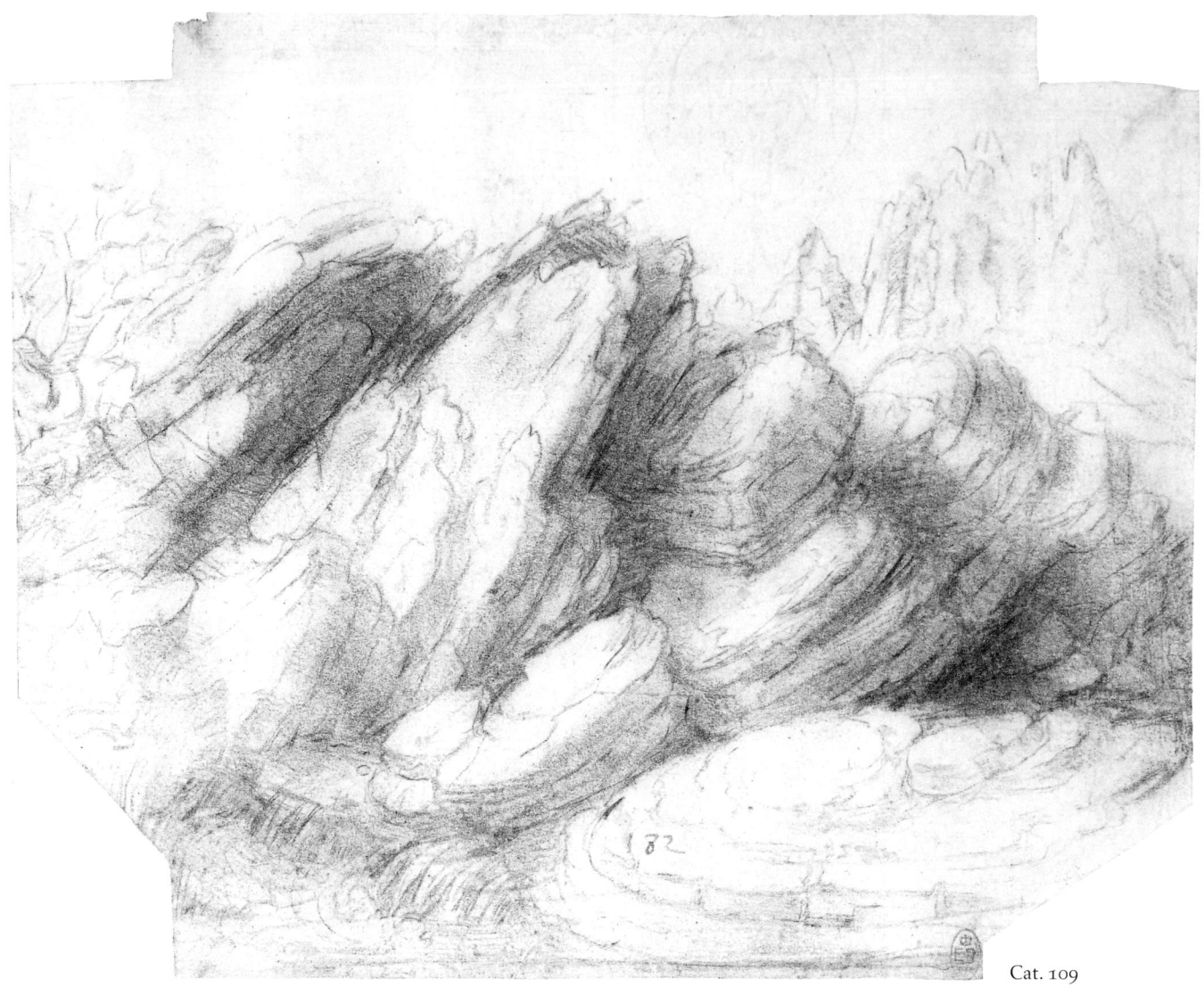

Cat. 109

Leonardo must have prepared the background landscape of the Louvre *Virgin and Child with Saint Anne* (fig. 23) in detailed and carefully rendered drawings such as this one, probably executed in plein air. On-site landscape drawings must have been much more numerous than what is now extant. Although the scale of some details is modified, the rocky landscape motif seen in this drawing can be connected with a passage in the background that is immediately to the left of Saint Anne's head in the oil painting (Clayton 1996). Leonardo also devoted considerable attention to a scientific study of rocks and to a retelling of their mythical origins, probably intending to compile his notes into an independent treatise on geology. Here, a great mass of rocks that seems to have burst forth from the earth and stratified as a diagonally slanting cluster spans the entire width of the middle ground of the sheet. It is an enormously dynamic compositional arrangement. As he often did in his late period, Leonardo selected only the main forms of the drawing to work up fully in sfumato technique—the imposing cluster of rocks at center is a breathtaking example of such pictorial calibration—leaving the rest of the forms only suggestively sketched. In the present drawing, small vertical peaks are lightly sketched in the depth of space toward the upper right, and these give a measure of the vast distance that Leonardo intended to suggest. In the foreground, close to the bottom border, the rocks are stratified horizontally, and from them a spring pours forth with a waterfall on the lower left.

CCB

LEONARDO DA VINCI

110. *Diagrams and Notes on Geometry; Allegorical Representations* (recto and verso)

Pen and dark brown ink, 294 × 206 mm (11 9/16 × 8 1/8 in.)
Inscribed on recto in pen and brown ink, in right-to-left script: *a b sono equali io po[n]ro dj sotto tal superfitie e ffaro la portione b c la / quale e doppia allo spatio o e djujdero p[er] equale essa portione b c ella / mettero in o coe jª portione intera equale a una meza erestera nel/lla medesima quantita dj pª dj poj io torro* [crossed out: *la*] *il settore o s equale allej / ella sopra porro* [crossed out: *a essa*] *colla sua portione alla portione o e cosj mj reste/ra la superfitie c e equale al* [triangle]*lo s essio rimetto* [crossed out: *e*] *la meza por/tione c inella co[n]caujta o io aro e o* [square]*to equale al* [triangle]*lo s.*; farther down: *io ho q[ueste] 3 superfitie equali inqua[n]tita le qualj sono . a b . he n p c b / he . f t . [p or e] io leuero n ello mettero in o eresta nella medesima / equalita . dj poi leuero p e tal superfitie ujene a ma[n]care desso p e co/si faro ma[n]care f t della sua portione f elleuero altrettanto alla / lunola che fia l e cosi restera[n] 3 superfitie equalj coe a b hel/l c c o.*; near center of sheet: *prima privato di moto che stanco / di giouare*; below that: *7 2 6 13*; under numbers: *manchera prima il moto che 'l giouame[n]to*; below emblem at left border: *prima morte che stanchezza——; no[n] mi sta[n]co nel giouare / è motto da carnovale;* [crossed out at left] *insatiabile serujtu;* [crossed out at right] *prima sta[n]cho chesso / tia dj serujre; no[n] mi satio di seruire;* in encircled emblem on left: *tutte le op[er]e, sine lassitudine, no[n] so[n] p[er] istancarmi;* in encircled emblem at center: *sine lassitudine;* at the right margin: *non mi stanco nel giouare;* at bottom left corner: *mani nelle quali fio/cca ducati e pietre p[r]e/tiose, queste mai si stu[n]/cano di seruire ma / tal seruitio e ssol p[er] sua vtilita e non e al no/stro proposito / naturalme[n]te / natura così mi dispone;* at lower border: *sine labore;* at bottom right corner: *sine lassitudine;* geometric studies inscribed with letters; on verso in pen and brown ink, in right-to-left script, vertically (from upper left corner down): *la intera por/tione fatta dj tu/ta la p[er]iffa dj g che / 1/16 dj tutto il suo cer/chio e simjle a 16 / portionj fatte dj / 16/16 del cerchio mj/nore a o. ; c e 2ˡᵃ al a coe tutto il suo cerchio onde la sua meta c / e pari a ttuto a e p[er] qvesto la sua meza portione n e /* [crossed out: *pari e] e pari a ttuta la portione* m *e ttuta la portione / n r e pari alle 2 portionj* m [with a line above] p [with a line above]. *Quando tu / tu faraj che g meza portione o 3ª e ffata dj piu por/tionj pichole nella sua p[er]iffa e che ttu possa provare tutte / esse portjonj essere equale attuta la portione* m *allo/ra leua vj a la portione* m *del suo sito e lleua / le piu portionj dellaltro sito g* [with a line above] *el rimane[n]te / del conjo sara pari al rimane[n]te del /* [circumscribed dot] *m ——.;* near center of upper border: *del ortogonjo* [crossed out: *il*] *dj / lati equali il cercio / che fatto su lipote/nissa vale li al/tri 2* [crossed out: *li*] *cerchi /*

fattj sulli altri / 2 lati [crossed out: *fatti*] */ del ortogonjo.;* within triangle: *i leuero vi/a il semjcirculo / al cerchio mjnore / e a cquello leuero le sua / 4 portionj el rimanente / resta* [square] *il quale* [square] *trarro della meta del cerchio / me[n]zano c. el suo rimane[n]te e pari alle 4 dette poʳ/tioni //. el simjle faro in* [crossed out: *d*] *nella meta dj d.;* to left: [crossed out: *". . ."*] *g e meza la portione g n / e co[n]tiene in se 4 portioni del / cerchio mjnore e jª portio/ne leueraj con tutta la cur/ua dj n che son 5 portionj / del cerchio mjnore che gliene / resta 3* [following the line that leads near the bottom of the right border] */ a esso mjnore cerchio e ttuto il suo resto e quadrato e* [square] *resta resta* [sic] *la piramjde / che rimane del g n colla parte rettilinja del* [triangle]*lo n il quale* [triangle]*lo e pari alle 3 / portionj che resstano del cerchio minore;* at upper right corner: *questa figura a b c d e f g h i . K e pari a / ttutto il cerchio a .p[er]che io* [crossed out: *lila*] *leuai al a* [following the line that leads upward] */* [crossed out: *8*] *le sue 8 portione elli rendo quj la portione b che co[n]tiene in se le dette 8 portionj del a / sequjta talj superfitie essere infalloro equali /. / tutto il cerchio a e pari al semjcirchulo / c e al 4° circhulo d e allottauo circhulo e onde* [crossed out: *a*] *la figura dj sotto a b c d e. ecc. e pari colla / sua parte* [square]*tu ul* [triangle]*lo e sanza. b e aguntole b detto k resta pari attutto h e.;* horizontally near bottom of sheet, from left to right and top to bottom: *verita / bugia / innoce[n]tia / malignita/ il sole, mascera / il foco distrugie* [crossed out: *la*] *la / bugia cioe il sofistico e / rende la uerita, scaccia[n]do / le teneb[r]e; la bugia mette mashera;* at lower left corner: *nulla ochulto sotto il sole;* [crossed out: *". . ."*] *Il foco e messo p[er] la verita, p[er]che destrug/ge o[g]ni soffistico e bugiu ella ma/scera [maschera?] p[er] la falsita e bugia ——, to right: ochultatrice del / uero.——;* in center: *verita; Il foco destrugie ogni soffistico c[i]oe lo [in]ga[n]no/ e ssol ma[n]tiene la verita c[i]oe l'oro. /* [unfinished word: *soffi (soffistico)*]*/ La uerita al fine no[n] si cela / no[n] ual simula[tione] simulatio[n] e fru/strata ava[n]ti a ta[n]to / giudice.;* at lower right corner: *Il foco e da essere messo p[er] co[n]suma/tore d'ogni sofistico e scopri/tore e dimostratore di uerita / p[er]che lui* [crossed out: *". . ."*] *e luce scaccia/tore delle teneb[r]e ochultatri/ci d'ogni essentia.;* geometric studies inscribed with letters and calculations

Lent by Her Majesty Queen Elizabeth II, Royal Library, Windsor Castle 12700

PROVENANCE: Windsor Leoni volume: 1519, Francesco Melzi, Milan and Rome (1491/93–ca. 1570); ca. 1570, Orazio Melzi; by 1590, Pompeo Leoni, Madrid and Milan (ca. 1533–1608; Lugt under 2885); ca. 1613, Thomas Howard, second earl of Arundel (1586–1646); before 1690, British Royal Collection (inventory of King George III's collection, ca. 1810).

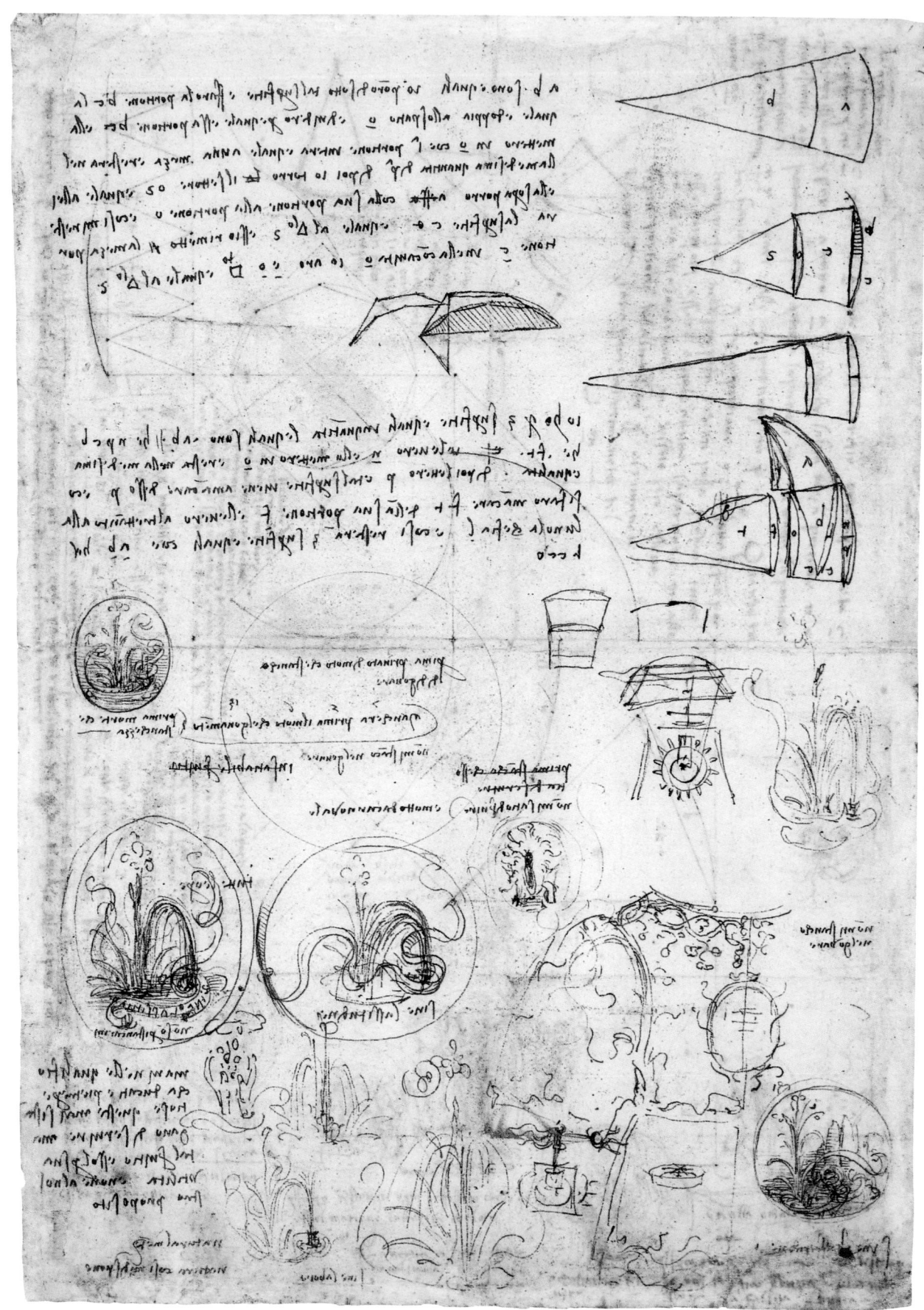

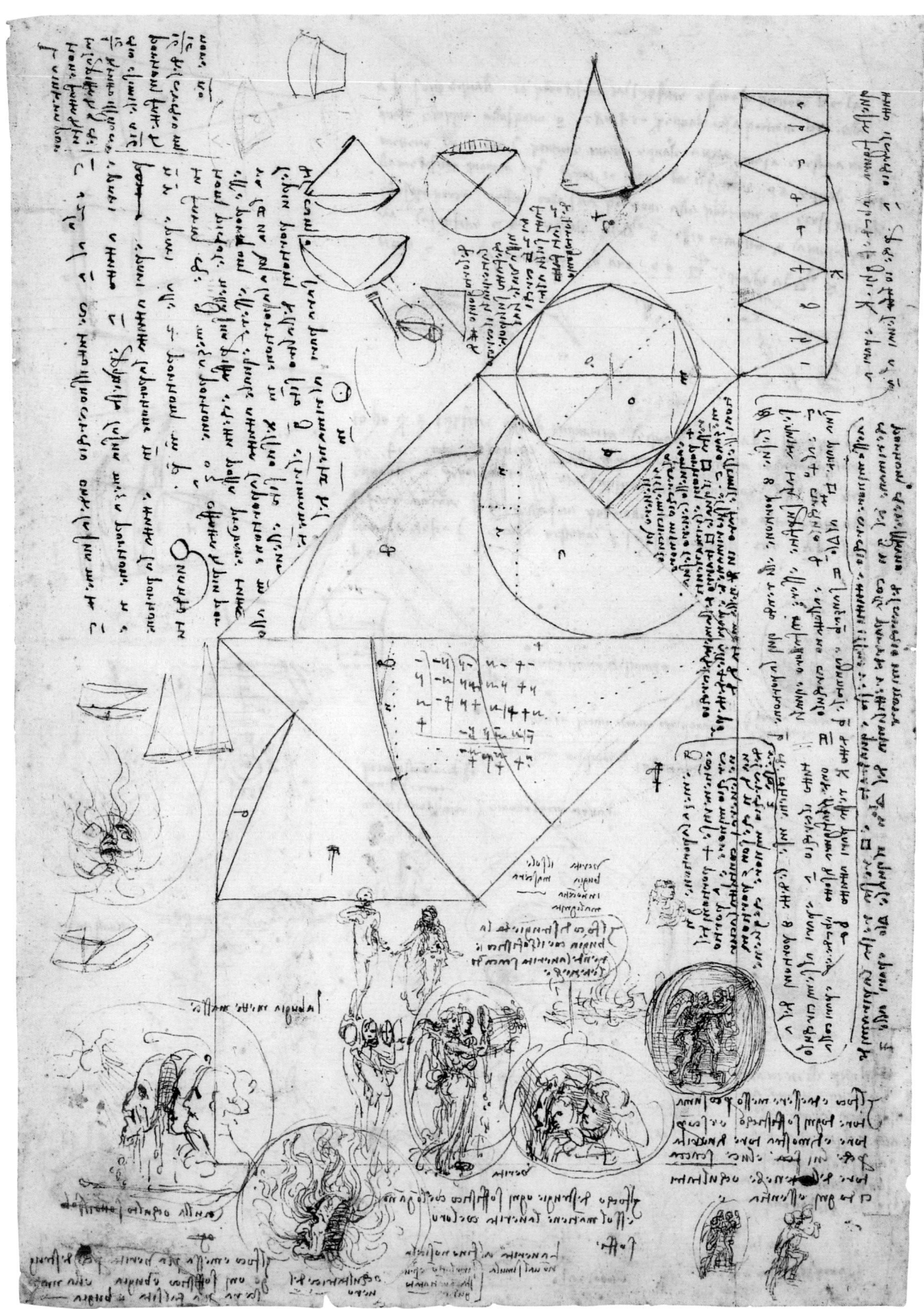

Literature: Richter 1883, vol. 1, pp. 356–57, nos. 684–85, pl. 63; Berenson 1903, vol. 2, p. 62, no. 1121; Seidlitz 1911, p. 289, nos. 848, 849; Solmi 1912, p. 509 n. 2; Commissione Vinciana 1928– , vol. 5, p. 22, pls. 193, 194; Bing 1937–38, pl. 47c; Berenson 1938, vol. 2, p. 124, no. 1121; Giglioli 1944, pl. 134; Reti 1959, pp. 42–54, pl. 7; Berenson 1961, vol. 2, p. 220, no. 1121; Clark and Pedretti 1968–69, vol. 1, pp. 177–79, no. 12700; Richter 1970, vol. 1, pp. 388–89 n., nos. 684–85, pl. 63; Gentile 1980, pp. 163–68; Kemp 1981, pp. 281–82, pl. 77; Pedretti 1982a, pp. 92, 114–15, figs. 67, 99–100; Kemp 1989a, pp. 244–45; Caroli 1991, p. 104; Popham 1994, no. 113 (verso); Clayton 1996–97, p. 109, under no. 59.

Although done in close succession, the diagrams and notes on geometry probably preceded the allegorical representations on this double-sided sheet. More so than many others, the complex sketches of emblems on both sides of the sheet illustrate Leonardo's "brainstorm" technique of composing images by variations of design, where one idea after another pours onto the paper. On the recto, below the diagrams and notes on geometry, at least six sketches take on the theme of a flower intertwined with a scroll inside a circle or oval. The flower has been identified as a lily (*Iris florentina* or fleur-de-lis). The motif in the extreme left is labeled "death before weariness" (*prima morte che stanchezza*), and other inscriptions allude similarly to the virtues of loyal service and constancy; here the motto "sine lassitudine" (without weariness) appears three times. The devices were clearly intended for a patron, and Leonardo explained much of their meaning in several lines of text toward the center of the page (here given in condensed form): "First deprived of movement than weary of being useful. Movement will fail sooner than usefulness. . . . I do not satiate from serving. . . . No labor is sufficient to tire me. Hands into which ducats and precious stones fall like snow, these [hands] never become tired of serving, but this service is only for its utility and is not to be for our purposes."

The emblems on the verso offer variations on the theme of Truth (*verita*) triumphant over Falsehood (*bugia*), who is represented by a mask. Within the cameos, Leonardo drew the beautiful, sinuous female figure of Truth holding the mask of Falsehood against the sun or flames, symbolizing the destruction of Falsehood by fire or light. The device toward the center of the left border portrays the mask of Falsehood burnt by flames as a close-up detail within the circular frame. As Leonardo explained in four paragraphs of notes toward the lower right of the verso (here given in condensed form): "Fire destroys falsehood, that is, sophistry, and reveals truth, dispelling the darkness. Fire is to be represented as the destroyer of all sophistry, and as the discoverer and demonstrator of truth, because it [fire] is light, the expeller of the darkness that obscures all essence. . . . Fire . . . maintains truth alone, that is, gold. Truth at last cannot be hidden. . . . Dissimulation is of no avail. Dissimulation fails before so great a judge. Falsehood puts on a mask."

The dating of the sheet presents some difficulty. Although the expressive figural sketches seem too abstract to rely entirely on the evidence of their drawing style and technique, comparisons can be made to the thumbnail sketches of figures for the Trivulzio monument on the lower right of catalogue number 111, from 1508–12. The iconography of the allegorical motifs offers little guidance, since such subject matter turns up in Leonardo's drawings from the late 1470s until his death in 1519 (see also cat. nos. 31 verso, 54). However, the evidence that Kenneth Clark and Carlo Pedretti rightly adduced—the paper, handwriting, ink, and diagrams of geometry—seems to confirm a dating of the Windsor sheet in 1508–9, and various comparisons can be made to the Codex Atlanticus, the Paris Ms. K, and the Codex Arundel. The Codex Leicester (cat. no. 114) offers another important touchstone for the question of the Windsor drawing's date. The dates proposed by previous scholars have ranged from about 1498 to 1502, the most significant hypothesis being that of Ladislao Reti, who related the emblems to Cesare Borgia, Leonardo's employer in 1502–3. (See Chronology.) According to A. E. Popham, this and the related drawings of allegories and emblems (Windsor, RL 12497, 12701) date to 1498. At least two of the cameos portrayed in this sheet seem to be inspired by antique gems.

CCB

LEONARDO DA VINCI

111. *Sketches for a Funerary Equestrian Monument to Gian Giacomo Trivulzio*

Pen and medium brown ink on coarse-fiber, buff or light tan paper,
278 × 198 mm (10 $\frac{15}{16}$ × 7 $\frac{13}{16}$ in.)
Lent by Her Majesty Queen Elizabeth II, Royal Library, Windsor
Castle 12355

PROVENANCE: Windsor Leoni volume: 1519, Francesco Melzi,
Milan and Rome (1491/93–ca. 1570); ca. 1570, Orazio Melzi; by
1590, Pompeo Leoni, Madrid and Milan (ca. 1533–1608; Lugt
under 2885); ca. 1613, Thomas Howard, second earl of Arundel
(1586–1646); before 1690, British Royal Collection (inventory of
King George III's collection, ca. 1810).

LITERATURE: Grosvenor Gallery 1878, vol. 2, p. 28; Richter 1883,
vol. 2, p. 6, pl. 66; Geymüller 1886, p. 161; Müller-Walde 1897,
pp. 108, 129, 131; Müller-Walde 1899, pp. 87 (bottom left), 92, 93
(left), 94 (bottom), 107, fig. 92; Venturi 1901–39, vol. 10, part 1,
fig. 55 (incorrect inv. no., as 12353), vol. 11, part 1, fig. 37; Berenson
1903, vol. 1, p. 155, vol. 2, p. 66, no. 1212; Seidlitz 1909, pl. 29;
Seidlitz 1911, p. 283, no. 606; Malaguzzi Valeri 1913–23, vol. 2,
p. 451, fig. 490; Meller 1916, pp. 219–20, no. 2; Poggi 1919, pl. 83;
Beltrami 1920, p. 84; Malaguzzi Valeri 1922, pp. 66–67, fig. 35;
Popp 1926–27, pp. 53, 60, no. 55; Commissione Vinciana 1928–,
vol. 6, p. 24, pl. 275.2; Popp 1928, pp. 8, 26, 42, no. 37; Sirén 1928,
p. 69, pl. 88; Suida 1929, p. 71, fig. 72; Bodmer 1931, pp. 324, 416;
Baroni 1935–39, fig. 60; Berenson 1938, vol. 1, p. 173, vol. 2, p. 134,
vol. 3, fig. 492, no. 1212; Palazzo dell'Arte 1939, p. 155; Royal
Academy of Arts 1952, p. 6, no. 182; Brugnoli 1954, pp. 365–66,
pl. 148, fig. 3; Clark 1954, pl. 42; Gould 1954b, p. 191; Heydenreich
1954, vol. 1, pp. 69–70, 134, vol. 2, p. 78, pl. 102; Maltese 1954,
p. 348, pl. 139, fig. 23; Heydenreich 1958b, col. 573, pl. 174;
Goldscheider 1959, pp. 179–80, pl. 111; Berenson 1961, vol. 1,
p. 253, vol. 2, p. 237, vol. 3, fig. 519, no. 1212; Chastel 1961, p. 13;
Pedretti 1962, pp. 61–64, fig. 26; Heydenreich 1965, figs. 2, 4b, 5b;
Castelfranco 1966, pp. 192–94, 238, figs. 43, 43; Clark and Pedretti
1968–69, vol. 1, pp. 43–44, no. 12355; Richter 1970, vol. 2, pl. 66;
Brugnoli 1974, p. 99, figs. 99/1, 99/2; Gould 1975, pp. 144–45, fig.
79; Visconti 1980, p. 108; Brugnoli 1982, pp. 98, 100–101, figs. 65,
66; Pedretti and Roberts 1984, p. 63, no. 35, colorpl. 10; Wasserman
1984, pp. 21–23, fig. 14; Pedretti 1987a, pp. 101–2, no. 133 recto;
Clark 1988, pp. 218–27, fig. 100; Agghházy 1989, p. 32, fig. 19; Martin
Clayton in Montreal Museum of Fine Arts 1992, no. 13; Cunnally
1993, p. 75, fig. 17; Marani 1994, p. 19; Popham 1994, no. 91; Clayton
1996–97, pp. 113–17, no. 64; Arasse 1998, pp. 251–52, fig. 185;
Marani 2000b, pp. 279–81; Ames-Lewis 2001b, p. 14, no. 28.

The classification of Leonardo's preliminary drawings for
equestrian monuments has caused considerable (and at
times chaotic) debate in the scholarly literature, and none
more so than the group of sketches and studies that can be
connected with Leonardo's second project for an equestrian
statue, that of Gian Giacomo Trivulzio. Scholars now unanimously agree that the present drawing was intended for the
Trivulzio project, especially on account of its drawing style
and technique. Yet this connection was not always so clear to
early scholars of Leonardo, and in 1926–27, for instance, the
able connoisseur Anny Popp still considered the present drawing to have been preparatory for Leonardo's first equestrian
project, the monument to Francesco Sforza, dating it to 1498.

Leonardo seems to have worked on the Trivulzio monument during his second Milanese period, from about 1508
until 1512, when the French domination of Milan came to an
end and he was forced to flee the city (see Chronology). The
project is entirely undocumented, other than a detailed but
undated note listing the materials and costs of making "the
funerary monument of *messer* Giovanni Jacomo da Trevulzo,"
written in Leonardo's hand.[1] The sheets of preliminary studies
related to the Sforza equestrian monument (see cat. nos. 53,
63, 64; figs. 166, 167) can now be dated more or less easily
within the period 1483 to 1495, based on drawing style and
technique. This dating is further supported by the evidence of
Leonardo's notes and other written sources. Quite the opposite
is true of the remaining sheets of equestrian subjects at
Windsor that exhibit a much later, and very disparate, drawing
style and technique. These sheets have recently been reassigned
to two groups, those pertaining to the Trivulzio equestrian
statue, and those pertaining to a third, much later equestrian
monument presumably done by Leonardo in his French period,
that is, in 1517–19.[2] The hypothesis of a third, French-period
equestrian monument (see cat. no. 118) seems extremely convincing on the basis of drawing style and technique, despite a
lack of supporting documents, while the group of drawings that is
now associated with the Trivulzio monument seems more
consistent.[3] As here, a few of the Trivulzio sheets are executed
in pen and a rather dark brown iron gall ink, with a somewhat
heavy-handed curved hatching technique, on coarse-fiber paper.

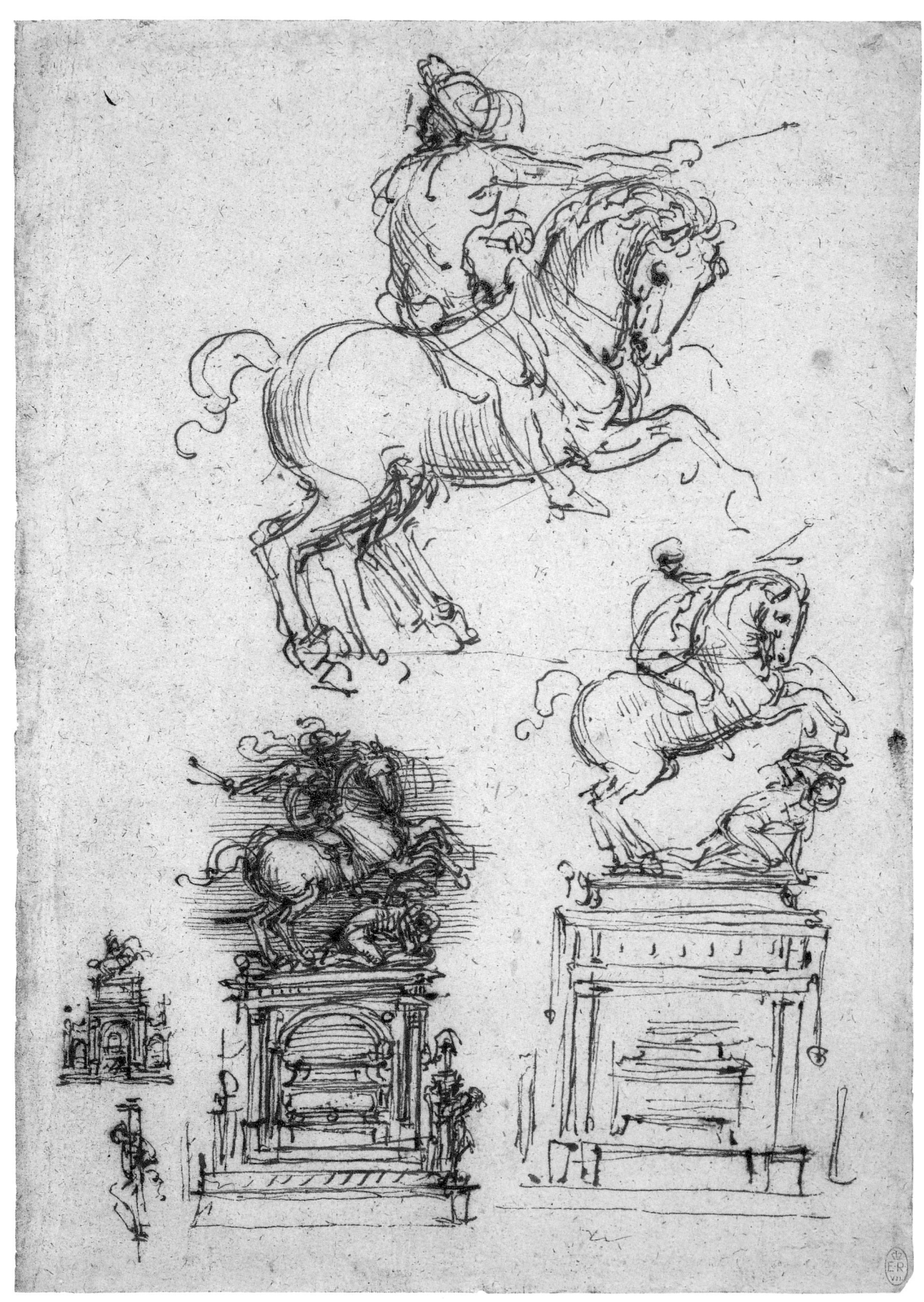

Cat. 111

The Milanese mercenary general Gian Giacomo Trivulzio (1441–1518) had led the French troops of King Louis XII that invaded Milan in 1499 (see Chronology). During the twelve years of the French occupation of Milan, Trivulzio rose in the ranks to become marshal of France, then marquis of Vigevano, and, after the death of Charles d'Amboise, governor of Milan, in 1511, joint governor with Gaston de Foix. Trivulzio's will of February 22, 1507, made provisions for a tomb and funerary chapel in the church of San Nazaro in Milan, and it can be assumed that Leonardo's preliminary drawings soon followed (whether these were commissioned or not). A document suggests that the actual building of the chapel began in 1511, to the design of Bramantino. It specifies that the horse and rider were to be lifesize (*grande al naturale*), but it does not mention Leonardo's involvement with the project.

Leonardo's list of costs for the materials and the labor of making the Trivulzio funerary monument breaks down expenses into three parts: for the casting of the lifesize horse and rider, for the cost of the marble, and for the carving of the marble. Although it is not specified, the metal of the horse and rider was surely to be bronze, judging from the materials of the models and the type of casting that were involved, as well as from the fact that the laborers polishing the metal sculptures were to be paid a considerable sum. From the list, it can also be deduced that the monumental marble base had opulent classical details (with some metal accents), a lifesize effigy reclining on a sarcophagus, eight figures, festoons and other ornaments, as well as six harpies bearing candelabra. More vividly than the list, the sketches on the lower half of the present sheet can suggest the grandeur of Leonardo's initial conception for the mausoleum. This sheet is also among the most informative drawings regarding Leonardo's ideas for the project, although the animated sketches portray the rider on a horse that is still in a rearing pose. In the final phase of design, and as with the Sforza monument, Leonardo would settle for a striding horse, in the majestic pose of such antique models as the so-called *Regisole* (now destroyed, but in Leonardo's time in the main square at Pavia) and Renaissance precursors like Donatello's *Gattamelata* or Andrea del Verrocchio's *Bartolommeo Colleoni* (figs. 125, 162). A red-chalk drawing, reworked with pen and dark brown ink, also at Windsor (fig. 197), shows Leonardo's final design, Trivulzio on a striding horse. Presumably the last that the artist prepared for the project, it shows an equestrian statue surmounting an elaborate antique-style base—not unlike the façade of a building or triumphal arch—which

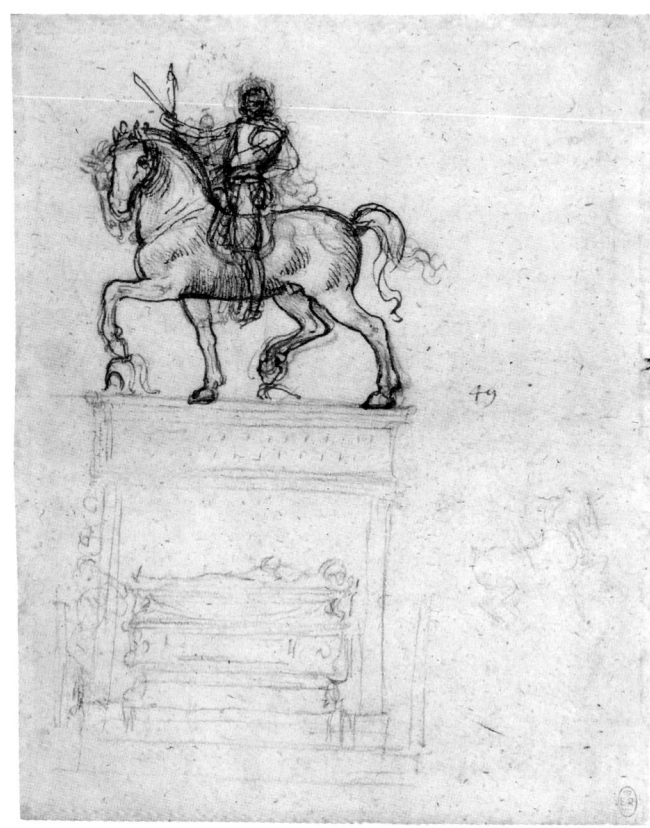

Fig. 197. Leonardo da Vinci, *Study for an Equestrian Monument*. Pen and brown ink, red chalk, 217 × 169 mm. The Royal Collection, H.M. Queen Elizabeth II, Windsor Castle RL 12356

housed the sarcophagus; on the sides stood the carved figures of captives shackled to columns, a motif that is reminiscent of the bound slaves on Michelangelo's project for the marble tomb of Pope Julius II (begun about 1506). The lower half of the present sheet offers three separate solutions for the elaborate architecture of the base, although it is not clear whether the design, at this stage of planning, was still for a freestanding monument, or whether the solutions here already imply the final intention of a wall tomb.   CCB

1. C.A., fol. 492r (formerly fol. 179v-a); Richter 1970, vol. 2, pp. 9–10, no. 725: "Sepulcro di messer Giovanni Jacomo da Trevulzo."
2. Clayton 1996–97, pp. 141–42.
3. In the author's opinion, the drawings to be connected with the Trivulzio equestrian monument are as follows: Windsor RL 12343, 12353, 12353A, 12355 (cat. no. 111), and 12356 (fig. 197). Although Martin Clayton connected RL 12343 with the French equestrian monument (Clayton 1996–97, pp. 142–49, no. 85), the sketch seems to me quite closely related in technique to RL 12356, which is considered to be one of the canonical Trivulzio drawings (Clayton 1996–97, pp. 113–17, fig. 16; Kemp and Roberts 1989, p. 68, no. 16).

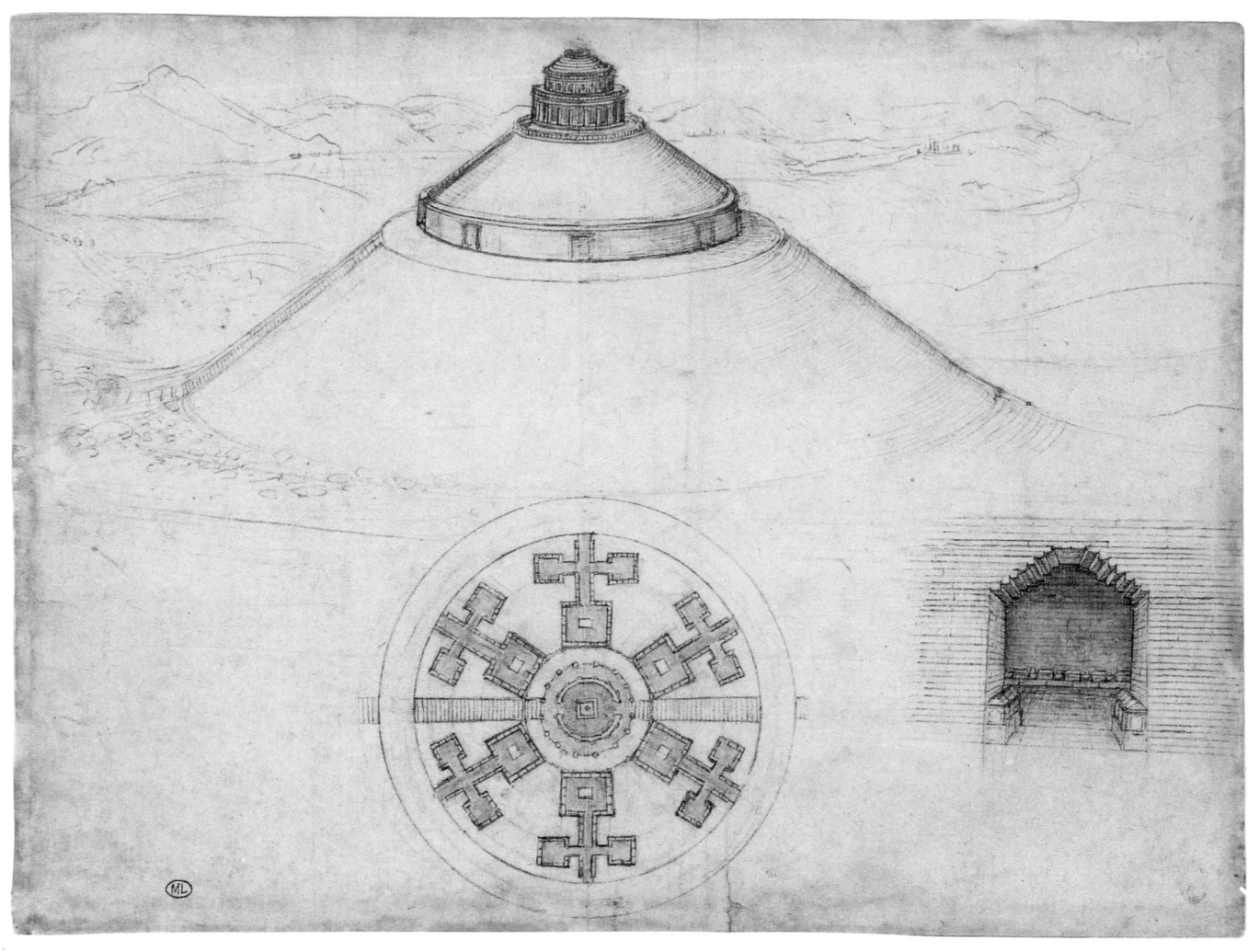

LEONARDO DA VINCI

112. *Project for a Mausoleum with Central Plan; Elevation, Plan, and Detail of a Funerary Chamber*

Pen and brown ink, brush and brown wash, on an underdrawing in black chalk, for the mausoleum; black-chalk wash for the funerary chamber; incised compass lines and traces of stylus for the plan, the funerary chamber, and the elevation axis, 199 × 267 mm (7⅞ × 10½ in.); on verso, three traces of vertical folds
Département des Arts Graphiques du Musée du Louvre, Paris 2386

PROVENANCE: Giuseppe Vallardi (Lugt 1223, in green on verso); 1856, acquired by the Musée du Louvre; museum mark (Lugt 1886a).

LITERATURE: Richter 1883, vol. 2, pp. 58–59, pl. 98; Geymüller 1886, vol. 2, p. 279; Müntz 1899, p. 521, no. 62; Seidlitz 1909, vol. 1, fig. p. 126 (with incorrect location); Poggi 1919, pl. 188, p. lxxiv; Sartoris 1952, p. 133, repr. p. 120; Chastel 1959, 1982, p. 69 and n. 6, repr. fig. 24 (attributed to Francesco di Giorgio); Heydenreich 1969, p. 146, fig. 24; Monnier 1972, no. 8; Jacob 1975, under no. 9 (Giuliano da Sangallo); Martelli 1977, pp. 58–61; Carpiceci 1978,

figs. 32, 43, 124, 130, 145, 224, p. 164; Musée National Message Biblique Marc Chagall 1982, no. 96; Galluzzi 1987; Guillaume 1987, p. 251, pl. 19; Pedretti 1988e, pp. 122–23; Kemp and Roberts 1989, no. 117; Pedretti 1989c, p. 129; Cristofani 1992, p. 276; Parronchi 1992, p. 103, fig. 6; Petrioli Tofani 1992, no. 11.1; Arasse 1997, p. 180, fig. 117; Bartoloni, forthcoming.

Giuseppe Vallardi's description and commentary[1] were adopted by Jean Paul Richter, who recognized an Etruscan "inspiration" behind the drawing. In spite of that, the attribution to Leonardo was refuted several times by art historians, who preferred to see the drawing as a work by Francesco di Giorgio or Giuliano da Sangallo. Today, this design for a mausoleum is no longer the subject of debate, primarily because the work of Marina Martelli (1977) and, very recently, Gilda Bartoloni (forthcoming) has made it possible to assess its innovative character and "archaeological" relevance.

A large tumulus stands in the center of the sheet with a round temple at its summit. Two stairways rise on opposite sides and, two-thirds of the way up, give access to six Latin-cross–shaped tombs, shown in the plan in the foreground. On the right is the cross section of a funerary chamber. Martelli has demonstrated that the drawing is related to an archaeological discovery in the early years of the sixteenth century in Tuscany in territory under the control of the Florentine Republic. A tumulus was discovered by chance on January 29, 1507, in Montecalvario near Castellina in the Chianti Mountains. At the summit of the hill stood a chapel, later destroyed, which Leonardo has re-created in his own way by the placement of the round temple. The background landscape of hills and a lake could be identifiable as the site at Castellina.[2]

The account of the discovery of the tumulus was given in several sixteenth-century sources, which describe the subterranean chamber as "twenty arms long, five high, and three wide." Francesco Giambullari, writing in 1546, and Santi Marmocchini, a scholar studying the Tuscan language, between 1541 and 1545,[3] enumerated the objects, statues, ornaments, and inscriptions that were found and that offered, for the first time, a genuine view into Etruscan civilization. The extraordi-

nary aspect of the ancient tomb lay in the fact that the vault was made up of successive overhangs, precisely the way Leonardo has shown the ceiling in his cross section of a funerary chamber. Bartoloni adds that even the layout of the urns and vases placed on the ledges corresponds to Marmocchini's description.

The technique of the drawing and its precision, the pen lines in the shaded area and in the landscape, and the preparation in stylus are all factors arguing for an unreserved attribution to Leonardo, although we do not know the circumstances under which he learned of the plans or notes relating to the Etruscan tomb.[4] Leonardo's presence in Florence in September 1507, upon his return from Milan, suggests that he may have seen the tomb site itself, which had been discovered the same year — whereas Francesco di Giorgio (one of the other artists to whom this work has been attributed) had been dead since 1502.

FV

1. Vallardi 1855, p. 39, fol. 182 (Leonardo da Vinci): "sopra carta bianca eseguito a penna ed a aquarello, offre il progetto di un grandioso monumento sepolcrale ad ordine jonico che s'innalza sopra un'artificiale collina di forma conica, cui si accede per scale laterali; il fondo del paese è montuoso con un laghetto. — Sotto havvi la relativa pianta e lo spaccato della cella. / Alto poll. 7.6. largo poll. 10.4. Questo pensiero comprova, como il Vinci fosse originale e grandioso anche ne' disegni architettonici monumentali."
2. Martelli 1977, fig. 2.
3. Martelli 1977, n. 10; Bartoloni, forthcoming.
4. See Martelli 1977, n. 15.

LEONARDO DA VINCI

113. *A Dead or Moribund Man in Bust Length; a Detail of the Jaw and Neck; the Muscular and Vascular Systems of the Shoulder and Arm* (recto)
Detail Section of the Mouth and Throat; the Muscular System of the Shoulder and Arm (verso)

Pen and dark brown ink, brush and brown wash, over leadpoint or black chalk on cream-white paper, 288 × 199 mm (11 3/8 × 7 7/8 in.) Inscribed in pen and brown ink on recto, in right-to-left script (from top to bottom) on left: *fighura p^a li musscholi del / chollo* [crossed out: *che*] *e spalla eppetto essoc/to lasella che movano lasspalla / poi li musscoli della spalla che / movano losso dellaiutorio ——— / dj poi li musscholi dellaiutori/o che pieghano e voltano il . b[raccio] . / e* [crossed out: *vltimo li*] *poi li musscholj / del . b[rac-cio] . che movano la mano elli / musscholi che movano lidjtj; vena basilicha; della vena m e si parte la vena e b / Laqual djsscende insino dal e al b / doue il . b[raccio] . sisspicha . dal pecto dal qual/le locho b sisspicha il ramo essiramj/ficha* [crossed out: *per la*

poppo da] infralla pelle el/la charne della poppa [crossed out: *el eess] eari / scontro nassce il ramo b il qual sira / mjficha infralla carne ella pelle della / paletta della sspatola sotto acqueste na/scie lauenu c che siramjficha infralla / charne ella pelle che uesste lecosste dallato / alquanto dj sotto s nassce lauena o che[n]/entra infral pessche del bracco ella sua / pelle ella uena maesstra donde tali ra/mjficationj si partano s[i] djmanda la basilicha;* anatomical studies inscribed with letters; at lower right corner by a sixteenth-century hand: *3;* at lower left corner by a sixteenth-century hand: *.Ma.;* on verso in pen and brown ink, in right-to-left script (from top to bottom, and left to right), at top: *Li principali ellj maggori ellj piu potentj musscholj chessieno nelluomo sono le sue natiche*

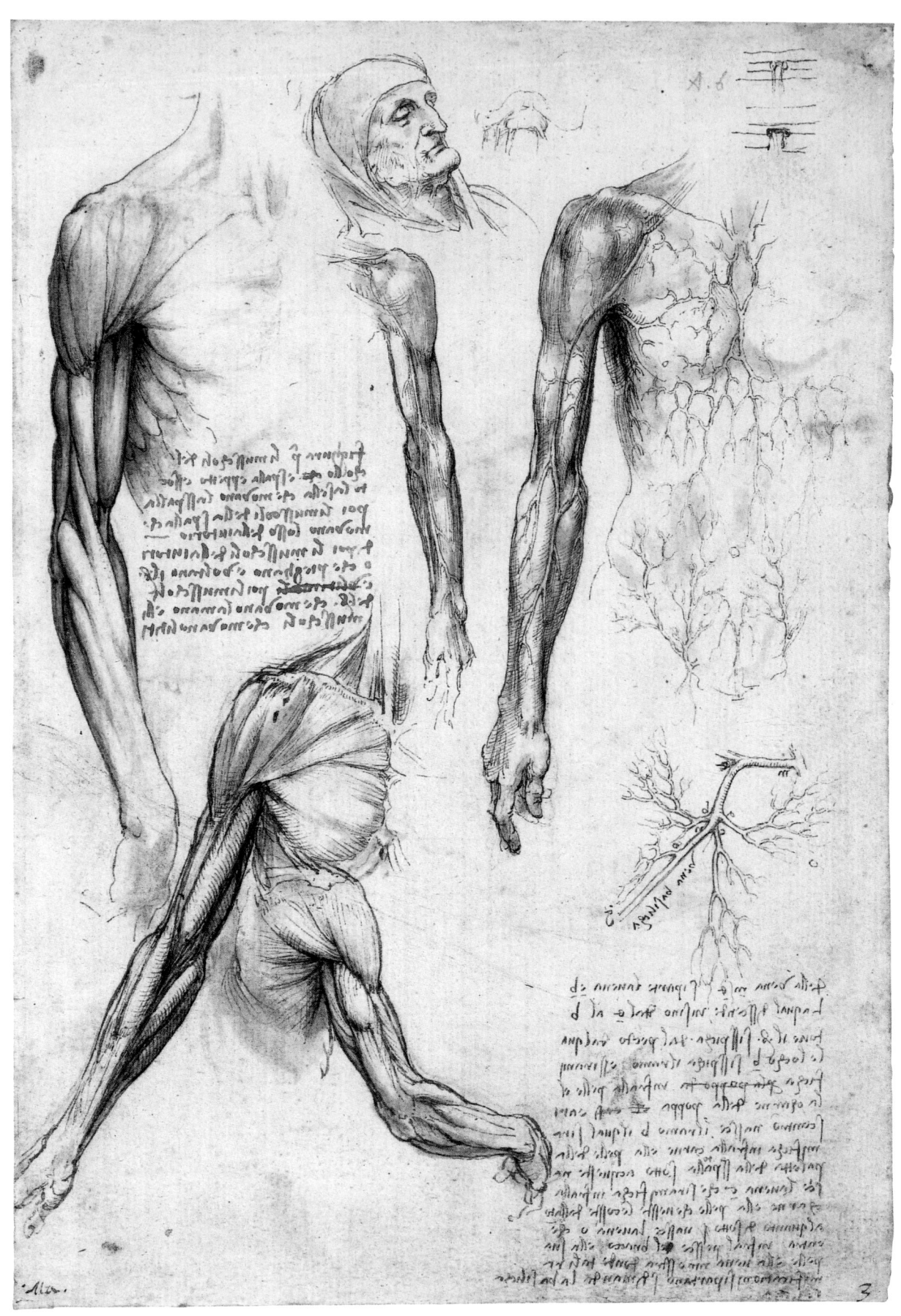

Cat. 113R

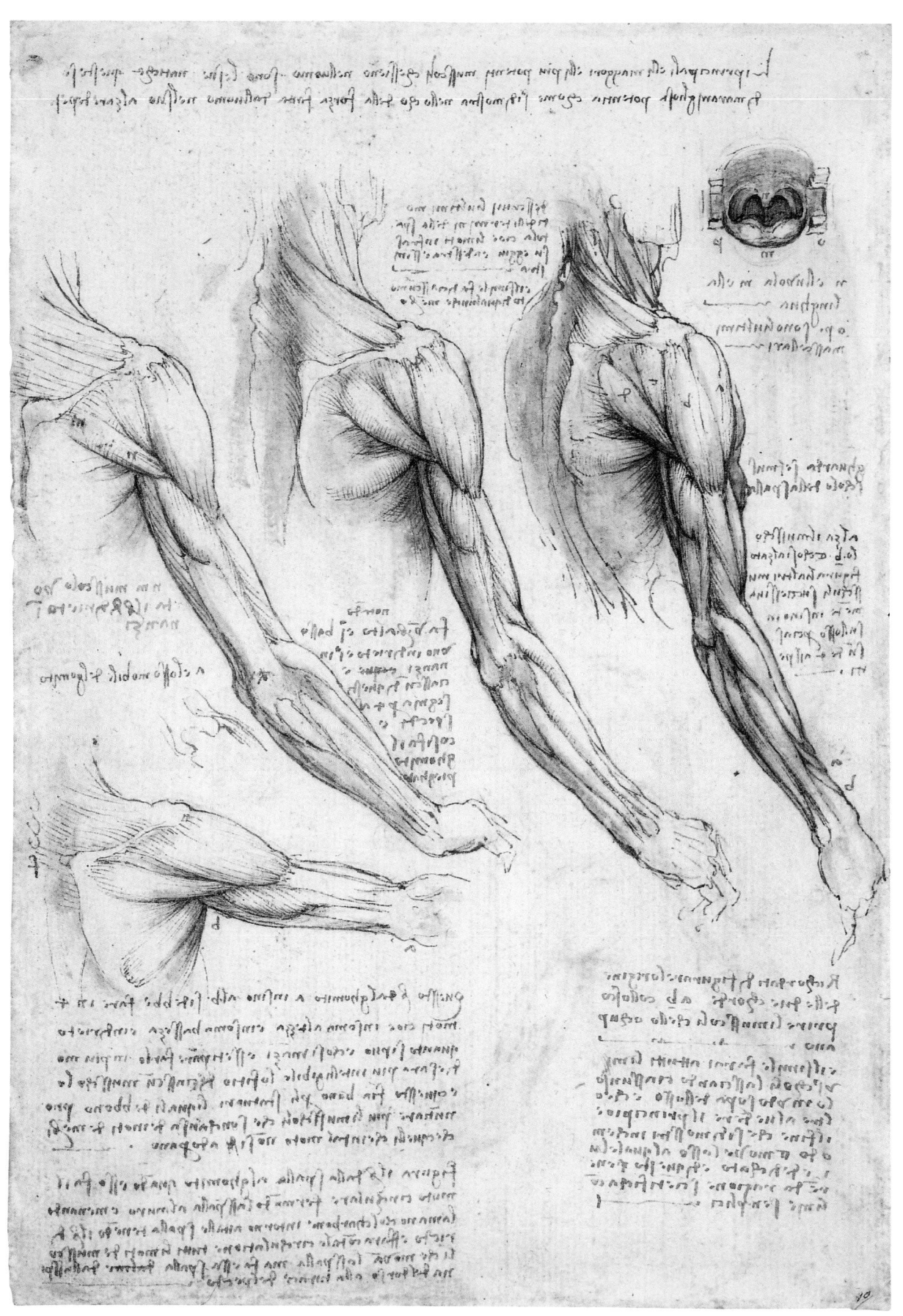

Cat. 113v

queste so[no] / dj maraujgliosa potentia chome sidjmostra nello cho della forza fatta dalluomo nel suo alzare de pesi; below at center: *desscriuj li ultimj mo/ti delli termjnj della spa/tola cioe li moti infras/su eggiu eadesstra essinj/stra—— / eilsimjle fa dj ciasscu[n] mo/to dj qualunche me[n]b[r]o;* at right border: *n elluvola m ella / linghua —— / o p . sono liultimj / masscellari ——;* at center of left border: *n m musscolo vo[l]/ta il b[raccio] dj djrietro j[n]/nanzi; a e losso mobile delgomjto;* at center: *nota[n]do/ fa v[n] . b[raccio] . alto e j° basso / vno indjrieto e j° in/nanzi* [crossed out: *e cque*] *e / ciasscu[n] dj questj / segnja p[er] 4 as/pectj e / cosi fa il / ghomjto / pieghato;* at the center of the right border: *ghuarda sel mus/cholo della spalla / alza il musscho/lo . b . e chosi alzato / figura li altri mu/sschulj successiua/me[n]te insino in / sullosso p[er]cias/s [c]u[n] de 4 asspe/ttj ——;* at bottom left corner: *Questo b[raccio] dal ghomito a insino al . b si debbe fare in 4 / motj cioe in soma altezza e in soma bassezza e indjrieto / quanto si puo echosi ina[n]zi essetipa[n]re farlo in piu mo/dj e sara piu intelligibile lofitio dj ciasscu[n] musschulo / e cquessto fia bono per li statuari liqualj debbono pro/nu[n]tiare piu limusscholj che sonchausa demotj de me[n]bri / che cquellj cheintal moto no[n]si* [crossed out: *d*] *adoprano . ——.; figura il b[raccio] dalla spalla al ghomjto qua[n]do esso fa il / moto circulare ferma[n]do lasspalla al muro emenando / lamano chol charbone intorno attale spalla tene[n]do il b[raccio] dj/ricto effara co[n]tale circhulatione tutti li moti de mussco/li che mova[n] lasspalla ma fa essa spalla* [crossed out: *dalame*] *dallasspi/na del dorso alla turace del pecto ——.;* at lower right corner: *Richordati dj figurare lorigine / delle due chorde* a b *collosco/prire limusscoli chello ochup/ano —— / e il simile farai attutti li m*[crossed out: *j*]*/vscholi lasscianda ciass[c]un so/lo invdo sopra dellosso e che o/ltre al uedere il principio e / il fine che si djmosstri in che m/odo e move losso al quale lu/i dedjchato e dj questo se ne / re[n]da ragione scie[n]tificha co[n] / linje senplici —— .;* anatomical studies inscribed with letters
Lent by Her Majesty Queen Elizabeth II, Royal Library, Windsor Castle 19005

PROVENANCE: Windsor Leoni volume: 1519, Francesco Melzi, Milan and Rome (1491/93–ca. 1570); ca. 1570, Orazio Melzi; by 1590, Pompeo Leoni, Madrid and Milan (ca. 1533–1608; Lugt under 2885); ca. 1613, Thomas Howard, second earl of Arundel (1586–1646); before 1690, British Royal Collection (inventory of King George III's collection, ca. 1810).

LITERATURE: Müntz 1898, vol. 2, p. 49 (verso); Müntz 1899, p. 309; Poggi 1919, pl. 165; O'Malley and Saunders 1952, pp. 130–35, nos. 45, 47; Esche 1954, pp. 104–5, figs. 105, 159; Heydenreich 1954, vol. 1, pp. 128, 169, vol. 2, p. 140, pl. 194; Clark and Pedretti 1968–69, vol. 3, p. 4, no. 19005; Keele 1976, pp. 42–43, no. 16; Royal Academy of Arts 1977, pp. 83–84, nos. 25A, 25B; Woodburne 1978, pp. 72, 316; Keele and Pedretti 1979–80, vol. 2, pp. 516–21, no. 141; Keele and Roberts 1983, pp. 95–97, nos. 25A, 25B; Philo 1985, pp. 115, 137, 101–27; Kemp and Roberts 1989, p. 172, no. 95; Clayton and Philo 1992, pp. 96–98, no. 15A, pp. 99–101, no. 15B; Arasse 1998, pp. 125–27, 274, 276, figs. 70, 195; Zwijnenberg 1999, pp. 167–70.

Toward the upper border of the recto is a reclining, gaunt old man with closed eyes and wearing a hood. He was probably the subject who was dissected for the myological and vascular studies of the arm in the lower portions of the recto and verso of this impressive double-sided sheet. On the recto, following his practice of drawing from right to left, Leonardo probably first undertook to represent the superficial dissection of the arms and torso at the upper right, showing a magnificent view of the courses of the various veins (cephalic, median, basilic, external and internal mammary, thoraco-epigastric, and superficial epigastric). The breathtaking accuracy of the rendition of the old man's veins—Leonardo had elsewhere noted that the veins of old men grow twisted in the manner of a snake—sharply contrasts with the fanciful abstraction seen in catalogue number 57, which is largely based on the writings of Galen (ca. A.D. 130–200/210), the most celebrated of the ancient Greek medical writers, and Avicenna (980–1037), the great Arab philosopher and physician. On the lower right, Leonardo portrayed an exquisitely drawn enlarged detail of the configuration of the basilic and axillary veins (as well as their tributaries), adding, immediately below, a paragraph description of the subject. He may then have proceeded to portray the superficial dissections of the muscles of the shoulder, arm, and elbow on the left half of the sheet, for which he described his procedure of illustration: "First draw the muscles of the neck, shoulder, and chest, and below the axilla that move the shoulder, then the muscles of the shoulder which move the humerus bone. . . . Then [follow with] the muscles of the humerus that bend and turn the arm, and then the muscles of the arm that move the hand, and the muscles that move the fingers."[1]

On the verso of the sheet, the rotated, sequential views of the surface dissection of the muscles of the neck, shoulders, and arms suggest a nearly cinematic effect of movement. A note toward the center of the sheet clarifies Leonardo's method of illustration: "Make an arm raised and one lowered, one [carried] backwards and one forwards. And draw each of these from four aspects, and do the same with the elbow bent."[2]

It is clear, from both the images and the inscribed texts on the double-sided Windsor sheet, that Leonardo here adapted the method of sculptors and architects to regard anatomical form in three dimensions, thereby revolutionizing the tradition of anatomical illustration. Before Leonardo, the Italian edition of the compendium known as Johannes de Ketham's *Fasciculo di medicina* (published in Venice in 1493/94; see discussion in cat. no. 57) had been the finest illustrated anatomical treatise of the Renaissance, including a selection of woodcuts by an anonymous Venetian artist directly influenced by Giovanni Bellini and Antonio del Pollaiuolo.

The present sheet and another, which portrays the bones of the leg as well as the muscles of the shoulder (Windsor, RL 19008), appear to have originally been part of the same page from Leonardo's so-called Anatomical Manuscript A (Windsor, RL 19000–19017). This notebook can be dated to 1510 from the inscription on a page in it by Leonardo: "In the winter of this year 1510, I expect to complete all this anatomy."[3] Before his untimely death in 1511, the brilliant young anatomist at the University of Pavia, Marcantonio della Torre, may well have directed Leonardo's method of dissection, for it reached a singular coherence of vision in the Anatomical Manuscript A. To judge from their neat, finished drawing technique and the careful disposition of image and text, these were not actual reportage-like sketches and notes made during dissections, but were clean, collated drafts.

Criticized for his undertaking, Leonardo passionately defended the purpose of his anatomical drawings in yet another page of notes that is not part of the Anatomical Manuscript A (Windsor, RL 19070 verso), adding there also that he had composed 120 books (chapters) on anatomy:

> And you who say that it would be better to watch an anatomist at work than to see these drawings, you would be right, if it were possible to observe all the things that are demonstrated in such drawings in a single figure, but in which you, with all your cleverness, will not see nor obtain knowledge of more than some few veins. To obtain a true and perfect knowledge, I have dissected more than ten human bodies, destroying all the other members, and removing the very minutest particles of the flesh by which these veins are surrounded, without causing them to bleed, except for the insensible bleeding of the capillary veins; and as one single body would not last so long, since it was necessary to proceed with several bodies by degrees, until I came to an end and had a complete knowledge; this I repeated twice, to learn the differences.[4]

In the extensive notes on the verso of another page (Windsor, RL 19027), Leonardo described the signs of bodily decay that accompany the natural aging process, such as changes in the hepatic arteries and the veins of old men and the results of these changes, adding also an eyewitness account of the death of an old man in Florence. While the dead man portrayed at the top of the recto in the present sheet of studies is most probably not to be directly identified with this eyewitness account, the artist's words offer nevertheless an enormously revealing glimpse of his motives: "And this old man, a few hours before his death, told me that he was over one hundred years old, and that he was conscious of no deficiency in his body other than feebleness. And thus while sitting on a bed in the hospital of Santa Maria Nuova in Florence, without any movement or other sign of distress, he passed from this life. And I made an anatomy of him to see the cause of so sweet a death."[5] The sheet detailing the death of the "centenarian" forms part of the small, so-called Anatomical Manuscript B (Windsor, RL 19018–19059). This notebook can probably be dated at least two years earlier than the present drawings from a related note on the changes of hepatic arteries and veins that is dated September 12, 1508 (Paris Ms. F).[6] From 1508 to 1510/11, Leonardo's anatomical drawings attained an unprecedented level of accuracy in description.   CCB

1. Translation quoted from Keele and Pedretti 1979–80, vol. 2, p. 156, no. 141r. See also O'Malley and Saunders 1952, p. 130, no. 45.

2. Translation quoted from Keele and Pedretti 1979–80, vol. 2, p. 518, no. 141v. See also O'Malley and Saunders 1952, p. 134, no. 47.

3. Windsor, RL 19016; Richter 1970, vol. 2, p. 345, no. 1376: "In questa vernata del mille 510 credo spedire tutta tal notomia."

4. Keele and Pedretti 1979–80, vol. 1, p. 362, no. 113r: "ettu che dj ess [*sic:* essere] me/glio il uedere fare / la notomja che uede/re taljdisegnj djre/sti bene se fussi [crossed out: be] / possibile veder tu/tte queste cose che / intal djsegnj sidj/mosstrano inuna / sola figura nella / quale con tutto il tu/o ingenjo non uedra / i e non araj la no/titia senon dalquan/te poche vene de / le qualj io per aver/ne [crossed out: v] vera e piena / notitia o djsfatti / piv dj dieci co/rpi vmani / distrugendo ognj / altri membri consi/mando con mjnuti/sime partichule / tutta la carne che / djntorno a esse / vene sitrovava / sanza insangui/narle se non dj/sensibile insan[:–:]guinamento delle vene capillare / e [crossed out: altrettante] e vnsol corpo non / bastava attanto tempo che biso/gnava procedere dj mano imano / in tanti corpi che sifinjssi lainte/re cognjtione la qual [crossed out: s] ripri/cai [crossed out: 4] 2 volte per uedere le djferentie." See also Richter 1970, vol. 2, p. 85, no. 796.

5. Keele and Pedretti 1979–80, vol. 1, p. 214, no. 69v: "ecquesto vechio dj poche ore inanzi lasua morte mj djsse lui / passare cento anni e chenonsi sentiua alcun manchamento ne/la persona altro che deboleza r vodi standosi assedere sopra / vno letto nello spedale djscan [*sic:* di santa] maria nova djfrenza sanza al/ltro movimento osegnjo dalcuno accidente oassi dj questa vita — / e io ne feci notomja per uedere lacausa djsi dolce morte." See Kemp and Roberts 1989a, p. 113.

6. Clark and Pedretti 1968–69, vol. 3, p. 13, no. 19027.

LEONARDO DA VINCI

114. *Eight Double-Sided Sheets from the Codex Leicester*

Collection of Bill and Melinda Gates, Seattle, Washington

PROVENANCE: Guglielmo della Porta, Milan and Rome (d. 1577; according to Vasari, vol. 7, p. 544); 1690, Giuseppe Ghezzi, Rome (1634–1721); 1717, Thomas William Coke, later first earl of Leicester (Coke of Norfolk), London and Norfolk (1697–1759), from Ghezzi (recorded 1719 in Holkham MS 735, account book of payments made by Casey for Thomas Coke, p. 67); thence by descent; sale, Christie's, London, December 12, 1980 (catalogue by Carlo Pedretti); 1980, Armand Hammer, New York and Los Angeles (1898–1990); sale, Christie's, London, November 11, 1994 (sold separately, no lot no.); 1994, Collection of Bill and Melinda Gates, Seattle, Washington.

LITERATURE: Richter 1883, vol. 2, nos. 864 (fol. 1r), 1082 (fol. 1v), 902 (fol. 2r), 985 (fol. 3r), 988 and 921 (fol. 9r), 989, 721, 1055 and 1061 (fol. 9v), 1472, 959, and 1008 (fol. 13r), 972 (fol. 15r), 920 (fol. 15v); Calvi 1909; Calvi 1925, pp. 215–32, 280–81; MacCurdy 1938, vol. 1, pp. 310–11, 347–48 (fol. 1), 312 (fol. 2), 348–49 (fol. 3), 351–56 (fol. 9), 360–61 (fol. 13), vol. 2, pp. 577 (fol. 2r), 148 and 578 (fol. 13r), 174–75 (fol. 13v), 105 (fol. 14v), 105–6 (fol. 15r,v); Royal Academy of Arts 1952, no. 410; Bassoli 1954, pp. 261–314; Pedretti 1964a, carta 86, 116 and carta 85, 116 (fol. 13r), carta 87, 119 and 120 and 86, 117 and 118 (fol. 14r), carta 75, 110 (fol. 15r); Hassall 1970, pp. 28–29, pls. 112–15; Pedretti 1977, notes to nos. 864 (fol. 1r), 4 (fols. 2v, 3r), 965A and 1471A (fol. 3r), 848 (fol. 3v), 920 (fol. 15v); Pedretti 1980b, pp. 17–43, 56–59, 64–67, 80–91; Pedretti 1987a (with complete bibliography to date of publication); Farago 1996b, pp. 35–179; Gingerich 1996, pp. 23–30; Kemp 1996, pp. 15–22; Pedretti 1996d; Fehrenbach 1997, pp. 220–27 and passim; Farago 1999b, vol. 4, pp. 417–60.

The numbering of the disassembled Codex Leicester follows the system established by Carlo Pedretti in the 1987 facsimile edition. Each of the eighteen sheets is labeled A and B, indicating the front and back, respectively.

In its bound form, each sheet was folded in the middle of the long side and the eighteen horizontally oriented bifolded sheets were stacked. The front side of each half sheet in its folded position in the stack, or signature, is numbered at the top right in keeping with the standard practice of numbering folios on the recto only. It follows that Sheet 1A comprises folio 36 verso (the unnumbered left side of the sheet) and folio 1 recto (the numbered right side of the sheet). Sheet 1B comprises folio 1 verso (the unnumbered left side of the sheet) and folio 36 recto (the numbered right side of the sheet). See figure 104 for a diagram of the nestling of the sheets.

SHEET 1
Sheet 1A (front) comprises folios 36 verso, 1 recto
Sheet 1B (back) comprises folios 1 verso, 36 recto
Pen with medium and dark brown ink over stylus ruling, pin-pricks, incised compass marks, and soft black chalk or lead-point, 298 × 448 mm (11 3/4 × 17 5/8 in.) maximum
Full transcription of Leonardo's extensive text in Pedretti 1987a, pp. 3–6.
Inscribed on front and back of page with sequential numbers in graphite by a modern hand (the compiler of a facsimile?)

Folio 1 recto of Sheet 1A, the first page of the manuscript in its bound form, concerns the sun, moon, and earth. Leonardo speculates on the composition of the moon, a central topic in the Aristotelian science of cosmology. This sheet exemplifies Leonardo's use of graphic methods to model situations by juxtaposing illustrations ranging from stereographic cross-sectional views to schematic geometric diagrams. Three large diagrams, among the most beautiful in the entire manuscript, show the relation of the sun and moon as sunlight strikes the moon, seen by a spectator positioned between the two heavenly bodies (center and bottom diagram).

The unresolved issue in Leonardo's day was whether a smooth, perfect sphere was responsible for the specific kind of light that the moon displays. The challenge was to explain why moonlight is less bright than sunlight. A number of explanations were offered, of which the two main variants addressed on folio 1 recto are (1) that the moon is, like the planets, transparent and crystalline, but to a lesser degree owing to its proximity to the earth, so that the light of the sun does not fully penetrate it; and (2) that the moon is composed of different densities through which light passes to relatively greater and lesser degrees. Leonardo's explanation, pursued on folios 1 verso, 2 recto, 5 recto, 7 recto and verso, 30 recto and verso, and 36 verso, is that the outer surface of the moon is made of water with standing waves that reflect some but not all of the sun's light. The text explains that the image of the sun reflected on the choppy water (bottom diagram) is broken up into many small images, and this condition, that is, the phenomenon of luster that moves as the position of the observer changes ("change as many places over those waters as are the places taken by the eye in observing it"), accounts for both the moon's subdued light and its lack of uniform brightness.

The text on Sheet 1A is organized like a Scholastic argument with propositions, objections (raised by imagined adversaries), and a concluding demonstration that proves the hypothesis—in this case, a geometric demonstration of the action of light moving in straight lines. Leonardo's main point, diagrammed on 1 recto and verso, is that the phenomenon of luster (that is, the glow of light reflected from a polished surface toward the observer) does not explain the moon's luminescence as well as the theory that its surface is covered by a sea with standing waves.

The scalloped edge of the sphere at the bottom of folio 1 recto represents the waves on the watery surface of the moon. Leonardo demonstrates that rays of light striking it and rebounding do not intermingle and become confused (as the adversary, whose views are recorded on the left side of Sheet 1A [36 verso], claims). The same point-to-point analysis of the action of light, in the tradition of Ibn al-Haytham (Alhazen), is the basis for Leonardo's defense of painting as a science of optics concerned with the graphic representation of appearances on a flat surface.

The lower part of folio 1 verso continues the discussion begun on folio 1 recto about the cause of the moon's brightness. In an imaginary debate with Master Andrea de Imola, tentatively identified as Andrea Cattaneo da Imola, a professor of philosophy and medicine at the University of Bologna, Leonardo argues that the surface of the moon is not as smooth as a mirror because it is covered by water, which has a textured, three-dimensional surface like the seas of earth. Therefore, sunlight lost in the shadows in the troughs of the waves accounts for the pale brilliance of the moon's glow.

This discussion of the composition of the moon ends on Sheet 1A, folio 36 verso, on the lower half of the page, in conjunction with observations about standing waves in the sea versus the descending flow of water in rivers. Leonardo explains his hypothesis to an imaginary adversary who denies that there is water on the surface of the moon. Leonardo suggests that the moon has its own gravity, a topic pursued at greater length on folio 2 recto of Sheet 2A. His discussion implies knowledge of Ptolemy's *Hypotheses on the Planets,* a

second-century revision of Aristotle's concept, generally accepted by scientists in Leonardo's day, that the university was arranged in fifty-five concentric spheres. According to Ptolemy, the planets revolved around eccentric orbits within concentric spheres, thus allowing for the possibility that each planet had its own center of gravity and hence its own concentric spheres of the four elements (air, water, fire, and earth) arranged according to their relative densities, with the densest element at the center.

On Sheet 1B, folio 36 recto, located at the end of the treatise when the notebook was bound, Leonardo discusses the composition of the earth. Textual traditions since antiquity associated the composition of the earth with that of the moon, the cause of tides and the reasons that fossils and other evidence of sea life are found on mountaintops. The main questions that Leonardo addresses on folio 36 recto, with the aid of sketches of the earth in cross section, concern the effect of the earth's gravity on the composite of its elements of water and land. Leonardo discusses the projection of land masses from the sphere of water. He constructs a mechanical model based on the balancing of weights. The discussion continues on folio 36 verso, on the top half of the page, which describes equilibrium in terms of a geometric model of a pyramid (representing the land masses) surrounded by a circle (representing the watery sphere). Similar notes are recorded in the Paris Ms. F, folio 27 recto, where Leonardo plays with Platonic configurations of the elements as distinct, interlocking geometric shapes.

Also on Sheet 1B, on the upper part of folio 1 verso, the discussion of the mingling of land and water in the body of the earth continues with the Danube, Europe's largest river, serving as a case in point. Leonardo considers whether the eroding action of rivers is responsible for lakes contained in underground channels as well as for the presence of seashells on the high slopes of the Carpathian Mountains. Elsewhere, on folio 4 recto, Leonardo describes his own expedition to the Alps. Throughout the treatise, he pursues two questions that also preoccupied his predecessors: (1) given that water, moving on its own, only descends, how do rivers reach the tops of mountains? and (2) does the biblical account of the Great Deluge adequately account for the presence of seashells and other aquatic fossils on the tops of mountains?[1] Leonardo approaches the first question with Aristotelian theories of movement; his response to the second question challenges the biblical account of the history of the earth on the basis of

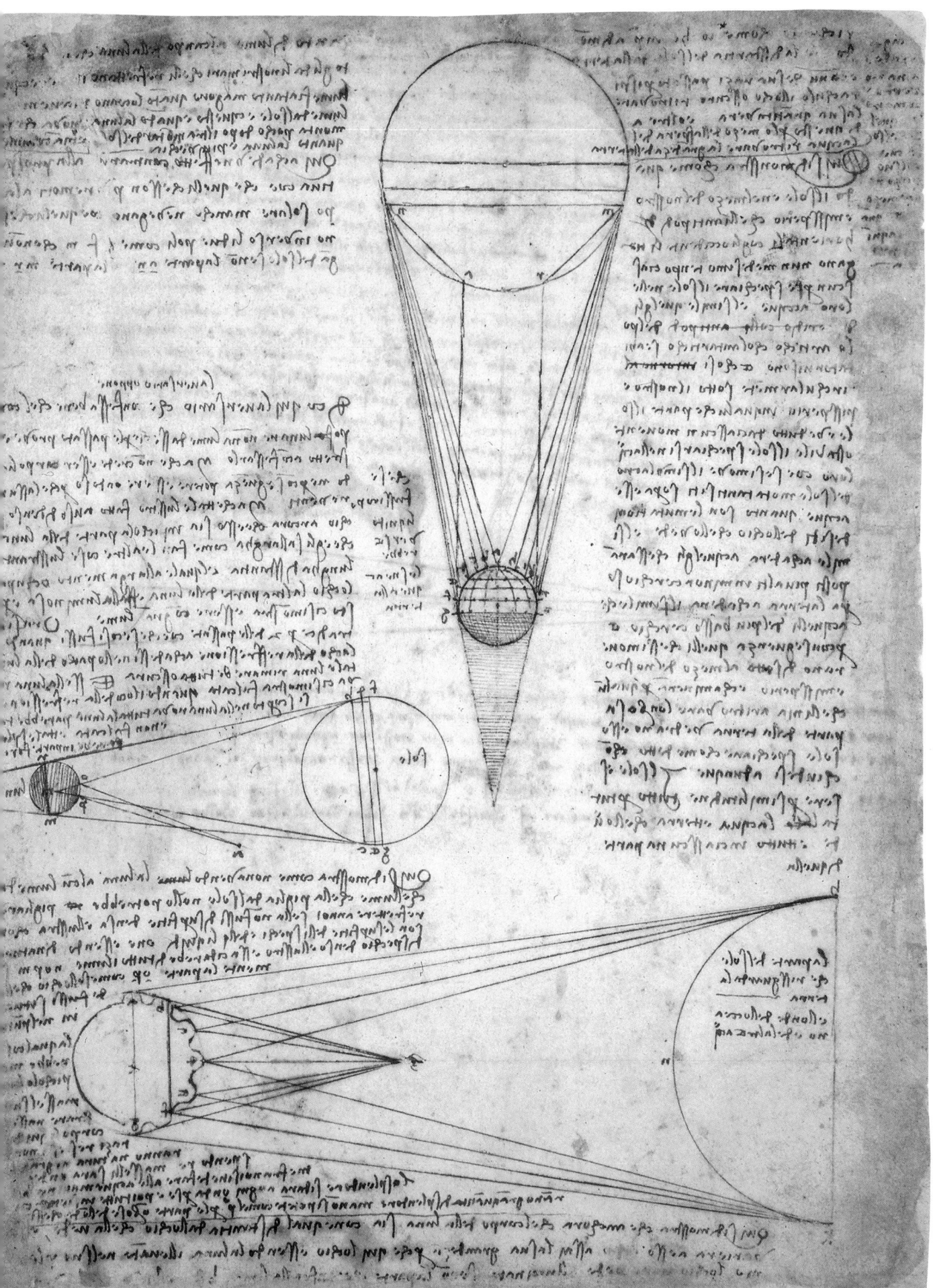

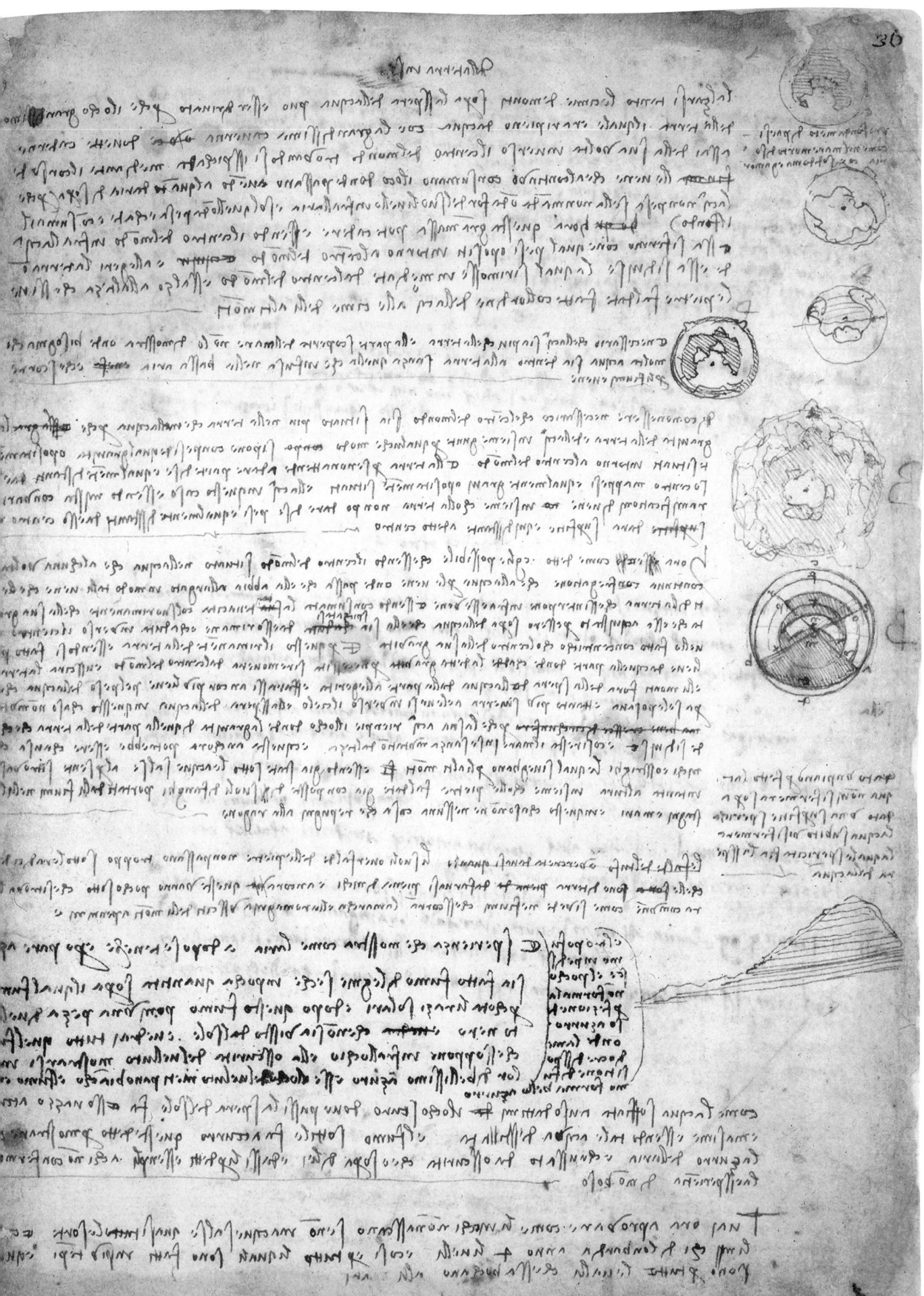

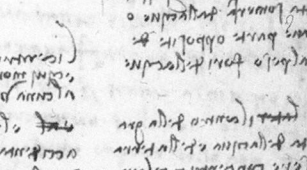

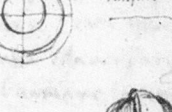

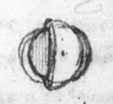

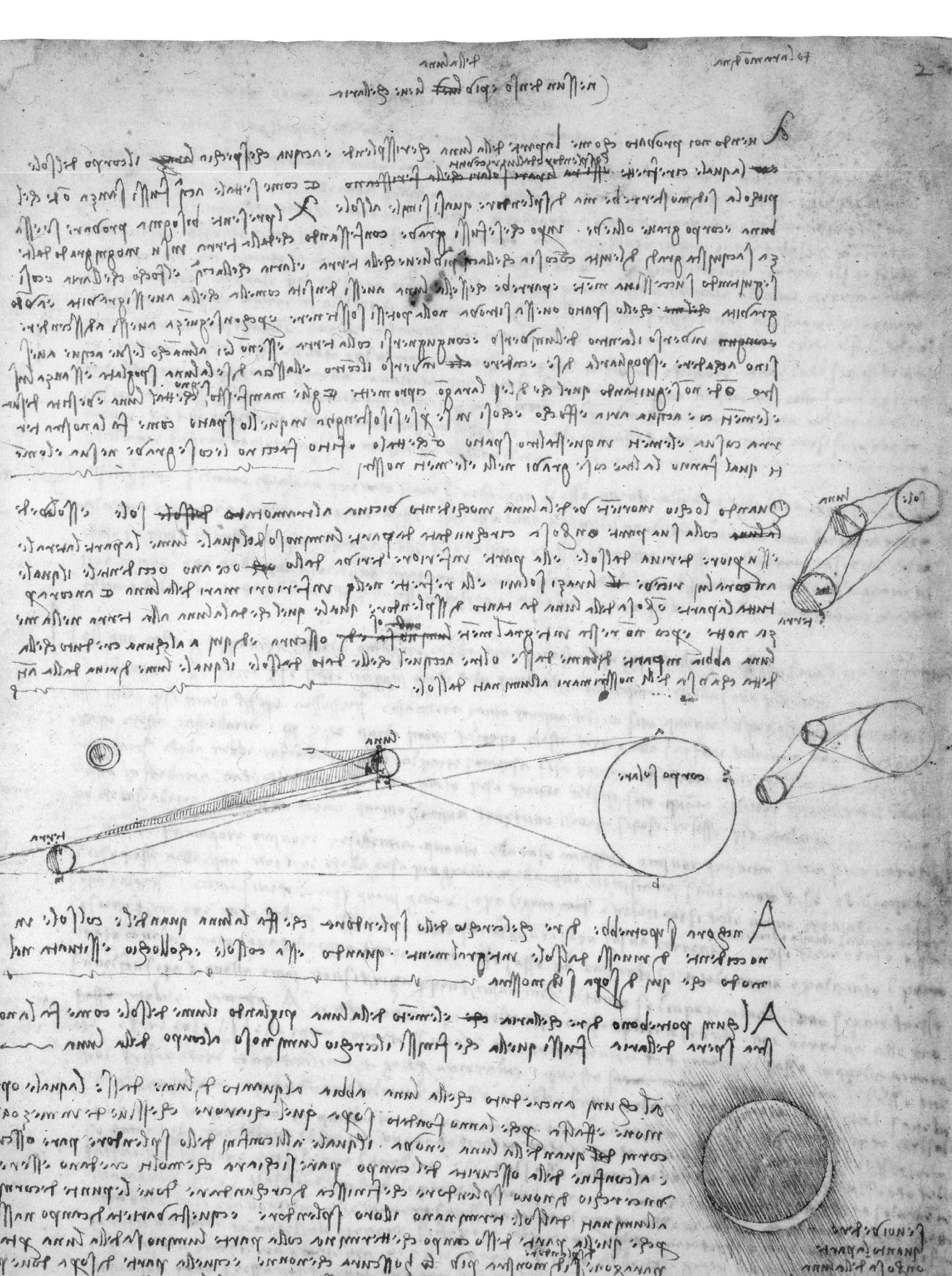

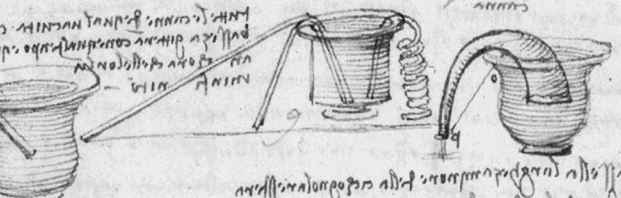
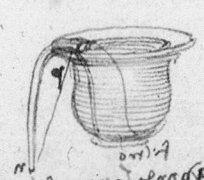
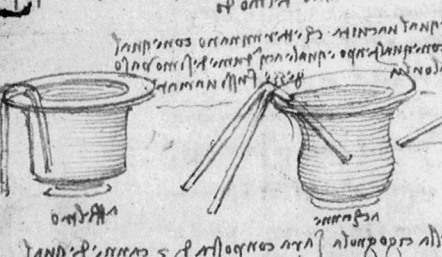
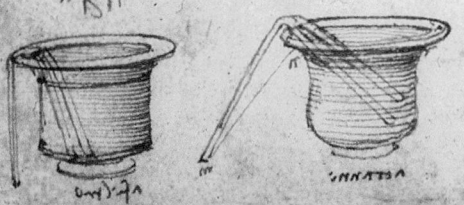

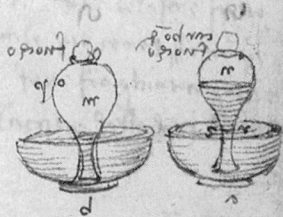

Cat. 114, SHEET 3B *(back)*, fol. 3v

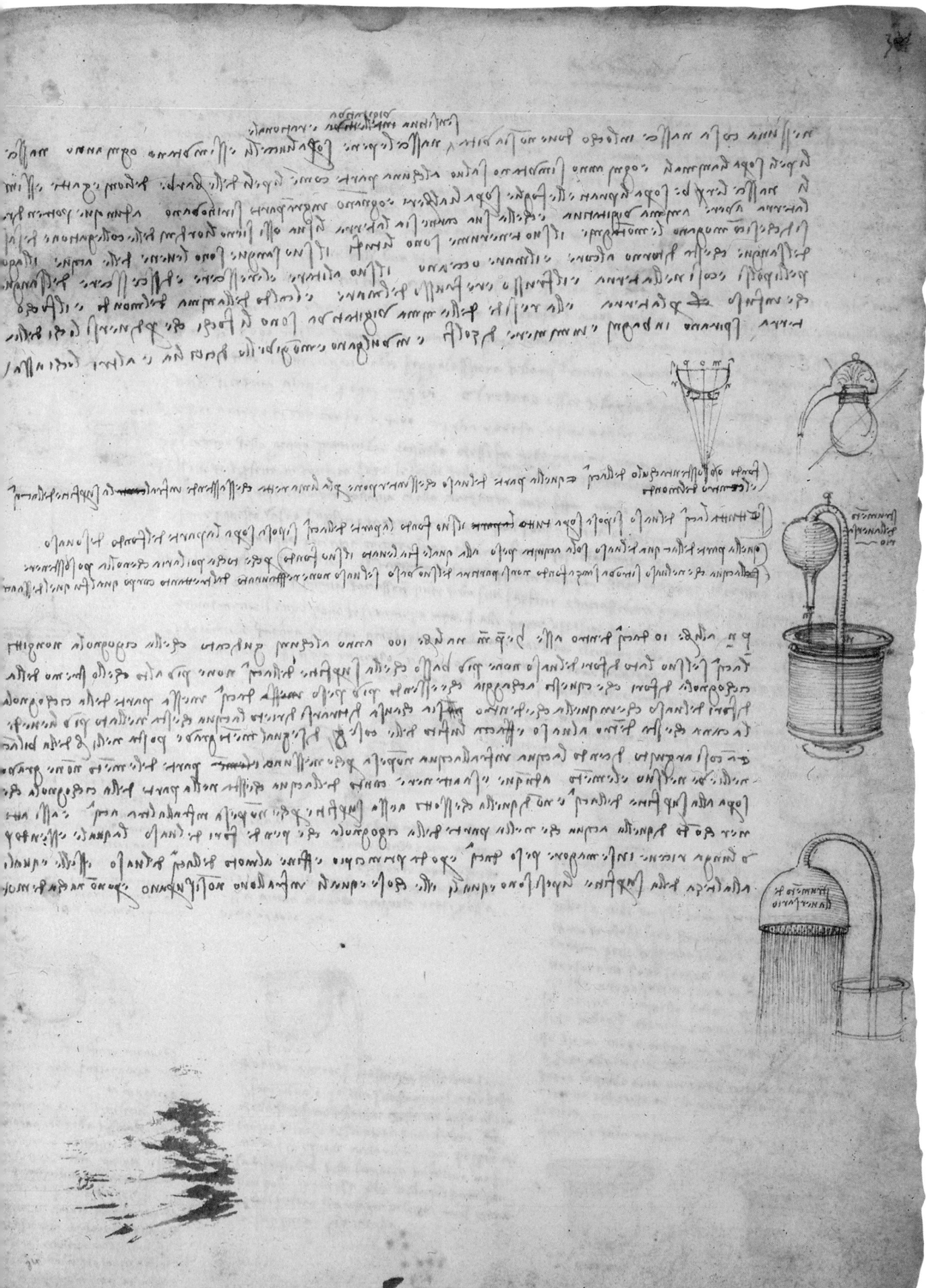

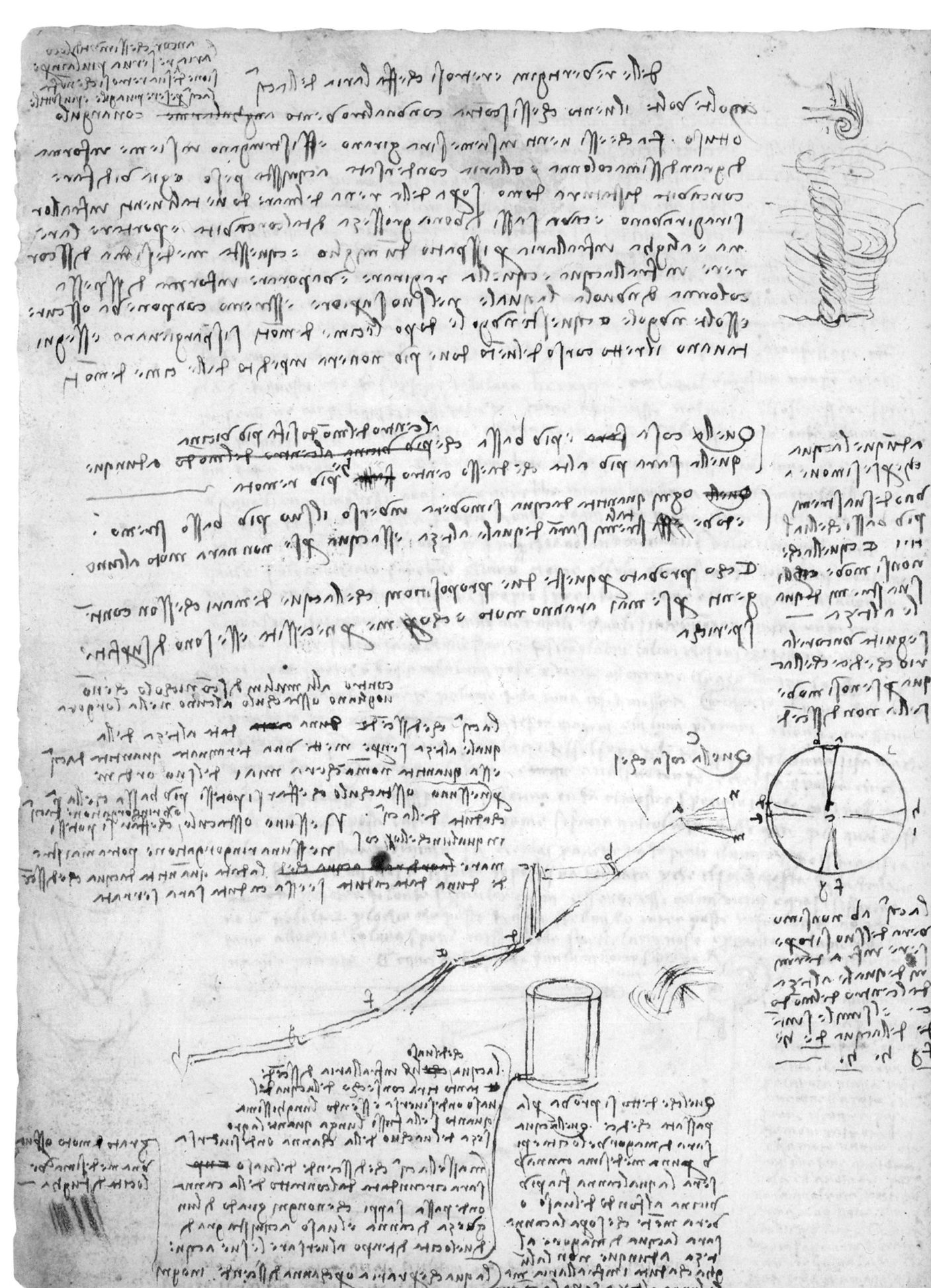

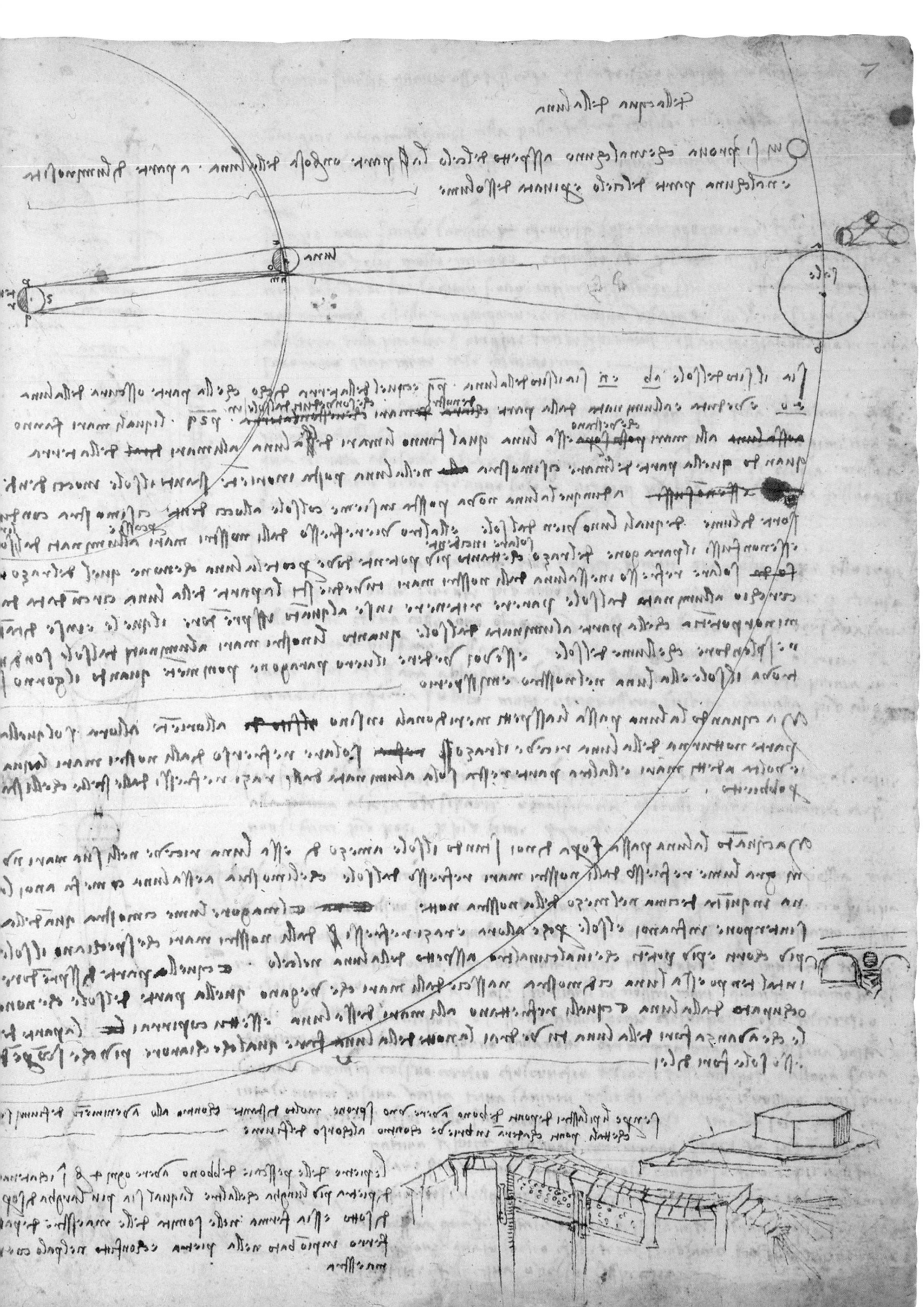

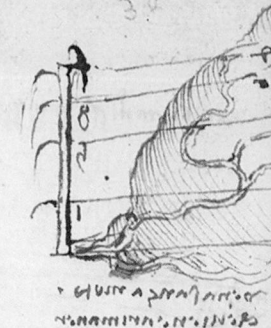

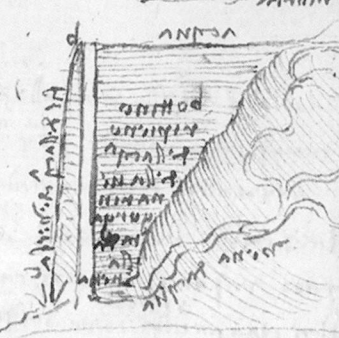

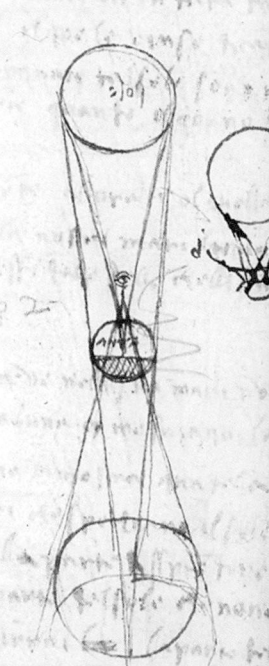

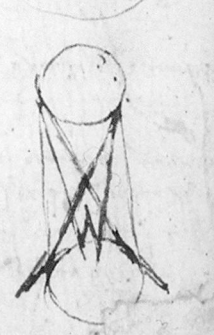

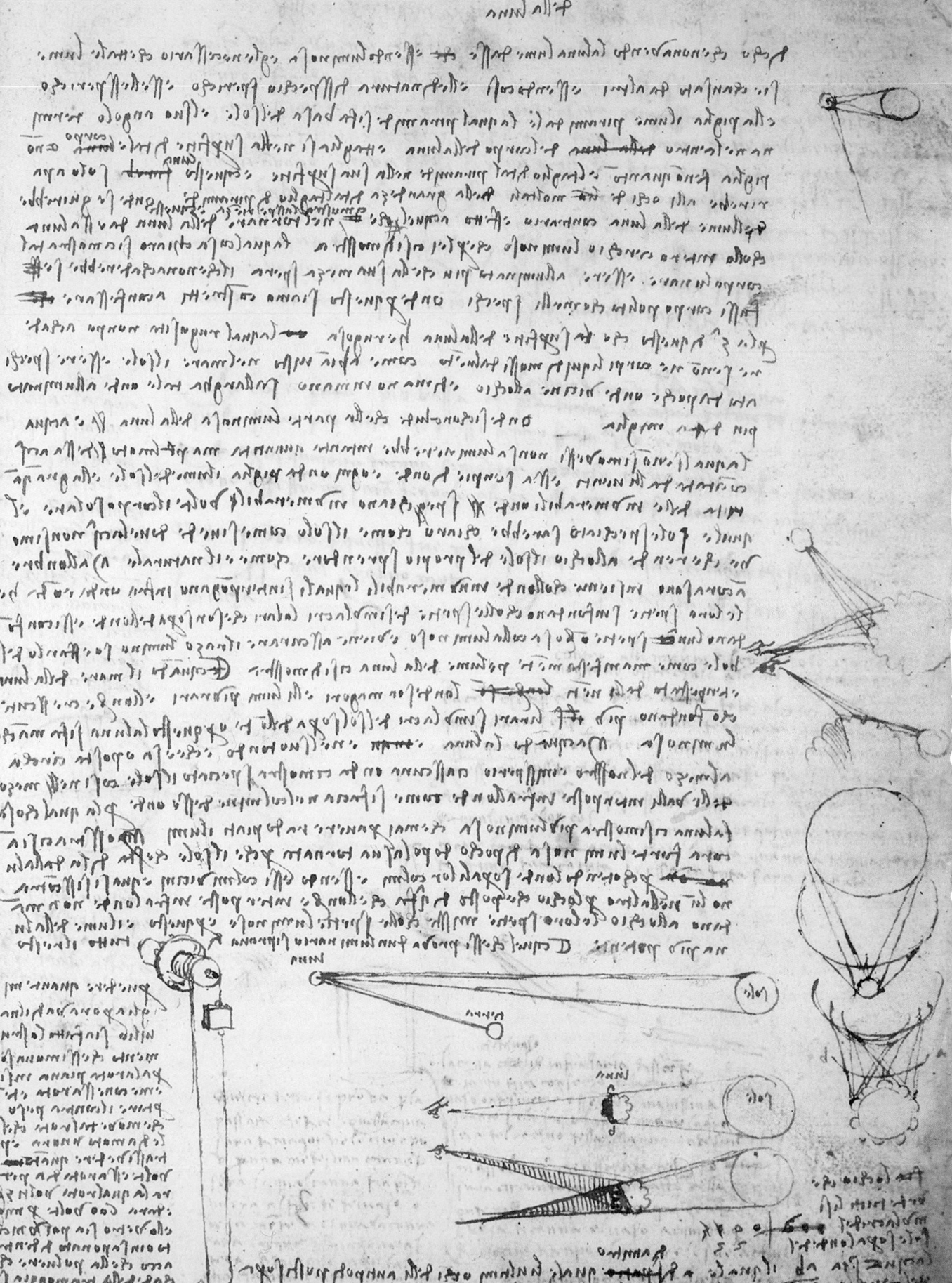

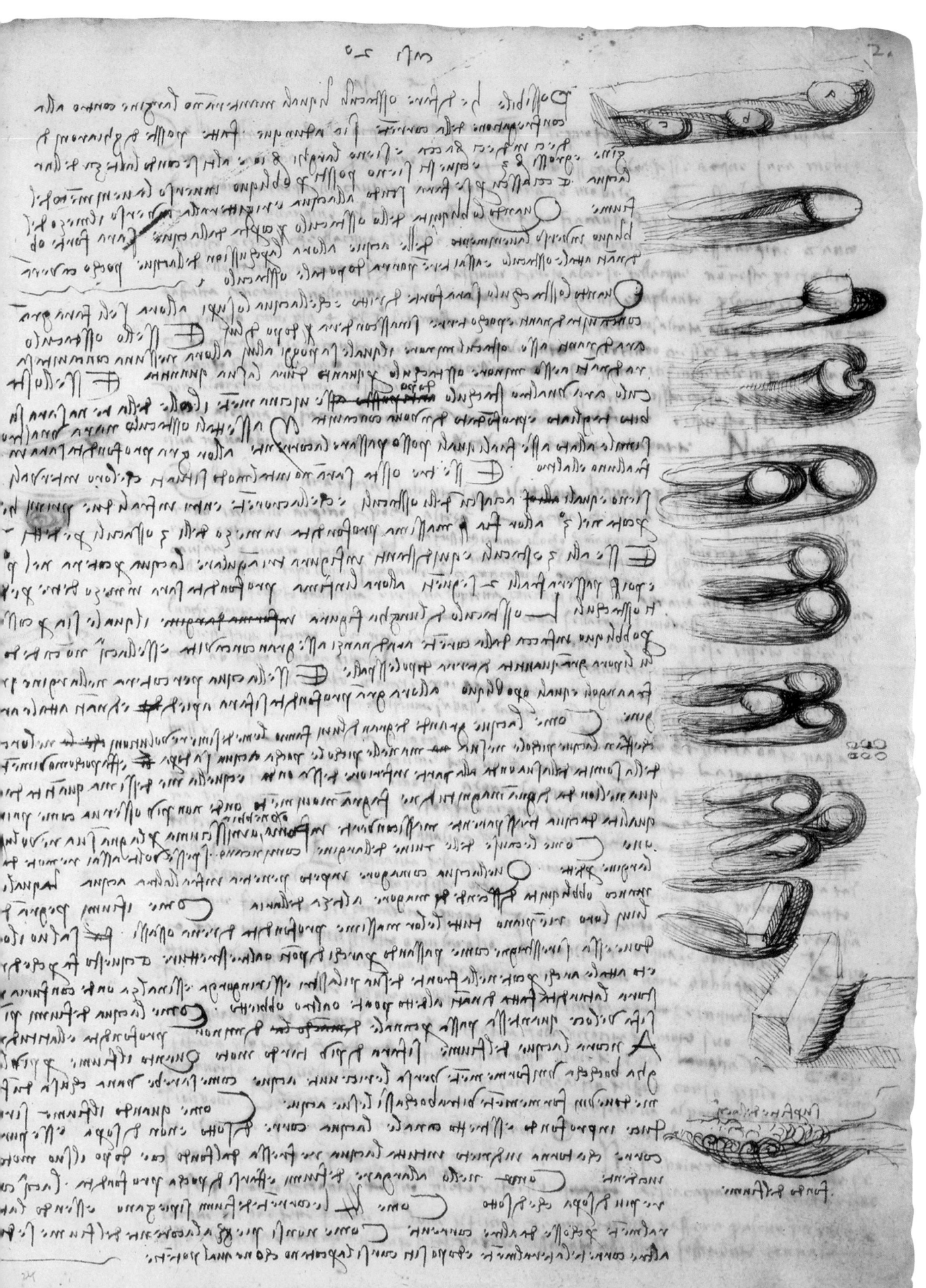

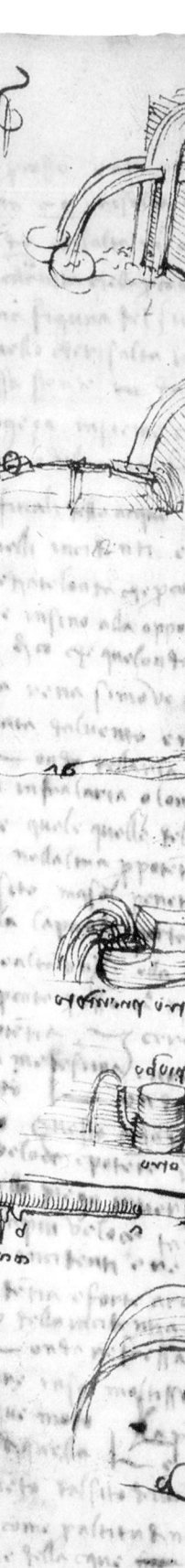

Cat. 114, SHEET 14A *(front)*, fol. 23v

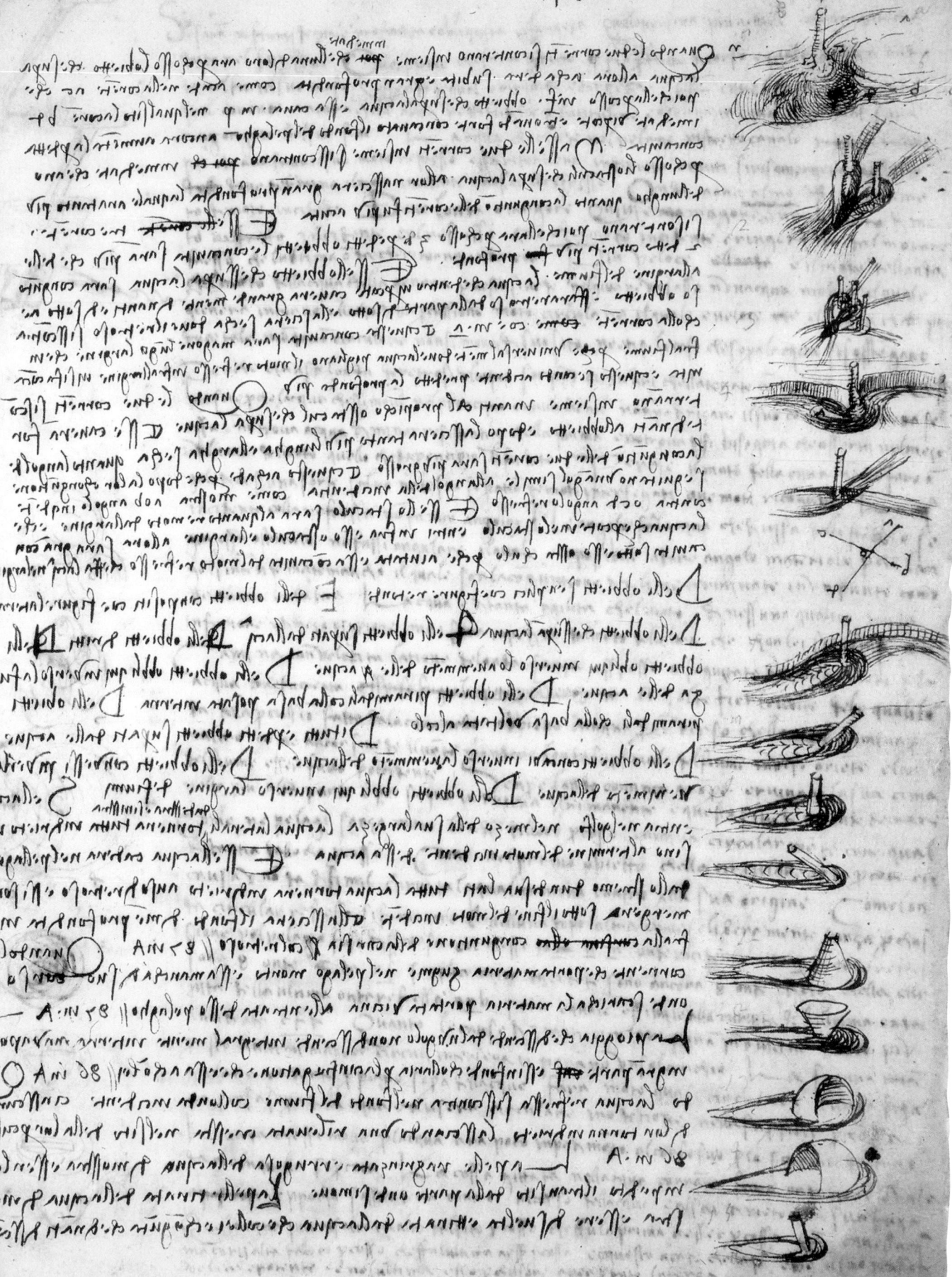

Cat. 114, SHEET 14A *(front)*, fol. 14R

Cat. 114, SHEET 14B *(back)*, fol. 14v

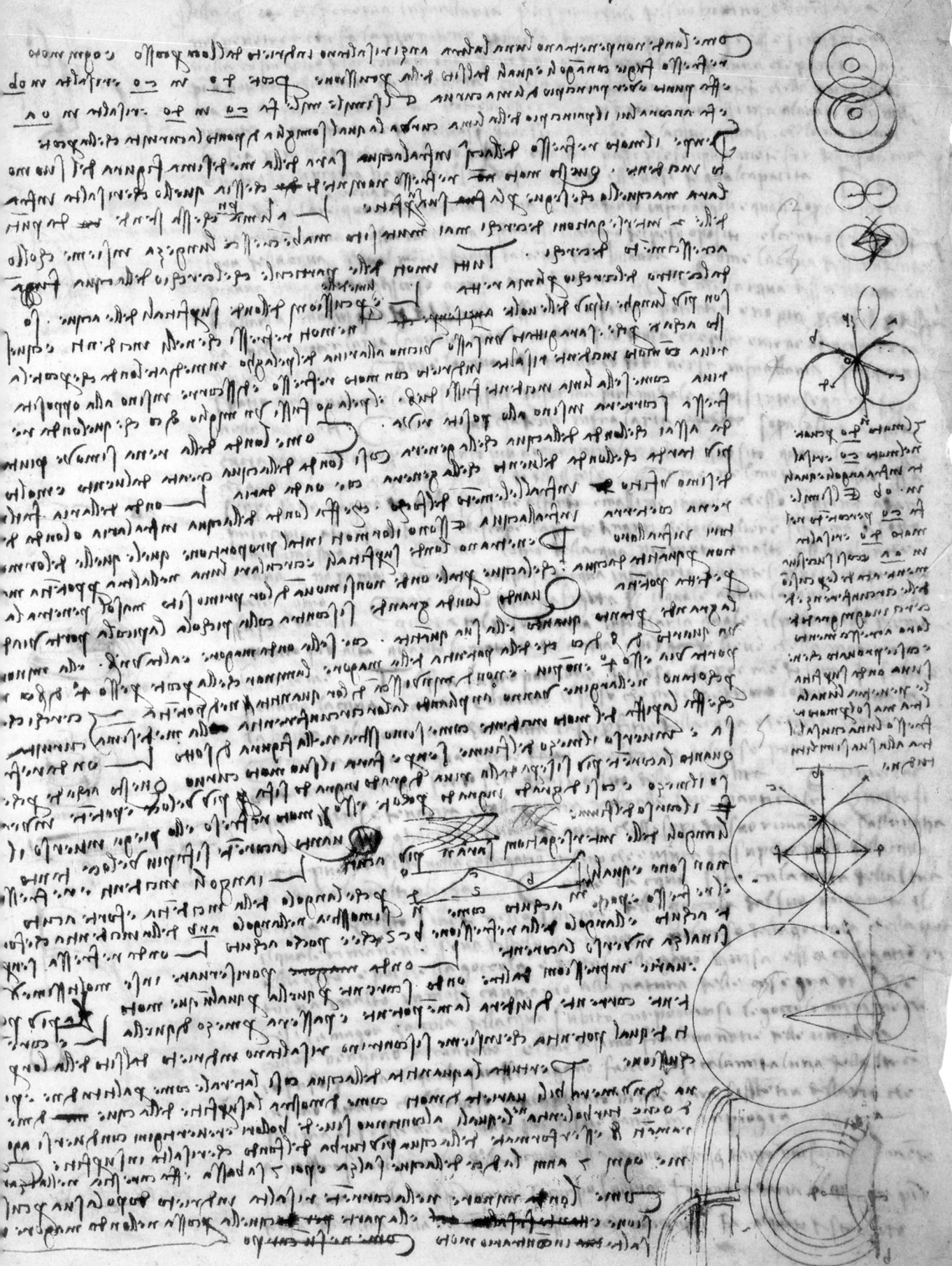

these theories. Although Leonardo knew nothing of the molecular action that changed shells into fossils, his explanation of erosion, sedimentation at the microscale, and the macroscale movement of land and water during earthquakes, tidal waves, and floods is largely correct.

The ancient Greek cosmic system built from the four elements, including the analogy of the macro- and microcosm, is key to the entire tradition upon which Leonardo develops his discussion of the effects of gravity on the circulation of water in the body of the earth. Plato's description of the earth as a macrocosm and his complementary idea of the human body as a microcosm or miniature cosmos have been known continuously since antiquity from the *Timaeus*, which sets forth a dynamic, concrete conception of the cosmic system in terms of the four elements as the building blocks of nature (an analogy that Plato borrowed from Empedocles). One of the most important aspects of Plato's macro/microcosm analogy is his comparison of blood to water (*Timaeus*, 80e – 81b) in which he states that just as the body feeds on blood, so the earth draws on water to replenish itself.[2]

Some historians have categorized differences among theories of the macrocosm deeply embedded in Western thought by the time Leonardo set down his scientific investigations of water, but in the present context, the differences are less significant than the commonalities. There are two main features, both amply demonstrated in the manuscript: (1) that the earth functions like a living creature, and (2) that the physical world as a whole (the cosmos), which is in a constant state of change (or becoming), is a copy of a divine, unchanging, eternal world. Leonardo, who did not apply the Platonic comparison between the macrocosm and the microcosm in a simplistic manner, grounded his observations and theories in the rich scientific tradition based on Aristotle's writings on the physical sciences, especially his treatise on cosmology, the study of the causes and effects of the cosmos. Leonardo understood nature to operate in the same manner on different scales and through different materials. Aristotelian science, in other words, justified his use of models to observe the forces of nature directly, without instruments, on a human scale.

The Platonic configuration of the elements worked out by the mathematician Fra Luca Pacioli with Leonardo's participation may have inspired his concept of the mingling of earth and water as a marbled mass, recorded on folio 36 recto of Sheet 1B, which contains the most innovative visual models

of the dynamic balance of the world in the entire codex. The sequence of discussion suggests that Leonardo combined more recent theories of gravity with the familiar theme of subterranean waters eroding the interior of the earth and causing caverns to collapse. His cross-sectional diagrams show how layers of earth and water continually fold in upon themselves, pulled toward the center by gravity and pushed toward the periphery by the lightening of their mass. The Platonic model of interlocked geometric shapes provides the perfect prototype for the plastic representation of these forces. Leonardo also developed theoretical models by observing the behavior of actual substances, such as the dewdrop discussed on Sheet 3 (see the entry below). The juxtaposition of natural phenomena and their eternal (geometrically describable) causes allowed Leonardo to pursue implications of Aristotelian science beyond anything that Aristotle had imagined. Leonardo made detailed, theoretical analyses of the action of water under many different circumstances. Knowledge of theories of the elements and of gravity, discussed in the following entry, was necessary to participate in this intellectual exercise.

SHEET 2
Sheet 2A (front) comprises folios 35 verso, 2 recto
Sheet 2B (back) comprises folios 2 verso, 35 recto
Pen with light and medium brown ink, brush and brown wash over stylus ruling and incised compass marks
298 × 448 mm (11¾ × 17⅝ in.) maximum
Full transcription of Leonardo's extensive text in Pedretti 1987a, pp. 11 – 21.
Inscribed on front of page with scattered numbers in graphite by a modern hand (the compiler of a facsimile?)

On folio 2 recto of sheet 2A, Leonardo restates in succinct terms arguments made on folio 1 recto and verso that if the moon were without waves, its radiance would be almost equal to the sun's. Moreover, the moon is clothed in its own elements, just like the earth, so that the moon "maintains its own space," that is, the moon has its own center of gravity. This is the question that most concerns Leonardo on folio 2 recto in a text accompanied by a hauntingly beautiful sketch of a crescent moon, based on an understanding of gravity quite different from modern theories. He takes up the subject of gravity at length on the facing half of Sheet 2A (on folio 35 verso), located at the end of the notebook in its bound form, and on Sheet 2B. On folio 2 recto, he also considers the challenge of accounting for "that glimmer visible in the middle between the horns of the [crescent] moon," or *lumen cinereum* as it was called in the scientific literature.[3] He argues that this ashen light is due to sunlight reflected from the seas of the earth onto the surface of the moon. This "glimmer" is darker than the illuminated portion of the moon but brighter than the heavens as a result of the mutual enhancement of light and dark when they are juxtaposed. On the same principle that informs Leonardo's compositional considerations of painting, he thus refutes an argument advanced by his main source of optical theory, Ibn al-Haytham, that the moon emits a weak light of its own. To test this hypothesis of the enhanced contrast of juxtaposed colors, Leonardo recommends covering up the bright part of the moon with one hand.

On the left side of Sheet 2A (on folio 35 verso) are found some of the most important discussions of theories of the composition of the world in the entire codex. The physical arrangement of notes on the page affords modern readers an invaluable glimpse into Leonardo's conceptualization of the dynamics of water. Here and on the part of Sheet 1B adjacent to it when the manuscript was bound (on folio 36 recto), several subsets of concerns are integrated with that of the circulation of water within the earth developed throughout the codex. Leonardo argues that, because the densities of material through which water circulates vary, an adequate theory must take into account the dynamics of water circulation and gravitational force.

How, Leonardo asks, can we account for the center of gravity, given that rock strata of various densities and water of various densities (depending on its location and depth, according to Leonardo) are intermingled inside the earth? Medieval interpretations of the Aristotelian scheme located the earth at the center of the universe. Accordingly, there would be three types of "gravity," each a kind of center: essential or geometric gravity, natural gravity, and accidental gravity. The first two depend on imagining the earth as a sphere at the center of a series of concentric spheres. Essential gravity is the geometric center of the sphere; natural gravity is the center of its mass. Accidental gravity, according to one of Leonardo's most sophisticated sources, Nicole Oresme, pertains to an object in motion — for instance, when a spinning top maintains its equilibrium, the central axis defines the center of its accidental gravity. The same principle can be applied to any object, regardlesss of shape, density, or weight: when the object is spinning in equilibrium, its accidental gravity is centered. By the same token,

an object at rest has no accidental gravity. It follows that if land projects in equal amounts on opposite sides of the earth, creating a balance, or if the earth is entirely surrounded by water on the outside, no matter what shape the land masses take, the fluid will fill the interstices and form a smooth outer surface due to gravitational force. The three centers of gravity will be at the same location under these conditions.

The second paragraph on Sheet 2B (on folio 2 verso) continues the discussion of the composition of the moon based on considerations of gravity. Leonardo was indebted to Archimedes' treatise on floating bodies and preserved fragments of it elsewhere in his notes (C.A. 153r-b, r-c, v-c). The subject interested him since the Paris Ms. A, folio 30 verso, of about 1492, but here he introduces a new level of complexity by including the role of light reflected from the earth's seas onto the moon's surface, as viewed from various positions during the day and night. These speculations, which are reminiscent of his studies about 1505 of the changing position of the sun, are entirely original.[4]

The right side of Sheet 2B, folio 35 recto, contains a passage on tides in which Leonardo rejects the theory that they originate from rivers in the depths of the sea; a comparison of ocean tides with the ebb and flow of canals; and a brief comment at the end of the page on the stratification of rocks created by the settling of silt in the sea. This appears to be an addition to the discussions of the earth's density and its center of gravity on folios 35 verso and 36 recto. That these related discussions (regarding the moon and the composition of the planet earth) appear on successive pages of the manuscript suggests that Leonardo added to these pages after the sheets were assembled in their bound order and after he had filled Sheet 3. The passages on folios 35 verso and 36 recto seem to be more complex considerations of the problem of the circulation of water in the earth discussed on Sheet 3.[5] They do not simply summarize those arguments, however, but integrate several subsets of concerns developed throughout the codex. Leonardo's original synthesis takes into account the dynamics of water circulation and gravitational force.

The order of compilation proposed above is corroborated by physical evidence, that is, by Pedretti's finding that a discussion about the body of the earth labeled B at the bottom of folio 35 verso, in a paragraph squeezed into the available space after the rest of the page was filled, refers to a diagram on Sheet 1 (on folio 36 recto).[6]

SHEET 3

Sheet 3A (front) comprises folios 34 verso, 3 recto
Sheet 3B (back) comprises folios 3 verso, 34 recto
Pen and light brown ink over traces of soft black chalk or
leadpoint
298 × 447 mm (11¾ × 17⅝ in.) maximum
Full transcription of Leonardo's extensive text in Pedretti
1987a, pp. 21–30.
Inscribed on front and back of page with sequential numbers
and framing outlines, and on lower left of front of page, "facsimile," all in graphite by a modern hand (the compiler of a
facsimile?)

Sheet 3 is without doubt the most significant in the entire
codex for documenting Leonardo's evolving thoughts on a single, tightly focused problem. On folio 34 verso of Sheet 3A, he
illustrates various kinds of siphons discussed on the facing
page, folio 3 recto; the same line of investigation continues on
the reverse of the sheet (Sheet 3B).

The context for Leonardo's considering the action of various
configurations of siphons is the problem of accounting for the
circulation of water in the earth, specifically the way water
reaches springs at the summits of mountains. Siphoning is the
drawing of a liquid through a tube or other conduit from one
reservoir into another at a lower level, over a barrier between
them that is higher than either reservoir. The history of the
theory is presented on folio 3 recto, derived from Ristoro
d'Arezzo's compendium *La composizione del mondo* (1282).
According to the argument that Leonardo summarizes (based
on book 6, chapter 7, of Ristoro's text), the formation of mountains and their weathering can be explained by the action of
water washing over the earth, descending from the mountains
in the form of rivers. The rivers bring with them gravel that
fills the valleys and raises their level of elevation. At the same
time, water in the form of subterranean rivers digs under the
valleys, carrying earth from one place to another on a sea-
sonal basis.

The discussion on folio 3 recto, which is the right side of
Sheet 3A, concerns the way water passes through various
densities and kinds of geologic strata. Leonardo takes up the
hypothesis that siphoning accounts for the presence of water
at the earth's highest points. Then, in true Scholastic style, he
raises several objections. Given the assumption that siphoning
action (taking place, according to Ristoro, in underground caverns that run from the oceans to the mountains) is the primary means by which water ascends to the tops of mountains,

Leonardo asks why there is not more water flowing in the
summer, when snows have melted, than in winter. In discussing the ways in which the earth's porous nature facilitates
the upward passage of water, he considers various densities of
soil. The actual composition of the earth in terms of the
stratification of rocks and soil is central to his study of water
dynamics. Leonardo's questioning leads him to consider
specific causes of water erosion. Even the traditional problem
of accounting for the presence of seashells on mountaintops,
discussed in the final paragraph on folio 3 recto, is interpreted
in the context of water erosion, as the result of underground
rivers that open up rock strata by carrying away rock of varying densities.

Folio 34 verso, constituting the left side of Sheet 3A, provides an excellent example of Leonardo's use of small-scale
models to explain principles of action on a much larger scale.
The main body of text contrasts two ways of calculating the
location of the center of the earth's sphere. Leonardo draws an
Aristotelian distinction between the "universal watery
sphere" and the "particular watery sphere" (like the tiniest
particles of dew), that is, between conditions pertaining to a
geometrically perfect sphere, of which the entire surface is
equidistant from the center and of which the mass is without
movement, and the conditions pertaining to an individual,
physically manifest sphere of water. Leonardo's underlying
assumption is that the defining forces of nature are geometric.
With characteristic precision and economy of visual means,
he describes the dynamics of a dewdrop (illustrated in the
right margin) to explain the location of the center in a "particular sphere of water." As the dewdrop increases in size, its
spherical shape flattens due to increasing internal pressure
on its skinlike surface. Text, accompanied by a diagram of concentric circles representing the increasing distension of the
surface, explains that as the dome of the drop flattens, the
drop approaches the perfect roundness of a "universal
sphere." In a closely related discussion in the Paris Ms. F,
folio 62 verso, contemporary with the Codex Leicester,
Leonardo adds that

> A drop of dew with its perfect curvature affords us an oppor-
> tunity to consider how the water sphere contains within itself
> the body of the earth without destruction of its sphericity of
> surface. If you take a cube of lead the size of a grain of millet,
> and by means of a very fine thread attached to it you sub-
> merge it in this drop, you will perceive that the drop will

not lose any of its original roundness, although it has been increased by an amount equal to the size of the cube which has been shut within it.[7]

Leonardo questions the siphon as explanation for the circulation of water throughout the earth by conceptualizing the problem in experimental terms. The cross-sectional diagram in the right margin of folio 34 verso showing the various densities of the earth's crust is related to the geometric diagram of the dewdrop directly below it. Leonardo's observations of a dewdrop address the traditional explanation for the circulation of water to mountain summits, which maintained that the height of the earth's seas is higher than the highest mountains (on which, see entry for Sheet 2). In a dozen pen-and-ink sketches of siphons scattered across the rest of the page, he considers how various configurations of siphons might account for raising water to the summits of mountains — but none do. Leonardo's draftsmanship on folio 34 verso, visually one of the most dramatic examples in the entire manuscript, can be especially appreciated today because of the freshness of the ink and the excellent condition of the ivory-colored paper.

In the main body of text on folio 34 verso, Leonardo asks whether the traditional explanation of siphoning action, first advanced by ancient writers such as Pliny the Elder and Seneca, adequately accounts for the differences between a spherical body subject to the actual forces of nature and a perfect "universal" sphere. The discussion continues on the reverse of the sheet, on folio 34 recto of Sheet 3B, in a short, cryptic paragraph and accompanying diagram at the center of the page, in which Leonardo illustrates the geometric principle in operation. The circumference of the circle in the diagram represents the surface of the earth. Lines (or, to use the mathematical term, chords) drawn through the circle intersect its circumference and mark off curved segments. The chords represent points of land, and the segment of the circumference between them represents sea. The diagram illustrates Ristoro's text, which argues that the sea is "higher than" the land because it bulges "above" the land. In the accompanying text, Leonardo questions Ristoro's geometry by drawing a concrete, easily accessible analogy with a bowl of water (not illustrated), which he imagines to be upside down to show that none of the water in the bowl rises "above" — that is, beyond — the bowl's outer surface. Therefore, anything that projects above the earth's surface, such as the mountains sketched in the diagram with the chords, is higher than any sea.

Sheet 3B, folio 3 verso, appears to contain the last set of notes that Leonardo wrote on the sheet. Here, it is again possible to follow Leonardo's line of thought as it moves between the visual and verbal registers. He considers other traditional explanations for the ability of water to reach the summits of mountains, such as evaporation within caverns that causes vapor to form in the same way that the sun generates clouds. Ristoro already made the analogy between this natural process and distillation, to which Leonardo adds that, under these conditions, heat generated at the center of the earth would also affect the level of the seas. The accompanying text and diagram describe an experiment recorded by Heron of Alexandria, one of Leonardo's known sources. In the ancient account, a piece of burning coal placed inside a vessel inverted over water consumes the air (oxygen) inside the vessel, and the water level rises. In Leonardo's retelling, the coal is described and shown "on top of the vessel" rather than within it. His explanation nonetheless is accurate in that the creation of a vacuum, not heat alone, causes the water level to rise.[8] The application of heat from above would draw air in but would not draw water up. The other two sketches in the right margin illustrate "instruments of the adversary" that incorrectly explain that water is drawn up by the use of siphons.

In summary, on Sheet 3, Leonardo questions traditional theories of the way water originates in mountain caverns by citing cases that contradict the assumption that caverns remain constantly full. This leads him to consider specific causes of water erosion. Closely related statements occur on folios 3 verso, 21 recto, 31 recto, and 34 recto and verso. The cohesive properties of the surface of the water drop, an important part of Leonardo's analysis of the dewdrop, are considered further on Sheet 10, where he lists twenty-three cases of cohesion resulting from the action of water and returns to the question of whether vaporization in caverns might be the cause of water circulating inside the earth. Related discussion about the circulation of water also occurs on Sheet 6, where Leonardo takes issue with the theory that seas are higher than mountains by observing the action of actual seas and rivers. The same dialectic between categories of the "universal" and the "particular" that takes place here recurs throughout the studies of water in the Codex Leicester.

SHEET 7
Sheet 7A (front) comprises folios 30 verso, 7 recto
Sheet 7B (back) comprises folios 7 verso, 30 recto

Pen and dark brown ink over stylus ruling and soft black chalk or leadpoint, 299 × 447 mm (11 ¾ × 17 ⅝ in.) maximum
Full transcription of Leonardo's extensive text in Pedretti 1987a, pp. 55–62.
Inscribed on lower left of front of page and on back of page with unrelated left-handed dashes in red chalk; front and back of page annotated with numbers in graphite by a modern hand (the compiler of a facsimile?)

This sheet continues the discussion on Sheets 1 and 2, beginning with the text on folio 30 verso of Sheet 7A, which (along with an illustrated discussion of the movement of water from the center of the earth) repeats arguments elsewhere that the radiance of the moon is softened by the contours of waves on its surface. This leads to the question discussed on folio 7 recto: under what conditions is the moon most luminous? On folio 7 recto of Sheet 7A, Leonardo takes into account the reflection of light from the earth's waters to explain variations in the radiance of the moon (also discussed on folios 2 verso and 5 recto). Summarizing these arguments with the help of geometric diagrams similar to those on folios 1 recto and 2 recto, Leonardo claims that the moon is brightest when it receives strong solar rays reflected from the oceans of the earth. The diagram shows that light from the sun (at right) reflected by the earth (at far left) onto the dark side of the moon (center) causes the ashen light that surrounds the lunar disk at the time of the crescent moon. Leonardo's aim is to account for variations in the brightness of the moon over the lunar cycle. The argument exemplifies his faith in the geometric structure of the universe, which encouraged such thought experiments based on analogies. Leonardo's proposal could not be verified then, but further questioning of the prevailing theory that the moon's surface is mirrorlike resulted, later in the sixteenth century, in Galileo's proposal, verified by telescopic observations of the moon's surface, that light from neighboring bodies affects the light of the moon (for Galileo's knowledge of Leonardo's manuscripts, see my essay in this volume).

Sheet 7, containing passages on various topics, is a disjointed compilation of odds and ends in comparison with the focused set of investigations recorded on the adjacent Sheet 3, for example. The three passages at the bottom of folio 7 recto, the last of which is fitted into the margins of the page and illustrated with delicately rendered stereographic views, deals with the placement of weirs in a way that protects a bridge's foundations by diverting currents that otherwise could cause erosion.[9] The behavior of descending water is discussed on folio 30 verso of Sheet 7A, with illustrations that refer to the gain in velocity as water descends in a pipe. The first passage at the top of this page, also illustrated, describes the action of a small tornado with its twisting column of air and sand.

Sheet 7B deals with practical problems of water erosion in general theoretical terms as well as experimentally ("Let ditches be made in that side along which the empty wells will quickly be filled"). The passage at the top of folio 7 verso contains observations about water descending through pipes and mountains, a topic also discussed on the opposite side of the sheet, on folio 30 verso.

The last paragraph on folio 7 verso of Sheet 7B, accompanied by four illustrations, revisits the problem of the composition of the moon explained in terms of its radiance. Leonardo observes that light travels in all directions, while the stationary observer sees only a small portion of the cosmic whole. His logic, driven by acute observation, is again directed against the traditional theory that the moon's surface is polished like a mirror. In that case, Leonardo argues, the observer would see one large image rather than many small images formed when the sun reflects on each facet of a surface in relief. This explanation supports the actual case, which is that the moon's surface shines with a soft radiance, unlike the brightness of a single large image reflected on a polished surface. The discussion on folio 30 recto of Sheet 7B is probably the codex's final passage on the composition of the moon—judging from its summary of points that Leonardo made on the pages located at the front of the codex in its bound form, on folios 1 recto and verso, 2 recto and verso, 5 recto, and 7 recto and verso. On folio 30 recto, Leonardo adds a new observation to corroborate his theory that the soft luminosity of the moon is due to its textured watery surface: he notes that the moon becomes less luminous whenever a storm arises at sea. The unrelated last paragraph on folio 30 recto, accompanied by an illustration, describes a water clock that would gauge the distance a ship travels in an hour (a related discussion occurs on folio 13 recto).

SHEET 9
Sheet 9A (front) comprises folios 28 verso, 9 recto
Sheet 9B (back) comprises folios 9 verso, 28 recto
Pen and dark brown ink, 298 × 446 mm (11 ¾ × 17 ½ in.) maximum
Full transcription of Leonardo's extensive text in Pedretti

1987a, pp. 72–83.
Inscribed on front and back of page with numbers in graphite by a modern hand (the compiler of a facsimile?)

Folio 9 recto of Sheet 9A, headed by Leonardo's notation that "10 sheets and 853 conclusions" follow, has sometimes been interpreted as signifying the beginning of a compilation on water. Yet the discussion on folio 9 recto is clearly a continuation of topics on the previous page, folio 8 verso of Sheet 8B; and the heading is an afterthought. The text concerns a subject frequently encountered in the codex, that of accounting for the presence of seashells on mountaintops. Drawing from his own experience as an engineer and referring to the geography of the Mediterranean basin (which he knew primarily from maps), Leonardo notes the resemblance between configurations of shells found on mountaintops and deposits of shells laid at the point where rivers "empty themselves into the sea."

On folio 9 recto, Leonardo's account of the formation of the gap at Gonfolina rock derives from Giovanni Villani's *Historiae* (1348), which argues that the gap was artificially made. After considering in detail how the churning of water associated with the Deluge would have affected the deposit of shells, Leonardo disagrees. He then discusses a variety of conditions that make water powerful and ends with the idea of writing an entire "book" on the places occupied by fresh water. The last part of the page gives practical advice, including a beautiful, detailed sketch of the way wooden bridge timbers should be set at a slant to avoid the direct impact of logs floating downriver.

The discussion of fossils continues on Sheet 9B, folio 9 verso, a page almost completely covered with text. Leonardo's thoughts move from water to fire in the form of heat and its part of the earth's system, and on to air in the form of wind. Altogether, this page is one of Leonardo's most comprehensive treatments of the macrocosm in terms of the four elements. The key passage on the page implies an alternate, cyclical theory for the composition of the earth based on the presence of seashells on mountaintops. Leonardo argues that mollusk shells were left on the Strait of Gibraltar by the Mediterranean Sea when the sea drained from its former, higher level to the level of the outer oceans. Next, a consideration of the action of waves at the shore leads to observations of nature and then to experiments in a specially constructed glass tank to explore the effects of waves and surface wind on objects in a body of water. A long tank, with an inlet on one end and an outlet on the other, has one of its long sides constructed of glass (illustrated in Paris Ms. F, folio 20 verso). This feature allows Leonardo to look into a stream of water from the side and from the top. He describes two experiments, sketched in the right margin, to predict the way that wind will affect an object submerged in water.

Leonardo plans to conduct two experiments in what he calls his testing "pit," which must refer to the canals near Milan given to him in 1508 by the French governor for the purpose of testing the movement of water. One experiment will show the effects of wind on a floating object in water; the other will determine whether small waves on the water's surface will "cause the water to move high above its bottom." Both experiments are intended to show that the action of neither wind nor waves could have washed shells up mountain slopes during the Deluge. Both tests utilize an apparatus, illustrated in greater detail in Paris Ms. I, folio 67, for studying the patterns of water flow and rebound. Only one of these tests uses a marker to make the movement clear, but elsewhere the use of dyes is described to mark the patterns of two currents mingling. Leonardo's ingenious approach is commonplace today.

Folio 28 recto of Sheet 9B and its verso (folio 28 verso of Sheet 9A) are devoted to further practical applications of the dynamics of water—driving piles and arranging the slope of a weir so that neither will be subject to erosion, for example. In this connection, an exquisite drawing of the complex action of water, in the lower right margin on folio 28 verso, might be described as a preliminary sketch for Leonardo's well-known magisterial drawing of the same subject at Windsor (RL 12660v). One of the most vivid images in the entire codex is not a drawing at all but a verbal description, on folio 28 recto, a page almost completely covered with text, comparing systems of ramification in the earth's body with those of animals. Here, Leonardo analyzes weather as a system involving the condensation and evaporation of water that creates clouds and hurricanes. His description in lucid detail of the formation of a thunderhead that he once observed is reminiscent of another well-known drawing, the red-chalk rendering made in 1506 of a storm forming over a valley (fig. 178). On the same page, he records an idea for using a waterwheel to measure wind and water velocity.

SHEET 13
Sheet 13A (front) comprises folios 24 verso, 13 recto
Sheet 13B (back) comprises folios 13 verso, 24 recto

Pen and dark brown ink, 297 × 445 mm (11 ¾ × 17 ½ in.) maximum
Full transcription of Leonardo's extensive text in Pedretti 1987a, pp. 113–22.
Inscribed on front and back of page with numbers in graphite by a modern hand (the compiler of a facsimile?)

The main topic on this sheet is the maintenance of navigable rivers and canals. The discussion apparently begins with the top paragraph on folio 13 recto of Sheet 13A, which concerns the effects of tides and river currents on the stability of water channels. It continues from upper right to lower left of Sheet 13A in the sequence Pedretti describes as Leonardo's standard procedure.[10]

Leonardo identified two passages on folio 13 recto and one on 24 verso (both on Sheet 13A) as being from Libro A, a lost manuscript reconstructed by Pedretti from passages incorporated into the Codex Urbinas Latinus 1270, the parent manuscript of Leonardo's projected treatise on painting.[11] The system of acknowledging the source document, while not in itself unusual, is the same as that used by the editors of the Codex Urbinas, except that Leonardo documents his sources within the body of the text rather than in marginal notes, as the editors did. Pedretti maintains that the folio numbers of the Codex Leicester are "almost certainly" by the same hand as the folio numbers of Paris Mss. C and L, although these notebooks are of much earlier date. In keeping with this evidence, which suggests the activities of Francesco Melzi or someone else who organized an entire collection of Leonardo manuscripts, Pedretti proposes, contra André Corbeau (who hypothesized that the codex passed through the hands of Pompeo Leoni), that the Codex Leicester belonged to Melzi before it went to Guglielmo della Porta by 1577.[12]

At the top of folio 13 recto, Leonardo added a memorandum referring to Leon Battista Alberti's treatise on ships and naval engineering, *De navis* (now lost), and to Frontinus's *De aquis urbis romae* (Rome, 1490), a classical text. The majority of the twenty-one "cases" on folio 24 verso that Leonardo describes, however, are based on his own experiences. Such topics as the behavior of water around obstacles lead him to consider, more generally, the varieties of underwater motion. Their confluence and intersection give rise to suggestions for preventing the erosion of riverbeds, illustrated on folio 13 recto by a section on the left bank of the Arno River in Florence, near the Ponte Vecchio.[13] Among other ideas, he

suggests suspending a small weight near the bottom of transparent water to study the motions below the surface.

On Sheet 13B, folio 24 recto, Leonardo records a novel idea for constructing obstacles to prevent the erosion of riverbanks. The series of pen-and-ink sketches in the right margin, among the most memorable graphics in the entire manuscript, continues on the left side of Sheet 13B (folio 13 verso), where Leonardo addresses theoretical considerations about the shape of obstacles relative to riverbeds. His method of quantification is rooted in geometric ratios, not in absolute units of measure. He is, typically, searching for ways to describe rates of change for two variables simultaneously.

Throughout the studies of water collected in the Codex Leicester, Leonardo proposes experiments that would permit him to see how surface obstacles affect river currents and the bottoms of streams. He adds dyes, fine seeds, and other particles to show the interaction of various currents. Studies are documented in the Codex Leicester and other notebooks, including Paris Mss. F, G, H, I, and in the posthumously compiled scrapbook known as the Codex Atlanticus. In the Codex Leicester, a glass-box water tank is mentioned specifically on folios 9 verso, 13 verso, and 29 verso, but many more sequences are based on the results of these experiments.

Diagrams in the margin of folio 24 recto show one of these experiments. Leonardo recognized not only the relationship between the surface of water and its bottom but also the dynamics of the intervening fluid mass. His account of the behavior of particles suspended in a medium were unprecedented then and are central to the science of fluid dynamics today. An experiment illustrated in the margins of Sheet 13B and also recorded on C.A. 81 recto uses millet seed in suspension to show currents interacting. In the Codex Atlanticus experiments, the glass box has an outlet at the bottom, and millet seed mixed with the water demonstrates the behavior of the water once the outlet is unplugged. The results prove that a faster, central water current develops under these conditions. With that observation, Leonardo explains the behavior of currents in a stream, for example, on folios 9 verso and 19 verso of the Codex Leicester.

SHEET 14
Sheet 14A (front) comprises folios 23 verso, 14 recto
Sheet 14B (back) comprises folios 14 verso, 23 recto
Pen and dark brown ink over some traces of black chalk or leadpoint (?), 300 × 448 mm (11 ¹³⁄₁₆ × 17 ⅝ in.) maximum

Full transcription of Leonardo's extensive text in Pedretti 1987a, pp. 122–30.
Inscribed on front of page with numbers and letters in graphite on back with numbers, all by a modern hand (the compiler of a facsimile?)

The eighty-five cases catalogued on this sheet all concern situations in which two or more currents meet. Four passages on folio 14 recto (Sheet 14A) are excerpted from Libro A. For the historian, folio 14 recto is one of the most interesting pages dealing with hydrodynamics, because it demonstrates the interdependence of Leonardo's aesthetic and scientific interests. Obstacles create beautiful stationary patterns in the fluid medium of water, as many famous examples in his drawing corpus testify. Leonardo used obstacles to experiment with prevention of riverbank erosion, as shown on all four sides of this sheet and Sheet 13, adjacent to it. We know from roughly contemporaneous notes in the Paris Ms. F that Leonardo planned to write a "book" on the ecology of maintaining waterways, which would have dealt with obstacles in water.

In the margins of the Codex Leicester, complex sets of obstacles are sketched in three major places: folios 15 verso, 24 recto, and 14 verso. A series of geometric shapes on folio 15 verso alongside the mention of the desire for a structured study makes clear that Leonardo planned a discussion of the control of rivers much broader than the existing one in regard to obstacles. On folio 24 recto of Sheet 13A, the text shifts from concerns with the proper placement of objects to controlling the river as a system in which obstacles play only a partial role. On folio 14 recto, the objects are again the focus; the discussion concerns complex interactions between multiple sets of currents and obstacles. The wide range of sources upon which Leonardo has drawn testifies to his ability to recognize key issues and bring together important information from various general principles. This includes a discussion of cloud formation from water vapor. Leonardo's concern with friction (*confregazione*) shows sensitivity to the physics as well as the geometry of water flow, an aspect of his work sometimes overlooked by modern scholars.

Sheet 14B, consisting of folios 14 verso and 23 recto, lists cases involving the percussion of waves, including standing waves in which impulses alone are transmitted. The accompanying diagrams of wave action illustrate emanating impulses that create circular standing patterns. A captivating series of drawings on folio 14 verso represents wave patterns rendered in stereographic view, as well as a variety of two-dimensional diagrams. Topics revolve around such concrete considerations as the way an elongated object produces circular waves in moving water.

Leonardo observes the particular actions of water as part of the entire system of the body of the earth. Even when these connections are not overtly made, they are present in the Aristotelian form of his text. Although the most visible use of geometry in his work is found in his diagrams and his sketches of devices, another geometric aspect is in the structure of his writing. Leonardo's sustained observations are often constructed as a series of linked axioms leading to a conclusion. Considered altogether, his series of words and images constitutes a type of geometric proof. Folio 14 recto is an excellent example, which considers the particular actions of water as belonging to the universal nature of water.

SHEET 15
Sheet 15A (front) comprises folios 22 verso, 15 recto
Sheet 15B (back) comprises folios 15 verso, 22 recto
Pen and dark brown ink, over traces of black chalk or leadpoint, 300×447 mm ($11\,^{13}/_{16} \times 17\,^{5}/_{8}$ in.) maximum
Full transcription of Leonardo's extensive text in Pedretti 1987a, pp. 130–40.
Inscribed on front of page with sequential numbers in graphite by a modern hand (the compiler of a facsimile?)

One of the most interesting aspects of the Codex Leicester is its documentation of the manner in which Leonardo applied his observations to practical, and sometimes highly imaginative, devices. The short descriptions of projects and natural phenomena on Sheet 15 represent many years of observations recorded in small notebooks. Among the myriad practical applications that Leonardo outlines are suggestions for maintaining riverbanks, setting piles in river bottoms, constructing and maintaining dams, and properly joining canals to rivers.

We also catch a glimpse of the historical connections between these experiments and attendant speculations, on the one hand, and Leonardo's consulting work as a water engineer. On folio 15 recto (Sheet 15A), he recommends a small experiment with sand to study what happens when streams of different sizes are united. Specific sites on the Arno River (at Refredi, Mugnone, and Ombrone), noted on sketches in the lower right margin refer to one of his first schemes to regulate and divert the flow of the river. This project of 1504 as recorded on RL 12277, C.A. fol. 46r-b, and elsewhere would have diverted the Arno toward Prato and Pistoia. Leonardo planned to go under the mountain pass at Serravalle, an engineering feat of unprecedented scale, and transform the huge, marshy valley of Chiana into an artificial lake. The lake was to serve as a retention basin connected to Lake Trasiveno by means of a tunnel under the hills between Mugnano and San Savino.[14]

On folio 22 verso of Sheet 15A, Leonardo diagrams one form of sluice to flush a canal bottom clear of silt and another to cause silt to be deposited before it could fill the mouth of a river with soil. His famous description of a simple snorkel for breathing under water—incompletely described to prevent man's "evil nature" from abusing the ability to remain under-water for extremely extended stays—is also given on folio 22 verso. Another part of this page tells how the flow of water can be controlled to "strike fear into the hearts of the enemy," how infantry troops might best ford a river using wineskin floats, and how a man can escape a whirlpool by simply seek-ing "the reflex current that will cast him out of the depths." Of course, one would need Leonardo's knowledge of the forms and action of eddies to apply that advice.

On folio 22 recto of Sheet 15B, he classifies categories of waves produced by various kinds of obstacles, illustrated in marginal sketches. On the other side of Sheet 15, in the upper right margin of folio 15 verso, Leonardo provides an outline for the book on water. It shows that he intended to define the science of water as deductive, issuing from first principles and descending from the general to the specific. Similar schemes are recorded on Paris Ms. F, folio 87 verso (1508), and else-where.[15] Because the main body of text is concerned with con-trolling water flow in canals by means of engineered "obstacles" in various shapes and sizes, we can reasonably infer that his thoughts once again developed while he experi-mented on a section of the Milanese canal donated to him for that purpose.

CF

1. Ligabue 1977 has most recently collected the evidence of Leonardo's field-work. Several maps, including Windsor, RL 12278 (of the plains of Arezzo); C.A., fol. 336v (the district of Luzio); and Windsor, RL 12688 (the Arno Valley), chart the places he visited looking for fossils.

2. For an overview of the cosmological tradition, see Barkan 1975, pp. 8ff.; Atlers 1944; and Kemp 1989b, pp. 93–143.

3. See Millosevich 1919, pp. 17–19; Pedretti 1987a, p. 13 n. 3, cites additional literature, noting that Kepler was the first to account for the light correctly in print, based on the ideas of his teacher Michael Maestlin, but Galileo also discussed it in 1610 in terms similar to those of Leonardo and Pietro Accolti; both Galileo and Accolti had access to Leonardo's manuscripts. See also Edgerton 1984; Reeves 1997.

4. On his studies of moving shadows about 1505, see Rzepinska 1962.

5. Leonardo recorded similar thoughts on the subject in the Paris Ms. F, especially folio 27 recto, where he played with Platonic configurations of the elements as distinct geometric states.

6. Pedretti 1987a, app. 5, pp. 182–83, summarizes the physical evidence of page correlation.

7. Translation from Kemp 1981, p. 313.

8. Many thanks to Michael Furr for explaining this experiment to me and for recognizing the ancient source.

9. See Pedretti 1987a, p. 56 n. 3; Di Teodoro and Barbi 1983.

10. Pedretti 1987a, pp. 182ff.

11. Pedretti 1964.

12. Pedretti 1987a, p. 165; Corbeau 1968.

13. Pedretti 1987a, p. 115 n. 4, summarizes Calvi and Richter; Vezzosi 1984 includes invaluable photographs of the sites that Leonardo sketched.

14. See further, Zammattio 1974.

15. C.A., fols. 74r-a, v-a, r-b, v-b, and 79r-a, v-b, also contemporary with the Codex Leicester, were first signaled by Calvi as Leonardo's earliest attempt to gather headings on water before compiling the codex. Within the Codex Leicester, the outline on folio 15 verso is the most extensive, but other schemes for organizing a treatise occur on folios 2 verso, 3 recto, 5 recto, 17 verso, 22 verso, 35 recto, and passim.

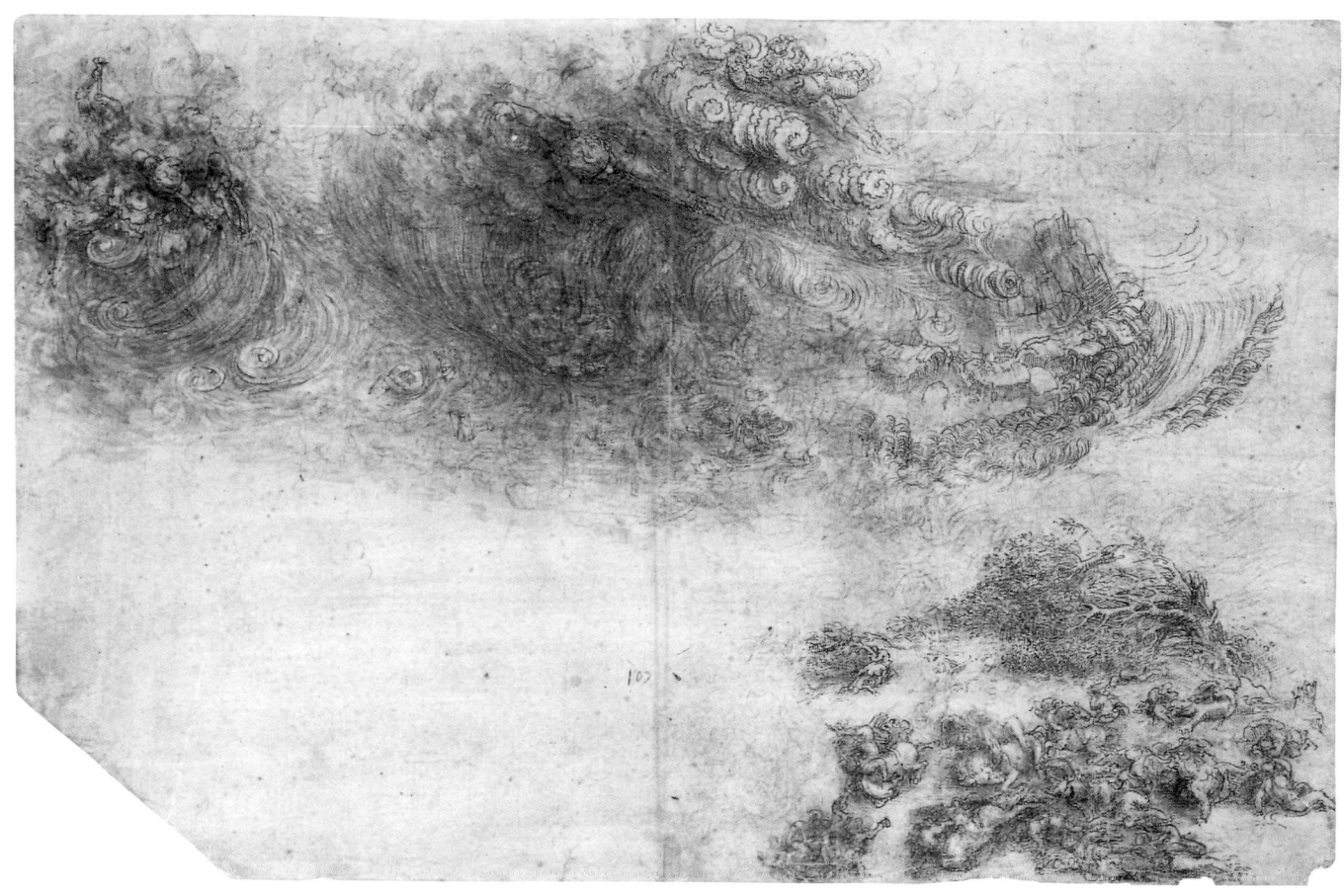

LEONARDO DA VINCI

115. *Cataclysmic Storm Striking a Landscape with a Cavalry*

Charcoal or soft black chalk reworked with pen and golden and dark brown ink, brush and brown wash, on cream-color paper smudged gray in many parts with charcoal; small traces of white gouache highlights on group at lower right, 266 × 409 mm (10½ × 16⅛ in.) maximum; lower left corner cropped

Lent by Her Majesty Queen Elizabeth II, Royal Library, Windsor Castle 12376

PROVENANCE: Windsor Leoni volume: 1519, Francesco Melzi, Milan and Rome (1491/93–ca. 1570); ca. 1570, Orazio Melzi; by 1590, Pompeo Leoni, Madrid and Milan (ca. 1533–1608; Lugt under 2885); ca. 1613, Thomas Howard, second earl of Arundel (1586–1646); before 1690, British Royal Collection (inventory of King George III's collection, ca. 1810).

LITERATURE: Richter 1883, vol. 1, pp. 305–7, nos. 606 n., 608 n., pl. 34; Müntz 1898, vol. 2, p. 25 (detail); Müntz 1899, p. 285; Berenson 1903, vol. 2, p. 67, no. 1240; Seidlitz 1911, p. 288, no. 793; Poggi 1919, pl. 126; Venturi 1919, p. 196, fig. 19; Venturi 1920, pp. 131–32, fig. 105; Venturi 1925, fig. 109; De Rinaldis 1926, p. 211, fig. 56; Commissione Vinciana 1928– , vol. 6, p. 24, pl. 253; Popp 1928, pp. 17, 53–54, no. 78; Sirén 1928, pl. 167; Popham 1930–31, p. 27, no. 92, pl. 86; Berenson 1938, vol. 1, p. 182, vol. 2, p. 137, no. 1240; MacCurdy 1939, vol. 2, pl. 21; Goldscheider 1952, pls. 57, 58; Gould 1952, figs. 20, 22; Royal Academy of Arts 1952, no. 221 (hors catalogue); Clark 1954, pl. 49; Heydenreich 1954, vol. 1, p. 155, vol. 2, p. 170, pl. 236; Gantner 1958, pp. 115, 184, 193, 200–201, 205, fig. 43; Goldscheider 1959, p. 174, pl. 82; Arthur Ewart Popham in Royal Academy of Arts 1960, p. 198, no. 485; Berenson 1961, vol. 2, p. 243, no. 1240; Eissler 1961, pp. 267–68, 270, 273, pl. 49; Clark and Pedretti 1968–69, vol. 1, pp. 52–53, no. 12376; Clark 1969–70, p. 36, no. 145; Richter 1970, vol. 1, pp. 351–52, nos. 606 n., 608 n., pl. 34; Lavagnino 1980, p. 129; Pedretti and Clark 1980–81, p. 50, no. 49; Kemp 1981, p. 321; Pedretti 1982a, pp. 138–40, no. 68 recto; Gombrich 1984, p. 19, pl. 12; Pedretti 1987a, pp. 116–17, 123, fig. 137; Clark 1988, pp. 241–46, fig. 115; Agghazy 1989, p. 69, fig. 83; Kemp and Roberts 1989, pp. 134–35, no. 64; Popham 1994, no. 290; Dolev 1995, p. 139, fig. 12; Pedretti 1996d, fig. 3; Letze and Buchsteiner 1997, p. 150; Marani 1997, pp. 179–80, figs. 12, 13;

627

Arasse 1998, pp. 442, 444, fig. 304; Graziella Federici Vescovini in Frosini 1998, fig. 1b; Marani 2000b, pp. 323–30; Clayton 2002–3, pp. 45–47, no. 10.

This haunting composition portrays the mythical destructive powers of water and is extremely similar in theme to ten other drawings representing the subject of the Deluge (see cat. no. 116; fig. 198).[1] Although it is clearly a direct precursor to these drawings, the present composition is technically not part of the series, as it is roughly twice their size and also includes a landscape with dying horsemen on the lower half of the pictorial field.

Leonardo's extensive notes on geology in the Codex Leicester (cat. no. 114), dating from 1508–12, as well as in shorter sections in the Codex Atlanticus and Codex Arundel, had attempted to arrive at an understanding of the causes and effects of the Deluge (diluvio) in scientific terms. He refuted at some length what he perceived to be pseudoscientific explanations of, for instance, the deposit of seashells in high mountains.[2] Yet when it came to pictorial representations of the Deluge, he reached for the storytelling devices of classical mythology: "Neptune will be seen in the midst of the waters with his trident, and let Aeolus with his winds be shown entangling the trees floating uprooted, and whirling in the huge waves."[3] His written descriptions and the series of Deluge drawings at Windsor evoke the imagery of destruction by wind and water that is the subject of a long passage in Ovid's Metamorphoses (1:260–312). The artist certainly owned the book, for he listed it in the Codex Madrid II (fols. 2v–3r) as among those "locked in the chest."

The verses from Ovid tell of the wrath of Jupiter, who unleashed the gods controlling the winds and commanded Neptune to flood the world: "The wrath of Jove is not content with the waters from his own sky; his sea-god brother [Neptune] aids him with auxiliary waves. . . . The rivers overleap all bounds and flood the open plains. And not alone orchards, crops and herds, men and dwellings, but shrines as well as their sacred contents do they sweep away. . . . And now the sea and land have no distinction. All is sea, and a sea without shore."[5]

The present drawing portrays a vision of the destructive forces of wind and waters in strong narrative terms, true to the spirit of Ovid and to the description of the diluvio in Leonardo's note, with a towering hurricane sweeping over men, horses, and trees on the lower right. Clearly unfinished, the drawing is extensively reworked with pen and brown ink and washes over an agitated, smoky underdrawing in charcoal or soft black chalk. At the upper center, to the right of the sheet's crease, appears the barely discernible sketchy foreshortened figure of a chubby putto, a god of the winds and storms, his arms outstretched. Blowing from his mouth, he unleashes the fury of the winds and the tidal waves that mercilessly swallow up rocks, trees, men, and horses in the scene below. It is quite possible that a grouping of Neptune commanding his quadriga of rearing sea horses, much as in the draft of the finished drawing presented to Antonio Segni (cat. no. 93), may be seen in underdrawn reinforcement lines on the left half of the sheet, about midpoint. On the lower right of the sheet, the arrangement of the tiny groups of struggling men and horses is not unlike that in the much earlier Battle of Anghiari. The model for the arrangement is thought to have been an antique gem or the Roman sarcophagus depicting the Fall of Phaeton (Villa Borghese, Rome) that was originally on the Aracoeli steps in Rome.

CCB

1. The sheets in the Windsor Deluge series include RL 12377, 12378 (cat. no. 116), 12379, 12380 (fig. 198), 12381, 12382, 12383, 12384, 12385, and 12386.
2. See Richter 1970, vol. 2, pp. 168–76, nos. 985–994A.
3. Paris Ms. G, fol. 6v; Richter 1970, vol. 1, p. 352, no. 607: "Nettuno si vedea in mezzo alle acque col tride[n]te e vedeasi Eolo colli sua ve[n]ti ravuilupare nota[n]ti pia[n]te diradicate miste colle imme[n]se o[n]de, l'orizzo[n]te con tutto lo emisperio era turbo e focoso per li ricie vuti vanpi delle continue saette."
4. See Ladislao Reti in Codex Madrid 1974, vol. 3, pp. 56–58, vol. 5, pp. 5–6.
5. Quoted from Ovid 1977 (1:274–91), pp. 21–23.

LEONARDO DA VINCI

116. *Cataclysmic Deluge Striking a Town*

Charcoal or soft black chalk over leadpoint on coarse-fiber paper (originally cream or light tan color), 161 × 210 mm (6⅜ × 8¼ in.) Lent by Her Majesty Queen Elizabeth II, Royal Library, Windsor Castle 12378

PROVENANCE: Windsor Leoni volume: 1519, Francesco Melzi, Milan and Rome (1491/93 – ca. 1570); ca. 1570, Orazio Melzi; by 1590, Pompeo Leoni, Madrid and Milan (ca. 1533 – 1608; Lugt under 2885); ca. 1613, Thomas Howard, second earl of Arundel (1586 – 1646); before 1690, British Royal Collection (inventory of King George III's collection, ca. 1810).

LITERATURE: Berenson 1903, vol. 2, p. 67, no. 1242; Commissione Vinciana 1928 – , vol. 6, p. 24, pl. 259.2; Popp 1928, pp. 12, 20, 55, no. 84; Berenson 1938, vol. 1, p. 182, vol. 2, p. 137, no. 1242; Goldscheider 1952, pl. 63; Royal Academy of Arts 1952, no. 219

(hors catalogue); Heydenreich 1954, vol. 1, pp. 158 – 59, vol. 2, p. 173, pl. 239; Gantner 1958, pp. 207, 215, fig. 48; Berenson 1961, vol. 2, p. 243, no. 1242; Eissler 1961, pp. 267 – 68, 270, pl. 52; Clark and Pedretti 1968 – 69, vol. 1, pp. 53 – 54, no. 12378; Clark 1969 – 70, p. 37, no. 147b; Pedretti and Clark 1980 – 81, p. 49, no. 44; Kemp 1981, pp. 320 – 22, pl. 85; Pedretti 1982a, p. 128, no. 62 recto; Clark 1988, pp. 241 – 46, fig. 112; Kemp and Roberts 1989a, p. 136, no. 66; Marani 1989, pp. 9 – 10, fig. 4; Pedretti 1990b, p. 36, fig. 36; Popham 1994, no. 296; Marani 1997, pp. 156 – 57, fig. 1; Arasse 1998, pp. 111, 114, fig. 60.

This and nine other drawings of closely similar size, style, and technique that are also at the Royal Library in Windsor offer variations on the theme of a cataclysmic deluge

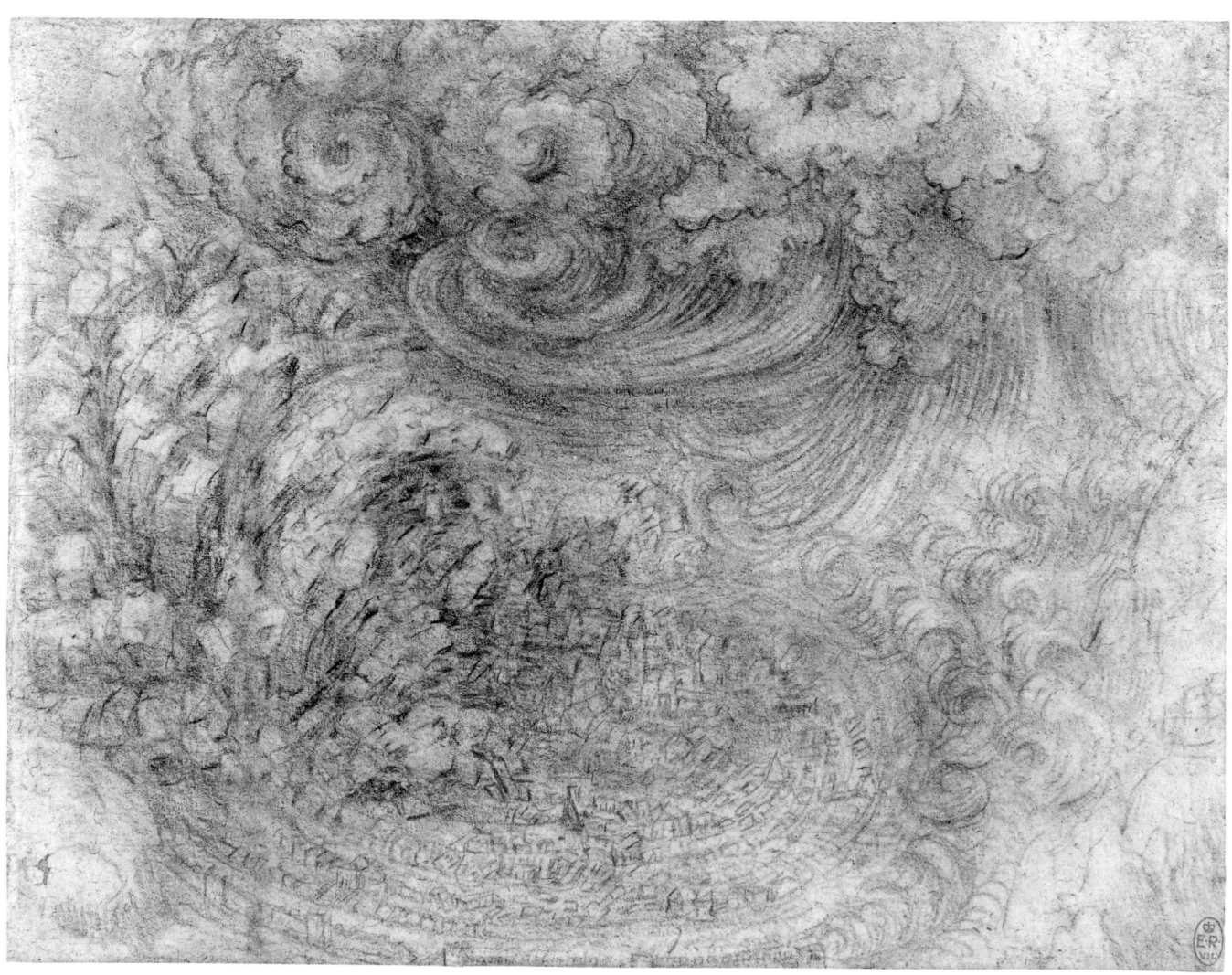

Cat. 116

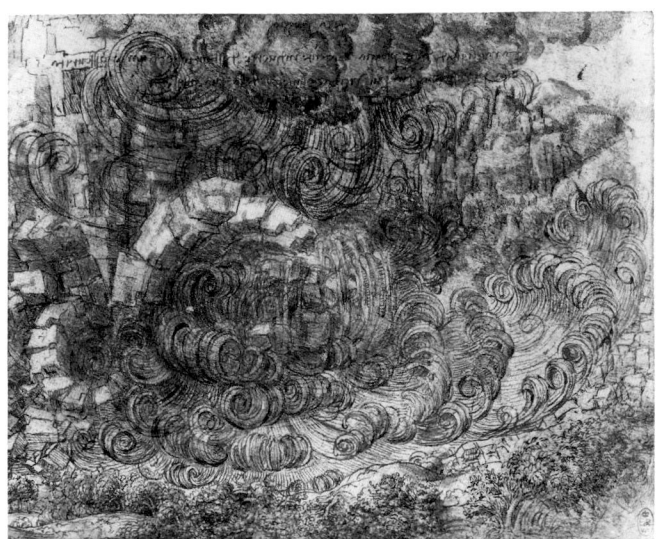

Fig. 198. Leonardo da Vinci, *Storm over a Hilly Landscape (Deluge)*. Pen with light brown and dark brown ink, black chalk, 162 × 203 mm. The Royal Collection, H.M. Queen Elizabeth II, Windsor Castle RL 12380

(*diluvio*), a subject that Leonardo amply described in his notes.[1] Like the present sheet, the nine other drawings are executed in charcoal or a soft black chalk, and two of these are also reworked with pen and ink (fig. 198 and Windsor, RL 12379). Catalogue number 115 has often been considered to be part of this *Deluge* series, but its size and technique are too remarkably different; its technique suggests that it is probably slightly earlier in date.

Here, the enormous tidal waves produced by a cataclysmic storm create a destructive vortex that envelops the falling rocks of a mountain on the left and a town seen in a distant valley, in the lower center. In its arresting power of evocation, the drawing offers a pictorial equivalent of one of Leonardo's descriptions of a deluge that swallows up cities and farmhouses. The mood suggests the artist succumbing to an apocalyptic vision, as he contemplates the destruction of the world from a distance. In pictures and in words, he conjures up a gradual descent into a chaotic underworld of Dantesque dimensions:

> And the ruins of a mountain fall into the depth of a valley, creating a shore for the swollen waters of its river, which, having already burst its banks, will rush onward with monstrous waves, the greatest of which will strike and destroy the walls of the cities and farmhouses in the valley. And the ruins of the high buildings in these cities will throw up immense dust that rises like smoke or wreathed clouds against the

falling rain. But the engorged waters will cascade around the pool that contains them, striking in eddying whirlpools against different obstacles, throwing up muddy foam as they leap into the air before falling back and then again being dashed into the air. And the whirling waves that flow from the site of percussion are impelled across other eddies going in opposite direction, and afterward their recoil will be tossed up into the air, without dashing off from the surface. And at the outlet where the water flows from the pool, the spent waves will be seen spreading out toward the outlet, and afterward, falling or pouring through the air, and gaining weight and impetuous movement, [this water] will hit the water below, pierce through it in a furious rush to reach bottom, and then being thrown back, the [water] returns to the surface of the lake, carrying with it the air that was submerged with it, and it remains at the outlet, its foam mingled with logs of wood and other things lighter than water. . . . The crests of the waves of the sea tumble down to their bases, whirling and falling with friction above the bubbles on their side.[2]

All this portrays, to quote yet another passage of Leonardo, a "cruel slaughter of the human race by the wrath of God."[3] Some scholars have regarded the *Deluge* as the artist's last graphic production (although, as usual with Leonardo, there is hardly a consensus), with the dates proposed for the drawings ranging widely, from 1512 to as late as 1517–18. On the basis of style and context, a date about 1515–17 seems convincing. Kenneth Clark and Carlo Pedretti have adduced as evidence for such dating a page with sketches that includes a description of winds and a mountain caving over a town;[4] the verso of that page contains a reference to a shipment of artillery from Venice to Lyons, presumably from the time of Francis I's expedition to Italy in 1515, although the date of the note is not certain. As proposed by Martin Clayton, there are aspects in the style and technique of the *Deluge* drawings that relates them to sheets from Leonardo's French period (1517–18). It is also not entirely clear to what extent Leonardo intended the ten Windsor *Deluge* drawings to form a series (the homogeneity of their theme and production would suggest so), or whether he meant them to be interpreted in terms of a narrative order. As Martin Kemp has rightly observed, the possible function of the *Deluge* drawings as a means for instruction may be surmised from the fact that Leonardo's notes for his projected painting treatise, or *Libro di pittura*, also offer highly descriptive advice to painters regarding the portrayals of a *diluvio* (deluge).[5] And one of the drawings from the series is inscribed by Leonardo with a brief note on how to depict rain and its varied darkness (fig. 198). The relatively finished character of the drawings suggests that he may have conceived them as works of art in and of themselves, as demonstration pieces independent from a treatise. A few of the compositions exhibit traces of framing outlines, and the versos of all of the sheets seem to be blank. Next to nothing, however, is known about the circumstances of their production. Without pressing the point too far, the *Deluge* drawings could have been conceived as presentation pieces; by the late fifteenth and early sixteenth centuries, many relatively finished drawings were intended for patrons and friends. Famous examples are Leonardo's presentation drawing of *Neptune Commanding His Quadriga of Sea Horses* for Antonio Segni (cat. no. 93), as well as the *teste divine* and other types of compositions by Michelangelo for Gherardo Perini, Tommaso de' Cavalieri, and Vittoria Colonna. Such a hypothesis certainly cannot be rejected on the grounds of provenance. It is true that Leonardo probably kept the drawings in his possession until his death, since it can be established that the Windsor *Deluge* drawings passed through the hands of Francesco Melzi and Pompeo Leoni (on their way to the British royal collection). Yet a patron cannot be excluded, for, if the series did not represent a completed project, then it would not have been presented to the intended recipient.[6]

CCB

1. The other nine closely related *Deluge* drawings are Windsor, RL 12377, 12379, 12380 (fig. 198), 12381, 12382, 12383, 12384, 12385, and 12386.
2. Windsor, RL 12665r; Richter 1970, vol. 1, pp. 355–56, no. 609: " E le ruine d'alcuni monti sien disciese nella profondita d'alcuna valle, e faccisi argine della ringorgata acqua del suo fiume, la quale argine gia rotta scorra con gra[n]dissime onde, delle quali le massime percuotino e ruinino le mura delle citta e ville di tal valle; E le ruine degli alti edifiti delle predette citta levino gra[n] polvere, la quale si levi in alto in forma di fumo, o di ravvi luppati nuvoli si movino contro alla disciende[n]te pioggia; Ma la ringorgata acqua si vada raggirando pel pelago, che de[n]tro a se la rinchiude, e con ritrosi revertiginosi in diversi obbietti percuotendo e risaltando in aria colla fangosa schiuma, poi ricadendo e faciendo reflettere in aria l'acqua percossal; E le onder circulari che si fuggono dal loco della percussione, caminando col suo inpeto in traverso sopra del moto dell'altre onde circulari, che contra di loro si muovono e dopo la fatta percussione risalgano in aria sanza spiccarsi dalle lor base; E all'uscita, che l'acqua fa di tal pelago, si vede le disfatte onde distendersi inverso la loro vscita, dopo la quale, cadendo over discie[n]dendo infra l'aria, acquista peso e moto inpetuoso, dopo il quale, penetrando la percossa acqua, quella apre e penetra con furore alla percussione del fondo, dal quale poi refflette[n]do risalta inverso la superfitie del pelago, accompagnata dall'aria che con lei si som[m]erse, e questa resta nella uscita colla schiuma mista co[n] legniami e altre cose piu lievi che l'acqua, . . . La cima delle onde del mare discende dina[n]zi alle lor base, battendosi e congrega[n]dosi sopra le globulentie della sua faccia."
3. Windsor, RL 12665v; Richter 1970, vol. 1, p. 353, no. 608: "il crudele stratio fatto della vmana spetie dall'ira di dio."
4. C.A., fol. 215r (formerly fol. 79r-c); Richter 1970, vol. 1, p. 357, no. 610.
5. Kemp 1992, pp. 285–86, under no. 188.
6. The famous example of this in Leonardo's oeuvre is the *Mona Lisa* (Musée du Louvre, Paris), a portrait not delivered to its intended patron, as it was probably unfinished for many years. The artist kept it until his death in France in 1519, when it was inherited by his pupil Salai (see Chronology).

LEONARDO DA VINCI

117. *Cats and a Dragon*

Pen and dark brown ink, brush with touches of wash, over soft black chalk or charcoal or leadpoint, some unrelated red-chalk offsetting, 271 × 205 mm (10 11/16 × 8 1/16 in.), irregular shape
Inscribed in pen and brown ink on recto, in right-to-left script, along bottom: *del pieghame[n]to / esstendimento / La spetie dj que[. . .]ssti anjmali della quale illione e principe p[er] avere le giu[n]ture delli sua spo[n]djlj atte al piegharsi.*
Lent by Her Majesty Queen Elizabeth II, Royal Library, Windsor Castle 12363

PROVENANCE: Windsor Leoni volume: 1519, Francesco Melzi, Milan and Rome (1491/93–ca. 1570); ca. 1570, Orazio Melzi; by 1590, Pompeo Leoni, Madrid and Milan (ca. 1533–1608; Lugt under 2885); ca. 1613, Thomas Howard, second earl of Arundel (1586–1646); before 1690, British Royal Collection (inventory of King George III's collection, ca. 1810, fol. 39, no. 196).

LITERATURE: Grosvenor Gallery 1878, vol. 2, p. 8; Müller-Walde 1889, p. 55, pl. 20; Müntz 1899, p. 447; Berenson 1903, vol. 2, p. 67, no. 1233; Seidlitz 1911, p. 286, no. 695; Poggi 1919, pl. 141; De Toni 1922, p. 115, fig. 27; Commissione Vinciana 1928– , vol. 6, p. 24, pl. 278.2; Popp 1928, p. 53; Bodmer 1931, pp. 321, 415; Berenson 1938, vol. 2, p. 137, no. 1233; Giglioli 1944, pl. 145; Royal Academy of Arts 1952, p. 45, no. 139; Heydenreich 1954, vol. 2, p. 148, pl. 204; Berenson 1961, vol. 2, p. 242, no. 1233; Chastel 1961, p. 54; Clark and Pedretti 1968–69, vol. 1, p. 49, no. 12363; Keele and Pedretti 1979–80, vol. 2, p. 570, fig. 30; Leinati 1980, p. 392; Pedretti 1982a, pp. 56, 117, 139, 143, fig. 141; Pedretti and Roberts 1984, pp. 73–74, no. 49; Wasserman 1984, p. 33, fig. 24; Pedretti 1987a, pp. 123–24, no. 157; Kemp and Roberts 1989a, pp. 96–97, no. 38; Kemp 1992d, p. 283, no. 183; Popham 1994, no. 87.

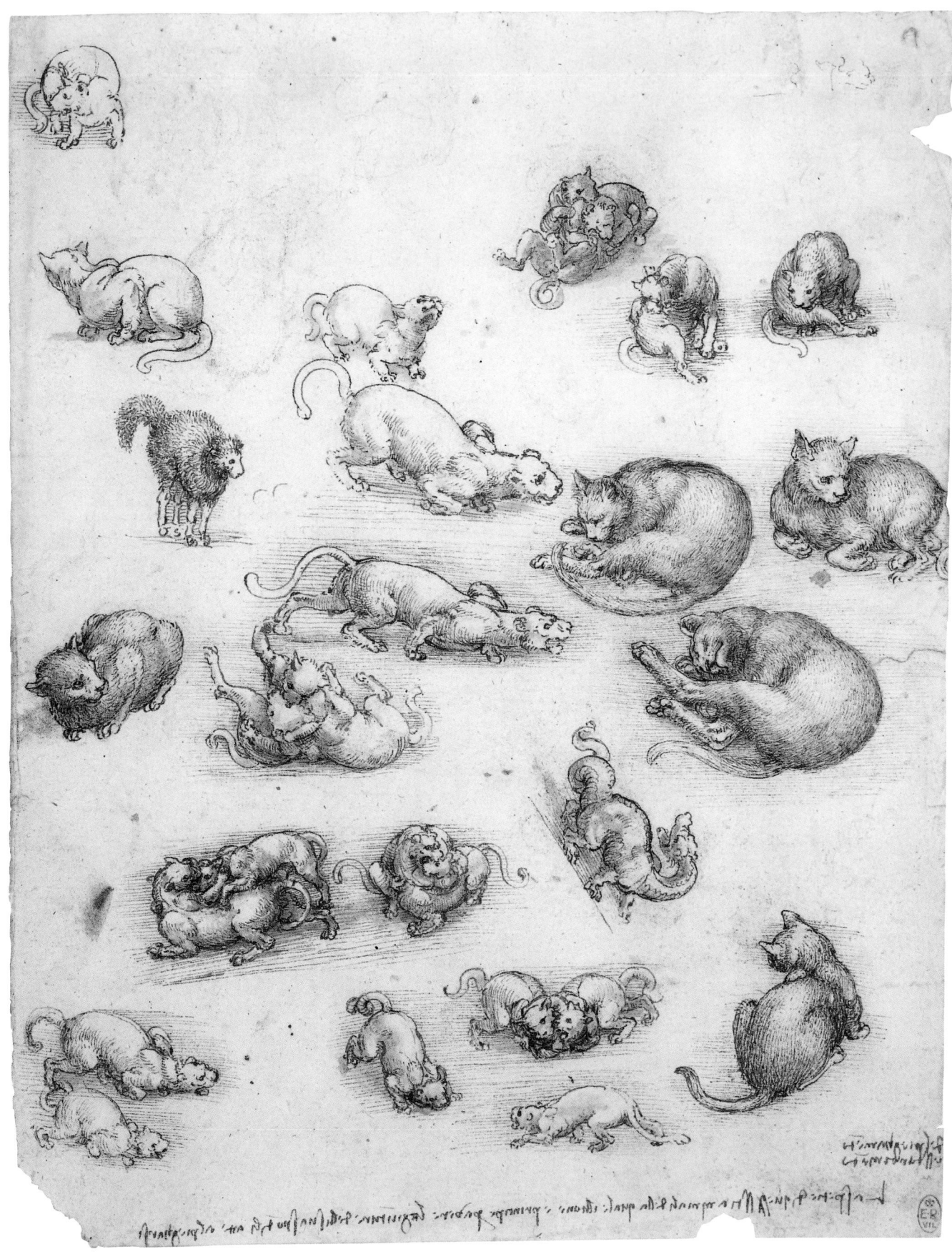

Cat. 117

In the bottom right corner of this page, Leonardo wrote the words "del pieghamento" (on contraction) and "esstendimento" (extension) to denote the types of motion that he was studying. This inscription and additional notes along the bottom of the sheet strongly confirm his intention in his late years to write a treatise on the movement of animals. The present drawing and another sheet of closely similar dimensions and technique (fig. 199) may well have been companion pages for the draft of this proposed treatise. This companion sheet portrays a cat and several horses in a variety of poses of somewhat exaggerated movement, as well as five designs for a rider (Saint George?) heatedly fighting a dragon. Along the upper border of the companion sheet, Leonardo inscribed a long note about the double coiling motions in the poses of animals ("il serpegiamento delle attitudine e principale actione . . . ed e duplo nelli movimenti delli animali"). It has been convincingly suggested that Leonardo drew at least the figures of the horses from small three-dimensional models

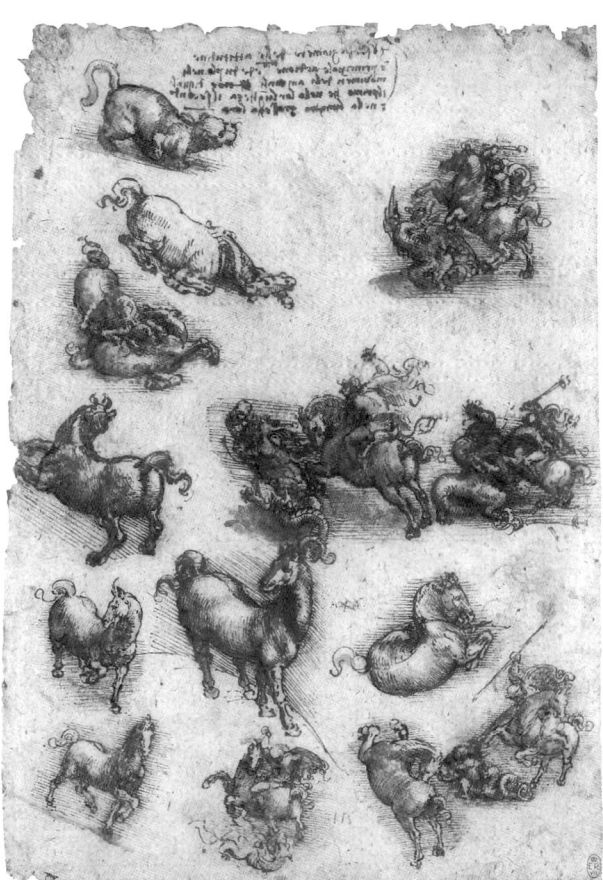

Fig. 199. Leonardo da Vinci, *Sketches of a Cat and Horses*. Pen and brown ink over faint traces of black chalk, on coarse paper, 298 × 212 mm. The Royal Collection, H.M. Queen Elizabeth II, Windsor Castle RL 12331

(made of either wax, clay, or plaster; see cat. nos. 84, 103), to judge from the somewhat lifeless, distorted, and squat proportions of the animals. It might, however, have been considerably more difficult for him to work from such models in drawing the cats in the present sheet.

Here, Leonardo drew more than twenty delightful sketches of cats in a variety of different poses, and with a clear, relatively orderly disposition on the page. The animals are seen pouncing, playing, prowling, sitting, lying asleep, licking themselves, fighting, and reacting with fright. Toward the upper left, the small sketch of a terrified cat on its tiptoes, with its back arched, its hair on end, and its bushy tail is worth a thousand words. In their variety, the poses are remarkably true to life, and the artist often illustrated two slightly different variants of movement for the same pose. It is not entirely clear, however, that he drew all the studies of the cats from life, freshly and directly onto the present page, as indicated by the immediacy of the sketch of the frightened animal with bushy tail. In the case of some of the other, more finished drawings, he may have tried out the animal's poses in rougher sketches on another sheet, since many of these sketches have the appearance of a somewhat cleaned-up draft. In fact, the motif of the prowling cat toward the upper center of the page seems to be a repetition of the cat portrayed at the top of the companion sheet (fig. 199), but with much less internal modeling. Toward the lower right of the present Windsor page, Leonardo drew a dragon moving down an inclined groundline, with its head turned sharply backward, a motif that relates to the explorations on the companion drawing of a possible *Saint George and the Dragon*.

These two Windsor sheets may be dated about 1513–17. The present drawing had been dated as early as 1480 and 1490, and Anny Popp, adducing succinctly the evidence of style and technique, was the first scholar to recognize it as a late work by Leonardo. Connoisseurs have often thought that some of the drawings of the cats on the Windsor sheet were possibly reworked by a pupil. As Kenneth Clark and Carlo Pedretti have noted, however, a certain dryness of line in the reworkings with pen and ink is frequent in securely autograph drawings by Leonardo. The dryness here is the inevitable result of Leonardo's method of producing illustrations, using motifs from other preparatory drawings (for example, to this end, he also frequently relied on techniques of semimechanical design transfer).   CCB

LEONARDO DA VINCI

118. *Studies for an Equestrian Monument*

Leadpoint and charcoal or soft black chalk on cream paper, reworked with pen and golden brown ink on bottom left study, 222 × 159 mm (8¾ × 6¼ in.)

Watermark: Cropped bunch of grapes (close to Briquet 13042) Lent by Her Majesty Queen Elizabeth II, Royal Library, Windsor Castle 12360

PROVENANCE: Windsor Leoni volume: 1519, Francesco Melzi, Milan and Rome (1491/93–ca. 1570); ca. 1570, Orazio Melzi; by 1590, Pompeo Leoni, Madrid and Milan (ca. 1533–1608; Lugt under 2885); ca. 1613, Thomas Howard, second earl of Arundel (1586–1646); before 1690, British Royal Collection (inventory of King George III's collection, ca. 1810).

LITERATURE: Grosvenor Gallery 1878, vol. 2, p. 33; Richter 1883, vol. 2, pp. 2–3, 5, pl. 69; Müller-Walde 1897, figs. pp. 101, 110, 112, 116 (Sforza); Müntz 1898, vol. 1, pp. 156–57 (detail), 160 (detail), vol. 2, p. 1 (detail); Müller-Walde 1899, pp. 86, 88–89, 98–99, 105 (Trivulzio); Müntz 1899, pp. 158, 261; Venturi 1901–39, X/1, fig. 39; Berenson 1903, vol. 2, p. 66, no. 1216; Seidlitz 1909, vol. 1, pp. 174, 180, pl. 31; Seidlitz 1911, p. 284, no. 632; Malaguzzi Valeri 1913–23, vol. 2, p. 456, fig. 511; Meller 1916, p. 220, fig. 3; Poggi 1919, pl. 77; Malaguzzi Valeri 1922, p. 73, fig. 48; Popp 1926, p. 61; Commissione Vinciana 1928– , vol. 4, p. 19, pl. 167; MacCurdy 1928, pl. 1; Popp 1928, pp. 10, 26, 51, fig. 68 (Trivulzio, ca. 1511); Sirén 1928, p. 63, pl. 84 (Sforza); Suida 1929, p. 70, fig. 42; Bodmer 1931, pp. 243, 401–2; Baroni 1935–39, fig. 61; Berenson 1938, vol. 2, p. 135, no. 1216; Giglioli 1944, pl. 77; Clark 1952, pp. 156–57, pl. 55; Royal Academy of Arts 1952, p. 16, no. 181; Brugnoli 1954, pp. 367, 373, pl. 151, fig. 10; Clark 1954, pl. 41; Gould 1954b, p. 191; Heydenreich 1954, vol. 1, pp. 69–70, 134, vol. 2, p. 79, pl. 103; Castelfranco 1957, pp. 527–28; Heydenreich 1957, pp. 157–58, fig. 14; Berenson 1961, vol. 2, p. 238, no. 1216; Heydenreich 1965, fig. 16; Castelfranco 1966, p. 118; Clark and Pedretti 1968–69, vol. 1, pp. 47–48, no. 12360; Clark 1969–70, p. 24, no. 104; Richter 1970, vol. 2, pl. 69; Gould 1975, pp. 145–46; Visconti 1980, p. 117; Hochstetler Meyer 1984, pp. 375, 380, fig. 25; Pedretti and Roberts 1984, p. 68, no. 44, colorpl. 11; Pedretti 1987a, pp. 107–8, no. 139 recto; Clark 1988, pp. 218–27, fig. 102; Marani 1990, p. 75, fig. 4; Zöllner 1991, p. 189, fig. 19; Cunnally 1993, p. 75, fig. 18; Popham 1994, no. 101; Clayton 1996–97, pp. 142–49, no. 84; Arasse 1998, pp. 254–55, fig. 187; Pedretti 1999, p. 137, fig. 9; Ames-Lewis 2001b, p. 14, no. 27.

Fig. 200. Leonardo da Vinci, *Studies for an Equestrian Monument.* Leadpoint on ivory prepared paper, 278 × 184 mm. The Royal Collection, H.M. Queen Elizabeth II, Windsor Castle RL 12342

An extended campaign of conservation and technical research on the Windsor Leonardo drawings (begun in the early 1970s and completed in 1992) brought to light at least five watermark types that point to France as the source of manufacture of the paper of various late drawings by Leonardo. The present sheet and two others of studies of horses also bear such French watermarks (fig. 200; Windsor RL 12344). In 1996, Martin Clayton redated these horse studies to Leonardo's French period (1517–19), based on style, technique, and watermarks, hypothesizing that the drawings may have been preparatory for an unknown (and presumably unexecuted) French equestrian monument. Before the evidence of the watermarks was given such weight, scholars had connected the studies to Leonardo's monument for Gian Giacomo

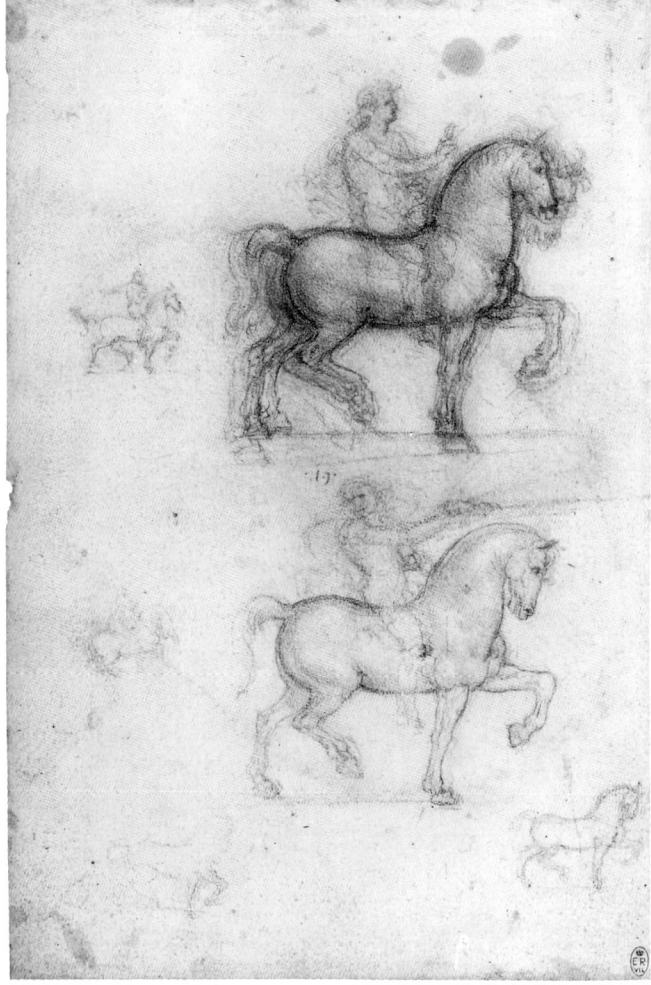

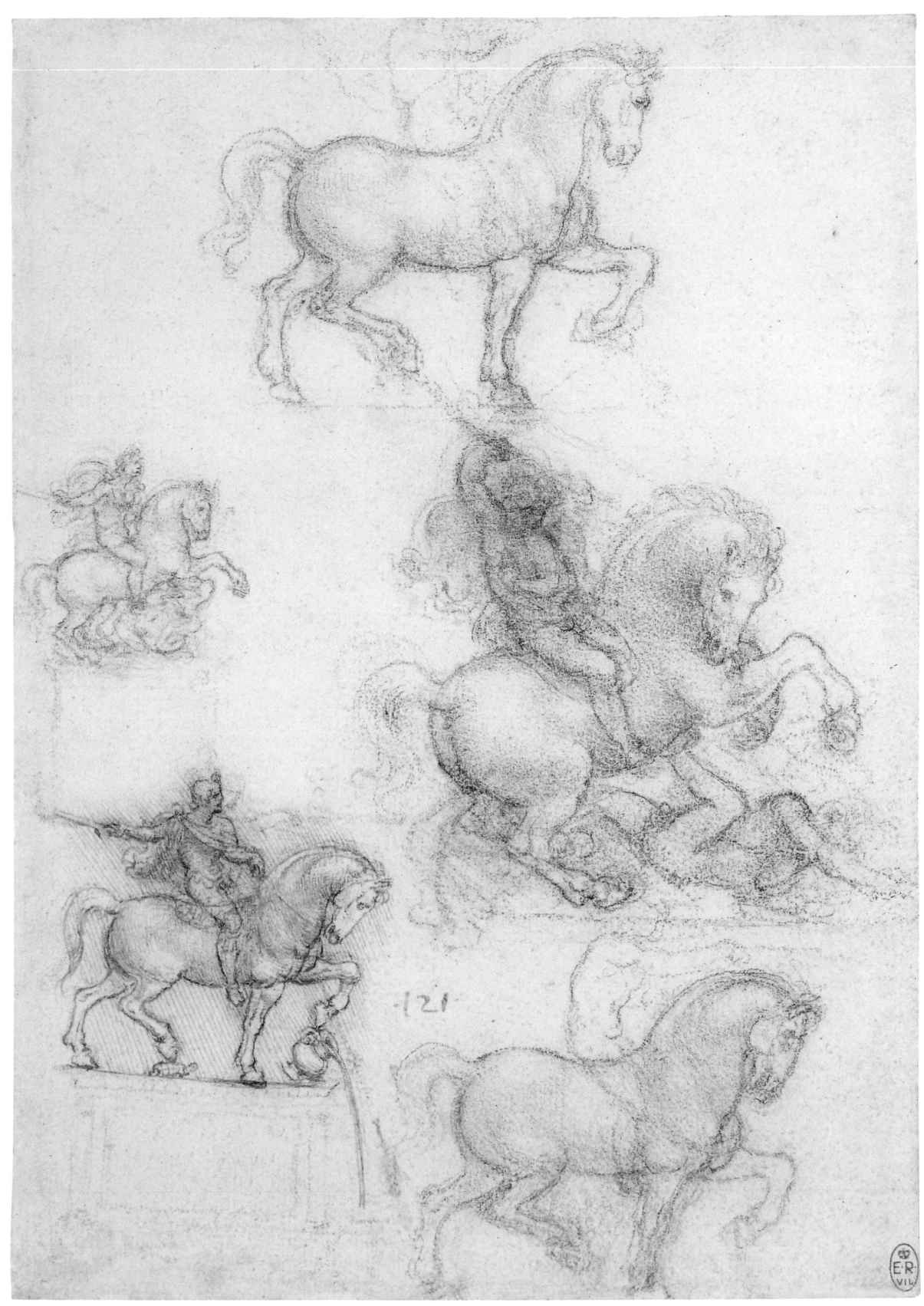

Cat. 118 *(actual size)*

Trivulzio (see cat. no. 111), thus dating them to 1508–12. In all justice, however, the apparent inconsistencies of style and technique among the drawings that were assumed to relate to the Trivulzio monument had certainly not gone unnoticed by earlier scholars. For example, the design toward the center right of the present sheet, showing a rider mounted on a rearing horse and violently attacking a fallen foe with a long weapon, is a variant of that found on another equestrian monument drawing (Windsor, RL 12354). In discussing the latter Windsor drawing in 1984, Carlo Pedretti had already intuited a possible French connection and date, noting that the design seemed destined for a portal. He compared the base for the statue in that drawing to the entranceway of the château of Écouen, "which appears topped by a rearing horse and rider in an engraving by Du Cerceau of 1579."[1]

The overall style of the "French" group of equestrian drawings is light in touch, with the forms soaring on the page. The charcoal, soft black chalk, or leadpoint medium tends to be silvery in hue, and the modeling of form, unified within fairly smudged outlines, seems atmospheric. Based on this evidence of style, the group of Windsor drawings associated with a presumed French equestrian monument may be revised, in the present author's opinion, to include nine sheets.[2] In contrast, the Trivulzio drawings exhibit a tightly plastic conception of form: the typical technique of 1508–12 is a use of the pen with a very dark brown ink, for a deep modeling of form, combined with rather pronounced curved hatching, over a black-chalk or red-chalk underdrawing (see cat. no. 111; fig. 197). The presumed French project by Leonardo would have constituted his third attempt at an equestrian statue, more than twenty years after the Sforza monument (cat. nos. 53, 63, 64; figs. 166, 167), and less than ten years after the Trivulzio monument (cat. no. 111; fig. 197). It is therefore not altogether surprising to find him here contemplating the old dilemma—a dynamic rider on a rearing horse or a majestic, antique-style rider on a striding horse—and revisiting the earlier solutions as alternatives on the same sheet. Leonardo refined the small, somewhat whimsical design on the lower left with pen and golden brown ink over the silvery underdrawing, suggesting that he considered it a finished solution. It shows the striding horse stepping on a turtle with its near hind hoof and toppling an amphora of water with its far front hoof. The suggestion that the motif may have been intended for a fountain does not seem implausible.   CCB

1. Pedretti and Roberts 1984, p. 68, no. 45.
2. Windsor, RL 12313, 12341, 12342 (fig. 200), 12343, 12344, 12354, 12359, 12360 (cat. no. 118), and 13042.

LEONARDO DA VINCI

119. *A Masquerader in the Guise of a Prisoner* (recto)
Slight Outline Drawing of a Nude Male Figure (verso)

Soft black chalk or charcoal, with some red-chalk offsetting (recto); black chalk (verso), 181 × 126 mm (7⅛ × 5 in.)
Watermark: Six-bladed Catherine wheel (close to Briquet 13278, 13280)
Lent by Her Majesty Queen Elizabeth II, Royal Library, Windsor Castle 12573

PROVENANCE: Windsor Leoni volume: 1519, Francesco Melzi, Milan and Rome (1491/93–ca. 1570); ca. 1570, Orazio Melzi; by 1590, Pompeo Leoni, Madrid and Milan (ca. 1533–1608; Lugt under 2885); ca. 1613, Thomas Howard, second earl of Arundel (1586–1646); before 1690, British Royal Collection (inventory of King George III's collection, ca. 1810).

LITERATURE: Chamberlaine 1812, pl. 13; Grosvenor Gallery 1878, vol. 2, p. 12; Müntz 1898, vol. 1, p. 137; Müntz 1899, p. 139; Berenson 1903, vol. 2, p. 63, no. 1132; Seidlitz 1909, vol. 1, p. 405 (note to no. 146); Seidlitz 1911, p. 274, nos. 125, 126; Bodmer 1931, pp. 207, 395–96; Berenson 1938, vol. 2, p. 126, no. 1132; Royal Academy of Arts 1952, no. 244 (hors catalogue); Heydenreich 1954, vol. 1, p. 61, vol. 2, p. 66, pl. 84; Arthur Ewart Popham in Royal Academy of Arts 1960, p. 198, no. 481; Berenson 1961, vol. 2, p. 223, no. 1132; Chastel 1961, p. 143; Castelfranco 1966, pp. 121–22; Clark and Pedretti 1968–69, vol. 1, p. 111, no. 12573; Clark 1969–70, p. 35, no. 139; Visconti 1980, p. 114; Bora 1982, p. 138, fig. 94; Wasserman 1984, p. 32, fig. 23; Caroli 1991, p. 83; Popham 1994, no. 118; Clayton 1996–97, pp. 150–54, no. 88; Arasse 1998, pp. 228, 233, fig. 159.

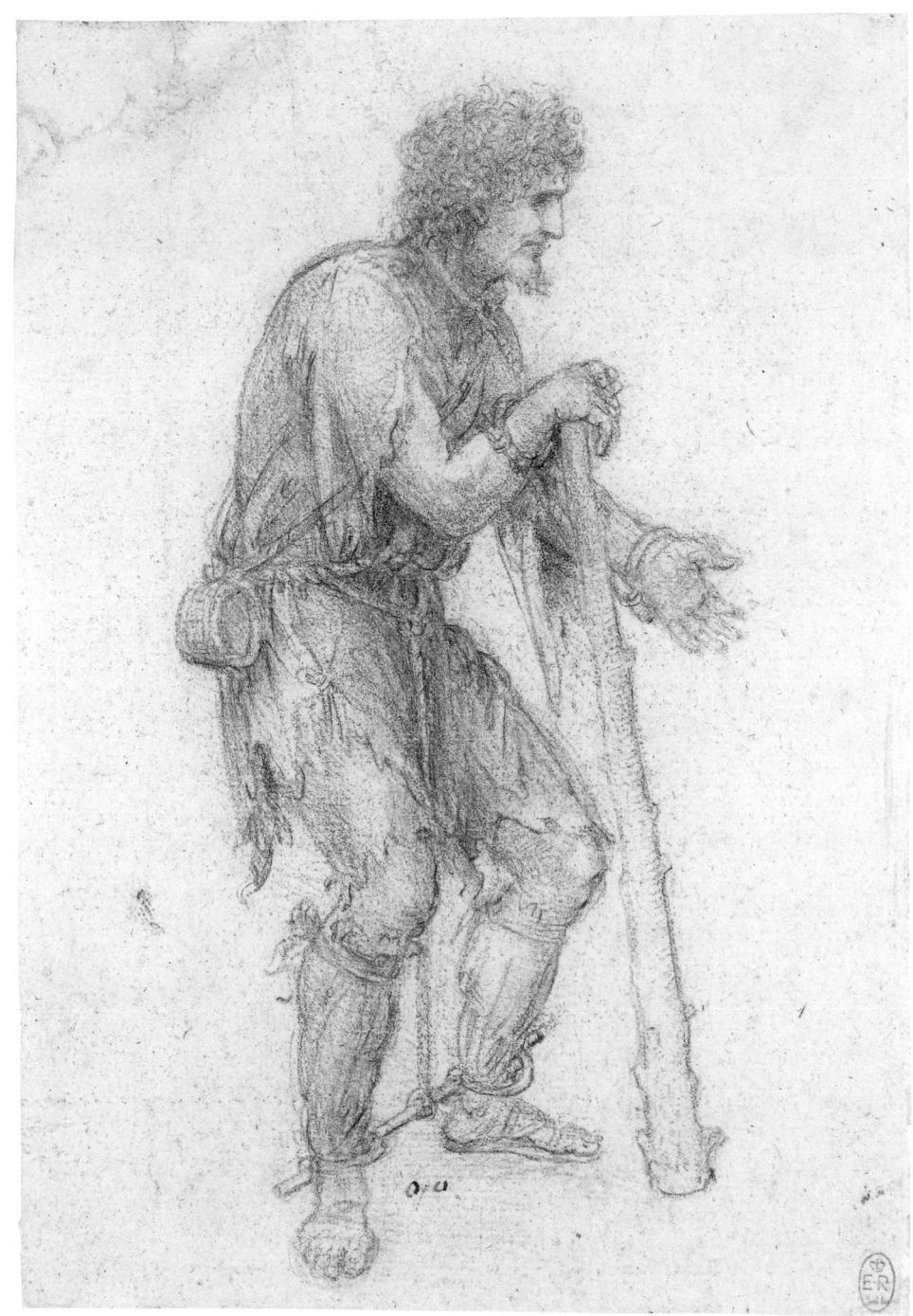

Cat. 119R *(actual size)*

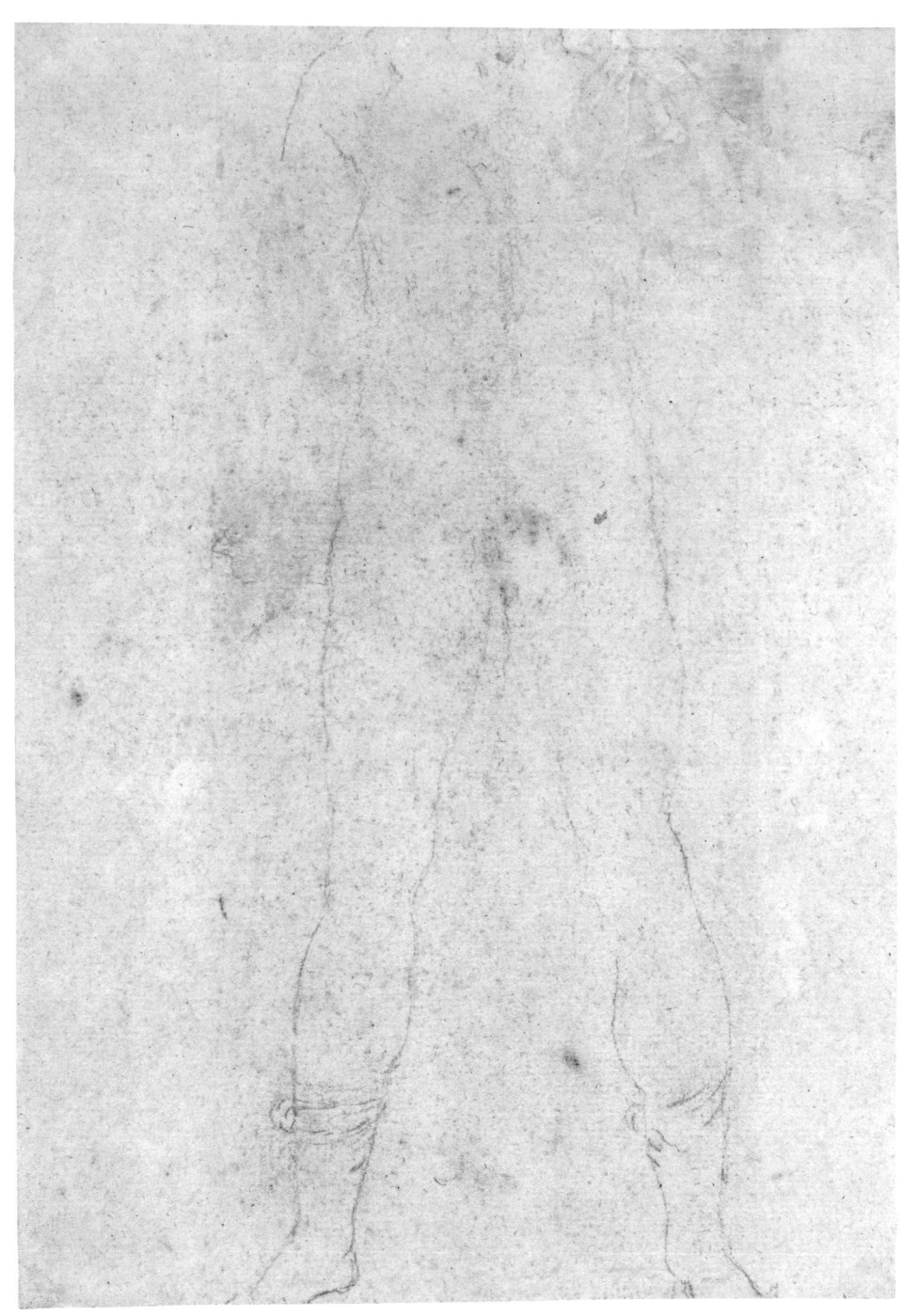

Cat. 119v *(actual size)*

That the hunched-over man in shackles and leaning on a long wood club is an actor, rather than an actual prisoner, can be inferred from his picturesque costume and declamatory pose with outstretched left hand. Leonardo portrayed the male figure in a standing pose turned in a three-quarter view for a descriptive purpose, conveying thereby the details of his costume and attributes with great clarity. Notice the rope noosed at the man's neck, wrists, and waist, and ingeniously connected like an axle to the metal shackles on his feet; the tunic of frilly rags; the small, somewhat courtly, agitated ribbons at his right hip and knees; and the beggar's cup hanging at the hip. Although Leonardo used or a soft black chalk or charcoal for a sfumato refinement of the modeling, some of his left-handed parallel hatching can still be seen underneath more deeply shaded areas. The passages of smudged red chalk on the sheet are not original to the production of the study and can be ignored, for they are the result of an accidental offset from the rubbed chalk of a drawing on another sheet (Leonardo's Windsor drawings were pasted into albums by the sculptor Pompeo Leoni).

The present drawing is part of a group of costume designs for masquerades, jousts, and other such entertainments that is now at Windsor, and of these at least seven seem very closely related in date, to judge from their elegantly ethereal conception and similarly delicate drawing technique in smoky charcoal or soft black chalk, sometimes reworked with brown ink and wash.[1] Martin Clayton recently redated these costume designs, as well as others, to Leonardo's late years, from 1517 to 1519, when the artist was in France, primarily on the basis of the watermarks of French origin found on the paper of some of the sheets.[2] Of the group, however, RL 12369 bears an Italian watermark. Aware of the French watermarks, Kenneth Clark and Carlo Pedretti dated the drawings between 1511 and 1513, reasoning that French paper could have been available in French-dominated Milan. But a French date for the present drawing and other costume designs had long ago also been proposed by the discerning connoisseur Anny Popp on the

basis of style. On this basis and that of technique, a date in the French period seems most probable.

As catalogue numbers 68 and 110 suggest, there is no question that Leonardo enjoyed his role as arbiter of taste and as designer of feasts, theatrical performances, and pageants. A context for the present costume study of a prisoner is found in one of Leonardo's notes from almost two decades earlier, from January 26, 1491, when the artist recorded that he was in the house of Galeazzo da Sanseverino, arranging the festival for his joust ("festa della sua giostra").[3] In the middle of the dress rehearsal, Salaì (Gian Giacomo Caprotti), the young scoundrel who had newly arrived from Oreno to join Leonardo's household as a servant and assistant, stole the money from the footmen who were trying on their costumes of wildmen ("omini salvatici"). The festival organized by Leonardo for Galeazzo da Sanseverino had apparently been to honor the wedding of Ludovico Sforza "Il Moro" and Beatrice d'Este.

Written sources amply attest to Leonardo's later activities as a designer of courtly entertainment during his second stay in Milan, during his service for Giuliano de' Medici at the papal court, and during his employment by Francis I, king of France (see Chronology). The drawings that Leonardo produced at the French court, whether these are the elegantly ethereal costume studies for masquerades or the project for an antique-style equestrian monument (cat. no. 118), seem magical in their silvery lightness on the page. It is hard to resist reading them as manifestations of the playful optimism that life at the French court probably held for the inventive great master in his twilight years.   CCB

1. Windsor RL 12369, 12508, 12573 (cat. no. 119), 12575, 12576, 12577, and 12581. Cat. no. 119, RL 12576, and RL 12577 are on the same type of paper, as noted by Clark and Pedretti 1968–69, vol. 2, p. 111, no. 12573.
2. Clayton 1996–97, pp. 140–42, 150–56, nos. 88–93.
3. Paris Ms. C, fol. 15v (1); Richter 1970, vol. 2, p. 363, no. 1458: "Item a dì di 26 di gienaro segue[n]te, essendo io in casa di messer Galeazzo da San Severino a ordinare la festa della sua giostra, e spogliandosi cierti staffieri per prouarsi alcune veste d'omini saluatici ch'a detta festa accadeano, Giacomo s'accostò alla scarsella d'uno di loro, la qual era ì[n] sul letto con altri panni, e tolse quelli dinari che de[n]tro vi trovò . . . Lire 2 S[oldi] 4."

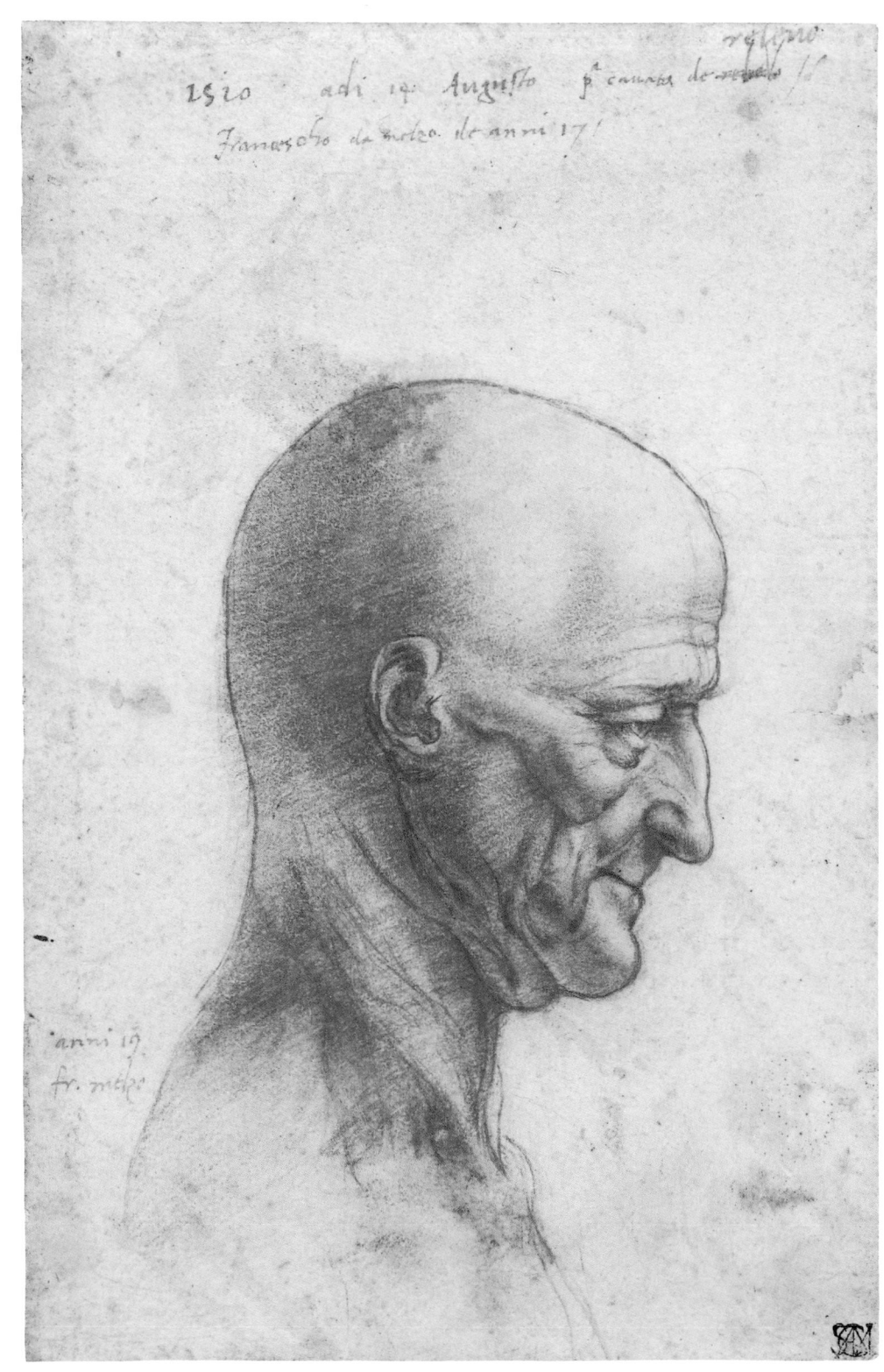

Cat. 120 *(actual size)*

640

(GIOVANNI) FRANCESCO MELZI

(? Milan, 1491/93 – Vaprio d'Adda, ca. 1570)

120. *Head of a Bald Man in Profile Facing to the Right*

Red chalk over traces of black chalk; glued onto secondary paper support, 202 × 130 mm (7 15/16 × 5 1/8 in.)
Inscribed in pen and brown ink on recto along the upper border: *1510 adi 14 Augusto p[rim]ᵃ cauata de* [crossed out: *revelo*] *relevo / Francescho da melzo . de anni 17*; close to lower left corner: *anni 19 / fr. melzo*.
Biblioteca Pinacoteca Ambrosiana, Milan Cod. F. 274 inf. 8

PROVENANCE: Part of the Accademia Ambrosiana (as suggested by the stamp of interlacing letters "ACAMSN"), possibly since the time of its opening in 1620–21 by Cardinal Federico Borromeo, Milan (1564–1631).

LITERATURE: Gerli 1784, p. 14, no. 44, pl. 44; Mantelli 1785, pl. 17; Gerli and Vallardi 1830, p. 15, pl. 45; Müntz 1899, pp. 471, 561, no. 41; Beltrami and Fumagalli 1904, p. 14, no. 20; Ratti 1907, p. 84, sala G; Beltrami 1909, p. 13; Malaguzzi Valeri 1913–23, vol. 2, p. 505, fig. 546; Calvi 1925, pp. 258–60 n. 3, 268–70, fig. 57; Suida 1929, p. 301; Palazzo dell'Arte 1939, p. 208; Kunstmuseum Lucerne 1946, p. 78, no. 154; De Hevesy 1952, p. 248; Pedretti 1964, pp. 97, 99–100, 260–62, pl. 13; Clark 1967, pp. 24–25, fig. 5; Clark and Pedretti 1968–69, vol. 1, pp. xvii, xviii, lxi; Garberi and Mucchi 1972, p. 222; Pedretti 1977, p. 9 n.; Pedretti 1979a, pp. 24, 27 n. 4, fig. 1; Bora 1980, pp. 12–13, no. 12; Mobilleau 1980, p. 146, Fiorio 1982, p. 17, fig. 21; Marinoni and Cogliati Arano 1982, p. 136, no. 42; Coleman 1984, pp. 58–59, no. 21; Cogliati Arano 1985, p. 61, fig. 9; Marani 1987a, pp. 60–61, fig. 53 (incorrect inventory number); Pietro C. Marani in Palazzo Reale 1987, pp. 92–93, no. 36; Pedretti 1987a, p. 59; Kemp 1988, p. 20, fig. 23; Norris 1988–89, pp. 18–19, no. 12; Pedretti 1989f, pp. 29–30; Kwakkelstein 1994, pp. 117, 126–28, pl. 85; *Libro di pittura* 1995, p. 22; Bora 1998, p. 116, fig. 4.36; Alessandro Rovetta in Ambrosiana 1998, pp. 114–15, no. 48.

Signed and dated August 14, 1510, this carefully rendered study of a bald old man in profile is the only securely autograph drawing by Francesco Melzi, the Milanese nobleman who came to live in Leonardo's household as a pupil and companion about 1508.[1] Melzi loyally stayed with the great master until his death in 1519. He became Leonardo's heir, as well as the great interpreter and protector of his artistic legacy. Although he is best known by the name of Francesco Melzi, his full name was actually Giovanni Francesco Melzi, as Carlo Pedretti demonstrated in 1964 based on archival research and a sample of a dated signature ("Joannes Franciscus Meltius

hic scripsit die xiij mensis Junij 1546").[2] The Ambrosiana study, although rendered with right-handed parallel hatching, re-creates Leonardo's red-chalk drawing technique fairly precisely. Melzi blended together the densely spaced, lightly drawn parallel strokes of the intial layer of tone almost seamlessly, working up the shadows and highlights for a pronounced sculptural effect within the emphatic outlines. The Ambrosiana drawing clearly derives from a well-known figural type by Leonardo, which the great master first developed in connection with the apostles of the *Last Supper* and the studies of human proportion (cat. nos. 66, 86) in the 1490s, and then revisited around the time of his studies for the *Battle of Anghiari* in 1503–6 (cat. no. 91).

The inscriptions by the young Melzi on the Ambrosiana sheet inconsistently state his age at the time he made the drawing—seventeen years old (written at the top) and nineteen years old (at the bottom). It was not unusual in this period for people to misremember their birthdates. Both passages are also signed with slightly different forms of the artist's name, but the brown ink and the hand seem the same. The inscription at the top also states the function of the drawing as a "first draft in relief" (*prima cavata in . . . relevo*), which suggests a pupil's drawing exercise. Melzi's study may well be based on an actual sculptural model, although the inscription does not necessarily indicate this. Martin Kemp and Michael Kwakkelstein identified the purported sculptural model as a lost terracotta bust (formerly Silberman Gallery, Vienna), known from a photograph published by Wilhelm Suida in 1929, which was attributed to Giovanni Francesco Rustici, Leonardo's friend and pupil in Florence in 1508. The lost terracotta was considered a preparatory *bozzetto* for the bald Levite in Rustici's bronze *Baptism of Christ* (Baptistery, Florence), executed in 1509.

The handwriting on the Ambrosiana drawing, nearly identical to that in the posthumously compiled manuscript of Leonardo's *Libro di pittura* (Codex Urbinas Latinus, 1270), also serves as a crucial means of authenticating Melzi's authorship.[3] Carlo Giuseppe Gerli knowingly included an illustration of Melzi's study of the bald man among the engravings reproducing drawings that he thought were by Leonardo in 1784, "because here [in Melzi's drawing] one sees the style of Leonardo, and because it is perhaps the only drawing by that valuable painter that survives."[4] CCB

1. See Chronology.
2. Pedretti 1964, pp. 260–64, with documents establishing the artist's full name.
3. Pedretti 1964, pp. 97–109, 260–64.
4. Gerli 1784, p. 14: "e perchè è forse vi si vede la maniera di Leonardo, e perchè è forse l'unico disegno che di quel valente dipintore ci rimane."

(GIOVANNI) FRANCESCO MELZI

121. *Two Grotesque Heads: An Old Woman with an Elaborate Headdress and a Man with Large Ears*

Pen and brown ink, 54 × 99 mm (2⅛ × 3⅞ in), lower margin irregular
The Metropolitan Museum of Art, New York; Gift of Mrs. Edward Fowles, in memory of Edward Fowles, 1975 1975.96

PROVENANCE: Earls of Pembroke (Lugt under 2183, under 2585, under 2957); Pembroke sale, Sotheby's, London, July 5–6, 9–10, 1917, part of lot 466 (as school of Leonardo); Bacri, Paris; Edward Fowles, New York; Mrs. Edward Fowles, New York.

LITERATURE: Strong 1900, part 2, no. 15 (as after Leonardo); Pedretti 1973a, p. 40; Bean 1982, pp. 135–36, no. 129 (as Francesco Melzi?); Pedretti and Trutty-Coohill 1993, pp. 67–71, no. 30i; Jaffé 1994, pp. 168–69, under nos. 820A–820C; Kwakkelstein 1994, pp. 107–8 n. 223, 114, fig. 57.

These two grotesque heads are copies after drawings by Leonardo, most likely made by his follower and artistic heir, Francesco Melzi. The attribution to Melzi was originally proposed by Carlo Pedretti in 1973 and was subsequently endorsed by Jacob Bean, Patricia Trutty-Coohill, and Michael Kwakkelstein. In attempting to copy the left-handed diagonal hatching technique of his master, Melzi used strokes that appear forced when viewed under great magnification, as he had to shift the paper continually in order to adapt the angle of his strokes.

While in the collection of the Earls of Pembroke at Wilton House, the drawing was mounted together with eleven other sheets of grotesques, all of which are copies after Leonardo.[1] Since the famous Pembroke sale in 1917, the twelve fragments have been divided among several collections. Three of the fragments are in the Fogg Art Museum, Harvard University, Cambridge, Massachusetts; two in the Elmer Belt Library of Vinciana, University of California, Los Angeles; two in the Pierpont Morgan Library, New York; one in the National Gallery of Art, Washington, D.C.; one in the Detroit Institute of Arts; one in a New York private collection; and still another

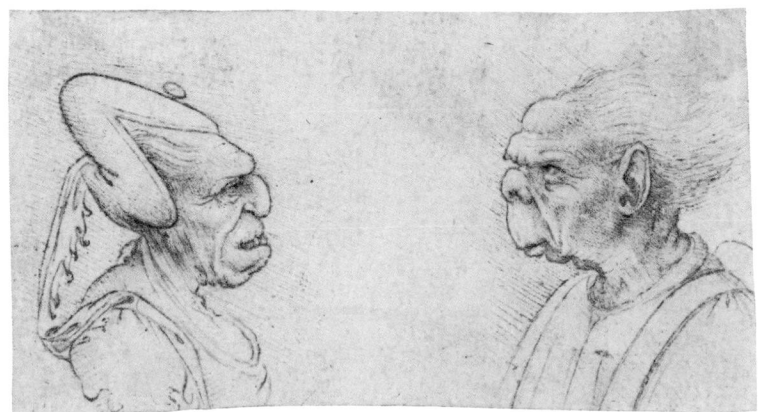

Cat. 121 *(actual size)*

642

sheet recently passed through the art market (Christie's, London, July 7, 1998, lot 59). The woman with the headdress in the present drawing is a copy after a caricature by Leonardo at Chatsworth (cat. no. 73b). While a few of the Pembroke fragments show groups of two or three male heads, the majority of these sheets contain pairs of facing male and female heads in profile. Some of the small-scale caricatures by Leonardo himself show such pairings (Windsor, RL 12453). Leonardo's role in Melzi's pairing of the grotesques, as in the present sheet, and the larger issue of the master's active involvement in the copying of his own work (the notion of "replacement copies") have been discussed by Kenneth Clark, Ernst Gombrich, Patricia Trutty-Coohill, Michael Kwakkelstein, and others.[2] Several additional copies of the individual heads portrayed in the present sheet survive, including those among the Spencer Grotesques bound in a

two-volume edition from 1669 of Rabelais's works (Spencer Collection I.10 and I.15, New York Public Library). The Spencer Grotesques are possibly by a Lombard artist of about 1590–1600; the watermarks suggest that the paper was manufactured in Italy in the late sixteenth century.[3] The two heads in the present drawing appear at the top of the sheet in catalogue number 136. A copy of the male head is also found in the album of the French collector Pierre-Jean Mariette (cat. no. 137), and thus an etched version appears in the album of the count of Caylus as number 31 (cat. no. 138).   AM

1. Illustrated in Kwakkelstein 1994, fig. 57.
2. Clark 1967, pp. 24–25; Clark and Pedretti 1968–69, vol. 1, pp. xviii–xix; Gombrich 1976, p. 66; Pedretti and Trutty-Coohill 1993, p. 66; Kwakkelstein 1994, p. 117.
3. For the locations of these dispersed copies, see Pedretti and Trutty-Coohill 1993, p. 70; and Scott-Elliot 1958, pp. 292–93.

MASTER OF THE SFORZA ALTARPIECE (MAESTRO DELLA PALA SFORZESCA)
(Milan, 1495–ca. 1520)

122. *Head of a Boy in Profile Facing to the Right (Massimiliano Sforza?)*

Metalpoint on blue-gray prepared paper, pricked for transfer and glued to secondary paper support, 205 × 156 mm (8 1/16 × 6 1/8 in.) Biblioteca Pinacoteca Ambrosiana, Milan Cod. F. 290 inf. 13

PROVENANCE: Part of the Accademia Ambrosiana (as suggested by the stamp of interlacing letters "ACAMSN"), possibly since the time of its opening in 1620–21 by Cardinal Federico Borromeo (1564–1631), Milan.

LITERATURE: Gerli 1784, pl. 7; Mantelli 1785, pl. 3; Morelli 1890, p. 250; Müntz 1899, no. 24; Loeser 1901, p. 66; Beltrami and Fumagalli 1904, p. 12, no. 3; Malaguzzi Valeri 1905, p. 46; Seidlitz 1906, p. 28, fig. 5; Ratti 1907, p. 84, sala G (Ambrogio de' Predis?); Jacobsen 1910, p. 53; Malaguzzi Valeri 1913–23, vol. 1, p. 440, vol. 3, pp. 19–22; Beltrami 1919b, pp. 170–71, 176, 213, fig. 44a; Suida 1919, p. 264; Parker 1927, p. 36, no. 69; Kunstmuseum Lucerne 1946, pp. 71–72, no. 123; Paredi, dell'Acqua, and Vitali 1967, pp. 110, 518, fig. 267; Kupferstichkabinett Berlin 1973, pp. 27–28; Cogliati Arano 1980, p. 21, no. 48; Cogliati Arano 1981, p. 21, no. 48; Marinoni and Cogliati Arano 1982, pp. 93, 141, no. 48; Bertelli 1983, pp. 191, 194 n. 8; Coleman 1984, pp. 42–43, no. 13; Piel 1986, p. 15; Bora 1987b, pp. 163–66; Marani 1987a, p. 75, fig. 60; Giulio Bora in Palazzo Reale 1987, pp. 58–59, no. 9; Marani 1988b, p. 325; Norris 1988–

89, pp. 18–19, no. 10 (as Master of the Pala Sforzesca or Ambrogio de' Predis); Marani 1990, p. 120; Cogliati Arano 1995, p. 27; Alessandro Rovetta in Ambrosiana 1998, pp. 106–7, no. 44; Bambach 1999a, pp. 110–11, 413–14 nn. 168–72, fig. 103; Fiorio 2000a, p. 150, under no. 1310.

This delicately rendered portrait in profile of a young boy from the Sforza family may have been drawn from life, to judge from the process of idealization that gradually took place as the artist drew the study. The paper is thinly coated with a blue-gray preparation applied with vertical strokes of the brush. With the metalpoint, the artist first sketched the boy's nose and chin slightly more bulbous. He went over and over the facial profile until he finally cleaned it up, unifying the various outlines of the profile into a single emphatic outline, almost incised in the paper. The boy's somewhat iconic features and fixed gaze are forcefully outlined, in contrast to the sketchiness of the hair and clothes. The contours along the ear and the back of the boy's neck and shoulders are also

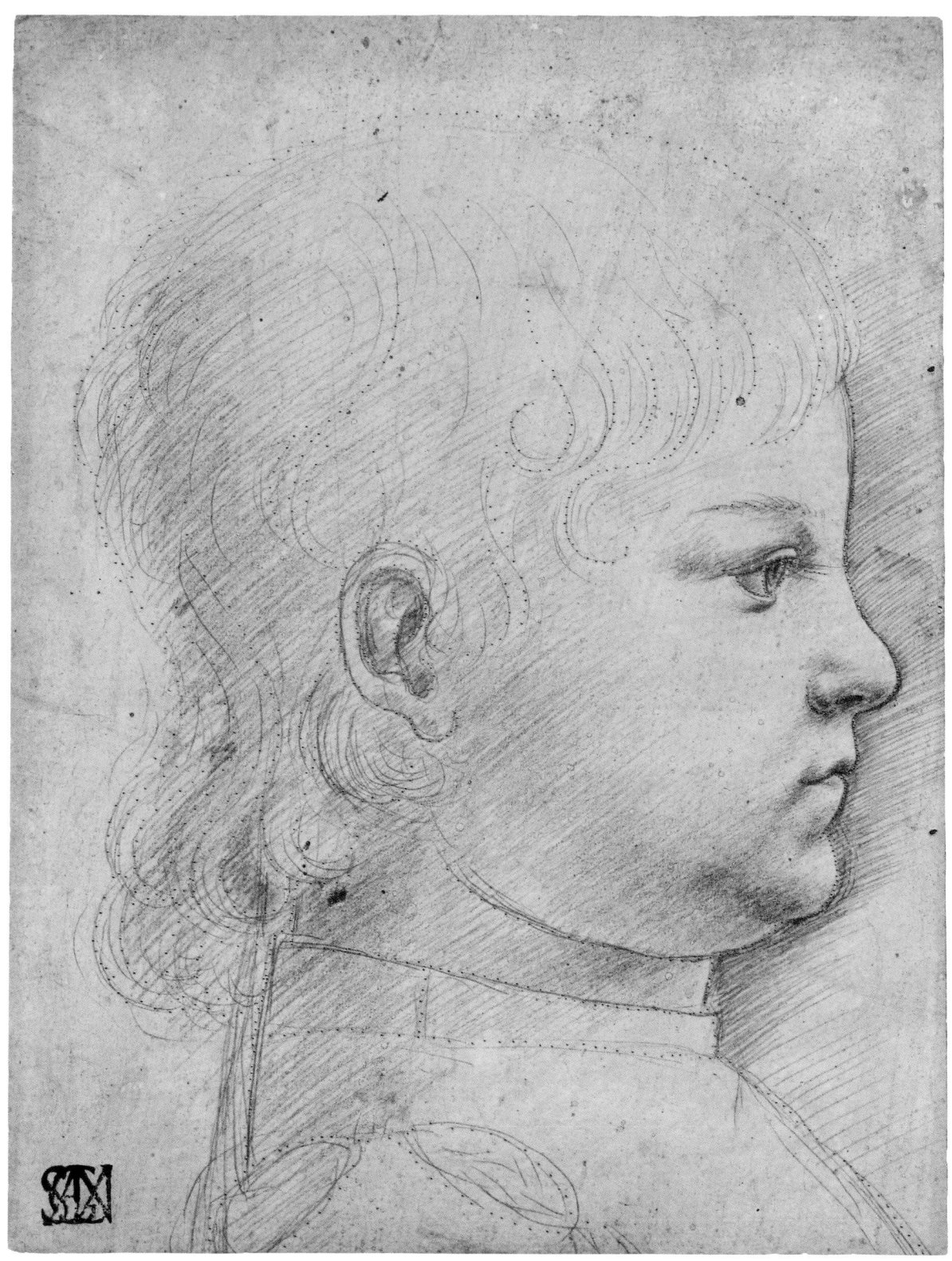

Cat. 122 *(actual size)*

repeatedly reinforced, while the facial outline is very densely and minutely pricked. This carefully drawn study served as a cartoon (full-scale drawing) for transferring the design by means of the technique of *spolvero* (pouncing). The artist pricked the outlines of the drawing finely, then presumably placed the pricked sheet on top of another surface and lightly rubbed powdered chalk through the perforated outlines, a procedure that left a dotted underdrawing (*spolvero*) on the surface underneath. At one point in its early history the present drawing seems to have exhibited the traces of rubbed red-chalk pouncing dust from the transfer process on both the recto and the verso, which means that the sheet was replicated more than once. This evidence has long since vanished with subsequent restorations.[1] The choice of a metalpoint medium on prepared blue-gray paper for a cartoon was common among Lombard artists of Leonardo's circle (see cat. no. 61), but the technique was rarely used for this type of drawing

elsewhere in Italy. Equally Leonardesque, the artist built up the background with a highly regular parallel-hatching to a tone that is much darker than the interior of the head, thereby creating a low-relief effect.

The precise identity of the young boy in the portrait is disputed. He has been identified both as Massimiliano, eldest son of Ludovico Sforza "Il Moro" by his wife, Beatrice d'Este, and as Cesare, the illegitimate but recognized son of Ludovico by his mistress, Cecilia Gallerani. The physiognomy of the boy in the Ambrosiana drawing is very similar to the securely documented portrait of Massimiliano Sforza on fol. 1 verso in the famous illuminated manuscript of Aelius Donatus's *Ars Minor: Disticha Cotonis; Istitutiones gramaticae* (Codex Trivulzianus 2167, Biblioteca Trivulziana, Castello Sforzesco, Milan). The boy in the Ambrosiana drawing appears in the same scale and design, paired with his father, Ludovico, and kneeling in the left foreground of the Sforza Altarpiece (the Pala Sforzesca;

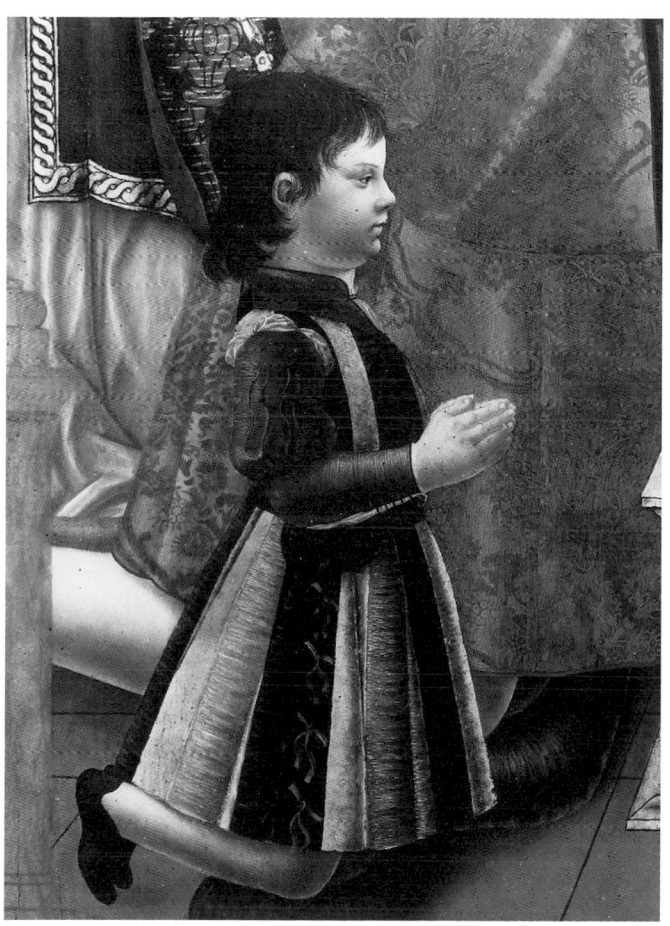

Fig. 201. Detail of fig. 202, showing a portrait of young Massimiliano Sforza

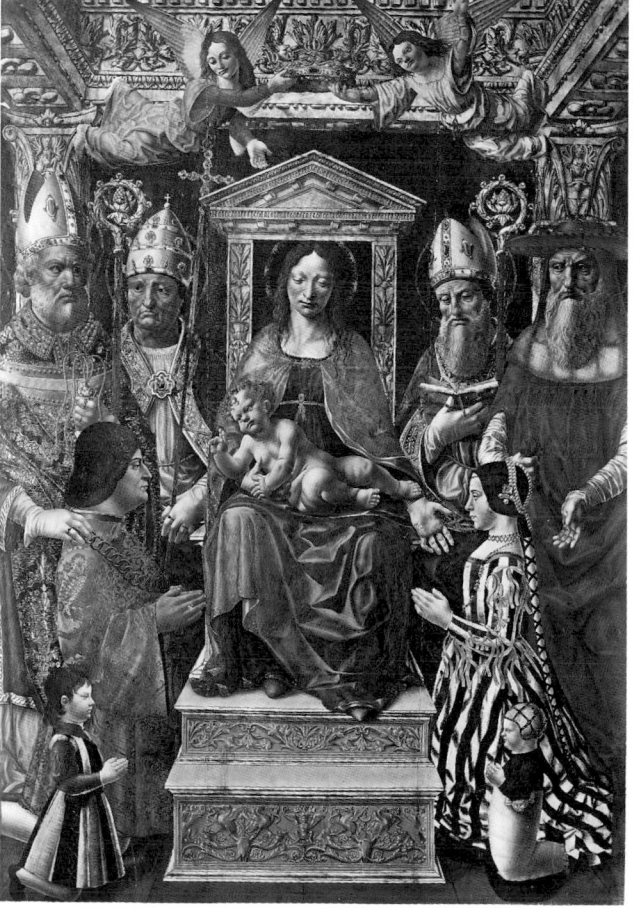

Fig. 202. Master of the Sforza Altarpiece, *The Enthroned Virgin and Child with Saints, Angels, and Donors from the Sforza Family.* Oil on wood, 230 × 165 cm. Pinacoteca di Brera, Milan Nap. 1

645

figs. 201, 202) by an anonymous Milanese master in Leonardo's circle. The style of this Master of the Sforza Altarpiece as a painter and draftsman (the present drawing is the most securely connected graphic work by him) is closely related to that of Ambrogio de' Predis and Giovanni Antonio Boltraffio. A boy similar to the one in the Ambrosiana drawing and in the Sforza Altarpiece also appears kneeling in the left foreground of the ruined underpainting of Giovanni Donato Montorfano's *Crucifixion* (Refectory of Santa Maria delle Grazie, Milan), which is signed and dated 1495. The iconic pairings of the donor portraits of the Sforza family are very similar in both the Sforza Altarpiece and Montorfano's *Crucifixion* mural. In the *Crucifixion*, the now virtually destroyed portraits of "Il Moro," his wife, Beatrice d'Este, and the two Sforza sons were added in oil pigments, as donor figures in the foreground, after the composition had been executed and finished in fresco.[2]

A case can be made either way regarding the identity of the two boys who are portrayed at the side of Ludovico Sforza and his wife in these two paintings, but it is more likely that the pair of children depicted in both works—panel and mural—portrays the legitimate progeny (Massimiliano and Francesco, rather than Cesare), because of the dynastic character of Ludovico's artistic enterprises. In the 1568 edition of Leonardo's vita, Giorgio Vasari attributed the portraits in Montorfano's *Crucifixion* mural to Leonardo and identified the boys as Massimiliano and Francesco, born to Beatrice in 1493 and 1495, respectively; the illegitimate Cesare was born in 1491.[3] As art historians have repeatedly noted, the unusual,

impermanent painting technique in this part of Montorfano's mural would tend to support Vasari's attribution to Leonardo.[4] Since these portraits were added later (Leonardo was at work on the *Last Supper* at the other end wall of the refectory until 1497/98), the date 1495 on the frescoed part by Montorfano is not difficult to reconcile with the ages of the boys. Ludovico Sforza, who used portraiture to further his dynastic ambitions, had commissioned the altarpiece in 1494 for Sant'Ambrogio ad Nemus (Milan) and was also the patron behind the decoration of the refectory of Santa Maria delle Grazie.[5] It seems quite possible that the present cartoon by the Master of the Sforza Altarpiece, which probably dates to 1494–98, was inspired by a lost original drawing by Leonardo. Archaeological evidence that has emerged from Renaissance paintings and drawings suggests that portraits such as the one of the Sforza boy seen here were among the types of designs that artists most frequently reproduced. To that purpose, Renaissance artists relied on sometimes complex uses and reuses of cartoons by means of the *spolvero* technique to perform these design replications.

CCB

1. Malaguzzi Valeri 1905, p. 46; the drawing is now glued down and the surface is quite clean.
2. Travers Newton 1983, pp. 86–87; Bertelli 1986, vol. 1, p. 40, vol. 2, pl. 83; Marani 1989, pp. 90–93, no. 17; Bambach 1999a, pp. 110–11, 413 nn. 168–69.
3. Vasari 1966– , vol. 3 (text), p. 27. Vasari visited the refectory of Santa Maria delle Grazie in 1566.
4. See Marani 1989, pp. 90–93, no. 17.
5. Only the precise date of the commission of the Sforza Altarpiece is documented, not the date of its completion: Marani 1987a, pp. 75–80, no. 3; Fabjan and Marani 1998, pp. 31–71; Romano 1978, pp. 7–23; Marani 1988a, pp. 325–30; and Baini 1995, pp. 158–67.

MASTER OF THE SFORZA ALTARPIECE (MAESTRO DELLA PALA SFORZESCA)

123. *Head of Man in Three-Quarter View Facing to the Right; Study of Profile; Doodles* (recto) *Study of a Hand* (verso)

Metalpoint with very light white highlights on blue-gray prepared paper (recto); black chalk (verso), 233 × 163 mm (9¼ × 6½ in.); reworked in stylus and metalpoint (?) on the right part of the outline of the face, and on the eyes, nose, and mouth; corners cut off, reconstituted, and colored green (recto), traces of former mount (verso)

Inscribed in pen and brown ink on verso by a later hand: *dun eleve de Leonard*

Département des Arts Graphiques du Musée du Louvre, Paris 2416

PROVENANCE: Giuseppe Vallardi, Milan (1784–1863; Lugt 1223, in green on verso);[1] 1856, acquired by the Musée du Louvre.

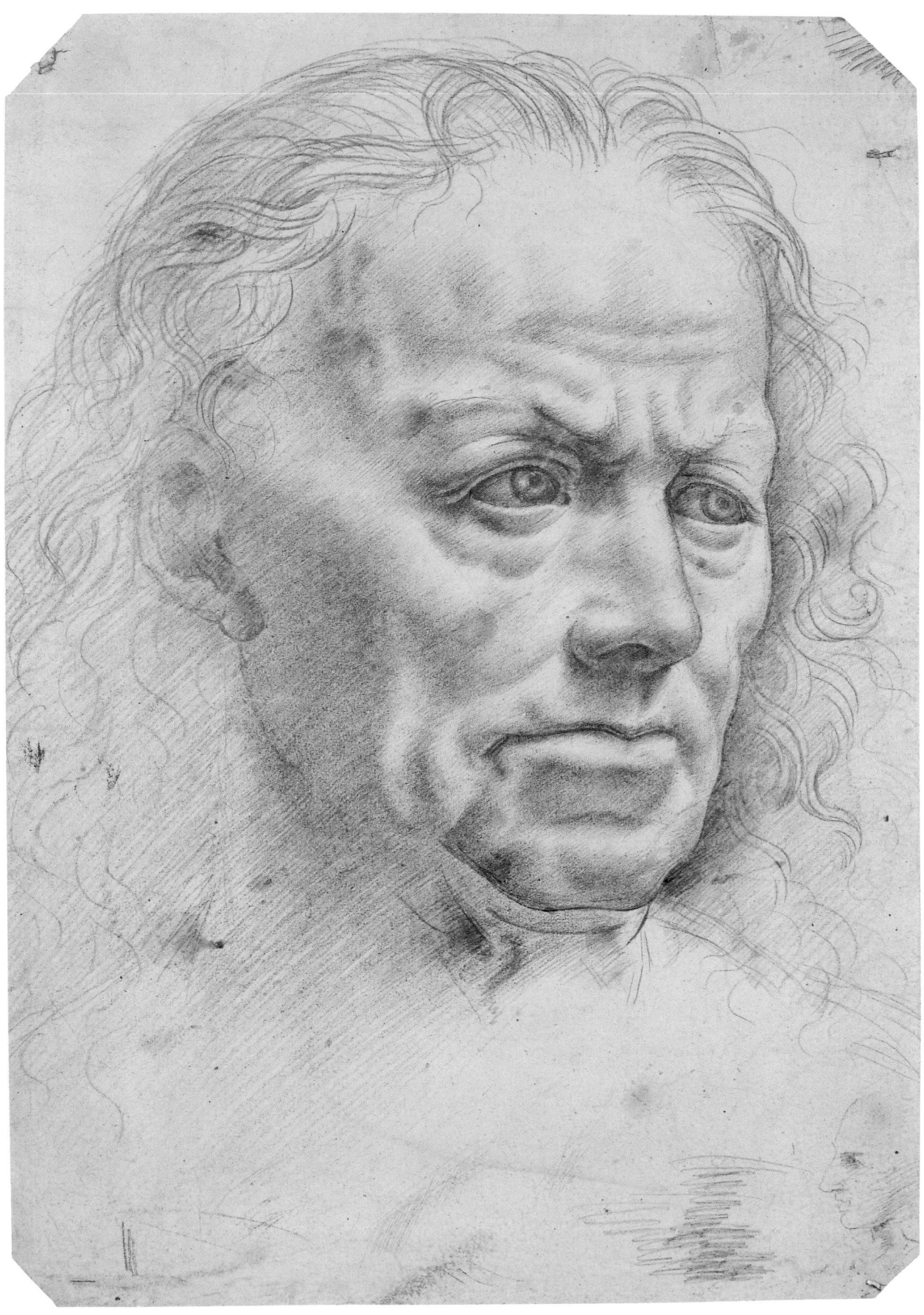

Cat. 123R *(actual size)*

Literature: Louvre 1888, no. 2027 (Leonardo); Münz 1899, pl. 14 (Leonardo); Seidlitz 1906–7, p. 10, fig. 7 (de' Predis); Louvre 1919, no. 25 (Leonardo); Demonts 1921, no. 20 and fig. 20 (attributed to Leonardo); Demonts 1922, no. 20 (attributed to Leonardo); Berenson 1938, vol. 1, p. 183 n. 1 (school of Leonardo); Palazzo dell'Arte 1939, p. 159 (Leonardo); Cogliati Arano 1985, p. 61, fig. 13 (de' Predis?); Bora 1987a, p. 19, fig. 12 (student after Leonardo); Pedretti 1990a, p. 36, fig. 99 (Bramante?); Kwakkelstein 1994, p. 116, fig. 87.

Like catalogue number 122, although more animated and of greater psychological presence, this carefully rendered study after life makes use of Leonardo's technique of metalpoint on blue-gray prepared paper (now discolored to a slightly green hue) that is also characteristic of drawings from the 1490s by Giovanni Antonio Boltraffio (cat. nos. 124–26) and Ambrogio de' Predis (Hamburger Kunsthalle, 21478). For Leonardo's studies in a similar medium, see catalogue numbers 53, 61, 63, and 66. Here, the artist focused attention on the intense physical movements of the man's face to articulate his *moti mentali* (motions of the mind) in what proves to be a somewhat exaggerated exercise of Leonardo's theories of physiognomic expression (compare cat. no. 66). The high polish of the drawing of the man's overwrought face dynamically contrasts with the impressionistic sketchiness of the shoulders and stringy hair, which serves as an effective framing element. The emphatic use of contours and the dense intermeshing of extremely fine, diagonal, parallel hatching in the deep chiaroscuro—as is seen here and in catalogue number 122—are hallmarks of the drawings by the Master of the Sforza Altarpiece.

The physiognomic type of the man in the present sheet, although beardless, of more poignant expression, and described in greater detail, seems comparable to that of the bishop-saint in the upper left of the much-discussed Sforza Altarpiece (the Pala Sforzesca; fig. 202). This is the painting that is mentioned in a letter of January 22, 1494, sent by the ducal secretary Marchesino Stanga to Ludovico Sforza "Il Moro" without stating the artist's name. A date of about 1494–98 for the altarpiece and the drawing seems plausible. It even seems possible that the present study served as a preparatory study for the head of the left bishop-saint (it would help explain the artist's relative unconcern with the man's hair, since in the painting it would have been covered by a miter), although the drawing is much freer and less stylized than the painting. The close connections of design of this drawing and catalogue number 122 to the Sforza Altarpiece make the attribution of the studies fairly certain, even if the name of the artist remains unknown. Greatly influenced by Ambrogio de' Predis, and showing certain affinities with the work of the young Boltraffio (see cat. nos. 124, 125), this anonymous master in Leonardo's circle is credited by most recent scholars with a corpus of about twenty paintings,[2] and of at least five other drawings dispersed among the collections of the Biblioteca Ambrosiana, the Musée du Louvre, the British Museum, and the Kupferstichkabinett, Berlin.[3] The attribution of the present drawing to the Master of the Sforza Altarpiece was also suggested by Michael Kwakkelstein in 1994.

CCB

1. Vallardi 1855, p. 46, fol. 209 (Leonardo da Vinci): "Disegno su carta preparata cenerognola, eseguito a matita nera ed a finissima penna, con qualche traccia di bianco: testa di uomo adulto, di carattere austero, a due terzi il naturale, veduta per due terzi dal lato destro. —Al basso in un angolo, piccolo profilo a sinistra forse della eguale testa. / Alto poll. 9 largo poll. 6.3."
2. Marani 1998d.
3. Discussed by Giulio Bora in Palazzo Reale 1987, pp. 58–63, nos. 9–12.

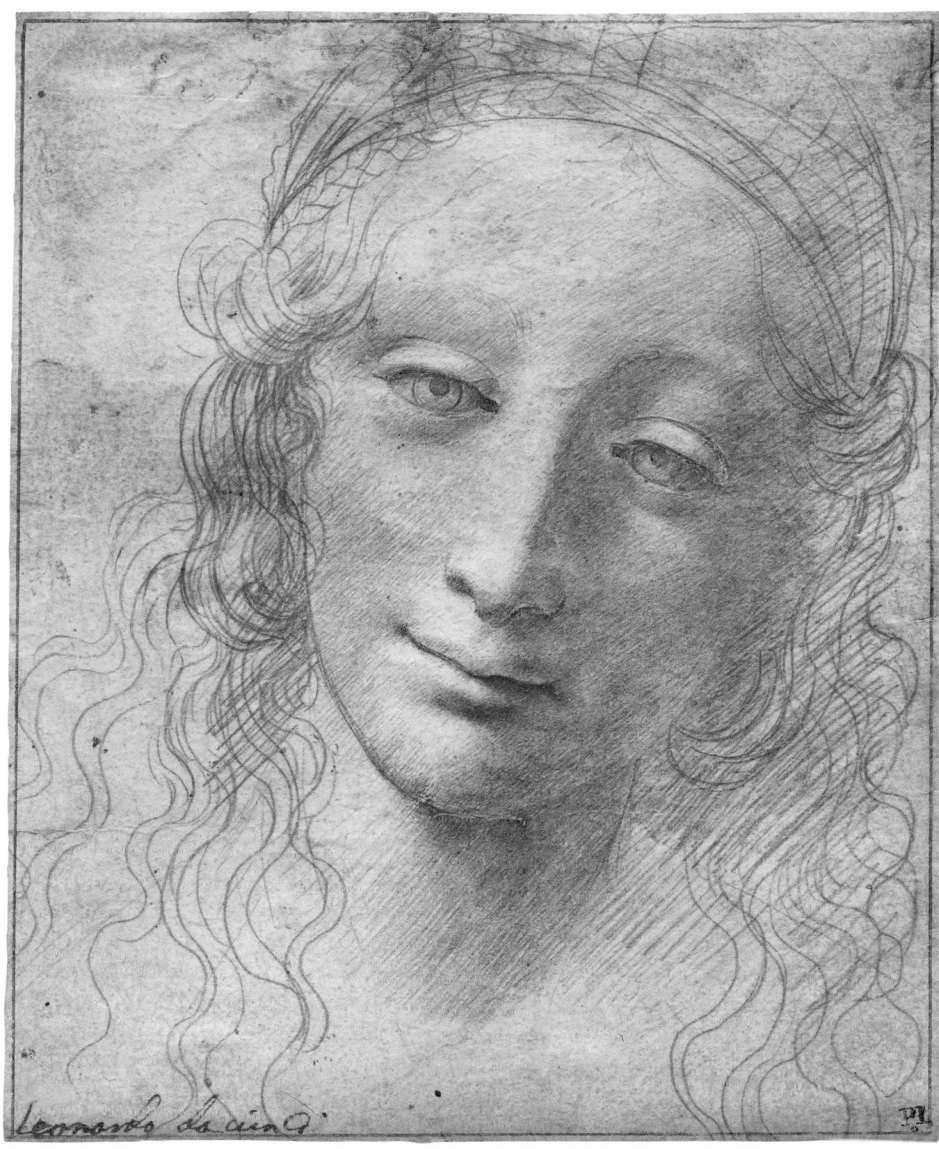

Cat. 124 *(actual size)*

GIOVANNI ANTONIO BOLTRAFFIO

(Milan, 1467–Milan, 1516)

124. *Head of a Young Woman in Front View*

Metalpoint on gray-green prepared paper, 150 × 124 mm
(5⅞ × 4⅞ in.)
Inscribed in (brown?) ink at lower left by a later hand: *Leonardo da vinci*
Sterling and Francine Clark Art Institute, Williamstown,
Massachusetts 1955.1470

PROVENANCE: Sir Peter Lely, London (1618–1680; Lugt 2092);
Ram Collection; [P&D Colnaghi, London]; Sterling Clark, 1917.

LITERATURE: Vasari Society 1905–15, vol. 10, no. 6; Suida 1929,
p. 189 (as Boltraffio); Clark Art Institute 1964, vol. 1, pp. 10 11,
no. 7 (as Leonardo follower); Bacall 1968, no. 20; Byam Shaw
1976, p. 273, under no. 1062; Byam Shaw 1983, vol. 1, p. 385,
under no. 388; Bora 1987d, pp. 13, 50 (as Boltraffio); Pedretti
1988a, p. 154; Brown 1989b, p. 29; Trutty-Coohill 1989, pp. 159–63;
Pedretti and Trutty-Coohill 1993, p. 50, no. 20; Fiorio 1998, p. 132;
Brown 1999, p. 133, under no. 4; Fiorio 2000a, pp. 142–43; Agosti
2001, p. 192, under no. 33.

Boltraffio was one of Leonardo's closest and most gifted pupils. Their affiliation, which endured for a decade or more, is attested by several contemporary sources: Leonardo himself mentioned Boltraffio in a note of 1491, in which the latter is familiarly referred to as "Gian Antonio";[1] the Bolognese poet Girolamo Casio, an intimate of Boltraffio, proclaimed (somewhat hyperbolically) that he was "the only student of Leonardo da Vinci";[2] and Vasari records that Boltraffio was a disciple of the master. Their association is borne out in Boltraffio's paintings and drawings of the 1490s, which are thoroughly indebted to Leonardo's example. Boltraffio is often credited with the execution of works designed by Leonardo and carried out under his tutelage, such as the *Madonna Litta* of about 1490 (fig. 82), while his independent paintings of this period are demonstrations of a pure Leonardesque idiom.[3] In his drawings, Boltraffio likewise emulated Leonardo's style and technique. According to Paolo Giovio, who described Leonardo's pedagogical method, the master cultivated such proficiency on the part of his pupils by having them execute drawings in his manner; only when full command of his technique was achieved was the pupil—who must also have attained at least twenty years of age—then permitted to paint.[4]

This beautiful study of a female head in the Clark Art Institute is dated to the early 1490s. Together with such stylistically related drawings as the similar head of a young woman at Christ Church, Oxford, it is the product of a period of "total dedication" to Leonardo on the part of Boltraffio.[5] The delicate, nuanced modeling, the idealized features, and the softly shadowed contours immediately summon to mind Leonardo's drawings (see cat. nos. 44, 61, 62). The figure's abstracted, vaguely wistful air and the summary treatment of the hair in comparison with the descriptively rendered physiognomy likewise find close precedents in the master's similar head studies. Finally, Boltraffio's fluent command of silverpoint is also derived from Leonardo, who was responsible for introducing this predominantly Florentine technique to Lombardy and promoting it among his pupils. The assured handling seen in the Clark drawing speaks of an artist who was not merely slavishly imitating his master, however, but had fully grasped the artistic and technical potential of the medium. Indeed, though not upheld by modern scholarship, the early attribu-

tion of the *Head of a Young Woman* to Leonardo, recorded at the lower left in an inscription that probably dates from the period of Sir Peter Lely's ownership, is entirely comprehensible. If, as Giovio recounts, the objective of his pupils was to strictly emulate Leonardo, Boltraffio's *Head of a Young Woman* must have been judged a resounding success.

Affinities between the Clark drawing and two paintings by Boltraffio from the 1490s, the *Madonna and Child* in Budapest and the slightly later painting of the same subject in the National Gallery, London, have been noted by various scholars.[6] The drawing's correspondence with the Madonna in both of these works is of a general rather than a precise nature, however, and Fiorio seems to be correct in surmising that the sheet is not directly connected with a specific painting by Boltraffio.[7] Neither a portrait drawing nor a preparatory study for a painting, it was presumably executed to demonstrate his mastery of Leonardo's style. Together with Boltraffio's other head studies of the 1490s, it also reflects his facility, acclaimed by Casio (who may again be suspected of employing a literary trope, although his praise was no doubt sincere), for improving on nature, transforming the merely real into the poetic and the ideal.[8]

LW-S

1. Bibliothèque de l'Institut de France, Paris, Ms. C, fol. 15v; see Richter 1970, vol. 2, pp. 438–39. The passage in question provides an eyewitness testimony of Boltraffio's use of silverpoint, the medium employed in this drawing and others by him: Leonardo here refers to the theft of Boltraffio's silverpoint stylus by his younger pupil Salaì, whom he derisively describes as a "thief, liar, obstinate, glutton."
2. Girolamo Casio, *Libro intitulato Cronica ove si tratta di epitaphii di amore e di virtute* (Bologna, 1525), carta 46; quoted in Fiorio 2000a, p. 132.
3. Frequently cited in this connection is the *Resurrection with Saint Leonard and Saint Lucy* (Gemäldegalerie, Berlin), a collaborative effort of Boltraffio and Marco d'Oggiono, another pupil of Leonardo; the kneeling saints in the lower section are Boltraffio's contribution. The figures are thoroughly Leonardesque in style and execution; indeed the altarpiece was at one time ascribed to Leonardo himself. See Fiorio 2000a, pp. 133–35.
4. See Fiorio 2000a, p. 132.
5. Inv. no. 0026; see Byam Shaw 1972, no. 1062. Byam Shaw suggests that the Christ Church and Clark drawings may portray the same model. The characterization of the 1490s as a period of Boltraffio's "total dedication" to Leonardo is Fiorio's (Fiorio 2000a, p. 151).
6. Suida 1929, Brown 1999; Bora 1987d, p. 13; Pedretti: NG, London. On the National Gallery painting, see Fiorio 2000a, pp. 105–6.
7. Fiorio 2000a, p. 143.
8. This point has been discussed in reference to Boltraffio's head studies by Ballarin and Agosti; see Agosti 2001, p. 193.

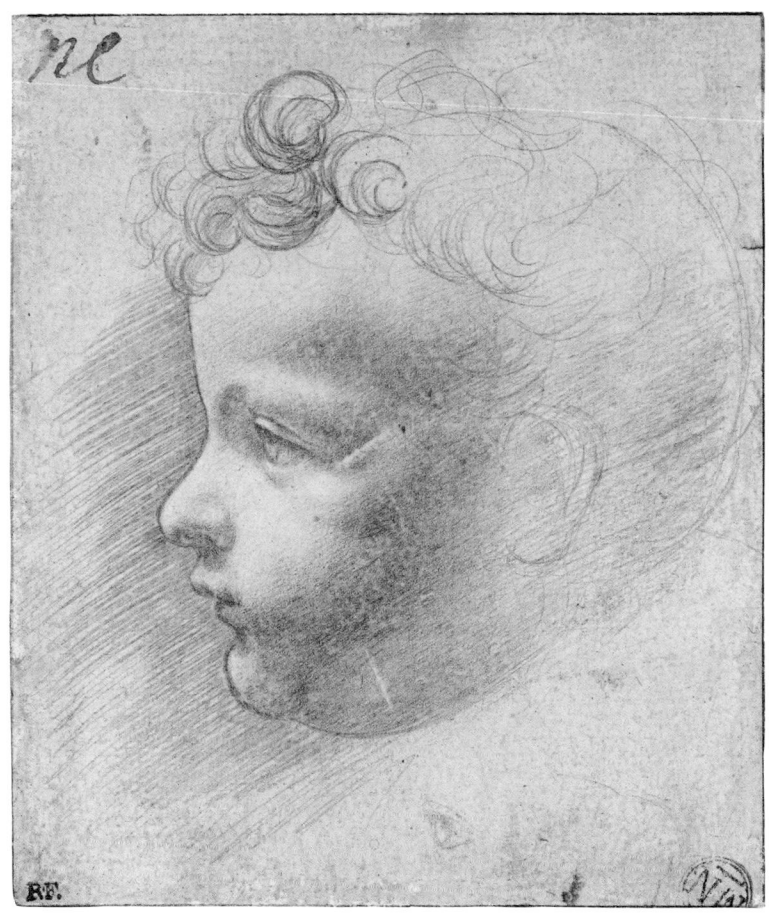

Cat. 125 *(actual size)*

GIOVANNI ANTONIO BOLTRAFFIO (ATTRIBUTED TO)

125. *Head of a Child in Profile*

Metalpoint on light beige prepared paper, with traces of white gouache and framing outlines in dark brown ink, 119 × 98 mm (4 11/16 × 3 7/8 in.)
Département des Arts Graphiques du Musée du Louvre, Paris 2250

PROVENANCE: Everard Jabach, Paris (1607/10–1695); 1671, acquired for the Cabinet du Roi; initials of Robert de Cotte, Paris (1656–1735; Lugt 1963); marks of the Commission du Museum (Lugt 1899) and of the Conservatoire (Lugt 2207); Morel d'Arleux, inv. MS 1, no. 52 (attributed to Leonardo da Vinci: "une tête d'enfant vue de profil dessin à la mine de plomb et rehaussé de blanc").

LITERATURE: Louvre 1866, no. 383 (Leonardo); Richter 1880, fig. p. 112 (Leonardo); Müller-Walde 1890, p. 110, fig. 62 (Leonardo); Gruyer 1891, p. 29 n. 4 (Leonardo; see 2347); Münz 1899, pp. 168, 213, pl. 7, p. 519, no. 6 (Leonardo); Seidlitz 1909, vol. 1, p. 169 (de' Predis); Malaguzzi Valeri, 1913–23, vol. 2, fig. 456 (de' Predis); Louvre 1919, no. 14 (Leonardo); Demonts 1921, p. 13, pl. 10 (de' Predis?); Demonts 1922, no. 10 (de' Predis?); Verne 1927, p. 627; Berenson 1938, vol. 1, p. 183 n. 1 (school of Leonardo); Cogliati Arano 1965, no. 4, fig. 63 (Solario); Cogliati Arano 1993, p. 40 (Solario); Sérullaz 1996, p. 565, fig. 5; Kwakkelstein 1999, p. 196 n. 32 (Maestro della Pala Sforzesca).

Early sources unanimously assigned this drawing of the head of an infant to Leonardo. His authorship was first questioned in 1909 by Woldemar von Seidlitz, whose reattribution to Ambrogio de' Predis initiated a debate that remains

651

unresolved nearly a century later. In addition to de' Predis, the range of alternative proposals has included Andrea Solario and the Master of the Pala Sforzesca, as well as the more generic and cautious appellation Leonardo school. The attribution to Giovanni Antonio Boltraffio has much to recommend it. The exquisitely delicate modeling of the features, which contrasts with the quick and summarily rendered curling locks of hair and reiterated eye at the lower right, is seen in other metalpoint drawings by Boltraffio in which the artist deftly emulated Leonardo's manner (see cat. no. 124). Both the technique and the subject matter are close to autograph drawings by Leonardo such as the *Head of a Child,* also in the Louvre (cat. no. 61), which, significantly for this discussion, is believed by one scholar to be by Boltraffio (Ballarin 1997). In the latter study, both left- and right-handed strokes are present, suggesting that a pupil—possibly Boltraffio—may have gone over Leonardo's drawing. Like other essays in a Leonardesque style and technique produced by Boltraffio, predominantly head studies such as this example and catalogue number 124, the sheet should be assigned to the 1490s.

The *Head of a Child in Profile* is closely based on the blessing Christ in Leonardo's *Virgin of the Rocks.* Of the two variants

of that celebrated composition, the Paris version with its more subtly inflected features of the infant provides the closest prototype (see fig. 23). That this figure was of particular interest to Boltraffio is attested to by his unfinished *Madonna and Child with Saint John the Baptist, Saint Sebastian, and a Donor (The Lodi Altarpiece),* now in the Szépmüvészeti Múzeum, Budapest, commissioned about 1508.[1] The blessing Christ Child in that work is directly quoted from the same figure in the *Virgin of the Rocks.*[2] Indeed, with its enveloping shadows, carefully described passages of flora, and enigmatic backdrop of rocky stalagmites, the *Lodi Altarpiece* has been regarded as an artistic ode to Leonardo. A recollection of the *Virgin of the Rocks,* the Louvre study of a *Head of a Child* may well have served as a model in this homage to the master by his former pupil.   LW-S

1. A closely related tondo by Boltraffio of the Madonna and Child in the Accademia Carrara, Bergamo (Fiorio 2000a, no. A24, pp. 133–34), essentially reprises the two central figures of the Madonna and Child from the *Lodi Altarpiece;* ultimately derived from the *Virgin of the Rocks,* the Christ Child in the tondo provides further visual evidence of Boltraffio's interest in Leonardo's prototype.

2. Fiorio 1998, pp. 159 fig. 33, 161; Fiorio 2000a, pp. 131–33, no. 123.

GIOVANNI ANTONIO BOLTRAFFIO (ATTRIBUTED TO)

126. *Young Man in Profile Facing to the Right*

Metalpoint on bluish gray prepared paper, 185 × 121 mm (7¼ by 4¾ in.)
Département des Arts Graphiques du Musée du Louvre, Paris 2251

PROVENANCE: Everard Jabach, Paris (1607/10–1695); 1671, acquired for the Cabinet du Roi; initials of Robert de Cotte, Paris (1656–1735; Lugt 1963); Morel d'Arleux, inv. MS 1, no. 67: "tête de jeune homme de profil couronné de feuilles de chêne, dessin à la plume et lavé" (copy of Leonardo da Vinci); museum mark (1886).

LITERATURE: Louvre 1866, no. 384 (Leonardo); Gruyer 1887, p. 92, fig. p. 93 (Leonardo); Morelli 1890, p. 207 n. 1 (Boltraffio); Müntz 1899, pp. 2, 520, no. 22 (Leonardo); Frizzoni 1904, p. 114, fig. 6; Seidlitz 1906–7, p. 30 n. 59; Louvre 1919, no. 23; Demonts 1921, no. 22 (school of Leonardo); Demonts 1922, no. 22 (school of Leonardo); Möller 1928, pp. 148–49, fig. 208 (Boltraffio); Suida 1929, p. 195, fig. 231 (Pseudo Boltraffio); Palazzo dell'Arte 1939,

p. 162 (school of Leonardo); Pedretti and Roberts 1981–83, p. 129 (attributed to Leonardo); Bora 1987–88, p. 14, fig. 6 (school of Leonardo); Pedretti 1988c, fig. 10 (Boltraffio); Pedretti 1990a, p. 37 n. 60, fig. 104 (Boltraffio?); Markova 1991, pp. 103–5, fig. 6 (Boltraffio?); Anderson 1995, p. 227, fig. 4 (with incorrect location and inv. no.; Boltraffio?); Marani 1995, p. 211, fig. 4 (Boltraffio?); Bora 1998c, p. 98; Fiorio 2000a, no. D39 (copy after Leonardo).

The image of an idealized youth with flowing locks of hair occurs frequently in works by members of Leonardo's circle, particularly Giovanni Antonio Boltraffio, who treated the subject in a number of drawings and paintings.[1] Among the former are a study of a young man seen in left profile in the Louvre (2248); a head of a youth crowned with branches

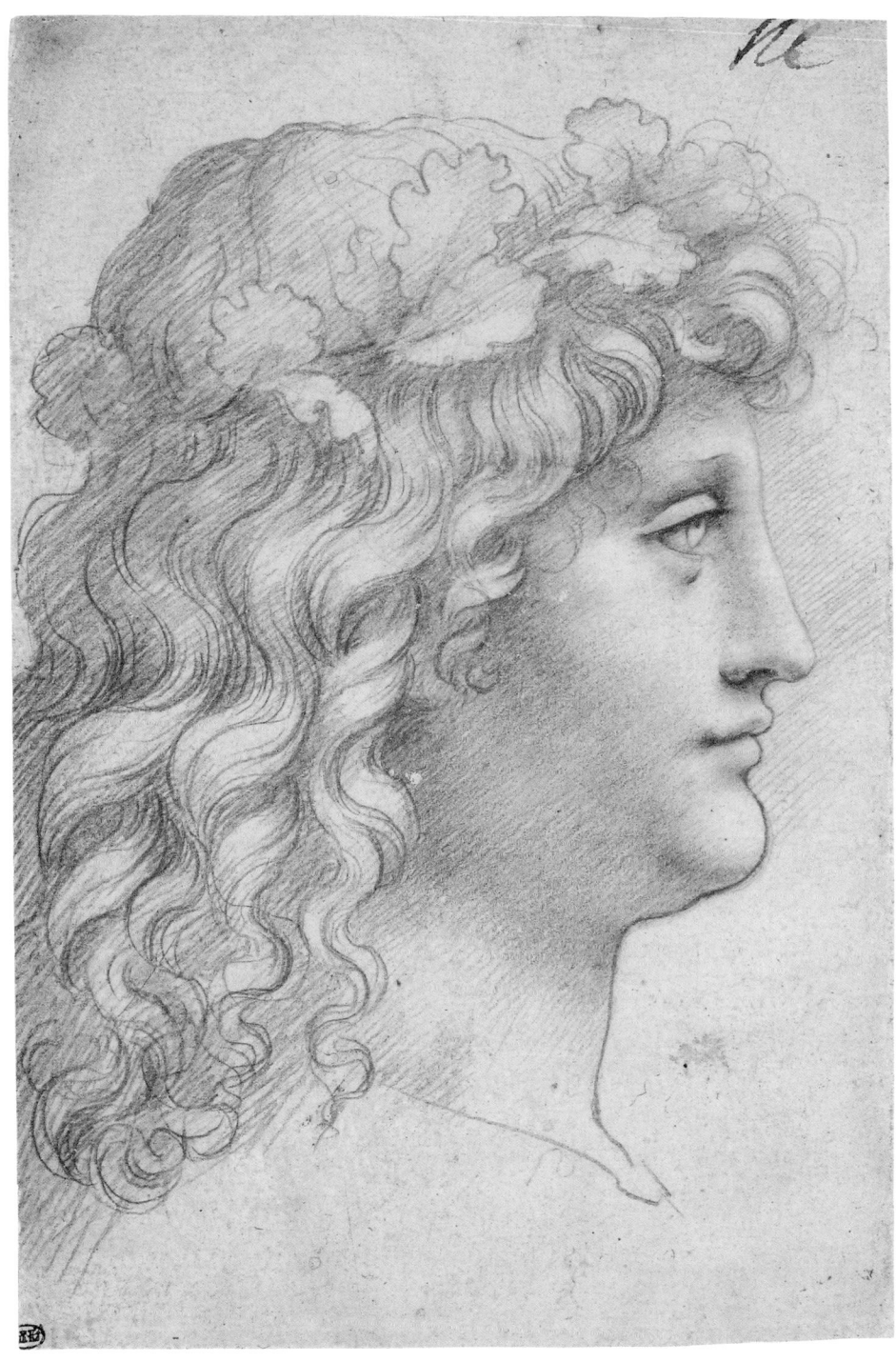

Cat. 126 *(actual size)*

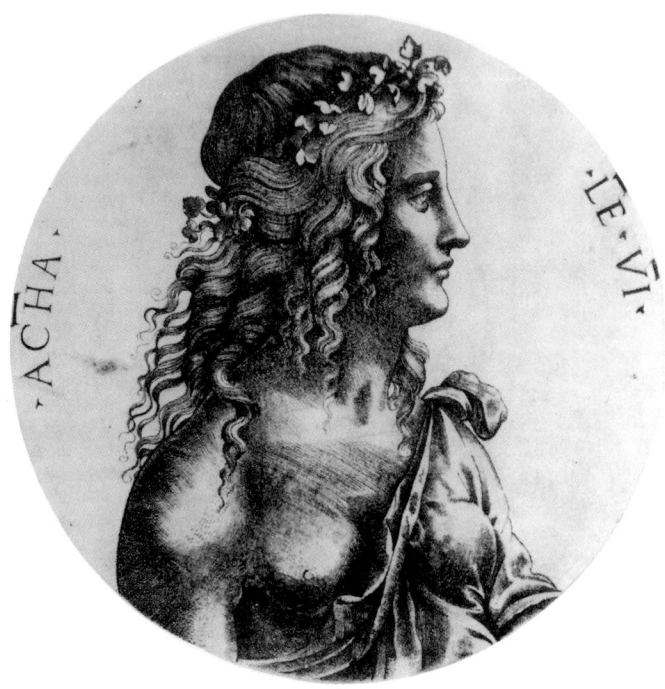

Fig. 203. School of Leonardo da Vinci, *Profile Bust of a Young Woman with a Garland of Ivy*. Engraving, H. 134 mm. The British Museum, London (Hind 13)

in the Uffizi (425 Er); a head of a youth (Christ or Bacchus?) wearing a crown of leaves and thorns in the Biblioteca Reale, Turin (15587 DC); and a head of a youth crowned with ivy (formerly Koenigs Collection, Haarlem). Boltraffio's painting of a young man in the guise of Saint Sebastian (Pushkin Museum, Moscow); a similar, though less clearly hagiographic, depiction of a youthful male sitter holding an arrow and crowned with laurel (Timken Art Gallery, San Diego); and an idealized portrait of his friend, the poet Girolamo Casio (Chatsworth, Duke of Devonshire), also exemplify this type, which finds parallels in the poetic portraits of Giorgione in Venice.[2] That these images by Boltraffio were likewise meant to convey broad poetic associations is suggested by the fact that in each case the young man depicted wears the poet's crown of laurel or oak leaves.

The Louvre's *Young Man in Profile Facing to the Right* self-evidently belongs to this category. As Giulio Bora first observed, it served as the model for an engraving produced as the emblem of the still-mysterious Achademia Leonardi Vinci that Leonardo is believed to have founded in Milan (fig. 203).[3] The androgynous figure in the drawing, described by Bora as an "image-cum-symbol of that subliminal beauty pursued by Leonardo," is transformed in the engraving into a classical female figure represented in a circular field evocative of a medal or antique cameo, thereby codifying the poetic, humanist allusions implicit in the source. Although by no means a literal portrait, the drawing may well be an idealized representation of an actual poet, possibly Casio, whom Boltraffio depicted on a number of occasions in both straightforward and idealized modes. The donor portrait in the votive painting of the *Madonna and Child with Saint John the Baptist and Saint Sebastian* (Musée du Louvre, Paris), known as the *Casio Altarpiece*, combines elements of both types, showing the poet in profile with shoulder-length hair crowned by a laurel wreath, but with distinctly individualized, slightly jowly features.

Though Boltraffio has most frequently been proposed as the author of this drawing, it has also been variously attributed to Gian Giacomo Caprotti, called Salaì, and to the Master of the Pala Sforzesca. Since 1990 the drawing has been published with the more cautionary "attributed to Boltraffio." Most recently, Maria Teresa Fiorio in her monograph on Boltraffio rejected the attribution to the artist, preferring the designation "school of Leonardo" and proposing that the sheet may be a copy with variations after a lost original by the master. The redrawn contours and somewhat frozen quality of the line, which have prompted the reservations about Boltraffio's authorship, may, however, as Bora observed, be explained by the fact that the drawing was produced, or subsequently employed, as a model for a print.   LW-S

1. Many of the paintings and drawings cited here are discussed by Markova 1991, pp. 100–107, who, while noting the derivation of the type from Leonardo, emphasizes that Boltraffio's works should be seen as products of the rarefied courtly culture of Milan.
2. According to Fiorio 1998, p. 143, all three paintings represent Casio. Parallels between Boltraffio's images and the lyric portraiture of Giorgione were noted by Ballarin 1979, pp. 241–42.
3. Bora 1998c, p. 98.

GIOVANNI ANTONIO BOLTRAFFIO

127. *Bust-Length Study of a Young Woman in Frontal View*

Brown, yellow ocher, red, and ivory pastel over charcoal on paper prepared with a cream-color ground; traces of stylus incisions on some outlines (?); traces of framing outlines in pen and dark brown ink and in brush and yellow ocher gouache, 533 × 405 mm (21 × 15 15/16 in.) maximum; losses along borders
Inscribed on recto toward upper corner in red chalk by a later hand: *x*; in charcoal: *xx*
Watermark: According to Maria Teresa Fiorio, eight-petaled flower (52 mm); according to Alessandro Rovetta, five-petaled flower (close to Briquet 6600); the watermark is not sufficiently distinctive, and a firm identification seems difficult.
Biblioteca Pinacoteca Ambrosiana, Milan Cod. F. 290 inf. 7

PROVENANCE: Part of the Accademia Ambrosiana (as suggested by the stamp of interlacing letters "ACAMSN"), possibly since the time of its opening in 1620–21 by Cardinal Federico Borromeo, Milan (1564–1631).

LITERATURE: Kugler 1869, p. 283; Frizzoni 1882, 17 agosto; Morelli 1890, p. 207; Frizzoni 1891, p. 350 n. 1; Rosenberg 1898, p. 111; Carotti 1899, vol. 4, pp. 319, 331; Morelli 1900, pp. 155–57, Layard 1902, p. 411; Malaguzzi Valeri 1904, 27 settembre; Cagnola 1907, pp. 21–22; Ratti 1907, sala G, p. 84; Clausse 1909, p. 457; Seidlitz 1909, vol. 3, p. 154; Pauli 1910, p. 257; Brinton 1911, p. 78; Malaguzzi Valeri 1913–23, vol. 3, pp. 78–79, fig. 68; Bock 1916, p. 163; De Schlegel 1917, p. 205; Suida 1920, p. 41; Dina 1921, p. 377; Schiparelli 1921, p. 154; Teall 1926, pp. 24, 94; Suida 1929, p. 191, fig. 207; Tea 1932, p. 14; Seidlitz 1935, p. 203; Bellani 1936, p. 199; De Hevesy 1936, pp. 323–29; Dussler 1938, p. 9; Kunstmuseum Lucerne 1946, p. 72, no. 124; Galbiati 1951, pp. 136, 146; Pischel Fraschini 1957, pp. 20–21, pl. 3; Paredi, dell'Acqua, and Vitali 1967, pp. 110, 518; Vitali 1967, p. 268; Cogliati Arano 1969, p. 360; Calder 1970, pp. 112, 283; Chiappo 1972, p. 182; De Logu and Marinelli 1975, p. 226; Bora 1980, pp. 8–9, no. 7; Cogliati Arano 1982; Marinoni and Cogliati Arano 1982, pp. 93, 126, no. 34; Precerutti Garberi 1982, pp. 197, 210–11, fig. 155; Coleman 1984, pp. 56–57, no. 20; Luisa Cogliati Arano in Palazzo Reale 1987, pp. 74–75, no. 22; Sannazaro and Shell 1987–93, p. 446; Cogliati Arano 1988, p. 119, fig. 6; McGrath 1994, pp. 64 n. 125, 140, app. pp. 20–22, fig. 70; Fiorio 1996b, p. 285; Fiorio 1997b, pp. 339–42, fig. 7; McGrath 1997, p. 29, n. 16; Bora 1998, pp. 102–3, 118 n. 14, fig. 4.13; McGrath 1998, p. 4 n. 14; Pedretti 1998c, p. 42; Alessandro Rovetta in Ambrosiana 1998, pp. 100–101, no. 41; Fiorio 2000a, pp. 152, under B12, 153–54, no. B13.

The composition of this exquisitely pictorial pastel drawing relates to Giovanni Antonio Boltraffio's monumental altarpiece of *Saint Barbara Standing in a Landscape* (fig. 204), commissioned in October 1502 for the chapel named after the saint in the church of Santa Maria presso San Satiro (Milan). Although an attribution to Boltraffio had already been correctly recognized by 1869, the connection to the painting was not noticed until the end of the nineteenth century. Were it not for the painting, however, the pastel drawing might pass for an independent portrait. The figure in both painting and pastel drawing is more or less lifesize in scale and is lit from the same direction, but in the painting the saint looks wide-eyed, directly at the viewer. It is possible that the idea for the figure of Saint Barbara in the painting occurred to Boltraffio in the process of designing this pastel drawing as an independent finished portrait. The large, slightly brown sheet of paper that the artist used has a horizontal fold at the center (such large paper originally came folded loosely in a quire) and is quite thick and sturdy, rather unlike ordinary drawing paper. A curi-

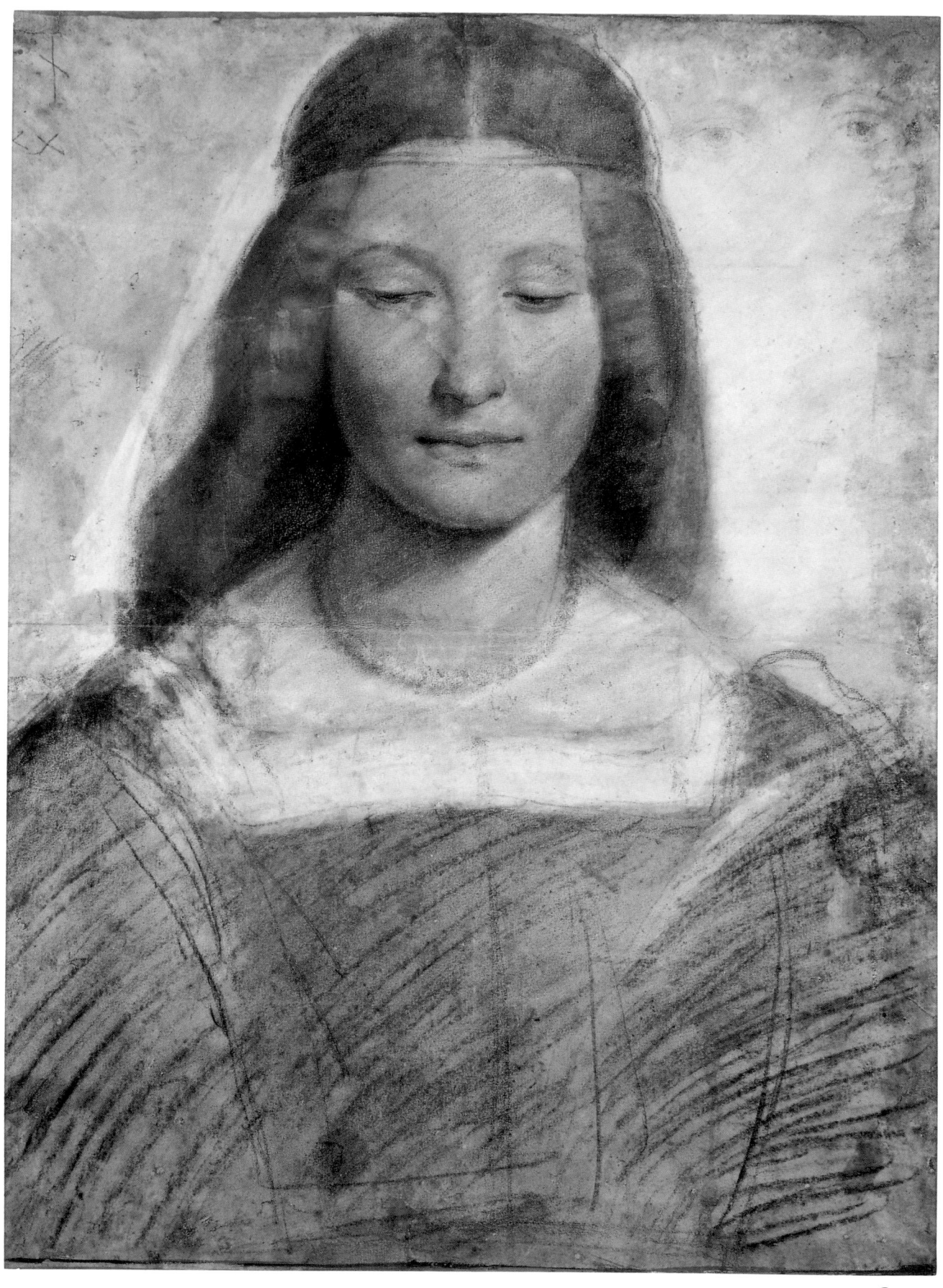

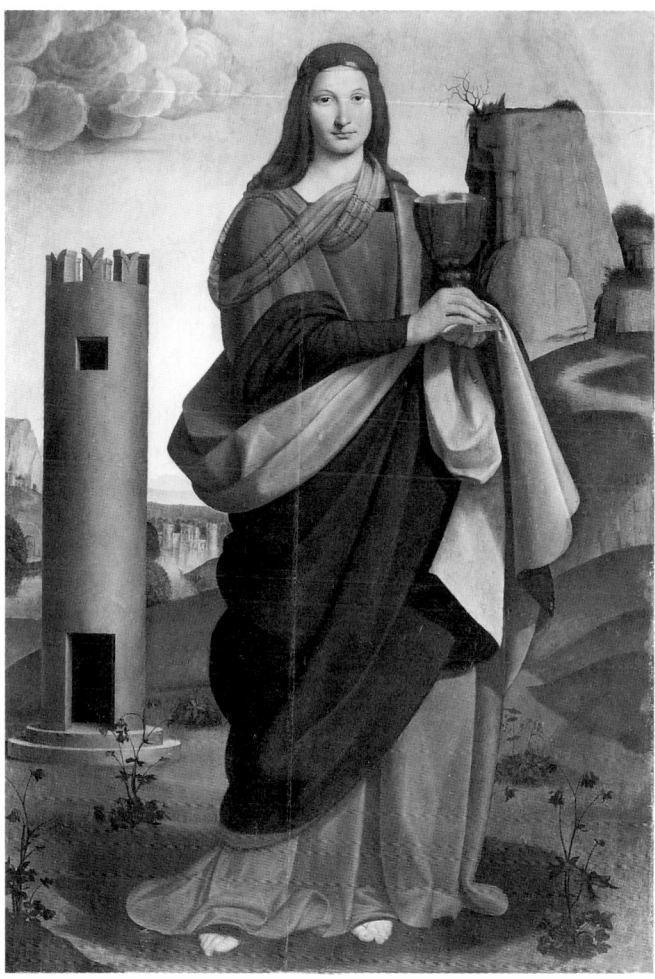

Fig. 204. Giovanni Antonio Boltraffio, *Saint Barbara Standing in a Landscape*. Oil on wood, 170 × 111 cm. Gemäldegalerie, Staatliche Museen zu Berlin—Preussischer Kulturbesitz 207

ous feature of the pastel drawing can be seen on the upper right, where the artist seems to have experimented by lightly sketching the woman's face, but with the same wide-eyed gaze as in the painting. The version of the face on the upper right, identical in scale with the main figure in the drawing, is heavily erased, although it seems difficult to determine whether the erasure was the artist's intention or the result of an early restoration. The artist drew the monumental figure at the center of the sheet, with her gaze modestly lowered. In contrast

to the painting, she wears a short, red, beaded necklace and a dress with a square white neckline, fitted high bodice, and wide sleeves, which render the figure more courtly and portrait-like. A much-disputed tradition suggests that the subject of Boltraffio's pastel portrait was the duchess Isabella of Aragon, wife of Gian Galeazzo Visconti. In a letter of June 13, 1498, Isabella expressed her high regard for Boltraffio's portraiture by asking her sister-in-law Isabella d'Este in Mantua to allow "Master Zo. Antonio Beltraffio, a painter most expert in his art," to make a copy of the portrait of her deceased brother Ferdinand, which the marchesa owned.[1]

Boltraffio's pastel drawing technique dazzles the eye with its dynamic contrasts of finish and unfinish (the "non finito" was one of Leonardo's aesthetics as a draftsman, even in large-scale drawings), serving to build up the sculptural presence of the figure.[2] He seamlessly stumped the lustrous modeling of the face, neck, and cleavage until the individual pastel strokes were hardly visible, but he left a remarkably bold staccato of unblended hatching on the bodice and sleeves. In the background the lighter hue that envelops the main figure almost like a halo does not seem original and may have been the result of restoration (stains or soil were probably erased, after which the treated area was covered with an ivory-hue pastel to harmonize it). The drawing surface appears to have also been slightly retouched in a few passages with a waxy chalk medium, but such interventions seem minor as well as inevitable in a drawing of this size, fragility, and complexity of technique. The ineffable pictorial effects of Boltraffio's pastel drawing technique would not have been possible without Leonardo's pioneering of the pastel medium. Yet the quality of this particular pastel by Boltraffio seems to go well beyond that of the only extant example by Leonardo, the cartoon portrait *Isabella d'Este* (Musée du Louvre, Paris; fig. 16), done by the master in 1500–1506, possibly even when he was passing through Mantua in the spring of 1500.   CCB

1. As transcribed in Fiorio 2000a, p. 221: "venendo lì ad Mantua M.ro Zo. Antonio Beltrafio depintore molto experto nel mestero suo."
2. Bambach 1999a, pp. 111–12, 249–76.

GIOVANNI ANTONIO BOLTRAFFIO

128. *Bust-Length Portrait of a Young Man in Three-Quarter View Facing to the Right and Pointing with His Right Hand*

Brown, yellow ocher, red, and ivory pastel over charcoal on paper prepared with a cream-color ground; traces of stylus incisions on some outlines; traces of framing outlines in pen and dark brown ink and in brush and yellow ocher gouache, 537 × 407 mm (21 ⅛ × 16 ¹⁄₁₆ in.)

Biblioteca Pinacoteca Ambrosiana, Milan Cod. F. 290 inf. 8

PROVENANCE: Part of the Accademia Ambrosiana (as suggested by the stamp of interlacing letters "ACAMSN"), possibly since the time of its opening in 1620–21 by Cardinal Federico Borromeo (1564–1631), Milan.

LITERATURE: Frizzoni 1882, 17 agosto; Morelli 1890, p. 207; Frizzoni 1891, p. 350 n. 1; Rosenberg 1898, p. 110; Carotti 1899, p. 325; Layard 1902, p. 411; Ratti 1907, pp. 84–85, sala G; Clausse 1909, p. 457; Pauli 1910, p. 257; Brinton 1911, p. 78; De Schlegel 1917, p. 197; Malaguzzi Valeri 1913–23, vol. 3, p. 89; Suida 1920, p. 141; Teall 1926, pp. 24, 94; Suida 1929, p. 191; Seidlitz 1935, p. 203; Kunstmuseum Lucerne 1946, p. 72, no. 125; Galbiati 1951, p. 146; De Hevesy 1952, p. 244; Pischel Fraschini 1957, pp. 22–23; Cogliati Arano 1969, p. 360; Bora 1980, p. 9, under no. 7; Marinoni and Cogliati Arano 1982, pp. 93, 127, no. 35; Coleman 1984, p. 56, under no. 20; Luisa Cogliati Arano in Palazzo Reale 1987, p. 76, no. 23; Cogliati Arano 1988, p. 119; Norris 1988–89, p. 19, no. 17; McGrath 1994, pp. 64 n. 125, 141, app. pp. 20–22, fig. 71; Fiorio 1996b, p. 285; Fiorio 1997b, pp. 339–42, fig. 8; Alessandro Rovetta in Ambrosiana 1998, pp. 102–3, no. 42; Vecce 1998, p. 416 n. 58; Fiorio 2000a, pp. 152, under no. 12, 155–56, no. B14.

The youth who intently gazes at the viewer in this pastel portrait has not been identified. Giovanni Morelli's correct attribution of the portrait to Boltraffio in 1890 was largely based on similarities with catalogue number 127. For instance, the pastel technique of soft sfumato rendering, though less subtle, nevertheless greatly resembles that of catalogue number 127, and the drawing is executed on a similarly

sturdy brown paper. When the portrait is examined in raking light, scattered traces of incisions are evident in the outlines, though much flattened (whether these are from a design transfer process, however, is difficult to determine). By way of contrast, this drawing exhibits a very bold, loosely sketched underdrawing in charcoal that is full of clues about the artist's design process and that, one suspects, was completely obscured by the pastel layers. Boltraffio seems to have first drawn the hat of the youth in a more frontal pose in charcoal. After deciding to narrow and foreshorten the hat into a three-quarter view, he reworked the design with dark brown pastel and strengthened the tones of the new design with a layer of brown wash. The condition of the pastel surface is similar to that of catalogue number 127, but with more retouching in waxy chalk, and the halo effect around the figure, the result of a lighter color pastel probably applied by an early restorer to harmonize the hues, is less noticeable. Although the lower portion of the drawing has suffered from considerable abrasion, especially along the youth's sleeve and pointing hand, the yellow ocher pastel on the zigzagging fringe is still fairly intact.

The drawing has not been convincingly connected to a finished painting. It is more than likely that it was conceived as an independent work, for it would seem impractical and redundant to the process of preliminary design for the artist to have prepared a fully colored and finished drawing in the same scale as the final easel painting. As a composition, the pastel drawing is complete in its details, and as a portrait type it has much in common with Boltraffio's paintings in Washington, Milan, Basel, and Florence.[1]   CCB

1. Illustrated and discussed in Fiorio 2000a, pp. 100–102, 107–9, 124–25, 128–29, nos. A11, A14, A20, A22.

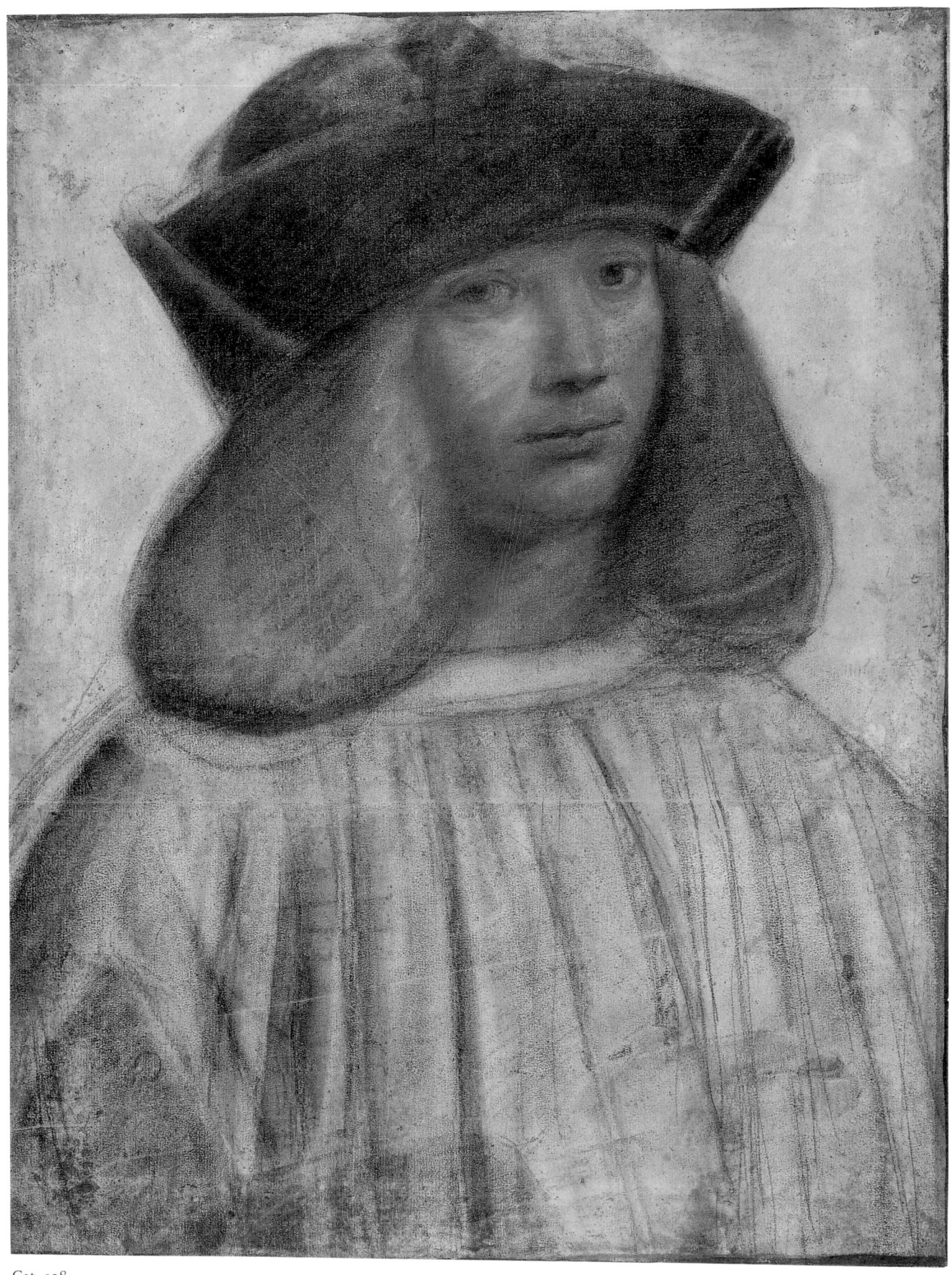

Cat. 128

ANDREA SOLARIO

(Milan, ca. 1465–Milan, 1524)

129. *Head of a Bearded Man*

Black, red, and yellow chalk on brownish paper; repaired losses,
374 × 273 mm (14¾ × 10¾ in.)
The Metropolitan Museum of Art, New York; Rogers Fund, 1906
06.1051.9

PROVENANCE: Samuel Woodburn, London (1786–1853; Lugt
2584, 2591; Suppl. 2378a), until 1854; Woodburn sale, Christie's,
London, June 16–25, 1854, lot 38 (as Bernardino Luini); purchased
in London by The Metropolitan Museum of Art in 1906.

LITERATURE: Suida 1945, pp. 18, 23, fig. 5; Cogliati Arano 1966,
p. 103; Bean 1982, p. 131, no. 122 (as Bernardino Luini); Béguin
1985, p. 91, under no. 53; Brown 1987, pp. 253, 270 n. 98, 288,
under no. 74, p. 289, no. 77, fig. 219; Griswold and Wolk-Simon
1994, pp. 50, 186, no. 45; McGrath 1994, pp. 64–65, 140–41,
app. pp. 123–24, fig. 29.

Andrea Solario figures prominently in the cadre of early-
sixteenth-century Lombard painters who were particularly attuned and responsive to the innovations of Leonardo.
This damaged but nonetheless imposing study of a bearded
man, which probably represents Christ or an apostle, reveals
the pervasive influence of the Florentine master. The unusual
use of colored chalks (a technique pioneered by Leonardo and
adopted by some of his followers, but widely employed only
later in the sixteenth century by such artists as Jacopo Bassano
and Federico Barocci), the softly modeled forms, and the
enveloping sfumato are all indebted to his example. The subject matter and the bust-length format of the figure likewise
have as their point of departure Leonardo's chalk drawings,
specifically the preparatory studies for Christ and the apostles
in the *Last Supper* that were singled out for particular mention by Giovanni Paolo Lomazzo.[1] In emulation of Leonardo's
paradigm, Solario's contemplative figure has an almost tangi-
ble presence and an emotive aspect that is communicated
through the tilted head and vaguely sketched hand deployed
in a rhetorical gesture of speech.

Solario's artistic personality has come into focus in recent
decades through the research of Sylvie Béguin and David Alan
Brown. For much of the twentieth century, however, his work
was confused with that of other artists working in Leonardo's
ambient in Milan such as Bernardino Luini, to whom the

Metropolitan Museum's *Head of a Bearded Man* was long
attributed, and Giovanni Antonio Boltraffio. The present sheet
is a case in point: even after Wilhelm Suida ascribed it to
Solario in 1945,[2] it continued to reside under the name of
Bernardino Luini. In 1956, an alternative attribution to
Gaudenzio Ferrari was advanced though not widely accepted.[3]
It was not until 1985 that the drawing was restored to Solario
by Béguin. Endorsing Solario's authorship, Brown connected
this study with the standing apostle at the far right of the
artist's *Assumption of the Virgin* in the Sacrestia Nuova of the
Certosa at Pavia.[4] (A late work, this altarpiece remained
unfinished at the time of Solario's death, evidently of the
plague, in the summer of 1524, and was completed only some
fifty years later by the Cremonese painter Bernardino Campi.)
The figure's inclined head and bearded countenance correspond
to the apostle in the *Assumption*, who indicates the Virgin's
empty sarcophagus. However, his gestures depart from the
drawing, which shows the figure's hand raised to his chest in
introverted self-acclamation. As the latter pose would have no
rhetorical resonance in the context of an Assumption, in
which all the assembled witnesses typically react in exaggerated amazement and disbelief to the sight of the vacated tomb,
it is worth considering the possibility that Solario executed
this drawing for some other purpose, or perhaps as a stock
type, and subsequently employed it as the model for the
apostle in the altarpiece.[5]

In addition to the Metropolitan's *Head of a Bearded Man*,
two other preparatory drawings by Solario (Musée du Louvre,
Paris) have been associated with the Pavia *Assumption*.[6]
Studies for the lateral wings, they each are executed in black
chalk and show a group of three apostles.   LW-S

1. Lomazzo 1584, vol. 1, pp. 80–81.
2. Suida 1945, p. 18.
3. Martin Weinberger, verbal communication to Claus Virch of The Metropolitan
   Museum of Art, 1956.
4. Brown 1987, p. 289.
5. McGrath's observation that the drawing has faint indications of squaring
   lines (1994, pp. 64, 123) is erroneous, thus negating his corollary postulate
   that its function as a preparatory study is thereby established.
6. Béguin 1985, pp. 90–91, no. 53.

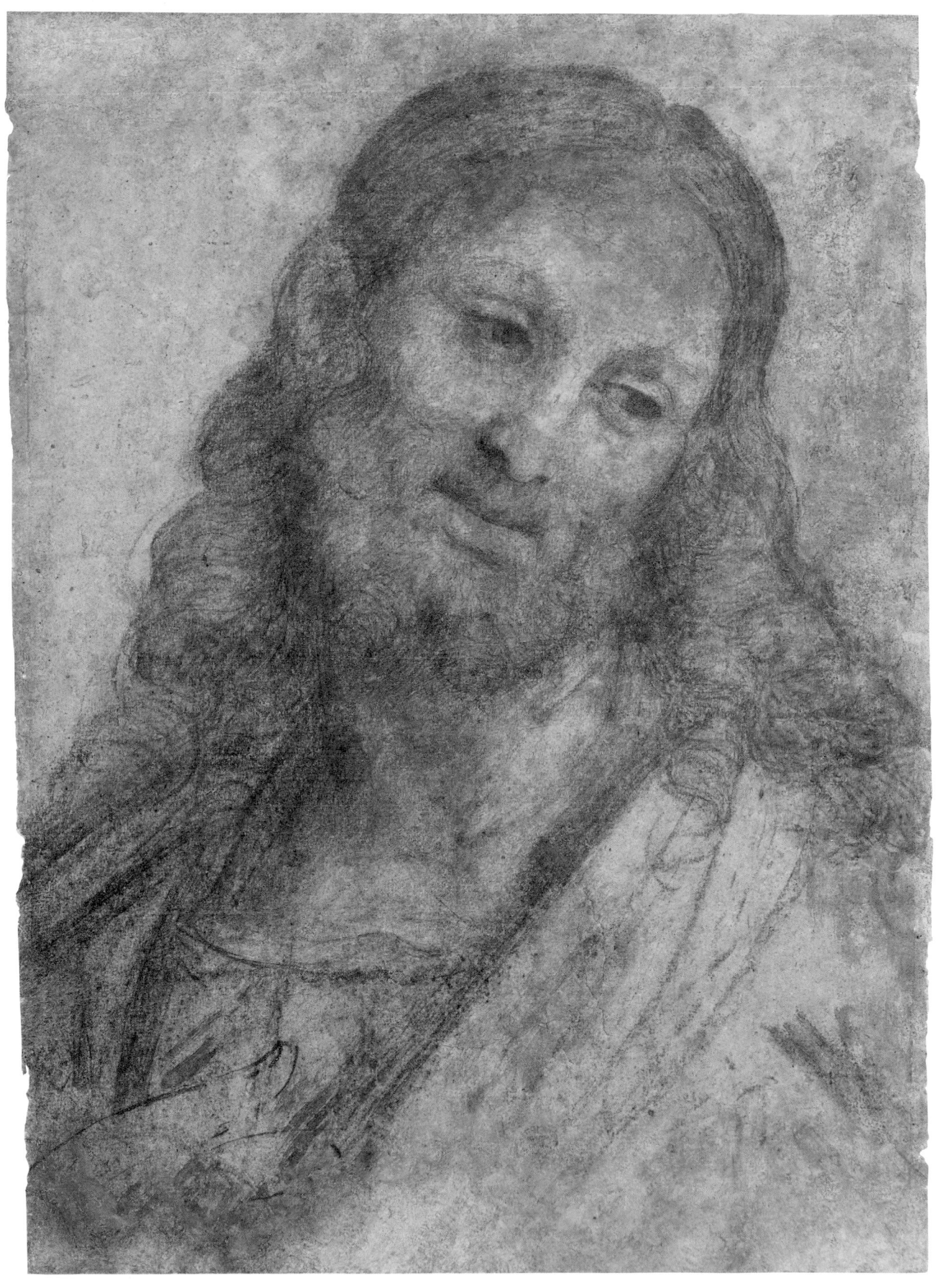

Cat. 129

661

GIOVANNI AGOSTINO DA LODI

(Lombardy, active ca. 1495–ca. 1520)

130. *Half-Length Study of Young Boy in Three-Quarter View Facing to the Right*

Red chalk, 100 × 83 mm (3¹⁵⁄₁₆ × 3¼ in.); perforations on the neck in center of sheet; folded in half
Inscribed in pen and brown ink at upper right by a later hand: *Lionardo 116*; on left: illegible (*sal* or *sol*? some have read *del.*)
Département des Arts Graphiques du Musée du Louvre, Paris 2252

PROVENANCE: Cabinet du Roi; Morel d'Arleux, inv. MS 1, no. 77 (Leonardo da Vinci): "Tête de jeune homme vue de 3/4 avec chevelure touffue dessin à la sanguine. Roy"; museum mark (Lugt 1886).

LITERATURE: Louvre 1866, no. 386 (Leonardo); Geymüller 1886, p. 375; Pater 1893, p. 121; Müntz 1899, pp. 520, 540, no. 23 (Leonardo); Louvre 1919, no. 21 (Leonardo); Demonts 1921, no. 24, pl. 24 (school of Leonardo); Demonts 1922, no. 24 (school of Leonardo); Palazzo dell'Arte 1939, p. 160 (Leonardo); Clark and Pedretti 1968–69, under no. 12494; Bora 1987b, pp. 146–48, fig. 2; Bora 1987–88, under no. 30; Simonetto 1988, p. 83 n. 57; Palazzo Grassi 1992, no. 81 with reproduction error: see p. 375 (Giovanni Augustino da Lodi)

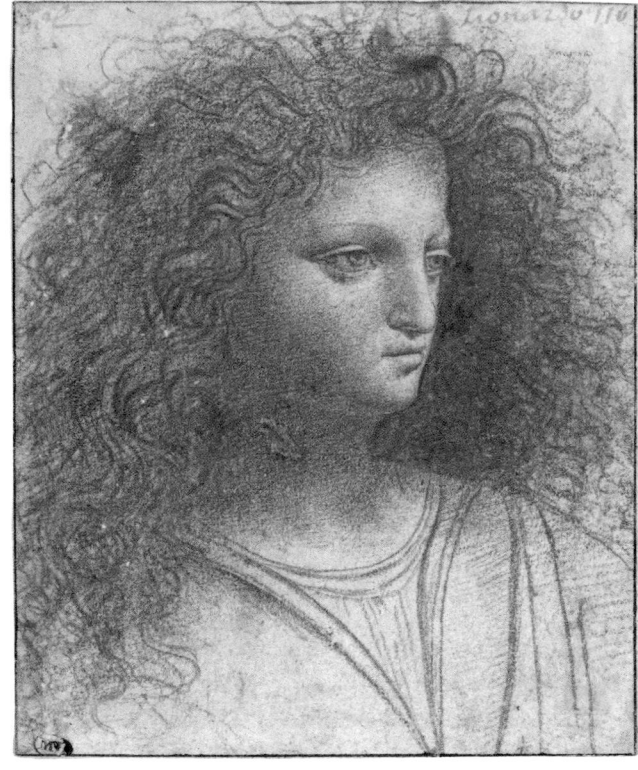

Cat. 130 *(actual size)*

This airily drawn study of a youth of slightly melancholic gaze and idealized facial features offset by a mane of hair is one of a number of such extant drawings of heads in red chalk by the brilliant though elusive painter Giovanni Agostino da Lodi (see essay by Pietro C. Marani in this volume). The precise purpose and iconography of this study remain unclear. Two documents of September 7, 1510, and May 13, 1511, prove the artist's residence in Milan (his native town of Lodi is nearby) during the later years of Leonardo's second stay in that city. Whether Giovanni Agostino was in direct contact with Leonardo, however, is not known. The delicate, somewhat stylized, androgynous face with large, elongated eyes, slightly aquiline nose, and pointy chin in this study seems more characteristic of his paintings from the first years of the sixteenth century. One finds such figural types in his *Portrait of a Youth* (formerly Viezzoli Collection, Genoa), *Virgin and Child with Two Donors* (Museo Nazionale di Capodimonte, Naples), and *Virgin and Child with a Donor* (Museo Isola San Lazzaro degli Armeni, Venice).[1] The *Christ Washing the Feet of the Apostles* (Gallerie dell'Accademia, Venice) from 1500, the only

dated picture by the artist, also integrates Leonardo's figural vocabulary and monumental style of chiaroscuro, and it offers a somewhat comparable youthful Saint John among the wide variety of physiognomic types of the apostles. Giovanni Agostino is recorded in Venice in 1504. Leonardo himself briefly visited Venice (as is recorded in a letter about him from March 13, 1500),[2] and Lombard artists from his circle had brought his artistic developments with them to Venice. Marco d'Oggiono (ca. 1475–1530) had worked in Venice in 1489, and Andrea Solario (cat. no. 129) in 1495. All that is known about the most mysterious of the Leonardesque painters, the idiosyncratic Francesco "Napoletano," is that he died in Venice in 1501.

The influence on Giovanni Agostino of Andrea Solario's early paintings, which blend German sources with a Leonardesque vocabulary, seems particularly strong. The use in the present study of a red-chalk technique, as well as the soft, luminous density of form and sfumato, suggests a more direct influence of Leonardo's style—at a point between 1505 and 1510—and the lessening of a purely Venetian idiom. The atmospheric treatment of the wild hair is typical of this imaginative artist and seems generally inspired by Leonardesque models (see Windsor, RL 12494, 12502, 12554; cat. nos. 69, 74), although none of the master's extant drawings offers an exact prototype. Few documents about Giovanni Agostino are extant, and until his identity was gradually discovered and reconstructed,[3] a homogeneous group of his paintings had been attributed to a master named the Pseudo Boccaccino (to distinguish him from Boccaccino Boccaccini) in an effort to define his unique assimilation of Leonardo's style, as well as of the pictorial traditions of Lombardy and Venice. Once thought to be by Leonardo himself (as is inscribed on the upper right of the sheet), the present drawing was correctly attributed to Giovanni Agostino by Philip Pouncey.

CCB

1. Illustrated in Berenson 1968, vol. 3, nos. 1445, 1449; Bora 1998b, pp. 260–61, figs. 144–45.
2. Letter of Lorenzo Gusnasco da Pavia to Isabella d'Este, transcribed in Villata 1999, pp. 130–31, no. 144; Marani 2000b, p. 349, no. 34.
3. See esp. discussion in Bora 1998b, pp. 251–74.

BERNARDINO LUINI

(Dumenza, sopra Luino, ca. 1480–Milan, 1532)

131. *Portrait of a Woman in Half-Length, Three-Quarter View Facing to the Left (Ippolita Bentivoglio?)*

Pastel (black, red, yellow, and white) and soft black chalk over charcoal, 414 × 284 mm (16 5/16 × 11 3/16 in.)
Graphische Sammlung Albertina, Vienna 59. (SR 71; B. 405)

PROVENANCE: Hofbibliothek; Albert von Sachsen-Teschen (1738–1822; Lugt 174).

LITERATURE: Wickhoff 1892, ScR. 71; Schönbrunner and Meder 1896, no. 352; Beltrami 1911, p. 360; Schaeffer 1911, p. 144; Meder 1923, pl. 26; Ottino della Chiesa 1956, p. 148, no. 41; Benesch 1964, p. 322, pl. 2; Albertina 1971, no. 52; Oberhuber and Walker 1973, p. 99, under no. 81 n. 3; Louvre 1975, pp. 104–5, no. 44; National Gallery of Art 1979, p. 283 n. 5, under no. 37; Macandrew 1980, p. 40, under no. 286A; National Gallery of Art 1984–85, pp. 232–33, no. 53; Brown 1987, under no. 44; Birke and Kertész 1992–97, vol. 1, pp. 32–33, inv. 59; McGrath 1994, p. 140, app. pp. 62–63, fig. 147; McGrath 1997a, p. 29 n. 16; Bora 1998c, pp. 115–16, fig. 4.33; McGrath 1998, p. 4 n. 15; Bandera and Fiorio 2000, pp. 56–57.

Although no known document to date states unequivocally that the enigmatic, brilliantly talented Bernardino Luini was a pupil or assistant of Leonardo, he is possibly the Lombard painter who may be credited with taking the great master's vocabulary of form and technique of sfumato to the most inspired heights (cat. nos. 132, 133). It is, therefore, no wonder that a number of early written sources refer to Luini as Leonardo's pupil. The artist's origins remain largely a mystery, however, and it is also not known in which workshop he received his earliest training. This portrait of a lovely, sumptuously dressed young woman by Luini has justly been regarded as one of the great masterpieces of pastel drawing of the sixteenth century. The sitter wears the fashionable northern Italian dress of the early 1520s, with a large, softly bulbous hat, a high, tight bodice, and voluminous puffed sleeves, and holds what may be a mirror or a fan upright in her right hand. The style of her dress is remarkably similar to that seen in two extant painted portraits, Lorenzo Lotto's *Lucina Brembati* (Accademia Carrara, Bergamo) and Luini's otherwise unidentified *Portrait of a Woman* (fig. 205).[1] The Albertina pastel drawing was long considered to be by Leonardo himself, until Gustavo Frizzoni correctly attributed it to Luini (note in the files of the Graphische Sammlung Albertina), and it is among the very few independent portraits by Luini that are extant.

Like catalogue numbers 127 and 128, the present drawing emanates from Leonardo's pioneering explorations of the pastel medium (*pastelli,* or fabricated colored chalks). Giovanni Paolo Lomazzo's treatise states that Leonardo first used

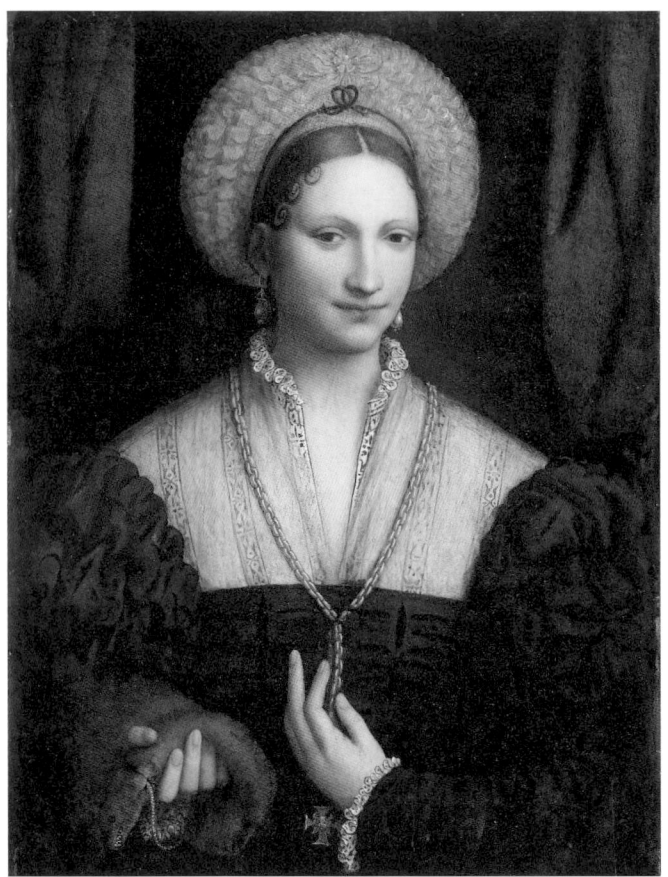

Fig. 205. Bernardino Luini, *Portrait of a Woman*. Oil on wood, 77.2 × 57.2 cm. National Gallery of Art, Washington, D.C.; Andrew W. Mellon Collection 1937.1.37 (PA)

pastelli for his studies of the heads of Christ and the apostles of the *Last Supper* (Refectory of Santa Maria delle Grazie, Milan). In the Albertina portrait, Luini accented only selective passages with color: the flesh, hair, and hat. He modeled the young woman's slender face to a high finish, diffusing the articulation of her facial features with a particularly soft sfumato technique (which complements the dreamy state of the young woman's gaze), while leaving much of her figure only suggestively sketched in the silvery, soft black chalk or charcoal of the underdrawing. This aspect of Luini's technique is similar to Leonardo's in the *Isabella d'Este* cartoon (fig. 16), dating to 1500–1501, which is executed in a delicate experimental technique combining colored chalks and pastel over leadpoint. As a result of the dynamic contrasts of finish and unfinish (*non finito*), the Albertina pastel drawing soars on the page with exquisite airiness, color, and light. As a portrait, it is also greatly indebted to the composition of Leonardo's *Isabella d'Este* cartoon, yet in its ineffable lightness of touch it far surpasses Leonardo's cartoon. Leonardo's pupils and followers could sometimes "out-Leonardo" the master himself.

In 1911 Luca Beltrami and Emil Schaeffer connected the Albertina pastel to the female figure that was frescoed by Luini in 1522–24 on the right part of the large dividing wall in the oratory church of San Maurizio al Monastero Maggiore

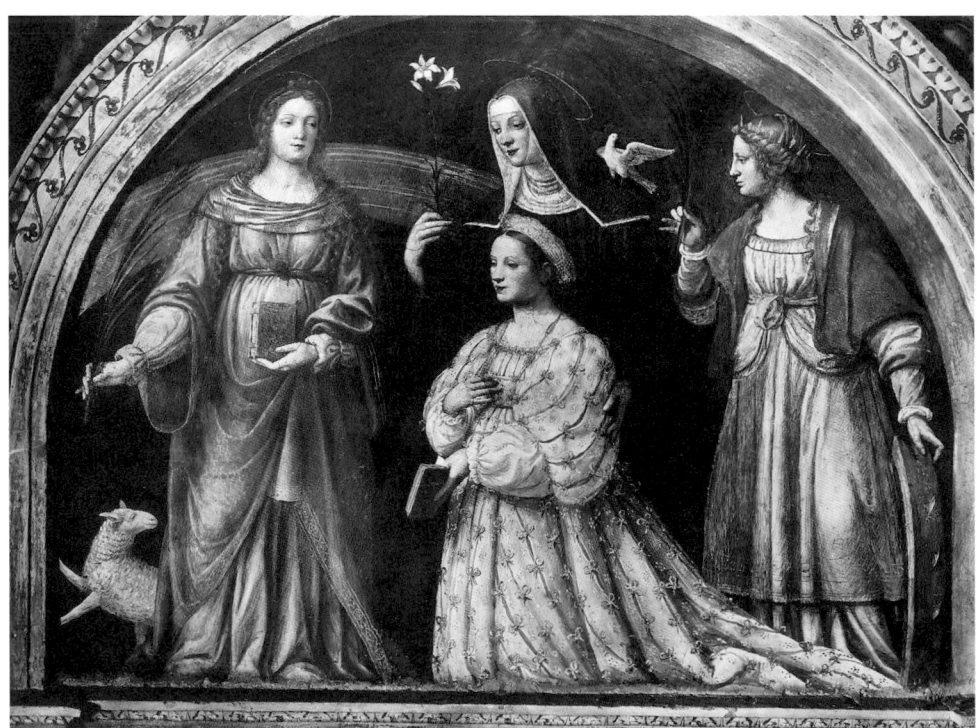

Fig. 206. Bernardino Luini, *Ippolita Sforza with Saints Scolastica, Agnes, and Lucy*. Fresco. San Maurizio al Monastero Maggiore, Milan

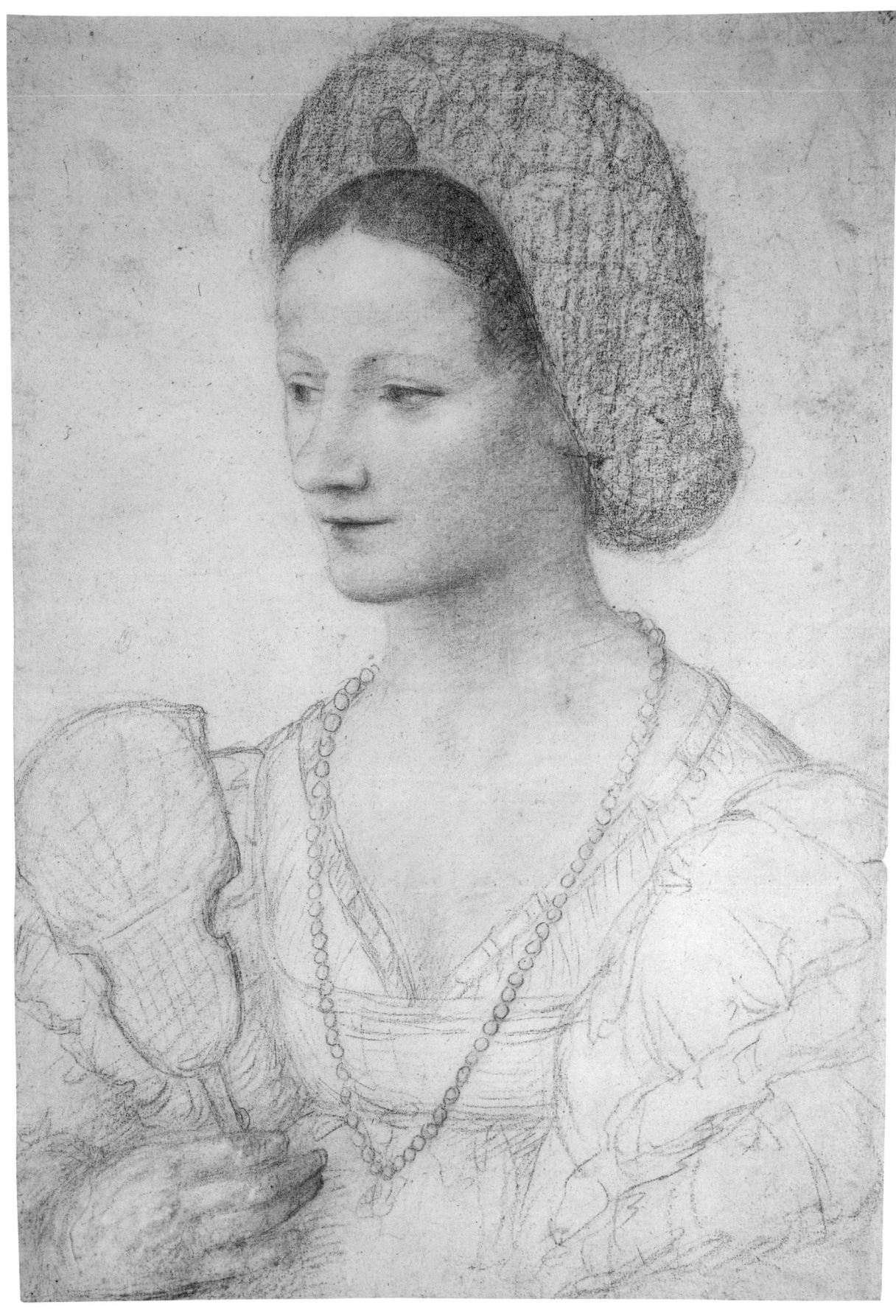

Cat. 131

in Milan (fig. 206). They identified the model for the Albertina portrait as Ippolita Sforza Bentivoglio (ca. 1481–ca. 1521), the cultivated wife of Alessandro Bentivoglio, who was himself a noted scholar of Latin and a prominent figure in Milanese society during the first two decades of the sixteenth century.[2] In 1492 Ippolita Sforza had married Alessandro, son of Giovanni II Bentivoglio, ruler of Bologna, and Ginevra Sforza. On the expulsion of the Bentivoglio from Bologna in 1506 by Pope Julius II, Alessandro closely allied his fortunes with Massimiliano Sforza, son of Ludovico Sforza "Il Moro," serving him as condottiere and helping him win the battle of Novara on June 6, 1513, with which the Sforza began regaining their power in Milan. Ippolita was herself a relative of Ludovico, Leonardo's patron from about 1482–83 until 1499, when he was expelled from Milan by the French. She was, along with her friend Cecilia Gallerani (Ludovico's mistress as a young woman, immortalized by Leonardo in his portrait *The Lady with the Ermine* (Muzeum Czartoryskich, Kraków), an important literary patron in her day. She was apparently one of the muses for the poet Matteo Bandello. According to Bandello himself, Ippolita's untimely death moved him to gather and begin writing some of his *Novelle* (about 1506–26), partly in tribute to her. As is well known, Bandello's *Novelle* also offer a rare eyewitness account of Leonardo at work both on the mural of the *Last Supper* at the Refectory of Santa Maria delle Grazie and on the model for the monumental "Sforza Horse" at the Corte Vecchia.

A manuscript by the painter known as Nucetus Johannes Ambrosius that is dedicated to Francis I, king of France, offers a rare, securely identified portrait of Ippolita Sforza Bentivoglio among twenty-seven such images of illustrious women (Codex Trivulzianus 2159, Biblioteca Trivulziana, Castello Sforzesco, Milan); it is labeled "Domina Hippolita Bentevolia."[3] This small portrait shows Ippolita in a fairly ungainly, strict profile view and seems quite unlike the portrait in the San Maurizio fresco. Because the female figure in the fresco exhibits a more ample girth (fig. 206), Otto Benesch and Konrad Oberhuber have repeatedly disputed either a connection of the Albertina pastel to the fresco or an identification of the sitter as Ippolita. Oberhuber has instead connected the likeness in the Albertina drawing to that of Luini's portrait in the National Gallery in Washington, D.C. That young lady, who

is represented in a frontal view and exhibits a *Mona Lisa* type of smile (fig. 205), offers a close resemblance in costume but, in the present author's opinion, not at all in facial features. In their recent study of the San Maurizio frescoes, Sandrina Bandera and Maria Teresa Fiorio have rightly restated the connection of the Albertina pastel to the fresco, noting again the striking resemblances of pose and physiognomy in the portraits of the women in both works. The corpulence of the frescoed figure is undeniable, but the distinctive, pleasingly angular facial features in both the fresco and the pastel are also rather similar, especially the thin lips and the long nose that curves upward (fig. 206). If not Ippolita herself, it is not to be ruled out that the sitter for the Albertina drawing may have been another member of her family.

Ippolita's husband, probably in the name of his recently deceased wife, commissioned the San Maurizio fresco cycle in 1521–22 from Luini, who left it unfinished at his death ten years later.[4] The commission celebrated the ties of the Bentivoglio family to the monastery of San Maurizio, for four of the patron's daughters would eventually take vows as nuns of the Benedictine order there; among them, his daughter Alessandra took her vows in 1522 and became abbess. In the San Maurizio fresco, Ippolita, holding her left hand to her chest and a book in her right, humbly kneels before the protecting Saints Agnes, Scolastica, and Lucy. Whether the Albertina pastel portrait is or is not a direct preparatory study for the fresco is not clear. The drawing has the character of an independent portrait, and, unlike the pious figure in the fresco, the sitter holds a courtly mirror or fan in her right hand. It is possible that the commission for the fresco inspired the pastel portrait as an independent work, and that the Albertina pastel represents an idealized posthumous likeness of Ippolita. The situation may have been similar to that regarding Giovanni Antonio Boltraffio's monumental pastel drawing that is also exhibited here (cat. no. 127), a young woman's portrait that seems to have been inspired by the artist's design of the altarpiece of Saint Barbara.

CCB

1. National Gallery of Art 1979, pp. 282–83, no. 37.
2. On Ippolita Sforza and Alessandro Bentivoglio as patrons, see Bandera and Fiorio 2000, pp. 56–58.
3. Illustrated and discussed in Beltrami 1911, p. 358.
4. Bandera and Fiorio 2000, p. 57.

BERNARDINO LUINI

132. *Cartoon Fragment of the Head of an Infant*

Charcoal, with some reworking in red and white chalk, on light brown paper, 212 × 187 mm (8 5/16 × 7 3/8 in.)

Département des Arts Graphiques du Musée du Louvre, Paris 6815

PROVENANCE: Cabinet du Roi; marks of the Commission du Museum (Lugt 1899) and of the Conservatoire (Lugt 2207); Morel d'Arleux, inv. MS 2, no. 1484 (Raphael).

LITERATURE: Louvre 1797 (AnV), no. 163 (Santi Raffaello); Louvre 1866, no. 237 (Luini); Bora 1980, under no. 16, p. 16; Bora 1987–88, under no. 124.

BERNARDINO LUINI

133. *Cartoon Fragment of the Head of an Infant*

Charcoal, with some reworking in red and white chalk, on light brown paper, 203 × 167 mm (8 × 6 9/16 in.)

Département des Arts Graphiques du Musée du Louvre, Paris 6816

PROVENANCE: Cabinet du Roi; marks of the Commission du Museum (Lugt 1889) and of the Conservatoire (Lugt 2207); Morel d'Arleux, inv. MS 2, no. 1596 (Raphael).

LITERATURE: Louvre 1866, no. 238; Bora 1980, under no. 16, p. 16; Bora 1987–88, under no. 124.

These virtually unknown studies of infants' heads entered the collection of the Louvre in the eighteenth century with an attribution to Raphael. One of the sheets (cat. no. 132) was exhibited in 1866 as the work of Bernardino Luini, whose authorship has never subsequently been challenged. Nonetheless, neither drawing has figured in the recent literature on the artist save the brief reference by Giulio Bora in the 1987 catalogue *Disegni e dipinti dalle collezioni milanesi*. The softly modeled features and delicately shadowed contours seen here and in certain other drawings by him recall Leonardo, whose influence also accounts for Luini's occasional use of red chalk.

Even though the contours are not incised or otherwise marked for transfer, the medium and physical condition of the paper of both drawings prompt the speculation that they are cartoon fragments. Both heads find close counterparts in the two musical angels at the left of the painting by Luini of the

Sleep of the Child Jesus in the Louvre (fig. 207), and they may well be preparatory to that work.[1] Luini's monumental frescoes and oil paintings do not exhibit a linear stylistic evolution, and his small-scale works created for private consumption are notoriously difficult, if not impossible, to arrange chronologically. Thus, no date can be inferred for the studies of infants' heads on the basis of the posited connection with the Louvre *Sleep of the Child Jesus*. A date after 1525 is nonetheless worth considering, given the drawings' manifest concern with "atmospheric values and contrasts between light and dark"—features that have been singled out as hallmarks of Luini's later graphic works.[2]   LW-S

1. The observation that these studies may be connected with the Louvre painting belongs to Carmen Bambach.
2. Bora 1998c, p. 116.

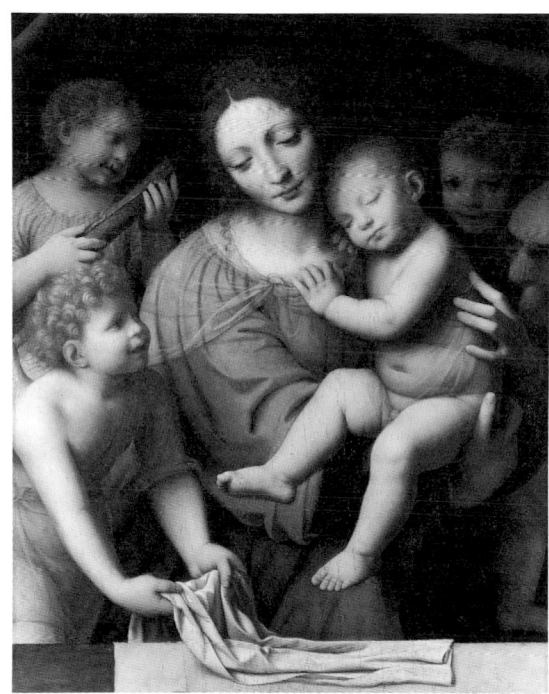

Fig. 207. Bernardino Luini, *The Sleep of the Child Jesus.* Oil on canvas, 92.5 × 73.5 cm. Musée du Louvre, Paris 360

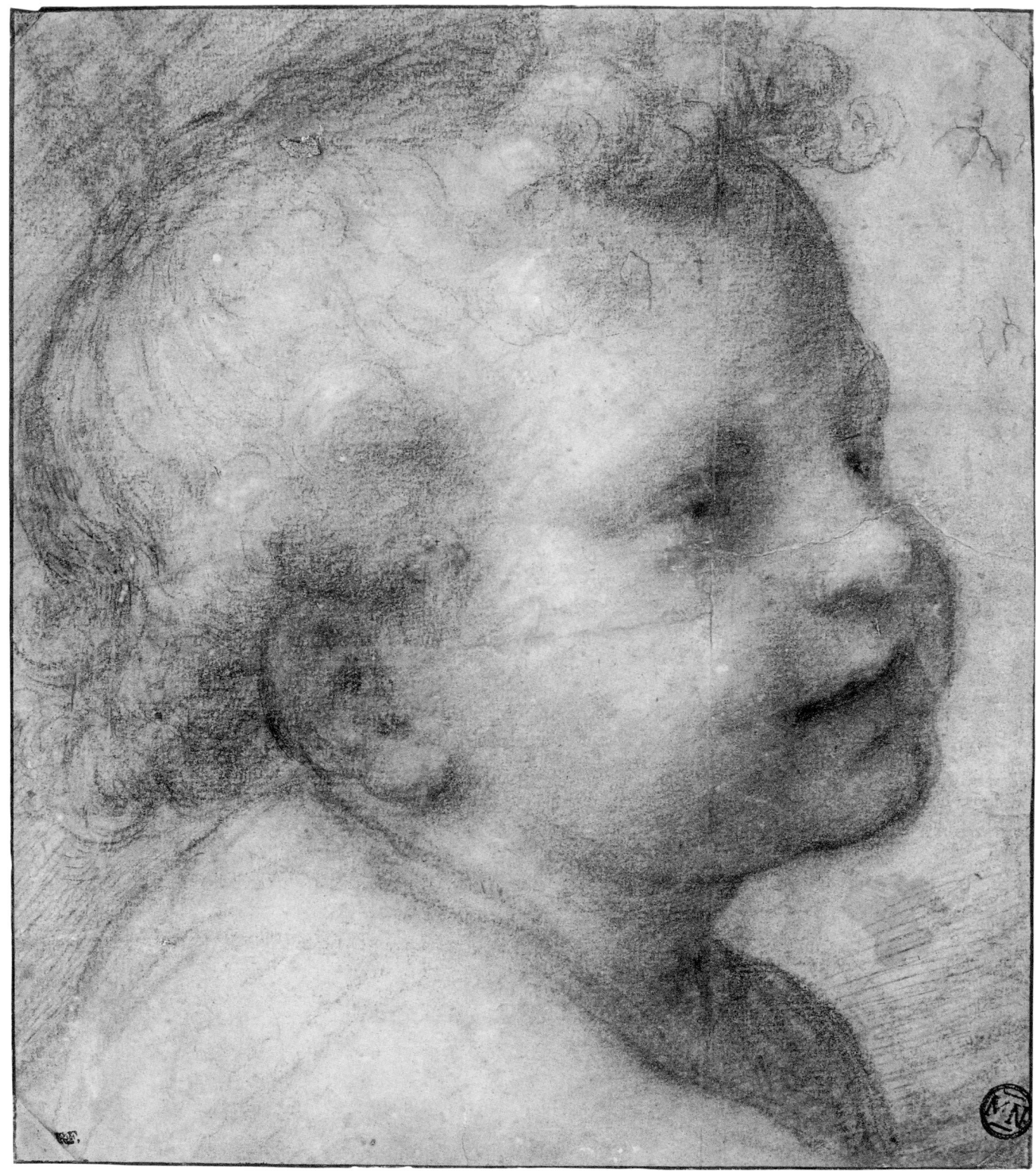

Cat. 132

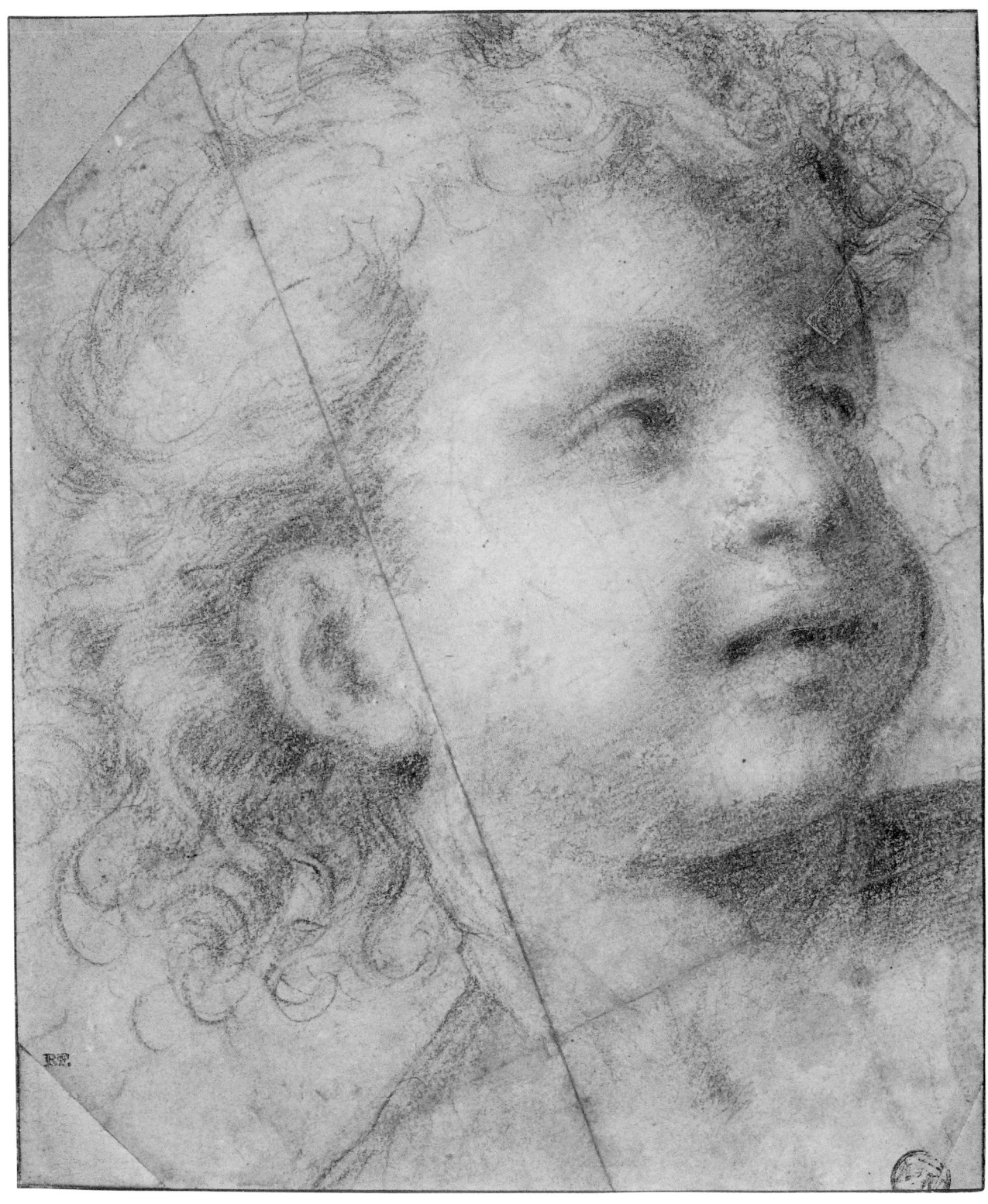

Cat. 133 *(actual size)*

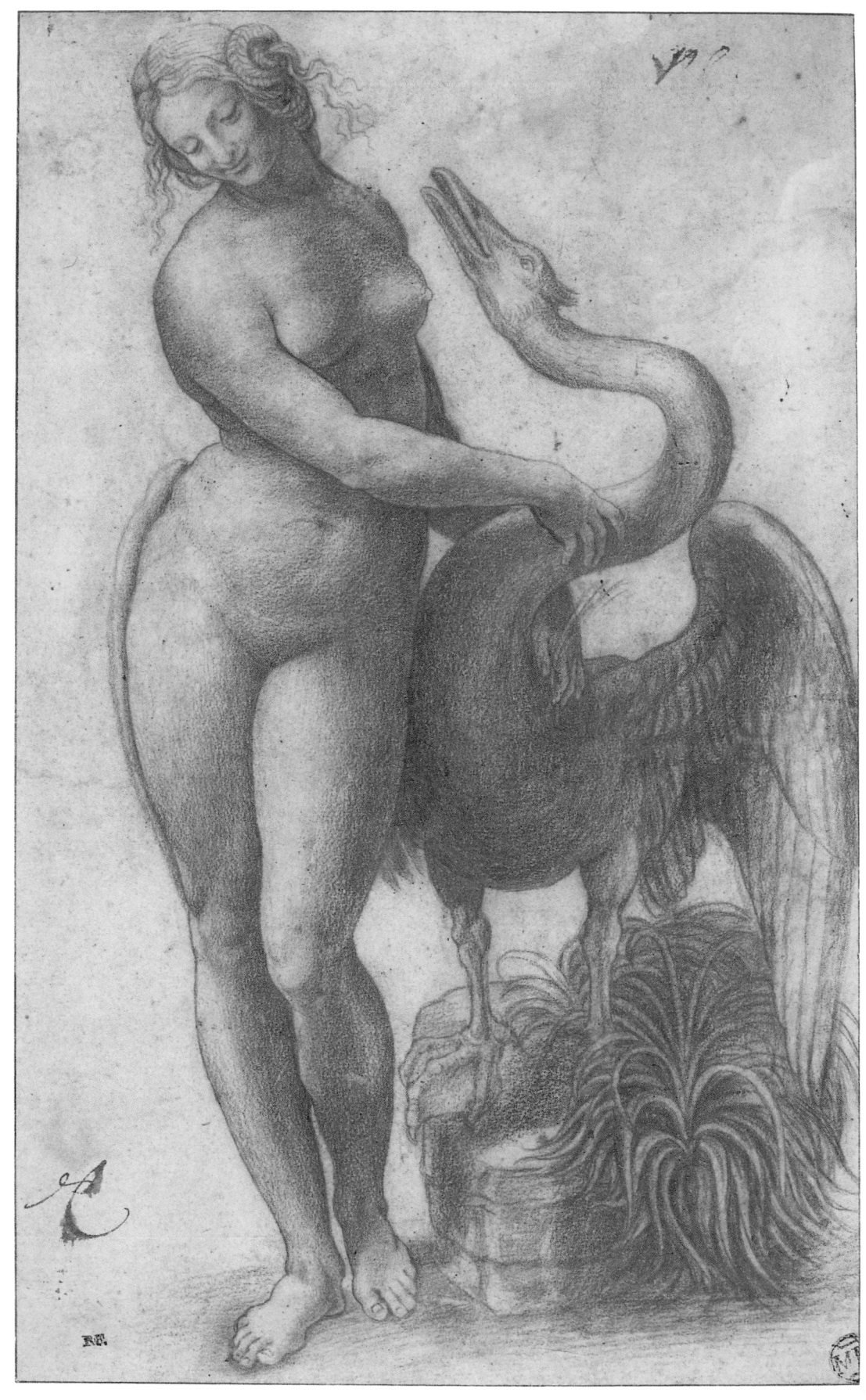

Cat. 134

AFTER LEONARDO DA VINCI

134. *Leda and the Swan*

Red chalk, 272 × 168 mm (10¾ × 6⅝ in.); framing outline in pen and brown ink
Département des Arts Graphiques du Musée du Louvre, Paris 2563

PROVENANCE: Everard Jabach (Lugt 2959); 1671, acquired for the Cabinet du Roi; initials of J.-Robert de Cotte (Lugt 1963) and C. Delamotte (Lugt 478); marks of the Commission du Museum (Lugt 1899) and of the Commission du Conservatoire (Lugt 2207); Morel d'Arleux, inv. MS 1, no. 499 (Andrea del Sarto).

LITERATURE: Suida 1929, pp. 158–59, fig. 165; Rosci 1978, fig. p. 136; Béguin 1983, p. 91; Vezzosi 1983–84a, pp. 85, 103, no. 173, pl. 33; Hochstetler Meyer 1990, p. 284, fig. 5; Nathan 1990, pp. 60, 62, 69, fig. 20; Costamagna 1994, under no. 61 (Florentine artist); Cox-Rearick 1995, under no. 4-4; Meyer zur Capellen 1996, pp. 109, 112, fig. 55; Arasse 1997, p. 425, fig. 287; Costamagna 1999, p. 106, fig. 6 (Baccio Bandinelli?); Giannattasio 1999, p. 40, fig. 25 (Pedro Fernàndez); Vezzosi 2000, fig. p. 73; Nanni 2001, p. 40, fig. 24.

Leonardo worked on two versions of the theme of Leda: in one of them, she is kneeling (see cat. nos. 88, 98, 99); in the other, standing. The pose chosen for the first version seems to have been abandoned in favor of a second interpretation, which is reflected in the Louvre drawing exhibited here. Our knowledge of a composition on the theme of Leda relies on a comment—"et anchora una Leda"—found in the *Libro di Antonio Billi,* compiled in 1518 and integrated into the Codice Magliabechiano.[1] In 1584 Lomazzo made the first mention of a work in Leonardo's hand depicting Leda: "Leda tutta ignuda co'l cigno in grembo, che vergognosamente, abbassa gl'occhi." In 1590 he returned to the subject, specifying this time that the painting was completed: "Il che chi desidera di veder nella pittura, miri l'opere finite . . . di Lionardo Vinci, come la Leda ignuda . . . nella Fontana di Beleo in Francia."[2] The presence of a painting that would have been in France in the seventeenth century was also attested by Cassiano del Pozzo in 1623. A large cartoon depicting a standing Leda seems to have remained in Milan until 1637.[3]

The copy drawn in chalk, exhibited here for the first time, is placed side by side with Leonardo's original studies for the crouching Leda. The copy of the standing Leda faithfully represents the composition of the painting in the Galleria Borghese in Rome (fig. 22).[4] A Florentine origin for the drawing has been convincingly argued by Philippe Costamagna, following a suggestion by Paul Joannides (Costamagna 1999).

FV

1. Vecce 1998a, p. 362.
2. See "La Leda di Vinci" in Vezzosi 1983–84b, pp. 79–116.
3. Vezzosi 1983–84a, pp. 84–85
4. Dalli Regoli, Nanni, and Natali 2001, no. 3.6.

ITALIAN 16TH-CENTURY COPY AFTER LEONARDO, RESTORED AND REWORKED BY PETER PAUL RUBENS
(Siegen, 1577–Antwerp, 1640), ca. 1615

135. *The Fight for the Standard*

Copy after Leonardo: black chalk, traces of white chalk highlights, pen and brown ink, 428 × 577 mm (16⅞ × 22¾ in.)
Entire drawing was remounted after 1805 on J Whatman Turkey Mill paper, bearing the firm's watermark
Reworking by Rubens: brush with brown and gray-black ink, gray wash, and white and bluish gray gouache, over copy inserted into a larger piece of paper, 453 × 636 mm (17⅞ × 25 1/16 in.)
Inscribed in pen and brown ink at bottom right by a later hand: *Leonhardo da Vinci;*[1] on verso: illegible words, *egisse*[?] and *Leonardo da Vinci*
Département des Arts Graphiques du Musée du Louvre, Paris 20.271

PROVENANCE: Peter Paul Rubens; Everard Jabach, Paris (1618–1695); Count Nicodemus Tessin, Stockholm (1654–1728); Count Carl Gustav Tessin, Stockholm (1695–1770); Count Nils Barck, Paris and Madrid (1820–1896); 1852, acquired by the Musée du Louvre; museum mark (Lugt 1886a).

LITERATURE: Tessin 1717, p. 213; Tessin 1730, p. 7 (as Leonardo); Montaiglon 1852, pp. 207–8; Louvre 1866, no. 565; Mantz 1882, pp. 16–17, ill. p. 17; Geymüller 1886, p. 160; Rooses 1886–92, vol. 5, no. 1395, pl. 399; Rosenberg 1898, p. 100, fig. 88; Michel 1899, vol. 1, p. 103, ill. on p. 56; Müntz 1899, pp. 273, 402–3, fig. p. 410; Wölfflin

1899, p. 39; Michel 1900, p. 56; Rooses 1904, vol. 1, pp. 102, 138; Seidlitz 1909, vol. 2, p. 74, pl. LXXX; Thiis 1913, pp. 209–10, fig. p. 208; Gronau 1914, fig. p. 86; Glück 1915, p. 9; Glück and Haberditzl 1928, no. 9, pl. 9; Suter 1929, p. 181; Suter 1930, p. 265, pl. IIA (ca. 1615); Bouchot-Saupique 1930–31, fig. p. 89; Bodmer 1931, p. 376, no. 103; Suter 1937, pp. 83–85, pl. XIII; Van Puyvelde 1939, p. 78; Van den Wijngaert 1940, under no. 170; Van Regteren Altena 1940, p. 199; Wilde 1944, pp. 65–81; Lugt 1949, no. 1084, pl. L; Neufeld 1949, pp. 170–83; Wilde 1953, p. 69; Terlinden 1953–54, pp. 371–72; Gould 1954, pp. 117–29; Heydenreich 1954, p. 50, fig. 64; Cederlöf 1959, p. 91, fig. 15; Held 1959, no. 161, pl. 173 (1600–1608); Cederlöf 1961, p. 85; Kurz 1962, p. 134; Burchard and d'Hulst 1963, under no. 50; Isermeyer 1964, pp. 91, 107–10, fig. 7; Müller Hofstede 1964, pp. 98, 101–3, fig. 13; Müller Hofstede 1965, pp. 73–74, 86, 130–32 and under n. 21; Clark and Pedretti 1968–69, under no. 12326; Rosand 1969, p. 35, n. 47; Richter 1970, vol. 1, p. 375; Pedretti 1973a, p. 83, fig. 85; Gould 1975; Bernhard 1977, pl. 153; Jaffé 1977, pp. 29–30, fig. 54; Müller Hofstede 1977, under no. 9, fig. K 9,2; Logan 1977, pp. 408–9; Sérullaz 1977–78, no. 79; Logan 1978, p. 433; Logan and Haverkamp Begemann 1978, p. 96; Kemp 1981, p. 239, fig. 65; Baumstark 1983, p. 183, n. 31; Béguin 1983, p. 86; Meller 1983, p. 128, fig. 24; Pedretti and Dalli Regoli 1985, p. 90, under no. 40; Held 1986, no. 49, pl. 50 (ca. 1612–15); Logan 1987, pp. 70–71; Clark 1988, p. 197, fig. 82; Joannides 1988, pp. 79–80, 84, fig. 10; Carroll 1989, p. 3, fig. 2; Roberts 1989, p. 39, fig. 32; Blass-Simmen 1991, p. 124, fig. 65; Zöllner 1991; Piel 1995, pp. 110–11, repr. in color; Simpson 1996, p. 47, fig. 15; Arasse 1997, p. 430, fig. 291; McGrath 1997a, under no. 58, fig. 227; Condorelli 1998, p. 348, fig. 4; Zentai 1998, under nos. 3–4, fig. 3; Zöllner 1998, p. 13, no. IX; Weil-Garris Brandt 1999, p. 31, fig. 67; Caracciolo 2001, pp. 675–76, fig. 6; Laurenza 2001, p. 180, fig. 91; Py 2001, p. 267; Wood 2002b, under no. 4.

This exceptionally large drawing of the *Fight for the Standard* is the most famous among the *ricordi* of Leonardo's *Battle of Anghiari* (see cat. nos. 81–91; figs. 18, 19) to commemorate the 1440 victory of the Florentines over the Milanese. The fierce struggle over possession of the Milanese standard, which would determine the victor, was central to the battle. Charging in from the right on a rearing horse is Pier Giampaolo Orsini, the captain-general leading the Florentines. He is apparently thrusting a spear toward Niccolò Piccinino, a Milanese condottiere, or mercenary general, identified as such by his cap. Orsini had the support of Pope Eugenius IV, whose militia was commanded by Ludovico degli Scarampi, the soldier behind Orsini at center right. Scarampi wears a turban and brandishes a sword in his right hand. Piccinino, his sword in his right hand over his head and his left hand grasping the pole of the standard, is assisted by his son, Francesco, the rider at the very left, in the effort to wrest the standard from under the Florentines.

The Louvre drawing has been discussed at length in the context of Leonardo's *Battle of Anghiari* and has traditionally been interpreted as a copy of a lost composition by Leonardo referred to in old documents as a "groppo de' cavalli e uomini" (tangle of horses and men). Some authors have considered the drawing to be a copy by Peter Paul Rubens after Leonardo's lost wall painting. However, since that unfinished battle piece was destroyed in the 1560s, Rubens cannot have seen the original during his Italian sojourn between 1600 and 1608. He had studied drawings by Leonardo in the collection of Pompeo Leoni, and he was so taken with them that he listed them individually in a manuscript in Latin, which unfortunately is lost. Roger de Piles still knew it at the end of the seventeenth century and quoted from it in his "Reflections on the Works of Leonardo da Vinci." Rubens was deeply impressed by the way Leonardo prepared himself for painting and marveled at Leonardo's command of anatomy, specifically that of the horse and the human body.[2] (For Leonardo's preliminary compositional studies for the *Fight for the Standard* and a discussion of Raphael's copy in Oxford after it, see cat. nos. 81–83).

The only dated copy based on Leonardo's lost battle composition known today is the engraving of 1558 by Lorenzo Zacchia the Younger (ca. 1524–after 1587), preserved in a unique impression in the Albertina, Vienna.[3] This print together with a large drawing in black chalk and gray wash partly accented with pen and brown ink, in the Koninklijk Huisarchief in The Hague,[4] and an equally large drawing in pen and brown ink, formerly in the Armand Hammer Museum in Los Angeles, have the most in common with the central, copy portion of the Louvre drawing.[5] The *Fight for the Standard* in The Hague is 435 by 565 millimeters (17 1/8 × 22 1/4 in.) and is annotated at bottom center *Leonardo da Vinci* [*fecit*; the latter crossed out] and *N° 2*. At bottom right we find an old (seventeenth-century?) annotation in red chalk, badly erased: *A V Dyk*. Sir Thomas Lawrence considered the drawing in The Hague to be by Rubens and copied after Leonardo's cartoon.[6] Thomas Dimsdale, its previous owner, believed it to be the design for Gerard Edelinck's engraving, according to the 1835 Lawrence exhibition catalogue of drawings by Rubens, which is incorrect. J. Q. van Regteren Altena supported the Rubens attribution in 1939, at the time of the Rubens exhibition

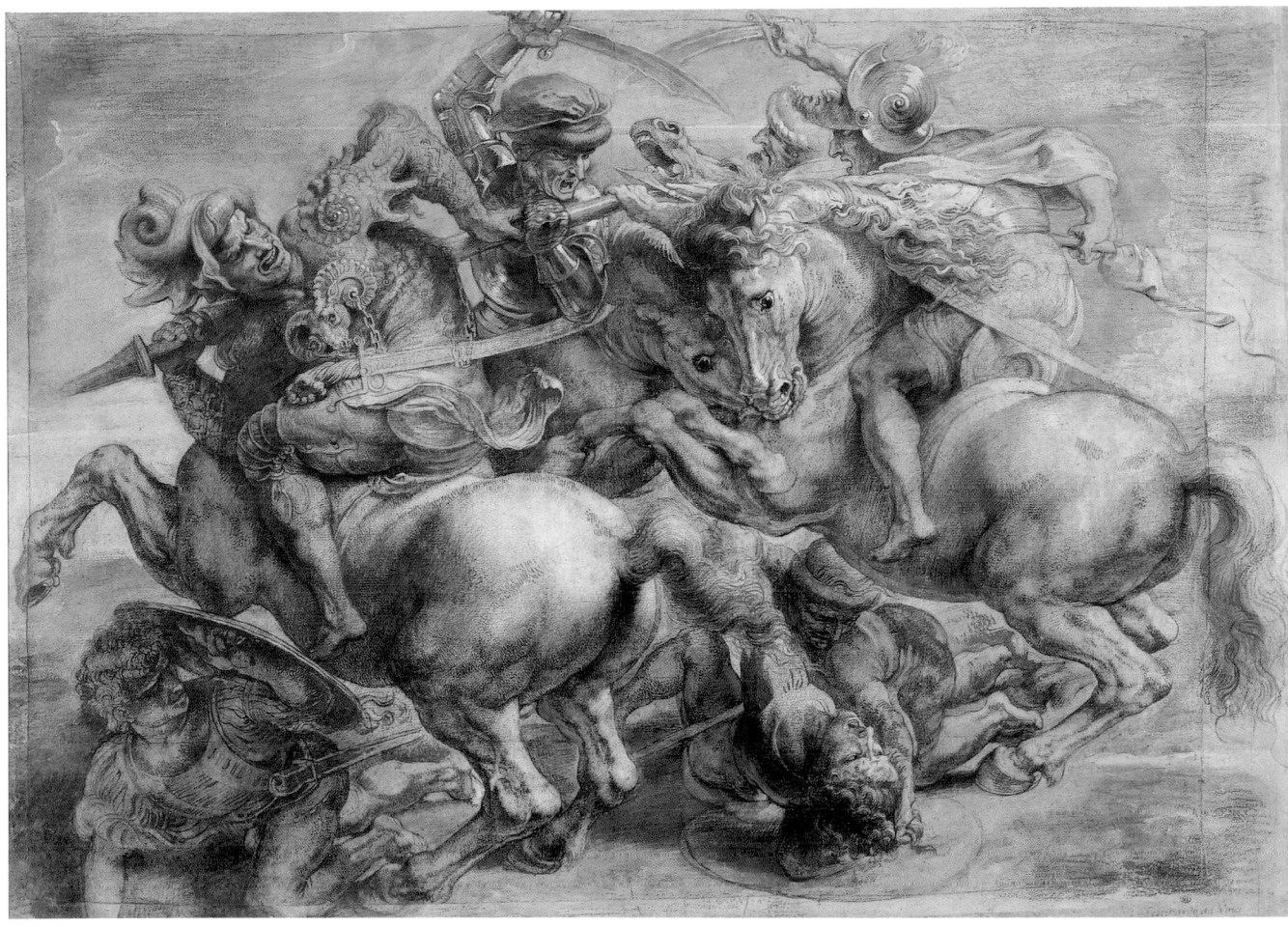

Cat. 135

in Rotterdam, and again in 1940.[7] The drawing last recorded in the Armand Hammer collection is on seventeenth-century paper (according to the Conservation Department at the Fogg Art Museum, Cambridge, Mass.) and measured 425 by 556 millimeters ($16\frac{3}{4} \times 21\frac{7}{8}$ in). It came from the collection of Benjamin West and was mounted on Whatman paper dating from 1829.[8]

Some authors have suggested that Rubens copied the *Fight for the Standard* now in the Louvre based on Zacchia's engraving.[9] This does not seem to be the case. Although the Louvre drawing is related to Zacchia's print (especially in the combatants in the foreground, who fight without daggers), it goes back to another prototype.[10] In the Louvre, Hague, and formerly Los Angeles drawings, the floating piece of drapery on the leftmost rider, which is scrolling up at its right, is almost identical. In contrast, Zacchia rendered here a tightly laced ver-

tical bundle. All three drawings also show a circular ending to the saddle of Orsini, at the right. Again Zacchia's print differs, for his saddle fits tightly around the captain's body. In addition, the three drawings show a vertical crease through the center, possibly reflecting the original, which might have been similarly folded,[11] although large sheets tend to show such a crease, which was caused during the drying of the paper.

In 1998, Frank Zöllner suggested that the drawings in The Hague and the Louvre might reflect a lost Leonardo cartoon or full-scale drawing rather than the painting, while the Los Angeles version in his opinion was an exact copy of the sheet in The Hague.[12] The slight differences between them might actually point to the existence not only of a cartoon proper ("ben finito cartone," according to Giovanni Battista Armenini), but also of a substitute cartoon, used for the final painting. Leonardo's paper purchases are documented through

673

payment records in the Archivio di Stato in Florence and published by Carmen Bambach.[13] She calculated that Leonardo's two orders on February 28, 1504, and April 30, 1505, amounted to some 1,025 sheets of the *reale* size, each measuring 438–52 by 605–17 millimeters, which was more than he would have needed for his painting on the wall of the Sala del Gran Consiglio in the Palazzo Vecchio in Florence. She therefore reasoned that Leonardo must have intended the two orders for two different types of cartoons or full-scale drawings. Since the later order of 525 sheets specified that the paper was to be used for the painting ("per la pictura"), she concluded that the first order of slightly more expensive, better-quality paper was intended for the cartoon proper. The slightly cheaper paper, ordered in 1505, therefore was for the substitute cartoon, which, according to Armenini, was part of the painting rather than the drawing process.[14] Just as a point of comparison, the Louvre drawing with Rubens's additions measures 453 by 636 millimeters and comes close to one sheet of the *reale* size of Bolognese paper Leonardo used for his cartoons.

There are two smaller pen-and-ink copies of the composition, one in the Uffizi, Florence (295 by 427 mm), and, according to Friedrich Piel, a tracing of it formerly in the Palazzo Rucellai, Florence.[15] Both show one of the combatants on the ground in the center threatening his enemy with a dagger that again differs from the Louvre version, where the fight is without weapons; furthermore, the soldier in the background is wearing a richly decorated helmet, not a turban. Judging from these copies, either the original part of the Louvre sheet is severely trimmed along the bottom and the right, or the Louvre, Hague, and formerly Los Angeles versions render a prototype that was heavily damaged. The areas now missing are the horse's tail at the right and the right hand and lower arm of the kneeling foot soldier at the lower left.

Regarding the various copies and Rubens's involvement, Julius Held's careful and detailed analysis and discussion of the *Fight for the Standard* in the Louvre, first published in 1959, still provides the best summary. Recently, a scientific examination of the Louvre sheet was undertaken by members of the Centre de Recherche et de Restauration des Musées de France, who investigated the media and techniques found in the drawing.[16] This examination clearly defined the pentimenti in the original black-chalk layer of the drawing, best visible in the forelegs of the horse at the left and in the rump

and hind legs of the horse at the right. Infrared reflectography also revealed that the cap of the struggling foot soldier in the center foreground, which came off in the fight, was obscured by Rubens's enlargement of the shield; thus this section was originally similar to the one in Zacchia's engraving and identical to the same area in the copy in The Hague. Rubens subsequently retraced part of the contour of the shield with brush and grayish gouache. The Centre de Recherche also distinguished two different types of brown ink, supporting the suggestion that the pen-and-ink work is not by Rubens, who introduced his dark brown ink changes with a brush. A thin gold band along the outer top edge of the drawing was analyzed as 95 percent pure, confirming Everard Jabach as an early owner (see below).

The *Fight for the Standard* in the Louvre thus appears to be the work of at least two but more likely three artists. The initial copy in black chalk cannot be attributed to Rubens but must be by an anonymous copyist who worked from a lost prototype that is also reflected in the copies in The Hague and formerly in Los Angeles. Another aspect of this core design in black chalk that previously has not been taken into consideration is the fact that it is drawn over squaring in black chalk, faintly visible at the top, especially at the left. The core of the Louvre drawing therefore cannot be a tracing of either the Hague or the formerly Los Angeles sheet. This core layer of the composition has been dated to the first half of the sixteenth century.[17] At a later time, another, possibly late-sixteenth-century, draftsman added the extensive drawing in pen and brown ink, accented with a few highlights in white gouache. The reworking with the pen is found only on the core of the drawing; it does not extend to the additions. Zöllner considered the draftsman of the black-chalk work and of the pen drawing probably one and the same person. This seems unlikely, since the pen drawing is much more pedantic and was added for a different purpose. The inclusion of small brown dots to indicate stippling strongly suggests that this layer was added by an engraver, possibly in preparation for a print, but no print derived from this core drawing is known. The black chalk is applied more freely, with pentimenti which are unsuitable for a print design.[18] Rubens's intervention came after this intermediary pen-and-ink stage. Some of his additions clearly cover the pen work; these are best visible in the highlights he placed on the armor worn by the condottiere Piccinino in the center.

This core section of the *Fight for the Standard* (428 by 577 mm) is very close to the versions in The Hague (435 by 565 mm) and formerly in Los Angeles (425 by 556 mm). All three copies render an almost identical battle scene, although the Hague and formerly Los Angeles versions lack pentimenti. One rather obvious difference among them exists, however, in the visor on the helmet worn by Orsini, at the right. On the Louvre and the formerly Los Angeles sheets this visor consists of a nose-length mask; it is analogous to the one in Zacchia's print. In the Hague version, on the other hand, the mask is a full face with a mustache, which eliminates it from being a direct copy or possibly a tracing of the Louvre one. (This detail actually looks almost as if the copyist included his own face as a "signature.") Frits Lugt rightly cautioned that the version in The Hague was dry and without pentimenti. The area in the center where the two horses meet is rather undifferentiated in the chalk lines; there is also a lack of any accentuation along the contours. This, together with a lack of "Rubenisms" such as more muscular arms or legs, speaks against Rubens's authorship of that copy. Therefore it is preferable to classify the version in The Hague as another anonymous copy[19] after a prototype that is also reflected in the black-chalk core of the Louvre drawing and the pen-and-ink drawing formerly in Los Angeles. There are enough differences between this last version and the core of the Louvre sheet — in addition to their sizes — for it to be either a direct copy or a tracing of that design. The formerly Los Angeles version, for example, does not include alterations to the rump of the horse at the right. Further, the armor protecting Niccolò Piccinino's left leg ends just below the knee instead of continuing downward, as it does in the Louvre example. In these details the copy formerly in Los Angeles is closer to the one in The Hague. We may therefore conclude that the underlying black-chalk drawing on the *Fight for the Standard* in the Louvre, together with the copies in The Hague and formerly in Los Angeles, have enough in common to give us a fairly reliable picture of a lost version of Leonardo's unfinished *Battle of Anghiari* commission. However, the Leonardesque aspect of the Louvre drawing, on the other hand, is due not to Rubens but to the cinquecento draftsman responsible for the black-chalk core, who, as Zöllner suggested, may have had access to Leonardo's composition.[20]

An examination of the Louvre drawing under high magnification clearly establishes that Rubens placed his additions and retouches on top of the core drawing in black chalk and the reinforcement in pen and brown ink. For his reworking with a brush he used bluish gray gouache that at times changes to white. Inserting the damaged sheet into a larger piece of paper (rather than enlarging it on each side) and extending missing details into the added margins is characteristic of Rubens's work when he restored drawings. If he copied another artist's work, however, he included his changes as he drew rather than going over and "editing" his own work.[21] Rubens's most conspicuous addition to the Louvre drawing is found at the right, where he completed the horse's tail. First he outlined it roughly in black chalk (the scientific examination could not distinguish two types of black chalk, but the looser application is characteristic of Rubens) and then highlighted it with brush and grayish gouache. His remaining additions, drawn freely with a brush and brownish gray ink, are clearly visible in the scientific examination.[22] These include: along the left margin the completion of the horse's hoof, at the bottom left the rounding of the footman's knee, and at the top the fingers of condottiere Piccinino's right hand holding the sword. Rubens even re-created the unusual ring on the middle finger of that hand (partly cut off in the Louvre drawing but fully visible in the copy of that sheet in the Fogg Art Museum, 1917.221).[23] He also added the bluish gray sky. The horizontal black-chalk and/or graphite (?) lines applied rather evenly over that section of blue sky, as well as in parts of the margin at the right, are incongruous with Rubens's working procedure and must have been done by restorers or in the remounting.[24] Entirely Rubens's invention is the addition of commander Ludovico degli Scarampi's right arm and hand brandishing a sword at top center right and extending into the margin. The result is a most dramatic high point of the fight, with Piccinino's and Scarampi's swords crossing in more or less the center of the composition. Rubens may well have been inspired in this solution by Giorgio Vasari's description of Leonardo's *Battle of Anghiari,* as has been suggested,[25] although it could have been his own idea. Further heavy alterations are found in the figure of Orsini, the victorious captain-general of the Florentines, at the right. Julius Held has already pointed out that the tip of the spear in the center was most likely part of the shaft that Orsini is thrusting toward his adversary.[26] The spear is also in the version in The Hague and in Zacchia's print. After Rubens's reworking of the composition, however, it lost its significance; Orsini's altered left hand is now firmly grasping the pole of the standard, the object of the right. With his right arm and hand, at the right of the composition, Orsini is breaking the pole at an angle.[27] To give credence to this action, Rubens greatly enhanced the musculature and strength of Orsini's right arm. He also modified the cape by wrapping it more tightly around the captain's shoulder. The cape may originally have extended somewhat at the right since Rubens covered that area with gouache; however, in the Hague copy the cape ends more or less as in the Louvre drawing. Rubens added a fluttering banner at the end of the pole at the right, all in brush and grayish black ink. He thus represented the banner itself, the object of the fight, for the first time; the known copies included just the pole to which the standard was attached. Less obvious but just as typical are alterations Rubens made to the plumage on Orsini's helmet and the small touches of white highlights he added on the helmet and visor. He also enlarged and rounded Orsini's lower back. Lastly, Rubens placed one dab of white at the top of Orsini's nose, making a pronounced aquiline profile. The heavy highlights Rubens superimposed with bluish gray gouache on the horses' flowing manes added volume and enhanced the idea of speed in this intense fight. Traces of whitish gray-blue gouache over some of the black-chalk additions along the rightmost horse's rump most likely were also his work. On the two foot soldiers in the center foreground, Rubens created the right arm and hand of the soldier on his back, and he altered the back of the soldier bent over him, pulling him to the ground by the hair to accommodate another arm and hand. Rubens also added a belt to that combatant and reconfigured his legs. He added touches of bluish gray gouache here and there in the horse's legs and those two warriors. In contrast, on the foot soldier at the lower left Rubens put only a few highlights, primarily with brush and grayish gouache. Considering the sum of these alterations, Rubens seems to have been much more involved in rethinking the action on the right half of the sheet, since on the left his retouches are more restrained and subtle.

Rubens's so-called retouched drawings are difficult to date. The *Fight for the Standard* in the Louvre traditionally has been placed in his Italian years, 1600–1608, and interpreted as the young Rubens in a dialogue with Leonardo. Suter (1937) and Held (1986) dated it later, about 1615 or 1612–15.[28] While Rubens could have obtained the copy in Italy and reworked it at that time, his rethinking Leonardo's admired composition and so drastically altering it may well reflect a more mature artist. This would favor the later date, or about

1615, when Rubens began his series of hunting scenes for members of the court and thus became interested in fierce battles. He may only then have searched for a *ricordo* of Leonardo's *Battle of Anghiari* for intensive study purposes. We know he did this with books that he purchased when he was embarking on a specific subject to familiarize himself with it.[29] Indeed, as mentioned, he may have derived the dramatically crossed swords in the Louvre sheet from reading Vasari.[30] Again inspired by Leonardo's *Battle of Anghiari*, Rubens created a drawing today in the British Museum, London, that is referred to as the *Battle of the Standard* and traditionally dated to the later Italian years.[31] In this we see a similar, although more tumultuous, fight between soldiers on rearing horses for a standard that includes figures reminiscent of Leonardo's.

The *Fight for the Standard* at the Louvre as retouched by Rubens was itself copied in three works. Sometime after Rubens's death in 1640, Gerard Edelinck (1640–1707) made an engraving (449 by 600 mm) of it.[32] A drawing in pen and brush and brown ink, highlighted with white and greenish white gouache on brownish paper, almost identical to the Louvre sheet in size (453 × 640 mm [17⅞ × 25¼ in.]), is in the Fogg Art Museum, Harvard University, Cambridge, Massachusetts (fig. 208).[33] This drawing has additional documentary value since it reflects the state of the Louvre sheet before its remounting in the early nineteenth century, when another hand introduced additional graphite (?) lines in the sky and added more areas of bluish gray wash. A painting based on the Louvre *Fight for the Standard* is in the Gemäldegalerie der Akademie der Bildenden Künste, Vienna.[34] In 1929, Friedrich Suter first attributed that painting to Rubens, an attribution that has generally been accepted and was supported most recently by Michael Jaffé,[35] although Robert Eigenberger listed it—in our opinion correctly—as a copy by a Flemish artist of the second half of the seventeenth century.[36]

Thanks to recent research by Varena Forcione, we now learn that the Louvre *Fight for the Standard* was once in the collection of Everard Jabach in Paris.[37] The two-millimeter-wide gold band still at the top of the drawing contains 95 percent gold, solid proof that the drawing belonged to Jabach because only he could afford such expensive mounts. The drawing was later purchased by Nicodemus Tessin in Stockholm; it is listed in a posthumous manuscript catalogue of his collection (ca. 1730; Stockholm) as a drawing by Leonardo da Vinci: "Combat d'hommes à cheval, grand et beau dessein de

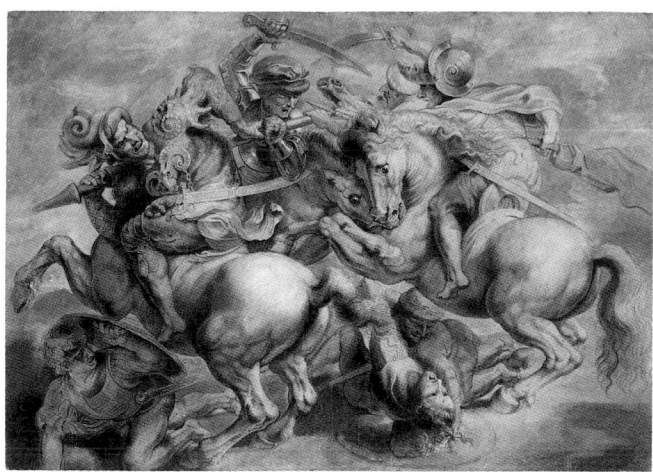

Fig. 208. Attributed to Gerard Edelinck, *Battle of Anghiari*. Pen and brown ink, brush and brown wash, highlighted with white and greenish white gouache on brownish paper, 453 × 640 mm. Fogg Art Museum, Harvard University Art Museums, Cambridge, Mass. 1917.221

Leonard da Vinci." We know from unpublished correspondence between Tessin and Daniel Cronström in Paris, dating from March–April 1699, that the latter was in contact with Gerard Edelinck, also in Paris, who was engraving a portrait of the Swedish queen Ulrika Eleonora.[38] The last letter in which Cronström mentioned Edelinck to Tessin dates from 1701, but the *Fight for the Standard* drawing is not referred to in any of this correspondence.[39] Edelinck, trained in Antwerp as an engraver and familiar with the reproductive prints produced under Rubens, may well have been commissioned to reproduce the drawing about that time in order to send a print to Tessin, possibly to entice him to buy the drawing. Tessin did purchase the drawing, which he treasured as "a large and beautiful drawing by Leonardo da Vinci."[40]

Until 1852, when this impressive drawing of the *Fight for the Standard* entered the Louvre, its composition was known only in reverse through Edelinck's engraving and admired as a vivid reminder of Leonardo da Vinci's lost *Battle of Anghiari*. The fact that Rubens was associated with it elicited even more praise. Since Rubens reworked the drawing so extensively we may assume that he knew he was not retouching an original design by Leonardo—he would have treated it with much more respect and most likely would have barely touched it. For Rubens the drawing more likely represented the challenge of an opportunity to study Leonardo's composition and engage in a direct dialogue with it, superimposing his own ideas.

Leonardo's *Fight for the Standard* deeply impressed Rubens and remained a lifelong inspiration. This is most evident in his numerous battle and hunting scenes dating primarily from the second decade of the seventeenth century that all reflect Leonardo's work.[41] For the research on Leonardo, however, only the core of the *Fight for the Standard* has validity. With regard to Rubens, on the other hand, it is only his reworking and restoring of the drawing that are of significance.

A-ML

1. Varena Forcione pointed out that the annotation is probably by the secretary of C. G. Tessin, who spelled Leonardo with an "h" in his manuscript catalogue of the Nicodemus Tessin collection; see Tessin 1730.
2. De Piles 1699, pp. 166–68.
3. 374 × 470 mm (14¾ × 18½ in.). Zöllner (1991, p. 187) questioned the reliability of Zacchia's print and its date. He also pointed out (1998, p. 36, under no. 15) that, being from Lucca, Zacchia may not have had access to Leonardo's drawings.
4. Inv. no. AL 29-13. Hinterding and Horsch 1989, p. 54.
5. For a discussion of these works, see Joannides 1988, pp. 76–86, figs. 1–18; Pedretti 1988e, pp. 87–88, figs. 1–9; Zöllner 1991, pp. 177–89, figs. 1–24; Zöllner 1998, App. pp. 31–39, figs. 1–26, esp. sec. B, pp. 33–34, figs. 8, 9 (probably derived from a Leonardo cartoon); Piel 1995, pp. 100–112, figs. 85–96.
6. Lawrence Gallery 1835–36, no. 23.
7. Van Regteren Altena 1940, pp. 194–200, pl. I, A.
8. Logan 1987, pp. 70–71, fig. 3; Zöllner 1991, p. 181, fig. 3. Carolyn Peter, assistant curator at the Armand Hammer Museum and Cultural Center, Los Angeles, informed me that the drawing no longer seems to be in the collection (February 2002). Zöllner (1991, p. 181; 1998, p. 38, fig. 21) considers it an exact copy after the version in The Hague.
9. Suter 1937, p. 82; Müller Hofstede 1964, p. 98.
10. Zöllner (1998, p. 36) suggested that the *tabella* Zacchia refers to in his engraving was a "trial painting" by Leonardo.
11. A document of March 1504 mentions a Leonardo cartoon; see Beltrami 1919a, nos. 137, 145; Isermeyer 1964, esp. pp. 94–98; Zöllner 1991, pp. 178–79.
12. Zöllner 1998, pp. 33–34, nos. 8, 9, p. 38, no. 21.
13. Bambach 1999b, esp. pp. 121–27.
14. Armenini 1587, 1977, pp. 99–104.
15. Piel 1995, p. 107, fig. 89. Zöllner (1998, p. 37) considers the Uffizi drawing the copy.
16. Contributors were Odile Guillon (photography), Elisabeth Ravaud (X ray), Alain Duval (macrophotography), and Patrick Le Chanu (reflectography). Hélène Guicharnaud and Alain Duval summarized the results in doc. C2RMF/R 4604, Lab. 13658, dated August 14, 2001, which was kindly shared with the author.
17. Zöllner 1991, p. 178.
18. Zöllner 1991, p. 183.
19. Müller Hofstede (1964, p. 101) also rejected the attribution to Rubens. Jaffé (1958, p. 416, n. 20), however, called it "unmistakably a Rubens drawing of the Italian period."
20. Zöllner 1991, p. 182.
21. An exception may be mentioned here: Rubens partly reworked two drawings after the *Garden of Love* in The Metropolitan Museum of Art, New York (acc. nos. 1958.96.1, 1958.96.2), after they had served for Christoffel Jegher's woodcut.

22. Centre de Recherche, doc. C2RMF/R 4604, Lab. 13658, fig. 9.

23. For the drawing at the Fogg, see Mongan and Sachs 1940, no. 473.

24. According to the scientific report it may be graphite, which certainly would exclude Rubens.

25. Joannides 1988, p. 80.

26. Held 1986, no. 49.

27. The broken shaft is made more explicit in the painted copy in the Akademie, Vienna, that is here attributed to an unidentified artist (see below).

28. Suter 1937, pp. 83–85, pl. 13; Held 1986, no. 49.

29. McGrath 1997a, pp. 59–67.

30. Rubens owned a copy of the 1568 edition of Vasari's *Vite*, presented to him in 1635 by Casp[erius] Gevartius. See Arents 2001, p. 104, no. B3; McGrath 1997a, pp. 56–57, n. 9. McGrath supposed Rubens must have owned a copy before that time.

31. British Museum 1996, no. 79 (with previous literature). The drawing bears an inscription by Rubens in Italian that is no longer fully legible. See also Wood 2002b, no. 5.

32. The engraving is inscribed on the plate, at left: *L. d' la finse, pin.*; and at center: *G. Edelinck Sc.* A proof impression before letters is in the Edmond de Rothschild collection in the Louvre, Paris.

33. See Mongan and Sachs 1940, no. 473, fig. 243, where it is described as "Edelinck's careful and exact copy after the drawing by Rubens in the Louvre."

34. Eigenberger 1927, p. 230.

35. Suter 1929, p. 181; Jaffé 1989, no. 47, dated ca. 1605.

36. Eigenberger 1927, p. 230. According to Jan de Maere, Brussels, another copy of the *Fight for the Standard* composition on panel is in a private collection in Ghent.

37. This addition to the drawing's provenance was established thanks to Bernadette Py and Varena Forcione, with the help of Linda Henriksson in Stockholm.

38. Weigert 1961, pp. 47–48. Tessin wrote that he would try to find work for Edelinck.

39. Weigert 1964, pp. 206, 225–26, 288.

40. Edelinck engraved another drawing in the Tessin collection, Pietro da Cortona's *Saint Margaret Presenting a Book to the Christ Child*, in the Rijksprentenkabinet, Amsterdam; see Py 2001, p. 226, no. 944.

41. Jaffé 1989, nos. 332, 340, 343–45, 355.

SIXTEENTH-CENTURY LOMBARD ARTIST AFTER LEONARDO DA VINCI

136. *Three Grotesque Couples*

Pen and brown ink, brush and touches of wash, 192 × 127 mm (7 9/16 × 5 in.); traces of framing lines in pen and brown ink; stains and perforations; old collection mark, faint and worn away, in lower right corner
Département des Arts Graphiques du Musée du Louvre, Paris 2296

PROVENANCE: Giuseppe Vallardi (Lugt 1223, in green on verso);[1] 1856, acquired by the Musée du Louvre; museum mark (Lugt 1886a).

LITERATURE: Gombrich 1954, 1976, p. 66, fig. 142 (detail); Pedretti and Trutty-Coohill 1993, under nos. 30a, 30i.

This sheet, which is exhibited here for the first time, became part of the Louvre collections in 1856, with an attribution to Leonardo da Vinci. In the album purchased from Giuseppe Vallardi, it was on the same folio as another sheet (fig. 114) that similarly displays grotesque figures after Leonardo. Both sheets bear, in the lower right-hand corner, a faint collection mark. Its diameter (80 mm; 3 3/16 in.) and the traces of still-visible black ink are not incompatible with Lugt number 545. That mark was identified as belonging to Modesto Genevosio, a Turin collector, known both as Count Gelosi and as Commendatore Genevosio, who was recently studied by Aidan Weston-Lewis (1994) and Piera Tordella (1996). The same mark is found on the drawing of the *Young Woman Bathing an Infant* in Oporto (cat. no. 21).

The couple in the upper register is found again in a drawing in The Metropolitan Museum of Art (cat. no. 121), and the same figures can be seen in isolation in the Mariette album (RF 28749 and RF 28765; cat. no. 137); for a list of related copies and prints, see the entry for catalogue number 137. The original of the old woman is at Chatsworth (cat. no. 73b); the

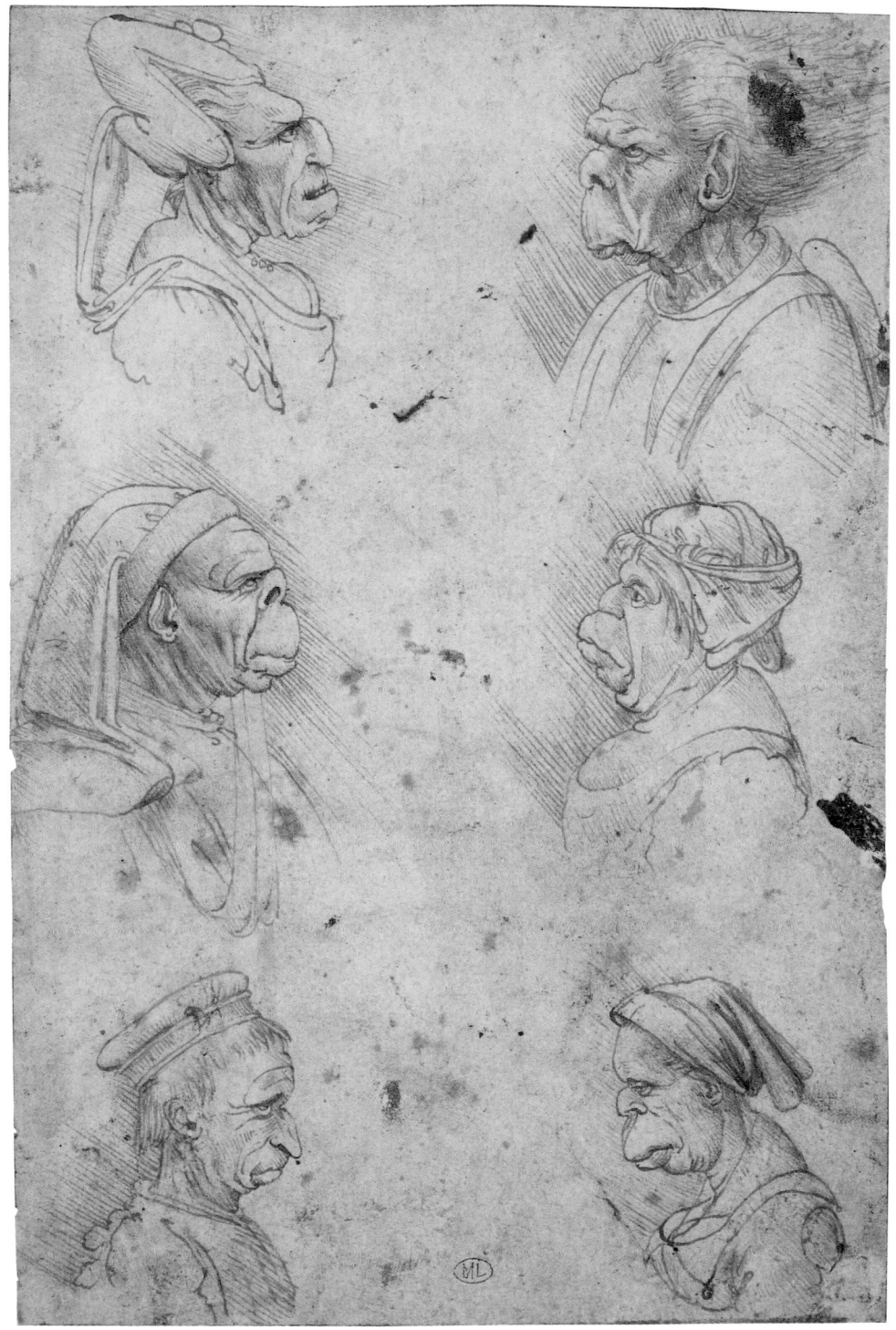

Cat. 136 *(actual size)*

original of the man has not been located. There are differences in detail in each of the three versions: the old woman has one pearl on her blouse in one version (RF 28749), three in the present sheet, and no pearl on the New York sheet (cat. no. 121). The man also displays minor variations in his hair and torso in each version.

The couple in the middle is reproduced on a sheet formerly in the Pembroke collection[2] and now in a private collection. The man is depicted in the Mariette album (RF 28757; cat. no. 137) with variations, whereas the woman is absent; for a list of related copies and prints, see the entry for the Mariette drawing (cat. no. 137). The original of the man, formerly at Chatsworth, is in a private collection (cat. no. 71); the original of the woman is still at Chatsworth (824D).

The couple in the lower register is not reproduced in the Pembroke sheets. The man is missing from the sheet in the Mariette album, whereas the woman is depicted (RF 28753; cat. no. 137), with different proportions; for a list of related copies and prints, see the entry for that sheet (cat. no. 137). The originals have not been located.

The somewhat hard, dry stroke in the drawing exhibited here can be connected to a sheet in the British Museum (1886-6-9-40),[3] which bears the Genevosio mark (Lugt 545), and to two others at the Accademia, Venice (fig. 113). The connection between the British Museum sheet and those at the Accademia has already been made by Luisa Cogliati Arano.[4] All these sheets depict grotesque heads executed in pen and brown ink and with very similar dimensions. This group, to which we can now add these two Louvre sheets (cat. no. 136 and fig. 114), can be attributed to a sixteenth-century Milanese hand copying Leonardo's originals. It is clear that this is not the much more subtle hand that drew the grotesque couples in pen and brown ink in the Windsor drawing (RL 12491) attributed to Franceso Melzi. VF

1. Vallardi 1855, p. 10, fol. 55 (Leonardo da Vinci): "Due disegni in carta bianca eseguiti a penna fina: undici caricature d'ambo i sessi.—Il primo ne contiene sei ed il secondo cinque. Alti ciascuno poll. 7 largo poll. 5. Le caricature di questo volume sono bastanti per confermare la sentenza del Lomazzo nel predetto Trattato dell Pittura Lib. I cap. 1 'che Leonardo studiavasi non solo di dipingere nei volti e negli atteggiamenti il bello od il deforme, ma ben anco di esprimervi le idee, gli affetti e l'anima stessa.'"
2. Pedretti and Trutty-Coohill 1993, no. 30a.
3. Popham and Pouncey 1950, no. 119.
4. Cogliati Arano 1980, no. 23.

137. *Mariette Album of Drawings after Leonardo da Vinci*

Binding in black shagreen, border of gold arabesques on upper and lower portions, edge decorated with gold threads and lozenges, 333 × 241 mm (13 ⅛ × 9 ½ in.)
Impressed with gilded letters on upper portion: TRONIEN / GETEKEND / DOOR / LIONARDO DA VINCI
Département des Arts Graphiques du Musée du Louvre, Paris
RF 28725–RF 28785

PROVENANCE: Siewert van der Schelling sale, Amsterdam, 1719; purchased by Gautier, "bric-a-brac salesman from Paris," for 374 guldens (740 francs); purchased from Gautier by Jean Mariette for one thousand francs; Pierre-Jean Mariette sale, Paris, 1775, no. 787; purchased by Remy[1] for 240 francs; Villeminot collection; given by Villeminot to Romain Deseze in January 1802; acquired by Willy Blumenthal in Frankfurt in 1885; acquired by the Société des Amis du Louvre with the cooperation of Albert Meyer and Jean Seligmann; gift to the Louvre, Comité of February 26, 1937; Louvre mark on each folio (Lugt 1886a).

LITERATURE: Dumesnil 1858, p. 39; Rocheblave 1889, p. 43; Lugt 1921, 1956, under no. 1852; Orangerie 1947–48, no. 174; Gombrich 1954, 1976, p. 57, p. 144 n. 4; Scott-Elliot 1958, p. 289; Bacou 1967, no. 76; Steinitz 1974, pp. 8–9; Cogliati Arano 1980, p. 15 n. 14; Bacou 1981, p. 76; Rezniceck 1981, p. 245; Alberici 1984, p. 131; Van Gelder and Jost 1985, p. 210 n. 62; Barryte 1990, p. 138; Cogliati Arano 1992b, p. 6; Paliaga 1995a, p. 240; Louvre 1997a, p. 232, nos. 132–92; Borea 2001, pp. 106–7; Plomp 2001, p. 131.

An early collector pasted together this album of thirty-two folios assembling drawings in different formats. The binding dates from about 1700 in Amsterdam (see my essay, n. 98). Circular cutouts were made of most of the pages in the album in order to insert the drawings, to allow view of the recto and verso. The folios bear two different numbers in the upper right-hand corner. The first set of numbers, from 1 to 54, is in pen and very faded brown ink, on the front and back of the pages, beginning with the frontispiece and ending with the last page containing drawings. The second set, from 1 to 32, is in black chalk. It was added later and was written on top of the earlier set; it begins and ends on the flyleaves, but the numbers are only on the front side of the pages. Folio num-

bers referred to here are to the second set. Numbers referring to the drawings engraved by the count of Caylus are
annotated in black chalk at the bottom, below the circular
cutouts, on the album page. These will be indicated in the
identifications below.

Thirty-nine drawings (RF 28725 to RF 28763), copies of
ones by Leonardo da Vinci, were executed by the same hand in
pen, brown ink, and gray wash. All but three (RF 28725, RF
28762, RF 28763) are on folios with drawings on front and
back. The original sheets containing the drawings were cut
into round shapes. Each drawing was surrounded by two concentric circles in pen and brown ink, which were traced with a
compass, as indicated by a perforation mark made by the compass in the center of the circle. The circles may have been later
additions, since the ink seems to be different from that of the
drawings. On certain sheets (for example, RF 28733, RF 28751)
the drawing of the head encroaches on the circles. Except for
the first of these (RF 28725), the cutout sheet containing the
drawing was inserted into the circular hole scooped out of the
album page. The cutout is slightly larger than the hole, but the
hole allowed both sides of the drawing to be seen, though one
drawing (RF 28762) bears on the reverse only an inscription
in Dutch. The last drawing to be surrounded by two concentric
circles (RF 28763) is also the last drawing copied from
Leonardo. Glued to its verso on the album page was a drawing
(RF 28764) that is not in the same medium or in the same
hand and also has different dimensions. Mariette (1730, p. 17)
believed that the last Leonardo drawing (RF 28763) may have
been the beginning of an earlier album of Leonardo's heads,
and that the preceding drawing (RF 28762), which bears the
Dutch annotation on its back concerning the number of original
sheets, was the last such sheet.

Drawings of differing dimensions and layout follow. The
first one (RF 28764), which is glued to the back of the final
Leonardo copy (RF 28763), is in a different medium—black
chalk—of larger dimensions, has cut-off corners, and, unlike
succeeding drawings, stands alone on the page. Three smaller
square drawings in pen and brown ink follow (RF 28765 to
RF 28767); they are glued to a single page, and there is no
drawing on the verso. On the next page are assembled five
even smaller square drawings in pen and brown ink (RF 28768
to RF 28772), which are glued to the same sheet with nothing
on the verso. Six little square drawings in pen and brown ink
follow (RF 28773 to RF 28778), glued to the same page; there

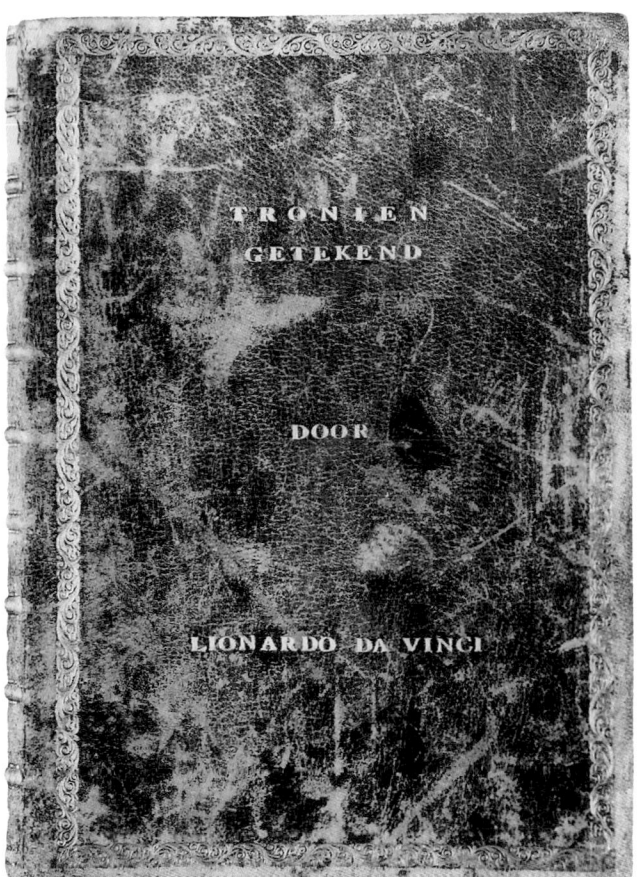

Cat. 137 (cover)

is nothing on the verso. It appears that each group was
designed to assemble drawings done by a similar hand.

From this point on, the drawings are again large and each is
in a different hand. The first (RF 28779), in pen and brown
ink, is alone on the album page, which has been cut out to its
dimensions. To its verso is affixed a drawing (RF 28780) in yet
another hand and in black chalk. The next album page has also
been cut to the dimensions of the drawing (RF 28781), which
is in a heavier black chalk. It is backed by a drawing (RF 28782)
in a lighter black chalk. The "Cigoli" (RF 28783), so called
because of the attribution noted on the back, follows in pen
and wash. It is glued to a mounting sheet that has been cut to
show the verso of the drawing; that mounting sheet is in turn
glued to the album page, which has been cut to its dimensions.

The two small drawings that close the album (RF 28784
and RF 28785), originally separate, have been glued, side by
side, to a large sheet bearing the mark of the collector
Nicolas Lanier (Lugt 2886). This sheet is glued to a larger

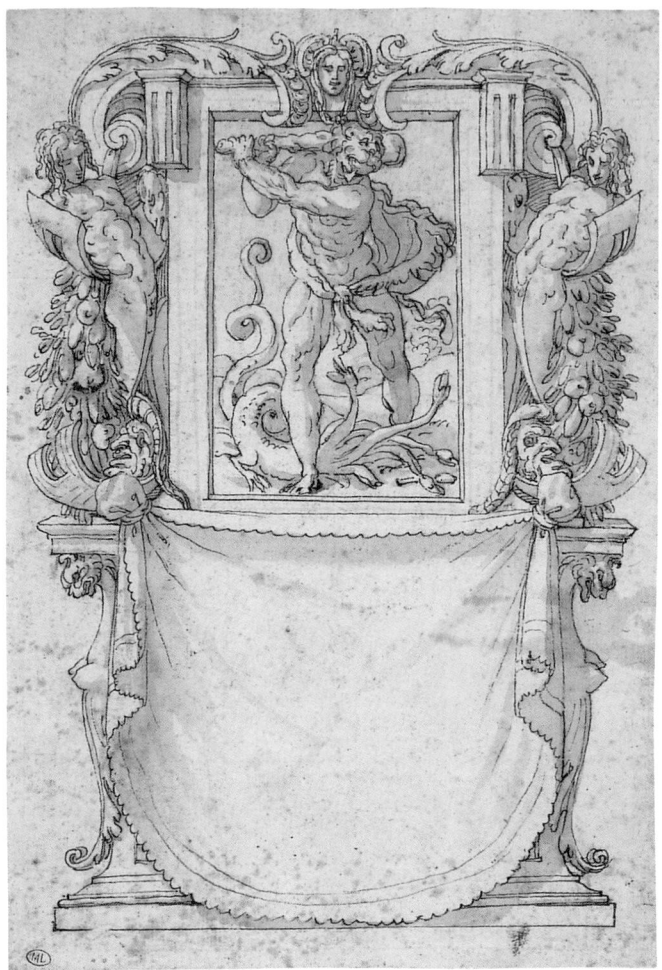

Cat. 137 *(title page)*, RF 28725

number from a sale at which the two volumes were to be auctioned off together] / *960* [crossed out] / *W 787* [crossed out; lot number of the Mariette sale, 1775]; these numbers are repeated at the bottom of the page; in center of page, in pen and brown ink: *Romain Deseze / Cette précieuse Collection m'a été donnée / par Monsieur Villeminot; Janvier 1802* (Romain Deseze / This precious collection was given to me / by Monsieur Villeminot; January 1802)

FOLIO 2
Inscribed at top of page in pen and brown ink: *Romain Deseze*

FOLIO 3
Blank

FOLIO 4 RECTO: RF 28725
Hercules Felling the Hydra of Lerna
Pen and brown ink, brown wash, 225 × 155 mm
(8⅞ × 6⅛ in.); glued to secondary support
Inscribed beneath drawing on album page, hence added when the album was bound: *Aug. Carrache*; not numbered by Caylus
LITERATURE: Bacou 1981, p. 79; Loisel 2000b, p. 125, fig. 88.

Catherine Loisel believes this is a copy after a lost drawing by Agostino Carracci for the fresco decoration of the Palazzo Sampieri in Bologna in about 1593–94.

FOLIO 5 RECTO: RF 28726
Monk, Half-Length, in Three-Quarter Profile to the Left
Pen, brown ink, and gray wash, inner circle 82.5 mm
(3¼ in.), outer circle 95 mm (3¾ in.); all the sheets bearing drawings, up to RF 28763 inclusive, are of the same dimensions
Caylus number 1

Original not located today but at Chatsworth in 1902 (Strong 1902, pl. 28 center). Copy at Musée Fabre, Montpellier, 870-1-192; Accademia copy, Venice, 227, paired with RF 28759.

The author will indicate when a drawing is paired with another head in an effort to identify the original couple. When the same pairing is made in several different old copies, one can make the assumption that this was the original pair.

In the drawings copied from Leonardo (up to RF 28763

sheet bearing the attribution to Leonardo, which in turn is glued to the album page.

When the album of engravings was executed, the drawings were engraved individually, most of them surrounded by two concentric circles and (in the Louvre copy of the Caylus album; cat. no. 138) grouped by twos on a single page, with the "Cigoli" (RF 28783) as the last image. As a result of the desire for regularity, the variety of layouts and hands was lost.

FOLIO 1
Inscribed at top of page in pen and brown ink: *N. N. 72 / 240 #* [price at the Mariette sale, 1775] / *N°. 134* [annotation identical to the one on the back of the flyleaf of the Caylus album of engravings in the Louvre (cat. no. 138); this is probably the lot

inclusive), the hatching was done in imitation of a left-handed artist, left to right; exceptions are noted here.

Folio 5 verso: RF 28727 (verso of RF 28726)

Old Man, Half-Length, in Profile to the Right, with a
Long Chin
Pen, brown ink, and gray wash
Caylus number 2

Original not located. Spencer copy, vol. 1, 7. Copied from the Mariette album by Gabriel de Saint Àubin in *Livre des Saint Aubin* (Book of the Saint Aubins), Louvre, RF 52456. Engraved and catalogued in the book on Hollar, Parthey 1853, no. 1743 (hereafter cited as P.), but not by Hollar according to Pennington 1982; not reversed, paired with RF 28728.

The Hollar engravings are generally reversed when compared to the drawings; it is indicated when that is not the case.

Berlin copy, Kupferstichkabinett, KdZ 17184. The series of twenty-eight copies after Leonardo in Berlin, in pen and brown ink (KdZ 17184 to 17211 — for KdZ 17183, a copy of RF 28758, see below), has an Italian provenance. The collector, Vincenzo Pacetti, is indicated by a P (Lugt 2057) on the drawings. According to Schulze Altcappenberg (1995), this mark is a provenance mark and not a collector's mark, since it was added when the collection arrived in 1843, after being purchased in Rome. Pacetti was president of the Accademia di San Luca in Rome, to which the sculptor Bartolomeo Cavaceppi bequeathed the ninety-five volumes of his collection of 7,350 drawings on his death in 1799. Among these drawings were those Cavaceppi had purchased in 1762 from the heirs of Valenti Gonzaga, and therefore probably the volume with Leonardo's grotesques to which Mariette and Bottari refer. Unfortunately, the Gonzaga volume cannot currently be located (for a discussion of the Gonzaga album, see my essay and Prosperi Valenti Rodinò 1996). The heads in the Berlin drawings were originally larger sheets and on the back bear fragments of drawings of different subjects, sometimes in red chalk. There were also several grotesque heads per page. The copies are simpler than the Leonardo originals, and they are very painstaking and labored. They may be studies executed, in the eighteenth century perhaps, by students at the Accademia di San Luca, since they are not all in the same hand. Of the Berlin grotesque heads, eighteen were etched by Caylus; of those not etched by Caylus, five are from originals in Chatsworth, three are copied in the Pembroke series, one is

copied in the Spencer series, and a version of one has not been located.

Folio 6 recto: RF 28728

Old Woman, Half-Length, in Profile to the Left
Pen, brown ink, and gray wash
Caylus number 3

Original not located. Spencer copy, vol. 1, 6; Chatsworth copy, 827A, where it is paired with RF 28745; Biblioteca Ambrosiana copy, Cod. F 274 inf. 45, paired with RF 28745. The copies of this sheet in the Ambrosiana seem to have been executed by a late hand, perhaps in the eighteenth century. Berlin copy, Kupferstichkabinett, KdZ 17185. Engraved P. 1591, paired with Chatsworth, 820C and P. 1743 (not by Hollar, according to Pennington 1982), not reversed, paired with RF 28727; engraved by Gerli, pl. 27.

Gerli (1784) engraved in the same direction as the drawings; only the exceptions will be indicated here.

Folio 6 verso: RF 28729 (verso of RF 28728)

Old Woman, Half-Length, in Profile to the Right
Pen, brown ink, and gray wash
Caylus number 4

Original not located. Spencer copy, vol. 2, 4; Chatsworth copy, 827B, paired with a man with a protruding lip (depicted on a copy in the Biblioteca Ambrosiana, Cod. F 274 inf. 45); Montpellier copy, Musée Fabre, 864-2-270; Berlin copy, Kupferstichkabinett, KdZ 17186. Engraved P. 1739 (not by Hollar, according to Pennington 1982), not reversed, paired with RF 28738.

Folio 7 recto: RF 28730

Old Woman, Half-Length in Profile to the Left, Shouting
Pen, brown ink, and gray wash
Caylus number 5

Original Chatsworth (sometimes contested; see Marani 1995–96, under no. 11), 825A. The Louvre copy is slightly larger than the original. Spencer copy, vol. 1, 32; Pembroke copy (Pedretti and Trutty-Coohill 1993, no. 30b, now in the Detroit Institute of Arts), paired with RF 28739; British Museum copy, 1886-6-9-40, paired with RF 28739; Montpellier copy, Musée Fabre, 864-2-271; copy auctioned at Christie's, New York, January 28, 2000. Engraved by Hollar, P. 1568.

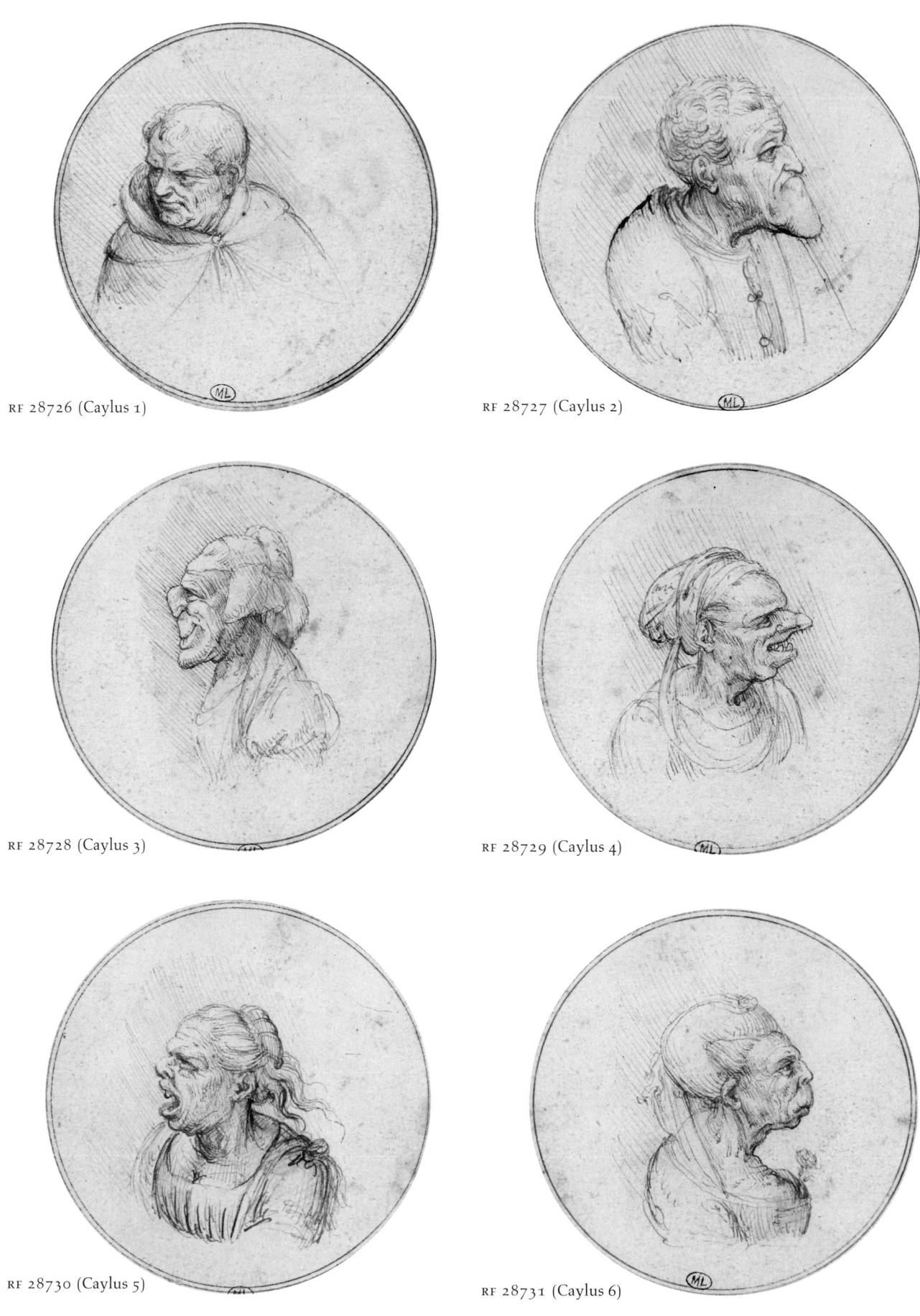

RF 28726 (Caylus 1)

RF 28727 (Caylus 2)

RF 28728 (Caylus 3)

RF 28729 (Caylus 4)

RF 28730 (Caylus 5)

RF 28731 (Caylus 6)

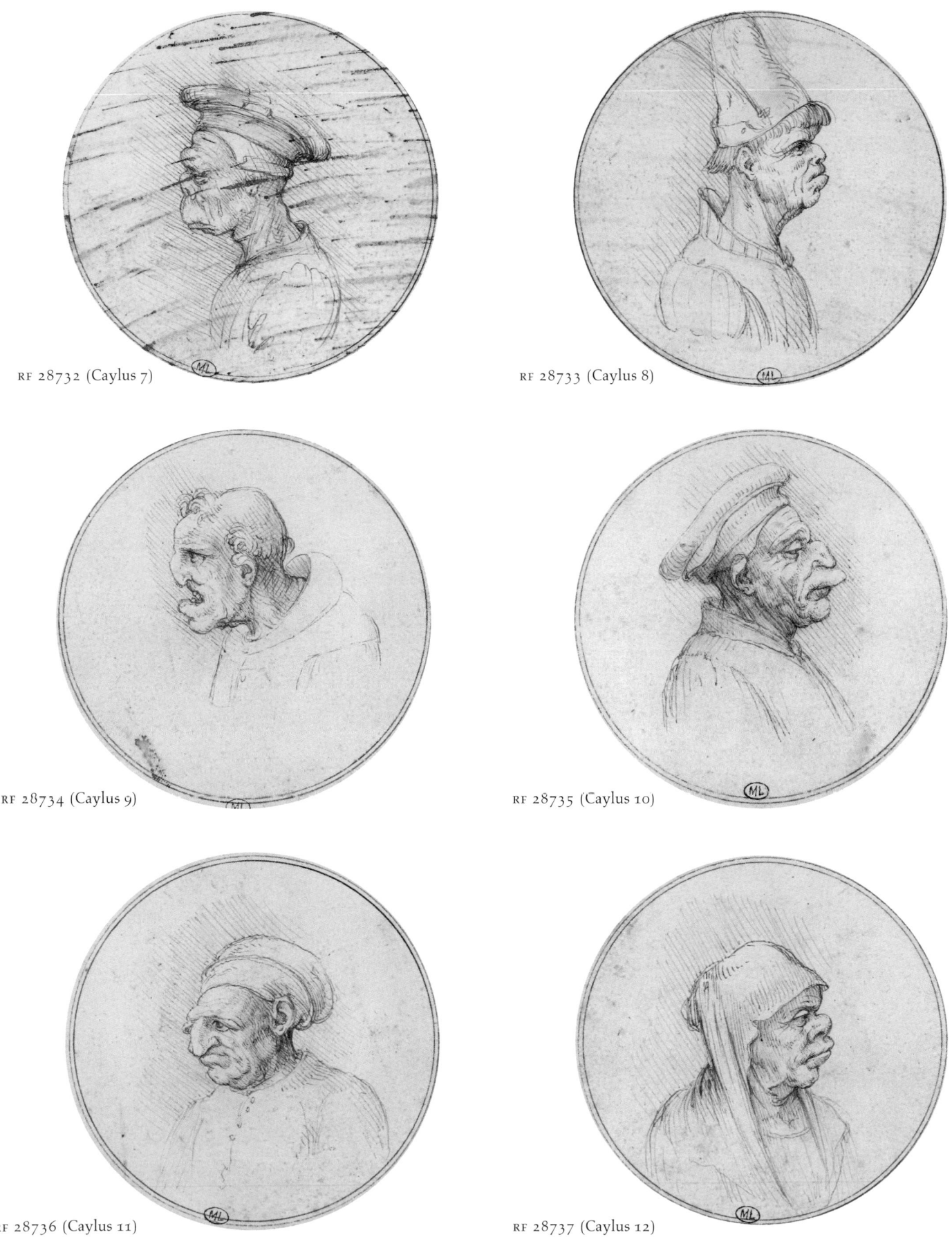

RF 28732 (Caylus 7)

RF 28733 (Caylus 8)

RF 28734 (Caylus 9)

RF 28735 (Caylus 10)

RF 28736 (Caylus 11)

RF 28737 (Caylus 12)

685

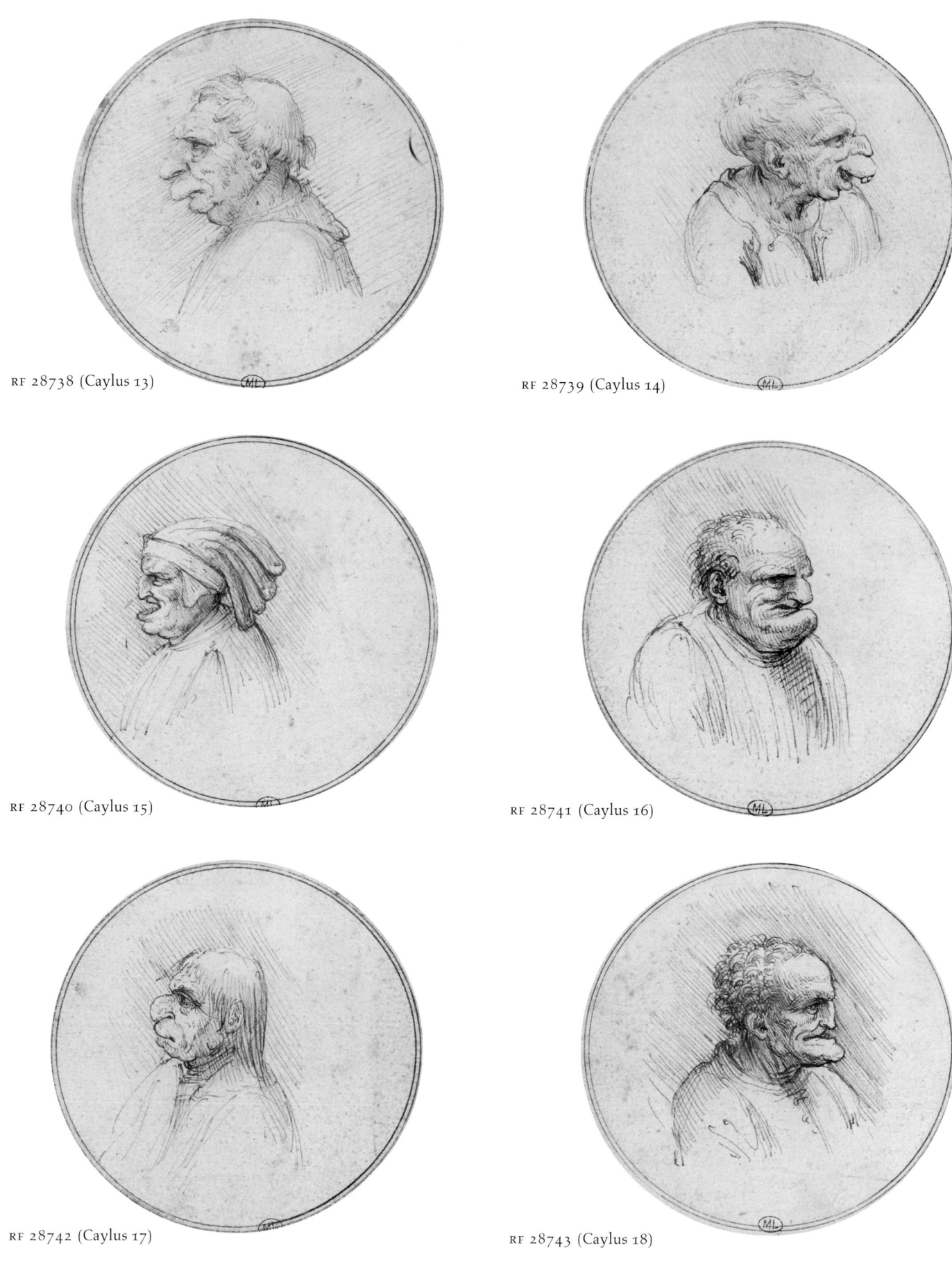

RF 28738 (Caylus 13)

RF 28739 (Caylus 14)

RF 28740 (Caylus 15)

RF 28741 (Caylus 16)

RF 28742 (Caylus 17)

RF 28743 (Caylus 18)

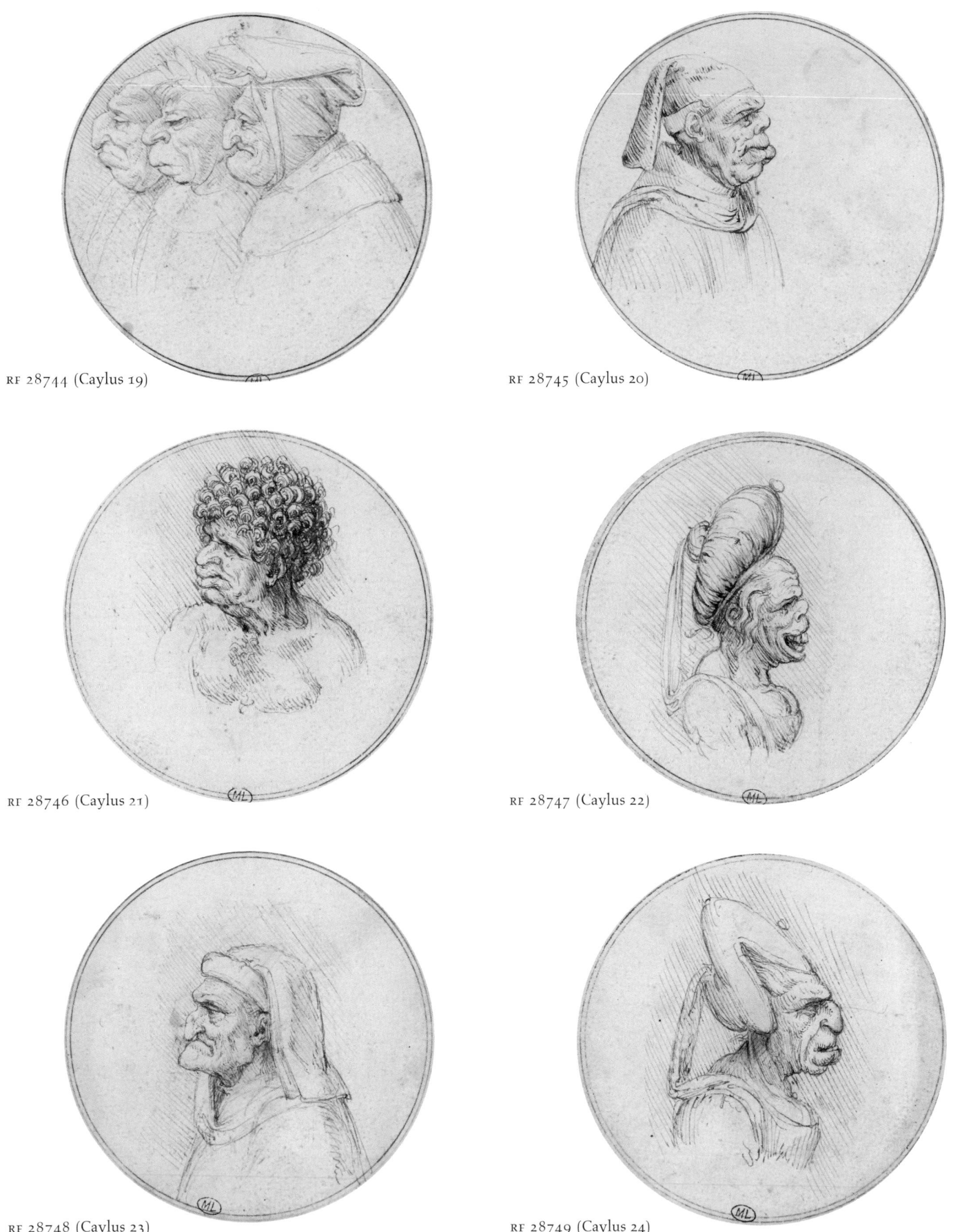

RF 28744 (Caylus 19)

RF 28745 (Caylus 20)

RF 28746 (Caylus 21)

RF 28747 (Caylus 22)

RF 28748 (Caylus 23)

RF 28749 (Caylus 24)

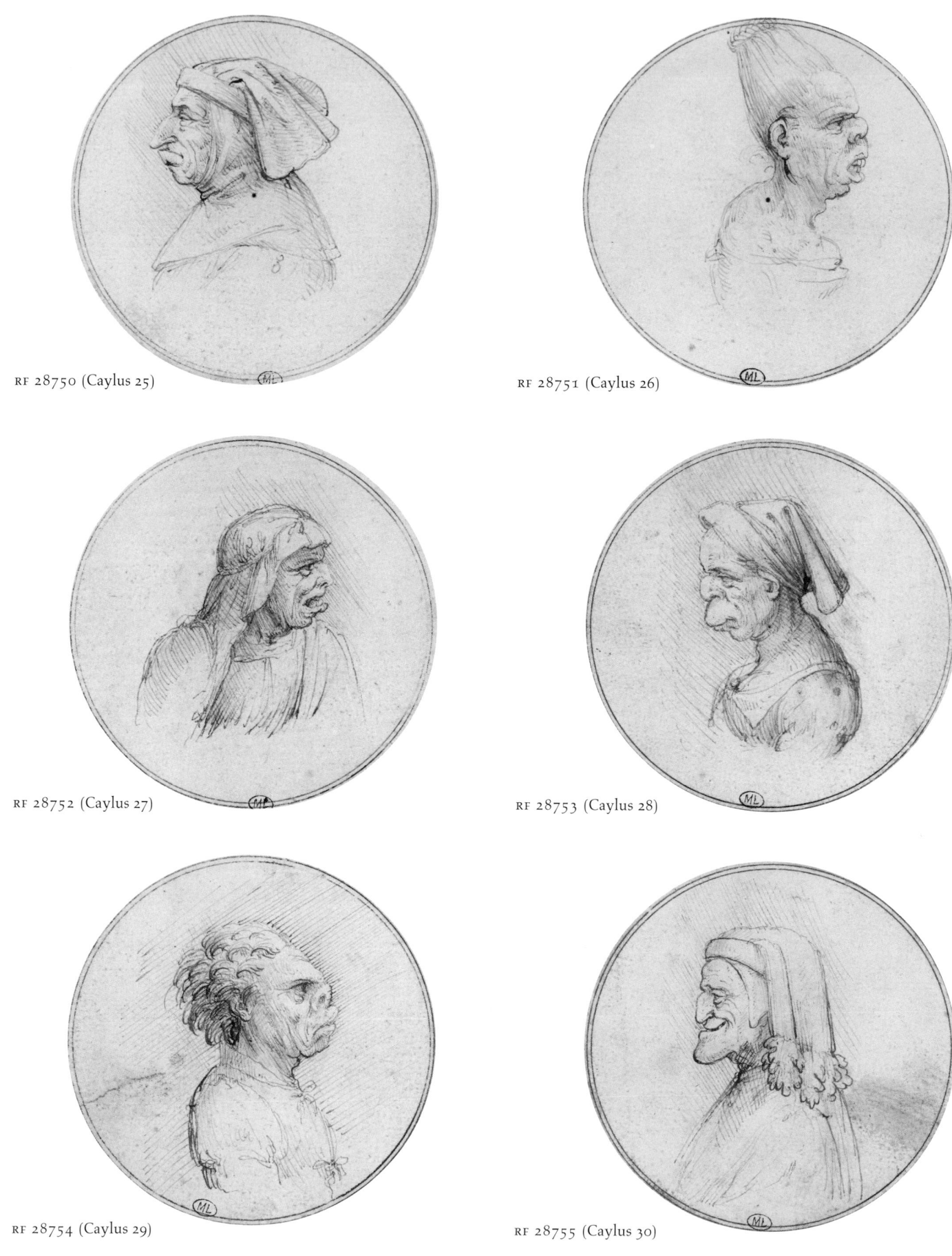

RF 28750 (Caylus 25)

RF 28751 (Caylus 26)

RF 28752 (Caylus 27)

RF 28753 (Caylus 28)

RF 28754 (Caylus 29)

RF 28755 (Caylus 30)

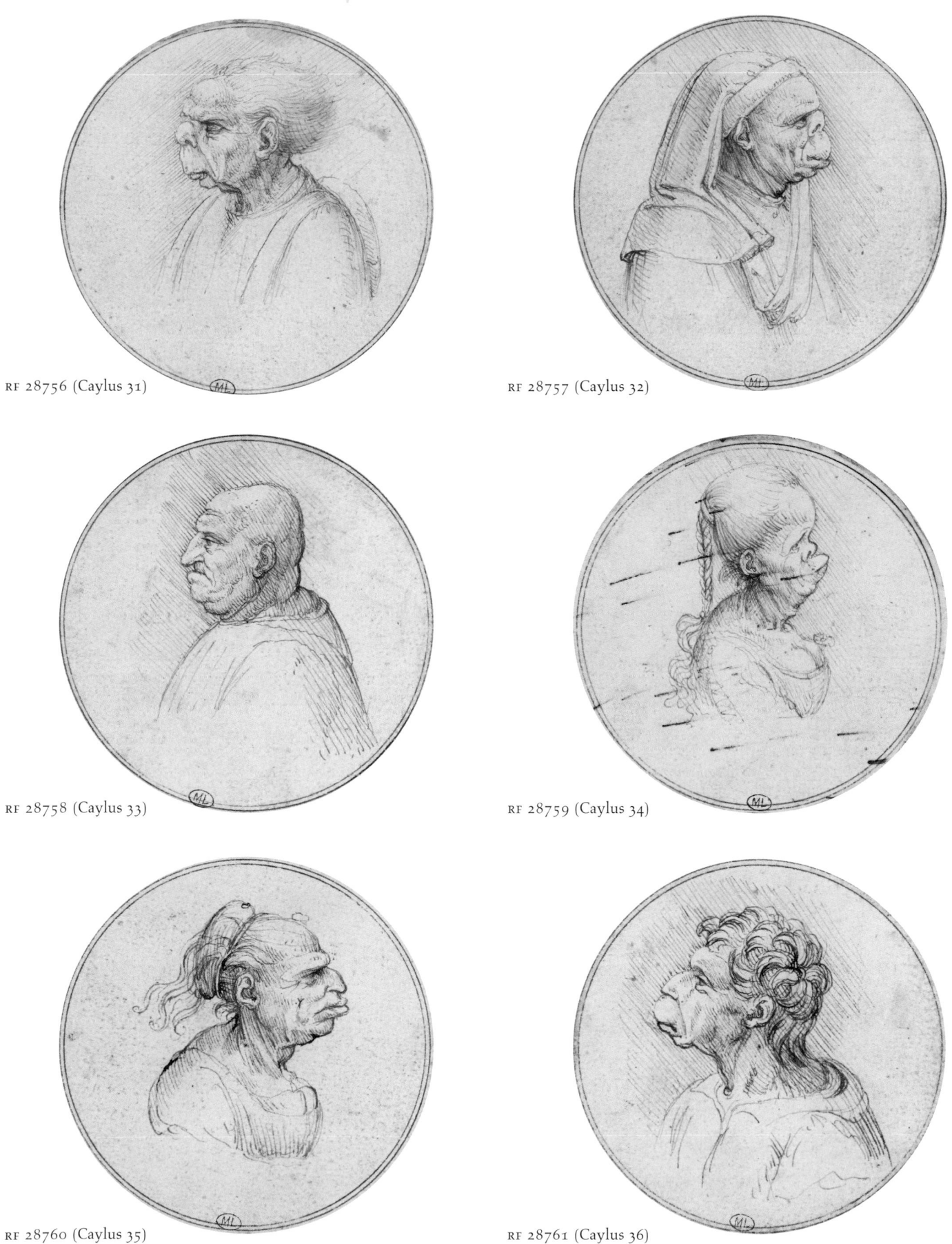

RF 28756 (Caylus 31)

RF 28757 (Caylus 32)

RF 28758 (Caylus 33)

RF 28759 (Caylus 34)

RF 28760 (Caylus 35)

RF 28761 (Caylus 36)

689

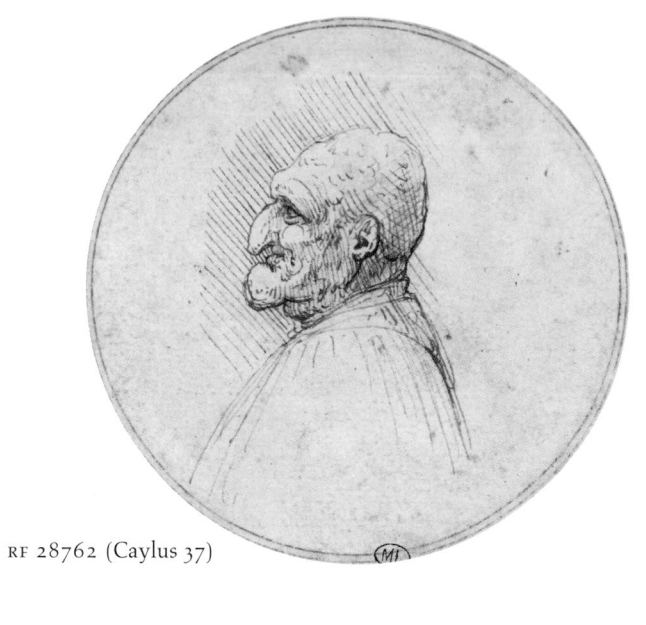

RF 28762 (Caylus 37)

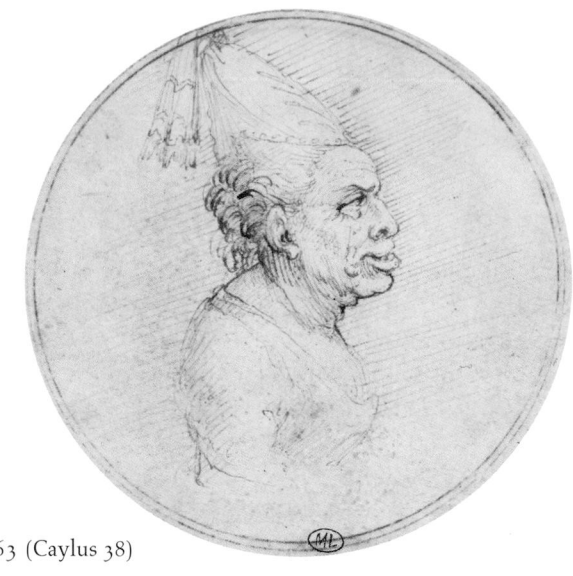

RF 28763 (Caylus 38)

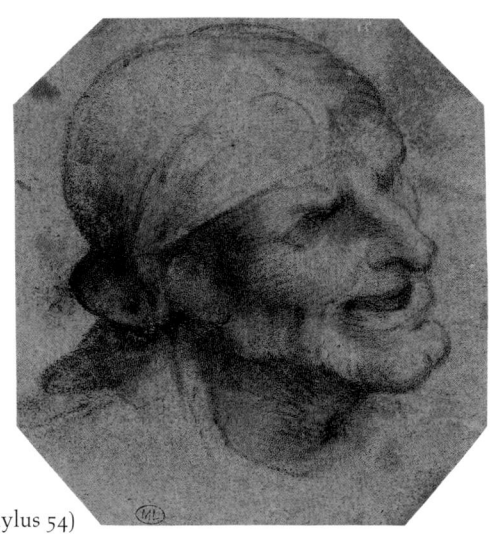

RF 28764 (Caylus 54)

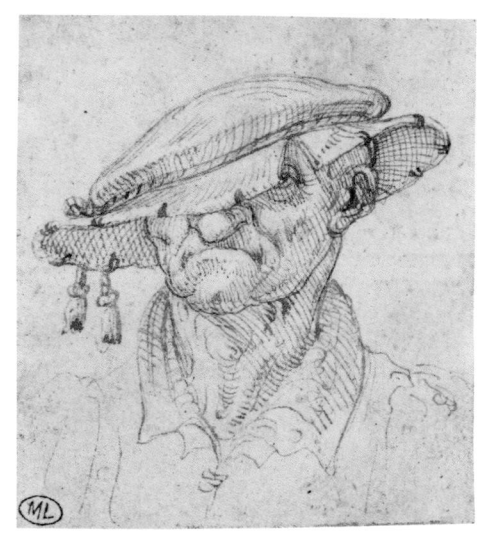

RF 28765 (Caylus 39)

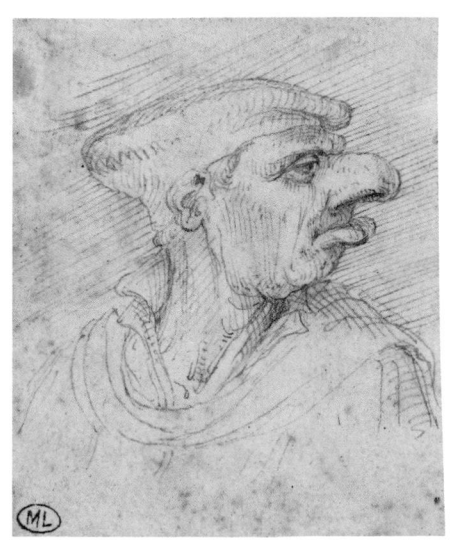

RF 28766 (Caylus 40)

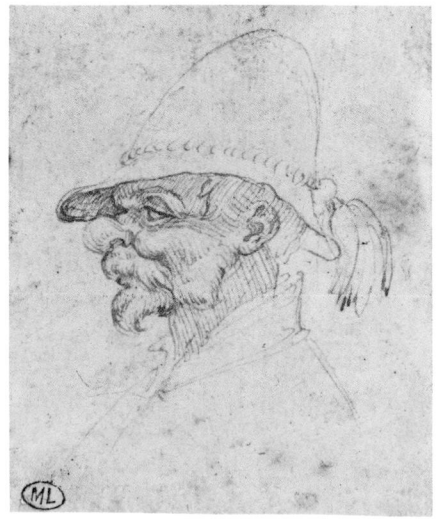

RF 28767 (Caylus 41)

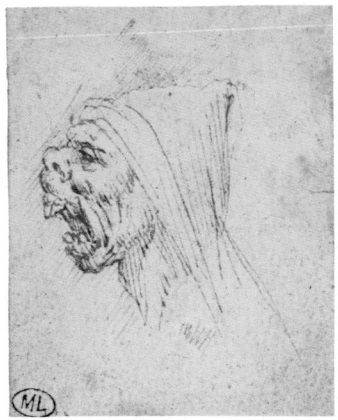

RF 28768 (Caylus 43)

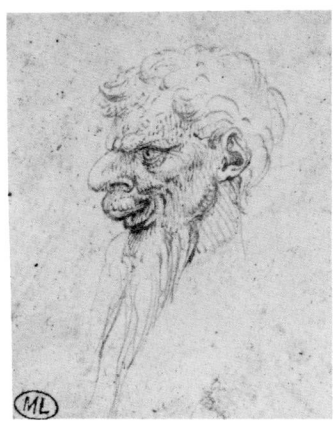

RF 28769 (Caylus 44)

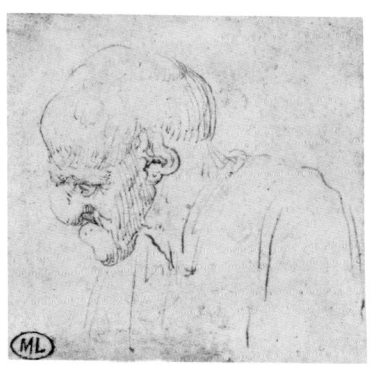

RF 28770 (Caylus 45)

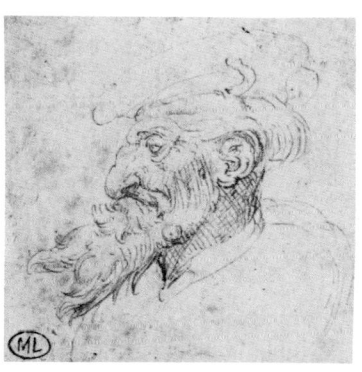

RF 28771 (Caylus 42)

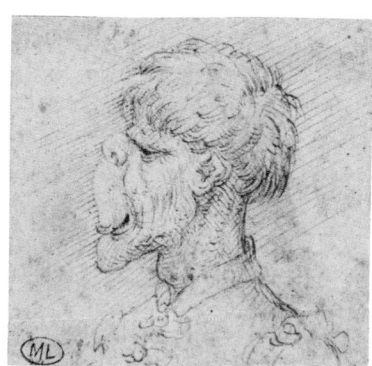

RF 28772 (Caylus 46)

RF 28773 (Caylus 47)

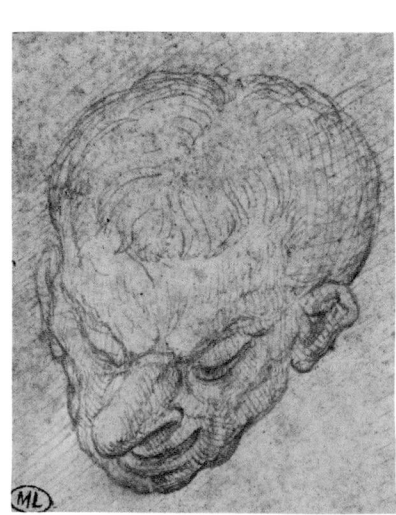

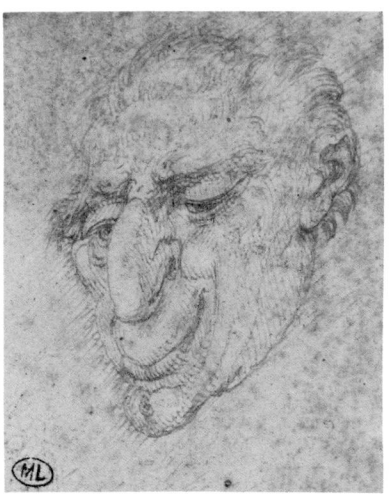

RF 28774 (Caylus 48)

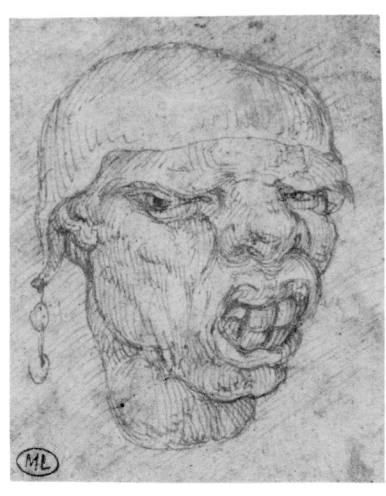

RF 28775 (Caylus 49)

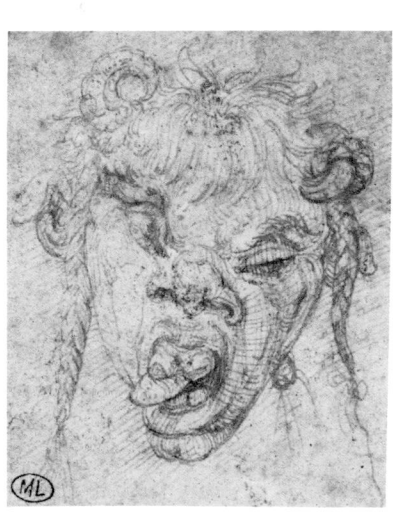

RF 28776 (Caylus 52)

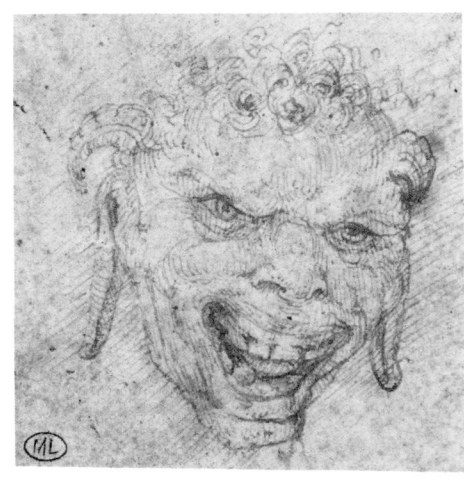

RF 28777 (Caylus 51)

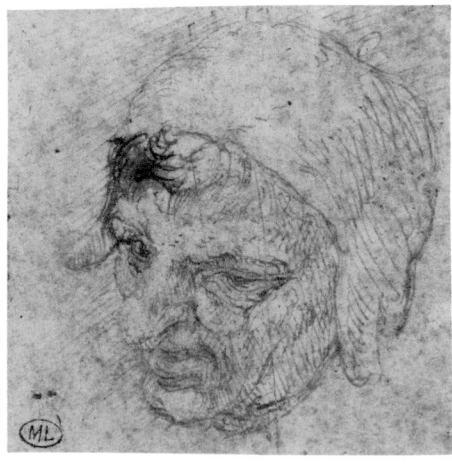

RF 28778 (Caylus 50)

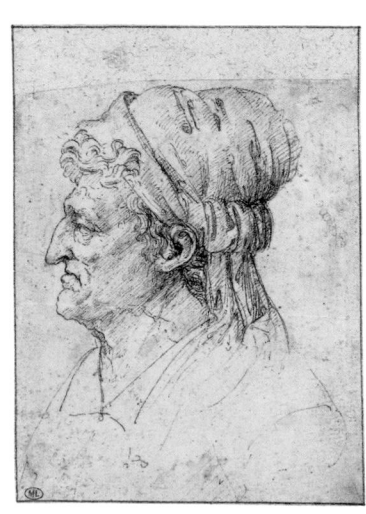

RF 28779 (Caylus 53)

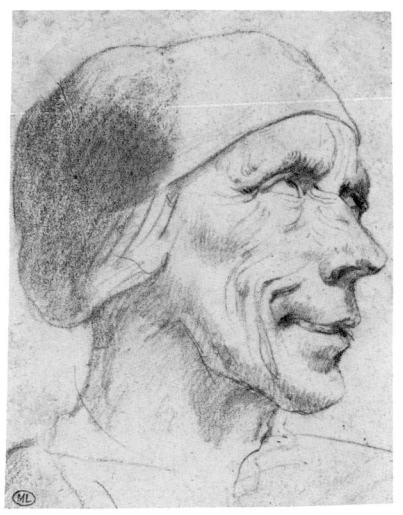

RF 28780 (no Caylus no.)

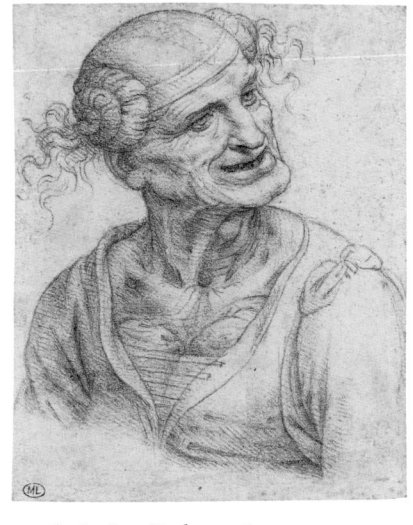

RF 28781 (no Caylus no.)

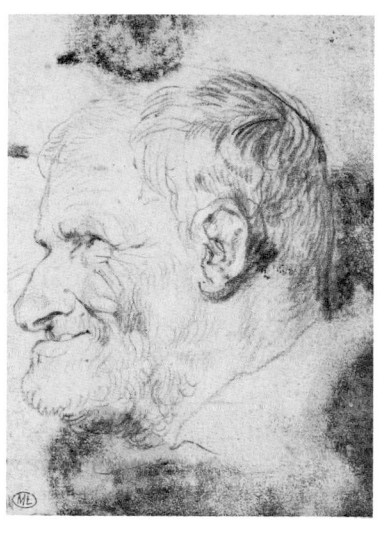

RF 28782 (no Caylus no.)

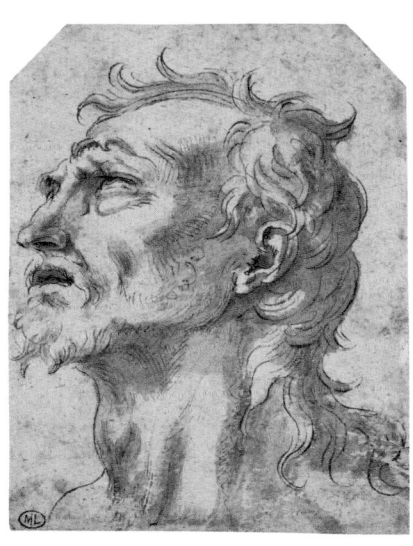

RF 28783 (no Caylus no.)

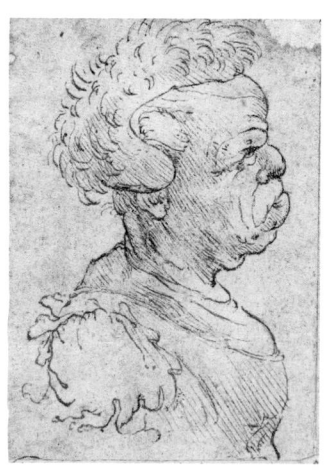

RF 28784 (no Caylus no.)

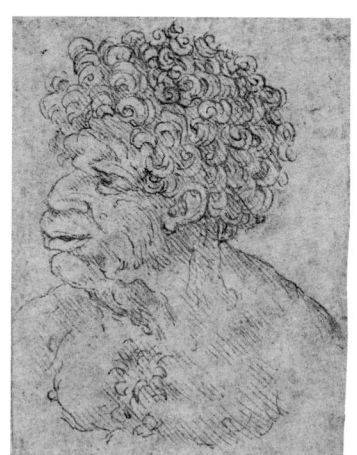

RF 28785 (no Caylus no.)

There is also a copy in Frankfurt, Städelsches Kunstinstitut, 4466, in pen and brown ink, surrounded by two circles; on the verso is the same old woman with carnation as on the Louvre sheet. The Frankfurt and Louvre sheets are executed in a similar hand. The Frankfurt sheet (as well as another in Berlin, identical to RF 28758 and its verso—see below) presents a difficult problem. It would seem there were several versions of the same sheet—but to what end?

FOLIO 7 VERSO: RF 28731 (VERSO OF RF 28730)
Old Woman, Half-Length, in Profile to the Right, with a Carnation at Her Neckline
Pen, brown ink, and gray wash
Caylus number 6

Original Chatsworth, 820A, now in the National Gallery, Washington, D.C. (cat. no. 72). The Louvre copy is slightly larger than the original. Spencer copy, vol. 1, 24 (fig. 174); Pembroke copy (Pedretti and Trutty-Coohill 1993, no. 30e, now in the National Gallery, Washington, D.C., Woodner Collections), paired with RF 28748; British Museum copy, 1886-6-9-40, paired with RF 28748; Berlin copy, Kupferstichkabinett, KdZ 17187; copy attributed to Quentin Metsys, Zeitlin and Ver Brugge sale, Los Angeles, 1977, no. 25; copy in Frankfurt, Städelsches Kunstinstitut, 4466 verso (see under RF 28730).

FOLIO 8 RECTO: RF 28732
Old Man, Half-Length, in Profile to the Left, with a Flattened Nose, Wearing a Flat Cap
Pen, brown ink, and gray wash, marked with green and black stains, traces of gold particles
Caylus number 7

Original Chatsworth, 823A (cat. no. 73a). The Louvre copy is slightly larger than the original. Spencer copy, vol. 1, 23; Pembroke copy (Pedretti and Trutty-Coohill 1993, no. 30k, now in the Fogg Art Museum, Cambridge), paired with RF 28760; Berlin copy, Kupferstichkabinett, KdZ 17188. Copied from the Mariette album by Gabriel de Saint Aubin in *Livre des Saint Aubin*, Louvre, RF 52455. Engraved, P. 1561 and P. 1740 (not by Hollar, according to Pennington 1982), not reversed, paired with RF 28735; engraved by Gerli, pl. 16.

FOLIO 8 VERSO: RF 28733 (VERSO OF RF 28732)
Man, Half-Length, in Right Profile to the Right, Wearing a

Pointed Cap with a Plume
Pen, brown ink, and gray wash
Caylus number 8

Original not located. Spencer copy, vol. 2, 5; copy former Béhague-Ravaisson collection (Pedretti and Trutty-Coohill 1993, p. 16, fig. 4).

FOLIO 9 RECTO: RF 28734
Monk, Half-Length, in Profile to the Left, Opening His Mouth
Pen, brown ink, and gray wash
Caylus number 9

Original Chatsworth, 823D (cat. no. 73d). The Louvre copy is slightly larger than the original. Spencer copy, vol. 1, 21; copy former Béhague-Ravaisson collection (Pedretti and Trutty-Coohill 1993, p. 16, fig. 4); New York copy, private collection (Pedretti and Trutty-Coohill 1993, p. 65, no. 29).

FOLIO 9 VERSO: RF 28735 (VERSO OF RF 28734)
Old Man, Half-Length, in Profile to the Right, with a Round Cap
Pen, brown ink, and gray wash
Caylus number 10

Original not located. Spencer copy, vol. 2, 38; copy former Béhague-Ravaisson collection (Pedretti and Trutty-Coohill 1993, p. 16, fig. 4); New York copy, private collection (Pedretti and Trutty-Coohill 1993, p. 65, no. 29). Engraved P. 1740 (not by Hollar, according to Pennington 1982), not reversed, paired with RF 28732.

FOLIO 10 RECTO: RF 28736
Old Man, Half-Length, in Three-Quarter Profile to the Left, with a Round Cap
Pen, brown ink, and gray wash
Caylus number 11

Original not located. Spencer copy, vol. 1, 29; Pembroke copy (Pedretti and Trutty-Coohill 1993, no. 30j; now in the Pierpont Morgan Library, in New York), paired with a woman not reproduced elsewhere; Montpellier copy, Musée Fabre, 864-2-270; Berlin copy, Kupferstichkabinett, KdZ 17189. Engraved P. 1741 (not by Hollar, according to Pennington 1982), not reversed, paired with RF 28749.

Folio 10 verso: RF 28737 (verso of RF 28736)
Old Woman, Half-Length, in Profile to the Right,
Wearing a Veil
Pen and brown ink
Caylus number 12

Original (sometimes considered a copy) British Museum,
London, Pp I-37; the Louvre copy is slightly larger.
Spencer copy, vol. 1, 28; Venice copy, Accademia, 227, paired
with RF 28758.

Folio 11 recto: RF 28738
Monk, Half-Length, in Profile to the Left
Pen, brown ink, and gray wash
Caylus number 13

Original Chatsworth, 826C; the Louvre copy is slightly
larger than the original. Hatching done by a right-handed
person. Spencer copy, vol. 2, 53. Engraved P. 1739 (not by
Hollar, according to Pennington 1982), not reversed, paired
with RF 28729.

Folio 11 verso: RF 28739 (verso of RF 28738)
Man, Half-Length, in Profile to the Right, Mouth Open
Pen, brown ink, and gray wash
Caylus number 14

Original Chatsworth, 825B; the Louvre copy is slightly larger
than the original. Spencer copy, vol. 1, 25; Pembroke copy
(Pedretti and Trutty-Coohill 1993, no. 30b, now in the Detroit
Institute of Arts), paired with RF 28730; London copy, British
Museum, 1886-6-9 40, paired with RF 28730; Berlin copy,
Kupferstichkabinett, KdZ 17190. Copied from the Mariette
album by Gabriel de Saint Aubin in *Livre des Saint Aubin,*
Louvre, RF 52460. Engraved P. 1563 and P. 1744 (not by
Hollar, according to Pennington 1982), not reversed, paired
with RF 28753.

Folio 12 recto: RF 28740
Man, Half-Length, in Profile to the Left, with a Hanging
Head Covering
Pen, brown ink, and gray wash
Caylus number 15

Original not located. Spencer copy, vol. 2, 41; Biblioteca
Ambrosiana copy, Cod. F 274 inf. 54. Engraved P. 1742 (not by

Hollar, according to Pennington 1982), not reversed, paired
with RF 28759; engraved by Gerli, pl. 26.

Folio 12 verso: RF 28741 (verso of RF 28740)
Man, Half-Length, in Three-Quarter Profile to the Right,
with an Enormous Chin
Pen, brown ink, and gray wash
Caylus number 16

Original not located, but probably cut from the Vienna fragment,
Albertina, 66 (see fig. 105 in my essay). Spencer copy, vol. 2, 30;
Pembroke copy (Pedretti and Trutty-Coohill 1993, no. 30d,
now in the Pierpont Morgan Library, New York), paired with
RF 28742 and RF 28746; Venice copy, Accademia, 227;
Biblioteca Ambrosiana copy, Cod. F 274 inf. 54; Montpellier
copy, Musée Fabre, 864-2-270. Engraved by Gerli, pl. 24;
engraved in *Characaturas* 1786, not reversed.

Folio 13 recto: RF 28742
Man, Half-Length, in Profile to the Left, with a Large Nose
Pen, brown ink, and gray wash
Caylus number 17

Original, fragment in Vienna, Albertina, 66, paired with
RF 28746 (fig. 105 in my essay); originally, the sheet also
contained the man reproduced in RF 28741. The Louvre copy
is larger and more complete than the original (fig. 106), which
omits the torso and on which the nose is hooked. Pembroke
copy (Pedretti and Trutty-Coohill 1993, no. 30d, now in the
Pierpont Morgan Library, New York), paired with RF 28741
and RF 28746, in the same layout as in the original (fig. 106).
British Museum copy, 1886-6-9-40, where the nose is closer
to the original. Engraved by Gerli, pl. 24.

Folio 13 verso: RF 28743 (verso of RF 28742)
Man, Half-Length, in Profile to the Right, with a Large
Protruding Chin
Pen, brown ink, and gray wash
Caylus number 18

Original Chatsworth, 822D. The Louvre copy is slightly larger
than the original. Spencer copy, vol. 2, 24; Louvre copy, 2571B;
Biblioteca Ambrosiana copy, Cod. F 274 inf. 54; Montpellier
copy, Musée Fabre, 864-2-270. Engraved by Gerli, pl. 25.

FOLIO 14 RECTO: RF 28744
Three Old Poets in Profile to the Left (Boccaccio, Petrarch, Dante?)
Pen and brown ink
Caylus number 19

Original not located. Spencer copies: Dante (figure on the right), vol. 2, 3; Petrarch (figure in the middle wearing a laurel wreath) and Boccaccio (figure on the left), vol. 2, 32. Pembroke copy (Pedretti and Trutty-Coohill 1993, no. 30h, now in the Fogg Art Museum, Cambridge); Venice copy, Accademia, 229 (fig. 113); Biblioteca Ambrosiana copy, Cod. F 274 inf. 54. Engraved by Gerli, pl. 24.

FOLIO 14 VERSO: RF 28745 (VERSO OF RF 28744)
Man, Half-Length, in Profile to the Right, Wearing a Cap Hanging Down in the Back
Pen, brown ink, and gray wash
Caylus number 20

Original not located. The Louvre copy has no hatching of the ground. Spencer copy, vol. 1, 3; Chatsworth copy, 827A, paired with RF 28728; Biblioteca Ambrosiana copy, Cod. F 274 inf. 45, paired with RF 28728; Berlin copy, Kupferstichkabinett, KdZ 17191. Engraved P. 1574 and P. 1738 (not by Hollar, according to Pennington 1982), not reversed, paired with RF 28761; engraved by Gerli, pl. 16.

FOLIO 15 RECTO: RF 28746
Black Man, Half-Length, in Three-Quarter Profile to the Left, Bare-Chested
Pen, brown ink, and gray wash
Caylus number 21
LITERATURE: Bacou 1981, p. 79, fig. 60.

Original Albertina, Vienna, 66, paired with RF 28742 (see fig. 105 in my essay). The Louvre copy is slightly larger than the original. Spencer copy, vol. 1, 17 (fig. 107); Pembroke copy (Pedretti and Trutty-Coohill 1993, no. 30d, now in the Pierpont Morgan Library, New York; fig. 106), with RF 28741 and RF 28742; copy at the Biblioteca Ambrosiana, Cod. F 274 inf. 54, paired, like the fragment now in the Albertina, with RF 28742; Berlin copy, Kupferstichkabinett, KdZ 17192. Engraved by Gerli, pl. 24; engraved in *Characaturas* 1786.

The same figure, copied by another hand, is depicted on RF 28785. Mariette does not mention this duplication in

"Lettre sur Léonard de Vinci," which serves as an introduction to Caylus's album of engravings (cat. no. 138).

FOLIO 15 VERSO: RF 28747 (VERSO OF RF 28746)
Old Woman, Half-Length, in Profile to the Right, with a Round Hat
Pen, brown ink, and brown wash
Caylus number 22

Original not located. Spencer copy, vol. 1, 12; Pembroke copy (Pedretti and Trutty-Coohill 1993, no. 30l, now in the Fogg Art Museum, Cambridge), paired with a man who is also depicted on the copy in the Biblioteca Ambrosiana, Cod. F 274 inf. 54; Montpellier copy, Musée Fabre, 864-2-271. Copied from the Mariette album by Gabriel de Saint Aubin in *Livre des Saint Aubin*, Louvre, RF 52459. Engraved by Gerli, pl. 22.

FOLIO 16 RECTO: RF 28748
Old Man, Half-Length, in Profile to the Left, with a Hooked Nose and a Head Covering
Pen, brown ink, and gray wash
Caylus number 23

Original Chatsworth, 822C. The Louvre copy is slightly larger than the original. Spencer copy, vol. 1, 10 (fig. 175); Pembroke copy (Pedretti and Trutty-Coohill 1993, no. 30e, now in the National Gallery, Washington, D.C.), paired with RF 28731; British Museum copy, 1886-6-9-40, also paired with RF 28731; Montpellier copy, Musée Fabre, 864-2-270; Berlin copy, Kupferstichkabinett, KdZ 17193.

FOLIO 16 VERSO: RF 28749 (VERSO OF RF 28748)
Old Woman, Half-Length, in Profile to the Right, Wearing a Hennin
Pen, brown ink, and gray wash; traces of lines gone over in drypoint for transfer onto copperplate
Caylus number 24

Original Chatsworth, 823B (cat. no. 73b). The Louvre copy is slightly larger than the original. Spencer copy, vol. 1, 10 (fig. 175); Pembroke copy (Pedretti and Trutty-Coohill 1993, no. 30i, now in The Metropolitan Museum of Art, New York; cat. no. 121), paired with RF 28756; Louvre copy, 2296 (cat. no. 136), paired with RF 28756; Berlin copy, Kupferstichkabinett, KdZ 17194; Montpellier copy, Musée Fabre, 864-2-271.

Engraved P. 1741 (not by Hollar, according to Pennington 1982), not reversed, paired with RF 28736.

FOLIO 17 RECTO: RF 28750
Man, Half-Length, in Profile to the Left, with a Pointed Nose, Wearing a Cap
Pen, brown ink, and gray wash
Caylus number 25

Original not located. Spencer copy, vol. 2, 23; Pembroke copy (Pedretti and Trutty-Coohill 1993, no. 30c, now in the Elmer Belt Library, Los Angeles), paired with Chatsworth, 820C (now in the J. Paul Getty Museum, Los Angeles); Venice copy, Accademia, 229 (see my essay, fig. 113), paired with Chatsworth, 820C; Biblioteca Ambrosiana copy, Cod. F 274 inf. 45, paired with Chatsworth, 820C; Louvre copy, 2571, paired with Chatsworth, 820C; copy, sometimes attributed to Hollar, in Edinburgh, National Gallery of Scotland, D 3505, paired with RF 28751. Engraved by Gerli, pl. 25; engraved in *Characaturas* 1786.

FOLIO 17 VERSO: RF 28751 (VERSO OF RF 28750)
Old Woman, Half-Length, in Profile to the Right, Hair Pulled Back in a Chignon
Pen, brown ink, and gray wash
Caylus number 26

Original Chatsworth, 824A. The Louvre copy is slightly larger than the original and has no hatching on the ground. Spencer copy, vol. 2, 6; Pembroke copy (Pedretti and Trutty-Coohill 1993, no. 30j; now in the Elmer Belt Library, Los Angeles), paired with an old man with pointed beard, which is copied in Louvre, 2571B; Venice copy, Accademia, 229 (see fig. 113 in my essay), in which the man with the pointed beard is placed at the bottom of the sheet; Biblioteca Ambrosiana copy, Cod. F274 inf. 54; British Museum copy, 1895-9-15-484; copy, sometimes attributed to Hollar, in Edinburgh, National Gallery of Scotland, D 3505, paired with RF 28750. Engraved by Gerli, pl. 25, reversed, the only case among the Caylus heads when Gerli does a reversed engraving.

FOLIO 18 RECTO: RF 28752
Old Woman, Half-Length, in Profile to the Right, Wearing a Veil
Pen, brown ink, and gray wash
Caylus number 27

Original Chatsworth, 819C. The Louvre copy is slightly larger than the original. Spencer copy, vol. 1, 16; Berlin copy, Kupferstichkabinett, KdZ 17195; Montpellier, Musée Fabre, 864-2-271.

FOLIO 18 VERSO: RF 28753 (VERSO OF RF 28752)
Old Woman, Half-Length, in Profile to the Left, Cocked Head Covered with a Cloth
Pen, brown ink, and gray wash
Caylus number 28

Original not located. Spencer copy, vol. 1, 38; Louvre copy, 2296, paired with a man with cocked head engraved by Gerli, pl. 17; Berlin copy, Kupferstichkabinett, KdZ 17196; Montpellier copy, Musée Fabre, 864-2-271. Copied from the Mariette album by Gabriel de Saint Aubin in *Livre des Saint Aubin*, Louvre, RF 52457.

FOLIO 19 RECTO: RF 28754
Man, Half-Length, in Profile to the Right, with a Crushed Nose
Pen, brown ink, and gray wash, traces of repair of tear at lower left
Caylus number 29

Original Chatsworth, 824B. The Louvre copy is slightly larger than the original, and the hatching was done by a right-handed person. Spencer copy, vol. 2, 19; Louvre copy, 2297 (fig. 114); Berlin copy, Kupferstichkabinett, KdZ 17207.

FOLIO 19 VERSO: RF 28755 (VERSO OF RF 28754)
Old Man, Half-Length, in Profile to the Left, with a Hooked Nose and a Head Covering Falling over His Shoulders
Pen, brown ink, and gray wash
Caylus number 30

Original (sometimes disputed) Chatsworth, 818A. The Louvre copy is slightly smaller than the original, the collar has been modified, and the torso finished. Spencer copy, vol. 1, 11; Chatsworth copy, 827C, paired with RF 28763; Windsor copy, RL 12493, paired with RF 28763. Copy paired with RF 28763 sold, Paris, Hôtel Drouot, June 13 – 14, 2002, no. 115. Engraved P. 1594, paired with a woman who is at upper left on Windsor RL 12493.

FOLIO 20 RECTO: RF 28756
Old Man, Half-Length, in Profile to the Left, Hair Blowing Backward
Pen, brown ink, and gray wash
Caylus number 31

The hatching was done by a right-handed person. Original not located. Spencer copy, vol. 1, 15; Pembroke copy (Pedretti and Trutty-Coohill 1993, no. 30i, now at The Metropolitan Museum of Art, New York; cat. no. 121), paired with RF 28749; Louvre copy, 2296 (cat. no. 136), paired with RF 28749; copy former Béhague-Ravaisson collection (Trutty-Coohill 1993, p. 16, fig. 4); Sacramento copy, Crocker Art Museum. Engraved P. 1593, not reversed, paired with the woman at upper right on Windsor RL 12491; engraved by Gerli, pl. 21.

FOLIO 20 VERSO: RF 28757 (VERSO OF RF 28756)
Old Man, Half-Length, in Profile to the Right, Wearing a Cloth on His Head That Falls over His Shoulders
Pen, brown ink, and gray wash
Caylus number 32

Original Chatsworth, 820A, now in a private collection (cat. no. 71). The Louvre copy is slightly larger than the original. Spencer copy, vol. 1, 35; Pembroke copy (Pedretti and Trutty-Coohill 1993, no. 30a, now in a private collection), paired with Chatsworth, 824D; Louvre copy, 2296, paired with Chatsworth, 824D; Sacramento copy, Crocker Art Museum; Berlin copy, Kupferstichkabinett, KdZ 17197. Engraved P. 1562; engraved by Hogarth, not reversed, lower right of sheet "Characters + Caricaturas," dated April 12, 1743; engraved by Gerli, pl. 27; engraved in *Characaturas* 1786.

FOLIO 21 RECTO: RF 28758
Bald Monk, Half-Length, in Profile to the Left
Pen, brown ink, and gray wash
Caylus number 33

Original (sometimes disputed) British Museum, Pp. I-38. The Louvre copy is slightly larger than the original; the torso is thinner. Spencer copy, vol. 2, 39; Venice copy, Accademia, 227, paired with RF 28737. Engraved in *Characaturas* 1786.

The copy in Berlin, Kupferstichkabinett, KdZ 17183 recto, is of the same dimensions and in the same medium as the Louvre copy, and in a very similar hand. The number 24 is inscribed in pen and brown ink at the top, between the two

concentric circles. The back of the Berlin sheet, like the verso of RF 28758, shows the woman with chignon and with lips resembling a beak (RF 28759); the number 25 is inscribed between the two circles. The variation between the two sheets is minimal; the difference in the color of the inks is limited to more yellow in the Louvre heads and darker circles in the Berlin copy. It is difficult to define the relation between the Louvre and the Berlin sheets. What is even more puzzling is that the Berlin sheet is probably of Pacetti and hence Valenti Gonzaga provenance (see entry for RF 28727 and the discussion of the Valenti Gonzaga album in my essay). What connection could it have to Leonardo's "original" album, which belonged, precisely, to Cardinal Valenti Gonzaga?

FOLIO 21 VERSO: RF 28759 (VERSO OF RF 28758)
Old Woman in Profile to the Right, with a Flower on Her Blouse and a Chignon Ending in a Braid
Pen, brown ink, marked with green and black stains
Caylus number 34

Original Chatsworth, 822A. The Louvre copy modifies the morphology of the original slightly, and it is also larger. Spencer copy, vol. 1, 26; Venice copy, Accademia, 227, paired with RF 28726; Berlin copy, Kupferstichkabinett, KdZ 17198. Painted copy attributed to Lomazzo, private collection (see exh. cat. Lugano 1998, no. 30). Engraved P. 1742 (not by Hollar, according to Pennington 1982), not reversed, paired with RF 28740; engraved in *Characaturas* 1786.

For the other copy in Berlin, KdZ 17183 verso, see under RF 28758.

FOLIO 22 RECTO: RF 28760
Old Woman, Half-Length, in Profile to the Right, Lips Jutting Out
Pen and brown ink
Caylus number 35

Original Chatsworth, 821A. The Louvre copy is slightly larger than the original and has no hatching on the ground. Spencer copy, vol. 1, 18; Pembroke copy (Pedretti and Trutty-Coohill 1993, no. 30k, now in the Fogg Art Museum, Cambridge), paired with RF 28732; Berlin copy, Kupferstichkabinett, KdZ 17199. Engraved P. 1565.

FOLIO 22 VERSO: RF 28761 (VERSO OF RF 28760)
Man, Half-Length, in Profile to the Left, with Simian Features
Pen and brown ink
Caylus number 36

Original Chatsworth, 821D. The Louvre copy is larger than the original, and the proportions of the head are greater. Spencer copy, vol. 1, 19; Pembroke copy (Pedretti and Trutty-Coohill 1993, no. 30f, now in a private collection), paired with RF 28784; Berlin copy, Kupferstichkabinett, KdZ 17200; Sacramento copy, Crocker Art Museum. Engraved P. 1738 (not by Hollar, according to Pennington 1982), not reversed, paired with RF 28745; engraved in *Characaturas* 1786.

FOLIO 23 RECTO: RF 28762
Old Man, Half-Length, in Profile to the Left, with a Hooked Nose
Pen, brown ink, and gray wash
Caylus number 37

Original and copies not located. According to Mariette (1730, p. 17 n. a), the inscription on the back suggests that this is the last page of a small book of Leonardo's grotesques.

FOLIO 23 VERSO
A circle in pen and brown ink marks where the sheet bearing the drawing was cut. An inscription in Dutch appears at the top. It has been transcribed by S. A. C. Dudok van Heel of the Municipal Archives in Amsterdam and translated by Peter Schatborn: *22 blate: D [. . .] banden sonden 43 angeschite geresen* (?) (22 sheets: D[. . .] albums would be 43 faces [?])

FOLIO 24 RECTO: RF 28763
Old Woman, Half-Length, in Profile to the Right, Wearing a Hennin
Pen, brown ink, and gray wash
Caylus number 38

Original not located. The Louvre copy has hatching done by a right-handed person. Spencer copy, vol. 1, 14; Chatsworth copy, 827C, paired with RF 28755; Windsor copy RL 12493, paired with RF 28755.
　　This is the last of the thirty-eight heads in the series after Leonardo done in the same hand. According to Mariette (1730, p. 17), since this drawing had no drawing on the back, it was

probably the first page in a small book of Leonardo's grotesques.

FOLIO 24 VERSO: RF 28764
Grimacing Head Wearing a Calotte
Black chalk and stump on bister paper, 99 × 92 mm ($3^{15}/_{16} × 3^{5}/_{8}$ in.); corners folded back
Caylus number 54

Variant of one of the five heads in the best known of Leonardo's sheet of grotesques, Windsor RL 12495. Copy (sometimes considered an original) at the Biblioteca Ambrosiana, Cod. F 263 inf. 71. Mariette himself (1730, p. 18) mentions that this is the only drawing that was not engraved by Caylus and writes that it depicts the head of Saint Elizabeth during the visit of the Blessed Virgin. Engraved by Gerli, pl. 14. According to Giulio Bora (oral communication, January 2002), it could be in a seventeenth-century northern European hand.

FOLIO 25 RECTO: RF 28765, RF 28766, AND RF 28767
Glued to secondary support
RF 28765
Head of Peasant Wearing a Hat with Pompons
Pen and brown ink, 67 × 61 mm ($2^{5}/_{8} × 2^{3}/_{8}$ in.)
Caylus number 39
LITERATURE: Strauss 1977, under no. 425; Reznicek 1981, p. 248 n. 9.

Reznicek has identified the xylograph attributed to Goltzius's circle (Strauss 1977, no. 425, dates it about 1600) from which this drawing was executed.

RF 28766
Man, Half-Length, in Profile to the Right, Wearing a Beret
Pen and brown ink, 68 × 58 mm ($2^{5}/_{8} × 2^{1}/_{4}$ in.)
Caylus number 40
LITERATURE: Reznicek 1981, p. 248 n. 9.

Original not located. Reznicek thinks this drawing and the following one are examples of Flemish drawings that have not yet been identified. Engraved in *Characaturas* 1786.

RF 28767
Head of Man in Profile to the Left Wearing a Hat with a Pompon
Pen and brown ink, 68 × 56 mm (2⅝ × 2¼ in.)
Caylus number 41
LITERATURE: Reznicek 1981, p. 248 n. 9.

Original not located.

FOLIO 26 RECTO: RF 28768, RF 28769, RF 28770, RF 28771, AND RF 28772
All in pen and brown ink; glued to secondary support

RF 28768
Head of Man in Profile to the Left, Mouth Open
54 × 43 mm (2⅛ × 1¹¹⁄₁₆ in.)
Caylus number 43

Original not located. Engraved in *Characaturas* 1786.

RF 28769
Head of Man in Profile to the Left with a Long Beard
54 × 43 mm (2⅛ × 1¹¹⁄₁₆ in.)
Caylus number 44

Original not located.

RF 28770
Man, Half-Length, in Profile to the Left, Head Cocked
46 × 48 mm (1¹³⁄₁₆ × 1⅞ in.)
Caylus number 45

Original not located.

RF 28771
Head of a Man in Profile to the Left with a Hat and a Long Beard
47 × 48 mm (1⅞ × 1⅞ in.)
Caylus number 42
LITERATURE: Reznicek 1981, pp. 248–49 n. 9.

Original not located. According to Reznicek, this is a "carniva-lesque" man "whom we might find in Joducus van Wingen," and he refers, as an example of the typology, to the figure of the very stooped old man on the left in Jan Muller's drawing *Masked Ball* (Louvre, 20900), dated about 1600.

RF 28772
Man in Profile to the Left with a Flattened Face
46 × 48 mm (1¹³⁄₁₆ × 1⅞ in.)
Caylus number 46

Original not located.

FOLIO 27 RECTO: RF 28773, RF 28774, RF 28775, RF 28776, RF 28777, AND RF 28778
All in pen and brown ink; glued to secondary support

In this series of grotesque masks, according to Mariette (1730, p. 18), "the pen is beautiful and flowing, but also more libertine." According to Reznicek (1981), they are of Flemish origin; Bora (oral communication, January 2002) mentions the possibility that they are drawings from the late sixteenth century. No originals have been located, and no other copies.

RF 28773
Man's Head, Foreshortened, Seen from Above
64 × 52 mm (2½ × 2¹⁄₁₆ in.)
Caylus number 47

RF 28774
Head of Man with a Roman Nose
64 × 52 mm (2½ × 2¹⁄₁₆ in.)
Caylus number 48

RF 28775
Head of Grimacing Man with a Calotte on His Head
63 × 50 mm (2½ × 2 in.)
Caylus number 49

RF 28776
Head of Grimacing Satyr with Two Small Ram's Horns
62 × 51 mm (2⁷⁄₁₆ × 2 in.)
Caylus number 52

RF 28777
Head of Smiling Satyr with Floppy Ears
60 × 59 mm (2⅜ × 2⅜ in.)
Caylus number 51

RF 28778
Head of Man, Seen from Above, Wearing a Cap
60 × 59 mm (2 ⅜ × 2 ⅜ in.)
Caylus number 50

FOLIO 28 RECTO: RF 28779
Woman, Half-Length, in Profile to the Left, with a Cloth Tied around Her Head
Pen and brown ink, 150 × 110 mm (5 ¹⁵⁄₁₆ × 4 ⅜ in.); strip added at the top; framing line in pen and brown ink
Inscribed in pen and brown ink on lower left: *(?) 1270*
Caylus number 53

Mariette (1730, p. 18) found the execution of this drawing "dry and cold." No other version has been located.

FOLIO 28 VERSO: RF 28780
Head of Man in Three-Quarter Profile to the Right Wearing a Calotte
Black chalk, 125 × 97 mm (4 ¹⁵⁄₁₆ × 3 ⅞ in.); oil stains (?)

No other version has been located. Bora (oral communication, January 2002) believes the hand is typically Flemish.

The Caylus engraving of this drawing was not inserted into the album, but is at the Bibliothèque Nationale de France, Richelieu location (Ed. 98c, vol. 1, folio 488 verso), where the counterproof is also located. It is inscribed in pen and brown ink at the lower right: "Van Dyk," with Caylus number 56 in pen and brown ink at the upper right.

FOLIO 29 RECTO: RF 28781
Old Woman, Half-Length, with an Emaciated Neck (Old Leda)
Black chalk, 130 × 106 mm (5 ⅛ × 4 ³⁄₁₆ in.)
LITERATURE: Möller 1928, p. 152; Scott-Elliot 1956, p. 17; Scott-Elliot 1958, pp. 285–86, fig. 2b; Białostocki 1959, p. 23 n. 35; Vezzosi 1983–84, fig. 162; Bora 1987–88, under no. 70; Barryte 1990, pp. 137–38, fig. 12; Vallese 1992, p. 46 n. 10, fig. 4; Kwakkelstein 1994, p. 110, fig. 67; Fabrizio-Costa 1997, p. 99 n. 42, fig. 2; Trutty-Coohill 1997, p. 191 n. 10.

Original not located. Variant, like RF 28764, of one of the heads on Windsor RL 12495, with the addition of an elaborate hairstyle that resembles that of the *Leda*. A copy attributed to Jacob Hoefnagel, *The Ill-Matched Couple*, is in the Albertina, Vienna (348a). In it the old woman is being kissed by a curly-haired young man wearing a calotte, who is taking her purse.

Engraved P. 1604, after the version of the Vienna drawing.

Möller wrote that Leonardo's original was probably in the collection of Emperor Rudolf II, who had purchased drawings from Lomazzo. According to Möller, Hoefnagel, who was an artist at the Rudolfine court, copied Leonardo's original at that time. The original then went to the earl of Arundel's home, where Hollar was able to engrave it.

Ever since Scott-Elliot published the Louvre drawing in her 1958 essay on the Spencer series, that drawing has been attributed to the Master of the Spencer Grotesques. Nevertheless, Scott-Elliot noted that she could not give any definitive opinion, since she had seen the Louvre drawing only in reproductions. In fact, *Old Leda* was executed by a skillful, very vibrant hand that used a great deal of hatching and pressure on the tip to vary the tonality of the black. The black chalk is different in nature, darker and thicker, than in the Spencer drawings. Philip Pouncey proposed an attribution to Giovanni Paolo Lomazzo, which is not to be ruled out. Alternatively, the drawing could be considered the work of a seventeenth-century northern European hand.

This drawing was not inserted into the Caylus album, although Caylus must have engraved it but chose not to keep it. In the volumes containing his engraved works at the Bibliothèque Nationale de France (Ed. 98c, vol. 1, folio 489 recto), he made an annotation on the engraving of RF 28782, which also does not appear in the album but which bears Caylus number 58, in pen and brown ink: "57 n'a pas été fait tant il était mauvais" (57 was so bad that it was not done).

FOLIO 29 VERSO: RF 28782
Head of Old Man in Profile to the Left
Pen and brown ink, brown wash, 121 × 89 mm (4 ¾ × 3 ½ in.); framing line in pen and brown ink; oil stains (?)
LITERATURE: Reznicek 1981, p. 248 n. 8.

No other version has been located. In 1966 Frits Lugt, cited by Reznicek, expressed the belief that this was an original early drawing by Jacob Jordaens. Reznicek indicates a painting in Raleigh, North Carolina, *Christ among the Scribes*, in which there is a similar figure, a type common for that artist.

The Caylus engraving from this drawing was not inserted in the album, but it is in the Bibliothèque Nationale de France, Richelieu location (Ed. 98c, vol. 1, folio 489 recto), where the counterproof is also located. It is inscribed in pen and brown ink at the lower right: "Van Dyck," with Caylus number 58 at the upper right. In addition, it bears the following annotation, which must refer to RF 28781: "57 n'a pas été fait tant il était mauvais" (57 was so bad that it was not done).

FOLIO 30 RECTO: RF 28783
Head of Man in Three-Quarter Profile to the Left, His Eyes Lifted ("Cigoli")
Pen and brown ink, brown wash, 109 × 87 mm (4⁵⁄₁₆ × 3⁷⁄₁₆ in.); upper corners cut
Inscribed in pen and brown ink on back of sheet: *di mano di Lodovico Cigoli* (in the hand of Lodovico Cigoli); and below: *av* (?) *ft f5*, perhaps the indication of a price

Inserted into Caylus's album of engravings with no Caylus number. In the engraving, the annotation on the back of the drawing has been moved to the front.

FOLIO 31 RECTO: RF 28784 AND RF 28785
Mark of Nicolas Lanier (Lugt 2886) between the two. Not engraved by Caylus
LITERATURE: Wood 2002a, fig. 2.

The two drawings are affixed side by side to a larger sheet, which contains the mark of Nicolas Lanier (Lugt 2886), a composer who was also the principal picture agent for the English king Charles I. This sheet is glued to a larger sheet that bears the attribution "Leonardo di Venci," which, in turn, is glued to the album page. Wood writes that the calligraphy making the attribution to Leonardo is typical of Lanier, as is the mount. In an

oral communication (December 2001), Wood even suggested that the Louvre copy may have been executed by Lanier.

RF 28784
Woman, Half-Length, in Profile to the Right
Pen and brown ink, 60 × 30 mm (2³⁄₈ × 1³⁄₁₆ in.); upper right corner reconstituted; strip added along the lower edge

Original (sometimes disputed; see Marani 1995–96, under no. 11) Chatsworth, 819D; Pembroke copy (Pedretti and Trutty-Coohill 1993, no. 30f, now in a private collection), paired with RF 28761. Engraved P. 1527; engraved by Gerli, pl. 28.

RF 28785
Black Man, Half-Length, in Three-Quarter Profile to the Left, Bare-Chested
Pen and brown ink, 60 × 43 mm (2³⁄₈ × 1¹¹⁄₁₆ in.)

This figure reproduces, in a different hand, the one depicted on RF 28746.

FOLIO 32
Blank

VF

1. Basan 1775, lot 787: "Vinci (Leonardo da). Florentine. Sixty heads and caricatures, done in pen and bister, known by the prints engraved from them by M. the C. of Caylus; they are glued to a small folio volume in black morocco." The Mariette sale catalogue in the Cabinet des Dessins in the Louvre is annotated in the left margin, in pen and brown ink: "240 Remy." Chennevières and Montaiglon 1851–60, vol. 3, p. 159 n. 2.

---

138. *Recueil / de Testes de caractere / & de Charges / dessinées / Par Leonard de Vinci / Florentin. / & gravées par M. le C. de C. / MDCCXXX*

Calf binding; double gold threads on the front cover; coat of arms of Louis-Antoine Crozat, baron of Thiers, on the upper and lower sections of the cover; 286 × 212 mm (11¼ × 8⁵⁄₁₆ in.)
On the edge, label in red leather with gold letters: *TEST DE CARAC*
Département des Arts Graphiques du Musée du Louvre, Paris
RF 28786

PROVENANCE: Louis-Antoine Crozat, baron of Thiers; his sale, February 1773, no. 829; acquired by the Société des Amis du Louvre with the cooperation of Albert Meyer and Jean Seligmann; gift to the Louvre, Comité of February 26, 1937.

LITERATURE: Mariette 1741, p. 2, under no. 8; Lugt 1921, 1956, under no. 1852; Orangerie, 1947–48, no. 175; Bacou 1981, p. 79; Reznicek 1981, p. 245; Bora 1991, p. 206; Muylle 2001, p. 174 n. 2.

The album, housed in the Département des Arts Graphiques at the Louvre, is composed of fifty-one folios.[1] Of its sixty-seven etchings, all but one (no. 54 by Charles-Antoine Coypel) are the work of Anne-Claude-Philippe de Thubières, de Grimoard, de Pestels, de Lévis, count of Caylus. The plates are numbered from 1 to 59 (with numbers 56–59 out of sequence

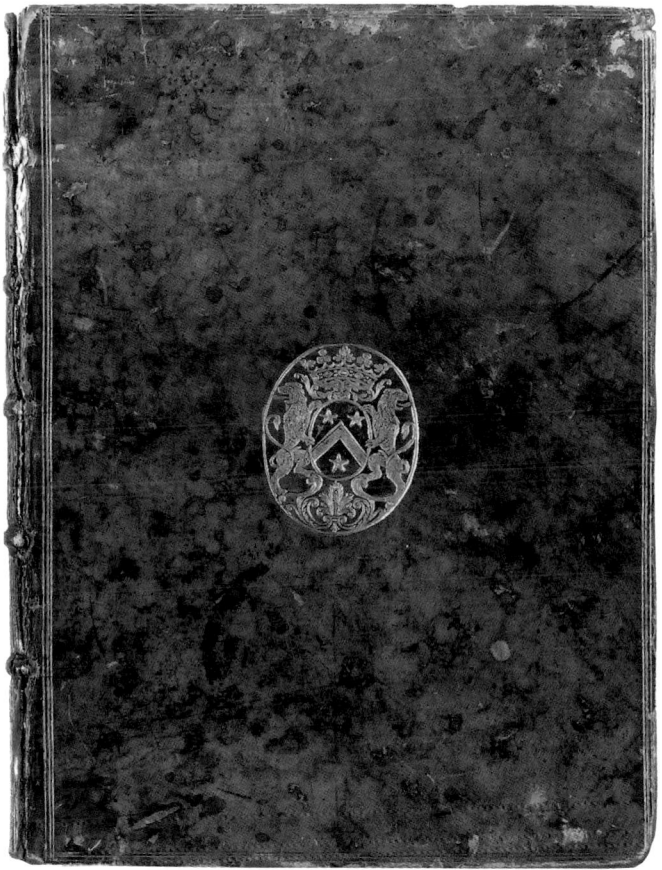

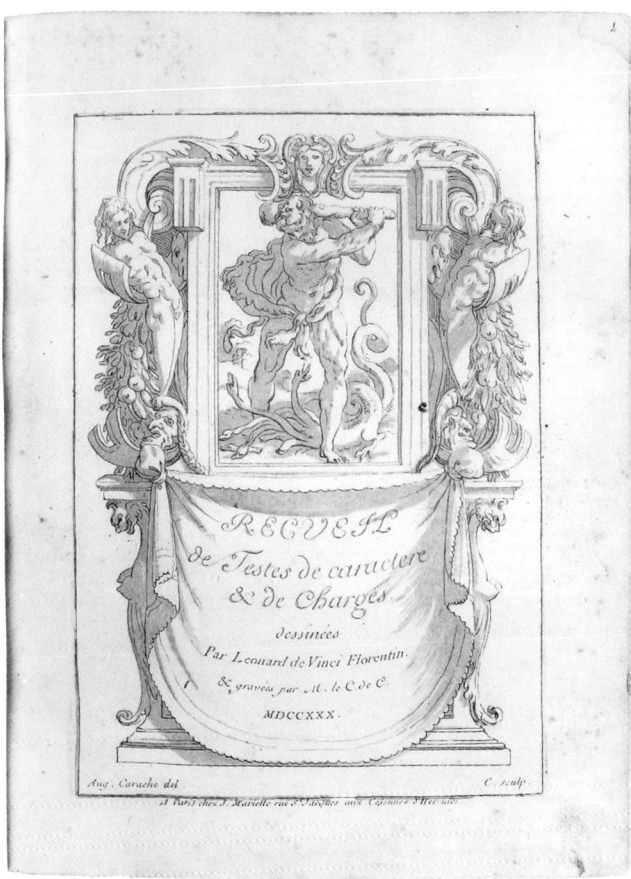

in the album), and numbers 1 to 54 (folios 14–41) and folio 45, the "Cigoli," were done from an album of drawings owned by Pierre-Jean Mariette (RF 28725–RF 28785; cat. no. 137). The etchings are reversed in relation to the drawings and respect the original dimensions. Their order also follows the order of the album of drawings up to number 38 (corresponding to drawing RF 28763), the last to be copied from drawings by Leonardo. Then there are a few etchings out of sequence, when compared to the drawings, as well as additions and repetitions of plates. The final three folios repeat the same image, the "Savonarola," three times, even though it is not found in the Mariette album. The six etchings placed at the end are not numbered. The etchings of the first thirty-eight drawings in the Mariette album reproduce the circular format of those drawings, and most bear the initial C for Caylus engraved at the bottom, sometimes inside, sometimes outside the circles surrounding the composition.

The plates are preceded by a twenty-two-page introductory text, "Lettre sur Léonard de Vinci peintre florentin A Monsieur le C. de C." (Letter concerning Leonardo da Vinci Florentine painter to monsieur the C. of C.), and by a two-page text titled "Catalogue des Pieces qui ont este' grave'es d'après les Tableaux, ou Desseins de Leonard de Vinci" (Catalogue of pieces that were engraved after the paintings or drawings of Leonardo da Vinci), in which Mariette discusses the album he had Caylus execute. The other copies of the 1730 edition of this album, consulted within the context of this research, all vary somewhat from one another. According to Steinitz (1974), such variation was common before the mechanization of printing. The copy in the Bibliothèque Nationale de France, Richelieu location (Ee 24 4°), contains, in addition to the text, only sixty etchings. It ends with the "Cigoli" plate, omitting the final six unnumbered Caylus engravings. Engraving 14 is also numbered 41; conversely, numbers 56 to 59 are in the proper order.

The copy at the Bibliothèque Nationale de France, Tolbiac location (Rare Books Room, Résac. V.10422), contains sixty-one etchings in addition to the prefatory text. This volume became part of the Bibliothèque Royale and was sent to the bindery on December 2, 1730.[2] Therefore, this copy very likely passed directly from Mariette to the Bibliothèque Royale. There are a few variations in content in comparison with the present album. The "Cigoli" is placed after the title page, Caylus number 14 is likewise numbered 41, and numbers 17 and 18 are reversed. The last Caylus number, 59, is located on the final folio (rather than the immediately preceding one, as in the Louvre museum).

The copy at the Bibliothèque d'Art et d'Archéologie, Fondation Jacques Doucet (4 Rés. 185), contains sixty-six etchings and has the same numbering error for 14. Number 55 is placed with the unnumbered etching of a Louvre album. Numbers 56 to 59 are in the proper order, after which the order of the plates deviates from that of the Louvre album. It begins with a sheet with two grotesques that are not in the Louvre album, followed by a *Caricature of a Man* and *Caricature of a Woman* (folios 47 and 48 in the Louvre) and "Savonarola" (folio 49). The last image is the "Cigoli."

In the copy at the Prentenkabinet in Leiden, which Jef Scaeps examined for me, etching 14 is numbered correctly, numbers 56 to 59 are in the proper order, and the last image is the "Cigoli." Steinitz (1974) mentions a copy in the Elmer Belt Library of Vinciana in Los Angeles, which is unique in that the etchings on the right-hand page are reversed on the facing left-hand page. Giulio Bora and Pietro C. Marani directed my attention to a copy in a private collection that is the object of a recent publication.[3] It contains forty-six etchings by Caylus, one per page, but unnumbered and in an order peculiar to it: for example, the first image is Caylus no. 21 and the last Caylus no. 44. Two cartouche drawings in pen and wash are bound in the front of the book.

Finally, at the Bibliothèque Nationale de France, Richelieu location, in the volumes that contain etchings by Caylus (Ed. 98b, vol. 1, folios 481 verso to 490 recto, then folio 492 recto; Ed. 98c, folios 581 and 659bis), are all the etchings from the Louvre album commissioned by Mariette (except for those on folios 47 and 48), each accompanied by a counterproof. They were cut out along the outline of the plate mark and glued onto the pages. There are even etchings of certain drawings (RF 28780, RF 28781, RF 28782) that were not included in the Mariette album. The proofs bear the number to assigned to the etching, annotated in pen and brown ink in the upper corner, sometimes on the left, sometimes on the right. This number does not always correspond to the Caylus number. The proofs are numbered up to 63. Annotations by the etcher, in pen and brown and ink, are placed on a few sheets as an aide-mémoire. These will be indicated in the pertinent entries.

FLYLEAF

Inscribed in pen and brown ink on verso at upper left: *N°. 134* and paraph. This annotation, without the paraph, is identical to the one on folio 1 in the Mariette album. It may be a lot number from a sale in which the two volumes were to be auctioned off together. Inscribed in pencil: *gravé par le Comte de Caylus. / Armes de Crozat, baron de Thiers* (engraved by the count of Caylus. / Coat of arms of Crozat, baron of Thiers)

TITLE PAGE

Etched from the first drawing (RF 28725) in the Mariette album (*Hercules Felling the Hydra of Lerna*), mixed media, etching and xylography for the bister wash color, 225 × 156 mm (8⅞ × 6⅛ in.); framing lines inside the plate mark
Inside the cartouche: *Recueil / de Testes de caractere / & de Charges / dessinés / Par Leonard de Vinci Florentin. / & gravées par M. le C. de C. / MDCCXXX.* (Album / of heads / and caricatures / drawn by Leonardo da Vinci Florentine / and engraved by M. the C. of C. / 1730.)
Inside the framing line, left: *Aug. Carache del.*; right: *C. sculp.*
Outside the framing line, center: *A Paris chez J. Mariette rue Sᵗ. Jaques aux Colonnes d'Hercules* (In Paris J. Mariette on rue Saint Jacques at the Columns of Hercules)

A proof and its counterproof are in the Bibliothèque Nationale de France, Richelieu location (Ed. 98b, vol. 1, fol. 481 verso and 482 recto), without the application of color by xylography. The proof bears an annotation at the bottom in pen and brown ink: *frontispice des tetes de Leonard de Mʳ Mariette* (frontispiece of Leonardo's heads by Mr. Mariette). On folio 492 recto there is another proof with the application of color.

Folios 2 recto to 12 verso (numbered 1 to 22): *Lettre / sur / Léonard de Vinci / peintre florentin / A Monsieur le C. de C.* (Letter / concerning / Leonardo da Vinci / Florentine Painter / to

Monsieur the C. of C.); fol. 13 recto and verso (no pagination): *Catalogue des Pieces qui ont este' grave'es / d'après les Tableaux, ou Desseins de Leonard de Vinci* (Catalogue of pieces that were engraved / after the paintings or drawings of Leonardo da Vinci)

Sixty-six etchings on thirty-eight folios follow:

Folio 14 recto: Caylus nos. 1 and 2 etched from RF 28726 and RF 28727. Circular, side by side, inside two double concentric circles.

Number 1
Plate mark: 98 × 100 mm (3 7/8 × 3 15/16 in.)
Image: 94 mm (3 3/4 in.)
C for Caylus
Bibliothèque Nationale de France, Richelieu location
(Ed. 98b, vol. 1, folio 481 verso)
Proof with page number 1, and counterproof

Number 2
Plate mark: 102 × 104 mm (4 × 4 1/8 in.)
Image: 93 mm (3 11/16 in.)
C for Caylus
Bibliothèque Nationale de France, Richelieu location (Ed. 98b, vol. 1, folio 481 verso). Folio 489 recto, two proofs and two counterproofs with the annotation: effacé (worn away)
Proof with number 2, and counterproof

Folio 15 recto: Caylus nos. 3 and 4 etched from RF 28728 and RF 28729. Circular, side by side, inside two double concentric circles.

Number 3
Plate mark: 98 × 100 mm (3 7/8 × 3 15/16 in.)
Image: 93 mm (3 11/16 in.)
C for Caylus
Bibliothèque Nationale de France, Richelieu location
(Ed. 98b, vol. 1, folio 482 recto)
Proof with number 3, and counterproof

Number 4
Plate mark: 96 × 100 mm (3 11/16 × 3 15/16 in.)
Image: 93 mm (3 11/16 in.)
C for Caylus

Bibliothèque Nationale de France, Richelieu location
(Ed. 98b, vol. 1, folio 482 recto)
Proof with number 4, and counterproof

Folio 16 recto: Caylus nos. 5 and 6 etched from RF 28730 and RF 28731. Circular, side by side, inside two double concentric circles.

Number 5
Plate mark: 100 × 99 mm (3 15/16 × 3 7/8 in.)
Image: 94 mm (3 3/4 in.)
C for Caylus
Bibliothèque Nationale de France, Richelieu location
(Ed. 98b, vol. 1, folio 482 verso)
Proof with number 5, and counterproof

Number 6
Plate mark: 98 × 100 mm (3 7/8 × 3 15/16 in.)
Image: 93 mm (3 11/16 in.)
C for Caylus
Bibliothèque Nationale de France, Richelieu location
(Ed. 98b, vol. 1, folio 482 verso)
Proof with number 6, and counterproof

Folio 17 recto: Caylus nos. 7 and 8 etched from RF 28732 and RF 28733. Circular, side by side, inside two double concentric circles.

Number 7
Plate mark: 98 × 102 mm (3 7/8 × 4 in.)
Image: 93 mm (3 11/16 in.)
C for Caylus
Bibliothèque Nationale de France, Richelieu location
(Ed. 98b, vol. 1, folio 482 verso)
Proof with number 7, and counterproof

Number 8
Plate mark: 97 × 100 mm (3 7/8 × 3 15/16 in.)
Image: 94 mm (3 3/4 in.)
C for Caylus
Bibliothèque Nationale de France, Richelieu location
(Ed. 98b, vol. 1, folio 482 verso)
Proof with number 8, and counterproof

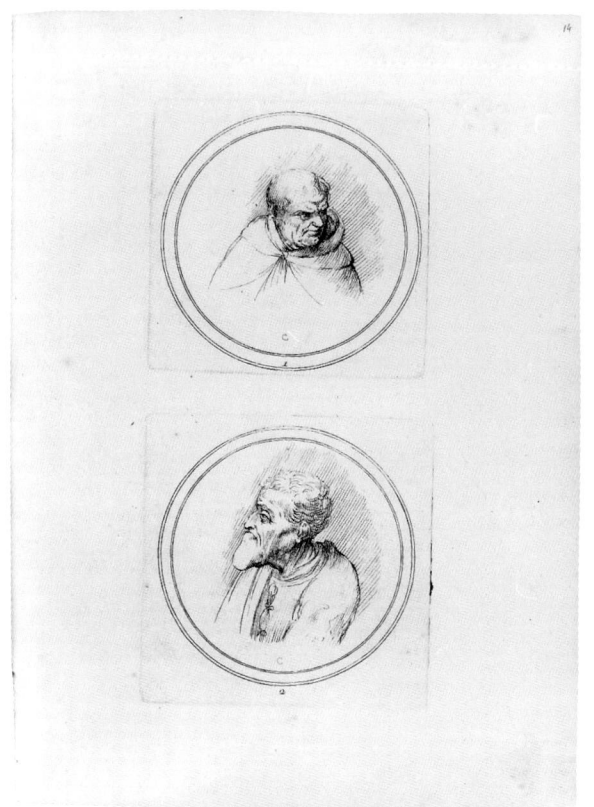

Fol. 14r (nos. 1, 2)

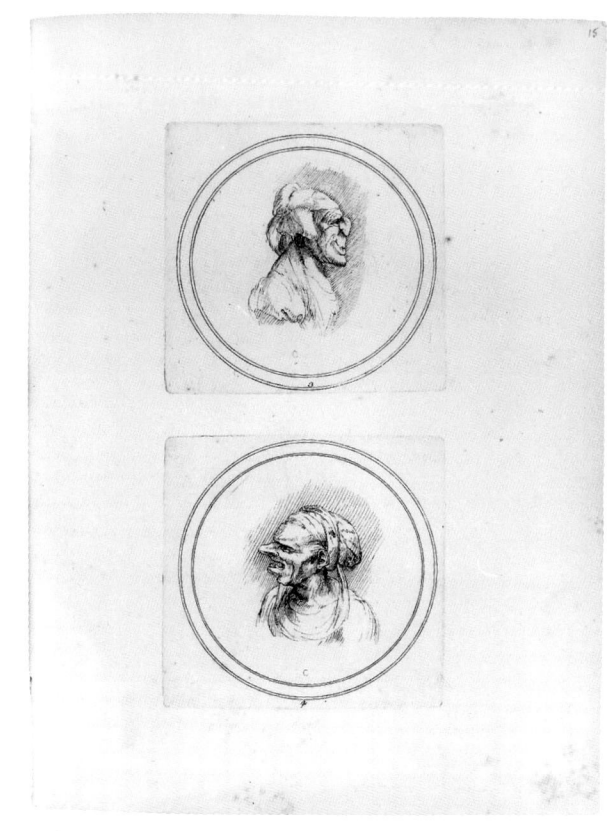

Fol. 15r (nos. 3, 4)

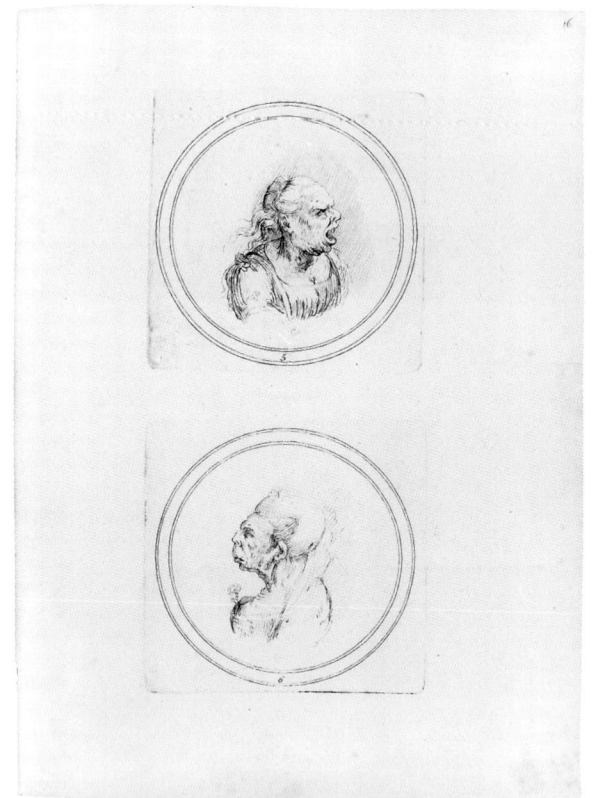

Fol. 16r (nos. 5, 6)

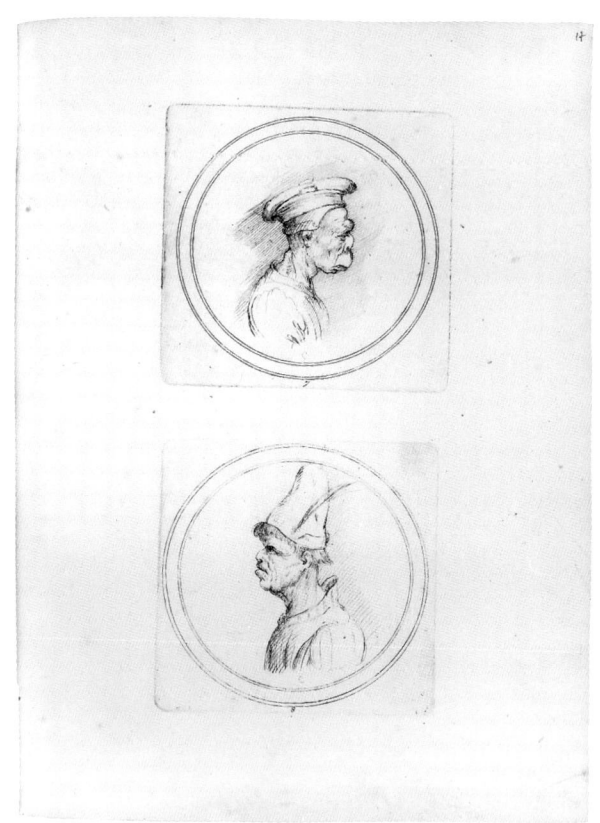

Fol. 17r (nos. 7, 8)

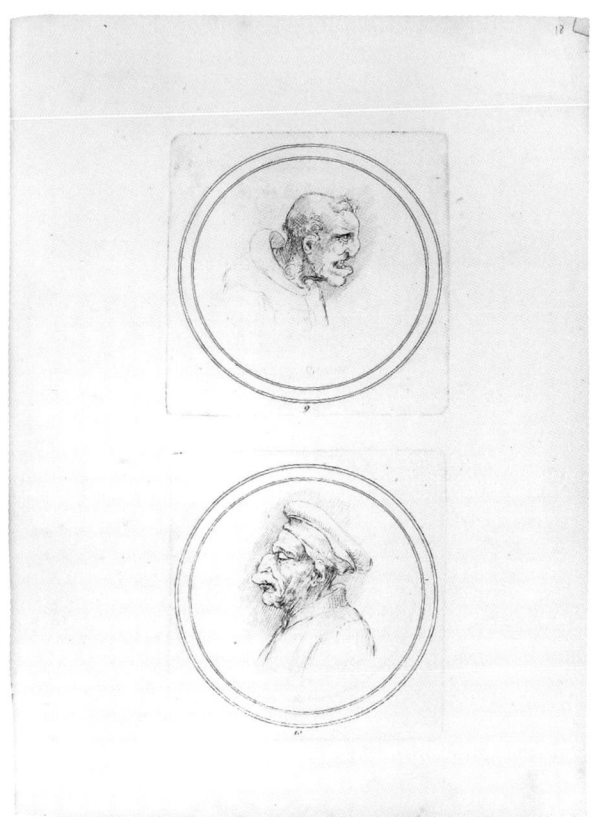

Fol. 18r (nos. 9, 10)

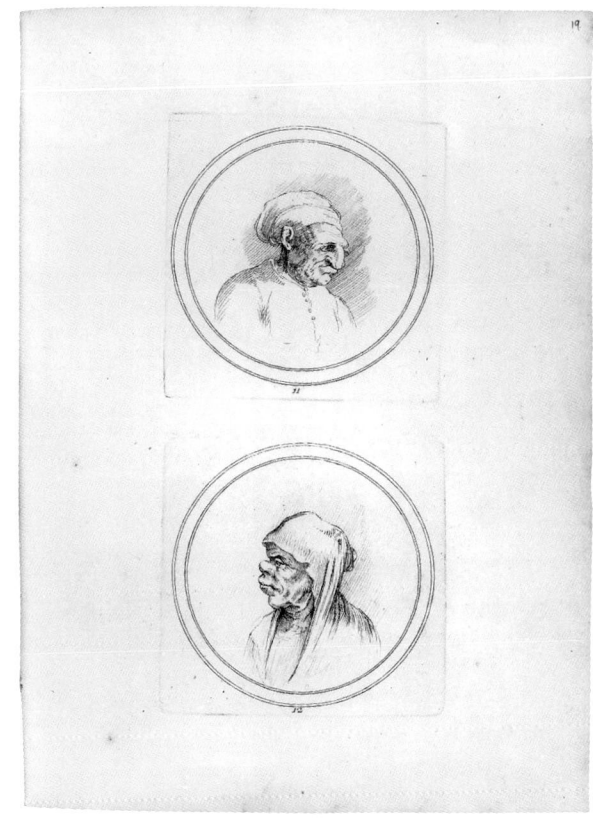

Fol. 19r (nos. 11, 12)

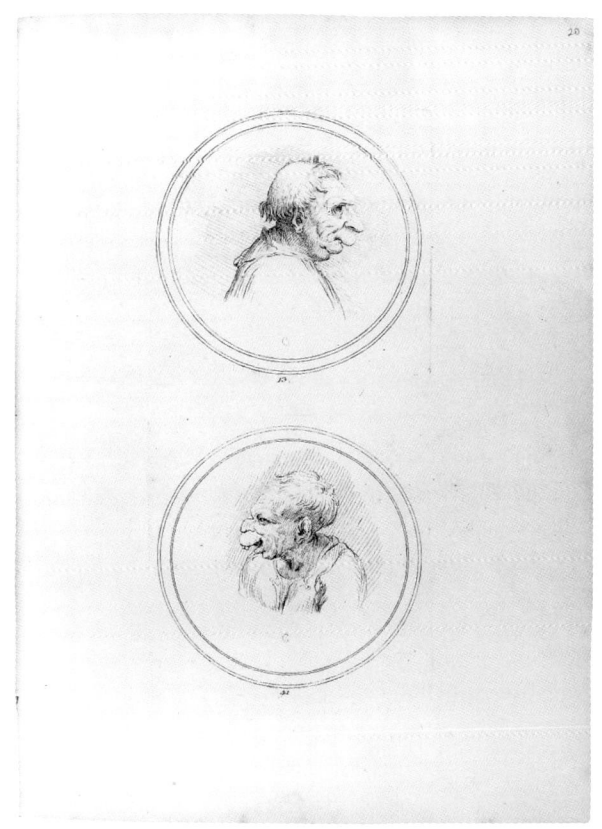

Fol. 20r (nos. 13, 14)

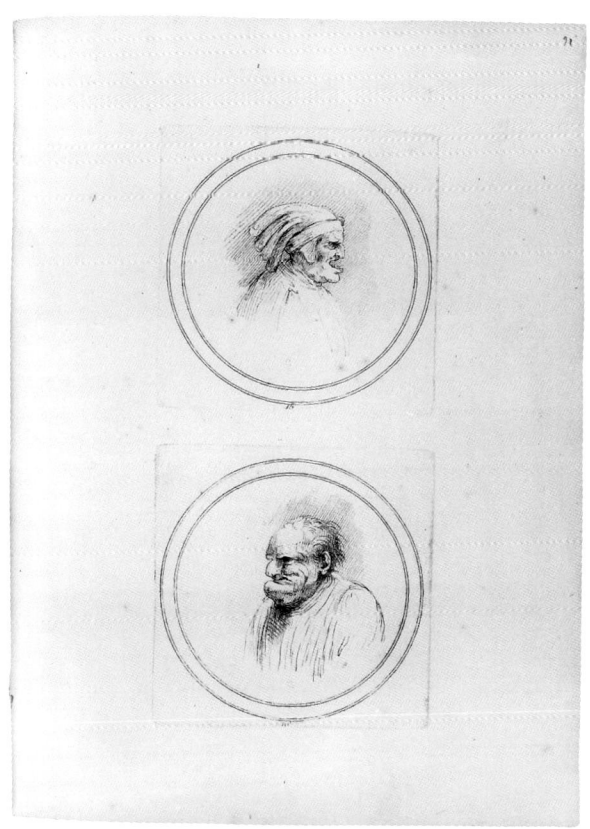

Fol. 21r (nos. 15, 16)

707

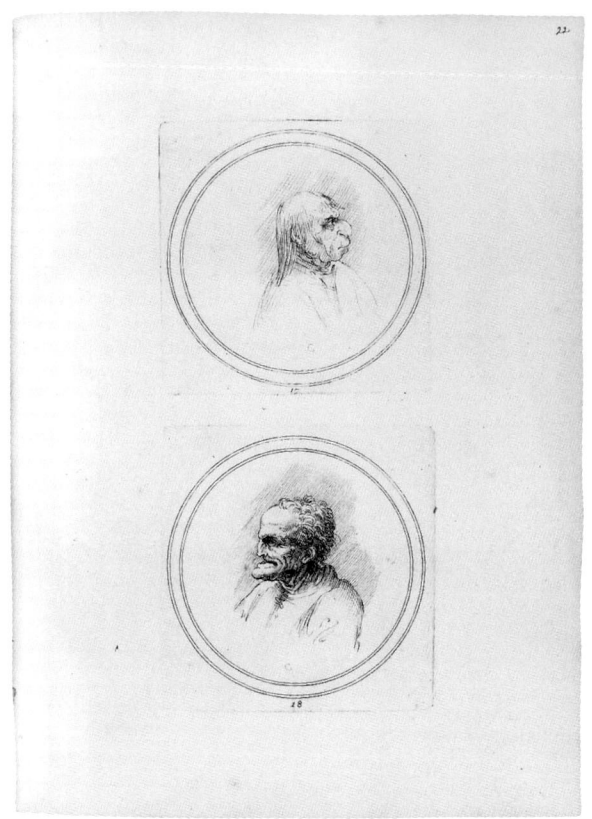

Fol. 22r (nos. 17, 18)

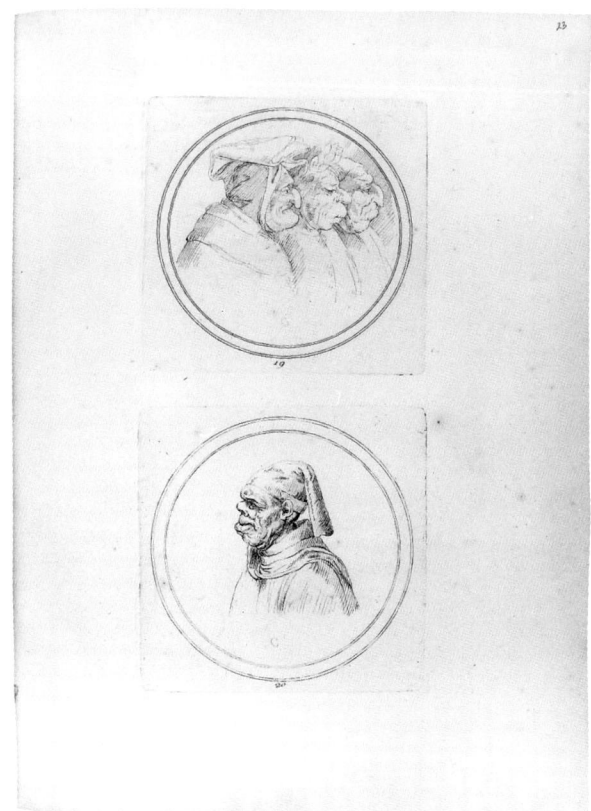

Fol. 23r (nos. 19, 20)

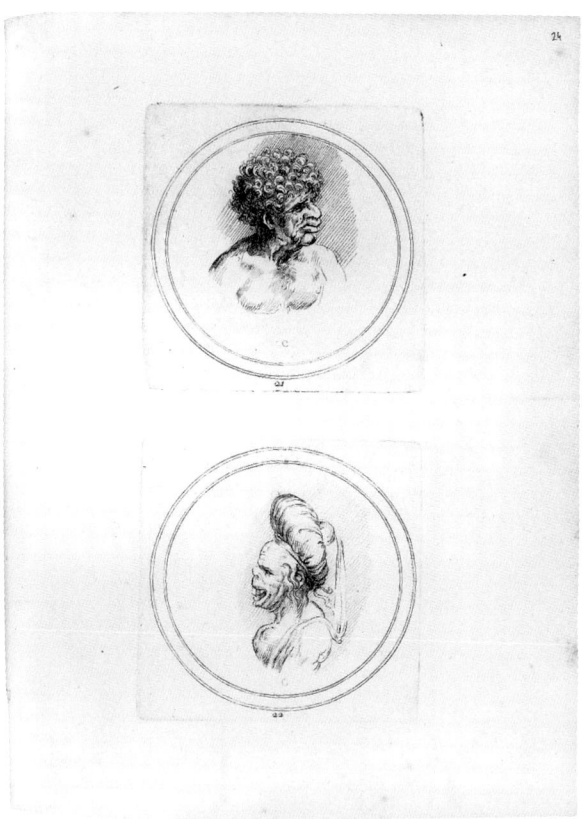

Fol. 24r (nos. 21, 22)

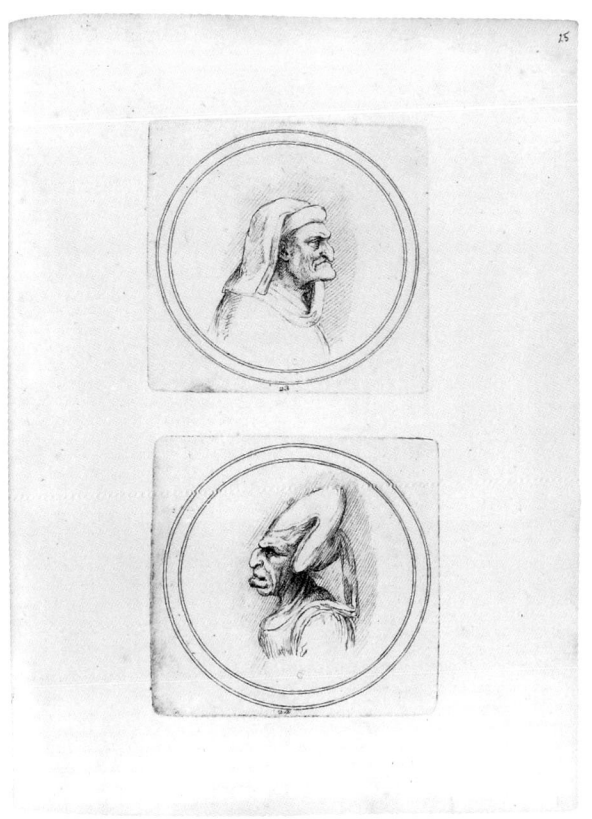

Fol. 25r (nos. 23, 24)

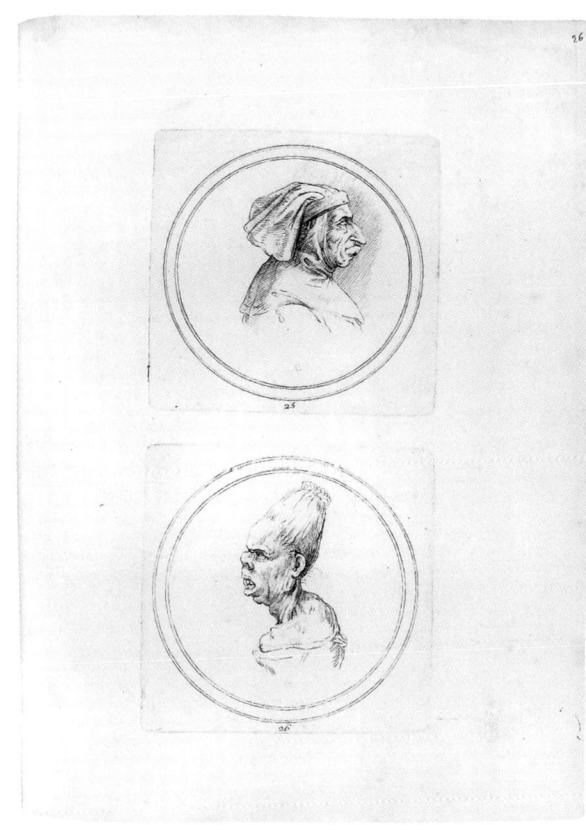

Fol. 26r (nos. 25, 26)

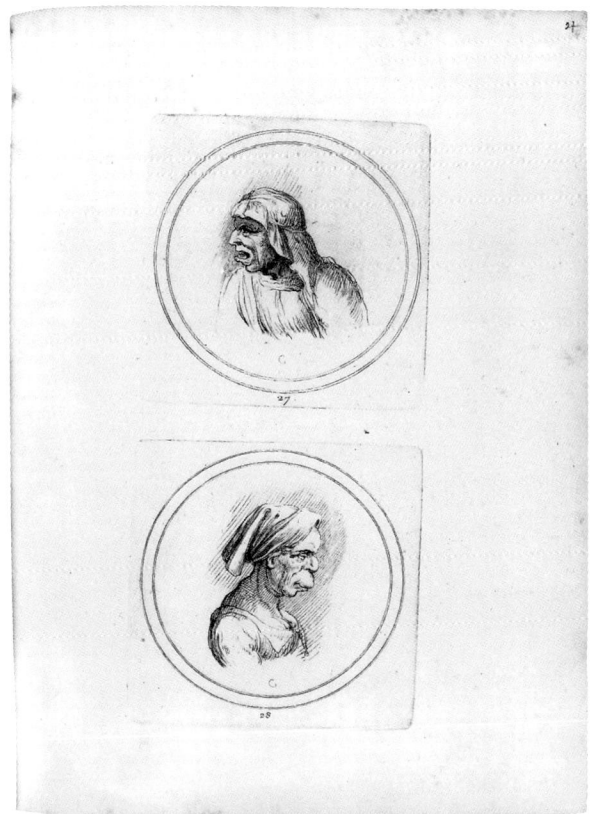

Fol. 27r (nos. 27, 28)

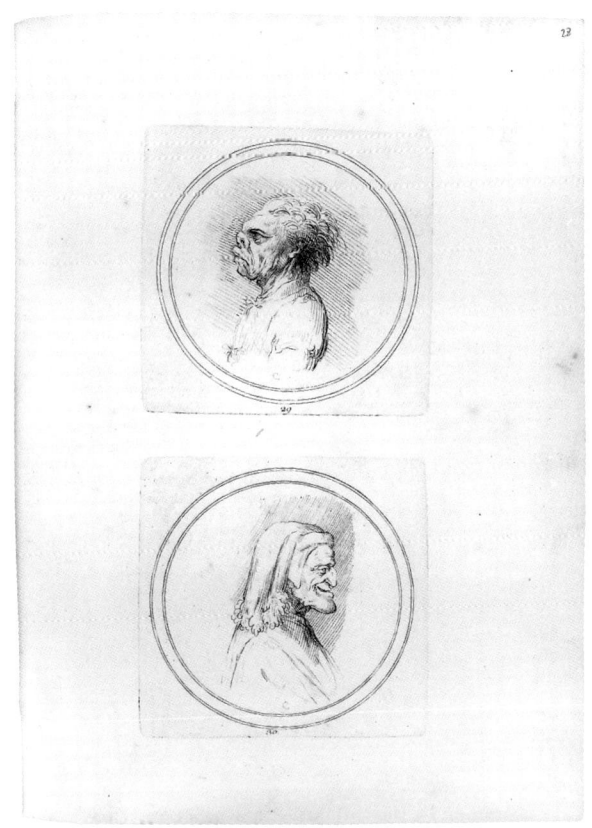

Fol. 28r (nos. 29, 30)

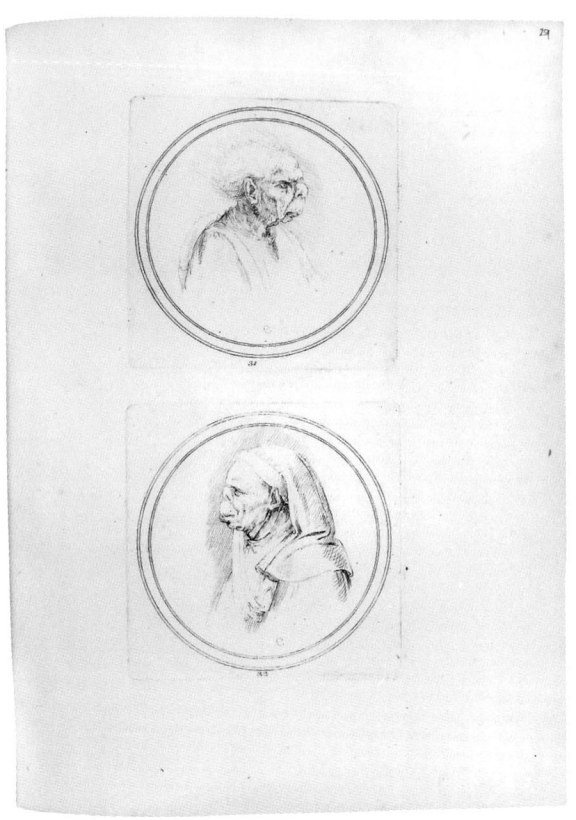

Fol. 29R (nos. 31, 32)

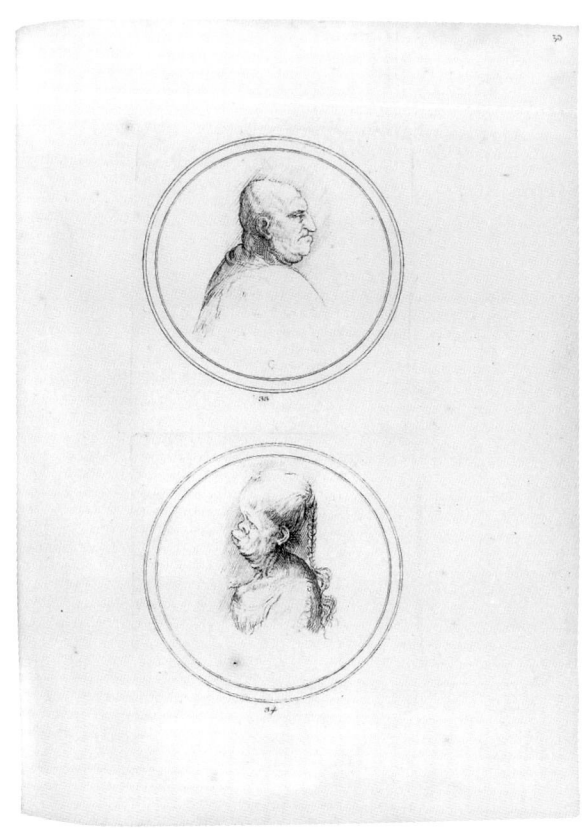

Fol. 30R (nos. 33, 34)

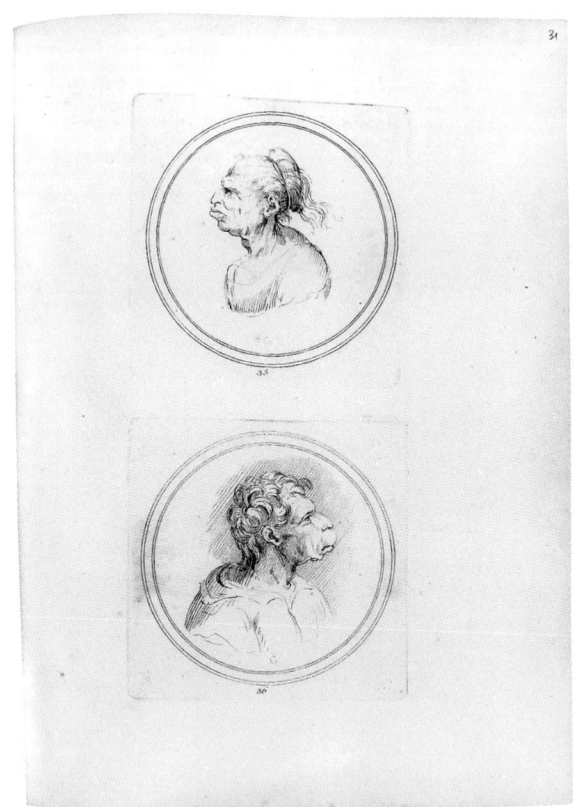

Fol. 31R (nos. 35, 36)

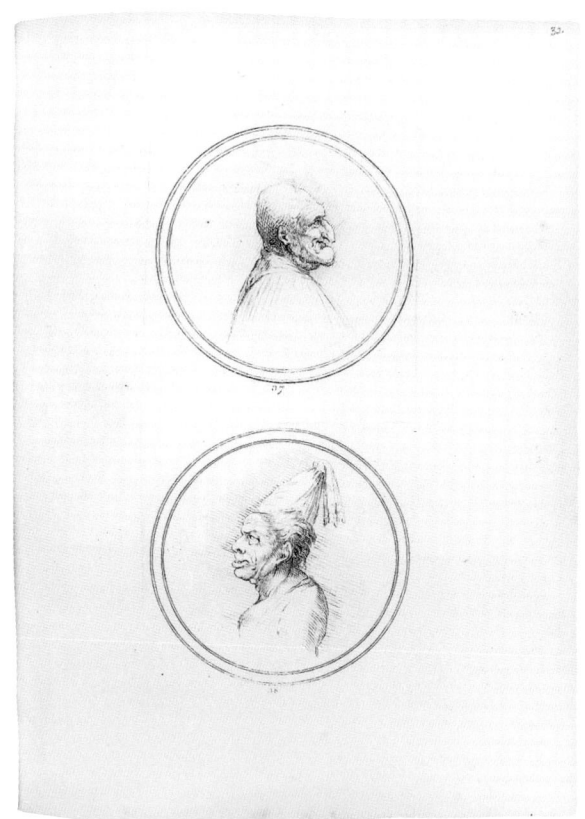

Fol. 32R (nos. 37, 38)

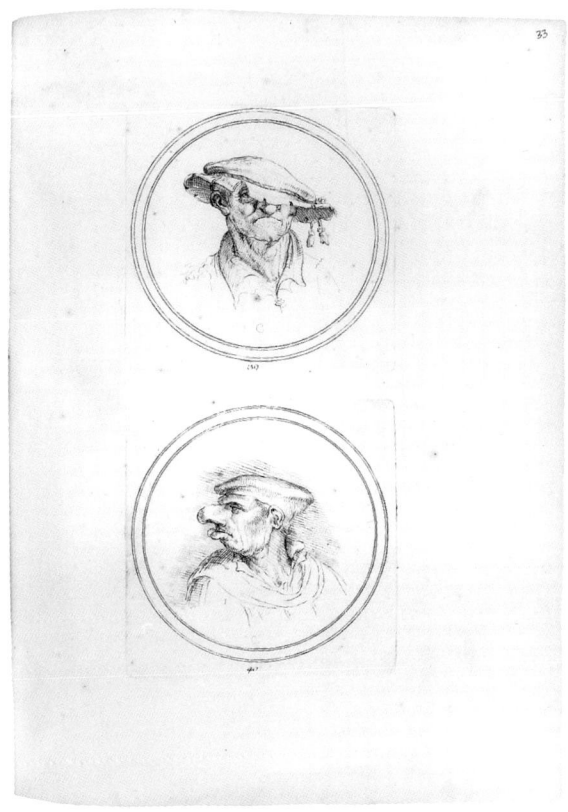

Fol. 33R (nos. 39, 40)

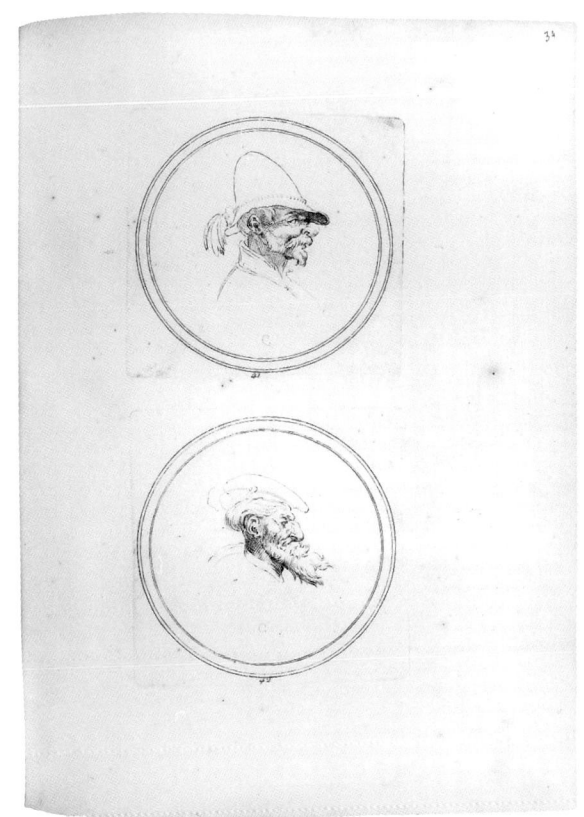

Fol. 34R (nos. 41, 42)

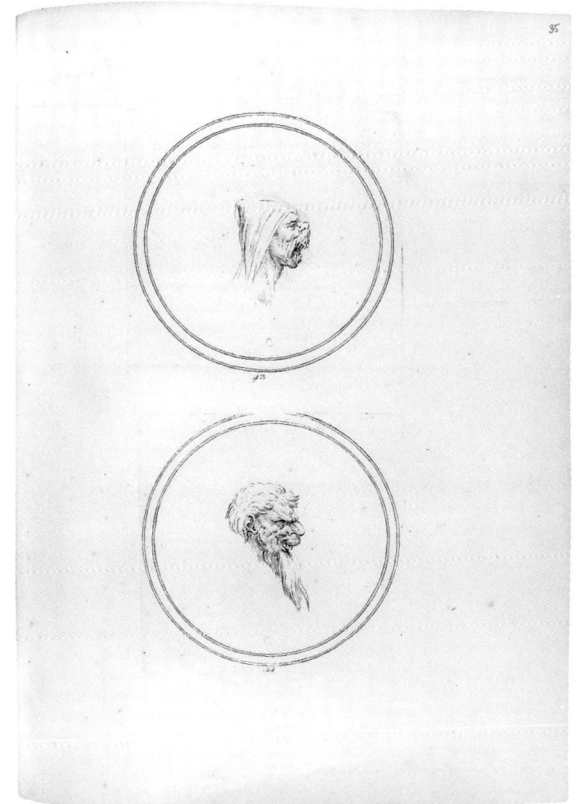

Fol. 35R (nos. 43, 44)

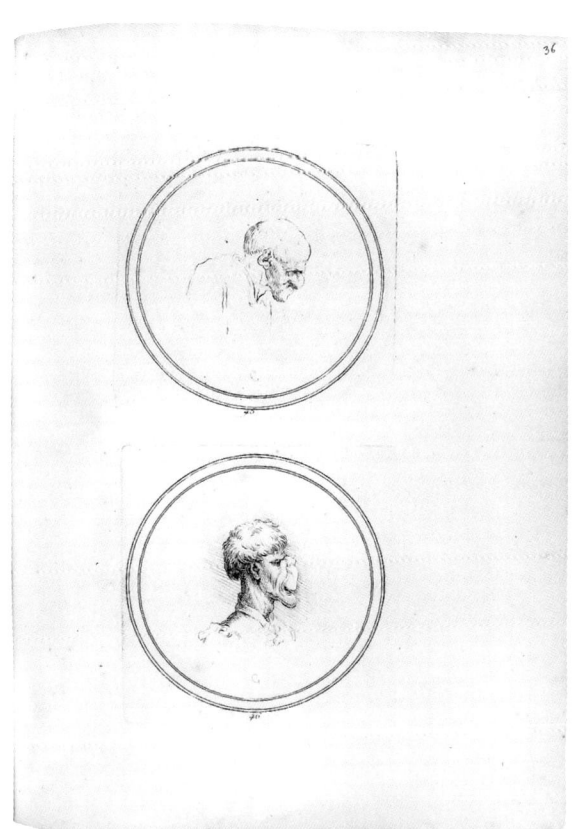

Fol. 36R (nos. 45, 46)

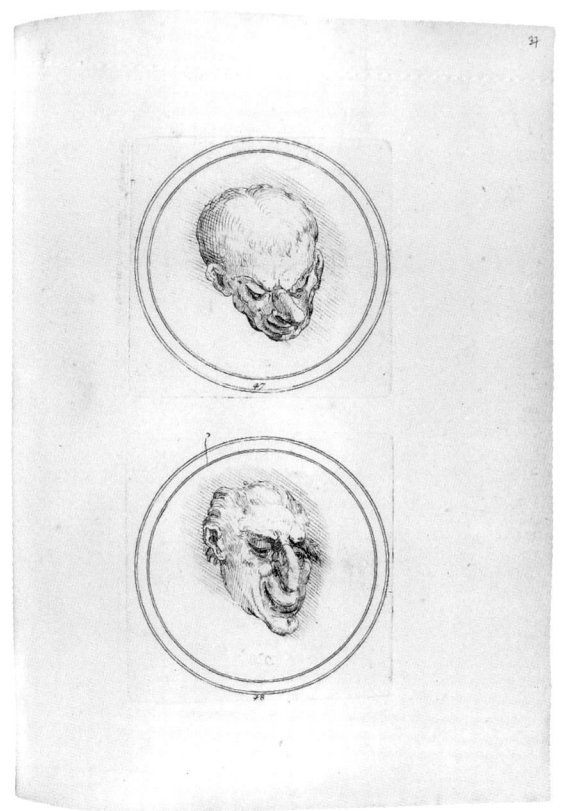

Fol. 37r (nos. 47, 48)

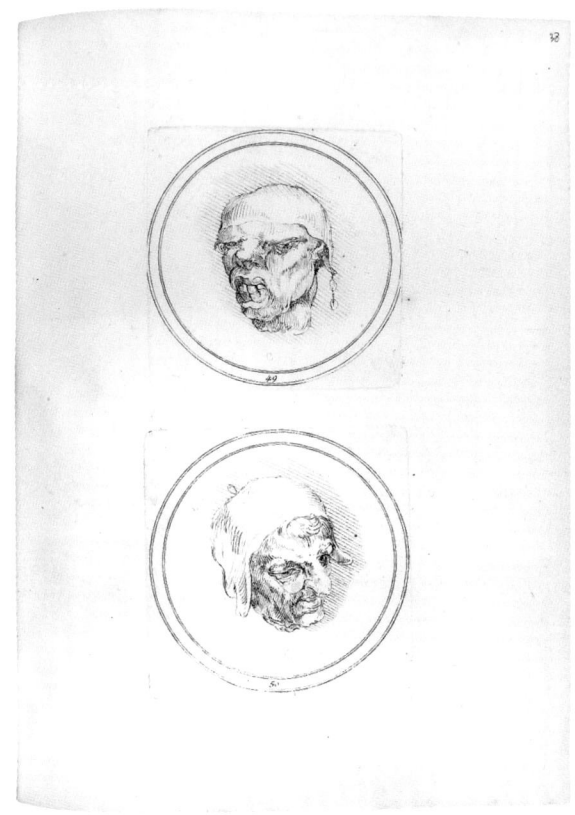

Fol. 38r (nos. 49, 50)

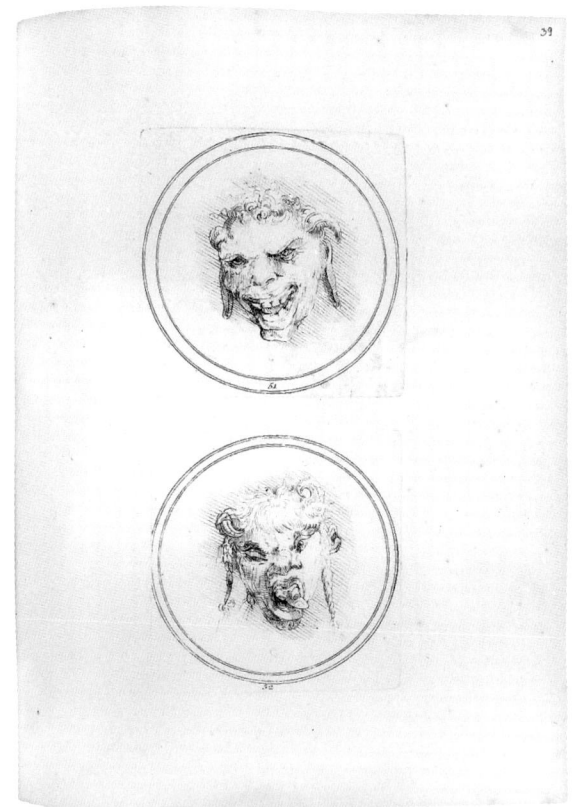

Fol. 39r (nos. 51, 52)

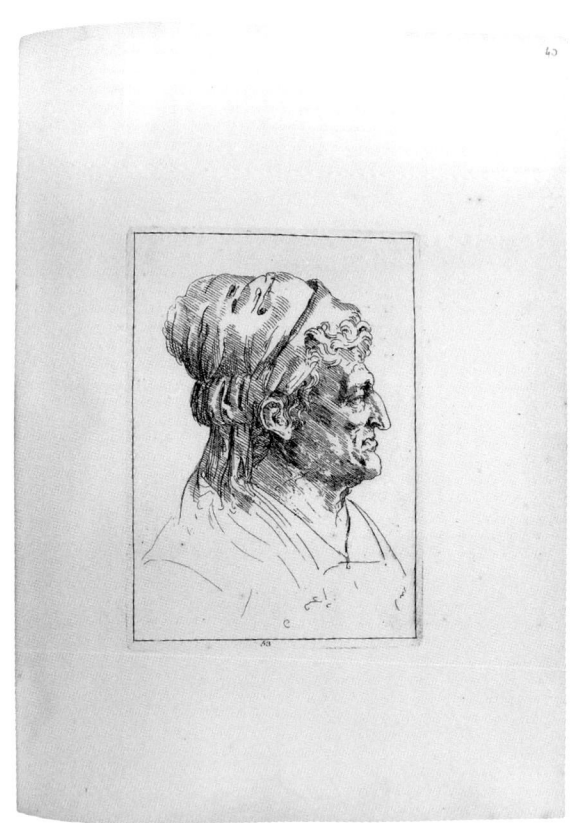

Fol. 40r (no. 53)

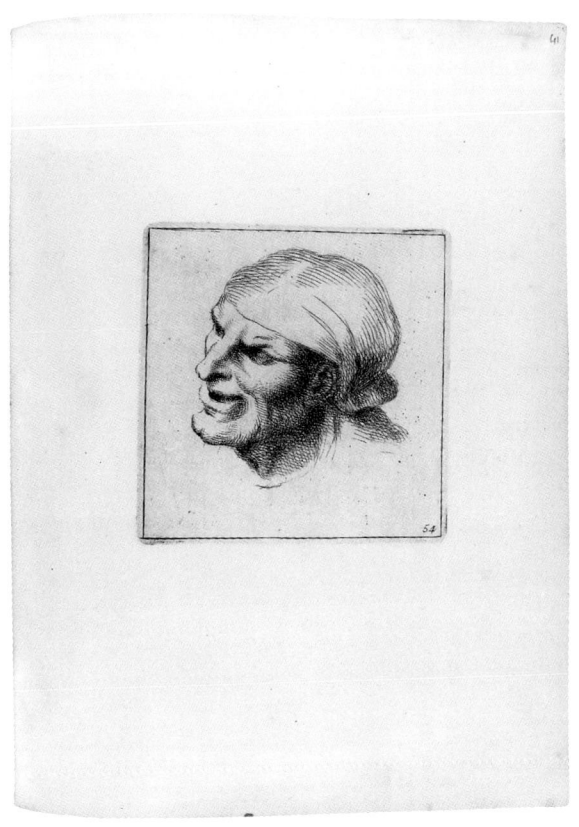

Fol. 41R (no. 54)

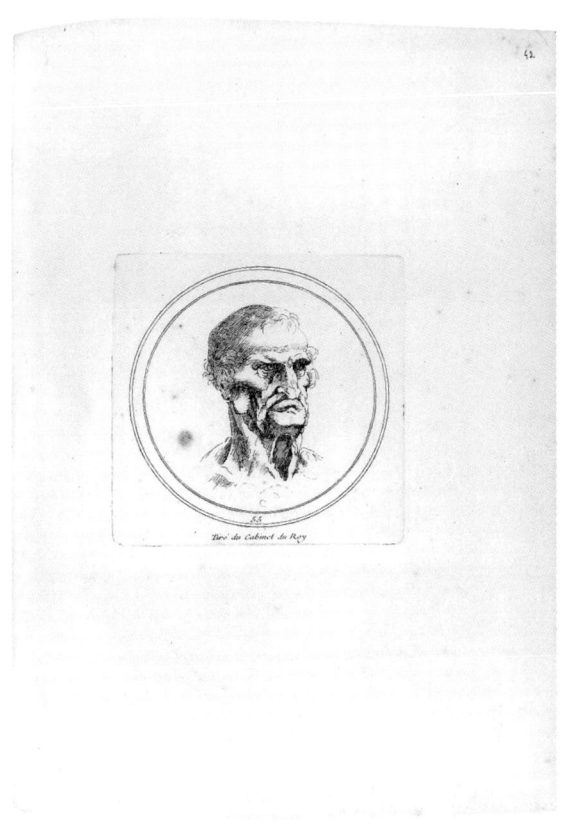

Fol. 42R (no. 55)

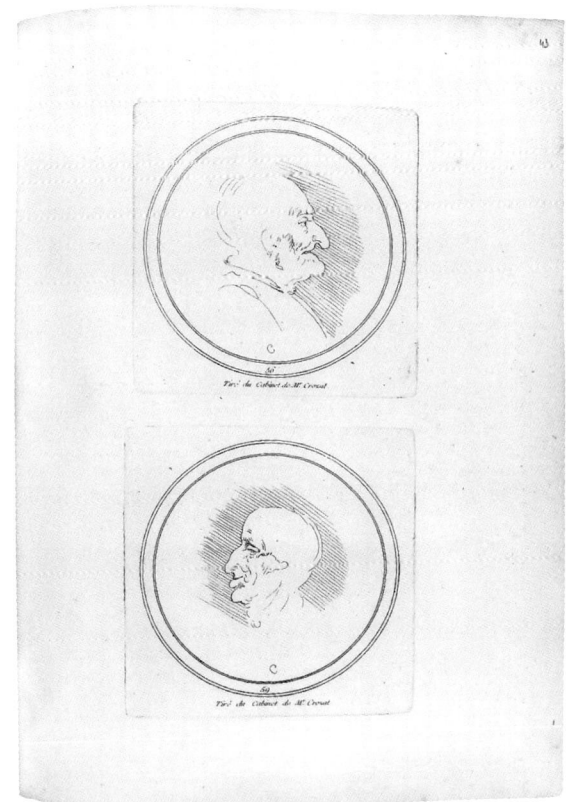

Fol. 43R (nos. 56, 59)

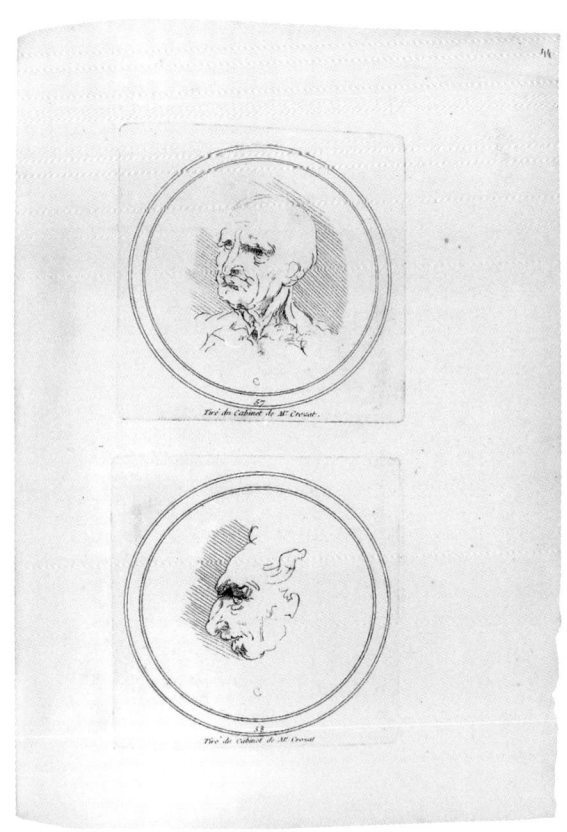

Fol. 44R (nos. 57, 58)

713

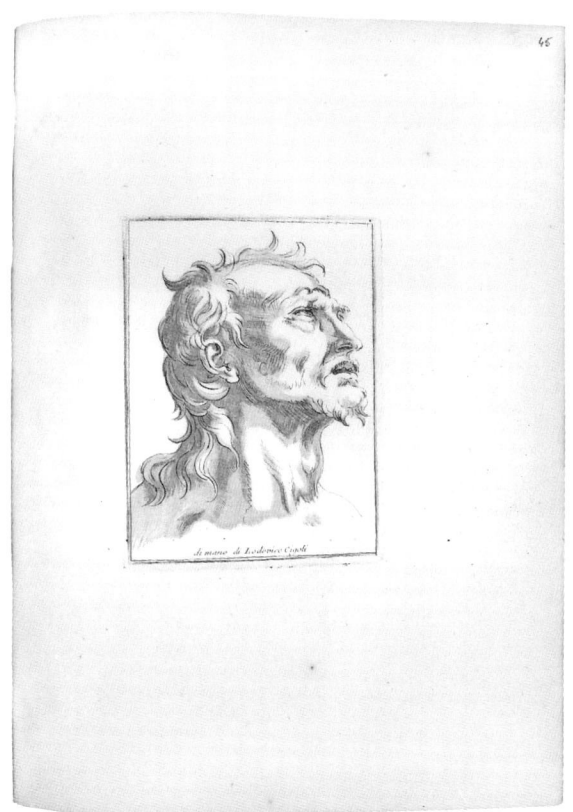

Fol. 45ʀ (no number)

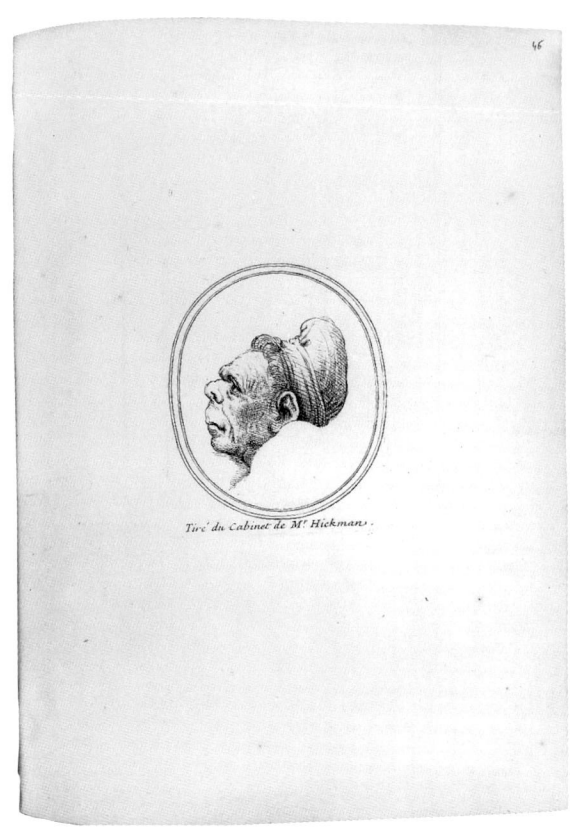

Fol. 46ʀ (no number)

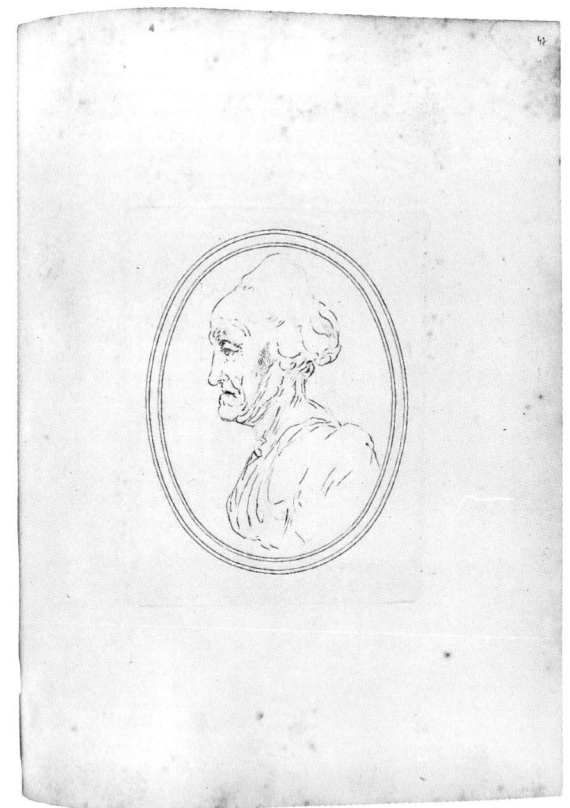

Fol. 47ʀ (no number)

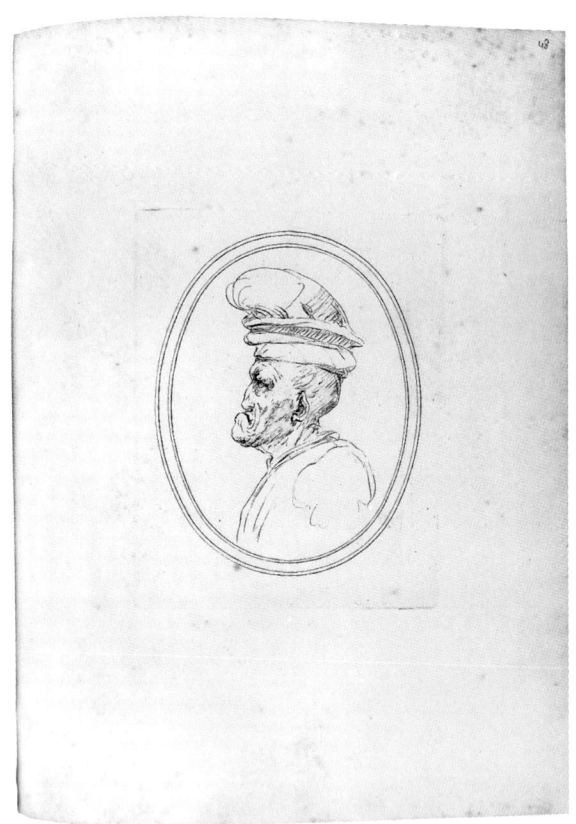

Fol. 48ʀ (no number)

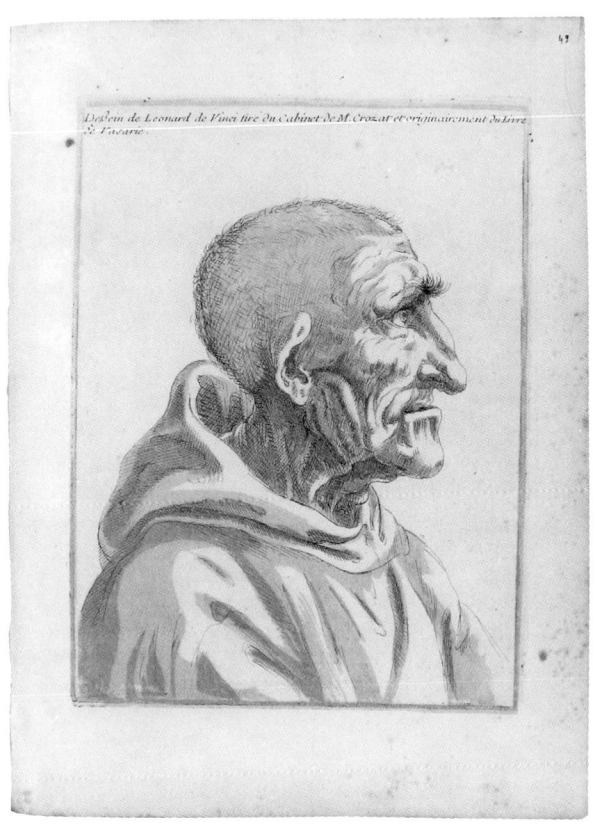

Fol. 49R (no number)

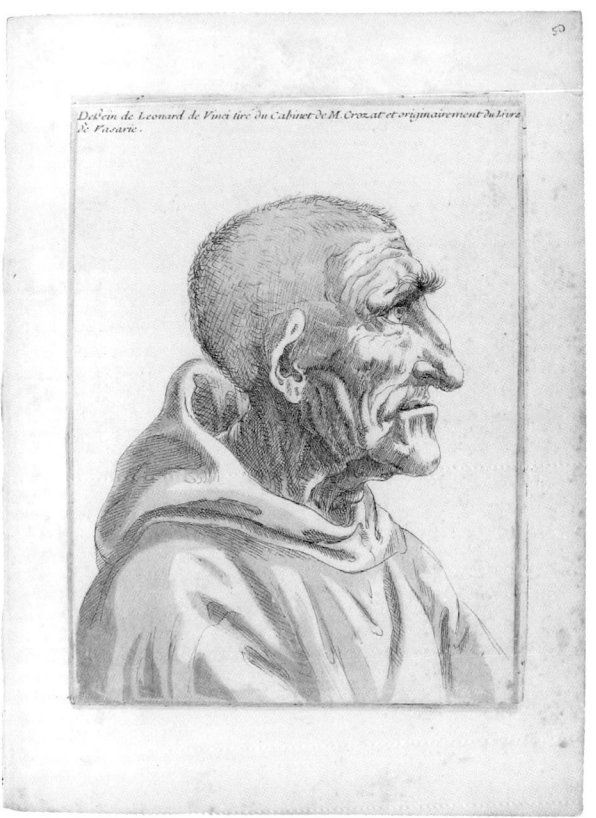

Fol. 50R (no number)

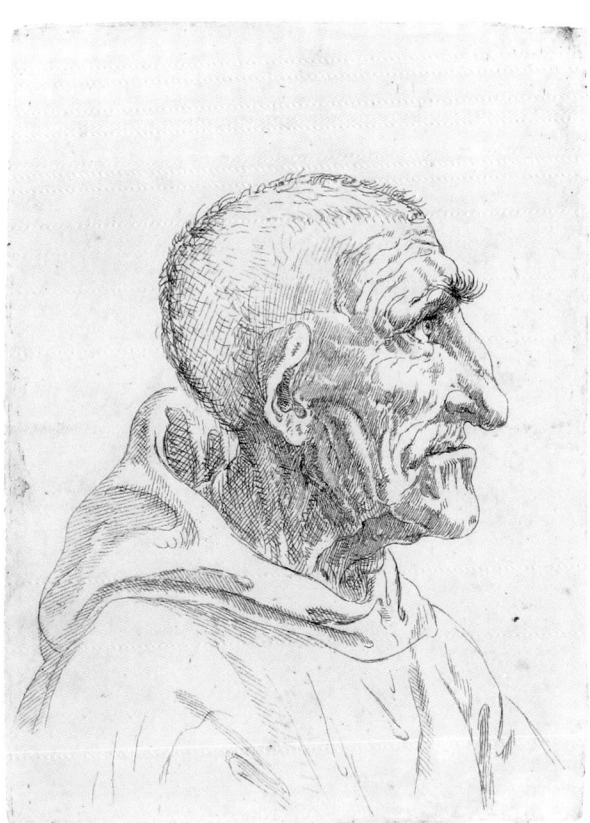

Fol. 51R (no number)

715

Folio 18 recto: Caylus nos. 9 and 10 etched from RF 28734 and RF 28735. Circular, side by side, inside two double concentric circles.

NUMBER 9
Plate mark: 100 × 100 mm (3 $\frac{15}{16}$ × 3 $\frac{15}{16}$ in.)
Image: 93 mm (3 $\frac{11}{16}$ in.)
C for Caylus
Bibliothèque Nationale de France, Richelieu location
(Ed. 98b, vol. 1, folio 483 recto)
Proof with number 9, and counterproof

NUMBER 10
Plate mark: 100 × 97 mm (3 $\frac{15}{16}$ × 3 $\frac{7}{8}$ in.)
Image: 93 mm (3 $\frac{11}{16}$ in.)
C for Caylus
Bibliothèque Nationale de France, Richelieu location
(Ed. 98b, vol. 1, folio 483 recto)
Proof with number 10, and counterproof

Folio 19 recto: Caylus nos. 11 and 12, etched from RF 28736 and RF 28737. Circular, side by side, inside two double concentric circles.

NUMBER 11
Plate mark: 101 × 98 mm (4 × 3 $\frac{7}{8}$ in.)
Image: 93 mm (3 $\frac{11}{16}$ in.)
C for Caylus
Bibliothèque Nationale de France, Richelieu location
(Ed. 98b, vol. 1, folio 483 recto)
Proof with number 11, and counterproof

NUMBER 12
Plate mark: 97 × 101 mm (3 $\frac{7}{8}$ × 4 in.)
Image: 100 mm (3 $\frac{15}{16}$ in.)
C for Caylus
Bibliothèque Nationale de France, Richelieu location
(Ed. 98b, vol. 1, folio 483 recto)
Proof with number 12, and counterproof

Folio 20 recto: Caylus nos. 13 and 14, etched from RF 28738 and RF 28739. Circular, side by side, inside two double concentric circles.

NUMBER 13
Plate mark: 97 × 98 mm (3 $\frac{7}{8}$ × 3 $\frac{7}{8}$ in.)
Image: 93 mm (3 $\frac{11}{16}$ in.)
C for Caylus
Bibliothèque Nationale de France, Richelieu location
(Ed. 98b, vol. 1, folio 483 verso)
Proof with number 13, and counterproof

NUMBER 14 (IDENTIFIED AS 41)
Plate mark: 100 × 98 mm (3 $\frac{15}{16}$ × 3 $\frac{7}{8}$ in.)
Image: 93 mm (3 $\frac{11}{16}$ in.)
C for Caylus
Bibliothèque Nationale de France, Richelieu location
(Ed. 98b, vol. 1, folio 483 verso)
Proof with number 14, and counterproof

Folio 21 recto: Caylus nos. 15 and 16, etched from RF 28740 and RF 28741. Circular, side by side, inside two double concentric circles.

NUMBER 15
Plate mark: 100 × 98 mm (3 $\frac{15}{16}$ × 3 $\frac{7}{8}$ in.)
Image: 93 mm (3 $\frac{11}{16}$ in.)
C for Caylus
Bibliothèque Nationale de France, Richelieu location
(Ed. 98b, vol. 1, folio 483 verso)
Proof with number 15, and counterproof

NUMBER 16
Plate mark: 100 × 98 mm (3 $\frac{15}{16}$ × 3 $\frac{7}{8}$ in.)
Image: 93 mm (3 $\frac{11}{16}$ in.)
C for Caylus
Bibliothèque Nationale de France, Richelieu location
(Ed. 98b, vol. 1, folio 483 verso)
Proof with number 16, and counterproof

Folio 22 recto: Caylus nos. 17 and 18, etched from RF 28742 and RF 28743. Circular, side by side, inside two double concentric circles.

NUMBER 17
Plate mark: 97 × 97 mm (3 $\frac{7}{8}$ × 3 $\frac{7}{8}$ in.)
Image: 93 mm (3 $\frac{11}{16}$ in.)
C for Caylus
Bibliothèque Nationale de France, Richelieu location

(Ed. 98b, vol. 1, folio 484 recto)
Proof with number 17, and counterproof

NUMBER 18
Plate mark: 99 × 98 mm ($3\,^{15}/_{16}$ × $3\,^{7}/_{8}$ in.)
Image: 93 mm ($3\,^{11}/_{16}$ in.)
C for Caylus
Bibliothèque Nationale de France, Richelieu location
(Ed. 98b, vol. 1, folio 484 recto)
Proof with number 18, and counterproof

Folio 23 recto: Caylus nos. 19 and 20, etched from RF 28744 and RF 28745. Circular, side by side, inside two double concentric circles.

NUMBER 19
Plate mark: 97 × 100 mm ($3\,^{7}/_{8}$ × $3\,^{15}/_{16}$ in.)
Image: 91 mm ($3\,^{5}/_{8}$ in.)
C for Caylus
Bibliothèque Nationale de France, Richelieu location
(Ed. 98b, vol. 1, folio 484 recto)
Proof with number 19, and counterproof

NUMBER 20
Plate mark: 99 × 100 mm ($3\,^{7}/_{8}$ × $3\,^{15}/_{16}$ in.)
Image: 93 mm ($3\,^{11}/_{16}$ in.)
C for Caylus
Bibliothèque Nationale de France, Richelieu location
(Ed. 98b, vol. 1, folio 484 recto)
Proof with number 20, and counterproof

Folio 24 recto: Caylus nos. 21 and 22, etched from RF 28746 and RF 28747. Circular, side by side, inside two double concentric circles.

NUMBER 21
Plate mark: 100 × 100 mm ($3\,^{15}/_{16}$ × $3\,^{15}/_{16}$ in.)
Image: 92 mm ($3\,^{5}/_{8}$ in.)
C for Caylus
Bibliothèque Nationale de France, Richelieu location
(Ed. 98b, vol. 1, folio 484 verso)
Proof with number 21, and counterproof

NUMBER 22
Plate mark: 100 × 98 mm ($3\,^{15}/_{16}$ × $3\,^{7}/_{8}$ in.)
Image: 93 mm ($3\,^{11}/_{16}$ in.)

C for Caylus
Bibliothèque Nationale de France, Richelieu location
(Ed. 98b, vol. 1, folio 484 verso)
Proof with number 22, and counterproof

Folio 25 recto: Caylus nos. 23 and 24, etched from RF 28748 and RF 28749. Circular, side by side, inside two double concentric circles.

NUMBER 23
Plate mark: 98 × 99 mm ($3\,^{7}/_{8}$ × $3\,^{7}/_{8}$ in.)
Image: 93 mm ($3\,^{11}/_{16}$ in.)
C for Caylus
Bibliothèque Nationale de France, Richelieu location
(Ed. 98b, vol. 1, folio 484 verso)
Proof with number 23, and counterproof

NUMBER 24
Plate mark: 99 × 100 mm ($3\,^{7}/_{8}$ × $3\,^{15}/_{16}$ in.)
Image: 94 mm ($3\,^{3}/_{4}$ in.)
C for Caylus
Bibliothèque Nationale de France, Richelieu location
(Ed. 98b, vol. 1, folio 484 verso)
Proof with number 24, and counterproof

Folio 26 recto: Caylus nos. 25 and 26, etched from RF 28750 and RF 28751. Circular, side by side, inside two double concentric circles.

NUMBER 25
Plate mark: 100 × 100 mm ($3\,^{15}/_{16}$ × $3\,^{15}/_{16}$ in.)
Image: 91 mm ($3\,^{5}/_{8}$ in.)
C for Caylus
Bibliothèque Nationale de France, Richelieu location
(Ed. 98b, vol. 1, folio 485 recto)
Proof with number 25, and counterproof

NUMBER 26
Plate mark: 100 × 102 mm ($3\,^{15}/_{16}$ × 4 in.)
Image: 93 mm ($3\,^{11}/_{16}$ in.)
C for Caylus
Bibliothèque Nationale de France, Richelieu location
(Ed. 98b, vol. 1, folio 485 recto)
Proof with number 26, and counterproof

Folio 27 recto: Caylus nos. 27 and 28, etched from RF 28752 and RF 28753. Circular, side by side, inside two double concentric circles.

NUMBER 27
Plate mark: 100 × 100 mm (3 $\frac{15}{16}$ × 3 $\frac{15}{16}$ in.)
Image: 93 mm (3 $\frac{11}{16}$ in.)
C for Caylus
Bibliothèque Nationale de France, Richelieu location
(Ed. 98b, vol. 1, folio 485 recto)
Proof with number 27, and counterproof

NUMBER 28
Plate mark: 100 × 100 mm (3 $\frac{15}{16}$ × 3 $\frac{15}{16}$ in.)
Image: 92 mm (3 $\frac{5}{8}$ in.)
C for Caylus
Bibliothèque Nationale de France, Richelieu location
(Ed. 98b, vol. 1, folio 485 recto)
Proof with number 28, and counterproof

Folio 28 recto: Caylus nos. 29 and 30, etched from RF 28754 and RF 28755. Circular, side by side, inside two double concentric circles.

NUMBER 29
Plate mark: 100 × 100 mm (3 $\frac{15}{16}$ × 3 $\frac{15}{16}$ in.)
Image: 92 mm (3 $\frac{5}{8}$ in.)
C for Caylus
Bibliothèque Nationale de France, Richelieu location
(Ed. 98b, vol. 1, folio 485 verso)
Proof with number 29, and counterproof

NUMBER 30
Plate mark: 100 × 100 mm (3 $\frac{15}{16}$ × 3 $\frac{15}{16}$ in.)
Image: 93 mm (3 $\frac{11}{16}$ in.)
C for Caylus
Bibliothèque Nationale de France, Richelieu location
(Ed. 98b, vol. 1, folio 485 verso)
Proof with number 30, and counterproof

Folio 29 recto: Caylus nos. 31 and 32, etched from RF 28756 and RF 28757. Circular, side by side, inside two double concentric circles.

NUMBER 31
Plate mark: 100 × 97 mm (3 $\frac{15}{16}$ × 3 $\frac{7}{8}$ in.)
Image: 92 mm (3 $\frac{5}{8}$ in.)
C for Caylus
Bibliothèque Nationale de France, Richelieu location
(Ed. 98b, vol. 1, folio 485 verso)
Proof with number 31, and counterproof

NUMBER 32
Plate mark: 97 × 100 mm (3 $\frac{7}{8}$ × 3 $\frac{15}{16}$ in.)
Image: 92 mm (3 $\frac{5}{8}$ in.)
C for Caylus
Bibliothèque Nationale de France, Richelieu location
(Ed. 98b, vol. 1, folio 485 verso)
Proof with number 32, and counterproof

Folio 30 recto: Caylus nos. 33 and 34, etched from RF 28758 and RF 28759. Circular, side by side, inside two double concentric circles.

NUMBER 33
Plate mark: 100 × 98 mm (3 $\frac{15}{16}$ × 3 $\frac{7}{8}$ in.)
Image: 92 mm (3 $\frac{5}{8}$ in.)
C for Caylus
Bibliothèque Nationale de France, Richelieu location
(Ed. 98b, vol. 1, folio 486 recto)
Proof with number 33, and counterproof

NUMBER 34
Plate mark: 100 × 100 mm (3 $\frac{15}{16}$ × 3 $\frac{15}{16}$ in.)
Image: 91 mm (3 $\frac{5}{8}$ in.)
C for Caylus
Bibliothèque Nationale de France, Richelieu location
(Ed. 98b, vol. 1, folio 486 recto)
Proof with number 34, and counterproof

Folio 31 recto: Caylus nos. 35 and 36, etched from RF 28760 and RF 28761. Circular, side by side, inside two double concentric circles.

NUMBER 35
Plate mark: 100 × 100 (3 $\frac{15}{16}$ × 3 $\frac{15}{16}$ in.)
Image: 91 mm (3 $\frac{5}{8}$ in.)
C for Caylus
Bibliothèque Nationale de France, Richelieu location
(Ed. 98b, vol. 1, folio 486 recto)
Proof with number 35, and counterproof

NUMBER 36
Plate mark: 100 × 100 mm (3 15/16 × 3 15/16 in.)
Image: 91 mm (3 5/8 in.)
C for Caylus
Bibliothèque Nationale de France, Richelieu location
(Ed. 98b, vol. 1, folio 486 recto)
Proof with number 36, and counterproof

Folio 32 recto: Caylus nos. 37 and 38, etched from RF 28762 and RF 28763. Circular, side by side, inside two double concentric circles.

NUMBER 37
Plate mark: 98 × 96 mm (3 7/8 × 3 13/16 in.)
Image: 92 mm (3 5/8 in.)
C for Caylus
Bibliothèque Nationale de France, Richelieu location
(Ed. 98b, vol. 1, folio 486 verso)
Proof with number 37, and counterproof

NUMBER 38
Plate mark: 96 × 99 mm (3 13/16 × 3 7/8 in.)
Image: 92 mm (3 5/8 in.)
C for Caylus
Bibliothèque Nationale de France, Richelieu location
(Ed. 98b, vol. 1, folio 486 verso)
Proof with number 39, and counterproof
LITERATURE: Reznicek 1981, p. 245, fig 2.
Reznicek links engraving no. 38 to one of the heads in the 1506 Dürer painting *Christ among the Doctors* (Museo Thyssen-Bornemisza, Madrid).

Folio 33 recto: Caylus nos. 39 and 40, etched from RF 28765 and RF 28766. Circular, side by side, inside two double concentric circles.

NUMBER 39
Plate mark: 96 × 96 mm (3 13/16 × 3 13/16 in.)
Image: 92 mm (3 5/8 in.)
C for Caylus
Bibliothèque Nationale de France, Richelieu location
(Ed. 98b, vol. 1, folio 486 verso)
Proof with number 41, and counterproof bearing the annotation "40 par Mr. Coypel à la pointe sèche" (40 by Mr. Coypel

in drypoint), referring to the plate bearing the number 54, engraved by Charles-Antoine Coypel from RF 28764.

NUMBER 40
Plate mark: 97 × 97 mm (3 7/8 × 3 7/8 in.)
Image: 92 mm (3 5/8 in.)
C for Caylus
Bibliothèque Nationale de France, Richelieu location
(Ed. 98b, vol. 1, folio 487 recto)
Proof with number 42, and counterproof

Folio 34 recto: Caylus nos. 41 and 42, etched from RF 28767 and RF 28771. Circular, side by side, inside two double concentric circles.

NUMBER 41
Plate mark: 95 × 97 mm (3 3/4 × 3 7/8 in.)
Image: 92 mm (3 5/8 in.)
C for Caylus
Bibliothèque Nationale de France, Richelieu location
(Ed. 98b, vol. 1, folio 487 recto)
Proof with number 43, and counterproof

NUMBER 42
Plate mark: 97 × 98 mm (3 7/8 × 3 7/8 in.)
Image: 92 mm (3 5/8 in.)
C for Caylus
Bibliothèque Nationale de France, Richelieu location
(Ed. 98b, vol. 1, folio 487 recto)
Proof with number 47, and counterproof

Folio 35 recto: Caylus nos. 43 and 44, etched from RF 28768 and RF 28769. Circular, side by side, inside two double concentric circles.

NUMBER 43
Plate mark: 96 × 96 mm (3 13/16 × 3 13/16 in.)
Image: 92 mm (3 5/8 in.)
C for Caylus
Bibliothèque Nationale de France, Richelieu location
(Ed. 98b, vol. 1, folio 487 recto)
Proof with number 44, and counterproof

NUMBER 44
Plate mark: 92 × 94 mm (3 ⅝ × 3 ¾ in.)
Image: 91 mm (3 ⅝ in.)
C for Caylus
Bibliothèque Nationale de France, Richelieu location
(Ed. 98b, vol. 1, folio 487 recto)
Proof with number 45, and counterproof

Folio 36 recto: Caylus nos. 45 and 46, etched from RF 28770 and RF 28772. Circular, side by side, inside two double concentric circles.

NUMBER 45
Plate mark: 95 × 96 mm (3 ¾ × 3 ¾ in.)
Image: 91 mm (3 ⅝ in.)
C for Caylus
Bibliothèque Nationale de France, Richelieu location
(Ed. 98b, vol. 1, folio 487 verso)
Proof with number 46, and counterproof

NUMBER 46
Plate mark: 98 × 96 mm (3 ⅞ × 3 ¹³⁄₁₆ in.)
Image: 92 mm (3 ⅝ in.)
C for Caylus
Bibliothèque Nationale de France, Richelieu location
(Ed. 98b, vol. 1, folio 487 verso)
Proof with number 48, and counterproof

Folio 37 recto: Caylus nos. 47 and 48, etched from RF 28773 and RF 28774. Circular, side by side, inside two double concentric circles.

NUMBER 47
Plate mark: 94 × 94 mm (3 ¾ × 3 ¾ in.)
Image: 92 mm (3 ⅝ in.)
C for Caylus
Bibliothèque Nationale de France, Richelieu location
(Ed. 98b, vol. 1, folio 487 verso)
Proof with number 49, and counterproof

NUMBER 48
Plate mark: 94 × 94 mm (3 ¾ × 3 ¾ in.)
Image: 92 mm (3 ⅝ in.)
C for Caylus

Bibliothèque Nationale de France, Richelieu location
(Ed. 98b, vol. 1, folio 488 recto)
Proof with number 50, and counterproof

Folio 38 recto: Caylus nos. 49 and 50, etched from RF 28775 and RF 28778. Circular, side by side, inside two double concentric circles.

NUMBER 49
Plate mark: 94 × 90 mm (3 ¾ × 3 ⁹⁄₁₆ in.)
Image: 90 mm (3 ⁹⁄₁₆ in.)
C for Caylus
Bibliothèque Nationale de France, Richelieu location
(Ed. 98b, vol. 1, folio 488 recto)
Proof with number 51, and counterproof

NUMBER 50
Plate mark: 93 × 94 mm (3 ¹¹⁄₁₆ × 3 ¾ in.)
Image: 92 mm (3 ⅝ in.)
C for Caylus
Bibliothèque Nationale de France, Richelieu location
(Ed. 98b, vol. 1, folio 488 verso)
Proof with number 54, and counterproof

Folio 39 recto: Caylus nos. 51 and 52, etched from RF 28777 and RF 28776. Circular, side by side, inside two double concentric circles.

NUMBER 51
Plate mark: 93 × 94 mm (3 ¹¹⁄₁₆ × 3 ¾ in.)
Image: 92 mm (3 ⅝ in.)
C for Caylus
Bibliothèque Nationale de France, Richelieu location
(Ed. 98b, vol. 1, folio 488 recto)
Proof with number 53, and counterproof

NUMBER 52
Plate mark: 94 × 90 mm (3 ¾ × 3 ⁹⁄₁₆ in.)
Image: 89 mm (3 ½ in.)
C for Caylus
Bibliothèque Nationale de France, Richelieu location
(Ed. 98b, vol. 1, folio 488 recto)
Proof with number 52, and counterproof

Folio 40 recto: Caylus no. 53, etched from RF 28779
Plate mark: 150 × 105 mm ($5^{15}/_{16}$ × $4^{1}/_{8}$ in.)
Framing line inside the plate mark
C for Caylus
Bibliothèque Nationale de France, Richelieu location
(Ed. 98b, vol. 1, folio 488 verso)
Proof with number 55 and the annotation: *copie* (copy), and
counterproof

Folio 41 recto: no. 54, etched from RF 28764 by Charles-Antoine Coypel
Plate mark: 114 × 109 mm ($4^{1}/_{2}$ × $4^{5}/_{16}$ in.)
Framing line inside the plate mark
At the Bibliothèque Nationale de France, Richelieu location
(Ed. 98b, vol. 1, folio 486 verso), for the etching by Caylus of
RF 28765, which bears the number 41, the counterproof bears
the annotation: *40 par Mr. Coypel à la pointe sèche* (40 by
Mr. Coypel in drypoint), referring to the plate bearing the
number 54.
LITERATURE: Mariette 1730, p. 18; Chennevières and
Montaiglon 1851–60, vol. 3, p. 159; Lefrançois 1994, p. 480,
no. G. 15.

Folio 42 recto: Caylus no. 55, etched from Louvre drawing 2249.
Circular, inside two double concentric circles.
Plate mark: 103 × 104 mm ($4^{1}/_{16}$ × $4^{1}/_{8}$ in.)
Image: 92 mm ($3^{5}/_{8}$ in.)
C for Caylus; inscribed bottom center: *Tiré du Cabinet du Roy*
(From the king's collection)
Bibliothèque de France, Richelieu location
(Ed. 98b, vol. 1, folio 489 verso)
Proof with the number 59, and counterproof with annotation
in pen and brown ink: *Cabinet du Roy* (The king's collection).
Another proof (Ed. 98b, vol. 2, folio 406 recto), without the
double concentric circles, bears the printed inscription:
Leonard de Vinci Cabinet du Roy C.s. Scul.; the counterproof
is on folio 405 verso.
LITERATURE: Mariette 1730, p. 19; Chennevières and
Montaiglon 1851–60, vol. 3, p. 161.

Folio 43 recto: Caylus nos. 56 and 59, etched from a sheet in
the Albertina, Vienna, 14179 (head center right and head

lower right). Circular, side by side, inside two double concentric
circles.

NUMBER 56
Plate mark: 104 × 100 mm ($4^{1}/_{8}$ × $3^{15}/_{16}$ in.)
Image: 93 mm ($3^{3}/_{4}$ in.)
C for Caylus. Inscribed bottom center: *Tiré du Cabinet de M^r
Crozat* (From the collection of Mr. Crozat)
Bibliothèque Nationale de France, Richelieu location
(Ed. 98b, vol. 1, folio 489 verso)
Proof with number 60, inscription in pen and brown ink,
stained: *n'a pas été fait . . . copie de cette table* (no copy was
made of this stone); and *Du Cab. de Crozat* (From the
col.[lection] of Crozat), and counterproof.

NUMBER 59
Plate mark: 103 × 100 mm ($4^{1}/_{16}$ × $3^{15}/_{16}$ in.)
Image: 93 mm ($3^{11}/_{16}$ in.)
C for Caylus. Inscribed bottom center: *Tiré du Cabinet de M^r
Crozat* (From the collection of Mr. Crozat)
Bibliothèque Nationale de France, Richelieu location
(Ed. 98b, vol. 1, folio 489 verso)
Proof with number 62, and counterproof
LITERATURE: Mariette 1730, pp. 18–19; Chennevières and
Montaiglon 1851–60, vol. 3, p. 160 and n. 1.

Folio 44 recto: Caylus nos. 57 and 58; etched from a sheet in
the Albertina, Vienna, 14179 (head center left, and head lower
left). Circular, side by side, inside two double concentric
circles.

NUMBER 57
Plate mark: 103 × 102 mm ($4^{1}/_{16}$ × 4 in.)
Image: 93 mm ($3^{11}/_{16}$ in.)
C for Caylus. Inscribed bottom center: *Tiré du Cabinet de M^r
Crozat* (From the collection of Mr. Crozat)
Bibliothèque Nationale de France, Richelieu location
(Ed. 98b, vol. 1, folio 489 verso)
Proof with number 61, and counterproof

NUMBER 58
Plate mark: 103 × 102 mm ($4^{1}/_{16}$ × 4 in.)
Image: 94 mm ($3^{3}/_{4}$ in.)
C for Caylus. Inscribed bottom center: *Tiré du Cabinet de M^r
Crozat* (From the collection of Mr. Crozat)

Bibliothèque Nationale de France, Richelieu location
(Ed. 98b, vol. 1, folio 490 recto)
Proof with number 63, and counterproof
LITERATURE: Mariette 1730, pp. 18–19; Chennevières and
Montaiglon 1851–60, vol. 3, p. 160 and n. 1.

Folio 45 recto: etched from RF 28783. Unnumbered, mixed
media, etching, and xylography for the bister wash color.
Plate mark: 125 × 96 mm (4^{15}/$_{16}$ × 3^{13}/$_{16}$ in.)
Framing line inside the platemark. Inscribed bottom center: *di
mano di Lodovico Cigoli* (in the hand of Lodovico Cigoli),
identical to inscription found on the back of the drawing.
Bibliothèque Nationale de France, Richelieu location
(Ed. 98b, vol. 1, folio 486 verso)
Proof with number 38 and the annotation: *chirofer* [?] *en bois*,
and counterproof, without the bister wash color. Folio 492
recto, proof with color applied by xylography.

Folio 46 recto: etched from an unidentified original.
Unnumbered, oval, inside two double concentric circles.
Plate mark: 98 × 82 mm (3^{7}/$_{8}$ × 3^{1}/$_{4}$ in.)
Image: 91 × 76 mm (3^{5}/$_{8}$ × 3 in.)
Inscribed bottom center: *Tiré du Cabinet de M^{r}. Hickman*
(From the collection of Mr. Hickman [unidentified collector])
Bibliothèque Nationale de France, Richelieu location
(Ed. 98, folio 556 recto)
Proof, unnumbered, with no concentric circles

Folio 47 recto: etched from a sheet in the Albertina, Vienna,
14179 (head upper left). Unnumbered, oval, inside two double
concentric circles.
Plate mark: 141 × 108 mm (5^{9}/$_{16}$ × 4^{1}/$_{4}$ in.)
Image: 124 × 96 mm (4^{7}/$_{8}$ × 3^{13}/$_{16}$ in.)
LITERATURE: Mariette 1730, pp. 18–19; Chennevières and
Montaiglon 1851–60, vol. 3, p. 160 and n. 1.

Folio 48 recto: etched from a sheet in the Albertina, Vienna,
14179 (head upper right). Unnumbered, oval, inside two
double concentric circles
Plate mark: 140 × 106 mm (5^{1}/$_{2}$ × 4^{3}/$_{16}$ in.)
Image: 124 × 95 mm (4^{7}/$_{8}$ × 3^{3}/$_{4}$ in.)
LITERATURE: Mariette 1730, pp. 18–19; Chennevières and
Montaiglon 1851–60, vol. 3, p. 160 and n. 1.

Folio 49 recto: etched from a sheet in the Albertina, Vienna, 61.
Unnumbered, mixed media, etching, and xylography for the
bister wash color.
Plate mark: 217 × 160 mm (8^{9}/$_{16}$ × 6^{5}/$_{16}$ in.); framing line inside
the platemark. Inscribed along the upper edge: *Dessein de
Leonard de Vinci tiré du Cabinet de M. Crozat et originairement
du Livre de Vasarie* (Drawing by Leonardo da Vinci from the
collection of Mr. Crozat and originally from the book by Vasari)
An identical proof is in the Bibliothèque Nationale de France,
Richelieu location (Ed. 98c, folio 659bis)
LITERATURE: Chennevières and Montaiglon 1851–60, vol. 3,
p. 160 and n. 1.

Folio 50 recto: Identical to the preceding number, with the
lines in a slightly darker ink.

Folio 51 recto: Like the two preceding numbers, but without
the bister wash color and without the inscription.
An identical proof is in the Bibliothèque Nationale de France,
Richelieu location (Ed. 98c, folio 581 recto).

FLYLEAF

1. My thanks to Pierrette Jean-Richard, for examining the album with me to
establish the medium, and to Maxime Préaud.
2. Jeanne-Marie Métivier of the Bibliothèque Nationale de France has
researched the binding of the volume in that collection. She informed me
that this copy appears on the list of volumes in the royal library sent, on
December 2, 1730, to the binder Antoine de Heuqueville, who is responsible
for the binding in lemon morocco, stamped with the coat of arms of the
royal library, which even today protects the volume.
3. See Guffanti 2001.

BIBLIOGRAPHY

Leonardo's Manuscripts: Abbreviations

Ar. = Codex Arundel 263, British Library, London. The diverse compilation of material dates from ca. 1478–1518.

C. A. = Codex Atlanticus, 12 vols., Biblioteca Ambrosiana, Milan. The drawings and notes pasted into these volumes also represent an amalgamation of material from dates that range from ca. 1478 to 1518. Here citations refer to the foliation of the codex both before its restoration in 1977–1980 (to correspond with Jean Paul Richter's anthology of Leonardo's notes; Richter 1883, 1970) and after restoration.

C. Urb. = Codex Urbinas Latinus 1270, Biblioteca Apostolica Vaticana. This is the *Libro di Pittura*, posthumously compiled by Francesco Melzi, based on Leonardo's notes. The anthology of precepts was produced between 1515 and 1570.

C.V. U. = Codice del Volo degli Uccelli, or Codex on the Flight of Birds, Biblioteca Reale Cod. Varia 95, Turin. This manuscript was originally part of Paris Ms. B, Institut de France, Paris, and was probably extracted in the theft by Count Guglielmo Libri (1803–1869) around 1840–47. The manuscript is dated 1505.

Fo. I, Fo. II, Fo. III = Codex Forster I, Codex Forster II, Codex Forster III, Victoria and Albert Museum, London. The first part of Forster I (fols. 1–40) is dated 1505, the second part (fols. 41–55) is probably from ca. 1487–90. The first part of Forster II (fols. 1–63) probably dates from ca. 1495–97, while the second part (fols. 64–159) dates from ca. 1494–97. Forster III appears to date from ca. 1490–97.

Leic. = Codex Leicester (formerly, Leicester 699, Holkham Hall; formerly called the Codex Hammer, when it was owned by Armand Hammer), Collection of Bill and Melinda Gates, Seattle, Washington. The codex dates from ca. 1508–12. See cat. no. 114 in the present catalogue.

Libro di Pittura = **C. Urb.** = Codex Urbinas Latinus 1270, Biblioteca Apostolica Vaticana (see C. Urb. above).

Ma. I, Ma. II = Codex Madrid I (8937), Codex Madrid II (8936), Biblioteca Nacional, Madrid.

Codex Madrid I dates from ca. 1493–99. Codex Madrid II bears the dates 1491, 1493, and other material in this volume seems to date ca. 1503–5.

Paris Ms. A = Manuscript A (2172; 2185), Institut de France, Paris. Sometime between ca. 1840 and 1847, the second part of this manuscript (fols. 81–114) was stolen by Count Guglielmo Libri, from whom it was bought by Lord Ashburnham in 1875 (designated as Ms. Ashburnham 1875/2). This part was acquired by the Bibliothèque Nationale as Ms. B.N. It. 2038 around 1888, and was then restituted to the Institut de France. Fols. 54, 65–80 were probably lost at the time of Libri's theft. The modern reconstitution of the two parts of the manuscript postdates the publication of the first edition of the famous anthology of Leonardo's notes by Jean Paul Richter (Richter 1883). In the early Leonardo literature, the second part of Paris Ms. A is referred to as Ms. Ashburnham II. In the later literature this second part is also designated as Ms. B.N. 2038 (the citation used in Richter 1939), while the recent Leonardo literature presents the foliation of the fully reconstituted manuscript. The first part of Paris Ms. A is dated 1492, but was begun earlier, ca. 1490–91.

Paris Ms. B = Manuscript B (2173; 2184), Institut de France, Paris. The second part of this manuscript (fols. 91–100) was also stolen ca. 1840–47 by Count Guglielmo Libri, and has the same history as the second part of Paris Ms. A, until it was acquired by the Bibliothèque Nationale as Ms. B.N. It. 2037, and then restituted to the Institut de France. When in Lord Ashburnham's collections, this part of Paris Ms. B was known as Ms. Ashburnham 1875/1. Fols. 3, 84–87 of Paris Ms. B were probably lost at the time of Libri's theft. The parts of Paris Ms. B were also reconstituted after the publication of the first edition of Richter's famous anthology. In the early Leonardo literature the second part of Paris Ms. B is referred to as Ashburnham I. In the later literature this second part is also designated as Ms. B.N. 2037, while the recent Leonardo literature presents the foliation of the fully reconstituted manuscript. Paris Ms. B dates from ca. 1486–90.

Paris Ms. C = Manuscript C (2174), Institut de France, Paris. This is dated 1490, 1491.

Paris Ms. D = Manuscript D (2175), Institut de France, Paris. The notebook seems to have been produced ca. 1508.

Paris Ms. E = Manuscript E (2176), Institut de France, Paris. Fols. 80–96 of this manuscript were lost probably at the time of Libri's theft ca. 1840–47. The manuscript seems to date from 1513–14.

Paris Ms. F = Manuscript F (2177), Institut de France, Paris. This is dated 1508.

Paris Ms. G = Manuscript G (2178), Institut de France, Paris. The material probably dates from 1510 to 1515.

Paris Ms. H = Manuscript H (2179), Institut de France, Paris. The first part (fols. 1–48) is dated March 1494, the second part (fols. 49–94) is dated January and February 1494, and the third part (fols. 95–142) is dated 1493, 1494.

Paris Ms. I = Manuscript I (2180), Institut de France, Paris. The first part (fols. 1–48) probably dates ca. 1497–99, while the second part (fols. 49–139) from ca. 1497.

Paris Ms. K = Manuscript K (2181), Institut de France, Paris. The first part (fols. 1–48) and second part (fols. 49–80) seem to date from ca. 1503–4 (and possibly 1505), while the third part (fols. 81–128) appears to be from ca. 1506–7 (and possibly 1508).

Paris Ms. L = Manuscript L (2182), Institut de France, Paris. Ms. L probably dates ca. 1497–1502 (and possibly 1504).

Paris Ms. M = Manuscript M (2183), Institut de France, Paris. The majority of the notebook probably dates from ca. 1498–1500, but was probably begun ca. 1495.

Tr. = Codex Trivulzianus N 2162, Castello Sforzesco, Milan. This codex dates ca. 1487–90.

All of Leonardo's manuscripts are now available in facsimile reproductions published by Giunti Barbèra–Giunti Gruppo Editoriale (the Giunti Publishing Group), Florence, under the direction of Carlo Pedretti. Earlier partial or full facsimile editions are listed in the Bibliography under the manuscript name.

Bibliography

Accordi 1987
Accordi, Bruno. *Conoscenze geologiche di Leonardo: Influssi sul suo ciclo pittorico. Atti della VII Giornata leonardiana, Brescia, 7 ottobre, 1984.* Brescia, 1987.

Ademollo and Passerini 1845
Ademollo, Agostino, and Luigi Passerini. *Marietta de'Ricci ovvero Firenze al tempo dell'assedio racconto storico.* 1840–41. 2d ed., 6 vols. Florence, 1845.

Adorno 1991
Adorno, Piero. *Il Verrocchio: Nuove proposte nella civiltà artistica del tempo di Lorenzo il Magnifico.* Florence, 1991.

Adriani 1980
Adriani, Gert. "Leonardo in Germany." In *Leonardo da Vinci* 1980, pp. 195–200.

Agghazy 1989
Agghazy, Mária G. *Leonardo's Equestrian Statuette.* Budapest, 1989.

Agnew 1967
Agnew, Geoffrey. *Agnew's, 1817–1967.* London, 1967.

Agosti 1990
Agosti, Giovanni. *Bambaia e il classicismo lombardo.* Turin, 1990.

Agosti 2001
Agosti, Giovanni. *Disegni del Rinascimento in Valpadana.* Exh. cat., Florence, Gabinetto Disegni e Stampe degli Uffizi. Florence, 2001.

Agosti and Farinella 1988–89
Agosti, Giovanni, and Vincenzo Farinella. "Qualche difficoltà nella carriera di Cesare da Sesto." *Prospettiva,* nos. 53–56 (April 1988–January 1989), pp. 325–33.

Ahl 1995
Ahl, Diane Cole, ed. *Leonardo da Vinci's Sforza Monument Horse: The Art and the Engineering.* Bethlehem, Pa., and London, 1995.

Alberici 1984
Alberici, Clelia. "Incisioni derivate da disegni di Leonardo." In Alberici and De Biasi 1984, pp. 129–40.

Alberici and De Biasi 1984
Alberici, Clelia, and Mariateresa De Biasi. *Leonardo e l'incisione: Stampe derivate da Leonardo e Bramante dal XV al XIX secolo.* Exh. cat., Milan, Castello Sforzesco. Milan, 1984.

Alberti 1966
Alberti, Leon Battista. *On Painting.* Translated and edited by John R. Spencer. 1956. Rev. ed. New Haven and London, 1966. Reprint, Westport, Conn., 1976.

Alberti 1992
Alberti, Leon Battista. *De la peinture—De pictura (1435).* Translated and annotated by Jean Louis Schefer. Introduction by Sylvie Deswarte-Rosa. [Paris], 1992.

Albertina 1971
Koschatzky, Walter, Konrad Oberhuber, and Eckhart Knab, eds. *Italian Drawings of the Albertina.* Milan, 1971. Italian edition: *I grandi disegni italiani dell'Albertina di Vienna.* 1972. References in this catalogue are to the English edition.

Alessandrini 1966
Alessandrini, A. "Benci, Ginevra." In *Dizionario biografico degli Italiani,* vol. 8, pp. 193–94. Rome, 1966.

Allison 1974
Allison, Ann H. "Antique Sources of Leonardo's Leda." *The Art Bulletin* 56, no. 3 (September 1974), pp. 375–84.

Almeida-Matos 1998
Almeida-Matos, Lúcia. "Desenhos de mestres na colecção do Museu da FBAUP: Leonardo da Vinci, Rapariga lavando os pés a uma criança." *Apontamentos* (Faculdade de Belas Artes da Universidade do Porto) 2 (1998), pp. 17–18, 25.

Alpatov 1984
Alpatov, Michele. "Leonardo da Vinci all'Ermitage." In Galleria degli Uffizi 1984, pp. 7–12.

Alpatov 1985
Alpatov, Michele. "Le opere di Leonardo nell'Ermitage." In *Leonardo: La pittura* 1985, pp. 45–48.

Amboise 1952
Le séjour de Léonard de Vinci en France. Exh. cat., Château d'Amboise. Amboise, 1952.

Ambrosiana 1998–99
Marani, Pietro C., Marco Rossi, and Alessandro Rovetta, eds. *L'Ambrosiana e Leonardo.* Exh. cat., Milan, Biblioteca-Pinacoteca Ambrosiana. Milan, 1998.

Ames 1962
Ames, Winslow. *Great Drawings of All Time.* Vol. 1, *Italian, Thirteenth through Nineteenth Century,* edited by Ira Moskowitz. New York, 1962.

Ames 1963
Ames, Winslow. *Italian Drawings from the Fifteenth to the Eighteenth Century.* London, 1963.

Ames-Lewis 1981
Ames-Lewis, Francis. *Drawing in Early Renaissance Italy.* New Haven and London, 1981.

Ames-Lewis 1989
Ames-Lewis, Francis. "Leonardo da Vinci's 'Kneeling Leda': The Evolution of an Expressive Figure-Composition." *Drawing* 11, no. 4 (November–December 1989), pp. 73–76.

Ames-Lewis 1990
Ames-Lewis, Francis. Review of *Leonardo da Vinci: Artist–Scientist–Inventor,* by Martin Kemp and Jane Roberts; and *Leonardo on Painting,* edited by Martin Kemp. *Master Drawings* 28, no. 1 (Spring 1990), pp. 80–82.

Ames-Lewis 1997
Ames-Lewis, Francis. "Leonardo's Botanical Drawings." *Achademia Leonardi Vinci: Journal of Leonardo Studies and Bibliography of Vinciana* 10 (1997), pp. 117–24, and unpaginated figures.

Ames-Lewis 1999
Ames-Lewis, Francis. *Drawing in Early Renaissance Italy.* 1981. 2d ed. New Haven and London, 1999.

Ames-Lewis 2001
Ames-Lewis, Francis. "Leonardo da Vinci e il disegno a matita." *Raccolta Vinciana,* no. 29 (2001), pp. 1–40.

Ames-Lewis 2002
Ames-Lewis, Francis. *La matita nera nella pratica di disegno di Leonardo da Vinci.* Lettura Vinciana, 41 (21 aprile 2001). Vinci and Florence, 2002.

Ames-Lewis and Bednarek 1990
Ames-Lewis, Francis, and Anka Bednarek, eds. *Nine Lectures on Leonardo da Vinci.* London, [1990].

Ames-Lewis and Wright 1983
Ames-Lewis, Francis, and Joanne Wright. *Drawing in the Italian Renaissance Workshop.* Exh. cat., Nottingham, University Art Gallery; London, Victoria and Albert Museum. London, 1983.

Amoretti 1804
Amoretti, Carlo. *Memorie storiche su la vita gli studi e le opere di Lionardo da Vinci.* Milan, 1804.

Amphiareo 1554
Amphiareo, Vespasiano. *Opera di frate vespa: Siano amphiareo da Ferrara del l'ordine minore conventvale, nella qvale si insegna a scrivere varie sorti di lettere, et massime vna lettera bastarda da lvi novamente con sva indvstria ritrovata, laqval serve al cancellaresco et mercantesco.* Venice, 1554. (The Metropolitan Museum of Art, acc. no. 28.106.5).

Andrews 1968
Andrews, Keith. *National Gallery of Scotland: Catalogue of Italian Drawings.* 2 vols. Cambridge, 1968.

Angiolillo 1979
Angiolillo, Marialuisa. *Leonardo: Feste e teatri.* Studi e testi di storia e critica dell'arte, 10. Naples, 1979.

Anglo 1989
Anglo, S. "The Man Who Taught Leonardo Darts: Pietro Monti and His 'Lost' Fencing Book." *The Antiquaries Journal* 59, no. 2 (1989), pp. 261–78.

Angoulvent 1933
Angoulvent, Paul-Joseph. *Musée National du Louvre: La Chalcographie du Louvre, Catalogue Général.* Paris, 1933.

Annesley 1995
Annesley, Noël. "Ian Woodner." *Drawing* 17, no. 3 (September–October 1995), p. 54.

Annoni 1980
Annoni, Ambrogio. "Leonardo as Decorator." In *Leonardo da Vinci* 1980, pp. 307–14.

Arasse 1978
Arasse, Daniel. *L'univers de Léonard de Vinci.* Paris, 1978.

Arasse 1985
Arasse, Daniel. "Ritratto di Isabella d'Este." In *Leonardo: La pittura* 1985, pp. 102–3.

Arasse 1997
Arasse, Daniel. *Léonard de Vinci: Le rythme du monde.* Paris, 1997.

Arasse 1998
Arasse, Daniel. *Leonardo da Vinci: The Rhythm of the World.* New York, 1998.

Arents 2001
Arents, Prosper. *De Biblioteek van Pieter Pauwel Rubens: Een reconstructie.* Edited by Alfons K. L. Thijs. Antwerp, 2001.

Argan 1985
Argan, Giulio Carlo. "5 Daghossto, 1473." In *Leonardo: La pittura* 1985, pp. 12–15.

Argentieri 1980
Argentieri, Domenico. "Leonardo's Optics." In *Leonardo da Vinci* 1980, pp. 405–36.

Armenini 1586, 1988
Armenini, Giovan Battista. *De' veri precetti della pittura.* 1586. Edited by Marina Gorreri; preface by Enrico Castelnuovo. Turin, 1988.

Armenini 1587, 1977
Armenini, Giovanni Battista. *On the True Precepts of the Art of Painting.* 1587. Translation, comment, and introduction by Edward J. Olszewski. New York, 1977.

Arnolds 1949
Arnolds, Günter. *Italienische Zeichnungen: Zeichnungen des Kupferstichkabinetts in Berlin.* Berlin, 1949.

Aronberg Lavin 1955
Aronberg Lavin, Marilyn. "Giovannino Battista: A Study in Renaissance Religion Symbolism." *The Art Bulletin* 37, no. 2 (June 1955), pp. 85–101.

Arquié-Bruley, Labbé, and Bicart-Sée 1987
Arquié-Bruley, Françoise, Jacqueline Labbé, and Lise Bicart-Sée. *La collection Saint-Morys au Cabinet des Dessins du musée du Louvre.* 2 vols. Paris, 1987.

Ashmolean Museum 1985–86
Howarth, David, et al. *Thomas Howard, Earl of Arundel: Patronage and Collecting in the Seventeenth Century.* Exh. cat., Oxford, Ashmolean Museum. Oxford, 1985.

Athenaeum 1835
The Athenaeum (London). May 30, 1835.

Athenaeum 1836
The Athenaeum (London). February 6, 1836.

Atlers 1944
Atlers, R. "Microcosmus from Anaximandros to Paracelsus." *Traditio* 2 (1944), pp. 319–407.

Bacall 1968
Bacall, B. "A Catalogue of the Drawings of Leonardo da Vinci and his School in the United States of America." M.A. thesis, directed by Carlo Pedretti. University of California, Los Angeles, 1968.

Bacou 1962
Bacou, Roseline. "Dessins italiens dans les collections hollandaises." *L'Œil*, no. 85 (January 1962), pp. 56–61.

Bacou 1967
Bacou, Roseline, et al. *Le cabinet d'un grand amateur, P.-J. Mariette, 1694–1774: Dessins du 15e au 18e siècle.* Exh. cat., Paris, Musée du Louvre, Galerie Mollien. Paris, 1967.

Bacou 1968
Bacou, Roseline, with Françoise Viatte. *Dessins du Louvre: École italienne.* Paris, 1968.

Bacou 1974
Bacou, Roseline. *Cartons d'artistes du XVe au XIXe siècle.* Exh. cat., Paris, Musée du Louvre. Paris, 1974.

Bacou 1981
Bacou, Roseline. *The Famous Italian Drawings from the Mariette Collection at the Louvre in Paris.* Milan, 1981.

Badt 1914
Badt, Kurt. *Andrea Solario, sein Leben und seine Werke: Ein Beitrag zur Kunstgeschichte der Lombardei.* Leipzig, 1914.

Baker 2002
Baker, Christopher. *Christ Church Picture Gallery.* Oxford, 2002.

Baldacci 1922–23
Baldacci, Antonio. "Le piante di Leonardo da Vinci nei codici della Biblioteca Reale del Castello di Windsor." *Memorie della R. Accademia delle Scienze dell'Istituto di Bologna, Classe di scienze naturali* 10 (1922–23), pp. 77–82.

Baldacci 1980
Baldacci, Antonio. "Da Vinci's Botany." In *Leonardo da Vinci* 1980, pp. 448–54.

Baldini 1988
Baldini, Umberto, ed. *Leonardo: Tutta la pittura.* La scheda d'arte. Florence, 1988.

Baldini 1992
Baldini, Umberto. *Un Leonardo inedito.* Florence, 1992.

Baldinotti 2000
Baldinotti, Andrea. "Lo specchio e l'orizzonte: *L'Annunciazione* di Leonardo, dal museo degli Uffizi al 'museo' della bibliografia." In *L'Annunciazione di Leonardo: La montagna sul mare*, edited by Antonio Natali, pp. 81–93. Cinisello Balsamo, 2000.

Balis 1986
Balis, Arnout. *Rubens Hunting Scenes.* Translated by P. S. Falla. Corpus Rubenianum Ludwig Burchard, 18, vol. 2. New York, 1986.

Ballarin 1985
Ballarin, Alessandro. "Problemi di leonardismo milanese tra Quattro e Cinquecento: Giovanni Antonio Boltraffio prima della pala Casio." Milan, Università Cattolica del Sacro Cuore, 1985.

Ballarin 1992
Ballarin, Alessandro. *Dosso Dossi e la pittura a Ferrara negli anni del ducato di Alfonso I.* Cittadella, 1992.

Ballarin 1998
Ballarin, Alessandro. "Milano nell'età di Ludovico il Moro: Problemi di leonardismo milanese di fine Quattrocento Giovanni Antonio Boltraffio prima della pala Casio." In *Pittura del Rinascimento nell'Italia settentrionale*, pp. 33–101. Cittadella, 1998.

Ballarin 2002
Ballarin, Alessandro. *Problemi di leonardismo milanese tra Quattro e Cinquecento: Giovanni Antonio Boltraffio prima della pala Casio.* Cittadella, 2002.

Bambach [Cappel] 1988
Bambach [Cappel], Carmen. "The Tradition of Pouncing Drawings in the Italian Renaissance Workshop: Innovation and Derivation." Ph.D. diss., Yale University, New Haven, 1988.

Bambach [Cappel] 1990
Bambach [Cappel], Carmen. "Pounced Drawings in the Codex Atlanticus." *Achademia Leonardi Vinci: Journal of Leonardo Studies and Bibliography of Vinciana* 3 (1990), pp. 129–31, and unpaginated figures.

Bambach [Cappel] 1991a
Bambach [Cappel], Carmen. "Foreshortened Letters." *Achademia Leonardi Vinci: Journal of Leonardo Studies and Bibliography of Vinciana* 4 (1991), pp. 99–106, and unpaginated figures.

Bambach [Cappel] 1991b
Bambach [Cappel], Carmen. "Leonardo, Tagliente, and Dürer: 'La scienza del far di groppi.'" *Achademia Leonardi Vinci: Journal of Leonardo Studies and Bibliography of Vinciana* 4 (1991), pp. 72–98, and unpaginated figures.

Bambach [Cappel] 1994a
Bambach [Cappel], Carmen. "On 'la testa proportionalmente degradata': Luca Signorelli, Leonardo, and Piero della Francesca's *De Prospectiva Pingendi*." In Cropper 1994, pp. 17–43, and unpaginated figures.

Bambach [Cappel] 1994b
Bambach [Cappel], Carmen. "Problemi di tecnica nei cartoni di Michelangelo per la Cappella Sistina." In *Michelangelo: La Cappella Sistina.* Vol. 3, *Atti del Convegno Internazionale di Studi, Rome, marzo 1990*, pp. 83–102, 355–60. Novara, 1994.

Bambach [Cappel] 1996
Bambach [Cappel], Carmen. "Piero della Francesca, The Study of Perspective and the Development of the Cartoon in the Quattrocento." In *Piero della Francesca tra arte e scienza: Atti del Convegno Internazionale di Studi, Arezzo, 8–11 ottobre 1992, Sansepolcro, 12 ottobre 1992*, edited by Marisa Dalai Emiliani and Valter Curzi, pp. 143–66, figs. 1–27 on unnumbered plates. Venice, 1996.

Bambach 1997
Bambach, Carmen C. "Technique and Workshop Practice in Filippino's Drawings." In Goldner and Bambach 1997, pp. 21–28.

Bambach 1999a
Bambach, Carmen C. *Drawing and Painting in the Italian Renaissance Workshop: Theory and Practice, 1300–1600.* Cambridge and New York, 1999.

Bambach 1999b
Bambach, Carmen C. "The Purchases of Cartoon Paper for Leonardo's *Battle of Anghiari* and Michelangelo's *Battle of Cascina*." In *I Tatti Studies: Essays in the Renaissance*, vol. 8, edited by Walter Kaiser, pp. 105–33. Florence, 1999.

Bambach 2001
Bambach, Carmen C. "A Leonardo Drawing for the Metropolitan Museum of Art; Studies for a Statue of *Hercules*." *Apollo* 153, no. 469 (March 2001), pp. 16–23.

Bambach [Cappel] and Whitaker 1991
Bambach [Cappel], Carmen, and Lucy Whitaker. "The Lost Knots." *Achademia Leonardi Vinci: Journal of Leonardo Studies and Bibliography of Vinciana* 4 (1991), pp. 107–10, and unpaginated figures.

Bandera and Fiorio 2000
Bandera, Sandrina, and Maria Teresa Fiorio, eds. *Bernardino Luini and Renaissance Painting in Milan: The Frescoes of San Maurizio al Monastero Maggiore.* Milan, 2000.

Bandini 1792
Bandini, A. M. *Biblioteca Leopoldina Lauretana . . .* Florence, 1792.

Baratta 1903
Baratta, Mario. *Leonardo da Vinci e I problemi della terra.* Turin, 1903.

Baratta 1905a
Baratta, Mario. *Curiosità Vinciane.* Turin, 1905.

Baratta 1905b
Baratta, Mario. "Leonardo da Vinci negli studi per la navigazione dell'Arno." *Bollettino della Società Geografica Italiana,* ser. 5, 6 (1905), pp. 739–61, 893–921.

Barkan 1975
Barkan, Leonard. *Nature's Work of Art: The Human Body as Image of the World.* New Haven, 1975.

Barocchi 1992
Barocchi, Paola, et al. *Il Giardino di San Marco: Maestri e compagni del giovane Michelangelo.* Exh. cat., Florence, Casa Buonarroti. Cinisello Balsamo, 1992.

Barocchi, Forlani, and Fossi Todorow 1961
Barocchi, Paola, Anna Forlani, and Maria Fossi Todorow, eds. *Mostra del disegno italiano di cinque secoli.* Exh. cat., Florence, Palazzo Strozzi, Florence, 1961.

Baroni 1934–39
Baroni, Constantino [*sic*]. "Leonardo, Bramantino ed il Mausoleo di G. Giacomo Trivulzio." *Raccolta Vinciana,* nos. 15–16 (1934–39), pp. 201–70.

Baroni 1980
Baroni, Costantino. "Leonardo as Architect." In *Leonardo da Vinci 1980,* pp. 238–60.

Baroni and Calvi 1980
Baroni, Costantino, and Ignazio Calvi. "The Birth of Leonardo." In *Leonardo da Vinci 1980,* pp. 6–7.

Barryte 1990
Barryte, Bernard. "The 'Ill-Matched Couple.'" *Achademia Leonardi Vinci: Journal of Leonardo Studies and Bibliography of Vinciana* 3 (1990), pp. 133–39, and unpaginated figures.

Bartoli 1998
Bartoli, Roberta. "La palestra del Verrocchio." In *Lo sguardo degli angeli: Verrocchio, Leonardo e il 'Battesimo di Cristo,'* edited Antonio Natali, pp. 11–37. Cinisello Balsamo, 1998.

Bartoloni forthcoming
Bartoloni, Gilda. " The Role of the Artist in the Rediscovery of Antiquity."

Bartsch 1794
Bartsch, Adam von. *Catalogue raisonné des dessins originaux . . . du Cabinet de feu Le Prince Charles de Ligne . . .* Vienna, 1794.

Bartsch 1803–21
Bartsch, Adam. *Le peintre graveur.* 21 vols. Vienna, 1803–21.

Basan 1775
Catalogue raisonné des différents objets de curiosités dans les Sciences et les Arts qui composaient le Cabinet de feu M. Mariette, Contrôleur Général de la Grande Chancellerie de France, Honoraire Amateur de l'Académie Rle de Peinture et de celle de Florence. Par F. Basan, graveur. Paris, 1775.

Bassi 1989
Bassi, Arturo. "Civitali." *Achademia Leonardi Vinci: Journal of Leonardo Studies and Bibliography of Vinciana* 2 (1989), pp. 113–14, and unpaginated figures.

Bassignana 1988
Bassignana, Pier Luigi. *Le Macchine di Valturio: Nei documenti dell'archivio storico amma.* Preface by Sergio Ricossa. Archivi di scienza e tecnica. Turin, 1988.

Bassoli 1954
Bassoli, Federico S. "Un pittore svizzero pioniere degli studi vinciani: Lodovico Antonio David." *Raccolta Vinciana,* no. 17 (1954), pp. 261–314.

Battaglia 1975
Battaglia, Salvatore. "Mancino." In *Grande dizionario della lingua italiana,* vol. 9, pp. 611–12. Turin, 1975.

Battaglia 1998
Battaglia, Salvatore. "Sinistro." In *Grande dizionario della lingua italiana,* vol. 19, pp. 73–76. Turin, 1998.

Baumstark 1983
Baumstark, Reinhold. "The Decius Mus Cycle of Tapestries at Vaduz." *The Ringling Museum of Art Journal. Papers presented at the International Rubens Symposium, April 14–16, 1982* (1983), pp. 178–87.

Baur 1984
Baur, Otto, Barbara Bott, Sigrid Braunfels-Esche, Kenneth D. Keele, Heinz Ladendorf, and Marielene Putscher. *Leonardo da Vinci: Anatomie, Physiognomik, Proportion und Bewegung.* Vol. 1. Cologne, 1984.

Bautier 1980
Bautier, Pietro. "Leonardo in Belgium." In *Leonardo da Vinci 1980,* pp. 186–90.

Baxandall 1980
Baxandall, Michael. *The Limewood Sculptors of Renaissance Germany.* New Haven, 1980.

Bayersdorfer 1893
Bayersdorfer, Adolf. *Zeichnungen alter Italiener in den Uffizien zu Florenz.* Munich, 1893.

Bean 1960
Bean, Jacob. *Les dessins italiens de la collection Bonnat.* Paris, 1960.

Bean 1964
Bean, Jacob. *100 European Drawings in The Metropolitan Museum of Art.* New York, [1964].

Bean 1982
Bean, Jacob, with Lawrence Turčić. *15th and 16th Century Italian Drawings in The Metropolitan Museum of Art.* New York, 1982.

Bean and Stampfle 1965
Bean, Jacob, and Felice Stampfle. *Drawings from New York Collections. I, The Italian Renaissance.* Exh. cat., New York, The Metropolitan Museum of Art. New York, 1965.

Becherucci 1985
Becherucci, Luisa. "L'Adorazione dei Magi." In *Leonardo: La pittura,* pp. 39–44.

Beck 1987
Beck, Hans-Ulrich. *Jan van Goyen: 1596–1656 (Ergänzungen zum Katalog der Handzeichnungen und Ergänzungen zum Katalog der Gemälde).* Doornspijk, 1987.

Beckerath 1904
Beckerath, Adolf von. "Notes on Some Florentine Drawings in the Print Room, Berlin." *The Burlington Magazine* 6, no. 21 (December 1904), pp. 234–40.

Beckerath 1905
Beckerath, A[dolf] v[on]. "Über einige Zeichnungen florentinischer Maler im königl. Kupferstichkabinett in Berlin." *Repertorium für Kunstwissenschaft* 28 (1905), pp. 104–26.

Béguin 1975
Béguin, Sylvie. *Le Studiolo d'Isabelle d'Este.* Exh. cat., Paris, Musée du Louvre. Les dossiers du département des peintures, 10. Paris, 1975.

Béguin 1983
Béguin, Sylvie. *Léonard de Vinci au Louvre.* Paris, 1983.

Béguin 1985
Béguin, Sylvie. *Andrea Solario en France.* Les dossiers du département des peintures, 31. Exh. cat., Paris, Musée du Louvre. Paris, 1985.

Béguin 1999
Béguin, Sylvie. "Andrea Solario en France." In Fabrizio-Costa and Le Goff 1999, pp. 81–98.

Bell 1914
Bell, Charles F. *Drawings by the Old Masters in the Library of Christ Church, Oxford.* Oxford, 1914.

Bell 1991
Bell, Janis. "Zaccolini and Leonardo's Manuscript A." In Fiorio and Marani 1991, pp. 183–93.

Bellani 1936
Bellani, Laura. "Giovanni Antonio Boltraffio." Tesi di laurea. Università di Milano, 1935–36.

Belt 1952
Belt, Elmer. "Leonardo da Vinci's Studies of the Aging Process." *Geriatrics* 7 (1952), pp. 205–10.

Beltrame Quattrocchi 1979
Beltrame Quattrocchi, Enrichetta. *Disegni Toscani e umbri del primo rinascimento dalle collezioni del Gabinetto Nazionale delle Stampe.* Exh. cat., Rome, Villa alla Farnesina alla Lungara. Rome, 1979.

Beltrami 1909
Beltrami, Luca. *La "destra mano" di Leonardo da Vinci e le lacune nella edizione del Codice Atlantico.* Analecta Ambrosiana, 2. Milan, 1909.

Beltrami 1911
Beltrami, Luca. *Bernardino Luini, 1512–1532.* Milan, 1911.

Beltrami 1919a
Beltrami, Luca, ed. *Documenti e memorie riguardanti la vita e le opere di Leonardo da Vinci in ordine cronologico.* Milan, 1919.

Beltrami 1919b
Beltrami, Luca. *Leonardo e i disfattisti suoi, con settanta illustrazioni e un'appendice "Leonardo architetto."* Milan, 1919.

Beltrami 1919c
B[eltrami], L[uca]. "La vita di Leonardo." *Emporium* 49, no. 293 (May 1919), pp. 227–71.

Beltrami 1920
Beltrami, Luca. "La ricostituzione del monumento

sepolcrale per il maresciallo Trivulzio in Milano di Leonardo da Vinci." *La Lettura* 20 (1920), pp. 84–90.

Beltrami and Fumagalli 1904
Beltrami, Luca, and Carlo Fumagalli. *Disegni di Leonardo e della sua scuola alla Biblioteca Ambrosiana.* Milan, 1904.

Benesch 1964
Benesch, Otto. *Meisterzeichnungen der Albertina.* Salzburg, 1964.

Benson 1994
Benson, Peter. "Freud and the Visual." *Representations* 45, (1994), pp. 101–16.

Berenson 1903
Berenson, Bernard. *The Drawings of the Florentine Painters Classified, Criticised and Studied as Documents in the History and Appreciation of the Tuscan Art, with a Copious Catalogue Raisonné.* 2 vols. London, 1903.

Berenson 1923
Berenson, Bernard. "Un possible Antonello da Messina ed uno impossibile." *Dedalo* 4 (1923), pp. 3–44.

Berenson 1933–34
Berenson, Bernhard. "Verrocchio e Leonardo: Leonardo e Credi." *Bollettino d'arte,* ser. 3, 27 (1933–34), pp. 193–214, 241–64.

Berenson 1938
Berenson, Bernard. *The Drawings of the Florentine Painters, Amplified Edition.* 3 vols. Chicago, 1938.

Berenson 1955
Berenson, Bernard. *Lorenzo Lotto.* London, 1955.

Berenson 1961
Berenson, Bernard. *I disegni dei pittori fiorentini.* Revised and enlarged edition. 3 vols. Translated by Luisa Vertova Nicolson. Milan, 1961.

Bernacchioni 1992
Bernacchioni, Annamaria. "Le botteghe di pittura: Luoghi, strutture e attività." In Palazzo Strozzi 1992–93, pp. 23–33.

Bernardi 1952
Bernardi, Marziano. *Leonardo a Milano.* Turin, 1952.

Bernhard 1977
Bernhard, Marianne. *Rubens: Handzeichnungen.* Munich, 1977.

Berra 1993
Berra, Giacomo. "La storia dei canoni proporzionali del corpo umano e gli sviluppi in area lombarda alla fine del cinquecento." *Raccolta Vinciana,* no. 25 (1993), pp. 158–310.

Berra 1998
Giacomo Berra. "Arcimboldi: Le teste 'caricate' leonardesche e le 'grillerie' dell'Accademia della Val di Blenio." In Museo Cantonale d'Arte 1998, pp. 57–67.

Bertelli 1983
Bertelli, Carlo. "Il Cenacolo vinciano." In *Santa Maria delle Grazie in Milano,* edited by A. Pizzi, pp. 188–95. Milan, 1983.

Bertelli 1986
Bertelli, Carlo. "Leonardo e l'*Ultima Cena* (ca. 1495–97)." In *Tecnica e stile: Esempi di pittura murale del Rinascimento Italiano,* edited by Eve

Borsook and Fiorella Superbi Gioffredi, vol. 1, pp. 31–42. Florence, 1986.

Bertelli 2001
Bertelli, Carlo. "Prima della *Cena.*" In Palazzo Reale 2001, pp. 39–46.

Berti and Baldini 1991
Berti, Luciano, and Umberto Baldini. *Filippino Lippi.* Florence, 1991.

Bertini 1935
Bertini, Aldo. "L'Arte del Verrocchio." *L'Arte* 38 (1935), pp. 433–73.

Bertini 1950a
Bertini, Aldo. "Disegni inediti nella Biblioteca reale di Torino." *Critica d'arte* 32 (1950), pp. 501–6.

Bertini 1950b
Bertini, Aldo, ed. *Prima mostra dei disegni italiani della Biblioteca reale, Torino.* Exh. cat., Turin, Biblioteca reale. Turin, 1950.

Bertini 1958
Bertini, Aldo. *I disegni italiani della Biblioteca reale di Torino.* Rome, 1958.

Bertini 1987
Bertini, Giuseppe. *La Galleria del Duca di Parma: Storia di una collezione.* Parma, 1987.

Beuys Wurmbach 1959
Beuys Wurmbach, Eva. *Die Landschaften in den Hintergründen der Gemälde Leonardos.* Monaco, 1959.

Biaggi 1980
Biaggi, Carlo Felice. "Anatomy in Art." In *Leonardo da Vinci* 1980, pp. 137–47.

Bialler 1992–93
Bialler, Nancy. *Chiaroscuro Woodcuts: Hendrick Goltzius (1558–1617) and his Time.* Exh. cat., Amsterdam, Rijksmuseum, Rijksprentenkabinett; Cleveland Museum of Art. Ghent, 1992.

Białostocki 1959
Białostocki, Jan. "'Opus Quinque dierum': Dürer's 'Christ among the Doctors' and its Sources." *Journal of the Warburg and Courtauld Institutes* 22 (1959), pp. 17–34.

Biblioteca Medicea Laurenziana 1952
Brunetti, Giulia, et al. *Quinto centenario della nascita di Leonardo da Vinci: Mostra di disegni, manoscritti e documenti.* Exh. cat., Florence, Biblioteca Medicea Laurenziana. Florence, 1952.

Bing 1937–38
Bing, Gertrud. "Nugae circa veritatem: Notes on Anton Francesco Doni." *Journal of the Warburg and Courtauld Institutes* 1 (1937–38), pp. 304–12.

Biringuccio 1942
Biringuccio, Vannoccio. *The Pirotechnia of Vannoccio Biringuccio.* Translation, introduction and notes by Cyril Stanley Smith and Martha Teach Gnudi. New York, 1942.

Birke 1991
Birke, Veronika. *Die italienischen Zeichnungen der Albertina: Zur Geschichte der Zeichnung in Italien.* Veröffentlichungen der Albertina, 29. Munich, 1991.

Birke and Kertész 1992–97
Birke, Veronika, and Janine Kertész. *Die italienischen Zeichnungen der Albertina: Generalverzeichnis.*

4 vols. Veröffentlichungen der Albertina, 33–36. Vienna, Cologne, and Weimar, 1992–97.

Birmingham Museum of Art 1978
Farmer, J. D. *Rubens and Humanism.* Exh. cat., Birmingham Museum of Art. Birmingham, 1978.

Blanc 1861
Blanc, Charles. "Une peinture de Léonard de Vinci." *Gazette des Beaux-Arts,* ser. 1, 9 (1861), pp. 65–74.

Blank, Miller, and von Voss 2000
Blank, R., V. Miller, and H. von Voss. "Human Motor Development and Hand Laterality: A Kinematic Analysis of Drawing Movements." *Neuroscience Letters,* no. 295 (2000), pp. 89–92.

Blass-Simmen 1991
Blass-Simmen, Birgit. *Sankt Georg: Drachenkampf in der Renaissance: Carpaccio, Raffael, Leonardo.* Berlin, 1991.

Bloch 1962
Bloch, Vitale. "Le dessin italien dans les collections hollandaises." *Pantheon* 20, no. 3 (1962), pp. 198–99.

Blum 1932
Blum, André. "Léonard de Vinci graveur." *Gazette des Beaux-Arts,* ser. 6, 8 (1932), pp. 89–104.

Blunt 1979–80
Blunt, Anthony. *Treasures From Chatsworth: The Devonshire Inheritance.* Exh. cat., Richmond, Museum of Fine Arts; Fort Worth, Kimbell Art Museum; Toledo Museum of Art; San Antonio, Museum Association; New Orleans, Museum of Art; San Francisco, California Palace of the Legion of Honor; London, Royal Academy of Arts. [Washington, D.C.], 1979.

Bober and Rubinstein 1986
Bober, Phyllis Pray, and Ruth Rubinstein. *Renaissance Artists and Antique Sculpture: A Handbook of Sources.* London and New York, 1986.

Bock 1916
Bock, Franz. "Leonardofragen." *Repertorium für Kunstwissenschaft* 39 (1916), pp. 153–65, 218–30.

Bock 1996
Bock, Henning, et al. *Gemäldegalerie Berlin: Gesamtverzeichnis.* Berlin, 1996.

Bode 1950
Bode, Wilhelm von. *Leonardo da Vinci: Ausgewählte Handzeichnungen.* Berlin, [1950].

Bode 1899
Bode, W[ilhelm von]. "Verrocchio und das Altarbild der Sacramentskapelle im Dom zu Pistoja." *Repertorium für Kunstwissenschaft* 22 (1899), pp. 390–94.

Bode 1921
Bode, Wilhelm von. *Studien über Leonardo da Vinci.* Berlin, 1921.

Bodmer 1931
Bodmer, Heinrich. *Leonardo: Des Meisters Gemälde und Zeichnungen.* Klassiker der Kunst in Gesamtausgaben, 37. Stuttgart and Berlin, 1931.

Bongioanni 1980
Bongioanni, Fausto M. "Studying Leonardo." In *Leonardo da Vinci* 1980, pp. 175–85.

Boorsch 1992
Boorsch, Suzanne. "Mantegna and his Printmakers." In Metropolitan Museum of Art and Royal Academy of Arts 1992, pp. 56–64.

Bora 1978
Bora, Giulio. *I disegni del Codice Resta.* Milan, 1978.

Bora 1980
Bora, Giulio. *I disegni lombardi e genovesi del Cinquecento.* Treviso, 1980.

Bora 1982
Bora, Giulio. "I disegni." In Dell'Aqua 1982, pp. 131–52.

Bora 1987a
Bora, Giulio. *Due tavole leonardesche: Nuove indagini sul musico e sul San Giovanni dell'Ambrosiana.* Vicenza, 1987.

Bora 1987b
Bora, Giulio. "Per un catalogo dei disegni dei leonardeschi lombardi: Indicazioni e problemi di metodo." *Raccolta Vinciana,* no. 22 (1987) pp. 139–82.

Bora 1987–88
Bora, Giulio. "I leonardeschi e il ruolo del disegno." In Palazzo Reale 1987–88, pp. 11–19.

Bora 1988
Bora, Giulio, et al. *I disegni della collezione Morelli.* Bergamo, 1988.

Bora 1989
Bora, Giulio. "Da Leonardo all'Accademia della Val di Bregno: Giovan Paolo [Gianpaolo] Lomazzo, Aurelio Luini e i disegni degli accademici." *Raccolta Vinciana,* no. 23 (1989), pp. 73–101.

Bora 1991
Bora, Giulio. "I disegni dei leonardeschi e il collezionismo milanese: Consistenza, fortuna, dispersione." In Fiorio and Marani 1991, pp. 206–17.

Bora 1994
Bora, Giulio. *Giovanni Morelli, collezionista di disegni: La donazione al Castello Sforzesco.* Milan, 1994.

Bora 1998a
Bora, Giulio. "Bernardino Luini." In *Legacy of Leonardo* 1998, pp. 325–70.

Bora 1998b
Bora, Giulio. "Giovanni Agostino da Lodi." In *Legacy of Leonardo* 1998, pp. 251–74.

Bora 1998c
Bora, Giulio. "The Leonardesque Circle and Drawing." In *Legacy of Leonardo* 1998, pp. 92–120.

Bora 1998d
Bora, Giulio. "Milano nell'età di Lomazzo e San Carlo: Riaffermazione e difficoltà di sopravvivenza di una cultura." In Museo Cantonale d'Arte 1998, pp. 37–56.

Borea 2001
Borea, Evelina. "Caylus e l'arte italiana." In *Mélanges Pierre Rosenberg: Peintures et dessins en France et en Italie, XVIIe–XVIIIe siècles,* pp. 103–13. Paris, 2001.

Borenius 1930
Borenius, Tancred. "Leonardo's *Madonna with the Children at Play.*" *The Burlington Magazine* 56, no. 324 (March 1930), pp. 142–47.

Borenius 1980
Borenius, Tancred. "Leonardo in England." In *Leonardo da Vinci* 1980, pp. 191–93.

Borne 2001
Borne, F[rançois] J. "*Horse and Rider*: A Mirror of Leonardo's Culture." In *Old Master Drawings, including Leonardo da Vinci's Horse and Rider.* Sale cat., Christie's, London, Tuesday, July 10, 2001, pp. 51–55.

Bossi 1810
Bossi, Giuseppe. *Del Cenacolo di Leonardo da Vinci, Libri Quattro.* Milan, 1810.

Bottari and Ticozzi 1822–25
Bottari, Gio[vanni Gaetano], and Stefano Ticozzi. *Raccolta di lettere sulla pittura scultura ed architettura: Scritte da' più celebri personaggi dei secoli XV, XVI e XVII, pubblicata da M. Gio. Bottari e continuate fino ai nostri giorni da Stefano Ticozzi.* 1757–73. 8 vols. Milan, 1822–25.

Bottari 1942
Bottari, Stefano. *Leonardo.* Bergamo, 1942.

Bottazzi 1980
Bottazzi, Filippo. "Leonardo as Physiologist." In *Leonardo da Vinci* 1980, pp. 373–87.

Bouchot-Saupique 1930–31
Bouchot-Saupique, Jacqueline. "Quelques dessins flamands du fonds au Musée du Louvre." *De Kunst der Nederlanden* (1930–31), pp. 90–91.

Bouchot-Saupique 1953–54
Bouchot-Saupique, Jacqueline. "Contribution à l'étude des dessins de Léonard de Vinci: Quelques notes relatives à des dessins des Musées nationaux et de l'École des Beaux-Arts de Paris." In *L'art et la pensée de Léonard de Vinci: Communications du Congrès International du Val de Loire (7–12 juillet 1952),* pp. 51–67. Paris and Algiers, 1953–54.

Bouchot-Saupique 1957
Bouchot-Saupique, Jacqueline. *L'enfant dans le dessin du XVe au XIXe siècle.* Exh. cat., Paris, Musée du Louvre. Paris, 1957.

Bovi 1952
Bovi, Arturo. *Leonardo, filosofo, artista, uomo.* Milan, 1952.

Bovi 1959
Bovi, Arturo. *L'opera di Leonardo per il monumento Sforza a Milano.* Florence, 1959.

Brachert 1970
Brachert, Thomas. "A Distinctive Aspect in the Painting Technique of the *Ginevra de' Benci* and of Leonardo's Early Works." *Report and Studies in the History of Art.* National Gallery of Art, Washington, D.C. (1970), pp. 85–103.

Brachert 1971
Brachert, Thomas. "A Musical Canon of Proportion in Leonardo da Vinci's *Last Supper.*" *The Art Bulletin* 53, no. 4 (December 1971), pp. 461–66.

Brady 2000
Old Master Drawings. Exh. cat., New York, W. M. Brady & Co. New York, 2000.

Brambilla Barcilon and Marani 1990
Brambilla Barcilon, Pinin, and Pietro C. Marani. *Le lunette di Leonardo nel Refettorio delle Grazie.* Quaderni del restauro, 7. Milan, 1990.

Brambilla Barcilon and Marani 1999
Brambilla Barcilon, Pinin, and Pietro C. Marani. *Leonardo: L'Ultima Cena.* Milan, 1999. Revised and expanded edition, Milan, 2000; English edition: *Leonardo: The Last Supper.* Translated by Harlow Tighe. Chicago and London, 2001. References in the catalogue entries are to the English edition.

Bramly 1991
Bramly, Serge. *Leonardo: Discovering the Life of Leonardo da Vinci.* Translated by Siân Reynolds. New York, 1991.

Bramly 1995
Bramly, Serge. *Mona Lisa.* Mémoire de l'art. Paris, 1995.

Brinton 1911
Brinton, Selwyn. *Leonardo at Milan.* London, 1911.

British Museum 1858
A Guide to the Drawings and Prints Exhibited . . . in the King's Library. Exh. cat., London, British Museum. London, 1858.

British Museum 1888–94
Reproductions of Drawings by Old Masters in the British Museum. London, 1888–94.

British Museum 1891
Guide to the Exhibition of Drawings . . . by Continental and British Masters in the Print and Drawing Gallery. Exh. cat., London, British Museum. London, 1891.

British Museum 1895
Colvin, Sidney. *Guide to the Exhibition of Drawings and Engravings by Old Masters, Principally from the Malcolm Collection.* Exh. cat., London, British Museum. London, 1895.

British Museum 1983
Italian Drawings from the Lugt Collection, Institut néerlandais, Paris. Exh. cat., London, British Museum. London, 1983.

British Museum 1996
Royalton-Kisch, Martin, Hugo Chapman, and Stephen Coppel, eds. *Old Master Drawings from the Malcolm Collection.* Exh. cat., London, British Museum. London, 1996.

British Museum 1998
Griffiths, Antony and Robert A. Gerard. *The Print in Stuart England, 1603–1689.* Exh. cat., London, British Museum. London, 1998.

British Museum and Metropolitan Museum of Art 2000–1
Bambach, Carmen C., et al. *Correggio and Parmigianino: Master Draughtsmen of the Renaissance.* Exh. cat., London, British Museum; New York, The Metropolitan Museum of Art. London, 2000.

Brizio 1951
Brizio, Anna Maria. "Primo libro delle acque." In *Scritti vari* (Facoltà di Magistero di Torino), vol. 2, pp. 93–111. Turin, 1951.

Brizio 1954
Brizio, Anna Maria. "Delle acque." In *Leonardo: Saggi e ricerche* 1954, pp. 275–89, pls. 117–23.

Brizio 1960
Brizio, A[nna] M[aria]. Review of *Studi Vinciani,* by C[arlo] Pedretti. *Raccolta Vinciana,* no. 18 (1960), pp. 260–63.

Brizio 1974a
Brizio, Anna Maria. "Arte e scienza in Leonardo." *Almanacco italiano* 75 (1975), pp. 324–30.

Brizio 1974b
Brizio, Anna Maria. "The Painter." In Reti 1974, pp. 20–55.

Brizio 1985
Brizio, Anna Maria. "Il Cenacolo." In *Leonardo: La pittura* 1985, pp. 75–89.

Brockhaus 1902
Brockhaus, Enrico. *Ricerche sopra alcuni capolavori d'arte fiorentina.* Milan, 1902.

Brown 1971
Brown, David Alan. "The Profile of a Youth and Leonardo's Annunciation." *Mitteilungen des Kunsthistorischen Institutes in Florenz* 15 (1971), pp. 265–72.

Brown 1981
Brown, Beverly Louise. "The Patronage and Building History of the Tribuna of SS. Annunziata in Florence: A Reappraisal in Light of New Documentation." *Mitteilungen des Kunsthistorischen Institutes in Florenz* 25, no. 1 (1981), pp. 59–146.

Brown 1983a
Brown, David Alan. "Leonardo and the Idealized Portrait in Milan." *Arte lombarda*, no. 67 (1983), pp. 102–16.

Brown 1983b
Brown, David Alan. *Leonardo's Last Supper: Precedents and Reflections. Leonardo's Last Supper: Before and After.* Exh. cat., Washington D.C., National Gallery of Art. Washington, D.C., 1983.

Brown 1983c
Brown, David Alan. *Leonardo's Last Supper: The Restoration. Leonardo's Last Supper: Before and After.* Exh. cat., Washington D.C., National Gallery of Art. Washington, D.C., 1983.

Brown 1983d
Brown, David Alan. *Raphael and America.* Exh. cat., Washington, D.C., National Gallery of Art. Washington, D.C., 1983.

Brown 1986
Brown, Deborah. "The *Apollo Belvedere* and the Garden of Giuliano Della Rovere at SS. Apostoli." *Journal of the Warburg and Courtauld Institutes* 49 (1986), pp. 235–38.

Brown 1987
Brown, David Alan. *Andrea Solario.* Milan, 1987.

Brown 1989a
Brown, David Alan. Review of *Leonardo e i leonardeschi a Brera*, by Pietro C. Marani; and *Disegni e dipinti leonardeschi dalle collezioni milanesi. The Burlington Magazine* 131, no. 1036 (July 1989), pp. 491–92.

Brown 1989b
Brown, David Alan. "Some Observations about the Exhibition 'Disegni e dipinti leonardeschi dalle collezioni milanesi.'" *Raccolta Vinciana*, no. 23 (1989), pp. 27–32.

Brown 1990a
Brown, David Alan. "Leonardo and the Ladies with the Ermine and the Book." *Artibus et historiae*, no. 22 (1990), pp. 47–61.

Brown 1990b
Brown, David Alan. *Madonna Litta.* Lettura Vinciana, 29 (15 aprile 1989). Vinci, 1990.

Brown 1991
Brown, David Alan. "The Master of the 'Madonna Litta.'" In Fiorio and Marani 1991, pp. 25–34.

Brown 1994a
Brown, David Alan. "Leonardo's 'Head of an Old Man' in Turin: Portrait or Self-Portrait?" In *Studi di storia dell'arte in onore di Mina Gregori*, edited by Miklós Boskovits, pp. 75–78. Milan, 1994.

Brown 1994b
Brown, David Alan. "Verrocchio and Leonardo: Studies for the *Giostra*." In Cropper 1994, pp. 99–109, and unpaginated figures.

Brown 1998a
Brown, David Alan. "Andrea Solario." In *Legacy of Leonardo* 1998, pp. 231–50.

Brown 1998b
Brown, David Alan. *Leonardo da Vinci: Origins of a Genius.* New Haven and London, 1998.

Brown 1999a
Brown, David Alan. "Giovanni Antonio Boltraffio." In *Von Raffael bis Tiepolo: Italienische Kunst aus der Sammlung des Fürstenhauses Esterházy*, edited by István Barkóczi, pp. 132–33. Exh. cat., Budapest, Szépművészeti Múzeum; Frankfurt, Schirn Kunsthalle. Munich, 1999.

Brown 1999b
Brown, David Alan. *Leonardo apprendista.* Lettura Vinciana, 39 (17 aprile 1999). Vinci, 1999.

Brown 2001–2
Brown, David Alan, et al. *Virtue and Beauty: Leonardo's* Ginevra de' Benci *and Renaissance Portraits of Women.* Exh. cat., Washington, D.C., National Gallery of Art. Washington, D.C., 2001.

Brugnoli 1954
Brugnoli, Maria Vittoria. "Documenti, notizie e ipotesi sulla scultura di Leonardo." In *Leonardo: Saggi e ricerche* 1954, pp. 359–89, pls. 146–58.

Brugnoli 1974
Brugnoli, Maria Vittoria. "Il Cavallo." In Reti 1974, pp. 86–109.

Brugnoli 1982
Brugnoli, Maria Vittoria. "Il Monumento Sforza e il Cavallo Colossale." In Dell'Acqua 1982, pp. 89–112.

Brummer 1993
Brummer, Hans Henrik. "The *editio princeps* of Leonardo da Vinci's Treatise on Painting Dedicated to Queen Christina." *Achademia Leonardi Vinci: Journal of Leonardo Studies and Bibliography of Vinciana* 6 (1993), pp. 117–25, and unpaginated figures.

Budny 1979–80
Budny, Virginia. "The Poses of the Child in the Composition Sketches by Leonardo da Vinci for *The Madonna and Child with a Cat* and in Other Works Related to this Group." *Weatherspoon Gallery Association Bulletin* (1979–80), pp. 4–12.

Budny 1983
Budny, Virginia. "The Sequence of Leonardo's Sketches for *The Virgin and Child with Saint Anne and Saint John the Baptist*." *The Art Bulletin* 65, no. 1 (March 1983), pp. 34–50.

Bule 1992
Bule, Steven, Alan Phipps Darr, and Fiorella Superbi Gioffredi, eds. *Verrocchio and Late Quattrocento Italian Sculpture.* Florence, 1992.

Bull 1992
Bull, David. "Two Portraits by Leonardo: *Ginevra de' Benci* and the *Lady with an Ermine*." *Artibus et historiae*, no. 25 (1992), pp. 67–83.

Burchard and d'Hulst 1963
Burchard, Ludwig, and Roger Adolf d'Hulst. *Rubens Drawings.* 2 vols. Brussels, 1963.

Burroughs 1918
B[urroughs], B[ryson]. "Drawings by Leonardo da Vinci on Exhibition." *The Metropolitan Museum of Art Bulletin* 13, no. 10 (October 1918), pp. 214–17.

Burroughs 1919
B[urroughs], B[ryson]. "Drawings from the Pembroke Collection." *The Metropolitan Museum of Art Bulletin* 14, no. 6 (June 1919), pp. 136–40.

Bush 1978
Bush, Virginia. "Leonardo's Sforza Monument and Cinquecento Sculpture." *Arte lombarda* 50 (1978), pp. 47–68.

Bush 1980
Bush, Virginia. "Bandinelli's *Hercules and Cacus* and Florentine Traditions." *Memoirs of the American Academy in Rome* 35 (1980), pp. 163–206.

Busignani 1970
Busignani, Alberto. *Pollaiolo.* Florence, 1970.

Butterfield 1997
Butterfield, Andrew. *The Sculptures of Andrea del Verrocchio.* New Haven and London, 1997.

Butterfield 2001
Butterfield, Andrew. "Leonardo: Draughtsman of Genius." In *Old Master Drawings, including Leonardo da Vinci's Horse and Rider.* Sale cat., Christie's, London, Tuesday, July 10, 2001, pp. 48–50.

Byam Shaw 1972–73
Byam Shaw, James. *Old Master Drawings from Christ Church, Oxford.* Exh. cat., Washington, D.C., National Gallery of Art; Philadelphia Museum of Art; New York, The Pierpont Morgan Library; Cleveland Museum of Art; St. Louis Art Museum. Washington, D.C., 1972.

Byam Shaw 1976a
Byam Shaw, James. *Drawings by Old Masters at Christ Church, Oxford.* 2 vols. Oxford, 1976.

Byam Shaw 1976b
Byam Shaw, James. "Master Draughtsmen of the Venetian *Settecento*." *Apollo* 104, no. 177 (November 1976), pp. 388–95.

Byam Shaw 1983
Byam Shaw, James. *The Italian Drawings of the Frits Lugt Collection.* 3 vols. Paris, 1983.

Byam Shaw 1984
Byam Shaw, James. *Dessins florentins et romains de la collection Frits Lugt.* Exh. cat., Paris, Institut Néerlandais, Fondation Custodia. Paris, 1984.

Cadogan 1983a
Cadogan, Jean K. "Linen Drapery Studies by

Verrocchio, Leonardo and Ghirlandaio." *Zeitschrift für Kunstgeschichte* 46, no. 1 (1983), pp. 27–62.

Cadogan 1983b
Cadogan, Jean K. "Reconsidering Some Aspects of Ghirlandaio's Drawings." *The Art Bulletin* 65, no. 2 (June 1983), pp. 274–90.

Cadogan 1983c
Cadogan, Jean K. "Verrocchio's Drawings Reconsidered." *Zeitschrift für Kunstgeschichte* 46, no. 4 (1983), pp. 367–400.

Cadogan 2000
Cadogan, Jean K. *Domenico Ghirlandaio, Artist and Artisan.* New Haven and London, 2000.

Caglioti 2000
Caglioti, F. *Donatello e i Medici.* Vol. 2. Florence, 2000.

Cagnola 1907
Cagnola, Guido. "Brevi note sulla Pinacoteca Ambrosiana riordinata." *Rassegna d'arte* 7, no. 2 (February 1907), pp. 17–22.

Calcani 1983–84
Calcani, Giuliana. "Un modello antico in Andrea del Castagno e in Leonardo." *Prospettiva,* nos. 33–36 (April 1983–January 1984), pp. 58–61.

Calder 1970
Calder, Ritchie. *Leonardo and the Age of the Eye.* London, 1970.

Calvesi 1980
Calvesi, Maurizio. *Il sogno di Polifilo.* Rome, 1980.

Calvesi 1985
Calvesi, Maurizio. "Leda." In *Leonardo: La pittura* 1985, pp. 137–53.

Calvi 1909
Calvi, Gerolamo. *Il codice di Leonardo da Vinci (idraulica e cosmografica) della Biblioteca di Lord Leicester in Holkham Hall.* Reale Istituto Lombardo di Scienze e Lettere. Milan, 1909.

Calvi 1916
Calvi, Gerolamo. "Contributi alla biografia di Leonardo da Vinci: (Periodo Sforzesco)." *Archivio storico lombardo* 43, no. 3 (1916), pp. 417–508.

Calvi 1919
Calvi, G[erolamo]. "L'Adorazione dei Magi di Leonardo da Vinci." *Raccolta Vinciana,* no. 10 (1919), pp. 1–44.

Calvi 1925a
Calvi, Gerolamo. *I manoscritti di Leonardo da Vinci dal punto di vista cronologico, storico e biografico.* Bologna, 1925.

Calvi 1925b
Calvi, G[erolamo]. "Pagine inedite del Codice Atlantico." *Raccolta Vinciana,* no. 12 (1925), pp. 163–72.

Calvi 1930–34
[Calvi, Gerolamo]. Review of *Leonardo da Vinci, the Artist,* by Edward MacCurdy. *Raccolta Vinciana,* no. 14 (1930–34), pp. 303–7.

Calvi 1934–39
Calvi, Ignazio. "Ritornando sul parallelismo tra la S. Anna di Leonardo ed il quadro luinesco all'Ambrosiana." *Raccolta Vinciana,* nos. 15–16 (1934–39), pp. 85–114.

Calvi 1943
Calvi, Ignazio. *L'architettura militare di Leonardo da Vinci.* Milan, 1943.

Calvi 1980
Calvi, Ignazio. "Military Engineering and Arms." In *Leonardo da Vinci* 1980, pp. 275–306.

Calvi 1982
Calvi, Girolamo. *I manoscritti di Leonardo da Vinci dal punto di vista cronologico, storico e biografico.* New edition, edited by Augusto Marinoni. Busto Arsizio, 1982.

Calvino 1992
Calvino, Italo. *Six Memos for the Next Millenium.* Translated by Patrick Creagh. London, 1992.

Camerota 2001–2
Camerota, Filippo, et al. *Nel segno di Masaccio: L'invenzione della prospettiva.* Exh. cat., Florence, Galleria degli Uffizi. Florence, 2001.

Campbell 1997
Campbell, Stephen. *Cosmè Tura of Ferrara: Style, Politics and the Renaissance City, 1450–1495.* New Haven and London, 1997.

Campbell 2002
Campbell, Stephen, et al. *Cosmè Tura: Painting and Design in Renaissance Ferrara.* Exh. cat., Boston, Isabella Stewart Gardner Museum. Boston, 2002.

Canestrini 1980
Canestrini, Giovanni. "Leonardo's Machines." In *Leonardo da Vinci* 1980, pp. 493–507.

Caracciolo 2001
Caracciolo, Maria Teresa. "Pour le Maître des Albums Egmont et ses sources." In *Francesco Salviati et la bella maniera: Actes des colloques de Rome et de Paris (1998),* edited by Catherine Monbeig Goguel, Philippe Costamagna, and Michel Hochmann, pp. 667–89. Rome, 2001.

Cardellini 1962
Cardellini, Ida. *Desiderio da Settignano.* Milan, 1962.

Carl 1982
Carl, Doris. "Zur Goldschmiedefamilie Dei mit neuen Dokumenten zu Antonio Pollaiuolo und Andrea Verrocchio." *Mitteilungen des Kunsthistorichen Institutes in Florenz* 26, no. 2 (1982), pp. 129–66.

Carminati 1990
Carminati, Marco. "Cesare da Sesto: Un ciclo di affreschi poco noto ed un riesame." *Arte cristiana* 77, no. 734 (September–October 1990), pp. 347–68.

Carminati 1994
Carminati, Marco. *Cesare da Sesto, 1477–1523.* Milan, 1994.

Carminati 1998
Carminati, Marco. "Cesare da Sesto." In *Legacy of Leonardo* 1998, pp. 305–24.

Caroli 1991
Caroli, Flavio. *Leonardo: Studi di fisiognomica.* Milan, 1991.

Caroli 1995
Caroli, Flavio. "Fisiognomica come nuovo Umaneisimo: Da Leonardo a Freud." *Achademia Leonardi Vinci: Journal of Leonardo Studies and Bibliography of Vinciana* 8 (1995), pp. 167–70, and unpaginated figures.

Carotti 1899
Carotti, Giulio. "R. Galleria di Brera in Milano. Giovanni Antonio Boltraffio (a proposito dell acquisto della tavola dei due divoti)." *Le Gallerie nazionali italiane: Notizie e documenti* 4 (1899), pp. 298–331.

Carotti 1905
Carotti, Giulio. *Le opere di Leonardo, Bramante e Raffaello.* Milan, 1905.

Carotti 1921
Carotti, Giulio. *Leonardo da Vinci, pittore, scultore, architetto: Studio biografico critico.* Turin, 1921.

Carpiceci 1978
Carpiceci, Alberto Carlo. *L'architettura di Leonardo: Indagine e ipotesi su tutta l'opera di Leonardo architetto.* Florence, 1978.

Carpiceci 1984
Carpiceci, Alberto Carlo. *L'architettura di Leonardo: Indagine e ipotesi su tutta l'opera di Leonardo architetto.* 2d edition, revised and enlarged. Florence, 1984.

Carroll 1989
Carroll, Margaret D. "The Erotics of Absolutism: Rubens and the Mystification of Sexual Violence." *Representations* 25 (1989), pp. 3–30.

Cartwright 1903
Cartwright, Julia. *Isabella d'Este Marchioness of Mantua, 1474–1539: A Study of the Renaissance.* 2 vols. London, 1903.

Carusi 1926
Carusi, Enrico. *Reale Commissione Vinciana: I fogli mancanti al codice di Leonardo da Vinci su'l volo degli uccelli nella Biblioteca reale di Torino.* 3 vols. Rome, 1926.

Carusi 1940
Carusi, Enrico. "Un incunabolo con disegni di scuola leonardesca." *Accademie e Biblioteche d'Italia* 14 (1940), pp. 145–53.

Carusi 1980
Carusi, Enrico. "Leonardo's Manuscripts." In *Leonardo da Vinci* 1980, pp. 157–62.

Carusi and Favaro 1923
Leonardo da Vinci. *Del moto e misura dell'acqua: Libri nove ordinati da F. Luigi Maria Arconati, editi sul codice archetipo barberiniano.* 1826. Critical edition edited by E[nrico] Carusi and A[ntonio] Favaro. Bologna, 1923.

Casamassima 1966
Casamassima, Emanuele. *Trattati di scritura del cinquecento italiano.* Milan, 1966.

Cast 1981
Cast, David. *The Calumny of Apelles: A Study in the Humanistic Tradition.* New Haven, 1981.

Castelfranco 1952a
Castelfranco, Giorgio. "Il canale Firenze-Mare nei progetti di Leonardo." *Civiltà delle macchine* 3 (1952), pp. 56–58.

Castelfranco 1952b
Castelfranco, Giorgio. *Leonardo: I grandi maestri del disegno.* Milan, 1952.

Castelfranco 1954a
Castelfranco, Giorgio. "Chiana e Trasimeno negli

studi geografici di Leonardo." *Bollettino d'arte* 39 (1954), pp. 273–77.

Castelfranco 1954b
Castelfranco, Giorgio. "Momenti della recente critica vinciana." In *Leonardo: Saggi e ricerche 1954*, pp. 415–77, pls. 159–74.

Castelfranco 1955
Castelfranco, Giorgio. "Il preventivo di Leonardo per il monumento sepolcrale di Giangiacomo Trivulzio." *Bollettino d'arte* 40 (1955), pp. 262–69.

Castelfranco 1956
Castelfranco, Giorgio. *La pittura di Leonardo da Vinci.* Milan, 1956.

Castelfranco 1957
Castelfranco, Giorgio. *Storia di Milano.* Vol. 8. Milan, 1957.

Castelfranco 1966
Castelfranco, Giorgio. *Studi vinciani.* Rome, 1966.

Castiglione 1560
Castiglione, Sabba da. *Ricordi di Monsignor Sabba da Castiglione Cavalier Gierosolimitano, di nuovo corretti, et ristampati.* 1546. Venice, 1560.

Cazort and Kornell 1996–97
Cazort, Mimi, and Monique Kornell. *The Ingenious Machine of Nature: Four Centuries of Art and Anatomy.* Exh. cat., Ottawa, The National Gallery of Canada; Vancouver Art Gallery; Philadelphia Museum of Art; Jerusalem, Israel Museum. Ottawa, 1996.

Cecchi 1984
Cecchi, Alessandro. "Una predella e altri contributi per l'Adorazione dei Magi di Filippino." In *I pittori della Brancacci agli Uffizi,* pp. 59–72. Gli Uffizi: Studi e ricerche, 5. Florence, 1984.

Cecchi 1996
Cecchi, Alessandro. "Niccolò Machiavelli o Marcello Virgilio Adriani? Sul programma e l'assetto compositivo delle 'Battaglie' di Leonardo e Michelangelo per la Sala del Maggior Consiglio in Palazzo Vecchio." *Prospettiva,* nos. 83–84 (July–October 1996), pp. 102–15.

Cecchi and Natali 1996–97
Cecchi, Alessandro, and Antonio Natali. *L'officina della maniera: Varietà e fierezza nell'arte fiorentina del Cinquecento fra le due repubbliche, 1494–1530.* Exh. cat., Florence, Galleria degli Uffizi. Florence, 1996.

Cecchi and Natali 2000
Cecchi, Alessandro, and Antonio Natali. "Viatico romano per Botticelli illustratore." In *Sandro Botticelli, pittore della Divina Commedia,* vol. 1, pp. 26–32. Exh. cat., Rome, Scuderie Papali al Quirinale. 2 vols. Milan, 2000.

Cederlöf 1959
Cederlöf, Olle. "Leonardos 'Kampen om standaret': En ikonografisk undersökning." *Konsthistorisk Tidskrift* 28 (1959), pp. 73–98.

Cederlöf 1961
Cederlöf, Olle. "Leonardos 'Kampen om standaret': En ikonologisk tolkning." *Konsthistorisk Tidskrift* 30 (1961), pp. 62–94.

Cellini 1971
Cellini, Benvenuto. *Opere di Benvenuto Cellini.* Edited by Giuseppe Guido Ferrero. Turin, 1971.

Cennini 1933
Cennini, Cennino. *The Craftsman's Handbook.* Translated by Daniel V. Thompson, Jr. New York, 1933.

Cennini 1991
Cennini, Cennino. *Il libro dell'arte.* Edited and annotated by Mario Serchi. Florence, 1991.

Cetto 1950
Cetto, Anna Maria. *Animal Drawings of Eight Centuries.* New York, 1950.

Chamberlaine 1812
Chamberlaine, John. *Original Designs of the Most Celebrated Masters in . . . His Majesty's Collection, Engraved by Bartolozzi . . .* London, 1812.

Characaturas 1786
Characaturas by Leonardo da Vinci, from Drawings by Winceslaus Hollar out of the Portland Museum, John Clarke, Nov. 1, 1786. [London], 1786.

Chastel 1950
Chastel, André. *Les dessins florentins du XIV au XVII siècle.* Paris, 1950.

Chastel 1955
Chastel, André. "Carta tinta." *L'Œil,* no. 12 (December 1955), pp. 26–31.

Chastel 1959, 1982
Chastel, André. *Art et humanisme à Florence au temps de Laurent le Magnifique: Études sur la Renaissance et l'humanisme platonicien.* 1952. 3d ed. Paris, 1982.

Chastel 1961
Chastel, André. *The Genius of Leonardo da Vinci: Leonardo da Vinci on Art and the Artist.* New York, 1961.

Chastel 1965
Chastel, André. *The Flowering of the Italian Renaissance.* Translated by Jonathan Griffin. New York, 1965.

Chastel 1979
Chastel, André. *Le Madonne di Leonardo.* Lettura Vinciana, 28 (15 aprile 1978). Florence, 1979. Reprinted in Chastel 1995.

Chastel 1980
Chastel, André. "Nota sul Codice Trivulziano." In Marinoni 1980b, pp. xxvii–xxxi.

Chastel 1995
Chastel, André. *Leonardo da Vinci: Studi e ricerche 1952–90.* Turin, 1995.

Chennevières 1879
Chennevières, Philippe de. "Les dessins de maîtres anciens exposés à l'École des Beaux-Arts." *Gazette des Beaux-Arts,* ser. 2, 19 (1879), pp. 505–35.

Chennevières and Montaiglon 1851–60
Chennevières, Ph. de, and A. de Montaiglon, *Abecedario de Mariette et autres notes inédites de cet amateur sur les arts et les artistes. Ouvrage d'après les manuscrits autographes conservés au Cabinet des Estampes de la Bibliothèque Impériale et annoté par Ph. de Chennevières et A. de Montaiglon.* 6 vols. Paris, 1851–60.

Chiappelli 1925–26
Chiappelli, Alessandro. "Il Verrocchio e Lorenzo di Credi a Pistoia." *Bollettino d'arte,* ser. 2, 5 (1925–26), pp. 49–68.

Chiappo 1972
Chiappo, Mabel. "Boltraffio, Giovan Antonio." In *Dizionario enciclopedico Bolaffi dei pittori e degli incisori italiani,* edited by Giulio Bolaffi, vol. 2, p. 182. Turin, 1972.

Chierici 1980
Chierici, Gino. "Dome Architecture." In *Leonardo da Vinci 1980,* pp. 232–37.

Chomentovskaja 1938
Chomentovskaja, O. "Le comput digital: Histoire d'un geste dan l'art de la Renaissance italienne." *Gazette des Beaux-Arts,* ser. 6, 20 (1938), pp. 157–72.

Christiansen 1990
Christiansen, Keith. "Letters: Leonardo's Drapery Studies." *The Burlington Magazine* 132, no. 1049 (August 1990), pp. 572–73.

Christie's 1997
Treasures for Everyone Saved by the National Art Collections Fund. Exhibition January 6–26, 1997. Exh. cat., London, Christie's. London, 1997.

Christie's, Manson and Woods 1896
Earl of Warwick Sale. Sale cat., London, Christie's, Manson and Woods. London, 1896.

Cianchi 1988
Cianchi, Marco, et al. *Leonardo's Machines.* Translated by Lisa Goldenberg Stoppato. Florence, 1988.

Cisotti 1980
Cisotti, Umberto. "The Mathematics of Leonardo." In *Leonardo da Vinci 1980,* pp. 201–3.

Civai 1990
Civai, A. *Dipinti e sculture in casa Martelli: Storia di una collezione patrizia fiorentina dal Quattrocento all'Ottocento.* Florence, 1990.

Clark 1929
Clark, Kenneth. "Florentine Sculptor." *Vasari Society,* ser. 2, 10, no. 3 (1929), pp. 7–9.

Clark 1933a
Clark, Kenneth. "Leonardo's *Adoration of the Shepherds* and *Dragon Fight.*" *The Burlington Magazine* 62, no. 358 (January 1933), pp. 20–26.

Clark 1933b
Clark, Kenneth. "The Madonna in Profile." *The Burlington Magazine* 62, no. 360 (March 1933), pp. 136–40.

Clark 1935
Clark, Kenneth. *A Catalogue of the Drawings of Leonardo da Vinci in the Collection of His Majesty the King, at Windsor Castle.* 2 vols. Cambridge, 1935.

Clark 1937
Clark, Kenneth. "Leonardo da Vinci (1452–1519): *Study of a Bear Walking . . .*" *Old Master Drawings* 11, no. 44 (March 1937), pp. 66–67, pl. 65.

Clark 1939
Clark, Kenneth. *Leonardo da Vinci: An Account of His Development as an Artist.* Cambridge, 1939.

Clark 1954
Clark, Kenneth. *Selected Drawings from Windsor Castle: Leonardo da Vinci.* London, 1954.

Clark 1967a
Clark, Kenneth. "Francesco Melzi as Preserver of Leonardo da Vinci's Drawings." In *Studies in Renaissance and Baroque Art Presented to*

Anthony Blunt on his 60th Birthday, edited by Michael Kitson and John Shearman, pp. 24–25. London and New York, 1967.

Clark 1967b
Clark, Kenneth. *Leonardo da Vinci: An Account of His Development as an Artist.* 1939; 1959. Rev. ed. with [further] revisions. Harmondsworth, 1967.

Clark 1969
Clark, Kenneth. "Leonardo and the Antique." In O'Malley 1969, pp. 1–34.

Clark 1969–70
Clark, Kenneth. *Leonardo da Vinci: An Exhibition of Drawings by Leonardo da Vinci from the Royal Collection, 1969–1970.* Exh. cat., London, The Queen's Gallery, Buckingham Palace. London, 1969.

Clark 1985
Clark, Kenneth. "La Sant'Anna." In *Leonardo: La pittura* 1985, pp. 106–12.

Clark 1988
Clark, Kenneth. *Leonardo da Vinci.* 1939; 1959. Revised edition with an introduction by Martin Kemp. London, 1988.

Clark and Pedretti 1968–69
Clark, Kenneth, and Carlo Pedretti. *The Drawings of Leonardo da Vinci in the Collection of Her Majesty the Queen at Windsor Castle.* 1935. 2d edition, revised. 3 vols. London, 1968–69.

Clark Art Institute 1964
Haverkamp-Begemann, Egbert, Standish D. Lawder, and Charles W. Talbot, Jr. *Drawings from the Clark Art Institute.* New Haven, 1964.

Clausse 1909
Clausse, Gustave. *Le Sforza et les Arts en Milanais: 1450–1530.* Paris, 1909.

Clayton 1996–97
Clayton, Martin. *Leonardo da Vinci: A Curious Vision.* Exh. cat., London, The Queen's Gallery, Buckingham Palace. New York and London, 1996.

Clayton 2001
Clayton, Martin. Review of *Leonardo da Vinci: The Complete Paintings,* by Pietro Marani. *Apollo* 153 (May 2001), p. 54.

Clayton 2002a
Clayton, Martin. "Leonardo's *Gypsies,* and the *Wolf and the Eagle.*" *Apollo* 155 (August 2002), pp. 27–33.

Clayton 2002b
Clayton, Martin. *Ten Drawings by Leonardo da Vinci: A Golden Jubilee Celebration.* Exh. cat., Exhibition travelling through Great Britain, sponsored by the Royal Collection. London, 2002.

Clayton 2002–3
Clayton, Martin. *Leonardo da Vinci: The Divine and the Grotesque.* Exh. cat., Edinburgh, The Queen's Gallery, Palace of Holyroodhouse; London, The Queen's Gallery, Buckingham Palace. London, 2002.

Clayton and Philo 1992–93
Clayton, Martin, and Ron Philo. *Leonardo da Vinci, The Anatomy of Man: Drawings from the Collection of Her Majesty Queen Elizabeth II.* Exh. cat., Houston, Museum of Fine Arts; Philadelphia Museum of Art; Boston, Museum of Fine Arts. Houston, 1992.

Clément 1881
Clément, Charles. *Michel Ange, Léonard de Vinci, Raphael.* 1861. Paris, [1881].

Cocke 1984
Cocke, Richard. "Art and Politics in a Drawing by Antonio Pollaiuolo." *Master Drawings* 22, no. 2 (Summer 1984), pp. 173–77, pls. 15–17.

Codex Arundel 1923–36
Reale Commissione Vinciana. *I manoscritti e i disegni di Leonardo da Vinci: Il Codice Arundel 263.* 3 vols. Rome, 1923–36.

Codex Atlanticus 1973–75
Il Codice Atlantico di Leonardo da Vinci nella Biblioteca Ambrosiana di Milano. Transcriptions and concordance by Augusto Marinoni. 12 vols. Florence, 1973–75.

Codex Atlanticus 2000. See Marinoni 2000.

Codex Forster 1930–36
Reale Commissione Vinciana. *I manoscritti e i disegni di Leonardo da Vinci: Il Codice Forster I . . .* 5 vols. Rome, 1930–36.

Codex Madrid 1974
Leonardo da Vinci: The Madrid Codices. Transcription, translation, and commentary by Ladislao Reti. 5 vols. New York, 1974.

Cogliati Arano 1963
Cogliati Arano, Luisa. "Andrea Solario e Jean Clouet." *Arte lombarda* 8, no. 2 (1963), pp. 147–56.

Cogliati Arano 1965
Cogliati Arano, Luisa. *Andrea Solario.* Milan, 1965.

Cogliati Arano 1966
Cogliati Arano, Luisa. *Andrea Solario.* 1965. 2d ed. Milan, 1966.

Cogliati Arano 1966–67
Cogliati Arano, Luisa. *Disegni di Leonardo e della sua cerchia alle Gallerie dell'Accademia.* Exh. cat., Venice, Gallerie dell'Accademia. Venice, 1966.

Cogliati Arano 1969
Cogliati Arano, Luisa. "Boltraffio." In *Dizionario biografico degli Italiani,* edited by Alberto M. Ghisalberti, vol. 11, pp. 360–62. Rome, 1969.

Cogliati Arano 1980
Cogliati Arano, Luisa. *Leonardo: Disegni di Leonardo e della sua cerchia alle Gallerie dell'Accademia.* Exh. cat., Venice, Gallerie dell'Accademia. Milan, 1980.

Cogliati Arano 1981
Cogliati Arano, Luisa. *Disegni di Leonardo e della sua cerchia alla Biblioteca Ambrosiana di Milano.* Milan, 1981.

Cogliati Arano 1982
Cogliati Arano, Luisa. *Moments of Lombard Leonardism: Two Portraits by Boltraffio.* Milan, 1982.

Cogliati Arano 1985a
Cogliati Arano, Luisa. "Cesare da Sesto tra Leonardo e Raffaello." *Arte cristiana* 73, no. 709 (July–August 1985), pp. 235–44.

Cogliati Arano 1985b
Cogliati Arano, Luisa. "Con Wart Arslan, studiando i fondi di disegni milanesi e la ritrattistica lombarda." In *Yewart Arslan: Una scuola di storici dell'arte,* pp. 59–63. Milan, 1985.

Cogliati Arano 1985c
Cogliati Arano, Luisa. "I fondi di disegni milanesi e la ritrattistica lombarda." In *Yewart Arslan: Una scuola di storici dell'arte.* Milan, 1985.

Cogliati Arano 1987a
Cogliati Arano, Luisa. "Andrea Solario en France: Mostra al *Département des Peintures,* Parigi, Louvre." *Raccolta Vinciana,* no. 22 (1987), pp. 183–200.

Cogliati Arano 1987b
Cogliati Arano, Luisa. "Un Boltraffio inedito alla Biblioteca Ambrosiana: La ritrattistica lombarda alla luce della moderna tecnologia." *Raccolta Vinciana,* no. 22 (1987), pp. 61–69.

Cogliati Arano 1988
Cogliati Arano, Luisa. "New Discoveries at the Ambrosiana." *Achademia Leonardi Vinci: Journal of Leonardo Studies and Bibliography of Vinciana* 1 (1988), pp. 118–19, and unpaginated figures.

Cogliati Arano 1992a
Cogliati Arano, Luisa. "Leonardo e i De Predis." In *Studi di storia dell'arte sul Medioevo e il Rinascimento nel centenario della nascita di Mario Salmi: Atti del Convegno Internazionale Arezzo–Firenze 16–19 Novembre 1989,* edited by Maria Grazia Ciardi Dupré Dal Poggetto, Alberto Fatucchi, and Maria Grazia Paolini, pp. 729–37. Florence, 1992.

Cogliati Arano 1992b
Cogliati Arano, Luisa. *Leonardo e la rappresentazione della terza età.* Lettura Vinciana, 31 (15 aprile 1991). Vinci, 1992.

Cogliati Arano 1993
Cogliati Arano, Luisa. "I disegni di Andrea Solario: Dal secondo lustro del Cinquecento al rientro dalla Francia." *Finantiquari* 2 (1993), pp. 36–45.

Cogliati Arano 1995
Cogliati Arano, Luisa. "Miniatori lombardi al tempo di Leonardo: I De Predis." *FIMA Antiquari, Arte viva* 7 (1995), pp. 14–32.

Colacicchi 1943
Colacicchi, Giovanni. *Antonio del Pollaiuolo.* Florence, 1943.

Colalucci 1993
Colalucci, Gianluigi. "Leonardo's 'St. Jerome': Notes on Technique, State of Conservation and its Restoration." In National Museum of Western Art 1993, English text supplement, pp. 109–10 (Japanese text, pp. 262–64, with figures).

Coleman 1984–85
Coleman, Robert Randolf, et al. *Renaissance Drawings from the Ambrosiana.* Exh. cat., Washington, D.C., National Gallery of Art; Notre Dame, Indiana, The Snite Museum of Art; Los Angeles County Museum of Art; Cleveland Museum of Art; Fort Worth, Kimbell Art Museum. Notre Dame, Indiana, 1984.

Colenbrander 1992
Colenbrander, Herman T. "Hands in Leonardo Portraiture." *Achademia Leonardi Vinci: Journal of Leonardo Studies and Bibliography of Vinciana* 5 (1992), pp. 37–43, and unpaginated figures.

Colvin 1907
Colvin, Sidney. *Drawings of the Old Masters in the*

University Galleries and in the Library of Christ Church, Oxford. 3 vols. Oxford, 1907.

Colvin 1912
Colvin, Sidney. "A Note on the Bénois *Madonna* of Leonardo da Vinci." *The Burlington Magazine* 20, no. 106 (January 1912), pp. 230–33.

Commissione Vinciana 1928–
Venturi Adolfo, ed. *I manoscritti e i disegni di Leonardo da Vinci pubblicati dalla Reale Commissione Vinciana sotto gli auspici del Ministero della istruzione pubblica. Disegni.* 8 vols. Vol. 1 (1928), *I disegni di Leonardo da Vinci dal 1470 al 1478.* Vol. 2 (1930), *I disegni di Leonardo da Vinci dal 1478 al 1481.* Vol. 3 (1934–42), *I disegni di Leonardo da Vinci dal 1482 al 1489.* Vol. 4 (1936–45), *I disegni di Leonardo da Vinci dal 1481–1499.* Vol. 5 (1939–47), *I disegni di Leonardo da Vinci dal 1489–1499.* Vol. 6 (1949), *I disegni di Leonardo da Vinci dalla fine del 1499 al 1519.* Vol. 7 (1952), *I disegni di Leonardo da Vinci di varie epoca.* Epilogue by Adolfo Venturi. Transcription and index by Nando De Toni. Fascicolo unico (1941–1970), *I disegni geografici di Leonardo da Vinci conservati nel castello di Windsor.* Transcription by Mario Baratta. Rome, 1928– .

Condorelli 1998
Condorelli, Adele. "Consideraciones sobre 'Ferrando Spagnuolo' y otros maestros ibéricos." *Archivo español de arte* 71, no. 284 (October–December 1998), pp. 345–60.

Conti 1992
Conti, Alessandro. "Osservazioni e appunti sulla 'Vita' di Leonardo di Giorgio Vasari." In *Kunst des Cinquecento in der Toskana,* edited by Monika Cämmerer, pp. 26–36. Munich, 1992.

Cook 1923
Cook, Theodore A. *Leonardo da Vinci, Sculptor: An Illustrated Essay on the Albizzi Madonna, Formerly Known as the Signa Madonna, Carved by Leonardo in 1478.* London, 1923.

Corbeau 1968
Corbeau, André. *Les manuscrits de Léonard de Vinci: Examen critique et historique del leurs elements extremes.* Caen, 1968.

Cordellier and Py 1992a
Cordellier, Dominique, and Bernadette Py. *Raphaël: Autour des dessins du Louvre.* Exh. cat., Académie de France à Rome, Villa Médicis. Rome, 1992.

Cordellier and Py 1992b
Cordellier, Dominique, and Bernadette Py. *Raphaël: Son atelier, ses copistes.* Musée du Louvre, Musée d'Orsay, Département des Arts Graphiques. Inventaire général des dessins italiens, 5. Paris, 1992.

Coren 1993
Coren, Stanley. *The Left-Hander Syndrome: The Causes and Consequences of Left-handedness.* 1992. Rev. ed. New York, 1993.

Cormio 1986
Cormio, Stefania. "Il Cardinale Silvio Valenti Gonzaga promotore e protettore delle scienze e delle Belle Arti." *Bollettino d'arte,* ser. 6, 35–36 (1986), pp. 49–66.

Costamagna 1994
Costamagna, Philippe. *Pontormo.* Paris, 1994.

Costamagna 1999
Costamagna, Philippe. "L'influence de Léonard de Vinci sur les artistes toscans et ses apports à la *maniera*: Le rôle du séjour français d'Andrea del Sarto." In Fabrizio-Costa and Le Goff 1999, pp. 99–116.

Courajod 1879
Courajod, Louis. "Léonard de Vinci et la statue de Francesco Sforza." *L'Arte* 4 (1879).

Courajod and Ravaisson-Mollien 1877
Courajod, Louis, and Charles Ravaisson-Mollien. "Conjectures à propos d'un buste en marbre de Béatrix d'Este au Musée du Louvre [et étude sur les connaissance botaniques de Léonard de Vinci]." *Gazette des Beaux-Arts,* ser. 2, 16 (1877), pp. 330–54.

Covi 1966
Covi, Dario A. "Four New Documents Concerning Andrea del Verrocchio." *The Art Bulletin* 48, no. 1 (March 1966), pp. 97–103.

Covi 1987
Covi, Dario [A]. "More About Verrocchio Documents and Verrocchio's Name." *Mitteilungen des Kunsthistorischen Institutes in Florenz* 31, no. 1 (1987), pp. 157–61.

Covi 1992a
Covi, Dario A. "The Current State of Verrocchio Study." In Bule 1992, pp. 7–23.

Covi 1992b
Covi, Dario A. "Per una giusta valutazione del Verrocchio." In Bule 1992, pp. 91–100, and figures.

Cox-Rearick 1995
Cox-Rearick, Janet. *Chefs d'œuvre de la Renaissance: La collection de François Ier.* Paris, 1995.

Cox-Rearick 1996
Cox-Rearick, Janet. *The Collection of Francis I: Royal Treasures.* Antwerp and New York, 1996.

Cremante 1998–99
Cremante, Simona. "Le 'Regole del Disegno' di Carlo Urbino: Il leonardesco Codice Huygens come documento per lo studio del rapporto fra arte e scienza nel Cinquecento." Università degli Studi di Firenze, Facoltà di lettere e filosogia, Tesi di laurea in Storia della Scienza, 1998–99.

Cresci 1570
Cresci, Giovanni Francesco. *Il Perfetto Scrittore . . . Doue si veggono i veri Caratteri, e le natural forme di tutte quelle sorti di lettere, che à vero scrittor si appartengono . . .* Rome, 1570. (The Metropolitan Museum of Art, acc. no. 28.106.6).

Cristofani 1992
Cristofani, Mauro. "Le mythe étrusque en Europe entre le XVIe et le XVIII siècle." In Grand Palais 1992, pp. 276–92.

Cropper 1994
Cropper, Elizabeth, ed. *Florentine Drawing at the Time of Lorenzo the Magnificent: Papers from a Colloquium held at the Villa Spellman, Florence, 1992.* Bologna, 1994.

Cruttwell 1904
Cruttwell, Maud. *Verrocchio.* London, 1904.

Cunnally 1988
Cunnally, John. "Leonardo and the Horses of Nero." *The Burlington Magazine* 130, no. 1026 (September 1988), pp. 689–90.

Cunnally 1993
Cunnally, John. "Numismatic Sources for Leonardo's Equestrian Monuments." *Achademia Leonardi Vinci: Journal of Leonardo Studies and Bibliography of Vinciana* 6 (1993), pp. 67–78, and unpaginated figures.

Cust 1911–12
Cust, Lionel. "Notes on the Collections formed by Thomas Howard, Earl of Arundel and Surrey, K.G." *The Burlington Magazine* 19, no. 101 (August 1911), pp. 278–86; 19, no. 104 (November 1911), pp. 97–100; 20, no. 106 (January 1912), pp. 233–36; 20, no. 108 (March 1912), pp. 341–43.

Cutry 1980
Cutry, Francesco. "The Flight of Birds." In *Leonardo da Vinci* 1980, pp. 336–46.

D'Achiardi 1913
D'Achiardi, Pietro. *Musei e Gallerie Pontificie: Guida della Pinacoteca Vaticana.* Vol. 3. Rome, 1913.

D'Achiardi 1914
D'Achiardi, Pietro. *La nuova Pinacoteca Vaticana.* Bergamo, 1914.

Dalli Regoli 1965
Dalli Regoli, Gigetta. "Problema di grafica crediana." *Critica d'arte* 12, no. 76 (December 1965), pp. 25–45.

Dalli Regoli 1966
Dalli Regoli, Gigetta. *Lorenzo di Credi.* Raccolta pisana di saggi e studi, 19. [Milan], 1966.

Dalli Regoli 1976
Dalli Regoli, Gigetta. "Il 'piegar de' panni.'" *Critica d'arte* 22, no. 150 (November–December 1976), pp. 35–48.

Dalli Regoli 1982
Dalli Regoli, Gigetta. "Leonardo intorno al 1501: Il tema del gioco." In Vezzosi 1982, pp. 25–31.

Dalli Regoli 1988
Dalli Regoli, Gigetta. "Order and Fantasy: Fra' Domenico de' Fossi and Leonardo." *Achademia Leonardi Vinci: Journal of Leonardo Studies and Bibliography of Vinciana* 1 (1988), pp. 11–15, and unpaginated figures.

Dalli Regoli 1991
Dalli Regoli, Gigetta. *Mito e scienza nella 'Leda' di Leonardo.* Lettura Vinciana, 30 (15 aprile 1990). Vinci, 1991.

Dalli Regoli 1994
Dalli Regoli, Gigetta. "Leonardo e Michelangelo: Il tema della 'Battaglia' agli inizi del Cinquecento." *Achademia Leonardi Vinci: Journal of Leonardo Studies and Bibliography of Vinciana* 7 (1994), pp. 98–106.

Dalli Regoli 1998
Dalli Regoli, Gigetta. "Leonardo e Sandro all'inizio degli anni Settanta: La forma degli alberi." In Frosini 1998, pp. 59–76.

Dalli Regoli, Nanni, and Natali 2001
Dalli Regoli, Gigetta, Romano Nanni, and Antonio Natali. *Leonardo e il mito di Leda: Modelli, memorie e metamorfosi di un'invenzione.* Exh. cat.,

Vinci, Palazzina Uzielli del Museo Leonardiano. Cinisello Balsamo, 2001.

Dan 1642
Dan, Pierre. *Le Trésor des Merveilles de la maison royale de Fontainebleau.* Paris, 1642. Facsimile in *Monographies des villes et villages de France.* Paris, 1990.

D'Arrigo 1940
D'Arrigo, Agatino. *Leonardo da Vinci e il regime della spiaggia di Cesenatico.* Rome, 1940.

Davies 1951
Davies, Martin. *National Gallery, Catalogue of the Earlier Italian School.* London, 1951.

Davies 1986
Davies, Martin. *National Gallery Catalogues: The Earlier Italian Schools.* 1951. London, 1986.

Davies and Hemsoll 1996
Davies, Paul, and David Hemsoll. "Bramante, Donato." In *The Dictionary of Art,* edited by Jane S. Turner, vol. 4, pp. 642–53. 34 vols. London, 1996.

Davis 1999
Davis, Whitney. "Freud's Leonardo and the Culture of Homosexuality." In *Biography and Early Art Criticism of Leonardo da Vinci,* edited by Claire Farago, pp. 484–97. New York, 1999.

Degenhart 1932a
Degenhart, Bernhard. "Di alcuni problemi di sviluppo della pittura nella bottega del Verrocchio, di Leonardo e di Lorenzo di Credi." *Rivista d'arte* 14 (1932), pp. 263–300, 403–44.

Degenhart 1932b
Degenhart, Bernhard. "Die Schüler des Lorenzo di Credi." *Münchner Jahrbuch der bildenden Kunst,* n.s., 9 (1932), pp. 95–161.

Degenhart 1934
Degenhart, Bernhard. "Eine Gruppe von Gewandstudien des jungen Fra Bartolommeo." *Münchner Jahrbuch der bildenden Kunst,* n.s., 11 (1934), pp. 222–31.

Degenhart 1939
Degenhart, Bernhard. "Unbekannte Zeichnungen Francescos di Giorgio." *Zeitschrift für Kunstgeschichte* 8, nos. 3–4 (1939), pp. 117–50.

Degenhart and Schmitt 1964
Degenhart, Bernhard, and Annegrit Schmitt. "Methoden Vasaris bei der Gestaltung seines 'Libro.'" In *Studien zur toskanischen Kunst: Festschrift für Ludwig Heinrich Heydenreich,* edited by Wolfgang Lotz and Lise Lotte Möller, pp. 45–64. Munich, 1964.

Degenhart and Schmitt 1967
Degenhart, Bernhard, and Annegrit Schmitt. *Italienische Zeichnungen, 15–18. Jahrhundert.* Exh. cat., Munich, Staatliche Graphische Sammlung. Munich, 1967.

Degenhart and Schmitt 1968
Degenhart, Bernhard, and Annegrit Schmitt. *Corpus der italienischen Zeichnungen, 1300–1450.* Part I, *Süd-und Mittelitalien.* 4 vols. Berlin, 1968.

Degl'innocenti 1978
Degl'innocenti, Giovanni. "Restituzioni prospettiche: Proposte e verifiche di un metodo." In *Leonardo architetto,* edited by Carlo Pedretti, pp. 274–89. Milan, 1978.

Del Badia 1886
Del Badia, J. "Appunti e notizie—Le botteghe di Donatello." In *Miscellanea fiorentina di erudizione e storia* 1 (1886), pp. 60–62.

De Liphart Rathshoff 1933
De Liphart Rathshoff, Rinaldo. "L'Ercole di Michelangelo e un disegno del Beccafumi." *Rivista d'arte* 15 (1933), pp. 93–104.

Dell'Aqua 1982
Dell'Aqua, Gian Alberto, ed. *Leonardo e Milano.* Milan, 1982.

Della Torre 1902
Della Torre, A. *Storia dell'Accademia Platonica di Firenze.* Florence, 1902.

De Logu and Marinelli 1975
De Logu, Giuseppe, and Guido Marinelli. *Il ritratto nella pittura italiana.* Vol. 1. Bergamo, 1975.

Demonts 1921
Demonts, Louis. *Dessins de Léonard de Vinci.* Paris, [1921].

Demonts 1922
Demonts, Louis. *Catalogue des dessins de Léonard de Vinci (1452–1519).* Exh. cat., Paris, Palais du Louvre. Paris, 1921.

Denison 1984–86
Denison, Cara Dufour. *21st Report to the Fellows of the Pierpont Morgan Library* (1984–86).

De Piles 1699
De Piles, Roger. *Abrégé de la Vie des peintres.* Paris, 1699.

De Rinaldis 1926
De Rinaldis, Aldo. *Storia dell'opera pittorica di Leonardo da Vinci.* Bologna, 1926.

De Roover 1970
De Roover, R. *Il Banco Medici dalle origini al declino (1397–1494).* Florence, 1970.

De Schlegel 1917
De Schlegel, Lisa. "Arte retrospettiva: Di alcuni dipinti di Giov. Antonio Boltraffio." *Emporium* 46 (1917), pp. 197–205.

Dethloff 1996
Dethloff, Diana. "The Executors' Account Book and the Dispersal of Sir Peter Lely's Collection." *Journal of the History of Collections* 8, no. 1 (1996), pp. 15–51.

De Tolnay 1943
De Tolnay, Charles. *History and Technique of Old Master Drawings: A Handbook.* New York, 1943.

De Tolnay 1962
De Tolnay, Charles. "Quelques dessins inedits de Léonard de Vinci." *Raccolta Vinciana,* no. 19 (1962), pp. 95–114.

De Tolnay 1969
De Tolnay, Charles. *The Youth of Michelangelo.* Princeton, N.J., 1969.

De Toni 1922
De Toni, Giovan Battista. *Le piante e gli animali in Leonardo da Vinci.* Bologna, 1922.

De Toni 1930–34
De Toni, Giovan Battista. "Saggio di onomastica vinciana." *Raccolta Vinciana,* no. 14 (1930–34), pp. 54–117.

De Toni 1967
De Toni, Nando. *Contributo alla conoscenza dei manoscritti vinciana 8936 e 8937 della Biblioteca nazionale di Madrid.* Florence, 1967.

De Toni 1975
De Toni, Giovan Battista. *Frammenti Vinciani XXXIII: Trascrizioni inedite del Manoscritto E 2176 dell'Istituto di Francia di Leonardo da Vinci.* Florence, 1975.

De Toni 1979
De Toni, Giovan Battista. "Attualità leonardiane: Due precisazioni sulla storia della *Battaglia.*" *Almanacco italiano* 79 (1979).

De Toni 1987
De Toni, Giovanni. *Macchine di Leonardo: Mostra di modelli.* Exh. cat., Brescia, Sale dell'Ateneo di Brescia. Brescia, 1987.

De Vecchi 1982
De Vecchi, Pier Luigi. "La Vergine delle Rocce." In Dell'Aqua 1982, pp. 41–60.

Dézallier d'Argenville 1752
[Dézallier d'Argenville, Antoine Joseph]. *Abrégé de la vie des plus fameux peintres. Supplement.* Paris, 1752.

Di Giampaolo 1994
Di Giampaolo, Mario, ed. *Philip Pouncey: Raccolta di Scritti (1937–1985).* Rimini, 1994.

Dillon 1994
Dillon, Gianvittorio. "Una serie di figure grottesche." In Cropper 1994, pp. 217–30, and unpaginated figures.

Dina 1921
Dina, Achille. "Isabella d'Aragona Duchessa di Milano e di Bari." *Archivio Storico Lombardo,* ser. 5, 48 (1921), pp. 269–457.

Di Teodoro 1992
Di Teodoro, Francesco P. "'Maestro Piero del Borgo.'" *Achademia Leonardi Vinci: Journal of Leonardo Studies and Bibliography of Vinciana* 5 (1992), pp. 58–62, and unpaginated figures.

Di Teodoro and Barbi 1983
Di Teodoro, Francesco, and Luciano Barbi. "Leonardo da Vinci: 'Del riparo a terremoti.'" *Physis* 25 (1983), pp. 5–39.

Dolev 1995
Dolev, Nevet. "Leonardo's Amorphous Imagery and the Arcimboldo Outcome." *Achademia Leonardi Vinci: Journal of Leonardo Studies and Bibliography of Vinciana* 8 (1995), pp. 129–42, and unpaginated figures.

Doménech and Sricchia Santoro 1998
Doménech, Fernando Benito, and Fiorella Sricchia Santoro. *Ferrando Spagnuolo e altri maestri iberici nell'Italia di Leonardo e Michelangelo.* Exh. cat., Florence, Casa Buonarroti. Florence, 1998.

Donato 1991
Donato, Maria Monica. "Hercules and the David in the Early Decoration of the Palazzo Vecchio: Manuscript Evidence." *Journal of the Warburg and Courtauld Institutes* 54 (1991), pp. 83–98.

Dossi 1999
Dossi, Barbara. *Albertina: The History of the Collection and Its Masterpieces.* Munich, London, and New York, 1999.

Douglas 1933
Douglas, Langston [sic] R. *Leonardo da Vinci: His*

"San Donato of Arezzo and the Tax-Collector."
[London, 1933].

Douglas 1944
Douglas, Langton R. *Leonardo da Vinci: His Life and his Pictures*. Chicago, 1944.

Dover 1980
Leonardo Drawings: 50 Works. Dover Art Library. New York, 1980.

Dragstra 1997
Dragstra, Rolf. "The Vitruvian Proportions for Leonardo's Construction of the 'Last Supper.'" *Raccolta Vinciana*, no. 27 (1997), pp. 83–104.

Draper 1992
Draper, James David. *Bertoldo di Giovanni, Sculptor of the Medici Household: Critical Reappraisal and Catalogue Raisonné*. Columbia, [Mo.], and London, 1992.

Draper 2002
D[raper], J[ames]. "Benedetto da Maiano: Saint Jerome in the Wilderness." *The Metropolitan Museum of Art Bulletin*, n.s, 60, no. 2 (Fall 2002), p. 14.

Dreyer 1979
Dreyer, Peter. *I grandi disegni italiani del Kupferstichkabinett di Berlino*. Milan, 1979.

Dumesnil 1858
Dumesnil, Jules-Antoine. *Histoire des plus célèbres amateurs français et de leurs rélations avec les artistes*. Vol. 1, *Pierre-Jean Mariette, 1694–1774*. Paris, 1858.

Dussler 1926
Dussler, L[uitpold]. "Verrocchio, Andrea del." In *Allgemeines Lexikon der bildenden Künstler von der Antike bis zur Gegenwart*, edited by Ulrich Thieme and Felix Becker, vol. 34, pp. 292–98. 37 vols. 1907–50. Leipzig, 1926.

Dussler 1938
Dussler, Luitpold. *Italienische Meisterzeichnungen*. Frankfurt, 1938.

Echinger-Maurach 1998
Echinger-Maurach, Claudia. "Ein Entwurf Michelangelos für den Tondo Pitti und seine Beziehungen zu Leonardo da Vinci, zu antiken Werken und zu Raphael." *Mitteilungen des Kunsthistorischen Institutes in Florenz* 42, nos. 2–3 (1998), pp. 274–310.

École des Beaux-Arts 1879
Catalogue descriptif des dessins de Maîtres anciens exposés à l'École des Beaux-Arts. Exh. cat., Paris, École nationale supérieure des Beaux-Arts. Paris, 1879.

École des Beaux-Arts 1935
Art italien des XVe et XVIe siècles: Exposition de dessins, manuscrits enluminés, livres et xylographies faisant partie des collections de l'École. Exh. cat., Paris, École nationale supérieure des Beaux-Arts. Paris, 1935.

École des Beaux-Arts 1958
La Renaissance italienne et ses prolongements européens. Exh. cat., Paris, École nationale supérieure des Beaux-Arts. Paris, 1958.

École des Beaux-Arts 1981–82
De Michel-Ange à Géricault: Dessins de la

Donation Armand-Valton. Exh. cat., Paris, École des Beaux-Arts; Malibu, The J. Paul Getty Museum; Hamburg, Hamburger Kunsthalle. Paris, 1981.

École des Beaux-Arts 1984
Brugerolles, Emmanuelle. *Les dessins de la collection Armand-Valton: La donation d'un grand collectionneur du XIXe siècle à l'École des Beaux-Arts*. Paris, 1984.

Edgerton 1984
Edgerton, Jr., Samuel Y. "Galileo, Florentine 'Disegno,' and the 'Strange Spottednesse' of the Moon." *The Art Journal* 44, no. 3 (Fall 1984), pp. 225–32.

Eichholz 1998
Eichholz, Georg. *Das Abendmahl Leonardo da Vincis: Eine systematische Bildmonographie*. Munich, 1998.

Eigenberger 1927
Eigenberger, Robert. *Die Gemäldegalerie der Akademie der bildenden Künste in Wien*. Vienna and Leipzig, 1927.

Eisler 1948
Eisler, Robert. "Letters: Leonardo's *Virgin of the Rocks*." and "Letters: [Response to Cecil Gould's letter, "Leonardo's 'Virgin of the Rocks.'" *The Burlington Magazine* 90, no. 545 (August 1948), pp. 239–40; no. 548 (November 1948), pp. 329–30.

Eisler 1979
Eisler, Colin. *The Master of the Unicorn: The Life and Work of Jean Duvet*. New York, 1979.

Eissler 1961
Eissler, Kurt R. *Leonardo da Vinci: Psychoanalytic Notes on the Enigma*. New York, 1961.

Elam 1992
Elam, Caroline. "Il giardino delle sculture di Lorenzo de' Medici." In Barocchi 1992, pp. 157–74.

Elam 1996a
Elam, Caroline. "Cronaca [Simone di Tomaso del Pollaiuolo]." In *The Dictionary of Art*, edited by Jane S. Turner, vol. 8, pp. 187–89. 34 vols. London, 1996.

Elam 1996b
Elam, Caroline. "Giuliano da Sangallo." In *Dictionary of Art*, edited by Jane S. Turner, vol. 27, pp. 733–39. 34 vols. London, 1996.

Elen 1995
Elen, Albert J. *Italian Late-Medieval and Renaissance Drawing-Books from Giovannino de' Grassi to Palma Giovane: A Codicological Approach*. Leiden, 1995.

Emanuelli 1980
Emanuelli, Pio. "Da Vinci's Astronomy." In *Leonardo da Vinci 1980*, pp. 204–8.

Emboden 1987
Emboden, William A. *Leonardo da Vinci on Plants and Gardens*. London, 1987.

Ephrussi 1882
Ephrussi, Charles. "Les dessins de la collection His de la Salle." *Gazette des Beaux-Arts*, ser. 2, 25 (1882), pp. 225–45, 297–309.

Esche 1954
Esche, Sigrid. *Leonardo da Vinci: Das anatomische Werk*. Basel, 1954.

***Etat des dessins . . . His de la Salle* 1872**
His de la Salle, Aimé-Charles-Horace. "Collection

de Mr. His de la Salle. Dessins. Etat des dessins et des tableaux légués par Monsieur His de la Salle au Musée du Louvre." Ms., 1872. Paris, Musée du Louvre, Cabinet des Dessins. Edited by Frédéric Reiset, Henry de Chennevières, and Both de Tauzia.

Ettlinger 1953
Ettlinger, L[eopold] D. "Pollaiuolo's Tomb of Pope Sixtus IV." *Journal of the Warburg and Courtauld Institutes* 16 (1953), pp. 239–74.

Ettlinger 1972
Ettlinger, Leopold D. "Hercules Florentinus." *Mitteilungen des Kunsthistorischen Institutes in Florenz* 16, no. 2 (1972), pp. 119–42.

Ettlinger 1978
Ettlinger, Leopold D. *Antonio and Piero Pollaiuolo: Complete Edition with a Critical Dialogue*. Oxford and New York, 1978.

Executors' Account Book 1679–91
"Executors' Account Book of Sir Peter Lely." London, British Library, Add. Ms. 16174.

Faber Kolb 1996
Faber Kolb, Arianne. "The Arundels' Printmakers: Four Approaches to the Reproduction of Drawings." *Apollo* 144, no. 414 (August 1996), pp. 57–62.

Fabjan 1986
Fabjan, Barbara, ed. *Perugino, Lippi e la Bottega di San Marco alla Certosa di Pavia, 1495–1511*. Exh. cat., Milan, Pinacoteca di Brera. Florence, 1986.

Fabjan and Marani 1998–99
Fabjan, Barbara, and Pietro Marani, eds. *Leonardo: La dama con l'ermellino*. Exh. cat., Rome, Palazzo del Quirinale; Milan, Pinacoteca di Brera; Florence, Palazzo Pitti. Cinisello Balsamo, 1998.

Fabrizio-Costa 1997
Fabrizio-Costa, Silvia. "'Elena quando si specchiava . . .'" *Achademia Leonardi Vinci: Journal of Leonardo Studies and Bibliography of Vinciana* 10 (1997), pp. 89–100, and unpaginated figures.

Fabrizio-Costa and Le Goff 1999
Fabrizio-Costa, Silvia, and Jean-Pierre Le Goff, eds. *Léonard de Vinci entre France et Italie, "miroir profond et sombre": Actes du Colloque international de l'Université de Caen (3–4 octobre 1996)*. Caen, 1999.

Fahy 1966
Fahy, Everett. "The Beginnings of Fra Bartolommeo." *The Burlington Magazine* 108, no. 762 (September 1966), pp. 456–63.

Fahy 1969
Fahy, Everett. "The Earliest Works of Fra Bartolommeo." *The Art Bulletin* 51, no. 2 (June 1969), pp. 142–54.

Fairbrother and Ishikawa 1997–98
Fairbrother, Trevor, and Chiyo Ishikawa, eds. *Leonardo Lives: The Codex Leicester and Leonardo da Vinci's Legacy of Art and Science*. Exh. cat., Seattle Art Museum. Seattle, 1997.

Falletti 1996
Falletti, Franca. *I Medici, Il Verrocchio e Pistoia—Storia e restauro di due capolavori nella cattedrale di S. Zeno: Il monumento al cardinale Noccolò Forteguerri, la Madonna di Piazza*. Livorno, 1996.

Fanti 1535
Fanti, Sigismondo. *Thesauro de Scrittori: Opera*

artificio sa laquale con grandissima arte si per practica come per geometria insegna a Scriuere diuerse sorte littere . . . [Rome?], 1535. (The Metropolitan Museum of Art, acc. no. 18.7.2).

Fara 1997
Fara, Amelio. *Leonardo e l'architettura militare.* Lettura Vinciana, 36 (15 aprile 1996). Florence, 1997.

Farago 1991
Farago, Claire J. "Leonardo's Color and Chiaroscuro Reconsidered: The Visual Force of Painted Images." *The Art Bulletin* 73, no. 1 (March 1991), pp. 63–88.

Farago 1992
Farago, Claire J. *Leonardo da Vinci's* Paragone: *A Critical Interpretation with a New Edition of the Text in the* Codex Urbinas. Leiden, 1992.

Farago 1993
Farago, Claire J. "Fractal Geometry in the Organization of Madrid MS. II." *Achademia Leonardi Vinci: Journal of Leonardo Studies and Bibliography of Vinciana* 6 (1993), pp. 47–55, and unpaginated figures.

Farago 1994
Farago, Claire J. "Leonardo's *Battle of Anghiari*: A Study in the Exchange between Theory and Practice." *The Art Bulletin* 76, no. 2 (June 1994), pp. 301–30.

Farago 1996a
Farago, Claire J. "The *Battle of Anghiari*: A Speculative Reconstruction of Leonardo's Design Process." *Achademia Leonardi Vinci: Journal of Leonardo Studies and Bibliography of Vinciana* 9 (1996), pp. 73–86, and unpaginated figures.

Farago 1996b
Farago, Claire [J.], et al. *Leonardo da Vinci: Codex Leicester, A Masterpiece of Science.* Based on the translation of the Codex Leicester by Carlo Pedretti. Introductory essays by Martin Kemp, Owen Gingerich, and Carlo Pedretti. Exh. cat., New York, American Museum of Natural History. New York, 1996.

Farago 1997
Farago, Claire J. "The Defense of Art and the Art of Defense." *Achademia Leonardi Vinci: Journal of Leonardo Studies and Bibliography of Vinciana* 10 (1997), pp. 13–22, and unpaginated figures.

Farago 1999a
Farago, Claire. "How Leonardo da Vinci's editors organized his Treatise on Painting and how Leonardo would have done it differently." In Farago 1999b, vol. 4, pp. 417–59.

Farago 1999b
Farago, Claire, ed. *Leonardo da Vinci: Selected Scholarship.* 5 vols. New York, 1999.

Favaro 1917
Favaro, Giuseppe. "Il canone di Leonardo da Vinci sulle proporzioni del corpo umano." *Atti del Reale Istituto Veneto di Scienze, Lettere ed Arti*, Venice, *1917–1918* 77, pt. 2 (1917), pp. 167–227.

Favaro 1930
Favaro, Giuseppe. "Come scriveva Leonardo." *Rivista di storia delle scienze mediche e naturali* 21, nos. 11–12 (November–December 1930), pp. 330–34.

Favaro 1980
Favaro, Giuseppe. "Anatomy and the Biological Sciences." In *Leonardo da Vinci* 1980, pp. 363–72.

Fehrenbach 1997
Fehrenbach, Frank. *Licht und Wasser: Zur Dynamik naturphilosophischer Leitbilder im Werk Leonardo da Vincis.* Tübingen, 1997.

Fenyö 1967
Fenyö, Ivan, ed. *Meisterzeichnungen aus dem Museum der Schönen Künste in Budapest.* Exh. cat., Vienna, Albertina. Vienna, 1967.

Ferino-Pagden 1982
Ferino-Pagden, Sylvia. Review of *Das Leonardo-Porträt in der Kgl. Bibliothek Turin und andere Fälschungen des Giuseppe Bossi*, by Hans Ost. *Kunst Chronik* 35, no. 1 (January 1982), pp. 34–40.

Ferri 1879–81
Ferri, Pasquale Nerino, ed. *Catalogo descrittivo dei disegni della R. Galleria degli Uffizi esposti al pubblico.* Florence, 1879–81.

Ferri 1890
Ferri, Pasquale Nerino, ed. *Catalogo riassuntivo della raccolta di disegni, antichi e moderni della R. Galleria degli Uffizi di Firenze.* Rome, 1890.

Ferri 1895–1901
Ferri, Pasquale Nerino, ed. *Catalogo dei disegni, cartoni e bozzetti esposti al pubblico nella R. Galleria degli Uffizi ed in altri Musei di Firenze compilato da Pasquale Nerino, ispettore preposto al Gabinetto dei disegni e delle stampe nella detta Galleria.* Florence, 1895–1901.

Ferri Piccaluga 1994
Ferri Piccaluga, Gabriella. "ΣΟΦΙΑ [Sophia];" and "Appendice I: La prima versione della *Vergine delle Rocce* riconsiderata nelle repliche." *Achademia Leonardi Vinci: Journal of Leonardo Studies and Bibliography of Vinciana* 7 (1994), pp. 13–50, and unpaginated figures.

Fesch Sale 1841
Camuccini, [Vincenzo], [Giovanni Battista] Borrani, [Tommaso] Minardi, [Filippo] Agricola, and [Luigi] Durantini. *Catalogue des tableaux composant la galerie de feu Son Eminence le Cardinal Fesch.* Rome, 1841.

Fesch Sale 1845
Galerie de feu S. E. le Cardinal Fesch . . . Catalogue des tableaux des écoles italiennes, et espagnole, par Georg, peintre, Commissaire-Expert du Musée royal du Louvre. Rome, 1845.

Filarete 1972
Filarete, [Antonio Averlino]. *Trattato di Architettura.* Edited and introduced by Liliana Grassi and Anna Maria Finoli. 2 vols. Milan, 1972.

Fiorani 1992
Fiorani, Francesca. "Abraham Bosse e le prime critiche al Trattato della Pittura di Leonardo." *Achademia Leonardi Vinci: Journal of Leonardo Studies and Bibliography of Vinciana* 5 (1992), pp. 78–95, and unpaginated figures.

Fiore and Marani 1996
Fiore, Francesco Paolo, and Pietro C. Marani. "Francesco (Maurizio) di Giorgio Martini (Pollaiolo)." In *The Dictionary of Art*, edited by Jane S. Turner, vol. 11, pp. 687–95. 34 vols. London, 1996.

Fiorio 1982
Fiorio, Maria Teresa. *Leonardeschi in Lombardia.* Milan, 1982.

Fiorio 1988
Fiorio, Maria Teresa. "La pittura del Cinquecento nei territori di Milano e Cremona." In *La Pittura in Italia: Il Cinquecento*, vol. 1, pp. 64–94. 2 vols. Milan, 1988.

Fiorio 1991
Fiorio, Maria Teresa. "Uno spunto leonardesco in un rilievo del Bambaia." In Fiorio and Marani 1991, pp. 87–99.

Fiorio 1996a
Fiorio, Maria Teresa. "Boltraffio [Beltraffio], Giovanni Antonio." In *The Dictionary of Art*, edited by Jane S. Turner, vol. 4, pp. 283–86. 34 vols. London, 1996.

Fiorio 1996b
Fiorio, Maria Teresa. "Melzi, Francesco." In *The Dictionary of Art*, edited by Jane S. Turner, vol. 21, pp. 99–100. 34 vols. London, 1996.

Fiorio 1997a
Fiorio, Maria Teresa. "Giovanni Antonio Boltraffio." In *Museo d'arte antica del Castello Sforzesco*, edited by Carlo Pirovano, vol. 1, pp. 262–65. Milan, 1997.

Fiorio 1997b
Fiorio, Maria Teresa. "Leonardo, Boltraffio e Jean Perréal." *Raccolta Vinciana*, no. 27 (1997), pp. 325–55.

Fiorio 1998a
Fiorio, Maria Teresa. "Bernardino de' Conti." In *Legacy of Leonardo* 1998, pp. 211–30.

Fiorio 1998b
Fiorio, Maria Teresa. "Cesare Magni." In *Legacy of Leonardo* 1998, pp. 385–96.

Fiorio 1998c
Fiorio, Maria Teresa. "Francesco Napoletano (and the Pseudo Francesco Napoletano)." In *Legacy of Leonardo* 1998, pp. 199–210.

Fiorio 1998d
Fiorio, Maria Teresa. "Giovanni Antonio Boltraffio." In *Legacy of Leonardo* 1998, pp. 131–62.

Fiorio 1998e
Fiorio, Maria Teresa. "The Many Faces of Leonardismo." In *Legacy of Leonardo* 1998, pp. 38–63.

Fiorio 2000a
Fiorio, Maria Teresa. *Giovanni Antonio Boltraffio: Un pittore milanese nel lume di Leonardo.* Milan and Rome, 2000.

Fiorio 2000b
Fiorio, Maria Teresa. "Spigolature leonardesche." In *'Hostinato rigore': Leonardiana in memoria di Augusto Marinoni*, edited by Pietro C. Marani, pp. 77–83. Milan, 2000.

Fiorio and Marani 1991
Fiorio, Maria Teresa, and Pietro C. Marani, eds. *I leonardeschi a Milano: Fortuna e collezionismo.* Atti del Convegno Internazionale, Milano 25–26 settembre 1990. Milan, 1991.

Fischer 1990–92a
Fischer, Chris. *Fra Bartolommeo, Master Draughtsman of the High Renaissance: A Selection from the Rotterdam Albums and Landscape Drawings from Various Collections.* Exh. cat., Rotterdam, Museum Boymans-Van Beuningen; Boston, Museum of Fine Arts; Fort Worth, Kimbell Art Museum; New York, The Pierpont Morgan Library. Seattle, 1990.

Fischer 1990–92b
Fischer, Chris. "Studies for 'St. George and the Dragon.'" In Fischer 1990–92a, pp. 170–77.

Fischer 1994
Fischer, Chris. "Ghirlandaio and the Origins of Cross-hatching." In Cropper 1994, pp. 245–53, and unpaginated figures.

Fitzwilliam Museum 1976–77
Jaffé, Michael. *European Drawings from the Fitzwilliam.* Exh. cat., New York, The Pierpont Morgan Library; Fort Worth, Kimbell Art Museum; The Baltimore Art Museum; The Minneapolis Museum of Art; Philadelphia Museum of Art. [Washington, D.C.], 1976.

Flammini 1891
Flammini, Francesco. *La lirica toscana del Rinascimento anteriore ai tempi del Magnifico.* Annali della R. Scuola Normale Superiore di Pisa. Filologia e filosofia, 8. Pisa, 1891.

Fleres 1896
Fleres, Ugo. "Il Gabinetto Nazionale delle Stampe di Roma." *Le Gallerie nazionali italiane: Notizie e documenti* 2 (1968), pp. 139–62.

Fletcher 1981–82
Fletcher, Jennifer M. "Isabella d'Este, Patron and Collector." In Victoria and Albert Museum 1981–82, pp. 51–64.

Fletcher 1989
Fletcher, Jennifer. "Bernardo Bembo and Leonardo's Portrait of Ginevra de' Benci." *The Burlington Magazine* 131, no. 1041 (December 1989), pp. 811–16.

Florisoone and Bacou 1952
Florisoone, Michel, and Roseline Bacou. *Hommage à Léonard de Vinci: Exposition en l'honneur du cinquième centenaire de sa naissance.* Exh. cat., Paris, Musée du Louvre. Paris, 1952.

Fogg Art Museum 1983
Italy in the Time of Raphael. Exh. cat., Cambridge, Mass., Fogg Art Museum, Harvard University. Cambridge, Mass., 1983.

Fogolari 1913
Fogolari, Gino. *I disegni delle R. Gallerie dell'Accademia di Venezia.* Milan, 1913.

Fontana 1988
Fontana, Vincenzo. *Fra' Giovanni Giocondo, Architetto 1433 – c. 1515.* Nuovi saggi e studi di storia dell'arte e della cultura, 2. Vicenza, 1988.

Ford 2002
Ford, Edward. "Interpretation of Marks from Draughting Tools in Some Italian Renaissance Drawings." Ph.D. diss., Oxford University, 2002.

Forlani 1963
Forlani, Anna. "Fra Muséer og Samlinger VII.

Italienske Mestertegninger I Uffiziene." *Kunst Kultur* (1963).

Forlani Tempesti 1970
Forlani Tempesti, Anna. *I disegni dei maestri: Capolavori del Rinascimento.* Milan, 1970.

Forlani Tempesti 1991
Forlani Tempesti, Anna. *The Robert Lehman Collection.* Vol. 5, *Italian Fifteenth to Seventeenth-Century Drawings.* New York, 1991.

Forlani Tempesti and Petrioli Tofani 1974
Forlani Tempesti, Anna, and Anna Maria Petrioli Tofani. *I grandi disegni italiani degli Uffizi di Firenze.* Milan, [1974].

Fornasari 2001
Fornasari, Liletta. "Introduzione: La cerchia del Verrocchio e 'i dintorni di Leonardo.'" In Palazzo del Comune, Arezzo 2001, pp. 12–90.

Fortuna 1952
Fortuna, A. "Addi 5 daghosto 1473: Con Leonardo a Montevettolini per la festa della Madonna delle Neve." *La Nazione* 5, no. 8 (1952), p. 4.

Francia 1960
Francia, Ennio. *Pinacoteca Vaticana.* Milan, 1960.

Franck 1997
Franck, Jacques. "The *Last Supper,* 1497–1997: The Moment of Truth." *Achademia Leonardi Vinci: Journal of Leonardo Studies and Bibliography of Vinciana* 10 (1997), pp. 165–82, and unpaginated figures.

Frangi 1991
Frangi, Francesco. "Qualche considerazione su un leonardesco eccentrico: Francesco Napoletano." In Fiorio and Marani 1991, pp. 71–86.

Franklin 2000
Franklin, David. "Francisco de Holanda's Collection of Drawings by Polidoro da Caravaggio." *Apollo* 151, no. 457 (March 2000), pp. 12–21.

Freedberg 1961
Freedberg, S. J. *Painting of the High Renaissance in Rome and Florence.* Cambridge, Mass., 1961.

Freud 1964
Freud, Sigmund. *Leonardo da Vinci and a Memory of his Childhood,* translated by Alan Tyson, edited by James Strachey, in collaboration with Anna Freud. New York, 1964.

Frey 1892
Frey, Karl. *Il Codice Magliabechiano . . . scritte da Anonimo Giorentino.* Berlin, 1892.

Frey 1909
Frey, Karl. "Studien zu Michelangiolo Buonarroti und zur Kunst seiner Zeit." *Jahrbuch der Koniglich Preuszischen Kunstsammlungen Berlin* 30 (1909), pp. 103–80.

Friedländer 1947
Friedländer, Max J. "Quentin Massys as a Painter of Genre Pictures." *The Burlington Magazine* 89, no. 530 (May 1947), pp. 115–19.

Frison 2000
Frison, Leonilo. *Il ritratto perduto di Isabella e l'enigma di un sorriso.* Vicenza, 2000.

Frizzoni 1882
Frizzoni, Gustavo. "Le pubbliche raccolte artistiche

in Milano a proposito di una recente opera critica." *La Perseveranza* (August 17, 1882).

Frizzoni 1891
Frizzoni, Gustavo. *Arte italiana del Rinascimento: Saggi critici.* Milan, 1891.

Frizzoni 1904
Frizzoni, Gustavo. "L'arte toscana studiata nei disegni dei maestri antichi." *Rassegna d'arte* 4, no. 7 (July 1904), pp. 97–99; no. 8 (August 1904), pp. 113–16.

Frizzoni 1905
Frizzoni, Gustavo. Review of *Drawings by Old Masters in the University Galleries and the Library of Christ Church, Oxford,* by Sidney Colvin. *Arte* 8 (1905), pp. 64–68.

Frizzoni 1910
Frizzoni, Gustavo. "Un disegno di Leonardo da Vinci alla Biblioteca Reale di Torino." *Raccolta Vinciana,* no. 6 (1910), pp. 123–26.

Frizzoni 1911
Frizzoni, Gustavo. "La raccolta Mond ed opere attinenti alla medesima." *Rassegna d'arte* 11, no. 2 (1911), pp. 25–48.

Frosini 1998
Frosini, Fabio, ed. *"Tutte le opere non son per istancarmi": Raccolta di scritti per i settant'anni di Carlo Pedretti.* Rome, 1998.

Fumagalli 1915
Fumagalli, Giuseppina, ed. *Leonardo prosatore . . .* Milan, 1915.

Fumagalli 1970
Fumagalli, Giuseppina, [ed]. *Leonardo omo sanza lettere.* 1938. Florence, 1970.

Fusco 1982
Fusco, Laurie. "The Use of Sculptural Models by Painters in Fifteenth-Century Italy." *The Art Bulletin* 64, no. 2 (June 1982), pp. 175–94.

Fusco and Corti 1992
Fusco, Laurie, and Gino Corti. "Lorenzo de' Medici on the Sforza Monument." *Achademia Leonardi Vinci: Journal of Leonardo Studies and Bibliography of Vinciana* 5 (1992), pp. 11–32, and unpaginated figures.

Gagné 1986
Gagné, Joan. "Du quadrivium aux scientiae mediae." In *Arts liberaux et philosophie au Moyen Age,* pp. 975–86. Montreal and Paris, 1986.

Galbiati 1951
Galbiati, Giovanni. *Itinerario per il visitatore della Biblioteca Ambrosiana, della Pinacoteca e dei monumenti annessi.* Milan, 1951.

Galichon 1865
Galichon, Émile. "De quelques estampes milanaises attribuées à Cesare da Sesto." *Gazette des Beaux-Arts,* ser. 1, 18 (1865), pp. 546–52.

Galichon 1867
Galichon, Emile. "Un dessin de Léonard de Vinci pour le tableau de l'Adoration des mages." *Gazette des Beaux-Arts,* ser. 1, 23 (1867), pp. 530–36.

Galleria degli Uffizi 1984
Berti, Luciano, et al. *La Madonna Benois di Leonardo da Vinci a Firenze: Il capolavoro dell'Ermitage in mostra agli Uffizi.* Galleria degli Uffizi. Florence, 1984.

Galluzzi 1982
Galluzzi, Paolo. "Leonardo, Pacioli e Savasorda." In Vezzosi 1982, pp. 87–93.

Galluzzi 1987
Galluzzi, Paolo, ed. *Leonardo da Vinci, Engineer and Architect.* Introduction by Carlo Pedretti. Exh. cat., The Montreal Museum of Fine Arts. Montreal, 1987.

Galluzzi 1991
Galluzzi, Paolo, ed. *Prima di Leonardo: Cultura delle macchine a Siena nel Rinascimento.* Exh. cat., Siena, Magazzini del Sale. Milan, 1991.

Galluzzi 1996
Galluzzi, Paolo. *Gli ingegneri del Rinascimento da Brunelleschi a Leonardo da Vinci.* Exh. cat., Florence, Palazzo Strozzi. Florence, 1996.

Galluzzi 1997
Galluzzi, Paolo. *Mechanical Marvels: Inventions in the Age of Leonardo.* Florence, 1997.

Galoppini 1988
Galoppini, Laura. "Fra' Domenico: From Design to Calligraphy." *Achademia Leonardi Vinci: Journal of Leonardo Studies and Bibliography of Vinciana* 1 (1988), pp. 16–20, and unpaginated figures.

Gamba 1957
Gamba, Carlo. "Due tavole del Museo Jacquemart André." *L'Arte* 21 (1957), pp. 3–5.

Gantner 1958
Gantner, Joseph. *Leonardos Visionen von der Sintflut und vom Untergang der Welt.* Bern, 1958.

Garberi and Mucchi 1972
Garberi, Merces Precerutti, and Ludovico Mucchi, eds. *Capolavori d'arte lombarda: I leonardeschi ai raggi 'X'. Mostra a cura della direzione Civiche Raccolta d'Arte.* Exh. cat., Milan, Castello Sforzesco. Milan, 1972.

Garzelli 1985
Garzelli, Annarosa. "Problemi del Ghirlandaio nella cappella di Santa Fina: Il ciclo figurativo nella cupola e i probabili disegni." *Antichità viva* 24, no. 4 (1985), pp. 11–25.

Gatteschi 1998
Gatteschi, Riccardo, ed. *Vita di Raffaello da Montelupo.* Florence, 1998.

Geddo 1992
Geddo, Cristina. "Le pale d'altare di Giampietrino: Ipotesi per un percorso stilistico." *Arte lombarda,* no. 101 (1992), pp. 67–82.

Geddo 1994
Geddo, Cristina. "La Madonna di Castel Vitoni del Giampietrino;" and "Appendice: Per i disegni del Giampietrino." *Achademia Leonardi Vinci: Journal of Leonardo Studies and Bibliography of Vinciana* 7 (1994), pp. 57–67, and unpaginated figures.

Geddo 1995
Geddo, Cristina. "La pala di Pavia del Giampietrino: Documenti sulle committenza." *Bollettino della Società Pavese di Storia Patria* 45, no. 47 (1995), pp. 23–253.

Gentile 1980
Gentile, Giovanni. "Leonardo's Thought." In *Leonardo da Vinci* 1980, pp. 163–74.

Gere and Turner 1983–84
Gere, John A., and Nicholas Turner. *Drawings by Raphael from the Royal Library, the Ashmolean, the British Museum, Chatsworth and Other English Collections.* Exh. cat., London, British Museum. London, 1983.

Gerli 1784
Gerli, Carlo Giuseppe. *Disegni di Leonardo da Vinci incisi e pubblicati da Carlo Giuseppe Gerli, milanese, con prefazione dell'Amoretti.* Milan, 1784.

Gerli and Vallardi 1830
Gerli, Carlo G., and Giuseppe Vallardi. *Disegni di Leonardo da Vinci incisi sugli originali da Carlo Giuseppe Gerli: Riprodotti con note illustrative da Giuseppe Vallardi.* Milan, 1830.

Gerszi 1999
Gerszi, Teréz, ed. *Dürer to Dalí: Master Drawings in the Budapest Museum of Fine Arts.* Budapest, 1999.

Geymüller 1881
Geymüller, Heinrich de. "Léonard de Vinci a-t-il été au Righi le 5 août 1473?" *Chroniques des arts* 23 (1881), pp. 186–87.

Geymüller 1886
Geymüller, Heinrich de. "Les derniers travaux sur Léonard de Vinci." *Gazette des Beaux-Arts,* ser. 2, 33 (1886), pp. 357–76; 34 (1886), pp. 143–64; 274–96.

Giacobello Bernard 1998
Giacobello Bernard, Giovanna. *Leonardo e le meraviglie della Biblioteca reale di Torino.* Exh. cat., Turin, Biblioteca reale. Turin, 1998.

Giannattasio 1999
Giannattasio, Paolo. "Sulla difficile relazione fra disegni e dipinti: Intorno a Cesare da Sesto, Pedro Fernández e Vincenzo da Pavia." *Dialoghi di storia dell'arte,* nos. 8–9 (1999), pp. 30–49.

Gibbes Museum of Art 1999
McInnis, Maurie D., et. al. *In Pursuit of Refinement: Charlestonians Abroad, 1740–1860.* Exh. cat., Charleston, S.C., Gibbes Museum of Art. Charleston, S.C., 1999.

Gibson 1991
Gibson, Eric. "Leonardo's *Ginevra de' Benci:* The Restoration of a Renaissance Masterpiece." *Apollo* 133, no. 349 (March 1991), pp. 161–65.

Giglioli 1928
Giglioli, Odoardo H. "Disegni italiani di paese nella Galleria degli Uffizi." *Dedalo* 9, no. 3 (August 1928), pp. 172–91.

Giglioli 1936
Giglioli, Odoardo H. "Alcuni disegni di Fra Bartolommeo attribuiti a Domenico Ghirlandaio nella raccolta degli Uffizi." *Bollettino d'arte,* ser. 3, 29 (1936), pp. 489–91.

Giglioli 1944
Giglioli, Odoardo H. *Leonardo: Iniziazione alla conoscenza di lui e delle questioni vinciane.* Florence, 1944.

Gilbert 1949
Gilbert, Felix. "Bernardo Rucellai and the Orti Oricellari: A Study on the Origin of Modern Political Thought." *Journal of the Warburg and Courtauld Institutes* 12 (1949), pp. 101–31.

Gille 1966
Gille, Bertrand. *Engineers of the Renaissance.* Cambridge, Mass., 1966.

Gingerich 1996
Gingerich, Owen. "Leonardo's Legacy in Science." In Farago 1996b, pp. 23–30.

Giusti et de Castris 1988
Giusti, Paola, and Pierluigi Leone de Castris. *Pittura del Cinquecento a Napoli, 1510–1540: Forastieri e regnicoli.* Naples, 1988.

Glasser 1977
Glasser, Hannelore. *Artists' Contracts of the Early Renaissance.* Garland Series of Outstanding Dissertations in the Fine Arts. New York and London, 1977.

Glück 1915
Glück, Gustav. "Jugendwerke von Rubens." *Jahrbuch der kunsthistorischen Sammlungen des allerhöchsten Kaiserhauses* 33 (1915), pp. 1–30.

Glück and Haberdtizl 1928
Glück, Gustav, and Franz Martin Haberdtizl. *Die Handzeichnungen von Peter Paul Rubens.* Berlin, 1928.

Goldner 1985
[Goldner, George]. "Drawings." *The J. Paul Getty Museum Journal* 13 (1985), pp. 185–98.

Goldner 1987
[Goldner, George]. "Drawings." *The J. Paul Getty Museum Journal* 15 (1987), pp. 188–209.

Goldner 1988
Goldner, George, with Lee Hendrix, and Gloria Williams. *European Drawings, 1: Catalogue of the Collections.* The J. Paul Getty Museum. Malibu, 1988.

Goldner and Bambach 1997
Goldner, George R., and Carmen C. Bambach et al. *The Drawings of Filippino Lippi and His Circle.* Exh. cat., New York, The Metropolitan Museum of Art. New York, 1997.

Goldner and Hendrix 1992
Goldner, George R., and Lee Hendrix. *European Drawings, 2: Catalogue of the Collections.* The J. Paul Getty Museum. Malibu, 1992.

Goldscheider 1943
Goldscheider, Ludwig. *Leonardo da Vinci.* London and New York, 1943.

Goldscheider 1945
Goldscheider, Ludwig. *Leonardo da Vinci: The Artist.* Oxford and London, 1945.

Goldscheider 1952
Goldscheider, Ludwig, ed. *Leonardo da Vinci: Landscapes and Plants.* New York, 1952.

Goldscheider 1959
Goldscheider, Ludwig. *Leonardo da Vinci: Life and Work, Paintings and Drawings, with the Leonardo Biography by Vasari, 1568.* 1943. 6th edition, revised. London, 1959.

Goldthwaite 1972
Goldthwaite, Richard. "Schools and Teaching of Commercial Arithmetic in Renaissance Florence." *Journal of European Economic History* 1 (1972), pp. 418–33.

Gombrich 1954
Gombrich, Ernst [H]. "Leonardo's Grotesque

Heads: Prolegomena to their Study." In *Leonardo: Saggi e ricerche* 1954, pp. 197–219, pls. 107–12.

Gombrich 1954, 1976
Gombrich, E[rnst] H. "The Grotesque Heads." 1954. In Gombrich 1976, pp. 57–75.

Gombrich 1966
Gombrich, E[rnst] H. "Leonardo's Method for Working Out Compositions." In *Norm and Form*, pp. 58–63. Studies in the Art of the Renaissance, 1. London, 1966.

Gombrich 1969, 1976
Gombrich, E[rnst] H. "The Form of Movement in Water and Air." In O'Malley 1969, pp. 171–204. Reprinted in Gombrich 1976, pp. 39–56.

Gombrich 1973
Gombrich, Ernst H. "I precetti di Leonardo per comporre delle storie." In *Norma e forma*, pp. 84–92. Turin, 1973.

Gombrich 1976
Gombrich, E[rnst] H. *The Heritage of Apelles*. Studies in the Art of the Renaissance, 3. Ithaca, 1976.

Gombrich 1984
Gombrich, Ernst H. *Leonardo e i maghi, polemiche e rivaltà*. Lettura Vinciana, 23 (16 aprile 1983). Florence, 1984.

Gombrich 1986a
Gombrich, Ernst H. *L'eredità di Apelle: Studi sull'arte del Rinascimento*. 2d ed. Turin, 1986.

Gombrich 1986b
Gombrich, Ernst H. "Il metodo di analisi e permutazione di Leonardo da Vinci." In Gombrich 1986a, pp. 51–106.

Gotti 1870
[Gotti, Aurelio]. *Catalogo della raccolta di disegni autografi antichi e moderni donata dal prof. Emilio Santarelli alla Reale Galleria di Firenze*. Florence, 1870.

Gould 1948
Gould, Cecil. "Letters: Leonardo's 'Virgin of the Rocks.'" *The Burlington Magazine* 90, no. 548 (November 1948), pp. 328–29.

Gould 1952
Gould, Cecil. "Leonardo's 'Neptune' Drawing." *The Burlington Magazine* 94, no. 595 (October 1952), pp. 289–95.

Gould 1954a
Gould, Cecil. "Leonardo's Great Battle-Piece: A Conjectural Reconstruction." *The Art Bulletin* 36, no. 2 (June 1954), pp. 117–29, figs. 1–19.

Gould 1954b
Gould, Cecil. "On the Critique of Leonardo's Drawings." In *Leonardo: Saggi e ricerche* 1954, pp. 187–95.

Gould 1975
Gould, Cecil. *Leonardo: The Artist and the Non-Artist*. Boston and London, 1975.

Gould 1985
Gould, Cecil. "La Vergine delle Rocce." In *Leonardo: La pittura* 1985, pp. 56–62.

Grabski and Walek 1991
Grabski, Josef, and Janusz Walek, eds. *Leonardo da Vinci (1452–1519): Lady with an Ermine from the*

Czartoryski Collection, National Museum, Cracow. Vienna, 1991.

Gramberg 1964
Gramberg, Werner. *Die Düsseldorfer Skizzenbücher des Guglielmo della Porta*. 2 vols. Berlin, 1964.

Grand Palais 1992
Les etrusques et l'Europe. Exh. cat., Paris, Galeries nationales du Grand Palais. Paris, 1992.

Grasselli 1995–96
Grasselli, Margaret Morgan, ed. *The Touch of the Artist: Master Drawings from the Woodner Collections*. Exh. cat., Washington D.C., National Gallery of Art. Washington, D.C., 1995.

Grassi 1956
Grassi, Luigi. *Il disegno italiano dal Trecento al Seicento*. Rome, [1956].

Grassi 1963
Grassi, Luigi. *I disegni italiani del Trecento e Quattrocento*. 1956. Venice, 1963.

Gratchenkov 1963
Gratchenkov, V. N. [Drawings of the Italian Renaissance (in Russian)]. Moscow, 1963.

Green 1992
Green, Andre. *Revelations de l'inachevement: A propos du carton de Londres de Leonard de Vinci*. Paris, 1992.

Grewenig and Letze 1995
Grewenig, Meinrad Maria, and Otto Letze, eds. *Leonardo da Vinci: Künstler, Erfinder, Wissenschaftler*. Exh. cat., Speyer, Historisches Museum der Pfalz. Speyer, 1995.

Griffiths 1998
Griffiths, Antony. "Charles I and his Circle." In British Museum 1998, pp. 71–104.

Griseri 1978
Griseri, Andreina. *I grandi disegni della Biblioteca reale di Torino*. Milan, 1978.

Griseri 1980
Griseri, Andreina. "Il disegno." *Storia dell'arte italiana* 9, no. 1 (1980), pp. 187–226.

Griswold and Wolk-Simon 1994
Griswold, William M., and Linda Wolk-Simon. *Sixteenth-Century Italian Drawings in New York Collections*. Exh. cat., New York, The Metropolitan Museum of Art. New York, 1994.

Gronau 1896
Gronau, Georg. "Über das sogenannte Skizzenbuch des Verrocchio." *Jahrbuch der Königlich Preussischen Kunstsammlungen* 17 (1896), pp. 65–72.

Gronau 1904
Gronau, Georg. Review of *Leonardo da Vinci*, by Edward MacCurdy. *Kunstchronik* 15 (1904), p. 547.

Gronau 1912
Gronau, Georg. "Ein Jugendwerk des Leonardo da Vinci." *Zeitschrift für bildende Kunst* 23, no. 10 (1912), pp. 253–59.

Gronau 1913
Gronau, Georg. "Credi, Lorenzo di." In *Allgemeines Lexikon der bildenden Künstler von der Antike bis zur Gegenwart*, edited by Ulrich Thieme and Felix Becker, vol. 8, pp. 73–77. 37 vols. 1907–50. Leipzig, 1913.

Gronau 1914
Gronau, Georg. *Leonardo da Vinci*. Chicago and New York, 1914.

Grossing 1989
Grossing, Helmuth. "Zu den Technikzeichnungen Leonardo da Vincis." In *Poesis et pictura: Studien zum Verhältnis von Text und Bild in Handschriften und alten Drucken*, edited by Stephan Fussel and Joachim Knape, pp. 107–29. Baden-Baden, 1989.

Grossman 1968
Grossman, Sheldon. "The *Madonna and Child with a Pomegranate* and Some New Paintings from the Circle of Verrocchio." *Report and Studies in the History of Art* 2 (1968), pp. 46–69.

Grossman 1972
Grossman, Sheldon. "An Anonymous Florentine Drawing and the 'So-Called Verrocchio Sketchbook.'" *Master Drawings* 10, no. 1 (Spring 1972), pp. 15–19, pl. 14.

Grossman 1974
Grossman, Sheldon. "An Early Drawing by Fra Bartolommeo." *Studies in the History of Art* 6 (1974), pp. 6–22.

Grossman 1979
Grossman, Sheldon. "Ghirlandaio's 'Madonna and Child' in Frankfurt and Leonardo's Beginnings as a Painter." *Städel-Jahrbuch* 7 (1979), pp. 100–125.

Grosvenor Gallery 1877
Winter Exhibition of Drawings by Old Masters. Exh. cat., London, Grosvenor Gallery. London, 1877.

Grosvenor Gallery 1878
The Royal Collection of Drawings at Windsor. 2 vols. Exh. cat., London, Grosvenor Gallery. London, 1878.

Gruyer 1887
Gruyer, [François-]A[natole]. "Léonard de Vinci au Musée du Louvre." *Gazette des Beaux-Arts*, ser. 2, 35 (1887), pp. 449–72; 36 (1887), pp. 89–107.

Gruyer 1891
Gruyer, François-Anatole. *Voyage autour du Salon Carré au musée du Louvre*. Paris, 1891.

Guffanti 2001
Guffanti, Mario Valentino. "Il Conte di Caylus e le Caricature di Leonardo." *Raccolta Vinciana*, no. 29 (2001), pp. 303–16.

Guicciardini 1984
Guicciardini, Francesco. *The History of Italy*. Translated, edited, with notes and an introduction by Sidney Alexander. Princeton, N.J., 1984.

Guillaume 1987
Guillaume, Jean. "Léonard et l'architecture." In Galluzzi 1987, pp. 207–86.

Habich 1892
Habich, Ernst. "Handzeichnungen italienischer Meister." *Kunstchronik* 31 (July 21, 1892).

Hadley 1968
Hadley, Rollin van N. *Drawings: Isabella Stewart Gardner Museum*. Boston, 1968.

Hager 1992
Hager, Serafina, ed. *Leonardo, Michelangelo, and Raphael in Renaissance Florence from 1500 to 1508*. Washington, D.C., 1992.

Hale 1965
Hale, John R. *Renaissance.* The Great Ages of Man. New York, 1965.

Halm, Degenhart, and Wegner 1958
Halm, Peter, Bernhard Degenhart, and Wolfgang Wegner. *Hundert Meisterzeichnungen aus der Staatlichen Graphischen Sammlung München.* Munich, 1958.

Hamburger Kunsthalle 1957
Stubbe, Wolf, ed. *Italienische Zeichnungen 1500– 1800 aus den Beständen des Kupferstichkabinettes.* Exh. cat., Hamburg, Hamburger Kunsthalle. Hamburg, 1957.

Hamburger Kunsthalle 1997
Italienische Zeichnungen der Renaissance aus dem Kupferstichkabinett der Hamburger Kunsthalle. Exh. cat., Hamburg, Hamburger Kunsthalle. Hamburg, 1997.

Hamburger Kunsthalle 2001
Stolzenburg, Andreas. *Von Dürer bis Goya: 100 Meisterzeichnungen aus dem Kupferstichkabinett der Hamburger Kunsthalle.* Exh. cat., Hamburg, Hamburger Kunsthalle. Hamburg, 2001.

Harding, Braham, Wyld, and Burnstock 1989
Harding, Eric, Allan Braham, Martin Wyld, and Aviva Burnstock. "The Restoration of the Leonardo Cartoon." *National Gallery Technical Bulletin* 13 (1989), pp. 4–27.

Harprath 1994
Harprath, Richard. "Ulteriori pensieri sul disegno di Michelangelo conservato a Monaco per l'Ercole di Fountainebleau." In Cropper 1994, pp. 91–98, and unpaginated figures.

Haskell and Penny 1981
Haskell, Francis, and Nicholas Penny. *Taste and the Antique: The Lure of Classical Sculpture, 1500– 1900.* New Haven and London, 1981.

Hassall 1970
Hassall, W. O., ed. *The Holkham Library.* Oxford, 1970.

Hasselt 1960
Hasselt, Carlos C. von. *15th and 16th Century Drawings.* Exh. cat., Cambridge, Fitzwilliam Museum. Cambridge, 1960.

Haus 1998
Haus, Anny-Claire. *Johann Wilhelm Baur 1607– 1642: Maniérisme et baroque en Europe.* Exh. cat., Strasbourg, Palais Rohan. Paris, 1998.

Haverkamp Begemann 1957
Haverkamp Begemann, Egbert. *Vijf Eeuwen Tekenkunst: Tekenigen van Europese Messters in Het Museum Boymans te Rotterdam.* Rotterdam, 1957.

Heijbroek 1982–83
Heijbroek, J. F., et al. *Met Huygens op Reis: Tekeningen en dagboeknotities van Constantijn Huygens jr. (1628–1697), secretaris van stadhouder-koning Willem III.* Exh. cat., Amsterdam, Rijks-prentenkabinet; Ghent, Museum voor Schone Kunsten. Zutphen, 1982.

Heil 1969
Heil, Walter. "A Marble Putto by Verrocchio." *Pantheon* 27, no. 4 (July–August 1969), pp. 271–82.

Held 1959
Held, Julius. *Rubens: Selected Drawings, with an Introduction and a Critical Catalogue.* 2 vols. London, 1959.

Held 1986
Held, Julius. *Rubens: Selected Drawings.* Oxford, 1986.

Hercolani 1574
Hercolani, Giuliantonio. *Lo scrittor' utile et brieue.* [Bologna], 1574. (The Metropolitan Museum of Art, acc. no. 29.72.3).

Hervey 1921
Hervey, Mary Fredericka. *The Life, Correspondence and Collections of Thomas Howard, Earl of Arundel.* Cambridge, 1921.

Herzfeld 1922
Herzfeld, Marie. "La rappresentazione della 'Danae' organizzata da Leonardo." *Raccolta Vinciana,* no. 11 (1920–22), pp. 226–28.

Herzfeld 1932
Herzfeld, Marie. "Über ein Skizzenblatt Leonardos als beitrag zur Charakterdeutung des Meisters." *Mitteilungen des Kunsthistorischen Institutes in Florenz* 4, no. 1 (July 1932), pp. 1–24.

Hevesy 1931
Hevesy, André de. "Autour de Léonard de Vinci oeuvres retrouvées—oeuvres perdues." *Gazette des Beaux-Arts,* ser. 6, 5 (1931), pp. 103–14.

Hevesy 1932
Hevesy, André de. "Dans l'atelier de Léonard de Vinci: Boltraffio et ses modèles." *L'amour de l'art* 13, no. 8 (October 1932), pp. 260–66.

Hevesy 1936
Hevesy, A[ndré] de. "Boltraffio." *Pantheon* 18, no. 10 (October 1936), pp. 323–29.

Hevesy 1952
Hevesy, André de. "Un compagno di Leonardo: Francesco Melzi." *Emporium* 116, no. 696 (December 1952), pp. 242–57.

Heydenreich 1933
Heydenreich, Ludwig-Heinrich. "La Sainte Anne de Léonard de Vinci." *Gazette des Beaux-Arts,* ser. 6, 10 (1933), pp. 205–19. Reprinted in *Leonardo-Studien,* Munich, 1988, pp. 13–22.

Heydenreich 1946
Heydenreich, Ludwig H. Review of *The Drawing of Leonardo da Vinci,* by A. E. Popham. *Phoebus* 1, nos. 3–4 (1946), pp. 181–84.

Heydenreich 1949
Heydenreich, Ludwig H., ed. *I disegni di Leonardo da Vinci e della sua scuola, conservati nella galleria dell'Accademia di Venezia.* Florence, 1949.

Heydenreich 1954
Heydenreich, Ludwig H. *Leonardo da Vinci.* 1943. 2 vols. New York and Basel, 1954.

Heydenreich 1957
Heydenreich, Ludwig H. "Marc Aurel und Regisole." In *Festschrift für Erich Meyer zum sechzigsten Geburtstag 29. Oktober 1957,* edited by Werner Gramberg et al., pp. 146–59. Hamburg, 1957.

Heydenreich 1958a
Heydenreich, Ludwig H. *Leonardo da Vinci: Das Abendmahl.* Stuttgart, 1958.

Heydenreich 1958b
Heydenreich, Ludwig H. "Leonardo da Vinci." In *Enciclopedia universale dell'arte,* vol. 8. Venice and Rome, 1958.

Heydenreich 1964
Heydenreich, Ludwig H. "Leonardo's 'Salvator Mundi.'" *Raccolta Vinciana,* no. 20 (1964), pp. 83–109.

Heydenreich 1965
Heydenreich, Ludwig H. "Bemerkungen zu den Entwürfen Leonardos für das Grabmal des Gian Giacomo Trivulzio." In *Studien zur Geschichte der europäischen Plastik: Festschrift Theodor Müller, zum 19. April 1965,* pp. 179–94. Munich, 1965.

Heydenreich 1969
Heydenreich, Ludwig H. "Leonardo and Bramante: Genius in Architecture." In O'Malley 1969, pp. 124–48.

Heydenreich 1974a
Heydenreich, Ludwig H. *Leonardo: The Last Supper.* Art in Context. New York, 1974.

Heydenreich 1974b
Heydenreich, Ludwig H. "The Military Architect." In Reti 1974, pp. 136–65.

Heydenreich 1977
Heydenreich, Ludwig H. "Qui è la veduta: Über einige Landschaftszeichnungen Leonardo da Vincis in Madrider skizzenbuch. (Cod. 8936)." In *Studies in Late Medieval and Renaissance Painting in Honor of Millard Meiss,* vol. 1, pp. 241–48. 2 vols. New York, 1977.

Heydenreich 1982
Heydenreich, Ludwig H. *Invito a Leonardo: L'Ultima Cena.* 1974. Milan, 1982.

Hibbard 1980
Hibbard, Howard. *The Metropolitan Museum of Art.* New York, 1980.

Hildebrandt 1927
Hildebrandt, Edmund. *Leonardo da Vinci.* Berlin, 1927.

Hills 1980
Hills, Paul. "Leonardo and Flemish Painting." *The Burlington Magazine* 122, no. 930 (September 1980), pp. 608–15.

Hind 1907
Hind, Charles Lewis. *Drawings of Leonardo da Vinci.* London, 1907.

Hind 1910
Hind, Arthur Mayger. *Catalogue of Early Italian Engravings, preserved in the Department of Prints and Drawings in the British Museum.* London, 1910.

Hind 1938–48
Hind, A[rthur] M[ayger]. *Early Italian Engraving. A Critical Catalogue with Complete Reproductions of all the Prints Described.* 7 vols. London, 1938–48.

Hind 1948
Hind, A[rthur] M[ayger]. *Early Italian Engraving: A Critical Catalogue with Complete Reproductions of all the Prints Described.* Vol. 5, part 2, *Known Masters other than Florentine Monogrammists and Anonymous.* London, 1948.

Hinterding and Horsch 1989
Hinterding, Erik, and Femy Horsch. "'A small but choice collection': The Art Gallery of King Willem II of the Netherlands (1792–1849)." *Simiolus* 19, nos. 1–2 (1989), pp. 4–122.

Hirst 1988
Hirst, Michael. *Michelangelo and his Drawings.* New Haven and London, 1988.

Hirst 2000
Hirst, Michael. "Michelangelo in Florence: 'David' in 1503 and 'Hercules' in 1506." *The Burlington Magazine* 142, no. 1169 (August 2000), pp. 487–92.

Hochstetler Meyer 1984
Hochstetler Meyer, Barbara. "Leonardo's *Battle of Anghiari*: Proposals for Some Sources and a Reflection." *The Art Bulletin* 66, no. 3 (September 1984), pp. 367–82.

Hochstetler Meyer 1990
Hochstetler Meyer, Barbara. "Leonardo's Hypothetical Painting of *Leda and the Swan.*" *Mitteilungen des Kunsthistorischen Institutes in Florenz* 34, no. 3 (1990), pp. 279–94.

Hochstetler Meyer and Glover 1989
Hochstetler Meyer, Barbara, and Alice Wilson Glover. "Botany and Art in Leonardo's *Leda and the Swan.*" *Leonardo* 22, no. 1 (1989), pp. 75–82.

Hohenstatt 1998
Hohenstatt, Peter. *Léonard de Vinci.* Cologne, 1998.

Holberton 1995
Holberton, Paul. Review of *Leonardo as a Physiognomist: Theory and Drawing Practice,* by Michael W. Kwakkelstein. *The Burlington Magazine* 137, no. 1104 (March 1995), pp. 188–89.

Hollstein 1962
Hollstein, F. W. H. *German Engravings, Etchings and Woodcuts, ca. 1400–1700.* Vol. 7, *Albrecht and Hans Dürer.* Amsterdam, 1962.

Holly 1996
Holly, Michael Ann. "Writing Leonardo Backwards." Chap. 5 in *Past Looking: Historical Imagination and the Rhetoric of the Image,* pp. 112–48. Ithaca and London, 1996.

Holst 1974
Holst, Christian von. *Francesco Granacci.* Munich, 1974.

Horne 1903
Horne, Herbert P. *The Life of Leonardo da Vinci by Giorgio Vasari, done into English . . . with a Commentary.* London, 1903.

Horne 1908
Horne, Herbert P. *Alessandro Filipepi, commonly called Sandro Botticelli, Painter of Florence.* London, 1908.

Horne 1909
Horne, Herbert P., ed. *Il Memoriale di Francesco Albertini.* London, 1909.

Houbraken 1753
Houbraken, Arnold. *De Groote Schouburgh der Nederlantsche Konstschilders en Schilderessen.* Amsterdam, 1753.

Hours 1954
Hours, Madeleine. "Étude analytique des tableaux de Léonard de Vinci au laboratoire du Musée du Louvre." In *Leonardo: Saggi e ricerche* 1954, pp. 13–26.

Howarth 1980
Howarth, David. "Lord Arundel as an Entrepreneur of the Arts." *The Burlington Magazine* 122, no. 931 (October 1980), pp. 690–92, 694.

Howarth 1998
Howarth, David. "The Patronage and Collecting of Aletheia, Countess of Arundel, 1606–54." *Journal of the History of Collections* 10, no. 2 (1998), pp. 125–37.

Howze and Mittler 2001
Howze, James D., and Gene A. Mittler. *Creating and Understanding Drawings.* New York, 2001.

Huygens 1888–1905
Huygens, Christiaan. *Œuvres complètes de Christiaan Huygens, publiées par la Société Hollandaise des Sciences.* 10 vols. The Hague, 1888–1905.

Huyghe 1960
Huyghe, René. *L'art et l'âme.* [Paris], 1960.

I leonardeschi: L'eredità di Leonardo in Lombardia.
See *Legacy of Leonardo* 1998 and essays by contributors under their names.

Institut néerlandais 1962
Le dessin italien dans les collections hollandaises. Exh. cat., Paris, Institut néerlandais, Fondation Custodia; Rotterdam, Museum Boymans-Van Beuningen; Haarlem, Teylers Museum. Paris, 1962.

Inventaire après décès 1695–96
"Mémoire Estat Inventaire & Reglement de droitz dans la famille de feu S Evrard Jabach, et de dame Anne Marie Deyroot sa veuve du 17 juillet 1696. Reconnu par devant notaire." Bibliothèque Centrale des Musées nationaux, Paris.

Inventaire 1848–52
"Inventaire 1848–1852. Musées Nationaux. République Française. Acquisitions et Dons." Départements des Arts graphiques du musée du Louvre, Paris.

Inventaire Napoléon 1812
Manuscript inventory of the drawings in the Louvre, compiled by 1812 by Louis-Marie-Joseph Morel d'Arleux, curator of the Cabinet des dessins du Louvre from 1797 to 1827. 9 vols. Départements des Arts graphiques du musée du Louvre, Paris.

Isermeyer 1964
Isermeyer, Christian Adolf. "Die Arbeiten Leonardos und Michelangelos für den Grossen Ratssaal in Florenz: Eine Revision der Bild- und Schriftquellen für ihre Rekonstruktion und Geschichte." In *Studien zur Toskanischen Kunst: Festschrift für Ludwig Heinrich Heydenreich.* Munich, 1964.

Jacob 1975
Jacob, Sabine. *Italienische Zeichnungen der Kunstbibliothek Berlin, Architektur und Decoration, (16 bis 18 Jahre).* Berlin, 1975.

Jacobsen 1904
Jacobsen, Emil. "Die Handzeichnungen der Uffizien in ihren Beziehungen zu Gemälden, Skulpturen und Gebäuden in Florenz." *Repertorium für Kunstwissenschaft* 27 (1904), pp. 113–32, 401–429.

Jacobsen 1906–7
Jacobsen, Emil. "Neues über Leonardo." *Kunstchronik* 28 (1906–7), pp. 194–97.

Jacobsen 1910
Jacobsen, Emil. "Un quadro e un disegno del maestro della Pala Sforzesca." *Rassegna d'arte* 10, no. 4 (April 1910), pp. 53–55.

Jaffé 1958
Jaffé, Michael. "Rubens in Italy: Rediscovered Works." *The Burlington Magazine* 100, no. 669 (December 1958), pp. 410–22.

Jaffé 1962
Jaffé, Michael. "Italian Drawings from Dutch Collections." *The Burlington Magazine* 104, no. 711 (June 1962), pp. 230–38.

Jaffé 1977
Jaffé, Michael. *Rubens and Italy.* Oxford, 1977.

Jaffé 1989
Jaffé, Michael. *Rubens: Catalogo completo.* Translated by Germano Mulazzani. Milan, 1989.

Jaffé 1993
Jaffé, Michael. *Old Master Drawings from Chatsworth.* London, 1993.

Jaffé 1994
Jaffé, Michael. *The Devonshire Collection of Italian Drawings: Venetian and Northern Italian Schools.* London, 1994.

Jaffé 1995–96
Jaffé Michael. *A Great Heritage: Renaissance and Baroque Drawings from Chatsworth.* Exh. cat., Washington, D.C., National Gallery of Art; New York, The Pierpont Morgan Library. Washington, D.C., 1995.

Jebb 1946
Jebb, Richard C., et al. "The Classical Renaissance." *The Metropolitan Museum of Art Bulletin,* n.s., 5, no. 3 (November 1946), pp. 73–100.

Jessop 1887
Jessop, Augustus. *The Autobiography of the Hon. Roger North.* London, 1887.

Joannides 1988
Joannides, Paul. "Leonardo da Vinci, Peter-Paul Rubens, Pierre-Nolasque Bergeret and the 'Fight for the Standard.'" *Achademia Leonardi Vinci: Journal of Leonardo Studies and Bibliography of Vinciana* 1 (1988), pp. 76–86, and unpaginated figures.

Jung 1977
Jung, Richard. "Über Zeichnungen linkshändiger Künstler von Leonardo bis Klee: Linkshänder Merkmale als Zuschreibungskriterien, Semper Attentus." *Beiträge für Heinz Götze zum 8. August 1977,* pp. 189–218. Berlin and Heidelberg, 1977.

Keele 1976
Keele, Kenneth D. *Leonardo da Vinci: Anatomical Drawings from the Queen's Collection at Windsor Castle.* Introduction by Anthony Blunt. Exh. cat., Washington, D.C., National Museum of History and Technology, Smithsonian Institution; Los Angeles County Museum of Art. Los Angeles, 1976.

Keele 1983
Keele, Kenneth D. *Leonardo da Vinci's Elements of*

the *Science of Man*. New York and London, 1983.

Keele and Pedretti 1979–80
Keele, Kenneth D., and Carlo Pedretti. *Leonardo da Vinci: Corpus of Anatomical Drawings in the Collection of Her Majesty the Queen*. 3 vols. London, 1979–80.

Keele and Roberts 1983
Keele, Kenneth D., and Jane Roberts. *Leonardo da Vinci: Anatomical Drawings from the Royal Library, Windsor Castle*. Exh. cat., New York, The Metropolitan Museum of Art. New York, 1983.

Keisch and Riemann-Reyher 1996–97
Keisch, Claude, and Marie Ursula Riemann-Reyher, eds. *Adolph Menzel, 1815–1905: Between Romanticism and Impressionism*. Exh. cat., Paris, Musée d'Orsay; Washington, D.C., National Gallery of Art; Berlin, Alte Nationalgalerie. New Haven and London, 1996.

Keller 1938
Keller, R. "Zwei berühmte Linkshänder." *Ciba Zeitschrift* 6 (1938), pp. 2153–55.

Kemp 1977
Kemp, Martin. "From 'Mimesis' to 'Fantasia': The Quattrocento Vocabulary of Creation, Inspiration and Genius in the Visual Arts." *Viator* 8 (1977), pp. 347–98, fig. 1.

Kemp 1978
Kemp, Martin. "Science, Non-Science and Nonsense: The Interpretation of Brunelleschi's Perspective." *Art History* 1, no. 2 (June 1978), pp. 134–61.

Kemp 1981
Kemp, Martin. *Leonardo da Vinci: The Marvellous Works of Nature and Man*. London, 1981.

Kemp 1982a
Kemp, Martin. "Exhibition Reviews: Vinci, Leonardo dopo Milano." *The Burlington Magazine* 124, no. 957 (December 1982), p. 788.

Kemp 1982b
Kemp, Martin. *Leonardo da Vinci: Le mirabili operazioni della natura e del'uomo*. Milan, 1982.

Kemp 1986
Kemp, Martin. "Analogy and Observation in the Codex Hammer." In *Studi vinciani in memoria di Nando de Toni*, pp. 103–34. Brescia, 1986.

Kemp 1987
Kemp, Martin. "'A Chaos of Intelligence': Leonardo's *Traité* and the Perspective Wars in the Académie Royale." In *"Il se rendit en Italie": Études offertes à André Chastel*, pp. 415–26. Paris, 1987.

Kemp 1988
Kemp, Martin. *Leonardo e lo spazio dello scultore*. Lettura Vinciana, 27 (20 aprile 1987). Vinci, 1988.

Kemp 1989a
Kemp, Martin J. "Geometrical Bodies as Exemplary Forms in Renaissance Space." In *World Art: Themes of Unity in Diversity*, edited by Irving Lavin, vol. 1, pp. 237–42. Acts of the XXVIth International Congress of the History of Art. 3 vols. University Park, Pa., and London, 1989.

Kemp 1989b
Kemp, Martin. *Leonardo da Vinci: The Marvellous Works of Nature and Man*. 1981. Reprint. London, 1989.

Kemp 1989c
Kemp, Martin, ed. *Leonardo on Painting: An Anthology of Writings by Leonardo da Vinci, with a Selection of Documents Relating to his Career as an Artist*. Translated by Martin Kemp and Margaret Walker. New Haven and London, 1989.

Kemp 1990a
Kemp, Martin. "Looking at Leonardo's *Last Supper*." In *Appearance, Opinion, Change: Evaluating the Look of Paintings*, pp. 14–21. London, 1990.

Kemp 1990b
Kemp, Martin. *The Science of Art: Optical Themes in Western Art from Brunelleschi to Seurat*. New Haven and London, 1990.

Kemp 1991
Kemp, Martin. "The 'Madonna of the Yarnwinder' in the Buccleuch Collection Reconsidered in the Context of Leonardo's Studio Practice." In Fiorio and Marani 1991, pp. 35–48.

Kemp 1992a
Kemp, Martin. "The 'Hammer Lecture' (1992): In the Beholder's Eye—Leonardo and the 'Errors of Sight' in Theory and Practice." *Achademia Leonardi Vinci: Journal of Leonardo Studies and Bibliography of Vinciana* 5 (1992), pp. 153–62, and unpaginated figures.

Kemp 1992b
Kemp, Martin. "Leonardo." In *Circa 1492: Art in the Age of Exploration*, edited by Jay Levenson, pp. 270–87. Exh. cat., Washington, D.C., National Gallery of Art. Washington, D.C., 1992.

Kemp 1992c
Kemp, Martin, ed. *Leonardo da Vinci: The Mystery of the* Madonna of the Yarnwinder. Exh. cat., Edinburgh, National Gallery of Scotland. Edinburgh, 1992.

Kemp 1992d
Kemp, Martin. "Leonardo da Vinci: The National Gallery of Scotland's First Leonardo." *National Art-Collections Fund Review* 88 (1992), pp. 16–20.

Kemp 1992e
Kemp, Martin. "Leonardo Verso 1500." In Palazzo Grassi 1992, pp. 45–54.

Kemp 1995
Kemp, Martin. "Leonardo's Drawings for 'Il Cavallo del Duca Francesco di Bronzo': The Program of Research." In Ahl 1995, pp. 64–78.

Kemp 1996a
Kemp, Martin. "The Body of the Earth." In Farago 1996b, pp. 15–22.

Kemp 1996b
Kemp, Martin. "Leonardo da Vinci." In *The Dictionary of Art*, edited by Jane Turner, vol. 19, pp. 180–99. 34 vols. London, 1996.

Kemp 1996c
Kemp, Martin. *Leonardo da Vinci*. CD-ROM. Bellevue, Wash.: Corbis Productions, 1996.

Kemp 1998
Kemp, Martin. "Verrocchio's 'San Donato' and the Chiesina della Virgine di Piazza in Pistoia." *Pantheon* 56 (1998), pp. 25–34.

Kemp and Roberts 1989
Kemp, Martin, and Jane Roberts. *Leonardo da Vinci*. Exh. cat., London, Hayward Gallery. Exhibition held by the South Bank Center. London, 1989.

Kemp and Smart 1980
Kemp, Martin, and Alastair Smart. "Leonardo's *Leda* and the Belvedere *River-Gods*: Roman Sources and a New Chronology." *Art History* 3, no. 2 (June 1980), pp. 182–93.

Kemp and Wallace 2000
Kemp, Martin, and Marina Wallace. *Spectacular Bodies: The Art and Science of the Human Body from Leonardo to Now*. Exh. cat., London, Hayward Gallery. London, 2000.

Kennedy 1938
Kennedy, Ruth W. *Alesso Baldovinetti: A Critical and Historical Study*. New Haven and London, 1938.

Kiang 1989
Kiang, Dawson. "Gasparo Visconti's *Pasitea* and the Sala delle Asse." *Achademia Leonardi Vinci: Journal of Leonardo Studies and Bibliography of Vinciana* 2 (1989), pp. 101–9, and unpaginated figures.

Kiang 1994
Kiang, Dawson. "Aristotle and Phyllis: Leonardo's Drawing of an *exemplum*." *Achademia Leonardi Vinci: Journal of Leonardo Studies and Bibliography of Vinciana* 7 (1994), pp. 75–80, and unpaginated figures.

Kirk and Kertesz 1989
Kirk, A., and A. Kertesz. "Hemispheric Contributions to Drawing." *Neuropsychologia* 27, no. 6 (1989), pp. 881–86.

Kirk and Kertesz 1993
Kirk, A., and A. Kertesz. "Subcortical Contributions to Drawing." *Brain and Cognition* 21, no. 1 (January 1993), pp. 57–70.

Kirwin 1995
Kirwin, W. Chandler, with Peter G. Rush. "The Bubble Reputation: In the Cannon's and the Horse's Mouth (or The Tale of Three Horses)." In Ahl 1995, pp. 87–110.

Koopmann 1891
Koopmann, W. "Einige weniger bekannte Handzeichnungen Raffaels." *Jahrbuch der Königlich Preussischen Kunstsammlungen* 12 (1891), pp. 40–49.

Kornell 1992
Kornell, Monique N. "Artists and the Study of Anatomy in Sixteenth-Century Italy." Ph.D. diss., University of London, Warburg Institute, 1992.

Koschatzky and Krasa 1969
Koschatzky, Walther, and S. Krasa. *200 Jahre Albertina: Herzog Albert von Sachsen-Teschen und seine Kunstsammlung*. Exh. cat., Vienna, Albertina. Vienna, 1969.

Kristeller 1913
Kristeller, Paul. *Die Lombardische Graphik der Renaissance*. Berlin, 1913.

Kristeller 1963
Kristeller, P. O. *Iter Italicum, I Italy*. London and Leiden, 1963.

Kugler 1869
Kugler, Franz T. *Handbook of Painting: The Italian Schools, National Gallery of Art.* Edited by C. L. Eastlake. London, 1869.

Kunsthalle, Basel 1937
Künstlerkopien. Exh. cat., Basel, Kunsthalle. Basel, 1937.

Kunsthistorisches Museum 1994
Ferino-Pagden, Sylvia. *"La prima donna del mondo": Isabella d'Este, Fürstin und Mäzenatin der Renaissance.* Exh. cat., Vienna, Kunsthistorisches Museum. Vienna, 1994.

Kunstmuseum Lucerne 1946
Italienische Kunst aus der Ambrosiana Mailand: Meisterwerke aus oberitalienischen Kirchen, Museen und Privatsammlungen. Exh. cat., Kunstmuseum Lucerne. Lucerne, 1946.

Kunst- und Austellungshalle 1999
Hoch Renaissance im Vatikan: Kunst und Kultur im Rom der Päpste I, 1503–1534. Exh. cat., Bonn, Kunst- und Austellungshalle der Bundesrepublik Deutschland. Bonn, 1999.

Kupferstichkabinett Berlin 1910
Zeichnungen alter Meister im Kupferstichkabinett der K. Museen zu Berlin. Vol. 1, *Italien-Frankreich.* Berlin, 1910.

Kupferstichkabinett Berlin 1973
Vom späten Mittelalter bis zu Jacques Louis David: Neuerworbene und neubestimmte Zeichnungen im Berliner Kupferstichkabinett. Exh. cat., Berlin, Kupferstichkabinett, Staatliche Museen zu Berlin–Preussischer Kulturbesitz. Berlin, 1973.

Kupferstichkabinett Berlin 1994
Dückers, Alexander, ed. *Das Kupferstichkabinett: Ein Handbuch zur Sammlung.* Berlin, 1994.

Küppers 1915
Küppers, Paul Erich. "Über den Zusammenhang einiger Handzeichnungen mit Domenico Ghirlandajo." *Monatsheft für Kunstwissenschaft* 8 (1915), pp. 293–95, pl. 72.

Kurz 1936
Kurz, Otto. "Shorter Notices: A Contribution to the History of the Leonardo Drawings." *The Burlington Magazine* 69, no. 402 (September 1936), p. 135.

Kurz 1937
Kurz, Otto. "Giorgio Vasari's 'Libro de' Disegni.'" *Old Master Drawings* 11, no. 45 (June 1937), pp. 1–15, pls. 1–16; 12, no. 47 (December 1937), pp. 32–44, pls. 34–49.

Kurz 1955
Kurz, Otto. "A Group of Florentine Drawings for an Altar." *Journal of the Warburg and Courtauld Institutes* 18 (1955), pp. 35–53.

Kurz 1962
Kurz, Otto. "An Early Copy of the "Battle of Anghiari.'" *Raccolta Vinciana*, no. 19 (1962), pp. 129–35.

Kustodieva 1984
Kustodieva, Tatiana. "Madonna Benois e Madonna Litta." In *Galleria degli Uffizi* 1984, pp. 13–21.

Kustodieva 1985
Kustodieva, Tatiana. "Madonna Benois e Madonna Litta." In *Leonardo: La pittura* 1985, pp. 49–55.

Kwakkelstein 1991
Kwakkelstein, Michael W. "Leonardo da Vinci's Grotesque Heads and the Breaking of the Physiognomic Mould." *Journal of the Warburg and Courtauld Institutes* 54 (1991), pp. 127–36.

Kwakkelstein 1993a
K[wakkelstein], M[ichael] W. "Gleanings: 1. The Master of the Spencer Grotesques." *Achademia Leonardi Vinci: Journal of Leonardo Studies and Bibliography of Vinciana* 6 (1993), p. 185, and unpaginated figures.

Kwakkelstein 1993b
Kwakkelstein, Michael W. "The Lost Book on 'moti mentali.'" *Achademia Leonardi Vinci: Journal of Leonardo Studies and Bibliography of Vinciana* 6 (1993), pp. 56–66, and unpaginated figures.

Kwakkelstein 1993c
Kwakkelstein, Michael W. "'Teste di vecchi in buon numero.'" *Raccolta Vinciana*, no. 25 (1993), pp. 39–62.

Kwakkelstein 1994
Kwakkelstein, Michael W. *Leonardo da Vinci as a Physiognomist: Theory and Drawing Practice.* Leiden, 1994.

Kwakkelstein 1999
Kwakkelstein, Michael W. "The Use of Sculptural Models by Italian Renaissance Painters: Leonardo da Vinci's *Madonna of the Rocks* Reconsidered in Light of his Working Procedures." *Gazette des Beaux-Arts*, ser. 6, 133 (1999), pp. 182–98.

Laclotte 1956
Laclotte, Michel. *De Giotto à Bellini.* Exh. cat., Paris, Musée national de l'Orangerie des Tuileries. Paris, 1956.

Lagrange 1862
Lagrange, Léon. "Catalogue des dessins de maîtres exposés dans la Galerie des Uffizii, à Florence." *Gazette des Beaux-Arts*, ser. 1, 12 (1862), pp 535–54; 13 (1862), pp. 277–84; 446–62.

Lambert 1999
Lambert, Gisèle. *Les premières gravures italiennes: Quattrocento début Cinquecento.* Paris, 1999.

Lambertini 1953
Lambertini, Gastone. "Leonardo anatomico." In *Atti del Convegno di Studi Vinciani*, pp. 289–309. Florence, 1953.

Landau and Parshall 1994
Landau, David, and Peter Parshall. *The Renaissance Print, 1470–1550.* New Haven and London, 1994.

Landucci 1927
Landucci, Luca. *A Florentine Diary from 1450 to 1516.* Translated by Alice de Rosen Jervis. London, 1927.

Langl 1889
Langl, Josef. "Das Testament der Angelica Kauffmann." *Zeitschrift für Bildende Kunst* 24 (1889), pp. 294–300.

L'Anthony 1995
L'Anthony, P. "Left-handed Painters." *Revue neurologique* 151, no. 3 (March 1995), pp. 165–70.

Laurenza 1996
Laurenza, Domenico. "La *fisionomia naturale* di Leonardo: Una traccia giovanile e alcuni sviluppi." *Achademia Leonardi Vinci: Journal of Leonardo Studies and Bibliography of Vinciana* 9 (1996), pp. 14–19, and unpaginated figures.

Laurenza 1997
Laurenza, Domenico. "*Corpus Mobile*: Tracce di patognomica in Leonardo." *Raccolta Vinciana*, no. 27 (1997), pp. 237–98.

Laurenza 1998
Laurenza, Domenico. "Gli studi leonardiana sul volo: Spunti per una reconsiderazione." In Frosini 1998, pp. 189–202.

Laurenza 2001
Laurenza, Domenico. *De figura umana: Fisiognomica, anatomia e arte in Leonardo.* Florence, 2001.

Laureti 1911
Laureti, Cesare. *Progetto del monumento a Dante Alighieri in Roma da un disegno di Leonardo da Vinci proposto da Cesare Laureti pittore.* Venice, 1911.

Lauts 1956
Lauts, Jan. *Isabella d'Este, fürstin der Renaissance.* Paris, 1956.

Lavagnino 1980
Lavagnino, Emilio. "Leonardo in Rome." In *Leonardo da Vinci* 1980, pp. 127–37.

Lawrence Gallery 1835–36
Woodburn, S. and A. *The Lawrence Gallery . . . Exhibition . . . of His . . . Collection . . . Forming Ten Exhibitions . . . Messrs. Woodburn . . . London.* Exh. cats., London, Lawrence Gallery. London, 1835–36.

Layard 1902
Layard, Austen H., ed. *The Italian Schools of Painting Based on the Handbook of Kugler.* 2 vols. London, 1902.

Lebel 1952
Lebel, Robert. *Léonard de Vinci ou la fin de l'humilité.* Paris, 1952.

Lefrançois 1994
Lefrançois, Thierry. *Charles Coypel: Peintre du roi (1694–1752).* Paris, 1994.

Legacy of Leonardo 1998
Bora, Giulio, et al. *The Legacy of Leonardo: Painters in Lombardy, 1490–1530*, edited by Francesco Porzio. Milan, 1998. Published simultaneously as *I leonardeschi: L'eredità di Leonardo in Lombardia*. References in this catalogue are to the English edition.

Leinati 1980
Leinati, Luigi. "Comparative Anatomy." In *Leonardo da Vinci* 1980, pp. 388–98.

Lenzuni 1992
Lenzuni, Anna, ed. *All'ombra del lauro: Documenti librari della cultura in eta laurenziana.* Exh. cat., Florence, Biblioteca Medicea Laurenziana. Florence, 1992.

Leonardo da Vinci 1980
Leonardo da Vinci. [1939]. Rev. ed. New York, [1980].

Leonardo da Vinci: Conference fiorentine 1910
Solmi, Edmondo, et al. *Leonardo da Vinci: Conference fiorentine.* Milan, 1910.

Leonardo: La pittura 1985
[Marani, Pietro, ed.]. *Leonardo: La pittura.* 1977.
Rev. ed. Florence, 1985.

Leonardo: Saggi e ricerche 1954
Comitato nazionale per le onoranze a Leonardo da
Vinci nel quinto centenario della nascita (1452–
1952). *Leonardo: Saggi e ricerche,* edited by Achille
Marazza. [Rome, 1954].

Leoni 1992
Leoni, Massimo. "La tecnica di fonderia ai tempi
del Verrocchio." In Bule 1992, pp. 157–61.

Lesca 1919
Lesca, Giuseppe. *Leonardo da Vinci: Saggio sulla
vita e le opere.* Bergamo, 1919.

Letze and Buchsteiner 1997
Letze, Otto, and Thomas Buchsteiner. *Leonardo da
Vinci: Scientist, Inventor, Artist.* Exh. cat., Boston,
Museum of Science, Tübingen, Institut für
Kulturaustausch. Tübingen, 1997.

Levenson, Oberhuber, and Sheehan 1973
Levenson, Jay A., Konrad Oberhuber, and
Jacquelyn L. Sheehan. *Early Italian Engravings
from the National Gallery of Art.* Washington,
D.C., 1973.

Levine 1974
Levine, Saul. "The Location of Michelangelo's
David: The Meeting of January 25, 1504." *The Art
Bulletin* 56, no. 1 (March 1974), pp. 31–49.

Libro di pittura 1995
Pedretti, Carlo, ed. *Leonardo da Vinci: Libro di pit-
tura. Codice Urbinate lat. 1270 nella Biblioteca
Apostolica Vaticana.* Critical transcription by Carlo
Vecce. 2 vols. Florence, 1995.

Lieb 1919
Lieb, J. W. "Elenco e analisi . . . : *Bulletin of the
Metropolitan Museum of Art,* New Jork, october
1918." *Raccolta Vinciana,* no. 10 (1919), pp. 259–64.

Ligabue 1977
Ligabue, Giancarlo. *Leonardo da Vinci e i fossili.*
Venice, 1977.

Lightbown 1978
Lightbown, Ronald. *Sandro Botticelli.* 2 vols.
London, 1978.

LIMC 1990
Lexicon Iconographicum Mythologiae Classicae.
Zurich and Munich, 1990.

LIMC 1994
Lexicon Iconographicum Mythologiae Classicae.
Zurich and Munich, 1994.

Lini and Sutera 1997
Lini, Domenico, and Salvatore Sutera, eds. *Museo
Nazionale della Scienza e della Tecnica Leonardo
da Vinci.* Milan, 1997.

Liphart 1912
Liphart, E. von. "Kritische Gänge und Reiseeindrücke." *Jahrbuch der Königlich Preuszischen
Kunstsammlungen* 33 (1912), pp. 193–224.

Lisner 1981
Lisner, Margrit. "Leonardos Anbetung der Könige:
Zum Sinngehalt und zur Komposition." *Zeitschrift
für Kunstgeschichte* 44, no. 3 (1981), pp. 201–42.

Loeser 1899
Loeser, Charles. "Die Handzeichnungen der

königlichen Bibliothek in Turin, mit besonderer
Berücksichtigung der italienischen Meister."
Repertorium für Kunstwissenschaft 22 (1899),
pp. 13–21.

Loeser 1901
Loeser, Charles. "Un'opera di Ambrogio de'Predis."
Rassegna d'arte 1, no. 5 (May 1901), pp. 65–67.

Loeser 1903a
Loeser, Charles. "La Collection Beckerath au
Cabinet des Estampes de Berlin [Part 2]." *Gazette
des Beaux-Arts,* ser. 3, 29 (1903), pp. 47–58.

Loeser 1903b
Loeser, Charles. "Note intorno ai disegni conservati
nelle R. Galleria di Venezia." *Rassegna d'arte* 3,
no. 12 (December 1903), pp. 177–84.

Logan 1977
Logan, Anne-Marie. "Reviews: Rubens Exhibitions,
1977." *Master Drawings* 15, no. 4 (Winter 1977),
pp. 403–17, pls. 46a–47b.

Logan 1978
Logan, Anne-Marie. "Reviews: Rubens Exhibitions,
1977–1978." *Master Drawings* 16, no. 4 (Winter
1978), pp. 419–50.

Logan 1987
Logan, Anne-Marie. Review of *Rubens: Selected
Drawings,* by Julius S. Held. *Master Drawings* 25,
no. 1 (Spring 1987), pp. 63–82.

Logan and Haverkamp-Begemann 1978
Logan, Anne-Marie, and Egbert Haverkamp-
Begeman[n]. "Dessins de Rubens." *Revue de l'art,*
no. 42 (1978), pp. 89–99.

Loisel 2000a
Loisel, Catherine, et al. *Gli affreschi dei Carracci:
Studi e disegni preparatori.* Exh. cat., Bologna,
Palazzo Magnani. Bologna, 2000.

Loisel 2000b
Loisel, Catherine. "Il disegno: Uno strumento priv-
ilegiato per i Carracci." In Loisel 2000a, pp. 51–131.

Lomazzo 1584
Lomazzo, Gian Paolo. *Trattato dell'arte de la pittura,
scoltura et architettura.* 1584. In Lomazzo 1973–74,
vol. 2.

Lomazzo 1590
Lomazzo, Gian Paolo. *Idea del tempio della pittura.*
1590. In Lomazzo 1973–74, vol. 1.

Lomazzo 1973–74
Lomazzo, Gian Paolo [Giovanni Paolo; Gianpaolo].
Scritti sulle arti. Edited and introduced by Roberto
Paolo Ciardi. 2 vols. Florence, 1973–74.

Longnon 1928
Longnon, Henry. *Dessins des maîtres étrangers,
Léonard.* Paris, 1928.

López-Rey 1935
López-Rey, José. *Antonio del Pollaiuolo y el fin del
'Quattrocento.'* Madrid, 1935.

Los Angeles County Museum of Art 1971
The Armand Hammer Collection. Exh. cat., Los
Angeles County Museum of Art. Los Angeles,
1971.

Los Angeles County Museum of Art 1976
Feinblatt, Ebria. *Old Master Drawings from
American Collections.* Exh. cat., Los Angeles
County Museum of Art. Los Angeles, 1976.

Louvre 1797 (An V)
*Notices des dessins originaux, cartons, gouaches,
pastels, émaux et miniatures du Musée Central
des Arts. Exposés pour la première fois dans la
Galerie d'Apollon. Le 28 Thermidor de l'an V de
la République Française. Première Partie.* Paris,
An V [1797].

Louvre 1802 (An X)
Foubert, Jacques. *Notice des dessins originaux,
esquisses peintes, cartons, gouaches, pastels,
émaux, miniatures et vases étrusques, Exposés au
Musée central des Arts, dans la Galerie d'Apollon,
En Messidor de l' an X de la République Française.
Seconde partie.* Paris, An X [1802].

Louvre 1811
[Morel d'Arleux, Louis-Marie-Joseph]. *Notices des
dessins, des peintures, des bas-reliefs et des bronzes
Exposés au Musée Napoléon, dans la Galerie
d'Apollon. Notice des tableaux anciens, des trois
écoles, Mis dans le Salon d'Exposition de Peinture
moderne, en juin de l'an 1811.* Paris, 1811.

Louvre 1814
[Morel d'Arleux, Louis-Marie-Joseph]. *Notice des
dessins, des peintures, des bas-reliefs et des bronzes
exposés au Musée Royal, dans la Galerie d'Apollon,
ouverte le 6 août 1814.* Paris, 1814. Reissued in 1815
as *Notice des dessins . . . au Musée Napoléon . . .*

Louvre 1817
[Morel d'Arleux, Louis-Marie-Joseph]. *Notice des
dessins, peintures, émaux et terres cuites émaillées
exposés au Musée Royal dans la Galerie
d'Apollon.* Paris, 1817. Reissued in 1818, 1819.

Louvre 1820
[Morel d'Arleux, Louis-Marie-Joseph]. *Notice des
dessins, peintures, émaux et terres cuites émaillées
exposés au Musée Royal, dans la Galerie
d'Apollon.* Paris, 1820.

Louvre 1838
[Cailleux, Alphonse de]. *Notice des dessins placés
dans les Galeries du Musée Royal au Louvre.* Paris,
1838. Reissued in 1839, 1841, 1845.

Louvre 1866
Reiset, Frédéric. *Notice des dessins, cartons, pastels,
miniatures et émaux exposés dans les salles du 1er
étage au Musée Impérial du Louvre. Première partie: Écoles d'Italie, Écoles Allemande, Flamande et
Hollandaise; précédée d'une introduction historique et du résumé de l'inventaire général des
dessins par M. Frédéric Reiset, conservateur des
peintures, des dessins et de la chalcographie.*
Reissued in 1871, 1872, 1876, 1878, 1879, 1887 as
Notice des dessins . . . au Musée national. Part 1,
nos. 1–644; Part 2, nos. 645–1513. Paris, 1866.

Louvre 1879
Tauzia, L. Both de. *Notice supplémentaire des
dessins, cartons, pastels et miniatures des diverses
écoles exposés depuis 1869 dans les salles du 1er
étage au musée national du Louvre, par le Vte L.
Both de Tauzia, Conservateur des Peintures, des
Dessins et de la Chalcographie.* Reissued in 1887,
1888. Nos. 1514–1958. Paris, 1879.

Louvre 1881
Tauzia, L. Both de. *Notice des dessins de la

Collection His de la Salle exposés au Louvre, catalogue par le Vte L. Both de Tauzia, Conservateur des Peintures, des Dessins et de la Chalcographie. Exh. cat., Paris, Musée du Louvre. Paris, 1881.

Louvre 1888
Tauzia, L. Both de. *Musée National du Louvre. Dessins, cartons, pastels, miniatures des diverses écoles, exposés, depuis 1879, dans les salles du 1er étage. Deuxième notice supplémentaire, par le Vte L. Both de Tauzia, Conservateur des Peintures, des Dessins et de la Chalcographie. Nos. 1959–2177.* Paris, 1888.

Louvre 1919
Exposition d'œuvres de Léonard de Vinci organisée à l'occasion du quatrième centenaire de sa mort au Château de Cloux, en France le 2 mai 1549. Exh. cat., Paris, Musée du Louvre. Paris, 1919.

Louvre 1952a
Dessins flamands du XVIIe siècle. Exh. cat., Paris, Musée du Louvre. Paris, 1952.

Louvre 1952b
Dessins florentins du Trecento et du Quattrocento. Exh. cat., Paris, Musée du Louvre. Paris, 1952.

Louvre 1955
Choix de dessins de maîtres florentins et siennois: Première moité du XVIe siècle. Exh. cat., Paris, Musée du Louvre. Paris, 1955.

Louvre 1959
Dessins de Pierre-Paul Rubens. Exh. cat., Paris, Musée du Louvre. Paris, 1959.

Louvre 1962
Première exposition des plus beaux dessins du Louvre et de quelques pièces célèbres des collections de Paris. Exh. cat., Paris, Musée du Louvre. Paris, 1962.

Louvre 1969
Pastels. Exh. cat., Paris, Musée du Louvre. Paris, 1969.

Louvre 1975
Koschatzky, Walther, Konrad Oberhuber, and Eckart Knab. *Dessins italiens de l'Albertina de Vienne.* Exh. cat., Paris, Musée du Louvre. Paris, 1975.

Louvre 1977
Le corps et son image: Anatomies, académies. Exh. cat., Paris, Musée du Louvre. Paris, 1977.

Louvre 1982
Pastels, gouaches, aquarelles, miniatures, emaux. Exh. cat., Paris, Musée du Louvre. Paris, 1982.

Louvre 1986
Les mots dans le dessin. Exh. cat., Paris, Musée du Louvre. Paris, 1986.

Louvre 1989
Les donateurs du Louvre. Exh. cat., Paris, Musée du Louvre. Paris, 1989.

Louvre 1989–90
Viatte, Françoise, with Catherine Monbeig Goguel, and Madeleine Pinault. *Léonard de Vinci: Les études de draperie.* Exh. cat., Paris, Musée du Louvre. Paris, 1989.

Louvre 1996
Cordellier, Dominique. *Pisanello: Le peintre aux sept vertus.* Exh. cat., Paris, Musée du Louvre. Paris, 1996.

Louvre 1997a
Des mécènes par milliers: Un siècle de dons par les Amis du Louvre. Exh. cat., Paris, Musée du Louvre. Paris, 1997.

Louvre 1997b
Kristeva, Julia. *Visions capitales.* Exh. cat., Paris, Musée du Louvre. Paris, 1998.

Lowe 1993
Lowe, K. J. P. *Church and Politics in Renaissance Italy: The Life and Career of Cardinal Francesco Soderini (1453–1524).* Cambridge, 1993.

Lucco 1989
Lucco, Mauro. "Le cosiddette 'Tre età dell'uomo' di Palazzo Pitti." In *Le tre età dell'uomo della Galleria Palatina,* pp. 11–28. Exh. cat., Florence, Palazzo Pitti. Florence, 1989.

Ludwig 1882
Ludwig, Heinrich. *Lionardo da Vinci. Das Buch von der Malerei, nach dem Codex Vaticanus (Urbinas) 1270 herausgegehnen, übersetzt und erläutert von Heinrich Ludwig.* 3 vols. Vienna, 1882.

Lugt 1921, 1956
Lugt, Frits. *Les marques de collections de dessins et d'estampes.* Amsterdam, 1921. *Supplément.* The Hague, 1956.

Lugt 1949
Lugt, Frits. *Inventaire général des dessins des écoles du nord publié sous les auspices du Cabinet des Dessin. Ecole Flamande.* 2 vols. Paris, 1949.

Luijten and Meij 1990–91
Luijten, Ger, and A. W. F. M. Meij. *From Pisanello to Cézanne: Master Drawings from the Museum Boymans-van Beuningen, Rotterdam.* Exh. cat., New York, The Pierpont Morgan Library; Forth Worth, Kimbell Art Museum; Cleveland Museum of Art. Rotterdam, 1990.

Luzio 1888
Luzio, Alessandro. "Nuovi Documenti: Ancora Leonardo da Vinci e Isabella d'Este." *Archivio storico dell'arte* 1, no. 5 (May 1888), pp. 181–84.

Luzio 1900
Luzio, Alessandro. "I ritratti di Isabella d'Este." *Emporium* 11, no. 65 (May 1900), pp. 344–59; 11, no. 66 (June 1900), pp. 427–42.

Luzio 1913
Luzio, Alessandro. *La Galleria dei Gonzaga venduta all'Inghilterra nel 1627–1628.* Milan, 1913.

Luzzati 1987
Luzzati, Michele. "Firenze e le origini della banca moderna." *Studi storici,* no. 2 (1987), pp. 423–34.

Lyonnet 1841
Lyonnet, Abbé [Jean Baptiste]. *Le Cardinal Fesch, Archevèque de Lyon, Primat des Gaules, etc. etc.: Fragments biographiques, politiques et religieux pour servir à l'histoire ecclésiastique contemporaine.* 2 vols. Lyon and Paris, 1841.

Mabilleau 1980
Mabilleau, Léopold. "Leonardo in France." In *Leonardo da Vinci 1980,* pp. 143–56.

Macandrew 1980
Macandrew, Hugh. *Catalogue of the Collection of Drawings, Ashmolean Museum, Oxford.* Vol. 3, *Italian Schools: Supplement.* Oxford, 1980.

Macandrew 1990–91
Macandrew, Hugh. *Old Master Drawings from the National Gallery of Scotland.* Exh. cat., Washington, D.C., National Gallery of Art; Fort Worth, Kimbell Art Museum. Washington, D.C., 1990.

Maccagni 1971
Maccagni, Carlo. *Riconsiderando il problema delle fonti di Leonardo: L' elenco di libri ai fogli 2 verso-3 recto del codice 8936 della Biblioteca Nacional di Madrid.* Lettura Vinciana, 10 (15 aprile 1970). Florence, 1971.

MacCurdy 1904
McCurdy [sic], Edward. *Leonardo da Vinci.* London, 1904.

MacCurdy 1928
MacCurdy, Edward. *The Mind of Leonardo da Vinci.* London, 1928.

MacCurdy 1930
McCurdy [sic], Edward. "The Drawings of Leonardo da Vinci." *Apollo* 12, no. 69 (September 1930), pp. 173–82; 12, no. 70 (October 1930), pp. 249–57.

MacCurdy 1938
MacCurdy, Edward, ed. *The Notebooks of Leonardo da Vinci.* 2 vols. London, 1938.

Machiavelli 1971
Machiavelli, Niccolò. *Tutte le opere.* Edited by Mario Martelli. Florence, 1971.

Mackowsky 1901
Mackowsky, Hans. *Verrocchio.* Leipzig, 1901.

Magasin Pittoresque 1858
"Recueil de dessins de Léonard de Vinci au musée du Louvre." *Magasin Pittoresque* 26 (January 1858), pp. 11–14.

Magni-Dufflocq 1980
Magni-Dufflocq, Enrico. "Da Vinci's Music." In *Leonardo da Vinci 1980,* pp. 227–31.

Maidani Gerard and Krause-Zimmer 1993
Maidani Gerard, Jean-Pierre, and Hella Krause-Zimmer. "Alter ego, 1501: L'agneau et le dévidoir." *Achademia Leonardi Vinci: Journal of Leonardo Studies and Bibliography of Vinciana* 6 (1993), pp. 79–89, and unpaginated figures.

Maison Ad. Braun 1896
Maison Ad. Braun & C. *Catalogue général des reproductions . . . d'après les originaux: Peintures fresques et dessins des musées d'Europe des galeries et collections particulières . . .* Paris and New York, 1896.

Malaguzzi Valeri 1904
Malaguzzi Valeri, Francesco. "Un quadro del Boltraffio e una data." *La Perseveranza* 27 (September 1904).

Malaguzzi Valeri 1905
Malaguzzi Valeri, Francesco. "Il Maestro della Pala Sforzesca." *Rassegna d'arte* 5, no. 3 (March 1905), pp. 44–48.

Malaguzzi Valeri 1908
Malaguzzi Valeri, Francesco. "Cesare da Sesto e un nuovo acquisto della Pinacoteca di Brera." *Rassegna d'arte* 8, no. 2 (February 1908), pp. 21–26, pl. facing p. 21.

Malaguzzi Valeri 1913–23
Malaguzzi Valeri, Francesco. *La corte di Lodovico il Moro*. 4 vols. Milan, 1913–23.

Malaguzzi Valeri 1922
Malaguzzi Valeri, Francesco. *Leonardo da Vinci e la scultura*. Bologna, 1922.

Maltese 1954
Maltese, Corrado. "Il pensiero architettonico e urbanistico di Leonardo." In *Leonardo: Saggi e ricerche* 1954, pp. 331–58, pls. 130–45.

Mancinelli 1993
Mancinelli, Fabrizio. "St. Jerome." In National Museum of Western Art 1993.

Mancinelli and Nahmad 1981
Mancinelli, Fabrizio, and Ezra Nahmad. *Vatican Museums: Pinacoteca*. Florence, 1981.

Manetti 1970
Manetti, Antonio di Tuccio. *The Life of Brunelleschi*. Introduction, notes and critical text edition by Howard Saalman. Translation of the Italian by Catherine Enggass. University Park, Pa., and London, 1970.

Mantelli 1785
Mantelli, Girolamo. *Raccolta di disegni incisi da Girolamo Mantelli di Canobio sugli originali esistenti nella Biblioteca Ambrosiana di mano di Leonardo da Vinci e de'suoi scolari lombardi*. Milan, 1785.

Mantz 1882
Mantz, Paul. "Rubens [Part 3]." *Gazette des Beaux-Arts*, ser. 2, 25 (1882), pp. 5–18.

Marani 1984
Marani, Pietro C. *L'Architettura fortificata negli studi di Leonardo da Vinci, con il catalogo completo dei disegni*. Florence, 1984.

Marani 1984–85
Marani, Pietro C. *Disegni di fortificazioni da Leonardo a Michelangelo*. Exh. cat., Florence, Casa Buonarroti. Florence, 1984.

Marani 1985a
Marani, Pietro C. *"Circulo dentato ortogonial-mente" (Ms. Madrid 8937, f. 177r.): Leonardo, gli ingegneri e alcune macchine lombarde*. Lettura Vinciana, 25 (13 aprile 1985). Florence, 1985.

Marani 1985b
Marani, Pietro C. "Trascrizione critica (Fogli 134–200)." In *Leonardo da Vinci. Corpus degli studi anatomici nella Collezione di Sua Maestà la Regina Elisabetta II nel Castello di Windsor*. Edited by Kenneth D. Keele and Carlo Pedretti, vol. 3, pp. 471–786. Florence, 1985.

Marani 1986a
Marani, Pietro C. *Il Cenacolo di Leonardo*. Milan, 1986.

Marani 1986b
Marani, Pietro C., with Roberto Cecchi and Germano Mulazzani. *Il Cenacolo e Santa Maria delle Grazie*. Milan, 1986.

Marani 1986c
Marani, Pietro C. *Disegni lombardi del Cinque e Seicento della Pinacoteca di Brera e dell' Arcivescovado di Milano*. Exh. cat., Milan, Pinacoteca di Brera. Florence, 1986.

Marani 1987a
Marani, Pietro C. *Leonardo e i leonardeschi a Brera*. Florence, 1987.

Marani 1987b
Marani, Pietro C. "Leonardo: Fortified Architecture and its Structural Problems." In Galluzzi 1987, pp. 303–14.

Marani 1988a
Marani, Pietro C. "L'architettura militare di Leonardo da Vinci fra tradizione, rinnovamento e ripensamento." In *Architettura militare nell'Europa del XVI secolo: Atti del Convegno di Studi, Firenze, 25–28 novembre 1986*, edited by Carlo Cresti, Amelio Fara and Daniela Lamberini, pp. 49–59. Siena, 1988.

Marani 1988b
Marani, Pietro C. *Pinacoteca di Brera*. Milan, 1988.

Marani 1989
Marani, Pietro C. *Leonardo: Catalogo completo dei dipinti*. Florence, 1989.

Marani 1990
Marani, Pietro C. *Leonardo e i leonardeschi nei musei della Lombardia*. Milan, 1990.

Marani 1992a
Marani, Pietro C. "I dipinti di Leonardo, 1500–1507: Per una cronologia." In Hager 1992, pp. 1–28.

Marani 1992b
Marani, Pietro C. "Tracce ed elementi Verrocchieschi nella tarda produzione grafica e pittorica di Leonardo." In Bule 1992, pp. 141–52 and figures.

Marani 1994
Marani, Pietro C. *Leonardo*. Milan, 1994.

Marani 1995
Marani, Pietro C. "The 'Hammer Lecture' (1994): Tivoli, Hadrian and Antinoüs, New Evidence of Leonardo's Relation to the Antique." *Achademia Leonardi Vinci: Journal of Leonardo Studies and Bibliography of Vinciana* 8 (1995), pp. 207–25, and unpaginated figures.

Marani 1996
Marani, Pietro. *La Madonna del Gatto di Leonardo in un dipinto della Pinacoteca di Brera: Nuove indagini e restauri*. Milan and Cremona, 1996.

Marani 1997
Marani, Pietro C. "Dalla natura al simbolo: Osservazione della natura, imitazione dell'antico e visualizzazione del moto nell'opera di Leonardo." *Raccolta Vinciana*, no. 27 (1997), pp. 155–85.

Marani 1998a
Marani, Pietro C. "Francesco Melzi." In *Legacy of Leonardo* 1998, pp. 371–84.

Marani 1998b
Marani, Pietro C. "Giovan Battista Belmonte." In *Legacy of Leonardo* 1998, pp. 301–4.

Marani 1998c
Marani, Pietro C. "Giovan Pietro Rizzoli, called Giampietrino." In *Legacy of Leonardo* 1998, pp. 275–300.

Marani 1998d
Marani, Pietro C. "Master of the Pala Sforzesca." In *Legacy of Leonardo* 1998, pp. 179–98.

Marani 1998e
Marani, Pietro C. "The Question of Leonardo's

Bottega: Practices and the Transmission of Leonardo's Ideas on Art and Painting." In *Legacy of Leonardo* 1998, pp. 8–37.

Marani 1999a
Marani, Pietro C. "Classical Masterpiece." *The Art Quarterly* (Winter 1999), pp. 44–47.

Marani 1999b
Marani, Pietro C. *Léonard de Vinci, une carrière de peintre*. Paris, 1999. This monograph was published in French, Italian, and English, referred to here as Marani 1999b, 1999c, and 2000b.

Marani 1999c
Marani, Pietro C. *Leonardo: Una carriera di pittore*. Milan, 1999.

Marani 2000a
Marani, Pietro C. "Gli affreschi di Bernardino Luini in San Maurizio fra circoli letterari, tradizione lombarda e classicismo centro-italiano." In *Bernardino Luini e la pittura del Rinascimento a Milano: Gli affreschi di San Maurizio al Monastero Maggiore*, by Sandrina Bandera and Maria Teresa Fiorio et al., pp. 53–73. Milan, 2000. For the English edition, see Bandera and Fiorio 2000.

Marani 2000b
Marani, Pietro C. *Leonardo da Vinci: The Complete Paintings*. New York, 2000.

Marani 2001a
Marani, Pietro C. "I disegni di Leonardo." In Palazzo Reale 2001, pp. 102–53.

Marani 2001b
Marani, Pietro C. "Leonardo e gli scultori: Un altro esempio di collaborazione col Rustici?" *Raccolta Vinciana*, no. 29 (2001), pp. 103–23.

Marani, Cecchi, and Mulazzani 1986
Marani, Pietro C., Roberto Cecchi, and Germano Mulazzani. *Il Cenacolo e Santa Maria delle Grazie*. Milan, 1986.

Marcheix 1909
Marcheix, Lucien. "Les nouveaux dessins de l'École des Beaux-Arts." *L'art et les artistes* 8 (1909), pp. 257–64.

Marchini 1985a
Marchini, Giuseppe. "L'Annunciazione." In *Leonardo: La pittura* 1985, pp. 23–29.

Marchini 1985b
Marchini, Giuseppe. "Leonardo e le scale." *Antichità viva* 24, nos. 1–3 (January–June 1985), pp. 180–85.

Marcolongo 1937
Marcolongo, Roberto. *Memorie sulla geometria e la meccanica di Leonardo da Vinci*. Studi Vinciani. Naples, 1937.

Marcolongo 1980
Marcolongo, Roberto. "Da Vinci's Mechanics." In *Leonardo da Vinci* 1980, pp. 483–92.

Mariette 1730
[Mariette, Pierre Jean]. "Lettre sur Léonard de Vinci, peintre florentin, a Monsieur le C. de C.," a text addressed by Mariette to Caylus that appears at the beginning of *Recueil de Testes de caractère & de Charges dessinées par Léonard de Vinci Florentin & gravées par M. le Cte de C[aylus], MDCCXXX, A Paris, chez J[ean] Mariette, rue St.*

Jacques, aux Colonnes d'Hercules, pp. 1–22. The letter is signed: "Votre très-humble & très obéissant Serviteur M***" (p. 22). Mariette's text was translated into Italian and included in Bottari and Ticozzi 1822–25, vol. 2, part 1, pp. 206–48. The second edition of the Caylus album was revised and augmented by Mariette and published by Jombert in 1767, the letter falling on pp. 4–29, and this revised text was published in Chennevières and Montaiglon 1851–60, vol. 3, pp. 139–75.

Mariette 1741
Mariette, Pierre Jean. *Description sommaire des desseins des grands maistres d'Italie, des Pays-Bas et de France, du Cabine de Feur M. Crozat. Avec des réflexions sur la manière de dessiner des principaux peintres.* Paris, 1741.

Marinoni 1944–55
Marinoni, Augusto. *Gli appunti grammaticali e lessicali di Leonardo da Vinci.* 2 vols. Milan, 1944–55.

Marinoni 1954a
Marinoni, Augusto. "I manoscritti di Leonardo da Vinci e le loro edizioni." In *Leonardo: Saggi e ricerche* 1954, pp. 229–74.

Marinoni 1954b
Marinoni, Augusto. *I rebus di Leonardo da Vinci raccolti e interpretati.* Florence, 1954.

Marinoni 1980a
Marinoni, Augusto. "Da Vinci's Philology." In *Leonardo da Vinci* 1980, pp. 215–26.

Marinoni 1980b
Marinoni, Augusto, with a note by André Chastel. *Leonardo da Vinci, Codice Trivulziano (Il Codice no. 2162 della Biblioteca Trivulziana di Milano).* Milan, 1980.

Marinoni 1982
Marinoni, Augusto. *La matematica di Leonardo da Vinci.* Milan, 1982.

Marinoni 1990
Marinoni, Augusto. *Leonardo da Vinci: I manocritti dell'Institut de France. Il manocritto A.* Florence, 1990.

Marinoni 1991
Marinoni, Augusto. "Interventi dei collezionisti sui manoscritti vinciani nei secoli XVI e XVII." In Fiorio and Marani 1991, pp. 163–65.

Marinoni 2000
Marinoni, Augusto. *Leonardo da Vinci, Il Codice Atlantico della Biblioteca Ambrosiana di Milano.* 3 vols. Florence, 2000.

Marinoni and Cogliati Arano 1982
Marinoni, Augusto, and Luisa Cogliati Arano. *Leonardo all'Ambrosiana: Il Codice Atlantico, i disegni di Leonardo e della sua cerchia.* Exh. cat., Milan, Biblioteca Ambrosiana. Milan, 1982.

Marinoni and Meneguzzo 1981a
Marinoni, Augusto, and Marco Meneguzzo. *I disegni di Leonardo.* Milan, 1981.

Marinoni and Meneguzzo 1981b
Marinoni, Augusto, and Marco Meneguzzo. *Leonardo da Vinci disegni.* Verona, 1981.

Markova 1991
Markova, Vittoria. "Il 'San Sebastiano' di Giovanni Antonio Boltraffio e alcuni disegni

dell'area leonardesca." In Fiorio and Marani 1991, pp. 100–107.

Marks 1882
Marks, Alfred. *The St. Anne of Leonardo da Vinci* [read to the Royal Society of Literature, June 28, 1882]. Reprinted from the Society's *Transactions*.

Marotte and Longon 1928
Marotte, Léon, and Henri Longon. *Léonardo da Vinci: Cinquante-six dessins reproduits en fac-similé.* Paris, 1928.

Martelli 1977
Martelli, Marina. "Un disegno attribuito a Leonardo e una scoperta archeologica degli inizi del Cinquecento." *Prospettiva*, no. 10 (July 1977), pp. 58–61.

Martindale 1966
Martindale, Andrew. *Man and the Renaissance: Landmarks of the World's Art.* New York and London, 1966.

Martineau 1981–82
Martineau, Jane. "Isabella d'Este, the Insatiable Collector." In Victoria and Albert Museum 1981–82, pp. 159–64.

Martinori 1918
Martinori, E. *Annali della Zecca di Roma.* Rome, 1918.

Marzi 1910
Marzi, Demetrio. *La Cancelleria della Repubblica Fiorentina.* 2 vols. Rocca San Casciano, 1910. Reprint, Florence, 1987.

Mathey 1951
Mathey, Jacques. *Bildnis und Gestalt der Frau in Meisterzeichnungen aus fünf Jahrhunderten.* Basel, 1951.

Matthiesen Gallery 1960
Paintings and Drawings from Christ Church, Oxford: An Exhibition in Aid of the Christ Church United Clubs, Kennington. Exh. cat., London, Matthiesen Gallery. London, 1960.

Mazenta 1919
Mazenta, [Giovanni] Ambrogio. *Le memorie su Leonardo da Vinci.* Milan, 1919.

Mazzini 1982
Mazzini, Franco. "Il Cenacolo e il cartone per la Sant'Anna." In Dell'Aqua 1982, pp. 61–82.

Mazzocchi Doglio 1983
Mazzocchi Doglio, Mariangela. "Leonardo 'apparatore' di spettacoli a Milano per la corte degli Sforza." In Mazzocchi Doglio and Tintori.. Exh. cat., Milan, Rotonda di Via Besana, pp. 41–75. 1983.

Mazzocchi Doglio and Tintori 1983
Mazzocchi Doglio, Mariangela, and Giampiero Tintori. *Leonardo e gli spettacoli del suo tempo.* Exh. cat., Milan, Rotonda di Via Besana. Milan, 1983.

Mazzucchelli 1753–63
Mazzucchelli, G. *Gli scrittori d'Italia cioè notizie storiche, e critiche intorno alle vite e agli scritti dei letterati italiani . . .* 6 parts in 2 vols. Brescia, 1753–63.

McClintock 1993
McClintock, M. J. In National Museum of Western Art 1993, English text supplement, pp. 106–8 (Japanese text, pp. 256–61, with figures).

McGrath 1994
McGrath, Thomas. "Disegno, colore and the dis-

egno colorito: The Use and Significance of Color in Italian Renaissance Drawings." Ph.D. diss., Harvard University, 1994.

McGrath 1997a
McGrath, Thomas. "Colour in Italian Renaissance Drawings: Reconciling Theory and Practice in Central Italy and Venice." *Apollo* 146, no. 429 (November 1997), pp. 22–30.

McGrath 1997b
McGrath, Elizabeth. *Rubens: Subjects from History.* 2 vols. Corpus Rubenianum Ludwig Burchard, 13. London, 1997.

McGrath 1998
McGrath, Thomas. "Federico Barocci and the History of *Pastelli* in Central Italy." *Apollo* 148, no. 441 (November 1998), pp. 3–9.

McLanathan 1966
McLanathan, Richard. *Images of the Universe. Leonardo da Vinci: The Artist as Scientist.* Garden City, N.Y., 1966.

McMahon 1956
Leonardo da Vinci: Treatise on Painting (Codex Urbinas Latinus 1270). Translated and annotated by A. Philip McMahon; introduced by Ludwig Heydenreich. 2 vols. Princeton, N.J., 1956.

Meder 1919
Meder, Joseph. *Die Handzeichnung, Ihre Technik und Entwicklung.* Vienna, 1919.

Meder 1923
Meder, Joseph. *Albertina-Faksimile: Handzeichnungen italienischer Meister des XV–XVIII. Jahrhunderts.* Vienna, 1923.

Meder and Ames 1978
Meder, Joseph. *The Mastery of Drawing.* 2 vols. Translated and revised by Winslow Ames. New York, 1978.

Meijer 1971
Meijer, Bert W. "Esempi del comico figurativo nel rinascimento lombardo." *Arte lombarda* 16 (1971), pp. 259–66.

Meijer 1988
Meijer, Bert W. "From Leonardo to Bruegel: Comic Art in Sixteenth-Century Europe." *Word and Image* 4, no.1 (1988), pp. 405–11.

Meijer 1998
Meijer, Bert W. "'L'arte non deve schernire': Sul comico e sul grottesco al Nord." In Museo Cantonale d'Arte 1998, pp. 69–76.

Meijer and van der Sman 2000
Meijer, Bert W., and Gert Jan van der Sman. *Da Leonardo a Mondrian: Disegni del Museum Boijmans van Beuningen, Rotterdam.* Exh. cat., Florence, Istituto Universitario Olandese di storia dell' Arte. Florence, 2000.

Meinhof 1931
Meinhof, Werner. "Leonardos Hieronymus." *Repertorium für Kunstwissenschaft* 52 (1931), pp. 101–24.

Méla 2002
Méla, Charles. "The Bodmeriana, A Growing Library." In *Master Drawings from the Martin Bodmer Foundation.* Sale cat., Christie's, New York, Wednesday, January, 23, 2002, pp. 8–13.

Meller 1916
Meller, Simon. "Die Reiterdarstellungen Leonardos und die Budapester Bronzestatuette." *Jahrbuch der Königlich Preuszischen Kunstsammlungen* 37 (1916), pp. 213–50, pl. facing p. 213.

Meller 1934
Meller, Simon. "I Progetti di Antonio Pollaiuolo per la Statua Equestre di Francesco Sforza." In *Hommage à Alexis Petrovics*, pp. 204–5. Budapest, 1934.

Meller 1948
Meller, Simon. "Leonardo Nachzeichnungen von Cesare da Sesto." *Phoebus* 2 (1948), pp. 12–14.

Meller 1955
Meller, Peter. "Leonardo da Vinci's Drawings to the Divine Comedy." *Acta Historiae Artium Academiae Scientiarum Hungaricae* (1955), pp. 135–66.

Meller 1977
Meller, Peter. "Tracce di Leonardo a Pistoia?" *Almanacco Italiano* 77 (1977), pp. 174–80.

Meller 1983
Meller, Peter. "Quello che Leonardo non ha scritto sulla figura umana: Dall'uomo di Vitruvio alla Leda." *Arte lombarda*, no. 67 (1983), pp. 117–33.

Meller 1985
Meller, Peter. "La Battaglia D'Anghiari." In *Leonardo: La pittura* 1985, pp. 130–36.

Meneguzzo and Marinoni, 1981
Meneguzzo, Marco, and Augusto Marinoni. *Leonardo da Vinci: Disegni, l'invenzione e l'arte nel linguaggio delle immagini.* Verona, 1981.

Mercator 1540
The Treatise of Gerard Mercator: Literarum Latinarum, quas Italicas, cursoriasque vocant, scribendarum ratio (Antwerp 1540). Edited by Jan Denucé, with a note by Stanley Morison. Facsimile edition. Antwerp and Paris, 1930.

Mercillon 1989
M[ercillon], H[enri]. "Les dessins de Vinci: L'intelligence et le regard." *Connaissance des arts*, no. 446 (April 1989), pp. 79–87.

Metropolitan Museum of Art 1942
European Drawings from the Collections of The Metropolitan Museum of Art. Vol. 1, *Italian Drawings (Portfolio of Collotype Reproductions).* New York, 1942.

Metropolitan Museum of Art 1944
European Drawings from the Collections of The Metropolitan Museum of Art: Italian, Flemish, Dutch, German, Spanish, French, and British Drawings (Portfolio of Collotype Reproductions). New York, 1944.

Metropolitan Museum of Art 1952
Art Treasures of The Metropolitan Museum of Art: A Selection from the European and Asiatic Collections of the Metropolitan Museum of Art. New York, 1952.

Metropolitan Museum of Art 1970
Masterpieces of Fifty Centuries. Introduction by Kenneth Clark. Exh. cat., New York, The Metropolitan Museum of Art. New York, 1970.

Metropolitan Museum of Art 1980
The Horses of San Marco. Supplementary exh. cat., New York, The Metropolitan Museum of Art. New York, 1980.

Metropolitan Museum of Art 1983
The Vatican Collections: The Papacy and Art. Organized by Philippe de Montebello, Carlo Pietrangeli, Olga Raggio, and Margaret E. Frazer. Exh. cat., New York, The Metropolitan Museum of Art; The Art Institute of Chicago; The Fine Arts Museums of San Francisco. New York, 1983.

Metropolitan Museum of Art 1987
The Renaissance in Italy and Spain. Introduction by Frederick Hartt. The Metropolitan Museum of Art Series, 4. New York, 1987.

Metropolitan Museum of Art 1990
Master Drawings from the Woodner Collections. Exh. cat., New York, The Metropolitan Museum of Art. New York, 1990.

Metropolitan Museum of Art 1993
Burn, Barbara, et al. *Masterpieces of The Metropolitan Museum of Art.* New York, 1993.

Metropolitan Museum of Art 2001
Walter Liedtke, Michiel Plomp, and A. Ruger. *Vermeer and the Delft School.* Exh. cat., New York, The Metropolitan Museum of Art. New York, 2001.

Metropolitan Museum of Art and Royal Academy of Arts 1992
Martineau, Jane, et al. *Andrea Mantegna.* Exh. cat., New York, The Metropolitan Museum of Art; London, Royal Academy of Arts. New York, 1992.

Meyer zur Capellen 1996
Meyer zur Capellen, Jürg. *Raphael in Florence.* London, 1996.

Michel 1899
Michel, Emile. *Rubens: His Life, his Work, and his Time.* 2 vols. Translated by Elizabeth Lee. New York, 1899.

Michel 1900
Michel, Emile. *Rubens: Sa vie, son œuvre, et son temps.* Paris, 1900.

Middeldorf 1934
Middeldorf, Ulrich. Review of *The Unfinished Monument by Andrea del Verrocchio to the Cardinal Niccolò Forteguerri at Pistoia*, by Elizabeth Wilder. Studies in the History and Criticism of Sculpture, 7. *Zeitschrift für Kunstgeschichte* 3 (1934), pp. 54–58.

Middeldorf 1958
Middeldorf, Ulrich. "Su alcuni bronzetti all'antica del Quattrocento." In *Il mondo antico del Rinascimento*, pp. 167–77. Florence, 1958.

Milan 1982. See Museo Poldi Pezzoli 1982–83.

Milanesi 1876
Milanesi, Gaetano. *La scrittura di artisti italiani (sec. XIV–XVII) riprodotta con la fotografia da Carlo Pini e corredata di notizie da Gaetano Milanesi.* 12 vols. Florence, 1876.

Milanesi 1879
Milanesi, Gaetano. "Commentario alla Vita di Leonardo da Vinci." In Vasari–Milanesi 1878–85, vol. 4.

Millosevich 1919
Millosevich, E. "Leonardo e la luce cinerea." In *Miscellanea Cermenati*, pp. 17–19. Bergamo, 1919.

Moffitt 1991
Moffitt, John F. "The *Evidentia* of Curling Waters and Whirling Winds: Leonardo's *Ekphraseis* of the Latin Weathermen." *Achademia Leonardi Vinci: Journal of Leonardo Studies and Bibliography of Vinciana* 4 (1991), pp. 11–33, and unpaginated figures.

Moffitt 1994
Moffitt, John F. "*Puer et Senex in Didactic Contrapositum*: Two Rhetorical Contexts for Leonardo's Grotesque Heads." *Achademia Leonardi Vinci: Journal of Leonardo Studies and Bibliography of Vinciana* 7 (1994), pp. 124–28, and unpaginated figures.

Möller 1918
Möller, Emil. "Zwei bisher unerkannte Bildnisse der Mona Lisa." *Monatshefte für Kunstwissenschaft* 11 (1918), pp. 1–14, pls. 1–4.

Möller 1926
Möller, Emil. "Wie sah Leonardo aus?" *Belvedere* 9–10 (1926), pp. 29–46.

Möller 1926–29
Möller, Emil. "Aggiunte e chiarimenti al tema 'La Madonna coi Bambini che Giuocano.'" *Raccolta Vinciana*, no. 13 (1926–29), pp. 63–66.

Möller 1928
Möller, Emil. "Salai und Leonardo da Vinci." *Jahrbuch der Kunsthistorischen Sammlungen in Wien*, n.s., 2 (1928), pp. 139–61.

Möller 1928–29
Möller, Emil. "Die Madonna mit den Spielenden Kindern aus der Werkstatt Leonardos." *Zeitschrift fur Bildende Kunst* 62 (1928–29), pp. 217–27.

Möller 1930–34
Möller, E[mil]. "Leonardo e il Verrocchio: Quattro rilievi di capitani antichi lavorati per re Mattia Corvino." *Raccolta Vinciana*, no. 14 (1930–34), pp. 3–38.

Möller 1935
Möller, Emil. "Shorter Notices: Verrocchio's Last Drawing." *The Burlington Magazine* 66, no. 385 (April 1935), pp. 192–95.

Möller 1937–38
Möller, Emil. Leonardos Bildnis der Ginevra dei Benci." *Münchner Jahrbuch der bildenden Kunst*, n.s., 12 (1937–38), pp. 185–209.

Möller 1952a
Möller, Emil. *Das Abendmahl des Lionardo da Vinci.* Veröffentlichungen des Instituts für Europäische Geschichte Mainz, 1. Baden-Baden, 1952.

Möller 1952b
Möller, Emil. Review of *The Drawings of Leonardo da Vinci*, by A. E. Popham. *Das Münster* 5 (1952), p. 341.

Monbeig Goguel 1988
Monbeig Goguel, Catherine. "Taste and Trade: The Retouched Drawings in the Everard Jabach Collection at the Louvre." *The Burlington Magazine* 130, no. 1028 (November 1988), pp. 821–35.

Monbeig Goguel 1992
Monbeig Goguel, Catherine. "Il disegno italiano del Cinquecento." In *La pittura in Italia.* Vol. 2, *Il Cinquecento*, pp. 593–614. 1987. Milan, 1992.

Mongan 1987
Mongan, Agnes. "On Silverpoint Drawings and the Subject of Left-handedness." In *Drawings Defined*, by Konrad Oberhuber et al., pp. 150–64. New York, 1987.

Mongan and Sachs 1940
Mangan, Agnes, and Paul J. Sachs. *Drawings in the Fogg Museum of Art*. Vol. 1. Cambridge, Mass., 1940.

Le Moniteur 1850
"Beaux-Arts." *Le Moniteur*, no. 252 (1850), pp. 2948–49.

Monnier 1972
Monnier, Geneviève. *Dessins d'architecture du XVe au XIXe siècle dans les collections du musée du Louvre*. Exh. cat., Paris, Musée du Louvre. Paris, 1972.

Montaiglon 1852
Montaiglon, Anatole de. "Des nouvelles acquisitions du Musée de dessins du Louvre. Ecole Allemande, Hollandaise et Flamande." *La lumière* 2, no. 52 (December 18, 1852), pp. 207–8; 2, no. 53 (December 31, 1852), pp. 211–12.

Monti 1966
Monti, Raffaele. *Andrea del Sarto*. Milan, 1966.

Montreal Museum of Fine Arts 1992
The Genius of the Sculptor in Michelangelo's Work. Exh. cat., Montreal Museum of Fine Arts. Montreal, 1992.

Moreira 1998
Moreira, Rafael. "Leonardo and Portugal." In Mosteiro dos Jeronimos 1998, pp. 25–39. 1998.

Morel d'Arleux
Manuscript inventory of the drawings in the Louvre, circa 1802, by Louis-Marie-Joseph Morel d'Arleux, curator of the Cabinet des dessins du Louvre from 1797 to 1827. 9 albums, Département des arts Graphiques du musée du Louvre, Paris.

Morelli 1890
Lermolieff, Ivan [Giovanni Morelli]. *Kunstkritische Studien über italienische Malerei: Die Galerien Borghese und Doria Panfili in Rom*. Leipzig, 1890.

Morelli 1893
Morelli, Giovanni (Ivan Lermolieff). *Italian Painters: Critical Studies of Their Works*. [Vol. 2], *The Galleries of Munich and Dresden*. London, 1893.

Morelli 1900
Morelli, Giovanni (Ivan Lermolieff). *Italian Painters: Critical Studies of Their Works*. [Vol. 1], *The Borghese and Doria-Pamfili Galleries in Rome*. 1892. London, 1900.

Morelli 1994
Morelli, Giovanni. *De la peinture italienne*. 1900. Paris, 1994.

Morley 1979
Morley, Brian. "The Plant Illustrations of Leonardo da Vinci." *The Burlington Magazine* 121, no. 918 (September 1979), pp. 553–62.

Morning Advertiser **1835**
The Morning Advertiser (London). May 27, 1835.

Moro 1987
Moro, Franco. *Pittura tra Adda e Serio, Lodi,*

Treviglio, Caravaggio, Crema. Edited by Mina Gregori. Milan, 1987.

Moro 1991
Moro, Franco. "Spunti sulla diffusione di un tema leonardesco tra Italia e Fiandra sino a Lanino." In Fiorio and Marani 1991, pp. 120–40.

Morolli 1990
Morolli, Gabriele. "Lorenzo, Leonardo e Giuliano—Da San Lorenzo al Duomo a Poggio a Caiano: Paralipomeni architettonici minimi in vista del semimillenario della morte del Magnifico." *Quasar* 3 (January 1990), pp. 5–14.

Moroni 1858
Moroni, G. *Dizionario di educazione storico-ecclesiastica*. Vol. 88. Venice, 1858.

Morozzi 1988–89
Morozzi, Luisa. "La 'Battaglia di Cascina' di Michelangelo: Nuova ipotesi sulla data di commissione." *Prospettiva*, nos. 53–56 (April 1988–January 1989), pp. 320–24.

Morrison 1892
Morrison, Alfred. *Catalogue of the Collection of Autograph Letters and Historical Documents Formed by Alfred Morrison*. 2d ser. 6 vols. London, 1892.

Moschini 1828
Moschini, Giovanni Antonio. *Memorie della vita di Antonio de Solario, detto il Zingaro, pittore viniziana*. Venice, 1828.

Moskovits 1962
Moskovits, Ira. *Great Drawings of All Time*. Vol. 1, *Italian Drawings*. New York, 1962.

Mosteiro dos Jeronimos 1998
Leonardo da Vinci, a Man on a World Scale, the World on a Human Scale . . . : Codex Leicester Exhibit. Exh. cat., Lisbon, Mosteiro dos Jerónimos. Lisbon, 1998.

Mraz and Galavics 1999
Mraz, Gerda, and Géza Galavics. *Von Bildern und anderen Schätzchen: Die Sammlung der Esterházy*. Vienna and Cologne, 1999.

Mss A-M 1881–91
Ravaisson-Mollien, Charles, ed. *Les Manuscrits de Léonard de Vinci, Manuscrit A (etc) de l'Institut de France*. 6 vols. Paris, 1881–91.

Müller Hofstede 1964
Müller Hofstede, Justus. "An Early Rubens *Conversion of St Paul*: The Beginning of his Preoccupation with Leonardo's *Battle of Anghiari*." *The Burlington Magazine* 106, no. 732 (March 1964), pp. 95–106.

Müller Hofstede 1965
Müller Hofstede, Justus. "Rubens' St. Georg und seine frühen Reiterbildnisse." *Zeitschrift für Kunstgeschichte* 28, nos. 1–2 (1965), pp. 69–112.

Müller Hofstede 1977
Müller Hofstede, Justus. *Peter Paul Rubens, 1577–1640. Rubens in Italien: Gemälde, Ölskizzen, Zeichnungen*. Exh. cat., Cologne, Wallraf-Richartz-Museum. Cologne, 1977.

Müller-Walde 1889
Müller-Walde, Paul. *Leonardo da Vinci: Lebensskizze und Forschungen über sein Verhältnis*

zur Florentiner Kunst und zu Rafael. Munich, 1889.

Müller-Walde 1897
Müller-Walde, Paul. "Beiträge zur Kenntnis des Leonardo da Vinci. I. Ein neues Dokument zur Geschichte des Reiterdenkmals für Francesco Sforza: Das erste Modell Leonardo's. II. Eine Skizze Leonardo's zur stehenden Leda; Eine Skizze nach Praxiteles und der Merkur im Kastell von Mailand." *Jahrbuch der Königlich Preussischen Kunstsammlungen* 18 (1897), pp. 92–136; 137–69.

Müller-Walde 1898
Müller-Walde, Paul. "Beiträge zur Kenntnis des Leonardo da Vinci. III. Vorbereitungen zum Hl. Johannes des Louvre unter Plänen zum Trivulzio-Grabmal und geometrischen Berechnungen. IV. Einige Darstellungen des Hl. Sebastian: Erinnerung an die Pollajuoli." *Jahrbuch der Königlich Preussischen Kunstsammlungen* 19 (1898), pp. 225–49; 2 unnumbered plates, pp. 250–66.

Müller-Walde 1899
Müller-Walde, Paul. "Beiträge zur Kenntnis des Leonardo da Vinci. V. Eine frühe Redaktion von Leonardo's Komposition der Madonna mit der Hl. Anna und dem Lamm. VI. Einige Anweisungen Leonardo's für den unterseeischen Schiffskampf, Taucherapparate und Torpedoboote: Leonardo's Erfindung der Schiffsschraube. VII. Leonardo da Vinci und die antike Reiterstatue des Regisole: Einige Entwürfe Leonardo's zum Reiterdenkmale für Gian Giacomo Trivulzio. Plaketten des Berliner K. Museums nach Studien Leonardo's zu Reiterdenkmälern und zur Darstellung der Reiterschlacht von Anghiari." *Jahrbuch der Königlich Preussischen Kunstsammlungen* 20 (1899), pp. 54–59; 60–80; 81–116.

Müntz 1886
Müntz, Eugène. "Le château de Fontainebleau en 1625, d'après le *Diarium* du Commandeur Cassiano del Pozzo." *Mémoires de la Société de l'Histoire de Paris et de l'Ile-de-France* 12 (1885), pp. 255–78.

Müntz 1892
Müntz, Eugène. "Studi leonardeschi. I. La Vergine delle Roccie. II. L'Adorazione dei Magi." *Archivio storico dell' arte* 5 (1892), pp. 26–32; 32–33.

Müntz 1898
Müntz, Eugène. *Leonardo da Vinci, Artist, Thinker, and Man of Science*. 2 vols. London and New York, 1898.

Müntz 1899
Müntz, Eugène. *Léonard de Vinci: L'artiste, le penseur, le savant*. Paris, 1899.

Musée Condé 1995
Lanfranc de Panthou, Caroline, and Benjamin Peronnet. *Dessins italiens du musée Condé à Chantilly. I. Autour de Pérugin, Filippino Lippi et Michel-Ange*. Exh. cat., Musée Condé, Château de Chantilly. Paris, 1995.

Musée d'Art et d'Histoire, Geneva 1998
Le corps à vif. Exh. cat., Geneva, Musée d'Art et d'Histoire. Geneva, 1998.

Musée des Beaux-Arts, Rennes 1990
Disegno, Les dessins italiens du Musée de Rennes:

Catalogue de l'exposition suivi d'un Inventaire de la Collection. Modène, Galleria Estense. Exh. cat., Rennes, Musée des Beaux-Arts. Rennes, 1990.

Musée national Message Biblique Marc Chagall 1982
Représentation de l'architecture sacrée. Le temple. Musée national Message Biblique Marc Chagall. Nice, 1982.

Musée Royal des Beaux-Arts 1977
P. P. Rubens. Peintures—Esquisses à l'huile—Dessins. Exh. cat., Antwerp, Musée Royal des Beaux-Arts. Antwerp, 1977.

Museo Cantonale d'Arte 1998
Rabisch—Il grottesco nell'arte del Cinquecento: L'Accademia della Val di Blenio, Lomazzo e l'ambiente milanese. Exh. cat., Lugano, Museo Cantonale d'Arte. Milan, 1998.

Museo Poldi Pezzoli 1982–83
Natale, Mauro. Zenale e Leonardo: Tradizione e rinnovamento della pittura lombarda. Exh. cat., Milan, Museo Poldi Pezzoli. Milan, 1982.

Museum Boymans-Van Beuningen 1962
Lugt, Frits, et al. Italiaanse tekeningen in Nederlands bezit. Exh. cat., Paris, Institut néerlandais; Rotterdam, Museum Boymans-Van Beuningen; Haarlem, Teylers Museum. Rotterdam, 1962.

Mussini 1991
Mussini, Massimo. Il Trattato di Francesco di Giorgio Martini e Leonardo: Il Codice Estense restituito. Parma, 1991.

Muylle 1994
Muylle, Jan. "Groteske koppen van Quinten Metsijs, Hieronymus Cock en Hans Liefrinck naar Leonardo da Vinci." Zeventiende eeuw 10, no. 2 (1994), pp. 252–65.

Muylle 2001
Muylle, Jan. "Tronies toegeschreven aan Pieter Bruegel: Fysionomie en expressie." De zeventiende eeuw 17, no. 2 (2001), pp. 174–204.

Nagel 1993
Nagel, Alexander. "Leonardo and Sfumato." Res, no. 24 (Autumn 1993), pp. 7–20.

Nanni 2001
Nanni, Romano. "Leonardo nella 'tradizione' di Leda." In Dalli Regoli, Nanni, and Natali 2001, pp. 23–45.

Narducci 1859
Narducci, Enrico, ed. La composizione del mondo di Ristoro d'Arezzo, testo italiano del 1282. Rome, 1859.

Natale 1982
Natale, M. Museo Poldi-Pezzoli: Dipinti. Milan, 1982.

Natali 1994
Natali, Antonio. "Il tempio e la radice." In Cropper 1994, pp. 147–56, and unpaginated figures.

Natali 1998a
Natali, Antonio. "Lo sguardo degli angeli." In Lo sguardo degli angeli: Verrocchio, Leonardo e il 'Battesimo di Cristo,' edited by Antonio Natali, pp. 60–94. Cinisello Balsamo, 1998.

Natali 1998b
Natali, Antonio. "Lo sguardo degli angeli: Tragitto indiziario per il Battesimo di Cristo di Verrocchio e

Leonardo." Mitteilungen des Kunsthistorischen Institutes in Florenz 42, nos. 2–3 (1998), pp. 252–73.

Natali 2000
Natali, Antonio. "Dubbi, difficoltà e disguidi nell' Annunciazione di Leonardo." In L'Annunciazione di Leonardo: La montagna sul mare, edited by Antonio Natali, pp. 36–59. Cinisello Balsamo, 2000.

Natali 2001
Natali, Antonio. "Le pose di Leda." In Dalli Regoli, Nanni, and Natali 2001, pp. 46–64.

Nathan 1990
Nathan, Johannes. "Workshop Practices of Leonardo da Vinci: Background Material and the Example of the Leda." M.A. Thesis, University of London, The Courtauld Institute of Art, 1990.

Nathan 1992
Nathan, Johannes. "Some Drawing Practices of Leonardo da Vinci: New Light on the St. Anne." Mitteilungen des Kunsthistorischen Institutes in Florenz 36, nos. 1–2 (1992), pp. 85–102.

Nathan 1996
Nathan, Johannes. "The Working Methods of Leonardo da Vinci and Their Relation to Previous Artistic Practice." Ph.D. diss., University of London, The Courtauld Institute of Art, 1996.

National Gallery of Art 1974
Recent Acquisitions and Promised Gifts. Exh. cat., Washington, D.C., National Gallery of Art. Washington, D.C., 1974.

National Gallery of Art 1978
Master Drawings from the Collection of the National Gallery of Art and Promised Gifts. Exh. cat., Washington, D.C., National Gallery of Art. Washington, D.C., 1978.

National Gallery of Art 1979
Shapley, Fern Rusk. Catalogue of Italian Paintings. Washington, D.C., 1979.

National Gallery of Art 1984–85
Koschatzky, Walther, A. Strobl, F. Koreny, and Veronika Birke. Old Master Drawings from the Albertina. Organized and circulated by the International Exhibitions Foundation, Washington, D.C. Exh. cat., Washington, D.C., National Gallery of Art; New York, Pierpont Morgan Library. Washington, D.C., 1984. German edition: Zeichnungen Alter Meister aus der Albertina. References in this catalogue are to the English edition.

National Gallery of Art 1987
[Robinson, Andrew, et al.] Master Drawings from the Armand Hammer Collection. Exh. cat., Washington, D.C., National Gallery of Art. Washington, D.C., 1987.

National Gallery of Scotland 1991
Saved for Scotland: Works of Art Acquired with the Help of the National Art Collections Fund. Exh. cat., Edinburgh, National Gallery of Scotland. Edinburgh, 1991.

National Gallery of Scotland 1999
The Draughtsman's Art: Master Drawings from the National Gallery of Scotland. Exh. cat., Edinburgh, National Gallery of Scotland; New York, Frick Collection; Houston, Museum of Fine Arts. Edinburgh, 1999.

National Gallery of Scotland and Hazlitt Gooden and Fox 1994
From Leonardo to Manet: Ten Years of Collecting Prints and Drawings. Exh. cat., Edinburgh, National Gallery of Scotland; London, Hazlitt Gooden and Fox. Edinburgh, 1994.

National Museum of Western Art 1993
Ishikawa, M., and M. J. McClintock, eds. High Renaissance in the Vatican: The Age of Julius II and Leo X. Exh. cat., Tokyo, National Museum of Western Art. Tokyo, 1993.

National Museum of Western Art 2001–2
Paolucci, Antonio, et al. Il Rinascimento in Italia: La Civiltà delle Corti. Exh. cat., Tokyo, National Museum of Western Art; Rome, Scuderie Papali al Quirinale. Tokyo, 2001.

Nationalmuseum Stockholm 1983
Leonardo da Vinci. Exh. cat., Stockholm, Nationalmuseum. Stockholm, 1983.

Nees 1978
Nees, Lawrence. "Le 'Quos Ego' de Marc-Antoine Raimondi: L'adaptation d'une source antique par Raphael." Nouvelles de l'estampe, nos. 40–41 (July–October 1978), pp. 18–29.

Nelson 1997
Nelson, Jonathan. "The High Altar-piece of SS.Annunziata in Florence : History, Form, and Function." The Burlington Magazine 139, no. 1127 (February 1997), pp. 84–94.

Nepi Scirè 1982
Nepi Scirè, Giovanna. Storia della collezione dei Disegni, Gallerie dell'Accademia di Venezia. Milan, 1982.

Nepi Scirè and Torrini 1999
Nepi Scirè, Giovanna, and Annalisa Perissa Torrini. Da Leonardo a Canaletto: Disegni delle Gallerie dell' Accademia. Exh. cat., Venice, Gallerie dell'Accademia. Milan, 1999.

Nesselrath 1999
Nesselrath, Arnold. "Leonardo da Vinci: Bühender hl. Hieronymus um 1482." In Hoch Renaissance im Vatikan: Kunst und Kultur im Rom der Päpste I, 1503–1534, pp. 552–53. Exh. cat., Bonn, Kunst- und Austellungshalle der Bundesrepublik Deutschland. Bonn, 1999.

Neufeld 1949
Neufeld, Günther. "Leonardo da Vinci's Battle of Anghiari: A Genetic Reconstruction." The Art Bulletin 33, no. 3 (September 1949), pp. 170–83.

New Gallery 1893–94
Exhibition of Early Italian Art from 1300–1550. Exh. cat., London, The New Gallery. London, 1893–94.

Newman 1980
Newman, John. "A Draft Will of the Earl of Arundel." The Burlington Magazine 122, no. 931 (October 1980), pp. 692–96.

Nicodemi 1939
Nicodemi, Giorgio. Leonardo da Vinci: Gemälde, Zeichnungen, Studien. Leipzig, 1939.

Nicodemi 1980a
Nicodemi, Giorgio. "The Life and Works of Leonardo." In Leonardo da Vinci 1980, pp. 18–87.

Nicodemi 1980b
Nicodemi, Giorgio. "The Portrait of Leonardo." In *Leonardo da Vinci* 1980, pp. 8–17.

Niessen 1868
Niessen, Johannes. *The Lord's Supper: Christ and His Twelve Disciples from the Original Crayon-drawings of Leonardo da Vinci in the Possession of Her Royal Highness the Grand Duchess of Saxe-Weimar.* Explanatory text by J. Sighart. London, 1868.

Nogara 1931
Nogara, Bartolomeo. "Gli ultimi restauri del S. Girolamo di Leonardo da Vinci." In *Miscellanea di Studi Lombardi in onore di Ettore Verga.* Milan, 1931.

Norris 1988-89
Norris, Andrea, ed. *The Sforza Court: Milan in the Renaissance, 1450–1535.* Exh. cat. Austin, Archer M. Huntington Art Gallery; University Art Museum, University of California, Berkeley; New Haven, Yale University Art Gallery. New Haven and London, 1988.

Oberhuber and Gnann 1999
Oberhuber, Konrad, and Achim Gnann. *Roma e lo stile classico di Raffaello, 1515–1527.* Exh. cat., Mantua, Palazzo Te; Vienna, Graphische Sammlung Albertina. Milan, 1999.

Oberhuber and Walker 1973
Oberhuber, Konrad, and Dean Walker. *Sixteenth Century Italian Drawings from the Collection of Janos Scholz.* Exh. cat., Washington, D.C., National Gallery of Art. Washington, D.C., 1973.

O'Malley 1969
O'Malley, C[harles] D., ed. *Leonardo's Legacy: An International Symposium.* Berkeley and Los Angeles, 1969.

O'Malley and Saunders 1952
O'Malley, Charles D., and J[ohn] B[ertrand] de C[usance] M[orant] Saunders. *Leonardo da Vinci on the Human Body: The Anatomical, Physiological, and Embryological Drawings of Leonardo da Vinci.* New York, 1952.

Orangerie 1931
Dessins Italiens. Exh. cat., Paris, Musée national de l'Orangerie des Tuileries. Paris, 1931.

Orangerie 1935
Portraits et figures de femme: Pastels et dessins. Exh. cat., Paris, Musée national de l'Orangerie des Tuileries. Paris, 1935.

Orangerie 1947–48
Cinquantenaire des "Amis du Louvre" 1897–1947. Exh. cat., Paris, Musée national de l'Orangerie des Tuileries. Paris, 1947.

Orangerie, 1954
Chefs-d'œuvre de la Collection Edmond de Rothschild. Exh. cat., Paris, Musée national de l'Orangerie des Tuileries. Paris, 1954.

Orangerie 1977–78
Collections de Louis XIV: Dessins, albums, manuscrits. Exh. cat., Paris, Musée national de l'Orangerie des Tuileries. Paris, 1977.

Oremland 1997
Oremland, Jerome D. *The Origins and Psychodynamics of Creativity: A Psychoanalytic Perspective.* Madison, 1997.

Ortolani 1948
Ortolani, Sergio. *Il Pollaiuolo.* Milan, 1948.

Ost 1975a
Ost, Hans. "Der vatikanische Hieronymus." In Ost 1975b, pp. 1–97.

Ost 1975b
Ost, Hans. *Leonardo-Studien.* Berlin and New York, 1975.

Ost 1980
Ost, Hans. *Das Leonardo Porträt in der Kgl. Bibliothek Turin und andere Fäschungen des Giuseppe Bossi.* Berlin, 1980.

Ottino della Chiesa 1956
Ottino della Chiesa, Angela. *Bernardino Luini.* Novara, 1956.

Ottino della Chiesa 1966
Ottino della Chiesa, Angela. *Bernardino Luini.* I maestri del colore, 141. Milan, 1966.

Ottino della Chiesa 1967
Ottino della Chiesa, Angela. "Apparati critici e filologici." In *L'opera completa di Leonardo pittore,* vol. 12. Milan, 1967.

Ottino della Chiesa 1985
Ottino della Chiesa, Angela. *L'opera completa di Leonardo pittore.* Preface by Mario Pomilio. Milan. 1967. English edition introduced by L. D. Ettlinger. London, 1985.

Ottley 1823
Ottley, William Young. *The Italian School of Design, being a series of fac-similes of original drawings, by the most eminent painters and sculptors of Italy; with biographical notices of the artists, and observations on their works.* London, 1823.

Ovid 1977
Ovid. *Metamorphoses.* Translation by Frank Justus Miller. 1916. 3d ed. Cambridge, Mass., 1977.

Paatz 1940–54
Paatz, Walter and Elisabeth. *Die Kirchen von Florenz: Ein Kunstgeschichtliches Handbuch.* Frankfurt a Main, 1940–54.

Pacioli 1509
Pacioli [da Borgo San Sepolcro], Fra Luca. *Divina proportione. Opera a tutti glingegni perspi caci e curiosi necessaria One cia scun studioso di Philosophia: Prospectiua Pitura Sculptura: Architectura: Musica: e altre Mathematice: sua uissima:sottile: e admirabile doctrina consequira: e de lectarassi co varie questione de secretissima scienta.* Venice, 1509. (The Metropolitan Museum of Art, acc. no. 19.50).

Pacioli 1997
Pacioli, Luca. *De viribus quantitatis.* Edited by Augusto Marinoni. Milan, 1997.

Palais de la Découverte 1952–53
Léonard de Vinci, homme de science, 1452–1519. Exh. cat., Paris, Palais de la Découverte. Paris, 1952.

Palais des Beaux-Arts and Museum Boymans–Van Beuningen 1938–39
Dessins de Rubens. Exh. cat., Brussels, Palais des Beaux-Arts; Rotterdam, Museum Boymans–Van Beuningen. Brussels, 1938.

Palais de Tokyo 1980
La grisaille. Exh. cat., Paris, Palais de Tokyo. Paris, 1980.

Palatino 1540
Palatino, Giovanni Battista. *Libro di M. Giovanbattista. Palatino cittadino romano, Nel qual s'insegna à Scriuer ogni sorte lettera, Antica, & Moderna, di qualunque natione, con le sue regole, & misure, & essempi . . .* Rome, 1540. (The Metropolitan Museum of Art, acc. no. 28.106.4).

Palatino 1547
Palatino, Giovanni Battista. *Libro di M. Giovanbattista. Palatino cittadino romano, Nel qual s'insegna à Scriuer ogni sorte lettera, Antica, & Moderna, di qualunque natione, con le sue regole, & misure, & essempi . . .* Rome, 1547. (The Metropolitan Museum of Art, acc. no. 30.23.2).

Palazzo del Comune, Arezzo 2001
*Verrocchio e l'atelier del Rinascimento. Leonardo e dintorni, 1.*Exh. cat., Arezzo, Palazzo del Comune. Florence, 2001.

Palazzo dell'Arte 1939
Mostra di Leonardo da Vinci. Exh. cat., Milan, Palazzo dell'Arte. Milan, 1939.

Palazzo del Podestà 1985
Pedretti, Carlo, et al. *Leonardo: Il Codice Hammer e la Mappa di Imola presentati da Carlo Pedretti. Arte e scienza a Bologna in Emilia e Romagna nel primo Cinquecento.* Exh. cat., Bologna, Palazzo del Podestà. Florence, 1985.

Palazzo Grassi 1992
Nepi Sciré, Giovanna, and Pietro C. Marani, eds. *Leonardo & Venice.* Exh. cat., Venice, Palazzo Grassi. Milan, 1992. Italian edition: *Leonardo & Venezia.* References in this catalogue are to the English edition.

Palazzo Reale 1981
I Cavalli di San Marco. Exh. cat., Milan, Palazzo Reale. Milan, 1981.

Palazzo Reale 1987–88
Bora, Giulio, et al. *Disegni e dipinti leonardeschi dalle collezioni milanesi.* Exh. cat., Milan, Palazzo Reale. Milan, 1987.

Palazzo Reale 1998–99
L'anima e il volto: Ritratto e fisiognomica da Leonardo a Bacon. Exh. cat., Milan, Palazzo Reale. Milan, 1998.

Palazzo Reale 2000
Caroli, Flavio, ed. *Il Cinquecento lombardo: Da Leonardo a Caravaggio.* Exh. cat., Milan, Palazzo Reale. Milan, 2000.

Palazzo Reale 2001
Marani, Pietro C., et al. *Il genio e le passioni—Leonardo e il Cenacolo: Precedenti, innovazioni, riflessi di un capolavoro.* Exh. cat., Milan, Palazzo Reale. Milan and Florence, 2001.

Palazzo Strozzi 1992–93
Gregori, Mina, et al. *Maestri e botteghe: Pittura a Firenze alla fine del Quattrocento.* Exh. cat., Florence, Palazzo Strozzi. Cinisello Balsamo, 1992.

Palazzo Vecchio 1979
Blunt, Anthony, et. al. *Leonardo da Vinci: Anatomical Drawings from the Royal Collection,*

Windsor Castle. Exh. cat., Florence, Palazzo Vecchio. Florence, 1979.

Paliaga 1995a
Paliaga, Franco. "Giovanni Ambrogio Brambilla, 'le teste di carattere' di Leonardo e la commedia dell'arte." *Raccolta Vinciana*, no. 26 (1995), pp. 219–54.

Paliaga 1995b
Paliaga, Franco. "Quattro persone che ridono con un gatto." *Achademia Leonardi Vinci: Journal of Leonardo Studies and Bibliography of Vinciana* 8 (1995), pp. 143–57, and unpaginated figures.

Panconcelli-Calzia 1980
Panconcelli-Calzia, G. "Leonardo's Work in Phonetics and Linguistics." In *Leonardo da Vinci* 1980, pp. 399–404.

Panofsky 1940
Panofsky, Erwin. *The Codex Huygens and Leonardo da Vinci's Art Theory: The Pierpont Morgan Library Codex M.A. 1139*. London, 1940.

Panzanelli Clignett 1993
Panzanelli Clignett, Roberta. "Gleanings." *Achademia Leonardi Vinci: Journal of Leonardo Studies and Bibliography of Vinciana* 6 (1993), pp. 185–88, and unpaginated figures.

Paredi, Dell'Acqua and Vitali 1967
Paredi, Angelo, Gian Alberto Dell'Acqua, and Lamberto Vitali. *L'Ambrosiana*. Milan, 1967.

Paris Ms. A. See Marinoni 1980.

Parker 1927
Parker, Karl T. *North Italian Drawings of the Quattrocento*. London, 1927.

Parker 1956
Parker, K[arl] T. *Catalogue of the Collection of Drawings in the Ashmolean Museum*. Vol. 2, *Italian Schools*. Oxford, 1956.

Parker 1972
Parker, Karl T. *Catalogue of the Collections of Drawings in the Ashmolean Museum: Italian Schools*. Vol. 2. 1956. Reprint. Oxford, 1972.

Parker 1983
Parker, Karl T. *The Drawings of Hans Holbein in the Collection of Her Majesty The Queen at Windsor Castle, with an Appendix to the Catalogue by Susan Foister*. Reprint. London, 1983.

Parks 1975
Parks, N. Randolph. "The Placement of Michelangelo's *David*: A Review of the Documents." *The Art Bulletin* 57, no. 4 (December 1975), pp. 560–70.

Parronchi 1979
Parronchi, Alessandro. "Paesaggio della prospettiva da Firenze a Venezia." In *Giorgione: Atti del convegno internazionale di studio per il 5 centenario della nascita (29–31 maggio 1978)*, pp. 119–26. Castelfranco Veneto, 1979.

Parronchi 1982
Parronchi, Alessandro. "E questo il luogo del suo premio disegno?" *Toscana qui* 2 (1982), pp. 49–52.

Parronchi 1989
Parronchi, Alessandro. "Nuove proposte per Leonardo scultore." *Achademia Leonardi Vinci: Journal of Leonardo Studies and Bibliography of*

Vinciana 2 (1989), pp. 40–67, and unpaginated figures.

Parronchi 1992a
Parronchi, Alessandro. "Un 'tondo' per il *San Girolamo*." *Achademia Leonardi Vinci: Journal of Leonardo Studies and Bibliography of Vinciana* 5 (1992), pp. 33–36, and unpaginated figures.

Parronchi 1992b
Parronchi, Alessandro. "Urbino, Baltimora, Berlino: Fronti di cassoni quattrocenteschi o modelli di scena del 1518?" In *Kunst des Cinquecento in der Toskana*, edited by Monika Cämmerer, pp. 100–106. Munich, 1992.

Parronchi and Pedretti 1988
Parronchi, Alessandro, and C[arlo] P[edretti]. "A Leonardesque Madonna with Dürer's Monogram." *Achademia Leonardi Vinci: Journal of Leonardo Studies and Bibliography of Vinciana* 1 (1988), pp. 21–26, and unpaginated figures.

Parthey 1853
Parthey, Gustav. *Kurzes Verzeichniss der Hollar'schen Kupferstiche*. Berlin, 1853.

Passavant 1836
Passavant, Johann D. *Tour of a German Artist in England: With Notices of Private Galleries, and Remarks on the State of Art*. 2 vols. London, 1836.

Passavant 1860
Passavant, J.-D. *Raphael d'Urbin et son père Giovanni Santi*. 2 vols. Paris, 1860.

Passavant 1864
Passavant, J.-D. *Le peintre-graveur*. Vol. 5. Leipzig, 1864.

Passavant 1959
Passavant, Günter. *Andrea del Verrocchio als Maler*. Düsseldorf, 1959.

Passavant 1969
Passavant, G[ünter]. *Verrocchio: Sculptures, Paintings, and Drawings, Complete Edition*. Translated by Katherine Watson. London, 1969.

Passerini 1870
Passerini, L. *Genealogia e storia della famiglia Niccolini*. Florence, 1870.

Pater 1893
Pater, Walter. *The Renaissance Studies in Art and Poetry*. 1873. London and New York, 1893.

Pauli 1910
Pauli, G[ustav]. "Boltraffio, Giovanni Antonio." In *Allgemeines Lexikon der bildenden Künstler von der Antike bis zur Gegenwart*, edited by Ulrich Thieme and Felix Becker, vol. 4, pp. 256–58. 37 vols. 1907–50. Leipzig, 1910.

Pauli 1927
Pauli, Gustav. *Zeichnungen alter Meister in der Kunsthalle zu Hamburg*. 3 vols. Frankfurt, 1927.

Paulicelli 1996
Paulicelli, Eugenia. *Parola e immagine: Sentieri della scrittura in Leonardo, Marino, Foscolo, Calvino*. Florence, 1996.

Payne 1979
Payne, Robert. *Leonardo*. London, 1979.

Pedretti 1951
Pedretti, Carlo. *Leonardo da Vinci e il poeta*

bolognese Gerolamo Pandolfi da Casio de' Medici. Bologne, 1951.

Pedretti 1953
Pedretti, Carlo. *Documenti e memorie riguardanti Leonardo da Vinci a Bologna e in Emilia*. Bologna, 1953.

Pedretti 1954
Pedretti, Carlo. "Leonardo's Allegories at Oxford explained by Lomazzo." *The Burlington Magazine* 96, no. 615 (June 1954), pp. 175–77.

Pedretti 1957a
Pedretti, Carlo. *Leonardo da Vinci: Fragments at Windsor Castle from the Codex Atlanticus*. London, 1957.

Pedretti 1957b
Pedretti, Carlo. *Studi Vinciani: Documenti, analisi e inediti leonardeschi*. Geneva, 1957.

Pedretti 1957, 1998
Pedretti, Carlo. "Studi vinciani: Documenti, analisi e inediti leonardeschi;" and appendix: "Saggio di una cronologia dei fogli del 'Codice Atlantico.'" In *Travaux d'Humanisme et Renaissance, 27, Genève, 1957*. *Mitteilungen des Kunsthistorischen Institutes in Florenz* 42 (1998), pp. 252–73.

Pedretti 1958a
Pedretti, Carlo. "L'Ercole di Leonardo." *L'Arte* 57 (1958), pp. 163–72.

Pedretti 1958b
Pedretti, Carlo. "Gli ultimi disegni di Leonardo." *Bibliothèque d'Humanisme et Renaissance* 20 (1958), pp. 565–68.

Pedretti 1959
Pedretti, Carlo. "Uno 'studio' per la Gioconda." *L'Arte* 58 (1959), pp. 155–223.

Pedretti 1962a
Pedretti, Carlo. *A Chronology of Leonardo da Vinci's Architectural Studies After 1500*. Geneva, 1962.

Pedretti 1962b
Pedretti, Carlo. "A New Grotesque after Leonardo." *Raccolta Vinciana*, no. 19 (1962), pp. 283–86.

Pedretti 1964a
Pedretti, Carlo. *Leonardo da Vinci on Painting: A Lost Book (Libro A) Reassembled from the Codex Vaticanus Urbinas 1270 and from the Codex Leicester*. Berkeley and Los Angeles, 1964.

Pedretti 1964b
Pedretti, Carlo. "The Missing Folio 3 of Ms. B." *Raccolta Vinciana* 20 (1964), pp. 211–24.

Pedretti 1968a
Pedretti, Carlo. "The Burlington House Cartoon." *The Burlington Magazine* 110, no. 778 (January 1968), pp. 22–28.

Pedretti 1968b
Pedretti, Carlo. *Leonardo da Vinci inedito: Tre saggi*. Florence, 1968.

Pedretti 1969
Pedretti, Carlo. "The 'Pointing Lady.'" *The Burlington Magazine* 111, no. 795 (June 1969), pp. 338–46.

Pedretti 1970
Pedretti, Carlo. "Leonardo da Vinci: Manuscripts and Drawings of the French Period, 1517–1518." *Gazette des Beaux-Arts*, ser. 6, 76 (1970), pp. 285–318.

Pedretti 1972a
Pedretti, Carlo. *Leonardo da Vinci: The Royal Palace at Romorantin.* Cambridge, Mass., 1972.

Pedretti 1972b
Pedretti, Carlo. "La Verruca. "*Renaissance Quarterly* 25, no. 4 (Winter 1972), pp. 417–25.

Pedretti 1973a
Pedretti, Carlo. *Leonardo: A Study in Chronology and Style.* Berkeley and Los Angeles, 1973.

Pedretti 1973b
Pedretti, Carlo. *Leonardo da Vinci: Studies for a Nativity and the 'Mona Lisa Cartoon,' with Drawings after Leonardo from the Elmer Belt Library of Vinciana. Exhibition in Honour of Elmer Belt, M.D. on the Occasion of His Eightieth Birthday.* Exh. cat., Belt Library, University of California, Los Angeles. Los Angeles, 1973.

Pedretti 1975a
Pedretti, Carlo. *Disegni di Leonardo da Vinci e della sua scuola alla Biblioteca Reale di Torino.* Florence, 1975.

Pedretti 1975b
Pedretti, Carlo. "*Eccetera, perché la minestra si fredda*": Codice Arundel, fol. 245 recto. Lettura Vinciana, 15 (15 aprile 1975). Florence, 1975.

Pedretti 1977
Pedretti, Carlo. *The Literary Works of Leonardo da Vinci, Compiled and Edited from the Original Manuscripts by Jean Paul Richter: Commentary.* 2 vols. Berkeley and Los Angeles, 1977.

Pedretti 1978a
Pedretti, Carlo. "Leonardo a Venezia." In *Giorgione 1478.1978. Guida alla mostra: I tempi di Giorgione,* edited by Paolo Carpeggiani, pp. 84–85. Exh. cat., Castelfranco Veneto. Venice, 1978.

Pedretti 1978b
Pedretti, Carlo. "Notes: Reconstruction of a Leonardo Drawing." *Master Drawings* 16, no. 2 (Summer 1978), pp. 151–56, pl. 26.

Pedretti 1978–79
Pedretti, Carlo. *The Codex Atlanticus of Leonardo da Vinci: A Catalogue of its Newly Restored Sheets.* 2 vols. New York, 1978–79.

Pedretti 1979a
Pedretti, Carlo. "Giorgione e il Cristo portacroce di Leonardo." *Almanacco italiano* 79 (1979), pp. 8–14.

Pedretti 1979b
Pedretti, Carlo. *Infra l'anatomia e 'l vivo.* Lettura Vinciana (13 September 1979). Florence, 1979.

Pedretti 1979c
Pedretti, Carlo. *Leonardo.* Bologna, 1979.

Pedretti 1979d
Pedretti, Carlo. "Notes: An Unpublished Leonardo Drawing." *Master Drawings* 17, no. 1 (Spring 1979), pp. 24–28, pls. 14a–14b.

Pedretti 1980a
Pedretti, Carlo. *The Codex Leicester by Leonardo da Vinci.* Sale cat., Christie, Manson and Woods, London, Friday, December 12, 1980.

Pedretti 1980b
Pedretti, Carlo. "Leonardo e la lettura del territorio." In *Lombardia: Il territorio, l'ambiente, il paesaggio,* edited by Carlo Pirovano, pp. 235–84. Milan, 1980.

Pedretti 1981a
Pedretti, Carlo. "Giorgione e Leonardo." In *Giorgione e l'Umanismo veneziano,* edited by Rodolfo Palluchini, vol. 2, pp. 485–512. Florence, 1981.

Pedretti 1981b
Pedretti, Carlo. *Leonardo architetto.* 1978. Rev. ed. Milan, 1981.

Pedretti 1982a
Pedretti, Carlo, ed. *The Drawings and Miscellaneous Papers of Leonardo da Vinci in the Collection of Her Majesty the Queen at Windsor Castle.* Vol. 1, *Landscapes, Plants, and Water Studies.* London and New York, 1982.

Pedretti 1982b
Pedretti, Carlo. "Foglio di Weimar." In Vezzosi 1982, pp. 82–85.

Pedretti 1982c
Pedretti, Carlo. "Introduzione." In Vezzosi 1982, pp. 11–23.

Pedretti 1982d
Pedretti, Carlo. *Leonardo da Vinci: Studi di natura dalla Biblioteca Reale nel Castello di Windsor.* Florence, 1982.

Pedretti 1983–84
Pedretti, Carlo. "Leonardo dopo Milano." In Vezzosi 1983–84b, pp. 43–59.

Pedretti 1984
Pedretti, Carlo. "Il linguaggio delle mani." In Galleria degli Uffizi 1984, pp. 23–35.

Pedretti 1985
Pedretti, Carlo. "La scapiliata." In *Leonardo: La pittura* 1985, pp. 140–52.

Pedretti 1986a
Pedretti, Carlo. "C'è a Firenze un 'Leonardo' che andrà all'asta a New York per più di 3 miliardi." *La Nazione* (October 3, 1986), p. 3.

Pedretti 1986b
Pedretti, Carlo. *Leonardo Architect.* 1981. London, 1986.

Pedretti 1987a
Pedretti, Carlo. *The Codex Hammer of Leonardo da Vinci.* Translated into English and annotated by Carlo Pedretti. Florence, 1987.

Pedretti 1987b
Pedretti, Carlo, ed. *The Drawings and Miscellaneous Papers of Leonardo da Vinci in the Collection of Her Majesty The Queen at Windsor Castle.* Vol. 2, *Horses and Other Animals.* London and New York, 1987.

Pedretti 1987c
Pedretti, Carlo. "Leonardo: Era giusto tentare." *Art e dossier* 10 (February 1987), pp. 4–5.

Pedretti 1988a
P[edretti], C[arlo]. "A Chronicle of Events, 1980–1987." *Achademia Leonardi Vinci: Journal of Leonardo Studies and Bibliography of Vinciana* 1 (1988), pp. 146–54.

Pedretti 1988b
P[edretti], C[arlo]. "The Getty 'TL Sheet.'" *Achademia Leonardi Vinci: Journal of Leonardo Studies and Bibliography of Vinciana* 1 (1988), p. 145, and unpaginated figures.

Pedretti 1988c
Pedretti, Carlo. "Gleanings: 12. The Androgynous."

Achademia Leonardi Vinci: Journal of Leonardo Studies and Bibliography of Vinciana 1 (1988), p. 130, and unpaginated figures.

Pedretti 1988d
P[edretti], C[arlo]. "A Gloss for L.C.A. and P.C.M." *Achademia Leonardi Vinci: Journal of Leonardo Studies and Bibliography of Vinciana* 1 (1988), p. 120, and unpaginated figures.

Pedretti 1988e
Pedretti, Carlo. *Léonard de Vinci, Architecte.* 1983. Paris, 1988.

Pedretti 1988f
P[edretti], C[arlo]. "Leonardo at the Morgan Library." *Achademia Leonardi Vinci: Journal of Leonardo Studies and Bibliography of Vinciana* 1 (1988), pp. 142–44, and unpaginated figures.

Pedretti 1988g
Pedretti, Carlo. "The 'libro dj medjcina dj cavallj.'" *Achademia Leonardi Vinci: Journal of Leonardo Studies and Bibliography of Vinciana* 1 (1988), pp. 91–95, and unpaginated figures.

Pedretti 1988h
Pedretti, Carlo. "MS. Saluzzo 312: Disegni di architettura militare di Leonardo da Vinci." *Achademia Leonardi Vinci: Journal of Leonardo Studies and Bibliography of Vinciana* 1 (1988), pp. 107–17, and unpaginated figures.

Pedretti 1988i
[Pedretti, Carlo]. "Previews: Drawings Worth a Chat." *Achademia Leonardi Vinci: Journal of Leonardo Studies and Bibliography of Vinciana* 1 (1988), pp. 155–56, and unpaginated figures.

Pedretti 1988j
P[edretti], C[arlo]. "Quae sunt Caesaris . . ." *Achademia Leonardi Vinci: Journal of Leonardo Studies and Bibliography of Vinciana* 1 (1988), pp. 121–22, and unpaginated figures.

Pedretti 1988k
P[edretti], C[arlo]. "Windsor Landscapes and Horses: Addenda and Corrigenda." *Achademia Leonardi Vinci: Journal of Leonardo Studies and Bibliography of Vinciana* 1 (1988), pp. 122–26, and unpaginated figures.

Pedretti 1989a
Pedretti, Carlo. "Leonardo as a Sculptor: A Bibliography." *Achademia Leonardi Vinci: Journal of Leonardo Studies and Bibliography of Vinciana* 2 (1989), pp. 131–47, and unpaginated figures.

Pedretti 1989b
P[edretti], C[arlo]. "Leonardo at the Städel Museum." *Achademia Leonardi Vinci: Journal of Leonardo Studies and Bibliography of Vinciana* 2 (1989), pp. 166–67, and unpaginated figures.

Pedretti 1989c
P[edretti], C[arlo]. "The Mock Sepulchre." *Achademia Leonardi Vinci: Journal of Leonardo Studies and Bibliography of Vinciana* 2 (1989), pp. 127–30, and unpaginated figures.

Pedretti 1989d
[Pedretti, Carlo]. "Previews: Drapery Studies at the Louvre." *Achademia Leonardi Vinci: Journal of Leonardo Studies and Bibliography of Vinciana* 2 (1989), p.178, and unpaginated figures.

Pedretti 1989e
Pedretti, Carlo. "Previews: The Vatican St. Jerome." *Achademia Leonardi Vinci: Journal of Leonardo Studies and Bibliography of Vinciana* 2 (1989), p. 178.

Pedretti 1989f
Pedretti, Carlo. "A Proem to Sculpture." *Achademia Leonardi Vinci: Journal of Leonardo Studies and Bibliography of Vinciana* 2 (1989), pp. 11–39, and unpaginated figures.

Pedretti 1990a
Pedretti, Carlo, ed. *Disegni di Leonardo da Vinci e della sua cerchia nella Biblioteca Reale di Torino.* Florence, 1990.

Pedretti 1990b
Pedretti, Carlo. "The Final Shot." *Achademia Leonardi Vinci: Journal of Leonardo Studies and Bibliography of Vinciana* 3 (1990), pp. 30–38, and unpaginated figures.

Pedretti 1990c
P[edretti], C[arlo]. "Gleanings: 2. A Cesare da Sesto Profile." *Achademia Leonardi Vinci: Journal of Leonardo Studies and Bibliography of Vinciana* 3 (1990), p.145, and unpaginated figure.

Pedretti 1990d
P[edretti], C[arlo]. "Gleanings: 3. The Spencer Grotesques." *Achademia Leonardi Vinci: Journal of Leonardo Studies and Bibliography of Vinciana* 3 (1990), pp. 145–46, and unpaginated figures.

Pedretti 1990e
P[edretti], C[arlo]. "Leonardo's 'Half Egg.'" *Achademia Leonardi Vinci: Journal of Leonardo Studies and Bibliography of Vinciana* 3 (1990), pp. 161–64, and unpaginated figures.

Pedretti 1990f
Pedretti, Carlo. "Leonardo's Late Notes on Drapery." *Achademia Leonardi Vinci: Journal of Leonardo Studies and Bibliography of Vinciana* 3 (1990), p. 168, and unpaginated figures.

Pedretti 1990g
Pedretti, Carlo. "Nec ense." *Achademia Leonardi Vinci: Journal of Leonardo Studies and Bibliography of Vinciana* 3 (1990), pp. 82–90, and unpaginated figures.

Pedretti 1991a
Pedretti, Carlo. "The 'Angel in the Flesh.'" *Achademia Leonardi Vinci: Journal of Leonardo Studies and Bibliography of Vinciana* 4 (1991), pp. 34–48, and unpaginated figures.

Pedretti 1991b
P[edretti], C[arlo]. "L'Anima e il volto." In *Leonardo: Studi di fisiognomica,* by F. Cardi, pp. 44–47. Milan, 1991.

Pedretti 1991c
Pedretti, Carlo. "Leonardo and the Antique: A Bibliography." *Achademia Leonardi Vinci: Journal of Leonardo Studies and Bibliography of Vinciana* 4 (1991), pp. 214–44, and unpaginated figures.

Pedretti 1991d
Pedretti, Carlo. "The Phallic Head." *Achademia Leonardi Vinci: Journal of Leonardo Studies and Bibliography of Vinciana* 4 (1991), pp. 48–51, and unpaginated figures.

Pedretti 1992a
P[edretti], C[arlo]. Appendice: "Un frammento di 'Uomo Vitruviano.'" *Achademia Leonardi Vinci: Journal of Leonardo Studies and Bibliography of Vinciana* 5 (1992), p. 112, and unpaginated figures.

Pedretti 1992b
P[edretti], C[arlo]. "Jacques Franck on the Restoration of the Louvre *St. Anne.*" *Achademia Leonardi Vinci: Journal of Leonardo Studies and Bibliography of Vinciana* 5 (1992), pp. 166–68.

Pedretti 1992c
Pedretti, Carlo. *Leonardo da Vinci: La Battaglia di Anghiari e le armi fantastiche.* Florence, 1992.

Pedretti 1992d
P[edretti], C[arlo]. "The Mysteries of a Leonardo Madonna, Mostly Unsolved." *Achademia Leonardi Vinci: Journal of Leonardo Studies and Bibliography of Vinciana* 5 (1992), pp. 169–75, and unpaginated figures.

Pedretti 1992e
Pedretti, Carlo. "Paolo di Leonardo." *Achademia Leonardi Vinci: Journal of Leonardo Studies and Bibliography of Vinciana* 5 (1992), pp. 120–22, and unpaginated figures.

Pedretti 1992f
[Pedretti, Carlo, ed.] "Views and Previews." *Achademia Leonardi Vinci: Journal of Leonardo Studies and Bibliography of Vinciana* 5 (1992), pp. 185–88, and unpaginated figures.

Pedretti 1993a
Pedretti, Carlo. "A.D. 1493." *Achademia Leonardi Vinci: Journal of Leonardo Studies and Bibliography of Vinciana* 6 (1993), pp. 131–41, and unpaginated figures.

Pedretti 1993b
Pedretti, Carlo. "Gleanings." *Achademia Leonardi Vinci: Journal of Leonardo Studies and Bibliography of Vinciana* 6 (1993), pp. 185–88, and unpaginated figures.

Pedretti 1993c
Pedretti, Carlo. "Three Texts on Color." *Achademia Leonardi Vinci: Journal of Leonardo Studies and Bibliography of Vinciana* 6 (1993), pp. 34–46, and unpaginated figures.

Pedretti 1994a
Pedretti, Carlo. "Excursus: Un gioco di simboli per bambini." *Achademia Leonardi Vinci: Journal of Leonardo Studies and Bibliography of Vinciana* 7 (1994), pp. 96–97, and unpaginated figures.

Pedretti 1994b
Pedretti, Carlo. *Leonardo a Venezia.* Rome, 1994.

Pedretti 1994c
Pedretti, Carlo. *The Leonardo da Vinci Codex Hammer.* Sale cat., Christie, Manson and Woods, New York, Friday, November 11, 1994.

Pedretti 1995a
Pedretti, Carlo. "The Sforza Horse in Context." In Ahl 1995, pp. 27–39.

Pedretti 1995b
Pedretti, Carlo. "The St. Jerome Restored." *Achademia Leonardi Vinci: Journal of Leonardo Studies and Bibliography of Vinciana* 8 (1995), p. 264, and unpaginated figures.

Pedretti 1995c
Pedretti, Carlo. "The Stockholm St. Jerome." *Achademia Leonardi Vinci: Journal of Leonardo Studies and Bibliography of Vinciana* 8 (1995), pp. 239–40, and unpaginated figures.

Pedretti 1996a
Pedretti, Carlo. "The Dart Caster." *Achademia Leonardi Vinci: Journal of Leonardo Studies and Bibliography of Vinciana* 9 (1996), pp. 55–72, and unpaginated figures.

Pedretti 1996b
Pedretti, Carlo. "Deluges after Leonardo: Basquiat and Matta." *Achademia Leonardi Vinci: Journal of Leonardo Studies and Bibliography of Vinciana* 9 (1996), p. 218, and unpaginated figures.

Pedretti 1996c
Pedretti, Carlo. "Quella puttana di Leonardo." *Achademia Leonardi Vinci: Journal of Leonardo Studies and Bibliography of Vinciana* 9 (1996), pp. 121–39, and unpaginated figures.

Pedretti 1996d
Pedretti, Carlo. "The Structure and Dating of the Codex Leicester." In Farago 1996b, pp. 31–33.

Pedretti 1996e
Pedretti, Carlo. "The Vatican St. Jerome Restored." *Achademia Leonardi Vinci: Journal of Leonardo Studies and Bibliography of Vinciana* 9 (1996), p. 234, and unpaginated figures.

Pedretti 1997a
Pedretti, Carlo. "Il disegno di Oporto." *Raccolta Vinciana,* no. 27 (1997), pp. 3–11.

Pedretti 1997b
Pedretti, Carlo. "Drawings Ruined in Restoration." *Achademia Leonardi Vinci: Journal of Leonardo Studies and Bibliography of Vinciana* 10 (1997), pp. 258–59, and unpaginated figures.

Pedretti 1997c
Pedretti, Carlo. "Leonardo a Urbino e il Libro di Pittura." *Achademia Leonardi Vinci: Journal of Leonardo Studies and Bibliography of Vinciana* 10 (1997), pp. 76–88, and unpaginated figures.

Pedretti 1998a
Pedretti, Carlo. "Il 'bagnetto' di Leonardo." *Il Sole–24 Ore,* January 11, 1998, p. 25.

Pedretti 1998b
Pedretti, Carlo. "O Desenho do Porto." *Apontamentos* (Faculdade de Belas Artes da Universidade do Porto) 2 (1998), pp. 22–24.

Pedretti 1998c
Pedretti, Carlo. "Leonardo: Il ritratto." *Art e dossier,* no. 138 (October 1998), p. 42.

Pedretti 1998–99
Pedretti, Carlo, ed. *Leonardo e la pulzella di Camaiore: Inediti vinciani e capolavori della scultura lucchese del primo Rinascimento.* Exh. cat., Camaiore, Museo di Arte Sacra. Florence, 1998.

Pedretti 1999a
Pedretti, Carlo. "Il cavallo come simbolo." In Fabrizio-Costa and Le Goff 1999, pp. 131–45.

Pedretti 1999b
Pedretti, Carlo. *Leonardo: The Machines.* Florence, 1999.

Pedretti 2001
Pedretti, Carlo. "La bocca della maraviglia." In Palazzo Reale 2001, pp. 363–65.

Pedretti and Clark 1980–81
Pedretti, Carlo, and Kenneth Clark. *Leonardo da Vinci: Nature Studies from the Royal Library at Windsor Castle.* Exh. cat., Malibu, The J. Paul Getty Museum; New York, The Metropolitan Museum of Art. [New York], 1980.

Pedretti and Clark 1983
Pedretti, Carlo. *Leonardo: Studies for the Last Supper from the Royal Library at Windsor Castle.* Introduction by Kenneth Clark. Exh. cat., Washington, D.C., National Gallery of Art; Milan, Castello Sforzesco. Washington, D.C., 1983. Italian edition: *Leonardo: Studi per il Cenacolo della Biblioteca Reale nel Castello di Windsor.* References in this catalogue are to the English edition.

Pedretti and Dalli Regoli 1985
Pedretti, Carlo, and Gigetta Dalli Regoli. *I disegni di Leonardo da Vinci e della sua cerchia nel Gabinetto Disegni e Stampe della Galleria degli Uffizi a Firenze.* Florence, 1985.

Pedretti and Hauser 1990
P[edretti], C[arlo], and E[nrique] H[auser]. "The 'Inhabited Draperies.'" *Achademia Leonardi Vinci: Journal of Leonardo Studies and Bibliography of Vinciana* 3 (1990), pp. 165–69, and unpaginated figures.

Pedretti and Marani 1988
Pedretti, Carlo, and Pietro C. Marani. *Leonardo da Vinci, architetto militare prima di Gradisca.* Milan, 1988.

Pedretti and Roberts 1981–83
Pedretti, Carlo, and Jane Roberts. *Leonardo da Vinci: The Codex Hammer, formerly The Codex Leicester.* Exh. cat., Washington, D.C., Corcoran Gallery of Art; Los Angeles County Museum of Art; London, Royal Academy of Arts; Florence, Palazzo Vecchio; Paris, Musée Jacquemart André; Edinburgh, Royal Scottish Academy; Stockholm, Nationalmuseum; Baltimore, The Walters Art Gallery; Moscow, Pushkin Museum of Fine Arts; Leningrad, Hermitage Museum. Los Angeles, 1981. Florentine and American editions: *The Codex Hammer of Leonardo da Vinci: The Waters, the Earth, the Universe*; Italian edition: *Il Codice Hammer di Leonardo da Vinci: Le acque, la terra, l'universo*; French edition: *Le Codex Hammer de Léonard de Vinci: Les eaux, la terre, l'univers.* Swedish and Russian editions were also published. References in this catalogue are to the English edition.

Pedretti and Roberts 1984–86
Pedretti, Carlo, and Jane Roberts. *Leonardo's Horses: Studies of Horses and Other Animals by Leonardo da Vinci from the Royal Library at Windsor Castle.* Exh. cat., Florence, Palazzo Vecchio; Washington, D.C., National Gallery of Art; Houston, The Museum of Fine Arts; The Fine Arts Museums of San Francisco. Florence and New York, 1984. American edition: *Leonardo da Vinci: Drawings of Horses and Other Animals from the Royal Library at Windsor Castle*; Italian edition: *I cavalli di Leonardo: Studi sul cavallo e altri animali di Leonardo da Vinci dalla Biblioteca Reale nel Castello di Windsor.*

Pedretti and Trutty-Coohill 1993
Pedretti, Carlo, and Patricia Trutty-Coohill. *The Drawings of Leonardo da Vinci and His Circle in America.* Florence, 1993.

Pedretti and Vecce 1998
Pedretti, Carlo, and Carlo Vecce. *Il Codice Arundel 263 nella British Library, Leonardo da Vinci: Edizione in facsimile nel riordinamento cronologico dei suoi fascicoli.* Florence, 1998.

Pembroke 1968
Sydney, 16th Earl of Pembroke. *A Catalogue of the Paintings and Drawings in the Collection at Wilton House, Salisbury Wiltshire.* London and New York, 1968.

Pennington 1982
Pennington, Richard. *A Descriptive Catalogue of the Etched Work of Wenceslaus Hollar, 1607–1677.* Cambridge, 1982.

Penny 1992
Penny, Nicholas. "Exhibition Reviews: National Gallery of Scotland, Leonardo's Madonna of the Yarnwinder." *The Burlington Magazine* 134, no. 1073 (August 1992), pp. 542–44.

Pereira Viana 1987
Pereira Viana, T. *Desenhos italianos, gravuras de Bartolozzi: Património da Escola Superior des Belas Artes do Porto de da Faculdade de Ciências da Universidade do Porto.* Section on prints by Bartolozzi by F. de Vasconcelos. Exh. cat., Porto, Museu Nacional de Soares dos Reis. Lisbon, 1987.

Perissa Torrini 1983
Perissa Torrini, Annalisa. "Considerazioni su Cesare da Sesto nel periodo romano." *Bollettino d'arte*, ser. 6, no. 22 (1983), pp. 75–96.

Perissa Torrini 1992
Perissa Torrini, Annalisa. "Cesare da Sesto: The Drawings in Venice." In Palazzo Grassi 1992, pp. 400–405.

Perrig 1997
Perrig, Alexander. "Das 'Zeitalter Michelangelos.'" In Saarland Museum 1997, pp. 10–28.

Petit Palais 1935
Escholier, Raymond. *L'art italien de Cimabue à Tiepolo.* Exh. cat., Paris, Musée du Petit Palais. 1935.

Petit Palais 1965–66
Chastel, André, et al. *Le XVI siècle européen, peintures et dessins dans les collections publiques françaises.* Exh. cat., Paris, Petit Palais. Paris, 1965.

Petit Palais 1968
Rome à Paris. Exh. cat., Paris, Petit Palais. Paris, 1968.

Petit Palais 1968–69
Baudelaire. Exh. cat., Paris, Petit Palais. Paris, 1968.

Petrioli Tofani 1980
Petrioli Tofani, Annamaria, ed. *Il Primato del Disegno, Firenze e la Toscana dei Medici nell'Europa del Cinquecento.* Exh. cat., Florence, Palazzo Strozzi. Florence, 1980.

Petrioli Tofani 1986
Petrioli Tofani, Annamaria, ed. *Gabinetto Disegni e Stampe degli Uffizi, Inventario 1: Disegni esposti.* Florence, 1986.

Petrioli Tofani 1987
Petrioli Tofani, Annamaria, ed. *Gabinetto Disegni e Stampe degli Uffizi, Inventario 2: Disegni esposti.* Florence, 1987.

Petrioli Tofani 1991
Petrioli Tofani, Annamaria, ed. *Gabinetto Disegni e Stampe degli Uffizi, Inventario disegni di figura, 1.* Florence, 1991.

Petrioli Tofani 1992
Petrioli Tofani, Annamaria, et al. *Il disegno fiorentino del tempo di Lorenzo il Magnifico.* Exh. cat., Florence, Uffizi, Gabinetto Disegni e Stampe. Cinisello Balsamo, 1992.

Pettorelli 1920
Pettorelli, Artù. "Leonardiana." *Rassegna d'arte* 7 (1920), pp. 197–99.

Philadelphia Museum of Art 1950
Diamond Jubilee Exhibition: Masterpieces of Drawing. Exh. cat., Philadelphia Museum of Art. Philadelphia, 1950.

Philipson 1966
Philipson, Morris. *Leonardo da Vinci: Aspects of the Renaissance Genius.* New York, 1966.

Philo 1985
Philo, Ron, et al. *Guide to Human Anatomy.* Philadelphia, 1985.

Piantanida 1980
Piantanida, Sandro. "The Codex on the Flight of Birds." In *Leonardo da Vinci* 1980, pp. 347–61.

Piantanida and Baroni 1939
Piantanida, Sandro, and Costantino Baroni. *Leonardo da Vinci: Edizione curata dalla Mostra di Leonardo da Vinci in Milano.* Novara, [1939].

Piel 1986
Piel, Friedrich, et al. *Die Sammlung Ian Woodner: Meisterzeichnungen aus sechs Jahrhunderten.* Exh. cat., Vienna, Graphische Sammlung Albertina; Munich, Haus der Kunst and Bayerische Staatsgemäldesammlungen; Madrid, Museo del Prado [see Rocha 1986–87]. Cologne, 1986.

Piel 1995
Piel, Friedrich. *Tavola Doria: Leonardo da Vinci's Modello zu seinem Wandgemälde der 'Anghiarischlacht': Materialien, Texte, Dokumente.* Published to accompany an exhibition in the Max Gandolph Library at the University of Salzburg. Munich, 1995.

Pietrangeli 1987
Pietrangeli, Carlo. "Un Leonardo in vendita a Roma." In *Roma, questa nostra città*, pp. 102–10 Originally published in *Strenna dei Romanisti* (1986). Rome, 1987.

Pietrangeli 1996
Pietrangeli, Carlo. *Paintings in the Vatican.* Udine, 1996.

Pignatti 1982
Pignatti, Terisio. *Le dessin dans l'histoire de l'art.* Paris, 1982.

Pinacoteca di Brera 1988
Zeri, Federico, et al. *Pinacoteca di Brera: Scuole lombarde e piemontese, 1300–1535.* Milan, 1988.

Pinacoteca Vaticana 1857a
Galleria dei quadri al terzo piano delle Logge Vaticane. Rome, 1857.

Pinacoteca Vaticana 1857b
Indicazione della Pinacoteca Pontificia nel Palazzo Apostolico Vaticano. Rome, 1857.

Pinacoteca Vaticana 1934
Guida della Pinacoteca Vaticana. Città del Vaticano, 1934.

Pinacoteca Vaticana 1992
Baldini, Umberto, et al. *Monumenti, Musei, Gallerie Pontificie: Pinacoteca Vaticana nella pittura l'espressione del messaggio divino nella luce la radice della creazione pittorica.* Milan, 1992.

Pinault Sørensen 2001
Pinault Sørensen, Madeleine. "Les recherches encyclopédiques en Europe: Pour une définition de l'homme." In *Les vies de Dominique-Vivant Denon: Actes du colloque organisé au musée du Louvre par le Service Culturel du 8 au 11 décembre 1999,* vol. 1, pp. 215–41. 2 vols. Paris, 2001.

Piochi 1984
Piochi, Brunetto. "Il trattato di Paolo dell'Abbaco." *Annali dell'Istituto e Museo di Storia della Scienza i Firenze* 9 (1984), pp. 21–40.

Pischel Fraschini 1957
Pischel Fraschini, Gina. *Pinacoteca Ambrosiana.* Bergamo, 1957.

Plato 2000
Plato. *The Laws.* Translated by Benjamin Jowett. New York, 2000.

Pliny the Elder 1968
Pliny the Elder. *Natural History.* Translated by H. Rackham. Vol. 9. Cambridge, 1968.

Plomp 2001
Plomp, Michiel. *Collectionner, passionnément: Les collectionneurs hollandais de dessins au XVIIIe siècle.* Paris, 2002.

Poggi 1910
Poggi, Giovanni. "Note su Filippino Lippi: La tavola per san Donato di Scopeto e l'Adorazione dei Magi di Leonardo da Vinci." *Rivista d'arte* 7 (1910), pp. 93–101.

Poggi 1912–21
Poggi, Giovanni. "I disegni di Leonardo." In *I disegni della R. Galleria degli Uffizi.* serie 5, fasc. 3. Florence, 1912–21.

Poggi 1919
Poggi, Giovanni. *Leonardo da Vinci: La 'Vita' di Giorgio Vasari, nuovamente commentata e illustrata con 2000 tavole.* Florence, 1919.

Polverini Fosi 1991
Polverini Fosi, Irene. "Pietà, devozione e politica: Due confraternite fiorentine nella Roma del Rinascimento." *Archivio storico italiano* 149 (1991), pp. 119–61.

Ponting 1979
Ponting, Kenneth G. *Leonardo da Vinci, Drawings of Textile Machines.* Bradford-on-Avon, 1979.

Pope-Hennessy 1985
Pope-Hennessy, John. *An Introduction to Italian Renaissance Sculpture.* Vol. 2, *Italian Renaissance Sculpture.* 1958. 3d ed. London, 1985.

Pope-Hennessy 1993
Pope-Hennessy, John. *Donatello Sculptor.* New York and London, 1993.

Pope-Hennessy 2000
Pope-Hennessy, John. *An Introduction to Italian Renaissance Sculpture.* Vol. 2, *Italian Renaissance Sculpture.* 1958. 4th ed. London, 2000.

Popham 1930–31
Popham, Arthur Ewart. *Italian Drawings Exhibited at the Royal Academy, Burlington House, London, 1930.* Oxford, 1931.

Popham 1937
Popham, A[rthur] E[wart]. "Shorter Notices: The Drawings at the Burlington Fine Arts Club." *The Burlington Magazine* 70, no. 407 (February 1937), pp. 87–88.

Popham 1945
Popham, Arthur Ewart. *The Drawings of Leonardo da Vinci.* New York, 1945.

Popham 1947
Popham, A[rthur] E[wart]. *The Drawings of Leonardo da Vinci.* London, 1945. 2d ed. London, 1947.

Popham 1948a
Popham, Arthur Ewart. An Exhibition of *Old Master Drawings from the Albertina Collection.* Exh. cat., London, The Arts Council of Great Britain. London, 1948.

Popham 1948b
Popham, A[rthur] E[wart]. Review of *Leonardo da Vinci: The Virgin of the Rocks in the National Gallery,* by Martin Davies. *The Burlington Magazine* 90, no. 544 (July 1948), p. 212.

Popham 1949
Popham, Arthur Ewart. *Old Master Drawings from Chatsworth.* Exh. cat., London, Arts Council. London, 1949.

Popham 1952
Popham, A[rthur] E[wart]. "The Reappearance of some Leonardo Drawings." *The Burlington Magazine* 94, no. 590 (May 1952), pp. 127–32.

Popham 1954
Popham, Arthur Ewart. "The Dragon-Fight." In *Leonardo: Saggi e ricerche* 1954, pp. 221–27, pls. 113–16.

Popham 1957
Popham, Arthur Ewart. *Leonardo da Vinci.* London, 1957.

Popham 1962
Popham, Arthur Ewart. *Old Master Drawings from Chatsworth.* Exh. cat., Washington, D.C., National Gallery of Art; New York, Pierpont Morgan Library; Boston, Museum of Fine Arts; Cleveland Museum of Art; Ottawa, National Gallery of Canada; The Art Institute of Chicago; San Francisco, California Palace of the Legion of Honor. Catalogue reprinted for exhibition at the Royal Academy of Arts, London, 1969. Washington, D.C., 1962.

Popham 1971
Popham, Arthur Ewart. *Catalogue of the Drawings of Parmigianino.* 3 vols. New Haven and London, 1971.

Popham 1994
Popham, A[rthur] E[wart]. *The Drawings of Leonardo da Vinci.* 1945. Revised and with an introductory essay by Martin Kemp. London, 1994.

Popham and Pouncey 1950
Popham, Arthur E., and Philip Pouncey. *Italian Drawings in the Department of Prints and Drawings in the British Museum: The Fourteenth and Fifteenth Centuries.* London, 1950.

Popham and Wilde 1949
Popham, Arthur E., and Johannes Wilde. *The Italian Drawings of the XV and XVI Centuries in the Collection of Her Majesty the Queen at Windsor Castle.* London, 1949.

Popp 1926–27
Popp, Anny E. "Leonardo's Reiterdenkmalprojekte." *Zeitschrift für bildende Kunst* 60 (1926–27), pp. 52–62.

Popp 1927a
Popp, Anny E. "Andrea Verrocchio (1435–1488)." *Old Master Drawings* 2, no. 7 (December 1927), p. 35, pls. 37–38.

Popp 1927b
Popp, Anny E. "Jacopino del Conte (1510–1598)." *Old Master Drawings* 2, no. 5 (June 1927), pp. 7–8, pl. 7.

Popp 1928
Popp, Anny E. *Leonardo da Vinci: Zeichnungen.* Munich, 1928.

Posèq 1994
Posèq, Avigdor W. G. "The Case of the Two-headed Figure and the Elusive Lamb." *Achademia Leonardi Vinci: Journal of Leonardo Studies and Bibliography of Vinciana* 7 (1994), pp. 81–95, and unpaginated figures.

Pouncey 1964
Pouncey, Philip. Review of *I disegni dei pittori fiorentini,* by Bernard Berenson. *Master Drawings* 2, no. 3 (1964), pp. 278–93, pls. 28–41b.

Pouncey 1978
Pouncey, Philip. "An Unknown Drawing by Leonardo da Vinci." *Apollo* 108, no. 202 (December 1978), p. 405.

Pouncey 1998
Pouncey, Philip. "Um desenho desconhecido de Leonard da Vinci." *Apontamentos* (Faculdade de Belas Artes da Universidade do Porto) 2 (1998), p. 19, figs. 1–3. Translation of Pouncy 1978.

Pouncey and Gere 1962
Pouncey, Philip, and John A. Gere. *The Italian Drawings in the Department of Prints and Drawings in the British Museum, Raphael and his Circle.* 2 vols. London, 1962.

Powell 1951
Powell, Nicolas. *The Drawings of Henry Fuseli.* London, 1951.

Precerutti Garberi 1982
Precerutti Garberi, Mercedes. "Se tu sarai solo tu sarai tutto tuo: L'eredità di Leonardo in Lombardia." In Dell'Aqua 1982, pp. 193–224.

Procacci 1968
Procacci, U. "L'uso dei documenti negli studi di storia dell'arte e le vicende politiche ed economiche in Firenze durante il primo Quattrocento nel loro rapporto con gli artisti." In *Donatello e il suo tempo:*

Atti dell'VIII Convegno Internazionale di Studi sul Rinascimento, Firenze–Padova, 25 settembre–1 ottobre 1966, pp. 11–39. Florence, 1968.

Propeck forthcoming
Propeck, Lina, and Laurence Linarès. "Signatures, marques et paraphes administratifs des dessins du Louvre, 1671–1796." Forthcoming in *La Revue du Louvre*.

Prosperi Valenti Rodinò 1978
Prosperi Valenti Rodinò, Simonetta. "Le lettere del Mariette a Giovanni Gaetano Bottari nella Biblioteca Corsiniana." *Paragone* 29, no. 339 (1978), pp. 35–62, pls. 25–30.

Prosperi Valenti Rodinò 1996
Prosperi Valenti Rodinò, Simonetta. "La collezione di grafica del cardinal Silvio Valenti Gonzaga." In *Artisti e Mecenati: Dipinti, disegni, sculture e carteggi nella Roma curiale*, edited by Elisa Debenedetti, pp. 131–78. Studi sul Settecento Romano, 12. Rome, 1996.

Puccinelli 1664
Puccinelli. *Istoria dell'eroiche attioni di Ugo il Grande duca della Toscana ec., con la Cronica dell'Abbadia di Fiorenza ec., la Galleria sepolcrale dell'Abbadia di Fiorenza— Aggiunta al Trattato de' Tumuli, con l'introduzione della devozione di S.Mauro abbate.* Milan, 1664.

Py 2001
Py, Bernadette. *Everhard Jabach Collectionneur (1618–1695): Les dessins de l'inventaire de 1695.* Paris, 2001.

Quaderni d'anatomia 1911–16
Fonahn, Adolf M., Halfdan Hopstock, and Ove C. L. Vangensten. *Leonardo da Vinci: Quaderni d'anatomia.* 6 vols. Vol. 1, *Tredici fogli della Royal Library di Windsor: Respirazione, Cuore, visceri addominali*; Vol. 2, *Ventiquattro fogli della Royal Library di Windsor: Cuore, anatomia e fisiologia*; Vol. 3, *Dodici fogli della Royal Library di Windsor: Organi della generazione, embrione*; Vol. 4, *Ventun fogli della Royal Library di Windsor: Sangue, cuore, fonetica, varie altre materie*; Vol. 5, *Ventisei fogli della Royal Library di Windsor: Vasi, muscoli, cervello e nervi, anatomia topografica e comparata*; Vol. 6, *Ventitre fogli della Royal Library di Windsor: Proporzioni, funzioni dei muscoli, anatomia delle superficie del corpo humano.* Christiana, 1911–16.

Queen's Gallery 1972–73
Drawings by Michelangelo Raphael & Leonardo and Their Contemporaries. Exh. cat., London, Queen's Gallery, Buckingham Palace. London,1972–73.

Radcliffe 1994
Radcliffe, A. *The Robert H. Smith Collection: Bronzes, 1500–1600.* London, 1994.

Ragghianti 1938
[Ragghianti, Carlo Ludovico]. "Notizie e letture: Un 'Corpus Photographicum' di disegni." *Critica d'arte* 3, nos. 4–6 (1938), pp. xxv–xxx.

Ragghianti 1954
Ragghianti, Carlo L. "Inizio di Leonardo." *Critica d'arte* (1954), no. 1, pp. 1–18; no. 2, pp. 102–18; no. 4, pp. 302–29.

Ragghianti and Dalli Regoli 1975
Ragghianti, Carlo L., and Gigetta Dalli Regoli. *Firenze 1470–1480: Disegni dal modello, Pollaiuolo, Leonardo, Botticelli, Filippino.* Pisa, 1975.

Ragghianti Collobi 1974
Ragghianti Collobi, Licia. *Il libro de'disegni del Vasari.* 2 vols. Florence, 1974.

Ramade 1987
Ramade, Patrick. *Première idée.* Exh. cat., Rennes, Musée des Beaux-Arts. Rennes, 1987.

Ramirez di Montalvo 1849
Ramirez di Montalvo, A. "Inventario manoscritto dei disegni degli Uffizi." Florence, 1849.

Ratti 1907
[Ratti, Achille]. *Guida sommaria per il visitatore della Biblioteca Ambrosiana e delle collezioni annesse.* Milan, 1907.

Ravaisson Mollien 1881
Ravaisson Mollien, Charles. "Les écrits de Léonard de Vinci." *Gazette des Beaux-Arts*, ser. 2, 23 (1881), pp. 225–48; 331–49.

Réau 1957
Réau, Louis. *Iconographie de l'art chrétien.* Vol. 2, *Iconographie de la Bible.* Part 2, *Nouveau Testament.* Paris, 1957.

Réau 1958
Réau, Louis. *Iconographie de l'art chrétien· Iconographie des saints.* Vol. 3, part 2. Paris, 1958.

Recueil Caylus
Suite of 223 engravings by Anne-Claude-Philippe, comte de Caylus, after drawings in the collection of the Cabinet du Roy (*Recueil Caylus*). Département des Arts graphiques, musée du Louvre.

Recueil de Ligne
Suite of etchings by M. le Prince Charles de Ligne, Chevalie (*Recueil de Ligne*).

Redig De Campos 1985
Redig De Campos, Deoclecio. "San Girolamo." In *Leonardo: La pittura* 1985, pp. 37–38.

Reeves 1997
Reeves, Eileen. *Painting the Heavens: Art and Science in the Age of Galileo.* Princeton, N.J., 1997.

Renouard 1966
Renouard, Y. "Benci, Giovanni." In *Dizionario biografico degli Italiani*, vol. 8, pp. 194–96. Rome, 1966.

Renouard and Ragni, 1966
Renouard, Y., and E. Ragni. "Benci, Amerigo." In *Dizionario biografico degli Italiani*, vol. 8, pp. 182–83. Rome, 1966.

Renouard de Bussierre 1991
Renouard de Bussierre, S. *Martin Schongauer: Maitre de la gravure rhenane vers 1450–1491.* Paris, 1991.

Repetti 1833–1846
Repetti, Emanuele. *Dizionario geografico fisico storico della Toscana contenente la descrizione di tutti i luoghi del granducato ducato di Lucca, Garfagnana e Lunigiana.* 5 vols. and appendix. Florence, 1833–46.

Reti 1959
Reti, Ladislao. "'Non si volta chi a stella è fisso': Le 'imprese' di Leonardo da Vinci." *Bibliothèque*

d'Humanisme et Renaissance 21 (1959), pp. 7–54.

Reti 1971
Reti, Ladislao. "Leonardo da Vinci and the Graphic Arts: The Early Invention of Relief-Etching." *The Burlington Magazine* 113, no. 817 (April 1971), pp. 188–95.

Reti 1974
Reti, Ladislao, ed. *The Unknown Leonardo.* New York, 1974.

Reti and Dibner 1969
Reti, Ladislao, and Bern Dibner. *Leonardo da Vinci, Technologist.* Norwalk, Conn., 1969.

Reuterswärd 1993
Reuterswärd, Patrik. "Left-handedness in Master Drawings." *Nationalmuseum Bulletin* (Stockholm) 17, no. 2 (1993), pp. 1–10.

Reymond 1892
Reymond, Marcel. "Cesare da Sesto." *Gazette des Beaux-Arts*, ser. 3, 7 (1892), pp. 314–33.

Reymond 1910
Reymond, Marcel. "L'éducation de Léonard." In *Leonardo da Vinci: Conferenze fiorentine*, 1910, pp. 49–79.

Reznicek 1981
Reznicek, E. K. J. "Alcune osservazioni a proposito degli studi patognomici di Leonardo da Vinci." *Ars Auro Prior: Studia Ioanni Białostocki sexagenario dicata.* Warsaw, 1981.

Ricci 1913
Ricci, Corrado. "Il 'Musicista' dell'Ambrosiana." *Bollettino d'arte*, ser. 1, 29 (1913), pp. 200–202.

Richardson and Richardson 1722
Richardson, Jonathan, father and son. *An Account of some of the Statues, Bas-reliefs, Drawings, and Pictures in Italy with Remarks.* London, 1722.

Richardson and Richardson 1728
Richardson, Jonathan, father and son. *Traité de la peinture, et de la sculpture.* 3 vols. Amsterdam, 1728. Reprint, Geneva, 1972.

Richter 1880
Richter, Jean Paul. *Leonardo.* London, 1880.

Richter 1883
Richter, Jean Paul. *The Literary Works of Leonardo da Vinci Compiled and Edited from the Original Manuscripts.* 2 vols. London, 1883.

Richter 1910
Richter, Jean Paul. *The Mond Collection, An Appreciation.* 2 vols. London, 1910.

Richter 1970
Richter, Jean Paul. *The Literary Works of Leonardo da Vinci Compiled and Edited from the Original Manuscripts.* 1883. 3d ed. 2 vols. London, 1970.

Rigaud and Brown 1877
A Treatise on Painting by Leonardo da Vinci translated from the the Italian by John Francis Rigaud, R.A., With a Life of Leonardo and an Account of his Works by John William Brown. Rev. ed. London, 1877.

Righi 1995
Righi, Nadia. "Una recente pubblicazione su Cesare da Sesto." *Critica d'arte*, no. 768 (1995), pp. 239–40.

Rigollot 1849
Rigollot, D. *Catalogue de l'oeuvre de Léonard de Vinci.* Paris, 1849.

Ritgen 1865
Ritgen, H. von. *Fünfzig Photographien nach Handzeichnungen alter Meister.* 1865.

Roberts 1986
Roberts, Jane. *Master Drawings in the Royal Collection From Leonardo to the Present Day.* London, 1986.

Roberts 1987
Roberts, Jane. *Italian Master Drawings, Leonardo to Canaletto, from the British Royal Collection.* Exh. cat., Washington, D.C., National Gallery of Art; The Fine Arts Museums of San Francisco; The Art Institute of Chicago. Washington, D.C., 1987.

Roberts 1988
Roberts, Jane. *A Study in Genius: Master Drawings and Watercolours from the Collection of Her Majesty the Queen in the Royal Library, Windsor Castle.* Exh. cat., Sydney, Art Gallery of New South Wales; Melbourne, National Gallery of Victoria; Brisbane, Queensland Art Gallery. Sydney, 1988.

Roberts 1989
Roberts, Jane. "The Life of Leonardo." In Kemp and Roberts 1989, pp. 23–41.

Roberts 1992
Roberts, Jane. "The Early History of the Collecting of Drawings by Leonardo da Vinci." In Palazzo Grassi 1992, pp. 155–78.

Roberts forthcoming
Roberts, Jane. *Thomas Howard, Earl of Arundel, and Leonardo's Drawings.* Forthcoming.

Roberts and Trent 1991
Roberts, Verne L., and Ivy Trent. *Bibliotheca Mechanica.* New York, 1991. Bibliography of the private library of Verne Roberts, Approximately 1200 items in fields of mechanics, biomechanics, and the history of technology from the 15th, 16th, and 17th centuries, with extensive descriptions that document the development of ideas in science and technology.

Robertson 1990
Robertson, Charles. "Bramantino as Painter and Designer." Ph.D. diss., University of London, The Courtauld Institute of Art, 1990.

Robinson 1869
Robinson, John C. *Descriptive Catalogue of Drawings by the Old Masters, Forming the Collection of John Malcolm of Poltalloch, Esq.* London, 1869.

Robinson 1876
Robinson, John C. *Descriptive Catalogue of Drawings by the Old Masters, Forming the Collection of John Malcolm of Poltalloch, Esq.* 1869. 2d ed. London, 1876.

Rocha 1986–87
Rocha, Francisco J., ed. *Dibujos de los siglos XIV al XX. Coleccion Woodner.* Exh. cat., Madrid, Museo del Prado. Madrid, 1986. See Peil 1986 for earlier venues.

Rocheblave 1889
Rocheblave, Samuel. *Essai sur le Comte de Caylus: L'homme, l'artiste, l'antiquaire.* Paris, 1889.

Romano 1978
Romano, Giovanni. *Studi sul paesaggio.* Turin, 1978.

Romano 1981
Romano, Giovanni. "Verso la maniera moderna, da Mantegna a Raffaello." In *Storia dell'arte italiana,* vol. 6, part 1, pp. 5–85. Turin, 1981.

Romano, Binaghi, and Collura 1978
Romano, Giovanni, Maria Teresa Binaghi, and Domenico Collura. "Il maestro della Pala sforzesca." In *Quaderni di Brera.* Florence, 1978.

Rooses 1886–92
Rooses, Max. *L'œuvre de P. P. Rubens: Histoire et description de ses tableaux et dessins.* 5 vols. Antwerp, 1886–92.

Rooses 1904
Rooses, Max. *Rubens.* 2 vols. London, 1904.

Rosand 1969
Rosand, David. "Rubens's Munich *Lion Hunt*: Its Sources and Significance." *The Art Bulletin* 51, no. 1 (March 1969), pp. 29–40.

Rosand 1988
Rosand, David. *The Meaning of the Mark: Leonardo and Titian.* The Franklin D. Murphy Lectures, 8. Spencer Museum of Art, The University of Kansas. [Lawrence, Ks.], 1988.

Rosand 1990
Rosand, David. "Leonardo da Vinci: Sul disegnare una linea." *Eidos,* no. 6 (July 1990), pp. 4–28.

Rosci 1977
Rosci, Marco. *The Hidden Leonardo.* Chicago, 1977.

Rosci 1978
Rosci, Marco. *Léonard de Vinci.* 1976. Paris, 1978.

Rosci 1979
Rosci, Marco. *Leonardo.* Milan, 1979.

Rosci 1980
Rosci, Marco. "The Madrid Manuscripts of Leonardo." In *Leonardo da Vinci* 1980, pp. 509–24.

Rosci 1982
Rosci, Marco. *Leonardo.* Milan, 1982.

Rosci 1984
Rosci, Marco. "Leonardo 'filosofo'—Lomazzo e Borghini 1584: Due linee di tradizione dei pensieri e precetti di Leonardo sull'arte." In *Fra Rinascimento Manierismo e realtà: Scritti di storia dell'arte in memoria di Anna Maria Brizio,* edited by Pietro C. Marani, pp. 53–77. Florence, 1984.

Rosenberg 1898
Rosenberg, Adolf. *Leonardo da Vinci.* Künstler-Monographien, 33. Bielefeld and Leipzig, 1898.

Rosenberg 1903
Rosenberg, Adolf. *Leonardo da Vinci.* Translated by J. Lohse. Monographs on Artists, 7. Bielefeld and Leipzig, 1903.

Rosenberg 1959
Rosenberg, Jakob. *Great Draughtsmen from Pisanello to Picasso.* Cambridge, Mass., 1959.

Rosenberg 1974
Rosenberg, Jakob. *Great Draughtsmen from Pisanello to Picasso.* 1959. Rev. ed. New York, 1974.

Rosini 1843
Rosini, Giovanni. *Storia della pittura italiana.* 11 vols. Pisa, 1843.

Rossi and Rovetta 1988
Rossi, Marco, and Alessandro Rovetta. *Il Cenacolo di Leonardo: Cultura domenicana, iconografia eucaristica e tradizione lombarda.* Milan, 1988.

Røsstad 1995
Røsstad, Anna. *Leonardo da Vinci, the Man and the Mystery.* Translated by Ann Zwick. Oslo, 1995.

Rousseau 1951
Rousseau Jr., Theodore. "Notes." *The Metropolitan Museum of Art Bulletin,* n.s., 10, no. 4 (December 1951), p. 112.

Rouvèyre 1901
Rouvèyre, Édouard. *Léonard da Vinci: Feuillets inédits, reproduit d'après les originaux conservés à la Bibliotèque du Château du Windsor.* 23 vols. Paris, 1901.

Roux 1940
Roux, Marcel. *Bibliothèque Nationale, Département des Estampes: Inventaire du Fonds Français, graveurs du XVIIIe siècle.* Vol. 4. Paris, 1940.

Rowlands and Bartrum 1993
Rowlands, John, with Giulia Bartrum. *Drawings by German Artists and Artist from German-Speaking Regions of Europe in the Department of Prints and Drawings in the British Museum.* 2 vols. London, 1993.

Royal Academy of Arts 1930
Exhibition of Italian Art, 1200–1900. Exh. cat., London, Royal Academy of Arts. London, 1930.

Royal Academy of Arts 1952
Leonardo da Vinci Drawings. Leonardo da Vinci, Quincentenary Exhibition, 1452–1952. Exh. cat., London, Royal Academy of Arts, Diploma Gallery. London, 1952.

Royal Academy of Arts 1960
Italian Art and Britain. Exh. cat., London, Royal Academy of Arts. London, 1960.

Royal Academy of Arts 1977
Leonardo da Vinci: Anatomical Drawings from the Royal Collection. Introduction by Carlo Pedretti. Exh. cat., London, Royal Academy of Arts. London, 1977.

Royal Academy of Arts 1987
Turner, Nicholas, et al. *Master Drawings: The Woodner Collection.* Edited by Jane Shoaf Turner. Exh. cat., London, Royal Academy of Arts. London, 1987.

Rubin 1990
Rubin, Patricia. Review of *Leonardo da Vinci,* by Martin Kemp and Jane Roberts. *Renaissance Studies* 4, no. 1 (March 1990), pp. 99–106.

Rubin and Wright 1999–2000
Rubin, Patricia Lee, and Alison Wright. *Renaissance Florence: The Art of the 1470's.* Exh. cat., London, National Gallery. London, 1999.

Rubinstein 1987
Rubinstein, Nicolai. "Classical Themes in the Decoration of the Palazzo Vecchio in Florence." *Journal of the Warburg and Courtauld Institutes* 50 (1987), pp. 29–43.

Rubinstein 1991
Rubinstein, Nicolai. "Machiavelli and the Mural Decoration of the Hall of the Great Council of Florence." In *Musagetes: Festschrift für Wolfram Prinz zu seinem 60. Geburtstag am 5. Februar 1989*, pp. 275–85. Berlin, 1991.

Rubinstein 1995
Rubinstein, Nicolai. *The Palazzo Vecchio, 1298–1532: Government, Architecture, and Imagery in the Civic Palace of the Florentine Republic.* Oxford, 1995.

Ruggeri 1976
Ruggeri, Ugo. *Maestri Lombardi e Lombardo-Veneti del Rinascimento, Biblioteca dei disegni.* Florence, 1976.

Ruggeri 1982
Ruggeri, Ugo. *Disegni Lombardi: Gallerie dell' Accademia di Venezia.* Milan, 1982.

Rzepińska 1962
Rzepińska, Maria. "Light and Shadow in the Late Writings of Leonardo da Vinci." *Raccolta Vinciana,* no. 19 (1962), pp. 259–66.

Rzepińska 1993
Rzepińska, Maria. "Leonardo's Colour Theory." *Achademia Leonardi Vinci: Journal of Leonardo Studies and Bibliography of Vinciana* 6 (1993), pp. 11–33, and unpaginated figures.

Saarland Museum 1997
Güse, Ernst-Gerhard, and Alexander Perrig, eds. *Zeichnungen aus der Toskana: Das Zeitalter Michelangelos.* Exh. cat., Saarbrücken, Saarland Museum. Munich, 1997.

Sabachnikoff, Piumati, and Ravaisson-Mollien 1893
Sabachnikoff, Teodoro, Giovanni Piumati, and Charles Lachner Ravaissno-Mollien, eds. *I Manoscritti di Leonardo da Vinci: Codice sul volo degli uccelli e varie altre materie, Biblioteca Reale, Turin.* Paris, 1893.

Sabatini 1944
Sabatini, Attilio. *Antonio e Piero del Pollaiuolo.* Florence, 1944.

Sacco 1980
Sacco, Federico. "Da Vinci's Geology and Geography." In *Leonardo da Vinci* 1980, pp. 455–66.

Salvini 1964
Salvini, Roberto. "Una possibile fonte medioevale di Leonardo e il suo autore." In *Studien zur toskanischen Kunst: Festschrift für Ludwig Heinrich Heydenreich,* edited by Wolfgang Lotz and Lise Lotte Möller, pp. 266–74. Munich, 1964.

Salvini 1977
Salvini, Roberto. "Paralipomena su Leonardo e Dürer." In *Studies in Late Medieval and Renaissance Painting in Honor of Millard Meiss,* vol. 1, pp. 377–91. 2 vols. New York, 1977.

Sanders 2001
Sanders, Marion. *Understanding Dyslexia and the Reading Process: A Guide for Educators and Parents.* Boston, London, and Toronto, 2001.

Sannazaro and Shell 1987–93
Sannazaro, Giovanni Battista, and Janice Shell. "Boltraffio." In *Dizionario della Chiesa ambrosiana,* vol. 1, pp. 445–46. 6 vols. Milan, 1987–93.

Sanpaolesi 1954
Sanpaolesi, Piero. "I dipinti di Leonardo agli Uffizi." In *Leonardo: Saggi e ricerche* 1954, pp. 27–46, pls. 35–52.

Sansum 2001
Sansum, James. *European Master Drawings, 1500–1900.* Sale cat., New York, L'Antiquaire and the Connoisseur. New York, 2001.

Sartoris 1952
Sartoris, Alberto. *Léonard architecte.* Paris, 1952.

Scaglia 1981
Scaglia, Gustina. *Alle origini degli studi tecnologici di Leonardo.* Lettura Vinciana, 20 (20 aprile 1980). Vinci, 1981.

Scaglia 1982
Scaglia, Gustina. "Leonardo's Non-inverted Writing and Verrocchio's Measured Drawing of a Horse." *The Art Bulletin* 64, no. 1 (March 1982), pp. 32–44.

Scaglia 1995
Scaglia, Gustina. "Leonardo da Vinci's Drawing in the Pierpont Morgan Library: Its Travels from Milan to La Rochelle (1519–1572)." *Arte lombarda,* nos. 113–15 (1995), pp. 27–36.

Scailliérez 1991
Scailliérez, Cécile. *Joos van Cleve au Louvre.* Exh. cat., Paris, Musée du Louvre. Paris, 1991.

Scailliérez 2000
Scailliérez, Cécile. "'La Vierge à l'Enfant avec sainte Anne' de Léonard de Vinci: Questions et hypothèses." In *Au Louvre avec Viviane Forrester: La Vierge à l'Enfant avec sainte Anne, Léonard de Vinci (1452–1519),* pp. 31–55. Paris, 2000.

Scalini 2001–2
Scalini, Mario, et al. *Pulchritudo, Amor, Voluptas: Pico della Mirandola alla corte del Magnifico.* Exh. cat., Mirandola, Centro Culturale Polivalente. Florence, 2001.

Scalino 1591
Scalino, da Camerino, Marcello. *Regole Nvove, et avertimenti di Marcello Scalino da Camerino Cittadino Romano.* Brescia, 1591. (The Metropolitan Museum of Art, acc. no. 28.106.7).

Scarpati 1982
Scarpati, Claudio. "Leonardo e i linguaggi." In *Studi sul Cinquecento italiano,* pp. 3–26. Milan, 1982.

Scarpati 1993
Leonardo da Vinci. *Il paragone delle arti.* Edited by C. Scarpati. Milan, 1993.

Scarpati 2001
Scarpati, Claudio. *Leonardo scrittore.* Milan, 2001.

Scarpellini 1984
Scarpellini, Pietro. *Perugino.* Milan, 1984.

Schaeffer 1911
Schaeffer, Emil. "Un disegno del Luini nell Albertina di Vienna." *Rassegna d'arte* 11, no. (1911), p. 144.

Schaeffer 1961
Schaeffer Galleries: Twenty-Fifth Anniversary, 1936–1961. New York, 1961.

Schapiro 1956
Schapiro, Meyer. "Leonardo and Freud: An Art Historical Study." *Journal of the History of Ideas* 17 (1956), pp. 303–39.

Schiaparelli 1921
Schiaparelli, Attilio. *Leonardo rittrattista.* Milan, 1921.

Schnapper 1974
Schnapper, Antoine. *Jean Jouvenet, 1644–1717, et la peinture d'histoire à Paris.* Paris, 1974.

Schneider Adams 1993
Schneider Adams, Laurie. *Art and Psychoanalysis.* New York, 1993.

Schofield 1989a
Schofield, Richard. "Exhibition Reviews: London, Hayward Gallery, Leonardo." *The Burlington Magazine* 131, no. 1033 (April 1989), pp. 306–7.

Schofield 1989b
Schofield, Richard. "Amadeo, Bramante, and Leonardo and the *Tiburio* of Milan Cathedral." *Achademia Leonardi Vinci: Journal of Leonardo Studies and Bibliography of Vinciana* 2 (1989), pp. 68–100, and unpaginated figures.

Schofield 1991
Schofield, Richard. "Leonardo's Milanese Architecture: Career, Sources, and Graphic Techniques." *Achademia Leonardi Vinci: Journal of Leonardo Studies and Bibliography of Vinciana* 4 (1991), pp. 111–57, and unpaginated figures.

Schofield and Shell 1996
Schofield, Richard, and Janice Shell. "Amadeo, Giovanni Antonio." In *The Dictionary of Art,* edited by Jane S. Turner, vol. 1, pp. 746–49. 34 vols. London, 1996.

Schönbrunner and Meder 1896
Schönbrunner, Joseph, and Joseph Meder. *Handzeichnungen Alter Meister aus der Albertina und anderen Sammlungen.* 12 vols. Vienna, 1896.

Schott 1979
Schott, G. D. "Some Neurological Observations on Leonardo da Vinci's Handwriting." *Journal of the Neurological Sciences* 42, no. 3 (August 1979), pp. 321–29.

Schott 1999
Schott, G. D. "Mirror Writing: Allen's Self Observations, Lewis Carroll's 'Looking-glass' Letters, and Leonardo da Vinci's Maps." *The Lancet* 354 (December 18–25, 1999), pp. 2158–61.

Schug 1968
Schug, Albert. "Zur Ikonographie von Leonardos Londoner Karton." *Pantheon* 26, no. 6 (November–December 1968), pp. 446–55.

Schulze Altcappenberg 1995
Schulze Altcappenberg, Hein-Th. *Die italienischen Zeichnungen des 14. und 15. Jahrhunderts im Berliner Kupferstichkabinett: Kritischer Katalog.* Berlin, 1995.

Sciolla 1985
Sciolla, Gianni Carlo, ed. *Le collezioni d'arte della Biblioteca Reale di Torino: Disegni, incisioni, manoscritti figurati.* Turin, 1985.

Sciolla 1990
Sciolla, Gianni Carlo, et al. *Da Leonardo a Rembrandt: Disegni della Biblioteca reale di Torino.* Exh. cat., Turin, Biblioteca reale di Torino. Turin, 1990.

Sciolla 1991a
Sciolla, Gianni Carlo, ed. *Nuove ricerche in margine alla mostra, Da Leonardo a Rembrandt: Disegni della Biblioteca reale di Torino. Atti del Convegno internazionale di studi. Torino, Vigna di Madama reale (Villa Abegg), 24–25 ottobre 1990.* Turin, 1991.

Sciolla 1991b
Sciolla, Gianni Carlo, Annamaria Petrioli Tofani, and Simonetta Prosperi Valenti Rodinò. *Die Zeichnung.* Vol. 1, *Formen, Techniken, Bedeutungen.* 3 vols. Turin, 1991.

Sciolla 1998
Sciolla, Gianni Carlo, ed. *Ambrogio da Fossano detto il Bergognone, un pittore per la Certosa.* Milan, 1998.

Scott-Elliot 1956
Scott-Elliot, A. H. "The Pompeo Leoni Volume of Leonardo Drawings at Windsor." *The Burlington Magazine* 98, no. 634 (January 1956), pp. 11–17.

Scott-Elliot 1958
Scott-Elliot, A. H. "Caricature Heads after Leonardo da Vinci in the Spencer Collection. *Bulletin of the New York Public Library* 62, no. 6 (June 1958), pp. 279–99.

Scrase 1990
Scrase, David. "Exhibition reviews: Paris and Lille Leonardo; Italian Drawings." Reviews of *Léonard de Vinci: Études de draperies,* by Françoise Viatte, André Chastel, and Carlo Pedretti; and *Renaissance et Baroque: Dessins italiens du Musée de Lille,* by Barbara Brejon de Lavergnée. *The Burlington Magazine* 132, no. 1043 (February 1990), pp. 151–54.

Scrase 2002
Scrase, David. *Chefs-d'oeuvre du Fitzwilliam Museum de Cambridge: Dix ans d'acquisitions de dessins de maîtres anciens.* Exh. cat., Paris, Artemis–C. G. Boerner. Paris, 2002.

Scuderie Papali al Quirinale 2001–2
Paolucci, Antonio, et al. *Rinascimento: Capolavori dei musei italiani, Tokyo-Roma 2001.* Exh. cat., Tokyo, National Museum of Western Art; Rome, Scuderie Papali al Quirinale. Milan, 2001.

Sedini 1989
Sedini, Domenico. *Marco d'Oggiono: Tradizione e rinnovamento in Lombardia tra Quattrocento e Cinquecento.* Milan and Rome, 1989.

Segre 1979
Segre, Cesare. "La descrizione al futuro: Leonardo da Vinci." In *Semiotica filologica: Testo e modelli culturali,* pp. 131–60. Turin, 1979.

Seidlitz 1906
Seidlitz, Woldemar von. "Ambrogio Preda und Leonardo da Vinci." *Jahrbuch der Kunsthistorischen Sammlungen des Allerhöchsten Kaiserhauses* 26, no. 1 (1906), pp. 1–48.

Seidlitz 1909
Seidlitz, Woldemar von. *Leonardo da Vinci: Der Wendepunkt der Renaissance.* 2 vols. Berlin, 1909.

Seidlitz 1911
Seidlitz, W[oldemar] von. "I disegni di Leonardo da Vinci a Windsor." *L'Arte* 14 (1911), pp. 269–89.

Seidlitz 1935
Seidlitz, Woldemar von. *Leonardo da Vinci: Der Wendepunkt der Renaissance.* Rev. ed. Vienna, 1935.

Sele Arte 1966
"Mostre a New York." *Sele Arte* 77–78 (1966), pp. 100–103.

Selvatico 1854
Selvatico, Pietro. *Catologo delle opere d'arte contenute nella Sala delle Sedute dell'Imperiale e Reale Accademia di Venezia.* Venice, 1854.

Sérullaz 1965
Sérullaz, Maurice, et al. *Le XVIe siècle européen, dessins du Louvre.* Exh. cat., Paris, Musée du Louvre. Paris, 1965.

Sérullaz 1977–78
Sérullaz, Arlette. *Rubens, ses maîtres, ses élèves.* Exh. cat., Paris, Musée du Louvre. Paris, 1977.

Sérullaz 1996
Sérullaz, Arlette and Maurice. " Delacroix and l'Italie." In *Hommage au dessin: Mélanges offerts à Roseline Bacou,* pp. 561–71. Rimini, 1996.

Seymour 1971
Seymour, Charles. *The Sculpture of Andrea del Verrocchio.* Greenwich, Conn., 1971.

Sgarbi 1985
Sgarbi, Vittorio. "Testimonianza per Johannes Ispanus." *Paragone,* nos. 419–23 (January–May 1985), pp. 151–56.

Shapley 1925
Shapley, John. "A Lost Cartoon for Leonardo's Madonna with St. Anne." *The Art Bulletin* 7, no. 3 (March 1925), pp. 96–102.

Shearman 1962
Shearman, John. "Leonardo's Colour and Chiaroscuro." *Zeitschrift für Kunstgeschichte* 25 no. 1 (1962), pp. 13–47.

Shell 1995
Shell, Janice. *Pittori in bottega: Milano nel rinascimento.* Turin, 1995.

Shell 1998a
Shell, Janice. "Ambrogio de Predis" In *Legacy of Leonardo* 1998, pp. 123–30.

Shell 1998b
Shell, Janice. "Gian Giacomo Caprotti, detto Salaì." In *Legacy of Leonardo* 1998, pp. 397–406.

Shell 1998c
Shell, Janice. "Leonardo and the Lombard Traditionalists." In *Legacy of Leonardo* 1998, pp. 64–91.

Shell 1998d
Shell, Janice. "Marco d'Oggiono." In *Legacy of Leonardo* 1998, pp. 163–78.

Shell and Sironi 1989a
Shell, Janice, and Grazioso Sironi. "Documents for Copies of the *Cenacolo* and the *Virgin of the Rocks* by Bramantino, Marco d'Oggiono, Bernardino de' Conti, and Cesare Magni." *Raccolta Vinciana,* no. 23 (1989), pp. 103–17.

Shell and Sironi 1989b
Shell, Janice, and Grazioso Sironi. "Giovanni Antonio Boltraffio and Marco d'Oggiono: The Berlin Resurrection of Christ with Sts Leonardo and Lucy." *Raccolta Vinciana,* no. 23 (1989), pp. 119–54.

Shell and Sironi 1991
Shell, Janice, and Grazioso Sironi. "Salaì and Leonardo's Legacy." *The Burlington Magazine* 133, no. 1055 (February 1991), pp. 95–108.

Shell and Sironi 2000
Shell, Janice, and Grazioso Sironi. "Un nuovo documento di pagamento per la 'Vergine delle Rocce' di Leonardo." In *'Hostinato rigore': Leonardiana in memoria di Augusto Marinoni,* edited by Pietro C. Marani, pp. 27–31. Milan, 2000.

Shell, Brown, and Brambilla Barcilon 1988
Shell, Janice, David Alan Brown, and Pinin Brambilla Barcilon. *Giampietrino e una copia cinquecentesca dell'ultima cena di Leonardo.* Milan, 1988.

Simon 1997
Simon, Robin. "Leonardo and Holbein (?)." *Apollo* 146, no. 429 (November 1997), pp. 20–21.

Simonetto 1988
Simonetto, Lucia. "Lo Pseudo Boccaccino fra Milano e Venezia: Certezze e dubbi di una cronologia." *Arte lombarda,* nos. 84–85 (1988), pp. 73–84.

Simpson 1996
Simpson, Otto von. *Peter Paul Rubens (1577–1640): Humanist, Maler und Diplomat.* Mainz, 1996.

Sirén 1911
Sirén, Osvald. *Leonardo da Vinci: Hans Lefnadsön, Bildverk, Personlighet och Mälarbok.* Stockholm, 1911.

Sirén 1916
Sirén, Osvald. *Leonardo da Vinci.* New Haven and London, 1916.

Sirén 1928
Sirén, Osvald. *Léonard de Vinci: L'artiste et l'homme: Édition entièrement refondue et mis à jour.* 3 vols. Paris and Brussels, 1928.

Sironi 1981
Sironi, Grazioso. *Nuovi documenti riguardanti la Vergine delle Rocce di Leonardo da Vinci.* Milan and Florence, 1981.

Smiraglia Scognamiglio 1900
Smiraglia Scognamiglio, Nino. *Ricerche e documenti sulla giovinezza di Leonardo da Vinci (1452–1482).* Naples, 1900.

Smyth 1979
Smyth, Craig Hugh. "Venice and the Emergence of the High Renaissance in Florence: Observations and Questions." In *Florence and Venice, Comparisons and Relations: Acts of Two Conferences at Villa I Tatti in 1976–77,* vol. 1, *Quattrocento,* edited by Sergio Bertelli et al., pp. 209–49. Florence, 1979.

Snow-Smith 1987
Snow-Smith, Joanne. "Leonardo's *Virgin of the Rocks* (Musée du Louvre): A Franciscan Interpretation." *Studies in Iconography* 11 (1987), pp. 35–94.

Solmi 1908
Solmi, Edmondo. "Le Fonti dei Manoscritti di Leonardo da Vinci." *Giornale Storico della Letturatura Italiana,* suppl. nos. 10–11 (1908), pp. 263–64 and in the same journal, "Nuovi Contributi," 58 (1911), pp. 297 ff.

Solmi 1911a
Solmi, Edmondo. "Leonardo da Vinci e Papa

Giulio II." *Archivio storico lombardo*, ser. 4, 38 (1911), pp. 390–411.

Solmi 1911b
Solmi, Edmondo. "Leonardo e la sollevazione d' Arezzo del 1502." *Raccolta Vinciana*, no. 7 (1911), pp. 133–37.

Solmi 1912a
Solmi, Edmondo. "Partecipazione di Leonardo da Vinci alla sollevazione d'Arezzo e della val di Chiana nel giugno del 1502." *Archivio Storico Italiano* 49 (1912), pp. 122–29.

Solmi 1912b
Solmi, Edmondo. "La politica di Lodovico il Moro nei simboli di Leonardo da Vinci (1489–1499)." In *Scritti varii di erudizione e di critica in onore di Rodolfo Renier*, pp. 491–509. Turin, 1912.

Solmi 1923
Solmi, Edmondo. *Leonardo (1452–1519)*. 1900. Florence, 1923.

Spagnolo 2000
Spagnolo, M. "La matita rocca come luce e colore: Verifiche sugli studi di teste di Leonardo e dei leonardeschi." *Polittico* 1 (2000), pp. 65–82.

Spencer 1972
Spencer, John. "Sources of Leonardo da Vinci's Sforza Monument." *Actes du XXIIe Congrès International d'Histoire de l'Art, Budapest 1969.* Vol. 2, *Evolution générale et dévelopments régionaux en histoire de l'art*, pp. 735–42. Budapest, 1972.

Spencer 1973
Spencer, John. "Il progetto per il cavallo di bronzo per Francesco Sforza." *Arte lombarda*, nos. 38–39 (1973), pp. 23–35.

Spinosa 1995
Spinosa, Nicola. *Museo e Gallerie Nazionali di Capodimonte: La Collezione Farnese.* Naples, 1995.

Starnazzi 1996a
Starnazzi, Carlo. "La gioconda nella valle dell'Arno." *Archeologia viva* 15, no. 57 (May–June 1996), pp. 42–51.

Starnazzi 1996b
Starnazzi, Carlo. "Leonardo da Vinci: La rappresentazione cartografica e pittorica del paesagio toscano." *L'universo* 5 (October 1996), pp. 695–704.

Starnazzi 1997
Starnazzi, Carlo. "Leonardo da Vinci e la Preistoria dal Valdarno." *Periodico del Laboratorio di Ecologia del Quaternario* 19 (1997), pp. 117–27.

Starnazzi 1998
Starnazzi, Carlo. "Leonardo da Vinci: Un cartografo tra Euclide e Tolomeo." *L'universo* 4 (1998), pp. 544–56.

Stedelijk Museum 1934
Italiaansche Kunst in Nederlandsch Bezit. Introduction by F. Schmidt-Degener. Exh. cat., Amsterdam, Staedelijk Museum, 1934.

Stedman Sheard 1978
Stedman Sheard, Wendy. "'Asa Adorna': The Prehistory of the Vendramin Tomb." *Jahrbuch der Berliner Museen* 20 (1978), pp. 117–56.

Stedman Sheard 1992
Stedman Sheard, Wendy. "Verrocchio's Medici Tomb and the Language of Materials, with a

Postscript on his Legacy in Venice." In Bule 1992, pp. 63–90 and figures.

Steinberg 1973
Steinberg, Leo. "Leonardo's *Last Supper.*" *The Art Quarterly* 36, no. 4 (Winter 1973), pp. 297–410.

Steinberg 2001
Steinberg, Leo. *Leonardo's Incessant Last Supper.* New York, 2001.

Steinitz 1948
Steinitz, Kate Trauman. *Manuscripts of Leonardo da Vinci: Their History, with a Description of the Manuscript Editions in Facsimile.* Los Angeles, 1948.

Steinitz 1964a
Steinitz, Kate Trauman. "Le Dessin de Léonard de Vinci pour la représentation de la Danae de Baldassare Taccone," In *Le lieu théâtral à la Renaissance*, edited by Jean Jacquot, pp. 35–40. Paris, 1964.

Steinitz 1964b
Steinitz, Kate T[rauman]. "The Leonardo Drawings at Weimar." *Raccolta Vinciana*, no. 20 (1964), pp. 339–49.

Steinitz 1970
Steinitz, Kate Trauman. *Leonardo architetto teatrale e organizzatore di feste . . . "Quando s'apre Il Paradiso di Plutone."* Lettura Vinciana, 9 (15 aprile 1969).Florence, 1970.

Steinitz 1974
Steinitz, Kate Trauman. *Pierre-Jean Mariette and le Comte de Caylus and their Concept of Leonardo da Vinci in the Eighteenth Century.* Los Angeles, 1974.

Sterling 1957
Sterling, Charles. *Exposition de la collection Lehman de New York.* Exh. cat., Paris, Musée du l'Orangerie. Paris, 1957.

Stites 1930
Stites, Raymond S. "The Bronzes of Leonardo da Vinci." *The Art Bulletin* 12, no. 3 (September 1930), pp. 254–69.

Stix and Fröhlich-Bum 1932
Stix, Alfred, and Lilli Fröhlich-Bum. *Die Zeichnungen der toskanischen, umbrischen und römischen Schulen.* Katalog der Albertina, vol. 3. Vienna, 1932.

Stix and Spitzmüller 1926–41
Stix, Alfred, and Anna Spitzmüller. *Beschreibender Katalog der Handzeichnungen in der Graphischen Sammlung Albertina.* 6 vols. Vienna, 1926–41.

Stock 1985
Stock, Julien, ed. *Il valore dei disegni antichi.* Turin, 1985.

Stock and Scrase 1985
Stock, Julien, and David Scrase. *The Achievement of a Connoisseur, Philip Pouncey: Italian Old Master Drawings.* First Sotheby Fitzwilliam Exhibition. Exh. cat., Cambridge, Fitzwilliam Museum. Cambridge, 1985.

Strauss 1977
Strauss, Walter L. *Hendrik Goltzius, 1558–1617: The Complete Engravings and Woodcuts.* New York, 1977.

Strong 1900
Strong, S. Arthur. *Reproductions in Facsimile of Drawings by Old Masters in the Collection of the

Earl of Pembroke and Montgomery at Wilton House.* London, 1900.

Strong 1902
Strong, S. Arthur. *Drawings by Old Masters in the Collection of the Duke of Devonshire at Chatsworth.* London, 1902.

Strong 1905
Strong, S. Arthur. *Critical Studies and Fragments.* London, 1905.

Strong 1988
Strong, Donald S. "The Painter in Despair: 'Trasparentia' and 'Rilievo' in Leonardo's Treatise on Painting." *Achademia Leonardi Vinci: Journal of Leonardo Studies and Bibliography of Vinciana* 1 (1988), pp. 35–48, and unpaginated figures.

Strzygowski 1895
Strzygowski, Josef. "Studien zu Leonardos Entwickelung als Maler." *Jahrbuch der Preussischen Kunstsammlungen* 16 (1895), pp. 159–75.

Stubbe 1967
Stubbe, Wolf. *Hundert Meisterzeichnungen aus der Hamburger Kunsthalle, 1500–1800.* Hamburg, 1967.

Suida 1919–20
Suida, Wilhelm. "Leonardo da Vinci und seine Schule in Mailand." *Monatshefte für Kunstwissenschaft* 12 (1919), pp. 257–78; 13 (1920), pp. 28–51, 251–97.

Suida 1929
Suida, Wilhelm. *Leonardo und sein Kreis.* Munich, 1929.

Suida 1945
Suida, William E. "Andrea Solario in the Light of Newly Discovered Documents and Unpublished Works." *The Art Quarterly* 8, no. 1 (Winter 1945), pp. 16–23.

Suida 1953
Suida, William [Wilhelm]. *Bramante pittore e il Bramantino.* Milan, 1953.

Suida 1954
Suida, Wilhelm. "Leonardo's Activity as a Painter—A Sketch." In *Leonardo: Saggi e ricerche 1954*, pp. 313–29, pls. 124–29.

Suida 1980
Suida, Guglielmo [Wilhelm]. "The School of Leonardo." In *Leonardo da Vinci 1980*, pp. 315–35.

Suter 1929
Suter, Karl Friedrich. "The Earliest Copy of Leonardo da Vinci's *Battle of Anghiari.*" *The Burlington Magazine* 55, no. 319 (October 1929), pp. 181–88.

Suter 1930
Suter, Karl Friedrich. "A Copy in Colour by Rubens of Leonardo's 'Battle of Anghiari.'" *The Burlington Magazine* 56, no. 327 (June 1930), pp. 257–71.

Suter 1937
Suter, Karl Friedrich. *Das Rätsel von Leonardos Schlachtenbild.* Strasburg, 1937.

Sutton 1947
Sutton, Denys. "Thomas Howard, Earl of Arundel and Surrey, as a Collector of Drawings." *The Burlington Magazine* 89, no. 526 (January 1947), pp. 3–9; no. 527 (February 1947), pp. 32–37; no. 528 (March 1947), pp. 75–77.

Sutton 1970
Sutton, Denys. *Italian Drawings from the Ashmolean Museum, Oxford.* Exh. cat., London, Wildenstein & Co. London, 1970.

Szabo 1975
Szabo, George. *The Robert Lehman Collection: A Guide.* New York, 1975.

Szabo 1978
Szabo, George. *15th Century Italian Drawings from the Robert Lehman Collection.* Exh. cat., New York, The Metropolitan Museum of Art. New York, 1978.

Szabo 1979
Szabo, George. *16th Century Italian Drawings from the Robert Lehman Collection.* Exh. cat., New York, The Metropolitan Museum of Art. New York, 1979.

Szabo 1981
Szabo, George. "Notes on XV-Century Italian Drawings of Equestrian Figures: Giambono, Pollaiuolo, and the Horses of San Marco." *Drawing* 3, no. 2 (July–August 1981), pp. 34–37.

Szabo 1983
Szabo, George. *Masterpieces of Italian Drawing in the Robert Lehman Collection.* Exh. cat., New York, The Metropolitan Museum of Art. New York, 1983.

Tagliente 1532
Tagliente, Giovanni Antonio. *Lo presente libro insegna la vera arte de lo excellente sevivere de diverse varie de litere le quali se fano poeometrica ragione . . . Opera del Tagliente.* Venice, 1532. (The Metropolitan Museum of Art, acc. no. 25.65.3).

Tanaka 1976–77
Tanaka, Hidemichi. "Leonardo's Isabella d'Este: A New Analysis of the *Mona Lisa* in the Louvre." *Annali dell'Istituto giapponese di cultura in Roma* 13 (1976–77), pp. 23–34.

Tanaka 1983
Tanaka, Hidemichi. *Leonardo da Vinci: La sua arte e la sua vita.* Tokyo, 1983.

Tarchiani 1980
Tarchiani, Nello. "Leonardo in Florence and Tuscany." In *Leonardo da Vinci* 1980, pp. 92–107.

Tardito 1988
Tardito, Rosalba. "Il Cenacolo di Leonardo." In *Problemi del restauro in Italia: Atti del convegno nazionale tenutosi a Roma,* edited by Corrado Maltese et al., pp. 275–85. Udine, 1988.

Tea 1932
Tea, Eva. *La Pinacoteca Ambrosiana di Milano.* Rome, 1932.

Teall 1926
Teall, Gardner. "Giovanni Antonio Boltraffio." *The International Studio* 85 (October 1926), pp. 21–25.

Terlinden 1953–54
Terlinden, Vicomte. "Léonard de Vinci dans la gravure flamande." In *L'art et la pensée de Léonard de Vinci: Communications du Congrès international du Val de Loire (7–12 juillet 1952),* pp. 361–74. Paris and Algiers, 1953–54.

Tessin 1717, 2002
Tessin, Nicodème. *Traicté dela [sic] decoration intérieure.* Edited by Patricia Waddy, et al. 1717. Stockholm, 2002.

Tessin 1730
Tessin, Carl Gustav. "Manuscript catalogue written between 1730–1739 on the collection of his father, Nicodemus Tessin the Younger." Nationalmuseum, Stockholm.

Testori 2001
Testori, E. *Dessins anciens de l'école lombarde.* London, 2001.

Teylers Museum and Institut néerlandais 2001–2
Berg-Gerbaud, Mària van, et al. *Collectionner, passionnément: Les plus beaux dessins dans les collections hollandaises du XVIIIe siècle/Hartstochtelijk Verzameld: Beroemde tekeningen in 18de-eeuwse Hollandse collecties.* Exh. cat., Haarlem, Teylers Museum; Paris, Institut néerlandais, Fondation Custodia. Paris and Bussum, 2001.

Thiis 1913
Thiis, Jens. *Leonardo da Vinci: The Florentine Years of Leonardo and Verrocchio.* 1909. Translated by Jessie Muir. London, 1913.

Tietze 1947
Tietze, Hans. *European Master Drawings in the United States.* New York, 1947.

Tietze 1973
Tietze, Hans. *European Master Drawings in the United States.* 1947. Reprint. New York, 1973.

Timpanaro 1980
Timpanaro, Sebastiano. "The Physics of da Vinci." In *Leonardo da Vinci* 1980, pp. 209–13.

Todd 1983
Todd, Edwin M. *The Neuroanatomy of Leonardo da Vinci.* Preface by Carlo Pedretti, foreword by Kenneth D. Keele. Santa Barbara, 1983.

Tomio 2002
Tomio, L. "Bramantino e gli arazzi dei Mesi Trivulzio: Dalla rustica classicità alla maniera moderna." *Rassegna di studi e notizie* 26 (2002).

Tordella 1995
Tordella, Piera Giovanna. "Un disegno di Ambrogio Figino per l'Erodiade di Cesare da Sesto." *Mitteilungen des Kunsthistorischen Institutes in Florenz* 39, nos. 2–3 (1995), pp. 409–25.

Tordella 1996a
Tordella, Piera Giovanna. "Il collezionismo dei disegni a Torino e in Piemonte da Emanuele Filiberto all'età napoleonica." In *". . . Quei leggierissimi tocchi di penna o matita . . .": Le collezioni di disegni in Piemonte,* edited by Gianni Carlo Sciolla, pp. 15–55. Milan, 1966.

Tordella 1996b
Tordella, Piera Giovanna. "La matita rossa nella pratica del disegno: Considerazioni sulle sperimentazioni preliminari del medium attraverso le fonti antichi." In *Conversazione dei materiali libriri, archivistici e grafici,* edited by Marina Regni and Piera Giovanna Tordella, pp. 187–207. Documenti, 3. Turin, 1996.

Torriti 1998
Torriti, Piero, et al. *Beccafumi.* Milan, 1998.

Tours 1956
Dessins et manuscrits de Léonard de Vinci. Exh. cat., Tours, Musée des Beaux-Arts. Tours, 1956.

Travers Newton 1983
Travers Newton, H. "Leonardo da Vinci as Mural Painter: Some Observations on his Materials and Working Methods." *Arte lombarda,* no. 66 (1983), pp. 71–88.

Travers Newton and Spencer 1982
Travers Newton, H., and John R. Spencer. "On the Location of Leonardo's *Battle of Anghiari.*" *The Art Bulletin* 64, no. 1 (March 1982), pp. 45–52.

Trichet du Fresne 1651
Trattato della pittura di Lionardo da Vinci. Nouamente dato in luce, con la vita dell'istesso autore, scritta da Rafaelle du Fresne. Si sono giunt i tre libri della pittura, & il trattato della statua di Leon Battista Alberti, con la vita del medesimo. Paris, 1651.

Trombetti 1929
Trombetti, Anna Maria. "Opere d'arte ignote o poco note: Un nuovo disegno di Lorenzo di Credi per la pala della capella Pappagalli nel Duomo di Pistoia." *Rivista d'arte* 11 (1929), pp. 205–11.

Trombetti 1936
Trombetti, Anna Maria. "Opere d'arte ignote o poco note: Disegni inediti di Lorenzo di Credi." *Rivista d'arte* 17 (1936), pp. 374–87.

Trutty-Coohill 1988
Trutty-Coohill, Patricia. "Narrative to Icon: The San Diego Luini and Leonardo's Language of the Dumb." *Achademia Leonardi Vinci: Journal of Leonardo Studies and Bibliography of Vinciana* 1 (1988), pp. 27–31, and unpaginated figures.

Trutty-Coohill 1989a
Trutty-Coohill, Patricia. "Appendix: The Gardner Adoration Study." *Achademia Leonardi Vinci: Journal of Leonardo Studies and Bibliography of Vinciana* 2 (1989), pp. 164–65, and unpaginated figures.

Trutty-Coohill 1989b
Trutty-Coohill, Patricia. "The Formation of American Collections of Drawings by Leonardo and his Circle." *Achademia Leonardi Vinci: Journal of Leonardo Studies and Bibliography of Vinciana* 2 (1989), pp. 159–63, and unpaginated figures.

Trutty-Coohill 1990
Trutty-Coohill, Patricia. "The Spanish Connection." *Achademia Leonardi Vinci: Journal of Leonardo Studies and Bibliography of Vinciana* 3 (1990), p. 132, and unpaginated figures.

Trutty-Coohill 1993
Trutty-Coohill, Patricia. "The Spencer Collection of Grotesques and Characatures after Leonardo." *Art lombarda,* nos. 2–4 (1993), p. 48–54.

Trutty-Coohill 1997
Trutty-Coohill, Patricia. "Making the Dead Laugh." *Achademia Leonardi Vinci: Journal of Leonardo Studies and Bibliography of Vinciana* 10 (1997), pp. 190–96, and unpaginated figures.

Trutty-Coohill 1998a
Trutty-Coohill, Patricia. "Bracketing Theory in Leonardo's *Five Grotesque Heads.*" In *Enjoyment: From Laughter to Delight in Philosophy, Literature, the Fine Arts, and Aesthetics,* edited by Anna-Teresa Tymieniecka, pp. 87–102. Analecta Husserliana, 56. Dordrecht and Boston, 1998.

Trutty-Coohill 1998b
Trutty-Coohill, Patricia. "Comic Rhythms in Leonardo da Vinci." In *Enjoyment: From Laughter to Delight in Philosophy, Literature, the Fine Arts, and Aesthetics*, edited by Anna-Teresa Tymieniecka, pp. 185–202. Analecta Husserliana, 56. Dordrecht and Boston, 1998.

Tryon Art Gallery 1941
Italian Drawings. Exh. cat., Northampton, Mass., Tryon Art Gallery, Smith College Museum of Art. Northampton, Mass., 1941.

Turner 1966
Turner, Richard. *The Vision of Landscape in Renaissance Italy*. Princeton, N.J., 1966.

Turner 1983
Turner, Richard. "Words and Pictures: The Birth and Death of Leonardo's Medusa." *Arte lombarda*, no. 66 (1983), pp. 103–11.

Turner 1993
Turner, A. Richard. *Inventing Leonardo*. New York, 1993.

Turner 1986
Turner, Nicholas. *Florentine Drawings of the Sixteenth Century*. Cambridge, 1986.

Turner 2000–1
Turner, Nicholas, in consultation with Manuela Fidalgo and José Alberto Seabra de Carvalho. *European Master Drawings from Portuguese Collections*. Exh. cat., Cambridge, Fitzwilliam Museum; Lisbon, Centro Cultural de Belém; Oporto, Museu Nacional Soares dos Reis. Lisbon, 2000.

Turner 2002
Turner, Nicholas, in consultation with Manuela Fidalgo and José Alberto Seabra Carvalho. *Dibujos de maestros europeos en las colecciones portuguesas, 1500–1800*. Exh. cat., Madrid, Museo Nacional Del Prado. Madrid, 2002.

Turner and Hendrix 1997
Turner, Nicholas, and Lee Hendrix. *Masterpieces of the J. Paul Getty Museum: Drawings*. Los Angeles, 1997.

Turotti 1857
Turotti, Felice. *Leonardo da Vinci e la sua scuola: Illustrazioni storiche e note pubblicate per cura di Felice Turotti colla traduzione dell'opera suddetta di [Alexis-] F[rançois] Rio*. Milan, 1857.

Tursini 1954
Tursini, Luigi. "Navi e scafandri negli studi di Leonardo." In *Leonardo: Saggie e ricerche 1954*, pp. 67–84.

Uccelli 1980
Uccelli, Arturo. "The Science of Structures." In *Leonardo da Vinci 1980*, pp. 261–74.

Uffizi 1793
"Indice generale dei volumi nei quali è compresa la raccolta dei disegni della R. Galeria disposto secondo l'ordine dei medesimi." 4 vols. Manuscript inventory of 1793. Gabinetto Disegni e Stampe degli Ufizzi, Florence.

Uffizi 1912–21
I disegni della R. Galleria degli Uffizi in Firenze. Florence, 1912–21.

Uffizi 1960
Mostra di disegni dei grandi maestri. Exh. cat., Florence, Gabinetto Disegni e Stampe degli Uffizi. Florence, 1960.

Uffizi 1979
Berti, Luciano, ed. *Gli Uffizi: Catalogo generale*. Florence, 1979.

Urbini 1919
Urbini, Giulio. "Leonardo." *Nuova Rivista storica* 3 (1919), pp. 257–90.

Uzielli 1872
Uzielli, Gustavo. *Ricerche intorno a Leonardo da Vinci*. Florence, 1872.

Uzielli 1884
Uzielli, Gustavo. *Ricerche intorno a Leonardo da Vinci*. Ser. 2. Rome, 1884.

Uzielli 1896
Uzielli, Gustavo. *Ricerche intorno a Leonardo da Vinci*. Ser. 2. 2d ed. Turin, 1896.

Valentiner 1930
Valentiner, W[ilhelm] R[einhold]. "Leonardo as Verrocchio's Coworker." *The Art Bulletin* 12, no. 1 (March 1930), pp. 43–89.

Valentiner 1933
Valentiner, W[ilhelm] R[einhold]. "Verrocchio's Lost Candlestick." *The Burlington Magazine* 62, no. 362 (May 1933), pp. 228–32.

Valentiner 1949
Valentiner, Wilhelm Reinhold, et al. *Leonardo da Vinci: Loan Exhibition 1452–1519*. Exh. cat., Los Angeles County Museum of Art. Los Angeles, 1949.

Valentiner 1950
Valentiner, Wilhelm Reinhold. *Studies of Italian Renaissance Sculpture*. London and New York, 1950.

Valentiner 1957
Valentiner, W[ilhelm] R[einhold]. "The Madonna of the Scales; La Vierge aux balances." *Gazette des Beaux-Arts*, ser. 6, 49 (1957), pp. 128–48.

Valentiner 1966
Valentiner, Wilhelm Reinhold. "Leonardo as Verrocchio's Coworker." In Philipson 1966, pp. 57–111. Reprint of Valentiner 1930.

Valeri 1980
Valeri, Diego. "Leonardo in Venice." In *Leonardo da Vinci 1980*, pp. 138–42.

Valéry 1894, 1957
Valéry, Paul. "Introduction à la méthode de Léonard de Vinci." *Variété*, 1894. In *Paul Valéry, Œuvres*, edited by Jean Hytier, vol. 1, pp. 1153–99. Paris, 1957.

Vallardi 1855
Vallardi, Giuseppe. *Disegni di Leonardo da Vinci*. Milan, 1855.

Vallese 1992
Vallese, Gloria. "Leonoard's *Malinchonia*." *Achademia Leonardi Vinci: Journal of Leonardo Studies and Bibliography of Vinciana* 5 (1992), pp. 44–51, and unpaginated figures.

Van Cleave 1994
Van Cleave, Claire. "Tradition and Innovation in the Early History of Black Chalk Drawing." In Cropper 1994, pp. 231–43, and unpaginated figures.

Van den Wijngaert 1940
Van den Wijngaert, Frank. *Inventaris van der Rubeniaansche Prentkunst*. Antwerp, 1940.

Van Egmond 1980
Van Egmond, Warren. *Practical Mathematics in the Italian Renaissance: A Catalog of Italian Abbacus Manuscripts and Printed Books to 1600*. Florence, 1980.

Van Gelder 1971
Van Gelder, Jan Gerrit. "Jan de Bisschop." *Oud Holland* 86, no. 4 (1971), pp. 1–88.

Van Gelder and Jost 1985
Van Gelder, Jan Gerrit, and Ingrid Jost, *Jan de Bisschop and his Icones and Paradigmata: Classical Antiquities and Italian Drawings for Artistic Instruction in Seventeenth Century Holland*. Doornspijk, 1985.

Van Gelder, Gerson, and de Gorter 1964
Van Gelder, Jan Gerrit, Horst Karl Gerson, and Sadi de Gorter. *Frits Lugt: Zijn leven en zijn verzamelingen, 1949–1964*. The Hague, 1964.

Van Groschwitz 1959
Van Groschwitz, G. *Lehman Collection*. Exh. cat., Cincinnati Art Museum, 1959.

Van Heel 1975
Van Heel, Dudok. "De kunstverzamelingen van Lennep met de Arundel-tekeningen," and "Honderdvijftig advertenties van kunstverkopinengen uit veertig jaargangen van de *Amsterdamsche Courant, 1671–1711*." *Zevenenzestigste Jaarboek van het Genootschap Amstelodamum* (1975), pp. 137–48; 149–64

Van Heel 1977
Van Heel, Dudok. "Ruim honderd advertenties van kunstverkopingen uit de *Amsterdamsche Courant, 1712–1725*." *Negenenzestigste Jaarboek van het Genootschap Amstelodamum* (1977), pp. 107–22.

Van Marle 1923–38
Van Marle, Raimond *The Development of the Italian Schools of Painting*. 19 vols. The Hague, 1923–38.

Vannini 1987
Vannini, Stefania. "Il Cardinale Fesch e la sua Collezione." *Studi sul Settecento Romano* 3 (1987), pp. 301–9.

Van Puyvelde 1939
Van Puyvelde, Leo. "Die Handzeichnungen des P. P. Rubens: Zu der Ausstellung in Brüssel." *Pantheon* 23 (January–June 1939), pp. 75–80.

Van Regteren Altena, 1940
Van Regteren Altena, J. Q. "Rubens as a Draughtsman. I. Relations to Italian Art." *The Burlington Magazine* 76, no. 447 (June 1940), pp. 194–200.

Vasari 1912–15
Vasari, Giorgio. *Lives of the Most Eminent Painters, Sculptors, and Architects*. 1568. Translated by Gaston Du C. de Vere. 10 vols. London, 1912–15.

Vasari 1966–
Vasari, Giorgio. *Le vite de' più eccellenti pittori, scultori e architettori nelle redazioni del 1550 e 1568*. Edited by Rosana Bettarini; annotated by Paola Barocchi. Florence, 1966– .

Vasari 1996
Vasari, Giorgio. *Lives of the Painters, Sculptors, and Architects.* 1568. Translated by Gaston Du C. de Vere. 1912–15. Introduction and notes by David Ekserdjian. Everyman's Library, 129. 2 vols. New York and Toronto, 1996.

Vasari–Milanesi 1878–85
Vasari, Giorgio. *Le vite de' più eccellenti pittori, scultori ed architettori scritte da Giorgio Vasari, pittore aretino, con nuove annotazioni e commenti di Gaetano Milanesi.* 1568. 9 vols. Florence, 1878–85.

Vasari–Milanesi 1906
Vasari, Giorgio. *Le vite de' più eccellenti pittori, scultori ed architettori scritte da Giorgio Vasari, pittore aretino, con nuove annotazioni e commenti di Gaetano Milanesi.* 1568; 1878–85. 2d ed. 9 vols. Florence, 1906.

Vasari Society 1905–15
The Vasari Society for the Reproduction of Drawings by Old Masters. First ser., 10 parts. London, 1905–15.

Vasari Society 1920–35
The Vasari Society for the Reproduction of Drawings by Old Masters. Second ser., 16 parts. Oxford, 1920–35.

Vasconcelos 1962–63
Vasconcelos, Florido de. *Desenhos: Sécs. XVI a XIX.* Introduction by C. Ramos. Exh. cat., Oporto, Escola Superior de Belas Artes da Porto; Lisbon, Coimbra and Évora. Lisbon, 1962.

Vasconcelos 1963
Vasconcelos, Florido de. "Uma notável colecção de desenhos italianos da Escola Superior de Belas Artes do Porto." *Colóquio,* ser. 1, 22 (1963), pp. 10–16.

Vayer 1957
Vayer, Lajos. *Meisterzeichnungen aus der Sammlung des Museums der Bildenden Künst in Budapest.* Budapest, 1957.

Vecce 1990
Vecce, Carlo. "La Gualanda." *Achademia Leonardi Vinci: Journal of Leonardo Studies and Bibliography of Vinciana* 3 (1990), pp. 51–72, and unpaginated figures.

Vecce 1992
Vecce, Carlo, ed. *Leonardo da Vinci: Scritti.* Milan, 1992.

Vecce 1993a
Vecce, Carlo. "Leonardo e il gioco." In *Passare il tempo: La letteratura del gioco e dell'intrattenimento dal XII al XVI secolo,* vol. 1, pp. 180–205. Rome, 1993.

Vecce 1993b
Vecce, Carlo. "Scritti di Leonardo da Vinci." In *Letteratura italiana: Le opere,* edited by Alberto Asor Rosa, vol. 2, pp. 95–124. Turin, 1993.

Vecce 1995
Vecce, Carlo. "La parola e l'icona: Dai rebus di Leonardo ai 'fermagli' di Fabricio Luna." *Achademia Leonardi Vinci: Journal of Leonardo Studies and Bibliography of Vinciana* 8 (1995), pp. 173–83, and unpaginated figures.

Vecce 1998a
Vecce, Carlo. *Leonardo.* Rome, 1998.

Vecce 1998b
Vecce, Carlo. "'Una voce chiamantemi a cena.'" In Frosini 1998, pp. 437–48.

Vecce 1998c
Vecce, Carlo. *Gli zibaldoni di Iacopo Sannazaro.* Messina, 1998.

Vecce 2000
Vecce, Carlo. "Parola e immagine nei manoscritti di Leonardo." In *Percorsi tra parole e immagini (1400–1600),* edited by A. Guidotti and M. Rossi, pp. 19–35. Lucca, 2000.

Vecce 2001
Vecce, Carlo. *Scritture: Per un manuale di comunicazione.* Naples, 2001.

Veltman 1993
Veltman, Kim H. *Leonardo's Method.* Brescia, 1993.

Veltman and Keele 1986
Veltman, Kim H., with Kenneth D. Keele. *Studies on Leonardo da Vinci: Linear Perspective and the Visual Dimensions of Science and Art.* Munich, 1986.

Venerella 1999–
Venerella, John, trans. and ed. *The Manuscripts of Leonardo da Vinci in the Institut de France.* Ente Raccolta Vinciana. Milan, 1999– . Manuscripts A through M in progress.

Vente record 1987
"Vente record de dessins." *L'estampille* 199 (January 1987), p. 26.

Ventura 1995
Ventura, Leandro. "Isabella d'Este: Committenza e collezionismo." *Civiltà mantovana* 30 (March–June 1995).

Venturelli 1994
Venturelli, Paola. "Percorso iconologico nell'oreficeria vinciana." *Achademia Leonardi Vinci: Journal of Leonardo Studies and Bibliography of Vinciana* 7 (1994), pp. 113–23, and unpaginated figures.

Venturi 1896
Venturi, Adolfo. "Raccolta di disegni delle Gallerie dell'Accademia di Venezia." *Le Gallerie nazionali italiane: Notizie e documenti* 2 (1896).

Venturi 1901–39
Venturi, Adolfo. *Storia dell'arte italiana.* 11 vols. Milan, 1901–39.

Venturi 1919
Venturi, Leonello. *La critica e l'arte di Leonardo da Vinci.* Bologna, 1919.

Venturi 1920
Venturi, Adolfo. *Leonardo da Vinci pittore.* Istituto di Studii Vinciani in Roma, 2. Bologna, 1920.

Venturi 1922
Venturi, Adolfo. "Per Leonardo da Vinci." *L'Arte* 25 (1922), pp. 1–6.

Venturi 1925
Venturi, Adolfo. *Storia dell'arte italiana.* Vol. 9, parts 1–2, *La pittura del Cinquecento.* Milan, 1925.

Venturi 1927
Venturi, Adolfo. *Memorie autobiografiche.* Milan, 1927.

Venturi 1939
Venturi, Adolfo. "L'uso della mano sinistra nella scrittura e nei disegni di Leonardo da Vinci." *L'Arte* 42 (1939), pp. 165–73.

Venturi 1942
Venturi, Adolfo. *Leonardo e la sua scuola.* Novara, 1942.

Venturi 1980
Venturi, Adolfo. "The Drawings of Leonardo." In *Leonardo da Vinci* 1980, pp. 89–91.

Verga 1926–29
Verga, E[ttore]. Review of "Die Madonna mit den spielenden Kindern aus der Werkstatt Leonardos," *Zeitschrift für bildende Kunst* (1929), by Emil Möller. *Raccolta Vinciana,* no. 13 (1926–29), pp. 219–23.

Verga 1931
Verga, Ettore. *Bibliografia vinciana, 1493–1930.* Bologna, 1931.

Verini 1527
Verini, Giovanni Battista. "Incipit liber pri mvs elementorum Litterarum Ioannis Baptiste de Verinis Florentini nouiter impressus [c. 1527]." (The Metropolitan Museum of Art, acc. no. 36.26.1).

Verne 1927
Verne, Henri. "Quelques réflections sur les musées." *Le Figaro artistique,* July 14, 1927, pp. 626–27.

Vertova 1976
Vertova, Luisa. *Biblioteca dei disegni.* Vol. 19, *Maestri toscani del Quattro e del primo Cinquecento.* Florence, 1976.

Vertova 1981
Vertova, Luisa. *Maestri toscani del Quattro e del primo Cinquecento: Finiguerra, Pollaiolo, Verrocchio, Ghirlandaio, Lorenzo di Credi, Francesco di Simone Ferrucci, Francesco di Giorgio,* edited by A. Boschetto and Ulrich Middledorf. Florence, 1981.

Vesalius 1555
Vesalius, Andrea. *Brvxellensis, Invietissimi Caroli V. Imperatoris medici, de Humani corporis fabrica Libri septem.* Basel, 1555. (The Metropolitan Museum of Art, acc. no. 53.682).

Vescovini 1998
Vescovini, Graziella Federici. "Note à propos de la tradition latine des livres de météorologie d'Alkindi et Léonard." In Frosini 1998, pp. 101-12.

Vezzosi 1980
Vezzosi, Alessandro, et al. *La raccolta leonardesca della contessa de Béhague.* Exh. cat., Città di Vinci, Castello di Conti Guidi. Vinci, 1980.

Vezzosi 1982
Vezzosi, Alessandro, et al. *Leonardo dopo Milano: La Madonna dei fusi (1501).* Exh. cat., Vinci, Castello dei Conti Guidi. Florence, 1982.

Vezzosi 1983–84a
Vezzosi, Alessandro. "Asterischi per una Nemesi, Leda stante e il cigno moro." In Vezzosi 1983–84b, pp. 85–114.

Vezzosi 1983–84b
Vezzosi, Alessandro, ed. *Leonardo e il leonardismo a Napoli e a Roma.* Exh. cat., Naples, Museo Nazionale di Capodimonte; Rome, Palazzo Venezia. Florence, 1983.

Vezzosi 1984
Vezzosi, Alessandro. *Toscana di Leonardo.* Florence, 1984.

Vezzosi 1987a
Vezzosi, Alessandro. *Il disegno dell'universo:*

Leonardo e la sua scuola nelle raccolte italiane. Introduced and coordinated by Carlo Pedretti. Exh. cat., Tokyo, 1987.

Vezzosi 1987b
Vezzosi, Alessandro. *Leonardo: Arte, Scienza e Utopia.* Exh. cat., Toronto, J. D. Carrier Art Gallery. Toronto, 1987.

Vezzosi 1988
Vezzosi, Alessandro, ed. *Leonardo scomparso e ritrovato.* Exh. cat., Florence, Palazzo Medici Riccardi. Florence, 1988.

Vezzosi 1996
Vezzosi, Alessandro. *Leonardo da Vinci: Arte e scienza dell'universo.* Milan, 1996.

Vezzosi 2000
Vezzosi, Alessandro, et al. *"Parleransi li omini . . .": Leonardo e l'Europa. Dal disegno delle idee alla profezia telematica.* Exh. cat., Assisi, Palazzo Vallemani; Naples, Archivio di Stato; San Benedetto del Tronto, Palacongressi. Perugia, 2000.

Viatte 1991
Viatte, Françoise, et al. *Repentirs.* Exh. cat., Paris, Musée du Louvre. Paris, 1991.

Viatte 1994
Viatte, Françoise. "Verrocchio et Leonardo da Vinci: À propos des 'têtes idéales.'" In Cropper 1994, pp. 45–53, and unpaginated figures.

Viatte 1999
Viatte, Françoise. *Léonard de Vinci—Isabelle d'Este.* Paris, 1999.

Vicentino 1522
Vicentino, Ludovico [Arrighi]. *La Operina di Ludouico Vicentino, da imparare di scriuere littera cancellarescha.* Rome, 1522. (The Metropolitan Museum of Art, acc. no. 28.106.2).

Vicentino 1523
Vicentino, Ludovico [Arrighi]. *Il Modo de Temperare le Penne. Con le uarie Sorti de littere ordinato per Ludouico Vicentino.* Rome, 1523. (The Metropolitan Museum of Art, acc. no. 28.106.3).

Victoria and Albert Museum 1981–82
Chambers, David, and Jane Martineau, eds. *Splendours of the Gonzaga.* Exh. cat., London, Victoria and Albert Museum. London, 1981.

Villata 1997
Villata, Edoardo. "Il San Giovanni Battista di Leonardo: Un' ipotesi per la cronologia e la committenza." *Raccolta Vinciana,* no. 27 (1997), pp. 187–236.

Villata 1999
Villata, Edoardo, ed. *Leonardo da Vinci: I documenti e le testimonianze contemporanee.* Milan, 1999.

Villata 2000
Villata, Edoardo. "'Ventiquattro storie romane.' Leonardo intorno al 'Cenacolo': Il ritratto di Bernardo Bellincioni e un progetto di decorazione all'antica." In *'Hostinato rigore': Leonardiana in memoria di Augusto Marinoni,* edited by Pietro C. Marani, pp. 61–70. Milan, 2000.

Virch 1962
Virch, Claus. *Master Drawings in the Collection of Walter C. Baker.* [New York], 1962.

Visconti 1980
Visconti, Alessandro. "Leonardo in Milan and Lombardy." In *Leonardo da Vinci* 1980, pp. 108–26.

Vitali 1967
Vitali, Lamberto. "I disegni e le stampe." In *L'Ambrosiana: Storia dell'Ambrosiana,* edited by Angelo Paredi. Milan, 1967.

Vitzthum 1966
Vitzthum, Walter. "Current and Forthcoming Exhibitions: Drawings from New York Collections." *The Burlington Magazine* 108, no. 755 (February 1966), pp. 109–10.

Vitzthum 1967
Vitzthum, Walter. Review of *17th and 18th Century European Drawings,* by Richard P. Wunder; *Italian Drawings in the Art Museum, Princeton University,* by J. Bean; and *Drawings from New York Collections. Vol. II, The Seventeenth Century in Italy,* by Felice Stampfle and Jacob Bean. *The Burlington Magazine* 109, no. 769 (April 1967), pp. 253–54.

Voragine 1969
Voragine, Jacobus de. *The Golden Legend.* Translated by Granger Ryan and Helmut Ripperger. New York, 1969.

Waagen 1854
Waagen, G. F. *Treasures of Art in Great Britain: Being an Account of the Chief Collections of Paintings, Drawings, Sculptures, Illuminated MSS.* London, 1854.

Wackernagel 1981
Wackernagel, Martin. *The World of the Florentine Artist.* Translated, introduced, and edited by Alison Luchs. Princeton, N.J., 1981.

Walcher Casotti 1960
Walcher Casotti, Maria. *Il Vignola.* Rome, 1960.

Walker 1984
Walker, John. *National Gallery of Art.* New York, 1984.

Walker 1987
Walker, R. "Da Vinci Drawing Tops Triumphant Gaines Sale." *Art News* 87 (1987), p. 16.

Walker Art Gallery 1964
Masterpieces from Christ Church: The Drawings. Exh. cat., Liverpool, Walker Art Gallery. Liverpool, 1964.

Wallraf-Richartz-Museum 1953
May, Helmut. *Frühe italienische Kunst des 13.–15. Jahrhunderts.* Exh. cat., Cologne, Wallraf-Richartz-Museum. Cologne, 1953.

Walpole 1849
Walpole, Horace. *Anecdotes of Painting in England with some Account of the Principal Artists and Incidental Notes on other Arts. Also, a Catalogue of Engravers who have been Born or Resided in England. Collected by the late George Vertue; Digested and Published from his original Mss by Horace Walpole; with Additions by the Rev. James Dallaway. A New Edition, Revised, With Additional Notes by Ralph N. Wornum.* 1762–71. 3 vols. London, 1849.

Walsh 2000
Walsh, Judith. "The Use of Paper Splitting in Old Master Print Restorations." *Print Quarterly* 17, no. 4 (2000), pp. 383–90.

Warburg 1893
Warburg, Aby. *Sandro Botticellis "Geburt der Venus" und "Frühling": Eine Untersuchung über die Vorstellungen von der Antike in der italienischen Frührenaissance.* Hamburg and Leipzig, 1893.

Ward 1988
Ward, Roger. *Baccio Bandinelli, 1493–1560: Drawings from British Collections.* Exh. cat., Cambridge, Fitzwilliam Museum. Cambridge, 1988.

Ward-Jackson 1979
Ward-Jackson, Peter. *Italian Drawings. Vol. I, 14th–16th Century.* Victoria and Albert Museum Catalogues. London, 1979.

Wasserman 1969
Wasserman, Jack. "Michelangelo's Virgin and Child with St Anne at Oxford." *The Burlington Magazine* 111, no. 792 (March 1969), pp. 122–31.

Wasserman 1970
Wasserman, Jack. "A Re-discovered Cartoon by Leonardo da Vinci," *The Burlington Magazine* 112, no. 805 (April 1970), pp. 194–204.

Wasserman 1971
Wasserman, Jack. "The Dating and Patronage of Leonardo's Burlington House Cartoon." *The Art Bulletin* 53, no. 3 (September 1971), pp. 312–25.

Wasserman 1978
Wasserman, Jack. "The Genesis of Raphael's 'Alba Madonna.'" *Studies in the History of Art* 8 (1978), pp. 35–61.

Wasserman 1984
Wasserman, Jack. *Leonardo da Vinci.* Abridged edition of *Leonardo,* 1975. New York, 1984.

Wasserman 1986
Wasserman, Jack. In *The Catalogue of the John R. Gaines Collection.* Sotheby's, London, November 17, 1986.

Wasserman 1989
Wasserman, Jack. "A Florentine 'Last Supper' Sketch: A Question of Gesture." *Achademia Leonardi Vinci: Journal of Leonardo Studies and Bibliography of Vinciana* 2 (1989), pp. 110–13, and unpaginated figures.

Watrous 1957
Watrous, James. *The Craft of Old-Master Drawings.* Madison, Wisc., 1957.

Watson 1944
Watson, F. J. B. "On the Early History of Collecting in England." *The Burlington Magazine* 85, no. 498 (September 1944), pp. 223–29.

Weigert 1961
Weigert, Roger-Armand. *Inventaire du fonds français: Graveurs du XVIIe siècle.* Vol. 4. Paris, 1961.

Weigert 1964
Weigert, Roger-Armand. *Les relations artistiques entre la France et la Suède, 1693–1718, Nicodème Tessin le jeune et Daniel Cronström: Correspondence (extraits).* Stockholm, 1964.

Weil-Garris Brandt 1999
Weil-Garris Brandt, Kathleen. *Leonardo e la scultura.* Lettura Vinciana, 38 (18 aprile 1998). Florence, 1999.

Weil-Garris Posner 1974
Weil-Garris Posner, Kathleen. *Leonardo and Central Italian Art, 1515–1550.* New York, 1974.

Weisheipl 1965
Weisheipl, John. "Classification of the Sciences in Medieval Thought." *Medieval Studies* 27 (1965), pp. 54–90.

Weller 1943
Weller, Allen Stuart. *Francesco di Giorgio, 1430–1501.* Chicago, 1943.

Westfehling 1986
Westfehling, Uwe. *Meisterzeichnungen von Leonardo bis zu Rodin: Eine Auswahl von Miniaturen, Handzeichnungen und Aquarellen aus der Graphischen Sammlung Museen der Städt Köln.* Exh. cat., Cologne, Wallraf-Richartz-Museum. Cologne, 1986.

Weston-Lewis 1994a
Weston-Lewis, Aidan. "Appendix: The Commendatore Genevosio as a Collector of Drawings." In Weston-Lewis 1994b, pp. 129–31.

Weston-Lewis 1994b
Weston-Lewis, Aidan. *Raphael: The Pursuit of Perfection.* Exh. cat., Edinburgh, National Gallery of Scotland. 1994.

Wethey 1987
Wethey, Harold E. *Titian and his Drawings.* Princeton, N.J., 1987.

Wey 1878
Wey, Francis. *I musei del Vaticano.* Milan, 1878.

White 1995
White, Christopher. *Anthony van Dyck: Thomas Howard, The Earl of Arundel.* Getty Museum Studies on Art. Malibu, 1995.

White, Whistler, and Harrison 1992
White, Christopher, Catherine Whistler, and Colin Harrison. *Old Master Drawings from the Ashmolean Museum.* Exh. cat., Rome, Palazzo Ruspoli; Oxford, Ashmolean Museum. Oxford, 1992.

Wickhoff 1892
Wickhoff, Franz. "Die römische Schule." Part 2 of "Die italienischen Handzeichnungen der Albertina." *Jahrbuch der kunsthistorischen Sammlungen des allerhöchsten Kaiserhauses* 13 (1892).

Wickhoff 1899
Wickhoff, Franz. "Über einige italienische Zeichnungen im British Museum." *Jahrbuch der Königlich Preussischen Kunstsammlungen* 20 (1899), pp. 202–15.

Wiemers 1996
Wiemers, Michael. *Bildform und Werkgenese: Studien zur zeichnerischen Bildworbereitung in der italienischen Malerei zwischen 1450 und 1490.* Munich and Berlin, 1996.

Wilde 1944
Wilde, J[ohannes]. "The Hall of the Great Council of Florence." *Journal of the Warburg and Courtauld Institutes* 7 (1944), pp. 65–81.

Wilde 1953
Wilde, Johannes. "Michelangelo and Leonardo." *The Burlington Magazine* 95, no. 600 (March 1953), pp. 65–77.

Wilson 1828
[Wilson, Thomas]. *A Catalogue Raisonné of the Select Collection of Engravings of an Amateur.* London, 1828

Wind 1939
Wind, Edgar. "Fresh Light on Two Well-Known Italian Drawings." *Old Master Drawings* 13, no. 52 (1939), pp. 49–51.

Winternitz 1982
Winternitz, Emanuel. *Leonardo da Vinci as a Musician.* New Haven and London, 1982.

Wirtz 1998
Wirtz, Rolf C. *Donatello, 1386–1466.* Cologne, 1998.

Wölfflin 1899
Wölfflin, Heinrich. *Die Klassische Kunst: Eine Einführung in die italienische Renaissance.* Munich, 1899.

Wood 1998
Wood, Jeremy. "Peter Oliver at the Court of Charles I: New Drawings and Documents." *Master Drawings* 36, no. 2 (Summer 1998), pp. 123–53.

Wood 2002a
Wood, Jeremy. "Nicholas Lanier (1588–1666) and the Origins of Drawing Collecting in Stuart England." In *Collecting Prints and Drawings in Europe, c. 1500–1750,* edited by Caroline Elam and Geneviève Warwick. Aldershot, 2002.

Wood 2002b
Wood, Jeremy. *Rubens Drawing on Italy.* Exh. cat., Edinburgh, National Gallery of Scotland. Edinburgh, 2002.

Woodburne 1978
Woodburne, Russell T. *Essentials of Human Anatomy.* 6th ed. New York, 1978.

Woodward 1870
Woodward, Bernard Bolingbroke. *Specimens of the Drawings of Ten Masters from the Royal Collection at Windsor Castle: Michelangelo, Perugino, Raphael, Julio Romano, Leonardo da Vinci, Giorgione, Paul Veronese, Poussin, Albert Durer, Holbein.* London, 1870.

Yakush 1985
Yakush, Mary, ed. *Leonardo to Van Gogh: Master Drawings from Budapest.* Translated from the Hungarian by Janos Scholz. Exh. cat., Budapest, Museum of Fine Arts; Washington, D.C., National Gallery of Art; The Art Institute of Chicago; Los Angeles County Museum of Art. Washington, D.C., 1985.

Yriarte 1888
Yriarte, Charles. "Les relations d'Isabelle d'Este avec Léonard de Vinci." *Gazette des Beaux-Arts,* ser. 2, 37 (1888), pp. 118–31.

Yriarte 1895
Yriarte, Charles. "Isabelle d'Este et les artistes de son temps." *Gazette des Beaux-Arts,* ser. 3, 13 (1895), pp. 13–32.

Zacharias and Kirk 1998
Zacharias, S., and A. Kirk. "Drawing with the Non-dominant Hand: Implications for the Study of Construction." *Canadian Journal of Neurological Sciences* 25, no. 4 (November 1998), pp. 306–9.

Zambrano 1990
Zambrano, Patrizia. "Un nuovo disegno del Sodoma per Monteoliveto Maggiore." *Paragone,* no. 487 (1990), pp. 59–63.

Zammattio 1974
Zammattio, Carlo. "The Mechanics of Water and Stone." In Reti 1974, pp. 190–215.

Zammattio 1980
Zammattio, Carlo. "Hydraulic and Nautical Engineering." In *Leonardo da Vinci 1980,* pp. 467–82.

Zammattio 1980
Zammattio, Carlo, ed. *Leonardo the Scientist.* New York, 1980.

Zentai 1998
Zentai, Loránd. *Sixteenth Century Italian Drawings.* Exh. cat., Budapest, Szépmüvészeti Múzeum. Budapest, 1998.

Zeri 1991
Zeri, Federico. "Rivedendo Piero di Cosimo." In *Giorno per giorno nella pittura: Scritti sull'arte toscana dal Trecento al primo Cinquecento.* Turin, 1991.

Zeri and Zuffi 1995
Zeri, Federico, and Stefano Zuffi. *Leonardo da Vinci: Della natura, peso e moto delle acque: Il Codice Leicester.* Exh. cat., Venice, Palazzo Querini-Dubois. Venice, 1995.

Zöllner 1987
Zöllner, Frank. *Vitruvs Proportionsfigur: Quellenkritische Studien zur Kunstliteratur im 15. und 16. Jahrhundert.* Worms, 1987.

Zöllner 1989a
Zöllner, Frank. "Die Bedeutung von Codex Huygens und Codex Urbinas für die Proportions- und Bewegungsstudien Leonardos da Vinci." *Zeitschrift für Kunstgeschichte* 52, no. 3 (1989), pp. 334–52.

Zöllner 1989b
Zöllner, Frank. "Ogni Pittore Dipinge se." In *Der Künstler über sich in seinem Werk. Internationales Symposium der Bibliotheca Hertziana.* Rome, 1989.

Zöllner 1989c
Zöllner, Frank. Review of *Leonardo-Studien,* by Ludwig H. Heydenreich. *The Burlington Magazine* 131, no. 1033 (April 1989), pp. 301–02.

Zöllner 1991
Zöllner, Frank. "Rubens Reworks Leonardo: 'The Fight for the Standard.'" *Achademia Leonardi Vinci: Journal of Leonardo Studies and Bibliography of Vinciana* 4 (1991), pp. 177–90, and unpaginated figures.

Zöllner 1994
Zöllner, Frank. *Leonardo da Vinci: Das Porträt der Lisa del Giocondo, Legende und Geschichte.* Frankfurt, 1994.

Zöllner 1998
Zöllner, Frank. *La Battaglia di Anghiari di Leonardo da Vinci fra mitologia e politica.* Lettura Vinciana, 37 (18 aprile 1997). Florence, 1998.

Zöllner 2000
Zöllner, Frank. *Leonardo da Vinci, 1452–1519.* Cologne, 2000.

Zöllner 2002
Zöllner, Frank. *Leonardo da Vinci, 1452–1519.* Rome, 2002.

Zubov 1968
Zubov, Vasilii P. *Leonardo da Vinci.* Cambridge, Mass., 1968.

Zucker 1980
Zucker, Mark J. *The Illustrated Bartsch: Early Italian Masters.* Vol. 25. Commentary, formerly vol. 13, part 2. New York, 1980.

Zwijnenberg 1995a
Zwijnenberg, Robert. "Denken op papier: De manuscripten van Leonardo da Vinci." Ph.D. diss., University of Amsterdam, 1995.

Zwijnenberg 1995b
Zwijnenberg, Robert. "De wetenschap der schilderkunst: Leonardo da Vinci's Paragone." In *Dans der muzen: de relatie tussen de kunsten gethematiseerd,* edited by C. G. Anneke, L. G. Korpel, and Kees Meerhoff, pp. 23–32. Hilversum, 1995.

Zwijnenberg 1999
Zwijnenberg, Robert. *The Writings and Drawings of Leonardo da Vinci: Order and Chaos in Early Modern Thought.* Translated by Caroline A. van Eck. Cambridge, 1999.

INDEX

Piccinino, Francesco, 672, *673*, *674*, *675*

Piccinino, Niccolò, 481, 484, 492, *506*, *507*, *507*, *672*, *673*, *675*; fig. 183, no. 91

Piccolomini, Francesco, Cardinal, 542

Piero di Cosimo, 442

Pietro da Novellara, Fra, 19, 141, 149, 151, 153, 233, 516, 519–20, 521–22, 523, 524, 562–64

Pistoia Cathedral altarpiece. *See* Lorenzo di Credi, attributed to, *Enthroned Madonna with Child and Saints*

Pius III, pope, 542

Plato, 131, 445, 618
  Laws, 51
  Timaeus, 492, 618

Plato of Tivoli, 519

Pliny the Elder, 60, 315, 621; *Historia naturalis*, 197, 361, 444, 447

Poliziano, Angelo, 68, 69, 131
  Giostra, 83
  Orfeo, 236
  Stanze, 65

Pollaiuolo, Antonio del (Antonio Benci), 13, 121, 157, 161, 270, 274, 275, 278, 312, 360, 374, 376, 387, 411, 583
  Adam and Eve studies, 274
  The Birth of Saint John the Baptist, silver relief for altar, Florence Baptistery, *300*, 302; fig. 134
  and Colleoni monument, 400
  Design for an Equestrian Monument to Francesco Sforza (Munich), *276*, 276–77, 399; fig. 127
  Design for an Equestrian Monument to Francesco Sforza (New York), 399
  Nude Man Seen from Three Angles, *410*, 411, 542; fig. 158
  Study for an Equestrian Monument, 13, 121, 270, **274–77**, *275*, *277*, 399; no. 11

Pollaiuolo, Antonio di Jacopo, 127

Pollaiuolo, Piero del, 121, 128, 228, 242, 374

Pollaiuolo, Simone "Il Cronaca," 232, 479

Pontormo, *Penitent Saint Jerome*, 376

Porta, Giacomo della, 193–94

Porta, Giovanni Battista della, 548

Porta, Guglielmo della, 6, 193–94, 624

pouncing (*spolvero*), 374

Pozzo, Cassiano del, 33, 534, 539, 671

Predis, Ambrogio de'. *See* Predis, Giovan Ambrogio de'

Predis, Evangelista de', 158, 229, 231, 235, 350

Predis, Giovan Ambrogio de', 163, 165, 183, 646, 648, 651–52
  altarpiece for chapel of the Confraternity of the Immaculate Conception, San Francesco Grande, Milan (jointly with Leonardo and with Evangelista de'

Predis), 158, 229–30, 231, 234, 235–36, 237, 350, 422; copy of, 237. *For the central panel, see* Leonardo da Vinci, *Virgin of the Rocks*
  Head of a Lady in Profile to the Left, 165
  Portrait of Maximilian I, 165
  studies for portraits: Bianca Maria Sforza, 165; Maximilian I, 165
  studies of a putto for *Madonna Litta*, 165

Predis, Giovan Ambrogio de', after Leonardo, *Young Man in Profile to the Right*, 165

Predis, Giovan Ambrogio de', attributed to, *Bust of a Child in Profile to the Left*, 173

prospettiva, 16, 24

Pseudo Boccaccino, 663

Ptolemy, 72; *Hypotheses on the Planets*, 585

quill pens, writing with, 48–49, 50, 51; figs. 37, 38

Rabelais, François, *Les oeuvres de M François Rabelais*, two-volume edition (1669) with drawings after Leonardo, by late-sixteenth-century Lombard artist (Spencer Grotesques), 39, 216–17, 419, 643. *See also* Spencer Grotesques

Raffaello da Montelupo, 31, 45–48, 73, 301; *Phaeton, Horses, and Other Studies*, 45, 48, 50; fig. 36

Raffaello d'Antonio di Biagio, 235

Raffaello Motta da Reggio (Raffaellino da Reggio), 88, 300–301

Raimondi, Marcantonio, engraving after Raphael, *Quos Ego*, 515

Ramolino, Maria Letizia, 378

Rampini d'Asti, Francesco di Jacopo, 132

Ramusio, Paolo, 68, 161, 302, 386, 390

Raphael, 83, 87, 141, 142, 169, 177, 206, 208, 213, 306, 515–16, 667
  Disputa, 83
  drawing of a papal procession, 181–82
  Judgment of Solomon, Stanza della Segnature, Vatican Palace, 552
  Madonna del Granduca, silverpoint studies for, 442
  Madonna of the Veil, silverpoint studies for, 442
  Quos Ego, 515
  Santa Cecilia, 83
  Triumph of Galatea, 513
  Vatican *stanze*, silverpoint studies for, 442

Raphael, after Leonardo
  Fight for the Standard, 484, 672
  Leda and the Swan (standing pose), 515, 535, 553

red-chalk drawings, 174, 175–77

Regisole, 400, 426–27, 577

Rembrandt, 208, 457

Resta, Padre Sebastiano, 521, 523, 564

Reynolds, Sir Joshua, 89

Ristoro d'Arezzo, *La composizione del mondo*, 197, 620, 621

Rizzoli, Giovanni Pietro. *See* Giampietrino

Robbia, Andrea della, 127

Robbia, Luca della, 278

Robbia workshop, 419; after Verrocchio, *Darius*, 308

Robertet, Florimond, 234, 236, 522

Rodinò, Simonetta Prosperi Valenti, 210

Rossellino, Bernardo, 278

Rubens, Peter Paul, 81–82, 204, 672, 675, 676, 677
  Battle of the Standard, 676
  Het Pelsken, 81–82

Rubens, Peter Paul, restored and reworked by, Italian 16th-century copy after Leonardo, *The Fight for the Standard*, 20, 480, 484, 486, 503, 507, **671–77**, *673*; no. 135

Rucellai, Bernardo, 133

Rudolf II, Holy Roman emperor, 701

Rufo, Giordano, *Liber de medicina veternaria*, 131

Rustici, Giovanni Francesco, 133, 543, 548; *Baptism of Christ*, Florence Baptistery, 641

Rustici, Giovanni Francesco, attributed to, terra-cotta bust of bald man, 641

Rutgers, Antoni, 203, 214; annotations in the Caylus album, 214, *214*, *215*; figs. 111, 112

Saint Aubin, Gabriel de, *Livre des Saint Aubin*, 683, 694, 695, 696, 697

Salaì (Gian Giacomo Caprotti di Oreno), 164, 230–31, 236, 238, 239, 240, 366, 442, 534, 639, 654

Salernitani, Masuccio, *Novellino*, 302

Saltarelli, Jacopo, 228

Salvetti, Fra Lorenzo di Antonio, 127

San Bartolomeo di Monteoliveto monastery, Florence, 127, 128

San Donato a Scopeto, Florence, altarpiece commissioned by, 123, 128–29, 142, 161, 302, 320–23, 331, 334, 346, 350, 372. *See also* Leonardo da Vinci, *Adoration of the Magi*

San Francesco Grande, Milan, 230; altarpiece for, *see* Leonardo da Vinci, *Virgin of the Rocks*

Sangallo, Aristotile da, after Michelangelo, *Copy of the Bathers*, 19, *21*, 543; fig. 20

Sangallo, Giuliano da, 231, 234, 238, 394, 433, 542, 543, 578
  Hercules, 542, *543*; fig. 189
  Palazzo Gondi, 228
  sketchbook, 352

PHOTOGRAPH CREDITS

Accademia di Belle Arti di Brera, Milan: fig. 81

© Alinari/Art Resource, New York: figs. 26, 57, 59, 125, 131, 134, 135, 136, 140, 162, 169, 179, 194, 202, 206

Ashmolean Museum, Oxford: cat. nos. 23, 26, 39, figs. 36, 183

Biblioteca Casanatense, Rome/photograph by Carlo Pedretti: fig. 154

Biblioteca Palatina, Parma: fig. 14

Biblioteca-Pinacoteca Ambrosiana, Milan: cat. nos. 59, 120, 122, 127, 128, fig. 9

Biblioteca Reale, Turin: cat. nos. 63, 102, 103, figs. 15, 80, 163

© The British Museum, London: cat. nos. 3, 19, 20, 31–34, 41, 96, figs. 33, 71, 72, 77, 85, 182, 203

Castello Sforzesco, Gabinetto dei Disegni, Milan: fig. 98

Chatsworth Photo Library, Chatsworth, Bakewell, Derbyshire, reproduced by permission of the Duke of Devonshire and the Chatsworth Settlement Trustees: cat. nos. 73, 99

By permission of the Governing Body of Christ Church, Oxford: cat. nos. 1, 54, 92, fig. 46

Christie's International: fig. 192

Sterling and Francine Clark Art Institute, Williamstown, Massachusetts: cat. no. 124

Collection of Bill and Melinda Gates, Seattle: cat. no. 114

Courtauld Institute Gallery, Somerset House, London: fig. 69

École Nationale Supérieure des Beaux-Arts, Paris: cat. nos. 30, 47, 50

Faculdade de Belas Artes, Universidade do Porto, Oporto/photograph by Jorge Coelho: cat. no. 21

Fitzwilliam Museum, University of Cambridge; reproduction by permission of the Syndics of the Fitzwilliam Museum, Cambridge: cat. nos. 6, 40, fig. 146

Fogg Art Museum, Harvard University Art Museums, Cambridge, Massachusetts: fig. 208

Reconstruction after Edward Ford: fig. 78

© Foto Marburg/Art Resource, New York: fig. 144

Gallerie dell'Accademia, Venice: cat. nos. 36, 37, 49, 62, 81–83, 86, 95, 105, figs. 26, 92, 93, 94, 95, 96, 97, 113

Gemäldegalerie, Staatliche Museen zu Berlin— Preussischer Kulturbesitz: figs. 83, 204

Gemäldegalerie, Staatliche Museen zu Berlin— Preussischer Kulturbesitz/photograph by Jörg P. Anders: fig. 116

© The J. Paul Getty Museum, Los Angeles: cat. nos. 69, 94

© Giraudon/Art Resource, New York: figs. 41, 42, 138, 187

Graphische Sammlung Albertina, Vienna: cat. nos. 66, 131, figs. 5, 102, 105

© Hamburger Kunsthalle: fig. 145

© Hamburger Kunsthalle/ photograph by Elke Walford: cat. nos. 25, 35, 38, 75

Marvin Hayes, New York: figs. 19, 104, 190

Kunsthistorisch Instituut, Universiteit Leiden: figs. 111, 112

Kupferstichkabinett, Staatliche Museen zu Berlin— Preussischer Kulturbesitz: fig. 83

© Erich Lessing/Art Resource, New York: figs. 10, 11, 12, 65, 118, 137, 207

Courtesy of Pietro C. Marani: figs. 100, 129, 130, 168

Ministero per i Beni e le Attività Culturali, Istituto Nazionale per la Grafica di Roma, Archivio Fotografico: cat. no. 10, figs. 55, 56

Monumenti e Gallerie Pontificie, Musei Vaticani, Archivio Fotografico: cat. no. 46, figs. 151, 152, 155

Museum Boijmans Van Beuningen, Rotterdam: cat. no. 98

Paolo Nannoni, Florence: fig. 8

Národní Galerie, Prague (courtesy of Varena Forcione): fig. 108

© The National Gallery, London; reproduced by courtesy of the Trustees of The National Gallery, London: figs. 17, 75, 76

National Gallery of Art, Washington, D.C.: figs. 67, 205

National Gallery of Art, Washington, D.C., The Armand Hammer Collection: cat. no. 24

National Gallery of Art, Washington, D.C., Ian Woodner Family Collection (The Woodner Collections on deposit at the National Gallery of Art, Washington): cat. no. 72

National Gallery of Scotland, Edinburgh: cat. nos. 8, 42

The New York Public Library; Spencer Collection: figs. 32, 107, 170, 171, 173–76

The Photograph Studio, The Metropolitan Museum of Art, New York (Barbara Bridgers, Rachel Mustalish, Mark Morosse, Chad Beer, Bruce Schwarz): cat. nos. 9, 11, 12, 43, 45, 60, 68, 101, 108, 121, 129, figs. 2, 3, 4, 13, 24, 25, 31, 34, 35a–d, 37, 38, 84, 126, 149, 153, 156, 157, 159, 172, 180

© Photo RMN (Michèle Bellot, J. G. Berizzi, Gérard Blot, C. Jean, Le Mage, R. G. Ojéda): cat. nos. 4, 7, 13–17, 22, 27, 29, 44, 48, 56, 61, 67, 76, 107, 112, 123, 125, 126, 130, 132–38, figs. 12, 40, 68, 99, 114, 120, 128, 143, 158, 195

© 2002 by The Pierpont Morgan Library, New York: cat. no. 55, fig. 106

Pinacoteca di Brera, Milan: figs. 54, 101, 103, 201

Pinacoteca di Brera, Milan (courtesy of Pietro C. Marani): figs. 129, 130

Printroom, Universiteit Leiden: figs. 109, 110

Private collection, United States: cat. nos. 18, 70, 71

© RMN/Art Resource, New York: fig. 23

© RMN/Art Resource, New York/photograph by Arnaudet: fig. 141

© RMN/Art Resource, New York/photograph by Michèle Bellot: fig. 16

© RMN/Art Resource, New York/photograph by Michèle Blot: fig. 186

© RMN/Art Resource, New York/photograph by Ojéda/Hubert: fig. 142

The Royal Collection © 2002, Her Majesty Queen Elizabeth II, Windsor Castle: figs. 27–30, 44, 45, 47, 53, 70, 73, 74, 87–91, 115, 124, 147, 160, 161, 164, 177, 178, 185, 188, 196–200

© Scala/Art Resource, New York: figs. 1, 6, 7, 18, 20, 22, 43, 49, 52, 66, 82, 117, 122, 132, 133, 166, 167, 184, 191, 193

Soprintendenza per i Beni Artistici e Storici per le Provincie di Firenze e Pistoia, Florence/ Archivio di Stato, Florence: figs. 60, 62, 63, 123

Soprintendenza per i Beni Artistici e Storici per le Provincie di Firenze e Pistoia, Florence/ Gabinetto Disegni e Stampe degli Uffizi, Florence: figs. 8, 39, 48, 50, 51, 58, 61, 64, 79, 86, 139

Soprintendenza per i Beni Artistici e Storici per le Provincie di Firenze e Pistoia, Florence/Galleria Palatina, Palazzo Pitti, Florence/ photograph by Paolo Tosi, Florence: fig. 150

Soprintendenza per i Beni Artistici e Storici per le Provincie di Firenze e Pistoia, Florence/Museo Horne, Florence: fig. 181

Soprintendenza per i Beni Artistici e Storici per le Provincie di Firenze e Pistoia, Florence/Palazzo Gondi, Florence: fig. 189

Staatliche Graphische Sammlung, Munich: fig. 127

© Staatliche Museen zu Berlin—Kupferstichkabinett, KdZ 5095/photograph by Jörg P. Anders: cat. no. 2

Szépművészeti Múzeum, Budapest: cat. nos. 90, 91, fig. 165

Teylers Museum, Haarlem: fig. 21

V & A Picture Library, The Victoria & Albert Museum, London: cat. no. 5

© Victoria & Albert Museum, London/Art Resource, New York: fig. 121

Wallraf-Richartz-Museum—Foundation Corboud, Cologne/Repro Rheinisches Bildarchiv, Köln: cat. no. 28

Windsor Castle, Royal Collection © Her Majesty Queen Elizabeth II: cat. nos. 51–53, 57, 58, 64, 65, 74, 77–80, 84, 85, 87–89, 93, 97, 100, 104, 106, 109–11, 113, 115–19

M. H. de Young Memorial Museum, San Francisco: fig. 119